WHITAKER'S CONCISE ALMANACK 2000

D1632781

AN

Almanack

For the Year of Our Lord

2000

ESTABLISHED 1868

BY

JOSEPH WHITAKER, FSA

CONTAINING AN ACCOUNT OF THE

ASTRONOMICAL AND OTHER PHENOMENA

AND

A vast Amount of INFORMATION respecting the
GOVERNMENT, FINANCES, POPULATION,
COMMERCE, and GENERAL STATISTICS of
the various Nations of the WORLD
with an INDEX containing
nearly 10,000
References

LONDON

OFFICE: 51 NINE ELMS LANE
LONDON SW8 5DR

The traditional design of the title page for Whitaker's Almanack which has appeared in each edition since 1868

Whitaker's Concise Almanack

2000

LONDON:

THE STATIONERY OFFICE

THE STATIONERY OFFICE LTD

51 Nine Elms Lane, London SW8 5DR

Whitaker's Almanack published annually since 1868

© 132nd edition The Stationery Office Ltd 1999

Concise Almanack (672 pages)

0 11 702254 3

Designed by Douglas Martin
Jacket designed by Compendium
Jacket photographs Telegraph Colour Library, PA News Ltd, Super Stock Ltd
Typeset, printed and bound in Great Britain by
William Clowes Ltd, Beccles, Suffolk

All rights reserved. No part of this publication may be
reproduced, stored in a retrieval system, or transmitted in
any form or by any means – electronic, mechanical,
photocopying, recording or otherwise – without prior written
permission of the publisher, to be obtained from the Contracts
and Rights Manager, St Crispins, Duke Street, Norwich NR3 IPD

Crown copyright material is reproduced with the
permission of the Controller of Her Majesty's
Stationery Office

Whitaker's Almanack is a registered trade mark of
J. Whitaker and Sons Ltd. Registered Trade Mark Nos:
(UK) 1322125/09; 1322126/16 and 1322127/41;
(EC) 19960401/09, 16, 41, licensed for use by The
Stationery Office Ltd

EDITORIAL CONSULTANTS
Sally Whitaker
Gyles Brandreth
Rupert Pennant-Rea

EDITORIAL STAFF
Lauren Hill (*Editor*)
Bridie Macmahon; Neil Mackay (*Assistant Editors, UK*)
Chris Sadowski (*Assistant Editor, International*)
Arlene Zuccolo (*Database Co-ordinator*)

Published by The Stationery Office and available from:

The Publications Centre
(mail, telephone and fax orders only)
PO Box 276, London SW8 5DT
General enquiries/Telephone orders 0870 600 5522
Fax orders 0870 600 5533

The Stationery Office Bookshops
123 Kingsway, London WC2B 6PQ
020-7242 6393   Fax 020-7242 6394
16 Arthur Street, Belfast BT1 4GD
028-9023 8451   Fax 028-9023 5401
68–69 Bull Street, Birmingham B4 6AD
0121-236 9696   Fax 0121-236 9699
33 Wine Street, Bristol BS1 2BQ
0117-926 4306   Fax 0117-929 4515
The Stationery Office Oriel Bookshop
18–19 High Street, Cardiff CF1 2BZ
029-2039 5548   Fax 029-2038 4347
71 Lothian Road, Edinburgh EH3 9AZ
0870-606 5566   Fax 0870-606 5588
9–21 Princess Street, Manchester M60 8AS
0161-834 7201   Fax 0161-833 0634

The Stationery Office's Accredited Agents
(*see* Yellow Pages)
and through good booksellers

Contents

CONTENTS CONTINUED

AVAILABLE IN WHITAKER'S ALMANACK
(1,291 pages, hardback, £40)

FINANCE

British currency, banking, mutual societies, national savings, insurance, financial regulation, Stock Exchange, stamp dutues, taxation

LEGAL NOTES

Consumer law, wills, divorce

MEDIA

Broadcasting, the press, book publishers, annual reference books

ORGANIZATIONS

Trade and employers' associations, trade unions, national academies of scholarship, research councils and associations, sports bodies, clubs, societies and institutions

INTERNATIONAL ORGANIZATIONS

European Union, the Commonwealth, CIS, United Nations

Preface

TO THE 132ND ANNUAL VOLUME

Welcome to *Whitaker's Almanack 2000*, the 132nd edition. As we enter a new millennium the world about us is changing ever more rapidly and the *Whitaker's Almanack* team have to work harder than ever to keep abreast of current affairs and maintain the high levels of accuracy and breadth of information that readers have come to expect.

I took over as Editor in July at the height of the researching and compilation of this edition. Developing *Whitaker's Almanack* and its associated titles presents an interesting and diverse challenge for me, and I very much hope that you enjoy this edition as much as I have enjoyed co-ordinating its production.

I would like to take this opportunity to thank the editorial team, the contributors and everyone else who works hard to ensure that *Whitaker's Almanack* is published to a consistently high standard. This preface would be incomplete without a further expression of gratitude from myself and The Stationery Office to Hilary Marsden, editor of Whitaker's Almanack for the past thirteen years, who has been most supportive during the transitional period.

I would also like to thank the many readers who take the time to contact us with comments and suggestions about the content of future editions. I hope that readers will continue to do this and contact details for the editorial department are given below.

Whitaker's Almanack now produces a quarterly newsletter, *Whit and Wisdom*, to provide readers with news, quizzes and a host of *Whitaker's Almanack*-related information throughout the year. If you would like further details of *Whit and Wisdom*, please contact Matt Brady at The Stationery Office, St Crispins, Duke Street, Norwich, NR3 1PD.

51 NINE ELMS LANE, LONDON SW8 5DR
TEL: 0171-873 8442 (editorial); 0870-600 5522 (customer services)
E-MAIL: whitakers.almanack@theso.co.uk
WEB: www.whitakers-almanack.co.uk

LAUREN HILL
Editor
OCTOBER 1999

NOTE – TELEPHONE AND FAX NUMBER CHANGES

As you will know, telephone and fax number codes are changing in some parts of the country. These changes are not reflected in this edition; however, details of the nature and timescale of the changes are as follows:

AREA	OLD CODE	NEW CODE	NUMBER PREFIX
Cardiff	01222	029	20
Coventry	01203	024	76
London	0171	020	7
London	0181	020	8
Northern Ireland	various	028	various
Portsmouth	01705	023	92
Southampton	01703	023	80

From 1 June 1999 parallel running was established and it is possible to dial these areas using either the old dialling codes and local numbers or the new numbers. Parallel running will be phased out between August and October 2000 depending on location, after which time only the new area codes and numbers will be available for use. These changes will, of course, be reflected throughout the next edition of *Whitaker's Almanack*.

The Year 2000

CHRONOLOGICAL CYCLES AND ERAS

Dominical Letter	BA
Epact	24
Golden Number (Lunar Cycle)	VI
Julian Period	6713
Roman Indiction	8
Solar Cycle	21

	Beginning
Japanese year Heisei 12	1 January
Chinese year of the Dragon	5 February
Regnal year 49	6 February
Hindu new year	5 April
Indian (Saka) year 1922	5 April
Muslim year AH 1421	6 April
Sikh new year	13 April
Jewish year AM 5761	30 September
Roman year 2753 AUC	

RELIGIOUS CALENDARS

CHRISTIAN

Epiphany	6 January
Presentation of Christ in the Temple	2 February
Ash Wednesday	8 March
The Annunciation	25 March
Maundy Thursday	20 April
Good Friday	21 April
Easter Day (western churches)	23 April
Easter Day (Eastern Orthodox)	30 April
Rogation Sunday	28 May
Ascension Day	1 June
Pentecost (Whit Sunday)	11 June
Trinity Sunday	18 June
Corpus Christi	22 June
All Saints' Day	1 November
Advent Sunday	3 December
Christmas Day	25 December

HINDU

Makara Sankranti	15 January
Vasant Panchami (Sarasvati-puja)	10 February
Mahashivaratri	4 March
Holi	19 March
Chaitra (Hindu new year)	5 April
Ramanavami	12 April
Raksha-bandhan	15 August
Janmashtami	22 August
Ganesh Chaturthi, first day	1 September
Ganesh festival, last day	12 September
Durga-puja	28 September
Navaratri festival, first day	28 September
Sarasvati-puja	5 October
Dasara	7 October
Diwali, first day	24 October
Diwali, last day	29 October

JEWISH

Passover, first day	20 April
Feast of Weeks, first day	9 June
Jewish new year	30 September
Yom Kippur (Day of Atonement)	9 October
Feast of Tabernacles, first day	14 October
Chanucah, first day	22 December

MUSLIM

Muslim new year	6 April
Ramadan, first day	28 November

SIKH

Birthday of Guru Gobind Singh Ji	14 January
Baisakhi Mela (Sikh new year)	13 April
Martyrdom of Guru Arjan Dev Ji	5 June
Birthday of Guru Nanak Dev Ji	11 November
Martyrdom of Guru Tegh Bahadur Ji	1 December

CIVIL CALENDAR

Accession of Queen Elizabeth II	6 February
Duke of York's birthday	19 February
St David's Day	1 March
Earl of Wessex's birthday	10 March
Commonwealth Day	13 March
St Patrick's Day	17 March
Birthday of Queen Elizabeth II	21 April
St George's Day	23 April
Europe Day	9 May
Coronation of Queen Elizabeth II	2 June
Duke of Edinburgh's birthday	10 June
The Queen's Official Birthday	17 June
Queen Elizabeth the Queen Mother's birthday	4 August
Princess Royal's birthday	15 August
Princess Margaret's birthday	21 August
Lord Mayor's Day	11 November
Remembrance Sunday	12 November
Prince of Wales's birthday	14 November
Wedding Day of Queen Elizabeth II	20 November
St Andrew's Day	30 November

LEGAL CALENDAR

LAW TERMS

Hilary Term	11 January to 19 April
Easter Term	2 May to 26 May
Trinity Term	6 June to 31 July
Michaelmas Term	2 October to 21 December

QUARTER DAYS

England, Wales and Northern Ireland

Lady	25 March
Midsummer	24 June
Michaelmas	29 September
Christmas	25 December

TERM DAYS

Scotland

Candlemas	28 February
Whitsunday	28 May
Lammas	28 August
Martinmas	28 November
Removal Terms	28 May, 28 November

2000

JANUARY

Sunday		2	9	16	23	30
Monday		3	10	17	24	31
Tuesday		4	11	18	25	
Wednesday		5	12	19	26	
Thursday		6	13	20	27	
Friday		7	14	21	28	
Saturday	1	8	15	22	29	

FEBRUARY

Sunday			6	13	20	27
Monday			7	14	21	28
Tuesday		1	8	15	22	29
Wednesday		2	9	16	23	
Thursday		3	10	17	24	
Friday		4	11	18	25	
Saturday		5	12	19	26	

MARCH

Sunday			5	12	19	26
Monday			6	13	20	27
Tuesday			7	14	21	28
Wednesday		1	8	15	22	29
Thursday		2	9	16	23	30
Friday		3	10	17	24	31
Saturday		4	11	18	25	

APRIL

Sunday		2	9	16	23	30
Monday		3	10	17	24	
Tuesday		4	11	18	25	
Wednesday		5	12	19	26	
Thursday		6	13	20	27	
Friday		7	14	21	28	
Saturday	1	8	15	22	29	

MAY

Sunday			7	14	21	28
Monday		1	8	15	22	29
Tuesday		2	9	16	23	30
Wednesday		3	10	17	24	31
Thursday		4	11	18	25	
Friday		5	12	19	26	
Saturday		6	13	20	27	

JUNE

Sunday			4	11	18	25
Monday			5	12	19	26
Tuesday			6	13	20	27
Wednesday			7	14	21	28
Thursday		1	8	15	22	29
Friday		2	9	16	23	30
Saturday		3	10	17	24	

JULY

Sunday		2	9	16	23	30
Monday		3	10	17	24	31
Tuesday		4	11	18	25	
Wednesday		5	12	19	26	
Thursday		6	13	20	27	
Friday		7	14	21	28	
Saturday	1	8	15	22	29	

AUGUST

Sunday			6	13	20	27
Monday			7	14	21	28
Tuesday		1	8	15	22	29
Wednesday		2	9	16	23	30
Thursday		3	10	17	24	31
Friday		4	11	18	25	
Saturday		5	12	19	26	

SEPTEMBER

Sunday			3	10	17	24
Monday			4	11	18	25
Tuesday			5	12	19	26
Wednesday			6	13	20	27
Thursday			7	14	21	28
Friday		1	8	15	22	29
Saturday		2	9	16	23	30

OCTOBER

Sunday		1	8	15	22	29
Monday		2	9	16	23	30
Tuesday		3	10	17	24	31
Wednesday		4	11	18	25	
Thursday		5	12	19	26	
Friday		6	13	20	27	
Saturday		7	14	21	28	

NOVEMBER

Sunday			5	12	19	26
Monday			6	13	20	27
Tuesday			7	14	21	28
Wednesday		1	8	15	22	29
Thursday		2	9	16	23	30
Friday		3	10	17	24	
Saturday		4	11	18	25	

DECEMBER

Sunday			3	10	17	24	31
Monday			4	11	18	25	
Tuesday			5	12	19	26	
Wednesday			6	13	20	27	
Thursday			7	14	21	28	
Friday		1	8	15	22	29	
Saturday		2	9	16	23	30	

PUBLIC HOLIDAYS

	England and Wales	Scotland	Northern Ireland
New Year	†3 January	3, †4 January	†3 January
St Patrick's Day	—	—	17 March
*Good Friday	21 April	21 April	21 April
Easter Monday	24 April	—	24 April
Early May	†1 May	1 May	†1 May
Spring	29 May	†29 May	29 May
Battle of the Boyne	—	—	‡12 July
Summer	28 August	7 August	28 August
*Christmas	25, 26 December	25, †26 December	25, 26 December

*In England, Wales and Northern Ireland, Christmas Day and Good Friday are common law holidays
In the Channel Islands, Liberation Day (9 May) is a bank and public holiday
†Subject to royal proclamation
‡Subject to proclamation by the Secretary of State for Northern Ireland

2001

JANUARY

Sunday		7	14	21	28
Monday	1	8	15	22	29
Tuesday	2	9	16	23	30
Wednesday	3	10	17	24	31
Thursday	4	11	18	25	
Friday	5	12	19	26	
Saturday	6	13	20	27	

FEBRUARY

Sunday		4	11	18	25
Monday		5	12	19	26
Tuesday		6	13	20	27
Wednesday		7	14	21	28
Thursday	1	8	15	22	
Friday	2	9	16	23	
Saturday	3	10	17	24	

MARCH

Sunday		4	11	18	25
Monday		5	12	19	26
Tuesday		6	13	20	27
Wednesday		7	14	21	28
Thursday	1	8	15	22	29
Friday	2	9	16	23	30
Saturday	3	10	17	24	31

APRIL

Sunday	1	8	15	22	29
Monday	2	9	16	23	30
Tuesday	3	10	17	24	
Wednesday	4	11	18	25	
Thursday	5	12	19	26	
Friday	6	13	20	27	
Saturday	7	14	21	28	

MAY

Sunday		6	13	20	27
Monday		7	14	21	28
Tuesday	1	8	15	22	29
Wednesday	2	9	16	23	30
Thursday	3	10	17	24	31
Friday	4	11	18	25	
Saturday	5	12	19	26	

JUNE

Sunday		3	10	17	24
Monday		4	11	18	25
Tuesday		5	12	19	26
Wednesday		6	13	20	27
Thursday		7	14	21	28
Friday	1	8	15	22	29
Saturday	2	9	16	23	30

JULY

Sunday	1	8	15	22	29
Monday	2	9	16	23	30
Tuesday	3	10	17	24	31
Wednesday	4	11	18	25	
Thursday	5	12	19	26	
Friday	6	13	20	27	
Saturday	7	14	21	28	

AUGUST

Sunday		5	12	19	26
Monday		6	13	20	27
Tuesday		7	14	21	28
Wednesday	1	8	15	22	29
Thursday	2	9	16	23	30
Friday	3	10	17	24	31
Saturday	4	11	18	25	

SEPTEMBER

Sunday		2	9	16	23	30
Monday		3	10	17	24	
Tuesday		4	11	18	25	
Wednesday		5	12	19	26	
Thursday		6	13	20	27	
Friday		7	14	21	28	
Saturday	1	8	15	22	29	

OCTOBER

Sunday		7	14	21	28
Monday	1	8	15	22	29
Tuesday	2	9	16	23	30
Wednesday	3	10	17	24	31
Thursday	4	11	18	25	
Friday	5	12	19	26	
Saturday	6	13	20	27	

NOVEMBER

Sunday		4	11	18	25
Monday		5	12	19	26
Tuesday		6	13	20	27
Wednesday		7	14	21	28
Thursday	1	8	15	22	29
Friday	2	9	16	23	30
Saturday	3	10	17	24	

DECEMBER

Sunday		2	9	16	23	30
Monday		3	10	17	24	31
Tuesday		4	11	18	25	
Wednesday		5	12	19	26	
Thursday		6	13	20	27	
Friday		7	14	21	28	
Saturday	1	8	15	22	29	

PUBLIC HOLIDAYS

	England and Wales	Scotland	Northern Ireland
New Year	†1 January	1, †2 January	†1 January
St Patrick's Day	—	—	‡19 March
*Good Friday	13 April	13 April	13 April
Easter Monday	16 April	—	16 April
Early May	†7 May	7 May	†7 May
Spring	28 May	†28 May	28 May
Battle of the Boyne	—	—	‡12 July
Summer	27 August	6 August	27 August
*Christmas	25, 26 December	25, †26 December	25, 26 December

FORTHCOMING EVENTS 2000

This is the UN International Year for the Culture of
Peace and the Arts Council Year of the Artist
The European Cities of Culture are Avignon, France;
Bologna, Italy; Prague, Czech Republic; Helsinki,
Finland; Bergen, Norway; Brussels, Belgium; Reykjavik,
Iceland; Santiago de Compostela, Spain; Cracow, Poland
*Provisional dates

6–16 January	London International Boat Show
	Earls Court, London
15 January–	The Year 1900: Art at the Crossroads
3 April	Royal Academy of Arts, London
9–12 March	Cruft's Dog Show
	National Exhibition Centre,
	Birmingham
11 March–29 May	Jean-Baptiste-Simeon Chardin
	Royal Academy of Arts, London
16 March–9 April	Ideal Home Exhibition
	Earls Court, London
17–19 March	Liberal Democrat Party Spring
	Conference
	Plymouth
19–21 March	London Book Fair
	Olympia, London
7 April–4 June	British Art Show 5
	Scottish National Gallery of Modern
	Art, Edinburgh
May–October	Chichester Festival Theatre season
*29 May–12 August	Royal Academy Summer Exhibition
	Piccadilly, London
19 May–4 June	Bath International Music Festival
22–27 May	Chelsea Flower Show
	Royal Hospital, Chelsea
26 May–4 June	Hay Festival of Literature
	Hay-on-Wye, Hereford
*9–25 June	Aldeburgh Festival of Music and Arts
	Suffolk
*17 June	Trooping the Colour
	Horse Guards Palace, London
22 June–22 July	York Millennium Mystery Plays
	York Minster
23 June–20 August	British Art Show 5
	City Art Gallery, Southampton
27–28 June	Wisley Flower Show
	RHS Garden, Wisley, Surrey
3–6 July	The Royal Show
	Stoneleigh Park, Kenilworth, Warks
4–9 July	Hampton Court Palace Flower Show
	East Molesey, Surrey
7–16 July	York Early Music Festival
13–23 July	Buxton Festival
	Buxton, Derbyshire
14 July–	Promenade Concerts Season
9 September	Royal Albert Hall, London
*20–29 July	Welsh Proms 2000
	St David's Hall, Cardiff
28 July–	Pitlochry Festival Theatre season
31 October	Tayside
4–26 August	Edinburgh Military Tattoo
	Edinburgh Castle
5–12 August	Royal National Eisteddfod of Wales
	Llanelli
10–11 August	Battle of the Flowers
	Jersey
13 August–	Edinburgh International Festival
2 September	Edinburgh
19–25 August	Three Choirs Festival
	Gloucester
22–23 August	Wisley Flower Show
	RHS Garden, Wisley, Surrey
27–28 August	Notting Hill Carnival
	London
1 September–	Blackpool Illuminations
5 November	
2 September	Braemar Royal Highland Gathering
	Aberdeenshire
8 September–	British Art Show 5
5 November	National Museum of Wales, Cardiff
11–14 September	TUC Annual Congress
	Glasgow
15–24 September	Southampton International Boat Show
	West Esplanade, Southampton
17–20 September	Liberal Democrat Party Autumn
	Conference
	Bournemouth
24–29 September	Labour Party Conference
	Brighton
2–5 October	Conservative Party Conference
	Blackpool
*2–19 November	London International Film Festival
	London
5 November	London to Brighton Veteran Car Run
11 November	Lord Mayor's Procession and Show
	City of London
	Two minute silence at 11 a.m.
15–26 November	Huddersfield Contemporary Music
	Festival
26–29 November	Smithfield Show
	Earls Court, London

SPORTS EVENTS

2–6 January	Cricket: 4th Test Match, England v.
	South Africa
	Cape Town, South Africa
14–18 January	Cricket: 5th Test Match, England v.
	South Africa
	Centurion, South Africa
17–30 January	Tennis: Australian Open
	Championships
	Melbourne, Australia
23 January	Cricket: One-day International,
	England v. South Africa
	Bloemfontein, South Africa
26 January	Cricket: One-day International,
	England v. South Africa
	Cape Town, South Africa
28 January	Cricket: One-day International,
	England v. Zimbabwe
	Paarl, South Africa
30 January	Cricket: One-day International,
	England v. Zimbabwe
	Kimberley, South Africa
4 February	Cricket: One-day International,
	England v. South Africa
	East London, South Africa
5 February	Rugby Union: England v. Ireland
	Twickenham, London
	Rugby Union: Wales v. France
	Cardiff
	Rugby Union: Italy v. Scotland
	Rome, Italy
16 February	Cricket: One-day International,
	England v. Zimbabwe
	Bulawayo, Zimbabwe

19 February	Rugby Union: Wales v. Italy
	Cardiff
	Rugby Union: Ireland v. Scotland
	Dublin, Republic of Ireland
	Rugby Union: France v. England
	Paris, France
	Cricket: One-day International,
	England v. Zimbabwe
	Harare, Zimbabwe
20 February	Cricket: One-day International,
	England v. Zimbabwe
	Harare, Zimbabwe
23 February	Cricket: One-day International,
	England v. Zimbabwe
	Harare, Zimbabwe
4 March	Rugby Union: England v. Wales
	Twickenham, London
	Rugby Union: Scotland v. France
	Edinburgh
	Rugby Union: Ireland v. Italy
	Dublin, Republic of Ireland
18 March	Rugby Union: Italy v. England
	Rome, Italy
	Rugby Union: Wales v. Scotland
	Cardiff
19 March	Rugby Union: France v. Ireland
	Paris, France
25 March	Rowing: Oxford and Cambridge Boat
	Race
	Putney to Mortlake, London
1 April	Rugby Union: Ireland v. Wales
	Dublin, Republic of Ireland
2 April	Rugby Union: Scotland v. England
	Edinburgh
*15 April–1 May	Snooker: World Professional
	Championship
	Crucible Theatre, Sheffield
16 April	London Marathon
29 April	Rugby League: Challenge Cup Final
	Murrayfield, Edinburgh
4 May	Badminton Horse Trials
	Badminton
7 May	Football: Welsh FA Cup Final
11–14 May	Royal Windsor Horse Show
	Home Park, Windsor
20 May	Football: FA Cup Final
	Wembley Stadium, London
	Rugby Union: Tetley's Bitter Cup
	Final
	Twickenham, London
27 May	Football: Scottish FA Cup Final
	Hampden Park, Glasgow
	Rugby Union: County Championship
	Final
	Twickenham, London
29 May–9 June	Motorcycle: TT Races
	Isle of Man
29 May–11 June	Tennis: French Open Championships
	Paris, France
24 June	Football: European Championships
	Quarter-Finals
	King Baudouin, Brussels, Belgium and
	Amsterdam, Netherlands
25 June	Football: European Championships
	Quarter-Finals
	Feijenoord, Rotterdam, Netherlands
	and Jan Breydel, Bruges, Belgium
26 June–9 July	Lawn Tennis: All-England
	Championships
	Wimbledon, London

28 June	Football: European Championships
	Semi-Final
	King Baudouin, Brussels, Belgium
28 June–2 July	Rowing: Henley Royal Regatta
	Henley-on-Thames, Oxon
29 June	Football: European Championships
	Semi-Final
	Amsterdam, Netherlands
*16 July	British Formula 1 Grand Prix
	Silverstone, Northants
2 July	Football: European Championship
	Final
	Feijenoord, Rotterdam, Netherlands
8–22 July	Shooting: NRA Imperial Meeting
	Bisley Camp, Woking, Surrey
20–23 July	Golf: The Open
	Old Course, St Andrews
29 July–5 August	Yachting: Cowes Week
	Isle of Wight
*12 August–	Yachting: Commodore Cup
19 August	Cowes, Isle of Wight
16–20 August	Golf: British Amateur Championship
	Royal Troon
28 August–	Tennis: US Open Championships
10 September	New York, USA
31 August–	Burghley Horse Trials
3 September	
September	Cricket: Natwest Trophy Final
	Lord's, London
19 September–	Summer Olympic Games
1 October	Sydney, Australia
27 September–	Horse of the Year Show
1 October	Wembley Arena, London
6–8 October	Golf: Solheim Cup
	Loch Lomond

HORSE-RACING*

*16 March	Cheltenham Gold Cup
*25 March	Lincoln Handicap
	Doncaster
*8 April	Grand National
	Aintree, Liverpool
*6 May	Two Thousand Guineas
	Newmarket
*7 May	One Thousand Guineas
	Newmarket
*9 June	The Oaks
	Epsom
*9 June	Coronation Cup
	Epsom
*10 June	The Derby
	Epsom
*20 June–23 June	Royal Ascot
*29 July	King George VI and Queen Elizabeth
	Diamond Stakes
	Ascot
*6 September	St Leger
	Doncaster
*30 September	Cambridgeshire Handicap
	Newmarket
*14 October	Cesarewitch
	Newmarket

CENTENARIES OF 2000

1400

| 14 February | Richard II, King 1377–99, killed |
| 25 October | Geoffrey Chaucer, poet, died |

1500

| 29 May | Bartolomeu Diaz, Portuguese navigator who sailed around the Cape of Good Hope, died |
| 1 November | Benvenuto Cellini, Italian sculptor and engraver, born |

1600

| 17 January | Pedro Caldéron de la Barca, Spanish playwright, born |
| 19 November | Charles I, King 1625–49, born |

1700

| 1 May | John Dryden, poet, died |

1800

24 January	Sir Edwin Chadwick, social reformer, born
11 February	William Fox Talbot, photography pioneer, born
25 April	William Cowper, poet, died
9 May	John Brown, American slavery abolitionist, born
14 June	Battle of Marengo
25 October	Thomas, Lord Macaulay, historian, born

1900

20 January	John Ruskin, author and art critic, died
24 January	Battle of Spion Kop, Boer War
22 February	Luis Buñuel, Spanish film director, born
27 February	Labour Party founded
28 February	Relief of Ladysmith, Boer War
2 March	Kurt Weill, German-born composer, born
2 March	Lord Cottesloe, soldier and philanthropist, born
5 April	Spencer Tracy, American actor, born
19 April	Richard Hughes, novelist, born
25 April	Gladwyn Jebb, diplomat, born
17 May	Relief of Mafeking, Boer War
28 May	Sir George Grove, musicologist, died
6 June	Arthur Askey, comedian, born
13 June	Boxer Rebellion broke out in China
25 June	Louis, Earl Mountbatten of Burma, born
2 July	Sir Tyrone Guthrie, theatre producer, born
4 July	Louis Armstrong, American trumpeter, born
10 July	Evelyn Laye, actress, born
4 August	Queen Elizabeth the Queen Mother born
25 August	Friedrich Nietzsche, philosopher, died
7 September	Joan Cross, opera singer, born
8 October	Sir Geoffrey Jellicoe, architect, born
16 October	Edward Ardizzone, illustrator, born
23 October	Douglas Jardine, cricketer, born
14 November	Aaron Copland, American composer, born
22 November	Sir Arthur Sullivan, composer, died
30 November	Oscar Wilde, novelist and playwright, died
16 December	Sir Victor Pritchett, author, born

CENTENARIES OF 2001

1501

| 17 January | Leonhard Fuchs, German botanist after whom the fuchsia was named, born |

1701

| 6 September | James II and VII, King 1685–9, died |
| 27 November | Anders Celsius, Swedish astronomer, born |

1801

11 January	Domenico Cimarosa, Italian composer, died
21 February	Cardinal John Henry Newman, churchman and man of letters, born
2 April	Battle of Copenhagen
28 April	Anthony Ashley Cooper, 7th Earl of Shaftesbury, politician, reformer and philanthropist, born
14 June	Benedict Arnold, American general and turncoat, died
3 August	Sir Joseph Paxton, architect and landscape gardener, born
3 November	Karl Baedeker, German publisher and founder of Baedeker guidebooks, born
3 November	Vincenzo Bellini, Italian composer, born

1901

16 January	Laura Riding, American poet and critic, born
22 January	Victoria, Queen 1837–1901, died
27 January	Giuseppe Verdi, Italian composer, died
1 February	Clark Gable, American actor, born
22 February	Stefan Lorant, Hungarian-born British photojournalist, first editor of Picture Post, born
28 February	Linus Pauling, American chemist, born
24 March	Charlotte Yonge, novelist, died
30 March	Sir John Stainer, composer, died
3 April	Richard D'Oyly Carte, producer of Gilbert and Sullivan operas and founder of the Savoy Theatre, died
15 April	Joe Davis, snooker player, born
7 May	Gary Cooper, American actor, born
12 June	Sir Norman Hartnell, couturier, born
13 July	Sir Reginald Goodall, conductor, born
20 July	Dilys Powell, film critic and reviewer, born
9 September	Henri de Toulouse-Lautrec, French painter, died
17 September	Sir Francis Chichester, yachtsman who made a solo circumnavigation of the world in 1966–7, born
10 October	Alberto Giacometti, Swiss sculptor and painter, born
6 November	Kate Greenaway, artist and illustrator, died
5 December	Walt Disney, American artist and animated film producer, born
10 December	Nobel Prizes awarded for the first time

Astronomy

The following pages give astronomical data for each month of the year 2000. There are four pages of data for each month. All data are given for 0h Greenwich Mean Time (GMT), i.e. at the midnight at the beginning of the day named. This applies also to data for the months when British Summer Time is in operation (for dates, *see* below).

The astronomical data are given in a form suitable for observation with the naked eye or with a small telescope. These data do not attempt to replace the *Astronomical Almanac* for professional astronomers.

A fuller explanation of how to use the astronomical data is given on pages 71–3.

CALENDAR FOR EACH MONTH

The calendar for each month shows dates of religious, civil and legal significance for the year 2000.

The days in bold type are the principal holy days and the festivals and greater holy days of the Church of England as set out in the calendar authorized for use from 1997. Observance of certain festivals and greater holy days is transferred if the day falls on a principal holy day. The calendar shows the date on which holy days and festivals are to be observed in 2000.

The days in small capitals are dates of significance in the calendars of non-Anglican denominations and non-Christian religions.

The days in italic type are dates of civil and legal significance. The royal anniversaries shown in italic type are the days on which the Union flag is to be flown.

The rest of the calendar comprises days of general interest and the dates of birth or death of well-known people.

Fuller explanations of the various calendars can be found under Time Measurement and Calendars (pages 81–9).

The zodiacal signs through which the Sun is passing during each month are illustrated. The date of transition from one sign to the next, to the nearest hour, is given under Astronomical Phenomena.

JULIAN DATE

The Julian date on 2000 January 0.0 is 2451543.5. To find the Julian date for any other date in 2000 (at 0h GMT), add the day-of-the-year number on the extreme right of the calendar for each month to the Julian date for January 0.0.

SEASONS

The seasons are defined astronomically as follows:

Spring from the vernal equinox to the summer solstice
Summer from the summer solstice to the autumnal equinox
Autumn from the autumnal equinox to the winter solstice
Winter from the winter solstice to the vernal equinox

The seasons in 2000 are:

Northern hemisphere

Vernal equinox	March 20d 08h GMT
Summer solstice	June 21d 02h GMT
Autumnal equinox	September 22d 17h GMT
Winter solstice	December 21d 14h GMT

Southern hemisphere

Autumnal equinox	March 20d 08h GMT
Winter solstice	June 21d 02h GMT
Vernal equinox	September 22d 17h GMT
Summer solstice	December 21d 14h GMT

The longest day of the year, measured from sunrise to sunset, is at the summer solstice. The longest day in the United Kingdom will fall on 21 June in 2000. *See also* page 81.

The shortest day of the year is at the winter solstice. The shortest day in the United Kingdom will fall on 21 December in 2000. *See also* page 81.

The equinox is the point at which day and night are of equal length all over the world. *See also* page 81.

In popular parlance, the seasons in the northern hemisphere comprise the following months:

Spring March, April, May
Summer June, July, August
Autumn September, October, November
Winter December, January, February

BRITISH SUMMER TIME

British Summer Time is the legal time for general purposes during the period in which it is in operation (*see also* page 75). During this period, clocks are kept one hour ahead of Greenwich Mean Time. The hour of changeover is 01h Greenwich Mean Time. The duration of Summer Time in 2000 is from March 26 01h GMT to October 29 01h GMT.

January 2000

FIRST MONTH, 31 DAYS. *Janus,* god of the portal, facing two ways, past and future

1	*Saturday*	**Naming and Circumcision of Jesus**	1
2	*Sunday*	**2nd S. of Christmas.** Sir Michael Tippett b. 1905	2
3	*Monday*	*Bank Holiday in UK.* J. R. R. Tolkien b. 1892	*week 1 day* 3
4	*Tuesday*	*Bank Holiday in Scotland.* Augustus John b. 1878	4
5	*Wednesday*	Twelfth Night. Lord Frederic Leighton d. 1896	5
6	*Thursday*	**The Epiphany.** Rudolf Nureyev d. 1993	6
7	*Friday*	Glasgow University founded 1450	7
8	*Saturday*	Galileo d. 1642. Sir Laurence Alma-Tadema b. 1936	8
9	*Sunday*	**Baptism of Christ. 1st S. of Epiphany**	9
10	*Monday*	Dame Barbara Hepworth b. 1903. Coco Chanel d. 1971	*week 2 day* 10
11	*Tuesday*	*Hilary Law Sittings begin.* Girolamo Mazzola b. 1503	11
12	*Wednesday*	John Singer Sargent b. 1856. Dame Agatha Christie d. 1976	12
13	*Thursday*	Jan van Goyen b. 1596. James Joyce d. 1941	13
14	*Friday*	Henri Fantin-Latour b. 1836. Jean Ingres d. 1867	14
15	*Saturday*	British Museum opened 1759. Molière b. 1622	15
16	*Sunday*	**2nd S. of Epiphany.** Anton Chekhov b. 1860	16
17	*Monday*	Pedro Calderón de la Barca d. 1600. T. H. White d. 1964	*week 3 day* 17
18	*Tuesday*	Captain Scott reaches South Pole 1912	18
19	*Wednesday*	William Congreve d. 1729. General Robert E. Lee b. 1807	19
20	*Thursday*	George Burns b. 1896. Sir Matthew Busby d. 1994	20
21	*Friday*	Christian Dior b. 1905. Benny Hill b. 1925	21
22	*Saturday*	August Strindberg b. 1847. Walter Sickert d. 1942	22
23	*Sunday*	**3rd S. of Epiphany.** Édouard Manet b. 1832	23
24	*Monday*	**Conversion of St Paul.** Amedeo Modigliani d. 1920	*week 4 day* 24
25	*Tuesday*	Edward III acceded to throne 1327	25
26	*Wednesday*	Théodore Géricault d. 1824. Jacqueline du Pré b. 1945	26
27	*Thursday*	Samuel Palmer b. 1805. Arthur Marshall d. 1989	27
28	*Friday*	Sir Francis Drake d. 1596. Jackson Pollock b. 1912	28
29	*Saturday*	W. C. Fields b. 1880. Alfred Sisley d. 1899	29
30	*Sunday*	**4th S. of Epiphany.** Vanessa Redgrave b. 1937	30
31	*Monday*	Anna Pavlova b. 1885. John Galsworthy d. 1933	*week 5 day* 31

ASTRONOMICAL PHENOMENA

d	h	
3	05	Venus in conjunction with Moon. Venus 3° S.
3	05	Earth at perihelion (147 million km)
6	05	Mercury in conjunction with Moon. Mercury 4° S.
10	20	Mars in conjunction with Moon. Mars 2° N.
12	05	Saturn at stationary point
14	18	Jupiter in conjunction with Moon. Jupiter 4° N.
15	18	Saturn in conjunction with Moon. Saturn 3° N.
16	01	Mercury in superior conjunction
20	18	Sun's longitude 300° ♒
21	05	Total eclipse of Moon (*see* page 71)
24	18	Neptune in conjunction

MINIMA OF ALGOL

d	h	d	h	d	h
1	19.7	13	07.0	24	18.2
4	16.5	16	03.8	27	15.1
7	13.3	19	00.6	30	11.9
10	10.1	21	21.4		

CONSTELLATIONS

The following constellations are near the meridian at

	d	h		d	h
December	1	24	January	16	21
December	16	23	February	1	20
January	1	22	February	15	19

Draco (below the Pole), Ursa Minor (below the Pole), Camelopardus, Perseus, Auriga, Taurus, Orion, Eridanus and Lepus

THE MOON

Phases, Apsides and Node	d	h	m
● New Moon	6	18	14
☽ First Quarter	14	13	34
○ Full Moon	21	04	40
☾ Last Quarter	28	07	57
Apogee (406,418 km)	4	12	23
Perigee (359,361 km)	19	22	47

Mean longitude of ascending node on January 1, 125°

THE SUN   s.d. 16′.3

Day	Right Ascension	Dec. −	Equation of time	Rise 52°	Rise 56°	Transit	Set 52°	Set 56°	Sidereal time	Transit of First Point of Aries
	h m s	° ′	m s	h m	h m	h m	h m	h m	h m s	h m s
1	18 42 54	23 04	− 3 03	8 08	8 31	12 03	15 59	15 35	6 39 51	17 17 18
2	18 47 19	23 00	− 3 31	8 08	8 31	12 04	16 00	15 37	6 43 48	17 13 22
3	18 51 44	22 54	− 3 59	8 08	8 31	12 04	16 01	15 38	6 47 44	17 09 26
4	18 56 08	22 49	− 4 27	8 08	8 30	12 05	16 02	15 39	6 51 41	17 05 30
5	19 00 32	22 42	− 4 55	8 07	8 30	12 05	16 03	15 41	6 55 38	17 01 35
6	19 04 56	22 36	− 5 22	8 07	8 29	12 06	16 04	15 42	6 59 34	16 57 39
7	19 09 19	22 29	− 5 48	8 07	8 29	12 06	16 06	15 43	7 03 31	16 53 43
8	19 13 42	22 21	− 6 15	8 06	8 28	12 06	16 07	15 45	7 07 27	16 49 47
9	19 18 04	22 14	− 6 40	8 06	8 28	12 07	16 08	15 47	7 11 24	16 45 51
10	19 22 26	22 05	− 7 05	8 05	8 27	12 07	16 10	15 48	7 15 20	16 41 55
11	19 26 47	21 56	− 7 30	8 05	8 26	12 08	16 11	15 50	7 19 17	16 37 59
12	19 31 08	21 47	− 7 54	8 04	8 25	12 08	16 13	15 52	7 23 13	16 34 03
13	19 35 27	21 38	− 8 17	8 03	8 24	12 08	16 14	15 53	7 27 10	16 30 07
14	19 39 47	21 28	− 8 40	8 03	8 23	12 09	16 16	15 55	7 31 07	16 26 11
15	19 44 05	21 17	− 9 02	8 02	8 22	12 09	16 17	15 57	7 35 03	16 22 15
16	19 48 23	21 06	− 9 24	8 01	8 21	12 10	16 19	15 59	7 39 00	16 18 20
17	19 52 41	20 55	− 9 44	8 00	8 20	12 10	16 20	16 01	7 42 56	16 14 24
18	19 56 57	20 43	−10 04	7 59	8 18	12 10	16 22	16 03	7 46 53	16 10 28
19	20 01 13	20 31	−10 24	7 58	8 17	12 11	16 24	16 04	7 50 49	16 06 32
20	20 05 28	20 19	−10 42	7 57	8 16	12 11	16 25	16 06	7 54 46	16 02 36
21	20 09 43	20 06	−11 00	7 56	8 14	12 11	16 27	16 08	7 58 43	15 58 40
22	20 13 56	19 53	−11 17	7 55	8 13	12 11	16 29	16 10	8 02 39	15 54 44
23	20 18 09	19 39	−11 34	7 54	8 12	12 12	16 30	16 12	8 06 36	15 50 48
24	20 22 21	19 25	−11 49	7 52	8 10	12 12	16 32	16 15	8 10 32	15 46 52
25	20 26 33	19 11	−12 04	7 51	8 08	12 12	16 34	16 17	8 14 29	15 42 56
26	20 30 43	18 56	−12 18	7 50	8 07	12 12	16 36	16 19	8 18 25	15 39 00
27	20 34 53	18 41	−12 31	7 48	8 05	12 13	16 37	16 21	8 22 22	15 35 05
28	20 39 02	18 26	−12 44	7 47	8 03	12 13	16 39	16 23	8 26 18	15 31 09
29	20 43 10	18 10	−12 55	7 46	8 02	12 13	16 41	16 25	8 30 15	15 27 13
30	20 47 18	17 54	−13 06	7 44	8 00	12 13	16 43	16 27	8 34 12	15 23 17
31	20 51 24	17 38	−13 16	7 43	7 58	12 13	16 45	16 29	8 38 08	15 19 21

DURATION OF TWILIGHT (in minutes)

Latitude	52°	56°	52°	56°	52°	56°	52°	56°
	1 January		11 January		21 January		31 January	
Civil	41	47	40	45	38	43	37	41
Nautical	84	96	82	93	80	90	78	87
Astronomical	125	141	123	138	120	134	117	130

THE NIGHT SKY

Mercury is unsuitably placed for observation throughout the month since superior conjunction occurs on the 16th.

Venus is a brilliant object in the south-eastern sky before dawn, magnitude −4.0, though the duration of its period of visibility shortens noticeably during the month. On the morning of the 3rd the old crescent Moon passes 2° north of Venus. On the 7th Venus passes 7° north of Antares.

Mars, magnitude +1.1, is visible in the south-western sky in the evenings. Its slightly reddish appearance is an aid to its identification. Mars is in the constellation of Aquarius, and south of the Square of Pegasus. The Moon, four days old, will be seen about 3° below Mars on the evening of the 10th.

Jupiter, magnitude −2.4, is an evening object, visible in the south-western quadrant of the sky shortly after sunset. Jupiter is in the constellation of Pisces. The Moon, at First Quarter, passes nearly 5° south of Jupiter on the evening of the 14th.

Saturn, magnitude +0.2, is visible in the southern and south-western sky until after local midnight. On the early evening of the 15th the planet will be seen about 4° above the gibbous Moon. Saturn is almost stationary in the constellation of Aries.

THE MOON

Day	RA	Dec.	Hor. par.	Semi-diam.	Sun's co-long.	PA of Bright Limb	Phase	Age	Rise 52°	Rise 56°	Transit	Set 52°	Set 56°
	h m	°	′	′	°	°	%	d	h m	h m	h m	h m	h m
1	14 27	− 9.0	54.7	14.9	202	111	27	24.1	2 41	2 50	8 01	13 11	13 02
2	15 13	−12.7	54.3	14.8	214	109	19	25.1	3 47	3 59	8 45	13 35	13 22
3	16 00	−15.8	54.1	14.7	226	107	12	26.1	4 51	5 06	9 30	14 03	13 47
4	16 49	−18.3	54.0	14.7	238	104	7	27.1	5 52	6 11	10 16	14 36	14 17
5	17 38	−20.0	54.0	14.7	250	102	3	28.1	6 50	7 11	11 04	15 16	14 55
6	18 29	−20.9	54.1	14.7	263	103	1	29.1	7 42	8 04	11 52	16 03	15 41
7	19 20	−20.8	54.2	14.8	275	234	0	0.2	8 28	8 49	12 41	16 57	16 36
8	20 11	−19.8	54.5	14.8	287	256	1	1.2	9 07	9 26	13 30	17 57	17 39
9	21 01	−17.8	54.8	14.9	299	255	5	2.2	9 40	9 56	14 17	19 02	18 47
10	21 51	−15.0	55.2	15.0	311	253	10	3.2	10 08	10 20	15 04	20 09	19 58
11	22 40	−11.6	55.7	15.2	324	251	16	4.2	10 33	10 41	15 51	21 19	21 11
12	23 29	− 7.5	56.2	15.3	336	249	24	5.2	10 55	11 00	16 37	22 30	22 27
13	0 18	− 3.1	56.9	15.5	348	248	34	6.2	11 17	11 18	17 23	23 43	23 44
14	1 07	+ 1.7	57.6	15.7	0	248	44	7.2	11 39	11 36	18 11	—	—
15	1 58	+ 6.4	58.4	15.9	12	249	55	8.2	12 03	11 55	19 01	0 58	1 03
16	2 51	+10.9	59.1	16.1	24	251	66	9.2	12 30	12 19	19 55	2 15	2 25
17	3 47	+15.0	59.9	16.3	36	254	76	10.2	13 04	12 48	20 52	3 35	3 49
18	4 47	+18.2	60.5	16.5	49	259	86	11.2	13 46	13 27	21 53	4 53	5 12
19	5 49	+20.3	60.9	16.6	61	264	93	12.2	14 40	14 19	22 56	6 08	6 29
20	6 54	+20.9	61.0	16.6	73	269	98	13.2	15 45	15 24	23 59	7 12	7 34
21	7 58	+20.1	60.8	16.6	85	269	100	14.2	17 00	16 41	—	8 06	8 25
22	9 00	+17.9	60.4	16.5	97	102	99	15.2	18 19	18 04	1 00	8 48	9 03
23	10 00	+14.5	59.7	16.3	109	106	95	16.2	19 38	19 28	1 57	9 21	9 32
24	10 55	+10.4	58.8	16.0	121	108	89	17.2	20 55	20 49	2 51	9 48	9 55
25	11 48	+ 5.8	57.9	15.8	134	110	82	18.2	22 09	22 08	3 40	10 12	10 15
26	12 38	+ 1.2	56.9	15.5	146	111	73	19.2	23 20	23 23	4 27	10 33	10 33
27	13 26	− 3.4	56.1	15.3	158	110	63	20.2	—	—	5 13	10 54	10 50
28	14 13	− 7.7	55.4	15.1	170	,109	53	21.2	0 28	0 35	5 57	11 16	11 08
29	15 00	−11.6	54.8	14.9	182	107	44	22.2	1 35	1 46	6 41	11 39	11 27
30	15 47	−15.0	54.4	14.8	194	104	34	23.2	2 40	2 55	7 26	12 06	11 50
31	16 35	−17.7	54.1	14.8	206	101	26	24.2	3 43	4 01	8 12	12 37	12 18

MERCURY

Day	RA	Dec.	Diam.	Phase	Transit	5° high 52°	5° high 56°
	h m	°	″	%	h m	h m	h m
1	18 05	−24.4	5	97	11 26	8 36	9 16
3	18 19	−24.5	5	98	11 32	8 43	9 24
5	18 32	−24.5	5	99	11 38	8 49	9 30
7	18 46	−24.5	5	99	11 44	8 54	9 35
9	19 00	−24.3	5	99	11 50	8 59	9 39
11	19 14	−24.1	5	100	11 57	9 03	9 42
13	19 29	−23.8	5	100	12 03	15 01	14 23
15	19 43	−23.3	5	100	12 09	15 11	14 35
17	19 57	−22.8	5	100	12 16	15 23	14 49
19	20 11	−22.2	5	100	12 22	15 35	15 03
21	20 25	−21.4	5	99	12 28	15 47	15 17
23	20 39	−20.6	5	99	12 34	16 01	15 33
25	20 54	−19.6	5	98	12 41	16 14	15 49
27	21 08	−18.6	5	97	12 47	16 28	16 05
29	21 21	−17.4	5	96	12 53	16 43	16 21
31	21 35	−16.2	5	94	12 58	16 57	16 37

VENUS

Day	RA	Dec.	Diam.	Phase	Transit	5° high 52°	5° high 56°
	h m	°	″	%	h m	h m	h m
1	15 57	−18.3	15	76	9 18	5 38	6 02
6	16 22	−19.6	14	77	9 23	5 52	6 19
11	16 48	−20.6	14	79	9 29	6 06	6 35
16	17 14	−21.5	14	80	9 35	6 19	6 50
21	17 40	−22.0	13	81	9 42	6 30	7 02
26	18 06	−22.3	13	83	9 48	6 39	7 13
31	18 33	−22.4	13	84	9 55	6 46	7 20

MARS

Day	RA	Dec.	Diam.	Phase	Transit	5° high 52°	5° high 56°
	h m	°	″	%	h m	h m	h m
1	22 01	−13.3	5	93	15 20	19 35	19 19
6	22 15	−11.9	5	93	15 15	19 38	19 24
11	22 30	−10.4	5	93	15 10	19 42	19 29
16	22 44	− 8.9	5	94	15 05	19 45	19 34
21	22 59	− 7.4	5	94	14 59	19 49	19 39
26	23 13	− 5.9	5	94	14 54	19 52	19 43
31	23 27	− 4.3	5	95	14 48	19 54	19 48

SUNRISE AND SUNSET

	London 0°05' 51°30'		Bristol 2°35' 51°28'		Birmingham 1°55' 52°28'		Manchester 2°15' 53°28'		Newcastle 1°37' 54°59'		Glasgow 4°14' 55°52'		Belfast 5°56' 54°35'	
	h m	h m	h m	h m	h m	h m	h m	h m	h m	h m	h m	h m	h m	h m
1	8 06	16 01	8 16	16 12	8 18	16 04	8 25	16 00	8 31	15 48	8 47	15 53	8 46	16 08
2	8 06	16 02	8 16	16 13	8 18	16 05	8 25	16 01	8 31	15 50	8 47	15 54	8 46	16 09
3	8 06	16 04	8 16	16 14	8 18	16 06	8 25	16 02	8 31	15 51	8 47	15 56	8 46	16 10
4	8 06	16 05	8 15	16 15	8 18	16 07	8 24	16 03	8 31	15 52	8 47	15 57	8 45	16 12
5	8 05	16 06	8 15	16 16	8 17	16 08	8 24	16 04	8 30	15 53	8 46	15 58	8 45	16 13
6	8 05	16 07	8 15	16 17	8 17	16 10	8 24	16 06	8 30	15 55	8 46	16 00	8 45	16 14
7	8 05	16 08	8 15	16 18	8 17	16 11	8 23	16 07	8 29	15 56	8 45	16 01	8 44	16 16
8	8 04	16 10	8 14	16 20	8 16	16 12	8 23	16 08	8 29	15 58	8 44	16 03	8 44	16 17
9	8 04	16 11	8 14	16 21	8 16	16 14	8 22	16 10	8 28	15 59	8 44	16 04	8 43	16 19
10	8 03	16 12	8 13	16 22	8 15	16 15	8 22	16 11	8 27	16 01	8 43	16 06	8 42	16 20
11	8 03	16 14	8 13	16 24	8 15	16 17	8 21	16 13	8 26	16 02	8 42	16 08	8 42	16 22
12	8 02	16 15	8 12	16 25	8 14	16 18	8 20	16 14	8 26	16 04	8 41	16 09	8 41	16 23
13	8 01	16 17	8 11	16 27	8 13	16 20	8 19	16 16	8 25	16 06	8 40	16 11	8 40	16 25
14	8 01	16 18	8 10	16 28	8 12	16 21	8 19	16 18	8 24	16 07	8 39	16 13	8 39	16 27
15	8 00	16 20	8 10	16 30	8 12	16 23	8 18	16 19	8 23	16 09	8 38	16 15	8 38	16 28
16	7 59	16 21	8 09	16 31	8 11	16 24	8 17	16 21	8 22	16 11	8 37	16 16	8 37	16 30
17	7 58	16 23	8 08	16 33	8 10	16 26	8 16	16 23	8 21	16 13	8 36	16 18	8 36	16 32
18	7 57	16 24	8 07	16 35	8 09	16 28	8 15	16 24	8 20	16 14	8 35	16 20	8 35	16 34
19	7 56	16 26	8 06	16 36	8 08	16 29	8 14	16 26	8 18	16 16	8 33	16 22	8 34	16 36
20	7 55	16 28	8 05	16 38	8 07	16 31	8 12	16 28	8 17	16 18	8 32	16 24	8 32	16 37
21	7 54	16 29	8 04	16 39	8 05	16 33	8 11	16 30	8 16	16 20	8 31	16 26	8 31	16 39
22	7 53	16 31	8 03	16 41	8 04	16 34	8 10	16 31	8 14	16 22	8 29	16 28	8 30	16 41
23	7 52	16 33	8 02	16 43	8 03	16 36	8 09	16 33	8 13	16 24	8 28	16 30	8 28	16 43
24	7 51	16 34	8 01	16 45	8 02	16 38	8 07	16 35	8 12	16 26	8 26	16 32	8 27	16 45
25	7 49	16 36	7 59	16 46	8 01	16 40	8 06	16 37	8 10	16 28	8 25	16 34	8 26	16 47
26	7 48	16 38	7 58	16 48	7 59	16 42	8 05	16 39	8 09	16 30	8 23	16 36	8 24	16 49
27	7 47	16 40	7 57	16 50	7 58	16 43	8 03	16 41	8 07	16 32	8 21	16 38	8 22	16 51
28	7 46	16 41	7 55	16 52	7 56	16 45	8 02	16 43	8 05	16 34	8 20	16 40	8 21	16 53
29	7 44	16 43	7 54	16 53	7 55	16 47	8 00	16 45	8 04	16 36	8 18	16 43	8 19	16 55
30	7 43	16 45	7 53	16 55	7 53	16 49	7 58	16 47	8 02	16 38	8 16	16 45	8 18	16 57
31	7 41	16 47	7 51	16 57	7 52	16 51	7 57	16 48	8 00	16 40	8 14	16 47	8 16	16 59

JUPITER

Day	RA	Dec.	Transit	5° high	
				52°	56°
	h m	° '	h m	h m	h m
1	1 35.4	+ 8 35	18 53	1 07	1 11
11	1 37.4	+ 8 50	18 15	0 31	0 35
21	1 40.6	+ 9 12	17 39	23 53	0 01
31	1 45.0	+ 9 39	17 04	23 21	23 25

Diameters – equatorial 41″ polar 38″

SATURN

Day	RA	Dec.	Transit	5° high	
				52°	56°
	h m	° '	h m	h m	h m
1	2 35.1	+12 37	19 52	2 27	2 34
11	2 34.6	+12 38	19 12	1 48	1 55
21	2 34.8	+12 42	18 33	1 09	1 16
31	2 35.7	+12 49	17 55	0 31	0 38

Diameters – equatorial 19″ polar 17″
Rings – major axis 42″ minor axis 14″

URANUS

Day	RA	Dec.	Transit	10° high	
				52°	56°
	h m	° '	h m	h m	h m
1	21 09.8	−17 02	14 28	17 34	17 03
11	21 11.9	−16 52	13 50	16 58	16 27
21	21 14.1	−16 42	13 13	16 22	15 52
31	21 16.4	−16 32	12 36	15 46	15 17

Diameter 4″

NEPTUNE

Day	RA	Dec.	Transit	10° high	
				52°	56°
	h m	° '	h m	h m	h m
1	20 21.7	−19 13	13 40	16 27	15 48
11	20 23.2	−19 08	13 02	15 50	15 12
21	20 24.7	−19 03	12 24	15 13	14 35
31	20 26.3	−18 58	11 46	14 36	13 58

Diameter 2″

February 2000

SECOND MONTH, 28 or 29 DAYS. *Februa,* Roman festival of Purification

1	*Tuesday*	Muriel Spark b. 1918. Buster Keaton d. 1966	32
2	*Wednesday*	**Presentation of Christ in the Temple (Candlemas)**	33
3	*Thursday*	George Crabbe d. 1832. Gertrude Stein b. 1874	34
4	*Friday*	Charles Lindbergh b. 1902. Karen Carpenter d. 1983	35
5	*Saturday*	*Chinese Year of the Dragon.* Sir John Pritchard b. 1921	36
6	*Sunday*	**5th S. before Lent.** *Queen's Accession 1952*	37
7	*Monday*	Charles Dickens b. 1812. King Hussein of Jordan d. 1999	*week 6 day* 38
8	*Tuesday*	Mary, Queen of Scots executed 1587	39
9	*Wednesday*	Alban Berg b. 1885. Bill Haley d. 1981	40
10	*Thursday*	Charles Montesquieu d. 1755. Boris Pasternak b. 1890	41
11	*Friday*	Sir Vivian Fuchs b. 1908. John Buchan d. 1940	42
12	*Saturday*	Immanuel Kant d. 1804. Franco Zeffirelli b. 1923	43
13	*Sunday*	**4th S. before Lent.** Accession of William III and Mary II 1689	44
14	*Monday*	St Valentine's Day. Captain James Cook d. 1779	*week 7 day* 45
15	*Tuesday*	Galileo b. 1564. Norman Parkinson d. 1990	46
16	*Wednesday*	Sonny Bono b. 1935. Angela Carter d. 1992	47
17	*Thursday*	Geronimo d. 1909. Ruth Rendell b. 1930	48
18	*Friday*	Mary I b. 1516. Gustave Charpentier d. 1956	49
19	*Saturday*	*Duke of York b. 1960.* Deng Xiaoping d. 1997	50
20	*Sunday*	**3rd S. before Lent.** Enzo Ferrari b. 1898	51
21	*Monday*	W. H. Auden b. 1907. Sir Frederick Banting d. 1941	*week 8 day* 52
22	*Tuesday*	Niki Lauda b. 1949. Elizabeth Bowen d. 1973	53
23	*Wednesday*	John Keats d. 1821. George Frideric Handel b. 1685	54
24	*Thursday*	William C. Russell b. 1844. Bobby Moore d. 1993	55
25	*Friday*	Anthony Burgess b. 1917. Tennessee Williams d. 1983	56
26	*Saturday*	Sir James Goldsmith b. 1933. Sir Harry Lauder d. 1950	57
27	*Sunday*	**2nd S. before Lent.** Elizabeth Taylor b. 1932	58
28	*Monday*	Linus Pauling b. 1901. Sir Stephen Spender b. 1909	*week 9 day* 59
29	*Tuesday*	John Whitgift d. 1604. Gioacchino Rossini b. 1792	60

ASTRONOMICAL PHENOMENA

d	h	
2	15	Venus in conjunction with Moon. Venus 1° S.
5	13	Partial eclipse of Sun (*see* page 71)
6	07	Uranus in conjunction
6	21	Mercury in conjunction with Moon. Mercury 2° N.
8	20	Mars in conjunction with Moon. Mars 4° N.
11	05	Jupiter in conjunction with Moon. Jupiter 4° N.
12	02	Saturn in conjunction with Moon. Saturn 3° N.
15	01	Mercury at greatest elongation E.18°
19	09	Sun's longitude 330° ♓
21	13	Mercury at stationary point

MINIMA OF ALGOL

d	h	d	h	d	h
2	08.7	13	20.0	25	07.3
5	05.5	16	16.8	28	04.1
8	02.4	19	13.6		
10	23.2	22	10.5		

CONSTELLATIONS

The following constellations are near the meridian at

	d	h		d	h
January	1	24	February	15	21
January	16	23	March	1	20
February	1	22	March	16	19

Draco (below the Pole), Camelopardus, Auriga, Taurus, Gemini, Orion, Canis Minor, Monoceros, Lepus, Canis Major and Puppis

THE MOON

Phases, Apsides and Node	d	h	m
● New Moon	5	13	03
☽ First Quarter	12	23	21
○ Full Moon	19	16	27
☾ Last Quarter	27	03	53
Apogee (405,608 km)	1	01	20
Perigee (364,494 km)	17	02	32
Apogee (404,615 km)	28	20	45

Mean longitude of ascending node on February 1, 123°

THE SUN   s.d. 16′.2

Day	Right Ascension	Dec. −	Equation of time	Rise 52°	Rise 56°	Transit	Set 52°	Set 56°	Sidereal time	Transit of First Point of Aries
	h m s	° ′	m s	h m	h m	h m	h m	h m	h m s	h m s
1	20 55 30	17 21	−13 26	7 41	7 56	12 14	16 47	16 32	8 42 05	15 15 25
2	20 59 35	17 04	−13 34	7 40	7 54	12 14	16 48	16 34	8 46 01	15 11 29
3	21 03 40	16 47	−13 42	7 38	7 52	12 14	16 50	16 36	8 49 58	15 07 33
4	21 07 43	16 29	−13 49	7 36	7 50	12 14	16 52	16 38	8 53 54	15 03 37
5	21 11 46	16 12	−13 55	7 35	7 48	12 14	16 54	16 40	8 57 51	14 59 41
6	21 15 47	15 54	−14 00	7 33	7 46	12 14	16 56	16 42	9 01 47	14 55 45
7	21 19 48	15 35	−14 04	7 31	7 44	12 14	16 58	16 45	9 05 44	14 51 50
8	21 23 49	15 17	−14 08	7 29	7 42	12 14	17 00	16 47	9 09 41	14 47 54
9	21 27 48	14 58	−14 11	7 28	7 40	12 14	17 01	16 49	9 13 37	14 43 58
10	21 31 46	14 38	−14 13	7 26	7 38	12 14	17 03	16 51	9 17 34	14 40 02
11	21 35 44	14 19	−14 14	7 24	7 36	12 14	17 05	16 53	9 21 30	14 36 06
12	21 39 41	13 59	−14 15	7 22	7 34	12 14	17 07	16 56	9 25 27	14 32 10
13	21 43 37	13 40	−14 14	7 20	7 31	12 14	17 09	16 58	9 29 23	14 28 14
14	21 47 33	13 19	−14 13	7 18	7 29	12 14	17 11	17 00	9 33 20	14 24 18
15	21 51 28	12 59	−14 11	7 16	7 27	12 14	17 13	17 02	9 37 16	14 20 22
16	21 55 21	12 39	−14 08	7 15	7 25	12 14	17 14	17 04	9 41 13	14 16 26
17	21 59 15	12 18	−14 05	7 13	7 22	12 14	17 16	17 07	9 45 09	14 12 30
18	22 03 07	11 57	−14 01	7 11	7 20	12 14	17 18	17 09	9 49 06	14 08 35
19	22 06 59	11 36	−13 56	7 09	7 18	12 14	17 20	17 11	9 53 03	14 04 39
20	22 10 50	11 15	−13 51	7 07	7 15	12 14	17 22	17 13	9 56 59	14 00 43
21	22 14 40	10 53	−13 45	7 04	7 13	12 14	17 24	17 15	10 00 56	13 56 47
22	22 18 30	10 31	−13 38	7 02	7 11	12 14	17 26	17 18	10 04 52	13 52 51
23	22 22 19	10 10	−13 30	7 00	7 08	12 13	17 27	17 20	10 08 49	13 48 55
24	22 26 08	9 48	−13 22	6 58	7 06	12 13	17 29	17 22	10 12 45	13 44 59
25	22 29 55	9 26	−13 14	6 56	7 03	12 13	17 31	17 24	10 16 42	13 41 03
26	22 33 43	9 03	−13 04	6 54	7 01	12 13	17 33	17 26	10 20 38	13 37 07
27	22 37 30	8 41	−12 55	6 52	6 58	12 13	17 35	17 28	10 24 35	13 33 11
28	22 41 16	8 18	−12 44	6 50	6 56	12 13	17 37	17 30	10 28 32	13 29 15
29	22 45 01	7 56	−12 33	6 47	6 53	12 12	17 38	17 33	10 32 28	13 25 20

DURATION OF TWILIGHT (in minutes)

Latitude	52°	56°	52°	56°	52°	56°	52°	56°
	1 February		11 February		21 February		28 February	
Civil	37	41	35	39	34	38	34	38
Nautical	77	86	75	83	74	81	73	81
Astronomical	117	130	114	126	113	125	112	124

THE NIGHT SKY

Mercury is visible low in the west-south-western sky at the end of evening civil twilight during the middle two weeks of the month, its magnitude decreasing during this period from −1.0 to +1.0. For observers in the northern hemisphere this is the most favourable evening apparition of the year. While Mercury is visible there will be three other planets visible in the south-western quadrant of the sky; moving to the left observers will see Mars, then Jupiter, with Saturn near the meridian.

Venus continues to be visible as a brilliant object in the morning skies, magnitude −4.0, though it will only be seen low above the south-eastern horizon for a short period of time, just before sunrise.

Mars, magnitude +1.2, continues to be visible as an evening object in the south-western sky. Mars is close to the three-day-old crescent Moon on the evening of the 8th, the Moon passing about 4° south of the planet.

Jupiter continues to be visible in the south-western sky in the early part of the evening, magnitude −2.2. The crescent Moon is near the planet on the evenings of the 10th and 11th. On the 11th the relative positions of Jupiter, Saturn and the Moon are of some interest since the Moon is almost at its maximum distance south of the ecliptic (5.2°) and thus well below the line joining the two planets. During February Jupiter moves from Pisces into Aries.

Saturn, magnitude +0.3, continues to be visible in the south-western quadrant of the sky in the evenings but is unlikely to be visible for long after 2200 hours by the end of the month.

Zodiacal Light. The evening cone may be observed stretching up from the western horizon, along the ecliptic, after the end of twilight, from the beginning of the month to the 7th and again after the 20th. This faint phenomenon is only visible under good conditions and in the absence of both moonlight and artificial lighting.

THE MOON

Day	RA	Dec.	Hor. par.	Semi-diam.	Sun's co-long.	PA of Bright Limb	Phase	Age	Rise 52°	Rise 56°	Transit	Set 52°	Set 56°
	h m	°	′	′	°	°	%	d	h m	h m	h m	h m	h m
1	17 24	−19.6	54.1	14.7	219	97	18	25.2	4 42	5 03	8 59	13 14	12 53
2	18 14	−20.7	54.1	14.7	231	92	11	26.2	5 37	5 58	9 47	13 58	13 36
3	19 05	−20.9	54.3	14.8	243	87	6	27.2	6 25	6 46	10 36	14 49	14 28
4	19 57	−20.1	54.6	14.9	255	81	2	28.2	7 07	7 26	11 25	15 48	15 29
5	20 48	−18.4	54.9	15.0	267	70	0	29.2	7 42	7 59	12 14	16 52	16 36
6	21 38	−15.8	55.3	15.1	280	269	0	0.5	8 12	8 25	13 02	17 59	17 47
7	22 28	−12.5	55.8	15.2	292	257	2	1.5	8 38	8 47	13 49	19 09	19 01
8	23 17	− 8.5	56.2	15.3	304	254	6	2.5	9 01	9 07	14 35	20 21	20 16
9	0 06	− 4.1	56.7	15.5	316	252	12	3.5	9 23	9 25	15 22	21 33	21 33
10	0 56	+ 0.6	57.2	15.6	328	251	20	4.5	9 44	9 42	16 09	22 47	22 51
11	1 46	+ 5.3	57.8	15.7	341	251	29	5.5	10 07	10 01	16 58	—	—
12	2 37	+ 9.9	58.3	15.9	353	253	39	6.5	10 33	10 23	17 49	0 02	0 11
13	3 31	+14.0	58.8	16.0	5	256	50	7.5	11 03	10 49	18 43	1 19	1 32
14	4 28	+17.4	59.3	16.2	17	260	62	8.5	11 40	11 22	19 40	2 36	2 53
15	5 27	+19.7	59.7	16.3	29	265	73	9.5	12 27	12 06	20 40	3 49	4 10
16	6 29	+20.9	60.0	16.4	41	271	82	10.5	13 25	13 03	21 41	4 56	5 18
17	7 32	+20.6	60.2	16.4	53	277	90	11.5	14 33	14 13	22 41	5 53	6 14
18	8 34	+19.0	60.1	16.4	66	285	96	12.5	15 49	15 33	23 40	6 39	6 57
19	9 33	+16.1	59.8	16.3	78	298	99	13.5	17 09	16 56	—	7 16	7 30
20	10 31	+12.3	59.2	16.1	90	79	100	14.5	18 27	18 20	0 35	7 46	7 56
21	11 25	+ 7.8	58.6	16.0	102	101	98	15.5	19 44	19 41	1 27	8 12	8 17
22	12 17	+ 3.1	57.8	15.7	114	106	93	16.5	20 58	20 59	2 16	8 35	8 36
23	13 07	− 1.7	57.0	15.5	126	107	87	17.5	22 10	22 15	3 03	8 56	8 53
24	13 55	− 6.2	56.2	15.3	138	107	79	18.5	23 19	23 29	3 49	9 18	9 11
25	14 43	−10.4	55.5	15.1	151	105	70	19.5	—	—	4 35	9 41	9 30
26	15 31	−14.0	54.9	15.0	163	103	61	20.5	0 27	0 40	5 20	10 06	9 52
27	16 19	−17.0	54.5	14.8	175	100	52	21.5	1 31	1 48	6 06	10 35	10 18
28	17 08	−19.2	54.3	14.8	187	96	42	22.5	2 32	2 52	6 53	11 10	10 50
29	17 58	−20.6	54.2	14.8	199	91	33	23.5	3 29	3 50	7 41	11 51	11 30

MERCURY

Day	RA	Dec.	Diam.	Phase	Transit	5° high 52°	5° high 56°
	h m	°	″	%	h m	h m	h m
1	21 42	−15.5	5	92	13 01	17 04	16 45
3	21 55	−14.2	5	89	13 06	17 18	17 01
5	22 08	−12.7	6	86	13 11	17 32	17 17
7	22 20	−11.2	6	81	13 15	17 45	17 32
9	22 31	− 9.8	6	75	13 19	17 57	17 45
11	22 42	− 8.3	6	68	13 21	18 07	17 57
13	22 51	− 6.8	7	60	13 22	18 16	18 07
15	22 59	− 5.5	7	51	13 21	18 21	18 14
17	23 04	− 4.4	8	42	13 18	18 24	18 17
19	23 08	− 3.5	8	32	13 13	18 23	18 17
21	23 09	− 2.8	9	23	13 06	18 18	18 13
23	23 08	− 2.4	9	15	12 56	18 10	18 04
25	23 04	− 2.4	10	9	12 44	17 57	17 52
27	22 59	− 2.7	10	4	12 30	17 41	17 35
29	22 52	− 3.3	10	2	12 15	17 23	17 16
31	22 44	− 4.0	11	1	12 00	17 03	16 56

VENUS

Day	RA	Dec.	Diam.	Phase	Transit	5° high 52°	5° high 56°
	h m	°	″	%	h m	h m	h m
1	18 38	−22.4	13	84	9 57	6 48	7 21
6	19 05	−22.1	12	85	10 03	6 52	7 24
11	19 31	−21.5	12	86	10 10	6 54	7 24
16	19 57	−20.7	12	87	10 17	6 53	7 22
21	20 23	−19.6	12	88	10 23	6 51	7 17
26	20 49	−18.3	11	89	10 29	6 47	7 11
31	21 14	−16.7	11	90	10 34	6 42	7 03

MARS

Day	RA	Dec.	Diam.	Phase	Transit	5° high 52°	5° high 56°
1	23 30	− 4.0	5	95	14 47	19 55	19 48
6	23 44	− 2.4	5	95	14 41	19 58	19 52
11	23 58	− 0.8	5	95	14 36	20 00	19 56
16	0 12	+ 0.8	4	96	14 30	20 02	20 00
21	0 26	+ 2.3	4	96	14 24	20 04	20 03
26	0 39	+ 3.9	4	96	14 18	20 06	20 07
31	0 53	+ 5.4	4	96	14 12	20 08	20 10

SUNRISE AND SUNSET

	London		Bristol		Birmingham		Manchester		Newcastle		Glasgow		Belfast	
	0°05′	51°30′	2°35′	51°28′	1°55′	52°28′	2°15′	53°28′	1°37′	54°59′	4°14′	55°52′	5°56′	54°35′
	h m	h m	h m	h m	h m	h m	h m	h m	h m	h m	h m	h m	h m	h m
1	7 40	16 49	7 50	16 59	7 50	16 53	7 55	16 50	7 59	16 42	8 13	16 49	8 14	17 01
2	7 38	16 50	7 48	17 00	7 49	16 55	7 54	16 52	7 57	16 44	8 11	16 51	8 12	17 03
3	7 37	16 52	7 47	17 02	7 47	16 56	7 52	16 54	7 55	16 46	8 09	16 53	8 11	17 05
4	7 35	16 54	7 45	17 04	7 45	16 58	7 50	16 56	7 53	16 48	8 07	16 56	8 09	17 07
5	7 33	16 56	7 43	17 06	7 44	17 00	7 48	16 58	7 51	16 50	8 05	16 58	8 07	17 09
6	7 32	16 58	7 42	17 08	7 42	17 02	7 47	17 00	7 49	16 53	8 03	17 00	8 05	17 11
7	7 30	16 59	7 40	17 10	7 40	17 04	7 45	17 02	7 47	16 55	8 01	17 02	8 03	17 13
8	7 28	17 01	7 38	17 11	7 38	17 06	7 43	17 04	7 45	16 57	7 59	17 04	8 01	17 15
9	7 27	17 03	7 37	17 13	7 37	17 08	7 41	17 06	7 43	16 59	7 57	17 06	7 59	17 18
10	7 25	17 05	7 35	17 15	7 35	17 10	7 39	17 08	7 41	17 01	7 54	17 09	7 57	17 20
11	7 23	17 07	7 33	17 17	7 33	17 12	7 37	17 10	7 39	17 03	7 52	17 11	7 55	17 22
12	7 21	17 09	7 31	17 19	7 31	17 14	7 35	17 12	7 37	17 05	7 50	17 13	7 53	17 24
13	7 19	17 10	7 29	17 21	7 29	17 15	7 33	17 14	7 35	17 07	7 48	17 15	7 51	17 26
14	7 18	17 12	7 27	17 22	7 27	17 17	7 31	17 16	7 33	17 09	7 46	17 17	7 49	17 28
15	7 16	17 14	7 26	17 24	7 25	17 19	7 29	17 18	7 31	17 12	7 43	17 20	7 47	17 30
16	7 14	17 16	7 24	17 26	7 23	17 21	7 27	17 20	7 28	17 14	7 41	17 22	7 45	17 32
17	7 12	17 18	7 22	17 28	7 21	17 23	7 25	17 22	7 26	17 16	7 39	17 24	7 42	17 34
18	7 10	17 20	7 20	17 30	7 19	17 25	7 23	17 24	7 24	17 18	7 37	17 26	7 40	17 36
19	7 08	17 21	7 18	17 31	7 17	17 27	7 21	17 26	7 22	17 20	7 34	17 28	7 38	17 38
20	7 06	17 23	7 16	17 33	7 15	17 29	7 19	17 28	7 19	17 22	7 32	17 30	7 36	17 40
21	7 04	17 25	7 14	17 35	7 13	17 31	7 16	17 30	7 17	17 24	7 30	17 33	7 33	17 42
22	7 02	17 27	7 12	17 37	7 11	17 32	7 14	17 32	7 15	17 26	7 27	17 35	7 31	17 44
23	7 00	17 29	7 10	17 39	7 09	17 34	7 12	17 34	7 12	17 28	7 25	17 37	7 29	17 46
24	6 58	17 30	7 08	17 40	7 07	17 36	7 10	17 36	7 10	17 30	7 22	17 39	7 27	17 48
25	6 56	17 32	7 06	17 42	7 05	17 38	7 08	17 38	7 08	17 32	7 20	17 41	7 24	17 50
26	6 54	17 34	7 03	17 44	7 02	17 40	7 05	17 40	7 05	17 34	7 17	17 43	7 22	17 52
27	6 51	17 36	7 01	17 46	7 00	17 42	7 03	17 42	7 03	17 37	7 15	17 45	7 20	17 54
28	6 49	17 38	6 59	17 48	6 58	17 44	7 01	17 43	7 01	17 39	7 13	17 48	7 17	17 56
29	6 47	17 39	6 57	17 49	6 56	17 45	6 58	17 45	6 58	17 41	7 10	17 50	7 15	17 59

JUPITER

Day	RA	Dec.	Transit	5° high	
				52°	56°
	h m	° ′	h m	h m	h m
1	1 45.4	+ 9 42	17 01	23 18	23 22
11	1 50.8	+10 15	16 27	22 46	22 52
21	1 57.1	+10 52	15 54	22 17	22 22
31	2 04.0	+11 31	15 22	21 48	21 54

Diameters – equatorial 37″ polar 35″

SATURN

Day	RA	Dec.	Transit	5° high	
				52°	56°
	h m	° ′	h m	h m	h m
1	2 35.9	+12 50	17 51	0 27	0 35
11	2 37.6	+13 01	17 13	23 47	23 55
21	2 39.9	+13 15	16 36	23 11	23 19
31	2 42.9	+13 31	16 00	22 37	22 45

Diameters – equatorial 18″ polar 16″
Rings – major axis 40″ minor axis 13″

URANUS

Day	RA	Dec.	Transit	10° high	
				52°	56°
	h m	° ′	h m	h m	h m
1	21 16.6	−16 31	12 33	9 22	9 52
11	21 18.9	−16 21	11 56	8 44	9 13
21	21 21.2	−16 10	11 19	8 06	8 34
31	21 23.4	−16 00	10 41	7 27	7 55

Diameter 4″

NEPTUNE

Day	RA	Dec.	Transit	10° high	
				52°	56°
	h m	° ′	h m	h m	h m
1	20 26.4	−18 57	11 42	8 53	9 30
11	20 28.0	−18 52	11 05	8 14	8 51
21	20 29.4	−18 47	10 27	7 36	8 12
31	20 30.8	−18 42	9 49	6 57	7 33

Diameter 2″

March 2000 ♈

THIRD MONTH, 31 DAYS. *Mars,* Roman god of battle

1	*Wednesday*	St David's Day. Yitzhak Rabin b. 1922	61
2	*Thursday*	Cardinal Basil Hume b. 1923. Lord Lloyd Webber b. 1948	62
3	*Friday*	James Michener b. 1907. Joe DiMaggio d. 1999	63
4	*Saturday*	Forth Railway Bridge opened 1890. Patrick Moore b. 1923	64
5	*Sunday*	**S. next before Lent.** Sir Rex Harrison b. 1908	65
6	*Monday*	Battle of the Alamo ended 1836. Davy Crockett d. 1836	*week* 10 *day* 66
7	*Tuesday*	Shrove Tuesday. Stanley Kubrick d. 1999	67
8	*Wednesday*	**Ash Wednesday.** William III d. 1702	68
9	*Thursday*	Imogen Holst d. 1984. George Burns d. 1996	69
10	*Friday*	*Earl of Wessex b. 1964.* Sir Charles Groves b. 1915	70
11	*Saturday*	Sir Henry Tate b. 1819. Outbreak of Russian Revolution 1917	71
12	*Sunday*	**1st S. of Lent.** Liza Minnelli b. 1946	72
13	*Monday*	Commonwealth Day. Tsar Alexander II d. 1881	*week* 11 *day* 73
14	*Tuesday*	Johann Strauss (elder) b. 1804. Fred Zinnemann d. 1997	74
15	*Wednesday*	Julius Caesar d. 44 BC. Aristotle Onassis d. 1975	75
16	*Thursday*	Georg Ohm b. 1789. Sir Austen Chamberlain d. 1937	76
17	*Friday*	St Patrick's Day. *Bank Holiday in Northern Ireland*	77
18	*Saturday*	Rudolph Diesel b. 1858. Joan Freeman d. 1998	78
19	*Sunday*	**2nd S. of Lent. St Joseph of Nazareth**	79
20	*Monday*	Sir Isaac Newton d. 1727. Dame Vera Lynn b. 1917	*week* 12 *day* 80
21	*Tuesday*	Ayrton Senna b. 1960. Ernie Wise d. 1999	81
22	*Wednesday*	Thomas Hughes d. 1896. Marcel Marceau b. 1923	82
23	*Thursday*	Princess Eugenie of York b. 1990. Joan Crawford b. 1906	83
24	*Friday*	Elizabeth I d. 1603. Charlotte Yonge d. 1901	84
25	*Saturday*	**The Annunciation.** Treaty of Rome 1957	85
26	*Sunday*	**3rd S. of Lent.** Beethoven d. 1827	86
27	*Monday*	Yuri Gagarin d. 1968. Sir Henry Royce b. 1863	*week* 13 *day* 87
28	*Tuesday*	St Teresa of Ávila b. 1515. Virginia Woolf d. 1941	88
29	*Wednesday*	Sir William Walton b. 1902. Carl Orff d. 1982	89
30	*Thursday*	Sean O'Casey b. 1880. Russia sold Alaska to USA 1867	90
31	*Friday*	John Donne d. 1631. Jesse Owens d. 1980	91

ASTRONOMICAL PHENOMENA

d	h	
1	15	Mercury in inferior conjunction
4	01	Venus in conjunction with Moon. Venus 0.6° N.
5	13	Mercury in conjunction with Moon. Mercury 6° N.
8	17	Mars in conjunction with Moon. Mars 5° N.
9	20	Jupiter in conjunction with Moon. Jupiter 4° N.
10	11	Saturn in conjunction with Moon. Saturn 3° N.
14	21	Mercury at stationary point
15	12	Pluto at stationary point
15	18	Venus in conjunction with Mercury. Venus 2° S.
20	08	Sun's longitude 0° ♈
28	21	Mercury at greatest elongation W.28°

MINIMA OF ALGOL

d	h	d	h	d	h
2	00.9	13	12.2	24	23.5
4	21.8	16	09.0	27	20.3
7	18.6	19	05.9	30	17.1
10	15.4	22	02.7		

CONSTELLATIONS

The following constellations are near the meridian at

	d	h		d	h
February	1	24	March	16	21
February	15	23	April	1	20
March	1	22	April	15	19

Cepheus (below the Pole), Camelopardus, Lynx, Gemini, Cancer, Leo, Canis Minor, Hydra, Monoceros, Canis Major and Puppis

THE MOON

Phases, Apsides and Node	d	h	m
● New Moon	6	05	17
☽ First Quarter	13	06	59
○ Full Moon	20	04	44
☾ Last Quarter	28	00	21
Perigee (369,533 km)	14	23	39
Apogee (404,167 km)	27	17	19

Mean longitude of ascending node on March 1, 122°

THE SUN

s.d. 16′.1

Day	Right Ascension	Dec.	Equation of time	Rise 52°	Rise 56°	Transit	Set 52°	Set 56°	Sidereal time	Transit of First Point of Aries
	h m s	° ′	m s	h m	h m	h m	h m	h m	h m s	h m s
1	22 48 47	− 7 33	−12 22	6 45	6 51	12 12	17 40	17 35	10 36 25	13 21 24
2	22 52 31	− 7 10	−12 10	6 43	6 48	12 12	17 42	17 37	10 40 21	13 17 28
3	22 56 16	− 6 47	−11 58	6 41	6 46	12 12	17 44	17 39	10 44 18	13 13 32
4	22 59 59	− 6 24	−11 45	6 39	6 43	12 12	17 46	17 41	10 48 14	13 09 36
5	23 03 43	− 6 01	−11 32	6 36	6 41	12 11	17 47	17 43	10 52 11	13 05 40
6	23 07 26	− 5 38	−11 18	6 34	6 38	12 11	17 49	17 45	10 56 07	13 01 44
7	23 11 08	− 5 15	−11 04	6 32	6 36	12 11	17 51	17 47	11 00 04	12 57 48
8	23 14 50	− 4 51	−10 50	6 30	6 33	12 11	17 53	17 49	11 04 01	12 53 52
9	23 18 32	− 4 28	−10 35	6 27	6 30	12 10	17 54	17 52	11 07 57	12 49 56
10	23 22 13	− 4 04	−10 19	6 25	6 28	12 10	17 56	17 54	11 11 54	12 46 01
11	23 25 54	− 3 41	−10 04	6 23	6 25	12 10	17 58	17 56	11 15 50	12 42 05
12	23 29 35	− 3 17	− 9 48	6 21	6 23	12 10	18 00	17 58	11 19 47	12 38 09
13	23 33 15	− 2 53	− 9 32	6 18	6 20	12 09	18 01	18 00	11 23 43	12 34 13
14	23 36 55	− 2 30	− 9 15	6 16	6 17	12 09	18 03	18 02	11 27 40	12 30 17
15	23 40 35	− 2 06	− 8 59	6 14	6 15	12 09	18 05	18 04	11 31 36	12 26 21
16	23 44 15	− 1 42	− 8 42	6 11	6 12	12 09	18 07	18 06	11 35 33	12 22 25
17	23 47 54	− 1 19	− 8 24	6 09	6 10	12 08	18 08	18 08	11 39 30	12 18 29
18	23 51 33	− 0 55	− 8 07	6 07	6 07	12 08	18 10	18 10	11 43 26	12 14 33
19	23 55 12	− 0 31	− 7 49	6 04	6 04	12 08	18 12	18 12	11 47 23	12 10 37
20	23 58 51	− 0 08	− 7 32	6 02	6 02	12 07	18 14	18 14	11 51 19	12 06 41
21	0 02 29	+ 0 16	− 7 14	6 00	5 59	12 07	18 15	18 16	11 55 16	12 02 46
22	0 06 08	+ 0 40	− 6 56	5 58	5 56	12 07	18 17	18 18	11 59 12	11 58 50
23	0 09 46	+ 1 04	− 6 37	5 55	5 54	12 06	18 19	18 20	12 03 09	11 54 54
24	0 13 25	+ 1 27	− 6 19	5 53	5 51	12 06	18 20	18 22	12 07 05	11 50 58
25	0 17 03	+ 1 51	− 6 01	5 51	5 48	12 06	18 22	18 25	12 11 02	11 47 02
26	0 20 41	+ 2 14	− 5 43	5 48	5 46	12 06	18 24	18 27	12 14 58	11 43 06
27	0 24 20	+ 2 38	− 5 25	5 46	5 43	12 05	18 26	18 29	12 18 55	11 39 10
28	0 27 58	+ 3 01	− 5 07	5 44	5 41	12 05	18 27	18 31	12 22 52	11 35 14
29	0 31 37	+ 3 25	− 4 48	5 41	5 38	12 05	18 29	18 33	12 26 48	11 31 18
30	0 35 15	+ 3 48	− 4 30	5 39	5 35	12 04	18 31	18 35	12 30 45	11 27 22
31	0 38 54	+ 4 11	− 4 13	5 37	5 33	12 04	18 32	18 37	12 34 41	11 23 26

DURATION OF TWILIGHT (in minutes)

Latitude	52°	56°	52°	56°	52°	56°	52°	56°
	1 March		11 March		21 March		31 March	
Civil	34	38	34	37	34	37	34	38
Nautical	73	81	73	80	74	82	76	84
Astronomical	112	124	113	125	116	129	120	136

THE NIGHT SKY

Mercury is too close to the Sun for observation, inferior conjunction occurring on the 1st.

Venus, magnitude −3.9, is a brilliant morning object at first, but only visible low in the east-south-eastern sky for a short time before dawn. On the morning of the 4th the old crescent Moon is in the vicinity of the planet, but this will be a very difficult observation to make as Venus is only about 5° above the horizon at sunrise. Thereafter the planet is too close to the Sun for observation.

Mars continues to be visible in the south-western sky in the early evenings, until about 2000 hours. The crescent Moon will be seen passing about 5° south of the planet on the evening of the 8th. Mars, magnitude +1.4, is in the constellation of Pisces.

Jupiter, magnitude −2.1, is still visible for a short time in the south-western sky after sunset.

Saturn is still an evening object in the western sky but moving closer to the Sun and only visible for a short time after sunset. Its magnitude is +0.3. The thin crescent Moon, only three days old, is near the planet on the evening of the 10th. By the end of the month Jupiter is only about 6° west of Saturn and, although nearer to the Sun, may be used as a guide to Saturn, which is over 2 magnitudes fainter.

Zodiacal Light. The evening cone may be observed, stretching up from the western horizon, along the ecliptic, after the end of twilight, from the beginning of the month up to the 7th, and again after the 22nd.

THE MOON

Day	RA	Dec.	Hor. par.	Semi-diam.	Sun's co-long.	PA of Bright Limb	Phase	Age	Rise 52°	Rise 56°	Transit	Set 52°	Set 56°
	h m	°	′	′	°	°	%	d	h m	h m	h m	h m	h m
1	18 49	−21.0	54.3	14.8	211	86	25	24.5	4 20	4 41	8 29	12 40	12 18
2	19 40	−20.5	54.6	14.9	224	81	17	25.5	5 04	5 24	9 18	13 36	13 16
3	20 31	−19.1	54.9	15.0	236	76	10	26.5	5 41	5 59	10 07	14 38	14 21
4	21 22	−16.8	55.4	15.1	248	69	5	27.5	6 13	6 28	10 55	15 45	15 31
5	22 13	−13.6	55.9	15.2	260	60	2	28.5	6 41	6 52	11 43	16 55	16 45
6	23 03	− 9.7	56.5	15.4	272	16	0	29.5	7 05	7 12	12 31	18 07	18 02
7	23 53	− 5.3	57.0	15.5	285	270	1	0.8	7 27	7 31	13 18	19 21	19 20
8	0 42	− 0.6	57.5	15.7	297	259	4	1.8	7 49	7 48	14 06	20 36	20 39
9	1 33	+ 4.3	58.0	15.8	309	256	9	2.8	8 12	8 07	14 55	21 52	22 00
10	2 25	+ 9.0	58.4	15.9	321	256	16	3.8	8 36	8 27	15 46	23 09	23 21
11	3 19	+13.2	58.7	16.0	333	258	25	4.8	9 05	8 52	16 39	—	—
12	4 15	+16.8	59.0	16.1	346	261	36	5.8	9 39	9 22	17 35	0 26	0 43
13	5 13	+19.4	59.2	16.1	358	266	47	6.8	10 22	10 02	18 32	1 40	2 00
14	6 13	+20.9	59.3	16.2	10	271	58	7.8	11 15	10 53	19 32	2 48	3 10
15	7 14	+21.0	59.3	16.2	22	277	69	8.8	12 18	11 57	20 31	3 47	4 08
16	8 14	+19.8	59.3	16.2	34	283	79	9.8	13 29	13 11	21 28	4 35	4 54
17	9 13	+17.3	59.1	16.1	47	289	88	10.8	14 46	14 31	22 23	5 14	5 30
18	10 10	+13.8	58.8	16.0	59	295	94	11.8	16 03	15 54	23 15	5 46	5 57
19	11 04	+ 9.6	58.4	15.9	71	305	98	12.8	17 20	17 15	—	6 12	6 19
20	11 56	+ 4.9	57.9	15.8	83	353	100	13.8	18 36	18 35	0 05	6 36	6 38
21	12 47	+ 0.1	57.3	15.6	95	88	99	14.8	19 49	19 52	0 53	6 57	6 56
22	13 36	− 4.6	56.6	15.4	107	99	96	15.8	21 01	21 08	1 40	7 19	7 14
23	14 24	− 9.0	56.0	15.2	119	101	91	16.8	22 10	22 22	2 26	7 41	7 32
24	15 13	−12.9	55.4	15.1	132	101	85	17.8	23 17	23 32	3 12	8 05	7 53
25	16 02	−16.2	54.9	15.0	144	98	77	18.8	—	—	3 58	8 33	8 17
26	16 51	−18.7	54.5	14.9	156	95	69	19.8	0 21	0 39	4 45	9 06	8 46
27	17 41	−20.4	54.3	14.8	168	91	60	20.8	1 20	1 41	5 33	9 44	9 23
28	18 32	−21.2	54.3	14.8	180	87	50	21.8	2 13	2 35	6 22	10 30	10 07
29	19 23	−21.0	54.4	14.8	192	82	41	22.8	3 00	3 21	7 10	11 23	11 01
30	20 14	−19.9	54.7	14.9	205	77	32	23.8	3 40	3 59	7 59	12 22	12 03
31	21 04	−17.8	55.2	15.0	217	73	23	24.8	4 13	4 30	8 47	13 27	13 11

MERCURY

Day	RA	Dec.	Diam.	Phase	Transit	5° high 52°	5° high 56°
	h m	°	″	%	h m	h m	h m
1	22 48	− 3.6	11	1	12 08	17 13	17 06
3	22 40	− 4.5	11	1	11 52	6 51	6 58
5	22 33	− 5.5	11	3	11 37	6 41	6 49
7	22 27	− 6.4	11	6	11 24	6 32	6 41
9	22 22	− 7.3	10	10	11 11	6 25	6 35
11	22 19	− 8.2	10	15	11 01	6 18	6 29
13	22 17	− 8.8	10	20	10 51	6 13	6 24
15	22 17	− 9.3	10	24	10 44	6 08	6 20
17	22 19	− 9.7	9	29	10 38	6 04	6 16
19	22 22	− 9.9	9	33	10 33	6 00	6 12
21	22 26	−10.0	9	38	10 30	5 57	6 09
23	22 31	− 9.9	8	41	10 27	5 53	6 06
25	22 37	− 9.7	8	45	10 26	5 50	6 03
27	22 44	− 9.3	8	48	10 25	5 48	5 59
29	22 51	− 8.9	8	52	10 25	5 45	5 56
31	23 00	− 8.3	7	55	10 25	5 42	5 53

VENUS

Day	RA	Dec.	Diam.	Phase	Transit	5° high 52°	5° high 56°
	h m	°	″	%	h m	h m	h m
1	21 09	−17.0	11	90	10 33	6 43	7 04
6	21 34	−15.3	11	91	10 38	6 37	6 55
11	21 58	−13.5	11	92	10 43	6 29	6 45
16	22 22	−11.4	11	93	10 47	6 21	6 35
21	22 45	− 9.3	11	93	10 50	6 12	6 24
26	23 09	− 7.0	11	94	10 54	6 03	6 12
31	23 32	− 4.6	10	95	10 57	5 53	6 01

MARS

Day	RA	Dec.	Diam.	Phase	Transit	5° high 52°	5° high 56°
1	0 51	+ 5.1	4	96	14 13	20 08	20 09
6	1 04	+ 6.6	4	97	14 07	20 10	20 12
11	1 18	+ 8.1	4	97	14 02	20 11	20 15
16	1 32	+ 9.5	4	97	13 56	20 13	20 18
21	1 46	+10.9	4	97	13 50	20 14	20 20
26	2 00	+12.2	4	98	13 44	20 16	20 23
31	2 14	+13.5	4	98	13 39	20 17	20 25

SUNRISE AND SUNSET

	London		Bristol		Birmingham		Manchester		Newcastle		Glasgow		Belfast	
	0°05′	51°30′	2°35′	51°28′	1°55′	52°28′	2°15′	53°28′	1°37′	54°59′	4°14′	55°52′	5°56′	54°35′
	h m	h m	h m	h m	h m	h m	h m	h m	h m	h m	h m	h m	h m	h m
1	6 45	17 41	6 55	17 51	6 54	17 47	6 56	17 47	6 56	17 43	7 08	17 52	7 12	18 01
2	6 43	17 43	6 53	17 53	6 51	17 49	6 54	17 49	6 53	17 45	7 05	17 54	7 10	18 03
3	6 41	17 45	6 51	17 55	6 49	17 51	6 52	17 51	6 51	17 47	7 03	17 56	7 08	18 05
4	6 38	17 46	6 48	17 56	6 47	17 53	6 49	17 53	6 48	17 49	7 00	17 58	7 05	18 07
5	6 36	17 48	6 46	17 58	6 45	17 55	6 47	17 55	6 46	17 51	6 57	18 00	7 03	18 09
6	6 34	17 50	6 44	18 00	6 42	17 56	6 45	17 57	6 44	17 53	6 55	18 02	7 00	18 10
7	6 32	17 52	6 42	18 02	6 40	17 58	6 42	17 59	6 41	17 55	6 52	18 04	6 58	18 12
8	6 30	17 53	6 40	18 03	6 38	18 00	6 40	18 01	6 39	17 57	6 50	18 07	6 55	18 14
9	6 27	17 55	6 37	18 05	6 35	18 02	6 37	18 02	6 36	17 59	6 47	18 09	6 53	18 16
10	6 25	17 57	6 35	18 07	6 33	18 04	6 35	18 04	6 34	18 01	6 45	18 11	6 51	18 18
11	6 23	17 59	6 33	18 09	6 31	18 05	6 33	18 06	6 31	18 03	6 42	18 13	6 48	18 20
12	6 21	18 00	6 31	18 10	6 28	18 07	6 30	18 08	6 29	18 05	6 39	18 15	6 46	18 22
13	6 18	18 02	6 28	18 12	6 26	18 09	6 28	18 10	6 26	18 07	6 37	18 17	6 43	18 24
14	6 16	18 04	6 26	18 14	6 24	18 11	6 25	18 12	6 23	18 09	6 34	18 19	6 41	18 26
15	6 14	18 05	6 24	18 15	6 21	18 13	6 23	18 14	6 21	18 11	6 32	18 21	6 38	18 28
16	6 12	18 07	6 22	18 17	6 19	18 14	6 21	18 15	6 18	18 13	6 29	18 23	6 36	18 30
17	6 09	18 09	6 19	18 19	6 17	18 16	6 18	18 17	6 16	18 15	6 26	18 25	6 33	18 32
18	6 07	18 10	6 17	18 20	6 14	18 18	6 16	18 19	6 13	18 17	6 24	18 27	6 31	18 34
19	6 05	18 12	6 15	18 22	6 12	18 20	6 13	18 21	6 11	18 19	6 21	18 29	6 28	18 36
20	6 03	18 14	6 13	18 24	6 10	18 21	6 11	18 23	6 08	18 21	6 19	18 31	6 26	18 38
21	6 00	18 16	6 10	18 26	6 07	18 23	6 09	18 25	6 06	18 23	6 16	18 33	6 23	18 40
22	5 58	18 17	6 08	18 27	6 05	18 25	6 06	18 27	6 03	18 24	6 13	18 35	6 21	18 42
23	5 56	18 19	6 06	18 29	6 03	18 27	6 04	18 28	6 01	18 26	6 11	18 37	6 18	18 44
24	5 53	18 21	6 03	18 31	6 00	18 28	6 01	18 30	5 58	18 28	6 08	18 39	6 15	18 45
25	5 51	18 22	6 01	18 32	5 58	18 30	5 59	18 32	5 55	18 30	6 05	18 41	6 13	18 47
26	5 49	18 24	5 59	18 34	5 56	18 32	5 56	18 34	5 53	18 32	6 03	18 43	6 10	18 49
27	5 47	18 26	5 57	18 36	5 53	18 34	5 54	18 36	5 50	18 34	6 00	18 45	6 08	18 51
28	5 44	18 27	5 54	18 37	5 51	18 35	5 52	18 37	5 48	18 36	5 58	18 47	6 05	18 53
29	5 42	18 29	5 52	18 39	5 49	18 37	5 49	18 39	5 45	18 38	5 55	18 49	6 03	18 55
30	5 40	18 31	5 50	18 41	5 46	18 39	5 47	18 41	5 43	18 40	5 52	18 52	6 00	18 57
31	5 37	18 32	5 47	18 42	5 44	18 41	5 44	18 43	5 40	18 42	5 50	18 54	5 58	18 59

JUPITER

Day	RA	Dec.	Transit	5° high	
				52°	56°
	h m	° ′	h m	h m	h m
1	2 03.3	+11 27	15 25	21 51	21 57
11	2 10.8	+12 09	14 53	21 23	21 29
21	2 18.9	+12 52	14 22	20 55	21 03
31	2 27.5	+13 36	13 51	20 28	20 36

Diameters – equatorial 35″ polar 32″

SATURN

Day	RA	Dec.	Transit	5° high	
				52°	56°
	h m	° ′	h m	h m	h m
1	2 42.6	+13 30	16 04	22 40	22 48
11	2 46.0	+13 48	15 28	22 06	22 14
21	2 49.9	+14 08	14 52	21 32	21 41
31	2 54.2	+14 28	14 17	20 59	21 08

Diameters – equatorial 17″ polar 15″
Rings – major axis 38″ minor axis 13″

URANUS

Day	RA	Dec.	Transit	10° high	
				52°	56°
	h m	° ′	h m	h m	h m
1	21 23.2	−16 01	10 45	7 31	7 59
11	21 25.3	−15 51	10 08	6 53	7 21
21	21 27.3	−15 42	9 30	6 14	6 42
31	21 29.0	−15 34	8 53	5 35	6 03

Diameter 4″

NEPTUNE

Day	RA	Dec.	Transit	10° high	
				52°	56°
	h m	° ′	h m	h m	h m
1	20 30.7	−18 42	9 53	7 01	7 37
11	20 31.9	−18 38	9 15	6 22	6 58
21	20 33.0	−18 34	8 36	5 44	6 19
31	20 34.0	−18 31	7 58	5 05	5 40

Diameter 2″

April 2000

FOURTH MONTH, 30 DAYS. *Aperire*, to open; Earth opens to receive seed

1	*Saturday*	Robert III d. 1406. Royal Air Force formed 1918	92
2	*Sunday*	**4th S. of Lent.** Mothering Sunday	93
3	*Monday*	Johannes Brahms d. 1897. Doris Day b. 1924	*week 14 day* 94
4	*Tuesday*	Edgar Wallace b. 1875. Sir Cuthbert Whitaker d. 1950	95
5	*Wednesday*	HINDU NEW YEAR. Howard Hughes d. 1976	96
6	*Thursday*	MUSLIM NEW YEAR. Richard I d. 1199	97
7	*Friday*	St Francis Xavier b. 1506. Jim Clark d. 1968	98
8	*Saturday*	Mary Pickford b. 1893. Pablo Picasso d. 1973	99
9	*Sunday*	**5th S. of Lent.** Sir Francis Bacon d. 1626	100
10	*Monday*	Battle of Toulouse 1814. General William Booth b. 1829	*week 15 day* 101
11	*Tuesday*	Sir Charles Hallé b. 1819. Josephine Baker d. 1975	102
12	*Wednesday*	Joe Louis d. 1981. Sugar Ray Robinson d. 1989	103
13	*Thursday*	SIKH NEW YEAR. Seamus Heaney b. 1939	104
14	*Friday*	Arnold Toynbee b. 1889. Dorothy Squires d. 1998	105
15	*Saturday*	*Titanic* sank 1912. John Curry d. 1994	106
16	*Sunday*	**Palm Sunday.** Wilbur Wright b. 1867	107
17	*Monday*	Nikita Krushchev b. 1894. Clare Francis b. 1946	*week 16 day* 108
18	*Tuesday*	Leopold Stokowski b. 1882. Albert Einstein d. 1955	109
19	*Wednesday*	*Hilary Law Sittings end.* Charles Darwin d. 1882	110
20	*Thursday*	**Maundy Thursday.** PASSOVER begins	111
21	*Friday*	**Good Friday.** *Bank Holiday in UK. Queen Elizabeth II b. 1926*	112
22	*Saturday*	Easter Eve. Immanuel Kant b. 1724	113
23	*Sunday*	**Easter Day** (Western churches). **St George**	114
24	*Monday*	*Bank Holiday in England, Wales and Northern Ireland*	*week 17 day* 115
25	*Tuesday*	Tchaikovsky b. 1840. Anna Sewell d. 1878	116
26	*Wednesday*	**St Mark.** Jill Dando d. 1999	117
27	*Thursday*	Ferdinand Magellan d. 1521. Cecil Day-Lewis b. 1904	118
28	*Friday*	Ferruccio Lamborghini b. 1916. Richard Hughes d. 1976	119
29	*Saturday*	Frank Auerbach b. 1931. Sir Alfred Hitchcock d. 1980	120
30	*Sunday*	**2nd S. of Easter.** EASTER DAY (Eastern Orthodox)	121

ASTRONOMICAL PHENOMENA

d h
2 14 Mercury in conjunction with Moon. Mercury 2° N.
3 08 Venus in conjunction with Moon. Venus 3° N.
6 07 Jupiter in conjunction with Mars. Jupiter 1° S.
6 13 Jupiter in conjunction with Moon. Jupiter 4° N.
6 13 Mars in conjunction with Moon. Mars 5° N.
6 23 Saturn in conjunction with Moon. Saturn 3° N.
15 20 Saturn in conjunction with Mars. Saturn 2° S.
19 19 Sun's longitude 30° ♉
28 13 Venus in conjunction with Mercury. Venus 0.3° N.

MINIMA OF ALGOL

d	h	d	h	d	h
2	14.0	14	01.2	25	12.5
5	10.8	16	22.1	28	09.3
8	07.6	19	18.9		
11	04.4	22	15.7		

CONSTELLATIONS

The following constellations are near the meridian at

	d	h		d	h
March	1	24	April	15	21
March	16	23	May	1	20
April	1	22	May	16	19

Cepheus (below the Pole), Cassiopeia (below the Pole), Ursa Major, Leo Minor, Leo, Sextans, Hydra and Crater

THE MOON

Phases, Apsides and Node

	d	h	m
● New Moon	4	18	12
☽ First Quarter	11	13	30
○ Full Moon	18	17	41
☾ Last Quarter	26	19	30
Perigee (368,258 km)	8	22	06
Apogee (404,558 km)	24	12	25

Mean longitude of ascending node on April 1, 120°

THE SUN   s.d. 16′.0

Day	Right Ascension	Dec. +	Equation of time	Rise 52°	Rise 56°	Transit	Set 52°	Set 56°	Sidereal time	Transit of First Point of Aries
	h m s	° ′	m s	h m	h m	h m	h m	h m	h m s	h m s
1	0 42 32	4 34	− 3 55	5 34	5 30	12 04	18 34	18 39	12 38 38	11 19 31
2	0 46 11	4 58	− 3 37	5 32	5 27	12 03	18 36	18 41	12 42 34	11 15 35
3	0 49 50	5 21	− 3 19	5 30	5 25	12 03	18 38	18 43	12 46 31	11 11 39
4	0 53 29	5 44	− 3 02	5 28	5 22	12 03	18 39	18 45	12 50 27	11 07 43
5	0 57 09	6 06	− 2 45	5 25	5 20	12 03	18 41	18 47	12 54 24	11 03 47
6	1 00 48	6 29	− 2 27	5 23	5 17	12 02	18 43	18 49	12 58 21	10 59 51
7	1 04 28	6 52	− 2 11	5 21	5 14	12 02	18 44	18 51	13 02 17	10 55 55
8	1 08 08	7 14	− 1 54	5 18	5 12	12 02	18 46	18 53	13 06 14	10 51 59
9	1 11 48	7 37	− 1 37	5 16	5 09	12 01	18 48	18 55	13 10 10	10 48 03
10	1 15 28	7 59	− 1 21	5 14	5 07	12 01	18 50	18 57	13 14 07	10 44 07
11	1 19 09	8 21	− 1 05	5 12	5 04	12 01	18 51	18 59	13 18 03	10 40 12
12	1 22 50	8 43	− 0 50	5 09	5 02	12 01	18 53	19 01	13 22 00	10 36 16
13	1 26 31	9 05	− 0 34	5 07	4 59	12 00	18 55	19 03	13 25 56	10 32 20
14	1 30 12	9 26	− 0 19	5 05	4 56	12 00	18 56	19 05	13 29 53	10 28 24
15	1 33 54	9 48	− 0 04	5 03	4 54	12 00	18 58	19 07	13 33 50	10 24 28
16	1 37 36	10 09	+ 0 10	5 01	4 51	12 00	19 00	19 09	13 37 46	10 20 32
17	1 41 18	10 30	+ 0 24	4 59	4 49	11 59	19 02	19 11	13 41 43	10 16 36
18	1 45 01	10 51	+ 0 38	4 56	4 46	11 59	19 03	19 13	13 45 39	10 12 40
19	1 48 45	11 12	+ 0 51	4 54	4 44	11 59	19 05	19 15	13 49 36	10 08 44
20	1 52 28	11 33	+ 1 04	4 52	4 42	11 59	19 07	19 18	13 53 32	10 04 48
21	1 56 12	11 53	+ 1 17	4 50	4 39	11 59	19 08	19 20	13 57 29	10 00 52
22	1 59 57	12 14	+ 1 29	4 48	4 37	11 58	19 10	19 22	14 01 25	9 56 57
23	2 03 42	12 34	+ 1 40	4 46	4 34	11 58	19 12	19 24	14 05 22	9 53 01
24	2 07 27	12 53	+ 1 51	4 44	4 32	11 58	19 13	19 26	14 09 19	9 49 05
25	2 11 13	13 13	+ 2 02	4 42	4 29	11 58	19 15	19 28	14 13 15	9 45 09
26	2 15 00	13 32	+ 2 12	4 40	4 27	11 58	19 17	19 30	14 17 12	9 41 13
27	2 18 47	13 52	+ 2 21	4 38	4 25	11 58	19 19	19 32	14 21 08	9 37 17
28	2 22 34	14 11	+ 2 31	4 36	4 22	11 57	19 20	19 34	14 25 05	9 33 21
29	2 26 22	14 29	+ 2 39	4 34	4 20	11 57	19 22	19 36	14 29 01	9 29 25
30	2 30 11	14 48	+ 2 47	4 32	4 18	11 57	19 24	19 38	14 32 58	9 25 29

DURATION OF TWILIGHT (in minutes)

Latitude	52°	56°	52°	56°	52°	56°	52°	56°
	1 April		11 April		21 April		30 April	
Civil	34	38	35	40	37	42	39	44
Nautical	76	85	79	90	84	96	89	105
Astronomical	121	137	128	148	138	167	152	200

THE NIGHT SKY

Mercury is unsuitably placed for observation throughout April.

Venus is unsuitably placed for observation throughout April.

Mars, magnitude +1.5, is visible for a short time, low above the western horizon in the evenings. It is coming towards the end of its evening apparition and will be lost in the lengthening evening twilight before the end of the month.

Jupiter is an evening object, magnitude −2.0, visible for a short time, low in the western sky shortly after sunset, for the first half of the month. Jupiter passes within 1° of Mars on the 5th to 6th, and could be a useful guide to locating the fainter planet. On the evening of the 5th Mars is 1.0° to the right of and 0.3° higher than Jupiter, while on the following evening Mars is 0.8° to the right and 0.8° higher than Jupiter. During these two evenings Saturn may be seen about 4° to the left and 4° above Jupiter, given good conditions. On the 6th the crescent Moon, only two days old, may be seen about 4° below and 1° to the left of Saturn. After Jupiter has disappeared from view no naked-eye planet is visible during the hours of darkness until about the last week of May.

Saturn, magnitude +0.3, is disappearing into the lengthening evening twilight in the west, and is unlikely to be seen with the naked eye after the first few days of the month. However, it may be possible to detect it with binoculars for a little longer as it remains about 4° or 5° above and to the left of Jupiter for some time.

THE MOON

Day	RA	Dec.	Hor. par.	Semi-diam.	Sun's co-long.	PA of Bright Limb	Phase	Age	Rise 52°	Rise 56°	Transit	Set 52°	Set 56°
	h m	°	'	'	°	°	%	d	h m	h m	h m	h m	h m
1	21 55	−14.9	55.7	15.2	229	68	15	25.8	4 42	4 55	9 35	14 36	14 24
2	22 45	−11.3	56.4	15.4	241	63	9	26.8	5 07	5 16	10 22	15 48	15 40
3	23 35	− 7.0	57.1	15.6	254	57	4	27.8	5 30	5 35	11 10	17 02	16 58
4	0 25	− 2.2	57.8	15.7	266	42	1	28.8	5 52	5 53	11 58	18 18	18 19
5	1 16	+ 2.7	58.4	15.9	278	305	0	0.2	6 14	6 11	12 47	19 35	19 41
6	2 09	+ 7.7	58.9	16.1	290	267	2	1.2	6 38	6 31	13 39	20 55	21 05
7	3 03	+12.3	59.3	16.1	302	262	7	2.2	7 06	6 54	14 33	22 14	22 29
8	4 00	+16.2	59.5	16.2	315	263	13	3.2	7 39	7 22	15 29	23 32	23 51
9	4 59	+19.1	59.5	16.2	327	266	22	4.2	8 19	7 59	16 27	—	—
10	5 59	+20.9	59.5	16.2	339	271	33	5.2	9 09	8 47	17 27	0 43	1 05
11	7 00	+21.3	59.3	16.2	351	276	44	6.2	10 09	9 47	18 26	1 45	2 07
12	8 01	+20.4	59.0	16.1	3	282	55	7.2	11 18	10 58	19 23	2 36	2 56
13	8 59	+18.2	58.7	16.0	16	287	66	8.2	12 32	12 16	20 18	3 17	3 33
14	9 55	+15.0	58.4	15.9	28	291	76	9.2	13 48	13 36	21 09	3 49	4 02
15	10 49	+11.0	57.9	15.8	40	295	85	10.2	15 04	14 57	21 59	4 16	4 25
16	11 41	+ 6.5	57.5	15.7	52	299	92	11.2	16 18	16 16	22 46	4 40	4 44
17	12 30	+ 1.7	57.0	15.5	64	305	97	12.2	17 31	17 33	23 33	5 01	5 02
18	13 19	− 3.0	56.5	15.4	77	321	99	13.2	18 43	18 49	—	5 22	5 18
19	14 08	− 7.6	56.0	15.3	89	52	100	14.2	19 54	20 04	0 19	5 43	5 36
20	14 56	−11.7	55.5	15.1	101	89	98	15.2	21 02	21 16	1 04	6 06	5 55
21	15 45	−15.3	55.0	15.0	113	94	95	16.2	22 08	22 26	1 51	6 32	6 17
22	16 34	−18.2	54.7	14.9	125	93	90	17.2	23 10	23 31	2 38	7 02	6 44
23	17 25	−20.2	54.4	14.8	137	91	83	18.2	—	—	3 26	7 38	7 17
24	18 15	−21.3	54.2	14.8	150	87	76	19.2	0 06	0 29	4 14	8 21	7 58
25	19 06	−21.4	54.2	14.8	162	83	67	20.2	0 56	1 18	5 03	9 11	8 48
26	19 57	−20.6	54.4	14.8	174	79	58	21.2	1 38	1 59	5 51	10 07	9 47
27	20 47	−18.9	54.7	14.9	186	75	48	22.2	2 14	2 32	6 39	11 10	10 52
28	21 37	−16.3	55.2	15.0	198	71	39	23.2	2 44	2 58	7 26	12 16	12 02
29	22 26	−12.9	55.9	15.2	211	67	29	24.2	3 10	3 20	8 13	13 26	13 16
30	23 16	− 8.9	56.6	15.4	223	64	20	25.2	3 33	3 40	9 00	14 38	14 33

MERCURY

Day	RA	Dec.	Diam.	Phase	Transit	5° high 52°	5° high 56°
	h m	°	"	%	h m	h m	h m
1	23 04	− 8.0	7	56	10 26	5 40	5 51
3	23 13	− 7.3	7	59	10 27	5 38	5 47
5	23 22	− 6.5	7	61	10 28	5 35	5 43
7	23 32	− 5.6	7	64	10 30	5 32	5 40
9	23 42	− 4.6	6	66	10 33	5 29	5 36
11	23 53	− 3.5	6	69	10 36	5 26	5 32
13	0 04	− 2.4	6	71	10 39	5 23	5 28
15	0 15	− 1.1	6	74	10 42	5 20	5 24
17	0 27	+ 0.2	6	76	10 46	5 17	5 20
19	0 39	+ 1.5	6	79	10 50	5 14	5 16
21	0 51	+ 3.0	6	81	10 55	5 11	5 12
23	1 04	+ 4.4	5	84	11 00	5 08	5 08
25	1 17	+ 6.0	5	87	11 05	5 06	5 04
27	1 31	+ 7.6	5	89	11 11	5 03	5 00
29	1 45	+ 9.2	5	92	11 18	5 01	4 57
31	2 00	+10.8	5	94	11 25	5 00	4 54

VENUS

Day	RA	Dec.	Diam.	Phase	Transit	5° high 52°	5° high 56°
	h m	°	"	%	h m	h m	h m
1	23 36	− 4.2	10	95	10 58	5 51	5 58
6	23 59	− 1.8	10	96	11 01	5 42	5 46
11	0 22	+ 0.7	10	96	11 04	5 32	5 35
16	0 44	+ 3.1	10	97	11 07	5 22	5 23
21	1 07	+ 5.5	10	97	11 10	5 13	5 12
26	1 30	+ 7.9	10	98	11 13	5 04	5 01
31	1 53	+10.2	10	98	11 16	4 56	4 51

MARS

Day	RA	Dec.	Diam.	Phase	Transit	5° high 52°	5° high 56°
1	2 17	+13.8	4	98	13 37	20 17	20 25
6	2 31	+15.0	4	98	13 32	20 18	20 27
11	2 45	+16.2	4	98	13 26	20 19	20 29
16	2 59	+17.2	4	99	13 21	20 19	20 31
21	3 14	+18.3	4	99	13 16	20 20	20 32
26	3 28	+19.2	4	99	13 10	20 20	20 34
31	3 43	+20.1	4	99	13 05	20 20	20 34

SUNRISE AND SUNSET

	London 0°05′ 51°30′		Bristol 2°35′ 51°28′		Birmingham 1°55′ 52°28′		Manchester 2°15′ 53°28′		Newcastle 1°37′ 54°59′		Glasgow 4°14′ 55°52′		Belfast 5°56′ 54°35′	
	h m	h m	h m	h m	h m	h m	h m	h m	h m	h m	h m	h m	h m	h m
1	5 35	18 34	5 45	18 44	5 42	18 42	5 42	18 45	5 38	18 44	5 47	18 56	5 55	19 01
2	5 33	18 36	5 43	18 46	5 39	18 44	5 39	18 47	5 35	18 46	5 44	18 58	5 53	19 03
3	5 31	18 37	5 41	18 47	5 37	18 46	5 37	18 48	5 33	18 48	5 42	19 00	5 50	19 05
4	5 28	18 39	5 38	18 49	5 35	18 48	5 35	18 50	5 30	18 50	5 39	19 02	5 48	19 07
5	5 26	18 41	5 36	18 51	5 32	18 49	5 32	18 52	5 28	18 52	5 37	19 04	5 45	19 08
6	5 24	18 42	5 34	18 52	5 30	18 51	5 30	18 54	5 25	18 54	5 34	19 06	5 43	19 10
7	5 22	18 44	5 32	18 54	5 28	18 53	5 28	18 56	5 23	18 56	5 32	19 08	5 40	19 12
8	5 20	18 46	5 30	18 56	5 25	18 55	5 25	18 58	5 20	18 58	5 29	19 10	5 38	19 14
9	5 17	18 47	5 27	18 57	5 23	18 56	5 23	18 59	5 18	19 00	5 26	19 12	5 36	19 16
10	5 15	18 49	5 25	18 59	5 21	18 58	5 20	19 01	5 15	19 02	5 24	19 14	5 33	19 18
11	5 13	18 51	5 23	19 01	5 19	19 00	5 18	19 03	5 13	19 03	5 21	19 16	5 31	19 20
12	5 11	18 52	5 21	19 02	5 16	19 02	5 16	19 05	5 10	19 05	5 19	19 18	5 28	19 22
13	5 09	18 54	5 19	19 04	5 14	19 03	5 13	19 07	5 08	19 07	5 16	19 20	5 26	19 24
14	5 06	18 56	5 16	19 06	5 12	19 05	5 11	19 08	5 05	19 09	5 14	19 22	5 23	19 26
15	5 04	18 57	5 14	19 07	5 10	19 07	5 09	19 10	5 03	19 11	5 11	19 24	5 21	19 28
16	5 02	18 59	5 12	19 09	5 07	19 09	5 07	19 12	5 00	19 13	5 09	19 26	5 19	19 30
17	5 00	19 01	5 10	19 11	5 05	19 10	5 04	19 14	4 58	19 15	5 06	19 28	5 16	19 31
18	4 58	19 02	5 08	19 12	5 03	19 12	5 02	19 16	4 56	19 17	5 04	19 30	5 14	19 33
19	4 56	19 04	5 06	19 14	5 01	19 14	5 00	19 18	4 53	19 19	5 01	19 32	5 12	19 35
20	4 54	19 06	5 04	19 16	4 59	19 15	4 57	19 19	4 51	19 21	4 59	19 34	5 09	19 37
21	4 52	19 07	5 02	19 17	4 57	19 17	4 55	19 21	4 49	19 23	4 56	19 36	5 07	19 39
22	4 49	19 09	5 00	19 19	4 54	19 19	4 53	19 23	4 46	19 25	4 54	19 38	5 05	19 41
23	4 47	19 11	4 58	19 21	4 52	19 21	4 51	19 25	4 44	19 27	4 52	19 40	5 02	19 43
24	4 45	19 12	4 56	19 22	4 50	19 22	4 49	19 27	4 42	19 29	4 49	19 42	5 00	19 45
25	4 43	19 14	4 54	19 24	4 48	19 24	4 47	19 28	4 39	19 31	4 47	19 44	4 58	19 47
26	4 41	19 16	4 52	19 26	4 46	19 26	4 44	19 30	4 37	19 33	4 44	19 46	4 56	19 49
27	4 39	19 17	4 50	19 27	4 44	19 28	4 42	19 32	4 35	19 35	4 42	19 48	4 53	19 51
28	4 38	19 19	4 48	19 29	4 42	19 29	4 40	19 34	4 33	19 37	4 40	19 50	4 51	19 52
29	4 36	19 21	4 46	19 31	4 40	19 31	4 38	19 36	4 30	19 38	4 38	19 52	4 49	19 54
30	4 34	19 22	4 44	19 32	4 38	19 33	4 36	19 37	4 28	19 40	4 35	19 54	4 47	19 56

JUPITER

Day	RA	Dec.	Transit	5° high	
				52°	56°
	h m	° ′	h m	h m	h m
1	2 28.3	+13 41	13 48	20 26	20 34
11	2 37.3	+14 25	13 18	19 59	20 08
21	2 46.5	+15 08	12 47	19 33	19 42
31	2 55.9	+15 50	12 17	19 07	19 17

Diameters – equatorial 33″ polar 31″

SATURN

Day	RA	Dec.	Transit	5° high	
				52°	56°
	h m	° ′	h m	h m	h m
1	2 54.6	+14 30	14 14	20 56	21 05
11	2 59.3	+14 52	13 39	20 23	20 32
21	3 04.1	+15 14	13 05	19 50	20 00
31	3 09.2	+15 35	12 30	19 18	19 28

Diameters – equatorial 16″ polar 15″
Rings – major axis 37″ minor axis 14″

URANUS

Day	RA	Dec.	Transit	10° high	
				52°	56°
	h m	° ′	h m	h m	h m
1	21 29.2	−15 33	8 49	5 32	5 59
11	21 30.7	−15 27	8 11	4 53	5 20
21	21 31.9	−15 21	7 33	4 14	4 41
31	21 32.8	−15 17	6 55	3 35	4 02

Diameter 4″

NEPTUNE

Day	RA	Dec.	Transit	10° high	
				52°	56°
	h m	° ′	h m	h m	h m
1	20 34.1	−18 30	7 54	5 01	5 36
11	20 34.8	−18 28	7 16	4 22	4 57
21	20 35.3	−18 26	6 37	3 43	4 18
31	20 35.6	−18 25	5 58	3 04	3 39

Diameter 2″

May 2000

FIFTH MONTH, 31 DAYS. *Maia,* goddess of growth and increase

1	*Monday*	**SS Philip and James.** *Bank Holiday in UK*	*week* 18 *day* 122
2	*Tuesday*	*Easter Law Sittings begin.* Dr Benjamin Spock b. 1903	123
3	*Wednesday*	Thomas Hood d. 1845. Golda Meir b. 1898	124
4	*Thursday*	Joseph Whitaker b. 1820. Sir Osbert Sitwell d. 1969	125
5	*Friday*	Søren Kierkegaard b. 1813. Karl Marx b. 1818	126
6	*Saturday*	Tony Blair b. 1953. Sigmund Freud b. 1856	127
7	*Sunday*	**3rd S. of Easter.** Johannes Brahms b. 1833	128
8	*Monday*	Antoine-Laurent Lavoisier d. 1794. Sir David Attenborough b. 1926	*week* 19 *day* 129
9	*Tuesday*	Europe Day. Channel Islands liberated 1945	130
10	*Wednesday*	Louis XV d. 1774. Karl Barth b. 1886	131
11	*Thursday*	Battle of Fontenoy 1745. Sir John Herschel d. 1871	132
12	*Friday*	Florence Nightingale b. 1820. Sir Alfred Beit d. 1894	133
13	*Saturday*	United Presbyterian Church of Scotland formed 1847	134
14	*Sunday*	**4th S. of Easter. St Matthias**	135
15	*Monday*	Edwin Muir b. 1887. Joseph Whitaker d. 1895	*week* 20 *day* 136
16	*Tuesday*	H. E. Bates b. 1905. Sammy Davis Jnr d. 1990	137
17	*Wednesday*	Edward Jenner b. 1749. Paul Dukas d. 1935	138
18	*Thursday*	Dame Margot Fonteyn b. 1919. Pope John Paul II b. 1920	139
19	*Friday*	William Gladstone d. 1898. Dr Edward de Bono b. 1933	140
20	*Saturday*	John Stuart Mill b. 1806. Gilbert Murray d. 1957	141
21	*Sunday*	**5th S. of Easter.** Christopher Columbus d. 1506	142
22	*Monday*	Sir Arthur Conan Doyle b. 1859. Lord Olivier b. 1907	*week* 21 *day* 143
23	*Tuesday*	Sir Samuel Curran b. 1912. Herbert Austin d. 1941	144
24	*Wednesday*	Nicolaus Copernicus d. 1543. Queen Victoria b. 1819	145
25	*Thursday*	The Venerable Bede d. 735. William Aitken b. 1879	146
26	*Friday*	*Easter Law Sittings end.* Queen Mary b. 1867	147
27	*Saturday*	Niccolò Paganini d. 1840. Arnold Bennett b. 1867	148
28	*Sunday*	**6th S. of Easter.** Rogation Sunday	149
29	*Monday*	*Bank Holiday in UK.* George I b. 1660	*week* 22 *day* 150
30	*Tuesday*	Joan of Arc d. 1431. Benny Goodman b. 1909	151
31	*Wednesday*	**Visit of Virgin Mary to Elizabeth.** Battle of Jutland 1916	152

ASTRONOMICAL PHENOMENA

d	h	
3	10	Venus in conjunction with Moon. Venus 4° N.
3	17	Mercury in conjunction with Moon. Mercury 4° N.
4	09	Jupiter in conjunction with Moon. Jupiter 4° N.
4	13	Saturn in conjunction with Moon. Saturn 3° N.
5	08	Mars in conjunction with Moon. Mars 5° N.
8	04	Jupiter in conjunction
8	13	Neptune at stationary point
8	19	Jupiter in conjunction with Mercury. Jupiter 0.8° S.
9	04	Mercury in superior conjunction
9	20	Saturn in conjunction with Mercury. Saturn 2° S.
10	20	Saturn in conjunction
17	11	Jupiter in conjunction with Venus. Jupiter 0.01° S.
18	13	Saturn in conjunction with Venus. Saturn 1° S.
19	12	Mars in conjunction with Mercury. Mars 1° S.
20	18	Sun's longitude 60° ♊
25	08	Uranus at stationary point
28	16	Saturn in conjunction with Jupiter. Saturn 1° S.

MINIMA OF ALGOL

Algol is inconveniently situated for observation during May.

CONSTELLATIONS

The following constellations are near the meridian at

	d	h		d	h
April	1	24	May	16	21
April	15	23	June	1	20
May	1	22	June	15	19

Cepheus (below the Pole), Cassiopeia (below the Pole), Ursa Minor, Ursa Major, Canes Venatici, Coma Berenices, Bootes, Leo, Virgo, Crater, Corvus and Hydra

THE MOON

Phases, Apsides and Node	d	h	m
● New Moon	4	04	12
☽ First Quarter	10	20	00
○ Full Moon	18	07	34
☾ Last Quarter	26	11	55
Perigee (363,169 km)	6	09	06
Apogee (405,428 km)	22	03	58

Mean longitude of ascending node on May 1, 119°

THE SUN   s.d. 15′.8

Day	Right Ascension	Dec. +	Equation of time	Rise 52°	Rise 56°	Transit	Set 52°	Set 56°	Sidereal time	Transit of First Point of Aries
	h m s	° ′	m s	h m	h m	h m	h m	h m	h m s	h m s
1	2 34 00	15 06	+ 2 55	4 30	4 16	11 57	19 25	19 40	14 36 54	9 21 33
2	2 37 50	15 24	+ 3 01	4 28	4 13	11 57	19 27	19 42	14 40 51	9 17 37
3	2 41 40	15 42	+ 3 08	4 26	4 11	11 57	19 29	19 44	14 44 48	9 13 42
4	2 45 31	15 59	+ 3 14	4 24	4 09	11 57	19 30	19 46	14 48 44	9 09 46
5	2 49 22	16 17	+ 3 19	4 22	4 07	11 57	19 32	19 48	14 52 41	9 05 50
6	2 53 14	16 34	+ 3 23	4 21	4 05	11 57	19 34	19 50	14 56 37	9 01 54
7	2 57 06	16 50	+ 3 28	4 19	4 03	11 57	19 35	19 52	15 00 34	8 57 58
8	3 00 59	17 07	+ 3 31	4 17	4 00	11 56	19 37	19 54	15 04 30	8 54 02
9	3 04 53	17 23	+ 3 34	4 15	3 58	11 56	19 38	19 56	15 08 27	8 50 06
10	3 08 47	17 39	+ 3 37	4 14	3 56	11 56	19 40	19 58	15 12 23	8 46 10
11	3 12 41	17 54	+ 3 39	4 12	3 54	11 56	19 42	20 00	15 16 20	8 42 14
12	3 16 37	18 09	+ 3 40	4 10	3 52	11 56	19 43	20 02	15 20 17	8 38 18
13	3 20 32	18 24	+ 3 41	4 09	3 50	11 56	19 45	20 03	15 24 13	8 34 22
14	3 24 29	18 39	+ 3 41	4 07	3 49	11 56	19 46	20 05	15 28 10	8 30 27
15	3 28 25	18 53	+ 3 41	4 06	3 47	11 56	19 48	20 07	15 32 06	8 26 31
16	3 32 23	19 07	+ 3 40	4 04	3 45	11 56	19 49	20 09	15 36 03	8 22 35
17	3 36 21	19 21	+ 3 38	4 03	3 43	11 56	19 51	20 11	15 39 59	8 18 39
18	3 40 19	19 34	+ 3 36	4 01	3 41	11 56	19 52	20 13	15 43 56	8 14 43
19	3 44 18	19 47	+ 3 34	4 00	3 40	11 56	19 54	20 14	15 47 52	8 10 47
20	3 48 18	20 00	+ 3 31	3 59	3 38	11 57	19 55	20 16	15 51 49	8 06 51
21	3 52 18	20 12	+ 3 27	3 57	3 36	11 57	19 57	20 18	15 55 46	8 02 55
22	3 56 19	20 24	+ 3 23	3 56	3 35	11 57	19 58	20 20	15 59 42	7 58 59
23	4 00 20	20 36	+ 3 18	3 55	3 33	11 57	19 59	20 21	16 03 39	7 55 03
24	4 04 22	20 47	+ 3 13	3 54	3 32	11 57	20 01	20 23	16 07 35	7 51 07
25	4 08 24	20 58	+ 3 07	3 53	3 30	11 57	20 02	20 25	16 11 32	7 47 12
26	4 12 27	21 08	+ 3 01	3 51	3 29	11 57	20 03	20 26	16 15 28	7 43 16
27	4 16 30	21 19	+ 2 55	3 50	3 28	11 57	20 05	20 28	16 19 25	7 39 20
28	4 20 34	21 28	+ 2 47	3 49	3 26	11 57	20 06	20 29	16 23 21	7 35 24
29	4 24 38	21 38	+ 2 40	3 48	3 25	11 57	20 07	20 31	16 27 18	7 31 28
30	4 28 43	21 47	+ 2 31	3 47	3 24	11 58	20 08	20 32	16 31 15	7 27 32
31	4 32 48	21 56	+ 2 23	3 47	3 23	11 58	20 09	20 33	16 35 11	7 23 36

DURATION OF TWILIGHT (in minutes)

Latitude	52°	56°	52°	56°	52°	56°	52°	56°
	1 May		11 May		21 May		31 May	
Civil	39	45	41	49	44	53	46	57
Nautical	90	106	97	121	106	143	116	TAN
Astronomical	154	209	179	TAN	TAN	TAN	TAN	TAN

THE NIGHT SKY

Unusually, until about the last week of the month, no naked-eye planet will be visible during the hours of darkness.

Mercury is unsuitably placed for most of the month, superior conjunction occurring on the 9th. However, during the last week of May it may be glimpsed as a difficult evening object low above the north-western horizon, though the lengthening twilight hinders observation. During this period its magnitude fades from −0.8 to −0.1.

Venus is too close to the Sun for observation throughout May.

Mars is unsuitably placed for observation.

Jupiter is too close to the Sun for observation, conjunction occurring on the 8th. Keen skywatchers will have noticed that before the two giant planets, Jupiter and Saturn, were lost in the evening twilight in April, Jupiter was west of Saturn. During May Jupiter overtakes Saturn and when they emerge from the morning twilight in June, Saturn will appear to the west of Jupiter.

Saturn is unsuitably placed for observation throughout May, conjunction occurring on the 10th.

THE MOON

Day	RA h m	Dec. °	Hor. par. ′	Semi-diam. ′	Sun's co-long. °	PA of Bright Limb °	Phase %	Age d	Rise 52° h m	Rise 56° h m	Transit h m	Set 52° h m	Set 56° h m
1	0 05	− 4.3	57.4	15.7	235	62	13	26.2	3 54	3 57	9 47	15 53	15 52
2	0 56	+ 0.7	58.3	15.9	247	58	6	27.2	4 16	4 15	10 36	17 10	17 14
3	1 48	+ 5.7	59.1	16.1	260	52	2	28.2	4 39	4 33	11 27	18 30	18 39
4	2 42	+10.6	59.7	16.3	272	8	0	29.2	5 05	4 55	12 20	19 52	20 05
5	3 39	+15.0	60.1	16.4	284	278	1	0.8	5 35	5 21	13 17	21 14	21 32
6	4 39	+18.4	60.4	16.4	296	270	5	1.8	6 13	5 54	14 17	22 31	22 52
7	5 41	+20.7	60.3	16.4	308	271	11	2.8	7 01	6 39	15 18	23 39	—
8	6 44	+21.6	60.1	16.4	321	275	20	3.8	7 59	7 36	16 19	—	0 02
9	7 46	+21.0	59.7	16.3	333	280	30	4.8	9 07	8 46	17 18	0 35	0 57
10	8 46	+19.1	59.2	16.1	345	285	41	5.8	10 21	10 03	18 15	1 20	1 38
11	9 43	+16.0	58.6	16.0	357	289	52	6.8	11 37	11 24	19 07	1 55	2 09
12	10 38	+12.2	58.0	15.8	10	293	63	7.8	12 53	12 44	19 57	2 23	2 33
13	11 29	+ 7.7	57.4	15.6	22	295	73	8.8	14 07	14 03	20 44	2 47	2 52
14	12 18	+ 3.1	56.8	15.5	34	297	82	9.8	15 19	15 19	21 30	3 08	3 10
15	13 07	− 1.7	56.3	15.3	46	299	89	10.8	16 31	16 35	22 15	3 28	3 26
16	13 54	− 6.3	55.8	15.2	58	301	95	11.8	17 41	17 49	23 00	3 48	3 42
17	14 42	−10.6	55.4	15.1	71	305	98	12.8	18 49	19 02	23 46	4 10	4 00
18	15 30	−14.4	55.0	15.0	83	335	100	13.8	19 57	20 13	—	4 34	4 20
19	16 19	−17.5	54.6	14.9	95	73	99	14.8	21 00	21 20	0 32	5 02	4 45
20	17 09	−19.8	54.4	14.8	107	86	97	15.8	22 00	22 22	1 20	5 35	5 15
21	18 00	−21.2	54.2	14.8	119	86	93	16.8	22 52	23 15	2 08	6 15	5 53
22	18 51	−21.7	54.1	14.7	131	84	88	17.8	23 37	23 59	2 57	7 02	6 39
23	19 42	−21.2	54.1	14.7	144	80	81	18.8	—	—	3 45	7 56	7 35
24	20 32	−19.7	54.3	14.8	156	76	73	19.8	0 15	0 35	4 33	8 56	8 37
25	21 21	−17.4	54.7	14.9	168	73	65	20.8	0 46	1 03	5 20	10 00	9 45
26	22 10	−14.3	55.2	15.0	180	70	55	21.8	1 13	1 26	6 06	11 08	10 56
27	22 59	−10.6	55.8	15.2	192	67	45	22.8	1 37	1 45	6 52	12 17	12 10
28	23 47	− 6.2	56.6	15.4	205	65	35	23.8	1 58	2 03	7 38	13 29	13 26
29	0 36	− 1.5	57.5	15.7	217	64	25	24.8	2 19	2 20	8 25	14 44	14 45
30	1 26	+ 3.5	58.4	15.9	229	64	17	25.8	2 40	2 37	9 13	16 02	16 08
31	2 19	+ 8.5	59.3	16.2	241	64	9	26.8	3 04	2 56	10 05	17 22	17 33

MERCURY

Day	RA h m	Dec. °	Diam. ″	Phase %	Transit h m	5° high 52° h m	5° high 56° h m
1	2 00	+10.8	5	94	11 25	5 00	4 54
3	2 15	+12.5	5	96	11 32	4 58	4 51
5	2 31	+14.1	5	98	11 40	4 58	4 49
7	2 47	+15.7	5	100	11 49	4 57	4 47
9	3 04	+17.3	5	100	11 58	4 58	4 46
11	3 21	+18.8	5	100	12 07	19 19	19 32
13	3 39	+20.2	5	98	12 17	19 36	19 52
15	3 57	+21.5	5	96	12 27	19 54	20 10
17	4 14	+22.6	5	92	12 37	20 10	20 28
19	4 32	+23.5	5	88	12 47	20 25	20 44
21	4 49	+24.3	6	83	12 56	20 39	20 59
23	5 06	+24.9	6	78	13 04	20 51	21 11
25	5 22	+25.3	6	73	13 13	21 01	21 22
27	5 37	+25.5	6	68	13 20	21 09	21 31
29	5 52	+25.6	6	63	13 26	21 16	21 38
31	6 05	+25.6	7	58	13 32	21 21	21 42

VENUS

Day	RA h m	Dec. °	Diam. ″	Phase %	Transit h m	5° high 52° h m	5° high 56° h m
1	1 53	+10.2	10	98	11 16	4 56	4 51
6	2 16	+12.4	10	99	11 20	4 48	4 41
11	2 40	+14.5	10	99	11 24	4 41	4 32
16	3 04	+16.4	10	99	11 29	4 35	4 24
21	3 29	+18.2	10	100	11 34	4 30	4 18
26	3 54	+19.7	10	100	11 39	4 27	4 13
31	4 20	+21.1	10	100	11 45	4 25	4 09

MARS

Day	RA h m	Dec. °	Diam. ″	Phase %	Transit h m	5° high 52° h m	5° high 56° h m
1	3 43	+20.1	4	99	13 05	20 20	20 34
6	3 57	+20.9	4	99	13 00	20 19	20 35
11	4 12	+21.6	4	99	12 55	20 19	20 35
16	4 27	+22.2	4	99	12 50	20 17	20 34
21	4 42	+22.8	4	100	12 45	20 16	20 33
26	4 56	+23.2	4	100	12 40	20 14	20 32
31	5 11	+23.6	4	100	12 35	20 11	20 30

SUNRISE AND SUNSET

	London 0°05' 51°30'		Bristol 2°35' 51°28'		Birmingham 1°55' 52°28'		Manchester 2°15' 53°28'		Newcastle 1°37' 54°59'		Glasgow 4°14' 55°52'		Belfast 5°56' 54°35'	
	h m	h m	h m	h m	h m	h m	h m	h m	h m	h m	h m	h m	h m	h m
1	4 32	19 24	4 42	19 34	4 36	19 34	4 34	19 39	4 26	19 42	4 33	19 56	4 45	19 58
2	4 30	19 26	4 40	19 36	4 34	19 36	4 32	19 41	4 24	19 44	4 31	19 58	4 43	20 00
3	4 28	19 27	4 38	19 37	4 32	19 38	4 30	19 43	4 22	19 46	4 29	20 00	4 41	20 02
4	4 26	19 29	4 36	19 39	4 30	19 40	4 28	19 45	4 20	19 48	4 26	20 02	4 38	20 04
5	4 25	19 31	4 35	19 40	4 28	19 41	4 26	19 46	4 18	19 50	4 24	20 04	4 36	20 06
6	4 23	19 32	4 33	19 42	4 27	19 43	4 24	19 48	4 16	19 52	4 22	20 06	4 34	20 07
7	4 21	19 34	4 31	19 44	4 25	19 45	4 22	19 50	4 13	19 54	4 20	20 08	4 32	20 09
8	4 19	19 35	4 29	19 45	4 23	19 46	4 20	19 52	4 12	19 56	4 18	20 10	4 31	20 11
9	4 18	19 37	4 28	19 47	4 21	19 48	4 19	19 53	4 10	19 57	4 16	20 12	4 29	20 13
10	4 16	19 38	4 26	19 48	4 20	19 50	4 17	19 55	4 08	19 59	4 14	20 14	4 27	20 15
11	4 14	19 40	4 24	19 50	4 18	19 51	4 15	19 57	4 06	20 01	4 12	20 16	4 25	20 17
12	4 13	19 42	4 23	19 51	4 16	19 53	4 13	19 58	4 04	20 03	4 10	20 18	4 23	20 18
13	4 11	19 43	4 21	19 53	4 15	19 54	4 12	20 00	4 02	20 05	4 08	20 20	4 21	20 20
14	4 10	19 45	4 20	19 54	4 13	19 56	4 10	20 02	4 00	20 07	4 06	20 22	4 19	20 22
15	4 08	19 46	4 18	19 56	4 11	19 58	4 08	20 03	3 58	20 08	4 04	20 23	4 18	20 24
16	4 07	19 48	4 17	19 57	4 10	19 59	4 07	20 05	3 57	20 10	4 03	20 25	4 16	20 25
17	4 05	19 49	4 15	19 59	4 08	20 01	4 05	20 07	3 55	20 12	4 01	20 27	4 14	20 27
18	4 04	19 50	4 14	20 00	4 07	20 02	4 04	20 08	3 53	20 13	3 59	20 29	4 13	20 29
19	4 03	19 52	4 13	20 02	4 06	20 04	4 02	20 10	3 52	20 15	3 57	20 31	4 11	20 30
20	4 01	19 53	4 11	20 03	4 04	20 05	4 01	20 11	3 50	20 17	3 56	20 32	4 10	20 32
21	4 00	19 55	4 10	20 05	4 03	20 07	3 59	20 13	3 49	20 18	3 54	20 34	4 08	20 34
22	3 59	19 56	4 09	20 06	4 02	20 08	3 58	20 14	3 47	20 20	3 53	20 36	4 07	20 35
23	3 58	19 57	4 08	20 09	4 00	20 09	3 57	20 16	3 46	20 22	3 51	20 37	4 05	20 37
24	3 56	19 59	4 07	20 09	3 59	20 11	3 55	20 17	3 44	20 23	3 50	20 39	4 04	20 38
25	3 55	20 00	4 05	20 10	3 58	20 12	3 54	20 19	3 43	20 25	3 48	20 41	4 03	20 40
26	3 54	20 01	4 04	20 11	3 57	20 13	3 53	20 20	3 42	20 26	3 47	20 42	4 01	20 41
27	3 53	20 03	4 03	20 12	3 56	20 15	3 52	20 21	3 40	20 28	3 45	20 44	4 00	20 43
28	3 52	20 04	4 02	20 14	3 55	20 16	3 51	20 23	3 39	20 29	3 44	20 45	3 59	20 44
29	3 51	20 05	4 01	20 15	3 54	20 17	3 50	20 24	3 38	20 31	3 43	20 47	3 58	20 45
30	3 50	20 06	4 00	20 16	3 53	20 18	3 49	20 25	3 37	20 32	3 42	20 48	3 57	20 47
31	3 49	20 07	4 00	20 17	3 52	20 20	3 48	20 27	3 36	20 33	3 41	20 50	3 56	20 48

JUPITER

Day	RA	Dec.	Transit	5° high 52°	5° high 56°
	h m	° '	h m	h m	h m
1	2 55.9	+15 50	12 17	5 28	5 18
11	3 05.4	+16 31	11 48	4 55	4 44
21	3 14.9	+17 10	11 18	4 21	4 10
31	3 24.4	+17 46	10 48	3 48	3 36

Diameters – equatorial 33" polar 31"

SATURN

Day	RA	Dec.	Transit	5° high 52°	5° high 56°
	h m	° '	h m	h m	h m
1	3 09.2	+15 35	12 30	5 43	5 33
11	3 14.3	+15 56	11 56	5 07	4 57
21	3 19.5	+16 16	11 22	4 31	4 20
31	3 24.6	+16 36	10 48	3 55	3 44

Diameters – equatorial 16" polar 15"
Rings – major axis 37" minor axis 14"

URANUS

Day	RA	Dec.	Transit	10° high 52°	10° high 56°
	h m	° '	h m	h m	h m
1	21 32.8	−15 17	6 55	3 35	4 02
11	21 33.5	−15 14	6 16	2 56	3 23
21	21 33.8	−15 13	5 37	2 17	2 43
31	21 33.8	−15 14	4 58	1 38	2 04

Diameter 4"

NEPTUNE

Day	RA	Dec.	Transit	10° high 52°	10° high 56°
	h m	° '	h m	h m	h m
1	20 35.6	−18 25	5 58	3 04	3 39
11	20 35.6	−18 25	5 18	2 24	3 00
21	20 35.4	−18 26	4 39	1 45	2 20
31	20 35.1	−18 27	3 59	1 05	1 41

Diameter 2"

June 2000

SIXTH MONTH, 30 DAYS. *Junius*, Roman *gens* (family)

1	*Thursday*	**Ascension Day.** Helen Keller d. 1968	153
2	*Friday*	*Coronation Day 1953.* Jesse Boot b. 1850	154
3	*Saturday*	Richard Cobden b. 1804. Samuel Plimsoll d. 1898	155
4	*Sunday*	**7th S. of Easter.** Battle of Magenta 1859	156
5	*Monday*	Adam Smith b. 1723. Stravinsky b. 1882	*week 23 day* 157
6	*Tuesday*	*Trinity Law Sittings begin.* Sir Isaiah Berlin d. 1997	158
7	*Wednesday*	Robert I d. 1329. Dennis Potter d. 1994	159
8	*Thursday*	Muhammad d. 632. Sir Norman Hartnell d. 1979	160
9	*Friday*	FEAST OF WEEKS begins. John Constable b. 1776	161
10	*Saturday*	*Duke of Edinburgh b. 1921. Queen's Official Birthday*	162
11	*Sunday*	**Pentecost (Whit Sunday). St Barnabas**	163
12	*Monday*	Harriet Martineau b. 1802. John Ireland d. 1962	*week 24 day* 164
13	*Tuesday*	W. B. Yeats b. 1865. Sir Eugene Goossens d. 1962	165
14	*Wednesday*	Harriet Beecher Stowe b. 1811. John Baird d. 1946	166
15	*Thursday*	Magna Carta sealed 1215. Ella Fitzgerald d. 1996	167
16	*Friday*	Stan Laurel b. 1890. Margaret Bondfield d. 1953	168
17	*Saturday*	Edward I b. 1239. Battle of Bunker Hill 1775	169
18	*Sunday*	**Trinity Sunday.** Battle of Waterloo 1815	170
19	*Monday*	Blaise Pascal b. 1623. The Duchess of Windsor b. 1896	*week 25 day* 171
20	*Tuesday*	William IV d. 1837. Dame Catherine Cookson b. 1906	172
21	*Wednesday*	Prince William of Wales b. 1982. Benazir Bhutto b. 1953	173
22	*Thursday*	**Corpus Christi.** Dame Cicely Saunders b. 1918	174
23	*Friday*	James Mill d. 1836. The Duke of Windsor b. 1894	175
24	*Saturday*	**John the Baptist.** Book of Common Prayer issued 1559	176
25	*Sunday*	**1st S. after Trinity.** Erskine Childers b. 1870	177
26	*Monday*	Joseph-Michel Montgolfier d. 1810. George IV d. 1830	*week 26 day* 178
27	*Tuesday*	Helen Keller b. 1880. Sir Alfred Ayer d. 1989	179
28	*Wednesday*	Treaty of Versailles signed 1919	180
29	*Thursday*	**SS Peter and Paul.** Lana Turner d. 1995	181
30	*Friday*	Sir Stanley Spencer b. 1891. Nancy Mitford d. 1973	182

ASTRONOMICAL PHENOMENA

d	h	
1	06	Saturn in conjunction with Moon. Saturn 3° N.
1	06	Jupiter in conjunction with Moon. Jupiter 4° N.
1	18	Pluto at opposition
2	08	Venus in conjunction with Moon. Venus 3° N.
3	02	Mars in conjunction with Moon. Mars 4° N.
4	04	Mercury in conjunction with Moon. Mercury 4° N.
9	13	Mercury at greatest elongation E.24°
11	11	Venus in superior conjunction
21	02	Sun's longitude 90° ♋
21	19	Mars in conjunction with Venus. Mars 0.3° N.
23	09	Mercury at stationary point
28	21	Saturn in conjunction with Moon. Saturn 2° N.
29	03	Jupiter in conjunction with Moon. Jupiter 3° N.

MINIMA OF ALGOL

Algol is inconveniently situated for observation during June.

CONSTELLATIONS

The following constellations are near the meridian at

	d	h		d	h
May	1	24	June	15	21
May	16	23	July	1	20
June	1	22	July	16	19

Cassiopeia (below the Pole), Ursa Minor, Draco, Ursa Major, Canes Venatici, Bootes, Corona, Serpens, Virgo and Libra

THE MOON

Phases, Apsides and Node	d	h	m
● New Moon	2	12	14
☽ First Quarter	9	03	29
○ Full Moon	16	22	27
☾ Last Quarter	25	01	00
Perigee (359,089 km)	3	13	18
Apogee (406,112 km)	18	12	57

Mean longitude of ascending node on June 1, 117°

THE SUN

s.d. 15′.8

Day	Right Ascension	Dec. +	Equation of time	Rise 52°	Rise 56°	Transit	Set 52°	Set 56°	Sidereal time	Transit of First Point of Aries
	h m s	° ′	m s	h m	h m	h m	h m	h m	h m s	h m s
1	4 36 54	22 04	+ 2 14	3 46	3 22	11 58	20 11	20 35	16 39 08	7 19 40
2	4 41 00	22 12	+ 2 04	3 45	3 21	11 58	20 12	20 36	16 43 04	7 15 44
3	4 45 06	22 19	+ 1 54	3 44	3 20	11 58	20 13	20 37	16 47 01	7 11 48
4	4 49 13	22 26	+ 1 44	3 44	3 19	11 58	20 14	20 39	16 50 57	7 07 52
5	4 53 20	22 33	+ 1 34	3 43	3 18	11 59	20 15	20 40	16 54 54	7 03 57
6	4 57 27	22 40	+ 1 23	3 42	3 17	11 59	20 16	20 41	16 58 50	7 00 01
7	5 01 35	22 46	+ 1 12	3 42	3 16	11 59	20 16	20 42	17 02 47	6 56 05
8	5 05 43	22 51	+ 1 00	3 41	3 16	11 59	20 17	20 43	17 06 44	6 52 09
9	5 09 51	22 56	+ 0 49	3 41	3 15	11 59	20 18	20 44	17 10 40	6 48 13
10	5 14 00	23 01	+ 0 37	3 40	3 15	11 59	20 19	20 45	17 14 37	6 44 17
11	5 18 08	23 05	+ 0 25	3 40	3 14	12 00	20 20	20 46	17 18 33	6 40 21
12	5 22 17	23 09	+ 0 13	3 40	3 14	12 00	20 20	20 46	17 22 30	6 36 25
13	5 26 26	23 13	0 00	3 40	3 14	12 00	20 21	20 47	17 26 26	6 32 29
14	5 30 35	23 16	− 0 12	3 39	3 13	12 00	20 21	20 48	17 30 23	6 28 33
15	5 34 44	23 19	− 0 25	3 39	3 13	12 01	20 22	20 48	17 34 19	6 24 37
16	5 38 54	23 21	− 0 38	3 39	3 13	12 01	20 22	20 49	17 38 16	6 20 41
17	5 43 03	23 23	− 0 51	3 39	3 13	12 01	20 23	20 49	17 42 13	6 16 46
18	5 47 13	23 24	− 1 03	3 39	3 13	12 01	20 23	20 50	17 46 09	6 12 50
19	5 51 22	23 25	− 1 16	3 39	3 13	12 01	20 23	20 50	17 50 06	6 08 54
20	5 55 32	23 26	− 1 29	3 40	3 13	12 02	20 24	20 50	17 54 02	6 04 58
21	5 59 41	23 26	− 1 42	3 40	3 13	12 02	20 24	20 50	17 57 59	6 01 02
22	6 03 51	23 26	− 1 55	3 40	3 13	12 02	20 24	20 51	18 01 55	5 57 06
23	6 08 00	23 26	− 2 08	3 40	3 14	12 02	20 24	20 51	18 05 52	5 53 10
24	6 12 10	23 25	− 2 21	3 41	3 14	12 02	20 24	20 51	18 09 48	5 49 14
25	6 16 19	23 23	− 2 34	3 41	3 15	12 03	20 24	20 51	18 13 45	5 45 18
26	6 20 28	23 21	− 2 47	3 41	3 15	12 03	20 24	20 50	18 17 42	5 41 22
27	6 24 37	23 19	− 2 59	3 42	3 16	12 03	20 24	20 50	18 21 38	5 37 26
28	6 28 46	23 16	− 3 12	3 43	3 16	12 03	20 24	20 50	18 25 35	5 33 31
29	6 32 55	23 13	− 3 24	3 43	3 17	12 03	20 24	20 50	18 29 31	5 29 35
30	6 37 04	23 10	− 3 36	3 44	3 18	12 04	20 23	20 49	18 33 28	5 25 39

DURATION OF TWILIGHT (in minutes)

Latitude	52°	56°	52°	56°	52°	56°	52°	56°
	1 June		11 June		21 June		30 June	
Civil	47	58	48	61	49	63	49	62
Nautical	117	TAN	125	TAN	128	TAN	125	TAN
Astronomical	TAN	TAN	TAN	TAN	TAN	TAN	TAN	TAN

THE NIGHT SKY

Mercury may be visible, though only as a difficult evening object. The long summer twilight will seriously hinder observation but under good conditions it may be possible to glimpse the planet during the first ten days of the month, very low above the north-western horizon at the end of evening civil twilight. During this period its magnitude fades from 0.0 to +1.0. Under very good conditions it may be possible to glimpse the thin crescent Moon, about 2.4 days old, about 10° to the left of the planet on the evening of the 4th.

Venus is at superior conjunction on the 11th, actually passing behind the disk of the Sun, and thus remaining too close to the Sun for observation throughout the month.

Mars is too close to the Sun for observation.

Jupiter, magnitude −2.1, becomes a morning object during the second half of the month, low in the eastern sky shortly before dawn. Both Jupiter and Saturn are moving eastwards in the western part of Taurus, with Jupiter about 3° further east. It will continue to be a useful guide to locating Saturn, which is over 2 magnitudes fainter.

Saturn is not visible for the first three weeks of June, but then begins to emerge from the long morning twilight and may be detected low above the east-north-eastern horizon before the sky gets too bright. The fact that in these latitudes even nautical twilight is continuous throughout the night means that Saturn will not be an easy object to locate. Its magnitude is +0.3.

Twilight. Reference to the section above shows that astronomical twilight lasts all night for a period around the summer solstice (i.e. in June and July), even in southern England. Under these conditions the sky never gets completely dark as the Sun is always less than 18° below the horizon.

THE MOON

Day	RA	Dec.	Hor. par.	Semi-diam.	Sun's co-long.	PA of Bright Limb	Phase	Age	Rise 52°	Rise 56°	Transit	Set 52°	Set 56°
	h m	°	′	′	°	°	%	d	h m	h m	h m	h m	h m
1	3 15	+13.2	60.1	16.4	254	63	4	27.8	3 31	3 19	11 00	18 45	19 01
2	4 14	+17.1	60.7	16.5	266	51	1	28.8	4 05	3 48	11 59	20 07	20 27
3	5 16	+20.0	61.0	16.6	278	289	0	0.5	4 48	4 28	13 01	21 22	21 45
4	6 20	+21.5	61.0	16.6	290	277	3	1.5	5 43	5 20	14 05	22 26	22 49
5	7 25	+21.5	60.8	16.6	303	279	9	2.5	6 49	6 27	15 07	23 17	23 37
6	8 28	+20.0	60.2	16.4	315	283	17	3.5	8 04	7 45	16 07	23 57	—
7	9 28	+17.2	59.5	16.2	327	287	27	4.5	9 22	9 07	17 03	—	0 13
8	10 24	+13.4	58.8	16.0	339	291	38	5.5	10 40	10 30	17 54	0 28	0 40
9	11 17	+ 9.0	58.0	15.8	352	293	49	6.5	11 56	11 50	18 43	0 53	1 01
10	12 08	+ 4.3	57.2	15.6	4	294	59	7.5	13 10	13 08	19 29	1 15	1 19
11	12 56	− 0.5	56.5	15.4	16	295	69	8.5	14 21	14 24	20 14	1 35	1 35
12	13 43	− 5.1	55.9	15.2	28	295	78	9.5	15 31	15 38	20 59	1 55	1 51
13	14 31	− 9.5	55.3	15.1	40	294	86	10.5	16 40	16 51	21 44	2 16	2 07
14	15 18	−13.4	54.9	15.0	53	292	92	11.5	17 47	18 02	22 29	2 39	2 26
15	16 07	−16.7	54.5	14.9	65	291	96	12.5	18 52	19 11	23 16	3 05	2 49
16	16 56	−19.3	54.3	14.8	77	294	99	13.5	19 53	20 14	—	3 36	3 16
17	17 46	−20.9	54.1	14.7	89	17	100	14.5	20 48	21 11	0 04	4 13	3 51
18	18 37	−21.7	54.0	14.7	101	79	99	15.5	21 36	21 58	0 53	4 57	4 34
19	19 28	−21.5	54.0	14.7	114	80	96	16.5	22 16	22 37	1 41	5 49	5 27
20	20 19	−20.3	54.1	14.7	126	78	92	17.5	22 50	23 07	2 29	6 47	6 27
21	21 08	−18.3	54.3	14.8	138	75	86	18.5	23 18	23 32	3 17	7 50	7 33
22	21 57	−15.4	54.7	14.9	150	72	79	19.5	23 42	23 52	4 03	8 55	8 42
23	22 45	−11.9	55.1	15.0	162	69	70	20.5	—	—	4 48	10 03	9 54
24	23 32	− 7.8	55.7	15.2	175	68	61	21.5	0 03	0 10	5 32	11 13	11 08
25	0 20	− 3.2	56.5	15.4	187	67	51	22.5	0 23	0 26	6 17	12 24	12 23
26	1 08	+ 1.6	57.3	15.6	199	66	40	23.5	0 44	0 42	7 04	13 38	13 42
27	1 58	+ 6.5	58.3	15.9	211	67	30	24.5	1 05	1 00	7 52	14 55	15 03
28	2 51	+11.2	59.2	16.1	224	69	20	25.5	1 30	1 20	8 44	16 15	16 28
29	3 48	+15.5	60.1	16.4	236	72	12	26.5	1 59	1 45	9 40	17 37	17 54
30	4 48	+18.9	60.8	16.6	248	76	5	27.5	2 36	2 18	10 41	18 56	19 17

MERCURY

Day	RA	Dec.	Diam.	Phase	Transit	5° high 52°	5° high 56°
	h m	°	″	%	h m	h m	h m
1	6 12	+25.6	7	56	13 34	21 23	21 44
3	6 24	+25.4	7	51	13 38	21 25	21 46
5	6 35	+25.1	7	47	13 41	21 26	21 46
7	6 46	+24.7	8	43	13 43	21 25	21 45
9	6 55	+24.2	8	39	13 44	21 22	21 42
11	7 03	+23.7	8	35	13 44	21 19	21 37
13	7 10	+23.2	9	31	13 43	21 14	21 31
15	7 15	+22.6	9	27	13 40	21 07	21 24
17	7 20	+22.0	10	24	13 36	21 00	21 16
19	7 23	+21.4	10	20	13 31	20 51	21 06
21	7 25	+20.9	10	17	13 25	20 41	20 56
23	7 25	+20.3	11	14	13 17	20 30	20 44
25	7 25	+19.8	11	10	13 08	20 18	20 31
27	7 23	+19.3	11	8	12 58	20 05	20 18
29	7 20	+18.9	12	5	12 47	19 51	20 04
31	7 16	+18.5	12	3	12 35	19 37	19 50

VENUS

Day	RA	Dec.	Diam.	Phase	Transit	5° high 52°	5° high 56°
	h m	°	″	%	h m	h m	h m
1	4 25	+21.3	10	100	11 47	19 09	19 25
6	4 51	+22.4	10	100	11 53	19 22	19 39
11	5 18	+23.2	10	100	12 00	19 34	19 52
16	5 44	+23.7	10	100	12 07	19 43	20 02
21	6 11	+23.9	10	100	12 14	19 52	20 11
26	6 38	+23.8	10	100	12 21	19 58	20 17
31	7 05	+23.4	10	100	12 28	20 02	20 21

MARS

Day	RA	Dec.	Diam.	Phase	Transit	5° high 52°	5° high 56°
1	5 14	+23.7	4	100	12 34	20 10	20 29
6	5 29	+23.9	4	100	12 30	20 07	20 26
11	5 44	+24.1	4	100	12 25	20 03	20 23
16	5 58	+24.2	4	100	12 20	19 59	20 18
21	6 13	+24.2	4	100	12 15	19 54	20 13
26	6 28	+24.1	4	100	12 10	19 48	20 07
31	6 42	+24.0	4	100	12 04	19 42	20 01

SUNRISE AND SUNSET

	London		Bristol		Birmingham		Manchester		Newcastle		Glasgow		Belfast	
	0°05′	51°30′	2°35′	51°28′	1°55′	52°28′	2°15′	53°28′	1°37′	54°59′	4°14′	55°52′	5°56′	54°35′
	h m	h m	h m	h m	h m	h m	h m	h m	h m	h m	h m	h m	h m	h m
1	3 49	20 08	3 59	20 18	3 51	20 21	3 47	20 28	3 35	20 34	3 40	20 51	3 55	20 49
2	3 48	20 09	3 58	20 19	3 50	20 22	3 46	20 29	3 34	20 36	3 39	20 52	3 54	20 50
3	3 47	20 10	3 57	20 20	3 49	20 23	3 45	20 30	3 33	20 37	3 38	20 53	3 53	20 52
4	3 47	20 11	3 57	20 21	3 49	20 24	3 44	20 31	3 32	20 38	3 37	20 55	3 52	20 53
5	3 46	20 12	3 56	20 22	3 48	20 25	3 44	20 32	3 31	20 39	3 36	20 56	3 51	20 54
6	3 45	20 13	3 56	20 23	3 47	20 26	3 43	20 33	3 31	20 40	3 35	20 57	3 51	20 55
7	3 45	20 14	3 55	20 24	3 47	20 27	3 42	20 34	3 30	20 41	3 34	20 58	3 50	20 56
8	3 44	20 15	3 55	20 25	3 46	20 28	3 42	20 35	3 29	20 42	3 34	20 59	3 49	20 57
9	3 44	20 16	3 54	20 25	3 46	20 28	3 41	20 36	3 29	20 43	3 33	21 00	3 49	20 58
10	3 44	20 16	3 54	20 26	3 45	20 29	3 41	20 37	3 28	20 44	3 33	21 01	3 48	20 58
11	3 43	20 17	3 53	20 27	3 45	20 30	3 40	20 37	3 28	20 45	3 32	21 02	3 48	20 59
12	3 43	20 18	3 53	20 28	3 45	20 31	3 40	20 38	3 28	20 45	3 32	21 02	3 48	21 00
13	3 43	20 18	3 53	20 28	3 45	20 31	3 40	20 39	3 27	20 46	3 31	21 03	3 47	21 01
14	3 43	20 19	3 53	20 29	3 44	20 32	3 40	20 39	3 27	20 47	3 31	21 04	3 47	21 01
15	3 43	20 19	3 53	20 29	3 44	20 32	3 40	20 40	3 27	20 47	3 31	21 04	3 47	21 02
16	3 42	20 20	3 53	20 30	3 44	20 33	3 39	20 40	3 27	20 48	3 31	21 05	3 47	21 02
17	3 42	20 20	3 53	20 30	3 44	20 33	3 39	20 41	3 27	20 48	3 31	21 05	3 47	21 03
18	3 43	20 21	3 53	20 30	3 44	20 33	3 39	20 41	3 27	20 49	3 31	21 06	3 47	21 03
19	3 43	20 21	3 53	20 31	3 44	20 34	3 40	20 41	3 27	20 49	3 31	21 06	3 47	21 03
20	3 43	20 21	3 53	20 31	3 45	20 34	3 40	20 42	3 27	20 49	3 31	21 06	3 47	21 04
21	3 43	20 21	3 53	20 31	3 45	20 34	3 40	20 42	3 27	20 49	3 31	21 06	3 47	21 04
22	3 43	20 21	3 53	20 31	3 45	20 34	3 40	20 42	3 27	20 50	3 31	21 07	3 47	21 04
23	3 43	20 22	3 54	20 31	3 45	20 34	3 40	20 42	3 28	20 50	3 32	21 07	3 48	21 04
24	3 44	20 22	3 54	20 31	3 46	20 35	3 41	20 42	3 28	20 50	3 32	21 07	3 48	21 04
25	3 44	20 22	3 54	20 31	3 46	20 35	3 41	20 42	3 29	20 50	3 33	21 07	3 49	21 04
26	3 45	20 22	3 55	20 31	3 46	20 34	3 42	20 42	3 29	20 49	3 33	21 06	3 49	21 04
27	3 45	20 21	3 55	20 31	3 47	20 34	3 42	20 42	3 30	20 49	3 34	21 06	3 50	21 04
28	3 46	20 21	3 56	20 31	3 48	20 34	3 43	20 42	3 30	20 49	3 34	21 06	3 50	21 04
29	3 46	20 21	3 56	20 31	3 48	20 34	3 43	20 41	3 31	20 49	3 35	21 06	3 51	21 03
30	3 47	20 21	3 57	20 31	3 49	20 34	3 44	20 41	3 32	20 48	3 36	21 05	3 52	21 03

JUPITER

Day	RA	Dec.	Transit	5° high	
				52°	56°
	h m	° ′	h m	h m	h m
1	3 25.3	+17 50	10 45	3 45	3 33
11	3 34.7	+18 23	10 15	3 12	2 59
21	3 43.8	+18 54	9 45	2 38	2 25
31	3 52.6	+19 21	9 14	2 05	1 52

Diameters – equatorial 34″ polar 32″

SATURN

Day	RA	Dec.	Transit	5° high	
				52°	56°
	h m	° ′	h m	h m	h m
1	3 25.1	+16 38	10 44	3 51	3 40
11	3 30.1	+16 55	10 10	3 15	3 04
21	3 34.8	+17 12	9 35	2 39	2 28
31	3 39.3	+17 26	9 01	2 03	1 51

Diameters – equatorial 17″ polar 15″
Rings – major axis 38″ minor axis 15″

URANUS

Day	RA	Dec.	Transit	10° high	
				52°	56°
	h m	° ′	h m	h m	h m
1	21 33.7	−15 14	4 54	1 34	2 00
11	21 33.4	−15 16	4 14	0 54	1 21
21	21 32.7	−15 19	3 34	0 15	0 42
31	21 31.8	−15 24	2 54	23 31	0 02

Diameter 4″

NEPTUNE

Day	RA	Dec.	Transit	10° high	
				52°	56°
	h m	° ′	h m	h m	h m
1	20 35.0	−18 27	3 55	1 01	1 37
11	20 34.4	−18 29	3 15	0 22	0 57
21	20 33.7	−18 32	2 35	23 38	0 18
31	20 32.8	−18 36	1 55	22 58	23 34

Diameter 2″

July 2000

SEVENTH MONTH, 31 DAYS. *Julius* Caesar, formerly *Quintilis,* fifth month of Roman pre-Julian calendar

1	*Saturday*	Diana, Princess of Wales b. 1961. Juan Perón d. 1974	183
2	*Sunday*	**2nd S. after Trinity.** Christoph Gluck b. 1714	184
3	*Monday*	**St Thomas.** Ken Russell b. 1927	*week* 27 *day* 185
4	*Tuesday*	Dr Thomas Barnardo b. 1845. Marie Curie d. 1934	186
5	*Wednesday*	Cecil Rhodes b. 1853. Salvation Army founded 1865	187
6	*Thursday*	Beatrix Potter b. 1866. Roy Rogers d. 1998	188
7	*Friday*	Georg Ohm d. 1854. Sir Arthur Conan Doyle d. 1930	189
8	*Saturday*	Edmund Burke d. 1797. Vivien Leigh d. 1967	190
9	*Sunday*	**3rd S. after Trinity.** Ann Radcliffe b. 1764	191
10	*Monday*	Hadrian d. 138 AD. George Stubbs d. 1806	*week* 28 *day* 192
11	*Tuesday*	Battle of Courtrai 1302. Paul Nash d. 1946	193
12	*Wednesday*	*Bank Holiday in Northern Ireland.* Julius Caesar b. 102 BC	194
13	*Thursday*	Jean-Paul Marat d. 1793. Sir George Scott b. 1811	195
14	*Friday*	Storming of the Bastille 1789. Leon Garfield d. 1921	196
15	*Saturday*	Rembrandt b. 1606. Versace d. 1997	197
16	*Sunday*	**4th S. after Trinity.** Roald Amundsen b. 1872	198
17	*Monday*	Jules-Henri Poincaré d. 1912. Juan Fangio d. 1995	*week* 29 *day* 199
18	*Tuesday*	Thomas Cook d. 1892. Spanish Civil War began 1936	200
19	*Wednesday*	A. J. Cronin b. 1896. Sir James Goldsmith d. 1997	201
20	*Thursday*	Andrew Lang b. 1912. Guglielmo Marconi d. 1937	202
21	*Friday*	Robert Burns d. 1796. Paul Reuter b. 1816	203
22	*Saturday*	**Mary Magdalene.** Battle of Falkirk 1298	204
23	*Sunday*	**5th S. after Trinity.** Haile Selassie b. 1891	205
24	*Monday*	Amelia Earhart b. 1897. Treaty of Lausanne 1923	*week* 30 *day* 206
25	*Tuesday*	**St James.** Samuel Taylor Coleridge d. 1834	207
26	*Wednesday*	Francesco Cilea b. 1866. Robert Graves b. 1895	208
27	*Thursday*	Sir Anton Dolin b. 1904. Gertrude Stein d. 1946	209
28	*Friday*	Thomas Cromwell exec. 1540. J. S. Bach d. 1750	210
29	*Saturday*	Mussolini b. 1883. Van Gogh d. 1890	211
30	*Sunday*	**6th S. after Trinity.** Henry Moore b. 1898	212
31	*Monday*	*Trinity Law Sittings end.* Sir George Allen b. 1902	*week* 31 *day* 213

ASTRONOMICAL PHENOMENA

d	h	
1	16	Mars in conjunction
1	19	Mars in conjunction with Moon. Mars 2° N.
1	19	Partial eclipse of Sun (*see* page 71)
2	05	Venus in conjunction with Moon. Venus 2° N.
2	06	Mercury in conjunction with Moon. Mercury 3° S.
2	18	Venus in conjunction with Mercury. Venus 5° N.
4	00	Earth at aphelion (152 million km)
6	12	Mercury in inferior conjunction
7	14	Mars in conjunction with Mercury. Mars 6° N.
16	14	Total eclipse of Moon (*see* page 71)
17	13	Mercury at stationary point
22	13	Sun's longitude 120° ♌
26	10	Saturn in conjunction with Moon. Saturn 2° N.
26	21	Jupiter in conjunction with Moon. Jupiter 3° N.
27	09	Mercury at greatest elongation W.20°
27	23	Neptune at opposition
29	17	Mercury in conjunction with Moon. Mercury 0.8° S.
30	12	Mars in conjunction with Moon. Mars 0.6° N.
31	02	Partial eclipse of Sun (*see* page 71)

MINIMA OF ALGOL

d	h	d	h	d	h
3	08.1	14	19.3	26	06.5
6	04.9	17	16.1	29	03.3
9	01.7	20	12.9		
11	22.5	23	09.7		

CONSTELLATIONS

The following constellations are near the meridian at

	d	h		d	h
June	1	24	July	16	21
June	15	23	August	1	20
July	1	22	August	16	19

Ursa Minor, Draco, Corona, Hercules, Lyra, Serpens, Ophiuchus, Libra, Scorpius and Sagittarius

THE MOON

Phases, Apsides and Node	d	h	m
● New Moon	1	19	20
☽ First Quarter	8	12	53
○ Full Moon	16	13	55
☾ Last Quarter	24	11	02
● New Moon	31	02	25
Perigee (357,362 km)	1	22	16
Apogee (406,200 km)	15	15	33
Perigee (358,375 km)	30	07	44

Mean longitude of ascending node on July 1, 115°

THE SUN   s.d. 15′.8

Day	Right Ascension	Dec. +	Equation of time	Rise 52°	Rise 56°	Transit	Set 52°	Set 56°	Sidereal time	Transit of First Point of Aries
	h m s	° ′	m s	h m	h m	h m	h m	h m	h m s	h m s
1	6 41 12	23 06	− 3 48	3 44	3 19	12 04	20 23	20 49	18 37 24	5 21 43
2	6 45 20	23 02	− 3 59	3 45	3 19	12 04	20 23	20 48	18 41 21	5 17 47
3	6 49 28	22 57	− 4 11	3 46	3 20	12 04	20 22	20 48	18 45 17	5 13 51
4	6 53 36	22 52	− 4 22	3 47	3 21	12 04	20 22	20 47	18 49 14	5 09 55
5	6 57 43	22 47	− 4 32	3 48	3 22	12 05	20 21	20 46	18 53 11	5 05 59
6	7 01 50	22 41	− 4 42	3 49	3 23	12 05	20 21	20 45	18 57 07	5 02 03
7	7 05 56	22 34	− 4 52	3 49	3 25	12 05	20 20	20 45	19 01 04	4 58 07
8	7 10 02	22 28	− 5 02	3 50	3 26	12 05	20 19	20 44	19 05 00	4 54 11
9	7 14 08	22 21	− 5 11	3 51	3 27	12 05	20 18	20 43	19 08 57	4 50 16
10	7 18 13	22 13	− 5 19	3 52	3 28	12 05	20 18	20 42	19 12 53	4 46 20
11	7 22 18	22 05	− 5 28	3 54	3 30	12 06	20 17	20 41	19 16 50	4 42 24
12	7 26 22	21 57	− 5 35	3 55	3 31	12 06	20 16	20 40	19 20 46	4 38 28
13	7 30 26	21 49	− 5 43	3 56	3 32	12 06	20 15	20 38	19 24 43	4 34 32
14	7 34 29	21 40	− 5 49	3 57	3 34	12 06	20 14	20 37	19 28 40	4 30 36
15	7 38 32	21 30	− 5 56	3 58	3 35	12 06	20 13	20 36	19 32 36	4 26 40
16	7 42 34	21 21	− 6 01	3 59	3 37	12 06	20 12	20 34	19 36 33	4 22 44
17	7 46 36	21 11	− 6 07	4 01	3 38	12 06	20 11	20 33	19 40 29	4 18 48
18	7 50 37	21 00	− 6 11	4 02	3 40	12 06	20 10	20 32	19 44 26	4 14 52
19	7 54 38	20 50	− 6 16	4 03	3 41	12 06	20 08	20 30	19 48 22	4 10 56
20	7 58 38	20 39	− 6 19	4 05	3 43	12 06	20 07	20 29	19 52 19	4 07 00
21	8 02 38	20 27	− 6 22	4 06	3 45	12 06	20 06	20 27	19 56 15	4 03 05
22	8 06 37	20 15	− 6 25	4 07	3 46	12 06	20 05	20 25	20 00 12	3 59 09
23	8 10 35	20 03	− 6 27	4 09	3 48	12 06	20 03	20 24	20 04 09	3 55 13
24	8 14 33	19 51	− 6 28	4 10	3 50	12 06	20 02	20 22	20 08 05	3 51 17
25	8 18 31	19 38	− 6 29	4 12	3 52	12 06	20 00	20 20	20 12 02	3 47 21
26	8 22 28	19 25	− 6 29	4 13	3 53	12 06	19 59	20 18	20 15 58	3 43 25
27	8 26 24	19 11	− 6 29	4 14	3 55	12 06	19 57	20 17	20 19 55	3 39 29
28	8 30 20	18 58	− 6 28	4 16	3 57	12 06	19 56	20 15	20 23 51	3 35 33
29	8 34 15	18 44	− 6 27	4 17	3 59	12 06	19 54	20 13	20 27 48	3 31 37
30	8 38 09	18 29	− 6 25	4 19	4 01	12 06	19 53	20 11	20 31 44	3 27 41
31	8 42 03	18 15	− 6 22	4 21	4 02	12 06	19 51	20 09	20 35 41	3 23 45

Duration of Twilight (in minutes)

Latitude	52°	56°	52°	56°	52°	56°	52°	56°
	1 July		11 July		21 July		31 July	
Civil	48	61	46	58	44	53	41	49
Nautical	124	TAN	116	TAN	107	144	98	122
Astronomical	TAN	TAN	TAN	TAN	TAN	TAN	180	TAN

THE NIGHT SKY

Mercury is unsuitably placed for observation for most of the month, inferior conjunction occurring on the 6th. However, for the last few days of July it may be glimpsed as a difficult morning object, low above the east-north-eastern horizon at the beginning of morning civil twilight. During this period its magnitude brightens from +0.6 to −0.3.

Venus is too close to the Sun for observation for most of July. However, during the last week of the month it may be glimpsed with difficulty for a short time after sunset, low above the west-north-western horizon. Its magnitude is −3.9.

Mars is unsuitably placed for observation as it passes through conjunction on the 1st.

Jupiter continues to be visible as a morning object in the south-eastern sky, magnitude −2.1. It is moving eastwards between the Pleiades and the Hyades. On the morning of the 27th the old crescent Moon will be seen near the planet.

Saturn, magnitude +0.3, is a difficult morning object at first. However, it is rising earlier each night and by the end of the month it may be detected low above the eastern horizon shortly after midnight. On the morning of the 26th, the gibbous Moon will be seen approaching the planet. Saturn is in Taurus.

Neptune is at opposition on the 27th, in Capricornus. It is not visible to the naked eye since its magnitude is +7.8.

THE MOON

Day	RA (h m)	Dec. (°)	Hor. par. (′)	Semi-diam. (′)	Sun's co-long. (°)	PA of Bright Limb (°)	Phase (%)	Age (d)	Rise 52° (h m)	Rise 56° (h m)	Transit (h m)	Set 52° (h m)	Set 56° (h m)
1	5 51	+21.1	61.2	16.7	260	78	1	28.5	3 25	3 03	11 44	20 07	20 30
2	6 57	+21.7	61.4	16.7	273	296	0	0.2	4 26	4 03	12 48	21 06	21 28
3	8 02	+20.8	61.2	16.7	285	281	2	1.2	5 39	5 18	13 51	21 52	22 10
4	9 05	+18.5	60.7	16.5	297	284	7	2.2	6 58	6 41	14 51	22 28	22 42
5	10 05	+14.9	59.9	16.3	309	287	15	3.2	8 20	8 07	15 46	22 57	23 06
6	11 01	+10.6	59.1	16.1	322	290	24	4.2	9 39	9 32	16 38	23 21	23 25
7	11 53	+ 5.8	58.2	15.8	334	292	34	5.2	10 56	10 53	17 26	23 42	23 42
8	12 43	+ 0.9	57.2	15.6	346	293	44	6.2	12 10	12 11	18 12	—	23 59
9	13 32	− 3.9	56.4	15.4	358	292	55	7.2	13 21	13 27	18 57	0 02	—
10	14 19	− 8.4	55.7	15.2	11	291	65	8.2	14 30	14 40	19 42	0 22	0 15
11	15 07	−12.4	55.1	15.0	23	289	74	9.2	15 38	15 52	20 28	0 44	0 33
12	15 55	−15.9	54.7	14.9	35	286	82	10.2	16 44	17 01	21 14	1 09	0 54
13	16 44	−18.7	54.3	14.8	47	282	89	11.2	17 46	18 07	22 01	1 38	1 20
14	17 34	−20.6	54.1	14.7	59	278	94	12.2	18 43	19 06	22 49	2 13	1 52
15	18 24	−21.6	54.0	14.7	72	273	98	13.2	19 33	19 56	23 38	2 55	2 32
16	19 15	−21.6	54.0	14.7	84	269	100	14.2	20 16	20 38	—	3 44	3 21
17	20 06	−20.7	54.1	14.7	96	83	100	15.2	20 52	21 11	0 26	4 40	4 19
18	20 56	−18.9	54.2	14.8	108	79	98	16.2	21 22	21 37	1 14	5 42	5 23
19	21 45	−16.2	54.5	14.8	120	76	95	17.2	21 47	21 59	2 01	6 47	6 32
20	22 33	−12.8	54.8	14.9	133	73	90	18.2	22 09	22 17	2 46	7 54	7 43
21	23 20	− 8.9	55.3	15.1	145	71	83	19.2	22 29	22 33	3 30	9 02	8 56
22	0 07	− 4.4	55.8	15.2	157	69	75	20.2	22 49	22 49	4 15	10 12	10 10
23	0 55	+ 0.2	56.5	15.4	169	69	65	21.2	23 09	23 05	5 00	11 23	11 25
24	1 43	+ 5.0	57.2	15.6	181	69	55	22.2	23 32	23 23	5 46	12 37	12 43
25	2 34	+ 9.7	58.0	15.8	194	71	44	23.2	23 58	23 45	6 35	13 53	14 04
26	3 27	+14.0	58.9	16.0	206	74	33	24.2	—	—	7 27	15 12	15 27
27	4 24	+17.6	59.7	16.3	218	78	23	25.2	0 30	0 13	8 23	16 30	16 50
28	5 25	+20.3	60.4	16.5	230	83	14	26.2	1 11	0 51	9 24	17 44	18 06
29	6 28	+21.6	60.9	16.6	243	90	7	27.2	2 05	1 42	10 27	18 49	19 11
30	7 33	+21.4	61.2	16.7	255	98	2	28.2	3 11	2 49	11 30	19 41	20 01
31	8 37	+19.7	61.1	16.7	267	142	0	29.2	4 28	4 09	12 32	20 23	20 39

MERCURY

Day	RA (h m)	Dec. (°)	Diam. (″)	Phase (%)	Transit (h m)	5° high 52° (h m)	56° (h m)
1	7 16	+18.5	12	3	12 35	19 37	19 50
3	7 11	+18.3	12	2	12 22	19 23	19 35
5	7 06	+18.1	12	1	12 09	19 09	19 21
7	7 00	+18.0	12	1	11 56	4 56	4 44
9	6 55	+18.0	12	2	11 43	4 43	4 31
11	6 51	+18.0	11	3	11 31	4 31	4 19
13	6 47	+18.2	11	5	11 20	4 18	4 06
15	6 45	+18.4	11	8	11 10	4 07	3 54
17	6 44	+18.7	10	11	11 01	3 57	3 44
19	6 44	+19.0	10	16	10 54	3 47	3 34
21	6 46	+19.4	9	20	10 49	3 40	3 26
23	6 50	+19.8	9	25	10 45	3 33	3 19
25	6 55	+20.1	8	31	10 43	3 29	3 14
27	7 02	+20.5	8	37	10 42	3 26	3 11
29	7 11	+20.7	7	44	10 44	3 25	3 10
31	7 21	+20.9	7	51	10 46	3 27	3 11

VENUS

Day	RA (h m)	Dec. (°)	Diam. (″)	Phase (%)	Transit (h m)	5° high 52° (h m)	56° (h m)
1	7 05	+23.4	10	100	12 28	20 02	20 21
6	7 31	+22.8	10	99	12 35	20 05	20 22
11	7 58	+21.8	10	99	12 42	20 04	20 19
16	8 24	+20.6	10	99	12 48	20 04	20 19
21	8 49	+19.2	10	98	12 53	20 01	20 14
26	9 14	+17.5	10	98	12 58	19 56	20 08
31	9 38	+15.6	10	97	13 03	19 50	20 00

MARS

Day	RA (h m)	Dec. (°)	Diam. (″)	Phase (%)	Transit (h m)	5° high 52° (h m)	56° (h m)
1	6 42	+24.0	4	100	12 04	4 27	4 08
6	6 57	+23.7	4	100	11 59	4 23	4 05
11	7 11	+23.4	4	100	11 54	4 20	4 02
16	7 25	+23.0	4	100	11 48	4 17	3 59
21	7 39	+22.5	4	100	11 42	4 14	3 57
26	7 53	+21.9	4	100	11 37	4 12	3 56
31	8 07	+21.3	4	100	11 31	4 10	3 54

SUNRISE AND SUNSET

	London		Bristol		Birmingham		Manchester		Newcastle		Glasgow		Belfast	
	0°05′	51°30′	2°35′	51°28′	1°55′	52°28′	2°15′	53°28′	1°37′	54°59′	4°14′	55°52′	5°56′	54°35′
	h m	h m	h m	h m	h m	h m	h m	h m	h m	h m	h m	h m	h m	h m
1	3 48	20 21	3 58	20 30	3 49	20 33	3 45	20 41	3 32	20 48	3 36	21 05	3 52	21 03
2	3 48	20 20	3 58	20 30	3 50	20 33	3 46	20 40	3 33	20 47	3 37	21 04	3 53	21 02
3	3 49	20 20	3 59	20 30	3 51	20 32	3 46	20 40	3 34	20 47	3 38	21 04	3 54	21 01
4	3 50	20 19	4 00	20 29	3 52	20 32	3 47	20 39	3 35	20 46	3 39	21 03	3 55	21 01
5	3 51	20 19	4 01	20 29	3 53	20 31	3 48	20 39	3 36	20 46	3 40	21 02	3 56	21 00
6	3 52	20 18	4 02	20 28	3 54	20 31	3 49	20 38	3 37	20 45	3 41	21 01	3 57	21 00
7	3 52	20 18	4 03	20 27	3 55	20 30	3 50	20 37	3 38	20 44	3 42	21 01	3 58	20 59
8	3 53	20 17	4 04	20 27	3 56	20 29	3 51	20 36	3 39	20 43	3 44	21 00	3 59	20 58
9	3 54	20 16	4 05	20 26	3 57	20 29	3 52	20 36	3 40	20 42	3 45	20 59	4 00	20 57
10	3 55	20 15	4 06	20 25	3 58	20 28	3 53	20 35	3 42	20 41	3 46	20 58	4 01	20 56
11	3 56	20 15	4 07	20 24	3 59	20 27	3 54	20 34	3 43	20 40	3 47	20 57	4 03	20 55
12	3 58	20 14	4 08	20 24	4 00	20 26	3 56	20 33	3 44	20 39	3 49	20 56	4 04	20 54
13	3 59	20 13	4 09	20 23	4 01	20 25	3 57	20 32	3 45	20 38	3 50	20 54	4 05	20 53
14	4 00	20 12	4 10	20 22	4 02	20 24	3 58	20 31	3 47	20 37	3 52	20 53	4 06	20 52
15	4 01	20 11	4 11	20 21	4 03	20 23	3 59	20 30	3 48	20 36	3 53	20 52	4 08	20 51
16	4 02	20 10	4 12	20 20	4 05	20 22	4 01	20 29	3 49	20 35	3 54	20 51	4 09	20 50
17	4 03	20 09	4 14	20 19	4 06	20 21	4 02	20 27	3 51	20 33	3 56	20 49	4 11	20 48
18	4 05	20 08	4 15	20 17	4 07	20 20	4 03	20 26	3 52	20 32	3 58	20 48	4 12	20 47
19	4 06	20 06	4 16	20 16	4 09	20 18	4 05	20 25	3 54	20 31	3 59	20 46	4 14	20 46
20	4 07	20 05	4 17	20 15	4 10	20 17	4 06	20 23	3 56	20 29	4 01	20 45	4 15	20 44
21	4 09	20 04	4 19	20 14	4 11	20 16	4 08	20 22	3 57	20 28	4 02	20 43	4 17	20 43
22	4 10	20 03	4 20	20 13	4 13	20 14	4 09	20 21	3 59	20 26	4 04	20 42	4 18	20 41
23	4 11	20 01	4 21	20 11	4 14	20 13	4 11	20 19	4 00	20 24	4 06	20 40	4 20	20 40
24	4 13	20 00	4 23	20 10	4 16	20 12	4 12	20 18	4 02	20 23	4 07	20 38	4 21	20 38
25	4 14	19 59	4 24	20 08	4 17	20 10	4 14	20 16	4 04	20 21	4 09	20 36	4 23	20 36
26	4 15	19 57	4 26	20 07	4 19	20 09	4 15	20 15	4 05	20 19	4 11	20 35	4 25	20 35
27	4 17	19 56	4 27	20 06	4 20	20 07	4 17	20 13	4 07	20 18	4 13	20 33	4 26	20 33
28	4 18	19 54	4 29	20 04	4 22	20 06	4 19	20 11	4 09	20 16	4 15	20 31	4 28	20 31
29	4 20	19 53	4 30	20 03	4 23	20 04	4 20	20 10	4 10	20 14	4 16	20 29	4 30	20 30
30	4 21	19 51	4 31	20 01	4 25	20 02	4 22	20 08	4 12	20 12	4 18	20 27	4 31	20 28
31	4 23	19 50	4 33	19 59	4 26	20 01	4 23	20 06	4 14	20 10	4 20	20 25	4 33	20 26

JUPITER

Day	RA	Dec.	Transit	5° high	
				52°	56°
	h m	° ′	h m	h m	h m
1	3 52.6	+19 21	9 14	2 05	1 52
11	4 01.0	+19 46	8 43	1 32	1 18
21	4 08.9	+20 07	8 12	0 58	0 44
31	4 16.2	+20 26	7 39	0 24	0 10

Diameters – equatorial 35″ polar 33″

SATURN

Day	RA	Dec.	Transit	5° high	
				52°	56°
	h m	° ′	h m	h m	h m
1	3 39.3	+17 26	9 01	2 03	1 51
11	3 43.5	+17 39	8 25	1 26	1 15
21	3 47.2	+17 50	7 50	0 50	0 38
31	3 50.5	+17 58	7 14	0 13	0 01

Diameters – equatorial 17″ polar 16″
Rings – major axis 39″ minor axis 16″

URANUS

Day	RA	Dec.	Transit	10° high	
				52°	56°
	h m	° ′	h m	h m	h m
1	21 31.8	−15 24	2 54	23 31	0 02
11	21 30.6	−15 30	2 13	22 51	23 19
21	21 29.3	−15 37	1 33	22 12	22 39
31	21 27.8	−15 44	0 52	21 32	22 00

Diameter 4″

NEPTUNE

Day	RA	Dec.	Transit	10° high	
				52°	56°
	h m	° ′	h m	h m	h m
1	20 32.8	−18 36	1 55	22 58	23 34
11	20 31.8	−18 39	1 15	22 19	22 55
21	20 30.7	−18 43	0 34	21 39	22 15
31	20 29.6	−18 47	23 50	20 59	21 36

Diameter 2″

August 2000

EIGHTH MONTH, 31 DAYS. *Augustus,* formerly *Sextilis,* sixth month of Roman pre-Julian calendar

1	*Tuesday*	Queen Anne d. 1714. Yves St Laurent b. 1936	214
2	*Wednesday*	John Pinkerton b. 1919. Alexander Graham Bell d. 1922	215
3	*Thursday*	James II d. 1460. Rupert Brooke b. 1887	216
4	*Friday*	*Queen Elizabeth the Queen Mother b. 1900*	217
5	*Saturday*	Thomas Newcomen d. 1729. Richard Burton d. 1984	218
6	*Sunday*	**7th S. after Trinity. The Transfiguration**	219
7	*Monday*	*Bank Holiday in Scotland.* Ossie Clark d. 1996	*week 32 day* 220
8	*Tuesday*	Princess Beatrice of York b. 1988. Sir Frank Whittle d. 1996	221
9	*Wednesday*	Thomas Telford b. 1757. Hermann Hesse d. 1962	222
10	*Thursday*	Greenwich Observatory founded 1675	223
11	*Friday*	Charlotte Yonge b. 1823. Cardinal Newman d. 1890	224
12	*Saturday*	George IV b. 1762. Viscount Stewart d. 1822	225
13	*Sunday*	**8th S. after Trinity.** Sir Alfred Hitchcock b. 1899	226
14	*Monday*	Japan surrenders 1945. Enzo Ferrari d. 1988	*week 33 day* 227
15	*Tuesday*	**Blessed Virgin Mary.** *Princess Royal b. 1950*	228
16	*Wednesday*	Robert Bunsen d. 1899. Elvis Presley d. 1977	229
17	*Thursday*	Construction of Berlin Wall began 1961	230
18	*Friday*	Genghis Khan d. 1227. Lord John Russell b. 1792	231
19	*Saturday*	Augustus d. 14 AD. Coco Chanel b. 1883	232
20	*Sunday*	**9th S. after Trinity.** Rajiv Gandhi b. 1944	233
21	*Monday*	*Princess Margaret b. 1930.* William IV b. 1765	*week 34 day* 234
22	*Tuesday*	Michael Collins d. 1922. Dr Jacob Bronowski d. 1974	235
23	*Wednesday*	Louis XVI b. 1754. Rudolf Valentino d. 1926	236
24	*Thursday*	**St Bartholomew.** First Edinburgh Festival 1947	237
25	*Friday*	David Hume d. 1776. Sir Frederick Herchel d. 1822	238
26	*Saturday*	Mother Teresa b. 1910. Sir Francis Chichester d. 1972	239
27	*Sunday*	**10th S. after Trinity.** Haile Selassie d. 1975	240
28	*Monday*	*Bank Holiday in England, Wales and Northern Ireland*	*week 35 day* 241
29	*Tuesday*	First motorcycle patented 1885. Eamon de Valera d. 1975	242
30	*Wednesday*	Maria Montessori b. 1870. Ernest Rutherford b. 1871	243
31	*Thursday*	Diana, Princess of Wales d. 1997	244

ASTRONOMICAL PHENOMENA

d	h	
1	02	Venus in conjunction with Moon. Venus 1° S.
10	13	Mars in conjunction with Mercury. Mars 0.06° N.
11	05	Uranus at opposition
20	23	Pluto at stationary point
22	01	Mercury in superior conjunction
22	20	Sun's longitude 150° ♍
22	20	Saturn in conjunction with Moon. Saturn 2° N.
23	11	Jupiter in conjunction with Moon. Jupiter 3° N.
28	03	Mars in conjunction with Moon. Mars 0.9° S.
30	00	Mercury in conjunction with Moon. Mercury 3° S.
31	01	Venus in conjunction with Moon. Venus 4° S.

MINIMA OF ALGOL

d	h	d	h	d	h
1	00.2	12	11.4	23	22.6
3	21.0	15	08.2	26	19.4
6	17.8	18	05.0	29	16.3
9	14.6	21	01.8		

CONSTELLATIONS

The following constellations are near the meridian at

	d	h		d	h
July	1	24	August	16	21
July	16	23	September	1	20
August	1	22	September	15	19

Draco, Hercules, Lyra, Cygnus, Sagitta, Ophiuchus, Serpens, Aquila and Sagittarius

THE MOON

Phases, Apsides and Node	d	h	m
☽ First Quarter	7	01	02
○ Full Moon	15	05	13
☾ Last Quarter	22	18	51
● New Moon	29	10	19
Apogee (405,652 km)	11	22	24
Perigee (361,906 km)	27	13	58

Mean longitude of ascending node on August 1, 114°

THE SUN   s.d. 15′.8

Day	Right Ascension	Dec. +	Equation of time	Rise 52°	Rise 56°	Transit	Set 52°	Set 56°	Sidereal time	Transit of First Point of Aries
	h m s	° ′	m s	h m	h m	h m	h m	h m	h m s	h m s
1	8 45 56	18 00	− 6 19	4 22	4 04	12 06	19 49	20 07	20 39 38	3 19 50
2	8 49 49	17 44	− 6 15	4 24	4 06	12 06	19 48	20 05	20 43 34	3 15 54
3	8 53 41	17 29	− 6 10	4 25	4 08	12 06	19 46	20 03	20 47 31	3 11 58
4	8 57 32	17 13	− 6 05	4 27	4 10	12 06	19 44	20 01	20 51 27	3 08 02
5	9 01 23	16 57	− 5 59	4 28	4 12	12 06	19 43	19 59	20 55 24	3 04 06
6	9 05 13	16 40	− 5 53	4 30	4 14	12 06	19 41	19 57	20 59 20	3 00 10
7	9 09 03	16 24	− 5 46	4 31	4 16	12 06	19 39	19 54	21 03 17	2 56 14
8	9 12 52	16 07	− 5 38	4 33	4 18	12 06	19 37	19 52	21 07 13	2 52 18
9	9 16 40	15 50	− 5 30	4 35	4 20	12 05	19 35	19 50	21 11 10	2 48 22
10	9 20 28	15 32	− 5 21	4 36	4 22	12 05	19 33	19 48	21 15 07	2 44 26
11	9 24 15	15 14	− 5 12	4 38	4 23	12 05	19 31	19 45	21 19 03	2 40 30
12	9 28 02	14 57	− 5 02	4 39	4 25	12 05	19 29	19 43	21 23 00	2 36 35
13	9 31 48	14 38	− 4 52	4 41	4 27	12 05	19 27	19 41	21 26 56	2 32 39
14	9 35 33	14 20	− 4 41	4 43	4 29	12 05	19 25	19 38	21 30 53	2 28 43
15	9 39 18	14 01	− 4 29	4 44	4 31	12 04	19 23	19 36	21 34 49	2 24 47
16	9 43 03	13 42	− 4 17	4 46	4 33	12 04	19 21	19 34	21 38 46	2 20 51
17	9 46 47	13 23	− 4 04	4 48	4 35	12 04	19 19	19 31	21 42 42	2 16 55
18	9 50 30	13 04	− 3 51	4 49	4 37	12 04	19 17	19 29	21 46 39	2 12 59
19	9 54 13	12 45	− 3 37	4 51	4 39	12 03	19 15	19 27	21 50 36	2 09 03
20	9 57 55	12 25	− 3 23	4 52	4 41	12 03	19 13	19 24	21 54 32	2 05 07
21	10 01 37	12 05	− 3 09	4 54	4 43	12 03	19 11	19 22	21 58 29	2 01 11
22	10 05 19	11 45	− 2 54	4 56	4 45	12 03	19 09	19 19	22 02 25	1 57 15
23	10 09 00	11 25	− 2 38	4 57	4 47	12 03	19 07	19 17	22 06 22	1 53 20
24	10 12 41	11 04	− 2 22	4 59	4 49	12 02	19 04	19 14	22 10 18	1 49 24
25	10 16 21	10 44	− 2 06	5 01	4 51	12 02	19 02	19 12	22 14 15	1 45 28
26	10 20 01	10 23	− 1 49	5 02	4 53	12 02	19 00	19 09	22 18 11	1 41 32
27	10 23 40	10 02	− 1 32	5 04	4 55	12 01	18 58	19 07	22 22 08	1 37 36
28	10 27 19	9 41	− 1 15	5 06	4 57	12 01	18 56	19 04	22 26 05	1 33 40
29	10 30 58	9 20	− 0 57	5 07	4 59	12 01	18 53	19 02	22 30 01	1 29 44
30	10 34 37	8 58	− 0 39	5 09	5 01	12 00	18 51	18 59	22 33 58	1 25 48
31	10 38 15	8 37	− 0 20	5 10	5 03	12 00	18 49	18 56	22 37 54	1 21 52

•

DURATION OF TWILIGHT (in minutes)

Latitude	52°	56°	52°	56°	52°	56°	52°	56°
	1 August		11 August		21 August		31 August	
Civil	41	48	39	45	37	42	35	40
Nautical	97	120	89	106	83	96	79	89
Astronomical	177	TAN	153	205	138	166	127	147

THE NIGHT SKY

Mercury is a morning object during the first week of the month, low above the east-north-eastern horizon at the (time of) beginning of morning civil twilight. During this period its magnitude increases from −0.4 to −1.1. For the remainder of August it is too close to the Sun for observation, superior conjunction occurring on the 22nd.

Venus, magnitude −3.9, is visible in the evenings at sunset, though only for a short time, extremely low above the western horizon. The further north the observer is in Britain, the greater the difficulty in locating the planet.

Mars, magnitude +1.8, gradually becomes visible as a difficult morning object towards the end of the month, low above the east-north-eastern horizon, about an hour before sunrise.

Jupiter, magnitude −2.3, is still a splendid morning object in the south-eastern sky. The Moon, at Last Quarter, will be seen about 7° to the right of the planet during the early hours of the 23rd, while Saturn is on the opposite side of the Moon.

Saturn continues to be visible as a morning object, magnitude +0.2. By the end of the month the planet is visible low in the eastern sky by 2200 hours. Saturn is in Taurus.

Uranus is at opposition on the 11th, in Capricornus. Uranus is barely visible to the naked eye as its magnitude is +5.7, but it is readily located with any small optical aid.

Meteors. The maximum of the famous Perseid meteor shower occurs on the morning of the 12th. Conditions are best between moonset (shortly after 0100 hours) and the beginning of morning twilight.

THE MOON

Day	RA	Dec.	Hor. par.	Semi-diam.	Sun's co-long.	PA of Bright Limb	Phase	Age	Rise 52°	Rise 56°	Transit	Set 52°	Set 56°
	h m	°	′	′	°	°	%	d	h m	h m	h m	h m	h m
1	9 39	+16.6	60.7	16.6	279	278	1	0.9	5 51	5 36	13 31	20 55	21 07
2	10 38	+12.4	60.1	16.4	292	285	5	1.9	7 14	7 04	14 26	21 22	21 29
3	11 33	+ 7.6	59.3	16.2	304	288	12	2.9	8 34	8 29	15 17	21 45	21 47
4	12 26	+ 2.6	58.4	15.9	316	290	20	3.9	9 52	9 51	16 06	22 06	22 04
5	13 16	− 2.4	57.4	15.6	328	290	30	4.9	11 06	11 10	16 52	22 27	22 21
6	14 05	− 7.1	56.5	15.4	340	289	40	5.9	12 18	12 26	17 38	22 48	22 39
7	14 53	−11.4	55.7	15.2	353	287	50	6.9	13 27	13 40	18 24	23 12	22 59
8	15 42	−15.1	55.1	15.0	5	284	60	7.9	14 35	14 51	19 11	23 40	23 23
9	16 31	−18.0	54.6	14.9	17	280	69	8.9	15 38	15 58	19 58	—	23 52
10	17 21	−20.2	54.3	14.8	29	276	77	9.9	16 37	16 59	20 46	0 13	—
11	18 11	−21.4	54.1	14.7	42	271	85	10.9	17 30	17 53	21 34	0 52	0 30
12	19 02	−21.7	54.0	14.7	54	265	91	11.9	18 15	18 37	22 23	1 39	1 16
13	19 53	−21.1	54.1	14.7	66	259	96	12.9	18 53	19 13	23 11	2 33	2 11
14	20 43	−19.4	54.3	14.8	78	250	99	13.9	19 25	19 42	23 58	3 33	3 14
15	21 33	−16.9	54.5	14.9	90	208	100	14.9	19 52	20 05	—	4 38	4 22
16	22 21	−13.7	54.8	14.9	102	89	99	15.9	20 15	20 24	0 44	5 45	5 33
17	23 09	− 9.8	55.2	15.0	115	78	97	16.9	20 36	20 41	1 29	6 54	6 46
18	23 56	− 5.4	55.7	15.2	127	74	92	17.9	20 55	20 56	2 14	8 03	8 00
19	0 43	− 0.8	56.2	15.3	139	72	86	18.9	21 15	21 12	2 58	9 14	9 15
20	1 31	+ 4.0	56.7	15.5	151	72	78	19.9	21 36	21 29	3 44	10 27	10 32
21	2 21	+ 8.6	57.3	15.6	163	73	69	20.9	22 00	21 49	4 31	11 41	11 50
22	3 12	+13.0	58.0	15.8	176	75	59	21.9	22 29	22 13	5 21	12 57	13 11
23	4 07	+16.8	58.6	16.0	188	79	48	22.9	23 05	22 46	6 14	14 13	14 31
24	5 04	+19.7	59.3	16.1	200	84	37	23.9	23 51	23 29	7 11	15 26	15 48
25	6 05	+21.4	59.8	16.3	212	89	26	24.9	—	—	8 11	16 33	16 56
26	7 08	+21.8	60.3	16.4	225	96	16	25.9	0 50	0 27	9 12	17 30	17 51
27	8 11	+20.6	60.5	16.5	237	103	8	26.9	2 01	1 40	10 14	18 15	18 33
28	9 13	+18.1	60.6	16.5	249	112	3	27.9	3 21	3 03	11 14	18 51	19 05
29	10 13	+14.3	60.3	16.4	261	138	0	28.9	4 43	4 31	12 10	19 20	19 29
30	11 10	+ 9.7	59.8	16.3	274	266	1	0.6	6 06	5 59	13 04	19 45	19 50
31	12 04	+ 4.7	59.1	16.1	286	282	4	1.6	7 27	7 24	13 54	20 07	20 07

MERCURY

Day	RA	Dec.	Diam.	Phase	Transit	5° high 52°	5° high 56°
	h m	°	″	%	h m	h m	h m
1	7 27	+21.0	7	54	10 48	3 28	3 13
3	7 39	+21.0	6	61	10 53	3 32	3 17
5	7 53	+20.9	6	69	10 59	3 39	3 24
7	8 07	+20.6	6	76	11 06	3 48	3 33
9	8 23	+20.2	6	82	11 14	3 58	3 44
11	8 39	+19.5	6	87	11 22	4 10	3 56
13	8 55	+18.7	5	92	11 30	4 23	4 10
15	9 12	+17.8	5	95	11 39	4 38	4 26
17	9 28	+16.7	5	98	11 47	4 52	4 42
19	9 44	+15.4	5	99	11 56	5 08	4 58
21	10 00	+14.1	5	100	12 03	18 42	18 50
23	10 15	+12.7	5	100	12 11	18 42	18 48
25	10 30	+11.2	5	99	12 17	18 41	18 46
27	10 44	+ 9.7	5	99	12 24	18 39	18 43
29	10 58	+ 8.2	5	98	12 30	18 37	18 40
31	11 12	+ 6.6	5	96	12 35	18 34	18 36

VENUS

Day	RA	Dec.	Diam.	Phase	Transit	5° high 52°	5° high 56°
	h m	°	″	%	h m	h m	h m
1	9 43	+15.3	10	97	13 04	19 49	19 58
6	10 07	+13.2	10	96	13 08	19 42	19 49
11	10 30	+10.9	10	96	13 12	19 34	19 39
16	10 54	+ 8.6	10	95	13 15	19 25	19 28
21	11 16	+ 6.2	10	94	13 18	19 15	19 17
26	11 39	+ 3.7	11	94	13 21	19 05	19 05
31	12 01	+ 1.1	11	93	13 23	18 55	18 52

MARS

Day	RA	Dec.	Diam.	Phase	Transit	5° high 52°	5° high 56°
1	8 10	+21.2	4	100	11 29	4 09	3 54
6	8 23	+20.5	4	100	11 23	4 07	3 53
11	8 36	+19.7	4	100	11 17	4 05	3 51
16	8 50	+18.9	4	99	11 10	4 04	3 51
21	9 03	+18.0	4	99	11 03	4 02	3 50
26	9 15	+17.1	4	99	10 57	4 00	3 49
31	9 28	+16.2	4	99	10 50	3 58	3 48

SUNRISE AND SUNSET

	London		Bristol		Birmingham		Manchester		Newcastle		Glasgow		Belfast	
	0°05′ 51°30′		2°35′ 51°28′		1°55′ 52°28′		2°15′ 53°28′		1°37′ 54°59′		4°14′ 55°52′		5°56′ 54°35′	
	h m	h m	h m	h m	h m	h m	h m	h m	h m	h m	h m	h m	h m	h m
1	4 24	19 48	4 34	19 58	4 28	19 59	4 25	20 04	4 16	20 09	4 22	20 23	4 35	20 24
2	4 26	19 46	4 36	19 56	4 29	19 57	4 27	20 03	4 17	20 07	4 24	20 21	4 37	20 22
3	4 27	19 45	4 37	19 54	4 31	19 55	4 28	20 01	4 19	20 05	4 26	20 19	4 38	20 20
4	4 29	19 43	4 39	19 53	4 33	19 54	4 30	19 59	4 21	20 03	4 28	20 17	4 40	20 18
5	4 30	19 41	4 41	19 51	4 34	19 52	4 32	19 57	4 23	20 01	4 29	20 15	4 42	20 16
6	4 32	19 39	4 42	19 49	4 36	19 50	4 33	19 55	4 25	19 59	4 31	20 13	4 44	20 14
7	4 34	19 37	4 44	19 47	4 37	19 48	4 35	19 53	4 27	19 57	4 33	20 11	4 45	20 12
8	4 35	19 36	4 45	19 46	4 39	19 46	4 37	19 51	4 28	19 54	4 35	20 09	4 47	20 10
9	4 37	19 34	4 47	19 44	4 41	19 44	4 39	19 49	4 30	19 52	4 37	20 06	4 49	20 08
10	4 38	19 32	4 48	19 42	4 42	19 42	4 40	19 47	4 32	19 50	4 39	20 04	4 51	20 06
11	4 40	19 30	4 50	19 40	4 44	19 40	4 42	19 45	4 34	19 48	4 41	20 02	4 53	20 04
12	4 41	19 28	4 51	19 38	4 46	19 38	4 44	19 43	4 36	19 46	4 43	20 00	4 55	20 02
13	4 43	19 26	4 53	19 36	4 47	19 36	4 45	19 41	4 38	19 44	4 45	19 57	4 56	19 59
14	4 45	19 24	4 55	19 34	4 49	19 34	4 47	19 39	4 39	19 41	4 47	19 55	4 58	19 57
15	4 46	19 22	4 56	19 32	4 51	19 32	4 49	19 37	4 41	19 39	4 49	19 53	5 00	19 55
16	4 48	19 20	4 58	19 30	4 52	19 30	4 51	19 35	4 43	19 37	4 51	19 50	5 02	19 53
17	4 49	19 18	4 59	19 28	4 54	19 28	4 52	19 32	4 45	19 34	4 53	19 48	5 04	19 50
18	4 51	19 16	5 01	19 26	4 56	19 26	4 54	19 30	4 47	19 32	4 55	19 45	5 05	19 48
19	4 52	19 14	5 03	19 24	4 57	19 24	4 56	19 28	4 49	19 30	4 56	19 43	5 07	19 46
20	4 54	19 12	5 04	19 22	4 59	19 22	4 58	19 26	4 51	19 27	4 58	19 41	5 09	19 44
21	4 56	19 10	5 06	19 20	5 01	19 20	4 59	19 24	4 53	19 25	5 00	19 38	5 11	19 41
22	4 57	19 08	5 07	19 18	5 02	19 17	5 01	19 21	4 54	19 23	5 02	19 36	5 13	19 39
23	4 59	19 06	5 09	19 16	5 04	19 15	5 03	19 19	4 56	19 20	5 04	19 33	5 15	19 37
24	5 00	19 04	5 11	19 14	5 06	19 13	5 05	19 17	4 58	19 18	5 06	19 31	5 17	19 34
25	5 02	19 01	5 12	19 11	5 07	19 11	5 06	19 14	5 00	19 16	5 08	19 28	5 18	19 32
26	5 04	18 59	5 14	19 09	5 09	19 09	5 08	19 12	5 02	19 13	5 10	19 26	5 20	19 29
27	5 05	18 57	5 15	19 07	5 11	19 06	5 10	19 10	5 04	19 11	5 12	19 23	5 22	19 27
28	5 07	18 55	5 17	19 05	5 12	19 04	5 12	19 07	5 06	19 08	5 14	19 21	5 24	19 25
29	5 08	18 53	5 18	19 03	5 14	19 02	5 13	19 05	5 08	19 06	5 16	19 18	5 26	19 22
30	5 10	18 51	5 20	19 00	5 16	19 00	5 15	19 03	5 09	19 03	5 18	19 16	5 28	19 20
31	5 12	18 48	5 22	18 58	5 17	18 57	5 17	19 00	5 11	19 01	5 20	19 13	5 29	19 17

JUPITER

Day	RA	Dec.	Transit	5° high	
				52°	56°
	h m	° ′	h m	h m	h m
1	4 16.9	+20 27	7 36	0 21	0 06
11	4 23.3	+20 42	7 03	23 43	23 28
21	4 28.8	+20 54	6 29	23 08	22 53
31	4 33.3	+21 03	5 55	22 32	22 17

Diameters – equatorial 38″ polar 36″

SATURN

Day	RA	Dec.	Transit	5° high	
				52°	56°
	h m	° ′	h m	h m	h m
1	3 50.7	+17 59	7 10	0 09	23 53
11	3 53.4	+18 06	6 33	23 28	23 16
21	3 55.4	+18 10	5 56	22 50	22 38
31	3 56.7	+18 12	5 18	22 12	22 00

Diameters – equatorial 18″ polar 16″
Rings – major axis 41″ minor axis 17″

URANUS

Day	RA	Dec.	Transit	10° high	
				52°	56°
	h m	° ′	h m	h m	h m
1	21 27.6	−15 45	0 48	4 04	3 36
11	21 26.1	−15 52	0 07	3 22	2 54
21	21 24.5	−16 00	23 22	2 40	2 12
31	21 23.0	−16 07	22 41	1 59	1 30

Diameter 4″

NEPTUNE

Day	RA	Dec.	Transit	10° high	
				52°	56°
	h m	° ′	h m	h m	h m
1	20 29.5	−18 48	23 46	2 41	2 04
11	20 28.4	−18 52	23 05	2 00	1 23
21	20 27.3	−18 55	22 25	1 19	0 42
31	20 26.4	−18 59	21 45	0 38	0 01

Diameter 2″

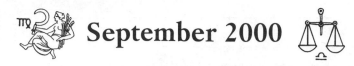

September 2000

NINTH MONTH, 30 DAYS. *Septem* (seven), seventh month of Roman pre-Julian calendar

1	*Friday*	Pope Adrian IV d. 1159. Great Fire of London 1666	245
2	*Saturday*	Frederick Soddy b. 1877. Henri Rousseau d. 1910	246
3	*Sunday*	**11th S. after Trinity.** Ferdinand Porsche b. 1875	247
4	*Monday*	Albert Schweitzer d. 1965. Professor Hans Eysenck d. 1997	*week 36 day* 248
5	*Tuesday*	Jesse James b. 1847. Mother Teresa d. 1997	249
6	*Wednesday*	Henry Walford Davies b. 1869. Austin Reed b. 1873	250
7	*Thursday*	Elizabeth I b. 1533. Sir Leonard Hutton d. 1990	251
8	*Friday*	Richard I b. 1157. Peter Sellers b. 1925	252
9	*Saturday*	Battle of Flodden 1513. Captain William Bligh b. 1754	253
10	*Sunday*	**12th S. after Trinity.** Arnold Palmer b. 1929	254
11	*Monday*	David Ricardo d. 1823. D. H. Lawrence b. 1885	*week 37 day* 255
12	*Tuesday*	Cleopatra's Needle erected 1878. Steve Biko d. 1977	256
13	*Wednesday*	British capture Quebec 1759. Roald Dahl b. 1916	257
14	*Thursday*	**Holy Cross Day.** Princess Grace of Monaco d. 1982	258
15	*Friday*	Battle of Britain Day. Prince Henry of Wales b. 1984	259
16	*Saturday*	Fire of Moscow 1812. Sir Gordon Newton b. 1907	260
17	*Sunday*	**13th S. after Trinity.** Laura Ashley d. 1985	261
18	*Monday*	Dr Samuel Johnson b. 1709. Jimi Hendrix d. 1970	*week 38 day* 262
19	*Tuesday*	Meyer Amschel Rothschild d. 1812. Sir William Golding b. 1911	263
20	*Wednesday*	Mungo Park b. 1771. Jacob Grimm d. 1863	264
21	*Thursday*	**St Matthew.** John McAdam b. 1756	265
22	*Friday*	Anne of Cleves b. 1515. Coronation of George III 1761	266
23	*Saturday*	Augustus b. 63 BC. Aldo Moro assassinated 1916	267
24	*Sunday*	**14th S. after Trinity.** Horace Walpole b. 1717	268
25	*Monday*	Transatlantic telephone service began 1956	*week 39 day* 269
26	*Tuesday*	Ivan Pavlov b. 1849. Sir Barnes Wallis b. 1887	270
27	*Wednesday*	Sir Martin Ryle b. 1918. *Queen Elizabeth I* launched 1938	271
28	*Thursday*	Edwin Hubble d. 1953. Miles Davis d. 1991	272
29	*Friday*	**St Michael and All Angels.** Lord Nelson b. 1758	273
30	*Saturday*	JEWISH NEW YEAR. James Dean d. 1955	274

ASTRONOMICAL PHENOMENA

d	h	
12	12	Saturn at stationary point
19	02	Saturn in conjunction with Moon. Saturn 2° N.
19	20	Jupiter in conjunction with Moon. Jupiter 2° N.
22	17	Sun's longitude 180° ♎
25	18	Mars in conjunction with Moon. Mars 2° S.
29	13	Jupiter at stationary point
29	18	Mercury in conjunction with Moon. Mercury 7° S.
30	04	Venus in conjunction with Moon. Venus 5° S.

MINIMA OF ALGOL

d	h	d	h	d	h
1	13.1	13	00.3	24	11.5
4	09.9	15	21.1	27	08.4
7	06.7	18	17.9	30	05.2
10	03.5	21	14.7		

CONSTELLATIONS

The following constellations are near the meridian at

	d	h		d	h
August	1	24	September	15	21
August	16	23	October	1	20
September	1	22	October	16	19

Draco, Cepheus, Lyra, Cygnus, Vulpecula, Sagitta, Delphinus, Equuleus, Aquila, Aquarius and Capricornus

THE MOON

Phases, Apsides and Node	d	h	m
☽ First Quarter	5	16	27
○ Full Moon	13	19	37
☾ Last Quarter	21	01	28
● New Moon	27	19	53
Apogee (404,761 km)	8	12	35
Perigee (366,961 km)	24	08	21

Mean longitude of ascending node on September 1, 112°

THE SUN

s.d. 15′.9

Day	Right Ascension	Dec.	Equation of time	Rise 52°	Rise 56°	Transit	Set 52°	Set 56°	Sidereal time	Transit of First Point of Aries
	h m s	° ′	m s	h m	h m	h m	h m	h m	h m s	h m s
1	10 41 52	+ 8 15	− 0 02	5 12	5 05	12 00	18 47	18 54	22 41 51	1 17 56
2	10 45 30	+ 7 53	+ 0 17	5 14	5 07	12 00	18 44	18 51	22 45 47	1 14 01
3	10 49 07	+ 7 31	+ 0 37	5 15	5 09	11 59	18 42	18 49	22 49 44	1 10 05
4	10 52 44	+ 7 09	+ 0 57	5 17	5 10	11 59	18 40	18 46	22 53 40	1 06 09
5	10 56 21	+ 6 47	+ 1 16	5 19	5 12	11 59	18 37	18 43	22 57 37	1 02 13
6	10 59 57	+ 6 24	+ 1 37	5 20	5 14	11 58	18 35	18 41	23 01 34	0 58 17
7	11 03 33	+ 6 02	+ 1 57	5 22	5 16	11 58	18 33	18 38	23 05 30	0 54 21
8	11 07 09	+ 5 40	+ 2 18	5 23	5 18	11 58	18 31	18 36	23 09 27	0 50 25
9	11 10 45	+ 5 17	+ 2 38	5 25	5 20	11 57	18 28	18 33	23 13 23	0 46 29
10	11 14 21	+ 4 54	+ 2 59	5 27	5 22	11 57	18 26	18 30	23 17 20	0 42 33
11	11 17 56	+ 4 31	+ 3 20	5 28	5 24	11 56	18 24	18 28	23 21 16	0 38 37
12	11 21 31	+ 4 09	+ 3 42	5 30	5 26	11 56	18 21	18 25	23 25 13	0 34 41
13	11 25 07	+ 3 46	+ 4 03	5 32	5 28	11 56	18 19	18 22	23 29 09	0 30 46
14	11 28 42	+ 3 23	+ 4 24	5 33	5 30	11 55	18 17	18 20	23 33 06	0 26 50
15	11 32 17	+ 3 00	+ 4 46	5 35	5 32	11 55	18 14	18 17	23 37 03	0 22 54
16	11 35 52	+ 2 37	+ 5 07	5 36	5 34	11 55	18 12	18 14	23 40 59	0 18 58
17	11 39 27	+ 2 13	+ 5 29	5 38	5 36	11 54	18 10	18 12	23 44 56	0 15 02
18	11 43 02	+ 1 50	+ 5 50	5 40	5 38	11 54	18 07	18 09	23 48 52	0 11 06
19	11 46 37	+ 1 27	+ 6 12	5 41	5 40	11 54	18 05	18 06	23 52 49	0 07 10
20	11 50 12	+ 1 04	+ 6 33	5 43	5 42	11 53	18 03	18 04	23 56 45	{ 0 03 14 / 23 59 18 }
21	11 53 48	+ 0 40	+ 6 54	5 45	5 44	11 53	18 00	18 01	0 00 42	23 55 22
22	11 57 23	+ 0 17	+ 7 15	5 46	5 46	11 53	17 58	17 58	0 04 38	23 51 26
23	12 00 59	− 0 06	+ 7 36	5 48	5 48	11 52	17 56	17 56	0 08 35	23 47 31
24	12 04 34	− 0 30	+ 7 57	5 50	5 49	11 52	17 53	17 53	0 12 31	23 43 35
25	12 08 10	− 0 53	+ 8 18	5 51	5 51	11 52	17 51	17 50	0 16 28	23 39 39
26	12 11 46	− 1 16	+ 8 39	5 53	5 53	11 51	17 49	17 48	0 20 25	23 35 43
27	12 15 22	− 1 40	+ 8 59	5 55	5 55	11 51	17 46	17 45	0 24 21	23 31 47
28	12 18 59	− 2 03	+ 9 19	5 56	5 57	11 51	17 44	17 43	0 28 18	23 27 51
29	12 22 35	− 2 27	+ 9 39	5 58	5 59	11 50	17 42	17 40	0 32 14	23 23 55
30	12 26 12	− 2 50	+ 9 59	6 00	6 01	11 50	17 39	17 37	0 36 11	23 19 59

DURATION OF TWILIGHT (in minutes)

Latitude	52°	56°	52°	56°	52°	56°	52°	56°
	1 September		11 September		21 September		30 September	
Civil	35	39	34	38	34	37	34	37
Nautical	79	89	76	84	74	82	73	80
Astronomical	127	146	120	135	115	129	113	126

THE NIGHT SKY

Mercury is unsuitably placed for observation throughout the month.

Venus, magnitude −3.9, continues to be visible as a difficult evening object for a short time after sunset, very low above the western horizon. Although it is farther from the Sun at the end of the month compared with the beginning, its rapid southward motion in declination compensates for this increase in elongation so that the time available for observation remains almost exactly the same throughout September.

Mars, magnitude +1.8, is a difficult morning object in the constellation of Leo, passing 1° north of Regulus on the 16th. The planet may be detected after about 0400 hours, low above the eastern horizon.

Jupiter, magnitude −2.5, continues to be visible as a splendid object in the southern half of the sky, from the late evening and through the night. Jupiter commences its retrograde motion after reaching its first stationary point on the 29th, in the constellation of Taurus. The gibbous Moon is near Jupiter and Saturn on the 19th.

Saturn, magnitude 0.0, is still a morning object, some 10° west of Jupiter. Saturn commences its retrograde motion after reaching its first stationary point on the 12th, in the constellation of Taurus.

Zodiacal Light. The morning cone may be seen reaching up from the eastern horizon along the ecliptic, before the beginning of morning twilight, from the beginning of the month to the 11th and again after the 25th.

THE MOON

Day	RA	Dec.	Hor. par.	Semi- diam.	Sun's co- long.	PA of Bright Limb	Phase	Age	Rise 52°	Rise 56°	Transit	Set 52°	Set 56°
	h m	°	′	′	°	°	%	d	h m	h m	h m	h m	h m
1	12 56	− 0.5	58.3	15.9	298	285	9	2.6	8 44	8 46	14 43	20 28	20 24
2	13 47	− 5.5	57.4	15.7	310	286	16	3.6	9 59	10 06	15 30	20 50	20 42
3	14 36	−10.1	56.6	15.4	322	285	24	4.6	11 12	11 23	16 17	21 13	21 01
4	15 26	−14.1	55.8	15.2	335	283	34	5.6	12 22	12 37	17 04	21 40	21 24
5	16 15	−17.3	55.2	15.0	347	280	43	6.6	13 28	13 47	17 52	22 11	21 51
6	17 06	−19.8	54.7	14.9	359	276	53	7.6	14 29	14 51	18 40	22 48	22 26
7	17 56	−21.3	54.4	14.8	11	271	63	8.6	15 25	15 48	19 29	23 32	23 09
8	18 47	−21.9	54.2	14.8	24	266	71	9.6	16 13	16 36	20 17	—	—
9	19 38	−21.5	54.2	14.8	36	261	80	10.6	16 53	17 14	21 06	0 24	0 01
10	20 29	−20.1	54.3	14.8	48	255	87	11.6	17 27	17 45	21 53	1 22	1 02
11	21 19	−17.8	54.6	14.9	60	249	92	12.6	17 55	18 09	22 40	2 26	2 09
12	22 08	−14.7	54.9	15.0	72	242	97	13.6	18 19	18 30	23 26	3 33	3 19
13	22 56	−10.9	55.4	15.1	84	226	99	14.6	18 41	18 47	—	4 42	4 33
14	23 44	− 6.6	55.8	15.2	97	131	100	15.6	19 01	19 03	0 11	5 52	5 47
15	0 31	− 1.9	56.3	15.3	109	86	98	16.6	19 20	19 19	0 56	7 04	7 03
16	1 20	+ 2.9	56.8	15.5	121	78	95	17.6	19 41	19 35	1 42	8 17	8 21
17	2 09	+ 7.7	57.3	15.6	133	77	89	18.6	20 04	19 54	2 29	9 31	9 40
18	3 00	+12.2	57.8	15.7	145	77	82	19.6	20 31	20 17	3 18	10 47	11 00
19	3 54	+16.2	58.2	15.9	157	80	72	20.6	21 04	20 45	4 10	12 03	12 21
20	4 50	+19.3	58.7	16.0	170	84	62	21.6	21 46	21 24	5 05	13 17	13 38
21	5 49	+21.3	59.0	16.1	182	89	51	22.6	22 39	22 16	6 03	14 25	14 48
22	6 50	+22.0	59.4	16.2	194	95	39	23.6	23 44	23 21	7 02	15 24	15 46
23	7 51	+21.3	59.6	16.2	206	101	29	24.6	—	—	8 02	16 11	16 31
24	8 52	+19.2	59.7	16.3	218	107	19	25.6	0 58	0 39	9 01	16 49	17 05
25	9 51	+15.9	59.7	16.3	231	113	11	26.6	2 18	2 03	9 57	17 20	17 31
26	10 48	+11.6	59.5	16.2	243	120	5	27.6	3 39	3 30	10 51	17 46	17 52
27	11 42	+ 6.7	59.1	16.1	255	135	1	28.6	5 00	4 55	11 42	18 08	18 11
28	12 35	+ 1.5	58.6	16.0	267	228	0	0.2	6 19	6 19	12 31	18 30	18 27
29	13 26	− 3.6	57.9	15.8	280	274	2	1.2	7 36	7 41	13 20	18 51	18 44
30	14 16	− 8.5	57.2	15.6	292	280	6	2.2	8 51	9 00	14 08	19 13	19 03

MERCURY

Day	RA	Dec.	Diam.	Phase	Transit	5° high 52°	5° high 56°
	h m	°	″	%	h m	h m	h m
1	11 18	+ 5.9	5	96	12 38	18 33	18 34
3	11 31	+ 4.3	5	94	12 42	18 29	18 29
5	11 43	+ 2.7	5	93	12 47	18 26	18 24
7	11 55	+ 1.2	5	92	12 51	18 22	18 19
9	12 07	− 0.3	5	90	12 55	18 18	18 14
11	12 19	− 1.8	5	89	12 58	18 14	18 08
13	12 30	− 3.3	5	87	13 01	18 09	18 02
15	12 41	− 4.7	5	86	13 04	18 04	17 56
17	12 51	− 6.1	5	84	13 07	17 59	17 50
19	13 02	− 7.5	5	82	13 10	17 54	17 44
21	13 12	− 8.8	6	80	13 12	17 49	17 38
23	13 22	−10.1	6	78	13 14	17 44	17 31
25	13 32	−11.3	6	76	13 16	17 39	17 24
27	13 41	−12.5	6	74	13 17	17 33	17 18
29	13 51	−13.6	6	72	13 19	17 28	17 11
31	14 00	−14.7	6	69	13 20	17 22	17 04

VENUS

Day	RA	Dec.	Diam.	Phase	Transit	5° high 52°	5° high 56°
	h m	°	″	%	h m	h m	h m
1	12 06	+ 0.6	11	93	13 24	18 53	18 49
6	12 28	− 2.0	11	92	13 27	18 42	18 36
11	12 50	− 4.5	11	91	13 29	18 31	18 23
16	13 13	− 7.1	11	90	13 32	18 20	18 10
21	13 35	− 9.6	11	89	13 35	18 09	17 56
26	13 58	−11.9	12	88	13 38	17 58	17 43
31	14 21	−14.2	12	87	13 42	17 48	17 30

MARS

Day	RA	Dec.	Diam.	Phase	Transit	5° high 52°	5° high 56°
1	9 31	+16.0	4	99	10 48	3 58	3 48
6	9 43	+15.0	4	99	10 41	3 56	3 47
11	9 55	+13.9	4	99	10 34	3 55	3 46
16	10 08	+12.8	4	98	10 26	3 53	3 46
21	10 20	+11.7	4	98	10 18	3 51	3 45
26	10 32	+10.6	4	98	10 11	3 49	3 44
31	10 44	+ 9.4	4	98	10 03	3 48	3 43

SUNRISE AND SUNSET

	London		Bristol		Birmingham		Manchester		Newcastle		Glasgow		Belfast	
	0°05′	51°30′	2°35′	51°28′	1°55′	52°28′	2°15′	53°28′	1°37′	54°59′	4°14′	55°52′	5°56′	54°35′
	h m	h m	h m	h m	h m	h m	h m	h m	h m	h m	h m	h m	h m	h m
1	5 13	18 46	5 23	18 56	5 19	18 55	5 19	18 58	5 13	18 58	5 22	19 10	5 31	19 15
2	5 15	18 44	5 25	18 54	5 21	18 53	5 20	18 56	5 15	18 56	5 24	19 08	5 33	19 12
3	5 16	18 42	5 26	18 52	5 22	18 50	5 22	18 53	5 17	18 53	5 26	19 05	5 35	19 10
4	5 18	18 39	5 28	18 49	5 24	18 48	5 24	18 51	5 19	18 51	5 28	19 03	5 37	19 07
5	5 20	18 37	5 30	18 47	5 26	18 46	5 25	18 48	5 21	18 48	5 30	19 00	5 38	19 05
6	5 21	18 35	5 31	18 45	5 27	18 43	5 27	18 46	5 22	18 46	5 32	18 57	5 40	19 02
7	5 23	18 33	5 33	18 43	5 29	18 41	5 29	18 44	5 24	18 43	5 34	18 55	5 42	19 00
8	5 24	18 30	5 34	18 40	5 31	18 39	5 31	18 41	5 26	18 41	5 35	18 52	5 44	18 57
9	5 26	18 28	5 36	18 38	5 32	18 36	5 32	18 39	5 28	18 38	5 37	18 50	5 46	18 55
10	5 28	18 26	5 38	18 36	5 34	18 34	5 34	18 36	5 30	18 36	5 39	18 47	5 48	18 52
11	5 29	18 23	5 39	18 33	5 36	18 32	5 36	18 34	5 32	18 33	5 41	18 44	5 49	18 50
12	5 31	18 21	5 41	18 31	5 37	18 29	5 38	18 32	5 34	18 30	5 43	18 42	5 51	18 47
13	5 32	18 19	5 42	18 29	5 39	18 27	5 39	18 29	5 35	18 28	5 45	18 39	5 53	18 45
14	5 34	18 17	5 44	18 27	5 41	18 25	5 41	18 27	5 37	18 25	5 47	18 36	5 55	18 42
15	5 36	18 14	5 46	18 24	5 42	18 22	5 43	18 24	5 39	18 23	5 49	18 34	5 57	18 40
16	5 37	18 12	5 47	18 22	5 44	18 20	5 45	18 22	5 41	18 20	5 51	18 31	5 59	18 37
17	5 39	18 10	5 49	18 20	5 46	18 17	5 46	18 19	5 43	18 18	5 53	18 28	6 00	18 35
18	5 40	18 07	5 50	18 17	5 47	18 15	5 48	18 17	5 45	18 15	5 55	18 26	6 02	18 32
19	5 42	18 05	5 52	18 15	5 49	18 13	5 50	18 14	5 47	18 12	5 57	18 23	6 04	18 29
20	5 43	18 03	5 53	18 13	5 51	18 10	5 52	18 12	5 48	18 10	5 59	18 21	6 06	18 27
21	5 45	18 00	5 55	18 10	5 52	18 08	5 53	18 09	5 50	18 07	6 01	18 18	6 08	18 24
22	5 47	17 58	5 57	18 08	5 54	18 06	5 55	18 07	5 52	18 05	6 03	18 15	6 10	18 22
23	5 48	17 56	5 58	18 06	5 56	18 03	5 57	18 05	5 54	18 02	6 05	18 13	6 11	18 19
24	5 50	17 54	6 00	18 04	5 57	18 01	5 59	18 02	5 56	18 00	6 06	18 10	6 13	18 17
25	5 51	17 51	6 02	18 01	5 59	17 58	6 00	18 00	5 58	17 57	6 08	18 07	6 15	18 14
26	5 53	17 49	6 03	17 59	6 01	17 56	6 02	17 57	6 00	17 54	6 10	18 05	6 17	18 12
27	5 55	17 47	6 05	17 57	6 02	17 54	6 04	17 55	6 02	17 52	6 12	18 02	6 19	18 09
28	5 56	17 44	6 06	17 54	6 04	17 51	6 06	17 52	6 04	17 49	6 14	17 59	6 21	18 07
29	5 58	17 42	6 08	17 52	6 06	17 49	6 07	17 50	6 05	17 47	6 16	17 57	6 23	18 04
30	6 00	17 40	6 10	17 50	6 07	17 47	6 09	17 48	6 07	17 44	6 18	17 54	6 24	18 02

JUPITER

Day	RA	Dec.	Transit	5° high	
				52°	56°
	h m	° ′	h m	h m	h m
1	4 33.7	+21 03	5 51	22 29	22 13
11	4 36.8	+21 09	5 15	21 52	21 36
21	4 38.7	+21 12	4 37	21 14	20 58
31	4 39.3	+21 12	3 58	20 35	20 19

Diameters – equatorial 42″ polar 39″

SATURN

Day	RA	Dec.	Transit	5° high	
				52°	56°
	h m	° ′	h m	h m	h m
1	3 56.8	+18 12	5 14	22 08	21 56
11	3 57.3	+18 11	4 35	21 29	21 17
21	3 57.0	+18 09	3 56	20 50	20 38
31	3 56.1	+18 04	3 15	20 10	19 58

Diameters – equatorial 19″ polar 17″
Rings – major axis 43″ minor axis 18″

URANUS

Day	RA	Dec.	Transit	10° high	
				52°	56°
	h m	° ′	h m	h m	h m
1	21 22.9	−16 07	22 37	1 54	1 26
11	21 21.5	−16 14	21 57	1 13	0 44
21	21 20.3	−16 19	21 16	0 32	0 03
31	21 19.4	−16 23	20 36	23 47	23 18

Diameter 4″

NEPTUNE

Day	RA	Dec.	Transit	10° high	
				52°	56°
	h m	° ′	h m	h m	h m
1	20 26.3	−18 59	21 41	0 34	23 52
11	20 25.5	−19 02	21 01	23 49	23 12
21	20 24.9	−19 04	20 21	23 09	22 31
31	20 24.5	−19 06	19 41	22 29	21 51

Diameter 2″

October 2000

TENTH MONTH, 31 DAYS. *Octo* (eighth), eighth month of Roman pre-Julian calendar

1	*Sunday*	**15th S. after Trinity.** Stanley Holloway b. 1890	275
2	*Monday*	*Michaelmas Law Sittings begin.* Lord Runcie b. 1921	*week* 40 *day* 276
3	*Tuesday*	William Morris d. 1896. A. L. Rowse d. 1997	277
4	*Wednesday*	Ken Wood b. 1916. Janis Joplin d. 1970	278
5	*Thursday*	Jacques Offenbach d. 1880. Oxfam founded 1942	279
6	*Friday*	Lord Tennyson d. 1892. Anwar Sadat d. 1981	280
7	*Saturday*	Battle of Lepanto 1571. Archbishop Laud b. 1573	281
8	*Sunday*	**16th S. after Trinity.** Clement Attlee d. 1967	282
9	*Monday*	YOM KIPPUR. Che Guevara d. 1967	*week* 41 *day* 283
10	*Tuesday*	Verdi b. 1813. Harold Pinter b. 1930	284
11	*Wednesday*	François Mauriac b. 1885. Anton Bruckner d. 1896	285
12	*Thursday*	Edward VI b. 1537. John Denver d. 1997	286
13	*Friday*	Antonio Canova d. 1822. Paul Simon b. 1941	287
14	*Saturday*	FEAST OF TABERNACLES begins. William Penn b. 1644	288
15	*Sunday*	**17th S. after Trinity.** Sarah, Duchess of York b. 1959	289
16	*Monday*	Houses of Parliament destroyed by fire 1834	*week* 42 *day* 290
17	*Tuesday*	John Wilkes b. 1727. Battle of Saratoga 1777	291
18	*Wednesday*	**St Luke.** Charles Babbage d. 1871	292
19	*Thursday*	Ernest Rutherford d. 1937. Jacqueline du Pré d. 1987	293
20	*Friday*	Sir Christopher Wren b. 1632. Sir Richard Burton d. 1890	294
21	*Saturday*	Battle of Trafalgar 1805. Alfred Nobel b. 1833	295
22	*Sunday*	**18th S. after Trinity.** Liszt b. 1811	296
23	*Monday*	First Parliament of Great Britain 1707. John Dunlop d. 1921	*week* 43 *day* 297
24	*Tuesday*	Jane Seymour d. 1537. Tchaikovsky d. 1893	298
25	*Wednesday*	Picasso b. 1881. Vincent Price d. 1993	299
26	*Thursday*	Domenico Scarlatti b. 1685. Igor Sikorsky d. 1972	300
27	*Friday*	Sir John Lennard-Jones b. 1894. Oliver Tambo b. 1917	301
28	*Saturday*	**SS Simon and Jude.** Statue of Liberty unveiled 1886	302
29	*Sunday*	**Last S. after Trinity.** Sir Walter Raleigh d. 1618	303
30	*Monday*	George II b. 1683. Edmund Cartwright d. 1823	*week* 44 *day* 304
31	*Tuesday*	Jan Vermeer b. 1632. Indira Gandhi assassinated 1984	305

ASTRONOMICAL PHENOMENA

d	h	
6	10	Mercury at greatest elongation E.26°
15	14	Neptune at stationary point
16	06	Saturn in conjunction with Moon. Saturn 2° N.
17	01	Jupiter in conjunction with Moon. Jupiter 2° N.
18	14	Mercury at stationary point
23	03	Sun's longitude 210° ♏
24	08	Mars in conjunction with Moon. Mars 3° S.
26	15	Uranus at stationary point
27	18	Mercury in conjunction with Moon. Mercury 6° S.
30	02	Mercury in inferior conjunction
30	10	Venus in conjunction with Moon. Venus 4° S.

MINIMA OF ALGOL

d	h	d	h	d	h
3	02.0	14	13.2	26	00.5
5	22.8	17	10.0	28	21.3
8	19.6	20	06.8	31	18.1
11	16.4	23	03.7		

CONSTELLATIONS

The following constellations are near the meridian at

	d	h		d	h
September	1	24	October	16	21
September	15	23	November	1	20
October	1	22	November	15	19

Ursa Major (below the Pole), Cepheus, Cassiopeia, Cygnus, Lacerta, Andromeda, Pegasus, Capricornus, Aquarius and Piscis Austrinus

THE MOON

Phases, Apsides and Node	d	h	m
☽ First Quarter	5	10	59
○ Full Moon	13	08	53
☾ Last Quarter	20	07	59
● New Moon	27	07	58
Apogee (404,170 km)	6	07	02
Perigee (370,115 km)	19	21	59

Mean longitude of ascending node on October 1, 111°

THE SUN

s.d. 16'.1

Day	Right Ascension h m s	Dec. ° '	Equation of time m s	Rise 52° h m	Rise 56° h m	Transit h m	Set 52° h m	Set 56° h m	Sidereal time h m s	Transit of First Point of Aries h m s
1	12 29 49	3 13	+10 18	6 01	6 03	11 50	17 37	17 35	0 40 07	23 16 03
2	12 33 27	3 36	+10 37	6 03	6 05	11 49	17 35	17 32	0 44 04	23 12 07
3	12 37 04	4 00	+10 56	6 05	6 07	11 49	17 32	17 29	0 48 00	23 08 11
4	12 40 42	4 23	+11 15	6 06	6 09	11 49	17 30	17 27	0 51 57	23 04 16
5	12 44 21	4 46	+11 33	6 08	6 11	11 48	17 28	17 24	0 55 54	23 00 20
6	12 47 59	5 09	+11 51	6 10	6 13	11 48	17 25	17 22	0 59 50	22 56 24
7	12 51 38	5 32	+12 08	6 11	6 15	11 48	17 23	17 19	1 03 47	22 52 28
8	12 55 18	5 55	+12 25	6 13	6 17	11 47	17 21	17 16	1 07 43	22 48 32
9	12 58 58	6 18	+12 42	6 15	6 19	11 47	17 19	17 14	1 11 40	22 44 36
10	13 02 38	6 40	+12 58	6 16	6 21	11 47	17 16	17 11	1 15 36	22 40 40
11	13 06 19	7 03	+13 14	6 18	6 23	11 47	17 14	17 09	1 19 33	22 36 44
12	13 10 00	7 26	+13 29	6 20	6 26	11 46	17 12	17 06	1 23 29	22 32 48
13	13 13 42	7 48	+13 44	6 22	6 28	11 46	17 10	17 04	1 27 26	22 28 52
14	13 17 24	8 10	+13 58	6 23	6 30	11 46	17 08	17 01	1 31 23	22 24 57
15	13 21 07	8 33	+14 12	6 25	6 32	11 46	17 05	16 59	1 35 19	22 21 01
16	13 24 50	8 55	+14 25	6 27	6 34	11 45	17 03	16 56	1 39 16	22 17 05
17	13 28 34	9 17	+14 38	6 29	6 36	11 45	17 01	16 54	1 43 12	22 13 09
18	13 32 19	9 39	+14 50	6 30	6 38	11 45	16 59	16 51	1 47 09	22 09 13
19	13 36 04	10 00	+15 01	6 32	6 40	11 45	16 57	16 49	1 51 05	22 05 17
20	13 39 50	10 22	+15 12	6 34	6 42	11 45	16 55	16 46	1 55 02	22 01 21
21	13 43 37	10 43	+15 22	6 36	6 44	11 45	16 53	16 44	1 58 58	21 57 25
22	13 47 24	11 05	+15 31	6 37	6 46	11 44	16 51	16 42	2 02 55	21 53 29
23	13 51 12	11 26	+15 40	6 39	6 48	11 44	16 49	16 39	2 06 52	21 49 33
24	13 55 00	11 47	+15 48	6 41	6 50	11 44	16 47	16 37	2 10 48	21 45 37
25	13 58 50	12 08	+15 55	6 43	6 53	11 44	16 45	16 35	2 14 45	21 41 42
26	14 02 40	12 28	+16 01	6 44	6 55	11 44	16 43	16 32	2 18 41	21 37 46
27	14 06 31	12 48	+16 07	6 46	6 57	11 44	16 41	16 30	2 22 38	21 33 50
28	14 10 22	13 09	+16 12	6 48	6 59	11 44	16 39	16 28	2 26 34	21 29 54
29	14 14 15	13 29	+16 16	6 50	7 01	11 44	16 37	16 25	2 30 31	21 25 58
30	14 18 08	13 48	+16 20	6 52	7 03	11 44	16 35	16 23	2 34 27	21 22 02
31	14 22 01	14 08	+16 23	6 53	7 05	11 44	16 33	16 21	2 38 24	21 18 06

DURATION OF TWILIGHT (in minutes)

Latitude	52°	56°	52°	56°	52°	56°	52°	56°
	1 October		11 October		21 October		31 October	
Civil	34	37	34	37	34	38	36	40
Nautical	73	80	73	80	74	81	75	83
Astronomical	113	125	112	124	113	124	114	126

THE NIGHT SKY

Mercury is unsuitably placed for observation throughout October, inferior conjunction occurring on the 30th.

Venus is a brilliant object in the early evenings, magnitude −4.0, though still very low in the south-western sky. By the end of the month it is visible for about half-an-hour after sunset, for observers in southern England.

Mars, magnitude +1.8, continues to be visible in the pre-dawn sky, low above the eastern horizon. On the morning of the 24th the old crescent Moon, only three days before New, passes 4° north of Mars.

Jupiter, magnitude −2.7, is in Taurus, about 5° north of Aldebaran. It is becoming visible for the greater part of the night, and by the end of the month is visible low in the east, shortly after 1800 hours. The four Galilean satellites are readily observable with a small telescope, or a good pair of binoculars provided that they are held rigidly. On the morning of the 17th the gibbous Moon passes 3° south of the planet.

Saturn is now visible for the greater part of the night as it approaches opposition next month, magnitude −0.2. The rings of Saturn present a beautiful spectacle to the observer with a small telescope. The Earth passed through the ring plane twice in 1995 and since then the rings have been slowly opening; the diameter of the minor axis is now 19 arcseconds, marginally greater than the polar diameter of the planet itself. The rings will not be at their maximum opening for a couple of years. The gibbous Moon passes 3° below the planet on the morning of the 16th.

THE MOON

Day	RA	Dec.	Hor. par.	Semi-diam.	Sun's co-long.	PA of Bright Limb	Phase	Age	Rise 52°	Rise 56°	Transit	Set 52°	Set 56°
	h m	°	'	'	°	°	%	d	h m	h m	h m	h m	h m
1	15 07	−12.8	56.5	15.4	304	280	12	3.2	10 04	10 17	14 55	19 38	19 24
2	15 57	−16.5	55.8	15.2	316	279	19	4.2	11 13	11 31	15 44	20 08	19 49
3	16 48	−19.3	55.2	15.0	328	275	27	5.2	12 18	12 39	16 33	20 43	20 21
4	17 39	−21.1	54.7	14.9	341	271	36	6.2	13 17	13 40	17 22	21 24	21 01
5	18 31	−22.0	54.4	14.8	353	267	46	7.2	14 08	14 32	18 10	22 13	21 50
6	19 22	−21.9	54.3	14.8	5	262	55	8.2	14 52	15 14	18 59	23 09	22 47
7	20 12	−20.8	54.3	14.8	17	257	64	9.2	15 28	15 47	19 47	—	23 52
8	21 02	−18.8	54.5	14.8	29	253	73	10.2	15 58	16 14	20 33	0 11	—
9	21 52	−16.0	54.8	14.9	42	248	81	11.2	16 23	16 35	21 19	1 17	1 02
10	22 40	−12.4	55.3	15.1	54	244	88	12.2	16 45	16 53	22 05	2 25	2 14
11	23 28	− 8.1	55.9	15.2	66	239	94	13.2	17 05	17 09	22 50	3 35	3 29
12	0 16	− 3.5	56.5	15.4	78	231	98	14.2	17 25	17 25	23 36	4 47	4 45
13	1 04	+ 1.5	57.1	15.6	90	200	100	15.2	17 45	17 41	—	6 01	6 04
14	1 54	+ 6.4	57.7	15.7	102	101	99	16.2	18 07	17 59	0 24	7 17	7 24
15	2 46	+11.2	58.2	15.8	115	85	97	17.2	18 33	18 20	1 13	8 35	8 46
16	3 40	+15.4	58.6	16.0	127	83	92	18.2	19 04	18 46	2 05	9 53	10 09
17	4 37	+18.8	58.9	16.0	139	85	85	19.2	19 43	19 22	3 00	11 09	11 30
18	5 36	+21.2	59.1	16.1	151	89	75	20.2	20 33	20 09	3 58	12 20	12 44
19	6 36	+22.2	59.2	16.1	163	94	65	21.2	21 34	21 11	4 57	13 22	13 45
20	7 38	+21.8	59.2	16.1	175	99	54	22.2	22 45	22 24	5 57	14 12	14 33
21	8 38	+20.1	59.2	16.1	188	105	43	23.2	—	23 45	6 54	14 52	15 09
22	9 36	+17.1	59.1	16.1	200	110	32	24.2	0 01	—	7 50	15 24	15 37
23	10 32	+13.1	58.9	16.0	212	114	22	25.2	1 21	1 09	8 43	15 50	15 58
24	11 25	+ 8.5	58.6	16.0	224	118	13	26.2	2 40	2 33	9 34	16 12	16 16
25	12 17	+ 3.4	58.2	15.9	236	122	7	27.2	3 58	3 56	10 23	16 33	16 33
26	13 08	− 1.8	57.8	15.7	249	129	2	28.2	5 15	5 17	11 11	16 53	16 49
27	13 58	− 6.8	57.2	15.6	261	161	0	29.2	6 30	6 37	11 58	17 14	17 06
28	14 48	−11.4	56.7	15.4	273	258	1	0.7	7 44	7 56	12 46	17 38	17 25
29	15 38	−15.4	56.1	15.3	285	273	3	1.7	8 56	9 12	13 34	18 05	17 48
30	16 29	−18.6	55.5	15.1	297	274	8	2.7	10 04	10 24	14 23	18 37	18 17
31	17 21	−20.8	55.0	15.0	310	271	14	3.7	11 07	11 30	15 13	19 16	18 53

MERCURY

Day	RA	Dec.	Diam.	Phase	Transit	5° high 52°	5° high 56°
	h m	°	"	%	h m	h m	h m
1	14 00	−14.7	6	69	13 20	17 22	17 04
3	14 08	−15.7	6	66	13 20	17 17	16 57
5	14 16	−16.6	7	63	13 21	17 11	16 49
7	14 24	−17.4	7	60	13 20	17 05	16 42
9	14 31	−18.1	7	56	13 19	16 59	16 35
11	14 37	−18.7	7	51	13 17	16 53	16 28
13	14 42	−19.2	8	47	13 14	16 47	16 21
15	14 46	−19.5	8	41	13 10	16 40	16 14
17	14 49	−19.6	8	35	13 04	16 34	16 07
19	14 49	−19.6	9	29	12 56	16 27	16 01
21	14 48	−19.3	9	22	12 46	16 20	15 55
23	14 45	−18.7	9	15	12 34	16 13	15 49
25	14 39	−17.8	10	9	12 20	16 06	15 43
27	14 31	−16.6	10	4	12 05	15 58	15 38
29	14 23	−15.3	10	1	11 48	7 47	8 05
31	14 13	−13.8	10	0	11 31	7 21	7 37

VENUS

Day	RA	Dec.	Diam.	Phase	Transit	5° high 52°	5° high 56°
	h m	°	"	%	h m	h m	h m
1	14 21	−14.2	12	87	13 42	17 48	17 30
6	14 45	−16.4	12	86	13 46	17 38	17 17
11	15 09	−18.3	12	84	13 50	17 29	17 04
16	15 34	−20.1	13	83	13 55	17 21	16 53
21	15 59	−21.7	13	82	14 01	17 14	16 42
26	16 25	−23.0	13	81	14 07	17 09	16 33
31	16 51	−24.1	14	79	14 13	17 06	16 26

MARS

Day	RA	Dec.	Diam.	Phase	Transit	5° high 52°	5° high 56°
1	10 44	+ 9.4	4	98	10 03	3 48	3 43
6	10 55	+ 8.3	4	98	9 55	3 46	3 42
11	11 07	+ 7.1	4	97	9 47	3 44	3 41
16	11 18	+ 5.9	4	97	9 39	3 42	3 40
21	11 30	+ 4.6	4	97	9 30	3 40	3 39
26	11 41	+ 3.4	4	96	9 22	3 38	3 38
31	11 53	+ 2.2	4	96	9 14	3 36	3 37

SUNRISE AND SUNSET

	London		Bristol		Birmingham		Manchester		Newcastle		Glasgow		Belfast	
	0°05′	51°30′	2°35′	51°28′	1°55′	52°28′	2°15′	53°28′	1°37′	54°59′	4°14′	55°52′	5°56′	54°35′
	h m	h m	h m	h m	h m	h m	h m	h m	h m	h m	h m	h m	h m	h m
1	6 01	17 38	6 11	17 48	6 09	17 44	6 11	17 45	6 09	17 42	6 20	17 52	6 26	17 59
2	6 03	17 35	6 13	17 45	6 11	17 42	6 13	17 43	6 11	17 39	6 22	17 49	6 28	17 57
3	6 05	17 33	6 15	17 43	6 13	17 40	6 15	17 40	6 13	17 37	6 24	17 46	6 30	17 54
4	6 06	17 31	6 16	17 41	6 14	17 37	6 16	17 38	6 15	17 34	6 26	17 44	6 32	17 52
5	6 08	17 28	6 18	17 38	6 16	17 35	6 18	17 36	6 17	17 32	6 28	17 41	6 34	17 49
6	6 10	17 26	6 19	17 36	6 18	17 33	6 20	17 33	6 19	17 29	6 30	17 39	6 36	17 47
7	6 11	17 24	6 21	17 34	6 19	17 30	6 22	17 31	6 21	17 27	6 32	17 36	6 38	17 44
8	6 13	17 22	6 23	17 32	6 21	17 28	6 24	17 28	6 23	17 24	6 34	17 33	6 39	17 42
9	6 15	17 20	6 24	17 30	6 23	17 26	6 25	17 26	6 25	17 22	6 36	17 31	6 41	17 39
10	6 16	17 17	6 26	17 27	6 25	17 24	6 27	17 24	6 27	17 19	6 38	17 28	6 43	17 37
11	6 18	17 15	6 28	17 25	6 26	17 21	6 29	17 21	6 29	17 17	6 40	17 26	6 45	17 35
12	6 20	17 13	6 30	17 23	6 28	17 19	6 31	17 19	6 30	17 14	6 42	17 23	6 47	17 32
13	6 21	17 11	6 31	17 21	6 30	17 17	6 33	17 17	6 32	17 12	6 44	17 21	6 49	17 30
14	6 23	17 09	6 33	17 19	6 32	17 15	6 34	17 14	6 34	17 09	6 46	17 18	6 51	17 27
15	6 25	17 07	6 35	17 17	6 33	17 12	6 36	17 12	6 36	17 07	6 48	17 16	6 53	17 25
16	6 26	17 04	6 36	17 14	6 35	17 10	6 38	17 10	6 38	17 05	6 50	17 13	6 55	17 23
17	6 28	17 02	6 38	17 12	6 37	17 08	6 40	17 08	6 40	17 02	6 53	17 11	6 57	17 20
18	6 30	17 00	6 40	17 10	6 39	17 06	6 42	17 05	6 42	17 00	6 55	17 08	6 59	17 18
19	6 31	16 58	6 41	17 08	6 41	17 04	6 44	17 03	6 44	16 58	6 57	17 06	7 01	17 16
20	6 33	16 56	6 43	17 06	6 42	17 02	6 46	17 01	6 46	16 55	6 59	17 04	7 03	17 13
21	6 35	16 54	6 45	17 04	6 44	16 59	6 48	16 59	6 48	16 53	7 01	17 01	7 05	17 11
22	6 37	16 52	6 47	17 02	6 46	16 57	6 49	16 57	6 50	16 51	7 03	16 59	7 07	17 09
23	6 38	16 50	6 48	17 00	6 48	16 55	6 51	16 54	6 52	16 48	7 05	16 57	7 09	17 06
24	6 40	16 48	6 50	16 58	6 50	16 53	6 53	16 52	6 54	16 46	7 07	16 54	7 11	17 04
25	6 42	16 46	6 52	16 56	6 51	16 51	6 55	16 50	6 56	16 44	7 09	16 52	7 13	17 02
26	6 44	16 44	6 54	16 54	6 53	16 49	6 57	16 48	6 58	16 42	7 11	16 50	7 15	17 00
27	6 45	16 42	6 55	16 52	6 55	16 47	6 59	16 46	7 00	16 39	7 13	16 47	7 17	16 58
28	6 47	16 40	6 57	16 50	6 57	16 45	7 01	16 44	7 02	16 37	7 16	16 45	7 19	16 56
29	6 49	16 38	6 59	16 48	6 59	16 43	7 03	16 42	7 04	16 35	7 18	16 43	7 21	16 53
30	6 51	16 37	7 01	16 47	7 01	16 41	7 05	16 40	7 07	16 33	7 20	16 41	7 23	16 51
31	6 52	16 35	7 02	16 45	7 02	16 39	7 07	16 38	7 09	16 31	7 22	16 38	7 25	16 49

JUPITER

Day	RA	Dec.	Transit	5° high	
				52°	56°
	h m	° ′	h m	h m	h m
1	4 39.3	+21 12	3 58	20 35	20 19
11	4 38.3	+21 10	3 18	19 55	19 39
21	4 36.0	+21 05	2 37	19 14	18 58
31	4 32.4	+20 57	1 54	18 32	18 16

Diameters – equatorial 46″ polar 43″

SATURN

Day	RA	Dec.	Transit	5° high	
				52°	56°
	h m	° ′	h m	h m	h m
1	3 56.1	+18 04	3 15	20 10	19 58
11	3 54.4	+17 58	2 34	19 30	19 18
21	3 52.1	+17 50	1 53	18 49	18 37
31	3 49.3	+17 41	1 11	18 08	17 56

Diameters – equatorial 20″ polar 18″
Rings – major axis 45″ minor axis 19″

URANUS

Day	RA	Dec.	Transit	10° high	
				52°	56°
	h m	° ′	h m	h m	h m
1	21 19.4	−16 23	20 36	23 47	23 18
11	21 18.7	−16 26	19 56	23 07	22 37
21	21 18.3	−16 27	19 16	22 27	21 57
31	21 18.3	−16 27	18 37	21 48	21 18

Diameter 4″

NEPTUNE

Day	RA	Dec.	Transit	10° high	
				52°	56°
	h m	° ′	h m	h m	h m
1	20 24.5	−19 06	19 41	22 29	21 51
11	20 24.3	−19 07	19 02	21 49	21 12
21	20 24.3	−19 07	18 22	21 10	20 32
31	20 24.5	−19 06	17 43	20 31	19 53

Diameter 2″

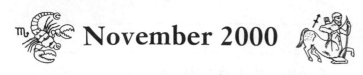

November 2000

ELEVENTH MONTH, 30 DAYS. *Novem* (nine), ninth month of Roman pre-Julian calendar

1	*Wednesday*	**All Saints' Day.** L. S. Lowry b. 1887	306
2	*Thursday*	Marie Antoinette b. 1755. Balfour Declaration 1917	307
3	*Friday*	Bellini b. 1801. Conor Cruise O'Brien b. 1917	308
4	*Saturday*	William III b. 1650. Wilfred Owen d. 1918	309
5	*Sunday*	**4th S. before Advent.** Sir John Hackett b. 1910	310
6	*Monday*	Adolphe Sax b. 1814. Jan Paderewski b. 1860	*week* 45 *day* 311
7	*Tuesday*	Sir Godfrey Kneller d. 1723. Marie Curie b. 1867	312
8	*Wednesday*	John Milton d. 1674. Prof. Christiaan Barnard b. 1922	313
9	*Thursday*	Edward VII b. 1841. Dylan Thomas d. 1953	314
10	*Friday*	William Hogarth b. 1697. Sir Gordon Richards d. 1986	315
11	*Saturday*	Armistice Day 1918. Dennis Wheatley d. 1977	316
12	*Sunday*	**3rd S. before Advent.** Remembrance Sunday	317
13	*Monday*	R. L. Stevenson b. 1850. Archbishop of Canterbury b. 1935	*week* 46 *day* 318
14	*Tuesday*	*Prince of Wales b. 1948.* Sir Frederick Banting b. 1841	319
15	*Wednesday*	Brazil becomes a Republic 1889. J. G. Ballard b. 1930	320
16	*Thursday*	Francis Danby b. 1793. John Walter d. 1812	321
17	*Friday*	Mary I d. 1558. Heitor Villa-Lobos d. 1959	322
18	*Saturday*	Sir William Gilbert b. 1836. Man Ray d. 1976	323
19	*Sunday*	**2nd S. before Advent.** Wolfe Tone d. 1798	324
20	*Monday*	*Queen's Wedding Day 1947.* Admiral Jellicoe d. 1935	*week* 47 *day* 325
21	*Tuesday*	Voltaire b. 1694. Natalia Makarova b. 1940	326
22	*Wednesday*	Sir Martin Frobisher d. 1594. J. F. Kennedy assassinated 1963	327
23	*Thursday*	Manuel de Falla b. 1876. Boris Karloff b. 1887	328
24	*Friday*	Ian Botham b. 1955. Freddie Mercury d. 1991	329
25	*Saturday*	Karl Benz b. 1844. Pope John XXIII b. 1881	330
26	*Sunday*	**Christ the King. S. next before Advent**	331
27	*Monday*	Anders Celsius b. 1701. Alexandre Dumas (younger) d. 1895	*week* 48 *day* 332
28	*Tuesday*	RAMADAN begins. William Blake b. 1757	333
29	*Wednesday*	Christian Doppler b. 1803. Ada Lovelace d. 1852	334
30	*Thursday*	**St Andrew.** Sir Winston Churchill b. 1874	335

ASTRONOMICAL PHENOMENA

d	h	
8	02	Mercury at stationary point
12	11	Saturn in conjunction with Moon. Saturn 2° N.
13	04	Jupiter in conjunction with Moon. Jupiter 2° N.
15	06	Mercury at greatest elongation W.19°
19	13	Saturn at opposition
21	21	Mars in conjunction with Moon. Mars 4° S.
22	00	Sun's longitude 240° ♐
24	13	Mercury in conjunction with Moon. Mercury 3° S.
28	02	Jupiter at opposition
29	18	Venus in conjunction with Moon. Venus 2° S.

MINIMA OF ALGOL

d	h	d	h	d	h
3	14.9	15	02.2	26	13.4
6	11.7	17	23.0	29	10.3
9	08.5	20	19.8		
12	05.4	23	16.6		

CONSTELLATIONS

The following constellations are near the meridian at

	d	h		d	h
October	1	24	November	15	21
October	16	23	December	1	20
November	1	22	December	16	19

Ursa Major (below the Pole), Cepheus, Cassiopeia, Andromeda, Pegasus, Pisces, Aquarius and Cetus

THE MOON

Phases, Apsides and Node	d	h	m
☽ First Quarter	4	07	27
○ Full Moon	11	21	15
☾ Last Quarter	18	15	24
● New Moon	25	23	11

	d	h	m
Apogee (404,377 km)	3	03	30
Perigee (366,047 km)	14	23	01
Apogee (405,273 km)	30	23	39

Mean longitude of ascending node on November 1, 109°

THE SUN

s.d. 16′.2

Day	Right Ascension	Dec. −	Equation of time	Rise 52°	Rise 56°	Transit	Set 52°	Set 56°	Sidereal time	Transit of First Point of Aries
	h m s	° ′	m s	h m	h m	h m	h m	h m	h m s	h m s
1	14 25 56	14 27	+16 24	6 55	7 07	11 44	16 31	16 19	2 42 21	21 14 10
2	14 29 51	14 46	+16 26	6 57	7 10	11 44	16 29	16 17	2 46 17	21 10 14
3	14 33 48	15 05	+16 26	6 59	7 12	11 44	16 28	16 15	2 50 14	21 06 18
4	14 37 45	15 24	+16 26	7 01	7 14	11 44	16 26	16 12	2 54 10	21 02 22
5	14 41 42	15 42	+16 24	7 02	7 16	11 44	16 24	16 10	2 58 07	20 58 27
6	14 45 41	16 00	+16 22	7 04	7 18	11 44	16 22	16 08	3 02 03	20 54 31
7	14 49 40	16 18	+16 19	7 06	7 20	11 44	16 21	16 06	3 06 00	20 50 35
8	14 53 41	16 36	+16 16	7 08	7 22	11 44	16 19	16 04	3 09 56	20 46 39
9	14 57 42	16 53	+16 11	7 10	7 25	11 44	16 17	16 03	3 13 53	20 42 43
10	15 01 44	17 10	+16 06	7 11	7 27	11 44	16 16	16 01	3 17 50	20 38 47
11	15 05 46	17 27	+16 00	7 13	7 29	11 44	16 14	15 59	3 21 46	20 34 51
12	15 09 50	17 43	+15 53	7 15	7 31	11 44	16 13	15 57	3 25 43	20 30 55
13	15 13 55	17 59	+15 45	7 17	7 33	11 44	16 11	15 55	3 29 39	20 26 59
14	15 18 00	18 15	+15 36	7 19	7 35	11 44	16 10	15 53	3 33 36	20 23 03
15	15 22 06	18 30	+15 26	7 20	7 37	11 45	16 08	15 52	3 37 32	20 19 07
16	15 26 13	18 45	+15 16	7 22	7 39	11 45	16 07	15 50	3 41 29	20 15 12
17	15 30 21	19 00	+15 05	7 24	7 41	11 45	16 06	15 48	3 45 25	20 11 16
18	15 34 30	19 14	+14 52	7 25	7 43	11 45	16 04	15 47	3 49 22	20 07 20
19	15 38 39	19 29	+14 39	7 27	7 45	11 45	16 03	15 45	3 53 19	20 03 24
20	15 42 50	19 42	+14 25	7 29	7 47	11 46	16 02	15 44	3 57 15	19 59 28
21	15 47 01	19 56	+14 11	7 30	7 49	11 46	16 01	15 42	4 01 12	19 55 32
22	15 51 13	20 09	+13 55	7 32	7 51	11 46	16 00	15 41	4 05 08	19 51 36
23	15 55 26	20 21	+13 39	7 34	7 53	11 47	15 59	15 40	4 09 05	19 47 40
24	15 59 40	20 34	+13 22	7 35	7 55	11 47	15 58	15 38	4 13 01	19 43 44
25	16 03 54	20 46	+13 04	7 37	7 57	11 47	15 57	15 37	4 16 58	19 39 48
26	16 08 09	20 57	+12 45	7 39	7 59	11 47	15 56	15 36	4 20 54	19 35 52
27	16 12 25	21 08	+12 26	7 40	8 00	11 48	15 55	15 35	4 24 51	19 31 57
28	16 16 42	21 19	+12 06	7 42	8 02	11 48	15 54	15 34	4 28 48	19 28 01
29	16 20 59	21 29	+11 45	7 43	8 04	11 48	15 53	15 33	4 32 44	19 24 05
30	16 25 17	21 39	+11 23	7 45	8 06	11 49	15 53	15 32	4 36 41	19 20 09

DURATION OF TWILIGHT (in minutes)

Latitude	52°	56°	52°	56°	52°	56°	52°	56°
	1 November		11 November		21 November		30 November	
Civil	36	40	37	41	38	43	39	45
Nautical	75	84	78	87	80	90	82	93
Astronomical	115	127	117	130	120	134	123	137

THE NIGHT SKY

Mercury is a morning object, visible low above the south-eastern horizon from after the first week of the month until almost the end of November. During this period its magnitude brightens from +1.1 to −0.7. On the morning of the 24th Mercury may be seen about 3° below the old crescent Moon, only 1.7 days old. This is the most favourable morning apparition of the year for observers in the northern hemisphere.

Venus continues to be visible as a brilliant object for a short time after sunset, low above the west-south-western horizon. By the end of the month it sets about two hours after the Sun. Its magnitude is −4.1. On the evening of the 29th the crescent Moon, four days old, passes about 1° north of the planet.

Mars is still a morning object, magnitude +1.7, moving steadily eastwards in the constellation of Virgo. The Moon is in the vicinity of the planet on the mornings of the 21st and 22nd.

Jupiter reaches opposition on the 28th and is therefore visible throughout the hours of darkness, magnitude −2.9. The Moon, just after Full, is near Jupiter on the nights of the 12th and 13th.

Saturn, magnitude −0.4, reaches opposition on the 19th and thus is visible throughout the hours of darkness. The Full Moon is near the planet on the nights of the 11th and 12th.

Meteors. The Leonid meteor shower, associated with Comet Tempel-Tuttle, does not usually provide a very noticeable display to the casual observer but on rare occasions spectacular displays of short duration have been observed. There is a possibility of such a display in the early morning hours of the 17th, though the Moon, near Last Quarter, will create some interference.

THE MOON

Day	RA	Dec.	Hor. par.	Semi-diam.	Sun's co-long.	PA of Bright Limb	Phase	Age	Rise 52°	Rise 56°	Transit	Set 52°	Set 56°
	h m	°	'	'	°	°	%	d	h m	h m	h m	h m	h m
1	18 13	−22.1	54.6	14.9	322	268	21	4.7	12 02	12 26	16 02	20 03	19 38
2	19 05	−22.3	54.3	14.8	334	264	29	5.7	12 49	13 13	16 51	20 56	20 33
3	19 56	−21.6	54.2	14.8	346	259	38	6.7	13 28	13 49	17 39	21 55	21 35
4	20 46	−19.9	54.3	14.8	358	255	47	7.7	14 00	14 18	18 26	22 59	22 42
5	21 35	−17.3	54.5	14.9	11	251	57	8.7	14 26	14 40	19 12	—	23 53
6	22 23	−14.0	54.9	15.0	23	248	66	9.7	14 49	14 59	19 57	0 06	—
7	23 10	−10.0	55.5	15.1	35	245	75	10.7	15 09	15 15	20 42	1 15	1 06
8	23 58	− 5.4	56.2	15.3	47	242	83	11.7	15 29	15 31	21 27	2 26	2 22
9	0 46	− 0.6	56.9	15.5	59	240	90	12.7	15 48	15 46	22 14	3 39	3 39
10	1 35	+ 4.5	57.7	15.7	71	238	95	13.7	16 09	16 02	23 03	4 54	4 59
11	2 26	+ 9.5	58.4	15.9	83	229	99	14.7	16 33	16 22	23 55	6 12	6 22
12	3 20	+14.1	59.1	16.1	96	145	100	15.7	17 02	16 46	—	7 32	7 47
13	4 18	+17.9	59.5	16.2	108	93	98	16.7	17 38	17 18	0 50	8 53	9 12
14	5 18	+20.8	59.8	16.3	120	90	94	17.7	18 25	18 02	1 49	10 09	10 32
15	6 20	+22.3	59.9	16.3	132	93	87	18.7	19 24	19 00	2 49	11 17	11 41
16	7 23	+22.3	59.8	16.3	144	98	79	19.7	20 33	20 11	3 50	12 12	12 35
17	8 24	+20.8	59.6	16.2	156	103	68	20.7	21 50	21 31	4 50	12 55	13 15
18	9 23	+18.1	59.2	16.1	168	108	57	21.7	23 09	22 55	5 47	13 29	13 44
19	10 20	+14.3	58.8	16.0	181	111	46	22.7	—	—	6 40	13 56	14 06
20	11 13	+ 9.8	58.4	15.9	193	114	35	23.7	0 27	0 19	7 31	14 19	14 25
21	12 04	+ 4.9	57.9	15.8	205	116	25	24.7	1 44	1 41	8 19	14 39	14 41
22	12 54	- 0.2	57.4	15.6	217	118	16	25.7	3 00	3 01	9 06	14 59	14 56
23	13 43	- 5.3	56.9	15.5	229	118	9	26.7	4 14	4 20	9 53	15 19	15 12
24	14 32	−10.0	56.4	15.4	242	119	4	27.7	5 28	5 38	10 39	15 41	15 29
25	15 22	−14.2	55.9	15.2	254	125	1	28.7	6 40	6 54	11 27	16 06	15 50
26	16 12	−17.6	55.5	15.1	266	197	0	0.0	7 50	8 08	12 16	16 35	16 16
27	17 04	−20.3	55.0	15.0	278	264	1	1.0	8 55	9 17	13 05	17 11	16 48
28	17 56	−21.9	54.7	14.9	290	267	4	2.0	9 54	10 18	13 55	17 54	17 30
29	18 48	−22.5	54.4	14.8	302	265	9	3.0	10 45	11 09	14 44	18 45	18 21
30	19 39	−22.1	54.2	14.8	315	261	15	4.0	11 27	11 50	15 33	19 42	19 20

MERCURY

Day	RA	Dec.	Diam.	Phase	Transit	5° high 52°	5° high 56°
	h m	°	"	%	h m	h m	h m
1	14 09	−13.0	10	1	11 23	7 08	7 24
3	14 02	−11.7	10	6	11 08	6 45	7 00
5	13 57	−10.6	9	13	10 56	6 27	6 40
7	13 54	- 9.9	9	22	10 46	6 13	6 25
9	13 55	- 9.6	8	32	10 39	6 04	6 16
11	13 57	- 9.6	8	41	10 35	6 00	6 12
13	14 02	−10.0	7	51	10 32	6 00	6 12
15	14 09	−10.6	7	59	10 32	6 02	6 15
17	14 17	−11.3	6	66	10 32	6 07	6 21
19	14 27	−12.2	6	72	10 34	6 14	6 29
21	14 37	−13.2	6	77	10 36	6 22	6 39
23	14 47	−14.2	6	81	10 39	6 31	6 49
25	14 58	−15.2	6	85	10 42	6 41	7 01
27	15 10	−16.2	5	88	10 46	6 52	7 13
29	15 22	−17.2	5	90	10 50	7 03	7 25
31	15 34	−18.2	5	92	10 55	7 14	7 38

VENUS

Day	RA	Dec.	Diam.	Phase	Transit	5° high 52°	5° high 56°
	h m	°	"	%	h m	h m	h m
1	16 56	−24.3	14	79	14 14	17 05	16 25
6	17 22	−25.0	14	78	14 21	17 05	16 22
11	17 49	−25.4	14	76	14 28	17 08	16 23
16	18 15	−25.5	15	75	14 35	17 14	16 28
21	18 42	−25.3	15	74	14 41	17 23	16 38
26	19 08	−24.9	16	72	14 48	17 35	16 53
31	19 34	−24.1	16	70	14 54	17 49	17 10

MARS

1	11 55	+ 1.9	4	96	9 12	3 35	3 37
6	12 06	+ 0.7	4	96	9 04	3 33	3 36
11	12 18	- 0.5	4	95	8 55	3 31	3 35
16	12 29	- 1.7	4	95	8 47	3 29	3 34
21	12 40	- 2.9	4	95	8 38	3 27	3 32
26	12 51	- 4.1	4	94	8 30	3 24	3 31
31	13 03	- 5.3	5	94	8 21	3 22	3 30

SUNRISE AND SUNSET

	London 0°05′ 51°30′		Bristol 2°35′ 51°28′		Birmingham 1°55′ 52°28′		Manchester 2°15′ 53°28′		Newcastle 1°37′ 54°59′		Glasgow 4°14′ 55°52′		Belfast 5°56′ 54°35′	
	h m	h m	h m	h m	h m	h m	h m	h m	h m	h m	h m	h m	h m	h m
1	6 54	16 33	7 04	16 43	7 04	16 37	7 08	16 36	7 11	16 29	7 24	16 36	7 27	16 47
2	6 56	16 31	7 06	16 41	7 06	16 36	7 10	16 34	7 13	16 27	7 26	16 34	7 29	16 45
3	6 58	16 29	7 08	16 39	7 08	16 34	7 12	16 32	7 15	16 25	7 28	16 32	7 31	16 43
4	7 00	16 28	7 09	16 38	7 10	16 32	7 14	16 30	7 17	16 23	7 30	16 30	7 33	16 41
5	7 01	16 26	7 11	16 36	7 12	16 30	7 16	16 28	7 19	16 21	7 32	16 28	7 35	16 39
6	7 03	16 24	7 13	16 34	7 13	16 29	7 18	16 27	7 21	16 19	7 35	16 26	7 37	16 37
7	7 05	16 23	7 15	16 33	7 15	16 27	7 20	16 25	7 23	16 17	7 37	16 24	7 39	16 36
8	7 07	16 21	7 17	16 31	7 17	16 25	7 22	16 23	7 25	16 15	7 39	16 22	7 41	16 34
9	7 08	16 19	7 18	16 30	7 19	16 23	7 24	16 21	7 27	16 13	7 41	16 20	7 43	16 32
10	7 10	16 18	7 20	16 28	7 21	16 22	7 26	16 20	7 29	16 11	7 43	16 18	7 45	16 30
11	7 12	16 16	7 22	16 26	7 23	16 20	7 27	16 18	7 31	16 09	7 45	16 16	7 47	16 28
12	7 14	16 15	7 23	16 25	7 24	16 19	7 29	16 16	7 33	16 08	7 47	16 14	7 49	16 27
13	7 15	16 13	7 25	16 24	7 26	16 17	7 31	16 15	7 35	16 06	7 49	16 13	7 50	16 25
14	7 17	16 12	7 27	16 22	7 28	16 16	7 33	16 13	7 37	16 04	7 51	16 11	7 52	16 23
15	7 19	16 11	7 29	16 21	7 30	16 14	7 35	16 12	7 39	16 03	7 53	16 09	7 54	16 22
16	7 20	16 09	7 30	16 19	7 31	16 13	7 37	16 10	7 41	16 01	7 55	16 08	7 56	16 20
17	7 22	16 08	7 32	16 18	7 33	16 12	7 39	16 09	7 43	16 00	7 57	16 06	7 58	16 19
18	7 24	16 07	7 34	16 17	7 35	16 10	7 40	16 07	7 45	15 58	7 59	16 04	8 00	16 17
19	7 25	16 06	7 35	16 16	7 37	16 09	7 42	16 06	7 47	15 57	8 01	16 03	8 02	16 16
20	7 27	16 04	7 37	16 15	7 38	16 08	7 44	16 05	7 48	15 55	8 03	16 01	8 04	16 14
21	7 29	16 03	7 39	16 13	7 40	16 07	7 46	16 04	7 50	15 54	8 05	16 00	8 06	16 13
22	7 30	16 02	7 40	16 12	7 42	16 05	7 48	16 02	7 52	15 53	8 07	15 58	8 08	16 12
23	7 32	16 01	7 42	16 11	7 43	16 04	7 49	16 01	7 54	15 51	8 09	15 57	8 09	16 11
24	7 34	16 00	7 43	16 10	7 45	16 03	7 51	16 00	7 56	15 50	8 11	15 56	8 11	16 09
25	7 35	15 59	7 45	16 09	7 47	16 02	7 53	15 59	7 58	15 49	8 13	15 55	8 13	16 08
26	7 37	15 58	7 47	16 09	7 48	16 01	7 54	15 58	7 59	15 48	8 15	15 53	8 15	16 07
27	7 38	15 58	7 48	16 08	7 50	16 01	7 56	15 57	8 01	15 47	8 17	15 52	8 16	16 06
28	7 40	15 57	7 50	16 07	7 51	16 00	7 58	15 56	8 03	15 46	8 18	15 51	8 18	16 05
29	7 41	15 56	7 51	16 06	7 53	15 59	7 59	15 55	8 05	15 45	8 20	15 50	8 20	16 04
30	7 43	15 55	7 52	16 05	7 54	15 58	8 01	15 55	8 06	15 44	8 22	15 49	8 21	16 03

JUPITER

Day	RA	Dec.	Transit	5° high	
				52°	56°
	h m	° ′	h m	h m	h m
1	4 32.0	+20 57	1 49	18 27	18 12
11	4 27.3	+20 47	1 05	17 44	17 29
21	4 21.8	+20 35	0 21	17 01	16 46
31	4 16.1	+20 22	23 31	16 17	16 02

Diameters – equatorial 48″ polar 45″

SATURN

Day	RA	Dec.	Transit	5° high	
				52°	56°
	h m	° ′	h m	h m	h m
1	3 49.0	+17 40	1 07	8 05	8 17
11	3 45.9	+17 29	0 24	7 22	7 34
21	3 42.6	+17 19	23 37	6 38	6 50
31	3 39.3	+17 09	22 55	5 55	6 06

Diameters – equatorial 20″ polar 18″
Rings – major axis 46″ minor axis 19″

URANUS

Day	RA	Dec.	Transit	10° high	
				52°	56°
	h m	° ′	h m	h m	h m
1	21 18.3	−16 27	18 33	21 44	21 14
11	21 18.7	−16 25	17 54	21 05	20 36
21	21 19.4	−16 21	17 15	20 27	19 58
31	21 20.4	−16 16	16 37	19 49	19 20

Diameter 4″

NEPTUNE

Day	RA	Dec.	Transit	10° high	
				52°	56°
	h m	° ′	h m	h m	h m
1	20 24.6	−19 06	17 39	20 27	19 50
11	20 25.0	−19 05	17 01	19 49	19 11
21	20 25.8	−19 02	16 22	19 11	18 33
31	20 26.7	−18 59	15 44	18 33	17 55

Diameter 2″

December 2000

TWELFTH MONTH, 31 DAYS. *Decem* (ten), tenth month of Roman pre-Julian calendar

1	*Friday*	Henry I d. 1135. David Ben-Gurion d. 1973	336
2	*Saturday*	Maria Callas b. 1923. Philip Larkin d. 1985	337
3	*Sunday*	**Advent Sunday.** Sir Rowland Hill b. 1795	338
4	*Monday*	Robert Jenkinson d. 1828. Vassily Kandinsky b. 1866	*week* 49 *day* 339
5	*Tuesday*	Mozart d. 1791. Lord Dainton d. 1997	340
6	*Wednesday*	Henry VI b. 1421. Joseph Gay-Lussac b. 1778	341
7	*Thursday*	Battle of Pearl Harbor 1941. Robert Graves d. 1985	342
8	*Friday*	Mary, Queen of Scots b. 1542. Golda Meir d. 1978	343
9	*Saturday*	Sir Anthony van Dyck b. 1641. Ralph Bunche d. 1951	344
10	*Sunday*	**2nd S. of Advent.** Ada Lovelace b. 1815	345
11	*Monday*	First motor show opened in Paris 1894	*week* 50 *day* 346
12	*Tuesday*	Sir Marc Brunel d. 1849. Frank Sinatra b. 1915	347
13	*Wednesday*	Abel Tasman discovered New Zealand 1642	348
14	*Thursday*	Nostradamus b. 1503. Sir Stanley Spencer d. 1959	349
15	*Friday*	Alexandre-Gustave Eiffel b. 1832. Sitting Bull d. 1890	350
16	*Saturday*	Beethoven b. 1770. Boston Tea Party 1773	351
17	*Sunday*	**3rd S. of Advent.** Dame Mary Cartwright b. 1900	352
18	*Monday*	Stradivari d. 1737. Steven Spielberg b. 1947	*week* 51 *day* 353
19	*Tuesday*	Vitus Bering d. 1741. Emily Brontë d. 1848	354
20	*Wednesday*	Artur Rubinstein d. 1982. Carl Sagan d. 1996	355
21	*Thursday*	*Michaelmas Law Sittings end.* Frank Zappa b. 1940	356
22	*Friday*	CHANUCAH begins. Puccini b. 1858	357
23	*Saturday*	Richard Arkwright b. 1732. Thomas Malthus d. 1834	358
24	*Sunday*	**4th S. of Advent.** Christmas Eve	359
25	*Monday*	**Christmas Day.** *Bank Holiday in the UK*	*week* 52 *day* 360
26	*Tuesday*	**St Stephen.** Boxing Day. *Bank Holiday in the UK*	361
27	*Wednesday*	**St John.** Louis Pasteur d. 1822	362
28	*Thursday*	**Holy Innocents.** Sir Arthur Eddington b. 1882	363
29	*Friday*	William Gladstone b. 1809. Jameson Raid 1895	364
30	*Saturday*	Robert Boyle d. 1691. Josephine Butler d. 1906	365
31	*Sunday*	**1st S. of Christmas.** John Flamsteed d. 1719	366

ASTRONOMICAL PHENOMENA

d	h	
4	14	Pluto in conjunction
9	18	Saturn in conjunction with Moon. Saturn 2° N.
10	08	Jupiter in conjunction with Moon. Jupiter 3° N.
20	10	Mars in conjunction with Moon. Mars 4° S.
21	14	Sun's longitude 270° ♑
25	17	Mercury in conjunction with Moon. Mercury 3° S.
25	17	Partial eclipse of Sun (*see* page 71)
25	19	Mercury in superior conjunction
30	00	Venus in conjunction with Moon. Venus 2° N.

MINIMA OF ALGOL

d	h	d	h	d	h
2	07.1	13	18.3	25	05.6
5	03.9	16	15.2	28	02.4
8	00.7	19	12.0	30	23.3
10	21.5	22	08.8		

CONSTELLATIONS

The following constellations are near the meridian at

	d	h		d	h
November	1	24	December	16	21
November	15	23	January	1	20
December	1	22	January	16	19

Ursa Major (below the Pole), Ursa Minor (below the Pole), Cassiopeia, Andromeda, Perseus, Triangulum, Aries, Taurus, Cetus and Eridanus

THE MOON

Phases, Apsides and Node	d	h	m
☽ First Quarter	4	03	55
○ Full Moon	11	09	03
☾ Last Quarter	18	00	41
● New Moon	25	17	22
Perigee (360,602 km)	12	22	21
Apogee (406,192 km)	28	15	05

Mean longitude of ascending node on December 1, 107°

THE SUN

s.d. 16'.3

Day	Right Ascension	Dec.	Equation of time	Rise 52°	Rise 56°	Transit	Set 52°	Set 56°	Sidereal time	Transit of First Point of Aries
	h m s	° ′	m s	h m	h m	h m	h m	h m	h m s	h m s
1	16 29 36	21 49	+11 01	7 46	8 07	11 49	15 52	15 31	4 40 37	19 16 13
2	16 33 55	21 58	+10 38	7 47	8 09	11 50	15 51	15 30	4 44 34	19 12 17
3	16 38 15	22 07	+10 15	7 49	8 10	11 50	15 51	15 29	4 48 30	19 08 21
4	16 42 36	22 15	+ 9 51	7 50	8 12	11 50	15 50	15 28	4 52 27	19 04 25
5	16 46 57	22 23	+ 9 27	7 51	8 14	11 51	15 50	15 28	4 56 23	19 00 29
6	16 51 18	22 30	+ 9 02	7 53	8 15	11 51	15 49	15 27	5 00 20	18 56 33
7	16 55 40	22 37	+ 8 36	7 54	8 16	11 52	15 49	15 27	5 04 17	18 52 37
8	17 00 03	22 43	+ 8 10	7 55	8 18	11 52	15 49	15 26	5 08 13	18 48 41
9	17 04 26	22 49	+ 7 44	7 56	8 19	11 52	15 49	15 26	5 12 10	18 44 46
10	17 08 50	22 55	+ 7 17	7 57	8 20	11 53	15 48	15 25	5 16 06	18 40 50
11	17 13 13	23 00	+ 6 49	7 58	8 21	11 53	15 48	15 25	5 20 03	18 36 54
12	17 17 38	23 05	+ 6 22	7 59	8 23	11 54	15 48	15 25	5 23 59	18 32 58
13	17 22 02	23 09	+ 5 54	8 00	8 24	11 54	15 48	15 25	5 27 56	18 29 02
14	17 26 27	23 13	+ 5 25	8 01	8 25	11 55	15 48	15 25	5 31 52	18 25 06
15	17 30 52	23 16	+ 4 57	8 02	8 26	11 55	15 49	15 25	5 35 49	18 21 10
16	17 35 18	23 19	+ 4 28	8 03	8 26	11 56	15 49	15 25	5 39 46	18 17 14
17	17 39 44	23 21	+ 3 58	8 03	8 27	11 56	15 49	15 25	5 43 42	18 13 18
18	17 44 10	23 23	+ 3 29	8 04	8 28	11 57	15 49	15 25	5 47 39	18 09 22
19	17 48 36	23 25	+ 2 59	8 05	8 29	11 57	15 50	15 26	5 51 35	18 05 26
20	17 53 02	23 26	+ 2 30	8 05	8 29	11 58	15 50	15 26	5 55 32	18 01 31
21	17 57 29	23 26	+ 2 00	8 06	8 30	11 58	15 51	15 27	5 59 28	17 57 35
22	18 01 55	23 26	+ 1 30	8 06	8 30	11 59	15 51	15 27	6 03 25	17 53 39
23	18 06 22	23 26	+ 1 00	8 07	8 31	11 59	15 52	15 28	6 07 21	17 49 43
24	18 10 48	23 25	+ 0 30	8 07	8 31	12 00	15 52	15 29	6 11 18	17 45 47
25	18 15 14	23 24	0 00	8 08	8 31	12 00	15 53	15 29	6 15 15	17 41 51
26	18 19 41	23 22	− 0 30	8 08	8 32	12 01	15 54	15 30	6 19 11	17 37 55
27	18 24 07	23 19	− 0 59	8 08	8 32	12 01	15 55	15 31	6 23 08	17 33 59
28	18 28 33	23 17	− 1 29	8 08	8 32	12 02	15 55	15 32	6 27 04	17 30 03
29	18 32 59	23 13	− 1 58	8 08	8 32	12 02	15 56	15 33	6 31 01	17 26 07
30	18 37 25	23 10	− 2 27	8 08	8 32	12 03	15 57	15 34	6 34 57	17 22 11
31	18 41 50	23 05	− 2 56	8 08	8 31	12 03	15 58	15 35	6 38 54	17 18 16

DURATION OF TWILIGHT (in minutes)

Latitude	52°	56°	52°	56°	52°	56°	52°	56°
	1 December		11 December		21 December		31 December	
Civil	40	45	41	47	41	47	41	47
Nautical	82	93	84	96	85	97	84	96
Astronomical	123	138	125	141	126	142	125	141

THE NIGHT SKY

Mercury is too close to the Sun for observation throughout the month, superior conjunction occurring on the 25th.

Venus is a magnificent object in the early evening sky, magnitude −4.2, low above the west-south-western horizon. By the end of the month it is visible for over three hours after sunset. The crescent Moon will be seen about 4° below the planet on the evening of the 29th.

Mars, magnitude +1.5, continues to be visible low in the east-south-eastern sky in the early mornings. Mars passes 4° north of Spica on the 11th. On the morning of the 20th the crescent Moon will be seen about 3° above the planet.

Jupiter, magnitude −2.8, is only just past opposition so that it is effectively visible throughout the hours of darkness until morning twilight begins. By the very end of the year it has sunk too low in the west to be visible shortly after 0400 hours. During the night of the 9th to 10th the Full Moon will be seen near Jupiter.

Saturn is an evening object, magnitude −0.2, visible from the end of evening twilight until the early hours of the morning. The Moon passes 2° south of Saturn on the evening of the 9th.

Meteors. The maximum of the well-known Geminid meteor shower occurs on the 13th. Conditions are not favourable since the bright gibbous Moon will be above the horizon.

THE MOON

Day	RA	Dec.	Hor. par.	Semi-diam.	Sun's co-long.	PA of Bright Limb	Phase	Age	Rise 52°	Rise 56°	Transit	Set 52°	Set 56°
	h m	°	'	'	°	°	%	d	h m	h m	h m	h m	h m
1	20 30	−20.7	54.1	14.7	327	257	22	5.0	12 02	12 21	16 20	20 44	20 26
2	21 19	−18.4	54.2	14.8	339	253	30	6.0	12 30	12 46	17 06	21 50	21 35
3	22 07	−15.4	54.4	14.8	351	250	39	7.0	12 53	13 05	17 50	22 57	22 46
4	22 54	−11.6	54.8	14.9	3	248	49	8.0	13 14	13 22	18 34	—	23 59
5	23 40	− 7.4	55.4	15.1	16	246	58	9.0	13 33	13 37	19 18	0 05	—
6	0 27	− 2.7	56.1	15.3	28	245	68	10.0	13 52	13 51	20 03	1 16	1 13
7	1 15	+ 2.3	57.0	15.5	40	244	77	11.0	14 11	14 07	20 50	2 28	2 31
8	2 04	+ 7.2	57.9	15.8	52	245	85	12.0	14 33	14 24	21 40	3 44	3 51
9	2 57	+12.1	58.8	16.0	64	246	92	13.0	14 58	14 45	22 33	5 03	5 15
10	3 53	+16.3	59.6	16.2	76	247	97	14.0	15 31	15 13	23 31	6 24	6 41
11	4 52	+19.8	60.3	16.4	88	235	100	15.0	16 13	15 51	—	7 45	8 06
12	5 55	+21.9	60.7	16.5	100	99	99	16.0	17 08	16 43	0 32	9 00	9 24
13	7 00	+22.6	60.8	16.6	113	96	96	17.0	18 15	17 52	1 36	10 03	10 27
14	8 04	+21.6	60.7	16.5	125	100	90	18.0	19 32	19 12	2 39	10 53	11 14
15	9 06	+19.2	60.3	16.4	137	105	82	19.0	20 53	20 38	3 39	11 32	11 48
16	10 05	+15.5	59.7	16.3	149	109	72	20.0	22 14	22 04	4 36	12 02	12 13
17	11 01	+11.1	59.0	16.1	161	112	62	21.0	23 33	23 28	5 28	12 26	12 33
18	11 53	+ 6.1	58.3	15.9	173	113	50	22.0	—	—	6 18	12 47	12 50
19	12 43	+ 1.0	57.6	15.7	185	114	40	23.0	0 50	0 49	7 05	13 07	13 05
20	13 32	− 4.0	56.9	15.5	198	114	30	24.0	2 04	2 08	7 51	13 26	13 20
21	14 21	− 8.8	56.3	15.3	210	113	21	25.0	3 17	3 25	8 37	13 47	13 37
22	15 09	−13.1	55.8	15.2	222	111	13	26.0	4 28	4 41	9 24	14 10	13 56
23	15 59	−16.7	55.3	15.1	234	108	7	27.0	5 38	5 55	10 11	14 37	14 19
24	16 49	−19.6	54.9	15.0	246	105	3	28.0	6 45	7 06	11 00	15 10	14 48
25	17 41	−21.6	54.6	14.9	259	105	1	29.0	7 46	8 10	11 49	15 50	15 26
26	18 33	−22.5	54.3	14.8	271	253	0	0.3	8 40	9 05	12 39	16 38	16 13
27	19 24	−22.4	54.1	14.7	283	263	1	1.3	9 26	9 49	13 28	17 33	17 10
28	20 15	−21.3	54.0	14.7	295	260	5	2.3	10 03	10 24	14 16	18 33	18 13
29	21 05	−19.3	54.0	14.7	307	257	9	3.3	10 33	10 51	15 02	19 38	19 21
30	21 53	−16.4	54.1	14.7	319	253	16	4.3	10 58	11 12	15 47	20 44	20 31
31	22 40	−12.9	54.3	14.8	332	251	23	5.3	11 19	11 29	16 30	21 51	21 43

MERCURY

Day	RA	Dec.	Diam.	Phase	Transit	5° high 52°	5° high 56°
	h m	°	"	%	h m	h m	h m
1	15 34	−18.2	5	92	10 55	7 14	7 38
3	15 47	−19.1	5	93	10 59	7 26	7 51
5	15 59	−20.0	5	95	11 04	7 37	8 05
7	16 12	−20.8	5	96	11 09	7 48	8 18
9	16 25	−21.6	5	97	11 14	7 59	8 31
11	16 38	−22.3	5	98	11 19	8 10	8 44
13	16 51	−22.9	5	98	11 25	8 21	8 57
15	17 05	−23.5	5	99	11 30	8 31	9 09
17	17 18	−23.9	5	99	11 36	8 41	9 20
19	17 32	−24.3	5	100	11 42	8 51	9 31
21	17 46	−24.6	5	100	11 48	8 59	9 41
23	17 59	−24.8	5	100	11 54	9 07	9 50
25	18 13	−25.0	5	100	12 00	14 45	14 02
27	18 27	−25.0	5	100	12 06	14 51	14 08
29	18 42	−24.9	5	100	12 12	14 58	14 16
31	18 56	−24.8	5	100	12 19	15 07	14 25

VENUS

Day	RA	Dec.	Diam.	Phase	Transit	5° high 52°	5° high 56°
	h m	°	"	%	h m	h m	h m
1	19 34	−24.1	16	70	14 54	17 49	17 10
6	19 59	−23.0	17	69	14 59	18 04	17 29
11	20 24	−21.7	17	67	15 04	18 20	17 50
16	20 48	−20.2	18	65	15 08	18 37	18 10
21	21 11	−18.4	19	63	15 12	18 53	18 30
26	21 33	−16.5	20	61	15 14	19 10	18 49
31	21 55	−14.4	21	59	15 16	19 25	19 08

MARS

1	13 03	− 5.3	5	94	8 21	3 22	3 30
6	13 14	− 6.4	5	94	8 13	3 20	3 29
11	13 25	− 7.5	5	93	8 04	3 18	3 28
16	13 36	− 8.6	5	93	7 56	3 16	3 27
21	13 48	− 9.7	5	93	7 48	3 13	3 25
26	13 59	−10.8	5	92	7 39	3 11	3 24
31	14 10	−11.8	5	92	7 31	3 08	3 23

SUNRISE AND SUNSET

	London		Bristol		Birmingham		Manchester		Newcastle		Glasgow		Belfast	
	0°05'	51°30'	2°35'	51°28'	1°55'	52°28'	2°15'	53°28'	1°37'	54°59'	4°14'	55°52'	5°56'	54°35'
	h m	h m	h m	h m	h m	h m	h m	h m	h m	h m	h m	h m	h m	h m
1	7 44	15 55	7 54	16 05	7 56	15 57	8 02	15 54	8 08	15 43	8 23	15 48	8 23	16 03
2	7 45	15 54	7 55	16 04	7 57	15 57	8 04	15 53	8 09	15 42	8 25	15 48	8 24	16 02
3	7 47	15 54	7 57	16 04	7 59	15 56	8 05	15 52	8 11	15 42	8 27	15 47	8 26	16 01
4	7 48	15 53	7 58	16 03	8 00	15 56	8 06	15 52	8 12	15 41	8 28	15 46	8 27	16 01
5	7 49	15 53	7 59	16 03	8 01	15 55	8 08	15 51	8 14	15 40	8 30	15 45	8 29	16 00
6	7 50	15 52	8 00	16 02	8 03	15 55	8 09	15 51	8 15	15 40	8 31	15 45	8 30	15 59
7	7 52	15 52	8 02	16 02	8 04	15 54	8 10	15 51	8 16	15 39	8 32	15 44	8 31	15 59
8	7 53	15 52	8 03	16 02	8 05	15 54	8 12	15 50	8 18	15 39	8 34	15 44	8 33	15 59
9	7 54	15 51	8 04	16 02	8 06	15 54	8 13	15 50	8 19	15 39	8 35	15 44	8 34	15 58
10	7 55	15 51	8 05	16 01	8 07	15 54	8 14	15 50	8 20	15 38	8 36	15 43	8 35	15 58
11	7 56	15 51	8 06	16 01	8 08	15 54	8 15	15 50	8 21	15 38	8 37	15 43	8 36	15 58
12	7 57	15 51	8 07	16 01	8 09	15 54	8 16	15 50	8 22	15 38	8 39	15 43	8 37	15 58
13	7 58	15 51	8 08	16 01	8 10	15 54	8 17	15 49	8 23	15 38	8 40	15 43	8 38	15 58
14	7 59	15 51	8 09	16 01	8 11	15 54	8 18	15 50	8 24	15 38	8 41	15 43	8 39	15 58
15	8 00	15 51	8 10	16 02	8 12	15 54	8 19	15 50	8 25	15 38	8 42	15 43	8 40	15 58
16	8 00	15 52	8 10	16 02	8 13	15 54	8 20	15 50	8 26	15 38	8 42	15 43	8 41	15 58
17	8 01	15 52	8 11	16 02	8 14	15 54	8 20	15 50	8 27	15 38	8 43	15 43	8 42	15 58
18	8 02	15 53	8 12	16 02	8 14	15 54	8 21	15 50	8 28	15 39	8 44	15 43	8 43	15 58
19	8 03	15 53	8 12	16 03	8 15	15 55	8 22	15 51	8 28	15 39	8 45	15 44	8 43	15 59
20	8 03	15 53	8 13	16 03	8 16	15 55	8 22	15 51	8 29	15 39	8 45	15 44	8 44	15 59
21	8 04	15 53	8 14	16 04	8 16	15 56	8 23	15 52	8 30	15 40	8 46	15 45	8 44	16 00
22	8 04	15 54	8 14	16 04	8 17	15 56	8 23	15 52	8 30	15 40	8 46	15 45	8 45	16 00
23	8 05	15 55	8 14	16 05	8 17	15 57	8 24	15 53	8 30	15 41	8 47	15 46	8 45	16 01
24	8 05	15 55	8 15	16 05	8 17	15 57	8 24	15 53	8 31	15 42	8 47	15 46	8 46	16 01
25	8 05	15 56	8 15	16 06	8 18	15 58	8 25	15 54	8 31	15 42	8 47	15 47	8 46	16 02
26	8 06	15 57	8 15	16 07	8 18	15 59	8 25	15 55	8 31	15 43	8 48	15 48	8 46	16 03
27	8 06	15 57	8 16	16 08	8 18	16 00	8 25	15 56	8 31	15 44	8 48	15 49	8 46	16 04
28	8 06	15 58	8 16	16 08	8 18	16 01	8 25	15 56	8 32	15 45	8 48	15 50	8 46	16 05
29	8 06	15 59	8 16	16 09	8 18	16 02	8 25	15 57	8 32	15 46	8 48	15 51	8 46	16 06
30	8 06	16 00	8 16	16 10	8 18	16 03	8 25	15 58	8 32	15 47	8 48	15 52	8 46	16 07
31	8 06	16 01	8 16	16 11	8 18	16 04	8 25	15 59	8 31	15 48	8 47	15 53	8 46	16 08

JUPITER

Day	RA	Dec.	Transit	5° high	
				52°	56°
	h m	° '	h m	h m	h m
1	4 16.1	+20 22	23 31	6 50	7 04
11	4 10.5	+20 10	22 46	6 04	6 18
21	4 05.5	+19 58	22 02	5 18	5 33
31	4 01.4	+19 49	21 19	4 34	4 48

Diameters – equatorial 48" polar 45"

SATURN

Day	RA	Dec.	Transit	5° high	
				52°	56°
	h m	° '	h m	h m	h m
1	3 39.3	+17 09	22 55	5 55	6 06
11	3 36.2	+17 00	22 12	5 12	5 23
21	3 33.5	+16 53	21 30	4 29	4 40
31	3 31.3	+16 47	20 49	3 47	3 58

Diameters – equatorial 20" polar 18"
Rings – major axis 46" minor axis 18"

URANUS

Day	RA	Dec.	Transit	10° high	
				52°	56°
	h m	° '	h m	h m	h m
1	21 20.4	−16 16	16 37	19 49	19 20
11	21 21.7	−16 10	15 59	19 12	18 43
21	21 23.2	−16 03	15 21	18 35	18 07
31	21 25.0	−15 54	14 44	17 59	17 31

Diameter 4"

NEPTUNE

Day	RA	Dec.	Transit	10° high	
				52°	56°
	h m	° '	h m	h m	h m
1	20 26.7	−18 59	15 44	18 33	17 55
11	20 27.8	−18 56	15 05	17 55	17 18
21	20 29.0	−18 52	14 27	17 18	16 41
31	20 30.4	−18 47	13 49	16 40	16 04

Diameter 2"

RISING AND SETTING TIMES

TABLE 1. SEMI-DIURNAL ARCS (HOUR ANGLES AT RISING/SETTING)

Dec.	Latitude 0°	10°	20°	30°	40°	45°	50°	52°	54°	56°	58°	60°	Dec.
	h m	h m	h m	h m	h m	h m	h m	h m	h m	h m	h m	h m	
0°	6 00	6 00	6 00	6 00	6 00	6 00	6 00	6 00	6 00	6 00	6 00	6 00	0°
1°	6 00	6 01	6 01	6 02	6 03	6 04	6 05	6 05	6 06	6 06	6 06	6 07	1°
2°	6 00	6 01	6 03	6 05	6 07	6 08	6 10	6 10	6 11	6 12	6 13	6 14	2°
3°	6 00	6 02	6 04	6 07	6 10	6 12	6 14	6 15	6 17	6 18	6 19	6 21	3°
4°	6 00	6 03	6 06	6 09	6 13	6 16	6 19	6 21	6 22	6 24	6 26	6 28	4°
5°	6 00	6 04	6 07	6 12	6 17	6 20	6 24	6 26	6 28	6 30	6 32	6 35	5°
6°	6 00	6 04	6 09	6 14	6 20	6 24	6 29	6 31	6 33	6 36	6 39	6 42	6°
7°	6 00	6 05	6 10	6 16	6 24	6 28	6 34	6 36	6 39	6 42	6 45	6 49	7°
8°	6 00	6 06	6 12	6 19	6 27	6 32	6 39	6 41	6 45	6 48	6 52	6 56	8°
9°	6 00	6 06	6 13	6 21	6 31	6 36	6 44	6 47	6 50	6 54	6 59	7 04	9°
10°	6 00	6 07	6 15	6 23	6 34	6 41	6 49	6 52	6 56	7 01	7 06	7 11	10°
11°	6 00	6 08	6 16	6 26	6 38	6 45	6 54	6 58	7 02	7 07	7 12	7 19	11°
12°	6 00	6 09	6 18	6 28	6 41	6 49	6 59	7 03	7 08	7 13	7 20	7 26	12°
13°	6 00	6 09	6 19	6 31	6 45	6 53	7 04	7 09	7 14	7 20	7 27	7 34	13°
14°	6 00	6 10	6 21	6 33	6 48	6 58	7 09	7 14	7 20	7 27	7 34	7 42	14°
15°	6 00	6 11	6 22	6 36	6 52	7 02	7 14	7 20	7 27	7 34	7 42	7 51	15°
16°	6 00	6 12	6 24	6 38	6 56	7 07	7 20	7 26	7 33	7 41	7 49	7 59	16°
17°	6 00	6 12	6 26	6 41	6 59	7 11	7 25	7 32	7 40	7 48	7 57	8 08	17°
18°	6 00	6 13	6 27	6 43	7 03	7 16	7 31	7 38	7 46	7 55	8 05	8 17	18°
19°	6 00	6 14	6 29	6 46	7 07	7 21	7 37	7 45	7 53	8 03	8 14	8 26	19°
20°	6 00	6 15	6 30	6 49	7 11	7 25	7 43	7 51	8 00	8 11	8 22	8 36	20°
21°	6 00	6 16	6 32	6 51	7 15	7 30	7 49	7 58	8 08	8 19	8 32	8 47	21°
22°	6 00	6 16	6 34	6 54	7 19	7 35	7 55	8 05	8 15	8 27	8 41	8 58	22°
23°	6 00	6 17	6 36	6 57	7 23	7 40	8 02	8 12	8 23	8 36	8 51	9 09	23°
24°	6 00	6 18	6 37	7 00	7 28	7 46	8 08	8 19	8 31	8 45	9 02	9 22	24°
25°	6 00	6 19	6 39	7 02	7 32	7 51	8 15	8 27	8 40	8 55	9 13	9 35	25°
26°	6 00	6 20	6 41	7 05	7 37	7 57	8 22	8 35	8 49	9 05	9 25	9 51	26°
27°	6 00	6 21	6 43	7 08	7 41	8 03	8 30	8 43	8 58	9 16	9 39	10 08	27°
28°	6 00	6 22	6 45	7 12	7 46	8 08	8 37	8 52	9 08	9 28	9 53	10 28	28°
29°	6 00	6 22	6 47	7 15	7 51	8 15	8 45	9 01	9 19	9 41	10 10	10 55	29°
30°	6 00	6 23	6 49	7 18	7 56	8 21	8 54	9 11	9 30	9 55	10 30	12 00	30°
35°	6 00	6 28	6 59	7 35	8 24	8 58	9 46	10 15	10 58	12 00	12 00	12 00	35°
40°	6 00	6 34	7 11	7 56	8 59	9 48	12 00	12 00	12 00	12 00	12 00	12 00	40°
45°	6 00	6 41	7 25	8 21	9 48	12 00	12 00	12 00	12 00	12 00	12 00	12 00	45°
50°	6 00	6 49	7 43	8 54	12 00	12 00	12 00	12 00	12 00	12 00	12 00	12 00	50°
55°	6 00	6 58	8 05	9 42	12 00	12 00	12 00	12 00	12 00	12 00	12 00	12 00	55°
60°	6 00	7 11	8 36	12 00	12 00	12 00	12 00	12 00	12 00	12 00	12 00	12 00	60°
65°	6 00	7 29	9 25	12 00	12 00	12 00	12 00	12 00	12 00	12 00	12 00	12 00	65°
70°	6 00	7 56	12 00	12 00	12 00	12 00	12 00	12 00	12 00	12 00	12 00	12 00	70°
75°	6 00	8 45	12 00	12 00	12 00	12 00	12 00	12 00	12 00	12 00	12 00	12 00	75°
80°	6 00	12 00	12 00	12 00	12 00	12 00	12 00	12 00	12 00	12 00	12 00	12 00	80°

TABLE 2. CORRECTION FOR REFRACTION AND SEMI-DIAMETER

	m	m	m	m	m	m	m	m	m	m	m	m	
0°	3	3	4	4	4	5	5	5	6	6	6	7	0°
10°	3	3	4	4	4	5	5	6	6	6	7	7	10°
20°	4	4	4	4	5	5	6	7	7	8	8	9	20°
25°	4	4	4	4	5	6	7	8	8	9	11	13	25°
30°	4	4	4	5	6	7	8	9	11	14	21	—	30°

NB: Regarding Table 1. If latitude and declination are of the same sign, take out the respondent directly. If they are of opposite signs, subtract the respondent from 12h.
Example:

Lat.	Dec.	Semi-diurnal arc
+52°	+20°	7h 51m
+52°	−20°	4h 09m

SUNRISE AND SUNSET

The local mean time of sunrise or sunset may be found by obtaining the hour angle from Table 1 and applying it to the time of transit. The hour angle is negative for sunrise and positive for sunset. A small correction to the hour angle, which always has the effect of increasing it numerically, is necessary to allow for the Sun's semi-diameter (16′) and for refraction (34′); it is obtained from Table 2. The resulting local mean time may be converted into the standard time of the country by taking the difference between the longitude of the standard meridian of the country and that of the place, adding it to the local mean time if the place is west of the standard meridian, and subtracting it if the place is east.

Example – Required the New Zealand Mean Time (12h fast on GMT) of sunset on May 23 at Auckland, latitude 36° 50′ S. (or minus), longitude 11h 39m E. Taking the declination as +20°.6 (page 33), we find

	h	m
Tabular entry for Lat. 30° and Dec. 20°, opposite signs	+ 5	11
Proportional part for 6° 50′ of Lat.	–	15
Proportional part for 0°.6 of Dec.	–	2
Correction (Table 2)	+	4
Hour angle	4	58
Sun transits (page 33)	11	57
Longitudinal correction	+	21
New Zealand Mean Time	17	16

MOONRISE AND MOONSET

It is possible to calculate the times of moonrise and moonset using Table 1, though the method is more complicated because the apparent motion of the Moon is much more rapid and also more variable than that of the Sun.

The parallax of the Moon, about 57′, is near to the sum of the semi-diameter and refraction but has the opposite effect on these times. It is thus convenient to neglect all three quantities in the method outlined below.

TABLE 3. LONGITUDE CORRECTION

X A h	40m	45m	50m	55m	60m	65m	70m
	m	m	m	m	m	m	m
1	2	2	2	2	3	3	3
2	3	4	4	5	5	5	6
3	5	6	6	7	8	8	9
4	7	8	8	9	10	11	12
5	8	9	10	11	13	14	15
6	10	11	13	14	15	16	18
7	12	13	15	16	18	19	20
8	13	15	17	18	20	22	23
9	15	17	19	21	23	24	26
10	17	19	21	23	25	27	29
11	18	21	23	25	28	30	32
12	20	23	25	28	30	33	35
13	22	24	27	30	33	35	38
14	23	26	29	32	35	38	41
15	25	28	31	34	38	41	44
16	27	30	33	37	40	43	47
17	28	32	35	39	43	46	50
18	30	34	38	41	45	49	53
19	32	36	40	44	48	51	55
20	33	38	42	46	50	54	58
21	35	39	44	48	53	57	61
22	37	41	46	50	55	60	64
23	38	43	48	53	58	62	67
24	40	45	50	55	60	65	70

Notation

φ = latitude of observer
λ = longitude of observer (measured positively towards the west)
T_{-1} = time of transit of Moon on previous day
T_0 = time of transit of Moon on day in question
T_1 = time of transit of Moon on following day
δ_0 = approximate declination of Moon
δ_R = declination of Moon at moonrise
δ_S = declination of Moon at moonset
h_0 = approximate hour angle of Moon
h_R = hour angle of Moon at moonrise
h_S = hour angle of Moon at moonset
t_R = time of moonrise
t_S = time of moonset

Method

1. With arguments φ, δ_0 enter Table 1 on page 64 to determine h_0 where h_0 is negative for moonrise and positive for moonset.

2. Form approximate times from
$$t_R = T_0 + \lambda + h_0$$
$$t_S = T_0 + \lambda + h_0$$

3. Determine δ_R, δ_S for times t_R, t_S respectively.

4. Re-enter Table 1 on page 64 with
   (a) arguments φ, δ_R to determine h_R
   (b) arguments φ, δ_S to determine h_S

5. Form $t_R = T_0 + \lambda + h_R + AX$
$$t_S = T_0 + \lambda + h_S + AX$$

where $A = (\lambda + h)$

and $X = (T_0 - T_{-1})$ if $(\lambda + h)$ is negative
$X = (T_1 - T_0)$ if $(\lambda + h)$ is positive

AX is the respondent in Table 3.

Example – To find the times of moonrise and moonset at Vancouver ($\varphi = +49°$, $\lambda = +8h$ 12m) on 2000 March 4. The starting data (page 26) are

T_{-1} = 10h 07m
T_0 = 10h 55m
T_1 = 11h 43m
δ_0 = −15°

1. h_0 = 4h 48m
2. Approximate values
   t_R = 4d 10h 55m+8h 12m+(−4h 48m)
   = 4d 14h 19m
   t_S = 4d 10h 55m+8h 12m+(+4h 48m)
   = 4d 23h 55m
3. δ_R = −14°.8
   δ_S = −13°.6
4. h_R = −4h 49m
   h_S = +4h 55m
5. t_R = 4d 10h 55m+8h 12m+(−4h 49m)+7m
   = 4d 14h 25m
   t_S = 4d 10h 55m+8h 12m+(+4h 55m)+26m
   = 5d 00h 28m

To get the LMT of the phenomenon the longitude is subtracted from the GMT thus:
Moonrise = 4d 14h 25m−8h 12m = 4d 06h 13m
Moonset = 5d 00h 28m−8h 12m = 4d 16h 16m

ECLIPSES AND OCCULTATIONS 2000

ECLIPSES

There will be six eclipses in 2000, four of the Sun and two of the Moon. (Penumbral eclipses are not mentioned in this section as they are too difficult to observe.)

1. A total eclipse of the Moon on January 21 is visible from northern and western Asia, Asia Minor, Africa, Europe (including the British Isles), Iceland, Greenland, the Atlantic Ocean, the Arctic Ocean, the Americas and the Pacific Ocean (except the western part). The eclipse begins at 03h 01m and ends at 06h 26m. Totality lasts from 04h 04m to 05h 22m.

2. A partial eclipse of the Sun on February 5 is visible from the Southern Ocean and Antarctica. The eclipse begins at 10h 56m and ends at 14h 43m. At maximum eclipse 58 per cent of the Sun is obscured.

3. A partial eclipse of the Sun on July 1 is visible from the South Pacific Ocean and southern South America. The eclipse begins at 18h 07m and ends at 20h 58m. At maximum eclipse 48 per cent of the Sun is obscured.

4. A total eclipse of the Moon on July 16 is visible from southern South America, western North America, the Pacific Ocean, Antarctica, Australasia, Asia, the Indian Ocean, the Middle East, and south and east Africa. The eclipse begins at 11h 57m and ends at 15h 54m. Totality lasts from 13h 02m to 14h 49m.

5. A partial eclipse of the Sun on July 31 is visible from northern Scandinavia, Finland, northern Asia, northern Greenland, the Arctic Ocean, northern and western North America, and the North Pacific Ocean. The eclipse begins at 00h 37m and ends at 03h 49m. At maximum eclipse 60 per cent of the Sun is obscured.

6. A partial eclipse of the Sun on December 25 is visible from the north-eastern part of the Pacific Ocean, North and Central America, southern Greenland, the Caribbean and the North Atlantic Ocean, including the Azores. The eclipse begins at 15h 27m and ends at 19h 43m. At maximum eclipse 72 per cent of the Sun is obscured.

LUNAR OCCULTATIONS

Observations of the times of occultations are made by both amateur and professional astronomers. Such observations are later analysed to yield accurate positions of the Moon; this is one method of determining the difference between ephemeris time and universal time.

Many of the observations made by amateurs are obtained with the use of a stop-watch which is compared with a time-signal immediately after the observation. Thus an accuracy of about one-fifth of a second is obtainable, though the observer's personal equation may amount to one-third or one-half of a second.

The list on page 67 includes most of the occultations visible under favourable conditions in the British Isles. No occultation is included unless the star is at least 10° above the horizon and the Sun sufficiently far below the horizon to permit the star to be seen with the naked eye or with a small telescope. The altitude limit is reduced from 10° to 2° for stars and planets brighter than magnitude 2.0 and such occultations are also predicted in daylight.

The column Phase shows (i) whether a disappearance (D) or reappearance (R) is to be observed; and (ii) whether it is at the dark limb (D) or bright limb (B). The column headed 'El. of Moon' gives the elongation of the Moon from the Sun, in degrees. The elongation increases from 0° at New Moon to 180° at Full Moon and on to 360° (or 0°) at New Moon again. Times and position angles (P), reckoned from the north point in the direction north, east,

south, west, are given for Greenwich (lat. 51° 30′, long. 0°) and Edinburgh (lat. 56° 00′, long. 3° 12′ west).

The coefficients a and b are the variations in the GMT for each degree of longitude (positive to the west) and latitude (positive to the north) respectively; they enable approximate times (to within about 1m generally) to be found for any point in the British Isles. If the point of observation is $\Delta\lambda$ degrees west and $\Delta\phi$ degrees north, the approximate time is found by adding $a.\Delta\lambda + b.\Delta\phi$ to the given GMT.

Example: the disappearance of ZC 364 on February 11 at Coventry, found from both Greenwich and Edinburgh.

	Greenwich	Edinburgh
	°	°
Longitude	0.0	+3.2
Long. of Coventry	+1.5	+1.5
$\Delta\lambda$	+1.5	−1.7
Latitude	+51.5	+56.0
Lat. of Coventry	+52.4	+52.4
$\Delta\phi$	+0.9	−3.6

	h	m	h	m
GMT	20	09.6	20	01.2
$a.\Delta\lambda$		−1.5		+1.5
$b.\Delta\phi$		−1.3		+3.2
	20	06.8	20	05.9

If the occultation is given for one station but not the other, the reason for the suppression is given by the following code:

N = star not occulted

A = star's altitude less than 10° (2° for bright stars and planets)

S = Sun not sufficiently below the horizon

G = occultation is of very short duration

In some cases the coefficients a and b are not given; this is because the occultation is so short that prediction for other places by means of these coefficients would not be reliable.

LUNAR OCCULTATIONS 2000

Date		ZC No.	Mag.	Phase	El. of Moon	GREENWICH UT	a	b	P	EDINBURGH UT	a	b	P
					°	h m	m	m	°	h m	m	m	°
January	11	3419	4.5	D.D.	56	18 7.1	0.0	2.0	6	N			
	11	3425	4.6	D.D.	56	18 49.0	−1.1	−1.1	84	18 41.7	−0.9	−0.7	69
	15	405	4.4	D.D.	107	21 51.3	−0.8	1.1	29	21 57.6	G		4
	16	526	6.9	D.D.	120	20 23.3	−1.4	0.3	75	20 21.6	−1.1	0.8	60
	19	888	6.0	D.D.	150	1 34.0	−0.9	−0.6	66	1 29.2	−0.9	−0.2	54
	19	895	5.9	D.D.	151	2 37.3	−0.4	−1.4	93	2 29.7	−0.5	−1.3	84
	19	913	5.2	D.D.	152	S				5 43.9	0.3	−1.3	96
	25	1733	5.2	R.D.	234	S				6 59.9	−1.0	−1.3	260
	27	1950	5.8	R.D.	257	5 21.6	G		218	5 23.7	G		232
	30	2291	5.5	R.D.	292	S				6 57.0	−1.1	−0.2	307
February	11	364	4.3	D.D.	76	20 9.6	−1.0	−1.5	93	20 1.2	−0.9	−0.9	77
	12	491	6.2	D.D.	89	N				21 21.5	G		142
	13	627	6.8	D.D.	101	18 59.1	−1.5	0.3	78	18 57.4	−1.2	0.8	63
	13	636	6.9	D.D.	102	20 49.0	−1.2	0.2	57	20 47.9	−1.1	0.9	40
	13	650	5.7	D.D.	103	22 45.2	−0.9	0.5	37	22 47.1	G		16
	14	800	7.5	D.D.	115	21 50.2	−1.2	−1.9	115	21 39.7	−1.1	−1.1	100
	15	991	6.1	D.D.	130	24 0.2	−1.3	0.3	46	23 59.8	G		29
	16	995	4.1	D.D.	130	0 20.9	−0.6	−1.8	108	0 11.4	−0.7	−1.5	98
	16	1113	5.2	D.D.	141	19 24.2	−0.9	2.8	45	19 39.8	G		16
	16	1127	5.9	D.D.	142	21 46.6	−1.5	0.4	79	21 45.1	−1.3	1.0	65
	26	2223	4.0	R.D.	258	1 36.8	−0.2	−0.2	328	A			
March	10	453	7.3	D.D.	57	18 47.5	−1.1	−1.7	101	S			
	10	462	5.9	D.D.	59	21 8.9	0.0	−3.5	133	20 55.3	−0.3	−2.4	114
	11	618	7.2	D.D.	73	22 59.1	0.0	−1.4	91	22 52.8	−0.1	−1.3	82
	12	764	5.0	D.D.	85	22 16.3	−0.5	−1.4	89	22 8.8	−0.6	−1.2	79
	13	915	4.7	D.D.	97	20 27.4	−1.2	−1.4	106	20 18.6	−1.2	−0.8	93
	14	1077	3.7	D.D.	110	19 47.8	−1.5	−0.1	89	19 44.3	−1.3	0.5	75
	16	1245	7.5	D.D.	127	1 37.9	G		169	1 25.0	0.3	−2.9	159
April	9	888	6.0	D.D.	68	22 7.4	G		158	21 53.4	0.2	−3.0	142
	9	892	6.6	D.D.	69	22 19.4	−0.4	−0.4	49	22 16.3	−0.6	−0.2	38
	9	894	4.6	D.D.	69	22 43.1	−0.3	−0.6	54	22 39.5	−0.4	−0.5	45
	11	1193	5.4	D.D.	95	22 25.9	−0.7	−1.3	88	22 17.8	−0.8	−1.2	81
	12	1205	6.3	D.D.	96	0 51.6	G		34	0 51.9	G		19
	12	1321	6.7	D.D.	107	20 13.4	−1.4	−0.9	107	20 6.0	−1.3	−0.4	97
	13	1345	7.1	D.D.	110	1 47.0	0.3	−1.9	132	1 39.3	0.2	−1.9	129
May	8	1150	6.8	D.D.	64	N				21 15.6	G		168
	9	1310	4.2	D.D.	79	24 3.0	0.3	−1.7	121	23 56.2	0.2	−1.7	118
	22	2747	5.0	R.D.	221	1 15.4	G		203	1 20.0	G		211
	22	2749	5.0	R.D.	222	2 10.5	−1.8	0.9	235	A			
June	6	1387	6.8	D.D.	61	21 59.9	0.0	−1.7	113	S			
	8	1625	5.9	D.D.	88	N				23 36.0	G		191
	9	1741	7.2	D.D.	100	23 17.1	−0.4	−2.0	127	23 7.1	−0.4	−1.9	124
	12	2072	6.7	D.D.	135	23 9.3	−1.9	−0.3	56	23 2.2	G		51
July	10	2148	7.6	D.D.	118	22 32.8	−1.4	−0.5	52	22 26.0	G		46
	11	2271	4.3	D.D.	130	23 52.9	−1.0	−1.6	101	23 42.8	−1.0	−1.5	97
	22	18	6.0	R.D.	241	0 53.8	−0.7	2.2	213	1 1.0	−0.6	2.0	219
	29	Mercury	0.0	D.B.	341	17 42.5	0.3	−1.3	92	17 37.1	0.2	−1.4	88
August	11	2762	6.0	D.D.	144	21 57.0	−1.7	0.1	70	21 52.7	−1.5	0.2	65
	21	364	4.3	R.D.	249	3 35.1	−1.0	1.8	220	3 39.0	−1.0	1.4	232
September	1	1950	5.8	D.D.	45	19 16.7	−0.5	−1.8	108	S			
October	8	3197	6.5	D.D.	128	23 42.2	−1.2	−1.7	100	A			
	14	405	4.4	R.D.	201	23 10.8	−0.3	2.7	197	23 19.9	−0.5	2.1	211
	18	881	5.9	R.D.	243	S				5 49.1	−1.2	0.1	245
	21	1322	6.1	R.D.	282	5 17.9	−1.4	2.1	240	5 21.2	−1.2	1.3	257
November	13	648	3.9	R.D.	197	2 56.2	−1.1	1.6	211	2 57.0	−1.1	0.5	229
	13	658	4.2	R.D.	198	4 30.8	−0.8	−1.2	267	4 21.8	−0.8	−1.7	280
	16	1129	5.3	R.D.	236	1 32.2	G		196	1 48.3	−0.8	2.7	225
	18	1418	5.9	R.D.	265	6 4.9	G		220	6 8.0	−1.7	1.3	240
	30	2961	6.0	D.D.	53	18 42.2	−0.8	−0.9	66	A			
December	1	3078	4.9	D.D.	63	16 38.8	−1.0	1.0	27	16 40.6	−0.7	1.1	17
	4	3458	6.5	D.D.	96	17 19.2	−1.4	1.2	61	17 20.8	−1.1	1.2	54
	7	291	7.1	D.D.	134	21 49.4	−2.0	−1.4	107	21 40.6	−1.5	−0.3	90
	8	306	6.9	D.D.	136	1 29.7	−0.5	0.0	43	1 29.3	−0.4	0.6	26
	8	405	4.4	D.D.	144	17 19.5	−0.5	1.7	76	17 25.9	−0.4	1.8	69
	12	1047	5.2	R.D.	200	20 21.8	−0.1	1.9	241	20 29.6	−0.1	1.7	253
	31	3413	6.4	D.D.	65	18 0.1	−1.7	−0.9	92	17 52.4	−1.3	−0.4	79

MEAN PLACES OF STARS 2000.5

Name	Mag.	RA h m	Dec. ° '	Spectrum
α And *Alpheratz*	2.1	0 08.4	+29 06	A0p
β Cassiopeiae *Caph*	2.3	0 09.2	+59 09	F5
γ Pegasi *Algenib*	2.8	0 13.3	+15 11	B2
β Mensae	2.9	0 25.8	−77 15	G0
α Phoenicis	2.4	0 26.3	−42 18	K0
α Cassiopeiae *Schedar*	2.2	0 40.5	+56 32	K0
β Ceti *Diphda*	2.0	0 43.6	−17 59	K0
γ Cassiopeiae*	Var.	0 56.7	+60 43	B0p
β *Andromedae Mirach*	2.1	1 09.8	+35 37	M0
δ Cassiopeiae	2.7	1 25.8	+60 14	A5
α Eridani *Achernar*	0.5	1 37.7	−57 14	B5
β Arietis *Sheratan*	2.6	1 54.7	+20 49	A5
γ Andromedae *Almak*	2.3	2 03.9	+42 20	K0
α Arietis *Hamal*	2.0	2 07.2	+23 28	K2
α Ursae Minoris *Polaris*	2.0	2 32.4	+89 16	F8
β Persei *Algol**	Var.	3 08.2	+40 57	B8
α Persei *Mirfak*	1.8	3 24.4	+49 52	F5
η Tauri *Alcyone*	2.9	3 47.5	+24 06	B5p
α Tauri *Aldebaran*	0.9	4 35.9	+16 31	K5
β Orionis *Rigel*	0.1	5 14.6	− 8 12	B8p
α *Aurigae Capella*	0.1	5 16.7	+46 00	G0
γ Orionis *Bellatrix*	1.6	5 25.2	+ 6 21	B2
β Tauri *Elnath*	1.7	5 26.3	+28 36	B8
δ Orionis	2.2	5 32.0	− 0 18	B0
α Leporis	2.6	5 32.8	−17 49	F0
ε Orionis	1.7	5 36.2	− 1 12	B0
ζ Orionis	1.8	5 40.8	− 1 57	B0
κ Orionis	2.1	5 47.8	− 9 40	B0
α Orionis *Betelgeuse**	Var.	5 55.2	+ 7 24	M0
β Aurigae *Menkalinan*	1.9	5 59.6	+44 57	A0p
β CMa *Mirzam*	2.0	6 22.7	−17 57	B1
α Carinae *Canopus*	−0.7	6 24.0	−52 42	F0
γ Geminorum *Alhena*	1.9	6 37.7	+16 24	A0
α Canis Majoris *Sirius*	−1.5	6 45.2	−16 43	A0
ε Canis Majoris	1.5	6 58.6	−28 58	B1
δ Canis Majoris	1.9	7 08.4	−26 24	F8p
α Geminorum *Castor*	1.6	7 34.6	+31 53	A0
α CMi *Procyon*	0.4	7 39.3	+ 5 13	F5
β Geminorum *Pollux*	1.1	7 45.3	+28 02	K0
ζ Puppis	2.3	8 03.6	−40 00	Od
γ Velorum	1.8	8 09.5	−47 20	Oap
ε Carinae	1.9	8 22.5	−59 31	K0
δ Velorum	2.0	8 44.7	−54 43	A0
λ Velorum *Suhail*	2.2	9 08.0	−43 26	K5
β Carinae	1.7	9 13.2	−69 43	A0
ι Carinae	2.2	9 17.1	−59 17	F0
κ Velorum	2.6	9 22.1	−55 01	B3
α Hydrae *Alphard*	2.0	9 27.6	− 8 40	K2
α Leonis *Regulus*	1.3	10 08.4	+11 58	B8
γ Leonis *Algeiba*	1.9	10 20.0	+19 50	K0
β Ursae Majoris *Merak*	2.4	11 01.9	+56 23	A0
α Ursae Majoris *Dubhe*	1.8	11 03.8	+61 45	K0
δ Leonis	2.6	11 14.1	+20 31	A3
β Leonis *Denebola*	2.1	11 49.1	+14 34	A2
γ Ursae Majoris *Phecda*	2.4	11 53.9	+53 42	A0
γ Corvi	2.6	12 15.8	−17 33	B8
α Crucis	1.0	12 26.6	−63 06	B1
γ Crucis	1.6	12 31.2	−57 07	M3
γ Centauri	2.2	12 41.5	−48 58	A0
γ Virginis	2.7	12 41.7	− 1 27	F0
β Crucis	1.3	12 47.8	−59 41	B1
ε Ursae Majoris *Alioth*	1.8	12 54.1	+55 57	A0p
α Canum Venaticorum	2.9	12 56.1	+38 19	A0p
ζ Ursae Majoris *Mizar*	2.1	13 23.9	+54 55	A2p
α Virginis *Spica*	1.0	13 25.2	−11 10	B2
ε Centauri	2.6	13 39.9	−53 28	B1
η Ursae Majoris *Alkaid*	1.9	13 47.6	+49 19	B3
β Centauri *Hadar*	0.6	14 03.9	−60 23	B1
θ Centauri	2.1	14 06.7	−36 22	K0
α Bootis *Arcturus*	0.0	14 15.7	+19 11	K0
α Centauri *Rigil Kent*	0.1	14 39.6	−60 50	G0
ε Bootis	2.4	14 45.0	+27 04	K0
β UMi *Kochab*	2.1	14 50.7	+74 09	K5
γ Ursae Minoris	3.1	15 20.7	+71 50	A2
α CrB *Alphecca*	2.2	15 34.7	+26 43	A0
β Trianguli Australis	3.0	15 55.2	−63 26	F0
δ Scorpii	2.3	16 00.4	−22 37	B0
β Scorpii	2.6	16 05.5	−19 48	B1
α Scorpii *Antares*	1.0	16 29.4	−26 26	M0
α Trianguli Australis	1.9	16 48.7	−69 02	K2
ε Scorpii	2.3	16 50.2	−34 18	K0
α Herculis†	Var.	17 14.7	+14 23	M3
λ Scorpii	1.6	17 33.6	−37 06	B2
α Ophiuchi *Rasalhague*	2.1	17 35.0	+12 34	A5
θ Scorpii	1.9	17 37.4	−43 00	F0
κ Scorpii	2.4	17 42.5	−39 02	B2
γ Draconis	2.2	17 56.6	+51 29	K5
ε Sgr *Kaus Australis*	1.9	18 24.2	−34 23	A0
α Lyrae *Vega*	0.0	18 37.0	+38 47	A0
σ Sagittarii	2.0	18 55.3	−26 18	B3
β Cygni *Albireo*	3.1	19 30.7	+27 58	K0
α Aquilae *Altair*	0.8	19 50.8	+ 8 52	A5
α Capricorni	3.8	20 18.1	−12 33	G5
γ Cygni	2.2	20 22.2	+40 16	F8p
α Pavonis	1.9	20 25.7	−56 44	B3
α Cygni *Deneb*	1.3	20 41.4	+45 17	A2p
α Cephei *Alderamin*	2.4	21 18.6	+62 35	A5
ε Pegasi	2.4	21 44.2	+ 9 53	K0
δ Capricorni	2.9	21 47.1	−16 07	A5
α Gruis	1.7	22 08.3	−46 58	B5
δ Cephei†	3.7	22 29.2	+58 25	†
β Gruis	2.1	22 42.7	−46 53	M3
α PsA *Fomalhaut*	1.2	22 57.7	−29 37	A3
β Pegasi *Scheat*	2.4	23 03.8	+28 05	M0
α Pegasi *Markab*	2.5	23 04.8	+15 12	A0

* γ Cassiopeiae, 1999 mag. 2.5. β Persei, mag. 2.1 to 3.4. α Orionis, mag. 0.1 to 1.2.

†α Herculis, mag. 3.1 to 3.9. δ Cephei, mag. 3.7 to 4.4, spectrum F5 to G0.

The positions of heavenly bodies on the celestial sphere are defined by two co-ordinates, right ascension and declination, which are analogous to longitude and latitude on the surface of the Earth. If we imagine the plane of the terrestrial equator extended indefinitely, it will cut the celestial sphere in a great circle known as the celestial equator. Similarly the plane of the Earth's orbit, when extended, cuts in the great circle called the ecliptic. The two intersections of these circles are known as the First Point of Aries and the First Point of Libra. If from any star a perpendicular be drawn to the celestial equator, the length of this perpendicular is the star's declination. The arc, measured eastwards along the equator from the First Point of Aries to the foot of this perpendicular, is the right ascension. An alternative definition of right ascension is that it is the angle at the celestial pole (where the Earth's axis, if prolonged, would meet the sphere) between the great circles to the First Point of Aries and to the star.

The plane of the Earth's equator has a slow movement, so that our reference system for right ascension and declination is not fixed. The consequent alteration in these quantities from year to year is called precession. In right ascension it is an increase of about 3 seconds a year for equatorial stars, and larger or smaller changes in either direction for stars near the poles, depending on the right ascension of the star. In declination it varies between $+20''$ and $-20''$ according to the right ascension of the star.

A star or other body crosses the meridian when the sidereal time is equal to its right ascension. The altitude is then a maximum, and may be deduced by remembering that the altitude of the elevated pole is numerically equal to the latitude, while that of the equator at its intersection with the meridian is equal to the co-latitude, or complement of the latitude.

Thus in London (lat. 51° 30′) the meridian altitude of Sirius is found as follows:

	°	′
Altitude of equator	38	30
Declination south	16	43
Difference	21	47

The altitude of Capella (Dec. +46° 00′) at lower transit is:

	°	′
Altitude of pole	51	30
Polar distance of star	44	00
Difference	7	30

The brightness of a heavenly body is denoted by its magnitude. Omitting the exceptionally bright stars Sirius and Canopus, the twenty brightest stars are of the first magnitude, while the faintest stars visible to the naked eye are of the sixth magnitude. The magnitude scale is a precise one, as a difference of five magnitudes represents a ratio of 100 to 1 in brightness. Typical second magnitude stars are Polaris and the stars in the belt of Orion. The scale is most easily fixed in memory by comparing the stars with Norton's *Star Atlas* (*see* page 71). The stars Sirius and Canopus and the planets Venus and Jupiter are so bright that their magnitudes are expressed by negative numbers. A small telescope will show stars down to the ninth or tenth magnitude, while stars fainter than the twentieth magnitude may be photographed by long exposures with the largest telescopes.

MEAN AND SIDEREAL TIME

Acceleration

h	m s	m s	s
1	0 10	0 00	0
2	0 20	3 02	1
3	0 30	9 07	2
4	0 39	15 13	3
5	0 49	21 18	4
6	0 59	27 23	5
7	1 09	33 28	6
8	1 19	39 34	7
9	1 29	45 39	8
10	1 39	51 44	9
11	1 48	57 49	10
12	1 58	60 00	
13	2 08		
14	2 18		
15	2 28		
16	2 38		
17	2 48		
18	2 57		
19	3 07		
20	3 17		
21	3 27		
22	3 37		
23	3 47		
24	3 57		

Retardation

h	m s	m s	s
1	0 10	0 00	0
2	0 20	3 03	1
3	0 29	9 09	2
4	0 39	15 15	3
5	0 49	21 21	4
6	0 59	27 28	5
7	1 09	33 34	6
8	1 19	39 40	7
9	1 28	45 46	8
10	1 38	51 53	9
11	1 48	57 59	10
12	1 58	60 00	
13	2 08		
14	2 18		
15	2 27		
16	2 37		
17	2 47		
18	2 57		
19	3 07		
20	3 17		
21	3 26		
22	3 36		
23	3 46		
24	3 56		

The length of a sidereal day in mean time is 23h 56m 04s.09. Hence 1h MT = 1h+9s.86 ST and 1h ST = 1h−9s.83 MT.

To convert an interval of mean time to the corresponding interval of sidereal time, enter the acceleration table with the given mean time (taking the hours and the minutes and seconds separately) and add the acceleration obtained to the given mean time. To convert an interval of sidereal time to the corresponding interval of mean time, take out the retardation for the given sidereal time and subtract.

The columns for the minutes and seconds of the argument are in the form known as critical tables. To use these tables, find in the appropriate left-hand column the two entries between which the given number of minutes and seconds lies; the quantity in the right-hand column between these two entries is the required acceleration or retardation. Thus the acceleration for 11m 26s (which lies between the entries 9m 07s and 15m 13s) is 2s. If the given number of minutes and seconds is a tabular entry, the required acceleration or retardation is the entry in the right-hand column above the given tabular entry, e.g. the retardation for 45m 46s is 7s.

Example – Convert 14h 27m 35s from ST to MT

	h	m	s
Given ST	14	27	35
Retardation for 14h		2	18
Retardation for 27m 35s			5
Corresponding MT	14	25	12

For further explanation, *see* pages 73–4.

ECLIPSES AND SHADOW TRANSITS OF JUPITER'S SATELLITES 2000

GMT d h m	Sat.	Phen.
JANUARY		
6 20 08	II	Ec.D
7 18 21	I	Sh.I
7 20 30	I	Sh.E
8 17 46	I	Ec.R
14 20 18	I	Sh.I
15 17 56	III	Sh.I
15 19 42	I	Ec.R
15 19 57	II	Sh.E
15 19 58	III	Sh.E
22 20 04	II	Sh.I
23 18 52	I	Sh.E
30 18 39	I	Sh.I
31 19 58	II	Ec.R
FEBRUARY		
7 19 57	I	Ec.R
7 20 04	II	Ec.D
9 19 55	III	Ec.D
JUNE		
25 02 21	III	Ec.R
JULY		
1 02 03	I	Sh.E
8 01 48	I	Sh.I
13 00 32	III	Sh.E
14 23 57	II	Sh.I
15 02 30	II	Sh.E
16 00 52	I	Ec.D
17 00 19	I	Sh.E
20 02 37	III	Sh.I
22 02 35	II	Sh.I
23 02 46	I	Ec.D
24 00 04	I	Sh.I
24 02 13	I	Sh.E
30 23 58	II	Ec.D
31 01 58	I	Sh.I
31 23 09	I	Ec.D
AUGUST		
1 22 35	I	Sh.E
7 00 28	III	Ec.D
7 02 24	III	Ec.R
7 02 32	II	Ec.D
8 01 03	I	Ec.D
8 22 20	I	Sh.I
8 23 41	II	Sh.E
9 00 29	I	Sh.E
15 02 57	I	Ec.D
15 23 45	II	Sh.I
16 00 14	I	Sh.I
16 02 18	II	Sh.E
16 02 22	I	Sh.E
23 02 07	I	Sh.I
23 02 22	II	Sh.I
23 23 20	I	Ec.D
24 22 37	III	Sh.I
24 22 44	I	Sh.E
24 23 30	II	Ec.R
25 00 32	III	Sh.E
30 04 01	I	Sh.I
31 01 14	I	Ec.D

GMT d h m	Sat.	Phen.
AUGUST		
31 22 29	I	Sh.I
31 23 31	II	Ec.D
SEPTEMBER		
1 00 38	I	Sh.E
1 02 04	II	Ec.R
1 02 36	III	Sh.I
2 20 51	II	Sh.I
7 03 08	I	Ec.D
8 00 23	I	Sh.I
8 02 05	II	Sh.I
8 02 31	I	Sh.E
8 04 39	II	Ec.R
8 21 37	I	Ec.D
9 20 54	I	Sh.I
9 20 59	I	Sh.E
9 23 28	II	Sh.E
11 20 28	III	Ec.D
11 22 26	III	Ec.R
15 02 16	I	Sh.I
15 04 25	I	Sh.E
15 04 39	II	Ec.D
15 23 31	I	Ec.D
16 20 45	I	Sh.I
16 22 53	I	Sh.E
16 23 31	II	Sh.I
17 02 05	I	Sh.E
18 20 30	I	Ec.R
19 00 28	III	Ec.D
19 02 27	III	Ec.R
22 04 10	I	Sh.I
23 01 25	I	Ec.D
23 22 38	I	Sh.I
24 00 47	I	Sh.E
24 02 08	II	Sh.I
24 04 42	II	Sh.E
24 19 54	I	Sh.E
25 19 15	I	Sh.E
25 20 30	II	Ec.D
26 04 28	III	Ec.D
29 20 32	III	Sh.E
30 03 19	I	Ec.D
OCTOBER		
1 00 31	I	Sh.I
1 02 40	I	Sh.E
1 21 48	I	Ec.D
2 19 00	I	Sh.I
2 21 09	I	Sh.E
2 23 04	II	Ec.D
4 20 38	II	Sh.E
6 22 33	III	Sh.I
7 00 32	III	Sh.E
8 02 25	I	Sh.I
8 23 42	I	Ec.D
9 20 53	I	Sh.I
9 23 02	I	Sh.E
10 01 39	II	Ec.D
11 20 40	II	Sh.I
11 23 14	II	Sh.E
14 02 33	III	Sh.I
16 01 37	I	Ec.D
16 22 47	I	Sh.I

GMT d h m	Sat.	Phen.
OCTOBER		
17 00 56	I	Sh.E
17 18 29	III	Ec.R
17 20 05	I	Ec.D
18 19 25	I	Sh.E
18 23 16	II	Sh.I
19 01 51	II	Sh.E
24 00 41	I	Sh.I
24 02 50	I	Sh.E
24 20 28	III	Ec.D
24 21 59	I	Ec.D
24 22 30	III	Ec.R
25 19 09	I	Sh.I
25 21 19	I	Sh.E
26 01 53	II	Sh.I
27 20 05	II	Ec.D
31 02 34	I	Sh.I
31 23 54	I	Ec.D
NOVEMBER		
1 00 28	III	Ec.D
1 21 03	I	Sh.I
1 23 13	I	Sh.E
2 18 22	I	Ec.D
3 22 40	II	Ec.D
5 17 47	II	Sh.I
5 20 23	II	Sh.E
8 01 48	I	Ec.D
8 22 57	I	Sh.I
9 01 07	I	Sh.E
9 20 17	I	Ec.D
10 19 36	I	Sh.E
11 01 16	II	Ec.D
11 18 31	III	Sh.I
11 20 34	III	Sh.E
12 20 24	II	Sh.I
12 23 00	II	Sh.E
16 00 51	I	Sh.I
16 22 11	I	Ec.D

GMT d h m	Sat.	Phen.
NOVEMBER		
17 19 20	I	Sh.I
17 21 30	I	Sh.E
18 22 31	III	Sh.I
19 00 35	III	Sh.E
19 23 00	II	Sh.I
24 00 06	I	Ec.D
24 21 14	I	Sh.I
24 23 25	I	Sh.E
25 18 35	I	Ec.D
26 17 53	I	Sh.E
28 22 22	II	Ec.R
29 18 35	III	Ec.R
30 17 31	II	Sh.E
DECEMBER		
1 23 09	I	Sh.I
2 22 40	I	Ec.R
3 17 37	I	Sh.I
3 19 48	I	Sh.E
6 22 36	III	Ec.R
7 17 32	II	Sh.I
7 20 08	II	Sh.E
10 19 32	I	Sh.I
10 21 43	I	Sh.E
11 19 04	I	Ec.R
14 20 08	II	Sh.I
14 22 44	II	Sh.E
17 21 27	I	Sh.I
18 20 59	I	Ec.R
19 18 07	I	Sh.E
21 22 45	II	Sh.I
23 19 31	II	Ec.R
24 18 34	III	Sh.I
24 20 41	III	Sh.E
25 22 54	I	Ec.R
26 17 51	I	Sh.I
26 20 02	I	Sh.E
30 22 08	II	Ec.R

Jupiter's satellites transit across the disk from east to west, and pass behind the disk from west to east. The shadows that they cast also transit across the disk. With the exception at times of Satellite IV, the satellites also pass through the shadow of the planet, i.e. they are eclipsed. Just before opposition the satellite disappears in the shadow to the west of the planet and reappears from occultation on the east limb. Immediately after opposition the satellite is occulted by the west limb and reappears from eclipse to the east of the planet. At times approximately two to four months before and after opposition, both phases of eclipses of Satellite III may be seen. When Satellite IV is eclipsed, both phases may be seen.

The times given refer to the centre of the satellite. As the satellite is of considerable size, the immersion and emersion phases are not instantaneous. Even when the satellite enters or leaves the shadow along a radius of the shadow, the phase can last for several minutes. With Satellite IV, grazing phenomena can occur so that the light from the satellite may fade and brighten again without a complete eclipse taking place.

The list of phenomena gives most of the eclipses and shadow transits visible in the British Isles under favourable conditions.

Ec. = Eclipse   R. = Reappearance
Sh. = Shadow transit   I. = Ingress
D. = Disappearance   E. = Egress

EXPLANATION OF ASTRONOMICAL DATA

Positions of the heavenly bodies are given only to the degree of accuracy required by amateur astronomers for setting telescopes, or for plotting on celestial globes or star atlases. Where intermediate positions are required, linear interpolation may be employed.

Definitions of the terms used cannot be given here. They must be sought in astronomical literature and textbooks. Probably the best source for the amateur is Norton's *Star Atlas and Reference Handbook* (Longman, 18th edition, 1989; £26.99), which contains an introduction to observational astronomy, and a series of star maps showing stars visible to the naked eye. Certain more extended ephemerides are available in the British Astronomical Association Handbook, an annual popular among amateur astronomers (Secretary: Burlington House, Piccadilly, London W1V 9AG).

A special feature has been made of the times when the various heavenly bodies are visible in the British Isles. Since two columns, calculated for latitudes 52° and 56°, are devoted to risings and settings, the range 50° to 58° can be covered by interpolation and extrapolation. The times given in these columns are Greenwich Mean Times for the meridian of Greenwich. An observer west of this meridian must add his/her longitude (in time) and vice versa.

In accordance with the usual convention in astronomy, + and − indicate respectively north and south latitudes or declinations.

All data are, unless otherwise stated, for 0h Greenwich Mean Time (GMT), i.e. at the midnight at the beginning of the day named. Allowance must be made for British Summer Time during the period that this is in operation (*see* pages 15 and 75).

PAGE ONE OF EACH MONTH

The calendar for each month is explained on page 15.

Under the heading Astronomical Phenomena will be found particulars of the more important conjunctions of the Sun, Moon and planets with each other, and also the dates of other astronomical phenomena of special interest.

Times of Minima of Algol are approximate times of the middle of the period of diminished light.

The Constellations listed each month are those that are near the meridian at the beginning of the month at 22h local mean time. Allowance must be made for British Summer Time if necessary. The fact that any star crosses the meridian 4m earlier each night or 2h earlier each month may be used, in conjunction with the lists given each month, to find what constellations are favourably placed at any moment. The table preceding the list of constellations may be extended indefinitely at the rate just quoted.

The principal phases of the Moon are the GMTs when the difference between the longitude of the Moon and that of the Sun is 0°, 90°, 180° or 270°. The times of perigee and apogee are those when the Moon is nearest to, and farthest from, the Earth, respectively. The nodes or points of intersection of the Moon's orbit and the ecliptic make a complete retrograde circuit of the ecliptic in about 19 years. From a knowledge of the longitude of the ascending node and the inclination, whose value does not vary much from 5°, the path of the Moon among the stars may be plotted on a celestial globe or star atlas.

PAGE TWO OF EACH MONTH

The Sun's semi-diameter, in arc, is given once a month.

The right ascension and declination (Dec.) is that of the true Sun. The right ascension of the mean Sun is obtained by applying the equation of time, with the sign given, to the right ascension of the true Sun, or, more easily, by applying 12h to the Sidereal Time. The direction in which the equation of time has to be applied in different problems is a frequent source of confusion and error. Apparent Solar Time is equal to the Mean Solar Time plus the Equation of Time. For example, at noon on August 8 the Equation of Time is −5m 34s and thus at 12h Mean Time on that day the Apparent Time is 12h−5m 34s = 11h 54m 26s.

The Greenwich Sidereal Time at 0h and the Transit of the First Point of Aries (which is really the mean time when the sidereal time is 0h) are used for converting mean time to sidereal time and vice versa.

The GMT of transit of the Sun at Greenwich may also be taken as the local mean time (LMT) of transit in any longitude. It is independent of latitude. The GMT of transit in any longitude is obtained by adding the longitude to the time given if west, and vice versa.

LIGHTING-UP TIME

The legal importance of sunrise and sunset is that the Road Vehicles Lighting Regulations 1989 (SI 1989 No. 1796) make the use of front and rear position lamps on vehicles compulsory during the period between sunset and sunrise. Headlamps on vehicles are required to be used during the hours of darkness on unlit roads or whenever visibility is seriously reduced. The hours of darkness are defined in these regulations as the period between half an hour after sunset and half an hour before sunrise.

In all laws and regulations 'sunset' refers to the local sunset, i.e. the time at which the Sun sets at the place in question. This common-sense interpretation has been upheld by legal tribunals. Thus the necessity for providing for different latitudes and longitudes, as already described, is evident.

SUNRISE AND SUNSET

The times of sunrise and sunset are those when the Sun's upper limb, as affected by refraction, is on the true horizon of an observer at sea-level. Assuming the mean refraction to be 34′, and the Sun's semi-diameter to be 16′, the time given is that when the true zenith distance of the Sun's centre is 90°+34′+16′ or 90° 50′, or, in other words, when the depression of the Sun's centre below the true horizon is 50′. The upper limb is then 34′ below the true horizon, but is brought there by refraction. An observer on a ship might see the Sun for a minute or so longer, because of the dip of the horizon, while another viewing the sunset over hills or mountains would record an earlier time. Nevertheless, the moment when the true zenith distance of the Sun's centre is 90° 50′ is a precise time dependent only on the latitude and longitude of the place, and independent of its altitude above sea-level, the contour of its horizon, the vagaries of refraction or the small seasonal change in the Sun's semi-diameter; this moment is suitable in every way as a definition of sunset (or sunrise) for all statutory purposes. (For further information, *see* footnote on page 72.)

TWILIGHT

Light reaches us before sunrise and continues to reach us for some time after sunset. The interval between darkness and sunrise or sunset and darkness is called twilight. Astronomically speaking, twilight is considered to begin or end when the Sun's centre is 18° below the horizon, as no light from the Sun can then reach the observer. As thus defined twilight may last several hours; in high latitudes at the summer solstice the depression of 18° is not reached, and twilight lasts from sunset to sunrise.

The need for some sub-division of twilight is met by dividing the gathering darkness into four stages.

(1) *Sunrise or Sunset*, defined as above
(2) *Civil twilight*, which begins or ends when the Sun's centre is 6° below the horizon. This marks the time when operations requiring daylight may commence or must cease. In England it varies from about 30 to 60 minutes after sunset and the same interval before sunrise
(3) *Nautical twilight*, which begins or ends when the Sun's centre is 12° below the horizon. This marks the time when it is, to all intents and purposes, completely dark
(4) *Astronomical twilight*, which begins or ends when the Sun's centre is 18° below the horizon. This marks theoretical perfect darkness. It is of little practical importance, especially if nautical twilight is tabulated

To assist observers the durations of civil, nautical and astronomical twilights are given at intervals of ten days. The beginning of a particular twilight is found by subtracting the duration from the time of sunrise, while the end is found by adding the duration to the time of sunset. Thus the beginning of astronomical twilight in latitude 52°, on the Greenwich meridian, on March 11 is found as 06h 23m−113m = 04h 30m and similarly the end of civil twilight as 17h 58m+34m = 18h 32m. The letters TAN (twilight all night) are printed when twilight lasts all night.

Under the heading The Night Sky will be found notes describing the position and visibility of the planets and other phenomena.

PAGE THREE OF EACH MONTH

The Moon moves so rapidly among the stars that its position is given only to the degree of accuracy that permits linear interpolation. The right ascension (RA) and declination (Dec.) are geocentric, i.e. for an imaginary observer at the centre of the Earth. To an observer on the surface of the Earth the position is always different, as the altitude is always less on account of parallax, which may reach 1°.

The lunar terminator is the line separating the bright from the dark part of the Moon's disk. Apart from irregularities of the lunar surface, the terminator is elliptical, because it is a circle seen in projection. It becomes the full circle forming the limb, or edge, of the Moon at New and Full Moon. The selenographic longitude of the terminator is measured from the mean centre of the visible disk, which may differ from the visible centre by as much as 8°, because of libration.

Instead of the longitude of the terminator the Sun's selenographic co-longitude (Sun's co-long.) is tabulated. It is numerically equal to the selenographic longitude of the morning terminator, measured eastwards from the mean centre of the disk. Thus its value is approximately 270° at New Moon, 360° at First Quarter, 90° at Full Moon and 180° at Last Quarter.

The Position Angle (PA) of the Bright Limb is the position angle of the midpoint of the illuminated limb, measured eastwards from the north point on the disk. The Phase column shows the percentage of the area of the Moon's disk illuminated; this is also the illuminated percentage of the diameter at right angles to the line of cusps. The terminator is a semi-ellipse whose major axis is the line of cusps, and whose semi-minor axis is determined by the tabulated percentage; from New Moon to Full Moon the east limb is dark, and vice versa.

The times given as moonrise and moonset are those when the upper limb of the Moon is on the horizon of an observer at sea-level. The Sun's horizontal parallax (Hor. par.) is about 9″, and is negligible when considering sunrise and sunset, but that of the Moon averages about 57′. Hence the computed time represents the moment when the true zenith distance of the Moon is 90° 50′ (as for the Sun) minus the horizontal parallax. The time required for the Sun or Moon to rise or set is about four minutes (except in high latitudes). *See also* page 65 and footnote below.

The GMT of transit of the Moon over the meridian of Greenwich is given; these times are independent of latitude but must be corrected for longitude. For places in the British Isles it suffices to add the longitude if west, and vice versa. For other places a further correction is necessary because of the rapid movement of the Moon relative to the stars. The entire correction is conveniently determined by first finding the west longitude λ of the place. If the place is in west longitude, λ is the ordinary west longitude; if the place is in east longitude λ is the complement to 24h (or 360°) of the longitude and will be greater than 12h (or 180°). The correction then consists of two positive portions, namely λ and the fraction $\lambda/24$ (or $\lambda°/360$) multiplied by the difference between consecutive transits. Thus for Christchurch, New Zealand, the longitude is 11h 31m east, so $\lambda = $ 12h 29m and the fraction $\lambda/24$ is 0.52. The transit on the local date 2000 June 17 is found as follows:

		d	h	m
GMT of transit at Greenwich	June	17	00	04
λ			12	29
0.52×(24h 04m−23h 16m)				25
GMT of transit at Christchurch		17	12	58
Corr. to NZ Standard Time			12	00
Local standard time of transit		18	00	58

As is evident, for any given place the quantities λ and the correction to local standard time may be combined permanently, being here 24h 29m.

Positions of Mercury are given for every second day, and those of Venus and Mars for every fifth day; they may be interpolated linearly. The diameter (Diam.) is given in seconds of arc. The phase is the illuminated percentage of the disk. In the case of the inner planets this approaches 100 at superior conjunction and 0 at inferior conjunction. When the phase is less than 50 the planet is crescent-shaped or horned; for greater phases it is gibbous. In the case of the exterior planet Mars, the phase approaches 100 at conjunction and opposition, and is a minimum at the quadratures.

Since the planets cannot be seen when on the horizon, the actual times of rising and setting are not given; instead, the time when the planet has an apparent altitude of 5°

SUNRISE, SUNSET AND MOONRISE, MOONSET

The tables have been constructed for the meridian of Greenwich and for latitudes 52° and 56°. They give Greenwich Mean Time (GMT) throughout the year. To obtain the GMT of the phenomenon as seen from any other latitude and longitude in the British Isles, first interpolate or extrapolate for latitude by the usual rules of proportion. To the time found, the longitude (expressed in time) is to be added if west (as it usually is in Great Britain) or subtracted if east. If the longitude is expressed in degrees and minutes of arc, it must be converted to time at the rate of 1°=4m and 15′=1m.

A method of calculating rise and set times for other places in the world is given on pages 64 and 65

has been tabulated. If the time of transit is between 00h and 12h the time refers to an altitude of 5° above the eastern horizon; if between 12h and 24h, to the western horizon. The phenomenon tabulated is the one that occurs between sunset and sunrise. The times given may be interpolated for latitude and corrected for longitude, as in the case of the Sun and Moon.

The GMT at which the planet transits the Greenwich meridian is also given. The times of transit are to be corrected to local meridians in the usual way, as already described.

PAGE FOUR OF EACH MONTH

The GMTs of sunrise and sunset for seven cities, whose adopted positions in longitude (W.) and latitude (N.) are given immediately below the name, may be used not only for these phenomena, but also for lighting-up times (*see* page 71 for a fuller explanation).

The particulars for the four outer planets resemble those for the planets on Page Three of each month, except that, under Uranus and Neptune, times when the planet is 10° high instead of 5° high are given; this is because of the inferior brightness of these planets. The diameters given for the rings of Saturn are those of the major axis (in the plane of the planet's equator) and the minor axis respectively. The former has a small seasonal change due to the slightly varying distance of the Earth from Saturn, but the latter varies from zero when the Earth passes through the ring plane every 15 years to its maximum opening half-way between these periods. The rings were last open at their widest extent (and Saturn at its brightest) in 1988; this will occur again in 2002. The Earth passed through the ring plane in 1995–6 and will do so again in 2009.

TIME

From the earliest ages, the natural division of time into recurring periods of day and night has provided the practical time-scale for the everyday activities of the human race. Indeed, if any alternative means of time measurement is adopted, it must be capable of adjustment so as to remain in general agreement with the natural time-scale defined by the diurnal rotation of the Earth on its axis. Ideally the rotation should be measured against a fixed frame of reference; in practice it must be measured against the background provided by the celestial bodies. If the Sun is chosen as the reference point, we obtain Apparent Solar Time, which is the time indicated by a sundial. It is not a uniform time but is subject to variations which amount to as much as a quarter of an hour in each direction. Such wide variations cannot be tolerated in a practical time-scale, and this has led to the concept of Mean Solar Time in which all the days are exactly the same length and equal to the average length of the Apparent Solar Day.

The positions of the stars in the sky are specified in relation to a fictitious reference point in the sky known as the First Point of Aries (or the Vernal Equinox). It is therefore convenient to adopt this same reference point when considering the rotation of the Earth against the background of the stars. The time-scale so obtained is known as Apparent Sidereal Time.

GREENWICH MEAN TIME

The daily rotation of the Earth on its axis causes the Sun and the other heavenly bodies to appear to cross the sky from east to west. It is convenient to represent this relative motion as if the Sun really performed a daily circuit

around a fixed Earth. Noon in Apparent Solar Time may then be defined as the time at which the Sun transits across the observer's meridian. In Mean Solar Time, noon is similarly defined by the meridian transit of a fictitious Mean Sun moving uniformly in the sky with the same average speed as the true Sun. Mean Solar Time observed on the meridian of the transit circle telescope of the Old Royal Observatory at Greenwich is called Greenwich Mean Time (GMT). The mean solar day is divided into 24 hours and, for astronomical and other scientific purposes, these are numbered 0 to 23, commencing at midnight. Civil time is usually reckoned in two periods of 12 hours, designated a.m. (*ante meridiem*, i.e. before noon) and p.m. (*post meridiem*, i.e. after noon).

UNIVERSAL TIME

Before 1925 January 1, GMT was reckoned in 24 hours commencing at noon; since that date it has been reckoned from midnight. To avoid confusion in the use of the designation GMT before and after 1925, since 1928 astronomers have tended to use the term Universal Time (UT) or Weltzeit (WZ) to denote GMT measured from Greenwich Mean Midnight.

In precision work it is necessary to take account of small variations in Universal Time. These arise from small irregularities in the rotation of the Earth. Observed astronomical time is designated UT0. Observed time corrected for the effects of the motion of the poles (giving rise to a 'wandering' in longitude) is designated UT1. There is also a seasonal fluctuation in the rate of rotation of the Earth arising from meteorological causes, often called the annual fluctuation. UT1 corrected for this effect is designated UT2 and provides a time-scale free from short-period fluctuations. It is still subject to small secular and irregular changes.

APPARENT SOLAR TIME

As mentioned above, the time shown by a sundial is called Apparent Solar Time. It differs from Mean Solar Time by an amount known as the Equation of Time, which is the total effect of two causes which make the length of the apparent solar day non-uniform. One cause of variation is that the orbit of the Earth is not a circle but an ellipse, having the Sun at one focus. As a consequence, the angular speed of the Earth in its orbit is not constant; it is greatest at the beginning of January when the Earth is nearest the Sun.

The other cause is due to the obliquity of the ecliptic; the plane of the equator (which is at right angles to the axis of rotation of the Earth) does not coincide with the ecliptic (the plane defined by the apparent annual motion of the Sun around the celestial sphere) but is inclined to it at an angle of 23° 26′. As a result, the apparent solar day is shorter than average at the equinoxes and longer at the solstices. From the combined effects of the components due to obliquity and eccentricity, the equation of time reaches its maximum values in February (−14 minutes) and early November (+16 minutes). It has a zero value on four dates during the year, and it is only on these dates (approximately April 15, June 14, September 1 and December 25) that a sundial shows Mean Solar Time.

SIDEREAL TIME

A sidereal day is the duration of a complete rotation of the Earth with reference to the First Point of Aries. The term sidereal (or 'star') time is a little misleading since the time-scale so defined is not exactly the same as that which would be defined by successive transits of a selected star, as there is a small progressive motion between the stars and the First Point of Aries due to the precession of the Earth's axis. This makes the length of the sidereal day shorter than the true period of rotation by 0.008 seconds. Superimposed on this steady precessional motion are small oscillations (nutation), giving rise to fluctuations in apparent sidereal time amounting to as much as 1.2 seconds. It is therefore customary to employ Mean Sidereal Time, from which these fluctuations have been removed. The conversion of GMT to Greenwich sidereal time (GST) may be performed by adding the value of the GST at 0h on the day in question (Page Two of each month) to the GMT converted to sidereal time using the table on page 69.

Example – To find the GST at August 8d 02h 41m 11s GMT

	h	m	s
GST at 0h	21	07	13
GMT	2	41	11
Acceleration for 2h			20
Acceleration for 41m 11s			7
Sum = GST =	23	48	51

If the observer is not on the Greenwich meridian then his/her longitude, measured positively westwards from Greenwich, must be subtracted from the GST to obtain Local Sidereal Time (LST). Thus, in the above example, an observer 5h east of Greenwich, or 19h west, would find the LST as 4h 48m 51s.

EPHEMERIS TIME

An analysis of observations of the positions of the Sun, Moon and planets taken over an extended period is used in preparing ephemerides. (An ephemeris is a table giving the apparent position of a heavenly body at regular intervals of time, e.g. one day or ten days, and may be used to compare current observations with tabulated positions.) Discrepancies between the positions of heavenly bodies observed over a 300-year period and their predicted positions arose because the time-scale to which the observations were related was based on the assumption that the rate of rotation of the Earth is uniform. It is now known that this rate of rotation is variable. A revised time-scale, Ephemeris Time (ET), was devised to bring the ephemerides into agreement with the observations.

The second of ET is defined in terms of the annual motion of the Earth in its orbit around the Sun (1/31556925.9747 of the tropical year for 1900 January 0d 12h ET). The precise determination of ET from astronomical observations is a lengthy process as the requisite standard of accuracy can only be achieved by averaging over a number of years.

In 1976 the International Astronomical Union adopted a new dynamical time-scale for general use whose scale unit is the SI second (*see* Atomic Time). ET is now of little more than historical interest.

TERRESTRIAL DYNAMICAL TIME

The uniform time system used in computing the ephemerides of the solar system is Terrestrial Dynamical Time (TDT), which has replaced ET for this purpose. Except for the most rigorous astronomical calculations, it may be assumed to be the same as ET. During 2000 the estimated difference TDT–UT is about 65 seconds.

ATOMIC TIME

The fundamental standards of time and frequency must be defined in terms of a periodic motion adequately uniform, enduring and measurable. Progress has made it possible to use natural standards, such as atomic or molecular oscillations. Continuous oscillations are generated in an electrical circuit, the frequency of which is then compared or brought into coincidence with the frequency

characteristic of the absorption or emission by the atoms or molecules when they change between two selected energy levels. The National Physical Laboratory (NPL) routinely uses clocks of high stability produced by locking a quartz oscillator to the frequencies defined by caesium or hydrogen atoms.

International Atomic Time (TAI), established through international collaboration, is formed by combining the readings of many caesium clocks and was set close to the astronomically based Universal Time (UT) near the beginning of 1958. It was formally recognized in 1971 and since 1988 January 1 has been maintained by the International Bureau of Weights and Measures (BIPM). The second markers are generated according to the International System (SI) definition adopted in 1967 at the 13th General Conference of Weights and Measures: 'The second is the duration of 9 192 631 770 periods of the radiation corresponding to the transition between the two hyperfine levels of the ground state of the caesium-133 atom.'

Civil time in almost all countries is now based on Co-ordinated Universal Time (UTC), which was adopted for scientific purposes on 1972 January 1. UTC differs from TAI by an integer number of seconds (determined from studies of the rate of rotation of the Earth) and was designed to make both atomic time and UT accessible with accuracies appropriate for most users. The UTC time-scale is adjusted by the insertion (or, in principle, omission) of leap seconds in order to keep it within ±0.9s of UT. These leap seconds are introduced, when necessary, at the same instant throughout the world, either at the end of December or at the end of June. So, for example, the 22nd leap second occurred at 0h UTC on 1999 January 1. All leap seconds so far have been positive, with 61 seconds in the final minute of the UTC month. The time 23h 59m 60s UTC is followed one second later by 0h 0m 00s of the first day of the following month. Notices concerning the insertion of leap seconds are issued by the International Earth Rotation Service (IERS) at the Observatoire de Paris.

RADIO TIME-SIGNALS

UTC is made generally available through time-signals and standard frequency broadcasts such as MSF in the UK, CHU in Canada and WWV and WWVH in the USA. These are based on national time-scales that are maintained in close agreement with UTC and provide traceability to the national time-scale and to UTC. The markers of seconds in the UTC scale coincide with those of TAI.

To disseminate the national time-scale in the UK, special signals are broadcast on behalf of the National Physical Laboratory from the BT (British Telecom) radio station at Rugby (call-sign MSF). The signals are controlled from a caesium beam atomic frequency standard and consist of a precise frequency carrier of 60 kHz which is switched off, after being on for at least half a second, to mark every second. The first second of the minute begins with a period of 500ms with the carrier switched off, to serve as a minute marker. In the other seconds the carrier is always off for at least one tenth of a second at the start and then it carries an on-off code giving the British clock time and date, together with information identifying the start of the next minute. Changes to and from summer time are made following government announcements. Leap seconds are inserted as announced by the IERS and information provided by them on the difference between UTC and UT is also signalled. Other broadcast signals in the UK include the BBC six pips signal, the BT Timeline ('speaking clock'), the NPL Truetime service for computers, and a coded time-signal on the BBC 198 kHz transmitters which is used for timing in the electricity supply industry. From 1972 January 1 the six pips on the BBC have consisted of five short pips from second 55 to second 59 (six pips in the case of a leap second) followed by one lengthened pip, the start of which indicates the exact minute. From 1990 February 5 these signals have been controlled by the BBC with seconds markers referenced to the satellite-based US navigation system GPS (Global Positioning System) and time and day referenced to the MSF transmitter. Formerly they were generated by the Royal Greenwich Observatory. The BT Timeline is compared daily with the National Physical Laboratory caesium beam atomic frequency standard at the Rugby radio station. The NPL Truetime service is directly connected to the national time-scale.

Accurate timing may also be obtained from the signals of international navigation systems such as the ground-based Omega, or the satellite-based American GPS or Russian GLONASS systems.

STANDARD TIME

Since 1880 the standard time in Britain has been Greenwich Mean Time (GMT); a statute that year enacted that the word 'time' when used in any legal document relating to Britain meant, unless otherwise specifically stated, the mean time of the Greenwich meridian. Greenwich was adopted as the universal meridian on 13 October 1884. A system of standard time by zones is used world-wide, standard time in each zone differing from that of the Greenwich meridian by an integral number of hours, either fast or slow. The large territories of the USA and Canada are divided into zones approximately 7.5° on either side of central meridians. (For time zones of countries of the world, see Index.)

Variations from the standard time of some countries occur during part of the year; they are decided annually and are usually referred to as Summer Time or Daylight Saving Time.

At the 180th meridian the time can be either 12 hours fast on Greenwich Mean Time or 12 hours slow, and a change of date occurs. The internationally recognized date or calendar line is a modification of the 180th meridian, drawn so as to include islands of any one group on the same side of the line, or for political reasons. The line is indicated by joining up the following co-ordinates:

Lat.	Long.	Lat.	Long.
60° S.	180°	48° N.	180°
51° S.	180°	53° N.	170° E.
45° S.	172.5° W.	65.5° N.	169° W.
15° S.	172.5° W.	75° N.	180°
5° S.	180°		

Changes to the date line would require an international conference.

BRITISH SUMMER TIME

In 1916 an Act ordained that during a defined period of that year the legal time for general purposes in Great Britain should be one hour in advance of Greenwich Mean Time. The Summer Time Acts 1922 and 1925 defined the period during which Summer Time was to be in force, stabilizing practice until the Second World War.

During the war the duration of Summer Time was extended and in the years 1941 to 1945 and in 1947 Double Summer Time (two hours in advance of Greenwich Mean Time) was in force. After the war, Summer Time was extended each year in 1948–52 and 1961–4 by Order in Council.

Between 1968 October 27 and 1971 October 31 clocks were kept one hour ahead of Greenwich Mean Time throughout the year. This was known as British Standard Time.

The most recent legislation is the Summer Time Act 1972, which enacted that 'the period of summer time for the purposes of this Act is the period beginning at two o'clock, Greenwich mean time, in the morning of the day after the third Saturday in March or, if that day is Easter Day, the day after the second Saturday in March, and ending at two o'clock, Greenwich mean time, in the morning of the day after the fourth Saturday in October.'

The duration of Summer Time can be varied by Order in Council and in recent years alterations have been made to bring the operation of Summer Time in Britain closer to similar provisions in other countries of the European Union; for instance, since 1981 the hour of changeover has been 01h Greenwich Mean Time.

The duration of Summer Time in the next two years is:

2000   March 26 01h GMT to October 29 01h GMT
2001   March 25 01h GMT to October 28 01h GMT

MEAN REFRACTION

Alt.	Ref.	Alt.	Ref.	Alt.	Ref.
° ′	′	° ′	′	° ′	′
1 20		3 12		7 54	
	21		13		6
1 30		3 34		9 27	
	20		12		5
1 41		4 00		11 39	
	19		11		4
1 52		4 30		15 00	
	18		10		3
2 05		5 06		20 42	
	17		9		2
2 19		5 50		32 20	
	16		8		1
2 35		6 44		62 17	
	15		7		0
2 52		7 54		90 00	
	14				
3 12					

The refraction table is in the form of a critical table (see page 69)

ASTRONOMICAL CONSTANTS

Solar parallax	8″.794
Astronomical unit	149597870 km
Precession for the year 2000	50″.291
Precession in right ascension	3s.075
Precession in declination	20″.043
Constant of nutation	9″.202
Constant of aberration	20″.496
Mean obliquity of ecliptic (2000)	23° 26′ 22″
Moon's equatorial hor. parallax	57′ 02″.70
Velocity of light in vacuo per second	299792.5 km
Solar motion per second	20.0 km
Equatorial radius of the Earth	6378.140 km
Polar radius of the Earth	6356.755 km

North galactic pole (IAU standard)
        RA 12h 49m (1950.0). Dec. 27°.4 N.
Solar apex   RA 18h 06m Dec.+30°

Length of year (in mean solar days)

Tropical	365.24219
Sidereal	365.25636
Anomalistic (perihelion to perihelion)	365.25964
Eclipse	346.62000

Length of month (mean values)

	d	h	m	s
New Moon to New	29	12	44	02.9
Sidereal	27	07	43	11.5
Anomalistic (perigee to perigee)	27	13	18	33.2

ELEMENTS OF THE SOLAR SYSTEM

Orb	Mean distance from Sun (Earth=1)	km 10⁶	Sidereal period days	Synodic period days	Incl. of orbit to ecliptic ° ′	Diameter km	Mass (Earth=1)	Period of rotation on axis days
Sun	—	—	—	—	—	1,392,530	332,946	25–35*
Mercury	0.39	58	88.0	116	7 00	4,879	0.0553	58.646
Venus	0.72	108	224.7	584	3 24	12,104	0.8150	243.019r
Earth	1.00	150	365.3	—	—	12,756e	1.0000	0.997
Mars	1.52	228	687.0	780	1 51	6,794e	0.1074	1.026
Jupiter	5.20	778	4,332.6	399	1 18	142,984e 133,708p	317.89	0.410e
Saturn	9.54	1427	10,759.2	378	2 29	120,536e 108,728p	95.18	0.426e
Uranus	19.18	2870	30,684.6	370	0 46	51,118e	14.54	0.718r
Neptune	30.06	4497	60,191.0	367	1 46	49,528e	17.15	0.671
Pluto	39.80	5954	91,708.2	367	17 09	2,302	0.002	6.387

e equatorial, p polar, r retrograde, * depending on latitude

THE SATELLITES

Name	Star mag.	Mean distance from primary	Sidereal period of revolution
EARTH		km	d
I Moon	—	384,400	27.322
MARS			
I Phobos	12	9,378	0.319
II Deimos	13	23,459	1.262
JUPITER			
XVI Metis	17	127,960	0.295
XV Adrastea	19	128,980	0.298
V Amalthea	14	181,300	0.498
XIV Thebe	16	221,900	0.675
I Io	5	421,600	1.769
II Europa	5	670,900	3.552
III Ganymede	5	1,070,000	7.155
IV Callisto	6	1,883,000	16.689
XIII Leda	20	11,094,000	239
VI Himalia	15	11,480,000	251
X Lysithea	18	11,720,000	259
VII Elara	17	11,737,000	260
XII Ananke	19	21,200,000	631r
XI Carme	18	22,600,000	692r
VIII Pasiphae	17	23,500,000	735r
IX Sinope	18	23,700,000	758r
SATURN			
XVIII Pan	—	133,583	0.575
XV Atlas	18	137,640	0.602
XVI Prometheus	16	139,353	0.613
XVII Pandora	16	141,700	0.629
XI Epimetheus	15	151,422	0.695
X Janus	14	151,472	0.695
I Mimas	13	185,520	0.942
II Enceladus	12	238,020	1.370
III Tethys	10	294,660	1.888
XIII Telesto	19	294,660	1.888
XIV Calypso	19	294,660	1.888
IV Dione	10	377,400	2.737
XII Helene	18	377,400	2.737
V Rhea	10	527,040	4.518
VI Titan	8	1,221,850	15.945
VII Hyperion	14	1,481,100	21.277

Name	Star mag.	Mean distance from primary	Sidereal period of revolution
SATURN		km	d
VIII Iapetus	11	3,561,300	79.330
IX Phoebe	16	12,952,000	550.48r
URANUS			
VI Cordelia	—	49,750	0.335
VII Ophelia	—	53,760	0.376
VIII Bianca	—	59,170	0.435
IX Cressida	—	61,780	0.464
X Desdemona	—	62,660	0.474
XI Juliet	—	64,360	0.493
XII Portia	—	66,100	0.513
XIII Rosalind	—	69,930	0.558
XIV Belinda	—	75,260	0.624
S/1986U10	—	77,000	0.638
XV Puck	—	86,000	0.762
V Miranda	17	129,800	1.413
I Ariel	14	191,200	2.520
II Umbriel	15	266,000	4.144
III Titania	14	435,800	8.706
IV Oberon	14	583,600	13.463
S/1997U1	—	7,164,600	579
S/1997U2	—	12,174,700	1,289
NEPTUNE			
III Naiad	25	48,230	0.294
IV Thalassa	24	50,070	0.311
V Despina	23	52,530	0.335
VI Galatea	22	61,950	0.429
VII Larissa	22	73,550	0.555
VIII Proteus	20	117,650	1.122
I Triton	13	354,760	5.877
II Nereid	19	5,513,400	360.136
PLUTO			
I Charon	17	19,600	6.387

THE EARTH

The shape of the Earth is that of an oblate spheroid or solid of revolution whose meridian sections are ellipses not differing much from circles, whilst the sections at right angles are circles. The length of the equatorial axis is about 12,756 km, and that of the polar axis is 12,714 km. The mean density of the Earth is 5.5 times that of water, although that of the surface layer is less. The Earth and Moon revolve about their common centre of gravity in a lunar month; this centre in turn revolves round the Sun in a plane known as the ecliptic, that passes through the Sun's centre. The Earth's equator is inclined to this plane at an angle of 23.4°. This tilt is the cause of the seasons. In mid-latitudes, and when the Sun is high above the Equator, not only does the high noon altitude make the days longer, but the Sun's rays fall more directly on the Earth's surface; these effects combine to produce summer. In equatorial regions the noon altitude is large throughout the year, and there is little variation in the length of the day. In higher latitudes the noon altitude is lower, and the days in summer are appreciably longer than those in winter.

The average velocity of the Earth in its orbit is 30 km a second. It makes a complete rotation on its axis in about 23h 56m of mean time, which is the sidereal day. Because of its annual revolution round the Sun, the rotation with respect to the Sun, or the solar day, is more than this by about four minutes (*see* page 73). The extremity of the axis of rotation, or the North Pole of the Earth, is not rigidly fixed, but wanders over an area roughly 20 metres in diameter.

TERRESTRIAL MAGNETISM

A magnetic compass points along the horizontal component of a magnetic line of force. These lines of force converge on the 'magnetic dip-poles', the places where a freely suspended magnetized needle would become vertical. Not only do these poles move with time, but their exact locations are ill-defined, particularly so in the case of the north dip-pole where the lines of force on the north side of it, instead of converging radially, tend to bunch into a channel. Although it is therefore unrealistic to attempt to specify the locations of the dip-poles exactly, the present approximate adopted positions are 80°.0 N., 107°.2 W. and 64°.6 S., 138°.4 E. The two magnetic dip-poles are thus not antipodal, the line joining them passing the centre of the Earth at a distance of about 1,250 km. The distances of the magnetic dip-poles from the north and south geographical poles are about 1,200 km and 2,800 km respectively.

There is also a 'magnetic equator', at all points of which the vertical component of the Earth's magnetic field is zero and a magnetized needle remains horizontal. This line runs between 2° and 10° north of the geographical equator in Asia and Africa, turns sharply south off the west African coast, and crosses South America through Brazil, Bolivia and Peru; it recrosses the geographical equator in mid-Pacific.

Reference has already been made to secular changes in the Earth's field. The following table indicates the changes in magnetic declination (or variation of the compass). Declination is the angle in the horizontal plane between the direction of true north and that in which a magnetic compass points. Similar, though much smaller, changes have occurred in 'dip' or magnetic inclination. Secular changes differ throughout the world. Although the London observations suggest a cycle with a period of several hundred years, an exact repetition is unlikely.

London		Greenwich	
1580	11° 15′ E.	1900	16° 29′ W.
1622	5° 56′ E.	1925	13° 10′ W.
1665	1° 22′ W.	1950	9° 07′ W.
1730	13° 00′ W.	1975	6° 39′ W.
1773	21° 09′ W.	1998	3° 32′ W.
1850	22° 24′ W.		

In order that up-to-date information on declination may be available, many governments publish magnetic charts on which there are lines (isogonic lines) passing through all places at which specified values of declination will be found at the date of the chart.

In the British Isles, isogonic lines now run approximately north-east to south-west. Though there are considerable local deviations due to geological causes, a rough value of magnetic declination may be obtained by assuming that at 50° N. on the meridian of Greenwich, the value in 2000 is 2° 37′ west and allowing an increase of 15′ for each degree of latitude northwards and one of 27′ for each degree of longitude westwards. For example, at 53° N., 5° W., declination will be about 2° 37′+45′+135′, i.e. 5° 37′ west. The average annual change at the present time is about 12′ decrease.

The number of magnetic observatories is about 200, irregularly distributed over the globe. There are three in Great Britain, run by the British Geological Survey: at Hartland, north Devon; at Eskdalemuir, Dumfriesshire; and at Lerwick, Shetland Islands. The following are some recent annual mean values of the magnetic elements for Hartland.

Year	Declination West ° ′	Dip or inclination ° ′	Horizontal force gauss	Vertical force gauss
1960	9 59	66 44	0.1871	0.4350
1965	9 30	66 34	0.1887	0.4354
1970	9 06	66 26	0.1903	0.4364
1975	8 32	66 17	0.1921	0.4373
1980	7 44	66 10	0.1933	0.4377
1985	6 56	66 08	0.1938	0.4380
1990	6 15	66 10	0.1939	0.4388
1995	5 33	66 07	0.1946	0.4395
1998	5 03	66 07	0.1949	0.4400

The normal worldwide terrestrial magnetic field corresponds approximately to that of a very strong small bar magnet near the centre of the Earth, but with appreciable smooth spatial departures. The origin and the slow secular change of the normal field are not fully understood but are generally ascribed to electric currents associated with fluid motions in the Earth's core. Superimposed on the normal field are local and regional anomalies whose magnitudes may in places approach that of the normal field; these are due to the influence of mineral deposits in the Earth's crust. A small proportion of the field is of external origin, mostly associated with electric currents in the ionosphere. The configuration of the external field and the ionization of the atmosphere depend on the incident particle and radiation flux from the Sun. There are, therefore, short-term and non-periodic as well as diurnal, 27-day, seasonal and 11-year periodic changes in the magnetic field, dependent upon the position of the Sun and the degree of solar activity.

MAGNETIC STORMS

Occasionally, sometimes with great suddenness, the Earth's magnetic field is subject for several hours to marked disturbance. During a severe storm in 1989 the declination at Lerwick changed by almost 8° in less than an hour. In many instances such disturbances are accompanied by widespread displays of aurorae, marked changes in the incidence of cosmic rays, an increase in the reception of 'noise' from the Sun at radio frequencies, and rapid changes in the ionosphere and induced electric currents within the Earth which adversely affect radio and telegraphic communications. The disturbances are caused by changes in the stream of ionized particles which emanates from the Sun and through which the Earth is continuously passing. Some of these changes are associated with visible eruptions on the Sun, usually in the region of sun-spots. There is a marked tendency for disturbances to recur after intervals of about 27 days, the apparent period of rotation of the Sun on its axis, which is consistent with the sources being located on particular areas of the Sun.

ARTIFICIAL SATELLITES

To consider the orbit of an artificial satellite, it is best to imagine that one is looking at the Earth from a distant point in space. The Earth would then be seen to be rotating about its axis inside the orbit described by the rapidly revolving satellite. The inclination of a satellite orbit to the Earth's equator (which generally remains almost constant throughout the satellite's lifetime) gives at once the maximum range of latitudes over which the satellite passes. Thus a satellite whose orbit has an inclination of 53° will pass overhead all latitudes between 53° S. and 53° N., but would never be seen in the zenith of any place nearer the poles than these latitudes. If we consider a particular place on the earth, whose latitude is less than the inclination of the satellite's orbit, then the Earth's rotation carries this place first under the northbound part of the orbit and then under the southbound portion of the orbit, these two occurrences being always less than 12 hours apart for satellites moving in direct orbits (i.e. to the east). (For satellites in retrograde orbits, the words 'northbound' and 'southbound' should be interchanged in the preceding statement.) As the value of the latitude of the observer increases and approaches the value of the inclination of the orbit, so this interval gets shorter until (when the latitude is equal to the inclination) only one overhead passage occurs each day.

OBSERVATION OF SATELLITES

The regression of the orbit around the Earth causes alternate periods of visibility and invisibility, though this is of little concern to the radio or radar observer. To the visual observer the following cycle of events normally occurs (though the cycle may start in any position): invisibility, morning observations before dawn, invisibility, evening observations after dusk, invisibility, morning observations before dawn, and so on. With reasonably high satellites and for observers in high latitudes around the summer solstice, the evening observations follow the morning observations without interruption as sunlight passing over the polar regions can still illuminate satellites which are passing over temperate latitudes at local midnight. At the moment all satellites rely on sunlight to make them visible, though a satellite with a flashing light has been suggested for a future launching. The observer must be in darkness or twilight in order to make any useful observations. (For durations of twilight; and sunrise and sunset times, *see* Page Two of each month.)

Some of the satellites are visible to the naked eye and much interest has been aroused by the spectacle of a bright satellite disappearing into the Earth's shadow. The event is even more interesting telescopically as the disappearance occurs gradually as the satellite traverses the Earth's penumbral shadow, and during the last few seconds before the eclipse is complete the satellite may change colour (in suitable atmospheric conditions) from yellow to red. This is because the last rays of sunlight are refracted through the denser layers of our atmosphere before striking the satellite.

Some satellites rotate about one or more axes so that a periodic variation in brightness is observed. This was particularly noticeable in several of the Soviet satellites.

Satellite research has provided some interesting results, including a revised value of the Earth's oblateness (1/298.2), and the discovery of the Van Allen radiation belts.

LAUNCHINGS

Apart from their names, e.g. Cosmos 6 Rocket, the satellites are also classified according to their date of launch. Thus 1961 α refers to the first satellite launching of 1961. A number following the Greek letter indicated the relative brightness of the satellites put in orbit. From the beginning of 1963 the Greek letters were replaced by numbers and the numbers by roman letters e.g. 1963–01A. For all satellites successfully injected into orbit the following table gives the designation and names of the main objects, the launch date and some initial orbital data. These are the inclination to the equator (i), the nodal period of revolution (P), and the apogee and perigee heights.

Although most of the satellites launched are injected into orbits less than 1,000 km high, there are an increasing number of satellites in geostationary orbits, i.e. where the orbital inclination is zero, the eccentricity close to zero, and the period of revolution is 1436.1 minutes. Thus the satellite is permanently situated over the equator at one selected longitude at a mean height of 35,786 km. This geostationary band is crowded. In one case there are four television satellites (Astra 1A, Astra 1B, Astra 1C and Astra 1D) orbiting within a few tens of kilometres of each other. In the sky they appear to be separated by only a few arc minutes.

In 1997 a number of *Iridium* satellites were launched into high inclination orbits. These are owned by the mobile telephone company Cellnet. For visual observers, these satellites have the interesting characteristic that the large flat aerials they carry can, when in exactly the right orientation with respect to the Sun and the observer, give off a 'flare' in brightness which can on occasion attain a magnitude of −6, much brighter than Venus. The flare can be visible to the naked eye for nearly a minute.

SPACE STATION MIR

The Russian Space Station, Mir, 1986–17A, which was launched in 1986, is likely to be decommissioned soon. When passing over Britain it has appeared to be almost as bright as Jupiter on favourable transits, though only visible for 4 or 5 minutes on each pass.

The new International Space Station, ISS, 1998–67A, is currently being assembled in an orbit of similar size and inclination. It is already nearly as bright as Mir and will eventually become brighter as more parts are added to it. Predictions for Mir and ISS can be found on the internet at http://www2.gsoc.dlr.de/scripts/satvis.

ARTIFICIAL SATELLITE LAUNCHES 1998–9

Desig-nation	Satellite	Launch date	P	i	Apogee height	Perigee height
1998–			m	°	km	km
015	Progress M, rocket	March 14	90.1	51.6	314	254
016	UHF FO 8	March 16	641.0	24.1	36106	414
017	SPOT 4, rocket	March 24	101.0	98.7	807	802
018	Iridium 51, 61, 55, 57, 58, 59, 60, rocket	March 25	97.3	86.4	636	622
020	TRACE, rocket	April 2	97.2	97.7	642	599
021	Iridium 62-68	April 6	94.9	86.7	522	499
022	STS-90	April 17	89.8	39.0	286	257
023	Globalstar 5-8, rocket	April 24	110.5	52.0	1261	1241
024	Nilesat, BSAT, rocket	April 28	1436.0	0.0	35800	35771
025	Cosmos 2350, rocket, platform, rocket	April 29	1439.6	2.2	35934	35781
026	Iridium XI	May 2	97.4	86.4	644	623
027	Cosmos 2351, platform, platform, platform	May 7	704.9	63.0	39204	514
028	Echostar 4, rocket, platform, rocket	May 7	794.3	15.4	35727	8346
029	USA139, rocket	May 9			(unknown)	
030	NOAA-K	May 13	101.3	98.7	824	809
031	Progress M39	May 14	90.0	51.6	298	254
032	Iridium 70, 72, 73, 74, 75, rocket	May 17	97.4	86.5	644	625
033	Chinastar 1, rocket	May 30	1798.0	24.3	65534	217
034	Shuttle 91	June 2	91.6	51.6	379	369
035	THOR 3, rocket	June 10	1422.3	0.1	36165	34870
036	Cosmos 2352-7, rocket	June 15	118.1	82.5	1875	1310
037	Intelsat 805, rocket	June 18	1045.4	3.2	35694	19798
038	Cosmos 2358, rocket	June 25	89.5	67.0	331	167
039	Cosmos 2359, rocket	June 26	89.9	64.9	302	241
040	Molniya 3-49, platform, rocket	July 1	90.3	62.7	373	208
041	Planet B, rocket	July 3	20896.1	27.3	489366	702
042	Tubsat, rocket	July 7	96.0	78.9	756	396
043	Resurs 01, Fasat-Bravo, TMSAT, Gurwin Techsat 1B, Westpac, SAFIR-2	July 10	101.0	98.8	815	812
044	Sinosat, rocket	July 18	1436.1	0.0	35828	570
045	Cosmos 2360, rocket	July 28	101.7	71.0	852	842
046	Orbcomm FM13-20	August 2	101.0	45.0	822	800
047	Soyuz TM-28	August 13	91.4	51.7	361	347
048	Iridium SV03, SV76	August 19	100.1	86.4	776	773
049	ST-1	August 25	1436.0	0.0	35794	35778
050	Astra 2A	August 30	1436.0	0.0	35847	35724
051	Iridium 82-77	September 8	95.4	86.1	552	544
052	PAS-7, rocket	September 16	1089.9	7.3	57262	169
053	Orbcomm FM21-28, rocket, rocket	September 23	101.3	45.1	834	825
054	Molniya 1-91, rocket, launcher, rocket	September 28	734.4	62.9	40933	2600
055	STEX/ATEX USA 140, rocket	October 3	98.5	85.1	713	681
056	Eutelsat W-2, Sirius 3, rocket, Spelda	October 5	1433.7	0.1	35768	35732
057	Hot Bird 5, rocket	October 9	1407.3	0.4	36649	33814
058	UHF F/O 9, rocket	October 20	1436.2	6.1	36778	34822
059	MAQSAT 3	October 21	641.3	7.1	35515	1018
060	SCD-2 (Brazil), rocket	October 23	100.0	25.0	782	755
061	Deep Space DS-1, SEDSAT-1, rocket, rocket	October 24			(unknown)	
062	Progress M-40, rocket	October 25	91.8	51.7	376	366
063	Afristar, GE-5, rocket	October 28	1430.4	0.1	35754	35616
064	STS-95 Discovery F15, PANSAT, Spartan	October 29	95.8	28.5	572	563
065	Panamsat PAS-8, rocket, launcher, rocket	November 4	768.9	17.3	35952	6916
066	Iridium 2, 86, 85, 84, 83, rocket	November 6	95.2	86.1	546	529
067	Zarya=International Space Station, 1st module, rocket	November 20	89.8	51.6	355	191
068	Bonum 1, rocket	November 22	670.4	19.5	36718	1297
069	STS-88 Endeavour F	December 4	89.7	51.6	336	203
070	Sat Mex 5, rocket	December 6	375.4	6.6	21516	224

ARTIFICIAL SATELLITE LAUNCHES 1998–9

Designation	Satellite	Launch date	P	i	Apogee height	Perigee height
1998–			m	°	km	km
071	SWAS, rocket	December 6	97.6	70.0	662	650
072	Nadezhda 5, Astrid 2, rocket	December 9	105.1	83.0	1025	99
073	Mars Climate Observer, rocket, rocket	December 11	(No elements available)			
074	Iridium 11A, 20A, rocket, Smart Dispenser	December 19	97.6	86.4	668	636
075	Panamsat PAS-6B, rocket	December 22	1197.7	0.7	35789	26195
076	Cosmos 2361, rocket	December 24	105.0	83.0	1026	982
077	Cosmos 2362-2364, rocket, platform, rocket	December 30	675.6	64.9	19147	19128
1999–						
001	Mars payload orbiter	January 3	(Selenocentric orbit)			
002	Rocsat-1	January 27	96.6	35.0	614	601
003	Stardust, rocket	February 7	(Selenocentric orbit)			
004	Globalstar M36, M23, M38 and M40	February 9	103.7	52.0	960	928
005	Telstar 6, rocket, launcher, rocket	February 15	940.5	7.9	35813	15051
006	JCSAT-06, rocket	February 16	2131.1	24.3	65534	267
007	Soyuz TM-29, rocket	February 20	91.7	51.7	377	359
008	Argos, Orsted, Sunsat, rocket	February 23	101.8	98.8	861	844
009	Arabsat 3A, Skynet 4E, rocket, Spelda	February 26	631.9	7.1	35818	234
010	Raduga 1094, rocket, platform, rocket	February 28	1480.3	1.7	36820	36496
011	Wire, rocket	March 5	96.0	97.6	606	552

Time Measurement and Calendars

MEASUREMENTS OF TIME

Measurements of time are based on the time taken by the earth to rotate on its axis (day); by the moon to revolve round the earth (month); and by the earth to revolve round the sun (year). From these, which are not commensurable, certain average or mean intervals have been adopted for ordinary use.

THE DAY

The day begins at midnight and is divided into 24 hours of 60 minutes, each of 60 seconds. The hours are counted from midnight up to 12 noon (when the sun crosses the meridian), and these hours are designated a.m. (*ante meridiem*); and again from noon up to 12 midnight, which hours are designated p.m. (*post meridiem*), except when the 24-hour reckoning is employed. The 24-hour reckoning ignores a.m. and p.m., numbering the hours 0 to 23 from midnight.

Colloquially the 24 hours are divided into day and night, day being the time while the sun is above the horizon (including the four stages of twilight defined on page 72). Day is subdivided into morning, the early part of daytime, ending at noon; afternoon, from noon to about 6 p.m.; and evening, which may be said to extend from 6 p.m. until midnight. Night, the dark period between day and day, begins at the close of astronomical twilight (*see* page 72) and extends beyond midnight to sunrise the next day.

The names of the days are derived from Old English translations or adaptations of the Roman titles.

Sunday	Sun	Sol
Monday	Moon	Luna
Tuesday	Tiw/Tyr (god of war)	Mars
Wednesday	Woden/Odin	Mercury
Thursday	Thor	Jupiter
Friday	Frigga/Freyja	Venus
	(goddess of love)	
Saturday	Saeternes	Saturn

THE MONTH

The month in the ordinary calendar is approximately the twelfth part of a year, but the lengths of the different months vary from 28 (or 29) days to 31.

THE YEAR

The equinoctial or tropical year is the time that the earth takes to revolve round the sun from equinox to equinox, i.e. 365.24219 mean solar days, or 365 days 5 hours 48 minutes and 45 seconds.

The calendar year usually consists of 365 days but a year containing 366 days is called bissextile (*see* Roman calendar, page 89) or leap year, one day being added to the month of February so that a date 'leaps over' a day of the week. In the Roman calendar the day that was repeated was the sixth day before the beginning of March, the equivalent of 24 February.

A year is a leap year if the date of the year is divisible by four without remainder, unless it is the last year of the century. The last year of a century is a leap year only if its number is divisible by 400 without remainder, e.g. the years 1800 and 1900 had only 365 days but the year 2000 has 366 days.

THE SOLSTICE

A solstice is the point in the tropical year at which the sun attains its greatest distance, north or south, from the Equator. In the northern hemisphere the furthest point north of the Equator marks the summer solstice and the furthest point south the winter solstice.

The date of the solstice varies according to locality. For example, if the summer solstice falls on 21 June late in the day by Greenwich time, that day will be the longest of the year at Greenwich though it may be by only a second, but it will fall on 22 June, local date, in Japan, and so 22 June will be the longest day there. The date of the solstice is also affected by the length of the tropical year, which is 365 days 6 hours less about 11 minutes 15 seconds. If a solstice happens late on 21 June in one year, it will be nearly six hours later in the next (unless the next year is a leap year), i.e. early on 22 June, and that will be the longest day.

This delay of the solstice does not continue because the extra day in leap year brings it back a day in the calendar. However, because of the 11 minutes 15 seconds mentioned above, the additional day in leap year brings the solstice back too far by 45 minutes, and the time of the solstice in the calendar is earlier, in a four-year pattern, as the century progresses. The last year of a century is in most cases not a leap year, and the omission of the extra day puts the date of the solstice later by about six hours too much. Compensation for this is made by the fourth centennial year being a leap year. The solstice has become earlier in date throughout this century and, because the year 2000 is a leap year, the solstice will get earlier still throughout the 21st century.

The date of the winter solstice, the shortest day of the year, is affected by the same factors as the longest day.

At Greenwich the sun sets at its earliest by the clock about ten days before the shortest day. The daily change in the time of sunset is due in the first place to the sun's movement southwards at this time of the year, which diminishes the interval between the sun's transit and its setting. However, the daily decrease of the Equation of Time causes the time of apparent noon to be continuously later day by day, which to some extent counteracts the first effect. The rates of the change of these two quantities are not equal or uniform; their combination causes the date of earliest sunset to be 12 or 13 December at Greenwich. In more southerly latitudes the effect of the movement of the sun is less, and the change in the time of sunset depends on that of the Equation of Time to a greater degree, and the date of earliest sunset is earlier than it is at Greenwich, e.g. on the Equator it is about 1 November.

THE EQUINOX

The equinox is the point at which the sun crosses the Equator and day and night are of equal length all over the world. This occurs in March and September.

DOG DAYS

The days about the heliacal rising of the Dog Star, noted from ancient times as the hottest period of the year in the northern hemisphere, are called the Dog Days. Their incidence has been variously calculated as depending on the Greater or Lesser Dog Star (Sirius or Procyon) and their duration has been reckoned as from 30 to 54 days. A generally accepted period is from 3 July to 15 August.

CHRISTIAN CALENDAR

In the Christian chronological system the years are distinguished by cardinal numbers before or after the birth of Christ, the period being denoted by the letters BC (Before Christ) or, more rarely, AC (*Ante Christum*), and AD (*Anno Domini* – In the Year of Our Lord). The correlative dates of the epoch are the fourth year of the 194th Olympiad, the 753rd year from the foundation of Rome, AM 3761 in Jewish chronology, and the 4714th year of the Julian period. The actual date of the birth of Christ is somewhat uncertain.

The system was introduced into Italy in the sixth century. Though first used in France in the seventh century, it was not universally established there until about the eighth century. It has been said that the system was introduced into England by St Augustine (AD 596), but it was probably not generally used until some centuries later. It was ordered to be used by the Bishops at the Council of Chelsea (AD 816).

THE JULIAN CALENDAR

In the Julian calendar (adopted by the Roman Empire in 45 BC, *see* page 89) all the centennial years were leap years, and for this reason towards the close of the 16th century there was a difference of ten days between the tropical and calendar years; the equinox fell on 11 March of the calendar, whereas at the time of the Council of Nicaea (AD 325), it had fallen on 21 March. In 1582 Pope Gregory ordained that 5 October should be called 15 October and that of the end-century years only the fourth should be a leap year (*see* page 81).

THE GREGORIAN CALENDAR

The Gregorian calendar was adopted by Italy, France, Spain and Portugal in 1582, by Prussia, the Roman Catholic German states, Switzerland, Holland and Flanders on 1 January 1583, by Poland in 1586, Hungary in 1587, the Protestant German and Netherland states and Denmark in 1700, and by Great Britain and Dominions (including the North American colonies) in 1752, by the omission of eleven days (3 September being reckoned as 14 September). Sweden omitted the leap day in 1700 but observed leap days in 1704 and 1708, and reverted to the Julian calendar by having two leap days in 1712; the Gregorian calendar was adopted in 1753 by the omission of eleven days (18 February being reckoned as 1 March). Japan adopted the calendar in 1872, China in 1912, Bulgaria in 1915, Turkey and Soviet Russia in 1918, Yugoslavia and Romania in 1919, and Greece in 1923.

In the same year that the change was made in England from the Julian to the Gregorian calendar, the beginning of the new year was also changed from 25 March to 1 January (*see* page 86).

THE ORTHODOX CHURCHES

Some Orthodox Churches still use the Julian reckoning but the majority of Greek Orthodox Churches and the Romanian Orthodox Church have adopted a modified 'New Calendar', observing the Gregorian calendar for fixed feasts and the Julian for movable feasts.

The Orthodox Church year begins on 1 September. There are four fast periods and, in addition to Pascha (Easter), twelve great feasts, as well as numerous commemorations of the saints of the Old and New Testaments throughout the year.

THE DOMINICAL LETTER

The dominical letter is one of the letters A–G which are used to denote the Sundays in successive years. If the first day of the year is a Sunday the letter is A; if the second, B; the third, C; and so on. A leap year requires two letters, the first for 1 January to 29 February, the second for 1 March to 31 December (*see* page 84).

EPIPHANY

The feast of the Epiphany, commemorating the manifestation of Christ, later became associated with the offering of gifts by the Magi. The day was of great importance from the time of the Council of Nicaea (AD 325), as the primate of Alexandria was charged at every Epiphany feast with the announcement in a letter to the churches of the date of the forthcoming Easter. The day was also of importance in Britain as it influenced dates, ecclesiastical and lay, e.g. Plough Monday, when work was resumed in the fields, fell on the Monday in the first full week after Epiphany.

LENT

The Teutonic word *Lent*, which denotes the fast preceding Easter, originally meant no more than the spring season; but from Anglo-Saxon times at least it has been used as the equivalent of the more significant Latin term Quadragesima, meaning the 'forty days' or, more literally, the fortieth day. Ash Wednesday is the first day of Lent, which ends at midnight before Easter Day.

PALM SUNDAY

Palm Sunday, the Sunday before Easter and the beginning of Holy Week, commemorates the triumphal entry of Christ into Jerusalem and is celebrated in Britain (when palm is not available) by branches of willow gathered for use in the decoration of churches on that day.

MAUNDY THURSDAY

Maundy Thursday is the day before Good Friday, the name itself being a corruption of *dies mandati* (day of the mandate) when Christ washed the feet of the disciples and gave them the mandate to love one another.

EASTER DAY

Easter Day is the first Sunday after the full moon which happens on, or next after, the 21st day of March; if the full moon happens on a Sunday, Easter Day is the Sunday after.

This definition is contained in an Act of Parliament (24 Geo. II c. 23) and explanation is given in the preamble to the Act that the day of full moon depends on certain tables that have been prepared. These tables are summarized in the early pages of the Book of Common Prayer. The moon referred to is not the real moon of the heavens, but a hypothetical moon on whose 'full' the date of Easter depends, and the lunations of this 'calendar' moon consist of twenty-nine and thirty days alternately, with certain necessary modifications to make the date of its full agree as nearly as possible with that of the real moon, which is known as the Paschal Full Moon.

A FIXED EASTER

In 1928 the House of Commons agreed to a motion for the third reading of a bill proposing that Easter Day shall, in the calendar year next but one after the commencement of the Act and in all subsequent years, be the first Sunday after the second Saturday in April. Easter would thus fall on the second or third Sunday in April, i.e. between 9 and 15 April (inclusive). A clause in the Bill provided that before it shall come into operation, regard shall be had to any opinion expressed officially by the various Christian churches. Efforts by the World Council of Churches to secure a unanimous choice of date for Easter by its member churches have so far been unsuccessful.

ROGATION DAYS

Rogation Days are the Monday, Tuesday and Wednesday preceding Ascension Day and from the fifth century were observed as public fasts with solemn processions and supplications. The processions were discontinued as religious observances at the Reformation, but survive in the ceremony known as 'beating the parish bounds'. Rogation Sunday is the Sunday before Ascension Day.

EMBER DAYS

The Ember Days at the four seasons are the Wednesday, Friday and Saturday (a) before the third Sunday in Advent,

(b) before the second Sunday in Lent, and (c) before the Sundays nearest to the festivals of St Peter and of St Michael and All Angels.

TRINITY SUNDAY

Trinity Sunday is eight weeks after Easter Day, on the Sunday following Pentecost (Whit Sunday). Subsequent Sundays are reckoned in the Book of Common Prayer calendar of the Church of England as 'after Trinity'.

Thomas Becket (1118–70) was consecrated Archbishop of Canterbury on the Sunday after Whit Sunday and his first act was to ordain that the day of his consecration should be held as a new festival in honour of the Holy Trinity. This observance spread from Canterbury throughout the whole of Christendom.

MOVABLE FEASTS TO THE YEAR 2035

Year	Ash Wednesday	Easter	Ascension	Pentecost (Whit Sunday)	Advent Sunday
2000	8 March	23 April	1 June	11 June	3 December
2001	28 February	15 April	24 May	3 June	2 December
2002	13 February	31 March	9 May	19 May	1 December
2003	5 March	20 April	29 May	8 June	30 November
2004	25 February	11 April	20 May	30 May	28 November
2005	9 February	27 March	5 May	15 May	27 November
2006	1 March	16 April	25 May	4 June	3 December
2007	21 February	8 April	17 May	27 May	2 December
2008	6 February	23 March	1 May	11 May	30 November
2009	25 February	12 April	21 May	31 May	29 November
2010	17 February	4 April	13 May	23 May	28 November
2011	9 March	24 April	2 June	12 June	27 November
2012	22 February	8 April	17 May	27 May	2 December
2013	13 February	31 March	9 May	19 May	1 December
2014	5 March	20 April	29 May	8 June	30 November
2015	18 February	5 April	14 May	24 May	29 November
2016	10 February	27 March	5 May	15 May	27 November
2017	1 March	16 April	25 May	4 June	3 December
2018	14 February	1 April	10 May	20 May	2 December
2019	6 March	21 April	30 May	9 June	1 December
2020	26 February	12 April	21 May	31 May	29 November
2021	17 February	4 April	13 May	23 May	28 November
2022	2 March	17 April	26 May	5 June	27 November
2023	22 February	9 April	18 May	28 May	3 December
2024	14 February	31 March	9 May	19 May	1 December
2025	5 March	20 April	29 May	8 June	30 November
2026	18 February	5 April	14 May	24 May	29 November
2027	10 February	28 March	6 May	16 May	28 November
2028	1 March	16 April	25 May	4 June	3 December
2029	14 February	1 April	10 May	20 May	2 December
2030	6 March	21 April	30 May	9 June	1 December
2031	26 February	13 April	22 May	1 June	30 November
2032	11 February	28 March	6 May	16 May	28 November
2033	2 March	17 April	26 May	5 June	27 November
2034	22 February	9 April	18 May	28 May	3 December
2035	7 February	25 March	3 May	13 May	2 December

NOTES

Ash Wednesday (first day in Lent) can fall at earliest on 4 February and at latest on 10 March

Mothering Sunday (fourth Sunday in Lent) can fall at earliest on 1 March and at latest on 4 April

Easter Day can fall at earliest on 22 March and at latest on 25 April

Ascension Day is forty days after Easter Day and can fall at earliest on 30 April and at latest on 3 June

Pentecost (Whit Sunday) is seven weeks after Easter and can fall at earliest on 10 May and at latest on 13 June

Trinity Sunday is the Sunday after Whit Sunday

Corpus Christi falls on the Thursday after Trinity Sunday

Sundays after Pentecost – there are not less than 18 and not more than 23

Advent Sunday is the Sunday nearest to 30 November

EASTER DAYS AND DOMINICAL LETTERS 1500 TO 2035

Dates up to and including 1752 are according to the Julian calendar. For dominical letters in leap years, *see* page 82

	1500–1599	1600–1699	1700–1799	1800–1899	1900–1999	2000–2035
March						
d 22	1573	1668	1761	1818		
e 23	1505/16	1600	1788	1845/56	1913	2008
f 24		1611/95	1706/99		1940	
g 25	1543/54	1627/38/49	1722/33/44	1883/94	1951	2035
A 26	1559/70/81/92	1654/65/76	1749/58/69/80	1815/26/37	1967/78/89	
b 27	1502/13/24/97	1608/87/92	1785/96	1842/53/64	1910/21/32	2005/16
c 28	1529/35/40	1619/24/30	1703/14/25	1869/75/80	1937/48	2027/32
d 29	1551/62	1635/46/57	1719/30/41/52	1807/12/91	1959/64/70	
e 30	1567/78/89	1651/62/73/84	1746/55/66/77	1823/34	1902/75/86/97	
f 31	1510/21/32/83/94	1605/16/78/89	1700/71/82/93	1839/50/61/72	1907/18/29/91	2002/13/24
April						
g 1	1526/37/48	1621/32	1711/16	1804/66/77/88	1923/34/45/56	2018/29
A 2	1553/64	1643/48	1727/38	1809/20/93/99	1961/72	
b 3	1575/80/86	1659/70/81	1743/63/68/74	1825/31/36	1904/83/88/94	
c 4	1507/18/91	1602/13/75/86/97	1708/79/90	1847/58	1915/20/26/99	2010/21
d 5	1523/34/45/56	1607/18/29/40	1702/13/24/95	1801/63/74/85/96	1931/42/53	2015/26
e 6	1539/50/61/72	1634/45/56	1729/35/40/60	1806/17/28/90	1947/58/69/80	
f 7	1504/77/88	1667/72	1751/65/76	1822/33/44	1901/12/85/96	
g 8	1509/15/20/99	1604/10/83/94	1705/87/92/98	1849/55/60	1917/28	2007/12
A 9	1531/42	1615/26/37/99	1710/21/32	1871/82	1939/44/50	2023/34
b 10	1547/58/69	1631/42/53/64	1726/37/48/57	1803/14/87/98	1955/66/77	
c 11	1501/12/63/74/85/96	1658/69/80	1762/73/84	1819/30/41/52	1909/71/82/93	2004
d 12	1506/17/28	1601/12/91/96	1789	1846/57/68	1903/14/25/36/98	2009/20
e 13	1533/44	1623/28	1707/18	1800/73/79/84	1941/52	2031
f 14	1555/60/66	1639/50/61	1723/34/45/54	1805/11/16/95	1963/68/74	
g 15	1571/82/93	1655/66/77/88	1750/59/70/81	1827/38	1900/06/79/90	2001
A 16	1503/14/25/36/87/98	1609/20/82/93	1704/75/86/97	1843/54/65/76	1911/22/33/95	2006/17/28
b 17	1530/41/52	1625/36	1715/20	1808/70/81/92	1927/38/49/60	2022/33
c 18	1557/68	1647/52	1731/42/56	1802/13/24/97	1954/65/76	
d 19	1500/79/84/90	1663/74/85	1747/67/72/78	1829/35/40	1908/81/87/92	
e 20	1511/22/95	1606/17/79/90	1701/12/83/94	1851/62	1919/24/30	2003/14/25
f 21	1527/38/49	1622/33/44	1717/28	1867/78/89	1935/46/57	2019/30
g 22	1565/76	1660	1739/53/64	1810/21/32	1962/73/84	
A 23	1508	1671		1848	1905/16	2000
b 24	1519	1603/14/98	1709/91	1859		2011
c 25	1546	1641	1736	1886	1943	

HINDU CALENDAR

The Hindu calendar is a luni-solar calendar of twelve months, each containing 29 days, 12 hours. Each month is divided into a light fortnight (Shukla or Shuddha) and a dark fortnight (Krishna or Vadya) based on the waxing and waning of the moon. In most parts of India the month starts with the light fortnight, i.e. the day after the new moon, although in some regions it begins with the dark fortnight, i.e. the day after the full moon.

The new year begins in the month of Chaitra (March/April) and ends in the month of Phalgun (March). The twelve months, Chaitra, Vaishakh, Jyeshtha, Ashadh, Shravan, Bhadrapad, Ashvin, Kartik, Margashirsh, Paush, Magh and Phalgun, have Sanskrit names derived from twelve asterisms (constellations). There are regional variations to the names of the months but the Sanskrit names are understood throughout India.

Every lunar month must have a solar transit and is termed pure (shuddha). The lunar month without a solar transit is impure (mala) and called an intercalary month. An intercalary month occurs approximately every 32 lunar months, whenever the difference between the Hindu year of 360 lunar days (354 days 8 hours solar time) and the 365 days 6 hours of the solar year reaches the length of one Hindu lunar month (29 days 12 hours).

The leap month may be added at any point in the Hindu year. The name given to the month varies according to when it occurs but is taken from the month immediately following it. No leap month occurs in 2000.

The days of the week are called Raviwar (Sunday), Somawar (Monday), Mangalwar (Tuesday), Budhawar (Wednesday), Guruwar (Thursday), Shukrawar (Friday) and Shaniwar (Saturday). The names are derived from the Sanskrit names of the Sun, the Moon and five planets, Mars, Mercury, Jupiter, Venus and Saturn.

Most fasts and festivals are based on the lunar calendar but a few are determined by the apparent movement of the Sun, e.g. Sankranti and Pongal (in southern India), which are celebrated on 14/15 January to mark the start of the Sun's apparent journey northwards and a change of season.

Festivals celebrated throughout India are Chaitra (the New Year), Raksha-bandhan (the renewal of the kinship bond between brothers and sisters), Navaratri (a nine-night festival dedicated to the goddess Parvati), Dasara (the victory of Rama over the demon army), Diwali (a festival of lights), Makara Sankranti, Shivaratri (dedicated to Shiva), and Holi (a spring festival).

Regional festivals are Durga-puja (dedicated to the goddess Durga (Parvati)), Sarasvati-puja (dedicated to the goddess Sarasvati), Ganesh Chaturthi (worship of Ganesh on the fourth day (Chaturthi) of the light half of Bhadrapad), Ramanavami (the birth festival of the god Rama) and Janmashtami (the birth festival of the god Krishna).

The main festivals celebrated in Britain are Navaratri, Dasara, Durga-puja, Diwali, Holi, Sarasvati-puja, Ganesh Chaturthi, Raksha-bandhan, Ramanavami and Janmashtami.

For dates of the main festivals in 2000, *see* page 9.

JEWISH CALENDAR

The story of the Flood in the Book of Genesis indicates the use of a calendar of some kind and that the writers recognized thirty days as the length of a lunation. However, after the diaspora, Jewish communities were left in considerable doubt as to the times of fasts and festivals. This led to the formation of the Jewish calendar as used today. It is said that this was done in AD 358 by Rabbi Hillel II, though some assert that it did not happen until much later.

The calendar is luni-solar, and is based on the lengths of the lunation and of the tropical year as found by Hipparchus (c.120 BC), which differ little from those adopted at the present day. The year AM 5760 (1999–2000) is the 3rd year of the 304th Metonic (Minor or Lunar) cycle of 19 years and the 20th year of the 206th Solar (or Major) cycle of 28 years since the Era of the Creation. Jews hold that the Creation occurred at the time of the autumnal equinox in the year known in the Christian calendar as 3760 BC (954 of the Julian period). The epoch or starting point of Jewish chronology corresponds to 7 October 3761 BC. At the beginning of each solar cycle, the Tekufah of Nisan (the vernal equinox) returns to the same day and to the same hour.

The hour is divided into 1080 minims, and the month between one new moon and the next is reckoned as 29 days, 12 hours, 793 minims. The normal calendar year, called a Regular Common year, consists of 12 months of 30 days and 29 days alternately. Since 12 months such as these comprise only 354 days, in order that each of them shall not diverge greatly from an average place in the solar year, a 13th month is occasionally added after the fifth month of the civil year (which commences on the first day of the month Tishri), or as the penultimate month of the ecclesiastical year (which commences on the first day of the month Nisan). The years when this happens are called Embolismic or leap years.

Of the 19 years that form a Metonic cycle, seven are leap years; they occur at places in the cycle indicated by the numbers 3, 6, 8, 11, 14, 17 and 19, these places being chosen so that the accumulated excesses of the solar years should be as small as possible.

A Jewish year is of one of the following six types:

Minimal Common	353 days
Regular Common	354 days
Full Common	355 days
Minimal Leap	383 days
Regular Leap	384 days
Full Leap	385 days

The Regular year has alternate months of 30 and 29 days. In a Full year, whether common or leap, Marcheshvan, the second month of the civil year, has 30 days instead of 29;

in Minimal years Kislev, the third month, has 29 instead of 30. The additional month in leap years is called Adar I and precedes the month called Adar in Common years. Adar II is called Adar Sheni in leap years, and the usual Adar festivals are kept in Adar Sheni. Adar I and Adar II always have 30 days, but neither this, nor the other variations mentioned, is allowed to change the number of days in the other months, which still follow the alternation of the normal twelve.

These are the main features of the Jewish calendar, which must be considered permanent because as a Jewish law it cannot be altered except by a great Sanhedrin.

The Jewish day begins between sunset and nightfall. The time used is that of the meridian of Jerusalem, which is 2h 21m in advance of Greenwich Mean Time. Rules for the beginning of sabbaths and festivals were laid down for the latitude of London in the 18th century and hours for nightfall are now fixed annually by the Chief Rabbi.

JEWISH CALENDAR 5760–1

AM 5760 (760) is a Full Leap year of 13 months, 55 sabbaths and 385 days. AM 5761 (761) is a Minimal Common year of 12 months, 50 sabbaths and 353 days.

Month (first day)	AM 5760	AM 5761
Tishri 1	11 September 1999	30 September 2000
Marcheshvan 1	11 October	30 October
Kislev 1	10 November	28 November
Tebet 1	10 December	27 December
Shebat 1	8 January 2000	25 January 2001
*Adar 1	7 February	24 February
†Adar II	8 March	
Nisan 1	6 April	25 March
Iyar 1	6 May	24 April
Sivan 1	4 June	23 May
Tammuz 1	4 July	22 June
Ab 1	2 August	21 July
Elul 1	1 September	20 August

*Known as Adar Rishon in leap years
†Known as Adar Sheni in leap years

JEWISH FASTS AND FESTIVALS

For dates of principal festivals in 2000, *see* page 9.

Tishri 1–2	Rosh Hashanah (New Year)
Tishri 3	*Fast of Gedaliah
Tishri 10	Yom Kippur (Day of Atonement)
Tishri 15–21	Succoth (Feast of Tabernacles)
Tishri 21	Hoshana Rabba
Tishri 22	Shemini Atseret (Solemn Assembly)
Tishri 23	Simchat Torah (Rejoicing of the Law)
Kislev 25	Chanucah (Dedication of the Temple) begins
Tebet 10	Fast of Tebet
†Adar 13	§Fast of Esther
†Adar 14	Purim
†Adar 15	Shushan Purim
Nisan 15–22	Pesach (Passover)
Sivan 6–7	Shavuot (Feast of Weeks)
Tammuz 17	*Fast of Tammuz
Ab 9	*Fast of Ab

*If these dates fall on the sabbath the fast is kept on the following day
†Adar Sheni in leap years
§This fast is observed on Adar 11 (or Adar Sheni 11 in leap years) if Adar 13 falls on a sabbath

THE MUSLIM CALENDAR

The Muslim era is dated from the *Hijrah*, or flight of the Prophet Muhammad from Mecca to Medina, the corresponding date of which in the Julian calendar is 16 July AD 622. The lunar *hijri* calendar is used principally in Iran, Egypt, Malaysia, Pakistan, Mauritania, various Arab states and certain parts of India. Iran uses the solar *hijri* calendar as well as the lunar *hijri* calendar. The dating system was adopted about AD 639, commencing with the first day of the month Muharram.

The lunar calendar consists of twelve months containing an alternate sequence of 30 and 29 days, with the intercalation of one day at the end of the twelfth month at stated intervals in each cycle of 30 years. The object of the intercalation is to reconcile the date of the first day of the month with the date of the actual new moon.

Some adherents still take the date of the evening of the first physical sighting of the crescent of the new moon as that of the first of the month. If cloud obscures the moon the present month may be extended to 30 days, after which the new month will begin automatically regardless of whether the moon has been seen. (Under religious law a month must have less than 31 days.) This means that the beginning of a new month and the date of religious festivals can vary from the published calendars.

In each cycle of 30 years, 19 years are common and contain 354 days, and 11 years are intercalary (leap years) of 355 days, the latter being called *kabish*. The mean length of the Hijrah years is 354 days 8 hours 48 minutes and the period of mean lunation is 29 days 12 hours 44 minutes.

To ascertain if a year is common or kabisah, divide it by 30: the quotient gives the number of completed cycles and the remainder shows the place of the year in the current cycle. If the remainder is 2, 5, 7, 10, 13, 16, 18, 21, 24, 26 or 29, the year is kabisah and consists of 355 days.

MUSLIM CALENDAR 1420–21

Hijrah year 1420 AH (remainder 10) is a kabisah year; 1421 AH (remainder 11) is a common year.

Month (length)	1420 AH	1421 AH
Muharram (30)	17 April 1999	6 April 2000
Safar (29)	17 May	6 May
Rabi' I (30)	15 June	4 June
Rabi' II (29)	15 July	4 July
Jumada I (30)	13 August	2 August
Jumada II (29)	12 September	1 September
Rajab (30)	11 October	30 September
Sha'ban (29)	10 November	30 October
Ramadân (30)	9 December	28 November
Shawwâl (29)	8 January 2000	28 December
Dhû'l-Qa'da (30)	6 February	26 January 2001
Dhû'l-Hijjah (29 or 30)	7 March	26 February

MUSLIM FESTIVALS

Ramadan is a month of fasting for all Muslims because it is the month in which the revelation of the *Qur'an* (Koran) began. During Ramadan Muslims abstain from food, drink and sexual pleasure from dawn until after sunset throughout the month.

The two major festivals are *Id al-Fitr* and *Id al-Adha*. Id al-Fitr marks the end of the Ramadan fast and is celebrated on the day after the sighting of the new moon of the following month. Id al-Adha, the festival of sacrifice (also known as the great festival), celebrates the submission of the Prophet Ibrahim (Abraham) to God. Id al-Adha falls on the tenth day of Dhul-Hijjah, coinciding with the day when those on *hajj* (pilgrimage to Mecca) sacrifice animals.

Other days accorded special recognition are:

Muharram 1	New Year's Day
Muharram 10	Ashura (the day Prophet Noah left the Ark and Prophet Moses was saved from Pharaoh (Sunni), the death of the Prophet's grandson Husain (Shi'ite))
Rabi'u-l-Awwal (*Rabi' I*) 12	Mawlid al-Nabi (birthday of the Prophet Muhammad)
Rajab 27	Laylat al-Isra' wa'l-Mi'raj (The Night of Journey and Ascension)
Ramadân One of the odd-numbered nights in the last 10 of the month	Laylat al-Qadr (Night of Power)
Dhû'l-Hijjah 10	Id al-Adha (Festival of Sacrifice)

THE SIKH CALENDAR

The Sikh calendar is a lunar calendar of 365 days divided into 12 months. The length of the months varies between 29 and 32 days.

There are no prescribed feast days and no fasting periods. The main celebrations are Baisakhi Mela (the new year and the anniversary of the founding of the Khalsa), Diwali Mela (festival of light), Hola Mohalla Mela (a spring festival held in the Punjab), and the Gurpurbs (anniversaries associated with the ten Gurus).

For dates of the major celebrations in 2000, *see* page 9.

CIVIL AND LEGAL CALENDAR

THE HISTORICAL YEAR

Before 1752, two calendar systems were used in England. The civil or legal year began on 25 March and the historical year on 1 January. Thus the civil or legal date 24 March 1658 was the same day as the historical date 24 March 1659; a date in that portion of the year is written as 24 March 165⅝, the lower figure showing the historical year.

THE NEW YEAR

In England in the seventh century, and as late as the 13th, the year was reckoned from Christmas Day, but in the 12th century the Church in England began the year with the feast of the Annunciation of the Blessed Virgin ('Lady Day') on 25 March and this practice was adopted generally in the 14th century. The civil or legal year in the British Dominions (exclusive of Scotland) began with Lady Day until 1751. But in and since 1752 the civil year has begun with 1 January. New Year's Day in Scotland was changed from 25 March to 1 January in 1600.

Elsewhere in Europe, 1 January was adopted as the first day of the year by Venice in 1522, German states in 1544, Spain, Portugal and the Roman Catholic Netherlands in 1556, Prussia, Denmark and Sweden in 1559, France in 1564, Lorraine in 1579, the Protestant Netherlands in 1583, Russia in 1725, and Tuscany in 1751.

REGNAL YEARS

Regnal years are the years of a sovereign's reign and each begins on the anniversary of his or her accession, e.g. regnal year 49 of the present Queen begins on 6 February 2000.

The system was used for dating Acts of Parliament until 1962. The Summer Time Act 1925, for example, is quoted as 15 and 16 Geo. V c. 64, because it became law in the parliamentary session which extended over part of both of these regnal years. Acts of a parliamentary session during which a sovereign died were usually given two year numbers, the regnal year of the deceased sovereign and the regnal year of his or her successor, e.g. those passed in 1952 were dated 16 Geo. VI and 1 Elizabeth II. Since 1962 Acts of Parliament have been dated by the calendar year.

QUARTER AND TERM DAYS

Holy days and saints days were the usual means in early times for setting the dates of future and recurrent appointments. The quarter days in England and Wales are the feast of the Nativity (25 December), the feast of the Annunciation (25 March), the feast of St John the Baptist (24 June) and the feast of St Michael and All Angels (29 September).

The term days in Scotland are Candlemas (the feast of the Purification), Whitsunday, Lammas (Loaf Mass), and Martinmas (St Martin's Day). These fell on 2 February, 15 May, 1 August and 11 November respectively. However, by the Term and Quarter Days (Scotland) Act 1990, the dates of the term days were changed to 28 February (Candlemas), 28 May (Whitsunday), 28 August (Lammas) and 28 November (Martinmas).

RED-LETTER DAYS

Red-letter days were originally the holy days and saints days indicated in early ecclesiastical calendars by letters printed in red ink. The days to be distinguished in this way were approved at the Council of Nicaea in AD 325.

These days still have a legal significance, as judges of the Queen's Bench Division wear scarlet robes on red-letter days falling during the law sittings. The days designated as red-letter days for this purpose are:

Holy and saints days (for dates, *see* pages 16, 20, etc.)
The Conversion of St Paul, the Purification, Ash Wednesday, the Annunciation, the Ascension, the feasts of St Mark, SS Philip and James, St Matthias, St Barnabas, St John the Baptist, St Peter, St Thomas, St James, St Luke, SS Simon and Jude, All Saints, St Andrew

Civil calendar (for dates, *see* page 9)
The anniversaries of The Queen's accession, The Queen's birthday and The Queen's coronation, The Queen's official birthday, the birthday of the Duke of Edinburgh, the birthday of Queen Elizabeth the Queen Mother, the birthday of the Prince of Wales, St David's Day and Lord Mayor's Day

PUBLIC HOLIDAYS

Public holidays are divided into two categories, common law and statutory. Common law holidays are holidays 'by habit and custom'; in England, Wales and Northern Ireland these are Good Friday and Christmas Day.

Statutory public holidays, known as bank holidays, were first established by the Bank Holidays Act 1871. They were, literally, days on which the banks (and other public institutions) were closed and financial obligations due on that day were payable the following day. The legislation currently governing public holidays in the UK, which is the Banking and Financial Dealings Act 1971, stipulates the days that are to be public holidays in England, Wales, Scotland and Northern Ireland.

Certain holidays (indicated by * below) are granted annually by royal proclamation, either throughout the UK or in any place in the UK. The public holidays are:

England and Wales
*New Year's Day
Easter Monday
*The first Monday in May
The last Monday in May
The last Monday in August
26 December, if it is not a Sunday
27 December when 25 or 26 December is a Sunday

Scotland
New Year's Day, or if it is a Sunday, 2 January
2 January, or if it is a Sunday, 3 January
Good Friday
The first Monday in May
*The last Monday in May
The first Monday in August
Christmas Day, or if it is a Sunday, 26 December
*Boxing Day – if Christmas Day falls on a Sunday, 26 December is given in lieu and an alternative day is given for Boxing Day

Northern Ireland
*New Year's Day
17 March, or if it is a Sunday, 18 March
Easter Monday
*The first Monday in May
The last Monday in May
*12 July, or if it is a Sunday, 13 July
The last Monday in August
26 December, if it is not a Sunday
27 December if 25 or 26 December is a Sunday

For dates of public holidays in 2000 and 2001, *see* pages 10–11.

CHRONOLOGICAL CYCLES AND ERAS

SOLAR (OR MAJOR) CYCLE

The solar cycle is a period of twenty-eight years in any corresponding year of which the days of the week recur on the same day of the month.

METONIC (LUNAR, OR MINOR) CYCLE

In 432 BC, Meton, an Athenian astronomer, found that 235 lunations are very nearly, though not exactly, equal in duration to 19 solar years and so after 19 years the phases of the Moon recur on the same days of the month (nearly). The dates of full moon in a cycle of 19 years were inscribed in figures of gold on public monuments in Athens, and the number showing the position of a year in the cycle is called the golden number of that year.

JULIAN PERIOD

The Julian period was proposed by Joseph Scaliger in 1582. The period is 7980 Julian years, and its first year coincides with the year 4713 BC. The figure of 7980 is the product of the number of years in the solar cycle, the Metonic cycle and the cycle of the Roman indiction (28 × 19 × 15).

ROMAN INDICTION

The Roman indiction is a period of fifteen years, instituted for fiscal purposes about AD 300.

EPACT

The epact is the age of the calendar Moon, diminished by one day, on 1 January, in the ecclesiastical lunar calendar.

CHINESE CALENDAR

A lunar calendar was the sole calendar in use in China until 1911, when the government adopted the new (Gregorian) calendar for official and most business activities. The Chinese tend to follow both calendars, the lunar calendar playing an important part in personal life, e.g. birth celebrations, festivals, marriages; and in rural villages the lunar calendar dictates the cycle of activities, denoting the change of weather and farming activities.

The lunar calendar is used in Hong Kong, Singapore, Malaysia, Tibet and elsewhere in south-east Asia. The calendar has a cycle of 60 years. The new year begins at the first new moon after the sun enters the sign of Aquarius, i.e. the new year falls between 21 January and 19 February in the Gregorian calendar.

Each year in the Chinese calendar is associated with one of 12 animals: the rat, the ox, the tiger, the rabbit, the dragon, the snake, the horse, the goat or sheep, the monkey, the chicken or rooster, the dog, and the pig.

The date of the Chinese new year and the astrological sign for the years 2000–2005 are:

2000	5 February	Dragon
2001	—	Snake
2002	—	Horse
2003	—	Goat or Sheep
2004	—	Monkey
2005	—	Chicken

COPTIC CALENDAR

In the Coptic calendar, which is used in parts of Egypt and Ethiopia, the year is made up of 12 months of 30 days each, followed, in general, by five complementary days. Every fourth year is an intercalary or leap year and in these years there are six complementary days. The intercalary year of the Coptic calendar immediately precedes the leap year of the Julian calendar. The era is that of Diocletian or the Martyrs, the origin of which is fixed at 29 August AD 284 (Julian date).

INDIAN ERAS

In addition to the Muslim reckoning, other eras are used in India. The Saka era of southern India, dating from 3 March AD 78, was declared the national calendar of the Republic of India with effect from 22 March 1957, to be used concurrently with the Gregorian calendar. As revised, the year of the new Saka era begins at the spring equinox, with five successive months of 31 days and seven of 30 days in ordinary years, and six months of each length in leap years. The year AD 2000 is 1922 of the revised Saka era.

The year AD 2000 corresponds to the following years in other eras:

Year 2057 of the Vikram Samvat era
Year 1407 of the Bengali San era
Year 1176 of the Kollam era
Vedanga Jyotisa year 6 of the five-yearly cycle (384th cycle of Paitamah Siddhanta)
Year 6001 of the Kaliyuga era
Year 2544 of the Buddha Nirvana era

JAPANESE CALENDAR

The Japanese calendar is essentially the same as the Gregorian calendar, the years, months and weeks being of the same length and beginning on the same days as those of the Gregorian calendar. The numeration of the years is different, based on a system of epochs or periods each of which begins at the accession of an Emperor or other important occurrence. The method is not unlike the British system of regnal years, except that each year of a period closes on 31 December. The Japanese chronology begins about AD 650 and the three latest epochs are defined by the reigns of Emperors, whose actual names are not necessarily used:

Epoch

Taishō   1 August 1912 to 25 December 1926
Shōwa   26 December 1926 to 7 January 1989
Heisei   8 January 1989

The year Heisei 12 begins on 1 January 2000.

The months are known as First Month, Second Month, etc., First Month being equivalent to January. The days of the week are Nichiyōbi (Sun-day), Getsuyōbi (Moon-day), Kayōbi (Fire-day), Suiyōbi (Water-day), Mokuyōbi (Wood-day), Kinyōbi (Metal-day), Doyōbi (Earth-day).

THE MASONIC YEAR

Two dates are quoted in warrants, dispensations, etc., issued by the United Grand Lodge of England, those for the current year being expressed as *Anno Domini* 2000 – *Anno Lucis* 6000. This *Anno Lucis* (year of light) is based on the Book of Genesis 1:3, the 4000-year difference being derived, in modified form, from *Ussher's Notation*, published in 1654, which places the Creation of the World in 4004 BC.

OLYMPIADS

Ancient Greek chronology was reckoned in Olympiads, cycles of four years corresponding with the periodic Olympic Games held on the plain of Olympia in Elis once every four years. The intervening years were the first, second, etc., of the Olympiad, which received the name of the victor at the Games. The first recorded Olympiad is that of Choroebus, 776 BC.

ZOROASTRIAN CALENDAR

Zoroastrians, followers of the Iranian prophet Zarathushtra (known to the Greeks as Zoroaster) are mostly to be found in Iran and in India, where they are known as Parsees.

The Zoroastrian era dates from the coronation of the last Zoroastrian Sasanian king in AD 631. The Zoroastrian calendar is divided into twelve months, each comprising 30 days, followed by five holy days of the Gathas at the end of each year to make the year consist of 365 days.

In order to synchronize the calendar with the solar year of 365 days, an extra month was intercalated once every 120 years. However, this intercalation ceased in the 12th century and the New Year, which had fallen in the spring, slipped back to August. Because intercalation ceased at different times in Iran and India, there was one month's difference between the calendar followed in Iran (Kadmi calendar) and that followed by the Parsees (Shenshai calendar). In 1906 a group of Zoroastrians decided to bring the calendar back in line with the seasons again and restore the New Year to 21 March each year (Fasli calendar).

The Shenshai calendar (New Year in August) is mainly used by Parsees. The Fasli calendar (New Year, 21 March) is mainly used by Zoroastrians living in Iran, in the Indian subcontinent, or away from Iran.

THE ROMAN CALENDAR

Roman historians adopted as an epoch the foundation of Rome, which is believed to have happened in the year 753 BC. The ordinal number of the years in Roman reckoning is followed by the letters AUC (*ab urbe condita*), so that the year 2000 is 2753 AUC (MMDCCLIII). The calendar that we know has developed from one said to have been established by Romulus using a year of 304 days divided into ten months, beginning with March. To this Numa added January and February, making the year consist of 12 months of 30 and 29 days alternately, with an additional day so that the total was 355. It is also said that Numa ordered an intercalary month of 22 or 23 days in alternate years, making 90 days in eight years, to be inserted after 23 February.

However, there is some doubt as to the origination and the details of the intercalation in the Roman calendar. It is certain that some scheme of this kind was inaugurated and

not fully carried out, for in the year 46 BC Julius Caesar found that the calendar had been allowed to fall into some confusion. He sought the help of the Egyptian astronomer Sosigenes, which led to the construction and adoption (45 BC) of the Julian calendar, and, by a slight alteration, to the Gregorian calendar now in use. The year 46 BC was made to consist of 445 days and is called the Year of Confusion.

In the Roman (Julian) calendar the days of the month were counted backwards from three fixed points, or days, and an intervening day was said to be so many days before the next coming point, the first and last being counted. These three points were the Kalends, the Nones, and the Ides. Their positions in the months and the method of counting from them will be seen in the table below. The year containing 366 days was called *bissextillis annus*, as it had a doubled sixth day (*bissextus dies*) before the March Kalends on 24 February – *ante diem sextum Kalendas Martias*, or a.d. VI Kal. Mart.

Present days of the month	*March, May, July, October have thirty-one days*		*January, August, December have thirty-one days*		*April, June, September, November have thirty days*		*February has twenty-eight days, and in leap year twenty-nine*	
1	Kalendis		Kalendis		Kalendis		Kalendis	
2	VI		IV	ante	IV	ante	IV	ante
3	V	ante	III	Nonas	III	Nonas	III	Nonas
4	IV	Nonas	pridie Nonas		pridie Nonas		pridie Nonas	
5	III		Nonis		Nonis		Nonis	
6	pridie Nonas		VIII		VIII		VIII	
7	Nonis		VII		VII		VII	
8	VIII		VI	ante	VI	ante	VI	ante
9	VII		V	Idus	V	Idus	V	Idus
10	VI	ante	IV		IV		IV	
11	V	Idus	III		III		III	
12	IV		pridie Idus		pridie Idus		pridie Idus	
13	III		Idibus		Idibus		Idibus	
14	pridie Idus		XIX		XVIII		XVI	
15	Idibus		XVIII		XVII		XV	
16	XVII		XVII		XVI		XIV	
17	XVI		XVI		XV		XIII	
18	XV		XV		XIV		XII	
19	XIV		XIV		XIII		XI	
20	XIII		XIII		XII	ante Kalendas	X	ante Kalendas
21	XII		XII	ante Kalendas	XI	(of the month	IX	Martias
22	XI	ante Kalendas	XI	(of the month	X	following)	VIII	
23	X	(of the month	X	following)	IX		VII	
24	IX	following)	IX		VIII		*VI	
25	VIII		VIII		VII		V	
26	VII		VII		VI		IV	
27	VI		VI		V		III	
28	V		V		IV		pridie Kalendas	
29	IV		IV		III			
30	III		III		pridie Kalendas			
31	pridie Kalendas (Aprilis, Iunias, Sextilis, Novembris)		pridie Kalendas (Februarias, Septembris, Iunuarias)		pridie Kalendas (Maias, Quinctilis, Octobris, Decembris)		* (repeated in leap year)	

Calendar for Any Year 1780–2040

To select the correct calendar for any year between 1780 and 2040,
consult the index below
* leap year

Year		Year		Year		Year		Year		Year	
1780	N*	1813	K	1846	I	1879	G	1912	D*	1945	C	1978	A	2011	M
1781	C	1814	M	1847	K	1880	J*	1913	G	1946	E	1979	C	2012	B*
1782	E	1815	A	1848	N*	1881	M	1914	I	1947	G	1980	F*	2013	E
1783	G	1816	D*	1849	C	1882	A	1915	K	1948	J*	1981	I	2014	G
1784	J*	1817	G	1850	E	1883	C	1916	N*	1949	M	1982	K	2015	I
1785	M	1818	I	1851	G	1884	F*	1917	C	1950	A	1983	M	2016	L*
1786	A	1819	K	1852	J*	1885	I	1918	E	1951	C	1984	B*	2017	A
1787	C	1820	N*	1853	M	1886	K	1919	G	1952	F*	1985	E	2018	C
1788	F*	1821	C	1854	A	1887	M	1920	J*	1953	I	1986	G	2019	E
1789	I	1822	E	1855	C	1888	B*	1921	M	1954	K	1987	I	2020	H*
1790	K	1823	G	1856	F*	1889	E	1922	A	1955	M	1988	L*	2021	K
1791	M	1824	J*	1857	I	1890	G	1923	C	1956	B*	1989	A	2022	M
1792	B*	1825	M	1858	K	1891	I	1924	F*	1957	E	1990	C	2023	A
1793	E	1826	A	1859	M	1892	L*	1925	I	1958	G	1991	E	2024	D*
1794	G	1827	C	1860	B*	1893	A	1926	K	1959	I	1992	H*	2025	G
1795	I	1828	F*	1861	E	1894	C	1927	M	1960	L*	1993	K	2026	I
1796	L*	1829	I	1862	G	1895	E	1928	B*	1961	A	1994	M	2027	K
1797	A	1830	K	1863	I	1896	H*	1929	E	1962	C	1995	A	2028	N*
1798	C	1831	M	1864	L*	1897	K	1930	G	1963	E	1996	D*	2029	C
1799	E	1832	B*	1865	A	1898	M	1931	I	1964	H*	1997	G	2030	E
1800	G	1833	E	1866	C	1899	A	1932	L*	1965	K	1998	I	2031	G
1801	I	1834	G	1867	E	1900	C	1933	A	1966	M	1999	K	2032	J*
1802	K	1835	I	1868	H*	1901	E	1934	C	1967	A	2000	N*	2033	M
1803	M	1836	L*	1869	K	1902	G	1935	E	1968	D*	2001	C	2034	A
1804	B*	1837	A	1870	M	1903	I	1936	H*	1969	G	2002	E	2035	C
1805	E	1838	C	1871	A	1904	L*	1937	K	1970	I	2003	G	2036	F*
1806	G	1839	E	1872	D*	1905	A	1938	M	1971	K	2004	J*	2037	I
1807	I	1840	H*	1873	G	1906	C	1939	A	1972	N*	2005	M	2038	K
1808	L*	1841	K	1874	I	1907	E	1940	D*	1973	C	2006	A	2039	M
1809	A	1842	M	875	K	1908	H*	1941	G	1974	E	2007	C	2040	B*
1810	C	1843	A	1876	N*	1909	K	1942	I	1975	G	2008	F*		
1811	E	1844	D*	1877	C	1910	M	1943	K	1976	J*	2009	I		
1812	H*	1845	G	1878	E	1911	A	1944	N*	1977	M	2010	K		

A

	January	February	March
Sun.	1 8 15 22 29	5 12 19 26	5 12 19 26
Mon.	2 9 16 23 30	6 13 20 27	6 13 20 27
Tue.	3 10 17 24 31	7 14 21 28	7 14 21 28
Wed.	4 11 18 25	1 8 15 22	1 8 15 22 29
Thur.	5 12 19 26	2 9 16 23	2 9 16 23 30
Fri.	6 13 20 27	3 10 17 24	3 10 17 24 31
Sat.	7 14 21 28	4 11 18 25	4 11 18 25
	April	May	June
Sun.	2 9 16 23 30	7 14 21 28	4 11 18 25
Mon.	3 10 17 24	1 8 15 22 29	5 12 19 26
Tue.	4 11 18 25	2 9 16 23 30	6 13 20 27
Wed.	5 12 19 26	3 10 17 24 31	7 14 21 28
Thur.	6 13 20 27	4 11 18 25	1 8 15 22 29
Fri.	7 14 21 28	5 12 19 26	2 9 16 23 30
Sat.	1 8 15 22 29	6 13 20 27	3 10 17 24
	July	August	September
Sun.	2 9 16 23 30	6 13 20 27	3 10 17 24
Mon.	3 10 17 24 31	7 14 21 28	4 11 18 25
Tue.	4 11 18 25	1 8 15 22 29	5 12 19 26
Wed.	5 12 19 26	2 9 16 23 30	6 13 20 27
Thur.	6 13 20 27	3 10 17 24 31	7 14 21 28
Fri.	7 14 21 28	4 11 18 25	1 8 15 22 29
Sat.	1 8 15 22 29	5 12 19 26	2 9 16 23 30
	October	November	December
Sun.	1 8 15 22 29	5 12 19 26	3 10 17 24 31
Mon.	2 9 16 23 30	6 13 20 27	4 11 18 25
Tue.	3 10 17 24 31	7 14 21 28	5 12 19 26
Wed.	4 11 18 25	1 8 15 22 29	6 13 20 27
Thur.	5 12 19 26	2 9 16 23 30	7 14 21 28
Fri.	6 13 20 27	3 10 17 24	1 8 15 22 29
Sat.	7 14 21 28	4 11 18 25	2 9 16 23 30

EASTER DAYS

March 26	1815, 1826, 1837, 1967, 1978, 1989
April 2	1809, 1893, 1899, 1961
April 9	1871, 1882, 1939, 1950, 2023, 2034
April 16	1786, 1797, 1843, 1854, 1865, 1911 1922, 1933, 1995, 2006, 2017
April 23	1905

B (LEAP YEAR)

	January	February	March
Sun.	1 8 15 22 29	5 12 19 26	4 11 18 25
Mon.	2 9 16 23 30	6 13 20 27	5 12 19 26
Tue.	3 10 17 24 31	7 14 21 28	6 13 20 27
Wed.	4 11 18 25	1 8 15 22 29	7 14 21 28
Thur.	5 12 19 26	2 9 16 23	1 8 15 22 29
Fri.	6 13 20 27	3 10 17 24	2 9 16 23 30
Sat.	7 14 21 28	4 11 18 25	3 10 17 24 31
	April	May	June
Sun.	1 8 15 22 29	6 13 20 27	3 10 17 24
Mon.	2 9 16 23 30	7 14 21 28	4 11 18 25
Tue.	3 10 17 24	1 8 15 22 29	5 12 19 26
Wed.	4 11 18 25	2 9 16 23 30	6 13 20 27
Thur.	5 12 19 26	3 10 17 24 31	7 14 21 28
Fri.	6 13 20 27	4 11 18 25	1 8 15 22 29
Sat.	7 14 21 28	5 12 19 26	2 9 16 23 30
	July	August	September
Sun.	1 8 15 22 29	5 12 19 26	2 9 16 23 30
Mon.	2 9 16 23 30	6 13 20 27	3 10 17 24
Tue.	3 10 17 24 31	7 14 21 28	4 11 18 25
Wed.	4 11 18 25	1 8 15 22 29	5 12 19 26
Thur.	5 12 19 26	2 9 16 23 30	6 13 20 27
Fri.	6 13 20 27	3 10 17 24 31	7 14 21 28
Sat.	7 14 21 28	4 11 18 25	1 8 15 22 29
	October	November	December
Sun.	7 14 21 28	4 11 18 25	2 9 16 23 30
Mon.	1 8 15 22 29	5 12 19 26	3 10 17 24 31
Tue.	2 9 16 23 30	6 13 20 27	4 11 18 25
Wed.	3 10 17 24 31	7 14 21 28	5 12 19 26
Thur.	4 11 18 25	1 8 15 22 29	6 13 20 27
Fri.	5 12 19 26	2 9 16 23 30	7 14 21 28
Sat.	6 13 20 27	3 10 17 24	1 8 15 22 29

EASTER DAYS

April 1	1804, 1888, 1956, 2040
April 8	1792, 1860, 1928, 2012
April 22	1832, 1984

C

	January	February	March
Sun.	7 14 21 28	4 11 18 25	4 11 18 25
Mon.	1 8 15 22 29	5 12 19 26	5 12 19 26
Tue.	2 9 16 23 30	6 13 20 27	6 13 20 27
Wed.	3 10 17 24 31	7 14 21 28	7 14 21 28
Thur.	4 11 18 25	1 8 15 22	1 8 15 22 29
Fri.	5 12 19 26	2 9 16 23	2 9 16 23 30
Sat.	6 13 20 27	3 10 17 24	3 10 17 24 31

	April	May	June
Sun.	1 8 15 22 29	6 13 20 27	3 10 17 24
Mon.	2 9 16 23 30	7 14 21 28	4 11 18 25
Tue.	3 10 17 24	1 8 15 22 29	5 12 19 26
Wed.	4 11 18 25	2 9 16 23 30	6 13 20 27
Thur.	5 12 19 26	3 10 17 24 31	7 14 21 28
Fri.	6 13 20 27	4 11 18 25	1 8 15 22 29
Sat.	7 14 21 28	5 12 19 26	2 9 16 23 30

	July	August	September
Sun.	1 8 15 22 29	5 12 19 26	2 9 16 23 30
Mon.	2 9 16 23 30	6 13 20 27	3 10 17 24
Tue.	3 10 17 24 31	7 14 21 28	4 11 18 25
Wed.	4 11 18 25	1 8 15 22 29	5 12 19 26
Thur.	5 12 19 26	2 9 16 23 30	6 13 20 27
Fri.	6 13 20 27	3 10 17 24 31	7 14 21 28
Sat.	7 14 21 28	4 11 18 25	1 8 15 22 29

	October	November	December
Sun.	7 14 21 28	4 11 18 25	2 9 16 23 30
Mon.	1 8 15 22 29	5 12 19 26	3 10 17 24 31
Tue.	2 9 16 23 30	6 13 20 27	4 11 18 25
Wed.	3 10 17 24 31	7 14 21 28	5 12 19 26
Thur.	4 11 18 25	1 8 15 22 29	6 13 20 27
Fri.	5 12 19 26	2 9 16 23 30	7 14 21 28
Sat.	6 13 20 27	3 10 17 24	1 8 15 22 29

EASTER DAYS

March 25	1883, 1894, 1951, 2035
April 1	1866, 1877, 1923, 1934, 1945, 2018, 2029
April 8	1787, 1798, 1849, 1855, 1917, 2007
April 15	1781, 1827, 1838, 1900, 1906, 1979, 1990, 2001
April 22	1810, 1821, 1962, 1973

E

	January	February	March
Sun.	6 13 20 27	3 10 17 24	3 10 17 24 31
Mon.	7 14 21 28	4 11 18 25	4 11 18 25
Tue.	1 8 15 22 29	5 12 19 26	5 12 19 26
Wed.	2 9 16 23 30	6 13 20 27	6 13 20 27
Thur.	3 10 17 24 31	7 14 21 28	7 14 21 28
Fri.	4 11 18 25	1 8 15 22	1 8 15 22 29
Sat.	5 12 19 26	2 9 16 23	2 9 16 23 30

	April	May	June
Sun.	7 14 21 28	5 12 19 26	2 9 16 23 30
Mon.	1 8 15 22 29	6 13 20 27	3 10 17 24
Tue.	2 9 16 23 30	7 14 21 28	4 11 18 25
Wed.	3 10 17 24	1 8 15 22 29	5 12 19 26
Thur.	4 11 18 25	2 9 16 23 30	6 13 20 27
Fri.	5 12 19 26	3 10 17 24 31	7 14 21 28
Sat.	6 13 20 27	4 11 18 25	1 8 15 22 29

	July	August	September
Sun.	7 14 21 28	4 11 18 25	1 8 15 22 29
Mon.	1 8 15 22 29	5 12 19 26	2 9 16 23 30
Tue.	2 9 16 23 30	6 13 20 27	3 10 17 24
Wed.	3 10 17 24 31	7 14 21 28	4 11 18 25
Thur.	4 11 18 25	1 8 15 22 29	5 12 19 26
Fri.	5 12 19 26	2 9 16 23 30	6 13 20 27
Sat.	6 13 20 27	3 10 17 24 31	7 14 21 28

	October	November	December
Sun.	6 13 20 27	3 10 17 24	1 8 15 22 29
Mon.	7 14 21 28	4 11 18 25	2 9 16 23 30
Tue.	1 8 15 22 29	5 12 19 26	3 10 17 24 31
Wed.	2 9 16 23 30	6 13 20 27	4 11 18 25
Thur.	3 10 17 24 31	7 14 21 28	5 12 19 26
Fri.	4 11 18 25	1 8 15 22 29	6 13 20 27
Sat.	5 12 19 26	2 9 16 23 30	7 14 21 28

EASTER DAYS

March 24	1799
March 31	1782, 1793, 1839, 1850, 1861, 1907, 1918, 1929, 1991, 2002, 2013
April 7	1822, 1833, 1901, 1985
April 14	1805, 1811, 1895, 1963, 1974
April 21	1867, 1878, 1889, 1935, 1946, 1957, 2019, 2030

D (LEAP YEAR)

	January	February	March
Sun.	7 14 21 28	4 11 18 25	3 10 17 24 31
Mon.	1 8 15 22 29	5 12 19 26	4 11 18 25
Tue.	2 9 16 23 30	6 13 20 27	5 12 19 26
Wed.	3 10 17 24 31	7 14 21 28	6 13 20 27
Thur.	4 11 18 25	1 8 15 22 29	7 14 21 28
Fri.	5 12 19 26	2 9 16 23	1 8 15 22 29
Sat.	6 13 20 27	3 10 17 24	2 9 16 23 30

	April	May	June
Sun.	7 14 21 28	5 12 19 26	2 9 16 23 30
Mon.	1 8 15 22 29	6 13 20 27	3 10 17 24
Tue.	2 9 16 23 30	7 14 21 28	4 11 18 25
Wed.	3 10 17 24	1 8 15 22 29	5 12 19 26
Thur.	4 11 18 25	2 9 16 23 30	6 13 20 27
Fri.	5 12 19 26	3 10 17 24 31	7 14 21 28
Sat.	6 13 20 27	4 11 18 25	1 8 15 22 29

	July	August	September
Sun.	7 14 21 28	4 11 18 25	1 8 15 22 29
Mon.	1 8 15 22 29	5 12 19 26	2 9 16 23 30
Tue.	2 9 16 23 30	6 13 20 27	3 10 17 24
Wed.	3 10 17 24 31	7 14 21 28	4 11 18 25
Thur.	4 11 18 25	1 8 15 22 29	5 12 19 26
Fri.	5 12 19 26	2 9 16 23 30	6 13 20 27
Sat.	6 13 20 27	3 10 17 24 31	7 14 21 28

	October	November	December
Sun.	6 13 20 27	3 10 17 24	1 8 15 22 29
Mon.	7 14 21 28	4 11 18 25	2 9 16 23 30
Tue.	1 8 15 22 29	5 12 19 26	3 10 17 24 31
Wed.	2 9 16 23 30	6 13 20 27	4 11 18 25
Thur.	3 10 17 24 31	7 14 21 28	5 12 19 26
Fri.	4 11 18 25	1 8 15 22 29	6 13 20 27
Sat.	5 12 19 26	2 9 16 23 30	7 14 21 28

EASTER DAYS

March 24	1940
March 31	1872, 2024
April 7	1844, 1912, 1996
April 14	1816, 1968

F (LEAP YEAR)

	January	February	March
Sun.	6 13 20 27	3 10 17 24	2 9 16 23 30
Mon.	7 14 21 28	4 11 18 25	3 10 17 24 31
Tue.	1 8 15 22 29	5 12 19 26	4 11 18 25
Wed.	2 9 16 23 30	6 13 20 27	5 12 19 26
Thur.	3 10 17 24 31	7 14 21 28	6 13 20 27
Fri.	4 11 18 25	1 8 15 22 29	7 14 21 28
Sat.	5 12 19 26	2 9 16 23	1 8 15 22 29

	April	May	June
Sun.	6 13 20 27	4 11 18 25	1 8 15 22 29
Mon.	7 14 21 28	5 12 19 26	2 9 16 23 30
Tue.	1 8 15 22 29	6 13 20 27	3 10 17 24
Wed.	2 9 16 23 30	7 14 21 28	4 11 18 25
Thur.	3 10 17 24	1 8 15 22 29	5 12 19 26
Fri.	4 11 18 25	2 9 16 23 30	6 13 20 27
Sat.	5 12 19 26	3 10 17 24 31	7 14 21 28

	July	August	September
Sun.	6 13 20 27	3 10 17 24 31	7 14 21 28
Mon.	7 14 21 28	4 11 18 25	1 8 15 22 29
Tue.	1 8 15 22 29	5 12 19 26	2 9 16 23 30
Wed.	2 9 16 23 30	6 13 20 27	3 10 17 24
Thur.	3 10 17 24 31	7 14 21 28	4 11 18 25
Fri.	4 11 18 25	1 8 15 22 29	5 12 19 26
Sat.	5 12 19 26	2 9 16 23 30	6 13 20 27

	October	November	December
Sun.	5 12 19 26	2 9 16 23 30	7 14 21 28
Mon.	6 13 20 27	3 10 17 24	1 8 15 22 29
Tue.	7 14 21 28	4 11 18 25	2 9 16 23 30
Wed.	1 8 15 22 29	5 12 19 26	3 10 17 24 31
Thur.	2 9 16 23 30	6 13 20 27	4 11 18 25
Fri.	3 10 17 24 31	7 14 21 28	5 12 19 26
Sat.	4 11 18 25	1 8 15 22 29	6 13 20 27

EASTER DAYS

March 23	1788, 1856, 2008
April 6	1828, 1980
April 13	1884, 1952, 2036
April 20	1924

G

	January	February	March
Sun.	5 12 19 26	2 9 16 23	2 9 16 23 30
Mon.	6 13 20 27	3 10 17 24	3 10 17 24 31
Tue.	7 14 21 28	4 11 18 25	4 11 18 25
Wed.	1 8 15 22 29	5 12 19 26	5 12 19 26
Thur.	2 9 16 23 30	6 13 20 27	6 13 20 27
Fri.	3 10 17 24 31	7 14 21 28	7 14 21 28
Sat.	4 11 18 25	1 8 15 22	1 8 15 22 29

	April	May	June
Sun.	6 13 20 27	4 11 18 25	1 8 15 22 29
Mon.	7 14 21 28	5 12 19 26	2 9 16 23 30
Tue.	1 8 15 22 29	6 13 20 27	3 10 17 24
Wed.	2 9 16 23 30	7 14 21 28	4 11 18 25
Thur.	3 10 17 24	1 8 15 22 29	5 12 19 26
Fri.	4 11 18 25	2 9 16 23 30	6 13 20 27
Sat.	5 12 19 26	3 10 17 24 31	7 14 21 28

	July	August	September
Sun.	6 13 20 27	3 10 17 24 31	7 14 21 28
Mon.	7 14 21 28	4 11 18 25	1 8 15 22 29
Tue.	1 8 15 22 29	5 12 19 26	2 9 16 23 30
Wed.	2 9 16 23 30	6 13 20 27	3 10 17 24
Thur.	3 10 17 24 31	7 14 21 28	4 11 18 25
Fri.	4 11 18 25	1 8 15 22 29	5 12 19 26
Sat.	5 12 19 26	2 9 16 23 30	6 13 20 27

	October	November	December
Sun.	5 12 19 26	2 9 16 23 30	7 14 21 28
Mon.	6 13 20 27	3 10 17 24	1 8 15 22 29
Tue.	7 14 21 28	4 11 18 25	2 9 16 23 30
Wed.	1 8 15 22 29	5 12 19 26	3 10 17 24 31
Thur.	2 9 16 23 30	6 13 20 27	4 11 18 25
Fri.	3 10 17 24 31	7 14 21 28	5 12 19 26
Sat.	4 11 18 25	1 8 15 22 29	6 13 20 27

EASTER DAYS

March 23	1845, 1913
March 30	1823, 1834, 1902, 1975, 1986, 1997
April 6	1806, 1817, 1890, 1947, 1958, 1969
April 13	1800, 1873, 1879, 1941, 2031
April 20	1783, 1794, 1851, 1862, 1919, 1930, 2003, 2014, 2025

I

	January	February	March
Sun.	4 11 18 25	1 8 15 22	1 8 15 22 29
Mon.	5 12 19 26	2 9 16 23	2 9 16 23 30
Tue.	6 13 20 27	3 10 17 24	3 10 17 24 31
Wed.	7 14 21 28	4 11 18 25	4 11 18 25
Thur.	1 8 15 22 29	5 12 19 26	5 12 19 26
Fri.	2 9 16 23 30	6 13 20 27	6 13 20 27
Sat.	3 10 17 24 31	7 14 21 28	7 14 21 28

	April	May	June
Sun.	5 12 19 26	3 10 17 24 31	7 14 21 28
Mon.	6 13 20 27	4 11 18 25	1 8 15 22 29
Tue.	7 14 21 28	5 12 19 26	2 9 16 23 30
Wed.	1 8 15 22 29	6 13 20 27	3 10 17 24
Thur.	2 9 16 23 30	7 14 21 28	4 11 18 25
Fri.	3 10 17 24	1 8 15 22 29	5 12 19 26
Sat.	4 11 18 25	2 9 16 23 30	6 13 20 27

	July	August	September
Sun.	5 12 19 26	2 9 16 23 30	6 13 20 27
Mon.	6 13 20 27	3 10 17 24 31	7 14 21 28
Tue.	7 14 21 28	4 11 18 25	1 8 15 22 29
Wed.	1 8 15 22 29	5 12 19 26	2 9 16 23 30
Thur.	2 9 16 23 30	6 13 20 27	3 10 17 24
Fri.	3 10 17 24 31	7 14 21 28	4 11 18 25
Sat.	4 11 18 25	1 8 15 22 29	5 12 19 26

	October	November	December
Sun.	4 11 18 25	1 8 15 22 29	6 13 20 27
Mon.	5 12 19 26	2 9 16 23 30	7 14 21 28
Tue.	6 13 20 27	3 10 17 24	1 8 15 22 29
Wed.	7 14 21 28	4 11 18 25	2 9 16 23 30
Thur.	1 8 15 22 29	5 12 19 26	3 10 17 24 31
Fri.	2 9 16 23 30	6 13 20 27	4 11 18 25
Sat.	3 10 17 24 31	7 14 21 28	5 12 19 26

EASTER DAYS

March 22	1818
March 29	1807, 1891, 1959, 1970
April 5	1795, 1801, 1863, 1874, 1885, 1931, 1942, 1953, 2015, 2026, 2037
April 12	1789, 1846, 1857, 1903, 1914, 1925, 1998, 2009
April 19	1829, 1835, 1981, 1987

H (LEAP YEAR)

	January	February	March
Sun.	5 12 19 26	2 9 16 23	1 8 15 22 29
Mon.	6 13 20 27	3 10 17 24	2 9 16 23 30
Tue.	7 14 21 28	4 11 18 25	3 10 17 24 31
Wed.	1 8 15 22 29	5 12 19 26	4 11 18 25
Thur.	2 9 16 23 30	6 13 20 27	5 12 19 26
Fri.	3 10 17 24 31	7 14 21 28	6 13 20 27
Sat.	4 11 18 25	1 8 15 22 29	7 14 21 28

	April	May	June
Sun.	5 12 19 26	3 10 17 24 31	7 14 21 28
Mon.	6 13 20 27	4 11 18 25	1 8 15 22 29
Tue.	7 14 21 28	5 12 19 26	2 9 16 23 30
Wed.	1 8 15 22 29	6 13 20 27	3 10 17 24
Thur.	2 9 16 23 30	7 14 21 28	4 11 18 25
Fri.	3 10 17 24	1 8 15 22 29	5 12 19 26
Sat.	4 11 18 25	2 9 16 23 30	6 13 20 27

	July	August	September
Sun.	5 12 19 26	2 9 16 23 30	6 13 20 27
Mon.	6 13 20 27	3 10 17 24 31	7 14 21 28
Tue.	7 14 21 28	4 11 18 25	1 8 15 22 29
Wed.	1 8 15 22 29	5 12 19 26	2 9 16 23 30
Thur.	2 9 16 23 30	6 13 20 27	3 10 17 24
Fri.	3 10 17 24 31	7 14 21 28	4 11 18 25
Sat.	4 11 18 25	1 8 15 22 29	5 12 19 26

	October	November	December
Sun.	4 11 18 25	1 8 15 22 29	6 13 20 27
Mon.	5 12 19 26	2 9 16 23 30	7 14 21 28
Tue.	6 13 20 27	3 10 17 24	1 8 15 22 29
Wed.	7 14 21 28	4 11 18 25	2 9 16 23 30
Thur.	1 8 15 22 29	5 12 19 26	3 10 17 24 31
Fri.	2 9 16 23 30	6 13 20 27	4 11 18 25
Sat.	3 10 17 24 31	7 14 21 28	5 12 19 26

EASTER DAYS

March 29	1812, 1964
April 5	1896
April 12	1868, 1936, 2020
April 19	1840, 1908, 1992

J (LEAP YEAR)

	January	February	March
Sun.	4 11 18 25	1 8 15 22 29	7 14 21 28
Mon.	5 12 19 26	2 9 16 23	1 8 15 22 29
Tue.	6 13 20 27	3 10 17 24	2 9 16 23 30
Wed.	7 14 21 28	4 11 18 25	3 10 17 24 31
Thur.	1 8 15 22 29	5 12 19 26	4 11 18 25
Fri.	2 9 16 23 30	6 13 20 27	5 12 19 26
Sat.	3 10 17 24 31	7 14 21 28	6 13 20 27

	April	May	June
Sun.	4 11 18 25	2 9 16 23 30	6 13 20 27
Mon.	5 12 19 26	3 10 17 24 31	7 14 21 28
Tue.	6 13 20 27	4 11 18 25	1 8 15 22 29
Wed.	7 14 21 28	5 12 19 26	2 9 16 23 30
Thur.	1 8 15 22 29	6 13 20 27	3 10 17 24
Fri.	2 9 16 23 30	7 14 21 28	4 11 18 25
Sat.	3 10 17 24	1 8 15 22 29	5 12 19 26

	July	August	September
Sun.	4 11 18 25	1 8 15 22 29	5 12 19 26
Mon.	5 12 19 26	2 9 16 23 30	6 13 20 27
Tue.	6 13 20 27	3 10 17 24 31	7 14 21 28
Wed.	7 14 21 28	4 11 18 25	1 8 15 22 29
Thur.	1 8 15 22 29	5 12 19 26	2 9 16 23 30
Fri.	2 9 16 23 30	6 13 20 27	3 10 17 24
Sat.	3 10 17 24 31	7 14 21 28	4 11 18 25

	October	November	December
Sun.	3 10 17 24 31	7 14 21 28	5 12 19 26
Mon.	4 11 18 25	1 8 15 22 29	6 13 20 27
Tue.	5 12 19 26	2 9 16 23 30	7 14 21 28
Wed.	6 13 20 27	3 10 17 24	1 8 15 22 29
Thur.	7 14 21 28	4 11 18 25	2 9 16 23 30
Fri.	1 8 15 22 29	5 12 19 26	3 10 17 24 31
Sat.	2 9 16 23 30	6 13 20 27	4 11 18 25

EASTER DAYS

March 28	1880, 1948, 2032
April 4	1920
April 11	1784, 1852, 2004
April 18	1824, 1976

K

January / February / March

Day	January	February	March
Sun.	3 10 17 24 31	7 14 21 28	7 14 21 28
Mon.	4 11 18 25	1 8 15 22	1 8 15 22 29
Tue.	5 12 19 26	2 9 16 23	2 9 16 23 30
Wed.	6 13 20 27	3 10 17 24	3 10 17 24 31
Thur.	7 14 21 28	4 11 18 25	4 11 18 25
Fri.	1 8 15 22 29	5 12 19 26	5 12 19 26
Sat.	2 9 16 23 30	6 13 20 27	6 13 20 27

April / May / June

Day	April	May	June
Sun.	4 11 18 25	2 9 16 23 30	6 13 20 27
Mon.	5 12 19 26	3 10 17 24 31	7 14 21 28
Tue.	6 13 20 27	4 11 18 25	1 8 15 22 29
Wed.	7 14 21 28	5 12 19 26	2 9 16 23 30
Thur.	1 8 15 22 29	6 13 20 27	3 10 17 24
Fri.	2 9 16 23 30	7 14 21 28	4 11 18 25
Sat.	3 10 17 24	1 8 15 22 29	5 12 19 26

July / August / September

Day	July	August	September
Sun.	4 11 18 25	1 8 15 22 29	5 12 19 26
Mon.	5 12 19 26	2 9 16 23 30	6 13 20 27
Tue.	6 13 20 27	3 10 17 24 31	7 14 21 28
Wed.	7 14 21 28	4 11 18 25	1 8 15 22 29
Thur.	1 8 15 22 29	5 12 19 26	2 9 16 23 30
Fri.	2 9 16 23 30	6 13 20 27	3 10 17 24
Sat.	3 10 17 24 31	7 14 21 28	4 11 18 25

October / November / December

Day	October	November	December
Sun.	3 10 17 24 31	7 14 21 28	5 12 19 26
Mon.	4 11 18 25	1 8 15 22 29	6 13 20 27
Tue.	5 12 19 26	2 9 16 23 30	7 14 21 28
Wed.	6 13 20 27	3 10 17 24	1 8 15 22 29
Thur.	7 14 21 28	4 11 18 25	2 9 16 23 30
Fri.	1 8 15 22 29	5 12 19 26	3 10 17 24 31
Sat.	2 9 16 23 30	6 13 20 27	4 11 18 25

EASTER DAYS

March 28	1869, 1875, 1937, 2027
April 4	1790, 1847, 1858, 1915, 1926, 1999, 2010, 2021
April 11	1819, 1830, 1841, 1909, 1971, 1982, 1993
April 18	1802, 1813, 1897, 1954, 1965
April 25	1886, 1943, 2038

M

January / February / March

Day	January	February	March
Sun.	2 9 16 23 30	6 13 20 27	6 13 20 27
Mon.	3 10 17 24 31	7 14 21 28	7 14 21 28
Tue.	4 11 18 25	1 8 15 22	1 8 15 22 29
Wed.	5 12 19 26	2 9 16 23	2 9 16 23 30
Thur.	6 13 20 27	3 10 17 24	3 10 17 24 31
Fri.	7 14 21 28	4 11 18 25	4 11 18 25
Sat.	1 8 15 22 29	5 12 19 26	5 12 19 26

April / May / June

Day	April	May	June
Sun.	3 10 17 24	1 8 15 22 29	5 12 19 26
Mon.	4 11 18 25	2 9 16 23 30	6 13 20 27
Tue.	5 12 19 26	3 10 17 24 31	7 14 21 28
Wed.	6 13 20 27	4 11 18 25	1 8 15 22 29
Thur.	7 14 21 28	5 12 19 26	2 9 16 23 30
Fri.	1 8 15 22 29	6 13 20 27	3 10 17 24
Sat.	2 9 16 23 30	7 14 21 28	4 11 18 25

July / August / September

Day	July	August	September
Sun.	3 10 17 24 31	7 14 21 28	4 11 18 25
Mon.	4 11 18 25	1 8 15 22 29	5 12 19 26
Tue.	5 12 19 26	2 9 16 23 30	6 13 20 27
Wed.	6 13 20 27	3 10 17 24 31	7 14 21 28
Thur.	7 14 21 28	4 11 18 25	1 8 15 22 29
Fri.	1 8 15 22 29	5 12 19 26	2 9 16 23 30
Sat.	2 9 16 23 30	6 13 20 27	3 10 17 24

October / November / December

Day	October	November	December
Sun.	2 9 16 23 30	6 13 20 27	4 11 18 25
Mon.	3 10 17 24 31	7 14 21 28	5 12 19 26
Tue.	4 11 18 25	1 8 15 22 29	6 13 20 27
Wed.	5 12 19 26	2 9 16 23 30	7 14 21 28
Thur.	6 13 20 27	3 10 17 24	1 8 15 22 29
Fri.	7 14 21 28	4 11 18 25	2 9 16 23 30
Sat.	1 8 15 22 29	5 12 19 26	3 10 17 24 31

EASTER DAYS

March 27	1785, 1842, 1853, 1910, 1921, 2005
April 3	1825, 1831, 1983, 1994
April 10	1803, 1814, 1887, 1898, 1955, 1966, 1977, 2039
April 17	1870, 1881, 1927, 1938, 1949, 2022, 2033
April 24	1791, 1859, 2011

L (LEAP YEAR)

January / February / March

Day	January	February	March
Sun.	3 10 17 24 31	7 14 21 28	6 13 20 27
Mon.	4 11 18 25	1 8 15 22 29	7 14 21 28
Tue.	5 12 19 26	2 9 16 23	1 8 15 22 29
Wed.	6 13 20 27	3 10 17 24	2 9 16 23 30
Thur.	7 14 21 28	4 11 18 25	3 10 17 24 31
Fri.	1 8 15 22 29	5 12 19 26	4 11 18 25
Sat.	2 9 16 23 30	6 13 20 27	5 12 19 26

April / May / June

Day	April	May	June
Sun.	3 10 17 24	1 8 15 22 29	5 12 19 26
Mon.	4 11 18 25	2 9 16 23 30	6 13 20 27
Tue.	5 12 19 26	3 10 17 24 31	7 14 21 28
Wed.	6 13 20 27	4 11 18 25	1 8 15 22 29
Thur.	7 14 21 28	5 12 19 26	2 9 16 23 30
Fri.	1 8 15 22 29	6 13 20 27	3 10 17 24
Sat.	2 9 16 23 30	7 14 21 28	4 11 18 25

July / August / September

Day	July	August	September
Sun.	3 10 17 24 31	7 14 21 28	4 11 18 25
Mon.	4 11 18 25	1 8 15 22 29	5 12 19 26
Tue.	5 12 19 26	2 9 16 23 30	6 13 20 27
Wed.	6 13 20 27	3 10 17 24 31	7 14 21 28
Thur.	7 14 21 28	4 11 18 25	1 8 15 22 29
Fri.	1 8 15 22 29	5 12 19 26	2 9 16 23 30
Sat.	2 9 16 23 30	6 13 20 27	3 10 17 24

October / November / December

Day	October	November	December
Sun.	2 9 16 23 30	6 13 20 27	4 11 18 25
Mon.	3 10 17 24 31	7 14 21 28	5 12 19 26
Tue.	4 11 18 25	1 8 15 22 29	6 13 20 27
Wed.	5 12 19 26	2 9 16 23 30	7 14 21 28
Thur.	6 13 20 27	3 10 17 24	1 8 15 22 29
Fri.	7 14 21 28	4 11 18 25	2 9 16 23 30
Sat.	1 8 15 22 29	5 12 19 26	3 10 17 24 31

EASTER DAYS

March 27	1796, 1864, 1932, 2016
April 3	1836, 1904, 1988
April 17	1808, 1892, 1960

N (LEAP YEAR)

January / February / March

Day	January	February	March
Sun.	2 9 16 23 30	6 13 20 27	5 12 19 26
Mon.	3 10 17 24 31	7 14 21 28	6 13 20 27
Tue.	4 11 18 25	1 8 15 22 29	7 14 21 28
Wed.	5 12 19 26	2 9 16 23	1 8 15 22 29
Thur.	6 13 20 27	3 10 17 24	2 9 16 23 30
Fri.	7 14 21 28	4 11 18 25	3 10 17 24 31
Sat.	1 8 15 22 29	5 12 19 26	4 11 18 25

April / May / June

Day	April	May	June
Sun.	2 9 16 23 30	7 14 21 28	4 11 18 25
Mon.	3 10 17 24	1 8 15 22 29	5 12 19 26
Tue.	4 11 18 25	2 9 16 23 30	6 13 20 27
Wed.	5 12 19 26	3 10 17 24 31	7 14 21 28
Thur.	6 13 20 27	4 11 18 25	1 8 15 22 29
Fri.	7 14 21 28	5 12 19 26	2 9 16 23 30
Sat.	1 8 15 22 29	6 13 20 27	3 10 17 24

July / August / September

Day	July	August	September
Sun.	2 9 16 23 30	6 13 20 27	3 10 17 24
Mon.	3 10 17 24 31	7 14 21 28	4 11 18 25
Tue.	4 11 18 25	1 8 15 22 29	5 12 19 26
Wed.	5 12 19 26	2 9 16 23 30	6 13 20 27
Thur.	6 13 20 27	3 10 17 24 31	7 14 21 28
Fri.	7 14 21 28	4 11 18 25	1 8 15 22 29
Sat.	1 8 15 22 29	5 12 19 26	2 9 16 23 30

October / November / December

Day	October	November	December
Sun.	1 8 15 22 29	5 12 19 26	3 10 17 24 31
Mon.	2 9 16 23 30	6 13 20 27	4 11 18 25
Tue.	3 10 17 24 31	7 14 21 28	5 12 19 26
Wed.	4 11 18 25	1 8 15 22 29	6 13 20 27
Thur.	5 12 19 26	2 9 16 23 30	7 14 21 28
Fri.	6 13 20 27	3 10 17 24	1 8 15 22 29
Sat.	7 14 21 28	4 11 18 25	2 9 16 23 30

EASTER DAYS

March 26	1780
April 2	1820, 1972
April 9	1944
April 16	2028
April 23	1848, 1916, 2000

GEOLOGICAL TIME

The earth is thought to have come into existence approximately 4,600 million years ago, but for nearly half this time, the Archean era, it was uninhabited. Life is generally believed to have emerged in the succeeding Proterozoic era. The Archean and the Proterozoic eras are often together referred to as the Precambrian.

Although primitive forms of life, e.g. algae and bacteria, existed during the Proterozoic era, it is not until the strata of Palaeozoic rocks is reached that abundant fossilized remains appear.

Since the Precambrian, there have been three great geological eras:

PALAEOZOIC ('ancient life')
c.570–c.245 million years ago

Cambrian – Mainly sandstones, slate and shales; limestones in Scotland. Shelled fossils and invertebrates, e.g. trilobites and brachiopods, appear
Ordovician – Mainly shales and mudstones, e.g. in north Wales; limestones in Scotland. First fishes
Silurian – Shales, mudstones and some limestones, found mostly in Wales and southern Scotland
Devonian – Old red sandstone, shale, limestone and slate, e.g. in south Wales and the West Country
Carboniferous – Coal-bearing rocks, millstone grit, limestone and shale. First traces of land-living life
Permian – Marls, sandstones and clays. First reptile fossils

There were two great phases of mountain building in the Palaeozoic era: the Caledonian, characterized in Britain by NE–SW lines of hills and valleys; and the later Hercyian, widespread in west Germany and adjacent areas, and in Britain exemplified in E.–W. lines of hills and valleys.

The end of the Palaeozoic era was marked by the extensive glaciations of the Permian period in the southern continents and the decline of amphibians. It was succeeded by an era of warm conditions.

MESOZOIC ('middle forms of life')
c.245–c.65 million years ago

Triassic – Mostly sandstone, e.g. in the West Midlands
Jurassic – Mainly limestones and clays, typically displayed in the Jura mountains, and in England in a NE–SW belt from Lincolnshire and the Wash to the Severn and the Dorset coast
Cretaceous – Mainly chalk, clay and sands, e.g. in Kent and Sussex

Giant reptiles were dominant during the Mesozoic era, but it was at this time that marsupial mammals first appeared, as well as *Archaeopteryx lithographica*, the earliest known species of bird. Coniferous trees and flowering plants also developed during the era and, with the birds and the mammals, were the main species to survive into the Cenozoic era. The giant reptiles became extinct.

CENOZOIC ('recent life')
from c.65 million years ago

Palaeocene ⎫ The emergence of new forms of life,
Eocene ⎬ including existing species
Oligocene – Fossils of a few still existing species
Miocene – Fossil remains show a balance of existing and extinct species
Pliocene – Fossil remains show a majority of still existing species
Pleistocene – The majority of remains are those of still existing species

Holocene – The present, post-glacial period. Existing species only, except for a few exterminated by man

In the last 25 million years, from the Miocene through the Pliocene periods, the Alpine-Himalayan and the circum-Pacific phases of mountain building reached their climax. During the Pleistocene period ice-sheets repeatedly locked up masses of water as land ice; its weight depressed the land, but the locking-up of the water lowered the sea-level by 100–200 metres. The glaciations and interglacials of the Ice Age are difficult to date and classify, but recent scientific opinion considers the Pleistocene period to have begun approximately 1.64 million years ago. The last glacial retreat, merging into the Holocene period, was 10,000 years ago.

HUMAN DEVELOPMENT

Any consideration of the history of mankind must start with the fact that all members of the human race belong to one species of animal, i.e. *Homo sapiens*, the definition of a species being in biological terms that all its members can interbreed. As a species of mammal it is possible to group man with other similar types, known as the primates. Amongst these is found a sub-group, the apes, which includes, in addition to man, the chimpanzees, gorillas, orang-utans and gibbons. All lack a tail, have shoulder blades at the back, and a Y-shaped chewing pattern on the surface of their molars, as well as showing the more general primate characteristics of four incisors, a thumb which is able to touch the fingers of the same hand, and finger and toe nails instead of claws. The factors available to scientific study suggest that human beings have chimpanzees and gorillas as their nearest relatives in the animal world. However, there remains the possibility that there once lived creatures, now extinct, which were closer to modern man than the chimpanzees and gorillas, and which shared with modern man the characteristics of having flat faces (i.e. the absence of a pronounced muzzle), being bipedal, and possessing large brains.

There are two broad groups of extinct apes recognized by specialists. The ramapithecines, the remains of which, mainly jaw fragments, have been found in east Africa, Asia, and Turkey, lived about 14 to 8 million years ago. From the evidence of their teeth it seems they chewed more in the manner of modern man than the other presently living apes. The second group, the australopithecines, have left more numerous remains amongst which sub-groups may be detected, although the geographic spread is limited to south and east Africa. Living between 5 and 1.5 million years ago, they were closer relatives of modern man to the extent that they walked upright, did not have an extensive muzzle and had similar types of pre-molars. The first australopithecine remains were recognized at Taung in South Africa in 1924 and subsequent discoveries include those at the Olduvai Gorge in Tanzania. The most impressive discovery was made at Hadar, Ethiopia, in 1974 when about half a skeleton, known as 'Lucy', was found.

Also in east Africa, between 2 million and 1.5 million years ago, lived a hominid group which not only walked upright, had a flat face, and a large brain case, but also made simple pebble and flake stone tools. On present evidence these habilines seem to have been the first people to make tools, however crude. This facility is related to the larger brain size and human beings are the only animals to make implements to be used in other processes. These early pebble tool users, because of their distinctive

GEOLOGICAL TIME

Era	Period	Epoch	Date began*	Evolutionary stages
Cenozoic	Quaternary	Holocene	0.01	Man
		Pleistocene	1.64	
	Tertiary	Pliocene	5.2	
		Miocene	23.3	
		Oligocene	35.4	
		Eocene	56.5	
		Palaeocene	65.0	
Mesozoic	Cretaceous		145.6	
	Jurassic		208.0	First birds
	Triassic		245.0	First mammals
Palaeozoic	Permian		290.0	First reptiles
	Carboniferous		362.5	First amphibians and insects
	Devonian		408.5	
	Silurian		439.0	
	Ordovician		510.0	First fishes
	Cambrian		570.0	First invertebrates
	Precambrian		4,600.0	First primitive life forms, e.g. algae and bacteria

*millions of years ago

characteristics, have been grouped as a separate sub-species, now extinct, of the genus *Homo* and are known as *Homo habilis*.

The use of fire, again a human characteristic, is associated with another group of extinct hominids whose remains, about a million years old, are found in south and east Africa, China, Indonesia, north Africa and Europe. Mastery of the techniques of making fire probably helped the colonization of the colder northern areas and in this respect the site of Vertesszollos in Hungary is of particular importance. *Homo erectus* is the name given to this group of fossils and it includes a number of famous individual discoveries, e.g. Solo Man, Heidelberg Man, and especially Peking Man who lived at the cave site at Choukoutien which has yielded evidence of fire and burnt bone.

The well-known group Neanderthal Man, or *Homo sapiens neandertalensis*, is an extinct form of modern man who lived between about 100,000 and 40,000 years ago, thus spanning the last Ice Age. Indeed, its ability to adapt to the cold climate on the edge of the ice-sheets is one of its characteristic features, the remains being found only in Europe, Asia and the Middle East. Complete neanderthal skeletons were found during excavations at Tabun in Israel, together with evidence of tool-making and the use of fire. Distinguished by very large brains, it seems that neanderthal man was the first to develop recognizable social customs, especially deliberate burial rites. Why the neanderthalers became extinct is not clear but it may be connected with the climatic changes at the end of the Ice Ages, which would have seriously affected their food supplies; possibly they became too specialized for their own good.

The Swanscombe skull is the only known human fossil remains found in England. Some specialists see Swanscombe Man (or, more probably, woman) as a neanderthaler. Others group these remains together with the Steinheim skull from Germany, seeing both as a separate sub-species. There is too little evidence as yet on which to form a final judgement.

Modern Man, *Homo sapiens sapiens*, the surviving sub-species of *Homo sapiens*, had evolved to our present physical condition and had colonized much of the world by about 30,000 years ago. There are many previously distinguished individual specimens, e.g. Cromagnon Man, which may now be grouped together as *Homo sapiens sapiens*. It was modern man who spread to the American continent by crossing the landbridge between Siberia and Alaska and thence moved south through North America and into South America. Equally it is modern man who over the last 30,000 years has been responsible for the major developments in technology, art and civilization generally.

One of the problems for those studying fossil man is the lack in many cases of sufficient quantities of fossil bone for analysis. It is important that theories should be tested against evidence, rather than the evidence being made to fit the theory. The Piltdown hoax is a well-known example of 'fossils' being forged to fit what was seen in some quarters as the correct theory of man's evolution.

CULTURAL DEVELOPMENT

The Eurocentric bias of early archaeologists meant that the search for a starting point for the development and transmission of cultural ideas, especially by migration, trade and warfare, concentrated unduly on Europe and the Near East. The Three Age system, whereby pre-history was divided into a Stone Age, a Bronze Age and an Iron Age, was devised by Christian Thomsen, curator of the National Museum of Denmark in the early 19th century, to facilitate the classification of the museum's collections. The descriptive adjectives referred to the materials from which the implements and weapons were made and came to be regarded as the dominant features of the societies to which they related. The refinement of the Three Age system once dominated archaeological thought and remains a generally accepted concept in the popular mind. However, it is now seen by archaeologists as an inadequate model for human development.

Common sense suggests that there were no complete breaks between one so-called Age and another, any more than contemporaries would have regarded 1485 as a complete break between medieval and modern English history. Nor can the Three Age system be applied universally. In some areas it is necessary to insert a Copper Age, while in Africa south of the Sahara there would seem to be no Bronze Age at all; in Australia, Old Stone Age societies survived, while in South America, New Stone Age communities existed into modern times. The civilizations in other parts of the world clearly invalidate a Eurocentric theory of human development.

The concept of the 'Neolithic revolution', associated with the domestication of plants and animals, was a development of particular importance in the human cultural pattern. It reflected change from the primitive hunter/gatherer economies to a more settled agricultural way of life and therefore, so the argument goes, made possible the development of urban civilization. However, it can no longer be argued that this 'revolution' took place only in one area from which all development stemmed. Though it appears that the cultivation of wheat and barley was first undertaken, together with the domestication of cattle and goats/sheep in the Fertile Crescent (the area bounded by the rivers Tigris and Euphrates), there is evidence that rice was first deliberately planted and pigs domesticated in south-east Asia, maize first cultivated in Central America and llamas first domesticated in South America. It has been recognized in recent years that cultural changes can take place independently of each other in different parts of the world at different rates and different times. There is no need for a general diffusionist theory.

Although scholars will continue to study the particular societies which interest them, it may be possible to obtain a reliable chronological framework, in absolute terms of years, against which the cultural development of any particular area may be set. The development and refinement of radio-carbon dating and other scientific methods of producing absolute chronologies is enabling the cross-referencing of societies to be undertaken. As the techniques of dating become more rigorous in application and the number of scientifically obtained dates increases, the attainment of an absolute chronology for prehistoric societies throughout the world comes closer to being achieved.

Tidal Tables

CONSTANTS

The constant tidal difference may be used in conjunction with the time of high water at a standard port shown in the predictions data (pages 98–103) to find the time of high water at any of the ports or places listed below.

These tidal differences are very approximate and should be used only as a guide to the time of high water at the places below. More precise local data should be obtained for navigational and other nautical purposes.

All data allow high water time to be found in Greenwich Mean Time; this applies also to data for the months when British Summer Time is in operation and the hour's time difference should be allowed for. Ports marked * are in a different time zone and the standard time zone difference also needs to be added/subtracted to give local time.

EXAMPLE

Required time of high water at Stranraer at 2 January 2000
Appropriate time of high water at Greenock

Afternoon tide 2 January	2026 hrs
Tidal difference	−0020 hrs
High water at Stranraer	2006 hrs

The columns headed 'Springs' and 'Neaps' show the height, in metres, of the tide above datum for mean high water springs and mean high water neaps respectively.

Port	Diff.		Springs	Neaps
		h m	m	m
Aberdeen	Leith	−1 19	4.3	3.4
*Antwerp (Prosperpolder)	London	+0 50	5.8	4.8
Ardrossan	Greenock	−0 15	3.2	2.6
Avonmouth	London	−6 45	13.2	9.8
Ayr	Greenock	−0 25	3.0	2.5
Barrow (Docks)	Liverpool	0 00	9.3	7.1
Belfast	London	−2 47	3.5	3.0
Blackpool	Liverpool	−0 10	8.9	7.0
*Boulogne	London	−2 44	8.9	7.2
*Calais	London	−2 04	7.2	5.9
*Cherbourg	London	−6 00	6.4	5.0
Cobh	Liverpool	−5 55	4.2	3.2
Cowes	London	−2 38	4.2	3.5
Dartmouth	London	+4 25	4.9	3.8
*Dieppe	London	−3 03	9.3	7.3
Douglas, IOM	Liverpool	−0 04	6.9	5.4
Dover	London	−2 52	6.7	5.3
Dublin	London	−2 05	4.1	3.4
Dun Laoghaire	London	−2 10	4.1	3.4
*Dunkirk	London	−1 54	6.0	4.9
Fishguard	Liverpool	−4 01	4.8	3.4
Fleetwood	Liverpool	0 00	9.2	7.3
*Flushing	London	−0 15	4.7	3.9
Folkestone	London	−3 04	7.1	5.7
Galway	Liverpool	−6 08	5.1	3.9
Glasgow	Greenock	+0 26	4.7	4.0
Harwich	London	−2 06	4.0	3.4
*Le Havre	London	−3 55	7.9	6.6
Heysham	Liverpool	+0 05	9.4	7.4
Holyhead	Liverpool	−0 50	5.6	4.4
*Hook of Holland	London	−0 01	2.1	1.7
Hull (Albert Dock)	London	−7 40	7.5	5.8
Immingham	London	−8 00	7.3	5.8
Larne	London	−2 40	2.8	2.5
Lerwick	Leith	−3 48	2.2	1.6
Londonderry	London	−5 37	2.7	2.1
Lowestoft	London	−4 25	2.4	2.1
Margate	London	−1 53	4.8	3.9
Milford Haven	Liverpool	−5 08	7.0	5.2
Morecambe	Liverpool	+0 07	9.5	7.4
Newhaven	London	−2 46	6.7	5.1
Oban	Greenock	+5 43	4.0	2.9
*Ostend	London	−1 32	5.1	4.2
Plymouth (Devonport)	London	+4 05	5.5	4.4
Portland	London	+5 09	2.1	1.4
Portsmouth	London	−2 38	4.7	3.8
Ramsgate	London	−2 32	5.2	4.1
Richmond Lock	London	+1 00	4.9	3.7
Rosslare Harbour	Liverpool	−5 24	1.9	1.4
Rosyth	Leith	+0 09	5.8	4.7
*Rotterdam	London	+1 45	2.0	1.7
St Helier	London	+4 48	11.0	8.1
St Malo	London	+4 27	12.2	9.2
St Peter Port	London	+4 54	9.3	7.0
Scrabster	Leith	−6 06	5.0	4.0
Sheerness	London	−1 19	5.8	4.7
Shoreham	London	−2 44	6.3	4.9
Southampton (1st high water)	London	−2 54	4.5	3.7
Spurn Head	London	−8 25	6.9	5.5
Stornoway	Liverpool	−4 16	4.8	3.7
Stranraer	Greenock	−0 20	3.0	2.4
Stromness	Leith	−5 26	3.6	2.7
Swansea	London	−7 35	9.5	7.2
Tees (River Entrance)	Leith	+1 09	5.5	4.3
Tilbury	London	−0 49	6.4	5.4
Tobermory	Liverpool	−5 11	4.4	3.3
Tyne River (North Shields)	London	−10 30	5.0	3.9
Ullapool	Leith	−7 40	5.2	3.9
Walton-on-the-Naze	London	−2 10	4.2	3.4
Wick	Leith	−3 26	3.5	2.8
*Zeebrugge	London	−0 55	4.8	3.9

PREDICTIONS

The data on pages 98–103 are daily predictions of the time and height of high water at London Bridge, Liverpool, Greenock and Leith. The time of the data is Greenwich Mean Time; this applies also to data for the months when British Summer Time is in operation and the hour's time difference should be allowed for. The datum of predictions for each port shows the difference of height, in metres, from Ordnance data (Newlyn).

The tidal information for London Bridge, Liverpool, Greenock and Leith is reproduced with the permission of the UK Hydrographic Office and the Controller of HMSO. Crown copyright reserved.

JANUARY 2000   *High water*   GMT

		LONDON BRIDGE				LIVERPOOL				GREENOCK				LEITH			
		*Datum of predictions 3.20 m below				*Datum of predictions 4.93 m below				*Datum of predictions 1.62 m below				*Datum of predictions 2.90 m below			
		hr	ht m	hr	ht m	hr	ht m	hr	ht m	hr	ht m	hr	ht m	hr	ht m	hr	ht m
1	Saturday	09 31	5.9	22 05	6.1	07 11	7.6	19 37	7.8	08 41	3.0	20 26	3.1	10 47	4.5	23 15	4.7
2	Sunday	10 32	6.0	23 01	6.2	08 11	7.9	20 35	8.0	09 46	3.1	21 45	3.1	11 48	4.6	—	—
3	Monday	11 28	6.2	23 53	6.4	09 02	8.2	21 25	8.3	10 37	3.2	22 42	3.1	00 14	4.8	12 42	4.8
4	Tuesday	—	—	12 20	6.4	09 46	8.6	22 07	8.5	11 21	3.3	23 29	3.2	01 05	4.9	13 26	4.9
5	Wednesday	00 39	6.6	13 07	6.6	10 25	8.8	22 45	8.7	—	—	12 01	3.4	01 49	5.0	14 03	5.1
6	Thursday	01 22	6.7	13 48	6.7	11 01	9.0	23 20	8.7	00 09	3.2	12 38	3.5	02 27	5.1	14 37	5.2
7	Friday	01 59	6.7	14 25	6.7	11 36	9.1	23 54	8.8	00 45	3.2	13 10	3.5	03 02	5.1	15 09	5.2
8	Saturday	02 33	6.7	15 00	6.6	—	—	12 11	9.1	01 18	3.2	13 40	3.5	03 36	5.2	15 41	5.3
9	Sunday	03 05	6.7	15 33	6.6	00 28	8.8	12 47	9.1	01 52	3.2	14 11	3.5	04 10	5.2	16 15	5.3
10	Monday	03 38	6.6	16 09	6.7	01 05	8.8	13 23	9.0	02 29	3.2	14 45	3.5	04 46	5.2	16 50	5.2
11	Tuesday	04 12	6.6	16 47	6.7	01 42	8.7	14 01	8.9	03 08	3.2	15 21	3.5	05 23	5.1	17 27	5.2
12	Wednesday	04 50	6.6	17 29	6.6	02 22	8.6	14 42	8.8	03 49	3.2	16 00	3.4	06 04	5.0	18 07	5.1
13	Thursday	05 32	6.5	18 14	6.5	03 05	8.4	15 28	8.6	04 31	3.1	16 42	3.3	06 48	4.9	18 51	5.0
14	Friday	06 19	6.4	19 05	6.4	03 55	8.1	16 22	8.4	05 17	3.0	17 29	3.2	07 38	4.8	19 43	4.9
15	Saturday	07 13	6.3	20 03	6.2	04 54	7.9	17 25	8.2	06 07	3.0	18 26	3.1	08 37	4.7	20 46	4.8
16	Sunday	08 17	6.2	21 09	6.1	06 03	7.8	18 33	8.2	07 06	2.9	19 38	3.0	09 45	4.7	22 00	4.8
17	Monday	09 28	6.2	22 19	6.2	07 14	8.0	19 43	8.4	08 22	3.0	21 07	3.0	10 53	4.8	23 13	5.0
18	Tuesday	10 42	6.3	23 26	6.4	08 23	8.5	20 51	8.8	09 44	3.1	22 21	3.2	11 57	5.0	—	—
19	Wednesday	11 50	6.6	—	—	09 23	9.0	21 50	9.3	10 47	3.3	23 21	3.3	00 19	5.2	12 55	5.3
20	Thursday	00 26	6.7	12 52	7.0	10 17	9.5	22 45	9.6	11 39	3.5	—	—	01 18	5.5	13 46	5.6
21	Friday	01 21	7.0	13 47	7.3	11 08	9.8	23 35	9.8	00 16	3.4	12 28	3.7	02 11	5.7	14 34	5.7
22	Saturday	02 12	7.2	14 38	7.5	11 56	10.0	—	—	01 09	3.5	13 14	3.8	03 00	5.8	15 21	5.8
23	Sunday	02 59	7.2	15 27	7.5	00 23	9.8	12 43	10.0	01 59	3.5	13 58	3.9	03 49	5.8	16 08	5.8
24	Monday	03 44	7.2	16 14	7.5	01 10	9.7	13 28	9.9	02 46	3.5	14 41	3.9	04 37	5.7	16 56	5.7
25	Tuesday	04 27	7.1	16 58	7.3	01 54	9.4	14 12	9.6	03 29	3.4	15 23	3.9	05 24	5.5	17 45	5.5
26	Wednesday	05 07	6.9	17 40	7.0	02 37	9.0	14 55	9.1	04 10	3.4	16 04	3.8	06 13	5.2	18 35	5.3
27	Thursday	05 46	6.7	18 22	6.6	03 19	8.5	15 39	8.6	04 51	3.3	16 46	3.6	07 02	4.9	19 28	5.0
28	Friday	06 26	6.4	19 06	6.2	04 05	8.0	16 27	8.0	05 34	3.1	17 31	3.4	07 54	4.6	20 25	4.7
29	Saturday	07 14	6.1	19 57	5.9	05 00	7.5	17 27	7.5	06 21	3.0	18 19	3.2	08 49	4.4	21 24	4.5
30	Sunday	08 18	5.7	21 02	5.7	06 08	7.3	18 41	7.3	07 15	2.9	19 14	3.0	09 48	4.3	22 28	4.4
31	Monday	09 40	5.6	22 11	5.7	07 24	7.4	19 57	7.4	08 37	2.9	20 27	2.8	10 54	4.3	23 37	4.4

FEBRUARY 2000   *High water*   GMT

		LONDON BRIDGE				LIVERPOOL				GREENOCK				LEITH			
1	Tuesday	10 51	5.8	23 13	5.9	08 29	7.7	20 57	7.7	10 03	3.0	22 13	2.9	—	—	12 03	4.5
2	Wednesday	11 50	6.0	—	—	09 20	8.2	21 45	8.1	10 56	3.1	23 10	2.9	00 40	4.6	13 00	4.7
3	Thursday	00 07	6.2	12 42	6.3	10 04	8.6	22 26	8.4	11 40	3.3	23 53	3.0	01 29	4.8	13 43	4.9
4	Friday	00 56	6.5	13 26	6.6	10 43	8.9	23 03	8.7	—	—	12 18	3.3	02 09	5.0	14 20	5.1
5	Saturday	01 38	6.7	14 07	6.7	11 19	9.1	23 38	8.8	00 30	3.0	12 52	3.4	02 44	5.1	14 53	5.2
6	Sunday	02 17	6.7	14 43	6.7	11 54	9.2	—	—	01 03	3.1	13 21	3.4	03 17	5.2	15 25	5.3
7	Monday	02 52	6.7	15 18	6.8	00 13	8.9	12 30	9.2	01 36	3.1	13 52	3.4	03 50	5.3	15 57	5.4
8	Tuesday	03 25	6.7	15 53	6.8	00 48	9.0	13 06	9.3	02 10	3.1	14 26	3.5	04 24	5.3	16 30	5.4
9	Wednesday	03 57	6.7	16 29	6.8	01 24	9.0	13 43	9.3	02 46	3.2	15 02	3.5	05 00	5.3	17 05	5.4
10	Thursday	04 33	6.8	17 08	6.8	02 01	9.0	14 21	9.2	03 23	3.2	15 39	3.4	05 38	5.2	17 43	5.3
11	Friday	05 12	6.8	17 51	6.7	02 41	8.8	15 04	9.0	04 01	3.2	16 18	3.4	06 20	5.0	18 26	5.2
12	Saturday	05 56	6.7	18 38	6.5	03 26	8.5	15 53	8.6	04 41	3.1	17 00	3.2	07 06	4.9	19 14	5.0
13	Sunday	06 46	6.4	19 31	6.2	04 20	8.1	16 53	8.2	05 26	3.0	17 50	3.1	08 01	4.7	20 14	4.8
14	Monday	07 46	6.2	20 35	5.9	05 28	7.8	18 05	7.9	06 19	2.9	18 55	2.9	09 09	4.6	21 32	4.7
15	Tuesday	08 59	6.0	21 52	5.9	06 46	7.7	19 24	8.0	07 30	2.8	20 42	2.8	10 26	4.6	22 56	4.8
16	Wednesday	10 22	6.0	23 07	6.1	08 06	8.1	20 40	8.4	09 19	2.9	22 14	3.0	11 39	4.8	—	—
17	Thursday	11 38	6.4	—	—	09 13	8.7	21 43	8.9	10 33	3.1	23 17	3.1	00 10	5.0	12 42	5.1
18	Friday	00 11	6.5	12 41	6.8	10 08	9.3	22 36	9.4	11 27	3.4	—	—	01 12	5.3	13 35	5.4
19	Saturday	01 07	6.9	13 36	7.2	10 57	9.7	23 24	9.7	00 11	3.3	12 16	3.6	02 03	5.5	14 22	5.7
20	Sunday	01 57	7.1	14 25	7.4	11 42	9.9	—	—	01 01	3.3	13 01	3.7	02 49	5.7	15 07	5.8
21	Monday	02 43	7.2	15 11	7.5	00 08	9.8	12 26	10.0	01 47	3.4	13 44	3.8	03 33	5.7	15 50	5.8
22	Tuesday	03 26	7.2	15 54	7.4	00 50	9.7	13 07	9.9	02 28	3.4	14 24	3.8	04 16	5.6	16 34	5.8
23	Wednesday	04 04	7.2	16 33	7.2	01 29	9.5	13 46	9.6	03 04	3.4	15 03	3.8	04 58	5.4	17 18	5.6
24	Thursday	04 40	7.0	17 08	7.0	02 06	9.1	14 23	9.2	03 39	3.4	15 40	3.7	05 40	5.2	18 01	5.3
25	Friday	05 14	6.9	17 42	6.7	02 43	8.7	15 01	8.7	04 13	3.3	16 17	3.6	06 22	4.9	18 47	5.0
26	Saturday	05 50	6.6	18 17	6.4	03 21	8.2	15 42	8.1	04 51	3.2	16 56	3.4	07 05	4.6	19 37	4.6
27	Sunday	06 30	6.3	18 58	6.1	04 06	7.7	16 32	7.5	05 32	3.0	17 39	3.1	07 55	4.4	20 34	4.3
28	Monday	07 19	5.9	19 49	5.7	05 05	7.2	17 41	7.0	06 20	2.9	18 29	2.9	08 53	4.2	21 38	4.2
29	Tuesday	08 24	5.5	20 56	5.5	06 27	7.0	19 10	6.9	07 20	2.7	19 30	2.7	09 58	4.1	22 51	4.2

MARCH 2000   *High water*   GMT

		LONDON BRIDGE *Datum of predictions 3.20 m below*				LIVERPOOL *Datum of predictions 4.93 m below*				GREENOCK *Datum of predictions 1.62 m below*				LEITH *Datum of predictions 2.90 m below*			
		hr	ht m	hr	ht m	hr	ht m	hr	ht m	hr	ht m	hr	ht m	hr	ht m	hr	ht m
1	Wednesday	10 00	5.4	22 25	5.6	07 50	7.3	20 27	7.3	09 07	2.7	21 06	2.6	11 13	4.2	—	—
2	Thursday	11 18	5.7	23 34	6.0	08 52	7.8	21 20	7.8	10 28	2.9	22 47	2.8	00 08	4.3	12 27	4.5
3	Friday	—	—	12 14	6.2	09 39	8.3	22 03	8.3	11 15	3.1	23 32	2.9	01 04	4.6	13 17	4.7
4	Saturday	00 28	6.3	13 02	6.5	10 20	8.7	22 41	8.6	11 53	3.2	—	—	01 45	4.9	13 55	5.0
5	Sunday	01 15	6.6	13 44	6.7	10 57	9.0	23 17	8.9	00 09	3.0	12 26	3.3	02 20	5.1	14 29	5.2
6	Monday	01 56	6.7	14 22	6.9	11 33	9.2	23 52	9.1	00 43	3.0	12 57	3.3	02 53	5.3	15 01	5.4
7	Tuesday	02 33	6.8	14 58	6.9	—	—	12 08	9.4	01 14	3.1	13 29	3.4	03 26	5.4	15 33	5.5
8	Wednesday	03 07	6.8	15 33	7.0	00 27	9.2	12 45	9.5	01 47	3.1	14 04	3.4	04 00	5.5	16 07	5.6
9	Thursday	03 40	6.9	16 09	7.0	01 03	9.3	13 22	9.5	02 21	3.2	14 41	3.5	04 35	5.5	16 43	5.6
10	Friday	04 16	7.0	16 47	7.0	01 40	9.2	14 01	9.4	02 56	3.3	15 19	3.5	05 14	5.4	17 23	5.5
11	Saturday	04 55	7.0	17 28	6.8	02 19	9.1	14 43	9.1	03 32	3.3	15 57	3.4	05 55	5.2	18 07	5.3
12	Sunday	05 38	6.8	18 12	6.5	03 02	8.7	15 31	8.6	04 11	3.2	16 39	3.2	06 41	5.0	18 57	5.1
13	Monday	06 26	6.5	19 03	6.1	03 55	8.2	16 31	8.0	04 54	3.1	17 28	3.0	07 35	4.7	19 59	4.8
14	Tuesday	07 25	6.1	20 07	5.7	05 04	7.7	17 48	7.6	05 47	2.9	18 33	2.8	08 45	4.5	21 21	4.6
15	Wednesday	08 43	5.8	21 34	5.7	06 29	7.5	19 16	7.7	06 56	2.8	20 42	2.7	10 08	4.5	22 49	4.7
16	Thursday	10 16	5.9	22 54	6.0	07 55	7.9	20 34	8.1	09 02	2.8	22 13	2.9	11 26	4.7	—	—
17	Friday	11 30	6.4	23 57	6.4	09 02	8.5	21 34	8.7	10 19	3.1	23 11	3.1	00 05	4.9	12 31	5.0
18	Saturday	—	—	12 29	6.9	09 56	9.1	22 23	9.2	11 12	3.3	—	—	01 05	5.2	13 23	5.3
19	Sunday	00 51	6.8	13 22	7.2	10 42	9.5	23 07	9.5	00 01	3.2	12 00	3.5	01 52	5.4	14 08	5.6
20	Monday	01 40	7.1	14 09	7.4	11 24	9.8	23 47	9.6	00 46	3.3	12 43	3.6	02 34	5.5	14 49	5.7
21	Tuesday	02 24	7.2	14 52	7.4	—	—	12 04	9.8	01 28	3.3	13 25	3.6	03 13	5.6	15 30	5.7
22	Wednesday	03 04	7.2	15 30	7.3	00 25	9.5	12 42	9.6	02 03	3.3	14 03	3.7	03 52	5.5	16 11	5.7
23	Thursday	03 40	7.1	16 04	7.1	01 01	9.4	13 18	9.4	02 35	3.3	14 39	3.6	04 30	5.3	16 51	5.5
24	Friday	04 13	7.0	16 35	6.9	01 35	9.1	13 52	9.0	03 06	3.3	15 14	3.6	05 07	5.1	17 31	5.2
25	Saturday	04 45	6.8	17 05	6.7	02 09	8.8	14 27	8.6	03 38	3.3	15 49	3.5	05 44	4.9	18 12	4.9
26	Sunday	05 20	6.6	17 40	6.5	02 44	8.4	15 05	8.0	04 13	3.2	16 26	3.3	06 24	4.7	18 58	4.6
27	Monday	05 59	6.3	18 19	6.2	03 24	7.9	15 49	7.5	04 51	3.1	17 08	3.0	07 09	4.5	19 52	4.3
28	Tuesday	06 45	6.0	19 06	5.9	04 15	7.3	16 49	6.9	05 37	2.9	17 58	2.8	08 05	4.2	20 54	4.1
29	Wednesday	07 40	5.6	20 04	5.6	05 29	7.0	18 18	6.7	06 34	2.7	18 58	2.6	09 10	4.1	22 02	4.1
30	Thursday	08 54	5.4	21 25	5.5	07 03	7.0	19 47	7.0	07 47	2.6	20 13	2.6	10 22	4.1	23 18	4.2
31	Friday	10 35	5.6	22 53	5.8	08 15	7.5	20 46	7.6	09 40	2.7	22 04	2.7	11 38	4.3	—	—

APRIL 2000   *High water*   GMT

		LONDON BRIDGE				LIVERPOOL				GREENOCK				LEITH			
1	Saturday	11 39	6.0	23 54	6.1	09 06	8.1	21 32	8.1	10 37	2.9	22 58	2.8	00 24	4.5	12 38	4.6
2	Sunday	—	—	12 29	6.5	09 49	8.6	22 11	8.6	11 16	3.1	23 37	3.0	01 10	4.9	13 21	4.9
3	Monday	00 43	6.5	13 14	6.8	10 27	9.0	22 48	8.9	11 51	3.2	—	—	01 47	5.1	13 57	5.2
4	Tuesday	01 27	6.7	13 54	7.0	11 05	9.3	23 24	9.2	00 12	3.0	12 26	3.3	02 23	5.4	14 32	5.4
5	Wednesday	02 06	6.9	14 33	7.1	11 42	9.5	—	—	00 47	3.1	13 03	3.3	02 57	5.5	15 06	5.6
6	Thursday	02 43	7.0	15 10	7.1	00 02	9.4	12 22	9.6	01 21	3.2	13 42	3.4	03 33	5.6	15 43	5.7
7	Friday	03 21	7.1	15 49	7.1	00 40	9.5	13 02	9.6	01 56	3.3	14 21	3.5	04 11	5.6	16 23	5.7
8	Saturday	04 00	7.2	16 28	7.0	01 20	9.4	13 43	9.5	02 32	3.4	15 01	3.5	04 51	5.5	17 06	5.6
9	Sunday	04 41	7.1	17 09	6.8	02 01	9.2	14 28	9.1	03 09	3.4	15 42	3.4	05 34	5.3	17 53	5.4
10	Monday	05 26	6.9	17 53	6.5	02 47	8.8	15 18	8.5	03 48	3.3	16 26	3.2	06 22	5.0	18 47	5.1
11	Tuesday	06 16	6.5	18 43	6.1	03 41	8.2	16 20	7.9	04 33	3.2	17 20	2.9	07 18	4.8	19 54	4.8
12	Wednesday	07 18	6.1	19 51	5.7	04 52	7.7	17 41	7.5	05 27	3.0	18 38	2.7	08 33	4.6	21 18	4.6
13	Thursday	08 43	5.9	21 23	5.7	06 19	7.6	19 07	7.6	06 41	2.8	20 45	2.7	09 56	4.5	22 41	4.7
14	Friday	10 09	6.1	22 37	6.0	07 40	7.9	20 18	8.1	08 45	2.9	22 01	2.9	11 11	4.7	23 53	4.9
15	Saturday	11 15	6.5	23 37	6.5	08 44	8.4	21 15	8.6	09 59	3.1	22 55	3.1	—	—	12 14	5.0
16	Sunday	—	—	12 11	7.0	09 36	8.9	22 02	9.0	10 52	3.3	23 42	3.2	00 51	5.1	13 06	5.3
17	Monday	00 30	6.8	13 02	7.3	10 21	9.3	22 44	9.3	11 38	3.4	—	—	01 36	5.3	13 49	5.5
18	Tuesday	01 19	7.1	13 48	7.4	11 02	9.4	23 22	9.3	00 24	3.2	12 21	3.4	02 15	5.4	14 30	5.6
19	Wednesday	02 02	7.1	14 28	7.3	11 40	9.4	23 58	9.3	01 02	3.3	13 01	3.4	02 51	5.4	15 09	5.6
20	Thursday	02 41	7.1	15 04	7.1	—	—	12 16	9.3	01 35	3.3	13 38	3.4	03 27	5.4	15 48	5.5
21	Friday	03 17	7.0	15 35	6.9	00 31	9.2	12 50	9.1	02 06	3.3	14 13	3.4	04 02	5.3	16 26	5.3
22	Saturday	03 49	6.8	16 03	6.8	01 05	9.0	13 23	8.8	02 36	3.3	14 48	3.4	04 37	5.1	17 04	5.1
23	Sunday	04 21	6.7	16 34	6.7	01 38	8.8	13 57	8.5	03 07	3.3	15 23	3.3	05 12	5.0	17 44	4.9
24	Monday	04 55	6.6	17 09	6.6	02 13	8.4	14 34	8.1	03 41	3.3	16 01	3.2	05 50	4.8	18 27	4.6
25	Tuesday	05 34	6.4	17 48	6.4	02 52	8.0	15 17	7.6	04 17	3.1	16 43	3.0	06 33	4.6	19 17	4.4
26	Wednesday	06 19	6.1	18 34	6.0	03 38	7.6	16 10	7.1	05 01	2.9	17 33	2.8	07 24	4.4	20 13	4.2
27	Thursday	07 11	5.8	19 28	5.7	04 40	7.2	17 23	6.8	05 56	2.7	18 33	2.7	08 26	4.2	21 17	4.2
28	Friday	08 15	5.6	20 37	5.6	06 04	7.1	18 52	7.0	07 03	2.6	19 40	2.6	09 35	4.2	22 24	4.3
29	Saturday	09 35	5.7	22 00	5.7	07 23	7.4	20 00	7.4	08 22	2.7	20 58	2.7	10 45	4.3	23 30	4.5
30	Sunday	10 51	6.0	23 08	6.0	08 22	7.9	20 51	8.0	09 38	2.8	22 08	2.8	11 47	4.6	—	—

MAY 2000 *High water* GMT

		London Bridge *Datum of predictions 3.20 m below				Liverpool *Datum of predictions 4.93 m below				Greenock *Datum of predictions 1.62 m below				Leith *Datum of predictions 2.90 m below			
		hr	ht m	hr	ht m	hr	ht m	hr	ht m	hr	ht m	hr	ht m	hr	ht m	hr	ht m
1	Monday	11 48	6.4	—	—	09 09	8.4	21 34	8.5	10 29	3.0	22 57	3.0	00 24	4.8	12 38	4.9
2	Tuesday	00 03	6.4	12 38	6.8	09 52	8.9	22 14	9.0	11 12	3.1	23 38	3.1	01 09	5.1	13 20	5.2
3	Wednesday	00 51	6.7	13 22	7.0	10 33	9.3	22 55	9.3	11 53	3.3	—	—	01 49	5.4	14 00	5.5
4	Thursday	01 36	6.9	14 05	7.2	11 15	9.6	23 35	9.5	00 17	3.2	12 37	3.3	02 28	5.6	14 39	5.7
5	Friday	02 19	7.1	14 47	7.2	11 58	9.7	——		00 56	3.3	13 20	3.4	03 07	5.7	15 21	5.8
6	Saturday	03 02	7.3	15 29	7.2	00 18	9.6	12 43	9.7	01 34	3.4	14 04	3.4	03 48	5.7	16 05	5.8
7	Sunday	03 46	7.3	16 12	7.1	01 02	9.5	13 29	9.5	02 13	3.5	14 48	3.4	04 31	5.6	16 52	5.7
8	Monday	04 32	7.2	16 55	6.9	01 48	9.3	14 18	9.1	02 52	3.5	15 34	3.3	05 17	5.4	17 44	5.4
9	Tuesday	05 20	7.0	17 41	6.6	02 37	8.9	15 11	8.6	03 34	3.5	16 25	3.1	06 08	5.2	18 41	5.1
10	Wednesday	06 13	6.7	18 34	6.2	03 34	8.4	16 15	8.1	04 21	3.3	17 28	2.9	07 08	4.9	19 50	4.9
11	Thursday	07 17	6.3	19 44	5.9	04 44	8.0	17 30	7.7	05 18	3.1	18 52	2.8	08 23	4.7	21 08	4.7
12	Friday	08 37	6.2	21 05	5.9	06 02	7.8	18 46	7.7	06 34	3.0	20 26	2.8	09 39	4.7	22 22	4.7
13	Saturday	09 49	6.3	22 12	6.2	07 14	8.0	19 52	8.0	08 16	3.0	21 35	2.9	10 49	4.8	23 31	4.8
14	Sunday	10 50	6.6	23 10	6.5	08 17	8.3	20 48	8.4	09 31	3.1	22 29	3.0	11 50	5.0	—	—
15	Monday	11 46	6.9			09 10	8.7	21 36	8.7	10 26	3.2	23 15	3.1	00 28	5.0	12 43	5.2
16	Tuesday	00 04	6.8	12 37	7.1	09 56	8.9	22 18	9.0	11 13	3.3	23 56	3.2	01 14	5.1	13 29	5.3
17	Wednesday	00 53	6.9	13 22	7.2	10 38	9.0	22 56	9.0	11 56	3.3	—	—	01 53	5.2	14 10	5.3
18	Thursday	01 38	7.0	14 03	7.1	11 16	9.0	23 31	9.0	00 34	3.2	12 36	3.3	02 29	5.2	14 49	5.3
19	Friday	02 19	6.9	14 38	6.9	11 52	8.9	—		01 08	3.2	13 13	3.2	03 04	5.3	15 27	5.3
20	Saturday	02 55	6.8	15 08	6.8	00 04	9.0	12 25	8.8	01 40	3.3	13 48	3.2	03 37	5.2	16 04	5.2
21	Sunday	03 28	6.7	15 37	6.7	00 38	8.9	12 58	8.6	02 10	3.3	14 23	3.2	04 10	5.1	16 41	5.0
22	Monday	04 00	6.6	16 08	6.6	01 12	8.7	13 33	8.4	02 42	3.3	15 00	3.1	04 45	5.0	17 20	4.9
23	Tuesday	04 35	6.5	16 44	6.6	01 48	8.5	14 11	8.2	03 15	3.3	15 39	3.0	05 22	4.9	18 01	4.7
24	Wednesday	05 14	6.4	17 23	6.4	02 27	8.2	14 52	7.8	03 50	3.2	16 22	2.9	06 04	4.7	18 46	4.5
25	Thursday	05 58	6.2	18 08	6.2	03 11	7.9	15 40	7.5	04 31	3.0	17 12	2.8	06 50	4.5	19 37	4.4
26	Friday	06 47	6.0	18 59	6.0	04 05	7.6	16 39	7.2	05 21	2.9	18 08	2.7	07 44	4.4	20 34	4.3
27	Saturday	07 45	5.9	20 00	5.8	05 10	7.4	17 50	7.2	06 23	2.7	19 07	2.7	08 47	4.4	21 36	4.4
28	Sunday	08 51	5.9	21 10	5.9	06 21	7.5	19 02	7.5	07 31	2.7	20 10	2.7	09 53	4.4	22 39	4.6
29	Monday	10 00	6.1	22 18	6.1	07 27	7.9	20 02	8.0	08 42	2.8	21 17	2.8	10 56	4.6	23 38	4.8
30	Tuesday	11 03	6.4	23 19	6.4	08 24	8.4	20 54	8.5	09 44	3.0	22 16	2.9	11 53	4.9	—	—
31	Wednesday	——		12 00	6.7	09 15	8.9	21 41	9.0	10 37	3.1	23 06	3.1	00 30	5.1	12 43	5.2

JUNE 2000 *High water* GMT

		London Bridge				Liverpool				Greenock				Leith			
1	Thursday	00 15	6.7	12 51	7.0	10 03	9.3	22 26	9.3	11 25	3.2	23 51	3.2	01 17	5.4	13 30	5.5
2	Friday	01 07	7.0	13 40	7.2	10 51	9.5	23 12	9.6	—	—	12 13	3.3	02 00	5.6	14 16	5.7
3	Saturday	01 56	7.2	14 26	7.2	11 39	9.7	23 59	9.7	00 34	3.4	13 03	3.4	02 44	5.7	15 03	5.8
4	Sunday	02 45	7.4	15 12	7.3	——		12 28	9.6	01 17	3.5	13 52	3.4	03 28	5.7	15 51	5.8
5	Monday	03 34	7.4	15 58	7.2	00 47	9.6	13 18	9.5	02 00	3.6	14 42	3.3	04 14	5.7	16 41	5.7
6	Tuesday	04 23	7.4	16 44	7.0	01 37	9.4	14 10	9.2	02 42	3.6	15 33	3.3	05 03	5.5	17 35	5.5
7	Wednesday	05 13	7.2	17 32	6.8	02 29	9.2	15 03	8.8	03 27	3.6	16 28	3.1	05 57	5.3	18 33	5.3
8	Thursday	06 07	6.9	18 24	6.5	03 25	8.8	16 01	8.4	04 15	3.4	17 30	3.0	06 58	5.1	19 38	5.0
9	Friday	07 07	6.6	19 27	6.2	04 26	8.4	17 05	8.0	05 11	3.3	18 37	2.9	08 07	4.9	20 46	4.8
10	Saturday	08 14	6.4	20 36	6.1	05 33	8.1	18 13	7.8	06 16	3.1	19 49	2.9	09 15	4.9	21 53	4.7
11	Sunday	09 20	6.4	21 40	6.2	06 41	8.0	19 18	7.9	07 34	3.0	20 57	2.9	10 19	4.8	22 57	4.7
12	Monday	10 19	6.5	22 39	6.4	07 44	8.1	20 16	8.1	08 53	3.0	21 55	3.0	11 21	4.9	23 57	4.8
13	Tuesday	11 15	6.7	23 34	6.6	08 40	8.3	21 07	8.4	09 55	3.1	22 44	3.0	—	—	12 17	5.0
14	Wednesday	——		12 07	6.8	09 30	8.5	21 51	8.6	10 47	3.1	23 28	3.1	00 47	4.9	13 07	5.0
15	Thursday	00 26	6.7	12 54	6.9	10 14	8.6	22 31	8.8	11 32	3.1	—	—	01 31	5.0	13 51	5.1
16	Friday	01 14	6.8	13 37	6.9	10 54	8.6	23 07	8.9	00 08	3.2	12 13	3.1	02 09	5.1	14 32	5.1
17	Saturday	01 57	6.8	14 14	6.8	11 30	8.6	23 42	8.9	00 45	3.2	12 51	3.0	02 44	5.1	15 09	5.1
18	Sunday	02 36	6.7	14 46	6.7	——		12 04	8.6	01 18	3.3	13 27	3.0	03 17	5.2	15 45	5.1
19	Monday	03 11	6.6	15 17	6.6	00 16	8.8	12 39	8.5	01 50	3.3	14 02	3.0	03 49	5.1	16 21	5.0
20	Tuesday	03 44	6.5	15 49	6.5	00 51	8.8	13 14	8.4	02 20	3.3	14 39	3.0	04 24	5.1	16 57	5.0
21	Wednesday	04 18	6.5	16 24	6.5	01 28	8.6	13 51	8.3	02 53	3.3	15 19	3.0	05 00	5.0	17 36	4.9
22	Thursday	04 56	6.4	17 02	6.4	02 06	8.5	14 30	8.1	03 28	3.2	16 02	2.9	05 39	4.9	18 17	4.7
23	Friday	05 38	6.4	17 44	6.3	02 48	8.3	15 13	7.9	04 07	3.1	16 48	2.9	06 21	4.8	19 03	4.6
24	Saturday	06 24	6.3	18 32	6.1	03 34	8.1	16 03	7.7	04 51	3.0	17 37	2.8	07 07	4.7	19 53	4.5
25	Sunday	07 16	6.2	19 26	6.1	04 29	7.9	17 02	7.6	05 43	2.9	18 30	2.8	08 00	4.6	20 51	4.5
26	Monday	08 15	6.1	20 29	6.1	05 31	7.9	18 08	7.6	06 44	2.8	19 25	2.8	09 01	4.6	21 53	4.6
27	Tuesday	09 19	6.2	21 35	6.2	06 36	8.0	19 14	7.9	07 53	2.8	20 29	2.8	10 07	4.7	22 55	4.8
28	Wednesday	10 24	6.3	22 40	6.3	07 40	8.3	20 16	8.4	09 05	2.9	21 37	2.9	11 11	4.9	23 54	5.0
29	Thursday	11 26	6.6	23 43	6.6	08 41	8.7	21 11	8.9	10 08	3.1	22 37	3.1	——		12 11	5.1
30	Friday	——		12 24	6.8	09 38	9.1	22 04	9.3	11 04	3.2	23 29	3.2	00 48	5.3	13 07	5.4

JULY 2000 *High water* GMT

		London Bridge				Liverpool				Greenock				Leith			
		*Datum of predictions 3.20 m below				*Datum of predictions 4.93 m below				*Datum of predictions 1.62 m below				*Datum of predictions 2.90 m below			
		hr	ht m	hr	ht m	hr	ht m	hr	ht m	hr	ht m	hr	ht m	hr	ht m	hr	ht m
1	Saturday	00 42	6.9	13 17	7.0	10 32	9.4	22 54	9.6	11 57	3.3	—	—	01 38	5.5	13 59	5.6
2	Sunday	01 38	7.2	14 08	7.2	11 24	9.6	23 44	9.7	00 18	3.4	12 51	3.3	02 25	5.7	14 49	5.8
3	Monday	02 30	7.4	14 56	7.3	—	—	12 16	9.6	01 04	3.5	13 45	3.3	03 12	5.8	15 39	5.9
4	Tuesday	03 22	7.5	15 44	7.3	00 34	9.8	13 07	9.6	01 50	3.6	14 38	3.3	04 00	5.8	16 30	5.8
5	Wednesday	04 12	7.5	16 31	7.2	01 25	9.7	13 57	9.4	02 34	3.7	15 29	3.3	04 50	5.7	17 22	5.6
6	Thursday	05 01	7.4	17 17	7.0	02 15	9.5	14 46	9.1	03 19	3.7	16 20	3.2	05 42	5.6	18 16	5.4
7	Friday	05 51	7.1	18 04	6.8	03 05	9.1	15 37	8.6	04 05	3.6	17 11	3.1	06 39	5.3	19 13	5.1
8	Saturday	06 43	6.8	18 56	6.5	03 58	8.7	16 31	8.2	04 53	3.5	18 03	3.0	07 40	5.1	20 13	4.8
9	Sunday	07 40	6.5	19 55	6.3	04 55	8.2	17 31	7.8	05 47	3.3	18 57	2.9	08 42	4.9	21 14	4.6
10	Monday	08 42	6.3	21 00	6.1	05 59	7.9	18 37	7.6	06 45	3.1	20 00	2.9	09 43	4.8	22 15	4.5
11	Tuesday	09 42	6.2	22 03	6.1	07 06	7.7	19 41	7.7	07 56	3.0	21 11	2.9	10 45	4.7	23 17	4.5
12	Wednesday	10 40	6.2	23 03	6.2	08 09	7.8	20 37	8.0	09 18	2.9	22 12	2.9	11 48	4.7	—	—
13	Thursday	11 34	6.4	23 59	6.4	09 04	8.0	21 26	8.3	10 23	2.9	23 02	3.1	00 17	4.7	12 45	4.8
14	Friday	—	—	12 25	6.6	09 52	8.2	22 09	8.6	11 13	3.0	23 45	3.2	01 08	4.8	13 34	4.9
15	Saturday	00 50	6.6	13 11	6.7	10 34	8.4	22 48	8.8	11 56	3.0	—	—	01 50	5.0	14 16	5.0
16	Sunday	01 37	6.7	13 52	6.8	11 12	8.5	23 24	8.9	00 25	3.2	12 35	2.9	02 26	5.1	14 53	5.0
17	Monday	02 18	6.7	14 28	6.7	11 48	8.5	23 58	8.9	01 01	3.3	13 11	2.9	03 00	5.1	15 27	5.1
18	Tuesday	02 55	6.6	15 02	6.7	—	—	12 22	8.5	01 32	3.3	13 45	2.9	03 32	5.2	16 00	5.1
19	Wednesday	03 29	6.6	15 34	6.6	00 33	8.9	12 56	8.6	02 01	3.3	14 20	3.0	04 05	5.2	16 35	5.1
20	Thursday	04 02	6.5	16 07	6.5	01 09	8.8	13 31	8.5	02 33	3.3	14 58	3.0	04 39	5.2	17 11	5.0
21	Friday	04 37	6.5	16 42	6.5	01 45	8.8	14 08	8.5	03 07	3.3	15 38	3.0	05 15	5.1	17 49	5.0
22	Saturday	05 16	6.5	17 20	6.5	02 23	8.7	14 46	8.4	03 44	3.2	16 18	3.0	05 53	5.0	18 31	4.9
23	Sunday	05 58	6.5	18 03	6.4	03 05	8.5	15 30	8.2	04 23	3.1	17 01	2.9	06 34	4.9	19 16	4.7
24	Monday	06 45	6.4	18 52	6.3	03 54	8.3	16 22	7.9	05 08	3.0	17 48	2.9	07 20	4.8	20 09	4.7
25	Tuesday	07 39	6.2	19 50	6.2	04 51	8.1	17 25	7.8	06 00	2.9	18 39	2.8	08 16	4.7	21 10	4.6
26	Wednesday	08 41	6.1	20 57	6.1	05 56	8.0	18 34	7.8	07 06	2.8	19 41	2.8	09 24	4.7	22 18	4.7
27	Thursday	09 49	6.1	22 08	6.2	07 06	8.1	19 45	8.1	08 29	2.8	21 00	2.9	10 39	4.8	23 25	4.9
28	Friday	10 58	6.3	23 19	6.4	08 17	8.4	20 50	8.6	09 49	3.0	22 15	3.0	11 49	5.0	—	—
29	Saturday	—	—	12 02	6.6	09 21	8.8	21 48	9.1	10 53	3.1	23 13	3.2	00 26	5.1	12 52	5.3
30	Sunday	00 25	6.8	12 59	6.9	10 19	9.2	22 41	9.6	11 50	3.2	—	—	01 21	5.4	13 47	5.6
31	Monday	01 24	7.1	13 52	7.1	11 13	9.5	23 31	9.8	00 04	3.4	12 45	3.3	02 10	5.7	14 37	5.8

AUGUST 2000 *High water* GMT

		London Bridge				Liverpool				Greenock				Leith			
		hr	ht m	hr	ht m	hr	ht m	hr	ht m	hr	ht m	hr	ht m	hr	ht m	hr	ht m
1	Tuesday	02 17	7.4	14 41	7.3	—	—	12 03	9.7	00 52	3.6	13 38	3.3	02 57	5.8	15 26	5.9
2	Wednesday	03 08	7.6	15 27	7.3	00 20	9.9	12 52	9.7	01 38	3.7	14 28	3.4	03 44	5.9	16 14	5.8
3	Thursday	03 56	7.6	16 12	7.3	01 07	9.9	13 38	9.5	02 22	3.8	15 14	3.3	04 32	5.9	17 02	5.7
4	Friday	04 42	7.5	16 54	7.2	01 53	9.7	14 22	9.2	03 05	3.8	15 57	3.3	05 21	5.7	17 51	5.4
5	Saturday	05 26	7.2	17 36	7.0	02 37	9.3	15 05	8.8	03 46	3.7	16 38	3.2	06 12	5.5	18 41	5.1
6	Sunday	06 10	6.8	18 17	6.7	03 22	8.8	15 49	8.3	04 28	3.6	17 19	3.1	07 05	5.2	19 33	4.8
7	Monday	06 55	6.4	19 03	6.3	04 10	8.2	16 39	7.8	05 12	3.4	18 03	3.0	08 03	4.9	20 29	4.5
8	Tuesday	07 47	6.1	20 03	6.0	05 07	7.6	17 43	7.4	06 00	3.1	18 53	2.9	09 03	4.6	21 27	4.4
9	Wednesday	08 51	5.8	21 18	5.7	06 18	7.3	18 58	7.3	06 55	2.9	19 58	2.8	10 06	4.5	22 31	4.4
10	Thursday	09 58	5.8	22 30	5.8	07 36	7.3	20 07	7.6	08 08	2.7	21 35	2.9	11 14	4.4	23 40	4.5
11	Friday	11 00	5.9	23 32	6.1	08 40	7.5	21 02	8.0	10 02	2.8	22 37	3.0	—	—	12 22	4.5
12	Saturday	11 55	6.2	—	—	09 31	7.9	21 48	8.4	10 59	2.9	23 24	3.2	00 42	4.7	13 15	4.7
13	Sunday	00 27	6.4	12 45	6.5	10 15	8.2	22 29	8.7	11 43	2.9	—	—	01 29	4.9	13 58	4.9
14	Monday	01 15	6.6	13 30	6.7	10 54	8.5	23 06	8.9	00 05	3.2	12 22	3.0	02 07	5.1	14 33	5.1
15	Tuesday	01 57	6.8	14 09	6.8	11 29	8.6	23 40	9.0	00 41	3.3	12 56	3.0	02 40	5.2	15 05	5.2
16	Wednesday	02 35	6.8	14 45	6.7	—	—	12 03	8.7	01 12	3.3	13 27	3.0	03 12	5.3	15 37	5.3
17	Thursday	03 09	6.7	15 18	6.7	00 14	9.0	12 36	8.7	01 40	3.3	13 59	3.0	03 43	5.4	16 10	5.3
18	Friday	03 42	6.7	15 48	6.6	00 47	9.1	13 09	8.8	02 10	3.3	14 33	3.1	04 15	5.4	16 45	5.3
19	Saturday	04 15	6.7	16 19	6.6	01 22	9.1	13 43	8.8	02 44	3.3	15 09	3.1	04 49	5.4	17 21	5.2
20	Sunday	04 51	6.7	16 55	6.7	01 58	9.0	14 19	8.7	03 20	3.3	15 46	3.1	05 26	5.3	18 01	5.1
21	Monday	05 30	6.6	17 36	6.6	02 37	8.8	15 00	8.5	03 57	3.3	16 24	3.0	06 06	5.2	18 44	4.9
22	Tuesday	06 13	6.4	18 23	6.5	03 23	8.5	15 49	8.1	04 37	3.2	17 06	3.0	06 52	5.0	19 34	4.8
23	Wednesday	07 03	6.2	19 18	6.2	04 18	8.2	16 50	7.8	05 24	3.0	17 55	2.9	07 46	4.8	20 35	4.6
24	Thursday	08 04	5.9	20 25	6.0	05 27	7.8	18 05	7.7	06 26	2.8	18 56	2.8	08 56	4.7	21 49	4.6
25	Friday	09 18	5.8	21 44	6.0	06 45	7.8	19 25	7.9	08 02	2.7	20 27	2.8	10 19	4.7	23 04	4.8
26	Saturday	10 37	6.0	23 05	6.2	08 05	8.1	20 39	8.4	09 43	2.9	22 00	3.0	11 37	4.9	—	—
27	Sunday	11 45	6.4	—	—	09 14	8.6	21 39	9.1	10 51	3.1	23 00	3.3	00 11	5.1	12 44	5.3
28	Monday	00 14	6.7	12 44	6.8	10 10	9.1	22 30	9.6	11 46	3.3	23 51	3.5	01 08	5.4	13 37	5.6
29	Tuesday	01 12	7.1	13 35	7.1	11 00	9.5	23 17	9.9	—	—	12 37	3.3	01 56	5.7	14 25	5.8
30	Wednesday	02 03	7.5	14 23	7.3	11 47	9.7	—	—	00 38	3.6	13 25	3.4	02 41	5.9	15 09	5.9
31	Thursday	02 51	7.6	15 07	7.4	00 02	10.0	12 31	9.7	01 23	3.7	14 10	3.4	03 25	6.0	15 53	5.8

SEPTEMBER 2000   *High water*   GMT

		LONDON BRIDGE				LIVERPOOL				GREENOCK				LEITH			
		*Datum of predictions 3.20 m below				*Datum of predictions 4.93 m below				*Datum of predictions 1.62 m below				*Datum of predictions 2.90 m below			
		hr m	ht m	hr m	ht m	hr m	ht m	hr m	ht m	hr m	ht m	hr m	ht m	hr m	ht m	hr m	ht m
1	Friday	03 35	7.6	15 48	7.3	00 45	9.9	13 12	9.5	02 04	3.8	14 49	3.4	04 10	5.9	16 37	5.6
2	Saturday	04 17	7.4	16 27	7.2	01 26	9.7	13 51	9.2	02 44	3.8	15 25	3.4	04 55	5.8	17 20	5.4
3	Sunday	04 55	7.1	17 03	7.0	02 06	9.3	14 29	8.8	03 22	3.8	16 00	3.4	05 41	5.5	18 05	5.1
4	Monday	05 31	6.8	17 39	6.7	02 45	8.7	15 07	8.3	03 59	3.6	16 36	3.3	06 30	5.1	18 51	4.8
5	Tuesday	06 05	6.4	18 17	6.4	03 25	8.1	15 49	7.8	04 38	3.4	17 16	3.2	07 22	4.8	19 41	4.5
6	Wednesday	06 43	6.1	19 04	5.9	04 14	7.5	16 44	7.3	05 21	3.1	18 02	3.0	08 20	4.5	20 39	4.4
7	Thursday	07 32	5.7	20 09	5.5	05 23	7.0	18 06	7.0	06 11	2.9	18 58	2.9	09 24	4.3	21 44	4.3
8	Friday	08 48	5.5	21 51	5.5	06 58	6.9	19 34	7.3	07 15	2.7	20 26	2.8	10 36	4.2	22 56	4.3
9	Saturday	10 20	5.6	23 03	5.8	08 14	7.2	20 36	7.8	09 38	2.7	22 09	3.0	11 53	4.4		
10	Sunday	11 24	6.0	——	——	09 08	7.7	21 24	8.3	10 41	2.9	22 59	3.2	00 09	4.6	12 51	4.7
11	Monday	00 00	6.2	12 17	6.4	09 52	8.2	22 05	8.7	11 23	3.0	23 39	3.3	01 02	4.8	13 33	4.9
12	Tuesday	00 49	6.6	13 04	6.6	10 30	8.5	22 42	9.0			12 00	3.1	01 41	5.1	14 07	5.1
13	Wednesday	01 32	6.8	13 45	6.8	11 05	8.7	23 16	9.1	00 15	3.3	12 33	3.1	02 14	5.3	14 39	5.3
14	Thursday	02 10	6.9	14 21	6.8	11 38	8.9	23 49	9.2	00 45	3.3	13 03	3.1	02 46	5.4	15 10	5.4
15	Friday	02 44	6.9	14 54	6.8	——	——	12 10	9.0	01 14	3.4	13 32	3.2	03 17	5.5	15 43	5.5
16	Saturday	03 17	6.9	15 25	6.8	00 22	9.3	12 43	9.0	01 46	3.4	14 05	3.3	03 49	5.6	16 17	5.5
17	Sunday	03 50	6.9	15 56	6.8	00 57	9.3	13 17	9.0	02 21	3.4	14 39	3.3	04 24	5.6	16 54	5.4
18	Monday	04 25	6.8	16 32	6.8	01 34	9.2	13 54	8.9	02 57	3.4	15 14	3.3	05 01	5.5	17 33	5.3
19	Tuesday	05 03	6.7	17 13	6.8	02 14	9.0	14 35	8.6	03 34	3.4	15 51	3.3	05 44	5.3	18 17	5.1
20	Wednesday	05 45	6.5	18 00	6.5	02 59	8.6	15 23	8.2	04 13	3.2	16 32	3.2	06 32	5.1	19 07	4.9
21	Thursday	06 32	6.1	18 54	6.2	03 56	8.0	16 25	7.8	04 59	3.0	17 21	3.1	07 29	4.9	20 10	4.7
22	Friday	07 31	5.7	20 04	5.8	05 09	7.6	17 46	7.5	06 02	2.8	18 24	2.9	08 43	4.7	21 30	4.6
23	Saturday	08 54	5.6	21 35	5.6	06 37	7.5	19 16	7.8	07 59	2.7	20 06	2.9	10 11	4.7	22 50	4.8
24	Sunday	10 23	5.8	22 58	6.2	08 02	8.0	20 31	8.4	09 46	2.9	21 46	3.1	11 31	5.0	23 58	5.1
25	Monday	11 31	6.3	——	——	09 06	8.6	21 27	9.1	10 47	3.2	22 45	3.4	——	——	12 34	5.3
26	Tuesday	00 02	6.8	12 27	6.8	09 57	9.2	22 15	9.6	11 36	3.3	23 34	3.6	00 53	5.4	13 25	5.6
27	Wednesday	00 57	7.2	13 16	7.1	10 43	9.5	22 59	9.9	——	——	12 22	3.4	01 39	5.7	14 08	5.7
28	Thursday	01 45	7.5	14 02	7.3	11 25	9.7	23 40	9.9	00 19	3.7	13 05	3.5	02 22	5.9	14 49	5.8
29	Friday	02 30	7.5	14 43	7.3	——	——	12 05	9.6	01 02	3.8	13 44	3.5	03 04	6.0	15 29	5.7
30	Saturday	03 11	7.4	15 22	7.3	00 20	9.8	12 43	9.5	01 42	3.8	14 18	3.5	03 46	5.9	16 09	5.6

OCTOBER 2000   *High water*   GMT

		LONDON BRIDGE				LIVERPOOL				GREENOCK				LEITH			
		hr m	ht m	hr m	ht m	hr m	ht m	hr m	ht m	hr m	ht m	hr m	ht m	hr m	ht m	hr m	ht m
1	Sunday	03 48	7.2	15 58	7.1	00 57	9.5	13 19	9.2	02 19	3.8	14 50	3.5	04 29	5.7	16 49	5.4
2	Monday	04 21	7.0	16 32	7.0	01 33	9.1	13 53	8.8	02 55	3.7	15 23	3.5	05 12	5.4	17 29	5.1
3	Tuesday	04 51	6.8	17 06	6.7	02 09	8.6	14 28	8.4	03 31	3.6	15 58	3.4	05 57	5.1	18 10	4.9
4	Wednesday	05 22	6.5	17 43	6.4	02 47	8.1	15 08	7.9	04 08	3.4	16 36	3.3	06 45	4.7	18 57	4.6
5	Thursday	05 59	6.2	18 27	6.0	03 31	7.5	15 56	7.4	04 49	3.2	17 21	3.1	07 40	4.4	19 53	4.4
6	Friday	06 41	5.9	19 20	5.6	04 31	6.9	17 07	7.0	05 39	2.9	18 16	3.0	08 42	4.2	20 58	4.3
7	Saturday	07 38	5.5	20 40	5.3	06 08	6.7	18 50	7.1	06 42	2.7	19 25	2.9	09 51	4.2	22 09	4.3
8	Sunday	09 18	5.4	22 24	5.6	07 39	7.0	20 02	7.5	08 07	2.7	21 21	2.9	11 07	4.3	23 23	4.5
9	Monday	10 45	5.7	23 25	6.0	08 36	7.6	20 53	8.1	10 07	2.9	22 23	3.1	——	——	12 12	4.6
10	Tuesday	11 42	6.1	——	——	09 21	8.1	21 34	8.6	10 52	3.1	23 05	3.3	00 22	4.8	12 57	4.9
11	Wednesday	00 15	6.4	12 30	6.5	09 59	8.6	22 11	9.0	11 29	3.2	23 39	3.4	01 05	5.0	13 33	5.2
12	Thursday	00 59	6.7	13 13	6.7	10 33	8.9	22 46	9.2	——	——	12 02	3.3	01 41	5.3	14 07	5.4
13	Friday	01 38	6.9	13 51	6.8	11 07	9.1	23 20	9.4	00 11	3.4	12 33	3.3	02 14	5.5	14 40	5.6
14	Saturday	02 14	7.0	14 26	6.9	11 41	9.2	23 56	9.5	00 45	3.4	13 04	3.4	02 47	5.6	15 14	5.6
15	Sunday	02 50	7.0	15 00	7.0	——	——	12 16	9.3	01 21	3.5	13 37	3.5	03 22	5.7	15 50	5.7
16	Monday	03 25	7.0	15 36	7.0	00 33	9.5	12 54	9.3	01 59	3.5	14 13	3.5	04 00	5.7	16 28	5.6
17	Tuesday	04 02	6.9	16 16	7.0	01 13	9.3	13 33	9.1	02 37	3.5	14 49	3.6	04 42	5.6	17 09	5.4
18	Wednesday	04 41	6.8	16 59	6.9	01 56	9.0	14 17	8.8	03 16	3.4	15 27	3.5	05 27	5.4	17 55	5.2
19	Thursday	05 23	6.5	17 47	6.6	02 45	8.6	15 08	8.3	03 58	3.3	16 09	3.4	06 19	5.2	18 47	4.9
20	Friday	06 10	6.1	18 44	6.2	03 44	8.0	16 12	7.9	04 48	3.1	16 59	3.3	07 19	4.9	19 54	4.7
21	Saturday	07 09	5.7	19 58	5.9	05 01	7.6	17 36	7.6	06 00	2.8	18 06	3.1	08 38	4.7	21 18	4.7
22	Sunday	08 43	5.6	21 30	5.9	06 32	7.6	19 04	7.9	08 08	2.8	19 53	3.1	10 04	4.8	22 36	4.9
23	Monday	10 07	5.9	22 43	6.4	07 49	8.0	20 14	8.4	09 36	3.0	21 26	3.2	11 19	5.0	23 41	5.2
24	Tuesday	11 10	6.4	23 43	6.9	08 48	8.6	21 09	9.0	10 31	3.3	22 24	3.5	——	——	12 20	5.3
25	Wednesday	——	——	12 04	6.8	09 38	9.1	21 56	9.4	11 18	3.4	23 13	3.6	00 35	5.4	13 09	5.5
26	Thursday	00 35	7.2	12 54	7.1	10 22	9.4	22 38	9.6	12 00	3.5	23 57	3.7	01 21	5.7	13 50	5.6
27	Friday	01 23	7.4	13 38	7.3	11 02	9.5	23 18	9.6	——	——	12 39	3.6	02 03	5.8	14 28	5.6
28	Saturday	02 06	7.4	14 20	7.2	11 39	9.5	23 55	9.5	00 39	3.7	13 15	3.6	02 43	5.8	15 05	5.6
29	Sunday	02 45	7.3	14 58	7.1	——	——	12 14	9.3	01 18	3.7	13 48	3.6	03 24	5.7	15 43	5.5
30	Monday	03 19	7.0	15 33	7.0	00 30	9.3	12 48	9.1	01 54	3.7	14 20	3.6	04 06	5.5	16 19	5.4
31	Tuesday	03 48	6.8	16 06	6.8	01 04	8.9	13 22	8.9	02 30	3.6	14 53	3.6	04 46	5.3	16 56	5.2

NOVEMBER 2000 *High water* GMT

		London Bridge				Liverpool				Greenock				Leith			
		*Datum of predictions 3.20 m below				*Datum of predictions 4.93 m below				*Datum of predictions 1.62 m below				*Datum of predictions 2.90 m below			
		hr	ht m	hr	ht m	hr	ht m	hr	ht m	hr	ht m	hr	ht m	hr	ht m	hr	ht m
1	Wednesday	04 16	6.7	16 40	6.6	01 39	8.6	13 57	8.6	03 05	3.5	15 27	3.6	05 28	5.0	17 34	5.0
2	Thursday	04 48	6.6	17 17	6.4	02 16	8.1	14 36	8.2	03 43	3.4	16 04	3.5	06 13	4.7	18 18	4.7
3	Friday	05 25	6.3	17 59	6.1	02 59	7.6	15 21	7.7	04 24	3.2	16 46	3.3	07 03	4.5	19 10	4.5
4	Saturday	06 07	6.0	18 49	5.8	03 52	7.1	16 20	7.3	05 14	3.0	17 38	3.1	08 00	4.3	20 12	4.4
5	Sunday	06 58	5.7	19 50	5.5	05 04	6.8	17 42	7.1	06 15	2.9	18 41	3.0	09 03	4.2	21 20	4.3
6	Monday	08 06	5.5	21 14	5.5	06 42	6.9	19 08	7.4	07 26	2.8	19 58	3.0	10 09	4.3	22 28	4.5
7	Tuesday	09 43	5.6	22 32	5.9	07 51	7.4	20 07	7.9	08 52	2.9	21 22	3.1	11 14	4.6	23 30	4.7
8	Wednesday	10 53	5.9	23 29	6.3	08 40	8.0	20 53	8.4	10 03	3.1	22 16	3.2	—		12 08	4.9
9	Thursday	11 46	6.3	—		09 20	8.5	21 34	8.9	10 48	3.2	22 58	3.3	00 20	5.0	12 53	5.2
10	Friday	00 17	6.6	12 33	6.6	09 58	8.9	22 12	9.2	11 26	3.3	23 37	3.4	01 03	5.2	13 32	5.4
11	Saturday	01 01	6.9	13 16	6.8	10 35	9.2	22 51	9.5	—		12 01	3.4	01 41	5.5	14 10	5.6
12	Sunday	01 43	7.0	13 57	7.0	11 13	9.4	23 32	9.6	00 17	3.5	12 37	3.5	02 19	5.7	14 47	5.7
13	Monday	02 23	7.1	14 38	7.1	11 53	9.5	—		00 58	3.5	13 14	3.6	02 59	5.8	15 26	5.7
14	Tuesday	03 03	7.1	15 21	7.2	00 14	9.6	12 35	9.5	01 41	3.6	13 52	3.7	03 41	5.8	16 06	5.7
15	Wednesday	03 44	7.0	16 05	7.2	00 59	9.5	13 20	9.3	02 23	3.5	14 31	3.8	04 27	5.7	16 50	5.5
16	Thursday	04 26	6.8	16 52	7.0	01 46	9.1	14 08	9.0	03 07	3.5	15 11	3.7	05 16	5.6	17 39	5.3
17	Friday	05 10	6.6	17 42	6.7	02 38	8.7	15 01	8.6	03 54	3.3	15 56	3.6	06 10	5.3	18 34	5.1
18	Saturday	05 58	6.2	18 40	6.4	03 39	8.2	16 05	8.2	04 52	3.1	16 49	3.4	07 13	5.0	19 43	4.9
19	Sunday	06 59	5.9	19 53	6.1	04 52	7.8	17 21	8.0	06 11	3.0	17 56	3.3	08 29	4.8	21 03	4.8
20	Monday	08 27	5.8	21 12	6.2	06 11	7.8	18 39	8.1	07 50	3.0	19 26	3.2	09 46	4.8	22 15	5.0
21	Tuesday	09 42	6.0	22 19	6.5	07 23	8.1	19 47	8.4	09 08	3.1	20 55	3.3	10 57	4.9	23 18	5.1
22	Wednesday	10 43	6.4	23 17	6.8	08 23	8.5	20 44	8.8	10 05	3.3	21 57	3.4	11 57	5.1	—	
23	Thursday	11 38	6.7	—		09 14	8.9	21 33	9.1	10 52	3.4	22 49	3.5	00 13	5.3	12 48	5.2
24	Friday	00 09	7.0	12 29	7.0	09 58	9.1	22 17	9.2	11 34	3.5	23 34	3.6	01 02	5.5	13 30	5.4
25	Saturday	00 58	7.2	13 15	7.1	10 38	9.3	22 56	9.3	—		12 13	3.5	01 45	5.5	14 08	5.4
26	Sunday	01 41	7.2	13 58	7.2	11 15	9.3	23 32	9.2	00 16	3.5	12 49	3.6	02 27	5.5	14 45	5.4
27	Monday	02 19	7.0	14 37	7.0	11 49	9.2	—		00 56	3.5	13 23	3.6	03 07	5.5	15 20	5.4
28	Tuesday	02 52	6.9	15 13	6.8	00 06	9.0	12 23	9.1	01 32	3.5	13 55	3.6	03 47	5.3	15 55	5.3
29	Wednesday	03 20	6.7	15 46	6.7	00 41	8.8	12 57	9.0	02 08	3.4	14 29	3.7	04 25	5.2	16 29	5.2
30	Thursday	03 49	6.6	16 19	6.5	01 16	8.6	13 33	8.7	02 44	3.4	15 03	3.6	05 04	5.0	17 06	5.1

DECEMBER 2000 *High water* GMT

		London Bridge				Liverpool				Greenock				Leith			
1	Friday	04 22	6.5	16 56	6.4	01 53	8.3	14 12	8.4	03 22	3.3	15 38	3.5	05 45	4.8	17 46	4.9
2	Saturday	04 59	6.4	17 37	6.2	02 34	7.9	14 55	8.1	04 04	3.2	16 18	3.4	06 30	4.6	18 33	4.7
3	Sunday	05 40	6.2	18 23	6.0	03 21	7.6	15 45	7.8	04 52	3.1	17 04	3.2	07 19	4.5	19 26	4.5
4	Monday	06 28	6.0	19 16	5.9	04 17	7.2	16 45	7.5	05 46	3.0	17 59	3.1	08 15	4.4	20 28	4.5
5	Tuesday	07 25	5.8	20 18	5.8	05 27	7.1	17 55	7.5	06 46	2.9	19 02	3.0	09 15	4.4	21 33	4.5
6	Wednesday	08 36	5.7	21 27	5.9	06 41	7.3	19 03	7.8	07 51	2.9	20 11	3.0	10 17	4.5	22 35	4.6
7	Thursday	09 50	5.9	22 34	6.2	07 44	7.8	20 02	8.2	08 59	3.0	21 20	3.1	11 16	4.8	23 32	4.9
8	Friday	10 54	6.2	23 32	6.5	08 36	8.3	20 53	8.7	10 00	3.1	22 17	3.2	—		12 10	5.0
9	Saturday	11 50	6.5	—		09 22	8.8	21 40	9.1	10 49	3.3	23 06	3.4	00 23	5.1	12 58	5.3
10	Sunday	00 25	6.8	12 43	6.8	10 06	9.2	22 26	9.5	11 32	3.4	23 53	3.5	01 11	5.4	13 41	5.5
11	Monday	01 14	7.0	13 32	7.1	10 50	9.5	23 12	9.7	—		12 14	3.6	01 56	5.6	14 23	5.7
12	Tuesday	02 00	7.1	14 20	7.2	11 35	9.7	—		00 40	3.5	12 56	3.7	02 41	5.8	15 06	5.7
13	Wednesday	02 45	7.1	15 08	7.4	00 00	9.7	12 22	9.7	01 28	3.5	13 38	3.8	03 27	5.9	15 50	5.8
14	Thursday	03 30	7.1	15 56	7.4	00 49	9.6	13 11	9.6	02 16	3.5	14 20	3.9	04 15	5.8	16 36	5.7
15	Friday	04 15	7.0	16 45	7.2	01 39	9.4	14 01	9.4	03 05	3.4	15 04	3.8	05 06	5.7	17 26	5.5
16	Saturday	05 01	6.8	17 36	7.0	02 32	9.0	14 54	9.1	03 56	3.3	15 50	3.8	06 00	5.4	18 22	5.3
17	Sunday	05 50	6.5	18 31	6.7	03 27	8.6	15 50	8.7	04 53	3.2	16 42	3.6	07 00	5.2	19 27	5.1
18	Monday	06 46	6.3	19 34	6.4	04 29	8.2	16 54	8.4	05 58	3.1	17 41	3.5	08 08	4.9	20 38	5.0
19	Tuesday	07 56	6.1	20 43	6.3	05 38	7.9	18 04	8.2	07 10	3.1	18 49	3.3	09 17	4.8	21 45	5.0
20	Wednesday	09 07	6.1	21 47	6.3	06 48	7.9	19 13	8.2	08 25	3.1	20 09	3.3	10 24	4.8	22 49	5.0
21	Thursday	10 10	6.2	22 45	6.5	07 52	8.1	20 15	8.3	09 29	3.2	21 24	3.3	11 27	4.8	23 49	5.0
22	Friday	11 08	6.4	23 40	6.6	08 47	8.4	21 10	8.6	10 22	3.3	22 24	3.3	—		12 23	4.9
23	Saturday	—		12 02	6.6	09 35	8.7	21 57	8.7	11 08	3.4	23 14	3.3	00 43	5.1	13 11	5.1
24	Sunday	00 30	6.8	12 53	6.8	10 17	8.9	22 38	8.8	11 49	3.5	23 58	3.3	01 31	5.2	13 52	5.2
25	Monday	01 16	6.8	13 38	6.8	10 55	9.1	23 15	8.9	—		12 28	3.5	02 14	5.2	14 29	5.2
26	Tuesday	01 56	6.8	14 20	6.8	11 30	9.1	23 50	8.8	00 39	3.3	13 04	3.6	02 54	5.2	15 04	5.3
27	Wednesday	02 31	6.7	14 57	6.7	—		12 05	9.1	01 16	3.3	13 38	3.6	03 32	5.2	15 37	5.3
28	Thursday	03 01	6.6	15 30	6.6	00 23	8.8	12 40	9.0	01 51	3.2	14 10	3.6	04 07	5.1	16 10	5.2
29	Friday	03 30	6.6	16 03	6.5	00 58	8.7	13 16	8.9	02 27	3.2	14 43	3.6	04 43	5.0	16 45	5.2
30	Saturday	04 02	6.5	16 38	6.5	01 35	8.5	13 53	8.8	03 04	3.2	15 17	3.5	05 20	4.9	17 22	5.0
31	Sunday	04 38	6.5	17 16	6.4	02 13	8.3	14 32	8.5	03 43	3.2	15 54	3.4	06 00	4.8	18 02	4.9

World Geographical Statistics

THE EARTH

The shape of the Earth is that of an oblate spheroid or solid of revolution whose meridian sections are ellipses, whilst the sections at right angles are circles.

DIMENSIONS

Equatorial diameter = 12,756.27 km (7,926.38 miles)
Polar diameter = 12,713.50 km (7,899.80 miles)
Equatorial circumference = 40,075.01 km (24,901.46 miles)
Polar circumference = 40,007.86 km (24,859.73 miles)

The equatorial circumference is divided into 360 degrees of longitude, which is measured in degrees, minutes and seconds east or west of the Greenwich meridian (0°) to 180°, the meridian 180° E. coinciding with 180° W. This was internationally ratified in 1884.

Distance north and south of the Equator is measured in degrees, minutes and seconds of latitude. The Equator is 0°, the North Pole is 90° N. and the South Pole is 90° S. The Tropics lie at 23° 26′ N. (Tropic of Cancer) and 23° 26′ S. (Tropic of Capricorn). The Arctic Circle lies at 66° 34′ N. and the Antarctic Circle at 66° 34′ S. (NB The Tropics and the Arctic and Antarctic circles are affected by the slow decrease in obliquity of the ecliptic, of about 0.47 arcseconds per year. The effect of this is that the Arctic and Antarctic circles are currently moving towards their respective poles by about 14 metres per century, while the Tropics move towards the Equator by the same amount.

AREA, ETC.

The surface area of the Earth is 510,069,120 km² (196,938,800 miles²), of which the water area is 70.92 per cent and the land area is 29.08 per cent.

The velocity of a given point on the Earth's surface at the Equator is 1,669.79 km per hour (1,037.56 m.p.h.). The Earth's mean velocity in its orbit around the Sun is 107,229 km per hour (66,629 m.p.h.). The Earth's mean distance from the Sun is 149,597,870 km (92,955,807 miles).

OCEANS

AREA

	km²	miles²
Pacific	166,240,000	64,186,300
Atlantic	86,550,000	33,420,000
Indian	73,427,000	28,350,500
Arctic	9,485,000	3,662,000

The division by the Equator of the Pacific into the North and South Pacific and the Atlantic into the North and South Atlantic makes a total of six oceans.

GREATEST DEPTHS

Greatest depth location	metres	feet
Mariana Trench, Pacific	10,920	35,827
Puerto Rico Trench, Atlantic	8,605	28,232
Java (Sunda) Trench, Indian	7,125	23,376
Molloy Deep, Arctic	5,680	18,399

SEAS

AREA

	km²	miles²
South China	2,974,600	1,148,500
Caribbean	2,515,900	971,400
Mediterranean	2,509,900	969,100
Bering	2,261,000	873,000
Gulf of Mexico	1,507,600	582,100
Okhotsk	1,392,000	537,500
Japan	1,012,900	391,100
Hudson Bay	730,100	281,900
East China	664,600	256,600
Andaman	564,880	218,100
Black Sea	507,900	196,100
Red Sea	453,000	174,900
North Sea	427,100	164,900
Baltic Sea	382,000	147,500
Yellow Sea	294,000	113,500
Persian/Arabian Gulf	230,000	88,800

GREATEST DEPTHS

	Maximum depth metres	feet
Caribbean	8,605	28,232
East China (Ryu Kyu Trench)	7,507	24,629
South China	7,258	23,812
Mediterranean (Ionian Basin)	5,150	16,896
Andaman	4,267	14,000
Bering	3,936	12,913
Gulf of Mexico	3,504	11,496
Okhotsk	3,365	11,040
Japan	3,053	10,016
Red Sea	2,266	7,434
Black Sea	2,212	7,257
North Sea	439	1,440
Hudson Bay	111	364
Baltic Sea	90	295
Yellow Sea	73	240
Persian Gulf	73	240

THE CONTINENTS

There are six geographic continents, although America is often divided politically into North and Central America, and South America.

AFRICA is surrounded by sea except for the narrow isthmus of Suez in the north-east, through which is cut the Suez Canal. Its extreme longitudes are 17° 20′ W. at Cape Verde, Senegal, and 51° 24′ E. at Ras Hafun, Somalia. The extreme latitudes are 37° 20′ N. at Cape Blanc, Tunisia, and 34° 50′ S. at Cape Agulhas, South Africa, about 4,400 miles apart. The Equator passes through the middle of the continent.

NORTH AMERICA, including Mexico, is surrounded by ocean except in the south, where the isthmian states of CENTRAL AMERICA link North America with South America. Its extreme longitudes are 168° 5′ W. at Cape Prince of Wales, Alaska, and 55° 40′ W. at Cape Charles,

Newfoundland. The extreme continental latitudes are the tip of the Boothia peninsula, NW Territories, Canada (71° 51′ N.) and 14° 22′ N. at Ocós in the south of Mexico.

SOUTH AMERICA lies mostly in the southern hemisphere; the Equator passes through the north of the continent. It is surrounded by ocean except where it is joined to Central America in the north by the narrow isthmus through which is cut the Panama Canal. Its extreme longitudes are 34° 47′ W. at Cape Branco in Brazil and 81° 20′ W. at Punta Pariña, Peru. The extreme continental latitudes are 12° 25′ N. at Punta Gallinas, Colombia, and 53° 54′ S. at the southernmost tip of the Brunswick peninsula, Chile. Cape Horn, on Cape Island, Chile, lies at 55° 59′ S.

ANTARCTICA lies almost entirely within the Antarctic Circle (66° 34′ S.) and is the largest of the world's glaciated areas. The continent has an area of 5.1 million square miles, 99 per cent of which is permanently ice-covered. The ice amounts to some 7.2 million cubic miles and represents more than 90 per cent of the world's fresh water. The environment is too hostile for unsupported human habitation. See also pages 790–1

ASIA is the largest continent and occupies 30 per cent of the world's land surface. The extreme longitudes are 26° 05′ E. at Baba Buran, Turkey and 169° 40′ W. at Mys Dežneva (East Cape), Russia, a distance of about 6,000 miles. Its extreme northern latitude is 77° 45′ N. at Cape Čeljuskin, Russia, and it extends over 5,000 miles south to about 1° 15′ N. of the Equator.

AUSTRALIA is the smallest of the continents and lies in the southern hemisphere. It is entirely surrounded by ocean. Its extreme longitudes are 113° 11′ E. at Steep Point and 153° 11′ E. at Cape Byron. The extreme latitudes are 10° 42′ S. at Cape York and 39° S. at South East Point, Tasmania.

EUROPE, including European Russia, is the smallest continent in the northern hemisphere. Its extreme latitudes are 71° 11′ N. at North Cape in Norway, and 36° 23′ N. at Cape Matapan in southern Greece, a distance of about 2,400 miles. Its breadth from Cabo Carvoeiro in Portugal (9° 34′ W.) in the west to the Kara River, north of the Urals (66° 30′ E.) in the east is about 3,300 miles. The division between Europe and Asia is generally regarded as the watershed of the Ural Mountains; down the Ural river to Gur'yev, Kazakhstan; across the Caspian Sea to Apsheronskiy Poluostrov, near Baku; along the watershed of the Caucasus Mountains to Anapa and thence across the Black Sea to the Bosporus in Turkey; across the Sea of Marmara to Çanakkale Boğazi (Dardanelles).

	Area km²	miles²
Asia	43,998,000	16,988,000
*America	41,918,000	16,185,000
Africa	29,800,000	11,506,000
Antarctica	13,209,000	5,100,000
†Europe	9,699,000	3,745,000
Australia	7,618,493	2,941,526

*North and Central America has an area of 24,255,000 km² (9,365,000 miles²)

†Includes 5,571,000 km² (2,151,000 miles²) of former USSR territory, including the Baltic states, Belarus, Moldova, the Ukraine, that part of Russia west of the Ural Mountains and Kazakhstan west of the Ural river. European Turkey (24,378 km²/9,412 miles²) comprises territory to the west and north of the Bosporus and the Dardanelles

GLACIATED AREAS

It is estimated that 15,915,000 km² (6,145,000 miles²) or 10.73 per cent of the world's land surface is permanently covered with ice.

	Area km²	miles²
South Polar regions	13,830,000	5,340,000
North Polar regions (incl. Greenland or Kalaallit Nunaat)	1,965,000	758,500
Alaska-Canada	58,800	22,700
Asia	37,800	14,600
South America	11,900	4,600
Europe	10,700	4,128
New Zealand	1,015	391
Africa	238	92

The largest glacier is the 515 km/320 mile-long Lambert-Fisher Ice Passage, Antarctica.

PENINSULAS

	Area km²	miles²
Arabian	3,250,000	1,250,000
Southern Indian	2,072,000	800,000
Alaskan	1,500,000	580,000
Labradorian	1,300,000	500,000
Scandinavian	800,300	309,000
Iberian	584,000	225,500

LARGEST ISLANDS

Island, and Ocean	Area km²	miles²
Greenland (Kalaallit Nunaat), Arctic	2,175,500	840,000
New Guinea, Pacific	821,030	317,000
Borneo, Pacific	725,450	280,100
Madagascar, Indian	587,040	226,658
Baffin Island, Arctic	507,451	195,928
Sumatra, Indian	427,350	165,000
Honshu, Pacific	227,413	87,805
*Great Britain, Atlantic	218,077	84,200
Victoria Island, Arctic	217,292	83,897
Ellesmere Island, Arctic	196,236	75,767
Sulawesi (Celebes), Indian	189,036	72,987
South Island, NZ, Pacific	151,213	58,384
Java, Indian	126,650	48,900
North Island, NZ, (Pacific)	115,777	44,702
Cuba, Atlantic	110,862	42,804
Newfoundland, Atlantic	108,855	42,030
Luzon, Pacific	105,880	40,880
Iceland, Atlantic	102,817	39,698
Mindanao, Pacific	95,247	36,775
Ireland, Atlantic	82,462	31,839

*Mainland only

LARGEST DESERTS

	Area (approx.)	
	km²	miles²
The Sahara, N. Africa	8,400,000	3,250,000
Australian Desert	1,550,000	600,000
Arabian Desert	1,200,000	470,000
The Gobi, Mongolia/China	1,040,000	400,000
Kalahari Desert, Botswana/ Namibia/S. Africa	520,000	200,000
Takla Makan, Mongolia/ China	320,000	125,000
*Kara Kum, Turkmenistan	310,000	120,000
Namib Desert, Namibia	285,000	110,000
Thar Desert, India/Pakistan	260,000	100,000
Somali Desert, Somalia	260,000	100,000
Atacama Desert, Chile	180,000	70,000
Sonoran Desert, USA/ Mexico	180,000	70,000
Dasht-e Lut, Iran	52,000	20,000
Mojave Desert, USA	38,850	15,000

*Together with the Kyzyl Kum known as the Turkestan Desert

DEEPEST DEPRESSIONS

	Maximum depth below sea level	
	metres	feet
Dead Sea, Jordan/Israel	408	1,338
Lake Assal, Djibouti	156	511
Turfan Depression, Sinkiang, China	153	505
Qattara Depression, Egypt	132	436
Mangyshlak peninsula, Kazakhstan	131	433
Danakil Depression, Ethiopia	116	383
Death Valley, California, USA	86	282
Salton Sink, California, USA	71	235
W. of Ustyurt plateau, Kazakhstan	70	230
Prikaspiyskaya Nizmennost', Russia/Kazakhstan	67	220
Lake Sarykamysh, Uzbekistan/ Turkmenistan	45	148
El Faiyûm, Egypt	44	147
Valdies peninsula, Lago Enriquillo, Dominican Republic	40	131
Lake Eyre, South Australia	16	52

The world's largest exposed depression is the Prikaspiyskaya Nizmennost' covering the hinterland of the northern third of the Caspian Sea, which is itself 28 m (92 ft) below sea level.

Western Antarctica and Central Greenland largely comprise crypto-depressions under ice burdens. The Antarctic Bentley subglacial trench has a bedrock 2,538 m (8,326 ft) below sea-level. In Greenland (lat. 73° N., long. 39° W.) the bedrock is 365 m (1,197 ft) below sea-level.

More than a quarter of the area of The Netherlands lies marginally below sea-level, an area of more than 10,000 km²/3,860 miles².

LONGEST MOUNTAIN RANGES

Range, and location	Length	
	km	miles
Cordillera de Los Andes, W. South America	7,200	4,500
Rocky Mountains, W. North America	4,800	3,000
Himalaya-Karakoram-Hindu Kush, S. Central Asia	3,800	2,400
Great Dividing Range, E. Australia	3,600	2,250
Trans-Antarctic Mts, Antarctica	3,500	2,200
Atlantic Coast Range, E. Brazil	3,000	1,900
West Sumatran-Javan Range, Indonesia	2,900	1,800
Aleutian Range, Alaska and NW Pacific	2,650	1,650
Tien Shan, S. Central Asia	2,250	1,400
Central New Guinea Range, Irian Jaya/Papua New Guinea	2,000	1,250

HIGHEST MOUNTAINS

The world's 8,000-metre mountains (with six subsidiary peaks) are all in the Himalaya-Karakoram-Hindu Kush ranges.

Mountain	Height	
	metres	feet
Mt Everest*	8,848	29,028
K2 (Chogori)†	8,607	28,238
Kangchenjunga	8,597	28,208
Lhotse	8,511	27,923
Makalu I	8,481	27,824
Lhotse Shar (II)	8,383	27,504
Dhaulagiri I	8,171	26,810
Manaslu I (Kutang I)	8,156	26,760
Cho Oyu	8,153	26,750
Nanga Parbat (Diamir)	8,125	26,660
Annapurna I	8,091	26,546
Gasherbrum I (Hidden Peak)	8,068	26,470
Broad Peak I	8,046	26,400
Shisham Pangma (Gosainthan)	8,046	26,400
Gasherbrum II	8,034	26,360
Makalu South-East	8,010	26,280
Broad Peak Central	8,000	26,246

*Named after Sir George Everest (1790–1866), Surveyor-General of India 1830–43, in 1863. He pronounced his name Eve-rest
†Formerly Godwin-Austin

The culminating summits in the other major mountain ranges are:

Mountain, by range or country	Height	
	metres	feet
Pik Pobedy, Tien Shan	7,439	24,406
Cerro Aconcagua, Cordillera de Los Andes	6,960	22,834
Mt McKinley (S. Peak), Alaska Range	6,194	20,320
Kilimanjaro (Kibo), Tanzania	5,894	19,340
Hkakabo Razi, Myanmar	5,881	19,296
El'brus, (W. Peak), Caucasus	5,642	18,510
Citlaltépetl (Orizaba), Sierra Madre Oriental, Mexico	5,610	18,405
Vinson Massif, E. Antarctica	4,897	16,066
Puncak Jaya, Central New Guinea Range	4,884	16,023

Mountain, by range or country	Height metres	feet
Mt Blanc, Alps	4,807	15,771
Klyuchevskaya Sopka, Kamchatka peninsula, Russia	4,750	15,584
Ras Dashan, Ethiopian Highlands	4,620	15,158
Zard Kūh, Zagros Mts, Iran	4,547	14,921
Mt Kirkpatrick, Trans Antarctic	4,529	14,860
Mt Belukha, Altai Mts, Russia/ Kazakhstan	4,505	14,783
Mt Elbert, Rocky Mountains	4,400	14,433
Mt Rainier, Cascade Range, N. America	4,392	14,410
Nevado de Colima, Sierra Madre Occidental, Mexico	4,268	14,003
Jebel Toubkal, Atlas Mts, N. Africa	4,165	13,665
Kinabalu, Crocker Range, Borneo	4,101	13,455
Kerinci, West Sumatran-Javan Range, Indonesia	3,800	12,467
Jabal an NabīShu'ayb, N. Tihāmat, Yemen	3,760	12,336
Mt Cook (Aorangi), Southern Alps, New Zealand	3,754	12,315
Teotepec, Sierra Madre del Sur, Mexico	3,703	12,149
Thaban Ntlenyana, Drakensberg, South Africa	3,482	11,425
Pico de Bandeira, Atlantic Coast Range	2,890	9,482
Shishaldin, Aleutian Range	2,861	9,387
Kosciusko, Great Dividing Range	2,228	7,310

HIGHEST VOLCANOES

Volcano (last major eruption), and location	Height metres	feet
Ojos del Salado (1981), Andes, Argentina	6,895	22,588
Llullaillaco (1877), Andes, Argentina/Chile	6,723	22,057
San Pedro (1960), Andes, Chile	6,199	20,325
Guallatiri (1960, 1993), Andes, Chile	6,071	19,918
Cotopaxi (1940, 1975), Andes, Ecuador	5,897	19,347
Tupungatito (1986), Andes, Chile	5,640	18,504
Láscar (1995), Andes, Chile	5,591	18,346
Popocatépetl (1998), Mexico	5,426	17,802
Nevado del Ruiz (1985, 1991), Colombia	5,321	17,457
Sangay (1998), Andes, Ecuador	5,188	17,021
Guagua Pichincha (1993), Andes, Ecuador	4,784	15,696
Purace (1977), Colombia	4,756	15,601
Klyuchevskaya Sopka (1997), Kamchatka peninsula, Russia	4,750	15,584
Galeras (1993), Colombia	4,275	14,028
Nevado de Colima (1991, 1994), Mexico	4,268	14,003
Mauna Loa (1984, 1987), Hawaii Is.	4,170	13,680
Cameroon (1982), Cameroon	4,095	13,435

OTHER NOTABLE VOLCANOES

	Height metres	feet
Erebus (1998), Ross Island, Antarctica	3,794	12,450
Fuji (1708), Honshu, Japan	3,775	12,388
Santa Maria (1902, 1998), Guatemala	3,768	12,362
Semeru (1995, 1998), Java, Indonesia	3,675	12,060
Mt Etna (1169, 1669, 1993, 1996, 1997, 1998), Sicily, Italy	3,350	10,990
Raung (1993, 1997), Java, Indonesia	3,322	10,932
Sheveluch (1964, 1997), Kamchatka, Russia	3,283	10,771
Llaima (1995), Chile	3,125	10,253
Mt St Helens (1980, 1986, 1991), Washington State, USA	2,549	8,363
Beerenberg (1985), Jan Mayen Island	2,546	8,347
Pinatubo (1991, 1995), Philippines	1,598	5,249
Hekla (1981, 1991), Iceland	1,491	4,892
Mt Unzen (1792, 1991, 1996), Kyushu, Japan	1,360	4,462
Vesuvius (AD 79, 1631, 1944), Italy	1,281	4,203
Kilauea (1996, 1997–8), Hawaii, USA	1,249	4,009
Soufrière (1979, 1997), St Vincent	1,234	4,048
Soufrière Hills (1997–8), Montserrat	942	3,091
Stromboli (1996, 1997), Lipari Is., Italy	926	3,038
Krakatau (1883, 1995), Sunda Strait, Indonesia	813	2,667
Santorini (Thíra) (1628 BC, 1950), Aegean Sea, Greece	564	1,850
Tristan da Cunha (1961), South Atlantic	243	800
Surtsey (1963–7), off Iceland	173	568

LARGEST LAKES

The areas of some of these lakes are subject to seasonal variation.

	Area km²	miles²	Length km	miles
Caspian Sea, Iran/ Azerbaijan/Russia/ Turkmenistan/ Kazakhstan	371,000	143,000	1,171	728
*Michigan–Huron, USA/Canada	117,610	45,300	1,010	627
Superior, Canada/ USA	82,100	31,700	563	350
Victoria, Uganda/ Tanzania/Kenya	69,500	26,828	362	225
Aral Sea, Kazakhstan/ Uzbekistan	40,000	15,444	134	217
Tanganyika, Dem. Rep. of Congo/ Tanzania/Zambia/ Burundi	32,900	12,665	725	450
Great Bear, Canada	31,328	12,096	309	192
†Baykal (Baikal), Russia	30,500	11,776	620	385
Malawi (Nyasa), Tanzania/Malawi/ Mozambique	29,600	11,150	580	360
Great Slave, Canada	28,570	11,031	480	298
Erie, Canada/USA	25,670	9,910	388	241

	Area km²	miles²	Length km	miles
Winnipeg, Canada	24,390	9,417	428	266
Ontario, Canada/USA	19,010	7,340	310	193
Balkhash, Kazakhstan	18,427	7,115	605	376
Ladozhskoye (*Ladoga*), Russia	17,700	6,835	193	120

*Lakes Michigan and Huron are regarded as lobes of the same lake. The Michigan lobe has an area of 57,750 km² (22,300 miles²) and the Huron lobe an area of 59,570 km² (23,000 miles²)
†World's deepest lake (1,940 m/6,365 ft)

UNITED KINGDOM, BY COUNTRY

	km²	miles²	km	miles
Lough Neagh, Northern Ireland	381.73	147.39	28.90	18.00
Loch Lomond, Scotland	71.12	27.46	36.44	22.64
Windermere, England	14.74	5.69	16.90	10.50
Lake Vyrnwy, Wales (artificial)	4.53	1.75	7.56	4.70
Llyn Tegid (*Bala*), Wales (natural)	4.38	1.69	5.80	3.65

LONGEST RIVERS

River, source and outflow	Length km	miles
Nile (*Bahr-el-Nil*), R. Luvironza, Burundi – E. Mediterranean Sea	6,670	4,145
Amazon (*Amazonas*), Lago Villafro, Peru – S. Atlantic Ocean	6,448	4,007
Yangtze-Kiang (*Chang Jiang*), Kunlun Mts, W. China – Yellow Sea	6,380	3,964
Mississippi-Missouri-Red Rock, Montana – Gulf of Mexico	5,970	3,710
Yenisey-Angara, W. Mongolia – Kara Sea	5,540	3,442
Huang He (*Yellow River*), Bayan Har Shan range, central China – Yellow Sea	5,463	3,395
Ob'-Irtysh, W. Mongolia – Kara Sea	5,410	3,362
Zaïre (*Congo*), R. Lualaba, Dem. Rep. of Congo-Zambia – S. Atlantic Ocean	4,700	2,920
Lena-Kirenga, R. Kirenga, W. of Lake Baykal – Laptev Sea, Arctic Ocean	4,400	2,734
Mekong, Lants'ang, Tibet – South China Sea	4,345	2,700
Amur-Argun, R. Argun, Khingan Mts, N. China – Sea of Okhotsk	4,345	2,700
Mackenzie-Peace, Tatlatui Lake, British Columbia – Beaufort Sea	4,240	2,635
Niger, Loma Mts, Guinea – Gulf of Guinea, E. Atlantic Ocean	4,168	2,590
Río de la Plata-Paraná, R. Paranáiba, central Brazil – S. Atlantic Ocean	4,000	2,485
Murray-Darling, SE Queensland – Lake Alexandrina, S. Australia	3,717	2,310
Volga, Valdai plateau – Caspian Sea	3,685	2,290

OTHER NOTABLE RIVERS

	km	miles
Rio Grande, USA–Mexian border	3,057	1,900
Ganges-Brahmaputra, R. Matsang, SW Tibet – Bay of Bengal	2,900	1,800
Indus, R. Sengge, SW Tibet – N. Arabian Sea	2,897	1,800
Danube (*Donau*), Black Forest, SW Germany – Black Sea	2,856	1,775

River, source and outflow	Length km	miles
Tigris-Euphrates, R. Murat, E. Turkey – Persian Gulf	2,800	1,740
Zambezi, NW Zambia – S. Indian Ocean	2,735	1,700
Irrawaddy, R. Mali Hka, Myanmar – Andaman Sea	2,151	1,337
Don, SE of Novomoskovsk – Sea of Azov	1,969	1,224

BRITISH ISLES

	km	miles
Shannon, Co. Cavan, Rep. of Ireland – Atlantic Ocean	386	240
Severn, Powys, Wales – Bristol Channel	354	220
Thames, Gloucestershire, England – North Sea	346	215
Tay, Perthshire, Scotland – North Sea	188	117
Clyde, Lanarkshire, Scotland – Firth of Clyde	158	98½
Tweed, Peeblesshire, Scotland – North Sea	155	96½
Bann (Upper and Lower), Co. Down, N. Ireland – Atlantic Ocean	122	76

GREATEST WATERFALLS – BY HEIGHT

Waterfall, river and location	Total drop metres	feet	Greatest single leap metres	feet
Saltó Angel, Carrao Auyán Tepuí, Venezuela	979	3,212	807	2,648
Tugela, Tugela, Natal, S. Africa	914	2,014	410	1,350
Utigård, Jostedal Glacier, Norway	800	2,625	600	1,970
Mongefossen, Monge, Norway	774	2,540	—	—
Yosemite, Yosemite Creek, USA	739	2,425	435	1,430
Østre Mardøla Foss, Mardals, Norway	656	2,154	296	974
Tyssestrengane, Tysso, Norway	646	2,120	289	948
Cuquenán, Arabopó, Venezuela	610	2,000	—	—
Sutherland, Arthur, NZ	580	1,904	248	815
*Kjellfossen (Kile), Naeröfjord, Norway	561	1,841	149	490

*Volume often so low the fall atomizes into a 'bridal veil'

BRITISH ISLES, BY COUNTRY

	metres	feet	metres	feet
Eas a' Chuàl Aluinn, Glas Bheinn, Sutherland, Scotland	200	658		
Powerscourt Falls, Dargle, Co. Wicklow, Rep. of Ireland	106	350		
Pistyll-y-Llyn, Powys/ Dyfed border, Wales	c.72	c.235	(cascades)	
Pistyll Rhyadr, Clwyd/ Powys border, Wales	71.5	235	(single leap)	
Caldron Snout, R. Tees, Cumbria/Durham, England	61	200	(cascades)	

GREATEST WATERFALLS – BY VOLUME

Waterfall, river and location	Mean annual flow	
	m³/sec	galls/sec
Inga (Congo dam site),		
Dem. Rep. of Congo	43,000	9,460,000
Khône, Mekong, Laos	42,500	9,350,000
Boyoma (Stanley), R. Lualaba,		
Dem. Rep. of Congo	c.17,000	c.3,750,000
Guayra (Sete Quedas), Brazil	13,000	2,860,000
Rio Paraná, Argentina/		
Paraguay	11,900	2,619,000
Niagara (Horseshoe), R.		
Niagara/Lake Erie–Lake		
Ontario	6,000	1,320,000
Paulo Afonso, R. São		
Francisco, Brazil	2,830	622,500
Urubupunga, Alto Paraná,		
Brazil	2,745	604,000
Cataratas del Iguazú, R.		
Iguaçu, Brazil/Argentina	1,743	380,000
Patos-Maribando, Rio Grande,		
Brazil	1,500	330,000
Churchill, R. Churchill,		
Canada	1,132	215,000
Victoria (Mosi-oa-tunya), R.		
Zambezi, Zambia/		
Zimbabwe	1,087	242,000

TALLEST DAMS

	metres	feet
*Rogun, R. Vakhsh, Tajikistan	335	1,098
Nurek, R. Vakhsh, Tajikistan	300	984
Grande Dixence, Switzerland	285	935
*Longtan, R. Hangshui, China	285	935
Inguri, Georgia	272	892
Manuel M. Torres, Chicoasén, Mexico	261	856
Tehri, R. Bhagivathi, India	261	856

*Under construction

The world's most massive dam is the Syncrude Tailings dam in Alberta, Canada, which will have a volume of 540 million cubic metres/706 million cubic yards.

The Three Gorges Chang Jiang (Yangtze) Dam, China, with a crest length of 1,983 m/6,505 ft, is due for completion in 2009.

The Yacyretá-Apipe dam across the River Paraná, Argentina-Paraguay, is being completed to a length of 69,600 m/43.24 miles.

TALLEST INHABITED BUILDINGS

Building and city	Height	
	metres	feet
Chongqing Tower, China	457	1,499
Petronas Towers I and II, Kuala		
Lumpur, Malaysia	451.9	1,482
Sears Tower, Chicago[1]	443	1,454
Jin Mao, Shanghai, China (1998)	420	1,378
One World Trade Center Tower, New		
York[2]	417	1,368
Plaza Rakyat, Kuala Lumpur, Malaysia	382	1,254
Empire State Building, New York[3]	381	1,250
Central Plaza, Hong Kong	373	1,227
Bank of China Tower, Hong Kong	368	1,209
T. & C. Tower, Kaohsiung, Taiwan	347	1,140
Amoco Building, Chicago	346	1,136
John Hancock Center, Chicago	343	1,127
Shun Hing Square, Shenzhen, China	325	1,066
Sky Central Plaza, Guangzhou, China	321	1,056
Chicago Beach Tower, Dubai	321	1,053
Baiyoke Tower, Bangkok, Thailand	320	1,050

1. With TV antennae, 520 m/1,707 ft
2. With TV antennae, 521.2 m/1,710 ft; Two World Trade Center Tower, 415 m/1,362 ft
3. With TV tower (added 1950–1), 430.9 m/1,414 ft

TALLEST STRUCTURES

Structure and location	Height	
	metres	feet
*Warszawa Radio Mast,		
Konstantynow, Poland	646	2,120
KTHI-TV Mast, Blanchard, North		
Dakota (guyed)	629	2,063
CN Tower, Metro Centre,		
Toronto, Canada	555	1,822
Ostankino Tower, Moscow	537	1,762

*Collapsed during renovation, August 1991

LONGEST BRIDGES – BY SPAN

Bridge and location	Length	
	metres	feet
SUSPENSION SPANS		
*Akashi-Kaikyo, Shikoku, Japan (1998)	1,990	6,529
Store Baelt East Bridge, Denmark	1,624	5,328
Humber Estuary, Humberside, England	1,410	4,626
*Jiangyin (Yangtze), China (1999)	1,385	4,544
Tsing Ma, Hong Kong, China	1,377	4,518
Verrazano Narrows, Brooklyn–Staten I,		
USA	1,298	4,260
Golden Gate, San Francisco Bay, USA	1,280	4,200
Hoga Kustan, Sweden	1,210	3,970
Mackinac Straits, Michigan, USA	1,158	3,800
Minami Bisan-Seto, Japan	1,100	3,609
Bosporus II, Istanbul, Turkey	1,089	3,576
Bosporus I, Istanbul, Turkey	1,074	3,524
George Washington, Hudson River, New		
York City, USA	1,067	3,500
Kurushima III, Japan	1,030	3,379
Kurushima II, Japan	1,020	3,346
Ponte 25 de Abril (Tagus), Lisbon,		
Portugal	1,013	3,323
Firth of Forth (road), nr Edinburgh,		
Scotland	1,006	3,300
Kita Bisan-Seto, Japan	990	3,248
Severn River, Severn Estuary, England	988	3,240

*Under construction

The main span of the 5.15 km/3.2 mile long Second Severn bridging, opened in 1996, is 456 m/1,496 ft.

Bridge and location	Length metres	feet

CANTILEVER SPANS

Bridge and location	metres	feet
Pont de Québec (rail-road), St Lawrence, Canada	548.6	1,800
Ravenswood, W. Virginia, USA	525.1	1,723
Firth of Forth (rail), nr Edinburgh, Scotland	521.2	1,710
Nanko, Osaka, Japan	510.0	1,673
Commodore Barry, Chester, Pennsylvania, USA	494.3	1,622
Greater New Orleans, Louisiana, USA	480.0	1,575
Howrah (rail-road), Calcutta, India	457.2	1,500

STEEL ARCH SPANS

	metres	feet
New River Gorge, Fayetteville, W. Virginia, USA	518.0	1,700
Bayonne (Kill van Kull), Bayonne, NJ – Staten I., USA	503.5	1,652
Sydney Harbour, Sydney, Australia	502.9	1,650

The 'floating' bridging at Evergreen Point, Seattle, Washington State, USA, is 3,839 m/12,596 ft long, of which 2,310 m/7,578 ft floats.

The longest stretch of bridgings of any kind is that carrying the Interstate 55 and Interstate 10 highways at Manchac, Louisiana, on twin concrete trestles over 55.21 km/34.31 miles.

LONGEST VEHICULAR TUNNELS

Tunnel and location	Length km	miles
*Seikan (rail), Tsugaru Channel, Japan	53.90	33.49
*Channel Tunnel, Cheriton, Kent – Sangatte, Calais	49.94	31.03
Moscow metro, Belyaevo – Bittsevsky, Moscow, Russia	37.90	23.50
Northern line tube, East Finchley – Morden, London	27.84	17.30
Oshimizu (rail), Honshū, Japan	22.17	13.78
Simplon II (rail), Brigue, Switzerland – Iselle, Italy	19.82	12.31
Simplon I (rail), Brigue, Switzerland – Iselle, Italy	19.80	12.30
*Shin-Kanmon (rail), Kanmon Strait, Japan	18.68	11.61
Great Appennine (rail), Vernio, Italy	18.49	11.49
St Gotthard (road), Göschenen – Airolo, Switzerland	16.32	10.14
Rokko (rail), Ōsaka – Kōbe, Japan	16.09	10.00

*Sub-aqueous

The longest non-vehicular tunnelling in the world is the Delaware Aqueduct in New York State, USA, constructed in 1937–44 to a length of 168.9 km/105 miles.

BRITAIN – RAIL TUNNELS

	miles	yards
Severn, Bristol – Newport	4	484
Totley, Manchester – Sheffield	3	950
Standedge, Manchester – Huddersfield	3	66
Sodbury, Swindon – Bristol	2	924
Disley, Stockport – Sheffield	2	346
Ffestiniog, Llandudno – Blaenau Ffestiniog	2	338
Bramhope, Leeds – Harrogate	2	241
Cowburn, Manchester – Sheffield	2	182

The longest road tunnel in Britain is the Mersey Road Tunnel, 3.42 km/2 miles 228 yards long. The longest canal tunnel, at Standedge, W. Yorks, is 5.13 km/3 miles 330 yards long; it was closed in 1944 but is currently being restored.

LONGEST SHIP CANALS

Canal (opening date)	Length km	miles	Min. depth metres	feet
White Sea-Baltic (formerly Stalin) (1933) Canalized river; canal 51.5 km/32 miles	227	141.00	5.0	16.5
*Suez (1869) Links Red and Mediterranean Seas	162	100.60	12.9	42.3
V. I. Lenin Volga-Don (1952) Links Black and Caspian Seas	100	62.20	n/a	n/a
Kiel (or North Sea) (1895) Links North and Baltic Seas	98	60.90	13.7	45.0
*Houston (1940) Links inland city with sea	91	56.70	10.4	34.0
Alphonse XIII (1926) Gives Seville access to sea	85	53.00	7.6	25.0
Panama (1914) Links Pacific Ocean and Caribbean Sea; lake chain, 78.9 km/49 miles dug	82	50.71	12.5	41.0
Manchester Ship (1894) Links city with Irish Channel	64	39.70	8.5	28.0
Welland (1932) Circumvents Niagara Falls and Rapids	43.5	27.00	8.8	29.0
Brussels (Rupel Sea) (1922) Renders Brussels an inland port	32	19.80	6.4	21.0

*Has no locks

The first section of China's Grand Canal, running 1,782 km/1,107 miles from Beijing to Hangzhou, was opened AD 610 and completed in 1283. Today it is limited to 2,000 tonne vessels.

The St Lawrence Seaway comprises Beauharnois, Welland and Welland Bypass and Seaway 54–59 canals, and allows access to Duluth, Minnesota, USA via the Great Lakes from the Atlantic end of Canada's Gulf of St Lawrence, a distance of 3,769 km/2,342 miles. The St Lawrence Canal, completed in 1959, is 293 km/182 miles long.

Distances from London by Air

The list of the distances in statute miles from London, Heathrow, to various cities (airport) abroad was supplied by the publishers of *IATA/Serco Aviation Services Air Distances Manual.*

To	Miles
Abidjan	3,197
Abu Dhabi (International)	3,425
Addis Ababa	3,675
Adelaide (International)	10,111
Aden	3,670
Algiers	1,035
Amman (Queen Alia)	2,287
Amsterdam	230
Ankara (Esenboga)	1,770
Athens	1,500
Atlanta	4,198
Auckland	11,404
Baghdad (Saddam)	2,551
Bahrain	3,163
Baku	2,485
Bangkok	5,928
Barbados	4,193
Barcelona (Muntadas)	712
Basle	447
Beijing (Capital)	5,063
Beirut	2,161
Belfast (Aldergrove)	325
Belgrade	1,056
Berlin (Tegel)	588
Bermuda	3,428
Berne	476
Bogotá	5,262
Bombay (Mumbai)	4,478
Boston	3,255
Brasilia	5,452
Bratislava	817
Brisbane (Eagle Farm)	10,273
Brussels	217
Bucharest (Otopeni)	1,307
Budapest	923
Buenos Aires	6,915
Cairo (International)	2,194
Calcutta	4,958
Calgary	4,357
Canberra	10,563
Cape Town	6,011
Caracas	4,639
Casablanca (Mohamed V)	1,300
Chicago (O'Hare)	3,941
Cologne	331
Colombo (Katunayake)	5,411
Copenhagen	608
Dakar	2,706
Dallas (Fort Worth)	4,736
Dallas (Lovefield)	4,732
Damascus (International)	2,223
Dar-es-Salaam	4,662
Darwin	8,613
Delhi	4,180
Denver	4,655
Detroit (Metropolitan)	3,754
Dhahran	3,143
Dhaka	4,976
Doha	3,253
Dubai	3,414

To	Miles
Dublin	279
Durban	5,937
Düsseldorf	310
Entebbe	4,033
Frankfurt (Main)	406
Freetown	3,046
Geneva	468
Gibraltar	1,084
Gothenburg (Landvetter)	664
Hamburg	463
Harare	5,156
Havana	4,647
Helsinki (Vantaa)	1,148
Hobart	10,826
Ho Chi Minh City	6,345
Hong Kong	5,990
Honolulu	7,220
Houston (Intercontinental)	4,821
Houston (William P. Hobby)	4,837
Islamabad	3,767
Istanbul	1,560
Jakarta (Halim Perdanakusuma)	7,295
Jeddah	2,947
Johannesburg	5,634
Kabul	3,558
Karachi	3,935
Kathmandu	4,570
Khartoum	3,071
Kiev (Borispol)	1,357
Kiev (Julyany)	1,337
Kingston, Jamaica	4,668
Kuala Lumpur (Subang)	6,557
Kuwait	2,903
Lagos	3,107
Larnaca	2,036
Lima	6,303
Lisbon	972
Lomé	3,129
Los Angeles (International)	5,439
Madras	5,113
Madrid	773
Malta	1,305
Manila	6,685
Marseille	614
Mauritius	6,075
Melbourne (Essendon)	10,504
Melbourne (Tullamarine)	10,499
Mexico City	5,529
Miami	4,414
Milan (Linate)	609
Minsk	1,176
Montego Bay	4,687
Montevideo	6,841
Montreal (Mirabel)	3,241
Moscow (Sheremetievo)	1,557
Munich (Franz Josef Strauss)	584
Muscat	3,621
Nairobi (Jomo Kenyatta)	4,248
Naples	1,011
Nassau	4,333
New York (J. F. Kennedy)	3,440
Nice	645
Oporto	806
Oslo (Fornebu)	722
Ottawa	3,321

To	Miles
Palma, Majorca (Son San Juan)	836
Paris (Charles de Gaulle)	215
Paris (Le Bourget)	215
Paris (Orly)	227
Perth, Australia	9,008
Port of Spain	4,404
Prague	649
Pretoria	5,602
Reykjavik (Domestic)	1,167
Reykjavik (Keflavik)	1,177
Rhodes	1,743
Rio de Janeiro	5,745
Riyadh (King Khaled) International	3,067
Rome (Fiumicino)	895
St John's, Newfoundland	2,308
St Petersburg	1,314
Salzburg	651
San Francisco	5,351
São Paulo	5,892
Sarajevo	1,017
Seoul (Kimpo)	5,507
Shanghai	5,725
Shannon	369
Singapore (Changi)	6,756
Sofia	1,266
Stockholm (Arlanda)	908
Suva	10,119
Sydney (Kingsford Smith)	10,568
Tangier	1,120
Tehran	2,741
Tel Aviv	2,227
Tokyo (Narita)	5,956
Toronto	3,544
Tripoli (International)	1,468
Tunis	1,137
Turin (Caselle)	570
Ulan Bator	4,340
Valencia	826
Vancouver	4,707
Venice (Tessera)	715
Vienna (Schwechat)	790
Vladivostok	5,298
Warsaw	912
Washington (Dulles)	3,665
Wellington	11,692
Yangon/Rangoon	5,582
Yokohama (Aomori)	5,647
Zagreb	848
Zürich	490

The United Kingdom

The United Kingdom comprises Great Britain (England, Wales and Scotland) and Northern Ireland. The Isle of Man and the Channel Islands are Crown dependencies with their own legislative systems, and not a part of the United Kingdom.

AREA AS AT 31 MARCH 1981

	Land miles²	km²	*Inland water miles²	km²	Total miles²	km²
United Kingdom	93,006	240,883	1,242	3,218	94,248	244,101
England	50,058	129,652	293	758	50,351	130,410
Wales	7,965	20,628	50	130	8,015	20,758
Scotland	29,767	77,097	653	1,692	30,420	78,789
†Northern Ireland	5,225	13,532	249	628	5,467	14,160
Isle of Man	221	572	—	—	221	572
Channel Islands	75	194	—	—	75	194

*Excluding tidal water
†Excluding certain tidal waters that are parts of statutory areas in Northern Ireland

POPULATION

The first official census of population in England, Wales and Scotland was taken in 1801 and a census has been taken every ten years since, except in 1941 when there was no census because of war. The last official census in the United Kingdom was taken on 21 April 1991 and the next is due in April 2001.

The first official census of population in Ireland was taken in 1841. However, all figures given below refer only to the area which is now Northern Ireland. Figures for Northern Ireland in 1921 and 1931 are estimates based on the censuses taken in 1926 and 1937 respectively.

Estimates of the population of England before 1801, calculated from the number of baptisms, burials and marriages, are:
1570 4,160,221   1670 5,773,646
1600 4,811,718   1700 6,045,008
1630 5,600,517   1750 6,517,035

Thousands	United Kingdom Total	Male	Female	England and Wales Total	Male	Female	Scotland Total	Male	Female	Northern Ireland Total	Male	Female
CENSUS RESULTS ;1801–1991												
1801	—	—	—	8,893	4,255	4,638	1,608	739	869	—	—	—
1811	13,368	6,368	7,000	10,165	4,874	5,291	1,806	826	980	—	—	—
1821	15,472	7,498	7,974	12,000	5,850	6,150	2,092	983	1,109	—	—	—
1831	17,835	8,647	9,188	13,897	6,771	7,126	2,364	1,114	1,250	—	—	—
1841	20,183	9,819	10,364	15,914	7,778	8,137	2,620	1,242	1,378	1,649	800	849
1851	22,259	10,855	11,404	17,928	8,781	9,146	2,889	1,376	1,513	1,443	698	745
1861	24,525	11,894	12,631	20,066	9,776	10,290	3,062	1,450	1,612	1,396	668	728
1871	27,431	13,309	14,122	22,712	11,059	11,653	3,360	1,603	1,757	1,359	647	712
1881	31,015	15,060	15,955	25,974	12,640	13,335	3,736	1,799	1,936	1,305	621	684
1891	34,264	16,593	17,671	29,003	14,060	14,942	4,026	1,943	2,083	1,236	590	646
1901	38,237	18,492	19,745	32,528	15,729	16,799	4,472	2,174	2,298	1,237	590	647
1911	42,082	20,357	21,725	36,070	17,446	18,625	4,761	2,309	2,452	1,251	603	648
1921	44,027	21,033	22,994	37,887	18,075	19,811	4,882	2,348	2,535	1,258	610	648
1931	46,038	22,060	23,978	39,952	19,133	20,819	4,843	2,326	2,517	1,243	601	642
1951	50,225	24,118	26,107	43,758	21,016	22,742	5,096	2,434	2,662	1,371	668	703
1961	52,709	25,481	27,228	46,105	22,304	23,801	5,179	2,483	2,697	1,425	694	731
1971	55,515	26,952	28,562	48,750	23,683	25,067	5,229	2,515	2,714	1,536	755	781
1981	55,848	27,104	28,742	49,155	23,873	25,281	5,131	2,466	2,664	*1,533	750	783
1991	56,467	27,344	29,123	49,890	24,182	25,707	4,999	2,392	2,607	1,578	769	809
†RESIDENT POPULATION: PROJECTIONS (MID-YEAR)												
2001	59,618	29,377	30,241	52,818	26,062	26,756	5,106	2,484	2,622	1,694	830	864
2011	60,929	30,206	30,723	54,151	26,881	27,269	5,059	2,476	2,583	1,720	848	872
2021	62,244	30,916	31,328	55,526	27,614	27,913	4,993	2,449	2,544	1,724	853	871

*Figures include 44,500 non-enumerated persons
† Projections are 1996 based

Source: The Stationery Office – *Annual Abstract 1998*; ONS – Census reports (Crown copyright)

ISLANDS: Census Results 1901–91

	Isle of Man			Jersey			*Guernsey		
	Total	Male	Female	Total	Male	Female	Total	Male	Female
1901	54,752	25,496	29,256	52,576	23,940	28,636	40,446	19,652	20,794
1911	52,016	23,937	28,079	51,898	24,014	27,884	41,858	20,661	21,197
1921	60,284	27,329	32,955	49,701	22,438	27,263	38,315	18,246	20,069
1931	49,308	22,443	26,865	50,462	23,424	27,038	40,643	19,659	20,984
1951	55,123	25,749	29,464	57,296	27,282	30,014	43,652	21,221	22,431
1961	48,151	22,060	26,091	57,200	27,200	30,000	45,068	21,671	23,397
1971	56,289	26,461	29,828	72,532	35,423	37,109	51,458	24,792	26,666
1981	64,679	30,901	33,778	77,000	37,000	40,000	53,313	25,701	27,612
1991	69,788	33,693	36,095	84,082	40,862	43,220	58,867	28,297	30,570

* Population of Guernsey, Herm, Jethou and Lithou. Figures for 1901–71 record all persons present on census night; census figures for 1981 and 1991 record all persons resident in the islands on census night
Source: 1991 Census

RESIDENT POPULATION

MID-YEAR ESTIMATE

	1987	1997
United Kingdom	57,009,000	59,009,000
England	47,488,000	49,284,000
Wales	2,833,000	2,927,000
Scotland	5,113,000	5,123,000
Northern Ireland	1,575,000	1,675,000

Source: The Stationery Office – Annual Abstract of Statistics 1999 (Crown copyright)

BY AGE AND SEX 1997

Males	Under 16	65 and over
United Kingdom	6,208,000	3,796,000
England	5,168,000	3,191,000
Wales	307,000	208,000
Scotland	522,000	311,000
Northern Ireland	212,000	86,000

Females	Under 16	60 and over
United Kingdom	5,895,000	6,894,000
England	4,903,000	5,748,000
Wales	293,000	375,000
Scotland	499,000	605,000
Northern Ireland	200,000	166,000

Source: The Stationery Office – Annual Abstract of Statistics 1999 (Crown copyright)

BY ETHNIC GROUP (1991 Census (Great Britain))

Ethnic group	Estimated population	As % of ethnic minority population
Caribbean	500,000	16.6
African	212,000	7
Other black	178,000	5.9
Indian	840,000	27.9
Pakistani	477,000	15.8
Bangladeshi	163,000	5.4
Chinese	157,000	5.2
Other Asian	198,000	6.6
Other	290,000	9.6
Total ethnic minority groups	3,015,000	100
White	51,874,000	—
All ethnic groups	54,889,000	—

Source: The Stationery Office – Population Trends 72 (Crown copyright)

AVERAGE DENSITY Persons per hectare

	1981	1991
England	3.55	3.61
Wales	1.34	1.36
Scotland	0.66	0.65
Northern Ireland	1.12	1.11

Sources: ONS – Census reports (Crown copyright)

IMMIGRATION 1997
Acceptances for settlement in the UK by nationality

Region	Number of persons
Europe: total	7,750
European Economic Area	110
Remainder of Europe	7,640
Americas: total	7,790
USA	3,900
Canada	980
Africa: total	13,200
Asia: total	25,610
Indian sub-continent	13,080
Middle East	4,160
Oceania: total	3,100
British Overseas Citizens	540
Stateless	740
Total	58,720

Source: The Stationery Office – Annual Abstract of Statistics 1999 (Crown copyright)

LIVE BIRTHS AND BIRTH RATES 1997

	Live births	Birth rate*
United Kingdom	726,000	12.3
England and Wales	642,000	12.3
Scotland	59,000	11.6
Northern Ireland	24,000	14.5

*Live births per 1,000 population
Source: The Stationery Office – Annual Abstract of Statistics 1999 (Crown copyright)

LEGAL ABORTIONS 1997p

Age group	England and Wales	Scotland
Under 16	3,430	289
16–19	29,927	2,428
20–34	113,917	7,929
35–44	22,249	1,410
45 and over	482	24
Total	182,085	

p provisional
Source: The Stationery Office – *Annual Abstract of Statistics 1999*
(Crown copyright)

BIRTHS OUTSIDE MARRIAGE (UK)

Age group	1987	1997
Under 20	48,000	47,000
20–24	68,000	78,000
25–29	37,000	70,000
Over 30	26,000	71,000
Total	179,000	266,000

Source: The Stationery Office – *Annual Abstract of Statistics 1999*
(Crown copyright)

MARRIAGE AND DIVORCE 1996p

	Marriages	Divorces
United Kingdom	317,514p	170,150
England and Wales	278,975p	155,310
Scotland	30,242	12,308
Northern Ireland	8,297	2,532

p provisional
Source: The Stationery Office – *Annual Abstract of Statistics 1999*
(Crown copyright)

DEATHS AND DEATH RATES 1997

Males	Deaths	Death rate*
United Kingdom	300,414	10.4
England and Wales	264,865	9.8
Scotland	28,305	11.4
Northern Ireland	7,244	8.8
Females		
United Kingdom	329,332	11.0
England and Wales	290,416	10.5
Scotland	31,189	11.8
Northern Ireland	7,727	9.0

* Deaths per 1,000 population
Sources: The Stationery Office – *Annual Abstract of Statistics 1999*
(Crown copyright); ONS; General Register Office for Scotland;
General Register Office (Northern Ireland)

INFANT MORTALITY 1997p
Deaths of infants under 1 year of age per 1,000 live births

	Number
United Kingdom	5.8
England and Wales	5.9
Scotland	5.3
Northern Ireland	5.6

p provisional
Source: The Stationery Office – *Annual Abstract of Statistics 1999*
(Crown copyright)

LIFE EXPECTANCY   LIFE TABLES 1994–96 (INTERIM FIGURES)

Age	England and Wales		Scotland		Northern Ireland	
	Male	Female	Male	Female	Male	Female
0	74.4	79.6	72.1	77.6	73.3	78.7
5	70.0	75.1	67.7	73.2	68.9	74.2
10	65.0	70.1	62.7	68.2	63.9	69.3
15	60.1	65.2	57.8	63.2	59.0	64.3
20	55.2	60.3	53.1	58.3	54.3	59.4
25	50.5	55.3	48.3	53.4	49.6	54.5
30	45.7	50.4	43.6	48.6	44.8	49.6
35	40.9	45.6	38.9	43.7	40.0	44.7
40	36.2	40.7	34.2	38.9	35.3	39.9
45	31.5	36.0	29.6	34.2	30.6	35.1
50	26.9	31.3	25.2	29.6	26.1	30.5
55	22.6	26.8	21.0	25.2	21.7	26.0
60	18.5	22.5	17.2	21.0	17.7	21.7
65	14.8	18.4	13.7	17.2	14.2	17.8
70	11.6	14.7	10.8	13.7	11.0	14.0
75	8.9	11.4	8.3	10.6	8.3	10.8
80	6.6	8.6	6.2	7.9	6.0	7.9
85	4.9	6.3	4.6	5.7	4.2	5.6

Source: The Stationery Office – *Annual Abstract of Statistics 1999* (Crown copyright)

DEATHS ANALYSED BY CAUSE 1997

	England and Wales	Scotland	N. Ireland
TOTAL DEATHS	555,281	59,494	14,967
Deaths from natural causes	536,422	56,932	14,274
Infectious and parasitic diseases	3,496	431	61
Neoplasms	137,618	15,054	3,667
Malignant neoplasm of stomach	6,613	710	171
Malignant neoplasm of trachea, bronchus and lung	29,976	4,106	772
Malignant neoplasm of breast	12,047	1,161	267
Malignant neoplasm of uterus	1,291	106	35
Malignant neoplasm of cervix	1,225	144	26
Benign and unspecified neoplasms	1,624	126	53
Leukaemia	3,587	291	107
Endocrine, nutritional and metabolic diseases and immunity disorders	7,383	727	106
Diabetes mellitus	5,890	510	77
Nutritional deficiencies	65	7	1
Other metabolic and immunity disorders	1,038	167	17
Diseases of blood and blood-forming organs	2,008	200	20
Anaemias	681	71	9
Mental disorders	9,725	1,611	138
Diseases of the nervous system and sense organs	9,772	900	234
Meningitis	224	17	8
Diseases of the circulatory system	228,446	25,911	6,505
Rheumatic heart disease	1,481	183	38
Hypertensive disease	3,084	294	73
Ischaemic heart disease	122,432	14,013	3,764
Diseases of pulmonary circulation and other forms of heart disease	26,609	2,900	635
Cerebrovascular disease	57,747	6,959	1,646
Diseases of the respiratory system	92,517	7,891	2,663
Influenza	347	83	8
Pneumonia	56,719	4,028	1,774
Bronchitis, emphysema	4,116	320	99
Asthma	1,439	113	32
Diseases of the digestive system	20,406	2,428	459
Ulcer of stomach and duodenum	3,959	306	95
Appendicitis	125	14	4
Hernia of the abdominal cavity and other intestinal obstruction	2,106	168	42
Chronic liver disease and cirrhosis	4,107	767	68
Diseases of the genitourinary system	6,757	904	245
Nephritis, nephrotic syndrome and nephrosis	2,930	576	175
Hyperplasia of prostate	247	9	4
Complications of pregnancy, childbirth and the puerperium	35	4	—
Abortion	2	—	—
Diseases of the skin and subcutaneous tissue	1,025	87	25
Diseases of the musculo-skeletal system	3,559	268	44
Congenital anomalies	1,283	182	57
Certain conditions originating in the perinatal period	131	140	69
Birth trauma, hypoxia, birth asphyxia and other respiratory conditions	99	71	26
Signs, symptoms and ill-defined conditions	12,292	383	92
Sudden infant death syndrome	327	52	8
Deaths from injury and poisoning	16,311	2,373	591
All accidents	10,661	1,398	427
Motor vehicle accidents	3,184	384	152
Suicide and self-inflicted injury	3,424	599	120
All other external causes	2,226	376	44

Source: The Stationery Office—*Annual Abstract of Statistics 1999* (Crown copyright)

The National Flag

The national flag of the United Kingdom is the Union Flag, generally known as the Union Jack.

The Union Flag is a combination of the cross of St George, patron saint of England, the cross of St Andrew, patron saint of Scotland, and a cross similar to that of St Patrick, patron saint of Ireland.

Cross of St George: cross Gules in a field Argent (red cross on a white ground)

Cross of St Andrew: saltire Argent in a field Azure (white diagonal cross on a blue ground)

Cross of St Patrick: saltire Gules in a field Argent (red diagonal cross on a white ground)

The Union Flag was first introduced in 1606 after the union of the kingdoms of England and Scotland under one sovereign. The cross of St Patrick was added in 1801 after the union of Great Britain and Ireland.

FLYING THE UNION FLAG

The correct orientation of the Union Flag when flying is with the broader diagonal band of white uppermost in the hoist (i.e. near the pole) and the narrower diagonal band of white uppermost in the fly (i.e. furthest from the pole).

It is the practice to fly the Union Flag daily on some customs houses. In all other cases, flags are flown on government buildings by command of The Queen.

Days for hoisting the Union Flag are notified to the Department for Culture, Media and Sport by The Queen's command and communicated by the department to the other government departments. On the days appointed, the Union Flag is flown on government buildings in the United Kingdom from 8 a.m. to sunset.

DAYS FOR FLYING FLAGS

The Queen's Accession	6 February
Birthday of The Duke of York	19 February
*St David's Day (in Wales only)	1 March
Birthday of The Prince Edward	10 March
Commonwealth Day** (2000)	13 March
Birthday of The Queen	21 April
*St George's Day (in England only)	23 April
†Europe Day	9 May
Coronation Day	2 June
Birthday of The Duke of Edinburgh	10 June
The Queen's Official Birthday (2000)	17 June
Birthday of Queen Elizabeth the Queen Mother	4 August
Birthday of The Princess Royal	15 August
Birthday of The Princess Margaret	21 August
Remembrance Sunday (2000)	12 November
Birthday of The Prince of Wales	14 November
The Queen's Wedding Day	20 November
*St Andrew's Day (in Scotland only)	30 November
‡The opening of Parliament by The Queen	
‡The prorogation of Parliament by The Queen	

*Where a building has two or more flagstaffs, the appropriate national flag may be flown in addition to the Union Flag, but not in a superior position

**Commonwealth Day is always the second Monday in March

†The Union Flag should fly alongside the European flag. On government buildings that have only one flagpole, the Union Flag should take precedence

‡Flags are flown whether or not The Queen performs the ceremony in person. Flags are flown only in the Greater London area

FLAGS AT HALF-MAST

Flags are flown at half-mast (i.e. two-thirds up between the top and bottom of the flagstaff) on the following occasions:

(a) From the announcement of the death up to the funeral of the Sovereign, except on Proclamation Day, when flags are hoisted right up from 11 a.m. to sunset

(b) The funerals of members of the royal family, subject to special commands from The Queen in each case

(c) The funerals of foreign rulers, subject to special commands from The Queen in each case

(d) The funerals of prime ministers and ex-prime ministers of the UK, subject to special commands from The Queen in each case

(e) Other occasions by special command of The Queen

On occasions when days for flying flags coincide with days for flying flags at half-mast, the following rules are observed. Flags are flown:

(a) although a member of the royal family, or a near relative of the royal family, may be lying dead, unless special commands are received from The Queen to the contrary

(b) although it may be the day of the funeral of a foreign ruler

If the body of a very distinguished subject is lying at a government office, the flag may fly at half-mast on that office until the body has left (provided it is a day on which the flag would fly) and then the flag is to be hoisted right up. On all other government buildings the flag will fly as usual.

THE ROYAL STANDARD

The Royal Standard is hoisted only when The Queen is actually present in the building, and never when Her Majesty is passing in procession.

The Royal Family

THE SOVEREIGN

ELIZABETH II, by the Grace of God, of the United Kingdom of Great Britain and Northern Ireland and of her other Realms and Territories Queen, Head of the Commonwealth, Defender of the Faith

Her Majesty Elizabeth Alexandra Mary of Windsor, elder daughter of King George VI and of HM Queen Elizabeth the Queen Mother
Born 21 April 1926, at 17 Bruton Street, London WI
Ascended the throne 6 February 1952
Crowned 2 June 1953, at Westminster Abbey
Married 20 November 1947, in Westminster Abbey, HRH The Prince Philip, Duke of Edinburgh
Official residences: Buckingham Palace, London SWIA IAA; Windsor Castle, Berks; Palace of Holyroodhouse, Edinburgh
Private residences: Sandringham, Norfolk; Balmoral Castle, Aberdeenshire

HUSBAND OF THE QUEEN

HRH THE PRINCE PHILIP, DUKE OF EDINBURGH, KG, KT, OM, GBE, AC, QSO, PC, Ranger of Windsor Park
Born 10 June 1921, son of Prince and Princess Andrew of Greece and Denmark (*see* page 129), naturalized a British subject 1947, created Duke of Edinburgh, Earl of Merioneth and Baron Greenwich 1947

CHILDREN OF THE QUEEN

HRH THE PRINCE OF WALES; (Prince Charles Philip Arthur George), KG, KT, GCB and Great Master of the Order of the Bath, AK, QSO, PC, ADC(P)
Born 14 November 1948, created Prince of Wales and Earl of Chester 1958, succeeded as Duke of Cornwall, Duke of Rothesay, Earl of Carrick and Baron Renfrew, Lord of the Isles and Prince and Great Steward of Scotland 1952
Married 29 July 1981 Lady Diana Frances Spencer (Diana, Princess of Wales (1961–97), youngest daughter of the 8th Earl Spencer and the Hon. Mrs Shand Kydd), marriage dissolved 1996
Issue:
(1) HRH Prince William of Wales (Prince William Arthur Philip Louis), *born* 21 June 1982
(2) HRH Prince Henry of Wales (Prince Henry Charles Albert David), *born* 15 September 1984
Residences of the Prince of Wales: St James's Palace, London SWIA IBS; Highgrove, Doughton, Tetbury, Glos GL8 8TN

HRH THE PRINCESS ROYAL (Princess Anne Elizabeth Alice Louise), KG, GCVO
Born 15 August 1950, declared The Princess Royal 1987
Married (1) 14 November 1973 Captain Mark Anthony Peter Phillips, CVO (*born* 22 September 1948); marriage dissolved 1992; (2) 12 December 1992 Captain Timothy James Hamilton Laurence, MVO, RN (*born* 1 March 1955)
Issue:
(1) Peter Mark Andrew Phillips, *born* 15 November 1977

(2) Zara Anne Elizabeth Phillips, *born* 15 May 1981
Residence: Gatcombe Park, Minchinhampton, Glos

HRH THE DUKE OF YORK (Prince Andrew Albert Christian Edward), CVO, ADC(P)
Born 19 February 1960, created Duke of York, Earl of Inverness and Baron Killyleagh 1986
Married 23 July 1986 Sarah Margaret Ferguson, now Sarah, Duchess of York (*born* 15 October 1959, younger daughter of Major Ronald Ferguson and Mrs Hector Barrantes), marriage dissolved 1996
Issue:
(1) HRH Princess Beatrice of York (Princess Beatrice Elizabeth Mary), *born* 8 August 1988
(2) HRH Princess Eugenie of York (Princess Eugenie Victoria Helena), *born* 23 March 1990
Residences: Buckingham Palace, London SWIA IAA; Sunninghill Park, Ascot, Berks

HRH THE EARL OF WESSEX (Prince Edward Antony Richard Louis), CVO
Born 10 March 1964, created Earl of Wessex, Viscount Severn 1999
Married 19 June 1999 Sophie Helen Rhys-Jones, now HRH The Countess of Wessex (*born* 20 January 1965, daughter of Mr and Mrs Christopher Rhys-Jones)
Residence: Bagshot Park, Bagshot, Surrey GU19 5PL

SISTER OF THE QUEEN

HRH THE PRINCESS MARGARET, COUNTESS OF SNOWDON, CI, GCVO, Royal Victorian Chain, Dame Grand Cross of the Order of St John of Jerusalem
Born 21 August 1930, younger daughter of King George VI and HM Queen Elizabeth the Queen Mother
Married 6 May 1960 Antony Charles Robert Armstrong-Jones, GCVO (*born* 7 March 1930, created Earl of Snowdon 1961), marriage dissolved 1978
Issue:
(1) David Albert Charles, Viscount Linley, *born* 3 November 1961, *married* 8 October 1993 the Hon. Serena Stanhope, and has issue, *born* 2 July 1999
(2) Lady Sarah Chatto (Sarah Frances Elizabeth), *born* 1 May 1964, *married* 14 July 1994 Daniel Chatto, and has issue, Samuel David Benedict Chatto, *born* 28 July 1996; Arthur Robert Nathaniel Chatto, *born* 5 February 1999
Residence: Kensington Palace, London W8 4PU

MOTHER OF THE QUEEN

HM QUEEN ELIZABETH THE QUEEN MOTHER (Elizabeth Angela Marguerite), Lady of the Garter, Lady of the Thistle, CI, GCVO, GBE, Dame Grand Cross of the Order of St John of Jerusalem, Royal Victorian Chain, Lord Warden and Admiral of the Cinque Ports and Constable of Dover Castle
Born 4 August 1900, youngest daughter of the 14th Earl of Strathmore and Kinghorne
Married 26 April 1923 (as Lady Elizabeth Bowes-Lyon) Prince Albert, Duke of York, afterwards King George VI (*see* page 127)

Residences: Clarence House, St James's Palace, London SWIA IBA; Royal Lodge, Windsor Great Park, Berks; Castle of Mey, Caithness

AUNT OF THE QUEEN

HRH PRINCESS ALICE, DUCHESS OF GLOUCESTER (Alice Christabel), GCB, CI, GCVO, GBE, Grand Cordon of Al Kamal
Born 25 December 1901, third daughter of the 7th Duke of Buccleuch and Queensberry
Married 6 November 1935 (as Lady Alice Montagu-Douglas-Scott) Prince Henry, Duke of Gloucester, third son of King George V (*see* page 127)
Residence: Kensington Palace, London W8 4PU

COUSINS OF THE QUEEN

HRH THE DUKE OF GLOUCESTER (Prince Richard Alexander Walter George), KG, GCVO, Grand Prior of the Order of St John of Jerusalem
Born 26 August 1944
Married 8 July 1972 Birgitte Eva van Deurs, now HRH The Duchess of Gloucester, GCVO (*born* 20 June 1946, daughter of Asger Henriksen and Vivian van Deurs)
Issue:
(1)   Earl of Ulster (Alexander Patrick Gregers Richard), *born* 24 October 1974
(2)   Lady Davina Windsor (Davina Elizabeth Alice Benedikte), *born* 19 November 1977
(3)   Lady Rose Windsor (Rose Victoria Birgitte Louise), *born* 1 March 1980
Residence: Kensington Palace, London W8 4PU

HRH THE DUKE OF KENT (Prince Edward George Nicholas Paul Patrick), KG, GCMG, GCVO, ADC(P)
Born 9 October 1935
Married 8 June 1961 Katharine Lucy Mary Worsley, now HRH The Duchess of Kent, GCVO (*born* 22 February 1933, daughter of Sir William Worsley, Bt.)
Issue:
(1)   Earl of St Andrews (George Philip Nicholas), *born* 26 June 1962, *married* 9 January 1988 Sylvana Tomaselli, and has issue, Edward Edmund Maximilian George, Baron Downpatrick, *born* 2 December 1988; Lady Marina Charlotte Alexandra Katharine Windsor, *born* 30 September 1992; Lady Amelia Sophia Theodora Mary Margaret Windsor, *born* 24 August 1995
(2)   Lady Helen Taylor (Helen Marina Lucy), *born* 28 April 1964, *married* 18 July 1992 Timothy Taylor, and has issue, Columbus George Donald Taylor, *born* 6 August 1994; Cassius Edward Taylor, *born* 26 December 1996
(3)   Lord Nicholas Windsor (Nicholas Charles Edward Jonathan), *born* 25 July 1970
Residence: Wren House, Palace Green, London W8 4PY

HRH PRINCESS ALEXANDRA, THE HON. LADY OGILVY (Princess Alexandra Helen Elizabeth Olga Christabel), GCVO
Born 25 December 1936
Married 24 April 1963 The Rt. Hon. Sir Angus Ogilvy, KCVO (*born* 14 September 1928, second son of 12th Earl of Airlie)
Issue:
(1)   James Robert Bruce Ogilvy, *born* 29 February 1964, *married* 30 July 1988 Julia Rawlinson, and has issue,

Flora Alexandra Ogilvy, *born* 15 December 1994; Alexander Charles Ogilvy, *born* 12 November 1996
(2)   Marina Victoria Alexandra, Mrs Mowatt, *born* 31 July 1966, *married* 2 February 1990 Paul Mowatt (marriage dissolved 1997), and has issue, Zenouska May Mowatt, *born* 26 May 1990; Christian Alexander Mowatt, *born* 4 June 1993
Residence: Thatched House Lodge, Richmond Park, Surrey

HRH PRINCE MICHAEL OF KENT (Prince Michael George Charles Franklin), KCVO
Born 4 July 1942
Married 30 June 1978 Baroness Marie-Christine Agnes Hedwig Ida von Reibnitz, now HRH Princess Michael of Kent (*born* 15 January 1945, daughter of Baron Gunther von Reibnitz)
Issue:
(1)   Lord Frederick Windsor (Frederick Michael George David Louis), *born* 6 April 1979
(2)   Lady Gabriella Windsor (Gabriella Marina Alexandra Ophelia), *born* 23 April 1981
Residences: Kensington Palace, London W8 4PU; Nether Lypiatt Manor, Stroud, Glos.

ORDER OF SUCCESSION

1   HRH The Prince of Wales
2   HRH Prince William of Wales
3   HRH Prince Henry of Wales
4   HRH The Duke of York
5   HRH Princess Beatrice of York
6   HRH Princess Eugenie of York
7   HRH The Earl of Wessex
8   HRH The Princess Royal
9   Peter Phillips
10   Zara Phillips
11   HRH The Princess Margaret, Countess of Snowdon
12   Viscount Linley
13   Hon. Charles Patrick Inigo Armstrong-Jones
14   Lady Sarah Chatto
15   Samuel Chatto
16   Arthur Chatto
17   HRH The Duke of Gloucester
18   Earl of Ulster
19   Lady Davina Windsor
20   Lady Rose Windsor
21   HRH The Duke of Kent
22   Baron Downpatrick
23   Lady Marina Charlotte Windsor
24   Lady Amelia Windsor
25   Lord Nicholas Windsor
26   Lady Helen Taylor
27   Columbus Taylor
28   Cassius Taylor
29   Lord Frederick Windsor
30   Lady Gabriella Windsor
31   HRH Princess Alexandra, the Hon. Lady Ogilvy
32   James Ogilvy
33   Alexander Ogilvy
34   Flora Ogilvy
35   Marina, Mrs Paul Mowatt
36   Christian Mowatt
37   Zenouska Mowatt
38   The Earl of Harewood

The Earl of St Andrews and HRH Prince Michael of Kent both lost the right of succession to the throne through marriage to a Roman Catholic. Their children remain in succession provided that they are in communion with the Church of England

Royal Households

THE QUEEN'S HOUSEHOLD

Office: Buckingham Palace, London SW1A 1AA
Tel: 0171-930 4832
Web: http://www.royal.gov.uk

The Lord Chamberlain is the most senior member of The Queen's Household and under him come the heads of the six departments: the Private Secretary, the Keeper of the Privy Purse, the Comptroller of the Lord Chamberlain's Office, the Master of the Household, the Crown Equerry, and the Director of the Royal Collection. Positions in these departments are full-time salaried posts.

There are also a number of honorary or now largely ceremonial appointments which carry no remuneration or a small honorarium. In the following list, most honorary appointments have been placed at the end; however, where this is not the case, such appointments are indicated by an asterisk.

GREAT OFFICERS OF STATE
Lord Chamberlain, The Lord Camoys, GCVO, PC
Lord Steward, The Viscount Ridley, KG, GCVO, TD
Master of the Horse, The Lord Vestey

LADIES-IN-WAITING AND EQUERRIES
Mistress of the Robes, The Duchess of Grafton, GCVO
Ladies of the Bedchamber, The Countess of Airlie, DCVO; The Lady Farnham, CVO
Women of the Bedchamber, Hon. Mary Morrison, DCVO; Lady Susan Hussey, DCVO; Lady Dugdale, DCVO; The Lady Elton, CVO; Mrs Christian Adams (temp.)
Equerry, Sqn. Ldr. S. Brailsford

THE PRIVATE SECRETARY'S OFFICE

Buckingham Palace, London SW1A 1AA

Private Secretary to The Queen, Sir Robin Janvrin, KCVO, CB
Deputy Private Secretary, vacant
Communications Secretary, S. Lewis
Assistant Private Secretary, T. Hitchens
Special Assistant to the Private Secretary, A. Dent
Chief Clerk, Mrs G. Middleburgh, MVO
Secretary to the Private Secretary, Miss E. Ash

PRESS OFFICE
Press Secretary, G. Crawford, LVO
Deputy Press Secretary, Miss P. Russell-Smith
Assistant Press Secretaries, R. Arbiter, LVO; D. Tuck

THE QUEEN'S ARCHIVES
Round Tower, Windsor Castle, Berks

Keeper of The Queen's Archives, Sir Robin Janvrin, KCVO, CB
Assistant Keeper, O. Everett, CVO
Registrar, Lady de Bellaigue, MVO

THE PRIVY PURSE AND TREASURER'S OFFICE

Buckingham Palace, London SW1A 1AA

Keeper of the Privy Purse and Treasurer to The Queen, Sir Michael Peat, KCVO
Director of Property Services, J. Tiltman, LVO
Director of Royal Travel, Air Cdre the Hon. T. Elworthy

Director of Finance, Property Services and Royal Travel, S. Cawley
Deputy Keeper of the Privy Purse and Deputy Treasurer, J. Parsons, CVO
Chief Accountant and Paymaster, I. McGregor
Personnel Officer, Miss P. Lloyd
Land Agent, Sandringham, M. O'Lone, FRICS
Resident Factor, Balmoral, P. Ord, FRICS

THE LORD CHAMBERLAIN'S OFFICE

Buckingham Palace, London SW1A 1AA

Comptroller, Lt.-Col. W. H. M. Ross, CVO, OBE
Assistant Comptroller, Lt.-Col. R. Cartwright
Secretary, J. Spencer, MVO
Assistant Secretary, Miss A. Krysztofiak
State Invitations Assistant, J. O. Hope

Marshal of the Diplomatic Corps, Vice-Adm. Sir James Weatherall, KBE
Vice-Marshal, Mrs K. Colvin

CENTRAL CHANCERY OF THE ORDERS OF KNIGHTHOOD
St James's Palace, London SW1A 1BS

Secretary, Lt.-Col. A. Mather, CVO, OBE
Assistant Secretary, Miss R. Wells, MVO

MASTER OF THE HOUSEHOLD'S DEPARTMENT

Buckingham Palace, London SW1A 1AA

Master of the Household, Maj.-Gen. Sir Simon Cooper, KCVO
Deputy Master of the Household, Lt.-Col. C. Richards
Assistants to the Master of the Household, M. T. Parker, MVO; A. Jarman; A. Smith
Chief Clerk, M. C. W. N. Jephson, LVO
Chief Housekeeper, Miss H. Colebrook, MVO
Palace Steward, P. S. Croasdale, RVM
Royal Chef, L. Mann, RVM
Superintendent, Windsor Castle, Maj. M. Davidson, MBE, BEM
Superintendent, The Palace of Holyroodhouse, Lt.-Col. D. Anderson, OBE

ROYAL MEWS DEPARTMENT

Buckingham Palace, London SW1W 0QH

Crown Equerry, Lt.-Col. S. Gilbart-Denham, CVO
Superintendent, Royal Mews, Buckingham Palace, Maj. I. Kelly

THE ROYAL COLLECTION

St James's Palace, London SW1A 1BS

Director of Royal Collection and Surveyor of The Queen's Works of Art, H. Roberts, CVO, FSA
Surveyor of The Queen's Pictures, C. Lloyd, LVO
Librarian, The Royal Library, Windsor Castle, O. Everett, CVO
Deputy Surveyor of The Queen's Works of Art, J. Marsden
Director of Media Affairs, R. Arbiter, LVO
Curator of the Print Room, The Hon. Mrs Roberts, LVO
Financial Director, M. Stevens
Financial Controller, Mrs G. Johnson, MVO
Administrator and Assistant to The Surveyors, D. Rankin-Hunt, MVO, TD
Senior Picture Restorer, Miss V. Pemberton-Pigott, MVO
Chief Restorer, Old Master Drawings, A. Donnithorne

Senior Furniture Restorer, E. Fancourt, LVO, RVM
Armourer, J. Jackson, RVM
Chief Binder, R. Day, MVO, RVM

ROYAL COLLECTION ENTERPRISES LTD
Managing Director, M. E. K. Hewlett, LVO

ECCLESIASTICAL HOUSEHOLD

*Clerk of the Closet, The Bishop of Derby
*Deputy Clerk of the Closet, Revd W. Booth, LVO
*Chaplains and Extra Chaplains to The Queen: approx. 30–40
*Dean of the Chapels Royal, The Bishop of London
Sub-Dean of the Chapels Royal, Revd W. Booth, LVO
*Organist, Choirmaster and Composer, R. J. Popplewell, MVO,
    FRCO, FRCM
Domestic Chaplain, Buckingham Palace, Revd W. Booth, LVO
Domestic Chaplain, Windsor Castle, The Dean of Windsor
Domestic Chaplain, Sandringham, Revd Canon G. R. Hall,
    LVO

MEDICAL HOUSEHOLD

*Head of the Medical Household and Physician to The Queen, R.
    Thompson, DM, FRCP
*Serjeant Surgeon, B. T. Jackson, FRCS
Apothecary to The Queen and to the Household,
    N. R. Southward, CVO
Apothecary to the Household at Windsor, J. Holliday
Apothecary to the Household at Sandringham, I. K. Campbell,
    D.Obst., FRCGP
*Coroner of The Queen's Household, J. Burton, CBE

OTHER HONORARY/CEREMONIAL
APPOINTMENTS

Lord High Almoner, The Bishop of Wakefield
Master of The Queen's Music, M. Williamson, CBE, AO
Poet Laureate (1999–2009), Prof. Andrew Motion
Keeper of the Royal Philatelic Collection, C. Goodwyn
Bargemaster, R. Crouch
Swan Warden, Prof. C. Perrins, LVO
Swan Marker, D. Barber

POLITICAL (GOVERNMENT WHIPS) (*see also* page 277)

*Captain, Honourable Corps of Gentlemen-at-Arms (Chief Whip in
    the Lords)*, The Lord Carter, PC
*Captain, Queen's Bodyguard of the Yeomen of the Guard (Deputy
    Chief Whip in the Lords)*, The Lord McIntosh of
    Haringey
Lords-in-Waiting, The Lord Burlison of Rowlands; The
    Lord Bach
Baronesses-in-Waiting, The Baroness Farrington of
    Ribbleton; The Baroness Ramsay of Cartvale; The
    Baroness Amos
*Treasurer of the Household (Deputy Chief Whip in the
    Commons)*, K. Bradley, MP
Comptroller of the Household, T. McAvoy, MP
Vice-Chamberlain, G. Allen, MP

ARMED FORCES

Gold Sticks, HRH The Princess Royal, KG, GCVO; Gen. Sir
    Charles Guthrie, GCB, LVO, OBE
Vice-Admiral of the United Kingdom, Adm. Sir Nicholas Hunt,
    GCB, LVO
Rear-Admiral of the United Kingdom, Adm. Sir Jeremy Black,
    GBE, KCB, DSO
First and Principal Naval Aide-de-Camp, Adm. Sir Michael
    Boyce, GCB, OBE
Flag Aide-de-Camp, Adm. Sir John Brigstocke, KCB

Aides-de-Camp-General, Gen. Sir Charles Guthrie, GCB,
    LVO, OBE; Gen. Sir Roger Wheeler, GCB, CBE; Gen. Sir
    Michael Walker, KCB, CMG, CBE; Gen. Sir Alex Harley,
    KBE, CB
Air Aides-de-Camp, Air Chief Marshal Sir Richard Johns,
    GCB, CBE, LVO; Air Chief Marshal Sir Peter Squire, KCB,
    DFC, AFC
Gentleman Usher to the Sword of State, Adm. Sir Michael
    Layard, KCB, CBE
Constable and Governor of Windsor Castle, vacant
Governor of Edinburgh Castle, Maj.-Gen. M. J. Strudwick,
    CBE

BODYGUARDS

THE HONOURABLE CORPS OF GENTLEMEN-AT-ARMS
Captain, The Lord Carter, PC
Lieutenant, Lt.-Col. R. Mayfield, DSO
Clerk of the Cheque and Adjutant, Col. D. Fanshawe, OBE;
Gentlemen of the Corps: 27
The Queen's Body Guard of the Yeomen of the Guard
Captain, The Lord McIntosh of Haringey
Lieutenant, Col. G. W. Tufnell
Clerk of the Cheque and Adjutant, Col. S. Longsdon
Yeomen of the Guard: 81

THE QUEEN'S HOUSEHOLD IN SCOTLAND

*Hereditary Lord High Constable of Scotland, The Earl of Erroll
*Hereditary Master of the Household in Scotland, The Duke of
    Argyll
Lord Lyon King of Arms, Sir Malcolm Innes of Edingight,
    KCVO, WS
*Hereditary Banner-Bearer for Scotland, The Earl of Dundee
*Hereditary Bearer of the National Flag of Scotland, The Earl of
    Lauderdale
*Hereditary Keeper of the Palace of Holyroodhouse, The Duke of
    Hamilton and Brandon
*Historiographer, Prof. T. C. Smout, CBE, FBA, FRSE, FSA Scot.
*Botanist, Prof. D. Henderson, CBE, FRSE
*Painter and Limner, vacant
*Sculptor in Ordinary, Prof. Sir Eduardo Paolozzi, CBE, RA
*Astronomer, Prof. J. Brown, Ph.D., FRSE
*Heralds and Pursuivants, see Government Departments

ECCLESIASTICAL HOUSEHOLD

*Dean of the Chapel Royal, Very Revd J. Harkness, CB, OBE
*Dean of the Order of the Thistle, Very Revd G. I. Macmillan,
    CVO
*Chaplains in Ordinary: 10
Domestic Chaplain, Balmoral, Revd R. P. Sloan

MEDICAL HOUSEHOLD

*Physicians in Scotland, P. Brunt, OBE, MD, FRCP; A. Toft, CBE,
    FRCPE
*Surgeons in Scotland, J. Engeset, FRCS; I. Macintyre
Apothecary to the Household at Balmoral, D. J. A. Glass
Apothecary to the Household at the Palace of Holyroodhouse, Dr J.
    Cormack, MD, FRCPE, FRCGP

**ROYAL COMPANY OF ARCHERS (QUEEN'S BODYGUARD
FOR SCOTLAND)

Captain-General and Gold Stick for Scotland, Maj. Sir Hew
    Hamilton-Dalrymple, Bt., KCVO
President of the Council and Silver Stick for Scotland, The
    Duke of Buccleuch and Queensberry, KT, VRD
Adjutant, Maj. the Hon. Sir Lachlan Maclean, Bt.
Secretary, Capt. J. D. B. Younger
Treasurer, J. M. Haldane of Gleneagles
Members on the active list: c.400

HOUSEHOLD OF THE PRINCE PHILIP, DUKE OF EDINBURGH

Office: Buckingham Palace, London SW1A 1AA
Tel: 0171-930 4832

Treasurer, Sir Brian McGrath, KCVO
Private Secretary, Brig. M. G. Hunt-Davis, CVO, CBE
Equerry, Sqh. Ldr. L. Johnson
Temporary Equerries, Capt. P. Wise; Lt.-Col. P. Denning;
   Capt. B. Hancock
Chief Clerk and Accountant, G. D. Partington

HOUSEHOLD OF QUEEN ELIZABETH THE QUEEN MOTHER

Office: Clarence House, St James's Palace, London SW1A 1BA
Tel: 0171-930 3141

Lord Chamberlain, The Earl of Crawford and Balcarres, KT,
   PC
Private Secretary, Comptroller and Equerry, Capt. Sir Alastair
   Aird, GCVO
Assistant Private Secretary and Equerry, Maj. R. Seymour,
   CVO
Treasurer and Extra Equerry, Hon. N. Assheton
Treasurer Emeritus and Equerry, Maj. Sir Ralph Anstruther,
   Bt., GCVO, MC
Equerry, Capt. W. de Rouet (temp.)
Apothecary to the Household, Dr N. Southward, CVO
Surgeon-Apothecary to the Household (Royal Lodge, Windsor), J.
   Holliday
Ladies of the Bedchamber, The Lady Grimthorpe, DCVO; The
   Countess of Scarbrough
Women of the Bedchamber, Dame Frances Campbell-Preston,
   DCVO; Lady Angela Oswald, LVO; The Hon. Mrs
   Rhodes; Mrs Michael Gordon-Lennox
Clerk Comptroller, A. Kirkpatrick-Smith
Information Officer, Mrs R. Murphy, LVO
Clerks, Miss F. Fletcher, LVO; Mrs W. Stevens

HOUSEHOLD OF THE PRINCE OF WALES

Office: St James's Palace, London SW1A 1BS
Tel: 0171-930 4832

Private Secretary and Treasurer, S. M. J. Lamport, CVO
Deputy Private Secretary, M. Bolland
Assistant Private Secretaries, N. S. Archer; Miss E. Buchanan
Press Secretary, Miss S. Henney
Deputy Press Secretary, Mrs C. Harris
Equerry, Lt. Cdr. W. N. Entwisle, RN
Secretary to the Duchy of Cornwall and Keeper of the Records, W.
   R. A. Ross

HOUSEHOLD OF THE DUKE OF YORK

Office: Buckingham Palace, London SW1A 1AA
Tel: 0171-930 4832

Private Secretary, Treasurer and Extra Equerry, Capt. R. N.
   Blair, LVO, RN
Comptroller and Deputy Private Secretary, Miss C. Manley,
   OBE
Equerry, Capt. R. L. Gerrard-Wright

HOUSEHOLD OF THE EARL OF WESSEX

Office: Buckingham Palace, London SW1A 1AA
Tel: 0171-930 4832

Private Secretary, Lt.-Col. S. G. O'Dwyer, LVO
Clerk, Mrs L. Sharp, MVO

HOUSEHOLD OF THE PRINCESS ROYAL

Office: Buckingham Palace, London SW1A 1AA
Tel: 0171-930 4832

Private Secretary, Col. T. Earl
Assistant Private Secretary, Mrs S. Gee
Ladies-in-Waiting, Lady Carew Pole, LVO; Mrs Andrew
   Feilden, LVO; The Hon. Mrs Legge-Bourke, LVO; Mrs
   William Nunneley, LVO; Mrs Timothy Holderness-
   Roddam, LVO; Mrs Charles Ritchie, LVO; Mrs David
   Bowes Lyon

HOUSEHOLD OF THE PRINCESS MARGARET, COUNTESS OF SNOWDON

Office: Kensington Palace, London W8 4PU
Tel: 0171-930 3141

Private Secretary, The Viscount Ullswater, PC
Treasurer, Maj. The Lord Napier and Ettrick, KCVO
Lady-in-Waiting, The Hon. Mrs Whitehead, LVO

HOUSEHOLD OF THE DUKE AND DUCHESS OF GLOUCESTER

Office: Kensington Palace, London W8 4PU
Tel: 0171-937 6374

Private Secretary, Comptroller and Equerry, Maj. N. M. L.
   Barne, LVO
Assistant Private Secretary to the Duchess of Gloucester, Miss S.
   Marland, LVO
Ladies-in-Waiting, Mrs Michael Wigley, CVO; Mrs Euan
   McCorquodale, LVO; Mrs Howard Page, LVO

HOUSEHOLD OF PRINCESS ALICE, DUCHESS OF GLOUCESTER

Office: Kensington Palace, London W8 4PU
Tel: 0171-937 6374

Private Secretary, Comptroller and Equerry, Maj. N. M. L.
   Barne, LVO
Ladies-in-Waiting, Dame Jean Maxwell-Scott, DCVO; Mrs
   Michael Harvey, LVO

HOUSEHOLD OF THE DUKE AND DUCHESS OF KENT

Office: York House, St James's Palace, London SW1 1BQ
Tel: 0171-930 4872

Private Secretary, N. C. Adamson, OBE
Temporary Equerry, Capt. D. Hampshire
Ladies-in-Waiting, Mrs Colin Marsh, LVO; Mrs Julian
   Tomkins; Mrs Peter Troughton; Mrs Richard Beckett

HOUSEHOLD OF PRINCE AND PRINCESS MICHAEL OF KENT

Office: Kensington Palace, London w8 4PU
Tel: 0171-938 3519

Private Secretary, N. Chance
Personal Secretaries, Miss C. Jenkins, Miss K. Garrod
Ladies-in-Waiting, The Hon. Mrs Sanders; Miss A. Frost;
   Mrs J. Fellowes

HOUSEHOLD OF PRINCESS ALEXANDRA, THE HON. LADY OGILVY

Office: Buckingham Palace, London SWIA IAA
Tel: 0171-930 1860

Comptroller and Private Secretary, Capt. N. Blair, LVO, RN
Lady-in-Waiting, Lady Mary Mumford, DCVO

Royal Salutes

ENGLAND

A salute of 62 guns is fired on the wharf at the Tower of London on the following occasions:
(a) the anniversaries of the birth, accession and coronation of the Sovereign
(b) the anniversary of the birth of HM Queen Elizabeth the Queen Mother
(c) the anniversary of the birth of HRH Prince Philip, Duke of Edinburgh

A salute of 41 guns only is fired on extraordinary and triumphal occasions, e.g. on the occasion of the Sovereign opening, proroguing or dissolving Parliament in person, or when passing through London in procession, except when otherwise ordered.

A salute of 41 guns is fired from the two saluting stations in London (the Tower of London and Hyde Park) on the occasion of the birth of a royal infant.

Constable of the Royal Palace and Fortress of London, Field Marshal the Lord Inge, GCB
Lieutenant of the Tower of London, Lt.-Gen. Sir Anthony Denison-Smith, KBE
Resident Governor and Keeper of the Jewel House, Maj.-Gen. G. Field, CB, OBE

Master Gunner of St James's Park, Field Marshal the Lord Vincent of Coleshill, GBE, KCB, DSO
Master Gunner within the Tower, Col. S. Lalor

SCOTLAND

Royal salutes are authorized at Edinburgh Castle and Stirling Castle, although in practice Edinburgh Castle is the only operating saluting station in Scotland.

A salute of 21 guns is fired on the following occasions:
(a) the anniversaries of the birth, accession and coronation of the Sovereign
(b) the anniversary of the birth of HM Queen Elizabeth the Queen Mother
(c) the anniversary of the birth of HRH Prince Philip, Duke of Edinburgh

A salute of 21 guns is fired in Edinburgh on the occasion of the opening of the General Assembly of the Church of Scotland.

A salute of 21 guns may also be fired in Edinburgh on the arrival of HM The Queen, HM Queen Elizabeth the Queen Mother, or a member of the royal family who is a Royal Highness on an official visit.

Royal Finances

FUNDING

THE CIVIL LIST

The Civil List dates back to the late 17th century. It was originally used by the sovereign to supplement hereditary revenues for paying the salaries of judges, ambassadors and other government officers as well as the expenses of the royal household. In 1760 on the accession of George III it was decided that the Civil List would be provided by Parliament to cover all relevant expenditure in return for the King surrendering the hereditary revenues of the Crown. At that time Parliament undertook to pay the salaries of judges, ambassadors, etc. In 1831 Parliament agreed also to meet the costs of the royal palaces in return for a reduction in the Civil List. Each sovereign has agreed to continue this arrangement.

The Civil List paid to The Queen is charged on the Consolidated Fund. Until 1972, the amount of money allocated annually under the Civil List was set for the duration of a reign. The system was then altered to a fixed annual payment for ten years but from 1975 high inflation made an annual review necessary. The system of payments reverted to the practice of a fixed annual payment for ten years from 1 January 1991.

The Civil List Acts provide for other members of the royal family to receive parliamentary annuities from government funds to meet the expenses of carrying out their official duties. Since 1975 The Queen has reimbursed the Treasury for the annuities paid to the Duke of Gloucester, the Duke of Kent and Princess Alexandra. Since 1993 The Queen has reimbursed all the annuities except those paid to herself, Queen Elizabeth the Queen Mother and the Duke of Edinburgh.

The Prince of Wales does not receive a parliamentary annuity. He derives his income from the revenues of the Duchy of Cornwall and these monies meet the official and private expenses of the Prince of Wales and his family.

The annual payments for the years 1991–2000 are:

The Queen	£7,900,000
Queen Elizabeth the Queen Mother	643,000
The Duke of Edinburgh	359,000
*The Duke of York	249,000
*†The Earl of Wessex	141,000
*The Princess Royal	228,000
*The Princess Margaret, Countess of Snowdon	219,000
*Princess Alice, Duchess of Gloucester	87,000
*The Duke of Gloucester	175,000
*The Duke of Kent	236,000
*Princess Alexandra	225,000
	10,462,000
*Refunded to the Treasury	1,560,000
Total	8,947,000

†The Earl of Wessex's annuity was increased from £96,000 upon his marriage in June 1999

GRANTS-IN-AID

The royal household receives grants-in-aid from several government departments to meet various official expenses. The Department for Culture, Media and Sport provides grant-in-aid to pay for the upkeep of English occupied royal palaces, which are used as offices, for official or ceremonial purposes and to which there is public access, and to meet the cost of media and information services.

Royal Travel grant-in-aid is provided by the Department of the Environment, Transport and the Regions to meet the cost of official royal travel by air and rail, using mainly aircraft from 32 (The Royal) Squadron, chartered commercial aircraft for major overseas state visits and the Royal Train.

Grant-in-aid for 1999–2000 is:

Property Services and Communications and Information	£15,000,000
Royal Travel	9,300,000

THE PRIVY PURSE

The funds received by the Privy Purse pay for official expenses incurred by The Queen as head of state and for some of The Queen's private expenditure. The revenues of the Duchy of Lancaster are the principal source of income for the Privy Purse. The revenues of the Duchy were retained by George III in 1760 when the hereditary revenues were surrendered in exchange for the Civil List.

PERSONAL INCOME

The Queen's personal income derives mostly from investments, and is used to meet private expenditure.

DEPARTMENTAL VOTES

Items of expenditure connected with the official duties of the royal family which fall directly on votes of government departments include:

Ministry of Defence – equerries

Foreign and Commonwealth Office – Marshal of the Diplomatic Corps; costs (other than travel costs) associated with overseas visits at the request of government departments

HM Treasury – Central Chancery of the Orders of Knighthood

The Post Office – postal services

TAXATION

The sovereign is not legally liable to pay income tax, capital gains tax or inheritance tax. After income tax was reintroduced in 1842, some income tax was paid voluntarily by the sovereign but over a long period these payments were phased out. In 1992 The Queen offered to pay tax on a voluntary basis from 6 April 1993, and the Prince of Wales to pay tax on a voluntary basis on his income from the Duchy of Cornwall. (He was already taxed in all other respects.)

The main provisions for The Queen and the Prince of Wales to pay tax, set out in a Memorandum of Understanding on Royal Taxation presented to Parliament on 11 February 1993, are that The Queen will pay income tax and capital gains tax in respect of her private income and assets, and on the proportion of the income and capital gains of the Privy Purse used for private purposes. Inheritance tax will be paid on The Queen's assets, except for those which pass to the next sovereign, whether automatically or by gift or bequest. The Prince of Wales will pay income tax on income from the Duchy of Cornwall used for private purposes.

The Prince of Wales has confirmed that he intends to pay tax on the same basis following his accession to the throne.

Other members of the royal family are subject to tax as for any taxpayer.

Military Ranks and Titles

THE QUEEN

Lord High Admiral of the United Kingdom

Colonel-in-Chief
The Life Guards; The Blues and Royals (Royal Horse Guards and 1st Dragoons); The Royal Scots Dragoon Guards (Carabiniers and Greys); The Queen's Royal Lancers; Royal Tank Regiment; Corps of Royal Engineers; Grenadier Guards; Coldstream Guards; Scots Guards; Irish Guards; Welsh Guards; The Royal Welch Fusiliers; The Queen's Lancashire Regiment; The Argyll and Sutherland Highlanders (Princess Louise's); The Royal Green Jackets; Adjutant General's Corps; The Royal Mercian and Lancastrian Yeomanry; The Governor General's Horse Guards (of Canada); The King's Own Calgary Regiment; Canadian Forces Military Engineers Branch; Royal 22e Regiment (of Canada); Governor-General's Foot Guards (of Canada); The Canadian Grenadier Guards; Le Regiment de la Chaudiere (of Canada); 2nd Bn Royal New Brunswick Regiment (North Shore); The 48th Highlanders of Canada; The Argyll and Sutherland Highlanders of Canada (Princess Louise's); The Calgary Highlanders; Royal Australian Engineers; Royal Australian Infantry Corps; Royal Australian Army Ordnance Corps; Royal Australian Army Nursing Corps; The Corps of Royal New Zealand Engineers; Royal New Zealand Infantry Regiment; Royal Malta Artillery; The Malawi Rifles

Affiliated Colonel-in-Chief
The Queen's Gurkha Engineers

Captain-General
Royal Regiment of Artillery; The Honourable Artillery Company; Combined Cadet Force Association; Royal Regiment of Canadian Artillery; Royal Regiment of Australian Artillery; Royal Regiment of New Zealand Artillery; Royal New Zealand Armoured Corps

Patron
Royal Army Chaplains' Department

Air Commodore-in-Chief
Royal Auxiliary Air Force; Royal Air Force Regiment; Air Reserve (of Canada); Royal Australian Air Force Reserve; Territorial Air Force (of New Zealand)

Commandant-in-Chief
Royal Air Force College, Cranwell

Hon. Air Commodore
RAF Marham

HRH THE PRINCE PHILIP, DUKE OF EDINBURGH

Admiral of the Fleet
Field Marshal
Marshal of the Royal Air Force

Admiral of the Fleet, Royal Australian Navy
Field Marshal, Australian Military Forces
Marshal of the Royal Australian Air Force

Admiral of the Fleet, Royal New Zealand Navy
Field Marshal, New Zealand Army
Marshal of the Royal New Zealand Air Force

Captain-General, Royal Marines

Admiral
Royal Canadian Sea Cadets

Colonel-in-Chief
The Royal Gloucestershire, Berkshire and Wiltshire Regiment; The Highlanders (Seaforth, Gordons and Camerons); Corps of Royal Electrical and Mechanical Engineers; Intelligence Corps; Army Cadet Force Association; The Royal Canadian Regiment; The Royal Hamilton Light Infantry (Wentworth Regiment) (of Canada); The Cameron Highlanders of Ottawa; The Queen's Own Cameron Highlanders of Canada; The Seaforth Highlanders of Canada; The Royal Canadian Army Cadets; The Royal Corps of Australian Electrical and Mechanical Engineers; The Australian Cadet Corps

Deputy Colonel-in-Chief
The Queen's Royal Hussars (Queen's Own and Royal Irish)

Colonel
Grenadier Guards

Hon. Colonel
City of Edinburgh Universities Officers' Training Corps; The Trinidad and Tobago Regiment

Air Commodore-in-Chief
Air Training Corps; Royal Canadian Air Cadets

Hon. Air Commodore
RAF Kinloss

HM QUEEN ELIZABETH THE QUEEN MOTHER

Colonel-in-Chief
1st The Queen's Dragoon Guards; The Queen's Royal Hussars (Queen's Own and Royal Irish); 9th/12th Royal Lancers (Prince of Wales's); The King's Regiment; The Royal Anglian Regiment; The Light Infantry; The Black Watch (Royal Highland Regiment); Royal Army Medical Corps; The Black Watch (Royal Highland Regiment) of Canada; The Toronto Scottish Regiment; Canadian Forces Medical Services; Royal Australian Army Medical Corps; Royal New Zealand Army Medical Corps

Hon. Colonel
The Royal Yeomanry; The London Scottish; Inns of Court and City Yeomanry

Commandant-in-Chief
Women in the Royal Navy; Women, Royal Air Force; Royal Air Force Central Flying School

HRH THE PRINCE OF WALES

Rear Admiral, Royal Navy
Major-General, Army
Air Vice-Marshal, Royal Air Force

Colonel-in-Chief
The Royal Dragoon Guards; The 22nd (Cheshire) Regiment; The Royal Regiment of Wales (24th/41st Foot); The Parachute Regiment; The Royal Gurkha Rifles; Army Air Corps; The Royal Canadian Dragoons; Lord Strathcona's Horse (Royal Canadians); Royal Regiment of Canada; Royal Winnipeg Rifles; Air Reserve

Group of Air Command (of Canada); Royal Australian Armoured Corps; The Royal Pacific Islands Regiment

Deputy Colonel-in-Chief
The Highlanders (Seaforth, Gordons and Camerons)

Colonel
Welsh Guards

Air Commodore-in-Chief
Royal New Zealand Air Force

Hon. Air Commodore
RAF Valley

HRH THE DUKE OF YORK

Commander, Royal Navy

Admiral
Sea Cadet Corps

Colonel-in-Chief
The Staffordshire Regiment (The Prince of Wales's); The Royal Irish Regiment (27th (Inniskilling), 83rd, 87th and The Ulster Defence Regiment); Royal New Zealand Army Logistic Regiment; The Queen's York Rangers (First Americans)

Hon. Air Commodore
RAF Lossiemouth

HRH THE PRINCESS ROYAL

Rear Admiral
Chief Commandant for Women in the Royal Navy

Colonel-in-Chief
The King's Royal Hussars; Royal Corps of Signals; The Royal Scots (The Royal Regiment); The Worcestershire and Sherwood Foresters Regiment (29th/45th Foot); The Royal Logistic Corps; 8th Canadian Hussars (Princess Louise's); Canadian Forces Communications and Electronics Branch; The Grey and Simcoe Foresters; The Royal Regina Rifle Regiment; Royal Australian Corps of Signals; Royal New Zealand Corps of Signals; Royal New Zealand Nursing Corps

Colonel
Blues and Royals

Affiliated Colonel-in-Chief
The Queen's Gurkha Signals; The Queen's Own Gurkha Transport Regiment

Hon. Colonel
University of London Officers' Training Corps

Hon. Air Commodore
RAF Lyneham; University of London Air Squadron

HRH THE PRINCESS MARGARET, COUNTESS OF SNOWDON

Colonel-in-Chief
The Light Dragoons; The Royal Highland Fusiliers (Princess Margaret's Own Glasgow and Ayrshire Regiment); Queen Alexandra's Royal Army Nursing Corps; The Highland Fusiliers of Canada; The Princess Louise Fusiliers (of Canada); The Bermuda Regiment

Deputy Colonel-in-Chief
The Royal Anglian Regiment

Hon. Air Commodore
RAF Coningsby

HRH PRINCESS ALICE, DUCHESS OF GLOUCESTER

Air Chief Marshal

Colonel-in-Chief
The King's Own Scottish Borderers; Royal Australian Corps of Transport

Deputy Colonel-in-Chief
The King's Royal Hussars; The Royal Anglian Regiment

Air Chief Commandant
Women, Royal Air Force

HRH THE DUKE OF GLOUCESTER

Hon. Air Marshal

Deputy Colonel-in-Chief
The Royal Gloucestershire, Berkshire and Wiltshire Regiment; The Royal Logistic Corps

Hon. Colonel
Royal Monmouthshire Royal Engineers (Militia)

Hon. Air Commodore
RAF Odiham

HRH THE DUCHESS OF GLOUCESTER

Colonel-in-Chief
Royal Australian Army Educational Corps; Royal New Zealand Army Educational Corps

Deputy Colonel-in-Chief
Adjutant-General's Corps

HRH THE DUKE OF KENT

Field Marshal
Hon. Air Chief Marshal

Colonel-in-Chief
The Royal Regiment of Fusiliers; The Devonshire and Dorset Regiment; The Lorne Scots (Peel, Dufferin and Hamilton Regiment)

Deputy Colonel-in-Chief
The Royal Scots Dragoon Guards (Carabiniers and Greys)

Colonel
Scots Guards

Hon. Air Commodore
RAF Leuchars

HRH THE DUCHESS OF KENT

Hon. Major-General
Colonel-in-Chief
The Prince of Wales's Own Regiment of Yorkshire

Deputy Colonel-in-Chief
The Royal Dragoon Guards; Adjutant-General's Corps; The Royal Logistic Corps

HRH PRINCE MICHAEL OF KENT

Major (retd), The Royal Hussars (Prince of Wales's Own)
Hon. Commodore
Royal Naval Reserve

HRH PRINCESS ALEXANDRA, THE HON. LADY OGILVY

Patron
Queen Alexandra's Royal Naval Nursing Service
Colonel-in-Chief
The King's Own Royal Border Regiment; The Queen's Own Rifles of Canada; The Canadian Scottish Regiment (Princess Mary's)
Deputy Colonel-in-Chief
The Queen's Royal Lancers; The Light Infantry
Deputy Hon. Colonel
The Royal Yeomanry
Patron and Air Chief Commandant
Princess Mary's Royal Air Force Nursing Service

The House of Windsor

King George V assumed by royal proclamation (17 July 1917) for his House and family, as well as for all descendants in the male line of Queen Victoria who are subjects of these realms, the name of Windsor.

KING GEORGE V (George Frederick Ernest Albert), second son of King Edward VII, *born* 3 June 1865; *married* 6 July 1893 HSH Princess Victoria Mary Augusta Louise Olga Pauline Claudine Agnes of Teck (Queen Mary, *born* 26 May 1867; *died* 24 March 1953); *succeeded* to the throne 6 May 1910; *died* 20 January 1936. *Issue:*

1. HRH PRINCE EDWARD Albert Christian George Andrew Patrick David, *born* 23 June 1894, *succeeded* to the throne as King Edward VIII, 20 January 1936; *abdicated* 11 December 1936; created *Duke of Windsor* 1937; *married* 3 June 1937, Mrs Wallis Simpson (Her Grace The Duchess of Windsor, *born* 19 June 1896; *died* 24 April 1986), *died* 28 May 1972

2. HRH PRINCE ALBERT Frederick Arthur George, *born* 14 December 1895, *created* Duke of York 1920; *married* 26 April 1923, Lady Elizabeth Bowes-Lyon, youngest daughter of the 14th Earl of Strathmore and Kinghorne (HM Queen Elizabeth the Queen Mother, *see* page 117), *succeeded* to the throne as King George VI, 11 December 1936; *died* 6 February 1952, having had issue (*see* page 117)

3. HRH PRINCESS (Victoria Alexandra Alice) MARY, *born* 25 April 1897, *created* Princess Royal 1932; *married* 28 February 1922, Viscount Lascelles, later the 6th Earl of Harewood (1882–1947), *died* 28 March 1965. *Issue:*
    (1) George Henry Hubert Lascelles, 7th Earl of Harewood, KBE, *born* 7 February 1923; *married* (1) 1949, Maria (Marion) Stein (marriage dissolved 1967); *issue,* (*a*) David Henry George,

Viscount Lascelles, *born* 1950; (*b*) James Edward, *born* 1953; (*c*) (Robert) Jeremy Hugh, *born* 1955; (2) 1967, Mrs Patricia Tuckwell; *issue,* (*d*) Mark Hubert, *born* 1964
    (2) Gerald David Lascelles (1924–98), *married* (1) 1952, Miss Angela Dowding (marriage dissolved 1978); *issue,* (*a*) Henry Ulick, *born* 1953; (2) 1978, Mrs Elizabeth Colvin; *issue,* (*b*) Martin David, *born* 1962

4. HRH PRINCE HENRY William Frederick Albert, *born* 31 March 1900, *created* Duke of Gloucester, Earl of Ulster and Baron Culloden 1928, *married* 6 November 1935, Lady Alice Christabel Montagu-Douglas-Scott, daughter of the 7th Duke of Buccleuch (HRH Princess Alice, Duchess of Gloucester, *see* page 118); *died* 10 June 1974. *Issue:*
    (1) HRH Prince William Henry Andrew Frederick, *born* 18 December 1941; *accidentally killed* 28 August 1972
    (2) HRH Prince Richard Alexander Walter George (HRH The Duke of Gloucester), *see* page 118

5. HRH PRINCE GEORGE Edward Alexander Edmund, *born* 20 December 1902, *created* Duke of Kent, Earl of St Andrews and Baron Downpatrick 1934, *married* 29 November 1934, HRH Princess Marina of Greece and Denmark (*born* 30 November OS, 1906; *died* 27 August 1968); *killed on active service,* 25 August 1942. *Issue:*
    (1) HRH Prince Edward George Nicholas Paul Patrick (HRH The Duke of Kent), *see* page 118
    (2) HRH Princess Alexandra Helen Elizabeth Olga Christabel (HRH Princess Alexandra, the Hon. Lady Ogilvy), *see* page 118
    (3) HRH Prince Michael George Charles Franklin (HRH Prince Michael of Kent), *see* page 118

6. HRH PRINCE JOHN Charles Francis, *born* 12 July 1905; *died* 18 January 1919

Descendants of Queen Victoria

QUEEN VICTORIA (Alexandrina Victoria), *born* 24 May 1819; *succeeded* to the throne 20 June 1837; *married* 10 February 1840 (Francis) Albert Augustus Charles Emmanuel, Duke of Saxony, Prince of Saxe-Coburg and Gotha (HRH Albert, Prince Consort, *born* 26 August 1819, *died* 14 December 1861); *died* 22 January 1901. *Issue:*
1. HRH PRINCESS VICTORIA Adelaide Mary Louisa (Princess Royal) (1840–1901), *m.* 1858, Friedrich III (1831–88), German Emperor March–June 1888. *Issue:*
    (1) HIM Wilhelm II (1859–1941), German Emperor 1888–1918, *m.* (1) 1881 Princess Augusta Victoria of Schleswig-Holstein-Sonderburg-Augustenburg (1858–1921); (2) 1922 Princess Hermine of Reuss (1887–1947). *Issue:*
        (*a*) Prince Wilhelm (1882–1951), *Crown Prince* 1888–1918, *m.* 1905 Duchess Cecilie of Mecklenburg-Schwerin; *issue:* Prince Wilhelm (1906–40); Prince Louis Ferdinand (1907–94), *m.* 1938 Grand Duchess Kira (*see* page 128); Prince Hubertus (1909–50); Prince Friedrich Georg (1911–66); Princess Alexandrine Irene (1915–80); Princess Cecilie (1917–75)
        (*b*) Prince Eitel-Friedrich (1883–1942), *m.* 1906 Duchess Sophie of Oldenburg (marriage dissolved 1926)
        (*c*) Prince Adalbert (1884–1948), *m.* 1914 Duchess Adelheid of Saxe-Meiningen; *issue:* Princess Victoria Marina (1917–81); Prince Wilhelm Victor (1919–89)
        (*d*) Prince August Wilhelm (1887–1949), *m.* 1908 Princess Alexandra of Schleswig-Holstein-Sonderburg-Glücksburg (marriage dissolved 1920); *issue:* Prince Alexander (1912–85)
        (*e*) Prince Oskar (1888–1958), *m.* 1914 Countess von Ruppin; *issue:* Prince Oskar (1915–39); Prince Burchard (1917–88); Princess Herzeleide (1918–89); Prince Wilhelm-Karl (*b.* 1922)
        (*f*) Prince Joachim (1890–1920), *m.* 1916 Princess Marie of Anhalt; *issue:* Prince (Karl) Franz Joseph (1916–75), and has issue

        (*g*) Princess Viktoria Luise (1892–1980), *m.* 1913 Ernst, Duke of Brunswick 1913–18 (1887–1953); *issue:* Prince Ernst (1914–87); Prince Georg (*b.* 1915), *m.* 1946 Princess Sophie of Greece (*see* page 128) and has issue (two sons, one daughter); Princess Frederika (1917–81), *m.* 1938 Paul I, King of the Hellenes (*see* page 128); Prince Christian (1919–81); Prince Welf Heinrich (*b.* 1923)
    (2) Princess Charlotte (1860–1919), *m.* 1878 Bernhard, Duke of Saxe-Meiningen 1914 (1851–1914). *Issue:*
        Princess Feodora (1879–1945), *m.* 1898 Prince Heinrich XXX of Reuss
    (3) Prince Heinrich (1862–1929), *m.* 1888 Princess Irene of Hesse (*see* page 128). *Issue:*
        (*a*) Prince Waldemar (1889–1945), *m.* Princess Calixta Agnes of Lippe
        (*b*) Prince Sigismund (1896–1978), *m.* 1919 Princess Charlotte of Saxe-Altenburg; *issue:* Princess Barbara (1920–94); Prince Alfred (*b.* 1924)
        (*c*) Prince Heinrich (1900–4)
    (4) Prince Sigismund (1864–6)
    (5) Princess Victoria (1866–1929), *m.* (1) 1890, Prince Adolf of Schaumburg-Lippe (1859–1916); (2) 1927 Alexander Zubkov
    (6) Prince Waldemar (1868–79)
    (7) Princess Sophie (1870–1932), *m.* 1889 Constantine I (1868–1923), King of the Hellenes 1913–17, 1920–3. *Issue:*
        (*a*) George II (1890–1947), King of the Hellenes 1923–4 and 1935–47, *m.* 1921 Princess Elisabeth of Roumania (marriage dissolved 1935) (*see* page 128)
        (*b*) Alexander I (1893–1920), King of the Hellenes 1917–20, *m.*

1919 Aspasia Manos; *issue*: Princess Alexandra (1921–93), *m.* 1944 King Petar II of Yugoslavia (*see* below)
(*c*) Princess Helena (1896–1982), *m.* 1921 King Carol of Roumania (*see* below), (marriage dissolved 1928)
(*d*) Paul I (1901–64), King of the Hellenes 1947–64, *m.* 1938 Princess Frederika of Brunswick (*see* page 127); *issue*: King Constantine II (*b.* 1940), *m.* 1964 Princess Anne-Marie of Denmark (*see* page 129), and has issue (three sons, two daughters); Princess Sophie (*b.* 1938), *m.* 1962 Juan Carlos I of Spain (*see* page 129); Princess Irene (*b.* 1942)
(*e*) Princess Irene (1904–74), *m.* 1939 4th Duke of Aosta; *issue*: Prince Amedeo, 5th Duke of Aosta (*b.* 1943)
(*f*) Princess Katherine (Lady Katherine Brandram) (*b.* 1913), *m.* 1947 Major R. C. A. Brandram, MC, TD; *issue*: R. Paul G. A. Brandram (*b.* 1948)
(8) Princess Margarethe (1872–1954), *m.* 1893 Prince Friedrich Karl of Hesse (1868–1940). *Issue*:
 (*a*) Prince Friedrich Wilhelm (1893–1916)
 (*b*) Prince Maximilian (1894–1914)
 (*c*) Prince Philipp (1896–1980), *m.* 1925 Princess Mafalda of Italy; *issue*: Prince Moritz (*b.* 1926); Prince Heinrich (*b.* 1927); Prince Otto (*b.* 1937); Princess Elisabeth (*b.* 1940)
 (*d*) Prince Wolfgang (1896–1989), *m.* (1) 1924 Princess Marie Alexandra of Baden; (2) 1948 Ottilie Möller
 (*e*) Prince Richard (1901–69)
 (*f*) Prince Christoph (1901–43), *m.* 1930 Princess Sophie of Greece (*see* below) and has issue (two sons, three daughters)

2. HRH PRINCE ALBERT EDWARD (HM KING EDWARD VII), *b.* 9 November 1841, *m.* 1863 HRH Princess Alexandra of Denmark (1844–1925), *succeeded* to the throne 22 January 1901, *d.* 6 May 1910. *Issue*:
(1) Albert Victor, Duke of Clarence and Avondale (1864–92)
(2) George (HM KING GEORGE V) (*see* page 127)
(3) Louise (1867–931) Princess Royal 1905–31, *m.* 1889 1st Duke of Fife (1849–1912). *Issue*:
 (*a*) Princess Alexandra, Duchess of Fife (1891–1959), *m.* 1913 Prince Arthur of Connaught (*see* page 129)
 (*b*) Princess Maud (1893–1945), *m.* 1923 11th Earl of Southesk (1893–1992); *issue*: The Duke of Fife (*b.* 1929)
(4) Victoria (1868–1935)
(5) Maud (1869–1938), *m.* 1896 Prince Carl of Denmark (1872–1957), later King Haakon VII of Norway 1905–57. *Issue*:
 (*a*) Olav V (1903–91), King of Norway 1957–91, *m.* 1929 Princess Märtha of Sweden (1901–54); *issue*: Princess Ragnhild (*b.* 1930); Princess Astrid (*b.* 1932); Harald V, King of Norway (*b.* 1937)
(6) Alexander (6–7 April 1871)

3. HRH PRINCESS ALICE Maud Mary (1843–78), *m.* 1862 Prince Ludwig (1837–92), Grand Duke of Hesse 1877–92. *Issue*:
(1) Victoria (1863–1950), *m.* 1884 *Admiral of the Fleet* Prince Louis of Battenberg (1854–1921), *cr.* 1st Marquess of Milford Haven 1917. *Issue*:
 (*a*) Alice (1885–1969), *m.* 1903 Prince Andrew of Greece (1882–1944); *issue*: Princess Margarita (1905–81), *m.* 1931 Prince Gottfried of Hohenlohe-Langenburg (*see* below); Princess Theodora (1906–69), *m.* Prince Berthold of Baden (1906–63) and has issue (two sons, one daughter); Princess Cecilie (1911–37), *m.* George, Grand Duke of Hesse (*see* below); Princess Sophie (*b.* 1914), *m.* (1) 1930 Prince Christoph of Hesse (*see* above); (2) 1946 Prince Georg of Hanover (*see* page 127); Prince Philip, Duke of Edinburgh (*b.* 1921) (*see* page 117)
 (*b*) Louise (1889–1965), *m.* 1923 Gustaf VI Adolf (1882–1973), King of Sweden 1950–73
 (*c*) George, 2nd Marquess of Milford Haven (1892–1938), *m.* 1916 Countess Nadejda, daughter of Grand Duke Michael of Russia; *issue*: Lady Tatiana (1917–88); David Michael, 3rd Marquess (1919–70)
 (*d*) Louis, 1st Earl Mountbatten of Burma (1900–79), *m.* 1922 Edwina Ashley, daughter of Lord Mount Temple; *issue*: Patricia, Countess Mountbatten of Burma (*b.* 1924), Pamela (*b.* 1929)
(2) Elizabeth (1864–1918), *m.* 1884 Grand Duke Sergius of Russia (1857–1905)
(3) Irene (1866–1953), *m.* 1888 Prince Heinrich of Prussia (*see* page 127)
(4) Ernst Ludwig (1868–1937), Grand Duke of Hesse 1892–1918, *m.* (1) 1894 Princess Victoria Melita of Saxe-Coburg (*see*

below) (marriage dissolved 1901); (2) 1905 Princess Eleonore of Solms-Hohensolmslich. *Issue*:
 (*a*) Princess Elizabeth (1895–1903)
 (*b*) George, Hereditary Grand Duke of Hesse (1906–37), *m.* Princess Cecilie of Greece (*see* above), and had issue, two sons, accidentally killed with parents 1937
 (*c*) Ludwig, Prince of Hesse (1908–68), *m.* 1937 Margaret, daughter of 1st Lord Geddes
(5) Frederick William (1870–3)
(6) Alix (Tsaritsa of Russia) (1872–1918), *m.* 1894 Nicholas II (1868–1918) Tsar of All the Russias 1894–1917, assassinated 16 July 1918. *Issue*:
 (*a*) Grand Duchess Olga (1895–1918)
 (*b*) Grand Duchess Tatiana (1897–1918)
 (*c*) Grand Duchess Marie (1899–1918)
 (*d*) Grand Duchess Anastasia (1901–18)
 (*e*) Alexis, Tsarevich of Russia (1904–18)
(7) Marie (1874–8)

4. HRH PRINCE ALFRED Ernest Albert, Duke of Edinburgh, *Admiral of the Fleet* (1844–1900), *m.* 1874 Grand Duchess Marie Alexandrovna of Russia (1853–1920); succeeded as Duke of Saxe-Coburg and Gotha 22 August 1893. *Issue*:
(1) Alfred, Prince of Saxe-Coburg (1874–99)
(2) Marie (1875–1938), *m.* 1893 Ferdinand (1865–1927), King of Roumania 1914–27. *Issue*:
 (*a*) Carol II (1893–1953), King of Roumania 1930–40, *m.* (2) 1921 Princess Helena of Greece (*see* above) (marriage dissolved 1928; *issue*: Michael (*b.* 1921), King of Roumania 1927–30, 1940–7, *m.* 1948 Princess Anne of Bourbon-Parma, and has issue (five daughters)
 (*b*) Elisabeth (1894–1956), *m.* 1921 George II, King of the Hellenes (*see* page 127)
 (*c*) Marie (1900–61), *m.* 1922 Alexander (1888–1934), King of Yugoslavia 1921–34; *issue*: Petar II (1923–70), King of Yugoslavia 1934–45, *m.* 1944 Princess Alexandra of Greece (*see* above) and has issue (Crown Prince Alexander, *b.* 1945); Prince Tomislav (*b.* 1928), *m.* (1) 1957 Princess Margarita of Baden (daughter of Princess Theodora of Greece and Prince Berthold of Baden, *see* above); (2) 1982 Linda Bonney; and has issue (three sons, one daughter); Prince Andrej (1929–90), *m.* (1) 1956 Princess Christina of Hesse (daughter of Prince Christoph of Hesse and Princess Sophie of Greece, *see* above); (2) 1963 Princess Kira-Melita of Leiningen (*see* below); and has issue (three sons, two daughters)
 (*d*) Prince Nicolas (1903–78)
 (*e*) Princess Ileana (1909–91), *m.* (1) 1931 Archduke Anton of Austria; (2) 1954 Dr Stefan Issarescu; *issue*: Archduke Stefan (*b.* 1932); Archduchess Maria Ileana (1933–59); Archduchess Alexandra (*b.* 1935); Archduke Dominic (*b.* 1937); Archduchess Maria Magdalena (*b.* 1939); Archduchess Elisabeth (*b.* 1942)
 (*f*) Prince Mircea (1913–16)
(3) Victoria Melita (1876–1936), *m.* (1) 1894 Grand Duke Ernst Ludwig of Hesse (*see* above) (marriage dissolved 1901); (2) 1905 the Grand Duke Kirill of Russia (1876–1938). *Issue*:
 (*a*) Marie Kirillovna (1907–51), *m.* 1925 Prince Friedrich Karl of Leiningen; *issue*: Prince Emich (1926–91); Prince Karl (1928–90); Princess Kira-Melita (*b.* 1930), *m.* Prince Andrej of Yugoslavia (*see* above); Princess Margarita (*b.* 1932); Princess Mechtilde (*b.* 1936); Prince Friedrich (*b.* 1938)
 (*b*) Kira Kirillovna (1909–67), *m.* 1938 Prince Louis Ferdinand of Prussia (*see* page 127); *issue*: Prince Friedrich Wilhelm (*b.* 1939); Prince Michael (*b.* 1940); Princess Marie (*b.* 1942); Princess Kira (*b.* 1943); Prince Louis Ferdinand (1944–77); Prince Christian (*b.* 1946); Princess Xenia (1949–92)
 (*c*) Vladimir Kirillovich (1917–92), *m.* 1948 Princess Leonida Bagration-Mukhransky; *issue*: Grand Duchess Maria (*b.* 1953), and has issue
(4) Alexandra (1878–1942), *m.* 1896 Ernst, Prince of Hohenlohe Langenburg. *Issue*:
 (*a*) Gottfried (1897–1960), *m.* 1931 Princess Margarita of Greece (*see* above); *issue*: Prince Kraft (*b.* 1935), Princess Beatrice (1936–97), Prince Georg Andreas (*b.* 1938), Prince Ruprecht (1944–76); Prince Albrecht (1944–92)
 (*b*) Maria (1899–1967), *m.* 1916 Prince Friedrich of Schleswig-Holstein-Sonderburg-Glücksburg; *issue*: Prince Peter (1922–80); Princess Marie (*b.* 1927)
 (*c*) Princess Alexandra (1901–63)

(d) Princess Irma (1902–86)
(5) Princess Beatrice (1884–1966), m. 1909 Alfonso of Orleans, Infante of Spain. Issue:
   (a) Prince Alvaro (b. 1910), m. 1937 Carla Parodi-Delfino; issue: Doña Gerarda (b. 1939); Don Alonso (1941–75); Doña Beatriz (b. 1943); Don Alvaro (b. 1947)
   (b) Prince Alonso (1912–36)
   (c) Prince Ataulfo (1913–74)

5. HRH PRINCESS HELENA Augusta Victoria (1846–1923), m. 1866 Prince Christian of Schleswig-Holstein-Sonderburg-Augustenburg (1831–1917). Issue:
(1) Prince Christian Victor (1867–1900)
(2) Prince Albert (1869–1931), Duke of Schleswig-Holstein 1921–31
(3) Princess Helena (1870–1948)
(4) Princess Marie Louise (1872–1956), m. 1891 Prince Aribert of Anhalt (marriage dissolved 1900)
(5) Prince Harold (12–20 May 1876)

6. HRH PRINCESS LOUISE Caroline Alberta (1848–1939), m. 1871 the Marquess of Lorne, afterwards 9th Duke of Argyll (1845–1914); without issue

7. HRH PRINCE ARTHUR William Patrick Albert, Duke of Connaught, Field Marshal (1850–1942), m. 1879 Princess Louisa of Prussia (1860–1917). Issue:
(1) Margaret (1882–1920), m. 1905 Crown Prince Gustaf Adolf (1882–1973), afterwards King of Sweden 1950–73. Issue:
   (a) Gustaf Adolf, Duke of Västerbotten (1906–47), m. 1932 Princess Sibylla of Saxe-Coburg-Gotha (see below); issue: Princess Margaretha (b. 1934); Princess Birgitta (b. 1937); Princess Désirée (b. 1938); Princess Christina (b. 1943); Carl XVI Gustaf, King of Sweden (b. 1946)
   (b) Count Sigvard Bernadotte (b. 1907), m.; issue: Count Michael (b. 1944)
   (c) Princess Ingrid (Queen Mother of Denmark) (b. 1910), m. 1935 Frederick IX (1899–1972), King of Denmark 1947–72; issue: Margrethe II, Queen of Denmark (b. 1940); Princess Benedikte (b. 1944); Princess Anne-Marie (b. 1946), m. 1964 Constantine II of Greece (see page 128)
   (d) Prince Bertil, Duke of Halland (1912–97), m. 1976 Mrs Lilian Craig
   (e) Count Carl Bernadotte (b. 1916), m. (1) 1946 Mrs Kerstin Johnson; (2) 1988 Countess Gunnila Bussler
(2) Arthur (1883–1938), m. 1913 HH the Duchess of Fife (see page 128). Issue:

Alastair Arthur, 2nd Duke of Connaught (1914–43)
(3) (Victoria) Patricia (1886–1974), m. 1919 Adm. Hon. Sir Alexander Ramsay. Issue:
Alexander Ramsay of Mar (b. 1919), m. 1956 Hon. Flora Fraser (Lady Saltoun)

8. HRH PRINCE LEOPOLD George Duncan Albert, Duke of Albany (1853–84), m. 1882 Princess Helena of Waldeck (1861–1922). Issue:
(1) Alice (1883–1981), m. 1904 Prince Alexander of Teck (1874–1957), cr. 1st Earl of Athlone 1917. Issue:
   (a) Lady May (1906–94), m. 1931 Sir Henry Abel-Smith, KCMG, KCVO, DSO; issue: Anne (b. 1932); Richard (b. 1933); Elizabeth (b. 1936)
   (b) Rupert, Viscount Trematon (1907–28)
   (c) Prince Maurice (March–September 1910)
(2) Charles Edward (1884–1954), Duke of Albany 1884 until title suspended 1917, Duke of Saxe-Coburg-Gotha 1900–18, m. 1905 Princess Victoria Adelheid of Schleswig-Holstein-Sonderburg-Glücksburg. Issue:
   (a) Prince Johann Leopold (1906–72), and has issue
   (b) Princess Sibylla (1908–72), m. 1932 Prince Gustav Adolf of Sweden (see above)
   (c) Prince Dietmar Hubertus (1909–43)
   (d) Princess Caroline (1912–83), and has issue
   (e) Prince Friedrich Josias (b. 1918), and has issue

9. HRH PRINCESS BEATRICE Mary Victoria Feodore (1857–1944), m. 1885 Prince Henry of Battenberg (1858–96). Issue:
(1) Alexander, 1st Marquess of Carisbrooke (1886–1960), m. 1917 Lady Irene Denison. Issue:
Lady Iris Mountbatten (1920–82), m.; issue: Robin A. Bryan (b. 1957)
(2) Victoria Eugénie (1887–1969), m. 1906 Alfonso XIII (1886–1941) King of Spain 1886–1931. Issue:
   (a) Prince Alfonso (1907–38)
   (b) Prince Jaime (1908–75), and has issue
   (c) Princess Beatrice (b. 1909), and has issue
   (d) Princess Maria (1911–96), and has issue
   (e) Prince Juan (1913–93), Count of Barcelona; issue: Princess Maria (b. 1936); Juan Carlos I, King of Spain (b. 1938), m. 1962 Princess Sophie of Greece (see page 128) and has issue (one son, two daughters); Princess Margarita (b. 1939)
   (f) Prince Gonzalo (1914–34)
(3) Major Lord Leopold Mountbatten (1889–1922)
(4) Maurice (1891–1914), died of wounds received in action

Kings and Queens

ENGLISH KINGS AND QUEENS 927 TO 1603

HOUSES OF CERDIC AND DENMARK

Reign
927–939 ÆTHELSTAN
Son of Edward the Elder, by Ecgwynn, and grandson of Alfred
Acceded to Wessex and Mercia c.924, established direct rule over Northumbria 927, effectively creating the Kingdom of England
Reigned 15 years

939–946 EDMUND I
Born 921, son of Edward the Elder, by Eadgifu
Married (1) Ælfgifu (2) Æthelflæd
Killed aged 25, reigned 6 years

946–955 EADRED
Son of Edward the Elder, by Eadgifu
Reigned 9 years

955–959 EADWIG
Born before 943, son of Edmund and Ælfgifu
Married Ælfgifu
Reigned 3 years

959–975 EDGAR I
Born 943, son of Edmund and Ælfgifu
Married (1) Æthelflæd (2) Wulfthryth (3) Ælfthryth
Died aged 32, reigned 15 years

975–978 EDWARD I (the Martyr)
Born c.962, son of Edgar and Æthelflæd
Assassinated aged c.16, reigned 2 years

978–1016 ÆTHELRED (the Unready)
Born c.968/969, son of Edgar and Ælfthryth
Married (1) Ælfgifu (2) Emma, daughter of Richard I, count of Normandy
1013–14 dispossessed of kingdom by Swegn Forkbeard (king of Denmark 987–1014)
Died aged c.47, reigned 38 years

1016 EDMUND II (Ironside)
Born before 993, son of Æthelred and Ælfgifu
Married Ealdgyth
Died aged over 23, reigned 7 months (April–November)

1016–1035 CNUT (Canute)
Born c.995, son of Swegn Forkbeard, king of Denmark, and Gunhild
Married (1) Ælfgifu (2) Emma, widow of Æthelred the Unready
Gained submission of West Saxons 1015, Northumbrians 1016, Mercia 1016, king of all

England after Edmund's death
King of Denmark 1019–35, king of Norway 1028–35
Died aged *c*.40, *reigned* 19 years

1035–1040   HAROLD I (Harefoot)
Born c.1016/17, son of Cnut and Ælfgifu
Married Ælfgifu
1035 recognized as regent for himself and his brother Harthacnut; 1037 recognized as king
Died aged *c*.23, *reigned* 4 years

1040–1042   HARTHACNUT
Born c.1018, son of Cnut and Emma
Titular king of Denmark from 1028
Acknowledged king of England 1035–7 with Harold I as regent; effective king after Harold's death
Died aged *c*.24, *reigned* 2 years

1042–1066   EDWARD II (the Confessor)
Born between 1002 and 1005, son of Æthelred the Unready and Emma
Married Eadgyth, daughter of Godwine, earl of Wessex
Died aged over 60, *reigned* 23 years

1066   HAROLD II (Godwinesson)
Born c.1020, son of Godwine, earl of Wessex, and Gytha
Married (1) Eadgyth (2) Ealdgyth
Killed in battle aged *c*.46, *reigned* 10 months (January–October)

THE HOUSE OF NORMANDY

1066–1087   WILLIAM I (the Conqueror)
Born 1027/8, son of Robert I, duke of Normandy; obtained the Crown by conquest
Married Matilda, daughter of Baldwin, count of Flanders
Died aged *c*.60, *reigned* 20 years

1087–1100   WILLIAM II (Rufus)
Born between 1056 and 1060, third son of William I; succeeded his father in England only
Killed aged *c*.40, *reigned* 12 years

1100–1135   HENRY I (Beauclerk)
Born 1068, fourth son of William I
Married (1) Edith or Matilda, daughter of Malcolm III of Scotland (2) Adela, daughter of Godfrey, count of Louvain
Died aged 67, *reigned* 35 years

1135–1154   STEPHEN
Born not later than 1100, third son of Adela, daughter of William I, and Stephen, count of Blois
Married Matilda, daughter of Eustace, count of Boulogne
1141 (February–November) held captive by adherents of Matilda, daughter of Henry I, who contested the crown until 1153
Died aged over 53, *reigned* 18 years

THE HOUSE OF ANJOU (PLANTAGENETS)

1154–1189   HENRY II (Curtmantle)
Born 1133, son of Matilda, daughter of Henry I, and Geoffrey, count of Anjou
Married Eleanor, daughter of William, duke of Aquitaine, and divorced queen of Louis VII of France
Died aged 56, *reigned* 34 years

1189–1199   RICHARD I (Coeur de Lion)
Born 1157, third son of Henry II
Married Berengaria, daughter of Sancho VI, king of Navarre
Died aged 42, *reigned* 9 years

1199–1216   JOHN (Lackland)
Born 1167, fifth son of Henry II
Married (1) Isabella or Avisa, daughter of William, earl of Gloucester (divorced) (2) Isabella, daughter of Aymer, count of Angoulême
Died aged 48, *reigned* 17 years

1216–1272   HENRY III
Born 1207, son of John and Isabella of Angoulême
Married Eleanor, daughter of Raymond, count of Provence
Died aged 65, *reigned* 56 years

1272–1307   EDWARD I (Longshanks)
Born 1239, eldest son of Henry III
Married (1) Eleanor, daughter of Ferdinand III, king of Castile (2) Margaret, daughter of Philip III of France
Died aged 68, *reigned* 34 years

1307–1327   EDWARD II
Born 1284, eldest surviving son of Edward I and Eleanor
Married Isabella, daughter of Philip IV of France
Deposed January 1327, *killed* September 1327 aged 43, *reigned* 19 years

1327–1377   EDWARD III
Born 1312, eldest son of Edward II
Married Philippa, daughter of William, count of Hainault
Died aged 64, *reigned* 50 years

1377–1399   RICHARD II
Born 1367, son of Edward (the Black Prince), eldest son of Edward III
Married (1) Anne, daughter of Emperor Charles IV (2) Isabelle, daughter of Charles VI of France
Deposed September 1399, *killed* February 1400 aged 33, *reigned* 22 years

THE HOUSE OF LANCASTER

1399–1413   HENRY IV
Born 1366, son of John of Gaunt, fourth son of Edward III, and Blanche, daughter of Henry, duke of Lancaster
Married (1) Mary, daughter of Humphrey, earl of Hereford (2) Joan, daughter of Charles, king of Navarre, and widow of John, duke of Brittany
Died aged *c*.47, *reigned* 13 years

1413–1422   HENRY V
Born 1387, eldest surviving son of Henry IV and Mary
Married Catherine, daughter of Charles VI of France
Died aged 34, *reigned* 9 years

1422–1471   HENRY VI
Born 1421, son of Henry V
Married Margaret, daughter of René, duke of Anjou and count of Provence
Deposed March 1461, *restored* October 1470
Deposed April 1471, *killed* May 1471 aged 49, *reigned* 39 years

THE HOUSE OF YORK

1461–1483   EDWARD IV
Born 1442, eldest son of Richard of York (grandson of Edmund, fifth son of Edward III, and son of Anne, great-granddaughter of Lionel, third son of Edward III)
Married Elizabeth Woodville, daughter of Richard, Lord Rivers, and widow of Sir John Grey
Acceded March 1461, *deposed* October 1470, *restored* April 1471
Died aged 40, *reigned* 21 years

1483   EDWARD V
Born 1470, eldest son of Edward IV
Deposed June 1483, *died* probably July–September 1483, aged 12, *reigned* 2 months (April–June)

1483–1485   RICHARD III
Born 1452, fourth son of Richard of York
Married Anne Neville, daughter of Richard, earl of Warwick, and widow of Edward, Prince of Wales, son of Henry VI
Killed in battle aged 32, *reigned* 2 years

THE HOUSE OF TUDOR

1485–1509   HENRY VII
Born 1457, son of Margaret Beaufort (great-granddaughter of John of Gaunt, fourth son of Edward III) and Edmund Tudor, earl of Richmond

Married Elizabeth, daughter of Edward IV
Died aged 52, *reigned* 23 years

1509–1547 HENRY VIII
Born 1491, second son of Henry VII
Married (1) Catherine, daughter of Ferdinand II, king of Aragon, and widow of his elder brother Arthur (divorced) (2) Anne, daughter of Sir Thomas Boleyn (executed) (3) Jane, daughter of Sir John Seymour (died in childbirth) (4) Anne, daughter of John, duke of Cleves (divorced) (5) Catherine Howard, niece of the Duke of Norfolk (executed) (6) Catherine, daughter of Sir Thomas Parr and widow of Lord Latimer
Died aged 55, *reigned* 37 years

1547–1553 EDWARD VI
Born 1537, son of Henry VIII and Jane Seymour
Died aged 15, *reigned* 6 years

1553 JANE
Born 1537, daughter of Frances (daughter of Mary Tudor, the younger daughter of Henry VII) and Henry Grey, duke of Suffolk
Married Lord Guildford Dudley, son of the Duke of Northumberland
Deposed July 1553, *executed* February 1554 aged 16, *reigned* 14 days

1553–1558 MARY I
Born 1516, daughter of Henry VIII and Catherine of Aragon
Married Philip II of Spain
Died aged 42, *reigned* 5 years

1558–1603 ELIZABETH I
Born 1533, daughter of Henry VIII and Anne Boleyn
Died aged 69, *reigned* 44 years

BRITISH KINGS AND QUEENS SINCE 1603

THE HOUSE OF STUART

Reign

1603–1625 JAMES I (VI OF SCOTLAND)
Born 1566, son of Mary, queen of Scots (granddaughter of Margaret Tudor, elder daughter of Henry VII), and Henry Stewart, Lord Darnley
Married Anne, daughter of Frederick II of Denmark
Died aged 58, *reigned* 22 years
(*see also* page 133)

1625–1649 CHARLES I
Born 1600, second son of James I
Married Henrietta Maria, daughter of Henry IV of France
Executed 1649 aged 48, *reigned* 23 years

COMMONWEALTH DECLARED 19 May 1649
1649–53 Government by a council of state
1653–8 Oliver Cromwell, *Lord Protector*
1658–9 Richard Cromwell, *Lord Protector*

1660–1685 CHARLES II
Born 1630, eldest son of Charles I
Married Catherine, daughter of John IV of Portugal
Died aged 54, *reigned* 24 years

1685–1688 JAMES II (VII of Scotland)
Born 1633, second son of Charles I
Married (1) Lady Anne Hyde, daughter of Edward, earl of Clarendon (2) Mary, daughter of Alphonso, duke of Modena
Reign ended with flight from kingdom December 1688
Died 1701 aged 67, *reigned* 3 years
INTERREGNUM 11 December 1688 to 12 February 1689

1689–1702 WILLIAM III
Born 1650, son of William II, prince of Orange, and Mary Stuart, daughter of Charles I
Married Mary, elder daughter of James II

Died aged 51, *reigned* 13 years
and

1689–1694 MARY II
Born 1662, elder daughter of James II and Anne
Died aged 32, *reigned* 5 years

1702–1714 ANNE
Born 1665, younger daughter of James II and Anne
Married Prince George of Denmark, son of Frederick III of Denmark
Died aged 49, *reigned* 12 years

THE HOUSE OF HANOVER

1714–1727 GEORGE I (Elector of Hanover)
Born 1660, son of Sophia (daughter of Frederick, elector palatine, and Elizabeth Stuart, daughter of James I) and Ernest Augustus, elector of Hanover
Married Sophia Dorothea, daughter of George William, duke of Lüneburg-Celle
Died aged 67, *reigned* 12 years

1727–1760 GEORGE II
Born 1683, son of George I
Married Caroline, daughter of John Frederick, margrave of Brandenburg-Anspach
Died aged 76, *reigned* 33 years

1760–1820 GEORGE III
Born 1738, son of Frederick, eldest son of George II
Married Charlotte, daughter of Charles Louis, duke of Mecklenburg-Strelitz
Died aged 81, *reigned* 59 years

REGENCY 1811–20
Prince of Wales regent owing to the insanity of George III

1820–1830 GEORGE IV
Born 1762, eldest son of George III
Married Caroline, daughter of Charles, duke of Brunswick-Wolfenbüttel
Died aged 67, *reigned* 10 years

1830–1837 WILLIAM IV
Born 1765, third son of George III
Married Adelaide, daughter of George, duke of Saxe-Meiningen
Died aged 71, *reigned* 7 years

1837–1901 VICTORIA
Born 1819, daughter of Edward, fourth son of George III
Married Prince Albert of Saxe-Coburg and Gotha
Died aged 81, *reigned* 63 years

THE HOUSE OF SAXE-COBURG AND GOTHA

1901–1910 EDWARD VII
Born 1841, eldest son of Victoria and Albert
Married Alexandra, daughter of Christian IX of Denmark
Died aged 68, *reigned* 9 years

THE HOUSE OF WINDSOR

1910–1936 GEORGE V
Born 1865, second son of Edward VII
Married Victoria Mary, daughter of Francis, duke of Teck
Died aged 70, *reigned* 25 years

1936 EDWARD VIII
Born 1894, eldest son of George V
Married (1937) Mrs Wallis Simpson
Abdicated 1936, *died* 1972 aged 77, *reigned* 10 months (20 January to 11 December)

1936–1952 GEORGE VI
Born 1895, second son of George V
Married Lady Elizabeth Bowes-Lyon, daughter of 14th Earl of Strathmore and Kinghorne (*see also* page 117)
Died aged 56, *reigned* 15 years

1952– ELIZABETH II
Born 1926, elder daughter of George VI
Married Philip, son of Prince Andrew of Greece (*see also* page 117)
WHOM GOD PRESERVE

KINGS AND QUEENS OF SCOTS 1016 TO 1603

Reign

1016–1034	**MALCOLM II** *Born c.*954, son of Kenneth II Acceded to Alba 1005, secured Lothian *c.*1016, obtained Strathclyde for his grandson Duncan *c.*1016, thus reigning over an area approximately the same as that governed by later rulers of Scotland *Died* aged *c.*80, *reigned* 18 years

THE HOUSE OF ATHOLL

1034–1040	**DUNCAN I** Son of Bethoc, daughter of Malcolm II, and Crinan, mormaer of Atholl *Married* a cousin of Siward, earl of Northumbria *Reigned* 5 years
1040–1057	**MACBETH** *Born c.*1005, son of a daughter of Malcolm II and Finlaec, mormaer of Moray *Married* Gruoch, granddaughter of Kenneth III *Killed* aged *c.*52, *reigned* 17 years
1057–1058	**LULACH** *Born c.*1032, son of Gillacomgan, mormaer of Moray, and Gruoch (and stepson of Macbeth) *Died* aged *c.*26, *reigned* 7 months (August–March)
1058–1093	**MALCOLM III** (Canmore) *Born c.*1031, elder son of Duncan I *Married* (1) Ingibiorg (2) Margaret (St Margaret), granddaughter of Edmund II of England *Killed* in battle aged *c.*62, *reigned* 35 years
1093–1097	**DONALD III BÁN** *Born c.*1033, second son of Duncan I *Deposed* May 1094, *restored* November 1094, *deposed* October 1097, *reigned* 3 years
1094	**DUNCAN II** *Born c.*1060, elder son of Malcolm III and Ingibiorg *Married* Octreda of Dunbar *Killed* aged *c.*34, *reigned* 6 months (May–November)
1097–1107	**EDGAR** *Born c.*1074, second son of Malcolm III and Margaret *Died* aged *c.*32, *reigned* 9 years
1107–1124	**ALEXANDER I** (The Fierce) *Born c.*1077, fifth son of Malcolm III and Margaret *Married* Sybilla, illegitimate daughter of Henry I of England *Died* aged *c.*47, *reigned* 17 years
1124–1153	**DAVID I** (The Saint) *Born c.*1085, sixth son of Malcolm III and Margaret *Married* Matilda, daughter of Waltheof, earl of Huntingdon *Died* aged *c.*68, *reigned* 29 years
1153–1165	**MALCOLM IV** (The Maiden) *Born c.*1141, son of Henry, earl of Huntingdon, second son of David I *Died* aged *c.*24, *reigned* 12 years
1165–1214	**WILLIAM I** (The Lion) *Born c.*1142, brother of Malcolm IV *Married* Ermengarde, daughter of Richard, viscount of Beaumont *Died* aged *c.*72, *reigned* 49 years
1214–1249	**ALEXANDER II** *Born* 1198, son of William I *Married* (1) Joan, daughter of John, king of England (2) Marie, daughter of Ingelram de Coucy *Died* aged 50, *reigned* 34 years
1249–1286	**ALEXANDER III** *Born* 1241, son of Alexander II and Marie *Married* (1) Margaret, daughter of Henry III of England (2) Yolande, daughter of the Count of Dreux *Killed* accidentally aged 44, *reigned* 36 years
1286–1290	**MARGARET** (The Maid of Norway) *Born* 1283, daughter of Margaret (daughter of Alexander III) and Eric II of Norway

Died aged 7, *reigned* 4 years

FIRST INTERREGNUM 1290–2
Throne disputed by 13 competitors. Crown
awarded to John Balliol by adjudication of Edward I
of England

THE HOUSE OF BALLIOL

1292–1296	**JOHN** (Balliol) *Born c.*1250, son of Dervorguilla, great-great- granddaughter of David I, and John de Balliol *Married* Isabella, daughter of John, earl of Surrey *Abdicated* 1296, *died* 1313 aged *c.*63, *reigned* 3 years

SECOND INTERREGNUM 1296–1306
Edward I of England declared John Balliol to have
forfeited the throne for contumacy in 1296 and took
the government of Scotland into his own hands

THE HOUSE OF BRUCE

1306–1329	**ROBERT I** (Bruce) *Born* 1274, son of Robert Bruce and Marjorie, countess of Carrick, and great-grandson of the second daughter of David, earl of Huntingdon, brother of William I *Married* (1) Isabella, daughter of Donald, earl of Mar (2) Elizabeth, daughter of Richard, earl of Ulster *Died* aged 54, *reigned* 23 years
1329–1371	**DAVID II** *Born* 1324, son of Robert I and Elizabeth *Married* (1) Joanna, daughter of Edward II of England (2) Margaret Drummond, widow of Sir John Logie (divorced) *Died* aged 46, *reigned* 41 years

1332 Edward Balliol, son of John Balliol, crowned
King of Scots September, expelled December
1333–6 Edward Balliol restored as King of Scots

THE HOUSE OF STEWART

1371–1390	**ROBERT II** (Stewart) *Born* 1316, son of Marjorie (daughter of Robert I) and Walter, High Steward of Scotland *Married* (1) Elizabeth, daughter of Sir Robert Mure of Rowallan (2) Euphemia, daughter of Hugh, earl of Ross *Died* aged 74, *reigned* 19 years
1390–1406	**ROBERT III** *Born c.*1337, son of Robert II and Elizabeth *Married* Annabella, daughter of Sir John Drummond of Stobhall *Died* aged *c.*69, *reigned* 16 years
1406–1437	**JAMES I** *Born* 1394, son of Robert III *Married* Joan Beaufort, daughter of John, earl of Somerset *Assassinated* aged 42, *reigned* 30 years
1437–1460	**JAMES II** *Born* 1430, son of James I *Married* Mary, daughter of Arnold, duke of Gueldres *Killed* accidentally aged 29, *reigned* 23 years
1460–1488	**JAMES III** *Born* 1452, son of James II *Married* Margaret, daughter of Christian I of Denmark *Assassinated* aged 36, *reigned* 27 years
1488–1513	**JAMES IV** *Born* 1473, son of James III *Married* Margaret Tudor, daughter of Henry VII of England *Killed* in battle aged 40, *reigned* 25 years
1513–1542	**JAMES V** *Born* 1512, son of James IV *Married* (1) Madeleine, daughter of Francis I of France (2) Mary of Lorraine, daughter of the Duc de Guise *Died* aged 30, *reigned* 29 years

1542–1567	MARY
	Born 1542, daughter of James V and Mary
	Married (1) the Dauphin, afterwards Francis II of France (2) Henry Stewart, Lord Darnley (3) James Hepburn, earl of Bothwell
	Abdicated 1567, prisoner in England from 1568, *executed* 1587, *reigned* 24 years
1567–1625	JAMES VI (and I of England)
	Born 1566, son of Mary, queen of Scots, and Henry, Lord Darnley
	Acceded 1567 to the Scottish throne, *reigned* 58 years
	Succeeded 1603 to the English throne, so joining the English and Scottish crowns in one person. The two kingdoms remained distinct until 1707 when the parliaments of the kingdoms became conjoined
	For British Kings and Queens since 1603, *see* page 131

WELSH SOVEREIGNS AND PRINCES

Wales was ruled by sovereign princes from the earliest times until the death of Llywelyn in 1282. The first English Prince of Wales was the son of Edward I, who was born in Caernarvon town on 25 April 1284. According to a discredited legend, he was presented to the Welsh chieftains as their prince, in fulfilment of a promise that they should have a prince who 'could not speak a word of English' and should be native born. This son, who afterwards became Edward II, was created 'Prince of Wales and Earl of Chester' at the Lincoln Parliament on 7 February 1301.

The title Prince of Wales is borne after individual conferment and is not inherited at birth, though some Princes have been declared and styled Prince of Wales but never formally so created (*s.*). The title was conferred on Prince Charles by The Queen on 26 July 1958. He was invested at Caernarvon on 1 July 1969.

INDEPENDENT PRINCES AD 844 TO 1282

844–878	Rhodri the Great
878–916	Anarawd, son of Rhodri
916–950	Hywel Dda, the Good
950–979	Iago ab Idwal (or Ieuaf)
979–985	Hywel ab Ieuaf, the Bad
985–986	Cadwallon, his brother
986–999	Maredudd ab Owain ap Hywel Dda
999–1008	Cynan ap Hywel ab Ieuaf
1018–1023	Llywelyn ap Seisyll
1023–1039	Iago ab Idwal ap Meurig
1039–1063	Gruffydd ap Llywelyn ap Seisyll
1063–1075	Bleddyn ap Cynfyn
1075–1081	Trahaern ap Caradog
1081–1137	Gruffydd ap Cynan ab Iago
1137–1170	Owain Gwynedd
1170–1194	Dafydd ab Owain Gwynedd
1194–1240	Llywelyn Fawr, the Great
1240–1246	Dafydd ap Llywelyn
1246–1282	Llywelyn ap Gruffydd ap Llywelyn

ENGLISH PRINCES SINCE 1301

1301	Edward (Edward II)
1343	Edward the Black Prince, son of Edward III
1376	Richard (Richard II), son of the Black Prince
1399	Henry of Monmouth (Henry V)
1454	Edward of Westminster, son of Henry VI
1471	Edward of Westminster (Edward V)
1483	Edward, son of Richard III (d. 1484)
1489	Arthur Tudor, son of Henry VII
1504	Henry Tudor (Henry VIII)
1610	Henry Stuart, son of James I (d. 1612)
1616	Charles Stuart (Charles I)

*c.*1638 (*s.*)	Charles Stuart (Charles II)
1688 (*s.*)	James Francis Edward Stuart (The Old Pretender), son of James II (d. 1766)
1714	George Augustus (George II)
1729	Frederick Lewis, son of George II (d. 1751)
1751	George William Frederick (George III)
1762	George Augustus Frederick (George IV)
1841	Albert Edward (Edward VII)
1901	George (George V)
1910	Edward (Edward VIII)
1958	Charles, son of Elizabeth II

PRINCESSES ROYAL

The style Princess Royal is conferred at the Sovereign's discretion on his or her eldest daughter. It is an honorary title, held for life, and cannot be inherited or passed on. It was first conferred on Princess Mary, daughter of Charles I, in approximately 1642.

*c.*1642	Princess Mary (1631–60), daughter of Charles I
1727	Princess Anne (1709–59), daughter of George II
1766	Princess Charlotte (1766–1828), daughter of George III
1840	Princess Victoria (1840–1901), daughter of Victoria
1905	Princess Louise (1867–1931), daughter of Edward VII
1932	Princess Mary (1897–1965), daughter of George V
1987	Princess Anne (b. 1950), daughter of Elizabeth II

Precedence

ENGLAND AND WALES

The Sovereign
The Prince Philip, Duke of
  Edinburgh
The Prince of Wales
The Sovereign's younger sons
The Sovereign's grandsons
The Sovereign's cousins
Archbishop of Canterbury
Lord High Chancellor
Archbishop of York
The Prime Minister
Lord President of the Council
Speaker of the House of Commons
Lord Privy Seal
Ambassadors and High
  Commissioners
Lord Great Chamberlain
Earl Marshal
Lord Steward of the Household
Lord Chamberlain of the Household
Master of the Horse
Dukes, according to their patent of
  creation:
  (1) of England
  (2) of Scotland
  (3) of Great Britain
  (4) of Ireland
  (5) those created since the Union
Ministers and Envoys
Eldest sons of Dukes of Blood Royal
Marquesses, according to their patent
  of creation:
  (1) of England
  (2) of Scotland
  (3) of Great Britain
  (4) of Ireland
  (5) those created since the Union
Dukes' eldest sons
Earls, according to their patent of
  creation:
  (1) of England
  (2) of Scotland
  (3) of Great Britain
  (4) of Ireland
  (5) those created since the Union
Younger sons of Dukes of Blood
  Royal
Marquesses' eldest sons
Dukes' younger sons
Viscounts, according to their patent
  of creation:
  (1) of England
  (2) of Scotland
  (3) of Great Britain
  (4) of Ireland
  (5) those created since the Union
Earls' eldest sons
Marquesses' younger sons
Bishops of London, Durham and
  Winchester
Other English Diocesan Bishops,
  according to seniority of
  consecration

Suffragan Bishops, according to
  seniority of consecration
Secretaries of State, if of the degree
  of a Baron
Barons, according to their patent of
  creation:
  (1) of England
  (2) of Scotland
  (3) of Great Britain
  (4) of Ireland
  (5) those created since the Union
Treasurer of the Household
Comptroller of the Household
Vice-Chamberlain of the Household
Secretaries of State under the degree
  of Baron
Viscounts' eldest sons
Earls' younger sons
Barons' eldest sons
Knights of the Garter
Privy Counsellors
Chancellor of the Exchequer
Chancellor of the Duchy of
  Lancaster
Lord Chief Justice of England
Master of the Rolls
President of the Family Division
Vice-Chancellor
Lords Justices of Appeal
Judges of the High Court
Viscounts' younger sons
Barons' younger sons
Sons of Life Peers
Baronets, according to date of patent
Knights of the Thistle
Knights Grand Cross of the Bath
Members of the Order of Merit
Knights Grand Cross of St Michael
  and St George
Knights Grand Commanders of the
  Indian Empire
Knights Grand Cross of the Royal
  Victorian Order
Knights Grand Cross of the British
  Empire
Companions of Honour
Knights Commanders of the Bath
Knights Commanders of St Michael
  and St George
Knights Commanders of the Indian
  Empire
Knights Commanders of the Royal
  Victorian Order
Knights Commanders of the British
  Empire
Knights Bachelor
Vice-Chancellor of the County
  Palatine of Lancaster
Official Referees of the Supreme
  Court
Circuit judges and judges of the
  Mayor's and City of London
  Court
Companions of the Bath
Companions of the Star of India

Companions of St Michael and St
  George
Companions of the Indian Empire
Commanders of the Royal Victorian
  Order
Commanders of the British Empire
Companions of the Distinguished
  Service Order
Lieutenants of the Royal Victorian
  Order
Officers of the British Empire
Companions of the Imperial Service
  Order
Eldest sons of younger sons of Peers
Baronets' eldest sons
Eldest sons of Knights, in the same
  order as their fathers
Members of the Royal Victorian
  Order
Members of the British Empire
Younger sons of the younger sons of
  Peers
Baronets' younger sons
Younger sons of Knights, in the same
  order as their fathers
Naval, Military, Air, and other
  Esquires by office

WOMEN

Women take the same rank as their
husbands or as their brothers; but the
daughter of a peer marrying a commoner retains her title as Lady or
Honourable. Daughters of peers rank
next immediately after the wives of
their elder brothers, and before their
younger brothers' wives. Daughters of
peers marrying peers of lower degree
take the same order of precedence as
that of their husbands; thus the daughter of a Duke marrying a Baron
becomes of the rank of Baroness only,
while her sisters married to common-
ers retain their rank and take precedence of the Baroness. Merely official
rank on the husband's part does not
give any similar precedence to the
wife.

Peeresses in their own right take
the same precedence as peers of the
same rank, i.e. from their date of
creation.

SCOTLAND

For precedence in Scotland, *see* Whitaker's Scottish Almanack.

Forms of address

It is only possible to cover here the forms of address for peers, baronets and knights, their wife and children, and Privy Counsellors. Greater detail should be sought in one of the publications devoted to the subject.

Both formal and social forms of address are given where usage differs; nowadays, the social form is generally preferred to the formal, which increasingly is used only for official documents and on very formal occasions.

F__ represents forename
S__ represents surname

BARON – *Envelope (formal)*, The Right Hon. Lord __; *(social)*, The Lord __. *Letter (formal)*, My Lord; *(social)*, Dear Lord __. *Spoken*, Lord __.

BARON'S WIFE – *Envelope (formal)*, The Right Hon. Lady __; *(social)*, The Lady __. *Letter (formal)*, My Lady; *(social)*, Dear Lady __. *Spoken*, Lady __.

BARON'S CHILDREN – *Envelope*, The Hon. F__ S__. *Letter*, Dear Mr/Miss/Mrs S__. *Spoken*, Mr/Miss/Mrs S__.

BARONESS IN OWN RIGHT – *Envelope*, may be addressed in same way as a Baron's wife or, if she prefers *(formal)*, The Right Hon. the Baroness __; *(social)*, The Baroness __. Otherwise as for a Baron's wife.

BARONET – *Envelope*, Sir F__ S__, Bt. *Letter (formal)*, Dear Sir; *(social)*, Dear Sir F__. *Spoken*, Sir F__.

BARONET'S WIFE – *Envelope*, Lady S__. *Letter (formal)*, Dear Madam; *(social)*, Dear Lady S__. *Spoken*, Lady S__.

COUNTESS IN OWN RIGHT – As for an Earl's wife.

COURTESY TITLES – The heir apparent to a Duke, Marquess or Earl uses the highest of his father's other titles as a courtesy title. (For list, *see* pages 165–6.) The holder of a courtesy title is not styled The Most Hon. or The Right Hon., and in correspondence 'The' is omitted before the title. The heir apparent to a Scottish title may use the title 'Master' (*see* below).

DAME – *Envelope*, Dame F__ S__, followed by appropriate post-nominal letters. *Letter (formal)*, Dear Madam; *(social)*, Dear Dame F__. *Spoken*, Dame F__.

DUKE – *Envelope (formal)*, His Grace the Duke of __; *(social)*, The Duke of __. *Letter (formal)*, My Lord Duke; *(social)*, Dear Duke. *Spoken (formal)*, Your Grace; *(social)*, Duke.

DUKE'S WIFE – *Envelope (formal)*, Her Grace the Duchess of __; *(social)*, The Duchess of __. *Letter (formal)*, Dear Madam; *(social)*, Dear Duchess. *Spoken*, Duchess.

DUKE'S ELDEST SON – *see* Courtesy titles.

DUKE'S YOUNGER SONS – *Envelope*, Lord F__ S__. *Letter (formal)*, My Lord; *(social)*, Dear Lord F__. *Spoken (formal)*, My Lord; *(social)*, Lord F__.

DUKE'S DAUGHTER – *Envelope*, Lady F__ S__. *Letter (formal)*, Dear Madam; *(social)*, Dear Lady F__. *Spoken*, Lady F__.

EARL – *Envelope (formal)*, The Right Hon. the Earl (of) __; *(social)*, The Earl (of) __. *Letter (formal)*, My Lord; *(social)*, Dear Lord __. *Spoken (formal)*, My Lord; *(social)*, Lord __.

EARL'S WIFE – *Envelope (formal)*, The Right Hon. the Countess (of) __; *(social)*, The Countess (of) __. *Letter (formal)*, Madam; *(social)*, Lady __. *Spoken (formal)*, Madam; *(social)*, Lady __.

EARL'S CHILDREN – *Eldest son, see* Courtesy titles. *Younger sons*, The Hon. F__ S__ (for forms of address, *see* Baron's children). *Daughters*, Lady F__ S__ (for forms of address, *see* Duke's daughter).

KNIGHT (BACHELOR) – *Envelope*, Sir F__ S__. *Letter (formal)*, Dear Sir; *(social)*, Dear Sir F__. *Spoken*, Sir F__.

KNIGHT (ORDERS OF CHIVALRY) – *Envelope*, Sir F__ S__, followed by appropriate post-nominal letters. Otherwise as for Knight Bachelor.

KNIGHT'S WIFE – As for Baronet's wife.

LIFE PEER – As for Baron/Baroness in own right.

LIFE PEER'S WIFE – As for Baron's wife.

LIFE PEER'S CHILDREN – As for Baron's children.

MARQUESS – *Envelope (formal)*, The Most Hon. the Marquess of __; *(social)*, The Marquess of __. *Letter (formal)*, My Lord; *(social)*, Dear Lord __. *Spoken (formal)*, My Lord; *(social)*, Lord __.

MARQUESS'S WIFE – *Envelope (formal)*, The Most Hon. the Marchioness of __; *(social)*, The Marchioness of __. *Letter (formal)*, Madam; *(social)*, Dear Lady __. *Spoken*, Lady __.

MARQUESS'S CHILDREN – *Eldest son, see* Courtesy titles. *Younger sons*, Lord F__ S__ (for forms of address, *see* Duke's younger sons). *Daughters*, Lady F__ S__ (for forms of address, *see* Duke's daughter).

MASTER – The title is used by the heir apparent to a Scottish peerage, though usually the heir apparent to a Duke, Marquess or Earl uses his courtesy title rather than 'Master'. *Envelope*, The Master of __. *Letter (formal)*, Dear Sir; *(social)*, Dear Master of __. *Spoken (formal)*, Master, or Sir; *(social)*, Master, or Mr S__.

MASTER'S WIFE – Addressed as for the wife of the appropriate peerage style, otherwise as Mrs S__.

PRIVY COUNSELLOR – *Envelope*, The Right (or Rt.) Hon. F__ S__. *Letter*, Dear Mr/Miss/Mrs S__. *Spoken*, Mr/Miss/Mrs S__. It is incorrect to use the letters PC after the name in conjunction with the prefix The Right Hon., unless the Privy Counsellor is a peer below the rank of Marquess and so is styled The Right Hon. because of his rank. In this case only, the post-nominal letters may be used in conjunction with the prefix The Right Hon.

VISCOUNT – *Envelope (formal)*, The Right Hon. the Viscount __; *(social)*, The Viscount __. *Letter (formal)*, My Lord; *(social)*, Dear Lord __. *Spoken*, Lord __.

VISCOUNT'S WIFE – *Envelope (formal)*, The Right Hon. the Viscountess __; *(social)*, The Viscountess __. *Letter (formal)*, Madam; *(social)*, Dear Lady __. *Spoken*, Lady __.

VISCOUNT'S CHILDREN – As for Baron's children.

The Peerage
and Members of the House of Lords

The rules which govern the creation and succession of peerages are extremely complicated. There are, technically, five separate peerages, the Peerage of England, of Scotland, of Ireland, of Great Britain, and of the United Kingdom. The Peerage of Great Britain dates from 1707 when an Act of Union combined the two kingdoms of England and Scotland and separate peerages were discontinued. The Peerage of the United Kingdom dates from 1801 when Great Britain and Ireland were combined under an Act of Union. Some Scottish peers have received additional peerages of Great Britain or of the United Kingdom since 1707, and some Irish peers additional peerages of the United Kingdom since 1801.

The Peerage of Ireland was not entirely discontinued from 1801 but holders of Irish peerages, whether pre-dating or created subsequent to the Union of 1801, are not entitled to sit in the House of Lords if they have no additional English, Scottish, Great Britain or United Kingdom peerage. However, they are eligible for election to the House of Commons and to vote in parliamentary elections. An Irish peer holding a peerage of a lower grade which enables him to sit in the House of Lords is introduced there by the title which enables him to sit, though for all other purposes he is known by his higher title.

In the Peerage of Scotland there is no rank of Baron; the equivalent rank is Lord of Parliament, abbreviated to 'Lord' (the female equivalent is 'Lady'). All peers of England, Scotland, Great Britain or the United Kingdom who are 21 years or over, and of British, Irish or Commonwealth nationality are entitled to sit in the House of Lords.

No fees for dignities have been payable since 1937. The House of Lords surrendered the ancient right of peers to be tried for treason or felony by their peers in 1948.

In 1999 the Government published a White Paper, *Modernizing Parliament: Reforming the House of Lords*, containing proposals including removing the right of hereditary peers to sit in the House of Lords. For more details, *see* White Papers section.

HEREDITARY WOMEN PEERS

Most hereditary peerages pass on death to the nearest male heir, but there are exceptions, and several are held by women (*see* pages 144 and 156).

A woman peer in her own right retains her title after marriage, and if her husband's rank is the superior she is designated by the two titles jointly, the inferior one second. Her hereditary claim still holds good in spite of any marriage whether higher or lower. No rank held by a woman can confer any title or even precedence upon her husband but the rank of a hereditary woman peer in her own right is inherited by her eldest son (or in some cases daughter).

Since the Peerage Act 1963, hereditary women peers in their own right have been entitled to sit in the House of Lords, subject to the same qualifications as men. The Government's proposals, once enacted, would also remove this right (*see* White Papers section).

LIFE PEERS

Since 1876 non-hereditary or life peerages have been conferred on certain eminent judges to enable the judicial functions of the House of Lords to be carried out. These Lords are known as Lords of Appeal or law lords and, to date, such appointments have all been male.

Since 1958 life peerages have been conferred upon distinguished men and women from all walks of life, giving them seats in the House of Lords in the degree of Baron or Baroness. They are addressed in the same way as hereditary Lords and Barons, and their children have similar courtesy titles.

PEERAGES EXTINCT SINCE THE LAST EDITION

EARLDOM: Lanesborough (*cr.* 1756)
VISCOUNTCY: Whitelaw (*cr.* 1983)
LIFE PEERAGES: Alport (*cr.* 1961); Beloff (*cr.* 1981); Brandon of Oakbrook (*cr.* 1981); Cayzer (*cr.* 1982); Dean of Beswick (*cr.* 1983); Denning (*cr.* 1957); Gillmore of Thamesfield (*cr.* 1996); Grade (*cr.* 1976); Hunt (*cr.* 1966); Lewin (*cr.* 1982); Lowry (*cr.* 1979); Menuhin (*cr.* 1993); Phillips of Ellesmere (*cr.* 1994); Robens of Woldingham (*cr.* 1961); Robson of Kiddington (*cr.* 1974); Sainsbury (*cr.* 1962); Soper (*cr.* 1965)

DISCLAIMER OF PEERAGES

The Peerage Act 1963 enables peers to disclaim their peerages for life. Peers alive in 1963 could disclaim within twelve months after the passing of the Act (31 July 1963); a person subsequently succeeding to a peerage may disclaim within 12 months (one month if an MP) after the date of succession, or of reaching 21, if later. The disclaimer is irrevocable but does not affect the descent of the peerage after the disclaimant's death, and children of a disclaimed peer may, if they wish, retain their precedence and any courtesy titles and styles borne as children of a peer. The disclaimer permits the disclaimant to sit in the House of Commons if elected as an MP. The Government's proposals (*see* White Papers section), once enacted, will permit hereditary peers to sit in the House of Commons without having to disclaim their titles.

The following peerages are currently disclaimed:

EARLDOMS: Durham (1970); Selkirk (1994)
VISCOUNTCIES: Camrose (1995); Hailsham (1963); Stansgate (1963)
BARONIES: Altrincham (1963); Merthyr (1977); Reith (1972); Sanderson of Ayot (1971); Silkin (1972)

PEERS WHO ARE MINORS (i.e. under 21 years of age)
MARQUESSES: Bristol (*b.* 1979)
EARLS: Craven (*b.* 1989)
BARONS: Elphinstone (*b.* 1980)

CONTRACTIONS AND SYMBOLS

s. Scottish title
I. Irish title
* The peer holds also an Imperial title, specified after the name by Engl., Brit. or UK
° there is no 'of' in the title
b. born
s. succeeded
m. married
w. widower or widow
M. minor
† heir not ascertained at time of going to press

Hereditary Peers

PEERS OF THE BLOOD ROYAL

Style, His Royal Highness The Duke of __/His Royal Highness the Earl of__
Style of address (formal) May it please your Royal Highness; (*informal*) Sir

Created	Title, order of succession, name, etc.	Heir
	Dukes	
1337	*Cornwall,* Charles, Prince of Wales, *s.* 1952 (*see* page 117)	‡
1398	*Rothesay,* Charles, Prince of Wales, *s.* 1952 (*see* page 117)	‡
1986	*York* (1st), The Prince Andrew, Duke of York (*see* page 117)	None
1928	*Gloucester* (2nd), Prince Richard, Duke of Gloucester, *s.* 1974 (*see* page 118)	Earl of Ulster (*see* page 118)
1934	*Kent* (2nd), Prince Edward, Duke of Kent, *s.* 1942 (*see* page 118)	Earl of St Andrews (*see* page 118)
	Earl	
1999	*Wessex* (1st), The Prince Edward, Earl of Wessex (*see* page 117)	None

‡ The title is not hereditary but is held by the Sovereign's eldest son from the moment of his birth or the Sovereign's accession

DUKES

Coronet, Eight strawberry leaves
Style, His Grace the Duke of __
Wife's style, Her Grace the Duchess of __
Eldest son's style, Takes his father's second title as a courtesy title
Younger sons' style, 'Lord' before forename and family name
Daughters' style, 'Lady' before forename and family name
For forms of address, *see* page 135

Created	Title, order of succession, name, etc.	Heir
1868 I.	*Abercorn* (5th), James Hamilton, KG, (6th *Brit. Marq., Abercorn,* 1790; 14th *Scott. Earl, Abercorn,* 1606) *b.* 1934, *s.* 1979, *m.*	Marquess of Hamilton, *b.* 1969
1701 S.*	*Argyll* (12th), Ian Campbell (5th *UK Duke, Argyll,* 1892), *b.* 1937, *s.* 1973, *m.*	Marquess of Lorne, *b.* 1968
1703 S.	*Atholl* (11th), John Murray, *b.* 1929, *s.* 1996, *m.*	Marquess of Tullibardine, *b.* 1960
1682	*Beaufort* (11th), David Robert Somerset, *b.* 1928, *s.* 1984, *w.*	Marquess of Worcester, *b.* 1952
1694	*Bedford* (13th), John Robert Russell, *b.* 1917, *s.* 1953, *m.*	Marquess of Tavistock, *b.* 1940
1663 S.*	*Buccleuch* (9th) and *Queensberry* (11th) (s. 1684), Walter Francis John Montagu Douglas Scott, KT, VRD (8th *Engl. Earl, Doncaster,* 1662), *b.* 1923, *s.* 1973, *m.*	Earl of Dalkeith, *b.* 1954
1694	*Devonshire* (11th), Andrew Robert Buxton Cavendish, KG, MC, PC, *b.* 1920, *s.* 1950, *m.*	Marquess of Hartington CBE, *b.* 1944
1947	*Edinburgh* (1st), HRH The Prince Philip, Duke of Edinburgh (see page 117).	The Prince of Wales (see page 117)
1900	*Fife* (3rd), James George Alexander Bannerman Carnegie (12th *Scott. Earl, Southesk,* 1633, *s.* 1992), *b.* 1929, *s.* 1959. (*see* page 128)	Earl of Southesk, *b.* 1961
1675	*Grafton* (11th), Hugh Denis Charles FitzRoy, KG, *b.* 1919, *s.* 1970, *m.*	Earl of Euston, *b.* 1947
1643 S.*	*Hamilton* (15th) and *Brandon* (12th) (*Brit.* 1711), Angus Alan Douglas Douglas-Hamilton, *b.* 1938, *s.* 1973. *Premier Peer of Scotland*	Marquess of Douglas and Clydesdale, *b.* 1978
1766 I.*	*Leinster* (8th), Gerald FitzGerald (8th *Brit. Visct., Leinster,* 1747), *b.* 1914, *s.* 1976, *m. Premier Duke and Marquess of Ireland*	Marquess of Kildare, *b.* 1948
1719	*Manchester* (12th), Angus Charles Drogo Montagu, *b.* 1938, *s.* 1985, *m.*	Viscount Mandeville, *b.* 1962
1702	*Marlborough* (11th), John George Vanderbilt Henry Spencer-Churchill, *b.* 1926, *s.* 1972, *m.*	Marquess of Blandford, *b.* 1955
1707 S.*	*Montrose* (8th), James Graham (6th *Brit. Earl, Graham,* 1722), *b.* 1935, *s.* 1992, *m.*	Marquess of Graham, *b.* 1973
1483	*Norfolk* (17th), Miles Francis Stapleton Fitzalan-Howard, KG, GCVO, CB, CBE, MC (12th *Engl. Baron, Beaumont,* 1309, *s.* 1971; 4th *UK Baron Howard of Glossop,* 1869, *s.* 1972), *b.* 1915, *s.* 1975, *m. Premier Duke and Earl Marshal*	Earl of Arundel and Surrey, *b.* 1956
1766	*Northumberland* (12th), Ralph George Algernon Percy, *b.* 1956, *s.* 1995, *m.*	Earl Percy, *b.* 1984

Created	Title, order of succession, name, etc.	Heir
1675	*Richmond* (10th) and *Gordon* (5th) (*UK* 1876), Charles Henry Gordon Lennox (10th *Scott. Duke, Lennox*, 1675), *b.* 1929, *s.* 1989, *m.*	Earl of March and Kinrara, *b.* 1955
1707 s.*	*Roxburghe* (10th), Guy David Innes-Ker (5th *UK Earl, Innes*, 1837), *b.* 1954, *s.* 1974, *m. Premier Baronet of Scotland*	Marquess of Bowmont and Cessford, *b.* 1981
1703	*Rutland* (11th), David Charles Robert Manners, *b.* 1959, *s.* 1999, *m.*	Hon. Edward J. F. M., *b.* 1965
1684	*St Albans* (14th), Murray de Vere Beauclerk, *b.* 1939, *s.* 1988, *m.*	Earl of Burford, *b.* 1965
1547	*Somerset* (19th), John Michael Edward Seymour, *b.* 1952, *s.* 1984, *m.*	Lord Seymour, *b.* 1982
1833	*Sutherland* (6th), John Sutherland Egerton, TD (5th *UK Earl, Ellesmere*, 1846, *s.* 1944), *b.* 1915, *s.* 1963, *m.*	Francis R. E., *b.* 1940
1814	*Wellington* (8th), Arthur Valerian Wellesley, KG, LVO, OBE, MC (9th *Irish Earl, Mornington*, 1760), *b.* 1915, *s.* 1972, *m.*	Marquess of Douro, *b.* 1945
1874	*Westminster* (6th), Gerald Cavendish Grosvenor, OBE, *b.* 1951, *s.* 1979, *m.*	Earl Grosvenor, *b.* 1991

MARQUESSES

Coronet, Four strawberry leaves alternating with four silver balls
Style, The Most Hon. the Marquess (of) __ . In Scotland the spelling 'Marquis' is preferred for pre-Union creations
Wife's style, The Most Hon. the Marchioness (of) __
Eldest son's style, Takes his father's second title as a courtesy title
Younger sons' style, 'Lord' before forename and family name
Daughters' style, 'Lady' before forename and family name
For forms of address, *see* page 135

Created	Title, order of succession, name, etc.	Heir
1916	*Aberdeen and Temair* (6th), Alastair Ninian John Gordon (12th *Scott. Earl, Aberdeen*, 1682), *b.* 1920, *s.* 1984, *m.*	Earl of Haddo, *b.* 1955
1876	*Abergavenny* (5th), John Henry Guy Nevill, KG, OBE, *b.* 1914, *s.* 1954, *m.*	Christopher G. C. N., *b.* 1955
1821	*Ailesbury* (8th), Michael Sidney Cedric Brudenell-Bruce, *b.* 1926, *s.* 1974.	Earl of Cardigan, *b.* 1952
1831	*Ailsa* (8th), Archibald Angus Charles Kennedy (20th *Scott. Earl, Cassillis*, 1509), *b.* 1956, *s.* 1994.	Lord David Kennedy, *b.* 1958
1815	*Anglesey* (7th), George Charles Henry Victor Paget, *b.* 1922, *s.* 1947, *m.*	Earl of Uxbridge, *b.* 1950
1789	*Bath* (7th), Alexander George Thynn, *b.* 1932, *s.* 1992, *m.*	Viscount Weymouth, *b.* 1974
1826	*Bristol* (8th), Frederick William Augustus Hervey, *b.* 1979, *s.* 1999, *M.*	Hon. Ronald F. W. H., *b.* 1919
1796	*Bute* (7th), John Colum Crichton-Stuart (12th *Scott. Earl, Dumfries*, 1633), *b.* 1958, *s.* 1993, *m.*	Earl of Dumfries, *b.* 1989
1812	° *Camden* (6th), David George Edward Henry Pratt, *b.* 1930, *s.* 1983.	Earl of Brecknock, *b.* 1965
1815	*Cholmondeley* (7th), David George Philip Cholmondeley (11th *Irish Visct., Cholmondeley*, 1661), *b.* 1960, *s.* 1990. *Lord Great Chamberlain*	Charles G. C., *b.* 1959
1816 I.*	° *Conyngham* (7th), Frederick William Henry Francis Conyngham (7th *UK Baron, Minster*, 1821), *b.* 1924, *s.* 1974, *m.*	Earl of Mount Charles, *b.* 1951
1791 I.*	*Donegall* (7th), Dermot Richard Claud Chichester, LVO (7th *Brit. Baron, Fisherwick*, 1790; 6th *Brit. Baron, Templemore*, 1831, *s.* 1953), *b.* 1916, *s.* 1975, *m.*	Earl of Belfast, *b.* 1952
1789 I.*	*Downshire* (8th), (Arthur) Robin Ian Hill (8th *Brit. Earl, Hillsborough*, 1772), *b.* 1929, *s.* 1989, *m.*	Earl of Hillsborough, *b.* 1959
1801 I.*	*Ely* (8th), Charles John Tottenham (8th *UK Baron, Loftus*, 1801), *b.* 1913, *s.* 1969, *m.*	Viscount Loftus, *b.* 1943
1801	*Exeter* (8th), (William) Michael Anthony Cecil, *b.* 1935, *s.* 1988, *m.*	Lord Burghley, *b.* 1970
1800 I.*	*Headfort* (6th), Thomas Geoffrey Charles Michael Taylour (4th *UK Baron, Kenlis*, 1831), *b.* 1932, *s.* 1960, *m.*	Earl of Bective, *b.* 1959
1793	*Hertford* (9th), Henry Jocelyn Seymour (10th *Irish Baron, Conway*, 1712), *b.* 1958, *s.* 1997, *m.*	Earl of Yarmouth, *b.* 1993
1599 s.*	*Huntly* (13th), Granville Charles Gomer Gordon (5th *UK Baron, Meldrum*, 1815), *b.* 1944, *s.* 1987, *m. Premier Marquess of Scotland*	Earl of Aboyne, *b.* 1973
1784	*Lansdowne* (9th), Charles Maurice Mercer Nairne Petty-Fitzmaurice (9th *Irish Earl, Kerry*, 1723), *b.* 1941, *s.* 1999, *m.*	Earl of Shelburne, *b.* 1970
1902	*Linlithgow* (4th), Adrian John Charles Hope (10th *Scott. Earl, Hopetoun*, 1703), *b.* 1946, *s.* 1987, *m.*	Earl of Hopetoun, *b.* 1971
1816 I.*	*Londonderry* (9th), Alexander Charles Robert Vane-Tempest-Stewart (6th *UK Earl, Vane*, 1823), *b.* 1937, *s.* 1955, *m.*	Viscount Castlereagh, *b.* 1972
1701 s.*	*Lothian* (12th), Peter Francis Walter Kerr, KCVO (6th *UK Baron, Kerr*, 1821), *b.* 1922, *s.* 1940, *m.*	Earl of Ancram PC, MP, *b.* 1945

Created	Title, order of succession, name, etc.	Heir
1917	*Milford Haven* (4th), George Ivar Louis Mountbatten, *b.* 1961, *s.* 1970, *m.*	Earl of Medina, *b.* 1991
1838	*Normanby* (5th), Constantine Edmund Walter Phipps (9th *Irish Baron, Mulgrave*, 1767), *b.* 1954, *s.* 1994, *m.*	Earl of Mulgrave, *b.* 1994
1812	*Northampton* (7th), Spencer Douglas David Compton, *b.* 1946, *s.* 1978, *m.*	Earl Compton, *b.* 1973
1682 s.	*Queensberry* (12th), David Harrington Angus Douglas, *b.* 1929, *s.* 1954.	Viscount Drumlanrig, *b.* 1967
1926	*Reading* (4th), Simon Charles Henry Rufus Isaacs, *b.* 1942, *s.* 1980, *m.*	Viscount Erleigh, *b.* 1986
1789	*Salisbury* (6th), Robert Edward Peter Cecil, *b.* 1916, *s.* 1972, *m.*	Viscount Cranborne PC, *b.* 1946 (*see also* Baron Cecil, page 139)
1800 I.*	*Sligo* (11th), Jeremy Ulick Browne (11th *UK Baron, Monteagle*, 1806), *b.* 1939, *s.* 1991, *m.*	Sebastian U. B., *b.* 1964
1787	° *Townshend* (7th), George John Patrick Dominic Townshend, *b.* 1916, *s.* 1921, *w.*	Viscount Raynham, *b.* 1945
1694 s.*	° *Tweeddale* (13th), Edward Douglas John Hay (4th *UK Baron Tweeddale*, 1881), *b.* 1947, *s.* 1979.	Lord Charles D. M. H., *b.* 1947
1789 I.*	*Waterford* (8th), John Hubert de la Poer Beresford (8th *Brit. Baron Tyrone*, 1786), *b.* 1933, *s.* 1934, *m.*	Earl of Tyrone, *b.* 1958
1551	*Winchester* (18th), Nigel George Paulet, *b.* 1941, *s.* 1968, *m.* Premier Marquess of England	Earl of Wiltshire, *b.* 1969
1892	*Zetland* (4th), Lawrence Mark Dundas (6th *UK Earl, Zetland*, 1838; 7th *Brit. Baron Dundas*, 1794), *b.* 1937, *s.* 1989, *m.*	Earl of Ronaldshay, *b.* 1965

EARLS

Coronet, Eight silver balls on stalks alternating with eight gold strawberry leaves
Style, The Right Hon. the Earl (of) _
Wife's style, The Right Hon. the Countess (of) _
Eldest son's style, Takes his father's second title as a courtesy title
Younger sons' style, 'The Hon.' before forename and family name
Daughters' style, 'Lady' before forename and family name
For forms of address, *see* page 135

Created	Title, order of succession, name, etc.	Heir
1639 s.	*Airlie* (13th), David George Coke Patrick Ogilvy, KT, GCVO, PC, Royal Victorian Chain, *b.* 1926, *s.* 1968, *m.*	Lord Ogilvy, *b.* 1958
1696	*Albemarle* (10th), Rufus Arnold Alexis Keppel, *b.* 1965, *s.* 1979.	Crispian W. J. K., *b.* 1948
1952	° *Alexander of Tunis* (2nd), Shane William Desmond Alexander, *b.* 1935, *s.* 1969, *m.*	Hon. Brian J. A., *b.* 1939
1662 s.	*Annandale and Hartfell.* (11th), Patrick Andrew Wentworth Hope Johnstone, *b.* 1941, claim established 1985, *m.*	Lord Johnstone, *b.* 1971
1789 I.	° *Annesley* (10th), Patrick Annesley, *b.* 1924, *s.* 1979, *m.*	Hon. Philip H. A., *b.* 1927
1785 I.	*Antrim* (9th), Alexander Randal Mark McDonnell, *b.* 1935, *s.* 1977, *m.*	Viscount Dunluce, *b.* 1967
1762 I.*	*Arran* (9th), Arthur Desmond Colquhoun Gore (5th *UK Baron Sudley*, 1884), *b.* 1938, *s.* 1983, *m.*	Paul A. G. CMG, CVO, *b.* 1921
1955	° *Attlee* (3rd), John Richard Attlee, *b.* 1956, *s.* 1991, *m.*	None
1714	*Aylesford* (11th), Charles Ian Finch-Knightley, *b.* 1918, *s.* 1958, *w.*	Lord Guernsey, *b.* 1947
1937	° *Baldwin of Bewdley* (4th), Edward Alfred Alexander Baldwin, *b.* 1938, *s.* 1976, *m.*	Viscount Corvedale, *b.* 1973
1922	*Balfour* (4th), Gerald Arthur James Balfour, *b.* 1925, *s.* 1968, *m.*	Eustace A. G. B., *b.* 1921
1772	° *Bathurst* (8th), Henry Allen John Bathurst, *b.* 1927, *s.* 1943, *m.*	Lord Apsley, *b.* 1961
1919	° *Beatty* (3rd), David Beatty, *b.* 1946, *s.* 1972, *m.*	Viscount Borodale, *b.* 1973
1797 I.	*Belmore* (8th), John Armar Lowry-Corry, *b.* 1951, *s.* 1960, *m.*	Viscount Corry, *b.* 1985
1739 I.*	*Bessborough* (11th), Arthur Mountifort Longfield Ponsonby (8th *UK Baron Duncannon*, 1834), *b.* 1912, *s.* 1993, *m.*	Viscount Duncannon, *b.* 1941
1815	*Bradford* (7th), Richard Thomas Orlando Bridgeman, *b.* 1947, *s.* 1981, *m.*	Viscount Newport, *b.* 1980
1469 s.*	*Buchan* (17th), Malcolm Harry Erskine (8th *UK Baron Erskine*, 1806), *b.* 1930, *s.* 1984, *m.*	Lord Cardross, *b.* 1960
1746	*Buckinghamshire* (10th), (George) Miles Hobart-Hampden, *b.* 1944, *s.* 1983, *m.*	Sir John Hobart, Bt., *b.* 1945
1800	° *Cadogan* (8th), Charles Gerald John Cadogan, *b.* 1937, *s.* 1997, *m.*	Viscount Chelsea, *b.* 1966
1878	° *Cairns* (6th), Simon Dallas Cairns, CBE, *b.* 1939, *s.* 1989, *m.*	Viscount Garmoyle, *b.* 1965
1455 s.	*Caithness* (20th), Malcolm Ian Sinclair, PC, *b.* 1948, *s.* 1965, *w.*	Lord Berriedale, *b.* 1981
1800 I.	*Caledon* (7th), Nicholas James Alexander, *b.* 1955, *s.* 1980, *m.*	Viscount Alexander, *b.* 1990

Created	Title, order of succession, name, etc.	Heir
1661	*Carlisle* (13th), George William Beaumont Howard (13th *Scott. Baron Ruthven of Freeland*, 1651), *b.* 1949, *s.* 1994.	Hon. Philip C. W. *H.*, *b.* 1963
1793	*Carnarvon* (7th), Henry George Reginald Molyneux Herbert, KCVO, KBE, *b.* 1924, *s.* 1987, *m.*	Lord Porchester, *b.* 1956
1748 I.*	*Carrick* (10th), David James Theobald Somerset Butler (4th *UK Baron Butler*, 1912), *b.* 1953, *s.* 1992, *m.*	Viscount Ikerrin, *b.* 1975
1800 I.	° *Castle Stewart* (8th), Arthur Patrick Avondale Stuart, *b.* 1928, *s.* 1961, *m.*	Viscount Stuart, *b.* 1953
1814	° *Cathcart* (7th), Charles Alan Andrew Cathcart (16th *Scott. Baron Cathcart*, 1447), *b.* 1952, *s.* 1999, *m.*	Lord Greenock, *b.* 1986
1647 I.	*Cavan*. The 12th Earl died in 1988. Heir had not established his claim to the title at the time of going to press	Roger C. *Lambart*, *b.* 1944
1827	° *Cawdor* (7th), Colin Robert Vaughan Campbell, *b.* 1962, *s.* 1993, *m.*	Hon. Frederick W. *C.*, *b.* 1965
1801	*Chichester* (9th), John Nicholas Pelham, *b.* 1944, *s.* 1944, *m.*	Richard A. H. *P.*, *b.* 1952
1803 I.*	*Clancarty* (9th), Nicholas Power Richard Le Poer Trench (8th *UK Visct. Clancarty*, 1823), *b.* 1952, *s.* 1995.	None
1776 I.*	*Clanwilliam* (7th), John Herbert Meade (5th *UK Baron Clanwilliam*, 1828), *b.* 1919, *s.* 1989, *m.*	Lord Gillford, *b.* 1960
1776	*Clarendon* (7th), George Frederick Laurence Hyde Villiers, *b.* 1933, *s.* 1955, *m.*	Lord Hyde, *b.* 1976
1620 I.*	*Cork* (14th) and *Orrery* (14th) (I. 1660), John William Boyle, DSC (10th *Brit. Baron Boyle of Marston*, 1711), *b.* 1916, *s.* 1995, *m.*	Viscount Dungarvan, *b.* 1945
1850	*Cottenham* (8th), Kenelm Charles Everard Digby Pepys, *b.* 1948, *s.* 1968, *m.*	Viscount Crowhurst, *b.* 1983
1762 I.*	*Courtown* (9th), James Patrick Montagu Burgoyne Winthrop Stopford (8th *Brit. Baron Saltersford*, 1796), *b.* 1954, *s.* 1975, *m.*	Viscount Stopford, *b.* 1988
1697	*Coventry* (11th), George William Coventry, *b.* 1934, *s.* 1940, *m.*	Francis H. *C.*, *b.* 1912
1857	° *Cowley* (7th), Garret Graham Wellesley, *b.* 1934, *s.* 1975, *m.*	Viscount Dangan, *b.* 1965
1892	*Cranbrook* (5th), Gathorne Gathorne-Hardy, *b.* 1933, *s.* 1978, *m.*	Lord Medway, *b.* 1968
1801	*Craven* (9th), Benjamin Robert Joseph Craven, *b.* 1989, *s.* 1990, *M.*	Rupert J. E. *C.*, *b.* 1926
1398 S.*	*Crawford* (29th) and *Balcarres* (12th) (S. 1651), Robert Alexander Lindsay, KT, PC (5th *UK Baron, Wigan*, 1826; *Baron Balniel* (life peerage), 1974), *b.* 1927, *s.* 1975, *m. Premier Earl on Union Roll*	Lord Balniel, *b.* 1958
1861	*Cromartie* (5th), John Ruaridh Blunt Grant Mackenzie, *b.* 1948, *s.* 1989, *m.*	Viscount Tarbat, *b.* 1987
1901	*Cromer* (4th), Evelyn Rowland Esmond Baring, *b.* 1946, *s.* 1991, *m.*	Viscount Errington, *b.* 1994
1633 S.*	*Dalhousie* (17th), James Hubert Ramsay (5th *UK Baron Ramsay*, 1875), *b.* 1948, *s.* 1999, *m.*	Lord Ramsay, *b.* 1981
1725 I.	*Darnley* (11th), Adam Ivo Stuart Bligh (20th *Engl. Baron Clifton of Leighton Bromswold*, 1608), *b.* 1941, *s.* 1980, *m.*	Lord Clifton, *b.* 1968
1711	*Dartmouth* (10th), William Legge, *b.* 1949, *s.* 1997.	Hon. Rupert *L.*, *b.* 1951
1761	° *De La Warr* (11th), William Herbrand Sackville, *b.* 1948, *s.* 1988, *m.*	Lord Buckhurst, *b.* 1979
1622	*Denbigh* (12th) and *Desmond* (11th) (I. 1622), Alexander Stephen Rudolph Feilding, *b.* 1970, *s.* 1995, *m.*	William D. *F.*, *b.* 1939
1485	*Derby* (19th), Edward Richard William Stanley, *b.* 1962, *s.* 1994, *m.*	Lord Stanley, *b.* 1998
1553	*Devon* (18th), Hugh Rupert Courtenay, *b.* 1942, *s.* 1998, *m.*	Lord Courtenay, *b.* 1975
1800 I.*	*Donoughmore* (8th), Richard Michael John Hely-Hutchinson (8th *UK Visct. Hutchinson*, 1821), *b.* 1927, *s.* 1981, *m.*	Viscount Suirdale, *b.* 1952
1661 I.*	*Drogheda* (12th), Henry Dermot Ponsonby Moore (3rd *UK Baron Moore*, 1954), *b.* 1937, *s.* 1989, *m.*	Viscount Moore, *b.* 1983
1837	*Ducie* (7th), David Leslie Moreton, *b.* 1951, *s.* 1991, *m.*	Lord Moreton, *b.* 1981
1860	*Dudley* (4th), William Humble David Ward, *b.* 1920, *s.* 1969, *m.*	Viscount Ednam, *b.* 1947
1660 S.*	*Dundee* (12th), Alexander Henry Scrymgeour (2nd *UK Baron Glassary*, 1954), *b.* 1949, *s.* 1983, *m.*	Lord Scrymgeour, *b.* 1982
1669 S.	*Dundonald* (15th), Iain Alexander Douglas Blair Cochrane, *b.* 1961, *s.* 1986, *m.*	Lord Cochrane, *b.* 1991
1686 S.	*Dunmore* (12th), Malcolm Kenneth Murray, *b.* 1946, *s.* 1995, *m.*	Hon. Geoffrey C. *M.*, *b.* 1949
1822 I.	*Dunraven and Mount-Earl* (7th), Thady Windham Thomas Wyndham-Quin, *b.* 1939, *s.* 1965, *m.*	None
1833	*Durham*. Disclaimed for life 1970. (*Antony Claud Frederick Lambton, b.*1922, *s.*1970, *m.*)	Hon. Edward R. *L.* (Baron Durham), *b.* 1961
1837	*Effingham* (7th), David Mowbray Algernon Howard (17th *Engl. Baron Howard of Effingham*, 1554), *b.* 1939, *s.* 1996, *m.*	Lord Howard of Effingham, *b.* 1971
1507 S.*	*Eglinton* (18th) and *Winton* (9th) (S. 1600), Archibald George Montgomerie (6th *UK Earl Winton*, 1859), *b.* 1939, *s.* 1966, *m.*	Lord Montgomerie, *b.* 1966
1733 I.*	*Egmont* (11th), Frederick George Moore Perceval (9th *Brit. Baron Lovel and Holland*, 1762), *b.* 1914, *s.* 1932, *m.*	Viscount Perceval, *b.* 1934
1821	*Eldon* (5th), John Joseph Nicholas Scott, *b.* 1937, *s.* 1976, *m.*	Viscount Encombe, *b.* 1962
1633 S.*	*Elgin* (11th) and *Kincardine* (15th) (S. 1647), Andrew Douglas Alexander Thomas Bruce, KT (4th *UK Baron, Elgin*, 1849), *b.* 1924, *s.* 1968, *m.*	Lord Bruce, *b.* 1961

Created	Title, order of succession, name, etc.	Heir
1789 I.*	*Enniskillen* (7th), Andrew John Galbraith Cole (5th *UK Baron, Grinstead*, 1815), *b.* 1942, *s.* 1989, *m.*	Arthur G. C., *b.* 1920
1789 I.*	*Erne* (6th), Henry George Victor John Crichton (3rd *UK Baron, Fermanagh*, 1876), *b.* 1937, *s.* 1940, *m.*	Viscount Crichton, *b.* 1971
1452 S.	*Erroll* (24th), Merlin Sereld Victor Gilbert Hay, *b.* 1948, *s.* 1978, *m.* Hereditary Lord High Constable and Knight Marischal of Scotland	Lord Hay, *b.* 1984
1661	*Essex* (10th), Robert Edward de Vere Capell, *b.* 1920, *s.* 1981, *m.*	Viscount Malden, *b.* 1944
1711	° *Ferrers* (13th), Robert Washington Shirley, PC, *b.* 1929, *s.* 1954, *m.*	Viscount Tamworth, *b.* 1952
1789	° *Fortescue* (8th), Charles Hugh Richard Fortescue, *b.* 1951, *s.* 1993, *m.*	Hon. Martin D. F., *b.* 1924
1841	*Gainsborough* (5th), Anthony Gerard Edward Noel, *b.* 1923, *s.* 1927, *m.*	Viscount Campden, *b.* 1950
1623 S.*	*Galloway* (13th), Randolph Keith Reginald Stewart (6th *Brit. Baron Stewart of Garlies*, 1796), *b.* 1928, *s.* 1978, *m.*	Andrew C. S., *b.* 1949
1703 S.*	*Glasgow* (10th), Patrick Robin Archibald Boyle (4th *UK Baron, Fairlie*, 1897), *b.* 1939, *s.* 1984, *m.*	Viscount of Kelburn, *b.* 1978
1806 I.*	*Gosford* (7th), Charles David Nicholas Alexander John Sparrow Acheson (5th *UK Baron, Worlingham*, 1835), *b.* 1942, *s.* 1966, *m.*	Hon. Patrick B. V. M. A., *b.* 1915
1945	*Gowrie* (2nd), Alexander Patric Greysteil Hore-Ruthven, PC (3rd *UK Baron Ruthven of Gowrie*, 1919), *b.* 1939, *s.* 1955, *m.*	Viscount Ruthven of Canberra, *b.* 1964
1684 I.*	*Granard* (10th), Peter Arthur Edward Hastings Forbes (5th *UK Baron, Granard*, 1806), *b.* 1957, *s.* 1992, *m.*	Viscount Forbes, *b.* 1981
1833	° *Granville* (6th), Granville George Fergus Leveson-Gower, *b.* 1959, *s.* 1996, *m.*	Hon. Niall J. L.-G., *b.* 1963
1806	° *Grey* (6th), Richard Fleming George Charles Grey, *b.* 1939, *s.* 1963, *m.*	Philip K. G., *b.* 1940
1752	*Guilford* (10th), Piers Edward Brownlow North, *b.* 1971, *s.* 1999, *m.*	Hon. Charles E N., *b.* 1918
1619 S.	*Haddington* (13th), John George Baillie-Hamilton, *b.* 1941, *s.* 1986, *m.*	Lord Binning, *b.* 1985
1919	° *Haig* (2nd), George Alexander Eugene Douglas Haig, OBE, *b.* 1918, *s.* 1928, *m.*	Viscount Dawick, *b.* 1961
1944	*Halifax* (3rd), Charles Edward Peter Neil Wood (5th *UK Visct., Halifax*, 1866), *b.* 1944, *s.* 1980, *m.*	Lord Irwin, *b.* 1977
1898	*Halsbury* (3rd), John Anthony Hardinge Giffard, FRS, FREng., *b.* 1908, *s.* 1943, *w.*	Adam E. G., *b.* 1934
1754	*Hardwicke* (10th), Joseph Philip Sebastian Yorke, *b.* 1971, *s.* 1974.	Charles E. Y., *b.* 1951
1812	*Harewood* (7th), George Henry Hubert Lascelles, KBE, *b.* 1923, *s.* 1947, *m.* (*see also* page 127)	Viscount Lascelles, *b.* 1950 (*see also* page 127)
1742	*Harrington* (11th), William Henry Leicester Stanhope (8th *Brit. Visct. Stanhope of Mahon*, 1717), *b.* 1922, *s.* 1929, *m.*	Viscount Petersham, *b.* 1945
1809	*Harrowby* (7th), Dudley Danvers Granville Coutts Ryder, TD, *b.* 1922, *s.* 1987, *m.*	Viscount Sandon, *b.* 1951
1605 S.	*Home* (15th), David Alexander Cospatrick Douglas-Home, CVO, *b.* 1943, *s.* 1995, *m.*	Lord Dunglass, *b.* 1987
1821	° *Howe* (7th), Frederick Richard Penn Curzon, *b.* 1951, *s.* 1984, *m.*	Viscount Curzon, *b.* 1994
1529	*Huntingdon* (16th), William Edward Robin Hood Hastings Bass, LVO, *b.* 1948, *s.* 1990, *m.*	Hon. Simon A. R. H. H. B., *b.* 1950
1885	*Iddesleigh* (4th), Stafford Henry Northcote, *b.* 1932, *s.* 1970, *m.*	Viscount St Cyres, *b.* 1957
1756	*Ilchester* (9th), Maurice Vivian de Touffreville Fox-Strangways, *b.* 1920, *s.* 1970, *m.*	Hon. Raymond G. F.-S., *b.* 1921
1929	*Inchcape* (4th), (Kenneth) Peter (Lyle) Mackay, *b.* 1943, *s.* 1994, *m.*	Viscount Glenapp, *b.* 1979
1919	*Iveagh* (4th), Arthur Edward Rory Guinness, *b.* 1969, *s.* 1992.	Hon. Rory M. B. G., *b.* 1974
1925	° *Jellicoe* (2nd), George Patrick John Rushworth Jellicoe, KBE, DSO, MC, PC, FRS, *b.* 1918, *s.* 1935, *m.*	Viscount Brocas, *b.* 1950
1697	*Jersey* (10th), (George Francis William Child Villiers (13th *Irish Visct. Grandison*, 1620), *b.* 1976, *s.* 1998.	Hon. Jamie C. V., *b.* 1994
1822 I.	*Kilmorey* (6th), Richard Francis Needham, KT, PC, *b.* 1942, *s.* 1977, *m.*	Viscount Newry and Morne, *b.* 1966
1866	*Kimberley* (4th), John Wodehouse, *b.* 1924, *s.* 1941, *m.*	Lord Wodehouse, *b.* 1951
1768 I.	*Kingston* (11th), Barclay Robert Edwin King-Tenison, *b.* 1943, *s.* 1948, *m.*	Viscount Kingsborough, *b.* 1969
1633 S.*	*Kinnoull* (15th), Arthur William George Patrick Hay (9th *Brit. Baron Hay of Pedwardine*, 1711), *b.* 1935, *s.* 1938, *m.*	Viscount Dupplin, *b.* 1962
1677 S.*	*Kintore* (13th), Michael Canning William John Keith (3rd *UK Visct. Stonehaven*, 1938), *b.* 1939, *s.* 1989, *m.*	Lord Inverurie, *b.* 1976
1914	° *Kitchener of Khartoum* (3rd), Henry Herbert Kitchener, TD, *b.* 1919, *s.* 1937.	None
1624 S.	*Lauderdale* (17th), Patrick Francis Maitland, *b.* 1911, *s.* 1968, *m.*	Viscount Maitland, *b.* 1937
1837	*Leicester* (7th), Edward Douglas Coke, *b.* 1936, *s.* 1994, *m.*	Viscount Coke, *b.* 1965
1641 S.*	*Leven* (14th) and *Melville* (13th) (S. 1690), Alexander Robert Leslie Melville, *b.* 1924, *s.* 1947, *m.*	Lord Balgonie, *b.* 1954
1831	*Lichfield* (5th), Thomas Patrick John Anson, *b.* 1939, *s.* 1960.	Viscount Anson, *b.* 1978
1803 I.*	*Limerick* (6th), Patrick Edmund Pery, KBE (6th *UK Baron Foxford*, 1815), *b.* 1930, *s.* 1967, *m.*	Viscount Glentworth, *b.* 1963

Created	Title, order of succession, name, etc.	Heir
1572	*Lincoln* (18th), Edward Horace Fiennes-Clinton, *b.* 1913, *s.* 1988, *m.*	Hon. Edward G. *F.-C., b.* 1943
1633 s.	*Lindsay* (16th), James Randolph Lindesay-Bethune, *b.* 1955, *s.* 1989, *m.*	Viscount Garnock, *b.* 1990
1626	*Lindsey* (14th) and *Abingdon* (9th) (1682), Richard Henry Rupert Bertie, *b.* 1931, *s.* 1963, *m.*	Lord Norreys, *b.* 1958
1776 I.	*Lisburne* (8th), John David Malet Vaughan, *b.* 1918, *s.* 1965, *m.*	Viscount Vaughan, *b.* 1945
1822 I.*	*Listowel* (6th), Francis Michael Hare (4th *UK Baron Hare,* 1869), *b.* 1964, *s.* 1997, *m.*	Hon. Timothy P. *H., b.* 1966
1905	*Liverpool* (5th), Edward Peter Bertram Savile Foljambe, *b.* 1944, *s.* 1969, *m.*	Viscount Hawkesbury, *b.* 1972
1945	° *Lloyd George of Dwyfor* (3rd), Owen Lloyd George, *b.* 1924, *s.* 1968, *m.*	Viscount Gwynedd, *b.* 1951
1785 I.*	*Longford* (7th), Francis Aungier Pakenham, KG, PC (6th *UK Baron, Silchester,* 1821; 1st *UK Baron Pakenham,* 1945), *b.* 1905, *s.* 1961, *m.*	Thomas F. D. *P., b.* 1933
1807	*Lonsdale* (7th), James Hugh William Lowther, *b.* 1922, *s.* 1953, *m.*	Viscount Lowther, *b.* 1949
1838	*Lovelace* (5th), Peter Axel William Locke King (12th *Brit. Baron King,* 1725), *b.* 1951, *s.* 1964, *m.*	None
1795 I.*	*Lucan* (7th), Richard John Bingham (3rd *UK Baron Bingham,* 1934), *b.* 1934, *s.* 1964, *m.*	Lord Bingham, *b.* 1967
1880	*Lytton* (5th), John Peter Michael Scawen Lytton (18th *Engl. Baron, Wentworth,* 1529), *b.* 1950, *s.* 1985, *m.*	Viscount Knebworth, *b.* 1989
1721	*Macclesfield* (9th), Richard Timothy George Mansfield Parker, *b.* 1943, *s.* 1992, *m.*	Hon. J. David G. *P., b.* 1945
1800	*Malmesbury* (6th), William James Harris, TD, *b.* 1907, *s.* 1950, *w.*	Viscount FitzHarris, *b.* 1946
1776 & 1792	*Mansfield and Mansfield* (8th), William David Mungo James Murray (14th *Scott. Visct. Stormont,* 1621), *b.* 1930, *s.* 1971, *m.*	Viscount Stormont, *b.* 1956
1565 s.*	*Mar* (14th) and *Kellie* (16th) (s. 1616), James Thorne Erskine, *b.* 1949, *s.* 1994, *m.*	Hon. Alexander D. *E., b.* 1952
1785 I.	*Mayo* (10th), Terence Patrick Bourke, *b.* 1929, *s.* 1962.	Lord Naas, *b.* 1953
1627 I.*	*Meath* (15th), John Anthony Brabazon (6th *UK Baron, Chaworth,* 1831), *b.* 1941, *s.* 1998, *m.*	Lord Ardee, *b.* 1977
1766 I.	*Mexborough* (8th), John Christopher George Savile, *b.* 1931, *s.* 1980, *m.*	Viscount Pollington, *b.* 1959
1813	*Minto* (6th), Gilbert Edward George Lariston Elliot-Murray-Kynynmound, OBE, *b.* 1928, *s.* 1975, *m.*	Viscount Melgund, *b.* 1953
1562 s.*	*Moray* (20th), Douglas John Moray Stuart (12th *Brit. Baron Stuart of Castle Stuart,* 1796), *b.* 1928, *s.* 1974, *m.*	Lord Doune, *b.* 1966
1815	*Morley* (6th), John St Aubyn Parker, KCVO, *b.* 1923, *s.* 1962, *m.*	Viscount Boringdon, *b.* 1956
1458 s.	*Morton* (22nd), John Charles Sholto Douglas, *b.* 1927, *s.* 1976, *m.*	Lord Aberdour, *b.* 1952
1789	*Mount Edgcumbe* (8th), Robert Charles Edgcumbe, *b.* 1939, *s.* 1982.	Piers V. *E., b.* 1946
1831	*Munster* (7th), Anthony Charles FitzClarence, *b.* 1926, *s.* 1983, *m.*	None
1805	° *Nelson* (9th), Peter John Horatio Nelson, *b.* 1941, *s.* 1981, *m.*	Viscount Merton, *b.* 1971
1660 s.	*Newburgh* (12th), Don Filippo Giambattista Camillo Francesco Aldo Ma Rospigliosi, *b.* 1942, *s.* 1986, *m.*	Princess Donna Benedetta F. M. *R., b.* 1974
1827 I.	*Norbury* (6th), Noel Terence Graham-Toler, *b.* 1939, *s.* 1955, *m.*	Viscount Glandine, *b.* 1967
1806 I.*	*Normanton* (6th), Shaun James Christian Welbore Ellis Agar (9th *Brit. Baron, Mendip,* 1794; 4th *UK Baron, Somerton,* 1873), *b.* 1945, *s.* 1967, *m.*	Viscount Somerton, *b.* 1982
1647 s.	*Northesk* (14th), David John MacRae Carnegie, *b.* 1954, *s.* 1994, *m.*	Lord Rosehill, *b.* 1980
1801	*Onslow* (7th), Michael William Coplestone Dillon Onslow, *b.* 1938, *s.* 1971, *m.*	Viscount Cranley, *b.* 1967
1696 s.	*Orkney* (9th), (Oliver) Peter St John, *b.* 1938, *s.* 1998, *m.*	Viscount Kirkwall, *b.* 1969
1328 I.*	*Ormonde and Ossory.* The 8th Marquess of Ormonde died in 1997, when the marquessate became extinct. The heir to his earldoms had not established his claim at the time of going to press	Viscount Mountgarret, *b.* 1936 (*see* page 146)
1925	*Oxford and Asquith* (2nd), Julian Edward George Asquith, KCMG, *b.* 1916, *s.* 1928, *w.*	Viscount Asquith OBE, *b.* 1952
1929	° *Peel* (3rd), William James Robert Peel (4th *UK Visct. Peel,* 1895), *b.* 1947, *s.* 1969, *m.*	Viscount Clanfield, *b.* 1976
1551	*Pembroke* (17th) and *Montgomery* (14th) (1605), Henry George Charles Alexander Herbert, *b.* 1939, *s.* 1969.	Lord Herbert, *b.* 1978
1605 s.	*Perth* (17th), John David Drummond, PC, *b.* 1907, *s.* 1951, *w.*	Viscount Strathallan, *b.* 1935
1905	*Plymouth* (3rd), Other Robert Ivor Windsor-Clive (15th *Engl. Baron, Windsor,* 1529), *b.* 1923, *s.* 1943, *m.*	Viscount Windsor, *b.* 1951
1785 I.	*Portarlington* (7th), George Lionel Yuill Seymour Dawson-Damer, *b.* 1938, *s.* 1959, *m.*	Viscount Carlow, *b.* 1965
1689	*Portland* (12th), Count Timothy Charles Robert Noel Bentinck, *b.* 1953, *s.* 1997, *m.*	Viscount Woodstock, *b.* 1984
1743	*Portsmouth* (10th), Quentin Gerard Carew Wallop, *b.* 1954, *s.* 1984, *m.*	Viscount Lymington, *b.* 1981
1804	*Powis* (8th), John George Herbert (9th *Irish Baron, Clive,* 1762), *b.* 1952, *s.* 1993, *m.*	Viscount Clive, *b.* 1979
1765	*Radnor* (8th), Jacob Pleydell-Bouverie, *b.* 1927, *s.* 1968, *m.*	Viscount Folkestone, *b.* 1955

Created	Title, order of succession, name, etc.	Heir
1831 I.*	*Ranfurly* (7th), Gerald Françoys Needham Knox (8th *UK Baron, Ranfurly,* 1826), *b.* 1929, *s.* 1988, *m.*	Edward J. *K., b.* 1957
1771 I.	*Roden* (10th), Robert John Jocelyn, *b.* 1938, *s.* 1993, *m.*	Viscount Jocelyn, *b.* 1989
1801	*Romney* (7th), Michael Henry Marsham, *b.* 1910, *s.* 1975, *m.*	Julian C. *M., b.* 1948
1703 S.*	*Rosebery* (7th), Neil Archibald Primrose (3rd *UK Earl Midlothian,* 1911), *b.* 1929, *s.* 1974, *m.*	Lord Dalmeny, *b.* 1967
1806 I.	*Rosse* (7th), William Brendan Parsons, *b.* 1936, *s.* 1979, *m.*	Lord Oxmantown, *b.* 1969
1801	*Rosslyn* (7th), Peter St Clair-Erskine, *b.* 1958, *s.* 1977, *m.*	Lord Loughborough, *b.* 1986
1457 S.	*Rothes* (21st), Ian Lionel Malcolm Leslie, *b.* 1932, *s.* 1975, *m.*	Lord Leslie, *b.* 1958
1861	° *Russell* (5th), Conrad Sebastian Robert Russell, FBA, *b.* 1937, *s.* 1987, *m.*	Viscount Amberley, *b.* 1968
1915	° *St Aldwyn* (3rd), Michael Henry Hicks Beach, *b.* 1950, *s.* 1992, *m.*	Hon. David S. *H. B., b.* 1955
1815	*St Germans* (10th), Peregrine Nicholas Eliot, *b.* 1941, *s.* 1988.	Lord Eliot, *b.* 1966
1660	*Sandwich* (11th), John Edward Hollister Montagu, *b.* 1943, *s.* 1995, *m.*	Viscount Hinchingbrooke, *b.* 1969
1690	*Scarbrough* (12th), Richard Aldred Lumley (13th *Irish Visct. Lumley,* 1628), *b.* 1932, *s.* 1969, *m.*	Viscount Lumley, *b.* 1973
1701 S.	*Seafield* (13th), Ian Derek Francis Ogilvie-Grant, *b.* 1939, *s.* 1969, *m.*	Viscount Reidhaven, *b.* 1963
1882	*Selborne* (4th), John Roundell Palmer, KBE, FRS, *b.* 1940, *s.* 1971, *m.*	Viscount Wolmer, *b.* 1971
1646 S.	*Selkirk.* Disclaimed for life 1994. (*see* Lord Selkirk of Douglas, page 161)	Hon. John A. *Douglas-Hamilton, b.* 1978
1672	*Shaftesbury* (10th), Anthony Ashley-Cooper, *b.* 1938, *s.* 1961, *m.*	Lord Ashley, *b.* 1977
1756 I.*	*Shannon* (9th), Richard Bentinck Boyle (8th *Brit. Baron Carleton,* 1786), *b.* 1924, *s.* 1963.	Viscount Boyle, *b.* 1960
1442	*Shrewsbury and Waterford* (22nd) (I. 1446), Charles Henry John Benedict Crofton Chetwynd Chetwynd-Talbot (7th *Engl. Earl Talbot,* 1784), *b.* 1952, *s.* 1980, *m. Premier Earl of England and Ireland*	Viscount Ingestre, *b.* 1978
1961	*Snowdon* (1st), Anthony Charles Robert Armstrong-Jones, GCVO, *b.* 1930, *m. Constable of Caernarfon Castle* (*see also* page 117)	Viscount Linley, *b.* 1961 (*see also* page 117)
1765	° *Spencer* (9th), Charles Edward Maurice Spencer, *b.* 1964, *s.* 1992.	Viscount Althorp, *b.* 1994
1703 S.*	*Stair* (14th), John David James Dalrymple (7th *UK Baron, Oxenfoord,* 1841), *b.* 1961, *s.* 1996.	Hon. David H. *D., b.* 1963
1984	*Stockton* (2nd), Alexander Daniel Alan Macmillan, MEP, *b.* 1943, *s.* 1986, *m.*	Viscount Macmillan of Ovenden, *b.* 1974
1821	*Stradbroke* (6th), Robert Keith Rous, *b.* 1937, *s.* 1983, *m.*	Viscount Dunwich, *b.* 1961
1847	*Strafford* (8th), Thomas Edmund Byng, *b.* 1936, *s.* 1984, *m.*	Viscount Enfield, *b.* 1964
1606 S.*	*Strathmore and Kinghorne* (18th), Michael Fergus Bowes Lyon (16th *Scott. Earl, Strathmore,* 1677; 18th *Scott. Earl, Kinghorne,* 1606; 5th *UK Earl, Strathmore and Kinghorne,* 1937), *b.* 1957, *s.* 1987, *m.*	Lord Glamis, *b.* 1986
1603	*Suffolk* (21st) and *Berkshire* (14th) (1626), Michael John James George Robert Howard, *b.* 1935, *s.* 1941, *m.*	Viscount Andover, *b.* 1974
1955	*Swinton* (2nd), David Yarburgh Cunliffe-Lister, *b.* 1937, *s.* 1972, *m.*	Hon. Nicholas J. *C.-L., b.* 1939
1714	*Tankerville* (10th), Peter Grey Bennet, *b.* 1956, *s.* 1980.	Revd the Hon. George A. G. *B., b.* 1925
1822	° *Temple of Stowe* (8th), (Walter) Grenville Algernon Temple-Gore-Langton, *b.* 1924, *s.* 1988, *m.*	Lord Langton, *b.* 1955
1815	*Verulam* (7th), John Duncan Grimston (11th *Irish Visct. Grimston,* 1719; 16th *Scott. Baron Forrester of Corstorphine,* 1633), *b.* 1951, *s.* 1973, *m.*	Viscount Grimston, *b.* 1978
1729	° *Waldegrave* (13th), James Sherbrooke Waldegrave, *b.* 1940, *s.* 1995, *m.*	Viscount Chewton, *b.* 1986
1759	*Warwick* (9th) and *Brooke* (9th) (*Brit.* 1746), Guy David Greville, *b.* 1957, *s.* 1996, *m.*	Lord Brooke, *b.* 1982
1633 S.*	*Wemyss* (12th) and *March* (8th) (S. 1697), Francis David Charteris, KT (5th *UK Baron Wemyss,* 1821), *b.* 1912, *s.* 1937, *m.*	Lord Neidpath, *b.* 1948
1621 I.	*Westmeath* (13th), William Anthony Nugent, *b.* 1928, *s.* 1971, *m.*	Hon. Sean C. W. *N., b.* 1965
1624	*Westmorland* (16th), Anthony David Francis Henry Fane, *b.* 1951, *s.* 1993, *m.*	Hon. Harry St C. *F., b.* 1953
1876	*Wharncliffe* (5th), Richard Alan Montagu Stuart Wortley, *b.* 1953, *s.* 1987, *m.*	Viscount Carlton, *b.* 1980
1801	*Wilton* (7th), Seymour William Arthur John Egerton, *b.* 1921, *s.* 1927, *m.*	Baron Ebury, *b.* 1934 (*see* page 149)
1628	*Winchilsea* (17th) and *Nottingham* (12th) (1681), Daniel James Hatfield Finch Hatton, *b.* 1967, *s.* 1999, *m.*	Robin Heneage *F.-H., b.* 1939
1766 I.	° *Winterton* (8th), (Donald) David Turnour, *b.* 1943, *s.* 1991, *m.*	Robert C. *T., b.* 1950
1956	*Woolton* (3rd), Simon Frederick Marquis, *b.* 1958, *s.* 1969, *m.*	None
1837	*Yarborough* (8th), Charles John Pelham, *b.* 1963, *s.* 1991, *m.*	Lord Worsley, *b.* 1990

COUNTESSES IN THEIR OWN RIGHT

Style, The Right Hon. the Countess (of) —
Husband, Untitled
Children's style, As for children of an Earl
For forms of address, *see* page 135

Created	Title, order of succession, name, etc.	Heir
1643 s.	*Dysart* (11th in line), Rosamund Agnes Greaves, *b.* 1914, *s.* 1975.	Lady Katherine *Grant of Rothiemurchus, b.* 1918
1633 s.	*Loudoun* (13th in line), Barbara Huddleston Abney-Hastings, *b.* 1919, *s.* 1960, *m.*	Lord Mauchline, *b.* 1942
c.1115 s.	*Mar* (31st in line), Margaret of Mar, *b.* 1940, *s.* 1975, *m. Premier Earldom of Scotland*	Mistress of Mar, *b.* 1963
1947	° *Mountbatten of Burma* (2nd in line), Patricia Edwina Victoria Knatchbull, CBE, *b.* 1924, *s.* 1979, *m.*	Lord Romsey, *b.* 1947 (*see also* page 148)
c.1235 s.	*Sutherland* (24th in line), Elizabeth Millicent Sutherland, *b.* 1921, *s.* 1963, *m.*	Lord Strathnaver, *b.* 1947

VISCOUNTS

Coronet, Sixteen silver balls
Style, The Right Hon. the Viscount —
Wife's style, The Right Hon. the Viscountess —
Children's style, 'The Hon.' before forename and family name
In Scotland, the heir apparent to a Viscount may be styled 'The Master of — (title of peer)'
For forms of address, *see* page 135

Created	Title, order of succession, name, etc.	Heir
1945	*Addison* (4th), William Matthew Wand Addison, *b.* 1945, *s.* 1992, *m.*	Hon. Paul W. *A., b.* 1973
1946	*Alanbrooke* (3rd), Alan Victor Harold Brooke, *b.* 1932, *s.* 1972.	None
1919	*Allenby* (3rd), Lt.-Col. Michael Jaffray Hynman Allenby, *b.* 1931, *s.* 1984, *m.*	Hon. Henry J. H. *A., b.* 1968
1911	*Allendale* (3rd), Wentworth Hubert Charles Beaumont, *b.* 1922, *s.* 1956.	Hon. Wentworth P. I. *B., b.* 1948
1642 s.	*of Arbuthnott* (16th), John Campbell Arbuthnott, KT, CBE, DSC, FRSE, *b.* 1924, *s.* 1966, *m.*	Master of Arbuthnott, *b.* 1950
1751 I.	*Ashbrook* (11th), Michael Llowarch Warburton Flower, *b.* 1935, *s.* 1995, *m.*	Hon. Rowland F. W. *F., b.* 1975
1917	*Astor* (4th), William Waldorf Astor, *b.* 1951, *s.* 1966, *m.*	Hon. William W. *A., b.* 1979
1781 I.	*Bangor* (8th), William Maxwell David Ward, *b.* 1948, *s.* 1993, *m.*	Hon. E. Nicholas *W., b.* 1953
1925	*Bearsted* (5th), Nicholas Alan Samuel, *b.* 1950, *s.* 1996, *m.*	Hon. Harry R. *S., b.* 1988
1963	*Blakenham* (2nd), Michael John Hare, *b.* 1938, *s.* 1982, *m.*	Hon. Caspar J. *H., b.* 1972
1935	*Bledisloe* (3rd), Christopher Hiley Ludlow Bathurst, *b.* 1934, *s.* 1979.	Hon. Rupert E. L. *B., b.* 1964
1712	*Bolingbroke* (7th) and *St John* (8th) (1716), Kenneth Oliver Musgrave St John, *b.* 1927, *s.* 1974.	Hon. Henry F. *St J., b.* 1957
1960	*Boyd of Merton* (2nd), Simon Donald Rupert Neville Lennox-Boyd, *b.* 1939, *s.* 1983, *m.*	Hon. Benjamin A. *L.-B., b.* 1964
1717 I.*	*Boyne* (11th), Gustavus Michael Stucley Hamilton-Russell (5th *UK Baron Brancepeth*, 1866), *b.* 1965, *s.* 1995, *m.*	Hon. Brian G. *H.-R., b.* 1940
1929	*Brentford* (4th), Crispin William Joynson-Hicks, *b.* 1933, *s.* 1983, *m.*	Hon. Paul W. *J.-H., b.* 1971
1929	*Bridgeman* (3rd), Robin John Orlando Bridgeman, *b.* 1930, *s.* 1982, *m.*	Hon. William O. C. *B., b.* 1968
1868	*Bridport* (4th), Alexander Nelson Hood (7th *Duke, Brontë in Sicily*, 1799; 6th *Irish Baron Bridport*, 1794), *b.* 1948, *s.* 1969, *m.*	Hon. Peregrine A. N. *H., b.* 1974
1952	*Brookeborough* (3rd), Alan Henry Brooke, *b.* 1952, *s.* 1987, *m.*	Hon. Christopher A. *B., b.* 1954
1933	*Buckmaster* (3rd), Martin Stanley Buckmaster, OBE, *b.* 1921, *s.* 1974.	Hon. Colin J. *B., b.* 1923
1939	*Caldecote* (2nd), Robert Andrew Inskip, KBE, DSC, FREng, *b.* 1917, *s.* 1947, *m.*	Hon. Piers J. H. *I., b.* 1947
1941	*Camrose.* Disclaimed for life 1995. (*see* Baron Hartwell, page 159)	Hon. Adrian M. *Berry, b.* 1937
1954	*Chandos* (3rd), Thomas Orlando Lyttelton, *b.* 1953, *s.* 1980, *m.*	Hon. Oliver A. *L., b.* 1986

Created	Title, order of succession, name, etc.	Heir
1665 I.*	*Charlemont* (14th), John Day Caulfeild (18th *Irish Baron Caulfeild of Charlemont*, 1620), b. 1934, s. 1985, m.	Hon. John D. C., b. 1966
1921	*Chelmsford* (3rd), Frederic Jan Thesiger, b. 1931, s. 1970, m.	Hon. Frederic C. P. T., b. 1962
1717 I.	*Chetwynd* (10th), Adam Richard John Casson Chetwynd, b. 1935, s. 1965, m.	Hon. Adam D. C., b. 1969
1911	*Chilston* (4th), Alastair George Akers-Douglas, b. 1946, s. 1982, m.	Hon. Oliver I. A.-D., b. 1973
1902	*Churchill* (3rd), Victor George Spencer (5th *UK Baron Churchill*, 1815), b. 1934, s. 1973.	None to Viscountcy. To Barony, Richard H. R. S., b. 1926
1718	*Cobham* (11th), John William Leonard Lyttelton (8th *Irish Baron Westcote*, 1776), b. 1943, s. 1977, m.	Hon. Christopher C. L., b. 1947
1902	*Colville of Culross* (4th), John Mark Alexander Colville, QC (13th *Scott. Baron Colville of Culross*, 1604), b. 1933, s. 1945, m.	Master of Colville, b. 1959
1826	*Combermere* (5th), Michael Wellington Stapleton-Cotton, b. 1929, s. 1969, m.	Hon. Thomas R. W. S.-C., b. 1969
1917	*Cowdray* (4th), Michael Orlando Weetman Pearson (4th *UK Baron Cowdray*, 1910), b. 1944, s. 1995, m.	Hon. Peregrine J. D. P., b. 1994
1927	*Craigavon* (3rd), Janric Fraser Craig, b. 1944, s. 1974.	None
1886	*Cross* (3rd), Assheton Henry Cross, b. 1920, s. 1932.	None
1943	*Daventry* (3rd), Francis Humphrey Maurice FitzRoy Newdegate, b. 1921, s. 1986, m.	Hon. James E. F. N., b. 1960
1937	*Davidson* (2nd), John Andrew Davidson, b. 1928, s. 1970, m.	Hon. Malcolm W. M. D., b. 1934
1956	*De L'Isle* (2nd), Philip John Algernon Sidney, MBE (7th *UK Baron De L'Isle and Dudley*, 1835), b. 1945, s. 1991, m.	Hon. Philip W. E. S., b. 1985
1776 I.*	*De Vesci* (7th), Thomas Eustace Vesey (8th *Irish Baron Knapton*, 1750), b. 1955, s. 1983, m.	Hon. Oliver I. V., b. 1991
1917	*Devonport* (3rd), Terence Kearley, b. 1944, s. 1973.	Chester D. H. K., b. 1932
1964	*Dilhorne* (2nd), John Mervyn Manningham-Buller, b. 1932, s. 1980, m.	Hon. James E. M.-B., b. 1956
1622 I.	*Dillon* (22nd), Henry Benedict Charles Dillon, b. 1973, s. 1982.	Hon. Richard A. L. D., b. 1948
1785 I.	*Doneraile* (10th), Richard Allen St Leger, b. 1946, s. 1983, m.	Hon. Nathaniel W. R. St J. St L., b. 1971
1680 I.*	*Downe* (11th), John Christian George Dawnay (4th *UK Baron Dawnay*, 1897), b. 1935, s. 1965, m.	Hon. Richard H. D., b. 1967
1959	*Dunrossil* (2nd), John William Morrison, CMG, b. 1926, s. 1961, m.	Hon. Andrew W. R. M., b. 1953
1964	*Eccles* (2nd), John Dawson Eccles, CBE, b. 1931, s. 1999, m.	Hon. William David E., b. 1960
1897	*Esher* (4th), Lionel Gordon Baliol Brett, CBE, b. 1913, s. 1963, m.	Hon. Christopher L. B. B., b. 1936
1816	*Exmouth* (10th), Paul Edward Pellew, b. 1940, s. 1970, m.	Hon. Edward F. P., b. 1978
1620 S.	*Falkland* (15th), Lucius Edward William Plantagenet Cary, b. 1935, s. 1984, m. *Premier Scottish Viscount on the Roll*	Master of Falkland, b. 1963
1720	*Falmouth* (9th), George Hugh Boscawen (26th *Engl. Baron Le Despencer*, 1264), b. 1919, s. 1962, m.	Hon. Evelyn A. H. B., b. 1955
1720 I.*	*Gage* (8th), (Henry) Nicolas Gage (7th *Brit. Baron Gage*, 1790), b. 1934, s. 1993, m.	Hon. Henry W. G., b. 1975
1727 I.	*Galway* (12th), George Rupert Monckton-Arundell, b. 1922, s. 1980, m.	Hon. J. Philip M.-A., b. 1952
1478 I.*	*Gormanston* (17th), Jenico Nicholas Dudley Preston (5th *UK Baron Gormanston*, 1868), b. 1939, s. 1940, w. *Premier Viscount of Ireland*	Hon. Jenico F. T. P., b. 1974
1816 I.	*Gort* (9th), Foley Robert Standish Prendergast Vereker, b. 1951, s. 1995, m.	Hon. Robert F. P. V., b. 1993
1900	*Goschen* (4th), Giles John Harry Goschen, b. 1965, s. 1977, m.	None
1849	*Gough* (5th), Shane Hugh Maryon Gough, b. 1941, s. 1951.	None
1937	*Greenwood* (3rd), Michael George Hamar Greenwood, b. 1923, s. 1998.	†
1929	*Hailsham*. Disclaimed for life 1963. (*see* Lord Hailsham of St Marylebone, page 159)	Rt. Hon. Douglas M. Hogg QC, MP, b. 1945
1891	*Hambleden* (4th), William Herbert Smith, b. 1930, s. 1948, m.	Hon. William H. B. S., b. 1955
1884	*Hampden* (6th), Anthony David Brand, b. 1937, s. 1975, m.	Hon. Francis A. B., b. 1970
1936	*Hanworth* (3rd), David Stephen Geoffrey Pollock, b. 1946, s. 1996, m.	Hon. Richard C. S. P., b. 1951
1791 I.	*Harberton* (10th), Thomas de Vautort Pomeroy, b. 1910, s. 1980, m.	Henry Robert P., b. 1958
1846	*Hardinge* (6th), Charles Henry Nicholas Hardinge, b. 1956, s. 1984, m.	Hon. Andrew H. H., b. 1960
1791 I.	*Hawarden* (9th), (Robert) Connan Wyndham Leslie Maude, b. 1961, s. 1991, m.	Hon. Varian J. C. E. M., b. 1997
1960	*Head* (2nd), Richard Antony Head, b. 1937, s. 1983, m.	Hon. Henry J. H., b. 1980
1550	*Hereford* (18th), Robert Milo Leicester Devereux, b. 1932, s. 1952. *Premier Viscount of England*	Hon. Charles R. de B. D., b. 1975
1842	*Hill* (8th), Antony Rowland Clegg-Hill, b. 1931, s. 1974, m.	Peter D. R. C. C.-H., b. 1945
1796	*Hood* (7th), Alexander Lambert Hood (7th *Irish Baron, Hood*, 1782), b. 1914, s. 1981, m.	Hon. Henry L. A. H., b. 1958
1956	*Ingleby* (2nd), Martin Raymond Peake, b. 1926, s. 1966, w.	None
1945	*Kemsley* (3rd), Richard Gomer Berry, b. 1951, s. 1999, m.	Hon. Edward A. M., B., b. 1960
1911	*Knollys* (3rd), David Francis Dudley Knollys, b. 1931, s. 1966, m.	Hon. Patrick N. M. K., b. 1962

Created	Title, order of succession, name, etc.	Heir
1895	*Knutsford* (6th), Michael Holland-Hibbert, *b.* 1926, *s.* 1986, *m.*	Hon. Henry T. *H.-H., b.* 1959
1945	*Lambert* (3rd), Michael John Lambert, *b.* 1912, *s.* 1989, *m.*	None
1954	*Leathers* (3rd), Christopher Graeme Leathers, *b.* 1941, *s.* 1996, *m.*	Hon. James F. *L., b.* 1969
1922	*Leverhulme* (3rd), Philip William Bryce Lever, KG,TD, *b.* 1915, *s.* 1949, *w.*	None
1781 I.	*Lifford* (9th), (Edward) James Wingfield Hewitt, *b.* 1949, *s.* 1987, *m.*	Hon. James T. W. *H., b.* 1979
1921	*Long* (4th), Richard Gerard Long, CBE, *b.* 1929, *s.* 1967, *m.*	Hon. James R. *L., b.* 1960
1957	*Mackintosh of Halifax* (3rd), (John) Clive Mackintosh, *b.* 1958, *s.* 1980, *m.*	Hon. Thomas H. G. *M., b.* 1985
1955	*Malvern* (3rd), Ashley Kevin Godfrey Huggins, *b.* 1949, *s.* 1978.	Hon. M. James *H., b.* 1928
1945	*Marchwood* (3rd), David George Staveley Penny, *b.* 1936, *s.* 1979, *w.*	Hon. Peter G. W. *P., b.* 1965
1942	*Margesson* (2nd), Francis Vere Hampden Margesson, *b.* 1922, *s.* 1965, *m.*	Maj. Hon. Richard F. D. *M., b.* 1960
1660 I.*	*Massereene* (14th) and *Ferrard* (7th) (1797), John David Clotworthy Whyte-Melville Foster Skeffington (7th *UK Baron, Oriel,* 1821), *b.* 1940, *s.* 1992, *m.*	Hon. Charles J. C. W.-M. F. *S., b.* 1973
1802	*Melville* (9th), Robert David Ross Dundas, *b.* 1937, *s.* 1971, *m.*	Hon. Robert H. K. *D., b.* 1984
1916	*Mersey* (4th), Richard Maurice Clive Bigham (13th *Scott. Lord Nairne,* 1681, *s.* 1995), *b.* 1934, *s.* 1979, *m.*	Hon. Edward J. H. *B.* Master of Nairne, *b.* 1966
1717 I.*	*Midleton* (12th), Alan Henry Brodrick (9th *Brit. Baron Brodrick of Peper Harow,* 1796), *b.* 1949, *s.* 1988, *m.*	Hon. Ashley R. *B., b.* 1980
1962	*Mills* (3rd), Christopher Philip Roger Mills, *b.* 1956, *s.* 1988, *m.*	None
1716 I.	*Molesworth* (12th), Robert Bysse Kelham Molesworth, *b.* 1959, *s.* 1997.	Hon. William J. C. *M., b.* 1960
1801 I.*	*Monck* (7th), Charles Stanley Monck (4th *UK Baron, Monck,* 1866), *b.* 1953, *s.* 1982. (does not use title)	Hon. George S. *M., b.* 1957
1957	*Monckton of Brenchley* (2nd), Maj.-Gen. Gilbert Walter Riversdale Monckton, CB, OBE, MC, *b.* 1915, *s.* 1965, *m.*	Hon. Christopher W. *M., b.* 1952
1946	*Montgomery of Alamein* (2nd), David Bernard Montgomery, CBE, *b.* 1928, *s.* 1976, *m.*	Hon. Henry D. *M., b.* 1954
1550 I.*	*Mountgarret* (17th), Richard Henry Piers Butler (4th *UK Baron Mountgarret,* 1911), *b.* 1936, *s.* 1966, *m.*	Hon. Piers J. R. *B., b.* 1961
1952	*Norwich* (2nd), John Julius Cooper, CVO, *b.* 1929, *s.* 1954, *m.*	Hon. Jason C. D. B. *C., b.* 1959
1651 S.	*of Oxfuird* (13th), George Hubbard Makgill, CBE, *b.* 1934, *s.* 1986, *m.*	Master of Oxfuird, *b.* 1969
1873	*Portman* (10th), Christopher Edward Berkeley Portman, *b.* 1958, *s.* 1999, *m.*	Hon. Luke O. B. *P., b.* 1984
1743 I.*	*Powerscourt* (10th), Mervyn Niall Wingfield (4th *UK Baron Powerscourt,* 1885), *b.* 1935, *s.* 1973, *m.*	Hon. Mervyn A. *W., b.* 1963
1900	*Ridley* (4th), Matthew White Ridley, KG, GCVO, TD, *b.* 1925, *s.* 1964, *m.* Lord Steward	Hon. Matthew W. *R., b.* 1958
1960	*Rochdale* (2nd), St John Durival Kemp, *b.* 1938, *s.* 1993, *m.*	Hon. Jonathan H. D. *K., b.* 1961
1919	*Rothermere* (4th), (Harold) Jonathan Esmond Vere Harmsworth, *b.* 1967, *s.* 1998, *m.*	Hon. Esmond Vyvyan *H., b.* 1967
1937	*Runciman of Doxford* (3rd), Walter Garrison Runciman (Garry), CBE, FBA (4th *UK Baron, Runciman,* 1933), *b.* 1934, *s.* 1989, *m.*	Hon. David W. *R., b.* 1967
1918	*St Davids* (3rd), Colwyn Jestyn John Philipps (20th *Engl. Baron Strange of Knokin,* 1299; 8th *Engl. Baron, Hungerford,* 1426; *Baron De Moleyns,* 1445), *b.* 1939, *s.* 1991, *m.*	Hon. Rhodri C. *P., b.* 1966
1801	*St Vincent* (7th), Ronald George James Jervis, *b.* 1905, *s.* 1940, *m.*	Hon. Edward R. J. *J., b.* 1951
1937	*Samuel* (3rd), David Herbert Samuel, OBE, PH.D., *b.* 1922, *s.* 1978, *m.*	Hon. Dan J. *S., b.* 1925
1911	*Scarsdale* (3rd), Francis John Nathaniel Curzon (7th *Brit. Baron Scarsdale,* 1761), *b.* 1924, *s.* 1977, *m.*	Hon. Peter G. N. *C., b.* 1949
1905	*Selby* (5th), Edward Thomas William Gully, *b.* 1967, *s.* 1997, *m.*	Hon. Christopher R. T. *G., b.* 1993
1805	*Sidmouth* (7th), John Tonge Anthony Pellew Addington, *b.* 1914, *s.* 1976, *m.*	Hon. Jeremy F. *A., b.* 1947
1940	*Simon* (3rd), Jan David Simon, *b.* 1940, *s.* 1993, *m.*	None
1960	*Slim* (2nd), John Douglas Slim, OBE, *b.* 1927, *s.* 1970, *m.*	Hon. Mark W. R. *S., b.* 1960
1954	*Soulbury* (2nd), James Herwald Ramsbotham, *b.* 1915, *s.* 1971, *w.*	Hon. Sir Peter E. *R.* GCMG, GCVO, *b.* 1919
1776 I.	*Southwell* (7th), Pyers Anthony Joseph Southwell, *b.* 1930, *s.* 1960, *m.*	Hon. Richard A. P. *S., b.* 1956
1942	*Stansgate.* Disclaimed for life 1963. (*Rt. Hon. Anthony Neil Wedgwood Benn,* MP, *b.*1925, *s.*1960, *m.*)	Stephen M. W. *B., b.* 1951
1959	*Stuart of Findhorn* (2nd), David Randolph Moray Stuart, *b.* 1924, *s.* 1971, *m.*	Hon. J. Dominic *S., b.* 1948
1957	*Tenby* (3rd), William Lloyd George, *b.* 1927, *s.* 1983, *m.*	Hon. Timothy H. G. L. *G., b.* 1962
1952	*Thurso* (3rd), John Archibald Sinclair, *b.* 1953, *s.* 1995, *m.*	Hon. James A. R. *S., b.* 1984
1721	*Torrington* (11th), Timothy Howard St George Byng, *b.* 1943, *s.* 1961, *m.*	John L. *B.,* MC, *b.* 1919
1936	*Trenchard* (3rd), Hugh Trenchard, *b.* 1951, *s.* 1987, *m.*	Hon. Alexander T. *T., b.* 1978
1921	*Ullswater* (2nd), Nicholas James Christopher Lowther, PC, *b.* 1942, *s.* 1949, *m.*	Hon. Benjamin J. *L., b.* 1975
1621 I.	*Valentia* (15th), Richard John Dighton Annesley, *b.* 1929, *s.* 1983, *m.*	Hon. Francis W. D. *A., b.* 1959

Created	*Title, order of succession, name, etc.*	*Heir*
1952	*Waverley* (3rd), John Desmond Forbes Anderson, *b.* 1949, *s.* 1990.	None
1938	*Weir* (3rd), William Kenneth James Weir, *b.* 1933, *s.* 1975, *m.*	Hon. James W. H. *W., b.* 1965
1918	*Wimborne* (4th), Ivor Mervyn Vigors Guest (5th *UK Baron Wimborne,* 1880), *b.* 1968, *s.* 1993.	Hon. Julian J. *G., b.* 1945
1923	*Younger of Leckie* (4th), George Kenneth Hotson Younger, KT, KCVO, TD, PC (*Baron Younger of Prestwick* (life peerage), 1992), *b.* 1931, *s.* 1997, *m.*	Hon. James E. G. *Y., b.* 1955

BARONS/LORDS

Coronet, Six silver balls
Style, The Right Hon. the Lord __. In the Peerage of Scotland there is no rank of Baron; the equivalent rank is Lord of Parliament (*see* page 136) and Scottish peers should always be styled 'Lord', never 'Baron'
Wife's style, The Right Hon. the Lady __
Children's style, 'The Hon.' before forename and family name
In Scotland, the heir apparent to a Lord may be styled 'The Master of __ (title of peer)'
For forms of address, *see* page 135

Created	*Title, order of succession, name, etc.*	*Heir*
1911	*Aberconway* (3rd), Charles Melville McLaren, *b.* 1913, *s.* 1953, *m.*	Hon. H. Charles *M., b.* 1948
1873	*Aberdare* (4th), Morys George Lyndhurst Bruce, KBE, PC, *b.* 1919, *s.* 1957, *m.*	Hon. Alastair J. L. *B., b.* 1947
1835	*Abinger* (8th), James Richard Scarlett, *b.* 1914, *s.* 1943, *m.*	Hon. James H. *S., b.* 1959
1869	*Acton* (4th), Richard Gerald Lyon-Dalberg-Acton, *b.* 1941, *s.* 1989, *m.*	Hon. John C. F. H. *L.-D.-A., b.* 1966
1887	*Addington* (6th), Dominic Bryce Hubbard, *b.* 1963, *s.* 1982.	Hon. Michael W. L. *H., b.* 1965
1896	*Aldenham* (6th) and *Hunsdon of Hunsdon* (4th) (1923), Vicary Tyser Gibbs, *b.* 1948, *s.* 1986, *m.*	Hon. Humphrey W. F. *G., b.* 1989
1962	*Aldington* (1st), Toby Austin Richard William Low, KCMG, CBE, DSO, TD, PC, *b.* 1914.	Hon. Charles H. S. *L., b.* 1948
1945	*Altrincham.* Disclaimed for life 1963. (*John Edward Poynder Grigg, b.* 1924, *s.* 1955, *m.*)	Hon. Anthony U. D. D. *G., b.* 1934
1929	*Alvingham* (2nd), Maj.-Gen. Robert Guy Eardley Yerburgh, CBE, *b.* 1926, *s.* 1955, *m.*	Capt. Hon. Robert R. G. *Y., b.* 1956
1892	*Amherst of Hackney* (4th), William Hugh Amherst Cecil, *b.* 1940, *s.* 1980, *m.*	Hon. H. William A. *C., b.* 1968
1881	*Ampthill* (4th), Geoffrey Denis Erskine Russell, CBE, PC, *b.* 1921, *s.* 1973.	Hon. David W. E. *R., b.* 1947
1947	*Amwell* (3rd), Keith Norman Montague, *b.* 1943, *s.* 1990, *m.*	Hon. Ian K. *M., b.* 1973
1863	*Annaly* (6th), Luke Richard White, *b.* 1954, *s.* 1990, *m.*	Hon. Luke H. *W., b.* 1990
1885	*Ashbourne* (4th), Edward Barry Greynville Gibson, *b.* 1933, *s.* 1983, *m.*	Hon. Edward C. d'O. *G., b.* 1967
1835	*Ashburton* (7th), John Francis Harcourt Baring, KG, KCVO, *b.* 1928, *s.* 1991, *m.*	Hon. Mark F. R. *B., b.* 1958
1892	*Ashcombe* (4th), Henry Edward Cubitt, *b.* 1924, *s.* 1962, *m.*	Mark E. *C., b.* 1964
1911	*Ashton of Hyde* (3rd), Thomas John Ashton, TD, *b.* 1926, *s.* 1983, *m.*	Hon. Thomas H. *A., b.* 1958
1800 I.	*Ashtown* (7th), Nigel Clive Crosby Trench, KCMG, *b.* 1916, *s.* 1990, *m.*	Hon. Roderick N. G. *T., b.* 1944
1956	*Astor of Hever* (3rd), John Jacob Astor, *b.* 1946, *s.* 1984, *m.*	Hon. Charles G. J. *A., b.* 1990
1789 I.*	*Auckland* (10th), Robert Ian Burnard Eden (10th *Brit. Baron Auckland,* 1793), *b.* 1962, *s.* 1997, *m.*	Hon. Ronald J. *E., b.* 1931
1313	*Audley.* The 25th Lord Audley died in July 1997, leaving three co-heiresses	
1900	*Avebury* (4th), Eric Reginald Lubbock, *b.* 1928, *s.* 1971, *m.*	Hon. Lyulph A. J. *L., b.* 1954
1718 I.	*Aylmer* (13th), Michael Anthony Aylmer, *b.* 1923, *s.* 1982, *m.*	Hon. A. Julian *A., b.* 1951
1929	*Baden-Powell* (3rd), Robert Crause Baden-Powell, *b.* 1936, *s.* 1962, *m.*	Hon. David M. *B.-P., b.* 1940
1780	*Bagot* (9th), Heneage Charles Bagot, *b.* 1914, *s.* 1979, *m.*	Hon. C. H. Shaun *B., b.* 1944
1953	*Baillieu* (3rd), James William Latham Baillieu, *b.* 1950, *s.* 1973, *m.*	Hon. Robert L. *B., b.* 1979
1607 S.	*Balfour of Burleigh* (8th), Robert Bruce, FRSE, *b.* 1927, *s.* 1967, *m.*	Hon. Victoria B., *b.* 1973
1945	*Balfour of Inchrye* (2nd), Ian Balfour, *b.* 1924, *s.* 1988, *m.*	None
1924	*Banbury of Southam* (3rd), Charles William Banbury, *b.* 1953, *s.* 1981, *m.*	None
1698	*Barnard* (11th), Harry John Neville Vane, TD, *b.* 1923, *s.* 1964.	Hon. Henry F. C. *V., b.* 1959
1887	*Basing* (5th), Neil Lutley Sclater-Booth, *b.* 1939, *s.* 1983, *m.*	Hon. Stuart W. *S.-B., b.* 1969
1917	*Beaverbrook* (3rd), Maxwell William Humphrey Aitken, *b.* 1951, *s.* 1985, *m.*	Hon. Maxwell F. *A., b.* 1977
1647 S.	*Belhaven and Stenton* (13th), Robert Anthony Carmichael Hamilton, *b.* 1927, *s.* 1961, *m.*	Master of Belhaven, *b.* 1953

Created	Title, order of succession, name, etc.	Heir

1848 I. *Bellew* (7th), James Bryan Bellew, *b.* 1920, *s.* 1981, *m.* — Hon. Bryan E. *B.*, *b.* 1943

1856 *Belper* (4th), (Alexander) Ronald George Strutt, *b.* 1912, *s.* 1956. — Hon. Richard H. *S.*, *b.* 1941

1938 *Belstead* (2nd), John Julian Ganzoni, PC, *b.* 1932, *s.* 1958. — None

1421 *Berkeley* (18th), Anthony Fitzhardinge Gueterbock, OBE, *b.* 1939, *s.* 1992, *m.* — Hon. Thomas F. *G.*, *b.* 1969

1922 *Bethell* (4th), Nicholas William Bethell, MEP, *b.* 1938, *s.* 1967, *m.* — Hon. James N. *B.*, *b.* 1967

1938 *Bicester* (3rd), Angus Edward Vivian Smith, *b.* 1932, *s.* 1968. — Hugh C. V. *S.*, *b.* 1934

1903 *Biddulph* (5th), (Anthony) Nicholas Colin Maitland Biddulph, *b.* 1959, *s.* 1988, *m.* — Hon. Robert J. *M. B.*, *b.* 1994

1938 *Birdwood* (3rd), Mark William Ogilvie Birdwood, *b.* 1938, *s.* 1962, *m.* — None

1958 *Birkett* (2nd), Michael Birkett, *b.* 1929, *s.* 1962, *m.* — Hon. Thomas *B.*, *b.* 1982

1907 *Blyth* (4th), Anthony Audley Rupert Blyth, *b.* 1931, *s.* 1977, *m.* — Hon. Riley A. J. *B.*, *b.* 1955

1797 *Bolton* (7th), Richard William Algar Orde-Powlett, *b.* 1929, *s.* 1963, *m.* — Hon. Harry A. N. *O.-P.*, *b.* 1954

1452 S. *Borthwick* (24th), John Hugh Borthwick, *b.* 1940, *s.* 1997, *m.* — Hon. James H. A. *B. of Glengelt*, *b.* 1940

1922 *Borwick* (4th), James Hugh Myles Borwick, MC, *b.* 1917, *s.* 1961, *m.* — Hon. Robin S. *B.*, *b.* 1927

1761 *Boston* (10th), Timothy George Frank Boteler Irby, *b.* 1939, *s.* 1978, *m.* — Hon. George W. E. B. *I.*, *b.* 1971

1942 *Brabazon of Tara* (3rd), Ivon Anthony Moore-Brabazon, *b.* 1946, *s.* 1974, *m.* — Hon. Benjamin R. *M.-B.*, *b.* 1983

1880 *Brabourne* (7th), John Ulick Knatchbull, CBE, *b.* 1924, *s.* 1943, *m.* — Lord Romsey, *b.* 1947 (*see* page 144)

1925 *Bradbury* (3rd), John Bradbury, *b.* 1940, *s.* 1994, *m.* — Hon. John *B.*, *b.* 1973

1962 *Brain* (2nd), Christopher Langdon Brain, *b.* 1926, *s.* 1966, *m.* — Hon. Michael C. *B.*, DM, FRCP, *b.* 1928

1938 *Brassey of Apethorpe* (3rd), David Henry Brassey, OBE, *b.* 1932, *s.* 1967, *m.* — Hon. Edward *B.*, *b.* 1964

1788 *Braybrooke* (10th), Robin Henry Charles Neville, *b.* 1932, *s.* 1990, *m.* — George *N.*, *b.* 1943

1957 *Bridges* (2nd), Thomas Edward Bridges, GCMG, *b.* 1927, *s.* 1969, *m.* — Hon. Mark T. *B.*, *b.* 1954

1945 *Broadbridge* (3rd), Peter Hewett Broadbridge, *b.* 1938, *s.* 1972, *m.* — Martin H. *B.*, *b.* 1929

1933 *Brocket* (3rd), Charles Ronald George Nall-Cain, *b.* 1952, *s.* 1967, *m.* — Hon. Alexander C. C. *N.-C.*, *b.* 1984

1860 *Brougham and Vaux* (5th), Michael John Brougham, CBE, *b.* 1938, *s.* 1967. — Hon. Charles W. *B.*, *b.* 1971

1945 *Broughshane* (3rd), (William) Kensington Davison, DSO, DFC, *b.* 1914, *s.* 1995. — None

1776 *Brownlow* (7th), Edward John Peregrine Cust, *b.* 1936, *s.* 1978, *m.* — Hon. Peregrine E. Q. *C.*, *b.* 1974

1942 *Bruntisfield* (2nd), John Robert Warrender, OBE, MC, TD, *b.* 1921, *s.* 1993, *m.* — Hon. Michael J. V. *W.*, *b.* 1949

1950 *Burden* (3rd), Andrew Philip Burden, *b.* 1959, *s.* 1995. — Hon. Fraser W. E. *B.*, *b.* 1964

1529 *Burgh* (7th), Alexander Peter Willoughby Leith, *b.* 1935, *s.* 1959, *m.* — Hon. A. Gregory D. *L.*, *b.* 1958

1903 *Burnham* (6th), Hugh John Frederick Lawson, *b.* 1931, *s.* 1993, *m.* — Hon. Harry F. A. *L.*, *b.* 1968

1897 *Burton* (3rd), Michael Evan Victor Baillie, *b.* 1924, *s.* 1962, *m.* — Hon. Evan M. R. *B.*, *b.* 1949

1643 *Byron* (13th), Robert James Byron, *b.* 1950, *s.* 1989, *m.* — Hon. Charles R. G. *B.*, *b.* 1990

1937 *Cadman* (3rd), John Anthony Cadman, *b.* 1938, *s.* 1966, *m.* — Hon. Nicholas A. J. *C.*, *b.* 1977

1945 *Calverley* (3rd), Charles Rodney Muff, *b.* 1946, *s.* 1971, *m.* — Hon. Jonathan E. *M.*, *b.* 1975

1383 *Camoys* (7th), (Ralph) Thomas Campion George Sherman Stonor, GCVO, PC, *b.* 1940, *s.* 1976, *m. Lord Chamberlain* — Hon. R. William R. T. *S.*, *b.* 1974

1715 I. *Carbery* (11th), Peter Ralfe Harrington Evans-Freke, *b.* 1920, *s.* 1970, *m.* — Hon. Michael P. *E.-F.*, *b.* 1942

1834 I.* *Carew* (7th), Patrick Thomas Conolly-Carew (7th *UK Baron, Carew*, 1838), *b.* 1938, *s.* 1994, *m.* — Hon. William P. *C.-C.*, *b.* 1973

1916 *Carnock* (4th), David Henry Arthur Nicolson, *b.* 1920, *s.* 1982. — Nigel *N.*, MBE, *b.* 1917

1796 I.* *Carrington* (6th), Peter Alexander Rupert Carington, KG, GCMG, CH, MC, PC (6th *Brit. Baron Carrington*, 1797), *b.* 1919, *s.* 1938, *m.* — Hon. Rupert F. J. *C.*, *b.* 1948

1812 I. *Castlemaine* (8th), Roland Thomas John Handcock, MBE, *b.* 1943, *s.* 1973, *m.* — Hon. Ronan M. E. *H.*, *b.* 1989

1936 *Catto* (2nd), Stephen Gordon Catto, *b.* 1923, *s.* 1959, *m.* — Hon. Innes G. *C.*, *b.* 1950

1918 *Cawley* (3rd), Frederick Lee Cawley, *b.* 1913, *s.* 1954, *m.* — Hon. John F. *C.*, *b.* 1946

1603 *Cecil.* A subsidiary title of the Marquess of Salisbury. His heir Viscount Cranborne, PC, was given a Writ in Acceleration in this title to enable him to sit in the House of Lords whilst his father is still alive (*see also* page 139)

1937 *Chatfield* (2nd), Ernle David Lewis Chatfield, *b.* 1917, *s.* 1967, *m.* — None

1858 *Chesham* (6th), Nicholas Charles Cavendish, *b.* 1941, *s.* 1989, *m.* — Hon. Charles G. C. *C.*, *b.* 1974

1945 *Chetwode* (2nd), Philip Chetwode, *b.* 1937, *s.* 1950, *m.* — Hon. Roger *C.*, *b.* 1968

1945 *Chorley* (2nd), Roger Richard Edward Chorley, *b.* 1930, *s.* 1978, *m.* — Hon. Nicholas R. D. *C.*, *b.* 1966

1858 *Churston* (5th), John Francis Yarde-Buller, *b.* 1934, *s.* 1991, *m.* — Hon. Benjamin F. A. *Y.-B.*, *b.* 1974

1946 *Citrine* (3rd), Ronald Eric Citrine, *b.* 1919, *s.* 1997, *m.* (does not use title) — None

1800 I. *Clanmorris* (8th), Simon John Ward Bingham, *b.* 1937, *s.* 1988, *m.* — Robert D. de B. *B.*, *b.* 1942

1672 *Clifford of Chudleigh* (14th), Thomas Hugh Clifford, *b.* 1948, *s.* 1988, *m.* — Hon. Alexander T. H. *C.*, *b.* 1985

1299 *Clinton* (22nd), Gerard Nevile Mark Fane Trefusis, *b.* 1934, *title called out of abeyance* 1965, *m.* — Hon. Charles P. R. F. *T.*, *b.* 1962

1955 *Clitheroe* (2nd), Ralph John Assheton, *b.* 1929, *s.* 1984, *m.* — Hon. Ralph C. *A.*, *b.* 1962

1919 *Clwyd* (3rd), (John) Anthony Roberts, *b.* 1935, *s.* 1987, *m.* — Hon. J. Murray *R.*, *b.* 1971

1948 *Clydesmuir* (3rd), David Ronald Colville, *b.* 1949, *s.* 1996, *m.* — Hon. Richard *C.*, *b.* 1980

Created	Title, order of succession, name, etc.	Heir
1960	*Cobbold* (2nd), David Antony Fromanteel Lytton Cobbold, *b.* 1937, *s.* 1987, *m.*	Hon. Henry F. *L. C., b.* 1962
1919	*Cochrane of Cults* (4th), (Ralph Henry) Vere Cochrane, *b.* 1926, *s.* 1990, *m.*	Hon. Thomas H. V. *C., b.* 1957
1954	*Coleraine* (2nd), (James) Martin (Bonar) Law, *b.* 1931, *s.* 1980, *m.*	Hon. James P. B. *L., b.* 1975
1873	*Coleridge* (5th), William Duke Coleridge, *b.* 1937, *s.* 1984, *m.*	Hon. James D. *C., b.* 1967
1946	*Colgrain* (3rd), David Colin Campbell, *b.* 1920, *s.* 1973, *m.*	Hon. Alastair C. L. *C., b.* 1951
1917	*Colwyn* (3rd), (Ian) Anthony Hamilton-Smith, CBE, *b.* 1942, *s.* 1966, *m.*	Hon. Craig P. *H.-S., b.* 1968
1956	*Colyton* (2nd), Alisdair John Munro Hopkinson, *b.* 1958, *s.* 1996, *m.*	Hon. James P. M. *H., b.* 1983
1841	*Congleton* (8th), Christopher Patrick Parnell, *b.* 1930, *s.* 1967, *m.*	Hon. John P. C. *P., b.* 1959
1927	*Cornwallis* (3rd), Fiennes Neil Wykeham Cornwallis, OBE, *b.* 1921, *s.* 1982, *m.*	Hon. F. W. Jeremy *C., b.* 1946
1874	*Cottesloe* (5th), Cdr. John Tapling Fremantle, *b.* 1927, *s.* 1994, *m.*	Hon. Thomas F. H. *F., b.* 1966
1929	*Craigmyle* (4th), Thomas Columba Shaw, *b.* 1960, *s.* 1998, *m.*	Hon. Alexander F. *S., b.* 1988
1899	*Cranworth* (3rd), Philip Bertram Gurdon, *b.* 1940, *s.* 1964, *m.*	Hon. Sacha W. R. *G., b.* 1970
1959	*Crathorne* (2nd), Charles James Dugdale, *b.* 1939, *s.* 1977, *m.*	Hon. Thomas A. J. *D., b.* 1977
1892	*Crawshaw* (5th), David Gerald Brooks, *b.* 1934, *s.* 1997, *m.*	Hon. John P. *B., b.* 1938
1940	*Croft* (3rd), Bernard William Henry Page Croft, *b.* 1949, *s.* 1997, *m.*	None
1797 I.	*Crofton* (7th), Guy Patrick Gilbert Crofton, *b.* 1951, *s.* 1989, *m.*	Hon. E. Harry P. *C., b.* 1988
1375	*Cromwell* (7th), Godfrey John Bewicke-Copley, *b.* 1960, *s.* 1982, *m.*	Hon. David G. *B.-C., b.* 1997
1947	*Crook* (2nd), Douglas Edwin Crook, *b.* 1926, *s.* 1989, *m.*	Hon. Robert D. E. *C., b.* 1955
1920	*Cullen of Ashbourne* (2nd), Charles Borlase Marsham Cokayne, MBE, *b.* 1912, *s.* 1932, *w.*	Hon. Edmund W. M. *C., b.* 1916
1914	*Cunliffe* (3rd), Roger Cunliffe, *b.* 1932, *s.* 1963, *m.*	Hon. Henry *C., b.* 1962
1927	*Daresbury* (4th), Peter Gilbert Greenall, *b.* 1953, *s.* 1996, *m.*	Hon. Thomas E. *G., b.* 1984
1924	*Darling* (2nd), Robert Charles Henry Darling, *b.* 1919, *s.* 1936, *m.*	Hon. R. Julian H. *D., b.* 1944
1946	*Darwen* (3rd), Roger Michael Davies, *b.* 1938, *s.* 1988, *m.*	Hon. Paul *D., b.* 1962
1932	*Davies* (3rd), David Davies, *b.* 1940, *s.* 1944, *m.*	Hon. David D. *D., b.* 1975
1299	*de Clifford* (27th), John Edward Southwell Russell, *b.* 1928, *s.* 1982, *m.*	Hon. William S. *R., b.* 1930
1851	*De Freyne* (7th), Francis Arthur John French, *b.* 1927, *s.* 1935, *m.*	Hon. Fulke C. A. J. *F., b.* 1957
1838	*de Mauley* (6th), Gerald John Ponsonby, *b.* 1921, *s.* 1962, *m.*	Hon. Col. Thomas M. *P.,* TD, *b.* 1930
1887	*De Ramsey* (4th), John Ailwyn Fellowes, *b.* 1942, *s.* 1993, *m.*	Hon. Freddie J. *F., b.* 1978
1264	*de Ros* (28th), Peter Trevor Maxwell, *b.* 1958, *s.* 1983, *m. Premier Baron of England*	Hon. Finbar J. *M., b.* 1988
1831	*de Saumarez* (7th), Eric Douglas Saumarez, *b.* 1956, *s.* 1991, *m.*	Hon. Victor T. *S., b.* 1956
1910	*de Villiers* (3rd), Arthur Percy de Villiers, *b.* 1911, *s.* 1934.	Hon. Alexander C. *de V., b.* 1940
1812 I.	*Decies* (7th), Marcus Hugh Tristram de la Poer Beresford, *b.* 1948, *s.* 1992, *m.*	Hon. Robert M. D. *de la P. B., b.* 1988
1821	*Delamere* (5th), Hugh George Cholmondeley, *b.* 1934, *s.* 1979, *m.*	Hon. Thomas P. G. *C., b.* 1968
1937	*Denham* (2nd), Bertram Stanley Mitford Bowyer, KBE, PC, *b.* 1927, *s.* 1948, *m.*	Hon. Richard G. G. *B., b.* 1959
1834	*Denman* (5th), Charles Spencer Denman, CBE, MC, TD, *b.* 1916, *s.* 1971, *w.*	Hon. Richard T. S. *D., b.* 1946
1885	*Deramore* (6th), Richard Arthur de Yarburgh-Bateson, *b.* 1911, *s.* 1964, *m.*	None
1881	*Derwent* (5th), Robin Evelyn Leo Vanden-Bempde-Johnstone, LVO, *b.* 1930, *s.* 1986, *m.*	Hon. Francis P. H. *V.-B.-J., b.* 1965
1930	*Dickinson* (2nd), Richard Clavering Hyett Dickinson, *b.* 1926, *s.* 1943, *m.*	Hon. Martin H. *D., b.* 1961
1620 I.*	*Digby* (12th), Edward Henry Kenelm Digby, KCVO (6th *Brit. Baron Digby,* 1765), *b.* 1924, *s.* 1964, *m.*	Hon. Henry N. K. *D., b.* 1954
1615	*Dormer* (17th), Geoffrey Henry Dormer, *b.* 1920, *s.* 1995, *m.*	Hon. William R. *D., b.* 1960
1943	*Dowding* (3rd), Piers Hugh Tremenheere Dowding, *b.* 1948, *s.* 1992.	Hon. Mark D. J. *D., b.* 1949
1800 I.	*Dufferin and Clandeboye.* The 10th Baron died in 1991. Heir had not established his claim to the title at the time of going to press	Sir John *Blackwood,* Bt., *b.* 1944
1929	*Dulverton* (3rd), (Gilbert) Michael Hamilton Wills, *b.* 1944, *s.* 1992.	Hon. Robert A. H. *W., b.* 1983
1800 I.	*Dunalley* (7th), Henry Francis Cornelius Prittie, *b.* 1948, *s.* 1992, *m.*	Hon. Joel H. *P., b.* 1981
1324 I.	*Dunboyne* (28th), Patrick Theobald Tower Butler, VRD, *b.* 1917, *s.* 1945, *m.*	Hon. John F. *B., b.* 1951
1892	*Dunleath* (6th), Brian Henry Mulholland, *b.* 1950, *s.* 1997, *m.*	Hon. Andrew H. *M., b.* 1981
1439 I.	*Dunsany* (20th), Edward John Carlos Plunkett, *b.* 1939, *s.* 1999, *m.*	Hon. Randal *P., b.* 1983
1780	*Dynevor* (9th), Richard Charles Uryan Rhys, *b.* 1935, *s.* 1962.	Hon. Hugo G. U. *R., b.* 1966
1857	*Ebury* (6th), Francis Egerton Grosvenor, *b.* 1934, *s.* 1957, *m.*	Hon. Julian F. M. *G., b.* 1959
1963	*Egremont* (2nd) and *Leconfield* (7th) (1859), John Max Henry Scawen Wyndham, *b.* 1948, *s.* 1972, *m.*	Hon. George R. V. *W., b.* 1983
1643	*Elibank* (14th), Alan D'Ardis Erskine-Murray, *b.* 1923, *s.* 1973, *w.*	Master of Elibank, *b.* 1964
1802	*Ellenborough* (8th), Richard Edward Cecil Law, *b.* 1926, *s.* 1945, *m.*	Maj. Hon. Rupert E. H. *L., b.* 1955
1509 S.*	*Elphinstone* (19th), Alexander Mountstuart Elphinstone (5th *UK Baron, Elphinstone,* 1885), *b.* 1980, *s.* 1994, *M.*	Hon. Angus J. *E., b.* 1982

Created	Title, order of succession, name, etc.	Heir
1934	*Elton* (2nd), Rodney Elton, TD, *b.* 1930, *s.* 1973, *m.*	Hon. Edward P. *E.*, *b.* 1966
1964	*Erroll of Hale* (1st), Frederick James Erroll, TD, PC, *b.* 1914, *m.*	None
1627 S.	*Fairfax of Cameron* (14th), Nicholas John Albert Fairfax, *b.* 1956, *s.* 1964, *m.*	Hon. Edward N. T. *F.*, *b.* 1984
1961	*Fairhaven* (3rd), Ailwyn Henry George Broughton, *b.* 1936, *s.* 1973, *m.*	Maj. Hon. James H. A. *B.*, *b.* 1963
1916	*Faringdon* (3rd), Charles Michael Henderson, *b.* 1937, *s.* 1977, *m.*	Hon. James H. *H.*, *b.* 1961
1756 I.	*Farnham* (12th), Barry Owen Somerset Maxwell, *b.* 1931, *s.* 1957, *m.*	Hon. Simon K. *M.*, *b.* 1933
1856 I.	*Fermoy* (6th), Patrick Maurice Burke Roche, *b.* 1967, *s.* 1984, *m.*	Hon. E. Hugh B. *R.*, *b.* 1972
1826	*Feversham* (6th), Charles Antony Peter Duncombe, *b.* 1945, *s.* 1963, *m.*	Hon. Jasper O. S. *D.*, *b.* 1968
1798 I.	*ffrench* (8th), Robuck John Peter Charles Mario ffrench, *b.* 1956, *s.* 1986, *m.*	Hon. John C. M. J. F. *ff.*, *b.* 1928
1909	*Fisher* (3rd), John Vavasseur Fisher, DSC, *b.* 1921, *s.* 1955, *m.*	Hon. Patrick V. *F.*, *b.* 1953
1295	*Fitzwalter* (21st), (Fitzwalter) Brook Plumptre, *b.* 1914, *title called out of abeyance* 1953, *m.*	Hon. Julian B. *P.*, *b.* 1952
1776	*Foley* (8th), Adrian Gerald Foley, *b.* 1923, *s.* 1927, *m.*	Hon. Thomas H. *F.*, *b.* 1961
1445 S.	*Forbes* (22nd), Nigel Ivan Forbes, KBE, *b.* 1918, *s.* 1953, *m. Premier Lord of Scotland*	Master of Forbes, *b.* 1946
1821	*Forester* (8th), (George Cecil) Brooke Weld-Forester, *b.* 1938, *s.* 1977, *m.*	Hon. C. R. George *W.-F.*, *b.* 1975
1922	*Forres* (4th), Alastair Stephen Grant Williamson, *b.* 1946, *s.* 1978, *m.*	Hon. George A. M. *W.*, *b.* 1972
1917	*Forteviot* (4th), John James Evelyn Dewar, *b.* 1938, *s.* 1993, *m.*	Hon. Alexander J. E. *D.*, *b.* 1971
1951	*Freyberg* (3rd), Valerian Bernard Freyberg, *b.* 1970, *s.* 1993.	None
1917	*Gainford* (3rd), Joseph Edward Pease, *b.* 1921, *s.* 1971, *m.*	Hon. George *P.*, *b.* 1926
1818 I.	*Garvagh* (5th), (Alexander Leopold Ivor) George Canning, *b.* 1920, *s.* 1956, *m.*	Hon. Spencer G. S. de R. *C.*, *b.* 1953
1942	*Geddes* (3rd), Euan Michael Ross Geddes, *b.* 1937, *s.* 1975, *m.*	Hon. James G. N. *G.*, *b.* 1969
1876	*Gerard* (5th), Anthony Robert Hugo Gerard, *b.* 1949, *s.* 1992, *m.*	Hon. Rupert B. C. *G.*, *b.* 1981
1824	*Gifford* (6th), Anthony Maurice Gifford, QC, *b.* 1940, *s.* 1961, *m.*	Hon. Thomas A. *G.*, *b.* 1967
1917	*Gisborough* (3rd), Thomas Richard John Long Chaloner, *b.* 1927, *s.* 1951, *m.*	Hon. T. Peregrine L. *C.*, *b.* 1961
1960	*Gladwyn* (2nd), Miles Alvery Gladwyn Jebb, *b.* 1930, *s.* 1996.	None
1899	*Glanusk* (5th), Christopher Russell Bailey, *b.* 1942, *s.* 1997, *m.*	Hon. Charles H. *B.*, *b.* 1976
1918	*Glenarthur* (4th), Simon Mark Arthur, *b.* 1944, *s.* 1976, *m.*	Hon. Edward A. *A.*, *b.* 1973
1911	*Glenconner* (3rd), Colin Christopher Paget Tennant, *b.* 1926, *s.* 1983, *m.*	Hon. Cody *T.*, *b.* 1994
1964	*Glendevon* (2nd), Julian John Somerset Hope, *b.* 1950, *s.* 1996.	Hon. Jonathan C. *H.*, *b.* 1952
1922	*Glendyne* (3rd), Robert Nivison, *b.* 1926, *s.* 1967, *m.*	Hon. John *N.*, *b.* 1960
1939	*Glentoran* (3rd), (Thomas) Robin (Valerian) Dixon, CBE, *b.* 1935, *s.* 1995, *m.*	Hon. Daniel G. *D.*, *b.* 1959
1909	*Gorell* (4th), Timothy John Radcliffe Barnes, *b.* 1927, *s.* 1963, *m.*	Hon. Ronald A. H. *B.*, *b.* 1931
1953	*Grantchester* (3rd), Christopher John Suenson-Taylor, *b.* 1951, *s.* 1995, *m.*	Hon. Jesse D. *S.-T.*, *b.* 1977
1782	*Grantley* (8th), Richard William Brinsley Norton, *b.* 1956, *s.* 1995.	Hon. Francis J. H. *N.*, *b.* 1960
1794 I.	*Graves* (9th), Evelyn Paget Graves, *b.* 1926, *s.* 1994, *m.*	Hon. Timothy E. *G.*, *b.* 1960
1445 S.	*Gray* (22nd), Angus Diarmid Ian Campbell-Gray, *b.* 1931, *s.* 1946, *m.*	Master of Gray, *b.* 1964
1950	*Greenhill* (3rd), Malcolm Greenhill, *b.* 1924, *s.* 1989.	None
1927	*Greenway* (4th), Ambrose Charles Drexel Greenway, *b.* 1941, *s.* 1975, *m.*	Hon. Mervyn S. K. *G.*, *b.* 1942
1902	*Grenfell* (3rd), Julian Pascoe Francis St Leger Grenfell, *b.* 1935, *s.* 1976, *m.*	Francis P. J. *G.*, *b.* 1938
1944	*Gretton* (4th), John Lysander Gretton, *b.* 1975, *s.* 1989.	None
1397	*Grey of Codnor* (6th), Richard Henry Cornwall-Legh, *b.* 1936, *s.* 1996, *m.*	Hon. Richard S. C. *C.-L.*, *b.* 1976
1955	*Gridley* (3rd), Richard David Arnold Gridley, *b.* 1956, *s.* 1996, *m.*	Hon. Carl R. *G.*, *b.* 1981
1964	*Grimston of Westbury* (2nd), Robert Walter Sigismund Grimston, *b.* 1925, *s.* 1979, *m.*	Hon. Robert J. S. *G.*, *b.* 1951
1886	*Grimthorpe* (4th), Christopher John Beckett, OBE, *b.* 1915, *s.* 1963, *m.*	Hon. Edward J. *B.*, *b.* 1954
1945	*Hacking* (3rd), Douglas David Hacking, *b.* 1938, *s.* 1971, *m.*	Hon. Douglas F. *H.*, *b.* 1968
1950	*Haden-Guest* (5th), Christopher Haden-Guest, *b.* 1948, *s.* 1996, *m.*	Hon. Nicholas *H.-G.*, *b.* 1951
1886	*Hamilton of Dalzell* (4th), James Leslie Hamilton, *b.* 1938, *s.* 1990, *m.*	Hon. Gavin G. *H.*, *b.* 1968
1874	*Hampton* (6th), Richard Humphrey Russell Pakington, *b.* 1925, *s.* 1974, *m.*	Hon. John H. A. *P.*, *b.* 1964
1939	*Hankey* (3rd), Donald Robin Alers Hankey, *b.* 1938, *s.* 1996, *m.*	Hon. Alexander M. A. *H.*, *b.* 1947
1958	*Harding of Petherton* (2nd), John Charles Harding, *b.* 1928, *s.* 1989, *m.*	Hon. William A. J. *H.*, *b.* 1969
1910	*Hardinge of Penshurst* (4th), Julian Alexander Hardinge, *b.* 1945, *s.* 1997.	Hon. Hugh F. *H.*, *b.* 1948
1876	*Harlech* (6th), Francis David Ormsby-Gore, *b.* 1954, *s.* 1985, *m.*	Hon. Jasset D. C. *O.-G.*, *b.* 1986
1939	*Harmsworth* (3rd), Thomas Harold Raymond Harmsworth, *b.* 1939, *s.* 1990, *m.*	Hon. Dominic M. E. *H.*, *b.* 1973
1815	*Harris* (8th), Anthony Harris, *b.* 1942, *s.* 1996, *m.*	Ronald G. T. *H.*, *b.* 1911
1954	*Harvey of Tasburgh* (2nd), Peter Charles Oliver Harvey, *b.* 1921, *s.* 1968, *w.*	Charles J. G. *H.*, *b.* 1951
1295	*Hastings* (22nd), Edward Delaval Henry Astley, *b.* 1912, *s.* 1956, *m.*	Hon. Delaval T. H. *A.*, *b.* 1960

Created	Title, order of succession, name, etc.	Heir
1835	*Hatherton* (8th), Edward Charles Littleton, *b.* 1950, *s.* 1985, *m.*	Hon. Thomas E. *L.*, *b.* 1977
1776	*Hawke* (11th), Edward George Hawke, TD, *b.* 1950, *s.* 1992, *m.*	Hon. William M. T. *H.*, *b.* 1995
1927	*Hayter* (3rd), George Charles Hayter Chubb, KCVO, CBE, *b.* 1911, *s.* 1967, *m.*	Hon. G. William M. *C.*, *b.* 1943
1945	*Hazlerigg* (2nd), Arthur Grey Hazlerigg, MC, TD, *b.* 1910, *s.* 1949, *w.*	Hon. Arthur G. *H.*, *b.* 1951
1943	*Hemingford* (3rd), (Dennis) Nicholas Herbert, *b.* 1934, *s.* 1982, *m.*	Hon. Christopher D. C. *H.*, *b.* 1973
1906	*Hemphill* (5th), Peter Patrick Fitzroy Martyn Martyn-Hemphill, *b.* 1928, *s.* 1957, *m.*	Hon. Charles A. M. *M.-H.*, *b.* 1954
1799 I.*	*Henley* (8th), Oliver Michael Robert Eden (6th *UK Baron Northington*, 1885), *b.* 1953, *s.* 1977, *m.*	Hon. John W. O. *E.*, *b.* 1988
1800 I.*	*Henniker* (8th), John Patrick Edward Chandos Henniker-Major, KCMG, CVO, MC (4th *UK Baron Hartismere*, 1866), *b.* 1916, *s.* 1980, *m.*	Hon. Mark I. P. C. *H.-M.*, *b.* 1947
1886	*Herschell* (3rd), Rognvald Richard Farrer Herschell, *b.* 1923, *s.* 1929, *m.*	None
1935	*Hesketh* (3rd), Thomas Alexander Fermor-Hesketh, KBE, PC, *b.* 1950, *s.* 1955, *m.*	Hon. Frederick H. *F.-H.*, *b.* 1988
1828	*Heytesbury* (6th), Francis William Holmes à Court, *b.* 1931, *s.* 1971, *m.*	Hon. James W. *H. à. C.*, *b.* 1967
1886	*Hindlip* (6th), Charles Henry Allsopp, *b.* 1940, *s.* 1993, *m.*	Hon. Henry W. *A.*, *b.* 1973
1950	*Hives* (3rd), Matthew Peter Hives, *b.* 1971, *s.* 1997.	Hon. Michael B. *H.*, *b.* 1926
1912	*Hollenden* (4th), Ian Hampden Hope-Morley, *b.* 1946, *s.* 1999, *m.*	Hon. Edward *H.-M.*, *b.* 1981
1897	*HolmPatrick* (4th), Hans James David Hamilton, *b.* 1955, *s.* 1991, *m.*	Hon. Ion H. J. *H.*, *b.* 1956
1797 I.	*Hotham* (8th), Henry Durand Hotham, *b.* 1940, *s.* 1967, *m.*	Hon. William B. *H.*, *b.* 1972
1881	*Hothfield* (6th), Anthony Charles Sackville Tufton, *b.* 1939, *s.* 1991, *m.*	Hon. William S. *T.*, *b.* 1977
1597	*Howard de Walden.* The 9th Baron Howard de Walden died in 1999, leaving four co-heiresses.	
1930	*Howard of Penrith* (2nd), Francis Philip Howard, *b.* 1905, *s.* 1939, *m.*	Hon. Philip E. *H.*, *b.* 1945
1960	*Howick of Glendale* (2nd), Charles Evelyn Baring, *b.* 1937, *s.* 1973, *m.*	Hon. David E. C. *B.*, *b.* 1975
1796 I.	*Huntingfield* (7th), Joshua Charles Vanneck, *b.* 1954, *s.* 1994, *m.*	Hon. Gerard C. A. *V.*, *b.* 1985
1866	*Hylton* (5th), Raymond Hervey Jolliffe, *b.* 1932, *s.* 1967, *m.*	Hon. William H. M. *J.*, *b.* 1967
1933	*Iliffe* (3rd), Robert Peter Richard Iliffe, *b.* 1944, *s.* 1996, *m.*	Hon. Edward R. *I.*, *b.* 1968
1543 I.	*Inchiquin* (18th), Conor Myles John O'Brien, *b.* 1943, *s.* 1982, *m.*	Murrough R. *O.*, *b.* 1910
1962	*Inchyra* (2nd), Robert Charles Reneke Hoyer Millar, *b.* 1935, *s.* 1989, *m.*	Hon. C. James C. H. *M.*, *b.* 1962
1964	*Inglewood* (2nd), (William) Richard Fletcher-Vane, MEP, *b.* 1951, *s.* 1989, *m.*	Hon. Henry W. F. *F.-V.*, *b.* 1990
1919	*Inverforth* (4th), Andrew Peter Weir, *b.* 1966, *s.* 1982.	Hon. John V. *W.*, *b.* 1935
1941	*Ironside* (2nd), Edmund Oslac Ironside, *b.* 1924, *s.* 1959, *m.*	Hon. Charles E. G. *I.*, *b.* 1956
1952	*Jeffreys* (3rd), Christopher Henry Mark Jeffreys, *b.* 1957, *s.* 1986, *m.*	Hon. Arthur M. H. *J.*, *b.* 1989
1906	*Joicey* (5th), James Michael Joicey, *b.* 1953, *s.* 1993, *m.*	Hon. William J. *J.*, *b.* 1990
1937	*Kenilworth* (4th), (John) Randle Siddeley, *b.* 1954, *s.* 1981, *m.*	Hon. William R. J. *S.*, *b.* 1992
1935	*Kennet* (2nd), Wayland Hilton Young, *b.* 1923, *s.* 1960, *m.*	Hon. W. A. Thoby *Y.*, *b.* 1957
1776 I.*	*Kensington* (8th), Hugh Ivor Edwardes (5th *UK Baron Kensington*, 1886), *b.* 1933, *s.* 1981, *m.*	Hon. W. Owen A. *E.*, *b.* 1964
1951	*Kenswood* (2nd), John Michael Howard Whitfield, *b.* 1930, *s.* 1963, *m.*	Hon. Michael C. *W.*, *b.* 1955
1788	*Kenyon* (6th), Lloyd Tyrell-Kenyon, *b.* 1947, *s.* 1993, *m.*	Hon. Lloyd N. *T.-K.*, *b.* 1972
1947	*Kershaw* (4th), Edward John Kershaw, *b.* 1936, *s.* 1962, *m.*	Hon. John C. E. *K.*, *b.* 1971
1943	*Keyes* (2nd), Roger George Bowlby Keyes, *b.* 1919, *s.* 1945, *m.*	Hon. Charles W. P. *K.*, *b.* 1951
1909	*Kilbracken* (3rd), John Raymond Godley, DSC, *b.* 1920, *s.* 1950.	Hon. Christopher J. *G.*, *b.* 1945
1900	*Killanin* (4th), (George) Redmond Fitzpatrick Morris, *b.* 1947, *s.* 1999, *m.*	Luke M. G. *M.*, *b.* 1975
1943	*Killearn* (3rd), Victor Miles George Aldous Lampson, *b.* 1941, *s.* 1996, *m.*	Hon. Miles H. M. *L.*, *b.* 1977
1789 I.	*Kilmaine* (7th), John David Henry Browne, *b.* 1948, *s.* 1978, *m.*	Hon. John F. S. *B.*, *b.* 1983
1831	*Kilmarnock* (7th), Alastair Ivor Gilbert Boyd, *b.* 1927, *s.* 1975, *m.*	Hon. Robin J. *B.*, *b.* 1941
1941	*Kindersley* (3rd), Robert Hugh Molesworth Kindersley, *b.* 1929, *s.* 1976, *m.*	Hon. Rupert J. M. *K.*, *b.* 1955
1223 I.	*Kingsale* (35th), John de Courcy, *b.* 1941, *s.* 1969. *Premier Baron of Ireland*	Nevinson R. *de C.*, *b.* 1920
1902	*Kinross* (5th), Christopher Patrick Balfour, *b.* 1949, *s.* 1985, *m.*	Hon. Alan I. *B.*, *b.* 1978
1951	*Kirkwood* (3rd), David Harvie Kirkwood, PH.D., *b.* 1931, *s.* 1970, *m.*	Hon. James S. *K.*, *b.* 1937
1800 I.	*Langford* (9th), Col. Geoffrey Alexander Rowley-Conwy, OBE, *b.* 1912, *s.* 1953, *m.*	Hon. Owain G. *R.-C.*, *b.* 1958
1942	*Latham* (2nd), Dominic Charles Latham, *b.* 1954, *s.* 1970.	Anthony M. *L.*, *b.* 1954
1431	*Latymer* (8th), Hugo Nevill Money-Coutts, *b.* 1926, *s.* 1987, *m.*	Hon. Crispin J. A. N. *M.-C.*, *b.* 1955
1869	*Lawrence* (5th), David John Downer Lawrence, *b.* 1937, *s.* 1968.	None
1947	*Layton* (3rd), Geoffrey Michael Layton, *b.* 1947, *s.* 1989, *m.*	Hon. David *L.*, MBE, *b.* 1914
1839	*Leigh* (5th), John Piers Leigh, *b.* 1935, *s.* 1979, *m.*	Hon. Christopher D. P. *L.*, *b.* 1960
1962	*Leighton of St Mellons* (3rd), Robert William Henry Leighton Seager, *b.* 1955, *s.* 1998.	Hon. Simon J. L. *S.*, *b.* 1957
1797	*Lilford* (7th), George Vernon Powys, *b.* 1931, *s.* 1949, *m.*	Hon. Mark V. *P.*, *b.* 1975
1945	*Lindsay of Birker* (3rd), James Francis Lindsay, *b.* 1945, *s.* 1994, *m.*	Alexander S. *L.*, *b.* 1940

Created	Title, order of succession, name, etc.	Heir

1758 I.   *Lisle* (8th), Patrick James Lysaght, *b.* 1931, *s.* 1998.   Hon. John N. G. *L.*, *b.* 1960

1850   *Londesborough* (9th), Richard John Denison, *b.* 1959, *s.* 1968, *m.*   Hon. James F. *D.*, *b.* 1990

1541 I.   *Louth* (16th), Otway Michael James Oliver Plunkett, *b.* 1929, *s.* 1950, *m.*   Hon. Jonathan O. *P.*, *b.* 1952

1458 S.*   *Lovat* (16th), Simon Fraser (5th *UK Baron, Lovat,* 1837), *b.* 1977, *s.* 1995.   Hon. Jack *F.*, *b.* 1984

1663   *Lucas* (11th) and *Dingwall* (14th) (S. 1609), Ralph Matthew Palmer, *b.* 1951, *s.* 1991, *m.*   Hon. Lewis E. *P.*, *b.* 1987

1946   *Lucas of Chilworth* (2nd), Michael William George Lucas, *b.* 1926, *s.* 1967, *m.*   Hon. Simon W. *L.*, *b.* 1957

1929   *Luke* (3rd), Arthur Charles St John Lawson-Johnston, *b.* 1933, *s.* 1996, *m.*   Hon. Ian J. St J. *L.-J.*, *b.* 1963

1914   *Lyell* (3rd), Charles Lyell, *b.* 1939, *s.* 1943.   None

1859   *Lyveden* (6th), Ronald Cecil Vernon, *b.* 1915, *s.* 1973, *m.*   Hon. Jack L. *V.*, *b.* 1938

1959   *MacAndrew* (3rd), Christopher Anthony Colin MacAndrew, *b.* 1945, *s.* 1989, *m.*   Hon. Oliver C. J. *M.*, *b.* 1983

1776 I.   *Macdonald* (8th), Godfrey James Macdonald of Macdonald, *b.* 1947, *s.* 1970, *m.*   Hon. Godfrey E. H. T. *M.*, *b.* 1982

1949   *Macdonald of Gwaenysgor* (2nd), Gordon Ramsay Macdonald, *b.* 1915, *s.* 1966, *m.*   None

1937   *McGowan* (3rd), Harry Duncan Cory McGowan, *b.* 1938, *s.* 1966, *m.*   Hon. Harry·J. C. *M.*, *b.* 1971

1922   *Maclay* (3rd), Joseph Paton Maclay, *b.* 1942, *s.* 1969, *m.*   Hon. Joseph P. *M.*, *b.* 1977

1955   *McNair* (3rd), Duncan James McNair, *b.* 1947, *s.* 1989, *m.*   Hon. William S. A. *M.*, *b.* 1958

1951   *Macpherson of Drumochter* (2nd), (James) Gordon Macpherson, *b.* 1924, *s.* 1965, *m.*   Hon. James A. *M.*, *b.* 1979

1937   *Mancroft* (3rd), Benjamin Lloyd Stormont Mancroft, *b.* 1957, *s.* 1987, *m.*   None

1807   *Manners* (5th), John Robert Cecil Manners, *b.* 1923, *s.* 1972, *m.*   Hon. John H. R. *M.*, *b.* 1956

1922   *Manton* (3rd), Joseph Rupert Eric Robert Watson, *b.* 1924, *s.* 1968, *m.*   Maj. Hon. Miles R. M. *W.*, *b.* 1958

1908   *Marchamley* (4th), William Francis Whiteley, *b.* 1968, *s.* 1994.   None

1964   *Margadale* (2nd), James Ian Morrison, TD, *b.* 1930, *s.* 1996, *m.*   Hon. Alastair J. *M.*, *b.* 1958

1961   *Marks of Broughton* (3rd), Simon Richard Marks, *b.* 1950, *s.* 1998, *m.*   Hon. Michael *M.*, *b.* 1989

1964   *Martonmere* (2nd), John Stephen Robinson, *b.* 1963, *s.* 1989.   David A. *R.*, *b.* 1965

1776 I.   *Massy* (9th), Hugh Hamon John Somerset Massy, *b.* 1921, *s.* 1958, *m.*   Hon. David H. S. *M.*, *b.* 1947

1935   *May* (3rd), Michael St John May, *b.* 1931, *s.* 1950, *m.*   Hon. Jasper B. St J. *M.*, *b.* 1965

1928   *Melchett* (4th), Peter Robert Henry Mond, *b.* 1948, *s.* 1973.   None

1925   *Merrivale* (3rd), Jack Henry Edmond Duke, *b.* 1917, *s.* 1951, *m.*   Hon. Derek J. P. *D.*, *b.* 1948

1911   *Merthyr.* Disclaimed for life 1977. (*Trevor Oswin Lewis,* Bt, CBE, *b.* 1935, *s.* 1977, *m.*)   David T. *L.*, *b.* 1977

1919   *Meston* (3rd), James Meston, *b.* 1950, *s.* 1984, *m.*   Hon. Thomas J. D. *M.*, *b.* 1977

1838   *Methuen* (7th), Robert Alexander Holt Methuen, *b.* 1931, *s.* 1994, *m.*   James Paul Archibald *Methuen-Campbell.*, *b.* 1952

1711   *Middleton* (12th), (Digby) Michael Godfrey John Willoughby, MC, *b.* 1921, *s.* 1970, *m.*   Hon. Michael C. J. *W.*, *b.* 1948

1939   *Milford* (3rd), Hugo John Laurence Philipps, *b.* 1929, *s.* 1993, *m.*   Hon. Guy W. *P.*, *b.* 1961

1933   *Milne* (2nd), George Douglass Milne, TD, *b.* 1909, *s.* 1948, *m.*   Hon. George A. *M.*, *b.* 1941

1951   *Milner of Leeds* (2nd), Arthur James Michael Milner, AE, *b.* 1923, *s.* 1967, *m.*   Hon. Richard J. *M.*, *b.* 1959

1947   *Milverton* (2nd), Revd Fraser Arthur Richard Richards, *b.* 1930, *s.* 1978, *m.*   Hon. Michael H. *R.*, *b.* 1936

1873   *Moncreiff* (5th), Harry Robert Wellwood Moncreiff, *b.* 1915, *s.* 1942, *w.*   Hon. Rhoderick H. W. *M.*, *b.* 1954

1884   *Monk Bretton* (3rd), John Charles Dodson, *b.* 1924, *s.* 1933, *m.*   Hon. Christopher M. *D.*, *b.* 1958

1885   *Monkswell* (5th), Gerard Collier, *b.* 1947, *s.* 1984, *m.*   Hon. James A. *C.*, *b.* 1977

1728   *Monson* (11th), John Monson, *b.* 1932, *s.* 1958, *m.*   Hon. Nicholas J. *M.*, *b.* 1955

1885   *Montagu of Beaulieu* (3rd), Edward John Barrington Douglas-Scott-Montagu, *b.* 1926, *s.* 1929, *m.*   Hon. Ralph *D.-S.-M.*, *b.* 1961

1839   *Monteagle of Brandon* (6th), Gerald Spring Rice, *b.* 1926, *s.* 1946, *m.*   Hon. Charles J. S. *R.*, *b.* 1953

1943   *Moran* (2nd), (Richard) John (McMoran) Wilson, KCMG, *b.* 1924, *s.* 1977, *m.*   Hon. James M. *W.*, *b.* 1952

1918   *Morris* (3rd), Michael David Morris, *b.* 1937, *s.* 1975, *m.*   Hon. Thomas A. S. *M.*, *b.* 1982

1950   *Morris of Kenwood* (2nd), Philip Geoffrey Morris, *b.* 1928, *s.* 1954, *m.*   Hon. Jonathan D. *M.*, *b.* 1968

1831   *Mostyn* (5th), Roger Edward Lloyd Lloyd-Mostyn, MC, *b.* 1920, *s.* 1965, *m.*   Hon. Llewellyn R. L. *L.-M.*, *b.* 1948

1933   *Mottistone* (4th), David Peter Seely, CBE, *b.* 1920, *s.* 1966, *m.*   Hon. Peter J. P. *S.*, *b.* 1949

1945   *Mountevans* (3rd), Edward Patrick Broke Evans, *b.* 1943, *s.* 1974, *m.*   Hon. Jeffrey de C. R. *E.*, *b.* 1948

1283   *Mowbray* (26th), *Segrave* (27th) (1283) and *Stourton* (23rd) (1448), Charles Edward Stourton, CBE, *b.* 1923, *s.* 1965, *m.*   Hon. Edward W. S. *S.*, *b.* 1953

1932   *Moyne* (3rd), Jonathan Bryan Guinness, *b.* 1930, *s.* 1992, *m.*   Hon. Jasper J. R. *G.*, *b.* 1954

1929   *Moynihan* (4th), Colin Berkeley Moynihan, *b.* 1955, *s.* 1997, *m.*   Hon. Nicholas E. B. *M.*, *b.* 1994

1781 I.   *Muskerry* (9th), Robert Fitzmaurice Deane, *b.* 1948, *s.* 1988, *m.*   Hon. Jonathan F. *D.*, *b.* 1986

1627 S.*   *Napier* (14th) and *Ettrick* (5th) (*UK* 1872), Francis Nigel Napier, KCVO, *b.* 1930, *s.* 1954, *m.*   Master of Napier, *b.* 1962

Created	Title, order of succession, name, etc.	Heir
1868	*Napier of Magdala* (6th), Robert Alan Napier, *b.* 1940, *s.* 1987, *m.*	Hon. James R. *N.*, *b.* 1966
1940	*Nathan* (2nd), Roger Carol Michael Nathan, *b.* 1922, *s.* 1963, *m.*	Hon. Rupert H. B. *N.*, *b.* 1957
1960	*Nelson of Stafford* (3rd), Henry Roy George Nelson, *b.* 1943, *s.* 1995, *m.*	Hon. Alistair W. H. *N.*, *b.* 1973
1959	*Netherthorpe* (3rd), James Frederick Turner, *b.* 1964, *s.* 1982, *m.*	Hon. Andrew J. E. *T.*, *b.* 1993
1946	*Newall* (2nd), Francis Storer Eaton Newall, *b.* 1930, *s.* 1963, *m.*	Hon. Richard H. E. *N.*, *b.* 1961
1776 I.	*Newborough* (8th), Robert Vaughan Wynn, *b.* 1949, *s.* 1998, *m.*	Hon. Charles H. R. *W.*, *b.* 1923
1892	*Newton* (5th), Richard Thomas Legh, *b.* 1950, *s.* 1992, *m.*	Hon. Piers R. *L.*, *b.* 1979
1930	*Noel-Buxton* (3rd), Martin Connal Noel-Buxton, *b.* 1940, *s.* 1980, *m.*	Hon. Charles C. *N.-B.*, *b.* 1975
1957	*Norrie* (2nd), (George) Willoughby Moke Norrie, *b.* 1936, *s.* 1977, *m.*	Hon. Mark W. J. *N.*, *b.* 1972
1884	*Northbourne* (5th), Christopher George Walter James, *b.* 1926, *s.* 1982, *m.*	Hon. Charles W. H. *J.*, *b.* 1960
1866	*Northbrook* (6th), Francis Thomas Baring, *b.* 1954, *s.* 1990, *m.*	None
1878	*Norton* (8th), James Nigel Arden Adderley, *b.* 1947, *s.* 1993, *m.*	Hon. Edward J. A. *A.*, *b.* 1982
1906	*Nunburnholme* (5th), Charles Thomas Wilson, *b.* 1935, *s.* 1998.	Hon. Stephen C. *W.*, *b.* 1973
	Oaksey. (see Trevethin and Oaksey, page 155)	
1950	*Ogmore* (2nd), Gwilym Rees Rees-Williams, *b.* 1931, *s.* 1976, *m.*	Hon. Morgan *R.-W.*, *b.* 1937
1870	*O'Hagan* (4th), Charles Towneley Strachey, *b.* 1945, *s.* 1961.	Hon. Richard T. *S.*, *b.* 1950
1868	*O'Neill* (4th), Raymond Arthur Clanaboy O'Neill, TD, *b.* 1933, *s.* 1944, *m.*	Hon. Shane S. C. *O'N.*, *b.* 1965
1836 I.*	*Oranmore and Browne* (4th), Dominick Geoffrey Edward Browne (2nd UK Baron, Mereworth, 1926), *b.* 1901, *s.* 1927, *m.*	Hon. Dominick G. T. *B.*, *b.* 1929
1933	*Palmer* (4th), Adrian Bailie Nottage Palmer, *b.* 1951, *s.* 1990, *m.*	Hon. Hugo B. R. *P.*, *b.* 1980
1914	*Parmoor* (4th), (Frederick Alfred) Milo Cripps, *b.* 1929, *s.* 1977.	Michael L. S. *C.*, *b.* 1942
1937	*Pender* (3rd), John Willoughby Denison-Pender, *b.* 1933, *s.* 1965, *m.*	Hon. Henry J. R. *D.-P.*, *b.* 1968
1866	*Penrhyn* (6th), Malcolm Frank Douglas-Pennant, DSO, MBE, *b.* 1908, *s.* 1967, *m.*	Hon. Nigel *D.-P.*, *b.* 1909
1603	*Petre* (18th), John Patrick Lionel Petre, *b.* 1942, *s.* 1989, *m.*	Hon. Dominic W. *P.*, *b.* 1966
1918	*Phillimore* (5th), Francis Stephen Phillimore, *b.* 1944, *s.* 1994, *m.*	Hon. Tristan A. S. *P.*, *b.* 1977
1945	*Piercy* (3rd), James William Piercy, *b.* 1946, *s.* 1981.	Hon. Mark E. P. *P.*, *b.* 1953
1827	*Plunket* (8th), Robin Rathmore Plunket, *b.* 1925, *s.* 1975, *m.*	Hon. Shaun A. F. S. *P.*, *b.* 1931
1831	*Poltimore* (7th), Mark Coplestone Bampfylde, *b.* 1957, *s.* 1978, *m.*	Hon. Henry A. W. *B.*, *b.* 1985
1690 S.	*Polwarth* (10th), Henry Alexander Hepburne-Scott, TD, *b.* 1916, *s.* 1944, *m.*	Master of Polwarth, *b.* 1947
1930	*Ponsonby of Shulbrede* (4th), Frederick Matthew Thomas Ponsonby, *b.* 1958, *s.* 1990.	None
1958	*Poole* (2nd), David Charles Poole, *b.* 1945, *s.* 1993, *m.*	Hon. Oliver J. *P.*, *b.* 1972
1852	*Raglan* (5th), FitzRoy John Somerset, *b.* 1927, *s.* 1964.	Hon. Geoffrey *S.*, *b.* 1932
1932	*Rankeillour* (4th), Peter St Thomas More Henry Hope, *b.* 1935, *s.* 1967.	Michael R. *H.*, *b.* 1940
1953	*Rathcavan* (3rd), Hugh Detmar Torrens O'Neill, *b.* 1939, *s.* 1994, *m.*	Hon. François H. N. *O'N.*, *b.* 1984
1916	*Rathcreedan* (3rd), Christopher John Norton, *b.* 1949, *s.* 1990, *m.*	Hon. Adam G. *N.*, *b.* 1952
1868 I.	*Rathdonnell* (5th), Thomas Benjamin McClintock-Bunbury, *b.* 1938, *s.* 1959, *m.*	Hon. William L. *M.-B.*, *b.* 1966
1911	*Ravensdale* (3rd), Nicholas Mosley, MC, *b.* 1923, *s.* 1966, *m.*	Hon. Shaun N. *M.*, *b.* 1949
1821	*Ravensworth* (8th), Arthur Waller Liddell, *b.* 1924, *s.* 1950, *m.*	Hon. Thomas A. H. *L.*, *b.* 1954
1821	*Rayleigh* (6th), John Gerald Strutt, *b.* 1960, *s.* 1988, *m.*	Hon. John F. *S.*, *b.* 1993
1937	*Rea* (3rd), John Nicolas Rea, MD, *b.* 1928, *s.* 1981, *m.*	Hon. Matthew J. *R.*, *b.* 1956
1628 S.	*Reay* (14th), Hugh William Mackay, *b.* 1937, *s.* 1963, *m.*	Master of Reay, *b.* 1965
1902	*Redesdale* (6th), Rupert Bertram Mitford, *b.* 1967, *s.* 1991, *m.*	None
1940	*Reith.* Disclaimed for life 1972. (*Christopher John Reith, b.1928, s.1971, m.*)	Hon. James H. J. *R.*, *b.* 1971
1928	*Remnant* (3rd), James Wogan Remnant, CVO, *b.* 1930, *s.* 1967, *m.*	Hon. Philip J. *R.*, *b.* 1954
1806 I.	*Rendlesham* (8th), Charles Anthony Hugh Thellusson, *b.* 1915, *s.* 1943, *w.*	Hon. Charles W. B. *T.*, *b.* 1954
1933	*Rennell* (3rd), (John Adrian) Tremayne Rodd, *b.* 1935, *s.* 1978, *m.*	Hon. James R. D. T. *R.*, *b.* 1978
1964	*Renwick* (2nd), Harry Andrew Renwick, *b.* 1935, *s.* 1973, *m.*	Hon. Robert J. *R.*, *b.* 1966
1885	*Revelstoke* (5th), John Baring, *b.* 1934, *s.* 1994.	Hon. James C. *B.*, *b.* 1938
1905	*Ritchie of Dundee* (5th), (Harold) Malcolm Ritchie, *b.* 1919, *s.* 1978, *m.*	Hon. C. Rupert R. *R.*, *b.* 1958
1935	*Riverdale* (3rd), Anthony Robert Balfour, *b.* 1960, *s.* 1998.	Hon. David R. *B.*, *b.* 1938
1961	*Robertson of Oakridge* (2nd), William Ronald Robertson, *b.* 1930, *s.* 1974, *m.*	Hon. William B. E. *R.*, *b.* 1975
1938	*Roborough* (3rd), Henry Massey Lopes, *b.* 1940, *s.* 1992, *m.*	Hon. Massey J. H. *L.*, *b.* 1969
1931	*Rochester* (2nd), Foster Charles Lowry Lamb, *b.* 1916, *s.* 1955, *m.*	Hon. David C. *L.*, *b.* 1944
1934	*Rockley* (3rd), James Hugh Cecil, *b.* 1934, *s.* 1976, *m.*	Hon. Anthony R. *C.*, *b.* 1961
1782	*Rodney* (10th), George Brydges Rodney, *b.* 1953, *s.* 1992, *m.*	Nicholas S. H. *R.*, *b.* 1947
1651 S.*	*Rollo* (14th), David Eric Howard Rollo (5th *UK Baron Dunning*, 1869), *b.* 1943, *s.* 1997, *m.*	Master of Rollo, *b.* 1972
1959	*Rootes* (3rd), Nicholas Geoffrey Rootes, *b.* 1951, *s.* 1992, *m.*	William B. *R.*, *b.* 1944
1796 I.*	*Rossmore* (7th), William Warner Westenra (6th *UK Baron, Rossmore*, 1838), *b.* 1931, *s.* 1958, *m.*	Hon. Benedict W. *W.*, *b.* 1983
1939	*Rotherwick* (3rd), (Herbert) Robin Cayzer, *b.* 1954, *s.* 1996, *m.*	Hon. H. Robin *C.*, *b.* 1989

Created	Title, order of succession, name, etc.	Heir
1885	*Rothschild* (4th), (Nathaniel Charles) Jacob Rothschild, GBE, *b.* 1936, *s.* 1990, *m.*	Hon. Nathaniel P. V. J. *R.*, *b.* 1971
1911	*Rowallan* (4th), John Polson Cameron Corbett, *b.* 1947, *s.* 1993.	Hon. Jason W. P. C. *C.*, *b.* 1972
1947	*Rugby* (3rd), Robert Charles Maffey, *b.* 1951, *s.* 1990, *m.*	Hon. Timothy J. H. *M.*, *b.* 1975
1919	*Russell of Liverpool* (3rd), Simon Gordon Jared Russell, *b.* 1952, *s.* 1981, *m.*	Hon. Edward C. S. *R.*, *b.* 1985
1876	*Sackville* (6th), Lionel Bertrand Sackville-West, *b.* 1913, *s.* 1965, *m.*	Hugh R. I. *S.-W.* MC, *b.* 1919
1964	*St Helens* (2nd), Richard Francis Hughes-Young, *b.* 1945, *s.* 1980, *m.*	Hon. Henry T. *H.-Y.*, *b.* 1986
1559	*St John of Bletso* (21st), Anthony Tudor St John, *b.* 1957, *s.* 1978, *m.*	Hon. Oliver B. *St J.*, *b.* 1995
1887	*St Levan* (4th), John Francis Arthur St Aubyn, DSC, *b.* 1919, *s.* 1978, *m.*	Hon. O. Piers *St. A*, MC, *b.* 1920
1885	*St Oswald* (6th), Charles Rowland Andrew Winn, *b.* 1959, *s.* 1999, *m.*	Hon. Rowland C. S. H. *W.*, *b.* 1986
1960	*Sanderson of Ayot.* Disclaimed for life 1971. (*Alan Lindsay Sanderson, b.* 1931, *s.* 1971, *m.*)	Hon. Michael *S.*, *b.* 1959
1945	*Sandford* (2nd), Revd John Cyril Edmondson, DSC, *b.* 1920, *s.* 1959, *m.*	Hon. James J. M. *E.*, *b.* 1949
1871	*Sandhurst* (5th), (John Edward) Terence Mansfield, DFC, *b.* 1920, *s.* 1964, *m.*	Hon. Guy R. J. *M.*, *b.* 1949
1802	*Sandys* (7th), Richard Michael Oliver Hill, *b.* 1931, *s.* 1961, *m.*	The Marquess of Downshire (*see* page 138)
1888	*Savile* (3rd), George Halifax Lumley-Savile, *b.* 1919, *s.* 1931.	Hon. Henry L. T. *L.-S.*, *b.* 1923
1447	*Saye and Sele* (21st), Nathaniel Thomas Allen Fiennes, *b.* 1920, *s.* 1968, *m.*	Hon. Richard I. *F.*, *b.* 1959
1826	*Seaford* (6th), Colin Humphrey Felton Ellis, *b.* 1946, *s.* 1999, *m.*	Benjamin F. T. *E.*, *b.* 1976
1932	*Selsdon* (3rd), Malcolm McEacharn Mitchell-Thomson, *b.* 1937, *s.* 1963, *m.*	Hon. Callum M. M. *M.-T.*, *b.* 1969
1489 S.	*Sempill* (21st), James William Stuart Whitemore Sempill, *b.* 1949, *s.* 1995, *m.*	Master of Sempill, *b.* 1979
1916	*Shaughnessy* (3rd), William Graham Shaughnessy, *b.* 1922, *s.* 1938, *w.*	Hon. Michael J. *S.*, *b.* 1946
1946	*Shepherd* (2nd), Malcolm Newton Shepherd, PC, *b.* 1918, *s.* 1954, *w.*	Hon. Graeme G. *S.*, *b.* 1949
1964	*Sherfield* (2nd), Christopher James Makins, *b.* 1942, *s.* 1996, *m.*	Hon. Dwight W. *M.*, *b.* 1951
1902	*Shuttleworth* (5th), Charles Geoffrey Nicholas Kay-Shuttleworth, *b.* 1948, *s.* 1975, *m.*	Hon. Thomas E. *K.-S.*, *b.* 1976
1950	*Silkin.* Disclaimed for life 1972. (*Arthur Silkin, b.* 1916, *s.* 1972, *m.*)	Hon. Christopher L. *S.*, *b.* 1947
1963	*Silsoe* (2nd), David Malcolm Trustram Eve, QC, *b.* 1930, *s.* 1976, *m.*	Hon. Simon R. T. *E.*, *b.* 1966
1947	*Simon of Wythenshawe* (2nd), Roger Simon, *b.* 1913, *s.* 1960, *m.*	Hon. Matthew *S.*, *b.* 1955
1449 S.	*Sinclair* (17th), Charles Murray Kennedy St Clair, CVO, *b.* 1914, *s.* 1957, *m.*	Master of Sinclair, *b.* 1968
1957	*Sinclair of Cleeve* (3rd), John Lawrence Robert Sinclair, *b.* 1953, *s.* 1985.	None
1919	*Sinha* (6th), Arup Kumar Sinha, *b.* 1966, *s.* 1999.	†
1828	*Skelmersdale* (7th), Roger Bootle-Wilbraham, *b.* 1945, *s.* 1973, *m.*	Hon. Andrew *B.-W.*, *b.* 1977
1916	*Somerleyton* (3rd), Savile William Francis Crossley, GCVO, *b.* 1928, *s.* 1959, *m.*	Hon. Hugh F. S. *C.*, *b.* 1971
1784	*Somers* (9th), Philip Sebastian Somers Cocks, *b.* 1948, *s.* 1995.	Alan B. *C.*, *b.* 1930
1780	*Southampton* (6th), Charles James FitzRoy, *b.* 1928, *s.* 1989, *m.*	Hon. Edward C. *F.*, *b.* 1955
1959	*Spens* (3rd), Patrick Michael Rex Spens, *b.* 1942, *s.* 1984, *m.*	Hon. Patrick N. G. *S.*, *b.* 1968
1640	*Stafford* (15th), Francis Melfort William Fitzherbert, *b.* 1954, *s.* 1986, *m.*	Hon. Benjamin J. B. *F.*, *b.* 1983
1938	*Stamp* (4th), Trevor Charles Bosworth Stamp, MD, FRCP, *b.* 1935, *s.* 1987, *m.*	Hon. Nicholas C. T. *S.*, *b.* 1978
1839	*Stanley of Alderley* (8th) and *Sheffield* (8th) (I. 1738), Thomas Henry Oliver Stanley (7th *UK Baron, Eddisbury*, 1848), *b.* 1927, *s.* 1971, *m.*	Hon. Richard O. *S.*, *b.* 1956
1318	*Strabolgi* (11th), David Montague de Burgh Kenworthy, *b.* 1914, *s.* 1953, *m.*	Andrew D. W. *K.*, *b.* 1967
1954	*Strang* (2nd), Colin Strang, *b.* 1922, *s.* 1978, *m.*	None
1955	*Strathalmond* (3rd), William Roberton Fraser, *b.* 1947, *s.* 1976, *m.*	Hon. William G. *F.*, *b.* 1976
1936	*Strathcarron* (2nd), David William Anthony Blyth Macpherson, *b.* 1924, *s.* 1937, *w.*	Hon. Ian D. P. *M.*, *b.* 1949
1955	*Strathclyde* (2nd), Thomas Galloway Dunlop du Roy de Blicquy Galbraith, PC, *b.* 1960, *s.* 1985, *m.*	Hon. Charles W. du R. de B. *G.*, *b.* 1962
1900	*Strathcona and Mount Royal* (4th), Donald Euan Palmer Howard, *b.* 1923, *s.* 1959, *m.*	Hon. D. Alexander S. *H.*, *b.* 1961
1836	*Stratheden* (6th) and *Campbell* (6th) (1841), Donald Campbell, *b.* 1934, *s.* 1987, *m.*	Hon. David A. *C.*, *b.* 1963
1884	*Strathspey* (6th), James Patrick Trevor Grant of Grant, *b.* 1943, *s.* 1992, *m.*	Hon. Michael P. F. *G.*, *b.* 1953
1838	*Sudeley* (7th), Merlin Charles Sainthill Hanbury-Tracy, *b.* 1939, *s.* 1941.	D. Andrew J. *H.-T.*, *b.* 1928
1786	*Suffield* (11th), Anthony Philip Harbord-Hamond, MC, *b.* 1922, *s.* 1951, *w.*	Hon. Charles A. A. *H.-H.*, *b.* 1953
1893	*Swansea* (4th), John Hussey Hamilton Vivian, *b.* 1925, *s.* 1934, *m.*	Hon. Richard A. H. *V.*, *b.* 1957
1907	*Swaythling* (5th), Charles Edgar Samuel Montagu, *b.* 1954, *s.* 1998, *m.*	Hon. Anthony T. S. *M.*, *b.* 1931

Created	Title, order of succession, name, etc.	Heir
1919	*Swinfen* (3rd), Roger Mynors Swinfen Eady, *b.* 1938, *s.* 1977, *m.*	Hon. Charles R. P. S. *E.*, *b.* 1971
1935	*Sysonby* (3rd), John Frederick Ponsonby, *b.* 1945, *s.* 1956.	None
1831 I.	*Talbot of Malahide* (10th), Reginald John Richard Arundell, *s.* 1987, *m.*	Hon. Richard J. T. *A.*, *b.* 1957
1946	*Tedder* (3rd), Robin John Tedder, *b.* 1955, *s.* 1994, *m.*	Hon. Benjamin J. *T.*, *b.* 1985
1884	*Tennyson* (5th), Cdr. Mark Aubrey Tennyson, DSC, *b.* 1920, *s.* 1991, *m.*	Lt.-Cdr. James A. *T.* DSC, *b.* 1913
1918	*Terrington* (5th), (Christopher) Montague Woodhouse, DSO, OBE, *b.* 1917, *s.* 1998, *w.*	Hon. Christopher R. J. *W.*, *b.* 1946
1940	*Teviot* (2nd), Charles John Kerr, *b.* 1934, *s.* 1968, *m.*	Hon. Charles R. *K.*, *b.* 1971
1616	*Teynham* (20th), John Christopher Ingham Roper-Curzon, *b.* 1928, *s.* 1972, *m.*	Hon. David J. H. I. *R.-C.*, *b.* 1965
1964	*Thomson of Fleet* (2nd), Kenneth Roy Thomson, *b.* 1923, *s.* 1976, *m.*	Hon. David K. R. *T.*, *b.* 1957
1792	*Thurlow* (8th), Francis Edward Hovell-Thurlow-Cumming-Bruce, KCMG, *b.* 1912, *s.* 1971, *w.*	Hon. Roualeyn R. *H.-T.-C.-B.*, *b.* 1952
1876	*Tollemache* (5th), Timothy John Edward Tollemache, *b.* 1939, *s.* 1975, *m.*	Hon. Edward J. H. *T.*, *b.* 1976
1564 S.	*Torphichen* (15th), James Andrew Douglas Sandilands, *b.* 1946, *s.* 1975, *m.*	Douglas R. A. *S.*, *b.* 1926
1947	*Trefgarne* (2nd), David Garro Trefgarne, PC, *b.* 1941, *s.* 1960, *m.*	Hon. George G. *T.*, *b.* 1970
1921	*Trevethin* (4th) and *Oaksey* (2nd) (1947), John Geoffrey Tristram Lawrence, OBE, *b.* 1929, *s.* 1971, *m.*	Hon. Patrick J. T. *L.*, *b.* 1960
1880	*Trevor* (5th), Marke Charles Hill-Trevor, *b.* 1970, *s.* 1997, *m.*	Hon. Iain R. *H.-T.*, *b.* 1971
1461 I.	*Trimlestown* (21st), Raymond Charles Barnewall, *b.* 1930, *s.* 1997.	None
1940	*Tryon* (3rd), Anthony George Merrik Tryon, *b.* 1940, *s.* 1976.	Hon. Charles G. B. *T.*, *b.* 1976
1935	*Tweedsmuir* (3rd), William de l'Aigle Buchan, *b.* 1916, *s.* 1996, *m.*	Hon. John W. H. de l'A. *B.*, *b.* 1950
1523	*Vaux of Harrowden* (10th), John Hugh Philip Gilbey, *b.* 1915, *s.* 1977, *m.*	Hon. Anthony W. *G.*, *b.* 1940
1800 I.	*Ventry* (8th), Andrew Wesley Daubeny de Moleyns, *b.* 1943, *s.* 1987, *m.*	Hon. Francis W. *D. de M.*, *b.* 1965
1762	*Vernon* (10th), John Lawrance Vernon, *b.* 1923, *s.* 1963, *m.*	Col. William R. D. *Vernon-Harcourt*, OBE, *b.* 1909
1922	*Vestey* (3rd), Samuel George Armstrong Vestey, *b.* 1941, *s.* 1954, *m.*	Hon. William G. *V.*, *b.* 1983
1841	*Vivian* (6th), Nicholas Crespigny Laurence Vivian, *b.* 1935, *s.* 1991, *m.*	Hon. Charles H. C. *V.*, *b.* 1966
1934	*Wakehurst* (3rd), (John) Christopher Loder, *b.* 1925, *s.* 1970, *m.*	Hon. Timothy W. *L.*, *b.* 1958
1723	*Walpole* (10th), Robert Horatio Walpole (8th *Brit. Baron Walpole of Wolterton*, 1756), *b.* 1938, *s.* 1989, *m.*	Hon. Jonathan R. H. *W.*, *b.* 1967
1780	*Walsingham* (9th), John de Grey, MC, *b.* 1925, *s.* 1965, *m.*	Hon. Robert *de. G.*, *b.* 1969
1936	*Wardington* (2nd), Christopher Henry Beaumont Pease, *b.* 1924, *s.* 1950, *m.*	Hon. William S. *P.*, *b.* 1925
1792 I.	*Waterpark* (7th), Frederick Caryll Philip Cavendish, *b.* 1926, *s.* 1948, *m.*	Hon. Roderick A. *C.*, *b.* 1959
1942	*Wedgwood* (4th), Piers Anthony Weymouth Wedgwood, *b.* 1954, *s.* 1970, *m.*	John *W.* CBE, MD, FRCP, *b.* 1919
1861	*Westbury* (5th), David Alan Bethell, CBE, MC, *b.* 1922, *s.* 1961, *m.*	Hon. Richard N. *B.*, MBE, *b.* 1950
1944	*Westwood* (3rd), (William) Gavin Westwood, *b.* 1944, *s.* 1991, *m.*	Hon. W. Fergus *W.*, *b.* 1972
1935	*Wigram* (2nd), (George) Neville (Clive) Wigram, MC, *b.* 1915, *s.* 1960, *w.*	Maj. Hon. Andrew F. C. *W.* MVO, *b.* 1949
1491	*Willoughby de Broke* (21st), Leopold David Verney, *b.* 1938, *s.* 1986, *m.*	Hon. Rupert G. *V.*, *b.* 1966
1946	*Wilson* (2nd), Patrick Maitland Wilson, *b.* 1915, *s.* 1964, *w.*	None
1937	*Windlesham* (3rd), David James George Hennessy, CVO, PC, *b.* 1932, *s.* 1962, *w.*	Hon. James R. *H.*, *b.* 1968
1951	*Wise* (2nd), John Clayton Wise, *b.* 1923, *s.* 1968, *m.*	Hon. Christopher J. C. *W.* Ph.D., *b.* 1949
1869	*Wolverton* (7th), Christopher Richard Glyn, *b.* 1938, *s.* 1988.	Hon. Andrew J. *G.*, *b.* 1943
1928	*Wraxall* (2nd), George Richard Lawley Gibbs, *b.* 1928, *s.* 1931.	Hon. Sir Eustace H. B. *G.*, KCVO, CMG, *b.* 1929
1915	*Wrenbury* (3rd), Revd John Burton Buckley, *b.* 1927, *s.* 1940, *m.*	Hon. William E. *B.*, *b.* 1966
1838	*Wrottesley* (6th), Clifton Hugh Lancelot de Verdon Wrottesley, *b.* 1968, *s.* 1977.	Hon. Stephen J. *W.*, *b.* 1955
1919	*Wyfold* (3rd), Hermon Robert Fleming Hermon-Hodge, ERD, *b.* 1915, *s.* 1942.	None
1829	*Wynford* (8th), Robert Samuel Best, MBE, *b.* 1917, *s.* 1943, *m.*	Hon. John P. R. *B.*, *b.* 1950
1308	*Zouche* (18th), James Assheton Frankland, *b.* 1943, *s.* 1965, *m.*	Hon. William T. A. *F.*, *b.* 1984

BARONESSES/LADIES IN THEIR OWN RIGHT

Style, The Right Hon. the Lady __, *or* The Right Hon. the Baroness __, according to her preference. Either style may be used, except in the case of Scottish titles (indicated by s.), which are not baronies (*see* page 136) and whose holders are always addressed as Lady
Husband, Untitled
Children's style, As for children of a Baron
For forms of address, *see* page 135

Created	Title, order of succession, name, etc.	Heir
1664	*Arlington,* Jennifer Jane Forwood, *b.* 1939, *title called out of abeyance* 1999, *m.*	Patrick John Dudley *F., b.* 1967
1455	*Berners* (16th in line), Pamela Vivien Kirkham, *b.* 1929, *title called out of abeyance* 1995, *m.*	Hon. Rupert W. T. *K., b.* 1953
1529	*Braye* (8th in line), Mary Penelope Aubrey-Fletcher, *b.* 1941, *s.* 1985, *m.*	Two co-heiresses
1321	*Dacre* (27th in line), Rachel Leila Douglas-Home, *b.* 1929, *title called out of abeyance* 1970, *w.*	Hon. James T. A. *D.-H., b.* 1952
1332	*Darcy de Knayth* (18th in line), Davina Marcia Ingrams, DBE, *b.* 1938, *s.* 1943, *w.*	Hon. Caspar D. *I., b.* 1962
1439	*Dudley* (14th in line), Barbara Amy Felicity Hamilton, *b.* 1907, *s.* 1972, *m.*	Hon. Jim A. H. *Wallace, b.* 1930
1490 s.	*Herries of Terregles* (14th in line), Anne Elizabeth Fitzalan-Howard, *b.* 1938, *s.* 1975, *m.*	Lady Mary *Mumford,* CVO, *b.* 1940
1602 s.	*Kinloss* (12th in line), Beatrice Mary Grenville Freeman-Grenville, *b.* 1922, *s.* 1944, *m.*	Master of Kinloss, *b.* 1953
1445 s.	*Saltoun* (20th in line), Flora Marjory Fraser, *b.* 1930, *s.* 1979, *m.*	Hon. Katharine I. M. I. *F., b.* 1957
1628	*Strange* (16th in line), (Jean) Cherry Drummond of Megginch, *b.* 1928, *title called out of abeyance* 1986, *m.*	Hon. Adam H. *D. of M., b.* 1953
1544/5	*Wharton* (11th in line), Myrtle Olive Felix Robertson, *b.* 1934, *title called out of abeyance* 1990, *m.*	Hon. Myles C. D. *R., b.* 1964
1313	*Willoughby de Eresby* (27th in line), (Nancy) Jane Marie Heathcote-Drummond-Willoughby, *b.* 1934, *s.* 1983.	Two co-heiresses

Life Peers

NEW LIFE PEERAGES *1 September 1998 to 31 August 1999*
NEW YEAR'S HONOURS (30 December 1998): Sir Peter Michael Imbert, QPM; Onora Sylvia O'Neill, CBE; Sir Narendrakumar Babubhai Patel; Sir Alexander Trotman; Sir David Francis Williamson, GCMG, CB
QUEEN'S BIRTHDAY HONOURS (12 June 1999): Rt. Hon. Sir Robert Fellowes, GCB, GCVO; Sir Norman Foster, OM; Sir Ronald Oxburgh, KBE; Usha Prashar, CBE; Sir Dennis Stevenson, CBE; Viven Stern, CBE
WORKING PEERS (19 June 1999): Catherine Ashton; Elizabeth Barker; May Blood, MBE; William Bradshaw; William Brett; Alexander Carlile, QC; Murray Elder; Richard Faulkner; David Filkin, CBE; Rt. Hon. Sir Michael Forsyth; Anita Gale; Robert Gavron, CBE; Peter Goldsmith, QC; Anthony Grabiner, QC; Joan Hanham, CBE; Angela Harris; Lyndon Harrison; Rosalind Howells, OBE; Tarsem King; Sir Graham Kirkham; John Laird; David Lea, OBE; David Lipsey; Genista McIntosh; Hector MacKenzie; Doreen Massey; Christopher Rennard, MBE; Dennis Rogan; Colin Sharman, OBE; Peter Smith; Rt. Hon. William Waldegrave; Diana Warwick; Alan Watson, CBE; Janet Whitaker; Rosalie Wilkins; Kenneth Woolmer

CREATED UNDER THE APPELLATE JURISDICTION ACT 1876 (AS AMENDED)

BARONS

Created
1986 *Ackner*, Desmond James Conrad Ackner, PC, *b.* 1920, *m.*
1980 *Bridge of Harwich*, Nigel Cyprian Bridge, PC, *b.* 1917, *m.*
1982 *Brightman*, John Anson Brightman, PC, *b.* 1911, *m.*
1991 *Browne-Wilkinson*, Nicolas Christopher Henry Browne-Wilkinson, PC, *b.* 1930, *m. Lord of Appeal in Ordinary*
1996 *Clyde*, James John Clyde, *b.* 1932, *m. Lord of Appeal in Ordinary*
1986 *Goff of Chieveley*, Robert Lionel Archibald Goff, PC, *b.* 1926, *m.*
1985 *Griffiths*, (William) Hugh Griffiths, MC, PC, *b.* 1923, *m.*
1998 *Hobhouse of Woodborough*, John Stewart Hobhouse, PC, *b.* 1932. *Lord of Appeal in Ordinary*
1995 *Hoffmann*, Leonard Hubert Hoffmann, PC, *b.* 1934, *m. Lord of Appeal in Ordinary*
1997 *Hutton*, (James) Brian (Edward) Hutton, PC, *b.* 1931, *m. Lord of Appeal in Ordinary*
1988 *Jauncey of Tullichettle*, Charles Eliot Jauncey, PC, *b.* 1925, *m.*
1977 *Keith of Kinkel*, Henry Shanks Keith, GBE, PC, *b.* 1922, *m.*
1979 *Lane*, Geoffrey Dawson Lane, AFC, PC, *b.* 1918, *m.*
1993 *Lloyd of Berwick*, Anthony John Leslie Lloyd, PC, *b.* 1929, *m. Lord of Appeal in Ordinary*
1998 *Millett*, Peter Julian Millett, PC, *b.* 1932, *m. Lord of Appeal in Ordinary*
1992 *Mustill*, Michael John Mustill, PC, *b.* 1931, *m.*
1994 *Nicholls of Birkenhead*, Donald James Nicholls, PC, *b.* 1933, *m. Lord of Appeal in Ordinary*
1994 *Nolan*, Michael Patrick Nolan, PC, *b.* 1928, *m.*

1986 *Oliver of Aylmerton*, Peter Raymond Oliver, PC, *b.* 1921, *m.*
1999 *Phillips of Worth Matravers*, Nicholas Addison Phillips, PC, *b.* 1938, *m. Lord of Appeal in Ordinary*
1997 *Saville of Newdigate*, Mark Oliver Saville, PC, *b.* 1936, *m. Lord of Appeal in Ordinary*
1977 *Scarman*, Leslie George Scarman, OBE, PC, *b.* 1911, *m.*
1992 *Slynn of Hadley*, Gordon Slynn, PC, *b.* 1930, *m. Lord of Appeal in Ordinary*
1995 *Steyn*, Johan van Zyl Steyn, PC, *b.* 1932, *m. Lord of Appeal in Ordinary*
1982 *Templeman*, Sydney William Templeman, MBE, PC, *b.* 1920, *m.*
1964 *Wilberforce*, Richard Orme Wilberforce, CMG, OBE, PC, *b.* 1907, *m.*
1992 *Woolf*, Harry Kenneth Woolf, PC, *b.* 1933, *m. Master of the Rolls*

CREATED UNDER THE LIFE PEERAGES ACT 1958

BARONS

Created
1998 *Ahmed*, Nazir Ahmed, *b.* 1957, *m.*
1996 *Alderdice*, John Thomas Alderdice, *b.* 1955, *m.*
1988 *Alexander of Weedon*, Robert Scott Alexander, QC, *b.* 1936, *m.*
1976 *Allen of Abbeydale*, Philip Allen, GCB, *b.* 1912, *m.*
1998 *Alli*, Waheed Alli.
1997 *Alton of Liverpool*, David Patrick Paul Alton, *b.* 1951, *m.*
1965 *Annan*, Noël Gilroy Annan, OBE, *b.* 1916, *m.*
1992 *Archer of Sandwell*, Peter Kingsley Archer, PC, QC, *b.* 1926, *m.*
1992 *Archer of Weston-super-Mare*, Jeffrey Howard Archer, *b.* 1940, *m.*
1988 *Armstrong of Ilminster*, Robert Temple Armstrong, GCB, CVO, *b.* 1927, *m.*
1992 *Ashley of Stoke*, Jack Ashley, CH, PC, *b.* 1922, *m.*
1993 *Attenborough*, Richard Samuel Attenborough, CBE, *b.* 1923, *m.*
1998 *Bach*, William Stephen Goulden Bach, *b.* 1946, *m.*
1997 *Bagri*, Raj Kumar Bagri, CBE, *b.* 1930, *m.*
1997 *Baker of Dorking*, Kenneth Wilfred Baker, CH, PC, *b.* 1934, *m.*
1974 *Balniel*, The Earl of Crawford and Balcarres. (*see* page 140)
1974 *Barber*, Anthony Perrinott Lysberg Barber, TD, PC, *b.* 1920, *m.*
1992 *Barber of Tewkesbury*, Derek Coates Barber, *b.* 1918, *m.*
1983 *Barnett*, Joel Barnett, PC, *b.* 1923, *m.*
1997 *Bassam of Brighton*, (John) Steven Bassam, *b.* 1953.
1982 *Bauer*, Prof. Peter Thomas Bauer, D.SC., FBA, *b.* 1915.
1967 *Beaumont of Whitley*, Revd Timothy Wentworth Beaumont, *b.* 1928, *m.*
1998 *Bell*, Timothy John Leigh Bell, *b.* 1941, *m.*
1979 *Bellwin*, Irwin Norman Bellow, *b.* 1923, *m.*
1997 *Biffen*, (William) John Biffen, PC, *b.* 1930, *m.*
1996 *Bingham of Cornhill*, Thomas Henry Bingham, PC, *b.* 1933, *m. Lord Chief Justice of England*

1997   *Blackwell*, Norman Roy Blackwell, *b.* 1952, *m.*
1971   *Blake*, Robert Norman William Blake, FBA, *b.* 1916, *w.*
1994   *Blaker*, Peter Allan Renshaw Blaker, KCMG, PC, *b.* 1922, *m.*
1978   *Blease*, William John Blease, *b.* 1914, *m.*
1995   *Blyth of Rowington*, James Blyth, *b.* 1940, *m.*
1980   *Boardman*, Thomas Gray Boardman, MC, TD, *b.* 1919, *m.*
1996   *Borrie*, Gordon Johnson Borrie, QC, *b.* 1931, *m.*
1976   *Boston of Faversham*, Terence George Boston, QC, *b.* 1930, *m.*
1996   *Bowness*, Peter Spencer Bowness, CBE, *b.* 1943, *m.*
1999   *Bradshaw*, William Peter Bradshaw, *b.* 1936, *m.*
1998   *Bragg*, Melvyn Bragg, *b.* 1939, *m.*
1992   *Braine of Wheatley*, Bernard Richard Braine, PC, *b.* 1914, *w.*
1987   *Bramall*, Edwin Noel Westby Bramall, KG, GCB, OBE, MC, *b.* 1923, *m.* Field Marshal
1999   *Brett*, William Henry Brett, *b.* 1942, *m.*
1976   *Briggs*, Asa Briggs, FBA, *b.* 1921, *m.*
1997   *Brooke of Alverthorpe*, Clive Brooke, *b.* 1942, *m.*
1975   *Brookes*, Raymond Percival Brookes, *b.* 1909, *m.*
1998   *Brookman*, David Keith Brookman, *b.* 1937, *m.*
1979   *Brooks of Tremorfa*, John Edward Brooks, *b.* 1927, *m.*
1974   *Bruce of Donington*, Donald William Trevor Bruce, *b.* 1912, *m.*
1976   *Bullock*, Alan Louis Charles Bullock, FBA, *b.* 1914, *m.*
1997   *Burlison*, Thomas Henry Burlison, *b.* 1936, *m.*
1998   *Burns*, Terence Burns, GCB, *b.* 1944, *m.*
1998   *Butler of Brockwell*, (Frederick Edward) Robin Butler, GCB, CVO, *b.* 1938, *m.*
1988   *Butterfield*, (William) John (Hughes) Butterfield, OBE, DM, FRCP, *b.* 1920, *m.*
1985   *Butterworth*, John Blackstock Butterworth, CBE, *b.* 1918, *m.*
1978   *Buxton of Alsa*, Aubrey Leland Oakes Buxton, KCVO, MC, *b.* 1918, *m.*
1987   *Callaghan of Cardiff*, (Leonard) James Callaghan, KG, PC, *b.* 1912, *m.*
1984   *Cameron of Lochbroom*, Kenneth John Cameron, PC, *b.* 1931, *m.*
1981   *Campbell of Alloway*, Alan Robertson Campbell, QC, *b.* 1917, *m.*
1974   *Campbell of Croy*, Gordon Thomas Calthrop Campbell, MC, PC, *b.* 1921, *m.*
1999   *Carlile of Berriew*, Alexander Charles Carlile, QC, *b.* 1948, *m.*
1987   *Carlisle of Bucklow*, Mark Carlisle, QC, PC, *b.* 1929, *m.*
1983   *Carmichael of Kelvingrove*, Neil George Carmichael, *b.* 1921.
1975   *Carr of Hadley*, (Leonard) Robert Carr, PC, *b.* 1916, *m.*
1987   *Carter*, Denis Victor Carter, PC, *b.* 1932, *m.*
1977   *Carver*, (Richard) Michael (Power) Carver, GCB, CBE, DSO, MC, *b.* 1915, *m.* Field Marshal
1990   *Cavendish of Furness*, (Richard) Hugh Cavendish, *b.* 1941, *m.*
1996   *Chadlington*, Peter Selwyn Gummer, *b.* 1942, *m.*
1964   *Chalfont*, (Alun) Arthur Gwynne Jones, OBE, MC, PC, *b.* 1919, *m.*
1985   *Chapple*, Francis (Frank) Joseph Chapple, *b.* 1921, *w.*
1978   *Charteris of Amisfield*, Martin Michael Charles Charteris, GCB, GCVO, OBE, PC, Royal Victorian Chain, *b.* 1913, *m.*
1987   *Chilver*, (Amos) Henry Chilver, FRS, FREng., *b.* 1926, *m.*

1977   *Chitnis*, Pratap Chidamber Chitnis, *b.* 1936, *m.*
1998   *Christopher*, Anthony Martin Grosvenor Christopher, CBE, *b.* 1925, *m.*
1992   *Clark of Kempston*, William Gibson Haig Clark, PC, *b.* 1917, *m.*
1998   *Clarke of Hampstead*, Anthony James Clarke, CBE, *b.* 1932, *m.*
1979   *Cledwyn of Penrhos*, Cledwyn Hughes, CH, PC, *b.* 1916, *m.*
1998   *Clement-Jones*, Timothy Francis Clement-Jones, CBE, *b.* 1949, *m.*
1990   *Clinton-Davis*, Stanley Clinton Clinton-Davis, PC, *b.* 1928, *m.*
1978   *Cockfield*, (Francis) Arthur Cockfield, PC, *b.* 1916, *w.*
1987   *Cocks of Hartcliffe*, Michael Francis Lovell Cocks, PC, *b.* 1929, *m.*
1980   *Coggan*, Rt. Revd (Frederick) Donald Coggan, PC, Royal Victorian Chain, *b.* 1909, *m.*
1981   *Constantine of Stanmore*, Theodore Constantine, CBE, AE, *b.* 1910, *w.*
1992   *Cooke of Islandreagh*, Victor Alexander Cooke, OBE, *b.* 1920, *m.*
1996   *Cooke of Thorndon*, Robin Brunskill Cooke, KBE, PC, PH.D., *b.* 1926, *m.*
1997   *Cope of Berkeley*, John Ambrose Cope, PC, *b.* 1937, *m.*
1997   *Cowdrey of Tonbridge*, (Michael) Colin Cowdrey, CBE, *b.* 1932, *m.*
1991   *Craig of Radley*, David Brownrigg Craig, GCB, OBE, *b.* 1929, *m.* Marshal of the Royal Air Force
1987   *Crickhowell*, (Roger) Nicholas Edwards, PC, *b.* 1934, *m.*
1978   *Croham*, Douglas Albert Vivian Allen, GCB, *b.* 1917, *w.*
1995   *Cuckney*, John Graham Cuckney, *b.* 1925, *m.*
1996   *Currie of Marylebone*, David Anthony Currie, *b.* 1946, *m.*
1979   *Dacre of Glanton*, Hugh Redwald Trevor-Roper, *b.* 1914, *w.*
1993   *Dahrendorf*, Ralf Dahrendorf, KBE, PH.D., D.PHIL., FBA, *b.* 1929, *m.*
1997   *Davies of Coity*, (David) Garfield Davies, CBE, *b.* 1935, *m.*
1997   *Davies of Oldham*, Bryan Davies, *b.* 1939, *m.*
1993   *Dean of Harptree*, (Arthur) Paul Dean, PC, *b.* 1924, *m.*
1998   *Dearing*, Ronald Ernest Dearing, CB, *b.* 1930, *m.*
1986   *Deedes*, William Francis Deedes, KBE MC, PC, *b.* 1913, *m.*
1991   *Desai*, Prof. Meghnad Jagdishchandra Desai, PH.D., *b.* 1940, *m.*
1997   *Dholakia*, Navnit Dholakia, OBE, *b.* 1937, *m.*
1970   *Diamond*, John Diamond, PC, *b.* 1907, *m.*
1997   *Dixon*, Donald Dixon, PC, *b.* 1929, *m.*
1993   *Dixon-Smith*, Robert William Dixon-Smith, *b.* 1934, *m.*
1988   *Donaldson of Lymington*, John Francis Donaldson, PC, *b.* 1920, *m.*
1985   *Donoughue*, Bernard Donoughue, D.PHIL., *b.* 1934.
1987   *Dormand of Easington*, John Donkin Dormand, *b.* 1919, *m.*
1994   *Dubs*, Alfred Dubs, *b.* 1932, *m.*
1995   *Eames*, Robert Henry Alexander Eames, PH.D., *b.* 1937, *m.*
1992   *Eatwell*, John Leonard Eatwell, *b.* 1945, *m.*
1983   *Eden of Winton*, John Benedict Eden, PC, *b.* 1925, *m.*
1999   *Elder*, Thomas Murray Elder.
1992   *Elis-Thomas*, Dafydd Elis Elis-Thomas, *b.* 1946, *m.*

1985   *Elliott of Morpeth*, Robert William Elliott, *b.* 1920, *m.*

1981   *Elystan-Morgan*, Dafydd Elystan Elystan-Morgan, *b.* 1932, *m.*

1980   *Emslie*, George Carlyle Emslie, MBE, PC, FRSE, *b.* 1919, *m.*

1997   *Evans of Parkside*, John Evans, *b.* 1930, *m.*

1998   *Evans of Watford*, David Charles Evans, *b.* 1942, *m.*

1992   *Ewing of Kirkford*, Harry Ewing, *b.* 1931, *m.*

1983   *Ezra*, Derek Ezra, MBE, *b.* 1919, *m.*

1997   *Falconer of Thoroton*, Charles Leslie Falconer, QC, *b.* 1951, *m.*

1983   *Fanshawe of Richmond*, Anthony Henry Fanshawe Royle, KCMG, *b.* 1927, *m.*

1999   *Faulkner of Worcester*, Richard Oliver Faulkner, *b.* 1946, *m.*

1996   *Feldman*, Basil Feldman, *b.* 1926, *m.*

1999   *Fellowes*, Robert Fellowes, PC, GCB, GCVO, *b.* 1941, *m.*

1999   *Filkin*, David Geoffrey Nigel Filkin, CBE, *b.* 1944.

1983   *Fitt*, Gerard Fitt, *b.* 1926, *w.*

1979   *Flowers*, Brian Hilton Flowers, FRS, *b.* 1924, *m.*

1967   *Foot*, John Mackintosh Foot, *b.* 1909, *m.*

1999   *Forsyth of Drumlean*, Michael Bruce Forsyth, *b.* 1954, *m.*

1982   *Forte*, Charles Forte, *b.* 1908, *m.*

1999   *Foster of Thames Bank*, Norman Robert Foster, OM, *b.* 1935, *m.*

1989   *Fraser of Carmyllie*, Peter Lovat Fraser, PC, QC, *b.* 1945, *m.*

1997   *Freeman*, Roger Norman Freeman, PC, *b.* 1942, *m.*

1982   *Gallacher*, John Gallacher, *b.* 1920, *m.*

1997   *Garel-Jones*, (William Armand) Thomas Tristan Garel-Jones, PC, *b.* 1941, *m.*

1999   *Gavron*, Robert Gavron, CBE, *b.* 1930, *m.*

1992   *Geraint*, Geraint Wyn Howells, *b.* 1925, *m.*

1975   *Gibson*, (Richard) Patrick (Tallentyre) Gibson, *b.* 1916, *m.*

1979   *Gibson-Watt*, (James) David Gibson-Watt, MC, PC, *b.* 1918, *m.*

1997   *Gilbert*, John William Gilbert, PC, PH.D., *b.* 1927, *m.*

1992   *Gilmour of Craigmillar*, Ian Hedworth John Little Gilmour, PC, *b.* 1926, *m.*

1994   *Gladwin of Clee*, Derek Oliver Gladwin, CBE, *b.* 1930, *m.*

1977   *Glenamara*, Edward Watson Short, CH, PC, *b.* 1912, *m.*

1999   *Goldsmith*, Peter Henry Goldsmith, QC, *b.* 1950, *m.*

1997   *Goodhart*, William Howard Goodhart, QC, *b.* 1933, *m.*

1997   *Gordon of Strathblane*, James Stuart Gordon, CBE, *b.* 1936, *m.*

1999   *Grabiner*, Anthony Stephen Grabiner, QC, *b.* 1945, *m.*

1983   *Graham of Edmonton*, (Thomas) Edward Graham, *b.* 1925, *m.*

1983   *Gray of Contin*, James (Hamish) Hector Northey Gray, PC, *b.* 1927, *m.*

1974   *Greene of Harrow Weald*, Sidney Francis Greene, CBE, *b.* 1910, *m.*

1974   *Greenhill of Harrow*, Denis Arthur Greenhill, GCMG, OBE, *b.* 1913, *m.*

1975   *Gregson*, John Gregson, *b.* 1924.

1968   *Grey of Naunton*, Ralph Francis Alnwick Grey, GCMG, GCVO, OBE, *b.* 1910, *w.*

1991   *Griffiths of Fforestfach*, Brian Griffiths, *b.* 1941, *m.*

1995   *Habgood*, Rt. Revd John Stapylton Habgood, PC, PH.D., *b.* 1927, *m.*

1970   *Hailsham of St Marylebone*, Quintin McGarel Hogg, KG, CH, PC, FRS, *b.* 1907, *w.*

1994   *Hambro*, Charles Eric Alexander Hambro, *b.* 1930, *m.*

1998   *Hamlyn*, Paul Bertrand Hamlyn, CBE, *b.* 1926, *m.*

1998   *Hanningfield*, Paul Edward Winston White, *b.* 1940

1983   *Hanson*, James Edward Hanson, *b.* 1922, *m.*

1997   *Hardie*, Andrew Rutherford Hardie, QC, PC, *b.* 1946, *m. Lord Advocate*

1997   *Hardy of Wath*, Peter Hardy, *b.* 1931, *m.*

1974   *Harmar-Nicholls*, Harmar Harmar-Nicholls, *b.* 1912, *m.*

1974   *Harris of Greenwich*, John Henry Harris, PC, *b.* 1930, *m.*

1998   *Harris of Haringey*, (Jonathan) Toby Harris, *b.* 1953, *m.*

1979   *Harris of High Cross*, Ralph Harris, *b.* 1924, *m.*

1996   *Harris of Peckham*, Philip Charles Harris, *b.* 1942, *m.*

1999   *Harrison*, Lyndon Henry Arthur Harrison, *b.* 1947, *m.*

1968   *Hartwell*, (William) Michael Berry, MBE, TD, *b.* 1911, *w.*

1993   *Haskel*, Simon Haskel, *b.* 1934, *m.*

1998   *Haskins*, Christopher Robin Haskins, *b.* 1937, *m.*

1990   *Haslam*, Robert Haslam, *b.* 1923, *m.*

1997   *Hattersley*, Roy Sidney George Hattersley, PC, *b.* 1932, *m.*

1992   *Hayhoe*, Bernard John (Barney) Hayhoe, PC, *b.* 1925, *m.*

1992   *Healey*, Denis Winston Healey, CH, MBE, PC, *b.* 1917, *m.*

1984   *Henderson of Brompton*, Peter Gordon Henderson, KCB, *b.* 1922, *m.*

1997   *Higgins*, Terence Langley Higgins, KBE, PC, *b.* 1928, *m.*

1979   *Hill-Norton*, Peter John Hill-Norton, GCB, *b.* 1915, *m. Admiral of the Fleet*

1997   *Hogg of Cumbernauld*, Norman Hogg, *b.* 1938, *m.*

1979   *Holderness*, Richard Frederick Wood, PC, *b.* 1920, *m.*

1991   *Hollick*, Clive Richard Hollick, *b.* 1945, *m.*

1990   *Holme of Cheltenham*, Richard Gordon Holme, CBE, *b.* 1936, *m.*

1979   *Hooson*, (Hugh) Emlyn Hooson, QC, *b.* 1925, *m.*

1995   *Hope of Craighead*, (James Arthur) David Hope, PC, *b.* 1938, *m. Lord of Appeal in Ordinary*

1992   *Howe of Aberavon*, (Richard Edward) Geoffrey Howe, CH, PC, QC, *b.* 1926, *m.*

1997   *Howell of Guildford*, David Arthur Russell Howell, PC, *b.* 1936, *m.*

1978   *Howie of Troon*, William Howie, *b.* 1924, *m.*

1997   *Hoyle*, (Eric) Douglas Harvey Hoyle, *b.* 1930, *w.*

1961   *Hughes*, William Hughes, CBE, PC, *b.* 1911, *w.*

1997   *Hughes of Woodside*, Robert Hughes, *b.* 1932, *m.*

1997   *Hunt of Kings Heath*, Philip Alexander Hunt, OBE, *b.* 1949, *m.*

1980   *Hunt of Tanworth*, John Joseph Benedict Hunt, GCB, *b.* 1919, *m.*

1997   *Hunt of Wirral*, David James Fletcher Hunt, MBE, PC, *b.* 1942, *m.*

1997   *Hurd of Westwell*, Douglas Richard Hurd, CH, CBE, PC, *b.* 1930, *m.*

1996   *Hussey of North Bradley*, Marmaduke James Hussey, *b.* 1923, *m.*

1978   *Hutchinson of Lullington*, Jeremy Nicolas Hutchinson, QC, *b.* 1915, *m.*

1999   *Imbert*, Peter Michael Imbert, QPM, *b.* 1933, *m.*

1997   *Inge*, Peter Anthony Inge, GCB, *b.* 1935, *m. Field Marshal*

1982   *Ingrow*, John Aked Taylor, OBE, TD, *b.* 1917, *m.*

1987   *Irvine of Lairg*, Alexander Andrew Mackay Irvine, PC, QC, *b.* 1940, *m. Lord High Chancellor*

1997   *Islwyn*, Royston John (Roy) Hughes, *b.* 1925, *m.*

1997   *Jacobs*, (David) Anthony Jacobs, *b.* 1931, *m.*

1988   *Jakobovits*, Immanuel Jakobovits, *b.* 1921, *m.*

1997   *Janner of Braunstone*, Greville Ewan Janner, QC, *b.* 1928, *w.*

1987   *Jenkin of Roding*, (Charles) Patrick (Fleeming) Jenkin, PC, *b.* 1926, *m.*

1987   *Jenkins of Hillhead*, Roy Harris Jenkins, OM, PC, *b.* 1920, *m.*

1981   *Jenkins of Putney*, Hugh Gater Jenkins, *b.* 1908, *w.*

1987   *Johnston of Rockport*, Charles Collier Johnston, TD, *b.* 1915, *m.*

1997   *Jopling*, (Thomas) Michael Jopling, PC, *b.* 1930, *m.*

1991   *Judd*, Frank Ashcroft Judd, *b.* 1935, *m.*

1980   *Keith of Castleacre*, Kenneth Alexander Keith, *b.* 1916, *m.*

1997   *Kelvedon*, (Henry) Paul Guinness Channon, PC, *b.* 1935, *m.*

1996   *Kilpatrick of Kincraig*, Robert Kilpatrick, CBE, *b.* 1926, *m.*

1985   *Kimball*, Marcus Richard Kimball, *b.* 1928, *m.*

1983   *King of Wartnaby*, John Leonard King, *b.* 1918, *m.*

1999   *King of West Bromwich*, Tarsem King.

1993   *Kingsdown*, Robert (Robin) Leigh-Pemberton, KG, PC, *b.* 1927, *m.*

1994   *Kingsland*, Christopher James Prout, TD, PC, QC, *b.* 1942.

1999   *Kirkham*, Graham Kirkham, *b.* 1944, *m.*

1975   *Kirkhill*, John Farquharson Smith, *b.* 1930, *m.*

1987   *Knights*, Philip Douglas Knights, CBE, QPM, *b.* 1920, *m.*

1991   *Laing of Dunphail*, Hector Laing, *b.* 1923, *m.*

1999   *Laird*, John Dunn Laird, *b.* 1944, *m.*

1998   *Laming*, (William) Herbert Laming, CBE, *b.* 1936, *m.*

1998   *Lamont of Lerwick*, Norman Stewart Hughson Lamont, PC, *b.* 1942.

1990   *Lane of Horsell*, Peter Stewart Lane, *b.* 1925, *w.*

1997   *Lang of Monkton*, Ian Bruce Lang, PC, *b.* 1940, *m.*

1992   *Lawson of Blaby*, Nigel Lawson, PC, *b.* 1932, *m.*

1999   *Lea of Crondall*, David Edward Lea, OBE, *b.* 1937.

1993   *Lester of Herne Hill*, Anthony Paul Lester, QC, *b.* 1936, *m.*

1997   *Levene of Portsoken*, Peter Keith Levene, KBE, *b.* 1941, *m.*

1997   *Levy*, Michael Abraham Levy, *b.* 1944, *m.*

1989   *Lewis of Newnham*, Jack Lewis, FRS, *b.* 1928, *m.*

1999   *Lipsey*, David Lawrence Lipsey, *b.* 1948, *m.*

1997   *Lloyd-Webber*, Andrew Lloyd Webber, *b.* 1948, *m.*

1997   *Lofthouse of Pontefract*, Geoffrey Lofthouse, *b.* 1925, *w.*

1974   *Lovell-Davis*, Peter Lovell Lovell-Davis, *b.* 1924, *m.*

1984   *McAlpine of West Green*, (Robert) Alistair McAlpine, *b.* 1942, *m.*

1988   *Macaulay of Bragar*, Donald Macaulay, QC, *b.* 1933, *m.*

1975   *McCarthy*, William Edward John McCarthy, D.Phil., *b.* 1925, *m.*

1976   *McCluskey*, John Herbert McCluskey, *b.* 1929, *m.*

1989   *McColl of Dulwich*, Ian McColl, CBE, FRCS, FRCSE, *b.* 1933, *m.*

1995   *McConnell*, Robert William Brian McConnell, PC (NI), *b.* 1922, *m.*

1998   *Macdonald of Tradeston*, Angus John Macdonald, CBE, *b.* 1940, *m.*

1991   *Macfarlane of Bearsden*, Norman Somerville Macfarlane, KT, FRSE, *b.* 1926, *m.*

1982   *McIntosh of Haringey*, Andrew Robert McIntosh, *b.* 1933, *m.*

1991   *Mackay of Ardbrecknish*, John Jackson Mackay, PC, *b.* 1938, *m.*

1979   *Mackay of Clashfern*, James Peter Hymers Mackay, KT, PC, FRSE, *b.* 1927, *m.*

1995   *Mackay of Drumadoon*, Donald Sage Mackay, PC, *b.* 1946, *m.*

1999   *MacKenzie of Culkein*, Hector Uisdean MacKenzie, *b.* 1940.

1998   *Mackenzie of Framwellgate*, Brian Mackenzie, OBE, *b.* 1943, *m.*

1988   *Mackenzie-Stuart*, Alexander John Mackenzie Stuart, *b.* 1924, *m.*

1974   *Mackie of Benshie*, George Yull Mackie, CBE, DSO, DFC, *b.* 1919, *m.*

1996   *MacLaurin*, Ian Charter MacLaurin, *b.* 1937, *w.*

1982   *MacLehose of Beoch*, (Crawford) Murray MacLehose, KT, GBE, KCMG, KCVO, *b.* 1917, *m.*

1995   *McNally*, Tom McNally, *b.* 1943, *m.*

1991   *Marlesford*, Mark Shuldham Schreiber, *b.* 1931, *m.*

1981   *Marsh*, Richard William Marsh, PC, *b.* 1928, *m.*

1998   *Marshall of Knightsbridge*, Colin Marsh Marshall, *b.* 1933, *m.*

1987   *Mason of Barnsley*, Roy Mason, PC, *b.* 1924, *m.*

1997   *Mayhew of Twysden*, Patrick Barnabas Burke Mayhew, QC, PC, *b.* 1929, *m.*

1992   *Merlyn-Rees*, Merlyn Merlyn-Rees, PC, *b.* 1920, *m.*

1978   *Mishcon*, Victor Mishcon, *b.* 1915, *m.*

1981   *Molloy*, William John Molloy, *b.* 1918.

1997   *Molyneaux of Killead*, James Henry Molyneaux, KBE, PC, *b.* 1920.

1997   *Monro of Langholm*, Hector Seymour Peter Monro, AE, PC, *b.* 1922, *m.*

1997   *Montague of Oxford*, Michael Jacob Montague, CBE, *b.* 1932.

1992   *Moore of Lower Marsh*, John Edward Michael Moore, PC, *b.* 1937, *m.*

1986   *Moore of Wolvercote*, Philip Brian Cecil Moore, GCB, GCVO, CMG, PC, *b.* 1921, *m.*

1990   *Morris of Castle Morris*, Brian Robert Morris, D.Phil., *b.* 1930, *m.*

1997   *Morris of Manchester*, Alfred Morris, PC, *b.* 1928, *m.*

1971   *Moyola*, James Dawson Chichester-Clark, PC (NI), *b.* 1923, *m.*

1985   *Murray of Epping Forest*, Lionel Murray, OBE, PC, *b.* 1922, *m.*

1979   *Murton of Lindisfarne*, (Henry) Oscar Murton, OBE, TD, PC, *b.* 1914, *m.*

1997   *Naseby*, Michael Wolfgang Laurence Morris, PC, *b.* 1936, *m.*

1997   *Neill of Bladen*, (Francis) Patrick Neill, QC, *b.* 1926, *m.*

1997   *Newby*, Richard Mark Newby, OBE, *b.* 1953, *m.*

1997   *Newton of Braintree*, Antony Harold Newton, OBE, PC, *b.* 1937, *m.*

1994   *Nickson*, David Wigley Nickson, KBE, FRSE, *b.* 1929, *m.*

1975   *Northfield*, (William) Donald Chapman, *b.* 1923.

1998   *Norton of Louth*, Philip Norton, *b.* 1951.

1997   *Onslow of Woking*, Cranley Gordon Douglas Onslow, KCMG, PC, *b.* 1926, *m.*

1976   *Oram*, Albert Edward Oram, *b.* 1913, *m.*

1997   *Orme*, Stanley Orme, PC, *b.* 1923, *m.*

1992   *Owen*, David Anthony Llewellyn Owen, CH, PC, *b.* 1938, *m.*

1999   *Oxburgh*, Ernest Ronald Oxburgh, KBE, FRS, Ph.D., *b.* 1934, *m.*

1991   *Palumbo*, Peter Garth Palumbo, *b.* 1935, *m.*

1992   *Parkinson*, Cecil Edward Parkinson, PC, *b.* 1931, *m.*

1975   *Parry,* Gordon Samuel David Parry, *b.* 1925, *m.*

1999   *Patel,* Narendrakumar Babubhai Patel, *b.* 1938.

1997   *Patten,* John Haggitt Charles Patten, PC, *b.* 1945, *m.*

1996   *Paul,* Swraj Paul, *b.* 1931, *m.*

1990   *Pearson of Rannoch,* Malcolm Everard MacLaren Pearson, *b.* 1942, *m.*

1979   *Perry of Walton,* Walter Laing Macdonald Perry, OBE, FRS, FRSE, *b.* 1921, *m.*

1987   *Peston,* Maurice Harry Peston, *b.* 1931, *m.*

1983   *Peyton of Yeovil,* John Wynne William Peyton, PC, *b.* 1919, *m.*

1998   *Phillips of Sudbury,* Andrew Wyndham Phillips, OBE, *b.* 1939, *m.*

1996   *Pilkington of Oxenford,* Revd Canon Peter Pilkington, *b.* 1933, *w.*

1992   *Plant of Highfield,* Prof. Raymond Plant, PH.D., *b.* 1945, *m.*

1959   *Plowden,* Edwin Noel Plowden, GBE, KCB, *b.* 1907, *m.*

1987   *Plumb,* (Charles) Henry Plumb, MEP, *b.* 1925, *m.*

1981   *Plummer of St Marylebone,* (Arthur) Desmond (Herne) Plummer, TD, *b.* 1914, *w.*

1990   *Porter of Luddenham,* George Porter, OM, FRS, *b.* 1920, *m.*

1992   *Prentice,* Reginald Ernest Prentice, PC, *b.* 1923, *m.*

1987   *Prior,* James Michael Leathes Prior, PC, *b.* 1927, *m.*

1982   *Prys-Davies,* Gwilym Prys Prys-Davies, *b.* 1923, *m.*

1997   *Puttnam,* David Terence Puttnam, CBE, *b.* 1941, *m.*

1987   *Pym,* Francis Leslie Pym, MC, PC, *b.* 1922, *m.*

1982   *Quinton,* Anthony Meredith Quinton, FBA, *b.* 1925, *m.*

1994   *Quirk,* Prof. (Charles) Randolph Quirk, CBE, FBA, *b.* 1920, *m.*

1997   *Randall of St Budeaux,* Stuart Jeffrey Randall, *b.* 1938, *m.*

1978   *Rawlinson of Ewell,* Peter Anthony Grayson Rawlinson, PC, QC, *b.* 1919, *m.*

1976   *Rayne,* Max Rayne, *b.* 1918, *m.*

1997   *Razzall,* (Edward) Timothy Razzall, CBE, *b.* 1943, *m.*

1987   *Rees,* Peter Wynford Innes Rees, PC, QC, *b.* 1926, *m.*

1988   *Rees-Mogg,* William Rees-Mogg, *b.* 1928, *m.*

1991   *Renfrew of Kaimsthorn,* (Andrew) Colin Renfrew, FBA, *b.* 1937, *m.*

1999   *Rennard,* Christopher John Rennard, MBE, *b.* 1960.

1979   *Renton,* David Lockhart-Mure Renton, KBE, TD, PC, QC, *b.* 1908, *w.*

1997   *Renton of Mount Harry,* (Ronald) Timothy Renton, PC, *b.* 1932, *m.*

1997   *Renwick of Clifton,* Robin William Renwick, KCMG, *b.* 1937, *m.*

1990   *Richard,* Ivor Seward Richard, PC, QC, *b.* 1932, *m.*

1979   *Richardson,* John Samuel Richardson, LVO, MD, FRCP, *b.* 1910, *w.*

1983   *Richardson of Duntisbourne,* Gordon William Humphreys Richardson, KG, MBE, TD, PC, *b.* 1915, *m.*

1992   *Rix,* Brian Norman Roger Rix, CBE, *b.* 1924, *m.*

1997   *Roberts of Conwy,* (Ieuan) Wyn (Pritchard) Roberts, PC, *b.* 1930, *m.*

1999   *Robertson of Port Ellen,* George Islay MacNeill Robertson, PC, *b.* 1946, *m.*

1992   *Rodger of Earlsferry,* Alan Ferguson Rodger, PC, QC, FBA, *b.* 1944.

1992   *Rodgers of Quarry Bank,* William Thomas Rodgers, PC, *b.* 1928, *m.*

1999   *Rogan,* Dennis Robert David Rogan, *b.* 1942, *m.*

1996   *Rogers of Riverside,* Richard George Rogers, RA, RIBA, *b.* 1933, *m.*

1977   *Roll of Ipsden,* Eric Roll, KCMG, CB, *b.* 1907, *w.*

1991   *Runcie,* Rt Revd Robert Alexander Kennedy Runcie, MC, PC, Royal Victorian Chain, *b.* 1921, *m.*

1997   *Russell-Johnston,* (David) Russell Russell-Johnston, *b.* 1932, *m.*

1975   *Ryder of Eaton Hastings,* Sydney Thomas Franklin (Don) Ryder, *b.* 1916, *m.*

1997   *Ryder of Wensum,* Richard Andrew Ryder, OBE, PC, *b.* 1949, *m.*

1996   *Saatchi,* Maurice Saatchi, *b.* 1946, *m.*

1989   *Sainsbury of Preston Candover,* John Davan Sainsbury, KG, *b.* 1927, *m.*

1997   *Sainsbury of Turville,* David John Sainsbury, *b.* 1940, *m.*

1987   *St John of Fawsley,* Norman Antony Francis St John-Stevas, PC, *b.* 1929.

1997   *Sandberg,* Michael Graham Ruddock Sandberg, CBE, *b.* 1927, *m.*

1985   *Sanderson of Bowden,* Charles Russell Sanderson, *b.* 1933, *m.*

1998   *Sawyer,* Lawrence (Tom) Sawyer.

1979   *Scanlon,* Hugh Parr Scanlon, *b.* 1913, *m.*

1978   *Sefton of Garston,* William Henry Sefton, *b.* 1915, *m.*

1997   *Selkirk of Douglas,* James Alexander Douglas-Hamilton, MSP, PC, QC, *b.* 1942, *m.*

1996   *Sewel,* John Buttifant Sewel, CBE, *b.* 1946.

1999   *Sharman,* Colin Morven Sharman, OBE, *b.* 1943, *m.*

1994   *Shaw of Northstead,* Michael Norman Shaw, *b.* 1920, *m.*

1959   *Shawcross,* Hartley William Shawcross, GBE, PC, QC, *b.* 1902, *m.*

1994   *Sheppard of Didgemere,* Allan John George Sheppard, KCVO, *b.* 1932, *m.*

1998   *Sheppard of Liverpool,* David Stuart Sheppard, *b.* 1929, *m.*

1997   *Shore of Stepney,* Peter David Shore, PC, *b.* 1924, *m.*

1980   *Sieff of Brimpton,* Marcus Joseph Sieff, OBE, *b.* 1913, *w.*

1971   *Simon of Glaisdale,* Jocelyn Edward Salis Simon, PC, *b.* 1911, *m.*

1997   *Simon of Highbury,* David Alec Gwyn Simon, CBE, *b.* 1939, *m.*

1997   *Simpson of Dunkeld,* George Simpson, *b.* 1942, *m.*

1991   *Skidelsky,* Robert Jacob Alexander Skidelsky, D.Phil., *b.* 1939, *m.*

1997   *Smith of Clifton,* Trevor Arthur Smith, *b.* 1937, *m.*

1999   *Smith of Leigh,* Peter Richard Charles Smith.

1990   *Soulsby of Swaffham Prior,* Ernest Jackson Lawson Soulsby, Ph.D., *b.* 1926, *m.*

1983   *Stallard,* Albert William Stallard, *b.* 1921, *m.*

1997   *Steel of Aikwood,* David Martin Scott Steel, PC, KBE, MSP, *b.* 1938, *m.*

1991   *Sterling of Plaistow,* Jeffrey Maurice Sterling, CBE, *b.* 1934, *m.*

1987   *Stevens of Ludgate,* David Robert Stevens, *b.* 1936, *m.*

1999   *Stevenson of Coddenham,* Henry Dennistoun Stevenson, CBE, *b.* 1945, *m.*

1992   *Stewartby,* (Bernard Harold) Ian (Halley) Stewart, RD, PC, FBA, FRSE, *b.* 1935, *m.*

1981   *Stodart of Leaston,* James Anthony Stodart, PC, *b.* 1916, *w.*

1983   *Stoddart of Swindon,* David Leonard Stoddart, *b.* 1926, *m.*

1969   *Stokes,* Donald Gresham Stokes, TD, FREng., *b.* 1914, *w.*

1997   *Stone of Blackheath,* Andrew Zelig Stone, *b.* 1942, *m.*

1971   *Tanlaw,* Simon Brooke Mackay, *b.* 1934, *m.*

1996   *Taverne,* Dick Taverne, QC, *b.* 1928, *m.*

1978   *Taylor of Blackburn*, Thomas Taylor, CBE, *b.* 1929, *m.*

1968   *Taylor of Gryfe*, Thomas Johnston Taylor, FRSE, *b.* 1912, *m.*

1996   *Taylor of Warwick*, John David Beckett Taylor, *b.* 1952, *m.*

1992   *Tebbit*, Norman Beresford Tebbit, CH, PC, *b.* 1931, *m.*

1996   *Thomas of Gresford*, Donald Martin Thomas, OBE, QC, *b.* 1937, *m.*

1987   *Thomas of Gwydir*, Peter John Mitchell Thomas, PC, QC, *b.* 1920, *w.*

1997   *Thomas of Macclesfield*, Terence James Thomas, CBE, *b.* 1937, *m.*

1981   *Thomas of Swynnerton*, Hugh Swynnerton Thomas, *b.* 1931, *m.*

1977   *Thomson of Monifieth*, George Morgan Thomson, KT, PC, *b.* 1921, *m.*

1990   *Tombs*, Francis Leonard Tombs, FREng., *b.* 1924, *m.*

1998   *Tomlinson*, John Edward Tomlinson, MEP, *b.* 1939.

1994   *Tope*, Graham Norman Tope, CBE, *b.* 1943, *m.*

1981   *Tordoff*, Geoffrey Johnson Tordoff, *b.* 1928, *m.*

1999   *Trotman*, Alexander Trotman, *b.* 1933.

1993   *Tugendhat*, Christopher Samuel Tugendhat, *b.* 1937, *m.*

1990   *Varley*, Eric Graham Varley, PC, *b.* 1932, *m.*

1996   *Vincent of Coleshill*, Richard Frederick Vincent, GBE, KCB, DSO, *b.* 1931, *m.* (Field Marshal)

1985   *Vinson*, Nigel Vinson, LVO, *b.* 1931, *m.*

1990   *Waddington*, David Charles Waddington, GCVO, PC, QC, *b.* 1929, *m.*

1990   *Wade of Chorlton*, (William) Oulton Wade, *b.* 1932, *m.*

1992   *Wakeham*, John Wakeham, PC, *b.* 1932, *m.*

1999   *Waldegrave of North Hill*, William Arthur Waldegrave, PC, *b.* 1946, *m.*

1997   *Walker of Doncaster*, Harold Walker, PC, *b.* 1927, *m.*

1992   *Walker of Worcester*, Peter Edward Walker, MBE, PC, *b.* 1932, *m.*

1974   *Wallace of Coslany*, George Douglas Wallace, *b.* 1906, *m.*

1995   *Wallace of Saltaire*, William John Lawrence Wallace, PH.D., *b.* 1941, *m.*

1989   *Walton of Detchant*, John Nicholas Walton, TD, FRCP, *b.* 1922, *m.*

1998   *Warner*, Norman Reginald Warner, *b.* 1940, *m.*

1997   *Watson of Invergowrie*, Michael Goodall Watson, MSP, *b.* 1949, *m.*

1999   *Watson of Richmond*, Alan John Watson, CBE, *b.* 1941, *m.*

1992   *Weatherill*, (Bruce) Bernard Weatherill, PC, *b.* 1920, *m.*

1977   *Wedderburn of Charlton*, (Kenneth) William Wedderburn, FBA, QC, *b.* 1927, *m.*

1976   *Weidenfeld*, (Arthur) George Weidenfeld, *b.* 1919, *m.*

1980   *Weinstock*, Arnold Weinstock, *b.* 1924, *m.*

1978   *Whaddon*, (John) Derek Page, *b.* 1927, *m.*

1996   *Whitty*, John Lawrence (Larry) Whitty, *b.* 1943, *m.*

1974   *Wigoder*, Basil Thomas Wigoder, QC, *b.* 1921, *m.*

1985   *Williams of Elvel*, Charles Cuthbert Powell Williams, CBE, *b.* 1933, *m.*

1992   *Williams of Mostyn*, Gareth Wyn Williams, QC, *b.* 1941, *m.*

1999   *Williamson of Horton*, David Francis Williamson, GCMG, CB, *b.* 1934, *m.*

1992   *Wilson of Tillyorn*, David Clive Wilson, GCMG, PH.D., *b.* 1935, *m.*

1995   *Winston*, Robert Maurice Lipson Winston, FRCOG, *b.* 1940, *m.*

1985   *Wolfson*, Leonard Gordon Wolfson, *b.* 1927, *m.*

1991   *Wolfson of Sunningdale*, David Wolfson, *b.* 1935, *m.*

1999   *Woolmer of Leeds*, Kenneth John Woolmer, *b.* 1940, *m.*

1994   *Wright of Richmond*, Patrick Richard Henry Wright, GCMG, *b.* 1931, *m.*

1978   *Young of Dartington*, Michael Young, PH.D., *b.* 1915, *m.*

1984   *Young of Graffham*, David Ivor Young, PC, *b.* 1932, *m.*

1992   *Younger of Prestwick*, The Viscount Younger of Leckie. (*see* page 147)

BARONESSES

Created

1997   *Amos*, Valerie Ann Amos, *b.* 1954.

1996   *Anelay of St Johns*, Joyce Anne Anelay, DBE, *b.* 1947, *m.*

1999   *Ashton of Upholland*, Catherine Margaret Ashton, *m.*

1999   *Barker*, Elizabeth Jean Barker, *b.* 1961.

1987   *Blackstone*, Tessa Ann Vosper Blackstone, PH.D., *b.* 1942.

1987   *Blatch*, Emily May Blatch, CBE, PC, *b.* 1937, *m.*

1999   *Blood*, May Blood, MBE, *b.* 1938.

1990   *Brigstocke*, Heather Renwick Brigstocke, *b.* 1929, *w.*

1964   *Brooke of Ystradfellte*, Barbara Muriel Brooke, DBE, *b.* 1908, *w.*

1998   *Buscombe*, Peta Jane Buscombe, *b.* 1954, *m.*

1996   *Byford*, Hazel Byford, DBE, *b.* 1941, *m.*

1982   *Carnegy of Lour*, Elizabeth Patricia Carnegy of Lour, *b.* 1925.

1990   *Castle of Blackburn*, Barbara Anne Castle, PC, *b.* 1910, *w.*

1992   *Chalker of Wallasey*, Lynda Chalker, PC, *b.* 1942, *m.*

1982   *Cox*, Caroline Anne Cox, *b.* 1937, *m.*

1998   *Crawley*, Christine Mary Crawley, MEP, *b.* 1950, *m.*

1990   *Cumberlege*, Julia Frances Cumberlege, CBE, *b.* 1943, *m.*

1978   *David*, Nora Ratcliff David, *b.* 1913, *w.*

1993   *Dean of Thornton-le-Fylde*, Brenda Dean, PC, *b.* 1943, *m.*

1974   *Delacourt-Smith of Alteryn*, Margaret Rosalind Delacourt-Smith, *b.* 1916, *m.*

1991   *Denton of Wakefield*, Jean Denton, CBE, *b.* 1935.

1990   *Dunn*, Lydia Selina Dunn, DBE, *b.* 1940, *m.*

1990   *Eccles of Moulton*, Diana Catherine Eccles, *b.* 1933, *m.*

1972   *Elles*, Diana Louie Elles, *b.* 1921, *m.*

1997   *Emerton*, Audrey Caroline Emerton, DBE, *b.* 1935.

1974   *Falkender*, Marcia Matilda Falkender, CBE, *b.* 1932.

1994   *Farrington of Ribbleton*, Josephine Farrington, *b.* 1940, *m.*

1974   *Fisher of Rednal*, Doris Mary Gertrude Fisher, *b.* 1919, *w.*

1990   *Flather*, Shreela Flather, *m.*

1997   *Fookes*, Janet Evelyn Fookes, DBE, *b.* 1936.

1999   *Gale*, Anita Gale, *b.* 1940.

1981   *Gardner of Parkes*, (Rachel) Trixie (Anne) Gardner, *b.* 1927, *m.*

1998   *Goudie*, Mary Teresa Goudie, *b.* 1946, *m.*

1993   *Gould of Potternewton*, Joyce Brenda Gould, *b.* 1932, *m.*

1991   *Hamwee*, Sally Rachel Hamwee, *b.* 1947.

1999   *Hanham*, Joan Brownlow Hanham, CBE, *b.* 1939, *m.*

1999   *Harris of Richmond*, Angela Felicity Harris, *b.* 1944.

1996   *Hayman*, Helene Valerie Hayman, *b.* 1949, *m.*

1991   *Hilton of Eggardon*, Jennifer Hilton, QPM, *b.* 1936.

1995   *Hogg,* Sarah Elizabeth Mary Hogg, *b.* 1946, *m.*
1990   *Hollis of Heigham,* Patricia Lesley Hollis, D.Phil., *b.* 1941, *m.*
1985   *Hooper,* Gloria Dorothy Hooper, *b.* 1939.
1999   *Howells of St Davids,* Rosalind Particia-Anne Howells.
1965   *Hylton-Foster,* Audrey Pellew Hylton-Foster, DBE, *b.* 1908, *w.*
1991   *James of Holland Park,* Phyllis Dorothy White (P. D. James), OBE, *b.* 1920, *w.*
1992   *Jay of Paddington,* Margaret Ann Jay, PC, *b.* 1939, *m. Lord Privy Seal*
1979   *Jeger,* Lena May Jeger, *b.* 1915, *w.*
1997   *Kennedy of the Shaws,* Helena Ann Kennedy, QC, *b.* 1950, *m.*
1997   *Knight of Collingtree,* (Joan Christabel) Jill Knight, DBE, *b.* 1923, *w.*
1997   *Linklater of Butterstone,* Veronica Linklater, *b.* 1943, *m.*
1996   *Lloyd of Highbury,* Prof. June Kathleen Lloyd, DBE, FRCP, FRCPE, FRCGP, *b.* 1928.
1978   *Lockwood,* Betty Lockwood, *b.* 1924, *w.*
1997   *Ludford,* Sarah Ann Ludford, MEP, *b.* 1951.
1979   *McFarlane of Llandaff,* Jean Kennedy McFarlane, *b.* 1926.
1999   *McIntosh of Hudnall,* Genista Mary McIntosh, *b.* 1946.
1971   *Macleod of Borve,* Evelyn Hester Macleod, *b.* 1915, *w.*
1997   *Maddock,* Diana Margaret Maddock, *b.* 1945, *m.*
1991   *Mallalieu,* Ann Mallalieu, QC, *b.* 1945, *m.*
1970   *Masham of Ilton,* Susan Lilian Primrose Cunliffe-Lister, *b.* 1935, *m. (Countess of Swinton)*
1999   *Massey of Darwen,* Doreen Elizabeth Massey, *b.* 1938, *m.*
1998   *Miller of Chilthorne Domer,* Susan Elizabeth Miller, *b.* 1954.
1993   *Miller of Hendon,* Doreen Miller, MBE, *b.* 1933, *m.*
1997   *Nicholson of Winterbourne,* Emma Harriet Nicholson, MEP, *b.* 1941, *m.*
1982   *Nicol,* Olive Mary Wendy Nicol, *b.* 1923, *m.*
1991   *O'Cathain,* Detta O'Cathain, OBE, *b.* 1938, *m.*
1999   *O'Neill of Bengarve,* Onora Sylvia O'Neill, CBE, PH.D., *b.* 1941.
1989   *Oppenheim-Barnes,* Sally Oppenheim-Barnes, PC, *b.* 1930, *m.*
1990   *Park of Monmouth,* Daphne Margaret Sybil Désirée Park, CMG, OBE, *b.* 1921.
1991   *Perry of Southwark,* Pauline Perry, *b.* 1931, *m.*
1974   *Pike,* (Irene) Mervyn (Parnicott) Pike, DBE, *b.* 1918.
1997   *Pitkeathley,* Jill Elizabeth Pitkeathley, OBE, *b.* 1940.
1981   *Platt of Writtle,* Beryl Catherine Platt, CBE, FREng., *b.* 1923, *m.*
1999   *Prashar,* Usha Kumari Prashar, CBE, *b.* 1948, *m.*
1996   *Ramsay of Cartvale,* Margaret Mildred (Meta) Ramsay, *b.* 1936.
1994   *Rawlings,* Patricia Elizabeth Rawlings, *b.* 1939.
1997   *Rendell of Babergh,* Ruth Barbara Rendell, CBE, *b.* 1930, *m.*
1998   *Richardson of Calow,* Kathleen Margaret Richardson, OBE, *b.* 1938, *m.*
1979   *Ryder of Warsaw,* Margaret Susan Cheshire (Sue Ryder), CMG, OBE, *b.* 1923, *w.*
1997   *Scotland of Asthal,* Patricia Janet Scotland, QC, *m.*
1991   *Seccombe,* Joan Anna Dalziel Seccombe, DBE, *b.* 1930, *m.*
1967   *Serota,* Beatrice Serota, DBE, *b.* 1919, *m.*
1998   *Sharp of Guildford,* Margaret Lucy Sharp, *m.*
1973   *Sharples,* Pamela Sharples, *b.* 1923, *m.*

1995   *Smith of Gilmorehill,* Elizabeth Margaret Smith, *b.* 1940, *w.*
1999   *Stern,* Vivien Helen Stern, CBE, *b.* 1941.
1996   *Symons of Vernham Dean,* Elizabeth Conway Symons, *b.* 1951.
1992   *Thatcher,* Margaret Hilda Thatcher, KG, OM, PC, FRS, *b.* 1925, *m.*
1994   *Thomas of Walliswood,* Susan Petronella Thomas, OBE, *b.* 1935, *m.*
1998   *Thornton,* (Dorothea) Glenys Thornton, *b.* 1952, *m.*
1980   *Trumpington,* Jean Alys Barker, PC, *b.* 1922, *w.*
1985   *Turner of Camden,* Muriel Winifred Turner, *b.* 1927, *m.*
1998   *Uddin,* Manzila Pola Uddin, *b.* 1959, *m.*
1985   *Warnock,* Helen Mary Warnock, DBE, *b.* 1924, *w.*
1999   *Warwick of Undercliffe,* Diana Mary Warwick, *b.* 1945, *m.*
1999   *Whitaker,* Janet Alison Whitaker.
1970   *White,* Eirene Lloyd White, *b.* 1909, *w.*
1996   *Wilcox,* Judith Ann Wilcox, *w.*
1999   *Wilkins,* Rosalie Catherine Wilkins, *b.* 1946.
1993   *Williams of Crosby,* Shirley Vivien Teresa Brittain Williams, PC, *b.* 1930, *m.*
1971   *Young,* Janet Mary Young, PC, *b.* 1926, *m.*
1997   *Young of Old Scone,* Barbara Scott Young, *b.* 1948.

Lords Spiritual

The Lords Spiritual are the Archbishops of Canterbury and York and 24 diocesan bishops of the Church of England. The Bishops of London, Durham and Winchester always have seats in the House of Lords; the other 21 seats are filled by the remaining diocesan bishops in order of seniority. The Bishop of Sodor and Man and the Bishop of Gibraltar are not eligible to sit in the House of Lords.

ARCHBISHOPS

Style, The Most Revd and Right Hon. the Lord
   Archbishop of __
Addressed as Archbishop, *or* Your Grace

Introduced to House of Lords
1991   *Canterbury* (103rd), George Leonard Carey, PC,
        PH.D., *b.* 1935, *m., cons.* 1987, *trans.* 1991
1990   *York* (96th), David Michael Hope, KCVO, PC,
        D.Phil., *b.* 1940, *cons.* 1985, *elected* 1985, *trans.*
        1991, 1995

BISHOPS

Style, The Right Revd the Lord Bishop of __
Addressed as My Lord
elected date of election as diocesan bishop

Introduced to House of Lords (as at mid-1999)
1996   *London* (132nd), Richard John Carew Chartres, *b.*
        1947, *m., cons.* 1992
1994   *Durham* (93rd), (Anthony) Michael (Arnold)
        Turnbull, *b.* 1935, *m., cons.* 1988, *elected* 1988,
        trans. 1994
1996   *Winchester* (96th), Michael Charles Scott-Joynt, *b.*
        1943, *m., cons.* 1987
1979   *Chichester* (102nd), Eric Waldram Kemp, DD, *b.*
        1915, *m., cons.* 1974, *elected* 1974
1989   *Lichfield* (97th), Keith Norman Sutton, *b.* 1934, *m.,*
        cons. 1978, *elected* 1984
1990   *Bristol* (54th), Barry Rogerson, *b.* 1936, *m., cons.*
        1979, *elected* 1985
1993   *Lincoln* (70th), Robert Maynard Hardy, *b.* 1936, *m.,*
        cons. 1980, *elected* 1986
1993   *Oxford* (41st), Richard Douglas Harries, *b.* 1936,
        m., cons. 1987, *elected* 1987
1994   *Birmingham* (7th), Mark Santer, *b.* 1936, *m., cons.*
        1981, *elected* 1987
1995   *Blackburn* (7th), Alan David Chesters, *b.* 1937, *m.,*
        cons. 1989, *elected* 1989
1996   *Carlisle* (65th), Ian Harland, *b.* 1932, *m., cons.* 1985,
        elected 1989
1997   *Hereford* (103rd), John Keith Oliver, *b.* 1935, *m.,*
        cons. 1990, *elected* 1990
1997   *Southwark* (9th), Thomas Frederick Butler, *b.* 1940,
        m., cons. 1985, *elected* 1991
1997   *Bath and Wells* (77th), James Lawton Thompson, *b.*
        1936, *m., cons.* 1978, *elected* 1991
1997   *Wakefield* (11th), Nigel Simeon McCulloch, *b.*
        1942, *m., cons.* 1986, *elected* 1992
1997   *Bradford* (8th), David James Smith, *b.* 1935, *m., cons.*
        1987, *elected* 1992
1997   *Manchester* (10th), Christopher John Mayfield, *b.*
        1935, *m., cons.* 1985, *elected* 1993

1998   *Salisbury* (77th), David Staffurth Stancliffe, *b.*
        1942, *m., cons.* 1993, *elected* 1993
1998   *Gloucester* (39th), David Edward Bentley, *b.* 1935,
        m., cons. 1986, *elected* 1993
1999   *Rochester* (106th), Michael James Nazir-Ali, PH.D.,
        b. 1949, *m., cons.* 1984, *elected* 1995
1999   *Guildford* (8th), John Warren Gladwin, *b.* 1942, *m.,*
        cons. 1994, *elected* 1994
1999   *Portsmouth* (8th), Kenneth William Stevenson, *b.*
        1949, *m., cons.* 1995, *elected* 1995
1999   *Derby* (6th), Jonathan Sansbury Bailey, *b.* 1940, *m.,*
        cons. 1992, *elected* 1995
1999   *St Albans* (9th), Christopher William Herbert, *b.*
        1944, *m., cons.* 1995, *elected* 1995

Bishops awaiting seats, in order of seniority (as at mid-1999)
    Chelmsford (8th), John Freeman Perry, *b.* 1935, *m.,*
        cons. 1989, *elected* 1996
    Peterborough (37th), Ian Cundy, *b.* 1945, *m., cons.*
        1992, *elected* 1996
    Chester (40th), Peter Robert Forster, PH.D., *b.* 1950,
        cons. 1996, *elected* 1996
    St Edmundsbury and Ipswich (9th), (John Hubert)
        Richard Lewis, *b.* 1943, *m., cons.* 1992, *elected*
        1997
    Truro (14th), William Ind, *b.* 1942, *m., cons.* 1987,
        elected 1997
    Worcester (112th), Peter Stephen Maurice Selby, *b.*
        1941, *cons.* 1984, *elected* 1997
    Newcastle (11th), (John) Martin Wharton, *b.* 1944,
        m., cons. 1992, *elected* 1997
    Sheffield (6th), John Nicholls, *b.* 1943, *m., cons.* 1990,
        elected 1997
    Coventry (8th), Colin J. Bennetts, *b.* 1940, *m., cons.*
        1994, *elected* 1997
    Liverpool (7th), James Jones, *b.* 1948, *m., cons.* 1994,
        elected 1998
    Leicester (6th), Timothy John Stevens, *b.* 1946, *m.,*
        cons. 1999, *elected* 1999
    Southwell (10th), George Henry Cassidy, *b.* 1942,
        m., cons. 1999, *elected* 1999

COURTESY TITLES

From this list it will be seen that, for example, the Marquess of Blandford is heir to the Dukedom of Marlborough, and Viscount Amberley to the Earldom of Russell. Titles of second heirs are also given, and the courtesy title of the father of a second heir is indicated by *; e.g. Earl of Burlington, eldest son of *Marquess of Hartington
For forms of address, see page 135

MARQUESSES
*Blandford – *Marlborough*, D.
Bowmont and Cessford – *Roxburghe*, D.
Douglas and Clydesdale – *Hamilton*, D.
*Douro – *Wellington*, D.
Graham – *Montrose*, D.
Hamilton – *Abercorn*, D.
*Hartington – *Devonshire*, D.
*Kildare – *Leinster*, D.
Lorne – *Argyll*, D.
*Tavistock – *Bedford*, D.
Tullibardine – *Atholl*, D.
*Worcester – *Beaufort*, D.

EARLS
Aboyne – *Huntly*, M.
Ancram – *Lothian*, M.
Arundel and Surrey – *Norfolk*, D.
*Bective – *Headfort*, M.
*Belfast – *Donegall*, M.
Brecknock – *Camden*, M.
Burford – *St Albans*, D.
Burlington – *Hartington*, M.
*Cardigan – *Ailesbury*, M.
Compton – *Northampton*, M.
*Dalkeith – *Buccleuch*, D.
Dumfries – *Bute*, M.
*Euston – *Grafton*, D.
Glamorgan – *Worcester*, M.
Grosvenor – *Westminster*, D.
*Haddo – *Aberdeen and Temair*, M.
Hillsborough – *Downshire*, M.
Hopetoun – *Linlithgow*, M.
March and Kinrara – *Richmond*, D.
Medina – *Milford Haven*, M.
*Mount Charles – *Conyngham*, M.
Mornington – *Douro*, M.
Mulgrave – *Normanby*, M.
Percy – *Northumberland*, D.
Ronaldshay – *Zetland*, M.
*St Andrews – *Kent*, D.
*Shelburne – *Lansdowne*, M.
*Southesk – *Fife*, D.
Sunderland – *Blandford*, M.
*Tyrone – *Waterford*, M.
Ulster – *Gloucester*, D.
*Uxbridge – *Anglesey*, M.

Wiltshire – *Winchester*, M.
Yarmouth – *Hertford*, M.

VISCOUNTS
Althorp – *Spencer*, E.
Amberley – *Russell*, E.
Andover – *Suffolk and Berkshire*, E.
Anson – *Lichfield*, E.
Asquith – *Oxford and Asquith*, E.
Boringdon – *Morley*, E.
Borodale – *Beatty*, E.
Boyle – *Shannon*, E.
Brocas – *Jellicoe*, E.
Campden – *Gainsborough*, E.
Carlow – *Portarlington*, E.
Carlton – *Wharncliffe*, E.
Castlereagh – *Londonderry*, M.
Chelsea – *Cadogan*, E.
Chewton – *Waldegrave*, E.
Chichester – *Belfast*, E.
Clanfield – *Peel*, E.
Clive – *Powis*, E.
Coke – *Leicester*, E.
Corry – *Belmore*, E.
Corvedale – *Baldwin of Bewdley*, E.
Cranborne – *Salisbury*, M.
Cranley – *Onslow*, E.
Crichton – *Erne*, E.
Crowhurst – *Cottenham*, E.
Curzon – *Howe*, E.
Dangan – *Cowley*, E.
Dawick – *Haig*, E.
Drumlanrig – *Queensberry*, M.
Duncannon – *Bessborough*, E.
Dungarvan – *Cork and Orrery*, E.
Dunluce – *Antrim*, E.
Dunwich – *Stradbroke*, E.
Dupplin – *Kinnoull*, E.
Ebrington – *Fortescue*, E.
Ednam – *Dudley*, E.
Encombe – *Eldon*, E.
Enfield – *Strafford*, E.
Erleigh – *Reading*, M.
Errington – *Cromer*, E.
FitzHarris – *Malmesbury*, E.
Folkestone – *Radnor*, E.
Forbes – *Granard*, E.
Garmoyle – *Cairns*, E.
Garnock – *Lindsay*, E.
Glandine – *Norbury*, E.
Glenapp – *Inchcape*, E.

Glentworth – *Limerick*, E.
Grimstone – *Verulam*, E.
Gwynedd – *Lloyd George of Dwyfor*, E.
Hawkesbury – *Liverpool*, E.
Hinchingbrooke – *Sandwich*, E.
Ikerrin – *Carrick*, E.
Ingestre – *Shrewsbury*, E.
Ipswich – *Euston*, E.
Jocelyn – *Roden*, E.
Kelburn – *Glasgow*, E.
Kilwarlin – *Hillsborough*, E.
Kingsborough – *Kingston*, E.
Kirkwall – *Orkney*, E.
Knebworth – *Lytton*, E.
Lascelles – *Harewood*, E.
Linley – *Snowdon*, E.
Loftus – *Ely*, M.
Lowther – *Lonsdale*, E.
Lumley – *Scarbrough*, E.
Lymington – *Portsmouth*, E.
Macmillan of Ovenden – *Stockton*, E.
Maitland – *Lauderdale*, E.
Malden – *Essex*, E.
Mandeville – *Manchester*, D.
Melgund – *Minto*, E.
Merton – *Nelson*, E.
Moore – *Drogheda*, E.
Newport – *Bradford*, E.
Newry and Mourne – *Kilmorey*, E.
Parker – *Macclesfield*, E.
Perceval – *Egmont*, E.
Petersham – *Harrington*, E.
Pollington – *Mexborough*, E.
Raynham – *Townshend*, M.
Reidhaven – *Seafield*, E.
Ruthven of Canberra – *Gowrie*, E.
St Cyres – *Iddesleigh*, E.
Sandon – *Harrowby*, E.
Savernake – *Cardigan*, E.
Slane – *Mount Charles*, E.
Somerton – *Normanton*, E.
Stopford – *Courtown*, E.
Stormont – *Mansfield*, E.
Strathallan – *Perth*, E.
Stuart – *Castle Stewart*, E.
Suirdale – *Donoughmore*, E.
Tamworth – *Ferrers*, E.
Tarbat – *Cromartie*, E.
Vaughan – *Lisburne*, E.
Weymouth – *Bath*, M.
Windsor – *Plymouth*, E.
Wolmer – *Selborne*, E.
Woodstock – *Portland*, E.

BARONS (LORD)
Aberdour – *Morton*, E.
Apsley – *Bathurst*, E.
Ardee – *Meath*, E.
Ashley – *Shaftesbury*, E.
Balgonie – *Leven and Melville*, E.
Balniel – *Crawford and Balcarres*, E.
Berriedale – *Caithness*, E.
Bingham – *Lucan*, E.
Binning – *Haddington*, E.
Brooke – *Warwick*, E.
Bruce – *Elgin*, E.
Buckhurst – *De La Warr*, E.
Burghley – *Exeter*, M.
Cardross – *Buchan*, E.
Carnegie – *Southesk*, E.
Clifton – *Darnley*, E.
Cochrane – *Dundonald*, E.
Courtenay – *Devon*, E.
Dalmeny – *Rosebery*, E.
Doune – *Moray*, E.
Downpatrick – *St Andrews*, E.
Dunglass – *Home*, E.
Eliot – *St Germans*, E.
Eskdail – *Dalkeith*, E.
Formartine – *Haddo*, E.
Gillford – *Clanwilliam*, E.
Glamis – *Strathmore*, E.
Greenock – *Cathcart*, E.
Guernsey – *Aylesford*, E.
Hay – *Erroll*, E.
Herbert – *Pembroke*, E.
Howard of Effingham – *Effingham*, E.
Howland – *Tavistock*, M.
Hyde – *Clarendon*, E.
Inverurie – *Kintore*, E.
Irwin – *Halifax*, E.
Johnstone – *Annandale and Hartfell*, E.
Kenlis – *Bective*, E.
Langton – *Temple of Stowe*, E.
La Poer – *Tyrone*, E.
Leslie – *Rothes*, E.
Loughborough – *Rosslyn*, E.
Maltravers – *Arundel and Surrey*, E.
Mauchline – *Loudoun*, C.
Medway – *Cranbrook*, E.
Montgomerie – *Eglinton and Winton*, E.
Moreton – *Ducie*, E.
Naas – *Mayo*, E.
Neidpath – *Wemyss and March*, E.
Norreys – *Lindsey and Abingdon*, E.
Ogilvy – *Airlie*, E.

Oxmantown – *Rosse, E.*
Paget de Beaudesert –
  *Uxbridge, E.
Porchester – *Carnarvon, E.*

Ramsay – *Dalhousie, E.*
Romsey – *Mountbatten of
  Burma, C.*
Rosehill – *Northesk, E.*

Scrymgeour – *Dundee, E.*
Seymour – *Somerset, D.*
Stanley – *Derby, E.*
Strathnaver – *Sutherland, C.*

Wodehouse – *Kimberley, E.*
Worsley – *Yarborough, E.*

PEERS' SURNAMES WHICH DIFFER FROM THEIR TITLES

The following symbols
indicate the rank of the
peer holding each title:

B. Baron/Baroness
C. Countess
D. Duke
E. Earl
M. Marquess
V. Viscount
* Life Peer

Abney-Hastings – *Loudoun,
  C.*
Acheson – *Gosford, E.*
Adderley – *Norton, B.*
Addington – *Sidmouth, V.*
Agar – *Normanton, E.*
Aitken – *Beaverbrook, B.*
Akers-Douglas – *Chilston, V.*
Alexander – *A. of Tunis, E.*
Alexander – *A. of Weedon,
  B.**
Alexander – *Caledon, E.*
Allen – *A. of Abbeydale, B.**
Allen – *Croham, B.**
Allsopp – *Hindlip, B.*
Alton – *A. of Liverpool, B.**
Anderson – *Waverley, V.*
Anelay – *A. of St Johns, B.**
Annesley – *Valentia, V.*
Anson – *Lichfield, E.*
Arbuthnott – *of Arbuthnott,
  V.*
Archer – *A. of Sandwell, B.**
Archer – *A. of Weston-super-
  Mare, B.**
Armstrong – *A. of Ilminster,
  B.**
Armstrong-Jones –
  Snowdon, E.
Arthur – *Glenarthur, B.*
Arundell – *T. of Malahide,
  B.*
Ashley – *A. of Stoke, B.**
Ashley-Cooper –
  Shaftesbury, E.
Ashton – *A. of Hyde, B.*
Ashton – *A. of Upholland, B.**
Asquith – *Oxford and
  Asquith, E.*
Assheton – *Clitheroe, B.*
Astley – *Hastings, B.*
Astor – *A. of Hever, B.*
Aubrey-Fletcher – *Braye, B.*
Bailey – *Glanusk, B.*
Baillie – *Burton, B.*
Baillie-Hamilton –
  Haddington, E.
Baker – *B. of Dorking, B.**
Balcarres – *Balniel, B.**
Baldwin – *B. of Bewdley, E.*
Balfour – *B. of Inchrye, B.*

Balfour – *Kinross, B.*
Balfour – *Riverdale, B.*
Bampfylde – *Poltimore, B.*
Banbury – *B. of Southam, B.*
Barber – *B. of Tewkesbury,
  B.**
Baring – *Ashburton, B.*
Baring – *Cromer, E.*
Baring – *H. of Glendale, B.*
Baring – *Northbrook, B.*
Baring – *Revelstoke, B.*
Barker – *Trumpington, B.**
Barnes – *Gorell, B.*
Barnewall – *Trimlestown, B.*
Bassam – *B. of Brighton, B.**
Bathurst – *Bledisloe, V.*
Beauclerk – *St Albans, D.*
Beaumont – *Allendale, V.*
Beaumont – *B. of Whitley,
  B.**
Beckett – *Grimthorpe, B.*
Bellow – *Bellwin, B.**
Benn – *Stansgate, V.*
Bennet – *Tankerville, E.*
Bentinck – *Portland, E.*
Beresford – *Waterford, M.*
Berry – *Hartwell, B.**
Berry – *Kemsley, V.*
Bertie – *Lindsey, E.*
Best – *Wynford, B.*
Bethell – *Westbury, B.*
Bewicke-Copley –
  Cromwell, B.
Bigham – *Mersey, V.*
Bingham – *B. of Cornhill, B.**
Bingham – *Clanmorris, B.*
Bingham – *Lucan, E.*
Bligh – *Darnley, E.*
Blyth – *B. of Rowington, B.**
Bootle-Wilbraham –
  Skelmersdale, B.
Boscawen – *Falmouth, V.*
Boston – *B. of Faversham, B.**
Bourke – *Mayo, E.*
Bowes Lyon – *Strathmore
  and Kinghorne, E.*
Bowyer – *Denham, B.*
Boyd – *Kilmarnock, B.*
Boyle – *Cork, E.*
Boyle – *Glasgow, E.*
Boyle – *Shannon, E.*
Brabazon – *Meath, E.*
Braine – *B. of Wheatley, B.**
Brand – *Hampden, V.*
Brassey – *B. of Apethorpe, B.*
Brett – *Esher, V.*
Bridge – *B. of Harwich, W.**
Bridgeman – *Bradford, E.*
Brodrick – *Midleton, V.*
Brooke – *Alanbrooke, V.*

Brooke – *B. of Alverthorpe,
  B.**
Brooke – *B. of Ystradfellte,
  B.**
Brooke – *Brookeborough, V.*
Brooks – *B. of Tremorfa, B.**
Brooks – *Crawshaw, B.*
Brougham – *Brougham and
  Vaux, B.*
Broughton – *Fairhaven, B.*
Browne – *Kilmaine, B.*
Browne – *Oranmore and
  Browne, B.*
Browne – *Sligo, M.*
Bruce – *Aberdare, B.*
Bruce – *B. of Burleigh, B.*
Bruce – *B. of Donington, B.**
Bruce – *Elgin, E.*
Brudenell-Bruce – *Ailesbury,
  M.*
Buchan – *Tweedsmuir, B.*
Buckley – *Wrenbury, B.*
Butler – *B. of Brockwell, B.**
Butler – *Carrick, E.*
Butler – *Dunboyne, B.*
Butler – *Mountgarret, V.*
Buxton – *B. of Alsa, B.**
Byng – *Strafford, E.*
Byng – *Torrington, V.*
Callaghan – *C. of Cardiff,
  B.**
Cameron – *C. of Lochbroom,
  B.**
Campbell – *Argyll, D.*
Campbell – *C. of Alloway,
  B.**
Campbell – *C. of Croy, B.**
Campbell – *Cawdor, E.*
Campbell – *Colgrain, B.*
Campbell – *Stratheden, B.*
Campbell-Gray – *Gray, B.*
Canning – *Garvagh, B.*
Capell – *Essex, E.*
Carington – *Carrington, B.*
Carlile – *C. of Berriew, B.**
Carlisle – *C. of Bucklow, B.**
Carmichael – *C. of
  Kelvingrove, B.**
Carnegie – *Fife, D.*
Carnegie – *Northesk, E.*
Carr – *C. of Hadley, B.**
Cary – *Falkland, V.*
Castle – *C. of Blackburn, B.**
Caulfeild – *Charlemont, V.*
Cavendish – *C. of Furness,
  B.**
Cavendish – *Chesham, B.*
Cavendish – *Devonshire, D.*
Cavendish – *Waterpark, B.*
Cayzer – *Rotherwick, B.*
Cecil – *A. of Hackney, B.*

Cecil – *Exeter, M.*
Cecil – *Rockley, B.*
Cecil – *Salisbury, M.*
Chalker – *C. of Wallasey, B.**
Chaloner – *Gisborough, B.*
Channon – *Kelvedon, B.**
Chapman – *Northfield, B.**
Charteris – *C. of Amisfield,
  B.**
Charteris – *Wemyss and
  March, E.*
Cheshire – *R. of Warsaw, B**
Chetwynd-Talbot –
  *Shrewsbury and Waterford,
  E.*
Chichester – *Donegall, M.*
Chichester-Clark – *Moyola,
  B.**
Child Villiers – *Jersey, E.*
Cholmondeley – *Delamere,
  B.*
Chubb – *Hayter, B.*
Clark – *C. of Kempston, B.**
Clarke – *C. of Hampstead,
  B.**
Clegg-Hill – *Hill, V.*
Clifford – *C. of Chudleigh, B.*
Cochrane – *C. of Cults, B.*
Cochrane – *Dundonald, E.*
Cocks – *C. of Hartcliffe, B.**
Cocks – *Somers, B.*
Cokayne – *C. of Ashbourne,
  B.*
Coke – *Leicester, E.*
Cole – *Enniskillen, E.*
Collier – *Monkswell, B.*
Colville – *Clydesmuir, B.*
Colville – *C. of Culross, V.*
Compton – *Northampton, M.*
Conolly-Carew – *Carew, B.*
Constantine – *C. of
  Stanmore, B.**
Cooke – *C. of Islandreagh,
  B.**
Cooke – *C. of Thorndon, B.**
Cooper – *Norwich, V.*
Cope – *C. of Berkeley, B.**
Corbett – *Rowallan, B.*
Cornwall-Legh – *G. of
  Codnor, B.*
Courtenay – *Devon, E.*
Cowdrey – *C. of Tonbridge,
  B.**
Craig – *C. of Radley, B.**
Craig – *Craigavon, V.*
Crichton – *Erne, E.*
Crichton-Stuart – *Bute, M.*
Cripps – *Parmoor, B.*
Crossley – *Somerleyton, B.*
Cubitt – *Ashcombe, B.*

Holmes à Court – *Heytesbury, B.*
Hood – *Bridport, V.*
Hope – *Glendevon, B.*
Hope – *H. of Craighead, B.**
Hope – *Linlithgow, M.*
Hope – *Rankeillour, B.*
Hope Johnstone – *Annandale and Hartfell, E.*
Hope-Morley – *Hollenden, B.*
Hopkinson – *Colyton, B.*
Hore-Ruthven – *Gowrie, E.*
Hovell-Thurlow-Cumming-Bruce – *Thurlow, B.*
Howard – *Carlisle, E.*
Howard – *Effingham, E.*
Howard – *H. of Penrith, B.*
Howard – *Strathcona and Mount Royal, B.*
Howard – *Suffolk and Berkshire, E.*
Howe – *H. of Aberavon, B.**
Howell – *H. of Guildford, B.**
Howells – *Geraint, B.**
Howells – *H. of St Davids, B.**
Howie – *H. of Troon, B.**
Hubbard – *Addington, B.*
Huggins – *Malvern, V.*
Hughes – *C. of Penrhos, B.**
Hughes – *H. of Woodside, B.**
Hughes – *Islwyn, B.**
Hughes-Young – *St Helens, B.*
Hunt – *H. of Kings Heath, B.**
Hunt – *H. of Tanworth, B.**
Hunt – *H. of Wirral, B.**
Hurd – *H. of Westwell, B.**
Hussey – *H. of North Bradley, B.**
Hutchinson – *H. of Lullington, B.**
Ingrams – *Darcy de Knayth, B.*
Innes-Ker – *Roxburghe, D.*
Inskip – *Caldecote, V.*
Irby – *Boston, B.*
Irvine – *I. of Lairg, B.**
Isaacs – *Reading, M.*
James – *J. of Holland Park, B.**
James – *Northbourne, B.*
Janner – *J. of Braunstone, B.**
Jauncey – *J. of Tullichettle, W.**
Jay – *J. of Paddington, B.**
Jebb – *Gladwyn, B.*
Jenkin – *J. of Roding, B.**
Jenkins – *J. of Hillhead, B.**
Jenkins – *J. of Putney, B.**
Jervis – *St Vincent, V.*
Jocelyn – *Roden, E.*
Johnston – *J. of Rockport, B.**
Jolliffe – *Hylton, B.*
Joynson-Hicks – *Brentford, V.*

Kay-Shuttleworth – *Shuttleworth, B.*
Kearley – *Devonport, V.*
Keith – *K. of Castleacre, B.**
Keith – *K. of Kinkel, W.**
Keith – *Kintore, E.*
Kemp – *Rochdale, V.*
Kennedy – *Ailsa, M.*
Kennedy – *K. of the Shaws, B.**
Kenworthy – *Strabolgi, B.*
Keppel – *Albemarle, E.*
Kerr – *Lothian, M.*
Kerr – *Teviot, B.*
Kilpatrick – *K. of Kincraig, B.**
King – *K. of Wartnaby, B.**
King – *K. of West Bromwich, B.**
King – *Lovelace, E.*
King-Tenison – *Kingston, E.*
Kirkham – *Berners, B.*
Kitchener – *K. of Khartoum, E.*
Knatchbull – *Brabourne, B.*
Knatchbull – *M. of Burma, C.*
Knight – *K. of Collingtree, B.**
Knox – *Ranfurly, E.*
Laing – *L. of Dunphail, B.**
Lamb – *Rochester, B.*
Lambton – *Durham, E.*
Lamont – *L. of Lerwick, B.**
Lampson – *Killearn, B.*
Lane – *L. of Horsell, B.*
Lang – *L. of Monkton, B.**
Lascelles – *Harewood, E.*
Law – *Coleraine, B.*
Law – *Ellenborough, B.*
Lawrence – *Trevethin, B.*
Lawson – *Burnham, B.*
Lawson – *L. of Blaby, B.**
Lawson-Johnston – *Luke, B.*
Lea – *L. of Crondall, B.**
Leckie – *Y. of Prestwick, B.**
Legge – *Dartmouth, E.*
Legh – *Newton, B.*
Leigh-Pemberton – *Kingsdown, B.**
Leith – *Burgh, B.*
Lennox-Boyd – *B. of Merton, V.*
Le Poer Trench – *Clancarty, E.*
Leslie – *Rothes, E.*
Leslie Melville – *Leven, E.*
Lester – *L. of Herne Hill, B.**
Levene – *L. of Portsoken, B.**
Lever – *Leverhulme, V.*
Leveson-Gower – *Granville, E.*
Lewis – *L. of Newnham, B.**
Lewis – *Merthyr, B.*
Liddell – *Ravensworth, B.*
Lindesay-Bethune – *Lindsay, E.*
Lindsay – *Crawford, E.*
Lindsay – *L. of Birker, B.*
Linklater – *L. of Butterstone, L.**

Littleton – *Hatherton, B.*
Lloyd – *L. of Berwick, W.**
Lloyd – *L. of Highbury, L.**
Lloyd George – *L. of Dwyfor, E.*
Lloyd George – *Tenby, V.*
Lloyd-Mostyn – *Mostyn, B.*
Loder – *Wakehurst, B.*
Lofthouse – *L. of Pontefract, B.**
Lopes – *Roborough, B.*
Lour – *C. of Lour, L.**
Low – *Aldington, B.*
Lowry-Corry – *Belmore, E.*
Lowther – *Lonsdale, E.*
Lowther – *Ullswater, V.*
Lubbock – *Avebury, B.*
Lucas – *L. of Chilworth, B.*
Lumley – *Scarbrough, E.*
Lumley-Savile – *Savile, B.*
Lyon-Dalberg-Acton – *Acton, B.*
Lysaght – *Lisle, B.*
Lyttelton – *Chandos, V.*
Lyttelton – *Cobham, V.*
Lytton Cobbold – *Cobbold, B.*
McAlpine – *M. of West Green, B.**
Macaulay – *M. of Bragar, B.**
McClintock-Bunbury – *Rathdonnell, B.*
McColl – *M. of Dulwich, B.**
Macdonald – *M. of Gwaenysgor, B.*
Macdonald – *M. of Tradeston, B.*
McDonnell – *Antrim, E.*
Macfarlane – *M. of Bearsden, B.**
McFarlane – *M. of Llandaff, B.**
McIntosh – *M. of Haringey, B.**
McIntosh – *M. of Hudnall, B.**
Mackay – *Inchcape, E.*
Mackay – *M. of Ardbrecknish, B.**
Mackay – *M. of Clashfern, B.**
Mackay – *M. of Drumadoon, B.**
Mackay – *Reay, B.*
Mackay – *Tanlaw, B.*
Mackenzie – *Cromartie, E.*
MacKenzie – *M. of Culkein, B.**
Mackenzie – *M. of Framwellgate, B.**
Mackie – *M. of Benshie, B.**
Mackintosh – *M. of Halifax, V.*
McLaren – *Aberconway, B.*
MacLehose – *M. of Beoch, B.**
Macleod – *M. of Borve, B.**
Macmillan – *Stockton, E.*

Macpherson – *M. of Drumochter, B.*
Macpherson – *Strathcarron, B.*
Maffey – *Rugby, B.*
Maitland – *Lauderdale, E.*
Maitland Biddulph – *Biddulph, B.*
Makgill – *of Oxfuird, V.*
Makins – *Sherfield, B.*
Manners – *Rutland, D.*
Manningham-Buller – *Dilhorne, V.*
Mansfield – *Sandhurst, B.*
Marks – *M. of Broughton, B.*
Marquis – *Woolton, E.*
Marshall – *M. of Knightsbridge, B.**
Marsham – *Romney, E.*
Martyn-Hemphill – *Hemphill, B.*
Mason – *M. of Barnsley, B.**
Massey – *M. of Darwen, B.**
Maude – *Hawarden, V.*
Maxwell – *de Ros, B.*
Maxwell – *Farnham, B.*
Mayhew – *M. of Twysden, B.**
Meade – *Clanwilliam, E.*
Mercer Nairne Petty-Fitzmaurice – *Lansdowne, M.*
Millar – *Inchyra, B.*
Miller – *M. of Chilthorne Domer, B.**
Miller – *M. of Hendon, B.**
Milner – *M. of Leeds, B.*
Mitchell-Thomson – *Selsdon, B.*
Mitford – *Redesdale, B.*
Molyneaux – *M. of Killead, B.**
Monckton – *M. of Brenchley, V.*
Monckton-Arundell – *Galway, V.*
Mond – *Melchett, B.*
Money-Coutts – *Latymer, B.*
Monro – *M. of Langholm, B.**
Montagu – *Manchester, D.*
Montagu – *Sandwich, E.*
Montagu – *Swaythling, B.*
Montagu Douglas Scott – *Buccleuch, D.*
Montagu Stuart Wortley – *Wharncliffe, E.*
Montague – *Amwell, B.*
Montague – *M. of Oxford, B.**
Montgomerie – *Eglinton, E.*
Montgomery – *M. of Alamein, V.*
Moore – *Drogheda, E.*
Moore – *M. of Lower Marsh, B.**
Moore – *M. of Wolvercote, B.**
Moore-Brabazon – *B. of Tara, B.*
Moreton – *Ducie, E.*

Temple-Gore-Langton –
T. *of Stowe, E.*
Tennant – *Glenconner, B.*
Thellusson – *Rendlesham, B.*
Thesiger – *Chelmsford, V.*
Thomas – *T. of Gresford, B.**
Thomas – *T. of Gwydir, B.**
Thomas – *T. of Macclesfield,*
*B.**
Thomas – *T. of Swynnerton,*
*B.**
Thomas – *T. of Walliswood,*
*B.**
Thomson – *T. of Fleet, B.*
Thomson – *T. of Monifieth,*
*B.**
Thynn – *Bath, M.*
Tottenham – *Ely, M.*
Trefusis – *Clinton, B.*
Trench – *Ashtown, B.*
Trevor-Roper – *D. of*
*Glanton, B.**
Tufton – *Hothfield, B.*
Turner – *Netherthorpe, B.*
Turner – *T. of Camden, B.**
Turnour – *Winterton, E.*
Tyrell-Kenyon – *Kenyon, B.*
Vanden-Bempde-Johnstone
– *Derwent, B.*
Vane – *Barnard, B.*
Vane-Tempest-Stewart –
Londonderry, M.
Vanneck – *Huntingfield, B.*
Vaughan – *Lisburne, E.*
Vereker – *Gort, V.*
Verney – *Willoughby de*
Broke, B.
Vernon – *Lyveden, B.*
Vesey – *De Vesci, V.*
Villiers – *Clarendon, E.*
Vincent – *V. of Coleshill, B.**
Vivian – *Swansea, B.*
Wade – *W. of Chorlton, B.**
Waldegrave – *W. of North*
*Hill, B.**
Walker – *W. of Doncaster,*
*B.**
Walker – *W. of Worcester,*
*B.**
Wallace – *W. of Coslany, B.**
Wallace – *W. of Saltaire, B.**
Wallop – *Portsmouth, E.*
Walton – *W. of Detchant, B.**
Ward – *Bangor, V.*
Ward – *Dudley, E.*
Warrender – *Bruntisfield, B.*
Warwick – *W. of Undercliffe,*
*B.**
Watson – *Manton, B.*
Watson – *W. of Invergowrie,*
*B.**
Watson – *W. of Richmond,*
*B.**
Webber – *Lloyd-Webber, B.**
Wedderburn – *W. of*
*Charlton, B.**
Weir – *Inverforth, B.*
Weld-Forester – *Forester, B.*
Wellesley – *Cowley, E.*
Wellesley – *Wellington, D.*

Westenra – *Rossmore, B.*
White – *Annaly, B.*
White – *Hanningfield, B.**
White – *J. of Holland Park,*
*B.**
Whiteley – *Marchamley, B.*
Whitfield – *Kenswood, B.*
Williams – *W. of Crosby, B.**
Williams – *W. of Elvel, B.**
Williams – *W. of Mostyn, B.**
Williamson – *Forres, B.*
Williamson – *W. of Horton,*
*B.**
Willoughby – *Middleton, B.*
Wills – *Dulverton, B.*
Wilson – *Moran, B.*
Wilson – *Nunburnholme, B.*
Wilson – *W. of Tillyorn, B.**
Windsor – *Gloucester, D.*
Windsor – *Kent, D.*
Windsor-Clive – *Plymouth,*
E.
Wingfield – *Powerscourt, V.*
Winn – *St Oswald, B.*
Wodehouse – *Kimberley, E.*
Wolfson – *W. of Sunningdale,*
*B.**
Wood – *Halifax, E.*
Wood – *Holderness, B.**
Woodhouse – *Terrington, B.*
Woolmer – *W. of Leeds, B.**
Wright – *W. of Richmond,*
*B.**
Wyndham – *Egremont, B.*
Wyndham-Quin –
Dunraven and Mount-Earl,
E.
Wynn – *Newborough, B.*
Yarde-Buller – *Churston, B.*
Yerburgh – *Alvingham, B.*
Yorke – *Hardwicke, E.*
Young – *Kennet, B.*
Young – *Y. of Dartington,*
*B.**
Young – *Y. of Graffham, B.**
Young – *Y. of Old Scone, B.**
Younger – *Y. of Leckie, V.*

Orders of Chivalry

THE MOST NOBLE ORDER OF THE GARTER (1348)

KG

Ribbon, Blue

Motto, Honi soit qui mal y pense (*Shame on him who thinks evil of it*)

The number of Knights Companions is limited to 24

SOVEREIGN OF THE ORDER
The Queen

LADIES OF THE ORDER

HM Queen Elizabeth the Queen Mother, 1936
HRH The Princess Royal, 1994

ROYAL KNIGHTS

HRH The Prince Philip, Duke of Edinburgh, 1947
HRH The Prince of Wales, 1958
HRH The Duke of Kent, 1985
HRH The Duke of Gloucester, 1997

EXTRA KNIGHTS COMPANIONS AND LADIES

HRH Princess Juliana of the Netherlands, 1958
HRH The Grand Duke of Luxembourg, 1972
HM The Queen of Denmark, 1979
HM The King of Sweden, 1983
HM The King of Spain, 1988
HM The Queen of the Netherlands, 1989
HIM The Emperor of Japan, 1998

KNIGHTS AND LADY COMPANIONS

The Earl of Longford, 1971
The Marquess of Abergavenny, 1974
The Duke of Grafton, 1976
The Duke of Norfolk, 1983
The Lord Richardson of Duntisbourne, 1983
The Lord Carrington, 1985
The Lord Callaghan of Cardiff, 1987
The Viscount Leverhulme, 1988
The Lord Hailsham of St Marylebone, 1988
The Duke of Wellington, 1990
Field Marshal the Lord Bramall, 1990
Sir Edward Heath, 1992
The Viscount Ridley, 1992
The Lord Sainsbury of Preston Candover, 1992
The Lord Ashburton, 1994
The Lord Kingsdown, 1994

Sir Ninian Stephen, 1994
The Baroness Thatcher, 1995
Sir Edmund Hillary, 1995
The Duke of Devonshire, 1996
Sir Timothy Colman, 1996
The Duke of Abercorn, 1999
Sir William Gladstone, 1999

Prelate, The Bishop of Winchester
Chancellor, The Lord Carrington, KG, GCMG, CH, MC
Register, The Dean of Windsor
Garter King of Arms, P. Gwynn-Jones, CVO
Gentleman Usher of the Black Rod, Gen. Sir Edward Jones, KCB, CBE
Secretary, D. H. B. Chesshyre, LVO

THE MOST ANCIENT AND MOST NOBLE ORDER OF THE THISTLE (REVIVED 1687)

KT

Ribbon, Green

Motto, Nemo me impune lacessit (*No one provokes me with impunity*)

The number of Knights is limited to 16

SOVEREIGN OF THE ORDER
The Queen

LADY OF THE THISTLE

HM Queen Elizabeth the Queen Mother, 1937

ROYAL KNIGHTS

HRH The Prince Philip, Duke of Edinburgh, 1952
HRH The Prince of Wales, Duke of Rothesay, 1977

KNIGHTS AND LADIES

The Earl of Wemyss and March, 1966
Sir Donald Cameron of Lochiel, 1973
The Duke of Buccleuch and Queensberry, 1978
The Earl of Elgin and Kincardine, 1981
The Lord Thomson of Monifieth, 1981
The Lord MacLehose of Beoch, 1983
The Earl of Airlie, 1985
Capt. Sir Iain Tennant, 1986
The Viscount Younger of Leckie, 1995

The Viscount of Arbuthnott, 1996
The Earl of Crawford and Balcarres, 1996
Lady Marion Fraser, 1996
The Lord Macfarlane of Bearsden, 1996
The Lord Mackay of Clashfern, 1997

Chancellor, The Duke of Buccleuch and Queensberry, KT, VRD
Dean, The Very Revd G. I. Macmillan, CVO
Secretary and Lord Lyon King of Arms, Sir Malcolm Innes of Edingight, KCVO, WS
Usher of the Green Rod, Rear-Adm. C. H. Layman, CB, DSO, LVO

THE MOST HONOURABLE ORDER OF THE BATH (1725)

GCB *Military*   GCB *Civil*

GCB   Knight (or Dame) Grand Cross
KCB   Knight Commander
DCB   Dame Commander
CB   Companion

Ribbon, Crimson

Motto, Tria juncta in uno (*Three joined in one*)

Remodelled 1815, and enlarged many times since. The Order is divided into civil and military divisions. Women became eligible for the Order from 1 January 1971

THE SOVEREIGN

GREAT MASTER AND FIRST OR PRINCIPAL KNIGHT GRAND CROSS
HRH The Prince of Wales, KG, KT, GCB

Dean of the Order, The Dean of Westminster
Bath King of Arms, Gen. Sir Brian Kenny, GCB, CBE
Registrar and Secretary, Rear-Adm. D. E. Macey, CB
Genealogist, P. Gwynn-Jones, CVO
Gentleman Usher of the Scarlet Rod, Air Vice-Marshal Sir Richard Peirse, KCVO, CB
Deputy Secretary, The Secretary of the Central Chancery of the Orders of Knighthood
Chancery, Central Chancery of the Orders of Knighthood, St James's Palace, London SW1A 1BH

THE ORDER OF MERIT (1902)

OM *Military*   OM *Civil*

OM

Ribbon, Blue and crimson

This Order is designed as a special distinction for eminent men and women without conferring a knighthood upon them. The Order is limited in numbers to 24, with the addition of foreign honorary members. Membership is of two kinds, military and civil, the badge of the former having crossed swords, and the latter oak leaves

THE SOVEREIGN

HRH The Prince Philip, Duke of Edinburgh, 1968
Sir George Edwards, 1971
Revd Prof. Owen Chadwick, KBE, 1983
Sir Andrew Huxley, 1983
Frederick Sanger, 1986
Prof. Sir Ernst Gombrich, 1988
Dr Max Perutz, 1988
Dame Cicely Saunders, 1989
The Lord Porter of Luddenham, 1989
The Baroness Thatcher, 1990
Dame Joan Sutherland, 1991
Prof. Francis Crick, 1991
Dame Ninette de Valois, 1992
Sir Michael Atiyah, 1992
Lucian Freud, 1993
The Lord Jenkins of Hillhead, 1993
Sir Aaron Klug, 1995
Sir John Gielgud, 1996
The Lord Foster of Thames Bank, 1997
Sir Denis Rooke, 1997
HE Cardinal Basil Hume, 1999 (died 1999)
Honorary Member, Nelson Mandela, 1995

Secretary and Registrar, Sir Edward Ford, GCVO, KCB, ERD
Chancery, Central Chancery of the Orders of Knighthood, St James's Palace, London SW1A 1BH

THE MOST DISTINGUISHED ORDER OF ST MICHAEL AND ST GEORGE (1818)

GCMG   KCMG

GCMG   Knight (or Dame) Grand Cross
KCMG   Knight Commander
DCMG   Dame Commander
CMG   Companion

Ribbon, Saxon blue, with scarlet centre
Motto, Auspicium melioris aevi (*Token of a better age*)

THE SOVEREIGN

GRAND MASTER
HRH The Duke of Kent, KG, GCMG, GCVO, ADC

Prelate, The Rt. Revd Simon Barrington-Ward
Chancellor, Sir Antony Acland, GCMG, GCVO
Secretary, The Permanent Under-Secretary of State at the Foreign and Commonwealth Office and Head of the Diplomatic Service
Registrar, Sir John Graham, Bt., GCMG
King of Arms, Sir Ewen Fergusson, GCMG, GCVO
Gentleman Usher of the Blue Rod, Sir John Margetson, KCMG
Dean, The Dean of St Paul's
Deputy Secretary, The Secretary of the Central Chancery of the Orders of Knighthood
Chancery, Central Chancery of the Orders of Knighthood, St James's Palace, London SW1A 1BH

THE MOST EMINENT ORDER OF THE INDIAN EMPIRE (1868)

GCIE   Knight Grand Commander
KCIE   Knight Commander
CIE   Companion

Ribbon, Imperial purple
Motto, Imperatricis auspiciis (*Under the auspices of the Empress*)

THE SOVEREIGN

Registrar, The Secretary of the Central Chancery of the Orders of Knighthood
No conferments have been made since 1947

THE IMPERIAL ORDER OF THE CROWN OF INDIA (1877) FOR LADIES

CI

Badge, the royal cipher in jewels within an oval, surmounted by an heraldic crown and attached to a bow of light blue watered ribbon, edged white
The honour does not confer any rank or title upon the recipient
No conferments have been made since 1947

HM The Queen, 1947
HM Queen Elizabeth the Queen Mother, 1931
HRH The Princess Margaret, Countess of Snowdon, 1947
HRH Princess Alice, Duchess of Gloucester, 1937

THE ROYAL VICTORIAN ORDER (1896)

GCVO   KCVO

GCVO   Knight or Dame Grand Cross
KCVO   Knight Commander
DCVO   Dame Commander
CVO   Commander
LVO   Lieutenant
MVO   Member

Ribbon, Blue, with red and white edges
Motto, Victoria

THE SOVEREIGN
GRAND MASTER
HM Queen Elizabeth the Queen Mother

Chancellor, The Lord Chamberlain
Secretary, The Keeper of the Privy Purse
Registrar, The Secretary of the Central Chancery of the Orders of Knighthood
Chaplain, The Chaplain of the Queen's Chapel of the Savoy
Hon. Genealogist, D. H. B. Chesshyre, LVO

THE MOST EXCELLENT ORDER OF THE BRITISH EMPIRE (1917)

GBE   KBE

The Order was divided into military and civil divisions in December 1918

GBE Knight or Dame Grand Cross
KBE Knight Commander
DBE Dame Commander
CBE Commander
OBE Officer
MBE Member

Ribbon, Rose pink edged with pearl grey with vertical pearl stripe in centre (military division); without vertical pearl stripe (civil division)
Motto, For God and the Empire

THE SOVEREIGN

GRAND MASTER
HRH The Prince Philip, Duke of Edinburgh, KG, KT, OM, GBE, PC

Prelate, The Bishop of London
King of Arms, Air Chief Marshal Sir Patrick Hine, GCB, GBE
Registrar, The Secretary of the Central Chancery of the Orders of Knighthood
Secretary, The Secretary of the Cabinet and Head of the Home Civil Service
Dean, The Dean of St Paul's
Gentleman Usher of the Purple Rod, Sir Robin Gillett, Bt., GBE, RD
Chancery, Central Chancery of the Orders of Knighthood, St James's Palace, London SW1A 1BH

ORDER OF THE COMPANIONS OF HONOUR (1917)

CH

Ribbon, Carmine, with gold edges

This Order consists of one class only and carries with it no title. The number of awards is limited to 65 (excluding honorary members)

Anthony, Rt. Hon. John, 1981
Ashley of Stoke, The Lord, 1975
Astor, Hon. David, 1993
Attenborough, Sir David, 1995
Baker, Dame Janet, 1993
Baker of Dorking, The Lord, 1992

Brenner, Sydney, 1986
Brook, Peter, 1998
Brooke, Rt. Hon. Peter, 1992
Carrington, The Lord, 1983
Cledwyn of Penrhos, The Lord, 1976
de Valois, Dame Ninette, 1981
De Chastelain, Gen. John, 1999
Doll, Prof. Sir Richard, 1995
Fraser, Rt. Hon. Malcolm, 1977
Freud, Lucian, 1983
Gielgud, Sir John, 1977
Glenamara, The Lord, 1976
Gorton, Rt. Hon. Sir John, 1971
Guinness, Sir Alec, 1994
Hailsham of St Marylebone, The Lord, 1974
Hawking, Prof. Stephen, 1989
Healey, The Lord, 1979
Heseltine, Rt. Hon. Michael, 1997
Hobsbawm, Prof. Eric, 1998
Hockney, David, 1997
Howe of Aberavon, The Lord, 1996
Hurd of Westwell, The Lord, 1995
Jones, James, 1977
King, Rt. Hon. Tom, 1992
Lange, Rt. Hon. David, 1989
Lasdun, Sir Denys, 1995
Major, Rt. Hon. John, 1999
Milstein, César, 1994
Owen, The Lord, 1994
Patten, Rt. Hon. Christopher, 1998
Perutz, Dr Max, 1975
Powell, Anthony, 1987
Powell, Sir Philip, 1984
Runciman, Hon. Sir Steven, 1984
Riley, Bridget, 1999
Sanger, Frederick, 1981
Sisson, Charles, 1993
Smith, Sir John, 1993
Somare, Rt. Hon. Sir Michael, 1978
Talboys, Rt. Hon. Sir Brian, 1981
Tebbit, The Lord, 1987
Trudeau, Rt. Hon. Pierre, 1984
Widdowson, Dr Elsie, 1993
Honorary Members, Lee Kuan Yew, 1970; Dr Joseph Luns, 1971

Secretary and Registrar, The Secretary of the Central Chancery of the Orders of Knighthood

THE DISTINGUISHED SERVICE ORDER (1886)

DSO

Ribbon, Red, with blue edges

Bestowed in recognition of especial services in action of commissioned officers in the Navy, Army and Royal Air Force and (since 1942) Mercantile Marine. The members are Companions only. A Bar may be awarded for any additional act of service

THE IMPERIAL SERVICE ORDER (1902)

ISO

Ribbon, Crimson, with blue centre

Appointment as Companion of this Order is open to members of the Civil Services whose eligibility is determined by the grade they hold. The Order consists of The Sovereign and Companions to a number not exceeding 1,900, of whom 1,300 may belong to the Home Civil Services and 600 to Overseas Civil Services. The then Prime Minister announced in March 1993 that he would make no further recommendations for appointments to the Order.

Secretary, The Secretary of the Cabinet and Head of the Home Civil Service
Registrar, The Secretary of the Central Chancery of the Orders of Knighthood, St James's Palace, London SW1A 1BH

THE ROYAL VICTORIAN CHAIN (1902)

It confers no precedence on its holders

HM THE QUEEN

HM Queen Elizabeth the Queen Mother, 1937

HRH Princess Juliana of the Netherlands, 1950
HM The King of Thailand, 1960
HM King Zahir Shah of Afghanistan, 1971
HM The Queen of Denmark, 1974
HM The King of Nepal, 1975
HM The King of Sweden, 1975
The Lord Coggan, 1980
HM The Queen of the Netherlands, 1982
Gen. Antonio Eanes, 1985
HM The King of Spain, 1986
HM The King of Saudi Arabia, 1987
HRH The Princess Margaret, Countess of Snowdon, 1990
The Lord Runcie, 1991
The Lord Charteris of Amisfield, 1992
HE Richard von Weizsäcker, 1992
HM The King of Norway, 1994
The Earl of Airlie, 1997

Baronetage and Knightage

BARONETS

Style, 'Sir' before forename and surname, followed by 'Bt.'
Wife's style, 'Lady' followed by surname
For forms of address, *see* page 135

There are five different creations of baronetcies: Baronets of England (creations dating from 1611); Baronets of Ireland (creations dating from 1619); Baronets of Scotland or Nova Scotia (creations dating from 1625); Baronets of Great Britain (creations after the Act of Union 1707 which combined the kingdoms of England and Scotland); and Baronets of the United Kingdom (creations after the union of Great Britain and Ireland in 1801).

Badge of Baronets of the United Kingdom

Badge of Baronets of Nova Scotia

Badge of Ulster

The patent of creation limits the destination of a baronetcy, usually to male descendants of the first baronet, although special remainders allow the baronetcy to pass, if the male issue of sons fail, to the male issue of daughters of the first baronet. In the case of baronetcies of Scotland or Nova Scotia, a special remainder of 'heirs male and of tailzie' allows the baronetcy to descend to heirs general, including women. There are four existing Scottish baronets with such a remainder.

The Official Roll of Baronets is kept at the Home Office by the Registrar of the Baronetage. Anyone who considers that he is entitled to be entered on the Roll may petition the Crown through the Home Secretary. Every person succeeding to a baronetcy must exhibit proofs of succession to the Home Secretary. A person whose name is not entered on the Official Roll will not be addressed or mentioned by the title of baronet in any official document, nor will he be accorded precedence as a baronet.

BARONETCIES EXTINCT SINCE THE LAST EDITION
Butt (*cr.* 1929); Edwards (*cr.* 1921); Gibson (*cr.* 1926)

Registrar of the Baronetage, Miss C. E. C. Sinclair
Assistant Registrar, Mrs F. G. Bright
Office, Home Office, 50 Queen Anne's Gate, London
SW1H 9AT. Tel: 0171-273 3498

KNIGHTS

Style, 'Sir' before forename and surname, followed by appropriate post-nominal initials if a Knight Grand Cross, Knight Grand Commander or Knight Commander
Wife's style, 'Lady' followed by surname

For forms of address, *see* page 135
The prefix 'Sir' is not used by knights who are clerics of the Church of England, who do not receive the accolade. Their wives are entitled to precedence as the wife of a knight but not to the style of 'Lady'.

ORDERS OF KNIGHTHOOD

Knight Grand Cross, Knight Grand Commander, and Knight Commander are the higher classes of the Orders of Chivalry (*see* pages 171–3). Honorary knighthoods of these Orders may be conferred on men who are citizens of countries of which The Queen is not head of state. As a rule, the prefix 'Sir' is not used by honorary knights.

KNIGHTS BACHELOR

The Knights Bachelor do not constitute a Royal Order, but comprise the surviving representation of the ancient State Orders of Knighthood. The Register of Knights Bachelor, instituted by James I in the 17th century, lapsed, and in 1908 a voluntary association under the title of The Society of Knights (now The Imperial Society of Knights Bachelor by Royal Command) was formed with the primary objects of continuing the various registers dating from 1257 and obtaining the uniform registration of every created Knight Bachelor. In 1926 a design for a badge to be worn by Knights Bachelor was approved and adopted; in 1974 a neck badge and miniature were added.

Knight Principal, Sir Conrad Swan, KCVO
Chairman of Council, Sir Richard Gaskell, Kt.
Prelate, Rt. Revd and Rt. Hon. The Bishop of London
Registrar, Sir Robert Balchin
Hon. Treasurer, Sir Paul Judge, Kt.
Clerk to the Council, R. M. Esden, MBE
Office, 21 Old Buildings, Lincoln's Inn, London WC2A 3UJ

LIST OF BARONETS AND KNIGHTS

Revised to 31 August 1999
Peers are not included in this list

†	Not registered on the Official Roll of the Baronetage at the time of going to press
()	The date of creation of the baronetcy is given in parenthesis
I	Baronet of Ireland
NS	Baronet of Nova Scotia
S	Baronet of Scotland

If a baronet or knight has a double-barrelled or hyphenated surname, he is listed under the final element of the name
A full entry in italic type indicates that the recipient of a knighthood died during the year in which the honour was conferred. The name is included for purposes of record

Abal, Sir Tei, Kt., CBE

Abbott, Sir Albert Francis, Kt., CBE

Abbott, *Adm.* Sir Peter Charles, GBE, KCB

Abdy, Sir Valentine Robert Duff, Bt. (1850)

Abel, Sir Seselo (Cecil) Charles Geoffrey, Kt., OBE

Abercromby, Sir Ian George, Bt. (s. 1636)

Acheson, *Prof.* Sir (Ernest) Donald, KBE

Ackers, Sir James George, Kt.

Ackroyd, Sir Timothy Robert Whyte, Bt. (1956)

Acland, Sir Antony Arthur, GCMG, GCVO

Acland, *Lt.-Col.* Sir (Christopher) Guy (Dyke), Bt., MVO (1890)

Acland, Sir John Dyke, Bt. (1644)

Acland, *Maj.-Gen.* Sir John Hugh Bevil, KCB, CBE

Adam, Sir Christopher Eric Forbes, Bt. (1917)

Adams, Sir Philip George Doyne, KCMG

Adams, Sir William James, KCMG

Adamson, Sir (William Owen) Campbell, Kt.

Adrien, *Hon.* Sir Maurice Latour-, Kt.

Adsetts, Sir William Norman, Kt., OBE

Adye, Sir John Anthony, KCMG

Agnew, Sir Crispin Hamlyn, Bt. (s. 1629)

Agnew, Sir John Keith, Bt. (1895)

Aiken, *Air Chief Marshal* Sir John Alexander Carlisle, KCB

Aikens, Sir Richard John Pearson, Kt., QC

Ainsworth, Sir (Thomas) David, Bt. (1916)

Aird, *Capt.* Sir Alastair Sturgis, GCVO

Aird, Sir (George) John, Bt. (1901)

Airey, Sir Lawrence, KCB

Airy, *Maj.-Gen.* Sir Christopher John, KCVO, CBE

Aitchison, Sir Charles Walter de Lancey, Bt. (1938)

Akehurst, *Gen.* Sir John Bryan, KCB, CBE

Albu, Sir George, Bt. (1912)

Alcock, *Air Chief Marshal* Sir (Robert James) Michael, GCB, KBE

Aldous, *Rt. Hon.* Sir William, Kt.

Alexander, Sir Charles Gundry, Bt. (1945)

Alexander, Sir Claud Hagart-, Bt. (1886)

Alexander, Sir Douglas, Bt. (1921)

Alexander, Sir (John) Lindsay, Kt.

Alexander, *Prof.* Sir Kenneth John Wilson, Kt.

Alexander, Sir Michael O'Donal Bjarne, GCMG

†Alexander, Sir Patrick Desmond William Cable-, Bt. (1809)

Allan, Sir Anthony James Allan Havelock-, Bt. (1858)

Allen, *Prof.* Sir Geoffrey, Kt., Ph.D., FRS

Allen, Sir John Derek, Kt., CBE

Allen, *Hon.* Sir Peter Austin Philip Jermyn, Kt.

Allen, Sir Thomas Boaz, Kt., CBE

Allen, Sir William Guilford, Kt.

Allen, Sir (William) Kenneth (Gwynne), Kt.

Alleyne, Sir George Allanmoore Ogarren, Kt.

Alleyne, *Revd* Sir John Olpherts Campbell, Bt. (1769)

Alliance, Sir David, Kt., CBE

Allinson, Sir (Walter) Leonard, KCVO, CMG

Alliott, *Hon.* Sir John Downes, Kt.

Allison, *Air Chief Marshal* Sir John Shakespeare, KCB, CBE

Alment, Sir (Edward) Anthony John, Kt.

Althaus, Sir Nigel Frederick, Kt.

Ambo, *Rt. Revd* George, KBE

Amet, *Hon.* Sir Arnold Karibone, Kt.

Amies, Sir (Edwin) Hardy, KCVO

Amory, Sir Ian Heathcoat, Bt. (1874)

Anderson, Sir John Anthony, KBE

Anderson, *Maj.-Gen.* Sir John Evelyn, KBE

Anderson, Sir John Muir, Kt., CMG

Anderson, *Hon.* Sir Kevin Victor, Kt.

Anderson, Sir Leith Reinsford Steven, Kt., CBE

Anderson, *Vice-Adm.* Sir Neil Dudley, KBE, CB

Anderson, *Prof.* Sir (William) Ferguson, Kt., OBE

Anderton, Sir (Cyril) James, Kt., CBE, QPM

Andrew, Sir Robert John, KCB

Andrews, Sir Derek Henry, KCB, CBE

Andrews, *Hon.* Sir Dormer George, Kt.

Angus, Sir Michael Richardson, Kt.

Annesley, Sir Hugh Norman, Kt., QPM

Anson, *Vice-Adm.* Sir Edward Rosebery, KCB

Anson, Sir John, KCB

Anson, *Rear-Adm.* Sir Peter, Bt., CB (1831)

Anstey, *Brig.* Sir John, Kt., CBE, TD

Anstruther, *Maj.* Sir Ralph Hugo, Bt., GCVO, MC (s. 1694)

Antico, Sir Tristan Venus, Kt.

Antrobus, Sir Charles James, GCMG, OBE

Antrobus, Sir Edward Philip, Bt. (1815)

Appleyard, Sir Leonard Vincent, KCMG

Appleyard, Sir Raymond Kenelm, KBE

Arbuthnot, Sir Keith Robert Charles, Bt. (1823)

Arbuthnot, Sir William Reierson, Bt. (1964)

Arbuthnott, *Prof.* Sir John Peebles, Kt., Ph.D., FRSE

Archdale, *Capt.* Sir Edward Folmer, Bt., DSC, RN (1928)

Arculus, Sir Ronald, KCMG, KCVO

Armitage, *Air Chief Marshal* Sir Michael John, KCB, CBE

Armour, *Prof.* Sir James, Kt., CBE

†Armstrong, Sir Christopher John Edmund Stuart, Bt., MBE (1841)

Armytage, Sir John Martin, Bt. (1738)

Arnold, *Rt. Hon.* Sir John Lewis, Kt.

Arnold, Sir Malcolm Henry, Kt., CBE

Arnold, Sir Thomas Richard, Kt.

Arnott, Sir Alexander John Maxwell, Bt. (1896)

Arnott, *Prof.* Sir (William) Melville, Kt., TD, MD

Arrindell, Sir Clement Athelston, GCMG, GCVO, QC

Arthur, *Lt.-Gen.* Sir (John) Norman Stewart, KCB

Arthur, Sir Stephen John, Bt. (1841)

Ash, *Prof.* Sir Eric Albert, Kt., CBE, FRS, FREng.

†Ashburnham, Sir James Fleetwood, Bt. (1661)

Ashe, Sir Derick Rosslyn, KCMG

Ashley, Sir Bernard Albert, Kt.

Ashmore, *Admiral of the Fleet* Sir Edward Beckwith, GCB, DSC

Ashmore, *Vice-Adm.* Sir Peter William Beckwith, KCB, KCVO, DSC

Ashworth, Sir Herbert, Kt.

Aske, *Revd* Sir Conan, Bt. (1922)

Askew, Sir Bryan, Kt.

Asscher, Prof. (Adolf) William, Kt., MD, FRCP

Astill, *Hon.* Sir Michael John, Kt.

Aston, Sir Harold George, Kt., CBE

Astor, *Hon.* Sir John Jacob, Kt., MBE

Astwood, *Hon.* Sir James Rufus, KBE

Atcherley, Sir Harold Winter, Kt.

Atiyah, Sir Michael Francis, Kt., OM, Ph.D., FRS

Atkins, *Rt. Hon.* Sir Robert James, Kt.

Atkinson, *Air Marshal* Sir David William, KBE

Atkinson, Sir Frederick John, KCB

Atkinson, Sir John Alexander, KCB, DFC

Atkinson, Sir Robert, Kt., DSC, FREng.

Atopare, Sir Sailas, GCMG

Attenborough, Sir David Frederick, Kt., CH, CVO, CBE, FRS

Atwill, Sir (Milton) John (Napier), Kt.

Audland, Sir Christopher John, KCMG

Audley, Sir George Bernard, Kt.

Augier, *Prof.* Sir Fitz-Roy Richard, Kt.

Auld, *Rt. Hon.* Sir Robin Ernest, Kt.

Austin, Sir Anthony Leonard, Bt. (1894)

Austin, *Vice-Adm.* Sir Peter Murray, KCB

Austin, *Air Marshal* Sir Roger Mark, KCB, AFC

Axford, Sir William Ian, Kt.

Ayckbourn, Sir Alan, Kt., CBE

Aykroyd, Sir James Alexander Frederic, Bt. (1929)
Aykroyd, Sir William Miles, Bt., MC (1920)
Aylmer, Sir Richard John, Bt. (I. 1622)
Bacha, Sir Bhinod, Kt., CMG
Backhouse, Sir Jonathan Roger, Bt. (1901)
Bacon, Sir Nicholas Hickman Ponsonby, Bt. *Premier Baronet of England* (1611 and 1627)
Bacon, Sir Sidney Charles, Kt., CB, FREng.
Baddeley, Sir John Wolsey Beresford, Bt. (1922)
Baddiley, *Prof.* Sir James, Kt., Ph.D., D.SC., FRS, FRSE
Badge, Sir Peter Gilmour Noto, Kt.
Badger, Sir Geoffrey Malcolm, Kt.
Baer, Sir Jack Mervyn Frank, Kt.
Bagge, Sir (John) Jeremy Picton, Bt. (1867)
Bagnall, *Air Marshal* Sir Anthony John Crowther, KCB, OBE
Bagnall, *Field Marshal* Sir Nigel Thomas, GCB, CVO, MC
Bailey, Sir Alan Marshall, KCB
Bailey, Sir Brian Harry, Kt., OBE
Bailey, Sir Derrick Thomas Louis, Bt., DFC (1919)
Bailey, Sir John Bilsland, KCB
Bailey, Sir Richard John, Kt., CBE
Bailey, Sir Stanley Ernest, Kt., CBE, QPM
Bailhache, Sir Philip Martin, Kt.
Baillie, Sir Gawaine George Hope, Bt. (1823)
Baines, *Prof.* Sir George Grenfell-, Kt., OBE
Baird, Sir David Charles, Bt. (1809)
†Baird, Sir James Andrew Gardiner, Bt. (S. 1695)
Baird, *Lt.-Gen.* Sir James Parlane, KBE, MD
Baird, *Air Marshal* Sir John Alexander, KBE
Baird, *Vice-Adm.* Sir Thomas Henry Eustace, KCB
Bairsto, *Air Marshal* Sir Peter Edward, KBE, CB
Baker, Sir Bryan William, Kt.
Baker, Sir Robert George Humphrey Sherston-, Bt. (1796)
Baker, *Hon.* Sir (Thomas) Scott (Gillespie), Kt.
Balchin, Sir Robert George Alexander, Kt.
Balcombe, *Rt. Hon.* Sir (Alfred) John, Kt.
Balderstone, Sir James Schofield, Kt.
Baldwin, *Prof.* Sir Jack Edward, Kt., FRS
Baldwin, Sir Peter Robert, KCB
Ball, *Air Marshal* Sir Alfred Henry Wynne, KCB, DSO, DFC
Ball, Sir Charles Irwin, Bt. (1911)
Ball, Sir Christopher John Elinger, Kt.
Ball, *Prof.* Sir Robert James, Kt., Ph.D.

Bamford, Sir Anthony Paul, Kt.
Banham, Sir John Michael Middlecott, Kt.
Bannerman, Sir David Gordon, Bt., OBE (S. 1682)
Bannister, Sir Roger Gilbert, Kt., CBE, DM, FRCP
Barber, Sir (Thomas) David, Bt. (1960)
Barbour, *Very Revd* Sir Robert Alexander Stewart, KCVO, MC
Barclay, Sir Colville Herbert Sanford, Bt. (S. 1668)
Barclay, Sir Peter Maurice, Kt., CBE
Barder, Sir Brian Leon, KCMG
Barker, Sir Alwyn Bowman, Kt., CMG
Barker, Sir Colin, Kt.
Barker, *Hon.* Sir (Richard) Ian, Kt.
Barlow, Sir Christopher Hilaro, Bt. (1803)
Barlow, Sir Frank, Kt., CBE
Barlow, Sir (George) William, Kt., FREng.
Barlow, Sir John Kemp, Bt. (1907)
Barlow, Sir Thomas Erasmus, Bt., DSC (1902)
Barnard, Sir Joseph Brian, Kt.
Barnes, Sir (James) David (Francis), Kt., CBE
Barnes, Sir Kenneth, KCB
Barnewall, Sir Reginald Robert, Bt. (I. 1623)
Baron, Sir Thomas, Kt., CBE
Barraclough, *Air Chief Marshal* Sir John, KCB, CBE, DFC, AFC
Barraclough, Sir Kenneth James Priestley, Kt., CBE, TD
Barran, Sir David Haven, Kt.
Barran, Sir John Napoleon Ruthven, Bt. (1895)
Barratt, Sir Lawrence Arthur, Kt.
Barratt, Sir Richard Stanley, Kt., CBE, QPM
Barrett, *Lt.-Gen.* Sir David William Scott-, KBE, MC
Barrett, Sir Stephen Jeremy, KCMG
Barrington, Sir Alexander (Fitzwilliam Croker), Bt. (1831)
Barrington, Sir Nicholas John, KCMG, CVO
Barron, Sir Donald James, Kt.
Barrow, *Capt.* Sir Richard John Uniacke, Bt. (1835)
Barrowclough, Sir Anthony Richard, Kt., QC
Barry, Sir (Lawrence) Edward (Anthony Tress), Bt. (1899)
†Bartlett, Sir Andrew Alan, Bt. (1913)
Barttelot, *Col.* Sir Brian Walter de Stopham, Bt., OBE (1875)
Batchelor, Sir Ivor Ralph Campbell, Kt., CBE
Bate, Sir David Lindsay, KBE
Bate, Sir (Walter) Edwin, Kt., OBE
Bates, Sir Geoffrey Voltelin, Bt., MC (1880)
Bates, Sir Malcolm Rowland, Kt.
Bates, Sir Richard Dawson Hoult, Bt. (1937)
Batho, Sir Peter Ghislain, Bt. (1928)

Bathurst, *Admiral of the Fleet* Sir (David) Benjamin, GCB
Bathurst, Sir Frederick John Charles Gordon Hervey-, Bt. (1818)
Bathurst, Sir Maurice Edward, Kt., CMG, CBE, QC
Batten, Sir John Charles, KCVO
Battersby, *Prof.* Sir Alan Rushton, Kt., FRS
Battishill, Sir Anthony Michael William, GCB
Batty, Sir William Bradshaw, Kt., TD
Baxendell, Sir Peter Brian, Kt., CBE, FREng.
Bayliss, Sir Richard Ian Samuel, KCVO, MD, FRCP
Bayne, Sir Nicholas Peter, KCMG
Baynes, Sir John Christopher Malcolm, Bt. (1801)
Bazley, Sir Thomas John Sebastian, Bt. (1869)
Beach, *Gen.* Sir (William Gerald) Hugh, GBE, KCB, MC
Beale, *Lt.-Gen.* Sir Peter John, KBE, FRCP
Beament, Sir James William Longman, Kt., SC.D., FRS
Beamish, Sir Adrian John, KCMG
Beattie, *Hon.* Sir Alexander Craig, Kt.
Beattie, *Hon.* Sir David Stuart, GCMG, GCVO
Beauchamp, Sir Christopher Radstock Proctor-, Bt. (1745)
Beaumont, *Capt.* the Hon. Sir (Edward) Nicholas (Canning), KCVO
Beaumont, Sir George (Howland Francis), Bt. (1661)
Beaumont, Sir Richard Ashton, KCMG, OBE
Beavis, *Air Chief Marshal* Sir Michael Gordon, KCB, CBE, AFC
Becher, Sir William Fane Wrixon, Bt. (1831)
Beck, Sir Edgar Charles, Kt., CBE, FREng.
Beck, Sir Edgar Philip, Kt.
Beckett, *Capt.* Sir (Martyn) Gervase, Bt., MC (1921)
Beckett, Sir Terence Norman, KBE, FREng.
Bedingfeld, *Capt.* Sir Edmund George Felix Paston-, Bt. (1661)
Bedser, Sir Alec Victor, Kt., CBE
Beecham, Sir Jeremy Hugh, Kt.
Beecham, Sir John Stratford Roland, Bt. (1914)
Beeley, Sir Harold, KCMG, CBE
Beetham, *Marshal of the Royal Air Force* Sir Michael James, GCB, CBE, DFC, AFC
Beevor, Sir Thomas Agnew, Bt. (1784)
Beith, Sir John Greville Stanley, KCMG
Beldam, *Rt. Hon.* Sir (Alexander) Roy (Asplan), Kt.
Belich, Sir James, Kt.
Bell, Sir Brian Ernest, KBE

Bell, Sir (George) Raymond, KCMG, CB

Bell, Sir John Lowthian, Bt. (1885)

Bell, *Hon.* Sir Rodger, Kt.

Bell, Sir (William) Ewart, KCB

Bell, Sir William Hollin Dayrell Morrison-, Bt. (1905)

Bellew, Sir Henry Charles Gratton-, Bt. (1838)

Bellinger, Sir Robert Ian, GBE

†Bellingham, Sir Anthony Edward Norman, Bt. (1796)

Bengough, *Col.* Sir Piers, KCVO, OBE

Benn, Sir (James) Jonathan, Bt. (1914)

Bennett, Sir Charles Moihi Te Arawaka, Kt., DSO

Bennett, *Air Vice-Marshal* Sir Erik Peter, KBE, CB

Bennett, *Rt. Hon.* Sir Frederic Mackarness, Kt.

Bennett, Sir Hubert, Kt.

Bennett, *Hon.* Sir Hugh Peter Derwyn, Kt.

Bennett, Sir John Mokonuiarangi, Kt.

Bennett, *Gen.* Sir Phillip Harvey, KBE, DSO

Bennett, Sir Reginald Frederick Brittain, Kt., VRD

Bennett, Sir Richard Rodney, Kt., CBE

Bennett, Sir Ronald Wilfrid Murdoch, Bt. (1929)

Benson, Sir Christopher John, Kt.

Benyon, Sir William Richard, Kt.

Beresford, Sir (Alexander) Paul, Kt., MP

Berger, *Vice-Adm.* Sir Peter Egerton Capel, KCB, LVO, DSC

Berghuser, *Hon.* Sir Eric, Kt., MBE

Berman, Sir Franklin Delow, KCMG

Bernard, Sir Dallas Edmund, Bt. (1954)

Berney, Sir Julian Reedham Stuart, Bt. (1620)

Berridge, *Prof.* Sir Michael John, Kt., FRS

Berrill, Sir Kenneth Ernest, GBE, KCB

Berriman, Sir David, Kt.

Berry, *Prof.* Sir Colin Leonard, Kt., FRCPath.

Berry, *Prof.* Sir Michael Victor, Kt., FRS

Berthon, *Vice-Adm.* Sir Stephen Ferrier, KCB

Berthoud, Sir Martin Seymour, KCVO, CMG

Best, Sir Richard Radford, KCVO, CBE

Bethune, *Hon.* Sir (Walter) Angus, Kt.

Bett, Sir Michael, Kt., CBE

Bevan, Sir Martyn Evan Evans, Bt. (1958)

Bevan, Sir Timothy Hugh, Kt.

Beverley, *Lt.-Gen.* Sir Henry York La Roche, KCB, OBE, RM

Bibby, Sir Derek James, Bt., MC (1959)

Bichard, Sir Michael George, KCB

Bick, *Hon.* Sir Martin James Moore-, Kt.

Bickersteth, *Rt. Revd* John Monier, KCVO

Biddulph, Sir Ian D'Olier, Bt. (1664)

Bide, Sir Austin Ernest, Kt.

Bidwell, Sir Hugh Charles Philip, GBE

Biggam, Sir Robin Adair, Kt.

Biggs, *Vice-Adm.* Sir Geoffrey William Roger, KCB

Biggs, Sir Norman Paris, Kt.

Bilas, Sir Angmai Simon, Kt., OBE

Billière, *Gen.* Sir Peter Edgar de la Cour de la, KCB, KBE, DSO, MC

Bingham, *Hon.* Sir Eardley Max, Kt., QC

Birch, Sir John Allan, KCVO, CMG

Birch, Sir Roger, Kt., CBE, QPM

Bird, Sir Richard Geoffrey Chapman, Bt. (1922)

Birkin, Sir John Christian William, Bt. (1905)

Birkin, Sir (John) Derek, Kt., TD

Birkmyre, Sir Archibald, Bt. (1921)

Birley, Sir Derek Sydney, Kt.

Birrell, Sir James Drake, Kt.

Birt, Sir John, Kt.

Birtwistle, Sir Harrison, Kt.

Bishop, Sir Frederick Arthur, Kt., CB, CVO

Bishop, Sir Michael David, Kt., CBE

Bisson, *Rt. Hon.* Sir Gordon Ellis, Kt.

Black, *Prof.* Sir Douglas Andrew Kilgour, Kt., MD, FRCP

Black, Sir James Whyte, Kt., FRCP, FRS

Black, *Adm.* Sir (John) Jeremy, GBE, KCB, DSO

Black, Sir Robert Brown, GCMG, OBE

Black, Sir Robert David, Bt. (1922)

Blackburne, *Hon.* Sir William Anthony, Kt.

Blacker, *Gen.* Sir (Anthony Stephen) Jeremy, KCB, CBE

Blacker, *Gen.* Sir Cecil Hugh, GCB, OBE, MC

Blackett, Sir Hugh Francis, Bt. (1673)

Blackham, *Vice-Adm.* Sir Jeremy Joe, KCB

Blacklock, *Surgeon Capt. Prof.* Sir Norman James, KCVO, OBE

Blackman, Sir Frank Milton, KCVO, OBE

Blackwell, Sir Basil Davenport, Kt., FREng.

Blackwood, Sir John Francis, Bt. (1814)

Blair, *Lt.-Gen.* Sir Chandos, KCVO, OBE, MC

Blair, Sir Edward Thomas Hunter, Bt. (1786)

Blake, Sir Alfred Lapthorn, KCVO, MC

Blake, Sir Francis Michael, Bt. (1907)

Blake, Sir Peter James, KBE

Blake, Sir (Thomas) Richard (Valentine), Bt. (I. 1622)

Blaker, Sir John, Bt. (1919)

Blakiston, Sir Ferguson Arthur James, Bt. (1763)

Blanch, Sir Malcolm, KCVO

Bland, Sir (Francis) Christopher (Buchan), Kt.

Bland, *Lt.-Col.* Sir Simon Claud Michael, KCVO

Blank, Sir Maurice Victor, Kt.

Blatherwick, Sir David Elliott Spiby, KCMG, OBE

Blelloch, Sir John Nial Henderson, KCB

Blennerhassett, Sir (Marmaduke) Adrian Francis William, Bt. (1809)

Blewitt, *Maj.* Sir Shane Gabriel Basil, GCVO

Blofeld, *Hon.* Sir John Christopher Calthorpe, Kt.

Blois, Sir Charles Nicholas Gervase, Bt. (1686)

Blomefield, Sir Thomas Charles Peregrine, Bt. (1807)

Bloomfield, Sir Kenneth Percy, KCB

Blosse, *Capt.* Sir Richard Hely Lynch-, Bt. (1622)

Blount, Sir Walter Edward Alpin, Bt., DSC (1642)

Blundell, Sir Thomas Leon, Kt., FRS

Blunden, Sir George, Kt.

†Blunden, Sir Philip Overington, Bt. (I. 1766)

Blunt, Sir David Richard Reginald Harvey, Bt. (1720)

Blyth, Sir Charles (Chay), Kt., CBE, BEM

Boardman, *Prof.* Sir John, Kt., FSA, FBA

Bodey, *Hon.* Sir David Roderick Lessiter, Kt., QC

Bodmer, Sir Walter Fred, Kt., Ph.D., FRS

Body, Sir Richard Bernard Frank Stewart, Kt., MP

Boevey, Sir Thomas Michael Blake Crawley-, Bt. (1784)

Bogan, Sir Nagora, KBE

Boileau, Sir Guy (Francis), Bt. (1838)

Boles, Sir Jeremy John Fortescue, Bt. (1922)

Boles, Sir John Dennis, Kt., MBE

Bolland, Sir Edwin, KCMG

Bollers, *Hon.* Sir Harold Brodie Smith, Kt.

Bolton, Sir Frederic Bernard, Kt., MC

Bona, Sir Kina, KBE

Bonallack, Sir Michael Francis, Kt., OBE

Bond, Sir John Reginald Hartnell, Kt.

Bond, Sir Kenneth Raymond Boyden, Kt.

Bond, *Prof.* Sir Michael Richard, Kt., FRCPsych., FRCPGlas., FRCSE

Bondi, *Prof.* Sir Hermann, KCB, FRS

Bonfield, Sir Peter Leahy, Kt., CBE, FREng.

Bonham, *Maj.* Sir Antony Lionel Thomas, Bt. (1852)

Bonington, Sir Christian John Storey, Kt., CBE

Bonsall, Sir Arthur Wilfred, KCMG, CBE

Bonsor, Sir Nicholas Cosmo, Bt. (1925)

Boolell, Sir Satcam, Kt.
Boord, Sir Nicolas John Charles, Bt. (1896)
Boorman, *Lt.-Gen.* Sir Derek, KCB
Booth, Sir Christopher Charles, Kt., MD, FRCP
Booth, Hon. Sir David Alwyn Gore-, KCMG, KCVO
Booth, Sir Douglas Allen, Bt. (1916)
Booth, Sir Gordon, KCMG, CVO
Booth, Sir Josslyn Henry Robert Gore-, Bt. (I. 1760)
Booth, Sir Michael Addison John Wheeler-, KCB
Boothby, Sir Brooke Charles, Bt. (1660)
Boreel, Sir Francis David, Bt. (1645)
Boreham, *Hon.* Sir Leslie Kenneth Edward, Kt.
Bornu, The Waziri of, KCMG, CBE
Borthwick, Sir John Thomas, Bt., MBE (1908)
Bossom, *Hon.* Sir Clive, Bt. (1953)
Boswall, Sir (Thomas) Alford Houstoun-, Bt. (1836)
Boswell, *Lt.-Gen.* Sir Alexander Crawford Simpson, KCB, CBE
Bosworth, Sir Neville Bruce Alfred, Kt., CBE
Bottomley, Sir James Reginald Alfred, KCMG
Boughey, Sir John George Fletcher, Bt. (1798)
Boulton, Sir Clifford John, GCB
Boulton, Sir (Harold Hugh) Christian, Bt. (1905)
Boulton, Sir William Whytehead, Bt., CBE, TD (1944)
Bourn, Sir John Bryant, KCB
Bourne, Sir (John) Wilfrid, KCB
Bovell, *Hon.* Sir (William) Stewart, Kt.
Bowater, Sir Euan David Vansittart, Bt. (1939)
Bowater, Sir (John) Vansittart, Bt. (1914)
Bowden, Sir Andrew, Kt., MBE
Bowden, Sir Frank, Bt. (1915)
Bowen, Sir Geoffrey Fraser, Kt.
Bowen, Sir Mark Edward Mortimer, Bt. (1921)
Bowett, *Prof.* Sir Derek William, Kt., CBE, QC, FBA
†Bowlby, Sir Richard Peregrine Longstaff, Bt. (1923)
Bowman, Sir Jeffery Haverstock, Kt.
Bowman, Sir Paul Humphrey Armytage, Bt. (1884)
Bowness, Sir Alan, Kt., CBE
Boyce, *Adm.* Sir Michael Cecil, GCB, OBE
Boyce, Sir Robert Charles Leslie, Bt. (1952)
Boyd, Sir Alexander Walter, Bt. (1916)
Boyd, Sir John Dixon Iklé, KCMG
Boyd, The Hon. Sir Mark Alexander Lennox-, Kt.
Boyd, *Prof.* Sir Robert Lewis Fullarton, Kt., CBE, D.SC., FRS

Boyes, Sir Brian Gerald Barratt-, KBE
Boyle, Sir Stephen Gurney, Bt. (1904)
Boynton, Sir John Keyworth, Kt., MC
Boys, *Rt. Hon.* Sir Michael Hardie, GCMG
Boyson, *Rt. Hon.* Sir Rhodes, Kt.
Brabham, Sir John Arthur, Kt., OBE
Bradbeer, Sir John Derek Richardson, Kt., OBE, TD
Bradbury, *Surgeon Vice-Adm.* Sir Eric Blackburn, KBE, CB
Bradford, Sir Edward Alexander Slade, Bt. (1902)
Bradman, Sir Donald George, Kt.
Bradshaw, Sir Kenneth Anthony, KCB
Bradshaw, *Lt.-Gen.* Sir Richard Phillip, KBE
Brain, Sir (Henry) Norman, KBE, CMG
Braithwaite, Sir (Joseph) Franklin Madders, Kt.
Braithwaite, *Rt. Hon.* Sir Nicholas Alexander, Kt., OBE
Braithwaite, Sir Rodric Quentin, GCMG
Bramley, *Prof.* Sir Paul Anthony, Kt.
Branigan, Sir Patrick Francis, Kt., QC
Bratza, Sir Nicolas Dušan, Kt., QC
Bray, Sir Theodor Charles, Kt., CBE
Brennan, *Hon.* Sir (Francis) Gerard, KBE
Brett, Sir Charles Edward Bainbridge, Kt., CBE
Brickwood, Sir Basil Greame, Bt. (1927)
Bridges, *Hon.* Sir Phillip Rodney, Kt., CMG
Brierley, Sir Ronald Alfred, Kt.
Bright, Sir Graham Frank James, Kt.
Bright, Sir Keith, Kt.
Brigstocke, *Adm.* Sir John Richard, KCB
Brinckman, Sir Theodore George Roderick, Bt. (1831)
†Brisco, Sir Campbell Howard, Bt. (1782)
Briscoe, Sir John Geoffrey James, Bt. (1910)
Brise, Sir John Archibald Ruggles-, Bt., CB, OBE, TD (1935)
Bristow, *Hon.* Sir Peter Henry Rowley, Kt.
Brittan, *Rt. Hon.* Sir Leon, Kt., QC
Brittan, Sir Samuel, Kt.
Britton, Sir Edward Louis, Kt., CBE
Broackes, Sir Nigel, Kt.
†Broadbent, Sir Andrew George, Bt. (1893)
Brocklebank, Sir Aubrey Thomas, Bt. (1885)
Brockman, *Vice-Adm.* Sir Ronald Vernon, KCB, CSI, CIE, CVO, CBE
Brodie, Sir Benjamin David Ross, Bt. (1834)
Broers, *Prof.* Sir Alec Nigel, Kt., PH.D., FRS
Bromhead, Sir John Desmond Gonville, Bt. (1806)
Bromley, Sir Michael Roger, KBE

Bromley, Sir Rupert Charles, Bt. (1757)
Bromley, Sir Thomas Eardley, KCMG
†Brooke, Sir Alistair Weston, Bt. (1919)
Brooke, Sir Francis George Windham, Bt. (1903)
Brooke, *Rt. Hon.* Sir Henry, Kt.
Brooke, Sir (Richard) David Christopher, Bt. (1662)
Brooksbank, Sir (Edward) Nicholas, Bt. (1919)
Broom, *Air Marshal* Sir Ivor Gordon, KCB, CBE, DSO, DFC, AFC
Broomfield, Sir Nigel Hugh Robert Allen, KCMG
†Broughton, Sir David Delves, Bt. (1661)
Broun, Sir William Windsor, Bt. (s. 1686)
Brown, Sir Allen Stanley, Kt., CBE
Brown, Sir (Austen) Patrick, KCB
Brown, *Adm.* Sir Brian Thomas, KCB, CBE
Brown, Sir (Cyril) Maxwell Palmer, KCB, CMG
Brown, *Vice-Adm.* Sir David Worthington, KCB
Brown, Sir Derrick Holden-, Kt.
Brown, Sir Douglas Denison, Kt.
Brown, *Hon.* Sir Douglas Dunlop, Kt.
Brown, Sir George Francis Richmond, Bt. (1863)
Brown, Sir George Noel, Kt.
Brown, Sir John Douglas Keith, Kt.
Brown, Sir John Gilbert Newton, Kt., CBE
Brown, Sir Mervyn, KCMG, OBE
Brown, Sir Peter Randolph, Kt.
Brown, *Hon.* Sir Ralph Kilner, Kt., OBE, TD
Brown, Sir Robert Crichton-, KCMG, CBE, TD
Brown, *Rt. Hon.* Sir Simon Denis, Kt.
Brown, *Rt. Hon.* Sir Stephen, GBE, Kt.
Brown, Sir Stephen David Reid, KCVO
Brown, Sir Thomas, Kt.
Brown, Sir William Brian Piggott-, Bt. (1903)
Browne, Sir (Edmund) John (Phillip), Kt., FREng.
Brownrigg, Sir Nicholas (Gawen), Bt. (1816)
Browse, *Prof.* Sir Norman Leslie, Kt., MD, FRCS
Bruce, Sir (Francis) Michael Ian, Bt. (s. 1628)
Bruce, Sir Hervey James Hugh, Bt. (1804)
Bruce, *Rt. Hon.* Sir (James) Roualeyn Hovell-Thurlow-Cumming-, Kt.
Brunner, Sir John Henry Kilian, Bt. (1895)
Brunton, Sir (Edward Francis) Lauder, Bt. (1908)
Brunton, Sir Gordon Charles, Kt.
Bryan, Sir Arthur, Kt.
Bryan, Sir Paul Elmore Oliver, Kt., DSO, MC

Bryce, *Hon.* Sir (William) Gordon, Kt., CBE

Bryson, *Adm.* Sir Lindsay Sutherland, KCB, FREng.

Buchan, Sir John, Kt., CMG

Buchanan, Sir Andrew George, Bt. (1878)

Buchanan, Sir Charles Alexander James Leith-, Bt. (1775)

Buchanan, *Prof.* Sir Colin Douglas, Kt., CBE

Buchanan, *Vice-Adm.* Sir Peter William, KBE

Buchanan, Sir (Ranald) Dennis, Kt., MBE

Buchanan, Sir Robert Wilson (Robin), Kt.

Buck, Sir (Philip) Antony (Fyson), Kt., QC

Buckland, Sir Ross, Kt.

Buckley, Sir John William, Kt.

Buckley, *Lt.-Cdr.* Sir (Peter) Richard, KCVO

Buckley, *Hon.* Sir Roger John, Kt.

Budd, Sir Alan Peter, Kt.

Bulkeley, Sir Richard Thomas Williams-, Bt. (1661)

Bull, Sir George Jeffrey, Kt.

Bull, Sir Simeon George, Bt. (1922)

Bullard, Sir Julian Leonard, GCMG

Bullus, Sir Eric Edward, Kt.

Bulmer, Sir William Peter, Kt.

Bultin, Sir Bato, Kt., MBE

Bunbury, Sir Michael William, Bt. (1681)

Bunbury, Sir (Richard David) Michael Richardson-, Bt. (I. 1787)

Bunch, Sir Austin Wyeth, Kt., CBE

Bunyard, Sir Robert Sidney, Kt., CBE, QPM

Burbidge, Sir Herbert Dudley, Bt. (1916)

Burgen, Sir Arnold Stanley Vincent, Kt., FRS

Burgess, *Gen.* Sir Edward Arthur, KCB, OBE

Burgess, Sir (Joseph) Stuart, Kt., CBE, Ph.D., FRSC

Burgh, Sir John Charles, KCMG, CB

Burke, Sir James Stanley Gilbert, Bt. (I. 1797)

Burke, Sir (Thomas) Kerry, Kt.

Burley, Sir Victor George, Kt., CBE

Burman, Sir (John) Charles, Kt.

Burnet, Sir James William Alexander (Sir Alastair Burnet), Kt.

Burnett, *Air Chief Marshal* Sir Brian Kenyon, GCB, DFC, AFC

Burnett, Sir David Humphery, Bt., MBE, TD (1913)

Burnett, Sir John Harrison, Kt.

Burnett, Sir Walter John, Kt.

Burney, Sir Cecil Denniston, Bt. (1921)

Burns, Sir (Robert) Andrew, KCMG

Burrell, Sir John Raymond, Bt. (1774)

Burrenchobay, Sir Dayendranath, KBE, CMG, CVO

Burrows, Sir Bernard Alexander Brocas, GCMG

Burston, Sir Samuel Gerald Wood, Kt., OBE

Burt, *Hon.* Sir Francis Theodore Page, KCMG

Burton, Sir Carlisle Archibald, Kt., OBE

Burton, Sir George Vernon Kennedy, Kt., CBE

Burton, *Lt.-Gen.* Sir Edmund Fortescue Gerard, KBE

Burton, Sir Graham Stuart, KCMG

Burton, Sir Michael John, Kt., QC

Burton, Sir Michael St Edmund, KCVO, CMG

Bush, *Adm.* Sir John Fitzroy Duyland, GCB, DSC

Butler, *Rt. Hon.* Sir Adam Courtauld, Kt.

Butler, *Hon.* Sir Arlington Griffith, KCMG

Butler, Sir Michael Dacres, GCMG

Butler, Sir (Reginald) Michael (Thomas), Bt. (1922)

Butler, *Hon.* Sir Richard Clive, Kt.

†Butler, Sir Richard Pierce, Bt. (1628)

Butter, *Maj.* Sir David Henry, KCVO, MC

Butterfield, *Hon.* Sir Alexander Neil Logie, Kt.

Buxton, Sir Jocelyn Charles Roden, Bt. (1840)

Buxton, *Rt. Hon.* Sir Richard Joseph, Kt.

Buzzard, Sir Anthony Farquhar, Bt. (1929)

Byatt, Sir Hugh Campbell, KCVO, CMG

Byers, Sir Maurice Hearne, Kt., CBE, QC

Byford, Sir Lawrence, Kt., CBE, QPM

Cable, Sir James Eric, KCVO, CMG

Cadbury, Sir (George) Adrian (Hayhurst), Kt.

Cadbury, Sir (Nicholas) Dominic, Kt.

Cadogan, *Prof.* Sir John Ivan George, Kt., CBE, FRS, FRSE

Cahn, Sir Albert Jonas, Bt. (1934)

Cain, Sir Henry Edney Conrad, Kt.

Caines, Sir John, KCB

Calcutt, Sir David Charles, Kt., QC

Calderwood, Sir Robert, Kt.

Caldwell, *Surgeon Vice-Adm.* Sir (Eric) Dick, KBE, CB

Callan, Sir Ivan Roy, KCVO, CMG

Callaway, *Prof.* Sir Frank Adams, Kt., CMG, OBE

Calman, *Prof.* Sir Kenneth Charles, KCB, MD, FRCP, FRCS, FRSE

Calne, *Prof.* Sir Roy Yorke, Kt., FRS

Calthorpe, Sir Euan Hamilton Anstruther-Gough-, Bt. (1929)

Cameron of Lochiel, Sir Donald Hamish, KT, CVO, TD

Cameron, Sir (Eustace) John, Kt., CBE

Cameron, Sir Hugh Roy Graham, Kt., QPM

Campbell, Sir Alan Hugh, GCMG

Campbell, *Prof.* Sir Colin Murray, Kt.

Campbell, *Prof.* Sir Donald, Kt., CBE, FRCS, FRCPGlas.

Campbell, Sir Ian Tofts, Kt., CBE, VRD

Campbell, Sir Ilay Mark, Bt. (1808)

Campbell, Sir James Alexander Moffat Bain, Bt. (S. 1668)

Campbell, Sir Lachlan Philip Kemeys, Bt. (1815)

Campbell, Sir Niall Alexander Hamilton, Bt. (1831)

Campbell, Sir Robin Auchinbreck, Bt. (S. 1628)

Campbell, Sir Thomas Cockburn-, Bt. (1821)

Campbell, *Hon.* Sir Walter Benjamin, Kt.

Campbell, *Rt. Hon.* Sir William Anthony, Kt.

†Carden, Sir Christopher Robert, Bt. (1887)

Carden, Sir John Craven, Bt. (I. 1787)

Carew, Sir Rivers Verain, Bt. (1661)

Carey, Sir Peter Willoughby, GCB

Carlisle, Sir James Beethoven, GCMG

Carlisle, Sir John Michael, Kt.

Carlisle, Sir Kenneth Melville, Kt.

Carmichael, Sir David Peter William Gibson-Craig-, Bt. (S. 1702 and 1831)

Carnac, *Revd Canon* Sir (Thomas) Nicholas Rivett-, Bt. (1836)

Carnegie, *Lt.-Gen.* Sir Robin Macdonald, KCB, OBE

Carnegie, Sir Roderick Howard, Kt.

Carnwath, Sir Robert John Anderson, Kt., CVO

Caro, Sir Anthony Alfred, Kt., CBE

Carpenter, *Lt.-Gen.* the Hon. Sir Thomas Patrick John Boyd-, KBE

Carr, Sir (Albert) Raymond (Maillard), Kt.

Carrick, *Hon.* Sir John Leslie, KCMG

Carrick, Sir Roger John, KCMG, LVO

Carsberg, *Prof.* Sir Bryan Victor, Kt.

Carswell, *Rt. Hon.* Sir Robert Douglas, Kt.

Carter, Sir Charles Frederick, Kt., FBA

Carter, *Prof.* Sir David Craig, Kt., FRCSE, FRCSGlas., FRCPE

Carter, Sir John, Kt., QC

Carter, Sir John Alexander, Kt.

Carter, Sir John Gordon Thomas, Kt.

Carter, Sir Philip David, Kt., CBE

Carter, Sir Richard Henry Alwyn, Kt.

Carter, Sir William Oscar, Kt.

Cartland, Sir George Barrington, Kt., CMG

Cartledge, Sir Bryan George, KCMG

Cary, Sir Roger Hugh, Bt. (1955)

Casey, *Rt. Hon.* Sir Maurice Eugene, Kt.

Cash, Sir Gerald Christopher, GCMG, GCVO, OBE

Cass, Sir Geoffrey Arthur, Kt.

Cassel, Sir Harold Felix, Bt., TD, QC (1920)

Cassels, Sir John Seton, Kt., CB

Cassels, *Adm.* Sir Simon Alastair Cassillis, KCB, CBE

Cassidi, *Adm.* Sir (Arthur) Desmond, GCB

Cater, Sir Jack, KBE

Catford, Sir (John) Robin, KCVO, CBE

Catherwood, Sir (Henry) Frederick (Ross), Kt.

Catling, Sir Richard Charles, Kt., CMG, OBE

Cave, Sir (Charles) Philip Haddon-, KBE, CMG

†Cave, Sir John Charles, Bt. (1896)

Cave, Sir Robert Cave-Browne-, Bt. (1641)

Cawley, Sir Charles Mills, Kt., CBE, Ph.D.

Cayley, Sir Digby William David, Bt. (1661)

Cayzer, Sir James Arthur, Bt. (1904)

Cazalet, *Hon.* Sir Edward Stephen, Kt.

Cazalet, Sir Peter Grenville, Kt.

Cecil, *Rear-Adm.* Sir (Oswald) Nigel Amherst, KBE, CB

Chacksfield, *Air Vice-Marshal* Sir Bernard Albert, KBE, CB

Chadwick, *Revd Prof.* Henry, KBE

Chadwick, *Rt. Hon.* Sir John Murray, Kt., ED

Chadwick, Sir Joshua Kenneth Burton, Bt. (1935)

Chadwick, *Revd Prof.* (William) Owen, OM, KBE, FBA

Chalstrey, Sir (Leonard) John, Kt., MD, FRCS

Chan, *Rt. Hon.* Sir Julius, GCMG, KBE

Chance, Sir (George) Jeremy ffolliott, Bt. (1900)

Chandler, Sir Colin Michael, Kt.

Chandler, Sir Geoffrey, Kt., CBE

Chaney, *Hon.* Sir Frederick Charles, KBE, AFC

Chantler, *Prof.* Sir Cyril, Kt., MD, FRCP

Chaplin, Sir Malcolm Hilbery, Kt., CBE

Chapman, Sir David Robert Macgowan, Bt. (1958)

Chapman, Sir George Alan, Kt.

Chapman, Sir Sidney Brookes, Kt., MP

Chapple, *Field Marshal* Sir John Lyon, GCB, CBE

Charles, *Hon.* Sir Arthur William Hessin, Kt

Charles, Sir George Frederick Lawrence, KCMG, CBE

Charlton, Sir Robert (Bobby), Kt., CBE

Charnley, Sir (William) John, Kt., CB, FREng.

Chataway, *Rt. Hon.* Sir Christopher, Kt.

Chatfield, Sir John Freeman, Kt., CBE

Chaytor, Sir George Reginald, Bt. (1831)

Checketts, *Sqn. Ldr.* Sir David John, KCVO

Checkland, Sir Michael, Kt.

Cheetham, Sir Nicolas John Alexander, KCMG

Cheshire, *Air Chief Marshal* Sir John Anthony, KBE, CB

Chessells, Sir Arthur David (Tim), Kt.

Chesterman, Sir (Dudley) Ross, Kt., Ph.D.

Chesterton, Sir Oliver Sidney, Kt., MC

Chetwood, Sir Clifford Jack, Kt.

Chetwynd, Sir Arthur Ralph Talbot, Bt. (1795)

Cheung, Sir Oswald Victor, Kt., CBE

Cheyne, Sir Joseph Lister Watson, Bt., OBE (1908)

Chichester, Sir (Edward) John, Bt. (1641)

Chilcot, Sir John Anthony, GCB

Child, Sir (Coles John) Jeremy, Bt. (1919)

Chilton, *Brig.* Sir Frederick Oliver, Kt., CBE, DSO

Chilwell, *Hon.* Sir Muir Fitzherbert, Kt.

Chinn, Sir Trevor Edwin, Kt., CVO

Chipperfield, Sir Geoffrey Howes, KCB

Chisholm, Sir John Alexander Raymond, Kt., FREng.

Chitty, Sir Thomas Willes, Bt. (1924)

Cholmeley, Sir Hugh John Frederick Sebastian, Bt. (1806)

Christie, Sir George William Langham, Kt.

Christie, Sir William, Kt., MBE

Christopherson, Sir Derman Guy, Kt., OBE, D.Phil., FRS, FREng.

Chung, Sir Sze-yuen, GBE, FREng.

Clapham, Sir Michael John Sinclair, KBE

Clark, Sir Francis Drake, Bt. (1886)

Clark, Sir John Allen, Kt.

Clark, Sir John Stewart-, Bt., MEP (1918)

Clark, Sir Jonathan George, Bt. (1917)

Clark, Sir Robert Anthony, Kt., DSC

Clark, Sir Robin Chichester-, Kt.

Clark, Sir Terence Joseph, KBE, CMG, CVO

Clark, Sir Thomas Edwin, Kt.

Clarke, *Hon.* Sir Anthony Peter, Kt.

Clarke, Sir Arthur Charles, Kt., CBE

Clarke, Sir (Charles Mansfield) Tobias, Bt. (1831)

Clarke, *Prof.* Sir Cyril Astley, KBE, MD, SC.D., FRS, FRCP

Clarke, Sir Ellis Emmanuel Innocent, GCMG

Clarke, Sir Jonathan Dennis, Kt.

Clarke, *Maj.* Sir Peter Cecil, KCVO

Clarke, Sir Robert Cyril, Kt.

Clarke, Sir Rupert William John, Bt., MBE (1882)

Clay, Sir Richard Henry, Bt. (1841)

Clayton, Sir David Robert, Bt. (1732)

Cleaver, Sir Anthony Brian, Kt.

Cleminson, Sir James Arnold Stacey, KBE, MC

Clerk, Sir John Dutton, Bt.,*CBE, VRD (s. 1679)

Clerke, Sir John Edward Longueville, Bt. (1660)

Clifford, Sir Roger Joseph, Bt. (1887)

Clothier, Sir Cecil Montacute, KCB, QC

Clucas, Sir Kenneth Henry, KCB

Clutterbuck, *Vice-Adm.* Sir David Granville, KBE, CB

Coates, Sir Anthony Robert Milnes, Bt. (1911)

Coates, Sir David Frederick Charlton, Bt. (1921)

Coats, Sir Alastair Francis Stuart, Bt. (1905)

Coats, Sir William David, Kt.

Cobham, Sir Michael John, Kt., CBE

Cochrane, Sir (Henry) Marc (Sursock), Bt. (1903)

Cockburn, Sir John Elliot, Bt. (s. 1671)

Cockcroft, Sir Wilfred Halliday, Kt., D.Phil.

Cockram, Sir John, Kt.

Cockshaw, Sir Alan, Kt., FREng.

Codrington, Sir Simon Francis Bethell, Bt. (1876)

Codrington, Sir William Alexander, Bt. (1721)

Coghill, Sir Egerton James Nevill Tobias, Bt. (1778)

Coghlin, *Hon.* Sir Patrick, Kt.

Cohen, Sir Edward, Kt.

Cohen, Sir Ivor Harold, Kt., CBE, TD

Cohen, *Prof.* Sir Philip, Kt., Ph.D, FRS

Cohen, Sir Stephen Harry Waley-, Bt. (1961)

Coldstream, Sir George Phillips, KCB, KCVO, QC

Cole, Sir (Alexander) Colin, KCB, KCVO, TD

Cole, Sir (Robert) William, Kt.

Coleman, Sir Timothy, KG

Coles, Sir (Arthur) John, GCMG

Colfox, Sir (William) John, Bt. (1939)

Collett, Sir Christopher, GBE

Collett, Sir Ian Seymour, Bt. (1934)

Collins, *Hon.* Sir Andrew David, Kt.

Collins, Sir Arthur James Robert, KCVO

Collins, Sir Bryan Thomas Alfred, Kt., OBE, QFSM

Collins, Sir John Alexander, Kt.

Collyear, Sir John Gowen, Kt., FREng.

Colman, *Hon.* Sir Anthony David, Kt.

Colman, Sir Michael Jeremiah, Bt. (1907)

Colquhoun of Luss, Sir Ivar Iain, Bt. (1786)

Colt, Sir Edward William Dutton, Bt. (1694)

Colthurst, Sir Richard La Touche, Bt. (1744)

Coltman, Sir (Arthur) Leycester Scott, KBE, CMG

Colvin, Sir Howard Montagu, Kt., CVO, CBE, FBA

Compston, *Vice-Adm.* Sir Peter Maxwell, KCB

Compton, *Rt. Hon.* Sir John George Melvin, KCMG

Conant, Sir John Ernest Michael, Bt. (1954)

Condon, Sir Paul Leslie, Kt., QPM

Connell, *Hon.* Sir Michael Bryan, Kt.

Conran, Sir Terence Orby, Kt.

Cons, *Hon.* Sir Derek, Kt.

Constable, Sir Frederic Strickland-, Bt. (1641)

Constantinou, Sir Georkios, Kt., OBE

Cook, *Prof.* Sir Alan Hugh, Kt.

Cook, Sir Christopher Wymondham Rayner Herbert, Bt. (1886)

Cooke, Sir Charles Fletcher-, Kt., QC

Cooke, *Col.* Sir David William Perceval, Bt. (1661)

Cooke, Sir Howard Felix Hanlan, GCMG, GCVO

Cooksey, Sir David James Scott, Kt.

Cooper, *Rt. Hon.* Sir Frank, GCB, CMG

Cooper, Sir (Frederick Howard) Michael Craig-, Kt., CBE, TD

Cooper, *Gen.* Sir George Leslie Conroy, GCB, MC

Cooper, Sir Louis Jacques Blom-, Kt., QC

Cooper, Sir Patrick Graham Astley, Bt. (1821)

Cooper, Sir Richard Powell, Bt. (1905)

Cooper, Sir Robert George, Kt., CBE

Cooper, *Maj.-Gen.* Sir Simon Christie, KCVO

Cooper, Sir William Daniel Charles, Bt. (1863)

Coote, Sir Christopher John, Bt., *Premier Baronet of Ireland* (I. 1621)

Copas, *Most Revd* Virgil, KBE, DD

Copisarow, Sir Alcon Charles, Kt.

Corbett, *Maj.-Gen.* Sir Robert John Swan, KCVO, CB

Corby, Sir (Frederick) Brian, Kt.

Corfield, *Rt. Hon.* Sir Frederick Vernon, Kt., QC

Corfield, Sir Kenneth George, Kt., FREng.

Cork, Sir Roger William, Kt.

Corley, Sir Kenneth Sholl Ferrand, Kt.

Cormack, Sir Magnus Cameron, KBE

Cormack, Sir Patrick Thomas, Kt., MP

Corness, Sir Colin Ross, Kt.

Cornforth, Sir John Warcup, Kt., CBE, D.Phil., FRS

Corry, Sir William James, Bt. (1885)

Cortazzi, Sir (Henry Arthur) Hugh, GCMG

Cory, Sir (Clinton Charles) Donald, Bt. (1919)

Cossons, Sir Neil, Kt., OBE

Cotter, *Lt.-Col.* Sir Delaval James Alfred, Bt., DSO (I. 1763)

Cotterell, Sir John Henry Geers, Bt. (1805)

Cotton, Sir John Richard, KCMG, OBE

Cotton, *Hon.* Sir Robert Carrington, KCMG

Cottrell, Sir Alan Howard, Kt., PH.D., FRS, FREng.

†Cotts, Sir Richard Crichton Mitchell, Bt. (1921)

Couper, Sir (Robert) Nicholas (Oliver), Bt. (1841)

Court, *Hon.* Sir Charles Walter Michael, KCMG, OBE

Cousins, *Air Chief Marshal* Sir David, KCB, AFC

Coutts, Sir David Burdett Money-, KCVO

Couzens, Sir Kenneth Edward, KCB

Covacevich, Sir (Anthony) Thomas, Kt., DFC

Cowan, *Gen.* Sir Samuel, KCB, CBE

Coward, *Vice-Adm.* Sir John Francis, KCB, DSO

Cowen, *Rt. Hon. Prof.* Sir Zelman, GCMG, GCVO, QC

Cowie, Sir Thomas (Tom), Kt., OBE

Cowperthwaite, Sir John James, KBE, CMG

Cox, Sir Alan George, Kt., CBE

Cox, *Prof.* Sir David Roxbee, Kt., FRS

Cox, Sir Geoffrey Sandford, Kt., CBE

Cox, *Vice-Adm.* Sir John Michael Holland, KCB

Cradock, *Rt. Hon.* Sir Percy, GCMG

Craig, Sir (Albert) James (Macqueen), GCMG

Craufurd, Sir Robert James, Bt. (1781)

Craven, Sir John Anthony, Kt.

Craven, *Air Marshal* Sir Robert Edward, KBE, CB, DFC

Crawford, *Prof.* Sir Frederick William, Kt., FREng.

Crawford, Sir (Robert) Stewart, GCMG, CVO

Crawford, *Vice-Adm.* Sir William Godfrey, KBE, CB, DSC

Creagh, *Maj.-Gen.* Sir (Kilner) Rupert Brazier-, KBE, CB, DSO

Cresswell, *Hon.* Sir Peter John, Kt.

Crill, Sir Peter Leslie, KBE

Cripps, Sir Cyril Humphrey, Kt.

Crisp, Sir (John) Peter, Bt. (1913)

Critchett, Sir Ian (George Lorraine), Bt. (1908)

Critchley, Sir Julian Michael Gordon, Kt.

Croft, Sir Owen Glendower, Bt. (1671)

Croft, Sir Thomas Stephen Hutton, Bt. (1818)

†Crofton, Sir Hugh Denis, Bt. (1801)

Crofton, *Prof.* Sir John Wenman, Kt.

Crofton, Sir Malby Sturges, Bt. (1838)

Croker, Sir Walter Russell, KBE

Crookenden, *Lt.-Gen.* Sir Napier, KCB, DSO, OBE

Cross, *Air Chief Marshal* Sir Kenneth Brian Boyd, KCB, CBE, DSO, DFC

Crossland, *Prof.* Sir Bernard, Kt., CBE, FREng.

Crossley, Sir Nicholas John, Bt. (1909)

Cruthers, Sir James Winter, Kt.

Cubbon, Sir Brian Crossland, GCB

Cubitt, Sir Hugh Guy, Kt., CBE

Cullen, Sir (Edward) John, Kt., FREng.

Cumming, Sir William Gordon Gordon-, Bt. (1804)

Cuninghame, Sir John Christopher Foggo Montgomery-, Bt. (NS 1672)

Cuninghame, Sir William Henry Fairlie-, Bt. (S. 1630)

Cunliffe, Sir David Ellis, Bt. (1759)

Cunningham, *Lt.-Gen.* Sir Hugh Patrick, KBE

Cunynghame, Sir Andrew David Francis, Bt. (S. 1702)

†Currie, Sir Donald Scott, Bt. (1847)

Currie, Sir Neil Smith, Kt., CBE

Curtis, Sir Barry John, Kt.

Curtis, Sir (Edward) Leo, Kt.

Curtis, *Hon.* Sir Richard Herbert, Kt.

Curtis, Sir William Peter, Bt. (1802)

Curtiss, *Air Marshal* Sir John Bagot, KCB, KBE

Curwen, Sir Christopher Keith, KCMG

Cuschieri, *Prof.* Sir Alfred, Kt.

Cutler, Sir (Arthur) Roden, VC, KCMG, KCVO, CBE

Cutler, Sir Charles Benjamin, KBE, ED

Dacie, *Prof.* Sir John Vivian, Kt., MD, FRS

Dain, Sir David John Michael, KCVO

Dale, Sir William Leonard, KCMG

Dalrymple, *Maj.* Sir Hew Fleetwood Hamilton-, Bt., KCVO (S. 1697)

Dalton, Sir Alan Nugent Goring, Kt., CBE

Dalton, *Vice-Adm.* Sir Geoffrey Thomas James Oliver, KCB

Daly, *Lt.-Gen.* Sir Thomas Joseph, KBE, CB, DSO

Dalyell, Sir Tam (Thomas), Bt., MP (NS 1685)

Daniel, Sir Goronwy Hopkin, KCVO, CB, D.Phil.

Daniel, Sir John Sagar, Kt., D.SC.

Daniell, Sir Peter Averell, Kt., TD

Darby, Sir Peter Howard, Kt., CBE, QFSM

Darell, Sir Jeffrey Lionel, Bt., MC (1795)

Dargie, Sir William Alexander, Kt., CBE

Dark, Sir Anthony Michael Beaumont-, Kt.

Darling, Sir Clifford, GCVO

Darvall, Sir (Charles) Roger, Kt., CBE

Dashwood, Sir Francis John Vernon Hereward, Bt., *Premier Baronet of Great Britain* (1707)

Dashwood, Sir Richard James, Bt. (1684)

Daunt, Sir Timothy Lewis Achilles, KCMG

Davey, *Hon.* Sir David Herbert Penry-, Kt.

David, Sir Jean Marc, Kt., CBE, QC

Duncombe, Sir Philip Digby Pauncefort-, Bt. (1859)
Dunham, Sir Kingsley Charles, Kt., ph.D., FRS, FRSE, FREng.
Dunlop, Sir Thomas, Bt. (1916)
Dunlop, Sir William Norman Gough, Kt.
Dunn, *Air Marshal* Sir Eric Clive, KBE, CB, BEM
Dunn, *Air Marshal* Sir Patrick Hunter, KBE, CB, DFC
Dunn, *Rt. Hon.* Sir Robin Horace Walford, Kt., MC
Dunne, Sir Thomas Raymond, KCVO
Dunning, Sir Simon William Patrick, Bt. (1930)
Dunstan, *Lt.-Gen.* Sir Donald Beaumont, KBE, CB
Dunt, *Vice-Adm.* Sir John Hugh, KCB
†Duntze, Sir Daniel Evans, Bt. (1774)
Dupre, Sir Tumun, Kt., MBE
Dupree, Sir Peter, Bt. (1921)
Durand, Sir Edward Alan Christopher David Percy, Bt. (1892)
Durant, Sir (Robert) Anthony (Bevis), Kt.
Durham, Sir Kenneth, Kt.
Durie, Sir Alexander Charles, Kt., CBE
Durkin, *Air Marshal* Sir Herbert, KBE, CB
Durrant, Sir William Alexander Estridge, Bt. (1784)
Duthie, *Prof.* Sir Herbert Livingston, Kt.
Duthie, Sir Robert Grieve (Robin), Kt., CBE
Dyer, *Prof.* Sir (Henry) Peter (Francis) Swinnerton-, Bt., KBE, FRS (1678)
Dyke, Sir David William Hart, Bt. (1677)
Dyson, *Hon.* Sir John Anthony, Kt.
Eady, *Hon.* Sir David, Kt.
Earle, Sir (Hardman) George (Algernon), Bt. (1869)
Easton, Sir Robert William Simpson, Kt., CBE
Eaton, *Adm.* Sir Kenneth John, GBE, KCB
Eberle, *Adm.* Sir James Henry Fuller, GCB
Ebrahim, Sir (Mahomed) Currimbhoy, Bt. (1910)
Echlin, Sir Norman David Fenton, Bt. (I. 1721)
Eckersley, Sir Donald Payze, Kt., OBE
Edge, *Capt.* Sir (Philip) Malcolm, KCVO
†Edge, Sir William, Bt. (1937)
Edmonstone, Sir Archibald Bruce Charles, Bt. (1774)
Edwardes, Sir Michael Owen, Kt.
Edwards, Sir Christopher John Churchill, Bt. (1866)
Edwards, Sir George Robert, Kt., OM, CBE, FRS, FREng.
Edwards, Sir Llewellyn Roy, Kt.

Edwards, *Prof.* Sir Samuel Frederick, Kt., FRS
Egan, Sir John Leopold, Kt.
Egerton, Sir John Alfred Roy, Kt.
Egerton, Sir (Philip) John (Caledon) Grey-, Bt. (1617)
Egerton, Sir Stephen Loftus, KCMG
Eggleston, *Hon.* Sir Richard Moulton, Kt.
Eichelbaum, *Rt. Hon.* Sir Thomas, GBE
Elias, Sir Patrick, Kt., QC
Eliott of Stobs, Sir Charles Joseph Alexander, Bt. (s. 1666)
Ellerton, Sir Geoffrey James, Kt., CMG, MBE
Elliot, Sir Gerald Henry, Kt.
Elliott, Sir Clive Christopher Hugh, Bt. (1917)
Elliott, Sir David Murray, KCMG, CB
Elliott, *Prof.* Sir John Huxtable, Kt., FBA
Elliott, Sir Randal Forbes, KBE
Elliott, *Prof.* Sir Roger James, Kt., FRS
Elliott, Sir Ronald Stuart, Kt.
Ellis, Sir Ronald, Kt., FREng.
Ellison, *Col.* Sir Ralph Harry Carr-, KCVO, TD
Elphinstone, Sir John, Bt. (s. 1701)
Elphinstone, Sir John Howard Main, Bt. (1816)
Elton, Sir Arnold, Kt., CBE
Elton, Sir Charles Abraham Grierson, Bt. (1717)
Elwes, Sir Jeremy Vernon, Kt., CBE
Elwood, Sir Brian George Conway, Kt., CBE
Elworthy, Sir Peter Herbert, Kt.
Elyan, Sir (Isadore) Victor, Kt.
Emery, *Rt. Hon.* Sir Peter Frank Hannibal, Kt., MP
Empey, Sir Reginald Norman Morgan, Kt., OBE
Engle, Sir George Lawrence Jose, KCB, QC
English, Sir Terence Alexander Hawthorne, KBE, FRCS
Epstein, *Prof.* Sir (Michael) Anthony, Kt., CBE, FRS
Errington, *Col.* Sir Geoffrey Frederick, Bt., OBE (1963)
Errington, Sir Lancelot, KCB
Erskine, Sir (Thomas) David, Bt. (1821)
Esmonde, Sir Thomas Francis Grattan, Bt. (I. 1629)
Espie, Sir Frank Fletcher, Kt., OBE
Esplen, Sir John Graham, Bt. (1921)
Essenhigh, *Adm.* Sir Nigel Richard, Kt.
Eustace, Sir Joseph Lambert, GCMG, GCVO
Evans, Sir Anthony Adney, Bt. (1920)
Evans, *Rt. Hon.* Sir Anthony Howell Meurig, Kt., RD
Evans, *Air Chief Marshal* Sir David George, GCB, CBE
Evans, *Air Chief Marshal* Sir David Parry-, GCB, CBE
Evans, *Hon.* Sir Haydn Tudor, Kt.

Evans, *Prof.* Sir John Grimley, Kt., FRCP
Evans, Sir Richard Harry, Kt., CBE
Evans, Sir Richard Mark, KCMG, KCVO
Evans, Sir Robert, Kt., CBE, FREng.
Evans, Sir (William) Vincent (John), GCMG, MBE, QC
Eveleigh, *Rt. Hon.* Sir Edward Walter, Kt., ERD
Everard, Sir Robin Charles, Bt. (1911)
Everson, Sir Frederick Charles, KCMG
Every, Sir Henry John Michael, Bt. (1641)
Ewans, Sir Martin Kenneth, KCMG
†Ewart, Sir William Michael, Bt. (1887)
Ewbank, *Hon.* Sir Anthony Bruce, Kt.
Ewin, Sir (David) Ernest Thomas Floyd, Kt., OBE, LVO
Ewing, Sir (Alistair) Simon Orr-, Bt. (1963)
Ewing, Sir Ronald Archibald Orr-, Bt. (1886)
Eyre, Sir Graham Newman, Kt., QC
Eyre, *Maj.-Gen.* Sir James Ainsworth Campden Gabriel, KCVO, CBE
Eyre, Sir Reginald Edwin, Kt.
Eyre, Sir Richard Charles Hastings, Kt., CBE
Faber, Sir Richard Stanley, KCVO, CMG
Fadahunsi, Sir Joseph Odeleye, KCMG
Fagge, Sir John William Frederick, Bt. (1660)
Fairbairn, Sir (James) Brooke, Bt. (1869)
Fairclough, Sir John Whitaker, Kt., FREng.
Fairhall, *Hon.* Sir Allen, KBE
Fairweather, Sir Patrick Stanislaus, KCMG
Falconer, *Hon.* Sir Douglas William, Kt., MBE
†Falkiner, Sir Benjamin Simon Patrick, Bt. (I. 1778)
Fall, Sir Brian James Proetel, GCVO, KCMG
Falle, Sir Samuel, KCMG, KCVO, DSC
Fang, *Prof.* Sir Harry, Kt., CBE
Fareed, Sir Djamil Sheik, Kt.
Farmer, Sir Thomas, Kt., CBE
Farndale, *Gen.* Sir Martin Baker, KCB
Farquhar, Sir Michael Fitzroy Henry, Bt. (1796)
Farquharson, *Rt. Hon.* Sir Donald Henry, Kt.
Farquharson, Sir James Robbie, KBE
Farrer, Sir (Charles) Matthew, GCVO
Farrington, Sir Henry Francis Colden, Bt. (1818)
Fat, Sir (Maxime) Edouard (Lim Man) Lim, Kt.
Faulkner, Sir (James) Dennis (Compton), Kt., CBE, VRD
Fawcus, Sir (Robert) Peter, KBE, CMG
Fawkes, Sir Randol Francis, Kt.

Fay, Sir (Humphrey) Michael Gerard, Kt.

Fayrer, Sir John Lang Macpherson, Bt. (1896)

Fearn, Sir (Patrick) Robin, KCMG

Feilden, Sir Bernard Melchior, Kt., CBE

Feilden, Sir Henry Wemyss, Bt., (1846)

Fell, Sir David, KCB

Fellowes, *Rt. Hon.* Sir Robert, GCB, GCVO

Fender, Sir Brian Edward Frederick, Kt., CMG, Ph.D.

Fenn, Sir Nicholas Maxted, GCMG

Fennell, *Hon.* Sir (John) Desmond Augustine, Kt., OBE

Fennessy, Sir Edward, Kt., CBE

Ferguson, Sir Alexander Chapman, Kt., CBE

Ferguson, Sir Ian Edward Johnson-, Bt. (1906)

Fergusson of Kilkerran, Sir Charles, Bt. (S. 1703)

Fergusson, Sir Ewan Alastair John, GCMG, GCVO

Fergusson, Sir James Herbert Hamilton Colyer-, Bt. (1866)

Feroze, Sir Rustam Moolan, Kt., FRCS

Ferris, *Hon.* Sir Francis Mursell, Kt., TD

ffolkes, Sir Robert Francis Alexander, Bt, OBE (1774)

Field, Sir Malcolm David, Kt.

Fielding, Sir Colin Cunningham, Kt., CB

Fielding, Sir Leslie, KCMG

Fieldsend, *Hon.* Sir John Charles Rowell, KBE

Fiennes, Sir Ranulph Twisleton-Wykeham-, Bt., OBE (1916)

Figg, Sir Leonard Clifford William, KCMG

Figgis, Sir Anthony St John Howard, KCVO, CMG

Figures, Sir Colin Frederick, KCMG, OBE

Fingland, Sir Stanley James Gunn, KCMG

Finlay, Sir David Ronald James Bell, Bt. (1964)

Finney, Sir Thomas, Kt., OBE

Firth, *Prof.* Sir Raymond William, Kt., Ph.D., FBA

Fisher, Sir George Read, Kt., CMG

Fisher, *Hon.* Sir Henry Arthur Pears, Kt.

Fison, Sir (Richard) Guy, Bt., DSC (1905)

†Fitzgerald, *Revd* (Sir) Daniel Patrick, Bt. (1903)

FitzGerald, Sir George Peter Maurice, Bt., MC (*The Knight of Kerry*) (1880)

FitzHerbert, Sir Richard Ranulph, Bt. (1784)

Fitzpatrick, *Gen.* Sir (Geoffrey Richard) Desmond, GCB, GCVO, DSO, MBE, MC

Fitzpatrick, *Air Marshal* Sir John Bernard, KBE, CB

Flanagan, Sir Ronald, Kt., OBE

Fletcher, Sir Henry Egerton Aubrey-, Bt. (1782)

Fletcher, Sir James Muir Cameron, Kt.

Fletcher, Sir Leslie, Kt., DSC

Floissac, *Hon.* Sir Vincent Frederick, Kt., CMG, OBE, QC

Floyd, Sir Giles Henry Charles, Bt. (1816)

Foley, *Lt.-Gen.* Sir John Paul, KCB, OBE, MC

Foley, Sir (Thomas John) Noel, Kt., CBE

Follett, *Prof.* Sir Brian Keith, Kt., FRS

Foot, Sir Geoffrey James, Kt.

Foots, Sir James William, Kt.

Forbes, *Hon.* Sir Alastair Granville, Kt.

Forbes, *Maj.* Sir Hamish Stewart, Bt., MBE, MC (1823)

Forbes of Craigievar, Sir John Alexander Cumnock, Bt. (S. 1630)

Forbes, *Vice-Adm.* Sir John Morrison, KCB

Forbes, *Hon.* Sir Thayne John, Kt.

†Forbes of Pitsligo, Sir William Daniel Stuart-, Bt. (S. 1626)

Ford, Sir Andrew Russell, Bt. (1929)

Ford, Sir David Robert, KBE, LVO, OBE

Ford, *Maj.* Sir Edward William Spencer, GCVO, KCB, ERD

Ford, *Air Marshal* Sir Geoffrey Harold, KBE, CB, FREng.

Ford, *Prof.* Sir Hugh, Kt., FRS, FREng.

Ford, Sir James Anson St Clair-, Bt. (1793)

Ford, Sir John Archibald, KCMG, MC

Ford, *Gen.* Sir Robert Cyril, GCB, CBE

Foreman, Sir Philip Frank, Kt., CBE, FREng.

Forman, Sir John Denis, Kt., OBE

Forrest, *Prof.* Sir (Andrew) Patrick (McEwen), Kt.

Forrest, *Rear-Adm.* Sir Ronald Stephen, KCVO

Forster, Sir Archibald William, Kt., FREng.

Forster, Sir Oliver Grantham, KCMG, LVO

Forte, Hon. Sir Rocco John Vincent, Kt.

Forwood, Sir Dudley Richard, Bt. (1895)

Foster, *Prof.* Sir Christopher David, Kt.

Foster, Sir John Gregory, Bt. (1930)

Foster, Sir Robert Sidney, GCMG, KCVO

Foulis, Sir Ian Primrose Liston-, Bt. (S. 1634)

Foulkes, Sir Nigel Gordon, Kt.

Fountain, *Hon.* Sir Cyril Stanley Smith, Kt.

Fowden, Sir Leslie, Kt., FRS

Fowke, Sir David Frederick Gustavus, Bt. (1814)

Fowler, Sir (Edward) Michael Coulson, Kt.

Fowler, *Rt. Hon.* Sir (Peter) Norman, Kt., MP

Fox, Sir (Henry) Murray, GBE

Fox, *Rt. Hon.* Sir (John) Marcus, Kt., MBE

Fox, *Rt. Hon.* Sir Michael John, Kt.

Fox, Sir Paul Leonard, Kt., CBE

France, Sir Christopher Walter, GCB

Francis, Sir Horace William Alexander, Kt., CBE, FREng.

Frank, Sir Douglas George Horace, Kt., QC

Frank, Sir Robert Andrew, Bt. (1920)

Franklin, Sir Michael David Milroy, KCB, CMG

Franks, Sir Arthur Temple, KCMG

Fraser, Sir Angus McKay, KCB, TD

Fraser, Sir Charles Annand, KCVO

Fraser, *Gen.* Sir David William, GCB, OBE

Fraser, *Air Marshal Revd* Sir (Henry) Paterson, KBE, CB, AFC

Fraser, Sir Iain Michael Duncan, Bt. (1943)

Fraser, Sir Ian James, Kt., CBE, MC

Fraser, Sir (James) Campbell, Kt.

Fraser, Sir William Kerr, GCB

Frederick, Sir Charles Boscawen, Bt. (1723)

Freeland, Sir John Redvers, KCMG

Freeman, Sir James Robin, Bt. (1945)

Freer, *Air Chief Marshal* Sir Robert William George, GBE, KCB

Freeth, *Hon.* Sir Gordon, KBE

French, *Hon.* Sir Christopher James Saunders, Kt.

Frere, *Vice-Adm.* Sir Richard Tobias, KCB

Fretwell, Sir (Major) John (Emsley), GCMG

Freud, Sir Clement Raphael, Kt.

Froggatt, Sir Leslie Trevor, Kt.

Froggatt, Sir Peter, Kt.

Frossard, Sir Charles Keith, KBE

Frost, Sir David Paradine, Kt., OBE

Frost, Sir Terence Ernest Manitou, Kt., RA

Fry, Sir Peter Derek, Kt.

Fry, *Hon.* Sir William Gordon, Kt.

Fuchs, Sir Vivian Ernest, Kt., Ph.D.

†Fuller, Sir James Henry Fleetwood, Bt. (1910)

Fuller, *Hon.* Sir John Bryan Munro, Kt.

Fung, *Hon.* Sir Kenneth Ping-Fan, Kt., CBE

Furness, Sir Stephen Roberts, Bt. (1913)

Gadsden, Sir Peter Drury Haggerston, GBE, FREng.

Gage, *Hon.* Sir William Marcus, Kt.

Gainsford, Sir Ian Derek, Kt., DDS

Gaius, *Rt. Revd* Saimon, KBE

Gallwey, Sir Philip Frankland Payne-, Bt. (1812)

Galsworthy, Sir Anthony Charles, KCMG

Gam, *Rt. Revd* Sir Getake, KBE

Gamble, Sir David Hugh Norman, Bt. (1897)

Gambon, Sir Michael John, Kt., CBE

Garden, *Air Marshal* Sir Timothy, KCB

Gardiner, Sir George Arthur, Kt.

Gardiner, Sir John Eliot, Kt., CBE

Gardner, Sir Edward Lucas, Kt., QC

Gardner, Sir Robert Henry Bruce-, Bt. (1945)

Garland, *Hon.* Sir Patrick Neville, Kt.

Garland, *Hon.* Sir Ransley Victor, KBE

Garlick, Sir John, KCB

Garner, Sir Anthony Stuart, Kt.

Garnett, *Vice-Adm.* Sir Ian David Graham, KCB

Garnier, *Rear-Adm.* Sir John, KCVO, CBE

Garrett, Sir Anthony Peter, Kt., CBE

Garrick, Sir Ronald, Kt., CBE, FREng.

Garrioch, Sir (William) Henry, Kt.

Garrod, *Lt.-Gen.* Sir (John) Martin Carruthers, KCB, OBE

Garthwaite, Sir (William) Mark (Charles), Bt. (1919)

Gaskell, Sir Richard Kennedy Harvey, Kt.

Gatehouse, *Hon.* Sir Robert Alexander, Kt.

Geno, Sir Makena Viora, KBE

George, Sir Arthur Thomas, Kt.

George, *Prof.* Sir Charles Frederick, MD, FRCP

George, Sir Richard William, Kt., CVO

Gerken, *Vice-Adm.* Sir Robert William Frank, KCB, CBE

Gery, Sir Robert Lucian Wade-, KCMG, KCVO

Gethin, Sir Richard Joseph St Lawrence, Bt. (I. 1665)

Getty, Sir (John) Paul, KBE

Ghurburrun, Sir Rabindrah, Kt.

Gibb, Sir Francis Ross (Frank), Kt., CBE, FREng.

Gibbings, Sir Peter Walter, Kt.

Gibbons, Sir (John) David, KBE

Gibbons, Sir William Edward Doran, Bt. (1752)

Gibbs, *Hon.* Sir Eustace Hubert Beilby, KCVO, CMG

Gibbs, *Rt. Hon.* Sir Harry Talbot, GCMG, KBE

Gibbs, *Lt.-Col.* Sir Peter Evan Wyldbore, KCVO

Gibbs, Sir Roger Geoffrey, Kt.

Gibbs, *Field Marshal* Sir Roland Christopher, GCB, CBE, DSO, MC

†Gibson, *Revd* Sir Christopher Herbert, Bt. (1931)

Gibson, *Vice-Adm.* Sir Donald Cameron Ernest Forbes, KCB, DSC

Gibson, Sir Ian, Kt., CBE

Gibson, *Rt. Hon.* Sir Peter Leslie, Kt.

Gibson, *Rt. Hon.* Sir Ralph Brian, Kt.

Giddings, *Air Marshal* Sir (Kenneth Charles) Michael, KCB, OBE, DFC, AFC

Gielgud, Sir (Arthur) John, Kt., OM, CH

Giffard, Sir (Charles) Sydney (Rycroft), KCMG

Gilbert, Sir Arthur, Kt.

Gilbert, *Air Chief Marshal* Sir Joseph Alfred, KCB, CBE

Gilbert, Sir Martin John, Kt., CBE

†Gilbey, Sir Walter Gavin, Bt. (1893)

Giles, *Rear-Adm.* Sir Morgan Charles Morgan-, Kt., DSO, OBE, GM

Gill, Sir Anthony Keith, Kt., FREng.

Gillam, Sir Patrick John, Kt.

Gillen, *Hon.* Sir John de Winter, Kt.

Gillett, Sir Robin Danvers Penrose, Bt., GBE, RD (1959)

Gilmour, *Col.* Sir Allan Macdonald, KCVO, OBE, MC

Gilmour, Sir John Edward, Bt., DSO, TD (1897)

Gina, Sir Lloyd Maepeza, KBE

Gingell, *Air Chief Marshal* Sir John, GBE, KCB, KCVO

Girolami, Sir Paul, Kt.

Girvan, *Hon.* Sir (Frederick) Paul, Kt.

Glasspole, Sir Florizel Augustus, GCMG, GCVO

Glen, Sir Alexander Richard, KBE, DSC

Glenn, Sir (Joseph Robert) Archibald, Kt., OBE

Glidewell, *Rt. Hon.* Sir Iain Derek Laing, Kt.

Glock, Sir William Frederick, Kt., CBE

Glover, *Gen.* Sir James Malcolm, KCB, MBE

Glover, Sir Victor Joseph Patrick, Kt.

Glyn, Sir Richard Lindsay, Bt. (1759 and 1800)

Goavea, Sir Sinaka Vakai, KBE

Godber, Sir George Edward, GCB, DM

Goff, Sir Robert (William) Davis-, Bt. (1905)

Gold, Sir Arthur Abraham, Kt., CBE

Gold, Sir Joseph, Kt.

Goldberg, *Prof.* Sir Abraham, Kt., MD, D.SC., FRCP

Goldberg, *Prof.* Sir David Paul Brandes, Kt.

Goldman, Sir Samuel, KCB

Gombrich, *Prof.* Sir Ernst Hans Josef, Kt., OM, CBE, Ph.D., FBA, FSA

Gooch, Sir Timothy Robert, Bt., MBE (1746)

Gooch, Sir Trevor Sherlock (Sir Peter), Bt. (1866)

Good, Sir John Kennedy-, KBE

Goodall, Sir (Arthur) David Saunders, GCMG

Goodenough, Sir Anthony Michael, KCMG

Goodenough, Sir William McLernon, Bt. (1943)

Goodhart, Sir Philip Carter, Kt.

Goodhart, Sir Robert Anthony Gordon, Bt. (1911)

Goodhew, Sir Victor Henry, Kt.

Goodison, Sir Alan Clowes, KCMG

Goodison, Sir Nicholas Proctor, Kt.

Goodlad, *Rt. Hon.* Sir Alastair Robertson, KCMG

Goodman, Sir Patrick Ledger, Kt., CBE

Goodson, Sir Mark Weston Lassam, Bt. (1922)

Goodwin, Sir Matthew Dean, Kt., CBE

†Goold, Sir George William, Bt. (1801)

Gordon, Sir Andrew Cosmo Lewis Duff-, Bt. (1813)

Gordon, Sir Charles Addison Somerville Snowden, KCB

Gordon, Sir Keith Lyndell, Kt., CMG

Gordon, Sir (Lionel) Eldred (Peter) Smith-, Bt. (1838)

Gordon, Sir Robert James, Bt. (S. 1706)

Gordon, Sir Sidney Samuel, Kt., CBE

Gordon Lennox, Lord Nicholas Charles, KCMG, KCVO

†Gore, Sir Nigel Hugh St George, Bt. (I. 1622)

Gorham, Sir Richard Masters, Kt., CBE, DFC

Goring, Sir William Burton Nigel, Bt. (1627)

Gorman, Sir John Reginald, Kt., CVO, CBE, MC

Gorst, Sir John Michael, Kt.

Gorton, *Rt. Hon.* Sir John Grey, GCMG, CH

Goschen, Sir Edward Christian, Bt., DSO (1916)

Gosling, Sir (Frederick) Donald, Kt.

Goswell, Sir Brian Lawrence, Kt.

Goulden, Sir (Peter) John, KCMG

Goulding, Sir (Ernest) Irvine, Kt.

Goulding, Sir Marrack Irvine, KCMG

Goulding, Sir (William) Lingard Walter, Bt. (1904)

Gourlay, *Gen.* Sir (Basil) Ian (Spencer), KCB, OBE, MC, RM

Gourlay, Sir Simon Alexander, Kt.

Govan, Sir Lawrence Herbert, Kt.

Gow, *Gen.* Sir (James) Michael, GCB

Gowans, Sir James Learmonth, Kt., CBE, FRCP, FRS

Graaff, Sir de Villiers, Bt., MBE (1911)

Grabham, Sir Anthony Henry, Kt.

Graham, Sir Alexander Michael, GBE

Graham, Sir James Bellingham, Bt. (1662)

Graham, Sir James Fergus Surtees, Bt. (1783)

Graham, Sir James Thompson, Kt., CMG

Graham, Sir John Alexander Noble, Bt., GCMG (1906)

Graham, Sir John Moodie, Bt. (1964)

Graham, Sir Norman William, Kt., CB

Graham, Sir Peter, KCB, QC

Graham, Sir Peter Alfred, Kt., OBE

Graham, *Lt.-Gen.* Sir Peter Walter, KCB, CBE

†Graham, Sir Ralph Stuart, Bt. (1629)

Graham, *Hon.* Sir Samuel Horatio, Kt., CMG, OBE

Grandy, *Marshal of the Royal Air Force* Sir John, GCB, GCVO, KBE, DSO
Grant, Sir Archibald, Bt. (s. 1705)
Grant, Sir Clifford, Kt.
Grant, Sir (John) Anthony, Kt.
Grant, Sir (Matthew) Alistair, Kt.
Grant, Sir Patrick Alexander Benedict, Bt. (s. 1688)
Grant, *Lt.-Gen.* Sir Scott Carnegie, KCB
Gray, *Hon.* Sir Charles Anthony St John, Kt., QC
Gray, *Prof.* Sir Denis John Pereira, Kt., OBE, FRCGP
Gray, Sir John Archibald Browne, Kt., Sc.D., FRS
Gray, Sir John Walton David, KBE, CMG
Gray, *Lt.-Gen.* Sir Michael Stuart, KCB, OBE
Gray, Sir Robert McDowall (Robin), Kt.
Gray, Sir William Hume, Bt. (1917)
Gray, Sir William Stevenson, Kt.
Graydon, *Air Chief Marshal* Sir Michael James, GCB, CBE
Grayson, Sir Jeremy Brian Vincent Harrington, Bt. (1922)
Green, Sir Allan David, KCB, QC
Green, Sir Andrew Fleming, KCMG
Green, *Hon.* Sir Guy Stephen Montague, KBE
Green, Sir Kenneth, Kt.
Green, Sir Owen Whitley, Kt.
†Green, Sir Stephen Lycett, Bt., TD (1886)
Greenaway, Sir John Michael Burdick, Bt. (1933)
Greenbury, Sir Richard, Kt.
Greene, Sir (John) Brian Massy-, Kt.
Greener, Sir Anthony Armitage, Kt.
Greengross, Sir Alan David, Kt.
Greening, *Rear-Adm.* Sir Paul Woollven, GCVO
Greenstock, Sir Jeremy Quentin, KCMG
Greenwell, Sir Edward Bernard, Bt. (1906)
Gregson, Sir Peter Lewis, GCB
Greig, Sir (Henry Louis) Carron, KCVO, CBE
Grenside, Sir John Peter, Kt., CBE
Grey, Sir Anthony Dysart, Bt. (1814)
Grierson, Sir Michael John Bewes, Bt. (s. 1685)
Grierson, Sir Ronald Hugh, Kt.
Griffin, *Maj.* Sir (Arthur) John (Stewart), KCVO
Griffin, Sir (Charles) David, Kt., CBE
Griffiths, Sir Eldon Wylie, Kt.
Griffiths, Sir John Norton-, Bt. (1922)
Grimwade, Sir Andrew Sheppard, Kt., CBE
Grindrod, *Most Revd* John Basil Rowland, KBE
Grinstead, Sir Stanley Gordon, Kt.
Grose, *Vice-Adm.* Sir Alan, KBE
Grossart, Sir Angus McFarlane McLeod, Kt., CBE

Grotrian, Sir Philip Christian Brent, Bt. (1934)
Grove, Sir Charles Gerald, Bt. (1874)
Grove, Sir Edmund Frank, KCVO
Grugeon, Sir John Drury, Kt.
Grylls, Sir (William) Michael (John), Kt.
Guinness, Sir Alec, Kt., CH, CBE
Guinness, Sir Howard Christian Sheldon, Kt., VRD
Guinness, Sir John Ralph Sidney, Kt., CB
Guinness, Sir Kenelm Ernest Lee, Bt. (1867)
Guise, Sir John Grant, Bt. (1783)
Gull, Sir Rupert William Cameron, Bt. (1872)
Gumbs, Sir Emile Rudolph, Kt.
Gunn, *Prof.* Sir John Currie, Kt., CBE
Gunn, Sir Robert Norman, Kt.
Gunn, Sir William Archer, KBE, CMG
†Gunning, Sir Charles Theodore, Bt. (1778)
Gunston, Sir John Wellesley, Bt. (1938)
Gurdon, *Prof.* Sir John Bertrand, Kt., D.Phil., FRS
Guthrie, *Gen.* Sir Charles Ronald Llewelyn, GCB, LVO, OBE
Guthrie, Sir Malcolm Connop, Bt. (1936)
Guy, *Gen.* Sir Roland Kelvin, GCB, CBE, DSO
Habakkuk, Sir John Hrothgar, Kt., FBA
Hadfield, Sir Ronald, Kt., QPM
Hadlee, Sir Richard John, Kt., MBE
Hadley, Sir Leonard Albert, Kt.
Hague, *Prof.* Sir Douglas Chalmers, Kt., CBE
Halberg, Sir Murray Gordon, Kt., MBE
Hall, Sir Arnold Alexander, Kt., FRS, FREng.
Hall, Sir Basil Brodribb, KCB, MC, TD
Hall, Sir Douglas Basil, Bt., KCMG (s. 1687)
Hall, Sir Ernest, Kt., OBE
Hall, Sir (Frederick) John (Frank), Bt. (1923)
Hall, Sir John, Kt.
Hall, Sir John Bernard, Bt. (1919)
Hall, Sir Peter Edward, KBE, CMG
Hall, *Prof.* Sir Peter Geoffrey, Kt., FBA
Hall, Sir Peter Reginald Frederick, Kt., CBE
Hall, Sir Robert de Zouche, KCMG
Hall, *Brig.* Sir William Henry, KBE, DSO, ED
Halliday, *Vice-Adm.* Sir Roy William, KBE, DSC
Halpern, Sir Ralph Mark, Kt.
Halsey, *Revd* Sir John Walter Brooke, Bt. (1920)
Halstead, Sir Ronald, Kt., CBE
Ham, Sir David Kenneth Rowe-, GBE
Hambling, Sir (Herbert) Hugh, Bt. (1924)

Hamburger, Sir Sidney Cyril, Kt., CBE
Hamer, *Hon.* Sir Rupert James, KCMG, ED
Hamill, Sir Patrick, Kt., QPM
Hamilton, *Rt. Hon.* Sir Archibald Gavin, Kt., MP
Hamilton, Sir Edward Sydney, Bt. (1776 and 1819)
Hamilton, Sir James Arnot, KCB, MBE, FREng.
Hamilton, Sir Malcolm William Bruce Stirling-, Bt. (s. 1673)
Hamilton, Sir Michael Aubrey, Kt.
Hamilton, Sir (Robert Charles) Richard Caradoc, Bt. (s. 1646)
Hammick, Sir Stephen George, Bt. (1834)
Hampel, Sir Ronald Claus, Kt.
Hampshire, Sir Stuart Newton, Kt., FBA
Hampson, Sir Stuart, Kt.
Hampton, Sir (Leslie) Geoffrey, Kt.
Hancock, Sir David John Stowell, KCB
Hancock, *Air Marshal* Sir Valston Eldridge, KBE, CB, DFC
Hand, *Most Revd* Geoffrey David, KBE
Handley, Sir David John Davenport-, Kt., OBE
Hanham, Sir Michael William, Bt., DFC (1667)
Hanley, *Rt. Hon.* Sir Jeremy James, KCMG
Hanley, Sir Michael Bowen, KCB
Hanmer, Sir John Wyndham Edward, Bt. (1774)
Hann, Sir James, Kt., CBE
Hannam, Sir John Gordon, Kt.
Hannay, Sir David Hugh Alexander, GCMG
Hanson, Sir (Charles) Rupert (Patrick), Bt. (1918)
Hanson, Sir John Gilbert, KCMG, CBE
Hardcastle, Sir Alan John, Kt.
Hardie, Sir Douglas Fleming, Kt., CBE
Harding, Sir Christopher George Francis, Kt.
Harding, Sir George William, KCMG, CVO
Harding, *Marshal of the Royal Air Force* Sir Peter Robin, GCB
Harding, Sir Roy Pollard, Kt., CBE
Hardman, Sir Henry, KCB
Hardy, Sir David William, Kt.
Hardy, Sir James Gilbert, Kt., OBE
Hardy, Sir Richard Charles Chandos, Bt. (1876)
Hare, Sir David, Kt., FRSL
Hare, Sir Philip Leigh, Bt. (1818)
Harford, Sir (John) Timothy, Bt. (1934)
Hargroves, *Brig.* Sir Robert Louis, Kt., CBE
Harington, *Gen.* Sir Charles Henry Pepys, GCB, CBE, DSO, MC
Harington, Sir Nicholas John, Bt. (1611)

Harland, *Air Marshal* Sir Reginald Edward Wynyard, KBE, CB

Harley, *Gen.* Sir Alexander George Hamilton, KBE, CB

Harman, *Gen.* Sir Jack Wentworth, GCB, OBE, MC

Harman, *Hon.* Sir Jeremiah LeRoy, Kt.

Harman, Sir John Andrew, Kt.

Harmsworth, Sir Hildebrand Harold, Bt. (1922)

Harris, *Prof.* Sir Alan James, Kt., CBE, FREng.

Harris, *Prof.* Sir Henry, Kt., FRCP, FRCPath., FRS

Harris, Sir Jack Wolfred Ashford, Bt. (1932)

Harris, *Air Marshal* Sir John Hulme, KCB, CBE

Harris, Sir William Gordon, KBE, CB, FREng.

Harrison, Sir David, Kt., CBE, FREng.

Harrison, *Prof.* Sir Donald Frederick Norris, Kt., FRCS

Harrison, Sir Ernest Thomas, Kt., OBE

Harrison, Sir Francis Alexander Lyle, Kt., MBE, QC

Harrison, *Surgeon Vice-Adm.* Sir John Albert Bews, KBE

Harrison, *Hon.* Sir (John) Richard, Kt., ED

Harrison, *Hon.* Sir Michael Guy Vicat, Kt.

Harrison, Sir Michael James Harwood, Bt. (1961)

Harrison, *Prof.* Sir Richard John, Kt., FRS

Harrison, Sir (Robert) Colin, Kt. (1922)

Harrison, Sir Terence, Kt., FREng

Harrop, Sir Peter John, KCB

Hart, Sir Graham Allan, KCB

Hart, *Hon.* Sir Michael Christopher Campbell, Kt.

Hartopp, *Lt. Cdr* Sir Kenneth Alston Cradock-, Bt., MBE, DSC (1796)

Hartwell, Sir (Francis) Anthony Charles Peter, Bt. (1805)

Harvey, Sir Charles Richard Musgrave, Bt. (1933)

Harvie, Sir John Smith, Kt., CBE

Haselhurst, *Rt. Hon.* Sir Alan Gordon Barraclough, Kt., MP

Haskard, Sir Cosmo Dugal Patrick Thomas, KCMG, MBE

Haslam, *Rear-Adm.* Sir David William, KBE, CB

Hassett, *Gen.* Sir Francis George, KBE, CB, DSO, LVO

Hastings, Sir Stephen Lewis Edmonstone, Kt., MC

Hatter, Sir Maurice, Kt.

Hatty, *Hon.* Sir Cyril James, Kt.

Haughton, Sir James, Kt., CBE, QPM

Havelock, Sir Wilfrid Bowen, Kt.

Hawkins, Sir Paul Lancelot, Kt., TD

†Hawkins, Sir Richard Caesar, Bt. (1778)

Hawley, Sir Donald Frederick, KCMG, MBE

†Hawley, Sir Henry Nicholas, Bt. (1795)

Haworth, Sir Philip, Bt. (1911)

Hawthorne, Sir Nigel Barnard, Kt., CBE

Hawthorne, *Prof.* Sir William Rede, Kt., CBE, SC.D., FRS, FREng.

Hay, Sir David Osborne, Kt., CBE, DSO

Hay, Sir David Russell, Kt., CBE, FRCP, MD

Hay, Sir Hamish Grenfell, Kt.

Hay, Sir James Brian Dalrymple-, Bt. (1798)

Hay, Sir John Erroll Audley, Bt. (S. 1663)

†Hay, Sir Ronald Frederick Hamilton, Bt. (S. 1703)

Haydon, Sir Walter Robert, KCMG

Hayes, Sir Brian, Kt., CBE, QPM

Hayes, Sir Brian David, GCB

Hayr, *Air Marshal* Sir Kenneth William, KCB, KBE, AFC

Hayward, Sir Anthony William Byrd, Kt.

Hayward, Sir Jack Arnold, Kt., OBE

Haywood, Sir Harold, KCVO, OBE

Head, Sir Francis David Somerville, Bt. (1838)

Healey, Sir Charles Edward Chadwyck-, Bt. (1919)

Heap, Sir Peter William, KCMG

Hearne, Sir Graham James, Kt., CBE

Heath, *Rt. Hon.* Sir Edward Richard George, KG, MBE, MP

Heath, Sir Mark Evelyn, KCVO, CMG

Heathcote, *Brig.* Sir Gilbert Simon, Bt., CBE (1733)

Heathcote, Sir Michael Perryman, Bt. (1733)

Heatley, Sir Peter, Kt., CBE

Heaton, Sir Yvo Robert Henniker-, Bt. (1912)

Heiser, Sir Terence Michael, GCB

Hellaby, Sir (Frederick Reed) Alan, Kt.

Henderson, Sir Denys Hartley, Kt.

Henderson, Sir (John) Nicholas, GCMG, KCVO

Henderson, Sir William MacGregor, Kt., D.SC., FRS

Henley, Sir Douglas Owen, KCB

Hennessy, Sir James Patrick Ivan, KBE, CMG

†Henniker, Sir Adrian Chandos, Bt. (1813)

Henry, Sir Denis Aynsley, Kt., OBE, QC

Henry, *Rt. Hon.* Sir Denis Robert Maurice, Kt.

Henry, *Hon.* Sir Geoffrey Arama, KBE

†Henry, Sir Patrick Denis, Bt. (1923)

Henry, *Hon.* Sir Trevor Ernest, Kt.

Hepburn, Sir John Alastair Trant Kidd Buchan-, Bt. (1815)

Herbecq, Sir John Edward, KCB

Herbert, *Adm.* Sir Peter Geoffrey Marshall, KCB, OBE

Hermon, Sir John Charles, Kt., OBE, QPM

Heron, Sir Conrad Frederick, KCB, OBE

Heron, Sir Michael Gilbert, Kt.

Hervey, Sir Roger Blaise Ramsay, KCVO, CMG

Heseltine, *Rt. Hon.* Sir William Frederick Payne, GCB, GCVO

Hetherington, Sir Arthur Ford, Kt., DSC, FREng.

Hetherington, Sir Thomas Chalmers, KCB, CBE, TD, QC

Hewetson, Sir Christopher Raynor, Kt., TD

Hewett, Sir Peter John Smithson, Bt., MM (1813)

Hewitt, Sir (Cyrus) Lenox (Simson), Kt., OBE

Hewitt, Sir Nicholas Charles Joseph, Bt. (1921)

Heygate, Sir Richard John Gage, Bt. (1831)

Heywood, Sir Peter, Bt. (1838)

Hezlet, *Vice-Adm.* Sir Arthur Richard, KBE, CB, DSO, DSC

Hibbert, Sir Jack, KCB

Hibbert, Sir Reginald Alfred, GCMG

Hickey, Sir Justin, Kt.

Hickman, Sir (Richard) Glenn, Bt. (1903)

Hicks, Sir Robert, Kt.

Hidden, *Hon.* Sir Anthony Brian, Kt.

Hielscher, Sir Leo Arthur, Kt.

Higgins, *Hon.* Sir Malachy Joseph, Kt.

Higginson, Sir Gordon Robert, Kt., Ph.D., FREng.

Hill, Sir Alexander Rodger Erskine-, Bt. (1945)

Hill, Sir Arthur Alfred, Kt., CBE

Hill, Sir Brian John, Kt.

Hill, Sir James Frederick, Bt. (1917)

Hill, Sir John McGregor, Kt., Ph.D., FREng.

Hill, Sir John Maxwell, Kt., CBE, DFC

†Hill, Sir John Rowley, Bt. (I. 1779)

Hill, *Vice-Adm.* Sir Robert Charles Finch, KBE, FREng.

Hillary, Sir Edmund, KG, KBE

Hillhouse, Sir (Robert) Russell, KCB

Hills, Sir Graham John, Kt.

Hine, *Air Chief Marshal* Sir Patrick Bardon, GCB, GBE

Hirsch, *Prof.* Sir Peter Bernhard, Kt., Ph.D., FRS

Hirst, *Rt. Hon.* Sir David Cozens-Hardy, Kt.

Hirst, Sir Michael William, Kt.

Hoare, Sir Peter Richard David, Bt. (1786)

Hoare, Sir Timothy Edward Charles, Bt., OBE (I. 1784)

Hobart, Sir John Vere, Bt. (1914)

Hobbs, *Maj.-Gen.* Sir Michael Frederick, KCVO, CBE

Hobday, Sir Gordon Ivan, Kt.

Hobhouse, Sir Charles John Spinney, Bt. (1812)

Hockaday, Sir Arthur Patrick, KCB, CMG

Hockley, *Gen.* Sir Anthony Heritage
Farrar-, GBE, KCB, DSO, MC
Hoddinott, Sir John Charles, Kt., CBE,
QPM
†Hodge, Sir Andrew Rowland, Bt.
(1921)
Hodge, Sir James William, KCVO,
CMG
Hodge, Sir Julian Stephen Alfred, Kt.
Hodges, *Air Chief Marshal* Sir Lewis
MacDonald, KCB, CBE, DSO, DFC
Hodgkin, Sir Gordon Howard Eliot,
Kt., CBE
Hodgkinson, *Air Chief Marshal* Sir
(William) Derek, KCB, CBE, DFC,
AFC
Hodgson, Sir Maurice Arthur Eric,
Kt., FREng.
Hodgson, *Hon.* Sir (Walter) Derek
(Thornley), Kt.
Hodson, Sir Michael Robin
Adderley, Bt. (I. 1789)
Hoffenberg, *Prof.* Sir Raymond, KBE
Hogg, Sir Christopher Anthony, Kt.
Hogg, *Vice-Adm.* Sir Ian Leslie
Trower, KCB, DSC
Hogg, Sir Michael David, Bt. (1846)
†Hogg, Sir Michael Edward Lindsay-,
Bt. (1905)
Holcroft, Sir Peter George Culcheth,
Bt. (1921)
Holden, Sir Edward, Bt. (1893)
Holden, Sir John David, Bt. (1919)
Holder, Sir John Henry, Bt. (1898)
Holder, *Air Marshal* Sir Paul Davie,
KBE, CB, DSO, DFC, ph.D.
Holdgate, Sir Martin Wyatt, Kt., CB,
ph.D.
Holland, *Hon.* Sir Alan Douglas, Kt.
Holland, *Hon.* Sir Christopher John,
Kt.
Holland, Sir Clifton Vaughan, Kt.
Holland, Sir Geoffrey, KCB
Holland, Sir Kenneth Lawrence, Kt.,
CBE, QFSM
Holland, Sir Philip Welsby, Kt.
Holliday, *Prof.* Sir Frederick George
Thomas, Kt., CBE, FRSE
Hollings, *Hon.* Sir (Alfred) Kenneth,
Kt., MC
Hollis, *Hon.* Sir Anthony Barnard, Kt.
Hollom, Sir Jasper Quintus, KBE
Holloway, *Hon.* Sir Barry Blyth, KBE
Holm, Sir Carl Henry, Kt., OBE
Holm, Sir Ian (Ian Holm Cuthbert),
Kt., CBE
Holman, *Hon.* Sir (Edward) James,
Kt.
Holmes, *Prof.* Sir Frank Wakefield,
Kt.
Holmes, Sir John Eaton, KBE, CMG,
CVO
Holmes, Sir Peter Fenwick, Kt., MC
Holroyd, *Air Marshal* Sir Frank
Martyn, KBE, CB, FREng.
Holt, *Prof.* Sir James Clarke, Kt.
Holt, Sir Michael, Kt., CBE
Home, Sir William Dundas, Bt. (S.
1671)

Honeycombe, *Prof.* Sir Robert
William Kerr, Kt., FRS, FREng.
Honywood, Sir Filmer Courtenay
William, Bt. (1660)
Hood, Sir Harold Joseph, Bt., TD
(1922)
Hookway, Sir Harry Thurston, Kt.
Hooper, *Hon.* Sir Anthony, Kt.
Hope, Sir Colin Frederick Newton,
Kt.
Hope, *Rt. Revd and Rt. Hon.* David
Michael, KCVO
Hope, Sir John Carl Alexander, Bt.
(S. 1628)
Hopkin, Sir (William Aylsham)
Bryan, Kt., CBE
Hopkins, Sir Anthony Philip, Kt., CBE
Hopkins, Sir Michael John, Kt., CBE,
RA, RIBA
Hopwood, *Prof.* Sir David Alan, Kt.,
FRS
Hordern, *Rt. Hon.* Sir Peter
Maudslay, Kt.
Horlick, *Vice-Adm.* Sir Edwin John,
KBE, FREng.
Horlick, Sir James Cunliffe William,
Bt. (1914)
Horlock, *Prof.* Sir John Harold, Kt.,
FRS, FREng.
Hornby, Sir Derek Peter, Kt.
Hornby, Sir Simon Michael, Kt.
Horne, Sir Alan Gray Antony, Bt.
(1929)
Horsfall, Sir John Musgrave, Bt., MC,
TD (1909)
Horsley, *Air Marshal* Sir (Beresford)
Peter (Torrington), KCB, CBE, LVO,
AFC
†Hort, Sir Andrew Edwin Fenton, Bt.
(1767)
Horton, Sir Robert Baynes, Kt.
Hosker, Sir Gerald Albery, KCB, QC
Hoskyns, Sir Benedict Leigh, Bt.
(1676)
Hoskyns, Sir John Austin
Hungerford Leigh, Kt.
Hotung, Sir Joseph Edward, Kt.
Houghton, Sir John Theodore, Kt.,
CBE, FRS
†Houldsworth, Sir Richard Thomas
Reginald, Bt. (1887)
Hounsfield, Sir Godfrey Newbold,
Kt., CBE
Hourston, Sir Gordon Minto, Kt.
House, *Lt.-Gen.* Sir David George,
GCB, KCVO, CBE, MC
Houssemayne du Boulay, Sir Roger
William, KCVO, CMG
Howard, Sir (Hamilton) Edward de
Coucey, Bt., GBE (1955)
Howard, *Prof.* Sir Michael Eliot, Kt.,
CBE, MC
Howard, *Maj.-Gen.* Lord Michael
Fitzalan-, GCVO, CB, CBE, MC
Howell, Sir Ralph Frederic, Kt.
Howells, Sir Eric Waldo Benjamin,
Kt., CBE
Howes, Sir Christopher Kingston,
KCVO, CB

Howlett, *Gen.* Sir Geoffrey Hugh
Whitby, KBE, MC
Hoyle, *Prof.* Sir Fred, Kt., FRS
Hoyos, *Hon.* Sir Fabriciano
Alexander, Kt.
Hudson, *Lt.-Gen.* Sir Peter, KCB, CBE
Huggins, *Hon.* Sir Alan Armstrong,
Kt.
Hughes, *Hon.* Sir Anthony Philip
Gilson, Kt.
Hughes, Sir David Collingwood, Bt.
(1773)
Hughes, *Prof.* Sir Edward Stuart
Reginald, Kt., CBE
Hughes, Sir Jack William, Kt.
Hughes, Sir Trevor Denby Lloyd-,
Kt.
Hughes, Sir Trevor Poulton, KCB
Hugo, *Lt.-Col.* Sir John Mandeville,
KCVO, OBE
Hull, *Prof.* Sir David, Kt.
Hulse, Sir Edward Jeremy Westrow,
Bt. (1739)
Hume, Sir Alan Blyth, Kt., CB
Humphreys, Sir (Raymond Evelyn)
Myles, Kt.
Hunt, Sir John Leonard, Kt.
Hunt, *Adm.* Sir Nicholas John
Streynsham, GCB, LVO
Hunt, Sir Rex Masterman, Kt., CMG
Hunt, Sir Robert Frederick, Kt., CBE,
FREng.
Hunter, Sir Alistair John, KCMG
Hunter, Sir Ian Bruce Hope, Kt., MBE
Hunter, *Prof.* Sir Laurence Colvin,
Kt., CBE, FRSE
Hurn, Sir (Francis) Roger, Kt.
Hurrell, Sir Anthony Gerald, KCVO,
CMG
Hurst, Sir Geoffrey Charles, Kt., MBE
Husbands, Sir Clifford Straugh,
GCMG
Hutchinson, *Hon.* Sir Ross, Kt., DFC
Hutchison, *Lt.-Cdr.* Sir (George) Ian
Clark, Kt., RN
Hutchison, *Rt. Hon.* Sir Michael, Kt.
Hutchison, Sir Peter Craft, Bt. (1956)
Hutchison, Sir Robert, Bt. (1939)
Huxley, *Prof.* Sir Andrew Fielding,
Kt., OM, FRS
Huxtable, *Gen.* Sir Charles Richard,
KCB, CBE
Hyatali, *Hon.* Sir Isaac Emanuel, Kt.
Hyslop, Sir Robert John (Robin)
Maxwell-, Kt.
Ibbs, Sir (John) Robin, KBE
Imray, Sir Colin Henry, KBE, CMG
Ingham, Sir Bernard, Kt.
Ingilby, Sir Thomas Colvin William,
Bt. (1866)
Inglis, Sir Brian Scott, Kt.
Inglis of Glencorse, Sir Roderick
John, Bt. (S. 1703)
Ingram, Sir James Herbert Charles,
Bt. (1893)
Ingram, Sir John Henderson, Kt., CBE
Inkin, Sir Geoffrey David, Kt., OBE
†Innes, Sir David Charles Kenneth
Gordon, Bt. (NS 1686)

Innes of Edingight, Sir Malcolm Rognvald, KCVO
Innes, Sir Peter Alexander Berowald, Bt. (s. 1628)
Irvine, Sir Donald Hamilton, Kt., CBE, MD, FRCGP
Irving, *Prof.* Sir Miles Horsfall, Kt., MD, FRCS, FRCSE
Isaacs, Sir Jeremy Israel, Kt.
Isham, Sir Ian Vere Gyles, Bt. (1627)
Jack, *Hon.* Sir Alieu Sulayman, Kt.
Jack, Sir David, Kt., CBE, FRS, FRSE
Jack, Sir David Emmanuel, GCMG, MBE
Jackson, Sir (John) Edward, KCMG
Jackson, Sir Kenneth Joseph, Kt.
Jackson, *Lt.-Gen.* Sir Michael David, KCB, CBE
Jackson, Sir Michael Roland, Bt. (1902)
Jackson, Sir Nicholas Fane St George, Bt. (1913)
Jackson, Sir Robert, Bt. (1815)
Jackson, *Hon.* Sir Rupert Matthew, Kt., QC
Jackson, Sir William Thomas, Bt. (1869)
Jacob, Sir Isaac Hai, Kt., QC
Jacob, *Hon.* Sir Robert Raphael Hayim (Robin), Kt.
Jacobi, Sir Derek George, Kt., CBE
Jacobi, *Dr* Sir James Edward, Kt., OBE
Jacobs, *Hon.* Sir Kenneth Sydney, KBE
Jacobs, Sir Piers, KBE
Jacobs, Sir Wilfred Ebenezer, GCMG, GCVO, OBE, QC
Jacomb, Sir Martin Wakefield, Kt.
Jaffray, Sir William Otho, Bt. (1892)
James, Sir Cynlais Morgan, KCMG
James, Sir Gerard Bowes Kingston, Bt. (1823)
James, Sir John Nigel Courtenay, KCVO, CBE
James, Sir Stanislaus Anthony, GCMG, OBE
Jamieson, *Air Marshal* Sir David Ewan, KBE, CB
Jansen, Sir Ross Malcolm, KBE
Janvrin, Sir Robin Berry, KCVO, CB
Jardine of Applegirth, Sir Alexander Maule, Bt. (s. 1672)
Jardine, Sir Andrew Colin Douglas, Bt. (1916)
Jardine, *Maj.* Sir (Andrew) Rupert (John) Buchanan-, Bt., MC (1885)
Jarman, *Prof.* Sir Brian, Kt., OBE
Jarratt, Sir Alexander Anthony, Kt., CB
Jarvis, Sir Gordon Ronald, Kt.
Jawara, *Hon.* Sir Dawda Kairaba, Kt.
Jay, Sir Antony Rupert, Kt., CVO
Jeewoolall, Sir Ramesh, Kt.
Jefferson, Sir George Rowland, Kt., CBE, FREng.
Jefferson, Sir Mervyn Stewart Dunnington-, Bt. (1958)
Jeffreys, *Prof.* Sir Alec John, Kt., FRS
Jeffries, *Hon.* Sir John Francis, Kt.
Jehangir, Sir Hirji, Bt. (1908)
Jejeebhoy, Sir Rustom, Bt. (1857)

Jenkins, Sir Brian Garton, GBE
Jenkins, Sir Elgar Spencer, Kt., OBE
Jenkins, Sir James Christopher, KCB, QC
Jenkins, Sir Michael Nicholas Howard, Kt., OBE
Jenkins, Sir Michael Romilly Heald, KCMG
Jenkinson, Sir John Banks, Bt. (1661)
†Jenks, Sir Maurice Arthur Brian, Bt. (1932)
Jennings, Sir John Southwood, Kt., CBE, FRSE
Jennings, *Prof.* Sir Robert Yewdall, Kt., QC
Jephcott, Sir (John) Anthony, Bt. (1962)
Jessel, Sir Charles John, Bt. (1883)
Jewkes, Sir Gordon Wesley, KCMG
John, Sir David Glyndwr, KCMG
John, Sir Elton Hercules (Reginald Kenneth Dwight), Kt., CBE
Johns, *Air Chief Marshal* Sir Richard Edward, GCB, CBE, LVO
Johnson, *Rt. Hon.* Sir David Powell Croom-, Kt., DSC, VRD
Johnson, *Gen.* Sir Garry Dene, KCB, OBE, MC
Johnson, Sir John Rodney, KCMG
†Johnson, Sir Patrick Eliot, Bt. (1818)
Johnson, Sir Peter Colpoys Paley, Bt. (1755)
Johnson, *Hon.* Sir Robert Lionel, Kt.
Johnson, Sir Vassel Godfrey, Kt., CBE
Johnston, Sir John Baines, GCMG, KCVO
Johnston, *Lt.-Col.* Sir John Frederick Dame, GCVO, MC
Johnston, *Lt.-Gen.* Sir Maurice Robert, KCB, OBE
Johnston, Sir Thomas Alexander, Bt. (s. 1626)
Johnston, Sir William Robert Patrick Knox- (Sir Robin), Kt., CBE, RD
Johnstone, Sir (George) Richard Douglas, Bt. (s. 1700)
Johnstone, Sir (John) Raymond, Kt., CBE
Jolliffe, Sir Anthony Stuart, GBE
Jones, *Gen.* Sir (Charles) Edward Webb, KCB, CBE
Jones, Sir Christopher Lawrence-, Bt. (1831)
Jones, Sir David Akers-, KBE, CMG
Jones, *Air Marshal* Sir Edward Gordon, KCB, CBE, DSO, DFC
Jones, Sir Ewart Ray Herbert, Kt., D.SC., Ph.D., FRS
Jones, Sir (John) Derek Alun-, Kt.
Jones, Sir John Henry Harvey-, Kt., MBE
Jones, Sir John Prichard-, Bt. (1910)
Jones, Sir Keith Stephen, Kt.
Jones, *Hon.* Sir Kenneth George Illtyd, Kt.
Jones, Sir Lyndon, Kt.
Jones, Sir (Owen) Trevor, Kt.
Jones, Sir (Peter) Hugh (Jefferd) Lloyd-, Kt.

Jones, Sir Richard Anthony Lloyd, KCB
Jones, Sir Robert Edward, Kt.
Jones, Sir Simon Warley Frederick Benton, Bt. (1919)
Jones, Sir (Thomas) Philip, Kt., CB
Jones, Sir (William) Emrys, Kt.
Jones, Sir Wynn Normington Hugh-, Kt., LVO
†Joseph, *Hon.* Sir James Samuel, Bt. (1943)
Jowitt, *Hon.* Sir Edwin Frank, Kt.
Joyce, *Lt.-Gen.* Sir Robert John Hayman-, KCB, CBE
Judge, *Rt. Hon.* Sir Igor, Kt.
Judge, Sir Paul Rupert, Kt.
Jugnauth, *Rt. Hon.* Sir Aneerood, KCMG, QC
Jungius, *Vice-Adm.* Sir James George, KBE
Jupp, *Hon.* Sir Kenneth Graham, Kt., MC
Kaberry, *Hon.* Sir Christopher Donald, Bt. (1960)
Kalms, Sir (Harold) Stanley, Kt.
Kalo, Sir Kwamala, Kt., MBE
Kan Yuet-Keung, Sir, GBE
Kapi, *Hon.* Sir Mari, Kt., CBE
Kaputin, Sir John Rumet, KBE, CMG
Katsina, The Emir of, KBE, CMG
Katz, Sir Bernard, Kt., FRS
Kausimae, Sir David Nanau, KBE
Kavali, Sir Thomas, Kt., OBE
Kawharu, *Prof.* Sir Ian Hugh, Kt.
Kay, *Prof.* Sir Andrew Watt, Kt.
Kay, *Hon.* Sir John William, Kt.
Kay, *Hon.* Sir Maurice Ralph, Kt.
Kaye, Sir John Phillip Lister Lister-, Bt. (1812)
Kaye, Sir Paul Henry Gordon, Bt. (1923)
Keane, Sir Richard Michael, Bt. (1801)
Keeble, Sir (Herbert Ben) Curtis, GCMG
Keene, *Hon.* Sir David Wolfe, Kt.
Keith, *Prof.* Sir James, KBE
Kellett, Sir Stanley Charles, Bt. (1801)
Kelly, Sir David Robert Corbett, Kt., CBE
Kelly, *Rt. Hon.* Sir (John William) Basil, Kt.
Kelly, Sir William Theodore, Kt., OBE
Kemball, *Air Marshal* Sir (Richard) John, KCB, CBE
Kemp, Sir (Edward) Peter, KCB
Kenilorea, *Rt. Hon.* Sir Peter, KBE
Kennard, *Lt.-Col.* Sir George Arnold Ford, Bt. (1891)
Kennaway, Sir John Lawrence, Bt. (1791)
Kennedy, Sir Francis, KCMG, CBE
Kennedy, *Hon.* Sir Ian Alexander, Kt.
Kennedy, Sir Ludovic Henry Coverley, Kt.
†Kennedy, Sir Michael Edward, Bt., (1836)

Kennedy, *Rt. Hon.* Sir Paul Joseph Morrow, Kt.

Kennedy, *Air Chief Marshal* Sir Thomas Lawrie, GCB, AFC

Kenny, Sir Anthony John Patrick, Kt., D.Phil., D.Litt., FBA

Kenny, *Gen.* Sir Brian Leslie Graham, GCB, CBE

Kentridge, Sir Sydney Woolf, KCMG, QC

Kenyon, Sir George Henry, Kt.

Kermode, Sir (John) Frank, Kt., FBA

Kermode, Sir Ronald Graham Quale, KBE

Kerr, *Hon.* Sir Brian Francis, Kt.

Kerr, *Adm.* Sir John Beverley, GCB

Kerr, Sir John Olav, KCMG

Kerr, *Rt. Hon.* Sir Michael Robert Emanuel, Kt.

Kerruish, Sir (Henry) Charles, Kt., OBE

Kerry, Sir Michael James, KCB, QC

Kershaw, Sir (John) Anthony, Kt., MC

Keswick, Sir John Chippendale Lindley, Kt.

Kidd, Sir Robert Hill, KBE, CB

Kikau, *Ratu* Sir Jone Latianara, KBE

Killen, *Hon.* Denis James, KCMG

Killick, Sir John Edward, GCMG

Kimber, Sir Charles Dixon, Bt. (1904)

King, Sir John Christopher, Bt. (1888)

King, *Vice-Adm.* Sir Norman Ross Dutton, KBE

King, Sir Wayne Alexander, Bt. (1815)

Kingman, *Prof.* Sir John Frank Charles, Kt., FRS

Kingsland, Sir Richard, Kt., CBE, DFC

Kinloch, Sir David, Bt. (s. 1686)

Kinloch, Sir David Oliphant, Bt. (1873)

Kipalan, Sir Albert, Kt.

Kirby, *Hon.* Sir Richard Clarence, Kt.

Kirkpatrick, Sir Ivone Elliott, Bt. (s. 1685)

Kirkwood, *Hon.* Sir Andrew Tristram Hammett, Kt.

Kitcatt, Sir Peter Julian, Kt., CB

Kitson, *Gen.* Sir Frank Edward, GBE, KCB, MC

Kitson, Sir Timothy Peter Geoffrey, Kt.

Kleinwort, Sir Richard Drake, Bt. (1909)

Klevan, *Hon.* Sir Rodney (Conrad), Kt., QC

Klug, Sir Aaron, Kt., OM

Kneller, Sir Alister Arthur, Kt.

Knight, Sir Arthur William, Kt.

Knight, Sir Harold Murray, KBE, DSC

Knight, *Air Chief Marshal* Sir Michael William Patrick, KCB, AFC

Knill, *Prof.* Sir John Lawrence, Kt., FREng.

†Knill, Sir Thomas John Pugin Bartholomew, Bt. (1893)

Knott, Sir John Laurence, Kt., CBE

Knowles, Sir Charles Francis, Bt. (1765)

Knowles, Sir Durward Randolph, Kt., OBE

Knowles, Sir Leonard Joseph, Kt., CBE

Knowles, Sir Richard Marchant, Kt.

Knox, Sir Bryce Muir, KCVO, MC, TD

Knox, Sir David Laidlaw, Kt.

Knox, *Hon.* Sir John Leonard, Kt.

Knox, *Hon.* Sir William Edward, Kt.

Koraea, Sir Thomas, Kt.

Kornberg, *Prof.* Sir Hans Leo, Kt., D.SC., SC.D., Ph.D., FRS

Korowi, Sir Wiwa, GCMG

Krebs, *Prof.* Sir John Richard, Kt., D.Phil., FRS

Kroto, *Prof.* Sir Harold Walter, Kt., FRS

Kulukundis, Sir Elias George (Eddie), Kt., OBE

Kurongku, *Most Revd* Peter, KBE

Lacon, Sir Edmund Vere, Bt. (1818)

Lacy, Sir Hugh Maurice Pierce, Bt. (1921)

Lacy, Sir John Trend, Kt., CBE

Laddie, *Hon.* Sir Hugh Ian Lang, Kt.

Laidlaw, Sir Christophor Charles Fraser, Kt.

Laing, Sir (John) Martin (Kirby), Kt., CBE

Laing, Sir (John) Maurice, Kt.

Laing, Sir (William) Kirby, Kt., FREng.

Laird, Sir Gavin Harry, Kt., CBE

Lake, Sir (Atwell) Graham, Bt. (1711)

Laker, Sir Frederick Alfred, Kt.

Lakin, Sir Michael, Bt. (1909)

Laking, Sir George Robert, KCMG

Lamb, Sir Albert (Larry), Kt.

Lamb, Sir Albert Thomas, KBE, CMG, DFC

Lambert, Sir Anthony Edward, KCMG

Lambert, Sir John Henry, KCVO, CMG

†Lambert, Sir Peter John Biddulph, Bt. (1711)

Lampl, Sir Frank William, Kt.

Landale, Sir David William Neil, KCVO

Landau, Sir Dennis Marcus, Kt.

Lang, *Lt.-Gen.* Sir Derek Boileau, KCB, DSO, MC

Langham, Sir James Michael, Bt. (1660)

Langlands, Sir Robert Alan, Kt.

Langley, *Hon.* Sir Gordon Julian Hugh, Kt.

Langley, *Maj.-Gen.* Sir Henry Desmond Allen, KCVO, MBE

Langrishe, Sir James Hercules, Bt. (I. 1777)

Lankester, Sir Timothy Patrick, KCB

Lapun, *Hon.* Sir Paul, Kt.

Larcom, Sir (Charles) Christopher Royde, Bt. (1868)

Large, Sir Andrew McLeod Brooks, Kt.

Large, Sir Peter, Kt., CBE

Lasdun, Sir Denys Louis, Kt., CH, CBE, FRIBA

Latham, *Hon.* Sir David Nicholas Ramsey, Kt.

Latham, Sir Michael Anthony, Kt.

Latham, Sir Richard Thomas Paul, Bt. (1919)

Latimer, Sir (Courtenay) Robert, Kt., CBE

Latimer, Sir Graham Stanley, KBE

Lauder, Sir Piers Robert Dick-, Bt. (s. 1690)

Laughton, Sir Anthony Seymour, Kt.

Laurantus, Sir Nicholas, Kt., MBE

Laurence, Sir Peter Harold, KCMG, MC

Laurie, Sir Robert Bayley Emilius, Bt. (1834)

Lauterpacht, Sir Elihu, Kt., CBE, QC

Lauti, *Rt. Hon.* Sir Toaripi, GCMG

Lavan, *Hon.* Sir John Martin, Kt.

Law, *Adm.* Sir Horace Rochfort, GCB, OBE, DSC

Lawes, Sir (John) Michael Bennet, Bt. (1882)

Lawler, Sir Peter James, Kt., OBE

Lawrence, Sir David Roland Walter, Bt. (1906)

Lawrence, Sir Guy Kempton, Kt., DSO, OBE, DFC

Lawrence, Sir Ivan John, Kt., QC

Lawrence, Sir John Patrick Grosvenor, Kt., CBE

Lawrence, Sir John Waldemar, Bt., OBE (1858)

Lawrence, Sir William Fettiplace, Bt. (1867)

Laws, *Rt. Hon.* Sir John Grant McKenzie, Kt.

Lawson, Sir Christopher Donald, Kt.

Lawson, *Col.* Sir John Charles Arthur Digby, Bt., DSO, MC (1900)

Lawson, Sir John Philip Howard-, Bt. (1841)

Lawson, *Gen.* Sir Richard George, KCB, DSO, OBE

Lawton, *Prof.* Sir Frank Ewart, Kt.

Lawton, *Rt. Hon.* Sir Frederick Horace, Kt.

Layard, *Adm.* Sir Michael Henry Gordon, KCB, CBE

Layfield, Sir Frank Henry Burland Willoughby, Kt., QC

Lea, *Vice-Adm.* Sir John Stuart Crosbie, KBE

Lea, Sir Thomas William, Bt. (1892)

Leach, *Admiral of the Fleet* Sir Henry Conyers, GCB

Leahy, Sir Daniel Joseph, Kt.

Leahy, Sir John Henry Gladstone, KCMG

Learmont, *Gen.* Sir John Hartley, KCB, CBE

Leask, *Lt.-Gen.* Sir Henry Lowther Ewart Clark, KCB, DSO, OBE

Leather, Sir Edwin Hartley Cameron, KCMG, KCVO

Leaver, Sir Christopher, GBE

Le Bailly, *Vice-Adm.* Sir Louis Edward Stewart Holland, KBE, CB

Le Cheminant, *Air Chief Marshal* Sir Peter de Lacey, GBE, KCB, DFC

Lechmere, Sir Berwick Hungerford, Bt. (1818)

Ledger, Sir Philip Stevens, Kt., CBE, FRSE

Lee, Sir Arthur James, KBE, MC

Lee, *Air Chief Marshal* Sir David John Pryer, GBE, CB

Lee, *Brig.* Sir Leonard Henry, Kt., CBE

Lee, Sir Quo-wei, Kt., CBE

Leeds, Sir Christopher Anthony, Bt. (1812)

Lees, Sir David Bryan, Kt.

Lees, Sir Thomas Edward, Bt. (1897)

Lees, Sir Thomas Harcourt Ivor, Bt. (1804)

Lees, Sir (William) Antony Clare, Bt. (1937)

Leese, Sir John Henry Vernon, Bt. (1908)

Le Fanu, *Maj.* Sir (George) Victor (Sheridan), KCVO

le Fleming, Sir David Kelland, Bt. (1705)

Legard, Sir Charles Thomas, Bt. (1660)

Legg, Sir Thomas Stuart, KCB, QC

Leggatt, *Rt. Hon.* Sir Andrew Peter, Kt.

Leggatt, Sir Hugh Frank John, Kt.

Leggett, Sir Clarence Arthur Campbell, Kt., MBE

Leigh, Sir Geoffrey Norman, Kt.

Leigh, Sir Richard Henry, Bt. (1918)

Leighton, Sir Michael John Bryan, Bt. (1693)

Leitch, Sir George, KCB, OBE

Leith, Sir Andrew George Forbes-, Bt. (1923)

Le Marchant, Sir Francis Arthur, Bt. (1841)

Lemon, Sir (Richard) Dawnay, Kt., CBE

Leng, *Gen.* Sir Peter John Hall, KCB, MBE, MC

Lennard, *Revd* Sir Hugh Dacre Barrett-, Bt. (1801)

Leon, Sir John Ronald, Bt. (1911)

Leonard, *Rt. Revd and Rt. Hon.* Graham Douglas, KCVO

Leonard, *Hon.* Sir (Hamilton) John, Kt.

Lepping, Sir George Geria Dennis, GCMG, MBE

Le Quesne, Sir (Charles) Martin, KCMG

Le Quesne, Sir (John) Godfray, Kt., QC

Leslie, Sir Colin Alan Bettridge, Kt.

Leslie, Sir John Norman Ide, Bt. (1876)

†Leslie, Sir (Percy) Theodore, Bt. (S. 1625)

Leslie, Sir Peter Evelyn, Kt.

Lester, Sir James Theodore, Kt.

Lethbridge, Sir Thomas Periam Hector Noel, Bt. (1804)

Lever, Sir Paul, KCMG

Lever, Sir (Tresham) Christopher Arthur Lindsay, Bt. (1911)

Levey, Sir Michael Vincent, Kt., LVO

Levine, Sir Montague Bernard, Kt.

Levinge, Sir Richard George Robin, Bt. (I. 1704)

Lewando, Sir Jan Alfred, Kt., CBE

Lewinton, Sir Christopher, Kt.

Lewis, Sir David Courtenay Mansel, KCVO

Lewthwaite, *Brig.* Sir Rainald Gilfrid, Bt., CVO, OBE, MC (1927)

Ley, Sir Ian Francis, Bt. (1905)

Leyland, Sir Philip Vyvyan Naylor-, Bt. (1895)

Lickiss, Sir Michael Gillam, Kt.

Liggins, *Prof.* Sir Graham Collingwood, Kt., CBE, FRS

Lightman, *Hon.* Sir Gavin Anthony, Kt.

Lighton, Sir Thomas Hamilton, Bt. (I. 1791)

Limon, Sir Donald William, KCB

Linacre, Sir (John) Gordon (Seymour), Kt., CBE, AFC, DFM

Lindop, Sir Norman, Kt.

Lindsay, Sir James Harvey Kincaid Stewart, Kt.

Lindsay, *Hon.* Sir John Edmund Frederic, Kt.

Lindsay, Sir Ronald Alexander, Bt., (1962)

Lipworth, Sir (Maurice) Sydney, Kt.

Lithgow, Sir William James, Bt. (1925)

Little, *Most Revd* Thomas Francis, KBE

Littler, Sir (James) Geoffrey, KCB

Livesay, *Adm.* Sir Michael Howard, KCB

Llewellyn, Sir Henry Morton, Bt., CBE (1922)

Llewelyn, Sir John Michael Dillwyn-Venables-, Bt. (1890)

Lloyd, *Prof.* Sir Geoffrey Ernest Richard, Kt., FBA

Lloyd, Sir Ian Stewart, Kt.

Lloyd, Sir Nicholas Markley, Kt.

Lloyd, *Rt. Hon.* Sir Peter Robert Cable, Kt., MP

Lloyd, Sir Richard Ernest Butler, Bt. (1960)

Lloyd, *Hon.* Sir Timothy Andrew Wigram, Kt.

Loader, Sir Leslie Thomas, Kt., CBE

Loane, *Most Revd* Marcus Lawrence, KBE

Lobo, Sir Rogerio Hyndman, Kt., CBE

Lockhart, Sir Simon John Edward Francis Sinclair-, Bt. (S. 1636)

†Loder, Sir Edmund Jeune, Bt. (1887)

Logan, Sir Donald Arthur, KCMG

Logan, Sir Raymond Douglas, Kt.

Lokoloko, Sir Tore, GCMG, GCVO, OBE

Lombe, *Hon.* Sir Edward Christopher Evans-, Kt.

Longmore, *Hon.* Sir Andrew Centlivres, Kt.

Loram, *Vice-Adm.* Sir David Anning, KCB, CVO

Lorimer, Sir (Thomas) Desmond, Kt.

Los, *Hon.* Sir Kubulan, Kt., CBE

Lovell, Sir (Alfred Charles) Bernard, Kt., OBE, FRS

Lovelock, Sir Douglas Arthur, KCB

Loveridge, Sir John Warren, Kt.

Lovill, Sir John Roger, Kt., CBE

Low, Sir Alan Roberts, Kt.

Low, Sir James Richard Morrison-, Bt. (1908)

Lowe, *Air Chief Marshal* Sir Douglas Charles, GCB, DFC, AFC

Lowe, Sir Thomas William Gordon, Bt. (1918)

Lowry, Sir John Patrick, Kt., CBE

Lowson, Sir Ian Patrick, Bt. (1951)

Lowther, *Col.* Sir Charles Douglas, Bt. (1824)

Lowther, Sir John Luke, KCVO, CBE

Loyd, Sir Francis Alfred, KCMG, OBE

Loyd, Sir Julian St John, KCVO

Lu, Sir Tseng Chi, Kt.

Lucas, Sir Cyril Edward, Kt., CMG, FRS

Lucas, Sir Thomas Edward, Bt. (1887)

Luce, *Rt. Hon.* Sir Richard Napier, Kt.

Lucy, Sir Edmund John William Hugh Cameron-Ramsay-Fairfax, Bt. (1836)

Luddington, Sir Donald Collin Cumyn, KBE, CMG, CVO

Lumsden, Sir David James, Kt.

Lus, *Hon.* Sir Pita, Kt., OBE

Lush, *Hon.* Sir George Hermann, Kt.

Lushington, Sir John Richard Castleman, Bt. (1791)

Luttrell, *Col.* Sir Geoffrey Walter Fownes, KCVO, MC

Lyell, *Rt. Hon.* Sir Nicholas Walter, Kt., QC, MP

Lygo, *Adm.* Sir Raymond Derek, KCB

Lyle, Sir Gavin Archibald, Bt. (1929)

Lyne, Sir Roderic Michael John, KBE, CMG

Lyons, Sir Edward Houghton, Kt.

Lyons, Sir James Reginald, Kt.

Lyons, Sir John, Kt.

McAlpine, Sir William Hepburn, Bt. (1918)

Macara, Sir Alexander Wiseman, Kt., FRCP, FRCGP

†Macara, Sir Hugh Kenneth, Bt. (1911)

Macartney, Sir John Barrington, Bt. (I. 1799)

McAvoy, Sir (Francis) Joseph, Kt., CBE

McCaffrey, Sir Thomas Daniel, Kt.

McCall, Sir (Charles) Patrick Home, Kt., MBE, TD

McCallum, Sir Donald Murdo, Kt., CBE, FREng.

McCamley, Sir Graham Edward, Kt., MBE

McCarthy, *Rt. Hon.* Sir Thaddeus Pearcey, KBE

McCartney, Sir (James) Paul, Kt., MBE

McClellan, *Col.* Sir Herbert Gerard Thomas, Kt., CBE, TD

McClintock, Sir Eric Paul, Kt.
McColl, Sir Colin Hugh Verel, KCMG
McCollum, *Rt. Hon.* Sir William, Kt.
McConnell, Sir Robert Shean, Bt. (1900)
McCorkell, *Col.* Sir Michael William, KCVO, OBE, TD
McCowan, *Rt. Hon.* Sir Anthony James Denys, Kt.
†McCowan, Sir David William, Bt. (1934)
McCullough, *Hon.* Sir (Iain) Charles (Robert), Kt.
MacDermott, *Rt. Hon.* Sir John Clarke, Kt.
McDermott, Sir (Lawrence) Emmet, KBE
Macdonald of Sleat, Sir Ian Godfrey Bosville, Bt. (s. 1625)
Macdonald, Sir Kenneth Carmichael, KCB
Macdonald, *Vice-Adm.* Sir Roderick Douglas, KBE
McDonald, Sir Tom, Kt., OBE
McDonald, Sir Trevor, Kt., OBE
MacDougall, Sir (George) Donald (Alastair), Kt., CBE, FBA
McDowell, Sir Eric Wallace, Kt., CBE
McDowell, Sir Henry McLorinan, KBE
Mace, *Lt.-Gen.* Sir John Airth, KBE, CB
McEwen, Sir John Roderick Hugh, Bt. (1953)
McFarland, Sir John Talbot, Bt. (1914)
Macfarlane, Sir (David) Neil, Kt.
Macfarlane, Sir George Gray, Kt., CB, FREng.
McFarlane, Sir Ian, Kt.
McGeoch, *Vice-Adm.* Sir Ian Lachlan Mackay, KCB, DSO, DSC
McGrath, Sir Brian Henry, KCVO
Macgregor, Sir Edwin Robert, Bt. (1828)
MacGregor of MacGregor, Sir Gregor, Bt. (1795)
McGregor, Sir Ian Alexander, Kt., CBE, FRS
McGrigor, *Capt.* Sir Charles Edward, Bt. (1831)
McIntosh, *Vice-Adm.* Sir Ian Stewart, KBE, CB, DSO, DSC
McIntosh, Sir Malcolm Kenneth, Kt., ph.D.
McIntosh, Sir Ronald Robert Duncan, KCB
McIntyre, Sir Donald Conroy, Kt., CBE
McIntyre, Sir Meredith Alister, Kt.
MacKay, *Prof.* Sir Donald Iain, Kt., FRSE
McKay, Sir John Andrew, Kt., CBE
Mackechnie, Sir Alistair John, Kt.
McKee, *Maj.* Sir (William) Cecil, Kt., ERD
McKellen, Sir Ian Murray, Kt., CBE
McKenzie, Sir Alexander, KBE
Mackenzie, Sir Alexander Alwyne Henry Charles Brinton Muir-, Bt. (1805)

†Mackenzie, Sir (James William) Guy, Bt. (1890)
Mackenzie, *Gen.* Sir Jeremy John George, GCB, OBE
†Mackenzie, Sir Peter Douglas, Bt. (s. 1673)
†Mackenzie, Sir Roderick McQuhae, Bt. (s. 1703)
McKenzie, Sir Roy Allan, KBE
Mackeson, Sir Rupert Henry, Bt. (1954)
MacKinlay, Sir Bruce, Kt., CBE
McKinnon, Sir James, Kt.
McKinnon, *Hon.* Sir Stuart Neil, Kt.
Mackintosh, Sir Cameron Anthony, Kt.
Macklin, Sir Bruce Roy, Kt., OBE
Mackworth, Sir Digby (John), Bt. (1776)
McLaren, Sir Robin John Taylor, KCMG
†Maclean of Dunconnell, Sir Charles Edward, Bt. (1957)
Maclean, Sir Donald Og Grant, Kt.
MacLean, *Vice-Adm.* Sir Hector Charles Donald, KBE, CB, DSC
Maclean, Sir Lachlan Hector Charles, Bt. (NS 1631)
McLeod, Sir Charles Henry, Bt. (1925)
McLeod, Sir Ian George, Kt.
MacLeod, Sir (John) Maxwell Norman, Bt. (1924)
Macleod, Sir (Nathaniel William) Hamish, KBE
McLintock, Sir (Charles) Alan, Kt.
McLintock, Sir Michael William, Bt. (1934)
Maclure, Sir John Robert Spencer, Bt. (1898)
McMahon, Sir Brian Patrick, Bt. (1817)
McMahon, Sir Christopher William, Kt.
Macmillan, Sir (Alexander McGregor) Graham, Kt.
MacMillan, *Lt.-Gen.* Sir John Richard Alexander, KCB, CBE
McMullin, *Rt. Hon.* Sir Duncan Wallace, Kt.
Macnaghten, Sir Patrick Alexander, Bt. (1836)
McNamara, *Air Chief Marshal* Sir Neville Patrick, KBE
Macnaughton, *Prof.* Sir Malcolm Campbell, Kt.
McNee, Sir David Blackstock, Kt., QPM
McNulty, Sir (Robert William) Roy, Kt., CBE
MacPhail, Sir Bruce Dugald, Kt.
Macpherson, Sir Ronald Thomas Steward (Tommy), CBE, MC, TD
Macpherson of Cluny, *Hon.* Sir William Alan, Kt., TD
McQuarrie, Sir Albert, Kt.
MacRae, Sir (Alastair) Christopher (Donald Summerhayes), KCMG
Macrae, *Col.* Sir Robert Andrew Scarth, KCVO, MBE

Macready, Sir Nevil John Wilfrid, Bt. (1923)
Mactaggart, Sir John Auld, Bt. (1938)
Macwhinnie, Sir Gordon Menzies, Kt., CBE
McWilliam, Sir Michael Douglas, KCMG
McWilliams, Sir Francis, GBE, FREng.
Madden, *Adm.* Sir Charles Edward, Bt., GCB (1919)
Maddocks, Sir Kenneth Phipson, KCMG, KCVO
Maddox, Sir John Royden, Kt.
Madel, Sir (William) David, Kt., MP
Madigan, Sir Russel Tullie, Kt., OBE
Magnus, Sir Laurence Henry Philip, Bt. (1917)
Maguire, *Air Marshal* Sir Harold John, KCB, DSO, OBE
Mahon, Sir (John) Denis, Kt., CBE
Mahon, Sir William Walter, Bt. (1819)
Maiden, Sir Colin James, Kt., D.phil.
Main, Sir Peter Tester, Kt., ERD
Maino, Sir Charles, KBE
†Maitland, Sir Charles Alexander, Bt. (1818)
Maitland, Sir Donald James Dundas, GCMG, OBE
Makins, Sir Paul Vivian, Bt. (1903)
Malcolm, Sir James William Thomas Alexander, Bt. (s. 1665)
Malet, Sir Harry Douglas St Lo, Bt. (1791)
Mallaby, Sir Christopher Leslie George, GCMG, GCVO
Mallick, *Prof.* Sir Netar Prakash, Kt., FRCP, FRCPEd.
Mallinson, Sir William James, Bt. (1935)
Malone, *Hon.* Sir Denis Eustace Gilbert, Kt.
Malpas, Sir Robert, Kt., CBE, FREng
Mamo, Sir Anthony Joseph, Kt., OBE
Mance, *Hon.* Sir Jonathan Hugh, Kt.
Manchester, Sir William Maxwell, KBE
Mander, Sir Charles Marcus, Bt. (1911)
Manduell, Sir John, Kt., CBE
Mann, *Rt. Revd* Michael Ashley, KCVO
Mann, Sir Rupert Edward, Bt. (1905)
Mansel, Sir Philip, Bt. (1622)
Mansfield, *Vice-Adm.* Sir (Edward) Gerard (Napier), KBE, CVO
Mansfield, *Prof.* Sir Peter, Kt., FRS
Mansfield, Sir Philip (Robert Aked), KCMG
Mantell, *Rt. Hon.* Sir Charles Barrie Knight, Kt.
Manton, Sir Edwin Alfred Grenville, Kt.
Manuella, Sir Tulaga, GCMG, MBE
Manzie, Sir (Andrew) Gordon, KCB
Mara, *Rt. Hon. Ratu* Sir Kamisese Kapaiwai Tuimacilai, GCMG, KBE
Margetson, Sir John William Denys, KCMG
Marjoribanks, Sir James Alexander Milne, KCMG

Mark, Sir Robert, GBE

Markham, Sir Charles John, Bt. (1911)

Marking, Sir Henry Ernest, KCVO, CBE, MC

Marling, Sir Charles William Somerset, Bt. (1882)

Marr, Sir Leslie Lynn, Bt. (1919)

Marriner, Sir Neville, Kt., CBE

Marriott, Sir Hugh Cavendish Smith-, Bt. (1774)

Marriott, Sir John Brook, KCVO

†Marsden, Sir Simon Neville Llewelyn, Bt. (1924)

Marsh, *Prof.* Sir John Stanley, Kt., CBE

Marshall, Sir Arthur Gregory George, Kt., OBE

Marshall, Sir Denis Alfred, Kt.

Marshall, *Prof.* Sir (Oshley) Roy, Kt., CBE

Marshall, Sir Peter Harold Reginald, KCMG

Marshall, Sir Robert Braithwaite, KCB, MBE

Marshall, Sir (Robert) Michael, Kt.

Martin, Sir George Henry, Kt., CBE

Martin, *Vice-Adm.* Sir John Edward Ludgate, KCB, DSC

Martin, *Prof.* Sir (John) Leslie, Kt., ph.D.

Martin, *Prof.* Sir Laurence Woodward, Kt.

Martin, Sir (Robert) Bruce, Kt., QC

Marychurch, Sir Peter Harvey, KCMG

Masefield, Sir Charles Beech Gordon, Kt.

Masefield, Sir Peter Gordon, Kt.

Masire, Sir Ketumile, GCMG

Mason, *Hon.* Sir Anthony Frank, KBE

Mason, Sir (Basil) John, Kt., CB, D.SC., FRS

Mason, *Prof.* Sir David Kean, Kt., CBE

Mason, Sir Frederick Cecil, KCVO, CMG

Mason, Sir Gordon Charles, Kt., OBE

Mason, Sir John Charles Moir, KCMG

Mason, Sir John Peter, Kt., CBE

Mason, *Prof.* Sir Ronald, KCB, FRS

Matane, Sir Paulias Nguna, Kt., CMG, OBE

Mather, Sir (David) Carol (Macdonell), Kt., MC

Mathers, Sir Robert William, Kt.

Matheson of Matheson, Sir Fergus John, Bt. (1882)

Matheson, Sir (James Adam) Louis, KBE, CMG, FREng.

Mathewson, Sir George Ross, Kt., CBE, ph.D., FRSE

Matthews, Sir Peter Alec, Kt.

Matthews, Sir Peter Jack, Kt., CVO, OBE, QPM

Matthews, Sir Stanley, Kt., CBE

Maud, The Hon. Sir Humphrey John Hamilton, KCMG

Mawhinney, *Rt. Hon.* Sir Brian Stanley, Kt., MP

Maxwell, Sir Michael Eustace George, Bt. (S. 1681)

Maxwell, Sir Nigel Mellor Heron-, Bt. (S. 1683)

May, *Rt. Hon.* Sir Anthony Tristram Kenneth, Kt.

May, Sir Kenneth Spencer, Kt., CBE

May, *Prof.* Sir Robert McCredie, Kt., FRS

Maynard, *Hon.* Sir Clement Travelyan, Kt.

Mayne, *Very Revd* Michael Clement Otway, KCVO

Meadow, *Prof.* Sir (Samuel) Roy, Kt., FRCP, FRCPE

Medlycott, Sir Mervyn Tregonwell, Bt. (1808)

Megarry, *Rt. Hon.* Sir Robert Edgar, Kt., FBA

Meinertzhagen, Sir Peter, Kt., CMG

Melhuish, Sir Michael Ramsay, KBE, CMG

Mellon, Sir James, KCMG

Melville, Sir Harry Work, KCB, ph.D., D.SC., FRS

Melville, Sir Leslie Galfreid, KBE

Melville, Sir Ronald Henry, KCB

Mensforth, Sir Eric, Kt., CBE, F.Eng.

Menter, Sir James Woodham, Kt., ph.D., SC.D., FRS

Menteth, Sir James Wallace Stuart-, Bt. (1838)

Meyer, Sir Anthony John Charles, Bt. (1910)

Meyer, Sir Christopher John Rome, KCMG

Meyjes, Sir Richard Anthony, Kt.

Meyrick, Sir David John Charlton, Bt. (1880)

Meyrick, Sir George Christopher Cadafael Tapps-Gervis-, Bt. (1791)

Miakwe, *Hon.* Sir Akepa, KBE

Michael, Sir Peter Colin, Kt., CBE

Middleton, Sir Peter Edward, GCB

Miers, Sir (Henry) David Alastair Capel, KBE, CMG

Milbank, Sir Anthony Frederick, Bt. (1882)

Milburn, Sir Anthony Rupert, Bt. (1905)

Mildmay, Sir Walter John Hugh St John-, Bt. (1772)

Miles, Sir Peter Tremayne, KCVO

Miles, Sir William Napier Maurice, Bt. (1859)

Millais, Sir Geoffrey Richard Everett, Bt. (1885)

Millar, Sir Oliver Nicholas, GCVO, FBA

Millard, Sir Guy Elwin, KCMG, CVO

Miller, Sir Donald John, Kt., FRSE, FREng.

Miller, Sir Harry Holmes, Bt. (1705)

Miller, Sir Hilary Duppa (Hal), Kt.

Miller, *Lt.-Col.* Sir John Mansel, GCVO, DSO, MC

Miller, Sir (Oswald) Bernard, Kt.

Miller, Sir Peter North, Kt.

Miller, Sir Ronald Andrew Baird, Kt., CBE

Miller of Glenlee, Sir Stephen William Macdonald, Bt. (1788)

Millett, *Rt. Hon.* Sir Peter Julian, Kt.

Millichip, Sir Frederick Albert (Bert), Kt.

Mills, *Vice-Adm.* Sir Charles Piercy, KCB, CBE, DSC

Mills, Sir Frank, KCVO, CMG

Mills, Sir John Lewis Ernest Watts, Kt., CBE

Mills, Sir Peter Frederick Leighton, Bt. (1921)

†Milman, Sir David Patrick, Bt. (1800)

Milne, Sir John Drummond, Kt.

Milner, Sir Timothy William Lycett, Bt. (1717)

Mirrlees, *Prof.* Sir James Alexander, Kt., FBA

Mitchell, *Air Cdre* Sir (Arthur) Dennis, KBE, CVO, DFC, AFC

Mitchell, Sir David Bower, Kt.

Mitchell, Sir Derek Jack, KCB, CVO

Mitchell, *Prof.* Sir (Edgar) William John, Kt., CBE, FRS

Mitchell, *Rt. Hon.* Sir James FitzAllen, KCMG

Mitchell, *Very Revd* Patrick Reynolds, KCVO

Mitchell, *Hon.* Sir Stephen George, Kt.

Moate, Sir Roger Denis, Kt.

Mobbs, Sir (Gerald) Nigel, Kt.

Moberly, Sir John Campbell, KBE, CMG

Moberly, Sir Patrick Hamilton, KCMG

Moffat, Sir Brian Scott, Kt., OBE

Moffat, *Lt.-Gen.* Sir (William) Cameron, KBE

Mogg, *Gen.* Sir (Herbert) John, GCB, CBE, DSO

†Moir, Sir Christopher Ernest, Bt. (1916)

Moller, *Hon.* Sir Lester Francis, Kt.

†Molony, Sir Thomas Desmond, Bt. (1925)

Monck, Sir Nicholas Jeremy, KCB

Montgomery, Sir (Basil Henry) David, Bt. (1801)

Montgomery, Sir (William) Fergus, Kt.

Mookerjee, Sir Birendra Nath, Kt.

Moollan, Sir Abdool Hamid Adam, Kt.

Moollan, *Hon.* Sir Cassam (Ismael), Kt.

Moon, Sir Peter Wilfred Giles Graham-, Bt. (1855)

†Moon, Sir Roger, Bt. (1887)

Moore, *Most Revd* Desmond Charles, KBE

Moore, Sir Francis Thomas, Kt.

Moore, Sir Henry Roderick, Kt., CBE

Moore, *Hon.* Sir John Cochrane, Kt.

Moore, *Maj.-Gen.* Sir (John) Jeremy, KCB, OBE, MC

Moore, Sir John Michael, KCVO, CB, DSC

Moore, *Vice Adm.* Sir Michael Antony Claës, KBE, LVO

Moore, *Prof.* Sir Norman Winfrid, Bt. (1919)

Moore, Sir Patrick William Eisdell, Kt., OBE

Moore, Sir William Roger Clotworthy, Bt., TD (1932)

Morauta, Sir Mekere, Kt.

Mordaunt, Sir Richard Nigel Charles, Bt. (1611)

Moreton, Sir John Oscar, KCMG, KCVO, MC

Morgan, *Vice-Adm.* Sir Charles Christopher, KBE

Morgan, *His Hon. Maj.-Gen.* Sir David John Hughes-, Bt., CB, CBE (1925)

Morgan, Sir John Albert Leigh, KCMG

Morison, *Hon.* Sir Thomas Richard Atkin, Kt.

Morland, *Hon.* Sir Michael, Kt.

Morland, Sir Robert Kenelm, Kt.

Morpeth, Sir Douglas Spottiswoode, Kt., TD

Morris, *Air Marshal* Sir Arnold Alec, KBE, CB, FREng.

Morris, Sir (James) Richard (Samuel), Kt., CBE, FREng.

Morris, *Rt. Hon.* Sir John, Kt., QC

Morris, Sir Keith Elliot Hedley, KBE, CMG

Morris, *Prof.* Sir Peter John, Kt., FRS

Morris, Sir Robert Byng, Bt. (1806)

Morris, Sir Trefor Alfred, Kt., CBE, QPM

Morris, *Very Revd* Sir William James, KCVO, ph.D.

Morrison, Sir (Alexander) Fraser, Kt., CBE

Morrison, *Hon.* Sir Charles Andrew, Kt.

Morrison, Sir Howard Leslie, Kt., OBE

Morritt, *Hon.* Sir (Robert) Andrew, Kt., CVO

Morrow, Sir Ian Thomas, Kt.

Morse, Sir Christopher Jeremy, KCMG

Mortimer, Sir John Clifford, Kt., CBE, QC

Morton, *Adm.* Sir Anthony Storrs, GBE, KCB

Morton, Sir (Robert) Alastair (Newton), Kt.

Moseley, Sir George Walker, KCB

Moser, *Prof.* Sir Claus Adolf, KCB, CBE, FBA

Moses, *Hon.* Sir Alan George, Kt.

†Moss, Sir David John Edwards-, Bt. (1868)

Moss, Sir David Joseph, KCVO, CMG

Mostyn, *Gen.* Sir (Joseph) David Frederick, KCB, CBE

†Mostyn, Sir William Basil John, Bt. (1670)

Mott, Sir John Harmer, Bt. (1930)

Mottram, Sir Richard Clive, KCB

†Mount, Sir (William Robert) Ferdinand, Bt. (1921)

Mountain, Sir Denis Mortimer, Bt. (1922)

Mountfield, Sir Robin, KCB

Mowbray, Sir John, Kt.

Mowbray, Sir John Robert, Bt. (1880)

Muir, Sir Laurence Macdonald, Kt.

†Muir, Sir Richard James Kay, Bt. (1892)

Mulcahy, Sir Geoffrey John, Kt.

Mullens, *Lt.-Gen.* Sir Anthony Richard Guy, KCB, OBE

Mummery, *Hon.* Sir John Frank, Kt.

Munn, Sir James, Kt., OBE

Munro, Sir Alan Gordon, KCMG

†Munro, Sir Kenneth Arnold William, Bt. (s. 1634)

†Munro, Sir Keith Gordon, Bt. (1825)

Munro, Sir Sydney Douglas Gun-, GCMG, MBE

Muria, *Hon.* Sir Gilbert John Baptist, Kt.

Murphy, Sir Leslie Frederick, Kt.

Murray, *Rt. Hon.* Sir Donald Bruce, Kt.

Murray, Sir James, KCMG

Murray, Sir John Antony Jerningham, Kt., CBE

Murray, *Prof.* Sir Kenneth, Kt., FRCPath., FRS, FRSE

Murray, Sir Nigel Andrew Digby, Bt. (s. 1628)

Murray, Sir Patrick Ian Keith, Bt. (s. 1673)

†Murray, Sir Rowland William, Bt. (s. 1630)

Mursell, Sir Peter, Kt., MBE

Musgrave, Sir Christopher Patrick Charles, Bt. (1611)

Musgrave, Sir Richard James, Bt. (I. 1782)

Musson, *Gen.* Sir Geoffrey Randolph Dixon, GCB, CBE, DSO

Myers, Sir Philip Alan, Kt., OBE, QPM

Myers, *Prof.* Sir Rupert Horace, KBE

Mynors, Sir Richard Baskerville, Bt. (1964)

Naipaul, Sir Vidiadhar Surajprasad, Kt.

Nairn, Sir Michael, Bt. (1904)

Nairn, Sir Robert Arnold Spencer-, Bt. (1933)

Nairne, *Rt. Hon.* Sir Patrick Dalmahoy, GCB, MC

Naish, Sir (Charles) David, Kt.

Nall, Sir Michael Joseph, Bt., RN (1954)

Namaliu, *Rt. Hon.* Sir Rabbie Langanai, Kt., CMG

†Napier, Sir Charles Joseph, Bt. (1867)

Napier, Sir John Archibald Lennox, Bt. (s. 1627)

Napier, Sir Oliver John, Kt.

Nasmith, *Prof.* Sir James Duncan Dunbar-, Kt., CBE, RIBA, FRSE

Neal, Sir Eric James, Kt., CVO

Neal, Sir Leonard Francis, Kt., CBE

Neale, Sir Gerrard Anthony, Kt.

Neave, Sir Paul Arundell, Bt. (1795)

Nedd, *Hon.* Sir Robert Archibald, Kt.

Needham, *Rt. Hon.* Sir Richard (The Earl of Kilmorey, *see* page 141)

Neill, *Rt. Hon.* Sir Brian Thomas, Kt.

Neill, *Rt. Hon.* Sir Ivan, Kt., PC (NI)

Neill, Sir (James) Hugh, KCVO, CBE, TD

†Nelson, Sir Jamie Charles Vernon Hope, Bt. (1912)

Nelson, *Hon.* Sir Robert Franklyn, Kt.

Nelson, *Air Marshal* Sir (Sidney) Richard (Carlyle), KCB, OBE, MD

Nepean, *Lt.-Col.* Sir Evan Yorke, Bt. (1802)

Neuberger, *Hon.* Sir David Edmond, Kt.

Neubert, Sir Michael John, Kt.

Neville, Sir Roger Albert Gartside, Kt., VRD

New, *Maj.-Gen.* Sir Laurence Anthony Wallis, Kt., CB, CBE

Newall, Sir Paul Henry, Kt., TD

Newington, Sir Michael John, KCMG

Newman, Sir Francis Hugh Cecil, Bt. (1912)

Newman, Sir Geoffrey Robert, Bt. (1836)

Newman, *Hon.* Sir George Michael, Kt.

Newman, Sir Kenneth Leslie, GBE, QPM

Newman, *Vice-Adm.* Sir Roy Thomas, KCB

Newman, *Col.* Sir Stuart Richard, CBE, TD

Newsam, Sir Peter Anthony, Kt.

Newton, Sir (Charles) Wilfred, Kt., CBE

Newton, Sir (Harry) Michael (Rex), Bt. (1900)

Newton, Sir Kenneth Garnar, Bt., OBE, TD (1924)

Ngata, Sir Henare Kohere, KBE

Nichol, Sir Duncan Kirkbride, Kt., CBE

Nicholas, Sir David, Kt., CBE

Nicholas, Sir John William, KCVO, CMG

Nicholls, *Air Marshal* Sir John Moreton, KCB, CBE, DFC, AFC

Nicholls, Sir Nigel Hamilton, KCVO, CBE

Nichols, Sir Richard Everard, Kt.

Nicholson, Sir Bryan Hubert, Kt.

†Nicholson, Sir Charles Christian, Bt. (1912)

Nicholson, *Rt. Hon.* Sir Michael, Kt.

Nicholson, Sir Paul Douglas, Kt.

Nicholson, Sir Robin Buchanan, Kt., ph.D., FRS, FREng.

Nicoll, Sir William, KCMG

Nightingale, Sir Charles Manners Gamaliel, Bt. (1628)

Nightingale, Sir John Cyprian, Kt., CBE, BEM, QPM

Nixon, Sir Simon Michael Christopher, Bt. (1906)

Nixon, Sir Edwin Ronald, Kt., CBE

Noble, Sir David Brunel, Bt. (1902)

Noble, Sir Iain Andrew, Bt., OBE (1923)

Noble, Sir (Thomas Alexander) Fraser, Kt., MBE

Nombri, Sir Joseph Karl, Kt., ISO, BEM

Norman, Sir Arthur Gordon, KBE, DFC

Norman, Sir Mark Annesley, Bt. (1915)

Norman, Sir Robert Henry, Kt., OBE

Norman, Sir Ronald, Kt., OBE

Norrington, Sir Roger Arthur Carver, Kt., CBE

Norris, *Air Chief Marshal* Sir Christopher Neil Foxley-, GCB, DSO, OBE

Norris, Sir Eric George, KCMG

North, Sir Peter Machin, Kt., CBE, QC, DCL, FBA

North, Sir Thomas Lindsay, Kt.

North, Sir (William) Jonathan (Frederick), Bt. (1920)

Norton, *Vice-Adm. Hon.* Sir Nicholas John Hill-, KCB

Norwood, Sir Walter Neville, Kt.

Nossal, Sir Gustav Joseph Victor, Kt., CBE

Nott, *Rt. Hon.* Sir John William Frederic, KCB

Nourse, *Rt. Hon.* Sir Martin Charles, Kt.

Nugent, Sir John Edwin Lavallin, Bt. (I. 1795)

Nugent, *Maj.* Sir Peter Walter James, Bt. (1831)

Nugent, Sir Robin George Colborne, Bt. (1806)

Nursaw, Sir James, KCB, QC

Nurse, Sir Paul Maxime, Kt., Ph.D.

Nuttall, Sir Nicholas Keith Lillington, Bt. (1922)

†Nutting, Sir John Grenfell, Bt., QC (1903)

Oakeley, Sir John Digby Atholl, Bt. (1790)

Oakes, Sir Christopher, Bt. (1939)

Oakshott, Hon. Sir Anthony Hendrie, Bt. (1959)

Oates, Sir Thomas, Kt., CMG, OBE

Obolensky, *Prof.* Sir Dimitri, Kt.

O'Brien, Sir Frederick William Fitzgerald, Kt.

O'Brien, Sir Richard, Kt., DSO, MC

O'Brien, Sir Timothy John, Bt. (1849)

O'Brien, *Adm.* Sir William Donough, KCB, DSC

O'Connell, Sir Maurice James Donagh MacCarthy, Bt. (1869)

O'Connor, *Rt. Hon.* Sir Patrick McCarthy, Kt.

O'Dea, Sir Patrick Jerad, KCVO

Odell, Sir Stanley John, Kt.

Odgers, Sir Graeme David William, Kt.

O'Dowd, Sir David Joseph, Kt., CBE, QPM

Ogden, Sir (Edward) Michael, Kt., QC

Ogilvy, *Rt. Hon.* Sir Angus James Bruce, KCVO

Ogilvy, Sir Francis Gilbert Arthur, Bt. (S. 1626)

Ognall, *Hon.* Sir Harry Henry, Kt.

Ohlson, Sir Brian Eric Christopher, Bt. (1920)

Okeover, *Capt.* Sir Peter Ralph Leopold Walker-, Bt. (1886)

Olewale, *Hon.* Sir Niwia Ebia, Kt.

Oliphant, Sir Mark (Marcus Laurence Elwin), KBE, FRS

O'Loghlen, Sir Colman Michael, Bt. (1838)

Olver, Sir Stephen John Linley, KBE, CMG

O'Neil, *Hon.* Sir Desmond Henry, Kt.

Ongley, *Hon.* Sir Joseph Augustine, Kt.

O'Nions, *Prof.* Sir Robert Keith, Kt., FRS, Ph.D.

Onslow, Sir John Roger Wilmot, Bt. (1797)

Oppenheim, Sir Duncan Morris, Kt.

Oppenheimer, Sir Michael Bernard Grenville, Bt. (1921)

Orde, Sir John Alexander Campbell-, Bt. (1790)

O'Regan, *Dr* Sir Stephen Gerard (Tipene), Kt.

Orlebar, Sir Michael Keith Orlebar Simpson-, KCMG

Orr, Sir David Alexander, Kt., MC

Osborn, Sir John Holbrook, Kt.

Osborn, Sir Richard Henry Danvers, Bt. (1662)

Osborne, Sir Peter George, Bt. (I. 1629)

Osifelo, Sir Frederick Aubarua, Kt., MBE

Osmond, Sir Douglas, Kt., CBE

Osmond, Sir (Stanley) Paul, Kt., CB

O'Sullevan, Sir Peter John, Kt., CBE

Oswald, *Admiral of the Fleet* Sir (John) Julian Robertson, GCB

Oswald, Sir (William Richard) Michael, KCVO

Otton, Sir Geoffrey John, KCB

Otton, *Rt. Hon.* Sir Philip Howard, Kt.

Oulton, Sir Antony Derek Maxwell, GCB, QC

Ouseley, Sir Herman George, Kt.

Outram, Sir Alan James, Bt. (1858)

Overall, Sir John Wallace, Kt., CBE, MC

Owen, Sir Geoffrey, Kt.

Owen, Sir Hugh Bernard Pilkington, Bt. (1813)

Owen, Sir Hugo Dudley Cunliffe-, Bt. (1920)

Owen, *Hon.* Sir John Arthur Dalziel, Kt.

Owo, The Olowo of, Kt.

Packard, *Lt.-Gen.* Sir (Charles) Douglas, KBE, CB, DSO

Page, Sir (Arthur) John, Kt.

Page, Sir Frederick William, Kt., CBE, FREng.

Page, Sir John Joseph Joffre, Kt., OBE

Paget, Sir Julian Tolver, Bt., CVO (1871)

Paget, Sir Richard Herbert, Bt. (1886)

Pain, *Lt.-Gen.* Sir (Horace) Rollo (Squarey), KCB, MC

Pain, *Hon.* Sir Peter Richard, Kt.

Paine, Sir Christopher Hammon, Kt., FRCP, FRCR

Palin, *Air Chief Marshal* Sir Roger Hewlett, KCB, OBE

Palliser, *Rt. Hon.* Sir (Arthur) Michael, GCMG

Palmar, Sir Derek James, Kt.

Palmer, Sir (Charles) Mark, Bt. (1886)

Palmer, *Gen.* Sir (Charles) Patrick (Ralph), KBE

Palmer, Sir Geoffrey Christopher John, Bt. (1660)

Palmer, *Rt. Hon.* Sir Geoffrey Winston Russell, KCMG

Palmer, Sir John Chance, Kt.

Palmer, Sir John Edward Somerset, Bt. (1791)

Palmer, *Maj.-Gen.* Sir (Joseph) Michael, KCVO

Palmer, Sir Reginald Oswald, GCMG, MBE

Pantlin, Sir Dick Hurst, Kt., CBE

Paolozzi, Sir Eduardo Luigi, Kt., CBE, RA

Parbo, Sir Arvi Hillar, Kt.

Park, *Hon.* Sir Andrew Edward Wilson, Kt.

Park, *Hon.* Sir Hugh Eames, Kt.

Parker, Sir (Arthur) Douglas Dodds-, Kt.

Parker, Sir Eric Wilson, Kt.

Parker, *Hon.* Sir Jonathan Frederic, Kt.

Parker, Sir Peter, KBE, LVO

Parker, Sir Richard (William) Hyde, Bt. (1681)

Parker, *Rt. Hon.* Sir Roger Jocelyn, Kt.

Parker, *Vice-Adm.* Sir (Wilfred) John, KBE, CB, DSC

Parker, Sir William Peter Brian, Bt. (1844)

Parkes, Sir Edward Walter, Kt., FREng.

Parkinson, Sir Nicholas Fancourt, Kt.

Parsons, Sir (John) Michael, Kt.

Parsons, Sir Richard Edmund (Clement Fownes), KCMG

Parsons, Sir William Clere Leonard Brendon Wilmer, Bt. (1677)

Partridge, Sir Michael John Anthony, KCB

Pascoe, *Gen.* Sir Robert Alan, KCB, MBE

Pasley, Sir John Malcolm Sabine, Bt. (1794)

Paterson, Sir Dennis Craig, Kt.

Paterson, Sir John Valentine Jardine, Kt.

Patnick, Sir (Cyril) Irvine, Kt., OBE

Pattie, *Rt. Hon.* Sir Geoffrey Edwin, Kt.

Pattinson, Sir (William) Derek, Kt.

Pattison, *Prof.* Sir John Ridley, Kt., DM, FRCpath.

Pattullo, Sir (David) Bruce, Kt., CBE
Paul, Sir John Warburton, GCMG,
  OBE, MC
Paul, *Air Marshal* Sir Ronald Ian
  Stuart-, KBE
Payne, Sir Norman John, Kt., CBE,
  FREng.
Peach, Sir Leonard Harry, Kt.
Peacock, *Prof.* Sir Alan Turner, Kt.,
  DSC
Pearce, Sir Austin William, Kt., CBE,
  Ph.D., FREng.
Pearce, Sir (Daniel Norton) Idris,
  Kt., CBE, TD
Pearse, Sir Brian Gerald, Kt.
Pearson, Sir Francis Nicholas Fraser,
  Bt. (1964)
Pearson, *Gen.* Sir Thomas Cecil
  Hook, KCB, CBE, DSO
Peart, *Prof.* Sir William Stanley, Kt.,
  MD, FRS
Pease, Sir (Alfred) Vincent, Bt.
  (1882)
Pease, Sir Richard Thorn, Bt. (1920)
Peat, Sir Gerrard Charles, KCVO
Peat, Sir Michael Charles Gerrard,
  KCVO
Peck, Sir Edward Heywood, GCMG
Peckham, *Prof.* Sir Michael John, Kt.,
  FRCP, FRCPGlas., FRCR, FRCPath.
Pedder, *Air Marshal* Sir Ian Maurice,
  KCB, OBE, DFC
Peek, *Vice-Adm.* Sir Richard Innes,
  KBE, CB, DSC
Peek, Sir William Grenville, Bt.
  (1874)
Peel, Sir John Harold, KCVO
Peel, Sir (William) John, Kt.
Peirse, Sir Henry Grant de la Poer
  Beresford-, Bt. (1814)
Peirse, *Air Vice-Marshal* Sir Richard
  Charles Fairfax, KCVO, CB
Pelgen, Sir Harry Friedrich, Kt., MBE
Peliza, Sir Robert John, KBE, ED
Pelly, Sir Richard John, Bt. (1840)
Pemberton, Sir Francis Wingate
  William, Kt., CBE
Penrose, *Prof.* Sir Roger, Kt., FRS
Pereira, Sir (Herbert) Charles, Kt.,
  D.SC., FRS
Perring, Sir John Raymond, Bt.
  (1963)
Perris, Sir David (Arthur), Kt., MBE
Perry, Sir David Howard, KCB
Perry, Sir (David) Norman, Kt., MBE
Perry, Sir Michael Sydney, Kt., CBE
Pervez, Sir Mohammed Anwar, Kt.,
  OBE
Pestell, Sir John Richard, KCVO
Peterkin, Sir Neville, Kt.
Peters, *Prof.* Sir David Keith, Kt.,
  FRCP
Petersen, Sir Jeffrey Charles, KCMG
Petersen, Sir Johannes Bjelke-, KCMG
Peterson, Sir Christopher Matthew,
  Kt., CBE, TD
†Petit, Sir Jehangir, Bt. (1890)
Peto, Sir Henry George Morton, Bt.
  (1855)

Peto, Sir Michael Henry Basil, Bt.
  (1927)
Peto, *Prof.* Sir Richard, Kt., FRS
Petrie, Sir Peter Charles, Bt., CMG
  (1918)
Pettigrew, Sir Russell Hilton, Kt.
Pettit, Sir Daniel Eric Arthur, Kt.
Pettitt, Sir Dennis, Kt.
Philips, *Prof.* Sir Cyril Henry, Kt.
Phillips, Sir Fred Albert, Kt., CVO
Phillips, Sir (Gerald) Hayden, KCB
Phillips, Sir Henry Ellis Isidore, Kt.,
  CMG, MBE
Phillips, Sir Horace, KCMG
Phillips, Sir Peter John, Kt., OBE
Phillips, Sir Robin Francis, Bt. (1912)
Pickard, Sir (John) Michael, Kt.
Pickering, Sir Edward Davies, Kt.
Pickthorn, Sir James Francis Mann,
  Bt. (1959)
Pidgeon, Sir John Allan Stewart, Kt.
†Piers, Sir James Desmond, Bt. (I.
  1661)
Pigot, Sir George Hugh, Bt. (1764)
Pigott, Sir Berkeley Henry Sebastian,
  Bt. (1808)
Pike, *Lt.-Gen.* Sir Hew William
  Royston, KCB, DSO, MBE
Pike, Sir Michael Edmund, KCVO,
  CMG
Pike, Sir Philip Ernest Housden, Kt.,
  QC
Pilditch, Sir Richard Edward, Bt.
  (1929)
Pile, Sir Frederick Devereux, Bt., MC
  (1900)
Pilkington, Sir Antony Richard, Kt.
Pilkington, Sir Thomas Henry
  Milborne-Swinnerton-, Bt. (S.
  1635)
Pill, *Rt. Hon.* Sir Malcolm Thomas,
  Kt.
Pindling, *Rt. Hon.* Sir Lynden Oscar,
  KCMG
Pinker, Sir George Douglas, KCVO
Pinsent, Sir Christopher Roy, Bt.
  (1938)
Pippard, *Prof.* Sir (Alfred) Brian, Kt.,
  FRS
Pirie, *Gp Capt* Sir Gordon Hamish,
  Kt., CVO, CBE
Pitakaka, Sir Moses Puibangara,
  GCMG
Pitcher, Sir Desmond Henry, Kt.
Pitman, Sir Brian Ivor, Kt.
Pitoi, Sir Sere, Kt., CBE
Pitt, Sir Harry Raymond, Kt., Ph.D.,
  FRS
Pitts, Sir Cyril Alfred, Kt.
Plastow, Sir David Arnold Stuart, Kt.
Platt, Sir Harold Grant, Kt.
Platt, *Prof.* Hon. Sir Peter, Bt. (1959)
Plowman, *Hon.* Sir John Robin, Kt.,
  CBE
Plumb, *Prof.* Sir John Harold, Kt.
Pohai, Sir Timothy, Kt., MBE
Pole, Sir (John) Richard (Walter
  Reginald) Carew, Bt. (1628)
Pole, Sir Peter Van Notten, Bt.
  (1791)

Polkinghorne, *Revd Canon* John
  Charlton, KBE, FRS
Pollen, Sir John Michael
  Hungerford, Bt. (1795)
Pollock, Sir George Frederick, Bt.
  (1866)
Pollock, Sir Giles Hampden
  Montagu-, Bt. (1872)
Pollock, *Admiral of the Fleet* Sir
  Michael Patrick, GCB, LVO, DSC
Ponsonby, Sir Ashley Charles Gibbs,
  Bt., KCVO, MC (1956)
Pontin, Sir Frederick William, Kt.
Poole, *Hon.* Sir David Anthony, Kt.
Poore, Sir Herbert Edward, Bt.
  (1795)
Pope, Sir Joseph Albert, Kt., D.SC.,
  Ph.D.
Popplewell, *Hon.* Sir Oliver Bury, Kt.
†Porritt, Sir Jonathon Espie, Bt. (1963)
Portal, Sir Jonathan Francis, Bt.
  (1901)
Porter, Sir John Simon Horsbrugh-,
  Bt. (1902)
Porter, Sir Leslie, Kt.
Porter, *Air Marshal* Sir (Melvin)
  Kenneth (Drowley), KCB, CBE
Porter, *Rt. Hon.* Sir Robert Wilson,
  Kt., PC (NI), QC
Posnett, Sir Richard Neil, KBE, CMG
Potter, *Rt. Hon.* Sir Mark Howard, Kt.
Potter, *Maj.-Gen.* Sir (Wilfrid) John,
  KBE, CB
Potts, *Hon.* Sir Francis Humphrey,
  Kt.
Pound, Sir John David, Bt. (1905)
Pountain, Sir Eric John, Kt.
Powell, Sir (Arnold Joseph) Philip,
  Kt., CH, OBE, RA, FRIBA
Powell, Sir Charles David, KCMG
Powell, Sir Nicholas Folliott
  Douglas, Bt. (1897)
Powell, Sir Raymond, Kt., MP
Powell, Sir Richard Royle, GCB, KBE,
  CMG
Power, Sir Alastair John Cecil, Bt.
  (1924)
Power, *Hon.* Sir Noel Plunkett, Kt.
Prance, *Prof.* Sir Ghillean Tolmie,
  Kt., FRS
Prendergast, Sir (Walter) Kieran,
  KCVO, CMG
Prentice, *Hon.* Sir William Thomas,
  Kt., MBE
Prescott, Sir Mark, Bt. (1938)
†Preston, Sir Philip Charles Henry
  Hulton, Bt. (1815)
Prevost, Sir Christopher Gerald, Bt.
  (1805)
Price, Sir Charles Keith Napier
  Rugge-, Bt. (1804)
Price, Sir David Ernest Campbell,
  Kt.
Price, Sir Francis Caradoc Rose, Bt.
  (1815)
Price, Sir Frank Leslie, Kt.
Price, Sir (James) Robert, KBE
Price, Sir Norman Charles, KCB
Price, Sir Robert John Green-, Bt.
  (1874)

Prickett, *Air Chief Marshal* Sir Thomas Other, KCB, DSO, DFC

Prideaux, Sir Humphrey Povah Treverbian, Kt., OBE

†Primrose, Sir John Ure, Bt. (1903)

Pringle, *Air Marshal* Sir Charles Norman Seton, KBE, FREng.

Pringle, *Hon.* Sir John Kenneth, Kt.

Pringle, *Lt.-Gen.* Sir Steuart (Robert), Bt., KCB, RM (S. 1683)

Pritchard, Sir Neil, KCMG

Proby, Sir Peter, Bt. (1952)

Prosser, Sir Ian Maurice Gray, Kt.

Pryke, Sir David Dudley, Bt. (1926)

Puapua, *Rt. Hon.* Sir Tomasi, KBE

Pugh, Sir Idwal Vaughan, KCB

Pullinger, Sir (Francis) Alan, Kt., CBE

Pumfrey, *Hon.* Sir Nicholas Richard, Kt.

Pumphrey, Sir (John) Laurence, KCMG

Purchas, *Rt. Hon.* Sir Francis Brooks, Kt.

Purves, Sir William, Kt., CBE, DSO

Purvis, *Vice-Adm.* Sir Neville, KCB

Quicke, Sir John Godolphin, Kt., CBE

Quigley, Sir (William) George (Henry), Kt., CB, Ph.D.

Quilliam, *Hon.* Sir (James) Peter, Kt.

Quilter, Sir Anthony Raymond Leopold Cuthbert, Bt. (1897)

Quinlan, Sir Michael Edward, GCB

Quinton, Sir James Grand, Kt.

Radcliffe, Sir Sebastian Everard, Bt. (1813)

Radzinowicz, *Prof.* Sir Leon, Kt., LL D

Rae, *Hon.* Sir Wallace Alexander Ramsay, Kt.

Raeburn, Sir Michael Edward Norman, Bt. (1923)

Raeburn, *Maj.-Gen.* Sir (William) Digby (Manifold), KCVO, CB, DSO, MBE

Raikes, *Vice-Adm.* Sir Iwan Geoffrey, KCB, CBE, DSC

Raison, *Rt. Hon.* Sir Timothy Hugh Francis, Kt.

Ralli, Sir Godfrey Victor, Bt., TD (1912)

Ramdanee, Sir Mookteswar Baboolall Kailash, Kt.

Ramphal, Sir Shridath Surendranath, GCMG

Ramphul, Sir Baalkhristna, Kt.

Ramphul, Sir Indurduth, Kt.

Ramsay, Sir Alexander William Burnett, Bt. (1806)

Ramsay, Sir Allan John (Hepple), KBE, CMG

Ramsbotham, *Gen.* Sir David John, GCB, CBE

Ramsbotham, *Hon.* Sir Peter Edward, GCMG, GCVO

Ramsden, Sir John Charles Josslyn, Bt. (1689)

Randle, *Prof.* Sir Philip John, Kt.

Rank, Sir Benjamin Keith, Kt., CMG

Rankin, Sir Ian Niall, Bt. (1898)

Rasch, Sir Simon Anthony Carne, Bt. (1903)

Rashleigh, Sir Richard Harry, Bt. (1831)

Ratford, Sir David John Edward, KCMG, CVO

Rattee, *Hon.* Sir Donald Keith, Kt.

Rattle, Sir Simon Dennis, Kt., CBE

Rault, Sir Louis Joseph Maurice, Kt.

Rawlins, *Surgeon Vice-Adm.* Sir John Stuart Pepys, KBE

Rawlins, *Prof.* Sir Michael David, Kt., FRCP, FRCPED.

Rawlinson, Sir Anthony Henry John, Bt. (1891)

Read, *Air Marshal* Sir Charles Frederick, KBE, CB, DFC, AFC

Read, *Gen.* Sir (John) Antony (Jervis), GCB, CBE, DSO, MC

Read, Sir John Emms, Kt.

†Reade, Sir Kenneth Ray, Bt. (1661)

Reay, *Lt.-Gen.* Sir (Hubert) Alan John, KBE

Redgrave, *Maj.-Gen.* Sir Roy Michael Frederick, KBE, MC

Redmayne, Sir Nicholas, Bt. (1964)

Redmond, Sir James, Kt., FREng.

Redwood, Sir Peter Boverton, Bt. (1911)

Reece, Sir Charles Hugh, Kt.

Reece, Sir James Gordon, Kt.

Rees, Sir (Charles William) Stanley, Kt., TD

Rees, Sir David Allan, Kt., Ph.D., D.SC., FRS

Rees, *Prof.* Sir Martin John, Kt., FRS

Reeve, Sir Anthony, KCMG, KCVO

Reeves, *Most Revd* Paul Alfred, GCMG, GCVO

Reffell, *Adm.* Sir Derek Roy, KCB

Refshauge, *Maj.-Gen.* Sir William Dudley, Kt., CBE

Reid, Sir Alexander James, Bt. (1897)

Reid, Sir (Harold) Martin (Smith), KBE, CMG

Reid, Sir Hugh, Bt. (1922)

Reid, Sir Norman Robert, Kt.

Reid, Sir Robert Paul, Kt.

Reid, Sir William Kennedy, KCB

Reiher, Sir Frederick Bernard Carl, KBE, CMG

Reilly, Sir (D'Arcy) Patrick, GCMG, OBE

Reilly, *Lt.-Gen.* Sir Jeremy Calcott, KCB, DSO

Renals, Sir Stanley, Bt. (1895)

Rennie, Sir John Shaw, GCMG, OBE

Renouf, Sir Clement William Bailey, Kt.

Renshaw, Sir (Charles) Maurice Bine, Bt. (1903)

Renwick, Sir Richard Eustace, Bt. (1921)

Reporter, Sir Shapoor Ardeshirji, KBE

Reynolds, Sir David James, Bt. (1923)

Reynolds, Sir Peter William John, Kt., CBE

Rhodes, Sir Basil Edward, Kt., CBE, TD

Rhodes, Sir John Christopher Douglas, Bt. (1919)

Rhodes, Sir Peregrine Alexander, KCMG

Rice, *Maj.-Gen.* Sir Desmond Hind Garrett, KCVO, CBE

Rice, Sir Timothy Miles Bindon, Kt.

Richard, Sir Cliff, Kt., OBE

Richards, Sir Brian Mansel, Kt., CBE, Ph.D.

Richards, Sir (Francis) Brooks, KCMG, DSC

Richards, *Lt.-Gen.* Sir John Charles Chisholm, KCB, KCVO, RM

Richards, Sir Rex Edward, Kt., D.SC., FRS

Richards, *Hon.* Sir Stephen Price, Kt.

Richardson, Sir Anthony Lewis, Bt. (1924)

Richardson, *Rt. Hon.* Sir Ivor Lloyd Morgan, Kt.

Richardson, Sir (John) Eric, Kt., CBE

Richardson, Sir Michael John de Rougemont, Kt.

Richardson, *Lt.-Gen.* Sir Robert Francis, KCB, CVO, CBE

Richardson, Sir Simon Alaisdair Stewart-, Bt. (S. 1630)

Richmond, Sir John Frederick, Bt. (1929)

Richmond, *Prof.* Sir Mark Henry, Kt., FRS

Ricketts, Sir Robert Cornwallis Gerald St Leger, Bt. (1828)

Riddell, Sir John Charles Buchanan, Bt., CVO (S. 1628)

Ridley, Sir Adam (Nicholas), Kt.

Ridsdale, Sir Julian Errington, Kt., CBE

Rifkind, *Rt. Hon.* Sir Malcolm Leslie, KCMG, QC

Rigby, Sir Anthony John, Bt. (1929)

Rimer, *Hon.* Sir Colin Percy Farquharson, Kt.

Ringadoo, *Hon.* Sir Veerasamy, GCMG

Ripley, Sir Hugh, Bt. (1880)

Risk, Sir Thomas Neilson, Kt.

Ritako, Sir Thomas Baha, Kt., MBE

Rix, *Hon.* Sir Bernard Anthony, Kt.

Rix, Sir John, Kt., MBE, FREng.

Robb, Sir John Weddell, Kt.

Roberts, *Hon.* Sir Denys Tudor Emil, KBE, QC

Roberts, Sir Derek Harry, Kt., CBE, FRS, FREng.

Roberts, Sir (Edward Fergus) Sidney, Kt., CBE

Roberts, *Prof.* Sir Gareth Gwyn, Kt., FRS

Roberts, Sir Gilbert Howland Rookehurst, Bt. (1809)

Roberts, Sir Gordon James, Kt., CBE

Roberts, Sir Samuel, Bt. (1919)

Roberts, Sir Stephen James Leake, Kt.

Roberts, Sir William James Denby, Bt. (1909)

Robertson, Sir John Fraser, KCMG, CBE

Robertson, Sir Lewis, Kt., CBE, FRSE

Robertson, *Prof.* Sir Rutherford Ness, Kt., CMG

Robins, Sir Ralph Harry, Kt., FREng.

Robinson, Sir Albert Edward Phineas, Kt.

†Robinson, Sir Christopher Philipse, Bt. (1854)

Robinson, Sir Dominick Christopher Lynch-, Bt. (1920)

Robinson, Sir John James Michael Laud, Bt. (1660)

Robinson, Sir Wilfred Henry Frederick, Bt. (1908)

Robson, *Prof.* Sir James Gordon, Kt., CBE

Robson, Sir John Adam, KCMG

Roch, *Rt. Hon.* Sir John Ormond, Kt.

Roche, Sir David O'Grady, Bt. (1838)

Roche, Sir Henry John, Kt.

Rodgers, Sir (Andrew) Piers (Wingate Aikin-Sneath), Bt. (1964)

Rodley, *Prof.* Sir Nigel, KBE

Rodrigues, Sir Alberto Maria, Kt., CBE, ED

Roe, *Air Chief Marshal* Sir Rex David, GCB, AFC

Rogers, Sir Frank Jarvis, Kt.

Rogers, *Air Chief Marshal* Sir John Robson, KCB, CBE

Rooke, Sir Denis Eric, Kt., OM, CBE, FRS, FREng.

Ropner, Sir John Bruce Woollacott, Bt. (1952)

Ropner, Sir Robert Douglas, Bt. (1904)

Roscoe, Sir Robert Bell, KBE

Rose, *Rt. Hon.* Sir Christopher Dudley Roger, Kt.

Rose, Sir Clive Martin, GCMG

Rose, Sir David Lancaster, Bt. (1874)

Rose, *Gen.* Sir (Hugh) Michael, KCB, CBE, DSO, QGM

Rose, Sir Julian Day, Bt. (1872 and 1909)

Ross, Sir (James) Keith, Bt., RD, FRCS (1960)

Ross, *Lt.-Col.* Sir Malcolm, KCVO

Ross, *Lt.-Gen.* Sir Robert Jeremy, KCB, OBE

Ross, *Lt.-Col.* Sir Walter Hugh Malcolm, KCVO, OBE

Rosser, Sir Melvyn Wynne, Kt.

Rossi, Sir Hugh Alexis Louis, Kt.

Rotblat, *Prof.* Joseph, KCMG, CBE, FRS

Roth, *Prof.* Sir Martin, Kt., MD, FRCP

Rothschild, Sir Evelyn Robert Adrian de, Kt.

Rougier, *Hon.* Sir Richard George, Kt.

Rowell, Sir John Joseph, Kt., CBE

Rowland, *Air Marshal* Sir James Anthony, KBE, DFC, AFC

Rowland, Sir (John) David, Kt.

Rowlands, *Air Marshal* Sir John Samuel, GC, KBE

Rowley, Sir Charles Robert, Bt. (1836) †(1786)

Roxburgh, *Vice-Adm.* Sir John Charles Young, KCB, CBE, DSO, DSC

Royden, Sir Christopher John, Bt. (1905)

Rudd, Sir (Anthony) Nigel (Russell), Kt.

Rumbold, Sir Henry John Sebastian, Bt. (1779)

Rumbold, Sir Jack Seddon, Kt.

Runchorelal, Sir (Udayan) Chinubhai Madhowlal, Bt. (1913)

Runciman, *Hon.* Sir James Cochran Stevenson (Sir Steven), Kt., CH

Rusby, *Vice-Adm.* Sir Cameron, KCB, LVO

†Russell, Sir (Arthur) Mervyn, Bt. (1812)

Russell, Sir Charles Dominic, Bt. (1916)

Russell, *Hon.* Sir David Sturrock West-, Kt.

Russell, Sir George, Kt., CBE

Russell, *Prof.* Sir Peter Edward Lionel, Kt., D.Litt., FBA

Russell, Sir (Robert) Mark, KCMG

Russell, *Rt. Hon.* Sir (Thomas) Patrick, Kt.

Rutter, Sir Frank William Eden, KBE

Rutter, *Prof.* Sir Michael Llewellyn, Kt., CBE, MD, FRS

Ryan, Sir Derek Gerald, Bt. (1919)

†Rycroft, Sir Richard John, Bt. (1784)

Ryrie, Sir William Sinclair, KCB

Sabola, *Hon.* Sir Joaquim Claudino Gonsalves-, Kt.

Sachs, *Hon.* Sir Michael Alexander Geddes, Kt.

Sainsbury, Sir Robert James, Kt.

Sainsbury, *Rt. Hon.* Sir Timothy Alan Davan, Kt.

†St Aubyn, Sir William Molesworth-, Bt. (1689)

†St George, Sir John Avenel Bligh, Bt. (I. 1766)

St Johnston, Sir Kerry, Kt.

Sainty, Sir John Christopher, KCB

Sakzewski, Sir Albert, Kt.

Salisbury, Sir Robert William, Kt.

Salt, Sir Patrick MacDonnell, Bt. (1869)

Salt, Sir (Thomas) Michael John, Bt. (1899)

Sampson, Sir Colin, Kt., CBE, QPM

Samuel, Sir John Michael Glen, Bt. (1898)

Samuelson, Sir (Bernard) Michael (Francis), Bt. (1884)

Samuelson, Sir Sydney Wylie, Kt., CBE

Sanders, Sir John Reynolds Mayhew-, Kt.

Sanders, Sir Robert Tait, KBE, CMG

Sanderson, Sir Frank Linton, Bt. (1920)

Sarei, Sir Alexis Holyweek, Kt., CBE

Sarell, Sir Roderick Francis Gisbert, KCMG, KCVO

Saunders, *Hon.* Sir John Anthony Holt, Kt., CBE, DSO, MC

Saunders, Sir Peter, Kt.

Savage, Sir Ernest Walter, Kt.

Savile, Sir James Wilson Vincent, Kt., OBE

Say, *Rt. Revd* Richard David, KCVO

Schiemann, *Rt. Hon.* Sir Konrad Hermann Theodor, Kt.

Scholar, Sir Michael Charles, KCB

Scholey, Sir David Gerald, Kt., CBE

Scholey, Sir Robert, Kt., CBE, FREng.

Scholtens, Sir James Henry, KCVO

Schubert, Sir Sydney, Kt.

Scipio, Sir Hudson Rupert, Kt.

Scoon, Sir Paul, GCMG, GCVO, OBE

Scott, Sir Anthony Percy, Bt. (1913)

Scott, Sir (Charles) Peter, KBE, CMG

Scott, Sir David Aubrey, GCMG

Scott, Sir Dominic James Maxwell-, Bt. (1642)

Scott, Sir Ian Dixon, KCMG, KCVO, CIE

Scott, Sir James Jervoise, Bt. (1962)

Scott, Sir Kenneth Bertram Adam, KCVO, CMG

Scott, Sir Michael, KCVO, CMG

Scott, *Rt. Hon.* Sir Nicholas Paul, KBE

Scott, Sir Oliver Christopher Anderson, Bt. (1909)

Scott, *Prof.* Sir Philip John, KBE

Scott, *Rt. Hon.* Sir Richard Rashleigh Folliott, Kt.

Scott, Sir Robert David Hillyer, Kt.

Scott, Sir Walter John, Bt. (1907)

Scott, *Rear-Adm.* Sir (William) David (Stewart), KBE, CB

Scowen, Sir Eric Frank, Kt., MD, D.SC., LL D, FRCP, FRCS

Seale, Sir John Henry, Bt. (1838)

Seaman, Sir Keith Douglas, KCVO, OBE

Sebastian, Sir Cuthbert Montraville, GCMG, OBE

†Sebright, Sir Peter Giles Vivian, Bt. (1626)

Seccombe, Sir (William) Vernon Stephen, Kt.

Secombe, Sir Harry Donald, Kt., CBE

Seconde, Sir Reginald Louis, KCMG, CVO

Sedley, *Rt. Hon.* Sir Stephen John, Kt.

Seely, Sir Nigel Edward, Bt. (1896)

Seeto, Sir Ling James, Kt., MBE

Seeyave, Sir Rene Sow Choung, Kt., CBE

Seligman, Sir Peter Wendel, Kt., CBE

Sellors, Sir Patrick John Holmes-, KCVO, FRCS

Sergeant, Sir Patrick, Kt.

Series, Sir (Joseph Michel) Emile, Kt., CBE

Serota, Sir Nicholas Andrew, Kt.

Serpell, Sir David Radford, KCB, CMG, OBE

†Seton, Sir Charles Wallace, Bt. (S. 1683)

Seton, Sir Iain Bruce, Bt. (S. 1663)

Severne, *Air Vice-Marshal* Sir John de Milt, KCVO, OBE, AFC

Seymour, *Cdr.* Sir Michael Culme-, Bt., RN (1809)

Shackleton, *Prof.* Sir Nicholas John, Kt., ph.D., FRS

Shakerley, Sir Geoffrey Adam, Bt. (1838)

Shakespeare, Sir Thomas William, Bt. (1942)

Shand, Sir James, Kt., MBE

Sharp, Sir Adrian, Bt. (1922)

Sharp, Sir George, Kt., OBE

Sharp, Sir Kenneth Johnston, Kt., TD

Sharp, Sir Leslie, Kt., QPM

Sharp, Sir Richard Lyall, KCVO, CB

†Sharp, Sir Samuel Christopher Reginald, Bt. (1920)

Sharpe, *Hon.* Sir John Henry, Kt., CBE

Sharples, Sir James, Kt., QPM

Shattock, Sir Gordon, Kt.

Shaw, Sir Brian Piers, Kt.

Shaw, Sir (Charles) Barry, Kt., CB, QC

Shaw, Sir (George) Neville Bowan-, Kt.

Shaw, *Prof.* Sir John Calman, Kt., CBE, FRSE

Shaw, Sir (John) Giles (Dunkerley), Kt.

Shaw, Sir John Michael Robert Best-, Bt. (1665)

Shaw, Sir Neil McGowan, Kt.

Shaw, Sir Robert, Bt. (1821)

Shaw, Sir Roy, Kt.

Shaw, Sir Run Run, Kt., CBE

Sheehy, Sir Patrick, Kt.

Sheen, *Hon.* Sir Barry Cross, Kt.

Sheffield, Sir Reginald Adrian Berkeley, Bt. (1755)

Shehadie, Sir Nicholas Michael, Kt., OBE

Sheil, *Hon.* Sir John, Kt.

Sheldon, *Hon.* Sir (John) Gervase (Kensington), Kt.

Shelley, Sir John Richard, Bt. (1611)

Shelton, Sir William Jeremy Masefield, Kt.

Shepheard, Sir Peter Faulkner, Kt., CBE

Shepherd, Sir Colin Ryley, Kt.

Shepperd, Sir Alfred Joseph, Kt.

Sherlock, Sir Philip Manderson, KBE

Sherman, Sir Alfred, Kt.

Sherman, Sir Louis, Kt., OBE

Shields, Sir Neil Stanley, Kt., MC

Shields, *Prof.* Sir Robert, Kt., MD

Shiffner, Sir Henry David, Bt. (1818)

Shillington, Sir (Robert Edward) Graham, Kt., CBE

Shinwell, Sir (Maurice) Adrian, Kt.

Shock, Sir Maurice, Kt.

Short, Sir Apenera Pera, KBE

Short, *Brig.* Sir Noel Edward Vivian, Kt., MBE, MC

Shuckburgh, Sir Rupert Charles Gerald, Bt. (1660)

Siaguru, Sir Anthony Michael, KBE

Siddall, Sir Norman, Kt., CBE, FREng.

Sidey, *Air Marshal* Sir Ernest Shaw, KBE, CB, MD

Sie, Sir Banja Tejan-, GCMG

Sieff, *Hon.* Sir David, Kt.

Simeon, Sir John Edmund Barrington, Bt. (1815)

Simmons, *Air Marshal* Sir Michael George, KCB, AFC

Simmons, Sir Stanley Clifford, Kt., FRCS, FRCOG

Simms, Sir Neville Ian, Kt., FREng.

Simon, Sir David Alec Gwyn, Kt., CBE

Simonet, Sir Louis Marcel Pierre, Kt., CBE

Simpson, *Hon.* Sir Alfred Henry, Kt.

Simpson, *Lt.-Gen.* Sir Roderick Alexander Cordy-, KBE, CB

Simpson, Sir William James, Kt.

Sims, Sir Roger Edward, Kt.

Sinclair, Sir Clive Marles, Kt.

Sinclair, Sir George Evelyn, Kt., CMG, OBE

Sinclair, Sir Ian McTaggart, KCMG, QC

Sinclair, *Air Vice-Marshal* Sir Laurence Frank, GC, KCB, CBE, DSO

Sinclair, Sir Patrick Robert Richard, Bt. (s. 1704)

Sinden, Sir Donald Alfred, Kt., CBE

Singer, *Prof.* Sir Hans Wolfgang, Kt.

Singer, *Hon.* Sir Jan Peter, Kt.

Singh, *Hon.* Sir Vijay Raghubir, Kt.

Sitwell, Sir (Sacheverell) Reresby, Bt. (1808)

Skeet, Sir Trevor Herbert Harry, Kt.

Skeggs, Sir Clifford George, Kt.

Skehel, Sir John James, Kt., FRS

Skingsley, *Air Chief Marshal* Sir Anthony Gerald, GBE, KCB

Skinner, Sir (Thomas) Keith (Hewitt), Bt. (1912)

Skipwith, Sir Patrick Alexander d'Estoteville, Bt. (1622)

Skyrme, Sir (William) Thomas (Charles), KCVO, CB, CBE, TD

Slack, Sir William Willatt, KCVO, FRCS

Slade, Sir Benjamin Julian Alfred, Bt. (1831)

Slade, *Rt. Hon.* Sir Christopher John, Kt.

Slaney, *Prof.* Sir Geoffrey, KBE

Slater, *Adm.* Sir John (Jock) Cunningham Kirkwood, GCB, LVO

Sleight, Sir Richard, Bt. (1920)

Sloan, Sir Andrew Kirkpatrick, Kt., QPM

Sloman, Sir Albert Edward, Kt., CBE

Smart, *Prof.* Sir George Algernon, Kt., MD, FRCP

Smart, Sir Jack, Kt., CBE

Smedley, *Hon.* Sir (Frank) Brian, Kt.

Smedley, Sir Harold, KCMG, MBE

Smiley, *Lt.-Col.* Sir John Philip, Bt. (1903)

Smith, Sir Alan, Kt., CBE, DFC

Smith, Sir Alexander Mair, Kt., Ph.D.

Smith, Sir Andrew Colin Hugh-, Kt.

Smith, *Lt.-Gen.* Sir Anthony Arthur Denison-, KBE

Smith, Sir Charles Bracewell-, Bt. (1947)

Smith, Sir Christopher Sydney Winwood, Bt. (1809)

Smith, *Prof.* Sir Colin Stansfield, Kt., CBE

Smith, Sir Cyril, Kt., MBE

Smith, *Prof.* Sir David Cecil, Kt., FRS

Smith, *Air Chief Marshal* Sir David Harcourt-, GBE, KCB, DFC

Smith, Sir David Iser, KCVO

Smith, Sir Douglas Boucher, KCB

Smith, Sir Dudley (Gordon), Kt.

Smith, *Prof.* Sir Eric Brian, Kt., Ph.D.

Smith, *Maj.-Gen.* Sir (Francis) Brian Wyldbore-, Kt., CB, DSO, OBE

Smith, *Prof.* Sir Francis Graham-, Kt., FRS

Smith, Sir Geoffrey Johnson, Kt., MP

Smith, Sir Graham William, Kt., CBE

Smith, Sir John Alfred, Kt., QPM

Smith, *Prof.* Sir John Cyril, Kt., CBE, QC, FBA

Smith, Sir John Hamilton-Spencer-, Bt. (1804)

Smith, Sir John Jonah Walker-, Bt. (1960)

Smith, Sir John Lindsay Eric, Kt., CH, CBE

Smith, Sir John Rathbone Vassar-, Bt. (1917)

Smith, Sir Joseph William Grenville, Kt., MD, FRCP

Smith, Sir Leslie Edward George, Kt.

Smith, *Maj.-Gen.* Sir Michael Edward Carleton-, Kt., CBE

Smith, Sir Michael John Llewellyn, KCVO, CMG

Smith, *Rt. Hon.* Sir Murray Stuart-, Kt.

Smith, Sir (Norman) Brian, Kt., CBE, Ph.D.

†Smith, Sir Peter Frank Graham Newson-, Bt. (1944)

Smith, Sir Raymond Horace, KBE

Smith, Sir Robert Courtney, Kt., CBE

Smith, Sir Robert Haldane, Kt

Smith, Sir Robert Hill, Bt., MP (1945)

Smith, *Prof.* Sir Roland, Kt.

Smith, *Air Marshal* Sir Roy David Austen-, KBE, CB, CVO, DFC

Smith, *Gen.* Sir Rupert Anthony, KCB, DSO, OBE, QGM

Smith, Sir (Thomas) Gilbert, Bt. (1897)

Smith, Sir (William) Antony (John) Reardon-, Bt. (1920)

Smith, Sir (William) Richard Prince-, Bt. (1911)

Smithers, Sir Peter Henry Berry Otway, Kt., VRD, D.Phil.

Smyth, Sir Thomas Weyland Bowyer-, Bt. (1661)

Smyth, Sir Timothy John, Bt. (1955)

Soakimori, Sir Frederick Pa-Nukuanca, KBE, CPM

Soame, Sir Charles John Buckworth-Herne-, Bt. (1697)

Sobers, Sir Garfield St Auburn, Kt.

Solomon, Sir Harry, Kt.

Somare, *Rt. Hon.* Sir Michael Thomas, GCMG, CH

Somers, *Rt. Hon.* Sir Edward Jonathan, Kt.

Somerville, *Brig.* Sir John Nicholas, Kt., CBE

Somerville, Sir Quentin Charles Somerville Agnew-, Bt. (1957)

Soulsby, Sir Peter Alfred, Kt.

Soutar, *Air Marshal* Sir Charles John Williamson, KBE

South, Sir Arthur, Kt.

Southby, Sir John Richard Bilbe, Bt. (1937)

Southern, Sir Richard William, Kt., FBA

Southern, Sir Robert, Kt., CBE

Southgate, Sir Colin Grieve, Kt.

Southgate, Sir William David, Kt.

Southward, Sir Leonard Bingley, Kt., OBE

Southwood, *Prof.* Sir (Thomas) Richard (Edmund), Kt., FRS

Souyave, *Hon.* Sir (Louis) Georges, Kt.

Sowrey, *Air Marshal* Sir Frederick Beresford, KCB, CBE, AFC

Sparkes, Sir Robert Lyndley, Kt.

Sparrow, Sir John, Kt.

Spearman, Sir Alexander Young Richard Mainwaring, Bt. (1840)

Spedding, *Prof.* Sir Colin Raymond William, Kt., CBE

Spedding, Sir David Rolland, KCMG, CVO, OBE

Speed, Sir (Herbert) Keith, Kt., RD

Speelman, Sir Cornelis Jacob, Bt. (1686)

Speight, *Hon.* Sir Graham Davies, Kt.

Spencer, Sir Derek Harold, Kt., QC

Spicer, Sir James Wilton, Kt.

Spicer, Sir Nicholas Adrian Albert, Bt., MB (1906)

Spicer, Sir (William) Michael Hardy, Kt., MP

Spiers, Sir Donald Maurice, Kt., CB, TD

Spooner, Sir James Douglas, Kt.

Spotswood, *Marshal of the Royal Air Force* Sir Denis Frank, GCB, CBE, DSO, DFC

Spratt, *Col.* Sir Greville Douglas, GBE, TD

Spring, Sir Dryden Thomas, Kt.

Squire, *Air Chief Marshal* Sir Peter Ted, KCB, DFC, AFC

Stabb, *Hon.* Sir William Walter, Kt., QC

Stainton, Sir (John) Ross, Kt., CBE

Stakis, Sir Reo Argiros, Kt.

Stamer, Sir (Lovelace) Anthony, Bt. (1809)

Stanbridge, *Air Vice-Marshal* Sir Brian Gerald Tivy, KCVO, CBE, AFC

Stanier, Sir Beville Douglas, Bt. (1917)

Stanier, *Field Marshal* Sir John Wilfred, GCB, MBE

Stanley, *Rt. Hon.* Sir John Paul, Kt., MP

†Staples, Sir Gerald James Arland, Bt. (I. 1628)

Stark, Sir Andrew Alexander Steel, KCMG, CVO

Starkey, Sir John Philip, Bt. (1935)

Starrit, Sir James, KCVO

Statham, Sir Norman, KCMG, CVO

Staughton, *Rt. Hon.* Sir Christopher Stephen Thomas Jonathan Thayer, Kt.

Staveley, Sir John Malfroy, KBE, MC

Stear, *Air Chief Marshal* Sir Michael James Douglas, KCB, CBE

Steel, Sir David Edward Charles, Kt., DSO, MC, TD

Steel, *Hon.* Sir David William, Kt.

Steele, Sir (Philip John) Rupert, Kt.

Steere, Sir Ernest Henry Lee-, KBE

Stephen, *Rt. Hon.* Sir Ninian Martin, KG, GCMG, GCVO, KBE

Stephens, Sir (Edwin) Barrie, Kt.

Stephenson, Sir Henry Upton, Bt. (1936)

Sternberg, Sir Sigmund, Kt.

Stevens, Sir Jocelyn Edward Greville, Kt., CVO

Stevens, Sir Laurence Houghton, Kt., CBE

Stevenson, *Vice-Adm.* Sir (Hugh) David, KBE

Stevenson, Sir Simpson, Kt.

Stewart, Sir Alan, KBE

Stewart, Sir Alan d'Arcy, Bt. (I. 1623)

Stewart, Sir David James Henderson-, Bt. (1957)

Stewart, Sir David John Christopher, Bt. (1803)

Stewart, Sir Edward Jackson, Kt.

Stewart, *Prof.* Sir Frederick Henry, Kt., Ph.D., FRS, FRSE

Stewart, Sir Houston Mark Shaw-, Bt., MC, TD (S. 1667)

Stewart, Sir James Douglas, Kt.

Stewart, Sir James Moray, KCB

Stewart, Sir (John) Simon (Watson), Bt. (1920)

Stewart, Sir Robertson Huntly, Kt., CBE

Stewart, Sir Robin Alastair, Bt. (1960)

Stewart, Sir Ronald Compton, Bt. (1937)

Stewart, *Prof.* Sir William Duncan Paterson, Kt., FRS, FRSE

Stibbon, *Gen.* Sir John James, KCB, OBE

Stirling, Sir Alexander John Dickson, KBE, CMG

Stirling, Sir Angus Duncan Aeneas, Kt.

Stockdale, Sir Arthur Noel, Kt.

Stockdale, Sir Thomas Minshull, Bt. (1960)

Stoddart, *Wg Cdr.* Sir Kenneth Maxwell, KCVO, AE

Stoker, *Prof.* Sir Michael George Parke, Kt., CBE, FRCP, FRS, FRSE

Stokes, Sir John Heydon Romaine, Kt.

Stones, Sir William Frederick, Kt., OBE

Stonhouse, *Revd* Sir Michael Philip, Bt. (1628)

Stonor, *Air Marshal* Sir Thomas Henry, KCB

Stoppard, Sir Thomas, Kt., CBE

Storey, *Hon.* Sir Richard, Bt., CBE (1960)

Stormonth Darling, Sir James Carlisle, Kt., CBE, MC, TD

Stott, Sir Adrian George Ellingham, Bt. (1920)

Stoute, Sir Michael Ronald, Kt.

Stow, Sir Christopher Philipson-, Bt., DFC (1907)

Stowe, Sir Kenneth Ronald, GCB, CVO

Stracey, Sir John Simon, Bt. (1818)

Strachan, Sir Curtis Victor, Kt., CVO

Strachey, Sir Charles, Bt. (1801)

Strawson, *Prof.* Sir Peter Frederick, Kt., FBA

Street, *Hon.* Sir Laurence Whistler, KCMG

Streeton, Sir Terence George, KBE, CMG

Stringer, Sir Donald Edgar, Kt., CBE

Strong, Sir Roy Colin, Kt., Ph.D., FSA

Stronge, Sir James Anselan Maxwell, Bt. (1803)

Stroud, *Prof.* Sir (Charles) Eric, Kt., FRCP

Strutt, Sir Nigel Edward, Kt., TD

Stuart, Sir James Keith, Kt.

Stuart, Sir Kenneth Lamonte, Kt.

†Stuart, Sir Phillip Luttrell, Bt. (1660)

Stubblefield, Sir (Cyril) James, Kt., D.SC., FRS

Stubbs, Sir James Wilfrid, KCVO, TD

Stubbs, Sir William Hamilton, Kt., Ph.D.

Stucley, *Lt.* Sir Hugh George Coplestone Bampfylde, Bt. (1859)

Studd, Sir Edward Fairfax, Bt. (1929)

Studd, Sir Peter Malden, GBE, KCVO

Studholme, Sir Henry William, Bt. (1956)

Style, *Lt.-Cdr.* Sir Godfrey William, Kt., CBE, DSC, RN

†Style, Sir William Frederick, Bt. (1627)

Sugden, Sir Arthur, Kt.

Sullivan, *Hon.* Sir Jeremy Mirth, Kt.

Sullivan, Sir Richard Arthur, Bt. (1804)

Sumner, *Hon.* Sir Christopher John, Kt.

Sutherland, Sir John Brewer, Bt. (1921)

Sutherland, Sir Maurice, Kt.

Sutherland, *Prof.* Sir Stewart Ross, Kt., FBA

Sutherland, Sir William George MacKenzie, Kt.

Suttie, Sir James Edward Grant-, Bt. (S. 1702)

Sutton, Sir Frederick Walter, Kt., OBE

Sutton, *Air Marshal* Sir John Matthias Dobson, KCB

Sutton, Sir Richard Lexington, Bt. (1772)

Swaffield, Sir James Chesebrough, Kt., CBE, RD

Swaine, Sir John Joseph, Kt., CBE

Swan, Sir Conrad Marshall John Fisher, KCVO, Ph.D.

Swan, Sir John William David, KBE

Swann, Sir Michael Christopher, Bt., TD (1906)

Swanwick, Sir Graham Russell, Kt., MBE

Swartz, Hon. Sir Reginald William Colin, KBE, ED

Sweetnam, Sir (David) Rodney, KCVO, CBE, FRCS

Swinburn, Lt.-Gen. Sir Richard Hull, KCB

Swinson, Sir John Henry Alan, Kt., OBE

Swinton, Maj.-Gen. Sir John, KCVO, OBE

Swire, Sir Adrian Christopher, Kt.

Swire, Sir John Anthony, Kt., CBE

Swynnerton, Sir Roger John Massy, Kt., CMG, OBE, MC

Sykes, Sir Francis John Badcock, Bt. (1781)

Sykes, Sir Hugh Ridley, Kt.

Sykes, Sir John Charles Anthony le Gallais, Bt. (1921)

Sykes, Prof. Sir (Malcolm) Keith, Kt.

Sykes, Sir Richard, Kt.

Sykes, Sir Tatton Christopher Mark, Bt. (1783)

Symington, Prof. Sir Thomas, Kt., MD, FRSE

Symons, Vice-Adm. Sir Patrick Jeremy, KBE

Synge, Sir Robert Carson, Bt. (1801)

Tait, Adm. Sir (Allan) Gordon, KCB, DSC

Talbot, Hon. Sir Hilary Gwynne, Kt.

Talboys, Rt. Hon. Sir Brian Edward, CH, KCB

Tancred, Sir Henry Lawson-, Bt. (1662)

Tangaroa, Hon. Sir Tangaroa, Kt., MBE

Tange, Sir Arthur Harold, Kt., CBE

Tapsell, Sir Peter Hannay Bailey, Kt., MP

Tate, Sir (Henry) Saxon, Bt. (1898)

Tavaiqia, Ratu Sir Josaia, KBE

Tavare, Sir John, Kt., CBE

Taylor, Lt.-Gen. Sir Allan Macnab, KBE, MC

Taylor, Sir (Arthur) Godfrey, Kt.

Taylor, Sir Cyril Julian Hebden, Kt.

Taylor, Sir Edward Macmillan (Teddy), Kt., MP

Taylor, Rt. Revd John Bernard, KCVO

Taylor, Sir John Lang, KCMG

Taylor, Sir Nicholas Richard Stuart, Bt. (1917)

Taylor, Prof. Sir William, Kt., CBE

Teagle, Vice-Adm. Sir Somerford Francis, KBE

Tebbit, Sir Donald Claude, GCMG

Telford, Sir Robert, Kt., CBE, FREng.

Temple, Sir Rawden John Afamado, Kt., CBE, QC

Temple, Maj. Sir Richard Anthony Purbeck, Bt., MC (1876)

Templeton, Sir John Marks, Kt.

Tenison, Sir Richard Hanbury-, KCVO

Tennant, Sir Anthony John, Kt.

Tennant, Capt. Sir Iain Mark, KT

Teo, Sir Fiatau Penitala, GCMG, GCVO, ISO, MBE

Terry, Air Marshal Sir Colin George, KBE, CB

Terry, Sir Michael Edward Stanley Imbert-, Bt. (1917)

Terry, Air Chief Marshal Sir Peter David George, GCB, AFC

Tett, Sir Hugh Charles, Kt.

Thatcher, Sir Denis, Bt., MBE, TD (1990)

Thesiger, Sir Wilfred Patrick, KBE, DSO

Thomas, Sir Derek Morison David, KCMG

Thomas, Sir Frederick William, Kt.

Thomas, Sir (Godfrey) Michael (David), Bt. (1694)

Thomas, Sir Jeremy Cashel, KCMG

Thomas, Sir (John) Alan, Kt.

Thomas, Sir John Maldwyn, Kt.

Thomas, Prof. Sir John Meurig, Kt., FRS

Thomas, Sir Keith Vivian, Kt.

Thomas, Sir Quentin Jeremy, Kt., CB

Thomas, Sir Robert Evan, Kt.

Thomas, Hon. Sir Roger John Laugharne, Kt.

Thomas, Hon. Sir Swinton Barclay, Kt.

Thomas, Sir William James Cooper, Bt., TD (1919)

Thomas, Sir (William) Michael (Marsh), Bt. (1918)

Thompson, Sir Christopher Peile, Bt. (1890)

Thompson, Sir Clive Malcolm, Kt.

Thompson, Sir Donald, Kt.

Thompson, Sir Gilbert Williamson, Kt., OBE

Thompson, Surgeon Vice-Adm. Sir Godfrey James Milton-, KBE

Thompson, Sir (Humphrey) Simon Meysey-, Bt. (1874)

Thompson, Prof. Sir Michael Warwick, Kt., D.SC

†Thompson, Sir Nicholas Annesley Marler, Bt. (1963)

Thompson, Sir Paul Anthony, Bt. (1963)

Thompson, Sir Peter Anthony, Kt.

Thompson, Sir (Thomas) Lionel Tennyson, Bt. (1806)

Thomson, Sir Adam, Kt., CBE

Thomson, Sir (Frederick Douglas) David, Bt. (1929)

Thomson, Sir John Adam, GCMG

Thomson, Sir John (Ian) Sutherland, KBE, CMG

Thomson, Sir Mark Wilfrid Home, Bt. (1925)

Thomson, Sir Thomas James, Kt., CBE, FRCP

Thorn, Sir John Samuel, Kt., OBE

Thorne, Maj.-Gen. Sir David Calthrop, KBE, CVO

Thorne, Sir Neil Gordon, Kt., OBE, TD

Thorne, Sir Peter Francis, KCVO, CBE

Thornton, Sir (George) Malcolm, Kt.

Thornton, Lt.-Gen. Sir Leonard Whitmore, KCB, CBE

Thornton, Sir Peter Eustace, KCB

Thornton, Sir Richard Eustace, KCVO, OBE

Thorold, Sir (Anthony) Oliver, Bt. (1642)

Thorpe, Hon. Sir Mathew Alexander, Kt.

Thouron, Sir John Rupert Hunt, KBE

Thwaites, Sir Bryan, Kt., ph.D.

Tibbits, Capt. Sir David Stanley, Kt., DSC

Tickell, Sir Crispin Charles Cervantes, GCMG, KCB, CBE

Tidbury, Sir Charles Henderson, Kt.

Tikaram, Sir Moti, KBE

Tilt, Sir Robin Richard, Kt.

Tims, Sir Michael David, KCVO

Tindle, Sir Ray Stanley, Kt., CBE

Tippet, Vice-Adm. Sir Anthony Sanders, KCB

†Tipping, Sir David Gwynne Evans-, Bt. (1913)

Tirvengadum, Sir Harry Krishnan, Kt.

Titman, Sir John Edward Powis, KCVO

Tod, Air Marshal Sir John Hunter Hunter-, KBE, CB

Tod, Vice-Adm. Sir Jonathan James Richard, KCB

Todd, Prof. Sir David, Kt., CBE

Todd, Sir Ian Pelham, KBE, FRCS

Todd, Hon. Sir (Reginald Stephen) Garfield, Kt.

Tollemache, Sir Lyonel Humphry John, Bt. (1793)

Tololo, Sir Alkan, KBE

Tomkins, Sir Edward Emile, GCMG, CVO

Tomkys, Sir (William) Roger, KCMG

Tomlinson, Prof. Sir Bernard Evans, Kt., CBE

Tooley, Sir John, Kt.

Tooth, Sir (Hugh) John Lucas-, Bt. (1920)

ToRobert, Sir Henry Thomas, KBE

Tory, Sir Geofroy William, KCMG

Touche, Sir Anthony George, Bt. (1920)

Touche, Sir Rodney Gordon, Bt. (1962)

Toulson, Hon. Sir Roger Grenfell, Kt.

Tovey, Sir Brian John Maynard, KCMG

ToVue, Sir Ronald, Kt., OBE

Towneley, Sir Simon Peter Edmund Cosmo William, KCVO

Townsend, Sir Cyril David, Kt.

Traill, Sir Alan Towers, GBE

Trant, Gen. Sir Richard Brooking, KCB

Travers, Sir Thomas à'Beckett, Kt.

Treacher, Adm. Sir John Devereux, KCB

Trehane, Sir (Walter) Richard, Kt.

Treitel, Prof. Sir Guenter Heinz, Kt., FBA, QC

Trelawny, Sir John Barry Salusbury-, Bt. (1628)

Trench, Sir Peter Edward, Kt., CBE, TD

Trescowthick, Sir Donald Henry, KBE

†Trevelyan, Sir Edward (Norman), Bt. (1662)

Trevelyan, Sir Geoffrey Washington, Bt. (1874)

Trewby, *Vice-Adm.* Sir (George Francis) Allan, KCB, FREng.

Trezise, Sir Kenneth Bruce, Kt., OBE

Trippier, Sir David Austin, Kt., RD

Tritton, Sir Anthony John Ernest, Bt. (1905)

Trollope, Sir Anthony Simon, Bt. (1642)

Trotter, Sir Neville Guthrie, Kt.

Trotter, Sir Ronald Ramsay, Kt.

Troubridge, Sir Thomas Richard, Bt. (1799)

Troup, *Vice-Adm.* Sir (John) Anthony (Rose), KCB, DSC

Trowbridge, *Rear-Adm.* Sir Richard John, KCVO

Truscott, Sir George James Irving, Bt. (1909)

Tuck, Sir Bruce Adolph Reginald, Bt. (1910)

Tucker, *Hon.* Sir Richard Howard, Kt.

Tuckey, *Hon.* Sir Simon Lane, Kt.

Tuita, Sir Mariano Kelesimalefo, Kt., OBE

Tuite, Sir Christopher Hugh, Bt., Ph.D. (1622)

Tuivaga, Sir Timoci Uluiburotu, Kt.

Tuke, Sir Anthony Favill, Kt.

Tumim, *His Hon.* Sir Stephen, Kt.

Tupper, Sir Charles Hibbert, Bt. (1888)

Turbott, Sir Ian Graham, Kt., CMG, CVO

Turing, Sir John Dermot, Bt. (S. 1638)

Turnberg, *Prof.* Sir Leslie Arnold, Kt., MD, FRCP

Turnbull, Sir Andrew, KCB, CVO

Turner, Sir Colin William Carstairs, Kt., CBE, DFC

Turner, *Hon.* Sir Michael John, Kt.

Turnquest, Sir Orville Alton, GCMG, QC

Tuti, *Revd* Dudley, KBE

Tweedie, *Prof.* Sir David Philip, Kt.

Tyree, Sir (Alfred) William, Kt., OBE

Tyrwhitt, Sir Reginald Thomas Newman, Bt. (1919)

Unsworth, *Hon.* Sir Edgar Ignatius Godfrey, Kt., CMG

Unwin, Sir (James) Brian, KCB

Ure, Sir John Burns, KCMG, LVO

Urquhart, Sir Brian Edward, KCMG, MBE

Urwick, Sir Alan Bedford, KCVO, CMG

Usher, Sir Andrew John, Bt. (1899)

Usher, Sir Leonard Gray, KBE

Ustinov, Sir Peter Alexander, Kt., CBE

Utting, Sir William Benjamin, Kt., CB

Vai, Sir Mea, Kt., CBE, ISO

Vallance, Sir Iain David Thomas, Kt.

Vallat, Sir Francis Aimé, GBE, KCMG, QC

Vallings, *Vice-Adm.* Sir George Montague Francis, KCB

Vanderfelt, Sir Robin Victor, KBE

Vane, Sir John Robert, Kt., D.Phil., D.Sc., FRS

van Straubenzee, Sir William Radcliffe, Kt., MBE

Vasquez, Sir Alfred Joseph, Kt., CBE, QC

Vaughan, Sir Gerard Folliott, Kt., FRCP

Vavasour, Sir Eric Michael Joseph Marmaduke, Bt. (1828)

Veale, Sir Alan John Ralph, Kt., FREng.

Verco, Sir Walter John George, KCVO

Vereker, Sir John Michael Medlicott, KCB

†Verney, Sir John Sebastian, Bt. (1946)

Verney, *Hon.* Sir Lawrence John, Kt., TD

Verney, Sir Ralph Bruce, Bt., KBE (1818)

Vernon, Sir James, Kt., CBE

Vernon, Sir Nigel John Douglas, Bt. (1914)

Vernon, Sir (William) Michael, Kt.

Vestey, Sir (John) Derek, Bt. (1921)

Vial, Sir Kenneth Harold, Kt., CBE

Vickers, *Lt.-Gen.* Sir Richard Maurice Hilton, KCB, CVO, OBE

Vincent, Sir William Percy Maxwell, Bt. (1936)

Vinelott, *Hon.* Sir John Evelyn, Kt.

Vines, Sir William Joshua, Kt., CMG

†Vyvyan, Sir Ralph Ferrers Alexander, Bt. (1645)

Waddell, Sir James Henderson, Kt., CB

Wade, *Prof.* Sir Henry William Rawson, Kt., QC, FBA

Wade, *Air Chief Marshal* Sir Ruthven Lowry, KCB, DFC

Waine, *Rt. Revd* John, KCVO

Waite, *Rt. Hon.* Sir John Douglas, Kt.

Wake, Sir Hereward, Bt., MC (1621)

Wakefield, Sir (Edward) Humphry (Tyrell), Bt. (1962)

Wakefield, Sir Norman Edward, Kt.

Wakefield, Sir Peter George Arthur, KBE, CMG

Wakeford, *Air Marshal* Sir Richard Gordon, KCB, OBE, LVO, AFC

Wakeley, Sir John Cecil Nicholson, Bt., FRCS (1952)

†Wakeman, Sir Edward Offley Bertram, Bt. (1828)

Walford, Sir Christopher Rupert, Kt.

Walker, *Revd* Alan Edgar, Kt., OBE

Walker, *Gen.* Sir Antony Kenneth Frederick, KCB

Walker, Sir Baldwin Patrick, Bt. (1856)

Walker, Sir (Charles) Michael, GCMG

Walker, Sir Colin John Shedlock, Kt., OBE

Walker, Sir David Alan, Kt.

Walker, Sir Gervas George, Kt.

Walker, Sir Harold Berners, KCMG

Walker, *Maj.* Sir Hugh Ronald, Bt. (1906)

Walker, Sir James Graham, Kt., MBE

Walker, Sir James Heron, Bt. (1868)

Walker, Sir John Ernest, Kt., D.Phil., FRS

Walker, *Air Marshal* Sir John Robert, KCB, CBE, AFC

Walker, *Gen.* Sir Michael John Dawson, KCB, CMG, CBE

Walker, Sir Michael Leolin Forestier-, Bt. (1835)

Walker, Sir Miles Rawstron, Kt., CBE

Walker, Sir Patrick Jeremy, KCB

Walker, *Rt. Hon.* Sir Robert, Kt.

Walker, Sir Rodney Myerscough, Kt.

Walker, *Hon.* Sir Timothy Edward, Kt.

Walker, *Gen.* Sir Walter Colyear, KCB, CBE, DSO

Wall, Sir (John) Stephen, KCMG, LVO

Wall, *Hon.* Sir Nicholas Peter Rathbone, Kt.

Wall, Sir Robert William, Kt., OBE

Wallace, *Lt.-Gen.* Sir Christopher Brooke Quentin, KBE

Wallace, Sir Ian James, Kt., CBE

Waller, *Hon.* Sir (George) Mark, Kt.

Waller, Sir Robert William, Bt. (I. 1780)

Walley, Sir John, KBE, CB

Wallis, Sir Peter Gordon, KCVO

Wallis, Sir Timothy William, Kt.

Walmsley, *Vice-Adm.* Sir Robert, KCB

Walsh, Sir Alan, Kt., D.SC., FRS

Walsh, *Prof.* Sir John Patrick, KBE

†Walsham, Sir Timothy John, Bt. (1831)

Walters, *Prof.* Sir Alan Arthur, Kt.

Walters, Sir Dennis Murray, Kt., MBE

Walters, Sir Frederick Donald, Kt.

Walters, Sir Peter Ingram, Kt.

Walters, Sir Roger Talbot, KBE, FRIBA

Walton, Sir John Robert, Kt.

Wamiri, Sir Akapite, KBE

Wan, Sir Wamp, Kt., MBE

Wanstall, *Hon.* Sir Charles Gray, Kt.

Ward, *Rt. Hon.* Sir Alan Hylton, Kt.

Ward, Sir John Devereux, Kt., CBE

Ward, Sir Joseph James Laffey, Bt. (1911)

Ward, *Maj.-Gen.* Sir Philip John Newling, KCVO, CBE

Ward, Sir Timothy James, Kt.

Wardale, Sir Geoffrey Charles, KCB

Wardlaw, Sir Henry (John), Bt. (S. 1631)

Waring, Sir (Alfred) Holburt, Bt. (1935)

Warmington, Sir David Marshall, Bt. (1908)

Warner, Sir (Edward Courtenay) Henry, Bt. (1910)

Warner, Sir Edward Redston, KCMG, OBE

Warner, *Prof.* Sir Frederick Edward, Kt., FRS, FREng.

Warner, Sir Gerald Chierici, KCMG

Warner, *Hon.* Sir Jean-Pierre Frank Eugene, Kt.

Warren, Sir (Frederick) Miles, KBE

Warren, Sir Kenneth Robin, Kt.

†Warren, Sir Michael Blackley, Bt. (1784)

Wass, Sir Douglas William Gretton, GCB

Waterhouse, *Hon.* Sir Ronald Gough, Kt.

Waterlow, Sir Christopher Rupert, Bt. (1873)

Waterlow, Sir (James) Gerard, Bt. (1930)

Waters, *Gen.* Sir (Charles) John, GCB, CBE

Waters, Sir (Thomas) Neil (Morris), Kt.

Wates, Sir Christopher Stephen, Kt.

Watkins, *Rt. Hon.* Sir Tasker, VC, GBE

†Watson, Sir Andrew Michael Milne-, Bt. (1937)

Watson, Sir Bruce Dunstan, Kt.

Watson, *Prof.* Sir David John, Kt., ph.D.

Watson, Sir (James) Andrew, Bt. (1866)

Watson, Sir John Forbes Inglefield-, Bt. (1895)

Watson, *Vice-Adm.* Sir Philip Alexander, KBE, LVO

Watson, Sir Ronald Matthew, Kt., CBE

Watt, *Surgeon Vice-Adm.* Sir James, KBE, FRCS

Watt, Sir James Harvie-, Bt. (1945)

Watts, Sir Arthur Desmond, KCMG

Watts, *Lt.-Gen.* Sir John Peter Barry Condliffe, KBE, CB, MC

Wauchope, Sir Roger (Hamilton) Don-, Bt. (S. 1667)

Weatherall, *Prof.* Sir David John, Kt., FRS

Weatherall, *Vice-Adm.* Sir James Lamb, KBE

Weatherstone, Sir Dennis, KBE

Weaver, Sir Tobias Rushton, Kt., CB

Webb, Sir Thomas Langley, Kt.

Webster, *Very Revd* Alan Brunskill, KCVO

Webster, *Vice-Adm.* Sir John Morrison, KCB

Webster, *Hon.* Sir Peter Edlin, Kt.

Wedderburn, Sir Andrew John Alexander Ogilvy-, Bt. (1803)

Wedgwood, Sir (Hugo) Martin, Bt. (1942)

Weekes, Sir Everton DeCourcey, KCMG, OBE

Weinberg, Sir Mark Aubrey, Kt.

Weir, Sir Michael Scott, KCMG

Weir, Sir Roderick Bignell, Kt.

Welby, Sir (Richard) Bruno Gregory, Bt. (1801)

Welch, Sir John Kemp-, Kt.

Welch, Sir John Reader, Bt. (1957)

Weldon, Sir Anthony William, Bt. (I. 1723)

Weller, Sir Arthur Burton, Kt., CBE

Wellings, Sir Jack Alfred, Kt., CBE

†Wells, Sir Christopher Charles, Bt. (1944)

Wells, Sir John Julius, Kt.

Wells, Sir William Henry Weston, Kt., FRICS

Westbrook, Sir Neil Gowanloch, Kt., CBE

Westerman, Sir (Wilfred) Alan, Kt., CBE

Weston, Sir Michael Charles Swift, KCMG, CVO

Weston, Sir (Philip) John, KCMG

Whalen, Sir Geoffrey Henry, Kt., CBE

Wheeler, Sir Harry Anthony, Kt., OBE

Wheeler, *Air Chief Marshal* Sir (Henry) Neil (George), GCB, CBE, DSO, DFC, AFC

Wheeler, *Rt. Hon.* Sir John Daniel, Kt.

Wheeler, Sir John Hieron, Bt. (1920)

Wheeler, *Gen.* Sir Roger Neil, GCB, CBE

Wheler, Sir Edward Woodford, Bt. (1660)

Whent, Sir Gerald Arthur, Kt., CBE

Whishaw, Sir Charles Percival Law, Kt.

Whitaker, Sir John James Ingham (Jack), Bt. (1936)

White, Sir Christopher Robert Meadows, Bt. (1937)

White, *Hon.* Sir Christopher Stuart Stuart-, Kt.

White, Sir David Harry, Kt.

White, Sir Frank John, Kt.

White, Sir George Stanley James, Bt. (1904)

White, *Wg Cdr.* Sir Henry Arthur Dalrymple-, Bt., DFC (1926)

White, *Adm.* Sir Hugo Moresby, GCB, CBE

White, *Hon.* Sir John Charles, Kt., MBE

White, Sir John Woolmer, Bt. (1922)

White, Sir Lynton Stuart, Kt., MBE, TD

White, Sir Nicholas Peter Archibald, Bt. (1802)

White, *Adm.* Sir Peter, GBE

Whitehead, Sir John Stainton, GCMG, CVO

Whitehead, Sir Rowland John Rathbone, Bt. (1889)

Whiteley, Sir Hugo Baldwin Huntington-, Bt. (1918)

Whiteley, *Gen.* Sir Peter John Frederick, GCB, OBE, RM

Whitfield, Sir William, Kt., CBE

Whitford, *Hon.* Sir John Norman Keates, Kt.

Whitmore, Sir Clive Anthony, GCB, CVO

Whitmore, Sir John Henry Douglas, Bt. (1954)

Whitney, Sir Raymond William, Kt., OBE, MP

Whittome, Sir (Leslie) Alan, Kt.

Wickerson, Sir John Michael, Kt.

Wicks, Sir Nigel Leonard, GCB, CVO, CBE

†Wigan, Sir Michael Iain, Bt. (1898)

Wiggin, Sir Alfred William (Jerry), Kt., TD

†Wiggin, Sir Charles Rupert John, Bt. (1892)

Wigram, *Revd Canon* Sir Clifford Woolmore, Bt. (1805)

Wilbraham, Sir Richard Baker, Bt. (1776)

Wilford, Sir (Kenneth) Michael, GCMG

Wilkes, *Gen.* Sir Michael John, KCB, CBE

Wilkins, Sir Graham John, Kt.

Wilkinson, Sir (David) Graham (Brook) Bt. (1941)

Wilkinson, *Prof.* Sir Denys Haigh, Kt., FRS

Wilkinson, Sir Peter Allix, KCMG, DSO, OBE

Wilkinson, Sir Philip William, Kt.

Willcocks, Sir David Valentine, Kt., CBE, MC

Williams, Sir Alastair Edgcumbe James Dudley-, Bt. (1964)

Williams, Sir Alwyn, Kt., ph.D., FRS, FRSE

Williams, Sir Arthur Dennis Pitt, Kt.

Williams, Sir (Arthur) Gareth Ludovic Emrys Rhys, Bt. (1918)

Williams, *Prof.* Sir Bernard Arthur Owen, Kt., FBA

Williams, *Prof.* Sir Bruce Rodda, KBE

Williams, Sir Daniel Charles, GCMG, QC

Williams, *Adm.* Sir David, GCB

Williams, *Prof.* Sir David Glyndwr Tudor, Kt.

Williams, Sir David Innes, Kt.

Williams, Sir David Reeve, Kt., CBE

Williams, *Hon.* Sir Denys Ambrose, KCMG

Williams, Sir Donald Mark, Bt. (1866)

Williams, *Prof.* Sir (Edward) Dillwyn, Kt., FRCP

Williams, *Hon.* Sir Edward Stratten, KCMG, KBE

Williams, Sir Francis Owen Garbett, Kt., CBE

Williams, *Prof.* Sir Glanmor, Kt., CBE, FBA

Williams, Sir Henry Sydney, Kt., OBE

Williams, Sir (John) Kyffin, Kt., OBE, DL, RA

Williams, Sir John Robert, KCMG

Williams, Sir (Lawrence) Hugh, Bt. (1798)

Williams, Sir Leonard, KBE, CB

Williams, Sir Osmond, Bt., MC (1909)

Williams, Sir Peter Michael, Kt.

Williams, *Prof.* Sir Robert Evan Owen, Kt., MD, FRCP

Williams, Sir (Robert) Philip Nathaniel, Bt. (1915)

Williams, Sir Robin Philip, Bt. (1953)

Williams, Sir (William) Maxwell (Harries), Kt.

Williamson, *Marshal of the Royal Air Force* Sir Keith Alec, GCB, AFC

Williamson, Sir (Nicholas Frederick) Hedworth, Bt. (1642)

Willink, Sir Charles William, Bt. (1957)

Willis, *Hon.* Sir Eric Archibald, KBE, CMG

Willis, *Vice-Adm.* Sir (Guido) James, KBE

Willis, *Air Chief Marshal* Sir John Frederick, GBE, KCB

Willison, *Lt.-Gen.* Sir David John, KCB, OBE, MC

Willison, Sir John Alexander, Kt., OBE

Wills, Sir David James Vernon, Bt. (1923)

Wills, Sir David Seton, Bt. (1904)

Wills, Sir (Hugh) David Hamilton, Kt., CBE, TD

Wilmot, Sir Henry Robert, Bt. (1759)

Wilmot, Sir Michael John Assheton Eardley-, Bt. (1821)

Wilsey, *Gen.* Sir John Finlay Willasey, GCB, CBE

Wilson, *Lt.-Gen.* Sir (Alexander) James, KBE, MC

Wilson, Sir Anthony, Kt.

Wilson, *Vice-Adm.* Sir Barry Nigel, KCB

Wilson, *Lt.-Col.* Sir Blair Aubyn Stewart-, KCVO

Wilson, Sir Charles Haynes, Kt.

Wilson, *Prof.* Sir Colin Alexander St John, Kt., RA, FRIBA

Wilson, Sir David, Bt. (1920)

Wilson, Sir David Mackenzie, Kt.

Wilson, Sir Geoffrey Masterman, KCB, CMG

Wilson, Sir James William Douglas, Bt. (1906)

Wilson, Sir John Foster, Kt., CBE

Wilson, *Brig.* Sir Mathew John Anthony, Bt., OBE, MC (1874)

Wilson, *Hon.* Sir Nicholas Allan Roy, Kt.

Wilson, Sir Patrick Michael Ernest David McNair-, Kt.

Wilson, Sir Richard Thomas James, KCB

Wilson, Sir Robert, Kt., CBE

Wilson, Sir Robert Donald, KBE

Wilson, *Rt. Revd* Roger Plumpton, KCVO, DD

Wilson, *Air Chief Marshal* Sir (Ronald) Andrew (Fellowes), KCB, AFC

Wilson, *Hon.* Sir Ronald Darling, KBE, CMG

Wilton, Sir (Arthur) John, KCMG, KCVO, MC

Wingate, *Capt.* Sir Miles Buckley, KCVO

Winkley, Sir David Ross, Kt.

Winnington, Sir Francis Salwey William, Bt. (1755)

Winskill, *Air Cdre* Sir Archibald Little, KCVO, CBE, DFC

Winterbottom, Sir Walter, Kt., CBE

Wiseman, Sir John William, Bt. (1628)

Wolfendale, *Prof.* Sir Arnold Whittaker, Kt., FRS

Wolfson, Sir Brian Gordon, Kt.

Wolseley, Sir Charles Garnet Richard Mark, Bt. (1628)

†Wolseley, Sir James Douglas, Bt. (I. 1745)

Wolstenholme, Sir Gordon Ethelbert Ward, Kt., OBE

Wombwell, Sir George Philip Frederick, Bt. (1778)

Womersley, Sir Peter John Walter, Bt. (1945)

Woo, Sir Leo Joseph, Kt.

Woo, Sir Po-Shing, Kt.

Wood, Sir Alan Marshall Muir, Kt., FRS, FREng.

Wood, Sir Andrew Marley, KCMG

Wood, Sir Anthony John Page, Bt. (1837)

Wood, Sir David Basil Hill-, Bt. (1921)

Wood, Sir Frederick Ambrose Stuart, Kt.

Wood, Sir Ian Clark, Kt., CBE

Wood, *Prof.* Sir John Crossley, Kt., CBE

Wood, *Hon.* Sir John Kember, Kt., MC

Wood, Sir Martin Francis, Kt., OBE

Wood, Sir Russell Dillon, KCVO, VRD

Wood, Sir William Alan, KCVO, CB

Woodard, *Rear Adm.* Sir Robert Nathaniel, KCVO

Woodcock, Sir John, Kt., CBE, QPM

Woodfield, Sir Philip John, KCB, CBE

Woodhead, *Vice-Adm.* Sir (Anthony) Peter, KCB

Woodhouse, *Rt. Hon.* Sir (Arthur) Owen, KBE, DSC

Wooding, Sir Norman Samuel, Kt., CBE

Woodroffe, *Most Revd* George Cuthbert Manning, KBE

Woodroofe, Sir Ernest George, Kt., Ph.D.

Woodruff, *Prof.* Sir Michael Francis Addison, Kt., D.SC., FRS, FRCS

Woods, Sir Colin Philip Joseph, KCVO, CBE

Woodward, *Hon.* Sir (Albert) Edward, Kt., OBE

Woodward, *Adm.* Sir John Forster, GBE, KCB

Worsley, *Gen.* Sir Richard Edward, GCB, OBE

Worsley, Sir (William) Marcus (John), Bt. (1838)

Worsthorne, Sir Peregrine Gerard, Kt.

Wratten, *Air Chief Marshal* Sir William John, GBE, CB, AFC

Wraxall, Sir Charles Frederick Lascelles, Bt. (1813)

Wrey, Sir George Richard Bourchier, Bt. (1628)

Wrigglesworth, Sir Ian William, Kt.

Wright, Sir Allan Frederick, KBE

Wright, Sir David John, KCMG, LVO

Wright, Sir Denis Arthur Hepworth, GCMG

Wright, Sir Edward Maitland, Kt., D.Phil., LL D, D.SC., FRSE

Wright, *Hon.* Sir (John) Michael, Kt.

Wright, Sir (John) Oliver, GCMG, GCVO, DSC

Wright, Sir Paul Hervé Giraud, KCMG, OBE

Wright, Sir Peter Robert, Kt., CBE

Wright, Sir Richard Michael Cory-, Bt. (1903)

Wrightson, Sir Charles Mark Garmondsway, Bt. (1900)

Wrigley, *Prof.* Sir Edward Anthony (Sir Tony), Kt., Ph.D., PBA

Wu, Sir Gordon Ying Sheung, KCMG

Wynn, Sir David Watkin Williams-, Bt. (1688)

Yacoub, *Prof.* Sir Magdi Habib, Kt., FRCS

Yaki, Sir Roy, KBE

Yang, *Hon.* Sir Ti Liang, Kt.

Yapp, Sir Stanley Graham, Kt.

Yardley, Sir David Charles Miller, Kt., LL D

Yarranton, Sir Peter George, Kt.

Yarrow, Sir Eric Grant, Bt., MBE (1916)

Yellowlees, Sir Henry, KCB

Yocklunn, Sir John (Soong Chung), KCVO

Yoo Foo, Sir (François) Henri, Kt.

Youens, Sir Peter William, Kt., CMG, OBE

Young, Sir Brian Walter Mark, Kt.

Young, Sir Colville Norbert, GCMG, MBE

Young, *Lt.-Gen.* Sir David Tod, KBE, CB, DFC

Young, Sir Dennis Charles, KCMG

Young, *Rt. Hon.* Sir George Samuel Knatchbull, Bt., MP (1813)

Young, *Hon.* Sir Harold William, KCMG

Young, Sir John Kenyon Roe, Bt. (1821)

Young, *Hon.* Sir John McIntosh, KCMG

Young, Sir John Robertson, KCMG

Young, Sir Leslie Clarence, Kt., CBE

Young, Sir Richard Dilworth, Kt.

Young, Sir Robert Christopher Mackworth-, GCVO

Young, Sir Roger William, Kt.

Young, Sir Stephen Stewart Templeton, Bt. (1945)

Young, Sir William Neil, Bt. (1769)

Younger, *Maj.-Gen.* Sir John William, Bt., CBE (1911)

Yuwi, Sir Matiabe, KBE

Zeeman, *Prof.* Sir (Erik) Christopher, Kt., FRS

Zissman, Sir Bernard Philip, Kt.

Zochonis, Sir John Basil, Kt.

Zoleveke, Sir Gideon Pitabose, KBE

Zunz, Sir Gerhard Jacob (Jack), Kt., FREng.

Zurenuoc, Sir Zibang, KBE

Dames Grand Cross and Dames Commanders

Style, 'Dame' before forename and surname, followed by appropriate post-nominal initials. Where such an award is made to a lady already in enjoyment of a higher title, the appropriate initials follow her name
Husband, Untitled
For forms of address, *see* page 135

Dame Grand Cross and Dame Commander are the higher classes for women of the Order of the Bath, the Order of St Michael and St George, the Royal Victorian Order, and the Order of the British Empire. Dames Grand Cross rank after the wives of Baronets and before the wives of Knights Grand Cross. Dames Commanders rank after the wives of Knights Grand Cross and before the wives of Knights Commanders.

Honorary Dames Commanders may be conferred on women who are citizens of countries of which The Queen is not head of state.

LIST OF DAMES
Revised to 31 August 1999

Women peers in their own right and life peers are not included in this list.

Female members of the royal family are not included in this list; details of the orders they hold are given on pages 117–8

If a dame has a double barrelled or hyphenated surname, she is listed under the final element of the name

A full entry in italic type indicates that the recipient of an honour died during the year in which the honour was conferred. The name is included for the purposes of record

Abaijah, Dame Josephine, DBE
Abel Smith, Lady, DCVO
Abergavenny, The Marchioness of, DCVO
Airlie, The Countess of, DCVO
Albemarle, The Countess of, DBE
Anderson, *Brig. Hon.* Dame Mary Mackenzie (Mrs Pihl), DBE
Anglesey, The Marchioness of, DBE
Anson, Lady (Elizabeth Audrey), DBE
Anstee, Dame Margaret Joan, DCMG
Arden, *Hon.* Dame Mary Howarth (Mrs Mance), DBE
Baker, Dame Janet Abbott (Mrs Shelley), CH, DBE
Ballin, Dame Reubina Ann, DBE
Barnes, Dame (Alice) Josephine (Mary Taylor), DBE, FRCP, FRCS
Barrow, Dame Jocelyn Anita (Mrs Downer), DBE
Barstow, Dame Josephine Clare (Mrs Anderson), DBE
Basset, Lady Elizabeth, DCVO
Bean, Dame Majorie Louise, DBE
Beaurepaire, Dame Beryl Edith, DBE
Beer, *Prof.* Dame Gillian Patricia Kempster, DBE, FBA
Bergquist, *Prof.* Dame Patricia Rose, DBE
Berry, Dame Alice Miriam, DBE
Blaize, Dame Venetia Ursula, DBE
Blaxland, Dame Helen Frances, DBE
Booth, *Hon.* Dame Margaret Myfanwy Wood, DBE
Bottomley, Dame Bessie Ellen, DBE
Bowman, Dame (Mary) Elaine Kellett-, DBE
Bowtell, Dame Ann Elizabeth, DCB
Boyd, Dame Vivienne Myra, DBE

Bracewell, *Hon.* Dame Joyanne Winifred (Mrs Copeland), DBE
Brain, Dame Margaret Anne (Mrs Wheeler), DBE
Brazill, Dame Josephine (Sister Mary Philippa), DBE
Bridges, Dame Mary Patricia, DBE
Browne, Lady Moyra Blanche Madeleine, DBE
Bryans, Dame Anne Margaret, DBE
Buttfield, Dame Nancy Eileen, DBE
Byatt, Dame Antonia Susan, DBE, FRSL
Bynoe, Dame Hilda Louisa, DBE
Caldicott, Dame Fiona, DBE, FRCP, FRCPsych.
Cartland, Dame Barbara Hamilton, DBE
Cartwright, Dame Silvia Rose, DBE
Casey, Dame Stella Katherine, DBE
Charles, Dame (Mary) Eugenia, DBE
Chesterton, Dame Elizabeth Ursula, DBE
Clark, *Prof.* Dame (Margaret) June, DBE, Ph.D.
Collins, Dame Diana Clavering, DBE
Clay, Dame Marie Mildred, DBE
Clayton, Dame Barbara Evelyn (Mrs Klyne), DBE
Cleland, Dame Rachel, DBE
Coll, Dame Elizabeth Anne Loosemore Esteve-, DBE
Collarbone, Dame Patricia, DBE
Corsar, The Hon. Dame Mary Drummond, DBE
Daws, Dame Joyce Margaretta, DBE
Dell, Dame Miriam Patricia, DBE
Dench, Dame Judith Olivia (Mrs Williams), DBE
de Valois, Dame Ninette, OM, CH, DBE
Devonshire, The Duchess of, DCVO
Digby, Lady, DBE
Donaldson, Dame (Dorothy) Mary (Lady Donaldson of Lymington), GBE
Dugdale, Kathryn, Lady, DCVO
Dumont, Dame Ivy Leona, DCMG
Dyche, Dame Rachael Mary, DBE
Ebsworth, *Hon.* Dame Ann Marian, DBE
Engel, Dame Pauline Frances (Sister Pauline Engel), DBE
Evans, Dame Lois Marie Browne-, DBE

Evison, Dame Helen June Patricia, DBE
Fenner, Dame Peggy Edith, DBE
Fielding, Dame Pauline, DBE
Fitton, Dame Doris Alice (Mrs Mason), DBE
Fort, Dame Maeve Geraldine, DCMG
Fraser, Dame Dorothy Rita, DBE
Friend, Dame Phyllis Muriel, DBE
Fritchie, Dame Irene Tordoff (Dame Rennie Fritchie), DBE
Frost, Dame Phyllis Irene, DBE
Fry, Dame Margaret Louise, DBE
Gallagher, Dame Monica Josephine, DBE
Gardiner, Dame Helen Louisa, DBE, MVO
Giles, *Air Comdt.* Dame Pauline (Mrs Parsons), DBE, RRC
Goodman, Dame Barbara, DBE
Gordon, Dame Minita Elmira, GCMG, GCVO
Gow, Dame Jane Elizabeth (Mrs Whiteley), DBE
Grafton, The Duchess of, GCVO
Grant, Dame Mavis, DBE
Green, Dame Mary Georgina, DBE
Grey, Dame Beryl Elizabeth (Mrs Svenson), DBE
Grimthorpe, The Lady, DCVO
Guilfoyle, Dame Margaret Georgina Constance, DBE
Guthardt, *Revd Dr* Dame Phyllis Myra, DBE
Haig, Dame Mary Alison Glen-, DBE
Hale, *Hon.* Dame Brenda Marjorie (Mrs Farrand), DBE
Hallett, Dame Heather Carol, DBE, QC
Harper, Dame Elizabeth Margaret Way, DBE
Heilbron, *Hon.* Dame Rose, DBE
Henderson, Dame Louise Etiennette Sidonie, DBE
Herbison, Dame Jean Marjory, DBE, CMG
Hercus, *Hon.* Dame (Margaret) Ann, DCMG
Hetet, Dame Rangimarie, DBE
Higgins, *Prof.* Dame Rosalyn, DBE, QC
Hill, *Air Cdre* Dame Felicity Barbara, DBE
Hiller, Dame Wendy (Mrs Gow), DBE
Hine, Dame Deirdre Joan, DBE, FRCP

Decorations and Medals

PRINCIPAL DECORATIONS AND MEDALS
In order of precedence

VICTORIA CROSS (VC), 1856 (*see* page 208)
GEORGE CROSS (GC), 1940 (*see* pages 208–9)
BRITISH ORDERS OF KNIGHTHOOD, ETC.
Baronet's Badge
Knight Bachelor's Badge

DECORATIONS
Conspicuous Gallantry Cross (CGC), 1995
Royal Red Cross Class I (RRC), 1883
Distinguished Service Cross (DSC), 1914. For all ranks for
    actions at sea
Military Cross (MC), December 1914. For all ranks for
    actions on land
Distinguished Flying Cross (DFC), 1918. For all ranks for
    acts of gallantry when flying in active operations
    against the enemy
Air Force Cross (AFC), 1918. For all ranks for acts of
    courage when flying, although not in active operations
    against the enemy
Royal Red Cross Class II (ARRC)
Order of British India
Kaisar-i-Hind Medal
Order of St John

MEDALS FOR GALLANTRY AND DISTINGUISHED
CONDUCT
Union of South Africa Queen's Medal for Bravery, in Gold
Distinguished Conduct Medal (DCM), 1854
Conspicuous Gallantry Medal (CGM), 1874
Conspicuous Gallantry Medal (Flying)
George Medal (GM), 1940
Queen's Police Medal for Gallantry
Queen's Fire Service Medal for Gallantry
Royal West African Frontier Force Distinguished Conduct Medal
King's African Rifles Distinguished Conduct Medal
Indian Distinguished Service Medal
Union of South Africa Queen's Medal for Bravery, in Silver
Distinguished Service Medal (DSM), 1914
Military Medal (MM), 1916
Distinguished Flying Medal (DFM), 1918
Air Force Medal (AFM)
Constabulary Medal (Ireland)
Medal for Saving Life at Sea
Sea Gallantry Medal
Indian Order of Merit (Civil)
Indian Police Medal for Gallantry
Ceylon Police Medal for Gallantry
Sierra Leone Police Medal for Gallantry
Sierra Leone Fire Brigades Medal for Gallantry
Colonial Police Medal for Gallantry (CPM)
Queen's Gallantry Medal, 1974
Royal Victorian Medal (RVM), Gold, Silver and Bronze
British Empire Medal (BEM), (formerly the Medal of the
    Order of the British Empire, for Meritorious Service;
    also includes the Medal of the Order awarded before 29
    December 1922)
Canada Medal
*Queen's Police (QPM) and Queen's Fire Service Medals
    (QFSM) for Distinguished Service*
Queen's Volunteer Reserves Medal
Queen's Medal for Chiefs

WAR MEDALS AND STARS (in order of date)
POLAR MEDALS (in order of date)
POLICE MEDALS FOR VALUABLE SERVICE
JUBILEE, CORONATION AND DURBAR MEDALS
*King George V, King George VI and Queen Elizabeth II Long and
    Faithful Service Medals*

EFFICIENCY AND LONG SERVICE DECORATIONS AND
MEDALS
Medal for Meritorious Service
Accumulated Campaign Service Medal
The Medal for Long Service and Good Conduct (Military)
Naval Long Service and Good Conduct Medal
Royal Marines Meritorious Service Medal
Royal Air Force Meritorious Service Medal
Royal Air Force Long Service and Good Conduct Medal
*Medal for Long Service and Good Conduct (Ulster Defence
    Regiment)*
Police Long Service and Good Conduct Medal
Fire Brigade Long Service and Good Conduct Medal
Colonial Police and Fire Brigades Long Service Medals
Colonial Prison Service Medal
Hong Kong Disciplined Services Medal
Army Emergency Reserve Decoration (ERD), 1952
Volunteer Officers' Decoration (VD)
Volunteer Long Service Medal
Volunteer Officers' Decoration for India and the Colonies
Volunteer Long Service Medal for India and the Colonies
Colonial Auxiliary Forces Officers' Decoration
Colonial Auxiliary Forces Long Service Medal
Medal for Good Shooting (Naval)
Militia Long Service Medal
Imperial Yeomanry Long Service Medal
Territorial Decoration (TD), 1908
Efficiency Decoration (ED)
Territorial Efficiency Medal
Efficiency Medal
Special Reserve Long Service and Good Conduct Medal
Decoration for Officers, Royal Navy Reserve (RD), 1910
Decoration for Officers, RNVR (VRD)
Royal Naval Reserve Long Service and Good Conduct Medal
RNVR Long Service and Good Conduct Medal
*Royal Naval Auxiliary Sick Berth Reserve Long Service and
    Good Conduct Medal*
Royal Fleet Reserve Long Service and Good Conduct Medal
*Royal Naval Wireless Auxiliary Reserve Long Service and Good
    Conduct Medal*
Air Efficiency Award (AE), 1942
Volunteer Reserves Service Medal
Ulster Defence Regiment Medal
Northern Ireland Home Service Medal
The Queen's Medal. For champion shots in the RN, RM,
    RNZN, Army, RAF
Cadet Forces Medal, 1950
Coastguard Auxiliary Service Long Service Medal (formerly
    Coast Life Saving Corps Long Service Medal)
Special Constabulary Long Service Medal
Royal Observer Corps Medal
Civil Defence Long Service Medal
*Ambulance Service (Emergency Duties) Long Service and Good
    Conduct Medal*
Rhodesia Medal
Royal Ulster Constabulary Service Medal
Service Medal of the Order of St John

Badge of the Order of the League of Mercy
Voluntary Medical Service Medal, 1932
Women's Voluntary Service Medal
Colonial Special Constabulary Medal

FOREIGN ORDERS, DECORATIONS AND MEDALS (IN
ORDER OF DATE)

THE VICTORIA CROSS (1856)
FOR CONSPICUOUS BRAVERY

VC

Ribbon, Crimson, for all Services (until 1918 it was blue for
the Royal Navy)

Instituted on 29 January 1856, the Victoria Cross was
awarded retrospectively to 1854, the first being held by Lt.
C. D. Lucas, RN, for bravery in the Baltic Sea on 21 June
1854 (gazetted 24 February 1857). The first 62 Crosses
were presented by Queen Victoria in Hyde Park, London,
on 26 June 1857.

The Victoria Cross is worn before all other decorations,
on the left breast, and consists of a cross-pattée of bronze,
one and a half inches in diameter, with the Royal Crown
surmounted by a lion in the centre, and beneath there is
the inscription *For Valour.* Holders of the VC receive a tax-
free annuity of £1,300, irrespective of need or other
conditions. In 1911, the right to receive the Cross was
extended to Indian soldiers, and in 1920 to matrons, sisters
and nurses, and the staff of the Nursing Services and other
services pertaining to hospitals and nursing, and to civilians
of either sex regularly or temporarily under the orders,
direction or supervision of the naval, military, or air forces
of the Crown.

SURVIVING RECIPIENTS OF THE VICTORIA CROSS
as at 31 August 1999

Agansing Rai, *Capt.,* MM (5th Royal Gurkha Rifles)
1944 *World War*
Annand, *Capt.* R. W. (Durham Light Infantry)
1940 *World War*
Bhan Bhagta Gurung, *Havildar* (2nd Gurkha Rifles)
1945 *World War*
Bhandari Ram, *Capt.* (10th Baluch Regiment)
1944 *World War*
Chapman, *Sgt.* E. T., BEM (Monmouthshire Regiment)
1945 *World War*
Cruickshank, *Flt. Lt.* J. A. (RAFVR)
1944 *World War*
Cutler, *Capt.* Sir Roden, AK, KCMG, KCVO, CBE (Australian
Military Forces, 2/5th Field Artillery)
1941 *World War*
Fraser, *Lt.-Cdr.* I. E., DSC (RNR)
1945 *World War*
Gaje Ghale, *Capt.* (5th Royal Gurkha Rifles)
1943 *World War*
Ganju Lama, *Capt.,* MM (7th Gurkha Rifles)
1944 *World War*
Gardner, *Capt.* P. J., MC (Royal Tank Regiment)
1941 *World War*
Gould, *Lt.* T. W. (RN)
1942 *World War*

Jamieson, *Maj.* D. A., CVO (Royal Norfolk Regiment)
1944 *World War*
Kenna, *Pte.* E. (Australian Military Forces, 2/4th (NSW))
1945 *World War*
Kenneally, *Guardsman* J. P. (Irish Guards)
1943 *World War*
Lachhiman Gurung, *Havildar* (8th Gurkha Rifles)
1945 *World War*
Merritt, *Lt.-Col.* C. C. I., CD (South Saskatchewan Regiment)
1942 *World War*
Norton, *Capt.* G. R., MM (South African Forces, Kaffrarian
Rifles)
1944 *World War*
Payne, *WO* K., DSC (USA) (Australian Army Training Team)
1969 *Vietnam*
Porteous, *Col.* P. A. (Royal Regiment of Artillery)
1942 *World War*
Rambahadur Limbu, *Capt.,* MVO (10th Princess Mary's
Gurkha Rifles)
1965 *Sarawak*
Reid, *Flt. Lt.* W. (RAFVR)
1943 *World War*
Smith, *Sgt.* E. A., CD (Seaforth Highlanders of Canada)
1944 *World War*
Speakman-Pitts, *Sgt.* W. (Black Watch)
1951 *Korea*
Tulbahadur Pun, *Lt.* (6th Gurkha Rifles)
1944 *World War*
Umrao Singh, *Sub Major* (Royal Indian Artillery)
1944 *World War*
Watkins, *Maj. Rt. Hon.* Sir Tasker, GBE (Welch Regiment)
1944 *World War*
Wilson, *Lt.-Col.* E. C. T. (East Surrey Regiment)
1940 *World War*

THE GEORGE CROSS (1940)
FOR GALLANTRY

GC

Ribbon, Dark blue, threaded through a bar adorned with
laurel leaves
Instituted 24 September 1940 (with amendments,
3 November 1942)

The George Cross is worn before all other decorations
(except the VC) on the left breast (when worn by a woman
it may be worn on the left shoulder from a ribbon of the
same width and colour fashioned into a bow). It consists of
a plain silver cross with four equal limbs, the cross having
in the centre a circular medallion bearing a design showing
St George and the Dragon. The inscription *For Gallantry*
appears round the medallion and in the angle of each limb
of the cross is the Royal cypher 'G VI' forming a circle
concentric with the medallion. The reverse is plain and
bears the name of the recipient and the date of the award.
The cross is suspended by a ring from a bar adorned with
laurel leaves on dark blue ribbon one and a half inches
wide.

The cross is intended primarily for civilians; awards to
the fighting services are confined to actions for which
purely military honours are not normally granted. It is

awarded only for acts of the greatest heroism or of the most conspicuous courage in circumstances of extreme danger. From 1 April 1965, holders of the Cross have received a tax-free annuity, which is now £1,300.

The royal warrant which ordained that the grant of the Empire Gallantry Medal should cease authorized holders of that medal to return it to the Central Chancery of the Orders of Knighthood and to receive in exchange the George Cross. A similar provision applied to posthumous awards of the Empire Gallantry Medal made after the outbreak of war in 1939. In October 1971 all surviving holders of the Albert Medal and the Edward Medal exchanged those decorations for the George Cross.

Surviving Recipients of the George Cross
as at 31 August 1999

If the recipient originally received the Empire Gallantry Medal (EGM), the Albert Medal (AM) or the Edward Medal (EM), this is indicated by the initials in parenthesis.

Archer, *Col.* B. S. T., GC, OBE, ERD, 1941
Baker, J. T., GC (EM), 1929
Bamford, J., GC, 1952
Beaton, J., GC, CVO, 1974
Bridge, *Lt.-Cdr.* J., GC, GM and BAR, 1944
Butson, *Lt.-Col.* A. R. C., GC, CD, MD (AM), 1948
Bywater, R. A. S., GC, GM, 1944
Errington, H., GC, 1941
Farrow, K., GC (AM), 1948
Flintoff, H. H., GC (EM), 1944
Gledhill, A. J., GC, 1967
Gregson, J. S., GC (AM), 1943
Hawkins, E., GC (AM), 1943
Johnson, *WO1 (SSM)* B., GC, 1990
Kinne, D. G., GC, 1954
Lowe, A. R., GC (AM), 1949
Lynch, J., GC, BEM (AM), 1948
Malta, GC, 1942
Manwaring, T. G., GC (EM), 1949
Moore, R. V., GC, CBE, 1940
Moss, B., GC, 1940
Naughton, F., GC (EGM), 1937
Pearson, Miss J. D. M., GC (EGM), 1940
Pratt, M. K., GC, 1978
Purves, Mrs M., GC (AM), 1949
Raweng, Awang anak, GC, 1951
Riley, G., GC (AM), 1944
Rowlands, *Air Marshal* Sir John, GC, KBE, 1943
Sinclair, *Air Vice-Marshal* Sir Laurence, GC, KCB, CBE, DSO, 1941
Stevens, H. W., GC, 1958
Stronach, *Capt.* G. P., GC, 1943
Styles, *Lt.-Col.* S. G., GC, 1972
Walker, C., GC, 1972
Walker, C. H., GC (AM), 1942
Walton, E. W. K., GC (AM), DSO, 1948
Wilcox, C., GC (EM), 1949
Wiltshire, S. N., GC (EGM), 1930
Wooding, E. A., GC (AM), 1945

Chiefs of Clans and Names in Scotland

Only chiefs of whole Names or Clans are included, except certain special instances (marked *) who, though not chiefs of a whole name, were or are for some reason (e.g. the Macdonald forfeiture) independent. Under decision (*Campbell-Gray*, 1950) that a bearer of a 'double or triple-barrelled' surname cannot be held chief of a part of such, several others cannot be included in the list at present.

THE ROYAL HOUSE: HM The Queen

AGNEW: Sir Crispin Agnew of Lochnaw, Bt., QC, 6 Palmerston Road, Edinburgh EH9 1TN

ANSTRUTHER: Sir Ralph Anstruther of that Ilk, Bt., GCVO, MC, Balcaskie, Pittenweem, Fife KY10 2RD

ARBUTHNOTT: The Viscount of Arbuthnott, KT, CBE, DSC, Arbuthnott House, Laurencekirk, Kincardineshire AB30 1PA

BARCLAY: Peter C. Barclay of Towie Barclay and of that Ilk, 28A Gordon Place, London W8 4JE

BORTHWICK: The Lord Borthwick, Crookston, Heriot, Midlothian EH38 5YS

BOYD: The Lord Kilmarnock, 194 Regent's Park Road, London NW1 8XP

BOYLE: The Earl of Glasgow, Kelburn, Fairlie, Ayrshire KA29 0BE

BRODIE: Ninian Brodie of Brodie, Brodie Castle, Forres, Morayshire IV36 0TE

BRUCE: The Earl of Elgin and Kincardine, KT, Broomhall, Dunfermline, Fife KY11 3DU

BUCHAN: David S. Buchan of Auchmacoy, Auchmacoy House, Ellon, Aberdeenshire

BURNETT: J. C. A. Burnett of Leys, Crathes Castle, Banchory, Kincardineshire

CAMERON: Sir Donald Cameron of Lochiel, KT, CVO, TD, Achnacarry, Spean Bridge, Inverness-shire

CAMPBELL: The Duke of Argyll, Inveraray, Argyll PA32 8XF

CARMICHAEL: Richard J. Carmichael of Carmichael, Carmichael, Thankerton, Biggar, Lanarkshire

CARNEGIE: The Duke of Fife, Elsick House, Stonehaven, Kincardineshire AB3 2NT

CATHCART: vacant

CHARTERIS: The Earl of Wemyss and March, KT, Gosford House, Longniddry, East Lothian EH32 0PX

CLAN CHATTAN: M. K. Mackintosh of Clan Chattan, Maxwell Park, Gwelo, Zimbabwe

CHISHOLM: Hamish Chisholm of Chisholm (*The Chisholm*), Elmpine, Beck Row, Bury St Edmunds, Suffolk

COCHRANE: The Earl of Dundonald, Lochnell Castle, Ledaig, Argyllshire

COLQUHOUN: Sir Ivar Colquhoun of Luss, Bt., Camstraddan, Luss, Dunbartonshire G83 8NX

CRANSTOUN: David A. S. Cranstoun of that Ilk, Corehouse, Lanark

CRICHTON: vacant

CUMMING: Sir William Cumming of Altyre, Bt., Altyre, Forres, Moray

DARROCH: Capt. Duncan Darroch of Gourock, The Red House, Branksome Park Road, Camberley, Surrey

DAVIDSON: Alister G. Davidson of Davidston, 21 Winscombe Street, Takapuna, Auckland, New Zealand

DEWAR: Kenneth Dewar of that Ilk and Vogrie, The Dower House, Grayshott, nr Hindhead, Surrey

DRUMMOND: The Earl of Perth, PC, Stobhall, Perth PH2 6DR

DUNBAR: Sir James Dunbar of Mochrum, Bt., 211 Gardenville Drive, Yorktown, VA 23693, USA

DUNDAS: David D. Dundas of Dundas, 8 Derna Road, Kenwyn 7700, South Africa

DURIE: Andrew Durie of Durie, Finnich Malise, Croftamie, Stirlingshire G63 0HA

ELIOTT: Mrs Margaret Eliott of Redheugh, Redheugh, Newcastleton, Roxburghshire

ERSKINE: The Earl of Mar and Kellie, Erskine House, Kirk Wynd, Alloa, Clackmannan FK10 4JF

FARQUHARSON: Capt. A. Farquharson of Invercauld, MC, Invercauld, Braemar, Aberdeenshire AB35 5TT

FERGUSSON: Sir Charles Fergusson of Kilkerran, Bt., Kilkerran, Maybole, Ayrshire

FORBES: The Lord Forbes, KBE, Balforbes, Alford, Aberdeenshire AB33 8DR

FORSYTH: Alistair Forsyth of that Ilk, Ethie Castle, by Arbroath, Angus DD11 5SP

FRASER: The Lady Saltoun, Inverey House, Aberdeenshire AB35 5YB

*FRASER (OF LOVAT): The Lord Lovat, Beaufort Lodge, Beauly, Inverness-shire IV4 7AZ

GAYRE: R. Gayre of Gayre and Nigg, Minard Castle, Minard, Inverary, Argyll PA32 8YB

GORDON: The Marquess of Huntly, Aboyne Castle, Aberdeenshire AB34 5JP

GRAHAM: The Duke of Montrose, Buchanan Auld House, Drymen, Stirlingshire

GRANT: The Lord Strathspey, The House of Lords, London SW1A 0PW

GRIERSON: Sir Michael Grierson of Lag, Bt., 40C Palace Road, London SW2 3NJ

HAIG: The Earl Haig, OBE, Bemersyde, Melrose, Roxburghshire TD6 9DP

HALDANE: Martin Haldane of Gleneagles, Gleneagles, Auchterarder, Perthshire

HANNAY: Ramsey Hannay of Kirkdale and of that Ilk, Cardoness House, Gatehouse-of-Fleet, Kirkcudbrightshire

HAY: The Earl of Erroll, Woodbury Hall, Sandy, Beds

HENDERSON: John Henderson of Fordell, 7 Owen Street, Toowoomba, Queensland, Australia

HUNTER: Pauline Hunter of Hunterston, Plovers Ridge, Lon Cecrist, Treaddur Bay, Holyhead, Gwynedd

IRVINE OF DRUM: David C. Irvine of Drum, Holly Leaf Cottage, Inchmarlo, Banchory, Aberdeenshire AB31 4BR

JARDINE: Sir Alexander Jardine of Applegirth, Bt., Ash House, Thwaites, Millom, Cumbria LA18 5HY

JOHNSTONE: The Earl of Annandale and Hartfell, Raehills, Lockerbie, Dumfriesshire

KEITH: The Earl of Kintore, The Stables, Keith Hall, Inverurie, Aberdeenshire AB51 0LD

KENNEDY: The Marquess of Ailsa, Cassillis House, Maybole, Ayrshire

KERR: The Marquess of Lothian, KCVO, Ferniehurst Castle, Jedburgh, Roxburghshire TN8 6NX

LAMONT: Peter N. Lamont of that Ilk, St Patrick's College, Manly, NSW 2095, Australia

LEASK: Madam Leask of Leask, 1 Vincent Road, Sheringham, Norfolk

LENNOX: Edward J. H. Lennox of that Ilk, Pools Farm, Downton on the Rock, Ludlow, Shropshire

LESLIE: The Earl of Rothes, Tanglewood, West Tytherley, Salisbury, Wilts SP5 1LX

LINDSAY: The Earl of Crawford and Balcarres, KT, PC, Balcarres, Colinsburgh, Fife

LOCKHART: Angus H. Lockhart of the Lee, Newholme, Dunsyre, Lanark

LUMSDEN: Gillem Lumsden of that Ilk and Blanerne, Stapely Howe, Hoe Benham, Newbury, Berks

MACALESTER: William St J. S. McAlester of Loup and Kennox, 2 Avon Road East, Christchurch, Dorset

McBAIN: J. H. McBain of McBain, 7025 North Finger Rock Place, Tucson, Arizona, USA

MACDONALD: The Lord Macdonald (*The Macdonald of Macdonald*), Kinloch Lodge, Sleat, Isle of Skye

*MACDONALD OF CLANRANALD: Ranald A. Macdonald of Clanranald, Mornish House, Killin, Perthshire FK21 8TX

*MACDONALD OF SLEAT (CLAN HUSTEAIN): Sir Ian Macdonald of Sleat, Bt., Thorpe Hall, Rudston, Driffield, N. Humberside YO25 0JE

*MACDONELL OF GLENGARRY: Ranald MacDonell of Glengarry, Elonbank, Castle Street, Fortrose, Ross-shire IV10 8TH

MACDOUGALL: vacant

MACDOWALL: Fergus D. H. Macdowall of Garthland, 9170 Ardmore Drive, North Saanich, British Columbia, Canada

MACGREGOR: Brig. Sir Gregor MacGregor of MacGregor, Bt., Bannatyne, Newtyle, Blairgowrie, Perthshire PH12 8TR

MACINTYRE: James W. MacIntyre of Glenoe, 15301 Pine Orchard Drive, Apartment 3H, Silver Spring, Maryland, USA

MACKAY: The Lord Reay, House of Lords, London SW1

MACKENZIE: The Earl of Cromartie, Castle Leod, Strathpeffer, Ross-shire IV14 9AA

MACKINNON: Madam Anne Mackinnon of Mackinnon, 16 Purleigh Road, Bridgwater, Somerset

MACKINTOSH: *The Mackintosh of Mackintosh*, Moy Hall, Inverness IV13 7YQ

MACLACHLAN: vacant

MACLAREN: Donald MacLaren of MacLaren and Achleskine, Achleskine, Kirkton, Balquhidder, Lochearnhead

MACLEAN: The Hon. Sir Lachlan Maclean of Duart, Bt., Arngask House, Glenfarg, Perthshire PH2 9QA

MACLENNAN: vacant

MACLEOD: John MacLeod of MacLeod, Dunvegan Castle, Isle of Skye

MACMILLAN: George MacMillan of MacMillan, Finlaystone, Langbank, Renfrewshire

MACNAB: J. C. Macnab of Macnab (*The Macnab*), Leuchars Castle Farmhouse, Leuchars, Fife KY16 0EY

MACNAGHTEN: Sir Patrick Macnaghten of Macnaghten and Dundarave, Bt., Dundarave, Bushmills, Co. Antrim

MACNEACAIL: Iain Macneacail of Macneacail and Scorrybreac, 12 Fox Street, Ballina, NSW, Australia

MACNEIL OF BARRA: Ian R. Macneil of Barra (*The Macneil of Barra*), 95/6 Grange Loan, Edinburgh

MACPHERSON: The Hon. Sir William Macpherson of Cluny, TD, Newtown Castle, Blairgowrie, Perthshire

MACTAVISH: E. S. Dugald MacTavish of Dunardry, c/o 2519 Vivaldi Lane, Four Seasons Estates, Gambrills, MD 21054, USA

MACTHOMAS: Andrew P. C. MacThomas of Finegand, c/o Roslin Cottage, Pitmedden, Aberdeenshire AB41 7NY

MAITLAND: The Earl of Lauderdale, 12 St Vincent Street, Edinburgh

MAKGILL: The Viscount of Oxfuird, Hill House, St Mary Bourne, Andover, Hants SP11 6BG

MALCOLM (MACCALLUM): Robin N. L. Malcolm of Poltalloch, Duntrune Castle, Lochgilphead, Argyll

MAR: The Countess of Mar, St Michael's Farm, Great Witley, Worcs WR6 6JB

MARJORIBANKS: Andrew Marjoribanks of that Ilk, 10 Newark Street, Greenock

MATHESON: Maj. Sir Fergus Matheson of Matheson, Bt., Old Rectory, Hedenham, Bungay, Suffolk NR35 2LD

MENZIES: David R. Menzies of Menzies, Wester Auchnagallin Farmhouse, Braes of Castle Grant, Grantown on Spey PH26 3PL

MOFFAT: Madam Moffat of that Ilk, St Jasual, Bullocks Farm Lane, Wheeler End Common, High Wycombe

MONCREIFFE: vacant

MONTGOMERIE: The Earl of Eglinton and Winton, Balhomie, Cargill, Perth PH2 6DS

MORRISON: Dr Iain M. Morrison of Ruchdi, Magnolia Cottage, The Street, Walberton, Sussex

MUNRO: Hector W. Munro of Foulis, Foulis Castle, Evanton, Ross-shire IV16 9UX

MURRAY: The Duke of Atholl, Blair Castle, Blair Atholl, Perthshire

NESBITT (or NISBET): Robert Nesbitt of that Ilk, Upper Roundhurst Farm, Roundhurst, Haslemere, Surrey

NICOLSON: The Lord Carnock, 90 Whitehall Court, London SW1A 2EL

OGILVY: The Earl of Airlie, KT, GCVO, PC, Cortachy Castle, Kirriemuir, Angus

RAMSAY: The Earl of Dalhousie, KT, GCVO, GBE, MC, Brechin Castle, Brechin, Angus DD7 6SH

RATTRAY: James S. Rattray of Rattray, Craighall, Rattray, Perthshire

ROBERTSON: Alexander G. H. Robertson of Struan (*Struan-Robertson*), The Breach Farm, Goudhurst Road, Cranbrook, Kent

ROLLO: The Lord Rollo, Pitcairns, Dunning, Perthshire

ROSE: Miss Elizabeth Rose of Kilravock, Kilravock Castle, Croy, Inverness

ROSS: David C. Ross of that Ilk, Shandwick, Perth Road, Sranley, Perthshire

RUTHVEN: The Earl of Gowrie, PC, 34 King Street, Covent Garden, London WC2

SCOTT: The Duke of Buccleuch and Queensberry, KT, VRD, Bowhill, Selkirk

SCRYMGEOUR: The Earl of Dundee, Birkhill, Cupar, Fife

SEMPILL: The Lord Sempill, 3 Vanburgh Place, Edinburgh, EH6 8AE

SHAW: John Shaw of Tordarroch, Newhall, Balblair, by Conon Bridge, Ross-shire

SINCLAIR: The Earl of Caithness, 137 Claxton Grove, London W6 8HB

SKENE: Danus Skene of Skene, Nether Pitlour, Strathmiglo, Fife

STIRLING: Fraser J. Stirling of Cader, 44A Oakley Street, London SW3 5HA

STRANGE: Maj. Timothy Strange of Balcaskie, Little Holme, Porton Road, Amesbury, Wilts

SUTHERLAND: The Countess of Sutherland, House of Tongue, Brora, Sutherland

SWINTON: John Swinton of that Ilk, 123 Superior Avenue SW, Calgary, Alberta, Canada

TROTTER: Alexander Trotter of Mortonhall, Charterhall, Duns, Berwickshire

URQUHART: Kenneth T. Urquhart of Urquhart, 507 Jefferson Park Avenue, Jefferson, New Orleans, Louisiana 70121, USA

WALLACE: Ian F. Wallace of that Ilk, 5 Lennox Street, Edinburgh EH4 1QB

WEDDERBURN OF THAT ILK: The Master of Dundee, Birkhill, Cupar, Fife

WEMYSS: David Wemyss of that Ilk, Invermay, Forteviot, Perthshire

The Privy Council

The Sovereign in Council, or Privy Council, was the chief source of executive power until the system of Cabinet government developed in the 18th century. Now the Privy Council's main functions are to advise the Sovereign and to exercise its own statutory responsibilities independent of the Sovereign in Council (*see also* page 215).

Membership of the Privy Council is automatic upon appointment to certain government and judicial positions in the United Kingdom, e.g. Cabinet ministers must be Privy Counsellors and are sworn in on first assuming office. Membership is also accorded by The Queen to eminent people in the UK and independent countries of the Commonwealth of which Her Majesty is Queen, on the recommendation of the British Prime Minister. Membership of the Council is retained for life, except for very occasional removals.

The administrative functions of the Privy Council are carried out by the Privy Council Office (*see* page 331) under the direction of the President of the Council, who is always a member of the Cabinet.

President of the Council, The Rt. Hon. Margaret Beckett, MP
Clerk of the Council, A. Galloway

MEMBERS *as at 31 August 1999*

HRH The Duke of Edinburgh, 1951
HRH The Prince of Wales, 1977

Aberdare, Lord, 1974
Ackner, Lord, 1980
Airlie, Earl of, 1984
Aldington, Lord, 1954
Aldous, Sir William, 1995
Alebua, Ezekiel, 1988
Alison, Michael, 1981
Alport, Lord, 1960
Ampthill, Lord, 1995
Ancram, Michael, 1996
Anthony, Douglas, 1971
Arbuthnot, James, 1998
Archer of Sandwell, Lord, 1977
Armstrong, Hilary, 1999
Arnold, Sir John, 1979
Arthur, Hon. Owen, 1995
Ashdown, Paddy, 1989
Ashley of Stoke, Lord, 1979
Atkins, Sir Robert, 1995
Auld, Sir Robin, 1995
Baker of Dorking, Lord, 1984
Balcombe, Sir John, 1985

Barber, Lord, 1963
Barnett, Lord, 1975
Beckett, Margaret, 1993
Beith, Alan, 1992
Beldam, Sir Roy, 1989
Belstead, Lord, 1983
Benn, Anthony, 1964
Bennett, Sir Frederic, 1985
Biffen, Lord, 1979
Bingham of Cornhill, Lord, 1986
Birch, William, 1992
Bisson, Sir Gordon, 1987
Blair, Anthony, 1994
Blaker, Lord, 1983
Blanchard, Peter, 1998
Blatch, Baroness, 1993
Blunkett, David, 1997
Boateng, Paul, 1999
Bolger, James, 1991
Booth, Albert, 1976
Boothroyd, Betty, 1992
Boscawen, Hon. Robert, 1992
Bottomley, Virginia, 1992
Boyson, Sir Rhodes, 1987
Braine of Wheatley, Lord, 1985
Brathwaite, Sir Nicholas, 1991
Bridge of Harwich, Lord, 1975
Brightman, Lord, 1979
Brittan, Sir Leon, 1981
Brook, Sir Henry, 1996
Brooke, Peter, 1988
Brown, Gordon, 1996
Brown, Nicholas, 1997
Brown, Sir Simon, 1992
Brown, Sir Stephen, 1983
Browne-Wilkinson, Lord, 1983
Butler, Sir Adam, 1984
Butler-Sloss, Dame Elizabeth, 1988
Buxton, Sir Richard, 1997
Byers, Stephen, 1998
Caborn, Richard, 1999
Caithness, Earl of, 1990
Callaghan of Cardiff, Lord, 1964
Cameron of Lochbroom, Lord, 1984
Camoys, Lord, 1997
Campbell of Croy, Lord, 1970
Campbell, Walter Menzies, 1998
Campbell, Sir William, 1999
Canterbury, The Archbishop of, 1991
Carlisle of Bucklow, Lord, 1979
Carr of Hadley, Lord, 1963
Carrington, Lord, 1959
Carswell, Sir Robert, 1993
Carter, Lord, 1997
Casey, Sir Maurice, 1986
Castle of Blackburn, Baroness, 1964
Chadwick, Sir John, 1997
Chalfont, Lord, 1964
Chalker of Wallasey, Baroness, 1987
Chan, Sir Julius, 1981
Charteris of Amisfield, Lord, 1972
Chataway, Sir Christopher, 1970

Clark, Alan, 1991
Clark, David, 1997
Clark, Helen, 1990
Clark of Kempston, Lord, 1990
Clarke, Sir Anthony, 1998
Clarke, Kenneth, 1984
Clarke, Thomas, 1997
Cledwyn of Penrhos, Lord, 1966
Clinton-Davis, Lord, 1998
Clyde, Lord, 1996
Cockfield, Lord, 1982
Cocks of Hartcliffe, Lord, 1976
Coggan, Lord, 1961
Colman, Fraser, 1986
Compton, Sir John, 1983
Concannon, John, 1978
Cook, Robin, 1996
Cooke of Thorndon, Lord, 1977
Cooper, Sir Frank, 1983
Cope of Berkeley, Lord, 1988
Corfield, Sir Frederick, 1970
Cowen, Sir Zelman, 1981
Cradock, Sir Percy, 1993
Cranborne, Viscount, 1994
Crawford and Balcarres, Earl of, 1972
Crickhowell, Lord, 1979
Croom-Johnson, Sir David, 1984
Cullen, *Hon.* Lord, 1997
Cumming-Bruce, Sir Roualeyn, 1977
Cunningham, Jack, 1993
Curry, David, 1996
Darling, Alistair, 1997
Davies, Denzil, 1978
Davies, Ronald, 1997
Davis, David, 1997
Davison, Sir Ronald, 1978
Dean of Harptree, Lord, 1991
Dean of Thornton-le-Fylde, Baroness, 1998
Deedes, Lord, 1962
Dell, Edmund, 1970
Denham, Lord, 1981
Devonshire, Duke of, 1964
Dewar, Donald, 1996
Diamond, Lord, 1965
Dillon, Sir Brian, 1982
Dixon, Lord, 1996
Dobson, Frank, 1997
Donaldson of Lymington, Lord, 1979
Dorrell, Stephen, 1994
Douglas, Sir William, 1977
du Cann, Sir Edward, 1964
Duff, Sir Antony, 1980
Dunn, Sir Robin, 1980
East, Paul, 1998
Eden of Winton, Lord, 1972
Eggar, Timothy, 1995
Eichelbaum, Sir Thomas, 1989
Emery, Sir Peter, 1993
Emslie, Lord, 1972
Erroll of Hale, Lord, 1960
Esquivel, Manuel, 1986
Evans, Sir Anthony, 1992

Eveleigh, Sir Edward, 1977
Farquharson, Sir Donald, 1989
Fellowes, Lord, 1990
Ferrers, Earl, 1982
Field, Frank, 1997
Floissac, Sir Vincent, 1992
Foot, Michael, 1974
Forsyth of Drumlean, The Lord, 1995
Forth, Eric, 1997
Foster, Derek, 1993
Fowler, Sir Norman, 1979
Fox, Sir Marcus, 1995
Fox, Sir Michael, 1981
Fraser, Malcolm, 1976
Fraser of Carmyllie, Lord, 1989
Freeman, John, 1966
Freeman, Lord, 1993
Freeson, Reginald, 1976
Garel-Jones, Lord, 1992
Gault, Thomas, 1992
George, Edward, 1999
Georges, Telford, 1986
Gibbs, Sir Harry, 1972
Gibson, Sir Peter, 1993
Gibson, Sir Ralph, 1985
Gibson-Watt, Lord, 1974
Gilbert, Lord, 1978
Gilmour of Craigmillar, Lord, 1973
Glenamara, Lord, 1964
Glidewell, Sir Iain, 1985
Goff of Chieveley, Lord, 1982
Goodlad, Sir Alastair, 1992
Gorton, Sir John, 1968
Gowrie, Earl of, 1984
Graham, Douglas, 1998
Graham of Edmonton, Lord, 1998
Gray of Contin, Lord, 1982
Griffiths, Lord, 1980
Gummer, John, 1985
Habgood, Rt. Revd Lord, 1983
Hague, William, 1995
Hailsham of St Marylebone, Lord, 1956
Hamilton, Sir Archie, 1991
Hanley, Sir Jeremy, 1994
Hardie, Lord, 1997
Hardie Boys, Sir Michael, 1989
Harman, Harriet, 1997
Harris of Greenwich, Lord, 1998
Harrison, Walter, 1977
Haselhurst, Sir Alan, 1999
Hattersley, Lord, 1975
Hayhoe, Lord, 1985
Healey, Lord, 1964
Heath, Sir Edward, 1955
Heathcoat-Amory, David, 1996
Henry, Sir Denis, 1993
Henry, John, 1996
Heseltine, Michael, 1979
Heseltine, Sir William, 1986
Hesketh, Lord, 1991
Higgins, Lord, 1979
Hirst, Sir David, 1992
Hobhouse, Sir John, 1993
Hoffmann, Lord, 1992
Hogg, Hon. Douglas, 1992
Holderness, Lord, 1959
Hollis of Heigham, Baroness, 1999
Hope of Craighead, Lord, 1989

Hordern, Sir Peter, 1993
Howard, Michael, 1990
Howe of Aberavon, Lord, 1972
Howell of Guildford, Lord, 1979
Hughes, Lord, 1970
Hunt, Jonathan, 1989
Hunt of Wirral, Lord, 1990
Hurd of Westwell, Lord, 1982
Hutchison, Sir Michael, 1995
Hutton, Lord, 1988
Ingraham, Hubert, 1993
Ingram, Adam, 1998
Irvine of Lairg, Lord, 1997
Jack, Michael, 1997
Janvrin, Sir Robin, 1998
Jauncey of Tullichettle, Lord, 1988
Jay of Paddington, Baroness, 1998
Jellicoe, Earl, 1963
Jenkin of Roding, Lord, 1973
Jenkins of Hillhead, Lord, 1964
Jones, Aubrey, 1955
Jones, Barry, 1999
Jopling, Lord, 1979
Jowell, Tessa, 1998
Judge, Sir Igor, 1996
Jugnauth, Sir Aneerood, 1987
Kaufman, Gerald, 1978
Keith, Sir Kenneth, 1998
Keith of Kinkel, Lord, 1976
Kelly, Sir Basil, 1984
Kelvedon, Lord, 1980
Kenilorea, Sir Peter, 1979
Kennedy, Sir Paul, 1992
Kerr, Sir Michael, 1981
King, Thomas, 1979
Kingsdown, Lord, 1987
Kingsland, Lord, 1994
Kinnock, Neil, 1983
Knight, Gregory, 1995
Lamont, Norman, 1986
Lane, Lord, 1975
Lang of Monkton, Lord, 1990
Lange, David, 1984
Lansdowne, Marquess of, 1964
Latasi, Kamuta, 1996
Lauti, Sir Toaripi, 1979
Laws, Sir John, 1999
Lawson of Blaby, Lord, 1981
Lawton, Sir Frederick, 1972
Leggatt, Sir Andrew, 1990
Leonard, Rt. Revd Graham, 1981
Liddell, Helen, 1998
Lilley, Peter, 1990
Lloyd of Berwick, Lord, 1984
Lloyd, Sir Peter, 1994
London, The Bishop of, 1995
Longford, Earl of, 1948
Louisy, Allan, 1981
Luce, Sir Richard, 1986
Lyell, Sir Nicholas, 1990
Mabon, Dickson, 1977
McCarthy, Sir Thaddeus, 1968
McCartney, Ian, 1999
McCollum, Sir Liam, 1997
McCowan, Sir Anthony, 1989
MacDermott, Sir John, 1987
Macdonald of Tradeston, Lord, 1999
MacGregor, John, 1985
MacIntyre, Duncan, 1980
Mackay, Andrew, 1998

McKay, Ian, 1992
Mackay of Ardbrecknish, Lord, 1996
Mackay of Clashfern, Lord, 1979
Mackay of Drumadoon, Lord, 1996
McKinnon, Donald, 1992
Maclean, David, 1995
Maclennan, Robert, 1997
McMullin, Sir Duncan, 1980
Major, John, 1987
Mance, Sir Jonathan, 1999
Mandelson, Peter, 1998
Mantell, Sir Charles, 1997
Mara, Ratu Sir Kamisese, 1973
Marsh, Lord, 1966
Mason of Barnsley, Lord, 1968
Maude, Hon. Francis, 1992
Mawhinney, Sir Brian, 1994
May, Sir Anthony, 1998
Mayhew of Twysden, Lord, 1986
Meacher, Michael, 1997
Megarry, Sir Robert, 1978
Mellor, David, 1990
Merlyn-Rees, Lord, 1974
Michael, Alun, 1998
Milburn, Alan, 1998
Millan, Bruce, 1975
Millett, Sir Peter, 1994
Mitchell, Sir James, 1985
Molyneaux of Killead, Lord, 1983
Monro of Langholm, Lord, 1995
Moore, Michael, 1990
Moore of Lower Marsh, Lord, 1986
Moore of Wolvercote, Lord, 1977
Morris, Charles, 1978
Morris, Sir John, 1970
Morris of Manchester, Lord, 1979
Morritt, Sir Robert, 1994
Mowlam, Marjorie, 1997
Moyle, Roland, 1978
Mummery, Sir John, 1996
Murphy, Paul, 1998
Murray, Hon. Lord, 1974
Murray, Sir Donald, 1989
Murray of Epping Forest, Lord, 1976
Murton of Lindisfarne, Lord, 1976
Mustill, Lord, 1985
Nairne, Sir Patrick, 1982
Namaliu, Sir Rabbie, 1989
Naseby, Lord, 1994
Needham, Sir Richard, 1994
Neill, Sir Brian, 1985
Newton of Braintree, Lord, 1988
Nicholls of Birkenhead, Lord, 1995
Nicholson, Sir Michael, 1995
Nolan, Lord, 1991
Nott, Sir John, 1979
Nourse, Sir Martin, 1985
Oakes, Gordon, 1979
O'Connor, Sir Patrick, 1980
O'Donnell, Turlough, 1979
O'Flynn, Francis, 1987
Ogilvy, Sir Angus, 1997
Oliver of Aylmerton, Lord, 1980
Onslow of Woking, Lord, 1988
Oppenheim-Barnes, Baroness, 1979
Orme, Lord, 1974
Otton, Sir Philip, 1995
Owen, Lord, 1976
Paeniu, Bikenibeu, 1991
Palliser, Sir Michael, 1983

Palmer, Sir Geoffrey, 1986
Parker, Sir Roger, 1983
Parkinson, Lord, 1981
Patten, Christopher, 1989
Patten, Lord, 1990
Patterson, Percival, 1993
Pattie, Sir Geoffrey, 1987
Perth, Earl of, 1957
Peters, Winston, 1998
Peyton of Yeovil, Lord, 1970
Phillips, Sir Nicholas, 1995
Pill, Sir Malcolm, 1995
Pindling, Sir Lynden, 1976
Portillo, Michael, 1992
Potter, Sir Mark, 1996
Prentice, Lord, 1966
Prescott, John, 1994
Price, George, 1982
Prior, Lord, 1970
Puapua, Sir Tomasi, 1982
Purchas, Sir Francis, 1982
Pym, Lord, 1970
Quin, Joyce, 1998
Radice, Giles, 1999
Raison, Sir Timothy, 1982
Ramsden, James, 1963
Rawlinson of Ewell, Lord, 1964
Redwood, John, 1993
Rees, Lord, 1983
Reid, John, 1998
Renton, Lord, 1962
Renton of Mount Harry, Lord, 1989
Richard, Lord, 1993
Richardson, Sir Ivor, 1978
Richardson of Duntisbourne, Lord, 1976
Rifkind, Sir Malcolm, 1986
Roberts of Conwy, Lord, 1991
Robertson of Port Ellen, Lord, 1997
Roch, Sir John, 1993
Rodger of Earlsferry, Lord, 1992
Rodgers of Quarry Bank, Lord, 1975
Rose, Sir Christopher, 1992
Ross, *Hon.* Lord, 1985
Rumbold, Dame Angela, 1991
Runcie, Lord, 1980
Russell, Sir Patrick, 1987

Ryder of Wensum, Lord, 1990
Sainsbury, Sir Timothy, 1992
St John of Fawsley, Lord, 1979
Sandiford, Erskine, 1989
Saville of Newdigate, Lord, 1994
Scarman, Lord, 1973
Schiemann, Sir Konrad, 1995
Scott, Sir Nicholas, 1989
Scott, Sir Richard, 1991
Seaga, Edward, 1981
Sedley, Sir Stephen, 1999
Selkirk of Douglas, Lord, 1996
Shawcross, Lord, 1946
Shearer, Hugh, 1969
Sheldon, Robert, 1977
Shephard, Gillian, 1992
Shepherd, Lord, 1965
Shipley, Jennifer, 1998
Shore of Stepney, Lord, 1967
Short, Clare, 1997
Simmonds, Kennedy, 1984
Simon of Glaisdale, Lord, 1961
Sinclair, Ian, 1977
Slade, Sir Christopher, 1982
Slynn of Hadley, Lord, 1992
Smith, Andrew, 1997
Smith, Christopher, 1997
Smith, Sir Geoffrey Johnson, 1996
Somare, Sir Michael, 1977
Somers, Sir Edward, 1981
Stanley, Sir John, 1984
Staughton, Sir Christopher, 1988
Steel of Aikwood, Lord, 1977
Stephen, Sir Ninian, 1979
Stephenson, Sir John, 1971
Stewartby, Lord, 1989
Steyn, Lord, 1992
Stodart of Leaston, Lord, 1974
Strang, Gavin, 1997
Strathclyde, Lord, 1995
Straw, Jack, 1997
Stuart-Smith, Sir Murray, 1988
Talboys, Sir Brian, 1977
Taylor, Ann, 1997
Tebbit, Lord, 1981
Templeman, Lord, 1978
Thatcher, Baroness, 1970

Thomas, Edmund, 1996
Thomas, Sir Swinton, 1994
Thomas of Gwydir, Lord, 1964
Thomson, David, 1981
Thomson of Monifieth, Lord, 1966
Thorpe, Jeremy, 1967
Thorpe, Sir Matthew, 1995
Tipping, Andrew, 1998
Tizard, Robert, 1986
Trefgarne, Lord, 1989
Trimble, David, 1997
Trumpington, Baroness, 1992
Tuckey, Sir Simon, 1998
Ullswater, Viscount, 1994
Varley, Lord, 1974
Waddington, Lord, 1987
Waite, Sir John, 1993
Wakeham, Lord, 1983
Waldegrave, William, 1990
Walker of Doncaster, Lord, 1979
Walker of Worcester, Lord, 1970
Walker, Sir Robert, 1997
Waller, Sir Mark, 1996
Ward, Sir Alan, 1995
Watkins, Sir Tasker, 1980
Weatherill, Lord, 1980
Wheeler, Sir John, 1993
Widdecombe, Ann, 1997
Wigley, Dafydd, 1997
Wilberforce, Lord, 1964
Williams, Alan, 1977
Williams of Crosby, Baroness, 1974
Williams of Mostyn, Lord
Windlesham, Lord, 1973
Wingti, Paias, 1987
Withers, Reginald, 1977
Woodhouse, Sir Owen, 1974
Woolf, Lord, 1986
Wylie, *Hon.* Lord, 1970
York, The Archbishop of, 1991
Young, Baroness, 1981
Young, Sir George, 1993
Young of Graffham, Lord, 1984
Younger of Leckie, Viscount, 1979
Zacca, Edward, 1992

The Privy Council of Northern Ireland

The Privy Council of Northern Ireland had responsibilities in Northern Ireland similar to those of the Privy Council in Great Britain until the Northern Ireland Act 1974 instituted direct rule and a UK Cabinet minister became responsible for the functions previously exercised by the Northern Ireland government.

Membership of the Privy Council of Northern Ireland is retained for life. The postnominal initials PC (NI) are used to differentiate its members from those of the Privy Council.

MEMBERS *as at 31 August 1999*

Bailie, Robin, 1971
Bleakley, David, 1971
Craig, William, 1963
Dobson, John, 1969
Kelly, Sir Basil, 1969
Kirk, Herbert, 1962
Long, William, 1966
Lowry, The Lord, 1971
McConnell, The Lord, 1964
McIvor, Basil, 1971
Moyola, The Lord, 1966

Neill, Sir Ivan, 1950
Porter, Sir Robert, 1969
Taylor, John, MP, 1970
West, Henry, 1960

Parliament

The United Kingdom constitution is not contained in any single document but has evolved in the course of time, formed partly by statute, partly by common law and partly by convention. A constitutional monarchy, the United Kingdom is governed by Ministers of the Crown in the name of the Sovereign, who is head both of the state and of the government.

The organs of government are the legislature (Parliament), the executive and the judiciary. The executive consists of HM Government (Cabinet and other Ministers) (*see* pages 272–3), government departments (*see* pages 276–350), local authorities (*see* Local Government), and public corporations operating nationalized industries or social or cultural services (*see* pages 276–350). The judiciary (*see* Law Courts and Offices) pronounces on the law, both written and unwritten, interprets statutes and is responsible for the enforcement of the law; the judiciary is independent of both the legislature and the executive.

THE MONARCHY

The Sovereign personifies the state and is, in law, an integral part of the legislature, head of the executive, head of the judiciary, commander-in-chief of all armed forces of the Crown and 'Supreme Governor' of the Church of England. The seat of the monarchy is in the United Kingdom. In the Channel Islands and the Isle of Man, which are Crown dependencies, the Sovereign is represented by a Lieutenant-Governor. In the member states of the Commonwealth of which the Sovereign is head of state, her representative is a Governor-General; in UK dependencies the Sovereign is usually represented by a Governor, who is responsible to the British Government.

Although in practice the powers of the monarchy are now very limited, restricted mainly to the advisory and ceremonial, there are important acts of government which require the participation of the Sovereign. These include summoning, proroguing and dissolving Parliament, giving royal assent to bills passed by Parliament, appointing important office-holders, e.g. government ministers, judges, bishops and governors, conferring peerages, knighthoods and other honours, and granting pardon to a person wrongly convicted of a crime. The Sovereign appoints the Prime Minister; by convention this office is held by the leader of the political party which enjoys, or can secure, a majority of votes in the House of Commons. In international affairs the Sovereign as head of state has the power to declare war and make peace, to recognize foreign states and governments, to conclude treaties and to annex or cede territory. However, as the Sovereign entrusts executive power to Ministers of the Crown and acts on the advice of her Ministers, which she cannot ignore, royal prerogative powers are in practice exercised by Ministers, who are responsible to Parliament.

Ministerial responsibility does not diminish the Sovereign's importance to the smooth working of government. She holds meetings of the Privy Council (*see* below), gives audiences to her Ministers and other officials at home and overseas, receives accounts of Cabinet decisions, reads dispatches and signs state papers; she must be informed and consulted on every aspect of national life; and she must show complete impartiality.

COUNSELLORS OF STATE

In the event of the Sovereign's absence abroad, it is necessary to appoint Counsellors of State under letters patent to carry out the chief functions of the Monarch, including the holding of Privy Councils and giving royal assent to acts passed by Parliament. The normal procedure is to appoint as Counsellors three or four members of the royal family among those remaining in the UK.

In the event of the Sovereign on accession being under the age of 18 years, or at any time unavailable or incapacitated by infirmity of mind or body for the performance of the royal functions, provision is made for a regency.

THE PRIVY COUNCIL

The Sovereign in Council, or Privy Council, was the chief source of executive power until the system of Cabinet government developed. Nowadays its main function is to advise the Sovereign to approve Orders in Council and to advise on the issue of royal proclamations. The Council's own statutory responsibilities (independent of the powers of the Sovereign in Council) include powers of supervision over the registering bodies for the medical and allied professions. A full Council is summoned only on the death of the Sovereign or when the Sovereign announces his or her intention to marry. (For full list of Counsellors, *see* pages 212–4.)

There are a number of advisory Privy Council committees, whose meetings the Sovereign does not attend. Some are prerogative committees, such as those dealing with legislative matters submitted by the legislatures of the Channel Islands and the Isle of Man or with applications for charters of incorporation; and some are provided for by statute, e.g. those for the universities of Oxford and Cambridge and the Scottish universities.

The Judicial Committee of the Privy Council is the final court of appeal from courts of the UK dependencies, courts of independent Commonwealth countries which have retained the right of appeal, courts of the Channel Islands and the Isle of Man, some professional and disciplinary committees, and church sources. The Committee is composed of Privy Counsellors who hold, or have held, high judicial office, although usually only three or five hear each case.

Administrative work is carried out by the Privy Council Office under the direction of the President of the Council, a Cabinet Minister.

PARLIAMENT

Parliament is the supreme law-making authority and can legislate for the UK as a whole or for any parts of it separately (the Channel Islands and the Isle of Man are Crown dependencies and not part of the UK). The main functions of Parliament are to pass laws, to provide (by voting taxation) the means of carrying on the work of government and to scrutinize government policy and administration, particularly proposals for expenditure.

International treaties and agreements are by custom presented to Parliament before ratification.

Parliament emerged during the late 13th and early 14th centuries. The officers of the King's household and the King's judges were the nucleus of early Parliaments, joined by such ecclesiastical and lay magnates as the King might summon to form a prototype 'House of Lords', and occasionally by the knights of the shires, burgesses and proctors of the lower clergy. By the end of Edward III's reign a 'House of Commons' was beginning to appear; the first known Speaker was elected in 1377.

Parliamentary procedure is based on custom and precedent, partly formulated in the Standing Orders of both Houses of Parliament, and each House has the right to control its own internal proceedings and to commit for contempt. The system of debate in the two Houses is similar; when a motion has been moved, the Speaker proposes the question as the subject of a debate. Members speak from wherever they have been sitting. Questions are decided by a vote on a simple majority. Draft legislation is introduced, in either House, as a bill. Bills can be introduced by a Government Minister or a private Member, but in practice the majority of bills which become law are introduced by the Government. To become law, a bill must be passed by each House (for parliamentary stages, *see* Bill, page 220) and then sent to the Sovereign for the royal assent, after which it becomes an Act of Parliament.

Proceedings of both Houses are public, except on extremely rare occasions. The minutes (called Votes and Proceedings in the Commons, and Minutes of Proceedings in the Lords) and the speeches (The Official Report of Parliamentary Debates, *Hansard*) are published daily. Proceedings are also recorded for transmission on radio and television and stored in the Parliamentary Recording Unit before transfer to the National Sound Archive. Television cameras have been allowed into the House of Lords since 1985 and into the House of Commons since 1989; committee meetings may also be televised.

By the Parliament Act of 1911, the maximum duration of a Parliament is five years (if not previously dissolved), the term being reckoned from the date given on the writs for the new Parliament. The maximum life has been prolonged by legislation in such rare circumstances as the two world wars (31 January 1911 to 25 November 1918; 26 November 1935 to 15 June 1945). Dissolution and writs for a general election are ordered by the Sovereign on the advice of the Prime Minister. The life of a Parliament is divided into sessions, usually of one year in length, beginning and ending most often in October or November.

DEVOLUTION

The Scottish Parliament elected in 1999 has legislative power over all devolved matters, i.e. matters not reserved to Westminster or otherwise outside its powers. The National Assembly for Wales elected in May 1999 has power to make secondary legislation in the areas where executive functions have been transferred to it. The New Northern Ireland Assembly elected in June 1998 was due to be formally established by legislation in 1999; this had not yet happened at time of going to press. It will have legislative authority in the fields currently administered by the Northern Ireland departments. For further details, *see* Regional Assemblies supplement and Local Government section.

THE HOUSE OF LORDS
London SW1A 0PW
Tel 0171-219 3000
Information Office: 0171–219 3107
E-mail: hlinfo@parliament.uk
Web site: http://www.parliament.uk

The House of Lords consists of the Lords Spiritual and Temporal. The Lords Spiritual are the Archbishops of Canterbury and York, the Bishops of London, Durham and Winchester, and the 21 senior diocesan bishops of the Church of England. The Lords Temporal currently consist of all hereditary peers of England, Scotland, Great Britain and the UK who have not disclaimed their peerages, life peers created under the Life Peerages Act 1958, and those Lords of Appeal in Ordinary created life peers under the Appellate Jurisdiction Act 1876, as amended (i.e. law lords). In January 1999 the Government introduced legislation removing the right of hereditary peers to sit in the House of Lords. An amendment to the legislation was later agreed that would allow 92 hereditary peers (42 Conservative, 28 cross-bench, three Liberal Democrat, two Labour, the Earl Marshal, the Lord Great Chamberlain and 15 others) to remain in the House of Lords until longer-term reform of the House had been carried out; elections to select those who would remain would be held in October and November 1999. At the time of going to press the legislation had passed through all its Commons stages and was awaiting its third reading in the House of Lords. The Government has also announced its intention of establishing an independent Appointments Commission to oversee the future nomination of life peers. A Royal Commission on the longer-term reform of the House of Lords was set up in February 1999 and is due to report by the end of 1999.

Disclaimants of a hereditary peerage lose their right to sit in the House of Lords but gain the right to vote at parliamentary elections and to offer themselves for election to the House of Commons. Those peers disqualified from sitting in the House include:

– aliens, i.e. any peer who is not a British citizen, a Commonwealth citizen (under the British Nationality Act 1981) or a citizen of the Republic of Ireland
– peers under the age of 21
– undischarged bankrupts or, in Scotland, those whose estate is sequestered
– peers convicted of treason

Peers who do not wish to attend sittings of the House of Lords may apply for leave of absence for the duration of a Parliament.

Until the beginning of this century the House of Lords had considerable power, being able to veto any bill submitted to it by the House of Commons, but those powers were greatly reduced by the Parliament Acts of 1911 and 1949 (*see* page 221).

Combined with its legislative role, the House of Lords has judicial powers as the ultimate Court of Appeal for courts in Great Britain and Northern Ireland, except for criminal cases in Scotland. These powers are exercised by the Lord Chancellor and the Lords of Appeal in Ordinary (the law lords) (*see* page 354).

Members of the House of Lords are unpaid. However, they are entitled to reimbursement of travelling expenses on parliamentary business within the UK and certain other expenses incurred for the purpose of attendance at sittings of the House, within a maximum for each day of £80.50 for overnight subsistence, £35.50 for day subsistence and incidental travel, and £34.50 for secretarial costs, postage and certain additional expenses.

COMPOSITION *as at 1 July 1999*

Archbishops and Bishops, 26
Peers by succession, 751 (17 women)
Hereditary peers of first creation (including the Prince of Wales), 8
Life peers under the Appellate Jurisdiction Act 1876, 27
Life peers under the Life Peerages Act 1958, 477 (87 women)
Total 1,289
Of whom:
    Peers without writs of summons, 67 (3 minors)
    Peers on leave of absence from the House, 57

STATE OF PARTIES *as at 1 July 1999**

More than half of the members of the House of Lords take the whip of one of the three main political parties. The other members have no political affiliations and more than 300 sit on the cross-benches as independents.

Conservative, 471
Labour, 176
Liberal Democrats, 66
Cross-bench, 339
Other (including Lords Spiritual), 113
* Excluding peers without writs of summons and peers on leave of absence from the House

OFFICERS

The House is presided over by the Lord Chancellor, who is *ex officio* Speaker of the House. A panel of deputy Speakers is appointed by Royal Commission. The first deputy Speaker is the Chairman of Committees, appointed at the beginning of each session, a salaried officer of the House who takes the chair in committee of the whole House and in some select committees. He is assisted by a panel of deputy chairmen, headed by the salaried Principal Deputy Chairman of Committees, who is also chairman of the European Communities Committee of the House.

The permanent officers include the Clerk of the Parliaments, who is in charge of the administrative and procedural staff collectively known as the Parliament Office; the Gentleman Usher of the Black Rod, who is also Serjeant-at-Arms in attendance upon the Lord Chancellor and is responsible for security and for accommodation and services in the House of Lords; and the Yeoman Usher who is Deputy Serjeant-at-Arms and assists Black Rod in his duties.

Speaker (£160,011), The Lord Irvine of Lairg, PC, QC
    Private Secretary, Ms E. Hutchinson
Chairman of Committees (£64,426), The Lord Boston of Faversham, QC
Principal Deputy Chairman of Committees (£60,032), The Lord Tordoff

DEPARTMENT OF THE CLERK OF THE PARLIAMENTS
Clerk of the Parliaments (£123,787), J. M. Davies
Clerk Assistant and Clerk of Legislation (£73,250–£110,300), P. D. G. Hayter, LVO
Reading Clerk and Principal Finance Officer (£61,110–£98,400), M. G. Pownall
Counsel to Chairman of Committees (£61,110–£98,400), Sir James Nursaw, KCB, QC: Dr C. S. Kerse; D. W. Saunders, CB *(Judicial Office and Fourth Clerk at the Table)*; B. P. Keith *(Journals)*; D. R. Beamish *(Committees and Overseas Office)*; R. H. Walters, D.Phil. *(Establishment Officer)*; Dr F. P. Tudor *(Private Bills)*; E. C. Ollard *(Public Bills)*; A. Makower; T. V. Mohan *(Select Committees)*

Senior Clerks (£31,283–£47,399), S. P. Burton; Miss M. B. Robertson *(seconded as Secretary to the Leader of the House and Chief Whip)*; T. E. Radice; D. J. Batt; E. R. Morgan; Dr E. A. Hopkins; Miss L. J. Mouland; J. A. Vaughan
Clerks (£16,306–£28,336), A. J. Mackersie; Miss K. S. Ball
Clerk of the Records (£45,810–£73,470), S. K. Ellison
Assistant Clerks of the Records (£30,431–£46,108), D. L. Prior; Dr C. Shenton
Librarian (£50,510–£82,650), D. L. Jones
Deputy Librarian (£35,427–£57,481), P. G. Davis, PH.D.
Senior Library Clerks (£31,283–£47,399), Miss I. L. Victory, PH.D.; S. Kennedy; H. C. Deadman
Library Clerk (£19,103–£25,022), I. S. Cruse
Examiners of Petitions for Private Bills, Dr F. P. Tudor; W. A. Proctor
Editor, Official Report (Hansard), (£45,810–£73,470), Mrs M. E. E. C. Villiers
Deputy Editor, Official Report (£34,462–£55,915), Mrs C. J. Boden

DEPARTMENT OF THE GENTLEMAN USHER OF THE BLACK ROD
Gentleman Usher of the Black Rod and Serjeant-at-Arms (£61,110–£98,400), Gen. Sir Edward Jones, KCB, CBE
Yeoman Usher of the Black Rod and Deputy Serjeant-at-Arms (£30,431–£46,108), Brig. H. D. C. Duncan, MBE

SELECT COMMITTEES

The main House of Lords select committees, as at 7 June 1999, are as follows:

European Communities – Sub-committees:
    A *(Economic and Financial Affairs, Trade and External Relations)* – *Chair,* The Lord Grenfell; *Clerk,* Dr E. A. Hopkins
    B *(Energy, Industry and Transport)* – *Chair,* The Lord Geddes; *Clerk,* R. Morgan
    C *(Environment, Transport and Consumer Protection)* – *Chair,* The Earl of Cranbrook; *Clerk,* T. Radice
    D *(Agriculture, Fisheries and Food)* – *Chair,* The Lord Reay; *Clerk,* J. A. Vaughan
    E *(Law and Institutions)* – *Chair,* The Lord Hope of Craighead, PC; *Clerk,* T. Radice
    F *(Social Affairs, Education and Home Affairs)* – *Chair,* The Lord Wallace of Saltaire, PH.D.; *Clerk,* T. V. Mohar
Science and Technology – *Chair,* The Lord Winston, FRCOG; *Clerk,* A. Makower
Delegated Powers and Deregulation – *Chair,* The Lord Alexander of Weedon, QC; *Clerk,* Dr F. P. Tudor
Monetary Policy Committee of the Bank of England – *Chair,* The Lord Peston; *Clerk,* D. J. Batt

THE HOUSE OF COMMONS

London SW1A 0AA
Tel 0171-219 3000
Information Office: 0171-219 4272
Forthcoming business: 0171-219 5532
E-mail: hcinfo@parliament.uk
Web site: http://www.parliament.uk

The members of the House of Commons are elected by universal adult suffrage. For electoral purposes, the United Kingdom is divided into constituencies, each of which returns one member to the House of Commons, the member being the candidate who obtains the largest number of votes cast in the constituency. To ensure equitable representation, the four Boundary Commissions *(see* page 283) keep constituency boundaries under review and recommend any redistribution of seats which may seem necessary because of population movements, etc. The number of seats was raised to 640 in 1945, reduced to 625 in 1948, and subsequently rose to 630 in 1955, 635 in 1970, 650 in 1983, 651 in 1992 and 659 in 1997. Of the present 659 seats, there are 529 for England, 40 for Wales, 72 for Scotland and 18 for Northern Ireland. The number of Scottish MPs at Westminster is to be cut by about 12 by 2007.

An electoral reform commission headed by Lord Jenkins of Hillhead proposed in October 1998 that the 'first-past-the-post' system of electing members of the House of Commons should be replaced by an alternative vote top-up system, under which 80–85 per cent of MPs would be elected by an alternative vote method and the remaining 15–20 per cent by an open-list system of proportional representation. A referendum will be held on the proposals at an unspecified future date.

ELECTIONS

Elections are by secret ballot, each elector casting one vote; voting is not compulsory. For entitlement to vote in parliamentary elections, *see* Legal Notes section. When a seat becomes vacant between general elections, a by-election is held.

British subjects and citizens of the Irish Republic can stand for election as Members of Parliament (MPs) provided they are 21 or over and not subject to disqualification. Those disqualified from sitting in the House include:

– undischarged bankrupts
– people sentenced to more than one year's imprisonment
– clergy of the Church of England, Church of Scotland, Church of Ireland and Roman Catholic Church
– members of the House of Lords
– holders of certain offices listed in the House of Commons Disqualification Act 1975, e.g. members of the judiciary, Civil Service, regular armed forces, police forces, some local government officers and some members of public corporations and government commissions

A candidate does not require any party backing but his or her nomination for election must be supported by the signatures of ten people registered in the constituency. A candidate must also deposit with the returning officer £500, which is forfeit if the candidate does not receive more than 5 per cent of the votes cast. All election expenses at a general election, except the candidate's personal expenses, are subject to a statutory limit of £4,965, plus 4.2 pence for each elector in a borough constituency or 5.6 pence for each elector in a county constituency.

See pages 226–33 for an alphabetical list of MPs, pages 236–68 for the results of the last general election, and page 233 for the results of by-elections since the general election.

STATE OF PARTIES *as at 26 July 1999*

Conservative, 162 (14 women)
Labour, 416 (101 women)
Liberal Democrats, 46 (3 women)
Plaid Cymru, 4
Scottish Labour, 1
Scottish Nationalist, 6 (2 women)
Sinn Fein, 2
Social Democratic and Labour, 3
Ulster Democratic Unionist, 2
Ulster Unionist, 10
United Kingdom Unionist, 1
Independent, 1
Member for Falkirk West (Dennis Canavan), 1
The Speaker and three Deputy Speakers, 4 (1 woman)
Total, 659 (121 women)
Government majority, 178

BUSINESS

The week's business of the House is outlined each Thursday by the Leader of the House, after consultation between the Chief Government Whip and the Chief Opposition Whip. A quarter to a third of the time will be taken up by the Government's legislative programme and the rest by other business. As a rule, bills likely to raise political controversy are introduced in the Commons before going on to the Lords, and the Commons claims exclusive control in respect of national taxation and expenditure. Bills such as the Finance Bill, which imposes taxation, and the Consolidated Fund Bills, which authorize expenditure, must begin in the Commons. A bill of which the financial provisions are subsidiary may begin in the Lords; and the Commons may waive its rights in regard to Lords' amendments affecting finance.

The Commons has a public register of MPs' financial and certain other interests; this is published annually as a House of Commons paper. Members must also disclose any relevant financial interest or benefit in a matter before the House when taking part in a debate, in certain other proceedings of the House, or in consultations with other MPs, with Ministers or with civil servants.

MEMBERS' PAY AND ALLOWANCES

Since 1911 members of the House of Commons have received salary payments; facilities for free travel were introduced in 1924. Salary rates since 1911 are as follows:

1911	£400 p.a.	1983 June	£15,308 p.a.
1931	360	1984 Jan	16,106
1934	380	1985 Jan	16,904
1935	400	1986 Jan	17,702
1937	600	1987 Jan	18,500
1946	1,000	1988 Jan	22,548
1954	1,250	1989 Jan	24,107
1957	1,750	1990 Jan	26,701
1964	3,250	1991 Jan	28,970
1972 Jan	4,500	1992 Jan	30,854
1975 June	5,750	1994 Jan	31,687
1976 June	6,062	1995 Jan	33,189
1977 July	6,270	1996 Jan	34,085
1978 June	6,897	1996 July	43,000
1979 June	9,450	1997 April	43,860
1980 June	11,750	1998 April	45,066
1981 June	13,950	1999 April	47,008
1982 June	14,510		

In 1969 MPs were granted an allowance for secretarial and research expenses, now known as the Office Costs Allowance. From April 1999 the allowance is £50,264 a year.

Since 1972 MPs have been able to claim reimbursement for the additional cost of staying overnight away from their main residence while on parliamentary business; this is known as the Additional Costs Allowance and from April 1999 is £12,984 a year.

Since 1980 each MP in receipt of the Office Costs Allowance has been able to contribute sums to an approved pension scheme for the provision of a pension, or other benefits, for or in respect of persons whose salary is met by him/her from the Office Costs Allowance.

MEMBERS' PENSIONS

Pension arrangements for MPs were first introduced in 1964. The arrangements currently provide a pension of one-fiftieth of salary for each year of pensionable service with a maximum of two-thirds of salary at age 65. Pension is payable normally at age 65, for men and women, or on later retirement. Pensions may be paid earlier, e.g. on retirement due to ill health or at age 60 after 20 years' service. The widow/widower of a former MP receives a pension of five-eighths of the late MP's pension. Pensions are index-linked. Members currently contribute 6 per cent of salary to the pension fund; there is an Exchequer contribution, currently slightly more than the amount contributed by MPs.

The House of Commons Members' Fund provides for annual or lump sum grants to ex-MPs, their widows or widowers, and children whose incomes are below certain limits or who are experiencing severe hardship. Members contribute £24 a year and the Exchequer £215,000 a year to the fund.

OFFICERS AND OFFICIALS

The House of Commons is presided over by the Speaker, who has considerable powers to maintain order in the House. A deputy Speaker, called the Chairman of Ways and Means, and two Deputy Chairmen may preside over sittings of the House of Commons; they are elected by the House, and, like the Speaker, neither speak nor vote other than in their official capacity.

The staff of the House are employed by a Commission chaired by the Speaker. The heads of the six House of Commons departments are permanent officers of the House, not MPs. The Clerk of the House is the principal adviser to the Speaker on the privileges and procedures of the House, the conduct of the business of the House, and committees. The Serjeant-at-Arms is responsible for security, ceremonial, and for accommodation in the Commons part of the Palace of Westminster.

Speaker (£111,315), The Rt. Hon. Betty Boothroyd, MP (West Bromwich West)
Chairman of Ways and Means (£80,367), The Rt. Hon. Sir Alan Haselhurst, MP (Saffron Walden)
First Deputy Chairman of Ways and Means (£76,326), Michael Martin, MP (Glasgow Springburn)
Second Deputy Chairman of Ways and Means (£76,326), Michael Lord, MP (Suffolk Central and Ipswich North)

OFFICES OF THE SPEAKER AND CHAIRMAN OF WAYS AND MEANS

Speaker's Secretary (£45,810–£73,470), N. Bevan, CB
Chaplain to the Speaker, Revd Canon R. Wright
Secretary to the Chairman of Ways and Means (£30,271 – £45,795), C. Stanton

DEPARTMENT OF THE CLERK OF THE HOUSE

Clerk of the House of Commons (£123,787), W. R. McKay, CB
Clerk Assistant (£66,900–£104,190), G. Cubie
Clerk of Committees (£66,900–£104,190), C. B. Winnifrith, CB
Clerk of Legislation (£66,900–£104,190), R. B. Sands
Principal Clerks (£61,110–£98,400)
  Journals, A. J. Hastings, CB
  Table Office, D. G. Millar
  Domestic Committees, M. R. Jack, PH.D.
Principal Clerks (£50,510–£82,650)
  Overseas Office, R. W. G. Wilson
  Bills, Ms H. E. Irwin
  Select Committees, Mrs J. Sharpe; F. A. Cranmer; R. J. Rogers
  Delegated Legislation, W. A. Proctor
Deputy Principal Clerks (£45,810–£73,470), Ms A. Barry; C. R. M. Ward, PH.D.; D. W. N. Doig; A. Sandall; D. L. Natzler; E. P. Silk; A. R. Kennon; L. C. Laurence Smyth; S. J. Patrick; D. J. Gerhold; C. J. Poyser; D. F. Harrison; S. J. Priestley; A. H. Doherty; P. A. Evans; R. I. S. Phillips; R. G. James, PH.D.; Ms P. A. Helme; D. R. Lloyd; B. M. Hutton; J. S. Benger, D.PHIL.; Ms E. C. Samson; N. P. Walker; M. D. Hamlyn; Mrs E. J. Flood; P. C. Seaward, D.PHIL.; A. Y. A. Azad

Senior Clerks (£30,271–£45,795), C. G. Lee; C. D. Stanton; C. A. Shaw; Ms L. M. Gardner; K. J. Brown; F. J. Reid; M. Hennessy; G. R. Devine; P. G. Moon; M. Clark; Mrs J. N. St J. Mulley; T. W. P. Healey; Mrs S. A. R. Davies; J. D. Whateley; K. C. Fox; J. D. W. Rhys; Ms J. A. Long; Miss E. S. Payne; Ms S. McGlashan; Ms J. Eldred (*acting*); S. T. Fiander (*acting*); D. H. Griffiths (*acting*); Ms R. Melling, CBE (*acting*); C. Wilson (*acting*)
Examiners of Petitions for Private Bills, Ms H. E. Irwin; Dr F. P. Tudor
Registrar of Members' Interests (£50,510–£82,650), R. J. Willoughby (*seconded to Speaker's Office*)
Taxing Officer, W. A. Proctor

Vote Office

Deliverer of the Vote (£45,810–£73,470), J. F. Collins
Deputy Deliverers of the Vote (£30,271–£45,795), vacant (*Distribution*); O. B. T. Sweeney (*Parliamentary*); F. W. Hallett (*Production*)

Speaker's Counsel

Speaker's Counsel (£61,110–£98,400), J. Mason, CB
Speaker's Counsel (European legislation) (£61,110–£98,400), J. E. G. Vaux
Speaker's Assistant Counsel (£45,810–£73,470), A. Akbar; J. R. Mallinson

DEPARTMENT OF THE SERJEANT-AT-ARMS

Serjeant-at-Arms (£61,110–£98,400), P. N. W. Jennings, CVO (until Dec. 1999); M. J. A. Cummins (from Jan. 2000)
Deputy Serjeant-at-Arms (£45,810–£73,470), M. J. A. Cummins (until Dec. 1999)
Assistant Serjeants-at-Arms (£34,283–£55,524), P. A. J. Wright; J. M. Robertson; M. Harvey

DEPARTMENT OF THE LIBRARY

Librarian (£61,110–£98,400), Miss J. B. Tanfield (until Dec. 1999); Miss P. Baines (from Jan. 2000)
Directors (£45,810–£73,470), Miss P. Baines (until Dec. 1999); K. G. Cuninghame; Mrs J. Wainwright; R. Clements; R. Ware, D.PHIL.
Heads of Sections (£34,283–£55,524), C. Pond, PH.D.; Mrs C. Andrews; Mrs J. Lourie; C. Barclay; Mrs J. Fiddick; Mrs C. Gillie; R. Twigger; Mrs G. Allen; R. Cracknell
Senior Library Clerks (£30,271–£45,795), Ms F. Poole; T. Edmonds; Ms O. Gay; Miss E. McInnes; Dr D. Gore; B. Winetrobe; Miss M. Baber; Ms A. Walker; Mrs H. Holden; Mrs P. Carling; Miss J. Seaton; Mrs K. Greener; Ms P. Strickland; Miss V. Miller; M. P. Hillyard; Ms J. Roll; Ms W. Wilson; S. Wise; E. Wood; P. Bowers, PH.D.; T. Dodd; A. Seely; Mrs J. Hough; G. Danby, PH.D.; Dr P. M. Richards; B. C. Morgan; Ms K. Wright; Miss L. Conway; C. Blair, PH.D.; G. Vidler; C. Sear; M. Oakes (*period*); D. Maddison (*period*); A. Presland (*period*); Ms F. Whittle (*acting*)

DEPARTMENT OF FINANCE AND ADMINISTRATION

Director of Finance and Administration (£61,110–£98,400), A. Walker
Head of the Establishments Office (£50,510–£82,650), B. Wilson
Head of the Fees Office (£45,810–£73,470), A. Cameron
Head of the Finance Office (£45,810–£73,470), M. Barram

DEPARTMENT OF THE OFFICIAL REPORT

Editor (£50,510–£82,650), I. Church
Deputy Editors (£41,550–£65,270), W. G. Garland; Miss L. Sutherland; Ms C. Fogarty

REFRESHMENT DEPARTMENT
Director of Catering Services (£50,510–£82,650), Mrs S.
Harrison
Operations Manager (£30,271–£45,795), vacant
Executive Chef (£30,271–£45,795), D. Dorricott
Financial Controller (£30,271–£45,795), Mrs J. Rissen

SELECT COMMITTEES

The more important committees, as at August 1999, are:

DEPARTMENTAL COMMITTEES
Agriculture – Chair, Peter Luff, MP; *Clerk*, Ms L. M.
Gardner
Culture, Media and Sport– Chair, Rt. Hon. Gerald Kaufman,
MP; *Clerks*, C. G. Lee; Ms T. H. L. Brufal
Defence – Chair, Bruce George, MP; *Clerks*, P. A. Evans; Ms
S. McGlashan
Education and Employment – Clerks, B. M. Hutton; K. C. Fox
Sub-committees: Education – Chair, Malcolm Wicks, MP;
Clerk, B. M. Hutton; *Employment – Chair*, Rt. Hon. Derek
Foster, MP; *Clerk*, T. W. P. Healey
Environment, Transport and the Regions – Chairs, Andrew
Bennett, MP; Gwyneth Dunwoody, MP; *Clerk*, D. F.
Harrison
Sub-committees: Environment – Chair, Andrew Bennett,
MP; *Clerk*, H. A. Yardley; *Transport – Chair*, Gwyneth
Dunwoody, MP; *Clerk*, G. R. Devine
Foreign Affairs – Chair, Donald Anderson, MP; *Clerks*, E. P.
Silk; one vacancy
Health – Chair, David Hinchliffe, MP; *Clerks*, J. S. Benger,
D.phil.; J. D. Whatley
Home Affairs – Chair, Chris Mullin, MP; *Clerks*, A. R.
Kennon; M. P. Atkins
International Development – Chair, Bowen Wells, MP; *Clerks*,
A. Y. A. Azad; Ms J. Hughes
Northern Ireland – Chair, Rt. Hon. Peter Brooke, CH, MP;
Clerk, C. R. M. Ward
Science and Technology – Chair, Dr Michael Clark, MP; *Clerk*,
Mrs J. N. St J. Mulley
Scottish Affairs – Chair, David Marshall, MP; *Clerk*, Ms A.
Barry
Social Security – Chair, Archy Kirkwood, MP; *Clerk*, L. C.
Laurence Smyth
Trade and Industry – Chair, Martin O'Neill, MP; *Clerks*, D.
L. Natzler; M. Egan
Treasury – Chair, Rt. Hon. Giles Radice, MP; *Clerks*, S. J.
Patrick; one vacancy
Treasury sub-committee: Chair, Sir Michael Spicer, MP;
Clerk, vacant
Welsh Affairs – Chair, Martyn Jones, MP; *Clerk*, Ms P. A.
Helme

NON-DEPARTMENTAL COMMITTEES
Deregulation – Chair, Peter Pike, MP; *Clerk*, J. D. W. Rhys
Environmental Audit – Chair, John Horam, MP; *Clerk*, F. J.
Reid
European Legislation – Chair, James Hood, MP; *Clerks*, Mrs E.
J. Flood; Mrs S. Craig
Modernization – Chair, Rt. Hon. Margaret Beckett, MP;
Clerks, C. B. Winnifrith, CB; A. Sandall
Procedure – Chair, Nicholas Winterton, MP; *Clerks*, Ms E. C.
Samson; S. Mark
Public Accounts – Chair, Rt. Hon. David Davis, MP; *Clerk*, K.
J. Brown, OBE
Public Administration – Chair, Tony Wright, MP; *Clerk*, Dr P.
C. Seaward
Standards and Privileges – Chair, Rt. Hon. Robert Sheldon,
MP; *Clerks*, A. Sandall; Mrs S. A. R. Davies

PARLIAMENTARY INFORMATION

The following is a short glossary of aspects of the work of
Parliament. Unless otherwise stated, references are to
House of Commons procedures.

BILL – Proposed legislation is termed a bill. The stages
of a public bill (for private bills, *see* page 221) in the House
of Commons are as follows:
First Reading: This stage nowadays merely constitutes an
order to have the bill printed
Second Reading: The debate on the principles of the bill
Committee Stage: The detailed examination of a bill, clause
by clause. In most cases this takes place in a standing
committee, or the whole House may act as a committee. A
special standing committee may take evidence before
embarking on detailed scrutiny of the bill. Very rarely, a
bill may be examined by a select committee (*see* page 221)
Report Stage: Detailed review of a bill as amended in
committee
Third Reading: Final debate on a bill
Public bills go through the same stages in the House of
Lords, except that in almost all cases the committee stage
is taken in committee of the whole House.
A bill may start in either House, and has to pass through
both Houses to become law. Both Houses have to agree
the same text of a bill, so that the amendments made by
the second House are then considered in the originating
House, and if not agreed, sent back or themselves amended,
until agreement is reached.

CHILTERN HUNDREDS – A nominal office of profit under
the Crown, the acceptance of which requires an MP to
vacate his/her seat. The Manor of Northstead is similar.
These are the only means by which an MP may resign.

CONSOLIDATED FUND BILL – A bill to authorize issue of
money to maintain Government services. The bill is dealt
with without debate.

EARLY DAY MOTION – A motion put on the notice paper
by an MP without in general the real prospect of its being
debated. Such motions are expressions of back-bench
opinion.

FATHER OF THE HOUSE – The Member whose continuous service in the House of Commons is the longest. The
present Father of the House is the Rt. Hon. Sir Edward
Heath, KG, MBE, MP, elected first in 1950.

HOURS OF MEETING – The House of Commons normally
meets Monday, Tuesday and Thursday at 2.30 p.m., and
on Wednesday and Friday at 9.30 a.m.; there are ten Fridays
without sittings in each session. From January 1999 until
the end of the 1999–2000 session the Commons is
experimenting with sitting from 11.30 a.m. on Thursdays.
(*See also* Westminster Hall Sittings, below). The House of
Lords normally meets at 2.30 p.m. Monday to Wednesday
and at 3 p.m. on Thursday. In the latter part of the session,
the House of Lords sometimes sits on Fridays at 11 a.m.

LEADER OF THE OPPOSITION – In 1937 the office of
Leader of the Opposition was recognized and a salary was
assigned to the post. Since April 1999 the salary has been
£105,957 (including parliamentary salary of £47,008). The
present Leader of the Opposition is the Rt. Hon. William
Hague, MP.

THE LORD CHANCELLOR – The Lord High Chancellor
of Great Britain is (*ex officio*) the Speaker of the House of
Lords. Unlike the Speaker of the House of Commons, he
is a member of the Government, takes part in debates and

votes in divisions. He has none of the powers to maintain order that the Speaker in the Commons has, these powers being exercised in the Lords by the House as a whole. The Lord Chancellor sits in the Lords on one of the Woolsacks, couches covered with red cloth and stuffed with wool. If he wishes to address the House in any way except formally as Speaker, he leaves the Woolsack.

NORTHERN IRELAND GRAND COMMITTEE – The Northern Ireland Grand Committee consists of all MPs representing constituencies in Northern Ireland, together with not more than 25 other MPs nominated by the Committee of Selection. The business of the committee includes questions, short debates, ministerial statements, bills, legislative proposals and other matters relating exclusively to Northern Ireland, and delegated legislation. In autumn 1999 the House will debate a proposal to suspend the work of the Committee during the experiment with sittings in Westminster Hall (*see* page 222).

The Northern Ireland Affairs Committee is one of the departmental select committees, empowered to examine the expenditure, administration and policy of the Northern Ireland Office and the administration and expenditure of the Crown Solicitor's Office.

OPPOSITION DAY – A day on which the topic for debate is chosen by the Opposition. There are 20 such days in a normal session. On 17 days, subjects are chosen by the Leader of the Opposition; on the remaining three days by the leader of the next largest opposition party.

PARLIAMENT ACTS 1911 AND 1949 – Under these Acts, bills may become law without the consent of the Lords, though the House of Lords has the power to delay a public bill for 13 months from its first second reading in the House of Commons.

PRIME MINISTER'S QUESTIONS – The Prime Minister answers questions from 3.00 to 3.30 p.m. on Wednesdays.

PRIVATE BILL – A bill promoted by a body or an individual to give powers additional to, or in conflict with, the general law, and to which a special procedure applies to enable people affected to object.

PRIVATE MEMBER'S BILL – A public bill promoted by a Member who is not a member of the Government.

PRIVATE NOTICE QUESTION – A question adjudged of urgent importance on submission to the Speaker (in the Lords, the Leader of the House), answered at the end of oral questions, usually at 3.30 p.m.

PRIVILEGE – The following are covered by the privilege of Parliament:
(i)   freedom from interference in going to, attending at, and going from, Parliament
(ii)   freedom of speech in parliamentary proceedings
(iii)   the printing and publishing of anything relating to the proceedings of the two Houses is subject to privilege
(iv)   each House is the guardian of its dignity and may punish any insult to the House as a whole

QUESTION TIME – Oral questions are answered by Ministers in the Commons from 2.30 to 3.30 p.m. every day except Friday. From January 1999 until the end of the 1999–2000 session the Commons is experimenting with taking questions on Thursdays from 11.30 a.m. to 12.30 p.m. Questions are taken at the start of the Lords sittings, with a daily limit of four oral questions.

ROYAL ASSENT – The royal assent is signified by letters patent to such bills and measures as have passed both Houses of Parliament (or bills which have been passed

under the Parliament Acts 1911 and 1949). The Sovereign has not given royal assent in person since 1854. On occasion, for instance in the prorogation of Parliament, royal assent may be pronounced to the two Houses by Lords Commissioners. More usually royal assent is notified to each House sitting separately in accordance with the Royal Assent Act 1967. The old French formulae for royal assent are then endorsed on the acts by the Clerk of the Parliaments.

The power to withhold assent resides with the Sovereign but has not been exercised in the UK since 1707.

SCOTTISH GRAND COMMITTEE – Established in its present form in 1957, the committee consists of all 72 MPs representing Scottish constituencies, with a quorum of ten. The functions of the committee are to consider the principle of all public bills relating exclusively to Scotland (constituting in effect the bill's second reading); to consider the Scottish estimates on not less than six days a session; and to consider matters relating exclusively to Scotland on not more than six days a session. From the beginning of the 1994–5 session, the committee's powers were enhanced to allow oral questions, short debates, ministerial statements, and consideration of appropriate statutory instruments. The committee can meet on appointed days at specified places in Scotland. In autumn 1999 the House will debate a proposal to suspend the work of the Committee during the experiment with sittings in Westminster Hall (*see* page 222).

The Scottish Affairs Committee, one of the departmental select committees, was empowered to examine the expenditure, administration and policy of the Scottish Office, and the expenditure and administration of the Lord Advocate's Office. Following devolution, the role of the select committee has been questioned. If it continues, it will be concerned with the role and responsibilities of the relevant Secretary of State and on occasion the policy of the UK departments as it affects Scotland.

SELECT COMMITTEES – Consisting usually of ten to 15 members of all parties, select committees are a means used by both Houses in order to investigate certain matters.

Most select committees in the House of Commons are tied to departments: each committee investigates subjects within a government department's remit. There are other select committees dealing with public accounts (i.e. the spending by the Government of money voted by Parliament) and European legislation, and also domestic committees dealing, for example, with privilege and procedure. Major select committees usually take evidence in public; their evidence and reports are published by The Stationery Office. House of Commons select committees are reconstituted after a general election. For main committees, *see* page 220.

The principal select committee in the House of Lords is that on the European Communities, which has, at present, six sub-committees dealing with all areas of Community policy. The House of Lords also has a select committee on science and technology, which appoints sub-committees to deal with specific subjects, and a select committee on delegated powers and deregulation. For committees, *see* page 217. In addition, *ad hoc* select committees have been set up from time to time to investigate specific subjects. There are also some joint committees of the two Houses, e.g. the committees on statutory instruments and on parliamentary privilege.

THE SPEAKER – The Speaker of the House of Commons is the spokesman and president of the Chamber. He or she is elected by the House at the beginning of each Parliament or when the previous Speaker retires or dies. The Speaker neither speaks in debates nor votes in divisions except when the voting is equal.

VACANT SEATS – When a vacancy occurs in the House of Commons during a session of Parliament, the writ for the by-election is moved by a Whip of the party to which the member whose seat has been vacated belonged. If the House is in recess, the Speaker can issue a warrant for a writ, should two members certify to him that a seat is vacant.

WELSH GRAND COMMITTEE – First appointed in the 1959–60 session, the committee consists of all 40 MPs representing Welsh constituencies plus not more than five other members nominated by the Committee of Selection. The functions of the committee are to consider the principle of all public bills referred to it (constituting in effect the second reading of such a bill); and to consider matters relating exclusively to Wales. Since 1996 the business of the committee may also include questions, ministerial statements and short debates. Since June 1996 members of the committee have been permitted to speak in Welsh. In autumn 1999 the House will debate a proposal to suspend the work of the Committee during the experiment with sittings in Westminster Hall (*see* below).

The Welsh Affairs Committee, one of the departmental select committees, was empowered to examine the expenditure, administration and policy of the Welsh Office. Following devolution, the role of the select committee has been questioned. If it continues, it will be concerned with the role and responsibilities of the relevant Secretary of State and on occasion the policy of the UK departments as it affects Wales.

WESTMINSTER HALL SITTINGS – Following a report by the Modernization of the House of Commons Select Committee, the Commons decided in May 1999 to set up a second debating forum for an experimental period from the start of the 1999–2000 session. It will be known as 'Westminster Hall' and sittings will be in the Grand Committee Room on Tuesdays from 10 a.m. to 1 p.m., Wednesdays from 9.30 a.m. to 2 p.m. and Thursdays from 2.30 p.m. for up to three hours. Sittings will be open to the public at the times indicated.

WHIPS – In order to secure the attendance of Members of a particular party in Parliament, particularly on the occasion of an important vote, Whips (originally known as 'Whippers-in') are appointed. The written appeal or circular letter issued by them is also known as a 'whip', its urgency being denoted by the number of times it is underlined. Failure to respond to a three-line whip is tantamount in the Commons to secession (at any rate temporarily) from the party. Whips are provided with office accommodation in both Houses, and Government and some Opposition Whips receive salaries from public funds.

PARLIAMENTARY EDUCATION UNIT – Norman Shaw Building (North), London SW1A 2TT. Tel: 0171-219 2105 E-mail: edunit@parliament.uk

GOVERNMENT OFFICE

The Government is the body of Ministers responsible for the administration of national affairs, determining policy and introducing into Parliament any legislation necessary to give effect to government policy. The majority of Ministers are members of the House of Commons but members of the House of Lords or of neither House may also hold ministerial responsibility. The Lord Chancellor is always a member of the House of Lords. The Prime Minister is, by current convention, always a member of the House of Commons.

THE PRIME MINISTER

The office of Prime Minister, which had been in existence for nearly 200 years, was officially recognized in 1905 and its holder was granted a place in the table of precedence. The Prime Minister, by tradition also First Lord of the Treasury and Minister for the Civil Service, is appointed by the Sovereign and is usually the leader of the party which enjoys, or can secure, a majority in the House of Commons. Other Ministers are appointed by the Sovereign on the recommendation of the Prime Minister, who also allocates functions amongst Ministers and has the power to obtain their resignation or dismissal individually.

The Prime Minister informs the Sovereign of state and political matters, advises on the dissolution of Parliament, and makes recommendations for important Crown appointments, the award of honours, etc.

As the chairman of Cabinet meetings and leader of a political party, the Prime Minister is responsible for translating party policy into government activity. As leader of the Government, the Prime Minister is responsible to Parliament and to the electorate for the policies and their implementation.

The Prime Minister also represents the nation in international affairs, e.g. summit conferences.

THE CABINET

The Cabinet developed during the 18th century as an inner committee of the Privy Council, which was the chief source of executive power until that time. The Cabinet is composed of about 20 Ministers chosen by the Prime Minister, usually the heads of government departments (generally known as Secretaries of State unless they have a special title, e.g. Chancellor of the Exchequer), the leaders of the two Houses of Parliament, and the holders of various traditional offices.

The Cabinet's functions are the final determination of policy, control of government and co-ordination of government departments. The exercise of its functions is dependent upon enjoying majority support in the House of Commons. Cabinet meetings are held in private, taking place once or twice a week during parliamentary sittings and less often during a recess. Proceedings are confidential, the members being bound by their oath as Privy Counsellors not to disclose information about the proceedings.

The convention of collective responsibility means that the Cabinet acts unanimously even when Cabinet Ministers do not all agree on a subject. The policies of departmental Ministers must be consistent with the policies of the Government as a whole, and once the Government's policy has been decided, each Minister is expected to support it or resign.

The convention of ministerial responsibility holds a Minister, as the political head of his or her department, accountable to Parliament for the department's work. Departmental Ministers usually decide all matters within their responsibility, although on matters of political importance they normally consult their colleagues collectively. A decision by a departmental Minister is binding on the Government as a whole.

POLITICAL PARTIES

Before the reign of William and Mary the principal officers of state were chosen by and were responsible to the Sovereign alone and not to Parliament or the nation at large. Such officers acted sometimes in concert with one another but more often independently, and the fall of one did not, of necessity, involve that of others, although all were liable to be dismissed at any moment.

In 1693 the Earl of Sunderland recommended to William III the advisability of selecting a ministry from the political party which enjoyed a majority in the House of Commons and the first united ministry was drawn in 1696 from the Whigs, to which party the King owed his throne. This group became known as the Junto and was regarded with suspicion as a novelty in the political life of the nation, being a small section meeting in secret apart from the main body of Ministers. It may be regarded as the forerunner of the Cabinet and in course of time it led to the establishment of the principle of joint responsibility of Ministers, so that internal disagreement caused a change of personnel or resignation of the whole body of Ministers.

The accession of George I, who was unfamiliar with the English language, led to a disinclination on the part of the Sovereign to preside at meetings of his Ministers and caused the appearance of a Prime Minister, a position first acquired by Robert Walpole in 1721 and retained by him without interruption for 20 years and 326 days.

DEVELOPMENT OF PARTIES

In 1828 the Whigs became known as Liberals, a name originally given to it by its opponents to imply laxity of principles, but gradually accepted by the party to indicate its claim to be pioneers and champions of political reform and progressive legislation. In 1861 a Liberal Registration Association was founded and Liberal Associations became widespread. In 1877 a National Liberal Federation was formed, with headquarters in London. The Liberal Party was in power for long periods during the second half of the 19th century and for several years during the first quarter of the 20th century, but after a split in the party the numbers elected were small from 1931. In 1988, a majority of the Liberals agreed on a merger with the Social Democratic Party under the title Social and Liberal Democrats; since 1989 they have been known as the Liberal Democrats. A minority continue separately as the Liberal Party.

Soon after the change from Whig to Liberal the Tory Party became known as Conservative, a name believed to have been invented by John Wilson Croker in 1830 and to have been generally adopted about the time of the passing of the Reform Act of 1832 to indicate that the preservation of national institutions was the leading principle of the party. After the Home Rule crisis of 1886 the dissentient Liberals entered into a compact with the Conservatives, under which the latter undertook not to contest their seats, but a separate Liberal Unionist organization was maintained until 1912, when it was united with the Conservatives.

Labour candidates for Parliament made their first appearance at the general election of 1892, when there were 27 standing as Labour or Liberal-Labour. In 1900 the Labour Representation Committee was set up in order to establish a distinct Labour group in Parliament, with its own whips, its own policy, and a readiness to co-operate with any party which might be engaged in promoting legislation in the direct interest of labour. In 1906 the LRC became known as the Labour Party.

The Council for Social Democracy was announced by four former Labour Cabinet Ministers in January 1981 and in March 1981 the Social Democratic Party was launched. Later that year the SDP and the Liberal Party formed an electoral alliance. In 1988 a majority of the SDP agreed on a merger with the Liberal Party but a minority continued as a separate party under the SDP title. In 1990 it was decided to wind up the party organization and its three sitting MPs were known as independent social democrats. None were returned at the 1992 general election.

Plaid Cymru was founded in 1926 to provide an independent political voice for Wales and to campaign for self-government in Wales.

The Scottish National Party was founded in 1934 to campaign for independence for Scotland.

The Social Democratic and Labour Party was founded in 1970, emerging from the civil rights movement of the 1960s, with the aim of promoting reform, reconciliation and partnership across the sectarian divide in Northern Ireland and of opposing violence from any quarter.

The Ulster Democratic Unionist Party was founded in 1971 to resist moves by the Ulster Unionist Party which were considered a threat to the Union. Its aim is to maintain Northern Ireland as an integral part of the UK.

The Ulster Unionist Council first met formally in 1905. Its objectives are to maintain Northern Ireland as an integral part of the UK and to promote the aims of the Ulster Unionist Party.

GOVERNMENT AND OPPOSITION

The government of the day is formed by the party which wins the largest number of seats in the House of Commons at a general election, or which has the support of a majority of members in the House of Commons. By tradition, the leader of the majority party is asked by the Sovereign to form a government, while the largest minority party becomes the official Opposition with its own leader and a 'Shadow Cabinet'. Leaders of the Government and Opposition sit on the front benches of the Commons with their supporters (the back-benchers) sitting behind them.

FINANCIAL SUPPORT

Financial support to Opposition parties in the House of Commons was introduced in 1975 and is commonly known as Short Money, after Edward Short, the Leader of the House at that time, who introduced the scheme. For 1999–2000 financial support is:

Conservative	£3,377,973
Liberal Democrats	1,085,010
Plaid Cymru	61,859
SNP	134,643
SDLP	54,112
Democratic Unionists	33,871
Ulster Unionsts	138,750

A specific allocation for the Leader of the Opposition's office was introduced in April 1999 and has been set at £500,000 a year.

Financial support to the Opposition parties in the House of Lords was introduced in 1996 and is commonly known as Cranborne Money.

The parties included here are those with MPs sitting in the House of Commons in the present Parliament. Addresses of other political parties may be found in the Societies and Institutions section.

CONSERVATIVE AND UNIONIST PARTY
Central Office, 32 Smith Square, London
SWIP 3HH
Tel 0171-222 9000; fax 0171-222 1135
E-mail: ccoffice@conservative-party.org.uk
Web: http://www.conservative-party.org.uk

Chairman, Rt. Hon. Michael Ancram, QC, MP
Deputy Chairman and Chief Executive, The Hon. David Prior,
   MP
Senior Vice-Chairman, Tim Collins, CBE, MP
Vice-Chairmen, N. Evans, MP (*Wales*); John Hayes, MP
Treasurer, M. Ashcroft
SHADOW CABINET *as at August 1999*
Leader of the Opposition, Rt. Hon. William Hague, MP
Agriculture, Fisheries and Food, Tim Yeo, MP
Cabinet Office, Duchy of Lancaster and Policy Renewal, Andrew
   Lansley, CBE, MP
Culture, Media and Sport, Peter Ainsworth, MP
Defence, Iain Duncan Smith, MP
Education and Employment, Theresa May, MP
Environment, Transport and the Regions, Rt. Hon. John
   Redwood, MP
Foreign and Commonwealth Affairs, John Maples, MP
Health, Dr Liam Fox, MP
Home Affairs, Rt. Hon. Ann Widdecombe, MP
International Development, Gary Streeter, MP
Leader of the House of Commons and Constitutional Affairs, Rt.
   Hon. Sir George Young, Bt., MP
Leader of the House of Lords and Constitutional Affairs, The
   Lord Strathclyde, PC
Northern Ireland, Rt. Hon. Andrew Mackay, MP
Social Security, David Willetts, MP
Trade and Industry, Angela Browning, MP
Transport, Bernard Jenkin, MP
Treasury, Rt. Hon. Francis Maude, MP
Chief Secretary to the Treasury, Rt. Hon. David Heathcoat-
   Amory, MP
Conservative Party Chairman, Rt. Hon. Michael Ancram, QC,
   MP

CHIEF WHIPS
House of Lords, The Lord Henley
House of Commons, Rt. Hon. James Arbuthnot, MP (*Chief
   Whip*); Patrick McLoughlin, MP (*Deputy Chief Whip*)

SCOTTISH CONSERVATIVE AND UNIONIST
CENTRAL OFFICE
Suite 1/1, 14 Links Place, Leith, Edinburgh
EH6 7EZ
Tel 0131-555 2900
E-mail: scuco@scottish.tory.org.uk

Chairman, R. Robertson
Deputy Chairman, Mrs K. Donald
Hon. Treasurer, D. Mitchell, CBE
Head of Campaigns and Operations, D. Canzini

LABOUR PARTY
Millbank Tower, Millbank, London SWIP 4GT
Tel 0171-802 1000; fax 0171-802 1234
E-mail: labour-party@geo2.poptel.org.uk
Web: http://www.labour.org.uk

Parliamentary Party Leader, Rt. Hon. Anthony Blair, MP
Deputy Party Leader, Rt. Hon. John Prescott, MP
Leader in the Lords, The Baroness Jay of Paddington
Chair, R. Rosser
Vice-Chair, Rt. Hon. Clare Short, MP
Treasurer, Ms M. Prosser
General Secretary, Ms M. McDonagh
General Secretary, Scottish Labour Party, A. Rowley

LIBERAL DEMOCRATS
4 Cowley Street, London SWIP 3NB
Tel 0171-222 7999; fax 0171-799 2170
E-mail: libedems@cix.co.uk
Web: http://www.libdems.org.uk

President, The Baroness Maddock
Hon. Treasurer, The Lord Razzall, CBE
Chief Executive, Ms E. Pamplin
Parliamentary Party Leader, Charles Kennedy, MP
Leader in the Lords, The Lord Rodgers of Quarry Bank, PC
LIBERAL DEMOCRAT SPOKESMEN *as at August 1999*
Deputy Leader, Home and Legal Affairs, Alan Beith, MP
Agriculture and Rural Affairs, Paul Tyler, MP
Culture, Media and Sport, Constitution, Rt. Hon. Robert
   Maclennan, MP
Education and Employment, Don Foster, MP
Environment and Transport, Matthew Taylor, MP
Foreign Affairs, Defence and Europe, Menzies Campbell, MP
Health, Simon Hughes, MP
Local Government and Housing, Paul Burstow, MP
Social Security and Welfare, David Rendel, MP
Trade and Industry, David Chidgey, MP
Treasury, Malcolm Bruce, MP
Women, Jackie Ballard, MP
Young People, Lembit Opik, MP
Northern Ireland, Lembit Opik, MP
Scotland, Jim Wallace, MP
Wales, Richard Livsey, MP

LIBERAL DEMOCRAT WHIPS
House of Lords, The Lord Harris of Greenwich, PC
House of Commons, Paul Tyler, MP (*Chief Whip*); Andrew
   Stunell, MP (*Deputy Whip*)

LIBERAL DEMOCRATS WALES
Bay View House, 102 Bute Street, Cardiff
CFI 6AD
Tel 01222-313400; fax 01222-313401
E-mail: ldwales@cix.co.uk

Party President, A. Carlile, QC
Party Leader, Richard Livsey, CBE, MP
Chairman, P. Lloyd
Treasurer, A. Joyce
Secretary, Ms K. Lloyd
Administrative Officer, Ms H. Northmore-Thomas

SCOTTISH LIBERAL DEMOCRATS
4 Clifton Terrace, Edinburgh EHI2 5DR
Tel 0131-337 2314; fax 0131-337 3566
E-mail: scotlibdem@cix.co.uk
Web: http://www.scotlibdems.org.uk

Party President, R. Thomson
Party Leader, Jim Wallace, MP, MSP
Convener, Cllr I. Yuill
Treasurer, D. R. Sullivan
Chief Executive, W. Rennie

PLAID CYMRU – THE PARTY OF WALES
18 Park Grove, Cardiff CF10 3BN
Tel 01222-646000; fax 01222-646001
E-mail: post@plaidcymru.org
Web: http://www.plaidcymru.org

Party President, Dafydd Wigley, MP
Chairman, M. Phillips
Hon. Treasurer, vacant
Chief Executive/General Secretary, K. Davies

SCOTTISH NATIONAL PARTY
6 North Charlotte Street, Edinburgh EH2 4JH
Tel 0131-226 3661; fax 0131-225 9597
Web: http://www.snp.org.uk

Parliamentary Party Leader, Alasdair Morgan, MP, MSP
Chief Whip, Alasdair Morgan, MP, MSP
National Convener, Alex Salmond, MP
Senior Vice-Convener, John Swinney, MP
National Treasurer, I. Blackford
National Secretary, Colin Campbell, MSP

NORTHERN IRELAND

SOCIAL DEMOCRATIC AND LABOUR
PARTY
121 Ormeau Road, Belfast BT7 1SH
Tel 01232-247700; fax 01232-236699
E-mail: sdlp@indigo.ie
Web: http://www.indigo.ie/sdlp

Parliamentary Party Leader, John Hume, MP, MEP
Deputy Leader, Seamus Mallon, MP
Chief Whip, Eddie McGrady, MP
Chairman, J. Lennon
Hon. Treasurer, H. Doherty
General Secretary, Mrs G. Cosgrove

ULSTER DEMOCRATIC UNIONIST PARTY
91 Dundela Avenue, Belfast BT4 3BU
Tel 01232-471155; fax 01232-471797
E-mail: info@dup.org.uk
Web: http://www.dup.org.uk

Parliamentary Party Leader, Ian Paisley, MP, MEP
Deputy Leader, Peter Robinson, MP
Chairman, W. J. McClure
Chief Executive, A. Ewart
Hon. Treasurer, G. Campbell
Party Secretary, N. Dodds

ULSTER UNIONIST PARTY
3 Glengall Street, Belfast BT12 5AE
Tel 01232-324601; fax 01232-246738
E-mail: uup@uup.org.uk
Web: http://www.uup.org

Party Leader, Rt. Hon. David Trimble, MP
Chief Whip, Revd Martin Smyth, MP

ULSTER UNIONIST COUNCIL
President, J. Cunningham
Chairman, The Lord Rogan
Hon. Treasurer, J. Allen, OBE
General Secretary, D. Boyd

MEMBERS OF PARLIAMENT AS AT 27 JULY 1999

For abbreviations, *see* page 235
* Member of last Parliament
† Elected at a by-election since the general election
For late amendments *see* Stop-press

*Abbott, Ms Diane J. (*b.* 1953) *Lab., Hackney North and Stoke Newington,* maj. 15,627

Adams, Gerard (Gerry) (*b.* 1948) *SF, Belfast West,* maj. 7,909

*Adams, Mrs K. Irene (*b.* 1948) *Lab., Paisley North,* maj. 12,814

*Ainger, Nicholas R. (*b.* 1949) *Lab., Carmarthen West and Pembrokeshire South,* maj. 9,621

*Ainsworth, Peter M. (*b.* 1956) *C., Surrey East,* maj. 15,093

*Ainsworth, Robert W. (*b.* 1952) *Lab., Coventry North East,* maj. 22,569

†Alexander, Douglas G. (*b.* 1967) *Lab., Paisley South,* maj. 2,731

Allan, Richard B. (*b.* 1966) *LD, Sheffield Hallam,* maj. 8,271

*Allen, Graham W. (*b.* 1953) *Lab., Nottingham North,* maj. 18,801

*Amess, David A. A. (*b.* 1952) *C., Southend West,* maj. 2,615

*Ancram, Rt. Hon. Michael A. F. J. K. (Earl of Ancram) (*b.* 1945) *C., Devizes,* maj. 9,782

*Anderson, Donald (*b.* 1939) *Lab., Swansea East,* maj. 25,569

*Anderson, Mrs Janet (*b.* 1949) *Lab., Rossendale and Darwen,* maj. 10,949

*Arbuthnot, Rt. Hon. James N. (*b.* 1952) *C., Hampshire North East,* maj. 14,398

*Armstrong, Miss Hilary J. (*b.* 1945) *Lab., Durham North West,* maj. 24,754

*Ashdown, Rt. Hon. J. J. D. (Paddy) (*b.* 1941) *LD, Yeovil,* maj. 11,403

*Ashton, Joseph W. (*b.* 1933) *Lab., Bassetlaw,* maj. 17,460

Atherton, Ms Candice K. (*b.* 1955) *Lab., Falmouth and Camborne,* maj. 2,688

Atkins, Ms Charlotte (*b.* 1950) *Lab., Staffordshire Moorlands,* maj. 10,049

*Atkinson, David A. (*b.* 1940) *C., Bournemouth East,* maj. 4,346

*Atkinson, Peter L. (*b.* 1943) *C., Hexham,* maj. 222

*Austin-Walker, John E. (*b.* 1944) *Lab., Erith and Thamesmead,* maj. 17,424

Baker, Norman J. (*b.* 1957) *LD, Lewes,* maj. 1,300

*Baldry, Antony B. (*b.* 1950) *C., Banbury,* maj. 4,737

Ballard, Mrs Jacqueline M. (*b.* 1953) *LD, Taunton,* maj. 2,443

*Banks, Anthony L. (*b.* 1943) *Lab., West Ham,* maj. 19,494

*Barnes, Harold (*b.* 1936) *Lab., Derbyshire North East,* maj. 18,321

*Barron, Kevin J. (*b.* 1946) *Lab., Rother Valley,* maj. 23,485

*Battle, John D. (*b.* 1951) *Lab., Leeds West,* maj. 19,771

*Bayley, Hugh (*b.* 1952) *Lab., City of York,* maj. 20,523

Beard, C. Nigel (*b.* 1936) *Lab., Bexleyheath and Crayford,* maj. 3,415

*Beckett, Rt. Hon. Margaret M. (*b.* 1943) *Lab., Derby South,* maj. 16,106

Begg, Ms Anne (*b.* 1955) *Lab., Aberdeen South,* maj. 3,365

*Beggs, Roy (*b.* 1936) *UUP, Antrim East,* maj. 6,389

*Beith, Rt. Hon. Alan J. (*b.* 1943) *LD, Berwick upon Tweed,* maj. 8,042

Bell, Martin, OBE (*b.* 1938) *Ind., Tatton,* maj. 11,077

*Bell, Stuart (*b.* 1938) *Lab., Middlesbrough,* maj. 25,018

*Benn, Rt. Hon. Anthony N. W. (*b.* 1925) *Lab., Chesterfield,* maj. 5,775

†Benn, Hilary J. (*b.* 1953) *Lab., Leeds Central,* maj. 2,293

*Bennett, Andrew F. (*b.* 1939) *Lab., Denton and Reddish,* maj. 20,311

*Benton, Joseph E. (*b.* 1933) *Lab., Bootle,* maj. 28,421

Bercow, John S. (*b.* 1963) *C., Buckingham,* maj. 12,386

*Beresford, Sir Paul (*b.* 1946) *C., Mole Valley,* maj. 10,221

*Bermingham, Gerald E. (*b.* 1940) *Lab., St Helens South,* maj. 23,739

*Berry, Roger L., D.PHIL. (*b.* 1948) *Lab., Kingswood,* maj. 14,253

Best, Harold (*b.* 1939) *Lab., Leeds North West,* maj. 3,844

*Betts, Clive J. C. (*b.* 1950) *Lab., Sheffield Attercliffe,* maj. 21,818

Blackman, Ms Elizabeth M. (*b.* 1949) *Lab., Erewash,* maj. 9,135

*Blair, Rt. Hon. Anthony C. L. (*b.* 1953) *Lab., Sedgefield,* maj. 25,143

Blears, Hazel A. (*b.* 1956) *Lab., Salford,* maj. 17,069

Blizzard, Robert J. (*b.* 1950) *Lab., Waveney,* maj. 12,453

*Blunkett, Rt. Hon. David (*b.* 1947) *Lab., Sheffield Brightside,* maj. 19,954

Blunt, Crispin J. R. (*b.* 1960) *C., Reigate,* maj. 7,741

*Boateng, Paul Y. (*b.* 1951) *Lab., Brent South,* maj. 19,691

*Body, Sir Richard (*b.* 1927) *C., Boston and Skegness,* maj. 647

*Boothroyd, Rt. Hon. Betty (*b.* 1929) *The Speaker, West Bromwich West,* maj. 15,423

Borrow, David S. (*b.* 1952) *Lab., Ribble South,* maj. 5,084

*Boswell, Timothy E. (*b.* 1942) *C., Daventry,* maj. 7,378

*Bottomley, Peter J. (*b.* 1944) *C., Worthing West,* maj. 7,713

*Bottomley, Rt. Hon. Virginia H. B. M. (*b.* 1948) *C., Surrey South West,* maj. 2,694

*Bradley, Keith J. C. (*b.* 1950) *Lab., Manchester Withington,* maj. 18,581

Bradley, Peter C. S. (*b.* 1953) *Lab., Wrekin, The,* maj. 3,025

Bradshaw, Benjamin P. J. (*b.* 1960) *Lab., Exeter,* maj. 11,705

Brady, Graham (*b.* 1967) *C., Altrincham and Sale West,* maj. 1,505

Brake, Thomas A. (*b.* 1962) *LD, Carshalton and Wallington,* maj. 2,267

Brand, Dr Peter (*b.* 1947) *LD, Isle of Wight,* maj. 6,406

*Brazier, Julian W. H., TD (*b.* 1953) *C., Canterbury,* maj. 3,964

Breed, Colin E. (*b.* 1947) *LD, Cornwall South East,* maj. 6,480

Brinton, Ms Helen R. (*b.* 1954) *Lab., Peterborough,* maj. 7,323

*Brooke, Rt. Hon. Peter L., CH (*b.* 1934) *C., Cities of London and Westminster,* maj. 4,881

*Brown, Rt. Hon. J. Gordon, PH.D. (*b.* 1951) *Lab., Dunfermline East,* maj. 18,751

*Brown, Nicholas H. (*b.* 1950) *Lab., Newcastle upon Tyne East and Wallsend,* maj. 23,811

Brown, Russell L. (*b.* 1951) *Lab., Dumfries,* maj. 9,643

Browne, Desmond (*b.* 1952) *Lab., Kilmarnock and Loudoun,* maj. 7,256

*Browning, Mrs Angela F. (*b.* 1946) *C., Tiverton and Honiton,* maj. 1,653

*Bruce, Ian C. (*b.* 1947) *C., Dorset South,* maj. 77

*Bruce, Malcolm G. (*b.* 1944) *LD, Gordon,* maj. 6,997

Buck, Ms Karen P. (*b.* 1958) *Lab., Regent's Park and Kensington North,* maj. 14,657

*Burden, Richard H. (*b.* 1954) *Lab., Birmingham Northfield,* maj. 11,443

Burgon, Colin (*b.* 1948) *Lab., Elmet,* maj. 8,779

*Burnett, John P. A. (*b.* 1945) *LD, Devon West and Torridge,* maj. 1,957

*Burns, Simon H. M. (*b.* 1952) *C., Chelmsford West,* maj. 6,691

Burstow, Paul K. (*b.* 1962) *LD, Sutton and Cheam,* maj. 2,097

Butler, Ms Christine M. (*b.* 1943) *Lab.*, *Castle Point*, maj. 1,116

*Butterfill, John V. (*b.* 1941) *C.*, *Bournemouth West*, maj. 5,710

*Byers, Rt. Hon. Stephen J. (*b.* 1953) *Lab.*, *Tyneside North*, maj. 26,643

Cable, Dr J. Vincent (*b.* 1943) *LD*, *Twickenham*, maj. 4,281

*Caborn, Richard G. (*b.* 1943) *Lab.*, *Sheffield Central*, maj. 16,906

Campbell, Alan (*b.* 1957) *Lab.*, *Tynemouth*, maj. 11,273

*Campbell, Mrs Anne (*b.* 1940) *Lab.*, *Cambridge*, maj. 14,137

*Campbell, Ronald (*b.* 1943) *Lab.*, *Blyth Valley*, maj. 17,736

*Campbell, Rt. Hon. W. Menzies, CBE, QC (*b.* 1941) *LD*, *Fife North East*, maj. 10,356

*Campbell-Savours, Dale N. (*b.* 1943) *Lab.*, *Workington*, maj. 19,656

*Canavan, Dennis A. (*b.* 1942) *Lab.*, *Falkirk West*, maj. 13,783

*Cann, James C. (*b.* 1946) *Lab.*, *Ipswich*, maj. 10,439

Caplin, Ivor K. (*b.* 1958) *Lab.*, *Hove*, maj. 3,959

Casale, Roger M. (*b.* 1960) *Lab.*, *Wimbledon*, maj. 2,980

*Cash, William N. P. (*b.* 1940) *C.*, *Stone*, maj. 3,818

Caton, Martin P. (*b.* 1951) *Lab.*, *Gower*, maj. 13,007

Cawsey, Ian A. (*b.* 1960) *Lab.*, *Brigg and Goole*, maj. 6,389

*Chapman, J. K. (Ben) (*b.* 1940) *Lab.*, *Wirral South*, maj. 7,004

*Chapman, Sir Sydney (*b.* 1935) *C.*, *Chipping Barnet*, maj. 1,035

Chaytor, David M. (*b.* 1949) *Lab.*, *Bury North*, maj. 7,866

*Chidgey, David W. G. (*b.* 1942) *LD*, *Eastleigh*, maj. 754

*Chisholm, Malcolm G. R. (*b.* 1949) *Lab.*, *Edinburgh North and Leith*, maj. 10,978

Chope, Christopher R., OBE (*b.* 1947) *C.*, *Christchurch*, maj. 2,165

*Church, Mrs Judith A. (*b.* 1953) *Lab.*, *Dagenham*, maj. 17,054

*Clapham, Michael (*b.* 1943) *Lab.*, *Barnsley West and Penistone*, maj. 17,267

*Clappison, W James (*b.* 1956) *C.*, *Hertsmere*, maj. 3,075

Clark, Rt. Hon. Alan K. M. (*b.* 1928) *C.*, *Kensington and Chelsea*, maj. 9,519

*Clark, Rt. Hon. David G., PH.D. (*b.* 1939) *Lab.*, *South Shields*, maj. 22,153

Clark, Ms Lynda M. (*b.* 1949) *Lab.*, *Edinburgh Pentlands*, maj. 4,862

*Clark, Dr Michael, PH.D. (*b.* 1935) *C.*, *Rayleigh*, maj. 10,684

Clark, Paul G. (*b.* 1957) *Lab.*, *Gillingham*, maj. 1,980

Clarke, Anthony R. (*b.* 1963) *Lab.*, *Northampton South*, maj. 744

Clarke, Charles R. (*b.* 1950) *Lab.*, *Norwich South*, maj. 14,239

*Clarke, Eric L. (*b.* 1933) *Lab.*, *Midlothian*, maj. 9,870

*Clarke, Rt. Hon. Kenneth H., QC (*b.* 1940) *C.*, *Rushcliffe*, maj. 5,055

*Clarke, Rt. Hon. Thomas, CBE (*b.* 1941) *Lab.*, *Coatbridge and Chryston*, maj. 19,295

*Clelland, David G. (*b.* 1943) *Lab.*, *Tyne Bridge*, maj. 22,906

*Clifton-Brown, Geoffrey R. (*b.* 1953) *C.*, *Cotswold*, maj. 11,965

*Clwyd, Mrs Ann (*b.* 1937) *Lab.*, *Cynon Valley*, maj. 19,755

Coaker, Vernon R. (*b.* 1953) *Lab.*, *Gedling*, maj. 3,802

*Coffey, Ms M. Ann (*b.* 1946) *Lab.*, *Stockport*, maj. 18,912

*Cohen, Harry M. (*b.* 1949) *Lab.*, *Leyton and Wanstead*, maj. 15,186

Coleman, Iain (*b.* 1958) *Lab.*, *Hammersmith and Fulham*, maj. 3,842

Collins, Timothy W. G. (*b.* 1964) *C.*, *Westmorland and Lonsdale*, maj. 4,521

Colman, Anthony (*b.* 1943) *Lab.*, *Putney*, maj. 2,976

*Colvin, Michael K. B. (*b.* 1932) *C.*, *Romsey*, maj. 8,585

*Connarty, Michael (*b.* 1947) *Lab.*, *Falkirk East*, maj. 13,385

*Cook, Francis (*b.* 1935) *Lab.*, *Stockton North*, maj. 21,357

*Cook, Rt. Hon. R. F. (Robin) (*b.* 1946) *Lab.*, *Livingston*, maj. 11,747

Cooper, Ms Yvette (*b.* 1969) *Lab.*, *Pontefract and Castleford*, maj. 25,725

*Corbett, Robin (*b.* 1933) *Lab.*, *Birmingham Erdington*, maj. 12,657

*Corbyn, Jeremy B. (*b.* 1949) *Lab.*, *Islington North*, maj. 19,955

*Cormack, Sir Patrick (*b.* 1939) *C.*, *Staffordshire South*, maj. 7,821

*Corston, Ms Jean A. (*b.* 1942) *Lab.*, *Bristol East*, maj. 16,159

Cotter, Brian J. (*b.* 1938) *LD*, *Weston-Super-Mare*, maj. 1,274

*Cousins, James M. (*b.* 1944) *Lab.*, *Newcastle upon Tyne Central*, maj. 16,480

*Cox, Thomas M. (*b.* 1930) *Lab.*, *Tooting*, maj. 15,011

*Cran, James D. (*b.* 1944) *C.*, *Beverley and Holderness*, maj. 811

Cranston, Ross F. (*b.* 1948) *Lab.*, *Dudley North*, maj. 9,457

Crausby, David A. (*b.* 1946) *Lab.*, *Bolton North East*, maj. 12,669

Cryer, Mrs C. Ann (*b.* 1939) *Lab.*, *Keighley*, maj. 7,132

Cryer, John R. (*b.* 1964) *Lab.*, *Hornchurch*, maj. 5,680

*Cummings, John S. (*b.* 1943) *Lab.*, *Easington*, maj. 30,012

*Cunliffe, Lawrence F. (*b.* 1929) *Lab.*, *Leigh*, maj. 24,496

*Cunningham, Rt. Hon. Dr. J. A. (Jack), PH.D. (*b.* 1939) *Lab.*, *Copeland*, maj. 11,944

*Cunningham, James D. (*b.* 1941) *Lab.*, *Coventry South*, maj. 10,953

*Cunningham, Ms Roseanna (*b.* 1951) *SNP*, *Perth*, maj. 3,141

*Curry, Rt. Hon. David M. (*b.* 1944) *C.*, *Skipton and Ripon*, maj. 11,620

Curtis-Tansley, Ms Claire (*b.* 1958) *Lab.*, *Crosby*, maj. 7,182

*Dafis, Cynog G. (*b.* 1938) *PC*, *Ceredigion*, maj. 6,961

*Dalyell, Tam (Sir Thomas Dalyell of the Binns, Bt.) (*b.* 1932) *Lab.*, *Linlithgow*, maj. 10,838

*Darling, Rt. Hon. Alistair M. (*b.* 1953) *Lab.*, *Edinburgh Central*, maj. 11,070

Darvill, Keith E. (*b.* 1948) *Lab.*, *Upminster*, maj. 2,770

Davey, Edward J. (*b.* 1965) *LD*, *Kingston and Surbiton*, maj. 56

Davey, Ms Valerie (*b.* 1940) *Lab.*, *Bristol West*, maj. 1,493

*Davidson, Ian G. (*b.* 1950) *Lab. Co-op.*, *Glasgow Pollok*, maj. 13,791

*Davies, Rt. Hon. D. J. Denzil (*b.* 1938) *Lab.*, *Llanelli*, maj. 16,039

Davies, Geraint R. (*b.* 1960) *Lab.*, *Croydon Central*, maj. 3,897

*Davies, J. Quentin (*b.* 1944) *C.*, *Grantham and Stamford*, maj. 2,692

*Davies, Rt. Hon. Ronald (*b.* 1946) *Lab.*, *Caerphilly*, maj. 25,839

*Davis, Rt. Hon. David M. (*b.* 1948) *C.*, *Haltemprice and Howden*, maj. 7,514

*Davis, Terence A. G. (*b.* 1938) *Lab.*, *Birmingham Hodge Hill*, maj. 14,200

Dawson, T. Hilton (*b.* 1953) *Lab.*, *Lancaster and Wyre*, maj. 1,295

*Day, Stephen R. (*b.* 1948) *C.*, *Cheadle*, maj. 3,189

Dean, Ms Janet E. A. (*b.* 1949) *Lab.*, *Burton*, maj. 6,330

*Denham, John Y. (*b.* 1953) *Lab.*, *Southampton Itchen*, maj. 14,209

*Dewar, Rt. Hon. Donald C. (*b.* 1937) *Lab.*, *Glasgow Anniesland*, maj. 15,154

Dismore, Andrew H. (*b.* 1954) *Lab.*, *Hendon*, maj. 6,155

Dobbin, James (*b.* 1941) *Lab. Co-op.*, *Heywood and Middleton*, maj. 17,542

*Dobson, Rt. Hon. Frank G. (*b.* 1940) *Lab.*, *Holborn and St Pancras*, maj. 17,903

Donaldson, Jeffrey M. (*b.* 1962) *UUP*, *Lagan Valley*, maj. 16,925

*Donohoe, Brian H. (*b.* 1948) *Lab.*, *Cunninghame South*, maj. 14,869

*Heathcoat-Amory, Rt. Hon. David P. (*b.* 1949) *C., Wells*, maj. 528

*Henderson, Douglas J. (*b.* 1949) *Lab., Newcastle upon Tyne North*, maj. 19,332

Henderson, Ivan J. (*b.* 1958) *Lab., Harwich*, maj. 1,216

Hepburn, Stephen (*b.* 1959) *Lab., Jarrow*, maj. 21,933

*Heppell, John B. (*b.* 1948) *Lab., Nottingham East*, maj. 15,419

*Heseltine, Rt. Hon. Michael R. D., CH (*b.* 1933) *C., Henley*, maj. 11,167

Hesford, Stephen (*b.* 1957) *Lab., Wirral West*, maj. 2,738

Hewitt, Ms Patricia H. (*b.* 1948) *Lab., Leicester West*, maj. 12,864

*Hill, T. Keith (*b.* 1943) *Lab., Streatham*, maj. 18,423

*Hinchliffe, David M. (*b.* 1948) *Lab., Wakefield*, maj. 14,604

*Hodge, Mrs Margaret E., MBE (*b.* 1944) *Lab., Barking*, maj. 15,896

*Hoey, Ms Catharine (Kate) L. (*b.* 1946) *Lab., Vauxhall*, maj. 18,660

*Hogg, Rt. Hon. Douglas M., QC (*b.* 1945) *C., Sleaford and North Hykeham*, maj. 5,123

*Home Robertson, John D. (*b.* 1948) *Lab., East Lothian*, maj. 14,221

*Hood, James (*b.* 1948) *Lab., Clydesdale*, maj. 13,809

*Hoon, Geoffrey W. (*b.* 1953) *Lab., Ashfield*, maj. 22,728

Hope, Philip I. (*b.* 1955) *Lab. Co-op., Corby*, maj. 11,860

Hopkins, Kelvin P. (*b.* 1941) *Lab., Luton North*, maj. 9,626

*Horam, John R. (*b.* 1939) *C., Orpington*, maj. 2,952

*Howard, Rt. Hon. Michael, QC (*b.* 1941) *C., Folkestone and Hythe*, maj. 6,332

*Howarth, Alan T., CBE (*b.* 1944) *Lab., Newport East*, maj. 13,523

*Howarth, George E. (*b.* 1949) *Lab., Knowsley North and Sefton East*, maj. 26,147

Howarth, J. Gerald D. (*b.* 1947) *C., Aldershot*, maj. 6,621

*Howells, Kim S., PH.D. (*b.* 1946) *Lab., Pontypridd*, maj. 23,129

Hoyle, Lindsay H. (*b.* 1957) *Lab., Chorley*, maj. 9,870

Hughes, Ms Beverley J. (*b.* 1950) *Lab., Stretford and Urmston*, maj. 13,640

*Hughes, Kevin M. (*b.* 1952) *Lab., Doncaster North*, maj. 21,937

*Hughes, Simon H. W. (*b.* 1951) *LD, Southwark North and Bermondsey*, maj. 3,387

Humble, Mrs Jovanka (Joan) (*b.* 1951) *Lab., Blackpool North and Fleetwood*, maj. 8,946

*Hume, John, MEP (*b.* 1937) *SDLP, Foyle*, maj. 13,664

*Hunter, Andrew R. F. (*b.* 1943) *C., Basingstoke*, maj. 2,397

Hurst, Alan A. (*b.* 1945) *Lab., Braintree*, maj. 1,451

*Hutton, John M. P. (*b.* 1955) *Lab., Barrow and Furness*, maj. 14,497

Iddon, Brian (*b.* 1940) *Lab., Bolton South East*, maj. 21,311

*Illsley, Eric E. (*b.* 1955) *Lab., Barnsley Central*, maj. 24,501

*Ingram, Rt. Hon. Adam P. (*b.* 1947) *Lab., East Kilbride*, maj. 17,384

*Jack, Rt. Hon. J. Michael (*b.* 1946) *C., Fylde*, maj. 8,963

*Jackson, Ms Glenda M., CBE (*b.* 1936) *Lab., Hampstead and Highgate*, maj. 13,284

*Jackson, Mrs Helen M. (*b.* 1939) *Lab., Sheffield Hillsborough*, maj. 16,451

*Jackson, Robert V. (*b.* 1946) *C., Wantage*, maj. 6,039

*Jamieson, David C. (*b.* 1947) *Lab., Plymouth Devonport*, maj. 19,067

*Jenkin, Hon. Bernard C. (*b.* 1959) *C., Essex North*, maj. 5,476

*Jenkins, Brian D. (*b.* 1942) *Lab., Tamworth*, maj. 7,496

Johnson, Alan A. (*b.* 1950) *Lab., Hull West and Hessle*, maj. 15,525

Johnson, Ms Melanie J. (*b.* 1955) *Lab., Welwyn Hatfield*, maj. 5,595

*Johnson Smith, Rt. Hon. Sir Geoffrey (*b.* 1924) *C., Wealden*, maj. 14,204

*Jones, Rt. Hon. S. Barry (*b.* 1938) *Lab., Alyn and Deeside*, maj. 16,403

Jones, Ms Fiona E. A. (*b.* 1957) *Lab., Newark*, maj. 3,016

Jones, Ms Helen M. (*b.* 1954) *Lab., Warrington North*, maj. 19,527

*Jones, Ieuan W. (*b.* 1949) *PC, Ynys Môn*, maj. 2,481

Jones, Ms Jennifer G. (*b.* 1948) *Lab., Wolverhampton South West*, maj. 5,118

*Jones, Jonathan O. (*b.* 1954) *Lab. Co-op., Cardiff Central*, maj. 7,923

*Jones, Ms Lynne M., PH.D. (*b.* 1951) *Lab., Birmingham Selly Oak*, maj. 14,088

*Jones, Martyn D. (*b.* 1947) *Lab., Clwyd South*, maj. 13,810

*Jones, Nigel D. (*b.* 1948) *LD, Cheltenham*, maj. 6,645

*Jowell, Rt. Hon. Tessa J. H. D. (*b.* 1947) *Lab., Dulwich and West Norwood*, maj. 16,769

*Kaufman, Rt. Hon. Gerald B. (*b.* 1930) *Lab., Manchester Gorton*, maj. 17,342

Keeble, Ms Sally C. (*b.* 1951) *Lab., Northampton North*, maj. 10,000

Keen, Mrs Ann L. (*b.* 1948) *Lab., Brentford and Isleworth*, maj. 14,424

*Keen, D. Alan (*b.* 1937) *Lab. Co-op., Feltham and Heston*, maj. 15,273

Keetch, Paul S. (*b.* 1961) *LD, Hereford*, maj. 6,648

Kelly, Ms Ruth M. (*b.* 1968) *Lab., Bolton West*, maj. 7,072

Kemp, Fraser (*b.* 1958) *Lab., Houghton and Washington East*, maj. 26,555

*Kennedy, Charles P. (*b.* 1959) *LD, Ross, Skye and Inverness West*, maj. 4,019

*Kennedy, Mrs Jane E. (*b.* 1958) *Lab., Liverpool Wavertree*, maj. 19,701

*Key, S. Robert (*b.* 1945) *C., Salisbury*, maj. 6,276

*Khabra, Piara S. (*b.* 1924) *Lab., Ealing Southall*, maj. 21,423

Kidney, David N. (*b.* 1955) *Lab., Stafford*, maj. 4,314

*Kilfoyle, Peter (*b.* 1946) *Lab., Liverpool Walton*, maj. 27,038

King, Andrew (*b.* 1948) *Lab., Rugby and Kenilworth*, maj. 495

King, Ms Oona T. (*b.* 1967) *Lab., Bethnal Green and Bow*, maj. 11,285

*King, Rt. Hon. Thomas J., CH (*b.* 1933) *C., Bridgwater*, maj. 1,796

Kingham, Ms Teresa J. (*b.* 1963) *Lab., Gloucester*, maj. 8,259

Kirkbride, Miss Julie (*b.* 1960) *C., Bromsgrove*, maj. 4,895

*Kirkwood, Archibald J. (*b.* 1946) *LD, Roxburgh and Berwickshire*, maj. 7,906

Kumar, Dr Ashok (*b.* 1956) *Lab., Middlesbrough South and Cleveland East*, maj. 10,607

Ladyman, Dr Stephen J. (*b.* 1952) *Lab., Thanet South*, maj. 2,878

Laing, Mrs Eleanor F. (*b.* 1958) *C., Epping Forest*, maj. 5,252

Lait, Ms Jacqueline A. H. (*b.* 1947) *C., Beckenham*, maj. 1,227

Lansley, Andrew D. (*b.* 1956) *C., Cambridgeshire South*, maj. 8,712

Lawrence, Mrs Jacqueline R. (*b.* 1948) *Lab., Preseli Pembrokeshire*, maj. 8,736

Laxton, Robert (*b.* 1944) *Lab., Derby North*, maj. 10,615

*Leigh, Edward J. E. (*b.* 1950) *C., Gainsborough*, maj. 6,826

Lepper, David (*b.* 1945) *Lab. Co-op., Brighton Pavilion*, maj. 13,181

Leslie, Christopher M. (*b.* 1972) *Lab., Shipley*, maj. 2,996

Letwin, Oliver (*b.* 1956) *C., Dorset West*, maj. 1,840

Levitt, Tom (*b.* 1954) *Lab., High Peak*, maj. 8,791

Lewis, Ivan (*b.* 1967) *Lab., Bury South*, maj. 12,433

Lewis, Dr Julian M. (*b.* 1951) *C., New Forest East*, maj. 5,215

*Lewis, Terence (*b.* 1935) *Lab., Worsley*, maj. 17,741

*Liddell, Rt. Hon. Helen (*b.* 1950) *Lab., Airdrie and Shotts*, maj. 15,412

*Lidington, David R., PH.D. (*b.* 1956) *C., Aylesbury*, maj. 8,419

*Lilley, Rt. Hon. Peter B. (*b.* 1943) *C., Hitchin and Harpenden,* maj. 6,671

Linton, J. Martin (*b.* 1944) *Lab., Battersea,* maj. 5,360

*Livingstone, Kenneth R. (*b.* 1945) *Lab., Brent East,* maj. 15,882

Livsey, Richard A. L., CBE (*b.* 1935) *LD, Brecon and Radnorshire,* maj. 5,097

*Lloyd, Anthony J. (*b.* 1950) *Lab., Manchester Central,* maj. 19,682

*Lloyd, Rt. Hon. Sir Peter (*b.* 1937) *C., Fareham,* maj. 10,358

*Llwyd, Elfyn (*b.* 1951) *PC, Meirionnydd nant Conwy,* maj. 6,805

Lock, David A. (*b.* 1960) *Lab., Wyre Forest,* maj. 6,946

*Lord, Michael N. (*b.* 1938) *C., Suffolk Central and Ipswich North,* maj. 3,538

Loughton, Timothy P. (*b.* 1962) *C., Worthing East and Shoreham,* maj. 5,098

Love, Andrew (*b.* 1949) *Lab. Co-op., Edmonton,* maj. 13,472

*Luff, Peter J. (*b.* 1955) *C., Worcestershire Mid,* maj. 9,412

*Lyell, Rt. Hon. Sir Nicholas, QC (*b.* 1938) *C., Bedfordshire North East,* maj. 5,883

*McAllion, John (*b.* 1948) *Lab., Dundee East,* maj. 9,961

*McAvoy, Thomas M. (*b.* 1943) *Lab. Co-op., Glasgow Rutherglen,* maj. 15,007

McCabe, Stephen J. (*b.* 1955) *Lab., Birmingham Hall Green,* maj. 8,420

*McCafferty, Ms Christine (*b.* 1945) *Lab., Calder Valley,* maj. 6,255

*McCartney, Ian (*b.* 1951) *Lab., Makerfield,* maj. 26,177

*McCartney, Robert L., QC (NI) (*b.* 1936) *UKU, Down North,* maj. 1,449

McDonagh, Ms Siobhain A. (*b.* 1960) *Lab., Mitcham and Morden,* maj. 13,741

*Macdonald, Calum A., PH.D. (*b.* 1956) *Lab., Western Isles,* maj. 3,576

McDonnell, John M. (*b.* 1951) *Lab., Hayes and Harlington,* maj. 14,291

*McFall, John (*b.* 1944) *Lab. Co-op., Dumbarton,* maj. 10,883

*McGrady, Edward K. (*b.* 1935) *SDLP, Down South,* maj. 9,933

*MacGregor, Rt. Hon. John R. R., OBE (*b.* 1937) *C., Norfolk South,* maj. 7,378

McGuinness, Martin (*b.* 1950) *SF, Ulster Mid,* maj. 1,883

McGuire, Mrs Anne (*b.* 1949) *Lab., Stirling,* maj. 6,411

McIntosh, Miss Anne C. B. (*b.* 1954) *C., Vale of York,* maj. 9,721

McIsaac, Ms Shona (*b.* 1960) *Lab., Cleethorpes,* maj. 9,176

*Mackay, Rt. Hon. Andrew J. (*b.* 1949) *C., Bracknell,* maj. 10,387

McKenna, Ms Rosemary (*b.* 1941) *Lab., Cumbernauld and Kilsyth,* maj. 11,128

*MacKinlay, Andrew S. (*b.* 1949) *Lab., Thurrock,* maj. 17,256

*Maclean, Rt. Hon. David J. (*b.* 1953) *C., Penrith and the Border,* maj. 10,233

*McLeish, Henry B. (*b.* 1948) *Lab., Fife Central,* maj. 13,713

*Maclennan, Rt. Hon. Robert A. R. (*b.* 1936) *LD, Caithness, Sutherland and Easter Ross,* maj. 2,259

*McLoughlin, Patrick A. (*b.* 1957) *C., Derbyshire West,* maj. 4,885

*McNamara, J. Kevin (*b.* 1934) *Lab., Hull North,* maj. 19,705

McNulty, Anthony J. (*b.* 1958) *Lab., Harrow East,* maj. 9,738

*MacShane, Denis, PH.D. (*b.* 1948) *Lab., Rotherham,* maj. 21,469

MacTaggart, Ms Fiona M. (*b.* 1953) *Lab., Slough,* maj. 13,071

McWalter, Tony (*b.* 1945) *Lab. Co-op., Hemel Hempstead,* maj. 3,636

*McWilliam, John D. (*b.* 1941) *Lab., Blaydon,* maj. 16,605

*Madel, Sir David (*b.* 1938) *C., Bedfordshire South West,* maj. 132

*Maginnis, Kenneth (*b.* 1938) *UUP, Fermanagh and South Tyrone,* maj. 13,688

*Mahon, Mrs Alice (*b.* 1937) *Lab., Halifax,* maj. 11,212

*Major, Rt. Hon. John, CH (*b.* 1943) *C., Huntingdon,* maj. 18,140

Malins, Humfrey J., CBE (*b.* 1945) *C., Woking,* maj. 5,678

Mallaber, Ms C. Judith (*b.* 1951) *Lab., Amber Valley,* maj. 11,613

*Mallon, Seamus (*b.* 1936) *SDLP, Newry and Armagh,* maj. 4,889

*Mandelson, Rt. Hon. Peter B. (*b.* 1953) *Lab., Hartlepool,* maj. 17,508

Maples, John C. (*b.* 1943) *C., Stratford-upon-Avon,* maj. 14,106

*Marek, John, PH.D. (*b.* 1940) *Lab., Wrexham,* maj. 11,762

*Marsden, Gordon (*b.* 1953) *Lab., Blackpool South,* maj. 11,616

Marsden, Paul W. B. (*b.* 1968) *Lab., Shrewsbury and Atcham,* maj. 1,670

*Marshall, David, PH.D (*b.* 1941) *Lab., Glasgow Shettleston,* maj. 15,868

*Marshall, James, PH.D. (*b.* 1941) *Lab., Leicester South,* maj. 16,493

Marshall-Andrews, Robert G., QC (*b.* 1944) *Lab., Medway,* maj. 5,354

*Martin, Michael J. (*b.* 1945) *Lab., Glasgow Springburn,* maj. 17,326

*Martlew, Eric A. (*b.* 1949) *Lab., Carlisle,* maj. 12,390

*Mates, Michael J. (*b.* 1934) *C., Hampshire East,* maj. 11,590

Maude, Rt. Hon. Francis A. A. (*b.* 1953) *C., Horsham,* maj. 14,862

*Mawhinney, Rt. Hon. Sir Brian, PH.D. (*b.* 1940) *C., Cambridgeshire North West,* maj. 7,754

*Maxton, John A. (*b.* 1936) *Lab., Glasgow Cathcart,* maj. 12,245

May, Mrs Theresa M. (*b.* 1956) *C., Maidenhead,* maj. 11,981

*Meacher, Rt. Hon. Michael H. (*b.* 1939) *Lab., Oldham West and Royton,* maj. 16,201

Meale, J. Alan (*b.* 1949) *Lab., Mansfield,* maj. 20,518

Merron, Ms Gillian J. (*b.* 1959) *Lab., Lincoln,* maj. 11,130

*Michael, Rt. Hon. Alun E. (*b.* 1943) *Lab. Co-op., Cardiff South and Penarth,* maj. 13,881

*Michie, Mrs J. Ray (*b.* 1934) *LD, Argyll and Bute,* maj. 6,081

*Michie, William (*b.* 1935) *Lab., Sheffield Heeley,* maj. 17,078

*Milburn, Rt. Hon. Alan (*b.* 1958) *Lab., Darlington,* maj. 16,025

*Miller, Andrew P. (*b.* 1949) *Lab., Ellesmere Port and Neston,* maj. 16,036

*Mitchell, Austin V., D.PHIL. (*b.* 1934) *Lab., Great Grimsby,* maj. 16,244

Moffatt, Mrs Laura J. (*b.* 1954) *Lab., Crawley,* maj. 11,707

*Moonie, Dr Lewis G. (*b.* 1947) *Lab. Co-op., Kirkcaldy,* maj. 10,710

Moore, Michael K. (*b.* 1965) *LD, Tweeddale, Ettrick and Lauderdale,* maj. 1,489

Moran, Ms Margaret (*b.* 1955) *Lab., Luton South,* maj. 11,319

Morgan, Alasdair N. (*b.* 1945) *SNP, Galloway and Upper Nithsdale,* maj. 5,624

*Morgan, H. Rhodri (*b.* 1939) *Lab., Cardiff West,* maj. 15,628

Morgan, Ms Julie (*b.* 1944) *Lab., Cardiff North,* maj. 8,126

*Morley, Elliot A. (*b.* 1952) *Lab., Scunthorpe,* maj. 14,173

*Morris, Ms Estelle (*b.* 1952) *Lab., Birmingham Yardley,* maj. 5,315

*Morris, Rt. Hon. John, QC (*b.* 1931) *Lab., Aberavon,* maj. 21,571

*Moss, Malcolm D. (*b.* 1943) *C., Cambridgeshire North East,* maj. 5,101

Mountford, Ms Kali C. J. (*b.* 1954) *Lab., Colne Valley,* maj. 4,840

*Mowlam, Rt. Hon. Marjorie, Ph.D. (b. 1949) Lab., Redcar, maj. 21,664

*Mudie, George E. (b. 1945) Lab., Leeds East, maj. 17,466

*Mullin, Christopher J. (b. 1947) Lab., Sunderland South, maj. 19,638

Murphy, Denis (b. 1948) Lab., Wansbeck, maj. 22,367

Murphy, James (b. 1967) Lab., Eastwood, maj. 3,236

*Murphy, Paul P. (b. 1948) Lab., Torfaen, maj. 24,536

Naysmith, J. Douglas (b. 1941) Lab. Co-op., Bristol North West, maj. 11,382

*Nicholls, Patrick C. M. (b. 1948) C., Teignbridge, maj. 281

Norman, Archibald J. (b. 1954) C., Tunbridge Wells, maj. 7,506

Norris, Dan (b. 1960) Lab., Wansdyke, maj. 4,799

Oaten, Mark (b. 1964) LD, Winchester, maj. 21,556

*O'Brien, Michael (b. 1954) Lab., Warwickshire North, maj. 14,767

†O'Brien, Stephen (b. 1957) C., Eddisbury, maj. 1,606

*O'Brien, William (b. 1929) Lab., Normanton, maj. 15,893

*O'Hara, Edward (b. 1937) Lab., Knowsley South, maj. 30,708

*Olner, William J. (b. 1942) Lab., Nuneaton, maj. 13,540

*O'Neill, Martin J. (b. 1945) Lab., Ochil, maj. 4,652

Opik, Lembit (b. 1965) LD, Montgomeryshire, maj. 6,303

Organ, Ms Diana M. (b. 1952) Lab., Forest of Dean, maj. 6,343

Osborne, Mrs Sandra C. (b. 1956) Lab., Ayr, maj. 6,543

*Ottaway, Richard G. J. (b. 1945) C., Croydon South, maj. 11,930

*Page, Richard L. (b. 1941) C., Hertfordshire South West, maj. 10,021

*Paice, James E. T. (b. 1949) C., Cambridgeshire South East, maj. 9,349

*Paisley, Revd Ian R. K., MEP (b. 1926) DUP, Antrim North, maj. 10,574

Palmer, Nicholas D. (b. 1950) Lab., Broxtowe, maj. 5,575

Paterson, Owen W. (b. 1956) C., Shropshire North, maj. 2,195

*Pearson, Ian P., Ph.D. (b. 1959) Lab., Dudley South, maj. 13,027

*Pendry, Thomas (b. 1934) Lab., Stalybridge and Hyde, maj. 14,806

Perham, Ms Linda (b. 1947) Lab., Ilford North, maj. 3,224

*Pickles, Eric J. (b. 1952) C., Brentwood and Ongar, maj. 9,690

*Pickthall, Colin (b. 1944) Lab., Lancashire West, maj. 17,119

*Pike, Peter L. (b. 1937) Lab., Burnley, maj. 17,062

Plaskitt, James A. (b. 1954) Lab., Warwick and Leamington, maj. 3,398

Pollard, Kerry P. (b. 1944) Lab., St Albans, maj. 4,459

Pond, Christopher R. (b. 1952) Lab., Gravesham, maj. 5,779

*Pope, Gregory J. (b. 1960) Lab., Hyndburn, maj. 11,448

Pound, Stephen P. (b. 1948) Lab., Ealing North, maj. 9,160

*Powell, Sir Raymond (b. 1928) Lab., Ogmore, maj. 24,447

*Prentice, Ms Bridget T. (b. 1952) Lab., Lewisham East, maj. 12,127

*Prentice, Gordon (b. 1951) Lab., Pendle, maj. 10,824

*Prescott, Rt. Hon. John L. (b. 1938) Lab., Hull East, maj. 23,318

*Primarolo, Ms Dawn (b. 1954) Lab., Bristol South, maj. 19,328

Prior, Hon. David G. L. (b. 1954) C., Norfolk North, maj. 1,293

Prosser, Gwynfor M. (b. 1943) Lab., Dover, maj. 11,739

*Purchase, Kenneth (b. 1939) Lab. Co-op., Wolverhampton North East, maj. 12,987

*Quin, Rt. Hon. Joyce G. (b. 1944) Lab., Gateshead East and Washington West, maj. 24,950

Quinn, Lawrence W. (b. 1956) Lab., Scarborough and Whitby, maj. 5,124

*Radice, Rt. Hon. Giles H. (b. 1936) Lab., Durham North, maj. 26,299

Rammell, William E. (b. 1959) Lab., Harlow, maj. 10,514

Randall, A. John (b. 1955) C., Uxbridge, maj. 3,766

Rapson, Sydney N. J. (b. 1942) Lab., Portsmouth North, maj. 4,323

*Raynsford, W. R. N. (Nick) (b. 1945) Lab., Greenwich and Woolwich, maj. 18,128

*Redwood, Rt. Hon. John A., D.Phil. (b. 1951) C., Wokingham, maj. 9,365

Reed, Andrew J. (b. 1964) Lab., Loughborough, maj. 5,712

*Reid, Rt. Hon. John, Ph.D. (b. 1947) Lab., Hamilton North and Bellshill, maj. 17,067

*Rendel, David D. (b. 1949) LD, Newbury, maj. 8,517

*Robathan, Andrew R. G. (b. 1951) C., Blaby, maj. 6,474

*Robertson, Rt. Hon. George I. M. (b. 1946) Lab., Hamilton South, maj. 15,878

Robertson, Laurence A. (b. 1958) C., Tewkesbury, maj. 9,234

*Robinson, Geoffrey (b. 1938) Lab., Coventry North West, maj. 16,601

*Robinson, Peter D. (b. 1948) DUP, Belfast East, maj. 6,754

*Roche, Mrs Barbara M. R. (b. 1954) Lab., Hornsey and Wood Green, maj. 20,499

*Roe, Mrs Marion A. (b. 1936) C., Broxbourne, maj. 6,653

*Rogers, Allan R. (b. 1932) Lab., Rhondda, maj. 24,931

*Rooker, Jeffrey W. (b. 1941) Lab., Birmingham Perry Barr, maj. 18,957

*Rooney, Terence H. (b. 1950) Lab., Bradford North, maj. 12,770

*Ross, Ernest (b. 1942) Lab., Dundee West, maj. 11,859

*Ross, William (b. 1936) UUP, Londonderry East, maj. 3,794

*Rowe, Andrew J. B. (b. 1935) C., Faversham and Kent Mid, maj. 4,173

*Rowlands, Edward (b. 1940) Lab., Merthyr Tydfil and Rhymney, maj. 27,086

Roy, Frank (b. 1958) Lab., Motherwell and Wishaw, maj. 12,791

Ruane, Christopher S. (b. 1958) Lab., Vale of Clwyd, maj. 8,955

*Ruddock, Mrs Joan M. (b. 1943) Lab., Lewisham Deptford, maj. 18,878

Ruffley, David L. (b. 1962) C., Bury St Edmunds, maj. 368

Russell, Ms Christine M. (b. 1945) Lab., City of Chester, maj. 10,553

Russell, Robert E. (b. 1946) LD, Colchester, maj. 1,581

Ryan, Ms Joan M. (b. 1955) Lab., Enfield North, maj. 6,822

St Aubyn, Nicholas F. (b. 1955) C., Guildford, maj. 4,791

*Salmond, Alexander E. A. (b. 1954) SNP, Banff and Buchan, maj. 12,845

Salter, Martin J. (b. 1954) Lab., Reading West, maj. 2,997

Sanders, Adrian M. (b. 1959) LD, Torbay, maj. 12

Sarwar, Mohammad (b. 1952) Lab., Glasgow Govan, maj. 2,914

Savidge, Malcolm K. (b. 1946) Lab., Aberdeen North, maj. 10,010

Sawford, Philip A. (b. 1950) Lab., Kettering, maj. 189

Sayeed, Jonathan (b. 1948) C., Bedfordshire Mid, maj. 7,090

*Sedgemore, Brian C. J. (b. 1937) Lab., Hackney South and Shoreditch, maj. 14,980

Shaw, Jonathan R. (b. 1966) Lab., Chatham and Aylesford, maj. 2,790

*Sheerman, Barry J. (b. 1940) Lab. Co-op., Huddersfield, maj. 15,848

*Sheldon, Rt. Hon. Robert E. (b. 1923) Lab., Ashton under Lyne, maj. 22,965

*Shephard, Rt. Hon. Gillian P. (b. 1940) C., Norfolk South West, maj. 2,464

*Shepherd, Richard C. S. (b. 1942) C., Aldridge-Brownhills, maj. 2,526

Shipley, Ms Debra A. (b. 1957) Lab., Stourbridge, maj. 5,645

*Short, Rt. Hon. Clare (b. 1946) Lab., Birmingham Ladywood, maj. 23,082

*Simpson, Alan J. (*b.* 1948) *Lab., Nottingham South*, maj. 13,364

Simpson, Keith (*b.* 1949) *C., Norfolk Mid*, maj. 1,336

Singh, Marsha (*b.* 1954) *Lab., Bradford West*, maj. 3,877

*Skinner, Dennis E. (*b.* 1932) *Lab., Bolsover*, maj. 27,149

*Smith, Rt. Hon. Andrew D. (*b.* 1951) *Lab., Oxford East*, maj. 16,665

Smith, Ms Angela E. (*b.* 1959) *Lab. Co-op., Basildon*, maj. 13,280

*Smith, Rt. Hon. Christopher R., PH.D. (*b.* 1951) *Lab., Islington South and Finsbury*, maj. 14,563

Smith, Ms Geraldine (*b.* 1961) *Lab., Morecambe and Lunesdale*, maj. 5,965

Smith, Ms Jacqueline J. (*b.* 1962) *Lab., Redditch*, maj. 6,125

Smith, John W. P. (*b.* 1951) *Lab., Vale of Glamorgan*, maj. 10,532

*Smith, Llewellyn T. (*b.* 1944) *Lab., Blaenau Gwent*, maj. 28,035

Smith, Sir Robert, Bt. (*b.* 1958) *LD, Aberdeenshire West and Kincardine*, maj. 2,662

*Smyth, Revd W. Martin (*b.* 1931) *UUP, Belfast South*, maj. 4,600

*Snape, Peter C. (*b.* 1942) *Lab., West Bromwich East*, maj. 13,584

*Soames, Hon. A. Nicholas W. (*b.* 1948) *C., Sussex Mid*, maj. 6,854

*Soley, Clive S. (*b.* 1939) *Lab., Ealing Acton and Shepherd's Bush*, maj. 15,647

Southworth, Ms Helen M. (*b.* 1956) *Lab., Warrington South*, maj. 10,807

*Spellar, John F. (*b.* 1947) *Lab., Warley*, maj. 15,451

Spelman, Mrs Caroline A. (*b.* 1958) *C., Meriden*, maj. 582

*Spicer, Sir Michael (*b.* 1943) *C., Worcestershire West*, maj. 3,846

*Spring, Richard J. G. (*b.* 1946) *C., Suffolk West*, maj. 1,867

*Squire, Ms Rachel A. (*b.* 1954) *Lab., Dunfermline West*, maj. 12,354

*Stanley, Rt. Hon. Sir John (*b.* 1942) *C., Tonbridge and Malling*, maj. 10,230

Starkey, Mrs Phyllis M. (*b.* 1947) *Lab., Milton Keynes South West*, maj. 10,292

*Steen, Sir Anthony (*b.* 1939) *C., Totnes*, maj. 877

*Steinberg, Gerald N. (*b.* 1945) *Lab., City of Durham*, maj. 22,504

*Stevenson, George W. (*b.* 1938) *Lab., Stoke-on-Trent South*, maj. 18,303

Stewart, David J. (*b.* 1956) *Lab., Inverness East, Nairn and Lochaber*, maj. 2,339

Stewart, Ian (*b.* 1950) *Lab., Eccles*, maj. 21,916

Stinchcombe, Paul D. (*b.* 1962) *Lab., Wellingborough*, maj. 187

Stoate, Howard G. A. (*b.* 1954) *Lab., Dartford*, maj. 4,328

*Stott, Roger, CBE (*b.* 1943) *Lab., Wigan*, maj. 22,643

*Strang, Rt. Hon. Gavin S., PH.D. (*b.* 1943) *Lab., Edinburgh East and Musselburgh*, maj. 14,530

*Straw, Rt. Hon. J. W. (Jack) (*b.* 1946) *Lab., Blackburn*, maj. 14,451

*Streeter, Gary N. (*b.* 1955) *C., Devon South West*, maj. 7,433

Stringer, Graham E. (*b.* 1950) *Lab., Manchester Blackley*, maj. 19,588

Stuart, Mrs Gisela G. (*b.* 1955) *Lab., Birmingham Edgbaston*, maj. 4,842

Stunell, Andrew (*b.* 1942) *LD, Hazel Grove*, maj. 11,814

*Sutcliffe, Gerard (*b.* 1953) *Lab., Bradford South*, maj. 12,936

Swayne, Desmond A. (*b.* 1956) *C., New Forest West*, maj. 11,332

Swinney, John R. (*b.* 1964) *SNP, Tayside North*, maj. 4,160

Syms, Robert A. R. (*b.* 1956) *C., Poole*, maj. 5,298

*Tapsell, Sir Peter (*b.* 1930) *C., Louth and Horncastle*, maj. 6,900

Taylor, Ms Dari J. (*b.* 1944) *Lab., Stockton South*, maj. 11,585

Taylor, David L. (*b.* 1946) *Lab., Leicestershire North West*, maj. 13,219

*Taylor, Sir Edward (Teddy) (*b.* 1937) *C., Rochford and Southend East*, maj. 4,225

*Taylor, Ian C., MBE (*b.* 1945) *C., Esher and Walton*, maj. 14,528

*Taylor, Rt. Hon. John D. (*b.* 1937) *UUP, Strangford*, maj. 5,852

*Taylor, John M. (*b.* 1941) *C., Solihull*, maj. 11,397

*Taylor, Matthew O. J. (*b.* 1963) *LD, Truro and St Austell*, maj. 12,501

*Taylor, Rt. Hon. W. Ann (*b.* 1947) *Lab., Dewsbury*, maj. 8,323

*Temple-Morris, Peter (*b.* 1938) *Lab., Leominster*, maj. 8,835

Thomas, Gareth (*b.* 1954) *Lab., Clwyd West*, maj. 1,848

Thomas, Gareth R. (*b.* 1967) *Lab., Harrow West*, maj. 1,240

Thompson, William J. (*b.* 1939) *UUP, Tyrone West*, maj. 1,161

*Timms, Stephen C. (*b.* 1955) *Lab., East Ham*, maj. 19,358

*Tipping, S. P. (Paddy) (*b.* 1949) *Lab., Sherwood*, maj. 16,812

Todd, Mark W. (*b.* 1954) *Lab., Derbyshire South*, maj. 13,967

Tonge, Dr Jennifer L. (*b.* 1941) *LD, Richmond Park*, maj. 2,951

*Touhig, J. Donnelly (Don) (*b.* 1947) *Lab. Co-op., Islwyn*, maj. 23,931

*Townend, John E. (*b.* 1934) *C., Yorkshire East*, maj. 3,337

*Tredinnick, David A. S. (*b.* 1950) *C., Bosworth*, maj. 1,027

*Trend, Hon. Michael St J., CBE (*b.* 1952) *C., Windsor*, maj. 9,917

*Trickett, Jon H. (*b.* 1950) *Lab., Hemsworth*, maj. 23,992

*Trimble, Rt. Hon. W. David (*b.* 1944) *UUP, Upper Bann*, maj. 9,252

Truswell, Paul A. (*b.* 1955) *Lab., Pudsey*, maj. 6,207

*Turner, Dennis (*b.* 1942) *Lab. Co-op., Wolverhampton South East*, maj. 15,182

Turner, Desmond S. (*b.* 1939) *Lab., Brighton Kemptown*, maj. 3,534

Turner, Dr George (*b.* 1940) *Lab., Norfolk North West*, maj. 1,339

Twigg, J. Derek (*b.* 1959) *Lab., Halton*, maj. 23,650

Twigg, Stephen (*b.* 1966) *Lab., Enfield Southgate*, maj. 1,433

*Tyler, Paul A., CBE (*b.* 1941) *LD, Cornwall North*, maj. 13,933

*Tyrie, Andrew G. (*b.* 1957) *C., Chichester*, maj. 9,734

*Vaz, N. Keith A. S. (*b.* 1956) *Lab., Leicester East*, maj. 18,422

*Viggers, Peter J. (*b.* 1938) *C., Gosport*, maj. 6,258

Vis, R. J. (Rudi) (*b.* 1941) *Lab., Finchley and Golders Green*, maj. 3,189

*Walker, A. Cecil (*b.* 1924) *UUP, Belfast North*, maj. 13,024

*Wallace, James R. (*b.* 1954) *LD, Orkney and Shetland*, maj. 6,968

*Walley, Ms Joan L. (*b.* 1949) *Lab., Stoke-on-Trent North*, maj. 17,392

Walter, Robert J. (*b.* 1948) *C., Dorset North*, maj. 2,746

Ward, Ms Claire M. (*b.* 1972) *Lab., Watford*, maj. 5,792

*Wardle, Charles F. (*b.* 1939) *C., Bexhill and Battle*, maj. 11,100

*Wareing, Robert N. (*b.* 1930) *Lab., Liverpool West Derby*, maj. 25,965

*Waterson, Nigel C. (*b.* 1950) *C., Eastbourne*, maj. 1,994

Watts, David L. (*b.* 1951) *Lab., St Helens North*, maj. 23,417

Webb, Prof. Steven J. (*b.* 1965) *LD, Northavon*, maj. 2,137

*Wells, Bowen (*b.* 1935) *C., Hertford and Stortford*, maj. 6,885

*Welsh, Andrew P. (*b.* 1944) *SNP, Angus*, maj. 10,189

White, Brian A. R. (*b.* 1957) *Lab., Milton Keynes North East*, maj. 240

Whitehead, Alan P. V. (*b.* 1950) *Lab., Southampton Test*, maj. 13,684

*Whitney, Sir Raymond, OBE (*b.* 1930) *C., Wycombe,* maj. 2,370

*Whittingdale, John F. L., OBE (*b.* 1959) *C., Maldon and Chelmsford East,* maj. 10,039

*Wicks, Malcolm H. (*b.* 1947) *Lab., Croydon North,* maj. 18,398

*Widdecombe, Rt. Hon. Ann N. (*b.* 1947) *C., Maidstone and the Weald,* maj. 9,603

*Wigley, Rt. Hon. Dafydd (*b.* 1943) *PC, Caernarfon,* maj. 7,949

*Wilkinson, John A. D. (*b.* 1940) *C., Ruislip-Northwood,* maj. 7,794

*Willetts, David L. (*b.* 1956) *C., Havant,* maj. 3,729

*Williams, Rt. Hon. Alan J. (*b.* 1930) *Lab., Swansea West,* maj. 14,459

*Williams, Dr Alan W. (*b.* 1945) *Lab., Carmarthen East and Dinefwr,* maj. 3,450

Williams, Mrs Betty H. (*b.* 1944) *Lab., Conwy,* maj. 1,596

Willis, G. Philip (*b.* 1941) *LD, Harrogate and Knaresborough,* maj. 6,236

Wills, Michael D. (*b.* 1952) *Lab., Swindon North,* maj. 7,688

*Wilshire, David (*b.* 1943) *C., Spelthorne,* maj. 3,473

*Wilson, Brian D. H. (*b.* 1948) *Lab., Cunninghame North,* maj. 11,039

*Winnick, David J. (*b.* 1933) *Lab., Walsall North,* maj. 12,588

*Winterton, Mrs J. Ann (*b.* 1941) *C., Congleton,* maj. 6,130

*Winterton, Nicholas R. (*b.* 1938) *C., Macclesfield,* maj. 8,654

Winterton, Ms Rosalie (*b.* 1958) *Lab., Doncaster Central,* maj. 17,856

*Wise, Mrs Audrey (*b.* 1935) *Lab., Preston,* maj. 18,680

Wood, Michael R. (*b.* 1946) *Lab., Batley and Spen,* maj. 6,141

Woodward, Shaun A. (*b.* 1958) *C., Witney,* maj. 7,028

Woolas, Philip J. (*b.* 1959) *Lab., Oldham East and Saddleworth,* maj. 3,389

*Worthington, Anthony (*b.* 1941) *Lab., Clydebank and Milngavie,* maj. 13,320

*Wray, James (*b.* 1938) *Lab., Glasgow Baillieston,* maj. 14,840

Wright, Anthony D. (*b.* 1954) *Lab., Great Yarmouth,* maj. 8,668

*Wright, Anthony W., D.Phil. (*b.* 1948) *Lab., Cannock Chase,* maj. 14,478

Wyatt, Derek M. (*b.* 1949) *Lab., Sittingbourne and Sheppey,* maj. 1,929

*Yeo, Timothy S. K. (*b.* 1945) *C., Suffolk South,* maj. 4,175

*Young, Rt. Hon. Sir George, Bt. (*b.* 1941) *C., Hampshire North West,* maj. 11,551

BY-ELECTIONS SINCE THE GENERAL ELECTION (*see also* Stop-press)

UXBRIDGE
(31 July 1997)
*E.*57,733 *T.*55.2%

J. Randall, *C.*	16,288
A. Slaughter, *Lab.*	12,522
K. Kerr, *LD*	1,792
'Lord Sutch', *Loony*	396
Ms J. Leonard, *Soc.*	259
Ms F. Taylor, *BNP*	205
I. Anderson, *Nat. Dem.*	157
J. McCauley, *NF*	110
H. Middleton, *Original Lib. Party*	69
J. Feisenberger, *UK Ind.*	39
R. Carroll, *Emerald Rainbow Islands Dream Ticket*	30
C. majority	3,766

PAISLEY SOUTH
(6 November 1997)
*E.*54,040 *T.*42%

D. Alexander, *Lab.*	10,346
I. Blackford, *SNP*	7,615
Ms E. McCartin, *LD*	2,582
Ms S. Laidlaw, *C.*	1,643
J. Deighan, *ProLife*	578
F. Curran, *Soc. All. Fighting Corruption*	306
C. McLauchlan, *Scottish Ind. Lab.*	155
C. Herriot, *Soc. Lab.*	153
K. Blair, *NLP*	57
Lab. majority	2,731

BECKENHAM
(20 November 1997)
*E.*72,807 *T.*43.7%

Ms J. Lait, *C.*	13,162
R. Hughes, *Lab.*	11,935
Ms R. Vetterlein, *LD*	5,864
P. Rimmer, *Lib.*	330
J. McAuley, *NF*	267
L. Mead, *New Britain Ref.*	237
T. Campion, *Social Foundation*	69
J. Small, *NLP*	44
C. majority	1,227

WINCHESTER
(20 November 1997)
*E.*78,884 *T.*68.7%

M. Oaten, *LD*	37,006
G. Malone, *C.*	15,450
P. Davies, *Lab.*	944
R. Page, *Ref./UK Ind. Alliance*	521
'Lord' Sutch, *Loony*	316
R. Huggett, *Literal Dem.*	59
Ms R. Barry, *NLP*	48
R. Everest, *European C.*	40
LD majority	21,556

LEEDS CENTRAL
(10 June 1999)
*E.*66,983 *T.*19.6%

H. Benn, *Lab.*	6,361
P. Wild, *LD*	4,068
E. Wild, *C.*	1,618
Lab. majority	2,293

EDDISBURY
(22 July 1999)
*E.*67,086 *T.*51.4 %

S. O'Brien, *C.*	15,465
Ms M. Hanson, *Lab.*	13,859
P. Roberts, *LD*	4,757
A. Hope, *Loony*	238
R. Everest, *Ind. Euro C.*	98
Ms D. Grice, *NLP*	80
C. majority	1,606

General Election statistics

PRINCIPAL PARTIES IN PARLIAMENT SINCE 1970

	1970	1974 Feb.	1974 Oct.	1979	1983	1987	1992	1997
Conservative	330*	296	276	339	397	375	336	165
Labour	287	301	319	268	209	229	270	418
Liberal/LD	6	14	13	11	17	17	20	46
Social Democrat	—	1	—	—	6	5	—	—
Independent	5†	1	1	2	—	—	—	1
Plaid Cymru	—	2	3	2	2	3	4	4
Scottish Nationalist	1	7	11	2	2	3	3	6
Democratic Unionist	—	—	—	3	3	3	3	2
SDLP	—	1	1	1	1	3	4	3
Sinn Fein	—	—	—	—	1	1	—	2
Ulster Popular Unionist	—	—	—	—	1	1	1	—
Ulster Unionist‡	*	11	10	6	10	9	9	10
UK Unionist	—	—	—	—	—	—	—	1
The Speaker	1	1	1	1	1	1	1	1
Total	630	635	635	635	650	650	651	659

* Including 8 Ulster Unionists
† Comprising: Independent Labour 1, Independent Unity 1, Protestant Unity 1, Republican Labour 1, Unity 1
‡ Comprises:
   1974 (February) United Ulster Unionist Council 11
   1974 (October) United Ulster Unionist 10
   1979 Ulster Unionist 5, United Ulster Unionist 1
   1983 Official Unionist 10

PARLIAMENTS SINCE 1970

		Duration		
Assembled	Dissolved	yr	m.	d.
29 June 1970	8 February 1974	3	7	10
6 March 1974	20 September 1974	0	6	14
22 October 1974	7 April 1979	4	5	16
9 May 1979	13 May 1983	4	0	4
15 June 1983	18 May 1987	3	11	3
17 June 1987	16 March 1992	4	8	28
27 April 1992	8 April 1997	4	11	12
7 May 1997				

MAJORITIES IN THE COMMONS SINCE 1970

Year	Party	Maj.
1970	Conservative	31
1974 Feb.	No majority	
1974 Oct.	Labour	5
1979	Conservative	43
1983	Conservative	144
1987	Conservative	102
1992	Conservative	21
1997	Labour	178

VOTES CAST 1992 AND 1997

	1992	1997
Conservative	14,089,722	9,600,940
Labour	11,567,764	13,517,911
Liberal Democrats	6,027,552	5,243,440
Scottish Nationalist	629,564	622,260
Plaid Cymru	154,390	161,030
N. Ireland parties	740,859	780,920
Others	401,239	1,361,701
Total	33,619,090	31,287,702

DISTRIBUTION OF SEATS BY COUNTRY 1997

	England	Wales	Scotland	N. Ireland
Conservative	165	—	—	—
Labour	328	34	56	—
Lib. Dem.	34	2	10	—
SNP	—	—	6	—
Plaid Cymru	—	4	—	—
Other	2*	—	—	18

* Includes the Speaker

SIZE OF ELECTORATE 1997

England	36,806,557
Wales	2,222,533
Scotland	3,984,406
Northern Ireland	1,190,198
Total	44,203,694

PARLIAMENTARY CONSTITUENCIES AS AT 1 MAY 1997 (see also Stop-press)

The results of voting in each parliamentary division at the general election of 1 May 1997 are given below. The majority in the 1992 general election, and any by-election between 1987 and 1992, is given below the 1992 result where the constituency covers the same area as in 1992. Where the boundaries of a constituency have changed since 1992, a notional result for 1992 is given.

Symbols

E.   Total number of electors in the constituency at the 1997 general election

T.   Turnout of electors at the 1997 general election

*   Member of the last Parliament in unchanged constituency

†   Member of the last Parliament in different constituency or one affected by boundary changes

Abbreviations

All.	Alliance Party (NI)
C.	Conservative
DUP	Democratic Unionist Party
Green	Green Party
Ind.	Independent
Lab.	Labour
Lab. Co-op.	Labour Co-operative
LD	Liberal Democrat
PC	Plaid Cymru
SDLP	Social Democratic and Labour Party
SF	Sinn Fein
SNP	Scottish National Party
UKU	United Kingdom Unionist
UUP	Ulster Unionist Party
ACA	Anti-Child Abuse
ACC	Anti-Corruption Candidate
Albion	Albion Party
Alt.	Alternative
ANP	All Night Party
Anti-maj.	Independent Anti-majority Democracy
AS	Anti-sleaze
Barts	Independent Save Barts Candidate
BDP	British Democratic Party
Beanus	Space Age Superhero from Planet Beanus
Beaut.	Independently Beautiful Party
Bert.	Berties Party
BFAIR	British Freedom and Individual Rights
BHMBCM	Black Haired Medium Build Caucasian Male
BHR	British Home Rule
B. Ind.	Beaconsfield Independent: Unity Through Electoral Reform
BIPF	British Isles People First Party
BNP	British National Party
Bypass	Newbury Bypass Stop Construction Now
Byro	Lord Byro versus the Scallywag Tories
Care	Care in the Community
CASC	Conservatives Against the Single Currency
CFSS	Country Field and Shooting Sports
Ch. D.	Christian Democrat
Ch. Nat.	Christian Nationalist
Choice	People's Choice
Ch. P.	Christian Party
Ch. U.	Christian Unity
Comm. L.	Communist League
Comm. P.	Communist Party of Britain
Constit.	Constitutionalist
Consult.	Independent Democracy Means Consulting the People
CRP	Community Representative Party
CSSPP	Common Sense Sick of Politicians Party
Cvty	Conservatory
D. Nat.	Democratic Nationalist
Dream	Rainbow Dream Ticket Party
Dynamic	First Dynamic Party
EDP	English Democratic Party
Embryo	Anti-Abortion Euthanasia Embryo Experiments
EUP	European Unity Party
Fair	Building a Fair Society
FDP	Fancy Dress Party
Fellowship	Fellowship Party for Peace and Justice
FEP	Full Employment Party
FP	Freedom Party
Glow	Glow Bowling Party
GRLNSP	Green Referendum Lawless Naturally Street Party
Heart	Heart 106.2 Alien Party
Hemp	Hemp Coalition
HR	Human Rights '97
Hum.	Humanist Party
IAC	Independent Anti-Corruption in Government/TGWU
Ind. AFE	Independent Against a Federal Europe
Ind. BB	Independent Back to Basics
Ind. CRP	Independent Conservative Referendum Party
Ind. Dean	Independent Royal Forest of Dean
Ind. Dem.	Independent Democrat
Ind. ECR	Independent English Conservative and Referendum
Ind. Euro C.	Independent Euro Conservative
Ind. F.	Independent Forester
Ind. Green	Independent Green: Your Children's Future
Ind. Hum.	English Independent Humanist Party
Ind. Is.	Island Independent
Ind. JRP	Justice and Renewal Independent Party
Ind. No	Independent No to Europe
IZB	Islam Zinda Baad Platform
JP	Justice Party
Juice	Juice Party
KBF	Keep Britain Free and Independent Party
Lab. Change	Labour Time for Change Candidate
LC	Loyal Conservative
LCP	Legalize Cannabis Party
LGR	Local Government Reform
Lib.	Liberal
Loc.	Local
Logic	Logic Party Truth Only Allowed
Loony	Monster Raving Loony Party
Mal	Mal Voice of the People Party
Miss M.	Miss Moneypenny's Glamorous One Party
MK	Mebyon Kernow
Mongolian	Mongolian Barbeque Great Place to Party
MRAC	Multi-racial Anti-Corruption Alliance
Nat. Dem.	National Democrat
New Way	New Millennium New Way Hemp Candidate
NF	National Front
NIFT	Former Captain NI Football Team
NIP	Northern Ireland Party
NI Women	Northern Ireland Women's Coalition
NLP	Natural Law Party
NLPC	New Labour Party Candidate
None	None of the Above Parties
NPC	Non-party Conservative
Pacifist	Pacifist for Peace, Justice, Co-operation, Environment
PAYR	Protecting All Your Rights Locally Effectively
PF	Pathfinders
PLP	People's Labour Party
Plymouth	Plymouth First Group
PP	People's Party
PPP	People's Party Party
ProLife	ProLife Alliance
PUP	Progressive Unionist Party
RA	Residents Association
Rain. Is.	Rainbow Connection Your Island Candidate
Rain. Ref.	Rainbow Referendum
R. Alt.	Radical Alternative
Ref.	Referendum Party
Ren. Dem.	Renaissance Democrat
Rep. GB	Republican Party of Great Britain
Rights	Charter for Basic Rights
Ronnie	Ronnie the Rhino Party
Route 66	Route 66 Party Posse Party
Scrapit	Scrapit Stop Avon Ring Road Now
SCU	Scottish Conservative Unofficial
SEP	Socialist Equality Party
SFDC	Stratford First Democratic Conservative
SG	Sub-genus Party
Shields	Pro Interests of South Shields People
SIP	Sheffield Independent Party
SLI	Scottish Labour Independent
Slough	People in Slough Shunning Useless Politicians
SLU	Scottish Labour Unofficial
Soc.	Socialist Party
Soc. Dem.	Social Democrat
Soc. Lab.	Socialist Labour Party
SPGB	Socialist Party of Great Britain
Spts All.	Sportsman's Alliance: Anything but Mellor
SSA	Scottish Socialist Alliance
Stan	Happiness Stan's Freedom to Party Party
Teddy	Teddy Bear Alliance Party
Top	Top Choice Liberal Democrat
21st Cent.	21st Century Independent Foresters
UA	Universal Alliance
UK Ind.	UK Independence Party
UKPP	UK Pensioners Party
WCCC	West Cheshire College in Crisis Party
Wessex	Wessex Regionalist
WP	Workers' Party
WRP	Workers' Revolutionary Party

ENGLAND

ALDERSHOT
E.76,189   T. 71.07%
G. Howarth, *C.*	23,119
A. Collett, *LD*	16,498
T. Bridgeman, *Lab.*	13,057
J. Howe, *UK Ind.*	794
A. Pendragon, *Ind.*	361
Dr D. Stevens, *BNP*	322
C. majority 6,621	
(Boundary change: notional C.)	

ALDRIDGE-BROWNHILLS
E.62,441   T. 74.26%
*R. Shepherd, *C.*	21,856
J. Toth, *Lab.*	19,330
Ms C. Downie, *LD*	5,184
C. majority 2,526	
(April 1992, C. maj. 11,024)	

ALTRINCHAM AND SALE WEST
E.70,625   T. 73.32%
G. Brady, *C.*	22,348
Ms J. Baugh, *Lab.*	20,843
M. Ramsbottom, *LD*	6,535
A. Landes, *Ref.*	1,348
J. Stephens, *ProLife*	313
Dr R. Mrozinski, *UK Ind.*	270
J. Renwick, *NLP*	125
C. majority 1,505	
(Boundary change: notional C.)	

AMBER VALLEY
E.72,005   T. 76.07%
Ms J. Mallaber, *Lab.*	29,943
†P. Oppenheim, *C.*	18,330
R. Shelley, *LD*	4,219
Mrs I. McGibbon, *Ref.*	2,283
Lab. majority 11,613	
(Boundary change: notional C.)	

ARUNDEL AND SOUTH DOWNS
E.67,641   T. 75.90%
H. Flight, *C.*	27,251
J. Goss, *LD*	13,216
R. Black, *Lab.*	9,376
J. Herbert, *UK Ind.*	1,494
C. majority 14,035	
(Boundary change: notional C.)	

ASHFIELD
E.72,269   T. 70.02%
†G. Hoon, *Lab.*	32,979
M. Simmonds, *C.*	10,251
W. Smith, *LD*	4,882
M. Betts, *Ref.*	1,896
S. Belshaw, *BNP*	595
Lab. majority 22,728	
(Boundary change: notional Lab.)	

ASHFORD
E.74,149   T. 74.57%
D. Green, *C.*	22,899
J. Ennals, *Lab.*	17,544
J. Williams, *LD*	10,901
C. Cruden, *Ref.*	3,201
R. Boden, *Green*	660
S. Tyrell, *NLP*	89
C. majority 5,355	
(April 1992, C. maj. 17,359)	

ASHTON UNDER LYNE
E.72,206   T. 65.48%
†Rt. Hon. R. Sheldon, *Lab.*	31,919
R. Mayson, *C.*	8,954
T. Pickstone, *LD*	4,603
Mrs L. Clapham, *Ref.*	1,346
Prince Cymbal, *Loony*	458
Lab. majority 22,965	
(Boundary change: notional Lab.)	

AYLESBURY
E.79,047   T. 72.81%
†D. Lidington, *C.*	25,426
Ms S. Bowles, *LD*	17,007
R. Langridge, *Lab.*	12,759
M. John, *Ref.*	2,196
L. Sheaff, *NLP*	166
C. majority 8,419	
(Boundary change: notional C.)	

BANBURY
E.77,456   T. 75.46%
†A. Baldry, *C.*	25,076
Ms H. Peperell, *Lab.*	20,339
Mrs C. Bearder, *LD*	9,761
J. Ager, *Ref.*	2,245
Ms B. Cotton, *Green*	530
Mrs L. King, *UK Ind.*	364
I. Pearson, *NLP*	131
C. majority 4,737	
(Boundary change: notional C.)	

BARKING
E.53,682   T. 61.41%
†Mrs M. Hodge, *Lab.*	21,698
K. Langford, *C.*	5,802
M. Marsh, *LD*	3,128
C. Taylor, *Ref.*	1,283
M. Tolman, *BNP*	894
D. Mearns, *ProLife*	159
Lab. majority 15,896	
(Boundary change: notional Lab.)	

BARNSLEY CENTRAL
E.61,133   T. 59.68%
†E. Illsley, *Lab.*	28,090
S. Gutteridge, *C.*	3,589
D. Finlay, *LD*	3,481
J. Walsh, *Ref.*	1,325
Lab. majority 24,501	
(Boundary change: notional Lab.)	

BARNSLEY EAST AND MEXBOROUGH
E.67,840   T. 63.88%
†J. Ennis, *Lab.*	31,699
Miss J. Ellison, *C.*	4,936
D. Willis, *LD*	4,489
K. Capstick, *Soc. Lab.*	1,213
A. Miles, *Ref.*	797
Ms J. Hyland, *SEP*	201
Lab. majority 26,763	
(Boundary change: notional Lab.)	

BARNSLEY WEST AND PENISTONE
E.64,894   T. 65.04%
*M. Clapham, *Lab.*	25,017
P. Watkins, *C.*	7,750
Mrs W. Knight, *LD*	7,613
Mrs J. Miles, *Ref.*	1,828
Lab. majority 17,267	
(April 1992, Lab. maj. 14,504)	

BARROW AND FURNESS
E.66,960   T. 72.03%
*J. Hutton, *Lab.*	27,630
R. Hunt, *C.*	13,133
Mrs A. Metcalfe, *LD*	4,264
J. Hamzeian, *PLP*	1,995
D. Mitchell, *Ref.*	1,208
Lab. majority 14,497	
(April 1992, Lab. maj. 3,578)	

BASILDON
E.73,989   T. 71.74%
Ms A. Smith, *Lab. Co-op.*	29,646
J. Baron, *C.*	16,366
Ms L. Granshaw, *LD*	4,608
C. Robinson, *Ref.*	2,462
Lab. Co-op. majority 13,280	
(Boundary change: notional C.)	

BASINGSTOKE
E.77,035   T. 74.16%
†A. Hunter, *C.*	24,751
N. Lickley, *Lab.*	22,354
M. Rimmer, *LD*	9,714
E. Selim, *Ind.*	310
C. majority 2,397	
(Boundary change: notional C.)	

BASSETLAW
E.68,101   T. 70.37%
†J. Ashton, *Lab.*	29,298
M. Cleasby, *C.*	11,838
M. Kerrigan, *LD*	4,950
R. Graham, *Ref.*	1,838
Lab. majority 17,460	
(Boundary change: notional Lab.)	

BATH
E.70,815   T. 76.24%
†D. Foster, *LD*	26,169
Ms A. McNair, *C.*	16,850
T. Bush, *Lab.*	8,828
A. Cook, *Ref.*	1,192
R. Scrase, *Green*	580
P. Sandell, *UK Ind.*	315
N. Pullen, *NLP*	55
LD majority 9,319	
(Boundary change: notional LD)	

BATLEY AND SPEN
E.64,209   T. 73.14%
M. Wood, *Lab.*	23,213
†Mrs E. Peacock, *C.*	17,072
Mrs K. Pinnock, *LD*	4,133
E. Wood, *Ref.*	1,691
R. Smith, *BNP*	472
C. Lord, *Green*	384
Lab. majority 6,141	
(Boundary change: notional C.)	

BATTERSEA
E.66,928   T. 70.82%
M. Linton, *Lab.*	24,047
†J. Bowis, *C.*	18,687
Ms P. Keaveney, *LD*	3,482
M. Slater, *Ref.*	804
R. Banks, *UK Ind.*	250
J. Marshall, *Dream*	127
Lab. majority 5,360	
(Boundary change: notional C.)	

BEACONSFIELD
*E.*68,959   *T.*72.80%

D. Grieve, *C.*	24,709
P. Mapp, *LD*	10,722
A. Hudson, *Lab.*	10,063
H. Lloyd, *Ref.*	2,197
C. Story, *CASC*	1,434
C. Cooke, *UK Ind.*	451
Ms G. Duval, *ProLife*	286
T. Dyball, *NLP*	193
R. Matthews, *B. Ind.*	146
C. majority 13,987	
(Boundary change: notional C.)	

BECKENHAM
*E.*72,807   *T.*74.65%

†P. Merchant, *C.*	23,084
R. Hughes, *Lab.*	18,131
Ms R. Vetterlein, *LD*	9,858
L. Mead, *Ref.*	1,663
P. Rimmer, *Lib.*	720
C. Pratt, *UK Ind.*	506
J. Mcauley, *NF*	388
C. majority 4,953	
(Boundary change: notional C.)	
See also page 233	

BEDFORD
*E.*66,560   *T.*73.53%

P. Hall, *Lab.*	24,774
R. Blackman, *C.*	16,474
C. Noyce, *LD*	6,044
P. Conquest, *Ref.*	1,503
Ms P. Saunders, *NLP*	149
Lab. majority 8,300	
(Boundary change: notional C.)	

BEDFORDSHIRE MID
*E.*66,979   *T.*78.41%

J. Sayeed, *C.*	24,176
N. Mallett, *Lab.*	17,086
T. Hill, *LD*	8,823
Mrs S. Marler, *Ref.*	2,257
M. Lorys, *NLP*	174
C. majority 7,090	
(Boundary change: notional C.)	

BEDFORDSHIRE NORTH EAST
*E.*64,743   *T.*77.83%

†Rt. Hon. Sir N. Lyell, *C.*	22,311
J. Lehal, *Lab.*	16,428
P. Bristow, *LD*	7,179
J. Taylor, *Ref.*	2,490
L. Foley, *Ind. C.*	1,842
B. Bence, *NLP*	138
C. majority 5,883	
(Boundary change: notional C.)	

BEDFORDSHIRE SOUTH WEST
*E.*69,781   *T.*75.76%

†Sir D. Madel, *C.*	21,534
A. Date, *Lab.*	21,402
S. Owen, *LD*	7,559
Ms R. Hill, *Ref.*	1,761
T. Wise, *UK Ind.*	446
A. Le Carpentier, *NLP*	162
C. majority 132	
(Boundary change: notional C.)	

BERWICK-UPON-TWEED
*E.*56,428   *T.*74.08%

*A. Beith, *LD*	19,007
P. Brannen, *Lab.*	10,965

N. Herbert, *C.*	10,056
N. Lambton, *Ref.*	1,423
I. Dodds, *UK Ind.*	352
LD majority 8,042	
(April 1992, LD maj. 5,043)	

BETHNAL GREEN AND BOW
*E.*73,008   *T.*61.20%

Ms O. King, *Lab.*	20,697
K. Choudhury, *C.*	9,412
S. N. Islam, *LD*	5,361
D. King, *BNP*	3,350
T. Milson, *Lib.*	2,963
S. Osman, *Real Lab.*	1,117
S. Petter, *Green*	812
M. Abdullah, *Ref.*	557
A. Hamid, *Soc. Lab.*	413
Lab. majority 11,285	
(Boundary change: notional Lab.)	

BEVERLEY AND HOLDERNESS
*E.*71,916   *T.*73.62%

†J. Cran, *C.*	21,629
N. O'Neill, *Lab.*	20,818
J. Melling, *LD*	9,689
D. Barley, *UK Ind.*	695
S. Withers, *NLP*	111
C. majority 811	
(Boundary change: notional C.)	

BEXHILL AND BATTLE
*E.*65,584   *T.*74.70%

†C. Wardle, *C.*	23,570
Mrs K. Field, *LD*	12,470
R. Beckwith, *Lab.*	8,866
Mrs V. Thompson, *Ref.*	3,302
J. Pankhurst, *UK Ind.*	786
C. majority 11,100	
(Boundary change: notional C.)	

BEXLEYHEATH AND CRAYFORD
*E.*63,334   *T.*76.14%

N. Beard, *Lab.*	21,942
†D. Evennett, *C.*	18,527
Mrs F. Montford, *LD*	5,391
B. Thomas, *Ref.*	1,551
Ms P. Smith, *BNP*	429
W. Jenner, *UK Ind.*	383
Lab. majority 3,415	
(Boundary change: notional C.)	

BILLERICAY
*E.*76,550   *T.*72.40%

†Mrs T. Gorman, *C.*	22,033
P. Richards, *Lab.*	20,677
G. Williams, *LD*	8,763
B. Hughes, *LC*	3,377
J. Buchanan, *ProLife*	570
C. majority 1,356	
(Boundary change: notional C.)	

BIRKENHEAD
*E.*59,782   *T.*65.78%

*F. Field, *Lab.*	27,825
J. Crosby, *C.*	5,982
R. Wood, *LD*	3,548
M. Cullen, *Soc. Lab.*	1,168
R. Evans, *Ref.*	800
Lab. majority 21,843	
(April 1992, Lab. maj. 17,613)	

BIRMINGHAM EDGBASTON
*E.*70,204   *T.*69.03%

Mrs G. Stuart, *Lab.*	23,554

A. Marshall, *C.*	18,712
J. Gallagher, *LD*	4,691
J. Oakton, *Ref.*	1,065
D. Campbell, *BDP*	443
Lab. majority 4,842	
(Boundary change: notional C.)	

BIRMINGHAM ERDINGTON
*E.*66,380   *T.*60.87%

†R. Corbett, *Lab.*	23,764
A. Tompkins, *C.*	11,107
I. Garrett, *LD*	4,112
G. Cable, *Ref.*	1,424
Lab. majority 12,657	
(Boundary change: notional Lab.)	

BIRMINGHAM HALL GREEN
*E.*58,767   *T.*71.16%

S. McCabe, *Lab.*	22,372
*A. Hargreaves, *C.*	13,952
A. Dow, *LD*	4,034
P. Bennett, *Ref.*	1,461
Lab. majority 8,420	
(April 1992, C. maj. 3,665)	

BIRMINGHAM HODGE HILL
*E.*56,066   *T.*60.91%

*T. Davis, *Lab.*	22,398
E. Grant, *C.*	8,198
H. Thomas, *LD*	2,891
P. Johnson, *UK Ind.*	660
Lab. majority 14,200	
(April 1992, Lab. maj. 7,068)	

BIRMINGHAM LADYWOOD
*E.*70,013   *T.*54.24%

†Ms C. Short, *Lab.*	28,134
S. Vara, *C.*	5,052
S. S. Marwa, *LD*	3,020
Mrs R. Gurney, *Ref.*	1,086
A. Carmichael, *Nat. Dem.*	685
Lab. majority 23,082	
(Boundary change: notional Lab.)	

BIRMINGHAM NORTHFIELD
*E.*56,842   *T.*68.34%

†R. Burden, *Lab.*	22,316
A. Blumenthal, *C.*	10,873
M. Ashall, *LD*	4,078
D. Gent, *Ref.*	1,243
K. Axon, *BNP*	337
Lab. majority 11,443	
(Boundary change: notional Lab.)	

BIRMINGHAM PERRY BARR
*E.*71,031   *T.*64.60%

†J. Rooker, *Lab.*	28,921
A. Dunnett, *C.*	9,964
R. Hassall, *LD*	4,523
S. Mahmood, *Ref.*	843
A. Baxter, *Lib.*	718
L. Windridge, *BNP*	544
A. S. Panesar, *Fourth Party*	374
Lab. majority 18,957	
(Boundary change: notional Lab.)	

BIRMINGHAM SELLY OAK
*E.*72,049   *T.*70.16%

*Dr L. Jones, *Lab.*	28,121
G. Greene, *C.*	14,033
D. Osborne, *LD*	6,121
L. Marshall, *Ref.*	1,520
Dr G. Gardner, *ProLife*	417

P. Sherriff-Knowles, *Loony* 253
H. Meads, *NLP* 85
Lab. majority 14,088
(April 1992, Lab. maj. 2,060)

BIRMINGHAM SPARKBROOK AND
SMALL HEATH
*E.*73,130 *T.* 57.11%
†R. Godsiff, *Lab.* 26,841
K. Hardeman, *C.* 7,315
R. Harmer, *LD* 3,889
A. Clawley, *Green* 959
R. Dooley, *Ref.* 737
P. Patel, *Fourth Party* 538
R. M. Syed, *PAYR* 513
Ms S. Bi, *Ind.* 490
C. Wren, *Soc. Lab.* 483
Lab. majority 19,526
(Boundary change: notional Lab.)

BIRMINGHAM YARDLEY
*E.*53,058 *T.* 71.22%
*Ms E. Morris, *Lab.* 17,778
J. Hemming, *LD* 12,463
Mrs A. Jobson, *C.* 6,736
D. Livingston, *Ref.* 646
A. Ware, *UK Ind.* 164
Lab. majority 5,315
(April 1992, Lab. maj. 162)

BISHOP AUCKLAND
*E.*66,754 *T.* 68.88%
†Rt. Hon. D. Foster, *Lab.* 30,359
Mrs J. Fergus, *C.* 9,295
L. Ashworth, *LD* 4,223
D. Blacker, *Ref.* 2,104
Lab. majority 21,064
(Boundary change: notional Lab.)

BLABY
*E.*70,471 *T.* 76.05%
†A. Robathan, *C.* 24,564
R. Willmott, *Lab.* 18,090
G. Welsh, *LD* 8,001
R. Harrison, *Ref.* 2,018
J. Peacock, *BNP* 523
T. Stokes, *Ind.* 397
C. majority 6,474
(Boundary change: notional C.)

BLACKBURN
*E.*73,058 *T.* 65.01%
*J. Straw, *Lab.* 26,141
Ms S. Sidhu, *C.* 11,690
S. Fenn, *LD* 4,990
D. Bradshaw, *Ref.* 1,892
Mrs T. Wingfield, *Nat. Dem.* 671
Mrs H. Drummond, *Soc. Lab.* 637
R. Field, *Green* 608
Mrs M. Carmichael-Grimshaw,
    KBF 506
W. Batchelor, *CSSPP* 362
Lab. majority 14,451
(April 1992, Lab. maj. 6,027)

BLACKPOOL NORTH AND
FLEETWOOD
*E.*74,989 *T.* 71.67%
Mrs J. Humble, *Lab.* 28,051
†H. Elletson, *C.* 19,105
Mrs B. Hill, *LD* 4,600
Ms K. Stacey, *Ref.* 1,704
J. Ellis, *BNP* 288

Lab. majority 8,946
(Boundary change: notional C.)

BLACKPOOL SOUTH
*E.*75,720 *T.* 67.80%
G. Marsden, *Lab.* 29,282
R. Booth, *C.* 17,666
Mrs D. Holt, *LD* 4,392
Lab. majority 11,616
(Boundary change: notional C.)

BLAYDON
*E.*64,699 *T.* 70.98%
*J. McWilliam, *Lab.* 27,535
P. Maughan, *LD* 10,930
M. Watson, *C.* 6,048
R. Rook, *Ind. Lab.* 1,412
Lab. majority 16,605
(April 1992, Lab. maj. 13,343)

BLYTH VALLEY
*E.*61,761 *T.* 68.78%
*R. Campbell, *Lab.* 27,276
A. Lamb, *LD* 9,540
Mrs B. Musgrave, *C.* 5,666
Lab. majority 17,736
(April 1992, Lab. maj. 8,044)

BOGNOR REGIS AND
LITTLEHAMPTON
*E.*66,480 *T.* 69.86%
N. Gibb, *C.* 20,537
R. Nash, *Lab.* 13,216
Dr J. Walsh, *LD* 11,153
G. Stride, *UK Ind.* 1,537
C. majority 7,321
(Boundary change: notional C.)

BOLSOVER
*E.*66,476 *T.* 71.32%
†D. Skinner, *Lab.* 35,073
R. Harwood, *C.* 7,924
I. Cox, *LD* 4,417
Lab. majority 27,149
(Boundary change: notional Lab.)

BOLTON NORTH EAST
*E.*67,930 *T.* 72.44%
D. Crausby, *Lab.* 27,621
R. Wilson, *C.* 14,952
Dr E. Critchley, *LD* 4,862
D. Staniforth, *Ref.* 1,096
W. Kelly, *Soc. Lab.* 676
Lab. majority 12,669
(Boundary change: notional Lab.)

BOLTON SOUTH EAST
*E.*66,459 *T.* 65.23%
B. Iddon, *Lab.* 29,856
P. Carter, *C.* 8,545
F. Harasiwka, *LD* 3,805
W. Pickering, *Ref.* 973
L. Walch, *NLP* 170
Lab. majority 21,311
(Boundary change: notional Lab.)

BOLTON WEST
*E.*63,535 *T.* 77.37%
Ms R. Kelly, *Lab.* 24,342
†T. Sackville, *C.* 17,270
Mrs B. Ronson, *LD* 5,309
Mrs D. Kelly, *Soc. Lab.* 1,374
Mrs G. Frankl-Slater, *Ref.* 865

Lab. majority 7,072
(Boundary change: notional C.)

BOOTLE
*E.*57,284 *T.* 66.73%
†J. Benton, *Lab.* 31,668
R. Mathews, *C.* 3,247
K. Reid, *LD* 2,191
J. Elliott, *Ref.* 571
P. Glover, *Soc.* 420
S. Cohen, *NLP* 126
Lab. majority 28,421
(Boundary change: notional Lab.)

BOSTON AND SKEGNESS
*E.*67,623 *T.* 68.87%
†Sir R. Body, *C.* 19,750
P. McCauley, *Lab.* 19,103
J. Dodsworth, *LD* 7,721
C. majority 647
(Boundary change: notional C.)

BOSWORTH
*E.*68,113 *T.* 76.57%
†D. Tredinnick, *C.* 21,189
A. Furlong, *Lab.* 20,162
J. Ellis, *LD* 9,281
S. Halborg, *Ref.* 1,521
C. majority 1,027
(Boundary change: notional C.)

BOURNEMOUTH EAST
*E.*61,862 *T.* 70.20%
†D. Atkinson, *C.* 17,997
D. Eyre, *LD* 13,651
Mrs J. Stevens, *Lab.* 9,181
A. Musgrave-Scott, *Ref.* 1,808
K. Benney, *UK Ind.* 791
C. majority 4,346
(Boundary change: notional C.)

BOURNEMOUTH WEST
*E.*62,028 *T.* 66.22%
†J. Butterfill, *C.* 17,115
Ms J. Dover, *LD* 11,405
D. Gritt, *Lab.* 10,093
R. Mills, *Ref.* 1,910
Mrs L. Tooley, *UK Ind.* 281
J. Morse, *BNP* 165
A. Springham, *NLP* 103
C. majority 5,710
(Boundary change: notional C.)

BRACKNELL
*E.*79,292 *T.* 74.52%
†A. Mackay, *C.* 27,983
Ms A. Snelgrove, *Lab.* 17,596
A. Hilliar, *LD* 9,122
J. Tompkins, *New Lab.* 1,909
W. Cairns, *Ref.* 1,636
L. Boxall, *UK Ind.* 569
Ms D. Roberts, *ProLife* 276
C. majority 10,387
(Boundary change: notional C.)

BRADFORD NORTH
*E.*66,228 *T.* 63.26%
*T. Rooney, *Lab.* 23,493
R. Skinner, *C.* 10,723
T. Browne, *LD* 6,083
H. Wheatley, *Ref.* 1,227
W. Beckett, *Loony* 369
Lab. majority 12,770
(April 1992, Lab. maj. 7,664)

BRADFORD SOUTH
E.68,391   T.65.88%
*G. Sutcliffe, *Lab.*	25,558
Mrs A. Hawkesworth, *C.*	12,622
A. Wilson-Fletcher, *LD*	5,093
Mrs M. Kershaw, *Ref.*	1,785

Lab. majority 12,936
(April 1992, Lab. maj. 4,902)
(June 1994, Lab. maj. 9,664)

BRADFORD WEST
E.71,961   T.63.32%
M. Singh, *Lab.*	18,932
M. Riaz, *C.*	15,055
Mrs H. Wright, *LD*	6,737
A. Khan, *Soc. Lab.*	1,551
C. Royston, *Ref.*	1,348
J. Robinson, *Green*	861
G. Osborn, *BNP*	839
S. Shah, *Soc.*	245

Lab. majority 3,877
(April 1992, Lab. maj. 9,502)

BRAINTREE
E.72,772   T.76.37%
A. Hurst, *Lab.*	23,729
†Rt. Hon. A. Newton, *C.*	22,278
T. Ellis, *LD*	6,418
N. Westcott, *Ref.*	2,165
J. Abbott, *Green*	712
M. Nolan, *New Way*	274

Lab. majority 1,451
(Boundary change: notional C.)

BRENT EAST
E.53,548   T.65.87%
†K. Livingstone, *Lab.*	23,748
M. Francois, *C.*	7,866
I. Hunter, *LD*	2,751
S. Keable, *Soc. Lab.*	466
A. Shanks, *ProLife*	218
Ms C. Warrilo, *Dream*	120
D. Jenkins, *NLP*	103

Lab. majority 15,882
(Boundary change: notional Lab.)

BRENT NORTH
E.54,149   T.70.50%
B. Gardiner, *Lab.*	19,343
†Rt. Hon. Sir R. Boyson, *C.*	15,324
P. Lorber, *LD*	3,104
A. Davids, *NLP*	204
G. Clark, *Dream*	199

Lab. majority 4,019
(Boundary change: notional C.)

BRENT SOUTH
E.53,505   T.64.48%
†P. Boateng, *Lab.*	25,180
S. Jackson, *C.*	5,489
J. Brazil, *LD*	2,670
Ms J. Phythian, *Ref.*	497
D. Edler, *Green*	389
C. Howard, *Dream*	175
Ms A. Mahaldar, *NLP*	98

Lab. majority 19,691
(Boundary change: notional Lab.)

BRENTFORD AND ISLEWORTH
E.79,058   T.71.00%
Mrs A. Keen, *Lab.*	32,249
†N. Deva, *C.*	17,825
Dr G. Hartwell, *LD*	4,613

J. Bradley, *Green*	687
Mrs B. Simmerson, *UK Ind.*	614
M. Ahmed, *NLP*	147

Lab. majority 14,424
(Boundary change: notional C.)

BRENTWOOD AND ONGAR
E.66,005   T.76.85%
†E. Pickles, *C.*	23,031
Mrs E. Bottomley, *LD*	13,341
M. Young, *Lab.*	11,231
Mrs A. Kilmartin, *Ref.*	2,658
Capt. D. Mills, *UK Ind.*	465

C. majority 9,690
(Boundary change: notional C.)

BRIDGWATER
E.73,038   T.74.79%
*Rt. Hon. T. King, *C.*	20,174
M. Hoban, *LD*	18,378
R. Lavers, *Lab.*	13,519
Ms F. Evens, *Ref.*	2,551

C. majority 1,796
(April 1992, C. maj. 9,716)

BRIGG AND GOOLE
E.63,648   T.73.53%
I. Cawsey, *Lab.*	23,493
D. Stewart, *C.*	17,104
Mrs M.-R. Hardy, *LD*	4,692
D. Rigby, *Ref.*	1,513

Lab. majority 6,389
(Boundary change: notional C.)

BRIGHTON KEMPTOWN
E.65,147   T.70.81%
D. Turner, *Lab.*	21,479
†Sir A. Bowden, *C.*	17,945
C. Gray, *LD*	4,478
D. Inman, *Ref.*	1,526
Ms H. Williams, *Soc. Lab.*	316
J. Bowler, *NLP*	172
Ms L. Newman, *Loony*	123
R. Darlow, *Dream*	93

Lab. majority 3,534
(Boundary change: notional C.)

BRIGHTON PAVILION
E.66,431   T.73.69%
D. Lepper, *Lab. Co-op.*	26,737
†Sir D. Spencer, *C.*	13,556
K. Blanshard, *LD*	4,644
P. Stocken, *Ref.*	1,304
P. West, *Green*	1,249
R. Huggett, *Ind. C.*	1,098
F. Stevens, *UK Ind.*	179
R. Dobbs, *SG*	125
A. Card, *Dream*	59

Lab. Co-op. majority 13,181
(Boundary change: notional C.)

BRISTOL EAST
E.68,990   T.69.87%
†Ms J. Corston, *Lab.*	27,418
E. Vaizey, *C.*	11,259
P. Tyzack, *LD*	7,121
G. Philp, *Ref.*	1,479
P. Williams, *Soc. Lab.*	766
J. McLaggan, *NLP*	158

Lab. majority 16,159
(Boundary change: notional Lab.)

BRISTOL NORTH WEST
E.75,009   T.73.65%
D. Naysmith, *Lab. Co-op.*	27,575
†M. Stern, *C.*	16,193
I. Parry, *LD*	7,263
C. Horton, *Ind. Lab.*	1,718
J. Quintanilla, *Ref.*	1,609
G. Shorter, *Soc. Lab.*	482
S. Parnell, *BNP*	265
T. Leighton, *NLP*	140

Lab. Co-op. majority 11,382
(Boundary change: notional Lab. Co-op.)

BRISTOL SOUTH
E.72,393   T.68.87%
†Ms D. Primarolo, *Lab.*	29,890
M. Roe, *C.*	10,562
S. Williams, *LD*	6,691
D. Guy, *Ref.*	1,486
J. Boxall, *Green*	722
I. Marshall, *Soc.*	355
Louis Taylor, *Glow*	153

Lab. majority 19,328
(Boundary change: notional Lab.)

BRISTOL WEST
E.84,870   T.73.81%
Ms V. Davey, *Lab.*	22,068
†Rt. Hon. W. Waldegrave, *C.*	20,575
C. Boney, *LD*	17,551
Lady M. Beauchamp, *Ref.*	1,304
J. Quinnell, *Green*	852
R. Nurse, *Soc. Lab.*	244
J. Brierley, *NLP*	47

Lab. majority 1,493
(Boundary change: notional C.)

BROMLEY AND CHISLEHURST
E.71,104   T.74.17%
†Rt. Hon. E. Forth, *C.*	24,428
R. Yeldham, *Lab.*	13,310
Dr P. Booth, *LD*	12,530
R. Bryant, *UK Ind.*	1,176
Ms F. Speed, *Green*	640
M. Stoneman, *NF*	369
G. Aitman, *Lib.*	285

C. majority 11,118
(Boundary change: notional C.)

BROMSGROVE
E.67,744   T.77.07%
Miss J. Kirkbride, *C.*	24,620
P. McDonald, *Lab.*	19,725
Mrs J. Davy, *LD*	6,200
Mrs D. Winsor, *Ref.*	1,411
Mrs G. Wetton, *UK Ind.*	251

C. majority 4,895
(Boundary change: notional C.)

BROXBOURNE
E.66,720   T.70.41%
†Mrs M. Roe, *C.*	22,952
B. Coleman, *Lab.*	16,299
Mrs J. Davies, *LD*	5,310
D. Millward, *Ref.*	1,633
D. Bruce, *BNP*	610
B. Cheetham, *Third Way*	172

C. majority 6,653
(Boundary change: notional C.)

BROXTOWE
E.74,144   T.78.41%
N. Palmer, *Lab.*	27,343

†Sir J. Lester, C. 21,768
T. Miller, LD 6,934
R. Tucker, Ref. 2,092
Lab. majority 5,575
(Boundary change: notional C.)

BUCKINGHAM
E.62,945 T.78.48%
J. Bercow, C. 24,594
R. Lehmann, Lab. 12,208
N. Stuart, LD 12,175
Dr G. Clements, NLP 421
C. majority 12,386
(Boundary change: notional C.)

BURNLEY
E.67,582 T.66.95%
*P. Pike, Lab. 26,210
W. Wiggin, C. 9,148
G. Birtwistle, LD 7,877
R. Oakley, Ref. 2,010
Lab. majority 17,062
(April 1992, Lab. maj. 11,491)

BURTON
E.72,601 T.75.08%
Ms J. Dean, Lab. 27,810
†Sir I. Lawrence, C. 21,480
D. Fletcher, LD 4,617
K. Sharp, Nat. Dem. 604
Lab. majority 6,330
(Boundary change: notional C.)

BURY NORTH
E.70,515 T.78.07%
D. Chaytor, Lab. 28,523
*A. Burt, C. 20,657
N. Kenyon, LD 4,536
R. Hallewell, Ref. 1,337
Lab. majority 7,866
(April 1992, C. maj. 4,764)

BURY SOUTH
E.66,568 T.75.60%
I. Lewis, Lab. 28,658
†D. Sumberg, C. 16,225
V. D'Albert, LD 4,227
B. Slater, Ref. 1,216
Lab. majority 12,433
(Boundary change: notional C.)

BURY ST EDMUNDS
E.74,017 T.75.02%
D. Ruffley, C. 21,290
M. Ereira-Guyer, Lab. 20,922
D. Cooper, LD 10,102
I. McWhirter, Ref. 2,939
Mrs J. Lillis, NLP 272
C. majority 368
(Boundary change: notional C.)

CALDER VALLEY
E.74,901 T.75.39%
Ms C. McCafferty, Lab. 26,050
*Sir D. Thompson, C. 19,795
S. Pearson, LD 8,322
A. Mellor, Ref. 1,380
Ms V. Smith, Green 488
C. Jackson, BNP 431
Lab. majority 6,255
(April 1992, C. maj. 4,878)

CAMBERWELL AND PECKHAM
E.50,214 T.56.71%
†Ms H. Harman, Lab. 19,734

K. Humphreys, C. 3,383
N. Williams, LD 3,198
N. China, Ref. 692
Ms A. Ruddock, Soc. Lab. 685
G. Williams, Lib. 443
Ms J. Barker, Soc. 233
C. Eames, WRP 106
Lab. majority 16,351
(Boundary change: notional Lab.)

CAMBRIDGE
E.71,669 T.71.63%
*Mrs A. Campbell, Lab. 27,436
D. Platt, C. 13,299
G. Heathcock, LD 8,287
W. Burrows, Ref. 1,262
Ms M. Wright, Green 654
Ms A. Johnstone, ProLife 191
R. Athow, WRP 107
Ms P. Gladwin, NLP 103
Lab. majority 14,137
(April 1992, Lab. maj. 580)

CAMBRIDGESHIRE NORTH EAST
E.76,056 T.72.87%
†M. Moss, C. 23,855
Mrs V. Bucknor, Lab. 18,754
A. Nash, LD 9,070
M. Bacon, Ref. 2,636
C. Bennett, Soc. Lab. 851
L. Leighton, NLP 259
C. majority 5,101
(Boundary change: notional C.)

CAMBRIDGESHIRE NORTH WEST
E.65,791 T.74.20%
†Rt. Hon. Dr B. Mawhinney, C. 23,488
L. Steptoe, Lab. 15,734
Mrs B. McCoy, LD 7,388
A.Watt, Ref. 1,939
W. Wyatt, UK Ind. 269
C. majority 7,754
(Boundary change: notional C.)

CAMBRIDGESHIRE SOUTH
E.69,850 T.76.85%
A. Lansley, C. 22,572
J. Quinlan, LD 13,860
A. Gray, Lab. 13,485
R. Page, Ref. 3,300
D. Norman, UK Ind. 298
F. Chalmers, NLP 168
C. majority 8,712
(Boundary change: notional C.)

CAMBRIDGESHIRE SOUTH EAST
E.75,666 T.75.08%
†J. Paice, C. 24,397
R. Collinson, Lab. 15,048
Ms S. Brinton, LD 14,246
J. Howlett, Ref. 2,838
K. Lam, Fair 167
P. While, NLP 111
C. majority 9,349
(Boundary change: notional C.)

CANNOCK CHASE
E.72,362 T.72.37%
†Dr A. Wright, Lab. 28,705
J. Backhouse, C. 14,227
R. Kirby, LD 4,537
P. Froggatt, Ref. 1,663

W. Hurley, New Lab. 1,615
M. Conroy, Soc. Lab. 1,120
M. Hartshorn, Loony 499
Lab. majority 14,478
(Boundary change: notional Lab.)

CANTERBURY
E.74,548 T.72.58%
†J. Brazier, C. 20,913
Ms C. Hall, Lab. 16,949
M. Vye, LD 12,854
J. Osborne, Ref. 2,460
G. Meaden, Green 588
J. Moore, UK Ind. 281
A. Pringle, NLP 64
C. majority 3,964
(Boundary change: notional C.)

CARLISLE
E.59,917 T.72.78%
†E. Martlew, Lab. 25,031
R. Lawrence, C. 12,641
C. Mayho, LD 4,576
A. Fraser, Ref. 1,233
W. Stevens, NLP 126
Lab. majority 12,390
(Boundary change: notional Lab.)

CARSHALTON AND
WALLINGTON
E.66,038 T.73.33%
T. Brake, LD 18,490
*N. Forman, C. 16,223
A. Theobald, Lab. 11,565
J. Storey, Ref. 1,289
P. Hickson, Green 377
G. Ritchie, BNP 261
L. Povey, UK Ind. 218
LD majority 2,267
(April 1992, C. maj. 9,943)

CASTLE POINT
E.67,146 T.72.34%
Ms C. Butler, Lab. 20,605
*Dr R. Spink, C. 19,489
D. Baker, LD 4,477
H. Maulkin, Ref. 2,700
Miss L. Kendall, Consult. 1,301
Lab. majority 1,116
(April 1992, C. maj. 16,830)

CHARNWOOD
E.72,692 T.77.28%
†Rt. Hon. S. Dorrell, C. 26,110
D. Knaggs, Lab. 20,210
R. Wilson, LD 7,224
H. Meechan, Ref. 2,104
M. Palmer, BNP 525
C. majority 5,900
(Boundary change: notional C.)

CHATHAM AND AYLESFORD
E.69,172 T.71.07%
J. Shaw, Lab. 21,191
R. Knox-Johnston, C. 18,401
R. Murray, LD 7,389
K. Riddle, Ref. 1,538
A. Harding, UK Ind. 493
T. Martel, NLP 149
Lab. majority 2,790
(Boundary change: notional C.)

CHEADLE
E.67,627   T.77.58%
†S. Day, C.	22,944
Mrs P. Calton, LD	19,755
P. Diggett, Lab.	8,253
P. Brook, Ref.	1,511

C. majority 3,189
(Boundary change: notional C.)

CHELMSFORD WEST
E.76,086   T.76.99%
†S. Burns, C.	23,781
M. Bracken, LD	17,090
Dr R. Chad, Lab.	15,436
T. Smith, Ref.	1,536
G. Rumens, Green	411
M. Levin, UK Ind.	323

C. majority 6,691
(Boundary change: notional C.)

CHELTENHAM
E.67,950   T.74.03%
†N. Jones, LD	24,877
J. Todman, C.	18,232
B. Leach, Lab.	5,100
Mrs A. Powell, Ref.	1,065
K. Hanks, Loony	375
G. Cook, UK Ind.	302
Ms A. Harriss, ProLife	245
Ms S. Brighouse, NLP	107

LD majority 6,645
(Boundary change: notional LD)

CHESHAM AND AMERSHAM
E.69,244   T.75.38%
†Mrs C. Gillan, C.	26,298
M. Brand, LD	12,439
P. Farrelly, Lab.	10,240
P. Andrews, Ref.	2,528
C. Shilson, UK Ind.	618
H. Godfrey, NLP	74

C. majority 13,859
(Boundary change: notional C.)

CHESTER, CITY OF
E.71,730   T.78.43%
Ms C. Russell, Lab.	29,806
†G. Brandreth, C.	19,253
D. Simpson, LD	5,353
R. Mullen, Ref.	1,487
I. Sanderson, Loony	204
J. Gerrard, WCCC	154

Lab. majority 10,553
(Boundary change: notional C.)

CHESTERFIELD
E.72,472   T.70.91%
*Rt. Hon. A. Benn, Lab.	26,105
A. Rogers, LD	20,330
M. Potter, C.	4,752
N. Scarth, Ind. OAP	202

Lab. majority 5,775
(April 1992, Lab. maj. 6,414)

CHICHESTER
E.74,489   T.74.88%
A. Tyrie, C.	25,895
Prof. P. Gardiner, LD	16,161
C. Smith, Lab.	9,605
D. Denny, Ref.	3,318
J. Rix, UK Ind.	800

C. majority 9,734
(Boundary change: notional C.)

CHINGFORD AND WOODFORD
GREEN
E.62,904   T.70.66%
†I. Duncan Smith, C.	21,109
T. Hutchinson, Lab.	15,395
G. Seeff, LD	6,885
A. Gould, BNP	1,059

C. majority 5,714
(Boundary change: notional C.)

CHIPPING BARNET
E.69,049   T.71.78%
†Sir S. Chapman, C.	21,317
G. Cooke, Lab.	20,282
S. Hooker, LD	6,121
V. Ribekow, Ref.	1,190
B. Miskin, Loony	253
B. Scallan, ProLife	243
Ms D. Dirksen, NLP	159

C. majority 1,035
(Boundary change: notional C.)

CHORLEY
E.74,387   T.77.58%
L. Hoyle, Lab.	30,607
†D. Dover, C.	20,737
S. Jones, LD	4,900
A. Heaton, Ref.	1,319
P. Leadbetter, NLP	143

Lab. majority 9,870
(Boundary change: notional C.)

CHRISTCHURCH
E.71,488   T.78.61%
C. Chope, C.	26,095
†Mrs D. Maddock, LD	23,930
C. Mannan, Lab.	3,884
R. Spencer, Ref.	1,684
R. Dickinson, UK Ind.	606

C. majority 2,165
(Boundary change: notional C.)

CITIES OF LONDON AND
WESTMINSTER
E.69,047   T.58.16%
†Rt. Hon. P. Brooke, C.	18,981
Ms K. Green, Lab.	14,100
M. Dumigan, LD	4,933
Sir A. Walters, Ref.	1,161
Ms P. Wharton, Barts	266
C. Merton, UK Ind.	215
R. Johnson, NLP	176
N. Walsh, Loony	138
G. Webster, Hemp	112
J. Sadowitz, Dream	73

C. majority 4,881
(Boundary change: notional C.)

CLEETHORPES
E.68,763   T.73.40%
Ms S. McIsaac, Lab.	26,058
†M. Brown, C.	16,882
K. Melton, LD	5,746
J. Berry, Ref.	1,787

Lab. majority 9,176
(Boundary change: notional C.)

COLCHESTER
E.74,743   T.69.58%
R. Russell, LD	17,886
S. Shakespeare, C.	16,305
R. Green, Lab.	15,891
J. Hazell, Ref.	1,776

Ms L. Basker, NLP	148

LD majority 1,581
(Boundary change: notional C.)

COLNE VALLEY
E.73,338   T.76.92%
Ms K. Mountford, Lab.	23,285
*G. Riddick, C.	18,445
N. Priestley, LD	12,755
A. Brooke, Soc. Lab.	759
A. Cooper, Green	493
J. Nunn, UK Ind.	478
Ms M. Staniforth, Loony	196

Lab. majority 4,840
(April 1992, C. maj. 7,225)

CONGLETON
E.68,873   T.77.56%
†Mrs A. Winterton, C.	22,012
Mrs J. Walmsley, LD	15,882
Ms H. Scholey, Lab.	14,714
J. Lockett, UK Ind.	811

C. majority 6,130
(Boundary change: notional C.)

COPELAND
E.54,263   T.76.19%
*Rt. Hon. Dr J. Cunningham, Lab.	24,025
A. Cumpsty, C.	12,081
R. Putnam, LD	3,814
C. Johnston, Ref.	1,036
G. Hanratty, ProLife	389

Lab. majority 11,944
(April 1992, Lab. maj. 2,439)

CORBY
E.69,252   T.77.91%
P. Hope, Lab. Co-op.	29,888
*W. Powell, C.	18,028
I. Hankinson, LD	4,045
S. Riley-Smith, Ref.	1,356
I. Gillman, UK Ind.	507
Ms J. Bence, NLP	133

Lab. Co-op. majority 11,860
(April 1992, C. maj. 342)

CORNWALL NORTH
E.80,076   T.73.16%
*P. Tyler, LD	31,186
N. Linacre, C.	17,253
Ms A. Lindo, Lab.	5,523
Ms F. Odam, Ref.	3,636
J. Bolitho, MK	645
R. Winfield, Lib.	186
N. Cresswell, NLP	152

LD majority 13,933
(April 1992, LD maj. 1,921)

CORNWALL SOUTH EAST
E.75,825   T.75.74%
C. Breed, LD	27,044
W. Lightfoot, C.	20,564
Mrs D. Kirk, Lab.	7,358
J. Wonnacott, UK Ind.	1,428
P. Dunbar, MK	573
W. Weights, Lib.	268
Ms M. Hartley, NLP	197

LD majority 6,480
(April 1992, C. maj. 7,704)

COTSWOLD
E.67,333   T.75.92%
†G. Clifton-Brown, C.	23,698

D. Gayler, *LD* 11,733
D. Elwell, *Lab.* 11,608
R. Lowe, *Ref.* 3,393
Ms V. Michael, *Green* 560
H. Brighouse, *NLP* 129
C. majority 11,965
(Boundary change: notional C.)

COVENTRY NORTH EAST
*E.*74,274   *T.*64.74%
†R. Ainsworth, *Lab.* 31,856
M. Burnett, *C.* 9,287
G. Sewards, *LD* 3,866
N. Brown, *Lib.* 1,181
R. Hurrell, *Ref.* 1,125
H. Khamis, *Soc. Lab.* 597
C. Sidwell, *Dream* 173
Lab. majority 22,569
(Boundary change: notional Lab.)

COVENTRY NORTH WEST
*E.*76,439   *T.*71.07%
†G. Robinson, *Lab.* 30,901
P. Bartlett, *C.* 14,300
Dr N. Penlington, *LD* 5,690
D. Butler, *Ref.* 1,269
D. Spencer, *Soc. Lab.* 940
R. Wheway, *Lib.* 687
P. Mills, *ProLife* 359
L. Francis, *Dream* 176
Lab. majority 16,601
(Boundary change: notional Lab.)

COVENTRY SOUTH
*E.*71,826   *T.*69.79%
†J. Cunningham, *Lab.* 25,511
P. Ivey, *C.* 14,558
G. MacDonald, *LD* 4,617
D. Nellist, *Soc.* 3,262
P. Garratt, *Ref.* 943
R. Jenking, *Lib.* 725
J. Astbury, *BNP* 328
Ms A.-M. Bradshaw, *Dream* 180
Lab. majority 10,953
(Boundary change: notional C.)

CRAWLEY
*E.*69,040   *T.*73.03%
Mrs L. Moffatt, *Lab.* 27,750
Miss J. Crabb, *C.* 16,043
H. de Souza, *LD* 4,141
R. Walters, *Ref.* 1,931
E. Saunders, *UK Ind.* 322
A. Kahn, *JP* 230
Lab. majority 11,707
(Boundary change: notional C.)

CREWE AND NANTWICH
*E.*68,694   *T.*73.67%
†Mrs G. Dunwoody, *Lab.* 29,460
M. Loveridge, *C.* 13,662
D. Cannon, *LD* 5,940
P. Astbury, *Ref.* 1,543
Lab. majority 15,798
(Boundary change: notional Lab.)

CROSBY
*E.*57,190   *T.*77.18%
Ms C. Curtis-Tansley, *Lab.* 22,549
†Sir M. Thornton, *C.* 15,367
P. McVey, *LD* 5,080
J. Gauld, *Ref.* 813
J. Marks, *Lib.* 233

W. Hite, *NLP* 99
Lab. majority 7,182
(Boundary change: notional C.)

CROYDON CENTRAL
*E.*80,152   *T.*69.62%
G. Davies, *Lab.* 25,432
†D. Congdon, *C.* 21,535
G. Schlich, *LD* 6,061
C. Cook, *Ref.* 1,886
M.-S. Barnsley, *Green* 595
J. Woollcott, *UK Ind.* 290
Lab. majority 3,897
(Boundary change: notional C.)

CROYDON NORTH
*E.*77,063   *T.*68.21%
†M. Wicks, *Lab.* 32,672
I. Martin, *C.* 14,274
M. Morris, *LD* 4,066
R. Billis, *Ref.* 1,155
J. Feisenberger, *UK Ind.* 396
Lab. majority 18,398
(Boundary change: notional C.)

CROYDON SOUTH
*E.*73,787   *T.*73.45%
†R. Ottaway, *C.* 25,649
C. Burling, *Lab.* 13,719
S. Gauge, *LD* 11,441
A. Barber, *Ref.* 2,631
P. Ferguson, *BNP* 354
A. Harker, *UK Ind.* 309
M. Samuel, *Choice* 96
C. majority 11,930
(Boundary change: notional C.)

DAGENHAM
*E.*58,573   *T.*61.74%
†Mrs J. Church, *Lab.* 23,759
J. Fairrie, *C.* 6,705
T. Dobrashian, *LD* 2,704
S. Kraft, *Ref.* 1,411
W. Binding, *BNP* 900
R. Dawson, *Ind.* 349
M. Hipperson, *Nat. Dem.* 183
Ms K. Goble, *ProLife* 152
Lab. majority 17,054
(Boundary change: notional Lab.)

DARLINGTON
*E.*65,140   *T.*73.95%
*A. Milburn, *Lab.* 29,658
P. Scrope, *C.* 13,633
L. Boxell, *LD* 3,483
M. Blakey, *Ref.* 1,399
Lab. majority 16,025
(April 1992, Lab. maj. 2,798)

DARTFORD
*E.*69,726   *T.*74.57%
H. Stoate, *Lab.* 25,278
†R. Dunn, *C.* 20,950
Mrs D. Webb, *LD* 4,827
P. McHale, *BNP* 428
P. Homden, *FDP* 287
J. Pollitt, *Ch. D.* 228
Lab. majority 4,328
(Boundary change: notional C.)

DAVENTRY
*E.*80,151   *T.*77.04%
†T. Boswell, *C.* 28,615

K. Ritchie, *Lab.* 21,237
J. Gordon, *LD* 9,233
Mrs B. Russocki, *Ref.* 2,018
B. Mahoney, *UK Ind.* 443
R. France, *NLP* 204
C. majority 7,378
(Boundary change: notional C.)

DENTON AND REDDISH
*E.*68,866   *T.*66.92%
†A. Bennett, *Lab.* 30,137
Ms B. Nutt, *C.* 9,826
I. Donaldson, *LD* 6,121
Lab. majority 20,311
(Boundary change: notional Lab.)

DERBY NORTH
*E.*76,116   *T.*73.76%
R. Laxton, *Lab.* 29,844
*Rt. Hon. G. Knight, *C.* 19,229
R. Charlesworth, *LD* 5,059
P. Reynolds, *Ref.* 1,816
J. Waters, *ProLife* 195
Lab. majority 10,615
(April 1992, C. maj. 4,453)

DERBY SOUTH
*E.*76,386   *T.*67.84%
†Rt. Hon. Mrs M. Beckett, *Lab.* 29,154
J. Arain, *C.* 13,048
J. Beckett, *LD* 7,438
J. Browne, *Ref.* 1,862
R. Evans, *Nat. Dem.* 317
Lab. majority 16,106
(Boundary change: notional Lab.)

DERBYSHIRE NORTH EAST
*E.*71,653   *T.*72.54%
*H. Barnes, *Lab.* 31,425
S. Elliott, *C.* 13,104
S. Hardy, *LD* 7,450
Lab. majority 18,321
(April 1992, Lab. maj. 6,270)

DERBYSHIRE SOUTH
*E.*76,672   *T.*78.21%
M. Todd, *Lab.* 32,709
†Mrs E. Currie, *C.* 18,742
R. Renold, *LD* 5,408
R. North, *Ref.* 2,491
Dr I. Crompton, *UK Ind.* 617
Lab. majority 13,967
(Boundary change: notional C.)

DERBYSHIRE WEST
*E.*72,716   *T.*78.23%
†P. McLoughlin, *C.* 23,945
S. Clamp, *Lab.* 19,060
C. Seeley, *LD* 9,940
J. Gouriet, *Ref.* 2,499
G. Meynell, *Ind. Green* 593
H. Price, *UK Ind.* 484
N. Delves, *Loony* 281
M. Kyslun, *Ind. BB* 81
C. majority 4,885
(Boundary change: notional C.)

DEVIZES
*E.*80,383   *T.*74.69%
†Rt. Hon. M. Ancram, *C.* 25,710
A. Vickers, *LD* 15,928
F. Jeffrey, *Lab.* 14,551
J. Goldsmith, *Ref.* 3,021

S. Oram, *UK Ind.* — 622
S. Haysom, *NLP* — 204
C. majority 9,782
(Boundary change: notional C.)

DEVON EAST
*E.*69,094   *T.*76.06%
†Rt. Hon. Sir P. Emery, *C.* — 22,797
Miss R. Trethewey, *LD* — 15,308
A. Siantonas, *Lab.* — 9,292
W. Dixon, *Ref.* — 3,200
G. Halliwell, *Lib.* — 1,363
C. Giffard, *UK Ind.* — 459
G. Needs, *Nat. Dem.* — 131
C. majority 7,489
(Boundary change: notional C.)

DEVON NORTH
*E.*70,350   *T.*77.94%
†N. Harvey, *LD* — 27,824
R. Ashworth, *C.* — 21,643
Mrs E. Brenton, *Lab.* — 5,367
LD majority 6,181
(Boundary change: notional LD)

DEVON SOUTH WEST
*E.*69,293   *T.*76.22%
†G. Streeter, *C.* — 22,695
C. Mavin, *Lab.* — 15,262
K. Baldry, *LD* — 12,542
R. Sadler, *Ref.* — 1,668
Mrs H. King, *UK Ind.* — 491
J. Hyde, *NLP* — 159
C. majority 7,433
(Boundary change: notional C.)

DEVON WEST AND TORRIDGE
*E.*75,919   *T.*77.91%
J. Burnett, *LD* — 24,744
I. Liddell-Grainger, *C.* — 22,787
D. Brenton, *Lab.* — 7,319
R. Lea, *Ref.* — 1,946
M. Jackson, *UK Ind.* — 1,841
M. Pithouse, *Lib.* — 508
LD majority 1,957
(Boundary change: notional C.)

DEWSBURY
*E.*61,523   *T.*70.01%
†Mrs A. Taylor, *Lab.* — 21,286
Dr P. McCormick, *C.* — 12,963
K. Hill, *LD* — 4,422
Ms F. Taylor, *BNP* — 2,232
Ms W. Goff, *Ref.* — 1,019
D. Daniel, *Ind. Lab.* — 770
I. McCourtie, *Green* — 383
Lab. majority 8,323
(Boundary change: notional Lab.)

DONCASTER CENTRAL
*E.*67,965   *T.*63.92%
Ms R. Winterton, *Lab.* — 26,961
D. Turtle, *C.* — 9,105
S. Tarry, *LD* — 4,091
M. Cliff, *Ref.* — 1,273
M. Kenny, *Soc. Lab.* — 854
J. Redden, *ProLife* — 697
P. Davies, *UK Ind.* — 462
Lab. majority 17,856
(April 1992, Lab. maj. 10,682)

DONCASTER NORTH
*E.*63,019   *T.*63.30%
†K. Hughes, *Lab.* — 27,843

P. Kennerley, *C.* — 5,906
M. Cook, *LD* — 3,369
R. Thornton, *Ref.* — 1,589
M. Swan, *AS Lab.* — 1,181
Lab. majority 21,937
(Boundary change: notional Lab.)

DON VALLEY
*E.*65,643   *T.*66.35%
Ms C. Flint, *Lab.* — 25,376
Mrs C. Gledhill, *C.* — 10,717
P. Johnston, *LD* — 4,238
P. Davis, *Ref.* — 1,379
N. Ball, *Soc. Lab.* — 1,024
S. Platt, *Green* — 493
Ms C. Johnson, *ProLife* — 330
Lab. majority 14,659
(Boundary change: notional Lab.)

DORSET MID AND POOLE NORTH
*E.*67,049   *T.*75.67%
C. Fraser, *C.* — 20,632
A. Leaman, *LD* — 19,951
D. Collis, *Lab.* — 8,014
D. Nabarro, *Ref.* — 2,136
C. majority 681
(Boundary change: notional C.)

DORSET NORTH
*E.*68,923   *T.*76.30%
R. Walter, *C.* — 23,294
Mrs P. Yates, *LD* — 20,548
J. Fitzmaurice, *Lab.* — 5,380
Mrs M. Evans, *Ref.* — 2,564
Revd D. Wheeler, *UK Ind.* — 801
C. majority 2,746
(Boundary change: notional C.)

DORSET SOUTH
*E.*66,318   *T.*74.16%
†I. Bruce, *C.* — 17,755
J. Knight, *Lab.* — 17,678
M. Plummer, *LD* — 9,936
P. McAndrew, *Ref.* — 2,791
Capt. M. Shakesby, *UK Ind.* — 861
G. Napper, *NLP* — 161
C. majority 77
(Boundary change: notional C.)

DORSET WEST
*E.*70,369   *T.*76.10%
O. Letwin, *C.* — 22,036
R. Legg, *LD* — 20,196
R. Bygraves, *Lab.* — 9,491
P. Jenkins, *UK Ind.* — 1,590
M. Griffiths, *NLP* — 239
C. majority 1,840
(Boundary change: notional C.)

DOVER
*E.*68,669   *T.*78.93%
G. Prosser, *Lab.* — 29,535
†D. Shaw, *C.* — 17,796
M. Corney, *LD* — 4,302
Mrs S. Anderson, *Ref.* — 2,124
C. Hyde, *UK Ind.* — 443
Lab. majority 11,739
(Boundary change: notional C.)

DUDLEY NORTH
*E.*68,835   *T.*69.45%
R. Cranston, *Lab.* — 24,471
C. MacNamara, *C.* — 15,014

G. Lewis, *LD* — 3,939
M. Atherton, *Soc. Lab.* — 2,155
S. Bavester, *Ref.* — 1,201
G. Cartwright, *NF* — 559
S. Darby, *Nat. Dem.* — 469
Lab. majority 9,457
(Boundary change: notional Lab.)

DUDLEY SOUTH
*E.*66,731   *T.*71.78%
†I. Pearson, *Lab.* — 27,124
M. Simpson, *C.* — 14,097
R. Burt, *LD* — 5,214
C. Birch, *Ref.* — 1,467
Lab. majority 13,027
(Boundary change: notional Lab.)

DULWICH AND WEST NORWOOD
*E.*69,655   *T.*65.49%
†Ms T. Jowell, *Lab.* — 27,807
R. Gough, *C.* — 11,038
Mrs S. Kramer, *LD* — 4,916
B. Coles, *Ref.* — 897
Dr A. Goldie, *Lib.* — 587
D. Goodman, *Dream* — 173
E. Pike, *UK Ind.* — 159
Capt. Rizz, *Rizz Party* — 38
Lab. majority 16,769
(Boundary change: notional Lab.)

DURHAM NORTH
*E.*67,891   *T.*69.48%
†G. Radice, *Lab.* — 33,142
M. Hardy, *C.* — 6,843
B. Moore, *LD* — 5,225
I. Parkin, *Ref.* — 1,958
Lab. majority 26,299
(Boundary change: notional Lab.)

DURHAM NORTH WEST
*E.*67,156   *T.*68.97%
†Miss H. Armstrong, *Lab.* — 31,855
Mrs L. St J. Howe, *C.* — 7,101
A. Gillings, *LD* — 4,991
R. Atkinson, *Ref.* — 2,372
Lab. majority 24,754
(Boundary change: notional Lab.)

DURHAM, CITY OF
*E.*69,340   *T.*70.86%
*G. Steinberg, *Lab.* — 31,102
R. Chalk, *C.* — 8,598
Dr N. Martin, *LD* — 7,499
Ms M. Robson, *Ref.* — 1,723
P. Kember, *NLP* — 213
Lab. majority 22,504
(April 1992, Lab. maj. 15,058)

EALING ACTON AND SHEPHERD'S BUSH
*E.*72,078   *T.*66.68%
†C. Soley, *Lab.* — 28,052
Mrs B. Yerolemou, *C.* — 12,405
A. Mitchell, *LD* — 5,163
C. Winn, *Ref.* — 637
J. Gilbert, *Soc. Lab.* — 635
J. Gomm, *UK Ind.* — 385
P. Danon, *ProLife* — 265
C. Beasley, *Glow* — 209
W. Edwards, *Ch. P.* — 163
K. Turner, *NLP* — 150
Lab. majority 15,647
(Boundary change: notional Lab.)

EALING NORTH
E.78,144   T.71.31%
S. Pound, *Lab.* ... 29,904
†H. Greenway, *C.* ... 20,744
A. Gupta, *LD* ... 3,887
G. Slysz, *UK Ind.* ... 689
Ms A. Siebe, *Green* ... 502
Lab. majority 9,160
(Boundary change: notional C.)

EALING SOUTHALL
E.81,704   T.66.88%
†P. Khabra, *Lab.* ... 32,791
J. Penrose, *C.* ... 11,368
Ms N. Thomson, *LD* ... 5,687
H. Brar, *Soc. Lab.* ... 2,107
N. Goodwin, *Green* ... 934
B. Cherry, *Ref.* ... 854
Ms K. Klepacka, *ProLife* ... 473
Dr R. Mead, *UK Ind.* ... 428
Lab. majority 21,423
(Boundary change: notional Lab.)

EASINGTON
E.62,518   T.67.01%
*J. Cummings, *Lab.* ... 33,600
J. Hollands, *C.* ... 3,588
J. Heppell, *LD* ... 3,025
R. Pulfrey, *Ref.* ... 1,179
S. Colborn, *SPGB* ... 503
Lab. majority 30,012
(April 1992, Lab. maj. 26,390)

EASTBOURNE
E.72,347   T.72.80%
†N. Waterson, *C.* ... 22,183
C. Berry, *LD* ... 20,189
D. Lines, *Lab.* ... 6,576
T. Lowe, *Ref.* ... 2,724
Mrs T. Williamson, *Lib.* ... 741
J. Dawkins, *UK Ind.* ... 254
C. majority 1,994
(Boundary change: notional C.)

EAST HAM
E.65,591   T.60.81%
†S. Timms, *Lab.* ... 25,779
Miss A. Bray, *C.* ... 6,421
I. Khan, *Soc. Lab.* ... 2,697
M. Sole, *LD* ... 2,599
C. Smith, *BNP* ... 1,258
Mrs J. McCann, *Ref.* ... 845
G. Hardy, *Nat. Dem.* ... 290
Lab. majority 19,358
(Boundary change: notional Lab.)

EASTLEIGH
E.72,155   T.76.91%
†D. Chidgey, *LD* ... 19,453
S. Reid, *C.* ... 18,699
A. Lloyd, *Lab.* ... 14,883
V. Eldridge, *Ref.* ... 2,013
P. Robinson, *UK Ind.* ... 446
LD majority 754
(Boundary change: notional C.)

ECCLES
E.69,645   T.65.60%
I. Stewart, *Lab.* ... 30,468
G. Barker, *C.* ... 8,552
R. Boyd, *LD* ... 4,905
J. De Roeck, *Ref.* ... 1,765

Lab. majority 21,916
(Boundary change: notional Lab.)

EDDISBURY
E.65,256   T.75.78%
†Rt. Hon. A. Goodlad, *C.* ... 21,027
Ms M. Hanson, *Lab.* ... 19,842
D. Reaper, *LD* ... 6,540
Ms N. Napier, *Ref.* ... 2,041
C. majority 1,185
(Boundary change: notional C.)
See also page 233

EDMONTON
E.63,718   T.70.37%
A. Love, *Lab. Co-op.* ... 27,029
*Dr I. Twinn, *C.* ... 13,557
A. Wiseman, *LD* ... 2,847
J. Wright, *Ref.* ... 708
B. Cowd, *BNP* ... 437
Mrs P. Weald, *UK Ind.* ... 260
Lab. Co-op. majority 13,472
(April 1992, C. maj. 593)

ELLESMERE PORT AND NESTON
E.67,573   T.77.79%
†A. Miller, *Lab.* ... 31,310
Mrs L. Turnbull, *C.* ... 15,274
Ms J. Pemberton, *LD* ... 4,673
C. Rodden, *Ref.* ... 1,305
Lab. majority 16,036
(Boundary change: notional Lab.)

ELMET
E.70,423   T.76.81%
C. Burgon, *Lab.* ... 28,348
*S. Batiste, *C.* ... 19,569
B. Jennings, *LD* ... 4,691
C. Zawadski, *Ref.* ... 1,487
Lab. majority 8,779
(April 1992, C. maj. 3,261)

ELTHAM
E.57,358   T.75.71%
C. Efford, *Lab.* ... 23,710
C. Blackwood, *C.* ... 13,528
Ms A. Taylor, *LD* ... 3,701
M. Clark, *Ref.* ... 1,414
H. Middleton, *Lib.* ... 584
W. Hitches, *BNP* ... 491
Lab. majority 10,182
(Boundary change: notional C.)

ENFIELD NORTH
E.67,680   T.70.43%
Ms J. Ryan, *Lab.* ... 24,148
M. Field, *C.* ... 17,326
M. Hopkins, *LD* ... 4,264
R. Ellingham, *Ref.* ... 857
Ms J. Griffin, *BNP* ... 590
Mrs J. O'Ware, *UK Ind.* ... 484
Lab. majority 6,822
(April 1992, Lab. maj. 9,430)

ENFIELD SOUTHGATE
E.65,796   T.70.72%
S. Twigg, *Lab.* ... 20,570
†Rt. Hon. M. Portillo, *C.* ... 19,137
J. Browne, *LD* ... 4,966
N. Luard, *Ref.* ... 1,342
A. Storkey, *Ch. D.* ... 289
A. Malakouna, *Mal* ... 229
Lab. majority 1,433
(Boundary change: notional C.)

EPPING FOREST
E.72,795   T.72.82%
Mrs E. Laing, *C.* ... 24,117
S. Murray, *Lab.* ... 18,865
S. Robinson, *LD* ... 7,074
J. Berry, *Ref.* ... 2,208
P. Henderson, *BNP* ... 743
C. majority 5,252
(Boundary change: notional C.)

EPSOM AND EWELL
E.73,222   T.74.00%
†Rt. Hon. Sir A. Hamilton, *C.* ... 24,717
P. Woodford, *Lab.* ... 13,192
J. Vincent, *LD* ... 12,380
C. Macdonald, *Ref.* ... 2,355
H. Green, *UK Ind.* ... 544
H. Charlton, *Green* ... 527
Ms K. Weeks, *ProLife* ... 466
C. majority 11,525
(Boundary change: notional C.)

EREWASH
E.77,402   T.77.95%
Ms E. Blackman, *Lab.* ... 31,196
†Mrs A. Knight, *C.* ... 22,061
Dr M. Garnett, *LD* ... 5,181
S. Stagg, *Ref.* ... 1,404
M. Simmons, *Soc. Lab.* ... 496
Lab. majority 9,135
(Boundary change: notional C.)

ERITH AND THAMESMEAD
E.62,887   T.66.13%
†J. Austin-Walker, *Lab.* ... 25,812
N. Zahawi, *C.* ... 8,388
A. Grigg, *LD* ... 5,001
J. Flunder, *Ref.* ... 1,394
V. Dooley, *BNP* ... 718
M. Jackson, *UK Ind.* ... 274
Lab. majority 17,424
(Boundary change: notional Lab.)

ESHER AND WALTON
E.72,382   T.74.14%
†I. Taylor, *C.* ... 26,747
Ms J. Reay, *Lab.* ... 12,219
G. Miles, *LD* ... 10,937
A. Cruickshank, *Ref.* ... 2,904
B. Collignon, *UK Ind.* ... 558
Ms S. Kay, *Dream* ... 302
C. majority 14,528
(Boundary change: notional C.)

ESSEX NORTH
E.68,008   T.75.30%
†B. Jenkin, *C.* ... 22,480
T. Young, *Lab.* ... 17,004
A. Phillips, *LD* ... 10,028
R. Lord, *UK Ind.* ... 1,202
Ms S. Ransome, *Green* ... 495
C. majority 5,476
(Boundary change: notional C.)

EXETER
E.79,154   T.78.16%
B. Bradshaw, *Lab.* ... 29,398
Dr A. Rogers, *C.* ... 17,693
D. Brewer, *LD* ... 11,148
D. Morrish, *Lib.* ... 2,062
P. Edwards, *Green* ... 643
Mrs C. Haynes, *UK Ind.* ... 638
J. Meakin, *UKPP* ... 282

Lab. majority 11,705
(Boundary change: notional C.)

FALMOUTH AND CAMBORNE
E.71,383   T.75.13%
Ms C. Atherton, *Lab.*		18,151
*S. Coe, *C.*		15,463
Mrs T. Jones, *LD*		13,512
P. de Savary, *Ref.*		3,534
J. Geach, *Ind. Lab.*		1,691
P. Holmes, *Lib.*		527
R. Smith, *UK Ind.*		355
Ms R. Lewarne, *MK*		238
G. Glitter, *Loony*		161

Lab. majority 2,688
(April 1992, C. maj. 3,267)

FAREHAM
E.68,787   T.75.85%
†Rt. Hon. Sir P. Lloyd, *C.*		24,436
M. Pryor, *Lab.*		14,078
Mrs G. Hill, *LD*		10,234
D. Markham, *Ref.*		2,914
W. O'Brien, *Ind. No*		515

C. majority 10,358
(Boundary change: notional C.)

FAVERSHAM AND KENT MID
E.67,490   T.73.50%
†A. Rowe, *C.*		22,016
A. Stewart, *Lab.*		17,843
B. Parmenter, *LD*		6,138
R. Birley, *Ref.*		2,073
N. Davidson, *Loony*		511
M. Cunningham, *UK Ind.*		431
D. Currer, *Green*		380
Ms C. Morgan, *GRLNSP*		115
N. Pollard, *NLP*		99

C. majority 4,173
(Boundary change: notional C.)

FELTHAM AND HESTON
E.71,093   T.65.58%
†A. Keen, *Lab. Co-op.*		27,836
P. Ground, *C.*		12,563
C. Penning, *LD*		4,264
R. Stubbs, *Ref.*		1,099
R. Church, *BNP*		682
D. Fawcett, *NLP*		177

Lab. Co-op. majority 15,273
(Boundary change: notional Lab.
Co-op.)

FINCHLEY AND GOLDERS GREEN
E.72,225   T.69.65%
R. Vis, *Lab.*		23,180
†J. Marshall, *C.*		19,991
J. Davies, *LD*		5,670
G. Shaw, *Ref.*		684
A. Gunstock, *Green*		576
D. Barraclough, *UK Ind.*		205

Lab. majority 3,189
(Boundary change: notional C.)

FOLKESTONE AND HYTHE
E.71,153   T.73.15%
†Rt. Hon. M. Howard, *C.*		20,313
D. Laws, *LD*		13,981
P. Doherty, *Lab.*		12,939
J. Aspinall, *Ref.*		4,188
J. Baker, *UK Ind.*		378
E. Segal, *Soc.*		182
R. Saint, *CFSS*		69

C. majority 6,332
(Boundary change: notional C.)

FOREST OF DEAN
E.63,465   T.79.07%
Ms D. Organ, *Lab.*		24,203
†P. Marland, *C.*		17,860
Dr A. Lynch, *LD*		6,165
J. Hopkins, *Ref.*		1,624
G. Morgan, *Ind. Dean*		218
C. Palmer, *21st Cent.*		80
S. Porter, *Ind. F.*		34

Lab. majority 6,343
(Boundary change: notional Lab.)

FYLDE
E.71,385   T.72.94%
†Rt. Hon. M. Jack, *C.*		25,443
J. Garrett, *Lab.*		16,480
W. Greene, *LD*		7,609
D. Britton, *Ref.*		2,372
T. Kerwin, *NLP*		163

C. majority 8,963
(Boundary change: notional C.)

GAINSBOROUGH
E.64,106   T.74.56%
†E. Leigh, *C.*		20,593
P. Taylor, *Lab.*		13,767
N. Taylor, *LD*		13,436

C. majority 6,826
(Boundary change: notional C.)

GATESHEAD EAST AND
WASHINGTON WEST
E.64,114   T.67.19%
†Miss J. Quin, *Lab.*		31,047
Miss J. Burns, *C.*		6,097
A. Ord, *LD*		4,622
M. Daley, *Ref.*		1,315

Lab. majority 24,950
(Boundary change: notional Lab.)

GEDLING
E.68,820   T.75.80%
V. Coaker, *Lab.*		24,390
*A. Mitchell, *C.*		20,588
R. Poynter, *LD*		5,180
J. Connor, *Ref.*		2,006

Lab. majority 3,802
(April 1992, C. maj. 10,637)

GILLINGHAM
E.70,389   T.72.00%
P. Clark, *Lab.*		20,187
†J. Couchman, *C.*		18,207
R. Sayer, *LD*		9,649
G. Cann, *Ref.*		1,492
C. MacKinlay, *UK Ind.*		590
D. Robinson, *Loony*		305
C. Jury, *BNP*		195
Ms G. Duguay, *NLP*		58

Lab. majority 1,980
(Boundary change: notional C.)

GLOUCESTER
E.78,682   T.73.61%
Ms T. Kingham, *Lab.*		28,943
†D. French, *C.*		20,684
P. Munisamy, *LD*		6,069
A. Reid, *Ref.*		1,482
A. Harris, *UK Ind.*		455
Ms M. Hamilton, *NLP*		281

Lab. majority 8,259
(Boundary change: notional C.)

GOSPORT
E.68,830   T.70.25%
*P. Viggers, *C.*		21,085
I. Gray, *Lab.*		14,827
S. Hogg, *LD*		9,479
A. Blowers, *Ref.*		2,538
P. Ettie, *Ind.*		426

C. majority 6,258
(April 1992, C. maj. 16,318)

GRANTHAM AND STAMFORD
E.72,310   T.73.25%
†Q. Davies, *C.*		22,672
P. Denning, *Lab.*		19,980
J. Sellick, *LD*		6,612
Ms M. Swain, *Ref.*		2,721
M. Charlesworth, *UK Ind.*		556
Ms R. Clark, *ProLife*		314
I. Harper, *NLP*		115

C. majority 2,692
(Boundary change: notional C.)

GRAVESHAM
E.69,234   T.76.92%
C. Pond, *Lab.*		26,460
†J. Arnold, *C.*		20,681
Dr M. Canet, *LD*		4,128
Mrs P. Curtis, *Ref.*		1,441
A. Leyshon, *Ind.*		414
D. Palmer, *Ind.*		129

Lab. majority 5,779
(Boundary change: notional C.)

GREAT GRIMSBY
E.65,043   T.66.26%
*A. Mitchell, *Lab.*		25,765
D. Godson, *C.*		9,521
A. De Freitas, *LD*		7,810

Lab. majority 16,244
(April 1992, Lab. maj. 7,504)

GREAT YARMOUTH
E.68,625   T.71.23%
A. Wright, *Lab.*		26,084
*M. Carttiss, *C.*		17,416
D. Wood, *LD*		5,381

Lab. majority 8,668
(April 1992, C. maj. 5,309)

GREENWICH AND WOOLWICH
E.61,352   T.65.85%
†N. Raynsford, *Lab.*		25,630
M. Mitchell, *C.*		7,502
Mrs C. Luxton, *LD*		5,049
D. Ellison, *Ref.*		1,670
R. Mallone, *Fellowship*		428
D. Martin-Eagle, *Constit.*		124

Lab. majority 18,128
(Boundary change: notional Lab.)

GUILDFORD
E.75,541   T.75.40%
N. St Aubyn, *C.*		24,230
Mrs M. Sharp, *LD*		19,439
J. Burns, *Lab.*		9,945
J. Gore, *Ref.*		2,650
R. McWhirter, *UK Ind.*		400
J. Morris, *Pacifist*		294

C. majority 4,791
(Boundary change: notional C.)

HACKNEY NORTH AND STOKE
NEWINGTON
E.62,045   T.52.95%
*Ms D. Abbott, *Lab.* ... 21,110
M. Lavender, *C.* ... 5,483
D. Taylor, *LD* ... 3,806
Yen Chit Chong, *Green* ... 1,395
B. Maxwell, *Ref.* ... 544
D. Tolson, *None* ... 368
Miss L. Lovebucket, *Rain. Ref.* ... 146
Lab. majority 15,627
(April 1992, Lab. maj. 10,727)

HACKNEY SOUTH AND
SHOREDITCH
E.61,728   T.54.67%
†B. Sedgemore, *Lab.* ... 20,048
M. Pantling, *LD* ... 5,068
C. O'Leary, *C.* ... 4,494
T. Betts, *New Lab.* ... 2,436
R. Franklin, *Ref.* ... 613
G. Callow, *BNP* ... 531
M. Goldman, *Comm. P.* ... 298
Ms M. Goldberg, *NLP* ... 145
W. Rogers, *WRP* ... 113
Lab. majority 14,980
(Boundary change: notional Lab.)

HALESOWEN AND ROWLEY REGIS
E.66,245   T.73.61%
Mrs S. Heal, *Lab.* ... 26,366
J. Kennedy, *C.* ... 16,029
Ms E. Todd, *LD* ... 4,169
P. White, *Ref.* ... 1,244
Ms K. Meeds, *Nat. Dem.* ... 592
T. Weller, *Green* ... 361
Lab. majority 10,337
(Boundary change: notional C.)

HALIFAX
E.71,701   T.70.51%
*Mrs A. Mahon, *Lab.* ... 27,465
R. Light, *C.* ... 16,253
E. Waller, *LD* ... 6,059
Mrs C. Whitaker, *UK Ind.* ... 779
Lab. majority 11,212
(April 1992, Lab. maj. 478)

HALTEMPRICE AND HOWDEN
E.65,602   T.75.53%
†Rt. Hon. D. Davis, *C.* ... 21,809
Ms D. Wallis, *LD* ... 14,295
G. McManus, *Lab.* ... 11,701
T. Pearson, *Ref.* ... 1,370
G. Bloom, *UK Ind.* ... 301
B. Stevens, *NLP* ... 74
C. majority 7,514
(Boundary change: notional C.)

HALTON
E.64,987   T.68.38%
D. Twigg, *Lab.* ... 31,497
P. Balmer, *C.* ... 7,847
Ms J. Jones, *LD* ... 3,263
R. Atkins, *Ref.* ... 1,036
D. Proffitt, *Lib.* ... 600
J. Alley, *Rep. GB* ... 196
Lab. majority 23,650
(Boundary change: notional Lab.)

HAMMERSMITH AND FULHAM
E.78,637   T.68.70%
I. Coleman, *Lab.* ... 25,262

†M. Carrington, *C.* ... 21,420
Ms A. Sugden, *LD* ... 4,728
Mrs M. Bremner, *Ref.* ... 1,023
W. Johnson-Smith, *New Lab.* ... 695
Ms E. Streeter, *Green* ... 562
G. Roberts, *UK Ind.* ... 183
A. Phillips, *NLP* ... 79
A. Elston, *Care* ... 74
Lab. majority 3,842
(Boundary change: notional C.)

HAMPSHIRE EAST
E.76,604   T.75.88%
†M. Mates, *C.* ... 27,927
R. Booker, *LD* ... 16,337
R. Hoyle, *Lab.* ... 9,945
J. Hayter, *Ref.* ... 2,757
I. Foster, *Green* ... 649
S. Coles, *UK Ind.* ... 513
C. majority 11,590
(Boundary change: notional C.)

HAMPSHIRE NORTH EAST
E.69,111   T.73.95%
†J. Arbuthnot, *C.* ... 26,017
I. Mann, *LD* ... 11,619
P. Dare, *Lab.* ... 8,203
D. Rees, *Ref.* ... 2,420
K. Jessavala, *Ind.* ... 2,400
C. Berry, *UK Ind.* ... 452
C. majority 14,398
(Boundary change: notional C.)

HAMPSHIRE NORTH WEST
E.73,222   T.74.66%
†Rt. Hon. Sir G. Young, Bt., *C.*
 ... 24,730
C. Fleming, *LD* ... 13,179
M. Mumford, *Lab.* ... 12,900
Mrs P. Callaghan, *Ref.* ... 1,533
T. Rolt, *UK Ind.* ... 1,383
W. Baxter, *Green* ... 486
H. Anscomb, *Bypass* ... 231
R. Dodd, *Ind.* ... 225
C. majority 11,551
(Boundary change: notional C.)

HAMPSTEAD AND HIGHGATE
E.64,889   T.67.86%
†Ms G. Jackson, *Lab.* ... 25,275
Miss E. Gibson, *C.* ... 11,991
Mrs B. Fox, *LD* ... 5,481
Ms M. Siddique, *Ref.* ... 667
J. Leslie, *NLP* ... 147
R. Carroll, *Dream* ... 141
Miss P. Prince, *UK Ind.* ... 123
R. J. Harris, *Hum.* ... 105
Capt. Rizz, *Rizz Party* ... 101
Lab. majority 13,284
(Boundary change: notional Lab.)

HARBOROUGH
E.70,424   T.75.27%
†E. Garnier, *C.* ... 22,170
M. Cox, *LD* ... 15,646
N. Holden, *Lab.* ... 13,332
N. Wright, *Ref.* ... 1,859
C. majority 6,524
(Boundary change: notional C.)

HARLOW
E.64,072   T.74.62%
W. Rammell, *Lab.* ... 25,861

†J. Hayes, *C.* ... 15,347
Ms L. Spenceley, *LD* ... 4,523
M. Wells, *Ref.* ... 1,422
G. Batten, *UK Ind.* ... 340
J. Bowles, *BNP* ... 319
Lab. majority 10,514
(Boundary change: notional C.)

HARROGATE AND
KNARESBOROUGH
E.65,155   T.73.14%
P. Willis, *LD* ... 24,558
†Rt. Hon. N. Lamont, *C.* ... 18,322
Ms B. Boyce, *Lab.* ... 4,159
J. Blackburn, *LC* ... 614
LD majority 6,236
(Boundary change: notional C.)

HARROW EAST
E.79,846   T.71.37%
A. McNulty, *Lab.* ... 29,927
†H. Dykes, *C.* ... 20,189
B. Sharma, *LD* ... 4,697
B. Casey, *Ref.* ... 1,537
A. Scholefield, *UK Ind.* ... 464
A. Planton, *NLP* ... 171
Lab. majority 9,738
(Boundary change: notional C.)

HARROW WEST
E.72,005   T.72.92%
G. Thomas, *Lab.* ... 21,811
*R. Hughes, *C.* ... 20,571
Mrs P. Nandhra, *LD* ... 8,127
H. Crossman, *Ref.* ... 1,997
Lab. majority 1,240
(Boundary change: notional C.)

HARTLEPOOL
E.67,712   T.65.65%
*P. Mandelson, *Lab.* ... 26,997
M. Horsley, *C.* ... 9,489
R. Clark, *LD* ... 6,248
Miss M. Henderson, *Ref.* ... 1,718
Lab. majority 17,508
(April 1992, Lab. maj. 8,782)

HARWICH
E.75,775   T.70.62%
I. Henderson, *Lab.* ... 20,740
†I. Sproat, *C.* ... 19,524
Mrs A. Elvin, *LD* ... 7,037
J. Titford, *Ref.* ... 4,923
R. Knight, *CRP* ... 1,290
Lab. majority 1,216
(Boundary change: notional C.)

HASTINGS AND RYE
E.70,388   T.69.71%
M. Foster, *Lab.* ... 16,867
*Mrs J. Lait, *C.* ... 14,307
M. Palmer, *LD* ... 13,717
C. McGovern, *Ref.* ... 2,511
Ms J. Amstad, *Lib.* ... 1,046
W. Andrews, *UK Ind.* ... 472
D. Howell, *Loony* ... 149
Lab. majority 2,560
(April 1992, C. maj. 6,634)

HAVANT
E.68,420   T.70.63%
†D. Willetts, *C.* ... 19,204
Ms L. Armstrong, *Lab.* ... 15,475

M. Kooner, *LD*	10,806
A. Green, *Ref.*	2,395
M. Atwal, *BIPF*	442
C. majority 3,729	
(Boundary change: notional C.)	

HAYES AND HARLINGTON
*E.*56,829   *T.*72.31%

J. McDonnell, *Lab.*	25,458
A. Retter, *C.*	11,167
A. Little, *LD*	3,049
F. Page, *Ref.*	778
J. Hutchins, *NF*	504
D. Farrow, *ANP*	135
Lab. majority 14,291	
(Boundary change: notional C.)	

HAZEL GROVE
*E.*63,694   *T.*77.46%

A. Stunell, *LD*	26,883
B. Murphy, *C.*	15,069
J. Lewis, *Lab.*	5,882
J. Stanyer, *Ref.*	1,055
G. Black, *UK Ind.*	268
D. Firkin-Flood, *Ind. Hum.*	183
LD majority 11,814	
(April 1992, C. maj. 929)	

HEMEL HEMPSTEAD
*E.*71,468   *T.*77.09%

A. McWalter, *Lab. Co-op.*	25,175
†R. Jones, *C.*	21,539
Mrs P. Lindsley, *LD*	6,789
P. Such, *Ref.*	1,327
Ms D. Harding, *NLP*	262
Lab. Co-op. majority 3,636	
(Boundary change: notional C.)	

HEMSWORTH
*E.*66,964   *T.*67.91%

†J. Trickett, *Lab.*	32,088
N. Hazell, *C.*	8,096
Ms J. Kirby, *LD*	4,033
D. Irvine, *Ref.*	1,260
Lab. majority 23,992	
(Boundary change: notional Lab.)	

HENDON
*E.*76,195   *T.*65.67%

A. Dismore, *Lab.*	24,683
†Sir J. Gorst, *C.*	18,528
W. Casey, *LD*	5,427
S. Rabbow, *Ref.*	978
B. Wright, *UK Ind.*	267
Ms S. Taylor, *WRP*	153
Lab. majority 6,155	
(Boundary change: notional C.)	

HENLEY
*E.*66,424   *T.*77.60%

†Rt. Hon. M. Heseltine, *C.*	23,908
T. Horton, *LD*	12,741
D. Enright, *Lab.*	11,700
S. Sainsbury, *Ref.*	2,299
Mrs S. Miles, *Green*	514
N. Barlow, *NLP*	221
T. Hibbert, *Whig Party*	160
C. majority 11,167	
(Boundary change: notional C.)	

HEREFORD
*E.*69,864   *T.*75.22%

P. Keetch, *LD*	25,198

†Sir C. Shepherd, *C.*	18,550
C. Chappell, *Lab.*	6,596
C. Easton, *Ref.*	2,209
LD majority 6,648	
(Boundary change: notional C.)	

HERTFORD AND STORTFORD
*E.*71,759   *T.*76.03%

†B. Wells, *C.*	24,027
S. Speller, *Lab.*	17,142
M. Wood, *LD*	9,679
H. Page Croft, *Ref.*	2,105
B. Smalley, *UK Ind.*	1,223
M. Franey, *ProLife*	259
D. Molloy, *Logic*	126
C. majority 6,885	
(Boundary change: notional C.)	

HERTFORDSHIRE NORTH EAST
*E.*67,161   *T.*77.42%

†O. Heald, *C.*	21,712
I. Gibbons, *Lab.*	18,624
S. Jarvis, *LD*	9,493
J. Grose, *Ref.*	2,166
C. majority 3,088	
(Boundary change: notional C.)	

HERTFORDSHIRE SOUTH WEST
*E.*71,671   *T.*77.31%

†R. Page, *C.*	25,462
M. Wilson, *Lab.*	15,441
Mrs A. Shaw, *LD*	12,381
T. Millward, *Ref.*	1,853
C. Adamson, *NLP*	274
C. majority 10,021	
(Boundary change: notional C.)	

HERTSMERE
*E.*68,011   *T.*74.03%

†J. Clappison, *C.*	22,305
Ms E. Kelly, *Lab.*	19,230
Mrs A. Gray, *LD*	6,466
J. Marlow, *Ref.*	1,703
R. Saunders, *UK Ind.*	453
N. Kahn, *NLP*	191
C. majority 3,075	
(Boundary change: notional C.)	

HEXHAM
*E.*58,914   *T.*77.52%

*P. Atkinson, *C.*	17,701
I. McMinn, *Lab.*	17,479
Dr P. Carr, *LD*	7,959
R. Waddell, *Ref.*	1,362
D. Lott, *UK Ind.*	1,170
C. majority 222	
(April 1992, C. maj. 13,438)	

HEYWOOD AND MIDDLETON
*E.*73,898   *T.*68.41%

J. Dobbin, *Lab. Co-op.*	29,179
S. Grigg, *C.*	11,637
D. Clayton, *LD*	7,908
Mrs C. West, *Ref.*	1,076
P. Burke, *Lib.*	750
Lab. Co-op. majority 17,542	
(Boundary change: notional Lab. Co-op.)	

HIGH PEAK
*E.*72,315   *T.*79.03%

T. Levitt, *Lab.*	29,052
†C. Hendry, *C.*	20,261

Mrs S. Barber, *LD*	6,420
C. Hanson-Orr, *Ref.*	1,420
Lab. majority 8,791	
(Boundary change: notional C.)	

HITCHIN AND HARPENDEN
*E.*67,219   *T.*77.99%

†Rt. Hon. P. Lilley, *C.*	24,038
Ms R. Sanderson, *Lab.*	17,367
C. White, *LD*	10,515
D. Cooke, *NLP*	290
J. Horton, *Soc.*	217
C. majority 6,671	
(Boundary change: notional C.)	

HOLBORN AND ST PANCRAS
*E.*63,037   *T.*60.28%

†F. Dobson, *Lab.*	24,707
J. Smith, *C.*	6,804
Ms J. McGuinness, *LD*	4,750
Mrs J. Carr, *Ref.*	790
T. Bedding, *NLP*	191
S. Smith, *JP*	173
Ms B. Conway, *WRP*	171
M. Rosenthal, *Dream*	157
P. Rice-Evans, *EUP*	140
B. Quintavalle, *ProLife*	114
Lab. majority 17,903	
(Boundary change: notional Lab.)	

HORNCHURCH
*E.*60,775   *T.*72.30%

J. Cryer, *Lab.*	22,066
*R. Squire, *C.*	16,386
R. Martins, *LD*	3,446
R. Khilkoff-Boulding, *Ref.*	1,595
Miss J. Trueman, *Third Way*	259
J. Sowerby, *ProLife*	189
Lab. majority 5,680	
(April 1992, C. maj. 9,165)	

HORNSEY AND WOOD GREEN
*E.*74,537   *T.*69.08%

*Mrs B. Roche, *Lab.*	31,792
Mrs H. Hart, *C.*	11,293
Ms L. Featherstone, *LD*	5,794
Ms H. Jago, *Green*	1,214
Ms R. Miller, *Ref.*	808
P. Sikorski, *Soc. Lab.*	586
Lab. majority 20,499	
(April 1992, Lab. maj. 5,177)	

HORSHAM
*E.*75,432   *T.*75.78%

Rt. Hon. F. Maude, *C.*	29,015
Mrs M. Millson, *LD*	14,153
Ms M. Walsh, *Lab.*	10,691
R. Grant, *Ref.*	2,281
H. Miller, *UK Ind.*	819
M. Corbould, *FEP*	206
C. majority 14,862	
(Boundary change: notional C.)	

HOUGHTON AND WASHINGTON EAST
*E.*67,343   *T.*62.10%

F. Kemp, *Lab.*	31,946
P. Booth, *C.*	5,391
K. Miller, *LD*	3,209
J. Joseph, *Ref.*	1,277
Lab. majority 26,555	
(Boundary change: notional Lab.)	

HOVE
E.69,016   T.69.72%
I. Caplin, *Lab.*		21,458
R. Guy, *C.*		17,499
T. Pearce, *LD*		4,645
S. Field, *Ref.*		1,931
J. Furness, *Ind. C.*		1,735
P. Mulligan, *Green*		644
J. Vause, *UK Ind.*		209

Lab. majority 3,959
(April 1992, C. maj. 12,268)

HUDDERSFIELD
E.65,824   T.67.69%
*B. Sheerman, *Lab. Co-op.*		25,171
W. Forrow, *C.*		9,323
G. Beever, *LD*		7,642
P. McNulty, *Ref.*		1,480
J. Phillips, *Green*		938

Lab. Co-op. majority 15,848
(April 1992, *Lab. majority* 7,258)

HULL EAST
E.68,733   T.58.90%
*Rt. Hon. J. Prescott, *Lab.*		28,870
A. West, *C.*		5,552
J. Wastling, *LD*		3,965
G. Rogers, *Ref.*		1,788
Ms M. Nolan, *ProLife*		190
D. Whitley, *NLP*		121

Lab. majority 23,318
(April 1992, Lab. maj. 18,719)

HULL NORTH
E.68,106   T.56.96%
*K. McNamara, *Lab.*		25,542
D. Lee, *C.*		5,837
D. Nolan, *LD*		5,667
A. Scott, *Ref.*		1,533
T. Brotheridge, *NLP*		215

Lab. majority 19,705
(April 1992, Lab. maj. 15,384)

HULL WEST AND HESSLE
E.65,840   T.58.25%
A. Johnson, *Lab.*		22,520
R. Tress, *LD*		6,995
C. Moore, *C.*		6,933
R. Bate, *Ref.*		1,596
B. Franklin, *NLP*		310

Lab. majority 15,525
(Boundary change: notional Lab.)

HUNTINGDON
E.76,094   T.74.86%
†Rt. Hon. J. Major, *C.*		31,501
J. Reece, *Lab.*		13,361
M. Owen, *LD*		8,390
D. Bellamy, *Ref.*		3,114
C. Coyne, *UK Ind.*		331
Ms V. Hufford, *Ch. D.*		177
D. Robertson, *Ind.*		89

C. majority 18,140
(Boundary change: notional C.)

HYNDBURN
E.66,806   T.72.26%
†G. Pope, *Lab.*		26,831
P. Britcliffe, *C.*		15,383
L. Jones, *LD*		4,141
P. Congdon, *Ref.*		1,627
J. Brown, *IAC*		290

Lab. majority 11,448
(Boundary change: notional Lab.)

ILFORD NORTH
E.68,218   T.71.60%
Ms L. Perham, *Lab.*		23,135
†V. Bendall, *C.*		19,911
A. Dean, *LD*		5,049
P. Wilson, *BNP*		750

Lab. majority 3,224
(Boundary change: notional C.)

ILFORD SOUTH
E.72,104   T.69.37%
†M. Gapes, *Lab. Co-op.*		29,273
Sir N. Thorne, *C.*		15,073
Ms A. Khan, *LD*		3,152
D. Hodges, *Ref.*		1,073
B. Ramsey, *Soc. Lab.*		868
A. Owens, *BNP*		580

Lab. Co-op. majority 14,200
(Boundary change: notional C.)

IPSWICH
E.66,947   T.72.24%
†J. Cann, *Lab.*		25,484
S. Castle, *C.*		15,045
N. Roberts, *LD*		5,881
T. Agnew, *Ref.*		1,637
W. Vinyard, *UK Ind.*		208
E. Kaplan, *NLP*		107

Lab. majority 10,439
(Boundary change: notional Lab.)

ISLE OF WIGHT
E.101,680   T.71.95%
Dr P. Brand, *LD*		31,274
A. Turner, *C.*		24,868
Ms D. Gardiner, *Lab.*		9,646
T. Bristow, *Ref.*		4,734
M. Turner, *UK Ind.*		1,072
H. Rees, *Ind. Is.*		848
P. Scivier, *Green*		544
C. Daly, *NLP*		87
J. Eveleigh, *Rain. Is.*		86

LD majority 6,406
(April 1992, C. maj. 1,827)

ISLINGTON NORTH
E.57,385   T.62.49%
*J. Corbyn, *Lab.*		24,834
J. Kempton, *LD*		4,879
S. Fawthrop, *C.*		4,631
C. Ashby, *Green*		1,516

Lab. majority 19,955
(April 1992, Lab. maj. 12,784)

ISLINGTON SOUTH AND FINSBURY
E.55,468   T.63.67%
†C. Smith, *Lab.*		22,079
Ms S. Ludford, *LD*		7,516
D. Berens, *C.*		4,587
Miss J. Bryett, *Ref.*		741
A. Laws, *ACA*		171
M. Creese, *NLP*		121
E. Basarik, *Ind.*		101

Lab. majority 14,563
(Boundary change: notional Lab.)

JARROW
E.63,828   T.68.84%
S. Hepburn, *Lab.*		28,497

M. Allatt, *C.*		6,564
T. Stone, *LD*		4,865
A. LeBlond, *Ind. Lab.*		2,538
P. Mailer, *Ref.*		1,034
J. Bissett, *SPGB*		444

Lab. majority 21,933
(Boundary change: notional Lab.)

KEIGHLEY
E.67,231   T.76.57%
Mrs A. Cryer, *Lab.*		26,039
*G. Waller, *C.*		18,907
M. Doyle, *LD*		5,064
C. Carpenter, *Ref.*		1,470

Lab. majority 7,132
(April 1992, C. maj. 3,596)

KENSINGTON AND CHELSEA
E.67,786   T.54.71%
Rt. Hon. A. Clark, *C.*		19,887
R. Atkinson, *Lab.*		10,368
R. Woodthorpe Browne, *LD*		5,668
Ms A. Ellis-Jones, *UK Ind.*		540
E. Bear, *Teddy*		218
G. Oliver, *UKPP*		176
Ms S. Hamza, *NLP*		122
P. Sullivan, *Dream*		65
P. Parliament, *Heart*		44

C. majority 9,519
(Boundary change: notional C.)
See also Stop-press

KETTERING
E.75,153   T.75.79%
P. Sawford, *Lab.*		24,650
†Rt. Hon. R. Freeman, *C.*		24,461
R. Aron, *LD*		6,098
A. Smith, *Ref.*		1,551
Mrs R. le Carpentier, *NLP*		197

Lab. majority 189
(Boundary change: notional C.)

KINGSTON AND SURBITON
E.73,879   T.75.35%
E. Davey, *LD*		20,411
†R. Tracey, *C.*		20,355
Ms S. Griffin, *Lab.*		12,811
Mrs G. Tchiprout, *Ref.*		1,470
Ms P. Burns, *UK Ind.*		418
C. Port, *Dream*		100
M. Leighton, *NLP*		100

LD majority 56
(Boundary change: notional C.)

KINGSWOOD
E.77,026   T.77.75%
†Dr R. Berry, *Lab.*		32,181
J. Howard, *C.*		17,928
Mrs J. Pinkerton, *LD*		7,672
Ms A. Reather, *Ref.*		1,463
P. Hart, *BNP*		290
A. Harding, *NLP*		238
A. Nicolson, *Scrapit*		115

Lab. majority 14,253
(Boundary change: notional C.)

KNOWSLEY NORTH AND SEFTON EAST
E.70,918   T.70.09%
†G. Howarth, *Lab.*		34,747
C. Doran, *C.*		8,600
D. Bamber, *LD*		5,499
C. Jones, *Soc. Lab.*		857

Lab. majority 26,147
(Boundary change: notional Lab.)

KNOWSLEY SOUTH
E.70,532   T.67.47%
†E. O'Hara, *Lab.*   36,695
G. Robertson, *C.*   5,987
C. Mainey, *LD*   3,954
A. Wright, *Ref.*   954
Lab. majority 30,708
(Boundary change: notional Lab.)

LANCASHIRE WEST
E.73,175   T.74.79%
†C. Pickthall, *Lab.*   33,022
C. Varley, *C.*   15,903
A. Wood, *LD*   3,938
M. Carter, *Ref.*   1,025
J. Collins, *NLP*   449
D. Hill, *Home Rule*   392
Lab. majority 17,119
(Boundary change: notional Lab.)

LANCASTER AND WYRE
E.78,168   T.75.30%
H. Dawson, *Lab.*   25,173
†K. Mans, *C.*   23,878
J. Humberstone, *LD*   6,802
Mrs V. Ivell, *Ref.*   1,516
J. Barry, *Green*   795
Dr J. Whittaker, *UK Ind.*   698
Lab. majority 1,295
(Boundary change: notional C.)

LEEDS CENTRAL
E.67,664   T.54.70%
†D. Fatchett, *Lab.*   25,766
E. Wild, *C.*   5,077
D. Freeman, *LD*   4,164
P. Myers, *Ref.*   1,042
D. Rix, *Soc. Lab.*   656
C. Hill, *Soc.*   304
Lab. majority 20,689
(Boundary change: notional Lab.)
See also page 233

LEEDS EAST
E.56,963   T.62.83%
*G. Mudie, *Lab.*   24,151
J. Emsley, *C.*   6,685
Mrs M. Kirk, *LD*   3,689
L. Parish, *Ref.*   1,267
Lab. majority 17,466
(April 1992, Lab. maj. 12,697)

LEEDS NORTH EAST
E.63,185   T.72.03%
F. Hamilton, *Lab.*   22,368
*T. Kirkhope, *C.*   15,409
Dr W. Winlow, *LD*   6,318
I. Rose, *Ref.*   946
Ms J. Egan, *Soc. Lab.*   468
Lab. majority 6,959
(April 1992, C. maj. 4,244)

LEEDS NORTH WEST
E.69,972   T.70.57%
H. Best, *Lab.*   19,694
*Dr K. Hampson, *C.*   15,850
Mrs B. Pearce, *LD*   11,689
S. Emmett, *Ref.*   1,325
R. Lamb, *Soc. Lab.*   335
R. Toone, *ProLife*   251

D. Duffy, *Ronnie*   232
Lab. majority 3,844
(April 1992, C. maj. 7,671)

LEEDS WEST
E.63,965   T.62.88%
*J. Battle, *Lab.*   26,819
J. Whelan, *C.*   7,048
N. Amor, *LD*   3,622
W. Finley, *Ref.*   1,210
D. Blackburn, *Green*   896
N. Nowosielski, *Lib.*   625
Lab. majority 19,771
(April 1992, Lab. maj. 13,828)

LEICESTER EAST
E.64,012   T.69.37%
*K. Vaz, *Lab.*   29,083
S. Milton, *C.*   10,661
J. Matabudul, *LD*   3,105
P. Iwaniw, *Ref.*   1,015
S. Sidhu, *Soc. Lab.*   436
N. Slack, *Glow*   102
Lab. majority 18,422
(April 1992, Lab. maj. 11,316)

LEICESTER SOUTH
E.71,750   T.67.06%
*J. Marshall, *Lab.*   27,914
C. Heaton-Harris, *C.*   11,421
B. Coles, *LD*   6,654
J. Hancock, *Ref.*   1,184
J. Dooher, *Soc. Lab.*   634
K. Sills, *Nat. Dem.*   307
Lab. majority 16,493
(April 1992, Lab. maj. 9,440)

LEICESTER WEST
E.64,570   T.63.36%
Ms P. Hewitt, *Lab.*   22,580
R. Thomas, *C.*   9,716
M. Jones, *LD*   5,795
W. Shooter, *Ref.*   970
G. Forse, *Green*   586
D. Roberts, *Soc. Lab.*   452
Ms J. Nicholls, *Soc.*   327
A. Belshaw, *BNP*   302
C. Potter, *Nat. Dem.*   186
Lab. majority 12,864
(April 1992, Lab. maj. 3,978)

LEICESTERSHIRE NORTH WEST
E.65,069   T.79.95%
D. Taylor, *Lab.*   29,332
R. Goodwill, *C.*   16,113
S. Heptinstall, *LD*   4,492
M. Abney-Hastings, *Ref.*   2,088
Lab. majority 13,219
(Boundary change: notional C.)

LEIGH
E.69,908   T.65.69%
†L. Cunliffe, *Lab.*   31,652
E. Young, *C.*   7,156
P. Hough, *LD*   5,163
R. Constable, *Ref.*   1,949
Lab. majority 24,496
(Boundary change: notional Lab.)

LEOMINSTER
E.65,993   T.76.60%
†P. Temple-Morris, *C.*   22,888
T. James, *LD*   14,053

R. Westwood, *Lab.*   8,831
A. Parkin, *Ref.*   2,815
Ms F. Norman, *Green*   1,086
R. Chamings, *UK Ind.*   588
J. Haycock, *BNP*   292
C. majority 8,835
(Boundary change: notional C.)

LEWES
E.64,340   T.76.42%
N. Baker, *LD*   21,250
†T. Rathbone, *C.*   19,950
Dr M. Patton, *Lab.*   5,232
Mrs L. Butler, *Ref.*   2,481
J. Harvey, *UK Ind.*   256
LD majority 1,300
(Boundary change: notional C.)

LEWISHAM DEPTFORD
E.58,141   T.57.87%
†Mrs J. Ruddock, *Lab.*   23,827
Mrs I. Kimm, *C.*   4,949
K. Appiah, *LD*   3,004
J. Mulrenan, *Soc. Lab.*   996
Ms S. Shepherd, *Ref.*   868
Lab. majority 18,878
(Boundary change: notional Lab.)

LEWISHAM EAST
E.56,333   T.66.41%
†Ms B. Prentice, *Lab.*   21,821
P. Hollobone, *C.*   9,694
D. Buxton, *LD*   4,178
S. Drury, *Ref.*   910
R. Croucher, *NF*   431
P. White, *Lib.*   277
Capt. Rizz, *Dream*   97
Lab. majority 12,127
(Boundary change: notional Lab.)

LEWISHAM WEST
E.58,659   T.64.00%
*J. Dowd, *Lab.*   23,273
Mrs C. Whelan, *C.*   8,936
Miss K. McGrath, *LD*   3,672
A. Leese, *Ref.*   1,098
N. Long, *Soc. Lab.*   398
Ms E. Oram, *Lib.*   167
Lab. majority 14,337
(April 1992, Lab. maj. 1,809)

LEYTON AND WANSTEAD
E.62,176   T.63.24%
†H. Cohen, *Lab.*   23,922
R. Vaudry, *C.*   8,736
C. Anglin, *LD*   5,920
S. Duffy, *ProLife*   488
A. Mian, *Ind.*   256
Lab. majority 15,186
(Boundary change: notional Lab.)

LICHFIELD
E.62,720   T.77.48%
†M. Fabricant, *C.*   20,853
Ms S. Woodward, *Lab.*   20,615
Dr P. Bennion, *LD*   5,473
G. Seward, *Ref.*   1,652
C. majority 238
(Boundary change: notional C.)

LINCOLN
E.65,485   T.71.08%
Ms G. Merron, *Lab.*   25,563

A. Brown, *C.* — 14,433
Ms L. Gabriel, *LD* — 5,048
J. Ivory, *Ref.* — 1,329
A. Myers, *NLP* — 175
Lab. majority 11,130
(Boundary change: notional Lab.)

LIVERPOOL GARSTON
*E.*66,755   *T.*65.14%
Ms M. Eagle, *Lab.* — 26,667
Ms F. Clucas, *LD* — 8,250
N. Gordon-Johnson, *C.* — 6,819
F. Dunne, *Ref.* — 833
G. Copeland, *Lib.* — 666
J. Parsons, *NLP* — 127
S. Nolan, *SEP* — 120
Lab. majority 18,417
(Boundary change: notional Lab.)

LIVERPOOL RIVERSIDE
*E.*73,429   *T.*51.93%
Ms L. Ellman, *Lab. Co-op.* — 26,858
Ms B. Fraenkel, *LD* — 5,059
D. Sparrow, *C.* — 3,635
Ms C. Wilson, *Soc.* — 776
D. Green, *Lib.* — 594
G. Skelly, *Ref.* — 586
Ms H. Neilson, *ProLife* — 277
D. Braid, *MRAC* — 179
G. Gay, *NLP* — 171
Lab. Co-op. majority 21,799
(Boundary change: notional Lab.
Co-op.)

LIVERPOOL WALTON
*E.*67,527   *T.*59.54%
*P. Kilfoyle, *Lab.* — 31,516
R. Roberts, *LD* — 4,478
M. Kotecha, *C.* — 2,551
C. Grundy, *Ref.* — 620
Ms L. Mahmood, *Soc.* — 444
Ms H. Williams, *Lib.* — 352
Ms V. Mearns, *ProLife* — 246
Lab. majority 27,038
(April 1992, Lab. maj. 28,299)

LIVERPOOL WAVERTREE
*E.*73,063   *T.*62.85%
†Ms J. Kennedy, *Lab.* — 29,592
R. Kemp, *LD* — 9,891
C. Malthouse, *C.* — 4,944
P. Worthington, *Ref.* — 576
K. McCullough, *Lib.* — 391
Ms R. Kingsley, *ProLife* — 346
Ms C. Corkhill, *WRP* — 178
Lab. majority 19,701
(Boundary change: notional Lab.)

LIVERPOOL WEST DERBY
*E.*68,682   *T.*61.38%
†R. Wareing, *Lab.* — 30,002
S. Radford, *Lib.* — 4,037
Ms A. Hines, *LD* — 3,805
N. Morgan, *C.* — 3,656
P. Forrest, *Ref.* — 657
Lab. majority 25,965
(Boundary change: notional Lab.)

LOUGHBOROUGH
*E.*68,945   *T.*75.95%
A. Reed, *Lab.* — 25,448
K. Andrew, *C.* — 19,736
Ms D. Brass, *LD* — 6,190

R. Gupta, *Ref.* — 991
Lab. majority 5,712
(Boundary change: notional C.)

LOUTH AND HORNCASTLE
*E.*68,824   *T.*72.58%
†Sir P. Tapsell, *C.* — 21,699
J. Hough, *Lab.* — 14,799
Mrs F. Martin, *LD* — 12,207
Ms R. Robinson, *Green* — 1,248
C. majority 6,900
(Boundary change: notional C.)

LUDLOW
*E.*61,267   *T.*75.55%
†C. Gill, *C.* — 19,633
I. Huffer, *LD* — 13,724
Ms N. O'Kane, *Lab.* — 11,745
T. Andrewes, *Green* — 798
E. Freeman-Keel, *UK Ind.* — 385
C. majority 5,909
(Boundary change: notional C.)

LUTON NORTH
*E.*64,618   *T.*73.25%
K. Hopkins, *Lab.* — 25,860
D. Senior, *C.* — 16,234
Mrs K. Newbound, *LD* — 4,299
C. Brown, *UK Ind.* — 689
A. Custance, *NLP* — 250
Lab. majority 9,626
(Boundary change: notional C.)

LUTON SOUTH
*E.*68,395   *T.*70.45%
Ms M. Moran, *Lab.* — 26,428
†Sir G. Bright, *C.* — 15,109
K. Fitchett, *LD* — 4,610
C. Jacobs, *Ref.* — 1,205
C. Lawman, *UK Ind.* — 390
M. Scheimann, *Green* — 356
Ms C. Perrin, *NLP* — 86
Lab. majority 11,319
(Boundary change: notional C.)

MACCLESFIELD
*E.*72,049   *T.*75.22%
†N. Winterton, *C.* — 26,888
Ms J. Jackson, *Lab.* — 18,234
M. Flynn, *LD* — 9,075
C. majority 8,654
(Boundary change: notional C.)

MAIDENHEAD
*E.*67,302   *T.*75.61%
Mrs T. May, *C.* — 25,344
A. Ketteringham, *LD* — 13,363
Ms D. Robson, *Lab.* — 9,205
C. Taverner, *Ref.* — 1,638
D. Munkley, *Lib.* — 896
N. Spiers, *UK Ind.* — 277
K. Ardley, *Glow* — 166
C. majority 11,981
(Boundary change: notional C.)

MAIDSTONE AND THE WEALD
*E.*72,466   *T.*73.98%
†Rt. Hon. Miss A. Widdecombe,
C. — 23,657
J. Morgan, *Lab.* — 14,054
Mrs J. Nelson, *LD* — 11,986
Ms S. Hopkins, *Ref.* — 1,998
Ms M. Cleator, *Soc. Lab.* — 979

Ms P. Kemp, *Green* — 480
Mrs R. Owen, *UK Ind.* — 339
J. Oldbury, *NLP* — 115
C. majority 9,603
(Boundary change: notional C.)

MAKERFIELD
*E.*67,358   *T.*66.83%
†I. McCartney, *Lab.* — 33,119
M. Winstanley, *C.* — 6,942
B. Hubbard, *LD* — 3,743
A. Seed, *Ref.* — 1,210
Lab. majority 26,177
(Boundary change: notional Lab.)

MALDON AND CHELMSFORD
EAST
*E.*66,184   *T.*76.13%
†J. Whittingdale, *C.* — 24,524
K. Freeman, *Lab.* — 14,485
G. Pooley, *LD* — 9,758
L. Overy-Owen, *UK Ind.* — 935
Ms E. Burgess, *Green* — 685
C. majority 10,039
(Boundary change: notional C.)

MANCHESTER BLACKLEY
*E.*62,227   *T.*57.46%
G. Stringer, *Lab.* — 25,042
S. Barclay, *C.* — 5,454
S. Wheale, *LD* — 3,937
P. Stanyer, *Ref.* — 1,323
Lab. majority 19,588
(Boundary change: notional Lab.)

MANCHESTER CENTRAL
*E.*63,815   *T.*52.55%
†A. Lloyd, *Lab.* — 23,803
Ms A. Firth, *LD* — 4,121
S. McIlwaine, *C.* — 3,964
F. Rafferty, *Soc. Lab.* — 810
J. Maxwell, *Ref.* — 742
T. Rigby, *Comm L.* — 97
Lab. majority 19,682
(Boundary change: notional Lab.)

MANCHESTER GORTON
*E.*64,349   *T.*56.43%
†Rt. Hon. G. Kaufman, *Lab.* — 23,704
Dr J. Pearcey, *LD* — 6,362
G. Senior, *C.* — 4,249
K. Hartley, *Ref.* — 812
Dr S. Fitz-Gibbon, *Green* — 683
T. Wongsam, *Soc. Lab.* — 501
Lab. majority 17,342
(Boundary change: notional Lab.)

MANCHESTER WITHINGTON
*E.*66,116   *T.*66.59%
†K. Bradley, *Lab.* — 27,103
J. Smith, *C.* — 8,522
Dr Y. Zalzala, *LD* — 6,000
M. Sheppard, *Ref.* — 1,079
S. Caldwell, *ProLife* — 614
Ms J. White, *Soc.* — 376
S. Kingston, *Dream* — 181
M. Gaskell, *NLP* — 152
Lab. majority 18,581
(Boundary change: notional Lab.)

MANSFIELD
*E.*67,057   *T.*70.72%
*A. Meale, *Lab.* — 30,556

T. Frost, *C.* 10,038
P. Smith, *LD* 5,244
W. Bogusz, *Ref.* 1,588
Lab. majority 20,518
(April 1992, Lab. maj. 11,724)

MEDWAY
*E.*61,736 *T.*72.47%
R. Marshall-Andrews, *Lab.* 21,858
*Dame P. Fenner, *C.* 16,504
R. Roberts, *LD* 4,555
J. Main, *Ref.* 1,420
Mrs S. Radlett, *UK Ind.* 405
Lab. majority 5,354
(April 1992, C. maj. 8,786)

MERIDEN
*E.*76,287 *T.*71.73%
Mrs C. Spelman, *C.* 22,997
B. Seymour-Smith, *Lab.* 22,415
A. Dupont, *LD* 7,098
P. Gilbert, *Ref.* 2,208
C. majority 582
(April 1992, C. maj. 14,699)

MIDDLESBROUGH
*E.*70,931 *T.*64.99%
†S. Bell, *Lab.* 32,925
L. Benham, *C.* 7,907
Miss A. Charlesworth, *LD* 3,934
R. Edwards, *Ref.* 1,331
Lab. majority 25,018
(Boundary change: notional Lab.)

MIDDLESBROUGH SOUTH AND
CLEVELAND EAST
*E.*70,481 *T.*76.03%
Dr A. Kumar, *Lab.* 29,319
†M. Bates, *C.* 18,712
H. Garrett, *LD* 4,004
R. Batchelor, *Ref.* 1,552
Lab. majority 10,607
(Boundary change: notional C.)

MILTON KEYNES NORTH EAST
*E.*70,395 *T.*72.78%
B. White, *Lab.* 20,201
†P. Butler, *C.* 19,961
G. Mabbutt, *LD* 8,907
M. Phillips, *Ref.* 1,492
A. Francis, *Green* 576
M. Simson, *NLP* 99
Lab. majority 240
(Boundary change: notional C.)

MILTON KEYNES SOUTH WEST
*E.*71,070 *T.*71.42%
Mrs P. Starkey, *Lab.* 27,298
*B. Legg, *C.* 17,006
P. Jones, *LD* 6,065
H. Kelly, *NLP* 389
Lab. majority 10,292
(April 1992, C. maj. 4,687)

MITCHAM AND MORDEN
*E.*65,385 *T.*73.33%
Ms S. McDonagh, *Lab.* 27,984
*Rt. Hon. Dame A. Rumbold, *C.*
14,243
N. Harris, *LD* 3,632
P. Isaacs, *Ref.* 810
Ms L. Miller, *BNP* 521
T. Walsh, *Green* 415

K. Vasan, *Ind.* 144
J. Barrett, *UK Ind.* 117
N. Dixon, *ACC* 80
Lab. majority 13,741
(April 1992, C. maj. 1,734)

MOLE VALLEY
*E.*69,140 *T.*78.86%
†Sir P. Beresford, *C.* 26,178
S. Cooksey, *LD* 15,957
C. Payne, *Lab.* 8,057
N. Taber, *Ref.* 2,424
R. Burley, *Ind. CRP* 1,276
Capt. I. Cameron, *UK Ind.* 435
Ms J. Thomas, *NLP* 197
C. majority 10,221
(Boundary change: notional C.)

MORECAMBE AND LUNESDALE
*E.*68,013 *T.*72.41%
Ms G. Smith, *Lab.* 24,061
†Sir M. Lennox-Boyd, *C.* 18,096
Mrs J. Greenwell, *LD* 5,614
I. Ogilvie, *Ref.* 1,313
D. Walne, *NLP* 165
Lab. majority 5,965
(Boundary change: notional C.)

MORLEY AND ROTHWELL
*E.*68,385 *T.*67.12%
†J. Gunnell, *Lab.* 26,836
A. Barraclough, *C.* 12,086
M. Galdas, *LD* 5,087
D. Mitchell-Innes, *Ref.* 1,359
R. Wood, *BNP* 381
Ms P. Sammon, *ProLife* 148
Lab. majority 14,750
(Boundary change: notional Lab.)

NEW FOREST EAST
*E.*65,717 *T.*74.64%
Dr J. Lewis, *C.* 21,053
G. Dawson, *LD* 15,838
A. Goodfellow, *Lab.* 12,161
C. majority 5,215
(Boundary change: notional C.)

NEW FOREST WEST
*E.*66,522 *T.*74.79%
D. Swayne, *C.* 25,149
R. Hale, *LD* 13,817
D. Griffiths, *Lab.* 7,092
Mrs M. Elliott, *Ref.* 2,150
M. Holmes, *UK Ind.* 1,542
C. majority 11,332
(Boundary change: notional C.)

NEWARK
*E.*69,763 *T.*74.50%
Ms F. Jones, *Lab.* 23,496
*R. Alexander, *C.* 20,480
P. Harris, *LD* 5,960
G. Creedy, *Ref.* 2,035
Lab. majority 3,016
(April 1992, C. maj. 8,229)

NEWBURY
*E.*73,680 *T.*76.65%
†D. Rendel, *LD* 29,887
R. Benyon, *C.* 21,370
P. Hannon, *Lab.* 3,107
E. Snook, *Ref.* 992
Ms R. Stark, *Green* 644

R. Tubb, *UK Ind.* 302
Ms K. Howse, *Soc. Lab.* 174
LD majority 8,517
(Boundary change: notional C.)

NEWCASTLE-UNDER-LYME
*E.*66,686 *T.*73.67%
*Mrs L. Golding, *Lab.* 27,743
M. Hayes, *C.* 10,537
Dr R. Studd, *LD* 6,858
Ms K. Suttle, *Ref.* 1,510
S. Mountford, *Lib.* 1,399
Ms B. Bell, *Soc. Lab.* 1,082
Lab. majority 17,206
(April 1992, Lab. maj. 9,839)

NEWCASTLE UPON TYNE
CENTRAL
*E.*69,781 *T.*66.05%
†J. Cousins, *Lab.* 27,272
B. Newmark, *C.* 10,792
Ms R. Berry, *LD* 6,911
C. Coxon, *Ref.* 1,113
Lab. majority 16,480
(Boundary change: notional Lab.)

NEWCASTLE UPON TYNE EAST
AND WALLSEND
*E.*63,272 *T.*65.73%
†N. Brown, *Lab.* 29,607
J. Middleton, *C.* 5,796
G. Morgan, *LD* 4,415
P. Cossins, *Ref.* 966
Ms B. Carpenter, *Soc. Lab.* 642
M. Levy, *Comm. P.* 163
Lab. majority 23,811
(Boundary change: notional Lab.)

NEWCASTLE UPON TYNE
NORTH
*E.*65,357 *T.*69.20%
*D. Henderson, *Lab.* 28,125
G. White, *C.* 8,793
P. Allen, *LD* 6,578
Mrs D. Chipchase, *Ref.* 1,733
Lab. majority 19,332
(April 1992, Lab. maj. 8,946)

NORFOLK MID
*E.*75,311 *T.*76.29%
K. Simpson, *C.* 22,739
D. Zeichner, *Lab.* 21,403
Mrs S. Frary, *LD* 8,617
N. Holder, *Ref.* 3,229
A. Park, *Green* 1,254
B. Parker, *NLP* 215
C. majority 1,336
(Boundary change: notional C.)

NORFOLK NORTH
*E.*77,113 *T.*76.27%
D. Prior, *C.* 21,456
N. Lamb, *LD* 20,163
M. Cullingham, *Lab.* 14,736
J. Allen, *Ref.* 2,458
C. majority 1,293
(April 1992, C. maj. 12,545)

NORFOLK NORTH WEST
*E.*77,083 *T.*74.72%
Dr G. Turner, *Lab.* 25,250
*H. Bellingham, *C.* 23,911
Ms E. Knowles, *LD* 5,513

R. Percival, *Ref.*   2,923
Lab. majority 1,339
(April 1992, C. maj. 11,564)

NORFOLK SOUTH
*E.*79,239   *T.*78.37%
†Rt. Hon. J. MacGregor, *C.*   24,935
Mrs B. Hacker, *LD*   17,557
Ms J. Ross, *Lab.*   16,188
Mrs P. Bateson, *Ref.*   2,533
Mrs S. Ross-Wagenknecht, *Green*   484
A. Boddy, *UK Ind.*   400
C. majority 7,378
(Boundary change: notional C.)

NORFOLK SOUTH WEST
*E.*80,236   *T.*73.28%
†Rt. Hon. Mrs G. Shephard, *C.*   24,694
A. Heffernan, *Lab.*   22,230
D. Buckton, *LD*   8,178
R. Hoare, *Ref.*   3,694
C. majority 2,464
(Boundary change: notional C.)

NORMANTON
*E.*62,980   *T.*68.28%
†W. O'Brien, *Lab.*   26,046
Miss F. Bulmer, *C.*   10,153
D. Ridgway, *LD*   5,347
K. Shuttleworth, *Ref.*   1,458
Lab. majority 15,893
(Boundary change: notional Lab.)

NORTHAMPTON NORTH
*E.*73,664   *T.*70.18%
Ms S. Keeble, *Lab.*   27,247
†A. Marlow, *C.*   17,247
Ms L. Dunbar, *LD*   6,579
D. Torbica, *UK Ind.*   464
B. Spivack, *NLP*   161
Lab. majority 10,000
(Boundary change: notional C.)

NORTHAMPTON SOUTH
*E.*79,384   *T.*71.94%
A. Clarke, *Lab.*   24,214
†Rt. Hon. M. Morris, *C.*   23,470
A. Worgan, *LD*   6,316
C. Petrie, *Ref.*   1,405
D. Clark, *UK Ind.*   1,159
G. Woollcombe, *NLP*   541
Lab. majority 744
(Boundary change: notional C.)

NORTHAVON
*E.*78,943   *T.*79.21%
Prof. S. Webb, *LD*   26,500
†Rt. Hon. Sir J. Cope, *C.*   24,363
R. Stone, *Lab.*   9,767
J. Parfitt, *Ref.*   1,900
LD majority 2,137
(Boundary change: notional C.)

NORWICH NORTH
*E.*72,521   *T.*75.92%
Dr I. Gibson, *Lab.*   27,346
Dr R. Kinghorn, *C.*   17,876
P. Young, *LD*   6,951
A. Bailey-Smith, *Ref.*   1,777
H. Marks, *LCP*   512
J. Hood, *Soc. Lab.*   495
Mrs D. Mills, *NLP*   100
Lab. majority 9,470
(Boundary change: notional C.)

NORWICH SOUTH
*E.*70,009   *T.*72.56%
C. Clarke, *Lab.*   26,267
B. Khanbhai, *C.*   12,028
A. Aalders-Dunthorne, *LD*   9,457
Dr D. Holdsworth, *Ref.*   1,464
H. Marks, *LCP*   765
A. Holmes, *Green*   736
B. Parsons, *NLP*   84
Lab. majority 14,239
(Boundary change: notional Lab.)

NOTTINGHAM EAST
*E.*65,581   *T.*60.60%
*J. Heppell, *Lab.*   24,755
A. Raca, *C.*   9,336
K. Mulloy, *LD*   4,008
B. Brown, *Ref.*   1,645
Lab. majority 15,419
(April 1992, Lab. maj. 7,680)

NOTTINGHAM NORTH
*E.*65,698   *T.*63.02%
*G. Allen, *Lab.*   27,203
Ms G. Shaw, *C.*   8,402
Ms R. Oliver, *LD*   3,301
J. Neal, *Ref.*   1,858
A. Belfield, *Soc.*   637
Lab. majority 18,801
(April 1992, Lab. maj. 10,743)

NOTTINGHAM SOUTH
*E.*72,418   *T.*67.00%
*A. Simpson, *Lab.*   26,825
B. Kirsch, *C.*   13,461
G. Long, *LD*   6,265
K. Thompson, *Ref.*   1,523
Ms S. Edwards, *Nat. Dem.*   446
Lab. majority 13,364
(April 1992, Lab. maj. 3,181)

NUNEATON
*E.*72,032   *T.*74.29%
*W. Olner, *Lab.*   30,080
R. Blunt, *C.*   16,540
R. Cockings, *LD*   4,732
R. English, *Ref.*   1,533
D. Bray, *Loc. Ind.*   390
P. Everitt, *UK Ind.*   238
Lab. majority 13,540
(April 1992, Lab. maj. 1,631)

OLD BEXLEY AND SIDCUP
*E.*68,044   *T.*75.53%
†Rt. Hon. Sir E. Heath, *C.*   21,608
R. Justham, *Lab.*   18,039
I. King, *LD*   8,284
B. Reading, *Ref.*   2,457
C. Bullen, *UK Ind.*   489
Ms V. Tyndall, *BNP*   415
R. Stephens, *NLP*   99
C. majority 3,569
(Boundary change: notional C.)

OLDHAM EAST AND
SADDLEWORTH
*E.*73,189   *T.*73.92%
P. Woolas, *Lab.*   22,546
†C. Davies, *LD*   19,157
J. Hudson, *C.*   10,666
D. Findlay, *Ref.*   1,116
J. Smith, *Soc. Lab.*   470
I. Dalling, *NLP*   146

Lab. majority 3,389
(Boundary change: notional C.)

OLDHAM WEST AND ROYTON
*E.*69,203   *T.*66.09%
†M. Meacher, *Lab.*   26,894
J. Lord, *C.*   10,693
H. Cohen, *LD*   5,434
G. Choudhury, *Soc. Lab.*   1,311
P. Etherden, *Ref.*   1,157
Mrs S. Dalling, *NLP*   249
Lab. majority 16,201
(Boundary change: notional Lab.)

ORPINGTON
*E.*78,749   *T.*76.40%
†J. Horam, *C.*   24,417
C. Maines, *LD*   21,465
Ms S. Polydorou, *Lab.*   10,753
D. Clark, *Ref.*   2,316
J. Carver, *UK Ind.*   526
R. Almond, *Lib.*   494
N. Wilton, *ProLife*   191
C. majority 2,952
(Boundary change: notional C.)

OXFORD EAST
*E.*69,339   *T.*69.05%
†A. Smith, *Lab.*   27,205
J. Djanogly, *C.*   10,540
G. Kershaw, *LD*   7,038
M. Young, *Ref.*   1,391
C. Simmons, *Green*   975
W. Harper-Jones, *Embryo*   318
Dr P. Gardner, *UK Ind.*   234
J. Thompson, *NLP*   108
P. Mylvaganam, *Anti-maj.*   68
Lab. majority 16,665
(Boundary change: notional Lab.)

OXFORD WEST AND ABINGDON
*E.*79,329   *T.*77.14%
Dr E. Harris, *LD*   26,268
L. Harris, *C.*   19,983
Ms S. Brown, *Lab.*   12,361
Mrs G. Eustace, *Ref.*   1,258
Dr M. Woodin, *Green*   691
R. Buckton, *UK Ind.*   258
Mrs L. Hodge, *ProLife*   238
Ms A.-M. Wilson, *NLP*   91
J. Rose, *LGR*   48
LD majority 6,285
(Boundary change: notional C.)

PENDLE
*E.*63,049   *T.*74.60%
*G. Prentice, *Lab.*   25,059
J. Midgeley, *C.*   14,235
A. Greaves, *LD*   5,460
D. Hockney, *Ref.*   2,281
Lab. majority 10,824
(April 1992, Lab. maj. 2,113)

PENRITH AND THE BORDER
*E.*66,496   *T.*73.63%
†Rt. Hon. D. Maclean, *C.*   23,300
G. Walker, *LD*   13,067
Mrs M. Meling, *Lab.*   10,576
C. Pope, *Ref.*   2,018
C. majority 10,233
(Boundary change: notional C.)

PETERBOROUGH
E.65,926 T.73.46%
Ms H. Brinton, *Lab.*	24,365
Mrs J. Foster, *C.*	17,042
D. Howarth, *LD*	5,170
P. Slater, *Ref.*	924
C. Brettell, *NLP*	334
J. Linskey, *UK Ind.*	317
S. Goldspink, *ProLife*	275

Lab. majority 7,323
(Boundary change: notional C.)

PLYMOUTH DEVONPORT
E.74,483 T.69.76%
†D. Jamieson, *Lab.*	31,629
A. Johnson, *C.*	12,562
R. Copus, *LD*	5,570
C. Norsworthy, *Ref.*	1,486
Mrs C. Farrand, *UK Ind.*	478
S. Ebbs, *Nat. Dem.*	238

Lab. majority 19,067
(Boundary change: notional Lab.)

PLYMOUTH SUTTON
E.70,666 T.67.43%
Mrs L. Gilroy, *Lab. Co-op.*	23,881
A. Crisp, *C.*	14,441
S. Melia, *LD*	6,613
T. Hanbury, *Ref.*	1,654
R. Bullock, *UK Ind.*	499
K. Kelway, *Plymouth*	396
F. Lyons, *NLP*	168

Lab. Co-op. majority 9,440
(Boundary change: notional C.)

PONTEFRACT AND CASTLEFORD
E.62,350 T.66.39%
Ms Y. Cooper, *Lab.*	31,339
A. Flook, *C.*	5,614
W. Paxton, *LD*	3,042
R. Wood, *Ref.*	1,401

Lab. majority 25,725
(April 1992, Lab. maj. 23,495)

POOLE
E.66,078 T.70.84%
R. Syms, *C.*	19,726
A. Tetlow, *LD*	14,428
H. White, *Lab.*	10,100
J. Riddington, *Ref.*	1,932
P. Tyler, *UK Ind.*	487
Mrs J. Rosta, *NLP*	137

C. majority 5,298
(Boundary change: notional C.)

POPLAR AND CANNING TOWN
E.67,172 T.58.46%
J. Fitzpatrick, *Lab.*	24,807
B. Steinberg, *C.*	5,892
Ms J. Ludlow, *LD*	4,072
J. Tyndall, *BNP*	2,849
I. Hare, *Ref.*	1,091
Ms J. Joseph, *Soc. Lab.*	557

Lab. majority 18,915
(Boundary change: notional Lab.)

PORTSMOUTH NORTH
E.64,539 T.70.14%
S. Rapson, *Lab.*	21,339
†P. Griffiths, *C.*	17,016
S. Sollitt, *LD*	4,788
S. Evelegh, *Ref.*	1,757
P. Coe, *UK Ind.*	298

C. Bex, *Wessex* 72
Lab. majority 4,323
(Boundary change: notional C.)

PORTSMOUTH SOUTH
E.80,514 T.64.21%
M. Hancock, *LD*	20,421
*D. Martin, *C.*	16,094
A. Burnett, *Lab.*	13,086
C. Trim, *Ref.*	1,629
J. Thompson, *Lib.*	184
Mrs J. Evans, *UK Ind.*	141
W. Treend, *NLP*	140

LD majority 4,327
(April 1992, C. maj. 242)

PRESTON
E.72,933 T.65.92%
†Mrs A. Wise, *Lab.*	29,220
P. Gray, *C.*	10,540
W. Chadwick, *LD*	7,045
J. C. Porter, *Ref.*	924
J. Ashforth, *NLP*	345

Lab. majority 18,680
(Boundary change: notional Lab.)

PUDSEY
E.70,922 T.74.35%
P. Truswell, *Lab.*	25,370
P. Bone, *C.*	19,163
Dr J. Brown, *LD*	7,375
D. Crabtree, *Ref.*	823

Lab. majority 6,207
(April 1992, C. maj. 8,972)

PUTNEY
E.60,176 T.73.11%
A. Colman, *Lab.*	20,084
*Rt. Hon. D. Mellor, *C.*	17,108
R. Pyne, *LD*	4,739
Sir J. Goldsmith, *Ref.*	1,518
W. Jamieson, *UK Ind.*	233
L. Beige, *Stan*	101
M. Yardley, *Spts All.*	90
J. Small, *NLP*	66
Ms A. Poole, *Beaut.*	49
D. Vanbraam, *Ren. Dem.*	7

Lab. majority 2,976
(April 1992, C. maj. 7,526)

RAYLEIGH
E.68,737 T.74.65%
†Dr M. Clark, *C.*	25,516
R. Ellis, *Lab.*	14,832
S. Cumberland, *LD*	10,137
A. Farmer, *Lib.*	829

C. majority 10,684
(Boundary change: notional C.)

READING EAST
E.71,586 T.70.15%
Ms J. Griffiths, *Lab.*	21,461
†J. Watts, *C.*	17,666
R. Samuel, *LD*	9,307
D. Harmer, *Ref.*	1,042
J. Buckley, *NLP*	254
Miss A. Thornton, *UK Ind.*	252
Ms B. Packer, *BNP*	238

Lab. majority 3,795
(Boundary change: notional C.)

READING WEST
E.69,073 T.70.05%
M. Salter, *Lab.*	21,841

N. Bennett, *C.*	18,844
Mrs D. Tomlin, *LD*	6,153
S. Brown, *Ref.*	976
I. Dell, *BNP*	320
D. Black, *UK Ind.*	255

Lab. majority 2,997
(Boundary change: notional C.)

REDCAR
E.68,965 T.70.99%
†Dr M. Mowlam, *Lab.*	32,972
A. Isaacs, *C.*	11,308
Ms J. Benbow, *LD*	4,679

Lab. majority 21,664
(Boundary change: notional Lab.)

REDDITCH
E.60,841 T.73.55%
Ms J. Smith, *Lab.*	22,280
Miss A. McIntyre, *C.*	16,155
M. Hall, *LD*	4,935
R. Cox, *Ref.*	1,151
P. Davis, *NLP*	227

Lab. majority 6,125
(Boundary change: notional C.)

REGENT'S PARK AND
KENSINGTON NORTH
E.73,752 T.64.19%
Ms K. Buck, *Lab.*	28,367
P. McGuinness, *C.*	13,710
Miss E. Gasson, *LD*	4,041
Ms S. Dangoor, *Ref.*	867
J. Hinde, *NLP*	192
Ms D. Sadowitz, *Dream*	167

Lab. majority 14,657
(Boundary change: notional Lab.)

REIGATE
E.64,750 T.74.40%
C. Blunt, *C.*	21,123
A. Howard, *Lab.*	13,382
P. Samuel, *LD*	9,615
†Sir G. Gardiner, *Ref.*	3,352
R. Higgs, *Ind.*	412
S. Smith, *UK Ind.*	290

C. majority 7,741
(Boundary change: notional C.)

RIBBLE SOUTH
E.71,670 T.77.06%
D. Borrow, *Lab.*	25,856
†Rt. Hon. R. Atkins, *C.*	20,772
T. Farron, *LD*	5,879
G. Adams, *Ref.*	1,475
N. Ashton, *Lib.*	1,127
Ms B. Leadbetter, *NLP*	122

Lab. majority 5,084
(Boundary change: notional C.)

RIBBLE VALLEY
E.72,664 T.78.75%
†N. Evans, *C.*	26,702
M. Carr, *LD*	20,062
M. Johnstone, *Lab.*	9,013
J. Parkinson, *Ref.*	1,297
Miss N. Holmes, *NLP*	147

C. majority 6,640
(Boundary change: notional C.)

RICHMOND (Yorks)
E.65,058 T.73.38%
†Rt. Hon. W. Hague, *C.*	23,326

S. Merritt, *Lab.* 13,275
Mrs J. Harvey, *LD* 8,773
A. Bentley, *Ref.* 2,367
C. majority 10,051
(Boundary change: notional C.)

RICHMOND PARK
E.71,572   T.79.43%
Dr J. Tonge, *LD* 25,393
†Rt. Hon. J. Hanley, *C.* 22,442
Ms S. Jenkins, *Lab.* 7,172
J. Pugh, *Ref.* 1,467
D. Beaupre, *Loony* 204
B. D'Arcy, *NLP* 102
P. Davies, *Dream* 73
LD majority 2,951
(Boundary change: notional C.)

ROCHDALE
E.68,529   T.70.16%
Ms L. Fitzsimons, *Lab.* 23,758
†Miss E. Lynne, *LD* 19,213
M. Turnberg, *C.* 4,237
G. Bergin, *BNP* 653
S. Mohammed, *IZB* 221
Lab. majority 4,545
(Boundary change: notional LD)

ROCHFORD AND SOUTHEND
EAST
E.72,848   T.63.97%
†Sir E. Taylor, *C.* 22,683
N. Smith, *Lab.* 18,458
Ms P. Smith, *LD* 4,387
B. Lynch, *Lib.* 1,070
C. majority 4,225
(Boundary change: notional C.)

ROMFORD
E.59,611   T.70.66%
Mrs E. Gordon, *Lab.* 18,187
†Sir M. Neubert, *C.* 17,538
N. Meyer, *LD* 3,341
S. Ward, *Ref.* 1,431
T. Hurlstone, *Lib.* 1,100
M. Carey, *BNP* 522
Lab. majority 649
(Boundary change: notional C.)

ROMSEY
E.67,306   T.76.99%
†M. Colvin, *C.* 23,834
M. Cooper, *LD* 15,249
Ms J. Ford, *Lab.* 9,623
Dr A. Sked, *UK Ind.* 1,824
M. Wigley, *Ref.* 1,291
C. majority 8,585
(Boundary change: notional C.)

ROSSENDALE AND DARWEN
E.69,749   T.73.42%
†Mrs J. Anderson, *Lab.* 27,470
Mrs P. Buzzard, *C.* 16,521
B. Dunning, *LD* 5,435
R. Newstead, *Ref.* 1,108
A. Wearden, *BNP* 674
Lab. majority 10,949
(Boundary change: notional Lab.)

ROTHER VALLEY
E.68,622   T.67.26%
*K. Barron, *Lab.* 31,184
S. Stanbury, *C.* 7,699

S. Burgess, *LD* 5,342
S. Cook, *Ref.* 1,932
Lab. majority 23,485
(April 1992, Lab. maj. 17,222)

ROTHERHAM
E.59,895   T.62.86%
*D. MacShane, *Lab.* 26,852
S. Gordon, *C.* 5,383
D. Wildgoose, *LD* 3,919
R. Hollibone, *Ref.* 1,132
A. Neal, *ProLife* 364
Lab. majority 21,469
(April 1992, Lab. maj. 17,561)

RUGBY AND KENILWORTH
E.79,384   T.77.10%
A. King, *Lab.* 26,356
†J. Pawsey, *C.* 25,861
J. Roodhouse, *LD* 8,737
M. Twite, *NLP* 251
Lab. majority 495
(Boundary change: notional C.)

RUISLIP-NORTHWOOD
E.60,393   T.74.24%
†J. Wilkinson, *C.* 22,526
P. Barker, *Lab.* 14,732
C. Edwards, *LD* 7,279
Ms C. Griffin, *NLP* 296
C. majority 7,794
(Boundary change: notional C.)

RUNNYMEDE AND WEYBRIDGE
E.72,177   T.71.44%
P. Hammond, *C.* 25,051
I. Peacock, *Lab.* 15,176
G. Taylor, *LD* 8,397
P. Rolt, *Ref.* 2,150
S. Slater, *UK Ind.* 625
J. Sleeman, *NLP* 162
C. majority 9,875
(Boundary change: notional C.)

RUSHCLIFFE
E.78,735   T.78.89%
*Rt. Hon. K. Clarke, *C.* 27,558
Ms J. Pettit, *Lab.* 22,503
S. Boote, *LD* 8,851
Miss S. Chadd, *Ref.* 2,682
J. Moore, *UK Ind.* 403
Ms A. Maszwska, *NLP* 115
C. majority 5,055
(April 1992, C. maj. 19,766)

RUTLAND AND MELTON
E.70,150   T.75.02%
†A. Duncan, *C.* 24,107
J. Meads, *Lab.* 15,271
K. Lee, *LD* 10,112
R. King, *Ref.* 2,317
J. Abbott, *UK Ind.* 823
C. majority 8,836
(Boundary change: notional C.)

RYEDALE
E.65,215   T.74.80%
†J. Greenway, *C.* 21,351
J. Orrell, *LD* 16,293
Ms A. Hiles, *Lab.* 8,762
J. Mackfall, *Ref.* 1,460
S. Feaster, *UK Ind.* 917
C. majority 5,058
(Boundary change: notional C.)

SAFFRON WALDEN
E.74,097   T.76.99%
†Sir A. Haselhurst, *C.* 25,871
M. Caton, *LD* 15,298
M. Fincken, *Lab.* 12,275
R. Glover, *Ref.* 2,308
I. Evans, *UK Ind.* 658
B. Tyler, *Ind.* 486
C. Edwards, *NLP* 154
C. majority 10,573
(Boundary change: notional C.)

ST ALBANS
E.65,560   T.77.49%
K. Pollard, *Lab.* 21,338
D. Rutley, *C.* 16,879
A. Rowlands, *LD* 10,692
J. Warrilow, *Ref.* 1,619
Ms S. Craigen, *Dream* 166
I. Docker, *NLP* 111
Lab. majority 4,459
(Boundary change: notional C.)

ST HELENS NORTH
E.71,380   T.68.97%
D. Watts, *Lab.* 31,953
P. Walker, *C.* 8,536
J. Beirne, *LD* 6,270
D. Johnson, *Ref.* 1,276
R. Waugh, *Soc. Lab.* 832
R. Rudin, *UK Ind.* 363
Lab. majority 23,417
(April 1992, Lab. maj. 16,244)

ST HELENS SOUTH
E.66,526   T.66.53%
†G. Bermingham, *Lab.* 30,367
Ms M. Russell, *C.* 6,628
B. Spencer, *LD* 5,919
W. Holdaway, *Ref.* 1,165
Ms H. Jump, *NLP* 179
Lab. majority 23,739
(Boundary change: notional Lab.)

ST IVES
E.71,680   T.75.20%
A. George, *LD* 23,966
W. Rogers, *C.* 16,796
C. Fegan, *Lab.* 8,184
M. Faulkner, *Ref.* 3,714
Mrs P. Garnier, *UK Ind.* 567
G. Stephens, *Lib.* 425
K. Lippiatt, *R. Alt.* 178
W. Hitchins, *BHMBCM* 71
LD majority 7,170
(April 1992, C. maj. 1,645)

SALFORD
E.58,610   T.56.51%
Ms H. Blears, *Lab.* 22,848
E. Bishop, *C.* 5,779
N. Owen, *LD* 3,407
R. Cumpsty, *Ref.* 926
Ms S. Herman, *NLP* 162
Lab. majority 17,069
(Boundary change: notional Lab.)

SALISBURY
E.78,973   T.73.75%
*R. Key, *C.* 25,012
Ms Y. Emmerson-Peirce, *LD* 18,736
R. Rogers, *Lab.* 10,242
N. Farage, *UK Ind.* 3,332

H. Soutar, *Green*	623
W. Holmes, *Ind.*	184
Mrs S. Haysom, *NLP*	110

C. majority 6,276
(April 1992, C. maj. 8,973)

SCARBOROUGH AND WHITBY
*E.*75,862   *T.*71.61%

L. Quinn, *Lab.*	24,791
*J. Sykes, *C.*	19,667
M. Allinson, *LD*	7,672
Ms S. Murray, *Ref.*	2,191

Lab. majority 5,124
(April 1992, C. maj. 11,734)

SCUNTHORPE
*E.*60,393   *T.*68.84%

†E. Morley, *Lab.*	25,107
M. Fisher, *C.*	10,934
G. Smith, *LD*	3,497
P. Smith, *Ref.*	1,637
B. Hopper, *Soc. Lab.*	399

Lab. majority 14,173
(Boundary change: notional Lab.)

SEDGEFIELD
*E.*64,923   *T.*72.57%

†Rt. Hon. A. Blair, *Lab.*	33,526
Mrs E. Pitman, *C.*	8,383
R. Beadle, *LD*	3,050
Miss M. Hall, *Ref.*	1,683
B. Gibson, *Soc. Lab.*	474

Lab. majority 25,143
(Boundary change: notional Lab.)

SELBY
*E.*75,141   *T.*74.95%

J. Grogan, *Lab.*	25,838
K. Hind, *C.*	22,002
E. Batty, *LD*	6,778
D. Walker, *Ref.*	1,162
P. Spence, *UK Ind.*	536

Lab. majority 3,836
(Boundary change: notional C.)

SEVENOAKS
*E.*66,474   *T.*75.44%

M. Fallon, *C.*	22,776
J. Hayes, *Lab.*	12,315
R. Walshe, *LD*	12,086
N. Large, *Ref.*	2,138
Ms M. Lawrence, *Green*	443
M. Ellis, *PF*	244
A. Hankey, *NLP*	147

C. majority 10,461
(Boundary change: notional C.)

SHEFFIELD ATTERCLIFFE
*E.*68,548   *T.*64.65%

*C. Betts, *Lab.*	28,937
B. Doyle, *C.*	7,119
Mrs G. Smith, *LD*	6,973
J. Brown, *Ref.*	1,289

Lab. majority 21,818
(April 1992, Lab. maj. 15,480)

SHEFFIELD BRIGHTSIDE
*E.*58,930   *T.*57.47%

*D. Blunkett, *Lab.*	24,901
F. Butler, *LD*	4,947
C. Buckwell, *C.*	2,850
B. Farnsworth, *Ref.*	624
P. Davidson, *Soc. Lab.*	482

R. Scott, *NLP*	61

Lab. majority 19,954
(April 1992, Lab. maj. 22,681)

SHEFFIELD CENTRAL
*E.*68,667   *T.*53.04%

†R. Caborn, *Lab.*	23,179
A. Qadar, *LD*	6,273
M. Hess, *C.*	4,341
A. D'Agorne, *Green*	954
A. Brownlow, *Ref.*	863
K. Douglas, *Soc.*	466
Ms M. Aitken, *ProLife*	280
M. Driver, *WRP*	63

Lab. majority 16,906
(Boundary change: notional Lab.)

SHEFFIELD HALLAM
*E.*62,834   *T.*72.38%

R. Allan, *LD*	23,345
†Sir I. Patnick, *C.*	15,074
S. Conquest, *Lab.*	6,147
I. Davidson, *Ref.*	788
P. Booler, *SIP*	125

LD majority 8,271
(Boundary change: notional C.)

SHEFFIELD HEELEY
*E.*66,599   *T.*64.96%

*W. Michie, *Lab.*	26,274
R. Davison, *LD*	9,196
J. Harthman, *C.*	6,767
D. Mawson, *Ref.*	1,029

Lab. majority 17,078
(April 1992, Lab. maj. 14,954)

SHEFFIELD HILLSBOROUGH
*E.*74,642   *T.*71.04%

*Mrs H. Jackson, *Lab.*	30,150
A. Dunworth, *LD*	13,699
D. Nuttall, *C.*	7,707
J. Rusling, *Ref.*	1,468

Lab. majority 16,451
(April 1992, Lab. maj. 7,068)

SHERWOOD
*E.*74,788   *T.*75.59%

*P. Tipping, *Lab.*	33,071
R. Spencer, *C.*	16,259
B. Moult, *LD*	4,889
L. Slack, *Ref.*	1,882
P. Ballard, *BNP*	432

Lab. majority 16,812
(April 1992, Lab. maj. 2,910)

SHIPLEY
*E.*69,281   *T.*76.32%

C. Leslie, *Lab.*	22,962
*Rt. Hon. Sir M. Fox, *C.*	19,966
J. Cole, *LD*	7,984
Dr S. Ellams, *Ref.*	1,960

Lab. majority 2,996
(April 1992, C. maj. 12,382)

SHREWSBURY AND ATCHAM
*E.*73,542   *T.*75.25%

P. Marsden, *Lab.*	20,484
*D. Conway, *C.*	18,814
Mrs A. Woolland, *LD*	13,838
D. Barker, *Ref.*	1,346
D. Rowlands, *UK Ind.*	477
A. Dignan, *CFSS*	257
A. Williams, *PPP*	128

Lab. majority 1,670
(April 1992, C. maj. 10,965)

SHROPSHIRE NORTH
*E.*70,852   *T.*72.71%

O. Paterson, *C.*	20,730
I. Lucas, *Lab.*	18,535
J. Stevens, *LD*	10,489
D. Allen, *Ref.*	1,764

C. majority 2,195
(Boundary change: notional C.)

SITTINGBOURNE AND SHEPPEY
*E.*63,850   *T.*72.30%

D. Wyatt, *Lab.*	18,723
†Sir R. Moate, *C.*	16,794
R. Truelove, *LD*	8,447
P. Moull, *Ref.*	1,082
C. Driver, *Loony*	644
N. Risi, *UK Ind.*	472

Lab. majority 1,929
(Boundary change: notional C.)

SKIPTON AND RIPON
*E.*72,042   *T.*75.44%

†Rt. Hon. D. Curry, *C.*	25,294
T. Mould, *LD*	13,674
R. Marchant, *Lab.*	12,171
Mrs N. Holdsworth, *Ref.*	3,212

C. majority 11,620
(Boundary change: notional C.)

SLEAFORD AND NORTH HYKEHAM
*E.*71,486   *T.*74.39%

†Rt. Hon. D. Hogg, *C.*	23,358
S. Harriss, *Lab.*	18,235
J. Marriott, *LD*	8,063
P. Clery, *Ref.*	2,942
R. Overton, *Ind.*	578

C. majority 5,123
(Boundary change: notional C.)

SLOUGH
*E.*70,283   *T.*67.91%

Ms F. MacTaggart, *Lab.*	27,029
Mrs P. Buscombe, *C.*	13,958
C. Bushill, *LD*	3,509
Ms A. Bradshaw, *Lib.*	1,835
T. Sharkey, *Ref.*	1,124
P. Whitmore, *Slough*	277

Lab. majority 13,071
(Boundary change: notional Lab.)

SOLIHULL
*E.*78,898   *T.*74.66%

†J. Taylor, *C.*	26,299
M. Southcombe, *LD*	14,902
Ms R. Harris, *Lab.*	14,334
M. Nattrass, *Ref.*	2,748
J. Caffery, *ProLife*	623

C. majority 11,397
(Boundary change: notional C.)

SOMERTON AND FROME
*E.*73,988   *T.*77.58%

D. Heath, *LD*	22,684
†M. Robinson, *C.*	22,554
R. Ashford, *Lab.*	9,385
R. Rodwell, *Ref.*	2,449
R. Gadd, *UK Ind.*	331

LD majority 130
(Boundary change: notional C.)

SOUTHAMPTON ITCHEN
E.76,869　T.70.06%
†J. Denham, *Lab.*　29,498
P. Fleet, *C.*　15,289
D. Harrison, *LD*　6,289
J. Clegg, *Ref.*　1,660
K. Rose, *Soc. Lab.*　628
C. Hoar, *UK Ind.*　172
G. Marsh, *Soc.*　113
Ms R. Barry, *NLP*　110
F. McDermott, *ProLife*　99
Lab. majority 14,209
(Boundary change: notional Lab.)

SOUTHAMPTON TEST
E.72,983　T.71.85%
A. Whitehead, *Lab.*　28,396
†Sir J. Hill, *C.*　14,712
A. Dowden, *LD*　7,171
P. Day, *Ref.*　1,397
H. Marks, *LCP*　388
A. McCabe, *UK Ind.*　219
P. Taylor, *Glow*　81
J. Sinel, *NLP*　77
Lab. majority 13,684
(Boundary change: notional Lab.)

SOUTHEND WEST
E.66,493　T.69.95%
†D. Amess, *C.*　18,029
Mrs N. Stimson, *LD*　15,414
A. Harley, *Lab.*　10,600
C. Webster, *Ref.*　1,734
B. Lee, *UK Ind.*　636
P. Warburton, *NLP*　101
C. majority 2,615
(April 1992, C. maj. 11,902)

SOUTH HOLLAND AND THE
DEEPINGS
E.69,642　T.71.98%
J. Hayes, *C.*　24,691
J. Lewis, *Lab.*　16,700
P. Millen, *LD*　7,836
G. Erwood, *NPC*　902
C. majority 7,991
(Boundary change: notional C.)

SOUTHPORT
E.70,194　T.72.08%
R. Fearn, *LD*　24,346
*M. Banks, *C.*　18,186
Ms S. Norman, *Lab.*　6,125
F. Buckle, *Ref.*　1,368
Ms S. Ashton, *Lib.*　386
E. Lines, *NLP*　93
M. Middleton, *Nat. Dem.*　92
LD majority 6,160
(April 1992, C. maj. 3,063)

SOUTH SHIELDS
E.62,261　T.62.60%
†Dr D. Clark, *Lab.*　27,834
M. Hoban, *C.*　5,681
D. Ord, *LD*　3,429
A. Loraine, *Ref.*　1,660
I. Wilburn, *Shields*　374
Lab. majority 22,153
(Boundary change: notional Lab.)

SOUTHWARK NORTH AND
BERMONDSEY
E.65,598　T.62.19%
†S. Hughes, *LD*　19,831

J. Fraser, *Lab.*　16,444
G. Shapps, *C.*　2,835
M. Davidson, *BNP*　713
W. Newton, *Ref.*　545
I. Grant, *Comm L.*　175
J. Munday, *Lib.*　157
Ms I. Yngvison, *Nat. Dem.*　95
LD majority 3,387
(Boundary change: notional LD)

SPELTHORNE
E.70,562　T.73.58%
*D. Wilshire, *C.*　23,306
K. Dibble, *Lab.*　19,833
E. Glynn, *LD*　6,821
B. Coleman, *Ref.*　1,495
J. Fowler, *UK Ind.*　462
C. majority 3,473
(April 1992, C. maj. 19,843)

STAFFORD
E.67,555　T.76.64%
D. Kidney, *Lab.*　24,606
D. Cameron, *C.*　20,292
Mrs P. Hornby, *LD*　5,480
S. Culley, *Ref.*　1,146
A. May, *Loony*　248
Lab. majority 4,314
(Boundary change: notional C.)

STAFFORDSHIRE MOORLANDS
E.66,095　T.77.34%
Ms C. Atkins, *Lab.*　26,686
Dr A. Ashworth, *C.*　16,637
Mrs C. Jebb, *LD*　6,191
D. Stanworth, *Ref.*　1,603
Lab. majority 10,049
(Boundary change: notional Lab.)

STAFFORDSHIRE SOUTH
E.68,896　T.74.19%
†Sir P. Cormack, *C.*　25,568
Ms J. LeMaistre, *Lab.*　17,747
Mrs J. Calder, *LD*　5,797
P. Carnell, *Ref.*　2,002
C. majority 7,821
(Boundary change: notional C.)

STALYBRIDGE AND HYDE
E.65,468　T.65.80%
†T. Pendry, *Lab.*　25,363
N. de Bois, *C.*　10,557
M. Cross, *LD*　5,169
R. Clapham, *Ref.*　1,992
Lab. majority 14,806
(Boundary change: notional Lab.)

STEVENAGE
E.66,889　T.76.82%
Ms B. Follett, *Lab.*　28,440
†T. Wood, *C.*　16,858
A. Wilcock, *LD*　4,588
J. Coburn, *Ref.*　1,194
D. Bundy, *ProLife*　196
A. Calcraft, *NLP*　110
Lab. majority 11,582
(Boundary change: notional C.)

STOCKPORT
E.65,232　T.71.54%
†Ms A. Coffey, *Lab.*　29,338
S. Fitzsimmons, *C.*　10,426
Mrs S. Roberts, *LD*　4,951

W. Morley-Scott, *Ref.*　1,280
G. Southern, *Soc. Lab.*　255
C. Newitt, *Loony*　213
C. Dronfield, *Ind.*　206
Lab. majority 18,912
(Boundary change: notional Lab.)

STOCKTON NORTH
E.64,380　T.69.08%
†F. Cook, *Lab.*　29,726
B. Johnston, *C.*　8,369
Mrs S. Fletcher, *LD*　4,816
K. McConnell, *Ref.*　1,563
Lab. majority 21,357
(Boundary change: notional Lab.)

STOCKTON SOUTH
E.68,470　T.76.12%
Ms D. Taylor, *Lab.*　28,790
†T. Devlin, *C.*　17,205
P. Monck, *LD*　4,721
J. Horner, *Ref.*　1,400
Lab. majority 11,585
(Boundary change: notional C.)

STOKE-ON-TRENT CENTRAL
E.64,113　T.62.77%
*M. Fisher, *Lab.*　26,662
N. Jones, *C.*　6,738
E. Fordham, *LD*　4,809
P. Stanyer, *Ref.*　1,071
M. Coleman, *BNP*　606
Ms F. Oborski, *Lib.*　359
Lab. majority 19,924
(April 1992, Lab. maj. 13,420)

STOKE-ON-TRENT NORTH
E.59,030　T.65.50%
†Ms J. Walley, *Lab.*　25,190
C. Day, *C.*　7,798
H. Jebb, *LD*　4,141
Ms J. Tobin, *Ref.*　1,537
Lab. majority 17,392
(Boundary change: notional Lab.)

STOKE-ON-TRENT SOUTH
E.69,968　T.66.08%
*G. Stevenson, *Lab.*　28,645
Mrs S. Scott, *C.*　10,342
P. Barnett, *LD*　4,710
R. Adams, *Ref.*　1,103
Mrs A. Micklem, *Lib.*　580
S. Batkin, *BNP*　568
B. Lawrence, *Nat. Dem.*　288
Lab. majority 18,303
(April 1992, Lab. maj. 6,909)

STONE
E.68,242　T.77.77%
†W. Cash, *C.*　24,859
J. Wakefield, *Lab.*　21,041
B. Stamp, *LD*　6,392
Ms A. Winfield, *Lib.*　545
Ms D. Grice, *NLP*　237
C. majority 3,818
(Boundary change: notional C.)

STOURBRIDGE
E.64,966　T.76.50%
Ms D. Shipley, *Lab.*　23,452
†W. Hawksley, *C.*　17,807
C. Bramall, *LD*　7,123
P. Quick, *Ref.*　1,319

Lab. majority 5,645
(Boundary change: notional C.)

STRATFORD-ON-AVON
E.81,434   T.76.26%

J. Maples, *C.*		29,967
Dr S. Juned, *LD*		15,861
S. Stacey, *Lab.*		12,754
A. Hilton, *Ref.*		2,064
J. Spilsbury, *UK Ind.*		556
J. Brewster, *NLP*		307
S. Marcus, *SFDC*		306
Ms S. Miller, *ProLife*		284

C. majority 14,106
(Boundary change: notional C.)

STREATHAM
E.74,509   T.60.24%

†K. Hill, *Lab.*		28,181
E. Noad, *C.*		9,758
R. O'Brien, *LD*		6,082
J. Wall, *Ref.*		864

Lab. majority 18,423
(Boundary change: notional Lab.)

STRETFORD AND URMSTON
E.69,913   T.69.65%

Ms B. Hughes, *Lab.*		28,480
J. Gregory, *C.*		14,840
J. Bridges, *LD*		3,978
Ms C. Dore, *Ref.*		1,397

Lab. majority 13,640
(Boundary change: notional Lab.)

STROUD
E.77,494   T.80.45%

D. Drew, *Lab. Co-op.*		26,170
†R. Knapman, *C.*		23,260
P. Hodgkinson, *LD*		9,502
J. Marjoram, *Green*		3,415

Lab. Co-op. majority 2,910
(Boundary change: notional C.)

SUFFOLK CENTRAL AND IPSWICH
NORTH
E.70,222   T.75.22%

†M. Lord, *C.*		22,493
Ms C. Jones, *Lab.*		18,955
Dr M. Goldspink, *LD*		10,886
Ms S. Bennell, *Ind.*		489

C. majority 3,538
(Boundary change: notional C.)

SUFFOLK COASTAL
E.74,219   T.75.80%

†Rt. Hon. J. Gummer, *C.*		21,696
M. Campbell, *Lab.*		18,442
Ms A. Jones, *LD*		12,036
S. Caulfield, *Ref.*		3,416
A. Slade, *Green*		514
Ms F. Kaplan, *NLP*		152

C. majority 3,254
(Boundary change: notional C.)

SUFFOLK SOUTH
E.67,323   T.77.20%

†T. Yeo, *C.*		19,402
P. Bishop, *Lab.*		15,227
Mrs K. Pollard, *LD*		14,395
C. de Chair, *Ref.*		2,740
Mrs A. Holland, *NLP*		211

C. majority 4,175
(Boundary change: notional C.)

SUFFOLK WEST
E.68,638   T.71.51%

†R. Spring, *C.*		20,081
M. Jefferys, *Lab.*		18,214
A. Graves, *LD*		6,892
J. Carver, *Ref.*		3,724
A. Shearer, *NLP*		171

C. majority 1,867
(Boundary change: notional C.)

SUNDERLAND NORTH
E.64,711   T.59.05%

†W. Etherington, *Lab.*		26,067
A. Selous, *C.*		6,370
G. Pryke, *LD*		3,973
M. Nicholson, *Ref.*		1,394
K. Newby, *Loony*		409

Lab. majority 19,697
(Boundary change: notional Lab.)

SUNDERLAND SOUTH
E.67,937   T.58.77%

†C. Mullin, *Lab.*		27,174
T. Schofield, *C.*		7,536
J. Lennox, *LD*		4,606
M. Wilkinson, *UK Ind.*		609

Lab. majority 19,638
(Boundary change: notional Lab.)

SURREY EAST
E.72,852   T.75.02%

†P. Ainsworth, *C.*		27,389
Ms B. Ford, *LD*		12,296
D. Ross, *Lab.*		11,573
M. Sydney, *Ref.*		2,656
A. Stone, *UK Ind.*		569
Ms S. Bartrum, *NLP*		173

C. majority 15,093
(Boundary change: notional C.)

SURREY HEATH
E.73,813   T.74.14%

†N. Hawkins, *C.*		28,231
D. Newman, *LD*		11,944
Ms S. Jones, *Lab.*		11,511
J. Gale, *Ref.*		2,385
R. Squire, *UK Ind.*		653

C. majority 16,287
(Boundary change: notional C.)

SURREY SOUTH WEST
E.72,350   T.78.03%

*Rt. Hon. Mrs V. Bottomley, *C.*		
		25,165
N. Sherlock, *LD*		22,471
Ms M. Leicester, *Lab.*		5,333
Mrs J. Clementson, *Ref.*		2,830
J. Kirby, *UK Ind.*		401
Ms J. Quintavalle, *ProLife*		258

C. majority 2,694
(April 1992, C. maj. 14,975)

SUSSEX MID
E.68,784   T.77.73%

†N. Soames, *C.*		23,231
Mrs M. Collins, *LD*		16,377
M. Hamilton, *Lab.*		9,969
T. Large, *Ref.*		3,146
J. Barnett, *UK Ind.*		606
E. Tudway, *Ind. JRP*		134

C. majority 6,854
(Boundary change: notional C.)

SUTTON AND CHEAM
E.62,785   T.75.01%

P. Burstow, *LD*		19,919
*Lady O. Maitland, *C.*		17,822
M. Allison, *Lab.*		7,280
P. Atkinson, *Ref.*		1,784
S. McKie, *UK Ind.*		191
Ms D. Wright, *NLP*		96

LD majority 2,097
(April 1992, C. maj. 10,756)

SUTTON COLDFIELD
E.71,864   T.72.92%

*Rt. Hon. Sir N. Fowler, *C.*		27,373
A. York, *Lab.*		12,488
J. Whorwood, *LD*		10,139
D. Hope, *Ref.*		2,401

C. majority 14,885
(April 1992, C. maj. 26,036)

SWINDON NORTH
E.65,535   T.73.66%

M. Wills, *Lab.*		24,029
G. Opperman, *C.*		16,341
M. Evemy, *LD*		6,237
Ms G. Goldsmith, *Ref.*		1,533
A. Fiskin, *NLP*		130

Lab. majority 7,688
(Boundary change: notional Lab.)

SWINDON SOUTH
E.70,207   T.72.87%

Ms J. Drown, *Lab.*		23,943
†S. Coombs, *C.*		18,298
S. Pajak, *LD*		7,371
D. Mackintosh, *Ref.*		1,273
R. Charman, *Route 66*		181
K. Buscombe, *NLP*		96

Lab. majority 5,645
(Boundary change: notional C.)

TAMWORTH
E.67,205   T.74.18%

†B. Jenkins, *Lab.*		25,808
Lady A. Lightbown, *C.*		18,312
Mrs J. Pinkett, *LD*		4,025
Mrs D. Livesey, *Ref.*		1,163
C. Lamb, *UK Ind.*		369
Ms C. Twelvetrees, *Lib.*		177

Lab. majority 7,496
(Boundary change: notional C.)

TATTON
E.63,822   T.76.45%

M. Bell, *Ind.*		29,354
†N. Hamilton, *C.*		18,277
S. Hill, *Ind.*		295
S. Kinsey, *Ind.*		187
B. Penhaul, *Miss M.*		128
J. Muir, *Albion*		126
M. Kennedy, *NLP*		123
D. Bishop, *Byro*		116
R. Nicholas, *Ind.*		113
J. Price, *Juice*		73

Ind. majority 11,077
(Boundary change: notional C.)

TAUNTON
E.79,783   T.76.47%

Mrs J. Ballard, *LD*		26,064
*D. Nicholson, *C.*		23,621
Ms E. Lisgo, *Lab.*		8,248
B. Ahern, *Ref.*		2,760

L. Andrews, *BNP* 318
LD majority 2,443
(April 1992, C. maj. 3,336)

TEIGNBRIDGE
*E.*81,667   *T.*77.08%
†P. Nicholls, *C.* 24,679
R. Younger-Ross, *LD* 24,398
Ms S. Dann, *Lab.* 11,311
S. Stokes, *UK Ind.* 1,601
N. Banwell, *Green* 817
Mrs L. Golding, *Dream* 139
C. majority 281
(Boundary change: notional C.)

TELFORD
*E.*56,558   *T.*65.62%
†B. Grocott, *Lab.* 21,456
B. Gentry, *C.* 10,166
N. Green, *LD* 4,371
C. Morris, *Ref.* 1,119
Lab. majority 11,290
(Boundary change: notional Lab.)

TEWKESBURY
*E.*68,208   *T.*76.46%
L. Robertson, *C.* 23,859
J. Sewell, *LD* 14,625
K. Tustin, *Lab.* 13,665
C. majority 9,234
(Boundary change: notional C.)

THANET NORTH
*E.*71,112   *T.*68.84%
*R. Gale, *C.* 21,586
Ms I. Johnston, *Lab.* 18,820
P. Kendrick, *LD* 5,576
M. Chambers, *Ref.* 2,535
Ms J. Haines, *UK Ind.* 438
C. majority 2,766
(April 1992, C. maj. 18,210)

THANET SOUTH
*E.*62,792   *T.*71.65%
Dr S. Ladyman, *Lab.* 20,777
†Rt. Hon. J. Aitken, *C.* 17,899
Ms B. Hewett-Silk, *LD* 5,263
C. Crook, *UK Ind.* 631
D. Wheatley, *Green* 418
Lab. majority 2,878
(Boundary change: notional C.)

THURROCK
*E.*71,600   *T.*65.94%
*A. MacKinlay, *Lab.* 29,896
A. Rosindell, *C.* 12,640
J. White, *LD* 3,843
P. Compobassi, *UK Ind.* 833
Lab. majority 17,256
(April 1992, Lab. maj. 1,172)

TIVERTON AND HONITON
*E.*75,744   *T.*78.06%
†Mrs A. Browning, *C.* 24,438
Dr J. Barnard, *LD* 22,785
J. King, *Lab.* 7,598
S. Lowings, *Ref.* 2,952
Mrs J. Roach, *Lib.* 635
Ms E. McIvor, *Green* 485
D. Charles, *Nat. Dem.* 236
C. majority 1,653
(Boundary change: notional C.)

TONBRIDGE AND MALLING
*E.*64,798   *T.*75.97%
†Rt. Hon. Sir J. Stanley, *C.* 23,640
Mrs B. Withstandley, *Lab.* 13,410
K. Brown, *LD* 9,467
J. Scrivenor, *Ref.* 2,005
Mrs B. Bullen, *UK Ind.* 502
G. Valente, *NLP* 205
C. majority 10,230
(Boundary change: notional C.)

TOOTING
*E.*66,653   *T.*69.17%
*T. Cox, *Lab.* 27,516
J. Hutchings, *C.* 12,505
S. James, *LD* 4,320
Mrs A. Husband, *Ref.* 829
J. Rattray, *Green* 527
P. Boddington, *BFAIR* 161
J. Koene, *Rights* 94
D. Bailey-Bond, *Dream* 83
P. Miller, *NLP* 70
Lab. majority 15,011
(April 1992, Lab. maj. 4,107)

TORBAY
*E.*72,258   *T.*73.79%
A. Sanders, *LD* 21,094
*R. Allason, *C.* 21,082
M. Morey, *Lab.* 7,923
G. Booth, *UK Ind.* 1,962
B. Cowling, *Lib.* 1,161
P. Wild, *Dream* 100
LD majority 12
(April 1992, C. maj. 5,787)

TOTNES
*E.*70,473   *T.*76.30%
†Sir A. Steen, *C.* 19,637
R. Chave, *LD* 18,760
V. Ellery, *Lab.* 8,796
Ms P. Cook, *Ref.* 2,552
C. Venmore, *Loc. C.* 2,369
H. Thomas, *UK Ind.* 999
A. Pratt, *Green* 548
J. Golding, *Dream* 108
C. majority 877
(Boundary change: notional C.)

TOTTENHAM
*E.*66,173   *T.*56.98%
*B. Grant, *Lab.* 26,121
A. Scantlebury, *C.* 5,921
N. Hughes, *LD* 4,064
P. Budge, *Green* 1,059
Ms E. Tay, *ProLife* 210
C. Anglin, *WRP* 181
Ms T. Kent, *SEP* 148
Lab. majority 20,200
(April 1992, Lab. maj. 11,968)

TRURO AND ST AUSTELL
*E.*76,824   *T.*73.87%
*M. Taylor, *LD* 27,502
N. Badcock, *C.* 15,001
M. Dooley, *Lab.* 8,697
C. Hearn, *Ref.* 3,682
A. Haithwaite, *UK Ind.* 576
Mrs D. Robinson, *Green* 482
D. Hicks, *MK* 450
Mrs L. Yelland, *PP* 240
P. Boland, *NLP* 117

LD majority 12,501
(April 1992, LD maj. 7,570)

TUNBRIDGE WELLS
*E.*65,259   *T.*74.10%
A. Norman, *C.* 21,853
A. Clayton, *LD* 14,347
P. Warner, *Lab.* 9,879
T. Macpherson, *Ref.* 1,858
M. Anderson Smart, *UK Ind.* 264
P. Levy, *NLP* 153
C. majority 7,506
(Boundary change: notional C.)

TWICKENHAM
*E.*73,281   *T.*79.34%
Dr V. Cable, *LD* 26,237
†T. Jessel, *C.* 21,956
Ms E. Tutchell, *Lab.* 9,065
Miss J. Harrison, *Ind. ECR* 589
T. Haggar, *Dream* 155
A. Hardy, *NLP* 142
LD majority 4,281
(Boundary change: notional C.)

TYNE BRIDGE
*E.*61,058   *T.*57.08%
†D. Clelland, *Lab.* 26,767
A. Lee, *C.* 3,861
Mrs M. Wallace, *LD* 2,785
G. Oswald, *Ref.* 919
Ms E. Brunskill, *Soc.* 518
Lab. majority 22,906
(Boundary change: notional Lab.)

TYNEMOUTH
*E.*66,341   *T.*77.11%
A. Campbell, *Lab.* 28,318
M. Callanan, *C.* 17,045
A. Duffield, *LD* 4,509
C. Rook, *Ref.* 819
Dr F. Rogers, *UK Ind.* 462
Lab. majority 11,273
(Boundary change: notional C.)

TYNESIDE NORTH
*E.*66,449   *T.*67.90%
†S. Byers, *Lab.* 32,810
M. McIntyre, *C.* 6,167
T. Mulvenna, *LD* 4,762
M. Rollings, *Ref.* 1,382
Lab. majority 26,643
(Boundary change: notional Lab.)

UPMINSTER
*E.*57,149   *T.*72.30%
K. Darvill, *Lab.* 19,085
†Sir N. Bonsor, *C.* 16,315
Mrs P. Peskett, *LD* 3,919
T. Murray, *Ref.* 2,000
Lab. majority 2,770
(Boundary change: notional C.)

UXBRIDGE
*E.*57,497   *T.*72.26%
†Sir M. Shersby, *C.* 18,095
D. Williams, *Lab.* 17,371
Dr A. Malyan, *LD* 4,528
G. Aird, *Ref.* 1,153
Ms J. Leonard, *Soc.* 398
C. majority 724
(Boundary change: notional C.)
See also page 233

VALE OF YORK
*E.*70,077   *T.*76.01%
Miss A. McIntosh, *C.* ... 23,815
M. Carter, *Lab.* ... 14,094
C. Hall, *LD* ... 12,656
C. Fairclough, *Ref.* ... 2,503
A. Pelton, *Soc. Dem.* ... 197
C. majority 9,721
(Boundary change: notional C.)

VAUXHALL
*E.*70,402   *T.*55.49%
†Ms K. Hoey, *Lab.* ... 24,920
K. Kerr, *LD* ... 6,260
R. Bacon, *C.* ... 5,942
I. Driver, *Soc. Lab.* ... 983
S. Collins, *Green* ... 864
R. Headicar, *SPGB* ... 97
Lab. majority 18,660
(Boundary change: notional Lab.)

WAKEFIELD
*E.*73,210   *T.*68.96%
†D. Hinchliffe, *Lab.* ... 28,977
J. Peacock, *C.* ... 14,373
D. Dale, *LD* ... 5,656
S. Shires, *Ref.* ... 1,480
Lab. majority 14,604
(Boundary change: notional Lab.)

WALLASEY
*E.*63,714   *T.*73.52%
*Ms A. Eagle, *Lab.* ... 30,264
Mrs P. Wilcock, *C.* ... 11,190
P. Reisdorf, *LD* ... 3,899
R. Hayes, *Ref.* ... 1,490
Lab. majority 19,074
(April 1992, Lab. maj. 3,809)

WALSALL NORTH
*E.*67,587   *T.*64.07%
*D. Winnick, *Lab.* ... 24,517
M. Bird, *C.* ... 11,929
Ms T. O'Brien, *LD* ... 4,050
D. Bennett, *Ref.* ... 1,430
M. Pitt, *Ind.* ... 911
A. Humphries, *NF* ... 465
Lab. majority 12,588
(April 1992, Lab. maj. 3,824)

WALSALL SOUTH
*E.*64,221   *T.*67.33%
*B. George, *Lab.* ... 25,024
L. Leek, *C.* ... 13,712
H. Harris, *LD* ... 2,698
Dr T. Dent, *Ref.* ... 1,662
Mrs L. Meads, *NLP* ... 144
Lab. majority 11,312
(April 1992, Lab. maj. 3,178)

WALTHAMSTOW
*E.*63,818   *T.*62.76%
†N. Gerrard, *Lab.* ... 25,287
Mrs J. Andrew, *C.* ... 8,138
Dr J. Jackson, *LD* ... 5,491
Revd G. Hargreaves, *Ref.* ... 1,139
Lab. majority 17,149
(Boundary change: notional Lab.)

WANSBECK
*E.*62,998   *T.*71.70%
D. Murphy, *Lab.* ... 29,569
A. Thompson, *LD* ... 7,202

WANSDYKE
*E.*69,032   *T.*79.27%
D. Norris, *Lab.* ... 24,117
M. Prisk, *C.* ... 19,318
J. Manning, *LD* ... 9,205
K. Clinton, *Ref.* ... 1,327
T. Hunt, *UK Ind.* ... 438
P. House, *Loony* ... 225
Ms S. Lincoln, *NLP* ... 92
Lab. majority 4,799
(Boundary change: notional C.)

WANTAGE
*E.*71,657   *T.*78.23%
*R. Jackson, *C.* ... 22,311
Ms C. Wilson, *Lab.* ... 16,272
Ms J. Riley, *LD* ... 14,822
S. Rising, *Ref.* ... 1,549
Ms M. Kennet, *Green* ... 640
Count N. Tolstoy-Miloslausky,
   UK Ind. ... 465
C. majority 6,039
(April 1992, C. maj. 16,473)

WARLEY
*E.*59,758   *T.*65.08%
†J. Spellar, *Lab.* ... 24,813
C. Pincher, *C.* ... 9,362
J. Pursehouse, *LD* ... 3,777
K. Gamre, *Ref.* ... 941
Lab. majority 15,451
(Boundary change: notional Lab.)

WARRINGTON NORTH
*E.*72,694   *T.*70.50%
Ms H. Jones, *Lab.* ... 31,827
Ms R. Lacey, *C.* ... 12,300
I. Greenhalgh, *LD* ... 5,308
Dr A. Smith, *Ref.* ... 1,816
Lab. majority 19,527
(Boundary change: notional Lab.)

WARRINGTON SOUTH
*E.*72,262   *T.*76.23%
Ms H. Southworth, *Lab.* ... 28,721
C. Grayling, *C.* ... 17,914
P. Walker, *LD* ... 7,199
G. Kelly, *Ref.* ... 1,082
S. Ross, *NLP* ... 166
Lab. majority 10,807
(Boundary change: notional C.)

WARWICK AND LEAMINGTON
*E.*79,374   *T.*75.71%
J. Plaskitt, *Lab.* ... 26,747
†Sir D. Smith, *C.* ... 23,349
N. Hicks, *LD* ... 7,133
Mrs V. Davis, *Ref.* ... 1,484
P. Baptie, *Green* ... 764
G. Warwick, *UK Ind.* ... 306
M. Gibbs, *EDP* ... 183
R. McCarthy, *NLP* ... 125
Lab. majority 3,398
(Boundary change: notional C.)

WARWICKSHIRE NORTH
*E.*72,602   *T.*74.71%
†M. O'Brien, *Lab.* ... 31,669

S. Hammond, *C.* ... 16,902
W. Powell, *LD* ... 4,040
R. Mole, *Ref.* ... 917
C. Cooke, *UK Ind.* ... 533
I. Moorecroft, *Bert.* ... 178
Lab. majority 14,767
(Boundary change: notional Lab.)

WATFORD
*E.*74,015   *T.*74.63%
Ms C. Ward, *Lab.* ... 25,019
R. Gordon, *C.* ... 19,227
A. Canning, *LD* ... 9,272
Dr P. Roe, *Ref.* ... 1,484
L. Davis, *NLP* ... 234
Lab. majority 5,792
(Boundary change: notional C.)

WAVENEY
*E.*75,266   *T.*75.21%
R. Blizzard, *Lab.* ... 31,846
†D. Porter, *C.* ... 19,393
C. Thomas, *LD* ... 5,054
N. Clark, *Ind.* ... 318
Lab. majority 12,453
(Boundary change: notional C.)

WEALDEN
*E.*79,519   *T.*74.32%
†Rt. Hon. Sir G. Johnson Smith,
   C. ... 29,417
M. Skinner, *LD* ... 15,213
N. Levine, *Lab.* ... 10,185
B. Taplin, *Ref.* ... 3,527
Mrs M. English, *UK Ind.* ... 569
P. Cragg, *NLP* ... 188
C. majority 14,204
(Boundary change: notional C.)

WEAVER VALE
*E.*66,011   *T.*73.17%
†M. Hall, *Lab.* ... 27,244
J. Byrne, *C.* ... 13,796
T. Griffiths, *LD* ... 5,949
R. Cockfield, *Ref.* ... 1,312
Lab. majority 13,448
(Boundary change: notional Lab.)

WELLINGBOROUGH
*E.*74,955   *T.*75.10%
P. Stinchcombe, *Lab.* ... 24,854
*Sir P. Fry, *C.* ... 24,667
P. Smith, *LD* ... 5,279
A. Ellwood, *UK Ind.* ... 1,192
Ms A. Lowrys, *NLP* ... 297
Lab. majority 187
(April 1992, C. maj. 11,816)

WELLS
*E.*72,178   *T.*78.11%
*Rt. Hon. D. Heathcoat-Amory,
   C. ... 22,208
Dr P. Gold, *LD* ... 21,680
M. Eavis, *Lab.* ... 10,204
Mrs P. Phelps, *Ref.* ... 2,196
Ms L. Royse, *NLP* ... 92
C. majority 528
(April 1992, C. maj. 6,649)

WELWYN HATFIELD
*E.*67,395   *T.*78.59%
Ms M. Johnson, *Lab.* ... 24,936
†D. Evans, *C.* ... 19,341

R. Schwartz, *LD* — 7,161
E. Cox, *RA* — 1,263
Ms H. Harold, *ProLife* — 267
Lab. majority 5,595
(Boundary change: notional C.)

WENTWORTH
*E.*63,951   *T.*65.33%
J. Healey, *Lab.* — 30,225
K. Hamer, *C.* — 6,266
J. Charters, *LD* — 3,867
A. Battley, *Ref.* — 1,423
Lab. majority 23,959
(April 1992, Lab. maj. 22,449)

WEST BROMWICH EAST
*E.*63,401   *T.*65.44%
†P. Snape, *Lab.* — 23,710
B. Matsell, *C.* — 10,126
M. Smith, *LD* — 6,179
G. Mulley, *Ref.* — 1,472
Lab. majority 13,584
(Boundary change: notional Lab.)

WEST BROMWICH WEST
*E.*67,496   *T.*54.37%
†Rt. Hon. Miss B. Boothroyd, *Speaker* — 23,969
R. Silvester, *Lab. Change* — 8,546
S. Edwards, *Nat. Dem.* — 4,181
Speaker majority 15,423
(Boundary change: notional Lab.)

WESTBURY
*E.*74,301   *T.*76.38%
†D. Faber, *C.* — 23,037
J. Miller, *LD* — 16,969
K. Small, *Lab.* — 11,969
G. Hawkins, *Lib.* — 1,956
N. Hawkings-Byass, *Ref.* — 1,909
R. Westbury, *UK Ind.* — 771
C. Haysom, *NLP* — 140
C. majority 6,068
(Boundary change: notional C.)

WEST HAM
*E.*57,058   *T.*58.99%
†A. Banks, *Lab.* — 24,531
M. MacGregor, *C.* — 5,037
Ms S. McDonough, *LD* — 2,479
K. Francis, *BNP* — 1,198
T. Jug, *Loony* — 300
J. Rainbow, *Dream* — 116
Lab. majority 19,494
(Boundary change: notional Lab.)

WESTMORLAND AND LONSDALE
*E.*68,389   *T.*74.29%
T. Collins, *C.* — 21,470
S. Collins, *LD* — 16,949
J. Harding, *Lab.* — 10,459
M. Smith, *Ref.* — 1,931
C. majority 4,521
(Boundary change: notional C.)

WESTON-SUPER-MARE
*E.*72,445   *T.*73.68%
B. Cotter, *LD* — 21,407
Mrs M. Daly, *C.* — 20,133
D. Kraft, *Lab.* — 9,557
T. Sewell, *Ref.* — 2,280
LD majority 1,274
(Boundary change: notional C.)

WIGAN
*E.*64,689   *T.*67.74%
†R. Stott, *Lab.* — 30,043
M. Loveday, *C.* — 7,400
T. Beswick, *LD* — 4,390
A. Bradborne, *Ref.* — 1,450
C. Maile, *Green* — 442
W. Ayliffe, *NLP* — 94
Lab. majority 22,643
(Boundary change: notional Lab.)
See also Stop-press

WILTSHIRE NORTH
*E.*77,237   *T.*75.11%
J. Gray, *C.* — 25,390
S. Cordon, *LD* — 21,915
N. Knowles, *Lab.* — 8,261
Ms M. Purves, *Ref.* — 1,774
A. Wood, *UK Ind.* — 410
Ms J. Forsyth, *NLP* — 263
C. majority 3,475
(Boundary change: notional C.)

WIMBLEDON
*E.*64,070   *T.*75.47%
R. Casale, *Lab.* — 20,674
*Dr C. Goodson-Wickes, *C.* — 17,694
Ms A. Willott, *LD* — 8,014
H. Abid, *Ref.* — 993
R. Thacker, *Green* — 474
Ms S. Davies, *ProLife* — 346
M. Kirby, *Mongolian* — 112
G. Stacey, *Dream* — 47
Lab. majority 2,980
(April 1992, C. maj. 14,761)

WINCHESTER
*E.*78,884   *T.*78.66%
M. Oaten, *LD* — 26,100
†G. Malone, *C.* — 26,098
P. Davies, *Lab.* — 6,528
P. Strand, *Ref.* — 1,598
R. Huggett, *Top* — 640
D. Rumsey, *UK Ind.* — 476
J. Browne, *Ind. AFE* — 307
P. Stockton, *Loony* — 307
LD majority 2
(Boundary change: notional C.)
See also page 233

WINDSOR
*E.*69,132   *T.*73.46%
†M. Trend, *C.* — 24,476
C. Fox, *LD* — 14,559
Mrs A. Williams, *Lab.* — 9,287
J. McDermott, *Ref.* — 1,676
P. Bradshaw, *Lib.* — 388
Mrs E. Bigg, *UK Ind.* — 302
Mr R. Parr, *Dynamic* — 93
C. majority 9,917
(Boundary change: notional C.)

WIRRAL SOUTH
*E.*59,372   *T.*81.01%
†B. Chapman, *Lab.* — 24,499
L. Byrom, *C.* — 17,495
P. Gilchrist, *LD* — 5,018
D. Wilcox, *Ref.* — 768
Ms J. Nielsen, *ProLife* — 264
G. Mead, *NLP* — 51
Lab. majority 7,004
(Boundary change: notional C.)

WIRRAL WEST
*E.*60,908   *T.*76.98%
S. Hesford, *Lab.* — 21,035
*Rt. Hon. D. Hunt, *C.* — 18,297
J. Thornton, *LD* — 5,945
D. Wharton, *Ref.* — 1,613
Lab. majority 2,738
(April 1992, C. maj. 11,064)

WITNEY
*E.*73,520   *T.*76.72%
S. Woodward, *C.* — 24,282
A. Hollingsworth, *Lab.* — 17,254
Mrs A. Lawrence, *LD* — 11,202
G. Brown, *Ref.* — 2,262
M. Montgomery, *UK Ind.* — 765
Ms S. Chapple-Perrie, *Green* — 636
C. majority 7,028
(Boundary change: notional C.)

WOKING
*E.*70,053   *T.*72.68%
H. Malins, *C.* — 19,553
P. Goldenberg, *LD* — 13,875
Ms K. Hanson, *Lab.* — 10,695
H. Bell, *Ind. C.* — 3,933
C. Skeate, *Ref.* — 2,209
M. Harvey, *UK Ind.* — 512
Miss D. Sleeman, *NLP* — 137
C. majority 5,678
(Boundary change: notional C.)

WOKINGHAM
*E.*66,161   *T.*75.74%
†Rt. Hon. J. Redwood, *C.* — 25,086
Dr R. Longton, *LD* — 15,721
Ms P. Colling, *Lab.* — 8,424
P. Owen, *Loony* — 877
C. majority 9,365
(Boundary change: notional C.)

WOLVERHAMPTON NORTH EAST
*E.*61,642   *T.*67.17%
K. Purchase, *Lab. Co-op.* — 24,534
D. Harvey, *C.* — 11,547
B. Niblett, *LD* — 2,214
C. Hallmark, *Lib.* — 1,560
A. Muchall, *Ref.* — 1,192
M. Wingfield, *Nat. Dem.* — 356
Lab. Co-op. majority 12,987
(Boundary change: notional Lab. Co-op.)

WOLVERHAMPTON SOUTH EAST
*E.*54,291   *T.*64.15%
*D. Turner, *Lab. Co-op.* — 22,202
W. Hanbury, *C.* — 7,020
R. Whitehouse, *LD* — 3,292
T. Stevenson-Platt, *Ref.* — 980
N. Worth, *Soc. Lab.* — 689
K. Bullman, *Lib.* — 647
Lab. Co-op. majority 15,182
(April 1992, Lab. maj. 10,240)

WOLVERHAMPTON SOUTH WEST
*E.*67,482   *T.*72.49%
Ms J. Jones, *Lab.* — 24,657
*N. Budgen, *C.* — 19,539
M. Green, *LD* — 4,012
M. Hyde, *Lib.* — 713
Lab. majority 5,118
(April 1992, C. maj. 4,966)

WOODSPRING
E.69,964   T.78.51%

†Dr L. Fox, *C.*	24,425
Mrs N. Kirsen, *LD*	16,691
Ms D. Sander, *Lab.*	11,377
R. Hughes, *Ref.*	1,614
Dr R. Lawson, *Green*	667
A. Glover, *Ind.*	101
M. Mears, *NLP*	52

C. majority 7,734
(Boundary change: notional C.)

WORCESTER
E.69,234   T.74.56%

M. Foster, *Lab.*	25,848
N. Bourne, *C.*	18,423
P. Chandler, *LD*	6,462
Mrs P. Wood, *UK Ind.*	886

Lab. majority 7,425
(Boundary change: notional C.)

WORCESTERSHIRE MID
E.68,381   T.74.32%

†P. Luff, *C.*	24,092
Mrs D. Smith, *Lab.*	14,680
D. Barwick, *LD*	9,458
T. Watson, *Ref.*	1,780
D. Ingles, *UK Ind.*	646
A. Dyer, *NLP*	163

C. majority 9,412
(Boundary change: notional C.)

WORCESTERSHIRE WEST
E.64,712   T.76.25%

†Sir M. Spicer, *C.*	22,223
M. Hadley, *LD*	18,377
N. Stone, *Lab.*	7,738
Ms S. Cameron, *Green*	1,006

C. majority 3,846
(Boundary change: notional C.)

WORKINGTON
E.65,766   T.75.08%

†D. Campbell-Savours, *Lab.*	31,717
R. Blunden, *C.*	12,061
P. Roberts, *LD*	3,967
G. Donnan, *Ref.*	1,412
C. Austin, *UA*	217

Lab. majority 19,656
(Boundary change: notional Lab.)

WORSLEY
E.68,978   T.67.82%

†T. Lewis, *Lab.*	29,083
D. Garrido, *C.*	11,342
R. Bleakley, *LD*	6,356

Lab. majority 17,741
(Boundary change: notional Lab.)

WORTHING EAST AND
SHOREHAM
E.70,771   T.72.87%

T. Loughton, *C.*	20,864
M. King, *LD*	15,766
M. Williams, *Lab.*	12,335
J. McCulloch, *Ref.*	1,683
Mrs R. Jarvis, *UK Ind.*	921

C. majority 5,098
(Boundary change: notional C.)

WORTHING WEST
E.71,329   T.72.12%

†P. Bottomley, *C.*	23,733
C. Hare, *LD*	16,020
J. Adams, *Lab.*	8,347
N. John, *Ref.*	2,313
T. Cross, *UK Ind.*	1,029

C. majority 7,713
(Boundary change: notional C.)

WREKIN, THE
E.59,126   T.76.56%

P. Bradley, *Lab.*	21,243
P. Bruinvels, *C.*	18,218
I. Jenkins, *LD*	5,807

Lab. majority 3,025
(Boundary change: notional C.)

WYCOMBE
E.73,589   T.71.10%

†Sir R. Whitney, *C.*	20,890
C. Bryant, *Lab.*	18,520
P. Bensilum, *LD*	9,678
A. Fulford, *Ref.*	2,394
J. Laker, *Green*	716
M. Heath, *NLP*	121

C. majority 2,370
(Boundary change: notional C.)

WYRE FOREST
E.73,063   T.75.35%

D. Lock, *Lab.*	26,843
†A. Coombs, *C.*	19,897
D. Cropp, *LD*	4,377
W. Till, *Ref.*	1,956
C. Harvey, *Lib.*	1,670
J. Millington, *UK Ind.*	312

Lab. majority 6,946
(Boundary change: notional C.)

WYTHENSHAWE AND SALE EAST
E.71,986   T.63.25%

P. Goggins, *Lab.*	26,448
P. Fleming, *C.*	11,429
Ms V. Tucker, *LD*	5,639
B. Stanyer, *Ref.*	1,060
J. Flannery, *Soc. Lab.*	957

Lab. majority 15,019
(Boundary change: notional Lab.)

YEOVIL
E.74,165   T.72.88%

†Rt. Hon. J. D. D. Ashdown, *LD*	26,349
N. Cambrook, *C.*	14,946
P. Conway, *Lab.*	8,053
J. Beveridge, *Ref.*	3,574
D. Taylor, *Green*	728
J. Archer, *Musician*	306
C. Hudson, *Dream*	97

LD majority 11,403
(Boundary change: notional LD)

YORK, CITY OF
E.79,383   T.73.50%

*H. Bayley, *Lab.*	34,956
S. Mallett, *C.*	14,433
A. Waller, *LD*	6,537
J. Sheppard, *Ref.*	1,083
M. Hill, *Green*	880
E. Wegener, *UK Ind.*	319
A. Lightfoot, *Ch. Nat.*	137

Lab. majority 20,523
(April 1992, Lab. maj. 6,342)

YORKSHIRE EAST
E.69,409   T.70.55%

†J. Townend, *C.*	20,904
I. Male, *Lab.*	17,567
D. Leadley, *LD*	9,070
R. Allerston, *Soc. Dem.*	1,049
M. Cooper, *Nat. Dem.*	381

C. majority 3,337
(Boundary change: notional C.)

WALES

ABERAVON
E.50,025   T.71.89%

*Rt. Hon. J. Morris, *Lab.*	25,650
R. McConville, *LD*	4,079
P. Harper, *C.*	2,835
P. Cockwell, *PC*	2,088
P. David, *Ref.*	970
Capt. Beany, *Beanus*	341

Lab. majority 21,571
(April 1992, Lab. maj. 21,310)

ALYN AND DEESIDE
E.58,091   T.72.21%

†B. Jones, *Lab.*	25,955
T. Roberts, *C.*	9,552
Mrs E. Burnham, *LD*	4,076
M. Jones, *Ref.*	1,627
Mrs S. Hills, *PC*	738

Lab. majority 16,403
(Boundary change: notional Lab.)

BLAENAU GWENT
E.54,800   T.72.32%

*L. Smith, *Lab.*	31,493
Mrs G. Layton, *LD*	3,458
Mrs M. Williams, *C.*	2,607
J. Criddle, *PC*	2,072

Lab. majority 28,035
(April 1992, Lab. maj. 30,067)

BRECON AND RADNORSHIRE
E.52,142   T.82.24%

R. Livsey, *LD*	17,516
*J. Evans, *C.*	12,419
C. Mann, *Lab.*	11,424
Ms E. Phillips, *Ref.*	900
S. Cornelius, *PC*	622

LD majority 5,097
(April 1992, C. maj. 130)

BRIDGEND
E.59,721   T.72.44%

*W. Griffiths, *Lab.*	25,115
D. Davies, *C.*	9,867
A. McKinlay, *LD*	4,968

T. Greaves, *Ref.*   1,662
D. Watkins, *PC*   1,649
Lab. majority 15,248
(April 1992, Lab. maj. 7,326)

CAERNARFON
E.46,815   T.72.65%
*D. Wigley, *PC*   17,616
E. Williams, *Lab.*   9,667
E. Williams, *C.*   4,230
Ms M. McQueen, *LD*   1,686
C. Collins, *Ref.*   811
PC majority 7,949
(April 1992, PC maj. 14,476)

CAERPHILLY
E.64,621   T.70.05%
*R. Davies, *Lab.*   30,697
R. Harris, *C.*   4,858
L. Whittle, *PC*   4,383
A. Ferguson, *LD*   3,724
M. Morgan, *Ref.*   1,337
Mrs C. Williams, *ProLife*   270
Lab. majority 25,839
(April 1992, Lab. maj. 22,672)

CARDIFF CENTRAL
E.60,354   T.70.01%
*J. Owen Jones, *Lab. Co-op.*   18,464
Mrs J. Randerson, *LD*   10,541
D. Melding, *C.*   8,470
T. Burns, *Soc. Lab.*   2,230
W. Vernon, *PC*   1,504
N. Lloyd, *Ref.*   760
C. James, *Loony*   204
A. Hobbs, *NLP*   80
Lab. Co-op. majority 7,923
(April 1992, Lab. maj. 3,465)

CARDIFF NORTH
E.60,430   T.80.24%
Ms J. Morgan, *Lab.*   24,460
*G. Jones, *C.*   16,334
R. Rowland, *LD*   5,294
Dr C. Palfrey, *PC*   1,201
E. Litchfield, *Ref.*   1,199
Lab. majority 8,126
(April 1992, C. maj. 2,969)

CARDIFF SOUTH AND PENARTH
E.61,838   T.68.57%
*A. Michael, *Lab. Co-op.*   22,647
Mrs C. Roberts, *C.*   8,766
Dr S. Wakefield, *LD*   3,964
J. Foreman, *New Lab.*   3,942
D. Haswell, *PC*   1,356
P. Morgan, *Ref.*   1,211
M. Shepherd, *Soc.*   344
Ms B. Caves, *NLP*   170
Lab. Co-op. majority 13,881
(April 1992, Lab. maj. 10,425)

CARDIFF WEST
E.58,198   T.69.21%
†R. Morgan, *Lab.*   24,297
S. Hoare, *C.*   8,669
Ms J. Gasson, *LD*   4,366
Ms G. Carr, *PC*   1,949
T. Johns, *Ref.*   996
Lab. majority 15,628
(Boundary change: notional Lab.)

CARMARTHEN EAST AND
DINEFWR
E.53,079   T.78.62%
†Dr A. Wynne Williams, *Lab.*   17,907
R. Thomas, *PC*   14,457
E. Hayward, *C.*   5,022
Mrs J. Hughes, *LD*   3,150
I. Humphreys-Evans, *Ref.*   1,196
Lab. majority 3,450
(Boundary change: notional Lab.)

CARMARTHEN WEST AND
PEMBROKESHIRE SOUTH
E.55,724   T.76.52%
†N. Ainger, *Lab.*   20,956
O. J. Williams, *C.*   11,335
R. Llewellyn, *PC*   5,402
K. Evans, *LD*   3,516
Mrs J. Poirrier, *Ref.*   1,432
Lab. majority 9,621
(Boundary change: notional Lab.)

CEREDIGION
E.54,378   T.73.90%
†C. Dafis, *PC*   16,728
R. Harris, *Lab.*   9,767
D. Davies, *LD*   6,616
Dr F. Aubel, *C.*   5,983
J. Leaney, *Ref.*   1,092
PC majority 6,961
(Boundary change: notional PC)

CLWYD SOUTH
E.53,495   T.73.62%
†M. Jones, *Lab.*   22,901
B. Johnson, *C.*   9,091
A. Chadwick, *LD*   3,684
G. Williams, *PC*   2,500
A. Lewis, *Ref.*   1,207
Lab. majority 13,810
(Boundary change: notional Lab.)

CLWYD WEST
E.53,467   T.75.29%
G. Thomas, *Lab.*   14,918
†R. Richards, *C.*   13,070
E. Williams, *PC*   5,421
G. Williams, *LD*   5,151
Ms H. Collins, *Ref.*   1,114
D. Neal, *Cvty*   583
Lab. majority 1,848
(Boundary change: notional C.)

CONWY
E.55,092   T.75.44%
Mrs B. Williams, *Lab.*   14,561
R. Roberts, *LD*   12,965
D. Jones, *C.*   10,085
R. Davies, *PC*   2,844
A. Barham, *Ref.*   760
R. Bradley, *Alt. LD*   250
D. Hughes, *NLP*   95
Lab. majority 1,596
(April 1992, C. maj. 995)

CYNON VALLEY
E.48,286   T.69.22%
*Mrs A. Clwyd, *Lab.*   23,307
A. Davies, *PC*   3,552
H. Price, *LD*   3,459
A. Smith, *C.*   2,262
G. John, *Ref.*   844

Lab. majority 19,755
(April 1992, Lab. maj. 21,364)

DELYN
E.53,693   T.74.02%
†D. Hanson, *Lab.*   22,300
Mrs K. Lumley, *C.*   10,607
P. Lloyd, *LD*   4,160
A. Drake, *PC*   1,558
Ms E. Soutter, *Ref.*   1,117
Lab. majority 11,693
(Boundary change: notional Lab.)

GOWER
E.57,691   T.75.12%
M. Caton, *Lab.*   23,313
A. Cairns, *C.*   10,306
H. Evans, *LD*   5,624
E. Williams, *PC*   2,226
R. Lewis, *Ref.*   1,745
A. Popham, *FP*   122
Lab. majority 13,007
(April 1992, Lab. maj. 7,018)

ISLWYN
E.50,540   T.72.03%
*D. Touhig, *Lab. Co-op.*   26,995
C. Worker, *LD*   3,064
R. Walters, *C.*   2,864
D. Jones, *PC*   2,272
Mrs S. Monaghan, *Ref.*   1,209
Lab. Co-op. majority 23,931
(April 1992, Lab. maj. 24,728)
(Feb. 1995, Lab. maj. 13,097)

LLANELLI
E.58,323   T.70.66%
†Rt. Hon. D. Davies, *Lab.*   23,851
M. Phillips, *PC*   7,812
A. Hayes, *C.*   5,003
N. Burree, *LD*   3,788
J. Willock, *Soc. Lab.*   757
Lab. majority 16,039
(Boundary change: notional Lab.)

MEIRIONNYDD NANT CONWY
E.32,345   T.75.98%
*E. Llwyd, *PC*   12,465
H. Rees, *Lab.*   5,660
J. Quin, *C.*   3,922
Mrs B. Feeley, *LD*   1,719
P. Hodge, *Ref.*   809
PC majority 6,805
(April 1992, PC maj. 4,613)

MERTHYR TYDFIL AND
RHYMNEY
E.56,507   T.69.27%
*T. Rowlands, *Lab.*   30,012
D. Anstey, *LD*   2,926
J. Morgan, *C.*   2,508
A. Cox, *PC*   2,344
A. Cowdell, *Old Lab.*   691
R. Hutchings, *Ref.*   660
Lab. majority 27,086
(April 1992, Lab. maj. 26,713)

MONMOUTH
E.60,703   T.80.76%
H. Edwards, *Lab.*   23,404
*R. Evans, *C.*   19,226
M. Williams, *LD*   4,689
N. Warry, *Ref.*   1,190

A. Cotton, *PC* — 516
Lab. majority 4,178
(April 1992, C. maj. 3,204)

MONTGOMERYSHIRE
*E.*42,618   *T.*74.91%
L. Opik, *LD* — 14,647
G. Davies, *C.* — 8,344
Ms A. Davies, *Lab.* — 6,109
Ms H. M. Jones, *PC* — 1,608
J. Bufton, *Ref.* — 879
Ms S. Walker, *Green* — 338
LD majority 6,303
(April 1992, LD maj. 5,209)

NEATH
*E.*55,525   *T.*74.28%
*P. Hain, *Lab.* — 30,324
D. Evans, *C.* — 3,583
T. Jones, *PC* — 3,344
F. Little, *LD* — 2,597
P. Morris, *Ref.* — 975
H. Marks, *LCP* — 420
Lab. majority 26,741
(April 1992, Lab. maj. 23,975)

NEWPORT EAST
*E.*50,997   *T.*73.06%
†A. Howarth, *Lab.* — 21,481
D. Evans, *C.* — 7,958
A. Cameron, *LD* — 3,880
A. Scargill, *Soc. Lab.* — 1,951
G. Davis, *Ref.* — 1,267
C. Holland, *PC* — 721
Lab. majority 13,523
(April 1992, Lab. maj. 9,899)

NEWPORT WEST
*E.*53,914   *T.*74.57%
*P. Flynn, *Lab.* — 24,331
P. Clarke, *C.* — 9,794
S. Wilson, *LD* — 3,907
C. Thompsett, *Ref.* — 1,199
H. Jackson, *PC* — 648
H. Moelwyn Hughes, *UK Ind.* — 323
Lab. majority 14,537
(April 1992, Lab. maj. 7,779)

OGMORE
*E.*52,078   *T.*73.10%
*Sir R. Powell, *Lab.* — 28,163
D. Unwin, *C.* — 3,716
Ms K. Williams, *LD* — 3,510
J. Rogers, *PC* — 2,679
Lab. majority 24,447
(April 1992, Lab. maj. 23,827)

PONTYPRIDD
*E.*64,185   *T.*71.44%
*Dr K. Howells, *Lab.* — 29,290
N. Howells, *LD* — 6,161
J. Cowen, *C.* — 5,910
O. Llewelyn, *PC* — 2,977
J. Wood, *Ref.* — 874
P. Skelly, *Soc. Lab.* — 380
R. Griffiths, *Comm. P.* — 178
A. Moore, *NLP* — 85
Lab. majority 23,129
(April 1992, Lab. maj. 19,797)

PRESELI PEMBROKESHIRE
*E.*54,088   *T.*78.40%
Mrs J. Lawrence, *Lab.* — 20,477
R. Buckland, *C.* — 11,741
J. Clarke, *LD* — 5,527
A. Lloyd Jones, *PC* — 2,683
D. Berry, *Ref.* — 1,574
Ms M. Scott Cato, *Green* — 401
Lab. majority 8,736
(Boundary change: notional C.)

RHONDDA
*E.*57,105   *T.*71.46%
*A. Rogers, *Lab.* — 30,381
Ms L. Wood, *PC* — 5,450
Dr R. Berman, *LD* — 2,307
S. Whiting, *C.* — 1,551
S. Gardiner, *Ref.* — 658
K. Jakeway, *Green* — 460
Lab. majority 24,931
(April 1992, Lab. maj. 28,816)

SWANSEA EAST
*E.*57,373   *T.*67.41%
*D. Anderson, *Lab.* — 29,151
Ms C. Dibble, *C.* — 3,582
E. Jones, *LD* — 3,440
Ms M. Pooley, *PC* — 1,308
Ms C. Maggs, *Ref.* — 904
R. Job, *Soc.* — 289
Lab. majority 25,569
(April 1992, Lab. maj. 23,482)

SWANSEA WEST
*E.*58,703   *T.*68.94%
*Rt. Hon. A. Williams, *Lab.* — 22,748
A. Baker, *C.* — 8,289
J. Newbury, *LD* — 5,872
D. Lloyd, *PC* — 2,675
D. Proctor, *Soc. Lab.* — 885
Lab. majority 14,459
(April 1992, Lab. maj. 9,478)

TORFAEN
*E.*60,343   *T.*71.67%
*P. Murphy, *Lab.* — 29,863
N. Parish, *C.* — 5,327
Ms J. Gray, *LD* — 5,249
Ms D. Holler, *Ref.* — 1,245
R. Gough, *PC* — 1,042
R. Coghill, *Green* — 519
Lab. majority 24,536
(April 1992, Lab. maj. 20,754)

VALE OF CLWYD
*E.*52,418   *T.*74.65%
C. Ruane, *Lab.* — 20,617
D. Edwards, *C.* — 11,662
D. Munford, *LD* — 3,425
Ms G. Kensler, *PC* — 2,301
S. Vickers, *Ref.* — 834
S. Cooke, *UK Ind.* — 293
Lab. majority 8,955
(Boundary change: notional C.)

VALE OF GLAMORGAN
*E.*67,213   *T.*80.21%
J. Smith, *Lab.* — 29,054
†W. Sweeney, *C.* — 18,522
Mrs S. Campbell, *LD* — 4,945
Ms M. Corp, *PC* — 1,393
Lab. majority 10,532
(Boundary change: notional C.)

WREXHAM
*E.*50,741   *T.*71.78%
Dr J. Marek, *Lab.* — 20,450
S. Andrew, *C.* — 8,688
A. Thomas, *LD* — 4,833
J. Cronk, *Ref.* — 1,195
K. Plant, *PC* — 1,170
N. Low, *NLP* — 86
Lab. majority 11,762
(Boundary change: notional Lab.)

YNYS MÔN
*E.*52,952   *T.*75.41%
*I. W. Jones, *PC* — 15,756
O. Edwards, *Lab.* — 13,275
G. Owen, *C.* — 8,569
D. Burnham, *LD* — 1,537
H. Gray Morris, *Ref.* — 793
PC majority 2,481

SCOTLAND

ABERDEEN CENTRAL
*E.*54,257   *T.*65.64%
F. Doran, *Lab.* — 17,745
Mrs J. Wisely, *C.* — 6,944
B. Topping, *SNP* — 5,767
J. Brown, *LD* — 4,714
J. Farquharson, *Ref.* — 446
Lab. majority 10,801
(Boundary change: notional Lab.)

ABERDEEN NORTH
*E.*54,302   *T.*70.74%
M. Savidge, *Lab.* — 18,389

B. Adam, *SNP* — 8,379
J. Gifford, *C.* — 5,763
M. Rumbles, *LD* — 5,421
A. Mackenzie, *Ref.* — 463
Lab. majority 10,010
(Boundary change: notional Lab.)

ABERDEEN SOUTH
*E.*60,490   *T.*72.84%
Ms A. Begg, *Lab.* — 15,541
N. Stephen, *LD* — 12,176
†R. Robertson, *C.* — 11,621

J. Towers, *SNP* — 4,299
R. Wharton, *Ref.* — 425
Lab. majority 3,365
(Boundary change: notional C.)

ABERDEENSHIRE WEST AND KINCARDINE
*E.*59,123   *T.*73.05%
Sir R. Smith, *LD* — 17,742
†G. Kynoch, *C.* — 15,080
Ms J. Mowatt, *SNP* — 5,639
Ms Q. Khan, *Lab.* — 3,923

S. Ball, *Ref.* 805
LD majority 2,662
(Boundary change: notional C.)

AIRDRIE AND SHOTTS
*E.*57,673   *T.*71.40%
†Mrs H. Liddell, *Lab.* 25,460
K. Robertson, *SNP* 10,048
Dr N. Brook, *C.* 3,660
R. Wolseley, *LD* 1,719
C. Semple, *Ref.* 294
Lab. majority 15,412
(Boundary change: notional Lab.)

ANGUS
*E.*59,708   *T.*72.14%
†A. Welsh, *SNP* 20,792
S. Leslie, *C.* 10,603
Ms C. Taylor, *Lab.* 6,733
Dr R. Speirs, *LD* 4,065
B. Taylor, *Ref.* 883
SNP majority 10,189
(Boundary change: notional SNP)

ARGYLL AND BUTE
*E.*49,451   *T.*72.23%
*Mrs R. Michie, *LD* 14,359
Prof. N. MacCormick, *SNP* 8,278
R. Leishman, *C.* 6,774
A. Syed, *Lab.* 5,596
M. Stewart, *Ref.* 713
LD majority 6,081
(April 1992, LD maj. 2,622)

AYR
*E.*55,829   *T.*80.17%
Mrs S. Osborne, *Lab.* 21,679
†P. Gallie, *C.* 15,136
I. Blackford, *SNP* 5,625
Miss C. Hamblen, *LD* 2,116
J. Enos, *Ref.* 200
Lab. majority 6,543
(Boundary change: notional Lab.)

BANFF AND BUCHAN
*E.*58,493   *T.*68.69%
†A. Salmond, *SNP* 22,409
W. Frain-Bell, *C.* 9,564
Ms M. Harris, *Lab.* 4,747
N. Fletcher, *LD* 2,398
A. Buchan, *Ref.* 1,060
SNP majority 12,845
(Boundary change: notional SNP)

CAITHNESS, SUTHERLAND AND
EASTER ROSS
*E.*41,566   *T.*70.18%
†R. Maclennan, *LD* 10,381
J. Hendry, *Lab.* 8,122
E. Harper, *SNP* 6,710
T. Miers, *C.* 3,148
Ms C. Ryder, *Ref.* 369
J. Martin, *Green* 230
M. Carr, *UK Ind.* 212
LD majority 2,259
(Boundary change: notional LD)

CARRICK, CUMNOCK AND DOON
VALLEY
*E.*65,593   *T.*74.96%
†G. Foulkes, *Lab. Co-op.* 29,398
A. Marshall, *C.* 8,336
Mrs C. Hutchison, *SNP* 8,190

D. Young, *LD* 2,613
J. Higgins, *Ref.* 634
Lab. Co-op. majority 21,062
(Boundary change: notional Lab.
Co-op.)

CLYDEBANK AND MILNGAVIE
*E.*52,092   *T.*75.03%
†A. Worthington, *Lab.* 21,583
J. Yuill, *SNP* 8,263
Ms N. Morgan, *C.* 4,885
K. Moody, *LD* 4,086
I. Sanderson, *Ref.* 269
Lab. majority 13,320
(Boundary change: notional Lab.)

CLYDESDALE
*E.*63,428   *T.*71.60%
*J. Hood, *Lab.* 23,859
A. Doig, *SNP* 10,050
M. Izatt, *C.* 7,396
Mrs S. Grieve, *LD* 3,796
K. Smith, *BNP* 311
Lab. majority 13,809
(April 1992, Lab. maj. 10,187)

COATBRIDGE AND CHRYSTON
*E.*52,024   *T.*72.30%
†T. Clarke, *Lab.* 25,697
B. Nugent, *SNP* 6,402
A. Wauchope, *C.* 3,216
Mrs M. Daly, *LD* 2,048
B. Bowsley, *Ref.* 249
Lab. majority 19,295
(Boundary change: notional Lab.)

CUMBERNAULD AND KILSYTH
*E.*48,032   *T.*75.00%
Ms R. McKenna, *Lab.* 21,141
C. Barrie, *SNP* 10,013
I. Sewell, *C.* 2,441
J. Biggam, *LD* 1,368
Ms J Kara, *ProLife* 609
K. McEwan, *SSA* 345
Ms P. Cook, *Ref.* 107
Lab. majority 11,128
(April 1992, Lab. maj. 9,215)

CUNNINGHAME NORTH
*E.*55,526   *T.*74.07%
*B. Wilson, *Lab.* 20,686
Mrs M. Mitchell, *C.* 9,647
Ms K. Nicoll, *SNP* 7,584
Ms K. Freel, *LD* 2,271
Ms L. McDaid, *Soc. Lab.* 501
I. Winton, *Ref.* 440
Lab. majority 11,039
(April 1992, Lab. maj. 2,939)

CUNNINGHAME SOUTH
*E.*49,543   *T.*71.54%
*B. Donohoe, *Lab.* 22,233
Mrs M. Burgess, *SNP* 7,364
Mrs P. Paterson, *C.* 3,571
E. Watson, *LD* 1,604
K. Edwin, *Soc. Lab.* 494
A. Martlew, *Ref.* 178
Lab. majority 14,869
(April 1992, Lab. maj. 10,680)

DUMBARTON
*E.*56,229   *T.*73.39%
*J. McFall, *Lab. Co-op.* 20,470

W. Mackechnie, *SNP* 9,587
P. Ramsay, *C.* 7,283
A. Reid, *LD* 3,144
L. Robertson, *SSA* 283
G. Dempster, *Ref.* 255
D. Lancaster, *UK Ind.* 242
Lab. Co-op. majority 10,883
(April 1992, Lab. maj. 6,129)

DUMFRIES
*E.*62,759   *T.*78.92%
R. Brown, *Lab.* 23,528
S. Stevenson, *C.* 13,885
R. Higgins, *SNP* 5,977
N. Wallace, *LD* 5,487
D. Parker, *Ref.* 533
Ms E. Hunter, *NLP* 117
Lab. majority 9,643
(Boundary change: notional C.)

DUNDEE EAST
*E.*58,388   *T.*69.41%
†J. McAllion, *Lab.* 20,718
Ms S. Robison, *SNP* 10,757
B. Mackie, *C.* 6,397
Dr G. Saluja, *LD* 1,677
E. Galloway, *Ref.* 601
H. Duke, *SSA* 232
Ms E. MacKenzie, *NLP* 146
Lab. majority 9,961
(Boundary change: notional Lab.)

DUNDEE WEST
*E.*57,346   *T.*67.67%
†E. Ross, *Lab.* 20,875
J. Dorward, *SNP* 9,016
N. Powrie, *C.* 5,105
Dr E. Dick, *LD* 2,972
Ms M. Ward, *SSA* 428
J. MacMillan, *Ref.* 411
Lab. majority 11,859
(Boundary change: notional Lab.)

DUNFERMLINE EAST
*E.*52,072   *T.*70.25%
†Rt. Hon. G. Brown, *Lab.* 24,441
J. Ramage, *SNP* 5,690
I. Mitchell, *C.* 3,656
J. Tolson, *LD* 2,164
T. Dunsmore, *Ref.* 632
Lab. majority 18,751
(Boundary change: notional Lab.)

DUNFERMLINE WEST
*E.*52,467   *T.*69.44%
†Ms R. Squire, *Lab.* 19,338
J. Lloyd, *SNP* 6,984
Mrs E. Harris, *LD* 4,963
K. Newton, *C.* 4,606
J. Bain, *Ref.* 543
Lab. majority 12,354
(Boundary change: notional Lab.)

EAST KILBRIDE
*E.*65,229   *T.*74.81%
†A. Ingram, *Lab.* 27,584
G. Gebbie, *SNP* 10,200
C. Herbertson, *C.* 5,863
Mrs K. Philbrick, *LD* 3,527
J. Deighan, *ProLife* 1,170
Ms J. Gray, *Ref.* 306
E. Gilmour, *NLP* 146

Lab. majority 17,384
(Boundary change: notional Lab.)

EAST LOTHIAN
*E.*57,441   *T.*75.61%
†J. Home Robertson, *Lab.*   22,881
M. Fraser, *C.*   8,660
D. McCarthy, *SNP*   6,825
Ms A. MacAskill, *LD*   4,575
N. Nash, *Ref.*   491
Lab. majority 14,221
(Boundary change: notional Lab.)

EASTWOOD
*E.*66,697   *T.*78.32%
J. Murphy, *Lab.*   20,766
P. Cullen, *C.*   17,530
D. Yates, *SNP*   6,826
Dr C. Mason, *LD*   6,110
D. Miller, *Ref.*   497
Dr M. Tayan, *ProLife*   393
D. McPherson, *UK Ind.*   113
Lab. majority 3,236
(Boundary change: notional C.)

EDINBURGH CENTRAL
*E.*63,695   *T.*67.09%
†A. Darling, *Lab.*   20,125
M. Scott-Hayward, *C.*   9,055
Ms F. Hyslop, *SNP*   6,750
Ms K. Utting, *LD*   5,605
Ms L. Hendry, *Green*   607
A. Skinner, *Ref.*   495
M. Benson, *Ind. Dem.*   98
Lab. majority 11,070
(Boundary change: notional Lab.)

EDINBURGH EAST AND
MUSSELBURGH
*E.*59,648   *T.*70.61%
†Dr G. Strang, *Lab.*   22,564
D. White, *SNP*   8,034
K. Ward, *C.*   6,483
Dr C. MacKellar, *LD*   4,511
J. Sibbet, *Ref.*   526
Lab. majority 14,530
(Boundary change: notional Lab.)

EDINBURGH NORTH AND LEITH
*E.*61,617   *T.*66.45%
†M. Chisholm, *Lab.*   19,209
Ms A. Dana, *SNP*   8,231
E. Stewart, *C.*   7,312
Ms H. Campbell, *LD*   5,335
A. Graham, *Ref.*   441
G. Brown, *SSA*   320
P. Douglas-Reid, *NLP*   97
Lab. majority 10,978
(Boundary change: notional Lab.)

EDINBURGH PENTLANDS
*E.*59,635   *T.*76.70%
Ms L. Clark, *Lab.*   19,675
†Rt. Hon. M. Rifkind, *C.*   14,813
S. Gibb, *SNP*   5,952
Dr J. Dawe, *LD*   4,575
M. McDonald, *Ref.*   422
R. Harper, *Green*   224
A. McConnachie, *UK Ind.*   81
Lab. majority 4,862
(Boundary change: notional C.)

EDINBURGH SOUTH
*E.*62,467   *T.*71.78%
†N. Griffiths, *Lab.*   20,993
Miss E. Smith, *C.*   9,541
M. Pringle, *LD*   7,911
Dr J. Hargreaves, *SNP*   5,791
I. McLean, *Ref.*   504
B. Dunn, *NLP*   98
Lab. majority 11,452
(Boundary change: notional Lab.)

EDINBURGH WEST
*E.*61,133   *T.*77.91%
D. Gorrie, *LD*   20,578
†Rt. Hon. Lord J. Douglas-
  Hamilton, *C.*   13,325
Ms L. Hinds, *Lab.*   8,948
G. Sutherland, *SNP*   4,210
Dr S. Elphick, *Ref.*   277
P. Coombes, *Lib.*   263
A. Jack, *AS*   30
LD majority 7,253
(Boundary change: notional C.)

FALKIRK EAST
*E.*56,792   *T.*73.24%
†M. Connarty, *Lab.*   23,344
K. Brown, *SNP*   9,959
M. Nicol, *C.*   5,813
R. Spillane, *LD*   2,153
S. Mowbray, *Ref.*   326
Lab. majority 13,385
(Boundary change: notional Lab.)

FALKIRK WEST
*E.*52,850   *T.*72.60%
†D. Canavan, *Lab.*   22,772
D. Alexander, *SNP*   8,989
Mrs C. Buchanan, *C.*   4,639
D. Houston, *LD*   1,970
Lab. majority 13,783
(Boundary change: notional Lab.)

FIFE CENTRAL
*E.*58,315   *T.*69.90%
†H. McLeish, *Lab.*   23,912
Mrs P. Marwick, *SNP*   10,199
J. Rees-Mogg, *C.*   3,669
R. Laird, *LD*   2,610
J. Scrymgeour-Wedderburn, *Ref.*   375
Lab. majority 13,713
(Boundary change: notional Lab.)

FIFE NORTH EAST
*E.*58,794   *T.*71.16%
*M. Campbell, *LD*   21,432
A. Bruce, *C.*   11,076
C. Welsh, *SNP*   4,545
C. Milne, *Lab.*   4,301
W. Stewart, *Ref.*   485
LD majority 10,356
(Boundary change: notional LD)

GALLOWAY AND UPPER
NITHSDALE
*E.*52,751   *T.*79.65%
A. Morgan, *SNP*   18,449
†Rt. Hon. I. Lang, *C.*   12,825
Ms K. Clark, *Lab.*   6,861
J. McKerchar, *LD*   2,700
R. Wood, *Ind.*   566
A. Kennedy, *Ref.*   428
J. Smith, *UK Ind.*   189

SNP majority 5,624
(Boundary change: notional C.)

GLASGOW ANNIESLAND
*E.*52,955   *T.*63.98%
†Rt. Hon. D. Dewar, *Lab.*   20,951
Dr W. Wilson, *SNP*   5,797
A. Brocklehurst, *C.*   3,881
C. McGinty, *LD*   2,453
A. Majid, *ProLife*   374
W. Bonnar, *SSA*   229
A. Milligan, *UK Ind.*   86
Ms G. McKay, *Ref.*   84
T. Pringle, *NLP*   24
Lab. majority 15,154
(Boundary change: notional Lab.)

GLASGOW BAILLIESTON
*E.*51,152   *T.*62.27%
†J. Wray, *Lab.*   20,925
Mrs P. Thomson, *SNP*   6,085
M. Kelly, *C.*   2,468
Ms S. Rainger, *LD*   1,217
J. McVicar, *SSA*   970
J. McClafferty, *Ref.*   188
Lab. majority 14,840
(Boundary change: notional Lab.)

GLASGOW CATHCART
*E.*49,312   *T.*69.17%
†J. Maxton, *Lab.*   19,158
Ms M. Whitehead, *SNP*   6,913
A. Muir, *C.*   4,248
C. Dick, *LD*   2,302
Ms Z. Indyk, *ProLife*   687
R. Stevenson, *SSA*   458
S. Haldane, *Ref.*   344
Lab. majority 12,245
(Boundary change: notional Lab.)

GLASGOW GOVAN
*E.*49,836   *T.*64.70%
M. Sarwar, *Lab.*   14,216
Ms N. Sturgeon, *SNP*   11,302
W. Thomas, *C.*   2,839
R. Stewart, *LD*   1,915
A. McCombes, *SSA*   755
P. Paton, *SLU*   325
I. Badar, *SLI*   319
Z. J. Abbasi, *SCU*   221
K. MacDonald, *Ref.*   201
J. White, *BNP*   149
Lab. majority 2,914
(Boundary change: notional Lab.)

GLASGOW KELVIN
*E.*57,438   *T.*56.85%
†G. Galloway, *Lab.*   16,643
Ms S. White, *SNP*   6,978
Ms E. Buchanan, *LD*   4,629
D. McPhie, *C.*   3,539
A. Green, *SSA*   386
R. Grigor, *Ref.*   282
V. Vanni, *SPGB*   102
G. Stidolph, *NLP*   95
Lab. majority 9,665
(Boundary change: notional Lab.)

GLASGOW MARYHILL
*E.*52,523   *T.*56.59%
†Ms M. Fyfe, *Lab.*   19,301
J. Wailes, *SNP*   5,037
Ms E. Attwooll, *LD*   2,119

S. Baldwin, *C.*	1,747
Ms L. Blair, *NLP*	651
Ms A. Baker, *SSA*	409
J. Hanif, *ProLife*	344
R. Paterson, *Ref.*	77
S. Johnstone, *SEP*	36

Lab. majority 14,264
(Boundary change: notional Lab.)

GLASGOW POLLOK
*E.*49,284   *T.*66.56%

†I. Davidson, *Lab. Co-op.*	19,653
D. Logan, *SNP*	5,862
T. Sheridan, *SSA*	3,639
E. Hamilton, *C.*	1,979
D. Jago, *LD*	1,137
Ms M. Gott, *ProLife*	380
D. Haldane, *Ref.*	152

Lab. Co-op. majority 13,791
(Boundary change: notional Lab. Co-op.)

GLASGOW RUTHERGLEN
*E.*50,646   *T.*70.14%

†T. McAvoy, *Lab. Co-op.*	20,430
I. Gray, *SNP*	5,423
R. Brown, *LD*	5,167
D. Campbell Bannerman, *C.*	3,288
G. Easton, *Ind. Lab.*	812
Ms R. Kane, *SSA*	251
Ms J. Kerr, *Ref.*	150

Lab. Co-op. majority 15,007
(Boundary change: notional Lab. Co-op.)

GLASGOW SHETTLESTON
*E.*47,990   *T.*55.87%

†D. Marshall, *Lab.*	19,616
H. Hanif, *SNP*	3,748
C. Simpson, *C.*	1,484
Ms K. Hiles, *LD*	1,061
Ms C. McVicar, *SSA*	482
R. Currie, *BNP*	191
T. Montguire, *Ref.*	151
J. Graham, *WRP*	80

Lab. majority 15,868
(Boundary change: notional Lab.)

GLASGOW SPRINGBURN
*E.*53,473   *T.*59.05%

†M. Martin, *Lab.*	22,534
J. Brady, *SNP*	5,208
M.Holdsworth, *C.*	1,893
J. Alexander, *LD*	1,349
J. Lawson, *SSA*	407
A. Keating, *Ref.*	186

Lab. majority 17,326
(Boundary change: notional Lab.)

GORDON
*E.*58,767   *T.*71.89%

†M. Bruce, *LD*	17,999
J. Porter, *C.*	11,002
R. Lochhead, *SNP*	8,435
Ms L. Kirkhill, *Lab.*	4,350
F. Pidcock, *Ref.*	459

LD majority 6,997
(Boundary change: notional C.)

GREENOCK AND INVERCLYDE
*E.*48,818   *T.*71.05%

†Dr N. Godman, *Lab.*	19,480
B. Goodall, *SNP*	6,440

R. Ackland, *LD*	4,791
H. Swire, *C.*	3,976

Lab. majority 13,040
(Boundary change: notional Lab.)

HAMILTON NORTH AND BELLSHILL
*E.*53,607   *T.*70.88%

†Dr J. Reid, *Lab.*	24,322
M. Matheson, *SNP*	7,255
G. McIntosh, *C.*	3,944
K. Legg, *LD*	1,924
R. Conn, *Ref.*	554

Lab. majority 17,067
(Boundary change: notional Lab.)

HAMILTON SOUTH
*E.*46,562   *T.*71.07%

†G. Robertson, *Lab.*	21,709
I. Black, *SNP*	5,831
R. Kilgour, *C.*	2,858
R. Pitts, *LD*	1,693
C. Gunn, *ProLife*	684
S. Brown, *Ref.*	316

Lab. majority 15,878
(Boundary change: notional Lab.)
See also Stop-press

INVERNESS EAST, NAIRN AND LOCHABER
*E.*65,701   *T.*72.71%

D. Stewart, *Lab.*	16,187
F. Ewing, *SNP*	13,848
S. Gallagher, *LD*	8,364
Mrs M. Scanlon, *C.*	8,355
Ms W. Wall, *Ref.*	436
M. Falconer, *Green*	354
D. Hart, *Ch. U.*	224

Lab. majority 2,339
(Boundary change: notional LD)

KILMARNOCK AND LOUDOUN
*E.*61,376   *T.*77.24%

D. Browne, *Lab.*	23,621
A. Neil, *SNP*	16,365
D. Taylor, *C.*	5,125
J. Stewart, *LD*	1,891
W. Sneddon, *Ref.*	284
W. Gilmour, *NLP*	123

Lab. majority 7,256
(April 1992, Lab. maj. 6,979)

KIRKCALDY
*E.*52,186   *T.*67.02%

†L. Moonie, *Lab. Co-op.*	18,730
S. Hosie, *SNP*	8,020
Miss C. Black, *C.*	4,779
J. Mainland, *LD*	3,031
V. Baxter, *Ref.*	413

Lab. Co-op. majority 10,710
(Boundary change: notional Lab. Co-op.)

LINLITHGOW
*E.*53,706   *T.*73.84%

†T. Dalyell, *Lab.*	21,469
K. MacAskill, *SNP*	10,631
T. Kerr, *C.*	4,964
A. Duncan, *LD*	2,331
K. Plomer, *Ref.*	259

Lab. majority 10,838
(Boundary change: notional Lab.)

LIVINGSTON
*E.*60,296   *T.*71.04%

†Rt. Hon. R. Cook, *Lab.*	23,510
P. Johnston, *SNP*	11,763
H. Craigie Halkett, *C.*	4,028
E. Hawthorn, *LD*	2,876
Ms H. Campbell, *Ref.*	444
M. Culbert, *SPGB*	213

Lab. majority 11,747
(Boundary change: notional Lab.)

MIDLOTHIAN
*E.*47,552   *T.*74.13%

†E. Clarke, *Lab.*	18,861
L. Millar, *SNP*	8,991
Miss A. Harper, *C.*	3,842
R. Pinnock, *LD*	3,235
K. Docking, *Ref.*	320

Lab. majority 9,870
(Boundary change: notional Lab.)

MORAY
*E.*58,302   *T.*68.21%

†Mrs M. Ewing, *SNP*	16,529
A. Findlay, *C.*	10,963
L. Macdonald, *Lab.*	7,886
Ms D. Storr, *LD*	3,548
P. Mieklejohn, *Ref.*	840

SNP majority 5,566
(Boundary change: notional SNP)

MOTHERWELL AND WISHAW
*E.*52,252   *T.*70.08%

F. Roy, *Lab.*	21,020
J. McGuigan, *SNP*	8,229
S. Dickson, *C.*	4,024
A. Mackie, *LD*	2,331
C. Herriot, *Soc. Lab.*	797
T. Russell, *Ref.*	218

Lab. majority 12,791
(Boundary change: notional Lab.)

OCHIL
*E.*56,572   *T.*77.40%

†M. O'Neill, *Lab.*	19,707
G. Reid, *SNP*	15,055
A. Hogarth, *C.*	6,383
Mrs A. Watters, *LD*	2,262
D. White, *Ref.*	210
I. McDonald, *D. Nat.*	104
M. Sullivan, *NLP*	65

Lab. majority 4,652
(Boundary change: notional Lab.)

ORKNEY AND SHETLAND
*E.*32,291   *T.*64.00%

*J. Wallace, *LD*	10,743
J. Paton, *Lab.*	3,775
W. Ross, *SNP*	2,624
H. Vere Anderson, *C.*	2,527
F. Adamson, *Ref.*	820
Ms C. Wharton, *NLP*	116
A. Robertson, *Ind.*	60

LD majority 6,968
(April 1992, LD maj. 5,033)

PAISLEY NORTH
*E.*49,725   *T.*68.65%

†Mrs I. Adams, *Lab.*	20,295
I. Mackay, *SNP*	7,481
K. Brookes, *C.*	3,267
A. Jelfs, *LD*	2,365
R. Graham, *ProLife*	531

E. Mathew, *Ref.*   196
Lab. majority 12,814
(Boundary change: notional Lab.)

PAISLEY SOUTH
*E.*54,040   *T.*69.12%
†G. McMaster, *Lab. Co-op.*   21,482
W. Martin, *SNP*   8,732
Ms E. McCartin, *LD*   3,500
R. Reid, *C.*   3,237
J. Lardner, *Ref.*   254
S. Clerkin, *SSA*   146
Lab. Co-op. majority 12,750
(Boundary change: notional Lab.
Co-op.)
See also page 233

PERTH
*E.*60,313   *T.*73.87%
†Ms R. Cunningham, *SNP*   16,209
J. Godfrey, *C.*   13,068
D. Alexander, *Lab.*   11,036
C. Brodie, *LD*   3,583
R. MacAuley, *Ref.*   366
M. Henderson, *UK Ind.*   289
SNP majority 3,141
(Boundary change: notional C.)

RENFREWSHIRE WEST
*E.*52,348   *T.*76.00%
†T. Graham, *Lab.*   18,525
C. Campbell, *SNP*   10,546
C. Cormack, *C.*   7,387
B. MacPherson, *LD*   3,045
S. Lindsay, *Ref.*   283
Lab. majority 7,979
(Boundary change: notional Lab.)

ROSS, SKYE AND INVERNESS
WEST
*E.*55,639   *T.*71.81%
†C. Kennedy, *LD*   15,472
D. Munro, *Lab.*   11,453
Mrs M. Paterson, *SNP*   7,821
Miss M. Macleod, *C.*   4,368
L. Durance, *Ref.*   535
A. Hopkins, *Green*   306
LD majority 4,019
(Boundary change: notional LD)

ROXBURGH AND BERWICKSHIRE
*E.*47,259   *T.*73.91%
†A. Kirkwood, *LD*   16,243
D. Younger, *C.*   8,337
Ms H. Eadie, *Lab.*   5,226
M. Balfour, *SNP*   3,959
J. Curtis, *Ref.*   922
P. Neilson, *UK Ind.*   202
D. Lucas, *NLP*   42
LD majority 7,906
(Boundary change: notional LD)

STIRLING
*E.*52,491   *T.*81.84%
Mrs A. McGuire, *Lab.*   20,382
†Rt. Hon. M. Forsyth, *C.*   13,971
E. Dow, *SNP*   5,752
A. Tough, *LD*   2,675
W. McMurdo, *UK Ind.*   154
Ms E. Olsen, *Value Party*   24
Lab. majority 6,411
(Boundary change: notional C.)

STRATHKELVIN AND BEARSDEN
*E.*62,974   *T.*78.94%
†S. Galbraith, *Lab.*   26,278

D. Sharpe, *C.*   9,986
G. McCormick, *SNP*   8,111
J. Morrison, *LD*   4,843
D. Wilson, *Ref.*   339
Ms J. Fisher, *NLP*   155
Lab. majority 16,292
(Boundary change: notional Lab.)

TAYSIDE NORTH
*E.*61,398   *T.*74.25%
J. Swinney, *SNP*   20,447
†W. Walker, *C.*   16,287
I. McFatridge, *Lab.*   5,141
P. Regent, *LD*   3,716
SNP majority 4,160
(Boundary change: notional C.)

TWEEDDALE, ETTRICK AND
LAUDERDALE
*E.*50,891   *T.*76.64%
M. Moore, *LD*   12,178
K. Geddes, *Lab.*   10,689
A. Jack, *C.*   8,623
I. Goldie, *SNP*   6,671
C. Mowbray, *Ref.*   406
J. Hein, *Lib.*   387
D. Paterson, *NLP*   47
LD majority 1,489
(Boundary change: notional LD)

WESTERN ISLES
*E.*22,983   *T.*70.08%
*C. Macdonald, *Lab.*   8,955
Dr A. Lorne Gillies, *SNP*   5,379
J. McGrigor, *C.*   1,071
N. Mitchison, *LD*   495
R. Lionel, *Ref.*   206
Lab. majority 3,576

NORTHERN IRELAND

ANTRIM EAST
*E.*58,963   *T.*58.26%
†R. Beggs, *UUP*   13,318
S. Neeson, *All.*   6,929
J. McKee, *DUP*   6,682
T. Dick, *C.*   2,334
W. Donaldson, *PUP*   1,757
D. O'Connor, *SDLP*   1,576
R. Mason, *Ind.*   1,145
Ms C. McAuley, *SF*   543
Ms M. McCann, *NLP*   69
UUP majority 6,389
(Boundary change: notional UUP)

ANTRIM NORTH
*E.*72,411   *T.*63.78%
*Revd I. Paisley, *DUP*   21,495
J. Leslie, *UUP*   10,921
S. Farren, *SDLP*   7,333
J. McCarry, *SF*   2,896
Dr D. Alderdice, *All.*   2,845
Ms B. Hinds, *NI Women*   580
J. Wright, *NLP*   116
DUP majority 10,574
(April 1992, DUP maj. 14,936)

ANTRIM SOUTH
*E.*69,414   *T.*57.91%
†C. Forsythe, *UUP*   23,108

D. McClelland, *SDLP*   6,497
D. Ford, *All.*   4,668
H. Smyth, *PUP*   3,490
H. Cushinan, *SF*   2,229
Ms B. Briggs, *NLP*   203
UUP majority 16,611
(Boundary change: notional UUP)

BELFAST EAST
*E.*61,744   *T.*63.21%
†P. Robinson, *DUP*   16,640
R. Empey, *UUP*   9,886
J. Hendron, *All.*   9,288
Miss S. Dines, *C.*   928
D. Corr, *SF*   810
Mrs P. Lewsley, *SDLP*   629
D. Dougan, *NIFT*   541
J. Bell, *WP*   237
D. Collins, *NLP*   70
DUP majority 6,754
(Boundary change: notional DUP)

BELFAST NORTH
*E.*64,577   *T.*64.19%
†C. Walker, *UUP*   21,478
A. Maginness, *SDLP*   8,454
G. Kelly, *SF*   8,375
T. Campbell, *All.*   2,221
P. Emerson, *Green*   539

P. Treanor, *WP*   297
Ms A. Gribben, *NLP*   88
UUP majority 13,024
(Boundary change: notional UUP)

BELFAST SOUTH
*E.*63,439   *T.*62.24%
†Revd M. Smyth, *UUP*   14,201
Dr A. McDonnell, *SDLP*   9,601
D. Ervine, *PUP*   5,687
S. McBride, *All.*   5,112
S. Hayes, *SF*   2,019
Ms A. Campbell, *NI Women*   1,204
Miss M. Boal, *C.*   962
N. Cusack, *Ind. Lab.*   292
P. Lynn, *WP*   286
J. Anderson, *NLP*   120
UUP majority 4,600
(Boundary change: notional UUP)

BELFAST WEST
*E.*61,785   *T.*74.27%
G. Adams, *SF*   25,662
†Dr J. Hendron, *SDLP*   17,753
F. Parkinson, *UUP*   1,556
J. Lowry, *WP*   721
L. Kennedy, *HR*   102
Ms M. Daly, *NLP*   91
SF majority 7,909
(Boundary change: notional SDLP)

Down North
E.63,010   T.58.03%
†R. McCartney, *UKU*   12,817
A. McFarland, *UUP*   11,368
Sir O. Napier, *All.*   7,554
L. Fee, *C.*   1,810
Miss M. Farrell, *SDLP*   1,602
Ms J. Morrice, *NI Women*   1,240
T. Mullins, *NLP*   108
R. Mooney, *NIP*   67
UKU majority 1,449
(Boundary change: notional Popular
Unionist)

Down South
E.69,855   T.70.84%
†E. McGrady, *SDLP*   26,181
D. Nesbitt, *UUP*   16,248
M. Murphy, *SF*   5,127
J. Crozier, *All.*   1,711
Ms R. McKeon, *NLP*   219
SDLP majority 9,933
(Boundary change: notional SDLP)

Fermanagh and South
Tyrone
E.64,600   T.74.75%
†K. Maginnis, *UUP*   24,862
G. McHugh, *SF*   11,174
T. Gallagher, *SDLP*   11,060
S. Farry, *All.*   977
S. Gillan, *NLP*   217
UUP majority 13,688
(Boundary change: notional UUP)

Foyle
E.67,620   T.70.71%
†J. Hume, *SDLP*   25,109
M. McLaughlin, *SF*   11,445
W. Hay, *DUP*   10,290
Mrs H.-M. Bell, *All.*   817
D. Brennan, *NLP*   154

SDLP majority 13,664
(Boundary change: notional SDLP)

Lagan Valley
E.71,225   T.62.21%
J. Donaldson, *UUP*   24,560
S. Close, *All.*   7,635
E. Poots, *DUP*   6,005
Ms D. Kelly, *SDLP*   3,436
S. Sexton, *C.*   1,212
Ms S. Ramsey, *SF*   1,110
Ms F. McCarthy, *WP*   203
H. Finlay, *NLP*   149
UUP majority 16,925
(Boundary change: notional UUP)

Londonderry East
E.58,831   T.64.77%
†W. Ross, *UUP*   13,558
G. Campbell, *DUP*   9,764
A. Doherty, *SDLP*   8,273
M. O'Kane, *SF*   3,463
Ms Y. Boyle, *All.*   2,427
J. Holmes, *C.*   436
Ms C. Gallen, *NLP*   100
I. Anderson, *Nat. Dem.*   81
UUP majority 3,794
(Boundary change: notional UUP)

Newry and Armagh
E.70,652   T.75.40%
†S. Mallon, *SDLP*   22,904
D. Kennedy, *UUP*   18,015
P. McNamee, *SF*   11,218
P. Whitcroft, *All.*   1,015
D. Evans, *NLP*   123
SDLP majority 4,889
(Boundary change: notional SDLP)

Strangford
E.69,980   T.59.47%
†Rt. Hon. J. Taylor, *UUP*   18,431

Mrs I. Robinson, *DUP*   12,579
K. McCarthy, *All.*   5,467
P. O'Reilly, *SDLP*   2,775
G. Chalk, *C.*   1,743
G. O Fachtna, *SF*   503
Mrs S. Mullins, *NLP*   121
UUP majority 5,852
(Boundary change: notional UUP)

Tyrone West
E.58,168   T.79.55%
W. Thompson, *UUP*   16,003
J. Byrne, *SDLP*   14,842
P. Doherty, *SF*   14,280
Ms A. Gormley, *All.*   829
T. Owens, *WP*   230
R. Johnstone, *NLP*   91
UUP majority 1,161
(Boundary change: notional DUP)

Ulster Mid
E.58,836   T.86.12%
M. McGuinness, *SF*   20,294
†Revd W. McCrea, *DUP*   18,411
D. Haughey, *SDLP*   11,205
E. Bogues, *All.*   460
Mrs M. Donnelly, *WP*   238
Ms M. Murray, *NLP*   61
SF majority 1,883
(Boundary change: notional DUP)

Upper Bann
E.70,398   T.67.88%
*D. Trimble, *UUP*   20,836
Ms B. Rodgers, *SDLP*   11,584
Ms B. O'Hagan, *SF*   5,773
M. Carrick, *DUP*   5,482
Dr W. Ramsay, *All.*   3,017
T. French, *WP*   554
B. Price, *C.*   433
J. Lyons, *NLP*   108
UUP majority 9,252

COMMONWEALTH PARLIAMENTARY ASSOCIATION (1911)

The Commonwealth Parliamentary Association consists of 143 branches in the national, state, provincial or territorial parliaments in the countries of the Commonwealth. Conferences and general assemblies are held every year in different countries of the Commonwealth.
President (1999–2000), Rt. Hon. Betty Boothroyd, MP, Speaker of the House of Commons, United Kingdom
Chairman of the Executive Committee (1996–9), Hon. Billie Miller, MP (Barbados)
Secretary-General, A. R. Donahoe, QC, Suite 700, Westminster House, 7 Millbank, London SWIP 3JA

UNITED KINGDOM BRANCH

Hon. Presidents, The Lord Chancellor; Madam Speaker
Chairman of Branch, Rt. Hon. Tony Blair, MP
Chairman of Executive Committee, Donald Anderson, MP

Secretary, A. Pearson, Westminster Hall, Houses of Parliament, London, SWIA OAA

THE INTER-PARLIAMENTARY UNION (1889)

The Union exists to facilitate personal contact between members of all parliaments in the promotion of representative institutions, peace and international co-operation.
Secretary-General, A. Johnsson, Place du Petit-Saconnex, CP 438, 1211 Geneva 19, Switzerland

BRITISH GROUP

Palace of Westminster, London SWIA OAA

Hon. Presidents, The Lord Chancellor; Madam Speaker
President, Rt. Hon. Tony Blair, MP
Chairman, David Marshall, MP
Secretary, D. Ramsay

European Parliament

European Parliament elections take place at five-yearly intervals; the first direct elections to the Parliament were held in 1979. In mainland Britain MEPs were elected in all constituencies on a first-past-the-post basis until the elections of June 1999; in Northern Ireland three MEPs have been elected by the single transferable vote system of proportional representation since 1979. From 1979 to 1994 the number of seats held by the UK in the European Parliament was 81. At the June 1994 election the number of seats increased to 87 (England 71, Wales 5, Scotland, 8, Northern Ireland 3).

At the European Parliament elections held on 10 June 1999, all British MEPs were elected under a 'closed-list' regional system of proportional representation, with England being divided into nine regions and Scotland and Wales each constituting a region. Parties submitted a list of candidates for each region in their own order of preference. Voters voted for a party or an independent candidate, and the first seat in each region was allocated to the party or candidate with the highest number of votes. The rest of the seats in each region were then allocated broadly in proportion to each party's share of the vote. Each region returned the following number of members: East Midlands, 6; Eastern, 8; London, 10; North East, 4; North West, 10; South East, 11; South West, 7; West Midlands, 8; Yorkshire and the Humber, 7; Wales, 5; Scotland, 8.

British subjects and citizens of the Irish Republic are eligible for election to the European Parliament provided they are 21 or over and not subject to disqualification. Since 1994, nationals of member states of the European Union have had the right to vote in elections to the European Parliament in the UK as long as they are entered on the electoral register.

MEPs currently receive a salary from the parliaments or governments of their respective member states, set at the level of the national parliamentary salary and subject to national taxation rules (for salary of British MPs, *see* page 218). A proposal that all MEPs should be paid the same rate of salary out of the EU budget, and subject to the EC tax rate, was under negotiation between the European Parliament and the Council of Ministers at the time of going to press.

UK MEMBERS AS AT 10 JUNE 1999

*Denotes membership of the last European Parliament

Atkins, Rt. Hon. Sir Robert (*b*. 1946), C., *North West*
Attwooll, Ms Elspeth M.-A. (*b*. 1943), LD, *Scotland*
*Balfe, Richard A. (*b*. 1944), *Lab.*, *London*
Beazley, Christopher J. P. (*b*. 1952), C., *Eastern*
Bethell, The Lord (*b*. 1938), C., *London*
*Bowe, David R. (*b*. 1955), *Lab.*, *Yorkshire and the Humber*
Bowis, John C., OBE (*b*. 1945), C., *London*
Bradbourn, Philip, OBE (*b*. 1951), C., *West Midlands*
Bushill-Matthews, Philip (*b*. 1943), C., *West Midlands*
Callanan, Martin (*b*. 1961), C., *North East*
Cashman, Michael (*b*. 1950), *Lab.*, *West Midlands*
*Chichester, Giles B. (*b*. 1946), C., *South West*
Clegg, Nicholas W. P. (*b*. 1967), LD, *East Midlands*
*Corbett, Richard (*b*. 1955), *Lab.*, *Yorkshire and the Humber*
*Corrie, John A. (*b*. 1935), C., *West Midlands*

Davies, Christopher G. (*b*. 1954), LD, *North West*
Deva, Niranjan J. A. (Nirj), FRSA (*b*. 1948), C., *South East*
*Donnelly, Alan J. (*b*. 1957), *Lab.*, *North East*
Dover, Den (*b*. 1938), C., *North West*
Duff, Andrew N. (*b*. 1950), LD, *Eastern*
*Elles, James E. M. (*b*. 1949), C., *South East*
Evans, Ms Jillian R. (*b*. 1959), PC, *Wales*
Evans, Jonathan P., FRSA (*b*. 1950), C., *Wales*
*Evans, Robert J. E. (*b*. 1956), *Lab.*, *London*
Farage, Nigel (*b*. 1964), UK Ind., *South East*
*Ford, J. Glyn (*b*. 1950), *Lab.*, *South West*
Foster, Mrs Jacqui (*b*. 1947), C., *North West*
Gill, Ms Neena (*b*. 1956), *Lab.*, *West Midlands*
Goodwill, Robert (*b*. 1956), C., *Yorkshire and the Humber*
*Green, Mrs Pauline (*b*. 1948), *Lab.*, *London*
Hannan, Daniel (*b*. 1971), C., *South East*
Harbour, Malcolm (*b*. 1947), C., *West Midlands*
Heaton-Harris, Christopher (*b*. 1967), C., *East Midlands*
Helmer, Roger (*b*. 1944), C., *East Midlands*
Holmes, Michael (*b*. 1938), UK Ind., *South West*
*Howitt, Richard (*b*. 1961), *Lab.*, *Eastern*
Hudghton, Ian (*b*. 1951), SNP, *Scotland*
*Hughes, Stephen S. (*b*. 1952), *Lab.*, *North East*
Huhne, Christopher M. P., OBE (*b*. 1954), LD, *South East*
*Hume, John, MP (*b*. 1937), SDLP, *Northern Ireland*
Inglewood, The Lord (*b*. 1951), C., *North West*
*Jackson, Mrs Caroline F., D.Phil. (*b*. 1946), C., *South West*
Khanbhai, Bashir (*b*. 1945), C., *Eastern*
*Kinnock, Mrs Glenys E. (*b*. 1944), *Lab.*, *Wales*
Kirkhope, Timothy J. R. (*b*. 1945), C., *Yorkshire and the Humber*
Lambert, Ms Jean D. (*b*. 1950), *Green, London*
Lucas, Ms Caroline, PH.D. (*b*. 1960), *Green, South East*
Ludford, The Baroness (*b*. 1951), LD, *London*
Lynne, Ms Elizabeth (*b*. 1948), LD, *West Midlands*
*McAvan, Ms Linda (*b*. 1962), *Lab.*, *Yorkshire and the Humber*
*McCarthy, Ms Arlene (*b*. 1960), *Lab.*, *North West*
MacCormick, Prof. D. Neil, FBA (*b*. 1941), SNP, *Scotland*
*McMillan-Scott, Edward H. C. (*b*. 1949), C., *Yorkshire and the Humber*
*McNally, Mrs Eryl M. (*b*. 1942), *Lab.*, *Eastern*
*Martin, David W. (*b*. 1954), *Lab.*, *Scotland*
*Miller, William (*b*. 1954), *Lab.*, *Scotland*
Moraes, Claude (*b*. 1965), *Lab.*, *London*
*Morgan, Ms Eluned (*b*. 1967), *Lab.*, *Wales*
*Murphy, Simon F., PH.D. (*b*. 1962), *Lab.*, *West Midlands*
Newton Dunn, William F. (Bill) (*b*. 1941), C., *East Midlands*
Nicholson of Winterbourne, The Baroness (*b*. 1941), LD, *South East*
*Nicholson, James F. (*b*. 1945), UUP, *Northern Ireland*
O'Toole, Ms Barbara M. (Mo) (*b*. 1960), *Lab.*, *North East*
*Paisley, Revd Ian R. K., MP (*b*. 1926), DUP, *Northern Ireland*
Parish, Neil (*b*. 1956), C., *South West*
*Perry, Roy J. (*b*. 1943), C., *South East*
*Provan, James L. C. (*b*. 1936), C., *South East*
Purvis, John R., CBE (*b*. 1938), C., *Scotland*
*Read, Ms I. M. (Mel) (*b*. 1939), *Lab.*, *East Midlands*
*Simpson, Brian (*b*. 1953), *Lab.*, *North West*
*Skinner, Peter W. (*b*. 1959), *Lab.*, *South East*
Stevenson, Struan (*b*. 1948), C., *Scotland*
Stockton, The Earl of (*b*. 1943), C., *South West*
*Sturdy, Robert W. (*b*. 1944), C., *Eastern*
Sumberg, David A. G. (*b*. 1941), C., *North West*
Tannock, Dr Charles (*b*. 1957), C., *London*

Taylor, Ms Catherine D. (*b.* 1973), *Lab., Scotland*
Titford, Jeffrey (*b.* 1933), *UK Ind., Eastern*
*Titley, Gary (*b.* 1950), *Lab., North West*
Van Orden, Geoffrey (*b.* 1945), *C., Eastern*
Villiers, Ms Theresa (*b.* 1968), *C., London*
Wallis, Ms Diana P. (*b.* 1954), *LD, Yorkshire and the Humber*

*Watson, Graham R. (*b.* 1956), *LD, South West*
*Watts, Mark F. (*b.* 1964), *Lab., South East*
*Whitehead, Philip (*b.* 1937), *Lab., East Midlands*
Wyn, Eurig (*b.* 1944), *PC, Wales*
*Wynn, Terence (*b.* 1946), *Lab., North West*

UK REGIONS AS AT 10 JUNE 1999

Abbreviations

ACPFCA	Anti-Corruption Pro Family Christian Alliance
AHRPE	Architect Human Rights Peace in Europe
Anti VAT	Independent Anti Value Added Tax
EFP	English Freedom Party
Ind. Profit	Independent Making a Profit in Europe
Ind. Stable	Independent Open Democracy for Stability
Lower Tax	Account for Lower Scottish Taxes
MEP Ind.	MEP Independent Labour
Soc. All.	Socialist Alliance
SSP	Scottish Socialist Party
WW	Weekly Worker

For other abbreviations, *see* page 235

EASTERN
(Bedfordshire; Cambridgeshire; Essex; Hertfordshire; Luton; Norfolk; Peterborough; Southend-on-Sea; Suffolk; Thurrock)
E.4,019,916   T.24.74%

C.	425,091 (42.75%)
Lab.	250,132 (25.15%)
LD	118,822 (11.95%)
UK Ind.	88,452 (8.89%)
Green	61,334 (6.17%)
Lib.	16,861 (1.70%)
Pro Euro C.	16,340 (1.64%)
BNP	9,356 (0.94%)
Soc. Lab.	6,143 (0.62%)
NLP	1,907 (0.19%)
C. majority	174,959

(June 1994, Lab. maj. 90,087)

MEMBERS ELECTED
*R. Sturdy, *C.*
C. Beazley, *C.*
B. Khanbhai, *C.*
G. Van Orden, *C.*
*Ms E. McNally, *Lab.*
*R. Howitt, *Lab.*
A. Duff, *LD*
J. Titford, *UK Ind.*

EAST MIDLANDS
(Derby; Derbyshire; Leicester; Leicestershire; Lincolnshire; Northamptonshire; Nottingham; Nottinghamshire; Rutland)
E.3,170,517   T.22.83%

C.	285,662 (39.47%)
Lab.	206,756 (28.57%)
LD	92,398 (12.77%)
UK Ind.	54,800 (7.57%)
Green	38,954 (5.38%)

Alt. Lab.	17,409 (2.41%)
Pro Euro C.	11,359 (1.57%)
BNP	9,342 (1.29%)
Soc. Lab.	5,528 (0.76%)
NLP	1,525 (0.21%)
C. majority	78,906

(June 1994, Lab. maj. 229,680)

MEMBERS ELECTED
R. Helmer, *C.*
W. Newton Dunn, *C.*
C. Heaton-Harris, *C.*
*Ms M. Read, *Lab.*
*P. Whitehead, *Lab.*
N. Clegg, *LD*

LONDON
E.4,940,493   T.23.10%

Lab.	399,466 (35.00%)
C.	372,989 (32.68%)
LD	133,058 (11.66%)
Green	87,545 (7.67%)
UK Ind.	61,741 (5.41%)
Soc. Lab.	19,632 (1.72%)
BNP	17,960 (1.57%)
Lib.	16,951 (1.49%)
Pro Euro C.	16,383 (1.44%)
AHRPE	4,851 (0.43%)
Anti VAT	2,596 (0.23%)
Hum.	2,586 (0.23%)
Hemp	2,358 (0.21%)
NLP	2,263 (0.20%)
WW	846 (0.07%)
Lab. majority	26,477

(June 1994, Lab. maj. 346,850)

MEMBERS ELECTED
Miss T. Villiers, *C.*
Dr C. Tannock, *C.*
The Lord Bethell, *C.*
J. Bowis, *C.*
*Ms P. Green, *Lab.*
C. Moraes, *Lab.*
*R. Evans, *Lab.*
*R. Balfe, *Lab.*
Ms S. Ludford, *LD*
Ms J. Lambert, *Green*

NORTH EAST
(Co. Durham; Darlington; Hartlepool; Middlesbrough; Northumberland; Redcar and Cleveland; Stockton-on-Tees; Tyne and Wear)
E.1,954,076   T.19.74%

Lab.	162,573 (42.15%)
C.	105,573 (27.37%)
LD	52,070 (13.50%)

UK Ind.	34,063 (8.83%)
Green	18,184 (4.71%)
Soc. Lab.	4,511 (1.17%)
BNP	3,505 (0.91%)
Pro Euro C.	2,926 (0.76%)
SPGB	1,510 (0.39%)
NLP	826 (0.21%)
Lab. majority	57,000

(June 1994, Lab. maj. 330,689)

MEMBERS ELECTED
M. Callanan, *C.*
*A. Donnelly, *Lab.*
*S. Hughes, *Lab.*
Ms M. O'Toole, *Lab.*

NORTHERN IRELAND
Northern Ireland forms a three-member seat with a single transferable vote system
E.1,190,160   T.57.77%
First Count

*Revd I. Paisley, *DUP*	192,762
*J. Hume, *SDLP*	190,731
*J. Nicholson, *UUP*	119,507
M. McLaughlin, *SF*	117,643
D. Ervine, *PUP*	22,494
R. McCartney, *UKU*	20,283
S. Neeson, *All.*	14,391
J. Anderson, *NLP*	998

MEMBERS ELECTED
*Revd I. Paisley, *DUP*
*J. Hume, *SDLP*
*J. Nicholson, *UUP* (elected on third count)

NORTH WEST
(Blackburn-with-Darwen; Blackpool; Cheshire; Cumbria; Greater Manchester; Halton; Lancashire; Merseyside; Warrington)
E.5,170,524   T.19.67%

C.	360,027 (35.39%)
Lab.	350,511 (34.46%)
LD	119,376 (11.74%)
UK Ind.	66,779 (6.57%)
Green	56,828 (5.59%)
Lib.	22,640 (2.23%)
BNP	13,587 (1.34%)
Soc. Lab.	11,338 (1.11%)
Pro Euro C.	9,816 (0.97%)
ACPFCA	2,251 (0.22%)
NLP	2,114 (0.21%)
Ind. Hum.	1,049 (0.10%)
WW	878 (0.09%)
C. majority	9,516

(June 1994, Lab. maj. 444,569)

MEMBERS ELECTED
The Lord Inglewood, *C.*
Sir Robert Atkins, *C.*
D. Sumberg, *C.*
D. Dover, *C.*
Mrs J. Foster, *C.*
*Ms A. McCarthy, *Lab.*
*G. Titley, *Lab.*
*T. Wynn, *Lab.*
*B. Simpson, *Lab.*
C. Davies, *LD*

SCOTLAND
*E.*3,979,845   *T.*24.83%

Lab.	283,490	(28.68%)
SNP	268,528	(27.17%)
C.	195,296	(19.76%)
LD	96,971	(9.81%)
Green	57,142	(5.78%)
SSP	39,720	(4.02%)
Pro Euro C.	17,781	(1.80%)
UK Ind.	12,549	(1.27%)
Soc. Lab.	9,385	(0.95%)
BNP	3,729	(0.38%)
NLP	2,087	(0.21%)
Lower Tax	1,632	(0.17%)
Lab. majority	14,962	

(June 1994, Lab. maj. 148,718)

MEMBERS ELECTED
S. Stevenson, *C.*
J. Purvis, *C.*
*D. Martin, *Lab.*
*W. Miller, *Lab.*
Ms C. Taylor, *Lab.*
Ms E. Attwooll, *LD*
*I. Hughdton, *SNP*
Prof. N. MacCormick, *SNP*

SOUTH EAST
(Bracknell Forest; Brighton and
Hove; Buckinghamshire; East Sussex;
Hampshire; Isle of Wight; Kent;
Medway; Milton Keynes;
Oxfordshire; Portsmouth; Reading;
Slough; Southampton; Surrey; West
Berkshire; West Sussex; Windsor and
Maidenhead; Wokingham)
*E.*5,972,945   *T.*24.95%

C.	661,931	(44.42%)
Lab.	292,146	(19.61%)
LD	228,136	(15.31%)
UK Ind.	144,514	(9.70%)
Green	110,571	(7.42%)
Pro Euro C.	27,305	(1.83%)
BNP	12,161	(0.82%)
Soc. Lab.	7,281	(0.49%)
NLP	2,767	(0.19%)
Ind. Stable	1,857	(0.12%)
Ind. Profit	1,400	(0.09%)
C. majority	369,785	

(June 1994, C. maj. 230,122)

MEMBERS ELECTED
*J. Provan, *C.*
*R. Perry, *C.*
D. Hannan, *C.*
*J. Elles, *C.*
N. Deva, *C.*
*P. Skinner, *Lab.*
*M. Watts, *Lab.*

The Baroness Nicholson of
Winterbourne, *LD*
C. Huhne, *LD*
Dr Caroline Lucas, *Green*
N. Farage, *UK Ind.*

SOUTH WEST
(Bath and North-East Somerset;
Bournemouth; Bristol; Cornwall;
Devon; Dorset; Gloucestershire;
North Somerset; Plymouth; Poole;
Scilly Isles; Somerset; South
Gloucestershire; Swindon; Torbay;
Wiltshire)
*E.*3,747,620   *T.*27.81%

C.	434,645	(41.70%)
Lab.	188,362	(18.07%)
LD	171,498	(16.45%)
UK Ind.	111,012	(10.65%)
Green	86,630	(8.31%)
Lib.	21,645	(2.08%)
Pro Euro C.	11,134	(1.07%)
BNP	9,752	(0.94%)
Soc. Lab.	5,741	(0.55%)
NLP	1,968	(0.19%)
C. majority	246,283	

(June 1994, LD maj. 3,796)

MEMBERS ELECTED
*Dr Caroline Jackson, *C.*
*G. Chichester, *C.*
The Earl of Stockton, *C.*
N. Parish, *C.*
*G. Ford, *Lab.*
*G. Watson, *LD*
M. Holmes, *UK Ind.*

WALES
*E.*2,211,162   *T.*28.33%

Lab.	199,690	(31.88%)
PC	185,235	(29.57%)
C.	142,631	(22.77%)
LD	51,283	(8.19%)
UK Ind.	19,702	(3.15%)
Green	16,146	(2.58%)
Pro Euro C.	5,834	(0.93%)
Soc. Lab.	4,283	(0.68%)
NLP	1,621	(0.26%)
Lab. majority	14,455	

(June 1994, Lab. maj. 368,271)

MEMBERS ELECTED
J. Evans, *C.*
*Ms G. Kinnock, *Lab.*
*Ms E. Morgan, *Lab.*
Ms J. Evans, *PC*
E. Wyn, *PC*

WEST MIDLANDS
(Herefordshire; Shropshire;
Staffordshire; Stoke-on-Trent;
Telford and Wrekin; Warwickshire;
West Midlands Metropolitan
County; Worcestershire)
*E.*4,001,942   *T.*21.21%

C.	321,719	(37.91%)
Lab.	237,671	(28.00%)
LD	95,769	(11.28%)
UK Ind.	49,621	(5.85%)
Green	49,440	(5.83%)
MEP Ind.	36,849	(4.34%)

Lib.	14,954	(1.76%)
BNP	14,344	(1.69%)
Pro Euro C.	11,144	(1.31%)
Soc. All.	7,203	(0.85%)
Soc. Lab.	5,257	(0.62%)
EFP	3,066	(0.36%)
NLP	1,647	(0.19%)
C. majority	84,048	

(June 1994, Lab. maj. 268,888)

MEMBERS ELECTED
*J. Corrie, *C.*
P. Bushill-Matthews, *C.*
M. Harbour, *C.*
P. Bradbourn, *C.*
*S. Murphy, *Lab.*
M. Cashman, *Lab.*
Ms N. Gill, *Lab.*
Ms E. Lynne, *LD*

YORKSHIRE AND THE HUMBER
(East Riding of Yorkshire; Kingston-
upon-Hull; North East Lincolnshire;
North Lincolnshire; North
Yorkshire; South Yorkshire; West
Yorkshire; York)
*E.*3,767,227   *T.*19.75%

C.	272,653	(36.64%)
Lab.	233,024	(31.32%)
LD	107,168	(14.40%)
UK Ind.	52,824	(7.10%)
Green	42,604	(5.73%)
Alt. Lab.	9,554	(1.28%)
BNP	8,911	(1.20%)
Pro Euro C.	8,075	(1.09%)
Soc. Lab.	7,650	(1.03%)
NLP	1,604	(0.22%)
C. majority	39,629	

(June 1994, Lab. maj. 344,310)

MEMBERS ELECTED
*E. McMillan-Scott, *C.*
T. Kirkhope, *C.*
R. Goodwill, *C.*
*Ms L. McAvan, *Lab.*
*D. Bowe, *Lab.*
*R. Corbett, *Lab.*
Ms D. Wallis, *LD*

BY-ELECTIONS SINCE THE LAST EDITION

SCOTLAND NORTH EAST
(26 November 1998)
E. 584,061   *T.* 20.53%

I. Hughdton, *SNP*	57,445
S. Stevenson, *C.*	23,744
Mrs K. Walker Shaw, *Lab.*	22,086
K. Raffar, *LD*	11,753
H. Duke, *SSP*	2,510
R. Harper, *Green*	2,067
SNP majority	33,701

The Government

Prime Minister, First Lord of the Treasury and Minister for the Civil Service
  The Rt. Hon. Anthony (Tony) Blair, MP, since May 1997
Deputy Prime Minister and Secretary of State for the Environment, Transport and the Regions
  The Rt. Hon. John Prescott, MP, since May 1997
Chancellor of the Exchequer
  The Rt. Hon. Gordon Brown, MP, since May 1997
Secretary of State for Foreign and Commonwealth Affairs
  The Rt. Hon. Robin Cook, MP, since May 1997
Lord Chancellor
  The Lord Irvine of Lairg, PC, QC, since May 1997
Secretary of State for the Home Department
  The Rt. Hon. Jack Straw, MP, since May 1997
Secretary of State for Education and Employment
  The Rt. Hon. David Blunkett, MP, since May 1997
President of the Council and Leader of the House of Commons
  The Rt. Hon. Margaret Beckett, MP, since July 1998
Minister for the Cabinet Office and Chancellor of the Duchy of Lancaster
  The Rt. Hon. Dr Jack Cunningham, MP, since July 1998
Secretary of State for Scotland
  The Rt. Hon. Dr John Reid, MP, since May 1999
Secretary of State for Defence
  The Lord Robertson of Port Ellen, PC (until October 1999), since May 1997
Secretary of State for Health
  The Rt. Hon. Frank Dobson, MP, since May 1997
Parliamentary Secretary to the Treasury (Chief Whip)
  The Rt. Hon. Ann Taylor, MP
Secretary of State for Culture, Media and Sport
  The Rt. Hon. Chris Smith, MP, since May 1997
Secretary of State for Northern Ireland
  The Rt. Hon. Dr Marjorie (Mo) Mowlam, MP, since May 1997
Secretary of State for Wales
  The Rt. Hon. Paul Murphy, MP, since July 1999
Secretary of State for International Development
  The Rt. Hon. Clare Short, MP, since May 1997
Secretary of State for Social Security
  The Rt. Hon. Alistair Darling, MP, since July 1998
Minister of Agriculture, Fisheries and Food
  The Rt. Hon. Nick Brown, MP, since July 1998
Leader of the House of Lords and Minister for Women
  The Baroness Jay of Paddington*, since July 1998
Secretary of State for Trade and Industry
  The Rt. Hon. Stephen Byers, MP, since January 1999
Chief Secretary to the Treasury
  The Rt. Hon. Alan Milburn, MP, since January 1999

The Minister of State at the Department of the Environment, Transport and the Regions with responsibility for Transport, and the Government Chief Whip in the House of Lords will attend Cabinet meetings although they are not members of the Cabinet.
* Appointed as Lord Privy Seal

LAW OFFICERS

Attorney-General
  The Lord Williams of Mostyn, QC, since July 1999
Lord Advocate
  The Lord Hardie, PC, QC, since May 1997
Solicitor-General
  Ross Cranston, MP, since July 1998
Solicitor-General for Scotland
  Colin Boyd, QC
Advocate-General for Scotland
  Lynda Clark, MP

MINISTERS OF STATE

Agriculture, Fisheries and Food
  The Rt. Hon. Joyce Quin, MP
  The Baroness Hayman
Cabinet Office
  The Lord Falconer of Thoroton, QC
  Ian McCartney, MP
Defence
  John Spellar, MP (*Armed Forces*)
  The Baroness Symons of Vernham Dean (*Defence Procurement*)
Education and Employment
  The Rt. Hon. Andrew Smith, MP (*Employment*)
  Estelle Morris, MP (*School Standards*)
  The Baroness Blackstone, Ph.D. (*Lifelong Learning*)
Environment, Transport and the Regions
  The Lord Macdonald of Tradeston (*Transport*)
  The Rt. Hon. Michael Meacher, MP (*Environment*)
  The Rt. Hon. Hilary Armstrong, MP (*Local Government, Regions*)
  The Rt. Hon. Nick Raynsford, MP (*Housing, Planning, London*)
Foreign and Commonwealth Office
  Geoffrey Hoon, MP (*Minister for Europe*)
  Peter Hain, MP
  John Battle, MP
Health
  John Denham, MP (*NHS Structure and Resources*)
  The Rt. Hon. Tessa Jowell, MP (*Public Health, Women's Issues*)
Home Office
  The Rt. Hon. Paul Boateng, MP
  Charles Clarke, MP
  Barbara Roche, MP
Northern Ireland Office
  The Rt. Hon. Adam Ingram, MP (*Security, Victims, Europe, Constitution*)
Scotland Office
  Brian Wilson, MP
Social Security
  Jeff Rooker, MP
Trade and Industry
  The Rt. Hon. Helen Liddell, MP (*Energy, Competitiveness in Europe*)
  The Rt. Hon. Richard Caborn, MP (*Trade*)
  Patricia Hewitt, MP

Treasury
Dawn Primarolo, MP (*Paymaster-General*)
Stephen Timms, MP (*Financial Secretary*)
Melanie Johnson, MP (*Economic Secretary*)

UNDER-SECRETARIES OF STATE

Agriculture, Fisheries and Food
Elliot Morley, MP
Culture, Media and Sport
Alan Howarth, MP (*Arts*)
Kate Hoey, MP (*Sport*)
Janet Anderson, MP (*Tourism, Film, Broadcasting*)
Defence
Peter Kilfoyle, MP
Education and Employment
Margaret Hodge, MP (*Employment, Under 5s*)
Malcolm Wicks, MP (*Lifelong Learning*)
Jacqui Smith, MP (*School Standards*)
Michael Wills, MP (*Information and Communications Technology*)
Environment, Transport and the Regions
The Lord Whitty
Keith Hill, MP
Chris Mullin, MP
Beverley Hughes, MP
Foreign and Commonwealth Office
The Baroness Scotland of Asthal
Health
John Hutton, MP
The Lord Hunt of Kings Heath
Gisela Stuart, MP
Home Office
Michael O'Brien, MP
The Lord Bassam of Brighton
International Development
George Foulkes, MP
Lord Chancellor's Department
Keith Vaz, MP
David Lock, MP
Northern Ireland Office
John McFall, MP (*Education, Economic Development*)
The Lord Dubs (*Environment, Agriculture*)
George Howarth, MP (*Political Development, Equality, Human Rights*)
Privy Council Office
Paddy Tipping, MP
Social Security
The Baroness Hollis of Heigham, D.Phil. (*Child Benefit, Child Support, War Pensions*)
Angela Eagle, MP (*Income-related Benefits, International and Green Issues*)
Hugh Bayley, MP (*Disability and Sickness Benefits, Deregulation, Independent Living Fund*)
Trade and Industry
Dr Kim Howells, MP (*Competition, Consumer Affairs*)
Alan Johnson, MP (*Employment Relations, the Post Office, Industry*)
The Lord Sainsbury of Turville§ (*Science*)
Welsh Office
David Hanson, MP
§ Unpaid

GOVERNMENT WHIPS

HOUSE OF LORDS

Captain of the Honourable Corps of Gentlemen-at-Arms (Chief Whip)
The Lord Carter, PC
Captain of The Queen's Bodyguard of the Yeoman of the Guard (Deputy Chief Whip)
The Lord McIntosh of Haringey
Lords-in-Waiting
The Lord Burlison; The Lord Bach
Baronesses-in-Waiting
The Baroness Farrington of Ribbleton; The Baroness Ramsay of Cartvale; The Baroness Amos

HOUSE OF COMMONS

Parliamentary Secretary to the Treasury (Chief Whip)
The Rt. Hon. Ann Taylor, MP
Treasurer of HM Household (Deputy Chief Whip)
Keith Bradley, MP
Comptroller of HM Household
Thomas McAvoy, MP
Vice-Chamberlain of HM Household
Graham Allen, MP
Lords Commissioners
Robert Ainsworth, MP; James Dowd, MP; Clive Betts, MP; David Jamieson, MP; Jane Kennedy, MP
Assistant Whips
David Clelland, MP; Kevin Hughes, MP; Anne McGuire, MP; Michael Hall, MP; Gregory Pope, MP; Gerry Sutcliffe, MP

Government Legislative Programme 1998–9 and Budget Summary

The Queen's Speech

The Queen's Speech was delivered in the House of Lords on 24 November 1998. It included the following main legislative proposals:
– a Bill to end the internal market, require hospitals to meet minimum standards of clinical care, abolish GP fundholding and create Primary Care Trusts
– a Bill to make it easier for hospitals to recover some of the costs of treating road accident victims from insurance companies
– a Bill to reform disability benefits and benefits for new widows and widowers, introduce stakeholder pensions and enable pensions to be split on divorce
– a Bill to guarantee a minimum income for working families, introduce a contribution to child care costs and replace the disability working allowance with a disabled person's tax credit
– a Bill to introduce a Disability Rights Commission
– a Bill to transfer the functions of the Contributions Agency to the Inland Revenue
– a Bill to modernize youth courts, introduce a 'contract of behaviour' for first-time offenders under 17 who plead guilty and are not discharged or jailed, and give greater protection to vulnerable witnesses
– a Bill to modernize the legal aid system
– a Bill to lower the age of consent for homosexuals to 16 in England, Wales and Scotland and 17 in Northern Ireland, and protect vulnerable teenagers from sexual advances by those in a position of trust or authority
– a Bill to remove the right of hereditary peers to sit and vote in the House of Lords as the first stage of reform of the Upper House
– a Bill to reform the treatment of asylum seekers with the aim of reducing the incentive to economic migration, and to restructure the appeals system and regulate immigration advisers
– a Bill to abolish compulsory competitive tendering in local authorities and require authorities to deliver 'best value' and review their services every five years
– a Bill to require local councils to adopt a code of conduct and set up a standards committee, and to enable them to have an elected mayor or a cabinet with a leader
– a Bill to establish a Greater London Authority headed by an elected mayor, transfer responsibility for policing in London from the Home Office to the Authority, and establish a transport executive and a development agency
– a Bill to give employees new rights, including greater protection against unfair dismissal, improved parental leave and the right to union recognition
– a Bill to close a loophole relating to the rating valuation of non-domestic properties
– a Bill to provide a fair basis for water charges and to remove from water companies the power to disconnect householders for non-payment
– a Bill to bring intensive pig farms, poultry batteries and other parts of the food industry under the control of pollution inspectors and establish a single pollution regime called Integrated Pollution Prevention and Control

– a Bill to increase the borrowing limit of Scottish Enterprise
– a Bill to establish the remit of the Financial Services Authority, a new single statutory regulatory body for the financial services industry, and set up a single ombudsman, compensation and appeals scheme
– a Bill to regulate electronic commerce
– a Bill to convert the Commonwealth Development Corporation into a public-private partnership
– a Bill to establish regional development agencies
The Queen's Speech also included the following pledges made on behalf of the Government:
– to continue with economic policies designed to build long-term stability
– to aim for high and stable levels of economic growth and employment
– to raise achievement in schools and improve standards of teaching, including the introduction of a consultation paper on the reform of the teaching profession
– to take forward proposals to establish a Food Standards Agency
– to increase expenditure on health and education
– to work for the successful establishment of the Scottish Parliament and the Welsh Assembly and the full implementation of all aspects of the Belfast Agreement
– to publish a White Paper setting out arrangements for a new system of appointing life peers and to establish a Royal Commission on the Reform of the House of Lords
– to publish a draft Freedom of Information Bill, to be subject to pre-legislative scrutiny in both Houses of Parliament
– to publish draft legislation on the reform of political party funding, the conduct of local councils' business and the establishment of a Strategic Rail Authority
– to tackle global poverty and promote sustainable development
– to play a leading role in preparing the EU for the challenge of enlargement, encouraging the reform of the CAP, making the EU's foreign and security policy more effective and ensuring that the EU meets the concerns of the UK's citizens
– to encourage preparations in the UK for the introduction of the Euro in other member states of the EU
– to ensure strong defence arrangements based on NATO and promote international peace and security
– to pursue reform of the UN and an early resolution of its financial crisis
– to promote human rights, fight against terrorism and serious crime and take a leading role in protecting the environment

The Budget

The Chancellor of the Exchequer (Gordon Brown) presented his Budget to the House of Commons on 9 March 1999. It included the following main points:
– a new 10p rate of income tax to be introduced on the first £1,500 of earnings from April 1999; the 20p tax rate to

be abolished; the basic rate of income tax to be cut from 23p to 22p from April 2000

– personal tax allowances for pensioners to be raised by more than the rate of inflation

– no national insurance to be paid on the first £87 per week of earnings from April 2001; the upper limit for NI contributions to be raised to £575 per week

– the married couple's tax allowance to be abolished from April 2001, except for pensioners, and replaced by a child tax credit worth £416 a year

– child benefit to be raised to £15 a week for the first child and £10 a week for subsequent children, from April 2000

– mortgage interest relief (MIRAS) to be abolished from April 2000

– stamp duty to be raised by 0.5 per cent for houses worth more than £250,000 from 16 March 1999

– pensioners' winter allowance to be raised from £20 to £100

– a guaranteed minimum income of £78 for a single pensioner and £121 for a couple

– petrol up 3.79p a litre for unleaded petrol and 4.25p a litre for leaded

– excise duty cut by £55 from June 1999 for cars with engines below 1,100 cc

– excise duty from autumn 2000 to be based on carbon dioxide emission rate

– cigarettes up 17.5p a packet from midnight on 9 March

– the capital gains tax threshold to be raised to £7,100 from April 1999

– the inheritance tax threshold to be raised to £231,000 from April 1999

– corporation tax to be cut by 1p from April 1999; a new 10p rate to be introduced for new small businesses from April 2000

– a new research and development tax credit for small businesses

– a new energy levy on industry from April 2001

– a new share ownership scheme for employees

– a 'computers for all' programme to be launched, including a national network of 1,000 computer learning centres

– a £60-a-week credit for over-50s moving off welfare into work

Government Departments and Public Offices

For changes notified after 31 August, *see* Stop-press

This section covers central government departments, executive agencies, regulatory bodies, other statutory independent organizations, and bodies which are government-financed or whose head is appointed by a government minister.

The Civil Service

Under the Next Steps programme, launched in 1988, many semi-autonomous executive agencies have been established to carry out much of the work of the Civil Service. Executive agencies operate within a framework set by the responsible minister which specifies policies, objectives and available resources. All executive agencies are set annual performance targets by their minister. Each agency has a chief executive, who is responsible for the day-to-day operations of the agency and who is accountable to the minister for the use of resources and for meeting the agency's targets. The minister accounts to Parliament for the work of the agency. Nearly 60 per cent of civil servants now work in executive agencies. Customs and Excise, the Inland Revenue, the Crown Prosecution Service and the Serious Fraud Office, which employ a further 17 per cent of civil servants, also operate on 'Next Steps' lines. In January 1999 there were about 463,700 permanent civil servants.

The Senior Civil Service was created in 1996 and comprises about 3,000 staff from Permanent Secretary to the former Grade 5 level, including all agency chief executives. All government departments and executive agencies are now responsible for their own pay and grading systems for civil servants outside the Senior Civil Service. In practice the grades of the former Open structure are still in use in some organizations. The Open structure represented the following:

Grade   Title
1   Permanent Secretary
1A   Second Permanent Secretary
2   Deputy Secretary
3   Under-Secretary
4   Chief Scientific Officer B, Professional and Technology Directing A
5   Assistant Secretary, Deputy Chief Scientific Officer, Professional and Technology Directing B
6   Senior Principal, Senior Principal Scientific Officer, Professional and Technology Superintending Grade
7   Principal, Principal Scientific Officer, Principal Professional and Technology Officer

SALARIES 1999–2000

Ministerial Salaries *from 1 April 1999*

Ministers who are Members of the House of Commons receive a parliamentary salary (£47,008) in addition to their ministerial salary.

*Prime Minister	£107,179
*Cabinet minister (Commons)	£64,307
*†Cabinet minister (Lords)	£83,560
Minister of State (Commons)	£33,359
Minister of State (Lords)	£64,426

Parliamentary Under-Secretary (Commons)	£25,319
Parliamentary Under-Secretary (Lords)	£55,631

* These ministers have yet to decide whether to take the full salaries provided for them for the financial year 1999–2000. For the time being they will draw the following ministerial salaries: Prime Minister, £62,760; Cabinet minister (Commons), £47,149; Cabinet minister (Lords), £70,608

† Except the Lord Chancellor, who receives a salary of £160,011

Special Advisers' Salaries *from 1 April 1999*

Special advisers to government ministers are paid out of public funds; their salaries are negotiated individually, but are usually in the range £26,728 to £78,186. At March 1999 there were 66 special advisers.

Civil Service Salaries *from 1 April 1999*
Senior Civil Service (SCS)

Secretary of the Cabinet and Head of the Home Civil Service	£98,400–£168,910
Permanent Secretary	£98,400–£168,910
Band 9	£87,460–£123,860
Band 8	£80,020–£116,860
Band 7	£73,250–£110,300
Band 6	£66,900–£104,190
Band 5	£61,110 –£98,400
Band 4	£55,750–£92,930
Band 3	£50,510–£82,650
Band 2	£45,810–£73,470
Band 1	£41,550–£65,270

Staff are placed in pay bands according to their level of responsibility and taking account of other factors such as experience and marketability. Movement within and between bands is based on performance. A recruitment and retention allowance of up to £3,000 may be paid in certain circumstances in addition to the salary ranges shown for bands 1 to 9.

Other Civil Servants

Following the delegation of responsibility for pay and grading to government departments and agencies from 1 April 1996, it is no longer possible to show service-wide pay rates for staff outside the Senior Civil Service. The following table will however give an indication of the percentage of civil servants at a given salary level.

*Non-Industrial Staff by Gross Salary Band
as at 1 April 1998*

Salary Band	Per Cent
£5,001–£10,000	8.9
£10,001–£15,000	38.8
£15,001–£20,000	23.4
£20,001–£25,000	16.1
£25,001–£30,000	5.5
£30,001–£35,000	2.7
£35,001–£40,000	1.9
£40,001–£45,000	1.0
£45,001–£50,000	0.6
£50,001–£55,000	0.4
£55,001–£60,000	0.2
£60,001–£65,000	0.1
£65,001–£70,000	0.1
£70,001–£75,000	0.0
£75,001 +	0.1

Source: Government Statistical Service – *Civil Service Statistics 1998*

ADJUDICATOR'S OFFICE
Haymarket House, 28 Haymarket, London SW1Y 4SP
Tel 0171-930 2292; fax 0171-930 2298

The Adjudicator's Office opened in 1993 and investigates complaints about the way the Inland Revenue (including the Valuation Office Agency) and Customs and Excise have handled an individual's affairs.
The Adjudicator, Dame Barbara Mills, DBE, QC
Head of Office, M. Savage

ADVISORY, CONCILIATION AND ARBITRATION SERVICE
Brandon House, 180 Borough High Street, London
SE1 1LW
Tel 0171-210 3613; fax 0171-210 3708

The Advisory, Conciliation and Arbitration Service (ACAS) was set up under the Employment Protection Act 1975 (the provisions now being found in the Trade Union and Labour Relations (Consolidation) Act 1992). ACAS is directed by a Council consisting of a full-time chairman and part-time employer, trade union and independent members, all appointed by the Secretary of State for Trade and Industry. The functions of the Service are to promote the improvement of industrial relations in general, to provide facilities for conciliation, mediation and arbitration as means of avoiding and resolving industrial disputes, and to provide advisory and information services on industrial relations matters to employers, employees and their representatives.

ACAS has regional offices in Birmingham, Bristol, Cardiff, Fleet, Glasgow, Leeds, Liverpool, London, Manchester, Newcastle upon Tyne and Nottingham.
Chairman, J. Hougham, CBE
Chief Conciliator (G4), D. Evans

MINISTRY OF AGRICULTURE, FISHERIES AND FOOD
Nobel House, 17 Smith Square, London SW1P 3JR
Tel 0171-238 6000; fax 0171-238 6591
E-mail: helpline@inf.maff.gov.uk
Web: http://www.maff.gov.uk/maffhome.htm

The Ministry of Agriculture, Fisheries and Food is responsible for government policies on agriculture, horticulture and fisheries in England and for policies relating to the safety and quality of food in the UK as a whole, including composition, labelling, additives, contaminants and new production processes. In association with the agriculture departments of the Scottish Executive, the National Assembly for Wales and the Northern Ireland Office and with the Intervention Board (*see* page 314), the Ministry is responsible for negotiations in the EU on the common agricultural and fisheries policies, and for single European market questions relating to its responsibilities. Its remit also includes international agricultural and food trade policy.

The Ministry exercises responsibilities for the protection and enhancement of the countryside and the marine environment, for flood defence and for other rural issues. It is the licensing authority for veterinary medicines and the registration authority for pesticides. It administers policies relating to the control of animal, plant and fish diseases. It provides scientific, technical and professional services and advice to farmers, growers and ancillary industries, and it commissions research to assist in the formulation and assessment of policy and to underpin applied research and development work done by industry. Responsibility for food safety and standards will be transferred to the new Food Standards Agency, expected to be in operation by mid 2000.

Minister of Agriculture, Fisheries and Food, The Rt. Hon. Nick Brown, MP
  Principal Private Secretary (G7), Ms S. Hendry
  Private Secretary (SEO), C. Porro
  Parliamentary Private Secretary, Ms R. Kelly, MP
Minister of State, The Rt. Hon. Joyce Quin, MP
  Private Secretary, Ms T. Hart
Minister of State, The Baroness Hayman
  Private Secretary, Mrs K. Lepper
Parliamentary Secretary, Elliot Morley, MP
  Private Secretary, M. Livesey
Parliamentary Clerk, M. Stickings
Permanent Secretary (SCS), R. J. Packer
  Private Secretary, A. Lawrence

ESTABLISHMENTS GROUP
Director of Establishments (SCS), R. A. Saunderson

ESTABLISHMENTS (GENERAL) AND OFFICE SERVICES DIVISION
Head of Division (SCS), Dr Mandy Bailey

PERSONNEL MANAGEMENT AND DEVELOPMENT DIVISION
Head of Division (SCS), vacant

BUILDING AND ESTATE MANAGEMENT
Eastbury House, 30–34 Albert Embankment,
London SE1 7TL
Tel 0171-238 6000
Head of Division (SCS), J. A. S. Nickson

INFORMATION TECHNOLOGY DIRECTORATE
Room 755, St Christopher House, Southwark Street,
London SE1 0UD
Tel 0171-921 1886

Director (SCS), A. G. Matthews

Government Buildings, Epsom Road, Guildford, Surrey
GU1 2LD
Tel 01483-403757

Head of Strategies (G6), P. Barber
Head of Applications (G6), D. D. Brown
Head of Infrastructure (G6), S. Soper

COMMUNICATIONS DIRECTORATE
Tel 0171-238 6000; helpline 0645-335577

Director of Communications (SCS), R. Lowson
Chief Press Officer (G7), M. Smith
Chief Publicity Officer (G7), N. Wagstaffe
Principal Librarian (G7), P. McShane

AGENCY OWNERSHIP UNIT
Head of Unit (SCS), Dr M. Tas

FINANCE DEPARTMENT
3–8 Whitehall Place (West Block), London SW1A 2HH
Tel 0171-238 6000
Principal Finance Officer (SCS), P. Elliott

FINANCIAL POLICY DIVISION
Head of Division (SCS), B. J. Harding

PROCUREMENT AND CONTRACTS DIVISION
19–29 Woburn Place, London WC1H 0LU
Tel 0171-273 3000

Head of Division (SCS), D. Rabey

AUDIT, CONSULTANCY AND MANAGEMENT SERVICES
19–29 Woburn Place, London WC1H 0LU
Tel 0171-273 3000

Director of Audit (SCS), D. V. Fisher

RESOURCE MANAGEMENT STRATEGY UNIT
19–29 Woburn Place, London WC1H 0LU
Tel 0171-273 3000

Head of Unit (SCS), D. V. Fisher

RESOURCE MANAGEMENT DIVISION
Foss House, Kings Pool, 1–2 Peasholme Green, York
YO1 7PX
Tel 01904-455328

Head of Division (G6), Mrs J. Flint

BUSINESS PLANNING UNIT
Head of Unit (G7), G. Holt

LEGAL DEPARTMENT
55 Whitehall, London SW1A 2EY
Tel 0171-238 6000

Legal Adviser and Solicitor (SCS), Miss K. M. S. Morton
Principal Assistant Solicitors (SCS), D. J. Pearson; Ms C. A.
Crisham

LEGAL DIVISIONS

Assistant Solicitor, Division A1 (SCS), P. Davis
Assistant Solicitor, Division A2 (SCS), P. Kent
Assistant Solicitor, Division A3 (SCS), C. Gregory
Assistant Solicitor, Division A4 (SCS), C. Allen
Assistant Solicitor, Division A5 (SCS), vacant
Assistant Solicitor, Division B1 (SCS), Dr Gisela Davis
Assistant Solicitor, Division B2 (SCS), Ms S. B. Spence
Assistant Solicitor, Division B3 (SCS), A. I. Corbett
Assistant Solicitor, Division B4 (SCS), N. Lambert

INVESTIGATION UNIT
Chief Investigation Officer, Miss J. Panting

ECONOMICS AND STATISTICS
3–8 Whitehall Place (West Block), London SW1A 2HH
Tel 0171-238 6000

Under-Secretary (SCS), D. Thompson

DIVISIONS

*Senior Economic Adviser, Economics and Statistics (Farm
Business) (G6)*, H. Fearn
Senior Economic Adviser, Economics (International) (SCS), N.
Atkinson
Senior Economic Adviser, Economics (Resource Use) (SCS), J. P.
Muriel

STATISTICS DIVISION
Foss House, Kings Pool, 1–2 Peasholme Green, York
YO1 7PX
Tel 01904-455332

Chief Statistician (Commodities and Food) (SCS), S. Platt
Chief Statistician (Census and Surveys) (SCS), P. F. Helm

CHIEF SCIENTIST'S GROUP
*St Christopher House, 80–112 Southwark Street, London
SE1 0UD
Tel 0171-928 3666

Chief Scientist (SCS), Dr D. W. F. Shannon

DIVISIONS

Head, Agriculture, Environment and Food Technology (SCS),
Dr J. C. Sherlock
Head, Veterinary, Food and Aquatic Science (SCS),
Dr K. J. MacOwan
Head, Research Policy and International (SCS), A. R. Burne

FISHERIES DEPARTMENT
Fisheries Secretary (SCS), S. Wentworth

DIVISIONS

Head, Fisheries I (SCS), P. M. Boyling
Head, Fisheries II (SCS), C. I. Llewellyn
Head, Fisheries III (SCS), Miss S. Brown
Head, Fisheries IV (SCS), B. S. Edwards
Chief Inspector, Sea Fisheries Inspectorate (G6), S. G. Ellson

AGRICULTURAL CROPS AND COMMODITIES DIRECTORATE
3–8 Whitehall Place (West Block), London SW1A 2HH
Tel 0171-238 6000

Deputy Secretary (SCS), Ms V. K. Timms, CB

EUROPEAN UNION AND INTERNATIONAL POLICY
Under-Secretary (SCS), A. J. Lebrecht

DIVISIONS

Head, European Union (SCS), Miss V. Smith
Head, Trade Policy and Tropical Foods (SCS), J. Robbs

AGRICULTURE GROUP
Head of Group (SCS), D. Hunter

DIVISIONS

Head, Horticulture, Potatoes and HMI (SCS), G. W. Noble
Head, New Crops and Sugar (SCS), H. B. Brown
Head, Arable Crops (SCS), A. Kuyk
Head, Beef and Sheep (SCS), R. Cowan
Head, Livestock Schemes (SCS), A. Taylor
Head, Milk, Pigs, Eggs and Poultry (SCS), P. Nash

FOOD INDUSTRY, COMPETITIVENESS AND CONSUMERS
Under-Secretary (SCS), N. Thornton

DIVISIONS

Head, Food and Drinks Industry (SCS), Miss C. J. Rabagliati
Head, International Relations and Export Promotion (SCS),
D. V. Orchard
Head, Agricultural Resources and Better Regulation (SCS), Mrs
A. Blackburn
Head, Marketing, Competition and Consumers (SCS), Ms J.
Allfrey
Heads, Inquiry Liaison Unit (SCS), D. Dawson; (G6), Mrs A.
Waters

REGIONAL SERVICES AND DEFENCE GROUP
3–8 Whitehall Place (West Block), London SW1A 2HH
Tel 0171-238 6000

Under-Secretary (SCS), Mrs K. J. A. Brown

DIVISIONS

*Head, Plant Health, and Plant Health and Seeds Inspectorate
(SCS)*, A. J. Perrins
Head, Flood and Coastal Protection (SCS), Dr J. Park
Head of CAP Schemes Management Division (SCS), Mrs J.
Purnell

PLANT VARIETY RIGHTS OFFICE AND SEEDS DIVISION
White House Lane, Huntingdon Road, Cambridge
CB3 0LF
Tel 01223-277151
Head of Office (SCS), D. A. Boreham

REGIONAL ORGANIZATION
Head, Regional Support Unit (G7), D. Putley
Regional Service Centres
ANGLIA REGION, Block B, Government Buildings,
Brooklands Avenue, Cambridge CB2 2DR. Tel: 01223-462727. *Regional Director*, M. Edwards
EAST MIDLANDS REGION, Block 7, Government
Buildings, Chalfont Drive, Nottingham NG8 3SN. Tel:
0115-929 0634. *Regional Director*, G. Norbury
NORTH-EAST REGION, Government Buildings, Crosby
Road, Northallerton, N. Yorks DL6 1AD. Tel: 01609-773751. *Regional Director*, P. Watson
NORTHERN REGION, Eden Bridge House, Lowther
Street, Carlisle, Cumbria CA3 8DX. Tel: 01228-523400.
Regional Director, I. G. Pearson
NORTH MERCIA REGION, Electra Way, Crewe Business
Park, Crewe, Cheshire CW1 6GL. Tel: 01270-754000. *Regional Director*, F. Whitehouse
SOUTH-EAST REGION, Block A, Government Buildings,
Coley Park, Reading, Berks RG1 6DT. Tel: 01889-581222. *Regional Director*, Mrs V. Silvester
SOUTH MERCIA REGION, Block C, Government
Buildings, Whittington Road, Worcester WR5 2LQ. Tel:
01905-763355. *Regional Director*, B. Davies
SOUTH-WEST REGION, Clyst House, Winslade Park,
Clyst St Mary, Exeter EX5 1DY. Tel: 01392-447400.
Regional Director, M. R. W. Highman
WESSEX REGION, Block 3, Government Buildings,
Burghill Road, Westbury-on-Trym, Bristol
BS10 6NJ. Tel: 0117-959 1000. *Regional Director*, Mrs
A. J. L. Ould

FOOD SAFETY AND ENVIRONMENT GROUP
Deputy Secretary (SCS), R. J. D. Carden, CB

ENVIRONMENT GROUP
Under-Secretary (SCS), D. J. Coates
Head, Rural Division (SCS), Ms L. Cornish
Head, Conservation Management Division (SCS), T. J.
Osmond
Head, Rural and Marine Environment (SCS), D. E. Jones

FOOD SAFETY AND STANDARDS GROUP
Under-Secretary (SCS), G. Podger

DIVISIONS
Head, Additives and Novel Foods (SCS), Dr J. R. Bell
Head, Food Contaminants (SCS), Dr R. Burt
Head, Food Labelling and Standards (SCS), G. F. Meekings
Head, Radiological Safety and Nutrition (SCS), Dr M. G. Segal
Head, Food Hygiene (SCS), R. J. Harding
Head, Meat Hygiene I (SCS), R. C. McIvor
Head, Meat Hygiene II (SCS), C. J. Lawson
Head, Food Standards Agency Division (SCS), Miss
E. J. Wordley

VETERINARY PUBLIC HEALTH UNIT
Assistant Chief Veterinary Officer (SCS), D. Taylor, CBE
Head of Unit (SCS), P. Hewson

ANIMAL HEALTH GROUP
*Government Buildings, Hook Rise South, Tolworth,
Surbiton, Surrey KT6 7NF
Tel 0181-330 4411
Under-Secretary (SCS), B. H. B. Dickinson

DIVISIONS
Head, Animal Health (BSE and International Trade) (SCS), T.
E. D. Eddy
Head, Animal Health (Disease Control) (SCS), T. D.
Rossington
Head, Services (G6), R. Gurd
Head, Animal Welfare (SCS), C. J. Ryder
Head, Bovine Tuberculosis (SCS), R. Hathaway

CHIEF VETERINARY OFFICER'S GROUP
*Government Buildings, Hook Rise South, Tolworth,
Surbiton, Surrey KT6 7NF
Tel 0181-330 8057
Chief Veterinary Officer (SCS), J. M. Scudamore
Assistant Chief Veterinary Officer (SCS), R. J. G. Cawthorne

DIVISIONS
Head, Veterinary International Trade Team (SCS), R. A. Bell
*Head, Veterinary Notifiable Disease Team (Exotic Diseases and
TSE) (SCS)*, Dr D. Matthews
*Head, Veterinary Notifiable Disease Team (Endemic Animal
Diseases and Zoonoses) (SCS)*, Dr Debby Reynolds
Head, Welfare Team (SCS), A. T. Turnbull

VETERINARY FIELD SERVICE
*Government Buildings, Hook Rise South, Tolworth,
Surbiton, Surrey KT15 3NB
Tel 0181-330 4411
Director of Veterinary Field Services (SCS), M. J. Atkinson
* During the autumn of 1999 staff at the Tolworth and St Christopher
House sites will begin to be relocated to: 1A Page Street, London
SW1P 4PQ. Tel: 0171-904 3000

EXECUTIVE AGENCIES
CENTRAL SCIENCE LABORATORY
Sand Hutton, York YO41 1LZ
Tel 01904-462000; fax 01904-462111
The agency provides MAFF with technical support and
policy advice on the protection and quality of the food
supply and on related environmental issues.
Chief Executive (G3), Prof. P. I. Stanley
Research Directors (G5), Prof. A. R. Hardy (*Agriculture and
Environment*); Prof. J. Gilbert (*Food*)

CENTRE FOR ENVIRONMENT, FISHERIES AND
AQUACULTURE SCIENCE
Pakefield Road, Lowestoft, Suffolk NR33 0HT
Tel 01502-562244; fax: 01502-513865
The Agency, established in April 1997, provides research
and consultancy services in fisheries science and manage-
ment, aquaculture, fish health and hygiene, environmental
impact assessment, and environmental quality assessment.
Chief Executive, Dr P. Greig-Smith

FARMING AND RURAL CONSERVATION AGENCY
Nobel House, 17 Smith Square, London SW1P 3JR
Tel 0171-238 5432; fax 0171-238 5588
The Agency, established in April 1997, is responsible
jointly to MAFF and the National Assembly for Wales. It
assists the Government in the design, development and
implementation of policies on the integration of farming
and conservation, environmental protection and the rural
economy. This includes agri-environment schemes such as

Environmentally Sensitive Areas, Countryside Stewardship and access schemes, rural development, milk hygiene
inspections and wildlife management.
Chief Executive (SCS), Miss S. Nason

INTERVENTION BOARD
— see page 314

MEAT HYGIENE SERVICE
Foss House, Kings Pool, 1–2 Peasholme Green, York
YOI 7PX
Tel 01904-455655; fax 01904-455502

The Agency was launched in April 1995. It protects public
health and promotes animal welfare through veterinary
supervision and meat inspection in licensed fresh meat
establishments.
Chief Executive (G4), J. McNeill

PESTICIDES SAFETY DIRECTORATE
Mallard House, Kings Pool, 3 Peasholme Green, York
YOI 7PX
Tel 01904-640500; fax 01904-455733

The Pesticides Safety Directorate is responsible for the
evaluation and approval of pesticides and the development
of policies relating to them, in order to protect consumers,
users and the environment.
Chief Executive (G4), G. K. Bruce
Director (Policy) (G5), J. A. Bainton
Director (Approvals) (G5), Dr A. D. Martin

VETERINARY LABORATORIES AGENCY
Woodham Lane, New Haw, Addlestone, Surrey KT15 3NB
Tel 01932-341111; fax 01932-347046

The Veterinary Laboratories Agency provides scientific
and technical expertise in animal and public health.
Chief Executive (G3), Dr T. W. A. Little
Director of Research (G5), Dr J. A. Morris
Director of Laboratory Services (G5), Dr S. Edwards
Director of Surveillance (G5), J. W. Harkness
Director of Finance (G6), I. Grattidge
Laboratory Secretary (G6), C. Edwards

VETERINARY MEDICINES DIRECTORATE
Woodham Lane, New Haw, Addlestone, Surrey KT15 3LS
Tel 01932-336911; fax 01932-336618

The Veterinary Medicines Directorate is responsible for
all aspects of the authorization and control of veterinary
medicines, including post-authorization surveillance of
residues in meat and animal products, and the provision of
policy advice to ministers.
Chief Executive and Director of Veterinary Medicines (G4),
Dr J. M. Rutter
Director (Policy) (G5), R. Anderson
Director (Licensing) (G5), S. Dean
Secretary and Head of Business Unit (G6), J. FitzGerald
Licensing Manager, Pharmaceuticals and Feed Additives (G6),
J. P. O'Brien
Licensing Manager, Immunologicals (G6), Dr D. J. K. Mackay

COLLEGE OF ARMS (OR HERALDS COLLEGE)
Queen Victoria Street, London EC4V 4BT
Tel 0171-248 2762; fax 0171-248 6448

The Sovereign's Officers of Arms (Kings, Heralds and
Pursuivants of Arms) were first incorporated by Richard
III. The powers vested by the Crown in the Earl Marshal
(the Duke of Norfolk) with regard to state ceremonial are
largely exercised through the College. The College is also
the official repository of the arms and pedigrees of English,
Welsh, Northern Irish and Commonwealth (except Canadian) families and their descendants, and its records include
official copies of the records of Ulster King of Arms, the
originals of which remain in Dublin. The 13 officers of the
College specialize in genealogical and heraldic work for
their respective clients.

Arms have been and still are granted by letters patent
from the Kings of Arms. A right to arms can only be
established by the registration in the official records of the
College of Arms of a pedigree showing direct male line
descent from an ancestor already appearing therein as
being entitled to arms, or by making application through
the College of Arms for a grant of arms. Grants are made
to corporations as well as to individuals.

The College of Arms is open Monday–Friday 10–4.

Earl Marshal, The Duke of Norfolk, KG, GCVO, CB, CBE, MC

KINGS OF ARMS
Garter, P. L. Gwynn-Jones, CVO, FSA
Clarenceux (and Registrar), D. H. B. Chesshyre, LVO, FSA
Norroy and Ulster, T. Woodcock, LVO, FSA

HERALDS
Richmond (and Earl Marshal's Secretary), P. L. Dickinson
York, H. E. Paston-Bedingfeld
Chester, T. H. S. Duke
Lancaster, R. J. B. Noel
Windsor, W. G. Hunt, TD

PURSUIVANTS
Rouge Croix, D. V. White
Rouge Dragon, C. E. A. Cheesman, PH.D.

COURT OF THE LORD LYON
HM New Register House, Edinburgh EH1 3YT
Tel 0131-556 7255; fax 0131-557 2148

The Court of the Lord Lyon is the Scottish Court of
Chivalry (including the genealogical jurisdiction of the *Ri-
Sennachie* of Scotland's Celtic Kings). The Lord Lyon King
of Arms has jurisdiction, subject to appeal to the Court of
Session and the House of Lords, in questions of heraldry
and the right to bear arms. The Court also administers the
Scottish Public Register of All Arms and Bearings and the
Public Register of All Genealogies. Pedigrees are established by decrees of Lyon Court and by letters patent. As
Royal Commissioner in Armory, the Lord Lyon grants
patents of arms (which constitute the grantee and heirs
noble in the Noblesse of Scotland) to 'virtuous and well-
deserving' Scotsmen and to petitioners (personal or
corporate) in The Queen's overseas realms of Scottish
connection, and issues birthbrieves.

Lord Lyon King of Arms, Sir Malcolm Innes of Edingight,
KCVO, WS

HERALDS
Albany, J. A. Spens, MVO, RD, WS
Rothesay, Sir Crispin Agnew of Lochnaw, Bt., QC
Ross, C. J. Burnett, FSA Scot.

PURSUIVANTS
Kintyre, J. C. G. George, FSA Scot.
Unicorn, Alastair Campbell of Airds, FSA Scot.
Carrick, Mrs C. G. W. Roads, MVO, FSA Scot.

Lyon Clerk and Keeper of Records, Mrs C. G. W. Roads, MVO,
FSA Scot.
Procurator-Fiscal, D. F. Murby, WS
Herald Painter, Mrs J. Phillips
Macer, A. M. Clark

ARTS COUNCILS

The Arts Council of Great Britain was established as an independent body in 1946 to be the principal channel for the Government's support of the arts. In 1994 the Scottish and Welsh Arts Councils became autonomous and the Arts Council of Great Britain became the Arts Council of England.

The Arts Councils are responsible for the distribution of the proceeds of the National Lottery allocated to the arts (*see* Lotteries and Gaming section).

ARTS COUNCIL OF ENGLAND
14 Great Peter Street, London SW1P 3NQ
Tel 0171-333 0100; fax 0171-973 6590

The Arts Council of England's objectives are to develop and improve the understanding and practice of the arts and to increase their accessibility to the public. The Council funds the major arts organizations in England and the ten Regional Arts Boards. It is funded by the Department for Culture, Media and Sport but operates at 'arm's length' from Government as regards artistic decision-making, although it is expected to account for such decisions to the Government and the public. The Council also provides advice, information and help to artists and arts organizations. Its members are unpaid.

The Council distributes an annual grant from the Department for Culture, Media and Sport; the grant for 1999–2000 is £218.8 million.
Chairman, G. Robinson
Members, D. Anderson; D. Brierley, CBE; Ms D. Bull, CBE; Prof. C. Frayling; A. Gormley; A. Kapoor; Prof. J. MacGregor; Prof. A. Motion; Ms P. Skene; Ms H. Strong
Chief Executive, P. Hewitt

REGIONAL ARTS BOARDS

EASTERN ARTS BOARD, Cherry Hinton Hall, Cherry Hinton Road, Cambridge CB1 8DW. Tel: 01223-215355. *Chair,* Prof. S. Timperley
EAST MIDLANDS ARTS BOARD, Mountfields House, Epinal Way, Loughborough, Leics LE11 0QE. Tel: 01509-218292. *Chair,* Prof. R. Cowell
LONDON ARTS BOARD, Elme House, 133 Long Acre, London WC2E 9AF. Tel: 0171-240 1313. *Chair,* T. Phillips, OBE
NORTHERN ARTS BOARD, 9–10 Osborne Terrace, Newcastle upon Tyne NE2 1NZ. Tel: 0191-281 6334. *Chair,* G. Loggie
NORTH-WEST ARTS BOARD, Manchester House, 22 Bridge Street, Manchester M3 3AB. Tel: 0161-834 6644. *Chair,* Prof. B. Cox, CBE, FRSL
SOUTH-EAST ARTS BOARD, Union House, Eridge Road, Tunbridge Wells, Kent TN4 8HF. Tel: 01892-507205. *Chair,* R. Reed
SOUTHERN ARTS BOARD, 13 St Clement Street, Winchester SO23 9DQ. Tel: 01962-855099. *Chair,* D. Astor
SOUTH-WEST ARTS BOARD, Bradninch Place, Gandy Street, Exeter EX4 3LS. Tel: 01392-218188. *Chair,* vacant
WEST MIDLANDS ARTS BOARD, 82 Granville Street, Birmingham B1 2LH. Tel: 0121-631 3121. *Chair,* R. Natkiel
YORKSHIRE ARTS BOARD, 21 Bond Street, Dewsbury, W. Yorks WF13 1AX. Tel: 01924-455555. *Chair,* C. Price

SCOTTISH ARTS COUNCIL
12 Manor Place, Edinburgh EH3 7DD
Tel 0131-226 6051; fax 0131-225 9833

The Scottish Arts Council funds arts organizations in Scotland and is funded directly by the Scottish Executive. The grant for 1999–2000 is £28.097 million.
Chairman, M. Linklater
Members, Ms S. Ainsley; H. Buchanan; Cllr Elizabeth Cameron; R. Chester; W. English; J. Faulds; Ms D. Idiens; Ms M. Marshall; Dr Ann Matheson, OBE; J. Scott Moncrieff; W. Speirs; Ms J. Urquart
Director, Ms T. Jackson

ARTS COUNCIL OF WALES
9 Museum Place, Cardiff CF1 3NX
Tel 01222-376500; fax 01222-221447

The Arts Council of Wales funds arts organizations in Wales and is funded by the National Assembly for Wales. The grant for 1999–2000 is about £14.7 million.
Chairman, Ms S. Crouch
Members, Ms E. Bennet; Ms A. Davies; R. Davies; K. Evans; Ms K. Gass; D. Johnston; G. S. Jones; L. Jones; G. Lewis; A. Lloyd; A. Roberts; Ms C. Thomas; Ms M. Vincentelli
Chief Executive, Ms J. Weston

ARTS COUNCIL OF NORTHERN IRELAND
MacNeice House, 77 Malone Road, Belfast BT9 6AQ
Tel 01232-385200; fax 01232-661715

The Arts Council of Northern Ireland is the prime distributor of government funds in support of the arts in Northern Ireland. It is funded by the Department of Education for Northern Ireland, and the grant for 1999–2000 is £6.89 million.
Chairman, Prof. B. Walker
Vice-Chairman, Ms M. O'Neill
Members, Cllr M. Bradley; W. Burns; S. Burnside; P. Donnelly; Dr Tess Hurson; Mrs R. McMullan; G. Patterson; Ms C. Poulter; Ms I. Sandford; A. Shortt
Chief Executive, B. Ferran

ART GALLERIES, ETC.

ROYAL FINE ART COMMISSION (former)
— *see* Commission for Architecture and the Built Environment

ROYAL FINE ART COMMISSION FOR SCOTLAND
Bakehouse Close, 146 Canongate, Edinburgh EH8 8DD
Tel 0131-556 6699; fax 0131-556 6633

The Commission was established in 1927 and advises ministers and local authorities on the visual impact and quality of design of construction projects. It is an independent body and gives its opinions impartially.
Chairman, The Lord Cameron of Lochbroom, PC, FRSE
Commissioners, Prof. G. Benson; W. A. Cadell; Mrs K. Dalyell; Ms J. Malvenan; R. G. Maund; M. Murray; D. Page; B. Rae; R. Russell; M. Turnbull; A. Wright
Secretary, C. Prosser

NATIONAL GALLERY
Trafalgar Square, London WC2N 5DN
Tel 0171-839 3321; fax 0171-747 2403

The National Gallery, which houses a permanent collection of western painting from the 13th to the 20th century, was founded in 1824, following a parliamentary grant of £60,000 for the purchase and exhibition of the Angerstein collection of pictures. The present site was first occupied in 1838; an extension to the north of the building with a public entrance in Orange Street was opened in 1975, and the Sainsbury wing was opened in 1991. Total government grant-in-aid for 1999–2000 is £19.478 million.

BOARD OF TRUSTEES
Chairman, P. Hughes, CBE
Trustees, Lady Bingham; Sir Mark Richmond, SC.D., FRS; Lady Monck; Sir Ewen Fergusson, GCMG, GCVO; R. Gavron, CBE; C. Le Brun; The Hon. R. G. H. Seitz; Dr D. Landau; Sir Colin Southgate; J. Snow; Prof. Dawn Ades; Lady Hopkins

OFFICERS
Director, R. N. MacGregor
Keeper, Dr N. Penny
Senior Curator, D. Jaffé
Chief Restorer, M. H. Wyld, CBE
Head of Exhibitions, M. J. Wilson
Scientific Adviser, Dr A. Roy
Director of Administration, J. MacAuslan
Head of Press and Public Relations, Miss J. Liddiard

NATIONAL PORTRAIT GALLERY
St Martin's Place, London WC2H OHE
Tel 0171-306 0055; fax 0171-306 0058

A grant was made in 1856 to form a gallery of the portraits of the most eminent persons in British history. The present building was opened in 1896 and an extension in 1933. There are four regional partnerships displaying portraits in appropriate settings: Montacute House, Gawthorpe Hall, Beningbrough Hall and Bodelwyddan Castle. Total government grant-in-aid for 1999–2000 is £4.997 million.

BOARD OF TRUSTEES
Chairman, H. Keswick
Trustees, The Lord President of the Council (*ex officio*); The President of the Royal Academy of Arts (*ex officio*); The Lord Morris of Castle Morris, D.phil.; Prof. N. Lynton; J. Tusa; Mrs J. E. Benson, LVO, OBE; Lady Tumim, OBE; Sir David Scholey, CBE; Mrs C. Tomalin; Baroness Willoughby de Eresby; M. Hastings; Prof. The Earl Russell, FBA; T. Phillips, RA; Prof. C. Matthew
Director (G3), C. Saumarez Smith, PH.D.

TATE GALLERY
Millbank, London SWIP 4RG
Tel 0171-887 8000; fax 0171-887 8007

The Tate Gallery comprises the national collections of British painting and 20th-century painting and sculpture. The Gallery was opened in 1897, the cost of erection (£80,000) being defrayed by Sir Henry Tate, who also contributed the nucleus of the present collection. The Turner wing was opened in 1910, galleries to contain the collection of modern foreign painting in 1926, and a new sculpture hall in 1937. In 1979 a further extension was built, and the Clore Gallery, for the Turner collection, was opened in 1987. The Tate Gallery Liverpool opened in 1988 and the Tate Gallery St Ives in 1993. The new Tate Gallery of Modern Art at Bankside is due to open in May 2000, with the Millbank gallery then being devoted to British art. Total government grant-in-aid for 1999–2000 is £19.727 million.

BOARD OF TRUSTEES
Chairman, D. Verey
Trustees, Prof. Dawn Ades; The Hon. Mrs J. de Botton; Sir Richard Carew Pole; Prof. M. Craig-Martin; P. Doig; Sir Christopher Mallaby, GCMG, GCVO; Sir Mark Richmond; Mrs P. Ridley, OBE; W. Woodrow

OFFICERS
Director, Sir Nicholas Serota
Director of National Programmes, S. Nairne

Director of Collections, J. Lewison
Director, Tate Gallery of Modern Art, L. Nittve
Director, Tate Gallery of British Art, S. Deuchar
Curator, Tate Gallery Liverpool, L. Biggs
Curator, Tate Gallery St Ives, M. Tooby

WALLACE COLLECTION
Hertford House, Manchester Square, London WIM 6BN
Tel 0171-935 0687; fax 0171-224 2155

The Wallace Collection was bequeathed to the nation by the widow of Sir Richard Wallace, Bt. in 1897, and Hertford House was subsequently acquired by the Government. Total government grant-in-aid for 1999–2000 is £2.453 million.

Director, Miss R. J. Savill
Head of Administration, A. W. Houldershaw

NATIONAL GALLERIES OF SCOTLAND
The Mound, Edinburgh EH2 2EL
Tel 0131-624 6200; fax 0131-343 3250

The National Galleries of Scotland comprise the National Gallery of Scotland, the Scottish National Portrait Gallery, the Scottish National Gallery of Modern Art and the Dean Gallery. There are also outstations at Paxton House, Berwickshire, and Duff House, Banffshire. Total government grant-in-aid for 1999–2000 is £10.197 million.

TRUSTEES
Chairman of the Trustees, The Countess of Airlie, CVO
Trustees, Ms V. Atkinson; J. H. Blair; G. J. N. Gemmell, CBE; Lord Gordon of Strathblane, CBE; A. P. Leitch; Prof. Christina Lodder; Dr I. McKenzie Smith, OBE; Dr M. Shea; G. Weaver; Prof. I. Whyte

OFFICERS
Director (G4), T. Clifford
Keeper of Conservation (G6), M. Gallagher
Head of Press and Information (G7), Mrs A. M. Wagener
Keeper of Education (G7), M. Cassin
Registrar (G7), Miss A. Buddle
Secretary (G6), Ms S. Edwards
Buildings (G7), R. Galbraith
Keeper, National Gallery of Scotland (G6), M. Clarke
Keeper, Scottish National Portrait Gallery (G6), J. Holloway
Curator of Photography, Miss S. F. Stevenson
Keeper, Scottish National Gallery of Modern Art and Dean Gallery (G6), R. Calvocoressi

ASSEMBLY OMBUDSMAN FOR NORTHERN IRELAND AND NORTHERN IRELAND COMMISSIONER FOR COMPLAINTS
Progressive House, 33 Wellington Place, Belfast BT1 6HN
Tel 01232-233821; fax 01232-234912

The Ombudsman is appointed under legislation with powers to investigate complaints by people claiming to have sustained injustice in consequence of maladministration arising from action taken by a Northern Ireland government department, or any other public body within his remit. Staff are presently seconded from the Northern Ireland Civil Service.
Ombudsman, G. Burns, MBE
Deputy Ombudsman, J. MacQuarrie
Directors, C. O'Hare; R. Doherty; H. Mallon

UK ATOMIC ENERGY AUTHORITY

Harwell, Didcot, Oxon OX11 ORA
Tel 01235-820220; fax 01235-436401

The UKAEA was established by the Atomic Energy Authority Act 1954 and took over responsibility for the research and development of the civil nuclear power programme. The Authority's commercial arm, AEA Technology PLC, was privatized in 1996. UKAEA is responsible for the safe management and decommissioning of its radioactive plant and for maximizing the income from the buildings and land on its sites. UKAEA also undertakes special nuclear tasks for the Government, including the UK's contribution to the international fusion programme.
Chairman, Adm. Sir Kenneth Eaton
Chief Executive, Dr J. McKeown

AUDIT COMMISSIONS

AUDIT COMMISSION FOR LOCAL AUTHORITIES AND THE NATIONAL HEALTH SERVICE IN ENGLAND AND WALES

1 Vincent Square, London SW1P 2PN
Tel 0171-828 1212; fax 0171-976 6187

The Audit Commission was set up in 1983 and is responsible for appointing external auditors to local authorities and local National Health Service bodies in England and Wales. It is also responsible for promoting the proper stewardship of public finances and value for money in the services provided by local authorities and health bodies.

The Commission has a chairman, a deputy chairman and up to 18 members who, though appointed by the Secretary of State for the Environment, Transport and the Regions in consultation with the Health Secretaries in England and Wales, are responsible to Parliament.
Chairman, Dame Helena Shovelton, DBE
Deputy Chairman, J. Orme
Controller of Audit, A. Foster
Commission Secretary, Ms C. Baldwinson
Chief Executive of District Audit Service, D. Prince

ACCOUNTS COMMISSION FOR SCOTLAND

18 George Street, Edinburgh EH2 2QU
Tel 0131-477 1234; fax 0131-477 4567

The Commission was set up in 1975. It is responsible for securing the audit of the accounts of Scottish local authorities and certain joint boards and joint committees, and for value-for-money audits of authorities. In 1995 it assumed responsibility for securing the audit of National Health Service bodies in Scotland. The Commission is required to deal with reports made by the Controller of Audit on items of account contrary to law; on incorrect accounting; and on losses due to misconduct, negligence and failure to carry out statutory duties.

Members are appointed by the First Minister.
Chairman, Prof. J. P. Percy, CBE
Controller of Audit, R. W. Black
Secretary, W. F. Magee

THE BANK OF ENGLAND

Threadneedle Street, London EC2R 8AH
Tel 0171-601 4444; fax 0171-601 4771

The Bank of England was incorporated in 1694 under royal charter. It is the banker of the Government and manages the note issue. Since May 1997 it has been operationally independent and its Monetary Policy Committee has had responsibility for setting short-term interest rates to meet the Government's inflation target. As the central reserve bank of the country, the Bank keeps the accounts of British banks, who maintain with it a proportion of their cash resources, and of most overseas central banks. The Bank is divided into two divisions, Monetary Stability and Financial Stability. Its responsibility for banking supervision has been transferred to the Financial Services Authority. (*See also* page 635).
Governor, The Rt. Hon. E. A. J. George
Deputy Governors, D. Clementi; M. A. King
Non-Executive Directors, C. J. Allsopp; R. Bailie, OBE; A. R. F. Buxton; Sir David Cooksey; H. J. Davies; Sir Ian Gibson; G. Hawker; Mrs F. A. Heaton; Sir John Keswick; Dame Sheila Masters, DBE; Ms S. McKechnie, OBE; W. Morris; J. Neill, CBE, Ph.D.; Ms K. O'Donovan; N. I. Simms; J. Stretton
Monetary Policy Committee, The Governor; the Deputy Governors; I. Plenderleith; Prof. C. Goodhart; Dr D. Julius; Prof. W. Buiter; J. Vickers; Dr S. Wadhwani
Advisers to the Governor, Sir Peter Petrie; L. Berkowitz; D. Brealey
Chief Cashier and Deputy Director, Banking and Market Services, Ms M. V. Lowther
Chief Registrar, G. P. Sparkes
General Manager, Printing Works, A. W. Jarvis
Secretary, P. D. Rodgers
The Auditor, K. Butler

BOUNDARY COMMISSIONS

The Commissions are constituted under the Parliamentary Constituencies Act 1986. The Speaker of the House of Commons is *ex officio* chairman of all four commissions in the UK. Each of the four commissions is required by law to keep the parliamentary constituencies in their part of the UK under review. The latest review was completed in 1995 and its proposals took effect at the 1997 general election. The next review is due to be completed between 2002 and 2006.

ENGLAND

1 Drummond Gate, London SW1V 2QQ
Tel 0171-533 5177; fax 0171-533 5176

Deputy Chairman, The Hon. Mr Justice Harrison
Joint Secretaries, R. Farrance; S. Limpkin

WALES

1 Drummond Gate, London SW1V 2QQ
Tel 0171-533 5172; fax 0171-533 5176

Deputy Chairman, The Hon. Mr Justice Kay
Joint Secretaries, R. Farrance; S. Limpkin

SCOTLAND

3 Drumsheugh Gardens, Edinburgh EH3 7QJ
Tel 0131-538 7200; fax 0131-538 7240

Deputy Chairman, The Hon. Lady Cosgrove
Secretary, R. Smith

NORTHERN IRELAND

REL Division, 11 Millbank, London SW1P 4PN
Tel 0171-210 6569

Deputy Chairman, The Hon. Mr Justice Coghlin
Secretary, Mrs L. Rogers

BRITISH BROADCASTING CORPORATION
Broadcasting House, Portland Place, London WIA IAA
Tel 0171-580 4468; fax 0171-637 1630
Television Centre, Wood Lane, London WI2 7RJ
Tel 0181-743 8000; fax 0181-749 7520

The BBC was incorporated under royal charter in 1926 as successor to the British Broadcasting Company Ltd. The BBC's current charter came into force on 1 May 1996 and extends to 31 December 2006. The chairman, vice-chairman and other governors are appointed by The Queen-in-Council. The BBC is financed by revenue from receiving licences for the home services and by grant-in-aid from Parliament for the World Service (radio). For services, *see* Broadcasting section.

BOARD OF GOVERNORS
Chairman (£67,420), Sir Christopher Bland
Vice-Chairman (£17,300), The Baroness Young of Old Scone
National Governors (each £17,300), Prof. F. Monds
  (*N. Ireland*); R. S. Jones, OBE (*Wales*); Sir Robert Smith (*Scotland*)
Chairman, English National Forum (£13,000), R. Sondhi
Governors (each £8,660), Sir David Scholey, CBE; Sir Richard Eyre, CBE; A. White, CBE; Dame Pauline Neville-Jones, DCMG; A. Young; Ms H. Rabbatts

BOARD OF MANAGEMENT
EXECUTIVE COMMITTEE
Director-General and Editor-in-Chief (£387,000), Sir John Birt (until April 2000); G. Dyke (from April 2000)
Chief Executives, M. Bannister (*BBC Production*); W. Wyatt (*BBC Broadcast*); T. Hall (*BBC News*); R. Lynch (*BBC Resources Ltd*); R. Gavin (*BBC Worldwide*); M. Byford (*World Service*)
Directors, Ms M. Salmon (*Personnel*); Ms P. Hodgson (*Policy and Planning*); J. Smith (*Finance*); C. Browne (*Corporate Affairs*)

OTHER BOARD OF MANAGEMENT MEMBERS
Directors, A. Yentob (*Television*); Ms J. Abramsky (*Radio*); Ms J. Drabble (*Education*); M. Thompson (*Regional Broadcasting*)

OTHER SENIOR STAFF
The Secretary, C. Graham
Director, Continuous News, R. Mosey
Controller, BBC1, P. Salmon
Controller, BBC2, Ms J. Root
Controller, Radio 1, A. Parfitt
Controller, Radio 2, J. Moir
Controller, Radio 3, R. Wright
Controller, Radio 4, J. Boyle
Controller, Radio 5 Live, R. Mosey
Controller, BBC Proms and Millennium Programmes, N. Kenyon
Controller, BBC Scotland, J. McCormick
Controller, BBC Wales, G. Talfan Davies
Controller, BBC N. Ireland, P. Loughrey
Controller, English Regions, A. Griffee

THE BRITISH COUNCIL
10 Spring Gardens, London SWIA 2BN
Tel 0171-930 8466; fax 0171-839 6347
Bridgewater House, 58 Whitworth Street, Manchester M15 4AA
Tel 0161-957 7755; fax 0161-957 7762
Arts Division: 11 Portland Place, London WIN 4EJ
Tel 0171-389 3001; fax 0171-389 3199

The British Council was established in 1934, incorporated by royal charter in 1940 and granted a supplemental charter in 1993. It is an independent, non-political organization which promotes Britain abroad. It is the UK's international network for education, culture and development services. The Council is represented in 230 towns and cities in 109 countries and runs 209 libraries, 95 teaching centres and 29 resource centres around the world.
  Total income in 1998–9, including Foreign and Commonwealth Office grants and contracted money, was £424.639 million.
Chairman, The Baroness Kennedy of The Shaws, QC
Deputy Chairman, Sir Tim Lankester, KCB
Director-General, D. Green

BRITISH FILM COMMISSION
70 Baker Street, London WIM IDJ
Tel 0171-224 5000; fax 0171-224 1013

The British Film Commission was set up in 1991 and is funded by the Department for Culture, Media and Sport. The Commission promotes the UK as an international production centre, encourages the use of locations, facilities, services and personnel, and provides, at no charge to the film makers, comprehensive advice and information relating to the practical aspects of filming in the UK.
  The Government has announced plans to establish a new film body by April 2000 which would incorporate the work currently undertaken by the Commision.
Commissioner and Chief Executive, S. Norris

BRITISH FILM INSTITUTE
21 Stephen Street, London WIP 2LN
Tel 0171-255 1444; fax 0171-436 7950

The British Film Institute was founded in 1933 and is now established by royal charter. It is the UK national agency with responsibility for encouraging the arts of film and television and conserving them in the national interest. The BFI has three main operating departments: bfi Collections, which runs the National Film and Television Archive; bfi Exhibition, which runs the National Film Theatre and the London Film Festival; and bfi Education, which comprises the National Library, publishing and education projects. Total government funding for 1999–2000 is £16.8 million.
  The Government has announced plans to establish a new film body by April 2000 which would incorporate the work currently undertaken by the Institute.
Chairman, A. Parker, CBE
Deputy Chairman, Ms J. Bakewell, CBE
Director, J. Woodward
Deputy Director, J. Teckman

BRITISH PHARMACOPOEIA COMMISSION
Market Towers, 1 Nine Elms Lane, London sw8 5NQ
Tel 0171-273 0561; fax 0171-273 0566

The British Pharmacopoeia Commission sets standards for medicinal products used in human and veterinary medicines and is responsible for publication of the British Pharmacopoeia (a publicly available statement of the standard that a product must meet throughout its shelf-life), the British Pharmacopoeia (Veterinary) and the selection of British Approved Names. It has 13 members who are appointed by the Secretary of State for Health, the Minister for Agriculture, Fisheries and Food, the Scottish ministers, the National Assembly for Wales, and the relevant Northern Ireland departments.
Chairman, Prof. D. Calam, OBE, D.phil.
Vice-Chairman, Prof. J. A. Goldsmith
Secretary and Scientific Director, Dr R. C. Hutton

BRITISH RAILWAYS BOARD and SHADOW STRATEGIC RAIL AUTHORITY
26 Old Queen Street, London swiH 9HP
Tel 0171-960 1500; fax 0171-960 1501

The British Railways Board came into being in 1963 under the terms of the Transport Act 1962. Under the Railways Act 1993, the activities of the Board were restructured and largely transferred to the private sector. Its residual responsibilities include disposing of surplus land and advising the Government on rail policy issues.

The Government announced in July 1998 that British Rail's residual functions would be taken over by a Strategic Rail Authority, which has been operating in shadow form since 1 April 1999 and will do so until the required legislation in enacted, probably in 2000. When the authority is set up it will also incorporate the functions of the Passenger Franchising Director and some functions currently exercised by the Rail Regulator and the Department of the Environment, Transport and the Regions. Its main responsibilities will be strategic planning, co-ordinating and supervising the activities of the rail industry, and the disbursement of public funds.
Chairman, British Railways Board and Shadow Strategic Rail Authority (£130,000), Sir Alastair Morton
Vice-Chairman, J. J. Jerram, CBE
Non-executive Members (part-time), M. J. Grant (The Franchising Director, *ex officio*); D. A. Begg; Miss K. T. Kantor
Secretary, P. Trewin

BRITISH STANDARDS INSTITUTION (BSI)
389 Chiswick High Road, London w4 4AL
Tel 0181-996 9000; fax 0181-996 7344

The British Standards Institution is the recognized authority in the UK for the preparation and publication of national standards for industrial and consumer products. About 90 per cent of its standards work is now internationally linked. British Standards are issued for voluntary adoption, though in a number of cases compliance with a British Standard is required by legislation. Industrial and consumer products certified as complying with the relevant British Standard may carry the Institution's certification trade mark, known as the 'Kitemark'.
Chairman, V. E. Thomas, CBE
Chief Executive, K. Tozzi

BRITISH TOURIST AUTHORITY
Thames Tower, Black's Road, London w6 9EL
Tel 0181-846 9000; fax 0181-563 0302

Established under the Development of Tourism Act 1969, the British Tourist Authority is responsible for promoting tourism to Great Britain from overseas. It also has a general responsibility for the promotion and development of tourism and tourist facilities within Great Britain as a whole, and for advising the Secretary of State for Culture, Media and Sport on tourism matters.
Chairman (part-time), D. Quarmby
Chief Executive, J. Hamblin

BRITISH WATERWAYS
Willow Grange, Church Road, Watford, Herts wDi 3QA
Tel 01923-226422; fax 01923-201400

British Waterways conserves and manages over 2,000 miles of canals and rivers in England, Scotland and Wales. It is responsible to the Secretary of State for the Environment, Transport and the Regions. Its responsibilities include maintaining the waterways and structures on and around them; looking after wildlife and the waterway environment; and ensuring that canals and rivers are safe and enjoyable places to visit.
Chairman (part-time), Dr G. Greener
Members (part-time), D. H. R. Yorke; Sir Neil Cossons; Ms J. Elvey; Ms J. Lewis-Jones; Ms C. Dobson; P. King; P. Soulsby; C. Christie
Chief Executive, D. Fletcher
Director of Corporate Services, R. J. Duffy

BROADCASTING STANDARDS COMMISSION
7 The Sanctuary, London swiP 3JS
Tel 0171-233 0544; fax 0171-233 0397

The Commission was established in April 1997 under the Broadcasting Act 1996. It is an independent organization representing the interests of the consumer, and its remit covers all television and radio broadcasting. The Commission considers the portrayal of violence and sexual conduct and matters of taste and decency. It also provides redress for people who believe they have been unfairly treated or subjected to unwarranted infringement of privacy. The Commission conducts research into standards and fairness in broadcasting and produces codes of practice, and it considers and adjudicates on complaints. Members of the Commission are appointed by the Secretary of State for Culture, Media and Sport. The appointments are part-time.
Chair (£45,210), vacant
Deputy Chairmen (£34,000–£36,000), Ms J. Leighton; Mrs S. Warner
Commissioners (each £14,960), Ms D. Barr; D. Boulton; Dame Fiona Caldicott, DBE; U. Dholakia; S. Heppel, CB; Revd Rose Hudson Wilkin; J. Mitchell; Ms S. O'Sullivan; M. Unger; Ms S. Wyn Thomas
Director, S. Whittle

BUILDING SOCIETIES COMMISSION
12th Floor, 25 The North Colonnade, Canary Wharf,
London E14 5HS
Tel 0171-676 1000

The Building Societies Commission was established by
the Building Societies Act 1986. The Commission is
responsible for the supervision of building societies and
administers the system of prudential regulation. It also
advises the Treasury and other government departments
on matters relating to building societies.

The Government has proposed to Parliament that the
functions of the Commission should pass to the Financial
Services Authority (*see* page 635) on implementation of the
Financial Services and Markets Bill.

BUILDING SOCIETIES COMMISSION
Chairman, G. E. Fitchew
Deputy Chairman, Ms C. Sergeant
Commissioners, S. Mundy; J. M. Palmer; *F. G. Sunderland;
*Sir James Birrell; *N. Fox Bassett; *F. E. Worsley
* part-time

COMMISSION STAFF
Assistant Commissioners, W. Champion; E. Engstrom
Secretary, G. Johnson

THE BROADS AUTHORITY
Thomas Harvey House, 18 Colegate, Norwich NR3 1BQ
Tel 01603-610734; fax 01603-765710

The Broads Authority is a special statutory authority set
up under the Norfolk and Suffolk Broads Act 1988. The
functions of the Authority are to conserve and enhance the
natural beauty of the Broads; to provide integrated
management of the land and water space of the area; to
promote the enjoyment of the Broads by the public; and to
protect the interests of navigation. The Authority comprises
35 members, appointed by the local authorities in the area
covered, environmental conservation bodies, the Environment
Agency, and the Great Yarmouth Port Authority.
Chairman, The Viscountess Knollys
Chief Executive, Prof. M. A. Clark, OBE

THE CABINET OFFICE
70 Whitehall, London SW1A 2AS
Tel 0171-270 3000
*Horse Guards Road, London SW1P 3AL
Tel 0171-270 1234
Web: http://www.open.gov.uk/co/

The Cabinet Office comprises the Secretariat, who support
Ministers collectively in the conduct of Cabinet business;
and units responsible for modernizing government and
helping to improve the quality, coherence and responsive-
ness of public services. It is also responsible for Senior
Civil Service and public appointments, market testing and
efficiency in the Civil Service, and Civil Service recruitment. The Cabinet Office supports the Prime Minister in
his capacity as Minister for the Civil Service, with
responsibility for day-to-day supervision delegated to the
Minister for the Cabinet Office, who is also responsible for
the Central Office of Information (*see* page 288).

Prime Minister and Minister for the Civil Service,
The Rt. Hon. Tony Blair, MP
*Minister for the Cabinet Office and Chancellor of the Duchy of
Lancaster,* The Rt. Hon. Dr Jack Cunningham, MP

Principal Private Secretary (SCS), Dr J. Fuller
Private Secretary, Ms B. Feeny
Special Advisers, T. Walker; Ms A. Healy
Minister of State, The Lord Falconer of Thoroton, QC
Private Secretary, M. Langdale
Parliamentary Private Secretary, C. Leslie, MP
Minister of State, Ian McCartney, MP
Private Secretary, Ms N. Pitts
Secretary of the Cabinet and Head of the Home Civil Service, Sir
Richard Wilson, KCB
Private Secretary (SCS), S. Wood
Second Permanent Secretary, B. Bender, CB
Private Secretary, M. Sweeney
Parliamentary Clerk, S. Brown
Chief Scientific Adviser, Sir Robert May, FRS

PRIME MINISTER'S OFFICE
10 Downing Street, London SW1A 2AA
Tel 0171-270 3000; fax 0171-925 0918
Web: http://www.number-10.gov.uk
Principal Private Secretary, J. J. Heywood
Chief of Staff (£91,014), J. Powell
Private Secretaries, J. Sawers (*Foreign Affairs*); R. Read
(*Parliamentary Affairs*); D. North (*Home Affairs*); O.
Barder (*Economic Affairs*); P. Barton (*Assistant on Foreign
Affairs*)
Diary Secretary, Ms K. Garvey
Special Assistant for Presentation and Planning, Ms A. Hunter
Assistant to Mrs Blair, Ms F. Millar
Political Secretary, Ms S. Morgan
Head of Policy Unit, D. Miliband
Policy Unit, G. Mulgan; R. Liddle; D. Scott; Ms E. Lloyd;
P. Hyman; J. Purnell; P. McFadden; R. Hill; G. Norris;
Ms S. White; A. Adonis
Parliamentary Private Secretary, B. Grocott, MP
Chief Press Secretary (£91,014), A. Campbell
Deputy Press Secretary, G. Smith
Special Advisers, Press Office, Ms H. Coffman; L. Price
Press Officers, P. Willinson; Ms L. McNeil; D. Peel; J.
Braithwaite; Mrs M. Cleaver
Strategic Communications Unit, A. Evans; P. Bassett; D.
Bradshaw; J. Humphreys; Ms S. Kenny; A. Silverman
*Secretary for Appointments, and Ecclesiastical Secretary to the
Lord Chancellor,* J. Holroyd, CB, CVO
Parliamentary Clerk, Mrs H. Murray

SECRETARIAT

ECONOMIC AND DOMESTIC SECRETARIAT
Head (SCS), W. Rickett
Deputy Heads (SCS), J. Gallagher; P. Britton
Adviser on Parliamentary Procedures (SCS), A. Kennon

DEFENCE AND OVERSEAS AFFAIRS SECRETARIAT
*Head of Secretariat and Chairman of Joint Intelligence Committee
(SCS),* The Hon. M. Pakenham, CMG
Deputy Head (SCS), D. Fisher
Head of Division (SCS), N. Sanderson
Chief of the Assessments Staff (SCS), R. Gozney

INTELLIGENCE CO-ORDINATION GROUP
Head (SCS), J. Alpass
Head of Security Division (SCS), Ms E. Chivers

EUROPEAN SECRETARIAT
Head (SCS), D. Bostock
Deputy Head (SCS), M. Donnelly
Head of Division (SCS), M. Kirk

CONSTITUTION SECRETARIAT
Head (SCS), Sir Quentin Thomas, CB
Head of Devolution Team (SCS), D. Brew
Head of Other Constitutional Reform Team (SCS), Ms J. Simpson
Head of Legal Advisers, Ms R. Jefferys

*CENTRAL SECRETARIAT
Head (SCS), D. A. Wilkinson, CB
Deputy Head (SCS), Ms S. Phippard

CEREMONIAL BRANCH
Ashley House, 2 Monck Street, London SWIP 2BQ
Tel 0171-270 1234
Honours Nomination Unit: Tel 0171-276 2775
Ceremonial Officer (SCS), A. J. Merifield, CB

PUBLIC SERVICE DELIVERY

*MODERNIZING PUBLIC SERVICES GROUP
Tel 0171-270 1838
Director (SCS), J. Rees
Deputy Directors (SCS), Mrs G. Craig; S. O'Leary, OBE; B. Avery

CENTRAL IT UNIT
53 Parliament Street, London SWIA 2NG
Tel 0171-238 2000
Director (SCS), D. Cooke
Deputy Directors (SCS), Ms M. Mayer; J. Crump; M. Gladwyn; Ms A. Steward; I. White; P. Waller

*REGULATORY IMPACT UNIT
Director (SCS), M. Stanley
Deputy Directors (SCS), M. Herron; P. Hayes; Ms A. French
Legal Adviser, P. Bovey

*MODERNIZING GOVERNMENT
Director, A. Wells
Head of Secretariat (SCS), J. Cowper

CIVIL SERVICE MANAGEMENT

*CIVIL SERVICE CORPORATE MANAGEMENT COMMAND
Senior Director (SCS), B. M. Fox, CB
Directors (SCS), J. Barker; Ms S. Hinkley, CBE
Deputy Directors (SCS), Ms A. Schofield; Ms J. Lemprière; C. J. Parry; Ms E. Goodison; D. G. Pain; S. Mitha

CENTRE FOR MANAGEMENT AND POLICY STUDIES
Director-General, Prof. R. Amman
Directors (SCS), R. Green; B. Behrens

GOVERNMENT INFORMATION AND COMMUNICATION
SERVICES
Head of Government Information and Communication Services (SCS), M. Granatt
Director, Development Centre (SCS), C. Skinner
Deputy Director, Ms S. Jenkins

*OFFICE OF THE COMMISSIONER FOR PUBLIC
APPOINTMENTS (OCPA)
Tel 0171-270 6472

The role of the Commissioner for Public Appointments (CPA) is to monitor, regulate and approve departmental procedures for ministerial appointments to advisory and executive non-departmental public bodies, public corporations, nationalized industries, regulators and NHS bodies. The Commissioner is appointed by Order-in-Council.
Commissioner, Dame Rennie Fritchie
Head of Office (SCS), J. Barron

*OFFICE OF THE CIVIL SERVICE COMMISSIONERS
(OCSC)
Tel 0171-270 5081; fax 0171-270 5967

First Commissioner, Sir Michael Bett, CBE
Commissioners (part-time), D. J. Burr; Ms S. Forbes; H. J. F. McLean, CBE; Sir Leonard Peach; J. Shrigley; K. Singh; C. Stevens, CB; Dame Rennie Fritchie
Secretary to the Commissioners and Head of the Office (SCS), J. Barron

CROSS-CUTTING ISSUES

*SOCIAL EXCLUSION UNIT
Tel 0171-270 5211
Director of Unit (SCS), Ms M. Wallace, OBE
Deputy Directors, J. Bright; Ms Z. Peatfield; M. Wheatley

*CENTRAL DRUGS CO-ORDINATION UNIT
Tel 0171-270 5399
UK Anti-Drugs Co-ordinator (£106,057), K. Hellawell
Deputy Co-ordinator, M. Trace
Head of Unit, J. Critchley

WOMEN'S UNIT
10 Great George Street, London SWIP 3AE
Tel 0171-273 8808
Head of Unit (SCS), Ms F. Reynolds, CBE
Deputy Director, K. Palmer

*PERFORMANCE AND INNOVATION UNIT
Tel 0171-270 1512
Director (SCS), S. Chakrabarti
Deputy Director (SCS), J. Rentoul
Chief Economist, S. Aldridge
Directors, J. Norton; D. Instone; A. Lean; G. Wilkinson; Ms J. Hutcheon

INFORMATION, ESTABLISHMENT AND ORGANIZATION

Queen Anne's Chambers, 28 Broadway, London SWIH 9JS
Director of Information (SCS), B. Sutlieff
Principal Establishment and Finance Officer (SCS), Mrs N. A. Oppenheimer
Deputy Directors (SCS), Miss E. Chennells; D. Brennan; R. Harris; K. Tolladay
Ministers' Adviser on Agencies, C. Brendish, CBE

HER MAJESTY'S STATIONERY OFFICE
St Clements House, 2–16 Colegate, Norwich NR3 1BQ
Tel 01603-621000
Controller (SCS), Mrs C. Tullo

EXECUTIVE AGENCIES

THE BUYING AGENCY
Royal Liver Building, Pier Head, Liverpool L3 1PE
Tel 0151-227 4262; fax 0151-227 3315

The Agency provides a professional purchasing service to government departments and other public bodies. From April 2000 it will be part of the new Office of Government Commerce reporting to the Chief Secretary to the Treasury.
Chief Executive (SCS), S. P. Sage

CCTA (CENTRAL COMPUTER AND TELECOMMUNICATIONS AGENCY)
Rosebery Court, St Andrew's Business Park, Norwich NR7 0HS
Tel 01603-704567; fax 01603-704817
Steel House, 11 Tothill Street, London SWIH 9NF
Tel 0171-273 6565; fax 0171-273 6555

---

* Unless otherwise stated, this is the address and telephone number of directorates of the Board

CCTA's objective is to develop, maintain and make available expertise about information technology which public sector organizations can draw on in order to operate more effectively and efficiently. From April 2000 it will be part of the new Office of Government Commerce reporting to the Chief Secretary to the Treasury.
Chief Executive, R. Assirati

CIVIL SERVICE COLLEGE
Sunningdale Park, Ascot, Berks SL5 0QE
Tel 01344-634000; fax 01344-634781
11 Belgrave Road, London SW1V 1RB
Tel 0171-834 6644; fax 01344-634451
199 Cathedral Street, Glasgow G4 0QU
Tel 0141-553 6021; fax 0141-553 6171
Suite 19, 1 St Colme Street, Edinburgh EH3 6AA
Tel 0131-220 8267; fax 0131-220 8367

The College provides training in management and professional skills for the public and private sectors.
Director (G3), E. Wooldridge
Business Executives (G5/G6), M. N. Barnes; R. Behrens; G. W. Llewellyn; Ms L. Oliver (*Non-Executive Director*); P. Tebby; M. Timmis; Dr A. Wyatt

GOVERNMENT CAR AND DESPATCH AGENCY
46 Ponton Road, London SW8 5AX
Tel 0171-217 3839; fax 0171-217 3840

The Agency provides secure transport and document transfers between government departments.
Chief Executive, N. Matheson

PROPERTY ADVISERS TO THE CIVIL ESTATE
6th Floor, Trevelyan House, Great Peter Street, London SW1P 2BY
Tel 0171-271 2626; fax 0171-271 2622

The Agency promotes co-operation between government departments to enable them to obtain best value for money in the management of their property assets. It also provides them with property guidance and other property-related services. From April 2000 it will be part of the new Office of Government Commerce reporting to the Chief Secretary to the Treasury.
Chief Executive, J. C. Locke, FRICS

CENTRAL ADJUDICATION SERVICES
Quarry House, Quarry Hill, Leeds LS2 7UB
Tel 0113-232 4000; fax 0113-232 4841
New Court, 48 Carey Street, London WC2A 2LS
Tel 0171-412 1504; fax 0171-412 1220

The Chief Adjudication Officer is appointed by the Secretary of State for Social Security to give advice to adjudication officers on making decisions for social security claims and to keep under review the standards of adjudication of the Benefits Agency and the Employment Service. He reports annually to the Secretary of State.

From 28 November 1999 under the Social Security Act 1998 all responsibility for standards of decision making will pass to the chief executives of the Benefits Agency and the Employment Service.
Chief Adjudication Officer, D. Petch (until 28 November 1999)

CENTRAL OFFICE OF INFORMATION
Hercules Road, London SE1 7DU
Tel 0171-928 2345; fax 0171-928 5037

The Central Office of Information (COI) is a government department which offers consultancy, procurement and project management services to central government for publicity. Though the majority of the COI's work is for government departments in the UK, it also procures a range of publicity materials for overseas consumption. Administrative responsibility for the COI rests with the Minister for the Cabinet Office.
Chief Executive (G3), Ms C. Fisher
    Senior Personal Secretary, Ms I. MacMull

MANAGEMENT BOARD
Members, K. Williamson; P. Buchanan; I. Hamilton; R. Haslam; Ms S. Whetton; M. Reid
Secretary, Ms I. MacMull

DIRECTORS
Director, Client Services (G6), I. Hamilton
Director, Marketing Communications (G6), P. Buchanan
Director, Films, Radio and Events (G6), S. Whetton
Director, Publications (G6), M. Reid
Director, Central Services (G5), K. Williamson
Director, Regional Network (G6), R. Haslam

NETWORK OFFICES
EASTERN, 2nd Floor, Block A1, Westbrook Centre, Milton Road, Cambridge CB4 1YG. *Network Director (G7)*, P. Powell
MIDLANDS EAST, 1st Floor, Severns House, 20 Middle Pavement, Nottingham NG1 7DW. *Network Director (G7)*, P. Smith
MIDLANDS WEST, Five Ways House, Islington Row, Middleway, Edgbaston, Birmingham B15 1SH. *Network Director (G6)*, B. Garner
NORTH-EAST, Wellbar House, Gallowgate, Newcastle upon Tyne NE1 4TB. *Network Director (G7)*, Ms L. Taylor
NORTH-WEST, Sunley Tower, Piccadilly Plaza, Manchester M1 4BD. *Network Director (G7)*, Mrs E. Jones
SOUTH-EAST, Hercules Road, London SE1 7DU. *Network Director (G6)*, Ms V. Burdon
SOUTH-WEST, The Pithay, Bristol BS1 2NF. *Network Director (G7)*, P. Whitbread
YORKSHIRE AND HUMBERSIDE, City House, New Station Street, Leeds LS1 4JG. *Network Director (G7)*, Ms W. Miller

---

CERTIFICATION OFFICE FOR TRADE UNIONS AND EMPLOYERS' ASSOCIATIONS
180 Borough High Street, London SE1 1LW
Tel 0171-210 3734/5; fax 0171-210 3612

The Certification Office is an independent statutory authority. The Certification Officer is appointed by the Secretary of State for Trade and Industry and is responsible for receiving and scrutinizing annual returns from trade unions and employers' associations; for investigating allegations of financial irregularities in the affairs of a trade union or employers' association; for dealing with complaints concerning trade union elections; for ensuring observance of statutory requirements governing political funds and trade union mergers; and for certifying the independence of trade unions.
Certification Officer, E. G. Whybrew
Assistant Certification Officer, G. S. Osborne

SCOTLAND
58 Frederick Street, Edinburgh EH2 1LN
Tel 0131-226 3224; fax 0131-200 1300
Assistant Certification Officer for Scotland, J. L. J. Craig

CHARITY COMMISSION

Harmsworth House, 13–15 Bouverie Street, London EC4Y 8DP
Tel 0870-333 0123; fax 0171-674 2310
2nd Floor, 20 King's Parade, Queen's Dock, Liverpool L3 4DQ
Tel 0151-703 1500; fax 0151-703 1557
Woodfield House, Tangier, Taunton, Somerset TA1 4BL
Tel 01823-345000; fax 01823-345008

The Charity Commission is established under the Charities Act 1993 with the general function of promoting the effective use of charitable resources in England and Wales. The Commission gives information and advice to charity trustees to make the administration of their charity more effective; investigates misconduct and the abuse of charitable assets, and takes or recommends remedial action; and maintains a public register of charities. The Commission does not have at its disposal any funds with which to make grants to organizations or individuals.

At the end of 1998 there were 186,248 registered charities.

Chief Commissioner (G3), J. Stoker
Legal Commissioner (G3), M. Carpenter
Commissioners (part-time) (G4), J. Bonds; Ms J. Warburton; Ms J. Unwin
Heads of Legal Sections (G5), J. A. Dutton; G. S. Goodchild; K. M. Dibble; S. Slack
Executive Director (G4), Ms L. Berry
Head of Policy Division (G5), R. Carter
Establishment Officer (G5), Ms C. Stewart
Information Systems Controller (G5), Ms G. Cruickshank

The offices responsible for charities in Scotland and Northern Ireland are:

SCOTLAND – Scottish Charities Office, Crown Office, 25 Chambers Street, Edinburgh EH1 1LA. Tel: 0131-226 2626
NORTHERN IRELAND – Department of Health and Social Services, Charities Branch, Annexe 3, Castle Buildings, Stormont Estate, Belfast BT4 3RA. Tel: 01232-522780

CHIEF ADJUDICATION OFFICER
— *see* Central Adjudication Services

CHILD SUPPORT AGENCY
— *see* page 342

CHURCH COMMISSIONERS
1 Millbank, London SW1P 3JZ
Tel 0171-222 7010; fax 0171-233 0171

The Church Commissioners were established in 1948 by the amalgamation of Queen Anne's Bounty (established 1704) and the Ecclesiastical Commissioners (established 1836). They are responsible for the management of most of the Church of England's assets, the income from which is predominantly used to pay, house and pension the clergy. The Commissioners own 51,000 acres of agricultural land, a number of residential estates in central London, and commercial property in Great Britain. They also carry out administrative duties in connection with pastoral reorganization and redundant churches.

The Commissioners are: the Archbishops of Canterbury and of York; four bishops, three clergy and four lay persons elected by the respective houses of the General Synod;

two deans or provosts elected by all the deans and provosts; three persons nominated by The Queen; three persons nominated by the Archbishops of Canterbury and York; three persons nominated by the Archbishops after consultation with others including the lord mayors of London and York and the vice-chancellors of the universities of Oxford and Cambridge; the First Lord of the Treasury; the Lord President of the Council; the Home Secretary; the Lord Chancellor; the Secretary of State for Culture, Media and Sport; and the Speaker of the House of Commons.

INCOME AND EXPENDITURE
for year ended 31 December 1998

	£ million
Total income	139.9
Net income	128.6
Investments	76.2
Property	45.9
Interest from loans, etc.	17.8
	158.9
Total expenditure	
Parochial ministry support	20.0
Bishop and cathedral clergy stipends	6.3
Bishops' housing	3.0
Grants to cathedrals	2.4
Financial provision for resigning clergy	1.8
Clergy pensions	108.2
Church buildings	1.1
Bishops' working cost	8.8
Commissioners' administration and administration of central church functions	5.3
Administration costs of other church bodies	2.0
Deficit for year	19.0

CHURCH ESTATES COMMISSIONERS
First, J. Sclater, CVO
Second, S. Bell, MP
Third, The Viscountess Brentford

OFFICERS
Secretary, H. H. Hughes
Deputy Secretary (Finance and Investment), C. W. Daws
Official Solicitor, N. I. Johnson
Assistant Secretaries:
 The Accountant, G. C. Baines
 Management Accountant, B. J. Hardy
 Chief Surveyor, A. C. Brown
 Computer Manager, J. W. Ferguson
 Bishoprics Secretary, E. G. Peacock
 Investments Manager, A. S. Hardy
 Pastoral, Houses and Redundant Churches, M. D. Elengorn
 Senior Architect, J. A. Taylor

CIVIL AVIATION AUTHORITY
CAA House, 45–59 Kingsway, London WC2B 6TE
Tel 0171-379 7311; fax: 0171-240 1153

The CAA is responsible for the economic regulation of UK airlines and for the safety regulation of UK civil aviation by the certification of airlines and aircraft and by licensing aerodromes, flight crew and aircraft engineers. Through its subsidiary company, National Air Traffic Services Ltd (NATS), it is also responsible for the provision of air traffic control and telecommunications services. The Government announced in July 1999 that it planned to separate safety regulation from service provision and sell 51 per cent of NATS to the private sector.

The CAA advises the Government on aviation issues,

represents consumer interests, conducts economic and scientific research, produces statistical data, and provides specialist services and other training and consultancy services to clients world-wide.

Chairman, Sir Malcolm Field
Secretary, R. J. Britton

THE COAL AUTHORITY
200 Lichfield Lane, Mansfield, Notts NG18 4RG
Tel 01623-427162; fax: 01623-622072

The Coal Authority was established under the Coal Industry Act 1994 to manage certain functions previously undertaken by British Coal, including ownership of unworked coal. It is responsible for licensing coal mining operations and for providing information on coal reserves and past and future coal mining. It settles subsidence claims not falling on coal mining operators. It deals with the management and disposal of property, and with surface hazards such as abandoned coal mine shafts.

Chairman, J. Harris
Chief Executive, K. J. Fergusson

COMMISSION FOR ARCHITECTURE AND THE BUILT ENVIRONMENT
7 St James's Square, London SW1Y 4JU
Tel 0171-839 6537; fax 0171-839 8475

The Commission for Architecture and the Built Environment (CABE) replaced the Royal Fine Art Commission (RFAC) in August 1999. It has taken over the RFAC's design review function, and is also responsible for promoting the importance of high quality architecture and urban design and encouraging the understanding of architecture through educational initiatives and grant programmes.

Chairman, S. A. Lipton
Secretary, F. Golding

COMMISSION FOR INTEGRATED TRANSPORT
Great Minster House, 76 Marsham Street, London SW1P 4DR
Tel 0171-890 4918/4453/4813; fax 0171-676 2167

The Commission for Integrated Transport was proposed in the 1998 Transport White Paper and was set up in June 1999. Its role is to provide independent expert advice to the Government in order to achieve a transport system that supports sustainable development. Members of the Commission are appointed by the Secretary of State for the Environment, Transport and the Regions.

Chairman (£25,000), Prof. D. Begg
Vice-Chairman (£17,500), Sir Trevor Chinn
Members (£5,000 each), Prof. B. Bradshaw; L. Christensen, CBE; N. Gavron; S. Joseph; D. Leeder; Ms L. Matson; W. Morris; J. O'Brien; Ms V. Palmer; M. Parker; N. Reilly
Ex-Officio Members, Sir Malcolm Field (*Chairman, Civil Aviation Authority*); L. Haynes (*Chief Executive, Highways Agency*); Sir Alastair Morton (*Chairman, British Railways Board and Head, Shadow Strategic Rail Authority*); Ms J. Wilmot (*Chair, Disabled Persons Transport Advisory Committee*)
Secretary (G7), P. Carey

COMMONWEALTH DEVELOPMENT CORPORATION
1 Bessborough Gardens, London SW1V 2JQ
Tel 0171-828 4488; fax 0171-828 6505

The Commonwealth Development Corporation (CDC) assists overseas countries in the development of their economies. Its sponsoring department is the Department for International Development. Its main activity is providing long-term finance, as loans and risk capital, for financially viable and developmentally sound business enterprises. CDC's area of operations includes UK overseas territories and, with ministerial approval, Commonwealth or other developing countries. At present, CDC is authorized to operate in more than 60 countries and territories. Its investments at the end of 1998 were US$2.4 billion.

Legislation was introduced in Parliament in November 1998 under which the CDC would become a public limited company and operate as a public/private partnership.

Chairman (*part-time*), The Earl Cairns, CBE
Deputy Chair (*part-time*), Ms J. Almond
Chief Executive, Dr R. Reynolds

COMMONWEALTH SECRETARIAT
— *see* Index

COMMONWEALTH WAR GRAVES COMMISSION
2 Marlow Road, Maidenhead, Berks SL6 7DX
Tel 01628-634221; fax 01628-771208

The Commonwealth War Graves Commission (formerly Imperial War Graves Commission) was founded by royal charter in 1917. It is responsible for the commemoration of 1,695,098 members of the forces of the Commonwealth who fell in the two world wars. More than one million graves are maintained in 23,216 burial grounds throughout the world. Over three-quarters of a million men and women who have no known grave or who were cremated are commemorated by name on memorials built by the Commission.

The funds of the Commission are derived from the six participating governments, i.e. the UK, Canada, Australia, India, New Zealand and South Africa.

President, HRH The Duke of Kent, KG, GCMG, GCVO, ADC
Chairman, The Secretary of State for Defence in the UK
Vice-Chairman, Adm. Sir John Kerr, GCB
Members, The High Commissioners in London for Canada, New Zealand, India, South Africa and Australia; The Viscount Ridley, KG, GCVO, TD; Prof. R. J. O'Neill, AO; Mrs L. Golding, MP; J. Wilkinson, MP; Sir John Gray, KBE, CMG; P. D. Orchard-Lisle, CBE, TD; Air Chief Marshal Sir Michael Stear, KCB, CBE; Gen. Sir John Wilsey, GCB, CBE
Director-General and Secretary to the Commission, D. Kennedy, CMG
Deputy Director-General, R. J. Dalley
Legal Adviser and Solicitor, G. C. Reddie
Directors, D. R. Parker (*Personnel*); A. Coombe (*Works*); R. D. Wilson (*Finance*); D. C. Parker (*Horticulture*); L. J. Hanna (*Information and Secretariat*)

IMPERIAL WAR GRAVES ENDOWMENT FUND
Trustees, The Lord Remnant, CVO, FCA (*Chairman*); A. C. Barker; Adm. Sir John Kerr, GCB
Secretary to the Trustees, R. D. Wilson

COMPETITION COMMISSION
New Court, 48 Carey Street, London wc2A 2JT
Tel 0171-271 0100; fax 0171-271 0367

The Commission was established in 1948 as the Monopolies and Restrictive Practices Commission (later the Monopolies and Mergers Commission); it became the Competition Commission in April 1999 under the Competition Act 1998. Its role is to investigate and report on matters which are referred to it by the Secretary of State for Trade and Industry or the Director-General of Fair Trading or, in the case of regulated utilities, by the appropriate regulator. It has no power to initiate its own investigations.

The Appeal Tribunals of the Competition Commission will hear appeals against decisions by the Director-General of Fair Trading and the utility regulators in respect of the prohibitions on anti-competitive agreements and abuse of a dominant position to be introduced in March 2000 under the Competition Act 1998.

The Commission has a full-time chairman, two part-time deputy chairmen and about 35 reporting panel members to carry out investigations. All are appointed by the Secretary of State for Trade and Industry.
Chairman (£123,600), D. Morris, Ph.D.
Deputy Chairmen (£54,106–£72,141), P. G. Corbett, CBE; Ms D. Kingsmill
President-designate, Appeal Tribunals, His Hon. Judge Bellamy, QC
Members (£15,628 each), H. Aldous; Prof. J. Beatson, QC; R. Bertram; Mrs S. Brown; Prof. M. Cave; A. T. Clothier; R. H. F. Croft, CB; C. Darke; N. H. Finney, OBE; Prof. P. Geroski; Prof. C. Graham; D. B. Hammond; Ms J. C. Hanratty; C. Henderson, CB; D. J. Jenkins, MBE; R. Lyons; P. MacKay, CB; Dr Elizabeth Monck; Ms K. M. H. Mortimer; R. J. Munson; Prof. D. M. G. Newbery, FBA; Dr Gill Owen; M. R. Prosser; A. Pryor, CB; R. Rawlinson; Prof. Judith Rees; T. S. Richmond, MBE; J. Rickford; Dame Helena Shovelton, DBE; G. H. Stacy, CBE; D. Start; Prof. A. Steele
Secretary, Miss P. Boys

COUNTRYSIDE AGENCY
John Dower House, Crescent Place, Cheltenham, Glos GL50 3RA
Tel 01242-521381; fax 01242-584270

The Countryside Agency was set up in April 1999 by the merger of the Countryside Commission with parts of the Rural Development Commission. It is an independent agency which promotes the conservation and enhancement of the countryside in England and undertakes activities aimed at stimulating job creation and the provision of essential services in the countryside. The Agency is funded by an annual grant from the Department of the Environment, Transport and the Regions, and board members are appointed by the Secretary of State.
Chairman, E. Cameron
Deputy Chair, Ms P. Warhurst
Members, Ms K. Ashbrook; Ms J. Bradbury; the Rt. Revd Bishop of Blackburn; M. Doughty; Dr Victoria Edwards, FRICS; Prof. P. Lowe; Ms C. Mack; M. Middleton, CBE, FCA; Ms F. Rowe; D. Woodhall, CBE
Chief Executive, R. G. Wakeford
Directors, Miss M. A. Clark, OBE; R. Clarke; D. Coleman

COUNTRYSIDE COUNCIL FOR WALES/CYNGOR CEFN GWLAD CYMRU
Plas Penrhos, Ffordd Penrhos, Bangor LL57 2LQ
Tel 01248-385500; fax 01248-385505

The Countryside Council for Wales is the Government's statutory adviser on sustaining natural beauty, wildlife and the opportunity for outdoor enjoyment in Wales and its inshore waters. It is funded by the National Assembly for Wales and accountable to the First Secretary, who appoints its members.
Chairman, E. M. W. Griffith, CBE
Chief Executive, P. E. Loveluck, CBE
Senior Director and Chief Scientist, Dr M. E. Smith
Director, Countryside Policy, Dr J. Taylor
Director, Conservation, Dr D. Parker

COVENT GARDEN MARKET AUTHORITY
Covent House, New Covent Garden Market, London SW8 5NX
Tel 0171-720 2211; fax 0171-622 5307

The Covent Garden Market Authority is constituted under the Covent Garden Market Acts 1961 to 1977, the members being appointed by the Minister of Agriculture, Fisheries and Food. The Authority owns and operates the 56-acre New Covent Garden Markets (fruit, vegetables, flowers) which have been trading since 1974.
Chairman (part-time), L. Mills, CBE
General Manager, Dr P. M. Liggins
Secretary, C. Farey

CRIMINAL CASES REVIEW COMMISSION
Alpha Tower, Suffolk Street Queensway, Birmingham B1 1TT
Tel 0121-633 1800; fax 0121-633 1823/1804

The Criminal Cases Review Commission is an independent body set up under the Criminal Appeal Act 1995. It is a non-departmental public body reporting to Parliament via the Home Secretary. It is responsible for investigating suspected miscarriages of justice in England, Wales and Northern Ireland, and deciding whether or not to refer cases back to an appeal court. Membership of the Commission is by royal appointment; the senior executive staff are appointed by the Commission.
Chairman, Sir Frederick Crawford, FREng.
Members, B. Capon; L. Elks; A. Foster; Ms J. Gort; Ms F. King; J. Knox; D. Kyle; J. Leckey; Prof. L. Leigh; J. MacKeith; K. Singh; B. Skitt; E. Weiss
Chief Executive, Ms G. Stacey
Director of Finance and Personnel, D. Robson
Legal Advisers, J. Wagstaff; M. Aspinall
Police Adviser, R. Barrington

For Scotland, *see* Scottish Criminal Cases Review Commission

CRIMINAL INJURIES COMPENSATION AUTHORITY AND BOARD
Morley House, Holborn Viaduct, London EC1A 2JQ
Tel 0171-842 6800; fax 0171-436 0804
Tay House, 300 Bath Street, Glasgow G2 4JR
Tel 0141-331 2726; fax 0141-331 2287

All applications for compensation for personal injury arising from crimes of violence in England, Scotland and

Wales are dealt with at the above locations. (Separate arrangements apply in Northern Ireland.) Applications received up to 31 March 1996 are assessed on the basis of common law damages under the 1990 compensation scheme by the Criminal Injuries Compensation Board (CICB), which was founded in 1964 under the prerogative powers of the Crown. The CICB also hears appeals. Applications received on or after 1 April 1996 are assessed under a tariff-based scheme, made under the Criminal Injuries Compensation Act 1995, by the Criminal Injuries Compensation Authority (CICA); there is a separate avenue of appeal to the Criminal Injuries Compensation Appeals Panel (CICAP). In 1998–9 total compensation paid was £194.5 million.

Chairman of the Criminal Injuries Compensation Board (part-time) (£36,951), The Lord Carlisle of Bucklow, PC, QC
Director of the Board and Chief Executive of the Criminal Injuries Compensation Authority, H. Webber
Head of Legal Services, Mrs A. M. Johnstone
Operations Manager, E. McKeown
Chairman of the Criminal Injuries Compensation Appeals Panel, M. Lewer, QC
Secretary to the Panel, Miss V. Jenson

CROFTERS COMMISSION
4–6 Castle Wynd, Inverness IV2 3EQ
Tel 01463-663450; fax 01463-711820

The Crofters Commission was established in 1955 under the Crofters (Scotland) Act. It advises the Scottish ministers on all matters relating to crofting. It seeks to develop and promote thriving crofting communities and to simplify relevant legislation. It administers the Crofting Counties Agricultural Grants Scheme, Livestock Improvement Schemes and the Croft Entrant Scheme. It also provides a free enquiry service.
Chairman, I. MacAskill
Secretary (G6), M. Grantham

CROWN ESTATE
16 Carlton House Terrace, London SW1Y 5AH
Tel 0171-210 4377; fax 0171-930 8187

The Crown Estate includes substantial blocks of urban property, primarily in London, almost 120,000 hectares of agricultural land and extensive marine holdings throughout the United Kingdom. Its origins go back to the reign of King Edward the Confessor and, until the accession of King George III, the Sovereign received its rents and profits. However, since 1760 the annual surplus, after deducting management expenses, has been surrendered by the Sovereign to Parliament to help meet the cost of civil government. In return, the Sovereign receives the Civil List and the Government meets other official expenditure incurred in support of the Sovereign.

In the year ended 31 March 1999, the gross revenue from the Crown Estate totalled £173.6 million and £125.8 million was paid to the Exchequer as surplus revenue.
First Commissioner and Chairman (part-time), Sir Denys Henderson
Second Commissioner and Chief Executive, Sir Christopher Howes, KCVO, CB
Commissioners (part-time), Mrs H. M. R. Chapman, CBE, FRICS; The Lord De Ramsey; I. D. Grant, CBE; D. E. G. Griffiths, CBE; J. H. M. Norris, CBE; R. R. Spinney, FRICS
Director of Finance and Administration, R. Bright

Director of Urban Estates, N. Borrett
Urban Estates Managers, D. A. Bickmore; M. W. Dillon; R. Wyatt
Development and Investment Manager, L. Colgan
Agricultural Estates Manager, C. Bourchier
Marine Estates Manager, F. G. Parrish
Finance Manager, J. G. Lelliott
Information Systems Manager, D. Kingston-Smith
Internal Audit Manager, J. E. Ford
Corporate Policy and Personnel Manager, M. J. Gravestock
Communications Manager, Miss I. Belcher

SCOTLAND
10 Charlotte Square, Edinburgh EH2 4BR
Tel 0131-226 7241; fax 0131-220 1366
Head of Scottish Estates, M. Cunliffe

WINDSOR ESTATE
The Great Park, Windsor, Berks SL4 2HT
Tel 01753-860222; fax 01753-859617
Deputy Ranger, P. Everrett

CROWN PROSECUTION SERVICE
— see pages 362–3

DEPARTMENT FOR CULTURE, MEDIA AND SPORT
2–4 Cockspur Street, London SW1Y 5DH
Tel 0171-211 6200; fax 0171-211 6032
E-mail: enquiries@culture.gov.uk
Web: http://www.culture.gov.uk

The Department for Culture, Media and Sport was established in July 1997 and is responsible for government policy relating to the arts, broadcasting, the press, museums and galleries, libraries, sport and recreation, historic buildings and ancient monuments, tourism, and the music industry. It is responsible for policy on the National Lottery and the Millennium, and sponsors the Millennium Commission.

Secretary of State for Culture, Media and Sport, The Rt. Hon. Chris Smith, MP
  Private Secretary, F. Muir
  Special Advisers, J. Newbigin; A. Burnham; B. Jefferson; R. Cotton; D. McGonigal
  Parliamentary Private Secretary, Ms F. Mactaggart, MP
Parliamentary Under-Secretaries, Alan Howarth, MP (*Arts*); Kate Hoey, MP (*Sport*); Janet Anderson, MP (*Tourism, Film and Broadcasting*)
  Private Secretaries, D. Fitzgerald; N. Hughes; D. Tambling
Parliamentary Clerk, T. English
Permanent Secretary (SCS), R. Young
  Private Secretary, K. Gibbins

MUSEUMS, GALLERIES, LIBRARIES AND HERITAGE GROUP
Head of Group (SCS), Ms A. Stewart
Head, Libraries and Information Division (SCS), N. MacKay
Head, Buildings, Monuments and Sites (SCS), N. Pittman
Head, Museums, Galleries and Cultural Property (SCS), H. Corner
Director, Government Art Collection (SCS), Ms P. Johnson

STRATEGY AND COMMUNICATION GROUP
Head of Group (SCS), P. Bolt
Head of News, I. Hepplewhite
Head of Information, G. Newsom
Head of Strategy, Ms Z. McNeill-Ritchie

CORPORATE SERVICES GROUP
Head of Group (SCS), A. Ramsay
Head, Finance Division (SCS), A. McLellan
Head, National Lottery Division (SCS), vacant
Head, Personnel and Central Services Division (SCS), Ms R. Siemaszko
Head, Central Appointments Unit, Ms R. Griggs
Head, Internal Audit, D. Rix

CREATIVE INDUSTRIES, MEDIA AND BROADCASTING GROUP
Head of Group (SCS), N. J. Kroll
Head, Broadcasting Division (SCS), Ms M. Leech
Head, Media Division (SCS), Ms J. Evans
Head, Creative Industries, A. Ferries

REGIONS, TOURISM, MILLENNIUM AND INTERNATIONAL GROUP
Head of Group, B. Leonard
Head, Tourism Division (SCS), S. Broadley
Head, Millennium Unit, Miss C. Pillman
Head, Local, Regional and International Division (SCS), P. Douglas

EDUCATION, TRAINING, ARTS AND SPORT
Head of Group, Ms P. Drew
Head, Arts Division (SCS), W. Nye
Head, Sports Division (SCS), vacant
Head, Education (SCS), A. Dyer

EXECUTIVE AGENCY

ROYAL PARKS AGENCY
The Old Police House, Hyde Park, London W2 2UH
Tel 0171-298 2000; fax 0171-298 2005

The Agency is responsible for maintaining and developing the royal parks.
Chief Executive (G5), D. Welch, CBE

BOARD OF CUSTOMS AND EXCISE
*New King's Beam House, 22 Upper Ground, London SE1 9PJ
Tel 0171-620 1313
Web: http://www.open.gov.uk/customs/c&ehome.htm

Commissioners of Customs were first appointed in 1671 and housed by the King in London. The Excise Department was formerly under the Inland Revenue Department and was amalgamated with the Customs Department in 1909.

HM Customs and Excise is responsible for collecting and administering customs and excise duties and VAT, and advises the Chancellor of the Exchequer on any matters connected with them. The Department is also responsible for preventing and detecting the evasion of revenue laws and for enforcing a range of prohibitions and restrictions on the importation of certain classes of goods. In addition, the Department undertakes certain agency work on behalf of other departments, including the compilation of UK overseas trade statistics from customs import and export documents.

THE BOARD
Chairman (G1), Dame Valerie Strachan, DCB
  Private Secretaries, Ms J. Mellon; P. Gerrard
Deputy Chairman, T. Walker

---

* Unless otherwise stated, this is the address and telephone number of directorates of the Board

Commissioners (G3), P. R. H. Allen; A. R. Rawsthorne; D. J. Howard; A. Paynter; M. R. Brown; R. N. McAfee; M. W. Norgrove; T. Byrne
Head of Board's Secretariat, J. Bone
Solicitor, D. Pickup

PUBLIC RELATIONS OFFICE
Tel 0171-865 5581

Head of Public Relations, P. Rose

CORPORATE SERVICES DIRECTORATE
Director, A. Paynter

INFORMATION SYSTEMS DIRECTORATE
Alexander House, 21 Victoria Avenue, Southend-on-Sea SS99 1AA
Tel 01702-348944
Director, vacant

CUSTOMS POLICY DIRECTORATE
Director, A. R. Rawsthorne

EXCISE AND CENTRAL POLICY DIRECTORATE
Director, D. J. Howard

VAT POLICY DIRECTORATE
Director, M. R. Brown

PERSONNEL AND FINANCE DIRECTORATE
Director, P. R. H. Allen

OUTFIELD
Director, R. N. McAfee
Tariff and Statistical Office
Portcullis House, 27 Victoria Avenue, Southend-on-Sea SS2 6AL
Tel 01702-348944
Controller, M. McDowall
Accounting Services Division
Alexander House, 21 Victoria Avenue, Southend-on-Sea SS99 1AA
Tel 01702-348944
Accountant and Comptroller-General, D. Robinson

OPERATIONS (COMPLIANCE) DIRECTORATE
Director, M. W. Norgrove

OPERATIONS (PREVENTION) DIRECTORATE
Director, T. Byrne
National Investigation Service
Custom House, Lower Thames Street, London EC3R 6EE
Tel 0171-283 5353
Chief Investigation Officer, P. Evans

SOLICITOR'S OFFICE
Solicitor, D. Pickup
Deputy Solicitor, G. Fotherby

COLLECTORS OF HM CUSTOMS AND EXCISE
(G5)
Anglia, M. Hill
Central England, D. Garlick
Eastern England, A. Durrant
London Airports, M. Peach
London Central, J. Maclean
Northern England, H. Peden
Northern Ireland, T. W. Logan
North-west England, A. Allen
Scotland, I. Mackay
South-east England, J. Tullberg
South London and Thames, J. Hendry
Southern England, H. Burnard
Thames Valley, J. Barnard
Wales, the West and Borders, B. Flavill

OFFICE OF THE DATA PROTECTION REGISTRAR
Wycliffe House, Water Lane, Wilmslow, Cheshire
SK9 5AF
Tel 01625-545745; fax 01625-524510

The Office of the Data Protection Registrar was created by the Data Protection Act 1984; the Registrar will be renamed the Data Protection Commissioner on 1 March 2000 under the Data Protection Act 1998, which will implement the EU Data Protection Directive (95/46/EC) in the UK. It is the Registrar's duty to compile and maintain the register of data users and computer bureaux and to provide facilities for members of the public to examine the register; to promote observance of data protection principles; to consider complaints made by data subjects; to disseminate information about the Data Protection Act; to encourage the production of codes of practice by trade associations and other bodies; to guide data users in complying with data protection principles; and to co-operate with other parties to the Council of Europe Convention and act as UK authority for the purposes of Article 13 of the Convention.
Registrar, Mrs E. France

DEER COMMISSION FOR SCOTLAND
Knowsley, 82 Fairfield Road, Inverness IV3 5LH
Tel 01463-231751; fax 01463-712931

The Deer Commission for Scotland has the general functions of furthering the conservation and control of deer in Scotland. It has the statutory duty, with powers, to prevent damage to agriculture, forestry and the habitat by deer. It is funded by the Scottish Executive.
Chairman (part-time), A. Raven
Director, A. Rinning
Technical Director, R. W. Youngson

MINISTRY OF DEFENCE
— *see* pages 384–96

DESIGN COUNCIL
34 Bow Street, London WC2E 7DL
Tel 0171-420 5200; fax 0171-420 5300

The Design Council is incorporated by royal charter and is a registered charity. It works with government, industry and academia to generate information and practical tools for uptake in industry and education which demonstrate the contribution, value and effectiveness of design. Its sponsoring department is the Department of Trade and Industry.
Chairman, J. Sorrell, CBE
Chief Executive, A. Summers

THE DUCHY OF CORNWALL
10 Buckingham Gate, London SW1E 6LA
Tel 0171-834 7346; fax 0171-931 9541

The Duchy of Cornwall was created by Edward III in 1337 for the support of his eldest son Edward, later known as the Black Prince. It is the oldest of the English duchies. The duchy is acquired by inheritance by the sovereign's eldest son either at birth or on the accession of his parent to the throne, whichever is the later. The primary purpose of the estate remains to provide an income for the Prince of Wales. The estate is mainly agricultural, consisting of 129,000 acres in 24 counties mainly in the south-west of England. The duchy also has some residential property, a number of shops and offices, and a Stock Exchange portfolio. Prince Charles is the 24th Duke of Cornwall.

THE PRINCE'S COUNCIL
Chairman, HRH The Prince of Wales, KG, KT, GCB
Lord Warden of the Stannaries, The Earl Peel
Receiver-General, The Earl Cairns, CBE
Attorney-General to the Prince of Wales, N. Underhill, QC
Secretary and Keeper of the Records, W. R. A. Ross
Other members, Earl of Shelburne; J. E. Pugsley;
    A. M. J. Galsworthy; C. Howes, CB; W. N. Hood, CBE; S. Lamport; R. Broadhurst

OTHER OFFICERS
Auditors, I. Brindle; R. Hughes
Sheriff (1999–2000), Lt.-Cdr. N. J. Trefusis

THE DUCHY OF LANCASTER
Lancaster Place, Strand, London WC2E 7ED
Tel 0171-836 8277; fax 0171-836 3098

The estates and jurisdiction known as the Duchy of Lancaster have belonged to the reigning monarch since 1399 when John of Gaunt's son came to the throne as Henry IV. As the Lancaster Inheritance it goes back as far as 1265 when Henry III granted his youngest son Edmund lands and possessions following the Baron's war. In 1267 Henry gave Edmund the County, Honor and Castle of Lancaster and created him the first Earl of Lancaster. In 1351 Edward III created Lancaster a County Palatine.

The Chancellor of the Duchy of Lancaster is responsible for the administration of the Duchy, the appointment of justices of the peace in Lancashire, Greater Manchester and Merseyside and ecclesiastical patronage in the Duchy gift.
Chancellor of the Duchy of Lancaster (and Minister for the Cabinet Office), The Rt. Hon. Dr Jack Cunningham, MP (*see also* page 286)
Attorney-General, R. G. B. McCombe, QC
Receiver-General, Sir Michael Peat, KCVO
Clerk of the Council, M. K. Ridley, CVO
Chief Clerk and Secretary for Appointments, Col. F. N. J. Davies

ECGD (EXPORT CREDITS GUARANTEE DEPARTMENT)
PO Box 2200, 2 Exchange Tower, Harbour Exchange Square, London E14 9GS
Tel 0171-512 7000; fax 0171-512 7649

ECGD (Export Credits Guarantee Department), the UK's official export credit insurer, is a government department responsible to the Secretary of State for Trade and Industry and functions under the Export and Investment Guarantees Act 1991. This enables ECGD to facilitate UK exports by making available export credit insurance to firms engaged in selling overseas and to guarantee repayment to banks providing finance for capital goods. The Act also empowers ECGD to insure UK companies investing overseas against political risks such as war, expropriation and restrictions on remittances.
Chief Executive, H. V. B. Brown

Group Directors (*G3*), V. P. Lunn-Rockliffe (*Asset Management*); J. R. Weiss (*Underwriting*); T. M. Jaffray (*Resource Management*)

DIVISIONS

Director, Finance (*G5*), R. J. Healey
Director, Central Services (*G5*), P. J. Callaghan
Directors, Underwriting Divisions (*G5*), G. G. W. Welsh (*Division 1*); J. C. W. Croall (*Division 2*); M. D. Pentecost (*Division 3*); R. Gotts (*Division 4*); S. R. Dodgson (*Division 5*); C. J. Leeds (*Division 6*)
Director, Office of the General Counsel (*G5*), N. Ridley
Director, International Debt (*G5*), Ms L. Woods
Director, Claims (*G5*), R. F. Lethbridge
Director, Treasury and Export Finance (*G5*), J. S. Snowdon
Director, Risk Management (*G5*), P. J. Radford
Director, External Relations (*G5*), Mrs M. E. Maddox
Director, IT Services (*G6*), E. J. Walsby
Director, Internal Audit (*G6*), G. Cassell
Director, Operational Research (*G6*), Ms R. Kaufman

EXPORT GUARANTEES ADVISORY COUNCIL
Chairman, D. H. A. Harrison
Other Members, Ms E. Airey; Dr A. K. Banerji; R. F. T. Binyon; A. Brown; S. J. Doughty; Ms L. Knox; G. W. Lynch, OBE; D. McLachlan; P. J. Mason; R. H. Maudslay; Sir David Wright, KCMG, LVO

DEPARTMENT FOR EDUCATION AND EMPLOYMENT
Sanctuary Buildings, Great Smith Street, London SW1P 3BT
Tel 0870-001 2345; fax 0171-925 6000
E-mail: info@dfee.gov.uk
Web: http://www.dfee.gov.uk
Caxton House, Tothill Street, London SW1H 9NF
Tel 0171-273 3000; fax 0171-273 5124
Moorfoot, Sheffield S1 4PQ
Tel 0114-275 3275; fax 0114-259 4724
Mowden Hall, Staindrop Road, Darlington DL3 9BG
Tel 01325-460155

The Department for Education and Employment was formed in July 1995, bringing together the functions of the former Department for Education with the training and labour market functions of the former Employment Department Group. It includes an executive agency, the Employment Service. The Department aims to support economic growth and improve the nation's competitiveness and quality of life by raising standards of educational achievement and skill and by promoting an efficient and flexible labour market.
Secretary of State for Education and Employment, The Rt. Hon. David Blunkett, MP
Principal Private Secretary, M. Wardle
Special Advisers, C. Ryan; Ms S. Linden; N. Pearce; T. Engel
Parliamentary Private Secretary, Ms J. Corston, MP
Minister of State, The Rt. Hon. Andrew Smith, MP (*Employment*)
Private Secretary, D. Nickerson
Parliamentary Private Secretary, Ms J. Ryan, MP
Minister of State, Estelle Morris, MP (*School Standards*)
Private Secretary, J. Whitfield
Minister in the Lords, The Baroness Blackstone, PH.D. (*Lifelong Learning*)
Private Secretary, E. Wilkinson
Parliamentary Private Secretary, T. McNulty, MP

Parliamentary Under-Secretaries of State, Margaret Hodge, MP (*Employment, Under 5s*); Malcolm Wicks, MP (*Lifelong Learning*); Jacqui Smith, MP (*School Standards*); Michael Wills, MP (*Information and Communications Technology*)
Private Secretaries, G. Walker; Ms J. Loosley; D. McGrath
Permanent Secretary, Sir Michael Bichard, KCB
Private Secretary, M. Doherty

EMPLOYMENT, LIFELONG LEARNING AND INTERNATIONAL DIRECTORATE
Director-General, N. Stuart

INTERNATIONAL
Director, C. Tucker, CB
Heads of Divisions, Ms W. Harris (*European Union*); Ms E. Trewartha (*European Social Fund*); B. Shaw (*International Relations*)

SKILLS AND LIFELONG LEARNING
Director, D. Grover, CB
Heads of Divisions, J. Temple (*Skills Unit*); vacant (*Individual Learning*); Mrs L. Ammon, CBE (*Learning at Work*); Dr J. Pugh (*University for Industry*)

EMPLOYMENT POLICY
Director, M. J. Richardson
Heads of Divisions, M. Neale (*Structural Unemployment Policy*); E. Galvin (*Employment and Benefits Policy*); C. Barnham (*Welfare to Work*); B. Wells (*Economy and Labour Market*)

EQUAL OPPORTUNITIES, TECHNOLOGY AND OVERSEAS LABOUR
Director, B. Niven
Heads of Divisions, Ms S. Trundle, OBE (*Childcare Unit*); Ms J. Eastabrook (*Sex and Race Equality*); Miss D. Fordham (*Disability Policy*); P. Chorley (*Family Friendly Employment*); N. Atkinson (*Overseas Labour Service*)

FINANCE AND ANALYTICAL SERVICES DIRECTORATE
Director-General, P. Shaw

FINANCE
Heads of Divisions, Mrs S. Todd (*Expenditure*); S. Burt (*Private Finance*); Mrs C. Hunter (*Programmes*); R. Wye (*Efficiency*); P. Connor (*Financial Accounting*); N. Thirtle (*Internal Audit*)

ANALYTICAL SERVICES
Director, D. Allnutt
Heads of Divisions, M. Britton (*Qualifications, Pupil Assessment and International*); J. Elliott (*Youth and Further Education*); S. Field (*Higher Education*); B. Butcher (*Employability and Adult Learning*); R. Bartholomew (*Equal Opportunities and Research Programmes*); Ms A. Brown (*Schools, Teachers and Resources*)

FURTHER AND HIGHER EDUCATION AND YOUTH TRAINING DIRECTORATE
Director-General, R. Dawe

QUALIFICATIONS
Director, R. Hull
Heads of Divisions, C. Johnson (*School and College Qualifications*); J. West (*Qualifications for Work*); A. Clarke (*Standards, Quality and Access*)

FURTHER EDUCATION AND YOUTH TRAINING
Director, D. Forrester

Heads of Divisions, Ms C. Tyler (*Investing in Young People*);
S. Geary (*Careers and Information*); S. Hillier (*Funding and
Organization*); A. Davies (*Partnership Skills and Young
People*)

HIGHER EDUCATION
Director, A. C. Clark
Heads of Divisions, M. Hipkins (*Higher Education Funding*);
N. Flint (*Student Support 1*); B. Evans (*Student Support 2*);
T. Fellowes (*Higher Education and Employment*)

LEGAL ADVISER'S OFFICE
Legal Adviser, D. Macrae
Heads of Divisions, F. Clarke; S. Harker; Miss D. Collins

OPERATIONS DIRECTORATE
Director, J. Hedger, CB
Heads of Divisions, P. Houten (*TECs Operational Policy,
Planning, Communications and Transition*); P. Lauener
(*Post-16 Review Group*); Ms S. Orr (*Quality and Finance
Assurance*); G. McKinsie (*Regional Development and
Government Offices*); J. Fuller (*National Training
Organizations*); P. Mucklow (*Structures and Learning Skills
Councils*); A. McCully (*Legislation*)

PERSONNEL AND SUPPORT SERVICES
DIRECTORATE
Director, Mrs H. Douglas
Heads of Divisions, R. Hinchcliffe (*Information Systems*); M.
Shipp (*Personnel*); P. Neill (*Procurement and Contracting*);
J. Gordon (*Training and Development*); L. Webb (*Facilities
Management*); G. Archer (*Corporate Change and Senior
Staff*); B. Hillon (*Senior Equal Opportunities Adviser*)

SCHOOLS DIRECTORATE
Director-General, D. Normington

SCHOOLS ORGANIZATION AND FUNDING
Director, Ms H. Williams
Heads of Divisions, Ms E. Wylie (*LEA Support*); A. Sevier
(*School Framework and Governance*); K. Beeton (*School
Capital and Buildings*); A. Wye (*Schools and LEA Funding*);
Ms C. Macready (*School Admissions and Organization*)

TEACHERS
Director, P. Makeham
Heads of Divisions, Ms A. Jackson (*Teachers' Pay and Policy*);
G. Holley (*Teacher Supply and Training*); Ms P. Jones
(*Teachers' Standards and Pensions*); Ms C. Bienkowska
(*Teacher Development and Leadership*)

PUPIL SUPPORT AND INCLUSION
Director, R. Smith
Heads of Divisions, P. Cohen (*School Inclusion*); C. Wells
(*Study Support, Business and Community Links and Youth*);
M. Phipps (*Pupil Support and Independent Schools*); S.
Crowne (*Special Educational Needs*); A. Cranston (*Early
Years*)
Head of Sure Start Unit, Ms N. Eisenstadt
Deputy Head of Sure Start Unit, Ms S. Thomson

CURRICULUM, COMMUNICATIONS, TECHNOLOGY AND
PARENTS
Director, Ms I. Wilde
Heads of Divisions, I. Berry (*Curriculum*); S. Edwards (*School
Communications*); R. Tabberer (*Education and Training
Technology*); N. Baxter (*Parents and Performance Tables*)

STANDARDS AND EFFECTIVENESS UNIT
Head of Unit, Prof. M. Barber
Heads of Divisions, S. Adamson (*Standards*); Ms S. Scales
(*LEA Effectiveness*); D. Sandeman (*School Effectiveness*)

STRATEGY AND COMMUNICATIONS
DIRECTORATE
Director, P. Wanless
Heads of Divisions, Ms J. Simpson (*Head of News*); T. Cook
(*Media Relations*); J. Ross (*Publicity*); R. Harrison (*Strategy
and Board Secretariat*); G. McKenzie (*Briefing*)

EXECUTIVE AGENCY

THE EMPLOYMENT SERVICE
Caxton House, Tothill Street, London SW1H 9NA
Tel 0171-273 6060; fax 0171-273 6099

The aims of the Employment Service are to contribute to
high levels of employment and growth by helping all
people without a job to find work and by helping employers
to fill their vacancies, and to help individuals lead rewarding
working lives.
Chief Executive, L. Lewis
Director of Jobcentre Services, J. Turner, CB
Director of Human Resources, K. White
Director of Welfare to Work Delivery, R. Foster
Director of Finance and Commercial Policy, P. Collis
Non-Executive Directors, R. Dykes; Ms L. de Groot; C. Cox
Regional Directors, M. Groves (*East Midlands and Eastern*); S.
Holt, OBE (*London and South-East*); P. Robson (*Northern*);
Ms M. John (*North-West*); K. Pascoe (*South-West*); Ms R.
Thew (*West Midlands*); R. Lasko (*Yorkshire and
Humberside*)
Director for Scotland, A. R. Brown
Director for Wales, Mrs S. Keyse

ELECTRICITY REGULATION, OFFICE OF
(former)
— *see* Gas and Electricity Markets, Office of

OFFICE FOR THE REGULATION OF
ELECTRICITY AND GAS
Brookmount Buildings, 42 Fountain Street, Belfast BT1 5EE
Tel 01232-311575 (*Electricity*); 01232-314212 (*Gas*); fax
01232-311740

The Office for the Regulation of Electricity and Gas
(OFREG) is the combined regulatory body for the
electricity and gas supply industries in Northern Ireland.
*Director-General of Electricity Supply and Director-General of
Gas for Northern Ireland*, D. B. McIldoon
Deputy Director-General of Electricity and Gas,
C. H. Coulthard

ENGLISH HERITAGE
— *see* Historic Buildings and Monuments Commission for
England

ENGLISH NATURE
Northminster House, Peterborough PE1 1UA
Tel 01733-455000; fax 01733-568834

English Nature (the Nature Conservancy Council for
England) was established in 1991 and is responsible for
advising the Secretary of State for the Environment,
Transport and the Regions on nature conservation in
England. It promotes, directly and through others, the
conservation of England's wildlife and natural features. It
selects, establishes and manages National Nature Reserves
and identifies and notifies Sites of Special Scientific Interest.
It provides advice and information about nature conservation, and supports and conducts research relevant to these

functions. Through the Joint Nature Conservation Committee (*see* page 326), it works with its sister organizations in Scotland and Wales on UK and international nature conservation issues.

Chairman, The Baroness Young of Old Scone
Chief Executive, Dr D. R. Langslow
Directors, Dr K. L. Duff; Miss C. E. M. Wood; Ms S. Collins

DEPARTMENT OF THE ENVIRONMENT, TRANSPORT AND THE REGIONS

Eland House, Bressenden Place, London SW1E 5DU
Great Minster House, 76 Marsham Street, London SW1P 4DR
Ashdown House, 123 Victoria Street, London SW1E 6DE
Tel 0171-890 3000
Web: http://www.detr.gov.uk

The Department of the Environment, Transport and the Regions (DETR) was formed in June 1997 by the merger of the Department of the Environment and the Department of Transport. It is responsible for policies relating to the environment, housing, transport services, rural affairs, planning, local government, regional development, regeneration, the construction industry and health and safety.

The Department's ministers are based at Eland House.

Deputy Prime Minister and Secretary of State for the Environment, Transport and the Regions, The Rt. Hon. John Prescott, MP
  Private Secretary, P. Unwin
  Special Advisers, J. Irvin; Ms J. Hammell
Minister for Transport, The Lord Macdonald of Tradeston
  Private Secretary, S. Davies
Minister of State, The Rt. Hon. Michael Meacher, MP (*Environment*)
  Private Secretary, C. Bird
  Parliamentary Private Secretary, T. Rooney, MP
Minister of State, The Rt. Hon. Hilary Armstrong, MP (*Local Government, Regions*)
  Private Secretary, N. Carter
  Special Adviser, D. Murphy
  Parliamentary Private Secretary, K. Hill, MP
Minister of State, Nick Raynsford, MP (*Housing, Planning, London*)
  Private Secretary, E. West
  Special Adviser, P. Hackett
  Parliamentary Private Secretary, B. Chapman, MP
Parliamentary Under-Secretaries of State, The Lord Whitty; Keith Hill, MP; Chris Mullin, MP; Beverley Hughes, MP
  Private Secretaries, Ms J. Borg; Ms K. Braddick; Ms J. Matthew; R. O'Donnell
Parliamentary Clerk, Ms P. Gaunt
Permanent Secretary (SCS), Sir Richard Mottram, KCB
  Private Secretary, Mrs S. Bishop

*DIRECTORATE OF COMMUNICATION
Director (SCS), vacant
Deputy Directors (SCS), C. Skinner (*Publicity*); D. Plews (*Press*)

†ENVIRONMENT PROTECTION GROUP
Director-General (SCS), Miss D. A. Nichols

ENERGY, ENVIRONMENT AND WASTE DIRECTORATE
Director (SCS), P. Ward
Heads of Divisions (SCS), L. Packer (*Sustainable Energy Policy*); D. Vincent (*Energy Environment and Best Practice*); H. Cleary (*Environment and Business 1–5*); B. Ryder (*Environment and Business 6–7*); Ms L. Simcock (*Waste Policy*); D. Prior (*Joint Environmental Markets Unit*)

ENVIRONMENT: RISK AND ATMOSPHERE DIRECTORATE
Director (SCS), H. Derwent
Heads of Divisions (SCS), Dr P. Hinchcliffe (*Chemicals and Biotechnology*); Dr S. Brown (*Radioactive Substances*); P. Betts (*Global Atmosphere*); M. Hurst (*Air and Environment Quality 1–5*); M. Williams (*Air and Environment Quality 6–10*)

ENVIRONMENT PROTECTION STRATEGY DIRECTORATE
Director (SCS), A. Burchell
Heads of Divisions (SCS), Mrs H. C. Hillier (*EP Statistics and Information Management*); B. Glicksman (*Environment Agency Sponsorship and Management*); Ms S. McCabe (*Environment Protection International*); R. Wilson (*Environment Protection Economics*); J. Adams (*Sustainable Development Unit*)

WATER AND LAND DIRECTORATE
Director (SCS), A. H. Davis
Heads of Divisions (SCS), M. Rouse (*Drinking Water Inspectorate*); A. Simcock (*Marine, Land and Liabilities*); S. Hoggan (*Water Quality*); B. Dinwiddy (*Water Supply and Regulation*)

†FINANCE GROUP
Director and Principal Finance Officer (SCS), J. Ballard
Heads of Divisions (SCS), R. Bennett (*Finance Programmes*); I. McBrayne (*Finance Sponsorship and Programme*); R. Anderson (*Finance Departmental Administration*); A. Beard (*Finance Accounting Services, Resource Accounting and Budgeting*); C. Arnott (*Internal Audit*)

*HOUSING, CONSTRUCTION, REGENERATION AND COUNTRYSIDE GROUP
Director-General (SCS), Mrs M. McDonald, CB

HOUSING
Director (SCS), M. Gahagan
Heads of Divisons (SCS), Mrs J. Littlewood (*Research, Analysis and Evaluation*); B. Oelman (*Housing Data and Statistics*); P. Cox (*Housing and Urban Economics*); Ms R. Sharpe (*Housing Policy, Renewal and Ownership*); M. Faulkner (*Housing Private Rented Sector*); Mrs H. Chipping (*Local Authority Housing Finance*); R. Horsman (*Housing Associations and Private Finance*); A. Allberry (*Homelessness and Housing Management*)

CONSTRUCTION DIRECTORATE
Director (SCS), J. Hobson
Heads of Divisions (SCS), N. Dorling (*Construction Industry Sponsorship*); J. Stambollouian (*Construction Innovation and Research Management*); R. Wood (*Export Promotion and Construction Materials*); P. Everall (*Building Regulations*); B. Davies (*Construction Market Intelligence*)

WILDLIFE AND COUNTRYSIDE DIRECTORATE
Director (SCS), Ms S. Lambert
Heads of Divisions (SCS), R. M. Pritchard (*European Wildlife*); R. Hepworth (*Global Wildlife*); Ms D. Kahn (*Rural Development*); Ms S. Carter (*Countryside*); C. Braun (*Countryside Legislation*)

REGENERATION DIRECTORATE
Director (SCS), P. Evans
Heads of Divisions (SCS), J. Roberts; W. Chapman; Ms L. Derrick; Ms H. Ghosh

---

* Based at Eland House
† Based at Ashdown House
‡ Based at Great Minster House

LONDON ROUGH SLEEPERS UNIT
Director (SCS), Ms L. Casey
Head of Division (SCS), Ms J. Bailey

*LEGAL GROUP
Director-General (SCS), D. Hogg

COUNTRYSIDE, PLANNING AND TRANSPORT
Director (SCS), Ms S. Unerman
Heads of Divisions (SCS), N. Lefton (*Countryside and Environmental Liability*); Ms G. Hedley-Dent (*Planning*); R. Lines (*Highways*); N. Thomas (*Road Traffic*); A. Jones (*Aviation*); C. Ingram (*Marine*); Ms J.-A. McKenzie (*Railways*)

COMMERCIAL, ENVIRONMENT, HOUSING AND LOCAL GOVERNMENT
Director (SCS), C. Muttukamaru
Heads of Divisions (SCS), J. Comber (*Environment (National)*); D. Jordan (*Local Government (Finance)*); Ms P. Conlon (*Local Government (General)*); K. Baublys (*Housing and Land*); Ms S. Headley (*Special Projects*); D. Aries (*Commercial and Establishments*); Ms D. Phillips (*Devolution and Regional Government*)

ENVIRONMENT (INTERNATIONAL AND EC)
Director (SCS), P. Szell
Head of Division (SCS), A. McGlone

LEGISLATIVE UNIT
Director (SCS), A. Roberts

*LOCAL AND REGIONAL GOVERNMENT GROUP
Director-General (SCS), P. Wood

LOCAL GOVERNMENT DIRECTORATE
Director (SCS), A. Whetnall
Heads of Divisions (SCS), P. Rowsell (*Local Government Sponsorship*); J. R. Footitt (*Local Government Competition and Quality*); T. Redpath (*Local Government Legislation*); T. Crossley (*Local Government Pensions*)

LOCAL GOVERNMENT FINANCE POLICY DIRECTORATE
Director (SCS), M. Lambirth
Heads of Divisions (SCS), R. J. Gibson (*Local Government Grant Distribution*); Mrs P. Penneck (*Local Government Finance Statistics*); Ms P. Williams (*Local Government Capital Finance*); S. Hughes (*Local Government Taxation*); I. Scotter (*Local Government Revenue Expenditure*)

GOVERNMENT OFFICES AND REGIONAL POLICY DIRECTORATE
Director (SCS), Miss L. Bell
Heads of Divisions (SCS), M. Coulshed; M. Ross; A. Murray; Mrs J. Scoones (*Government Offices Central Unit*)

REGIONAL OFFICES
— see pages 303–4

‡PLANNING, ROADS AND LOCAL TRANSPORT
Director-General (SCS), C. J. S. Brearley, CB

MOBILITY UNIT
Head of Unit (SCS), Miss E. A. Frye, OBE

PLANNING DIRECTORATE
Director (SCS), J. Jacobs
Heads of Divisions (SCS), J. Channing (*Planning and Policies*); C. Bowden (*Development Control Policy*); M. R. Ash (*Plans and Compensation*); J. Zetter (*Environmental Assessment, International and Research*); A. M. Oliver (*Planning and Land Use Statistics*); L. Hicks (*Minerals and Waste Planning*); J. M. Leigh-Pollitt (*Land and Property*)

NATIONAL ROADS POLICY DIRECTORATE
Director (SCS), Ms D. Phillips
Heads of Divisions (SCS), T. Worsley (*Highways, Economics and Traffic Appraisal*); N. McDonald (*Roads Policy*); M. Talbot (*Traffic Management and Tolls*); R. Donachie (*Transport Statistics: Roads*)

INTEGRATED AND LOCAL TRANSPORT
Director (SCS), R. Bird
Heads of Divisions (SCS), E. C. Neve (*Buses and Taxis*); P. McCarthy (*Local Transport Policy*); A. S. D. Whybrow (*Charging and Local Transport*); M. Walsh (*Economics, Local Transport and General*); P. Capell (*Transport Statistics: Personal Travel*)

ROAD AND VEHICLE SAFETY
Director (SCS), J. Plowman
Heads of Divisions (SCS), M. Fendick (*Vehicle Standards and Engineering*); R. Peal (*Road Safety*); R. Jones (*Licensing and Enforcement*); Dr T. Carter (*Chief Medical Adviser*); M. Brasher (*Driver, Vehicle Operator Task Force*); I. Todd (*Vehicle, Environment and Taxation*)

‡RAILWAYS, AVIATION LOGISTICS AND MARITIME
Director-General (SCS), D. Rowlands

RAILWAYS
Director (SCS), vacant
Heads of Divisions (SCS), M. Fuhr, OBE (*Channel Tunnel Rail Link*); S. Connolly (*Railways Economics and Finance*); P. Thomas (*Railways International and General*); B. Linnard (*Railways Sponsorship*)

AVIATION
Director (SCS), R. Griffins
Heads of Divisions (SCS), M. Fawcett (*Airports Policy*); M. C. Mann (*Economics, Aviation, Maritime and International*); Ms E. Duthie (*Aviation Environmental*); M. Smethers (*Multilateral*); A. T. Baker (*International Aviation*); D. McMillan (*Civil Aviation*)

AIR ACCIDENTS INVESTIGATION BRANCH
Defence Evaluation and Research Agency, Farnborough, Hants GU14 6TD
Tel 01252-510300

Chief Inspector of Air Accidents, K. P. R. Smart, CBE
Deputy Chief Inspector, R. McKinlay

LOGISTICS AND MARITIME TRANSPORT
Director (SCS), B. Wadsworth
Heads of Divisions (SCS), Ms A. Moss (*Road Haulage*); M. Hughes (*Transport Statistics Freight*); D. Liston-Jones (*Traffic Area Network Unit*); D. Cooke (*Shipping Policy 1*); G. D. Rowe (*Shipping Policy 2*); J. F. Wall, CMG (*Shipping Policy 3*); C. Young (*Radioactive Materials Transport*); S. Reeves (*Ports*)

MARINE ACCIDENTS INVESTIGATION BRANCH
5–7 Brunswick Place, Southampton SO1 2AN
Tel 01703-395500

Chief Inspector of Marine Accidents, Rear-Adm. J. Lang
Deputy Chief Inspector, S. Harwood

TRANSPORT SECURITY
Director (SCS), D. Lord
Head of Division and Deputy Director (SCS), W. Gillan

---

* Based at Eland House
† Based at Ashdown House
‡ Based at Great Minster House

*STRATEGY AND CORPORATE SERVICES
GROUP
Director-General (SCS), R. S. Dudding
Heads of Divisions (SCS), I. Heawood (*Information Management*); I. Harris (*Working Environment*); P. Walton (*Corporate, Business and Agencies*); G. Jones (*Procurement, Policy and Advice*); J. O'Callaghan (*IT Services*)

PERSONNEL AND CHANGE MANAGEMENT
Director (SCS), Ms J. Cotton
Heads of Divisions (SCS), M. Bailey (*Personnel Support*); E. Gibbons (*Group Facing Teams*); K. Arnold (*Pay and Industrial Relations*); B. Meakins (*Change Management, Development and Training*)

CHIEF ECONOMIST
Director and Chief Economist (SCS), C. Riley
Head of Division (SCS), vacant (*Central Economics and Policy*)

CENTRAL STRATEGY (AND CHIEF SCIENTIST)
Director (and Chief Scientist) (SCS), D. Fisk
Heads of Divisions (SCS), J. Stevens (*Europe, Transport and General*); M. Devine (*Health and Safety Sponsorship*); A. Apling (*Science and Technology Policy*); Ms B. Hill (*Transport Strategy and Awareness*)

EXECUTIVE AGENCIES

DRIVER AND VEHICLE LICENSING AGENCY
Longview Road, Morriston, Swansea SA6 7JL
Tel 01792-772151 (*drivers*); 01792-772134 (*vehicles*)

The Agency issues driving licences, registers and licenses vehicles, and collects excise duty.
Chief Executive, Dr S. J. Ford, CBE

DRIVING STANDARDS AGENCY
Stanley House, Talbot Street, Nottingham NG1 5GU
Tel 0115-947 4222; fax 0115-955 7334

The Agency's role is to carry out driving tests and approve driving instructors.
Chief Executive, vacant

HIGHWAYS AGENCY
St Christopher House, Southwark Street, London SE1 0TE
Tel 0645-556575

The Agency is responsible for the operation, management and maintenance of the motorway and trunk road network and for road construction and improvement.
Chief Executive, L. J. Haynes

MARITIME AND COASTGUARD AGENCY
Spring Place, 105 Commercial Road, Southampton
SO15 1EG
Tel 01703-329100

The Agency was formed in April 1998 by the merger of the Coastguard Agency and the Marine Safety Agency. Its role is to develop, promote and enforce high standards of marine safety; to minimize loss of life amongst seafarers and coastal users; and to minimize pollution from ships of the sea and coastline.
Chief Executive, M. Storey
Chief Coastguard, J. Astbury

PLANNING INSPECTORATE
Tollgate House, Houlton Street, Bristol BS2 9DJ
Tel 0117-987 8000

The Inspectorate is responsible for casework involving planning, housing, roads, environmental and related legislation. It is a joint executive agency of the Department of the Environment, Transport and the Regions and the National Assembly for Wales.
Chief Executive and Chief Planning Inspector, C. Shepley

QUEEN ELIZABETH II CONFERENCE CENTRE
Broad Sanctuary, London SW1P 3EE
Tel 0171-222 5000; fax 0171-798 4200

The Centre provides conference and banqueting facilities for both private sector and government use.
Chief Executive, M. C. Buck

VEHICLE CERTIFICATION AGENCY
1 Eastgate Office Centre, Eastgate Road, Bristol BS5 6XX
Tel 0117-951 5151; fax 0117-952 4103

The Agency tests and certificates vehicles to UK and international standards.
Chief Executive, D. W. Harvey

VEHICLE INSPECTORATE
Berkeley House, Croydon Street, Bristol BS5 0DA
Tel 0117-954 3200; fax 0117-954 3212

The Agency carries out annual testing and inspection of heavy goods and other vehicles and administers the MOT testing scheme.
Chief Executive, R. J. Oliver

TRAFFIC AREA OFFICES AND
COMMISSIONERS
Senior Traffic Commissioner, M. W. Betts, CBE

Eastern, G. Simms
North-Eastern and North-Western, K. R. Waterworth
Scottish, M. W. Betts, CBE
South-Eastern and Metropolitan, Brig. M. H. Turner
Wales, D. Dixon
Western, C. Heaps
West Midlands, D. Dixon

TRAFFIC DIRECTOR FOR LONDON
College House, Great Peter Street, London SW1P 3LN
Tel 0171-222 4545; fax 0171-976 8640

The Traffic Director for London is a non-departmental public body which is independent from the Department of the Environment, Transport and the Regions but is responsible to the Secretary of State and to Parliament. Its role is to co-ordinate the Priority (Red) Route Network in London and monitor its operation.
Traffic Director for London, D. Turner

THE ENVIRONMENT AGENCY
25th Floor, Millbank Tower, 21–24 Millbank, London
SW1P 4XL
Tel 0171-863 8600; fax 0171-863 8650
Rio House, Waterside Drive, Aztec West, Almondsbury, Bristol BS32 4UD
Tel 01454-624400; fax 01454-624409

The Environment Agency was established in 1996 under the Environment Act 1995 and is a non-departmental public body sponsored by the Department of the Environment, Transport and the Regions, MAFF and the National Assembly for Wales. The Agency is responsible for pollution prevention and control in England and Wales, and for the management and use of water resources, including flood defences, fisheries and navigation. It has head offices in London and Bristol and eight regional offices.

THE BOARD
Chairman, The Lord De Ramsey (until Dec. 1999)

Deputy Chairman, Sir John Harman
Members, C. Beardwood; A. J. P. Dalton; A. Dare, CBE;
    E. Gallagher; N. Haigh, OBE; C. Hampson, CBE; Prof. R.
    Macrory; Prof. Jacqueline McGlade; G. Manning, OBE;
    Dr A. Powell; Prof. D. Ritchie; A. Rogers; G. Wardell

THE EXECUTIVE
Chief Executive, E. Gallagher
Director of Finance, N. Reader
Director of Personnel, G. Duncan
Director of Environmental Protection, Dr P. Leinster
Director of Water Management, G. Mance
Director of Operations, A. Robertson
Director of Corporate Affairs, M. Wilson
Director of Legal Services, R. Navarro
Chief Scientist, J. Pentreath

ROYAL COMMISSION ON ENVIRONMENTAL POLLUTION
1st Floor, Steel House, 11 Tothill Street, London
SW1H 9RE
Tel 0171-273 6635

The Commission was set up in 1970 to advise on national
and international matters concerning the pollution of the
environment.
Chairman, Prof. Sir Thomas Blundell
Members, Sir Geoffrey Allen, FRS; Revd Prof. M. C.
    Banner; Prof. G. S. Boulton, FRS, FRSE; Prof. R. Clift,
    OBE, FREng.; J. Flemming; Sir Martin Holdgate, CB; Prof.
    B. Hoskins, CBE, FRS; Prof. R. Macrory; Prof.
    M. G. Marmot, PH.D.; Prof. J. G. Morris, CBE, FRS; Dr
    Susan Owens, OBE; J. Roberts; Dr Penelope A. Rowlatt
Secretary, D. R. Lewis

EQUAL OPPORTUNITIES COMMISSION
Overseas House, Quay Street, Manchester M3 3HN
Tel 0161-833 9244; fax 0161-835 1657

Press Office, 36 Broadway, London SW1H 0XH. Tel: 0171-
222 1110
Other Offices, Stock Exchange House, 7 Nelson Mandela
Place, Glasgow G2 1QW. Tel: 0141-248 5833; Windsor
House, Windsor Place, Cardiff. Tel: 01222-343552

The Commission was set up in 1975 as a result of the
passing of the Sex Discrimination Act. It works towards
the elimination of discrimination on the grounds of sex or
marital status and to promote equality of opportunity
between men and women generally. It is responsible to the
Department for Education and Employment.
Chair, Ms J. Mellor
Deputy Chairs, Mrs E. Hodder; Ms G. James
Members, P. Smith; Ms M. Berg; R. Grayson; Dr J. Stringer;
    Prof. T. Rees; R. Penn; Ms J. Rubin; Prof. M. Schofield;
    Ms K. Carberry; Ms J. Watson; Ms T. Woodcraft
Chief Executive (*acting*), F. Spencer

EQUAL OPPORTUNITIES COMMISSION FOR NORTHERN
IRELAND
Chamber of Commerce House, 22 Great Victoria Street,
Belfast BT2 7BA
Tel 01232-242752; fax 01232-331047

Chair, Mrs J. Smyth, CBE
Chief Executive, Ms E. Collins

OFFICE OF FAIR TRADING
Field House, Bream's Buildings, London EC4A 1PR
(from the end of 1999) Fleetbank House, 2–6 Salisbury
Square, London EC4Y 8JX
Tel 0171-211 8000; fax 0171-211 8800

The Office of Fair Trading is a non-ministerial government
department headed by the Director-General of Fair
Trading. It keeps commercial activities in the UK under
review and seeks to protect consumers against unfair
trading practices. The Director-General's consumer protection duties under the Fair Trading Act 1973, together
with his responsibilities under the Consumer Credit Act
1974, the Estate Agents Act 1979, the Control of Misleading
Advertisements Regulations 1988, and the Unfair Terms
in Consumer Contracts Regulations 1994, are administered
by the Office's Consumer Affairs Division. The Competition Policy Division is concerned with monopolies and
mergers (under the Fair Trading Act 1973) and the
Director-General's other responsibilities for competition
matters, including those under the Restrictive Trade
Practices Acts 1976 and 1977, the Resale Prices Act 1976,
the Competition Act 1980, the Financial Services Act 1986
and the Broadcasting Act 1990. In March 2000 the new
provisions in the Competition Act 1998 will replace the
Restrictive Trade Practices Acts 1976 and 1977, the Resale
Prices Act 1976 and most of the Competition Act 1980.
The Office is the UK competent authority on the
application of the European Commission's competition
rules, and also liaises with the Commission on consumer
protection initiatives.
Director-General, J. Bridgeman

CONSUMER AFFAIRS DIVISION
Director (*G3*), Miss C. Banks
Assistant Directors (*G5*), R. Watson; M. Graham; D. Wray

COMPETITION POLICY DIVISION
Director (*G3*), Mrs M. J. Bloom
Assistant Directors (*G5*), A. J. White; H. L. Emden;
    E. L. Whitehorn; S. Wood; P. G. A. Bamford

LEGAL DIVISION
Director (*G3*), Miss P. Edwards
Assistant Directors (*G5*), M. A. Khan; S. Brindley
Establishment and Finance Officer (*G5*), Mrs R. Heyhoe
Chief Information Officer (*G6*), D. Hill

FOREIGN AND COMMONWEALTH OFFICE
Downing Street, London SW1A 2AL
Tel 0171-270 3000
Web: http://www.fco.gov.uk

The Foreign and Commonwealth Office provides, mainly
through diplomatic missions, the means of communication
between the British Government and other governments
and international governmental organizations for the
discussion and negotiation of all matters falling within the
field of international relations. It is responsible for alerting
the Government to the implications of developments
overseas; for protecting British interests overseas; for
protecting British citizens abroad; for explaining British
policies to, and cultivating friendly relations with, governments overseas; and for the discharge of British responsibilities to the UK overseas territories.
Secretary of State for Foreign and Commonwealth Affairs, The
    Rt. Hon. Robin Cook, MP

Principal Private Secretary, S. L. Cowper-Coles, CMG, LVO
Private Secretaries, T. Barrow, LVO; A. Patrick
Special Advisers, A. Hood; D. Clark
Parliamentary Private Secretary, K. Purchase, MP
Minister for Europe, Geoffrey Hoon, MP
Private Secretary, N. Hopton
Minister of State, Peter Hain, MP
Minister of State, John Battle, MP
Private Secretaries to the Ministers of State, F. Baker; Ms P. Phillips
Parliamentary Under-Secretary of State, The Baroness Scotland of Asthal
Private Secretary, C. Newns
Permanent Under-Secretary of State and Head of HM Diplomatic Service, Sir John Kerr, KCMG
Private Secretary, D. Frost
Chief Executive, †*British Trade International*, Sir David Wright, KCMG, LVO
Deputy Under-Secretaries, C. Hum, CMG (*Chief Clerk*); C. Budd, CMG (*EU/Economic Director*); E. Jones Parry, CMG (*Political Director*); D. Manning, CMG; J. Shepherd, CMG; Sir Franklin Berman, KCMG, QC (*Legal Adviser*)
Directors, Ms A. Grant, CMG (*Africa and Commonwealth*); P. J. Westmacott, CMG (*Americas/Overseas Territories*); P. Ricketts, CMG, CVO (*International Security*); S. J. L. Wright, CMG (*Wider Europe*); N. E. Sheinwald, CMG (*European Union*); R. E. Dibble (*Chief Executive, FCO Services*); A. R. Brenton (*Global Issues*); C. Crawford (*Deputy Political Director*); D. Plumbly, CMG (*Middle East/North Africa*); R. F. Cooper (*Asia, Pacific*); D. Hall, CMG (*Export Promotion*); R. Dalton (*Personnel*); D. N. Reddaway, CMG, MBE (*Public Services*); P. S. Collecott (*Resources*); C. Butler (*Chief Economic Adviser*)

HEADS OF DEPARTMENTS

African Department (Equatorial), J. Bevan
African Department (Southern), N. R. Chrimes
Aviation and Maritime Department, N. A. Ling
Central and North-West European Department, Sir John Ramsden, Bt.
Change Management Unit, Ms S. Matthews
China/Hong Kong Department, D. A. Warren
Common Foreign and Security Policy Department, C. Roberts
Commonwealth Co-ordination Department, C. C. Bright
Consular Division, D. J. R. Taylor
Counter-Terrorism Policy Department, V. Fean
Cultural Relations Department, Ms A. W. Lewis
Devolved Administration Department, Dr J. Milligan
Drugs and International Crime Department, M. Ryder
Eastern Department, A. F. Pringle
Eastern Adriatic Department, T. R. V. Phillips
Economic Relations Department, C. Butler
Environment, Science and Energy Department, J. Ashton
European Union Department (Bi-lateral), J. Cresswell, CVO
European Union Department (External), S. Featherstone
European Union Department (Internal), M. J. Lyall-Grant
FCO Services, N. Hook (*Head, Conference and Visits Group*); Ms V. Life (*Head, Consultancy Group*); J. Elgie (*Head, Estates Group*); J. Thompson, MBE (*Head, Information Management Group*); Ms J. Link (*Head, Resource Management Group*); M. Carr (*Head, Support Group*); N. Stickells (*Head, Technical Group*)
Financial Compliance Unit, M. Purves
Financial Policy Department, M. J. Brown
Honours Department, R. M. Sands
Human Rights Policy Department, R. A. E. Gordon, OBE
Information Department, P. J. Dun
**Internal Audit Department*, R. A. Elias
†*Invest in Britain Bureau*, A. Fraser (*Chief Executive*)

†*Joint Export Promotion Directorate*, D. Hall, CMG
Latin America and Caribbean Department, H. G. Hogger
Middle East Department, E. G. M. Chaplin
Migration and Visa Department, R. M. White, MBE
Near East and North Africa Department, C. N. R. Prentice
News Department, N. K. Darroch, CMG
Non-Proliferation Department, P. W. Hare, LVO
North America Department, P. J. Priestley, CBE
North-East Asia and Pacific Department, P. Carter
OSCE and Council of Europe Department, A. E. Huckle
Parliamentary Relations Department, A. Henderson (*Head*); P. R. O. Bromley (*Deputy Head and Parliamentary Clerk*)
Personnel Command, P. Jones (*Asst. Director, Personnel Management*); T. Simmons (*Asst. Director, Performance Issues*); Ms E. Kennedy (*Asst. Director, *Medical and Welfare*); S. Wightman (*Asst. Director, Personnel Policy*); R. T. Fell, CVO (*Asst. Director, Personnel Services*); C. Edgerton, OBE, T. Malcomson (*Asst. Directors, Prosper*); Ms A. Cookson-Hall (*Head, Recruitment*); Dr Vanessa Davies (*Head, Diplomatic Service Language Centre*); Mrs C. Dharwarker (*Head, Training*); Ms J. Bennet, Ms A. Kirk (*Heads, Grading Review Team*)
Policy Planning Staff, Mrs A. M. Leslie
Protocol Department, M. B. L. Dalton, LVO, OBE (*Head of Department and First Assistant Marshal of the Diplomatic Corps*)
Purchasing Directorate, M. J. H. Gower
Republic of Ireland Department, G. Fergusson
Research Analysts, R. D. Lavers
Royal Matters Department, B. England
Security Strategy Unit, T. J. Duggin
Security Policy Department, A. M. Thompson
South Asian Department, S. N. Evans, OBE
South-East Asian Department, N. J. Cox
Southern European Department, J. Hill
United Nations Department, Ms R. M. Marsden
Whitehall Liaison Department, L. Parker

EXECUTIVE AGENCY

WILTON PARK CONFERENCE CENTRE
Wiston House, Steyning, W. Sussex BN44 3DZ
Tel 01903-815020; fax 01903-816373

The Centre organizes international affairs conferences and is hired out to government departments and commercial users.
Chief Executive and Director, C. B. Jennings

CORPS OF QUEEN'S MESSENGERS

Support Group, Foreign and Commonwealth Office, London SW1
Tel 0171-270 2779

Superintendent of the Corps of Queen's Messengers, A. C. Brown
Queen's Messengers, P. Allen; R. Allen; Maj. A. N. D. Bols; Lt.-Cdr. K. E. Brown; Lt.-Col. W. P. A. Bush; Lt.-Col. M. B. de S. Clayton; Maj. P. C. H. Dening-Smitherman; Sqn. Ldr. J. S. Frizzell; Capt. N. C. E. Gardner; Maj. D. A. Griffiths; A. Hill; R. Long; A. Rix; Maj. K. J. Rowbottom; Maj. M. R. Senior; Cdr. K. M. C. Simmons, AFC; Maj. P. M. O. Springfield; Maj. J. S. Steele

---

* Joint Foreign and Commonwealth Office/Department for International Development department
† Joint Foreign and Commonwealth Office/Department of Trade and Industry directorate

FOREIGN COMPENSATION COMMISSION
Room 3.G.9, 1 Palace Street, London SW1E 5HE
Tel 0171-238 4419; fax 0171-238 4594

The Commission was set up by the Foreign Compensation Act 1950 primarily to distribute, under Orders in Council, funds received from other governments in accordance with agreements to pay compensation for expropriated British property and other losses sustained by British nationals.
Chairman, A. W. E. Wheeler, CBE
Secretary, A. N. Grant

FORESTRY COMMISSION
231 Corstorphine Road, Edinburgh EH12 7AT
Tel 0131-334 0303; fax 0131-334 3047

The Forestry Commission is the government department responsible for forestry policy in Great Britain. It reports directly to forestry ministers (i.e. the Minister of Agriculture, Fisheries and Food, the Scottish ministers and the National Assembly for Wales), to whom it is responsible for advice on forestry policy and for the implementation of that policy.

The Commission's principal objectives are to protect Britain's forests and woodlands; expand Britain's forest area; enhance the economic value of the forest resources; conserve and improve the biodiversity, landscape and cultural heritage of forests and woodlands; develop opportunities for woodland recreation; and increase public understanding of and community participation in forestry. Forest Enterprise, a trading body operating as an executive agency of the Commission, manages its forestry estate on a multi-use basis.
Chairman (part-time), Sir Peter Hutchison, Bt., CBE
Director-General and Deputy Chairman (G2), D. J. Bills
Secretary to the Commissioners (G5), F. Strang

FOREST ENTERPRISE HEADQUARTERS, 231
Corstorphine Road, Edinburgh EH12 7AT. Tel: 0131-334
0303. *Chief Executive,* Dr B. McIntosh
FOREST RESEARCH, Alice Holt Lodge, Wrecclesham,
Farnham, Surrey GU10 4LU. Tel: 01420-222555;
Northern Research Station, Roslin, Midlothian
EH25 9SY. Tel: 0131-445 2176. *Chief Executive,* J. Dewar

FRANCHISING, OFFICE OF PASSENGER RAIL
— *see* Transport section

REGISTRY OF FRIENDLY SOCIETIES
Victory House, 30–34 Kingsway, London WC2B 6ES
Tel 0171-663 5282/5124/5269/5299

The Registry of Friendly Societies is a non-ministerial government department now comprising the Registry of Friendly Societies and the Assistant Registrar of Friendly Societies for Scotland.

The Central Office of the Registry of Friendly Societies provides a public registry for mutual organizations registered under the Building Societies Act 1986, the Friendly Societies Acts 1974 and 1992, and the Industrial and Provident Societies Act 1965. The Chief Registrar is responsible for the supervision of credit unions, and advises the Government on issues affecting them.

The Registry of Friendly Societies will be subsumed into the Financial Services Authority (*see* page 635) at a date to be fixed following the enactment of the Financial Services and Markets Bill.

CENTRAL OFFICE OF THE REGISTRY
Chief Registrar, G. E. Fitchew
Assistant Registrars, A. J. Perrett; Ms S. Eden; S. Mundy; E.
Engstrom; N. Fawcett
Legal Adviser, A. J. Perrett
Establishment and Finance Officer, R. E. Merrick

REGISTRY OF FRIENDLY SOCIETIES, SCOTLAND
58 Frederick Street, Edinburgh EH2 1NB
Tel 0131-226 3224
Assistant Registrar (G5), J. L. J. Craig, WS

FRIENDLY SOCIETIES COMMISSION
15th Floor, 25 The North Colonnade, Canary Wharf,
London E14 5HS
Tel 0171-676 1000; fax 0171-676 0059

The Friendly Societies Commission was established by the Friendly Societies Act 1992. It is responsible for the supervision of friendly societies and administers the system of prudential regulation. It also advises the Treasury and other government departments on matters relating to friendly societies.

The Government has proposed to Parliament that the functions of the Commission should pass to the Financial Services Authority (*see* page 635) on implementation of the Financial Services and Markets Bill.

FRIENDLY SOCIETIES COMMISSION
Chairman, *M. Roberts
Commissioners, F. da Rocha; *B. Richardson; *J. A. Geddes;
*Ms S. Brown; *Ms P. Triggs
* part-time

SECRETARIAT
Secretary, Ms J. Erskine

GAMING BOARD FOR GREAT BRITAIN
Berkshire House, 168–173 High Holborn, London
WC1V 7AA
Tel 0171-306 6200; fax 0171-306 6266

The Board was established in 1968 and is responsible to the Home Secretary. It is the regulatory body for casinos, bingo clubs, gaming machines and the larger society and all local authority lotteries in Great Britain. Its functions are to ensure that those involved in organizing gaming and lotteries are fit and proper to do so and to keep gaming free from criminal infiltration; to ensure that gaming and lotteries are run fairly and in accordance with the law; and to advise the Home Secretary on developments in gaming and lotteries.
Chairman (part-time) (£37,650), P. Dean, CBE
Secretary, T. Kavanagh

OFFICE OF GAS AND ELECTRICITY MARKETS
Stockley House, 130 Wilton Road, London SW1V 1LQ
Tel 0171-828 0898; fax 0171-932 1600
SCOTLAND: Regent Court, 70 West Regent Street,
Glasgow G2 2QZ
Tel 0141-331 2678; fax 0141-331 2777

The Office of Gas and Electricity Markets (Ofgem) was formed in 1999 by the merger of the separate regulators for electricity and gas set up under the Electricity Act 1989 and the Gas Act 1986 respectively. It is headed by the Director-General for Electricity and Gas Supply and is the independent regulatory body for the electricity and gas supply industries in England, Scotland and Wales. Its functions are to promote competition and to protect customers' interests in relation to prices, security of supply and quality of services.

Director-General for Electricity and Gas Supply, C. McCarthy
Deputy Directors-General, A. J. Boorman (*Customers*); Dr Eileen Marshall, CBE (*Supply Chain*); R. Morse (*Electricity and Gas Transportation Regulation*)
Chief Operating Officer, Ms G. Whittington
Director, Public Affairs, Ms S. Harrison
Legal Adviser, W. Sprigge

GOVERNMENT ACTUARY'S DEPARTMENT
New King's Beam House, 22 Upper Ground, London SE1 9RJ
Tel 0171-211 2600; fax 0171-211 2640

The Government Actuary provides a consulting service to government departments, the public sector, and overseas governments. The actuaries advise on social security schemes and superannuation arrangements in the public sector at home and abroad, on population and other statistical studies, and on government supervision of insurance companies, friendly societies and pension funds.

Government Actuary, C. D. Daykin, CB
Directing Actuaries, D. G. Ballantine; T. W. Hewitson; A. G. Young
Chief Actuaries, E. I. Battersby; A. J. M. Chamberlain; Ms C. Cresswell; Mrs B. J. Hall; A. I. Johnston; D. Lewis; J. C. A. Rathbone; G. T. Russell

---

GOVERNMENT HOSPITALITY FUND
8 Cleveland Row, London SW1A 1DH
Tel 0171-210 4282; fax 0171-930 1148

The Government Hospitality Fund was instituted in 1908 for the purpose of organizing official hospitality on a regular basis with a view to the promotion of international goodwill. It is responsible to the Foreign and Commonwealth Office.

Minister in Charge, The Baroness Symons of Vernham Dean
Secretary, Col. T. Earl

GOVERNMENT OFFICES FOR THE REGIONS

The Government Offices for the Regions were established in 1994. The regional directors are accountable to the Secretary of State for the Environment, Transport and the Regions, the Secretary of State for Trade and Industry, and the Secretary of State for Education and Employment. The offices' role is to promote a coherent approach to competitiveness, sustainable economic development and regeneration using public and private resources.

CENTRAL UNIT, 1st Floor, Eland House, Bressenden Place, London SW1E 5DU
Tel 0171-890 5157; fax 0171-890 5019

Director (*G3*), Miss L. Bell
Head of Unit (*G5*), Mrs J. Scoones

EAST MIDLANDS
Secretariat: The Belgrave Centre, Stanley Place, Talbot Street, Nottingham NG1 5GG
Tel 0115-971 9971; fax 0115-971 2769

Regional Director (*G3*), D. Morrison
Directors (*G5*), Dr S. Kennett (*Environment and Community Development*); R. Poole (*Competitiveness and European Policy*); P. Mucklow (*Skills and Enterprise*); (*G6*), K. Lussey (*Corporate Affairs*)

EAST OF ENGLAND
Secretariat: Building A, Westbrook Centre, Milton Road, Cambridge CB4 1YG
Tel 01223-346700; fax 01223-346701

Regional Director (*G3*), A. Riddell
Directors (*G5*), C. Dunabin (*Housing, Environment and Regeneration*); Ms C. Bowdler (*Planning and Transport*); M. Oldham (*Economic Development*); J. Street (*Skills and Enterprise*); (*G6*), vacant (*Strategy and Resources*)

LONDON
Secretariat: Riverwalk House, 157–161 Millbank, London SW1P 4RR
Tel 0171-217 3456; fax 0171-217 3450

Director of Office (*G2*), Miss E. C. Turton, CB
Directors (*G3*), J. A. Owen (*Skills, Education and Regeneration*); S. Lord (*Transport and Regeneration*); R. Allan (*New London Governance*); (*G5*), A. Sargent (*Skills and Education*); Mrs J. Bridges (*Planning*); Ms A. Munro (*Transport Division*); K. Timmins (*Enterprise and North-West*); Ms M. Winckler (*London East and European Programmes*); S. Gooding (*London Transport Division*); P. Sanders (*Transport for London Bill Division*); A. Melville (*Greater London Authority Implementation*); Ms E. Meek (*GLA Division*); A. Weedon (*Transport Task Force*); Ms C. Lyons (*Corporate*); J. Sienkiewicz (*London Development Unit*); R. Wragg (*Operations and Business Management*); N. Robinson (*Exports and Trade, and Business Development*); P. Fiddeman (*Regeneration London South*); B. Mann (*Home Office Liaison*); Z. Kowalczyk (*London Readiness 2000/Millennium Access*); I. Jordan (*Transport for London Project Division*)

NORTH-EAST
Secretariat: Wellbar House, Gallowgate, Newcastle upon Tyne NE1 4TD
Tel 0191-201 3300; fax 0191-202 3744

Regional Director (*G3*), Dr R. Dobbie
Directors (*G5*), J. Darlington (*Planning, Environment and Transport*); Miss D. Caudle (*Education, Skills, Enterprise and Regeneration*); A. Dell (*Europe, Industry, Trade and Technology*); (*G6*), Mrs D. Pearce (*Strategy and Resources*)

NORTH-WEST
Secretariat: 12th Floor, Sunley Tower, Piccadilly Plaza, Manchester M1 4BE
Tel 0161-952 4000; fax 0161-952 4099

Regional Director (*G3*), Ms M. Neville-Rolfe
Directors, (*G5*), Dr B. Isherwood (*Strategy and Regional Issues*); P. Styche (*Environment and Transport*); Dr D. Higham (*Business and Europe*); D. Duff (*Skills and Enterprise*); (*G6*), Ms E. Hughes (*Planning*); I. Jamieson (*Europe, Manchester*); Ms S. Yates (*Europe, Liverpool*); D. Hopewell (*Corporate Services*); N. Burke (*Operations, Skills and Enterprise*) (*acting*)

SOUTH-EAST
Secretariat: 2nd Floor, Bridge House, 1 Walnut Tree Close, Guildford, Surrey GU1 4GA
Tel 01483-882481; fax 01483-882259

Regional Director (*G3*), D. Saunders

Directors (*G5*), Ms L. Robinson (*Hants/IOW*); N. Wilson (*Berks/Oxon/Bucks*); A. Campbell (*Kent*); D. Andrews (*Surrey/E. and W. Sussex*); Mrs C. Dixon (*Regional Strategy Team*)

SOUTH-WEST
Secretariat: 4th Floor, The Pithay, Bristol BS1 2PB
Tel 0117-900 1792; fax 0117-900 1900

Regional Director (*G3*), Ms J. Henderson
Directors (*G5*), R. Bayly (*Devon and Cornwall*); Ms B. Houlden (*Environment and Regeneration*); T. Shearer (*Competitiveness and Skills*); Ms C. Carrington (*Corporate Services*)

WEST MIDLANDS
Secretariat: 6th Floor, 77 Paradise Circus, Queensway, Birmingham B1 2DT
Tel 0121-212 5000; fax 0121-212 5456

Regional Director (*G3*), D. Ritchie
Directors (*G5*), C. Marsh (*Policy Co-ordination and Europe Division*); Mrs P. Holland (*Local Government Division*); D. Way (*Business and Learning*); (*G6*), K. Griffiths (*Resource Management Division*)

YORKSHIRE AND THE HUMBER
Secretariat: PO Box 213, City House, New Station Street, Leeds LS1 4US
Tel 0113-280 0600; fax 0113-283 6394

Regional Director (*G3*), Mrs F. Everiss
Directors (*G5*), G. Dyche (*Strategy and Europe*); S. Perryman (*Business, Enterprise and Skills*); (*G6*), J. Jarvis (*Planning and Transport*); M. Doxey (*Personnel and Resources*); Ms M. Jackson (*Regeneration*) (*acting*)

DEPARTMENT OF HEALTH
Richmond House, 79 Whitehall, London SW1A 2NL
Tel 0171-210 2000
Web: http://www.open.gov.uk/doh/dhhome.htm

The Department of Health is responsible for the provision of the National Health Service in England and for social care, including oversight of personal social services run by local authorities in England for children (except day care, which is now the responsibility of the DfEE), the elderly, the infirm, the handicapped and other persons in need. It is responsible for health promotion and has functions relating to public and environmental health, food safety and nutrition. The Department is also responsible for the ambulance and emergency first aid services, under the Civil Defence Act 1948. The Department represents the UK at the European Union and other international organizations including the World Health Organization. It also supports UK-based healthcare and pharmaceutical industries.

Responsibility for food safety will be transferred to the new Food Standards Agency, expected to be in operation by mid 2000.

Secretary of State for Health, The Rt. Hon. Frank Dobson, MP
  Principal Private Secretary, J. Grauberg
  Private Secretaries, H. Rogers; M. Ferrero
  Special Advisers, J. McCrea; S. Stevens
  Parliamentary Private Secretary, Mrs A. Keen, MP
Minister of State, John Denham, MP (*NHS Structure and Resources*)
  Private Secretary, J. Adedji
  Parliamentary Private Secretary, P. Goggins, MP
Minister of State, The Rt. Hon. Tessa Jowell, MP (*Public Health, Women's Issues*)
  Private Secretary, R. Carter

  Parliamentary Private Secretary, J. Ennis, MP
Parliamentary Under-Secretaries of State, John Hutton, MP; The Lord Hunt of Kings Heath; Gisela Stuart, MP
  Private Secretaries, N. Paterson; Ms H. McLain; vacant
  Parliamentary Clerk, J. Fowles
Permanent Secretary (*SCS*), C. Kelly
  Private Secretary, Miss S. Foster
Chief Medical Officer (*SCS*), Prof. L. Donaldson, QHP, FRCSED., FRCP
Chief Executive, NHS Executive (*SCS*), Sir Alan Langlands
Deputy Chief Medical Officers (*SCS*), Dr Patricia Troop; Dr Sheila Adam

REGIONAL CHAIRMEN'S MEETING
Chairman, The Secretary of State for Health
Members, John Denham, MP (*Minister of State*); The Rt. Hon. Tessa Jowell, MP (*Minister of State*); John Hutton, MP (*Parliamentary Under-Secretary*); The Lord Hunt of Kings Heath (*Parliamentary Under-Secretary*); Gisela Stuart, MP (*Parliamentary Under-Secretary*); Prof. L. Donaldson, QHP, FRCSED., FRCP (*Chief Medical Officer*); Sir Alan Langlands (*Chief Executive, NHS Executive*); C. Kelly (*Permanent Secretary*); vacant (*Chief Nursing Officer*); C. Wilkinson; Mrs Z. Manzoor, CBE; P. Hammersley; Mrs R. Varley; Miss J. Trotter, OBE; I. Mills; W. Wells; Prof. A. Breckenridge, CBE; A. D. M. Liddell, CBE

CORPORATE MANAGEMENT DIRECTORATE GROUP
Head of Group (*SCS*), Ms A. Perkins

STATISTICS DIVISION
Director of Statistics (*SCS*), J. Fox
Chief Statisticians (*SCS*), R. K. Willmer; A. Roberts (*acting*)

PERSONNEL SERVICES
Director of Personnel (*SCS*), F. Goldhill
Heads of Branches (*SCS*), C. Muir; I. Forsyth; S. Redmond

INFORMATION SERVICES DIVISION
Head of Division (*SCS*), Dr A. A. Holt
Heads of Branches, Mrs L. Wishart; C. Horsey; M. Rainsford; Mrs J. Dainty; R. Long; P. G. Cobb; P. Charman

RESOURCE MANAGEMENT AND FINANCE
Head of Division (*SCS*), D. Clark
Heads of Branches, P. Kendall; B. Burleigh; J. Stopes-Roe; A. McNeil

ECONOMICS AND OPERATIONAL RESEARCH DIVISION (HEALTH)
Chief Economic Adviser (*SCS*), C. H. Smee, CB
Heads of Branches, Dr S. Harding; Dr G. Royston; A. Hare; N. York

COMMUNICATIONS DIRECTORATE
Director of Communications (*SCS*), Mrs H. McCallum
Deputy Directors, vacant (*Media Centre*); W. Roberts (*Publicity*); P. Addison-Child (*NHS Communications*) (*acting*)

POLICY MANAGEMENT UNIT
Head of Branch (*acting*), R. Walsh

SOLICITOR'S OFFICE
Solicitor (*SCS*), M. Morgan
Director of Legal Services (*SCS*), Mrs G. S. Kerrigan

PUBLIC HEALTH POLICY GROUP
PROTECTION OF HEALTH DIVISION
Head of Division (*SCS*), Dr Eileen Rubery, CB
Head of Branches, Dr E. Smales; A. Smith; J. Walden

JOINT FOOD SAFETY AND STANDARDS DIVISION
Head of Division (SCS), G. Podger
Heads of Branches, Dr R. Skinner; Ms P. Stewart; Miss J. Wordley; S. Catling

HEALTH PROMOTION DIVISION
Head of Division (SCS), D. P. Walden
Heads of Branches (SCS), Miss A. Mithani; M. Fry; Miss A. Edwards; E. Waterhouse

SOCIAL CARE GROUP
Chief Social Services Inspector, Ms D. Platt
Head of Social Care Policy, D. Walden
Deputy Chief Inspectors, D. Gilroy; Ms A. Nottage
Heads of Branches (SCS), S. Mitchell; N. Boyd; J. Kennedy; T. Jeffery; Miss A. Stephenson; R Wilson (*Section Head*)
Assistant Chief Inspector (HQ), J. Cleary
Assistant Chief Inspectors (Regions), S. Allard; J. Cypher; B. Riddell; A. Jones; Mrs P. K. Hall; C. P. Brearley; J. Fraser; Mrs L. Hoare; Ms J. Owen; Miss F. McCabe

NURSING GROUP
Chief Nursing Officer/Director of Nursing (SCS), vacant
Assistant Chief Nursing Officers (SCS), Mrs G. Stephens; D. Moore; Mrs E. Fradd

RESEARCH AND DEVELOPMENT DIVISION
Director of Research and Development, Prof. Sir John Pattison
Deputy Director of Research and Development (SCS), Dr C. Henshall
Heads of Branches (SCS), Dr P. Greenaway; Mrs J. Griffin; Ms A. Kauder; M. Taylor

NHS EXECUTIVE
Quarry House, Quarry Hill, Leeds LS2 7UE
Tel 0113-254 5000
Chief Executive, Sir Alan Langlands
Director of Human Resources, H. Taylor
Director of Finance and Performance, C. Reeves, CBE
Medical Director, Dr Sheila Adam
Chief Nursing Officer, vacant
Director of Research and Development, Prof. Sir John Pattison
Director of Planning and Performance Management, A. D. M. Liddell, CBE
Director of NHS Clinical Governance Support Team, Prof. A. Halligan

CORPORATE AFFAIRS
Head of Corporate Affairs (SCS), M. Staniforth

HUMAN RESOURCES
Deputy Director of Human Resources (SCS), S. Barnett

INFORMATION POLICY UNIT
Head of Unit (SCS), Dr P. Drury

PLANNING DIRECTORATE
Director (SCS), A. D. M. Liddell, CBE
Chief Economic Adviser, C. Smee, CB
Head of Planning, L. Bradley
Head of Communications, vacant
Director of Statistics, J. Fox

HEALTH SERVICES DIRECTORATE
Director (SCS), Dr Sheila Adam
Heads of Branches, M. Brown; Mrs L. Wolstenholme; Ms J. McKessack; L. Percival; Dr G. Radford; D. Hewlett; Ms K. Tyson

PRIMARY CARE DIVISION
Head of Division, A. McKeon
Fraud Supremo, J. Gee
Chief Dental Officer, J. R. Wild

Chief Pharmaceutical Officer (acting), Mrs J. Howe
Heads of Branches, Miss H. Robinson (*Dental and Optical Services*); K. Guinness (*Pharmacy and Prescribing*); Miss H. Gwynn (*White Paper Implementation Team*); M. Farrar (*General Medical Services*)

FINANCE AND PERFORMANCE DIRECTORATE
Director (SCS), C. L. Reeves
Deputy Directors, R. Douglas; B. McCarthy
Heads of Branches, J. Lawler; Dr S. Peck; M. Sturges; A. Angilley; M. A. Harris, CBE; J. Thomlinson; P. Coates; J. Copeland

REGIONAL OFFICES
– *see* Social Welfare section

ADVISORY COMMITTEES

ADVISORY COMMITTEE ON THE MICROBIOLOGICAL SAFETY OF FOOD, Room 502A, Skipton House, 80 London Road, London SE1 6LH. Tel: 0171-972 5050. *Chairman*, Prof. D. Georgarla, CBE, PH.D.
COMMITTEE ON THE SAFETY OF MEDICINES, Market Towers, 1 Nine Elms Lane, London SW8 5NQ. Tel: 0171-273 0451. *Chairman*, Prof. A. M. Breckenridge, CBE, FRCP, FRCPed., FRSE
MEDICINES COMMISSION, Market Towers, 1 Nine Elms Lane, London SW8 5NQ. Tel: 0171-273 0652. *Chairman*, Prof. D. H. Lawson, CBE, FRCPed., FRCP(Glas.)

SPECIAL HEALTH AUTHORITIES

DENTAL VOCATIONAL TRAINING AUTHORITY, Master's House, Temple Grove, Compton Place Road, Eastbourne, E. Sussex BN20 8AD. Tel: 01323-431189. *Chairman*, R. Davies; *Secretary*, Ms J. Verity
FAMILY HEALTH SERVICES APPEAL AUTHORITY, 30 Victoria Avenue, Harrogate HG1 5PR. Tel: 01423-535415. *Chief Executive*, D. J. Laverick
HEALTH EDUCATION AUTHORITY, Trevelyan House, 30 Great Peter Street, London SW1P 2HW. Tel: 0171-222 5300. *Chair*, Ms Y. Buckland; *Chief Executive*, S. Fortescue
MENTAL HEALTH ACT COMMISSION – *see* page 320
MICROBIOLOGICAL RESEARCH AUTHORITY, Porton Down, Salisbury, Wilts SP4 0JG. Tel: 01980-612100. *Chairman*, Sir William Stewart, FRS; *Director*, Dr R. H. Gilmour
NATIONAL BLOOD AUTHORITY, Oak House, Reeds Crescent, Watford, Herts WD1 1QH. Tel: 01923-486800. *Chairman*, M. Fogden; *Chief Executive*, M. Gorham
NATIONAL INSTITUTE OF CLINICAL EXCELLENCE, 90 Long Acre, London WC2E 9RZ. Tel: 0171-849 3444. *Chairman*, Sir Michael Rawlins; *Chief Executive*, A. Dillon
NHS INFORMATION AUTHORITY, 15 Frederick Road, Edgbaston, Birmingham B15 1JD. Tel: 0121-625 1992. *Chairman*, Prof. A. Bellingham, CBE; *Chief Executive*, N. Bell
NHS LITIGATION AUTHORITY, 5 Pemberton Row, London EC4A 3BA. Tel: 0171-936 4400. *Chairman*, Sir Bruce Martin, QC; *Chief Executive*, S. Walker
NHS SUPPLIES, Premier House, 60 Caversham Road, Reading, Berks RG1 7EB. Tel 0118-980 8600. *Chairman*, D. Hall, CBE, TD; *Chief Executive*, T. Hunt, CBE
PRESCRIPTION PRICING AUTHORITY, Bridge House, 152 Pilgrim Street, Newcastle upon Tyne NE1 6SN. Tel: 0191-232 5371. *Chairman*, Prof. D. J. Johns; *Chief Executive*, N. Scholte

UK Transplant Support Service Authority, Fox Den Road, Stoke Gifford, Bristol BS34 8RR. Tel: 0117-975 7575. *Chairman,* J. F. Shaw; *Chief Executive,* Mrs R. Balderson

SPECIAL HOSPITALS

Ashworth Hospital, Parkbourn, Maghull, Merseyside L31 1HW. Tel: 0151-473 0303. *Chief Executive (acting),* P. Clarke
Broadmoor Hospital, Crowthorne, Berks RG45 7EG. Tel: 01344-773111. *Chief Executive,* Dr J. Hollyman
Rampton Hospital, Retford, Notts DN22 0PD. Tel: 01777-248321. *Chief Executive,* Mrs S. Foley

EXECUTIVE AGENCIES

Medicines Control Agency
Market Towers, 1 Nine Elms Lane, London SW8 5NQ
Tel 0171-273 0000; fax 0171-273 0353

The Agency controls medicines through licensing, monitoring and inspection, and enforces safety standards.
Chief Executive, Dr K. H. Jones, CB

Medical Devices Agency
Hannibal House, Elephant and Castle, London SE1 6TQ
Tel 0171-972 8000; fax 0171-972 8108

The Agency safeguards the performance, quality and safety of medical devices and ensures that they comply with relevant EU directives.
Chief Executive, A. Kent

NHS Estates
1 Trevelyan Square, Boar Lane, Leeds LS1 6AE
Tel 0113-254 7000; fax 0113-254 7299

NHS Estates provides advice and support in the area of healthcare estate functions to the NHS and the healthcare industry.
Chief Executive, Mrs K. Priestley

NHS Pensions
Hesketh House, 200–220 Broadway, Fleetwood, Lancs FY7 8LG
Tel 01253-774774; fax 01253-774860

NHS Pensions administers the NHS occupational pension scheme.
Chief Executive, A. F. Cowan

HEALTH AND SAFETY COMMISSION
Rose Court, 2 Southwark Bridge, London SE1 9HS
Tel 0171-717 6000; fax 0171-717 6717

The Health and Safety Commission was created under the Health and Safety at Work etc. Act 1974, with duties to reform health and safety law, to propose new regulations, and generally to promote the protection of people at work and of the public from hazards arising from industrial and commercial activity, including major industrial accidents and the transportation of hazardous materials. The members of the Commission are appointed by the Secretary of State for the Environment, Transport and the Regions. The Commission is made up of representatives of employers, trades unions and local authorities, and has a full-time chairman.
Chairman, W. Callaghan
Members, Ms A. Gibson; Dr M. McKiernan; Ms J. Edmond-Smith; G. Brumwell; Ms M. Burns; S. Hamid; A. Chowdry; O. Tudor; R. Symons, CBE
Secretary, T. A. Gates

HEALTH AND SAFETY EXECUTIVE
Rose Court, 2 Southwark Bridge, London SE1 9HS
Tel 0171-717 6000; fax 0171-717 6717

The Health and Safety Executive is the Health and Safety Commission's major instrument. Through its inspectorates it enforces health and safety law in the majority of industrial premises. The Executive advises the Commission in its major task of laying down safety standards through regulations and practical guidance for many industrial processes. The Executive is also the licensing authority for nuclear installations and the reporting officer on the severity of nuclear incidents in Britain, and it is responsible for the Channel Tunnel Safety Authority.
Director-General, Miss J. H. Bacon, CB
Deputy Director-General, D. C. T. Eves, CB (*HM Chief Inspector of Factories*)
Director, Field Operations Directorate, Dr A. Ellis
Director, Science and Technology, Dr J. McQuaid, CB
Director, Safety Policy, C. Norris
Director, Health Directorate, Dr P. J. Graham
Director, Resources and Planning, R. Hillier
HM Chief Inspector of Nuclear Installations, Dr L. G. Williams
HM Chief Inspector of Mines, B. Langdon, CBE
HM Chief Inspecting Officer of Railways, V. Coleman

HIGHLANDS AND ISLANDS ENTERPRISE
Bridge House, 20 Bridge Street, Inverness IV1 1QR
Tel 01463-234171; fax 01463-244241

Highlands and Islands Enterprise (HIE) was set up under the Enterprise and New Towns (Scotland) Act 1991. Its role is to design, direct and deliver enterprise development, training, environmental and social projects and services. HIE is made up of a strategic core body and ten Local Enterprise Companies (LECs) to which many of its individual functions are delegated.
Chairman, Dr J. Hunter
Chief Executive, I. A. Robertson, CBE

HISTORIC BUILDINGS AND MONUMENTS COMMISSION FOR ENGLAND (ENGLISH HERITAGE)
23 Savile Row, London W1X 1AB
Tel 0171-973 3000; fax 0171-973 3001

English Heritage was established under the National Heritage Act 1983, and its duties are to offer expert advice and skills and give grants to secure the preservation of listed buildings, cathedrals, churches, archaeological sites, ancient monuments and historic houses in England; to encourage the imaginative re-use of historic buildings to aid regeneration of the centres of cities, towns and villages; to manage the historic houses and monuments in its care; and to promote access to and enjoyment of ancient monuments and historic buildings in England. It is funded by the Department for Culture, Media and Sport.

On 1 April 1999 English Heritage merged with the Royal Commission on the Historical Monuments of England (RCHME). It is therefore now responsible for the National Monuments Record, which includes all the material gathered since the formation of the RCHME in 1908 and now contains over 12 million photographs, maps and drawings.
Chairman, Sir Jocelyn Stevens, CVO (until March 2000)

Commissioners, Miss A. Arrowsmith; Ms B. Cherry; Cllr P. Davis; A. Fane; The Lord Faringdon; Prof. E. Fernie, CBE; Lady Gass; HRH The Duke of Gloucester, KG, GCVO; L. Grossman; Mrs C. Lycett-Green; Ms K. McLeod; Prof. R. Morris, FSA; Miss S. Underwood
Chief Executive, Ms P. Alexander

NATIONAL MONUMENTS RECORD, National Monuments Record Centre, Kemble Drive, Swindon SN2 2GZ. Tel: 01793-414600; fax: 01793-414606. *London Search Room:* 55 Blandford Street, London WIH 3AF. Tel: 0171-208 8200; fax: 0171-224 5333

HISTORIC BUILDINGS COUNCIL FOR SCOTLAND
Longmore House, Salisbury Place, Edinburgh EH9 ISH
Tel 0131-668 8600; fax 0131-668 8788

The Historic Buildings Council for Scotland is the advisory body to the Scottish ministers on matters related to buildings of special architectural or historical interest and in particular to proposals for awards by them of grants for the repair of buildings of outstanding architectural or historical interest or lying within outstanding conservation areas.
Chairman, Sir Raymond Johnstone, CBE
Members, R. Cairns; Mrs P. Chalmers; Mrs A. Dundas-Bekker; Dr J. Frew; D. Gauci; J. Hunter Blair; E. Jamieson; K. Martin; Revd C. Robertson; Mrs P. Robertson; Ms F. Sinclair
Secretary, Ms S. Adams

HISTORIC BUILDINGS COUNCIL FOR WALES
Cathays Park, Cardiff CF1 3NQ
Tel 01222-500200; fax 01222-826375

The Council's function is to advise the National Assembly for Wales on the built heritage through Cadw: Welsh Historic Monuments (*see* page 350), which is an executive agency of the Assembly.
Chairman, T. Lloyd, FSA
Members, Dr P. Morgan; Mrs S. Furse; Dr S. Unwin; Dr E. Wiliam; Miss E. Evans; Dr R. Wools
Secretary, Mrs J. Booker

HISTORIC ROYAL PALACES
Hampton Court Palace, East Molesey, Surrey KT8 9AU
Tel 0181-781 9500; fax 0181-781 9754

Historic Royal Palaces was formerly an executive agency of the Department for Culture, Media and Sport; it now has charitable trust status. The Secretary of State for Culture, Media and Sport is still accountable to Parliament for the care and presentation of the palaces, which are owned by the Sovereign in right of the Crown. The chairman of the trustees is appointed by The Queen on the advice of the Secretary of State.
Historic Royal Palaces is responsible for the Tower of London, Hampton Court Palace, Kensington Palace State Apartments and the Royal Ceremonial Dress Collection, Kew Palace with Queen Charlotte's Cottage, and the Banqueting House, Whitehall.

TRUSTEES
Chairman, The Earl of Airlie, KT, GCVO, PC

Appointed by The Queen, The Lord Camoys, GCVO, PC; Sir Michael Peat, KCVO; H. Roberts, CVO, FSA
Appointed by the Secretary of State, M. Herbert; Ms A. Heylin; S. Jones; Ms J. Sharman
Ex officio, Field Marshal the Lord Inge, GCB (*Constable of the Tower of London*)

OFFICERS
Chief Executive, A. Coppin
Director of Finance, Ms A. McLeish
Director of Human Resources, M. Bridger
Surveyor of the Fabric, R. Davidson
Curator, Historic Royal Palaces, Dr E. Impey
Director, Palaces Group, D. McGuinnes
Resident Governor, HM Tower of London, Maj.-Gen. G. Field, CB, OBE

Royal Commission on the Historical Monuments of England (former)
— *see* Historic Buildings and Monuments Commission for England (English Heritage)

ROYAL COMMISSION ON THE ANCIENT AND HISTORICAL MONUMENTS OF SCOTLAND
John Sinclair House, 16 Bernard Terrace, Edinburgh EH8 9NX
Tel 0131-662 1456; fax 0131-662 1477

The Royal Commission was established in 1908 and is appointed to provide for the survey and recording of ancient and historical monuments connected with the culture, civilization and conditions of life of the people in Scotland from the earliest times. It is funded by the Scottish Executive. The Commission compiles and maintains the National Monuments Record of Scotland as the national record of the archaeological and historical environment. The National Monuments Record is open for reference Monday–Thursday 9.30–4.30, Friday 9.30–4.
Chairman, Sir William Fraser, GCB, FRSE
Commissioners, Prof. J. M. Coles, Ph.D., FBA; Prof. Rosemary Cramp, CBE, FSA; Prof. T. C. Smout, CBE, FRSE, FBA; Dr Deborah Howard, FSA; Prof. R. A. Paxton, FRSE; Dr Barbara Crawford, FSA, FSA Scot.; Miss A. Riches; J. Simpson, FSA Scot.; Ms M. Mackay, Ph.D.
Secretary, R. J. Mercer, FSA, FRSE

ROYAL COMMISSION ON THE ANCIENT AND HISTORICAL MONUMENTS OF WALES
Crown Building, Plas Crug, Aberystwyth SY23 INJ
Tel 01970-621200; fax 01970-627701

The Royal Commission was established in 1908 and is currently empowered by a royal warrant of 1992 to survey, record, publish and maintain a database of ancient and historical and maritime sites and structures, and landscapes in Wales. The Commission is funded by the National Assembly for Wales and is also responsible for the National Monuments Record of Wales, which is open daily for public reference, for the supply of archaeological information to the Ordnance Survey, for the co-ordination of archaeological aerial photography in Wales, and for sponsorship of the regional Sites and Monuments Records.

Chairman, Prof. R. A. Griffiths, ph.D., D.Litt.
Commissioners, D. Gruffyd Jones; Prof. G. B. D. Jones,
    D.phil., FSA; Mrs A. Nicol; Prof. P. Sims-Williams, FBA;
    Prof. G. J. Wainwright, MBE, ph.D., FSA; E. Wiliam, ph.D.,
    FSA
Secretary, P. R. White, FSA

ANCIENT MONUMENTS BOARD FOR SCOTLAND
Longmore House, Salisbury Place, Edinburgh EH9 ISH
Tel 0131-668 8764; fax 0131-668 8765

The Ancient Monuments Board for Scotland advises the
Scottish ministers on the exercise of their functions, under
the Ancient Monuments and Archaeological Areas Act
1979, of providing protection for monuments of national
importance.
Chairman, Prof. M. Lynch, ph.D., FRSE, PSA scot.
Members, A. Wright, FRSA; Mrs K. Dalyell, FSA scot.; P.
    Clarke, FSA; Ms A. Ritchie, OBE, ph.D., FSA, FSA scot.;
    Prof. C. D. Morris, FRSE, FSA, FSA scot.; R. J. Mercer,
    FRSE, FSA, FSA scot.; Miss L. M. Thoms, FSA scot.; J.
    Higgitt, FSA; Ms C. Swanson, ph.D., FSA scot.; M.
    Baughan; Ms J. Cannizzo, ph.D.; S. Peake , ph.D.; M.
    Taylor; Ms J. Harden, FSA scot.
Secretary, R. A. J. Dalziel
Assessor, D. J. Breeze, ph.D., FRSE, FSA, FSA scot.

ANCIENT MONUMENTS BOARD FOR WALES
Cathays Park, Cardiff CFI 3NQ
Tel 01222-500200; fax 01222-826375

The Ancient Monuments Board for Wales advises the
National Assembly for Wales on its statutory functions in
respect of ancient monuments.
Chairman, Prof. R. R. Davies, CBE, D.phil., FBA
Members, R. G. Keen; Mrs F. M. Lynch Llewellyn, FSA;
    Prof. W. H. Manning, ph.D., FSA; Prof. Wendy Davies,
    ph.D., FBA; M. J. Garner; Prof. R. A. Griffiths, ph.D., D.Litt.
Secretary, Mrs J. Booker

HOME-GROWN CEREALS AUTHORITY
Caledonia House, 223 Pentonville Road, London NI 9NG
Tel 0171-520 3926; fax 0171-520 3954

Set up under the Cereals Marketing Act 1965, the Authority
consists of seven members representing UK cereal growers,
seven representing dealers in, or processors of, grain and
two independent members. The Authority's functions are
to improve the production and marketing of UK-grown
cereals and oilseeds through a research and development
programme, to provide a market information service, and
to promote UK cereals in export markets.
Chairman (part-time) (£21,324), A. Pike
Chief Executive, P. V. Biscoe

HOME OFFICE
50 Queen Anne's Gate, London SWIH 9AT
Tel 0171-273 4000; fax 0171-273 2190
E-mail: gen.ho@gtnet.gov.uk
Web: http://www.homeoffice.gov.uk

The Home Office deals with those internal affairs in
England and Wales which have not been assigned to other
government departments. The Home Secretary is particularly concerned with the administration of justice; criminal
law; the treatment of offenders, including probation and
the prison service; the police; immigration and nationality;
passport policy matters; community relations; certain
public safety matters; and fire and civil emergencies
services. The Home Secretary personally is the link
between The Queen and the public, and exercises certain
powers on her behalf, including that of the royal pardon.
    Other subjects dealt with include electoral arrangements;
ceremonial and formal business connected with honours;
scrutiny of local authority by-laws; granting of licences for
scientific procedures involving animals; cremations, burials
and exhumations; firearms; dangerous drugs and poisons;
general policy on laws relating to shops, liquor licensing,
gaming and marriage; theatre and cinema licensing; and
race relations policy.
    The Home Secretary is also the link between the UK
government and the governments of the Channel Islands
and the Isle of Man.
Secretary of State for the Home Department, The Rt. Hon. Jack
    Straw, MP
    Principal Private Secretary (SCS), Ms H. Jackson
    Private Secretaries, Ms C. Sumner; S. Harrison; Ms M.
        Goldstein
    Special Advisers, E. Owen; J. Russell
Minister of State, The Rt. Hon. Paul Boateng, MP
    Private Secretary, S. Hayes
Minister of State, Charles Clarke, MP
    Private Secretary, Ms C. French
Minister of State, Barbara Roche, MP
    Private Secretary, J. Payne
Parliamentary Under-Secretaries of State, Michael O'Brien,
    MP; The Lord Bassam of Brighton
    Private Secretaries, T. Wright; P. Morrison
Parliamentary Clerk, Mrs J. Thorne
Permanent Under-Secretary of State (SCS), D. B. Omand
    Private Secretary, Miss A. Rutherford
Chief Medical Officer (at Department of Health), Prof. L.
    Donaldson, QHP, FRCSEd., FRCP

COMMUNICATION DIRECTORATE
Director (SCS), B. Butler
Deputy Head of Communication (Head of News) (SCS), Ms P.
    Teare
Head of Publicity and Corporate Services (SCS), Miss A. Nash
Assistant Director, News (G6), vacant
Assistant Director and Head of Information Services Group (G6),
    P. Griffiths

CONSTITUTIONAL AND COMMUNITY POLICY DIRECTORATE
Director (SCS), Miss C. Sinclair
Heads of Units (SCS), Mrs G. Catto; R. Evans; M. de
    Pulford; E. Grant; L. Hughes; Ms S. Marshall; N.
    Varney

ANIMALS (SCIENTIFIC PROCEDURES) INSPECTORATE
Chief Inspector (SCS), Dr J. Richmond
Superintendent Inspector (SCS), Dr J. Anderson
Inspectors (G6), Dr R. Curtis; Dr V. Navaratnam; Dr C.
    Wilkins

GAMING BOARD FOR GREAT BRITAIN
— *see* page 302

CORPORATE DEVELOPMENT DIRECTORATE
Director (SCS), Dr D. Pepper
Heads of Units (SCS), T. Edwards; Ms S. Rae; Ms E.
    Sparrow; C. Welsh; S. Wharton

Senior Principals (G6), Mrs C. Burrows; S. Thornton; T. Williams

CORPORATE RESOURCES DIRECTORATE
Grenadier House, 99–105 Horseferry Road, London SW1P 2DD
Tel 0171-273 4000
Queen Anne's Gate, London SW1H 9AT
Tel 0171-273 4000
Director (SCS), Ms L. Lockyer
Heads of Units (SCS), T. Cobley; Ms E. Moody
Senior Principals (G6), R. Creedon; A. Ford; J. G. Jones; D. Rigby

CRIMINAL POLICY group
Directors (SCS), J. Halliday, CB; W. Fittall; Mrs S. Street
Heads of Units (SCS), S. Atkins; M. Boyle; Ms K. Bramwell; Ms C. Byrne; I. Chisholm; J. Duke-Evans; S. Hickson; H. Marriage; A. Norbury; J. Powls; Miss C. Stewart; J. Thompson; H. Webber
Senior Principals (G6), J. Furniss; Mrs A. Johnstone; A. Macfarlane; J. Nicholson; Ms L. Rogerson; S. Thornton

HOME OFFICE CRIME PREVENTION COLLEGE
The Hawkhills, Easingwold, York YO6 3EG
Tel 01347-825060
Director, S. Trimmins

HM INSPECTORATE OF PROBATION
Chief Inspector (SCS), Sir Graham Smith, CBE
Assistant Chief Inspector (G6), G. Childs

FIRE AND EMERGENCY PLANNING DIRECTORATE
Horseferry House, Dean Ryle Street, London SW1P 2AW
Tel 0171-273 4000
50 Queen Anne's Gate, London SW1H 9AT
Tel 0171-273 4000
Director (SCS), C. Everett
Heads of Units (SCS), P. Davies; E. Guy; Mrs V. Harris; Miss S. Hart; Dr D. Peace

HM FIRE SERVICE INSPECTORATE
HM Chief Inspector, G. Meldrum, CBE, QFSM
HM Territorial Inspectors, A. R. Currie, OBE, QFSM; P. Morphew, QFSM; A. Rule, QFSM; J. G. Russel, QFSM
Lay Inspector, vacant
HM Inspectors, R. A. M. Baillie, QFSM; D. Berry; G. P. Bowles; S. D. Christian; D. Kent; C. Moseley; R. Pearce; E. G. Pearn, OBE, QFSM; K. Phillips; M. Robinson; B. J. Unger; A. C. Wells, QFSM
Principal (G7), Miss G. Kirton

EMERGENCY PLANNING COLLEGE
The Hawkhills, Easingwold, Yorks YO6 3EG
Tel 01347-821406

IMMIGRATION AND NATIONALITY DIRECTORATE, AND EU AND INTERNATIONAL UNIT
Whitgift Centre, Block A, 15 Wellesley Road, Croydon, Surrey CR9 3LY
Tel 0181-686 7766
Apollo House, 36 Wellesley Road, Croydon, Surrey CR9 3RR
Tel 0181-686 0333
50 Queen Anne's Gate, London SW1H 9AT
Tel 0171-273 4000
India Buildings, 3rd Floor, Water Street, Liverpool L2 0QN
Tel 0151-237 5200

Director-General (SCS), S. Boys Smith
Deputy Directors-General (SCS), M. J. Eland (*Policy*); Miss K. Collins (*Operations*); Dr C. Mace (*Projects*)
Heads of Directorates (SCS), J. Acton; Miss V. M. Dews; B. Eagle; Mrs E. C. L. Pallett; J. Potts; R. M. Whalley; R. G. Yates
Senior Principals (G6), P. Dawson; B. Downie; P. Wheelhouse

IMMIGRATION SERVICE
Director (Ports) (SCS), T. Farrage, CBE
Deputy Director (G6), V. Hogg
Director (Enforcement) (SCS), I. Boon
Deputy Director (G6), C. Harbin

EU AND INTERNATIONAL UNIT
Head of Unit (SCS), P. Edwards

LEGAL ADVISERS' BRANCH
Legal Adviser (SCS), Miss J. Wheldon, CB
Deputy Legal Advisers (SCS), Mrs S. A. Evans; T. Middleton
Assistant Legal Advisers (SCS), R. J. Clayton; J. R. O'Meara; R. Green; S. A. Parker

ORGANIZED AND INTERNATIONAL CRIME DIRECTORATE
Director (SCS), J. Warne

PLANNING AND FINANCE DIRECTORATE
50 Queen Anne's Gate, London SW1H 9AT
Tel 0171-273 4000
Horseferry House, Dean Ryle Street, London SW1P 2AW
Tel 0171-273 4000
Director (SCS), R. Fulton
Heads of Units (SCS), C. Harnett; A. Mortimer
Senior Principal (G6), P. Dare

POLICE POLICY DIRECTORATE
Director (SCS), J. Lyon
Heads of Units (SCS), N. Benger; Miss D. Loudon
Senior Principal (G6), R. Ginman

NATIONAL DIRECTORATE OF POLICE TRAINING
National Director of Police Training, P. Hermitage, QPM

Corporate Services
Senior Principal (G6), S. Wells

NATIONAL POLICE TRAINING
Bramshill House, Bramshill, Hook, Hants RG27 0JW
Tel 01256-602100
Head of Higher Training, I. McDonald

HENDON DATA CENTRE
Aerodrome Road, Colindale, London NW9 5LN
Tel 0181-200 2424

Head of Unit (G6), J. Ladley

POLICE SCIENTIFIC DEVELOPMENT BRANCH
Sandridge, St Albans, Herts AL4 9HQ
Tel 01727-865051

Director (SCS), B. R. Coleman, OBE
Chief Scientist/Deputy Director (G6), Dr P. Young

Langhurst House, Langhurstwood Road, Nr Horsham, W. Sussex RH12 4WX
Tel 01403-255451
Head of Langhurst Facility (G6), Dr G. Thomas

HM INSPECTORATE OF CONSTABULARY
HM Chief Inspector of Constabulary (SCS), Sir David O'Dowd, CBE, QPM

HM Inspectors (SCS), D. Crompton, CBE, QPM; K. Povey, QPM; C. Smith, CBE, CVO, QPM; P. J. Winship, CBE, QPM; D. Blakey, CBE, QPM
Senior Principal (G6), L. Davidoff

METROPOLITAN POLICE COMMITTEE AND SECRETARIAT
Clive House, Petty France, London SW1H 9HD
Tel 0171-273 4000
Head of Secretariat (SCS), P. Honour

RESEARCH, DEVELOPMENT AND STATISTICS DIRECTORATE
Director (SCS), Dr P. Wiles
Heads of Units (SCS), Dr G. Laycock; C. Lewis; D. Moxon; R. Price; P. Ward; Dr J. Youell
Senior Principals (G6), G. Barclay; Ms M. Colledge; P. Collier; Mrs P. Dowdeswell; Ms M. FitzGerald; P. Goldblatt; Mrs C. Lehman; Mrs P. Mayhew, OBE; R. Walmsley; B. Webb

STRATEGY UNIT
Head of Unit (SCS), R. Weatherill

HM INSPECTORATE OF PRISONS
HM Chief Inspector, Gen. Sir David Ramsbotham, GCB, CBE
HM Deputy Chief Inspector, C. Allen
HM Inspectors (Governor 1), R. Jacques; G. Hughes

PRISONS OMBUDSMAN
— *see* page 331

PAROLE BOARD FOR ENGLAND AND WALES
— *see* page 329

HM PRISON SERVICE
— *see* pages 380–2

FIRE SERVICE COLLEGE
Moreton-in-Marsh, Glos GL56 0RH
Tel 01608-650831

An executive agency of the Home Office.
Chief Executive and Commandant, T. Glossop, QFSM
College Secretary, P. Taylor

UK PASSPORT AGENCY
Clive House, Petty France, London SW1H 9HD
Tel 0171-799 2728

An executive agency of the Home Office.
Chief Executive (SCS), B. L. Herdan
Deputy Chief Executive and Director of Operations (G6), K. J. Sheehan
Director of Systems (G6), J. Davies

CRIMINAL RECORDS BUREAU, Room 466/68, India Buildings, Water Street, Liverpool L2 0UZ. Tel: 0151-224 8068. *Programme Manager (G6)*, G. Ryan

HORSERACE TOTALISATOR BOARD
74 Upper Richmond Road, London SW15 2SU
Tel 0181-874 6411; fax 0181-874 6107

The Horserace Totalisator Board (the Tote) was established by the Betting, Gaming and Lotteries Act 1963. Its function is to operate totalisators on approved racecourses in Great Britain, and it also provides on- and off-course cash and credit offices. Under the Horserace Totalisator and Betting Levy Board Act 1972, it is further empowered to offer bets at starting price (or other bets at fixed odds) on any sporting event, and under the Horserace Totalisator Board Act 1997 to take bets on any event, except the National Lottery. The chairman and members of the Board are appointed by the Home Secretary.

The Government announced in May 1999 that the Tote would be made available for sale, subject to the necessary legislation going through Parliament.
Chairman (£78,225), P. I. Jones
Chief Executive, W. J. Heaton

HOUSE OF LORDS, ROYAL COMMISSION ON THE REFORM OF
— *see* Royal Commission on the Reform of the House of Lords

HOUSING CORPORATION
149 Tottenham Court Road, London W1P 0BN
Tel 0171-393 2000; fax 0171-393 2111

Established by Parliament in 1964, the Housing Corporation regulates, funds and promotes the proper performance of registered social landlords, which are non-profit making bodies run by voluntary committees. There are over 2,200 registered social landlords, most of which are housing associations, and they now provide homes for more than 1.5 million people. Under the Housing Act 1996, the Corporation's regulatory role was widened to embrace new types of landlords, in particular local housing companies. The Corporation is funded by the Department of the Environment, Transport and the Regions.
Chairman, The Baroness Dean of Thornton-le-Fylde, PC
Deputy Chairman, E. Armitage
Chief Executive, A. Mayer

HUMAN FERTILIZATION AND EMBRYOLOGY AUTHORITY
Paxton House, 30 Artillery Lane, London E1 7LS
Tel 0171-377 5077; fax 0171-377 1871

The Human Fertilization and Embryology Authority (HFEA) was established under the Human Fertilization and Embryology Act 1990. Its function is to license persons carrying out any of the following activities: the creation or use of embryos outside the body in the provision of infertility treatment services; the use of donated gametes in infertility treatment; the storage of gametes or embryos; and research on human embryos. It maintains a confidential database of all such treatments and of egg and sperm donors, and provides information to patients, clinics and the public. The HFEA also keeps under review information about embryos and, when requested to do so, gives advice to the Secretary of State for Health.
Chairman, Mrs R. Deech
Deputy Chairman, Mrs J. Denton
Members, Prof. Brenda Almond; Dr G. Bahadur; Prof. D. Barlow; Mrs M. E. Coath; Prof. Christine Gosden; Prof. A. Grubb; Prof. H. Leese; Prof. S. Lewis; Dr B. Lieberman; Dr Anne McLaren; Dr S. Muhammed; Ms S. Nathan; Ms S. Nebhrajani; The Rt. Revd Bishop of Rochester; Dr Joan Stringer; Prof. A. Templeton; Julia, Lady Tugendhat; Prof. J. Williams
Chief Executive, Mrs S. McCarthy

HUMAN GENETICS ADVISORY COMMISSION
Room 1/5, Albany House, 94–98 Petty France, London
SW1H 9ST
Tel 0171-271 2131; fax 0171-271 2028

The Human Genetics Advisory Commission was established in 1996. It is an advisory body with the remit of taking a broad view of developments in human genetics and advising ministers on ways to build public confidence in the application of the new science. Members of the Commission are appointed by the Secretary of State for Trade and Industry and the Secretary of State for Health.
Chairman, The Baroness O'Neill, CBE, FBA
Members, Prof. C. Aitken, CBE; Dr Michaela Aldred; Prof.
  M. Bobrow; Mrs D. Littlejohn, CBE; Prof. N. Nevin; Dr
  G. Poste, FRS; Revd Dr J. Polkinghorne, KBE, FRS; Ms
  M. Stuart
Head of Secretariat, Dr Amanda Goldin

INDEPENDENT COMMISSION FOR POLICE COMPLAINTS FOR NORTHERN IRELAND
Chamber of Commerce House, 22 Great Victoria Street,
Belfast BT2 7LP
Tel 01232-244821; fax 01232-248563

The Independent Commission for Police Complaints was established under the Police (Northern Ireland) Order 1987. It has powers to supervise the investigation of certain categories of serious complaints, can direct that disciplinary charges be brought, and has oversight of the informal resolution procedure for less serious complaints.
  Under the Police (Northern Ireland) Act 1998 the Commission will be replaced by a Police Ombudsman. This is expected to happen in early 2000.
Chairman, P. A. Donnelly
Chief Executive, B. McClelland

INDEPENDENT HOUSING OMBUDSMAN
Norman House, 105–109 Strand, London WC2R 0AA
Tel 0171-836 3630; 0345-125973; fax 0171-836 3900

The Independent Housing Ombudsman was established in 1997 under the Housing Act 1996. The Ombudsman deals with complaints against registered social landlords (not including local authorities).
Ombudsman, R. Jefferies
Chair of Board, Ms P. Brown
General Manager, L. Greenberg

INDEPENDENT INTERNATIONAL COMMISSION ON DECOMMISSIONING
Dublin Castle, Block M, Ship Street, Dublin 2
Tel 00 353 1-478 0111; fax 00 353 1-478 0600
Rosepark House, Upper Newtownards Road, Belfast BT4
3NX
Tel 01232-488600; fax 01232-488601

The Commission was established by agreement between the British and Irish governments in August 1997. Its objective is to facilitate the decommissioning of illegally-held firearms and explosives in accordance with the relevant legislation in both jurisdictions. Its members are appointed jointly by the two governments; staff are appointed by the Commission. All are drawn from countries other than the UK and the Republic of Ireland.
Chairman, Gen. J. de Chastelain (Canada)
Commissioners, Brig. T. Nieminen (Finland); Ambassador
  D. C. Johnson (USA)
Chief of Staff, C. E. Garrard (Canada)

INDEPENDENT REVIEW SERVICE FOR THE SOCIAL FUND
4th Floor, Centre City Podium, 5 Hill Street, Birmingham
B5 4UB
Tel 0121-606 2100; fax 0121-606 2180

The Social Fund Commissioner is appointed by the Secretary of State for Social Security. The Commissioner appoints Social Fund Inspectors, who provide an independent review of decisions made by Social Fund Officers in the Benefits Agency of the Department of Social Security.
Social Fund Commissioner, J. Scampion

INDEPENDENT TELEVISION COMMISSION
33 Foley Street, London W1P 7LB
Tel 0171-255 3000; fax 0171-306 7800

The Independent Television Commission replaced the Independent Broadcasting Authority in 1991. The Commission is responsible for licensing and regulating all commercially funded television services broadcast from the UK. Members are appointed by the Secretary of State for Culture, Media and Sport.
Chairman (£67,420), Sir Robin Biggam
Deputy Chairman (£17,300), The Lord Holme of
  Cheltenham, CBE
Members (*part-time*) (£12,980), A. Balls, CB; Dr J. Beynon,
  FREng.; Sir Michael Checkland; Ms J. Goffe; Dr Maria
  Moloney; Prof. D. L. Morgan, D.Phil. (*Member for Wales*);
  J. Ranelagh; Dr M. Shea, CVO (*Member for Scotland*)
Chief Executive (£175,000), P. Rogers
Secretary and Director of Administration, M. Redley

INDUSTRIAL INJURIES ADVISORY COUNCIL
6th Floor, The Adelphi, 1–11 John Adam Street, London
WC2N 6HT
Tel 0171-962 8066; fax 0171-712 2255

The Industrial Injuries Advisory Council is a statutory body under the Social Security Administration Act 1992 which considers and advises the Secretary of State for Social Security on regulations and other questions relating to industrial injuries benefits or their administration.
Chairman, Prof. A. J. Newman Taylor, OBE, FRCP
Secretary, A. Packer

BOARD OF INLAND REVENUE
Somerset House, Strand, London WC2R 1LB
Tel 0171-438 6622

The Board of Inland Revenue was constituted under the Inland Revenue Board Act 1849. The Board administers and collects direct taxes – income tax, corporation tax, capital gains tax, inheritance tax, stamp duty, and petroleum revenue tax – and advises the Chancellor of the Exchequer on policy questions involving them. The Department's Valuation Office is an executive agency responsible for valuing property for tax purposes. The Contributions Agency of the Department of Social Security, which is responsible for the collection of contributions under the National Insurance scheme, became part of the Inland Revenue in April 1999 and is now an executive office called the National Insurance Contributions Office. The Contributions Unit of the Social Security Agency in Northern Ireland also transferred to the Inland Revenue in April 1999.

THE BOARD

Chairman (*G1*), N. Montagu, CB
  Private Secretary, Ms C. Lunney
Deputy Chairmen (*G2*), S. C. T. Matheson, CB; G. H. Bush, CB
Director-General (*G2*), T. J. Flesher

DIVISIONS

Director, Human Resources Division (*G3*), J. Gant
Director, Business and Management Services Division (*G3*), J. Yard
Head, Strategy and Planning Division, P. Wardle
Principal Finance Officer (*G3*), R. R. Martin
Director, Business Operations Division (*G3*), D. A. Smith
Director, Statistics and Economics Division (*G3*), R. G. Ward
Director, Business Tax Division (*G3*), Ms J. Williams
Director, Management Services Unit (*G3*), K. Hodgson
Director, International Division (*G3*), G. Makhlouf
Director, Compliance Division (*G3*), E. J. Gribbon
Director, Personal Tax Division (*G3*), B. A. Mace
Director, Capital and Savings Division (*G3*), D. Hartnett

EXECUTIVE OFFICES

ACCOUNTS OFFICE (CUMBERNAULD), St Mungo's Road, Cumbernauld, Glasgow G70 5TR. *Director*, A. Geddes, OBE
ACCOUNTS OFFICE (SHIPLEY), Shipley, Bradford, W. Yorks BD98 8AA. *Director*, R. J. Warner
CAPITAL TAXES OFFICE, Ferrers House, PO Box 38, Castle Meadow Road, Nottingham NG2 1BB. *Director*, E. McKeegan
CAPITAL TAXES OFFICE (SCOTLAND), Mulberry House, 16 Picardy Place, Edinburgh EH1 3NB. *Registrar*, Mrs J. Templeton
COMMUNICATIONS UNITS, North-West Wing, Bush House, London WC2B 4PP. *Head of External Communications Unit*, P. Whyatt; *Head of Internal Communications Unit*, Ms N. Walters
ENFORCEMENT OFFICE, Durrington Bridge House, Barrington Road, Worthing, W. Sussex BN12 4SE. *Director*, Mrs C. A. Mellor
FINANCIAL ACCOUNTING OFFICE, South Block, Barrington Road, Worthing, W. Sussex BN12 4XH. *Director*, J. D. Easey
FINANCIAL INTERMEDIARIES AND CLAIMS OFFICE, St John's House, Merton Road, Bootle L26 9BB; Fitz Roy House, PO Box 46, Castle Meadow, Nottingham NG2 1BD. *Director*, J. Johnson
INTERNAL AUDIT OFFICE, North-West Wing, Bush House, London WC2B 4PP. *Director*, N. R. Buckley
NATIONAL INSURANCE CONTRIBUTIONS OFFICE, DSS Longbenton, Benton Park Road, Newcastle upon Tyne NE98 1YX. *Chief Executive* (*G3*), G. Bertram, CB
OIL TAXATION OFFICE, Melbourne House, Aldwych, London WC2B 4LL. *Director*, G. Nield

PENSION SCHEME OFFICE, Yorke House, PO Box 62, Castle Meadow Road, Nottingham NG2 1BG. *Director*, S. J. McManus
SOLICITOR'S OFFICE, East Wing, Somerset House, London WC2R 1LB. *Solicitor* (*G2*), P. Ridd
SOLICITOR'S OFFICE (SCOTLAND), Clarendon House, 114–116 George Street, Edinburgh EH2 4LH. *Solicitor*, I. K. Laing
SPECIAL COMPLIANCE OFFICE, Angel Court, 199 Borough High Street, London SE1 1HZ. *Director*, F. J. Brannigan
STAMP OFFICE, South-West Wing, Bush House, Strand, London WC2B 4QN. *Director*, K. S. Hodgson, OBE
TRAINING OFFICE, Lawress Hall, Riseholme Park, Lincoln LN2 2BJ. *Director*, T. Kuczys

REGIONAL EXECUTIVE OFFICES

INLAND REVENUE EAST, Churchgate, New Road, Peterborough PE1 1TD. *Director*, M. J. Hodgson
INLAND REVENUE LARGE BUSINESS OFFICE, 6th Floor, North-West Wing, Bush House, Strand, London WC2B 4BB. *Director*, Mrs M. E. Williams
INLAND REVENUE LONDON, New Court, Carey Street, London WC2A 2JE. *Director*, J. F. Carling
INLAND REVENUE NORTH, Ground Floor, Regent House, 10 Commercial Street, Darlington DL3 6JF. *Director*, R. Cooke
INLAND REVENUE NORTH-WEST, The Triad, Stanley Road, Bootle, Merseyside L75 2DD. *Director*, G. W. Lunn
INLAND REVENUE SOUTH-EAST, Dukes Court, Dukes Street, Woking GU21 5XR. *Director*, T. Sleeman
INLAND REVENUE SOUTH-WEST, 3rd Floor, Longbrook House, New North Road, Exeter EX4 4UA. *Director*, R. S. Hurcombe
INLAND REVENUE SOUTH YORKSHIRE, Concept House, 5 Young Street, Sheffield S1 4LF. *Director*, Ms M. Hay
INLAND REVENUE WALES AND MIDLANDS, 1st Floor, Phase II Building, Ty Glas Avenue, Llanishen, Cardiff CF4 5TS; 550 Streetsbrook Road, Solihull, West Midlands B91 1QU. *Director*, M. W. Kirk
INLAND REVENUE SCOTLAND, Clarendon House, 114–116 George Street, Edinburgh EH2 4LH. *Director*, I. S. Gerrie
INLAND REVENUE NORTHERN IRELAND, Dorchester House, 52–58 Great Victoria Street, Belfast BT2 7QE. *Director*, D. Hinstridge

VALUATION OFFICE AGENCY

New Court, 48 Carey Street, London WC2A 2JE
Tel 0171-506 1700; fax 0171-506 1998
50 Frederick Street, Edinburgh EH2 1NG
Tel 0131-465 0700; fax 0131-465 0799

Chief Executive, M. A. Johns
Chief Valuer, Scotland, A. Ainslie

ADJUDICATOR'S OFFICE
— *see* page 277

INTELLIGENCE SERVICES TRIBUNAL

PO Box 4823, London SW1A 9XD
Tel 0171-273 4383

The Intelligence Services Act 1994 established a tribunal of three senior members of the legal profession, independent of the Government and appointed by The Queen, to investigate complaints from any person about anything which they believe the Secret Intelligence Service or the

Government Communications Headquarters has done to them or to their property.
President, The Rt. Hon. Lord Justice Simon Brown
Vice-President, Sheriff J. McInnes, QC
Member, Sir Richard Gaskell
Secretary, N. Brooks

INTERCEPTION COMMISSIONER

c/o PO Box 12376, London SW1P 1XU
Tel 0171-273 4096

The Commissioner is appointed by the Prime Minister. He keeps under review the issue by Secretaries of State of warrants under the Interception of Communications Act 1985 and safeguards made in respect of intercepted material obtained through the use of such warrants. He is also required to give all such assistance as the Interception of Communications Tribunal may require to enable it to carry out its functions, and to submit an annual report to the Prime Minister with respect to the carrying out of his functions.
Commissioner, The Lord Nolan, PC
  Private Secretary, N. Brooks

INTERCEPTION OF COMMUNICATIONS TRIBUNAL

PO Box 12376, London SW1P 1XU
Tel 0171-273 4096

Under the Interception of Communications Act 1985, the Tribunal is required to investigate complaints from any person who believes that communications sent to or by them have been intercepted in the course of their transmission by post or by means of a public telecommunications system. The Tribunal comprises senior members of the legal profession, who are appointed by The Queen.
President, Sir William Macpherson of Cluny
Vice-President, Sir David Calcutt, QC
Members, P. Scott, QC; R. Seabrook, QC; W. Carmichael
Secretary, N. Brooks

DEPARTMENT FOR INTERNATIONAL DEVELOPMENT

94 Victoria Street, London SW1E 5JL
Tel 0171-917 7000; fax 0171-917 0016
Web: http://www.dfid.gov.uk
Abercrombie House, Eaglesham Road, East Kilbride, Glasgow G75 8EA
Tel 01355-844000; fax 01355-844099

The Department for International Development (DFID) was established in May 1997 from the former Overseas Development Administration of the Foreign and Commonwealth Office. It takes the lead on British policy towards developing countries. It also manages the development assistance budget, including financial aid and technical assistance (specialist staff abroad and training facilities in the UK), whether provided directly to developing countries or through the various multilateral aid organizations, including the EU, the World Bank and the UN agencies.
Secretary of State for International Development, The Rt. Hon. Clare Short, MP
  Private Secretary, A. Smith
  Special Advisers, D. Harris; D. Mepham
  Parliamentary Private Secretary, D. Turner, MP

Parliamentary Under-Secretary, George Foulkes, MP
Permanent Secretary (SCS), Sir John Vereker, KCB
  Private Secretary, M. James

PROGRAMMES

Director-General (SCS), B. R. Ireton
Head, Conflict and Humanitarian Affairs Department (SCS), Dr M. Kapila

AFRICA
Director (SCS), P. D. M. Freeman
Heads of Departments (SCS), Mrs B. M. Kelly, CBE (*Africa, Greater Horn and Co-ordination*); B. Thomson (*West and North Africa*); D. Fish (*Nairobi*); J. R. Drummond (*Harare*); J. H. S. Chard (*Pretoria*)

ASIA
Director (SCS), S. Unsworth
Heads of Departments (SCS), C. Myhill (*East Asia and Pacific*); R. Graham-Harrison (*India*); Ms M. H. Vowles (*Western Asia*); A. K. C. Wood (*South-East Asia*); K. L. Sparkhall (*Bangladesh*); Ms S. Wardell (*Nepal*); Ms J. Creighton (*Pacific*)

EASTERN EUROPE AND WESTERN HEMISPHERE
Director (SCS), J. Kerby
Heads of Departments (SCS), A. Coverdale (*Eastern Europe and Central Asia*); J. S. Laing (*Central and South-Eastern Europe*); B. P. Thomson (*Caribbean*)
Heads of Departments, D. R. Curran (*Latin America, Caribbean and Atlantic*); J. D. Moye (*EBRD Unit*)

ECONOMICS, STATISTICS AND ENTERPRISE
Director, and Chief Economic Adviser (SCS), A. Coverdale
Chief Statistician (SCS), A. B. Williams
Head, Asia Regional and Economic Policy, P. J. Ackroyd
Head, Africa Policy and Economics, P. J. Landymore
Head, Development Economics Research (SCS), P. D. Grant
Head, Enterprise Development, D. L. Wright
Head, Governance Department (SCS), R. J. Wilson

HUMAN RESOURCE DEVELOPMENT
Chief Health and Population Adviser (acting), Ms J. Cleves
Chief Social Development Adviser (SCS), Dr R. Eyben
Chief Education Adviser (SCS), Ms M. A. Harrison

RURAL LIVELIHOODS AND ENVIRONMENT
Director, and Chief Natural Resources Adviser (SCS), A. J. Bennett, CMG
Head, Environment Policy Department (SCS), D. P. Turner
Head, Natural Resources Policy and Advisory Department, and Deputy Chief Natural Resources Adviser (SCS), J. M. Scott
Head, Natural Resources Research Department (SCS), Dr J. Tarbit, OBE
Senior Environment and Research Adviser, Ms L. C. Brown
Senior Fisheries Adviser, R. W. Beales
Senior Forestry Advisers, J. M. Hudson; I. A. Napier
Senior Animal Health Advisers, G. G. Freeland; Ms L. M. Bell
Chief Engineering Adviser and Head, Infrastructure and Urban Development Department (SCS), J. W. Hodges

RESOURCES
Director-General (SCS), R. G. Manning
Heads of Departments (SCS), M. J. Dinham (*Head of Personnel and Principal Establishment Officer*); D. Sands-Smith (*Procurement, Appointments and NGO*); R. Calvert (*Information*); G. M. Stegmann (*Head, Aid Policy and Resources and Principal Finance Officer*); A. D. Davis (*Information Systems and Services*); R. A. Elias (*Internal Audit Unit*); C. P. Raleigh (*Evaluation*)
Head of Department, R. Plumb (*Overseas Pensions*)

INTERNATIONAL DEVELOPMENT AFFAIRS
Director (SCS), J. A. L. Faint
Heads of Departments (SCS), M. Lowcock (*European Union*);
D. J. Batt (*International Economic Policy*); G. Toulmin
(*United Nations and Commonwealth*); M. E. Cund
(*International Financial Institutions*)

INTERVENTION BOARD
PO Box 69, Reading RGI 3YD
Tel 0118-958 3626; fax 0118-953 1370

The Intervention Board was established as a government department in 1972 and became an executive agency in 1990. The Board is responsible for the implementation of European Union regulations covering the market support arrangements of the Common Agricultural Policy. Members are appointed by and are responsible to the four agriculture ministers in the UK.
Chairman, I. Kent
Chief Executive (G3), G. Trevelyan
Directors (G5), H. MacKinnon (*Operations*); J. P. Bradbury (*Operations*, Newcastle); Mrs A. Parker (*Corporate Services*); P. Kent (*Legal*); G. Trantham (*Finance*)

LAND REGISTRIES

HM LAND REGISTRY
Lincoln's Inn Fields, London WC2A 3PH
Tel 0171-917 8888; fax 0171-955 0110

The registration of title to land was first introduced in England and Wales by the Land Registry Act 1862; HM Land Registry operates today under the Land Registration Acts 1925 to 1988. The object of registering title to land is to create and maintain a register of landowners whose title is guaranteed by the state and so to simplify the transfer, mortgage and other dealings with real property. Registration on sale is now compulsory throughout England and Wales. The register has been open to inspection by the public since 1990.

HM Land Registry is an executive agency administered under the Lord Chancellor by the Chief Land Registrar.

HEADQUARTERS OFFICE
Chief Land Registrar and Chief Executive, P. Collis
Solicitor to Land Registry, C. J. West
Director of Corporate Services, E. G. Beardsall
Senior Land Registrar, J. V. Timothy
Director of Operations, A. Howarth
Director of Information Technology, P. J. Smith, OBE
Director of Management Services, P. R. Laker
Land Registrar, M. L. Wood
Deputy Establishment Officer, J. Hodder
Controller of Operations Development, P. Norman
Head of Legal Practice, P. Morris
Head of Survey and Plans Practice, M. K. Brown

COMPUTER SERVICES DIVISION
Burrington Way, Plymouth PL5 3LP
Tel 01752-635600
Head of IT Services Division, P. A. Maycock
Head of IT Development Division, J. Formby
Head of National Land Information Service (NLIS), P. Sizer
Head of IT Management Services, K. Deards

LAND CHARGES AND AGRICULTURAL CREDITS DEPARTMENT
Burrington Way, Plymouth PL5 3LP
Tel 01752-635600

Superintendent of Land Charges, J. Hughes

DISTRICT LAND REGISTRIES
BIRKENHEAD (OLD MARKET HOUSE) – Old Market House, Hamilton Street, Birkenhead L41 5FL. Tel: 0151-473 1110. *District Land Registrar*, P. J. Brough
BIRKENHEAD (ROSEBRAE COURT) – Rosebrae Court, Woodside Ferry Approach, Birkenhead L41 6DU. Tel: 0151-472 6666. *District Land Registrar*, M. G. Garwood
COVENTRY – Leigh Court, Torrington Avenue, Coventry CV4 9XZ. Tel: 01203-860860. *District Land Registrar*, T. H. O. Lewis
CROYDON – Sunley House, Bedford Park, Croydon CR9 3LE. Tel: 0181-781 9100. *District Land Registrar*, F. M. Twambley
DURHAM (BOLDON HOUSE) – Boldon House, Wheatlands Way, Pity Me, Durham DH1 5GJ. Tel: 0191-301 2345. *District Land Registrar*, R. B. Fearnley
DURHAM (SOUTHFIELD HOUSE) – Southfield House, Southfield Way, Durham DH1 5TR. Tel: 0191-301 3500. *District Land Registrar*, P. J. Timothy
GLOUCESTER – Twyver House, Bruton Way, Gloucester GL1 1DQ. Tel: 01452-511111. *District Land Registrar*, W. W. Budden
HARROW – Lyon House, Lyon Road, Harrow, Middx HA1 2EU. Tel: 0181-235 1181. *District Land Registrar*, C. Tate
KINGSTON UPON HULL – Earle House, Portland Street, Hull HU2 8JN. Tel: 01482-223244. *District Land Registrar*, S. R. Coveney
LANCASHIRE – Birkenhead House, East Beach, Lytham, Lancs FY8 5AB. Tel: 01253-849849. *District Land Registrar*, Mrs L. Wallwork
LEICESTER – Westbridge Place, Leicester LE3 5DR. Tel: 0116-265 4000. *District Land Registrar*, Mrs J. A. Goodfellow
LYTHAM – Birkenhead House, East Beach, Lytham, Lancs FY8 5AB. Tel: 01253-849849. *District Land Registrar*, J. G. Cooper
NOTTINGHAM (EAST) – Robins Wood Road, Nottingham NG8 3RQ. Tel: 0115-906 5353. *District Land Registrar*, P. A. Brown
NOTTINGHAM (WEST) – Chalfont Drive, Nottingham NG8 3RN. Tel: 0115-935 1166. *District Land Registrar*, Ms A. M. Goss
PETERBOROUGH – Touthill Close, City Road, Peterborough PE1 1XN. Tel: 01733-288288. *District Land Registrar*, C. W. Martin
PLYMOUTH – Plumer House, Tailyour Road, Crownhill, Plymouth PL6 5HY. Tel: 01752-636000. *District Land Registrar*, A. J. Pain
PORTSMOUTH – St Andrews Court, St Michael's Road, Portsmouth PO1 2JH. Tel: 01705-768888. *District Land Registrar*, S. R. Sehrawat
STEVENAGE – Brickdale House, Swingate, Stevenage, Herts SG1 1XG. Tel: 01438-788888. *District Land Registrar*, M. Croker
SWANSEA – Ty Bryn Glas, High Street, Swansea SA1 1PW. Tel: 01792-458877. *District Land Registrar*, T. M. Lewis
TELFORD – Parkside Court, Hall Park Way, Telford TF3 4LR. Tel: 01952-290355. *District Land Registrar*, A. M. Lewis
TUNBRIDGE WELLS – Forest Court, Forest Road, Tunbridge Wells, Kent TN2 5AQ. Tel: 01892-510015. *District Land Registrar*, G. R. Tooke
WALES – Ty Cwm Tave, Phoenix Way, Llansamlet, Swansea SA7 9FQ. Tel: 01792-355000. *District Land Registrar*, G. A. Hughes
WEYMOUTH – Melcombe Court, 1 Cumberland Drive, Weymouth, Dorset DT4 9TT. Tel: 01305-363636. *District Land Registrar*, Mrs P. M. Reeson

YORK – James House, James Street, York YO1 3YZ. Tel: 01904-450000. *District Land Registrar*, Mrs R. F. Lovel

REGISTERS OF SCOTLAND
Meadowbank House, 153 London Road, Edinburgh EH8 7AU
Tel 0131-659 6111; fax 0131-479 3688

Registers of Scotland is an executive agency of the Scottish Executive. It is responsible for framing and maintaining records relating to property and other legal documents. The agency holds 15 registers: two property registers (General Register of Sasines and Land Register of Scotland) and 13 chancery and judicial registers (Register of Deeds in the Books of Council and Session; Register of Protests; Register of Judgments; Register of Service of Heirs; Register of the Great Seal; Register of the Quarter Seal; Register of the Prince's Seal; Register of Crown Grants; Register of Sheriffs' Commissions; Register of the Cachet Seal; Register of Inhibitions and Adjudications; Register of Entails; and Register of Hornings).

Chief Executive and Keeper of the Registers of Scotland, A. W. Ramage
Deputy Keeper, A. G. Rennie
Managing Director, F. Manson

LAW COMMISSION
Conquest House, 37–38 John Street, London WC1N 2BQ
Tel 0171-453 1220; fax 0171-453 1297

The Law Commission was set up in 1965, under the Law Commissions Act 1965, to make proposals to the Government for the examination of the law in England and Wales and for its revision where it is unsuited for modern requirements, obscure, or otherwise unsatisfactory. It recommends to the Lord Chancellor programmes for the examination of different branches of the law and suggests whether the examination should be carried out by the Commission itself or by some other body. The Commission is also responsible for the preparation of Consolidation and Statute Law (Repeals) Bills.

Chairman, The Hon. Mr Justice Carnwath, CVO
Commissioners, C. Harpum; A. S. Burrows; Miss D. Faber; S. Silber, QC
Secretary, M. W. Sayers

SCOTTISH LAW COMMISSION
140 Causewayside, Edinburgh EH9 1PR
Tel 0131-668 2131; fax 0131-662 4900

The Commission keeps the law in Scotland under review and makes proposals for its development and reform. It is responsible to the Scottish Courts Administration (*see* pages 364–5).

Chairman (part-time), The Hon. Lord Gill
Commissioners (full-time), Dr E. M. Clive; N. R. Whitty; (*part-time*) Prof. K. G. C. Reid; P. S. Hodge, QC
Secretary, N. Raven

LAW OFFICERS' DEPARTMENTS
Legal Secretariat to the Law Officers, Attorney-General's Chambers, 9 Buckingham Gate, London SW1E 6JP
Tel 0171-271 2400; fax 0171-271 2434
Attorney-General's Chambers, Royal Courts of Justice, Belfast BT1 3JY
Tel 01232-235111; fax 01232-546049

The Law Officers of the Crown for England and Wales are the Attorney-General and the Solicitor-General. The Attorney-General, assisted by the Solicitor-General, is the chief legal adviser to the Government and is also ultimately responsible for all Crown litigation. He has overall responsibility for the work of the Law Officers' Departments (the Treasury Solicitor's Department, the Crown Prosecution Service, the Serious Fraud Office and the Legal Secretariat to the Law Officers). He has a specific statutory duty to superintend the discharge of their duties by the Director of Public Prosecutions (who heads the Crown Prosecution Service) and the Director of the Serious Fraud Office. The Director of Public Prosecutions for Northern Ireland is also responsible to the Attorney-General for the performance of his functions. The Attorney-General has additional responsibilities in relation to aspects of the civil and criminal law.

Attorney-General (*£68,332), The Lord Williams of Mostyn, QC
Private Secretary, R. Cazalet
Parliamentary Private Secretary, M. Foster, MP
Solicitor-General (*£56,031), Ross Cranston, MP
Private Secretary, R. Cazalet
Legal Secretary (G2), D. Seymour
Deputy Legal Secretary (G3), S. Parkinson
* In addition to a parliamentary salary of £47,008

LEGAL AID BOARD
85 Gray's Inn Road, London WC1X 8AA
Tel 0171-813 1000

The Legal Aid Board has the general function of ensuring that advice, assistance, mediation and representation are available to those who need them within the framework of the Legal Aid Act 1988. In 1989 the Board took over from the Law Society responsibility for administering legal aid. The Board is a non-departmental government body whose members are appointed by the Lord Chancellor.

Chairman, Sir Tim Chessells
Deputy Chairman, H. Hodge, OBE
Members, S. Orchard, CBE (*Chief Executive*); M. Barnes, CBE; Ms D. Charnock; Ms J. Dunkley; P. Ely; B. Harvey; Mrs S. Hewitt; P. Hollingworth; J. Shearer

SCOTTISH LEGAL AID BOARD
44 Drumsheugh Gardens, Edinburgh EH3 7SW
Tel 0131-226 7061; fax 0131-220 4878

The Scottish Legal Aid Board was set up under the Legal Aid (Scotland) Act 1986. It is responsible for ensuring that advice, assistance and representation are available in accordance with the Act. Members are appointed by the First Minister.

Chairman, Mrs J. Couper
Members, B. C. Adair; Mrs K. Blair; Prof. P. H. Grinyer; Sheriff A. Jessop; N. Kuenssberg; D. O'Carroll; Mrs Y. Osman; Ms M. Scanlan; M. C. Thomson, QC; A. F. Wylie, QC
Chief Executive, L. Montgomery

OFFICE OF THE LEGAL SERVICES OMBUDSMAN
22 Oxford Court, Oxford Street, Manchester M2 3WQ
Tel 0161-236 9532; fax 0161-236 2651

The Legal Services Ombudsman is appointed by the Lord Chancellor under the Courts and Legal Services Act 1990

to oversee the handling of complaints against solicitors, barristers, licensed conveyancers and legal executives by their professional bodies. A complainant must first complain to the relevant professional body before raising the matter with the Ombudsman. The Ombudsman is independent of the legal profession and her services are free of charge.
Legal Services Ombudsman, Ms A. Abraham
Secretary, S. D. Entwisle

OFFICE OF THE SCOTTISH LEGAL SERVICES OMBUDSMAN
Mulberry House, 16–22 Picardy Place, Edinburgh EH1 3JT
Tel 0131-556 5574; fax 0131-556 1519
Scottish Legal Services Ombudsman, G. S. Watson

LIBRARIES

LIBRARY AND INFORMATION COMMISSION
19–29 Woburn Place, London WC1H 0LU
Tel 0171-273 8700; fax 0171-273 8701

The Commission is an independent body set up in 1995 to advise the Government and others on library and information matters, notably in the areas of research strategy and international links. It also aims to promote co-operation and co-ordination between different types of information services.
The Commission will merge with the Museums and Galleries Commission in 2000 to form the Museums, Libraries and Archives Council.
Chairman, M. Evans, CBE
Commissioners, Cllr E. Arram; Mrs L. Brindley; Sir Charles Chadwyck-Healey; Prof. M. Collier; Prof. Judith Elkin; Prof. W. Ewart, OBE; Ms G. Kempster, OBE; Dr B. Lang (*ex officio*); D. Law; Dr R. McKee; Ms C. Rayner, OBE; Dr Sandra Ward; M. Wood
Chief Executive, Ms M. Haines

THE BRITISH LIBRARY
96 Euston Road, London NW1 2DB
Tel 0171-412 7000

The British Library was established in 1973. It is the UK's national library and occupies a key position in the library and information network. The Library aims to serve scholarship, research, industry, commerce and all other major users of information. Its services are based on collections which include over 18 million volumes, 1 million discs, and 55,000 hours of tape recordings. The Library is now based at two sites: London (St Pancras and Colindale) and Boston Spa, W. Yorks. Government grant-in-aid to the British Library in 1999–2000 is £83.2 million. The Library's sponsoring department is the Department for Culture, Media and Sport.
Access to the reading rooms at St Pancras is limited to holders of a British Library Reader's Pass; information about eligibility is available from the Reader Admissions Office. The exhibition galleries and public areas are open to all, free of charge.
Opening hours of services vary; some services may close for one week each year. Specific information should be checked by telephone.
In April 1999 the British Library's research function was transferred to the Library and Information Commission.

BRITISH LIBRARY BOARD
Chairman, Dr J. M. Ashworth
Chief Executive and Deputy Chairman, Dr B. Lang
Deputy Chief Executive, D. Russon
Director-General, Collections and Services, D. Bradbury

Part-time Members, The Hon. E. Adeane, CVO; Prof. M. Anderson, FBA, FRSE; Sir Matthew Farrer, GCVO; C. G. R. Leach, PH.D.; Mrs P. M. Lively, OBE; B. Naylor; Dr Jessica Rawson, CBE, FBA; J. Ritblat; The Viscount Runciman of Doxford, CBE, FBA; P. Scherer

BRITISH LIBRARY, BOSTON SPA
Boston Spa, Wetherby, W. Yorks LS23 7BQ
Tel 01937-546000

BIBLIOGRAPHIC SERVICES AND DOCUMENT SUPPLY, *Director,* M. Smith
NATIONAL BIBLIOGRAPHIC SERVICE. Tel: 01937-546585. *Director,* R. Smith
London Unit, 96 Euston Road, London NW1 2DB. Tel: 0171-412 7077
COLLECTION MANAGEMENT, *Director,* S. Ede
INFORMATION SYSTEMS. Tel: 01937-546879. *Director,* J. R. Mahoney

BRITISH LIBRARY, ST PANCRAS
96 Euston Road, London NW1 2DB
Tel 0171-412 7000

PLANNING AND RESOURCES. Tel: 0171-412 7132
PRESS AND PUBLIC RELATIONS. Tel: 0171-412 7111
EXHIBITIONS SERVICE, EDUCATION SERVICE AND VISITOR SERVICES. Tel: 0171-412 7332

READER SERVICES AND COLLECTION DEVELOPMENT. *Director,* M. J. Crump
Reader Admissions. Tel: 0171-412 7677
Reader Services. Tel: 0171-412 7676
West European Collections, Slavonic and East European Collections, English Language Collections. Tel: 0171-412 7676
Newspaper Library, Colindale Avenue, London NW9 5HE. Tel: 0171-412 7353

PRESERVATION SERVICE (NATIONAL PRESERVATION OFFICE). Tel: 0171-412 7612

SPECIAL COLLECTIONS. Tel: 0171-412 7513. *Director,* Dr A. Prochaska
Oriental and India Office Collections. Tel: 0171-412 7873
Western Manuscripts. Tel: 0171-412 7513
Map Library. Tel: 0171-412 7700
Music Library. Tel: 0171-412 7635
Philatelic Collections. Tel: 0171-412 7729
National Sound Archive. Tel: 0171-412 7440

SCIENCE, TECHNOLOGY AND BUSINESS
Science and Technology. Tel: 0171-412 7494/7496
British and EPO Patents. Tel: 0171-412 7919
Foreign Patents. Tel: 0171-412 7902
Business. Tel: 0171-412 7454
Social Policy Information Service. Tel: 0171-412 7536

NATIONAL LIBRARY OF SCOTLAND
George IV Bridge, Edinburgh EH1 1EW
Tel 0131-226 4531; fax 0131-622 4803

The Library, which was founded as the Advocates' Library in 1682, became the National Library of Scotland in 1925. It is funded by the Scottish Executive. It contains about six million books and pamphlets, 18,000 current periodicals, 230 newspaper titles and 100,000 manuscripts. It has an unrivalled Scottish collection.
The Reading Room is for reference and research which cannot conveniently be pursued elsewhere. Admission is by ticket issued to an approved applicant. Opening hours: Reading Room, weekdays, 9.30–8.30 (Wednesday, 10–8.30); Saturday 9.30–1. Map Library, weekdays, 9.30–5 (Wednesday, 10–5); Saturday 9.30–1. Exhibition, weekdays,

10–5; Saturday 10–5; Sunday 2–5. Scottish Science Library, weekdays, 9.30–5 (Wednesday, 10–8.30).
Chairman of the Trustees, The Earl of Crawford and Balcarres, PC
Librarian and Secretary to the Trustees (*G4*), I. D. McGowan
Secretary of the Library (*G6*), M. C. Graham
Keeper of Printed Books (*G6*), Ms A. Matheson, OBE, Ph.D.
Keeper of Manuscripts (*G6*), I. C. Cunningham
Director of Public Services (*G6*), A. M. Marchbank, Ph.D.

NATIONAL LIBRARY OF WALES/LLYFRGELL GENEDLAETHOL CYMRU
Aberystwyth SY23 3BU
Tel 01970-632800; fax 01970-615709

The National Library of Wales was founded by royal charter in 1907, and is funded by the National Assembly for Wales. It contains about four million printed books, 40,000 manuscripts, four million deeds and documents, numerous maps, prints and drawings, and a sound and moving image collection. It specializes in manuscripts and books relating to Wales and the Celtic peoples. It is the repository for pre-1858 Welsh probate records, manorial records and tithe documents, and certain legal records. Readers' room open weekdays, 9.30–6 (Saturday 9.30–5); closed first week of October. Admission by reader's ticket.
President, Dr R. Brinley Jones
Librarian (*G4*), A. M. W. Green
Heads of Departments (*G6*), M. W. Mainwaring (*Administration and Technical Services*); G. Jenkins (*Manuscripts and Records*); Dr W. R. M. Griffiths (*Printed Books*); Dr D. H. Owen (*Pictures and Maps*)

LIGHTHOUSE AUTHORITIES

CORPORATION OF TRINITY HOUSE
Trinity House, Tower Hill, London EC3N 4DH
Tel 0171-481 6900; fax 0171-480 7662

Trinity House, the first general lighthouse and pilotage authority in the kingdom, was granted its first charter by Henry VIII in 1514. The Corporation is the general lighthouse authority for England, Wales and the Channel Islands and maintains 72 lighthouses, 13 major floating aids to navigation (e.g. light vessels) and more than 420 buoys. The Corporation also has certain statutory jurisdiction over aids to navigation maintained by local harbour authorities and is responsible for dealing with wrecks dangerous to navigation, except those occurring within port limits or wrecks of HM ships.

The Trinity House Lighthouse Service is maintained out of the General Lighthouse Fund which is provided from light dues levied on ships calling at ports of the UK and the Republic of Ireland. The Corporation is also a deep-sea pilotage authority and a charitable organization.

The affairs of the Corporation are controlled by a board of Elder Brethren and the Secretary. A separate board, which comprises Elder Brethren, senior staff and outside representatives, currently controls the Lighthouse Service. The Elder Brethren also act as nautical assessors in marine cases in the Admiralty Division of the High Court of Justice.

ELDER BRETHREN
Master, HRH The Prince Philip, Duke of Edinburgh, KG, KT
Deputy Master, Rear-Adm. P. B. Rowe, CBE, LVO
Wardens, Capt. C. M. C. Stewart; Sir Brian Shaw

Elder Brethren, HRH The Prince of Wales, KG, KT; HRH The Duke of York, CVO, ADC; Capt. Sir David Tibbits, DSC, RN; Capt. D. A. G. Dickins; Capt. J. E. Bury; Capt. J. A. N. Bezant, DSC, RD, RNR (retd.); Capt. D. J. Cloke; Capt. Sir Miles Wingate, KCVO; The Rt. Hon. Sir Edward Heath, KG, MBE, MP; Capt. I. R. C. Saunders; Capt. P. F. Mason, CBE; Capt. T. Woodfield, OBE; The Lord Simon of Glaisdale, PC; Capt. D. T. Smith, RN; Cdr. Sir Robin Gillett, Bt., GBE, RD, RNR; Capt. Sir Malcolm Edge, KCVO; The Lord Cuckney; Capt. D. J. Orr; The Lord Carrington, KG, GCMG, CH, MC, PC; The Lord Mackay of Clashfern, KT, PC; Sir Adrian Swire; Capt. P. H. King; The Lord Sterling of Plaistow, CBE, RNR; Cdr. M. J. Rivett-Carnac, RN; Adm. Sir Jock Slater, GCB, LVO, ADC; Capt. J. R. Burton-Hall, RD; Capt. I. Gibb, FRSA; Cdre P. J. Melson, CBE, RN; Capt. D. C. Glass

OFFICERS
Secretary, R. F. Dobb
Director of Finance, K. W. Clark
Director of Engineering, M. G. B. Wannell
Director of Administration, D. I. Brewer
Human Resources Manager, C. A. Jameson
Legal and Insurance Manager, J. D. Price
Navigation Manager, Mrs K. Hossain
Head of Management Services, S. J. W. Dunning
Deputy Director of Engineering, P. N. Hyde
Senior Inspector of Shipping, J. R. Dunnett
Media and Communication Officer, H. L. Cooper

NORTHERN LIGHTHOUSE BOARD
84 George Street, Edinburgh EH2 3DA
Tel 0131-473 3100; fax 0131-220 2093

The Lighthouse Board is the general lighthouse authority for Scotland and the Isle of Man. The board owes its origin to an Act of Parliament passed in 1786. At present the Commissioners operate under the Merchant Shipping Act 1894 and are 19 in number.

The Commissioners control 84 major automatic lighthouses, 116 minor lights and many lighted and unlighted buoys. They have a fleet of two motor vessels.

COMMISSIONERS
The Lord Advocate; the Solicitor-General for Scotland; the Lord Provosts of Edinburgh, Glasgow and Aberdeen; the Provost of Inverness; the Convener of Argyll and Bute Council; the Sheriffs-Principal of North Strathclyde, Tayside, Central and Fife, Grampian, Highlands and Islands, South Strathclyde, Dumfries and Galloway, Lothians and Borders, and Glasgow and Strathkelvin; A. J. Struthers; W. F. Hay, CBE; Capt. D. M. Cowell; Adm. Sir Michael Livesay, KCB; The Lord Maclay

OFFICERS
Chief Executive, Capt. J. B. Taylor, RN
Director of Finance, D. Gorman
Director of Engineering, W. Paterson
Director of Operations and Navigational Requirements, P. J. Christmas

LOCAL COMMISSIONERS

COMMISSION FOR LOCAL ADMINISTRATION IN ENGLAND
21 Queen Anne's Gate, London SW1H 9BU
Tel 0171-915 3210; fax 0171-233 0396

Local Commissioners (local government ombudsmen) are responsible for investigating complaints from members of the public against local authorities (but not town and parish councils); police authorities; the Commission for New Towns (housing functions); education appeal committees and certain other authorities. The Commissioners are appointed by the Crown on the recommendation of the Secretary of State for the Environment, Transport and the Regions.

Certain types of action are excluded from investigation, including personnel matters and commercial transactions unless they relate to the purchase or sale of land. Complaints can be sent direct to the Local Government Ombudsman or through a councillor, although the Local Government Ombudsman will not consider a complaint unless the council has had an opportunity to investigate and reply to a complainant.

A free leaflet *Complaint about the council? How to complain to the Local Government Ombudsman* is available from the Commission's office.

Chairman and Chief Executive of the Commission and Local Commissioner (£123,787), E. B. C. Osmotherly, CB
Vice-Chairman and Local Commissioner (£93,810), Mrs P. A. Thomas
Local Commissioner (£92,810), J. R. White
Member (*ex officio*), The Parliamentary Commissioner for Administration
Deputy Chief Executive and Secretary (£59,059), N. J. Karney

COMMISSION FOR LOCAL ADMINISTRATION IN WALES
Derwen House, Court Road, Bridgend CF31 1BN
Tel 01656-661325; fax 01656-658317

The Local Commissioner for Wales has similar powers to the Local Commissioners in England. The Commissioner is appointed by the Crown on the recommendation of the First Secretary. A free leaflet *Your Local Ombudsman in Wales* is available from the Commission's office.

Local Commissioner, E. R. Moseley
Secretary, D. Bowen
Member (*ex officio*), The Parliamentary Commissioner for Administration

COMMISSIONER FOR LOCAL ADMINISTRATION IN SCOTLAND
23 Walker Street, Edinburgh EH3 7HX
Tel 0131-225 5300; fax 0131-225 9495

The Local Commissioner for Scotland has similar powers to the Local Commissioners in England, and is appointed by the Crown on the recommendation of the First Minister.

Local Commissioner, F. C. Marks, OBE
Deputy Commissioner and Secretary, Ms J. H. Renton

LONDON REGIONAL TRANSPORT
55 Broadway, London SW1H 0BD
Tel 0171-222 5600

Subject to the financial objectives and principles approved by the Secretary of State for the Environment, Transport and the Regions, London Regional Transport has a general duty to provide or secure the provision of public transport services for Greater London.

Chairman (*non-executive*), Sir Malcolm Bates
Chief Executive, D. Tunnicliffe, CBE
Member, and Managing Director of London Transport Buses, C. Hodson, CBE
Member, and Managing Director of London Underground Ltd, D. Smith

OFFICE OF THE LORD ADVOCATE
Crown Office, 25 Chambers Street, Edinburgh EH1 1LA
Tel 0131-226 2626; fax 0131-226 6910

The Law Officers for Scotland are the Lord Advocate and the Solicitor-General for Scotland.
Lord Advocate, The Lord Hardie, PC, QC
Solicitor-General for Scotland, Colin Boyd, QC
Private Secretary to the Law Officers, J. Gibbons

LORD CHANCELLOR'S DEPARTMENT
Selborne House, 54–60 Victoria Street, London SW1E 6QW
Tel 0171-210 8500
E-mail: enquiries.lcdhq@gtnet.gov.uk
Web: http://www.open.gov.uk/lcd

The Lord Chancellor appoints Justices of the Peace (except in the Duchy of Lancaster) and advises the Crown on the appointment of most members of the higher judiciary. He is responsible for promoting general reforms in the civil law, for the procedure of the civil courts and for legal aid. He is a member of the Cabinet. He also has ministerial responsibility for magistrates' courts, which are administered locally. Administration of the Supreme Court and county courts in England and Wales was taken over by the Court Service, an executive agency of the department, in 1995.

The Lord Chancellor is also responsible for ensuring that letters patent and other formal documents are passed in the proper form under the Great Seal of the Realm, of which he is the custodian. The work in connection with this is carried out under his direction in the Office of the Clerk of the Crown in Chancery.

The Lord Chancellor is also the senior Lord of Appeal in Ordinary and speaker of the House of Lords.

Lord Chancellor (£160,011), The Lord Irvine of Lairg, PC, QC
  Principal Private Secretary, Ms J. Rowe
  Special Adviser, G. Hart
Parliamentary Secretaries, Keith Vaz, MP; David Lock, MP
  Private Secretaries, R. Moore; Ms D. Hulin
Permanent Secretary (SCS), Sir Hayden Phillips, KCB
  Private Secretary, M. Camley

CROWN OFFICE
House of Lords, London SW1A 0PW
Tel 0171-219 4713

Clerk of the Crown in Chancery (SCS), Sir Hayden Phillips, KCB
Deputy Clerk of the Crown in Chancery (SCS), M. Huebner, CB
Clerk of the Chamber, C. I. P. Denyer

JUDICIAL GROUP
Tel 0171-210 8500

Head of Group (SCS), M. Huebner, CB
Heads of Divisions (SCS), D. E. Staff (*Policy and Conditions of Service*); Mrs M. Pigott (*Senior Appointment and Silk*); Miss J. Killick (*Senior Appointment and Silk*); J. Tanner (*District Bench and Tribunals*); S. Humphries (*Magistrates' Appointments*); P. L. Jacob (*Judicial Policy*)

Judicial Studies Board
9th Floor, Millbank Tower, London SW1P 4QW
Tel 0171-925 4762

Secretary (SCS), E. S. Adams

POLICY GROUP
Tel 0171-210 8719

Director-General (SCS), Ms J. MacNaughton
Heads of Divisions (SCS), A. Cogbill (*Civil Justice and Legal Services Directorate*); D. Gladwell (*Civil Justice*); R. Sams (*Civil Law Development*); D. A. Hill (*Access to Justice Bill Team*); C. Myerscough (*Community Legal Services*); Ms A. Finlay (*Public and Private Rights Directorate*); W. Arnold (*Family Policy*); A. Shaw (*Administrative Justice*); M. Ormerod (*Magistrates' Courts and Criminal Policy Directorate*); P. White (*Magistrates' Courts IT*); vacant (*Human Rights Act Implementation Team*); vacant (*Criminal Policy*); Mrs K. Allen (*Policy Group Secretariat and Agency Monitoring Unit*); Mrs J. Brown (*Social Policy Unit*)

LEGAL ADVISER'S GROUP
Tel 0171-210 0711

Legal Adviser (SCS), P. Jenkins
Heads of Divisions (SCS), M. H. Collon (*Legal Advice and Litigation*); A. Wallace (*International and Common Law Services*); M. Kron (*Drafting Services*)

COMMUNICATIONS GROUP
Tel 0171-210 8672

Director of Communications (SCS), A. Percival, LVO

CORPORATE SERVICES GROUP
Tel 0171-210 8503

Director of Corporate Services and Principal Establishment and Finance Officer (SCS), Mrs E. Grimsey
Heads of Divisions (SCS), Mrs S. Anderson (*Personnel Management*); Mrs S. Webber (*Personnel Management*); S. Smith (*Finance*); K. Cregeen, OBE (*Facilities and Support Services*); A. Rummins (*Internal Assurance*); K. Garrett (*Statutory Publications Office*)

ECCLESIASTICAL PATRONAGE
10 Downing Street, London SW1A 2AA
Tel 0171-930 4433

Secretary for Ecclesiastical Patronage, J. H. Holroyd, CB
Assistant Secretary for Ecclesiastical Patronage, N. C. Wheeler

HM MAGISTRATES' COURTS' SERVICE INSPECTORATE
Southside, 105 Victoria Street, London SW1E 6QJ
Tel 0171-210 1655

Chief Inspector (SCS), C. J. A. Chivers
Senior Inspectors (SCS), D. Gear; C. Monson; Ms S. Steel

LORD CHANCELLOR'S ADVISORY COMMITTEE ON STATUTE LAW
67 Tufton Street, London SW1P 3QS
Tel 0171-210 2615

The Advisory Committee advises the Lord Chancellor on all matters relating to the revision, modernization and publication of the statute book.
Chairman, The Lord Chancellor
Deputy Chairman, Sir Hayden Phillips, KCB
Members, The Hon. Mr Justice Carnwath, CVO; The Hon. Lord Gill; Sir James Jenkins, KCB, QC; Mrs E. Grimsey; J. M. Davies; J. C. McCluskie, CB, QC; A. H. Hammond, CB, QC; R. Henderson; P. Jenkins; Mrs C. Tullo; W. R. McKay, CB; K. Garrett; C. Carey; First Legislative Counsel of Northern Ireland
Secretary (acting), M. Heseltine

EXECUTIVE AGENCIES

THE COURT SERVICE
Southside, 105 Victoria Street, London SW1E 6QT
Tel 0171-210 1672; fax 0171-210 1797

The Court Service provides administrative support to the Supreme Court of England and Wales, county courts and a number of tribunals.

Chief Executive (SCS), I. Magee
Director of Operational Policy (SCS), Miss B. Kenny
Director of Finance (SCS), vacant
Change Director (SCS), K. Pogson
Director of Purchasing and Contract Management (SCS), vacant
Head of Information Services Division (SCS), Ms A. Vernon
Head of Personnel and Training (SCS), Ms H. Dudley
Director of Civil and Family Operations (SCS), S. Smith
Director of Criminal Operations (SCS), N. J. Smedley
Director of Tribunals (SCS), P. Stockton

Supreme Court Group
Strand, London WC2A 2LL
Tel 0171-936 6000
Director (SCS), I. Hyams

For Supreme Court departments and offices and circuit administrators, *see* Law Courts and Offices section

HM LAND REGISTRY
— *see* page 314

PUBLIC RECORD OFFICE
— *see* page 333

PUBLIC TRUST OFFICE
— *see* page 332

LORD GREAT CHAMBERLAIN'S OFFICE
House of Lords, London SW1A 0PW
Tel 0171-219 3100; fax 0171-219 2500

The Lord Great Chamberlain is a Great Officer of State, the office being hereditary since the grant of Henry I to the family of De Vere, Earls of Oxford. It is now a joint hereditary office between the Cholmondeley and Carington families. The Lord Great Chamberlain is responsible for the royal apartments of the Palace of Westminster, i.e. The Queen's Robing Room, the Royal Gallery and, in conjunction with the Lord Chancellor and the Speaker, Westminster Hall. The Lord Great Chamberlain has particular responsibility for the internal administrative arrangements within the House of Lords for State Openings of Parliament.
Lord Great Chamberlain, The Marquess of Cholmondeley
Secretary to the Lord Great Chamberlain, Gen. Sir Edward Jones, KCB, CBE
Clerks to the Lord Great Chamberlain, Miss C. J. Bostock; Miss R. M. Wilkinson

---

LORD PRIVY SEAL'S OFFICE
Privy Council Office, 68 Whitehall, London SW1A 2AT
Tel 0171-270 3000

The Lord Privy Seal is a member of the Cabinet and Leader of the House of Lords. She has no departmental portfolio, but is a member of a number of domestic and economic Cabinet committees. She is responsible to the Prime Minister for the organization of government business in the House and has a responsibility to the House itself to advise it on procedural matters and other difficulties which arise.
Lord Privy Seal, Leader of the House of Lords and Minister for Women, The Baroness Jay of Paddington, PC
Principal Private Secretary, W. Connon
Private Secretary (House of Lords), Miss M. Robertson
Special Adviser, Ms J. Gibbons

LOTTERY COMMISSION, NATIONAL
— *see* page 325

OFFICE OF MANPOWER ECONOMICS
Oxford House, 76 Oxford Street, London WIN 9FD
Tel 0171-467 7244; fax 0171-467 7248

The Office of Manpower Economics was set up in 1971. It is an independent non-statutory organization which is responsible for servicing independent review bodies which advise on the pay of various public service groups (*see* Review Bodies, pages 334–5), the Pharmacists Review Panel and the Police Negotiating Board. The Office is also responsible for servicing *ad hoc* bodies of inquiry and for undertaking research into pay and associated matters as requested by the Government.
OME Director, M. J. Horsman
Director, Health Secretariat, and OME Deputy Director, G. S. Charles
Director, Armed Forces' and Teachers' Secretariats, G. McGregor
Director, Senior Salaries Secretariat, Mrs C. Haworth
Press Liaison Officer, M. C. Cahill

MENTAL HEALTH ACT COMMISSION
Maid Marian House, 56 Hounds Gate, Nottingham
NG1 6BG
Tel 0115-943 7100; fax 0115-943 7101

The Mental Health Act Commission was established in 1983. Its functions are to keep under review the operation of the Mental Health Act 1983; to visit and meet patients detained under the Act; to investigate complaints falling within the Commission's remit; to operate the consent to treatment safeguards in the Mental Health Act; to publish a biennial report on its activities; to monitor the implementation of the Code of Practice; and to advise ministers. Commissioners are appointed by the Secretary of State for Health.
Chairman (acting), G. Lakes
Vice-Chairman, Prof. R. Williams
Chief Executive (G6), W. Bingley

MILLENNIUM COMMISSION
Portland House, Stag Place, London SWIE 5EZ
Tel 0171-880 2001; fax 0171-880 2000

The Millennium Commission was established in February 1994 and is accountable to the Department for Culture, Media and Sport. It is an independent body which distributes money from National Lottery proceeds to projects to mark the millennium.
Chairman, The Rt. Hon. Chris Smith, MP
Members, The Rt. Hon. Dr Jack Cunningham, MP; Prof. Heather Couper, FRAS; Earl of Dalkeith; The Lord Glentoran, CBE; Sir John Hall; The Rt. Hon. M. Heseltine, MP; S. Jenkins; The Baroness Scotland of Asthal, QC
Director, M. O'Connor

MONOPOLIES AND MERGERS COMMISSION (FORMER)
— *see* Competition Commission

MUSEUMS

MUSEUMS AND GALLERIES COMMISSION
16 Queen Anne's Gate, London SWIH 9AA
Tel 0171-233 4200; fax 0171-233 3686

Established in 1931 as the Standing Commission on Museums and Galleries, the Commission was renamed in 1981. Its sponsor department is the Department for Culture, Media and Sport. The Commission advises the Government, and the relevant ministers in Scotland, Wales and Northern Ireland, on museum affairs. Commissioners are appointed by the Prime Minister.

The Commission's executive functions include providing the services of the Museums Security Adviser; allocating grants to the seven Area Museum Councils in England; funding and monitoring the work of the Museum Documentation Association; and administering grant schemes for non-national museums. The Commission administers the arrangements for government indemnities and the acceptance of works of art in lieu of inheritance tax, and its Conservation Unit advises on conservation and environmental standards. A registration scheme for museums in the UK is operated by the Commission.

The Commission will merge with the Library and Information Commission in 2000 to form the Museums, Libraries and Archives Council.
Chairman, J. Joll
Members, Prof. P. Bateson, FRS (*Vice-Chairman*); The Baroness Brigstocke; Prof. R. Buchanan; Ms R. Butler; Penelope, Viscountess Cobham; R. Foster; L. Grossman; R. Hiscox; Adm. Sir John Kerr, GCB; Dr I. McKenzie Smith, RSA; A. Warhurst, CBE; Mrs C. Wilson
Director and Secretary, T. Mason

THE BRITISH MUSEUM
Great Russell Street, London WCIB 3DG
Tel 0171-636 1555; fax 0171-323 8614

The British Museum houses the national collection of antiquities, ethnography, coins and paper money, medals, and prints and drawings. The British Museum may be said to date from 1753, when Parliament approved the holding of a public lottery to raise funds for the purchase of the collections of Sir Hans Sloane and the Harleian manuscripts, and for their proper housing and maintenance. The building (Montagu House) was opened in 1759. The present buildings were erected between 1823 and the present day, and the original collection has increased to its present dimensions by gifts and purchases. Total government grant-in-aid for 1999–2000 is £34.7 million.

BOARD OF TRUSTEES
Appointed by the Sovereign, HRH The Duke of Gloucester, KG, GCVO
Appointed by the Prime Minister, N. Barber; Prof. Gillian Beer, FBA; Sir John Boyd; E. J. P. Browne, FREng.; Sir Matthew Farrer, GCVO; Sir Michael Hopkins, CBE, RA, RIBA; Sir Joseph Hotung; Prof. M. Kemp, FBA; S. Keswick; Hon. Mrs M. Marten, OBE; Sir John Morgan, KCMG; The Rt. Hon. Sir Timothy Raison; Sir Martin Rees, FRS; Prof. Sir Gunter Treitel, DCL, FBA, QC
Nominated by the Learned Societies, Prof. Jean Thomas, CBE (*Royal Society*); A. Jones, RA (*Royal Academy*); Sir Claus Moser, KCB, CBE, FBA (*British Academy*); The Lord Renfrew of Kaimsthorn, FBA, FSA (*Society of Antiquaries*)
Appointed by the Trustees of the British Museum, G. C. Greene, CBE (*Chairman*); Sir David Attenborough, CH, CVO, CBE, FRS; Prof. Rosemary Cramp, CBE, FSA; The Lord Egremont; Dr Jennifer Montagu, FBA

OFFICERS
Director, Dr R. G. W. Anderson, FRSC, FSA
Managing Director, Ms S. Taverne
Director of Marketing and Public Affairs, Dr C. Homden
Director of Finance and Resources, A. B. Blackstock
Secretary, Mrs C. Nihoul Parker
Head of Public Services, G. A. L. House
Head of Press and Public Relations, A. E. Hamilton
Head of Design, Miss M. Hall, OBE
Head of Education, J. F. Reeve
Head of Administration, C. E. I. Jones
Head of Building Development and Planning, K. T. Stannard
Head of Building Management, T. R. A. Giles
Head of Finance, Miss S. E. Davies
Head of Personnel and Office Services, Miss B. A. Hughes

KEEPERS
Keeper of Prints and Drawings, A. V. Griffiths
Keeper of Coins and Medals, Dr A. M. Burnett
Keeper of Egyptian Antiquities, W. V. Davies
Keeper of Western Asiatic Antiquities, Dr J. E. Curtis
Keeper of Greek and Roman Antiquities, Dr D. J. R. Williams
Keeper of Medieval and Later Antiquities, J. Cherry
Keeper of Prehistoric and Romano-British Antiquities, Dr T. M. Potter
Keeper of Japanese Antiquities, V. T. Harris
Keeper of Oriental Antiquities, R. J. Knox
Keeper of Ethnography, B. J. Mack
Keeper of Scientific Research, Dr S. G. E. Bowman
Keeper of Conservation, W. A. Oddy

NATURAL HISTORY MUSEUM
Cromwell Road, London SW7 5BD
Tel 0171-942 5000
The Natural History Museum originates from the natural history departments of the British Museum, which grew extensively during the 19th century; in 1860 the natural history collection was moved from Bloomsbury to a new location. Part of the site of the 1862 International Exhibition in South Kensington was acquired for the new museum, and the Museum opened to the public in 1881. In 1963 the Natural History Museum became completely independent with its own board of trustees. The Walter Rothschild Zoological Museum, Tring, bequeathed by the second Lord Rothschild, has formed part of the Museum since 1938. The Geological Museum merged with the Natural History Museum in 1985. Total government grant-in-aid for 1999–2000 is £29.583 million.

BOARD OF TRUSTEES
Appointed by the Prime Minister, The Lord Oxburgh, KBE, PH.D., FRS (*Chairman*); Sir Crispin Tickell, GCMG, KCVO; Dame Anne McLaren, DBE, FRS, FRCOG; Sir Richard Sykes, FRS; Miss J. Mayhew; Ms J. Bennett; Prof. M. Hassell, FRS; O. Stocken
Appointed by the Secretary of State for Culture, Media and Sport, Prof. C. Leaver, FRS, FRSE
Appointed by the Trustees of the Natural History Museum, The Lord Palumbo; Prof. K. O'Nions, FRS; Prof. Linda Partridge, FRS, FRSE

SENIOR STAFF
Director, N. R. Chalmers, PH.D.
Director of Science, Prof. P. Henderson, D.Phil.
Head of Audit and Review, D. Thorpe
Keeper of Botany, S. Blackmore, PH.D.
Head of Development and Marketing, Ms T. Burman
Keeper of Entomology, Dr R. Vane-Wright
Head of Estates, G. Pellow
Head of Education and Exhibitions, Dr G. Clarke
Head of Finance, N. Greenwood

Head of Library and Information Services, Dr R. G. Lester
Keeper of Mineralogy, Prof. A. Fleet
Keeper of Palaeontology, Prof. S. K. Donovan
Head of Human Resources, Mrs J. Rowe
Head of Visitor Services, M. Baron
Keeper of Zoology, Prof. P. Rainbow
Policy and Planning Co-ordinator, P. Kirkman
Director, Tring Zoological Museum, Mrs T. Wild

THE SCIENCE MUSEUM
Exhibition Road, London SW7 2DD
Tel 0171-938 8000; fax 0171-938 8112

The Science Museum, part of the National Museum of Science and Industry, houses the national collections of science, technology, industry and medicine. The Museum began as the science collection of the South Kensington Museum and first opened in 1857. In 1883 it acquired the collections of the Patent Museum and in 1909 the science collections were transferred to the new Science Museum, leaving the art collections with the Victoria and Albert Museum.

Some of the Museum's commercial aircraft, agricultural machinery, and road and rail transport collections are at Wroughton, Wilts. The National Museum of Science and Industry also incorporates the National Railway Museum, York and the National Museum of Photography, Film and Television, Bradford.

Total government grant-in-aid for 1999–2000 is £20.759 million.

BOARD OF TRUSTEES
Chairman, Sir Peter Williams, CBE, PH.D., FREng.
Members, HRH The Duke of Kent, KG, GCMG, GCVO, ADC; Dr M. Archer; G. Dyke; Dr A. Grocock; Mrs A. Higham, OBE; Mrs J. Kennedy, OBE; Dame Bridget Ogilvie, DBE; The Lord Puttnam, CBE; Sir Michael Quinlan, GCB; D. E. Rayner, CBE; Sir Christopher Wates

OFFICERS
Director, Sir Neil Cossons, OBE, FSA
Assistant Director and Head of Resource Management Division, J. Tucker
Head of Personnel and Legal Services, vacant
Head of Finance, Ms A. Caine
Head of Information Systems, S. Gordon
Head of Estates, J. Bevin
Assistant Director and Head of Collections Division, D. Swade
Head of Physical Sciences and Engineering Group (acting), Dr A. Q. Morton
Head of Life and Communications Technologies Group, Dr R. F. Bud
Head of Collections Management Group, Dr S. Keene
Assistant Director and Head of Public Affairs Division, C. M. Pemberton
Head of Corporate Relations, F. Kirk
Head of Commercial Development, M. Sullivan
Head of Marketing and Communications, H. Roderick
Head of Wellcome Wing Commercial and Access, B. Jones
Assistant Director, Wellcome Wing Project Director and Head of Science Communication Division, Prof. J. R. Durant
Head of Education and Programmes, Dr R. Jackson
Head of Exhibition and Wellcome Wing Content, Dr G. Farmelo
Head of Design, T. Molloy
Head of National Railway Museum, A. Scott
Head of National Museum of Photography, Film and Television, Ms A. Nevill

VICTORIA AND ALBERT MUSEUM
Cromwell Road, London SW7 2RL
Tel 0171-942 2000

The Victoria and Albert Museum is the national museum of fine and applied art and design. It descends directly from the Museum of Manufactures, which opened in Marlborough House in 1852 after the Great Exhibition of 1851. The Museum was moved in 1857 to become part of the South Kensington Museum. It was renamed the Victoria and Albert Museum in 1899. It also houses the National Art Library and Print Room.

The Museum administers three branch museums: the National Museum of Childhood in Bethnal Green, the Theatre Museum in Covent Garden, and the Wellington Museum at Apsley House. The museum in Bethnal Green was opened in 1872 and the building is the most important surviving example of the type of glass and iron construction used by Paxton for the Great Exhibition. Total government grant-in-aid for 1999–2000 is £30.084 million.

BOARD OF TRUSTEES
Chairman, Mrs P. Ridley
Deputy Chairman, J. Scott, CBE, FSA
Members, Miss N. Campbell; Penelope, Viscountess
    Cobham; Lady Copisarow; R. Fitch, CBE;
    Prof. C. Frayling, PH.D.; Sir Terence Heiser, GCB; Mrs A.
    Heseltine; A. Irby III; A. Snow; Prof. J. Steer, FSA, DLitt.;
    A. Wheatley; Prof. C. White, CVO, FBA
Secretary to the Board of Trustees, P. A. Wilson

OFFICERS
Director, Dr A. C. N. Borg, CBE, FSA
Assistant Directors, T. J. Stevens (*Collections*); J. W. Close
    (*Administration*)
Head of Buildings and Estate, R. P. Whitehouse
Chief Curator, Ceramics and Glass, Dr O. Watson
Head of Conservation, Dr J. Ashley-Smith
Head of Education, D. Anderson, OBE
Chief Curator, Far Eastern, Miss R. Kerr
Head of Finance and Central Services, Miss R. M. Sykes
Chief Curator, Furniture and Woodwork, C. Wilk
Chief Curator, Indian and South-East Asian, Dr D. Swallow
Head of Information Systems Services, A. Cooper
Head of Major Projects, Mrs G. F. Miles
Chief Curator, Metalwork, Silver and Jewellery, vacant
Chief Librarian, National Art Library, J. F. van den Wateren
Head of Personnel, Mrs G. Henchley
Chief Curator, Prints, Drawings and Paintings,
    Miss S. B. Lambert
Head of Public Services, R. Cole-Hamilton
Head of Records and Collections Services, A. Seal
Head of Research, P. Greenhalgh
Head of Safety and Security, R. Bland
Chief Curator, Sculpture, Dr P. E. D. Williamson
Chief Curator, Textiles and Dress, Mrs V. D. Mendes
Managing Director, V. and A. Enterprises Ltd, M. Cass
Director of Development, vacant
Head of National Museum of Childhood (*acting*), Dr S.
    Laurence
Head of Theatre Museum, Miss M. Benton
Head of Wellington Museum, Miss A. Robinson

MUSEUM OF LONDON
London Wall, London EC2Y 5HN
Tel 0171-600 3699; fax 0171-600 1058

The Museum of London illustrates the history of London from prehistoric times to the present day. It opened in 1976 and is based on the amalgamation of the former Guildhall Museum and London Museum. The Museum is controlled by a Board of Governors, appointed (nine each) by the Government and the Corporation of London. The Museum is currently funded jointly by the Department for Culture, Media and Sport and the Corporation of London, each contributing £4.360 million in 1999–2000.
Chairman of Board of Governors, R. Hambro
Director, Dr S. Thurley

COMMONWEALTH INSTITUTE
Kensington High Street, London W8 6NQ
Tel 0171-603 4535; fax 0171-602 7374

The Commonwealth Institute is responsible for promoting the Commonwealth in the UK and other member countries through exhibitions, educational programmes, publications, resources and information. The Institute houses the Commonwealth Resource Centre (CRC) and Literature Library and a Conference and Events Centre.

The Institute was established in 1958 and is an independent statutory body funded by the British government with contributions from other Commonwealth governments. It is controlled by a board of governors which includes the high commissioners of all Commonwealth countries represented in London.
Chairman, D. A. Thompson
Director-General, D. French
Administrative and Commercial Director, P. Kennedy
Director of Education, S. Brace
Director of Public Affairs, G. Carter

IMPERIAL WAR MUSEUM
Lambeth Road, London SE1 6HZ
Tel 0171-416 5000; fax 0171-416 5374

The Museum, founded in 1917, illustrates and records all aspects of the two world wars and other military operations involving Britain and the Commonwealth since 1914. It was opened in its present home, formerly Bethlem Hospital or Bedlam, in 1936. The Museum also administers HMS *Belfast* in the Pool of London, Duxford Airfield near Cambridge and the Cabinet War Rooms in Westminster.

Total government grant-in-aid for 1999–2000 is £11.662 million.

OFFICERS
Director-General, R. W. K. Crawford
Secretary, J. J. Chadwick, OBE
Assistant Directors, D. A. Needham (*Administration*); Miss
    K. J. Carmichael (*Collections*); G. Marsh (*Planning and
    Development*)
Director of Duxford Airfield, E. O. Inman, OBE
Director of HMS Belfast, E. J. Wenzel

KEEPERS
Department of Museum Services, C. Dowling, D.Phil.
Department of Documents, R. W. A. Suddaby
Department of Exhibits and Firearms, D. J. Penn
Department of Printed Books, R. Golland
Department of Art, Miss A. H. Weight
Department of Film, R. B. N. Smither
Department of Photographs, Ms B. Kinally
Department of Sound Records, Mrs M. A. Brooks
Department of Marketing and Trading, Miss A. Godwin
Curator of the Cabinet War Rooms, P. Reed

NATIONAL MARITIME MUSEUM
Greenwich, London SE10 9NF
Tel 0181-858 4422; fax 0181-312 6632

Established by Act of Parliament in 1934, the National Maritime Museum illustrates the maritime history of Great Britain in the widest sense, underlining the importance of the sea and its influence on the nation's power, wealth, culture, technology and institutions. The Museum is in three groups of buildings in Greenwich Park – the main building, the Queen's House (built by Inigo Jones, 1616–35) and the Royal Observatory (including Wren's Flamsteed House). Total government grant-in-aid for 1999–2000 is £10.425 million.

Director, R. L. Ormond

NATIONAL ARMY MUSEUM
Royal Hospital Road, London SW3 4HT
Tel 0171-730 0717; fax 0171-823 6573

The National Army Museum covers the history of five centuries of the British Army. It was established by royal charter in 1960. Total government grant-in-aid for 1999–2000 is £3.2 million.

Director, I. G. Robertson
Assistant Directors, D. K. Smurthwaite; A. J. Guy;
  Maj. P. R. Bateman

ROYAL AIR FORCE MUSEUM
Grahame Park Way, London NW9 5LL
Tel 0181-205 2266; fax 0181-200 1751

Situated on the former airfield at RAF Hendon, the Museum illustrates the development of aviation from before the Wright brothers to the present-day RAF. Total government grant-in-aid for 1999–2000, including funding for the aerospace museum at Cosford, is £3.5 million.

Director, Dr M. A. Fopp
Assistant Directors, H. Hall; A. Wright
Senior Keeper, P. Elliott

NATIONAL MUSEUMS AND GALLERIES ON MERSEYSIDE
PO Box 33, 127 Dale Street, Liverpool L69 3LA
Tel 0151-207 0001; fax 0151-478 4190

The Board of Trustees of the National Museums and Galleries on Merseyside is responsible for the Liverpool Museum, the Merseyside Maritime Museum (incorporating HM Customs and Excise National Museum), the Museum of Liverpool Life, the Lady Lever Art Gallery, the Walker Art Gallery and Sudley House, and the Conservation Centre. Total government grant-in-aid for 1999–2000 is £13.6 million.

Chairman of the Board of Trustees, D. McDonnell
Director, R. Foster
Keeper of Art Galleries, J. Treuherz
Keeper of Conservation, A. Durham
Keeper, Liverpool Museum, Ms L. Knowles
Keeper, Merseyside Maritime Museum and Museum of Liverpool Life, M. Stammers

NATIONAL MUSEUMS AND GALLERIES OF WALES/AMGUEDDFEYDD AC ORIELAU CENEDLAETHOL CYMRU
Cathays Park, Cardiff CF1 3NP
Tel 01222-573500; fax 01222-577010

The National Museums and Galleries of Wales comprise the National Museum and Gallery, the Museum of Welsh Life, the Roman Legionary Museum, Turner House Gallery, the Welsh Slate Museum, the Segontium Roman Museum and the Museum of the Welsh Woollen Industry. Total funding from the National Assembly for Wales for 1999–2000 is £13.516 million.

President, M. C. T. Prichard, CBE
Vice-President, A. Thomas

OFFICERS
Director, A. Southall

Assistant Directors, C. Thomas (*Public Affairs*); I. Fell (*Exhibitions and Interpretation*); Dr E. William (*Collections and Education and Deputy Director*); J. Williams-Davies (*Social and Industrial History, and Keeper, Museum of Welsh Life*); M. Tooby (*Arts and Sciences, and Keeper, National Museum and Gallery*)
Keeper of Geology, M. G. Bassett, PH.D.
Keeper of Bio-diversity and Systematic Biology, Dr P. G. Oliver
Keeper of Art, O. Fairclough
Keeper of Archaeology, R. Brewer
Manager, Roman Legionary Museum, vacant
Keeper in Charge, Turner House Gallery, O. Fairclough
Keeper, Welsh Slate Museum and Segontium Roman Museum, D. Roberts, PH.D.
Manager, Museum of the Welsh Woollen Industry, S. Moss

NATIONAL MUSEUMS OF SCOTLAND
Chambers Street, Edinburgh EH1 1JF
Tel 0131-225 7534; fax 0131-220 4819

The National Museums of Scotland comprise the Royal Museum of Scotland, the Scottish United Services Museum, the Scottish Agricultural Museum, the Museum of Flight, Shambellie House Museum of Costume and the Museum of Scotland. Total funding from the Scottish Executive for 1999–2000 is £19.9 million.

BOARD OF TRUSTEES
Chairman, Sir Robert Smith, FSA Scot.
Members, Prof. T. Devine; Dr L. Glasser, MBE, FRSE; S. G. Gordon, CBE; Dr V. van Heyingen, FRSE; G. Johnston, OBE, TD; Ms C. Macaulay; N. McIntosh, CBE; Prof. A. Manning, OBE; Prof. J. Murray; Sir William Purves, CBE, DSO; Dr A. Ritchie, OBE; The Countess of Rosebery; I. Smith; The Lord Wilson of Tillyorn, GCMG

OFFICERS
Director, M. Jones, FSA, FSA Scot., FRSA
Depute Director (Resources) and Project Director, Museum of Scotland, I. Hooper, FSA Scot.
Depute Director (Collections) and Keeper of History and Applied Art, Miss D. Idiens, FRSA, FSA Scot.
Development Director, C. McCallum
Keeper of Archaeology, D. V. Clarke, PH.D., FSA, FSA Scot.
Keeper of Geology and Zoology, M. Shaw, D.Phil.
Keeper of Social and Technological History, G. Sprott
Head of Public Affairs, Ms M. Bryden
Head of Museum Services, S. R. Elson, FSA Scot.
Head of Administration, A. G. Young
Keeper, Scottish United Services Museum, S. C. Wood
Curator, Scottish Agricultural Museum, G. Sprott
Curator, Museum of Flight, A. Smith
Keeper, Shambellie House Museum of Costume, Miss N. Tarrant

NATIONAL ASSEMBLY FOR WALES
— see Wales, National Assembly for

NATIONAL AUDIT OFFICE
157–197 Buckingham Palace Road, London SW1W 9SP
Tel 0171-798 7000; fax 0171-828 3774
22 Melville Street, Edinburgh EH3 7NS
Tel 0131-244 2736; fax 0131-244 2721
Audit House, 23–24 Park Place, Cardiff CF1 3BA
Tel 01222-378661; fax 01222-388415

The National Audit Office came into existence under the National Audit Act 1983 to replace and continue the work of the former Exchequer and Audit Department. The Act reinforced the Office's total financial and operational independence from the Government and brought its head, the Comptroller and Auditor-General, into a closer relationship with Parliament as an officer of the House of Commons.

The National Audit Office provides independent information, advice and assurance to Parliament and the public about all aspects of the financial operations of government departments and many other bodies receiving public funds. It does this by examining and certifying the accounts of these organizations and by regularly publishing reports to Parliament on the results of its value for money investigations of the economy, efficiency and effectiveness with which public resources have been used. The National Audit Office is also the auditor by agreement of the accounts of certain international and other organizations. In addition, the Office authorizes the issue of public funds to government departments.

Comptroller and Auditor-General, Sir John Bourn, KCB
   Private Secretary, M. Davies
Deputy Comptroller and Auditor-General, R. N. Le Marechal, CB
Assistant Auditors-General, T. Burr; J. Colman; L. H. Hughes, CB; J. Marshall; Miss C. Mawhood; M. C. Pfleger; M. Sinclair
Directors, Mrs C. Allen; Miss J. Angus; J. Ashcroft; T. Banfield; Ms G. Body; A. Burchell; P. Cannon; J. Cavanagh; D. Clarke; M. Daynes; S. Doughty; R. Eales; A. Fiander; R. Frith; N. Gale; F. Grogan; Mrs A. Hands; K. Hawkeswell; J. Jones; J. Jones; Mrs P. Leahy; J. McEwen; R. Maggs; G. Miller; R. Parker; J. Pearce; Ms M. Radford; J. Rickleton; A. Roberts; J. Robertson; N. Sloan; Mrs P. Smith; I. Summers; R. Swan; J. Thorpe; Miss J. Wheeler; M. Whitehouse; D. Woodward; P. Woodward

NATIONAL CONSUMER COUNCIL
20 Grosvenor Gardens, London SW1W 0DH
Tel 0171-730 3469; fax 0171-730 0191

The National Consumer Council was set up by the Government in 1975 to give an independent voice to consumers in the UK. Its role is to advocate the consumer interest to decision-makers in national and local government, industry and regulatory bodies, business and the professions. It does this through a combination of research and campaigning. It is largely funded by grant-in-aid from the Department of Trade and Industry.
Chairman, D. Hatch, CBE
Vice-Chairman, Mrs D. Hutton, CBE
Director, Ms A. Bradley

NATIONAL DEBT OFFICE
— *see* National Investment and Loans Office

NATIONAL ENDOWMENT FOR SCIENCE, TECHNOLOGY AND THE ARTS
1st Floor, Gainsborough House, 33 Throgmorton Street, London EC2N 2BR
Tel 0171-861 9670; fax 0171-861 9675

The National Endowment for Science, Technology and the Arts (NESTA) was established under the National Lottery Act 1998 with a £200 million endowment from the proceeds of the National Lottery. Its aims are to help talented individuals; to enable innovative ideas to be successfully commercially exploited; and to promote public knowledge of science, technology and the arts.
Chairman, The Lord Puttnam, CBE
Trustees, Dame Bridget Ogilvie, DBE; Prof. Sir Martin Rees, FRS; Dr C. Evans, OBE; Ms C. Vorderman; D. Wardell; F. Matarasso; C. Gillinson; The Baroness McIntosh of Hudnall; Ms C. McKeever; Ms J. Kirkpatrick; Ms S. Hunter; D. Alexander
Chief Executive, J. Newton

NATIONAL HERITAGE MEMORIAL FUND
7 Holbein Place, London SW1W 8NR
Tel 0171-591 6000; fax 0171-591 6001

The National Heritage Memorial Fund is an independent body established in 1980 as a memorial to those who have died for the UK. The Fund is empowered by the National Heritage Act 1980 to give financial assistance towards the cost of acquiring, maintaining or preserving land, buildings, works of art and other objects of outstanding interest which are also of importance to the national heritage. The Fund is administered by 15 trustees who are appointed by the Prime Minister.

The National Lottery Act 1993 designated the Fund as distributor of the heritage share of proceeds from the National Lottery. As a result, the Fund now operates two funds: the Heritage Memorial Fund and the Heritage Lottery Fund. The Heritage Memorial Fund receives an annual grant from the Department for Culture, Media and Sport; the grant for 1999–2000 is £2.5 million.
Chairman, Dr E. Anderson
Trustees, Prof. C. Baines; R. Boas; Sir Richard Carew Pole, Bt.; Sir Angus Grossart; Sir Ernest Hall; Mrs C. Hubbard; J. Keegan; Mrs P. Lankester; Prof. P. J. Newbould; Miss S. Palmer; Mrs C. Porteous; Prof. T. Pritchard; Ms M. A. Sieghart; Dame Sue Tinson, DBE
Director, Ms A. Case

NATIONAL INSURANCE JOINT AUTHORITY
The Adelphi, 1–11 John Adam Street, London WC2N 6HT
Tel 0171-962 8529; fax 0171-962 8647

The Authority's function is to co-ordinate the operation of social security legislation in Great Britain and Northern Ireland, including the necessary financial adjustments between the two National Insurance Funds.
Members, The Secretary of State for Social Security; the Head of the Department of Health and Social Services for Northern Ireland
Secretary, vacant

NATIONAL INVESTMENT AND LOANS OFFICE
1 King Charles Street, London SW1A 2AP
Tel 0171-270 3861; fax 0171-270 6075

The National Investment and Loans Office is a non-ministerial government department which was set up in 1980 by the merger of the National Debt Office and the Public Works Loan Board. The Office provides the staff and administrative support for the National Debt Commissioners, the Public Works Loan Commissioners and the Office of HM Paymaster-General. The National Debt

Office is responsible for managing the investment portfolios of certain public funds and the management of some residual operations relating to the national debt. The function of the Public Works Loan Board is to make loans from the National Loans Fund to local authorities and certain other statutory bodies, primarily for capital purposes.

The Office of HM Paymaster-General has continuously existed in its present form since 1836; the Paymaster-General has responsibilities assigned from time to time by the Prime Minister and is currently a Treasury minister. The Assistant Paymaster-General is responsible for the banking and financial information services provided to the Government and public sector bodies by the Office of HM Paymaster-General.
Director, I. H. Peattie
Establishment Officer, A. Lawrie

NATIONAL DEBT OFFICE
0171-270 3868

Comptroller-General, I. H. Peattie

PUBLIC WORKS LOAN BOARD
0171-270 3874

Chairman, A. D. Loehnis, CMG
Deputy Chairman, Miss V. J. Di Palma, OBE
Other Commissioners, Dame Sheila Masters, DBE; Mrs R. V. Hale; R. Burton; J. A. Parkes, CBE; J. Andrews; B. Tanner, CBE; T. Fellowes; Mrs R. Terry; D. W. Midgley; L. M. Nippers
Secretary, I. H. Peattie
Assistant Secretary, D. Hockey

OFFICE OF HM PAYMASTER-GENERAL
0171-270 6074

Paymaster-General, Dawn Primarolo, MP
Assistant Paymaster-General, I. H. Peattie
Head of Banking, L. Palmer

BANKING OPERATIONS, National Investment and Loans Office, Sutherland House, Russell Way, Crawley, W. Sussex RH10 1UH. Tel: 01293-604410. *Banking Manager*, P. Harris

NATIONAL LOTTERY CHARITIES BOARD
St Vincent House, 16 Suffolk Street, London SW1Y 4NL
Tel 0171-747 5299; fax 0171-747 5347

The Board was set up under the National Lottery Act 1993 to distribute funds from the Lottery to support charitable, benevolent and philanthropic organizations. The chairman and members are appointed by the Secretary of State for Culture, Media and Sport. The Board's main aim is to help meet the needs of those at greatest disadvantage in society and to improve the quality of life in the community through grants programmes in the UK and an international grants programme for UK-based agencies working abroad.
Chair, Lady Brittan, CBE
Deputy Chairman, Sir Adam Ridley
Members, Mrs T. Baring, CBE; A. Bhatia, OBE; S. Burkeman; J. Carroll; Mrs A. Clark; Ms K. Hampton; T. Jones, OBE; Ms A. Jordan; Mrs B. Lowndes, MBE; R. Martineau; W. Osborne; R. Partington; J. Simpson, OBE; N. Stewart, OBE; Mrs E. Watkins
Chief Executive, T. Hornsby

NATIONAL LOTTERY COMMISSION
2 Monck Street, London SW1P 2BQ
Tel 0171-227 2000; fax 0171-227 2005

The National Lottery Commission replaced the Office of the National Lottery (OFLOT) in April 1999 under the National Lottery Act 1998. The Commission is responsible for the granting, varying and enforcing of licences to run the National Lottery. Its duties are to ensure that the National Lottery is run with all due propriety, that the interests of players are protected, and, subject to these two objectives, that returns to the 'good causes' are maximized.
Chairman, B. Pomeroy
Commissioners, Ms H. Blume; Dame Helena Shovelton, DBE; Ms H. Spicer; R. Squire
Chief Executive, M. Harris
Director of Operations, K. Jones

For details of National Lottery operations, *see* National Lottery section

NATIONAL PHYSICAL LABORATORY
Queens Road, Teddington, Middx TW11 0LW
Tel 0181-977 3222; fax 0181-943 6458

The Laboratory is the UK's national standards laboratory. It develops, maintains and disseminates national measurement standards for physical quantities such as mass, length, time, temperature, voltage, force and pressure. It also conducts underpinning research on engineering materials and information technology and disseminates good measurement practice. It is government-owned but contractor-operated.
Managing Director, Dr J. Rae
Director of Marketing and Communications, D. C. Richardson

NATIONAL RADIOLOGICAL
PROTECTION BOARD
Chilton, Didcot, Oxon OX11 0RQ
Tel 01235-831600; fax 01235-833891

The National Radiological Protection Board is an independent statutory body created by the Radiological Protection Act 1970. It is the national point of authoritative reference on radiological protection for both ionizing and non-ionizing radiations, and has issued recommendations on limiting human exposure to electromagnetic fields and radiation from a range of sources, including X-rays, the Sun and power generators. Its sponsoring department is the Department of Health.
Chairman, Sir Walter Bodmer, PH.D., FRCPath., FRS
Director, Prof. R. H. Clarke

NATIONAL SAVINGS
Charles House, 375 Kensington High Street, London W14 8SD
Tel 0171-605 9300; fax 0171-605 9438

National Savings was established as a government department in 1969. It became an executive agency of the Treasury in 1996 and is responsible for the design, marketing and administration of savings and investment products for personal savers and investors. In April 1999 the German electronics group Siemens took over all the back office functions at National Savings.

Chief Executive, P. Bareau
Personnel Director, D. S. Speedie
Finance Director, R. Douglas
Commercial Director, C. Moxey
Funding Director, M. Corcoran
Sourcing Director, Ms J. Bevan

For details of schemes, *see* National Savings section

OFFICE FOR NATIONAL STATISTICS
1 Drummond Gate, London SW1V 2QQ
Tel 0171-533 6363; fax 0171-533 5719

The Office for National Statistics was created in 1996 by the merger of the Central Statistical Office and the Office of Population, Censuses and Surveys. It is an executive agency of the Treasury and is responsible for preparing and interpreting key economic statistics for government policy; collecting and publishing business statistics; publishing annual and monthly statistical digests; providing researchers, analysts and other customers with a statistical service; administration of the marriage laws and local registration of births, marriages and deaths in England and Wales; provision of population estimates and projections and statistics on health and other demographic matters in England and Wales; population censuses in England and Wales; surveys for government departments and public bodies; and promoting these functions within the UK, the European Union and internationally to provide a statistical service to meet European Union and international requirements.

The Office for National Statistics is also responsible for establishing and maintaining a central database of key economic and social statistics produced to common classifications, definitions and standards.

Chief Executive, Registrar-General for England and Wales and Head of the Government Statistical Service, Prof. T. Holt (until the end of 1999)
Directors (G3), J. Calder (*Methods and Quality*); vacant (*Census, Population and Health*); J. Kidgell (*Economic Statistics*); D. Roberts (*Administration and Registration*); M. Pepper (*Business Statistics*); J. Pullinger (*Social Statistics*)
Principal Establishment Officer (G5), E. Williams
Principal Finance Officer (G5), P. Murphy
Head of Information (G6), I. Scott
Parliamentary Clerk, L. Land

FAMILY RECORDS CENTRE, 1 Myddelton Street, London EC1R 1UW. Tel: 0181-392 5300. Open Mon., Wed., Fri. 9 a.m.–5 p.m.; Tues. 10 a.m.–7 p.m.; Thurs. 9 a.m.–7 p.m.; Sat. 9.30 a.m.–5 p.m.

JOINT NATURE CONSERVATION COMMITTEE
Monkstone House, City Road, Peterborough PE1 1JY
Tel 01733-562626; fax 01733-555948

The Committee was established under the Environmental Protection Act 1990. It advises the Government and others on UK and international nature conservation issues and disseminates knowledge on these subjects. It establishes common standards for the monitoring of nature conservation and research, and provides guidance to English Nature, Scottish Natural Heritage, the Countryside Council for Wales and the Department of the Environment for Northern Ireland.

Chairman, Sir Angus Stirling
Managing Director, D. Steer
Director, Dr M. A. Vincent

NEW OPPORTUNITIES FUND
Dacre House, Dacre Street, London SW1H 0DH
Tel 0171-222 3084; fax 0171-222 3085

The New Opportunities Fund was established under the National Lottery Act 1998 and is responsible for distributing funds allocated from the proceeds of the National Lottery to health, education and environment projects within initiatives determined by the Government.

Chair of the Board, The Baroness Pitkeathley
Members of the Board, Ms J. Barrow; Prof. E. Bolton, CB; Ms N. Clarke; Prof. A. Patmore, CBE; D. Mackie; D. Campbell; Ms J. Hutt; Dr S. Griffiths; Ms R. McDonough
Chief Executive, S. Dunmore

NORTHERN IRELAND AUDIT OFFICE
106 University Street, Belfast BT7 1EU
Tel 01232-251000; fax 01232-251106

The primary aim of the Northern Ireland Audit Office is to provide independent assurance, information and advice to Parliament on the proper accounting for Northern Ireland departmental and certain other public expenditure, revenue, assets and liabilities; on regularity and propriety; and on the economy, efficiency and effectiveness of the use of resources.

Comptroller and Auditor-General for Northern Ireland, J. M. Dowdall

NORTHERN IRELAND HUMAN RIGHTS COMMISSION
Temple Court, 39–41 North Street, Belfast BT1 1NA
Tel 01232-243987; fax 01232-247844

The Northern Ireland Human Rights Commission was set up in March 1999. Its main functions are to keep under the review the law and practice relating to human rights in Northern Ireland, to advise the Government and to promote an awareness of human rights in Northern Ireland. The Commission consists of one full-time commissioner and nine part-time commissioners, all appointed by the Secretary of State for Northern Ireland.

Chief Commissioner (£55,000), Prof. B. Dickson
Commissioners (£8,000 each), Ms C. Bell; Ms M-A. Dinsmore, QC; T. Donnelly, MBE; The Revd H. Good, OBE; Prof. T. Hadden; Ms A. Hegarty; Ms P. Kelly; Ms I. McCormack; F. McGuinness

NORTHERN IRELAND OFFICE
11 Millbank, London SW1P 4PN
Tel 0171-210 3000
Castle Buildings, Stormont, Belfast BT4 3SG
Tel 01232-520700; fax 01232-528195
Web: http://www.nics.gov.uk/centgov/nio/nio.htm

The Northern Ireland Office was established in 1972, when the Northern Ireland (Temporary Provisions) Act transferred the legislative and executive powers of the Northern

Ireland Parliament and Government to the UK Parliament and a Secretary of State.

The Northern Ireland Office is responsible primarily for security issues, law and order and prisons, and for matters relating to the political and constitutional future of the province. It also deals with international issues as they affect Northern Ireland. The Northern Ireland departments are responsible for the administration of social, industrial and economic policies.

Under the terms of the 1998 Belfast Agreement, power was due to be devolved to the New Northern Ireland Assembly in 1999; the Assembly would then take on responsibility for the relevant areas of work currently undertaken by the departments of the Northern Ireland Office. In December 1998 the creation of ten new departments was agreed: agriculture and rural development; the environment; regional development; social development; education; higher education, training and employment; enterprise, trade and investment; culture, arts and leisure; health, social services and public safety; and finance and personnel. Each department would be headed by a member of the power-sharing executive (three each by the UUP and the SDLP and two each by the DUP and Sinn Fein), which would be headed by the First Minister and Deputy First Minister. Six cross-border implementation bodies would also be established, dealing with inland waterways, food safety, trade and business development, EU programmes, language, and aquaculture.

It is anticipated that the number of ministers at the Northern Ireland Office would be reduced in the event of devolution.

The names of most civil servants are not listed for security reasons.

Secretary of State for Northern Ireland, The Rt. Hon. Dr Marjorie (Mo) Mowlam, MP
  Special Advisers, N. Warner; A. Lappin
  Parliamentary Private Secretary, H. Jackson, MP
Minister of State, The Rt. Hon. Adam Ingram, MP (*Security, Victims, Europe, Constitution*)
  Parliamentary Private Secretary, T. Colman, MP
Parliamentary Under-Secretaries of State, The Lord Dubs (*Environment, Agriculture*); John McFall, MP (*Education, Economic Development*); George Howarth, MP (*Political Development, Equality, Human Rights*)
Permanent Under-Secretary of State (*SCS*), J. Pilling, CB
Second Permanent Under-Secretary of State, Head of the Northern Ireland Civil Service, J. Semple, CB

LONDON
SCS, (Political Director)
SCS, (Associate Political Director); (International and Planning); (Constitutional and Political); (Rights and European); (Personnel and Office Services)
SCS, (Director of Information Services)

BELFAST
SCS, (Political Director)
SCS, (Associate Political Director); (Security); (Criminal Justice); (Political); (Personnel and Finance)

NORTHERN IRELAND INFORMATION SERVICE
Castle Buildings, Stormont, Belfast BT4 3SG
Tel 01232-520700

Director of Communications

EXECUTIVE AGENCIES

COMPENSATION AGENCY, Royston House, Upper Queen Street, Belfast BT1 6FD. Tel: 01232-2499444
FORENSIC SCIENCE AGENCY, Seapark, 151 Belfast Road, Carrickfergus, Co. Antrim BT38 8PL. Tel: 01232-365744
NORTHERN IRELAND PRISON SERVICE, *see* page 383

DEPARTMENT OF AGRICULTURE FOR NORTHERN IRELAND
Dundonald House, Upper Newtownards Road, Belfast BT4 3SB
Tel 01232-520100; fax 01232-525015

Parliamentary Under-Secretary of State, The Lord Dubs
Permanent Secretary (*SCS*)
Under-Secretaries (*SCS*), (Central Services and Rural Development); (Food, Farm and Environmental Policy); (Veterinary); (Science); (Agri-Food Development)

EXECUTIVE AGENCIES
INTERVENTION BOARD
— *see* page 314
RIVERS AGENCY, 4 Hospital Road, Belfast BT8 8JP. Tel: 01232-253355
FOREST SERVICE, Dundonald House, Upper Newtownards Road, Belfast BT4 3SB. Tel: 01232-524480

DEPARTMENT OF ECONOMIC DEVELOPMENT NORTHERN IRELAND
Netherleigh, Massey Avenue, Belfast BT4 2JP
Tel 01232-529900; fax 01232-529550

Parliamentary Under-Secretary of State, John McFall, MP
Permanent Secretary (*SCS*)
Under-Secretaries (*SCS*), (Resources Group); (Regulatory Services Group)
INDUSTRIAL DEVELOPMENT BOARD, IDB House, 64 Chichester Street, Belfast BT1 4JX. Tel: 01232-233233

EXECUTIVE AGENCIES
INDUSTRIAL RESEARCH AND TECHNOLOGY UNIT, 17 Antrim Road, Lisburn BT28 3AL. Tel: 01846-623000
TRAINING AND EMPLOYMENT AGENCY (NORTHERN IRELAND), Adelaide House, Adelaide Street, Belfast BT2 8FD. Tel: 01232-257777

DEPARTMENT OF EDUCATION FOR NORTHERN IRELAND
Rathgael House, Balloo Road, Bangor, Co. Down BT19 7PR
Tel 01247-279279; fax 01247-279100

Parliamentary Under-Secretary of State, John McFall, MP
Permanent Secretary (*SCS*)
Deputy Secretaries (*SCS*), (Schools); (Finance and Corporate Services)
Chief Inspector (*SCS*), (Education and Training Inspectorate)

DEPARTMENT OF THE ENVIRONMENT FOR NORTHERN IRELAND
Clarence Court, 10–18 Adelaide Street, Belfast BT2 8GB
Tel 01232-540540

Parliamentary Under-Secretary of State, The Lord Dubs
Permanent Secretary (*SCS*)
Under-Secretaries (*SCS*), (Personnel, Finance, Housing and Local Government); (Rural and Urban Affairs); (Roads, Water and Transport); (Planning, Works and Environment)

EXECUTIVE AGENCIES
CONSTRUCTION SERVICE, Churchill House, Victoria Square, Belfast BT1 4QW. Tel: 01232-250284
DRIVER AND VEHICLE LICENSING AGENCY (NORTHERN IRELAND), County Hall, Castlerock Road, Coleraine, Co. Londonderry BT51 3HS. Tel: 01265-41200

DRIVER AND VEHICLE TESTING AGENCY (NORTHERN IRELAND), Balmoral Road, Belfast BT12 6QL. Tel: 01232-681831

ENVIRONMENT AND HERITAGE SERVICE, Commonwealth House, Castle Street, Belfast BT1 1GU. Tel: 01232-251477

LAND REGISTERS OF NORTHERN IRELAND, Lincoln Building, 27–45 Great Victoria Street, Belfast BT2 7SL. Tel: 01232-251515

ORDNANCE SURVEY OF NORTHERN IRELAND, Colby House, Stranmillis Court, Belfast BT9 5BJ. Tel: 01232-255755

PLANNING SERVICE, Clarence Court, 10–18 Adelaide Street, Belfast BT2 8GB. Tel: 01232-540540

PUBLIC RECORD OFFICE (NORTHERN IRELAND) – *see* page 334

RATE COLLECTION AGENCY (NORTHERN IRELAND), Oxford House, 49–55 Chichester Street, Belfast BT1 4HH. Tel: 01232-252252

ROADS SERVICE, Clarence Court, 10–18 Adelaide Street, Belfast BT2 8GB. Tel: 01232-540540

WATER SERVICE, Northland House, 3 Frederick Street, Belfast BT1 2NR. Tel: 01232-244711

ADVISORY BODIES

HISTORIC BUILDINGS COUNCIL FOR NORTHERN IRELAND, c/o Environment and Heritage Service, Historic Monuments and Buildings, Commonwealth House, Castle Street, Belfast BT1 1GU. Tel: 01232-251477

COUNCIL FOR NATURE CONSERVATION AND THE COUNTRYSIDE, c/o Environment and Heritage Service, Commonwealth House, Castle Street, Belfast BT1 1GU. Tel: 01232-251477

DEPARTMENT OF FINANCE AND PERSONNEL

Parliament Buildings, Stormont, Belfast BT4 3SG
Tel 01232-520400

Minister of State, The Rt. Hon. Adam Ingram, MP
Permanent Secretary (*SCS*)
Under-Secretaries (*SCS*), (Supply Group); (Resources Control and Professional Services Group); (Central Personnel Group); (Government Purchasing Service)

NORTHERN IRELAND CIVIL SERVICE (NICS)
Parliament Buildings, Stormont, Belfast BT4 3TT
Tel 01232-520700

Head of Civil Service (*SCS*), J. Semple, CB
Under-Secretaries (*SCS*), (Central Secretariat); (Legal Services); (Office of the Legislative Council)

GENERAL REGISTER OFFICE (NORTHERN IRELAND), Oxford House, 49–65 Chichester Street, Belfast BT1 4HL. Tel: 01232-252000. *Registrar-General* (*G6*)

EXECUTIVE AGENCIES

BUSINESS DEVELOPMENT SERVICE, Craigantlet Buildings, Stoney Road, Belfast BT4 3SX. Tel: 01232-520400

GOVERNMENT PURCHASING AGENCY, Rosepark House, Upper Newtownards Road, Belfast BT4 3NR. Tel: 01232-520400

NORTHERN IRELAND STATISTICS AND RESEARCH AGENCY, The Arches Centre, 11–13 Bloomfield Avenue, Belfast BT5 5HD. Tel: 01232-526093

VALUATION AND LANDS AGENCY, Queen's Court, 56–66 Upper Queen Street, Belfast BT4 6FD. Tel: 01232-250700

DEPARTMENT OF HEALTH AND SOCIAL SERVICES NORTHERN IRELAND

Castle Buildings, Stormont, Belfast BT4 3PP
Tel 01232-520000; fax 01232-520572

Parlimentary Under-Secretary of State, George Howarth, MP
Permanent Secretary (*SCS*)
Chief Medical Officer (*SCS*)
Under-Secretaries (*SCS*), (Health and Social Services Executive); (Health and Social Policy); (Medical and Allied Services); (Central Management and Social Security Policy Group)

HEALTH AND SOCIAL SERVICES BOARDS
— *see* Social Welfare section

EXECUTIVE AGENCIES

NORTHERN IRELAND CHILD SUPPORT AGENCY, Great Northern Tower, 17 Great Victoria Street, Belfast BT2 7AD. Tel: 01232-339000

NORTHERN IRELAND HEALTH AND SOCIAL SERVICES ESTATES AGENCY, Stoney Road, Dundonald, Belfast BT16 1US. Tel: 01232-520025

NORTHERN IRELAND SOCIAL SECURITY AGENCY, Castle Buildings, Stormont, Belfast BT4 3SJ. Tel: 01232-520520

OCCUPATIONAL PENSIONS REGULATORY AUTHORITY

Invicta House, Trafalgar Place, Brighton BN1 4DW
Tel 01273-627600; fax 01273-627688

The Occupational Pensions Regulatory Authority (OPRA) was set up under the Pensions Act 1995 and became fully operational on 6 April 1997. It is the independent, statutory regulator of occupational pension schemes in the UK.
Chairman, J. Hayes, CBE
Chief Executive, Mrs C. Instance

OMBUDSMEN

— *see* Local Commissioners *and* Parliamentary Commissioner. For non-statutory Ombudsmen, *see* Index

ORDNANCE SURVEY

Romsey Road, Maybush, Southampton SO16 4GU
Tel 01703-792000; fax 01703-792452

Ordnance Survey is the national mapping agency for Britain. It is a government department funded by parliamentary vote, and reports to the Secretary of State for the Environment, Transport and the Regions.
Director-General and Chief Executive, Prof. D. Rhind

PARADES COMMISSION

12th Floor, Windsor House, 6–12 Bedford Street, Belfast BT2 7EL
Tel 01232-895900; fax 01232-322988

The Parades Commission was set up under the Public Processions (Northern Ireland) Act 1998. Its function is to encourage and facilitate local accommodation on contentious parades; where this is not possible, the Commission is empowered to make legal determinations about such parades, which may include imposing conditions on aspects of the notified parade.
    The chairman and members are appointed by the

Secretary of State for Northern Ireland; the membership must, as far as is practicable, be representative of the community in Northern Ireland.
Chairman, A. Graham
Members, D. Hewitt, CBE; Mrs R. A. McCormick; A. Canavan; F. Guckian, CBE; W. Martin; Dr Barbara Erwin
Secretary (*G5*), Mrs H. Robinson

OFFICE OF THE PARLIAMENTARY COMMISSIONER FOR ADMINISTRATION AND HEALTH SERVICE COMMISSIONER
Millbank Tower, Millbank, London SW1P 4QP
Tel 0845-015 4033; fax 0171-217 4000

The Parliamentary Commissioner for Administration (the Parliamentary Ombudsman) is independent of Government and is an officer of Parliament. He is responsible for investigating complaints referred to him by MPs from members of the public who claim to have sustained injustice in consequence of maladministration by or on behalf of government departments and certain non-departmental public bodies. In March 1999 an additional 158 public bodies were brought within the jurisdiction of the Parliamentary Commissioner. Certain types of action by government departments or bodies are excluded from investigation. The Parliamentary Commissioner is also responsible for investigating complaints, referred by MPs, alleging that access to official information has been wrongly refused under the Code of Practice on Access to Government Information 1994.

The Health Service Commissioners (the Health Service Ombudsmen) for England, for Scotland and for Wales are responsible for investigating complaints against National Health Service authorities and trusts that are not dealt with by those authorities to the satisfaction of the complainant. Complaints can be referred direct by the member of the public who claims to have sustained injustice or hardship in consequence of the failure in a service provided by a relevant body, failure of that body to provide a service or in consequence of any other action by that body. The Ombudsmens' jurisdiction now covers complaints about family doctors, dentists, pharmacists and opticians, and complaints about actions resulting from clinical judgment. The Health Service Ombudsmen are also responsible for investigating complaints that information has been wrongly refused under the Code of Practice on Openness in the National Health Service 1995. The three offices are presently held by the Parliamentary Commissioner.
Parliamentary Commissioner and Health Service Commissioner (*G1*), M. S. Buckley
Deputy Parliamentary Commissioner (*G3*), J. E. Avery, CB
Deputy Health Service Commissioner (*G3*), Ms H. Scott
Directors, Parliamentary Commissioner (*G5*), Ms J. Binstead; N. Cleary; Mrs S. P. Maunsell; G. Monk; A. Watson
Directors, Health Service Commissioners (*G5*), Ms H. Bainbridge; N. J. Jordan; D. R. G. Pinchin; R. Tyrrell
Finance and Establishment Officer (*G5*), J. Stevens

For Scotland, *see* Scottish Parliamentary Commissioner for Administration

For Wales, *see* Welsh Administration Ombudsman

PARLIAMENTARY COMMISSIONER FOR STANDARDS
House of Commons, London SW1A 0AA
Tel 0171-219 0320

Following recommendations of the Committee on Standards in Public Life, the House of Commons agreed to the appointment of an independent Parliamentary Commissioner for Standards with effect from November 1995. The Commissioner has responsibility for maintaining and monitoring the operation of the Register of Members' Interests; advising Members of Parliament and the select committee on standards and privileges, on the interpretation of the rules on disclosure and advocacy, and on other questions of propriety; and receiving and, if she thinks fit, investigating complaints about the conduct of MPs.
Parliamentary Commissioner for Standards, Miss E. Filkin

PARLIAMENTARY COUNSEL
36 Whitehall, London SW1A 2AY
Tel 0171-210 6637; fax 0171-210 6632

Parliamentary Counsel draft all government bills (i.e. primary legislation) except those relating exclusively to Scotland, the latter being drafted by the Lord Advocate's Department. They also advise on all aspects of parliamentary procedure in connection with such bills and draft government amendments to them as well as any motions (including financial resolutions) necessary to secure their introduction into, and passage through, Parliament.
First Counsel (*SCS*), E. G. Caldwell, CB
Counsel (*SCS*), E. G. Bowman, CB; G. B. Sellers, CB; E. R. Sutherland, CB; P. F. A. Knowles, CB; S. C. Laws, CB; R. S. Parker, CB; Miss C. E. Johnston; P. J. Davies; J. M. Sellers

PAROLE BOARD FOR ENGLAND AND WALES
Abell House, John Islip Street, London SW1P 4LH
Tel 0171-217 5314; 0171-217 5793

The Board was constituted under the Criminal Justice Act 1967 and continued under the Criminal Justice Act 1991. It is an executive non-departmental public body and its duty is to advise the Home Secretary with respect to matters referred to it by him which are connected with the early release or recall of prisoners. Its functions include giving directions concerning the release on licence of prisoners serving discretionary life sentences and of certain prisoners serving long-term determinate sentences.
Chairman, The Baroness Prashar, CBE
Vice-Chairman, The Hon. Mr Justice Tucker
Chief Executive, J. Casey

PAROLE BOARD FOR SCOTLAND
Saughton House, Broomhouse Drive, Edinburgh EH11 3XD
Tel 0131-244 8755; fax 0131-244 6974

The Board directs and advises the First Minister on the release of prisoners on licence, and related matters.
Chairman, I. McNee
Vice-Chairmen, Sheriff G. Shiach; Ms J. Freeman
Secretary, H. P. Boyle

PATENT OFFICE

Concept House, Cardiff Road, Newport NP9 1RH
Tel 0645-500505; fax 01633-814444

The Patent Office is an executive agency of the Department of Trade and Industry. The duties of the Patent Office are to administer the Patent Acts, the Registered Designs Act and the Trade Marks Act, and to deal with questions relating to the Copyright, Designs and Patents Act 1988. The Search and Advisory Service carries out commercial searches through patent information. In 1997 the Office granted 2,792 patents and registered 9,592 designs and 27,897 trade marks.

Comptroller-General, Ms A. Brimelow
Director, Intellectual Property Policy Directorate, G. Jenkins
Director, Patents and Designs, R. J. Marchant
Director and Assistant Registrar of Trade Marks, P. Lawrence
Director, Administration and Resources and Secretary to the Patent Office, C. Octon
Director, Copyright, J. Startup
Director, Finance, J. Thompson

HM PAYMASTER-GENERAL, OFFICE OF
— *see* National Investment and Loans Office

PENSIONS COMPENSATION BOARD

11 Belgrave Road, London SW1V 1RB
Tel 0171-828 9794; fax 0171-931 7239

The Pensions Compensation Board was established under the Pensions Act 1995 and is funded by a levy paid by all eligible occupational pension schemes. Its function is to compensate occupational pension schemes for losses due to dishonesty where the employer is solvent.

Chairman, Dr J. T. Farrand, QC
Secretary, M. Lydon

OFFICE OF THE PENSIONS OMBUDSMAN

6th Floor, 11 Belgrave Road, London SW1V 1RB
Tel 0171-834 9144; fax 0171-821 0065

The Pensions Ombudsman is appointed under the Pension Schemes Act 1993 as amended by the Pensions Act 1995. He investigates and decides complaints and disputes concerning occupational pension schemes. Complaints concerning personal pensions would normally be dealt with only if outside the jurisdiction of the Personal Investment Authority. The Ombudsman is completely independent and there is no charge for bringing a complaint or dispute to him.

Pensions Ombudsman, Dr J. T. Farrand, QC

POLICE COMPLAINTS AUTHORITY

10 Great George Street, London SW1P 3AE
Tel 0171-273 6450; fax 0171-273 6401

The Police Complaints Authority was established under the Police and Criminal Evidence Act 1984 to provide an independent system for dealing with complaints by members of the public against police officers in England and Wales. It is funded by the Home Office. The authority has powers to supervise the investigation of certain categories of serious complaints and certain statutory functions in relation to the disciplinary aspects of complaints. It does not deal with police operational matters; these are usually dealt with by the Chief Constable of the relevant force.

Chairman, P. Moorhouse
Deputy Chairman, Ms M. Meacher
Members, Mrs L. Allan; I. Bynoe; Ms J. Dobry; J. Elliott; Miss M. Mian; Mrs C. Mitchell; A. Potts; Mrs M. Scorer; Ms L. Whyte; A. Williams, MBE

INDEPENDENT COMMISSION FOR POLICE COMPLAINTS FOR NORTHERN IRELAND
— *see* page 311

POLITICAL HONOURS SCRUTINY COMMITTEE

Ashley House, 2 Monck Street, London SW1P 2BQ
Tel 0171-276 2770; fax 0171-276 2766

The function of the Political Honours Scrutiny Committee (a committee of Privy Councillors) was last set out in full in an Order in Council in May 1997. Subsequent Orders in Council have been made announcing changes in the committee's membership. The Prime Minister submits certain particulars to the Committee about persons proposed to be recommended for honour for their political services. The Committee, after such enquiry as it thinks fit, reports to the Prime Minister whether, so far as it believes, the persons whose names are submitted are fit and proper persons to be recommended.

Chairman, The Lord Thomson of Monifieth, KT, PC
Members, The Baroness Dean of Thornton-le-Fylde, PC; The Lord Hurd of Westwell, CH, CBE
Secretary, A. J. Merifield, CB

PORT OF LONDON AUTHORITY

Devon House, 58–60 St Katharine's Way, London E1 9LB
Tel 0171-265 2656; fax 0171-265 2699

The Port of London Authority is a public trust constituted under the Port of London Act 1908 and subsequent legislation. It is the governing body for the Port of London, covering the tidal portion of the River Thames from Teddington to the seaward limit. The Board comprises a chairman and up to seven but not less than four non-executive members appointed by the Secretary of State for the Environment, Transport and the Regions, and up to four but not less than one executive members appointed by the Board.

Chairman, Sir Brian Shaw
Vice-Chairman, J. H. Kelly, CBE
Chief Executive, S. Cuthbert
Secretary, G. E. Ennals

THE POST OFFICE

148 Old Street, London EC1V 9HQ
Tel 0171-490 2888

Crown services for the carriage of government dispatches were set up in about 1516. The conveyance of public correspondence began in 1635 and the mail service was made a parliamentary responsibility with the setting up of a Post Office in 1657. Telegraphs came under Post Office control in 1870 and the Post Office Telephone Service began in 1880. The National Girobank service of the Post

Office began in 1968. The Post Office ceased to be a government department in 1969 when responsibility for the running of the postal, telecommunications, giro and remittance services was transferred to a public authority called The Post Office. The 1981 British Telecommunications Act separated the functions of the Post Office, making it solely responsible for postal services and Girobank. Girobank was privatized in 1990. In July 1999 the Government announced plans to turn the Post Office into a public limited company, give it greater commercial freedom and set up an independent regulator to protect consumer interests.

The chairman, chief executive and members of the Post Office Board are appointed by the Secretary of State for Trade and Industry but responsibility for the running of the Post Office as a whole rests with the Board in its corporate capacity.

FINANCIAL RESULTS £m	1997–8	1998–9
Post Office Group		
Turnover	6,759	7,010
Profit before tax	664	608
Royal Mail		
Turnover	5,411	5,570
Profit before tax	560	485
Parcelforce		
Turnover	465	474
Profit (loss) before tax	(14)	(25)
Post Office Counters		
Turnover	1,130	1,148
Profit before tax	33	22

POST OFFICE BOARD
Chairman, Dr N. Bain
Chief Executive, J. Roberts, CBE
Members, R. Close (*Managing Director, Finance*); J. Cope (*Managing Director, Strategy and Personnel*)
Secretary, R. Adams

For postal services, *see* Communications section

PRIME MINISTER'S OFFICE
— *see* page 286

PRISONS OMBUDSMAN FOR ENGLAND AND WALES
Ashley House, 2 Monck Street, London SW1P 2BQ
Tel 0171-276 2876; fax 0171-276 2860

The post of Prisons Ombudsman was instituted in 1994. The Ombudsman is appointed by the Home Secretary and is an independent point of appeal for prisoners' grievances about their lives in prison, including disciplinary issues. The Ombudsman cannot investigate grievances relating to issues which are the subject of litigation or criminal proceedings, the merits of decisions taken by ministers (although from May 1999 he may investigate the advice upon which ministers' decisions were made), or actions of bodies outside the prison service.
Prisons Ombudsman, S. Shaw

For Scotland, *see* Scottish Prisons Complaints Commission

PRIVY COUNCIL OFFICE
2 Carlton Gardens, London SW1Y 5AA
Tel 0171-270 0474; fax 0171-270 0109

The Office is responsible for the arrangements leading to the making of all royal proclamations and Orders in Council; for certain formalities connected with ministerial changes; for considering applications for the granting (or amendment) of royal charters; for the scrutiny and approval of by-laws and statutes of chartered bodies; and for the appointment of high sheriffs and many Crown and Privy Council appointments to governing bodies.
President of the Council (and Leader of the House of Commons),
  The Rt. Hon. Margaret Beckett, MP
  Private Secretary, Ms V. A. Scarborough
Parliamentary Secretary, Paddy Tipping, MP
Clerk of the Council, A. K. Galloway
Deputy Clerk of the Council, G. C. Donald
Senior Clerk, Miss M. A. McCullagh
Registrar, J. A. C. Watherston

PROCURATOR FISCAL SERVICE
— *see* page 366

PUBLIC HEALTH LABORATORY SERVICE
61 Colindale Avenue, London NW9 5DF
Tel 0181-200 1295; fax 0181-200 8130

The Public Health Laboratory Service comprises nine groups of laboratories, the Central Public Health Laboratory, the Communicable Disease Surveillance Centre and the Headquarters. The PHLS seeks to protect the population from infection through detection, diagnosis, surveillance, prevention and control of infections and communicable diseases. It keeps track of what infections are appearing where, advises on remedial or preventive action and provides clinical diagnostic services.
Chairman (£15,125), Prof. Sir Leslie Turnberg, MD
Deputy Chairman, R. Tabor
Director, Dr Diana Walford, FRCP, FRCPath.
Deputy Directors, Prof. B. I. Duerden, MD, FRCPath.
  (*Programmes*); K. M. Saunders (*Corporate Planning and Resources*)
Board Secretary, K. M. Saunders

CENTRAL PUBLIC HEALTH LABORATORY
Colindale Avenue, London NW9 5HT
Director, Prof. S. P. Borriello

COMMUNICABLE DISEASES SURVEILLANCE CENTRE
Colindale Avenue, NW9 5EQ
Director, Dr C. L. R. Bartlett

PHLS GROUPS OF LABORATORIES AND GROUP DIRECTORS
East, Dr P. M. B. White
Midlands, Dr R. E. Warren
North, Dr N. F. Lightfoot
North-West, Prof. P. Morgan-Capner
South-West, Prof. K. A. V. Cartwright
Thames, Dr R. Gross
Trent, Dr P. J. Wilkinson
Wessex, Dr S. A. Rousseau
Wales, Dr A. J. Howard

OTHER SPECIAL LABORATORIES AND UNITS

ANAEROBE REFERENCE UNIT, Public Health Laboratory, Cardiff. *Head,* Prof. B. I. Duerden

ANTIVIRAL SUSCEPTIBILITY REFERENCE UNIT, Public Health Laboratory, Birmingham. *Head*, Dr D. P. Pillay
CRYPTOSPRORIDIUM REFERENCE UNIT, Public Health Laboratory, Rhyl. *Head*, Dr D. Casemore
FOOD MICROBIOLOGY RESEARCH UNIT, Public Health Laboratory, Exeter. *Head*, Prof. T. J. Humphrey
GENITO-URINARY INFECTIONS REFERENCE LABORATORY, Public Health Laboratory, Bristol. *Head*, Dr A. J. Herring
LEPTOSPIRA REFERENCE LABORATORY, Public Health Laboratory, Hereford. *Director*, Dr T. J. Coleman
LYME DISEASE REFERENCE UNIT, Public Health Laboratory, Southampton. *Head*, Dr S. O'Connell
MALARIA REFERENCE LABORATORY, London School of Hygiene and Tropical Medicine, London WCIE 7HT. *Directors*, Prof. D. J. Bradley; Dr D. C. Warhurst
MENINGOCOCCAL REFERENCE LABORATORY, Public Health Laboratory, Manchester. *Director*, Dr B. A. Oppenheim
MYCOBACTERIUM REFERENCE UNIT, Public Health Laboratory, Dulwich, London. *Director*, Dr F. Drobniewski
MYCOLOGY REFERENCE LABORATORY, Public Health Laboratory, Bristol. *Head*, Dr D. Warnock; University of Leeds. *Head*, Prof. E. G. V. Evans
PARASITOLOGY REFERENCE LABORATORY, Hospital for Tropical Diseases, London. *Director*, Dr P. L. Chiodini
TOXOPLASMA REFERENCE LABORATORY, Public Health Laboratory, Swansea. *Head*, D. H. M. Joynson
WATER AND ENVIRONMENTAL MICROBIOLOGY RESEARCH UNIT, Public Health Laboratory, Nottingham. *Head*, Dr J. V. Lee

REGISTRAR OF PUBLIC LENDING RIGHT
Bayheath House, Prince Regent Street, Stockton-on-Tees TSI8 IDF
Tel 01642-604699; fax 01642-615641

Under the Public Lending Right system, in operation since 1983, payment is made from public funds to authors whose books are lent out from public libraries. Payment is made once a year and the amount each author receives is proportionate to the number of times (established from a sample) that each registered book has been lent out during the previous year. The Registrar of PLR, who is appointed by the Secretary of State for Culture, Media and Sport, compiles the register of authors and books. Only living authors resident in the UK or Germany are eligible to apply. (The term 'author' covers writers, illustrators, translators, and some editors/compilers.)

A payment of 2.07 pence was made in 1998–9 for each estimated loan of a registered book, up to a top limit of £6,000 for the books of any one registered author; the money for loans above this level is used to augment the remaining PLR payments. In February 1999, the sum of £4.159 million was made available for distribution to 17,192 registered authors and assignees as the annual payment of PLR.
Registrar, Dr J. G. Parker
Chairman of Advisory Committee, M. Holroyd

PUBLIC RECORD OFFICE
— *see* page 333

PUBLIC TRUST OFFICE
Stewart House, 24 Kingsway, London WC2B 6JX
Tel 0171-664 7000; fax 0171-664 7702
COURT FUNDS OFFICE, 22 Kingsway, London WC2B 6LE
Tel 0171-936 6000

The Public Trust Office became an executive agency of the Lord Chancellor's Department in 1994. The chief executive of the agency holds the statutory titles of Public Trustee and Accountant-General of the Supreme Court.

The Public Trustee is a trust corporation created to undertake the business of executorship and trusteeship; she can act as executor or administrator of the estate of a deceased person, or as trustee of a will or settlement. The Public Trustee is also responsible for the performance of all the administrative, but not the judicial, tasks required of the Court of Protection under Part VII of the Mental Health Act 1983, relating to the management and administration of the property and affairs of persons suffering from mental disorder. The Public Trustee also acts as Receiver when so directed by the Court, usually where there is no other person willing or able so to act. It also deals with the registration of Enduring Powers of Attorney.

The Accountant-General of the Supreme Court, through the Court Funds Office, is responsible for the investment and accounting of funds in court for persons under a disability, monies in court subject to litigation and statutory deposits.
Chief Executive (Public Trustee and Accountant-General), Ms J. C. Lomas
Assistant Public Trustee, vacant
Investment Manager, H. Stevenson
Chief Property Adviser, A. Nightingale

MENTAL HEALTH SECTOR
Director of Mental Health, Mrs H. M. Bratton
Principal of Receivership Division, W. K. Middleton
Principal of Protection Division, P. L. Hales

TRUSTS AND FUNDS SECTOR
Director of Trusts and Funds, F. J. Eddy
Divisional Manager, Court Funds Office, P. MacDermott
Divisional Manager, Trust Division, M. Munt
Finance Officer, M. Guntrip

PLANNING AND PAY POLICY
Head of Human Resources and Planning, D. Adams

PUBLIC WORKS LOAN BOARD
— *see* National Investment and Loans Office

QUEST (THE QUALITY, EFFICIENCY AND STANDARDS TEAM)
c/o Department for Culture, Media and Sport, 2-4 Cockspur Street, London SW1Y 5DH
Tel 0171-211 6200; fax 0171-211 6032

Quest was established in 1999. Its role is to monitor efficiency and financial management in organizations sponsored by the Department for Culture, Media and Sport and to provide independent advice to the Secretary of State.
Chairman, K. Oates
Chief Executive, T. Suter

COMMISSION FOR RACIAL EQUALITY
Elliot House, 10–12 Allington Street, London SW1E 5EH
Tel 0171-828 7022; fax 0171-630 7605

The Commission was established in 1977 under the Race Relations Act 1976. Its duties are to work towards the elimination of discrimination and promote equality of opportunity, to encourage good relations between different racial groups and to monitor the working of the Race Relations Act. It is funded by the Home Office.
Chairman, Sir Herman Ouseley (until Jan. 2000)
Deputy Chairmen, H. Harris; Dr M. Jogee
Commissioners, M. Amran; Dr R. Chandran; M. Hastings; S. Malik; Ms J. Mellor; P. Passley; Ms S. Patel; R. Purkiss; Ms C. Short; Dr J. Singh; R. Singh
Chief Executive, Ms S. Parsons

THE RADIO AUTHORITY
Holbrook House, 14 Great Queen Street, London WC2B 5DG
Tel 0171-430 2724; fax 0171-405 7062

The Radio Authority was established in 1991 under the Broadcasting Act 1990. It is the regulator and licensing authority for all independent radio services. Members of the Authority are appointed by the Secretary of State for Culture, Media and Sport; senior executive staff are appointed by the Authority.
Chairman, Sir Peter Gibbings
Deputy Chairman, M. Moriarty, CB
Members, Lady Sheil; A. Reid; Mrs H. Tennant; F. Sharkey; Ms S. Hewitt; D.Witherow; Ms S. Nathan
Chief Executive, A. Stoller
Deputy Chief Executive, D. Vick
Secretary to the Authority and Head of Legal Affairs, Ms E. Salomon

OFFICE OF THE RAIL REGULATOR
1 Waterhouse Square, 138–142 Holborn, London EC1N 2TQ
Tel 0171-282 2000; fax 0171-282 2040

The Office of the Rail Regulator was set up under the Railways Act 1993. The Regulator's main functions are the licensing of operators of railway assets; the approval of agreements for access by those operators to track, stations and light maintenance depots; the enforcement of domestic competition law; and consumer protection. The Regulator also sponsors a network of Rail Users' Consultative Committees, which represent the interests of passengers.

Subject to parliamentary approval of the necessary legislation, the consumer protection function of the Rail Regulator will be taken over by the new Strategic Rail Authority when it is set up, and the Rail Regulator will become subject to strategic guidance from the Secretary of State.
Rail Regulator, T. Winsor
Director, Economic Regulation Group, vacant
Director, Railway Network Group, M. Beswick
Director, Passenger Services Group, vacant
Chief Legal Adviser, M. R. Brocklehurst
Chief Economic Adviser, vacant
Director, Resources and RUCC Sponsorship, vacant
Director, Communications, K. R. Webb

RECORD OFFICES

ADVISORY COUNCIL ON PUBLIC RECORDS
Secretariat: Public Record Office, Kew, Richmond, Surrey TW9 4DU
Tel 0181-876 3444 ext. 2351; fax 0181-392 5295

Council members are appointed by the Lord Chancellor, under the Public Records Act 1958, to advise him on matters concerning public records in general and, in particular, on those aspects of the work of the Public Record Office which affect members of the public who make use of it.
Chairman, The Master of the Rolls
Secretary, T. R. Padfield

THE PUBLIC RECORD OFFICE
Kew, Richmond, Surrey TW9 4DU
Tel 0181-876 3444; fax 0181-878 8905

The Public Record Office, originally established in 1838 under the Master of the Rolls, was placed under the direction of the Lord Chancellor in 1958; it became an executive agency in 1992. The Lord Chancellor appoints a Keeper of Public Records, whose duties are to co-ordinate and supervise the selection of records of government departments and the law courts for permanent preservation, to safeguard the records and to make them available to the public. There is a separate record office for Scotland, now called the National Archives of Scotland (*see* page 334).

The Office holds records of central government dating from the Domesday Book (1086) to the present. Under the Public Records Act 1967 they are normally open to inspection when 30 years old, and are then available, without charge, in the reading rooms (Monday, Wednesday, Friday, Saturday, 9.30–5; Tuesday 10–7; Thursday 9.30–7).
Keeper of Public Records (G3), Mrs S. Tyacke, CB
Director, Public Services Division (G5), Dr E. Hallam Smith
Director, Government, Corporate and Information Services Division (G5), Dr D. Simpson

HOUSE OF LORDS RECORD OFFICE (THE PARLIAMENTARY ARCHIVES)
House of Lords, London SW1A 0PW
Tel 0171-219 3074; fax 0171-219 2570

Since 1497, the records of Parliament have been kept within the Palace of Westminster. They are in the custody of the Clerk of the Parliaments. In 1946 a record department was established to supervise their preservation and their availability to the public. The search room of the office is open to the public Monday–Friday, 9.30–5 (Tuesday to 8, by appointment).

Some three million documents are preserved, including Acts of Parliament from 1497, journals of the House of Lords from 1510, minutes and committee proceedings from 1610, and papers laid before Parliament from 1531. Amongst the records are the Petition of Right, the Death Warrant of Charles I, the Declaration of Breda, and the Bill of Rights. The House of Lords Record Office also has charge of the journals of the House of Commons (from 1547), and other surviving records of the Commons (from 1572), including documents relating to private bill legislation from 1818. Among other documents are the records of the Lord Great Chamberlain, the political papers of certain members of the two Houses, and documents relating to Parliament acquired on behalf of the nation. A permanent exhibition was established in the Royal Gallery in 1979.
Clerk of the Records, S. K. Ellison
Assistant Clerks of the Records, D. L. Prior; Dr C. Shenton

ROYAL COMMISSION ON HISTORICAL MANUSCRIPTS
Quality House, Quality Court, Chancery Lane, London WC2A 1HP
Tel 0171-242 1198; fax 0171-831 3550

The Commission was set up by royal warrant in 1869 to enquire and report on collections of papers of value for the study of history which were in private hands. In 1959 a new warrant enlarged these terms of reference to include all historical records, wherever situated, outside the Public Records and gave it added responsibilities as a central co-ordinating body to promote, assist and advise on their proper preservation and storage. The Commission is sponsored by the Department for Culture, Media and Sport.

The Commission also maintains the National Register of Archives (NRA), which contains over 41,000 unpublished lists and catalogues of manuscript collections describing the holdings of local record offices, national and university libraries, specialist repositories and others in the UK and overseas. The NRA can be searched using computerized indices which are available in the Commission's search room.

The Commission also administers the Manorial and Tithe Documents Rules on behalf of the Master of the Rolls.

Chairman, The Lord Bingham of Cornhill, PC
Commissioners, Sir Patrick Cormack, FSA, MP; The Lord Egremont and Leconfield; Sir Matthew Farrer, GCVO; Sir John Sainty, KCB, FSA; Very Revd H. E. C. Stapleton, FSA; Sir Keith Thomas, FBA; Mrs C. M. Short; The Earl of Scarbrough; Mrs A. Dundas-Bekker; G. E. Aylmer, D.Phil, FBA; Mrs S. J. Davies, Ph.D.; Mrs A. Prochaska, Ph.D.; Prof. H. C. G. Matthew, D.Phil, FBA; Miss R. Dunhill, FSA; Dr Caroline Barron, FSA; Prof. T. C. Smout, CBE, Ph.D., FBA, FRSE, FSAScot.
Secretary, C. J. Kitching, Ph.D., FSA

SCOTTISH RECORDS ADVISORY COUNCIL
HM General Register House, Edinburgh EH1 3YY
Tel 0131-535 1314; fax 0131-535 1360

The Council was established under the Public Records (Scotland) Act 1937. Its members are appointed by the First Minister and it may submit proposals or make representations to the First Minister, the Lord Justice General or the Lord President of the Court of Session on questions relating to the public records of Scotland.
Chairman, Prof. Anne Crowther
Secretary, Ms A. Rosie

NATIONAL ARCHIVES OF SCOTLAND
HM General Register House, Edinburgh EH1 3YY
Tel 0131-535 1314; fax 0131-535 1360

The history of the national archives of Scotland can be traced back to the 13th century. The National Archives of Scotland (formerly the Scottish Record Office) is an executive agency of the Scottish Executive and keeps the administrative records of pre-Union Scotland, the registers of central and local courts of law, the public registers of property rights and legal documents, and many collections of local and church records and private archives. Certain groups of records, mainly the modern records of government departments in Scotland, the Scottish railway records, the plans collection, and private archives of an industrial or commercial nature, are preserved in the branch repository at the West Register House in Charlotte Square. The search rooms in both buildings are open Monday–Friday, 9–4.45. A permanent exhibition at the West Register

House and changing exhibitions at the General Register House are open to the public on weekdays, 10–4. The National Register of Archives (Scotland) is based in the West Register House.
Keeper of the Records of Scotland, P. M. Cadell
Deputy Keeper, Dr P. D. Anderson

PUBLIC RECORD OFFICE (NORTHERN IRELAND)
66 Balmoral Avenue, Belfast BT9 6NY
Tel 01232-251318; fax 01232-255999

The Public Record Office (Northern Ireland) is responsible for identifying and preserving Northern Ireland's archival heritage and making it available to the public. It is an executive agency of the Department of the Environment for Northern Ireland. The search room is open on weekdays, 9.15–4.15 (Thursday, 9.15–8.45).
Chief Executive, vacant

CORPORATION OF LONDON RECORDS OFFICE
Guildhall, London EC2P 2EJ
Tel 0171-332 1251; fax 0171-710 8682

The Corporation of London Records Office contains the municipal archives of the City of London which are regarded as the most complete collection of ancient municipal records in existence. The collection includes charters of William the Conqueror, Henry II, and later kings and queens to 1957; ancient custumals: Liber Horn, Dunthorne, Custumarum, Ordinacionum, Memorandorum and Albus, Liber de Antiquis Legibus, and collections of statutes; continuous series of judicial rolls and books from 1252 and Council minutes from 1275; records of the Old Bailey and Guildhall sessions from 1603; financial records from the 16th century; the records of London Bridge from the 12th century; and numerous subsidiary series and miscellanea of historical interest. The Readers' Room is open Monday–Friday, 9.30–4.45.
Keeper of the City Records, The Town Clerk
City Archivist, J. R. Sewell
Deputy City Archivist, Mrs J. M. Bankes

RESEARCH COUNCILS
— *see* Organizations section

REVIEW BODIES

The secretariat for these bodies is provided by the Office of Manpower Economics (*see* page 320)

ARMED FORCES PAY
The Review Body on Armed Forces Pay was appointed in 1971 to advise the Prime Minister on the pay and allowances of members of naval, military and air forces of the Crown and of any women's service administered by the Defence Council.
Chairman, The Baroness Dean of Thornton-le-Fylde, PC
Members, Mrs K. Coleman, OBE; J. Davies; Vice-Adm. Sir Toby Frere, KCB; The Lord Gladwin of Clee, CBE; Prof. D. Greenaway; Ms G. Haskins; M. Ward

DOCTORS' AND DENTISTS' REMUNERATION
The Review Body on Doctors' and Dentists' Remuneration was set up in 1971 to advise the Government on the remuneration of doctors and dentists taking any part in the National Health Service.
Chairman, C. B. Gough

Members, Mrs M. Alderson; Prof. N. Bourne; A. Hawksworth; Miss C. Hui; Dr G. Jones; C. King, CBE; Prof. Sheila McLean; D. Penton

NURSING STAFF, MIDWIVES, HEALTH VISITORS AND PROFESSIONS ALLIED TO MEDICINE

The Review Body for nursing staff, midwives, health visitors and professions allied to medicine was set up in 1983 to advise the Government on the remuneration of nursing staff, midwives and health visitors employed in the National Health Service; and also of physiotherapists, radiographers, occupational therapists, orthoptists, chiropodists, dietitians and related grades employed in the National Health Service.

Chairman, Prof. C. Booth

Members, Ms U. Bannerjee; J. Bartlett; Mrs M. Davies; Mrs S. Gleig; M. Malone-Lee, CB; K. Miles; C. Monks, OBE; Prof. G. Raab; Prof. P. Weetman

SCHOOL TEACHERS

The School Teachers' Review Body (STRB) was set up under the School Teachers' Pay and Conditions Act 1991. It is required to examine and report on such matters relating to the statutory conditions of employment of school teachers in England and Wales as may be referred to it by the Secretary of State for Education and Employment.

Chairman, A. R. Vineall

Members, P. Gedling; M. Harding; V. Harris; Miss J. Langdon; R. Pearson; J. Singh; Mrs P. Sloane

SENIOR SALARIES

The Senior Salaries Review Body (formerly the Top Salaries Review Body) was set up in 1971 to advise the Prime Minister on the remuneration of the judiciary, senior civil servants and senior officers of the armed forces. In 1993 its remit was extended to cover the pay, pensions and allowances of MPs, ministers and others whose pay is determined by a Ministerial and Other Salaries Order, and the allowances of peers.

Chairman, Sir Michael Perry, CBE

Members, The Hon. M. Beloff, QC; D. Clayman; Prof. S. Dawson; Mrs R. Day; The Baroness Dean of Thornton-le-Fylde, PC; Sir Terry Heiser, GCB; Sir Sydney Lipworth, QC; Miss P. Mann, OBE; Prof. Sir David Williams, QC

ROYAL BOTANIC GARDEN EDINBURGH

20A Inverleith Row, Edinburgh EH3 5LR
Tel 0131-552 7171; fax 0131-248 2901

The Royal Botanic Garden Edinburgh (RBGE) originated as the Physic Garden, established in 1670 beside the Palace of Holyroodhouse. The Garden moved to its present 28-hectare site at Inverleith, Edinburgh, in 1821. There are also three specialist gardens: Younger Botanic Garden Benmore, near Dunoon, Argyllshire; Logan Botanic Garden, near Stranraer, Wigtownshire; and Dawyck Botanic Garden, near Stobo, Peeblesshire. Since 1986 RBGE has been administered by a board of trustees established under the National Heritage (Scotland) Act 1985. It receives an annual grant from the Rural Affairs Department of the Scottish Executive.

RBGE is an international centre for scientific research on plant diversity and for horticulture education and conservation. It has an extensive library and a herbarium with over two million dried plant specimens. Public opening hours: Edinburgh site, daily (except Christmas Day and New Year's Day) November–January 9.30–4; February and October 9.30–5; March and September 9.30–6; April–August 9.30–7; specialist gardens, 1 March–31 October 9.30–6. Admission free to Edinburgh site; admission charge to specialist gardens.

Chairman of the Board of Trustees, Dr P. Nicholson

Regius Keeper, Prof. S. Blackmore

ROYAL BOTANIC GARDENS KEW

Richmond, Surrey TW9 3AB
Tel 0181-332 5000; fax 0181-332 5197
Wakehurst Place, Ardingly, nr Haywards Heath, W. Sussex RH17 6TN
Tel 01444-894066; fax 01444-894069

The Royal Botanic Gardens (RBG) Kew were originally laid out as a private garden for Kew House for George III's mother, Princess Augusta, in 1759. They were much enlarged in the 19th century, notably by the inclusion of the grounds of the former Richmond Lodge. In 1965 the garden at Wakehurst Place was acquired; it is owned by the National Trust and managed by RBG Kew. Under the National Heritage Act 1983 a board of trustees was set up to administer the gardens, which in 1984 became an independent body supported by grant-in-aid from the Ministry of Agriculture, Fisheries and Food.

The functions of RBG Kew are to carry out research into plant sciences, to disseminate knowledge about plants and to provide the public with the opportunity to gain knowledge and enjoyment from the gardens' collections. There are extensive national reference collections of living and preserved plants and a comprehensive library and archive. The main emphasis is on plant conservation and bio-diversity.

The gardens are open daily (except Christmas Day and New Year's Day) from 9.30 a.m. (Wakehurst, 10 a.m.). The closing hour varies from 4 p.m. in mid-winter to 6 p.m. on weekdays and 7.30 p.m. on Sundays and Bank Holidays in mid-summer. Admission, 1999, £5.00; concessionary schemes available. Glasshouses (Kew only), 9.30–4.30 (winter); 9.30–5.30 (summer). No dogs except guide-dogs for the blind.

BOARD OF TRUSTEES

Chairman, The Viscount Blakenham

Members, Sir Jeffery Bowman (*Queen's Trustee*); R. P. Bauman; Miss M. Black, CBE; Prof. M. Crawley; Prof. H. Dickinson; Miss A. Ford; Ms R. Franklin; S. de Grey, CBE; R. Lapthorne; Lady Lennox-Boyd; I. Oag; Prof. J. S. Parker; Prof. C. Payne, OBE

Director, Prof. P. Crane

ROYAL COMMISSION FOR THE EXHIBITION OF 1851

Sherfield Building, Imperial College of Science, Technology and Medicine, London SW7 2AZ
Tel 0171-594 8790; fax 0171-594 8794

The Royal Commission was incorporated by supplemental charter as a permanent commission after winding up the affairs of the Great Exhibition of 1851. Its object is to promote scientific and artistic education by means of funds derived from its Kensington estate, purchased with the surplus left over from the Great Exhibition. Annual charitable expenditure on educational grants is about £1 million.

President, HRH The Prince Philip, Duke of Edinburgh,
KG, KT, PC
Chairman, Board of Management, Sir Denis Rooke, OM,
CBE, FRS, FREng.
Secretary to Commissioners, J. P. W. Middleton, CB

ROYAL COMMISSION ON THE REFORM OF THE HOUSE OF LORDS
4 Central Buildings, Matthew Parker Street, London SW1H 9NL
Tel 0171-210 0450; fax 0171-210 0451

The Royal Commission was established by Royal Warrant dated 18 February 1999. Its terms of reference are to consider and make recommendations on the role and functions of a second chamber; to make recommendations on the method or combination of methods of composition required to constitute a second chamber fit for that role and those functions; and to report by 31 December 1999.
Chairman, The Lord Wakeham, PC
Members, Ms A. Beynon; The Lord Butler of Brockwell, GCB, CVO; The Baroness Dean of Thornton-le-Fylde, PC; The Rt. Revd R. Harries; The Lord Hurd of Westwell, CH, CBE, PC; G. Kaufman, PC, MP; Prof. A. King; W. Morris; K. Munro; Prof. Dawn Oliver; Sir Michael Wheeler-Booth, CB
Secretary, D. J. R. Hill

THE ROYAL MINT
Llantrisant, Pontyclun CF72 8YT
Tel 01443-623000; fax 01443-623190

The prime responsibility of the Royal Mint is the provision of United Kingdom coinage, but it actively competes in world markets for a share of the available circulating coin business and about two-thirds of the 18,000 tonnes of coins it produces annually are exported. The Mint also manufactures special proof and uncirculated quality coins in gold, silver and other metals; military and civil decorations and medals; commemorative and prize medals; and royal and official seals.
The Royal Mint became an executive agency of the Treasury in 1990. The Government announced in July 1999 that the Royal Mint would be given greater commercial freedom to expand its business into new areas and develop partnerships with the private sector.
Master of the Mint, The Chancellor of the Exchequer (*ex officio*)
Deputy Master and Comptroller, R. de L. Holmes

ROYAL NATIONAL THEATRE BOARD
South Bank, London, SE1 9PX
Tel 0171-452 3333; fax 0171-452 3344

The chairman and members of the Board of the Royal National Theatre are appointed by the Secretary of State for Culture, Media and Sport.
Chairman, Sir Christopher Hogg
Members, Ms J. Bakewell, CBE; The Hon. P. Benson; Gabrielle Lady Greenbury; Sir David Hancock, KCB; G. Hutchings; Ms K. Jones; Ms S. MacGregor, OBE; Sir Ian McKellen; M. Oliver; Sir Tom Stoppard, CBE; P. Wiegand
Company Secretary, Mrs M. McGregor
Director, T. Nunn, CBE
Executive Director, The Baroness McIntosh of Hudnall

SCOTLAND OFFICE
Dover House, Whitehall, London SW1A 2AU
Tel 0171-270 3000; fax 0171-270 6730

The Scotland Office is the Office of the Secretary of State for Scotland, who represents Scottish interests in the Cabinet on matters reserved to the UK Parliament, i.e. national financial and economic matters, social security, defence and international relations, and employment. *See also* Scottish Executive.
Secretary of State for Scotland, The Rt. Hon. Dr John Reid, MP
Private Secretary (SCS), Ms J. Coulquhoun
Minister of State, Brian Wilson, MP
Private Secretary, D. Ferguson
Advocate-General for Scotland, Lynda Clark, MP
Head of Office (SCS), I. Gordon

SCOTTISH COURTS ADMINISTRATION
— *see* page 364–5

SCOTTISH CRIMINAL CASES REVIEW COMMISSION
5th Floor, Portland House, 17 Renfield Street, Glasgow G2 5AH
Tel 0141-730 7030; fax 0141-730 7040

The Commission is a non-departmental public body which started operating on 1 April 1999. It took over from the Secretary of State for Scotland powers to consider alleged miscarriages of justice in Scotland and refer cases meeting the relevant criteria to the Appeal Court for review. Members are appointed by the First Minister; senior executive staff are appointed by the Commission.
Chairperson (£360 per day), Prof. Sheila McLean
Members (£210 per day), A. Bonnington; Prof. P. Duff; The Very Revd G. Forbes; A. Gallen; Sheriff G. Gordon, CBE, QC; W. Taylor, QC
Chief Executive, R. Eadie

SCOTTISH ENTERPRISE
120 Bothwell Street, Glasgow G2 7JP
Tel 0141-248 2700; fax 0141-221 3217

Scottish Enterprise was established in 1991 and its purpose is to create jobs and prosperity for the people of Scotland. It is funded largely by the Scottish Executive and is responsible to the Scottish ministers. Working in partnership with the private and public sectors, Scottish Enterprise aims to further the development of Scotland's economy, to enhance the skills of the Scottish workforce and to promote Scotland's international competitiveness. Through Locate in Scotland (*see* page 338), Scottish Enterprise is concerned with attracting firms to Scotland, and through Scottish Trade International (*see* page 338) it helps Scottish companies to compete in world export markets. Scottish Enterprise has a network of 13 Local Enterprise Companies that deliver economic development services at local level.
Chairman (£31,567), Sir Ian Wood, CBE
Chief Executive, C. Beveridge, CBE

SCOTTISH ENVIRONMENT PROTECTION AGENCY
Erskine Court, The Castle Business Park, Stirling FK9 4TR
Tel 01786-457700; fax 01786-446885

The Scottish Environment Protection Agency came into being on 1 April 1996 under the Environment Act 1995. It is responsible for controlling pollution to land, air and water in Scotland. It receives funding from the Scottish Executive.
Chairman, K. Collins
Chief Executive, A. Paton
Director of Finance, J. Ford
Director of Environmental Strategy, Ms P. Henton
Director, North Region, Prof. D. Mackay
Director, East Region, W. Halcrow
Director, West Region, J. Beveridge

SCOTTISH EXECUTIVE
St Andrew's House, Edinburgh EH1 3DG
Tel 0131-556 8400; fax 0131-244 8240
E-mail: ceu@scotland.gov.uk
Web: http://www.scotland.gov.uk

The Scottish Executive is responsible in Scotland for all matters not reserved to Westminster under devolution, including education, health, social work, law and order, agriculture and the environment. In addition there are a number of Scottish departments for which the Executive has some degree of responsibility; these include the Scottish Courts Administration, the General Register Office, the National Archives of Scotland (formerly the Scottish Record Office) and the Department of the Registers of Scotland. *See also* Scotland Office and National Assemblies supplement.
First Minister, The Rt. Hon. Donald Dewar, MP, MSP
Deputy First Minister and Minister for Justice, Jim Wallace, QC, MP, MSP
Finance Minister, Jack McConnell, MSP
Minister for Health and Community Care, Susan Deacon, MSP
Minister for Communities, Wendy Alexander, MSP
Minister for Transport and the Environment, Sarah Boyack, MSP
Minister for Enterprise and Lifelong Learning, Henry McLeish, MP, MSP
Minister for Rural Affairs, Ross Finnie, MSP
Minister for Education and Children, Sam Galbraith, MP, MSP
Minister for Parliament and Chief Whip, Tom McCabe, MSP
Lord Advocate, The Lord Hardie, PC, QC

SCOTTISH EXECUTIVE CORPORATE SERVICES
16 Waterloo Place, Edinburgh EH1 3DN
Tel 0131-556 8400
Principal Establishment Officer (*SCS*), C. C. MacDonald, CB
Head of Personnel (*SCS*), D. F. Middleton

DIRECTORATE OF ADMINISTRATIVE SERVICES
Saughton House, Broomhouse Drive, Edinburgh EH11 3DX
Tel 0131-556 8400
Director of Administrative Services (*SCS*), A. M. Brown
Chief Estates Officer, J. A. Andrew
Head of Information Technology (*SCS*), Ms M. McGinn
Director of Telecommunications, K. Henderson, OBE
Chief Quantity Surveyor (*SCS*), A. J. Wyllie

James Craig Walk, Edinburgh EH1 3BA
Head of Purchasing and Supplies (*SCS*), N. Bowd

SCOTTISH EXECUTIVE FINANCE
Victoria Quay, Edinburgh EH6 6QQ
Tel 0131-556 8400
Principal Finance Officer (*SCS*), Dr P. S. Collings
Assistant Secretaries (*SCS*), M. T. S. Batho; J. G. Henderson; D. G. N. Reid; W. T. Tait
Head of Accountancy Services Unit, I. M. Smith
Assistant Director of Finance Strategy, I. A. McLeod

SCOTTISH EXECUTIVE SECRETARIAT
St Andrew's House, Regent Road, Edinburgh EH1 3DG
Tel 0131-556 8400
Head of Secretariat, R. S. B. Gordon
Constitutional Policy, J. A. Ewing
Scotland Act Implementation (*SCS*), W. G. Burgess
Functions and Whitehall Negotiations (*SCS*), I. N. Walford
Legal Adviser, J. L. Jamieson, CBE

MANAGEMENT GROUP SUPPORT STAFF UNIT
Head of Unit (*SCS*), P. J. Rycroft

SCOTTISH EXECUTIVE INFORMATION DIRECTORATE
For the Scottish Executive and certain UK services in Scotland
Head of Information Directorate (*SCS*), R. Williams

SOLICITOR'S OFFICE
For the Scottish Executive
Solicitor (*SCS*), R. M. Henderson
Deputy Solicitor (*SCS*), J. S. G. Maclean
Divisional Solicitors (*SCS*), R. Bland (*seconded to Scottish Law Commission*); G. C. Duke; I. H. Harvie; H. F. Macdiarmid; J. G. S. Maclean; N. Raven; Mrs L. A. Towers

SCOTTISH EXECUTIVE RURAL AFFAIRS DEPARTMENT
Pentland House, 47 Robb's Loan, Edinburgh EH14 1TY
Tel 0131-556 8400
Secretary (*SCS*), J. S. Graham
Under-Secretaries (*SCS*), T. A. Cameron (*Agriculture*); S. F. Hampson (*Environment*)
Fisheries Secretary (*SCS*), Dr P. Brady
Assistant Secretaries (*SCS*), I. R. Anderson; D. R. Dickson; D. Feeley; Ms I. M. Low; Ms J. Polley; A. J. Rushworth; Dr P. Rycroft; G. M. D. Thomson; J. R. Wildgoose
Chief Agricultural Officer (*SCS*), A. J. Robertson
Assistant Chief Agricultural Officers, W. A. Aitken; J. Henderson; A. Robb
Chief Agricultural Economist, D. J. Greig
Chief Food and Dairy Officer, S. D. Rooke
Senior Principal Scientific Officers, Mrs L. A. D. Turl; Dr R. Waterhouse

ENVIRONMENTAL AFFAIRS GROUP
Head of Group (*SCS*), S. F. Hampson
Heads of Divisions (*SCS*), A. G. Dickson; Ms B. Campbell
Chief Water Engineer, P. Wright
Ecological Adviser, Dr J. Miles

STRATEGY AND CO-ORDINATION UNIT
Head of Unit, A. J. Cameron

EXECUTIVE AGENCIES

FISHERIES RESEARCH SERVICES
Marine Laboratory, PO Box 101, Victoria Road, Aberdeen AB11 9DB
Tel 01224-876544; fax 01224-295511

The Agency provides scientific information and advice on

marine and freshwater fisheries, aquaculture and the protection of the aquatic environment and its wildlife.
Director, Dr A. D. Hawkins
Deputy Director, Dr J. M. Davies

FRESHWATER FISHERIES LABORATORY
Faskally, Pitlochry, Perthshire PH6 5LB
Tel 01796-472060

Senior Principal Scientific Officers, Dr R. M. Cook; Dr J. M. Davies; Dr A. E. Ellis; R. G. J. Shelton; Dr R. Stagg; Dr P. A. Stewart; Dr C. S. Wardle
Inspector of Salmon and Freshwater Fisheries for Scotland, D. A. Dunkley

INTERVENTION BOARD
— *see* page 314

SCOTTISH AGRICULTURAL SCIENCE AGENCY
East Craig, Edinburgh EH12 8NJ
Tel 0131-244 8890; fax 0131-244 8988

The Agency provides scientific information and advice on agricultural and horticultural crops and the environment, and has various statutory and regulatory functions.
Director, Dr R. K. M. Hay
Deputy Director, S. R. Cooper
Senior Principal Scientific Officer, W. J. Rennie

SCOTTISH FISHERIES PROTECTION AGENCY
Pentland House, 47 Robb's Loan, Edinburgh EH14 1TY
Tel 0131-556 8400; fax 0131-244 6086

The Agency enforces fisheries law and regulations in Scottish waters and ports.
Chief Executive, Capt. P. Du Vivier, RN
Director of Corporate Strategy and Resources, J. B. Roddin
Director of Operational Enforcement, R. J. Walker
Marine Superintendent, Capt. W. A. Brown

SCOTTISH EXECUTIVE DEVELOPMENT DEPARTMENT

Victoria Quay, Edinburgh EH6 6QQ
Tel 0131-556 8400

Head of Department (SCS), K. MacKenzie
Heads of Groups (SCS), D. J. Belfall; J. S. B. Martin
Heads of Divisions (SCS), M. T. Affolter; A. M. Burnside; E. C. Davidson; J. D. Gallacher; R. A. Grant; D. S. Henderson; Mrs D. Mellon; W. J. R. McQueen; R. Tait
Senior Economic Adviser (SCS), C. L. Wood

PROFESSIONAL STAFF
Chief Planner (SCS), A. Mackenzie, CBE
Deputy Chief Architect (SCS), Dr J. P. Cornish
Chief Statistician (SCS), C. R. MacLean

INQUIRY REPORTERS
Robert Stevenson House, 2 Greenside Lane, Edinburgh
EH1 3AG
Tel 0131-244 5680

Chief Reporter (SCS), R. M. Hickman
Deputy Chief Reporter (SCS), J. M. McCulloch

NATIONAL ROADS DIRECTORATE
Victoria Quay, Edinburgh EH6 6QQ
Tel 0131-556 8400

Deputy Chief Engineers (SCS), J. A. Howison (*Roads*); N. B. MacKenzie (*Bridges*)

SCOTTISH EXECUTIVE EDUCATION DEPARTMENT

Victoria Quay, Edinburgh EH6 6QQ
Tel 0131-556 8400

Secretary (SCS), J. Elvidge

Under-Secretaries (SCS), D. J. Crawley; Mrs G. Stewart
Assistant Secretaries (SCS), R. N. Irvine; J. W. L. Lonie; S. Y. MacDonald; A. K. MacLeod; G. McHugh; Mrs R. Menlowe; Ms J. Morgan
Chief Statistician (SCS), C. R. MacLean
Chief Architect (SCS), J. E. Gibbons, PH.D., FSA SCOT.
Chief Inspector of Social Work Services, A. Skinner
Assistant Chief Inspectors, Mrs G. Ottley; D. Pia; I. C. Robertson

HM INSPECTORS OF SCHOOLS
Senior Chief Inspector (SCS), D. A. Osler
Depute Senior Chief Inspectors (SCS), F. Crawford; G. H. C. Donaldson
Chief Inspectors (SCS), P. Banks; J. Boyes; Miss K. M. Fairweather; D. E. Kelso; J. J. McDonald; A. S. McGlynn; H. M. Stalker
There are 79 Grade 6 Inspectors

EXECUTIVE AGENCIES

HISTORIC SCOTLAND
Longmore House, Salisbury Place, Edinburgh EH9 1SH
Tel 0131-668 8600; fax 0131-668 8699

The agency's role is to protect Scotland's historic monuments, buildings and lands, and to promote public understanding and enjoyment of them.
Chief Executive (G3), G. N. Munro
Directors (G5), F. J. Lawrie; I. Maxwell; B. Naylor; B. O'Neil; L. Wilson
Chief Inspector of Ancient Monuments, Dr D. J. Breeze
Chief Inspector, Historic Buildings, R. Emerson, FSA, FSASCot.

SCOTTISH PUBLIC PENSIONS AGENCY
St Margaret's House, 151 London Road, Edinburgh
EH8 7TG
Tel 0131-556 8400; fax 0131-244 3334

The Agency is responsible for the pension arrangements of some 300,000 people, mainly NHS and teaching services employees and pensioners.
Chief Executive, R. Garden
Directors, G. Mowat (*Policy*); A. M. Small (*Operations*); M. J. McDermott (*Resources and Customer Services*)

SCOTTISH EXECUTIVE ENTERPRISE AND LIFELONG LEARNING DEPARTMENT

Victoria Quay, Edinburgh EH6 6QQ
Tel 0131-556 8400

Secretary (SCS), E. Frizzell
Under-Secretaries (SCS), E. J. Weeple; M. B. Foulis
Assistant Secretaries (SCS), C. Smith; J. A. Brown; I. McGhee; D. A. Stewart; G. F. Dickson; C. M. Reeves

INDUSTRIAL EXPANSION
Meridian Court, 5 Cadogan Street, Glasgow G2 6AT
Tel 0141-248 2855

Under-Secretary (SCS), G. Robson
Industrial Adviser, D. Blair
Scientific Adviser, Prof. D. J. Tedford
Assistant Secretaries (SCS), W. Malone; J. K. Mason; Dr J. Rigg

LOCATE IN SCOTLAND
120 Bothwell Street, Glasgow G2 7JP
Tel 0141-248 2700

Director (SCS), M. Togneri

SCOTTISH TRADE INTERNATIONAL
120 Bothwell Street, Glasgow G2 7JP
Tel 0141-248 2700

Director, D. Taylor

EXECUTIVE AGENCY

STUDENT AWARDS AGENCY FOR SCOTLAND
Gyleview House, 3 Redheughs Rigg, Edinburgh EH12 9HH
Tel 0131-476 8212; fax 0131-244 5887
Chief Executive, K. MacRae

SCOTTISH EXECUTIVE HEALTH DEPARTMENT
St Andrew's House, Edinburgh EH1 3DG
Tel 0131-556 8400

NATIONAL HEALTH SERVICE IN SCOTLAND
MANAGEMENT EXECUTIVE
Chief Executive (SCS), G. R. Scaife, CB
Director of Purchasing (SCS), Dr K. J. Woods
Director of Primary Care (SCS), Mrs A. Robson
Director of Finance (SCS), J. Aldridge
Director of Human Resources (SCS), G. Marr
Director of Nursing, Miss A. Jarvie
Director of Community Care, Ms E. Lewis
Medical Director (SCS), Dr A. Fraser
Director of Trusts (SCS), P. Wilson
Director of Information Services, NHS, C. B. Knox
Director of Estates, H. R. McCallum
Chief Pharmacist (SCS), W. Scott
Chief Scientist, Prof. G. R. D. Catto
Chief Dental Officer, T. R. Watkins

PUBLIC HEALTH POLICY UNIT
Head of Unit and Chief Medical Officer (SCS), Prof. Sir David
    Carter, FRCSE, FRCSGlas., FRCPE
Deputy Chief Medical Officer (SCS), Dr A. Fraser
Head of Group (SCS), Mrs N. Munro
Assistant Secretary (SCS), J. T. Brown
Principal Medical Officers, Dr J. B. Louden (*part-time*); Dr A.
    MacDonald (*part-time*); Dr R. Skinner; Dr E. Sowler
Senior Medical Officers, Dr Angela Anderson; Dr E.
    Bashford; Dr K. G. Brotherston; Dr D. Campbell; Dr J.
    Cumming; Dr B. Davis; Dr D. J. Ewing; Dr D. Findlay;
    Dr G. R. Foster; Dr A. Keel; Dr Patricia Madden; Dr H.
    Whyte; Dr D. Will

STATE HOSPITAL
Carstairs Junction, Lanark ML11 8RP
Tel 01555-840293
Chairman, D. N. James
General Manager, R. Manson

COMMON SERVICES AGENCY
Trinity Park House, South Trinity Road, Edinburgh
EH5 3SE
Tel 0131-552 6255
Chairman, G. R. Scaife, CB
General Manager, Dr F. Gibb

HEALTH BOARDS
— *see* Social Welfare section

SCOTTISH EXECUTIVE JUSTICE DEPARTMENT
Saughton House, Broomhouse Drive, Edinburgh EH11 3XD
Tel 0131-556 8400

Secretary (SCS), J. Hamill, CB
Under-Secretaries (SCS), C. Baxter; N. G. Campbell
Assistant Secretaries (SCS), Mrs M. H. Brannan; Mrs M. B.
    Gunn; R. S. T. MacEwen
Chief Research Officer, Dr C. P. A. Levein
Senior Principal Research Officer, Mrs A. Millar

SCOTTISH COURTS ADMINISTRATION
— *see* pages 364–5

SOCIAL WORK SERVICES GROUP
James Craig Walk, Edinburgh EH1 3BA
Tel 0131-556 8400
Under-Secretary (SCS), N. G. Campbell
Assistant Secretaries (SCS), G. A. Anderson; Dr J. M. Francis;
    Mrs V. M. Macniven

OTHER APPOINTMENTS
HM Chief Inspector of Constabulary, W. Taylor, QPM
HM Chief Inspector of Prisons, C. Fairweather, OBE
Commandant, Scottish Police College, H. I. Watson, OBE, QPM
HM Chief Inspector of Fire Services, D. Davis, CBE, QFSM
Commandant, Scottish Fire Service Training School, D. Grant,
    QFSM

OFFICE OF THE SCOTTISH PARLIAMENTARY COUNSEL
Victoria Quay, Edinburgh EH6 6QQ
Tel 0131-556 8400

First Scottish Parliamentary Counsel, J. C. McCluskie, CB, QC
Scottish Parliamentary Counsel, G. M. Clark; C. A. M. Wilson
Depute Scottish Parliamentary Counsel, J. D. Harkness; Miss
    M. Mackenzie
Assistant Scottish Parliamentary Counsel, A. C. Gordon

PRIVATE LEGISLATION OFFICE UNDER THE PRIVATE LEGISLATION PROCEDURE (SCOTLAND) ACT 1936
50 Frederick Street, Edinburgh EH2 1EN
Tel 0131-226 6499

Senior Counsel, G. S. Douglas, QC
Junior Counsel, N. M. P. Morrison

EXECUTIVE AGENCIES

NATIONAL ARCHIVES OF SCOTLAND
— *see* page 334

REGISTERS OF SCOTLAND
— *see* page 315

SCOTTISH PRISON SERVICE
— *see* pages 382–3

GENERAL REGISTER OFFICE FOR SCOTLAND
New Register House, Edinburgh EH1 3YT
Tel 0131-334 0380; fax 0131-314 4400

The General Register Office for Scotland is a department forming part of the Scottish Executive. It is the office of the Registrar-General for Scotland, who has responsibility for civil registration and the taking of censuses in Scotland and has in his custody the following records: the statutory registers of births, deaths, still births, adoptions, marriages and divorces; the old parish registers (recording births, deaths and marriages, etc., before civil registration began in 1855); and records of censuses of the population in Scotland. Hours of public access: Monday–Friday 9–4.30.
Registrar-General (SCS), J. N. Randall
Deputy Registrar-General, B. V. Philp
Census Manager, D. A. Orr
Heads of Branches, D. B. L. Brownlee; R. C. Lawson;
    F. D. Garvie; G. Compton; G. W. L. Jackson;
    F. G. Thomas

MENTAL WELFARE COMMISSION FOR SCOTLAND
K Floor, Argyle House, 3 Lady Lawson Street, Edinburgh
EH3 9SH
Tel 0131-222 6111

Chairman, Sir William Reid, KCB
Vice-Chairman, Mrs N. Bennie
Commissioners (part-time), C. Campbell, QC; Mrs F. Cotter;
    W. Gent; Dr P. Jauhar; Dr Shainool Jiwa; Dr
    Elizabeth McCall-Smith; D. J. Macdonald; Dr J.
    Morrow; M. D. Murray; Dr Linda Pollock; A. Robb;
    Mrs M. Ross; Dr Margaret Thomas; Dr M. Whoriskey
Director, Dr J. A. T. Dyer

SCOTTISH HOMES
Thistle House, 91 Haymarket Terrace, Edinburgh
EH12 5HE
Tel 0131-313 0044; fax 0131-313 2680

Scottish Homes, the national housing agency for Scotland,
aims to improve the quality and variety of housing available
in Scotland by working in partnership with the public and
private sectors. The agency is a major funder of new and
improved housing provided by housing associations and
private developers. It is currently transferring its own
rented houses to alternative landlords. It is also involved in
housing research. Board members are appointed by the
First Minister.
Chairman, J. Ward, CBE
Chief Executive, P. McKinlay, CBE

SCOTTISH NATURAL HERITAGE
12 Hope Terrace, Edinburgh EH9 2AS
Tel 0131-447 4784; fax 0131-446 2277

Scottish Natural Heritage was established in 1992 under
the Natural Heritage (Scotland) Act 1991. It provides
advice on nature conservation to all those whose activities
affect wildlife, landforms and features of geological interest
in Scotland, and seeks to develop and improve facilities for
the enjoyment and understanding of the Scottish countryside. It is funded by the Scottish Executive.
Chairman, Dr J. Markland, CBE
Chief Executive, R. Crofts
Chief Scientific Adviser, M. B. Usher
Directors of Operations, J. Thomson (*West*); I. Jardine (*East*); J.
    Watson (*North*)
Director of Corporate Services, vacant

SCOTTISH OFFICE (former)
— *see* Scotland Office

SCOTTISH PARLIAMENTARY
COMMISSIONER FOR ADMINISTRATION
28 Thistle Street, Edinburgh EH2 1EN
Tel 0845-601 0456; fax 0131-226 4447

The Scottish Parliamentary Commissioner for Administration was appointed in July 1999 to investigate complaints
made to him by Members of the Scottish Parliament on
behalf of members of the public who have suffered an
injustice through maladministration by the Scottish Executive and a wide range of public bodies involved in
devolved Scottish affairs.
Scottish Parliamentary Commissioner for Administration, M. S.
    Buckley

SCOTTISH PRISONS COMPLAINTS
COMMISSION
Government Buildings, Broomhouse Drive, Edinburgh
EH11 3XD
Tel 0131-244 8423; fax 0131-244 8430

The Commission was established in 1994. It is an
independent body to which prisoners in Scottish prisons
can make application in relation to any matter where they
have failed to obtain satisfaction from the Prison Service's
internal grievance procedures. Clinical judgments made by
medical officers, matters which are the subject of legal
proceedings and matters relating to sentence, conviction
and parole decision-making are excluded from the Commission's jurisdiction. The Commissioner is appointed by
the First Minister.
Commissioner, Dr J. McManus

SEA FISH INDUSTRY AUTHORITY
18 Logie Mill, Logie Green Road, Edinburgh EH7 4HG
Tel 0131-558 3331; fax 0131-558 1442

Established under the Fisheries Act 1981, the Authority is
required to promote the efficiency of the sea fish industry.
It carries out research relating to the industry and gives
advice on related matters. It provides training, promotes
the marketing, consumption and export of sea fish and sea
fish products, and may provide financial assistance for the
improvement of fishing vessels in respect of essential safety
equipment. It is responsible to the Ministry of Agriculture,
Fisheries and Food.
Chairman, E. Davey
Chief Executive, A. C. Fairbairn

THE SECURITY AND INTELLIGENCE
SERVICES

Under the Intelligence Services Act 1994, the Intelligence
and Security Committee of Parliamentarians was established to oversee the work of GCHQ, MI5 and MI6; in
1999 an Investigator was appointed to the committee in
order to reinforce the authority of its findings and establish
public confidence in the oversight system. The Act also
established the Intelligence Services Tribunal (*see* pages
312–3), which hears complaints made against GCHQ and
MI6. The Security Service Tribunal and Commissioner
(*see* below) investigate complaints about MI5.

DEFENCE INTELLIGENCE STAFF
— *see* Defence section

GOVERNMENT COMMUNICATIONS
HEADQUARTERS (GCHQ)
Priors Road, Cheltenham, Glos GL52 5AJ
Tel 01242-221491; fax 01242-226816

GCHQ produces signals intelligence in support of national
security and the UK's economic wellbeing, and in the
prevention or detection of serious crime. It also provides
advice and assistance to government departments, the
armed forces and other national infrastructure bodies on
the security of their communications and information
systems. It was placed on a statutory footing by the
Intelligence Services Act 1994 and is headed by a director
who is directly accountable to the Foreign Secretary.
Director, F. N. Richards, CVO, CMG

NATIONAL CRIMINAL INTELLIGENCE SERVICE
PO Box 8000, London SE11 5EN
Tel: 0171-238 8000

The National Criminal Intelligence Service (NCIS) provides intelligence about serious and organized crime to law enforcement, government and other relevant national and international agencies. On 1 April 1998 NCIS was placed on a statutory footing. It is accountable to the NCIS Service Authority.

Director-General, J. Abbott, QPM
Deputy Director-General (Director (Intelligence)),
R. Gaspar, QPM
Director, International Division, N. Bailey
Director, UK Division, V. Harvey
Director, Resources Division, J. Bamfield

SERVICE AUTHORITY
PO Box 2600, London SW1V 2WG
Tel: 0171-238 2600

The Service Authority for NCIS is responsible for ensuring its effective operation. It operates with the Service Authority for the National Crime Squad (*see* page 374). There are 26 members of the authorities, of whom the chairman and nine others serve as 'core members' on both authorities.

Chairman, Rt. Hon. Sir John Wheeler
Clerk, T. Simmons
Treasurer, P. Derrick

THE SECRET INTELLIGENCE SERVICE (MI6)
PO Box 1300, London SE1 1BD

The Secret Intelligence Service produces secret intelligence in support of the Government's security, defence, foreign and economic policies. It was placed on a statutory footing by the Intelligence Services Act 1994 and is headed by a chief, known as 'C', who is directly accountable to the Foreign Secretary.

Chief, R. B. Dearlove, OBE

THE SECURITY SERVICE (MI5)
Thames House, PO Box 3255, London SW1P 1AE
Tel 0171-930 9000

The function of the Security Service is the protection of national security, in particular against threats from espionage, terrorism, sabotage and the proliferation of weapons of mass destruction, from the activities of agents of foreign powers, and from actions intended to overthrow or undermine parliamentary democracy by political, industrial or violent means. It is also the Service's function to safeguard the economic well-being of the UK against threats posed by the actions or intentions of persons outside the British Islands. Under the Security Service Act 1996, the Service's role was extended to support the police and customs in the prevention and detection of serious crime.

The Security Service was placed on a statutory footing by the Security Service Act 1989 and is headed by a director-general who is directly accountable to the Home Secretary.

Director-General, S. Lander

SECURITY SERVICE COMMISSIONER
c/o PO Box 18, London SE1 0TZ
Tel 0171-273 4095

The Commissioner is appointed by the Prime Minister. He keeps under review the issue of warrants by the Home Secretary under the Intelligence Services Act 1994, and is required to help the Security Service Tribunal by investigating complaints which allege interference with property and by offering all such assistance in discharging its functions as it may require. He is also required to submit an annual report on the discharge of his functions to the Prime Minister.

Commissioner, The Rt. Hon. Lord Justice Stuart-Smith
  Private Secretary, N. R. Brooks

SECURITY SERVICE TRIBUNAL
PO Box 18, London SE1 0TZ
Tel 0171-273 4095

The Security Service Act 1989 established a tribunal of three to five senior members of the legal profession, independent of the Government and appointed by The Queen, to investigate complaints from any person about anything which they believe the Security Service has done to them or to their property.

President, The Rt. Hon. Lord Justice Simon Brown
Vice-President, Sheriff J. McInnes, QC
Member, Sir Richard Gaskell
Secretary, N. R. Brooks

SENTENCE REVIEW COMMISSIONERS
PO Box 1011, Belfast BT2 7SR
Tel 01232-549412; fax 01232-549427

The Sentence Review Commissioners are appointed by the Secretary of State for Northern Ireland to consider applications from prisoners serving sentences in Northern Ireland for declarations that they are entitled to early release in accordance with the provisions of the Northern Ireland (Sentences) Act 1998. The commissioners have been appointed until 31 July 2000 and are served by staff seconded from the Northern Ireland Office.

Joint Chairmen, Sir John Belloch, KCB; B. Currin
Commissioners, Dr Silvia Casale; Dr P. Curran; I. Dunbar, CB; Mrs M. Gilpin; Dr A. Grounds; Ms C. McGrory; Dr D. Morrow; D. Wall
Secretary (SCS)

SERIOUS FRAUD OFFICE
Elm House, 10–16 Elm Street, London WC1X 0BJ
Tel 0171-239 7272; fax 0171-837 1689

The Serious Fraud Office works under the superintendence of the Attorney-General. Its remit is to investigate and prosecute serious and complex fraud. (Other fraud cases are handled by the fraud divisions of the Crown Prosecution Service.) The scope of its powers covers England, Wales and Northern Ireland. The staff includes lawyers, accountants and other support staff; investigating teams work closely with the police.

Director, Mrs R. Wright

DEPARTMENT OF SOCIAL SECURITY
Richmond House, 79 Whitehall, London SW1A 2NS
Tel 0171-238 0800

The Department of Social Security (DSS) is responsible for the payment of benefits including child benefit, one-parent benefit, income support and family credit. It administers the Social Fund, and is responsible for assessing the means of applicants for legal aid. It is also responsible for the payment of war pensions and the operation of the child maintenance system. Responsibility for the operation of the national insurance contributions scheme was transferred from the DSS to the Inland Revenue in April 1999.

Secretary of State for Social Security, The Rt. Hon. Alistair Darling, MP
  Principal Private Secretary, R. Clark
  Special Advisers, J. McTernan; A. Maugham
  Parliamentary Private Secretary, Ms A. Coffey, MP
Minister of State, Jeff Rooker, MP
  Private Secretary, D. Higlett
Parliamentary Under-Secretaries of State, The Baroness Hollis of Heigham, D.Phil. (*Family Policy, Child Benefit, Child Support, War Pensions*); Angela Eagle, MP (*Income-related Benefits, International and Green Issues*); Hugh Bayley, MP (*Disability and Sickness Benefits, Deregulation, Independent Living Fund*)
  Private Secretaries, B. Stayte; D. Topping; Ms V. Hutchinson; Ms H. McCarthy; R. Sanguinaza; Ms L. Wright
Permanent Secretary (*SCS*), Ms R. Lomax
  Private Secretary, C. Jackson

CORPORATE MANAGEMENT GROUP
Director (*SCS*), J. Tross

PERSONNEL AND HQ SUPPORT SERVICES DIRECTORATE
Director, S. Hewitt
Section Heads (*SCS*), T. Perl; (*G7*), R. Yeats; B. Glew; J. Elliott

ANALYTICAL SERVICES DIVISION
The Adelphi, 1–11 John Adam Street, London WC2N 6HT
Tel 0171-962 8000

Director (*SCS*), D. Stanton
Chief Statistician (*SCS*), N. Dyson
Senior Economic Advisers (*SCS*), J. Ball; G. Harris; R. D'Souza
Deputy Chief Scientific Officer (*SCS*), D. Barnbrook
Chief Research Officers (*SCS*), Ms S. Duncan; S. Rice

FINANCE DIVISION
Grade 3, S. Lord

INFORMATION DIRECTORATE
Director of Information (*SCS*), S. MacDowall
Deputy Head of Information (*G6*), J. Bretherton
Chief Press Officer (*G7*), Ms S. Lewis
Chief Publicity Officer (*G7*), Mrs A. Hall

SOCIAL SECURITY POLICY GROUP
Head of Policy Group (*SCS*), P. R. C. Gray
Policy Directors (*SCS*), M. Cayley; Miss M. Peirson, CB; D. Brereton; U. Brennan
Policy Managers (*SCS*), L. Richards; C. Ramsden; B. O'Gorman; M. Street; J. Groombridge; Mrs C. Rookes; B. Calderwood; D. Allsop, CBE; C. Evans; J. Hughes; P. Cleasby; P. Morgan; Mrs L. Richards; Ms J. Shersby; (*G6*), B. Layton; I. Williams; P. Barrett; J. Griffiths-Chayes; K. Sadler; N. Ward

SOLICITOR'S OFFICE
Solicitor (*SCS*), Mrs M. A. Morgan, CB

SOLICITOR'S DIVISION A
New Court, 48 Carey Street, London WC2A 2LS
Tel 0171-412 1466
Principal Assistant Solicitor (*SCS*), J. A. Catlin

Assistant Solicitors (*SCS*), J. M. Swainson; Mrs G. Massiah; Mrs F. A. Logan; C. Cooper; H. Connell; P. Milledge

SOLICITOR'S DIVISION B
New Court, 48 Carey Street, London WC2A 2LS
Tel 0171-412 1528
Solicitor (*SCS*), Mrs M. A. Morgan, CB
Assistant Solicitors (*SCS*), R. G. S. Aitken; Ms S. Edwards; S. Cooper

SOLICITOR'S DIVISION C
New Court, 48 Carey Street, London WC2A 2LS
Tel 0171-412 1342

Principal Assistant Solicitor (*SCS*), Mrs G. S. Kerrigan
Assistant Solicitors (*SCS*), R. J. Dormer; Miss M. E. Trefgarne; Mrs S. Walker; G. Aitkin

BENEFITS FRAUD INSPECTORATE
Berkeley House, 12A North Park Road, Harrogate HG1 5QA
Tel 01423-832922

Director-General (*SCS*), C. Bull

EXECUTIVE AGENCIES

APPEALS SERVICE AGENCY
— *see* Tribunals

BENEFITS AGENCY
Quarry House, Quarry Hill, Leeds LS2 7UA
Tel 0113-232 4000

The Agency administers claims for and payments of social security benefits.
Chief Executive, P. Mathison
  Private Secretary, R. Baldwin
Directors, J. Codling (*Finance*); M. Fisher (*Personnel and Communications*); S. Heminsley (*Strategic and Planning*); A. Cleveland (*Operations Support*); N. Haighton (*Projects*)
Medical Policy
Principal Medical Officers, Dr M. Aylward; Dr P. Dewis; Dr P. Sawney; Dr A. Braidwood; Dr P. Stidolph

CHILD SUPPORT AGENCY
DSS Long Benton, Benton Park Road, Newcastle upon Tyne NE98 1YX
Tel 0191-213 5000

The Agency was set up in April 1993. It is responsible for the administration of the Child Support Act and for the assessment, collection and enforcement of maintenance payments for all new cases.
Chief Executive, Ms F. Boardman
Directors, M. Davison; C. Peters; M. Isaacs; T. Read

INFORMATION TECHNOLOGY SERVICES AGENCY
4th Floor, Verulam Point, Station Way, St Albans, Herts AL1 5HE
Tel 01727-815835; fax 01727-833740

The Agency maintains and oversees policies on information technology strategy, procurement, technical standards and security.
Chief Executive, G. McCorkell
Directors, J. Thomas; J. Brewood; G. Brown; B. Barnes; B. Gormley; J. Delamere; C. Nicholls
Non-Executive Directors, K. Pfotzer; K. Bogg

WAR PENSIONS AGENCY
Norcross, Blackpool, Lancs FY5 3WP
Tel 01253-856123

The Agency administers the payment of war disablement and war widows' pensions and provides welfare services and support to war disablement pensioners, war widows and their dependants and carers.

Chief Executive, G. Hextall

Central Advisory Committee on War Pensions
6th Floor, The Adelphi, 1–11 John Adam Street, London WC2N 6HT
Tel 0171-962 8062

Secretary, C. Pike

ADVISORY BODIES

NATIONAL DISABILITY COUNCIL, Level 4, Caxton House, Tothill Street, London SW1H 9NA. Tel: 0171-273 5636. *Chairman,* D. Grayson, OBE; *Secretary,* R. Timm

SOCIAL SECURITY ADVISORY COMMITTEE, New Court, Carey Street, London WC2A 2LS. Tel 0171-412 1508. *Chairman,* Lt.-Gen. Sir Thomas Boyd-Carpenter, KBE; *Secretary,* Ms G. Saunders

SPORTS COUNCIL
— *see* United Kingdom Sports Council

OFFICE FOR STANDARDS IN EDUCATION (OFSTED)
Alexandra House, 33 Kingsway, London WC2B 6SE
Tel 0171-421 6800; fax 0171-421 6707

The Office is a non-ministerial government department established in 1992 to keep the Secretary of State and the public informed about the standards and management of schools in England, and to establish and monitor an independent inspection system for maintained schools in England. *See also* Education section.

HM Chief Inspector, C. Woodhead
Directors of Inspection, M. J. Tomlinson, CBE; D. Taylor
Director of Policy, Planning and Resources, Miss J. M. Phillips, CBE

DIVISION MANAGERS

Personnel Management, C. Payne
Contracts, C. Bramley
Communications, Media and Public Relations, J. Lawson
Information Systems, M. Worthy
Administrative Support and Estate Management, K. Francis
Inspection Quality, P. Matthews
LEA Reviews, Reorganization Proposals, D. Singleton
School Improvement, Ms E. Passmore, OBE
Nursery and Primary, K. Lloyd
Secondary and Independent, vacant
Post-Compulsory, D. West
Special Educational Needs, C. Marshall
Research, Analysis and International, Ms C. Agambar
Teacher Education and Training, C. Gould
Nursery Education Scheme, D. Bradley
Subject Specialist Advisers, N. Bufton; B. Ponchaud;
  A. Dobson; M. Ive; P. Smith; Ms J. Mills; G. Clay; P.
  Jones; J. Hertrich; Ms B. Wintersgill; S. Harrison

There are about 200 HM Inspectors

COMMITTEE ON STANDARDS IN PUBLIC LIFE
Horse Guards Road, London SW1P 3AL
Tel 0171-270 5875; fax 0171-270 5874

The Committee on Standards in Public Life was set up in October 1994. It is a standing body whose chairman and members are appointed by the Prime Minister; three members are nominated by the leaders of the three main political parties. The committee's remit is to examine concerns about standards of conduct of all holders of public office, including arrangements relating to financial and commercial activities, and to make recommendations as to any changes in present arrangements which might be required to ensure the highest standards of propriety in public life. It is also charged with reviewing issues in relation to the funding of political parties. The committee does not investigate individual allegations of misconduct.

Chairman, The Lord Neill of Bladen, QC
Members, Sir Clifford Boulton, GCB; Prof. Alice Brown; Sir Anthony Cleaver; The Lord Goodhart, QC; Ms F. Heaton; Prof. A. King; The Rt. Hon. J. MacGregor, OBE, MP; The Lord Shore of Stepney, PC; Sir William Utting, CB; Ms D. Warwick
Secretary (SCS), Mrs S. Tyerman

STRATEGIC RAIL AUTHORITY (SHADOW)
— *see* British Railways Board

OFFICE OF TELECOMMUNICATIONS
50 Ludgate Hill, London EC4M 7JJ
Tel 0171-634 8700; fax 0171- 634 8943

The Office of Telecommunications (Oftel) is a non-ministerial government department responsible for supervising telecommunications activities and broadcast transmission in the UK. Its goal is to achieve the best deal for UK telecommunications customers in terms of quality, choice and value for money. It is responsible for ensuring that holders of telecommunications licences comply with their licence conditions and for maintaining and promoting effective competition in telecommunications.

The Director-General has powers to deal with anti-competitive practices and monopolies. He also has a duty to consider all reasonable complaints and representations about telecommunication apparatus and services.

Director-General, D. Edmonds
Director of Operations, Miss A. Lambert
Director of Regulatory Policy, Mrs A. Taylor
Director of Compliance, Mrs J. Whittles
Director of Technology, P. Walker
Director of Strategy and Forecasting, A. Bell
Director of Business Support, D. Smith
Director of Communications, D. Stroud

TOURIST BOARDS
(For British Tourist Authority, *see* page 285)

The English Tourism Council, the Scottish Tourist Board, the Wales Tourist Board and the Northern Ireland Tourist Board are responsible for developing and marketing the tourist industry in their respective countries.

ENGLISH TOURISM COUNCIL, Thames Tower, Black's Road, London W6 9EL. Tel: 0181-846 9000. *Chief Executive (acting),* Ms E. Noble

SCOTTISH TOURIST BOARD, 23 Ravelston Terrace, Edinburgh EH4 3EU. Tel: 0131-332 2433; Thistle House, Beechwood Park North, Inverness IV2 3ED. Tel: 01463-716996. *Chief Executive,* T. Buncle

WALES TOURIST BOARD, Brunel House, 2 Fitzalan Road, Cardiff CF2 1UY. Tel: 01222-475272. *Chief Executive,* J. Jones

NORTHERN IRELAND TOURIST BOARD, St Anne's Court, 59 North Street, Belfast BTI INB. Tel: 01232-231221. *Chief Executive*, I. Henderson

---

DEPARTMENT OF TRADE AND INDUSTRY
1 Victoria Street, London SWIH OET
Tel 0171-215 5000; fax 0171-222 2629
Web: http://www.dti.gov.uk

The Department is responsible for international trade policy, including the promotion of UK trade interests in the European Union, GATT, OECD, UNCTAD and other international organizations; the promotion of UK exports and assistance to exporters; policy in relation to industry and commerce, including industrial relations policy; policy towards small firms; regional industrial assistance; legislation and policy in relation to the Post Office; competition policy and consumer protection; the development of national policies in relation to all forms of energy and the development of new sources of energy, including international aspects of energy policy; policy on science and technology research and development; space policy; standards, quality and design; and company legislation.

Secretary of State for Trade and Industry, The Rt. Hon. Stephen Byers, MP
Principal Private Secretary, A. Phillipson
Private Secretaries, C. Woolard; E. Barker
Minister of State, The Rt. Hon. Helen Liddell, MP (*Energy, Competitiveness in Europe*)
Minister of State, The Rt. Hon. Richard Caborn, MP (*Trade*)
Minister of State, Patricia Hewitt, MP
Parliamentary Under-Secretaries of State, Dr Kim Howells, MP (*Competition, Consumer Affairs*); Alan Johnson, MP (*Employment Relations, the Post Office, Industry*); The Lord Sainsbury of Turville (*Science*)
Private Secretaries, Ms D. Parr; Ms P. Ciniewicz; S. Evans
Parliamentary Clerk, T. Williams
Permanent Secretary, Sir Michael Scholar, KCB
Private Secretary, Ms J. Dav
Chief Scientific Adviser and Head of Office of Science and Technology, Sir Robert May, FRS
Private Secretary, R. Clay
British Trade International Chief Executive, Sir David Wright, KCMG, LVO
Directors-General, Dr J. Taylor, OBE, FREng., FRS (*Director-General of the Research Councils*); A. Hutton, CB (*Trade Policy*); D. Durie, CMG (*Enterprise and Regions*); Dr C. Bell (*Corporate and Consumer Affairs*); D. Nissen, CB (*The Solicitor*); Ms A. Walker (*Energy*); J. Spencer (*Resources and Services*); A. Macdonald, CB (*Industry*)

DIVISIONAL ORGANIZATION

†BRITISH NATIONAL SPACE CENTRE
Director-General (*SCS*), D. R. Davis
Deputy Director-General (*SCS*), D. Leadbeater
Directors (*SCS*), A. Cooper; Dr P. Murdin; Dr D. Lumley

BUSINESS LINK DIRECTORATE
Director of Business Link (*SCS*), P. Waller
Directors (*SCS*), P. Bentley; Mrs P. Jackson; T. Evans; Ms H. Merrifield

CENTRAL DIRECTORATE
Director of Competitiveness Unit (*SCS*), D. Evans
Directors (*SCS*), Ms S. Chambers; J. Reynolds

†CHEMICALS AND BIOTECHNOLOGY DIRECTORATE

Director of Chemicals and Biotechnology (*SCS*), M. Baker
Directors (*SCS*), Ms G. Alliston; Ms M. Darnbrough

COMMUNICATIONS DIRECTORATE
Director of News (*SCS*), M. Tee
Director of Publicity and Internal Communications (*SCS*), P. Burke

†COMMUNICATIONS AND INFORMATION INDUSTRIES DIRECTORATE
Director of Communications and Information Industries (*SCS*), W. MacIntyre
Directors (*SCS*), N. Worman; D. Lumley; D. Love; C. Holmes; P. Williams; S. Price

COMPANY LAW AND INVESTIGATIONS DIRECTORATE
Director of Company Law and Investigations (*SCS*), R. Rogers
Directors (*SCS*), J. Grewe; G. Harp; J. Gardner; J. Sibley; R. Burns; Ms B. Chase; A. Robertshaw

COMPETITION POLICY AND UTILITIES REVIEW TEAM
Director of Team (*SCS*), Ms R. Anderson
Directors (*SCS*), Dr A. Eggington; D. Miner; J. May; R. Bent

CONSUMER AFFAIRS DIRECTORATE
Director of Consumer Affairs (*SCS*), S. Haddrill
Directors (*SCS*), P. Mason; Ms J. Munday; H. Ewing; A. Willcocks

CONSUMER GOODS, BUSINESS AND POSTAL SERVICES DIRECTORATE
Director of Consumer Goods, Business and Postal Services (*SCS*), M. Baker
Directors (*SCS*), B. Hopson; Ms J. Britton

ECONOMICS AND STATISTICS DIRECTORATE
Chief Economic Adviser (*SCS*), D. R. Coates
Directors (*SCS*), K. Warwick; Ms J. Dougharty; M. Bradbury

EMPLOYMENT RELATIONS DIRECTORATE
Director of Industrial Relations (*SCS*), P. Salvidge
Directors (*SCS*), Dr E. Baker; R. Niblett; Ms N. Carter; K. Masson; M. Beatson

ENERGY POLICY, ANALYSIS, TECHNOLOGY AND COAL DIRECTORATE
Director of Energy Policy, Analysis, Technology and Coal (*SCS*), N. Hirst
Directors (*SCS*), G. C. White; N. Peace; G. Bevan; M. Atkinson; A. Wright

†ENGINEERING INDUSTRIES DIRECTORATE
Director of Engineering Industries (*SCS*), M. O'Shea
Directors (*SCS*), J. Neilson; M. Ralph; R. Kingcombe; H. Brown; R. Poole; A. Vinall; Ms A. Wilks

ENGINEERING INSPECTORATE
Director of Engineering Inspectorate (*SCS*), Dr P. Fenwick

†ENVIRONMENT DIRECTORATE
Director of Environment (*SCS*), Dr C. Hicks
Director (*SCS*), D. Prior

†ESTATES AND FACILITIES MANAGEMENT DIRECTORATE
Director (*SCS*), M. Coolican

EUROPEAN POLICY DIRECTORATE
Kingsgate House, 66–74 Victoria Street, London SWIE 6SW
Director (*SCS*), N. McMillan, CMG

EXPORT CONTROL AND NON-PROLIFERATION DIRECTORATE
Kingsgate House, 66–74 Victoria Street, London SWIE 6SW

Director of Export Control and Non-Proliferation (SCS), Dr R. Heathcote
Directors (SCS), J. Neve; S. Haird

EXPORT PROMOTION DIRECTORATES
Kingsgate House, 66–74 Victoria Street, London SW1E 6SW

Director, Markets and Sectors (SCS), M. Gibson
Directors (SCS), M. Mowlam (*The Americas*); M. Cohen (*Asia Pacific*); K. Levinson (*Central and Eastern Europe*); S. Lyle Smythe (*Business in Europe*); M. Khan (*Middle East, Near East and North Africa*); V. Fean (*Sub-Saharan Africa and South Asia*); R. Lamb (*Sectors, Services and Outward Investment*)

EXPORT SERVICES DIRECTORATE
Kingsgate House, 66–74 Victoria Street, London SW1E 6SW

Director (SCS), A. Reynolds

FINANCE AND RESOURCE MANAGEMENT DIRECTORATE
Director of Finance and Resource Management (SCS), J. Phillips
Directors (SCS), E. Hosker; K. Hills; N. Nandra; H. Savill

‡INDUSTRY ECONOMICS AND STATISTICS DIRECTORATE
Director (SCS), Dr N. Owen

†INFORMATION MANAGEMENT AND PROCESS ENGINEERING DIRECTORATE
Director (SCS), R. Wheeler

INFRASTRUCTURE AND ENERGY PROJECTS DIRECTORATE
Director of Infrastructure and Energy Projects (SCS), J. Rhodes
Directors (SCS), G. Atkinson; Dr K. Forrest; B. Gallagher; J. Campbell

†INNOVATION POLICY AND STANDARDS DIRECTORATE
Director of Innovation Policy and Standards (SCS), R. Foster
Directors (SCS), J. M. Barber; J. Hobday; D. Reed; P. Bunn

†INNOVATION UNIT
Director (SCS), Dr A. Keddie

†INTERNAL AUDIT DIRECTORATE
Director of Internal Audit (SCS), R. Louth

INTERNATIONAL ECONOMICS DIRECTORATE
Kingsgate House, 66–74 Victoria Street, London SW1E 6SW

Director (SCS), C. Moir

INVEST IN BRITAIN BUREAU (FCO/DTI)
Chief Executive (SCS), A. Fraser

JOINT EXPORT PROMOTION DIRECTORATE (FCO/DTI)
Kingsgate House, 66–74 Victoria Street, London SW1E 6SW

Director (SCS), D. Hall, CMG

LEGAL RESOURCE MANAGEMENT AND BUSINESS LAW UNIT
10 Victoria Street, London SW1H 0NN

The Solicitor and Director-General (SCS), D. Nissen, CB
Director (SCS), P. Burke

LEGAL SERVICES DIRECTORATE A
10 Victoria Street, London SW1H 0NN

Director of Legal A (SCS), J. Stanley
Legal Directors (SCS), J. Roberts; Miss N. O'Flynn; S. Hyett; Miss G. Richmond

LEGAL SERVICES DIRECTORATE B
10 Victoria Street, London SW1H 0NN

Director of Legal B (SCS), P. Bovey
Legal Directors (SCS), R. Baker; B. Welch; R. Perkins; Ms S. Hardy; C. Raikes; Ms N. Arora

LEGAL SERVICES DIRECTORATE C
10 Victoria Street, London SW1H 0NN

Director of Legal C (SCS), Ms A. Brett-Holt
Legal Directors (SCS), M. Bucknill; A. Woods; C. Osborne; T. Susman

LEGAL SERVICES DIRECTORATE D
10 Victoria Street, London SW1H 0NN

Director of Legal D (SCS), Mrs T. Dunstan
Directors (SCS), S. Milligan; L. Nawbatt

MANAGEMENT BEST PRACTICE
Director of Management Best Practice, Dr K. Poulter
Deputy Director (SCS), Dr I. Harrison

NEW ISSUES AND DEVELOPING COUNTRIES
Kingsgate House, 66–74 Victoria Street, London SW1E 6SW

Director (SCS), C. Bridge

NUCLEAR INDUSTRIES DIRECTORATE
Director of Nuclear Industries (SCS), H. Leiser
Directors (SCS), Dr M. Draper; Dr E. Drage; I. Downing; S. Bowen; D. Walker

OFFICE OF SCIENCE AND TECHNOLOGY: SCIENCE AND ENGINEERING BASE DIRECTORATE
Albany House, 84–86 Petty France, London SW1H 9ST

Director, Science and Engineering Base (SCS), A. Quigley
Directors (SCS), Ms F. Price; Dr K. Root

OFFICE OF SCIENCE AND TECHNOLOGY: TRANSDEPARTMENTAL SCIENCE AND TECHNOLOGY DIRECTORATE
Albany House, 84–86 Petty France, London SW1H 9ST

Director, Transdepartmental Science and Technology (SCS), Ms J. Durning
Directors (SCS), S. Spivey; Mrs P. Sellers; M. Parker; Ms J. Darrell

OIL AND GAS DIRECTORATE
1 Victoria Street, London SW1H 0ET

Director of Oil and Gas (SCS), G. Dart
Directors (SCS), J. R. V. Brooks, CBE; G. Riggs; S. Toole; M. Graham

Atholl House, 86–88 Guild Street, Aberdeen AB11 6AR
Tel 01224-254059

Director of Oil and Gas (SCS), S. Toole

REGIONAL ASSISTANCE DIRECTORATE
Director of Regional Assistance (SCS), A. Steele
Director (SCS), S. Robins

REGIONAL EUROPEAN FUNDS DIRECTORATE
Director (SCS), vacant

REGIONAL POLICY DIRECTORATE
Director (SCS), D. Smith

SENIOR STAFF MANAGEMENT DIRECTORATE
Director (SCS), Ms K. Elliott

SMALL AND MEDIUM-SIZED ENTERPRISES (SME) POLICY DIRECTORATE
Director (SCS), C. Johnston

SMALL AND MEDIUM-SIZED ENTERPRISES (SME) TECHNOLOGY DIRECTORATE
Director (SCS), R. Allpress

STAFF PERSONNEL OPERATIONS DIRECTORATE
Director (SCS), R. Wright

---

† At 151 Buckingham Palace Road, London SW1W 9SS

STAFF POLICY AND PAY DIRECTORATE
Director (SCS), Ms B. Habberjam

TRADE FACILITATION AND IMPORT POLICY
DIRECTORATE
Kingsgate House, 66–74 Victoria Street, London SW1E 6SW
Director (SCS), A. Berry

TRADE POLICY DIRECTORATE
Kingsgate House, 66–74 Victoria Street, London SW1E 6SW
Director (SCS), J. Hunt

BRITISH TRADE INTERNATIONAL
Kingsgate House, 66–74 Victoria Street, London SW1E 6SW
Tel 0171-215 5000

British Trade International replaced the British Overseas Trade Board in June 1999. It is responsible for international trade promotion and development.
Chairmen, Brian Wilson, MP (*Minister for Trade, DTI*); Geoffrey Hoon, MP (*Minister of State, FCO*)
Vice-Chairmen, HRH The Duke of Kent, KG, GCMG, GCVO; Sir Martin Laing, CBE
Chief Executive, Sir David Wright, KCMG, LVO
Members, R. Turner, OBE; V. Brown; J. Shepherd, CMG; A. Summers; Ms G. Goucher, MBE; Sir David John; R. Orgill; K. Pathak; W. Thomson; G. Robson; D. Jones; M. Bohill; D. Durie, CMG

REGIONAL OFFICES
— *see* pages 303–4

EXECUTIVE AGENCIES

COMPANIES HOUSE
Companies House, Crown Way, Cardiff CF4 3UZ
Tel 01222-380801; fax 01222-380900
London Information Centre, 21 Bloomsbury Street, London WC1B 3XD
37 Castle Terrace, Edinburgh EH1 2EB
Tel 0131-535 5800; fax 0131-535 5820

Companies House incorporates companies, registers company documents and provides company information.
Registrar of Companies for England and Wales, J. Holden
Registrar for Scotland, J. Henderson

EMPLOYMENT TRIBUNALS SERVICE
19–29 Woburn Place, London WC1H 0LU
Tel 0171-273 8666; fax 0171-273 8670

The Service became an executive agency in 1997 and brought together the administrative support for the employment tribunals and the Employment Appeal Tribunal.
Chief Executive, I. Jones

THE INSOLVENCY SERVICE
PO Box 203, 21 Bloomsbury Street, London WC1B 3QW
Tel 0171-637 1110; fax 0171-636 4709

The Service administers and investigates the affairs of bankrupts and companies in compulsory liquidation; deals with the disqualification of directors in all corporate failures; regulates insolvency practitioners and their professional bodies; provides banking and investment services for bankruptcy and liquidation estates; and advises ministers on insolvency policy issues.
Inspector-General and Chief Executive, P. R. Joyce
Deputy Inspectors-General, D. J. Flynn; L. T. Cramp

NATIONAL WEIGHTS AND MEASURES LABORATORY
Stanton Avenue, Teddington, Middx TW11 0JZ
Tel 0181-943 7272; fax 0181-943 7270

The Laboratory administers weights and measures legislation, carries out type examination, calibration and testing, and runs courses on metrological topics.
Chief Executive, Dr S. Bennett

PATENT OFFICE
— *see* page 330

RADIOCOMMUNICATIONS AGENCY
Wyndham House, 189 Marsh Wall, London E14 9SX
Tel 0171-211 0211; fax 0171-211 0507

The Agency is responsible for the management of the radio spectrum used for civilian purposes within the UK. It also represents UK radio interests internationally.
Chief Executive, D. Hendon

HM TREASURY
Parliament Street, London SW1P 3AG
Tel 0171-270 5000
Web: http://www.hm-treasury.gov.uk

The Office of the Lord High Treasurer has been continuously in commission for well over 200 years. The Lord High Commissioners of HM Treasury are the First Lord of the Treasury (who is also the Prime Minister), the Chancellor of the Exchequer and five junior Lords (who are government whips in the House of Commons). This Board of Commissioners is assisted at present by the Chief Secretary, the Parliamentary Secretary who is also the government Chief Whip, the Paymaster-General, the Financial Secretary, the Economic Secretary, the Minister of State and the Permanent Secretary.

The Prime Minister is not primarily concerned in the day-to-day aspects of Treasury business; the management of the Treasury devolves upon the Chancellor of the Exchequer and the other Treasury ministers.

The Chief Secretary is responsible for public expenditure planning and control; public sector pay; value for money in the public services; public/private partnerships and procurement policy; strategic oversight of banking, financial services and insurance; departmental investment strategies; welfare reform; devolution; and resource accounting and budgeting. From April 2000 he will be responsible for a new Office of Government Commerce which will centralize government procurement activities.

The Paymaster-General is responsible for the Inland Revenue, Customs and Excise and the Treasury, with overall responsibility for the Finance Bill. She leads on personal and business taxation, VAT and European/international tax issues. The Paymaster-General's Office is part of the National Investment and Loans Office (*see* pages 324–5).

The Financial Secretary is responsible for growth and productivity; small firms and venture capital; science, research and development; competition and deregulation policy; environmental issues; export credit; most Customs and Excise taxes; vehicle excise duty; and parliamentary financial business.

The Economic Secretary is responsible for National Savings, the Debt Management Office, the National Investment and Loans Office, the Office for National Statistics, the Royal Mint, and the Government Actuary's Department; banking, financial services and insurance; foreign exchange reserves; debt management policy; women's issues; and charity taxation.
Prime Minister and First Lord of the Treasury, The Rt. Hon. Tony Blair, MP
Chancellor of the Exchequer, The Rt. Hon. Gordon Brown, MP

---

† At 151 Buckingham Palace Road, London SW1W 9SS

Principal Private Secretary, T. Scholar
Private Secretaries, J. Papps; Ms T. Finkelstein
Special Advisers, E. Balls; E. Miliband; S. Livermore; I. Austin
Council of Economic Advisers, C. Wales; P. Gregg; Ms S. Vadera
Parliamentary Private Secretary, vacant
Chief Secretary to the Treasury, The Rt. Hon. Alan Milburn, MP
  Private Secretary, P. Schofield
Paymaster-General, Dawn Primarolo, MP
  Private Secretary, Ms S. Knight
  Parliamentary Private Secretary, A. Johnson, MP
Financial Secretary to the Treasury, Stephen Timms, MP
  Private Secretary, S. Field
Economic Secretary, Melanie Johnson, MP
  Private Secretary, Ms A. King
Parliamentary Secretary to the Treasury and Government Chief Whip (*£64,307), The Rt. Hon. Ann Taylor, MP
  Private Secretary, M. Maclean
Treasurer of HM Household and Deputy Chief Whip (*£33,359), Keith Bradley, MP
Comptroller of HM Household (*£21,467), Thomas McAvoy, MP
Vice-Chamberlain of HM Household (*21,467), Graham Allen, MP
Lord Commissioners of the Treasury (*£21,467), Robert Ainsworth, MP; James Dowd, MP; Clive Betts, MP; David Jamieson, MP; Jane Kennedy, MP
Assistant Whips (*£21,467), David Clelland, MP; Kevin Hughes, MP; Greg Pope, MP; Anne McGuire, MP; Michael Hall, MP; Gerry Sutcliffe, MP
Parliamentary Clerk, D. S. Martin
Permanent Secretary to the Treasury, Sir Andrew Turnbull, KCB, CVO
  Private Secretary, Ms S. Riach
Head of Government Accountancy Service and Chief Accountancy Adviser to the Treasury, A. Likierman

DIRECTORATES

Leader, Ministerial Support Team (*SCS*), T. Scholar
Leader, Communications Team (*SCS*), J. Kingman
Leader, Strategy Team (*SCS*), Dr R. Kosmin

MACROECONOMIC POLICY AND PROSPECTS
Director, and Head of the Government Economic Service (*SCS*), A. O'Donnell
Deputy Directors (*SCS*), J. Grice; J. Taylor
Team Leaders (*SCS*), M. Bradbury; D. Deaton; C. M. Kelly; Ms S. Killen; A. Kilpatrick; D. Ramsden

INTERNATIONAL FINANCE
Director (*SCS*), Sir Nigel Wicks, GCB, CVO, CBE
Deputy Directors (*SCS*), J. Cunliffe; P. McIntyre
Team Leaders (*SCS*), S. Brooks; A. Gibbs; D. Lawton; M. Richardson; R. Todd

BUDGET AND PUBLIC FINANCES
Director (*SCS*), R. Culpin
Deputy Directors (*SCS*), N. Macpherson; C. J. Mowl
Team Leaders (*SCS*), P. Curwen; Ms M. Dawes; S. N. Matthews; D. Savage; M. Swan; I. Taylor; M. Williams; P. Wynn Owen

PUBLIC SERVICES
Director (*SCS*), E. J. W. Gieve, CB
Deputy Directors (*SCS*), †N. Glass; Miss G. M. Noble, CB; P. N. Sedgwick; A. Sharples

is entitled to the ministerial salary shown but in common with other Cabinet ministers takes only £47,149
Team Leaders (*SCS*), Ms A. Charlesworth; T. Dowse; E. Evans; D. Franklin; N. Holgate; A. Hudson; P. Kane; Ms B. Kelly; J. Moore; M. Parkinson; A. Ritchie; P. Sedgwick; A. Sharples; Ms C. Slocock; Ms A. Tuffs

FINANCIAL MANAGEMENT, REPORTING AND AUDIT
Director (*Chief Accountancy Adviser*) (*SCS*), A. Likierman
Deputy Director (*SCS*), †J. E. Mortimer
Team Leaders (*SCS*), J. Breckenbridge; C. Butler; Mrs R. M. Dunn; Dr R. Kosmin; Ms A. M. Jones; D. Loweth; K. Ross

FINANCE, REGULATION AND INDUSTRY
Director (*SCS*), S. Robson, CB
Deputy Directors (*SCS*), H. J. Bush; R. Fellgett; B. Rigby; M. Roberts
Team Leaders (*SCS*), R. Allen; Ms S. Beckett; M. Burt; P. Casey; J. Colling; Mrs P. C. Diggle; C. Farthing; C. Ford; D. Griffiths; J. Halligan; Mrs S. Lewis; J. May; C. R. Pickering; D. Roe; P. Rutman; P. Schofield; Ms C. Speck; J. Whitlock; T. Wilson

PERSONNEL, ACCOMMODATION AND INFORMATION SERVICES
Director (*SCS*), Ms M. O'Mara
Team Leaders (*SCS*), I. Cooper; J. Dodds; J. Hibberd
† Combined deputy director and head of team

EXECUTIVE AGENCIES

NATIONAL SAVINGS
— see page 325–6

OFFICE FOR NATIONAL STATISTICS
— see pages 326

ROYAL MINT
— see page 336

UNITED KINGDOM DEBT MANAGEMENT OFFICE
Cheapside House, 138 Cheapside, London EC2V 6BB
Tel 0171-862 6500; fax 0171 862 6509

The UK Debt Management Office was launched as an executive agency of the Treasury in April 1998 after the transfer from the Bank of England to the Treasury of responsibility for debt management, the sale of gilts and oversight of the gilts market. It will in due course take over responsibility for the management of the Exchequer's daily cash flow.
Chief Executive, M. L. Williams

THE TREASURY SOLICITOR
DEPARTMENT OF HM PROCURATOR-GENERAL AND TREASURY SOLICITOR
Queen Anne's Chambers, 28 Broadway, London SW1H 9JS
Tel 0171-210 3000; fax 0171-210 3004

The Treasury Solicitor's Department provides legal services for many government departments. Those without their own lawyers are provided with legal advice, and both they and other departments are provided with litigation services. The Treasury Solicitor is also the Queen's Proctor, and is responsible for collecting Bona Vacantia on behalf of the Crown. The Department became an executive agency in 1996.
HM Procurator-General and Treasury Solicitor (*SCS*), A. H. Hammond, CB
Deputy Treasury Solicitor (*SCS*), A. M. Inglese

---

* In addition to a parliamentary salary of £47,008; the Chief Whip

LITIGATION DIVISION
SCS, R. Aitken; Mrs D. Babar; D. Brummell; A. D. Lawton; A. Leithead; B. McKay; P. R. Messer; Ms L. Nicoll; Mrs J. B. C. Oliver; D. Palmer; S. Parkinson; R. J. Phillips; A. J. Sandal

QUEEN'S PROCTOR DIVISION
Queen's Proctor (SCS), A. H. Hammond, CB
Assistant Queen's Proctor (SCS), Mrs D. Babar

RESOURCES AND SERVICES DIVISION
Principal Establishment and Finance Officer and Security Officer (SCS), J. P. Burnett
Deputy Establishment Officer (G7), Ms H. Donnelly
Finance Officer (G7), C. A. Woolley
Information Systems Manager (G7), M. Gabbidon
Business Support Manager (SEO), E. Blishen

BONA VACANTIA DIVISION
SCS, Ms L. Addison

EUROPEAN DIVISION
SCS, J. E. Collins; A. Ridout; M. C. P. Thomas

CULTURE, MEDIA AND SPORT DIVISION
SCS, Ms I. Letwin

CABINET OFFICE AND CENTRAL ADVISORY DIVISION
SCS, M. C. L. Carpenter; P. Kilgarriff

MINISTRY OF DEFENCE ADVISORY DIVISION
Metropole Building, Northumberland Avenue, London WC2N 5BL
Tel 0171-218 4691
SCS, N. Beach; Mrs V. Collett; M. Hemming; Ms F. Nash

DEPARTMENT FOR EDUCATION AND EMPLOYMENT ADVISORY DIVISION
Caxton House, Tothill Street, London SW1H 9NF
Tel 0171-273 3000
SCS, F. D. W. Clarke; Ms D. Collins; S. T. Harker; C. House; N. A. D. Lambert; D. Macrae

HM TREASURY ADVISORY DIVISION
Treasury Chambers, Parliament Street, London SW1P 3AG
Tel 0171-270 3000
SCS, M. A. Blythe; J. R. J. Braggins; Ms R. Ford; J. Jones; R. Ricks; Miss J. V. Stokes

CONSTITUTIONAL REFORM DIVISION
70 Whitehall, London SW1A 2AS
Tel 0171-270 6093
SCS, Miss R. A. Jeffreys

COUNCIL ON TRIBUNALS
7th Floor, 22 Kingsway, London WC2B 6LE
Tel 0171-936 7045; fax 0171-936 7044

The Council on Tribunals is an independent body that operates under the Tribunals and Inquiries Act 1992. It consists of 16 members appointed by the Lord Chancellor and the Lord Advocate; one member is appointed to represent the interests of people in Wales. The Scottish Committee of the Council generally considers Scottish tribunals and matters relating only to Scotland.

The Council advises on and keeps under review the constitution and working of administrative tribunals, and considers and reports on administrative procedures relating to statutory inquiries. Some 70 tribunals are currently under the Council's supervision. It is consulted by and advises government departments on a wide range of subjects relating to adjudicative procedures.

Chairman, vacant
Members, The Parliamentary Commissioner for Administration (*ex officio*); R. J. Elliot, WS (*Chairman of the Scottish Committee*); Mrs C. Berkeley; S. M. D. Brown; S. R. Davie, CB; J. H. Eames; Mrs A. Galbraith; ; Mrs S. R. Howdle; I. J. Irvine; S. Jones, CBE; Prof. T. M. Partington; I. D. Penman, CB; D. G. Readings; E. P. Roberts; P. A. A. Waring
Secretary, Mrs P. J. Fairbairn

SCOTTISH COMMITTEE OF THE COUNCIL ON TRIBUNALS
44 Palmerston Place, Edinburgh EH12 5BJ
Tel 0131-220 1236; fax 0131-225 4271
Chairman, R. J. Elliot, WS
Members, The Parliamentary Commissioner for Administration (*ex officio*); Mrs P. Y. Berry, MBE; Mrs B. Bruce; I. J. Irvine; Mrs A. Middleton; I. D. Penman, CB; Mrs H. Sheerin, OBE
Secretary, Mrs E. M. MacRae

TRIBUNALS
— *see* pages 370–3

UNITED KINGDOM SPORTS COUNCIL (UK SPORT)
Walkden House, 10 Melton Street, London NW1 2EB
Tel 0171-380 8000; fax 0171-380 8010

The UK Sports Council (UK Sport) was established by Royal Charter in January 1997. Its role is to focus on high performance sport at UK level, with the aim of achieving sporting excellence in world competition. It promotes the development of sport and fosters the provision of sporting facilities. It works to combat drug misuse, deals with international relations and organizes major events. It also distributes the funds allocated to sport from the proceeds of the National Lottery.
Chairman, Sir Rodney Walker
Chief Executive, R. Callicott

UNRELATED LIVE TRANSPLANT REGULATORY AUTHORITY
Department of Health, c/o Room 311, Wellington House, 133–155 Waterloo Road, London SE1 8UG
Tel 0171-972 4812; fax 0171-972 4852

The Unrelated Live Transplant Regulatory Authority (ULTRA) is a statutory body established in 1990. In every case where the transplant of an organ within the definition of the Human Organ Transplants Act 1989 is proposed between a living donor and a recipient who are not genetically related, the proposal must be referred to ULTRA. Applications must be made by registered medical practitioners.

The Authority comprises a chairman and ten members appointed by the Secretary of State for Health. The secretariat is provided by Department of Health officials.
Chairman, Prof. R. N. M. MacSween
Members, Mrs J. H. Callman; Dr J. F. Douglas; Dr H. Draper; Miss P. M. Franklin; Dr S. Fuggle; A. J. Hooker; S. G. Macpherson; Prof. Sir Netar Mallick; Prof. A. Rees; Mrs S. J. Sullivan
Administrative Secretary, E. Scarlett
Medical Secretary, Dr P. Doyle

NATIONAL ASSEMBLY FOR WALES
Cathays Park, Cardiff CF1 3NQ
Tel 01222-825111
National Assembly Information Line: 01222-898200
E-mail: webmaster@wales.gov.uk
Web: http://www.wales.gov.uk

The National Assembly for Wales has responsibility in Wales for ministerial functions relating to health and personal social services; education, except for terms and conditions of service and student awards; training; the Welsh language, arts and culture; the implementation of the Citizen's Charter in Wales; local government; housing; water and sewerage; environmental protection; sport; agriculture and fisheries; forestry; land use, including town and country planning and countryside and nature conservation; new towns; non-departmental public bodies and appointments in Wales; ancient monuments and historic buildings and the Welsh Arts Council; roads; tourism; financial assistance to industry; the Strategic Development Scheme in Wales and the Programme for the Valleys; and the operation of the European Regional Development Fund in Wales and other European Union matters. *See also* Welsh Office, and National Assemblies supplement.

First Secretary of the Assembly, The Rt. Hon. Alun Michael, MP, AM
   Private Secretary, Ms A. Coleman
   Special Advisers, Ms J. Crowley; A. Bold
Secretary for Economic Development, Rhodri Morgan, MP, AM
Secretary for Education Up to Age 16, Rosemary Butler, AM
Secretary for Health and Social Services, Jane Hutt, AM
Secretary for Post-16 Education and Training, Tom Middlehurst, AM
Secretary for Agriculture and the Rural Economy, Christine Gwyther, AM
Secretary for the Environment, Peter Law, AM
Trefnydd Manager, Andrew Davies, AM
Finance Secretary, Edwina Hart, AM
Permanent Secretary (G1), J. D. Shortridge
Clerk to the Assembly, J. W. Lloyd, CB

OFFICE OF THE PRESIDING OFFICER
Deputy Clerk (G3), B. J. Mitchell

COMMITTEE SECRETARIAT
Grade 5, Ms M. Knox

CABINET SECRETARIAT
Grade 5, L. Conway

OFFICE OF THE COUNSEL GENERAL
Counsel General, W. Roddick, QC

COMMUNICATIONS DIRECTORATE
Head of Publicity (G7), W. J. Edwards
Chief Press Officer (G7), D. Clifford

ESTABLISHMENT GROUP
Principal Establishment Officer (G3), Mrs B. Wilson
Heads of Divisions (G5), Dr A. G. Thornton; Ms K. Cassidy; Mrs M. Evans; N. Finlayson
Chief Statistician (G5), W. R. L. Alldritt
Head of Health Statistics and Analysis Unit (G6), P. Demery

FINANCE GROUP
Principal Finance Officer (G3), D. T. Richards
Head of Division (G5), L. A. Pavelin
Senior Economic Adviser (G5), M. G. Phelps
Head of Internal Audit (G6), D. A. McNeill

ECONOMIC AFFAIRS
Deputy Secretary (G2), D. W. Jones

AGRICULTURE DEPARTMENT
Head of Department (G3), H. D. Brodie

ECONOMIC DEVELOPMENT GROUP
Head of Group (G3), M. J. Cochlin
Heads of Divisions (G5), A. D. Lansdown; L. Conway; P. Fullerton

INDUSTRY AND TRAINING DEPARTMENT
Director (G3), D. W. Jones
Industrial Director (G4), vacant
Heads of Divisions (G5), R. Keveren; N. E. Thomas; W. G. Davies; *(G6)*, Dr R. J. Loveland

SOCIAL POLICY
Deputy Secretary (G2), G. C. G. Craid

EDUCATION DEPARTMENT
Head of Department (G3), R. J. Davies
†*Heads of Divisions (G5)*, R. Thomas; D. R. Adams; J. Howells; Mrs E. A. Taylor

OFFICE OF HM CHIEF INSPECTOR FOR SCHOOLS IN WALES
†*Chief Inspector (G4)*, Miss S. Lewis
†*Staff Inspectors (G5)*, M. G. Haines; C. Abbott
There are 45 Grade 6 Inspectors.
Head of Administration (G7), Mrs S. Howells

LOCAL GOVERNMENT GROUP
Head of Group (G3), Mrs H. F. O. Thomas
Heads of Divisions (G5), M. J. Shanahan; J. Atkins
Chief Inspector, Social Services Inspectorate (Wales) (G5), G. Williams
Deputy Chief Inspectors, R. Tebboth; R. C. Woodward; Mrs P. E. White

NHS DIRECTORATE
Director (G3), P. R. Gregory
Heads of Divisions (G5), B. Wilcox; R. C. Williams; Ms S. Beaver; J. Morgan

HEALTH PROTECTION AND IMPROVEMENT DIRECTORATE
Chief Medical Officer (G3), Dr R. Hall
Principal Medical Officers (G4), Dr B. Fuge; Dr M. Pontin
Senior Medical Officers (G5), Dr J. Ludlow; Dr H. N. Williams; Dr D. Salter
Chief Dental Officer (G5), P. Langmaid
Chief Scientific Adviser (G5), Dr J. A. V. Pritchard
Deputy Scientific Adviser (G6), Dr E. O. Crawley
Chief Pharmaceutical Adviser (G5), Miss C. W. Howells
Chief Environmental Health Adviser (G5), R. Alexander
Deputy Environmental Health Adviser (G6), D. Worthington

NURSING DIVISION
Chief Nursing Officer, Miss R. Kennedy
Nursing Officers, P. Johnson; M. F. Tonkin; Mrs H. Wood; Mrs R. Johnson

TRANSPORT, PLANNING AND ENVIRONMENT GROUP
Head of Group (G3), M. L. Evans
Director of Highways (G4), K. J. Thomas, CBE
Heads of Divisions (G5), J. R. Rees (*Roads Construction*); G. A. Thomas (*Transport Policy*); *(G6)*, R. J. Shaw (*Network Management*); B. H. Hawker, OBE (*Roads Major Projects*)
Grade 7, R. H. Powell; I. P. Davies; R. K. Cones; K. J. A. Tengy; T. J. Collins; S. C. Shouler; M. J. Gilbert; T. C. Dorken; M. J. A. Parker; I. A. Grindulis; A. D. Perry; Dr M. C. Dunn

† Based at Ty Glas Road, Llanishen, Cardiff CF4 5LE. Tel: 01222-761456

HEALTH AUTHORITIES

— *see* Social Welfare section

EXECUTIVE AGENCIES

CADW: WELSH HISTORIC MONUMENTS
Crown Building, Cathays Park, Cardiff CF1 3NQ
Tel 01222-500200; fax 01222-826375

Cadw supports the preservation, conservation, appreciation and enjoyment of the built heritage in Wales.
Chief Executive, T. Cassidy
Director of Policy and Administration, R. W. Hughes
Conservation Architect, J. D. Hogg
Principal Inspector of Ancient Monuments and Historic Buildings, J. R. Avent
Head of Presentation, A. J. Hood
Head of Corporate Services, J. Jenkins
Head of Administration, Mrs J. Booker
National Manager, Cadwraeth Cymru, M. B. R. Watkins

FARMING AND RURAL CONSERVATION AGENCY
— *see* page 279–80

INTERVENTION BOARD
— *see* pages 314

PLANNING INSPECTORATE
Crown Buildings, Cathays Park, Cardiff CF1 3NQ
Tel 01222-823892; fax 01222-825150

The Inspectorate is a joint executive agency of the Department of the Environment, Transport and the Regions and the National Assembly for Wales.
Chief Executive and Chief Planning Inspector (G3), C. Shepley
Director (G5), R. Davies

WALES YOUTH AGENCY

Leslie Court, Lon-y-Llyn, Caerphilly CF83 1BQ
Tel 01222-855700; fax 01222-855701

The Wales Youth Agency is an independent organization funded by the National Assembly for Wales. Its functions include the encouragement and development of the partnership between statutory and voluntary agencies relating to young people; the promotion of staff development and training; and the extension of marketing and information services in the relevant fields. The board of directors do not receive a salary.
Chairman of the Board of Directors, R. Noble
Vice-Chairman of the Board of Directors, Dr H. Williamson
Chief Executive, B. Williams

OFFICE OF WATER SERVICES

Centre City Tower, 7 Hill Street, Birmingham B5 4UA
Tel 0121-625 1300; fax 0121-625 1400

The Office of Water Services (Ofwat) was set up under the Water Act 1989 and is a non-ministerial government department headed by the Director-General of Water Services. It is the independent economic regulator of the water and sewerage companies in England and Wales. Ofwat's main duties are to ensure that the companies can finance and carry out the functions specified in the Water Industry Act 1991 and to protect the interests of water customers. There are ten regional customer service committees which are concerned solely with the interests of water customers. Representation of customer interests at national level is the responsibility of the Ofwat National Customer Council (ONCC).
Director-General of Water Services, I. C. R. Byatt
Chairman, Ofwat National Customer Council, Ms S. Reiter

WELSH ADMINISTRATION OMBUDSMAN

5th Floor, Capital Tower, Greyfriars Road, Cardiff CF10 3AG
Tel 0845-601 0987; fax 01222-226909

The Welsh Administration Ombudsman was appointed in July 1999 to investigate complaints by members of the public who have suffered an injustice through maladministration by the National Assembly for Wales and certain public bodies involved in devolved Welsh affairs.
Welsh Administration Ombudsman, M. S. Buckley

WELSH DEVELOPMENT AGENCY

Principality House, The Friary, Cardiff CF10 3FE
Tel 01443-845500; fax 01443-845589

The Agency was established under the Welsh Development Agency Act 1975. Its remit is to help further the regeneration of the economy and improve the environment in Wales. Under the Government of Wales Act 1998, the Land Authority for Wales and the Development Board for Rural Wales merged with the Welsh Development Agency. The Agency is sponsored by the National Assembly for Wales.

The Agency's priorities are to create new businesses and to encourage existing small firms to grow. Its main activities include promoting Wales as a location for inward investment, helping to boost the growth, profitability and competitiveness of indigenous Welsh companies, providing investment capital for industry, encouraging investment by the private sector in property development, grant-aiding land reclamation, and stimulating quality urban and rural development.
Chairman, D. Rowe-Beddoe
Deputy Chairman, G. Hawker
Chief Executive, W. B. Willott, CB

WELSH OFFICE

Gwydyr House, Whitehall, London SW1A 2ER
Tel 0171-270 3000

The Welsh Office is the Office of the Secretary of State for Wales, who represents Welsh interests in the Cabinet. *See also* National Assembly for Wales.
Secretary of State for Wales, The Rt. Hon. Paul Murphy, MP
Parliamentary Under-Secretary, David Hanson, MP
Head of Department, Ms A. Jackson

WOMEN'S NATIONAL COMMISSION

Room 56/4, Cabinet Office, Horse Guards Road, London SW1P 3AL
Tel 0171-238 0386; fax 0171-238 0387

The Women's National Commission is an independent advisory committee to the Government. Its remit is to ensure that the informed opinions of women are given their due weight in the deliberations of the Government and in public debate on matters of public interest including those of special interest to women. The Commission's sponsoring department is the Cabinet Office.
Chair, Miss V. Evans, CBE
Secretary, Ms J. Veitch

Prime Ministers since 1782

Over the centuries there has been some variation in the determination of the dates of appointment of Prime Ministers. Where possible, the date given is that on which a new Prime Minister kissed the Sovereign's hands and accepted the commission to form a ministry. However, until the middle of the 19th century the dating of a commission or transfer of seals could be the date of taking office. Where the composition of the Government changed, e.g. became a coalition, but the Prime Minister remained the same, the date of the change of government is given.

The Marquess of Rockingham, *Whig*, 27 March 1782
The Earl of Shelburne, *Whig*, 4 July 1782
The Duke of Portland ,*Coalition*, 2 April 1783
William Pitt, *Tory*, 19 December 1783
Henry Addington, *Tory*, 17 March 1801
William Pitt, *Tory*, 10 May 1804
The Lord Grenville, *Whig*, 11 February 1806
The Duke of Portland ,*Tory*, 31 March 1807
Spencer Perceval, *Tory*, 4 October 1809
The Earl of Liverpool, *Tory*, 8 June 1812
George Canning ,*Tory*, 10 April 1827
Viscount Goderich, *Tory*, 31 August 1827
The Duke of Wellington, *Tory*, 22 January 1828
The Earl Grey, *Whig*, 22 November 1830
The Viscount Melbourne, *Whig*, 16 July 1834
The Duke of Wellington, *Tory*, 17 November 1834
Sir Robert Peel, *Tory*, 10 December 1834
The Viscount of Melbourne, *Whig*, 18 April 1835
Sir Robert Peel, *Tory*, 30 August 1841
Lord John Russell (subsequently the Earl Russell), *Whig*, 30 June 1846
The Earl of Derby, *Tory*, 23 February 1852
The Earl of Aberdeen, *Peelite*, 19 December 1852
The Viscount Palmerston, *Liberal*, 6 February 1855
The Earl of Derby, *Conservative*, 20 February 1858
The Viscount Palmerston, *Liberal*, 12 June 1859
The Earl Russell, *Liberal*, 29 October 1865

The Earl of Derby, *Conservative*, 28 June 1866
Benjamin Disraeli, *Conservative*, 27 February 1868
William Gladstone, *Liberal*, 3 December 1868
Benjamin Disraeli, *Conservative*, 20 February 1874
William Gladstone, *Liberal*, 23 April 1880
The Marquess of Salisbury, *Conservative*, 23 June 1885
William Gladstone, *Liberal*, 1 February 1886
The Marquess of Salisbury, *Conservative*, 25 July 1886
William Gladstone, *Liberal*, 15 August 1892
The Earl of Rosebery, *Liberal*, 5 March 1894
The Marquess of Salisbury, *Conservative*, 25 June 1895
Arthur Balfour, *Conservative*, 12 July 1902
Sir Henry Campbell-Bannerman, *Liberal*, 5 December 1905
Herbert Asquith, *Liberal*, 7 April 1908
Herbert Asquith, *Coalition*, 25 May 1915
David Lloyd-George, *Coalition*, 7 December 1916
Andrew Bonar Law, *Conservative*, 23 October 1922
Stanley Baldwin, *Conservative*, 22 May 1923
Ramsay MacDonald, *Labour*, 22 January 1924
Stanley Baldwin, *Conservative*, 4 November 1924
Ramsay MacDonald, *Labour*, 5 June 1929
Ramsay MacDonald, *Coalition*, 24 August 1931
Stanley Baldwin, *Coalition*, 7 June 1935
Neville Chamberlain, *Coalition*, 28 May 1937
Winston Churchill, *Coalition*, 10 May 1940
Winston Churchill, *Conservative*, 23 May 1945
Clement Attlee, *Labour*, 26 July 1945
Sir Winston Churchill, *Conservative*, 26 October 1951
Sir Anthony Eden, *Conservative*, 6 April 1955
Harold Macmillan, *Conservative*, 10 January 1957
Sir Alec Douglas-Home, *Conservative*, 19 October 1963
Harold Wilson, *Labour*, 16 October 1964
Edward Heath, *Conservative*, 19 June 1970
Harold Wilson, *Labour*, 4 March 1974
James Callaghan, *Labour*, 5 April 1976
Margaret Thatcher, *Conservative*, 4 May 1979
John Major, *Conservative*, 28 November 1990
Anthony Blair, *Labour*, 2 May 1997

Speakers of the Commons since 1708

The date of appointment given is the day on which the Speaker was first elected by the House of Commons. The appointment requires royal approbation before it is confirmed and this is usually given within a few days. The present Speaker is the 155th.

PARLIAMENT OF GREAT BRITAIN

Sir Richard Onslow (*Lord Onslow*), 16 November 1708
William Bromley, 25 November 1710
Sir Thomas Hanmer, 16 February 1714
Spencer Compton (*Earl of Wilmington*), 17 March 1715
Arthur Onslow, 23 January 1728
Sir John Cust, 3 November 1761
Sir Fletcher Norton (*Lord Grantley*), 22 January 1770
Charles Cornwall, 31 October 1780
Hon. William Grenville (*Lord Grenville*), 5 January 1789
Henry Addington (*Viscount Sidmouth*), 8 June 1789

PARLIAMENT OF THE UNITED KINGDOM

Sir John Mitford (*Lord Redesdale*), 11 February 1801
Charles Abbot (*Lord Colchester*), 10 February 1802
Charles Manners-Sutton (*Viscount Canterbury*), 2 June 1817

James Abercromby (*Lord Dunfermline*), 19 February 1835
Charles Shaw-Lefevre (*Viscount Eversley*), 27 May 1839
J. Evelyn Denison (*Viscount Ossington*), 30 April 1857
Sir Henry Brand (*Viscount Hampden*), 9 February 1872
Arthur Wellesley Peel (*Viscount Peel*), 26 February 1884
William Gully (*Viscount Selby*), 10 April 1895
James Lowther (*Viscount Ullswater*), 8 June 1905
John Whitley, 27 April 1921
Hon. Edward Fitzroy, 20 June 1928
Douglas Clifton-Brown (*Viscount Ruffside*), 9 March 1943
William Morrison (*Viscount Dunrossil*), 31 October 1951
Sir Harry Hylton-Foster, 20 October 1959
Horace King (*Lord Maybray-King*), 26 October 1965
Selwyn Lloyd (*Lord Selwyn-Lloyd*), 12 January 1971
George Thomas (*Viscount Tonypandy*), 2 February 1976
Bernard Weatherill (*Lord Weatherill*), 15 June 1983
Betty Boothroyd, 27 April 1992

CIVIL SERVICE STAFF

BY MAIN DEPARTMENTS *as at 1 April 1998*

	Total	Of whom in agencies
Agriculture, Fisheries and Food	9,657	3,844
Cabinet Office (including Office of Public Service)	2,477	1,413
Culture, Media and Sport	612	231
Customs and Excise	23,400	—
Defence	104,163	59,526
Education and Employment	33,117	28,612
Environment, Transport and the Regions	15,215	10,457
Foreign Office	5,449	37
Health	4,596	1,104
HM Prison Service	39,363	39,363
Home Office	10,840	2,767
Inland Revenue	53,412	4,029
International Development	1,055	—
Lord Chancellor's Department	10,048	9,213
Northern Ireland Office	205	—
Scottish Departments	13,098	8,200
Social Security	87,218	84,448
Trade and Industry	8,493	4,059
Treasury	893	—
Welsh Office	2,110	170
Other departments	37,845	20,008
TOTAL	463,266	*277,481

*Excluding Inland Revenue (other than Valuation Office), Customs and Excise, Crown Prosecution Service and the Serious Fraud Office, which operate on Next Steps lines.
Source: Government Statistical Service – *Civil Service Statistics 1998* (Crown copyright)

Law Courts and Offices

THE JUDICIAL COMMITTEE OF THE PRIVY COUNCIL

The Judicial Committee of the Privy Council is primarily the final court of appeal for the United Kingdom overseas and those independent Commonwealth countries which have retained the avenue of appeal upon achieving independence (Antigua and Barbuda, The Bahamas, Barbados, Belize, Brunei, Dominica, Jamaica, Kiribati, Mauritius, New Zealand, St Christopher and Nevis, St Lucia, St Vincent and the Grenadines, Trinidad and Tobago, and Tuvalu). The Committee also hears appeals from the Channel Islands and the Isle of Man and the disciplinary and health committees of the medical and allied professions. It has a limited jurisdiction to hear appeals under the Pastoral Measure 1983. In 1998 the Judicial Committee heard 58 appeals and 85 petitions for special leave to appeal.

Following devolution, the Judicial Committee assumes a new role as Scotland's principal constitutional court and will be the final arbiter in disputes between the UK and Scottish Parliaments regarding legislative competence.

The members of the Judicial Committee include the Lord Chancellor, the Lords of Appeal in Ordinary (*see* page 354), other Privy Counsellors who hold or have held high judicial office and certain judges from the Commonwealth.

PRIVY COUNCIL OFFICE (JUDICIAL COMMITTEE), Downing Street, London SW1A 2AJ. Tel: 0171-270 0483. *Registrar of the Privy Council*, J. A. C. Watherston; *Chief Clerk*, F. G. Hart

The Judicature of England and Wales

The legal system of England and Wales is separate from those of Scotland and Northern Ireland and differs from them in law, judicial procedure and court structure, although there is a common distinction between civil law (disputes between individuals) and criminal law (acts harmful to the community).

The supreme judicial authority for England and Wales is the House of Lords, which is the ultimate Court of Appeal from all courts in Great Britain and Northern Ireland (except criminal courts in Scotland) for all cases except those concerning the interpretation and application of European Community law, including preliminary rulings requested by British courts and tribunals, which are decided by the European Court of Justice (*see* pages 773–81). Under the Human Rights Act 1998, which is due to come into force on 2 October 2000, the European Convention on Human Rights will be incorporated into British law; unresolved cases will still be referred to the European Court of Human Rights. As a Court of Appeal the House of Lords consists of the Lord Chancellor and the Lords of Appeal in Ordinary (law lords).

The Supreme Court of Judicature comprises the Court of Appeal, the High Court of Justice and the Crown Court. The High Court of Justice is the superior civil court and is divided into three divisions. The Chancery Division is concerned mainly with equity, bankruptcy and contentious probate business. The Queen's Bench Division deals with commercial and maritime law, serious personal injury and medical negligence cases, cases involving a breach of contract and professional negligence actions. The Family Division deals with matters relating to family law. Sittings are held at the Royal Courts of Justice in London or at 126 district registries outside the capital. High Court judges sit alone to hear cases at first instance. Appeals from lower courts are heard by two or three judges, or by single judges of the appropriate division. The Restrictive Practices Court, set up under the Restrictive Trade Practices Act 1956, and the Technology and Construction Court, which deals with cases which require expert evidence on technical and other issues concerning mainly the construction industry, defective products, property valuations, and landlord and tenant disputes, are also currently part of the High Court, although the Restrictive Practices Court is due to be abolished following the establishment of the Competition Commission (*see* page 291). Appeals from the High Court are heard in the Court of Appeal (Civil Division), presided over by the Master of the Rolls, and may go on to the House of Lords.

CRIMINAL CASES

In criminal matters the decision to prosecute in the majority of cases rests with the Crown Prosecution Service, the independent prosecuting body in England and Wales (*see* pages 362–3). The Service is headed by the Director of Public Prosecutions, who works under the superintendence of the Attorney-General. Certain categories of offence continue to require the Attorney-General's consent for prosecution.

The Crown Court sits in about 90 centres, divided into six circuits, and is presided over by High Court judges, full-time circuit judges, and part-time recorders and assistant recorders, sitting with a jury in all trials which are contested. There were 266 assistant recorders at 30 June 1999. The Crown Court deals with trials of the more serious criminal offences, the sentencing of offenders committed for sentence by magistrates' courts (when the magistrates consider their own power of sentence inadequate), and appeals from magistrates' courts. Magistrates usually sit with a circuit judge or recorder to deal with appeals and committals for sentence. Appeals from the Crown Court, either against sentence or conviction, are made to the Court of Appeal (Criminal Division), presided over by the Lord Chief Justice. A further appeal from the Court of Appeal to the House of Lords can be brought if a point of law of general public importance is considered to be involved.

Minor criminal offences (summary offences) are dealt with in magistrates' courts, which usually consist of three unpaid lay magistrates (justices of the peace) sitting without a jury, who are advised on points of law and procedure by a legally-qualified clerk to the justices. There were 30,260 justices of the peace at 1 January 1999. In busier courts a full-time, salaried and legally-qualified stipendiary magistrate presides alone. Cases involving people under 18 are heard in youth courts, specially constituted magistrates' courts which sit apart from other courts. Preliminary proceedings in a serious case to decide whether there is evidence to justify committal for trial in the Crown Court are also dealt with in the magistrates' courts. Appeals from magistrates' courts against sentence or conviction are made to the Crown Court. Appeals upon a point of law are made to the High Court, and may go on to the House of Lords.

CIVIL CASES

Most minor civil cases are dealt with by the county courts, of which there are about 270 (details may be found in the local telephone directory). Cases are heard by circuit judges or district judges. There were 356 district judges at 31 May 1999. For cases involving small claims there are special simplified procedures. Where there are financial limits on county court jurisdiction, claims which exceed those limits may be tried in the county courts with the consent of the parties, or in certain circumstances on transfer from the High Court. Outside London, bankruptcy proceedings can be heard in designated county courts. Magistrates' courts can deal with certain classes of civil case and committees of magistrates license public houses, clubs and betting shops. For the implementation of the Children Act 1989, a new structure of hearing centres was set up in 1991 for family proceedings cases, involving magistrates' courts (family proceedings courts), divorce county courts, family hearing centres and care centres. Appeals in family matters heard in the family proceedings courts go to the Family Division of the High Court; affiliation appeals and appeals from decisions of the licensing committees of magistrates go to the Crown Court. Appeals from county courts are heard in the Court of Appeal (Civil Division), and may go on to the House of Lords.

CORONERS' COURTS

Coroners' courts investigate violent and unnatural deaths or sudden deaths where the cause is unknown. Cases may be brought before a local coroner (a senior lawyer or doctor) by doctors, the police, various public authorities or members of the public. Where a death is sudden and the cause is unknown, the coroner may order a post-mortem examination to determine the cause of death rather than hold an inquest in court.

Judicial appointments are made by The Queen; the most senior appointments are made on the advice of the Prime Minister and other appointments on the advice of the Lord Chancellor.

Under the provisions of the Criminal Appeal Act 1995, a Commission was set up to direct and supervise investigations into possible miscarriages of justice and to refer cases to the courts on the grounds of conviction and sentence (*see* page 291); these functions were formerly the responsibility of the Home Secretary.

THE HOUSE OF LORDS
AS FINAL COURT OF APPEAL

The Lord High Chancellor (£160,011)
The Rt. Hon. the Lord Irvine of Lairg, *born* 1940, *apptd* 1997

LORDS OF APPEAL IN ORDINARY (each £147,214)
Style, The Rt. Hon. Lord —

Rt. Hon. Lord Browne-Wilkinson, *born* 1930, *apptd* 1991

Rt. Hon. Lord Slynn of Hadley, *born* 1930, *apptd* 1992
Rt. Hon. Lord Nicholls of Birkenhead, *born* 1933, *apptd* 1994
Rt. Hon. Lord Steyn, *born* 1932, *apptd* 1995
Rt. Hon. Lord Hoffman, *born* 1934, *apptd* 1995
Rt. Hon. Lord Hope of Craighead, *born* 1938, *apptd* 1996
Rt. Hon. Lord Clyde, *born* 1932, *apptd* 1996
Rt. Hon. Lord Hutton, *born* 1931, *apptd* 1997
Rt. Hon. Lord Saville of Newdigate, *born* 1936, *apptd* 1997
Rt. Hon. Lord Hobhouse of Woodborough, *born* 1932, *apptd* 1998
Rt. Hon. Lord Millett, *born* 1932, *apptd* 1998
Rt. Hon. Lord Phillips of Worth Matravers, *born* 1938, *apptd* 1999

Judicial Office of the House of Lords, House of Lords, London SWIA OPW. Tel: 0171-219 3111
Registrar, The Clerk of the Parliaments (*see* page 217)

SUPREME COURT OF JUDICATURE

COURT OF APPEAL

The Master of the Rolls (£147,214), The Rt. Hon. Lord Woolf, *born* 1933, *apptd* 1996
Secretary, Mrs L. Grace
Clerk, Ms J. Jones

LORDS JUSTICES OF APPEAL (each £139,931)
Style, The Rt. Hon. Lord/Lady Justice [surname]

Rt. Hon. Sir Martin Nourse, *born* 1932, *apptd* 1985
Rt. Hon. Sir Murray Stuart-Smith, *born* 1927, *apptd* 1988
Rt. Hon. Sir Roy Beldam, *born* 1925, *apptd* 1989
Rt. Hon. Sir Paul Kennedy, *born* 1935, *apptd* 1992
Rt. Hon. Sir Simon Brown, *born* 1937, *apptd* 1992
Rt. Hon. Sir Anthony Evans, *born* 1934, *apptd* 1992
Rt. Hon. Sir Christopher Rose, *born* 1937, *apptd* 1992
Rt. Hon. Sir John Roch, *born* 1934, *apptd* 1993
Rt. Hon. Sir Peter Gibson, *born* 1934, *apptd* 1993
Rt. Hon. Sir Denis Henry, *born* 1931, *apptd* 1993
Rt. Hon. Sir Swinton Thomas, *born* 1931, *apptd* 1994
Rt. Hon. Sir Andrew Morritt, CVO, *born* 1938, *apptd* 1994
Rt. Hon. Sir Philip Otton, *born* 1933, *apptd* 1995
Rt. Hon. Sir Robin Auld, *born* 1937, *apptd* 1995
Rt. Hon. Sir Malcolm Pill, *born* 1938, *apptd* 1995
Rt. Hon. Sir William Aldous, *born* 1936, *apptd* 1995
Rt. Hon. Sir Alan Ward, *born* 1938, *apptd* 1995
Rt. Hon. Sir Konrad Schiemann, *born* 1937, *apptd* 1995
Rt. Hon. Sir Mathew Thorpe, *born* 1938, *apptd* 1995
Rt. Hon. Sir Mark Potter, *born* 1937, *apptd* 1996
Rt. Hon. Sir Henry Brooke, *born* 1936, *apptd* 1996
Rt. Hon. Sir Igor Judge, *born* 1941, *apptd* 1996
Rt. Hon. Sir Mark Waller, *born* 1940, *apptd* 1996
Rt. Hon. Sir John Mummery, *born* 1938, *apptd* 1996
Rt. Hon. Sir Charles Mantell, *born* 1937, *apptd* 1997
Rt. Hon. Sir John Chadwick, ED, *born* 1941, *apptd* 1997
Rt. Hon. Sir Robert Walker, *born* 1938, *apptd* 1997
Rt. Hon. Sir Richard Buxton, *born* 1938, *apptd* 1997
Rt. Hon. Sir Anthony May, *born* 1940, *apptd* 1997
Rt. Hon. Sir Simon Tuckey, *born* 1941, *apptd* 1998
Rt. Hon. Sir Anthony Clarke, *born* 1943, *apptd* 1998
Rt. Hon. Sir John Laws, *born* 1945, *apptd* 1999
Rt. Hon. Sir Stephen Sedley, *born* 1939, *apptd* 1999
Rt. Hon. Sir Jonathan Mance, *born* 1943, *apptd* 1999
Rt. Hon. Dame Brenda Hale, *born* 1945, *apptd* 1999

Ex officio Judges, The Lord High Chancellor; the Lord Chief Justice of England; the Master of the Rolls; the President of the Family Division; and the Vice-Chancellor

COURT OF APPEAL (CRIMINAL DIVISION)

Vice-President, The Rt. Hon. Lord Justice Rose
Judges, The Lord Chief Justice of England; the Master of
the Rolls; Lords Justices of Appeal; and Judges of the
High Court of Justice

COURTS-MARTIAL APPEAL COURT

Judges, The Lord Chief Justice of England; the Master of
the Rolls; Lords Justices of Appeal; and Judges of the
High Court of Justice

HIGH COURT OF JUSTICE
CHANCERY DIVISION

President, The Lord High Chancellor
The Vice-Chancellor (£139,931), The Rt. Hon. Sir Richard
Scott, *born* 1934, *apptd* 1994
Clerk, W. Northfield, BEM

JUDGES (each £123,787)
Style, The Hon. Mr/Mrs Justice [surname]

Hon. Sir Donald Rattee, *born* 1937, *apptd* 1989
Hon. Sir Francis Ferris, TD, *born* 1932, *apptd* 1990
Hon. Sir Jonathan Parker, *born* 1937, *apptd* 1991
Hon. Sir John Lindsay, *born* 1935, *apptd* 1992
Hon. Dame Mary Arden, DBE, *born* 1947, *apptd* 1993
Hon. Sir Edward Evans-Lombe, *born* 1937, *apptd* 1993
Hon. Sir Robin Jacob, *born* 1941, *apptd* 1993
Hon. Sir William Blackburne, *born* 1944, *apptd* 1993
Hon. Sir Gavin Lightman, *born* 1939, *apptd* 1994
Hon. Sir Robert Carnwath, *born* 1945, *apptd* 1994
Hon. Sir Colin Rimer, *born* 1944, *apptd* 1994
Hon. Sir Hugh Laddie, *born* 1946, *apptd* 1995
Hon. Sir Timothy Lloyd, *born* 1946, *apptd* 1996
Hon. Sir David Neuberger, *born* 1948, *apptd* 1996
Hon. Sir Andrew Park, *born* 1939, *apptd* 1997
Hon. Sir Nicholas Pumfrey, *born* 1951, *apptd* 1997
Hon. Sir Michael Hart, *born* 1948, *apptd* 1998

HIGH COURT OF JUSTICE IN BANKRUPTCY

Judges, The Vice-Chancellor and judges of the Chancery
Division of the High Court

COMPANIES COURT

Judges, The Vice Chancellor and judges of the Chancery
Division of the High Court

PATENT COURT (APPELLATE SECTION)

Judge, The Hon. Mr Justice Jacob

QUEEN'S BENCH DIVISION

The Lord Chief Justice of England (£157,511) The Rt. Hon.
the Lord Bingham of Cornhill, *born* 1933, *apptd* 1996
Private Secretary, E. Adams
Clerk, J. Bond
Vice-President, The Rt. Hon. Lord Justice Kennedy

JUDGES (each £123,787)
Style, The Hon. Mr/Mrs Justice [surname]

Hon. Sir Oliver Popplewell, *born* 1927, *apptd* 1983
Hon. Sir Richard Tucker, *born* 1930, *apptd* 1985
Hon. Sir Patrick Garland, *born* 1929, *apptd* 1985
Hon. Sir Michael Turner, *born* 1931, *apptd* 1985
Hon. Sir John Alliott, *born* 1932, *apptd* 1986
Hon. Sir Harry Ognall, *born* 1934, *apptd* 1986
Hon. Sir John Owen, *born* 1925, *apptd* 1986
Hon. Sir Humphrey Potts, *born* 1931, *apptd* 1986
Hon. Sir Richard Rougier, *born* 1932, *apptd* 1986
Hon. Sir Ian Kennedy, *born* 1930, *apptd* 1986

Hon. Sir Stuart McKinnon, *born* 1938, *apptd* 1988
Hon. Sir Scott Baker, *born* 1937, *apptd* 1988
Hon. Sir Edwin Jowitt, *born* 1929, *apptd* 1988
Hon. Sir Douglas Brown, *born* 1931, *apptd* 1996
Hon. Sir Michael Morland, *born* 1929, *apptd* 1989
Hon. Sir Roger Buckley, *born* 1939, *apptd* 1989
Hon. Sir Anthony Hidden, *born* 1936, *apptd* 1989
Hon. Sir Michael Wright, *born* 1932, *apptd* 1990
Hon. Sir John Blofeld, *born* 1932, *apptd* 1990
Hon. Sir Peter Cresswell, *born* 1944, *apptd* 1991
Hon. Dame Ann Ebsworth, DBE, *born* 1937, *apptd* 1992
Hon. Sir David Latham, *born* 1942, *apptd* 1992
Hon. Sir Christopher Holland, *born* 1937, *apptd* 1992
Hon. Sir John Kay, *born* 1943, *apptd* 1992
Hon. Sir Richard Curtis, *born* 1933, *apptd* 1992
Hon. Dame Janet Smith, DBE, *born* 1940, *apptd* 1992
Hon. Sir Anthony Colman, *born* 1938, *apptd* 1992
Hon. Sir John Dyson, *born* 1943, *apptd* 1993
Hon. Sir Thayne Forbes, *born* 1938, *apptd* 1993
Hon. Sir Michael Sachs, *born* 1932, *apptd* 1993
Hon. Sir Stephen Mitchell, *born* 1941, *apptd* 1993
Hon. Sir Rodger Bell, *born* 1939, *apptd* 1993
Hon. Sir Michael Harrison, *born* 1939, *apptd* 1993
Hon. Sir Bernard Rix, *born* 1944, *apptd* 1993
Hon. Dame Heather Steel, DBE, *born* 1940, *apptd* 1993
Hon. Sir William Gage, *born* 1938, *apptd* 1993
Hon. Sir Andrew Longmore, *born* 1944, *apptd* 1993
Hon. Sir Thomas Morison, *born* 1939, *apptd* 1993
Hon. Sir David Keene, *born* 1941, *apptd* 1994
Hon. Sir Andrew Collins, *born* 1942, *apptd* 1994
Hon. Sir Maurice Kay, *born* 1942, *apptd* 1995
Hon. Sir Brian Smedley, *born* 1934, *apptd* 1995
Hon. Sir Anthony Hooper, *born* 1937, *apptd* 1995
Hon. Sir Alexander Butterfield, *born* 1942, *apptd* 1995
Hon. Sir George Newman, *born* 1941, *apptd* 1995
Hon. Sir David Poole, *born* 1938, *apptd* 1995
Hon. Sir Martin Moore-Bick, *born* 1946, *apptd* 1995
Hon. Sir Gordon Langley, *born* 1943, *apptd* 1995
Hon. Sir Roger Thomas, *born* 1947, *apptd* 1996
Hon. Sir Robert Nelson, *born* 1942, *apptd* 1996
Hon. Sir Roger Toulson, *born* 1946, *apptd* 1996
Hon. Sir Michael Astill, *born* 1938, *apptd* 1996
Hon. Sir Alan Moses, *born* 1945, *apptd* 1996
Hon. Sir Timothy Walker, *born* 1946, *apptd* 1996
Hon. Sir David Eady, *born* 1943, *apptd* 1997
Hon. Sir Jeremy Sullivan, *born* 1945, *apptd* 1997
Hon. Sir David Penry-Davey, *born* 1942, *apptd* 1997
Hon. Sir Stephen Richards, *born* 1950, *apptd* 1997
Hon. Sir David Steel, *born* 1943, *apptd* 1998
Hon. Sir Rodney Klevan, *born* 1940, *apptd* 1998
Hon. Sir Charles Gray, *born* 1942, *apptd* 1998
Hon. Sir Nicolas Bratza, *born* 1945, *apptd* 1998
Hon. Sir Michael Burton, *born* 1946, *apptd* 1998
Hon. Sir Rupert Jackson, *born* 1948, *apptd* 1998
Hon. Dame Heather Hallett, *born* 1949, *apptd* 1999
Hon. Sir Patrick Elias, *born* 1947, *apptd* 1999
Hon. Sir Richard Aikens, *born* 1948, *apptd* 1999

FAMILY DIVISION

President (£139,931), The Rt. Hon. Dame Elizabeth Butler-
Sloss, DBE, *born* 1933, *apptd* 1999
Secretary, Mrs S. Leung
Clerk, Mrs S. Bell

JUDGES (each £123,787)
Style, The Hon. Mr/Mrs Justice [surname]

Hon. Sir Edward Cazalet, *born* 1936, *apptd* 1988
Hon. Sir Robert Johnson, *born* 1933, *apptd* 1989
Hon. Dame Joyanne Bracewell, DBE, *born* 1934, *apptd* 1990

Hon. Sir Michael Connell, *born* 1939, *apptd* 1991
Hon. Sir Peter Singer, *born* 1944, *apptd* 1993
Hon. Sir Nicholas Wilson, *born* 1945, *apptd* 1993
Hon. Sir Nicholas Wall, *born* 1945, *apptd* 1993
Hon. Sir Andrew Kirkwood, *born* 1944, *apptd* 1993
Hon. Dame Brenda Hale, DBE, *born* 1945, *apptd* 1994
Hon. Sir Hugh Bennett, *born* 1943, *apptd* 1995
Hon. Sir Edward Holman, *born* 1947, *apptd* 1995
Hon. Dame Mary Hogg, DBE, *born* 1947, *apptd* 1995
Hon. Sir Christopher Sumner, *born* 1939, *apptd* 1996
Hon. Sir Anthony Hughes, *born* 1948, *apptd* 1997
Hon. Sir Arthur Charles, *born* 1948, *apptd* 1998
Hon. Sir David Bodey, *born* 1947, *apptd* 1998

RESTRICTIVE PRACTICES COURT
Room 410, Thomas More Building, Royal Courts of
Justice, Strand, London WC2A 2LL
Tel 0171-936 6727

President, The Hon. Mr Justice Buckley
Judges, The Hon. Mr Justice Ferris; The Hon. Mr Justice
Lightman
Lay Members, B. M. Currie; Sir Lewis Robertson, CBE; R.
Garrick, CBE; S. J. Ahearne; J. A. Graham; Mrs D. H.
Hatfield; J. A. Scott; B. D. Colgate; J. A. C. King
Clerk of the Court, M. Buckley

TECHNOLOGY AND CONSTRUCTION COURT
St Dunstan's House, 133–137 Fetter Lane, London
EC4A 1HD
Tel 0171-936 7427

JUDGES (each £100,209)
The Hon. Mr Justice Dyson (*Presiding Judge*)
His Hon. Judge Bowsher, QC
His Hon. Judge Hicks, QC
His Hon. Judge Havery, QC
His Hon. Judge Lloyd, QC
His Hon. Judge Newman, QC
His Hon. Judge Thornton, QC
His Hon. Judge Wilcox
His Hon. Judge Toulmin, CMG, QC

Court Manager, Miss B. Joy

LORD CHANCELLOR'S DEPARTMENT
— *see* Government Departments and Public Offices

SUPREME COURT DEPARTMENTS AND OFFICES
Royal Courts of Justice, London WC2A 2LL
Tel 0171-936 6000

DIRECTOR'S OFFICE

Director, I. Hyams
Group Manager and Deputy Director, J. Selch
Group Manager, Family Proceedings and Probate Service, R. P.
Knight
Finance and Performance Officer, K. T. Fairweather

ADMIRALTY AND COMMERCIAL REGISTRY AND
MARSHAL'S OFFICE
Registrar (£74,464), P. Miller
Admiralty Marshal and Court Manager, K. Houghton

BANKRUPTCY DEPARTMENT
Chief Registrar (£92,810), M. C. B. Buckley

Bankruptcy Registrars (£74,464), W. S. James; J. A.
Simmonds; P. J. S. Rawson; S. Baister; G. W. Jaques
Court Manager, M. A. Brown

CENTRAL OFFICE OF THE SUPREME COURT
Senior Master of the Supreme Court (*QBD*), *and Queen's
Remembrancer* (£92,810), R. L. Turner
Masters of the Supreme Court (*QBD*) (£74,464), D. L. Prebble;
G. H. Hodgson; J. Trench; M. Tennant; P. Miller; N. O.
G. Murray; I. H. Foster; G. H. Rose; P. G. A. Eyre; H. J.
Leslie; J. G. G. Ungley
Senior Court Manager, P. Emery

CHANCERY DIVISION
Senior Court Manager, P. Emery

CHANCERY CHAMBERS
Chief Master of the Supreme Court (£92,810), J. I. Winegarten
Masters of the Supreme Court (£74,464), J. A. Moncaster; R.
A. Bowman; N. W. Bragge; T. J. Bowles
Court Manager, G. Robinson
Conveyancing Counsel of the Supreme Court, W. D. Ainger; H.
M. Harrod; A. C. Taussig

COMPANIES COURT
Registrar (£74,464), M. Buckley
Court Manager, M. A. Brown

COURT OF APPEAL CIVIL DIVISION
Head of the Civil Appeals Office (£92,810), R. Venne
Court Manager, Miss H. M. Goddard

COURT OF APPEAL CRIMINAL DIVISION
Registrar (£92,810), M. McKenzie, CB, QC
Deputy Registrar, Mrs L. G. Knapman
Chief Clerk, M. Bishop

COURTS-MARTIAL APPEALS OFFICE
Registrar (£92,810), M. McKenzie, CB, QC
Chief Clerk, M. Bishop

CROWN OFFICE OF THE SUPREME COURT
Master of the Crown Office, and Queen's Coroner and Attorney
(£92,810), M. McKenzie, CB, QC
Head of Crown Office, Mrs L. G. Knapman
Chief Clerk, M. Bishop

EXAMINERS OF THE COURT
Empowered to take examination of witnesses in all
Divisions of the High Court
A. G. Dyer; A. W. Hughes; Mrs G. M. Kenne; R. M.
Planterose; Miss V. E. I. Selvaratnam

RESTRICTIVE PRACTICES COURT
Clerk of the Court, M. Buckley
Court Manager, M. A. Brown

SUPREME COURT COSTS OFFICE
Senior Cost Judge (£92,810), P. T. Hurst
Masters of the Supreme Court (£74,464), M. Ellis; T. H.
Seager Berry; C. C. Wright; P. R. Rogers; G. N. Pollard;
J. E. O'Hare; C. D. N. Campbell
Court Manager, Mrs H. Oakey

COURT OF PROTECTION
Stewart House, 24 Kingsway, London WC2B 6HD
Tel 0171-664 7000
Master (£92,810), D. A. Lush

ELECTION PETITIONS OFFICE
Room E113, Royal Courts of Justice, Strand, London
WC2A 2LL

Tel 0171-936 6131

The office accepts petitions and deals with all matters relating to the questioning of parliamentary, European Parliament and local government elections, and with applications for relief under the Representation of the People legislation.
Prescribed Officer, R. L. Turner
Chief Clerk, Miss J. L. Waine

OFFICE OF THE LORD CHANCELLOR'S VISITORS
Stewart House, 24 Kingsway, London WC2B 6HD
Tel 0171-664 7317
Legal Visitor, A. R. Tyrrell
Medical Visitors, K. Khan; W. B. Sprey; E. Mateu; S. E. Mahapatra; A. Bailey; A. Kaeser

OFFICIAL RECEIVERS' DEPARTMENT
21 Bloomsbury Street, London WC1B 3SS
Tel 0171-323 3090
Senior Official Receiver, M. C. A. Osborne
Official Receivers, M. J. Pugh; L. T. Cramp; J. Norris

OFFICIAL SOLICITOR'S DEPARTMENT
81 Chancery Lane, London WC2B 6HD
Tel 0171-911 7105
Official Solicitor to the Supreme Court, P. M. Harris
Deputy Official Solicitor, H. J. Baker
Chief Clerk, R. Lancaster

PRINCIPAL REGISTRY (FAMILY DIVISION)
First Avenue House, 42–49 High Holborn, London WC1V 6NP
Tel 0171-936 6000
Senior District Judge (£92,810), G. B. N. A. Angel
District Judges (£74,464), B. P. F. Kenworthy-Browne; Mrs K. T. Moorhouse; M. J. Segal; R. Conn; Miss I. M. Plumstead; G. J. Maple; Miss H. C. Bradley; K. J. White; A. R. S. Bassett-Cross; N. A. Grove; M. C. Berry; Miss S. M. Bowman; C. Million; P. Waller; Miss P. Cushing; R. Harper; G. C. Brasse; Miss D. C. Redgrave
Family and Probate Service Group Manager, R. P. Knight

District Probate Registrars

Birmingham and Stoke-on-Trent, C. Marsh
Brighton and Maidstone, P. Ellwood
Bristol, Exeter and Bodmin, R. H. P. Joyce
Cardiff, Bangor and Carmarthen, R. F. Yeldam
Ipswich, Norwich and Peterborough, D. N. Mee
Leeds, Lincoln and Sheffield, A. P. Dawson
Liverpool, Lancaster and Chester, C. Fox
Manchester and Nottingham, M. A. Moran
Newcastle, Carlisle, York and Middlesbrough, P. Sanderson
Oxford, Gloucester and Leicester, R. R. Da Costa
Winchester, A. K. Biggs

JUDGE ADVOCATES

OFFICE OF THE JUDGE ADVOCATE OF THE FLEET
c/o Group Manager's Office, The Court Service, Concorde House, 10–12 London Road, Maidstone ME16 8QA
Tel 01622-200120
Judge Advocate of the Fleet (£92,810), His Hon. Judge Sessions

OFFICE OF THE JUDGE ADVOCATE-GENERAL OF THE FORCES
(*Joint Service for the Army and the Royal Air Force*)
22 Kingsway, London WC2B 6LE

Tel 0171-218 8079
Judge Advocate-General (£100,209), His Hon. Judge J. W. Rant, CB, QC
Vice-Judge Advocate-General (£89,306), E. G. Moelwyn-Hughes
Judge Advocates (£74,464), D. M. Berkson; M. A. Hunter; J. P. Camp; Miss S. E. Woollam; R. C. C. Seymour; I. H. Pearson; R. G. Chapple; J. F. T. Bayliss
Style for Judge Advocates, Judge Advocate [surname]

HIGH COURT AND CROWN COURT CENTRES

First-tier centres deal with both civil and criminal cases and are served by High Court and circuit judges. Second-tier centres deal with criminal cases only and are served by High Court and circuit judges. Third-tier centres deal with criminal cases only and are served only by circuit judges.

MIDLAND AND OXFORD CIRCUIT
First-tier – Birmingham, Lincoln, Nottingham, Oxford, Stafford, Warwick
Second-tier – Leicester, Northampton, Shrewsbury, Worcester
Third-tier – Coventry, Derby, Grimsby, Hereford, Peterborough, Stoke-on-Trent, Wolverhampton
Circuit Administrator, P. Handcock, The Priory Courts, 6th Floor, 33 Bull Street, Birmingham B4 6DS. Tel: 0121-681 3000
Group Managers: Birmingham Group, Mrs K. Hoyte; *Coventry Group,* Mrs D. Ponsonby; *Lincoln Group,* A. Phillips; *Northampton Group,* K. Dickerson; *Nottingham Group,* Mrs E. A. Folman; *Stafford Group,* D. Bennett

NORTH-EASTERN CIRCUIT
First-tier – Leeds, Newcastle upon Tyne, Sheffield, Teesside
Second-tier – Bradford, York
Third-tier – Doncaster, Durham, Kingston-upon-Hull
Circuit Administrator, P. J. Farmer, 18th Floor, West Riding House, Albion Street, Leeds LS1 5AA. Tel: 0113-251 1200
Group Managers: Bradford Group, F. Taylor; *Leeds Group,* P. M. Norris; *Newcastle upon Tyne Group,* Miss S. Proudlock; *Sheffield Group,* G. Bingham, OBE; *Teesside Group,* Miss E. Yates

NORTHERN CIRCUIT
First-tier – Carlisle, Liverpool, Manchester (Crown Square), Preston
Third-tier – Barrow-in-Furness, Bolton, Burnley, Lancaster; Manchester (Minshull Street)
Circuit Administrator, R. A. Vincent, 15 Quay Street, Manchester M60 9FD. Tel: 0161-833 1005
Group Managers: Liverpool Group, Mrs J. Roche; *Manchester Central Group,* Mrs C. A. Mayer; *Outer Manchester Group,* S. Townley; *Preston Group,* B. Wilson

SOUTH-EASTERN CIRCUIT
First-tier – Chelmsford, Croydon, Lewes, Norwich
Second-tier – Chichester, Ipswich, London (Central Criminal Court), Luton, Maidstone, Reading, St Albans
Third-tier – Aylesbury, Basildon, Bury St Edmunds, Cambridge, Canterbury, Guildford, Hove, King's Lynn, London (Blackfriars, Harrow, Inner London Sessions House, Isleworth, Kingston, Knightsbridge, Middlesex Guildhall, Snaresbrook, Southend, Southwark, Wood Green, Woolwich)

Circuit Administrator, R. J. Clarke, New Cavendish House, 18 Maltravers Street, London WC2R 3EU. Tel: 0171-936 7235

Provincial Administrator, J. Powell, 1st Floor, Steeple House, Church Lane, Chelmsford CM1 1NH. Tel: 01245-257425

Group Managers: Chelmsford Group, M. Littlewood; *Kingston Group*, D. Thompson; *Lewes Group*, B. Macbeth; *London Group* (*Civil*), D. Marsh; *London Group* (*Crime*), K. Budgen; *Luton Group*, M. McIver; *Maidstone Group*, Mrs L. Lennon

The High Court in Greater London sits at the Royal Courts of Justice.

WALES AND CHESTER CIRCUIT

First-tier – Caernarfon, Cardiff, Chester, Mold, Swansea
Second-tier – Carmarthen, Merthyr Tydfil, Newport, Welshpool
Third-tier – Dolgellau, Haverfordwest, Knutsford, Warrington
Circuit Administrator, P. Risk, Churchill House, Churchill Way, Cardiff CF10 4HH. Tel: 01222-415501
Group Managers: Cardiff Group, G. Pickett; *Chester Group*, G. Kenney; *Swansea Group*, Mrs D. Thomas

WESTERN CIRCUIT

First-tier – Bristol, Exeter, Truro, Winchester
Second-tier – Dorchester, Gloucester, Plymouth, Weymouth
Third-tier – Barnstaple, Bournemouth, Newport (IOW), Portsmouth, Salisbury, Southampton, Swindon, Taunton
Circuit Administrator, D. Ryan, Bridge House, Sion Place, Clifton, Bristol BS8 4BN. Tel: 0117-974 3763
Group Managers: Bristol Group, N. Jeffery; *Exeter Group*, D. Gentry; *Winchester Group*, A. Bean

CIRCUIT JUDGES

*Senior Circuit Judges, each £100,209
Circuit Judges at the Central Criminal Court, London (*Old Bailey Judges*), each £100,209
Circuit Judges, each £92,810
Style, His/Her Hon. Judge [surname]

Senior Presiding Judge, The Rt. Hon. Lord Justice Judge
MIDLAND AND OXFORD CIRCUIT

Presiding Judges, The Hon. Mr Justice Jowitt; The Hon. Mr Justice Astill

F. A. Allan; Miss C. Alton; B. J. Appleby, QC; D. P. Bennett; R. S. A. Benson; J. G. Boggis, QC; R. W. A. Bray; D. W. Brunning; N. B. Cameron Coles, QC; J. J. Cavell; F. A. Chapman; P. N. R. Clark; M. F. Coates; R. R. B. Cole; T. G. E. Corrie; P. F. Crane; *P. J. Crawford, QC (*Recorder of Birmingham*); Mrs P. A. Deeley; P. N. de Mille; T. M. Dillon, QC; C. H. Durman; B. A. Farrer, QC; Miss E. N. Fisher; J. E. Fletcher; A. C. Geddes; R. J. H. Gibbs, QC; J. Hall; V. E. Hall; D. R. D. Hamilton; S. T. Hammond; G. C. W. Harris, QC; M. J. Heath; Miss E. J. Hindley, QC; C. R. Hodson; J. R. Hopkin; Mrs H. M. Hughes; R. H. Hutchinson; R. A. G. Inglis; A. A. Jenkins; R. P. V. Jenkins; A. W. P. King; M. K. Lee, QC; D. L. McCarthy; A. W. McCreath; A. G. MacDuff; D. D. McEvoy, QC; J. V. Machin; M. H. Mander; L. Marshall; K. Matthewman, QC; W. D. Matthews; H. R. Mayor, QC; N. J. Mitchell; D. P. Morrell; J. I. Morris; M. D. Mott; A. J. D. Nicholl; R. T. N. Orme; R. C. C. O'Rorke; J. F. F. Orrell; D. S. Perrett, QC; C. J. Pitchers; R. F. D. Pollard; D. P. Pugsley; J. R. Pyke; R. J. Rubery; J. A. O. Shand; D. P. Stanley; P. J. Stretton; G.

C. Styler; A. B. Taylor; J. J. Teare; R. S. W. F. Tonking; J. J. Wait; J. C. Warner; H. Wilson; J. W. Wilson

NORTH-EASTERN CIRCUIT

Presiding Judges, The Hon. Mr Justice Hooper; The Hon. Mr Justice Bennett

J. R. S. Adams; J. Altman; P. M. Baker, QC; T. W. Barber; J. E. Barry; G. N. Barr Young; R. Bartfield; C. O. J. Behrens; D. R. Bentley, QC; P. H. Bowers; A. N. J. Briggs; D. M. A. Bryant; J. W. M. Bullimore; B. Bush; M. C. Carr; M. L. Cartlidge; P. J. Charlesworth; P. J. Cockroft; G. J. K. Coles, QC; J. Crabtree; M. T. Cracknell; W. H. R. Crawford, QC; Mrs J. Davies; I. J. Dobkin; E. J. Faulks; P. J. Fox, QC; A. N. Fricker, QC; M. S. Garner; A. R. Goldsack, QC; R. A. Grant; S. P. Grenfell; S. J. Gullick; G. F. R. Harkins; T. S. A. Hawkesworth, QC; P. J. M. Heppel, QC; *T. D. T. Hodson (*Recorder of Newcastle upon Tyne*); P. M. L. Hoffman; D. P. Hunt; A. E. Hutchinson, QC; N. H. Jones, QC; R. A. Jordan; G. H. Kamil; T. D. Kent-Jones, TD; G. M. Lightfoot; R. P. Lowden; A. G. McCallum; C. I. McGonigal; M. K. Mettyear; R. J. Moore; A. L. Myerson, QC; D. A. Orde; Miss H. E. Paling; J. Prophet; P. E. Robertshaw; R. M. Scott; A. Simpson; L. Spittle; Mrs L. Sutcliffe; J. A. Swanson; M. J. Taylor; R. C. Taylor; J. D. G. Walford; M. Walker; P. H. C. Walker; *B. Walsh, QC; C. T. Walton; G. Whitburn, QC; J. S. Wolstenholme; D. R. Wood

NORTHERN CIRCUIT

Presiding Judge, The Hon. Mr Justice Forbes; The Hon. Mr Justice Douglas Brown

M. P. Allweis; J. F. Appleton; S. W. Baker; A. W. Bell; R. C. W. Bennett; Miss I. Bernstein; M. S. Blackburn; A. N. H. Blake; C. Bloom, QC; R. Brown; J. K. Burke, QC; I. B. Campbell; B. Carter, QC; B. I. Caulfield; D. Clark; *D. C. Clarke, QC (*Recorder of Liverpool*); G. M. Clifton; I. W. Crompton; *R. E. Davies, QC (*Recorder of Manchester*); Miss A. E. Downey; B. R. Duckworth; S. B. Duncan; Miss D. B. Eaglestone; T. K. Earnshaw; G. A. Ensor; D. M. Evans, QC; S. J. D. Fawcus; P. S. Fish; J. R. B. Geake; D. S. Gee; W. George; J. A. D. Gilliland, QC; J. A. Hammond; M. Hedley; T. B. Hegarty, QC; M. J. Henshell; F. R. B. Holloway; R. C. Holman; N. J. G. Howarth; G. W. Humphries; C. E. F. James; P. M. Kershaw, QC (*Commercial Circuit Judge*); H. L. Lachs; P. M. Lakin; B. W. Lewis; R. J. D. Livesey, QC; D. Lynch; D. I. Mackay; J. B. Macmillan; D. G. Maddison; B. C. Maddocks; C. J. Mahon; J. A. Morgan; W. P. Morris; T. J. Mort; *C. P. L. Openshaw, QC; F. D. Owen, TD; J. A. Phillips; J. C. Phipps; D. A. Pirie; A. J. Proctor; J. H. Roberts; Miss G. D. Ruaux; H. S. Singer; E. Slinger; A. C. Smith; W. P. Smith; Miss E. M. Steel; D. R. Swift; C. B. Tetlow; J. P. Townend; I. J. C. Trigger; P. W. G. Urquhart; K. H. P. Wilkinson; B. Woodward

SOUTH-EASTERN CIRCUIT

Presiding Judges, The Hon. Mr Justice Gage; The Hon. Mr Justice Moses

J. D. R. Adams; M. F. Addison; P. C. Ader; Mrs S. C. Andrew; A. R. L. Ansell; M. G. Anthony; S. A. Anwyl, QC; M. F. Baker, QC; A. F. Balston; G. S. Barham; C. J. A. Barnett, QC; W. E. Barnett, QC; R. A. Barratt, QC; K. Bassingthwaighte; *G. A. Bathurst Norman; P. J. L. Beaumont, QC; N. E. Beddard; Mrs C. V. Bevington; M. G. Binning; J. E. Bishop; B. M. B. Black; H. O. Blacksell, QC; J. G. Boal, QC; A. V. Bradbury; P. N. Brandt; R. G. Brown; J. M. Bull, QC; *N. M. Butter, QC; The Hon. C. W. Byers; H. J. Byrt, QC; C. V. Callman; J. Q. Campbell; M. J. Carroll; B. E. F. Catlin; *B. L. Charles, QC; P. C. L. Clark; P. C. Clegg; Miss S. Coates; N. J. Coleman; S. H. Colgan; P. H. Collins;

C. C. Colston, QC; S. S. Coltart; Viscount Colville of Culross, QC; J. S. Colyer, QC; C. D. Compston; T. A. C. Coningsby, QC; J. G. Connor; R. D. Connor; M. J. Cook; R. A. Cooke; M. R. Coombe; P. E. Copley; Dr E. Cotran; P. R. Cowell; R. C. Cox; M. L. S. Cripps; J. F. Crocker; D. L. Croft, QC; H. M. Crush; D. M. Cryan; P. Curl; G. L. Davies; I. H. Davies, TD; W. L. M. Davies, QC; M. Dean, QC; W. N. Denison, QC (*Common Serjeant*); J. E. Devaux; M. N. Devonshire, TD; P. H. Downes; W. H. Dunn, QC; C. M. Edwards; D. F. Elfer, QC; D. R. Ellis; R. C. Elly; C. Elwen; F. P. L. Evans; J. D. Farnworth; P. Fingret; P. E. J. Focke, QC; P. Ford; G. C. F. Forrester; Ms D. A. Freedman; R. Gee; L. Gerber; C. A. H. Gibson; Miss A. F. Goddard, QC; S. A. Goldstein; C. G. M. Gordon; J. B. Gosschalk; M. Graham, QC; B. S. Green, QC; D. J. Griffiths; G. D. Grigson; R. B. Groves, TD, VRD; N. T. Hague, QC; D. F. Hallett; A. B. R. Hallgarten; QC; Miss G. Hallon; J. Hamilton; Miss S. Hamilton, QC; C. R. H. Hardy; B. Hargrove, OBE, QC; M. F. Harris; A. M. Harvey; R. G. Hawkins, QC; J. M. Haworth; R. J. Haworth; R. M. Hayward; A. N. Hitching; D. Holden; J. F. Holt; A. C. W. Hordern, QC; K. A. D. Hornby; M. Hucker; Sir David Hughes-Morgan, Bt., CB, CBE; J. G. Hull, QC; M. J. Hyam (*Recorder of London*); D. A. Inman; A. B. Issard-Davies; Dr P. J. E. Jackson; T. J. C. Joseph; I. G. F. Karsten, QC; S. S. Katkhuda; C. J. B. Kemp; M. Kennedy, QC; A. M. Kenny; T. R. King; B. J. Knight, QC; L. G. Krikler; L. H. C. Lait; P. St J. H. Langan, QC; Capt. J. B. R. Langdon, RN; P. H. Latham; R. Laurie; T. Lawrence; D. M. Levy, QC; C. C. D. Lindsay, QC; S. H. Lloyd; F. R. Lockhart; Mrs C. M. Ludlow; Capt. S. Lyons; A. G. McDowall; R. J. McGregor-Johnson; K. M. McHale; K. A. Machin, QC; R. G. McKinnon; W. N. McKinnon; K. C. Macrae; T. Maher; F. J. M. Marr-Johnson; D. N. N. Martineau; N. A. Medawar, QC; D. B. Meier; D. J. Mellor; G. D. Mercer; D. Q. Miller; Miss A. E. Mitchell; F. I. Mitchell; H. M. Morgan; D. Morton Jack; R. T. Moss; Miss M. J. S. Mowat; T. M. E. Nash; M. H. D. Neligan; Mrs M. F. Norrie; Brig. A. P. Norris, OBE; P. W. O'Brien; M. A. Oppenheimer; D. C. J. Paget; D. J. Parry; Mrs N. Pearce; Prof. D. S. Pearl; Miss V. A. Pearlman; B. P. Pearson; J. R. Peppitt, QC; N. A. J. Philpot; T. D. Pillay; D. C. Pitman; J. R. Platt; J. R. Playford, QC; P. B. Pollock; T. G. Pontius; W. D. C. Poulton; H. C. Pownall, QC; S. Pratt; R. J. C. V. Prendergast; J. E. Previté, QC; B. H. Pryor, QC; J. E. Pullinger; D. W. Radford; J. W. Rant, CB, QC; E. V. P. Reece; J. R. Reid, QC; M. P. Reynolds; G. K. Rice; M. S. Rich, QC; N. P. Riddell; G. Rivlin, QC; S. D. Robbins; D. A. H. Rodwell, QC; G. H. Rooke, TD, QC; W. M. Rose; P. C. R. Rountree; J. H. Rucker; T. R. G. Ryland; J. E. A. Samuels, QC; R. B. Sanders; A. R. G. Scott-Gall; J. S. Sennitt; D. Serota, QC; J. L. Sessions; D. R. A. Sich; A. G. Simmons; K. T. Simpson; P. R. Simpson; M. Singh, QC; S. P. Sleeman; C. M. Smith, QC; S. A. R. Smith; R. J. Southan; S. B. Spence; S. M. Stephens, QC; N. A. Stewart; W. F. C. Thomas; J. Thompson; A. G. Y. Thorpe; C. H. Tilling; C. J. M. Tyrer; Mrs A. P. Uziell-Hamilton; J. E. van der Werff; A. O. R. Vick, QC; T. L. Viljoen; Miss A. P. Wakefield; R. Wakefield; R. Walker; S. P. Waller; D. B. Watling, QC; A. R. Webb; C. S. Welchman; A. F. Wilkie, QC; S. R. Wilkinson; R. J. Winstanley; D. Worsley; E. G. Wrintmore; M. P. Yelton; K. H. Zucker, QC

WALES AND CHESTER CIRCUIT

Presiding Judges, The Hon. Mr Justice Maurice Kay; The Hon. Mr Justice Connell; The Hon. Mr Justice Thomas

K. E. Barnett; M. R. Burr; G. H. F. Carson; S. P. Clarke; T. R. Crowther, QC; J. T. Curran; Miss J. M. P. Daley; G. H. M. Daniel; D. T. A. Davies; J. B. S. Diehl, QC; R. T.

Dutton; D. E. H. Edwards; G. O. Edwards, QC; The Lord Elystan-Morgan; *D. R. Evans, QC; M. R. Furness; J. W. Gaskell; D. R. Halbert; D. J. Hale; Miss J. E. Hayward; R. P. Hughes; P. J. Jacobs; G. J. Jones; H. D. H. Jones; G. E. Kilfoil; C. G. Masterman; D. G. Morgan; D. G. Morris; D. C. Morton; T. H. Moseley, QC; P. J. Price, QC; E. J. Prosser, QC; D. W. Richards; J. M. T. Rogers, QC; A. A. Wallace

WESTERN CIRCUIT

Presiding Judges, The Hon. Mr Justice Butterfield; The Hon. Mr Justice Toulson

P. R. Barclay; J. F. Beashel; R. H. Bond; Miss J. A. M. Bonvin; C. L. Boothman; M. J. L. Brodrick; J. M. J. Burford, QC; R. D. H. Bursell, QC; A. V. Chubb; M. G. Cotterill; G. W. A. Cottle; K. C. Cutler; P. M. Darlow; S. C. Darwall Smith; Mrs S. P. Darwall Smith; Mrs L. H. Davies; *M. Dyer; Ms J. A. Exton; J. D. Foley; D. L. Griffiths; J. D. Griggs; Mrs C. M. A. Hagen; P. J. C. R. Hooton; G. B. Hutton; R. E. Jack, QC; A. G. H. Jones; T. Longbotham; T. N. Mackean; Miss S. M. D. McKinney; I. S. McKintosh; J. G. McNaught; The Lord Meston, QC; T. J. Milligan; J. Neligan; S. K. O'Malley; S. K. Overend; R. Price; R. C. Pryor, QC; M. W. Roach; J. N. P. Rudd; A. Rutherford; Miss A. O. H. Sander; D. H. D. Selwood; R. M. Shawcross; D. A. Smith, QC; W. E. M. Taylor; P. M. Thomas; A. A. R. Thompson, QC; D. K. Ticehurst, QC; D. M. Webster, QC; J. H. Weeks, QC; J. S. Wiggs; J. A. J. Wigmore; J. C. Willis

RECORDERS
(each £422 per day)

F. A. Abbott; R. D. I. Adam; J. F. Akast; D. J. Ake; R. Akenhead, QC; I. D. G. Alexander, QC; C. D. Allan, QC; C. J. Alldis; J. H. Allen, QC; D. M. Altaras; A. J. Anderson, QC; W. P. Andreae-Jones, QC; Mrs E. H. Andrew; P. J. Andrews, QC; R. A. Anelay, QC; J. M. Appleby; Miss L. E. Appleby, QC; B. J. Argyle; E. K. Armitage, QC; P. J. B. Armstrong; G. K. Arran; S. J. Ashurst; E. G. Aspley; P. Atherton; R. K. Atherton; N. J. Atkinson, QC; D. J. M. Aubrey, QC; D. S. Aubrey; M. G. Austin-Smith, QC; M. J. S. Axtell; W. S. Aylen, QC; P. D. Babb; J. F. Badenoch, QC; P. G. N. Badge; Miss P. H. Badley; E. H. Bailey; A. B. Baillie; N. R. J. Baker, QC; Miss A. Ball, QC; C. G. Ball, QC; A. Barker, QC; B. J. Barker, QC; G. E. Barling, QC; D. N. Barnard; H. J. Barnes; T. P. Barnes, QC; A. J. Barnett; Miss F. J. Baron, QC; D. A. Bartlett; G. R. Bartlett, QC; J. C. T. Barton, QC; D. C. Bate, QC; S. D. Batten, QC; P. D. Batty, QC; J. J. Baughan, QC; J. F. T. Bayliss; R. A. Bayliss; D. M. Bean; J. Beatson; S. J. Bedford; R. V. M. E. Behar; R. W. Belben; J. K. Benson; P. C. Benson; R. A. Benson, QC; H. L. Bentham, QC; D. M. Berkson; C. R. Berry; M. Bethel, QC; J. P. V. Bevan; Mrs M. O. Bickford-Smith; N. Bidder; I. G. Bing; P. V. Birkett, QC; M. I. Birnbaum; W. J. Birtles; P. W. Birts, QC; Mrs J. M. Black, QC; M. J. Black, QC; B. G. D. Blair, QC; W. J. L. Blair, QC; P. E. Bleasdale; R. H. L. Blomfield, TD; D. J. Blunt, QC; O. S. P. Blunt, QC; Miss B. M. Bolton; D. T. K. Boney, QC; Ms C. Booth, QC; J. J. Boothby; D. J. Boulton; S. N. Bourne-Arton, QC; M. J. Bowerman; Ms M. R. Bowron; W. Boyce; S. C. Boyd, QC; J. J. Boyle; D. L. Bradshaw; W. T. S. Braithwaite, QC; G. B. Breen; D. J. Brennan, QC; M. L. Brent, QC; G. J. B. G. Brice, QC; A. J. Brigden; D. R. Bright; R. P. Brittain; R. A. Britton; J. Bromley-Davenport; L. F. M. Brown; S. C. Brown, QC; D. J. M. Browne, QC; J. N. Browne; A. J. N. Brunner, QC; R. V. Bryan; Miss B. M. Bucknall, QC; J. E. Bullen; J. P. Burke, QC; L. S. Burn; H. W. Burnett, QC; R. H. Burns; S. J. Burnton, QC; F. G. Burrell, QC; K. Bush; A. J. Butcher, QC; C. M. Butler; Miss J. Butler; M. D. Byrne; D. W. Caddick;

D. Calvert-Smith, QC; R. Camden Pratt, QC; Miss S. M. C. Cameron, QC; A. N. Campbell, QC; J. M. Caplan, QC; G. M. C. Carey, QC; A. C. Carlile, QC, MP; H. B. H. Carlisle, QC; J. J. Carter-Manning, QC; R. Carus, QC; Mrs J. R. Case; P. D. Cattan; Miss M. T. Catterson; R. M. Challinor; N. M. Chambers, QC; Miss D. C. Champion; C. B. Chandler; V. R. Chapman; J. M. Cherry, QC; A. C. Chippindall; C. F. Chruszcz, QC; C. H. Clark, QC; C. S. C. S. Clarke, QC; P. W. Clarke; P. R. J. Clarkson, QC; T. Clayson; A. S. L. Cleary; W. Clegg, QC; P. Clements; G. Cliffe; T. A. Clover; W. P. Coates; D. J. Cocks, QC; J. J. Coffey, QC; T. A. Coghlan, QC; J. L. Cohen; L. F. R. Cohen, QC; W. J. Coker, QC; A. J. S. Coleman; P. J. D. Coleridge, QC; A. R. Collender, QC; P. N. Collier, QC; M. G. Collins, QC; I. Collis; Mrs J. R. Comyns; D. G. Conlin; A. D. Conrad; C. S. Cook; J. L. Cooke, QC; N. O. Cooke; K. B. Coonan, QC; A. E. M. Cooper; P. J. Cooper, QC; C. J. Cornwall; P. J. Cosgrove, QC; Miss D. R. Cotton, QC; J. S. Coward, QC; T. G. Cowling; Mrs L. M. Cox, QC; P. Crampin, QC; L. S. Crawford; N. Crichton; D. I. Crigman, QC; C. A. Critchlow; D. R. Crome; S. R. Crookenden, QC; Mrs J. E. Crowley; J. D. Crowley, QC; T. S. Culver; Miss E. A. M. Curnow, QC; P. D. Curran; J. W. O. Curtis, QC; M. J. Curwen; A. J. G. Dalziel; Mrs P. M. T. Dangor; A. M. Darroch; C. P. M. Davidson; A. M. Davies; A. R. M. Davies; H. Davies; J. T. L. Davies; Miss N. V. Davies, QC; R. L. Davies, QC; N. A. L. Davis, QC; W. E. Davis; A. W. Dawson; D. H. Day, QC; P. G. Dedman; Ms M. R. de Haas, QC; P. A. de la Piquerie; M. A. de Navarro, QC; R. L. Denyer, QC; H. A. D. de Silva; P. N. Digney; C. E. Dines; A. D. Dinkin, QC; D. R. Dobbin; R. S. Dodds; P. Dodgson; R. A. M. Doggett; Ms B. Dohmann, QC; D. T. Donaldson, QC; A. M. Donne, QC; A. F. S. Donovan; A. K. Dooley; Ms J. M. R. Dowell; J. Dowse; M. J. Dudley; J. R. Duggan; P. R. Dunkels, QC; J. D. Durham Hall, QC; R. M. Eades; H. W. P. Eccles, QC; C. N. Edelman, QC; A. J. C. Edis, QC; A. H. Edwards; Miss S. M. Edwards, QC; A. J. C. Edwards-Stuart, QC; A. J. Elleray, QC; G. Elias, QC; E. A. Elliott; J. A. Elvidge; R. M. Englehart, QC; D. A. Evans, QC; D. H. Evans, QC; F. W. H. Evans, QC; G. J. Evans; G. W. R. Evans, QC; I. Evans; M. Evans, QC; M. J. Evans; M. A. Everall, QC; Miss D. Faber; T. M. Faber; R. B. Farley, QC; P. M. Farmer, QC; D. J. Farrer, QC; P. E. Feinberg, QC; J. F. Q. Fenwick, QC; R. Fernyhough, QC; M. C. Field; R. A. Field, QC; J. E. Finestein; Miss A. C. Finnerty; D. T. Fish; D. P. Fisher, QC; G. D. Flather, CBE, QC; R. A. Flowerdew; N. M. Ford, QC; R. A. Fordham, QC; B. C. Forster; M. D. P. Fortune; D. R. Foskett, QC; I. H. Foster; J. R. Foster, QC; D. P. Friedman, QC; S. A. Furst, QC; C. J. E. Gardner, QC; P. R. Garlick, QC; C. R. Garside, QC; R. C. Gaskell; J. B. Gateshill; S. A. G. L. Gault; A. H. Gee, QC; I. W. Geering, QC; D. S. Geey; C. R. George, QC; S. M. Gerlis; D. C. Gerrey; J. S. Gibbons, QC; A. J. Gilbart, QC; F. H. S. Gilbert, QC; N. J. Gilchrist; K. Gillance; N. B. D. Gilmour, QC; L. Giovenne; R. P. Glancy, QC; A. T. Glass, QC; M. G. J. Gledhill; H. B. Globe, QC; Miss E. Gloster, QC; H. K. Goddard, QC; H. A. Godfrey, QC; Ms L. S. Godfrey, QC; J. J. Goldberg, QC; I. S. Goldrein, QC; J. B. Goldring, QC; P. H. Goldsmith, QC; A. J. Goldstaub, QC; L. C. Goldstone, QC; A. J. J. Gompertz, QC; Miss R. M. Goode; J. R. W. Goss; T. J. C. Goudie, QC; A. A. Goymer; G. Gozem; The Lord Grabiner, QC; H. Green, QC; Miss J. E. G. Greenberg, QC; A. E. Greenwood; J. C. Greenwood; J. G. Grenfell, QC; D. E. Griffith-Jones; R. H. Griffith-Jones; J. P. G. Griffiths, QC; M. G. Grills; M. S. E. Grime, QC; P. Grobel; P. H. Gross, QC; B. P. Gulbenkian; J. D. Guthrie, QC; A. S. Hacking, QC; J. W. Haines; N. J. Hall; S. J. Hall; J. P. N. Hallam; A. N. R. Hamilton; G. M. Hamilton, TD, QC; I. M. Hamilton; P. L. Hamlin; J. L. Hand, QC; G. T. Harrap; M. K. Harington; P. J. Harrington; D. M.

Harris, QC; R. D. Harrison; R. M. Harrison, QC; H. M. Harrod; J. M. Harrow; C. A. Hart-Leverton, QC; B. Harvey; J. G. Harvey; M. L. T. Harvey, QC; D. W. Hatton, QC; A. M. D. Havelock-Allan, QC; The Hon. P. N. Havers, QC; W. G. Hawkesworth; R. W. P. H. Hay; Prof. D. J. Hayton; R. Hayward-Smith, QC; R. Hedgeland; A. T. Hedworth, QC; R. A. Henderson, QC; R. H. Q. Henriques, QC; R. C. Herman; M. S. Heslop, QC; T. Hewitt; G. R. Hickinbottom; J. W. Hillyer; A. J. H. Hilton, QC; J. W. Hirst, QC; W. T. J. Hirst; J. D. Hitchen; S. A. Hockman, QC; H. E. G. Hodge, OBE; A. J. C. Hoggett, QC; T. V. Holroyde, QC; R. M. Hone; G. A. J. Hooper; A. D. Hope; S. J. Hopkins; M. A. P. Hopmeier; M. Horowitz, QC; Miss R. Horwood-Smart; C. P. Hotten, QC; B. F. Houlder, QC; M. N. Howard, QC; C. I. Howells; M. J. Hubbard, QC; D. L. Hughes; Miss J. C. A. Hughes, QC; Miss K. L. Hughes; P. T. Hughes, QC; T. M. Hughes, QC; L. D. Hull; Capt. D. R. Humphrey, RN; W. G. B. Hungerford; D. R. N. Hunt, QC; P. J. Hunt, QC; I. G. A. Hunter, QC; M. A. Hunter; G. N. N. Huskinson; M. Hussain, QC; J. G. K. Hyland; R. Ibbotson; M. D. Inman, QC; P. R. Isaacs; S. L. Isaacs, QC; S. M. Jack; D. G. A. Jackson; M. R. Jackson; I. E. Jacob; N. F. B. Jarman, QC; J. M. Jarvis, QC; J. R. Jarvis; A. H. Jeffreys; D. A. Jeffreys, QC; J. D. Jenkins, QC; Miss A. M. Jolles; D. A. F. Jones; D. L. Jones; N. G. Jones; P. H. F. Jones; S. E. Jones, QC; W. J. Jones; R. C. Jose; Ms W. R. Joseph, QC; H. M. Joy; P. S. L. Joyce, QC; R. W. S. Juckes; M. L. Kallipetis, QC; Miss L. N. R. Kamill; R. G. Kaye, QC; C. B. Kealy; K. R. Keen, QC; Mrs S. M. Keen; B. R. Keith, QC; W. A. Kennedy; D. Kennett Brown; D. M. Kerr; L. D. Kershen, QC; M. I. Khan; G. M. P. F. Khayat, QC; C. A. Kinch; T. R. A. King, QC; Mrs F. M. Kirkham; M. S. Knott; Miss P. E. Knowles; C. J. Knox; Miss J. C. M. Korner, QC; S. E. Kramer, QC; Miss L. J. Kushner, QC; P. E. Kyte, QC; N. R. W. Lambert; D. C. Lamdin; A. T. Lancaster; D. A. Landau; D. G. Lane, QC; B. F. J. Langstaff, QC; R. B. Latham, QC; S. W. Lawler, QC; Sir Ivan Lawrence, QC; Miss E. A. Lawson, QC; M. H. Lawson, QC; G. S. Lawson-Rogers, QC; P. L. O. Leaver, QC; D. Lederman, QC; B. W. T. Leech; I. Leeming, QC; C. H. de V. Leigh, QC; H. B. G. Lett; B. L. Lever; B. H. Leveson, QC; A. E. Levy, QC; M. E. Lewer, QC; J. A. Lewis; K. M. J. Lewison, QC; S. J. Linehan, QC; R. A. Lissack, QC; G. W. Little; B. J. E. Livesey, QC; C. G. Llewellyn-Jones, QC; L. J. R. Lobo; C. J. Lockhart-Mummery, QC; A. J. C. Lodge, QC; D. C. Lovell-Pank, QC; A. C. Lowcock; G. W. Lowe; J. A. M. Lowen; Rt. Hon. Sir Nicholas Lyell, QC, MP; A. P. Lyon; P. G. McCahill, QC; R. G. B. McCombe, QC; G. F. McDermott; A. E. McFarlane, QC; K. M. P. Macgill; R. D. Machell, QC; B. M. McIntyre; C. C. Mackay, QC; D. L. Mackie; N. A. McKittrick; I. A. B. McLaren, QC; I. McLeod; R. B. Macleod, QC; A. G. Mainds; A. H. R. Maitland; A. R. Malcolm; H. J. Malins; M. E. Mann, QC; The Hon. G. R. J. Mansfield; R. L. Marks; J. W. Marrin, QC; A. L. Marriott, QC; G. M. Marriott; A. S. Marron, QC; P. Marsh; R. G. Marshall-Andrews, QC; G. C. Marson; H. R. A. Martineau; A. S. Maskrey, QC; C. P. Mather; D. Matheson, QC; P. R. Matthews; Mrs S. P. Matthews, QC; P. B. Mauleverer, QC; R. B. Mawrey, QC; J. F. M. Maxwell; R. Maxwell, QC; Mrs P. R. May; R. M. J. Meeke; G. M. Mercer; N. F. Merriman, QC; C. S. J. Metcalf; J. T. Milford; K. S. H. Miller; P. W. Miller; R. A. Miller; S. M. Miller, QC; C. J. Millington; C. E. Million; J. B. M. Milmo, QC; D. C. Milne, QC; C. J. M. Miskin, QC; Miss C. M. Miskin; A. P. Mitchell; A. R. Mitchell, QC; C. R. Mitchell; D. C. Mitchell; J. R. Mitchell; J. E. Mitting, QC; F. R. Moat; E. G. Moelwyn-Hughes; C. R. D. Moger, QC; Mrs J. P. Moir; D. R. P. Mole, QC; M. G. C. Moorhouse; A. G. Moran, QC; D. W. Morgan; P. B. Morgan; A. P. Morris, QC; C. Morris-Coole; H. A. C. Morrison, OBE; R. F. Morrison; G. E. Morrow, QC; M. G.

M. Morse; C. J. Moss, QC; P. C. Mott, QC; R. W. Moxon-Brown, QC; J. H. Muir; F. J. Muller, QC; A. H. Munday, QC; G. S. Murdoch, QC; I. P. Murphy, QC; M. J. A. Murphy, QC; A. C. Murray; C. M. Murray; N. O. G. Murray; N. J. Mylne, QC; H. G. Narayan; A. R. H. Newman, QC; Miss L. A. Newton; A. I. Niblett; G. Nice, QC; A. E. R. Noble; B. Nolan, QC; M. C. Norman; J. M. Norris; P. H. Norris; G. Nuttall; J. G. Nutting, QC; D. P. O'Brien, QC; Mrs F. M. T. Oldham; M. D. Oldham; S. Oliver-Jones, QC; R. W. Onions; M. N. O'Sullivan; D. B. W. Ouseley, QC; N. D. Padfield, QC; Miss A. M. Page, QC; S. R. Page; A. O. Palmer, QC; A. W. Palmer, QC; D. P. Pannick, QC; A. D. W. Pardoe, QC; S. A. B. Parish; P. L. Parker; G. C. Parkins, QC; G. E. Parkinson; M. P. Parroy; D. J. T. Parry; E. O. Parry; N. S. K. Pascoe, QC; A. Patience, QC; Miss A. E. H. Pauffley, QC; J. G. Paulusz; W. E. Pawlak; F. M. Pearce; D. J. Pearce-Higgins, QC; R. J. Pearse Wheatley; The Hon. I. J. C. Peddie, QC; J. V. Pegden; J. Perry, QC; M. Pert, QC; N. M. Peters, QC; J. R. D. Philips; D. J. Phillips, QC; W. B. Phillips; M. A. Pickering, QC; J. K. Pickup; C. J. Pitchford, QC; The Hon. B. M. D. Pitt; Miss E. F. Platt, QC; R. Platts; R. O. Plender, QC; Miss J. C. Plumptre; Miss I. M. Plumstead; S. D. Popat; A. R. Porten, QC; L. R. Portnoy; J. R. L. Posnansky, QC; Mrs R. M. Poulet, QC; S. R. Powles, QC; D. Price; G. A. L. Price, QC; J. A. Price, QC; J. C. Price; N. P. L. Price, QC; R. Price Lewis; R. B. L. Prior; F. S. K. Privett; H. W. Prosser; A. C. Pugh, QC; G. V. Pugh, QC; G. F. Pulman, QC; C. P. B. Purchas, QC; R. M. Purchas, QC; N. R. Purnell, QC; P. O. Purnell, QC; Q. C. W. Querelle; N. P. Quinn; D. A. Radcliffe; Mrs N. P. Radford, QC; Ms A. J. Rafferty, QC; T. W. H. Raggatt, QC; Miss E. A. Ralphs; J. Y. Randall, QC; A. D. Rawley, QC; J. E. Rayner James, QC; P. R. Raynor, QC; J. H. Reddihough; M. H. Redfern, QC; A. R. F. Redgrave, QC; D. W. Rees; G. W. Rees; P. Rees; C. E. Reese, QC; P. C. Reid; D. J. Rennie; R. E. Rhodes, QC; D. J. Richardson; T. Rigby; S. V. Riordan, QC; G. Risius; Miss J. H. Ritchie, QC; J. M. Roberts; J. M. G. Roberts, QC; T. D. Roberts; A. J. Robertson; G. R. Robertson, QC; V. Robinson, QC; D. E. H. Robson, QC; G. W. Roddick, QC; Miss M. B. Roddy; Miss D. J. Rodgers; P. F. G. Rook, QC; J. G. Ross; J. G. Ross Martyn; P. C. Rouch; J. J. Rowe, QC; R. J. Royce, QC; M. W. Rudland; P. E. B. M. Rueff; A. A. Rumbelow, QC; N. J. Rumfitt, QC; R. J. Rundell; J. R. T. Rylance; C. R. A. Sallon, QC; C. N. Salmon; D. A. Salter; G. R. Sankey, QC; N. L. Sarony; J. H. B. Saunders, QC; M. P. Sayers, QC; R. J. Scholes, QC; T. J. W. Scott; Miss P. Scriven, QC; R. J. Seabrook, QC; C. Seagroatt, QC; W. P. L. Sellick; O. M. Sells, QC; R. W. Seymour, QC; A. J. Seys-Llewellyn; A. R. F. Sharp; P. P. Shears; S. J. Sher, QC; Miss D. A. Sherwin; Miss J. Shipley; S. R. Silber, QC; P. C. H. Simon, QC; Miss E. A. Slade, QC; A. C. Smith, QC; A. T. Smith, QC; D. Smith; P. W. Smith, QC; R. D. H. Smith, QC; Ms Z. P. Smith; C. J. Smyth; R. C. Southwell, QC; R. C. E. Southwell; M. H. Spence, QC; Sir Derek Spencer, QC; J. Spencer, QC; M. G. Spencer, QC; R. G. Spencer; S. M. Spencer, QC; R. V. Spencer Bernard; D. P. Spens, QC; R. W. Spon-Smith; D. Steer, QC; M. T. Steiger, QC; Mrs L. J. Stern, QC; A. W. Stevenson, TD; J. S. H. Stewart, QC; S. P. Stewart, QC; W. R. Stewart Smith; A. C. Steynor; G. J. C. Still; D. A. Stockdale, QC; Mrs D. M. Stocken; D. M. A. Stokes, QC; M. G. T. Stokes, QC; J. B. Storey, QC; T. M. F. Stow, QC; D. M. A. Strachan, QC; M. Stuart-Moore, QC; J. H. Stuart-Smith, QC; F. R. C. Such; A. B. Suckling, QC; Ms L. E. Sullivan, QC; D. M. Sumner; J. P. C. Sumption, QC; M. A. Supperstone, QC; P. J. Susman; R. P. Sutton, QC; N. H. Sweeney; Miss C. J. Swift, QC; M. R. Swift, QC; Miss H. H. Swindells, QC; P. Sycamore; C. J. M. Symons, QC; J. P. Tabor, QC; J. A. Tackaberry, QC; P. J. Talbot, QC; R. K. K. Talbot; R. B. Tansey, QC; J. B. C. Tanzer; Miss S. A. M. Tapping; G. F. Tattersall, QC; E. T. H. Teague; N. J. M. Teare, QC; R. H. Tedd, QC; A. D. Temple, QC; V. B. A. Temple, QC; M. H. Tennant; The Lord Thomas of Gresford, OBE, QC; P. A. Thomas; R. L. Thomas, QC; R. M. Thomas; R. U. Thomas, QC; Miss S. M. Thomas; C. F. J. Thompson; R. E. T. Thorn, QC; A. R. Thornhill, QC; P. R. Thornton, QC; A. C. Tickle; M. B. Tillett, QC; J. W. Tinnion; R. N. Titheridge, QC; S. M. Tomlinson, QC; P. J. H. Towler; J. B. S. Townend, QC; C. M. Treacy, QC; H. B. Trethowan; A. D. H. Trollope, QC; M. G. Tugendhat, QC; H. W. Turcan; D. A. Turner, QC; J. Turner; P. A. Twigg, QC; J. F. Uff, QC; R. P. A. Ullstein, QC; N. E. Underhill, QC; J. G. G. Ungley; H. V. C. Vagg; N. P. Valios, QC; N. C. van der Bijl; D. A. J. Vaughan, QC; M. J. D. Vere-Hodge, QC; C. J. Vosper; J. P. Wadsworth, QC; S. P. Waine; R. M. Wakerley, QC; Mrs E. A. Walker; R. A. Walker, QC; R. J. Walker, QC; Sir Jonah Walker-Smith, Bt; T. M. Walsh; J. J. Wardlow; B. B. Warner; J. Warren, QC; N. J. Warren; N. R. Warren, QC; D. E. B. Waters; Miss B. J. Watson; Sir James Watson, Bt; B. J. Waylen; A. S. Webster, QC; M. R. West; L. J. West-Knights; G. B. N. White; W. J. M. White; D. R. B. Whitehouse, QC; R. P. Whitehurst; P. G. Whiteman, QC; P. J. M. Whiteman, TD; A. Whitfield, QC; S. J. P. Widdup; C. T. Wide, QC; R. Wigglesworth; Mrs M. Wilby; N. V. M. Wilkinson; Miss E. Willers; G. H. G. Williams, QC; Miss J. A. Williams; J. G. Williams, QC; J. L. Williams, QC; M. J. Williams; W. L. Williams, QC; Miss H. E. Williamson, QC; S. W. Williamson, QC; A. J. D. Wilson, QC; A. M. Wilson, QC; I. K. R. Wilson; C. Wilson-Smith, QC; G. W. Wingate-Saul, QC; Miss S. E. Wollam; H. Wolton, QC; M. M. Wood, QC; N. A. Wood; R. L. J. Wood, QC; W. R. Wood; Miss S. Woodley, QC; J. T. Woods; W. C. Woodward, QC; Miss S. E. Woollam; A. P. L. Woolman; T. H. Workman; Miss A. M. Worrall, QC; P. F. Worsley, QC; J. J. Wright; N. A. Wright; D. E. M. Young, QC; M. K. Zeidman, QC

STIPENDIARY MAGISTRATES

PROVINCIAL
(each £74,464)

Cheshire, P. K. Dodd, OBE, *apptd* 1991

Derbyshire, M. J. Friel, *apptd* 1997; Mrs J. H. Alderson, *apptd* 1997

Devon, P. H. Wassall, *apptd* 1994

Dorset, P. R. Farmer, *apptd* 1998

East and West Sussex, P. C. Tain, *apptd* 1992

Essex, K. A. Gray, *apptd* 1995

Greater Manchester, A. Berg, *apptd* 1994; C. R. Darnton, *apptd* 1994; M. A. Abelson, *apptd* 1998

Hampshire, T. G. Cowling, *apptd* 1989; J. I. Woollard, *apptd* 1998

Humberside, N. H. White, *apptd* 1985

Lancashire/Merseyside, J. Finestein, *apptd* 1992

Leicestershire, D. M. Meredith, *apptd* 1995; R. Holland, *apptd* 1999

Merseyside, D. R. G. Tapp, *apptd* 1992; P. S. Ward, *apptd* 1994; P. J. Firth, *apptd* 1994

Middlesex, N. A. McKittrick, *apptd* 1989; S. N. Day, *apptd* 1991; C. S. Wiles, *apptd* 1996

Mid Glamorgan, Miss P. J. Watkins, *apptd* 1995

Norfolk, N. P. Heley, *apptd* 1994

North-East London, G. E. Cawdron, *apptd* 1993

Nottinghamshire, P. F. Nuttall, *apptd* 1991; M. L. R. Harris, *apptd* 1991

Shropshire, P. H. R. Browning, *apptd* 1994

South Glamorgan, G. R. Watkins, *apptd* 1993

South Wales and Gwent, D. V. Manning-Davies, *apptd* 1996; Miss P. J. Watkins, *apptd* 1995

South Yorkshire, J. A. Browne, *apptd* 1992; W. D. Thomas, *apptd* 1989; M. A. Rosenberg, *apptd* 1993; P. H. F. Jones, *apptd* 1995; Mrs S. E. Driver, *apptd* 1995
Staffordshire, P. G. G. Richards, *apptd* 1991
West Midlands, W. M. Probert, *apptd* 1983; B. Morgan, *apptd* 1989; I. Gillespie, *apptd* 1991; M. F. James, *apptd* 1991; C. M. McColl, *apptd* 1994; J. A. Jellema, *apptd* 1998; D. J. Chinery, *apptd* 1998
West Yorkshire, Mrs P. A. Hewitt, *apptd* 1990; G. A. K. Hodgson, *apptd* 1993; N. R. Cadbury, *apptd* 1997

METROPOLITAN

Chief Metropolitan Stipendiary Magistrate and Chairman of Magistrates' Courts Committee for Inner London Area (£92,810), G. E. Parkinson, *apptd* 1997 (*Bow Street*)
Magistrates (each £74,464)
Bow Street, The Chief Magistrate; R. D. Bartle, *apptd* 1972; C. L. Pratt, *apptd* 1990; H. N. Evans, *apptd* 1994
Camberwell Green, C. P. M. Davidson, *apptd* 1984; B. Loosley, *apptd* 1989; H. Gott, *apptd* 1992; Miss E. Roscoe, *apptd* 1994; R. House, *apptd* 1995; Miss C. S. R. Tubbs, *apptd* 1996
Greenwich, D. A. Cooper, *apptd* 1991; M. Kelly, *apptd* 1992; P. S. Wallis, *apptd* 1993; H. C. F. Riddle, *apptd* 1995
Highbury Corner, M. A. Johnstone, *apptd* 1980; Miss D. Quick, *apptd* 1986; J. M. Baker, *apptd* 1990; A. T. Evans, *apptd* 1990; Mrs L. Morgan, *apptd* 1995; P. A. M. Clark, *apptd* 1996
Horseferry Road, A. R. Davies, *apptd* 1985; G. Breen, *apptd* 1986; T. Workman, *apptd* 1986; Mrs K. R. Keating, *apptd* 1987; Mrs E. Rees, *apptd* 1994
Inner London and City Family Proceedings Court, N. Crichton, *apptd* 1987
Marylebone, D. Kennett Brown, *apptd* 1982; K. Maitland-Davies, *apptd* 1984; A. C. Baldwin, *apptd* 1990; Ms G. Babington-Browne, *apptd* 1991
South-Western, C. D. Voelcker, *apptd* 1982; A. W. Ormerod, *apptd* 1988; Miss D. Wickham, *apptd* 1989
Thames, Mrs J. Comyns, *apptd* 1982; S. E. Dawson, *apptd* 1984; G. Wicks, *apptd* 1987; I. G. Bing, *apptd* 1989; W. A. Kennedy, *apptd* 1991
Tower Bridge, C. S. F. Black, *apptd* 1993; M. Read, *apptd* 1993; S. Somjee, *apptd* 1995
West London Magistrates' Court, Miss A. Jennings, *apptd* 1972; T. English, *apptd* 1986; J. Philips, *apptd* 1989; D. L. Thomas, *apptd* 1990; D. Simpson, *apptd* 1993; J. Coleman, *apptd* 1995
'Floaters', Miss D. Lachhar, *apptd* 1996; J. V. Perkins, *apptd* 1999; K. Grant, *apptd* 1999

MAGISTRATES' COURTS COMMITTEE FOR THE INNER LONDON AREA
65 Romney Street, London SW1P 3RD
Tel 0171-799 3332

Justices' Chief Executive and Clerk to the Committee (£84,015), Miss C. Glenn
Justices' Clerk (*Training*) (£26,305–£35,546), vacant

CROWN PROSECUTION SERVICE
50 Ludgate Hill, London EC4M 7EX
Tel 0171-273 8000

The Crown Prosecution Service (CPS) is responsible for the independent review and conduct of criminal proceedings instituted by police forces in England and Wales, with the exception of cases conducted by the Serious Fraud Office (*see* page 341) and certain minor offences.
The Service is headed by the Director of Public Prosecutions (DPP), who works under the superintendence of the Attorney-General, and a chief executive. The Service was reorganized in April 1999 and now comprises a headquarters office and 42 Areas, each Area corresponding to a police area in England and Wales. Each Area is headed by a Chief Crown Prosecutor, supported by an Area Business Manager.

Director of Public Prosecutions (*SCS*), D. Calvert-Smith, QC
Chief Executive (*SCS*), M. E. Addison
Directors (*SCS*), C. Newell (*Casework*); G. Patten (*Policy*); J. Graham (*Finance*); L. Carey (*Business Information Systems*); Ms T. Newell (*acting*) (*Personnel Strategy*); Ms T. Fisher (*acting*) (*Personnel Operations*)
Head of Communications (*SCS*), Ms L. Salisbury

CPS AREAS

ENGLAND

CPS AVON AND SOMERSET, 1st Floor, Froomsgate House, Rupert Street, Bristol BS1 2QJ. Tel: 0117-930 2800. *Chief Crown Prosecutor* (*SCS*), D. Archer; *Area Business Manager,* Ms L. Burton
CPS BEDFORDSHIRE, Sceptre House, 7–9 Castle Street, Luton LU1 3AJ. Tel: 01582-816600. *Chief Crown Prosecutor* (*SCS*), Ms M. Townsend; *Area Business Manager,* Ms J. Altham
CPS CAMBRIDGESHIRE, Justinian House, Spitfire Close, Ermine Business Park, Huntingdon, Cambs PE18 6XY. Tel: 01480-825200. *Chief Crown Prosecutor* (*SCS*), R. Crowley; *Area Business Manager,* I. Farrell
CPS CHESHIRE, 2nd Floor, Windsor House, Pepper Street, Chester CH1 1TD. Tel: 01244-408600. *Chief Crown Prosecutor* (*SCS*), B. Hughes; *Area Business Manager,* Ms E. Sherwood
CPS CLEVELAND, Linthorpe Road, Middlesbrough, Cleveland TS1 1TX. Tel: 01642-204500. *Chief Crown Prosecutor* (*SCS*), D. Magson; *Area Business Manager,* Ms M. Phillips
CPS CUMBRIA, 1st Floor, Stocklund House, Castle Street, Carlisle CA3 8SY. Tel: 01228-882900. *Chief Crown Prosecutor* (*SCS*), D. Farmer; *Area Business Manager,* J. Pears
CPS DERBYSHIRE, 5th Floor, St Peter's House, Gower Street, Derby DE1 1SB. Tel: 01332-614000. *Chief Crown Prosecutor* (*SCS*), D. Adams; *Area Business Manager,* Ms A. Clarke
CPS DEVON AND CORNWALL, Hawkins House, Pynes Hill, Rydon Lane, Exeter EX2 5SS. Tel: 01392-288000. *Chief Crown Prosecutor* (*SCS*), A. Cresswell; *Area Business Manager,* J. Nettleton
CPS DORSET, 1st Floor, Oxford House, Oxford Road, Bournemouth BH8 8HA. Tel: 01202-498700. *Chief Crown Prosecutor* (*SCS*), J. Revell; *Area Business Manager,* J. Putman
CPS DURHAM, Elvet House, Hallgarth Street, Durham DH1 3AT. Tel: 0191-383 5800. *Chief Crown Prosecutor* (*SCS*), J. Corringham; *Area Business Manager,* B. Feetham
CPS ESSEX, County House, 100 New London Road, Chelmsford CM2 0RG. Tel: 01245-455800. *Chief Crown Prosecutor* (*SCS*), J. Bell; *Area Business Manager,* P. Overett
CPS GLOUCESTERSHIRE, 2 Kimbrose Way, Gloucester GL1 2DB. Tel: 01452-872400. *Chief Crown Prosecutor* (*SCS*), W. Cole; *Area Business Manager,* W. Hollins
CPS GREATER MANCHESTER, PO Box 237, 8th Floor, Sunlight House, Quay Street, Manchester M60 3PS. Tel: 0161-827 4700. *Chief Crown Prosecutor* (*SCS*), T. Taylor; *Area Business Manager,* K. Fox

CPS HAMPSHIRE, 3rd Floor, Black Horse House, 8–10 Leigh Road, Eastleigh, Hants SO50 9FH. Tel: 01703-673800. *Chief Crown Prosecutor (SCS)*, R. Daw; *Area Business Manager*, M. Sunderland

CPS HERTFORDSHIRE, Queen's House, 58 Victoria Street, St Albans, Herts AL1 3HZ. Tel: 01727-798700. *Chief Crown Prosecutor (SCS)*, C. Ingham; *Area Business Manager*, L. Carroll

CPS HUMBERSIDE, 2nd Floor, King William House, Lowgate, Hull HU1 1RS. Tel: 01482-621000. *Chief Crown Prosecutor (SCS)*, B. Marshall; *Area Business Manager*, Ms C. Skidmore

CPS KENT, Priory Gate, 29 Union Street, Maidstone, Kent ME14 1PT. Tel: 01622-356600. *Chief Crown Prosecutor (SCS)*, Ms E. Howe; *Area Business Manager*, K. Mitchell

CPS LANCASHIRE, 3rd Floor, Unicentre, Lord's Walk, Preston PR1 1DH. Tel: 01772-208100. *Chief Crown Prosecutor (SCS)*, D. Dickenson; *Area Business Manager*, G. Rankin

CPS LEICESTERSHIRE, Princes Court, 34 York Road, Leicester LE1 5TU. Tel: 0116-204 6700. *Chief Crown Prosecutor (SCS)*, M. Howard; *Area Business Manager*, Ms L. Jones

CPS LINCOLNSHIRE, Crosstrent House, 10A Newport, Lincoln LN1 3DF. Tel: 01633-261100. *Chief Crown Prosecutor (SCS)*, Ms A. Kerr; *Area Business Manager*, Ms A. Garbett

CPS LONDON (METROPOLITAN), 4th Floor, 50 Ludgate Hill, London EC4M 7EX. Tel: 0171-796 8000. *Chief Crown Prosecutor (SCS)*, P. Boeuf; *Assistant Chief Crown Prosecutors (SCS)*, Ms A. Saunders; Ms M. Werrett; H. Cohen; *Area Business Manager*, A. Machray

CPS MERSEYSIDE, 7th Floor (South), Royal Liver Building, Pier Head, Liverpool L3 1HN. Tel: 0151-239 6400. *Chief Crown Prosecutor (SCS)*, J. Holt; *Area Business Manager*, Ms D. King

CPS NORFOLK, Haldin House, Old Bank of England Court, Queen Street, Norwich NR2 4SX. Tel: 01603-693000. *Chief Crown Prosecutor (SCS)*, P. Tidey; *Area Business Manager*, A. Mardell

CPS NORTH YORKSHIRE, 6th Floor, Ryedale Building, 60 Piccadilly, York YO1 1NS. Tel: 01904-731700. *Chief Crown Prosecutor (SCS)*, B. Turnbull; *Area Business Manager*, R. Cragg

CPS NORTHAMPTONSHIRE, Beaumont House, Cliftonville, Northampton NN1 5BE. Tel: 01604-823600. *Chief Crown Prosecutor (SCS)*, C. Chapman; *Area Business Manager*, J. Stephenson

CPS NORTHUMBRIA, 1st Floor, Benton House, 136 Sandyford Road, Newcastle upon Tyne NE2 1QE. Tel: 0191-260 4200. *Chief Crown Prosecutor (SCS)*, Ms N. Reasbeck; *Area Business Manager*, S. Guy

CPS NOTTINGHAMSHIRE, 2 King Edward Court, King Edward Street, Nottingham NG1 1EL. Tel: 0115-852 3300. *Chief Crown Prosecutor (SCS)*, P. Lewis; *Area Business Manager*, Ms G. Pessol

CPS SOUTH YORKSHIRE, Greenfield House, 32 Scotland Street, Sheffield S3 7DQ. Tel: 0114-229 8600. *Chief Crown Prosecutor (SCS)*, Ms J. Bermingham; *Area Business Manager*, C. Day

CPS STAFFORDSHIRE, 11A Princes Street, Stafford ST16 2EU. Tel: 01785-272200. *Chief Crown Prosecutor (SCS)*, H. Ireland; *Area Business Manager*, B. Laybourne

CPS SUFFOLK, Saxon House, 1 Cromwell Square, Ipswich IP1 1TS. Tel: 01473-282100. *Chief Crown Prosecutor (SCS)*, C. Yule; *Area Business Manager*, Ms D. Waddington

CPS SURREY, One Onslow Street, Guildford, Surrey GU1 4YA. Tel: 01483-468200. *Chief Crown Prosecutor (SCS)*, Ms S. Hebblethwaite; *Area Business Manager*, M. Wray

CPS SUSSEX, Unit 3, Clifton Mews, Clifton Hill, Brighton BN1 3HR. Tel: 01273-765600. *Chief Crown Prosecutor (SCS)*, M. Kennedy; *Area Business Manager*, B. Shepherd

CPS THAMES VALLEY, The Courtyard, Lombard Street, Abingdon, Oxon OX14 5SE. Tel: 01235-551900. *Chief Crown Prosecutor (SCS)*, S. Clements; *Area Business Manager*, G. Choldcroft

CPS WARWICKSHIRE, Rossmore House, 10 Newbold Terrace, Leamington Spa, Warks CV32 4EA. Tel: 01926-450088. *Chief Crown Prosecutor (SCS)*, M. Lynn; *Area Business Manager*, Ms S. Petyt

CPS WEST MERCIA, Artillery House, Heritage Way, Droitwich, Worcester WR9 8YB. Tel: 01905-825000. *Chief Crown Prosecutor (SCS)*, J. England; *Area Business Manager*, L. Sutton

CPS WEST MIDLANDS, 14th Floor, Colmore Gate, 2 Colmore Row, Birmingham B3 2QA. Tel: 0121-262 1300. *Chief Crown Prosecutor (SCS)*, D. Blundell; *Area Business Manager*, M. Grist

CPS WEST YORKSHIRE, 4–5 South Parade, Wakefield, W. Yorks WF1 1LR. Tel: 01924-205200. *Chief Crown Prosecutor (SCS)*, N. Franklin; *Area Business Manager*, R. Stevenson

CPS WILTSHIRE, 2nd Floor, Fox Talbot House, Bellinger Close, Malmesbury Road, Chippenham, Wilts SN15 1BN. Tel: 01249-766100. *Chief Crown Prosecutor (SCS)*, N. Hawkins; *Area Business Manager*, N. Nabi

WALES

CPS DYFED-POWYS, Heol Penlanffos, Tanerdy, Carmarthen, Dyfed SA31 2EZ. Tel: 01267-242100. *Chief Crown Prosecutor (SCS)*, S. Rowlands; *Area Business Manager*, Ms C. Jones

CPS GWENT, 7th Floor, Chartist Tower, Dock Street, Newport, Gwent NP9 1DW. Tel: 01633-241100. *Chief Crown Prosecutor (SCS)*, C. Woolley; *Area Business Manager*, B. Fullerton

CPS NORTH WALES, Llys Eirias, Heritage Gate, Abergele Road, Colwyn Bay, Conwy LL29 8BW. Tel: 01492-806800. *Chief Crown Prosecutor (SCS)*, P. Whittaker; *Area Business Manager*, Ms A. Walsh

CPS SOUTH WALES, 21st Floor, Capital Tower, Greyfriars Road, Cardiff CF1 3PL. Tel: 01222-803800. *Chief Crown Prosecutor (SCS)*, H. Heycock; *Area Business Manager*, I. Edmondson

The Scottish Judicature

Scotland has a legal system separate from and differing greatly from the English legal system in enacted law, judicial procedure and the structure of courts.

In Scotland the system of public prosecution is headed by the Lord Advocate and is independent of the police, who have no say in the decision to prosecute. The Lord Advocate, discharging his functions through the Crown Office in Edinburgh, is responsible for prosecutions in the High Court, sheriff courts and district courts. Prosecutions in the High Court are prepared by the Crown Office and conducted in court by one of the law officers, by an advocate-depute, or by a solicitor advocate. In the inferior courts the decision to prosecute is made and prosecution is preferred by procurators fiscal, who are lawyers and full-time civil servants subject to the directions of the Crown Office. A permanent legally-qualified civil servant known as the Crown Agent is responsible for the running of the Crown Office and the organization of the Procurator Fiscal Service, of which he is the head.

Scotland is divided into six sheriffdoms, each with a full-time sheriff principal. The sheriffdoms are further divided into sheriff court districts, each of which has a legally-qualified resident sheriff or sheriffs, who are the judges of the court.

In criminal cases sheriffs principal and sheriffs have the same powers; sitting with a jury of 15 members, they may try more serious cases on indictment, or, sitting alone, may try lesser cases under summary procedure. Minor summary offences are dealt with in district courts which are administered by the district and the islands local government authorities and presided over by lay justices of the peace (of whom there are about 4,000) and, in Glasgow only, by stipendiary magistrates. Juvenile offenders (children under 16) may be brought before an informal children's hearing comprising three local lay people. The superior criminal court is the High Court of Justiciary which is both a trial and an appeal court. Cases on indictment are tried by a High Court judge, sitting with a jury of 15, in Edinburgh and on circuit in other towns. Appeals from the lower courts against conviction or sentence are heard also by the High Court, which sits as an appeal court only in Edinburgh. There is no further appeal to the House of Lords in criminal cases.

In civil cases the jurisdiction of the sheriff court extends to most kinds of action. Appeal against decisions of the sheriff may be made to the sheriff principal and thence to the Court of Session, or direct to the Court of Session, which sits only in Edinburgh. The Court of Session is divided into the Inner and the Outer House. The Outer House is a court of first instance in which cases are heard by judges sitting singly, sometimes with a jury of 12. The Inner House, itself subdivided into two divisions of equal status, is mainly an appeal court. Appeals may be made to the Inner House from the Outer House as well as from the sheriff court. An appeal may be made from the Inner House to the House of Lords.

The judges of the Court of Session are the same as those of the High Court of Justiciary, the Lord President of the Court of Session also holding the office of Lord Justice General in the High Court. Senators of the College of Justice are Lords Commissioners of Justiciary as well as judges of the Court of Session. On appointment, a Senator takes a judicial title, which is retained for life. Although styled 'The Hon./Rt. Hon. Lord —', the Senator is not a peer.

The office of coroner does not exist in Scotland. The local procurator fiscal inquires privately into sudden or suspicious deaths and may report findings to the Crown Agent. In some cases a fatal accident inquiry may be held before the sheriff.

COURT OF SESSION AND HIGH COURT OF JUSTICIARY

The Lord President and Lord Justice General (£147,214)
The Rt. Hon. the Lord Rodger of Earlsferry, *born* 1944, *apptd* 1996
Secretary, A. Maxwell

INNER HOUSE

Lords of Session (each £139,931)
FIRST DIVISION
The Lord President
Hon. Lord Sutherland (Ranald Sutherland), *born* 1932, *apptd* 1985
Hon. Lord Prosser (William Prosser), *born* 1934, *apptd* 1986
Hon. Lord Caplan (Philip Caplan), *born* 1929, *apptd* 1989

SECOND DIVISION
Lord Justice Clerk (£139,931), The Rt. Hon. Lord Cullen (William Cullen), *born* 1935, *apptd* 1997
Rt. Hon. The Lord McCluskey, *born* 1929, *apptd* 1984
Hon. Lord Kirkwood (Ian Kirkwood), *born* 1932, *apptd* 1987
Hon. Lord Coulsfield (John Cameron), *born* 1934, *apptd* 1987

OUTER HOUSE

Lords of Session (each £123,787)

Hon. Lord Milligan (James Milligan), *born* 1934, *apptd* 1988
Rt. Hon. The Lord Cameron of Lochbroom, *born* 1931, *apptd* 1989
Hon. Lord Marnoch (Michael Bruce), *born* 1938, *apptd* 1990
Hon. Lord MacLean (Ranald MacLean), *born* 1938, *apptd* 1990
Hon. Lord Penrose (George Penrose), *born* 1938, *apptd* 1990
Hon. Lord Osborne (Kenneth Osborne), *born* 1937, *apptd* 1990
Hon. Lord Abernethy (Alistair Cameron), *born* 1938, *apptd* 1992
Hon. Lord Johnston (Alan Johnston), *born* 1942, *apptd* 1994
Hon. Lord Gill (Brian Gill), *born* 1942, *apptd* 1994
Hon. Lord Hamilton (Arthur Hamilton), *born* 1942, *apptd* 1995
Hon. Lord Dawson (Thomas Dawson), *born* 1948, *apptd* 1995
Hon. Lord Macfadyen (Donald Macfadyen), *born* 1945, *apptd* 1995
Hon. Lady Cosgrove (Hazel Aronson), *born* 1946, *apptd* 1996
Hon. Lord Nimmo Smith (William Nimmo Smith), *born* 1942, *apptd* 1996
Hon. Lord Philip (Alexander Philip), *born* 1942, *apptd* 1996
Hon. Lord Kingarth (Derek Emslie), *born* 1949, *apptd* 1997
Hon. Lord Bonomy (Iain Bonomy), *born* 1946, *apptd* 1997
Hon. Lord Eassie (Ronald Mackay), *born* 1945, *apptd* 1997
Hon. Lord Reed (Robert Reed), *born* 1956, *apptd* 1998

COURT OF SESSION AND HIGH COURT OF JUSTICIARY
Parliament House, Parliament Square, Edinburgh EH1 1HQ
Tel 0131-225 2595

Principal Clerk of Session and Justiciary (£32,293–£53,879), J. L. Anderson
Deputy Principal Clerk of Justiciary and Administration (£28,314–£43,873), T. Fyffe
Deputy Principal Clerk of Session and Principal Extractor (£28,314–£43,873), G. McKeand
Deputy Principal Clerk (Keeper of the Rolls) (£28,314–£43,873), T. Thomson
Depute Clerks of Session and Justiciary (£21,613–£28,414), N. J. Dowie; I. F. Smith; T. Higgins; T. B. Cruickshank; Q. A. Oliver; F. Shannly; A. S. Moffat; G. G. Ellis; W. Dunn; A. M. Finlayson; C. C. Armstrong; R. Jenkins; J. O. McLean; M. Weir; R. M. Sinclair; E. G. Appelbe; B. Watson; D. W. Cullen; D. J. Cullum; I. D. Martin; N. McGinley; J. Lynn; E. Dickson; K. D. Carter; F. Petrie

SCOTTISH COURTS ADMINISTRATION

Hayweight House, 23 Lauriston Street, Edinburgh
EH3 9DQ
Tel 0131-229 9200

The Scottish Courts Administration is responsible to the Scottish Ministers for the performance of the Scottish Court Service and central administration pertaining to the judiciary in the Supreme and Sheriff Courts. It is also responsible for policy in relation to civil court procedures and jurisdiction, the law of diligence, evidence, arbitration and dispute resolution, private international law, law reform and other matters.

Director, J. Hamill, CB
Deputy Director (Legal Policy) (Assistant Solicitor) (G5), P. M. Beaton
Deputy Director (Resources and Liaison), D. Stewart

SCOTTISH COURT SERVICE

Hayweight House, 23 Lauriston Street, Edinburgh
EH3 9DQ
Tel 0131-229 9200

The Scottish Court Service became an executive agency within the Scottish Courts Administration in 1995. It is responsible to the Scottish Ministers for the provision of staff, court houses and associated services for the Supreme and Sheriff Courts.

Chief Executive, M. Ewart

SHERIFF COURT OF CHANCERY

27 Chambers Street, Edinburgh EH1 1LB
Tel 0131-225 2525

The Court deals with service of heirs and completion of title in relation to heritable property.

Sheriff of Chancery, C. G. B. Nicholson, QC

HM COMMISSARY OFFICE

27 Chambers Street, Edinburgh EH1 1LB
Tel 0131-225 2525

The Office is responsible for issuing confirmation, a legal document entitling a person to execute a deceased person's will, and other related matters.

Commissary Clerk, J. M. Ross

SCOTTISH LAND COURT

1 Grosvenor Crescent, Edinburgh EH12 5ER
Tel 0131-225 3595

The court deals with disputes relating to agricultural and crofting land in Scotland.

Chairman (£100,209), The Hon. Lord McGhie (James McGhie), QC
Members, D. J. Houston; D. M. Macdonald; J. Kinloch (*part-time*)
Principal Clerk, K. H. R. Graham, WS

SHERIFFDOMS

SALARIES

Sheriff Principal	£100,209
Sheriff	£92,810
Area Director	£32,293–£63,490
Sheriff Clerk	£12,719–£43,873

*Floating Sheriff

GRAMPIAN, HIGHLANDS AND ISLANDS

Sheriff Principal, D. J. Risk, QC
Area Director North, J. Robertson

SHERIFFS AND SHERIFF CLERKS

Aberdeen and Stonehaven, D. Kelbie; L. A. S. Jessop; A. Pollock; Mrs A. M. Cowan; C. J. Harris, QC; I. H. L. Miller; *G. K. Buchanan; *Sheriff Clerks*, Mrs E. Laing (*Aberdeen*); B. McBride (*Stonehaven*)
Peterhead and Banff, K. A. McLernan; *Sheriff Clerk*, A. Hempseed (*Peterhead*); *Sheriff Clerk Depute*, Mrs F. L. MacPherson (*Banff*)
Elgin, N. McPartlin; *Sheriff Clerk*, M. McBey
Inverness, Lochmaddy, Portree, Stornoway, Dingwall, Tain, Wick and Dornoch, W. J. Fulton; D. Booker-Milburn; J. O. A. Fraser; I. A. Cameron; *Sheriff Clerks*, J. Robertson (*Inverness*); W. Cochrane (*Dingwall*); *Sheriff Clerks Depute*, Miss M. Campbell (*Lochmaddy and Portree*); Miss A. B. Armstrong (*Stornoway*); L. MacLachlan (*Tain*); Mrs J. McEwan (*Wick*); K. Kerr (*Dornoch*)
Kirkwall and Lerwick, C. S. Mackenzie; *Sheriff Clerks Depute*, vacant (*Kirkwall*); M. Flanagan (*Lerwick*)
Fort William, C. G. McKay (also *Oban*); *Sheriff Clerk Depute*, D. Hood

TAYSIDE, CENTRAL AND FIFE

Sheriff Principal, J. F. Wheatley, QC
Area Director East, M. Bonar

SHERIFFS AND SHERIFF CLERKS

Arbroath and Forfar, K. A. Veal; *C. N. R. Stein; *Sheriff Clerks*, M. Herbertson (*Arbroath*); S. Munro (*Forfar*)
Dundee, R. A. Davidson; A. L. Stewart, QC; *J. P. Scott; G. J. Evans (also *Cupar*); *Sheriff Clerk*, D. Nicoll
Perth, J. C. McInnes, QC; Mrs F. L. Reith, QC; *Sheriff Clerk*, J. Murphy
Falkirk, A. V. Sheehan; A. J. Murphy; *Sheriff Clerk*, R. McMillan
Stirling, The Hon. R. E. G. Younger; *Sheriff Clerk*, J. Clark
Alloa, W. M. Reid; *Sheriff Clerk*, R. G. McKeand
Cupar, G. J. Evans (also *Dundee*); *Sheriff Clerk*, R. Hughes
Dunfermline, J. S. Forbes; C. W. Palmer; *Sheriff Clerk*, W. McCulloch
Kirkcaldy, F. J. Keane; Mrs L. G. Patrick; *I. D. Dunbar; *B. G. Donald; *Sheriff Clerk*, W. Jones

LOTHIAN AND BORDERS

Sheriff Principal, C. G. B. Nicholson, QC
Area Director East, M. Bonar

SHERIFFS AND SHERIFF CLERKS

Edinburgh, R. G. Craik, QC (also *Peebles*); R. J. D. Scott (also *Peebles*); Miss I. A. Poole; A. M. Bell; J. M. S. Horsburgh, QC; G. W. S. Presslie (also *Haddington*); J. A. Farrell; *A. Lothian; I. D. Macphail, QC; C. N. Stoddart; A. B. Wilkinson, QC; Mrs D. J. B. Robertson; N. M. P. Morrison, QC; *Miss M. M. Stephen; Mrs M. L. E. Jarvie, QC; *Sheriff Clerk*, J. Ross
Peebles, R. G. Craik, QC (also *Edinburgh*); R. J. D. Scott (also *Edinburgh*); *Sheriff Clerk Depute*, M. L. Kubeczka
Linlithgow, H. R. MacLean; G. R. Fleming; *K. A. Ross; *Sheriff Clerk*, R. D. Sinclair
Haddington, G. W. S. Presslie (also *Edinburgh*); *Sheriff Clerk*, J. O'Donnell
Jedburgh and Duns, J. V. Paterson; *Sheriff Clerk*, I. W. Williamson
Selkirk, J. V. Paterson; *Sheriff Clerk Depute*, L. McFarlane

NORTH STRATHCLYDE

Sheriff Principal, B. A. Kerr, QC
Area Director West, I. Scott

SHERIFFS AND SHERIFF CLERKS

Oban, C. G. McKay (also *Fort William*); *Sheriff Clerk Depute*, J. G. Whitelaw

Dumbarton, J. T. Fitzsimons; T. Scott; S. W. H. Fraser; *Sheriff Clerk*, P. Corcoran

Paisley, J. Spy; C. K. Higgins; N. Douglas; D. J. Pender; *W. Dunlop; G. C. Kavanagh (also *Campbeltown*); *Sheriff Clerk*, Miss S. Hindes

Greenock, J. Herald (also *Rothesay*); Sir Stephen Young; *Sheriff Clerk*, J. Tannahill

Kilmarnock, T. M. Croan; D. B. Smith; T. F. Russell; *Sheriff Clerk*, G. Waddell

Dunoon, Mrs C. M. A. F. Gimblett; *Sheriff Clerk Depute*, Mrs C. Carson

Campbeltown, *W. Dunlop (also *Paisley*); *Sheriff Clerk Depute*, P. G. Hay

Rothesay, J. Herald (also *Greenock*); *Sheriff Clerk Depute*, Mrs C. K. McCormick

GLASGOW AND STRATHKELVIN

Sheriff Principal, E. F. Bowen, QC
Area Director West, I. Scott

SHERIFFS AND SHERIFF CLERKS

Glasgow, B. Kearney; G. H. Gordon, CBE, PH.D., QC; B. A. Lockhart; Mrs A. L. A. Duncan; A. C. Henry; J. K. Mitchell; A. G. Johnston; J. P. Murphy; Miss S. A. O. Raeburn, QC; D. Convery; J. McGowan; I. A. S. Peebles, QC; C. W. McFarlane, QC; K. M. Maciver; H. Matthews, QC; J. A. Baird; Miss R. E. A. Rae, QC; T. A. K. Drummond, QC; Mrs P. M. M. Bowman; A. W. Noble; *J. D. Friel; *Mrs D. M. MacNeill, QC; J. A. Taylor; C. A. L. Scott; *Sheriff Clerk*, R. Cockburn

SOUTH STRATHCLYDE, DUMFRIES AND GALLOWAY

Sheriff Principal, G. L. Cox, QC
Area Director West, I. Scott

SHERIFFS AND SHERIFF CLERKS

Hamilton, L. Cameron; D. C. Russell; V. J. Canavan (also *Airdrie*); W. E. Gibson; J. H. Stewart; H. S. Neilson; S. C. Pender; *Sheriff Clerk*, P. Feeney

Lanark, J. D. Allan; *Sheriff Clerk*, A. Whyte

Ayr, N. Gow, QC; R. G. McEwan, QC; *C. B. Miller; *Sheriff Clerk*, Miss C. D. Cockburn

Stranraer and Kirkcudbright, J. R. Smith (also *Dumfries*); *Sheriff Clerks*, W. McIntosh (*Stranraer*); B. Lindsay (*Kirkcudbright*)

Dumfries, K. G. Barr; M. J. Fletcher; J. R. Smith (also *Stranraer and Kirkcudbright*); *Sheriff Clerk*, P. McGonigle

Airdrie, V. J. Canavan (also *Hamilton*); R. H. Dickson; I. C. Simpson; J. C. Morris, QC; *Sheriff Clerk*, D. Forrester

STIPENDIARY MAGISTRATES

GLASGOW

R. Hamilton, *apptd* 1984; J. B. C. Nisbet, *apptd* 1984; R. B. Christie, *apptd* 1985; Mrs J. A. M. MacLean, *apptd* 1990

PROCURATOR FISCAL SERVICE

CROWN OFFICE
25 Chambers Street, Edinburgh EH1 1LA
Tel 0131-226 2626

Crown Agent (£80,020–£116,860), A. C. Normand
Deputy Crown Agent (£55,750–£92,930), F. R. Crowe

PROCURATORS FISCAL

SALARIES

Regional Procurator Fiscal – grade 3	£61,110–£98,400
Regional Procurator Fiscal – grade 4	£55,750–£92,930
Procurator Fiscal – upper level	£41,550–£65,270
Procurator Fiscal – lower level	£36,000–£43,822

GRAMPIAN, HIGHLANDS AND ISLANDS REGION

Regional Procurator Fiscal, L. A. Higson (*Aberdeen*)
Procurators Fiscal, E. K. Barbour (*Stonehaven*); A. J. M. Colley (*Banff*); A. N. Perry (*Peterhead*); D. J. Dickson (*Elgin*); A. N. Perry (*Wick*); J. Bamber (*Portree, Lochmaddy*); F. Redman (*Stornoway*); G. Napier (*Inverness*); R. W. Urquhart (*Kirkwall, Lerwick*); D. J. Buchanan (*Fort William*); A. N. MacDonald (*Dingwall, Tain*)

TAYSIDE, CENTRAL AND FIFE REGION

Regional Procurator Fiscal, B. K. Heywood (*Dundee*)
Procurators Fiscal, J. I. Craigen (*Forfar*); I. A. McLeod (*Perth*); W. J. Gallacher (*Falkirk*); C. Ritchie (*Stirling and Alloa*); E. B. Russell (*Cupar*); R. G. Stott (*Dunfermline*); Miss H.. M. Clark (*Kirkcaldy*)

LOTHIAN AND BORDERS REGION

Regional Procurator Fiscal, N. McFadyen (*Edinburgh*)
Procurators Fiscal, Miss L. M. Ruxton (*Linlithgow*); A. J. P. Reith (*Haddington*); A. R. G. Fraser (*Duns, Jedburgh*); D. MacNeill (*Selkirk*)

NORTH STRATHCLYDE REGION

Regional Procurator Fiscal, W. A. Gilchrist (*Paisley*)
Procurators Fiscal, I. Henderson (*Campbeltown*); C. C. Donnelly (*Dumbarton*); W. S. Carnegie (*Greenock*); D. L. Webster (*Dunoon*); J. G. MacGlennan (*Kilmarnock*); B. R. Maguire (*Oban*)

GLASGOW AND STRATHKELVIN REGION

Regional Procurator Fiscal, A. D. Vannet (*Glasgow*)

SOUTH STRATHCLYDE, DUMFRIES AND GALLOWAY REGION

Regional Procurator Fiscal, D. A. Brown (*Hamilton*)
Procurators Fiscal, S. R. Houston (*Lanark*); J. T. O'Donnell (*Ayr*); F. R. Crowe (*Stranraer*); A. S. Kennedy (*Stranraer, Kirkcudbright*); D. J. Howdle (*Dumfries*); D. Spiers (*Airdrie*)

Northern Ireland Judicature

In Northern Ireland the legal system and the structure of courts closely resemble those of England and Wales; there are, however, often differences in enacted law.

The Supreme Court of Judicature of Northern Ireland comprises the Court of Appeal, the High Court of Justice and the Crown Court. The practice and procedure of these courts is similar to that in England. The superior civil court is the High Court of Justice, from which an appeal lies to the Northern Ireland Court of Appeal; the House of Lords is the final civil appeal court.

The Crown Court, served by High Court and county court judges, deals with criminal trials on indictment. Cases are heard before a judge and, except those involving offences specified under emergency legislation, a jury. Appeals from the Crown Court against conviction or sentence are heard by the Northern Ireland Court of Appeal; the House of Lords is the final court of appeal.

The decision to prosecute in cases tried on indictment and in summary cases of a serious nature rests in Northern Ireland with the Director of Public Prosecutions, who is responsible to the Attorney-General. Minor summary offences are prosecuted by the police.

Minor criminal offences are dealt with in magistrates' courts by a legally qualified resident magistrate and, where an offender is under 17, by juvenile courts each consisting of a resident magistrate and two lay members specially qualified to deal with juveniles (at least one of whom must be a woman). On 6 August 1999 there were 937 justices of the peace in Northern Ireland. Appeals from magistrates' courts are heard by the county court, or by the Court of Appeal on a point of law or an issue as to jurisdiction.

Magistrates' courts in Northern Ireland can deal with certain classes of civil case but most minor civil cases are dealt with in county courts. Judgments of all civil courts are enforceable through a centralized procedure administered by the Enforcement of Judgments Office.

SUPREME COURT OF JUDICATURE

The Royal Courts of Justice, Belfast BT1 3JF
Tel 01232-235111
Lord Chief Justice of Northern Ireland (£147,214)
The Rt. Hon. Sir Robert Carswell, *born* 1934, *apptd* 1997
  Principal Secretary, G. W. Johnston

LORDS JUSTICES OF APPEAL (each £139,931)
Style, The Rt. Hon. Lord Justice [surname]

Rt. Hon. Sir Michael Nicholson, *born* 1933, *apptd* 1995
Rt. Hon. Sir William McCollum, *born* 1933, *apptd* 1997
Rt. Hon. Sir Anthony Campbell, *born* 1936, *apptd* 1998

PUISNE JUDGES (each £123,787)
Style, The Hon. Mr Justice [surname]

Hon. Sir John Sheil, *born* 1938, *apptd* 1989
Hon. Sir Brian Kerr, *born* 1948, *apptd* 1993
Hon. Sir John Pringle, *born* 1929, *apptd* 1993
Hon. Sir Malachy Higgins, *born* 1944, *apptd* 1993
Hon. Sir Paul Girvan, *born* 1948, *apptd* 1995
Hon. Sir Patrick Coghlin, *born* 1945, *apptd* 1997
Hon. Sir John Gillen, *born* 1947, *apptd* 1998

MASTERS OF THE SUPREME COURT (each £74,464)
Master, Queen's Bench and Appeals and Clerk of the Crown, J. W. Wilson, QC
Master, High Court, Mrs D. M. Kennedy
Master, Office of Care and Protection, F. B. Hall
Master, Chancery Office, R. A. Ellison
Master, Bankruptcy and Companies Office, C. W. G. Redpath
Master, Probate and Matrimonial Office, Miss M. McReynolds
Master, Taxing Office, J. C. Napier

OFFICIAL SOLICITOR
Official Solicitor to the Supreme Court of Northern Ireland, Miss B. M. Donnelly

COUNTY COURTS

JUDGES (each £100,209)
Style, His/Her Hon. Judge [surname]

Judge Curran, QC; Judge Gibson, QC; Judge Petrie, QC; Judge Smyth, QC; Judge Markey, QC; Judge McKay, QC; Judge Martin, QC (*Chief Social Security and Child Support Commissioner*); Judge Brady, QC; Judge Rodgers; Judge Foote, QC; Her Hon. Judge Philpott, QC; Judge McFarland; Judge Lockie

RECORDERS (each £100,209)
Belfast, Judge Hart, QC
Londonderry, Judge Burgess

MAGISTRATES' COURTS

RESIDENT MAGISTRATES (each £74,464)
There are 17 resident magistrates in Northern Ireland.

CROWN SOLICITOR'S OFFICE
PO Box 410, Royal Courts of Justice, Belfast BT1 3JY
Tel 01232-542555

Crown Solicitor, N. P. Roberts

DEPARTMENT OF THE DIRECTOR OF PUBLIC PROSECUTIONS
Royal Courts of Justice, Belfast BT1 3NX
Tel 01232-542444

Director of Public Prosecutions, A. Fraser, CB, QC
Deputy Director of Public Prosecutions, W. R. Junkin

NORTHERN IRELAND COURT SERVICE
Windsor House, Bedford Street, Belfast BT2 7LT
Tel 01232-328594

Director (*G3*)

Ecclesiastical Courts

Original jurisdiction is exercised by the consistory court of each diocese in England, presided over by the Chancellor of that diocese. Appellate jurisdiction is exercised by the provincial courts detailed below, by the Court for Ecclesiastical Causes Reserved, and by commissions of review (the membership of these being newly constituted for each case).

COURT OF ARCHES (PROVINCE OF CANTERBURY)
Registry, 16 Beaumont Street, Oxford OX1 2LZ
Tel 01865-241974

Dean of the Arches, The Rt. Worshipful Sir John Owen

COURT OF THE VICAR-GENERAL OF THE PROVINCE OF CANTERBURY
Registry, 16 Beaumont Street, Oxford OX1 2LZ
Tel 01865-241974

Vicar-General, The Rt. Worshipful Miss S. Cameron, QC

CHANCERY COURT OF YORK
Registry, Stamford House, Piccadilly, York YO1 9PP
Tel 01904-623487

Auditor, The Rt. Worshipful Sir John Owen

THE VICAR-GENERAL OF THE PROVINCE OF YORK
Registry, Stamford House, Piccadilly, York YO1 9PP
Tel 01904-623487

Vicar-General, His Honour the Worshipful Judge
  T. A. C. Coningsby, QC

COURT OF FACULTIES
Registry, 1 The Sanctuary, London SW1P 3JT
Tel 0171-222 5381

Office for the issue of special and common marriage licences, appointment of notaries public, etc. Office hours, Monday–Friday, 10–4.
Master of the Faculties, The Rt. Worshipful Sir John Owen

The Probation Service

ENGLAND AND WALES

The Probation Service is currently organized into 54 areas. It is employed in each area by an independent committee and it provides a professional service to the courts, with responsibility for a wide range of duties which include:

(a) a pre-sentence report service for the criminal courts
(b) provision of a range of non-custodial measures involving the supervision of offenders in the community
(c) supervision of offenders released from custody, together with work in penal establishments and help for the families of those serving sentences
(d) an enquiry, conciliation and supervision service in the divorce and domestic courts
(e) support for and promotion of preventive and containment measures in the community designed to reduce the level of crime and domestic breakdown

It is a direct grant service funded 80 per cent from the Home Office and 20 per cent from the relevant local authority. In April 1999 the Government announced plans to reform the Probation Service for England and Wales. A new, unified Probation Service will be led by a Director, responsible to the Home Secretary. There will be 42 local service areas, matching existing police force boundaries. Local Probation Boards are to take a more strategic role, and the Service will be entirely funded by central government.

Its national representative bodies are:

THE CENTRAL PROBATION COUNCIL, 4th Floor, 8–9 Grosvenor Place, London SW1X 7SH. Tel: 0171-245 9364. *Director*, M. Wargent

THE ASSOCIATION OF CHIEF OFFICERS OF PROBATION, 4th Floor, 8–9 Grosvenor Place, London SW1X 7SH. Tel: 0171-823 2551. *Chair*, G. Dobson

THE NATIONAL ASSOCIATION OF PROBATION OFFICERS, 4 Chivalry Road, London SW11 1HT. Tel: 0171-223 4887. *General Secretary*, Ms J. McKnight

SCOTLAND

The probation service in Scotland is a statutory duty of local authorities under section 27 of the Social Work (Scotland) Act 1968. Social workers supervise and provide advice, guidance and assistance to those persons living in their area who are subject to a court's supervision order. This is done by social workers as part of their normal duties and not by a separate probation staff.

NORTHERN IRELAND

The Probation Board for Northern Ireland provides a probation service throughout Northern Ireland. Its function and range of duties is similar to that of the Probation Service in England and Wales (*see* above), except that in Northern Ireland work in divorce and domestic courts is the responsibility of the social services and not the Probation Board. The Probation Board is a statutory body whose 14 members are appointed by the Secretary of State for Northern Ireland and it receives its funding from the Northern Ireland Office.

Tribunals

AGRICULTURAL LAND TRIBUNALS
c/o Rural and Marine Environment Division,
Ministry of Agriculture, Fisheries and Food, Nobel
House, 17 Smith Square, London SW1P 3JR
Tel 0171-238 6991

Agricultural Land Tribunals settle disputes and other
issues between agricultural landlords and tenants, and
drainage disputes between neighbours.
    There are seven tribunals covering England and one
covering Wales. For each tribunal the Lord Chancellor
appoints a chairman and one or more deputies (barristers
or solicitors of at least seven years standing). The Lord
Chancellor also appoints lay members to three statutory
panels: the 'landowners' panel, the 'farmers' panel and the
'drainage' panel.
    Each tribunal is an independent statutory body with
jurisdiction only within its own area. A separate tribunal is
constituted for each case, and consists of a chairman (who
may be the chairman or one of the deputy chairmen) and
two lay members nominated by the chairman.
Chairmen (England) (£271 a day), W. D. Greenwood;
   K. J. Fisher; P. A. de la Piquerie; A. G. Donn; His
   Hon. Judge Lee; G. L. Newsom; His Hon. Judge Robert
   Taylor
Chairman (Wales) (£271 a day), W. J. Owen

THE APPEALS SERVICE
Whittington House, 19–30 Alfred Place, London
WC1E 7LW
Tel 0171-814 6520

The Service (formerly the Independent Tribunal Service)
is responsible for the functioning of tribunals hearing
appeals concerning child support assessments, social
security benefits and vaccine damage payments. Judicial
authority for the Service rests with the President, while
administrative responsibility is exercised by the Appeals
Service Agency, which is an executive agency of the
Department of Social Security.
President, His Hon. Judge Michael Harris
Chief Executive, Appeals Service Agency, N. Ward

COMMONS COMMISSIONERS
Room 818, Tollgate House, Houlton Street, Bristol
BS2 9DJ
Tel 0117-987 8928

The Commons Commissioners are responsible for deciding
disputes arising under the Commons Registration Act 1965
and the Common Land (Rectification of Registers) Act
1989. They also enquire into the ownership of unclaimed
common land. Commissioners are appointed by the Lord
Chancellor.
Chief Commons Commissioner (part-time) (£37,164),
   D. M. Burton
Commissioner, I. L. R. Romer
Clerk, H. Thomas

COPYRIGHT TRIBUNAL
Harmsworth House, 13–15 Bouverie Street, London
EC4Y 8DP
Tel 0171-596 6510; fax 0171-596-6526

The Copyright Tribunal resolves disputes over copyright
licences, principally where there is collective licensing.
    The chairman and two deputy chairmen are appointed
by the Lord Chancellor. Up to eight ordinary members are
appointed by the Secretary of State for Trade and Industry.
Chairman (£316 a day), C. P. Tootal
Secretary, Miss J. E. M. Durdin

DATA PROTECTION TRIBUNAL
c/o The Home Office, Queen Anne's Gate, London
SW1H 9AT
Tel 0171-273 3755

The Data Protection Tribunal determines appeals against
decisions of the Data Protection Registrar (Commissioner
from March 2000) (*see* page 294). The chairman and deputy
chairman are appointed by the Lord Chancellor and must
be legally qualified. Lay members are appointed by the
Home Secretary to represent the interests of data users or
data subjects. A tribunal consists of a legally-qualified
chairman sitting with equal numbers of the lay members
appointed to represent the interests of data users and data
subjects.
Chairman (£394 a day), J. A. C. Spokes, QC
Secretary, R. Hartley

EMPLOYMENT TRIBUNALS

CENTRAL OFFICE (ENGLAND AND WALES)
19–29 Woburn Place, London WC1H 0LU
Tel 0171-273 8666

Employment Tribunals for England and Wales sit in 11
regions. The tribunals deal with matters of employment
law, redundancy, dismissal, contract disputes, sexual, racial
and disability discrimination, and related areas of dispute
which may arise in the workplace. A central registration
unit records all applications and maintains a public register
at Southgate Street, Bury St Edmunds, Suffolk IP33 2AQ.
The tribunals are funded by the Department of Trade and
Industry; administrative support is provided by the
Employment Tribunals Service (*see* page 346).
    Chairmen, who may be full-time or part-time, are legally
qualified. They are appointed by the Lord Chancellor.
Tribunal members are appointed by the Secretary of State
for Trade and Industry.
President, His Hon. Judge Prophet

CENTRAL OFFICE (SCOTLAND)
Eagle Building, 215 Bothwell Street, Glasgow G2 7TS
Tel 0141-204 0730

Tribunals in Scotland have the same remit as those in
England and Wales. Chairmen are appointed by the Lord
President of the Court of Session and lay members by the
Secretary of State for Trade and Industry.
President (£100,209), Mrs D. Littlejohn, CBE

EMPLOYMENT APPEAL TRIBUNAL
Central Office: Audit House, 58 Victoria Embankment, London EC4Y ODS
Tel 0171-273 1041
Divisional Office: 52 Melville Street, Edinburgh EH3 7HF
Tel 0131-225 3963

The Employment Appeal Tribunal hears appeals on a question of law arising from any decision of an employment tribunal. A tribunal consists of a high court judge and two lay members, one from each side of industry. They are appointed by The Queen on the recommendation of the Lord Chancellor and the Secretary of State for Trade and Industry. Administrative support is provided by the Employment Tribunals Service (*see* page 346).
President, The Hon. Mr Justice Lindsay
Scottish Chairman, The Hon. Lord Johnston
Registrar, Miss V. J. Selio

IMMIGRATION APPELLATE AUTHORITIES
Taylor House, 88 Rosebery Avenue, London
EC1R 4QU
Tel 0171-862 4200

The Immigration Appeal Adjudicators hear appeals from immigration decisions concerning the need for, and refusal of, leave to enter or remain in the UK, refusals to grant asylum, decisions to make deportation orders and directions to remove persons subject to immigration control from the UK. The Immigration Appeal Tribunal hears appeals direct from decisions to make deportation orders in matters concerning conduct contrary to the public good, and from refusals to grant asylum. Its principal jurisdiction is, however, the hearing of appeals from adjudicators by the party (Home Office or individual) who is aggrieved by the decision. Appeals are subject to leave being granted by the tribunal.

An adjudicator sits alone. The tribunal sits in divisions of three, normally a legally qualified member and two lay members. Members of the tribunal and adjudicators are appointed by the Lord Chancellor.

IMMIGRATION APPEAL TRIBUNAL
President, The Hon. Mr Justice Collins
Vice-Presidents, Mrs J. Chatwani; A. F. Hatt; M. Rapinet; A. O'Brien-Quinn

IMMIGRATION APPEAL ADJUDICATORS
Chief Adjudicator, His Hon. Judge Dunn, QC
Deputy Chief Adjudicator, J. Latter

INDUSTRIAL TRIBUNALS AND THE FAIR EMPLOYMENT TRIBUNAL (NORTHERN IRELAND)
Long Bridge House, 20–24 Waring Street, Belfast
BT1 2EB
Tel 01232-327666

The industrial tribunal system in Northern Ireland was set up in 1965 and has a similar remit to the employment tribunals in the rest of the UK. There is also in Northern Ireland a Fair Employment Tribunal, which hears and determines individual cases of alleged religious or political discrimination in employment. Employers can appeal to the Fair Employment Tribunal if they consider the directions of the Fair Employment Commission to be

unreasonable, inappropriate or unnecessary, and the Fair Employment Commission can make application to the Tribunal for the enforcement of undertakings or directions with which an employer has not complied.

The president, vice-president and part-time chairmen of the Fair Employment Tribunal are appointed by the Lord Chancellor. The full-time chairman and the part-time chairmen of the industrial tribunals and the panel members to both the industrial tribunals and the Fair Employment Tribunal are appointed by the Department of Economic Development Northern Ireland.
President of the Industrial Tribunals and the Fair Employment Tribunal (£100,209), J. Maguire, CBE
Vice-President of the Industrial Tribunals and the Fair Employment Tribunal, Mrs M. P. Price
Secretary, Mrs P. McVeigh

LANDS TRIBUNAL
48–49 Chancery Lane, London WC2A 1JR
Tel 0171-936 7200

The Lands Tribunal is an independent judicial body which determines questions relating to the valuation of land, rating appeals from valuation tribunals, the discharge or modification of restrictive covenants, and compulsory purchase compensation. The tribunal may also arbitrate under references by consent. The president and members are appointed by the Lord Chancellor.
President, G. R. Bartlett, QC
Members (£92,810), P. H. Clarke, FRICS; N. J. Rose, FRICS; P. R. Francis
Member (part-time), His Hon. Judge Rich, QC
Member (part-time) (£400 a day), A. P. Musto, FRICS
Registrar, C. A. McMullan

LANDS TRIBUNAL FOR SCOTLAND
1 Grosvenor Crescent, Edinburgh EH12 5ER
Tel 0131-225 7996

The Lands Tribunal for Scotland has the same remit as the tribunal for England and Wales but also covers questions relating to tenants' rights. The president is appointed by the Lord President of the Court of Session.
President, The Hon. Lord McGhie, QC
Members (£92,810), J. Devine, FRICS; A. R. MacLeary, FRICS
Members (part-time) (£33,409), Sheriff A. C. Henry; R. A. Edwards, CBE, WS
Clerk, N. M. Tainsh

MENTAL HEALTH REVIEW TRIBUNALS
Secretariat: Health Service Directorate, Room 302A Wellington House, 133–155 Waterloo Road, London SE1 8UG
Tel 0171-972 4503

The Mental Health Review Tribunals are independent judicial bodies which review the cases of patients compulsorily detained under the provisions of the Mental Health Act 1983. They have the power to discharge the patient, to recommend leave of absence, delayed discharge, transfer to another hospital or that a guardianship order be made, to reclassify both restricted and unrestricted patients, and to recommend consideration of a supervision application. There are four tribunals in England, each headed by a regional chairman who is appointed by the Lord Chancellor on a part-time basis. Each tribunal is made up of at least three members, and must include a lawyer, who acts as president (£239 a day), a medical member (£226 a day) and a lay member (£97 a day).

There are five regional offices:

LIVERPOOL, 3rd Floor, Cressington House, 249 St Mary's Road, Garston, Liverpool L19 0NF. Tel: 0151-494 0095

LONDON (NORTH), Spur 3, Block 1, Government Buildings, Honeypot Lane, Stanmore, Middx HA7 1AY. Tel: 0171-972 3734

LONDON (SOUTH), Block 3, Crown Offices, Kingston Bypass Road, Surbiton, Surrey KT6 5QN. Tel: 0181-268 4520

NOTTINGHAM, Spur A, Block 5, Government Buildings, Chalfont Drive, Western Boulevard, Nottingham NG8 3RZ. Tel: 0115-929 4222

WALES, 4th Floor, Crown Buildings, Cathays Park, Cardiff CF1 3NQ. Tel: 01222-825328

NATIONAL HEALTH SERVICE TRIBUNAL

The NHS Tribunal considers representations that the continued inclusion of a doctor, dentist, optician or pharmacist on a health authority's list would be prejudicial to the efficiency of the service concerned. The tribunal sits when required, about eight times a year, and usually in London. The chairman is appointed by the Lord Chancellor and members by the Secretary of State for Health.
Chairman, A. Whitfield, QC
Deputy Chairmen, Miss E. Platt, QC; Dr R. N. Ough
Clerk, I. D. Keith, East Hookers, Twineham, nr Haywards Heath, W. Sussex RH17 5NN. Tel: 01444-881345

NATIONAL HEALTH SERVICE TRIBUNAL (SCOTLAND)
Clerk: 66 Queen Street, Edinburgh EH2 4NE
Tel 0131-226 4771

The tribunal considers representations that the continued inclusion of a doctor, dentist, optometrist or pharmacist on a health board's list would be prejudicial to the efficiency of the service concerned. The tribunal sits when required and is composed of a chairman, one lay member, and one practitioner member drawn from a representative professional panel. The chairman is appointed by the Lord President of the Court of Session, and the lay member and the members of the professional panel are appointed by the First Minister.
Chairman, M. G. Thomson, QC
Lay member, J. D. M. Robertson
Clerk to the Tribunal, D. G. Brash, WS

PENSIONS APPEAL TRIBUNALS

CENTRAL OFFICE (ENGLAND AND WALES)
48–49 Chancery Lane, London WC2A 1JR
Tel 0171-936 7032/3/4

The Pensions Appeal Tribunals are responsible for hearing appeals from ex-servicemen or women and widows who have had their claims for a war pension rejected by the Secretary of State for Social Security. The Entitlement Appeal Tribunals hear appeals in cases where the Secretary of State has refused to grant a war pension. The Assessment Appeal Tribunals hear appeals against the Secretary of State's assessment of the degree of disablement caused by an accepted condition. The tribunal members are appointed by the Lord Chancellor.
President (£74,464), Dr H. M. G. Concannon
Secretary, Miss N. Collins

PENSIONS APPEAL TRIBUNALS FOR SCOTLAND
20 Walker Street, Edinburgh EH3 7HS
Tel 0131-220 1404
President (£298 a day), C. N. McEachran, QC

OFFICE OF THE SOCIAL SECURITY AND CHILD SUPPORT COMMISSIONERS
5th Floor, Newspaper House, 8–16 Great New Street, London EC4A 3BN
Tel 0171-353 5145
23 Melville Street, Edinburgh EH3 7PW
Tel 0131-225 2201

The Social Security Commissioners are the final statutory authority to decide appeals relating to entitlement to social security benefits. The Child Support Commissioners are the final statutory authority to decide appeals relating to child support. Appeals may be made in relation to both matters only on a point of law. The Commissioners' jurisdiction covers England, Wales and Scotland. There are 17 commissioners; they are all qualified lawyers.
Chief Social Security Commissioner and Chief Child Support Commissioner, His Hon. Judge Machin, QC
Secretary, S. Hill (*London*); Mrs M. Watts (*Edinburgh*)

OFFICE OF THE SOCIAL SECURITY COMMISSIONERS AND CHILD SUPPORT COMMISSIONERS FOR NORTHERN IRELAND
Lancashire House, 5 Linenhall Street, Belfast BT2 8AA
Tel 01232-332344

The role of Northern Ireland Social Security Commissioners and Child Support Commissioners is similar to that of the Commissioners in Great Britain. There are two commissioners for Northern Ireland.
Chief Commissioner, His Hon. Judge Martin, QC
Registrar of Appeals, W. D. Pollock

THE SOLICITORS' DISCIPLINARY TRIBUNAL
113 Chancery Lane, London WC2A 1PL
Tel 0171-242 0219

The Solicitors' Disciplinary Tribunal is an independent statutory body whose members are appointed by the Master of the Rolls. The tribunal considers applications made to it alleging either professional misconduct and/or a breach of the statutory rules by which solicitors are bound against an individually named solicitor, former solicitor, registered foreign lawyer, or solicitor's clerk. The president and solicitor members do not receive remuneration.
President, G. B. Marsh
Clerk, Mrs S. C. Elson

THE SCOTTISH SOLICITORS' DISCIPLINE TRIBUNAL
22 Rutland Square, Edinburgh EH1 2BB
Tel 0131-229 5860

The Scottish Solicitors' Discipline Tribunal is an independent statutory body with a panel of 18 members, ten of whom are solicitors; members are appointed by the Lord President of the Court of Session. Its principal function is to consider complaints of misconduct against solicitors in Scotland.
Chairman, J. W. Laughland
Clerk, J. M. Barton, WS

SPECIAL COMMISSIONERS OF INCOME TAX
15–19 Bedford Avenue, London WC1B 3AS
Tel 0171-631 4242

The Special Commissioners are an independent body appointed by the Lord Chancellor to hear complex appeals against decisions of the Board of Inland Revenue and its officials. In addition to the Presiding Special Commissioner there are two full-time and 13 deputy special commissioners; all are legally qualified.
Presiding Special Commissioner, His Hon. Stephen Oliver, QC
Special Commissioners (£92,810), T. H. K. Everett; one vacancy
Clerk, R. P. Lester

SPECIAL IMMIGRATION APPEALS COMMISSION
Taylor House, 88 Rosebery Avenue, London EC1R 4QU
Tel 0171-862 4200

The Commission was set up under the Special Immigration Appeals Commission Act 1998. Its main function is to consider appeals against orders for deportations in cases which involve, in the main, considerations of national security. Members are appointed by the Lord Chancellor.
Chairman, The Hon. Mr Justice Potts
Secretary, Ms P. Dews

TRAFFIC COMMISSIONERS
c/o Scottish Traffic Area, Argyle House, 3 Lady Lawson Street, Edinburgh EH3 9SE
Tel 0131-529 8500

The Traffic Commissioners are responsible for licensing operators of heavy goods and public service vehicles. They also have responsibility for appeals relating to the licensing of operators and for disciplinary cases involving the conduct of drivers of these vehicles. There are six Commissioners in the seven traffic areas covering Britain. Each Traffic Commissioner constitutes a tribunal for the purposes of the Tribunals and Inquiries Act 1971. For Traffic Area Offices and Commissioners, *see* page 299.
Senior Traffic Commissioner (£59,431), M. W. Betts, CBE

TRANSPORT TRIBUNAL
48–49 Chancery Lane, London WC2A 1JR
Tel 0171-936 7493

The Transport Tribunal hears appeals against decisions made by Traffic Commissioners at public inquiries. The tribunal consists of a legally-qualified president, two legal members who may sit as chairmen, and five lay members. The president and legal members are appointed by the Lord Chancellor and the lay members by the Secretary of State for the Environment, Transport and the Regions.
President (part-time), H. B. H. Carlisle, QC
Legal member (part-time) (£290 a day), His Hon. Judge Brodrick
Lay members (£232 a day), D. Yeomans; J. W. Whitworth; Ms P. Steel; P. Rogers; L. Milliken
Secretary, P. J. Fisher

VALUATION TRIBUNALS
c/o Warwickshire Valuation Tribunal, 2nd Floor, Walton House, 11 Parade, Leamington Spa, Warks CV32 4DG
Tel 01926-421875

The Valuation Tribunals hear appeals concerning the council tax, non-domestic rating and land drainage rates in England and Wales, and have residual jurisdiction to hear appeals concerning the community charge, the pre-1990 rating list, disabled rating and mixed hereditaments. There are 56 tribunals in England and eight in Wales; those in England are funded by the Department of the Environment, Transport and the Regions and those in Wales by the National Assembly for Wales. A separate tribunal is constituted for each hearing, and normally consists of a chairman and two other members. Members are appointed by the local authorities and serve on a voluntary basis. A National Association of Valuation Tribunals considers all matters affecting valuations tribunals in England, and the Council of Wales Valuation Tribunals performs the same function in Wales.
President, National Association of Valuation Tribunals, P. Wood
Valuation Tribunals National Officer, B. P. Massen
President, Council of Wales Valuation Tribunals, J. H. Owens

VAT AND DUTIES TRIBUNALS
15–19 Bedford Avenue, London WC1B 3AS
Tel 0171-631 4242

VAT and Duties Tribunals are administered by the Lord Chancellor in England and Wales, and by the First Minister in Scotland. They are independent, and decide disputes between taxpayers and Customs and Excise. In England and Wales, the president and chairmen are appointed by the Lord Chancellor and members by the Treasury. Chairmen in Scotland are appointed by the Lord President of the Court of Session.
President, His Hon. Stephen Oliver, QC
Vice-President, England and Wales (£92,810), A. W. Simpson
Vice-President, Scotland (£92,810), T. G. Coutts, QC
Vice-President, Northern Ireland (£92,810), His Hon. J. McKee, QC
Registrar, R. P. Lester

The Police Service

There are 52 police forces in the United Kingdom, each responsible for policing in its area. Most forces' area is coterminous with one or more local authority areas. Policing in London is carried out by the Metropolitan Police and the City of London Police; in Northern Ireland by the Royal Ulster Constabulary; and by the Isle of Man, States of Jersey, and Guernsey forces in their respective islands and bailiwicks. National services include the National Missing Persons Bureau and the National Crime Squad.

The police authorities of English and Welsh forces comprise local councillors, magistrates and independent members. In Scotland, there are six joint police boards made up of local councillors; the other two police authorities are councils. In London the authority for the Metropolitan Police is the Home Secretary, advised by the Metropolitan Police Committee; for the City of London Police the authority is a committee of the Corporation of London and includes councillors and magistrates. In Northern Ireland the Secretary of State appoints the police authority.

Police authorities are financed by central and local government grants and a precept on the council tax. Subject to the approval of the Home Secretary (in England and Wales) and to regulations, they appoint the chief constable. In England and Wales they are responsible for publishing annual policing plans and annual reports, setting local objectives and a budget, and levying the precept. The police authorities in Scotland are responsible for setting a budget, providing the resources necessary to police the area adequately, appointing officers of the rank of Assistant Chief Constable and above, and determining the number of officers and civilian staff in the force. The structure and responsibilities of the police authority in Northern Ireland are under review.

The Home Secretary, the Secretary of State for Northern Ireland and the Scottish Executive are responsible for the organization, administration and operation of the police service. They make regulations covering matters such as police ranks, discipline, hours of duty, and pay and allowances. All police forces are subject to inspection by HM Inspectors of Constabulary, who report to the Home Secretary, Scottish Executive or Secretary of State for Northern Ireland. In Scotland, a review of the structure of police forces began in April 1998. In Northern Ireland a commission on policing was established by the Belfast Agreement in April 1998. It made recommendations to the Secretary of State in September 1999.

In April 1999 the Home Secretary set targets for recruitment of officers from ethnic minorities for each force in England and Wales to achieve within ten years. From 2000 targets for promotion and retention of these officers will also be set.

COMPLAINTS

The investigation and resolution of a serious complaint against a police officer in England and Wales is subject to the scrutiny of the Police Complaints Authority. An officer who is dismissed, required to resign or reduced in rank, whether as a result of a complaint or not, may appeal to a police appeals tribunal established by the relevant police authority. In Scotland, chief constables are obliged to investigate a complaint against one of their officers; if there is a suggestion of criminal activity, the complaint is investigated by an independent public prosecutor. In Northern Ireland complaints are investigated by the Independent Commission for Police Complaints, which will be replaced by the Police Ombudsman in by April 2000.

BASIC RATES OF PAY
since 1 September 1998

Chief Constable	
No fixed term	£71,058–£101,613
Fixed term appointment	£74,616–£106,569
Assistant Chief Constable – designated Deputy	
No fixed term	80% of their Chief Constable's pay or £68,064, whichever is higher
Fixed term appointment	80% of their Chief Constable's pay or £71,466, whichever is higher
Assistant Chief Constable	
No fixed term	£59,292–£68,064
Fixed term appointment	£62,259–£71,466
Superintendent	£43,143–£53,556
Chief Inspector	£35,454–£38,307
Inspector	£31,719–£36,918
Sergeant	£24,525–£28,605
Constable	£16,056–£25,410
Metropolitan Police	
Metropolitan Commissioner	£121,300–£137,000
Deputy Commissioner	£99,570–£112,509
Assistant Commissioner	£90,036–£99,129
Commander	£59,292–£71,466

The rank of Chief Superintendent was abolished in April 1995. Existing appointments continue and receive the higher ranges of the pay scale for Superintendents
1999 pay negotiations still in progress at time of going to press

THE SPECIAL CONSTABULARY

Each police force has its own special constabulary, made up of volunteers who work in their spare time. Special Constables have full police powers within their force and adjoining force areas, and assist regular officers.

NATIONAL CRIME SQUAD

The National Crime Squad (NCS) was established on 1 April 1998, replacing the six regional crime squads in England and Wales. It investigates national and international organized and serious crime. It also supports police forces investigating serious crime. The squad is accountable to the National Crime Squad Service Authority.
Headquarters: PO Box 2500, London
SW1V 2WF. Tel: 0171-238 2500
Director General, Roy Penrose, OBE, QPM

NCS SERVICE AUTHORITY

The Service Authority is responsible for ensuring the effective operation of the National Crime Squad. It fulfills a similar role to a police authority. It works alongside the National Criminal Intelligence Service Service Authority. There are 26 members, of whom the chairman and nine others serve as 'core members' on both authorities.

Headquarters: PO Box 2600, London SW1V 2WG. Tel: 0171-238 2600
Chairman, Rt. Hon. Sir John Wheeler
Clerk, T. Simmons
Treasurer, P. Derrick

NATIONAL MISSING PERSONS BUREAU

The Police National Missing Persons Bureau (PNMPB) acts as a central clearing house of information, receiving reports about vulnerable missing persons that are still outstanding after 28 days and details of unidentified persons or remains within 48 hours of being found from all forces in England and Wales. Reports are also received from Scottish police forces, the RUC, and foreign police forces via Interpol.
Headquarters: New Scotland Yard, Broadway, London SW1H 0BG. Tel: 0171-230 1212
Director, C. J. Coombes

POLICE INFORMATION TECHNOLOGY ORGANIZATION

The Police Information Technology Organization (PITO) became a non-departmental public body on 1 April 1998. It develops and manages the delivery of national police information technology services, such as the Police National Computer, co-ordinates the development of local information technology systems where common standards and systems are needed, and provides a procurement service.
Headquarters: Horseferry House, Dean Ryle Street, London SW1P 2AW. Tel: 0181-358 5497
Chairman, Sir Trefor Morris
Chief Executive, vacant

FORENSIC SCIENCE SERVICE

The Forensic Science Service (FSS) provides forensic science support to the police forces in England and Wales for the investigation of scenes of crime, scientific analysis of material, and interpretation of scientific results. The FSS is organized into serious crime, volume crime, drugs and specialist services, supported by intelligence and consultancy services. Laboratories are located at Birmingham., Chepstow, Chorley, Huntingdon, London and Wetherby.
Headquarters: Priory House, Gooch Street North, Birmingham B5 6QQ. Tel: 0121-607 6800
Chief Executive, Dr J. Thompson

POLICE FORCES AND AUTHORITIES

Strength: actual strength of force as at mid 1999
Chair: chairman/convener of the police authority/police committee/joint police board

ENGLAND

AVON AND SOMERSET CONSTABULARY, *HQ,* PO Box 37, Valley Road, Portishead, Bristol BS20 8QJ. Tel: 01275-818181. *Strength,* 3,016; *Chief Constable,* S. Pilkington, QPM; *Chair,* J. Cristenson
BEDFORDSHIRE POLICE, *HQ,* Woburn Road, Kempston, Bedford MK43 9AX. Tel: 01234-841212. *Strength,* 1,054; *Chief Constable,* M. O'Byrne, QPM; *Chair,* A. Heffernan
CAMBRIDGESHIRE CONSTABULARY, *HQ,* Hinchingbrooke Park, Huntingdon, Cambs PE18 8NP. Tel: 01480-456111. *Strength,* 1,295; *Chief Constable,* D. G. Gunn, QPM; *Chair,* J. Reynolds
CHESHIRE CONSTABULARY, *HQ,* Nuns Road, Chester CH1 2PP. Tel: 01244-350000. *Strength,* 2,053; *Chief Constable,* N. Burgess, QPM; *Chair,* Mrs M. Chapman

CLEVELAND POLICE, *HQ,* PO Box 70, Ladgate Lane, Middlesbrough TS8 9EH. Tel: 01642-326326. *Strength,* 1,400 *Chief Constable,* B. D. D. Shaw, QPM; *Chair,* K. Walker
CUMBRIA CONSTABULARY, *HQ,* Carleton Hall, Penrith, Cumbria CA10 2AU. Tel: 01768-891999. *Strength,* 1,118; *Chief Constable,* C. Phillips, QPM; *Chair,* R. Watson
DERBYSHIRE CONSTABULARY, *HQ,* Butterley Hall, Ripley, Derbyshire DE5 3RS. Tel: 01773-570100. *Strength,* 1,770; *Chief Constable,* J. F. Newing, CBE, QPM; *Chair,* K. Wilkinson
DEVON AND CORNWALL CONSTABULARY, *HQ,* Middlemoor, Exeter EX2 7HQ. Tel: 0990-777444. *Strength,* 2,871; *Chief Constable,* J. S. Evans, QPM; *Chair,* O. May
DORSET POLICE FORCE, *HQ,* Winfrith, Dorchester, Dorset DT2 8DZ. Tel: 01929-462727. *Strength,* 1,284; *Chief Constable,* Mrs J. Stichbury; *Chair,* P. I. Jones
DURHAM CONSTABULARY, *HQ,* Aykley Heads, Durham DH1 5TT. Tel: 0191-386 4929. *Strength,* 1,570; *Chief Constable,* G. Hedges, QPM; *Chair,* J. Knox
ESSEX POLICE, *HQ,* PO Box 2, Springfield, Chelmsford CM2 6DA. Tel: 01245-491491. *Strength,* 2,928; *Chief Constable,* D. F. Stevens, QPM; *Chair,* E. A. Peel
GLOUCESTERSHIRE CONSTABULARY, *HQ,* Holland House, Lansdown Road, Cheltenham, Glos GL51 6QH. Tel: 01242-521321. *Strength,* 1,122; *Chief Constable,* A. J. P. Butler, QPM; *Chair,* Brig. M. A. Browne, CBE
GREATER MANCHESTER POLICE, *HQ,* PO Box 22 (S. West PDO), Chester House, Boyer Street, Manchester M16 0RE. Tel: 0161-872 5050. *Strength,* 6,840; *Chief Constable,* D. Wilmot, QPM; *Chair,* S. Murphy
HAMPSHIRE CONSTABULARY, *HQ,* West Hill, Winchester, Hants SO22 5DB. Tel: 01962-841500. *Strength,* 3,468; *Chief Constable,* Sir John Hoddinott, CBE, QPM; *Chair,* W. H. Wheeler
HERTFORDSHIRE CONSTABULARY, *HQ,* Stanborough Road, Welwyn Garden City, Herts AL8 6XF. Tel: 01707-354200. *Strength,* 1,767; *Chief Constable,* P. Sharpe, QPM; *Chair,* P. Holland
HUMBERSIDE POLICE, *HQ,* Queens Gardens, Kingston upon Hull HU1 3DJ. Tel: 01482-326111. *Strength,* 1,975; *Chief Constable,* D. Westwood; *Chair,* K. Townsend
KENT CONSTABULARY, *HQ,* Sutton Road, Maidstone, Kent ME15 9BZ. Tel: 01622-690690. *Strength,* 3,300; *Chief Constable,* J. D.Phillips, QPM; *Chair,* Mrs P. F. Stubbs
LANCASHIRE CONSTABULARY, *HQ,* PO Box 77, Hutton, Preston, Lancs PR4 5SB. Tel: 01772-614444. *Strength,* 3,299; *Chief Constable,* Mrs P. A. Clare, QPM; *Chair,* Dr R. B. Henig
LEICESTERSHIRE CONSTABULARY, *HQ,* St Johns, Narborough, Leicester LE9 5BX. Tel: 0116-222 2222. *Strength,* 1,896; *Chief Constable,* D. J. Wyrko, QPM; *Chair,* D. J. Saville
LINCOLNSHIRE POLICE, *HQ,* PO Box 999, Lincoln LN5 7PH. Tel: 01522-532222. *Strength,* 1,139; *Chief Constable,* R. J. N. Childs, QPM; *Chair,* M. D. Kennedy
MERSEYSIDE POLICE, *HQ,* PO Box 59, Canning Place, Liverpool L69 1JD. Tel: 0151-709 6010. *Strength,* 4,211; *Chief Constable,* N. Bettison; *Chair,* Ms C. Gustafson
NORFOLK CONSTABULARY, *HQ,* Martineau Lane, Norwich NR1 2DJ. Tel: 01603-768769. *Strength,* 1,394; *Chief Constable,* K. R. Williams, QPM; *Chair,* B. J. Landale
NORTHAMPTONSHIRE POLICE, *HQ,* Wootton Hall, Northampton NN4 0JQ. Tel: 01604-700700. *Strength,* 1,150; *Chief Constable,* C. Fox, QPM; *Chair,* Dr M. Dickie
NORTHUMBRIA POLICE, *HQ,* Ponteland, Newcastle upon Tyne NE20 0BL. Tel: 01661-872555. *Strength,* 3,800; *Chief Constable,* C. Strachan, QPM; *Chair,* G. Gill

NORTH YORKSHIRE POLICE, *HQ,* Newby Wiske Hall, Newby Wiske, Northallerton, N. Yorks DL7 9HA. Tel: 01609-783131. *Strength,* 1,353; *Chief Constable,* D. R. Kenworthy, QPM; *Chair,* Mrs A. F. Harris

NOTTINGHAMSHIRE POLICE, *HQ,* Sherwood Lodge, Arnold, Nottingham NG5 8PP. Tel: 0115-967 0999. *Strength,* 2,234; *Chief Constable,* C. F. Bailey, QPM; *Chair,* R. A. Hassett

SOUTH YORKSHIRE POLICE, *HQ,* Snig Hill, Sheffield S3 8LY. Tel: 0114-220 2020. *Strength,* 3,195; *Chief Constable,* M. Hedges; *Chair,* C. Swindell

STAFFORDSHIRE POLICE, *HQ,* Cannock Road, Stafford ST17 0QG. Tel: 01785-257717. *Strength,* 2,255; *Chief Constable,* J. W. Giffard, QPM; *Chair,* J. T. Meir

SUFFOLK CONSTABULARY, *HQ,* Martlesham Heath, Ipswich IP5 3QS. Tel: 01473-613500. *Strength,* 1,185; *Chief Constable,* P. J. Scott-Lee, QPM; *Chair,* M. N. Smith

SURREY POLICE, *HQ,* Mount Browne, Sandy Lane, Guildford, Surrey GU3 1HG. Tel: 01483-571212. *Strength,* 1,690; *Chief Constable,* I. Blair, QPM; *Chair,* A. Peirce

SUSSEX POLICE, *HQ,* Malling House, Church Lane, Lewes, E. Sussex BN7 2DZ. Tel: 0845-6070999. *Strength,* 3,038; *Chief Constable,* P. Whitehouse, QPM; *Chair,* K. C. Bodfish

THAMES VALLEY POLICE, *HQ,* Oxford Road, Kidlington, Oxon OX5 2NX. Tel: 01865-846000. *Strength,* 3,800; *Chief Constable,* C. Pollard, QPM; *Chair,* G. Maybury

WARWICKSHIRE CONSTABULARY, *HQ,* PO Box 4, Leek Wootton, Warwick CV35 7QB. Tel: 01926-415000. *Strength,* 923; *Chief Constable,* A. C. Timpson; *Chair,* J. Rennie

WEST MERCIA CONSTABULARY, *HQ,* Hindlip Hall, PO Box 55, Hindlip, Worcester WR3 8SP. Tel: 01905-723000. *Strength,* 2,007; *Chief Constable,* P. Hampson, QPM; *Chair,* D. B. Watkins

WEST MIDLANDS POLICE, *HQ,* PO Box 52, Lloyd House, Colmore Circus, Queensway, Birmingham B4 6NQ. Tel: 0121-626 5000. *Strength,* 7,322; *Chief Constable,* E. Crew, QPM; *Chair,* R. Jones

WEST YORKSHIRE POLICE, *HQ,* PO Box 9, Laburnum Road, Wakefield, W. Yorks WF1 3QP. Tel: 01924-375222. *Strength,* 4,982; *Chief Constable,* G. Moore, QPM; *Chair,* N. Taggart

WILTSHIRE CONSTABULARY, *HQ,* London Road, Devizes, Wilts SN10 2DN. Tel: 01380-722341. *Strength,* 1,085; *Chief Constable,* Miss E. Neville, QPM, PH.D.; *Chair,* H. A. Woolnough

WALES

DYFED-POWYS POLICE, *HQ,* PO Box 99, Llangunnor, Carmarthen SA31 2PF. Tel: 01267-222020. *Strength,* 1,021; *Chief Constable,* R. White, CBE, QPM; *Chair,* Ms M. Roberts

GWENT POLICE, *HQ,* Croesyceiliog, Cwmbran NP44 2XJ. Tel: 01633-838111. *Strength,* 1,200; *Chief Constable (acting),* K. Turner; *Chair,* D. Turnbull

NORTH WALES POLICE, *HQ,* Glan-y-don, Colwyn Bay, Conwy LL29 8AW. Tel: 01492-517171. *Strength,* 1,414; *Chief Constable,* M. J. Argent, QPM; *Chair,* J. Anderson, OBE

SOUTH WALES POLICE, *HQ,* Cowbridge Road, Bridgend CF31 3SU. Tel: 01656-655555. *Strength,* 2,999; *Chief Constable,* A. T. Burden, QPM; *Chair,* R. Thomas

SCOTLAND

CENTRAL SCOTLAND POLICE, *HQ,* Randolphfield, Stirling FK8 2HD. Tel: 01786-456000. *Strength,* 713; *Chief Constable,* W. J. M. Wilson, QPM; *Convener,* I. Miller

DUMFRIES AND GALLOWAY CONSTABULARY, *HQ,* Cornwall Mount, Dumfries DG1 1PZ. Tel: 01387-252112. *Strength,* 439; *Chief Constable,* W. Rae, QPM; *Chair,* B. Conchie

FIFE CONSTABULARY, *HQ,* Detroit Road, Glenrothes, Fife KY6 2RJ. Tel: 01592-418888. *Strength,* 840; *Chief Constable,* J. P. Hamilton, QPM; *Chair,* A. Keddie

GRAMPIAN POLICE, *HQ,* Queen Street, Aberdeen AB10 1ZA. Tel: 01224-386000. *Strength,* 1,220; *Chief Constable,* A. G. Brown, QPM; *Chair,* Ms M. Stewart

LOTHIAN AND BORDERS POLICE, *HQ,* Fettes Avenue, Edinburgh EH4 1RB. Tel: 0131-311 3131. *Strength,* 2,615; *Chief Constable,* Sir R. Cameron, QPM; *Convenor,* Ms L. Hinds

NORTHERN CONSTABULARY, *HQ,* Old Perth Road, Inverness IV2 3SY. Tel: 01463-715555. *Strength,* 659; *Chief Constable,* W. A. Robertson, QPM; *Chair,* Mrs J. Home

STRATHCLYDE POLICE, *HQ,* 173 Pitt Street, Glasgow G2 4JS. Tel: 0141-532 2000. *Strength,* 7,008; *Chief Constable,* J. Orr, OBE, QPM; *Chair,* W. Timoney

TAYSIDE POLICE, *HQ,* PO Box 59, West Bell Street, Dundee DD1 9JU. Tel: 01382-223200. *Strength,* 1,150; *Chief Constable,* W. A. Spence, QPM; *Chair,* J. Corrigan

NORTHERN IRELAND

ROYAL ULSTER CONSTABULARY, *HQ,* Brooklyn, Knock Road, Belfast BT5 6LD. Tel: 01232-650222. *Strength,* 8,450; *Chief Constable,* Sir Ronald Flanagan, OBE; *Chair,* P. Armstrong

ISLANDS

ISLAND POLICE FORCE, *HQ,* Hospital Lane, St Peter Port, Guernsey GY1 2QN. Tel: 01481-725111. *Strength,* 147; *Chief Officer,* M. H. Wyeth; *President, States Committee for Home Affairs,* M. W. Torode

STATES OF JERSEY POLICE, *HQ,* Rouge Bouillon, PO Box 789, St Helier, Jersey JE4 8ZD. Tel: 01534-612612. *Strength,* 241; *Chief Officer,* R. H. Le Breton; *President, Defence Committee,* M. Wavell

ISLE OF MAN CONSTABULARY, *HQ,* Glencrutchery Road, Douglas, Isle of Man IM2 4RG. Tel: 01624-631212. *Strength,* 226; *Chief Constable,* R. E. N. Oake, QPM; *Chairman, Police Committee,* Hon. A. R. Bell

---

METROPOLITAN POLICE SERVICE
New Scotland Yard, Broadway, London SW1H 0BG
Tel 0171-230 1212

Establishment, 26,425

Commissioner, (until January 2000) Sir Paul Condon, QPM; (from January 2000) J. Stevens, QPM
Deputy Commissioner (until January 2000), J. Stevens, QPM
Receiver, P. Fletcher
Chair, Sir John Quinton

OPERATIONAL AREAS
Assistant Commissioners, A. Dunn, QPM (*North London*); P. A. Manning, QPM (*Realignment Programme*); W. I. R. Johnston, QPM (*Central London*); D. F. O'Connor, QPM (*South London*)
Deputy Assistant Commissioner, R. Clark, QPM; D. Flanders, QPM; J. G. D. Grieve, QPM; W. I. Griffiths, BEM, QPM; J. Townsend, QPM; A. S. Trotter; B. Wilding; M. Todd

Commanders, M. Briggs, QPM; M. R. Campbell; P. J. Clarke; M. Craik; D. N. Croll, QPM; R. Culzen; R. Currie, QPM; R. Gaspar; P. C. Hagen; A. C. Hayman; C. A. Howlett; G. P. James; D. M. T. Kendrick, OBE, QPM; T. D. Laidlaw, LVO, QPM; M. Messinger; S. C. Pilkington; D. A. Ray, QPM; S. Roberts; A. L. Rowe, QPM; A. G. Shave; D. L. Smith;

SPECIALIST OPERATIONS DEPARTMENT
Assistant Commissioner, D. C. Veness, QPM
Deputy Assistant Commissioner, A. G. Fry, QPM
Commanders, B. G. Moss, QPM; N. G. Mulvihill, QPM; R. C. Pearce

COMPLAINTS INVESTIGATION BUREAU
Commander, I. G. Quinn, QPM

INSPECTORATE
Commander, B. J. Luckhurst, QPM

OTHER DEPARTMENTS
Director, Strategic Co-ordination, Commander T. C. Lloyd, QPM
Director, Personnel, Mrs P. Woods
Director, Consultancy and Information Services, Mrs S. Merchant
Director, Public Affairs, R. Fedorcio
Solicitor, D. Hamilton
Director, Technology, N. Boothman
Director, Property Services, T. G. Lawrence

CITY OF LONDON POLICE
26 Old Jewry, London EC2R 8DJ
Tel 0171-601 2222

Strength, 778
The City of London Police is responsible for policing the City of London. Though small, the area includes one of the most important financial centres in the world and the force has particular expertise in areas such as fraud investigation as well as the areas required of any police force.

The force has a wholly elected police authority, the police committee of the Corporation of London, which appoints the Commissioner.
Commissioner (£99,129), P. Nove, QPM
Assistant Commissioner (acting) (£79,302), J. Hart, QPM
Commander (acting) (£71,466), J. Davison
Chairman of Police Committee, L. St J. T. Jackson

BRITISH TRANSPORT POLICE
15 Tavistock Place, London WC1H 9SJ
Tel 0171-388 7541

Strength (March 1999), 2,106
British Transport Police is the national police force for the railways in England, Wales and Scotland, including the London Underground system, the Docklands Light Railway and the Midland Metro Tram system. The Chief Constable reports to the British Transport Police Committee. The members of the Committee are appointed by the British Railways Board and include representatives of Railtrack and London Underground Ltd as well as independent members. Officers are paid the same as other police forces.
Chief Constable, D. J. Williams, QPM
Deputy Chief Constable, A. Parker, QPM

MINISTRY OF DEFENCE POLICE
MDP Wethersfield, Braintree, Essex CM7 4AZ
Tel 01371-854000

Strength (March 1999), 3,577
The Ministry of Defence Police is an agency of the Ministry of Defence. It is a national civilian police force whose officers are appointed by the Secretary of State for Defence. It is responsible for the policing of all military land, stations and establishments in the United Kingdom. The agency also has certain responsibilities for the civilian Ministry of Defence Guard Service.
Chief Constable, W. E. E. Boreham, OBE
Deputy Chief Constable, A. V. Comben
Head of Secretariat, P. A. Crowther

ROYAL PARKS CONSTABULARY
The Old Police House, Hyde Park, London W2 2UH
Tel 0171-298 2000

Strength (July 1999), 155
The Royal Parks Constabulary is maintained by the Royal Parks Agency, an executive agency of the Department for Culture, Media and Sport, and is responsible for the policing of eight royal parks in and around London. These comprise an area in excess of 6,300 acres. Officers of the force are appointed under the Parks Regulations Act 1872 as amended and are paid around 85 per cent of the Metropolitan Police rate.
Chief Officer, W. Ross, OBE
Deputy Chief Officer, A. McLean

UK ATOMIC ENERGY AUTHORITY CONSTABULARY
Building E6, Culham Science Centre, Abingdon, Oxon OX14 3DB
Tel 01235-463760

Strength (June 1999), 498
The Constabulary is responsible for policing UK Atomic Energy Authority and British Nuclear Fuels PLC establishments and for escorting nuclear material between establishments. The Chief Constable is responsible, through the Atomic Energy Authority Police Authority, to the President of the Board of Trade. Officers are paid around 95 per cent of the rate paid to other police forces.
Chief Constable, W. F. Pryke
Assistant Chief Constable, P. P. Crossan

STAFF ASSOCIATIONS

Police officers are not permitted to join a trade union or to take strike action. All ranks have their own staff associations.
ASSOCIATION OF CHIEF POLICE OFFICERS OF ENGLAND, WALES AND NORTHERN IRELAND, 7th Floor, 25 Victoria Street, London SW1H 0EX. Tel: 0171-227 3434. Represents Chief Constables, Deputy and Assistant Chief Constables in England, Wales and Northern Ireland; officers of the rank of Commander and above in the Metropolitan and City of London Police and senior civilian members of these forces.
General Secretary, Miss M. C. E. Barton, OBE

THE POLICE SUPERINTENDENTS' ASSOCIATION OF
ENGLAND AND WALES, 67A Reading Road,
Pangbourne, Reading RG8 7JD. Tel: 0118-984 4005.
Represents officers of the rank of Superintendent.
Secretary, Supt. P. Williams

THE POLICE FEDERATION OF ENGLAND AND WALES,
15–17 Langley Road, Surbiton, Surrey KT6 6LP. Tel:
0181-399 2224. Represents officers up to and including
the rank of Chief Inspector. *General Secretary*, J. Moseley

ASSOCIATION OF CHIEF POLICE OFFICERS IN
SCOTLAND, Police Headquarters, Fettes Avenue,
Edinburgh EH4 IRB. Tel: 0131-311 3051. Represents the
Chief Constables, Deputy and Assistant Chief
Constables of the Scottish police forces. *Hon. Secretary*,
H. R. Cameron, QPM

THE ASSOCIATION OF SCOTTISH POLICE
SUPERINTENDENTS, Secretariat, 173 Pitt Street,
Glasgow G2 4JS. Tel: 0141-221 5796. Represents officers
of the rank of Superintendent. *President*, Chief Supt. S.
Davidson

THE SCOTTISH POLICE FEDERATION, 5 Woodside
Place, Glasgow G3 7QF. Tel: 0141-332 5234. Represents
officers up to and including the rank of Chief Inspector.
General Secretary, D. J. Keil, QPM

THE SUPERINTENDENTS' ASSOCIATION OF
NORTHERN IRELAND, RUC Training Centre,
Garnerville Road, Belfast BT4 2NX. Tel: 01232-700660.
Represents Superintendents and Chief Superintendents
in the RUC. *Hon. Secretary*, Supt. W. T. Brown

THE POLICE FEDERATION FOR NORTHERN IRELAND,
Royal Ulster Constabulary, Garnerville, Garnerville
Road, Belfast BT4 2NX. Tel: 01232-760831. Represents
officers up to and including the rank of Chief Inspector.
Secretary, D. A. McClurg

POLICE STRENGTHS 1999

	Male	Female	Total
ENGLAND AND WALES p			
Total officers	105,973	20,123	126,096
Ethnic minority officers	2,016	529	2,545
Special constables	10,860	5,624	16,484
Civilians	20,441	32,590	53,031
SCOTLAND*			
Officers	12,762	2,226	14,988
Special constables	–	–	1,723
Support staff	–	–	4,670
NORTHERN IRELAND			
Officers	7,512	957	8,469
Special constables	785	424	1,209
Civilians	1,192	2,314	3,506

p provisional
* Figures for Scotland as at 31 March 1998
Sources: Home Office; Scottish Office; RUC

The Prison Service

The prison services in the United Kingdom are the responsibility of the Home Secretary, the Scottish Executive Justice Department and the Secretary of State for Northern Ireland. The chief executive officers of the Prison Service, the Scottish Prison Service and the Northern Ireland Prison Service are responsible for the day-to-day running of the system.

There are 135 prison establishments (136 from December 1999) in England and Wales, 23 in Scotland and four in Northern Ireland. Convicted prisoners are classified according to their assessed security risk and are housed in establishments appropriate to that level of security. There are no open prisons in Northern Ireland. Female prisoners are housed in women's establishments or in separate wings of mixed prisons. Remand prisoners are, where possible, housed separately from convicted prisoners. Offenders under the age of 21 are usually detained in a young offenders' institution, which may be a separate establishment or part of a prison.

Seven prisons are now run by the private sector, and in England and Wales all escort services have been contracted out to private companies. Four prisons are being built and financed under the Private Finance Initiative and will also be run by private contractors. In Scotland, one prison (Kilmarnock) was built and financed by the private sector and is being operated by private contractors.

There are independent prison inspectorates in England and Wales (*see* page 310) and Scotland (*see* page 339) which report annually on conditions and the treatment of prisoners. HM Chief Inspector of Prisons for England and Wales also performs an inspectorate role for prisons in Northern Ireland. Every prison establishment also has an independent board of visitors or visiting committee made up of local volunteers. Any prisoner whose complaint is not satisfied by the internal complaints procedures may complain to the Prisons Ombudsman for England and Wales (*see* page 331) or the Scottish Prisons Complaints Commission (*see* page 340). There is no Prisons Ombudsman for Northern Ireland, but complaints by prisoners regarding maladministration may be made to the Parliamentary Commissioner for Administration (*see* page 329).

AVERAGE PRISON POPULATION 1998–9 (UK)

	Remand	Sentenced	Other
ENGLAND AND WALES*			
Male	11,900	49,700	—
Female	700	2,400	—
Total	12,600	52,100	600
SCOTLAND			
Male	n/a	n/a	—
Female	n/a	n/a	—
Total	971	5,057	—
N. IRELAND			
Male	340	1,028	9
Female	9	15	1
Total	349	1,043	10
UK TOTAL	13,920	58,200	610

* 1998 figures

The projected prison population for 2006 in England and Wales is 66,700 if custody rates and sentence lengths remain at 1998 levels

Sources: Home Office – *Statistical Bulletin 1/99*; Scottish Prison Service – *Annual Report and Accounts 1998–9*; Northern Ireland Prison Service – *Annual Report 1998–9*

SENTENCED PRISON POPULATION BY SEX AND OFFENCE (ENGLAND AND WALES)
as at June 1997

	Male	Female
Violence against the person	9,836	387
Sexual offences	3,973	9
Burglary	7,642	96
Robbery	6,069	154
Theft, handling, fraud and forgery	5,068	453
Drugs offences	6,309	675
Other offences	5,242	193
Offence not known	2,599	100
Total	46,739	2,066

Source: Home Office – *Statistical Bulletin 5/98*

AVERAGE SENTENCED POPULATION BY LENGTH OF SENTENCE 1997 (ENGLAND AND WALES)

	Adults	Young Offenders
Up to 18 months	9,724	3,267
18 months–4 years	10,777	3,019
Over 4 years	19,950	1,534
Total	40,451	7,820

Source: HMSO – *Annual Abstract of Statistics 1999*

AVERAGE DAILY SENTENCED POPULATION BY LENGTH OF SENTENCE 1998–9 (SCOTLAND)

	Adults	Young Offenders
Less than 4 years	2,036	518
4 years or over (including life)	2,312	191
Total	4,348	710

Source: Scottish Prison Service – *Annual Report and Accounts 1998–9*

PRISON SUICIDES 1998–9 (ENGLAND AND WALES)

Adults	71
Young offenders	11
Total	82

Source: HM Prison Service – *Annual Report and Accounts 1998–9*

AVERAGE NUMBER OF PRISON SERVICE STAFF 1998–9 (GREAT BRITAIN)

	England and Wales	Scotland
No. of prison service staff	41,196	4,974

Sources: HM Prison Service – *Annual Report and Accounts 1998–9*; Scottish Prison Service – *Annual Report and Accounts 1998–9*

OPERATING COSTS OF PRISON SERVICE IN ENGLAND AND WALES 1998–9

	£ million
Staff costs	995.2
Other operating costs	859.0
Operating income	(16.8)
Net operating costs before notional charge on capital employed	1,837.4
Charge on capital employed	251.7
Net operating costs	2,089.1
Average cost per prisoner place (reflecting establishment costs only)	£22,649

Source: HM Prison Service – *Annual Report and Accounts 1998–9*

OPERATING COSTS OF SCOTTISH PRISON SERVICE
1998–9

	£
Total income	1,996,000
Total expenditure	183,137,000
Staff costs	119,760,000
Running costs	45,284,000
Other current expenditure	18,093,000
Operating deficit	(181,141,000)
Cost of capital charges	(22,925,000)
Interest payable and similar charges	(14,000)
Interest receivable	105,000
Deficit for financial year	(203,975,000)
Average annual cost per prisoner per place	£26,912

Source: Scottish Prison Service – *Annual Report and Accounts 1998–9*

OPERATING COSTS OF NORTHERN IRELAND PRISON
SERVICE 1998–9

	£
Custodial	117,975,548
Non-custodial	5,489,720
Headquarters	7,269,975
Total	130,735,243
Average annual cost per prisoner place	73,612

Source: Northern Ireland Prison Service

THE PRISON SERVICES

HM PRISON SERVICE

Cleland House, Page Street, London SW1P 4LN
Tel 0171-217 6000; Fax 0171-217 6403
SALARIES 1998–9

Governor 1	£52,349–£54,156
Governor 2	£47,270–£48,721
Governor 3	£40,823–£41,977
Governor 4	£34,233–£36,055
Governor 5	£29,596–£32,295

For civil service salaries, *see* page 276

THE PRISON SERVICE STRATEGY BOARD

Chairman, The Rt. Hon. Paul Boateng, MP (*Home Office minister for prisons and probation*)
Director-General (*SCS*), M. Narey
 Private Secretary, Ms R. Goodwin
 Staff Officer, J. Heavens
Deputy Director-General (*SCS*), P. Wheatley
Director of High Security Prisons (*SCS*), B. Clark
Director of Security (*SCS*), Ms E. Bailey
Director of Personnel (*SCS*), G. Hadley
Director of Finance (*SCS*), J. Le Vay
Director of Corporate Affairs (*SCS*), Ms C. Pelham
Director of Regimes (*SCS*), K. D. Sutton
Director of Health Care (*SCS*), Dr M. Longfield (until end 1999)
Non-Executive Members, Sir Duncan Nichol, CBE; Mrs R. Thomson, CBE; Mrs P. A. Clare, QPM; P. Carter
Board Secretary and Head of Secretariat, Ms C. Checksfield
Chaplain-General and Archdeacon of the Prison Service, Ven. D. Fleming
Senior Roman Catholic Chaplain, Mgr J. Branson

AREA MANAGERS (*SCS*)

Central, J. Dring; *East Midlands,* M. Egan; *Kent,* T. Murtagh, OBE; *London North and East Anglia,* I. Ward; *London South,* P. Atherton; *Mercia,* D. Curtis; *Mersey and Manchester,* A. Fitzpatrick; *North-East,* R. Mitchell; *North-West,* D. I. Lockwood; *South Coast,* A. Smith; *Wales and the West,* J. May; *Yorkshire,* P. Earnshaw

PRISON ESTABLISHMENTS

CNA Average number of in use certified normal accommodation places without overcrowding 1998–9
Prisoners/Young Offenders Average number of prisoners/young offenders 1998–9

ACKLINGTON, Morpeth, Northumberland NE65 9XH. *CNA,* 662. *Prisoners,* 631. *Governor,* Ms H. Banks
ALBANY, Newport, Isle of Wight PO30 5RS. *CNA,* 436. *Prisoners,* 429. *Governor,* K. Munns
ALTCOURSE (private prison), Higher Lane, Fazakerley, Liverpool L9 7AG. *CNA,* 600. *Prisoners,* 669. *Director,* W. MacGowan
†‡ASHFIELD (from December 1999), Shortwood Road, Pucklechurch, Bristol BS16 9QT. *CNA,* 400. *Director,* N. Pascoe
ASHWELL, Oakham, Leics LE15 7LF. *CNA,* 484. *Prisoners,* 491. *Governor,* C. Bushell
*‡ASKHAM GRANGE, Askham Richard, York YO2 3PT. *CNA,* 130. *Prisoners and Young Offenders,* 121. *Governor,* H. E. Crew
‡AYLESBURY, Bierton Road, Aylesbury, Bucks HP20 1EH. *CNA,* 433. *Young Offenders,* 443. *Governor,* S. Bryans
BEDFORD, St Loyes Street, Bedford MK40 1HG. *CNA,* 352. *Prisoners,* 400. *Governor,* T. Ireson
†BELMARSH, Western Way, Thamesmead, London SE28 0EB. *CNA,* 843. *Prisoners,* 788. *Governor,* W. S. Duff
BIRMINGHAM, Winson Green Road, Birmingham B18 4AS. *CNA,* 734. *Prisoners,* 1,100. *Governor,* C. Scott, OBE
BLAKENHURST (private prison), Hewell Lane, Redditch, Worcs B97 6QS. *CNA,* 647. *Prisoners,* 850. *Director,* P. Siddons
BLANTYRE HOUSE, Goudhurst, Cranbrook, Kent TN17 2NH. *CNA,* 120. *Prisoners,* 120. *Governor,* E. McLennan-Murray
BLUNDESTON, Lowestoft, Suffolk NR32 5BG. *CNA,* 352. *Prisoners,* 385. *Governor,* S. Robinson
†‡BRINSFORD, New Road, Featherstone, Wolverhampton WV10 7PY. *CNA,* 477. *Young Offenders,* 509. *Governor,* C. Davidson
BRISTOL, Cambridge Road, Bristol BS7 8PS. *CNA,* 487. *Prisoners,* 602. *Governor,* N. Wall
BRIXTON, PO Box 369, Jebb Avenue, London SW2 5XF. *CNA,* 693. *Prisoners,* 659. *Governor,* R. Chapman
*†‡BROCKHILL, Redditch, Worcs B97 6RD. *CNA,* 159. *Prisoners and Young Offenders,* 159. *Governor,* V. Bird
BUCKLEY HALL (private prison), Buckley Farm Lane, Rochdale, Lancs OL12 9DP. *CNA,* 350. *Prisoners,* 382. *Director,* S. Mitson
BULLINGDON, PO Box 50, Bicester, Oxon OX6 0PR. *CNA,* 773. *Prisoners,* 897. *Governor,* J. Cann
*‡BULLWOOD HALL, High Road, Hockley, Essex SS5 4TE. *CNA,* 140. *Prisoners and Young Offenders,* 140. *Governor,* Mrs V. Hart
CAMP HILL, Newport, Isle of Wight PO30 5PB. *CNA,* 460. *Prisoners,* 472. *Governor,* W. Preston
CANTERBURY, 46 Longport, Canterbury CT1 1PJ. *CNA,* 196. *Prisoners,* 283. *Governor,* Ms J. Galbally
†‡CARDIFF, Knox Road, Cardiff CF2 1UG. *CNA,* 525. *Prisoners and Young Offenders,* 722. *Governor,* J. Thomas-Ferrand
‡CASTINGTON, Morpeth, Northumberland NE65 9XG. *CNA,* 450. *Young Offenders,* 398. *Governor,* M. Lees
CHANNINGS WOOD, Denbury, Newton Abbott, Devon TQ12 6DW. *CNA,* 594. *Prisoners,* 615. *Governor,* R. Mullen
†‡CHELMSFORD, 200 Springfield Road, Chelmsford, Essex CM2 6LQ. *CNA,* 388. *Prisoners and Young Offenders,* 409. *Governor,* Ms A. Gomme
COLDINGLEY, Bisley, Woking, Surrey GU24 9EX. *CNA,* 286. *Prisoners,* 290. *Governor,* E. R. Butt

*COOKHAM WOOD, Rochester, Kent ME1 3LU. *CNA,* 120. *Prisoners,* 149. *Governor,* Miss C. Kershaw

DARTMOOR, Princetown, Yelverton, Devon PL20 6RR. *CNA,* 671. *Prisoners,* 692. *Governor,* J. Lawrence

‡DEERBOLT, Bowes Road, Barnard Castle, Co. Durham DL12 9BG. *CNA,* 450. *Young Offenders,* 405. *Governor,* P. Atkinson

†‡DONCASTER (private prison), Off North Bridge, Marshgate, Doncaster DN5 8UX. *CNA,* 771. *Prisoners and Young Offenders,* 1,052. *Director,* H. Jones

†‡DORCHESTER, North Square, Dorchester DT1 1JD. *CNA,* 213. *Prisoners and Young Offenders,* 230. *Governor,* Mrs D. Calvert

‡DOVER, The Citadel, Western Heights, Dover CT17 9DR. *CNA,* 264. *Young Offenders,* 247. *Governor,* B. Pollett

DOWNVIEW, Sutton Lane, Sutton, Surrey SM2 5PD. *CNA,* 327. *Prisoners,* 340. *Governor,* C. Lambert

*‡DRAKE HALL, Eccleshall, Staffs ST21 6LQ. *CNA,* 295. *Prisoners and Young Offenders,* 295. *Governor,* P. Tidball

*†DURHAM, Old Elvet, Durham DH1 3HU. *CNA,* 686. *Prisoners,* 902. *Governor,* M. Newell

*‡EAST SUTTON PARK, Sutton Valence, Maidstone, Kent ME17 3DF. *CNA,* 94. *Prisoners and Young Offenders,* 79. *Governor,* Revd R. Carter

*†‡EASTWOOD PARK, Falfield, Wotton-under-Edge, Glos GL12 8DB. *CNA,* 255. *Prisoners and Young Offenders,* 288. *Governor,* P. Winkley.

ELMLEY, Church Road, Eastchurch, Sheerness, Kent ME12 4AY. *CNA,* 763. *Prisoners,* 886. *Governor,* A. Smith

ERLESTOKE HOUSE, Devizes, Wilts SN10 5TU. *CNA,* 310. *Prisoners,* 300. *Governor (acting),* I. Acheson

EVERTHORPE, Brough, E. Yorks HU15 1RB. *CNA,* 438. *Prisoners,* 464. *Governor,* P. Midgley

†‡EXETER, New North Road, Exeter EX4 4EX. *CNA,* 321. *Prisoners and Young Offenders,* 527. *Governor,* N. Evans

FEATHERSTONE, New Road, Wolverhampton WV10 7PU. *CNA,* 599. *Prisoners,* 599. *Governor,* M. Pascoe

†‡FELTHAM, Bedfont Road, Feltham, Middx TW13 4ND. *CNA,* 802. *Prisoners and Young Offenders,* 878. *Governor,* C. Welsh

FORD, Arundel, W. Sussex BN18 0BX. *CNA,* 501. *Prisoners,* 355. *Governor,* K. Kan

FOREST BANK (from December 1999), Agecroft Road, Pendlebury, Manchester M27 8UE. *CNA,* 800. *Director,* M. Goodwin

*‡FOSTON HALL, Foston, Derbys DE65 5DN. *CNA,* 174. *Prisoners and Young Offenders,* 174. *Governor,* Ms P. Scriven

FRANKLAND, Brasside, Durham DH1 5YD. *CNA,* 655. *Prisoners,* 530. *Governor,* I. Woods

FULL SUTTON, Full Sutton, York YO41 1PS. *CNA,* 602. *Prisoners,* 530. *Governor,* D. Roberts

GARTH, Ulnes Walton Lane, Leyland, Preston PR5 3NE. *CNA,* 633. *Prisoners,* 646. *Governor,* W. Rose-Quirie, OBE

GARTREE, Gallow Field Road, Market Harborough, Leics LE16 7RP. *CNA,* 366. *Prisoners,* 366. *Governor,* S. Rimmer

†‡GLEN PARVA, Tigers Road, Wigston, Leicester LE8 4TN. *CNA,* 720. *Young Offenders,* 845. *Governor,* B. Payling

†‡GLOUCESTER, Barrack Square, Gloucester GL1 2JN. *CNA,* 235. *Prisoners and Young Offenders,* 327. *Governor,* R. Booty

GRENDON/SPRING HILL, HMP Grendon, Grendon Underwood, Aylesbury, Bucks HP18 0TL. *CNA,* 497. *Prisoners,* 489. *Governor,* T. C. Newell

‡GUYS MARSH, Shaftesbury, Dorset SP7 0AH. *CNA,* 487. *Prisoners and Young Offenders,* 507. *Governor,* D. Godfrey

§HASLAR, 2 Dolphin Way, Gosport, Hants PO12 2AW. *CNA,* 160. *Prisoners,* 142. *Governor,* R. Oliver

†HATFIELD, Thorne Road, Hatfield, Doncaster DN7 6EL. *CNA,* 180. *Young Offenders,* 155. *Governor,* Ms C. Davies

HAVERIGG, Millom, Cumbria LA18 4NA. *CNA,* 530. *Prisoners,* 530. *Governor,* G. Brunskill

HEWELL GRANGE, Redditch, Worcs B97 6QQ. *CNA,* 203. *Prisoners,* 203. *Governor,* N. Croft

HIGH DOWN, Sutton Lane, Sutton, Surrey SM2 5PJ. *CNA,* 649. *Prisoners,* 779. *Governor,* D. Wilson

*HIGHPOINT, Stradishall, Newmarket, Suffolk CB8 9YG. *CNA,* 649. *Prisoners,* 836. *Governor,* R. Woolford

†‡HINDLEY, Gibson Street, Bickershaw, Wigan, Lancs WN2 5TH. *CNA,* 531. *Prisoners and Young Offenders,* 493. *Governor,* C. Sheffield

‡HOLLESLEY BAY COLONY, Woodbridge, Suffolk IP12 3JW. *CNA,* 365. *Prisoners and Young Offenders,* 353. *Governor,* J. Forster

*†‡HOLLOWAY, Parkhurst Road, London N7 0NU. *CNA,* 477. *Prisoners and Young Offenders,* 492. *Governor,* D. Lancaster

HOLME HOUSE, Holme House Road, Stockton-on-Tees TS18 2QU. *CNA,* 971. *Prisoners,* 944. *Governor,* D. Crouch

†‡HULL, Hedon Road, Hull HU9 5LS. *CNA,* 572. *Prisoners and Young Offenders,* 494. *Governor,* S. Wagstaffe

‡HUNTERCOMBE, Huntercombe Place, Nuffield, Henley-on-Thames RG9 5SB. *CNA,* 368. *Young Offenders,* 376. *Governor,* P. Manwaring

KINGSTON, 122 Milton Road, Portsmouth PO3 6AS. *CNA,* 193. *Prisoners,* 175. *Governor,* S. McLean

KIRKHAM, Freckleton Road, Preston PR4 2RA. *CNA,* 702. *Prisoners,* 658. *Governor,* A. F. Jennings, OBE

KIRKLEVINGTON GRANGE, Yarm, Cleveland TS15 9PA. *CNA,* 183. *Prisoners,* 178. *Governor,* Ms S. Anthony

LANCASTER, The Castle, Lancaster LA1 1YL. *CNA,* 218. *Prisoners,* 216. *Governor,* J. Illingsworth

†‡LANCASTER FARMS, Far Moor Lane, Stone Row Head, off Quernmore Road, Lancaster LA1 3QZ. *CNA,* 496. *Prisoners and Young Offenders,* 456. *Governor,* D. Thomas

LATCHMERE HOUSE, Church Road, Ham Common, Richmond, Surrey TW10 5HH. *CNA,* 193. *Prisoners,* 171. *Governor,* T. Hinchliffe

LEEDS, Armley, Leeds LS12 2TJ. *CNA,* 1,056. *Prisoners,* 1,233. *Governor,* R. Daly

LEICESTER, Welford Road, Leicester LE2 7AJ. *CNA,* 219. *Prisoners,* 331. *Governor,* D. Bamber

†‡LEWES, Brighton Road, Lewes, E. Sussex BN7 1EA. *CNA,* 485. *Prisoners and Young Offenders,* 483. *Governor,* J. F. Dixon

LEYHILL, Wotton-under-Edge, Glos GL12 8BT. *CNA,* 410. *Prisoners,* 422. *Governor,* D. T. Williams

LINCOLN, Greetwell Road, Lincoln LN2 4BD. *CNA,* 360. *Prisoners,* 430. *Governor,* B. McCourt

LINDHOLME, Bawtry Road, Hatfield Woodhouse, Doncaster DN7 6EE. *CNA,* 686. *Prisoners,* 666. *Governor,* A. Holman

LITTLEHEY, Perry, Huntingdon, Cambs PE18 0SR. *CNA,* 624. *Prisoners,* 648. *Governor,* C. Morris

LIVERPOOL, 68 Hornby Road, Liverpool L9 3DF. *CNA,* 1,216. *Prisoners,* 1,510. *Governor,* W. Abbott

LONG LARTIN, South Littleton, Evesham, Worcs WR11 5TZ. *CNA,* 456. *Prisoners,* 344. *Governor,* J. Mullen

LOWDHAM GRANGE (private prison), Lowdham, Notts NG14 7TA. *CNA,* 504. *Prisoners,* 498. *Director,* R. Tasker

---

* Women's establishment or establishment with units for women
† Remand Centre or establishment with units for remand prisoners
‡ Young Offender Institution or establishment with units for young offenders
§ Immigration Holding Centre

*†‡LOW NEWTON, Brasside, Durham DH1 5SD. *CNA,* 215. *Prisoners and Young Offenders,* 295. *Governor,* M. Kirby

MAIDSTONE, 36 County Road, Maidstone ME14 1UZ. *CNA,* 551. *Prisoners,* 541. *Governor,* M. Conway

MANCHESTER, Southall Street, Manchester M60 9AH. *CNA,* 953. *Prisoners,* 1,074. *Governor,* J. Smith

‡MOORLAND, Bawtry Road, Hatfield Woodhouse, Doncaster DN7 6BW. *CNA,* 740. *Prisoners and Young Offenders,* 760. *Governor,* D. J. Waplington, OBE

MORTON HALL, Swinderby, Lincoln LN6 9PS. *CNA,* 208. *Prisoners,* 158. *Governor,* M. Murphy

THE MOUNT, Molyneaux Avenue, Bovingdon, Hemel Hempstead HP3 0NZ. *CNA,* 705. *Prisoners,* 745. *Governor,* P. Wailen

*†‡NEW HALL, Dial Wood, Flockton, Wakefield WF4 4AX. *CNA,* 327. *Prisoners and Young Offenders,* 366. *Governor,* M. Shepherd

†‡NORTHALLERTON, 15A East Road, Northallerton, N. Yorks DL6 1NW. *CNA,* 152. *Prisoners and Young Offenders,* 271. *Governor,* D. P. G. Appleton

NORTH SEA CAMP, Freiston, Boston, Lincs PE22 0QX. *CNA,* 177. *Prisoners,* 197. *Governor,* M. A. Lewis

†‡NORWICH, Mousehold, Norwich NR1 4LU. *CNA,* 564. *Prisoners and Young Offenders,* 744. *Governor,* M. Spurr

NOTTINGHAM, Perry Road, Sherwood, Nottingham NG5 3AG. *CNA,* 466. *Prisoners,* 431. *Governor,* K. Beaumont

‡ONLEY, Willoughby, Rugby, Warks CV23 8AP. *CNA,* 400. *Young Offenders,* 400. *Governor,* J. N. Brooke

†‡PARC (private prison), Heol Hopcyn John, Bridgend CF35 6AR. *CNA,* 800. *Prisoners and Young Offenders,* 411. *Director,* R. Dixon

PARKHURST, Newport, Isle of Wight PO30 5NX. *CNA,* 482. *Prisoners,* 443. *Governor,* D. M. Morrison

PENTONVILLE, Caledonian Road, London N7 8TT. *CNA,* 897. *Prisoners,* 1,175. *Governor,* R. Duncan

‡PORTLAND, Easton, Portland, Dorset DT5 1DL. *CNA,* 516. *Young Offenders,* 534. *Governor,* K. Lockyer

‡PRESCOED, 47 Maryport Street, Usk, Gwent NP5 1XP. *CNA, see* Usk. *Prisoners and Young Offenders, see* Usk. *Governor,* R. J. Comber

PRESTON, 2 Ribbleton Lane, Preston PR1 5AB. *CNA,* 445. *Prisoners,* 679. *Governor,* A. Scott

RANBY, Ranby, Retford, Notts DN22 8EV. *CNA,* 710. *Prisoners,* 720. *Governor,* J. Slater

†‡READING, Forbury Road, Reading RG1 3HY. *CNA,* 203. *Prisoners and Young Offenders,* 245. *Governor,* C. Norman

*RISLEY, Risley, Warrington WA3 6BP. *CNA,* 851. *Prisoners,* 868. *Governor,* C. Sheffield

†‡ROCHESTER, 1 Fort Road, Rochester, Kent ME1 3QS. *CNA,* 433. *Prisoners and Young Offenders,* 366. *Governor,* T. Robson

*SEND, Ripley Road, Send, Woking, Surrey GU23 7LJ. *CNA,* 80. *Prisoners,* 80. *Governor,* T. Beeston

SHEPTON MALLET, Cornhill, Shepton Mallet, Somerset BA4 5LU. *CNA,* 162. *Prisoners,* 224. *Governor,* R. Bennett

SHREWSBURY, The Dana, Shrewsbury SY1 2HR. *CNA,* 323. *Prisoners,* 323. *Governor,* A. Bramley

STAFFORD, 54 Gaol Road, Stafford ST16 3AW. *CNA,* 627. *Prisoners,* 627. *Governor,* P. Wright

STANDFORD HILL, Church Road, Eastchurch, Isle of Sheppey, Kent ME12 4AA. *CNA,* 384. *Prisoners,* 217. *Governor,* K. Naisbitt

STOCKEN, Stocken Hall Road, Stretton, nr Oakham, Leics LE15 7RD. *CNA,* 556. *Prisoners,* 576. *Governor,* R. Curtis

‡STOKE HEATH, Stoke Heath, Market Drayton, Shropshire TF9 2JL. *CNA,* 646. *Young Offenders,* 633. *Governor,* J. Alldridge

*‡STYAL, Wilmslow, Cheshire SK9 4HR. *CNA,* 284. *Prisoners and Young Offenders,* 280. *Governor,* Ms M. Moulden

SUDBURY, Ashbourne, Derbys DE6 5HW. *CNA,* 511. *Prisoners,* 492. *Governor,* P. E. Salter

SWALESIDE, Brabazon Road, Eastchurch, Isle of Sheppey, Kent ME12 4AX. *CNA,* 632. *Prisoners,* 616. *Governor,* J. Podmore

†SWANSEA, 200 Oystermouth Road, Swansea SA1 3SR. *CNA,* 251. *Prisoners,* 336. *Governor,* G. Deighton

‡SWINFEN HALL, Lichfield, Staffs WS14 9QS. *CNA,* 255. *Young Offenders,* 295. *Governor,* Ms J. P. Francis

‡THORN CROSS, Arley Road, Appleton Thorn, Warrington WA4 4RL. *CNA,* 316. *Young Offenders,* 224. *Governor,* I. Windebank

USK, 47 Maryport Street, Usk, Gwent NP5 1XP. *CNA (Usk and Prescoed),* 206. *Prisoners (Usk and Prescoed),* 281. *Governor,* R. J. Comber

THE VERNE, Portland, Dorset DT5 1EQ. *CNA,* 552. *Prisoners,* 570. *Governor,* M. Cook

WAKEFIELD, 5 Love Lane, Wakefield WF2 9AG. *CNA,* 747. *Prisoners,* 555. *Governor,* D. Shaw

WANDSWORTH, Heathfield Road, London SW18 3HS. *CNA,* 1,102. *Prisoners,* 1,094. *Governor,* M. Knight

WAYLAND, Griston, Thetford, Norfolk IP25 6RL. *CNA,* 618. *Prisoners,* 648. *Governor,* Mrs K. Crawley

WEALSTUN, Wetherby, W. Yorks LS23 7AZ. *CNA,* 632. *Prisoners,* 603. *Governor,* S. Tasker

WEARE, Portland Dock, Castletown, Portland, Dorset DT5 1PZ. *CNA,* 400. *Prisoners,* 312. *Governor,* Ms S. F. McCormick

WELLINGBOROUGH, Millers Park, Doddington Road, Wellingborough, Northants NN8 2NH. *CNA,* 368. *Prisoners,* 338. *Governor,* E. Willetts

‡WERRINGTON, Werrington, Stoke-on-Trent ST9 0DX. *CNA,* 188. *Young Offenders,* 106. *Governor,* S. Habgood

‡WETHERBY, York Road, Wetherby, W. Yorks LS22 5ED. *CNA,* 360. *Young Offenders,* 347. *Governor,* D. Hall

WHATTON, 14 Cromwell Road, Nottingham NG13 9FQ. *CNA,* 275. *Prisoners,* 272. *Governor,* D. Walmesley

WHITEMOOR, Longhill Road, March, Cambs PE15 0PR. *CNA,* 522. *Prisoners,* 454. *Governor,* T. Williams

*WINCHESTER, Romsey Road, Winchester SO22 5DF. *CNA,* 463. *Prisoners,* 576. *Governor,* R. J. Gaines

THE WOLDS (private prison), Everthorpe, Brough, E. Yorks HU15 2JZ. *CNA,* 360. *Prisoners,* 399. *Director,* D. McDonnell

†‡§WOODHILL, Tattenhoe Street, Milton Keynes MK4 4DA. *CNA,* 672. *Prisoners and Young Offenders,* 693. *Governor,* Mrs M. Boon

WORMWOOD SCRUBS, PO Box 757, Du Cane Road, London W12 0AE. *CNA,* 746. *Prisoners,* 1,122. *Governor,* S. Moore

WYMOTT, Ulnes Walton Lane, Leyland, Preston PR5 3LW. *CNA,* 809. *Prisoners,* 797. *Governor,* R. Doughty

SCOTTISH PRISON SERVICE
Calton House, 5 Redheughs Rigg, Edinburgh EH12 9HW
Tel 0131-556 8400

SALARIES 1998–9

Senior managers in the Scottish Prison Service, including governors and deputy governors of prisons, are paid across three pay bands:

Band I	£36,000–£55,600
Band H	£30,000 –£46,350
Band G	£25,100–£38,150

Chief Executive of Scottish Prison Service (SCS), E. W. Frizzell
Director of Custody, J. Durno, OBE
Director, Human Resources, P. Russell

Director, Finance and Information Systems, W. Pretswell
Director, Strategy and Corporate Affairs, Ms J. Hutchison
Deputy Director, Regime Services and Supplies, J. McNeill
Deputy Director, Estates and Buildings, B. Paterson
Area Director, South and West, M. Duffy
Area Director, North and East, P. Withers
Head of Training, Scottish Prison Service College, J. Matthews
Head of Communications, M. Mulford

PRISON ESTABLISHMENTS

Prisoners/Young Offenders Average number of
prisoners/young offenders 1998–9

*ABERDEEN, Craiginches, Aberdeen AB9 2HN. *Prisoners,* 181.
Governor, I. Gunn
BARLINNIE, Barlinnie, Glasgow G33 2QX. *Prisoners,* 1,124.
Governor, R. L. Houchin
CASTLE HUNTLY, Castle Huntly, Longforgan, nr
Dundee DD2 5HL. *Prisoners,* 106. *Governor,* K. Rennie
*‡CORNTON VALE, Cornton Road, Stirling FK9 5NY.
Prisoners and Young Offenders, 180. *Governor,* Mrs K.
Donegan
*‡DUMFRIES, Terregles Street, Dumfries DG2 9AX. *Young
Offenders,* 137. *Governor,* G. Taylor
DUNGAVEL, Dungavel House, Strathaven, Lanarkshire
ML10 6RF. *Prisoners,* 113. *Governor,* T. Pitt
EDINBURGH, 33 Stenhouse Road, Edinburgh EH1 3LN.
Prisoners, 731. *Governor,* A. Spencer
FRIARTON, Friarton, Perth PH2 8DW. *Prisoners,* 77.
Governor, Mrs A. Mooney
‡GLENOCHIL, King O'Muir Road, Tullibody,
Clackmannanshire FK10 3AD. *Prisoners and Young
Offenders,* 573. *Governor,* L. McBain, OBE
GREENOCK, Gateside, Greenock PA16 9AH. *Prisoners,* 236.
Governor, R. MacCowan
*INVERNESS, Porterfield, Inverness IV2 3HH. *Prisoners,* 122.
Governor, H. Ross
KILMARNOCK (private prison), Bowhouse, Mauchline
Road, Kilmarnock KA1 5JH. *Prisoners,* 500. *Director,* J.
Bywalec
LONGRIGGEND, Longriggend, nr Airdrie, Lanarkshire
ML6 7TL. *Prisoners,* 158. *Governor,* Ms R. Kite
LOW MOSS, Low Moss, Bishopbriggs, Glasgow G64 2QB.
Prisoners, 362. *Governor,* E. Murch
NATIONAL INDUCTION UNIT, Shotts ML7 4LE. *Prisoners,*
48. *Governor,* J. Gerrie
NORANSIDE, Noranside, Fern, by Forfar, Angus DD8 3QY.
Prisoners, 102. *Governor,* A. MacDonald
PENNINGHAME, Penninghame, Newton Stewart DG8 6RG.
Prisoners, 89. *Governor,* S. Swan
PERTH, 3 Edinburgh Road, Perth PH2 8AT. *Prisoners,* 477.
Governor, W. Millar
PETERHEAD, Salthouse Head, Peterhead, Aberdeenshire
AB4 6YY. *Prisoners,* 297. *Governor,* W. Rattray; *Governor,
Peterhead Unit,* B. McConnell
‡POLMONT, Brightons, Falkirk, Stirlingshire FK2 0AB.
Young Offenders, 443. *Governor,* D. Gunn
SHOTTS, Shotts ML7 4LF. *Prisoners,* 467. *Governor,* W.
McKinlay; *Governor, Shotts Unit,* G. Storer

NORTHERN IRELAND PRISON SERVICE

Dundonald House, Upper Newtownards Road, Belfast
BT4 3SU
Tel 01232-520700; fax 01232-525160

SALARIES 1998–9

Governor 1	£52,349
Governor 2	£47,270
Governor 3	£40,923
Governor 4	£34,233–£35,107
Governor 5	£29,596–£31,810

A Northern Ireland allowance is also payable

PRISON ESTABLISHMENTS

Prisoners/Young Offenders Average number of
prisoners/young offenders 1998–9

‡HYDEBANK WOOD, Hospital Road, Belfast BT8 8NA.
Young Offenders, 173
*‡MAGHABERRY, Old Road, Ballinderry Upper, Lisburn,
Co. Antrim BT28 2PT. *Prisoners and Young Offenders,* 502
MAGILLIGAN, Point Road, Magilligan, Co. Londonderry
BT49 0LR. *Prisoners,* 340
MAZE, Halftown Road, Maze, Lisburn, Co. Antrim
BT27 5RF (due to close by late 2000). *Prisoners,* 387

---

* Women's establishment or establishment with units for women
† Remand Centre or establishment with units for remand prisoners
‡ Young Offender Institution or establishment with units for young
offenders
§ Immigration Holding Centre

Defence

The armed forces of the United Kingdom comprise the Royal Navy, the Army and the Royal Air Force. The Queen is commander-in-chief of all the armed forces. The Ministry of Defence, headed by a Secretary of State, provides the support structure for the armed forces. Within the Ministry of Defence, the Defence Council has overall responsibility for running the armed forces. The Chief of Staff of each service reports through the Chief of the Defence Staff to the Secretary of State on matters relating to the running of his service. The Chief of Staff also chairs the executive committee of the appropriate service board, which manages the service in accordance with centrally determined objectives and budgets. The military-civilian Central Staffs, headed by the Vice-Chief of the Defence Staff and the Second Permanent Under-Secretary of State, are responsible for policy, operational requirements, commitments, financial management, resource planning and civilian personnel management. The Defence Procurement Agency is responsible for purchasing equipment. The Defence Scientific Staff and the Defence Intelligence Staff also form part of the Ministry of Defence.

A permanent Joint Headquarters for the conduct of joint operations was set up at Northwood in 1996. The Joint Headquarters connects the policy and strategic functions of the MoD Head Office with the conduct of operations and is intended to strengthen the policy/executive division. A Joint Rapid Deployment Force was established in August 1996 and a Joint Rapid Reaction Force was set up in April 1999 and will be fully in place by October 2001.

Britain pursues its defence and security policies through its membership of NATO (to which most of its armed forces are committed), the Western European Union, the European Union, the Organization for Security and Co-operation in Europe and the UN (*see* International Organizations section).

ARMED FORCES STRENGTHS *as at 1 April 1999*

All Services	208,600
Men	192,500
Women	16,100
Royal Naval Services	43,700
Army	109,700
Royal Air Force	55,200

Source: The Stationery Office: *UK Defence Statistics 1999*

SERVICE PERSONNEL

1 April

	Royal Navy	Army	RAF	All Services
1975 strength	76,200	167,100	95,000	338,300
1990 strength	63,200	152,800	89,700	305,700
1999 strength	43,700	109,700	55,200	208,600

Source: The Stationery Office: *UK Defence Statistics 1999*

CIVILIAN PERSONNEL

1 April

1975 level	316,700
1990 level	172,300
1999 level	117,700

Source: The Stationery Office: *UK Defence Statistics 1999*

DEPLOYMENT OF UK PERSONNEL

Service personnel in UK *as at 1 July 1998*	173,400
England	144,600
Wales	3,200
Scotland	14,200
N. Ireland	11,000
Service personnel overseas *as at 1 April 1999*	49,924
Royal Naval Services	5,454
Army	31,412
Royal Air Force	8,650

Forces overseas were deployed in Continental Europe, Gibraltar, Cyprus and elsewhere in the Mediterranean, the Near East, the Gulf, the Far East and other locations.

There were also 3,977 locally entered army personnel as at 1 April 1999, of whom 2,087 were deployed in the UK, 352 in Gibraltar, 853 in Brunei and 685 in Nepal.

At 1 August 1998 there were 11,646 US forces personnel based in the UK (including 9,000 Air Force, 1,540 Navy and 376 Army personnel).

Sources: Ministry of Defence; *The Military Balance 1998–9* (OUP)

NUCLEAR FORCES

Britain's nuclear forces comprise four ballistic missile submarines carrying Trident missiles and equipped with nuclear warheads. All nuclear free-fall bombs have been taken out of service.

ARMS CONTROL

The 1990 Conventional Armed Forces in Europe Treaty (the CFE Treaty), which is currently being revised, commits all NATO and former Warsaw Pact members to limiting five major classes of conventional weapons. In 1968 Britain signed the Nuclear Non-Proliferation Treaty, which was indefinitely and unconditionally extended in 1995. In 1996 it signed a Comprehensive Nuclear Test Ban Treaty. Britain was a party to the 1972 Biological and Toxin Weapons Convention, which provides for a world-wide ban on biological weapons, and the 1993 Chemical Weapons Convention, which came into force in 1997 and provides for a world-wide ban on chemical weapons. In 1997 Britain signed the Ottawa Convention, which provides for an immediate ban on the use, production and transfer of anti-personnel land-mines; Britain ratified the Convention on 31 July 1998 and it came into force on 1 March 1999.

DEFENCE BUDGET

	£ million
1998–9 estimated outturn	22,549
1999–2000 estimated outturn	22,280

The Government estimated in July 1998 that defence expenditure as a percentage of GDP would fall from 2.7 per cent in 1998–9 to 2.4 per cent by 2001–2.

Sources: The Stationery Office: *UK Defence Statistics 1999*; Ministry of Defence: *The Strategic Defence Review*

MINISTRY OF DEFENCE
Main Building, Whitehall, London SW1A 2HB
Tel 0171-218 9000
Public Enquiry Office: Tel 0171-218 6645
Web http://www.mod.uk

For ministerial and civil service salaries, *see* page 276
For Services salaries, *see* pages 394–6
Officers promoted in an acting capacity to a more senior

rank are listed under the more senior rank. Promotion to five-star rank is no longer usual in peacetime.
For changes after 31 August 1999, *see* Stop-press

Secretary of State for Defence, The Lord Robertson of Port Ellen, PC (until Oct. 1999)
  Private Secretary (SCS), T. C. McKane
  Special Advisers, A. McGowan; B. Gray
  Parliamentary Private Secretary, Ms S. Heal, MP
Minister of State for the Armed Forces, John Spellar, MP
  Private Secretary (SCS), D. Applegate
Minister of State for Defence Procurement, The Baroness Symons of Vernham Dean
  Private Secretary (SCS), D. Hatcher
Parliamentary Under-Secretary of State, Peter Kilfoyle, MP
  Private Secretary (SCS), A. Dwyer
Permanent Under-Secretary of State (SCS), K. R. Tebbit, CMG
Chief of the Defence Staff, Gen. Sir Charles Guthrie, GCB, LVO, OBE, ADC (*Gen.*)

THE DEFENCE COUNCIL

The Defence Council is responsible for running the Armed Forces. It is chaired by the Secretary of State for Defence and consists of: the Ministers of State; the Parliamentary Under-Secretary of State; the Chief of the Defence Staff; the Permanent Under-Secretary of State; the Chief of the Naval Staff; the Chief of the General Staff; the Chief of the Air Staff; the Vice-Chief of the Defence Staff; the Chief Scientific Adviser; the Chief of Defence Procurement; and the Second Permanent Under-Secretary of State.

CHIEFS OF STAFF

CHIEF OF THE NAVAL STAFF

Chief of the Naval Staff and First Sea Lord, Adm. Sir Michael Boyce, GCB, OBE, ADC
Asst Chief of the Naval Staff, Rear-Adm. J. M. Burnell-Nugent (from 6 Dec. 1999)
Secretariat (Naval Staff) (SCS), C. Verey

CHIEF OF THE GENERAL STAFF

Chief of the General Staff, Gen. Sir Roger Wheeler, GCB, CBE, ADC (*Gen.*) (until April 2000); Gen. Sir Michael Walker, KCB, CMG, CBE, ADC (*Gen.*) (from April 2000)
Asst Chief of the General Staff, Maj.-Gen. K. O'Donoghue, CBE
Director-General, Development and Doctrine, Maj.-Gen. A. D. Pigott, CBE (until Feb. 2000); Maj.-Gen. C. L. Elliott, CB, MBE (from Feb. 2000)

CHIEF OF THE AIR STAFF

Chief of the Air Staff, Air Chief Marshal Sir Richard Johns, GCB, CBE, LVO, ADC
Asst Chief of the Air Staff, Air Vice-Marshal G. E. Stirrup, AFC
Secretariat (Air Staff) (SCS), M. J. D. Fuller
British-American Community Relations Co-ordinator, Air Marshal Sir John Kemball, KCB, CBE, RAF (retd)
Chief Executive, National Air Traffic Services (SCS), D. J. McLauchlan
Director, Airspace Policy, Air Vice-Marshal J. R. D. Arscott

CENTRAL STAFFS

Vice-Chief of the Defence Staff, Adm. Sir Peter Abbott, GBE, KCB
Second Permanent Under-Secretary of State (SCS), R. T. Jackling, CB, CBE
Deputy CDS (Equipment Capability), Vice-Adm. Sir Jeremy Blackham, KCB
Asst CDS, Operational Requirements (Sea Systems), Rear-Adm. R. J. G. Ward

Asst CDS, Operational Requirements (Land Systems), Maj.-Gen. P. J. Russell-Jones, OBE
Asst CDS, Operational Requirements (Air Systems), Air Vice-Marshal S. M. Nicholl, CBE, AFC
Deputy CDS (Personnel), Air Marshal M. D. Pledger, OBE, AFC
Asst CDS (Programmes), Maj.-Gen. J. P. Kiszely, MC
Asst Under-Secretary of State (Service Personnel Policy) (SCS), D. Bowen
Defence Housing Executive (SCS), C. J. I. James
Surgeon-General, Air Marshal Sir John Baird, KBE, QHP (until Feb. 2000); Lt.-Gen. R. C. Menzies, OBE, QHS (from Feb. 2000)
Chief of Staff to the Surgeon-General, Rear-Adm. C. D. Stanford
Chief Executive, Defence Medical Training Organization, and Chief Executive, Defence Secondary Care Agency, Maj.-Gen. C. G. Callow, OBE, QHP
Deputy Under-Secretary of State (Resources, Programmes and Finance) (SCS), C. V. Balmer
Asst Under-Secretary of State (Programmes) (SCS), T. A. Woolley
Asst Under-Secretary of State (Systems) (SCS), N. K. J. Witney
Asst Under-Secretary of State (Financial Management) (SCS), D. G. Jones
Asst Under-Secretary of State (General Finance) (SCS), C. Sanders
Defence Services Secretary, Rear-Adm. R. B. Lees
Deputy CDS (Commitments), Air Marshal Sir John Day, KCB, OBE
Asst CDS (Operations), Rear-Adm. S. Moore
Asst Under-Secretary of State (Home and Overseas) (SCS), E. V. Buckley, CB
Chief of Defence Logistics, Gen. Sir Samuel Cowan, KCB, CBE
Chief of Staff to the Chief of Defence Logistics, Air Vice-Marshal I. Brackenbury, OBE
Deputy to the Chief of Defence Logistics, J. R. C. Oughton
Asst CDS (Logistics), Air Vice-Marshal D. C. Couzens
Director of Policy (SCS), R. P. Hatfield, CBE
Asst CDS (Policy), Maj.-Gen. C. F. Drewry, CBE
Deputy Under-Secretary of State (Civilian Management) (SCS), J. Howe
Asst Under-Secretary of State, Civilian Management (Personnel) (SCS), B. A. E. Taylor
Chief Constable, MOD Police, W. E. E. Boreham, OBE
Asst Under-Secretary of State (Security and Support) (SCS), A. G. Rucker
Legal Adviser (SCS), M. J. Hemming
Director-General, Information and Communications Services (SCS), A. C. Sleigh
Defence Estate Organization (SCS), B. L. Hirst
Commandant, Joint Services Command and Staff College, Maj.-Gen. T. J. Granville-Chapman, CBE

DEFENCE INFORMATION STAFF

Director-General of Corporate Communications (SCS), J. Pitt-Brooke
Director, Information Strategy and News (SCS), Ms O. Muirhead
Director, Internal Communications and Media Training (SCS), A. Boardman
Director, Public Relations (Navy), Cdre H. Edelston
Director, Public Relations (Army), Brig. S. Roberts
Director, Public Relations (RAF), Air Cdre D. Walker

DEFENCE INTELLIGENCE STAFF

Old War Office Building, Whitehall, London SW1A 2EU
Tel 0171-218 6645; fax 0171-218 1562
Chief of Defence Intelligence, Vice-Adm. A. W. J. West, DSC

Deputy Chief of Defence Intelligence and Head of Defence Intelligence Analysis Staff (SCS), J. N. L. Morrison
Director, Intelligence Programmes and Resources (SCS), P. I. Bailey
Director, Defence Intelligence Secretariat and Communications Information Systems (SCS), R. C. Hack
Director, Regional Assessments, Brig. N. J. Cottam, OBE
Director, Intelligence Global Issues (SCS), J. M. Cunningham
Director-General, Intelligence and Geographic Resources, Air Vice-Marshal J. C. French, CBE

DEFENCE SCIENTIFIC STAFF

Chief Scientific Adviser (SCS), Prof. Sir David Davies, KBE (until Jan. 2000); Prof. Sir Keith O'Nions, FRS (from Jan. 2000)
Chief Scientist (SCS), G. H. B. Jordan
Deputy Chief Scientists (Scrutiny and Analysis) (SCS), M. J. Earwicker; P. M. Sutcliffe
Asst Chief Scientific Adviser (Nuclear) (SCS), P. W. Roper
Nuclear Weapon Safety Adviser (SCS), Dr A. Ferguson

SECOND SEA LORD/COMMANDER-IN-CHIEF NAVAL HOME COMMAND

Second Sea Lord and C.-in-C. Naval Home Command, Adm. Sir John Brigstocke, KCB, ADC
Director-General, Naval Personnel (Strategy and Plans) and Chief of Staff to Second Sea Lord and C.-in-C. Naval Home Command, Rear-Adm. P. A. Dunt
Asst Under-Secretary of State (Naval Personnel) (SCS), B. Miller
Flag Officer Training and Recruiting and Chief Executive, Naval Recruiting and Training Agency, Rear-Adm. J. Chadwick
Naval Secretary and Chief Executive, Naval Manning Agency, Rear-Adm. J. M. de Halpert
Director-General, Naval Medical Services, vacant
Director-General, Naval Chaplaincy Services, Revd Dr C. Stewart

NAVAL SUPPORT COMMAND

Chief of Fleet Support, Vice-Adm. Sir John Dunt, KCB
Director-General, Fleet Support (Operations and Plans), Rear-Adm. M. G. Wood, CBE
Asst Under-Secretary of State (Fleet Support) (SCS), D. J. Gould
Chief Executive, Ships Support Agency (SCS), J. Coles
Chief Executive, Naval Bases and Supply Agency,, Rear-Adm. B. B. Perowne
Chief Naval Engineering Officer, Rear-Adm. J. A. Burch, CBE
Director-General, Aircraft (Navy), vacant
Flag Officer Scotland, N. England and N. Ireland, and Naval Base Commander Clyde, Rear-Adm. A. M. Gregory, OBE

COMMANDER-IN-CHIEF FLEET

C.-in-C. Fleet, Adm. Sir Nigel Essenhigh, KCB
Deputy Commander Fleet, Vice-Adm. F. M. Malbon
Chief of Staff (Operations) and Flag Officer Submarines, Rear-Adm. R. P. Stevens, OBE
Flag Officer Surface Flotilla, Rear-Adm. P. M. Franklyn, CB, MVO (until Feb. 2000); Rear-Adm. I. A. Forbes, CBE (from Feb. 2000)
Flag Officer Sea Training, Rear-Adm. A. K. Backus, OBE
Commander, UK Task Group/Commander, Anti-Submarine Warfare Strike Force, Rear-Adm. I. A. Forbes, CBE (until Feb. 2000); Rear-Adm. S. R. Meyer (from Feb. 2000)
Flag Officer Naval Aviation, Rear-Adm. I. R. Henderson, CBE
Commandant-General, Royal Marines, Maj.-Gen. R. H. G. Fulton

QUARTERMASTER-GENERAL'S DEPARTMENT

Quartermaster-General, Lt.-Gen. Sir Scott Grant, KCB
Chief of Staff, Maj.-Gen. C. L. Elliott, CB, MBE (until Feb. 2000)
Asst Under-Secretary (Quartermaster) (SCS), N. H. R. Evans
Director of Contracts (Army) (SCS), P. D. Batt
Director-General, Logistic Support (Army), Maj.-Gen. A. W. Lyons, CBE
Director-General, Equipment Support (Army), Maj.-Gen. D. L. Judd

ADJUTANT-GENERAL'S DEPARTMENT

Adjutant-General, Gen. Sir Alexander Harley, KBE, CB, ADC
Chief of Staff, Maj-Gen. A. P. N. Currie
Head, Command Secretariat (SCS), M. E. McLoughlin
Director-General, Army Training and Recruiting and Chief Executive, Army Training and Recruiting Agency, Maj.-Gen. A. M. D. Palmer, CBE
Chaplain-General, Revd Dr V. Dobbin, MBE, QHC
Director-General, Army Medical Services, Maj.-Gen. R. C. Menzies, OBE, QHS (until Feb. 2000)
Director, Army Legal Services, Maj.-Gen. G. Risius
Military Secretary and Chief Executive, Army Personnel Centre, Maj.-Gen. A. S. H. Irwin, CBE
Commandant, Royal Military Academy, Sandhurst, Maj.-Gen. A. G. Denaro, CBE
Commandant, Royal Military College of Science, Maj.-Gen. J. C. B. Sutherell

COMMANDER-IN-CHIEF LAND COMMAND

C.-in-C., Land Command, Gen. Sir Michael Walker, KCB, CMG, CBE, ADC (Gen.) (until April 2000); Gen. Sir Michael Jackson, KCB, CBE (from April 2000)
Deputy C.-in-C., Land Command, and Inspector-General, Territorial Army, Lt.-Gen. Sir John Deverell, KCB, OBE
Chief of Staff, HQ Land Command, Maj.-Gen. P. C. C. Trousdell
Deputy Chief of Staff, HQ Land Command, Maj.-Gen. P. A. Chambers, MBE

HQ STRIKE COMMAND

Air Officer Commanding-in-Chief, Air Chief Marshal Sir Peter Squire, KCB, DFC, AFC, ADC
Chief of Staff and Deputy C.-in-C., Air Marshal T. I. Jenner, CB
Senior Air Staff Officer and Air Officer Commanding, No. 38 Group, Air Vice-Marshal P. O. Sturley, MBE
Air Officer Logistics and Communications Information Systems, Air Vice-Marshal P. J. Scott
Air Officer Administration, Air Vice-Marshal A. J. Burton
Head, Command Secretariat (SCS), C. J. Wright
Air Officer Commanding, No. 1 Group, Air Vice-Marshal J. H. Thompson
Air Officer Commanding, No. 11/18 Group, Air Vice-Marshal B. K. Burridge, CBE

HQ LOGISTICS COMMAND

Air Officer Commanding-in-Chief, Air Vice-Marshal G. Skinner, CBE
Chief of Staff (Air Officer Commanding Directly Administered Units), vacant
Command Secretary (SCS), H. Griffiths
Air Officer Communications Information Systems and Support Services, Air Vice-Marshal P. Liddell
Director-General, Support Management (RAF), Air Vice-Marshal P. W. Henderson, MBE

HQ PERSONNEL AND TRAINING COMMAND

Air Member for Personnel and Air Officer Commanding-in-Chief,
Air Marshal Sir Anthony Bagnall, KCB, OBE
Chief of Staff, Air Vice-Marshal R. A. Wright, AFC
Chief Executive, Training Group Defence Agency, Air Vice-Marshal A. J. Stables, CBE
Commandant, RAF College, Cranwell, Air Vice-Marshal T. W. Rimmer, OBE
Air Secretary and Chief Executive, RAF Personnel Management Agency, Air Vice-Marshal I. M. Stewart, AFC
Director-General, Medical Services (RAF), Air Vice-Marshal C. J. Sharples, QHP
Director, Legal Services (RAF), Air Vice-Marshal J. Weeden
Chaplain-in-Chief (RAF), Revd A. P. Bishop, QHC
Command Secretary (SCS), L. D. Kyle

DEFENCE PROCUREMENT AGENCY

MOD Abbey Wood, Bristol BS34 8JH
Tel 0117-913 0000

Chief of Defence Procurement and Chief Executive, Defence Procurement Agency, Vice-Adm. Sir Robert Walmsley, KCB
Deputy Chief of Defence Procurement (Operations) and Controller of the Navy, Air Marshal P. C. Norriss, CB, AFC
Deputy Chief Executive (SCS), J. F. Howe, CB, OBE
Executive Director 1 (SCS), I. Fauset
Executive Director 2, Maj.-Gen. D. J. M. Jenkins, CBE
Executive Director 3 (SCS), G. N. Beaven
Executive Director 4, Rear-Adm. P. Spencer (until Jan. 2000); Rear-Adm. N. C. F. Guild (from Jan. 2000)
Executive Director 5 (SCS), S. Porter
Executive Director 6 (SCS), S. Webb
Change Adviser (SCS), J. Allen
Integration and Aerospace Adviser, Air Vice-Marshal A. A. Nicholson, CBE, LVO
Engineering Adviser, Maj.-Gen. L. D. Curran
Head of Defence Export Services (SCS), L. A. Edwards

OTHER DEFENCE AGENCIES

ARMED FORCES PERSONNEL ADMINSTRATION AGENCY, Building 182, RAF Innsworth, Gloucester GL3 1HW. Tel: 01452-712612 ext. 7347. *Chief Executive,* T. S. Lord
ARMY BASE REPAIR ORGANIZATION, Building 200, Monxton Road, Andover, Hants SP11 8HT. Tel: 01264-383295. *Chief Executive,* J. R. Drew, CBE
ARMY PERSONNEL CENTRE, Kentigern House, 65 Brown Street, Glasgow G2 8EX. Tel: 0141-248 7890. *Chief Executive,* Maj.-Gen. A. S. H. Irwin, CBE
ARMY TECHNICAL SUPPORT AGENCY, Room 60/1, HQ QMG, Monxton Road, Andover, Hants SP11 8HT. Tel: 01264-383161. *Chief Executive,* Brig. A. D. Ball, CBE
ARMY TRAINING AND RECRUITING AGENCY, Trenchard Lines, Upavon, Pewsey, Wilts SN9 6BE. Tel: 01980-615024. *Chief Executive,* Maj.-Gen. A. M. D. Palmer, CBE
BRITISH FORCES POST OFFICE, Inglis Barracks, Mill Hill, London NW7 1PX. Tel: 0181-818 6313. *Director and Chief Executive,* Brig. B. J. Cash
DEFENCE ANALYTICAL SERVICES AGENCY, Northumberland House, Northumberland Avenue, London WC2N 5BP. Tel: 0171-218 0729. *Chief Executive,* C. Youngson
DEFENCE AVIATION REPAIR AGENCY, DARA Head Office, Building 145, St Athan, Barry, Vale of Glamorgan CF62 4WA. Tel: 01446-798893. *Chief Executive,* S. R. Hill, OBE

DEFENCE BILLS AGENCY, Room 410, Mersey House, Drury Lane, Liverpool L2 7PX. Tel: 0151-242 2234. *Chief Executive,* I. S. Elrick
DEFENCE CLOTHING AND TEXTILES AGENCY, Skimmingdish Lane, Caversfield, Oxon OX6 9TS. Tel: 01869-875501. *Chief Executive,* Brig. M. J. Roycroft
DEFENCE CODIFICATION AIR LOGISTICS DOCUMENTATION, Defence Codification, Room 2.4.23, Kentigern House, 65 Brown Street, Glasgow G2 8EX. Tel: 0141-224 2066. *Chief Executive,* K. A. Bradshaw
DEFENCE COMMUNICATION SERVICES AGENCY, Building 111, Basil Hill Barracks, Park Lane, Corsham, Wilts SN13 9NR. Tel: 01225-814886. *Chief Executive,* Maj-Gen. A. J. Raper, CBE
DEFENCE DENTAL AGENCY, RAF Halton, Aylesbury, Bucks HP22 5PG. Tel: 01296-623535, ext. 6851. *Chief Executive,* Air Vice-Marshal I. G. McIntyre, QHDS
DEFENCE ESTATES, St George's House, Blakemore Drive, Sutton Coldfield, W. Midlands B95 7RL. Tel: 0121-311 2140. *Chief Executive,* I. Andrews, CBE
DEFENCE EVALUATION AND RESEARCH AGENCY, Ively Road, Farnborough, Hants GU14 0LX. Tel: 01252-394500. *Chief Executive,* Sir John Chisholm
DEFENCE HOUSING EXECUTIVE, 8th Floor, St Christopher House, Southwark Street, London SE1 0TE. Tel: 0171-921 1033. *Chief Executive,* J. Wilson
DEFENCE INTELLIGENCE AND SECURITY CENTRE, Chicksands, Shefford, Beds SG17 5PR. Tel: 01462-752125. *Chief Executive,* Brig. C. G. Holtom
DEFENCE MEDICAL TRAINING ORGANIZATION, Building 87, Fort Blockhouse, Gosport, Hants PO12 2AB. Tel: 01705-765284/765438. *Chief Executive,* Maj.-Gen. C. G. Callow, OBE, QHP
DEFENCE SECONDARY CARE AGENCY, Room 564, St Giles Court, 1–13 St Giles High Street, London WC2H 8LD. Tel: 0171-305 6190. *Chief Executive,* Maj.-Gen. C. G. Callow, OBE, QHP
DEFENCE STORAGE AND DISTRIBUTION AGENCY, Ploughley Road, Lower Arncott, Bicester, Oxon OX6 0LD. Tel: 01869-256840. *Chief Executive,* Brig. P. D. Foxton
DEFENCE TRANSPORT AND MOVEMENTS AGENCY, Monxton Road, Andover, Hants SP11 8HT. Tel: 01264-382537. *Chief Executive,* Air Cdre P. T. W. Leaning
DEFENCE VETTING AGENCY, Room 4/54, Metropole Building, Northumberland Avenue, London WC2N 5BL. Tel: 0171-807 0435. *Chief Executive,* M. P. B. G. Wilson
DISPOSAL SALES AGENCY, 7th Floor, 6 Hercules Road, London SE1 7DJ. Tel: 0171-261 8853. *Chief Executive,* S. Taylor
JOINT AIR RECONNAISSANCE INTELLIGENCE CENTRE, RAF Brampton, Huntingdon, Cambs PE18 8QL. Tel: 01480-52151, ext. 7837. *Chief Executive,* Gp Capt S. J. Lloyd
LOGISTIC INFORMATION SYSTEMS AGENCY, Monxton Road, Andover, Hants SP11 8HT. Tel: 01264-382025. *Chief Executive,* Brig. P. A. Flanagan
MEDICAL SUPPLIES AGENCY, Drummond Barracks, Ludgershall, Andover, Hants SP11 9RU. Tel: 01980-608606. *Chief Executive,* B. E. Nimick
METEOROLOGICAL OFFICE, London Road, Bracknell, Berks RG12 2SZ. Tel: 01344-420242. *Chief Executive,* P. D. Ewins, CB, FEng.
MILITARY SURVEY, Elmwood Avenue, Feltham, Middx TW13 7AH. Tel: 0181-818 2181. *Chief Executive,* Brig. P. R. Wildman, OBE
MINISTRY OF DEFENCE POLICE, Wethersfield, Braintree, Essex CM7 4AZ. Tel: 01371-854000. *Chief Executive,* Chief Constable W. E. E. Boreham, OBE

NAVAL BASES AND SUPPLY AGENCY, Room 8, C Block, Ensleigh, Bath BAI 5AB. Tel: 01225-467400. *Chief Executive,* Rear-Adm. B. B. Perowne

NAVAL MANNING AGENCY, Victory Building, HM Naval Base, Portsmouth POI 3LS. Tel: 01705-727402. *Chief Executive,* Rear-Adm. J. M. de Halpert

NAVAL RECRUITING AND TRAINING AGENCY, Victory Building, HM Naval Base, Portsmouth POI 3LS. Tel: 01705-727602. *Chief Executive,* Rear-Adm. J. Chadwick

PAY AND PERSONNEL AGENCY, Warminster Road, Bath BAI 5AA. Tel: 01225-828533. *Chief Executive,* M. A. Rowe

RAF LOGISTICS SUPPORT SERVICES, H014, RAF Wyton, PO Box 70, Huntingdon, Cambs PE17 2PY. Tel: 01480-52451, ext. 6604. *Chief Executive,* Air Cdre I. Sloss

RAF PERSONNEL MANAGEMENT AGENCY, RAF Innsworth, Gloucester GL3 IEZ. Tel: 01452-712612, ext. 7010. *Chief Executive,* Air Vice-Marshal I. M. Stewart, AFC

RAF SIGNALS ENGINEERING ESTABLISHMENT, RAF Henlow, Beds SG16 6DN. Tel: 01462-851515, ext. 7625. *Chief Executive,* Air Cdre C. M. Davison

SERVICE CHILDREN'S EDUCATION, HQ SCE, Building 5, Wegberg Military Complex, BFPO 40. Tel: 00-49 2161-908 2372. *Chief Executive,* D. G. Wadsworth

SHIPS SUPPORT AGENCY, B Block, Room 102, Foxhill, Bath BAI 5AB. Tel: 01225-882348. *Chief Executive,* J. D. Coles

TRAINING GROUP DEFENCE AGENCY, RAF Innsworth, Gloucester GL3 IEZ. Tel: 01452-712612, ext. 5344. *Chief Executive,* Air Vice-Marshal A. J. Stables, CBE

UNITED KINGDOM HYDROGRAPHIC OFFICE, Admiralty Way, Taunton, Somerset TAI 2DN. Tel: 01823-337900. *Chief Executive, and Hydrographer of the Royal Navy,* Rear-Adm. J. P. Clarke, CB, LVO, MBE

The Royal Navy

LORD HIGH ADMIRAL OF THE UNITED KINGDOM
HM The Queen

ADMIRALS OF THE FLEET

HRH The Prince Philip, Duke of Edinburgh, KG, KT, OM, GBE, AC, QSO, PC, *apptd* 1953
The Lord Hill-Norton, GCB, *apptd* 1971
Sir Michael Pollock, GCB, LVO, DSC, *apptd* 1974
Sir Edward Ashmore, GCB, DSC, *apptd* 1977
Sir Henry Leach, GCB, *apptd* 1982
Sir Julian Oswald, GCB, *apptd* 1993
Sir Benjamin Bathurst, GCB, *apptd* 1995

ADMIRALS

Boyce, Sir Michael, GCB, OBE, ADC (*Chief of the Naval Staff and First Sea Lord*)
Abbott, Sir Peter, GBE, KCB (*Vice-Chief of the Defence Staff*)
Brigstocke, Sir John, KCB, ADC (*C.-in-C. Naval Home Command and Second Sea Lord*)
Essenhigh, Sir Nigel, KCB (*C.-in-C. Fleet, C.-in-C. Eastern Atlantic Area and Commander Allied Forces North-Western Europe*)

VICE-ADMIRALS

Dunt, Sir John, KCB (*Chief of Fleet Support*)
Garnett, Sir Ian, KCB (*Chief of Joint Operations*)
Haddacks, P. K. (*UK Military Rep. at NATO HQ*)
Blackham, Sir Jeremy, KCB (*Deputy CDS (Equipment Capability)*)
Blackburn, D. A. J., CB, LVO (*Chief of Staff, Commander Naval Forces South Atlantic*)

West, A. W. J., DSC (*Chief of Defence Intelligence*)
McAnally, J. H. S., LVO (*Commandant, Royal College of Defence Studies*)
Malbon, F. M. (*Deputy Commander Fleet*)
Band, J. (*Team Leader, Defence Training and Education Study*) (from 11 Jan. 2000)

REAR-ADMIRALS

Clarke, J. P., CB, LVO, MBE (*Hydrographer of the Navy and Chief Executive, UK Hydrographic Office*)
Franklyn, P. M., CB, MVO (*Flag Officer Surface Flotilla*) (until Feb. 2000)
Perowne, J. F., OBE (*Dep. SACLANT*)
Lees, R. B. (*Defence Services Secretary*)
Spencer, P. (*Executive Director 4, Defence Procurement Agency*) (until Jan. 2000)
Ross, A. B., CB, CBE (*Asst Director Operations Divn International Military Staff*)
Perowne, B. B. (*Chief Executive, Naval Bases and Supply Agency*)
Forbes, I. A., CBE (*Commander, UK Task Group/ Commander, Anti-Submarine Warfare Strike Force*) (until Feb. 2000); (*Flag Officer Surface Flotilla*) (from Feb. 2000)
Gough, A. B. (*Asst CDS (Policy and Requirements) to Supreme Allied Commander Europe*)
Lippiett, R. J., MBE (*Chief of Staff to Commander, Allied Naval Forces Southern Europe, and Senior British Officer Southern Region*)
Gregory, A. M., OBE (*Flag Officer Scotland, N. England and N. Ireland, and Naval Base Commander Clyde*)
Moore, S. (*Asst CDS (Operations)*)
Dunt, P. A. (*Director-General, Naval Personnel (Strategy and Plans) and Chief of Staff to Second Sea Lord and C.-in-C. Naval Home Command*)
Burch, J. A., CBE (*Chief Naval Engineering Officer*)
Rickard, H. W. (*Senior Directing Staff (Naval), Royal College of Defence Studies*)
Stevens, R. P., OBE (*Chief of Staff (Operations), Flag Officer Submarines,   COMSUBEASTLANT   and COMSUBNORTHWEST*)
Henderson, I. R., CBE (*Flag Officer Naval Aviation*)
Chadwick, J. (*Flag Officer Training and Recruiting and Chief Executive, Naval Recruiting and Training Agency*)
de Halpert, J. M. (*Naval Secretary/Chief Executive, Naval Manning Agency*)
HRH The Prince of Wales, KG, KT, GCB and Great Master of the Order of the Bath, AK, QSO, PC, ADC(P)
Wood, M. G., CBE (*Director-General, Fleet Support (Operations and Plans)*)
Stanford, C. D. (*Chief of Staff to the Surgeon-General*)
Burnell-Nugent, J. M. (*Asst Chief of the Naval Staff*) (from 6 Dec. 1999)
Meyer, S. R. (*Military Adviser to the High Representative in Sarajevo*) (until Feb. 2000); (*Commander, UK Task Group/ Commander, Anti-Submarine Warfare Strike Force*) (from Feb. 2000)
Backus, A. K., OBE (*Flag Officer Sea Training*)
Clare, R. A. G. (*Director of Operational Management, NATO Regional Command North*)
Guild, N. C. F. (*Executive Director 4, Defence Procurement Agency*) (from Jan. 2000)
Ward, R. J. G. (*Asst CDS Operational Requirements (Sea Systems)*)

Enquiries regarding records of serving officers should be directed to The Naval Secretary, Room 161, Victory Building, HM Naval Base, Portsmouth, Hants POI 3LS. Tel: 01705-727431.

HM FLEET *as at autumn 1999*

SUBMARINES

Trident	Vanguard, Vengeance, Victorious, Vigilant
Fleet	Sceptre, Sovereign, Spartan, Splendid, Superb, Talent, Tireless, Torbay, Trafalgar, Trenchant, Triumph, Turbulent
ANTI-SUBMARINE WARFARE CARRIERS	Ark Royal, Illustrious, Invincible
ASSAULT SHIPS	Fearless, Intrepid
LANDING PLATFORM HELICOPTER	Ocean
DESTROYERS	
Type 42	Birmingham, Cardiff, Edinburgh, Exeter, Glasgow, Gloucester, Liverpool, Manchester, Newcastle, Nottingham, Southampton, York
FRIGATES	
Type 23	Argyll, Grafton, Iron Duke, Lancaster, Marlborough, Monmouth, Montrose, Norfolk, Northumberland, Richmond, Somerset, Sutherland, Westminster
Type 22	Brave, Campbeltown, Chatham, Cornwall, Coventry, Cumberland, Sheffield
OFFSHORE PATROL	
Castle Class	Dumbarton Castle, Leeds Castle
Island Class	Alderney, Anglesey, Guernsey, Lindisfarne, Shetland
MINEHUNTERS	
Hunt Class	Atherstone, Berkeley, Bicester, Brecon, Brocklesby, Cattistock, Chiddingfold, Cottesmore, Dulverton, Hurworth, Ledbury, Middleton, Quorn
Sandown Class	Bridport, Cromer, Grimsby, Inverness, Pembroke, Penzance, Sandown, Walney
PATROL CRAFT	
River Class	Orwell
Coastal Training Craft*	Archer, Biter, Blazer, Charger, Dasher, Example, Exploit, Explorer, Express, Puncher, Pursuer, Raider, Smiter, Tracker
Gibraltar Search and Rescue Craft	Ranger, Trumpeter
ICE PATROL SHIP	Endurance
SURVEY SHIPS	Beagle, Bulldog, Gleaner, Herald, Roebuck, Scott
SOLD/DECOMMISSIONED 1998–9	Arun, Beaver, Blackwater, Boxer, London, Orkney, Spey

* Operated by the University Royal Naval Units

OTHER PARTS OF THE NAVAL SERVICE

ROYAL MARINES

The Royal Marines were formed in 1664 and are part of the Naval Service. Their primary purpose is to conduct amphibious and land warfare. The principal operational units are 3 Commando Brigade Royal Marines, an amphibious all-arms brigade trained to operate in arduous environments, which is a core element of the UK's Joint Rapid Reaction Force; Comacchio Group Royal Marines, which is responsible for the security of nuclear weapon facilities; and Special Boat Service Royal Marines, the maritime special forces. The Royal Marines also provide detachments for warships and land-based naval parties as required. The Royal Marines Band Service provides military musical support for the Naval Service. The headquarters of the Royal Marines is at Portsmouth, along with the Royal Marines School of Music, and principal bases are at Plymouth, Arbroath, Poole, Taunton and Chivenor. The Corps of Royal Marines is about 6,500 strong.

Commandant-General, Royal Marines, Maj.-Gen. R. H. G. Fulton

Chief of Staff, NATO Joint Headquarters North, Maj.-Gen. D. Wilson, OBE (from Dec. 1999)

Director-General, Joint Doctrine and Concepts Centre, Maj.-Gen. A. A. Milton, OBE, ADC

ROYAL MARINES RESERVE (RMR)

The Royal Marines Reserve is a commando-trained volunteer force with the principal role, when mobilized, of supporting the Royal Marines. There are RMR centres in London, Glasgow, Bristol, Liverpool and Newcastle. The current strength of the RMR is about 1,000.

Director, RMR, Lt.-Col. A. W. MacCormick

ROYAL FLEET AUXILIARY SERVICE (RFA)

The Royal Fleet Auxiliary Service is a civilian-manned flotilla of 22 ships. Its primary role is to supply the Royal Navy at sea with food, fuel, ammunition and spares, enabling it to maintain operations away from its home ports. In addition the RFA provides the Royal Navy with sea-borne aviation training facilities as well as secure logistic support and amphibious operations capability for the Army and Royal Marines.

FLEET AIR ARM

The Fleet Air Arm was founded in 1914 as the Royal Naval Air Service and operates some 240 fixed wing aircraft and helicopters for the Royal Navy. Sea Harrier fighters provide air defence/strike capability for the fleet, and Sea King and Lynx helicopters provide commando support, anti-submarine, anti-surface, airborne early warning and search and rescue capability. In 1999 the strength of the FAA was 5,600.

ROYAL NAVAL RESERVE (RNR)

The Royal Naval Reserve is an integral part of the Naval Service. It comprises up to 3,850 men and women nationwide who volunteer to train in their spare time to enable the Royal Navy to meet its operational commitments, at sea and ashore, in crisis or war.

The standard annual training commitment is 24 days, including 12 days' continuous training. Daily pay scales range from £35 to £110 for officers and from £22 to £56 for ratings. A single bounty is also payable, the amount depending on the length of service.

Director, Naval Reserves, Capt J. A. Rimington, RN

QUEEN ALEXANDRA'S ROYAL NAVAL NURSING SERVICE

The first nursing sisters were appointed to naval hospitals in 1884 and the Queen Alexandra's Royal Naval Nursing Service (QARNNS) gained its current title in 1902. Nursing ratings were introduced in 1960 and men were integrated into the Service in 1982; both men and women serve as officers and ratings. Female medical assistants were introduced in 1987.

Patron, HRH Princess Alexandra, the Hon. Lady Ogilvy, GCVO

Matron-in-Chief, Capt. P. M. Hambling, QHNS

The Army

THE QUEEN

FIELD MARSHALS

HRH The Prince Philip, Duke of Edinburgh, KG, KT, OM, GBE, AC, QSO, PC, *apptd* 1953
The Lord Carver, GCB, CBE, DSO, MC, *apptd* 1973
Sir Roland Gibbs, GCB, CBE, DSO, MC, *apptd* 1979
The Lord Bramall, KG, GCB, OBE, MC, *apptd* 1982
Sir John Stanier, GCB, MBE, *apptd* 1985
Sir Nigel Bagnall, GCB, CVO, MC, *apptd* 1988
The Lord Vincent of Coleshill, GBE, KCB, DSO (Col. Cmdt. RA), *apptd* 1991
Sir John Chapple, GCB, CBE, *apptd* 1992
HRH The Duke of Kent, KG, GCMG, GCVO, ADC, *apptd* 1993
The Lord Inge, GCB (Col. Green Howards, Col. Cmdt. APTC), *apptd* 1994

GENERALS

Guthrie, Sir Charles, GCB, LVO, OBE, ADC (*Gen.*), Col. LG (*Chief of the Defence Staff*)
Wheeler, Sir Roger, GCB, CBE, ADC (*Gen.*), Col. Cmdt. Int. Corps, Col. R. Irish (*Chief of the General Staff*) (until April 2000)
Walker, Sir Michael, KCB, CMG, CBE, ADC (*Gen.*), Col. Cmdt. The Queen's Division, Col. Cmdt. AAC (*C.-in-C., Land*) (until April 2000); (*Chief of the General Staff*) (from April 2000)
Harley, Sir Alexander, KBE, CB, ADC (*Gen.*), Col. Cmdt. RHA (*Adjutant-General*)
Cowan, Sir Samuel, KCB, CBE, Col. Cmdt. Bde of Gurkhas (*Chief of Defence Logistics*)
Smith, Sir Rupert, KCB, DSO, OBE, QGM, Col. Cmdt. REME (*D. SACEUR*)

LIEUTENANT-GENERALS

Pike, Sir Hew, KCB, DSO, MBE (*GOC Northern Ireland*)
Grant, Sir Scott, KCB, Col. Cmdt. King's Division, Col. Cmdt. RE, Chief Royal Engineer (*Quartermaster-General*)
Jackson, Sir Michael, KCB, CBE, Col. Cmdt. Parachute Regiment, Col. Cmdt. AG Corps (*Commander ACE Rapid Reaction Corps*) (until April 2000); (*C.-in-C., Land*) (in the rank of General, from April 2000)
Burton, Sir Edmund, KBE, Col. Cmdt. RA (until early 2000)
Deverell, Sir John, KCB, OBE, Col. LI, Col. Cmdt. SASC (*Deputy C.-in-C., Land Command, and Inspector-General, Territorial Army*)
Willcocks, M. A., CB (*Deputy Commander (Operations) SFOR Bosnia-Hercegovina*)

MAJOR-GENERALS

Cordingley, P. A. J., DSO (*Senior British Loan Service Officer, Oman*)
Pigott, A. D., CBE, Col. The Queen's Gurkha Engineers, Col. Cmdt. RE (*Director-General, Development and Doctrine*) (until Feb. 2000)
McAfee, R. W. M., CB, Col. Cmdt. RTR (*Commander Multinational Divn Central (Airmobile)*)
Vyvyan, C. G. C., CB, CBE, Col. Cmdt. RGJ (*Head of British Defence Staff, Washington*)
Jenkins, D. J. M., CBE, Col. Cmdt. REME, Col. Cmdt. RAC, Col. QRH (*Executive Director 2, Defence Procurement Agency*)
Granville-Chapman, T. J., CBE (*Commandant, Joint Services Command and Staff College*)
Drewienkiewicz, K. J., CB, Col. Cmdt. RE (*Head of British Contingent to Kosovo Monitoring Mission*)
Sulivan, T. J., CBE (*GOC HQ 4 Divn*)
Drewry, C. F., CBE (*Asst CDS (Policy)*)
Elliott, C. L., CB, MBE (*Chief of Staff, HQ Quartermaster-General*) (until Feb. 2000); (*Director-General, Development and Doctrine*) (from Feb. 2000)
Kiszely, J. P., MC (*Asst CDS (Programmes)*)
O'Donoghue, K., CBE (*Asst Chief of the General Staff*)
Webb-Carter, E. J., OBE, Col. DWR (*GOC London District*)
Callow, C. G., OBE, QHP (*Chief Executive, Defence Medical Training Organization, and Chief Executive, Defence Secondary Care Agency*)
Denaro, A. G., CBE (*Commandant, RMAS*)
Irwin, A. S. H., CBE (*Military Secretary and Chief Executive, Army Personnel Centre*)
Trousdell, P. C. C., Col. The Queen's Own Gurkha Transport Regiment (*Chief of Staff, HQ Land Command*)
Besgrove, P. V. R., CBE, Col. Cmdt. REME
Searby, R. V. (*GOC HQ 5 Divn*)
Russell-Jones, P. J., OBE (*Asst CDS, Operational Requirements (Land Systems)*)
Risius, G. (*Director, Army Legal Services*)
Chambers, P. A., MBE (*Deputy Chief of Staff, HQ Land Command*)
Reith, J. G., CBE (*Commander Allied Command Europe Mobile Force*)
Milne, J. (*Director Support, HQ Allied Land Forces Central Europe*)
Pringle, A. R. D., CBE, Col. Cmdt. RGJ (*Chief of Staff to Chief of Joint Operations*)
Raper, A. J., CBE (*Chief Executive, Defence Communications Services Agency*)
Truluck, A. E. G., CBE (*Executive Assistant to the Chief of Staff Supreme HQ Allied Powers Europe*)
Ridgway, A. P., CBE (*Chief of Staff HQ ACE Rapid Reaction Corps*)
Watt, C. R., CBE (*GOC 1 (UK) Armd Divn*)
Ramsay, A. I., CBE, DSO, Col. Cmdt. RHF (*Commander British Forces Cyprus*)
Strudwick, M. J., CBE, Col. Cmdt. The Scottish Division (*GOC Scotland*)
Currie, A. P. N. (*Chief of Staff to Adjutant-General*)
Lyons, A. W., CBE (*Director-General, Logistic Support (Army)*)
HRH The Prince of Wales, KG, KT, GCB and Great Master of the Order of the Bath, AK, QSO, PC, ADC(P)
Curran, L. D. (*Engineering Adviser, Defence Procurement Agency*)
Dannatt, F. R., CBE, MC (*GOC 3 (UK) Divn*)
Grant Peterkin, A. P., OBE (*Senior Army Member, Royal College of Defence Studies*)
Palmer, A. M. D., CBE (*Director-General, Army Training and Recruiting and Chief Executive, Army Training and Recruiting Agency*)
Delves, C. N. G. (*Chief of Joint Forces Operational Readiness and Training*)

Sutherell, J. C. B. (*Commandant, RMCS*)

Viggers, F. R., MBE (*Comd. Multinational Divn (SW) SFOR Bosnia-Hercegovina*)

Menzies, R. C., OBE, QHS (*Director-General, Army Medical Services*) (until Feb. 2000); (*Surgeon-General*) (in the rank of Lieutenant-General, from Feb. 2000)

Gordon, R. D. S., CBE (*GOC HQ 2 Divn*)

Moore-Bick, J. D., CBE (*Leader, Study into the Future of Shrivenham/Watchfield*)

Judd, D. L. (*Director-General, Equipment Support (Army)*)

CONSTITUTION OF THE ARMY

The regular forces include the following arms, branches and corps. They are listed in accordance with the order of precedence within the British Army. All enquiries with regard to records of serving personnel (Regular and Territorial Army) should be directed to Relations with the Public, Army Personnel Office, Kentigern House, 65 Brown Street, Glasgow G2 8EX. Tel: 0141-224 8883/8880/8881/8884.

THE ARMS

HOUSEHOLD CAVALRY – The Household Cavalry Regiment (The Life Guards and The Blues and Royals)

ROYAL ARMOURED CORPS – Cavalry Regiments: 1st The Queen's Dragoon Guards; The Royal Scots Dragoon Guards (Carabiniers and Greys); The Royal Dragoon Guards; The Queen's Royal Hussars (The Queen's Own and Royal Irish); 9th/12th Royal Lancers (Prince of Wales's); The King's Royal Hussars; The Light Dragoons; The Queen's Royal Lancers; Royal Tank Regiment, comprising two regular regiments

ARTILLERY – Royal Regiment of Artillery

ENGINEERS – Corps of Royal Engineers

SIGNALS – Royal Corps of Signals

THE INFANTRY

The Foot Guards and regiments of Infantry of the Line are grouped in divisions as follows:

GUARDS DIVISION – Grenadier, Coldstream, Scots, Irish and Welsh Guards. *Divisional Office,* HQ Infantry, Imber Road, Warminster, Wilts. *Training Centre,* Infantry Training Centre, Vimy Barracks, Catterick, N. Yorks

SCOTTISH DIVISION – The Royal Scots (The Royal Regiment); The Royal Highland Fusiliers (Princess Margaret's Own Glasgow and Ayrshire Regiment); The King's Own Scottish Borderers; The Black Watch (Royal Highland Regiment); The Highlanders (Seaforth, Gordons and Camerons); The Argyll and Sutherland Highlanders (Princess Louise's). *Divisional Office,* HQ Infantry, Imber Road, Warminster, Wilts. *Training Centre,* Infantry Training Centre, Vimy Barracks, Catterick, N. Yorks

QUEEN'S DIVISION – The Princess of Wales's Royal Regiment (Queen's and Royal Hampshire's); The Royal Regiment of Fusiliers; The Royal Anglian Regiment. *Divisional Office,* HQ Infantry, Imber Road, Warminster, Wilts. *Training Centre,* Infantry Training Centre, Vimy Barracks, Catterick, N. Yorks

KING'S DIVISION – The King's Own Royal Border Regiment; The King's Regiment; The Prince of Wales's Own Regiment of Yorkshire; The Green Howards (Alexandra, Princess of Wales's Own Yorkshire Regiment); The Queen's Lancashire Regiment; The Duke of Wellington's Regiment (West Riding). *Divisional Office,* HQ Infantry, Imber Road, Warminster, Wilts. *Training Centre,* Infantry Training Centre, Vimy Barracks, Catterick, N. Yorks

THE ROYAL IRISH REGIMENT (one general service and six home service battalions) – 27th (Inniskilling), 83rd, 87th and the Ulster Defence Regiment. *Regimental HQ* and *Training Centre,* St Patrick's Barracks, BFPO 808

PRINCE OF WALES'S DIVISION – The Devonshire and Dorset Regiment; The Cheshire Regiment; The Royal Welch Fusiliers; The Royal Regiment of Wales (24th/41st Foot); The Royal Gloucestershire, Berkshire and Wiltshire Regiment; The Worcestershire and Sherwood Foresters Regiment (29th/45th Foot); The Staffordshire Regiment (The Prince of Wales's). *Divisional Office,* HQ Infantry, Imber Road, Warminster, Wilts. *Training Centre,* Infantry Training Centre, Vimy Barracks, Catterick, N. Yorks

LIGHT DIVISION – The Light Infantry; The Royal Green Jackets. *Divisional Office,* HQ Infantry, Imber Road, Warminster, Wilts. *Training Centre,* Infantry Training Centre, Vimy Barracks, Catterick, N. Yorks

BRIGADE OF GURKHAS – The Royal Gurkha Rifles; The Queen's Gurkha Engineers; Queen's Gurkha Signals; The Queen's Own Gurkha Transport Regiment. *Regimental HQ,* Queen Elizabeth Barracks, Church Crookham, Fleet, Aldershot, Hants. *Gurkha Training Wing,* Infantry Training Centre, Vimy Barracks, Catterick, N. Yorks

THE PARACHUTE REGIMENT (three regular battalions) – *Regimental HQ,* Browning Barracks, Aldershot, Hants. *Training Centre,* Infantry Training Centre, Vimy Barracks, Catterick, N. Yorks

SPECIAL AIR SERVICE REGIMENT – *Regimental HQ* and *Training Centre,* Stirling Lines, Hereford

ARMY AIR CORPS – *Regimental HQ* and *Training Centre,* Middle Wallop, Stockbridge, Hants

SERVICES/ARMS*

Royal Army Chaplains' Department – *Regimental HQ,* HQ AG, Upavon, Pewsey, Wilts. *Training Centre,* Armed Forces Chaplaincy Centre, Amport House, Amport, Andover, Hants

The Royal Logistic Corps – *Regimental HQ,* Blackdown Barracks, Deepcut, Camberley, Surrey. *Training Centre,* Princess Royal Barracks, Deepcut, Camberley, Surrey

Royal Army Medical Corps – *Regimental HQ,* Keogh Barracks, Ash Vale, Aldershot, Hants. *Training Centre,* Defence Medical Services Training Centre, Keogh Barracks, Ash Vale, Aldershot, Hants

Corps of Royal Electrical and Mechanical Engineers – *Regimental HQ* and *Training Centre,* Hazebrouck Barracks, Isaac Newton Road, Arborfield, Reading, Berks

Adjutant-General's Corps – *Corps HQ* and *Training Centre,* Worthy Down, Winchester, Hants

Royal Army Veterinary Corps – *Regimental HQ,* Keogh Barracks, Ash Vale, Aldershot, Hants. *Training Centre,* Defence Animal Centre, Welby Lane, Melton Mowbray, Leics

Small Arms School Corps – *Corps HQ* and *Training Centre,* School of Infantry, Imber Road, Warminster, Wilts

Royal Army Dental Corps – *Regimental HQ,* Keogh Barracks, Ash Vale, Aldershot, Hants. *Training Centre,* Defence Dental Agency Training Establishment, Evelyn Woods Road, Aldershot, Hants

*Intelligence Corps – *Corps HQ* and *Training Centre,* Chicksands, Shefford, Beds

Army Physical Training Corps – *Regimental HQ* and *Depot,* Queen's Avenue, Aldershot, Hants

General Service Corps

Queen Alexandra's Royal Army Nursing Corps – *Regimental HQ,* Keogh Barracks, Ash Vale, Aldershot, Hants. *Training Centre,* Health Studies Division, Royal Defence Medical College, Vulcan Block, Fort Blockhouse, Gosport, Hants

Corps of Army Music – *Corps HQ* and *Training Centre*, Army School of Music, Kneller Hall, Kneller Road, Twickenham, Middx

ARMY EQUIPMENT HOLDINGS *as at August 1999*

Tanks	373
Armoured combat vehicles	2,920
Artillery pieces	406
Large landing craft	2
Helicopters	232

THE TERRITORIAL ARMY (TA)

The Territorial Army provides formed units and individuals as an essential part of the Army's order of battle for operations across all military tasks in order to ensure that the Army is capable of mounting and sustaining operations at nominated states of readiness. It also provides a basis for regeneration, while at the same time maintaining links with the local community and society at large. From 1 July 1999 its established strength is 41,204.

Members of the TA receive pay at the rate appropriate to their rank. From 1 April 1999, the minimum daily rates of pay for officers range between £28.26 and £86.27, and for soldiers between £25.34 and £60.38. Members who complete their annual training requirements (27 and 19 days respectively for members of the Independent and Specialist TA) and are certified as efficient receive a single bounty ranging from £100 to £1,050.

Inspector-General, Lt.-Gen. Sir John Deverell, KCB, OBE

QUEEN ALEXANDRA'S ROYAL ARMY NURSING CORPS

The Queen Alexandra's Royal Army Nursing Corps (QARANC) was founded in 1902 as Queen Alexandra's Imperial Military Nursing Service (QAIMNS) and gained its present title in 1949. The QARANC has trained nurses for the register since 1950 and also trains and employs health care assistants. Qualified Registered General Nurses are also recruited. Since 1992 men have been eligible to join the QARANC. Members of the Corps serve in military hospitals in the UK and abroad and in MOD hospital units in the UK.

Colonel-in-Chief, HRH The Princess Margaret, Countess of Snowdon, GCVO, CI

Matron-in-Chief (Army) and Director, Army Nursing Services, Col. B. C. McEvilly, QHNS

The Royal Air Force

THE QUEEN

MARSHALS OF THE ROYAL AIR FORCE

HRH The Prince Philip, Duke of Edinburgh, KG, KT, OM, GBE, AC, QSO, PC, *apptd* 1953
Sir John Grandy, GCB, GCVO, KBE, DSO, *apptd* 1971
Sir Denis Spotswood, GCB, CBE, DSO, DFC, *apptd* 1974
Sir Michael Beetham, GCB, CBE, DFC, AFC, *apptd* 1982
Sir Keith Williamson, GCB, AFC, *apptd* 1985
The Lord Craig of Radley, GCB, OBE, *apptd* 1988

AIR CHIEF MARSHALS

Johns, Sir Richard, GCB, CBE, LVO, ADC (*Chief of the Air Staff*)
Cheshire, Sir John, KBE, CB (*C.-in-C. Allied Forces NW Europe*)
Squire, Sir Peter, KCB, DFC, AFC, ADC (*Air Officer Commanding-in-Chief, HQ Strike Command, and Commander Allied Air Forces NW Europe*)

AIR MARSHALS

Bagnall, Sir Anthony, KCB, OBE (*Air Member for Personnel and Air Officer C.-in-C., HQ Personnel and Training Command*)
Baird, Sir John, KBE, QHP (*Surgeon-General*) (until Feb. 2000)
Day, Sir John, KCB, OBE (*Deputy CDS (Commitments)*)
Coville, C. C. C., CB (*Deputy C.-in-C. Allied Forces Central Europe*)
Jenner, T. I., CB (*Chief of Staff and Deputy C.-in-C., HQ Strike Command*)
Norriss, P. C., CB, AFC (*Deputy Chief of Defence Procurement (Operations) and Controller of the Navy*)
Pledger, M. D., OBE, AFC (*Deputy CDS (Personnel)*)
Goodall, R. H., CB, CBE, AFC (*Chief of Staff, Component Command Air North*)

AIR VICE-MARSHALS

Stables, A. J., CBE (*Chief Executive, Training Group Defence Agency*)
French, J. C., CBE (*Director-General, Intelligence and Geographic Resources*)
Spink, C. R., CBE (*Director-General, Saudi Arabia Armed Forces Project*)
Thompson, J. H. (*AOC No. 1 Group*)
Stewart, I. M., AFC (*Air Secretary and Chief Executive, RAF Personnel Management Agency*)
Weeden, J. (*Director, Legal Services (RAF)*)
Stirrup, G. E., AFC (*Asst Chief of the Air Staff*)
Wright, R. A., AFC (*Chief of Staff, HQ Personnel and Training Command*)
McIntyre, I. G., QHDS (*Chief Executive, Defence Dental Agency*)
Sharples, C. J., QHP (*Director-General, Medical Services (RAF)*)
Burridge, B. K., CBE (*AOC No. 11/18 Group*)
Filbey, K. D., CBE (*Senior Directing Staff (Air), Royal College of Defence Studies*)
Sturley, P. O., MBE (*Senior Air Staff Officer, HQ Strike Command, and AOC No. 38 Group*)
Brackenbury, I., OBE (*Chief of Staff to Chief of Defence Logistics*)
Henderson, P. W., MBE (*Director-General, Support Management, HQ Logistics Command*)
Nicholl, S. M., CBE, AFC (*Asst CDS Operational Requirements (Air Systems)*)
Niven, D. M., CBE (*Commander, Joint Helicopter Command*)
Scott, P. J. (*Air Officer Logistics and Communications Information Systems, HQ Strike Command*)
Burton, A. J., OBE (*Air Officer Administration, HQ Strike Command*)
Rimmer, T. W., OBE (*Commandant, RAF College, Cranwell*)
Nicholson, A. A., CBE, LVO (*Integration and Aerospace Adviser, Defence Procurement Agency*)
HRH The Prince of Wales, KG, KT, GCB and Great Master of the Order of the Bath, AK, QSO, PC, ADC(P)
Gardiner, M. J., OBE (*Deputy Commander, Interim Combined Air Operations Centre No. 4*)
Couzens, D. C. (*Asst CDS (Logistics)*)
Liddell, P. (*Air Officer Communications Information Systems and Support Services*)
Harris, P. V., AFC
Arscott, J. R. D. (*Director, Airspace Policy*)
Skinner, G., CBE (*Air Officer C.-in-C., HQ Logistics Command*)

CONSTITUTION OF THE ROYAL AIR FORCE

The RAF consists of three commands: Strike Command, Personnel and Training Command and Logistics Command. Strike Command is responsible for all the RAF's front-line forces. Its roles include strike/attack, air defence, reconnaissance, maritime patrol, strategic air transport, air-to-air refuelling, search and rescue, and aero-medical facilities. Personnel and Training Command is responsible for personnel administration and training in the RAF. Logistics Command is responsible for all logistics, engineering and materiel support.

Enquiries regarding records of serving officers should be directed to the RAF Personnel Management Agency (*see* Defence Agencies, above).

RAF EQUIPMENT *as at 1 July 1999*

AIRCRAFT

Tornado ADV	93
Tornado IDS	127
Harrier	64
Jaguar	53
Canberra	7
Nimrod	27
VC10	24
Tristar	9
Hercules	55
BAe 125	6
BAe 146	3
Sentry	7
Hawk	107
Bulldog	105
Domenie	10
Islander	2
Jetstream	11
Tucano	86

HELICOPTERS

Chinook	38
Puma	41
Sea King	25
Wessex	15
Gazelle	1

ROYAL AUXILIARY AIR FORCE (RAuxAF)

Formed in 1924, the Auxiliary Air Force received the prefix 'Royal' in 1947 in recognition of its war record. The RAuxAF amalgamated with the Royal Air Force Volunteer Reserve in 1997. The RAuxAF supports the RAF in many roles, including maritime air operations, air and ground defence of airfields, air movements, aero-medical evacuation, intelligence and public relations. In May 1999 there were 1,715 reservists in the RAuxAF; under the Strategic Defence Review, the Reserve Air Forces' establishment is expected to increase to 2,920 (these figures include elements of the Royal Air Force Reserve).

The minimum annual commitment for reservists is 27 days, including 15 days' continuous training. Pay scales are equivalent to regular rates less a percentage, made on a pro-rata daily basis. A single bounty is also payable, the amount depending on the length of service.

Air Commodore-in-Chief, HM The Queen
Controller of Reserve Forces (RAF), Air Cdre C. Davison, MBE

PRINCESS MARY'S ROYAL AIR FORCE NURSING SERVICE

The Princess Mary's Royal Air Force Nursing Service (PMRAFNS) offers commissions to Registered General Nurses (RGN) with a minimum of two years experience after obtaining RGN and normally with a second qualification. RGNs with no additional experience or qualification are recruited as non-commissioned officers in the grade of Staff Nurse.

Air Chief Commandant, HRH Princess Alexandra, the Hon. Lady Ogilvy, GCVO
Matron-in-Chief, Air Cdre R. H. Williams, QHNS

SERVICE SALARIES

The following rates of pay apply from 1 April 1999. Annual salaries are derived from daily rates in whole pence and rounded to the nearest £.

The pay rates shown are for Army personnel. The rates apply also to personnel of equivalent rank and pay band in the other services (*see* page 395 for table of relative ranks).

OFFICERS' SALARIES

MAIN SCALE

Rank	Daily	Annual	Rank	Daily	Annual
Second Lieutenant	£43.12	£15,782	Lieutenant-Colonel *contd*		
			After 4 years in the rank or with 21 years' service	£136.61	£49,999
Lieutenant			After 6 years in the rank or with 23 years' service	140.03	51,251
On appointment	57.00	20,862			
After 1 year in the rank	58.50	21,411	After 8 years in the rank or with 25 years' service	143.45	52,503
After 2 years in the rank	60.00	21,960			
After 3 years in the rank	61.50	22,509	Colonel		
After 4 years in the rank	63.00	23,058	On appointment	150.85	55,211
			After 2 years in the rank	154.82	56,664
Captain			After 4 years in the rank	158.79	58,117
On appointment	72.71	26,612	After 6 years in the rank	162.76	59,570
After 1 year in the rank	74.67	27,329	After 8 years in the rank	166.73	61,023
After 2 years in the rank	76.63	28,047			
After 3 years in the rank	78.59	28,764	Brigadier	184.79	67,633
After 4 years in the rank	80.55	29,481	Major-General		
After 5 years in the rank	82.51	30,199	Range 1	195.68	71,423
After 6 years in the rank	84.47	30,916	Range 2	200.98	73,358
			Range 3	207.85	75,865
Major					
On appointment	92.02	33,679	Lieutenant-General		
After 1 year in the rank	94.29	34,510	Range 4	223.00	81,396
After 2 years in the rank	96.56	35,341	Range 5	240.12	87,642
After 3 years in the rank	98.83	36,172			
After 4 years in the rank	101.10	37,003	General		
After 5 years in the rank	103.37	37,833	Range 6	298.82	109,069
After 6 years in the rank	105.64	38,664	Range 7	314.32	114,727
After 7 years in the rank	107.91	39,495	Range 8	384.49	140,339
After 8 years in the rank	110.18	40,326			
Special List Lieutenant-Colonel	127.23	46,566			
Lieutenant-Colonel					
On appointment with less than 19 years' service	129.77	47,496			
After 2 years in the rank or with 19 years' service	133.19	48,746			

Field Marshal – appointments to this rank will not usually be made in peacetime. The salary for existing holders of the rank is equivalent to the salary of a range 8 General

---

SALARIES OF OFFICERS COMMISSIONED FROM THE RANKS (LIEUTENANTS AND CAPTAINS ONLY)

YEARS OF COMMISSIONED SERVICE

YEARS OF NON-COMMISSIONED SERVICE FROM AGE 18

	Less than 12 years		12 years but less than 15 years		15 years or more	
	Daily	Annual	Daily	Annual	Daily	Annual
On commissioning	£80.07	£29,306	£84.16	£30,803	£88.25	£32,300
After 1 year's service	82.11	30,052	86.20	31,549	89.72	32,838
After 2 years' service	84.16	30,803	88.25	32,300	91.04	33,321
After 3 years' service	86.20	31,549	89.72	32,838	92.36	33,804
After 4 years' service	88.25	32,300	91.04	33,321	93.68	34,287
After 5 years' service	89.72	32,838	92.36	33,804	95.00	34,770
After 6 years' service	91.04	33,321	93.68	34,287	96.32	35,253
After 8 years' service	92.36	33,804	95.00	34,770	97.64	35,736
After 10 years' service	93.68	34,287	96.32	35,253	97.64	35,736
After 12 years' service	95.00	34,770	97.64	35,736	97.64	35,736
After 14 years' service	96.32	35,253	97.64	35,736	97.64	35,736
After 16 years' service	97.64	35,736	97.64	35,736	97.64	35,736

SOLDIERS' SALARIES

The pay structure below officer level is divided into pay bands. Jobs at each rank are allocated to bands according to their score in the job evaluation system. Length of service is from age 18.

Scale A: committed to serve for less than 6 years, or those with less than 9 years' service who are serving on Open Engagement

Scale B: committed to serve for 6 years but less than 9 years

Scale C: committed to serve for 9 years or more, or those with more than 9 years' service who are serving on Open Engagement

Daily rates of pay effective from 1 April 1999 are:

RANK — SCALE A

	Band 1	Band 2	Band 3	
Private				
Class 4	£27.05	£ —	£ —	
Class 3	30.44	35.33	40.76	
Class 2	34.02	38.95	44.38	
Class 1	37.00	41.92	47.34	
Lance Corporal				
Class 3	37.00	41.92	47.34	
Class 2	39.38	44.30	50.15	
Class 1	42.36	47.28	53.13	
Corporal				
Class 2	45.26	50.16	56.00	
Class 1	48.59	53.47	59.31	
	Band 4	Band 5	Band 6	Band 7
Sergeant	£53.44	£58.75	£64.54	£ —
Staff Sergeant	56.50	61.80	67.63	74.63
Warrant Officer				
Class 2	60.41	65.73	72.88	80.05
Class 1	64.42	69.73	76.98	84.12

SCALE B

	Band 1	Band 2	Band 3	
Private				
Class 4	£27.35	£ —	£ —	
Class 3	30.74	35.63	41.06	
Class 2	34.32	39.25	44.68	
Class 1	37.30	42.22	47.64	
Lance Corporal				
Class 3	37.30	42.22	47.64	
Class 2	39.68	44.60	50.45	
Class 1	42.66	47.58	53.43	
Corporal				
Class 2	45.56	50.46	56.30	
Class 1	48.89	53.77	59.61	
	Band 4	Band 5	Band 6	Band 7
Sergeant	£53.74	£59.05	£64.84	£ —
Staff Sergeant	56.80	62.10	67.93	74.93
Warrant Officer				
Class 2	60.71	66.03	73.18	80.35
Class 1	64.72	70.03	77.28	84.42

SCALE C

	Band 1	Band 2	Band 3	
Private				
Class 4	£27.80	£ —	£ —	
Class 3	31.19	36.08	41.51	
Class 2	34.77	39.70	45.13	
Class 1	37.75	42.67	48.09	
Lance Corporal				
Class 3	37.75	42.67	48.09	
Class 2	40.13	45.05	50.90	
Class 1	43.11	48.03	53.88	
Corporal				
Class 2	46.01	50.91	56.75	
Class 1	49.34	54.22	60.06	
	Band 4	Band 5	Band 6	Band 7
Sergeant	£54.19	£59.50	£65.29	£ —
Staff Sergeant	57.25	62.55	68.38	75.38
Warrant Officer				
Class 2	61.16	66.48	73.63	80.80
Class 1	65.17	70.48	77.73	84.87

RELATIVE RANK – ARMED FORCES

	Royal Navy		Army		Royal Air Force
1	Admiral of the Fleet	1	Field Marshal	1	Marshal of the RAF
2	Admiral (Adm.)	2	General (Gen.)	2	Air Chief Marshal
3	Vice-Admiral (Vice-Adm.)	3	Lieutenant-General (Lt.-Gen.)	3	Air Marshal
4	Rear-Admiral (Rear-Adm.)	4	Major-General (Maj.-Gen.)	4	Air Vice-Marshal
5	Commodore (Cdre)	5	Brigadier (Brig.)	5	Air Commodore (Air Cdre)
6	Captain (Capt.)	6	Colonel (Col.)	6	Group Captain (Gp Capt)
7	Commander (Cdr.)	7	Lieutenant-Colonel (Lt.-Col.)	7	Wing Commander (Wg Cdr.)
8	Lieutenant-Commander (Lt.-Cdr.)	8	Major (Maj.)	8	Squadron Leader (Sqn Ldr)
9	Lieutenant (Lt.)	9	Captain (Capt.)	9	Flight Lieutenant (Flt. Lt.)
10	Sub-Lieutenant (Sub-Lt.)	10	Lieutenant (Lt.)	10	Flying Officer (FO)
11	Acting Sub-Lieutenant (Acting Sub-Lt.)	11	Second Lieutenant (2nd Lt.)	11	Pilot Officer (PO)

SERVICE RETIRED PAY ON COMPULSORY RETIREMENT

Those who leave the services having served at least five years, but not long enough to qualify for the appropriate immediate pension, now qualify for a preserved pension and terminal grant, both of which are payable at age 60. The tax-free resettlement grants shown below are payable on release to those who qualify for a preserved pension and who have completed nine years service from age 21 (officers) or 12 years from age 18 (other ranks).

The annual rates for army personnel are given. The rates apply also to personnel of equivalent rank in the other services, including the nursing services.

OFFICERS

Applicable to officers who give full pay service on the active list on or after 31 March 1999. Senior officers (*) can elect to receive a pension calculated as a percentage of their pensionable earnings.

No. of years reckonable service over age 21	Capt. and below	Major	Lt.-Col.	Colonel	Brigadier	Major-General*	Lieutenant-General*	General*
16	£ 8,811	£10,546	£13,893	£ —	£ —	£ —	£ —	£ —
17	9,219	11,047	14,536	—	—	—	—	—
18	9,628	11,547	15,179	17,643	—	—	—	—
19	10,036	12,048	15,821	18,390	—	—	—	—
20	10,445	12,549	16,464	19,137	—	—	—	—
21	10,853	13,049	17,107	19,884	—	—	—	—
22	11,262	13,550	17,750	20,631	23,784	—	—	—
23	11,670	14,051	18,393	21,378	24,536	—	—	—
24	12,079	14,551	19,036	22,125	25,287	27,535	—	—
25	12,487	15,052	19,678	22,873	26,039	28,353	—	—
26	12,895	15,553	20,321	23,620	26,790	29,171	—	—
27	13,304	16,053	20,964	24,367	27,542	29,990	34,418	—
28	13,712	16,554	21,607	25,114	28,293	30,808	35,357	—
29	14,121	17,055	22,250	25,861	29,045	31,626	36,296	—
30	14,529	17,555	22,893	26,608	29,796	32,444	37,235	49,298
31	14,938	18,056	23,535	27,355	30,548	33,263	38,174	50,541
32	15,346	18,557	24,178	28,102	31,299	34,081	39,114	51,784
33	15,755	19,057	24,821	28,849	32,051	34,899	40,053	53,027
34	16,163	19,558	25,464	29,596	32,802	35,717	40,992	54,271

*Field Marshal** − active list half pay at the rate of £70,170 a year

WARRANT OFFICERS, NCOs AND PRIVATES

Applicable to soldiers who give full pay service on or after 31 March 1999.

No. of years reckonable service	Below Corporal	Corporal	Sergeant	Staff Sergeant	Warrant Officer Class II	Warrant Officer Class I
22	£5,121	£6,499	£ 7,198	£ 8,194	£ 8,470	£ 9,364
23	5,300	6,726	7,449	8,480	8,770	9,701
24	5,478	6,953	7,701	8,766	9,070	10,037
25	5,657	7,180	7,952	9,052	9,370	10,374
26	5,836	7,406	8,203	9,338	9,670	10,710
27	6,015	7,633	8,454	9,624	9,970	11,047
28	6,193	7,860	8,706	9,910	10,270	11,383
29	6,372	8,087	8,957	10,196	10,570	11,720
30	6,551	8,314	9,208	10,482	10,871	12,056
31	6,730	8,541	9,459	10,768	11,171	12,393
32	6,908	8,768	9,711	11,054	11,471	12,729
33	7,087	8,995	9,962	11,340	11,771	13,066
34	7,266	9,221	10,213	11,626	12,071	13,402
35	7,445	9,448	10,464	11,912	12,371	13,739
36	7,623	9,675	10,716	12,198	12,671	14,075
37	7,802	9,902	10,967	12,484	12,971	14,412

RESETTLEMENT GRANTS

Terminal grants are in each case three times the rate of retired pay or pension. There are special rates of retired pay for certain other ranks not shown above. Lower rates are payable in cases of voluntary retirement.

A gratuity of £2,995 is payable for officers with short service commissions for each year completed. Resettlement grants are: officers £10,305; non-commissioned ranks £6,771.

Religion in the UK

There are two established, i.e. state, churches in the United Kingdom: the Church of England and the Church of Scotland. There are no established churches in Wales or Northern Ireland, though the Church in Wales, the Scottish Episcopal Church and the Church of Ireland are members of the Anglican Communion.

About 65 per cent of the population of the UK (38.1 million people) would call itself broadly Christian (in the Trinitarian sense), with 45 per cent (26.1 million) identifying with Anglican churches, 10 per cent (5.7 million) with the Roman Catholic Church, 4 per cent (2.6 million) with Presbyterian Churches, 2 per cent (1.3 million) with the Methodist Churches and 4 per cent (2.6 million) with other Christian churches; but only about 8.7 per cent of the population of Great Britain (3.98 million people) regularly attends a Christian church. Church attendance in Northern Ireland is estimated at 30–35 per cent of the population.

About 2 per cent of the population (1.3 million people) is affiliated to non-Trinitarian churches, e.g. Jehovah's Witnesses, the Church of Jesus Christ of Latter-Day Saints (Mormons), the Church of Christ, Scientist and the Unitarian churches.

A further 5 per cent of the population (3.25 million people) are adherents of other faiths, including Hinduism, Islam, Judaism and Sikhism.

About 28 per cent of the population is non-religious.

ADHERENTS TO RELIGIONS IN UK (millions)

	1975	1985	1995
Christian (Trinitarian)	40.2	39.1	38.1
Non-Trinitarian	0.7	1.0	1.3
Hindu	0.3	0.4	0.4
Jew	0.4	0.3	0.3
Muslim	0.4	0.9	1.2
Sikh	0.2	0.3	0.6
Other	0.1	0.3	0.3
Total	42.3	42.3	42.2

PERCENTAGE OF UK POPULATION ADHERING TO RELIGIONS

	1975	1985	1995
Christian (Trinitarian)	72	69	65
Non-Trinitarian	1	2	2
Non-Christian religions	3	3	5
All religions	76	74	72

Source: Christian Research/Paternoster Publishing – UK Christian Handbook Religious Trends No. 1 1998–9; figures in text are for 1995

INTER-CHURCH AND INTER-FAITH CO-OPERATION

The main umbrella body for the Christian churches in the UK is the Churches Together in Britain and Ireland (formerly the Council of Churches for Britain and Ireland). There are also ecumenical bodies in each of the constituent countries of the UK: Churches Together in England, Action of Churches Together in Scotland, CYTUN (Churches Together in Wales), and the Irish Council of Churches. The Free Churches' Council comprises most of the Free Churches in England and Wales, and the Evangelical Alliance represents evangelical Christians.

The Inter Faith Network for the United Kingdom promotes co-operation between faiths, and the Council of Christians and Jews works to improve relations between the two religions. Churches Together in Britain and Ireland also has a Commission on Inter Faith Relations.

ACTION OF CHURCHES TOGETHER IN SCOTLAND, Scottish Churches House, Kirk Street, Dunblane, Perthshire FK15 0AJ. Tel: 01786-823588. General Secretary, Revd Dr K. Franz

CHURCHES TOGETHER IN BRITAIN AND IRELAND, Inter-Church House, 35–41 Lower Marsh, London SE1 7RL. Tel: 0171-620 4444. General Secretary, Dr D. Goodbourn

CHURCHES TOGETHER IN ENGLAND, 101 Queen Victoria Street, London EC4V 4EN. Tel: 0171-332 8230. Administration Officer, Ms J. Lampard

COUNCIL OF CHRISTIANS AND JEWS, Drayton House, 30 Gordon Street, London WC1H 0AN. Tel: 0171-388 3322. Director, Sr M. Shepherd, NDS

CYTUN (CHURCHES TOGETHER IN WALES) - Ty John Penri, 11 St Helen's Road, Swansea SA1 4AL. Tel: 01792-460876. General Secretary, Revd G. Abraham-Williams

EVANGELICAL ALLIANCE, Whitefield House, 186 Kennington Park Road, London SE11 4BT. Tel: 0171-207 2100. General Director, Revd J. Edwards

FREE CHURCHES' COUNCIL, 27 Tavistock Square, London WC1H 9HH. Tel: 0171-387 8413. General Secretary, Revd G. H. Roper

INTER FAITH NETWORK FOR THE UNITED KINGDOM, 5–7 Tavistock Place, London WC1H 9SN. Tel: 0171-388 0008. Director, B. Pearce

IRISH COUNCIL OF CHURCHES, Inter-Church Centre, 48 Elmwood Avenue, Belfast BT9 6AZ. Tel: 01232-663145. General Secretary, Dr R. D. Stevens

Christianity

The faith was slowly formulated in the first millennium of the Christian era. Between AD 325 and 787 there were seven Oecumenical Councils at which bishops from the entire Christian world assembled to resolve various doctrinal disputes. The estrangement between East and West began after Constantine moved the centre of the Roman Empire from Rome to Constantinople, and it gained momentum after the temporal administration was divided. Linguistic and cultural differences between Greek East and Latin West served to encourage separate ecclesiastical developments which became pronounced in the tenth and early 11th centuries.

Administration of the church was divided between five ancient patriarchates: Rome and all the West, Constantinople (the imperial city – the 'New Rome'), Jerusalem and all Palestine, Antioch and all the East, and Alexandria and all Africa. Of these, only Rome was in the Latin West and after the schism in 1054, Rome developed a structure of authority centralized on the Papacy, while the Orthodox East maintained the style of localized administration.

Papal authority over the doctrine and jurisdiction of the Church in western Europe was unrivalled after the split with the Eastern Orthodox Church until the Protestant Reformation in the 16th century.

CHRISTIANITY IN BRITAIN

A Church of England already existed when Pope Gregory sent Augustine to evangelize the English in AD 596. Conflicts between Church and State during the Middle Ages culminated in the Act of Supremacy in 1534, which repudiated papal supremacy and declared King Henry VIII to be the supreme head of the Church in England. Since 1559 the English monarch has been termed the Supreme Governor of the Church of England.

In 1560 the jurisdiction of the Roman Catholic Church in Scotland was abolished and the first assembly of the

Church of Scotland ratified the Confession of Faith, drawn up by a committee including John Knox. In 1592 Parliament passed an Act guaranteeing the liberties of the Church and its presbyterian government. King James VI (James I of England) and later Stuart monarchs attempted to reintroduce episcopacy, but a presbyterian church was finally restored in 1690 and secured by the Act of Settlement (1690) and the Act of Union (1707).

PORVOO DECLARATION

The Porvoo Declaration was drawn up by representatives of the British and Irish Anglican churches and the Nordic and Baltic Lutheran churches and was approved by the General Synod of the Church of England in July 1995. Churches that approve the Declaration regard baptized members of each other's churches as members of their own, and allow free interchange of episcopally ordained ministers within the rules of each church.

For Christian churches in the UK, *see* pages 401–423

Non-Christian Religions

BUDDHISM

Buddhism originated in northern India, in the teachings of Siddharta Gautama, who was born near Kapilavastu about 560 BC.

Fundamental to Buddhism is the concept that there is no such thing as a permanent soul or self; when someone dies, consciousness is the only one of the elements of which they were composed which is lost. All the other elements regroup in a new body and carry with them the consequences of the conduct of the earlier life (known as the law of *karma*). This cycle of death and rebirth is broken only when the state of *nirvana* has been reached. Buddhism steers a middle path between belief in personal immortality and belief in death as the final end.

The Four Noble Truths of Buddhism (*dukkha*, suffering; *tanha*, a thirst or desire for continued existence which causes dukkha; *nirvana*, the final liberation from desire and ignorance; and *ariya*, the path to nirvana) are all held to be universal and to sum up the *dhamma* or true nature of life. Necessary qualities to promote spiritual development are *sila* (morality), *samadhi* (meditation) and *panna* (wisdom).

There are two main schools of Buddhism: *Theravada* Buddhism, the earliest extant school, which is more traditional, and *Mahayana* Buddhism, which began to develop about 100 years after the Buddha's death and is more liberal; it teaches that all people may attain Buddahood. Important schools which have developed within Mahayana Buddhism are *Zen* Buddhism, *Nichiren* Buddhism and Pure Land Buddhism or *Amidism*. There are also distinctive Tibetan forms of Buddhism. Buddhism began to establish itself in the West in the early 20th century.

The scripture of Theravada Buddhism is the *Pali Canon*, which dates from the first century BC. Mahayana Buddhism uses a Sanskrit version of the Pali Canon but also has many other works of scripture.

There is no set time for Buddhist worship, which may take place in a temple or in the home. Worship centres around *paritta* (chanting), acts of devotion centering on the image of the Buddha, and, where possible, offerings to a relic of the Buddha. Buddhist festivals vary according to local traditions and within Theravada and Mahayana Buddhism. For religious purposes Buddhists use solar and lunar calendars, the New Year being celebrated in April. Other festivals mark events in the life of the Buddha. There is no supreme governing authority in Buddhism.

In the United Kingdom communities representing all schools of Buddhism have developed and operate independently. The Buddhist Society was established in 1924; it runs courses and lectures, and publishes books about Buddhism. It represents no one school of Buddhism.

There are estimated to be at least 300 million Buddhists world-wide, and more than 500 groups and centres, an estimated 25,000 adherents and up to 20 temples or monasteries in the UK.

THE BUDDHIST SOCIETY, 58 Eccleston Square, London SW1V 1PH. Tel: 0171-834 5858. *General Secretary*, R. C. Maddox

HINDUISM

Hinduism has no historical founder but had become highly developed in India by about 1200 BC. Its adherents originally called themselves Aryans; Muslim invaders first called the Aryans 'Hindus' (derived from 'Sindhu', the name of the river Indus) in the eighth century.

Most Hindus hold that *satya* (truthfulness), *ahimsa* (non-violence), honesty, physical labour and tolerance of other faiths are essential for good living. They believe in one supreme spirit (*Brahman*), and in the transmigration of *atman* (the soul). Most Hindus accept the doctrine of *karma* (consequences of actions), the concept of *samsara* (successive lives) and the possibility of all atmans achieving *moksha* (liberation from samsara) through *jnana* (knowledge), *yoga* (meditation), *karma* (work or action) and *bhakti* (devotion).

Most Hindus offer worship to *murtis* (images or statues) representing different aspects of Brahman, and follow their *dharma* (religious and social duty) according to the traditions of their *varna* (social class), *ashrama* (stage in life), *jati* (caste) and *kula* (family).

Hinduism's sacred texts are divided into *shruti* ('heard' or divinely inspired), including the *Vedas*; or *smriti* ('remembered' tradition), including the *Ramayana*, the *Mahabharata*, the *Puranas* (ancient myths), and the sacred law books. Most Hindus recognize the authority of the *Vedas*, the oldest holy books, and accept the philosophical teachings of the *Upanishads*, the *Vedanta Sutras* and the *Bhagavad-Gita*.

Brahman is formless, limitless and all-pervading, and is represented in worship by murtis which may be male or female and in the form of a human, animal or bird. Brahma, Vishnu and Shiva are the most important gods worshipped by Hindus; their respective consorts are Saraswati, Lakshmi and Durga or Parvati, also known as Shakti. There are believed to have been ten *avatars* (incarnations) of Vishnu, of whom the most important are Rama and Krishna. Other popular gods are Ganesha, Hanuman and Subrahmanyam. All gods are seen as aspects of the supreme God, not as competing deities.

Orthodox Hindus revere all gods and goddesses equally, but there are many sects, including the Hare-Krishna movement (ISKCon), the Arya Samaj, the Swami Narayan Hindu mission and the Satya Sai-Baba movement, in which worship is concentrated on one deity to the exclusion of others. In some sects a human *guru* (spiritual teacher) is revered more than the deity, while in other sects the guru is seen as the source of spiritual guidance.

Hinduism does not have a centrally-trained and ordained priesthood. The pronouncements of the *shankaracharyas* (heads of monasteries) of Shringeri, Puri, Dwarka and Badrinath are heeded by the orthodox but may be ignored by the various sects.

The commonest form of worship is a *puja*, in which offerings of red and yellow powders, rice grains, water, flowers, food, fruit, incense and light are made to the *murti* (image) of a deity. Puja may be done either in a home shrine or a *mandir* (temple). Many British Hindus celebrate life-cycle rituals with Sanskrit mantras for naming a baby, the sacred thread (an initiation ceremony), marriage and cremation. For details of the Hindu calendar, main festivals etc, *see* pages 84–5.

The largest communities of Hindus in Britain are in Leicester, London, Birmingham and Bradford, and developed as a result of immigration from India, eastern Africa and Sri Lanka.

There are an estimated 800 million Hindus world-wide; there are about 360,000 adherents and over 150 temples in the UK.

ARYA PRATINIDHI SABHA (UK) AND ARYA SAMAJ LONDON, 69A Argyle Road, London WI3 0LY. Tel: 0181-991 1732. *President*, Prof. S. N. Bharadwaj

BHARATIYA VIDYA BHAVAN, Institute of Indian Art and Culture, 4A Castletown Road, London W14 9HQ. Tel: 0171-381 4608. *Executive Director*, Dr M. N. Nandakumara

INTERNATIONAL SOCIETY FOR KRISHNA CONSCIOUSNESS (ISKCon), Bhaktivedanta Manor, Dharam Marg, Hilfield Lane, Aldenham, Watford, Herts WD2 8EZ. Tel: 01923-857244. *Governing Body Commissioner*, P. Latai

NATIONAL COUNCIL OF HINDU TEMPLES (UK), Bhakrivedanta Manor, Dharam Marg, Hilfield Lane, Aldenham, Watford WD2 8EZ. Tel: 01923-856269. *Secretary*, V. P. Aery

SWAMINARAYAN HINDU MISSION, 105–119 Brentfield Road, London NWI0 8JP. Tel: 0181-965 2651. *Chairman*, Sadhu Atmaswarup Das

VISHWA HINDU PARISHAD (UK), 48 Wharfedale Gardens, Thornton Heath, Surrey CR7 6LB. Tel: 0181-684 9716. *General Secretary*, K. Ruparelia

---

ISLAM

Islam (which means 'peace arising from submission to the will of Allah' in Arabic) is a monotheistic religion which was taught in Arabia by the Prophet Muhammad, who was born in Mecca (Makkah) in AD 570. Islam spread to Egypt, North Africa, Spain and the borders of China in the century following the prophet's death, and is now the predominant religion in Indonesia, the Near and Middle East, northern and parts of western Africa, Pakistan, Bangladesh, Malaysia and some of the former Soviet republics. There are also large Muslim communities in other countries.

For Muslims (adherents of Islam), there is one God (*Allah*), who holds absolute power. His commands were revealed to mankind through the prophets, who include Abraham, Moses and Jesus, but his message was gradually corrupted until revealed finally and in perfect form to Muhammad through the angel *Jibril* (Gabriel) over a period of 23 years. This last, incorruptible message has been recorded in the *Qur'an* (Koran), which contains 114 divisions called *surahs*, each made up of *ayahs*, and is held to be the essence of all previous scriptures. The *Ahadith* are the records of the Prophet Muhammad's deeds and sayings (the *Sunnah*) as recounted by his immediate followers. A culture and a system of law and theology gradually developed to form a distinctive Islamic civilization. Islam makes no distinction between sacred and worldly affairs and provides rules for every aspect of human life. The *Shari'ah* is the sacred law of Islam based upon prescriptions derived from the Qur'an and the Sunnah of the Prophet.

The 'five pillars of Islam' are *shahadah* (a declaration of faith in the oneness and supremacy of Allah and the messengership of Muhammad); *salat* (formal prayer, to be performed five times a day facing the Ka'bah (sacred house)

in the holy city of Mecca); *zakat* (welfare due); *sawm* (fasting during the month of Ramadan); and *hajj* (pilgrimage to Mecca); some Muslims would add *jihad* (striving for the cause of good and resistance to evil).

Two main groups developed among Muslims. *Sunni* Muslims accept the legitimacy of Muhammad's first four *caliphs* (successors as head of the Muslim community) and of the authority of the Muslim community as a whole. About 90 per cent of Muslims are Sunni Muslims. *Shi'ites* recognize only Muhammad's son-in-law Ali as his rightful successor and the *Imams* (descendants of Ali, not to be confused with *imams* (prayer leaders or religious teachers)) as the principal legitimate religious authority. The largest group within Shi'ism is *Twelver Shi'ism*, which has been the official school of law and theology in Iran since the 16th century; other subsects include the *Ismailis* and the *Druze*, the latter being an offshoot of the Ismailis and differing considerably from the main body of Muslims.

There is no organized priesthood, but learned men such as *ulama*, *imams* and *ayatollahs* are accorded great respect. The *Sufis* are the mystics of Islam. Mosques are centres for worship and teaching and also for social and welfare activities. For details of the Muslim calendar and festivals, *see* page 86.

Islam was first known in western Europe in the eighth century AD when 800 years of Muslim rule began in Spain. Later, Islam spread to eastern Europe. More recently, Muslims came to Europe from Africa, the Middle East and Asia in the late 19th century. Both the Sunni and Shi'ah traditions are represented in Britain, but the majority of Muslims in Britain adhere to Sunni Islam.

There is no central organization, but the Islamic Cultural Centre, which is the London Central Mosque, and the Imams and Mosques Council are influential bodies; there are many other Muslim organizations in Britain.

There are about 1,000 million Muslims world-wide, with more than one million adherents and about 900 mosques in Britain.

IMAMS AND MOSQUES COUNCIL, 20–22 Creffield Road, London W5 3RP. Tel: 0181-992 6636. *Director of the Council and Principal of the Muslim College*, Dr M. A. Z. Badawi

ISLAMIC CULTURAL CENTRE, 146 Park Road, London NW8 7RG. Tel: 0171-724 3363. *Director*, H. Al-Majed

MUSLIM COUNCIL OF BRITAIN, P.O. Box 52, Wembley, Middx HA9 7AL. Tel: 0181-903 9024. *Secretary-General*, Iqbal Sacranie

MUSLIM WORLD LEAGUE, 46 Goodge Street, London WIP IFJ. Tel: 0171-636 7568. *Deputy Director*, G. Rahman

UNION OF MUSLIM ORGANIZATIONS OF THE UK AND EIRE, 109 Campden Hill Road, London W8 7TL. Tel: 0171-229 0538. *General Secretary*, Dr S. A. Pasha

---

JUDAISM

Judaism is the oldest monotheistic faith. The primary authority of Judaism is the Hebrew Bible or *Tanakh*, which records how the descendants of Abraham were led by Moses out of their slavery in Egypt to Mount Sinai where God's law (*Torah*) was revealed to them as the chosen people. The *Talmud*, which consists of commentaries on the *Mishnah* (the first text of rabbinical Judaism), is also held to be authoritative, and may be divided into two main categories: the *halakah* (dealing with legal and ritual matters) and the *Aggadah* (dealing with theological and ethical matters not directly concerned with the regulation of conduct). The *Midrash* comprises rabbinic writings containing biblical interpretations in the spirit of the Aggadah. The *halakah* has become a source of division; Orthodox Jews regard Jewish law as derived from God and therefore unalterable; Reform and Liberal Jews seek to interpret it in the light of contemporary considerations; and Conservative Jews aim to maintain most of the traditional rituals but to allow changes in accordance with tradition. Reconstructionist Judaism, a 20th-century movement, regards Judaism as a culture rather than a theological system and accepts all forms of Jewish practice.

The family is the basic unit of Jewish ritual, with the synagogue playing an important role as the centre for public worship and religious study. A synagogue is led by a group of laymen who are elected to office. The Rabbi is primarily a teacher and spiritual guide. The Sabbath is the central religious observance. For details of the Jewish calendar, fasts and festivals, *see* page 85. Most British Jews are descendants of either the *Ashkenazim* of central and eastern Europe or the *Sephardim* of Spain and Portugal.

The Chief Rabbi of the United Hebrew Congregations of the Commonwealth is appointed by a Chief Rabbinate Conference, and is the rabbinical authority of the Orthodox sector of the Ashkenazi Jewish community. His authority is not recognized by the Reform Synagogues of Great Britain (the largest progressive group), the Union of Liberal and Progressive Synagogues, the Union of Orthodox Hebrew Congregations, the Federation of Synagogues, the Sephardi community, or the Assembly of Masorti Synagogues. He is, however, generally recognized both outside the Jewish community and within it as the public religious representative of the totality of British Jewry. The Chief Rabbi is President of the *Beth Din* of the United Synagogue.

A *Beth Din* (Court of Judgment) is a rabbinic court. The *Dayanim* (Assessors) adjudicate in disputes or on matters of Jewish law and tradition; they also oversee dietary law administration.

The Board of Deputies of British Jews, established in 1760, is the representative body of British Jewry. The basis of representation is mainly synagogal, but communal organizations are also represented. It watches over the interests of British Jewry, acts as the central voice of the community and seeks to counter anti-Jewish discrimination and antisemitic activities.

In November 1998 a Consultative Committee was established comprising representatives of the Assembly of Masorti Synagogues, Reform Synagogues of Great Britain, Union of Liberal and Progressive Synagogues and the United Synagogue. The Committee holds discussions to further communal harmony and development.

There are over 12.5 million Jews world-wide; in Great Britain and Ireland there are an estimated 285,000 adherents and about 365 synagogues. Of these, 191 congregations and about 150 rabbis and ministers are under the jurisdiction of the Chief Rabbi; 99 orthodox congregations have a more independent status; and 75 congregations do not recognize the authority of the Chief Rabbi.

CHIEF RABBINATE, 735 High Road, London N12 0US. Tel: 0181-343 6301. *Chief Rabbi,* Prof. Jonathan Sacks; *Executive Director,* Mrs S. Weinberg

BETH DIN (COURT OF THE CHIEF RABBI), 735 High Road, London N12 0US. Tel: 0181-343 6280. *Registrar,* vacant; *Dayanim,* Rabbi C. Ehrentreu; Rabbi I. Binstock; Rabbi C. D. Kaplin; Rabbi M. Gelley

BOARD OF DEPUTIES OF BRITISH JEWS, Commonwealth House, 1–19 New Oxford Street, London WC1A INF. Tel: 0171-543 5400. *President,* E. Tabachnik, QC; *Director-General,* N. A. Nagler

ASSEMBLY OF MASORTI SYNAGOGUES, 1097 Finchley Road, London NW11 0PU. Tel: 0181-201 8772. *Director,* H. Freedman

FEDERATION OF SYNAGOGUES, 65 Watford Way, London NW4 3AQ. Tel: 0181-202 2263. *Head of Administration,* G. D. Coleman

BETH DIN OF THE FEDERATION OF SYNAGOGUES, 65 Watford Way, London NW4 3AQ. Tel: 0181-202 2263. *Registrar,* Rabbi S. Zaiden; *Dayanim,* Dayan Y. Y. Lichtenstein, Dayan B. Berkovits, Dayan M. D. Elzas

REFORM SYNAGOGUES OF GREAT BRITAIN, The Sternberg Centre for Judaism, 80 East End Road, London N3 2SY. Tel: 0181-349 4731. *Chief Executive,* Rabbi T. Bayfield

SPANISH AND PORTUGUESE JEWS' CONGREGATION, 2 Ashworth Road, London W9 IJY. Tel: 0171-289 2573. *Chief Administrator and Secretary,* H. Miller

UNION OF LIBERAL AND PROGRESSIVE SYNAGOGUES, The Montagu Centre, 21 Maple Street, London W1P 6DS. Tel: 0171-580 1663. *Executive Director,* Rabbi Dr C. H. Middleburgh

UNION OF ORTHODOX HEBREW CONGREGATIONS, 140 Stamford Hill, London N16 6QT. Tel: 0181-802 6226.

UNITED SYNAGOGUE HEAD OFFICE, 735 High Road, London N12 0US. Tel: 0181-343 8989. *Chief Executive,* George Willman

---

SIKHISM

The Sikh religion dates from the birth of Guru Nanak in the Punjab in 1469. 'Guru' means teacher but in Sikh tradition has come to represent the divine presence of God giving inner spiritual guidance. Nanak's role as the human vessel of the divine guru was passed on to nine successors, the last of whom (Guru Gobind Singh) died in 1708. The immortal guru is now held to reside in the sacred scripture, *Guru Granth Sahib,* and so to be present in all Sikh gatherings.

Guru Nanak taught that there is one God and that different religions are like different roads leading to the same destination. He condemned religious conflict, ritualism and caste prejudices. The fifth Guru, Guru Arjan Dev, largely compiled the Sikh Holy Book, a collection of hymns (*gurbani*) known as the *Adi Granth.* It includes the writings of the first five Gurus and the ninth Guru, and selected writings of Hindu and Muslim saints whose views are in accord with the Gurus' teachings. Guru Arjan Dev also built the Golden Temple at Amritsar, the centre of Sikhism. The tenth Guru, Guru Gobind Singh, passed on the guruship to the sacred scripture, Guru Granth Sahib. He also founded the *Khalsa,* an order intended to fight against tyranny and injustice. Male initiates to the order added 'Singh' to their given names and women added 'Kaur'. Guru Gobind Singh also made five symbols obligatory: *kaccha* (a special undergarment), *kara* (a steel bangle), *kirpan* (a small sword), *kesh* (long unshorn hair, and consequently the wearing of a turban), and *kangha* (a comb). These practices are still compulsory for those Sikhs who are initiated into the Khalsa (the *Amritdharis*). Those who do not seek initiation are known as *Sehajdharis.*

There are no professional priests in Sikhism; anyone with a reasonable proficiency in the Punjabi language can conduct a service. Worship can be offered individually or communally, and in a private house or a *gurdwara* (temple). Sikhs are forbidden to eat meat prepared by ritual slaughter; they are also asked to abstain from smoking, alcohol and other intoxicants. Such abstention is compulsory for the *Amritdharis.* For details of the Sikh calendar and main celebrations, *see* page 86.

There are about 20 million Sikhs world-wide and about 400,000 adherents and 250 gurdwaras in Great Britain. Every gurdwara manages its own affairs and there is no central body in the UK. The Sikh Missionary Society provides an information service.

The Churches

For changes notified after 31 August, *see* Stop-press

The Church of England

The Church of England is the established (i.e. state) church in England and the mother church of the Anglican Communion. The Thirty-Nine Articles, a set of doctrinal statements which, together with the Book of Common Prayer of 1662 and the Ordinal, define the position of the Church of England, were adopted in their final form in 1571 and include the emphasis on personal faith and the authority of the scriptures common to the Protestant Reformation throughout Europe.

THE ANGLICAN COMMUNION

The Anglican Communion consists of 38 independent provincial or national Christian churches throughout the world, many of which are in Commonwealth countries and originated from missionary activity by the Church of England. Every ten years all the bishops in the Communion meet at the Lambeth Conference, convened by the Archbishop of Canterbury. The Conference has no policy-making authority but is an important forum for the discussion of issues of common concern. The Anglican Consultative Council was set up in 1968 to liaise between the member churches and provinces of the Anglican Communion. It meets every two to three years. Meetings of the Anglican primates have taken place every two years since 1979.

There are about 70 million Anglicans and 800 archbishops and bishops world-wide.

STRUCTURE

The Church of England is divided into the two provinces of Canterbury and York, each under an archbishop. The two provinces are subdivided into 44 dioceses.

Decisions on matters concerning the Church of England are made by the General Synod, established in 1970. It also discusses and expresses opinion on any other matter of religious or public interest. The General Synod has 574 members in total, divided between three houses: the House of Bishops, the House of Clergy and the House of Laity. It is presided over jointly by the Archbishops of Canterbury and York and normally meets twice a year. The Synod has the power, delegated by Parliament, to frame statute law (known as a Measure) on any matter concerning the Church of England. A Measure must be laid before both Houses of Parliament, who may accept or reject it but cannot amend it. Once accepted the Measure is submitted for royal assent and then has the full force of law. There are a number of committees, boards and councils answerable to the Synod, which deal with, or advise on, a wide range of matters. In addition to the General Synod, there are synods of clergy and laity at diocesan level.

The Archbishops' Council was established in January 1999. Its creation was the result of changes to the Church of England's national structure proposed in 1995 and subsequently approved by the Synod and Parliament. The Council undertakes strategic planning, co-ordinates the work of all the central institutions and oversees the internal and external affairs of the Church of England. It reports frequently to the General Synod and seeks Synodical approval of its decisions. The Archbishops' Council comprises seven *ex-officio* members: the Archbishops of

Canterbury and York (joint Presidents), the prolocutors of the Convocations of Canterbury and York, the chairman and vice-chairman of the House of Laity and a Church Estates Commissioner; six elected members: two bishops, two clergy and two lay members each elected by their respective Houses of the General Synod and up to six members appointed by the two archbishops.

GENERAL SYNOD OF THE CHURCH OF ENGLAND, Church House, Great Smith Street, London SWIP 3NZ. Tel: 0171-222 9011. *Secretary-General*, P. Mawer

HOUSE OF BISHOPS: *Chairman*, The Archbishop of Canterbury; *Vice-Chairman*, The Archbishop of York

HOUSE OF CLERGY: *Chairmen (alternating)*, Canon J. Stanley; Canon H. Wilcox

HOUSE OF LAITY: *Chairman*, Dr Christina Baxter; *Vice-Chairman*, Dr P. Giddings

ARCHBISHOPS' COUNCIL, Church House, Great Smith Street, London SWIP 3NZ. Tel: 0171-222 9011. *Secretary-General*, P. Mawer

THE ORDINATION OF WOMEN

The canon making it possible for women to be ordained to the priesthood was promulged in the General Synod in February 1994 and the first 32 women priests were ordained on 12 March 1994.

MEMBERSHIP

In 1997 the Church of England had an electoral roll membership of 1.3 million, and each week about 1 million people attended Sunday services. At mid-1999 there were two archbishops and 106 diocesan, suffragan and (stipendiary) assistant bishops. In 1998 there were 8,984 other male and 919 female full-time stipendiary clergy, and over 16,000 churches and places of worship. (The Diocese in Europe is not included in these figures.)

FULL-TIME DIOCESAN CLERGY 1998 AND CHURCH ELECTORAL ROLLS 1997

| | Clergy | | Membership |
	Male	Female	
Bath and Wells	223	25	42,500
Birmingham	189	31	19,600
Blackburn	233	12	37,700
Bradford	112	9	13,200
Bristol	133	24	19,800
Canterbury	171	13	21,600
Carlisle	140	12	25,100
Chelmsford	375	39	52,500
Chester	266	19	49,400
Chichester	336	7	60,000
Coventry	132	16	17,900
Derby	170	13	21,300
Durham	206	30	27,700
Ely	141	20	20,900
Europe	–	–	8,800
Exeter	245	13	34,100
Gloucester	147	14	26,500
Guildford	169	26	31,000
Hereford	103	15	19,400
Leicester	140	18	16,600

	Clergy		Membership
	Male	Female	
Lichfield	332	42	53,500
Lincoln	197	40	32,100
Liverpool	220	34	32,900
London	500	48	55,600
Manchester	267	28	39,000
Newcastle	141	11	17,800
Norwich	180	15	26,400
Oxford	393	67	62,200
Peterborough	147	15	19,900
Portsmouth	103	9	18,400
Ripon	136	24	19,600
Rochester	208	25	31,900
St Albans	248	42	44,900
St Edmundsbury			
and Ipswich	151	15	25,600
Salisbury	214	19	45,800
Sheffield	174	23	21,000
Sodor and Man	22	0	2,900
Southwark	316	63	45,500
Southwell	159	29	18,500
Truro	125	3	18,000
Wakefield	159	16	23,700
Winchester	230	15	43,000
Worcester	144	18	22,600
York	256	26	38,300
TOTAL	8,653	983	1,324,700

STIPENDS 1999–2000

Archbishop of Canterbury	£53,370
Archbishop of York	£46,760
Bishop of London	£43,580
Other diocesan bishops	£28,930
Suffragan bishops	£23,790
Deans and provosts	£23,790
Residentiary canons	£19,460
Incumbents and clergy of similar status	£15,910*

*national average, provisional estimate

CANTERBURY

103RD ARCHBISHOP AND PRIMATE OF ALL ENGLAND
Most Revd and Rt. Hon. George L. Carey, PH.D., cons. 1987, trans. 1991, apptd 1991; Lambeth Palace, London SE1 7JU. Signs George Cantuar:

BISHOPS SUFFRAGAN
Dover, Rt. Revd Stephen S. Venner, cons 1994, apptd 1999; Upway, St Martin's Hill, Canterbury, Kent CT1 1PR
Maidstone, Rt. Revd Gavin H. Reid, cons. 1992, apptd 1992; Bishop's House, Pett Lane, Charing, Ashford, Kent TN27 0DL
Ebbsfleet, Rt. Revd Michael A. Houghton, cons. 1998, apptd 1998 (provincial episcopal visitor); 8 Goldney Avenue, Bristol BS8 4RA
Richborough, Rt. Revd Edwin Barnes, cons. 1995, apptd 1995 (provincial episcopal visitor); 14 Hall Place Gardens, St Albans, Herts AL1 3SP

DEAN
Very Revd John Arthur Simpson, apptd 1986

CANONS RESIDENTIARY
P. Brett, apptd 1983; R. H. C. Symon, apptd 1994; Dr M. Chandler, apptd 1995; Ven. J. Pritchard, apptd 1996

Organist, D. Flood, FRCO, apptd 1988

ARCHDEACONS
Canterbury, Ven. J. Pritchard, apptd 1996
Maidstone, Ven. P. Evans, apptd 1989

Vicar-General of Province and Diocese, Chancellor S. Cameron, QC
Commissary-General, His Hon. Judge Richard Walker
Joint Registrars of the Province, F. E. Robson, OBE; B. J. T. Hanson, CBE
Diocesan Registrar and Legal Adviser, R. H. B. Sturt
Diocesan Secretary, D. Kemp, Diocesan House, Lady Wootton's Green, Canterbury CT1 1NQ. Tel: 01227-459401

YORK

96TH ARCHBISHOP AND PRIMATE OF ENGLAND
Most Revd and Rt. Hon. David M. Hope, KCVO, D.phil., LL D, cons. 1985, trans. 1995, apptd 1995; Bishopthorpe, York YO23 2GE. Signs David Ebor:

BISHOPS SUFFRAGAN
Hull, Rt. Revd Richard M. C. Frith, cons. 1998, apptd 1998; Hullen House, Woodfield Lane, Hessle, Hull HU13 0ES
Selby, Rt. Revd Humphrey V. Taylor, cons. 1991, apptd 1991; 10 Precentor's Court, York YO1 2ES
Whitby, Rt. Revd Robert S. Ladds, cons. 1999, apptd 1999; 60 West Green, Stokesley, Middlesbrough TS9 5BD
Beverley, Rt. Revd John Gaisford, cons. 1994, apptd 1994 (provincial episcopal visitor); 3 North Lane, Roundhay, Leeds LS8 2QJ

DEAN
Very Revd Raymond Furnell, apptd 1994

CANONS RESIDENTIARY
G. Webster., apptd 1999; R. Metcalfe, apptd 1988; P. J. Ferguson, apptd 1995; E. R. Norman, PH.D., DD, apptd 1999

Organist, P. Moore, FRCO, apptd 1983

ARCHDEACONS
Cleveland, Ven. C. J. Hawthorn, apptd 1991
East Riding, Ven. P. R. W. Harrison, apptd 1998
York, Ven. R. Seed, apptd 1999

Official Principal and Auditor of the Chancery Court, Sir John Owen, QC
Chancellor of the Diocese, His Hon. Judge Coningsby, QC, apptd 1977
Vicar-General of the Province and Official Principal of the Consistory Court, His Hon. Judge Coningsby, QC
Registrar and Legal Secretary, L. P. M. Lennox
Diocesan Secretary, C. Sheppard, Church House, Ogleforth, York YO1 7JE. Tel: 01904-611696

LONDON (Province of Canterbury)

132ND BISHOP
Rt. Revd and Rt. Hon Richard J. C. Chartres, cons. 1992, apptd. 1995; The Old Deanery, Dean's Court, London EC4V 5AA. Signs Richard Londin:

AREA BISHOPS
Edmonton, Rt. Revd Peter W. Wheatley, cons. 1999, apptd 1999; 27 Thurlow Road, London NW3 5PP
Kensington, Rt. Revd Michael Colclough, cons. 1996, apptd 1996; 19 Campden Hill Square, London W8 7JY
Stepney, Rt. Revd Dr John M. Sentamu, cons. 1996, apptd 1996; 63 Coborn Road, London E3 2DB

Willesden, Rt. Revd Graham G. Dow, *cons.* 1992, *apptd* 1992; 173 Willesden Lane, London NW6 7YN

BISHOP SUFFRAGAN
Fulham, Rt. Revd John Broadhurst, *cons.* 1996, *apptd* 1996; 26 Canonbury Park South, London NI 2FN

DEAN OF ST PAUL'S
Very Revd John H. Moses, PH.D., *apptd* 1996

CANONS RESIDENTIARY
R. J. Halliburton, *apptd* 1990; M. J. Saward, *apptd* 1991; S. J. Oliver, *apptd* 1997

Registrar and Receiver of St Paul's, Brig. R. W. Acworth, CBE
Organist, J. Scott, FRCO, *apptd* 1990

ARCHDEACONS
Charing Cross, Ven. Dr W. Jacob, *apptd* 1996
Hackney, Ven. L. Dennen, *apptd* 1999
Hampstead, Ven. M. Lawson, *apptd* 1999
London, Middlesex, Ven. M. Colmer, *apptd* 1996
Northolt, Ven. P. Broadbent, *apptd* 1995

Chancellor, Miss S. Cameron, QC, *apptd* 1992
Registrar and Legal Secretary, P. C. E. Morris
Diocesan Secretary, vacant

DURHAM (Province of York)

70TH BISHOP
Rt. Revd A. Michael A. Turnbull, *cons.* 1988, *apptd* 1994; Auckland Castle, Bishop Auckland DL14 7NR. *Signs* Michael Dunelm:

BISHOP SUFFRAGAN
Jarrow, Rt. Revd Alan Smithson, *cons.* 1990, *apptd* 1990; The Old Vicarage, Hallgarth, Pittington, Durham DH6 IAB

DEAN
Very Revd John R. Arnold, *apptd* 1989

CANONS RESIDENTIARY
D. W. Brown, *apptd* 1990; T. Willmott, *apptd* 1997; M. Kitchen, *apptd* 1997; D. J. Whittington, *apptd* 1998; N. Stock, *apptd* 1998

Organist, J. B. Lancelot, FRCO, *apptd* 1985

ARCHDEACONS
Auckland, Ven. G. G. Gibson, *apptd* 1993
Durham, Ven. T. Willmott, *apptd* 1997
Sunderland, Ven. F. White, *apptd* 1997

Chancellor, His Hon. Judge Bursell, QC, *apptd* 1989
Registrar and Legal Secretary, A. N. Fairclough
Diocesan Secretary, J. P. Cryer, Auckland Castle, Bishop Auckland, Co. Durham DL14 7QJ. Tel: 01388-604515

WINCHESTER (Canterbury)

96TH BISHOP
Rt. Revd Michael C. Scott-Joynt, *cons.* 1987, *trans.* 1995, *apptd* 1995; Wolvesey, Winchester SO23 9ND. *Signs* Michael Winton:

BISHOPS SUFFRAGAN
Basingstoke, Rt. Revd Dr. Geoffrey Rowell, *cons.* 1994, *apptd* 1994; Bishopswood End, Kingswood Rise, Four Marks, Alton, Hants GU34 5BD
Southampton, Rt. Revd Jonathan M. Gledhill, *cons.* 1996, *apptd* 1996; Ham House, The Crescent, Romsey SO51 7NG

DEAN
Very Revd Michael Till, *apptd* 1996

Dean of Jersey (*A Peculiar*), Very Revd John Seaford, *apptd* 1993
Dean of Guernsey (*A Peculiar*), Very Revd Marc Trickey, *apptd* 1995

CANONS RESIDENTIARY
A. K. Walker, *apptd* 1987; P. B. Morgan, *apptd* 1994; C. Stewart, *apptd* 1997; Ven. J. A. Guille, *apptd* 1998

Organist, D. Hill, FRCO, *apptd* 1988

ARCHDEACONS
Basingstoke, Ven. J. A. Guille, *apptd* 1998
Winchester, Ven. A. G. Harbidge, *apptd* 1998

Chancellor, C. Clark, *apptd* 1993
Registrar and Legal Secretary, P. M. White
Diocesan Secretary, R. Anderton, Church House, 9 The Close, Winchester, Hants SO23 9LS. Tel: 01962-844644

BATH AND WELLS (Canterbury)

76TH BISHOP
Rt. Revd James L. Thompson, *cons.* 1978, *apptd* 1991; The Palace, Wells BA5 2PD. *Signs* James Bath & Wells

BISHOP SUFFRAGAN
Taunton, Rt. Revd Andrew John Radford, *cons.* Dec. 1998, *apptd* 1998; The Bishop's Lodge, Monkton Heights, West Monkton, Taunton, Somerset TA2 8LU

DEAN
Very Revd Richard Lewis, *apptd* 1990

CANONS RESIDENTIARY
R. Acworth, *apptd* 1993;
P. G. Walker, *apptd* 1994; M. W. Matthews, *apptd* 1997

Organist, M. Archer, *apptd* 1996

ARCHDEACONS
Bath, Ven. R. J. S. Evens, *apptd* 1996
Taunton, Ven. J. P. C. Reed, *apptd* 1999
Wells, Ven. R. Acworth, *apptd* 1993

Chancellor, T. Briden, *apptd* 1993
Registrar and Legal Secretary, T. Berry
Diocesan Secretary, N. Denison, The Old Deanery, Wells, Somerset BA5 2UG. Tel: 01749-670777

BIRMINGHAM (Canterbury)

7TH BISHOP
Rt. Revd Mark Santer, *cons.* 1981, *apptd* 1987; Bishop's Croft, Harborne, Birmingham B17 0BG. *Signs* Mark Birmingham

BISHOP SUFFRAGAN
Aston, Rt. Revd John Austin, *cons.* 1992, *apptd* 1992; Strensham House, 8 Strensham Hill, Moseley, Birmingham B13 8AG

PROVOST
vacant

CANONS RESIDENTIARY
Ven. C. J. G. Barton, *apptd* 1990; Revd D. Lee, *apptd* 1996; Revd G. O'Neill, *apptd* 1997

Organist, M. Huxley, FRCO, *apptd* 1986

ARCHDEACONS
Aston, Ven. C. J. G. Barton, *apptd* 1990
Birmingham, Ven. J. F. Duncan, *apptd* 1985

Chancellor, His Hon. Judge Aglionby, *apptd* 1970
Registrar and Legal Secretary, H. Carslake
Diocesan Secretary, J. Drennan, 175 Harborne Park Road, Harborne, Birmingham B17 0BH. Tel: 0121-427 5141

BLACKBURN (York)

7TH BISHOP
Rt. Revd Alan D. Chesters, *cons.* 1989, *apptd* 1989; Bishop's House, Ribchester Road, Blackburn BB1 9EF. *Signs* Alan Blackburn

BISHOPS SUFFRAGAN
Burnley, Rt. Revd Martyn W. Jarrett, *cons.* 1994, *apptd* 1994; Dean House, 449 Padiham Road, Burnley BB12 6TE
Lancaster, Rt. Revd Stephen Pedley, *cons.* 1998, *apptd* 1997; The Vicarage, Shireshead, Forton, Preston PR3 0AE

PROVOST
Very Revd David Frayne, *apptd* 1992

CANONS RESIDENTIARY
D. M. Galilee, *apptd* 1995; A. D. Hindley, *apptd* 1996; P. J. Ballard, *apptd* 1998

Organist, R. Tanner, *apptd* 1998

ARCHDEACONS
Blackburn, Ven. F. J. Marsh, *apptd* 1996
Lancaster, vacant

Chancellor, J. W. M. Bullimore, *apptd* 1990
Registrar and Legal Secretary, T. A. Hoyle
Diocesan Secretary, Revd M. J. Wedgeworth, Diocesan Office, Cathedral Close, Blackburn BB1 5AA. Tel: 01254-54421

BRADFORD (York)

8TH BISHOP
Rt. Revd David J. Smith, *cons.* 1987, *apptd* 1992; Bishopscroft, Ashwell Road, Heaton, Bradford BD9 4AU. *Signs* David Bradford

PROVOST
Very Revd John S. Richardson, *apptd* 1990

CANONS RESIDENTIARY
C. G. Lewis, *apptd* 1993; G. Smith, *apptd* 1996

Organist, A. Horsey, FRCO, *apptd* 1986

ARCHDEACONS
Bradford, Ven. G. A. Wilkinson, *apptd* 1999
Craven, Ven. M. L. Grundy, *apptd* 1994

Chancellor, J. de G. Walford, *apptd* 1999
Registrar and Legal Secretary, J. G. H. Mackrell
Diocesan Secretary, M. Halliday, Cathedral Hall, Stott Hill, Bradford BD1 4ET. Tel: 01274-725958

BRISTOL (Canterbury)

54TH BISHOP
Rt. Revd Barry Rogerson, *cons.* 1979, *apptd* 1985; Bishop's House, Clifton Hill, Bristol BS8 1BW. *Signs* Barry Bristol

BISHOP SUFFRAGAN
Swindon, Rt. Revd Michael Doe, *cons.* 1994, *apptd* 1994; Mark House, Field Rise, Old Town, Swindon SN1 4HP

DEAN
Very Revd Robert W. Grimley, *apptd* 1997

CANONS RESIDENTIARY
P. F. Johnson, *apptd* 1990; D. R. Holt, *apptd* 1998; B. D. Clover, *apptd* 1999

Organist, M. Lee, *apptd* 1998

ARCHDEACONS
Bristol, Ven. T. E. McClure, *apptd* 1999
Swindon, Ven. A. F. Hawker, *apptd* 1998

Chancellor, Sir David Calcutt, QC, *apptd* 1971
Registrar and Legal Secretary, T. Berry
Diocesan Secretary, Mrs L. Farrall, Diocesan Church House, 23 Great George Street, Bristol, Avon BS1 5QZ. Tel: 0117-921 4411

CARLISLE (York)

65TH BISHOP
Rt. Revd Ian Harland, *cons.* 1985, *apptd* 1989; Rose Castle, Dalston, Carlisle CA5 7BZ. *Signs* Ian Carliol:

BISHOP SUFFRAGAN
Penrith, Rt. Revd Richard Garrard, *cons.* 1994, *apptd* 1994; Holm Croft, Castle Road, Kendal, Cumbria LA9 7AU

DEAN
Very Revd Graeme P. Knowles, *apptd* 1998

CANONS RESIDENTIARY
R. A. Chapman, *apptd* 1978; Ven. D. C. Turnbull, *apptd* 1993; D. W. V. Weston, *apptd* 1994; C. Hill, *apptd* 1996

Organist, J. Suter, FRCO, *apptd* 1991

ARCHDEACONS
Carlisle, Ven. D. C. Turnbull, *apptd* 1993
West Cumberland, Ven. A. N. Davis, *apptd* 1996
Westmorland and Furness, vacant

Chancellor, His Hon. Judge Aglionby, *apptd* 1991
Registrar and Legal Secretary, Mrs S. Holmes
Diocesan Secretary, Canon C. Hill, Church House, West Walls, Carlisle CA3 8UE. Tel: 01228-522573

CHELMSFORD (Canterbury)

8TH BISHOP
Rt. Revd John F. Perry, *cons.* 1989, *apptd* 1996; Bishopscourt, Margaretting, Ingatestone CM4 0HD. *Signs* John Chelmsford

BISHOPS SUFFRAGAN
Barking, Rt. Revd Roger F. Sainsbury, *cons.* 1991, *apptd* 1991; 110 Capel Road, Forest Gate, London E7 0JS
Bradwell, Rt. Revd Laurence Green, *cons.* 1993, *apptd* 1993; The Vicarage, Orsett Road, Horndon-on-the-Hill, Stanford-le-Hope, Essex SS17 8NS
Colchester, Rt. Revd Edward Holland, *cons.* 1986, *apptd* 1995; 1 Fitzwalter Road, Lexden, Colchester CO3 3SS

PROVOST
Very Revd Peter S. M. Judd, *apptd* 1997

CANONS RESIDENTIARY
T. Thompson, *apptd* 1988; B. P. Thompson, *apptd* 1988; D. Knight, *apptd* 1991; A. Knowles, *apptd* 1998

Master of Music, Dr G. Elliott, ph.d., frco, *apptd* 1981

ARCHDEACONS
Colchester, Ven. M. W. Wallace, *apptd* 1997
Harlow, Ven. P. F. Taylor, *apptd* 1996
Southend, Ven. D. Jennings, *apptd* 1992
West Ham, Ven. M. J. Fox, *apptd* 1996

Chancellor, Miss S. M. Cameron, qc, *apptd* 1970
Registrar and Legal Secretary, B. Hood
Diocesan Secretary, D.Phillips, 53 New Street, Chelmsford, Essex cmi iat. Tel: 01245-266731

CHESTER (York)

40TH BISHOP
Rt. Revd Peter R. Forster, ph.d., *cons.* 1996, *apptd* 1996; Bishop's House, Chester chi 2jd. *Signs* Peter Cestr:

BISHOPS SUFFRAGAN
Birkenhead, (until March 2000) Rt. Revd Michael L. Langrish, *cons.* 1993, *apptd* 1993; Bishop's Lodge, 67 Bidston Road, Oxton, Birkenhead ch43 6tr
Stockport, Rt. Revd Geoffrey M. Turner, *cons.* 1994, *apptd* 1994; Bishop's Lodge, Back Lane, Dunham Town, Altrincham, Cheshire wa14 4sg

DEAN
Very Revd Dr Stephen S. Smalley, *apptd* 1986

CANONS RESIDENTIARY
R. M. Rees, *apptd* 1990; O. A. Conway, *apptd* 1991; Dr T. J. Dennis, *apptd* 1994; J. W. S. Newcome, *apptd* 1994

Organist and Director of Music, D. G. Poulter, frco, *apptd* 1997

ARCHDEACONS
Chester, Ven. C. Hewetson, *apptd* 1994
Macclesfield, Ven. R. J. Gillings, *apptd* 1994

Chancellor, D. G. P. Turner, *apptd* 1998
Registrar and Legal Secretary, A. K. McAllester
Diocesan Secretary, S. P. A. Marriott, Church House, Lower Lane, Aldford, Chester ch3 6hp. Tel: 01244-620444

CHICHESTER (Canterbury)

102ND BISHOP
Rt. Revd Eric W. Kemp, dd, *cons.* 1974, *apptd* 1974; The Palace, Chichester po19 1py. *Signs* Eric Cicestr:

BISHOPS SUFFRAGAN
Horsham, Rt. Revd Lindsay G. Urwin, *cons.* 1993, *apptd* 1993; Bishop's House, 21 Guildford Road, Horsham, W. Sussex rh12 1lu
Lewes, Rt. Revd Wallace P. Benn, *cons.* 1997, *apptd* 1997; 16a Prideaux Road, Eastbourne, E. Sussex bn21 2nb

DEAN
Very Revd John D. Treadgold, lvo, *apptd* 1989

CANONS RESIDENTIARY
R. T. Greenacre, *apptd* 1975; F. J. Hawkins, *apptd* 1981; P. G. Atkinson, *apptd* 1997; C. Lansdale, *apptd.* 1999; D. McKittrick, *apptd.* 1999

Organist, A. J. Thurlow, frco, *apptd* 1980

ARCHDEACONS
Chichester, Ven. M. Brotherton, *apptd* 1991
Horsham, Ven. W. C. L. Filby, *apptd* 1983
Lewes and Hastings, Ven. N. S. Reade, *apptd* 1997

Chancellor, vacant
Registrar and Legal Secretary, C. Butcher
Diocesan Secretary, J. Prichard, Diocesan Church House, 211 New Church Road, Hove, E. Sussex bn3 4ed. Tel: 01273-421021

COVENTRY (Canterbury)

8TH BISHOP
Rt. Revd Colin J. Bennetts; *cons.* 1994, *apptd* 1997; The Bishop's House, 23 Davenport Road, Coventry cv5 6pw. *Signs* Colin Coventry

BISHOP SUFFRAGAN
Warwick, Rt. Revd Anthony M. Priddis, *cons.* 1996, *apptd* 1996; 139 Kenilworth Road, Coventry cv4 7af

PROVOST
Very Revd John F. Petty, *apptd* 1987

CANONS RESIDENTIARY
V. Faull, *apptd* 1994; J. C. Burch, *apptd* 1995; A. White, *apptd* 1998

Director of Music, R. Jeffcoat, *apptd* 1997

ARCHDEACONS
Coventry, Ven. H. I. L. Russell, *apptd* 1989
Warwick, Ven. M. J. J. Paget-Wilkes, *apptd* 1990

Chancellor, Sir William Gage, *apptd* 1980
Registrar and Legal Secretary, D. J. Dumbleton
Diocesan Secretary, Mrs I. Chapman, Church House, Palmerston Road, Coventry cv5 6fj. Tel: 01203-674328

DERBY (Canterbury)

6TH BISHOP
Rt. Revd Jonathan S. Bailey, *cons.* 1992, *apptd* 1995; Derby Church House, Full Street, Derby dei 3dr. *Signs* Jonathan Derby

BISHOP SUFFRAGAN
Repton, Rt. Revd David C. Hawtin, *cons.* 1999, *apptd* 1999; Repton House, Lea, Matlock, Derbys de4 5jp

PROVOST
Very Revd Michael F. Perham, *apptd* 1998

CANONS RESIDENTIARY
G. A. Chesterman, *apptd* 1989; Ven. I. Gatford, *apptd* 1992; G. O. Marshall, *apptd* 1992; D. C. Truby, *apptd* 1998

Organist, P. Gould, *apptd* 1982

ARCHDEACONS
Chesterfield, Ven. D. C. Garnett, *apptd* 1996
Derby, Ven. I. Gatford, *apptd* 1992

Chancellor, J. W. M. Bullimore, *apptd* 1981
Registrar and Legal Secretary, J. S. Battie
Diocesan Secretary, R. J. Carey, Derby Church House, Full Street, Derby dei 3dr. Tel: 01332-382233

ELY (Canterbury)

BISHOP
vacant

BISHOP SUFFRAGAN
Huntingdon, Rt. Revd John R. Flack, *cons.* 1997, *apptd* 1996; 14 Lynn Road, Ely, Cambs cb6 1da

DEAN
Very Revd Michael Higgins, *apptd* 1991

CANONS RESIDENTIARY
J. Inge, *apptd* 1996

Organist, P. Trepte, FRCO, *apptd* 1991

ARCHDEACONS
Ely, Ven. J. Watson, *apptd* 1993
Huntingdon, Ven. J. Beer, *apptd* 1997
Wisbech, Ven. J. Rone, *apptd* 1995

Chancellor, W. Gage, QC
Joint Registrars, W. H. Godfrey; P. F. B. Beesley (*Legal Secretary*)
Diocesan Secretary, Dr M. Lavis, Bishop Woodford House, Barton Road, Ely, Cambs CB7 4DX. Tel: 01353-652701

EXETER (Canterbury)

70TH BISHOP
(from March 2000) Rt. Revd Michael L. Langrish, *cons.* 1993, *apptd* 2000; The Palace, Exeter, EX1 1HY. *Signs* Michael Exon

BISHOPS SUFFRAGAN
Crediton, Rt. Revd Richard S. Hawkins, *cons.* 1988, *apptd* 1996;,10 The Close, Exeter EX1 1EZ
Plymouth, Rt. Revd John H. Garton, *cons.* 1996, *apptd* 1996; 31 Riverside Walk, Tamerton Foliot, Plymouth PL5 4AQ

DEAN
Very Revd Keith B. Jones, *apptd* 1996

CANONS RESIDENTIARY
K. C. Parry, *apptd* 1991; N. Collings, *apptd* 1999

Organist, L. A. Nethsingha, FRCO, *apptd* 1973

ARCHDEACONS
Barnstaple, Ven. T. Lloyd, *apptd* 1989
Exeter, Ven. A. F. Tremlett, *apptd* 1994
Plymouth, Ven. R. G. Ellis, *apptd* 1982
Totnes, Preb. R. T. Gilpin, *apptd* 1996

Chancellor, Sir David Calcutt, QC, *apptd* 1971
Registrar and Legal Secretary, R. K. Wheeler
Diocesan Secretary, M. Beedell, Diocesan House, Palace Gate, Exeter, Devon EX1 1HX. Tel: 01392-72686

GIBRALTAR IN EUROPE (Canterbury)

BISHOP
Rt. Revd John Hind, *cons.* 1991, *apptd* 1993; 14 Tufton Street, London SW1P 3QZ

BISHOP SUFFRAGAN
In Europe Rt. Revd Henry Scriven, *cons.* 1995, *apptd* 1994; 14 Tufton Street, London SW1P 3QZ

Dean, Cathedral Church of the Holy Trinity, Gibraltar, Very Revd W. G. Reid
Chancellor, Pro-Cathedral of St Paul, Valletta, Malta, Canon A. Woods
Chancellor, Pro-Cathedral of the Holy Trinity, Brussels, Belgium, Canon N. Walker

ARCHDEACONS
Eastern, Ven. S. J. B. Peake
North-West Europe, Ven. G. G. Allen

France, Ven. M. Draper, OBE
Gibraltar, Ven. K. Robinson
Italy, Ven. W. E. Edebohls
Scandinavia and Germany, Ven. D. Ratcliff
Switzerland, Ven. P. J. Hawker, OBE

Chancellor, Sir David Calcutt, QC
Registrar and Legal Secretary, J. G. Underwood
Diocesan Secretary, A. C. Mumford, 14 Tufton Street, London SW1P 3QZ. Tel: 0171-976 8001

GLOUCESTER (Canterbury)

39TH BISHOP
Rt. Revd David Bentley, *cons.* 1986, *apptd* 1993; Bishopscourt, Gloucester GL1 2BQ. *Signs* David Gloucestr

BISHOP SUFFRAGAN
Tewkesbury, Rt. Revd John S. Went, *cons.* 1995, *apptd* 1995; Green Acre, Hempsted, Gloucester GL2 6LG

DEAN
Very Revd Nicholas A. S. Bury, *apptd* 1997

CANONS RESIDENTIARY
R. D. M. Grey, *apptd* 1982; N. Chatfield, *apptd* 1992; N. Heavisides, *apptd* 1993; C. H. Morgan, *apptd* 1996

Organist, D. Briggs, FRCO, *apptd* 1994

ARCHDEACONS
Cheltenham, Ven. H. S. Ringrose, *apptd* 1998
Gloucester, Ven. C. J. H. Wagstaff, *apptd* 1982

Chancellor and Vicar-General, Ms D. J. Rodgers, *apptd* 1990
Registrar and Legal Secretary, C. G. Peak
Diocesan Secretary, M. Williams, Church House, College Green, Gloucester GL1 2LY. Tel: 01452-410022

GUILDFORD (Canterbury)

8TH BISHOP
Rt. Revd John W. Gladwin, *cons.* 1994, *apptd* 1994; Willow Grange, Woking Road, Guildford GU4 7QS. *Signs* John Guildford

BISHOP SUFFRAGAN
Dorking, Rt. Revd Ian Brackley, *cons.* 1996, *apptd* 1995; Dayspring, 13 Pilgrims Way, Guildford GU4 8AD

DEAN
Very Revd Alexander G. Wedderspoon, *apptd* 1987

CANONS RESIDENTIARY
Dr Maureen Palmer, *apptd* 1996

Organist, A. Millington, FRCO, *apptd* 1982

ARCHDEACONS
Dorking, Ven. M. Wilson, *apptd* 1995
Surrey, Ven. R. Reiss, *apptd* 1995

Chancellor, His Hon. Judge Goodman
Registrar and Legal Secretary, P. F. B. Beesley
Diocesan Secretary, vacant

HEREFORD (Canterbury)

103RD BISHOP
Rt. Revd John Oliver, *cons.* 1990, *apptd* 1990; The Palace, Hereford HR4 9BN. *Signs* John Hereford

BISHOP SUFFRAGAN
Ludlow, Rt. Revd Dr John Saxbee, *cons.* 1994, *apptd* 1994;
Bishop's House, Halford, Craven Arms, Shropshire
SY7 9BT

DEAN
Very Revd Robert A. Willis, *apptd* 1992

CANONS RESIDENTIARY
P. Iles, *apptd* 1983; J. Tiller, *apptd* 1984; M. W. Hooper,
apptd 1997

Organist, Dr R. Massey, FRCO, *apptd* 1974

ARCHDEACONS
Hereford, Ven. M. W. Hooper, *apptd* 1997
Ludlow, Rt. Revd J. C. Saxbee, *apptd* 1992

Chancellor, J. M. Henty
Joint Registrars and Legal Secretaries, V. T. Jordan; P. F. B.
Beesley
Diocesan Secretary, Miss S. Green, The Palace, Hereford
HR4 9BL. Tel: 01432-353863

LEICESTER (Canterbury)

6TH BISHOP
Rt. Revd Timothy J. Stevens, *cons.* 1995, *apptd* 1999;
Bishop's Lodge, 10 Springfield Road, Leicester LE2 3BD.
Signs Timothy Leicester

STIPENDIARY ASSISTANT BISHOP
Rt. Revd William Down, *cons.* 1990, *apptd* 1995

PROVOST
Vacant

CANONS RESIDENTIARY
M. T. H. Banks, *apptd* 1988; M. Wilson, *apptd* 1988

Organist, J. T. Gregory, *apptd* 1994

ARCHDEACONS
Leicester, Ven. M. Edson, *apptd* 1994
Loughborough, Ven. I. Stanes, *apptd* 1992

Chancellor, N. Seed, *apptd* 1989
Registrars and Legal Secretaries, P. C. E. Morris; R. H. Bloor
Diocesan Secretary, A. Howard; Church House, 3–5 St
Martin's East, Leicester LE1 5FX. Tel: 0116-262 7445

LICHFIELD (Canterbury)

97TH BISHOP
Rt. Revd Keith N. Sutton, *cons.* 1978, *apptd* 1984; Bishop's
House, The Close, Lichfield WS13 7LG. *Signs* Keith
Lichfield

BISHOPS SUFFRAGAN
Shrewsbury, Rt. Revd David M. Hallatt, *cons.* 1994, *apptd*
1994; 68 London Road, Shrewsbury SY2 6PG
Stafford, Rt. Revd Christopher J. Hill, *cons.* 1996, *apptd*
1996; Ash Garth, Broughton Crescent, Barlaston, Staffs
ST12 9DD
Wolverhampton, Rt. Revd Michael G. Bourke, *cons.* 1993,
apptd 1993; 61 Richmond Road, Wolverhampton
WV3 9JH

DEAN
Very Revd Michael Yorke, *apptd* 1999

CANONS RESIDENTIARY
A. N. Barnard, *apptd* 1977; C. W. Taylor, *apptd* 1995; Ven.
G. Frost, *apptd* 1998

Organist, A. Lumsden, *apptd* 1992

ARCHDEACONS
Lichfield, Ven. G. Frost, *apptd* 1998
Salop, Ven . J. B. Hall, *apptd* 1998
Stoke-on-Trent, Ven. A. G. C. Smith, *apptd* 1997
Walsall, Ven. A. G. Sadler, *apptd* 1997

Chancellor, His Hon. Judge Shand
Registrar and Legal Secretary, J. P. Thorneycroft
Diocesan Secretary, D. R. Taylor, St Mary's House, The
Close, Lichfield, Staffs WS13 7LD. Tel: 01543-306030

LINCOLN (Canterbury)

70TH BISHOP
Rt. Revd Robert M. Hardy, *cons.* 1980, *apptd* 1987; Bishop's
House, Eastgate, Lincoln LN2 1QQ. *Signs* Robert Lincoln

BISHOPS SUFFRAGAN
Grantham, Rt. Revd Alastair L. J. Redfern, *cons.* 1997, *apptd*
1997; Fairacre, 234 Barrowby Road, Grantham, Lincs
NG31 8NP
Grimsby, Rt. Revd David Tustin, *cons.* 1979, *apptd* 1979;
Bishop's House, Church Lane, Irby-upon-Humber,
Grimsby DN37 7JR

DEAN
Very Revd Alexander F. Knight, *apptd* 1998

CANONS RESIDENTIARY
B. R. Davis, *apptd* 1977; A. J. Stokes, *apptd* 1992; V. White,
apptd 1994

Organist, C. S. Walsh, FRCO, *apptd* 1988

ARCHDEACONS
Lincoln, Ven. A. Hawes, *apptd* 1995
Lindsey, vacant
Stow, Ven. R. J. Wells, *apptd* 1989

Chancellor, Peter N. Collier, QC, *apptd* 1999
Registrar and Legal Secretary, D. M. Wellman
Diocesan Secretary, P. Hamlyn Williams, The Old Palace,
Lincoln LN2 1PU. Tel: 01522-529241

LIVERPOOL (York)

7TH BISHOP
Rt. Revd James Jones, *cons.* 1994, *apptd* 1998; Bishop's
Lodge, Woolton Park, Liverpool L25 6DT. *Signs* James
Liverpool

BISHOP SUFFRAGAN
Warrington, Rt. Revd John Packer, *cons.* 1996, *apptd* 1996;
34 Central Avenue, Eccleston Park, Prescot, Merseyside
L34 2QP

DEAN
(from February 2000) Rt. Revd Dean Dr Rupert W. N.
Hoare

CANONS RESIDENTIARY
D. J. Hutton, *apptd* 1983; M. C. Boyling, *apptd* 1994; N. T.
Vincent, *apptd* 1995; C. Byworth, *apptd* 1999

Organist, Prof. I. Tracey, *apptd* 1980

ARCHDEACONS
Liverpool, Ven. R. L. Metcalf, *apptd* 1994
Warrington, Ven. C. D. S. Woodhouse, *apptd* 1981

Chancellor, R. G. Hamilton
Registrar and Legal Secretary, R. H. Arden

Diocesan Secretary, K. Cawdron, Church House, 1 Hanover Street, Liverpool LI 3DW. Tel: 0151-709 9722

MANCHESTER (York)

10TH BISHOP
Rt. Revd Christopher J. Mayfield, *cons.* 1985, *apptd* 1993; Bishopscourt, Bury New Road, Manchester M7 4LE. *Signs* Christopher Manchester

BISHOPS SUFFRAGAN
Bolton, Rt. Revd David K. Gillett, *cons.* 1999, *apptd* 1999; 4 Bishop's Lodge, Bolton Road, Hawkshaw, Bury BL8 4JN
Hulme, Rt. Revd Stephen R. Lowe, *cons.* 1999, *apptd.* 1999; 14 Moorgate Avenue, Withington, Manchester M20 IHE
Middleton, vacant

DEAN
Very Revd Kenneth Riley, *apptd* 1993

CANONS RESIDENTIARY
J. R. Atherton, PH.D., *apptd* 1984; A. E. Radcliffe, *apptd* 1991; P. Denby, *apptd* 1995
Organist, C. Stokes, *apptd* 1992

ARCHDEACONS
Bolton, Ven. L. M. Davies, *apptd* 1992
Manchester, Ven A. Wolstencroft, *apptd* 1998
Rochdale, Ven. J. M. M. Dalby, *apptd* 1991

Chancellor, J. Holden, *apptd* 1997
Registrar and Legal Secretary, M. Darlington
Diocesan Secretary, Mrs J. Park, Diocesan Church House, 90 Deansgate, Manchester M3 2GH. Tel: 0161-833 9521

NEWCASTLE (York)

11TH BISHOP
Rt. Revd J. Martin Wharton, *cons.* 1992, *apptd* 1997; Bishop's House, 29 Moor Road South, Gosforth, Newcastle upon Tyne NE3 IPA. *Signs* Martin Newcastle

STIPENDIARY ASSISTANT BISHOP
Rt. Revd Paul Richardson, *cons.* 1987, *apptd* 1999

PROVOST
Very Revd Nicholas G. Coulton, *apptd* 1990

CANONS RESIDENTIARY
R. Langley, *apptd* 1985; P. R. Strange, *apptd* 1986; Ven. P. Elliott, *apptd* 1993; G. V. Miller, *apptd* 1999
Organist, T. G. Hone, FRCO, *apptd* 1987

ARCHDEACONS
Lindisfarne, Ven. M. E. Bowering, *apptd* 1987
Northumberland, Ven. P. Elliott, *apptd* 1993

Chancellor, Prof. D. McClean, *apptd* 1998
Registrar and Legal Secretary, Mrs B. J. Lowdon
Diocesan Secretary, P. Davies, Church House, Grainger Park Road, Newcastle upon Tyne NE4 8SX. Tel: 0191-273 0120

NORWICH (Canterbury)

71ST BISHOP
vacant; (from January 2000) Rt Revd Graham R. James, *cons.* 1993, *apptd* 2000; Bishop's House, Norwich NR3 ISB. *Signs* Graham Norvic

BISHOPS SUFFRAGAN
Lynn, Rt. Revd A. C. Foottit, *cons.* 1999, *apptd* 1999
Thetford, Rt. Revd Hugo F. de Waal, *cons.* 1992, *apptd* 1992; Rectory Meadow, Bramerton, Norwich NR14 7DW

DEAN
Very Revd Stephen Platten, *apptd* 1995

CANONS RESIDENTIARY
J. M. Haselock, *apptd* 1998; Ven. C. J. Offer, *apptd* 1994; R. J. Hanmer, *apptd* 1994; M. Kitchener, *apptd* 1999
Organist, D. Dunnett, *apptd* 1996

ARCHDEACONS
Lynn, Ven. M. C. Gray, *apptd* 1999
Norfolk, Ven. A. M. Handley, *apptd* 1993
Norwich, Ven. C. J. Offer, *apptd* 1994

Chancellor, The Hon. Mr Justice Blofeld, *apptd* 1998
Registrar and Legal Secretary, J. W. F. Herring
Diocesan Secretary, D. Adeney, Diocesan House, 109 Dereham Road, Easton, Norwich, Norfolk NR9 5ES. Tel: 01603-880853

OXFORD (Canterbury)

41ST BISHOP
Rt. Revd Richard D. Harries, *cons.* 1987, *apptd* 1987; Diocesan Church House, North Hinksey, Oxford OX2 ONB. *Signs* Richard Oxon:

AREA BISHOPS
Buckingham, Rt. Revd Michael A. Hill *cons.* 1998, *apptd* 1998; 28 Church Street, Great Missenden, Bucks HP16 OAZ
Dorchester, Rt. Revd Anthony J. Russell, *cons.* 1988, *apptd* 1988; Holmby House, Sibford Ferris, Banbury, Oxon OX15 5RG
Reading, Rt. Revd Dominic Walker, *cons.* 1997, *apptd* 1997; Bishop's House, Tidmarsh Lane, Tidmarsh, Reading RG8 8HA

DEAN OF CHRIST CHURCH
Very Revd John H. Drury, *apptd* 1991

CANONS RESIDENTIARY
O. M. T. O'Donovan, D.Phil., *apptd* 1982; J. M. Pierce, *apptd* 1987; J. S. K. Ward, *apptd* 1991; R. Jeffery, *apptd* 1996; Prof. J. Webster, *apptd* 1996; Prof. H. M. R. E. Mayr-Harting, *apptd* 1997; Ven. J. A. Morrison, *apptd* 1998
Organist, S. Darlington, FRCO, *apptd* 1985

ARCHDEACONS
Berkshire, Ven. N. A. Russell, *apptd* 1998
Buckingham, Ven. D. Goldie, *apptd* 1998
Oxford, Ven. J. A. Morrison, *apptd* 1998

Chancellor, P. T. S. Boydell, QC, *apptd* 1958
Registrar and Legal Secretary, Dr F. E. Robson
Diocesan Secretary, R. Pearce, Diocesan Church House, North Hinksey, Oxford OX2 ONB. Tel: 01865-208202

PETERBOROUGH (Canterbury)

37TH BISHOP
Rt. Revd Ian P. M. Cundy, *cons.* 1992, *apptd* 1996; The Palace, Peterborough PEI IYA. *Signs* Ian Petriburg:

BISHOP SUFFRAGAN
Brixworth, Rt. Revd Paul E. Barber, *cons.* 1989, *apptd* 1989; 4 The Avenue, Dallington, Northampton NNI 4RZ

DEAN
Very Revd Michael Bunker, *apptd* 1992

CANONS RESIDENTIARY
T. R. Christie, *apptd* 1980; J. Higham, *apptd* 1983; P. A. Spence, *apptd* 1998
Organist, C. S. Gower, FRCO, *apptd* 1977

ARCHDEACONS
Northampton, Ven. M. R. Chapman, *apptd* 1991
Oakham, vacant

Chancellor, T. A. C. Coningsby, QC, *apptd* 1989
Registrar and Legal Secretary, R. Hemingray
Diocesan Secretary, Revd Canon R. J. Cattle, The Palace, Peterborough, Cambs PE1 1YB. Tel: 01733-64448

PORTSMOUTH (Canterbury)

8TH BISHOP
Rt. Revd Dr Kenneth W. Stevenson, *cons.* 1995, *apptd* 1995; Bishopsgrove, 26 Osborn Road, Fareham, Hants PO16 7DQ. *Signs* Kenneth Portsmouth

PROVOST
vacant

CANONS RESIDENTIARY
D. T. Isaac, *apptd* 1990; Jane B. Hedges, *apptd* 1993; G. Kirk, *apptd* 1998; I. Jagger, *apptd* 1998
Organist, D. J. C. Price, *apptd* 1996

ARCHDEACONS
Isle of Wight, Ven. K. M. L. H. Banting, *apptd* 1996
Portsmouth, Ven. C. Lowson, *apptd* 1999

Chancellor, His Hon. Judge Aglionby, *apptd* 1978
Registrar and Legal Secretary, Miss H. A. G. Tyler
Diocesan Secretary, M. F. Jordan, Cathedral House, St Thomas's Street, Portsmouth, Hants PO1 2HA. Tel: 01705-825731

RIPON (York)

BISHOP
vacant

BISHOP SUFFRAGAN
Knaresborough, Rt. Revd Frank V. Weston, *cons.* 1997, *apptd* 1997; 16 Shaftesbury Avenue, Roundhay, Leeds LS8 1DT

DEAN
Very Revd John Methuen, *apptd* 1995

CANONS RESIDENTIARY
M. R. Glanville-Smith, *apptd* 1990; K. Punshon, *apptd* 1996; J. Bell, *apptd* 1997
Organist, K. Beaumont, FRCO, *apptd* 1994

ARCHDEACONS
Leeds, Ven. J. M. Oliver, *apptd* 1992
Richmond, Ven. K. Good, *apptd* 1993

Chancellor, His Hon. Judge Grenfell, *apptd* 1992
Registrars and Legal Secretaries, C. T. Tunnard, Mrs N. Harding
Diocesan Secretary, P. M. Arundel, Diocesan Office, St Mary's Street, Leeds LS9 7DP. Tel: 0113-248 7487

ROCHESTER (Canterbury)

106TH BISHOP
Rt. Revd Dr Michael Nazir-Ali, *cons.* 1984, *apptd* 1994; Bishopscourt, Rochester ME1 1TS. *Signs* Michael Roffen:

BISHOP SUFFRAGAN
Tonbridge, Rt. Revd Brian A. Smith, *cons.* 1993, *apptd* 1993; Bishop's Lodge, 48 St Botolph's Road, Sevenoaks TN13 3AG

DEAN
Very Revd Edward F. Shotter, *apptd* 1990

CANONS RESIDENTIARY
E. R. Turner, *apptd* 1981; J. M. Armson, *apptd* 1989; N. L. Warren, *apptd* 1989; C. J. Meyrick, *apptd* 1998
Organist, R. Sayer, FRCO, *apptd* 1995

ARCHDEACONS
Bromley, Ven. G. Norman, *apptd* 1994
Rochester, Ven. N. L. Warren, *apptd* 1989
Tonbridge, Ven. Judith Rose, *apptd* 1996

Chancellor, His Hon. Judge Goodman, *apptd* 1971
Registrar and Legal Secretary, M. Thatcher
Diocesan Secretary, P. Law, St Nicholas Church, Boley Hill, Rochester ME1 1SL. Tel: 01634-830333

ST ALBANS (Canterbury)

9TH BISHOP
Rt. Revd Christopher W. Herbert, *cons.* 1995, *apptd* 1995; Abbey Gate House, St Albans AL3 4HD. *Signs* Christopher St Albans

BISHOPS SUFFRAGAN
Bedford, Rt. Revd John H. Richardson, *cons.* 1994, *apptd* 1994; 168 Kimbolton Road, Bedford MK41 8DN
Hertford, Rt. Revd Robin J. N. Smith, *cons.* 1990, *apptd* 1990; Hertford House, Abbey Mill Lane, St Albans AL3 4HE

DEAN
Very Revd Christopher Lewis, *apptd* 1993

CANONS RESIDENTIARY
G. R. S. Ritson, *apptd* 1987; M. Sansom, *apptd* 1988; C. R. J. Foster, *apptd* 1994
Organist, A. Lucas, *apptd* 1998

ARCHDEACONS
Bedford, Ven. M. L. Lesiter, *apptd* 1993
Hertford, Ven. T. P. Jones, *apptd* 1997
St Albans, Ven. R. I. Cheetham, *apptd* 1999

Chancellor, His Hon. Judge Bursell, QC, *apptd* 1992
Registrar and Legal Secretary, D. N. Cheetham
Diocesan Secretary, L. Nicholls, Holywell Lodge, 41 Holywell Hill, St Albans AL1 1HE. Tel: 01727-854532

ST EDMUNDSBURY AND IPSWICH (Canterbury)

9TH BISHOP
Rt. Revd J. H. Richard Lewis, *cons.* 1992, *apptd* 1997; Bishop's House, 4 Park Road, Ipswich IP1 3ST. *Signs* Richard St Edmundsbury and Ipswich

BISHOP SUFFRAGAN
Dunwich, Rt. Revd Clive Young, *cons.* 1999, *apptd* 1999; 28
    Westerfield Road, Ipswich IP4 2UJ

PROVOST
Very Revd J. Atwell, *apptd* 1995

CANONS RESIDENTIARY
A. M. Shaw, *apptd* 1989; M. E. Mingins, *apptd* 1993; J. Parr,
apptd 1999

Organist, J. Thomas, *apptd* 1997

ARCHDEACONS
Ipswich, Ven. T. A. Gibson, *apptd* 1987
Sudbury, Ven. J. Cox, *apptd* 1995
Suffolk, Ven. G. Arrand, *apptd* 1994

Chancellor, The Hon. Mr Justice Blofeld, *apptd* 1974
Registrar and Legal Secretary, J. Hall
Diocesan Secretary, N. Edgell, 13–15 Tower Street, Ipswich
    IP1 3BG. Tel: 01473-211028

SALISBURY (Canterbury)

77TH BISHOP
Rt. Revd David S. Stancliffe, *cons.* 1993, *apptd* 1993; South
    Canonry, The Close, Salisbury SP1 2ER. *Signs* David
    Sarum

BISHOPS SUFFRAGAN
Ramsbury, Rt. Revd Peter F. Hullah, *cons.* 1999, *apptd* 1999
Sherborne, Rt. Revd John D. G. Kirkham, *cons.* 1976, *apptd*
    1976; Little Bailie, Sturminster Marshall, Wimborne
    BH21 4AD

DEAN
Very Revd Derek Watson, *apptd* 1996

CANONS RESIDENTIARY
D. J. C. Davies, *apptd* 1985; D. M. K. Durston, *apptd* 1992;
June Osborne, *apptd* 1995

Organist, S. R. A. Lole, *apptd* 1997

ARCHDEACONS
Dorset, Ven. G. E. Walton, *apptd* 1982
Sherborne, Ven. P. C. Wheatley, *apptd* 1991
Wilts, Ven. B. J. Hopkinson, *apptd* 1986 (Sarum), 1998
    (Wilts)

Chancellor, His Hon. Judge Wiggs, *apptd* 1997
Registrar and Legal Secretary, A. Johnson
Diocesan Secretary, Revd Karen Curnock, Church House,
    Crane Street, Salisbury SP1 2QB. Tel: 01722-411922

SHEFFIELD (York)

6TH BISHOP
Rt. Revd John (Jack) Nicholls, *cons.* 1990, *apptd* 1997;
    Bishopscroft, Snaithing Lane, Sheffield S10 3LG. *Signs*
    Jack Sheffield

BISHOP SUFFRAGAN
Doncaster, Rt. Revd Michael F. Gear, *cons.* 1993, *apptd*
    1993; Bishops Lodge, Hooton Roberts, Rotherham
    S65 4PF

PROVOST
Very Revd Michael Sadgrove, *apptd* 1995

CANONS RESIDENTIARY
T. M. Page, *apptd* 1982; C. M. Smith, *apptd* 1991; Jane E. M.
Sinclair, *apptd* 1993; Ven. R. F. Blackburn, *apptd* 1999

Organist, N. Taylor, *apptd* 1997

ARCHDEACONS
Doncaster, Ven. B. L. Holdridge, *apptd* 1994
Sheffield, Ven. R. F. Blackburn, *apptd* 1999

Chancellor, Prof. J. D. McClean, *apptd* 1992
Registrar and Legal Secretary, Mrs M. Myers
Diocesan Secretary, C. A. Beck, FCIS, Diocesan Church
    House, 95–99 Effingham Street, Rotherham S65 1BL.
    Tel: 01709-511116

SODOR AND MAN (York)

79TH BISHOP
Rt. Revd Noel D. Jones, CB, *cons.* 1989, *apptd* 1989; The
    Bishop's House, Quarterbridge Road, Douglas, Isle of
    Man IM2 3RF. *Signs* Noel Sodor and Man

CANONS
B. H. Kelly, *apptd* 1980; F. H. Bird, *apptd* 1993; D.
Whitworth, *apptd* 1996; M. Convery, *apptd* 1999

ARCHDEACON
Isle of Man, Ven. B. H. Partington, *apptd* 1996

Vicar-General and Chancellor, Ms C. Faulds
Registrar and Legal Secretary, C. J. Callow
Diocesan Secretary, The Hon. C. Murphy, c/o 26 The
    Fountains, Ramsey, Isle of Man IM8 1NN. Tel: 01624-
    816545

SOUTHWARK (Canterbury)

9TH BISHOP
Rt. Revd Thomas F. Butler, PH.D, LL D, *cons.* 1985, *apptd*
    1998; Bishop's House, 38 Tooting Bec Gardens,
    London SW16 1QZ. *Signs* Thomas Southwark

AREA BISHOPS
Croydon, Rt. Revd Dr Wilfred D. Wood, DD, *cons.* 1985,
    apptd 1985; St Matthew's House, George Street,
    Croydon CR0 1PE
Kingston upon Thames, Rt Revd Peter B. Price, *cons.* 1997,
    apptd 1998; Kingston Episcopal Area Office, Whitelands
    College, West Hill, London SW15 3SN
Woolwich, Rt. Revd Colin O. Buchanan, *cons.* 1985, *apptd*
    1996; 37 South Road, Forest Hill, London SE23 2UJ

PROVOST
Very Revd Colin B. Slee, *apptd* 1994

CANONS RESIDENTIARY
D. Painter, *apptd* 1991; Helen Cunliffe, *apptd* 1995; J. John,
apptd 1997; B. Saunders, *apptd* 1997; A. P. Nunn, *apptd* 1999

Organist, P. Wright, FRCO, *apptd* 1989

ARCHDEACONS
Croydon, Ven. V. A. Davies, *apptd* 1994
Lambeth, Ven. C. R. B. Bird, *apptd* 1988
Lewisham, Ven. D. J. Atkinson, *apptd* 1996
Reigate, Ven. M. Baddeley, *apptd* 1996
Southwark, Ven. D. L. Bartles-Smith, *apptd* 1985
Wandsworth, Ven. D. Gerrard, *apptd* 1989

Chancellor, C. George, QC
Registrar and Legal Secretary, P. Morris
Diocesan Secretary, S. Parton, Trinity House, 4 Chapel
    Court, Borough High Street, London SE1 1HW. Tel:
    0171-403 8686

SOUTHWELL (York)

10TH BISHOP
Rt. Revd George H. Cassidy, *cons.* 1999, *apptd* 1999;
  Bishop's Manor, Southwell NG25 0JR. *Signs* George
  Southwell

BISHOP SUFFRAGAN
Sherwood, Rt. Revd Alan W. Morgan, *cons.* 1989, *apptd* 1989;
  Sherwood House, High Oakham Road, Mansfield
  NG18 5AJ

PROVOST
Very Revd David Leaning, *apptd* 1991

CANONS RESIDENTIARY
I. G. Collins, *apptd* 1985; G. A. Hendy *apptd* 1997

Organist, P. Hale, *apptd* 1989

ARCHDEACONS
Newark, Ven. N. Peyton, *apptd* 1999
Nottingham, Ven. G. Ogilvie, *apptd* 1996

Chancellor, J. Shand, *apptd* 1981
Registrar and Legal Secretary, C. C. Hodson
Diocesan Secretary, P. Prentis, Dunham House, Westgate,
  Southwell, Notts NG25 0JL. Tel: 01636-814331

TRURO (Canterbury)

14TH BISHOP
Rt. Revd William Ind, *cons.* 1987, *apptd* 1997; Lis Escop,
  Truro TR3 6QQ. *Signs* William Truro

BISHOP SUFFRAGAN
St Germans, vacant

DEAN
Very Revd Michael A. Moxon, LVO, *apptd* 1998

CANONS RESIDENTIARY
P. R. Gay, *apptd* 1994; K. P. Mellor, *apptd* 1994; P. D.
  Goodridge, *apptd* 1996; P. Robson, *apptd* 1999

Organist, A. Nethsingha, FRCO, *apptd* 1994

ARCHDEACONS
Cornwall, (until 31 December 1999)Ven. J. T. McCabe,
  apptd 1996; (from 1 January 2000) Ven. R. D. C.
  Whiteman
Bodmin, vacant

Chancellor, T. Briden, *apptd* 1998
Registrar and Legal Secretary, M. J. Follett
Diocesan Secretary, B. C. Laite, Diocesan House, Kenwyn,
  Truro TR1 3DU. Tel: 01872-274351

WAKEFIELD (York)

11TH BISHOP
Rt. Revd Nigel S. McCulloch, *cons.* 1986, *apptd* 1992;
  Bishop's Lodge, Woodthorpe Lane, Wakefield WF2 6JL.
  Signs Nigel Wakefield

BISHOP SUFFRAGAN
Pontefract, Rt. Revd David C. James, *cons.* 1998, *apptd* 1998;
  Pontefract House, 181A Manygates Lane, Wakefield
  WF2 7DR

PROVOST
Very Revd George P. Nairn-Briggs, *apptd* 1997

CANONS RESIDENTIARY
R. Capper, *apptd* 1997; R. Gage, *apptd* 1997; I. Gaskell,
  apptd 1998; J. Holmes, *apptd* 1998

Organist, J. Bielby, FRCO, *apptd* 1972

ARCHDEACONS
Halifax, Ven. R. Inwood, *apptd* 1995
Pontefract, Ven. A. Robinson, *apptd* 1997

Chancellor, P. Collier, QC, *apptd* 1992
Registrar and Legal Secretary, L. Box
Diocesan Secretary, A. W. Ellis, Church House, 1 South
  Parade, Wakefield WF1 1LP. Tel: 01924-371802

WORCESTER (Canterbury)

112TH BISHOP
Rt. Revd Dr Peter S. M. Selby, *cons.* 1984, *apptd* 1997; The
  Bishop's House, Hartlebury Castle, Kidderminster
  DY11 7XX. *Signs* Peter Wigorn:

BISHOP SUFFRAGAN
Dudley, (until February 2000) Rt. Revd Dr Rupert Hoare,
  cons. 1993, *apptd* 1993; The Bishop's House, Brooklands,
  Halesowen Road, Cradley Heath B64 7JF

DEAN
Very Revd Peter J. Marshall, *apptd* 1997

CANONS RESIDENTIARY
I. M. MacKenzie, *apptd* 1989; B. Ruddock, *apptd.* 1999; J. D.
  Tetley, *apptd* 1999

Organist, A. Lucas, *apptd* 1996

ARCHDEACONS
Dudley, Ven. J. Gathercole, *apptd* 1987
Worcester, Ven. Dr J. Tetley

Chancellor, C. Mynors, *apptd* 1999
Registrar and Legal Secretary, M. Huskinson
Diocesan Secretary, R. Higham, The Old Palace, Deansway,
  Worcester WR1 2JE. Tel: 01905-20537

ROYAL PECULIARS

WESTMINSTER
The Collegiate Church of St Peter

Dean, Very Revd Dr A. W. Carr, *apptd* 1997
Sub Dean and Archdeacon, A. E. Harvey, *apptd* 1987
Canons of Westminster, D. H. Hutt, *apptd* 1995; M. J.
  Middleton, *apptd* 1997; R. Wright, *apptd* 1998
Chapter Clerk and Receiver-General, Maj.-Gen. D. Burden,
  CB, CBE
Organist, J. O'Donnell
Registrar, S. J. Holmes, MVO, 20 Dean's Yard, London
  SW1P 3PA
Legal Secretary, C. L. Hodgetts

WINDSOR
*The Queen's Free Chapel of St George within Her Castle of
Windsor*

Dean, Rt. Revd D. J. Conner, *apptd* 1998
Canons Residentiary, J. A. White, *apptd* 1982; L. F. P.
  Gunner, *apptd* 1996; B. P. Thompson, PH.D., *apptd* 1998;
  J. A. Ovenden, *apptd* 1998
Chapter Clerk, Lt.-Col. N. J. Newman, *apptd* 1990, Chapter
  Office, The Cloisters, Windsor Castle, Windsor, Berks
  SL4 1NJ
Organist, J. Rees-Williams, FRCO, *apptd* 1991

Other Anglican Churches

THE CHURCH IN WALES

The Anglican Church was the established church in Wales from the 16th century until 1920, when the estrangement of the majority of Welsh people from Anglicanism resulted in disestablishment. Since then the Church in Wales has been an autonomous province consisting of six sees. The bishops are elected by an electoral college comprising elected lay and clerical members, who also elect one of the diocesan bishops as Archbishop of Wales.

The legislative body of the Church in Wales is the Governing Body, which has 365 members divided between the three orders of bishops, clergy and laity. Its President is the Archbishop of Wales and it meets twice annually. Its decisions are binding upon all members of the Church. The Church's property and finances are the responsibility of the Representative Body. There are about 96,000 members of the Church in Wales, with about 700 stipendiary clergy and 1,142 parishes.

THE GOVERNING BODY OF THE CHURCH IN WALES,
39 Cathedral Road, Cardiff CF1 9XF. Tel: 01222-231638.
Secretary-General, J. W. D. McIntyre

10TH ARCHBISHOP OF WALES, vacant

BISHOPS
Bangor (79*th*), vacant
Llandaff (102nd), Rt. Revd Dr Barry C. Morgan, b. 1947, *cons.* 1993, *elected* 1999; Llys Esgob, The Cathedral Green, Llandaff, Cardiff CF5 2YE. *Signs* Barry Landav. *Stipendiary clergy,* 164
Monmouth (8*th*), Rt. Revd Rowan D. Williams, *b* 1950, *cons.* 1992, *elected* 1992; Bishopstow, Stow Hill, Newport NP2 4EA. *Signs* Rowan Monmouth. *Stipendiary clergy,* 115
St Asaph (74*th*), Rt. Revd John S. Davies, *b.* 1943, *cons.* 1999, *elected* 1999; Esgobty, St Asaph, Clwyd LL17 0TW. *Signs* Cambrensis. *Stipendiary clergy,* 112
St David's (126*th*), Rt. Revd D. Huw Jones, *b.* 1934, *cons.* 1993, *elected* 1995; Llys Esgob, Abergwili, Carmarthen SA31 2JG. *Signs* Huw St Davids. *Stipendiary clergy,* 135
Swansea and Brecon (8*th*), Rt. Revd Anthony E. Pierce, *b.* 1941, *cons.* 1999, *elected* 1999; Ely Tower, Brecon, Powys LD3 9DE. *Signs* Anthony Swansea & Brecon. *Stipendiary clergy,* 100

The stipend of a diocesan bishop of the Church in Wales is £26,674 a year from 1998

THE SCOTTISH EPISCOPAL CHURCH

The Scottish Episcopal Church was founded after the Act of Settlement (1690) established the presbyterian nature of the Church of Scotland. The Scottish Episcopal Church is in full communion with the Church of England but is autonomous. The governing authority is the General Synod, an elected body of 180 members which meets once a year. The diocesan bishop who convenes and presides at meetings of the General Synod is called the Primus and is elected by his fellow bishops.

There are 51,353 members of the Scottish Episcopal Church, of whom 32,047 are communicants. There are seven bishops, 175 stipendiary clergy, and 320 churches and places of worship.

THE GENERAL SYNOD OF THE SCOTTISH EPISCOPAL CHURCH, 21 Grosvenor Crescent, Edinburgh EH12 5EE. Tel: 0131-225 6357. *Secretary-General,* J. F. Stuart

PRIMUS OF THE SCOTTISH EPISCOPAL CHURCH, Most Revd Richard F. Holloway (Bishop of Edinburgh), *elected* 1992

BISHOPS
Aberdeen and Orkney, A. Bruce Cameron, *b.* 1941, *cons.* 1992, *elected* 1992. *Clergy,* 23
Argyll and the Isles, Douglas M. Cameron, *b.* 1935, *cons.* 1993, *elected* 1992. *Clergy,* 8
Brechin, Neville Chamberlain, *b.* 1939, *cons.* 1997, *elected* 1997. *Clergy,* 16
Edinburgh, Richard F. Holloway, *b.* 1933, *cons.* 1986, *elected* 1986. *Clergy,* 52
Glasgow and Galloway, Idris Jones, *b.* 1943, *cons.* 1998, *elected* 1998. *Clergy,* 41
Moray, Ross and Caithness, John Crook, *b.* 1940, *Bishop Elect.* *Clergy,* 10
St Andrews, Dunkeld and Dunblane, Michael H. G. Henley, *b.* 1938, *cons.* 1995, *elected* 1995. *Clergy,* 25

The minimum stipend of a diocesan bishop of the Scottish Episcopal Church was £22,410 in 1998 (i.e. 1.5 × the minimum clergy stipend of £14,940)

THE CHURCH OF IRELAND

The Anglican Church was the established church in Ireland from the 16th century but never secured the allegiance of a majority of the Irish and was disestablished in 1871. The Church in Ireland is divided into the provinces of Armagh and Dublin, each under an archbishop. The provinces are subdivided into 12 dioceses.

The legislative body is the General Synod, which has 660 members in total, divided between the House of Bishops and the House of Representatives. The Archbishop of Armagh is elected by the House of Bishops; other episcopal elections are made by an electoral college.

There are about 375,000 members of the Church of Ireland, with two archbishops, ten bishops, about 600 clergy and about 1,000 churches and places of worship.

CENTRAL OFFICE, Church of Ireland House, Church Avenue, Rathmines, Dublin 6. Tel: 00-353-1-4978422. *Chief Officer and Secretary of the Representative Church Body,* R. H. Sherwood; *Assistant Secretary of the General Synod,* V. F. Beatty

PROVINCE OF ARMAGH

ARCHBISHOP OF ARMAGH AND PRIMATE OF ALL IRELAND, Most Revd Robert H. A. Eames, PH.D., *b.* 1937, *cons.* 1975, *trans.* 1986. *Clergy,* 51
BISHOPS
Clogher, Brian D. A. Hannon, *b.* 1936, *cons.* 1986, *apptd* 1986. *Clergy,* 32
Connor, James E. Moore, *b.* 1933, *cons.* 1995, *apptd* 1995. *Clergy,* 106
Derry and Raphoe, James Mehaffey, PH.D., *b.* 1931, *cons.* 1980, *apptd* 1980. *Clergy,* 50
Down and Dromore, Harold C. Miller, *b.* 1950, *cons.* 1997, *apptd* 1997. *Clergy,* 109
Kilmore, Elphin and Ardagh, Michael H. G. Mayes, *b.* 1941, *cons.* 1993, *apptd* 1993. *Clergy,* 24
Tuam, Killala and Achonry, Richard C. A. Henderson, *b.* 1957, *cons.* 1998, *apptd* 1998. *Clergy,* 12

PROVINCE OF DUBLIN

ARCHBISHOP OF DUBLIN, BISHOP OF GLENDALOUGH, AND PRIMATE OF IRELAND, Most Revd Walton N. F. Empey, b. 1934, cons. 1981, trans. 1985, 1996. Clergy, 90

BISHOPS

Cashel and Ossory, John R. W. Neill, b. 1945, cons. 1986, trans. 1997. Clergy, 37

Cork, Cloyne and Ross, W. Paul Colton, b. 1960, cons. 1999, apptd 1999. Clergy, 28

Limerick and Killaloe, Edward F. Darling, b. 1933, cons. 1985, apptd 1985. Clergy, 23

Meath and Kildare, (Most Revd) Robert L. Clarke, PH.D., b. 1949, cons. 1996, apptd 1996. Clergy, 23

OVERSEAS

PRIMATES

PRIMATE AND PRESIDING BISHOP OF AOTEAROA, NEW ZEALAND AND POLYNESIA, Rt. Revd John Paterson (Bishop of Auckland), cons. 1995, apptd 1998

PRIMATE OF AUSTRALIA, (until November 1999; election due February 2000) Most Revd Keith Rayner (Archbishop of Melbourne), cons. 1969, apptd 1991

PRIMATE OF BRAZIL, Most Revd Glauco Soares de Lima (Bishop of São Paulo), cons. 1989, apptd 1994

ARCHBISHOP OF THE PROVINCE OF BURUNDI, Most Revd Samuel Ndayisenga (Bishop of Buye), apptd 1998

ARCHBISHOP AND PRIMATE OF CANADA, Most Revd Michael G. Peers, cons. 1977, elected 1986

ARCHBISHOP OF THE PROVINCE OF CENTRAL AFRICA, Most Revd Walter P. K. Makhulu (Bishop of Botswana), cons. 1979, apptd 1980

PRIMATE OF THE CENTRAL REGION OF AMERICA, Most Revd Cornelius J. Wilson (Bishop of Costa Rica), cons. 1978, apptd 1998

ARCHBISHOP OF THE PROVINCE OF CONGO, Most Revd Byankya Njojo (Bishop of Boga), cons. 1980, apptd 1992

PRIMATE OF THE PROVINCE OF HONG KONG SHENG KUNG HUI, Most Revd Peter Kwong (Bishop of Hong Kong Island), cons.1981, apptd 1998

ARCHBISHOP OF THE PROVINCE OF THE INDIAN OCEAN, Most Revd Remi Rabenirina (Bishop of Antananarivo), cons. 1984, apptd 1995

PRIMATE OF JAPAN, Rt. Revd John M. Takeda (Bishop of Tokyo), cons. 1988, apptd 1998

PRESIDENT-BISHOP OF JERUSALEM AND THE MIDDLE EAST, (until May 2000) Rt. Revd Ghais A. Malik (Bishop of Egypt), cons. 1984, apptd 1996

ARCHBISHOP OF THE PROVINCE OF KENYA, Most Revd Dr David M. Gitari (Bishop of Nairobi), cons. 1975, apptd 1996

ARCHBISHOP OF THE PROVINCE OF KOREA, Most Revd Matthew Chul Bum Chung (Bishop of Seoul), cons. 1995, apptd 1998

ARCHBISHOP OF THE PROVINCE OF MELANESIA, Most Revd Ellison L. Pogo (Bishop of Central Melanesia), cons. 1981, apptd 1994

ARCHBISHOP OF MEXICO, Most Revd Samuel Espinoza (Bishop of Western Mexico), cons. 1981, elected 1995

ARCHBISHOP OF THE PROVINCE OF MYANMAR, Most Revd Andrew Mya Han (Bishop of Yangon), cons. 1988, apptd 1988

ARCHBISHOP OF THE PROVINCE OF NIGERIA, (until December 1999) Most Revd Joseph Adetiloye (Bishop of Lagos), cons. 1970, apptd 1991

ARCHBISHOP OF PAPUA NEW GUINEA, Most Revd James Ayong (Bishop of Aipo Rongo), cons. 1995, elected 1996

PRIME BISHOP OF THE PHILIPPINES, Most Revd Ignacio C. Soliba, cons. 1991, apptd 1997

ARCHBISHOP OF THE PROVINCE OF RWANDA, Most Revd Kolini Mboni (Bishop of Kigali), cons. 1980, apptd 1997

PRIMATE OF THE PROVINCE OF SOUTH EAST ASIA, Most Revd Moses Tay (Bishop of Singapore), cons. 1982 apptd 1996

METROPOLITAN OF THE PROVINCE OF SOUTHERN AFRICA, Most Revd Winston H. N. Ndungane (Archbishop of Cape Town), cons. 1991, trans. 1996

PRESIDING BISHOP OF THE SOUTHERN CONE OF AMERICA, Rt. Revd Maurice Sinclair (Bishop of Northern Argentina), cons. 1990

ARCHBISHOP OF THE PROVINCE OF THE SUDAN, vacant; election due February 2000

ARCHBISHOP OF THE PROVINCE OF TANZANIA, Most Revd Donald L. Mtetemela (Bishop of Ruaha), cons. 1982, apptd 1998

ARCHBISHOP OF THE PROVINCE OF UGANDA, Most Revd Mpalanyi-Nkoyoyo. cons. 1980

PRESIDING BISHOP AND PRIMATE OF THE USA, Most Revd Frank T. Griswold III, cons. 1985, apptd 1997

ARCHBISHOP OF THE PROVINCE OF WEST AFRICA, Most Revd Robert Okine (Bishop of Koforidua), cons. 1981, apptd 1993

ARCHBISHOP OF THE PROVINCE OF THE WEST INDIES, Most Revd Drexel Wellington Gomez (Bishop of Nassau and the Bahamas), cons. 1972, apptd 1998

OTHER CHURCHES AND EXTRA-PROVINCIAL DIOCESES

ANGLICAN CHURCH OF BERMUDA, Rt. Revd Ewen Ratteray, apptd 1996

CHURCH OF CEYLON: This Church comes under the Metropolitical authority of the Archbishop of Canterbury.
Bishop of Colombo, Rt. Revd. Kenneth Michael James Fernando, cons. 1992
Bishop of Kurunagala, Rt. Revd Andrew O. Kumarage, cons. 1984

EPISCOPAL CHURCH OF CUBA, Rt. Revd Jorge Perera Hurtado, apptd 1995

LUSITANIAN CHURCH (Portuguese Episcopal Church), Rt. Revd Fernando da Luz Soares, apptd 1971

SPANISH REFORMED EPISCOPAL CHURCH, Rt. Revd Carlos Lozano Lopez, apptd 1995

EXTRA-PROVINCIAL TO PROVINCE IX OF THE EPISCOPAL CHURCH IN THE USA:
PUERTO RICO, Rt. Revd David Andres Alvarez-Velazquez, cons. 1987
VENEZUELA, Rt. Revd Orlando Guerrero, cons. 1995

MODERATORS OF CHURCHES IN FULL COMMUNION WITH THE ANGLICAN COMMUNION

CHURCH OF NORTH INDIA, Rt. Revd Vinod Anandrao R. Peter (Bishop of Nagpur), apptd 1998

CHURCH OF SOUTH INDIA, Most Revd William Moses (Bishop of Coimbatore), cons. 1987, apptd 1998

CHURCH OF PAKISTAN, Rt. Revd Samuel Azariah, Bishop of Raiwind

CHURCH OF BANGLADESH, Rt. Revd Barnabas Mondal, cons. 1975, apptd 1975

The Church of Scotland

The Church of Scotland is the established (i.e. national) church of Scotland. The Church is Reformed and evangelical in doctrine, and presbyterian in constitution, i.e. based on a hierarchy of councils of ministers and elders and, since 1990, of members of a diaconate. At local level the kirk session consists of the parish minister and ruling elders. At district level the presbyteries, of which there are 47, consist of all the ministers in the district, one ruling elder from each congregation, and those members of the diaconate who qualify for membership. The General Assembly is the supreme authority, and is presided over by a Moderator chosen annually by the Assembly. The Sovereign, if not present in person, is represented by a Lord High Commissioner who is appointed each year by the Crown.

The Church of Scotland has about 700,000 members, 1,200 ministers and 1,600 churches. There are about 100 ministers and other personnel working overseas.

Lord High Commissioner (1999), The Lord Hogg of Cumbernauld
Moderator of the General Assembly (1999), The Rt. Revd John B. Cairns
Principal Clerk, Revd F. A. J. Macdonald
Depute Clerk, Revd M. A. MacLean
Procurator, R. A. Dunlop, QC
Law Agent and Solicitor of the Church, Mrs J. S. Wilson
Parliamentary Agent, I. McCulloch (*London*)
General Treasurer, D. F. Ross
Secretary, Church and Nation Committee, Revd Dr D. Sinclair
CHURCH OFFICE, 121 George Street, Edinburgh
EH2 4YN. Tel: 0131-225 5722

PRESBYTERIES AND CLERKS

Edinburgh, Revd W. P. Graham
West Lothian, Revd D. Shaw
Lothian, J. D. McCulloch

Melrose and Peebles, Revd J. H. Brown
Duns, Revd A. C. D. Cartwright
Jedburgh, Revd A. D. Reid

Annandale and Eskdale, Revd C. B. Haston
Dumfries and Kirkcudbright, Revd G. M. A. Savage
Wigtown and Stranraer, Revd D. Dutton

Ayr, Revd J. Crichton
Irvine and Kilmarnock, Revd C. G. F. Brockie
Ardrossan, Revd D. Broster

Lanark, Revd I. D. Cunningham
Paisley, Revd D. Kay
Greenock, Revd D. Mill
Glasgow, Revd A. Cunningham
Hamilton, Revd J. H. Wilson
Dumbarton, Revd D. P. Munro

South Argyll, M. A. J. Gossip
Dunoon, Revd R. Samuel
Lorn and Mull, Revd W. Hogg

Falkirk, Revd D. E. McClements
Stirling, Revd B. W. Dunsmore

Dunfermline, Revd W. E. Farquhar
Kirkcaldy, Revd B. L. Tomlinson
St Andrews, Revd P. Meager

Dunkeld and Meigle, Revd A. B. Reid
Perth, Revd A. M. Millar
Dundee, Revd J. A. Roy
Angus, Revd M. I. G. Rooney

Aberdeen, Revd A. Douglas
Kincardine and Deeside, Revd J. W. S. Brown
Gordon, Revd I. U. Thomson
Buchan, Revd R. Neilson
Moray, Revd D. J. Ferguson

Abernethy, Revd J. A. I. MacEwan
Inverness, Revd A. S. Younger
Lochaber, Revd A. Ramsay

Ross, Revd R. M. MacKinnon
Sutherland, Revd J. L. Goskirk
Caithness, Revd M. G. Mappin
Lochcarron/Skye, Revd A. I. Macarthur
Uist, Revd M. Smith
Lewis, Revd T. S. Sinclair

Orkney (*Finstown*), Revd T. Hunt
Shetland (*Lerwick*), Revd N. R. Whyte
England (*London*), Revd W. A. Cairns

Europe (*Geneva*), Revd J. W. McLeod

The minimum stipend of a minister in the Church of Scotland in 1998 was £16,737

The Roman Catholic Church

The Roman Catholic Church is one world-wide Christian Church acknowledging as its head the Bishop of Rome, known as the Pope (Father). The Pope is held to be the successor of St Peter and thus invested with the power which was entrusted to St Peter by Jesus Christ. A direct line of succession is therefore claimed from the earliest Christian communities. With the fall of the Roman Empire the Pope also became an important political leader. His temporal power is now limited to the 107 acres of the Vatican City State.

The Pope exercises spiritual authority over the Church with the advice and assistance of the Sacred College of Cardinals, the supreme council of the Church. He is also advised about the concerns of the Church locally by his ambassadors, who liaise with the Bishops' Conference in each country.

In addition to advising the Pope, those members of the Sacred College of Cardinals who are under the age of 80 also elect a successor following the death of a Pope. The assembly of the Cardinals at the Vatican for the election of a new Pope is known as the Conclave in which, in complete seclusion, the Cardinals elect by a secret ballot; a two-thirds majority is necessary before the vote can be accepted as final. When a Cardinal receives the necessary votes, the Dean of the Sacred College formally asks him if he will accept election and the name by which he wishes to be known. On his acceptance of the office the Conclave is dissolved and the First Cardinal Deacon announces the election to the assembled crowd in St Peter's Square. On the first Sunday or Holyday following the election, the new Pope assumes the pontificate at High Mass in St Peter's Square. A new pontificate is dated from the assumption of the pontificate.

The number of cardinals was fixed at 70 by Pope Sixtus V in 1586, but has been steadily increased since the pontificate of John XXIII and at the end of June 1999 stood at 157, plus two cardinals created 'in pectore' (their names being kept secret by the Pope for fear of persecution; they are thought to be Chinese).

The Roman Catholic Church universally and the Vatican City State are run by the Curia, which is made up of the Secretariat of State, the Sacred Council for the Public Affairs of the Church, and various congregations, secretariats and tribunals assisted by commissions and offices. The congregations are permanent commissions for conducting the affairs of the Church and are made up of cardinals, one of whom occupies the office of prefect. Below the Secretariat of State and the congregations are the secretariats and tribunals, all of which are headed by cardinals. (The Curial cardinals are analagous to ministers in charge of government departments.)

The Vatican State has its own diplomatic service, with representatives known as nuncios. Papal nuncios with full diplomatic recognition are given precedence over all other ambassadors to the country to which they are appointed; where precedence is not recognized the Papal representative is known as a pro-nuncio. Where the representation is only to the local churches and not to the government of a country, the Papal representative is known as an apostolic delegate. The Roman Catholic Church has an estimated 890.9 million adherents world-wide.

SOVEREIGN PONTIFF

His Holiness Pope John Paul II (Karol Wojtyla), *born* Wadowice, Poland, 18 May 1920; *ordained priest* 1946; *appointed Archbishop* of Krakow 1964; *created Cardinal* 1967; *assumed pontificate* 16 October 1978

SECRETARIAT OF STATE

Secretary of State, HE Cardinal Angelo Sodano
First Section (General Affairs), Mgr G. Re (Archbishop of Vescovio)
Second Section (Relations with other states), Mgr J. L. Tauran (Archbishop of Telepte)

BISHOPS' CONFERENCE

The Roman Catholic Church in England and Wales is governed by the Bishops' Conference, membership of which includes the Diocesan Bishops, the Apostolic Exarch of the Ukrainians, the Bishop of the Forces and the Auxiliary Bishops. The Conference is headed by the President and Vice-President. There are five departments, each with an episcopal chairman: the Department for Christian Life and Worship (the Archbishop of Southwark), the Department for Mission and Unity (the Bishop of Arundel and Brighton), the Department for Catholic Education and Formation (the Bishop of Leeds), the Department for Christian Responsibility and Citizenship (the Bishop of Plymouth), and the Department for International Affairs.

The Bishops' Standing Committee, made up of all the Archbishops and the chairman of each of the above departments, has general responsibility for continuity and policy between the plenary sessions of the Conference. It prepares the Conference agenda and implements its decisions. It is serviced by a General Secretariat. There are also agencies and consultative bodies affiliated to the Conference.

The Bishops' Conference of Scotland has as its president Archbishop Winning of Glasgow and is the permanently constituted assembly of the Bishops of Scotland. To promote its work, the Conference establishes various agencies which have an advisory function in relation to the Conference. The more important of these agencies are called Commissions and each one has a Bishop President who, with the other members of the Commissions, are appointed by the Conference.

The Irish Episcopal Conference has as its acting president Archbishop Connell of Dublin. Its membership comprises all the Archbishops and Bishops of Ireland and it appoints various Commissions to assist it in its work.

There are three types of Commissions: (a) those made up of lay and clerical members chosen for their skills and experience, and staffed by full-time expert secretariats; (b) Commissions whose members are selected from existing institutions and whose services are supplied on a part-time basis; and (c) Commissions of Bishops only.

The Roman Catholic Church in Britain and Ireland has an estimated 8,992,000 members, 11 archbishops, 67 bishops, 11,260 priests, and 8,588 churches and chapels open to the public.

Bishops' Conferences secretariats:

ENGLAND AND WALES, 39 Eccleston Square, London SW1V 1PD. Tel: 0171-630 8220. *General Secretary*, The Rt. Revd Arthur Roche

SCOTLAND, Candida Casa, 8 Corsehill Road, Ayr, Scotland KA7 2ST. Tel: 01292-256750. *General Secretary*, The Rt. Revd Maurice Taylor (Bishop of Galloway)

IRELAND, Iona, 65 Newry Road, Dundalk, Co. Louth. *Executive Secretary*, Revd Hugh G. Connelly

---

GREAT BRITAIN

APOSTOLIC NUNCIO TO GREAT BRITAIN
The Most Revd Pablo Puente, 54 Parkside, London SW19 5NE. Tel: 0181-946 1410

ENGLAND AND WALES

THE MOST REVD ARCHBISHOPS
Westminster, vacant
  Auxiliaries, Vincent Nichols, *cons.* 1992; James J. O'Brien, *cons.* 1977; Patrick O'Donoghue, *cons.* 1993
  Clergy, 789
  Archbishop's Residence, Archbishop's House, Ambrosden Avenue, London SW1P 1QJ. Tel: 0171-798 9033
Birmingham, vacant
  Auxiliaries, Philip Pargeter, *cons.* 1990
  Clergy, 490
  Diocesan Curia, Cathedral House, St Chad's Queensway, Birmingham B4 6EX. Tel: 0121-236 5535
Cardiff, John A. Ward, *cons.* 1980, *apptd* 1983
  Clergy, 137
  Diocesan Curia, Archbishop's House, 41–43 Cathedral Road, Cardiff CF1 9HD. Tel: 01222-220411
Liverpool, Patrick Kelly, *cons.* 1984, *apptd* 1996
  Auxiliary, Vincent Malone, *cons.* 1989
  Clergy, 533
  Diocesan Curia, 152 Brownlow Hill, Liverpool L3 5RQ. Tel: 0151-709 4801
Southwark, Michael Bowen, *cons.* 1970, *apptd* 1977
  Auxiliaries, Charles Henderson, *cons.* 1972; Howard Tripp, *cons.* 1980; John Jukes, *cons.* 1980
  Clergy, 516
  Diocesan Curia, Archbishop's House, 150 St George's Road, London SE1 6HX. Tel: 0171-928 5592

THE RT. REVD BISHOPS
Arundel and Brighton, Cormac Murphy-O'Connor, *cons.* 1977. *Clergy*, 313. *Diocesan Curia*, Bishop's House, The Upper Drive, Hove, E. Sussex BN3 6NE. Tel: 01273-506387
Brentwood, Thomas McMahon, *cons.* 1980, *apptd* 1980. *Clergy*, 174. *Bishop's Office*, Cathedral House, Ingrave Road, Brentwood, Essex CM15 8AT. Tel: 01277-232266
Clifton, Mervyn Alexander, *cons.* 1972, *apptd* 1974. *Clergy*, 251. *Diocesan Curia*, Egerton Road, Bishopston, Bristol BS7 8HU. Tel: 0117-983 3907

East Anglia, Peter Smith, *cons.* 1995, *apptd* 1995. *Clergy*, 173. *Diocesan Curia*, The White House, 21 Upgate, Poringland, Norwich NR14 7SH. Tel: 01508-492202

Hallam, John Rawsthorne, *cons.* 1981, *apptd* 1997. *Clergy*, 89. *Bishop's Residence*, 'Quarters', Carsick Hill Way, Sheffield S10 3LY. Tel: 0114-230 9101

Hexham and Newcastle, Michael Ambrose Griffiths, *cons.* 1992. *Clergy*, 259. *Diocesan Curia*, Bishop's House, East Denton Hall, 800 West Road, Newcastle upon Tyne NE5 2BJ. Tel: 0191-228 0003

Lancaster, John Brewer, *cons.* 1971, *apptd* 1985. *Clergy*, 256. *Bishop's Residence*, Bishop's House, Cannon Hill, Lancaster LA1 5NG. Tel: 01524-32231

Leeds, David Konstant, *cons.* 1977, *apptd* 1985. *Clergy*, 253. *Diocesan Curia*, 7 St Marks Avenue, Leeds LS2 9BN. Tel: 0113-244 4788

Menevia (*Wales*), Daniel Mullins, *cons.* 1970, *apptd* 1987. *Clergy*, 61. *Diocesan Curia*, 27 Convent Street, Swansea SA1 2BX. Tel: 01792-644017

Middlesbrough, John Crowley, *cons.* 1986, *apptd* 1992. *Clergy*, 187. *Diocesan Curia*, 50A The Avenue, Linthorpe, Middlesbrough, Cleveland TS5 6QT. Tel: 01642-850505

Northampton, Patrick Leo McCartie, *cons.* 1977, *apptd* 1990. *Clergy*, 154. *Diocesan Curia*, Bishop's House, Marriott Street, Northampton NN2 6AW. Tel: 01604-715635

Nottingham, James McGuinness, *cons.* 1972, *apptd* 1974. *Clergy*, 217. *Diocesan Curia*, Willson House, Derby Road, Nottingham NG1 5AW. Tel: 0115-953 9800

Plymouth, Christopher Budd, *cons.* 1986. *Clergy*, 143. *Diocesan Curia*, Bishop's House, 31 Wyndham Street West, Plymouth PL1 5RZ. Tel: 01752-224414

Portsmouth, F. Crispian Hollis, *cons.* 1987, *apptd* 1989. *Clergy*, 268. *Bishop's Residence*, Bishop's House, Edinburgh Road, Portsmouth, Hants PO1 3HG. Tel: 01705-820894

Salford, Terence J. Brain, *cons.* 1991, *apptd* 1997. *Clergy*, 394. *Diocesan Curia*, Cathedral House, 250 Chapel Street, Salford M3 5LL. Tel: 0161-834 9052

Shrewsbury, Brian Noble, *cons.* 1995, *apptd* 1995. *Clergy* 196. *Diocesan Curia*, 2 Park Road South, Birkenhead, Merseyside L43 4UX. Tel: 0151-652 9855

Wrexham (*Wales*), Edwin Regan, *apptd* 1994. *Clergy*, 86. *Diocesan Curia*, Bishop's House, Sontley Road, Wrexham, Clwyd LL13 7EW. Tel: 01978-262726

SCOTLAND

THE MOST REVD ARCHBISHOPS
St Andrews and Edinburgh, Keith Patrick O'Brien, *cons.* 1985 *Clergy*, 192 *Diocesan Curia*, 113 Whitehouse Loan, Edinburgh EH9 1BD. Tel: 0131-452 8244

Glasgow, HE Cardinal Thomas Winning, *cons.* 1971, *apptd* 1974 *Clergy*, 253 *Diocesan Curia*, 196 Clyde Street, Glasgow G1 4JY. Tel: 0141-226 5898

THE RT. REVD BISHOPS
Aberdeen, Mario Conti, *cons.* 1977. *Clergy*, 58. *Bishop's Residence*, 3 Queen's Cross, Aberdeen AB2 6BR. Tel: 01224-319154

Argyll and the Isles, vacant. *Clergy*, 33. *Diocesan Curia*, St Columba's Cathedral, Esplanade, Oban, Argyll PA34 5AB. Tel: 01631-571003

Dunkeld, Vincent Logan, *cons.* 1981. *Clergy*, 51. *Diocesan Curia*, 29 Roseangle, Dundee DD1 4LR. Tel: 01382-25453

Galloway, Maurice Taylor, *cons.* 1981. *Clergy*, 66. *Diocesan Curia*, 8 Corsehill Road, Ayr KA7 2ST. Tel: 01292-266750

Motherwell, Joseph Devine, *cons.* 1977, *apptd* 1983. *Clergy*, 168. *Diocesan Curia*, Coursington Road, Motherwell ML1 1PW. Tel: 01698-269114

Paisley, John A. Mone, *cons.* 1984, *apptd* 1988. *Clergy*, 86. *Diocesan Curia*, Cathedral House, 8 East Buchanan Street, Paisley, Renfrewshire PA1 1HS. Tel: 0141-889 3601

BISHOPRIC OF THE FORCES

Francis Walmsley, *cons.* 1979. Administration: AGPDO, Middle Hill, Aldershot, Hants GU11 1PP. Tel: 01252-349004

IRELAND

There is one hierarchy for the whole of Ireland. Several of the dioceses have territory partly in the Republic of Ireland and partly in Northern Ireland.

APOSTOLIC NUNCIO TO IRELAND
Most Revd Giovanni Ceirano (titular Archbishop of Tigimma), 183 Navan Road, Dublin 7. Tel: 00 353 1-380577

THE MOST REVD ARCHBISHOPS
Armagh, Sean Brady, *cons.* 1995, *apptd* 1996 *Auxiliary*, Gerard Clifford, *cons.* 1991 *Clergy*, 183 *Diocesan Curia*, Ara Coeli, Armagh BT61 7QY. Tel: 01861-522045

Cashel, Dermot Clifford, *cons.* 1986, *apptd* 1988 *Clergy*, 136 *Archbishop's Residence*, Archbishop's House, Thurles, Co. Tipperary. Tel: 00 353 504-21512

Dublin, Desmond Connell, *cons.* 1988, *apptd* 1988 *Auxiliaries*, James Moriarty, *cons.* 1991; Eamonn Walsh, *cons.* 1990; Fiachra O'Ceallaigh, *cons* 1994; Martin Drennan, *cons.* 1997; Raymond Field, *cons.* 1997 *Clergy*, 994 *Archbishop's Residence*, Archbishop's House, Drumcondra, Dublin 9. Tel: 00 353 1-8373732

Tuam, Michael Neary, *cons.* 1992, *apptd* 1995 *Clergy*, 180 *Archbishop's Residence*, Archbishop's House, Tuam, Co. Galway. Tel: 00 353 93-24166

THE MOST REVD BISHOPS
Achonry, Thomas Flynn, *cons.* 1975. *Clergy*, 62. *Bishop's Residence*, Bishop's House, Ballaghadaderreen, Co. Roscommon. Tel: 00 353 907-60021

Ardagh and Clonmacnois, Colm O'Reilly, *cons.* 1983. *Clergy*, 100. *Diocesan Office*, Bishop's House, St Michael's, Longford, Co. Longford. Tel: 00 353 43-46432

Clogher, Joseph Duffy, *cons.* 1979. *Clergy*, 108. *Bishop's Residence*, Bishop's House, Monaghan. Tel: 00 353 47-81019

Clonfert, Joseph Kirby, *cons.* 1988. *Clergy*, 71. *Bishop's Residence*, St Brendan's, Coorheen, Loughrea, Co. Galway. Tel: 00 353 91-41560

Cloyne, John Magee, *cons.* 1987. *Clergy*, 158. *Diocesan Centre*, Cobh, Co. Cork. Tel: 00 353 21-811430

Cork and Ross, John Buckley, *cons.* 1984, *apptd* 1998. *Clergy*, 338. *Diocesan Office*, Bishop's House, Redemption Road, Cork. Tel: 00 353 21-301717

Derry, Seamus Hegarty, *cons.* 1984, *apptd* 1994. *Clergy*, 157. *Bishop's Residence*, Bishop's House, St Eugene's Cathedral, Derry BT48 9AP. Tel: 01504-262302 *Auxiliary*, Francis Lagan, *cons.* 1988

Down and Connor, Patrick J. Walsh, *cons.* 1983, *apptd* 1991. *Clergy*, 248. *Bishop's Residence*, Lisbreen, 73 Somerton Road, Belfast, Co. Antrim DT15 4DE. Tel: 01232-776185 *Auxiliaries*, Anthony Farquhar, *cons.* 1983; Michael Dallat, *cons.* 1994

Dromore, Francis Brooks, *cons.* 1976. *Clergy*, 78. *Bishop's Residence*, Bishop's House, Violet Hill, Newry, Co. Down BT35 6PN. Tel: 01693-62444

Elphin, Christopher Jones, *cons.* 1994. *Clergy*, 101. *Bishop's Residence*, St Mary's, Sligo. Tel: 00 353 71-62670

Ferns, Brendon Comiskey, *cons.* 1980. *Clergy*, 161. *Bishop's Office*, Bishop's House, Summerhill, Wexford. Tel: 00 353 53-22177

Galway and Kilmacduagh, James McLoughlin, *cons.* 1993. *Clergy*, 90. *Diocesan Office*, The Cathedral, Galway. Tel: 00 353 91-63566

Kerry, William Murphy, *cons.* 1995. *Clergy*, 149. *Bishop's Residence*, Bishop's House, Killarney, Co. Kerry. Tel: 00 353 64-31168

Kildare and Leighlin, Laurence Ryan, *cons.* 1984. *Clergy*, 136. *Bishop's Residence*, Bishop's House, Carlow. Tel: 00 353 503-31102

Killala, Thomas Finnegan, *cons.* 1970. *Clergy*, 62. *Bishop's Residence*, Bishop's House, Ballina, Co. Mayo. Tel: 00 353 96-21518

Killaloe, William Walsh, *cons.* 1994. *Clergy*, 149. *Bishop's Residence*, Westbourne, Ennis, Co. Clare. Tel: 00 353 65-28638

Kilmore, Francis McKiernan, *cons.* 1972. *Coadjutor*, Leo O'Reilly. *Clergy*, 115. *Bishop's Residence*, Bishop's House, Cullies, Co. Cavan. Tel: 00 353 49-31496

Limerick, Donal Murray, *cons.* 1996. *Clergy*, 152. *Diocesan Offices*, 66 O'Connell Street, Limerick. Tel: 00 353 61-315856

Meath, Michael Smith, *cons.* 1984, *apptd* 1990. *Clergy*, 141. *Bishop's Residence*, Bishop's House, Dublin Road, Mullingar, Co. Westmeath. Tel: 00 353 44-48841

Ossory, Laurence Forristal, *cons.* 1980. *Clergy*, 111. *Bishop's Residence*, Sion House, Kilkenny. Tel: 00 353 56-62448

Raphoe, Philip Boyce, *cons.* 1994. *Clergy*, 96. *Bishop's Residence*, Ard Adhamhnáin, Letterkenny, Co. Donegal. Tel: 00 353 74-21208

Waterford and Lismore, William Lee, *cons.* 1993. *Clergy*, 130. *Bishop's Residence*, Woodleigh, Summerville Avenue, Waterford. Tel: 00 353 51-71432

PATRIARCHS IN COMMUNION WITH THE ROMAN CATHOLIC CHURCH

Alexandria, HB Stephanos II Ghattas (Patriarch for Catholic Copts)

Antioch, HB Ignace Antoine II Hayek (Patriarch for Syrian rite Catholics); HB Maximos V. Hakim (Patriarch for Greek Melekite rite Catholics); HE Cardinal Nasrallah Pierre Sfeir (Patriarch for Maronite rite Catholics)

Jerusalem, HB Michel Sabbah (Patriarch for Latin rite Catholics); HB Maximos V. Hakim (Patriarch for Greek Melekite rite Catholics)

Babilonia of the Chaldeans, HB Raphael I Bidawid

Cilicia of the Armenians, HB Jean Pierre XVIII Kasparian (Patriarch for Armenian rite Catholics)

Oriental India, Archbishop Raul Nicolau Gonsalves

Lisbon, vacant

Venice, HE Cardinal Marco Ce

Other Churches in the UK

AFRICAN AND AFRO-CARIBBEAN CHURCHES

There are more than 160 Christian churches or groups of African or Afro-Caribbean origin in the UK. These include the Apostolic Faith Church, the Cherubim and Seraphim Church, the New Testament Church Assembly, the New Testament Church of God, the Wesleyan Holiness Church and the Aladura Churches.

The Afro-West Indian United Council of Churches and the Council of African and Afro-Caribbean Churches UK (which was initiated as the Council of African and Allied Churches in 1979 to give one voice to the various Christian churches of African origin in the UK) are the media through which the member churches can work jointly to provide services they cannot easily provide individually.

There are about 70,000 adherents of African and Afro-Caribbean churches in the UK, and about 1,000 congregations. The Afro-West Indian United Council of Churches has about 30,000 individual members, 135 ministers and 65 places of worship. The Council of African and Afro-Caribbean Churches UK has about 17,000 members, 250 ministers and 75 congregations.

AFRO-WEST INDIAN UNITED COUNCIL OF CHURCHES,
c/o New Testament Church of God, Arcadian Gardens, High Road, London N22 5AA. Tel: 0181-888 9427. *Secretary*, Bishop E. Brown

COUNCIL OF AFRICAN AND AFRO-CARIBBEAN CHURCHES UK, 31 Norton House, Sidney Road, London SW9 0UJ. Tel: 0171-274 5589. *Chairman*, His Grace The Most Revd Father Olu A. Abiola

ASSOCIATED PRESBYTERIAN CHURCHES OF SCOTLAND

The Associated Presbyterian Churches came into being in 1989 as a result of a division within the Free Presbyterian Church of Scotland. Following two controversial disciplinary cases, the culmination of deepening differences within the Church, a presbytery was formed calling itself the Associated Presbyterian Churches (APC). The Associated Presbyterian Churches has about 1,000 members, 15 ministers and 20 churches.

Clerk of the Scottish Presbytery, Revd Dr M. MacInnes, Drumalin, 16 Drummond Road, Inverness IV2 4NB. Tel: 01463-223983

THE BAPTIST CHURCH

Baptists trace their origins to John Smyth, who in 1609 in Amsterdam reinstituted the baptism of conscious believers as the basis of the fellowship of a gathered church. Members of Smyth's church established the first Baptist church in England in 1612. They came to be known as 'General' Baptists and their theology was Arminian, whereas a later group of Calvinists who adopted the baptism of believers came to be known as 'Particular' Baptists. The two sections of the Baptists were united into one body, the Baptist Union of Great Britain and Ireland, in 1891. In 1988 the title was changed to the Baptist Union of Great Britain.

Baptists emphasize the complete autonomy of the local church, although individual churches are linked in various kinds of associations. There are international bodies (such as the Baptist World Alliance) and national bodies, but some Baptist churches belong to neither. However, in Great Britain the majority of churches and associations belong to the Baptist Union of Great Britain. There are also Baptist Unions in Wales, Scotland and Ireland which are much smaller than the Baptist Union of Great Britain, and there is some overlap of membership.

There are over 40 million Baptist church members world-wide; in the Baptist Union of Great Britain there are 147,089 members, 1,780 pastors and 2,114 churches. In the Baptist Union of Scotland there are 13,587 members, 140 pastors and 171 churches. In the Baptist Union of Wales there are 21,800 members, 110 pastors and 527 churches. In the Association of Baptist Churches (formerly the Baptist Union of Ireland) there are 8,378 members, 90 pastors and 110 churches.

President of the Baptist Union of Great Britain (1999–2000), Revd M. I. Bochenski

General Secretary, Revd D. R. Coffey, Baptist House, PO Box 44, 129 Broadway, Didcot, Oxon OX11 8RT. Tel: 01235-517700

THE CONGREGATIONAL FEDERATION

The Congregational Federation was founded by members of Congregational churches in England and Wales who did not join the United Reformed Church (see p. 422) in 1972. There are also churches in Scotland and Australia affiliated to the Federation. The Federation exists to encourage congregations of believers to worship in free assembly, but it has no authority over them and emphasizes their right to independence and self-government.

The Federation has 11,923 members, 71 recognized ministers and 313 churches in England, Wales and Scotland.

President of the Federation (1999–2000), Revd. R. Waddington

General Secretary, G. M. Adams, The Congregational Centre, 4 Castle Gate, Nottingham NG1 7AS. Tel: 0115-911 1460

THE FREE CHURCH OF ENGLAND

The Free Church of England is a union of two bodies in the Anglican tradition, the Free Church of England, founded in 1844 as a protest against the Oxford Movement in the established Church, and the Reformed Episcopal Church, founded in America in 1873 but which also had congregations in England. As both Churches sought to maintain the historic faith, tradition and practice of the Anglican Church since the Reformation, they decided to unite as one body in England in 1927. The historic episcopate was conferred on the English Church in 1876 through the line of the American bishops, who had pioneered an open table Communion policy towards members of other denominations.

The Free Church of England has 1,500 members, 42 ministers and 25 churches in England. It also has three house churches and three ministers in New Zealand, two churches and one minister in Queensland, Australia, and one church and one minister in St Petersburg, Russia.

General Secretary, Revd W. J. Lawler, 45 Broughton Road, Wallasey, Merseyside CH44 4DT. Tel: 0151-638 2564

THE FREE CHURCH OF SCOTLAND

The Free Church of Scotland was formed in 1843 when over 400 ministers withdrew from the Church of Scotland as a result of interference in the internal affairs of the church by the civil authorities. In 1900, all but 26 ministers joined with others to form the United Free Church (most of which rejoined the Church of Scotland in 1929). In 1904 the remaining 26 ministers were recognized by the House of Lords as continuing the Free Church of Scotland.

The Church maintains strict adherence to the Westminster Confession of Faith (1648) and accepts the Bible as the sole rule of faith and conduct. Its General Assembly meets annually. It also has links with Reformed Churches overseas. The Free Church of Scotland has 6,000 members, 110 ministers and 140 churches.

General Treasurer, I. D. Gill, The Mound, Edinburgh EH1 2LS. Tel: 0131-226 5286

THE FREE PRESBYTERIAN CHURCH OF SCOTLAND

The Free Presbyterian Church of Scotland was formed in 1893 by two ministers of the Free Church of Scotland who refused to accept a Declaratory Act passed by the Free Church General Assembly in 1892. The Free Presbyterian Church of Scotland is Calvinistic in doctrine and emphasizes observance of the Sabbath. It adheres strictly to the Westminster Confession of Faith of 1648.

The Church has about 3,000 members in Scotland and about 4,000 in overseas congregations. It has 20 ministers and 50 churches.

Moderator, Revd G. G. Hutton, Free Presbyterian Manse, Broadford, Isle of Skye IV49 4AQ

Clerk of Synod, Revd J. MacLeod, 16 Matheson Road, Stornoway, Isle of Lewis HS1 2LA. Tel: 01851-702755

THE INDEPENDENT METHODIST CHURCHES

The Independent Methodist Churches seceded from the Wesleyan Methodist Church in 1805 and remained independent when the Methodist Church in Great Britain was formed in 1932. They are mainly concentrated in industrial areas of the north of England.

The churches are Methodist in doctrine but their organization is congregational. All the churches are members of the Independent Methodist Connexion of Churches. The controlling body of the Connexion is the Annual Meeting, to which churches send delegates. The Connexional President is elected annually. Between annual meetings the affairs of the Connexion are handled by departmental committees. Ministers are appointed by the churches and trained through the Connexion. The ministry is open to both men and women and is unpaid.

There are 3,050 members, 106 ministers and 98 churches in Great Britain.

Connexional President (1999–2000), J. Dolan

General Secretary, J. M. Day, The Old Police House, Croxton, Stafford ST21 6PE. Tel: 0163-062 0671

THE LUTHERAN CHURCH

Lutheranism is based on the teachings of Martin Luther, the German leader of the Protestant Reformation. The authority of the scriptures is held to be supreme over Church tradition and creeds, and the key doctrine is that of justification by faith alone.

Lutheranism is one of the largest Protestant denominations and it is particularly strong in northern Europe and the USA. Some Lutheran churches are episcopal, while others have a synodal form of organization; unity is based on doctrine rather than structure. Most Lutheran churches are members of the Lutheran World Federation, based in Geneva.

Lutheran services in Great Britain are held in seventeen languages to serve members of different nationalities. English-language congregations are members either of the Lutheran Church in Great Britain, or of the Evangelical Lutheran Church of England. The Lutheran Church in Great Britain and other Lutheran churches in Britain are members of the Lutheran Council of Great Britain.

There are over 70 million Lutherans world-wide; in Great Britain there are about 50,000 members, 50 clergy and 100 congregations.

General Secretary of the Lutheran Council of Great Britain,
Revd T. Bruch, 30 Thanet Street, London WC1H 9QH. Tel: 0171-383 3081

THE METHODIST CHURCH

The Methodist movement started in England in 1729 when the Revd John Wesley, an Anglican priest, and his brother Charles met with others in Oxford and resolved to conduct their lives and study by 'rule and method'. In 1739 the Wesleys began evangelistic preaching and the first Methodist chapel was founded in Bristol in the same year. In 1744 the first annual conference was held, at which the Articles of Religion were drawn up. Doctrinal emphases included repentance, faith, the assurance of salvation, social concern and the priesthood of all believers. After John Wesley's death in 1791 the Methodists withdrew from the established Church to form the Methodist Church. Methodists gradually drifted into many groups, but in 1932 the Wesleyan Methodist Church, the United Methodist Church and the Primitive Methodist Church united to form the Methodist Church in Great Britain as it now exists.

The governing body and supreme authority of the Methodist Church is the Conference, but there are also 33 district synods, consisting of all the ministers and selected lay people in each district, and circuit meetings of the ministers and lay people of each circuit.

There are over 60 million Methodists world-wide; in Great Britain (1998 figures) there are 353,330 members, 3,727 ministers, 10,746 lay preachers and 6,452 churches.

President of the Conference in Great Britain (1999–2000), Revd S. Burgess
Vice-President of the Conference (1999–2000), B. Thornton
Secretary of the Conference, Revd Dr N. T. Collinson,
Methodist Church, Conference Office, 25 Marylebone Road, London NW1 5JR. Tel: 0171-486 5502

THE METHODIST CHURCH IN IRELAND

The Methodist Church in Ireland is closely linked to British Methodism but is autonomous. It has 16,956 members, 201 ministers, 290 lay preachers and 228 churches.

President of the Methodist Church in Ireland (1999–2000),
Revd Dr K. A. Wilson, 137 Wheatfield, Bray, Co. Wicklow, Republic of Ireland. Tel: 1-286 9647

Secretary of the Methodist Church in Ireland, Revd E. T. I. Mawhinney, 1 Fountainville Avenue, Belfast BT9 6AN. Tel: 01232-324554

THE (EASTERN) ORTHODOX CHURCH

The Eastern (or Byzantine) Orthodox Church is a communion of self-governing Christian churches recognizing the honorary primacy of the Oecumenical Patriarch of Constantinople.

The position of Orthodox Christians is that the faith was fully defined during the period of the Oecumenical Councils. In doctrine it is strongly trinitarian, and stresses the mystery and importance of the sacraments. It is episcopal in government. The structure of the Orthodox Christian year differs from that of western Churches (*see* page 82).

Orthodox Christians throughout the world are estimated to number about 300 million.

PATRIARCHS OF THE EASTERN ORTHODOX CHURCH
Archbishop of Constantinople, New Rome and Oecumenical Patriarch, Bartholomew, *elected* 1991
Pope and Patriarch of Alexandria and All Africa, Petros VII, *elected* 1997
Patriarch of Antioch and All the East, Ignatios IV, *elected* 1979
Patriarch of Jerusalem and All Palestine, Diodoros, *elected* 1981
Patriarch of Moscow and All Russia, Alexei II, *elected* 1990
Archbishop of Pec, Metropolitan of Belgrade and Karlovci, Patriarch of Serbia, Pavle, *elected* 1990
Archbishop of Bucharest and Patriarch of Romania, Teoctist, *elected* 1986
Metropolitan of Sofia and Patriarch of Bulgaria, Maxim, *elected* 1971
Archbishop of Tbilisi and Mtskheta, Catholicos-Patriarch of All Georgia, Ilia II, *elected* 1977

HEADS OF AUTOCEPHALOUS ORTHODOX CHURCHES
Archbishop of Cyprus, Chrysostomos, *elected* 1977
Archbishop of Athens and All Greece, Christodoulos, *elected* 1998
Metropolitan of Warsaw and All Poland, Sawa, *elected* 1998
Archbishop of Tirana and All Albania, Anastas, *elected* 1992
Archbishop of Prague and All the Czech Lands and Slovakia, Dorotej, *elected* 1964

EASTERN ORTHODOX CHURCHES IN THE UK

THE PATRIARCHATE OF ANTIOCH
There are ten parishes served by 13 clergy. In Great Britain the Patriarchate is represented by the Revd Fr Samir Gholam, 1A Redhill Street, London NW1 4BG. Tel: 0171-383 0403.

THE GREEK ORTHODOX CHURCH (PATRIARCHATE OF CONSTANTINOPLE)

The presence of Greek Orthodox Christians in Britain dates back at least to 1677 when Archbishop Joseph Geogirenes of Samos fled from Turkish persecution and came to London. The present Greek cathedral in Moscow Road, Bayswater, was opened for public worship in 1879 and the Diocese of Thyateira and Great Britain was established in 1922. There are now 110 parishes and other communities (including monasteries) in Great Britain, served by six bishops, 95 clergy and about 100 churches.

In Great Britain the Patriarchate of Constantinople is

represented by Archbishop Gregorios of Thyateira and Great Britain, 5 Craven Hill, London w2 3EN. Tel: 0171-723 4787.

THE RUSSIAN ORTHODOX CHURCH (PATRIARCHATE OF MOSCOW) AND THE RUSSIAN ORTHODOX CHURCH OUTSIDE RUSSIA

The records of Russian Orthodox Church activities in Britain date from the visit to England of Tsar Peter I in the early 18th century. Clergy were sent from Russia to serve the chapel established to minister to the staff of the Imperial Russian Embassy in London.

In Great Britain the Patriarchate of Moscow is represented by Metropolitan Anthony of Sourozh, 67 Ennismore Gardens, London SW7 1NH. Fax only: 0171-584 9864. He is assisted by one archbishop, one vicar bishop and 26 clergy. There are 27 parishes and smaller communities.

The Russian Orthodox Church Outside Russia is represented by Archbishop Mark of Berlin, Germany and Great Britain, c/o 57 Harvard Road, London w4 4ED. Tel: 0181-742 3493. There are eight communities, including two monasteries, served by eight clergy.

THE SERBIAN ORTHODOX CHURCH (PATRIARCHATE OF SERBIA)

There are 33 parishes and smaller communities in Great Britain served by 12 clergy. The Patriarchate of Serbia is represented by the Episcopal Vicar, the Very Revd Milenko Zebic, 131 Cob Lane, Bournville, Birmingham B30 1QE. Tel: 0121-458 5273.

OTHER NATIONALITIES

Most of the Ukrainian parishes in Britain have joined the Patriarchate of Constantinople, leaving a small number of Ukrainian parishes in Britain under the care of other patriarchates (not all of which are recognized by the other Orthodox churches). The Latvian, Polish and some Belorussian parishes are also under the care of the Patriarchate of Constantinople. The Patriarchate of Romania has one parish served by two clergy. The Patriarchate of Bulgaria has one parish served by one priest. The Belorussian Autocephalous Orthodox Church has five parishes served by two priests.

THE ORIENTAL ORTHODOX CHURCHES

The term 'Oriental Orthodox Churches' is now generally used to describe a group of six ancient eastern churches which reject the Christological definition of the Council of Chalcedon (AD 451) and use Christological terms in different ways from the Eastern Orthodox Church. There are about 34 million members of the Oriental Orthodox Churches.

PATRIARCHS OF THE ORIENTAL ORTHODOX CHURCHES

ARMENIAN ORTHODOX CHURCH – *Supreme Patriarch Catholicos of All Armenians (Etchmiadzin)*, vacant; *Catholicos of Cilicia*, Aram I, *elected* 1995; *Patriarch of Jerusalem*, Torkom II, *elected* 1994; *Patriarch of Constantinople*, Mesrob II, *elected* 1998

COPTIC ORTHODOX CHURCH – *Pope of Alexandria and Patriarch of the See of St Mark*, Shenouda III, *elected* 1971

ERITREAN ORTHODOX CHURCH – *Patriarch of Eritrea*, Philipos I, *elected* 1998

ETHIOPIAN ORTHODOX CHURCH – *Patriarch of Ethiopia*, Paulos, *elected* 1992

MALANKARA ORTHODOX SYRIAN CHURCH – *Catholicos of the East*, Basilios Mar Thoma Mathews II, *elected* 1991

SYRIAN ORTHODOX CHURCH – *Patriarch of Antioch and All the East*, Ignatius Zakka I, *elected* 1980

ORIENTAL ORTHODOX CHURCHES IN THE UK

THE ARMENIAN ORTHODOX CHURCH (PATRIARCHATE OF ETCHMIADZIN)

The Armenian Orthodox Church is the longest-established Oriental Orthodox community in Great Britain. It is represented by Archbishop Yeghishe Gizirian, Armenian Primate of Great Britain, Armenian Vicarage, Iverna Gardens, London w8 6TP. Tel: 0171-937 0152.

THE COPTIC ORTHODOX CHURCH

The Coptic Orthodox Church is the largest Oriental Orthodox community in Great Britain. It has four dioceses (Birmingham; Scotland, Ireland and North-East England; the British Orthodox Church; and churches directly under Pope Shenouda III). The senior bishop in Great Britain is Metropolitan Seraphim, 10 Heathwood Gardens, London SE7 8EP. Tel: 0181-854 3090.

THE ERITREAN ORTHODOX CHURCH

In Great Britain the Eritrean Orthodox Church is represented by Bishop Markos, 11 Anfield Close, Weir Road, London SW12 0NT. Tel: 0181-675 5115.

THE ETHIOPIAN ORTHODOX CHURCH

The acting head of the Ethiopian Orthodox Church in Europe is Revd Berhanu Beserat, 33 Jupiter Crescent, London NW1 8HA. Tel: 0956-513700.

THE MALANKARA ORTHODOX SYRIAN CHURCH

The Malankara Orthodox Syrian Church is part of the Diocese of Europe under Metropolitan Thomas Mar Makarios. His representative in Great Britain is Fr M. S. Skariah, Paramula House, 44 Newbury Road, Newbury Park, Ilford, Essex IG2 7HD. Tel: 0181-599 3836.

THE SYRIAN ORTHODOX CHURCH

The Syrian Orthodox Church in Great Britain comes under the Patriarchal Vicar, whose representative is Fr Touma Hazim Dakkama, Antiochian, 5 Canning Road, Croydon CR0 6QA. Tel: 0181-654 7531. The Indian congregation under the Syrian Patriarch of Antioch is represented by Fr Eldhose Koungampillil, 1 Roslyn Court, Roslyn Avenue, East Barnet, Herts EN4 8DJ. Tel: 0181-368 2794.

THE COUNCIL OF ORIENTAL ORTHODOX CHURCHES, 34 Chertsey Road, Church Square, Shepperton, Middx TW17 9LF. Tel: 0181-368 8447. *Secretary*, Deacon Aziz M. A. Nour

PENTECOSTAL CHURCHES

Pentecostalism is inspired by the descent of the Holy Spirit upon the apostles at Pentecost. The movement began in Los Angeles, USA, in 1906 and is characterized by baptism with the Holy Spirit, divine healing, speaking in tongues (glossolalia), and a literal interpretation of the scriptures. The Pentecostal movement in Britain dates from 1907. Initially, groups of Pentecostalists were led by laymen and did not organize formally. However, in 1915 the Elim Foursquare Gospel Alliance (more usually called the Elim Pentecostal Church) was founded in Ireland by George Jeffreys and in 1924 about 70 independent assemblies formed a fellowship, the Assemblies of God in Great Britain and Ireland. The Apostolic Church grew out of the

1904–5 revivals in South Wales and was established in 1916, and the New Testament Church of God was established in England in 1953. In recent years many aspects of Pentecostalism have been adopted by the growing charismatic movement within the Roman Catholic, Protestant and Eastern Orthodox churches.

There are about 105 million Pentecostalists world-wide, with about 200,000 adult adherents in Great Britain and Ireland.

THE APOSTOLIC CHURCH, International Administration Offices, PO Box 389, 24–27 St Helens Road, Swansea SAI IZH. Tel: 01792-473992. *President*, Pastor R. W. Jones; *Administrator*, Pastor A. Saunders. The Apostolic Church has about 130 churches, 5,500 adherents and 83 ministers

THE ASSEMBLIES OF GOD IN GREAT BRITAIN AND IRELAND, General Offices, 16 Bridgford Road, West Bridgford, Nottingham NG2 6AF. Tel: 0115-981 1188. *General Superintendent*, P.C. Weaver; *General Administrator*, D. H. Gill. The Assemblies of God has 640 churches, about 75,000 adherents (including children) and 860 accredited ministers

THE ELIM PENTECOSTAL CHURCH, PO Box 38, Cheltenham, Glos GL50 3HN. Tel: 01242-519904. *General Superintendent*, Pastor I. W. Lewis; *Administrator*, Pastor B. Hunter. The Elim Pentecostal Church has 600 churches, 68,500 adherents and 650 accredited ministers

THE NEW TESTAMENT CHURCH OF GOD, Main House, Overstone Park, Overstone, Northampton NN6 0AD. Tel: 01604-643311. *National Overseer*, Revd Dr R. O. Brown. The New Testament Church of God has 110 organized congregations, 7,971 baptized members, about 20,000 adherents and 242 accredited ministers

THE PRESBYTERIAN CHURCH IN IRELAND

The Presbyterian Church in Ireland is Calvinistic in doctrine and presbyterian in constitution. Presbyterianism was established in Ireland as a result of the Ulster plantation in the early 17th century, when English and Scottish Protestants settled in the north of Ireland.

There are 21 presbyteries and five regional synods under the chief court known as the General Assembly. The General Assembly meets annually and is presided over by a Moderator who is elected for one year. The ongoing work of the Church is undertaken by 18 boards under which there are a number of specialist committees.

There are about 290,000 Presbyterians in Ireland, mainly in the north, in 562 congregations and with 400 ministers.
Moderator (1999–2000), Rt. Revd J. Lockington
Clerk of Assembly and General Secretary, Very Revd Dr S. Hutchinson, Church House, Belfast BTI 6DW. Tel: 01232-322284

THE PRESBYTERIAN CHURCH OF WALES

The Presbyterian Church of Wales or Calvinistic Methodist Church of Wales is Calvinistic in doctrine and presbyterian in constitution. It was formed in 1811 when Welsh Calvinists severed the relationship with the established church by ordaining their own ministers. It secured its own confession of faith in 1823 and a Constitutional Deed in 1826, and since 1864 the General Assembly has met annually, presided over by a Moderator elected for a year. The doctrine and constitutional structure of the

Presbyterian Church of Wales was confirmed by Act of Parliament in 1931–2.

The Church has 47,535 members, 127 ministers and 894 churches.
Moderator (1999–2000), Revd G. Tudwal Jones
General Secretary, Revd W. G. Edwards, 53 Richmond Road, Cardiff CF24 3WJ. Tel: 01222-494913

THE RELIGIOUS SOCIETY OF FRIENDS (QUAKERS)

Quakerism is a movement, not a church, which was founded in the 17th century by George Fox and others in an attempt to revive what they saw as 'primitive Christianity'. The movement was based originally in the Midlands, Yorkshire and north-west England, but there are now Quakers in 36 countries around the world. The colony of Pennsylvania, founded by William Penn, was originally Quaker.

Emphasis is placed on the experience of God in daily life rather than on sacraments or religious occasions. There is no church calendar. Worship is largely silent and there are no appointed ministers; the responsibility for conducting a meeting is shared equally among those present. Social reform and religious tolerance have always been important to Quakers, together with a commitment to non-violence in resolving disputes.

There are 213,800 Quakers world-wide, with over 19,000 in Great Britain and Ireland. There are about 490 meeting houses in Great Britain.

CENTRAL OFFICES: (GREAT BRITAIN) Friends House, Euston Road, London NW1 2BJ. Tel: 0171-663 1000;
(IRELAND) Swanbrook House, Morehampton Road, Dublin 4. Tel: 00 353 1-683684

THE SALVATION ARMY

The Salvation Army was founded by a Methodist minister, William Booth, in the east end of London in 1865, and has since become established in 104 countries world-wide. It was first known as the Christian Mission, and took its present name in 1878 when it adopted a quasi-military command structure intended to inspire and regulate its endeavours and to reflect its view that the Church was engaged in spiritual warfare. Salvationists emphasize evangelism, social work and the relief of poverty.

The world leader, known as the General, is elected by a High Council composed of the Chief of the Staff and senior ranking officers known as commissioners.

There are about 1.5 million members, 17,201 active officers (full-time ordained ministers) and 15,670 worship centres and outposts world-wide. In Great Britain and Ireland there are 62,836 members, 1,638 active officers and 810 worship centres.
General, J. Gowans
UK Territorial Commander, A. Hughes
TERRITORIAL HEADQUARTERS, 101 Newington Causeway, London SE1 6BN. Tel: 0171-367 4500

THE SEVENTH-DAY ADVENTIST CHURCH

The Seventh-day Adventist Church was founded in 1863 in the USA. Its members look forward to the second coming of Christ and observe the Sabbath (the seventh day) as a day of rest, worship and ministry. The Church bases its faith and practice wholly on the Bible and has developed 27 fundamental beliefs.

The World Church is divided into 12 divisions, each made up of unions of churches. The Seventh-day Adventist Church in the British Isles is known as the British Union of Seventh-day Adventists and is a member of the Trans-European Division. In the British Isles the administrative organization of the church is arranged in three tiers: the local churches; the regional conferences for south England, north England, Wales, Scotland and Ireland; and the national 'union' conference.

There are about 9 million Adventists and 42,321 churches in 204 countries world-wide. In the UK and Ireland there are 19,702 members, 152 ministers and 238 churches.
President of the British Union Conference, Pastor C. R. Perry
BRITISH ISLES HEADQUARTERS, Stanborough Park, Watford WD2 6JP. Tel: 01923-672251

UNDEB YR ANNIBYNWYR CYMRAEG
The Union of Welsh Independents

The Union of Welsh Independents was formed in 1872 and is a voluntary association of Welsh Congregational Churches and personal members. It is entirely Welsh-speaking. Congregationalism in Wales dates back to 1639 when the first Welsh Congregational Church was opened in Gwent. Member churches are Calvinistic in doctrine and congregationalist in organization. Each church has complete independence in the government and administration of its affairs.

The Union has 39,174 members, 231 ministers and 535 member churches.
President of the Union (1999–2000), C. Evans
General Secretary, Revd D. Myrddin Hughes, Tŷ John Penry, 11 Heol Sant Helen, Swansea SA1 4AL. Tel: 01792-652542

THE UNITED REFORMED CHURCH

The United Reformed Church was formed by the union of most of the Congregational churches in England and Wales with the Presbyterian Church of England in 1972.

Congregationalism dates from the mid 16th century. It is Calvinistic in doctrine, and its followers form independent self-governing congregations bound under God by covenant, a principle laid down in the writings of Robert Browne (1550–1633). From the late 16th century the movement was driven underground by persecution, but the cause was defended at the Westminster Assembly in 1643 and the Savoy Declaration of 1658 laid down its principles. Congregational churches formed county associations for mutual support and in 1832 these associations merged to form the Congregational Union of England and Wales.

The Presbyterian Church in England also dates from the mid 16th century, and was Calvinistic and evangelical in its doctrine. It was governed by a hierarchy of courts.

In the 1960s there was close co-operation locally and nationally between Congregational and Presbyterian Churches. This led to union negotiations and a Scheme of Union, supported by Act of Parliament in 1972. In 1981 a further unification took place, with the Reformed Association of Churches of Christ becoming part of the URC. In its basis the United Reformed Church reflects local church initiative and responsibility with a conciliar pattern of oversight. The General Assembly is the central body, and is made up of equal numbers of ministers and lay members. The United Reformed Church is divided into 12 Synods,

each with a Synod Moderator, and 75 Districts. There are 96,917 members, 650 full-time stipendiary ministers, 190 non-stipendiary ministers and 1,739 local churches.
General Secretary, Revd A. G. Burnham, 86 Tavistock Place, London WC1H 9RT. Tel: 0171-916 2020

THE WESLEYAN REFORM UNION

The Wesleyan Reform Union was founded by Methodists who left or were expelled from Wesleyan Methodism in 1849 following a period of internal conflict. Its doctrine is conservative evangelical and its organization is congregational, each church having complete independence in the government and administration of its affairs. The main concentration of churches is in Yorkshire.

The Union has 2,187 members, 22 ministers, 125 lay preachers and 113 churches.
President (1999–2000), J. B. Kay
General Secretary, Revd A. J. Williams, Wesleyan Reform Church House, 123 Queen Street, Sheffield S1 2DU. Tel: 0114-272 1938

Non-Trinitarian Churches

THE CHURCH OF CHRIST, SCIENTIST

The Church of Christ, Scientist was founded by Mary Baker Eddy in the USA in 1879 to 'reinstate primitive Christianity and its lost element of healing'. Christian Science teaches the need for spiritual regeneration and salvation from sin, but is best known for its reliance on prayer alone in the healing of sickness. Adherents believe that such healing is a law, or Science, and is in direct line with that practised by Jesus Christ (revered, not as God, but as the Son of God) and by the early Christian Church.

The denomination consists of The First Church of Christ, Scientist, in Boston, Massachusetts, USA (the Mother Church) and its branch churches in over 60 countries world-wide. Branch churches are democratically governed by their members, while a five-member Board of Directors, based in Boston, is authorized to transact the business of the Mother Church. The Bible and Mary Baker Eddy's book, *Science and Health with Key to the Scriptures*, are used at services; there are no clergy. Those engaged in full-time healing are called practitioners, of whom there are 3,500 world-wide.

No membership figures are available, since Mary Baker Eddy felt that numbers are no measure of spiritual vitality and ruled that such statistics should not be published. There are over 2,400 branch churches world-wide, including nearly 200 in the UK.
CHRISTIAN SCIENCE COMMITTEE ON PUBLICATION, 2 Elysium Gate, 126 New Kings Road, London SW6 4LZ. Tel: 0171-371 0600. *District Manager for Great Britain and Ireland*, H. Joynes

THE CHURCH OF JESUS CHRIST OF LATTER-DAY SAINTS

The Church (often referred to as 'the Mormons') was founded in New York State, USA, in 1830, and came to Britain in 1837. The oldest continuous branch in the world is to be found in Preston, Lancs. Mormons are Christians who claim to belong to the 'Restored Church' of Jesus Christ. They believe that true Christianity died when the last original apostle died, but that it was given back to the world by God and Christ through Joseph Smith, the Church's founder and first president. They accept and use the Bible as scripture, but believe in continuing revelation from God and use additional scriptures, including *The Book of Mormon: Another Testament of Jesus Christ*. The importance of the family is central to the Church's beliefs and practices. Church members set aside Monday evenings as Family Home Evenings when Christian family values are taught. Polygamy was formally discontinued in 1890.

The Church has no paid ministry; local congregations are headed by a leader chosen from amongst their number. The world governing body, based in Utah, USA, is the three-man First Presidency, assisted by the Quorum of the Twelve Apostles.

There are more than 10 million members world-wide, with about 180,000 adherents in Britain in over 350 congregations.

President of the Europe North Area (including Britain), Elder S. J. Condie

BRITISH HEADQUARTERS, Church Offices, 751 Warwick Road, Solihull, W. Midlands B91 3DQ. Tel: 0121-712 1202

JEHOVAH'S WITNESSES

The movement now known as Jehovah's Witnesses grew from a Bible study group formed by Charles Taze Russell in 1872 in Pennsylvania, USA. In 1896 it adopted the name of the Watch Tower Bible and Tract Society, and in 1931 its members became known as Jehovah's Witnesses. Jehovah's (God's) Witnesses believe in the Bible as the word of God, and consider it to be inspired and historically accurate. They take the scriptures literally, except where there are obvious indications that they are figurative or symbolic, and reject the doctrine of the Trinity. Witnesses also believe that the earth will remain for ever and that all those approved of by Jehovah will have eternal life on a cleansed and beautified earth; only 144,000 will go to heaven to rule with Christ. They believe that the second coming of Christ began in 1914 and his thousand-year reign on earth is imminent, and that Armageddon (a final battle in which evil will be defeated) will precede Christ's rule of peace. They refuse to take part in military service, and do not accept blood transfusions. They publish two magazines, *The Watchtower* and *Awake!*

The 12-member world governing body is based in New York, USA. Witnesses world-wide are divided into branches, countries or areas, districts, circuits and congregations. There are overseers at each level, and two assemblies are held annually for each circuit. There is no paid ministry, but each congregation has elders assigned to look after various duties and every Witness is assigned homes to visit in their congregation.

There are over 5 million Jehovah's Witnesses world-wide, with 130,000 Witnesses in the UK organized into over 1,400 congregations.

BRITISH ISLES HEADQUARTERS, Watch Tower House, The Ridgeway, London NW7 1RN. Tel: 0181-906 2211

UNITARIAN AND FREE CHRISTIAN CHURCHES

Unitarianism has its historical roots in the Judaeo-Christian tradition but rejects the deity of Christ and the doctrine of the trinity. It allows the individual to embrace insights from all the world's faiths and philosophies, as there is no fixed creed. It is accepted that beliefs may evolve in the light of personal experience.

Unitarian communities first became established in Poland and Transylvania in the 16th century. The first avowedly Unitarian place of worship in the British Isles opened in London in 1774. The General Assembly of Unitarian and Free Christian Churches came into existence in 1928 as the result of the amalgamation of two earlier organizations. There are about 7,000 Unitarians in Great Britain and Ireland, and 150 Unitarian ministers. About 200 self-governing congregations and fellowship groups, including a small number overseas, are members of the General Assembly.

GENERAL ASSEMBLY OF UNITARIAN AND FREE CHRISTIAN CHURCHES, Essex Hall, 1–6 Essex Street, Strand, London WC2R 3HY. Tel: 0171-240 2384. *General Secretary*, J. J. Teagle

Education

For addresses of national education departments, *see* Government Departments and Public Offices. For other addresses, *see* Education Directory

Responsibility for education in England lies with the Secretary of State for Education and Employment; in Wales, with the First Secretary of the National Assembly for Wales; in Scotland, with the Scottish Ministers ; and in Northern Ireland, with the Secretary of State for Northern Ireland.

The main concerns of the education departments (the Department for Education and Employment (DfEE), the National Assembly for Wales Education Department, the Scottish Executive Education Department and Enterprise and Lifelong Learning Department and the Department of Education for Northern Ireland (DENI)) are the formulation of national policies for education and the maintenance of consistency in educational standards. They are responsible for the broad allocation of resources for education, for the rate and distribution of educational building and for the supply, training and superannuation of teachers.

EXPENDITURE

In the UK in 1996–7, expenditure on education was (£ million):

Schools	21,650.2
Further and higher education	9,543.5
Other education and related expenditure	1,445.8

Most of this expenditure is incurred by local authorities, which make their own expenditure decisions according to their local situations and needs. Expenditure on education by central government departments, in real terms, was (£ million):

	1998–9 estimated outturn	1999–2000 planned
DfEE	14,451	15,606
Welsh Office (now National Assembly for Wales)	451.5	523.1
SOEID (now Scottish Executive Education Dept.)	1,309	1,450
DENI	1,336	1,429

The bulk of direct expenditure by the DfEE, the National Assembly for Wales and the Scottish Executive is directed towards supporting higher education in universities and colleges through the Higher Education Funding Councils (HEFCs) and further education and sixth form colleges through the Further Education Funding Councils (FEFCs). In addition, the DfEE funds student support in England and Wales, the City Technology Colleges (CTCs), the City College for the Technology of the Arts, and pays grants under the specialist schools programme. In Wales the National Assembly also funds curriculum development, educational services and research and supports bilingual education. In Scotland the main elements of central government expenditure, in addition to those outlined above, are grant-aided special schools, student awards and bursaries (through the Student Awards Agency for Scotland), teachers, curriculum development, special educational needs, community education and further and higher education through the Funding Councils. The Department of Education for Northern Ireland directly funds higher education, teacher education, teacher salaries and superannuation, student awards, further education, grant-maintained integrated schools, and voluntary grammar schools.

Current net expenditure on education by local education authorities in England, Wales, and Scotland, and education and library boards in Northern Ireland is (£ million):

	1998–9 estimated outturn	1999–2000 planned
England	20,032	20,400
Wales	1,355	1,427
Scotland	2,475	2,605
Northern Ireland	913	938

LOCAL EDUCATION ADMINISTRATION

In England and Wales the education service is administered by local education authorities (LEAs), which carry the day-to-day responsibility for providing most state primary and secondary education in their areas. They share with the FEFCs the duty to provide adult education to meet local needs.

The LEAs own and maintain most schools and some colleges, build new ones and provide equipment. LEAs are financed largely from the council tax and aggregate external finance (AEF) from the Department for the Environment, Transport and the Regions in England and the National Assembly for Wales.

All LEA-maintained schools manage their own budgets. The LEA allocates funds to the school, largely on the basis of pupil numbers, and the school governing body is responsible for overseeing spending and for most aspects of staffing, including appointments and dismissals. LEAs have powers to monitor, maintain and improve standards. An Education Association can be set up to take over the management of failing schools where both the LEA and the governing body have not brought about improvements identified as necessary by inspection.

The duty of providing education locally in Scotland rests with the education authorities. They are responsible for the construction of buildings, the employment of teachers and other staff and the provision of equipment and materials. Devolved School Management is in place for all primary, secondary and special schools.

Education authorities are required to establish school boards consisting of parents and teachers as well as co-opted members, responsible among other things for the appointment of staff.

Education is administered locally in Northern Ireland by five education and library boards, whose costs are met in full by DENI. All grant-aided schools include elected parents and teachers on their boards of governors. Provision has been made for schools wishing to provide integrated education to have grant-maintained integrated status from the outset. All schools and colleges of further education have full responsibility for their own budgets, including staffing costs. The Council for Catholic Maintained Schools forms an upper tier of management for Catholic schools and provides advice on matters relating to management and administration.

THE INSPECTORATE

The Office for Standards in Education (OFSTED) is a non-ministerial government department in England headed by HM Chief Inspector of Schools (HMCI). OFSTED's remit is regularly to inspect and report on all maintained and independent schools; local education authorities (on a five-year cycle from 2000, supported by the Audit Commission); initial teacher training; adult and youth education and nursery education providers using independent registered nursery education inspectors. All state schools are inspected by teams of OFSTED-trained accredited inspectors, including educationalists and lay people and headed by registered inspectors. The inspection is carried out according to the *Framework for Inspection of Schools* to ensure consistency in the process of inspection and the criteria used. HM Inspectors (HMI) within OFSTED report on good practice in schools and on other educational issues based on inspection evidence. From 1997 for secondary and from 1998 for primary, schools are inspected once every six years or more frequently if there is cause. A summary of the inspection report must be sent to the parents of each pupil by the school, followed by a copy of the governors' action plan thereon. The inspection of further and higher education in England is the responsibility of inspectors appointed to the respective Funding Councils.

There are 200 HMIs on OFSTED's permanent staff, 2,000 trained registered inspectors and 9,500 team inspectors.

Estyn: Arolygiaeth Ei Mawrhydi Dros Addysg A Hyfforddiant yng Nghymru (Her Majesty's Inspectorate for Education and Training in Wales) has a similar remit to OFSTED and carries out the inspection of funded nursery provision, maintained and independent schools on a five-year cycle. Estyn also inspects establishments of further education at the request of the Further Education Funding Council for Wales. Its remit also includes advice to government on education and training matters.

There are 38 HMIs, about 350 registered inspectors and 820 team members in Wales.

HM Inspectors of Schools in Scotland inspect schools and publish reports on further education institutions and community education, and are involved in assessing the quality of teacher education. HMIs work in teams alongside lay people and associate assessors, who are practising teachers seconded for the inspection. The inspection of higher education is the responsibility of inspectors appointed to the Higher Education Funding Council for Scotland.

There are 83 HMIs and eight Chief Inspectors in Scotland.

Inspection is carried out in Northern Ireland by the Department of Education's Education and Training Inspectorate, using teams which, on occasion, include lay people. The Inspectorate also performs an advisory function to the Secretary of State for Northern Ireland. From September 1999 a seven-year cycle of inspection was introduced.

There is one Chief Inspector and 62 members of the Inspectorate in Northern Ireland.

SCHOOLS AND PUPILS

Schooling is compulsory in Great Britain for all children between five years and 16 years and between four and 16 years in Northern Ireland. Provision is being increased for pre-school children and many pupils remain at school after the minimum leaving age. No fees are charged in any publicly maintained school in England, Wales and Scotland. In Northern Ireland, fees may be charged in voluntary schools and are paid by pupils in preparatory departments of grammar schools, but pupils admitted to the secondary departments of grammar schools, unless they come from outside the province, do not pay fees.

The 'Parents' Charter', available free from education departments, is a booklet telling parents about the education system. Schools are now required to make available information about themselves, their truancy rates, destinations of leavers, their public examination and (in England, Wales and Northern Ireland) national test results. Parents in England and Wales must receive a written yearly progress report on all aspects of their child's achievements. There is a similar commitment for Northern Ireland. In Scotland the school report card gives parents information on their child's progress.

FALL AND RISE IN NUMBERS

In nursery and primary education, and increasingly in secondary education, pupil numbers in the UK declined through the 1980s. In maintained nursery and primary schools they reached their lowest figure of 4.6 million in 1986, had risen to 5.2 million by 1998 and are expected to decline to 5.1 million by 2002. In secondary schools pupil numbers peaked at 4.6 million in 1981, had fallen to 3.7 million by 1998 but are projected to rise to about 4 million by 2006.

ENGLAND AND WALES

There are two main types of school in England and Wales: publicly maintained schools, which charge no fees; and independent schools, which charge fees (*see* page 428). Publicly maintained schools, with the exception of City Technology Colleges, are maintained by local education authorities.

From September 1999, all existing publicly funded schools were incorporated into a new school framework comprising community, voluntary (subdivided into voluntary controlled and voluntary aided) and foundation schools. They are non-denominational and provide primary and secondary education. The voluntary category is retained as before but now comprises two categories, voluntary controlled and voluntary aided, the latter now includes the former special agreement schools. Voluntary schools provide primary and secondary education. Although the buildings are in many cases provided by the voluntary bodies (mainly religious denominations), they are financially maintained by an LEA. In the case of voluntary controlled schools the LEA bears all costs. In voluntary aided schools, although the managers or governors are responsible for repairs, improvements and alterations to the building, central government may reimburse up to 85 per cent of approved capital expenditure, while the LEA pays for internal maintenance and other running costs. In the case of former special agreement schools, the LEA may, by special agreement, pay between one-half and three-quarters of the cost of building a new, or extending an existing, school, usually a secondary school. Most grant-maintained schools (*see* below) have been categorised as foundation schools. It is proposed that schools have the opportunity to change category.

The number of schools by category in 1998 was:

	England	Wales
Maintained schools	27,487	2,210
County	13,917	1,628
Voluntary	6,785	291
controlled	2,805	121
aided	3,942	170
special agreement*	38	–
Grant-maintained	1,177	18
CTCs and CCTAs*	15	–
Independent schools	2,227	59
TOTAL	30,906	2,287

* In England only

Under the Local Management of Schools (LMS) initiative, LEAs are required, from April 2000, to delegate the entire school budget, including staffing costs, directly to those schools that wish it. LEAs continue to retain responsibility for various common services, including transport and special educational needs units. The LEA acts as admission authority for most community and some voluntary schools.

Governing bodies – All publicly maintained schools have a governing body, usually made up of a number of parent and local community representatives, governors appointed by the LEA if the school is LEA maintained, the headteacher (unless he or she chooses otherwise), and serving teachers. Schools can appoint up to four sponsor governors from business who will be expected to provide financial and managerial assistance. Governing bodies are responsible for the overall policies of schools and their academic aims and objectives. They also control matters of school discipline, the appointment and dismissal of staff and act as the admission authority for voluntary aided and all foundation schools. Governing bodies select inspectors for their schools, are responsible for action as a result of inspection reports and are required to make those reports and their action plans thereon available to parents.

The Specialist Schools Programme – The programme is open to all state secondary schools in England which teach the national curriculum and wish to specialise in the teaching of technology, mathematics and science (technology colleges), modern foreign languages (language colleges), sports colleges and arts colleges. In addition to the normal funding arrangements, the schools receive business sponsorship (up to four sponsor governors may sit on governing bodies) and complementary capital grants up to £100,000 from central government, together with extra annual funding of £100 a pupil to assist the delivery of an enhanced curriculum. By September 1999, there were 242 technology colleges, 61 language colleges, 33 sports colleges and 29 arts colleges.

Grant-maintained (GM) schools – Under the previous administration all secondary and primary schools, whether maintained or independent, were eligible to apply for grant-maintained status subject to a ballot of parents. GM schools were initially maintained directly by the Secretary of State (through the Funding Agency for Schools) and the former Welsh Office, not the LEA; those arrangements no longer apply and they are now included in LEA funding arrangements. They are wholly run by their own governing body. About 60 per cent of GM schools were secondary schools. From 1 September 1999, the name and status of GM schools changed. Those schools originally in the county and voluntary controlled categories and those established by the Funding Agency for Schools became foundation schools, while former voluntary aided and special agreement schools and those founded by promoters entered the voluntary aided subdivision of the voluntary category, with an option to express a preference as to category.

City Technology Colleges (CTCs) and *City Colleges for the Technology of the Arts (CCTAs)* are state-aided but independent of LEAs. Their aim is to widen the choice of secondary education in disadvantaged urban areas and to teach a broad curriculum with an emphasis on science, technology, business understanding and arts technologies. Capital costs are shared by government and business sponsors, and running costs are covered by a per capita grant from the DfEE in line with comparable costs in an LEA maintained school. The first city technology college opened in 1988 in Solihull. The first CCTA, known as Britschool, opened in Croydon in 1991.

SCOTLAND

Education authority schools (known as public schools) are financed by local government, partly through revenue support grants from central government, and partly from local taxation. Devolved management from the local authority to the school is in place for more than 88 per cent of all school level expenditure. A small number of grant-aided schools, mainly in the special sector, are conducted by boards of managers and receive grants direct from the Scottish Executive Education Department. There are, in addition, two self-governing schools in the public sector which are managed entirely by a board of management. At present they are funded by direct government grant but it is proposed to return them to the education authority framework. Independent schools receive no direct grant and charge fees, but are subject to inspection and registration.

Education authorities are required to establish school boards to participate in the administration and management of schools. These boards consist of elected parents and staff members as well as co-opted members.

The number of schools by category in 1998 was:

Publicly maintained schools:	
Education authority	3,711
Self-governing	2
Independent schools	114
TOTAL	3,827

NORTHERN IRELAND

Controlled schools are maintained by the education and library boards with all costs paid from public funds. Voluntary maintained schools, mainly under Roman Catholic management, receive grants towards capital costs and running costs in whole or in part. Voluntary grammar schools may be under denominational or non-denominational management and receive grants from DENI. Voluntary maintained and voluntary grammar schools can apply for designation as a new category of voluntary school, which is eligible for a 100 per cent as opposed to 85 per cent grant. Such schools are managed by a board of governors on which no single interest group has a majority of nominees. All grant-aided schools include elected parents and teachers on their boards of governors, whose responsibilities also include financial management under the Local Management of Schools (LMS) initiative. All schools now have fully delegated budgets. The majority of children in Northern Ireland are educated in schools which in practice are segregated on religious lines. Integrated schools exist to educate Protestant and Roman Catholic children together. There are two types: grant-maintained integrated schools which are funded by DENI; and controlled integrated schools funded by the education and library boards. Procedures are in place for balloting parents in existing segregated schools to determine whether they want instead to have integrated schools, subject to the satisfaction of certain criteria. By September 1999, 43 integrated schools had been established, 16 of them secondary.

The number of schools by category in 1998–9 was:

Grant-aided schools:
Controlled	653
Voluntary maintained	547
Voluntary grammar	54
Integrated schools	40
Independent schools	22
TOTAL	1,316

THE STATE SYSTEM

NURSERY EDUCATION – Nursery education is for children from two to five years and is not compulsory, although a free place is available for each four-year-old who requires it and free provision for three-year-olds is being increased. Northern Ireland has a compulsory school starting age of four as of September each year but there too pre-school provision is being increased. Nursery education takes place in nursery schools (1,685 in the public sector in 1998) or, in England, nursery classes in primary schools. The number of children receiving nursery education in the UK in 1997—8 was (thousands):

In maintained nursery schools	78.4
In primary schools	994.3
In non-maintained nursery schools	69.3
In special schools	8.0
TOTAL	1,150.0

Education authorities are responsible for planning, co-ordinating and delivering nursery education in their areas using a range of providers on the basis of an Early Years Development Plan, in partnership with parents and the private and voluntary sectors. All providers of pre-school education are subject to inspection.

PRIMARY EDUCATION – Primary education begins at five years in Great Britain and four years in Northern Ireland, and is almost always co-educational. In England, Wales and Northern Ireland the transfer to secondary school is generally made at 11 years. In Scotland, the primary school course lasts for seven years and pupils transfer to secondary courses at about the age of 12.

Primary schools consist mainly of infant schools for children aged five to seven, junior schools for those aged seven to 11, and combined junior and infant schools for both age groups. First schools in some parts of England cater for ages five to ten as the first stage of a three-tier system: first, middle and secondary. Many primary schools provide nursery classes for children under five (*see* above).

Primary schools (UK) 1997	8
No. of primary schools	23,213
No. of pupils (thousands)	5,413.8
Pupils under five years	379.0

Pupil-teacher ratios in maintained primary schools were:

	1996–7	1997–8
England	23.4	23.7
Wales	22.6	n/a
Scotland	19.6	19.9
Northern Ireland	19.8	19.9
UK	21.3	21.2

The average size of classes 'as taught' was 25.6 in 1997 .

MIDDLE SCHOOLS – Middle schools (which take children from first schools), mostly in England, cover varying age ranges between eight and 14 and usually lead on to comprehensive upper schools.

SECONDARY EDUCATION – Secondary schools are for children aged 11 to 16 and for those who choose to stay on to 18. At 16, many students prefer to move on to tertiary or sixth form colleges (*see* page 432–3). Most secondary schools in England, Wales and Scotland are co-educational. The largest secondary schools have over 1,500 pupils but only 31.3 per cent of the schools take over 1,000 pupils.

Secondary schools 1998

	England and Wales	Scotland	N. Ireland
No. of pupils (000s)	30,273.1	314.9	153.1
% 16 and 17 years old	74.1%	53.6%	45.5%
Average class size	42.5	19.2	n/a
Pupil-teacher ratio	32.6	13.2	14.5

In England and Wales the main types of maintained secondary schools are: comprehensive schools (86.7 per cent of pupils in England, 100 per cent in Wales), whose admission arrangements are without reference to ability or aptitude; deemed middle schools for children aged variously between eight and 14 years who then move on to senior comprehensive schools at 12, 13 or 14 (5.1 per cent of pupils in England); secondary modern schools (2.7 per cent of pupils in England) providing a general education with a practical bias; secondary grammar schools (4.2 per cent of pupils in England) with selective intake providing an academic course from 11 to 16–18 years; and technical schools (0.2 per cent of pupils in England), providing an integrated academic and technical education.

In Scotland all pupils in education authority secondary schools attend schools with a comprehensive intake. Most of these schools provide a full range of courses appropriate to all levels of ability from first to sixth year.

In most areas of Northern Ireland there is a selective system of secondary education with pupils transferring either to grammar schools (40.4 per cent of pupils in 1999) or secondary schools (59.6 per cent of pupils in 1999) at 11–12 years of age. Parents can choose the school they would like their children to attend and all those who apply must be admitted if they meet the criteria. If a school is over-subscribed beyond its statutory admissions number, selection is on the basis of published criteria, which, for most grammar schools, place emphasis on performance in the transfer procedure tests which are set and administered by the Northern Ireland Council for the Curriculum, Examinations and Assessment. When parents consider that a school has not applied its criteria fairly they have access to independent appeals tribunals. Grammar schools provide an academic type of secondary education with A-levels at the end of the seventh year, while secondary non-grammar schools follow a curriculum suited to a wider range of aptitudes and abilities.

SPECIAL EDUCATION – Special education is provided for children with special educational needs. Wherever possible, such children are educated in ordinary schools, taking the parents' wishes into account, and schools are required to publish their policy for pupils with special educational needs. LEAs in England and Wales and Education and Library Boards in Northern Ireland are required to identify and secure provision for the needs of children with learning difficulties, to involve the parents in any decision and draw up a formal statement of the child's special educational needs and how they intend to meet them, all within statutory time limits. Parents have a right to appeal to a Special Educational Needs (SEN) Tribunal if they disagree with the statement. In Scotland, school placing is a matter of agreement between education authorities and parents. Parents have the right to say which school they want their child to attend, and a right of appeal where their wishes are not being met. Whenever possible, children with special needs are integrated into ordinary schools.

Maintained special schools are run by education authorities which pay all the costs of maintenance, but under the terms of Local Management of Schools (LMS), those able and wishing to manage their own budgets may choose to do so. Non-maintained special schools are run by voluntary bodies; they may receive some grant from central government for capital expenditure and for equipment but their current expenditure is met primarily from the fees charged to education authorities for pupils placed in the schools. Some independent schools provide education wholly or mainly for children with special educational needs and are required to meet similar standards to those for maintained and non-maintained special schools. It is intended that pupils with special educational needs should have access to as much of the national curriculum as possible, but there is provision for them to be exempt from it or for it to be modified to suit their capabilities.

The number of pupils with statements of special needs in January 1998 was (thousands):

In special schools: total	101.7
England	87.9
Wales	3.5
Scotland	6.4
N. Ireland	3.8
In public sector primary and secondary	
schools: total	166.0
England	141.0
Wales	12.7
Scotland	8.2
N. Ireland	4.1

ALTERNATIVE PROVISION

There is no legal obligation on parents in the UK to educate their children at school provided that the local education authority is satisfied that the child is receiving full-time education suited to its age, abilities and aptitudes. The education authority need not be informed that a child is being educated at home unless the child is already registered at a state school. In this case the parents must arrange for the child's name to be removed from the school's register (by writing to the headteacher) before education at home can begin. Failure to do so leaves the parents liable to prosecution for condoning non-attendance.

INDEPENDENT SCHOOLS

Independent schools charge fees and are owned and managed under special trusts, with profits being used for the benefit of the schools concerned. There is a wide variety of provision, from kindergartens to large day and boarding schools, and from experimental schools to traditional institutions. A number of independent schools have been instituted by religious and ethnic minorities.

All independent schools in the UK are open to inspection by approved inspectors (see page 425) and must register with the appropriate government education department. The education departments lay down certain minimum standards and can make schools remedy any unacceptable features of their building or instruction and exclude any unsuitable teacher or proprietor. Most independent schools offer a similar range of courses to state schools and enter pupils for the same public examinations. Introduction of the national curriculum and the associated education targets and assessment procedures is not obligatory in the independent sector.

The term public schools is often applied to those independent schools in membership of the Headmasters'

and Headmistresses' Conference, the Governing Bodies Association or the Governing Bodies of Girls' Schools Association. Most public schools are single-sex but there are some mixed schools and an increasing number of schools have mixed sixth forms.

Preparatory schools are so-called because they prepare pupils for the common entrance examination to senior independent schools. Most cater for pupils from about seven to 13 years. The common entrance examination is set by the Common Entrance Examination Board, but marked by the independent school to which the pupil intends to go. It is taken at 13 by boys, and between 11 and 13 by girls.

The number of schools and pupils in 1997–8 was:

	No. of schools	No. of pupils (000s)	% of school population	Pupil-teacher ratio
England	2,231	572.2	6.9	10.2
Wales	59	9.9	1.9	10.0
Scotland	176	31.7	3.7	10.7
N. Ireland	22	1.2	0.3	9.3

Most independent schools in Scotland follow the same examination system as England, Wales and Northern Ireland, i.e. GCSE followed by A-levels, although some take the Scottish Certificate of Education examinations.

ASSISTED PLACES SCHEME

The Assisted Places Scheme ceased to operate after September 1997 and is being phased out. Pupils in secondary education holding their places at the beginning of the 1997–8 school year will keep them until they have completed their education at their current school. Those at the primary stage will hold them until they have completed that phase of their education, although some may exceptionally be allowed to so for a further period to complete their secondary education. The scheme enables children to attend independent secondary schools which their parents could not otherwise afford. It provides help with tuition fees and other expenses, except boarding costs, on a sliding scale depending on the family's income. The proportion of pupils receiving full fee remission is about 42.5 per cent. In the 1998–9 academic year, about 30,600 places were offered at the 466 participating schools in England and Wales. In Scotland about 2,800 pupils participated in the scheme in 50 schools in 1998–9.

The scheme is administered and funded in England by the DfEE and in Wales and Scotland by the respective education departments. The scheme does not operate in Northern Ireland as the independent sector admits non-fee-paying pupils. There is, however, a similar scheme known as the Talented Children's Scheme to help pupils gifted in music and dance.

Further information can be obtained from the Independent Schools Information Service (see Education Directory).

THE CURRICULUM

ENGLAND AND WALES

The national curriculum was introduced in primary and secondary schools between autumn 1989 and autumn 1996, for the period of compulsory schooling from five to 16. It is mandatory in all maintained schools. As originally proposed, it was widely criticised for being too prescriptive and time-consuming. Following revision in 1994 its requirements were substantially reduced; the revisions were implemented in August 1995 for key stages one to three and from August 1996 for key stage four. A review of the curriculum is under way and the new courses/structures will be introduced in schools from September 2000 including, for the first time, Citizenship. As a first step, primary schools have been allowed greater flexibility in teaching the non-core curriculum subjects (which remain compulsory) in order to allow priority to be given to literacy and numeracy.

The statutory subjects at key stages one and two (five–11-year olds) are:

Core subjects	Foundation subjects
English	Design and technology
Welsh (Welsh-speaking schools in Wales)	Information technology
Mathematics	History
Science	Geography
	Welsh (generally a second language in non-Welsh-speaking schools in Wales)
	Art
	Music
	PE

At key stage three (11- to 14-year-olds) all pupils must study a modern foreign language. At key stage four (14- to 16-year-olds) pupils are required to continue to study the core subjects, PE and, in England only, a modern foreign language, design and technology and information technology. Other foundation subjects are optional. Religious education must be taught across all key stages, following a locally agreed syllabus; parents have the right to remove their children if they wish. In Wales the national curriculum has separate and distinctive characteristics which are reflected, where appropriate, in the programmes of study.

Statutory assessment takes place on entry to primary school and national tests and tasks in English, Welsh (in Welsh-speaking schools in Wales) and mathematics at key stage one, with the addition of science at key stages two and three, are in place. Teachers make their own assessments of their pupils' progress to set alongside the test results. At key stage four the GCSE and vocational equivalents are the main form of assessment.

The DfEE and the National Assembly for Wales publish tables showing pupils' performance in A-level, AS-level, GCSE and GNVQ examinations school by school. In England only, local education authorities are required to publish similar information in November each year showing the results of national curriculum tests and teacher assessments for seven-, 11- and 14-year-olds. Approximately 600,000 pupils in each of the age groups take the tests each year in England and Wales (38,000).

NATIONAL TESTING AND TEACHERS' ASSESSMENT RESULTS IN CORE SUBJECTS 1998
Percentage of pupils reaching the expected level of performance at that age:

	Key stage 1 7-year olds (level 2)	Key stage 2 11-year olds (level 4)	Key stage 3 14-year olds (level 5)
ENGLAND			
English	81.0	65.0	58.5
Mathematics	84.5	62.0	62.0
Science	86.0	70.0	60.5
WALES			
English	80.0	65.0	62.0
Welsh (first language)	86.0	63.0	71.0
Mathematics	84.0	65.0	64.0
Science	85.0	71.0	60.0

National targets have been set for 11-year-olds in England: 80 per cent to reach level four in the English test and 75 per cent to reach level four in the mathematics test by 2002. In Wales the targets are: 70–80 per cent to reach the expected level of performance for that age at key stages two and three in English, Welsh, mathematics and science by 2002.

In Wales, Welsh is a compulsory subject for all pupils at key stages one, two and three where it is taught either as a first or second language. It is now compulsory also at key stage four in both Welsh-speaking and non Welsh-speaking schools. In 1997 some 27 per cent of primary schools used Welsh as the sole or main medium of instruction and a further 6 per cent used it for part of the curriculum. Nearly 22 per cent of secondary schools taught Welsh both as a first and second language.

In October 1997 in England the Qualifications and Curriculum Authority (QCA) was formed by the amalgamation of the School Curriculum and Assessment Authority and the National Council for Vocational Qualifications. An independent government agency funded by the DfEE, its remit ranges from the under-fives to higher level vocational qualifications. It is responsible for ensuring that the curriculum and qualifications available to young people and adults are of high quality, coherent and flexible. In Wales, Awdurdod Cymwysterau, Cwricwlwm ac Asesu Cymru (ACCAC)/the Qualifications, Curriculum and Assessment Authority for Wales exercises similar functions. ACCAC is funded by the National Assembly for Wales.

SCOTLAND

The content and management of the curriculum in Scotland are not prescribed by statute but are the responsibility of education authorities and individual headteachers. Advice and guidance are provided by the Scottish Executive Education Department and the Scottish Consultative Council on the Curriculum, which also has a developmental role. Guidance for the pre-school sector describes the nature of the pre-school experience, sets out features of learning in key aspects of the child's early development and identifies appropriate learning experiences for children and opportunities for collaboration with other agencies. For the five–14 age group there are guidelines on the structure and balance of the curriculum as well as for each of the curriculum areas, although they are currently under review. There are also guidelines on assessment across the whole curriculum, on reporting to parents, and on standardised national tests for English language and mathematics at five levels. The curriculum for 14- to 16-year-olds includes study within each of eight modes: language and communication, mathematical studies, science, technology, social studies, creative activities, physical education, and religious and moral education. There are recommendations for the percentage of time to be devoted to each area over the two years. Provision is made for teaching in Gaelic in Gaelic-speaking areas. Testing is carried out on a voluntary basis when the teacher deems it appropriate; most pupils are expected to move from one level to the next at roughly two-year intervals. National testing is largely in place in most primary schools but secondary school participation rates are lower.

For 16- to 18-year-olds, there is available a modular system of vocational courses, certificated by the Scottish Qualifications Authority (SQA), in addition to academic courses. A new unified framework of courses and awards, known as 'Higher Still', which will bring together both academic and vocational courses was introduced in 1999 (*see* page 431). The SQA will award the new certificates.

NORTHERN IRELAND

A curriculum common to all grant-aided schools exists. Pupils are required to study religious education and, depending on which key stage they have reached, certain subjects from six broad areas of study: English, mathematics, science and technology; the environment and society; creative and expressive studies and, in key stages three and four, language studies. The statutory curriculum requirements at key stages one to three have been revised and new programmes of study were introduced in September 1996. Six cross-curricular educational themes, which include information technology and education for mutual understanding, are woven through the main subjects of the curriculum. Irish is a foundation subject in schools that use it as a medium of instruction.

The assessment of pupils is broadly in line with practice in England and Wales and takes place at the ages of eight, 11 and 14. The GCSE is used to assess 16-year-olds.

NATIONAL TESTING AND TEACHERS' ASSESSMENT

RESULTS IN CORE SUBJECTS 1999 (1998 KEY STAGE 3)
Percentage of pupils reaching the expected level of performance at that age (at key stage 3, teacher assessed level (test level in brackets)):

	Key stage 1 8-year olds (level 2)	Key stage 2 11-year olds (level 4)	Key stage 3 14-year olds (level 5)
English	93	68	73(69)
Mathematics	93	73	70(66)
Science	—	—	70(66)

National targets have been set for 11-year-olds: 80 per cent to reach level four in English and mathematics by 2002.

The Northern Ireland Council for the Curriculum, Examinations and Assessment (NICCEA) monitors and advises DENI and teachers on all matters relating to the curriculum, assessment arrangements and examinations in grant-aided schools. It conducts GCSE, A- and AS-level examinations, pupil assessment at key stages one, two and three and administers the transfer procedure tests.

THE PUBLIC EXAMINATION SYSTEM

ENGLAND, WALES AND NORTHERN IRELAND

Until the end of 1987, secondary school pupils at the end of compulsory schooling around the age of 16, and others, took the General Certificate of Education (GCE) Ordinary-level or the Certificate of Secondary Education (CSE). From 1988 these were replaced by a single system of examinations, the General Certificate of Secondary Education (GCSE), which is usually taken after five years of secondary education. The GCSE is the main method of assessing the performance of pupils at age 16 in all national curriculum subjects required to be assessed at the end of compulsory schooling. The structure of the examination is being adapted in accordance with national curriculum requirements; new subject criteria were published in 1995 to govern GCSE syllabuses introduced in 1996 for first examination in 1998. GCSE short-course qualifications are available in some subjects. As a rule the syllabus takes half the time of a full GCSE course.

The GCSE differs from its predecessors in that there are syllabuses based on national criteria covering course objectives, content and assessment methods; differentiated assessment (i.e. different papers or questions for different ranges of ability) and grade-related criteria (i.e. grades awarded on absolute rather than relative performance). The GCSE certificates are awarded on a seven-point scale, A to G. From 1994 there has been an additional 'starred' A grade (A*), to recognise the achievement of the highest attainers at GCSE. Grades A to C are the equivalent of the corresponding O-level grades A to C or CSE grade 1. Grades D, E, F and G record achievement at least as high

as that represented by CSE grades 2 to 5. All GCSE syllabuses, assessments and grading procedures are monitored by the Qualifications and Curriculum Authority (*see* page 429) to ensure that they conform to the national criteria

In the UK in 1997–8, 94.5 per cent of all 16-year-olds achieved one or more graded GCSE, SCE Standard Grade, or equivalent result, while 48.4 per cent achieved five or more GCSEs at grade C or better (England, Wales and Northern Ireland).

In Wales the Certificate of Education is intended for 16-year-olds for whom no suitable examination exists. In 1997, 27,520 candidates took the examination, of whom 94.4 per cent obtained pass or better.

Many maintained schools offer BTEC Firsts (*see* page 433) and an increasing number offer BTEC Nationals. National Vocational Qualifications in the form of General NVQs are also available to students in schools (*see* page 434). The Part 1 GNVQ is a shortened version of the full GNVQ. Designed for 14- to 16-year-olds, it is a two-year course at foundation and intermediate levels, the former broadly equivalent to two GCSEs at grades D to G, the latter at grades A* to C. It has been piloted from 1995 and has been available in schools since September 1999.

Advanced (A-level) examinations are taken by those who choose to continue their education after GCSE. A-level courses last two years and have traditionally provided the foundation for entry to higher education. Revised A-level syllabuses from September 2000 will offer candidates the choice between end-of-course or staged assessment, with limits on coursework. A-levels are marked on a seven-point scale: pass, from A to E; N (narrow failure) which will be phased out; and U (unclassified), which is not certificated.

Advanced Supplementary level (AS-level) examinations were introduced in 1987 as an alternative to, and to complement, A-level examinations. AS-levels are for full-time A-level students but are also open to other students. An AS-level syllabus has heretofore covered not less than half the amount of ground covered by the corresponding A-level syllabus and, where possible, has been related to it. An AS-level course lasts two years and requires not less than half the teaching time of the corresponding A-level course, and two AS-levels are equivalent to one A-level. From September 2000 a new AS (Advanced Subsidiary) qualification will represent the first half of a full A-level. AS-level passes are graded A to E, with grade standards related to the A-level grades.

In the UK in 1996–7, 296,000 students (45.3 per cent boys, 54.7 per cent girls) achieved one or more passes at A-level or SCE H-grade (an increase of 4.3 per cent on the previous year). Of those in Great Britain who entered for at least one A-level, or at least two SCE H-grades, 32 per cent studied sciences (59 per cent boys, 41 per cent girls) and 68 per cent studied arts/social studies (43.5 per cent of boys, 56.5 per cent of girls).

Most examining boards allow the option of an additional paper of greater difficulty to be taken by A-level candidates to obtain what is known as a Special-level or Scholarship-level qualification. S-level papers are available in most of the traditional academic subjects and are marked on a three-point scale. From September 2000 they will be replaced by 'world class test' special papers.

The City & Guilds Diploma of Vocational Education is intended for a wide ability range. The Diploma provides recognition of achievement at two levels: foundation at pre-16 and intermediate at post-16. The intermediate level is being phased out in favour of the corresponding GNVQs. Within guidelines and to meet specified criteria, schools and colleges design their own courses, which stress activity-based learning, core skills which include application of number, communication and information technology, and work experience. The Diploma is of value to those who want to find out what aptitudes they may have and to prepare themselves for work, but who may not yet be committed to a particular occupation. At foundation level, it can be taken alongside GCSEs and can provide a context for the introduction of GNVQ units into the key stage four curriculum.

The various examining boards in England have combined into three unitary awarding bodies, which offer both academic and vocational qualifications: GNVQs, GCSEs and A-levels. The new bodies are Edexcel, the Assessment and Qualifications Alliance (AQA), and Oxford, Cambridge and RSA Examinations (OCR). At present the existing examination boards are still separate bodies, working in alliance to develop single courses.

SCOTLAND

Scotland has its own system of public examinations. At the end of the fourth year of secondary education, at about the age of 16, or earlier if appropriate, pupils take the Standard Grade of the Scottish Certificate of Education. Standard Grade courses and examinations have been designed to suit every level of ability, with assessment against nationally determined standards of performance.

For most courses there are three separate examination papers at the end of the two-year Standard Grade course. They are set at Credit (leading to awards at grade 1 or 2), General (leading to awards at grade 3 or 4) and Foundation (leading to awards at grade 5 or 6) levels. Grade 7 is available to those who, although they have completed the course, have not attained any of these levels. Normally pupils will take examinations covering two pairs of grades, either grades 1–4 or grades 3–6. Most candidates take seven or eight Standard Grade examinations.

Above Standard Grade, Higher Grade will be available after a one-year course in the fifth or sixth year of secondary school until 2000/1. The one-year Certificate of Sixth Year Studies (CSYS) will be available until 2001–2.

A new system of courses and qualifications is being phased in under the "Higher Still" reforms, bringing together academic and vocational qualifications. It will replace Highers, CSYS and National Certificate modules, for everyone studying beyond Standard Grade in Scottish schools, and for non-advanced students in further education colleges. Qualifications will be available at five levels: Access, Intermediate 1, Intermediate 2, Higher, and Advanced Higher, the latter not available until 2000–1. Courses will be made up of internally assessed units with external assessment of the full course determining the grade (A to C). Students possessing a number of units and courses may be able to build them into a Scottish Group Award. The core skills of communication, numeracy, problem-solving, information technology and working with others are embedded in the Higher Still qualifications, although the skills and levels covered vary between subjects; there will also be separate core skills units.

All of these qualifications are awarded by the Scottish Qualifications Authority (SQA), which on 1 April 1997 assumed the functions of the Scottish Examinations Board and the Scottish Vocational Education Council.

THE INTERNATIONAL BACCALAUREATE

The International Baccalaureate is an internationally recognised two-year pre-university course and examination designed to facilitate the mobility of students and to promote international understanding. Candidates must offer one subject from each of six subject groups, at least three at higher level and the remainder at subsidiary level. Single subjects can be offered, for which a certificate is received. There are 33 schools and colleges in the UK which offer the International Baccalaureate diploma.

RECORDS OF ACHIEVEMENT

The National Record of Achievement (NRA) is under review. Subject to evaluation, it will be replaced in England, Wales and Northern Ireland by the 'Progress file' after a three year trial period starting in July 1999. It is not compulsory in Scotland where, from 1999–2000, the Scottish Qualifications Authority will issue a Scottish Qualifications Certificate recording all qualifications achieved at all levels which it has either awarded or accredited.

TEACHERS

ENGLAND AND WALES

To obtain Qualified Teacher Status (QTS) it is necessary to have successfully completed a course of initial teacher training, traditionally either a Bachelor of Education (B Ed) degree or the Postgraduate Certificate of Education (PGCE) at an accredited institution. New entrants to the profession are statutorily required to serve a one-year induction period during which they will have a structured programme of support. In recent years various employment-based routes to teaching have been developed. The Graduate Teacher Programme allows graduates with teaching experience to undergo between one term's and one year's school-based training. The Registered Teacher Scheme is designed to attract into the teaching profession entrants over 24 years of age without formal teaching qualifications but with relevant training and experience; entrants are paid a salary and undertake one to two years higher education depending on whether they possess relevant teaching experience. Teachers in further education are not required to have Qualified Teacher Status, though roughly half have a teaching qualification and most have industrial, commercial or professional experience. A mandatory qualification for aspiring head-teachers, the National Professional Qualification for Headship (NPQH), was introduced in September 1997.

The national curriculum for initial teacher training is in place in both England and Wales in all core subjects of the national curriculum.

Teacher training is now largely school-based, with student teachers on secondary PGCE courses spending two-thirds of their training in the classroom. Changes have also been made to primary phase teacher training to make it more school-based and to give schools a role in course design and delivery. Individual schools or consortia of schools and CTCs can bid for funds from the DfEE to carry out their own teacher training, including recruitment of students, subject to approval of their proposed training programme by the Teacher Training Agency (TTA) and monitoring and evaluation by OFSTED and Estyn. Funds are given to schools to meet the costs of designing and delivering the courses.

The TTA funds all types of teacher training in England, whether run by universities, colleges or schools, and some educational research. In Wales funding is undertaken by the Higher Education Funding Council for Wales. On an integrated England and Wales basis the TTA also acts as a central source of information and advice about entry to teaching, and has responsibilities relating to the continuing professional development of teachers. An independent professional council, the General Teaching Council, is to be established to advise the Secretary of State and the TTA, with a separate council for Wales.

The Specialist Teacher Assistant (STA) scheme was introduced in September 1994 to provide trained support to qualified teachers in the teaching of reading, writing and arithmetic to young pupils.

SHORTAGE SUBJECTS

Because of a shortage of teachers in certain secondary subjects, from September 1999 a £5,000 incentive was introduced for graduates training for a PGCE who then take up a post as teachers of mathematics or science. Furthermore, providers of initial teacher training in England and Wales may receive funds from the TTA to help promote courses in certain subjects and to offer students on courses in those subjects financial support. The subjects are: science; mathematics; modern languages (including Welsh in Wales); design and technology; information technology; religious education; music, and geography.

SCOTLAND

The General Teaching Council (GTC) for Scotland advises central government on matters relating to teachers and teacher education. All teachers in maintained schools must be registered with the GTC, initially for a two-year probationary period which can be extended if necessary. Only graduates are accepted as entrants to the profession; primary school teachers undertake either a four-year vocational degree course or a one-year postgraduate course, while teachers of academic subjects in secondary schools undertake the latter. Most initial teacher training is classroom-based. The Scottish Qualification for Headship has been introduced for aspiring head teachers. The colleges of education provide both in-service and pre-service training for teachers which is subject to inspection by HM Inspectors. All pre-service courses must be approved by the Scottish Executive Education Department and, if appropriate, validated by a higher education institution and accredited by the GTC. The colleges are funded by the Scottish Higher Education Funding Council.

NORTHERN IRELAND

All new entrants to teaching in grant-aided schools are graduates and hold an approved teaching qualification. Teacher training is provided by the two universities and two colleges of education. The colleges are concerned with teacher education mainly for the primary school sector. They also provide B Ed courses for intending secondary school teachers of religious education, commercial studies, and craft, design and technology. With these exceptions, the professional training of teachers for secondary schools is provided in the education departments of the universities. A review of primary and secondary teacher training has taken place as a result of which all student teachers spend more time in the classroom. All newly qualified teachers undertake a two-year induction period. The General Teaching Council for Northern Ireland is in the process of being established to advise government on professional issues, to maintain a register of teachers and to act as a disciplinary body.

ACCREDITATION OF TRAINING INSTITUTIONS

Advice to central government on the accreditation, content and quality of initial teacher training courses is given in England by the TTA, in Wales by the HEFCW and in Northern Ireland by validating bodies (by the General Teaching Council for Northern Ireland when established). These bodies also monitor and disseminate good practice, assisted in Northern Ireland by the Teacher Education Committee. In Scotland the General Teaching Council advises the Scottish Executive Education Department on the professional suitability of all training courses in colleges of education.

SERVING TEACHERS 1996–7 (full-time and part-time) (thousands)

	All	% graduate
Public sector schools	450.0	56.6
Nursery and primary	211.0	52.0
Secondary	222.0	74.0
Special	17.0	44.0
FE and HE establishments	133.0	82.0
TOTAL	583.0	69.3

SALARIES

Qualified teachers in England, Wales and Northern Ireland, other than heads and deputy heads, are paid on an 18-point scale. Entry points and placement depend on qualifications, experience, responsibilities, excellence and recruitment and retention factors as calculated by the relevant body, i.e. the governing body or the LEA. A new career grade of 'Advanced Skills Teacher' has been introduced to enhance prospects in the classroom for the most able teachers. There is a statutory superannuation scheme in maintained schools.

Teachers in Scotland are paid on a ten-point scale. The entry point depends on type of qualification, and additional allowances are payable under certain circumstances.

Salaries from 1 September 1999*

	England, Wales and N. Ireland	Scotland
Head	£31,155–£70,002	£27,846–£51,582
Deputy head	£27,258–£44,841	£27,846–£38,589
Advanced skills teacher	£26,082–£41,607	
Teacher	£13,830–£37,041	£13,206–£28,893

* From 1 April 1998 for Scotland: award pending

FURTHER EDUCATION

Further education is defined as all provision outside schools to people aged over 16 of education up to and including A-level and its equivalent.

ENGLAND AND WALES

Further education and sixth form colleges are funded directly by central government through the Further Education Funding Council for England (FEFCE) and the Further Education Funding Council for Wales (FEFCW). The Councils have a duty to secure provision of adequate facilities in their areas and are also responsible for the assessment of quality, in which their inspectorates play a key role. The colleges are controlled by autonomous further education corporations, which include substantial representation from industry and commerce, and which own their own assets and employ their own staff. Their funding is determined in part by the number of students enrolled and their level of achievement.

In England and Wales further education courses are taught at a variety of institutions. These include universities which were formerly polytechnics, colleges of higher education, colleges of further education (some of which also offer higher education courses) and tertiary colleges and sixth form colleges, which concentrate on the provision of normal sixth form school courses as well as a range of vocational courses. A number of institutions specific to a particular form of training, e.g. the Royal College of Music, are also involved.

Teaching staff in further education establishments are not necessarily required to have teaching qualifications although many do so, but they are subject to regular appraisal of teaching performance. It is planned to introduce a mandatory professional qualification for college principals.

Further education tends to be broadly vocational in purpose and employers are often involved in designing courses. It ranges from lower-level technical and commercial courses and government-sponsored training, through courses for those aiming at higher-level posts in industry, commerce and administration, to professional courses. Facilities exist for GCE A- and AS-levels, GCSEs, GNVQs and a full range of vocational qualifications (see pages 430–1). These courses can form the foundation for progress to higher education qualifications. Many students attend part-time, either through day or block release from employment, or in the evenings.

The main courses and examinations in the vocational field, all of which link in with the National Vocational Qualification (NVQ) framework (see page 434), are offered by the following bodies, but there are also many others.

The Edexcel Foundation was formed by the merger of the Business and Technology Education Council (BTEC) and London Examinations. It provides programmes of study across a wide range of subject areas. The main qualifications offered are GCSEs, A-levels, GNVQs, NVQs, BTEC First, National and Higher National diplomas and certificates, key skills and entry certificates.

City & Guilds specialize in developing qualifications and assessments for work-related and leisure qualifications. They offer nationally and internationally recognized certificates in over 500 vocational qualifications. The progressive structure of awards spans seven levels, from foundation to the highest level of professional competence.

RSA Examinations Board schemes cover a wide range of vocational qualifications, including accounting, business administration, customer service, management, language schemes, information technology and teaching qualifications. A wide range of NVQs and GNVQs are offered and a policy operates of credit accumulation, so that candidates can take a single unit or complete qualifications.

There are 453 further education establishments (of which 110 are sixth form colleges) in England and 26 in Wales. In England (1998–9) there were 746.9 thousand full-time and sandwich-course students and 1,618.5 thousand part-time students. In Wales (1996–7) there were 39.9 thousand full-time and sandwich students and 103.8 thousand part-time students.

SCOTLAND

Further education comprises non-advanced courses up to SCE Higher Grade, occasionally GCE A-level and GSVQ work-based awards. Courses are taught mainly at colleges of further education, but may also be provided in schools, in higher education institutions and in the workplace.

Responsibility for further education lies with the Scottish Executive under the Minister for Enterprise and Lifelong Learning through the Scottish Further Education Funding Council. There are 47 further education colleges of which 43 are self-governing incorporated colleges run by their own boards of management. The boards include the principal, staff and student representatives among their ten to 16 members; at least half the members must have experience of commerce, industry or the practice of a profession. Two colleges, on Orkney and Shetland, are under Islands Council control and two further colleges, Sabhal Mor Ostaig (the Gaelic college on Skye) and Newbattle Abbey are run by trustees.

The Scottish Qualifications Authority (SQA) awards qualifications for most occupations. It awards at non-advanced level the National Certificate, which is available in over 4,000 individual modules and covers the whole range of non-advanced further education provision. Students may study for the National Certificate on a full-time, part-time, open learning or work-based learning basis. National Certificate modules can be taken in further education colleges, secondary schools and other centres, normally from the age of 16 onwards. New unified qualifications for non-advanced post-16 education began to be phased in from August 1999 under the Higher Still reforms, which bring together academic and vocational qualifications. Higher Still courses will be available at five levels, (Access, Intermediate 1, Intermediate 2, Higher and Advanced Higher) and will replace Higher Grades, CSYS, General Scottish Vocational Qualifications (GSVQ) and National Certificate modules, but not Standard Grade or Scottish Vocational Qualifications (SVQ).

The SQA also offers modular advanced-level HNC/HND qualifications, which are available in further education colleges and higher education institutions. SQA accredits and awards SVQs which have mutual recognition with the NVQs available in the rest of the UK. SVQs are work-place assessed, but can also be taken in further education colleges and other centres where work-place conditions can be simulated. The SQA will issue the Scottish Qualifications Certificate from 1999–2000, which replaces the National Record of Achievement in Scotland (see above).

In the academic year 1997–8 there were 35,750 full-time and sandwich-course students and 249,215 part-time students on non-advanced vocational courses of further education in further education colleges (excluding Newbattle Abbey College).

NORTHERN IRELAND

All further education colleges are free-standing corporate bodies like their counterparts in the rest of the UK. Planning is the responsibility of the Department of Education for Northern Ireland, which funds the colleges directly. The colleges own their own property, are responsible for their own services and employ their own staff.

The governing bodies of the colleges must include at least 50 per cent membership from the professions, local business or industry, or other fields of employment relevant to the activities of the college.

In 1998–9 Northern Ireland had 17 institutions of further education, and there were 20,594 full-time students and 55,827 part-time students on non-advanced vocational courses of further education.

STUDENT SUPPORT

At present 16 to 19-year-olds may receive means-tested discretionary payments from LEAs, while adults may apply for access funds allocated by central government through the FEFCs. New arrangements are being piloted comprising the means-tested Education Maintenance Allowance (EMA) for 16 to 18-year-old students in both schools and colleges and extension of the access fund scheme.

COURSE INFORMATION

Applications for further education courses are generally made directly to the colleges concerned.

NATIONAL VOCATIONAL QUALIFICATIONS

National Vocational Qualifications (NVQs) are work-place based occupational qualifications. In September 1992 General National Vocational Qualifications (GNVQs) were introduced into colleges and schools as a vocational alternative to academic qualifications. They cover six broad categories in the NVQ framework and are aimed at those wishing to familiarize themselves with a range of opportunities. Advanced GNVQ, sometimes known as the "vocational A-level" is equivalent to two A-levels; from September 2000 a revised version equivalent to a single A-level is to be introduced. Intermediate GNVQ is equivalent to four GCSEs at A* to C grade. Foundation GNVQ is equivalent to four GCSEs at D to G grade.

Bodies responsible for the regulation of GNVQs and NVQs in the UK are: in England, the Qualifications and Curriculum Authority (QCA); in Wales, Awdurdod Cymwysterau, Cwricwlwm ac Asesu Cymru (ACCAC)/ the Curriculum and Assessment Authority; in Northern Ireland, the Council for the Curriculum, Examinations and Assessment (NICCEA); and in Scotland, the Scottish Qualifications Authority (SQA). With the exception of the SQA those bodies do not award qualifications but accredit NVQs, GNVQs and core skills. Assessment is carried out through awarding bodies who bestow the qualifications where candidates reach the required standards.

HIGHER EDUCATION

The term higher education is used to describe education above A-level, Higher and Advanced Higher Grade and their equivalent, which is provided in universities, colleges of higher education and in some further education colleges.

The Further and Higher Education Act 1992 and parallel legislation in Scotland removed the distinction between higher education provided by the universities and that provided in England and Wales by the former polytechnics and colleges of higher education and in Scotland by the former central institutions and others, allowing all polytechnics, and other higher education institutions which satisfy the necessary criteria, to award their own taught course and research degrees and to adopt the title of university. All the polytechnics, art colleges and some colleges of higher education have since adopted the title of university. The change of name does not affect the legal constitution of the institutions. Funding is by the Higher Education Funding Councils for England, Wales and Scotland and directly by the Department of Education in Northern Ireland.

The number of students in higher education in the UK in 1997–8 was (thousands):

Full-time, sandwich	1,230.4
% female	51.7%
Part-time	708.0
% female	54.2%
TOTAL	1,938.4
of which overseas	10.8%

The proportion of 18- to 21-year-olds undertaking full-time and part-time courses in higher education in the UK was 34 per cent in 1997–8. The number of mature entrants (those aged 21 and over when starting an undergraduate course and 25 and over when starting a postgraduate course) to higher education in Great Britain in 1997–8 (including those at the Open University) was 1,070.9 thousand. The number of full-time and part-time students on science courses (excluding medicine and related courses) in 1997–8 was 421.5 thousand, of whom 31.4 per cent were female.

UNIVERSITIES AND COLLEGES

The universities are self-governing institutions established in most cases by royal charter or Act of Parliament. They have academic freedom and are responsible for their own academic appointments, curricula and student admissions and award their own degrees.

Responsibility for universities rests in England with the Secretary of State for Education and Employment, in their territories with the Secretaries of State for Wales and Northern Ireland and with the Scottish Executive. Advice to government on matters relating to the universities is provided by the Higher Education Funding Councils for England, Wales and Scotland, and by the Higher Education Council in Northern Ireland. The HEFCs receive a block grant from central government which they allocate to the universities and colleges. The grant is allocated directly to institutions by central government in Northern Ireland on the advice of the Northern Ireland Higher Education Council.

There are now 88 universities in the UK, where only 47 existed prior to the Further and Higher Education Acts 1992. Of the 88, 71 are in England (including one federal university), two (one a federal institution) in Wales, 13 in Scotland and two in Northern Ireland.

The pre-1992 universities each have their own system of internal government but broad similarities exist. Most are run by two main bodies: the senate, which deals primarily with academic issues and consists of members elected from within the university; and the council, which is the supreme body and is responsible for all appointments and promotions, and bidding for and allocation of financial resources. At least half the members of the council are drawn from outside the university. Joint committees of senate and council are becoming increasingly common.

Those universities which were formerly polytechnics (38) or other higher education institutions (three) and the colleges of higher education (60) are run by higher education corporations (HECs), which are controlled by boards of governors. At least half the members of each board must be drawn from industry, business, commerce and the professions.

ENGLAND AND WALES

In 1997–8 full-time and part-time student enrolments were (thousands):

England

Undergraduates	1,173.2
% overseas	9.3%
Postgraduates	323.6
% overseas	21%

Wales

Undergraduates	76.2
% overseas	8.5%
Postgraduates	16.9
% overseas	22.7%

Higher education courses funded by the respective HEFCs are also taught in some further education colleges. In England in 1997–8 there were about 35.6 thousand students (2.3 per cent of total higher education student numbers) on such courses and about 500 (0.5 per cent of higher education student numbers) in Wales.

SCOTLAND

The Scottish Higher Education Funding Council (SHEFC) funds 21 institutions of higher education, including 13 universities. The universities are broadly managed as described above and the remaining colleges are managed by independent governing bodies which include representatives of industrial, commercial, professional and educational interests. Most of the courses outside the universities have a vocational orientation and a substantial number are sandwich courses.

Student enrolments in 1997–8 in universities and other higher education institutions were (thousands):

Undergraduates	130.9
% overseas	8.9%
Postgraduates	37.9
% overseas	23.8%

There were 38.4 thousand students on higher education courses in further education colleges, 22.9 per cent of total higher education students.

NORTHERN IRELAND

In Northern Ireland advanced courses are provided by 17 colleges of further education, the two universities and the two colleges of education. As well as offering first and postgraduate degrees, the University of Ulster offers courses leading to the BTEC Higher National Diploma and professional qualifications. Applications to undertake courses of higher education other than degree courses are made to the institutions direct. Higher education student enrolments in 1997–8 were (thousands):

Undergraduates	32.8
% overseas	13.4%
Postgraduates	9.6
% overseas	15.5%

There were 9,879 students enrolled on advanced courses of higher education in the institutions of further education, 23.3 per cent of higher education student numbers.

The non-residential Open University provides courses nationally leading to degrees. Teaching is through a combination of television and radio programmes, correspondence, tutorials, short residential courses and local audio-visual centres. No qualifications are needed for entry. The Open University offers a modular programme of undergraduate courses by credit accumulation and post-experience and postgraduate courses, including a programme of higher degrees which comprises BPhil, MPhil and PhD through research, and MA, MBA and MSc through taught courses. The Open University throughout the UK is funded by the Higher Education Funding Council for England, although Scottish students, from 2000–1, will be funded by the Scottish Higher Education Funding Council. Its recurrent grant for 1997–8 was £116.9 million from the Higher Education Funding Council for England and £6.6 million from the Teacher Training Agency. In 1999, about 113,000 undergraduates were registered of whom about 53 per cent were women. Estimated cost (1999) of a six-credit degree was around £4,200 including course fees of about £3,000.

The independent University of Buckingham provides a two-year course leading to a bachelor's degree and its tuition fees were £9,996 for 1999. It receives no capital or recurrent income from the Government. Its academic year consists of four terms of ten weeks each.

ACADEMIC STAFF

Each university and college appoints its own academic staff on its own conditions. However, there is a common salary structure and, except for Oxford and Cambridge, a common career structure in those universities formerly funded by the UFC and a common salary structure for the former PCFC sector. The Universities and Colleges Employers Association (UCEA) acts as a pay agency for universities and colleges.

Teaching staff in higher education require no formal teaching qualification, but the Institute of Teaching and Learning in Higher Education, funded by the Higher Education Funding Councils, has been established to set up an accreditation scheme for higher education teachers and to encourage innovation in teaching and learning. Teacher trainers are required to spend a certain amount of time in schools to ensure that they have sufficient recent practical experience.

In 1997–8, there were 102,517 full-time and part-time teaching and research staff (UK nationals) in institutions of higher education in the UK.

Salary scales for staff in the pre-1992 universities sector differ from those in the former polytechnics and colleges; it is planned eventually to amalgamate them. The salary scales for non-clinical academic staff in universities formerly funded by the UFC are:

Professor	from £35,120
Senior lecturer	£30,498–£34,464
Lecturer grade B	£22,726–£29,048
Lecturer grade A	£15,735 –£21,815

The salaries of clinical academic staff are kept broadly comparable to those of doctors and dentists in the National Health Service.

Salary scales for lecturers in the former polytechnics, now universities, and colleges of higher education in England, Wales and Northern Ireland are:

	March 1999
Head of Department	from £26,304
Principal lecturer	£27,746–£35,204
Senior lecturer	£22,400–£29,600
Lecturer	£14,398–£24,002

The salary scales for such staff in Scotland are determined at individual college level.

FINANCE

Although universities and colleges are expected to look to a wider range of funding sources than before, and to generate additional revenue in collaboration with industry, they are still largely financed, directly or indirectly, from government resources.

In 1997–8 the total income of institutions of higher education in the UK was £11,616.7 million (£11,049.9 million in 1996–7). Grants from the funding councils amounted to £4,507.6 million (£4,371.8 million in 1996–7), forming 38.8 per cent of total income (39.5 per cent in 1996–7). Income from research grants and contracts was £1,733.3 million, 14.9 per cent of total income (14.7 per cent in 1996–7).

In the academic year 1997–8 the HEFCs' recurrent grant to institutions outside their sector for the provision of higher education courses was £62.8 million.

COURSES

In the UK all universities, including the Open University, and some colleges award their own degrees and other qualifications and may act as awarding and validating bodies for neighbouring colleges which are not yet accredited. The Quality Assurance Agency for Higher Education, funded by institutional contributions, advises government on applications for degree-awarding powers.

Higher education courses last full-time for at least four weeks or, if part-time, involve more than 60 hours of instruction. Facilities exist for full-time and part-time study, day release, sandwich or block release. Credit accumulation and transfer (CATS) is a system of study which is becoming widely available. It allows a student to achieve a final qualification by accumulating credits for courses of study successfully achieved, or even professional experience, over a period. Credit transfer information and values are carried on an electronic database called ECCTIS 2000, which is available in most careers offices and many schools and colleges.

Higher education courses comprise: first degree and postgraduate (including research); Diploma in Higher Education (DipHE); Higher National Diploma (HND) and Higher National Certificate (HNC); and preparation for professional examinations. The in-service training of teachers is also included, but from September 1994 has been funded in England by the TTA (*see* page 431), not the HEFCE.

The Diploma of Higher Education (DipHE) is a two-year diploma usually intended to serve as a stepping-stone to a degree course or other further study. The DipHE is awarded by the institution itself if it is accredited; by an accredited institution of its choice if not. The BTEC Higher National Certificate (HNC) is awarded after two years part-time study. The BTEC Higher National Diploma (HND) is awarded after two years full-time, or three years sandwich-course or part-time study.

With the exception of certain Scottish universities where master is sometimes used for a first degree in arts subjects, undergraduate courses lead to the title of Bachelor, Bachelor of Arts (BA) and Bachelor of Science (BSc) being the most common. For a higher degree the titles are: Master of Arts (MA), Master of Science (MSc) (usually taught courses) and the research degrees of Master of Philosophy (MPhil) and Doctor of Philosophy (PhD or, at a few universities, DPhil).

Most undergraduate courses at universities and colleges of higher education run for three years, but some take four years or more.

Postgraduate studies vary in length. Taught courses such as certificates, diplomas or masters degrees usually take one year full-time or two years part-time. Research degrees take from two to three years full-time. Details of taught courses and research degree opportunities can be found in the *Directory of Graduate Studies*, published annually for the Careers Research and Advisory Centre (CRAC).

Post-experience short courses are forming an increasing part of higher education provision, reflecting the need to update professional and technical training. Most of these courses fund themselves.

ADMISSIONS

The target number of students entering full-time higher education is 31 to 33 per cent of the 18- to 19-year-old age group in 1999–2000. Institutions suffer financial penalties if the number of students laid down for them by the Funding Councils is exceeded, but the individual university or college decides which students to accept. The formal entry requirements to most degree courses are two A-levels at grade E or above (or equivalent), and to HND courses one A-level (or equivalent). In practice, most offers of places require qualifications in excess of this, higher requirements usually reflecting the popularity of a course. These requirements do not, however, exclude applications from students with a variety of non-GCSE qualifications or unquantified experience and skills.

For admission to a degree, DipHE or HND, potential students apply through a central clearing house, Universities and Colleges Admission Service (UCAS). Applicants are supplied with an application form and a *UCAS Handbook*, available from schools, colleges and careers offices or directly from UCAS, and may apply to a maximum of six institutions/courses. The only exception among universities is the Open University, which conducts its own admissions.

Applications for undergraduate teacher training courses are made through UCAS. Details of initial teacher training courses in Scotland can be obtained from colleges of education and those universities offering such courses, and

from the Committee of Scottish Higher Education Principals (COSHEP).

For admission as a postgraduate student, universities and colleges normally require a good first degree in a subject related to the proposed course of study or research, but other experience and qualifications will be considered on merit. Most applications are made to individual institutions but there are two clearing houses of relevance. Postgraduate teacher training courses in England and Wales utilize the Graduate Teacher Training Registry. Applications to postgraduate teacher training courses in Scotland are made through the Teacher Education Admissions Clearing House (TEACH). Applications for PGCE courses at institutions in Northern Ireland are made to the Department of Education for Northern Ireland. For social work the Social Work Admissions System operates.

FEES

From September 1998 new entrants to undergraduate courses have paid, directly to the institution, an annual contribution to their fees (up to £1,025 in 1999–2000) depending on their own level of income and that of their spouse or parents. Among the classes of students exempt from payment are: existing students with mandatory awards (*see below*), for whom the grant-awarding body pays; postgraduate certificate of education students; Scottish and EU students in the fourth year of a four-year degree course at a Scottish institution; and medical students in the fifth year of their course. Students from EU member countries pay fees at home student rates and will also be liable to make an annual contribution to fees assessed against family income.

Universities and colleges are free to set their own charges for students from non-EU countries, whose fees are meant to cover the cost of their education. Financial help is available under a number of schemes. Information about them is available from British Council offices world-wide.

For postgraduate students, the maximum tuition fee that will be reimbursed through the awards system is £2,675 in 1999–2000.

STUDENT SUPPORT

STUDENT GRANTS

Students in the UK who started a full-time or sandwich undergraduate course of higher education since the academic year commencing in September 1998 are no longer eligible for a grant. Grants for such students have been replaced by loans which are partly income-contingent, although some students, such as single parents and those with dependants, are entitled to a means-tested grant for help in meeting certain living costs. Disabled students are eligible for non means-tested disabled students allowances. Students who started their courses before September 1998 continue to be eligible for means-tested maintenance grants, from which a parental contribution is deductible on a sliding scale dependent on income or, for married students, from their spouse's income. However, a parental contribution is not deducted from the grant to students over 25 years of age who have been self-supporting for at least three years. The main rates of mandatory grant have been frozen since 1991–2, while the amount available as a loan has increased in compensation.

Grants are paid by the local education authority for the area in which the student lives in England, Wales and Northern Ireland. The cost is reimbursed by central government. For students resident in Scotland grants are made by central government through the Student Awards Agency.

The means-tested maintenance grant, usually paid once a term, covers periods of attendance during term as well as the Christmas and Easter vacations, but not the summer vacation. The basic grant rates for 1999–2000 (rates for Scottish students in parentheses) are:

Living in

College/lodgings in London area	£2,280 (£2,200)
College/lodgings outside London area	£1,855 (£1,780)
Parental home	£1,515 (£1,360)

Additional allowances are available if, for example, the course requires a period of study abroad.

Expenditure on student fees and maintenance in 1997–8 was £2,378.7 million; about 943 thousand mandatory awards were made.

STUDENT LOANS

In the academic year 1999–2000 students are eligible to apply for interest-free but indexed loans of up to £4,480 through LEAs in England and Wales, education and library boards in Northern Ireland and the Student Awards Agency in Scotland.

Loans are available to students on designated courses, which are those full-time or sandwich courses leading to: a degree; the Diploma of Higher Education; the Higher National Diploma; initial teacher-training courses, including those for the postgraduate certificate of education and the art teachers' certificate or diploma; a university certificate or diploma course lasting at least three years and other qualifications which are specifically designated as being comparable to first degree courses. Certain residency conditions also apply. From autumn 2000 loans of up to £500 will be available to part-time students on low incomes. In 1997–8, 615.1 thousand loans were taken up, to the value of £941.0 million. Repayment arrangements differ for students who embarked upon higher education courses before the 1998–99 academic year and those starting thereafter. The former normally repay over five to seven years, although repayment can be deferred if annual income is at or below 85 per cent of national average earnings (£17,784 at 31 August 1999). The latter will not be required to make repayments if their annual income is below £10,000; otherwise a percentage of the income above that amount is taken to repay the loan.

ACCESS FUNDS

Access funds are allocated by central government to the appropriate Funding Councils in England, Wales and Scotland and administered by further and higher education institutions. In Northern Ireland they are allocated by central government directly to the institution. They are available to students whose access to education might otherwise be inhibited by financial considerations or where real financial difficulties are faced. For the academic year 1999–2000, provision in the UK is £72 million.

POSTGRADUATE AWARDS

Grants for postgraduate study are of two types, both discretionary: 30-week bursaries, which are means-tested and are available for certain vocational and diploma courses; and studentship awards, which cover students undertaking research degrees or taught masters degrees, are dependent on the class of first degree (especially for research degrees) and are not means-tested. Postgraduate students, with the exception of students on loan-bearing diploma courses such as teacher training, are not eligible to apply for student loans. For students resident in England and Wales funding is provided by the DfEE, research councils, the Ministry of Agriculture, Fisheries and Food and the British Academy.

In Scotland postgraduate funding is provided by central government through the Student Awards Agency for Scotland, the Scottish Executive Rural Affairs Department and the research councils as in England and Wales.

Awards in Northern Ireland are made by DENI, the Department of Agriculture for Northern Ireland and the Medical Research Council.

The rates for 30-week bursaries for non loan-bearing courses of professional and vocational training in 1999–2000 (Scottish rates in parenthesis) are:

Living in

College/lodgings in London area	£4,010* (£3,749)
College/lodgings outside London area	£3,085 (£2,958)
Parental home	£2,585 (£2,235)

*1998–9 rate

Studentship awards are payable at between £5,455 and £7,060 a year (1999–2000).

ADULT AND CONTINUING EDUCATION

The term adult education covers a broad spectrum of educational activities. In the UK, the responsibility for securing adult and continuing education leading to academic or vocational qualifications is statutory. In England, Wales and Scotland it is shared between various bodies: the Further Education Funding Councils are responsible for and fund those courses which take place in their sector and lead to academic and vocational qualifications, prepare students to undertake further or higher education courses, or confer basic skills; the Higher Education Funding Councils fund advanced courses of continuing education. The LEAs have the power, although not the duty, to provide those courses which do not fall within the remit of the Funding Councils. Funding in Northern Ireland is through the education and library boards.

Adult education takes place in 'area' adult education centres (England and Wales), vocational further education colleges (47 in 1998) and evening centres (Scotland), community schools (Northern Ireland), the adult studies departments of colleges of further and higher education and universities.

The involvement of universities in adult education and continuing education has diversified considerably. Birkbeck College in the University of London caters solely for part-time students. Those institutions and colleges formerly in the PCFC sector in England and Wales, because of their range of courses and flexible patterns of student attendance, provide opportunities in the field of adult and continuing education. The Forum for the Advancement of Continuing Education (FACE) promotes collaboration between institutions of higher education active in this area. The Open University, in partnership with the BBC, provides distance teaching leading to first degrees, and also offers post-experience and higher degree courses.

Of the voluntary bodies, the biggest is the Workers' Educational Association (WEA) which operates throughout the UK, reaching about 150,000 adult students annually. The FEFCs and LEAs make grants towards provision.

NIACE, the national organisation for adult learning has a broad remit to promote lifelong learning opportunities for adults. NIACE works to develop increased participation in education and training. It does this through research and project work, conferences, publications and the provision of an information service to educational providers. NIACE Cymru, the Welsh committee, receives financial support from the National Assembly for Wales, support in kind from local authorities, and advises government, voluntary bodies and education providers on adult continuing education and training matters in Wales. In Scotland advice on adult and community education, and promotion thereof, is provided by the Scottish Community Education Council. Following the demise of the Northern Ireland Council for Adult Education, its functions have been taken over by DENI until a successor body can be set up.

The Universities' Association for Continuing Education (UACE) represents the continuing education community within higher education and is open to universities and higher education institutions in the UK with additional provision for international, associate and individual members.

COURSES

Although lengths vary, most courses are part-time. Long-term residential colleges in England and Wales are grant-aided by the FEFCs and provide full-time courses lasting one or two years. Some colleges and centres offer short-term residential courses in a wide range of subjects. Local education authorities directly sponsor many of the colleges, while others are sponsored by universities or voluntary organizations. A directory of learning holidays, *Time to Learn*, is published by NIACE.

GRANTS

Adult education bursaries for students at the long-term residential colleges of adult education are the responsibility of the colleges themselves. The awards are administered for the colleges by the Awards Officer of the Residential Colleges Committee for students resident in England and are funded by the FEFC for England in English colleges; for colleges in Wales they are funded and administered by the FEFC for Wales; for colleges in Scotland they are funded by central government and administered by the Scottish FEFCs; and for colleges in Northern Ireland they are funded by central government and administered by the education and library boards.

Education Directory

LOCAL EDUCATION AUTHORITY

ENGLAND

County Councils

BEDFORDSHIRE, County Hall, Cauldwell Street, Bedford MK42 9AP. Tel: 01234-363222. *Director*, P. Brett

BUCKINGHAMSHIRE, County Hall, Walton Street, Aylesbury HP20 1UA. Tel: 01296-382602. *Director*, D. McGahey

CAMBRIDGESHIRE, Education Information Office, Box ELH 1500, Shire Hall, Cambridge CB3 0AP. Tel: 01223-717667. *Director*, A. Baxter

CHESHIRE, County Hall, Chester CHI 1SQ. Tel: 01244-602201. *Director*, D. Cracknell

CORNWALL, County Hall, Truro TRI 3AY. Tel: 01872-322000. *Director*, J. Harris

CUMBRIA, 5 Portland Square, Carlisle CAI 1PU. Tel: 01228-606868. *Director*, J. Nellist

DERBYSHIRE, County Hall, Matlock DE4 3AG. Tel: 01629-585641. *Director (acting)*, R. V. Taylor

DEVON, County Hall, Topsham Road, Exeter EX2 4QD. Tel: 01392-382059. *Director of Education, Arts and Libraries*, A Smith

DORSET, County Hall, Colliton Park, Dorchester DTI 1XJ. Tel: 01305-224171. *Director*, R. Ely

DURHAM, County Hall, Durham DHI 5UL. Tel: 0191-383 3319. *Director*, K. Mitchell

EAST SUSSEX, County Hall, St Anne's Crescent, Lewes BN7 1SG. Tel: 01273-481316. *County Education Officer*, D. Mallen, CBE

ESSEX, PO Box 47, Victoria Road South, Chelmsford CMI 1LD. Tel: 01245-492211. *Director of Learning Services*, P. A. Lincoln

GLOUCESTERSHIRE, Shire Hall, Westgate Street, Gloucester GLI 2TG. Tel: 01452-425300. *Director*, R. Crouch

HAMPSHIRE, The Castle, Winchester SO23 8UG. Tel: 01962-841841. *County Education Officer*, A. J. Seber

HERTFORDSHIRE, County Hall, Pegs Lane, Hertford SGI3 8DE. Tel: 01992-555827. *Director*, R. Shostak

ISLE OF WIGHT, County Hall, High Street, Newport PO30 1UD. Tel: 01983-823400. *Director*, A. Kaye

KENT, Sessions House, County Hall, Maidstone MEI4 1XQ. Tel: 01622-671411. *Director*, N. Henwood

LANCASHIRE, PO Box 61, County Hall, Preston PRI 8RJ. Tel: 01772-254868. *Director of Education and Cultural Services*, C. J. Trinick

LEICESTERSHIRE, County Hall, Glenfield, Leicester LE3 8RF. Tel: 0116-265 6634. *Director*, Mrs J. A. M. Strong

LINCOLNSHIRE, County Offices, Newland, Lincoln LNI 1YL. Tel: 01522-552222. *Director of Education and Cultural Services*, N. J. Riches

NORFOLK, County Hall, Martineau Lane, Norwich NRI 2DH. Tel: 01603-222146. *Director*, Dr B. C. Slater

NORTHAMPTONSHIRE, Education and Community Learning Directorate, PO Box 149, County Hall, Northampton NNI 1AU. Tel: 01604-236252. *Director*, Mrs B. Bignold

NORTHUMBERLAND, County Hall, Morpeth NE6I 2EF. Tel: 01670-533601. *Director*, Dr L. Davis

NORTH YORKSHIRE, County Hall, Northallerton, N. Yorks DL7 8AE. Tel: 01609-780780. *Director*, Miss C. Welburn

NOTTINGHAMSHIRE, County Hall, West Bridgford, Nottingham NG2 7QP. Tel: 0115-982 3823. *Director*, R. Valentine

OXFORDSHIRE, Macclesfield House, New Road, Oxford OXI 1NA. Tel: 01865-815449. *Chief Education Officer*, G. Badman

SHROPSHIRE, The Shirehall, Abbey Foregate, Shrewsbury SY2 6ND. Tel: 01743-254307. *Director*, Mrs C. Adams

SOMERSET, County Hall, Taunton TAI 4DY. Tel: 01823-355790. *Director*, M. Jennings

STAFFORDSHIRE, Tipping Street, Stafford STI6 2DH. Tel: 01785-223121. *Director*, Dr P. J. Hunter

SUFFOLK, St Andrew House, County Hall, Ipswich IPI4 1LJ. Tel: 01473-584627. *Director*, D. J. Peachey

SURREY, County Hall, Penrhyn Road, Kingston upon Thames KTI 2DN. Tel: 0181-541 9500. *Director*, Dr P. Gray

WARWICKSHIRE, PO Box 24, 22 Northgate Street, Warwick CV34 4SR. Tel: 01926-410410. *Director*, E. Wood

WEST SUSSEX, County Hall, Chichester PO19 1RF. Tel: 01243-777129. *Director*, R. D. C. Bunker

WILTSHIRE, County Hall, By The Sea Road, Trowbridge BAI4 8JB. Tel: 01225-713750. *Director*, vacant

WORCESTERSHIRE, County Hall, Spetchley Road, Worcester WR5 2NP. Tel: 01905-763763. *Director of Educational Services*, J. Kramer

Unitary Councils

BARNSLEY, Berneslai Close, Barnsley S70 2HS. Tel: 01226-773500. *Director*, D. Dalton

BATH AND NORTH-EAST SOMERSET, PO Box 25, Riverside, Temple Street, Keynsham, Bristol BS31 1DN. Tel: 01225-477000. *Strategic Director (Education and Culture)*, R. Jones

BIRMINGHAM, Margaret Street, Birmingham B3 3BU. Tel: 0121-303 2590. *Director*, Prof. T. Brighouse

BLACKBURN WITH DARWEN, Town Hall, Blackburn BBI 7DY. Tel: 01254-585541. *Director*, Dr M. Pattison

BLACKPOOL, Progress House, Clifton Road, Blackpool FY4 4US. Tel: 01253-476555. *Director*, Dr D. Sanders

BOLTON, Paderborn House, Civic Centre, Bolton BLI 1RU. Tel: 01204-522311. *Director*, Mrs M. Blenkinsop

BOURNEMOUTH, Dorset House, 20–22 Christchurch Road, Bournemouth BHI 3NL. Tel: 01202-451451. *Director*, K. Shaikh

BRACKNELL FOREST, Edward Elgar House, Skimped Hill Lane, Bracknell, Berks RGI2 1LY. Tel: 01344-424642. *Director*, A. Eccleston

BRADFORD, Flockton House, Flockton Road, Bradford BD7 7RY. Tel: 01274-751840. *Director*, Mrs D. Cavanagh

BRIGHTON AND HOVE, PO Box 2503, Kings House, Grand Avenue, Hove BN3 2SU. Tel: 01273-290000. *Director*, D. Hawker

BRISTOL, The Council House, College Green, Bristol BSI 5TR. Tel: 0117-903 7961. *Director*, R. Riddell

BURY, Athenaeum House, Market Street, Bury BL9 0SW. Tel: 0161-253 5652. *Director*, H. Williams

CALDERDALE, Northgate House, Northgate, Halifax HXI 1UN. Tel: 01422-357257. *Director*, Ms C. White

COVENTRY, Council Offices, Earl Street, Coventry CVI 5RS. Tel: 01203-831500. *Director*, Ms C. Goodwin

DARLINGTON, Town Hall, Darlington DLI 5QT. Tel: 01325-380651. *Director*, G. Pennington

DERBY, Middleton House, 27 St Mary's Gate, Derby DEI 3NN. Tel: 01332-716924. *Director,* vacant

DONCASTER, 7th Floor, The Council House, College Road, Doncaster DN1 3AD. Tel: 01302-737103. *Executive Director,* M. Simpson

DUDLEY, Westox House, 1 Trinity Road, Dudley DY1 1DQ. Tel: 01384-814225. *Chief Education Officer,* R. P. Colligan

EAST RIDING OF YORKSHIRE, County Hall, Beverley HU17 9BA. Tel: 01482-887700. *Director,* J. Ginnever

GATESHEAD, Civic Centre, Regent Street, Gateshead NE8 1HH. Tel: 0191-477 1011. *Director,* B. H. Edwards

HALTON, Grosvenor House, Halton Lea, Runcorn WA7 2ED. Tel: 0151-424 2061. *Director,* G. Talbot

HARTLEPOOL, Civic Centre, Victoria Road, Hartlepool TS24 8AY. Tel: 01429-266522. *Director,* J. J. Fitt

HEREFORDSHIRE, PO Box 185, Blackfriars Street, Hereford HR4 9ZR. Tel: 01432-260908. *Director,* Dr E. Oram

KINGSTON UPON HULL, Essex House, Manor Street, Hull HU1 1YD. Tel: 01482-613161. *Director,* Miss J. E. Taylor

KIRKLEES, Oldgate House, 2 Oldgate, Huddersfield HD1 6QW. Tel: 01484-225242. *Chief Education Officer,* G. Tonkin

KNOWSLEY, Huyton Hey Road, Huyton, Knowsley L36 9YH. Tel: 0151-443 3220. *Director,* P. Wylie

LEEDS, Merrion House, Merrion Way, Leeds LS2 8DT. Tel: 0113-247 5876. *Director,* K. Burton

LEICESTER, Marlborough House, 38 Welford Road, Leicester LE2 7AA. Tel: 0116-252 7807. *Director,* T. Warren

LIVERPOOL, 14 Sir Thomas Street, Liverpool L1 6BJ. Tel: 0151-233 3000. *Director,* M. F. Cogley

LUTON, Unity House, 111 Stuart Street, Luton LU1 5NP. Tel: 01582-546000. *Director,* T. Dessent

MANCHESTER, Cumberland House, Crown Square, Manchester M60 3BB. Tel: 0161-234 7125. *Director,* D. Johnston

MEDWAY, Compass Centre, Chatham Maritime, Chatham, Kent ME7 4OD. Tel: 01634-881638. *Director,* R Bolsin

MIDDLESBROUGH, PO Box 69, Vancouver House, Gurney Street, Middlesborough TS1 1QP. Tel: 01642-262001. *Corporate Director of Education and Leisure,* Ms C. Berry

MILTON KEYNES, Saxon Court, 502 Avebury Boulevard, Milton Keynes MK9 3HS. Tel: 01908-253325. *Director,* A. Flack

NEWCASTLE UPON TYNE, Civic Centre, Newcastle upon Tyne NE1 8PU. Tel: 0191-232 8520 ext. 5301. *Director,* D. Bell

NORTH EAST LINCOLNSHIRE, 7 Eleanor Street, Grimsby DN32 9DU. Tel: 01472-324021. *Director,* G. Hill

NORTH LINCOLNSHIRE, PO Box 35, Hewson House, Station Road, Brigg DN20 8XJ. Tel: 01724-297011. *Director,* T. Thomas

NORTH SOMERSET, Town Hall, Weston-super-Mare BS23 1AE. Tel: 01934-888822. *Director,* J. Simpson

NORTH TYNESIDE, Town Hall, High Street East, Wallsend, Tyne & Wear NE28 7RR. Tel: 0191-200 6565. *Executive Director,* L. Watson

NOTTINGHAM CITY, Sandfield Centre, Sandfield Road, Nottingham NG7 1QH. Tel: 0115-915 5555. *Director,* P. Roberts

OLDHAM, PO Box 40, Civic Centre, West Street, Oldham OL1 1XJ. Tel: 0161-911 4200. *Director,* M. Willis

PETERBOROUGH, Bayard Place, Broadway, Peterborough PE1 1FB. Tel: 01733-748000. *Director,* W. Goodwin

PLYMOUTH, Civic Centre, Armada Way, Plymouth PL1 2EW. Tel: 01752-307461. *Director,* S. Faruqi

POOLE, Civic Centre, Poole, Dorset BH15 2RU. Tel: 01202-633203. *Director,* F. Davies

PORTSMOUTH, Civic Offices, Guildhall Square, Portsmouth PO1 2AL. Tel: 01705-822251. *Director,* J. Gaskin

READING, Civic Centre, Reading RG1 7TD. Tel: 0118-939 0900. *Director,* A. Daykin

REDCAR AND CLEVELAND, Council Offices, Kirkleatham Street, Redcar TS10 1YA. Tel: 01642-444342. *Director,* P. Scott

ROCHDALE, PO Box 70, Municipal Offices, Smith Street, Rochdale OL16 1YD. Tel: 01706-647474. *Director,* B. Atkinson

ROTHERHAM, Norfolk House, Walker Place, Rotherham S60 1QT. Tel: 01709-822500. *Director,* H. C. Bower

RUTLAND, Catmose, Oakham, Rutland LE15 6HP. Tel: 01572-772700. *Head of Education Service,* Ms C. Chambers

ST HELENS, Rivington Centre, Rivington Road, St Helens WA10 4ND. Tel: 01744-456000. *Director,* C. Hilton

SALFORD, Chapel Street, Salford M3 5TL. Tel: 0161-832 9751. *Director of Education and Leisure,* M. Carriline

SANDWELL, PO Box 41, Shaftesbury House, 402 High Street, West Bromwich B70 9LT. Tel: 0121-525 7366. *Director,* S. Gallacher

*SEFTON, Town Hall, Trinity Road, Bootle, Merseyside L20 7AE. Tel: 0151-922 4040. *Director,* B. Marsh

SHEFFIELD, Leopold Street, Sheffield S1 1RJ. Tel: 0114-273 5722. *Director,* J. Crossley-Holland

SLOUGH, Town Hall, Bath Road, Slough SL1 3UQ. Tel: 01753-875712. *Chief Officer,* J. Christie

SOLIHULL, PO Box 19, Council House, Solihull B91 3QT. Tel: 0121-704 6656. *Director,* D. Nixon

SOUTHAMPTON, Civic Centre, Southampton SO14 7LY. Tel: 01703-832771. *Director,* R. Hogg

SOUTH GLOUCESTERSHIRE, Bowling Hill, Chipping Sodbury, S. Glos BS37 6JX. Tel: 01454-863253. *Director,* Ms T. Gillespie

SOUTHEND, Civic Centre, Victoria Avenue, Southend-on-Sea SS2 6ER. Tel: 01702-215890. *Director,* S. Hay

SOUTH TYNESIDE, Town Hall and Civic Offices, Westoe Road, South Shields NE33 2RL. Tel: 0191-427 1717. *Director,* I. Reid

STOCKPORT, Town Hall, Stockport SK1 3XE. Tel: 0161-474 3808. *Director,* M. K. J. Hunt

STOCKTON-ON-TEES, Municipal Buildings, Church Road, Stockton-on-Tees TS18 1LD. Tel: 01642-393441. *Director,* S. T. Bradford

STOKE-ON-TRENT, PO Box 758, Swann House, Boothen Road, Stoke-on-Trent ST4 1RU. Tel: 01782-234567. *Director,* N. Rigby

SUNDERLAND, PO Box 100, Civic Centre, Sunderland SR2 7DN. Tel: 0191-553 1355. *Director,* Dr J. W. Williams, ph.D

SWINDON, Civic Offices, Euclid Street, Swindon SN1 2JH. Tel: 01793-463069. *Director,* M. Lusty

TAMESIDE, Council Offices, Wellington Road, Ashton under Lyne, Lancs OL6 6DL. Tel: 0161-342 2201. *Director of Education and Leisure Services,* P. Lawday

TELFORD AND WREKIN, Civic Offices, Telford, Shropshire TF3 4LD. Tel: 01952-202402. *Director,* Ms C. Davies

THURROCK, PO Box 118, Grays, Essex RM17 6GF. Tel: 01375-652283. *Director,* R. Wilkins

TORBAY, Oldway Mansion, Paignton, Devon TQ3 2TE. Tel: 01803-208208. *Director,* G. Cane

TRAFFORD, PO Box 40, Trafford Town Hall, Talbot Road, Stretford, Trafford, Greater Manchester M32 0EL. Tel: 0161-912 1212. *Director Education, Arts and Leisure,* C. Pratt

WAKEFIELD, County Hall, Wakefield WF1 2QW. Tel: 01924-305500. *Director,* J. McLeod

WALSALL, Civic Centre, Darwall Street, Walsall WS1 1TP. Tel: 01922-652301. *Director,* T. Howard

WARRINGTON, New Town House, Buttermarket Street, Warrington, Cheshire WA1 2NH. Tel: 01925-442901. *Director,* M. Roxborgh

WEST BERKSHIRE, Avon Bank House, West Street, Newbury, Berks RG14 1BZ. Tel: 01635-519722. *Director,* J. Mercer

WIGAN, Gateway House, Standishgate, Wigan, Lancs WN1 1AE. Tel: 01942-828891. *Director,* R. J. Clark

WINDSOR AND MAIDENHEAD, Town Hall, St Ives Road, Maidenhead, Berks SL6 1RF. Tel: 01628-796367. *Director,* M. Peckham

WIRRAL, Hamilton Building, Conway Street, Birkenhead CH41 4FD. Tel: 0151-666 2121. *Director,* C. Rice

WOKINGHAM, PO Box 156, Shute End, Wokingham, Berks RG40 1WN. Tel: 0118-974 6100. *Director,* Mrs J. Griffin

WOLVERHAMPTON, Civic Centre, St Peter's Square, Wolverhampton WV1 1RR. Tel: 01902-554100. *Director,* R. Lockwood

YORK, 10–12 George Hudson Street, York YO1 1ZG. Tel: 01904-613161. *Director,* M. Peters

LONDON

*Inner London borough

BARKING AND DAGENHAM, Town Hall, Barking, Essex IG11 7LU. Tel: 0181-592 4500. *Director,* A. Larbalestier

BARNET, The Old Town Hall, Friern Barnet Lane, London N11 3DL. Tel: 0181-359 3004. *Head of Education,* Ms L. Stone

BEXLEY, Hill View, Hill View Drive, Welling, Kent DA16 3RY. Tel: 0181-303 7777. *Director,* P. McGee

BRENT, Chesterfield House, 9 Park Lane, Wembley, Middx HA9 7RW. Tel: 0181-937 3190. *Director,* vacant

BROMLEY, Civic Centre, Stockwell Close, Bromley BR1 3UH. Tel: 0181-313 4066. *Director,* K. Davis

*CAMDEN, Crowndale Centre, 218–220 Eversholt Street, London NW1 1BD. Tel: 0171-911 1505. *Director,* R. Litchfield

*CITY OF LONDON, Education Department, Corporation of London, PO Box 270, Guildhall, London EC2P 2EJ. Tel: 0171-332 1750. *City Education Officer,* D. Smith

*CITY OF WESTMINSTER, City Hall, 64 Victoria Street, London SW1E 6QP. Tel: 0171-641 1947. *Director,* J. Harris

CROYDON, Taberner House, Park Lane, Croydon CR9 3JS. Tel: 0181-760 5555. *Director,* D. Sands

EALING, Perceval House, 14–16 Uxbridge Road, London W5 2HL. Tel: 0181-758 5410. *Director,* A. Parker

ENFIELD, PO Box 56, Civic Centre, Silver Street, Enfield, Middx EN1 3XQ. Tel: 0181-379 3200. *Director,* Ms E. Graham

*GREENWICH, Riverside House, Woolwich High Street, London SE18 6DN. Tel: 0181-312 5638. *Director,* G. Gyte

*HACKNEY, Edith Cavell Building, Enfield Road, London N1 5BA. Tel: 0181-356 5000. *Director,* Ms E. Reid

*HAMMERSMITH AND FULHAM, Cambridge House, Cambridge Grove, London W6 0LE. Tel: 0181-748 3020. *Director,* Ms C. Whatford

HARINGEY, 48 Station Road, Wood Green, London N22 4TY. Tel: 0181-489 0000. *Director,* Ms F. Magee

HARROW, PO Box 22, Civic Centre, Station Road, Harrow HA1 2UW. Tel: 0181-424 1304. *Director,* P. Osburn

HAVERING, The Broxhill Centre, Broxhill Road, Harold Hill, Romford RM14 1XN. Tel: 01708-773839. *Executive Director Children and Lifelong Learning,* S. Evans

HILLINGDON, Civic Centre, High Street, Uxbridge UB8 1UW. Tel: 01895-250528. *Director,* P. O'Hear

HOUNSLOW, Civic Centre, Lampton Road, Hounslow, Middx TW3 4DN. Tel: 0181-862 5352. *Director,* J. D. Tricket

*ISLINGTON, Laycock Street, Islington, London N1 1TH. Tel: 0171-527 5753. *Director,* A. Roberts

*KENSINGTON AND CHELSEA, Town Hall, Hornton Street, London W8 7NX. Tel: 0171-361 3303. *Director,* R. Wood

KINGSTON UPON THAMES, Guildhall 2, Kingston upon Thames KT1 1EU. Tel: 0181-547 5220. *Director,* J. Braithwaite

*LAMBETH, International House, Canterbury Crescent, London SW9 7QE. Tel: 0171-926 1000. *Director,* Ms H. Du Quesnay

*LEWISHAM, 3rd Floor, Laurence House, 1 Catford Road, London SE6 4RU. Tel: 0181-314 8527. *Director,* Ms A. Efunshile

MERTON, Civic Centre, London Road, Morden, Surrey SM4 5DX. Tel: 0181-545 3251. *Director,* Ms J. Cairns

NEWHAM, Broadway House, 322 High Street, Stratford, London E15 1AJ. Tel: 0181-555 5552. *Director,* I. Harrison

REDBRIDGE, Lynton House, 255–259 High Road, Ilford, Essex IG1 1NY. Tel: 0181-478 3020. *Chief Education Officer,* D. Capper

RICHMOND UPON THAMES, 1st Floor, Regal House, London Road, Twickenham TW1 3QS. Tel: 0181-891 7500. *Chief Executive (acting),* R. Hancock

*SOUTHWARK, 1 Bradenham Close, London SE17 2QA. Tel: 0171-525 5050. *Director Education and Leisure Services,* G. Mott

SUTTON, The Grove, Carshalton, Surrey SM5 3AL. Tel: 0181-770 5000. *Strategic Director,* Dr I. Birnbaum

*TOWER HAMLETS, Mulberry Place, 5 Clove Crescent, London E14 2BG. Tel: 0171-364 5000. *Director of Education and Community Services,* Ms C. Gilbert

WALTHAM FOREST, Leyton Municipal Offices, High Road, Leyton, London E10 5QJ. Tel: 0181-527 5544 ext. 5001. *Chief Education Officer,* A. Lockhart

*WANDSWORTH, Town Hall, Wandsworth High Street, London SW18 2PU. Tel: 0181-871 8013. *Director,* P. Robinson

WALES

ANGLESEY, Swyddfa'r Sir, Llangefni, Anglesey LL77 7EY. Tel: 01248-752921. *Director,* R. P. Jones

BLAENAU GWENT, Festival House, Victoria Business Park, Ebbw Vale NP23 6ER. Tel: 01495-355434. *Director,* B. Mawby

BRIDGEND, Sunnyside, Sunnyside Road, Bridgend CF31 4AR. Tel: 01656-642600. *Director,* D. Matthews

CAERPHILLY, Council Offices, Caerphilly Road, Ystrad Mynach, Hengoed CF82 7EP. Tel: 01443-815588. *Director,* N. Harries

CARDIFF, County Hall, Atlantic Wharf, Cardiff CF1 5UW. Tel: 01222-872700. *Director,* T. Davies

CARMARTHENSHIRE, Pibwrlwyd, Carmarthen SA31 2NH. Tel: 01267-224501. *Director,* K. Davies

CEREDIGION, Swyddfa'r Sir, Marine Terrace, Aberystwyth SY23 2DE. Tel: 01970-633600. *Director,* R. Williams

CONWY, Government Buildings, Dinerth Road, Rhos-on-Sea LL28 4UL. Tel: 01492-575031. *Director,* R. E. Williams

DENBIGHSHIRE, Phase 4, County Hall, Mold, Flintshire CH7 6GR. Tel: 01824-706777. *Director,* E. Lewis

FLINTSHIRE, County Hall, Mold CH7 6NW. Tel: 01352-704010. *Director of Education, Libraries and Information,* K. McDonogh

GWYNEDD, Shirehall Street, Caernarfon LL55 1SH. Tel: 01286-677162. *Director,* D. Whittall

MERTHYR TYDFIL, Ty Keir Hardie, Riverside Court, Avenue De Clichy, Merthyr Tydfil CF47 8XD. Tel: 01685-724614. *Director*, D. Jones

MONMOUTHSHIRE, County Hall, Cwmbran NP44 2XH. Tel: 01633-644487. *Director*, D. Young

NEATH PORT TALBOT, Civic Centre, Port Talbot SA13 1PJ. Tel: 01639-763298. *Director*, V. Thomas

NEWPORT, Civic Centre, Newport NP20 4UR. Tel: 01633-232204. *Director*, G. Bingham

PEMBROKESHIRE, County Hall, Haverfordwest SA61 1TP. Tel: 01437-764551. *Director*, G. Davies

POWYS, County Hall, Llandrindod Wells LD1 5LG. Tel: 01597-826000. *Director*, M. Barker

RHONDDA, CYNON, TAFF, Education Centre, Grawen Street, Porth CF39 0BU. Tel: 01443-687666. *Director*, vacant

SWANSEA, County Hall, Oystermouth Road, Swansea SA1 3SN. Tel: 01792-636351. *Director*, R. Parry

TORFAEN, County Hall, Croesyceiliog, Cwmbran, Torfaen NP44 2WR. Tel: 01633-648069. *Director*, M. de Val

VALE OF GLAMORGAN, Civic Offices, Holton Road, Barry CF63 4RU. Tel: 01446-709138. *Director*, A. Davies

WREXHAM, Roxburgh House, Hill Street, Wrexham LL11 1SN. Tel: 01978-297420. *Director*, T. Garner

SCOTLAND

ABERDEEN CITY, Summerhill Education Centre, Stronsay Drive, Aberdeen AB15 6JA. Tel: 01224-346060. *Director*, J. Stodter

ABERDEENSHIRE, Woodhill House, Westburn Road, Aberdeen AB16 5GB. Tel: 01224-665420. *Director*, M. White

ANGUS, County Buildings, Market Street, Forfar DD8 3WE. Tel: 01307-461460. *Director*, J. Anderson

ARGYLL AND BUTE, Argyll House, Alexandra Parade, Dunoon PA23 8AG. Tel: 01369-704000. *Director*, A. Morton

CITY OF EDINBURGH, Wellington Court, 10 Waterloo Place, Edinburgh EH1 3EG. Tel: 0131-469 3000. *Director*, R. Jobson

CLACKMANNANSHIRE, Lime Tree House, Alloa FK10 1EX. Tel: 01259-452431. *Director*, K. Bloomer

DUMFRIES AND GALLOWAY, Education Department, 30 Edinburgh Road, Dumfries DG1 1JG. Tel: 01387-260000. *Director (acting)*, F. Sanderson

DUNDEE CITY, 8th Floor, Tayside House, Crichton Street, Dundee DD1 3RJ. Tel: 01382-434000. *Director*, Ms A. Wilson

EAST AYRSHIRE, Council Headquarters, London Road, Kilmarnock KA3 7BU. Tel: 01563-576017. *Director*, J. Mulgrew

EAST DUNBARTONSHIRE, Boclair House, 100 Milngavie Road, Bearsden, Glasgow G61 2TQ. Tel: 0141-578 8000. *Director*, I. Mills

EAST LOTHIAN, John Muir House, Haddington EH41 3HA. Tel: 01620-827562. *Director*, A. Blackie

EAST RENFREWSHIRE, Council Offices, Eastwood Park, Rouken Glen Road, Giffnock G46 6UG. Tel: 0141-577 3431. *Director*, Mrs E. J. Currie

EILEAN SIAR/WESTERN ISLES, Council Offices, Sandwick Road, Stornoway, Isle of Lewis HS1 2BW. Tel: 01851-703773. *Director (acting)*, M. Macleod

FALKIRK, McLaren House, Marchmont Avenue, Polmont, Falkirk FK2 0NZ. Tel: 01324-506600. *Director*, Dr G. Young

FIFE, Rothesay House, North Street, Glenrothes KY7 5PN. Tel: 01592-413656. *Director*, A. McKay

GLASGOW CITY, Nye Bevan House, 20 India Street, Glasgow G2 4PF. Tel: 0141-287 6898. *Director*, K. Corsar

HIGHLAND, Council Buildings, Glenurquhart Road, Inverness IV3 5NX. Tel: 01463-702802. *Director*, B. Robertson

INVERCLYDE, 105 Dalrymple Street, Greenock PA15 1HT. Tel: 01475-712824. *Director*, B. McLeary

MIDLOTHIAN, Fairfield House, 8 Lothian Road, Dalkeith EH22 3ZJ. Tel: 0131-270 7500. *Director*, D. MacKay

MORAY, Council Offices, High Street, Elgin IV30 1BX. Tel: 01343-563170. *Director*, K. Gavin

NORTH AYRSHIRE, Cunninghame House, Irvine KA12 8EE. Tel: 01294-324400. *Director*, J. Travers

NORTH LANARKSHIRE, Municipal Buildings, Kildonan Street, Coatbridge ML5 3BT. Tel: 01236-812222. *Director*, M. O'Neill

ORKNEY ISLANDS, Council Offices, School Place, Kirkwall, Orkney KW15 1NY. Tel: 01856-873535. *Director*, L. Manson

PERTH AND KINROSS, Blackfriars, Perth PH1 5LU. Tel: 01738-476200. *Director*, R. McKay

RENFREWSHIRE, Council Headquarters, South Building, Cotton Street, Paisley PA1 1LE. Tel: 0141-842 5601. *Director*, Ms S. Rae

SCOTTISH BORDERS, Council Headquarters, Newtown St Boswells, Melrose, Roxburghshire TD6 0SA. Tel: 01835-824000. *Director*, J. Christie

SHETLAND ISLANDS, Hayfield House, Hayfield Lane, Lerwick, Shetland ZE1 0QD. Tel: 01595-744000. *Director*, J. Halcrow

SOUTH AYRSHIRE, County Buildings, Wellington Square, Ayr KA7 1DR. Tel: 01292-612000. *Director*, M. McCabe

SOUTH LANARKSHIRE, Council Headquarters, Almada Street, Hamilton ML3 0AA. Tel: 01698-454545. *Executive Director*, Ms M. Allan

STIRLING, Viewforth, Stirling FK8 2ET. Tel: 01786-442678. *Director*, G. Jeyes

WEST DUNBARTONSHIRE, Garshake Road, Dumbarton G82 3PU. Tel: 01389-737301. *Director*, I. McMurdo

WEST LOTHIAN, Lindsay House, South Bridge Street, Bathgate EH48 1TS. Tel: 01506-776000. *Corporate Manager*, R. Stewart

NORTHERN IRELAND

EDUCATION AND LIBRARY BOARDS

BELFAST, 40 Academy Street, Belfast BT1 2NQ. Tel: 01232-564122. *Chief Executive*, D. Cargo

NORTH, County Hall, 182 Galgorm Road, Ballymena, Co. Antrim BT42 1HN. Tel: 01266-653333. *Chief Executive*, G. Topping

SOUTH EASTERN, Grahamsbridge Road, Dundonald BT16 2HS. Tel: 01232-381188. *Chief Executive*, J. B. Fitzsimons

SOUTHERN, 3 Charlemont Place, The Mall, Armagh BT61 9AX. Tel: 01861-512200. *Chief Executive*, Mrs H. McClenagahan

WESTERN, 1 Hospital Road, Omagh, Co. Tyrone BT79 0AW. Tel: 01662-411411. *Chief Executive*, P. J. Martin

ISLANDS

GUERNSEY, Grange Road, St Peter Port, Guernsey GY1 1RQ. Tel: 01481-710821. *Director*, D. T. Neale

JERSEY, PO Box 142, Jersey JE4 8QJ. Tel: 01534-509500. *Director*, T. W. McKeon

ISLE OF MAN, Murray House, 5–11 Mount Havelock, Douglas, Isle of Man IM1 2SG. Tel: 01624-685820. *Director*, R. B. Cowin

ISLES OF SCILLY, Town Hall, St Mary's, Isles of Scilly TR21 0LW. Tel: 01720-422537 ext. 145. *Secretary for Education*, P. S. Hygate

ADVISORY BODIES

SCHOOLS

EDUCATION OTHERWISE, PO Box 7420, London N9 9SG.
Tel: Helpline: 0870-730 0074

BRITISH EDUCATIONAL COMMUNICATIONS AND
TECHNOLOGY AGENCY (formerly National Council
for Educational Technology), Milburn Hill Road,
Science Park, Coventry CV4 7JJ. Tel: 01203-416994.
Chief Executive, O. Lynch

INTERNATIONAL BACCALAUREATE ORGANIZATION,
Peterson House, Fortran Road, St Mellons, Cardiff
CF3 0WB. Tel: 01222-774000. *Director of Academic Affairs,*
Dr H. Drennen

NATIONAL ADVISORY COUNCIL FOR EDUCATION AND
TRAINING TARGETS, Dunford Lodge, Storth Lane,
Ranmoor, Sheffield S10 3HN. Tel: 0114-259 7887.
Director, J. Dewsbury

SCOTTISH COUNCIL FOR EDUCATIONAL
TECHNOLOGY, 74 Victoria Crescent Road, Glasgow
G12 9JN. Tel: 0141-337 5000. *Chief Executive,* R. Pietrasik

SPECIAL EDUCATIONAL NEEDS TRIBUNAL, 7th Floor,
Windsor House, 50 Victoria Street, London SW1H 0NW.
Tel: 0171-925 6925. *President,* T. Aldridge; *Secretary,*
P. Craggs

INDEPENDENT SCHOOLS

GOVERNING BODIES ASSOCIATION, The Ancient
Foresters, Bush End, Takeley, Bishop's Stortford, Herts
CM22 6NN. Tel: 01279-871865. *Chief Executive,*
F. V. Morgan

GOVERNING BODIES OF GIRLS' SCHOOLS
ASSOCIATION, The Ancient Foresters, Bush End,
Takeley, Bishop's Stortford, Herts CM22 6NN. Tel:
01279-871865. *Chief Executive,* F. V. Morgan

INDEPENDENT SCHOOLS COUNCIL, Grosvenor Gardens
House, 35–37 Grosvenor Gardens, London SW1W 0BS.
Tel: 0171-798 1590. *General Secretary,* Dr A. B. Cooke

INDEPENDENT SCHOOLS EXAMINATIONS BOARD,
Jordan House, Christchurch Road, New Milton, Hants
BH25 6QJ. Tel: 01425-621111. *Secretary-General,*
Mrs J. Williams

INDEPENDENT SCHOOLS INFORMATION SERVICE, 21
Melville Street, Edinburgh EH3 7PE. Tel: 0131-220 2106.
Administrator, Mrs F. Valpy

INDEPENDENT SCHOOLS INFORMATION SERVICE, 35-
37 Grosvenor Gardens, London SW1W 0BS. Tel: 0171-
798 1500. *Secretary,* Mrs C. Parrish

SCOTTISH COUNCIL OF INDEPENDENT SCHOOLS, 21
Melville Street, Edinburgh EH3 7PE. Tel: 0131-220 2106.
Director, Mrs J. Sischy

FURTHER EDUCATION

FURTHER EDUCATION DEVELOPMENT AGENCY
(FEDA), Citadel Place, Tinworth Street, London
SE11 5EH. Tel: 0171-840 5400. *Chief Executive,* C. Hughes

Regional Advisory Councils

ASSOCIATION OF COLLEGES IN THE EASTERN REGION,
Merlin Place, Milton Road, Cambridge CB4 0DP. Tel:
01223-424022. *Chief Executive,* J. Graystone

CENTRA (EDUCATION AND TRAINING SERVICES) LTD,
Duxbury Park, Duxbury Hall Road, Chorley, Lancs
PR7 4AT. Tel: 01257-241428. *Chief Executive,* P. Wren;
Chairman, R. Chapman

EMFEC (East Midland Further Education Council),
Robins Wood House, Robins Wood Road, Aspley,
Nottingham NG8 3NH. Tel: 0115-929 3291. *Chief
Executive,* Ms J. Gardiner

NCFE (formerly Northern Council for Further
Education), Portland House, 2nd Floor, Block D, New
Bridge Street, Newcastle upon Tyne NE1 8AN. Tel:
0191-201 3100. *Chief Executive,* J. F. Pearce

SOUTHERN REGIONAL COUNCIL FOR EDUCATION AND
TRAINING, Building 33, The University of Reading,
London Road, Reading RG1 5AQ. Tel: 0118-931 6320.
Chief Executive, B. J. Knowles

SOUTH WEST ASSOCIATION FOR EDUCATION AND
TRAINING, Bishops Hull House, Bishops Hull,
Taunton, Somerset TA1 5RA. Tel: 01823-335491. *Chief
Executive,* Ms L. McGrath

WELSH JOINT EDUCATION COMMITTEE, 245 Western
Avenue, Cardiff CF5 2YX. Tel: 01222-265000.
Examinations Secretary, B. Evans

YORKSHIRE AND HUMBERSIDE ASSOCIATION FOR
FURTHER AND HIGHER EDUCATION, 13 Wellington
Road East, Dewsbury, W. Yorks WF13 1XG. Tel: 01924-
450900. *Director (acting),* C. Daniel

HIGHER EDUCATION

ASSOCIATION OF COMMONWEALTH UNIVERSITIES,
John Foster House, 36 Gordon Square, London
WC1H 0PF. Tel: 0171-387 8572. *Secretary-General,*
Prof. M. G. Gibbons

COMMITTEE OF SCOTTISH HIGHER EDUCATION
PRINCIPALS (COSHEP), 53 Hanover Street,
Edinburgh EH2 2PJ. Tel: 0131-226 1111. *Secretary,*
Dr R. L. Crawford

COMMITTEE OF VICE-CHANCELLORS AND PRINCIPALS
OF THE UNIVERSITIES OF THE UNITED KINGDOM,
Woburn House, 20 Tavistock Square, London
WC1H 9HQ. Tel: 0171-419 4111. *Chairman,* H. Newby;
Chief Executive, Ms D. Warwick

NORTHERN IRELAND HIGHER EDUCATION COUNCIL,
Rathgael House, Balloo Road, Bangor BT19 7PR. Tel:
01247-279333. *Chairman,* Sir Kenneth Bloomfield, KCB

QUALITY ASSURANCE AGENCY FOR HIGHER
EDUCATION, Southgate House, Southgate Street,
Gloucester GL1 1UB. Tel: 01452-557000. *Chief Executive,*
J. Randall

SCOTTISH STUDENTSHIP ADVISORY GROUP, c/o
Student Awards Agency for Scotland, Gyleview House,
3 Redheughs Rigg, Edinburgh EH12 9HH. Tel: 0131-244
5846. *Chairman,* Prof. D. Harding; *Secretary,*
Mrs A. Hampson

CURRICULUM COUNCILS

AWDURDOD CYMWYSTERAU CWRICWLWM AC ASESU
CYMRU/QUALIFICATIONS, CURRICULUM AND
ASSESSMENT AUTHORITY FOR WALES, Castle
Buildings, Womanby Street, Cardiff CF1 9SX. Tel:
01222-375400. *Chief Executive,* J. V. Williams

NORTHERN IRELAND COUNCIL FOR THE
CURRICULUM, EXAMINATIONS AND ASSESSMENT,
Clarendon Dock, 29 Clarendon Road, Belfast BT1 3BG.
Tel: 01232-261200. *Acting Chief Executive,* Dr A. Hamill

QUALIFICATIONS AND CURRICULUM AUTHORITY, 29
Bolton Street, London W1Y 7PD. Tel: 0171-509 5555.
Chairman, Sir William Stubbs, PH.D.

SCOTTISH CONSULTATIVE COUNCIL ON THE
CURRICULUM, Gardyne Road, Broughty Ferry,
Dundee DD5 1NY. Tel: 01382-455053. *Chief Executive,*
M. Baughan

EXAMINING BODIES

UNITARY AWARDING BODIES

ASSESSMENT AND QUALIFICATIONS ALLIANCE (AQA). Tel: 0161-953 1180. *Publicity Officer,* Ms H. Hallett

THE EDEXCEL FOUNDATION, Stewart House, 32 Russell Square, London WC1B 5DN. Tel: 0171-393 4444. *Chief Executive,* Ms C. Townsend, PH.D.

OXFORD, CAMBRIDGE AND RSA EXAMINATIONS (OCR), 1 Regent Street, Cambridge CB2 1GG. Tel: 01223-552552. *Chief Executive,* B. Swift; *Chairman,* Dr K. Pretty

GCSE

THE EDEXCEL FOUNDATION, *see above*

NORTHERN EXAMINATIONS AND ASSESSMENT BOARD, Devas Street, Manchester M15 6EX. Tel: 0161-953 1180. *Chief Executive,* Miss H. M. James

NORTHERN IRELAND COUNCIL FOR THE CURRICULUM, EXAMINATIONS AND ASSESSMENT. Tel: 01232-261200. *Chief Executive,* Dr A. Hamill

OXFORD, CAMBRIDGE AND RSA EXAMINATIONS

SEG (SOUTHERN EXAMINING GROUP), Stag Hill House, Guildford, Surrey GU2 5XJ. Tel: 01483-506506. *Secretary-General,* Dr C. P. Hughes

WELSH JOINT EDUCATION COMMITTEE, 245 Western Avenue, Cardiff CF5 2YX. Tel: 01222-265000. *Chief Executive,* I. Hume

A-LEVEL

THE ASSOCIATED EXAMINING BOARD, Stag Hill House, Guildford, Surrey GU2 5XJ. Tel: 01483-506506. *Secretary-General,* Dr C. P. Hughes

THE EDEXCEL FOUNDATION, *see above*

NORTHERN EXAMINATIONS AND ASSESSMENT BOARD, Devas Street, Manchester M15 6EX. Tel: 0161-953 1180. *Chief Executive,* Ms H. M. James; *Secretary,* J. Coote

NORTHERN IRELAND COUNCIL FOR THE CURRICULUM, EXAMINATIONS AND ASSESSMENT, Clarendon Dock, 29 Clarendon Road, Belfast BT1 3BG. Tel: 01232-261200. *Chief Executive,* Mrs C. Coxhead

OXFORD, CAMBRIDGE AND RSA EXAMINATIONS

WELSH JOINT EDUCATION COMMITTEE, 245 Western Avenue, Cardiff CF5 2YX. Tel: 01222-265000. *Chief Executive,* I. Hume

SCOTLAND

SCOTTISH QUALIFICATIONS AUTHORITY, Hanover House, 24 Douglas Street, Glasgow G2 7NQ. Tel: 0141-248 7900. *Chief Executive,* R. Tuck; *Chairman,* D. Miller

FURTHER EDUCATION

CITY & GUILDS, 1 Giltspur Street, London EC1A 9DD. Tel: 0171-294 2468. *Director-General,* N. Carey, PH.D.

THE EDEXCEL FOUNDATION, *see above*

OXFORD, CAMBRIDGE AND RSA EXAMINATIONS

FUNDING COUNCILS

SCHOOLS

FUNDING AGENCY FOR SCHOOLS, Albion Wharf, 25 Skeldergate, York YO1 2XL. Tel: 01904-661661. *Chairman,* Vice-Adm. Sir Antony Tippett, KCB

FURTHER EDUCATION

FURTHER EDUCATION FUNDING COUNCIL FOR ENGLAND, Cheylesmore House, Quinton Road, Coventry CV1 2WT. Tel: 01203-863000. *Chief Executive,* Prof. D. Melville

FURTHER EDUCATION FUNDING COUNCIL FOR WALES, Linden Court, The Orchards, Ty Glas Avenue, Cardiff CF14 5DZ. Tel: 01222-761861. *Chief Executive,* Prof. J. Andrews

SCOTTISH FURTHER EDUCATION FUNDING COUNCIL, Donaldson House, 97 Haymarket Terrace, Edinburgh EH12 5HD. Tel: 0131-313 6590. *Chief Executive,* Prof. J. Sizer, CBE

HIGHER EDUCATION

HIGHER EDUCATION FUNDING COUNCIL FOR ENGLAND, Northavon House, Coldharbour Lane, Bristol BS16 1QD. Tel: 0117-931 7317. *Chief Executive,* Sir Brian Fender, Kt.

HIGHER EDUCATION FUNDING COUNCIL FOR WALES, Linden Court, The Orchards, Ty Glas Avenue, Cardiff CF14 5DZ. Tel: 01222-761861. *Chief Executive,* Prof. J. A. Andrews

SCOTTISH HIGHER EDUCATION FUNDING COUNCIL, Donaldson House, 97 Haymarket Terrace, Edinburgh EH12 5HD. Tel: 0131-313 6500. *Chief Executive,* Prof. J. Sizer, CBE; *Secretary,* L. Howells

STUDENT AWARDS AGENCY FOR SCOTLAND, Gyleview House, 3 Redheughs Rigg, Edinburgh EH12 9HH. Tel: 0131-244 5868. *Chief Executive,* K. MacRae

STUDENT LOANS COMPANY LTD, 100 Bothwell Street, Glasgow G2 7JD. Tel: 0141-306 2000. *Chief Executive,* C. Ward

TEACHER TRAINING AGENCY, Portland House, Stag Place, London SW1E 5TT. Tel: 0171-925 3700. *Chairman,* Prof. C. Booth

ADMISSIONS AND COURSE INFORMATION

CAREERS RESEARCH AND ADVISORY CENTRE, Sheraton House, Castle Park, Cambridge CB3 0AX. Tel: 01223-460277. *Chief Executive,* D. McGregor

COMMITTEE OF SCOTTISH HIGHER EDUCATION PRINCIPALS (COSHEP), St Andrew House, 141 West Nile Street, Glasgow G1 2RN. Tel: 0141-353 1880. *Secretary,* Dr R. L. Crawford

GRADUATE TEACHER TRAINING REGISTRY, Rosehill, New Barn Lane, Cheltenham, Glos GL52 3LZ. Tel: 01242-544600. *Registrar,* Mrs M. Griffiths; *Chief Executive,* Ms A. Millett

SOCIAL WORK ADMISSIONS SYSTEM, Rosehill, New Barn Lane, Cheltenham, Glos GL52 3LZ. Tel: 01242-544600. *Admissions Officer,* Mrs M. Griffiths

UNIVERSITIES AND COLLEGES ADMISSIONS SERVICE, Rosehill, New Barn Lane, Cheltenham, Glos GL52 3LZ. Tel: 01242-222444. *Chief Executive,* M. A. Higgins, PH.D.

UNIVERSITIES

THE UNIVERSITY OF ABERDEEN (1495)
Regent Walk, Aberdeen AB24 3FX
Tel 01224-272000
Full-time students (1998–9), 11,061
Chancellor, The Lord Wilson of Tillyorn, GCMG (1997)
Vice-Chancellor and Principal, Prof. C. D. Rice
Secretary, S. Cannon
Rector, Miss C. Dickson Wright

THE UNIVERSITY OF ABERTAY DUNDEE (1994)
Bell Street, Dundee DD1 1HG
Tel 01382-308000
Full-time students (1998–9), 3,957
Chancellor, The Earl of Airlie, KT, GCVO, PC (1994)
Vice-Chancellor and Principal, Prof. B. King
Registrar, Dr D. Button
Secretary, D. Hogarth

ANGLIA POLYTECHNIC UNIVERSITY (1992)
Bishop Hall Lane, Chelmsford CM1 1SQ
Tel 01245-493131
Full-time students (1998–9), 16,800
Chancellor, The Lord Prior, PC (1992)
Vice-Chancellor, M. Malone-Lee, CB
Secretary, S. G. Bennett

ASTON UNIVERSITY (1966)
Aston Triangle, Birmingham B4 7ET
Tel 0121-359 3611
Full-time students (1998–9), 4,710
Chancellor, Sir Adrian Cadbury (1979)
Vice-Chancellor, Prof. M. Wright
Registrar and Secretary, R. D. A. Packham

THE UNIVERSITY OF BATH (1966)
Claverton Down, Bath BA2 7AY
Tel 01225-826826
Full-time students (1998–9), 7,475
Chancellor, The Lord Tugendhat (1998)
Vice-Chancellor, Prof. V. D. Vandelinde
Registrar, J. A. Bursey

THE UNIVERSITY OF BIRMINGHAM (1900)
Edgbaston, Birmingham B15 2TT
Tel 0121-414 3344
Full-time students (1998–9), 20,000
Chancellor, Sir Alexander Jarratt, CB (1983)
Vice-Chancellor, Prof. M. Irvine, PH.D., FRSE
Registrar and Secretary, D. J. Allen

BOURNEMOUTH UNIVERSITY (1992)
Talbot Campus, Fern Barrow, Poole BH12 5BB
Tel 01202-524111
Full-time students (1998–9), 7,714
Chancellor, The Baroness Cox (1992)
Vice-Chancellor, Prof. G. Slater
Registrar, N. O. G. Richardson

THE UNIVERSITY OF BRADFORD (1966)
Bradford BD7 1DP
Tel 01274-232323
Full-time students (1998–9), 7,517
Chancellor, The Baroness Lockwood (1997)
Vice-Chancellor, Prof. C. Bell
Registrar and Secretary, N. J. Andrew

THE UNIVERSITY OF BRIGHTON (1992)
Mithras House, Lewes Road, Brighton BN2 4AT
Tel 01273-600900
Full-time students (1998–9), 9,750
Academic Registrar, P. Reynolds
Deputy Director, D. E. House
Director, Prof. Sir David Watson
Rector, C. Lawlor

THE UNIVERSITY OF BRISTOL (1909)
Senate House, Tyndall Avenue, Bristol BS8 1TH
Tel 0117-928 9000
Full-time students (1998–9), 12,224
Chancellor, Sir Jeremy Morse, KCMG (1989)
Vice-Chancellor, Sir John Kingman, FRS

Registrar, D. Pretty
Secretary, Ms K. E. McKenzie, D.PHIL.

BRUNEL UNIVERSITY (1966)
Uxbridge, Middx UB8 3PH
Tel 01895-274000
Full-time students (1998–9), 12,320
Chancellor, The Lord Wakeham, PC (1998)
Vice-Chancellor and Principal, Prof. M. J. H. Sterling, PH.D, FRENG.
Academic Registrar, J. B. Alexander

THE UNIVERSITY OF BUCKINGHAM (1983)
Buckingham MK18 1EG
Tel 01280-814080
Full-time students (1998–9), 584
Chancellor, Sir Martin Jacomb (1998)
Vice-Chancellor, Prof. R. H. Taylor
Registrar and Secretary, S. Cooksey

THE UNIVERSITY OF CAMBRIDGE
University Offices, The Old Schools, Cambridge CB2 1TN
Tel 01223-337733
Undergraduates (1998–9) 17,350

UNIVERSITY OFFICERS, ETC.
Chancellor, HRH The Prince Philip, Duke of Edinburgh, KG, KT, OM, GBE, PC (1977)
Vice-Chancellor, Prof. Sir Alec Broers, FRS (1996)
High Steward, The Lord Runcie, PC, DD (1991)
Deputy High Steward,
    The Lord Richardson of Duntisbourne, MBE, TD, PC (1983)
Commissary, The Lord Oliver of Aylmerton (*Trinity Hall*), PC (1989)
Orator, A. J. Bowen (*Jesus*), (1993)
Librarian, P. K. Fox (*Selwyn*), (1994)
Director of the Fitzwilliam Museum, D. D. Robinson (*Clare*), (1995)
Registrary, T. J. Mead (*Wolfson*), PH.D. (1997)
Secretary-General of the Faculties, D. A. Livesey (*Emmanuel*), PH.D. (1992)
Treasurer, Mrs J. Womack (*Trinity Hall*), (1993)

COLLEGES AND HALLS, ETC.
with dates of foundation
CHRIST'S (1505), *Master,* A. J. Munro, PH.D. (1995)
CHURCHILL (1960), *Master,* Sir John Boyd, KCMG (1996)
CLARE (1326), *Master,* Prof. B. A. Hepple, LLD (1993)
CLARE HALL (1966), *President,*
    Prof. Dame Gillian Beer, DBE, Litt.D., FBA (1994)
CORPUS CHRISTI (1352), *Master,*
    Prof. Sir Tony Wrigley, PH.D. (1994)
DARWIN (1964), *Master,*
    Prof. Sir Geoffrey Lloyd, PH.D., FBA (1989)
DOWNING (1800), *Master,* Prof. D. A. King, FRS (1995)
EMMANUEL (1584), *Master,* Prof. J. E. Ffowcs-Williams, SC.D. (1996)
FITZWILLIAM (1966), *Master,* Prof. B. F. G. Johnston
GIRTON (1869), *Mistress,* Prof. A. M. Strathern, PH.D. (1998)
GONVILLE AND CAIUS (1348), *Master,* N. McKendrick (1996)
HOMERTON (1824) (for B.Ed. Students), *Principal,* Mrs K. B. Pretty, PH.D. (1991)
HUGHES HALL (1885) (for post-graduate students), *President,* Prof. P. Richards (1998)
JESUS (1496), *Master,* Prof. D. G. Crighton, SC.D., FRS (1997)
KING'S (1441), *Provost,* Prof. P. P. G. B. Bateson, SC.D., FRS (1987)

*Lucy Cavendish College (1965) (for women
   research students and mature and affiliated
   undergraduates), *President,*
   The Baroness Perry of Southwark (1994)
Magdalene (1542), *Master,*
   Prof. Sir John Gurdon, d.phil., frs (1995)
*New Hall (1954), *President,* Mrs A. Lonsdale (1996)
*Newnham (1871), *Principal,* Baroness O'Neill, cbe (1992)
Pembroke (1347), *Master,* Sir Roger Tomkys, kcmg
   (1992)
Peterhouse (1284), *Master,*
   Prof. Sir John Meurig Thomas, frs (1993)
Queens' (1448), *President,* The Lord Eatwell
Robinson (1977), *Warden,*
   Prof. the Lord Lewis of Newnham, sc.d., frs (1977)
Selwyn (1882), *Master,*
   Sir David Harrison, cbe, sc.d., freng. (1993)
Sidney Sussex (1596), *Master,* Prof. S. N. Dawson (1999)
St Catharine's (1473), *Master,*
   Prof. Sir Terence English (1993)
St Edmund's (1896), *Master,* Prof. R. B. Heap, sc.d.
   (1996)
St John's (1511), *Master,* Prof. P. Goddard, ph.d., frs
   (1994)
Trinity (1546), *Master,* Prof. A. K. Sen (1998)
Trinity Hall (1350), *Master,* Sir John Lyons, ph.d.
   (1984)
Wolfson (1965), *President,* G. Johnson ph.d. (1994)
*College for women only

UNIVERSITY OF CENTRAL ENGLAND IN
   BIRMINGHAM (1992)
Perry Barr, Birmingham b42 2su
Tel 0121-331 5000
Full-time students (1998–9), 10,750
Chancellor, I. McArdle
Vice-Chancellor, Dr P. C. Knight, cbe
Registrar and Secretary, Ms M. Penlington

UNIVERSITY OF CENTRAL LANCASHIRE (1992)
Preston pr1 2he
Tel 01772-201201
Full-time students (1998–9), 15,450
Chancellor, Sir Francis Kennedy, kcmg, cbe (1995)
Vice-Chancellor, Dr M. McVicar
Registrar, Ms L. Munro
Secretary, Mrs P. M. Ackroyd

CITY UNIVERSITY (1966)
Northampton Square, London ec1v 0hb
Tel 0171-477 8000
Full-time students (1998–9), 7,729
Chancellor, The Rt. Hon. the Lord Mayor of London
Vice-Chancellor, Prof. D. W. Rhind
Academic Registrar, A. H. Seville, ph.d.
Secretary, M. M. O'Hara

COVENTRY UNIVERSITY (1992)
Priory Street, Coventry cv1 5fb
Tel 01203-887688
Full-time students (1998–9), 16,000
Chancellor, The Lord Plumb, mep (1995)
Vice-Chancellor, Dr M. Goldstein, cbe, ph.d., d.sc.
Academic Registrar, Dr J. Gledhill, ph.d.
Secretary, Mrs L. Arlidge

CRANFIELD UNIVERSITY (1969)
Cranfield, Beds mk43 0al
Tel 01234-750111
Full-time students (1998–9), 2,248

Chancellor, The Lord Vincent of Coleshill, gbe, kcb, dso
   (1998)
Vice-Chancellor, Prof. F. R. Hartley, d.sc.
Academic Registrar and Secretary, D. J. Buck

DE MONTFORT UNIVERSITY (1992)
The Gateway, Leicester le1 9bh
Tel 0116-255 1551
Full-time students (1998–9), 17,350
Chancellor, Dr J. White (1998)
Vice-Chancellor, Prof. P. Tasker
Academic Registrar, V. E. Critchlow

UNIVERSITY OF DERBY (1993)
Kedleston Road, Derby de22 1gb
Tel 01332-622222
Full-time students (1998–9), 14,000
Chancellor, Sir Christopher Ball, frsa
Vice-Chancellor, Prof. R. Waterhouse
Registrar, Mrs J. Fry
Secretary, R. Gillis, frsa

THE UNIVERSITY OF DUNDEE (1967)
Dundee dd1 4hn
Tel 01382-344000
Full-time students (1998–9), 8,355
Chancellor, Sir James Black, frcp, frs (1992)
Vice-Chancellor and Principal, Dr I. J. Graham-Bryce
Secretary, R. Seaton
Rector, T. Slattery, 1998–2001

THE UNIVERSITY OF DURHAM
Old Shire Hall, Durham dh1 3hp
Tel 0191-374 2000
Full-time students (1998–9), 9,902
Chancellor, Sir Peter Ustinov, cbe, frsl
Vice-Chancellor, Prof. Sir Kenneth Calman, kcb, md, frcp,
   frcgp, frcr, frse, ph.d.
Registrar and Secretary, J. V. Hogan, ph.d.

Colleges

Collingwood *Principal,* Prof. G. H. Blake, ph.d.
Graduate Society *Principal,* M. Richardson, ph.d.
Grey *Master,* V. E. Watts
Hatfield *Master,* Prof. T. P. Burt, ph.d.
St Aidan's *Principal,* J. S. Ashworth
St Chad's *Principal,* Revd J. P. M. Cassidy, ph.d.
St Cuthbert's Society *Principal,* vacant
St Hild and St Bede *Principal,*
   Revd Prof. D. J. Davies, ph.d.
St John's *Principal,* Rt. Revd S. W. Sykes
St Mary's *Principal,* Miss J. L. Hobbs
Trevelyan *Principal,* Prof. M. Todd, d.litt
University *Master,* Prof. M. E. Tucker, ph.d.
Ushaw *President,* Revd J. O'Keefe
Van Mildert *Principal,* Prof. I. R. Taylor, ph.d.

THE UNIVERSITY OF EAST ANGLIA (1963)
Norwich nr4 7tj
Tel 01603-456161
Full-time students (1998–9), 11,730
Chancellor, Sir Geoffrey Allen, frs, freng. (1994)
Vice-Chancellor, V. Watts
Registrar and Secretary, B. Summers

UNIVERSITY OF EAST LONDON (1992)
Longbridge Road, Dagenham, Essex rm8 2as
Tel 0181-223 3000
Full-time students (1998–9), 12,500
Chancellor, The Lord Rix, cbe (1997)
Vice-Chancellor, Prof. F. W. Gould
Registrar and Secretary, A. Ingle

THE UNIVERSITY OF EDINBURGH (1583)
Old College, South Bridge, Edinburgh EH8 9YL
Tel 0131-650 1000
Full-time students (1998–9), 18,300
Chancellor, HRH The Prince Philip, Duke of Edinburgh,
    KG, KT, OM, GBE, PC, FRS (1952)
Vice-Chancellor and Principal, Prof. Sir Stewart Sutherland,
    FBA, FRSE
Secretary, M. J. B. Lowe, PH.D.
Rector, J. Colquhoun (1997–2000)

THE UNIVERSITY OF ESSEX (1964)
Wivenhoe Park, Colchester CO4 3SQ
Tel 01206-873333
Full-time students (1998–9), 5,710
Chancellor, The Lord Nolan, PC (1997)
Vice-Chancellor, Prof. I. Crewe
Registrar and Secretary, T. Rich, PH.D.

THE UNIVERSITY OF EXETER (1955)
Northcote House, The Queen's Drive, Exeter EX4 4QJ
Tel 01392-263263
Full-time students (1998–9), 9,140
Chancellor, The Lord Alexander of Weedon, QC (1998)
Vice-Chancellor, Sir Geoffrey Holland, KCB
Registrar and Secretary, I. H. C. Powell

UNIVERSITY OF GLAMORGAN (1992)
Treforest, Pontypridd CF37 1DL
Tel 01443-480480
Full-time students (1998–9), 10,657
Chancellor, The Lord Merlyn-Rees, PC, QC (1994)
Vice-Chancellor, Prof. A. L. Webb
Registrar, J. O'Shea
Secretary, J. L. Bracegirdle

THE UNIVERSITY OF GLASGOW (1451)
University Avenue, Glasgow G12 8QQ
Tel 0141-339 8855
Full-time students (1998–9), 19,900
Chancellor, Sir William Fraser, GCB, FRSE
Vice-Chancellor, Prof. Sir Graeme Davies, FREng, FRSE
Secretary, D. Mackie, FRSA
Rector, R. Kemp, 1999–2002

GLASGOW CALEDONIAN UNIVERSITY (1993)
Cowcaddens Road, Glasgow G4 0BA
Tel 0141-331 3000
Full-time students (1998–9), 8,500
Chancellor, The Lord Nickson, KBE (1993)
Vice-Chancellor and Principal, Dr I. A. Johnston, PH.D., CB
Head of Academic Registration, E. B. Ferguson

UNIVERSITY OF GREENWICH (1992)
Bexley Road, Eltham, London SE9 2PQ
Tel 0181-331 8000
Full-time students (1998–9), 14,007
Chancellor, Lord Holme of Cheltenham, CBE
Vice-Chancellor, Dr D. E. Fussey
Secretary, J. M. Charles

HERIOT-WATT UNIVERSITY (1966)
Riccarton, Edinburgh EH14 4AS
Tel 0131-449 5111
Full-time students (1998–9), 5,800, plus 9,000 full-time
    distance learning students
Chancellor, The Lord Mackay of Clashfern, PC, QC, FRSE
    (1979)
Vice-Chancellor and Principal, Prof. J. S. Archer, FREng.
Secretary, P. L. Wilson

UNIVERSITY OF HERTFORDSHIRE (1992)
College Lane, Hatfield, Herts AL10 9AB
Tel 01707-284000
Full-time students (1998–9), 18,015
Chancellor, The Lord MacLaurin of Knebworth (1996)
Vice-Chancellor, Prof. N. K. Buxton
Registrar and Secretary, P. G. Jeffreys

UNIVERSITY OF HUDDERSFIELD (1992)
Queensgate, Huddersfield HD1 3DH
Tel 01484-422288
Full-time students (1998–9), 17,000
Chancellor, Sir Ernest Hall, OBE (1996)
Vice-Chancellor, Prof. J. R. Tarrant
Registrar and Secretary, Mrs M. H. Andrew

THE UNIVERSITY OF HULL (1954)
Cottingham Road, Hull HU6 7RX
Tel 01482-346311
Full-time students (1998–9), 10,800
Chancellor, The Lord Armstrong of Ilminster, GCB, CVO
    (1994)
Vice-Chancellor, Prof. D. N. Dilks, FRSL
Registrar and Secretary, D. J. Lock

KEELE UNIVERSITY (1962)
Newcastle under Lyme, Staffs ST5 5BG
Tel 01782-621111
Full-time students (1998–9), 6,400
Chancellor, Sir Claus Moser, KCB, CBE, FBA (1986)
Vice-Chancellor, Prof. J. V. Finch, CBE
Registrar and Secretary, S. J. Morris

THE UNIVERSITY OF KENT AT CANTERBURY
    (1965)
Canterbury CT2 7NZ
Tel 01227-764000
Full-time students (1998–9), 7,185
Chancellor, Sir Crispin Tickell, GCMG, KCVO
Vice-Chancellor, Prof. R. Sibson, PH.D.
Registrar and Secretary, N. A. McHard

KINGSTON UNIVERSITY (1992)
Kingston upon Thames, Surrey KT1 1LQ
Tel 0181-547 2000
Full-time students (1998–9), 14,000
Chancellor, Sir Frank Lampl
Vice-Chancellor, Prof. P. Scott
Registrar, Ms A. M. Stokes
Secretary, R. S. Abdulla, MBE

THE UNIVERSITY OF LANCASTER (1964)
Bailrigg, Lancaster LA1 4YW
Tel 01524-65201
Full-time students (1998–9), 8,684
Chancellor, HRH Princess Alexandra, the Hon. Lady Ogilvy,
    GCVO (1964)
Vice-Chancellor, Prof. W. Ritchie, OBE
Academic Registrar, Mrs M. McClintock
Secretary, Ms F. Aiken

THE UNIVERSITY OF LEEDS (1904)
Leeds LS2 9JT
Tel 0113-243 1751
Full-time students (1998–9), 23,244
Chancellor, Lord Bragg
Vice-Chancellor, Prof. A. G. Wilson
Registrar and Secretary, D. S. Robinson, PH.D.

LEEDS METROPOLITAN UNIVERSITY (1992)
Calverley Street, Leeds LS1 3HE
Tel 0113-283 2600
Full-time students (1998–9), 14,000
Chancellor, L. Silver (1989)
Vice-Chancellor, Prof. L. Wagner
Registrar, Ms C. Orange
Secretary, M. Wilkinson

THE UNIVERSITY OF LEICESTER (1957)
University Road, Leicester LE1 7RH
Tel 0116-252 2522
Full-time students (1998–9), 8,476
Chancellor, Sir Michael Atiyah, OM, FRS, Ph.D., D.SC (1995)
Vice-Chancellor, Prof. R. Burgess, Ph.D.
Registrar and Secretary, K. J. Julian

**UNIVERSITY OF LINCOLNSHIRE AND
    HUMBERSIDE**
Humberside campus: Hull HU6 7RT
Tel 01482-440550
Lincoln campus: Lincoln LN2 4VF
Tel 01522-882000
Full-time students (1998–9), 7,000
Chancellor, Dr J. H. Hooper, CBE
Vice-Chancellor, Prof. R. P. King
Registrar, F. Marks
Secretary, R. Graham

THE UNIVERSITY OF LIVERPOOL (1903)
Senate House, Abercromby Square, Liverpool L69 3BX
Tel 0151-794 2000
Full-time students (1998–9), 13,200
Chancellor, The Lord Owen, CH, PC (1996)
Vice-Chancellor, Prof. P. N. Love, CBE
Registrar and Secretary, M. D. Carr

LIVERPOOL JOHN MOORES UNIVERSITY (1992)
Rodney House, 70 Mount Pleasant, Liverpool L3 5UX
Tel 0151-231 2121
Full-time students (1998–9), 20,000
Chancellor, Ms C. Booth, QC
Vice-Chancellor, Prof. P. Toyne
Registrar and Secretary, Ms A. Wild

THE UNIVERSITY OF LONDON (1836)
Senate House, Malet Street, London WC1E 7HU
Tel 0171-862 8000
Internal students (1998–9), 102,000; External students,
    26,000
Chancellor, HRH The Princess Royal, KG, GCVO, FRS (1981)
Vice-Chancellor, Prof. G. Zellick, Ph.D.
Academic Registrar, Mrs G. F. Roberts
Director of Administration, J. R. Davidson
Chairman of the Council, The Lord Woolf, PC
Chairman of Convocation, D. D. A. Leslie
Visitor, HM The Queen in Council

COLLEGES

BIRKBECK COLLEGE, Malet Street, London WC1E 7HX.
    Master, Prof. T. O'Shea
CHARING CROSS AND WESTMINSTER MEDICAL
    SCHOOL, *see* Imperial College of Science, Technology
    and Medicine
GOLDSMITHS COLLEGE, Lewisham Way, New Cross,
    London SE14 6NW. *Warden,* Prof. B. Pimlott, FBA
HEYTHROP COLLEGE, Kensington Square, London
    W8 5HQ. *Principal,* Revd Dr J. McBade, SJ

IMPERIAL COLLEGE OF SCIENCE, TECHNOLOGY AND
    MEDICINE (includes Imperial College Schools of
    Medicine at Charing Cross, Hammersmith and St
    Mary's hospitals and at the National Heart and Lung
    Institute), South Kensington, London SW7 2AZ. *Rector,*
    Prof. Sir Ronald Oxburgh, KBE, FRS
KING'S COLLEGE LONDON, (includes King's College
    School of Medicine and Dentistry, United Medical and
    Dental Schools of Guy's and St Thomas' Hospitals),
    Strand, London WC2R 2LS. *Principal,* Prof. A. Lucas, Ph.D.
LONDON BUSINESS SCHOOL, Sussex Place, Regent's
    Park, London NW1 4SA. *Principal,* Prof. J. Quelch
THE LONDON HOSPITAL MEDICAL COLLEGE, *see*
    Queen Mary and Westfield College
LONDON SCHOOL OF ECONOMICS AND POLITICAL
    SCIENCE, Houghton Street, London WC2A 2AE. *Director,*
    Prof. A. Giddens
LONDON SCHOOL OF HYGIENE AND TROPICAL
    MEDICINE, Keppel Street, London WC1E 7HT. *Dean,*
    Prof. H. Spencer
LONDON SCHOOL OF JEWISH STUDIES, 44A Albert
    Road, London NW4 2SJ. *Principal,* Prof. D. H. Ruben
QUEEN MARY AND WESTFIELD COLLEGE,
    (incorporating St Bartholomew's and the Royal London
    School of Medicine and Dentistry and the London
    Hospital Medical College), Mile End Road, London
    E1 4NS. *Principal,* Prof. A. Smith
ROYAL FREE HOSPITAL SCHOOL OF MEDICINE, *see*
    University College London
ROYAL HOLLOWAY, Egham Hill, Egham, Surrey TW20
    0EX. *Principal,* Prof. N. Gower (until Feb 2000);
    Prof. D. Bone (from Feb 2000)
ROYAL POSTGRADUATE MEDICAL SCHOOL, *see* Imperial
    College of Science, Technology and Medicine
ROYAL VETERINARY COLLEGE, Royal College Street,
    London NW1 0TU. *Principal and Dean,*
    Prof. L. E. Lanyon, Ph.D.
SCHOOL OF ORIENTAL AND AFRICAN STUDIES,
    Thornhaugh Street, Russell Square, London WC1H 0XG.
    Director, Sir Tim Lankester, KCB
SCHOOL OF PHARMACY, 29–39 Brunswick Square,
    London WC1N 1AX. *Dean,*
    Prof. A. T. Florence, CBE, Ph.D., FRSE
ST BARTHOLOMEW'S AND THE ROYAL LONDON
    SCHOOL OF MEDICINE AND DENTISTRY, *see* Queen
    Mary and Westfield College
ST GEORGE'S HOSPITAL MEDICAL SCHOOL, Cranmer
    Terrace, London SW17 0RE. *Dean,* Prof. R. Boyd, FRCP
UNITED MEDICAL AND DENTAL SCHOOLS OF GUY'S
    AND ST THOMAS' HOSPITALS, *see* King's College
    London
UNIVERSITY COLLEGE LONDON, (including UCL
    Medical School), Gower Street, London WC1E 6BT.
    Provost, Prof. C. Llewellyn-Smith, FRS
WYE COLLEGE, Wye, near Ashford, Kent TN25 5AH.
    Principal, Prof. J. H. D. Prescott, Ph.D.

INSTITUTES

BRITISH INSTITUTE IN PARIS, 9–11 rue de Constantine,
    75340 Paris Cedex 07, France. *Director,*
    Prof. C. L. Campos, CBE, Ph.D. *London office:* Senate House,
    Malet Street, London WC1E 7HU
CENTRE FOR DEFENCE STUDIES, King's College
    London, Strand, London WC2R 2LS. *Director,*
    Prof. L. Freedman, CBE, FBA
COURTAULD INSTITUTE OF ART, North Block,
    Somerset House, Strand, London WC2R 0RN. *Director,*
    Prof. E. C. Fernie, CBE, FSA, FRSE
UNIVERSITY MARINE BIOLOGICAL STATION
    MILLPORT, Isle of Cumbrae, Scotland KA28 0EG.
    Director, Dr R. Ormond

School of Advanced Study, Senate House, Malet Street, London WCIE 7HU. *Dean*, Prof. T. C. Daintith Comprises:
Institute of Advanced Legal Studies, Charles Clore House, 17 Russell Square, London WCIB 5DR. *Director*, Prof. B. A. K. Rider
Institute of Cancer Research, Royal Cancer Hospital, Chester Beatty Laboratories, 17A Onslow Gardens, London SW7 3AL. *Chief Executive*, Dr P. Rigby
Institute of Classical Studies, Senate House, Malet Street, London WCIE 7HU. *Director*, Prof. G. B. Waywell, FSA
Institute of Commonwealth Studies, 27–28 Russell Square, London WCIB 5DS. *Director*, Prof. P. Caplan
Institute of Education, 20 Bedford Way, London WCIH 0AL. *Director*, Prof. P. Mortimore, OBE
Institute of English Studies, Senate House, Malet Street, London WCIE 7HU. *Director*, Prof. W. Gould
Institute of Germanic Studies, 29 Russell Square, London WCIB 5DP. *Director*, Prof. R. Görner
Institute of Historical Research, Senate House, Malet Street, London WCIE 7HU. *Director*, Prof. D. Cannadine
Institute of Latin American Studies, 31 Tavistock Square, London WCIH 9HA. *Director*, Prof. J. Dunkerley
Institute of Psychiatry, De Crespigny Park, Denmark Hill, London SE5 8AF. *Dean*, Prof. S. Checkley
Institute of Romance Studies, Senate House, Malet Street, London WCIE 7HU. *Director*, Prof. J. Labanyi
Institute of United States Studies, Senate House, Malet Street, London WCIE 7HU. *Director*, Prof. G. L. McDowell, PH.D.
Warburg Institute, Woburn Square, London WCIH 0AB. *Director*, Prof. C. N. J. Mann, PH.D., CBE

Associate Institutions

Institute of Zoology, Royal Zoological Society, Regent's Park, London NWI 4RY. *Director*, Prof. M. Gosling
Royal Academy of Music, Marylebone Road, London NWI 2BS. *Director*, Dr C. Price
Trinity College of Music, 11–13 Mandeville Place, London WIM 6AQ. *Principal*, G. Henderson

LONDON GUILDHALL UNIVERSITY (1993)
31 Jewry Street, London EC3N 2EY
Tel 0171-320 1000
Full-time students (1998–9), 14,387
Academic Registrar, Ms J. Grinstead
Deputy Provost, M. Weaver
Patron, HRH The Prince Philip, Duke of Edinburgh, KG, KT, OM, GBE, PC (1952)
Provost, Prof. R. Floud, D.phil.

LOUGHBOROUGH UNIVERSITY (1966)
Loughborough, Leics LEII 3TU
Tel 01509-263171
Full-time students (1998–9), 9,757
Chancellor, Sir Denis Rooke, CBE, FRS, FREng. (1989)
Vice-Chancellor, Prof. D.Wallace, FRS, FRSE
Registrar, vacant

UNIVERSITY OF LUTON (1993)
Park Square, Luton LUI 3JU
Tel 01582-734111
Full-time students (1998–9), 10,000
Chancellor, Sir David Plastow
Vice-Chancellor, Dr D. John
Registrar, R. Harris
Secretary, vacant

THE UNIVERSITY OF MANCHESTER
Manchester M13 9PL
Tel 0161-275 2000
Full-time students (1998–9), 18,968
Chancellor, The Lord Flowers, FRS (1994)
Vice-Chancellor, Prof. M. B. Harris, CBE, PH.D.
Registrar and Secretary, E. Newcomb

UNIVERSITY OF MANCHESTER INSTITUTE OF SCIENCE AND TECHNOLOGY (UMIST) (1824)
PO Box 88, Manchester M60 1QD
Tel 0161-236 3311
Full-time students (1998–9), 6,747
Chancellor, Prof. Sir Roland Smith, PH.D. (1995)
Vice-Chancellor, Prof. R. F. Boucher, FREng., PH.D.
Registrar and Secretary, P. C. C. Stephenson

MANCHESTER METROPOLITAN UNIVERSITY (1992)
All Saints, Manchester M15 6BH
Tel 0161-247 2000
Full-time students (1998–9), 20,000
Chancellor, The Duke of Westminster, OBE, TD (1993)
Vice-Chancellor, Mrs A. V. Burslem, OBE
Academic Registrar, J. D. M. Karczewski-Slowikowski
Secretary, T. A. Hendley

MIDDLESEX UNIVERSITY (1992)
White Hart Lane, London N17 8HR
Tel 0181-362 5000
Full-time students (1998–9), 19,365
Chancellor, The Baroness Platt of Writtle (1993)
Vice-Chancellor, Prof. M. Driscoll
Registrar, G. Jones

NAPIER UNIVERSITY (1992)
219 Colinton Road, Edinburgh EH14 1DJ
Tel 0131-444 2266
Full-time students (1998–9), 10,387
Chancellor, The Viscount Younger of Leckie, KT, KCVO, TD, PC, FRSE (1993)
Vice-Chancellor and Principal, Prof. J. Mavor
Secretary, Dr G. Webber

THE UNIVERSITY OF NEWCASTLE UPON TYNE
6 Kensington Terrace, Newcastle upon Tyne NEI 7RU
Tel 0191-222 6000
Full-time students (1998–9), 12,321
Chancellor, Rt. Hon. C. Patten, CH
Vice-Chancellor, J. R. G. Wright
Registrar, D. E. T. Nicholson

UNIVERSITY OF NORTH LONDON (1992)
166–220 Holloway Road, London N7 8DB
Tel 0171-607 2789
Full-time students (1998–9), 13,189
Vice-Chancellor, B. A. Roper
Registrar, Ms M. Storey
Secretary, J. McParland

UNIVERSITY OF NORTHUMBRIA AT
NEWCASTLE (1992)
Ellison Place, Newcastle upon Tyne NE1 8ST
Tel 0191-232 6002
Full-time students (1998–9), 13,500
Chancellor, The Lord Glenamara, CH, PC (1984)
Vice-Chancellor, Prof. G. Smith
Registrar, Ms C. Penna
Secretary, R. A. Bott
Rector, Revd. A. Shipton

THE UNIVERSITY OF NOTTINGHAM (1948)
University Park, Nottingham NG7 2RD
Tel 0115-951 5151
Full-time students (1998–9), 15,000
Chancellor, The Lord Dearing, CB (1993)
Vice-Chancellor, Prof. Sir Colin Campbell
Registrar, K. H. Jones

NOTTINGHAM TRENT UNIVERSITY (1992)
Burton Street, Nottingham NG1 4BU
Tel 0115-948 8418
Full-time students (1998–9), 20,838
Vice-Chancellor, Prof. R. Cowell, PH.D.
Academic Registrar, D. W. Samson
Secretary, D. Skellett

THE UNIVERSITY OF OXFORD
University Offices, Wellington Square, Oxford OX1 2JD
Tel 01865-270000
Students in residence 1998–9, 16,185
Chancellor, The Lord Jenkins of Hillhead (*Balliol*), *elected*
1987, OM, PC
Vice-Chancellor, Dr C. R. Lucas (*Balliol*), *elected* 1997
High Steward, The Lord Goff of Chieveley (*Lincoln* and
New College), *elected* 1990, PC
Proctors, Dr R. H. A. Jenkyns (*Lady Margaret Hall*); P. W.
Smith (*Pembroke*), *elected* 1999
Assessor, Prof. R. A. Mayou (*Nuffield*), *elected* 1999
Public Orator, Prof. J. Griffin (*Balliol*), *elected* 1992
Bodley's Librarian, R. P. Carr (*Balliol*), *elected* 1997
Keeper of Archives, D. G. Vaisey (*Exeter*), *elected* 1995
Director of the Ashmolean Museum, Dr C. Brown (*Worcester*),
elected 1998
Registrar of the University, D. R. Holmes (*St John's*), *elected*
1998
Surveyor to the University, P. M. R. Hill (*St Cross*), *elected*
1993
Secretary of Faculties, A. P. Weale (*Worcester*), *elected* 1984
Secretary of the Chest, J. R. Clements (*Merton*), *elected* 1995

OXFORD COLLEGES AND HALLS
with dates of foundation

ALL SOULS (1438), *Warden,* Prof. J. Davis, FBA, PH.D.
(1995)
BALLIOL (1263), *Acting Master,* A. Graham (1998)
BLACKFRIARS (1221), *Regent,* Revd F. G. Kerr (1998)
BRASENOSE (1509), *Principal,* The Lord Windlesham, BT,
CVO, PC, D.Litt (1989)
CAMPION HALL (1896), *Master,* Revd G. J. Hughes,
D.phil. (1998)
CHRIST CHURCH (1546), *Dean,* Very Revd J. H. Drury
(1991)
CORPUS CHRISTI (1517), *President,* Prof. Sir Keith
Thomas, FBA (1986)
EXETER (1314), *Rector,* Dr M. Butler (1993)
GREEN (1979), *Warden,* Sir John Hanson, KCMG, CBE
(1997)
GREYFRIARS (1910), *Warden,* Revd T. G. Weinandy, PH.D.
(1996)

HARRIS MANCHESTER (1786), *Principal,* Revd R. Waller,
PH.D. (1990)
HERTFORD (1874), *Principal,* Sir Walter Bodmer, FRS,
FRCpath. (1996)
JESUS (1571), *Principal,* Sir Peter North, CBE, QC, FBA
(1984)
KEBLE (1868), *Warden,* Dr A. Cameron, FBA, FSA (1994)
KELLOGG (1990), *President,* Dr G. P. Thomas (1990)
LADY MARGARET HALL (1878), *Principal,* Sir Brian Fall,
GVCO, KCMG (1995)
LINACRE (1962), *Principal,* Dr P. A. Slack, FBA (1996)
LINCOLN (1427), *Rector,* Dr W. E. K. Anderson, FRSE
(1994)
MAGDALEN (1458), *President,* A. D. Smith, CBE (1988)
MANSFIELD (1886), *Principal,* Prof. D. I. Marquand (1996)
MERTON (1264), *Warden,* Dr. J Rawson, CBE, FBA (1994)
NEW COLLEGE (1379), *Warden,* Dr. A. J. Ryan, FBA (1996)
NUFFIELD (1958), *Warden,* A. Atkinson, FBA (1994)
ORIEL (1326), *Provost,* Dr E. W. Nicholson, DD, FBA (1990)
PEMBROKE (1624), *Master,* Dr R. Stevens, DCL (1993)
QUEEN'S (1340), *Provost,* Sir Alan Budd (1999)
REGENT'S PARK (1810), *Principal,* Revd P. S. Fiddes,
D.phil. (1989)
SOMERVILLE (1879), *Principal,* Dame Fiona Caldicott,
DBE, FRCP, FRCPsych., FRCPI (1996)
ST ANNE'S (1952 (Society of Oxford Home-Students
(1879)), *Principal,* Mrs R. L. Deech (1991)
ST ANTONY'S (1953), *Warden,* Sir Marrack Goulding,
KCMG (1997)
ST BENET'S HALL (1897), *Master,* Revd H. Wansbrough,
OSB (1991)
ST CATHERINE'S (1963), *Master,* The Lord Plant of
Highfield (1994)
ST CROSS (1965), *Master,* Dr R. C. Repp (1987)
ST EDMUND HALL (*c.*1278), *Principal,* Prof. D. M. P.
Mingos (1999)
*ST HILDA'S (1893), *Principal,* Miss E. Llewellyn-Smith,
CB (1990)
ST HUGH'S (1886), *Principal,* D. Wood, CBE, QC (1991)
ST JOHN'S (1555), *President,* Dr W. Hayes (1987)
ST PETER'S (1929), *Master,* Dr J. P. Barron, FSA (1991)
TEMPLETON (1965), *President,* Sir David Rowland (1998)
TRINITY (1554), *President,* The Hon. Michael J. Beloff, QC
(1996)
UNIVERSITY (1249), *Master,* Baron Butler of Brockwell,
GCB, CVO (1998)
WADHAM (1610), *Warden,* J. S. Flemming, FBA (1993)
WOLFSON (1966), *President,* Sir David Smith, D.phil., FRS,
FRSE (1994)
WORCESTER (1714), *Provost,* R. G. Smethurst (1991)
WYCLIFFE HALL (1877), *Principal,* Revd A. E. McGrath,
D.phil. (1995)
*College for women only

OXFORD BROOKES UNIVERSITY (1993)
Headington, Oxford OX3 0BP
Tel 01865-484851
Full-time students (1998–9), 10,200
Chancellor, Baroness Kennedy of the Shaws, QC
Vice-Chancellor, Prof. G. Upton
Academic Registrar, Ms E. N. Winders

UNIVERSITY OF PAISLEY (1992)
Paisley PA1 2BE
Tel 0141-848 3000
Full-time students (1998–9), 8,500
Chancellor, Sir Robert Easton, CBE (1993)
Vice-Chancellor, Prof. R. W. Shaw, CBE
Registrar, D. Rigg
Secretary, J. Fraser

UNIVERSITY OF PLYMOUTH (1992)
Drake Circus, Plymouth PL4 8AA
Tel 01752-600600
Full-time students (1998–9), 15,424
Vice-Chancellor, Prof. J. Bull
Academic Registrar and Secretary, Miss J. Hopkinson

UNIVERSITY OF PORTSMOUTH (1992)
University House, Winston Churchill Avenue,
    Portsmouth PO1 2UP
Tel 01705-848484
Full-time students (1998–9), 14,500
Chancellor, The Lord Palumbo (1992)
Vice-Chancellor, Prof. J. Craven
Academic Registrar, A. Rees
Secretary, Dr M. Bateman

THE QUEEN'S UNIVERSITY OF BELFAST (1908)
Belfast BT7 1NN
Tel 01232-245133
Full-time students (1995–6), 14,500
Chancellor, Sen. G. Mitchell
Vice-Chancellor, Prof. G. Bain
Registrar, J. Town

THE UNIVERSITY OF READING (1926)
Whiteknights, PO Box 217, Reading RG6 6AH
Tel 0118-987 5123
Full-time students (1998–9), 12,000
Chancellor, The Lord Carrington, KG, GCMG, CH, MC, PC
    (1992)
Vice-Chancellor, Prof. R. Williams
Registrar, D. C. R. Frampton

THE ROBERT GORDON UNIVERSITY (1992)
Schoolhill, Aberdeen AB10 1FR
Tel 01224-262000
Full-time students (1998–9), 7,582
Chancellor, Sir Bob Reid (1993)
Vice-Chancellor and Principal, Prof. W. Stevely
Secretary, D. Caldwell

ROYAL COLLEGE OF MUSIC
London SW7 2BS
Tel 0171-589 3643
Full-time students (1998–9), 610
Registrar and Secretary, K. A. Porter
Dean and Deputy Director, Dr J. Cox
Director, Dr J. Ritterman

THE UNIVERSITY OF ST ANDREWS (1411)
College Gate, St Andrews KY16 9AJ
Tel 01334-476161
Full-time students (1998–9), 5,843
Chancellor, Sir Kenneth Dover, DLitt., FRSE, FBA (1981)
Vice-Chancellor and Principal, Prof. S. Arnott, CBE, FRS, FRSE
Secretary and Registrar, D. J. Corner
Rector, D. R. Findlay, QC, FRSA (1996–1999)

THE UNIVERSITY OF SALFORD (1967)
Salford M5 4WT
Tel 0161-295 5000
Full-time students (1998–9), 20,000
Chancellor, Sir Walter Bodmer, Ph.D., FRS
Vice-Chancellor, Prof. M. Harloe
Registrar, Dr M. D. Winton, Ph.D.

THE UNIVERSITY OF SHEFFIELD (1905)
Western Bank, Sheffield S10 2TN
Tel 0114-222 2000
Full-time students (1998–9), 15,639
Chancellor, Sir Peter Middleton, GCB
Vice-Chancellor, Prof. Sir Gareth Roberts, Kt, FRS, Ph.D.
Registrar and Secretary, D. Fletcher, Ph.D.

SHEFFIELD HALLAM UNIVERSITY (1992)
Howard Street, Sheffield S1 1WB
Tel 0114-225 5555
Full-time students (1998–9), 17,147
Chancellor, Sir Bryan Nicholson (1992)
Vice-Chancellor, Ms D. Green
Registrar, Ms J. Tory
Secretary, Ms S. Neocosmos

THE UNIVERSITY OF SOUTHAMPTON (1952)
Highfield, Southampton SO17 1BJ
Tel 01703-595000
Full-time students (1998–9), 15,777
Chancellor, The Earl of Selbourne, KBE, FRS (1996)
Vice-Chancellor, Prof. H. Newby, CBE, Ph.D.
Registrar and Secretary, J. F. D. Lauwerys
Academic Registrar, R. Knight

SOUTH BANK UNIVERSITY (1992)
103 Borough Road, London SE1 0AA
Tel 0171-928 8989
Full-time students (1998–9), 10,594
Chancellor, Sir Trevor McDonald
Vice-Chancellor, Prof. G. Bernbaum
Registrar, R. Phillips
Secretary, Mrs L. Gander

STAFFORDSHIRE UNIVERSITY (1992)
College Road, Stoke-on-Trent ST4 2DE
Tel 01782-294000
Full-time students (1998–9), 11,734
Chancellor, The Lord Ashley of Stoke, CH, PC (1993)
Vice-Chancellor, Prof. C. E. King, Ph.D.
Academic Registrar, Ms F. Francis
Secretary, K. Sproston

THE UNIVERSITY OF STIRLING (1967)
Stirling FK9 4LA
Tel 01786-473171
Full-time students (1998–9), 5,887
Chancellor, Dame Diana Rigg, DBE
Vice-Chancellor, Prof. A. Miller, CBE, FRSE
Academic Registrar, D. G. Wood
Secretary, K. J. Clarke

THE UNIVERSITY OF STRATHCLYDE (1964)
McCance Building, John Anderson Campus, Glasgow
    G1 1XQ
Tel 0141-552 4400
Full-time students (1998–9), 16,528
Chancellor, The Lord Hope of Craighead, PC (1998)
Vice-Chancellor and Principal, Prof. Sir John Arbuthnott,
    FRSE, FRCPath
Secretary, P. W. A. West

UNIVERSITY OF SUNDERLAND (1992)
Langham Tower, Ryhope Road, Sunderland SR2 7EE
Tel 0191-515 2000
Full-time students (1998–9), 11,587
Chancellor, The Lord Puttnam, CBE (1998)
Vice-Chancellor, Prof. P. Fidler, MBE
Academic Registrar, S. Porteous
Secretary, J. D. Pacey

THE UNIVERSITY OF SURREY (1966)
Guildford, Surrey GU2 5XH
Tel 01483-300800
Full-time students (1998–9), 9,100
Chancellor, HRH The Duke of Kent, KG, GCMG, GCVO
  (1977)
Vice-Chancellor, Prof. P. J. Dowling, FRS, FREng.
Registrar, P. J. Beardsley
Secretary, H. W. B. Davies

THE UNIVERSITY OF SUSSEX (1961)
Falmer, Brighton BN1 9RH
Tel 01273-606755
Full-time students (1998–9), 9,176
Chancellor, The Lord Attenborough (1998)
Vice-Chancellor, Prof. M. A. M. Smith
Registrar (acting), G. Ivey

UNIVERSITY OF TEESSIDE (1992)
Middlesbrough TS1 3BA
Tel 01642-218121
Full-time students (1997–8), 8,216
Chancellor, The Rt. Hon. Sir Leon Brittan, QC (1993)
Vice-Chancellor, Prof. D. Fraser
Registrar, Ms J. Walters
Secretary, J. M. McClintock

THAMES VALLEY UNIVERSITY (1992)
St Mary's Road, Ealing, London W5 5RF
Tel 0181-579 5000
Full-time students (1997–8), 5,793
Chancellor, The Lord Hamlyn, CBE
Secretary, S. Denton
Vice-Chancellor (acting), Sir William Taylor

THE UNIVERSITY OF ULSTER (1984)
Cromore Road, Coleraine BT52 1SA
Tel 01265-44141
Full-time students (1998–9), 20,042
Chancellor, Rabbi J. Neuberger (1993)
Vice-Chancellor, Prof. P. G. McKenna, PH.D.
Academic Registrar, Dr K. I. Miller, PH.D.

THE UNIVERSITY OF WALES (1893)
King Edward VII Avenue, Cathays Park, Cardiff CF10 3NS
Tel 01222-382656
Students (1998–9), 48,017
Chancellor, HRH The Prince of Wales, KG, KT, GCB, PC
  (1976)
Senior Vice-Chancellor, Prof. K. G. Robbins, FRSE, D.Litt
Secretary-General, J. D. Pritchard

MEMBER INSTITUTIONS

UNIVERSITY OF WALES BANGOR, Bangor LL57 2DG. Tel:
  01248-351151. *Vice-Chancellor,* Prof. H. R. Evans, PH.D.,
  FREng. (1995)
UNIVERSITY OF WALES COLLEGE OF MEDICINE, Heath
  Park, Cardiff CF14 4XN. Tel: 01222-747747. *Vice-
  Chancellor,* Prof. I. R. Cameron, DM, FRCP (1994)
UNIVERSITY OF WALES COLLEGE, NEWPORT, Caerleon
  Campus, PO Box 179, Newport NP6 1YG. Tel: 01633-
  430088. *Principal,* Prof. K. J. Overshott, PH.D. (1990)
UNIVERSITY OF WALES INSTITUTE, CARDIFF, Llandaff
  Centre, Western Avenue, Cardiff CF5 2SG. Tel: 01222-
  506070. *Principal,* A. J. Chapman, PH.D. (1998)
UNIVERSITY OF WALES SWANSEA, Singleton Park,
  Swansea SA2 8PP. Tel: 01792-205678. *Vice-Chancellor,*
  Prof. R. H. Williams, PH.D., D.SC, FRS (1994)
UNIVERSITY OF WALES, ABERYSTWYTH, Old College,
  King Street, Aberystwyth SY23 2AX. Tel: 01970-623111.
  Vice-Chancellor, Prof. D. Llwyd Morgan, D.Phil, D.Litt

UNIVERSITY OF WALES, CARDIFF, PO Box 920, Cardiff
  CF10 3XP. Tel: 01222-874000. *Vice-Chancellor,* Prof. Sir
  Brian Smith, PH.D., D.SC. (1993)
UNIVERSITY OF WALES, LAMPETER, Lampeter SA48 7ED.
  Tel: 01570-422351. *Vice-Chancellor,* Prof. K. G. Robbins,
  D.Litt., D.Phil., FRSE (1992)

THE UNIVERSITY OF WARWICK (1965)
Coventry CV4 7AL
Tel 01203-523523
Full-time students (1998–9), 15,900
Chancellor, Sir Shridath Surendranath Ramphal, GCMG, QC
  (1989)
Vice-Chancellor, Prof. Sir Brian Follett, FRS
Registrar, Dr J. W. Nicholls

UNIVERSITY OF WESTMINSTER (1992)
309 Regent Street, London W1R 8AL
Tel 0171-911 5000
Full-time students (1998–9), 10,947
Vice-Chancellor and Rector, Dr G. M. Copland (1996)
Academic Registrar, Ms E. Green
Secretary, A. Strang

UNIVERSITY OF THE WEST OF ENGLAND (1992)
Coldharbour Lane, Bristol BS16 1QY
Tel 0117-965 6261
Full-time students (1998–9), 16,630
Chancellor, The Rt. Hon. Dame Elizabeth Butler-Sloss, DBE
  (1993)
Vice-Chancellor, A. C. Morris
Assistant Academic Registrar, Ms M. J. Carter
Academic Secretary, Ms C. Webb

THE UNIVERSITY OF WOLVERHAMPTON (1992)
Wulfruna Street, Wolverhampton WV1 1SB
Tel 01902-321000
Full-time students (1998–9), 14,170
Chancellor, vacant
Vice-Chancellor, Prof. J. S. Brooks, PH.D.
Registrar, J. F. Baldwin
Secretary, A. W. Lee

THE UNIVERSITY OF YORK (1963)
Heslington, York YO10 5DD
Tel 01904-430000
Full-time students (1998–9), 7,000
Chancellor, Dame Janet Baker, CH, DBE (1991)
Vice-Chancellor, Prof. R. U. Cooke, PH.D., D.SC.
Registrar and Secretary, D. J. Foster

THE OPEN UNIVERSITY (1969)
Walton Hall, Milton Keynes MK7 6AA
Tel 01908-274066
Students and clients (1999), *c.*165,000
Chancellor, The Rt. Hon. Betty Boothroyd, MP
Vice-Chancellor, Sir John Daniel
Secretary, F. Woodburn
Registry, H. Niven

ROYAL COLLEGE OF ART (1837)
Kensington Gore, London SW7 2EU
Tel 0171-590 4444
Students (1998–9), 780 (all postgraduate)
Registrar, A. Selby
Director of Administration, G. Philpott
Provost, The Earl of Snowdon, GCVO (1995)
Rector and Vice-Provost, Prof. C. Frayling

COLLEGES

It is not possible to name here all the colleges offering courses of higher or further education. The list does not include colleges forming part of a polytechnic or a university. The English colleges that follow are confined to those in the Higher Education Funding Council for England sector; there are many more colleges in England providing higher education courses, some with HEFCFE funding.

The list of colleges in Wales, Scotland and Northern Ireland includes institutions providing at least one full-time course leading to a first degree granted by an accredited validating body.

ENGLAND

BATH SPA UNIVERSITY COLLEGE, Newton Park, Newton St Loe, Bath BA2 9BN. Tel 01225-875875. *Director,* F. Morgan

BISHOP GROSSETESTE COLLEGE, Lincoln LN1 3DY. Tel 01522-527347. *Principal,* Prof. E. Baker

BOLTON INSTITUTE OF HIGHER EDUCATION, Deane Road, Bolton BL3 5AB. Tel 01204-528851. *Principal,* Ms M. Temple

BRETTON HALL, West Bretton, Wakefield, W. Yorks WF4 4LG. Tel 01924-830261. *Principal,* Prof. G. H. Bell

BUCKINGHAMSHIRE CHILTERNS UNIVERSITY COLLEGE, Queen Alexandra Road, High Wycombe, Bucks HP11 2JZ. Tel 01494-522141. *Director,* Prof. P. B. Mogford

CANTERBURY CHRIST CHURCH UNIVERSITY COLLEGE, North Holmes Road, Canterbury, Kent CT1 1QU. Tel 01227-767700. *Principal,* Prof. M. Wright

THE CENTRAL SCHOOL OF SPEECH AND DRAMA, Embassy Theatre, 64 Eton Avenue, London NW3 3HY. Tel 0171-722 8183. *Principal,* Prof. R. S. Fowler

CHELTENHAM AND GLOUCESTER COLLEGE OF HIGHER EDUCATION, PO Box 220, The Park, Cheltenham, Glos GL50 2QF. Tel 01242-532700. *Director,* Miss J. O. Trotter, OBE

THE COLLEGE OF RIPON AND YORK ST JOHN, Lord Mayor's Walk, York YO31 7EX. Tel 01904-656771. *Principal,* Prof. D. Willcocks

DARTINGTON COLLEGE OF ARTS, Totnes, Devon TQ9 6EJ. Tel 01803-862224. *Principal,* Prof. K. Thompson

EDGE HILL COLLEGE OF HIGHER EDUCATION, St Helens Road, Ormskirk, Lancs L39 4QP. Tel 01695-575171. *Chief Executive,* Dr J. Cater

FALMOUTH COLLEGE OF ARTS, Woodlane, Falmouth, Cornwall TR11 4RH. Tel 01326-211077. *Principal,* Prof. A. G. Livingston

HARPER ADAMS UNIVERSITY COLLEGE, Newport, Shropshire TF10 8NB. Tel 01952-820280. *Principal,* Prof. E. W. Jones

HOMERTON COLLEGE, Cambridge CB2 2PH. Tel 01223-507111. *Principal,* Dr K. Pretty, PH.D.

KENT INSTITUTE OF ART AND DESIGN, Oakwood Park, Maidstone, Kent ME16 8AG. Tel 01622-757286. *Director,* Prof. V. Grylls

KING ALFRED'S COLLEGE, Sparkford Road, Winchester, Hants SO22 4NR. Tel 01962-841515. *Principal,* Prof. J. P. Dickinson

LIVERPOOL HOPE UNIVERSITY COLLEGE, Hope Park, Liverpool L16 9JD. Tel 0151-291 3000. *Rector and Chief Executive,* Prof. S. Lee

THE LONDON INSTITUTE, 65 Davies Street, London W1Y 2AA. Tel 0171-514 6000. *Rector,* Sir William Stubbs

NEWMAN COLLEGE OF HIGHER EDUCATION, Genners Lane, Bartley Green, Birmingham B32 3NT. Tel 0121-476 1181. *Principal,* Prof. B. Ray

RCN INSTITUTE, The Royal College of Nursing, 20 Cavendish Square, London W1M 0AB. Tel 0171-647 3700. *Director,* Prof. A. L. Kitson

ROEHAMPTON INSTITUTE LONDON, Whitelands College, West Hill, London SW15 3SN. Tel 0181-392 3232. *Rector,* Dr B. Porter

ROSE BRUFORD COLLEGE, Lamorbey Park, Sidcup, Kent DA15 9DF. Tel 0181-300 3024. *Principal,* Prof. R. Ely

ROYAL AGRICULTURAL COLLEGE, Cirencester, Glos GL7 6JS. Tel 01285-652531. *Principal,* Prof. J. B. Dent

ROYAL NORTHERN COLLEGE OF MUSIC, 124 Oxford Road, Manchester M13 9RD. Tel 0161-907 5200. *Principal,* Prof. E. Gregson

SOUTHAMPTON INSTITUTE, East Park Terrace, Southampton SO14 0YN. Tel 01703-319000. *Principal,* Dr R. Brown

SURREY INSTITUTE OF ART AND DESIGN, UNIVERSITY COLLEGE, Falkner Road, Farnham, Surrey GU9 7DS. Tel 01252-722441. *Director,* Prof. N. J. Taylor

TRINITY AND ALL SAINTS' COLLEGE, Brownberrie Lane, Horsforth, Leeds LS18 5HD. Tel 0113-283 7100. *Principal,* Dr M. J. Coughlan

THE UNIVERSITY OF BIRMINGHAM, WESTHILL, Weoley Park Road, Selly Oak, Birmingham B29 6LL. Tel 0121-472 7245. *Principal and Vice-Chancellor,* Prof. J. H. Y. Briggs

UNIVERSITY COLLEGE CHESTER, Parkgate Road, Chester CH1 4BJ. Tel 01244-375444. *Principal,* Prof. T. J. Wheeler

UNIVERSITY COLLEGE CHICHESTER, College Lane, Chichester, W. Sussex PO19 4PE. Tel 01243-816000. *Director,* P. E. D. Robinson

UNIVERSITY COLLEGE NORTHAMPTON, Park Campus, Boughton Green Road, Northampton NN2 7AL. Tel 01604-733500. *Rector,* Dr S. M. Gaskell

UNIVERSITY COLLEGE OF ST MARK AND ST JOHN, Derriford Road, Plymouth PL6 8BH. Tel 01752-636700. *Principal,* Dr W. J. Rea

UNIVERSITY COLLEGE OF ST MARTIN, Lancaster LA1 3JD. Tel 01524-384384. *Principal,* Prof. C. J. Carr

UNIVERSITY COLLEGE SCARBOROUGH, Filey Road, Scarborough YO11 3AZ. Tel 01723-362392. *Principal,* Dr. R. A. Withers

UNIVERSITY COLLEGE WORCESTER, Henwick Grove, Worcester WR2 6AJ. Tel 01905-855000. *Principal,* Ms D. Urwin

WESTMINSTER COLLEGE, Oxford OX2 9AT. Tel 01865-247644. *Principal,* Revd Dr R. Ralph

WINCHESTER SCHOOL OF ART, Park Avenue, Winchester, Hants SO23 8DL. Tel 01703-596900. *Principal,* P. Pilgrim

WALES

CARMARTHENSHIRE COLLEGE, Graig Campus, Sandy Road, Llanelli SA15 4DN. Tel 01554-748000. *Principal,* B. Robinson

LLANDRILLO COLLEGE, Llandudno Road, Rhos-on-Sea, Colwyn Bay, Conwy LL28 4HZ. Tel 01492-546666. *Principal,* W. S. H. Evans

NORTH EAST WALES INSTITUTE OF HIGHER EDUCATION, Plas Coch, Mold Road, Wrexham LL11 2AW. Tel 01978-290666. *Principal,* Prof. J. O. Williams

SWANSEA INSTITUTE OF HIGHER EDUCATION, Mount Pleasant, Swansea SA1 6ED. Tel 01792-481000. *Principal,* Prof. D. Warner

TRINITY COLLEGE, Carmarthen SA31 3EP. Tel 01267-676767. *Principal*, D. C. Jones-Davies, OBE

UNIVERSITY OF WALES INSTITUTE CARDIFF, Llandaff Campus, Western Avenue, Cardiff CF5 2YB. Tel 01222-416070. *Principal*, Prof A. J. Chapman, ph.D.

WELSH COLLEGE OF MUSIC AND DRAMA, Castle Grounds, Cathays Park, Cardiff CF10 3ER. Tel 01222-342854. *Principal*, E. Fivet

SCOTLAND

BELL COLLEGE OF TECHNOLOGY, Almada Street, Hamilton, Lanarkshire ML3 0JB. Tel 01698-283100. *Principal*, Dr K. J. MacCallum

DUMFRIES AND GALLOWAY COLLEGE, Heathhall, Dumfries DG1 3QZ. Tel 01387-261261. *Principal*, J. Neil

FIFE COLLEGE OF FURTHER AND HIGHER EDUCATION, St Brycedale Avenue, Kirkcaldy, Fife KY1 1EX. Tel 01592-268591. *Principal*, Mrs J. S. R. Johnston

GLASGOW SCHOOL OF ART, 167 Renfrew Street, Glasgow G3 6RQ. Tel 0141-353 4500. *Director*, Ms S. Reid

INVERNESS COLLEGE, Longman Road, Inverness IV1 1SA. Tel 01463-236681. *Principal*, Dr G. Clark

LEWS CASTLE COLLEGE, Stornoway, Isle of Lewis HS2 0XR. Tel 01851-703311. *Principal*, D. Green

MORAY COLLEGE, Moray Street, Elgin, Moray IV30 1JJ. Tel 01343-554321. *Principal*, Dr R. J. Chalmers

NORTHERN COLLEGE, Hilton Place, Aberdeen AB24 4FA. Tel 01224-283500. *Principal*, D. Adams

ORKNEY COLLEGE, Kirkwall, Orkney KW15 1LX. Tel 01856-872839. *Principal*, P. Scott

QUEEN MARGARET UNIVERSITY COLLEGE, Duke Street, Edinburgh EH6 8HF. Tel 0131-317 3000. *Principal*, Dr J. Stringer

ROYAL SCOTTISH ACADEMY OF MUSIC AND DRAMA, 100 Renfrew Street, Glasgow G2 3DB. Tel 0141-332 4101. *Principal*, Sir Philip Ledger, Kt., CBE, FRSE

SABHAL MOR OSTAIG, Sleat, Isle of Skye IV44 8RQ. Tel 01471-844373. *Director*, N. N. Gillies

SAC (SCOTTISH AGRICULTURAL COLLEGE), Central Office, West Mains Road, Edinburgh EH9 3JG. Tel 0131-535 4000. *Principal*, K. A. Linklater

THURSO COLLEGE, Ormlie Road, Thurso, Caithness KW14 7EE. Tel 01847-896161. *Principal*, R. Murray

NORTHERN IRELAND

EAST DOWN INSTITUTE OF FURTHER AND HIGHER EDUCATION, Market Street, Downpatrick, Co. Down BT30 6ND. Tel 01396-615815.

ST MARY'S UNIVERSITY COLLEGE, 191 Falls Road, Belfast BT12 6FE. Tel 01232-327678. *Principal*, Very Revd Prof. M. O'Callaghan

STRANMILLIS COLLEGE, Stranmillis Road, Belfast BT9 5DY. Tel 01232-381271.

ADULT CONTINUING EDUCATION

FORUM FOR THE ADVANCEMENT OF CONTINUING EDUCATION (FACE), Centre for Access, Advice and Continuing Education, University of East London, Romford Road, London E15 4LZ. Tel 0181-849 3696. *Joint Chairs*, J. Storan; Ms L. Chiswick

NATIONAL INSTITUTE OF ADULT CONTINUING EDUCATION, 21 De Montfort Street, Leicester LE1 7GE. Tel 0116-204 4200

NIACE CYMRU, 245 Western Avenue, Cardiff CF5 2YX. Tel 01222-265002. *Director for Wales*, Ms A. Poole

THE RESIDENTIAL COLLEGES COMMITTEE, c/o Ruskin College, Oxford OX1 2HE. Tel 01865-556360. *Awards Officer*, Mrs F. A. Bagchi

COMMUNITY LEARNING SCOTLAND, Rosebery House, 9 Haymarket Terrace, Edinburgh EH12 5EZ. Tel 0131-313 2488. *Chief Executive*, C. McConnell

THE UNIVERSITIES ASSOCIATION FOR CONTINUING EDUCATION, University of Cambridge Board of Continuing Education, Madingley Hall, Madingley, Cambridge CB3 8AQ. Tel 01954-280279. *Administrator*, Ms S. Irwin

WORKERS' EDUCATIONAL ASSOCIATION, Temple House, 17 Victoria Park Square, London E2 9PB. Tel 0181-983 1515. *General Secretary*, R. Lochrie

LONG-TERM RESIDENTIAL COLLEGES FOR ADULT EDUCATION

COLEG HARLECH, Harlech, Gwynedd LL46 2PU. Tel 01766-780363. *Warden (Acting)*, Dr D. Wiltshire

CO-OPERATIVE COLLEGE, Stanford Hall, Loughborough, Leics LE12 5QP. Tel 01509-857218. *Chief Executive*, R. Wildgust

FIRCROFT COLLEGE, 1018 Bristol Road, Selly Oak, Birmingham B29 6LH. Tel 0121-472 0116. *Principal*, Ms F. Larden

HILLCROFT COLLEGE, South Bank, Surbiton, Surrey KT6 6DF. Tel 0181-399 2688. *Principal*, Ms J. Ireton

NEWBATTLE ABBEY COLLEGE, Dalkeith, Midlothian EH22 3LL. Tel 0131-663 1921. *Principal*, W. M. Conboy

NORTHERN COLLEGE, Wentworth Castle, Stainborough, Barnsley, S. Yorks S75 3ET. Tel 01226-776000. *Principal*, Dr J. A. Jowitt

PLATER COLLEGE, Pullens Lane, Oxford OX3 0DT. Tel 01865-740500. *Principal*, M. Blades

RUSKIN COLLEGE, Walton Street, Oxford OX1 2HE. Tel 01865-554331. *Principal*, J. Durcan

PROFESSIONAL EDUCATION
Excluding postgraduate study

The organizations listed below are those which, by providing specialist training or conducting examinations, control entry into a profession, or are responsible for maintaining a register of those with professional qualifications in their sector.

Many professions now have a largely graduate entry, and possession of a first degree can exempt entrants from certain of the professional examinations. Enquiries about obtaining professional qualifications should be made to the relevant professional organization(s). Details of higher education providers of first degrees may be found in *University and College Entrance: Official Guide* (available from UCAS, *see* page 444).

EC RECOGNITION

It is now possible for those with professional qualifications obtained in the UK to have these recognized in other European Union countries. A booklet, *Europe Open for Professions*, and further information can be obtained from:

DEPARTMENT OF TRADE AND INDUSTRY, Bay 212, Kingsgate House, 66–74 Victoria Street, London SW1E 6SW. Tel: 0171-215 4648. *Contact*, Ms A. Wilson

ACCOUNTANCY

The main bodies granting membership on examination after a period of practical work are:

ASSOCIATION OF CHARTERED CERTIFIED
ACCOUNTANTS (ACCA), 29 Lincoln's Inn Fields,
London WC2A 3EE. Tel: 0171-242 6855. *Chief Executive*,
Mrs A. L. Rose

CHARTERED INSTITUTE OF MANAGEMENT
ACCOUNTANTS, 63 Portland Place, London WIN 4AB.
Tel: 0171-637 2311. *Secretary*, J. S. Chester, OBE

CHARTERED INSTITUTE OF PUBLIC FINANCE AND
ACCOUNTANCY (CIPFA), 3 Robert Street, London
WC2N 6BH. Tel: 0171-543 5600. *Chief Executive*, D.
Adams

INSTITUTE OF CHARTERED ACCOUNTANTS IN
ENGLAND AND WALES, Chartered Accountants' Hall,
PO Box 433, Moorgate Place, London EC2P 2BJ. Tel:
0171-920 8100. *Chief Executive*, J. Collier

INSTITUTE OF CHARTERED ACCOUNTANTS OF
SCOTLAND, 27 Queen Street, Edinburgh EH2 ILA. Tel:
0131-225 5673. *Chief Executive*, P. W. Johnston

ACTUARIAL SCIENCE

Two professional organizations grant qualifications after
examination:

FACULTY OF ACTUARIES IN SCOTLAND, 18 Dublin
Street, Edinburgh EHI 3PP. Tel: 0131-240 1300. *Secretary*,
W. W. Mair

INSTITUTE OF ACTUARIES, Staple Inn Hall, High
Holborn, London WCIV 7QJ. Tel: 0171-632 2100.
Secretary-General, G. B. L. Campbell. Education
enquiries to Napier House, 4 Worcester Street, Oxford
OXI 2AW. Tel: 01865-268200

ARCHITECTURE

The Education Committee of the Royal Institute of British
Architects sets standards and guides the whole system of
architectural education throughout the UK. RIBA recognizes courses at 35 schools of architecture in the UK for
exemption from their own examinations as well as 65
courses overseas.

ARCHITECTS REGISTRATION BOARD, 73 Hallam Street,
London WIN 6EE. Tel: 0171-580 5861. *Chief Officer and
Registrar*, A. Finch

THE ROYAL INSTITUTE OF BRITISH ARCHITECTS, 66
Portland Place, London WIN 4AD. Tel: 0171-580 5533.
Information Unit: 0891-234400. *President*, M.
Goldschmied; *Director-General*, A. Reid, PH.D.

Schools of architecture outside the universities include:

THE ARCHITECTURAL ASSOCIATION, 34–36 Bedford
Square, London WCIB 3ES. Tel: 0171-887 4000. *Secretary*,
E. A. Le Maistre

THE SCHOOL OF ARCHITECTURE AND THE BUILDING
ARTS, 14–15 Gloucester Gate, London NWI 4HG. Tel:
0171-916 7380. *Director*, Prof. A. Gale

BANKING

Professional organizations granting qualifications after
examination are:

CHARTERED INSTITUTE OF BANKERS, 90 Bishopsgate,
London EC2N 4AS. Tel: 0171-444 7111. *Chief Executive*,
G. Shreeve

CHARTERED INSTITUTE OF BANKERS IN SCOTLAND,
Drumsheugh House, 38B Drumsheugh Gardens,
Edinburgh EH3 7SW. Tel: 0131-473 7777. *Chief Executive*,
C. W. Munn

BUILDING

Examinations are conducted by:

CHARTERED INSTITUTE OF BUILDING, Englemere,
King's Ride, Ascot, Berks SL5 7TB. Tel: 01344-630700.
Chief Executive, K. Banbury

INSTITUTE OF BUILDING CONTROL, 92–104 East Street,
Epsom, Surrey KTI7 IEB. Tel: 01372-745577. *Chief
Executive*, G. Parrott

INSTITUTE OF CLERKS OF WORKS OF GREAT BRITAIN,
41 The Mall, London W5 3TJ. Tel: 0181-579 2917/8.
Secretary, vacant

BUSINESS, MANAGEMENT AND
ADMINISTRATION

Professional bodies conducting training and/or examinations in business, administration, management or commerce include:

AMETS (ASSOCIATION FOR MANAGEMENT
EDUCATION AND TRAINING IN SCOTLAND), c/o
Cottrell Building, University of Stirling, Stirling
FK9 4LA. Tel: 01786-450906. *Chairman*, Prof. F.
Pignatelli

THE ASSOCIATION OF MBAS, 15 Duncan Terrace,
London NI 8BZ. Tel: 0171-837 3375. Publishes a
directory giving details of MBA programmes world-
wide. *Director*, M. Jones

CAM FOUNDATION (COMMUNICATIONS,
ADVERTISING AND MARKETING EDUCATION
FOUNDATION), Abford House, 15 Wilton Road,
London SWIV INJ. Tel: 0171-828 7506. *Chief Executive*, D.
Royston-Lee

CHARTERED INSTITUTE OF HOUSING, Octavia House,
Westwood Business Park, Westwood Way, Coventry
CV4 8JP. Tel: 01203-851700. *Chief Executive*, D. Butler

CHARTERED INSTITUTE OF MARKETING, Moor Hall,
Cookham, Maidenhead, Berks SL6 9QH. Tel: 01628-
427500. *Chief Executive*, J. Stubbs

CHARTERED INSTITUTE OF PURCHASING AND SUPPLY,
Easton House, Easton on the Hill, Stamford, Lincs
PE9 3NZ. Tel: 01780-756777. *Chief Executive*, C. Holden

CHARTERED INSTITUTE OF TRANSPORT, 80 Portland
Place, London WIN 4DP. Tel: 0171-467 9400. *Director*,
Mrs D. de Carvalho

HENLEY MANAGEMENT COLLEGE, Greenlands,
Henley-on-Thames, Oxon RG9 3AU. Tel: 01491-571454.
Principal, Prof. R. Wild, PH.D., D.SC.

INSTITUTE OF ADMINISTRATIVE MANAGEMENT, 40
Chatsworth Parade, Petts Wood, Orpington, Kent
BR5 IRW. Tel: 01689-875555. *Chief Executive*, Prof.
G. Robinson

INSTITUTE OF CHARTERED SECRETARIES AND
ADMINISTRATORS, 16 Park Crescent, London
WIN 4AH. Tel: 0171-580 4741. *Chief Executive*,
M. J. Ainsworth

INSTITUTE OF CHARTERED SHIPBROKERS, 3 St Helen's
Place, London EC3A 6EJ. Tel: 0171-628 5559. *Director*,
Ms B. Fletcher

INSTITUTE OF EXPORT, Export House, 64 Clifton Street,
London EC2A 4HB. Tel: 0171-247 9812. *Director-General*,
I. J. Campbell

INSTITUTE OF HEALTHCARE MANAGEMENT, 7–10
Chandos Street, London WIM 9DE. Tel: 0171-460 7654.
Director, S. Marples

INSTITUTE OF MANAGEMENT, Management House,
Cottingham Road, Corby, Northants NNI7 ITT. Tel:
01536-204222. *Director-General*, Mrs M. Chapman

INSTITUTE OF PERSONNEL AND DEVELOPMENT, IPD
House, Camp Road, London SWI9 4UX. Tel: 0181-971
9000. *Director-General*, G. Armstrong

INSTITUTE OF PRACTITIONERS IN ADVERTISING, 44 Belgrave Square, London SW1X 8QS. Tel: 0171-235 7020. *Secretary*, J. Raad

INSTITUTE OF QUALITY ASSURANCE, 12 Grosvenor Crescent, London SW1X 7EE. Tel: 0171-245 6722. *Chief Executive*, Frank Steer, MBE

CHIROPRACTIC

Chiropractic is accorded statutory regulation by the Chiropractic Act 1994. There were previously four professional associations operating voluntary registration schemes. These registers were replaced by the General Chiropractic Council, which opened a new register in June 1999, although the Associations still exist. It is illegal for anyone to call themselves a chiropractor unless they have undertaken a recognized course of training and are registered with the General Chiropractic Council.

There are currently five training centres for chiropractic. Two of these provide four-year part-time training programmes leading to internal academic awards; the other three provide full-time training leading to a B.Sc. and M.Sc. in chiropractic. In future, the General Chiropractic Council will determine the training requirements to qualify for registration and accredit courses.

BRITISH CHIROPRACTIC ASSOCIATION, Blagrave House, 17 Blagrave Street, Reading RG1 1QB. Tel: 0118-950 5950. *Executive Director*, Ms S. A. Wakefield

GENERAL CHIROPRACTIC COUNCIL, 3rd Floor, North Wing, 344–354 Gray's Inn Road, London WC1X 8BP. Tel: 0171-713 5155. *Chief Executive and Registrar*, Mrs M. Coats

SCOTTISH CHIROPRACTIC ASSOCIATION, St Boswells Chiropractic Clinic, 16 Jenny Moores Road, St Boswells, Melrose TD6 0AL. Tel: 01835-823645. *Secretary*, Dr C. I. How

DANCE

The Council for Dance Education and Training (CDET) has accredited courses at the following: Arts Education Schools, Tring Park and London; Central School of Ballet; Doreen Bird College of Performing Arts; Elmhurst–The School for Dance and Performing Arts; English National Ballet School; The Hammond School; The Italia Conti Academy of Theatre Arts Ltd; Laban Centre, London; Laine Theatre Arts Ltd; London Contemporary Dance School; London Studio Centre; Midlands Academy of Dance and Drama; Merseyside Dance and Drama Centre; Northern Ballet School; Performers College; Stella Mann College; Studios La Pointe; Royal Academy of Dancing; The Urdang Academy.

The accreditation of a course in a school does not necessarily imply that other courses of a different type or duration in the same school are also accredited.

CDET has approved the teacher registration systems of the following: Association of American Dancing; British Ballet Organization; British Theatre Dance Association; Cecchetti Society; Imperial Society of Teachers of Dancing; Royal Academy of Dancing.

COUNCIL FOR DANCE EDUCATION AND TRAINING (UK), Studio 8, The Glasshouse, 49A Goldhawk Road, London W12 8QP. Tel: 0181-746 0076. *Chairman*, Clive Priestley, CB

IMPERIAL SOCIETY OF TEACHERS OF DANCING, Imperial House, 22–26 Paul Street, London EC2A 4QE. Tel: 0171-377 1577. *Chief Executive*, M. J. Browne

INTERNATIONAL DANCE TEACHERS' ASSOCIATION, International House, 76 Bennett Road, Brighton BN2 5JL. Tel: 01273-685652. *Chief Executive*, J. Dearling

ROYAL ACADEMY OF DANCING, 36 Battersea Square, London SW11 3RA. Tel: 0171-223 0091. *Chief Executive*, L. Rittner; *Artistic Director*, Miss L. Wallis

ROYAL BALLET SCHOOL, 155 Talgarth Road, London W14 9DE. Tel: 0181-748 6335. Also at White Lodge, Richmond Park, Surrey TW10 5HR. Tel: 0181-876 5547. *Director*, Ms G. Stock

DEFENCE

ROYAL COLLEGE OF DEFENCE STUDIES, Seaford House, 37 Belgrave Square, London SW1X 8NS. Tel: 0171-915 4800. Prepares selected senior officers and officials for responsibilities in the direction and management of defence, security and related areas. *Commandant*, Vice-Adm. J. H. S. McAnally, LVO

JOINT SERVICES COMMAND AND STAFF COLLEGE, Bracknell, Berks RG12 9DD. Tel: 01344-454593. *Commandant*, Maj.-Gen. T. J. Granville-Chapman, CBE; *Dean of Academic Studies*, Prof. G. Till, PH.D.

ROYAL NAVAL COLLEGE

BRITANNIA ROYAL NAVAL COLLEGE, Dartmouth, Devon TQ6 0HJ. Tel: 01803-832141. Provides professional training and education for all new entry RN officers and officers from foreign and Commonwealth navies. *Commodore*, Cdre M. W. G. Kerr

MILITARY COLLEGES

DIRECTORATE OF EDUCATIONAL AND TRAINING SERVICES, Trenchard Lines, Upavon, Pewsey, Wilts SN9 6BE. Tel: 01980-618719. *Director*, Brig. P. S. Purves, DSC

ROYAL MILITARY ACADEMY SANDHURST, Camberley, Surrey GU15 4PQ. Tel: 01276-63344. *Commandant*, Maj.-Gen. A. G. Denaro, CBE

ROYAL MILITARY COLLEGE OF SCIENCE, Shrivenham, Swindon, Wilts SN6 8LA. Tel: 01793-785435. Students from UK and overseas study from degree to postgraduate levels in engineering, management, science and technology. The College is a faculty of Cranfield University. *Commandant*, Maj.-Gen. J. C. B. Sutherall, CBE; *Principal*, Prof. P. Hutchinson

ROYAL AIR FORCE COLLEGES

ROYAL AIR FORCE COLLEGE, Cranwell, Sleaford, Lincs. NG34 8HB. Provides initial training for all officer entrants to the RAF. Also provides initial specialist and postgraduate training for engineering and supply officers. The RAF College is the site of the Joint Elementary Flying School for pilots of all three services, Number 3 Flying Training School and the RAF Central Flying School. It is also the headquarters for the RAF University Air Squadrons, and is responsible for supervision of the Air Cadet Organization. *Air Officer Commanding and Commandant*, Air Vice-Marshal T. W. Rimmer, OBE

ROYAL AIR FORCE TRAINING, DEVELOPMENT AND SUPPORT UNIT, RAF Halton, Aylesbury, Bucks HP22 5PG. Tel: 01296-623535. *Commanding Officer*, Gp Capt. A. Harris

DENTISTRY

In order to practise in the UK, a dentist must be entered in the Dentists Register. To be registered, a person must hold the degree or diploma in dental surgery of a university in the UK or the diploma of any of the licensing authorities (the Royal Colleges of Surgeons of England and of Edinburgh, and the Royal College of Physicians and Surgeons of Glasgow). Nationals of EU or European

Economic Area member states holding an appropriate European diploma, and holders of certain overseas diplomas, may also be registered. Temporary registration may be available for those dentists who do not hold a diploma described above. The Dentists Register is maintained by:

THE GENERAL DENTAL COUNCIL, 37 Wimpole Street, London WIM 8DQ. Tel: 0171-887 3800. *Chief Executive and Registrar,* Mrs R. M. J. Hepplewhite

DIETETICS

See also FOOD AND NUTRITION SCIENCE

The professional association is the British Dietetic Association. Full membership is open to dietitians holding a recognized qualification, who may also become State Registered Dietitians through the Council for Professions Supplementary to Medicine (*see* Medicine).

THE BRITISH DIETETIC ASSOCIATION, 5th Floor, Elizabeth House, 22 Suffolk Street, Queensway, Birmingham BI ILS. Tel: 0121-616 4900. *Secretary,* J. Grigg

DRAMA

The national validating body for courses providing training in drama for the professional theatre is the National Council for Drama Training. It currently has accredited courses at the following: Academy of Live and Recorded Arts; Arts Educational Schools; Birmingham School of Speech Training and Dramatic Art; Bristol Old Vic Theatre School; Central School of Speech and Drama; Drama Centre, London; Drama Studio, London; Guildford School of Acting; Guildhall School of Music and Drama, London; London Academy of Music and Dramatic Art; Manchester Metropolitan University School of Theatre; Mountview Theatre School; Oxford School of Drama, Woodstock; Queen Margaret University College, Edinburgh; Rose Bruford College, Sidcup; Royal Academy of Dramatic Art, London; Royal Scottish Academy of Music and Drama; Webber Douglas Academy of Dramatic Art, London; Welsh College of Music and Drama.

The accreditation of a course in a school does not necessarily imply that other courses of different type or duration in the same school are also accredited.

THE NATIONAL COUNCIL FOR DRAMA TRAINING, 5 Tavistock Place, London WCIH 9SS. *Executive Secretary,* Mrs A. Bailey

ENGINEERING

The Engineering Council supervises the engineering profession through the 39 nominated engineering institutions who are represented on its Board for Engineers' Regulation. Working with and through the institutions, the Council sets the standards for the registration of individuals, and also the accreditation for academic courses in universities and colleges and the practical training in industry.

THE ENGINEERING COUNCIL, 10 Maltravers Street, London WC2R 3ER. Tel: 0171-240 7891. *Director-General,* M. Shirley

The principal qualifying bodies are:

BRITISH COMPUTER SOCIETY, 1 Sanford Street, Swindon SNI IHJ. Tel: 01793-417417. *Chief Executive,* Mrs J. M. Scott

BRITISH INSTITUTE OF NON-DESTRUCTIVE TESTING, 1 Spencer Parade, Northampton NNI 5AA. Tel: 01604-630124. *Secretary,* M. E. Gallagher

CHARTERED INSTITUTION OF BUILDING SERVICES ENGINEERS, 222 Balham High Road, London SW12 9BS. Tel: 0181-675 5211. *Secretary,* R. John

INSTITUTION OF AGRICULTURAL ENGINEERS, West End Road, Silsoe, Bedford MK45 4DU. Tel: 01525-861096. *Chief Executive,* J. H. Neville

INSTITUTE OF BRITISH FOUNDRYMEN, Bordesley Hall, The Holloway, Alvechurch, Birmingham B48 7QA. Tel: 01527-596100. *Secretary,* G. A. Schofield

INSTITUTION OF CHEMICAL ENGINEERS, Davis Building, 165–189 Railway Terrace, Rugby, Warks CV21 3HQ. Tel: 01788-578214. *Chief Executive,* Dr T. J. Evans

INSTITUTION OF CIVIL ENGINEERS, 1 Great George Street, London SW1P 3AA. Tel: 0171-222 7722. *Director-General,* M. Casebourne

INSTITUTION OF ELECTRICAL ENGINEERS, Savoy Place, London WC2R 0BL. Tel: 0171-240 1871. *Chief Executive,* Dr A. Roberts

INSTITUTE OF ENERGY, 18 Devonshire Street, London WIN 2AU. Tel: 0171-580 7124. *Secretary and Chief Executive,* Ms L. Evans

INSTITUTION OF ENGINEERING DESIGNERS, Courtleigh, Westbury Leigh, Westbury, Wilts BA13 3TA. Tel: 01373-822801. Secretary, M. Osborne

INSTITUTION OF FIRE ENGINEERS, 148 New Walk, Leicester LEI 7QB. Tel: 0116-255 3654. *General Secretary,* D. W. Evans

INSTITUTION OF GAS ENGINEERS, 21 Portland Place, London WIN 3AF. Tel: 0171-636 6603. *Secretary,* Ms J. Sedgwick

INSTITUTE OF HEALTHCARE ENGINEERING AND ESTATE MANAGEMENT, 2 Abingdon House, Cumberland Business Centre, Northumberland Road, Portsmouth PO5 IDS. Tel: 01705-823186. *Secretary,* W. R. Pym

INSTITUTION OF INCORPORATED ENGINEERS, Savoy Hill House, Savoy Hill, London WC2R 0BS. Tel: 0171-836 3357. *Chief Executive,* P. F. Wason

INSTITUTION OF INCORPORATED EXECUTIVE ENGINEERS, Wix Hill House, West Horsley, Surrey KT24 6DZ. Tel: 01483-222383. *Secretary,* D. Dacam, OBE

INSTITUTE OF LIGHTING ENGINEERS, Lennox House, 9 Lawford Road, Rugby CV21 2DZ. Tel: 01788-576492. *Chief Executive,* R. G. Frost

INSTITUTE OF MARINE ENGINEERS, 80 Coleman Street, London EC2R 5BJ. Tel: 0171-382 2600. *Director-General,* K. F. Read

INSTITUTE OF MATERIALS, 1 Carlton House Terrace, London SW1Y 5DB. Tel: 0171-451 7300. *Chief Executive,* Dr B. A. Rickinson

INSTITUTE OF MEASUREMENT AND CONTROL, 87 Gower Street, London WCIE 6AA. Tel: 0171-387 4949. *Secretary,* M. J. Yates

INSTITUTION OF MECHANICAL ENGINEERS, 1 Birdcage Walk, London SW1H 9JJ. Tel: 0171-222 7899. *Director-General,* Sir Michael Moore, KBE, LVO

INSTITUTION OF MINING AND METALLURGY, Danum House, 6A South Parade, Doncaster DNI 2DY. Tel: 01302-320486. *Secretary,* Dr G. J. M. Woodrow

INSTITUTION OF NUCLEAR ENGINEERS, 1 Penerley Road, London SE6 2LQ. Tel: 0181-698 1500. *Secretary,* W. J. Hurst

INSTITUTION OF PHYSICS, 76 Portland Place, London WIN 3DH. Tel: 0171-470 4800. *Chief Executive,* Dr A. D. W. Jones

INSTITUTION OF PLANT ENGINEERS, 77 Great Peter Street, London SW1P 2EZ. Tel: 0171-233 2855. *Secretary,* P. F. Tye

INSTITUTE OF PLUMBING, 64 Station Lane, Hornchurch, Essex RM12 6NB. Tel: 01708-472791. *Chief Executive,* W. A. Watts, MBE

INSTITUTE OF QUALITY ASSURANCE, 12 Grosvenor Crescent, London SW1X 7EE. Tel: 0171-245 6722. *Secretary-General*, D. Campbell

INSTITUTION OF STRUCTURAL ENGINEERS, 11 Upper Belgrave Street, London SW1X 8BH. Tel: 0171-235 4535. *Chief Executive*, Dr K. J. Eaton.

INSTITUTION OF WATER OFFICERS, Heriot House, 12 Summerhill Terrace, Newcastle upon Tyne NE4 6EB. Tel: 0191-230 5150. *Company Secretary (acting)*, Ms L. Harding

ROYAL AERONAUTICAL SOCIETY, 4 Hamilton Place, London W1V 0BQ. Tel: 0171-499 3515. *Director*, K. Mans

ROYAL INSTITUTION OF NAVAL ARCHITECTS, 10 Upper Belgrave Street, London SW1X 8BQ. Tel: 0171-235 4622. *Chief Executive*, T. Blakeley

THE WELDING INSTITUTE, Abington Hall, Abington, Cambridge CB1 6AL. Tel: 01223-891162. *Chief Executive*, B. Braithwaite, OBE

FILM AND TELEVISION

Postgraduate training for those intending to make a career in film and television production is provided by the National Film and Television School, which provides courses in television producing and direction, animation direction, documentary direction, fiction direction, screenwriting, screen design, editing, cinematography, screen sound, art direction and screen music. Short courses to enable professionals to update or expand their skills are also provided.

NATIONAL FILM AND TELEVISION SCHOOL, Beaconsfield Studios, Station Road, Beaconsfield, Bucks HP9 1LG. Tel: 01494-671234. Web: http://www.nftsfilm-tv.ac.uk. *Director*, S. Bayly

FOOD AND NUTRITION SCIENCE
See also DIETETICS

Scientific and professional bodies include:

INSTITUTE OF FOOD SCIENCE & TECHNOLOGY, 5 Cambridge Court, 210 Shepherd's Bush Road, London W6 7NJ. Tel: 0171-603 6316. *Chief Executive*, Ms H. G. Wild

FORESTRY AND TIMBER STUDIES

Professional organizations include:

COMMONWEALTH FORESTRY ASSOCIATION, c/o Oxford Forestry Institute, South Parks Road, Oxford OX1 3RB. Tel: 01865-271037. *Chairman*, Dr J. S. Maini

INSTITUTE OF CHARTERED FORESTERS, 7A St Colme Street, Edinburgh EH3 6AA. Tel: 0131-225 2705. *Secretary*, Ms L. Kennedy

ROYAL FORESTRY SOCIETY OF ENGLAND, WALES AND NORTHERN IRELAND, 102 High Street, Tring, Herts HP23 4AF. Tel: 01442-822028. *Director*, J. E. Jackson, PH.D.

ROYAL SCOTTISH FORESTRY SOCIETY, The Stables, Dalkeith Country Park, Dalkeith, Midlothian EH22 2NA. Tel: 0131-660 9480. *Director*, M. Osborne

FUEL AND ENERGY SCIENCE

The principal professional bodies are:

INSTITUTE OF ENERGY, 18 Devonshire Street, London W1N 2AU. Tel: 0171-580 7124. *Secretary*, Mrs D. Davy

INSTITUTION OF GAS ENGINEERS, 21 Portland Place, London W1N 3AF. Tel: 0171-636 6603. *Secretary*, Mrs S. M. Raine

INSTITUTE OF PETROLEUM, 61 New Cavendish Street, London W1M 8AR. Tel: 0171-467 7100. *Director-General*, J. G. Pym

HOTELKEEPING, CATERING AND INSTITUTIONAL MANAGEMENT
See also DIETETICS, AND FOOD AND NUTRITION SCIENCE

The qualifying professional body in these areas is:

HOTEL AND CATERING INTERNATIONAL MANAGEMENT ASSOCIATION, 191 Trinity Road, London SW17 7HN. Tel: 0181-672 4251. *Chief Executive*, D. Wood

INDUSTRIAL AND VOCATIONAL TRAINING

The NTO National Council represents the network of employer-led national training organizations (NTOs). NTOs represent the education and training interests of their respective sectors to government and ensure the development and adoption of occupational standards, particularly through National and Scottish Vocational Qualifications and learning initiatives including Modern Apprenticeship and National Traineeship.

NTO NATIONAL COUNCIL, 10 Meadowcourt, Amos Road, Sheffield S9 1BX. Tel: 0114-261 9926. *Chief Executive*, Dr. A. Powell

INSURANCE

Organizations conducting examinations and awarding diplomas are:

ASSOCIATION OF AVERAGE ADJUSTERS, 200 Aldersgate Street, London EC1A 4JJ. Tel: 0171-956 0099. *Secretary*, D. W. Taylor

CHARTERED INSTITUTE OF LOSS ADJUSTERS, Manfield House, 1 Southampton Street, London WC2R 0LR. Tel: 0171-240 1496. *Director*, G. L. Cave

CHARTERED INSURANCE INSTITUTE, 20 Aldermanbury, London EC2V 7HY. Tel: 0171-417 4425. *Director-General*, Prof. D. E. Bland

JOURNALISM

Courses for trainee newspaper journalists are available at 30 centres. One-year full-time courses are available for selected students and 18-week courses for graduates. Particulars of all these courses are available from the National Council for the Training of Journalists. Short courses for mid-career development can be arranged, as can various distance learning courses. The NCTJ also offers Assessor, Internal Verifier (IV) and Accreditation of Prior Achievement (APA) training, and NVQs.

For periodical journalists, there are nine centres running courses approved by the Periodicals Training Council (PTC). The PTC also offers NVQs and information on best practice training.

THE NATIONAL COUNCIL FOR TRAINING OF JOURNALISTS, Latton Bush Centre, Southern Way, Harlow, Essex CM18 7BL. Tel: 01279-430009. *Chief Executive*, R. Selwood

THE PERIODICALS TRAINING COUNCIL, Queen's House, 55–56 Lincoln's Inn Fields, London WC2A 3LJ. Tel: 0171-404 4168. *Director*, Ms J. Butcher

LAW

THE BAR

Admission to the Bar of England and Wales is controlled by the Inns of Court, admission to the Bar of Northern Ireland by the Honorable Society of the Inn of Court of Northern Ireland and admission as an Advocate of the Scottish Bar is controlled by the Faculty of Advocates. The governing body of the barristers' branch of the legal profession in England and Wales is the General Council of the Bar (the Bar Council). The governing body in Northern Ireland is the Honorable Society of the Inn of Court of Northern Ireland, and the Faculty of Advocates is the governing body of the Scottish Bar. The education and examination of students training for the Bar of England and Wales is regulated by the General Council of the Bar. Those who intend to practise at the Bar of England and Wales must pass the Bar's vocational course. The Inns of Court School of Law is the largest provider of initial training for those wishing to practise at the Bar, but seven other institutions have been validated to provide the course. Applications are handled by the Bar Council's Centralised Applications Clearing House (CACH).

FACULTY OF ADVOCATES, Advocates Library, Parliament House, Edinburgh EH1 1RF. Tel: 0131-226 5071. *Dean*, G. N. H. Emslie, QC; *Clerk*, I. G. Armstrong

THE GENERAL COUNCIL OF THE BAR, 3 Bedford Row, London WC1R 4DB. Tel: 0171-242 0082. *Chairman*, D. Brennan, QC; *Chief Executive*, N. Morison

CACH, Education and Training Department, 2–3 Cursitor Street, London EC4A 1NE. Tel: 0171-440 4000

THE HONORABLE SOCIETY OF THE INN OF COURT OF NORTHERN IRELAND, Royal Courts of Justice, Belfast BT1 3JF. Tel: 01232-235111. *Treasurer* (1999), Hon. Mr Justice Kerr; *Under-Treasurer*, J. W. Wilson, QC

INNS OF COURT SCHOOL OF LAW, 4 Gray's Inn Place, Gray's Inn, London WC1R 5DX. Tel: 0171-404 5787. *Chairman*, The Hon. Mr Justice Hooper; *Principal*, Prof. R. Stone

The Inns of Court

GRAY'S INN, 8 South Square, London WC1R 5EU. Tel: 0171-458 7900. *Treasurer*, Rt. Hon. Sir Anthony Evans, Kt., QC; *Under-Treasurer*, D. Machin

THE INNER TEMPLE, London EC4Y 7HL. Tel: 0171-797 8250. *Treasurer*, The Rt. Hon. The Lord Lloyd of Berwick; *Sub-Treasurer*, Brig. P. A. Little, CBE

LINCOLN'S INN, London WC2A 3TL. Tel: 0171-405 1393. *Treasurer*, The Rt. Hon. Sir John Balcombe, Kt., QC; *Under-Treasurer*, Col. D. H. Hills, MBE

THE MIDDLE TEMPLE, London EC4Y 9AT. Tel: 0171-427 4800. *Treasurer*, Hon. Sir Charles McCullough, Kt., QC; *Under-Treasurer*, Brig. C. T. J. Wright

SOLICITORS

Qualifications for solicitors are obtainable only from one of the Law Societies, which control the education and examination of trainee solicitors and the admission of solicitors.

THE COLLEGE OF LAW provides courses for the Common Professional Examination and Legal Practice Course at Braboeuf Manor, St Catherine's, Guildford, Surrey GU3 1HA; 14 Store Street, London WC1E 7DE; Christleton Hall, Chester CH3 7AB; Bishopthorpe Road, York YO23 2GA. The college also provides the Bar Vocational Course at its London branch

LAW SOCIETY OF ENGLAND AND WALES, 113 Chancery Lane, London WC2A 1PL. Tel: 0171-242 1222. *President* (1999–2000), R. Sayer; *Secretary-General*, Mrs J. M. Betts

LAW SOCIETY OF NORTHERN IRELAND, Law Society House, 98 Victoria Street, Belfast BT1 3JZ. Tel: 01232-231614. *Chief Executive*, J. W. Bailie

LAW SOCIETY OF SCOTLAND, 26 Drumsheugh Gardens, Edinburgh EH3 7YR. Tel: 0131-226 7411. *President* (1999–2000), M. Scanlan; *Secretary*, D. R. Mill

OFFICE FOR THE SUPERVISION OF SOLICITORS, Victoria Court, 8 Dormer Place, Leamington Spa, Warks CV32 5AE. Tel: 01926-820082. The Office is an establishment of the Law Society set up to handle complaints about solicitors and regulate solicitors' practices

LIBRARIANSHIP AND INFORMATION SCIENCE/MANAGEMENT

The Library Association accredits degree and postgraduate courses in library and information science which are offered by 17 universities in the UK. A full list of accredited degree and postgraduate courses is available from its Information Services and on its web site (*see* below). The Association also maintains a professional register of Chartered Members open to graduate ordinary members of the Association.

THE LIBRARY ASSOCIATION, 7 Ridgmount Street, London WC1E 7AE. Tel: 0171-636 7543. Web: http://www.la-hq.org.uk. *Chief Executive*, Dr R. McKee

MATERIALS STUDIES

The qualifying body is:

INSTITUTE OF MATERIALS, 1 Carlton House Terrace, London SW1Y 5DB. Tel: 0171-451 7300. *Chief Executive*, Dr B. A. Rickinson

MEDICINE

All doctors must be registered with the General Medical Council. In order to register, medical students must complete an undergraduate medical degree at one of the 19 universities with medical schools, followed by a year of general clinical training. Once registered, doctors undertake general professional and basic specialist training as senior house officers. Further specialist training is provided by the royal colleges, faculties and societies listed below. The General Medical Council keeps a register of those doctors who have been awarded Certificates of Completion of Specialist Training.

The United Examining Board holds qualifying examinations for candidates who have trained overseas. These candidates must also have spent a period at a UK medical school.

GENERAL MEDICAL COUNCIL, 178 Great Portland Street, London W1N 6JE. Tel: 0171-580 7642. *President*, Sir Donald Irvine, CBE, MD, FRGCP; *Chief Executive*, F. Scott

UNITED EXAMINING BOARD, Apothecaries Hall, Black Friars Lane, London EC4V 6EJ. Tel: 0171-236 1180. *Chairman*, Prof. J. S. P. Lumley, FRCS; *Registrar*, A. M. Wallington-Smith

COLLEGES/SOCIETIES HOLDING POSTGRADUATE MEMBERSHIP AND DIPLOMA EXAMINATIONS

FACULTY OF ACCIDENT AND EMERGENCY MEDICINE, Royal College of Surgeons of England, 35–43 Lincoln's Inn Fields, London WC2A 3PN. Tel: 0171-405 7071. *President (from 2 December 1999)*, I. W. R. Anderson

FACULTY OF OCCUPATIONAL MEDICINE, 6 St Andrew's Place, London NW1 4LB. Tel: 0171-317 5890. *Secretary*, Ms F. M. Quinn

FACULTY OF PHARMACEUTICAL MEDICINE, 1 St Andrew's Place, London NW1 4LB. Tel: 0171-224 0343. *Administrator*, Ms K. Wright

FACULTY OF PUBLIC HEALTH MEDICINE, 4 St Andrew's Place, London NW1 4LB. Tel: 0171-935 0243. *Secretary*, P. Scourfield

ROYAL COLLEGE OF ANAESTHETISTS, 48–49 Russell Square, London WC1B 4JY. Tel: 0171-813 1900. *President*, Prof. L. Strunin; *Chief Executive*, Ms W. Cogger

ROYAL COLLEGE OF GENERAL PRACTITIONERS, 14 Princes Gate, London SW7 1PU. Tel: 0171-581 3232. *President*, Prof. Sir Denis Gray, Kt., OBE, FRCGP; *Secretary* (from Nov. 1999), Dr M. Baker, FRCGP

ROYAL COLLEGE OF OBSTETRICIANS AND GYNAECOLOGISTS, 27 Sussex Place, London NW1 4RG. Tel: 0171-772 6200. *President*, Prof. R. W. Shaw; *Secretary*, P. A. Barnett

ROYAL COLLEGE OF PAEDIATRICS AND CHILD
HEALTH, 50 Hallam Street, London WIN 6DE. Tel:
0171-307 5600. *President*, Prof. J. D. Baum; *Secretary*, L.
Tyler

ROYAL COLLEGE OF PATHOLOGISTS, 2 Carlton House
Terrace, London SW1Y 5AF. Tel: 0171-930 5861.
President (from November 1999), Prof. J. Lilleyman; *Deputy
Secretary*, Ms E. Evans

ROYAL COLLEGE OF PHYSICIANS, 11 St Andrew's Place,
London NW1 4LE. Tel: 0171-935 1174. *President*, Prof. K.
G. M. M. Alberti, FRCP; *Secretary*, P. Masterton-Smith

ROYAL COLLEGE OF PHYSICIANS AND SURGEONS OF
GLASGOW, 232–242 St Vincent Street, Glasgow G2 5RJ.
Tel: 0141-221 6072. *President*, C. Mackay; *Hon. Secretary*,
Dr C. Semple

ROYAL COLLEGE OF PHYSICIANS OF EDINBURGH,
9 Queen Street, Edinburgh EH2 1JQ. Tel: 0131-225 7324.
President, Prof. J. C. Petrie; *Secretary*, Dr A. C. Parker

ROYAL COLLEGE OF PSYCHIATRISTS, 17 Belgrave
Square, London SW1X 8PG. Tel: 0171-235 2351. *President*,
Prof. J. Cox; *Secretary*, Mrs V. Cameron

ROYAL COLLEGE OF RADIOLOGISTS, 38 Portland Place,
London WIN 4QJ. Tel: 0171-636 4432. *President*, Prof. P.
Armstrong; *General Secretary*, A. J. Cowles

ROYAL COLLEGE OF SURGEONS OF EDINBURGH,
Nicolson Street, Edinburgh EH8 9DW. Tel: 0131-527
1600. *President*, Prof. A. G. D. Maran; *Executive Secretary*,
Ms A. S. Campbell

ROYAL COLLEGE OF SURGEONS OF ENGLAND, 35–43
Lincoln's Inn Fields, London WC2A 3PN. Tel: 0171-405
3474. *President*, B. T. Jackson, FRCS; *Secretary*, C. Duncan

SOCIETY OF APOTHECARIES OF LONDON, 14 Black
Friars Lane, London EC4V 6EJ. Tel: 0171-236 1189.
Clerk, Lt.-Col. R. J. Stringer

PROFESSIONS SUPPLEMENTARY TO MEDICINE

The standard of professional education in art, drama and
music therapies, biomedical sciences, chiropody, dietetics,
occupational therapy, orthoptics, prosthetics and orthotics,
physiotherapy and radiography is the responsibility of nine
professional boards, which also publish an annual register
of qualified practitioners. The work of the boards is co-
ordinated by the Council for Professions Supplementary
to Medicine.

In June 1999 the Government announced that three new
boards would be established, covering speech and language
therapists, clinical scientists and paramedics.

THE COUNCIL FOR PROFESSIONS SUPPLEMENTARY TO
MEDICINE, Park House, 184 Kennington Park Road,
London SE11 4BU. Tel: 0171-582 0866. *Registrar*, M. D.
Hall

ART, DRAMA AND MUSIC THERAPIES

A postgraduate qualification in the relevant therapy is
required. There are five institutions in the UK offering
courses in art therapy and six offering courses in music
therapy.

BRITISH ASSOCIATION OF ART THERAPISTS, Mary
Ward House, 5 Tavistock Place, London WC1H 9SN.
Tel: 0171-383 3774. *Administrator*, Ms. D. Haworth

ASSOCIATION OF PROFESSIONAL MUSIC THERAPISTS,
26 Hamlyn Road, Glastonbury, Somerset BA6 8HT
(enquirers should enclose a stamped addressed
envelope). Tel: 01458-834919

BRITISH ASSOCIATION OF DRAMATHERAPISTS, 41
Broomhouse Lane, London SW6 3DP (enquirers should
enclose a stamped addressed envelope). Tel: 0171-731
0160

BIOMEDICAL SCIENCES

Qualifications from higher education establishments and
training in medical laboratories are required for membership of the Institute of Biomedical Science.

INSTITUTE OF BIOMEDICAL SCIENCE, 12 Coldbath
Square, London EC1R 5HL. Tel: 0171-713 0214. *Chief
Executive*, A. Potter

CHIROPODY

Professional recognition is granted by the Society of
Chiropodists and Podiatrists to students who are awarded
B.Sc. degrees in Podiatry or Podiatric Medicine after
attending a course of full-time training for three or four
years at one of the 14 recognized schools in the UK (11 in
England and Wales, two in Scotland and one in Northern
Ireland). Qualifications granted and degrees recognized by
the Society are approved by the Chiropodists Board for
the purpose of State Registration, which is a condition of
employment within the National Health Service.

THE SOCIETY OF CHIROPODISTS AND PODIATRISTS,
53 Welbeck Street, London WIM 7HE. Tel: 0171-486
3381. *Chief Executive*, Ms H. de Lyon

See also DIETETICS

OCCUPATIONAL THERAPY

The professional qualification may be obtained upon
successful completion of a validated course in any of the
28 institutions approved by the College of Occupational
Therapists. The courses are normally degree-level courses
based in higher education institutions.

COLLEGE OF OCCUPATIONAL THERAPISTS, 106–114
Borough High Street, London SE1 1LB. Tel: 0171-357
6480. *Secretary*, J. Thompson

ORTHOPTICS

Orthoptists undertake the diagnosis and treatment of all
types of squint and other anomalies of binocular vision,
working in close collaboration with ophthalmologists. The
training and maintenance of professional standards are the
responsibility of the Orthoptists Board of the Council for
the Professions Supplementary to Medicine. The professional body is the British Orthoptic Society. Training is at
degree level.

THE BRITISH ORTHOPTIC SOCIETY, Tavistock House
North, Tavistock Square, London WC1H 9HX. Tel: 0171-
387 7992. *Hon. Secretary*, Ms R. Auld

PHYSIOTHERAPY

Full-time three- or four-year degree courses are available
at 29 recognized schools in the UK. Information about
courses leading to eligibility for Membership of the
Chartered Society of Physiotherapy and to State Registration is available from the Chartered Society of Physiotherapy.

THE CHARTERED SOCIETY OF PHYSIOTHERAPY, 14
Bedford Row, London WC1R 4ED. Tel: 0171-306 6666.
Chief Executive, P. Gray

PROSTHETICS AND ORTHOTICS

Prosthetists provide artificial limbs, while orthotists provide
devices to support or control a part of the body. It is
necessary to obtain an honours degree to become a
prosthetist or orthotist. Courses are available at two
institutions in the UK.

BRITISH ASSOCIATION OF PROSTHETISTS AND
ORTHOTISTS, Sir James Clark Building, Abbey Mill
Business Centre, Paisley PA1 1TJ. Tel: 0141-561 7217

RADIOGRAPHY AND RADIOTHERAPY

In order to practise both diagnostic and therapeutic radiography in the UK, it is necessary to have successfully completed a course of education and training recognized by the Privy Council. Such courses are offered by universities throughout the UK and lead to the award of a degree in radiography. Further information is available from the college.

THE COLLEGE OF RADIOGRAPHERS, 2 Carriage Row, 183 Eversholt Street, London NW1 1BU. Tel: 0171-391 4500. *Chief Executive*, S. Evans

COMPLEMENTARY MEDICINE

Professional courses are validated by:
INSTITUTE FOR COMPLEMENTARY MEDICINE, PO Box 194, London SE16 1QZ. Tel: 0171-237 5165. *Director*, A. Baird

MERCHANT NAVY TRAINING SCHOOLS

OFFICERS

WARSASH MARITIME CENTRE, Southampton Institute, Newtown Road, Warsash, Southampton SO31 9ZL. Tel: 01489-576161. *Dean*, Capt. G. B. Angas

SEAFARERS

NATIONAL SEA TRAINING CENTRE, North West Kent College, Dering Way, Gravesend, Kent DA12 2JJ. Tel: 01322-629600. *Director of Faculty*, R. MacDonald

MUSIC

ASSOCIATED BOARD OF THE ROYAL SCHOOLS OF MUSIC, 14 Bedford Square, London WC1B 3JG. Tel: 0171-636 5400. The Board conducts graded music examinations in over 80 countries and provides other services to music education through its professional development department and publishing company. *Chief Executive*, R. Morris

GUILDHALL SCHOOL OF MUSIC AND DRAMA, Silk Street, London EC2Y 8DT. Tel: 0171-628 2571. *Principal*, I. Horsbrugh

LONDON COLLEGE OF MUSIC AND MEDIA, Thames Valley University, St Mary's Road, London W5 5RF. Tel: 0181-231 2304. *Dean*, Mrs P. Thompson

ROYAL ACADEMY OF MUSIC, Marylebone Road, London NW1 5HT. Tel: 0171-873 7373. *Principal*, Prof. C. Price

ROYAL COLLEGE OF ORGANISTS, 7 St Andrew Street, London EC4A 3LQ. Tel: 0171-936 3606. *Senior Executive*, A. Dear

ROYAL NORTHERN COLLEGE OF MUSIC, 124 Oxford Road, Manchester M13 9RD. Tel: 0161-907 5200. *Principal*, Prof. E. Gregson

ROYAL SCOTTISH ACADEMY OF MUSIC AND DRAMA, 100 Renfrew Street, Glasgow G2 3DB. Tel: 0141-332 4101. *Principal*, Dr P. Ledger, CBE, FRSE

TRINITY COLLEGE OF MUSIC, 11–13 Mandeville Place, London W1M 6AQ. Tel: 0171-935 5773. *Principal*, G. Henderson

NURSING

All nurses must be registered with the UK Central Council for Nursing, Midwifery and Health Visiting. Courses leading to registration as a nurse are at least three years in length. There are also some programmes which are combined with degrees. Students study in colleges of nursing or in institutions of higher education. Courses offer a combination of theoretical and practical experience in a variety of settings. Different courses lead to different types of registration, including: Registered Nurse (RN), Registered Mental Nurse (RMN), Registered Mental Handicap Nurse (RMHN), Registered Sick Children's Nurse (RSCN), Registered Midwife (RM) and Registered Health Visitor (RHV). The various national boards, listed below, are responsible for validating courses in nursing. In February 1999 the Government announced plans to replace these boards and the UK Central Council with a single UK-wide body. Health visitors will continue to have separate registration and representation on the new body.

The Royal College of Nursing is the largest professional union representing nurses and provides higher education through its Institute.

ENGLISH NATIONAL BOARD FOR NURSING, MIDWIFERY AND HEALTH VISITING, Victory House, 170 Tottenham Court Road, London W1P 0HA. Tel: 0171-388 3131. *Chief Executive*, A. P. Smith, CBE

NATIONAL BOARD FOR NURSING, MIDWIFERY AND HEALTH VISITING FOR NORTHERN IRELAND, Centre House, 79 Chichester Street, Belfast BT1 4JE. Tel: 01232-238152. *Chief Executive*, Prof. O. D'A. Slevin, Ph.D.

NATIONAL BOARD FOR NURSING, MIDWIFERY AND HEALTH VISITING FOR SCOTLAND, 22 Queen Street, Edinburgh EH2 1NT. Tel: 0131-226 7371. *Chief Executive*, D. C. Benton

THE ROYAL COLLEGE OF NURSING OF THE UNITED KINGDOM, 20 Cavendish Square, London W1M 0AB. Tel: 0171-409 3333. *General Secretary*, Miss C. Hancock; *Director of the RCN Institute*, Prof. A. Kitson

WELSH NATIONAL BOARD FOR NURSING, MIDWIFERY AND HEALTH VISITING, 2nd Floor, Golate House, 101 St Mary Street, Cardiff CF10 1DX. Tel: 01222-261400. *Chief Executive*, D. A. Ravey

UK CENTRAL COUNCIL FOR NURSING, MIDWIFERY AND HEALTH VISITING, 23 Portland Place, London W1N 4JT. Tel: 0171-637 7181. *Chief Executive and Registrar*, Ms S. Norman

OPHTHALMIC AND DISPENSING OPTICS

Professional bodies are:
THE ASSOCIATION OF BRITISH DISPENSING OPTICIANS, 6 Hurlingham Business Park, Sulivan Road, London SW6 3DU. Tel: 0171-736 0088. Grants qualifications as a dispensing optician. *Registrar*, D. G. Baker

THE COLLEGE OF OPTOMETRISTS, 42 Craven Street, London WC2N 5NG. Tel: 0171-839 6000. Grants qualifications as an optometrist. *General Secretary*, P. D. Leigh

OSTEOPATHY

Osteopathy is accorded statutory regulation by the Osteopaths Act 1993. The existing voluntary registration schemes were taken over by the General Osteopathic Council, which opened a new statutory register on 9 May 1998. From 2000 it will be an offence for anyone who is not on the statutory register to call themselves an osteopath.

The General Osteopathic Council is now responsible for regulating, developing and promoting the profession. Osteopathic education is currently undergoing considerable change. Courses vary in length from four to six years, granting various qualifications from diploma to honours degree. Shorter courses are available for qualified doctors. Details of accrediting institutions and courses can be obtained from the General Osteopathic Council.

GENERAL OSTEOPATHIC COUNCIL, Osteopathy House, 176 Tower Bridge Road, London SE1 3LU. Tel: 0171-357 6655. *Chief Executive and Registrar*, Miss M. Craggs

PHARMACY

Information may be obtained from the Secretary and Registrar of the Royal Pharmaceutical Society of Great Britain.

ROYAL PHARMACEUTICAL SOCIETY OF GREAT BRITAIN, 1 Lambeth High Street, London SE1 7JN. Tel: 0171-735 9141. *Secretary and Registrar*, A. Lewis, OBE

PHOTOGRAPHY

The professional body is:

BRITISH INSTITUTE OF PROFESSIONAL PHOTOGRAPHY, Fox Talbot House, Amwell End, Ware, Herts SG12 9HN. Tel: 01920-464011. *Chief Executive*, A. Mair

PRINTING

Details of training courses in printing can be obtained from the Institute of Printing and the British Printing Industries Federation. In addition to these examining and organizing bodies, examinations are held by various independent regional examining boards in further education.

BRITISH PRINTING INDUSTRIES FEDERATION, 11 Bedford Row, London WC1R 4DX. Tel: 0171-242 6904. *Chief Executive*, T. P. E. Machin

INSTITUTE OF PRINTING, The Mews, Hill House, Clanricarde Road, Tunbridge Wells, Kent TN1 1PJ. Tel: 01892-538118. *Secretary-General*, D. Freeland

SCIENCE

Professional qualifications are awarded by:

GEOLOGICAL SOCIETY, Burlington House, Piccadilly, London W1V 0JU. Tel: 0171-434 9944. *Chief Executive*, E. Nickless

INSTITUTE OF BIOLOGY, 20–22 Queensberry Place, London SW7 2DZ. Tel: 0171-581 8333. *President*, Dr J. Norris; *Chief Executive*, Prof. A. Malcolm

INSTITUTE OF PHYSICS, 76 Portland Place, London W1N 3DH. Tel: 0171-470 4800. *Chief Executive*, Dr A. D. W. Jones

ROYAL SOCIETY OF CHEMISTRY, Burlington House, Piccadilly, London W1V 0BN. Tel: 0171-437 8656. *President*, Prof. A. Ledwith, CBE, FRS; *Secretary-General*, T. D. Inch, PH.D., D.SC.

SOCIAL WORK

The Central Council for Education and Training in Social Work promotes education and training for social work and social care in the UK. It approves education and training programmes, including those leading to its qualifying award, the Diploma in Social Work.

THE CENTRAL COUNCIL FOR EDUCATION AND TRAINING IN SOCIAL WORK, Derbyshire House, St Chad's Street, London WC1H 8AD. Tel: 0171-278 2455. *Chairperson*, Ms Z. Alexander; *Chief Executive*, J. Bernard

SPEECH AND LANGUAGE THERAPY

The Royal College of Speech and Language Therapists provides details of courses leading to qualification as a speech and language therapist. Other professionals may become Affiliates of the College. A directory of registered members is published annually.

THE ROYAL COLLEGE OF SPEECH AND LANGUAGE THERAPISTS, 7 Bath Place, Rivington Street, London EC2A 3SU. Tel: 0171-613 3855. *Director*, Mrs P. Evans

SURVEYING

The qualifying professional bodies include:

ARCHITECTURE AND SURVEYING INSTITUTE, St Mary House, 15 St Mary Street, Chippenham, Wilts SN15 3WD. Tel: 01249-444505. *Chief Executive*, I. N. Norris

ASSOCIATION OF BUILDING ENGINEERS, Jubilee House, Billing Brook Road, Weston Favell, Northampton NN3 8NW. Tel: 01604-404121. *Chief Executive*, D. R. Gibson

INCORPORATED SOCIETY OF VALUERS AND AUCTIONEERS (1968), 3 Cadogan Gate, London SW1X 0AS. Tel: 0171-235 2282. *Chief Executive*, C. Evans

INSTITUTE OF REVENUES, RATING AND VALUATION, 41 Doughty Street, London WC1N 2LF. Tel: 0171-831 3505. *Director*, Ms K. Aldred

ROYAL INSTITUTION OF CHARTERED SURVEYORS (incorporating The Institute of Quantity Surveyors), 12 Great George Street, London SW1P 3AD. Tel: 0171-222 7000. *Chief Executive*, J. H. A. J. Armstrong

TEACHING

Teachers in maintained schools must acquire Qualified Teacher Status (QTS) by completing a programme of Initial Teacher Training. Those without a first degree may take a Bachelor of Education (B.Ed) or a Bachelor of Arts/Science (BA/B.Sc) with QTS, full-time for three or four years, depending on the programme followed. These degrees combine subject and professional studies with teaching practice. Shortened courses of these degrees are available for those who have successfully completed one or two years of higher education. Flexible routes into teaching are increasing, including part-time, distance learning and modular courses. Alternatively, teachers can gain QTS through employment-based training, following individual training plans while in post.

For those who already have a first degree, the most common route is through a one-year Postgraduate Certificate of Education (PGCE). This may be taken full-time or part-time, or as a distance-learning programme. Postgraduates may also gain QTS through training in a school (School-Centred Initial Teacher Training). Since January 1998, graduates have been able to join the Graduate Teacher Programme which provides teaching and training for one year.

Details of courses in England and Wales are contained in the *NATFHE Handbook of Initial Teacher Training in England and Wales 1999*, in *University and College Entrance: 1999 (The Big Book)* published by UCAS and on the UCAS website. Further information about teaching in England and Wales is available from the Teaching Information Line, 01245-454454. Details of courses in Scotland can be obtained from universities and the Graduate Teacher Training Registry (GTTR). Each university chooses whether to receive applications direct or through the GTTR. Details of courses in Northern Ireland can be obtained from the Department of Education for Northern Ireland. Applications for teacher training courses in Northern Ireland are made to the institutions direct.

TEACHER TRAINING AGENCY COMMUNICATION CENTRE, PO Box 3210, Chelmsford, Essex CM1 3WA

UCAS WEB: http://www.ucas.ac.uk

TEXTILES

THE TEXTILE INSTITUTE, 4th Floor, St James's Buildings, Oxford Street, Manchester M1 6FQ. Tel: 0161-237 1188. *Director-General*, T. Hennessey

THEOLOGICAL COLLEGES

The number of students training for the ministry in the academic year 1998-9 is shown in parenthesis. Those marked * show figures for 1997-8.

ANGLICAN

COLLEGE OF THE RESURRECTION, Mirfield, W. Yorks WF14 0BW. Tel: 01924-481910. (40). *Principal*, Revd C. Irvine

CRANMER HALL, St John's College, Durham DH1 3RJ. Tel: 0191-374 3579. (69). *Principal*, Rt. Revd S. W. Sykes

OAK HILL COLLEGE, Chase Side, London N14 4PS. Tel: 0181-449 0467. (90). *Principal*, Revd Dr D. Peterson

RIDLEY HALL, Cambridge CB3 9HG. Tel: 01223-741080. (60). *Principal*, Revd G. A. Cray

RIPON COLLEGE, Cuddesdon, Oxford OX44 9EX. Tel: 01865-874427. (75). *Principal*, Revd J. Clarke

ST JOHN'S COLLEGE, Chilwell Lane, Bramcote, Nottingham NG9 3DS. Tel: 0115-925 1114. (70). *Principal*, Revd Canon Dr C. Baxter

ST MICHAEL'S THEOLOGICAL COLLEGE, Llandaff, Cardiff CF5 2YJ. Tel: 01222-563379. (40). *Principal*, Revd Dr J. I. Holdsworth

ST STEPHEN'S HOUSE, 16 Marston Street, Oxford OX4 1JX. Tel: 01865-247874. (c.60). *Principal*, Revd Dr J. P. Sheehy

THEOLOGICAL INSTITUTE OF THE SCOTTISH EPISCOPAL CHURCH, Old Coates House, 32 Manor Place, Edinburgh EH3 7EB. Tel: 0131-220 2272. (28).

TRINITY COLLEGE, Stoke Hill, Bristol BS9 1JP. Tel: 0117-968 2803. (200). *Principal*, Revd Dr F. Bridges (from Nov. 1999)

WESTCOTT HOUSE, Jesus Lane, Cambridge CB5 8BP. Tel: 01223-741000. (65). *Principal*, Revd M. G. V. Roberts

WYCLIFFE HALL, 54 Banbury Road, Oxford OX2 6PW. Tel: 01865-274200. (70). *Principal*, Revd Dr A. E. McGrath

BAPTIST

BRISTOL BAPTIST COLLEGE, The Promenade, Clifton, Bristol BS8 3NF. Tel: 0117-946 7050. (26). *Principal*, Revd Dr B. Haymes

NORTHERN BAPTIST COLLEGE, Luther King House, Brighton Grove, Rusholme, Manchester M14 5JP. Tel: 0161-224 2214. (30). *Principal*, Revd Dr R. L. Kidd

NORTH WALES BAPTIST COLLEGE, Ffordd Ffriddoedd, Bangor LL57 2EH. Tel: 01248-362608. (5*). *Warden*, Revd Dr D. D. Morgan

REGENT'S PARK COLLEGE, Oxford OX1 2LB. Tel: 01865-288120. (25). *Principal*, Revd Dr P. S. Fiddes

THE SCOTTISH BAPTIST COLLEGE, 12 Aytoun Road, Glasgow G41 5RN. Tel: 0141-424 0747. (14). *Principal*, Revd Dr K. B. E. Roxburgh

SOUTH WALES BAPTIST COLLEGE, 54 Richmond Road, Cardiff CF24 3UR. Tel: 01222-256066. (26). *Principal*, Revd D. H. Matthews

CHURCH OF SCOTLAND

TRINITY COLLEGE, Faculty of Divinity, University of Glasgow, Glasgow G12 8QQ. Tel: 0141-330 6840. (20). *Principal*, Revd Dr D. M. Murray

CONGREGATIONAL

SCOTTISH CONGREGATIONAL COLLEGE, 340 Catherdral Street, Glasgow G1 2BQ. Tel: 0141-332 7667. (4) *Principal*, Revd Dr J. W. Dyce

METHODIST

EDGHILL THEOLOGICAL COLLEGE, 9 Lennoxvale, Belfast BT9 5BY. Tel: 01232-665870. (25). *Principal*, Revd Dr W. D. D. Cooke

HARTLEY VICTORIA COLLEGE, Luther King House, Brighton Grove, Manchester M14 5JP. Tel: 0161-224 2215. (30). *Principal*, Revd Dr J. A. Harrod

WESLEY COLLEGE, College Park Drive, Henbury Road, Bristol BS10 7QD. Tel: 0117-959 1200. (49*). *Principal*, Revd Dr N. Richardson

WESLEY HOUSE, Jesus Lane, Cambridge CB5 8BJ. Tel: 01223-741033. (30). *Principal*, Revd Dr P. Luscombe

WESLEY STUDY CENTRE, 55 The Avenue, Durham DH1 4EB. Tel: 0191-374 3580. (20). *Director*, Revd R. Walton

NON-DENOMINATIONAL

CHRIST'S COLLEGE, 25 High Street, Old Aberdeen AB24 3EE. Tel: 01224-272380. (30). *Master*, Very Revd Prof. A. Main

NEW COLLEGE, Mound Place, Edinburgh EH1 2LX. Tel: 0131-650 8916. (15). *Principal*, Revd Dr D. Lyall

QUEENS' COLLEGE, Somerset Road, Edgbaston, Birmingham B15 2QH. Tel: 0121-454 1527. (56). *Principal*, Revd P. Fisher

ST MARY'S COLLEGE, The University, St Andrews, Fife KY16 9JU. Tel: 01334-462850. (7*). *Principal*, Dr R. A. Piper

SPURGEON'S COLLEGE, South Norwood Hill, London SE25 6DJ. Tel: 0181-653 0850. (100). *Principal*, Revd Dr M. J. Quicke

PRESBYTERIAN

UNION THEOLOGICAL COLLEGE, 108 Botanic Avenue, Belfast BT7 1JT. Tel: 01232-205080. (200). *Principal*, Revd Prof. J. C. McCullough

PRESBYTERIAN CHURCH OF WALES

UNITED THEOLOGICAL COLLEGE, Aberystwyth SY23 2LT. Tel: 01970-624574. (3). *Principal*, Revd Dr J. T. Williams

ROMAN CATHOLIC

ALLEN HALL, 28 Beaufort Street, London SW3 5AA. Tel: 0171-351 1296. (35). *Principal*, Revd J. Overton, STL

CAMPION HOUSE COLLEGE, 112 Thornbury Road, Isleworth, Middx TW7 4NN. Tel: 0181-560 1924. (c.12). *Principal*, Revd M. Barrow, SJ

OSCOTT COLLEGE, Chester Road, Sutton Coldfield, W. Midlands B73 5AA. Tel: 0121-354 7117. (40). *Rector*, Very Revd Mgr K. McDonald

ST JOHN'S SEMINARY, Wonersh, Guildford, Surrey GU5 0QX. Tel: 01483-892217. (45). *Rector*, Revd K. Haggerty, STL

SCOTUS COLLEGE, 2 Chesters Road, Bearsden, Glasgow G61 4AG. Tel: 0141-942 8384. (25). *Rector*, Revd N. Donnachie

USHAW COLLEGE, Durham DH7 9RH. Tel: 0191-373 1366. (32). *President*, Revd J. P. O'Keefe

UNITARIAN

UNITARIAN COLLEGE, Luther King House, Brighton Grove, Rusholme, Manchester M14 5JP. Tel: 0161-224 2849. (5). *Principal*, Revd Dr L. Smith

UNITED REFORMED

MANSFIELD COLLEGE, Mansfield Road, Oxford OX1 3TF. Tel: 01865-270999. (20). *Principal*, Prof. D. Marquand

NORTHERN COLLEGE, Luther King House, Brighton Grove, Rusholme, Manchester M14 5JP. Tel: 0161-224 4381. (44). *Principal*, Revd Dr D. R. Peel

WESTMINSTER COLLEGE, Madingley Road, Cambridge CB3 0AA. Tel: 01223-741084. (45). *Principal*, Revd Dr D. G. Cornick

JEWISH

JEWS' COLLEGE, Schaller House, Albert Road, London NW4 2SJ. Tel: 0181-203 6427. (6). *Director*, Prof. D. H. Ruben

LEO BAECK COLLEGE, Sternberg Centre for Judaism, 80 East End Road, London N3 2SY. Tel: 0181-349 4525. (27). *Principal*, Rabbi Prof. J. Magonet

TOWN AND COUNTRY PLANNING

Degree and diploma courses in town planning are accredited by the Royal Town Planning Institute.

THE ROYAL TOWN PLANNING INSTITUTE, 26 Portland Place, London W1N 4BE. Tel: 0171-636 9107. *Secretary-General*, R. Upton

TRANSPORT

Qualifying examinations in transport management and logistics leading to professional status are conducted by the Institute of Logistics and Transport.

THE INSTITUTE OF LOGISTICS AND TRANSPORT, 80 Portland Place, London W1N 4DP. Tel: 0171-467 9400. *Director*, Mrs D. de Carvalho

VETERINARY MEDICINE

The regulatory body for veterinary medicine is the Royal College of Veterinary Surgeons, which keeps the register of those entitled to practise veterinary medicine. In order to be registered, a person must complete a five-year undergraduate degree (BVetMed, BVSc., BVMS, BVM and S) at one of the six authorized institutions in the UK.

The British Veterinary Association is the professional body representing veterinary surgeons. The British Veterinary Nursing Association is the professional body representing veterinary nurses who are also registered with the Royal College of Veterinary Surgeons.

BRITISH VETERINARY ASSOCIATION, 7 Mansfield Street, London W1M 0AT. Tel: 0171-636 6541. *Chief Executive*, J. Baird

BRITISH VETERINARY NURSING ASSOCIATION, Level 15, Terminus House, Terminus Street, Harlow, Essex CM20 1XA. Tel: 01279-450567. *Chairman*, Ms J. More

ROYAL COLLEGE OF VETERINARY SURGEONS, Belgravia House, 62–64 Horseferry Road, London SW1P 2AF. Tel: 0171-222 2001. *President*, Prof A. R. Michell; *Registrar*, Miss J. C. Hern

Independent Schools

The following pages list those independent schools whose
Head is a member of the Headmasters' and Headmistress'
Conference, the Society of Headmasters and
Headmistresses of Independent Schools or the Girls'
Schools Association

THE HEADMASTERS' AND HEADMISTRESSES' CONFERENCE

Chairman (1990), J. Sabben-Clare (Winchester College)
  T. D. Wheare (Bryanston) (from Jan. 2000)
Secretary, V. S. Anthony, 130 Regent Road, Leicester LEI 7PG.
  Tel: 0116-285 4810
Membership Secretary, D. E. Prince. Tel: 0116-255 1567
The annual meeting is held early in October

* Woodard Corporation School, 1 The Sanctuary, London
  SWIP 3JT. Tel: 0171-222 5381
† Girls in VI form
‡ Co-educational

Name of School	Foun-ded	No. of pupils	Annual fees £		Head (with date of appointment)
			Boarding	Day	
ENGLAND AND WALES					
Abbotsholme School, Rocester	1889	134‡	13,860	9,270	Dr S. Tommis (1999)
Abingdon School, Oxon	1256	790	12,294	6,669	M. St J. Parker (1975)
Ackworth School, W. Yorks	1779	340‡	11,406	6,486	M. J. Dickinson (1995)
Aldenham School, Elstree, Herts	1597	405†	13,890	9,615	S. R. Borthwick (1994)
Alleyn's School, London SE22	1619	917‡	—	7,005	Dr C. H. R. Niven (1992)
Ampleforth College (*RC*), N. Yorks	1802	483†	14,805	7,644	Revd G. F. L. Chamberlain, OSB (1993)
*Ardingly College, Haywards Heath	1858	420‡	13,455	10,185	J. Franklin (1998)
Arnold School, Blackpool	1896	800‡	—	4,635	W. T. Gillen (1993)
Ashville College, Harrogate	1877	586‡	11,010	5,916	M. H. Crosby (1987)
Bablake School, Coventry	1560	850‡	—	4,497	Dr S. Nuttall (1991)
Bancroft's School, Woodford Green, Essex	1727	780‡	—	6,915	Dr P. R. Scott (1996)
Barnard Castle School, Co. Durham	1883	470‡	10,548	6,243	M. D. Featherstone (1997)
Batley Grammar School, W. Yorks	1612	503‡	—	4,887	B. Battye (1998)
Bedales School, Petersfield	1893	400‡	15,798	12,078	Mrs A. A. Willcocks (1995)
Bedford Modern School	1566	1,100	11,325	6,114	S. Smith (1997)
Bedford School	1552	688	13,440	8,460	Dr I. P. Evans (1990)
Berkhamsted Collegiate School, Herts	1541	1,000†	12,834	8,067	Dr P. Chadwick (*Principal*) (1996)
Birkdale School, Sheffield	1904	520†	—	5,364	R. J. Court (1998)
Birkenhead School, Merseyside	1860	620	—	4,776	S. J. Haggett (1988)
Bishop's Stortford College, Herts	1868	350‡	12,075	8,706	J. G. Trotman (1997)
*Bloxham School, Banbury	1860	345‡	15,150	11,460	D. K. Exham (1991)
Blundell's School, Tiverton	1604	370‡	14,070	8,580	J. Leigh (1992)
Bolton School	1641	850	—	5,298	A. W. Wright (1983)
Bootham School, York	1823	373‡	12,150	7,950	I. M. Small (1988)
Bradfield College, Reading	1850	580‡	15,105	11,328	P. B. Smith (1985)
Bradford Grammar School	1662	1,068‡	—	5,300	S. R. Davidson (1996)
Brentwood School, Essex	1557	1,080‡	11,991	6,891	J. A. B. Kelsall (1993)
Brighton College, E. Sussex	1845	540‡	14,724	9,498	Dr A. F. Seldon (1997)
Bristol Cathedral School	1140	470†	—	4,362	K. J. Riley (1993)
Bristol Grammar School	1532	1,030‡	—	4,776	Dr D. J. Mascord (1999)
Bromsgrove School, Worcs	1553	650‡	12,075	7,470	T. M. Taylor (1986)
Bryanston School, Blandford Forum	1928	640‡	15,807	11,382	T. D. Wheare (1983)
Bury Grammar School, Lancs	1634	650	—	4,470	K. Richards (1990)
Canford School, Wimbourne	1923	570‡	15,270	11,460	J. D. Lever (1992)
Caterham School, Surrey	1811	690‡	13,914	7,458	R. A. E. Davey (1995)
Charterhouse, Godalming	1611	675†	15,588	12,882	Revd J. S. Witheridge (1996)
Cheadle Hulme School, Cheshire	1855	1,083‡	—	5,085	D. J. Wilkinson (1990)
Cheltenham College, Glos	1841	520‡	14,700	11,055	P. A. Chamberlain (1997)
Chetham's School of Music, Manchester	1653	270‡	17,595	13,620	Mrs C. Moreland (1999)
Chigwell School, Essex	1629	400‡	11,571	7,611	D. F. Gibbs (1996)
Christ College, Brecon	1541	300‡	12,102	9,378	D. P. Jones (1996)

Name of School	Foun-ded	No. of pupils	Annual fees £		Head (with date of appointment)
			Boarding	Day	
Christ's Hospital, Horsham	1552	800‡	13,067	—	Dr P. C. D. Southern (1996)
Churcher's College, Petersfield	1722	560‡	—	6,180	G. W. Buttle (1988)
City of London Freemen's School, Ashtead	1854	400‡	11,997	7,497	D. C. Haywood (1986)
City of London, London EC4	1442	875	—	7,137	D. Levin (1999)
Clifton College, Bristol	1862	667‡	14,790	10,140	A. H. Monro (1990)
Colfe's School, London SE12	1652	669‡	—	6,345	Dr D. J. Richardson (1990)
Colston's Collegiate School, Bristol	1710	500‡	10,800	4,700	D. G. Crawford (1995)
Cranleigh School, Surrey	1865	480‡	14,535	10,755	G. Waller (1997)
Culford School, Bury St Edmunds	1881	365‡	13,038	8,484	J. S. Richardson (1992)
Dame Allan's Boys' School, Newcastle upon Tyne	1705	810†	—	4,692	D. W. Welsh (*Principal*) (1996)
Dauntsey's School, Devizes	1542	660‡	13,119	8,001	S. B. Roberts (1997)
Dean Close School, Cheltenham	1886	440‡	14,865	10,380	Revd T. M. Hastie-Smith (1998)
*Denstone College, Uttoxeter	1868	350‡	10,650	7,050	D. M. Derbyshire (1997)
Downside School (*RC*), Somerset	1606	280	13,368	6,786	Revd Dom. A. Sutch (1995)
Dulwich College, London SE21	1619	1,200	14,805	7,575	G. G. Able (*Master*) (1997)
*Durham School	1414	272‡	12,966	8,487	N. G. Kern (1997)
Eastbourne College	1867	500‡	14,460	9,690	C. M. P. Bush (1993)
*Ellesmere College, Shropshire	1884	435‡	12,900	8,541	B. J. Wignall (1996)
Eltham College, London SE9	1842	590‡	14,150	6,850	D. M. Green (1990)
Emanuel School, London SW11	1594	760‡	—	6,384	Mrs A-M. Sutcliffe (1998)
Epsom College, Surrey	1853	655‡	14,415	10,710	A. H. Beadles (1992)
Eton College, Windsor	1440	1,288	15,660	—	J. E. Lewis (1994)
Exeter School	1633	670‡	9,900	5,220	N. W. Gamble (1992)
Felsted School, Dunmow, Essex	1564	390‡	14,970	11,790	S. C. Roberts (1993)
Forest School, London E17	1834	1,000‡	11,001	7,008	A. G. Boggis (*Warden*) (1992)
Framlingham College, Woodbridge, Suffolk	1864	420‡	12,111	7,773	Mrs. G. M. Randall (1994)
Frensham Heights, Farnham	1925	300‡	13,800	9,000	P. M. de Voil (1993)
Giggleswick School, Settle	1499	325‡	14,394	9,552	A. P. Millard (1993)
The Grange School, Northwich, Cheshire	1933	650‡	—	4,215	Mrs J. E. Stephen (1997)
Gresham's School, Holt, Norfolk	1555	520‡	14,670	10,455	J. H. Arkell (1991)
Haberdashers' Aske's School, Elstree, Herts	1690	1,100	—	7,164	J. W. R. Goulding (1996)
Haileybury, Hertford	1862	620‡	15,510	11,220	S. A. Westley (*Master*) (1996)
Hampton School, Middx	1556	950	—	6,555	B. R. Martin (1997)
Harrow School, Middx	1572	790	15,900	—	B. J. Lenon (1999)
Hereford Cathedral School	1384	620‡	—	5,535	Dr H. C. Tomlinson (1987)
Highgate School, London N6	1565	575	—	8,640	R. P. Kennedy (1989)
Hulme Grammar School, Oldham	1611	648	—	4,455	T. J. Turvey (1995)
*Hurstpierpoint College, Hassocks, W. Sussex	1849	350‡	13,830	10,710	S. D. A. Meek (1995)
Hymers College, Hull	1889	740‡	—	4,518	J. C. Morris (1990)
Ipswich School	1390	585‡	10,599	6,144	I. G. Galbraith (1993)
John Lyon School, Harrow	1876	524	—	6,870	Revd T. J. Wright (1986)
Kelly College, Tavistock	1877	350‡	13,815	8,685	M. Turner (1995)
Kent College, Canterbury	1885	480‡	13,005	7,242	E. B. Halse (1995)
Kimbolton School, Huntingdon	1600	560‡	11,205	6,615	R. V. Peel (1987)
King Edward VI School, Southampton	1553	950‡	—	5,925	P. B. Hamilton (1996)
King Edward VII and Queen Mary School, Lytham St Annes	1908	795‡	—	4,500	P. J. Wilde, *Principal* (1999)
King Edward's School, Bath	1552	685‡	—	5,631	P. J. Winter (1993)
King Edward's School, Birmingham	1552	883	—	5,523	R. M. Dancey (*Chief Master*) (1998)
King Edward's School, Witley, Surrey	1553	480‡	11,385	7,785	R. J. Fox (1988)
King Henry VIII School, Coventry	1545	799‡	—	4,497	D. N. Ireland (*Acting Head*) (1999)
*King's College, Taunton	1879	430‡	13,950	9,180	R. S. Funnell (1988)
King's College School, London SW19	1829	700	—	8,400	A. C. V. Evans (1997)
King's School, Bruton, Somerset	1519	360‡	13,050	9,435	R. I. Smyth (1993)
King's School, Canterbury	600	754‡	15,780	11,010	Revd Canon K. H. Wilkinson (1996)
King's School, Chester	1541	540†	—	5,112	A. R. D. Wickson (1981)
King's School, Ely	973	395‡	13,325	9,150	R. H. Youdale (1992)
King's School, Gloucester	1541	300‡	11,000	7,500	P. Lacey (1992)
King's School, Macclesfield	1502	1,050‡	—	5,010	A. G. Silcock (1987)
King's School, Rochester, Kent	604	327‡	14,808	8,538	Dr I. R. Walker (1987)

Name of School	Founded	No. of pupils	Annual fees £ Boarding	Day	Head (with date of appointment)
*King's School, Tynemouth	1860	628‡	—	4,851	Dr D. Younger (1993)
King's School, Worcester	1541	788‡	—	6,273	T. H. Keyes (1998)
Kingston Grammar School, Surrey	1561	605‡	—	6,897	C. D. Baxter (1991)
Kingswood School, Bath	1748	486‡	13,999	7,954	G. M. Best (1987)
*Lancing College, W. Sussex	1848	463†	14,850	11,100	P. M. Tinniswood (1998)
Latymer Upper School, London w6	1624	950†	—	7,560	C. Diggory (1991)
Leeds Grammar School	1552	1,010	—	6,204	Dr M. Bailey (1999)
Leicester Grammar School	1981	650‡	—	5,250	J. B. Sugden (1989)
Leighton Park School, Reading	1890	340‡	13,455	9,414	J. Dunston (1996)
The Leys School, Cambridge	1875	500‡	13,680	10,080	Revd Dr J. C. A. Barrett (1990)
Liverpool College	1840	700‡	—	5,685	J. P. Siviter (*Principal*) (1997)
Llandovery College, Carmarthenshire	1848	210‡	11,652	7,737	Dr C. E. Evans (*Warden*) (1988)
Lord Wandsworth College, Long Sutton, Hants	1912	485‡	14,445	9,675	I. G. Power (1997)
Loughborough Grammar School	1495	970	9,504	5,238	P. B. Fisher (1998)
Magdalen College School, Oxford	1480	540	—	6,033	A. D. Halls (*Master*) (1998)
Malvern College, Worcs	1862	551‡	15,030	10,920	H. C. K. Carson (1997)
Manchester Grammar School	1515	1,425	—	5,040	Dr G. M. Stephen (*High Master*) (1994)
Marlborough College, Wilts	1843	800‡	15,555	11,670	E. J. H. Gould (*Master*) (1993)
Merchant Taylors' School, Liverpool	1620	728	—	4,599	S. J. R. Dawkins (1986)
Merchant Taylors' School, Northwood, Middx	1561	775	13,500	8,000	J. R. Gabitass (1991)
Millfield, Street, Somerset	1935	1,215‡	15,855	10,455	P. M. Johnson (1998)
Mill Hill School, London NW7	1807	565‡	14,085	9,225	W. R. Winfield (1995)
Monkton Combe School, Bath	1868	330‡	14,460	9,870	M. J. Cuthbertson (1990)
Monmouth School	1614	570	10,368	6,222	T. H. P. Haynes (1995)
Mount St Mary's College (*RC*), Sheffield	1842	280‡	10,920	6,270	P. MacDonald (1998)
Newcastle-under-Lyme School	1872	1,100‡	—	4,488	Dr R. M. Reynolds (*Principal*) (1990)
Norwich School	1156	615†	—	5,610	C. D. Brown, MA (1984)
Nottingham High School	1513	832	—	5,688	C. S. Parker (1995)
Oakham School, Rutland	1584	778‡	14,190	8,490	A. R. M. Little (1996)
The Oratory School (*RC*), Woodcote, Berks	1859	382	14,460	10,125	S. W. Barrow (1991)
Oundle School, Northants	1556	830‡	15,273	—	Dr R. Townsend (1999)
Pangbourne College, Berks	1917	320‡	13,920	9,750	A. B. E. Hudson (1988)
Perse School, Cambridge	1615	570†	—	6,078	N. P. V. Richardson (1994)
Plymouth College	1877	598‡	11,316	5,745	A. J. Morsley (1992)
Pocklington School, York	1514	585‡	10,000	6,200	J. N. D. Gray (1992)
Portsmouth Grammar School	1732	800‡	—	5,595	Dr T. R. Hands, D.Phil. (1997)
Prior Park College (*RC*), Bath	1830	500‡	12,765	7,062	Dr R. G. G. Mercer, D.Phil. (1996)
Queen Elizabeth GS, Wakefield	1591	680†	—	5,307	R. P. Mardling (1985)
Queen Elizabeth's GS, Blackburn	1567	908†	—	4,977	Dr D. S. Hempsall (1995)
Queen Elizabeth's Hospital, Bristol	1590	540	9,015	4,815	Dr R. Gliddon (1985)
Queen's College, Taunton	1843	473‡	11,340	7,434	C. T. Bradnock (1991)
Radley College, Abingdon	1847	620	15,375	—	R. M. Morgan (*Warden*) (1991)
Ratcliffe College (*RC*), Leicester	1844	495‡	10,899	7,269	P. Farrar (1999)
Reading Blue Coat School	1646	607†	11,760	6,450	S. J. W. McArthur (1997)
Reed's School, Cobham, Surrey	1813	320†	12,690	9,591	D. W. Jarrett (1997)
Reigate Grammar School, Surrey	1675	802‡	—	6,324	P. V. Dixon (1996)
Rendcomb College, Cirencester	1920	250‡	12,420	9,840	G. Holden (1999)
Repton School, Derby	1557	542‡	14,250	10,620	G. E. Jones (1987)
Rossall School, Fleetwood, Lancs	1844	390‡	13,500	5,025	R. D. W. Rhodes (1987)
Royal Grammar School, Guildford	1509	840	—	7,311	T. M. S. Young (1992)
Royal Grammar School, Newcastle upon Tyne	1545	925	—	4,842	J. F. X. Miller (1994)
Royal Grammar School, Worcester	1291	731	—	5,436	W. A. Jones (1993)
Royal Hospital School, Ipswich	1712	690‡	10,452	6,774	N. K. D. Ward (1995)
Rugby School	1567	719‡	15,375	9,225	M. B. Mavor, CVO (1990)
Rydal Penrhos School, Colwyn Bay	1885	452‡	11,577	7,674	M. S. James (1998)
Ryde School with Upper Chine, Isle of Wight	1921	420‡	10,290	5,040	Dr N. J. England (1997)
St Albans School	948	680†	—	6,900	A. R. Grant (1993)
St Bede's College (*RC*), Manchester	1876	1,002‡	—	4,170	J. Byrne (1983)
St Bees School, Cumbria	1583	300‡	13,425	9,075	Mrs J. D. Pickering (1998)

Name of School	Founded	No. of pupils	Annual fees £ Boarding	Annual fees £ Day	Head (with date of appointment)
St Benedict's School (RC), London w5	1902	548†	—	6,135	Dr A. J. Dachs (1986)
St Dunstan's College, London SE6	1888	930‡	—	6,480	D. I. Davies (1998)
St Edmund's College (RC), Ware, Herts	1568	373‡	11,985	7,575	D. J. J. McEwen (1984)
St Edmund's School, Canterbury	1749	270‡	14,688	9,480	A. N. Ridley (1994)
St Edward's School, Oxford	1863	569‡	15,150	10,995	D. Christie (Warden) (1988)
St George's College (RC), Addlestone, Surrey	1869	986‡	—	7,650	J. A. Peake (1994)
St John's School, Leatherhead, Surrey	1851	420†	13,200	9,300	C. H. Tongue (1993)
St Lawrence College in Thanet, Ramsgate	1879	370‡	14,595	9,360	M. Slater (1996)
St Mary's College (RC), Liverpool	1919	620‡	—	4,500	W. Hammond (1991)
St Paul's School, London SW13	1509	778	14,910	9,810	R. S. Baldock (High Master) (1992)
St Peter's School, York	627	500‡	12,228	7,119	A. F. Trotman (1995)
Sedbergh School, Cumbria	1525	288	14,760	10,920	C. H. Hirst (1995)
Sevenoaks School, Kent	1432	960‡	15,213	9,651	T. R. Cookson (1996)
Sherborne School, Dorset	1550	500	15,525	11,640	P. H. Lapping (1988)
Shrewsbury School	1552	700	15,150	10,665	F. E. Maidment (1988)
Silcoates School, Wakefield	1820	450‡	—	6,354	A. P. Spillane (1992)
Solihull School	1560	799†	—	5,277	P. S. J. Derham (1996)
Stamford School, Lincs	1532	511	10,500	5,400	Dr P. R. Mason (Principal) (1997)
Stockport Grammar School	1487	1,005‡	—	4,833	I. Mellor (1996)
Stonyhurst College (RC), Clitheroe	1593	400‡	14,028	8,466	A. J. F. Aylward (1996)
Stowe School, Bucks	1923	575†	15,690	11,760	J. G. L. Nichols (1989)
Sutton Valence School, Kent	1576	400‡	13,830	8,850	N. A. Sampson (1994)
Taunton School	1846	465†	13,185	8,460	J. P. Whiteley (1997)
Tettenhall College, Wolverhampton	1863	300‡	10,800	6,594	Dr P. C. Bodkin (1994)
Tonbridge School, Kent	1553	710	15,846	11,196	J. M. Hammond (1990)
Trent College, Nottingham	1868	640‡	12,382	7,628	J. S. Lee (1988)
Trinity School, Croydon	1596	860	—	6,828	C. J. Tarrant (1999)
Truro School	1880	752‡	10,668	5,571	G. A. G. Dodd (1993)
University College School, London NW3	1830	700	—	8,475	K. J. Durham (1996)
Uppingham School, Oakham, Rutland	1584	660†	15,420	10,800	Dr S. C. Winkley, D.Phil. (1991)
Warwick School	914	800	11,667	5,466	Dr P. J. Cheshire (1988)
Wellingborough School, Northants	1595	348‡	—	6,570	F. R. Ullmann (1993)
Wellington College, Crowthorne, Berks	1859	805†	15,525	11,400	C. J. Driver (Master) (1989)
Wellington School, Somerset	1837	556‡	9,828	5,388	A. J. Rogers (1990)
Wells Cathedral School, Somerset	909	568‡	12,306	7,308	J. S. Baxter (1985)
West Buckland School, Barnstaple, Devon	1858	489‡	10,350	6,210	J. F. Vick (1997)
Westminster School, London SW1	1560	652†	16,068	11,130	T. Jones-Parry (1998)
Whitgift School, South Croydon	1596	1,100	—	7,269	C. A. Barnett, D.Phil. (1991)
William Hulme's GS, Manchester	1887	660‡	—	4,785	B. J. Purvis (1997)
Winchester College	1382	680	16,110	12,474	J. P. Sabben-Clare (1985)
Wisbech Grammar School, Cambs	1379	702‡	—	5,685	R. S. Repper (1988)
Wolverhampton Grammar School	1512	760‡	—	6,000	Dr B. Trafford (1990)
Woodbridge School, Suffolk	1662	547‡	11,640	6,846	S. H. Cole (1994)
Woodhouse Grove School, Bradford	1812	600‡	10,995	6,420	D. C. Humphreys (1996)
*Worksop College, Notts	1895	380‡	12,930	8,865	R. A. Collard (1994)
Worth School (RC), Crawley	1959	405	13,971	9,861	Fr C. Jamison (1994)
Wrekin College, Telford	1880	310‡	13,740	8,310	S. G. Drew (1998)
Wycliffe College, Stonehouse, Glos	1882	400‡	15,750	10,035	Dr R. A. Collins (1998)
Yarm School, Stockton-on-Tees	1978	560†	—	6,141	D. M. Dunn (1999)

SCOTLAND

Name of School	Founded	No. of pupils	Annual fees £ Boarding	Annual fees £ Day	Head (with date of appointment)
Daniel Stewart's and Melville College, Edinburgh	1855	760†	10,650	5,436	P. J. F. Tobin (Principal) (1989)
Dollar Academy, Clackmannanshire	1818	749‡	11,340	5,121	J. S. Robertson (Rector) (1994)
The High School of Dundee	1239	720‡	—	4,950	A. M. Duncan (1997)
The Edinburgh Academy	1824	463†	12,645	5,931	J. V. Light (Rector) (1995)
Fettes College, Edinburgh	1870	392‡	14,886	10,044	M. C. B. Spens (1998)
George Heriot's School, Edinburgh	1628	885‡	—	4,815	A. G. Hector (1998)
George Watson's College, Edinburgh	1741	1,273‡	10,662	5,133	F. E. Gerstenberg (Principal) (1985)
Glasgow Academy	1845	600‡	—	5,142	D. Comins (Rector) (1994)
Glenalmond College, Perth	1841	366‡	14,370	9,585	I. G. Templeton (Warden) (1992)

Name of School	Foun-ded	No. of pupils	Annual fees £		Head (with date of appointment)
			Boarding	Day	
Gordonstoun School, Elgin	1935	430‡	14,241	9,192	M. C. Pyper (1990)
High School of Glasgow	1124	668‡	—	5,175	R. G. Easton (Rector) (1983)
Hutcheson's Grammar School, Glasgow	1641	1,250‡	—	4,617	J. Knowles (Rector) (1999)
Kelvinside Academy, Glasgow	1878	320‡	—	5,400	J. L. Broadfoot (Rector) (1998)
Loretto School, Musselburgh	1827	290‡	14,385	9,600	K. J. Budge (1995)
Merchiston Castle School, Edinburgh	1833	350	14,280	9,675	A. R. Hunter (1998)
Morrison's Academy, Crieff	1860	362‡	12,825	4,950	G. H. Edwards (Rector) (1996)
Robert Gordon's College, Aberdeen	1729	960‡	—	5,060	B. R. W. Lockhart (1996)
St Aloysius' College, Glasgow	1859	847‡	—	3,975	Fr. A. Porter, SJ (1995)
St Colomba's School, Kilmacolm	1897	360‡	—	4,713	A. H. Livingstone (1987)
Strathallan School, Perth	1912	400‡	14,040	9,672	A. W. McPhail (1993)
NORTHERN IRELAND					
Bangor Grammar School	1856	494	—	245	N. D. Argent (1998)
Belfast Royal Academy	1785	1,387‡	—	80	W. M. Sillery (1980)
Campbell College, Belfast	1894	690	6,759	1,389	Dr R. J. I. Pollock (1987)
Coleraine Academical Institution	1860	406	—	75	R. S. Forsythe (1984)
Methodist College, Belfast	1865	570‡	6,940	3,390	T. W. Mulryne (Principal) (1988)
Portora Royal School, Enniskillen	1608	110	—	42	R. L. Bennett (1983)
Royal Belfast Academical Institution	1810	1,050	—	510	R. M. Ridley (Principal) (1990)
CHANNEL ISLANDS AND ISLE OF MAN					
Elizabeth College, Guernsey	1563	500†	7,815	3,090	D. E. Toze (1998)
King William's College, Isle of Man	1668	280‡	13,545	9,630	P. K. Fulton-Peebles (Principal) (1996)
Victoria College, Jersey	1852	617†	—	2,268	vacant
EUROPE					
Aiglon College, Switzerland	1949	230‡	Fr.60,460	Fr.39,560	R. McDonald (1994)
British School in The Netherlands	1935	590‡	—	Gld.21,950	J. Hollis (1997)
British School of Brussels	1969	560‡	—	Euro.17,798	Ms J. M. Bray (Principal) (1990)
British School of Paris	1954	360‡	Fr.119,000	Fr.86,000	M. W. Honour (Principal) (1992)
The International School of Geneva	1924	1,140‡	—	Fr.19,615	G. Walker, OBE (Director-General) (1991)
King's College, Madrid	1969	600‡	Pesetas2.07m	Pesetas1.3m	C. T. Gill Leech (1996)
St Columba's College, Dublin	1843	305‡	Ir£7,140	Ir£4,125	T. E. Macey (1988)
St Edward's College, Malta	1929	330†	—	LM.858	W. Dimech (1997)
St George's English School, Rome	1958	280‡	—	L.21.2m	Mrs B. Gardner (Principal) (1994)

OTHER OVERSEAS MEMBERS

AFRICA

DIOCESAN COLLEGE, Rondebosch, SA. Head, C. N. Watson

FALCON COLLEGE, Esigodini, Zimbabwe. Head, P. N. Todd

HILTON COLLEGE, Kwazulu-Natal, SA. Head, M. J. Nicholson

MICHAELHOUSE, Balgowan, SA. Head, R. D. Forde

PETERHOUSE, Marondera, Zimbabwe. Head, M. W. Bawden

ST ANDREW'S COLLEGE, Grahamstown, SA. Head, A. R. Clark

ST GEORGE'S COLLEGE, Harare, Zimbabwe. Head, acting head

ST STITHIAN'S COLLEGE, Transvaal, SA. Head, D. B. Wylde

AUSTRALIA

BALLARAT AND CLARENDON COLLEGE, Ballarat, Victoria. Head, D. S. Shepherd

BRIGHTON GRAMMAR SCHOOL, Brighton, Victoria. Head, M. S. Urwin

BRISBANE BOYS' COLLEGE, Toowong, Queensland. Head, M. Norris

CAMBERWELL GRAMMAR SCHOOL, Deepdene DC, Victoria. Head, C. F. Black

CANBERRA GRAMMAR SCHOOL, Red Hill, ACT. Head, T. C. Murray

CAULFIELD GRAMMAR SCHOOL, Elsternwick, Victoria. Head, S. H. Newton

CHRIST CHURCH GRAMMAR SCHOOL, Claremont, W. Australia. Head, J. J. S. Madin

CRANBROOK SCHOOL, Bellevue Hill, NSW. Head, Dr B. N. Carter

THE GEELONG COLLEGE, Newtown, Victoria. Head, Dr P. Turner

GEELONG GRAMMAR SCHOOL, Corio, Victoria. Head, L. Hannah

GUILDFORD GRAMMAR SCHOOL, Guildford, W. Australia. Head, K. Walton

HAILEYBURY COLLEGE, Keysborough, Victoria. Head, A. H. M. Aikman

THE HALE SCHOOL, Wembley Downs, W. Australia. *Head,* R. J. Inverarity, MBE

IVANHOE GRAMMAR SCHOOL, Ivanhoe, Victoria. *Head,* R. D. Fraser

KINROSS WOLAROI SCHOOL, Orange, NSW. *Head,* A. E. S. Anderson

KNOX GRAMMAR SCHOOL, Wahroonga, NSW. *Head,* Dr I. Paterson

MELBOURNE GRAMMAR SCHOOL, South Yarra, Victoria. *Head,* A. P. Sheahan

MENTONE GRAMMAR SCHOOL, Mentone, Victoria. *Head,* N. Clark

NEWINGTON COLLEGE, Sydney, NSW. *Head,* M. H. Smee

ST PETER'S COLLEGE, St Peter's, S. Australia. *Head,* R. L. Burchnall

SCOTCH COLLEGE, Torrens Park, S. Australia. *Head,* K. Webb

SCOTCH COLLEGE, Hawthorn, Victoria. *Head,* Dr F. G. Donaldson

THE SCOTS COLLEGE, Bellevue Hill, NSW. *Head,* Dr R. L. Iles

THE SOUTHPORT SCHOOL, Southport, Queensland. *Head,* B. A. Cook

SYDNEY CHURCH OF ENGLAND GRAMMAR SCHOOL, North Sydney, NSW. *Head,* R. A. I. Grant

SYDNEY GRAMMAR SCHOOL, Darlinghurst, NSW. *Head,* Dr R. D. Townsend

TRINITY GRAMMAR SCHOOL, Summer Hill, NSW. *Head,* G. M. Cujes

WESLEY COLLEGE, Prahran, Victoria. *Head,* D. Loader

WESTBOURNE GRAMMAR SCHOOL, Werribee, Victoria. *Head,* G. G. Ryan

BERMUDA

SALTUS GRAMMAR SCHOOL, Hamilton. *Head,* R. T. Rowell

CANADA

BRENTWOOD COLLEGE SCHOOL, Mill Bay, BC. *Head,* W. T. Ross

GLENLYON-NORFOLK SCHOOL, Victoria, BC. *Head,* C. E. G. Peacock

HILLFIELD STRATHALLAN COLLEGE, Hamilton, Ontario. *Head,* W. S. Boyer

RIDLEY COLLEGE, St Catharines, Ontario. *Head,* R. D. Lane

ST ANDREW'S COLLEGE, Aurora, Ontario. *Head,* E. Staunton

UPPER CANADA COLLEGE, Toronto, Ontario. *Head,* J. D. Blakey

HONG KONG

ISLAND SCHOOL, Borrett Road. *Head,* D. J. James

KING GEORGE V SCHOOL, Kowloon. *Head,* M. J. Behennah

INDIA

BISHOP COTTON SCHOOL, Shimla. *Head,* K. K. Mustafi

THE CATHEDRAL AND JOHN CONNON SCHOOL, Bombay. *Head,* Mrs M. Isaacs

THE LAWRENCE SCHOOL, Sanawar. *Head,* Dr H. S. Dhillon

THE SCINDIA SCHOOL, Gwalior. *Head,* A. N. Dar

INDONESIA

THE BRITISH INTERNATIONAL SCHOOL, Jakarta. *Head,* J. Birchall

MALAYSIA

KOLEJ TUANKU JA'AFAR, Negeri Sembilan. *Head,* P. D. Briggs

MIDDLE EAST

THE INDIAN SCHOOL, Sultanate of Oman. *Head,* B. S. Bhatnagar

NEW ZEALAND

CHRIST'S COLLEGE, Christchurch. *Head,* R. A. Zordan

KING'S COLLEGE, Auckland. *Head,* J. S. Taylor

ST ANDREW'S COLLEGE, Christchurch. *Head,* B. J. Maister

WANGANUI COLLEGIATE SCHOOL, Wanganui. *Head,* J. R. Hensman

PAKISTAN

AITCHISON COLLEGE, Lahore. *Head,* S. Khan

KARACHI GRAMMAR SCHOOL, Karachi. *Head,* H. H. A. Pullan

SOUTH AND CENTRAL AMERICA

ACADEMIA BRITANICA CUSCATLECA, Santa Tecla, El Salvador. *Head,* R. Braund

THE BRITISH SCHOOLS, Montevideo, Uruguay. *Head,* C. D. T. Smith

MARKHAM COLLEGE, Lima, Peru. *Head,* W. J. Baker

ST ANDREW'S SCOTS SCHOOL, Buenos Aires, Argentina. *Head,* A. G. F. Fisher

ST GEORGE'S COLLEGE, Buenos Aires, Argentina. *Head,* N. P. O. Green

ST PAUL'S SCHOOL, São Paulo, Brazil. *Head,* M. T. M. C. McCann

USA

ST MARK'S COLLEGE, Southborough, Massachusetts. *Head,* A. J de V. Hill

SOCIETY OF HEADMASTERS AND HEADMISTRESSES OF INDEPENDENT SCHOOLS

The Society was founded in 1961 and, in general, represents smaller boarding schools.

General Secretary, I. D. Cleland, Celedston, Rhosesmor Road, Halkyn, Holywell CH8 8DL. Tel: 01352-781102

Headmasters/mistresses of the following schools are members of both HMC and SHMIS; details of these schools appear in the HMC list: Abbotsholme School, Ackworth School, Bedales School, Churcher's College, Colston's Collegiate School, King's School, Gloucester, King's School, Tynemouth, Leighton Park School, Lord Wandsworth College, Pangbourne College, Reading Blue Coat School, Reed's School, Rendcomb College, Royal Hospital School, Rydal Penrhos School, Ryde School, St George's College, Shiplake College, Silcoates School, Tettenhall College, Wisbech Grammar School, Yarm School

The Headmistress of King Edward VI High School for Girls is a member of both SHMIS and GSA; details of the school are given in the GSA list

CSC   Church Schools Company, Church Schools House, Chapel Street, Titchmarsh, Kettering, Northants NN14 3DA. Tel: 01832-735105

* Woodard Corporation School

† Girls in VI form

‡ Co-educational

Name of School	Foun-ded	No. of pupils	Annual fees £ Boarding	Day	Head (with date of appointment)
ENGLAND AND WALES					
Abbey Gate College, Saighton, Chester	1977	248‡	—	5,085	E. W. Mitchell (1991)
Austin Friars School (*RC*), Carlisle	1951	295‡	—	5,565	Revd D. Middleton (1996)
Battle Abbey School, E. Sussex	1912	130‡	11,100	6,900	R. Clark (1998)
Bearwood College, Wokingham	1827	250‡	12,225	7,170	S. G. G. Aiano (1998)
Bedstone College, Bucknell, Shropshire	1948	165‡	11,994	6,450	M. S. Symonds (1990)
Bentham Grammar School, N. Yorks	1726	183‡	10,950	5,550	Miss R. E. Colman (1999)
Bethany School, Cranbrook, Kent	1866	290‡	11,136	7,125	N. Dorey (1998)
Box Hill School, Dorking	1959	290‡	12,219	7,110	Dr R. A. S. Atwood (1987)
Claremont Fan Court School, Esher	1932	300‡	11,415	7,425	Mrs. P. B. Farrar (*Principal*) (1994)
Clayesmore School, Blandford Forum	1896	299‡	13,335	9,450	D. J. Beeby (1986)
Cokethorpe School, Witney, Oxon	1957	280‡	13,850	4,620	P. J. S. Cantwell (1995)
Duke of York's Royal Military School, Dover	1803	500‡	900	—	J. Cummings (1999)
Elmhurst - The School for Dance and Performing Arts, Camberley	1922	61‡	11,490	8,427	J. McNamara (*Principal*) (1995)
Embley Park School, Romsey, Hants	1946	285‡	11,395	6,870	D. F. Chapman (1987)
Ewell Castle School, Epsom	1926	300	—	5,205	R. A. Fewtrell (*Principal*) (1983)
Friends' School, Saffron Walden	1702	200‡	12,285	7,371	Ms J. E. Laing (1996)
Fulneck School, Pudsey, W. Yorks	1753	260‡	10,485	5,685	Mrs H. Gordon, (*Principal*) (1996)
*Grenville College, Bideford	1954	270‡	11,631	5,760	Dr M. C. V. Cane (1992)
Halliford School, Shepperton, Middx	1921	320†	—	5,550	J. R. Crook (1984)
Hipperholme Grammar School, Halifax	1648	320‡	—	4,620	C. C. Robinson (1988)
Keil School, Dumbarton	1915	180‡	11,805	6,618	T. S. Smith (1999)
Kingham Hill School, Chipping Norton	1886	230‡	11,874	7,128	M. H. Payne (1990)
Kirkham Grammar School, Preston	1549	620‡	8,895	4,590	B. Stacey (1991)
Langley School, Norwich	1910	270‡	12,630	6,555	J. G. Malcolm (1997)
Lincoln Minster School (*CSC*)	1996	285‡	10,512	5,556	C. Rickart (1999)
Lomond School, Helensburgh, Argyll and Bute	1977	385‡	11,865	5,535	A. D. Macdonald (1986)
Milton Abbey School, Blandford Forum	1954	80	14,175	10,275	W. J. Hughes-D'Aeth (1995)
Oswestry School, Shropshire	1407	310‡	12,120	7,230	P. K. Smith (1995)
The Purcell School (music), Harrow	1962	119‡	16,677	9,993	J. Tolputt (1999)
Rannoch School, Rannoch, By Pitlochry	1959	220‡	13,230	6,930	Dr J. D. Halliday (1997)
Rishworth School, W. Yorks	1724	350‡	11,250	5,340	R. A. Baker (1999)
Rougemont School, Newport	1974	330‡	—	5,163	I. Brown (1995)
Royal Russell School, Croydon	1853	485‡	12,480	6,540	Dr J. R. Jennings (1996)
Royal School, Dungannon, N. Ireland	1608	630‡	4,069	110	P. D. Hewitt (1984)
Royal Wolverhampton School	1850	303‡	12,675	6,210	Mrs B. A. Evans (1995)
Ruthin School, Denbighshire	1574	170‡	11,685	7,485	J. S. Rowlands (1993)
St Bede's School, Hailsham	1978	530‡	13,650	8,265	R. A. Perrin (1978)
St Christopher School, Letchworth	1915	360‡	13,317	7,548	C. Reid (1980)
St David's College, Llandudno	1965	220‡	11,658	7,581	W. Seymour (1991)
St Edward's School, Cheltenham	1987	450‡	—	6,390	A. J. Martin (1991)
Scarborough College, N. Yorks	1898	355‡	10,959	5,943	T. L. Kirkup (1996)
Seaford College, Petworth, W. Sussex	1884	302‡	12,600	8,400	T. J. Mullins (1997)

Name of School	Foun- ded	No. of pupils	Annual fees £		Head (with date of appointment)
			Boarding	Day	
Shebbear College, North Devon	1841	200‡	11,478	6,174	L. D. Clark (1997)
Shiplake College, Henley-on-Thames	1959	290†	13,590	9,165	N. V. Bevan (1988)
Sibford School, Banbury	1842	250‡	12,120	6,015	Ms S. Freestone (1997)
Sidcot School, North Somerset	1808	342‡	11,850	6,840	A. Slesser (1997)
Stafford Grammar School	1982	300‡	—	4,710	M. Darley (1998)
Stanbridge Earls School, Romsey, Hants	1952	190‡	14,175	10,560	H. Moxon (1984)
Sunderland High School (CSC)	1884	300‡	—	4,170	Dr A. Slater (1998)
Thetford Grammar School, Norfolk	1119	200‡	—	5,112	J. R. Weeks (1990)
Warminster School, Wilts	1707	300‡	11,160	6,300	D. Dowdles (1998)
Yehudi Menuhin School (music), Surrey	1963	51‡	varies	—	P. N. Chisholm (1988)

GIRLS' SCHOOLS ASSOCIATION

THE GIRL'S SCHOOLS ASSOCIATION, 130 Regent Road, Leicester LE1 7PG. Tel: 0116-254 1619
President, Mrs L. Warrington (from 1.1.2000)
Secretary, Ms S. Cooper

Headmasters/mistresses of the following schools are members of both HMC and GSA; details of these schools appear in the HMC list: Berkhamsted Collegiate School, Rydal Penrhos School, Stamford Endowed Schools

CSC Church Schools Company
§ Girls Day School Trust, 100 Rochester Row, London SW1P 1JP. Tel: 0171-393 6666
* Woodard Corporation School
† Boys in VI form
‡ Co-educational

Name of School	Foun- ded	No. of pupils	Annual fees £		Head (with date of appointment)
ENGLAND AND WALES			Boarding	Day	
Abbey School, Reading	1887	673	—	5,385	Miss B. C. L. Sheldon (1991)
Abbot's Hill, Hemel Hempstead	1912	164	12,525	7,500	Mrs K. Lewis (1997)
Adcote School for Girls, Shrewsbury	1907	80	11,460	6,585	Mrs A. E. Read (1997)
Alderley Edge School for Girls	1880	100	—	4,635	Ms P. A. Bristow (1997)
Alice Ottley School, Worcester	1883	500	—	6,678	Ms M. Chapman (1999)
Amberfield School, Ipswich	1952	151	—	4,410	Mrs L. A. Lewis (1992)
Ashford School, Kent	1910	340	13,671	7,869	Mrs J. Burnett (1997)
§Atherley School, Southampton (CSC)	1926	200	—	4,992	Mrs M. Bradley (1999)
Badminton School, Bristol	1858	380	13,425	7,425	Mrs J. A. Scarrow (1997)
Bedford High School	1882	668	10,890	5,832	Mrs B. E. Stanley (1995)
Bedgebury School, Goudhurst, Kent	1860	259	13,230	8,220	Mrs L. J. Griffin (until Dec 1999); vacant (from Jan 2000)
Beechwood Sacred Heart (RC), Tunbridge Wells	1915	130	12,540	7,680	N. R. Beesley (1999)
Benenden School, Cranbrook, Kent	1923	450	15,870	—	Mrs G. D. du Charme (1985)
Bolton School	1877	794	—	5,298	Miss E. J. Panton (1994)
Bradford Girls' Grammar School	1875	641	—	5,130	Mrs L. J. Warrington (1987)
Brigidine School, Windsor	1948	150	—	5,820	Mrs M. B. Cairns (1986)
Bruton School, Somerset	1900	457	10,035	5,445	Mrs B. Bates (1999)
Burgess Hill School, W. Sussex	1906	370	11,265	6,660	Mrs R. F. Lewis (1992)
Bury Grammar School, Lancs	1884	761	—	4,470	Miss C. H. Thompson (1998)
Casterton School, Carnforth, Lancs	1823	354	11,403	7,254	A. F. Thomas (1990)
Channing School, London N6	1885	350	—	6,735	Mrs E. Radice (1999)
Cheltenham Ladies' College, Glos	1853	840	14,340	9,105	Mrs A. V. Tuck (*Principal*) (1996)
City of London School for Girls, London EC2	1894	546	—	6,795	Mrs Y. A. Burne, PH.D. (1995)
Clifton High School, Bristol	1877	345	9,060	5,250	Mrs M. C. Culligan (1998)
Cobham Hall, Kent	1962	200	13,500	7,500	Mrs R. J. McCarthy (1989)
Colston's Girls' School, Bristol	1891	456	—	4,545	Mrs J. P. Franklin (1989)
Combe Bank School, Sevenoaks	1868	218	—	7,380	Miss N. Spurr (1993)
Cranford House School, Moulsford, Oxon	1931	87	—	5,850	Mrs A. B. Gray (1992)
Croham Hurst School, South Croydon	1899	350	—	5,850	Miss S. C. Budgen (1994)
Dame Alice Harpur School, Bedford	1882	721	—	5,769	Mrs R. Randle (1990)
Dame Allan's Girls' School, Newcastle upon Tyne	1705	430†	—	4,692	D. W. Welsh (*Principal*) (1996)

Name of School	Founded	No. of pupils	Annual fees £		Head (with date of appointment)
			Boarding	Day	
*Derby High School for Girls	1892	300	—	5,070	Dr G. H. Goddard, ph.d. (1983)
Downe House, Newbury	1907	551	14,955	10,842	Mrs E. McKendrick (1997)
Dunottar School, Reigate	1926	255	—	6,090	Miss M. J. Skinner (1997)
Durham High School for Girls	1884	256	—	5,592	Mrs A. J. Templeman (1998)
Edgbaston Church of England College, Birmingham	1886	149	—	5,100	Mrs A. Varley-Tipton (1992)
Edgbaston High School for Girls, Birmingham	1876	500	—	5,085	Miss E. M. Mullenger (1998)
*Elmslie Girls' School, Blackpool	1918	130	—	5,100	Miss S. J. Woodward (1997)
Farlington School, Horsham	1896	250	11,745	7,275	Mrs P. M. Mawer (1992)
Farnborough Hill, Hants	1889	500	—	5,802	Miss J. Thomas (1997)
Farringtons and Stratford House, Chislehurst	1911	280	12,480	6,330	Mrs C. E. James (1999)
Francis Holland School, London NW1	1878	375	—	2,265	Mrs G. Low (1998)
Francis Holland School, London SW1	1881	250	—	7,605	Miss S. J. Pattenden (1997)
Gateways School, Harewood, W. Yorks	1941	190	—	5,094	Mrs D. Davidson (1997)
Godolphin and Latymer School, London W6	1905	700	—	6,996	Miss M. Rudland (1986)
Godolphin School, Salisbury	1726	395	13,164	7,887	Miss M. J. Horsburgh (1996)
Greenacre School, Banstead	1933	225	—	6,000	Mrs P. M. Wood (1990)
§Guildford High School (CSC)	1888	570	—	6,390	Mrs S. H. Singer (1991)
Haberdashers' Aske's School for Girls, Elstree, Herts	1873	834	—	5,400	Mrs P. Penney (1991)
Haberdashers' Monmouth School	1891	575	10,422	5,937	Dr B. Despontin, ph.d. (1997)
Harrogate Ladies' College	1893	360	11,700	7,170	Dr M. J. Hustler (1996)
Headington School, Oxford	1915	543	11,925	6,525	Mrs H. A. Fender (1996)
Heathfield School, Ascot, Berks	1899	235	15,450	—	Mrs J. M. Benammar (1992)
Hethersett Old Hall School, Norwich	1928	183	11,295	5,670	Mrs B. M. Garrard (acting) (until Dec 1999); Mrs J. Mark (from Jan 2000)
Highclare School, Birmingham	1932	205†	—	4,875	Mrs C. A. Hanson (1974)
Hollygirt School, Nottingham	1877	231	—	4,305	Mrs M. I. Connolly (1997)
Holy Child School, Birmingham	1936	152	—	5,367	Mrs J. M. C. Hill (1993)
Holy Trinity College, Bromley	1886	222	—	5,274	Mrs D. A. Bradshaw (1994)
Holy Trinity School, Kidderminster	1903	170	—	4,650	Mrs E. L. Thomas (1998)
Howell's School, Denbigh	1859	220	11,085	7,485	Mrs S. Gordon (1998)
§Hull High School (CSC)	1890	164	—	4,824	Mrs M. A. Benson (1994)
Hulme Grammar School, Oldham	1895	511	—	4,455	Miss M. S. Smolenski (1992)
James Allen's Girls' School, London SE22	1741	740	—	7,059	Mrs M. O. Gibbs (1994)
Kent College, Tunbridge Wells	1886	240	13,740	8,100	Miss B. J. Crompton (1990)
King Edward VI High School for Girls, Birmingham	1883	543	—	5,385	Ms S. H. Evans (1996)
King's High School for Girls, Warwick	1879	547	—	5,355	Mrs J. M. Anderson (1987)
Kingsley School, Leamington Spa	1884	460	—	4,725	Mrs Mannion Watson (1997)
Lady Eleanor Holles School, Hampton, Middx	1710	719	—	7,062	Miss E. M. Candy (1981)
La Retraite School, Salisbury	1953	92‡	—	5,625	Mrs R. A. Simmons (1994)
La Sagesse High School, Newcastle upon Tyne	1906	320	—	5,058	Miss L. Clark (1994)
Lavant House and Rosemead, Chichester	1952	95	12,060	6,780	Mrs S. E. Watkins (1996)
Leeds Girls' High School	1876	615	—	5,511	Mrs S. Fishburn (1997)
Leicester High School	1906	297	—	5,235	Mrs P. A. Watson (1992)
Lodge School, Purley, Surrey	1916	120	—	5,430	Miss P. Maynard (1998)
Loughborough High School	1850	558	—	4,995	Miss J. E. L. Harvatt (1978)
Luckley-Oakfield School, Wokingham	1895	283	11,103	6,507	R. C. Blake (1984)
Malvern Girls' College, Worcs	1893	430	13,800	9,210	Mrs P. M. C. Leggate (1997)
Manchester High School	1874	729	—	4,830	Mrs C. Lee-Jones (1998)
Manor House School, Little Bookham, Surrey	1927	170	8,848	6,543	Mrs L. A. Mendes (1989)
Marymount International School, Kingston upon Thames	1955	242	16,335	9,510	Sr R. Sheridan (1990)
Maynard School, Exeter	1877	429	—	5,310	Miss F. Murdin (1980)
Merchant Taylors' School, Liverpool	1888	660	—	4,356	Mrs J. I. Mills (1994)
Moira House School, Eastbourne	1875	210	13,500	8,400	Mrs A. Harris (Principal) (1997)
More House School, London SW1	1953	220	—	6,660	Mrs L. Falconer (1999)
Moreton Hall, Oswestry	1913	260	14,085	9,660	J. Forster (1992)
Mount School, York	1785	265	12,075	7,575	Miss B. J. Windle (1986)
Newcastle upon Tyne Church High School	1885	372	—	4,845	Mrs L. G. Smith (1995)

Name of School	Foun-ded	No. of pupils	Annual fees £ Boarding	Day	Head (with date of appointment)
New Hall School, Chelmsford	1642	395	12,720	8,280	Sr Anne-Marie (1996)
Northampton High School	1878	570	—	5,040	Mrs L. A. Mayne (1988)
North Foreland Lodge, Hook	1909	180	14,550	8,700	Miss S. Cameron (1996)
North London Collegiate School, Edgware	1850	760	—	6,360	Mrs B. McCabe (1997)
Northwood College, Middx	1878	448	—	6,108	Mrs A. Mayou (1991)
Notre Dame Senior School, Cobham, Surrey	1937	330	—	5,625	Mrs M. McSwiggan (1999)
Ockbrook School, Derby	1799	430	8,505	4,635	Miss D. P. Bolland (1995)
Old Palace School, Croydon	1889	547	—	5,298	Miss K. L. Hilton (1974)
Palmers Green High School, London N21	1905	140	—	5,625	Mrs S. Grant (1989)
Parsons Mead, Ashtead, Surrey	1897	160	11,688	6,600	Miss E. B. Plant (1990)
Perse School for Girls, Cambridge	1881	530	—	5,862	Miss H. S. Smith (1989)
*Peterborough High School	1895	160	10,623	5,289	Mrs S. A. Dixon (1999)
Pipers Corner School, High Wycombe	1930	270	11,670	6,990	Mrs V. M. Stattersfield (1996)
Polam Hall School, Darlington	1848	289	11,595	5,391	Mrs H. C. Hamilton (1987)
Princess Helena College, Hitchin, Herts	1820	150	12,285	8,385	Mrs A. M. Hodgkiss (1997)
Prior's Field, Godalming	1902	235	11,670	7,800	Mrs J. Dwyer (1999)
Queen Anne's School, Reading	1894	320	14,010	9,180	Mrs D. Forbes (1993)
*Queen Ethelburga's College, York	1912	200	13,497	8,325	Mrs E. I. E. Taylor (1997)
*Queen Margaret's School, York	1901	365	12,594	7,980	Dr G. A. H. Chapman (1993)
Queen's College, London W1	1848	80	—	7,410	Miss M. M. Connell (1999)
Queen's Gate School, London SW7	1891	250	—	6,750	Mrs A. M. Holyoak (*Principal*) (1989)
Queen's School, Chester	1878	468	—	5,145	Miss D. M. Skilbeck (1989)
Queenswood, Hatfield, Herts	1894	371	14,430	8,940	Ms C. Farr (*Principal*) (1996)
Redland High School for Girls, Bristol	1882	490	—	4,944	Mrs C. Lear (1971)
Red Maids' School, Bristol	1634	495	8,940	4,470	Miss S. Hampton (1987)
Roedean School, Brighton	1885	410	15,750	9,750	Mrs P. Metham (1997)
Royal Masonic School, Herts	1788	520	9,876	6,009	Mrs I. M. Andrews (1992)
Rye St Antony School (*RC*), Oxford	1930	330	10,455	5,985	Mrs A. M. Jones (1990)
St Albans High School	1889	556	—	5,940	Mrs C. Y. Daly (1994)
St Andrew's School, Bedford	1897	154	—	5,007	Mrs J. M. Mark (1995)
St Anne's School, Windermere	1863	150‡	11,385	6,845	R. D. Hunter (1996)
St Antony's-Leweston School (*RC*), Sherborne	1891	240	13,023	8,580	H. J. MacDonald (*Acting Head*) (1999)
St Catherine's School, Guildford	1885	490	11,865	7,230	Mrs C. M. Oulton (1994)
St David's School, Ashford, Middx	1716	234†	11,550	6,390	Ms P. A. Bristow (1999)
St Dunstan's Abbey School, Plymouth	1850	160†	10,365	5,580	Mrs B. K. Brown (1998)
*St Elphin's School, Matlock	1844	160	11,670	6,798	Mrs V. E. Fisher (1995)
St Felix School, Southwold, Suffolk	1897	150	12,015	7,950	R. Williams (1998)
St Francis' College (*RC*), Letchworth	1933	182	12,210	6,270	Miss M. Hegarty (1993)
St Gabriel's School, Newbury	1929	187	—	6,108	D. J. Cobb (1990)
St George's School, Ascot, Berks	1923	280	14,070	8,970	Mrs J. Grant Peterkin (1999)
School of St Helen and St Katharine, Abingdon	1903	590	—	5,574	Mrs C. L. Hall (1993)
St Helen's School, Northwood, Middx	1899	634	11,610	6,108	Mrs D. M. Jefkins (1994)
St James' School, West Malvern	1896	150	13,890	8,070	Mrs S. Kershaw (1998)
St Joseph's Convent School (*RC*), Reading	1894	330	—	5,220	Mrs V. Brookes (1990)
St Leonards-Mayfield School, Mayfield	1872	460	12,900	8,600	Sr J. Sinclair (1980)
St Margaret's School, Bushey, Herts	1749	320	11,775	7,056	Miss M. de Villiers (1992)
*St Margaret's School, Exeter	1904	356	—	5,085	Mrs M. D'Albertanson (1993)
St Martin's School, Solihull	1941	240	—	5,250	Mrs S. J. Williams (1988)
*School of S. Mary and S. Anne, Abbots Bromley, Staffs	1874	186	12,675	8,136	Mrs M. Steel (1998)
St Mary's Convent School, Worcester	1934	200	—	4,230	C. Garner (1997)
St Mary's Hall, Brighton	1836	240	10,833	6,975	Mrs S. M. Meek (1997)
St Mary's School (*RC*), Ascot, Berks	1885	353	14,310	9,390	Mrs M. Breen (1999)
St Mary's School, Calne, Wilts	1872	300	14,490	9,150	Mrs C. J. Shaw (1996)
St Mary's School, Cambridge	1898	460	9,985	5,520	Mrs G. Piotrowska (1998)
St Mary's School, Colchester	1908	225	—	4,665	Mrs G. M. G. Mouser (1981)
St Mary's School, Gerrards Cross	1872	148	—	5,900	Mrs F. Balcombe (1995)
St Mary's School (*RC*), Shaftesbury	1945	316	12,150	7,875	Mrs S. Pennington (1998)
St Mary's School, Wantage, Oxon	1873	200	13,950	9,300	Mrs S. Bodinham (1994)
St Nicholas' School, Fleet, Hants	1935	156	—	5,340	Mrs A. V. Whatmough (1995)
St Paul's Girls' School, London W6	1904	657	—	7,782	Miss E. Diggory (*High Mistress*) (1998)

Name of School	Foun-ded	No. of pupils	Annual fees £		Head (with date of appointment)
			Boarding	Day	
St Swithun's School, Winchester	1884	462	13,620	8,250	Dr H. L. Harvey (1995)
St Teresa's School, Dorking	1928	360	11,700	6,450	Mrs M. E. Prescott (1997)
Sherborne School for Girls, Dorset	1899	390	14,970	11,250	Mrs G. Kerton-Johnson (1999)
Sir William Perkins's School, Chertsey, Surrey	1725	583	—	5,430	Miss S. Ross (1994)
Stonar School, Melksham, Wilts	1921	325	11,205	6,225	Mrs C. Homan (1997)
Stover School, Newton Abbot	1932	210	10,485	5,235	P. E. Bujak (1994)
§Surbiton High School, Kingston-upon-Thames (CSC)	1884	612	—	6,060	Miss M. G. Perry (1993)
Talbot Heath, Bournemouth	1886	398	10,650	6,150	Mrs C. Dipple (1991)
Teesside High School, Stockton-on-Tees	1970	350	—	4,965	Miss J. F. Hamilton (1995)
Tormead School, Guildford	1905	522	—	6,330	Mrs H. E. M. Alleyne (1992)
Truro High School	1880	380	9,795	5,355	J. Graham-Brown (1992)
Tudor Hall School, Banbury	1850	262	12,780	7,980	Miss N. Godfrey (1984)
Wakefield Girls' High School	1878	717†	—	5,300	Mrs P. A. Langham (1988)
Walthamstow Hall, Sevenoaks	1838	250	14,220	8,010	Mrs J. S. Lang (1984)
Wentworth College, Bournemouth	1871	235	10,545	6,615	Miss S. D. Coe (1991)
Westfield School, Newcastle upon Tyne	1962	235	—	5,085	Mrs M. Farndale (1991)
Westholme School, Blackburn	1923	685	—	4,305	Mrs L. Croston (Principal) (1988)
Westonbirt School, Tetbury, Glos	1928	200	13,728	9,180	Mrs M. Henderson (1999)
Wispers School, Haslemere, Surrey	1946	115	11,460	7,374	L. H. Beltran (1980)
Withington Girls' School, Manchester	1890	530	—	4,710	Mrs M. Kenyon (1986)
Woldingham School, Surrey	1842	550	14,085	8,523	Mrs M. M. Ribbins (1997)
Wychwood School, Oxford	1897	138	8,820	5,550	Mrs S. Wingfield Digby (1997)
Wycombe Abbey School, High Wycombe	1896	513	15,000	11,250	Mrs P. E. Davies (1998)
Wykeham House School, Fareham, Hants	1913	150	—	4,824	Mrs R. M. Kamaryc (1995)
SCOTLAND					
Kilgraston School, Bridge of Earn, Perth	1920	200	12,720	7,500	Mrs J. L. Austin (1993)
Laurel Park School, Glasgow	1996	465	—	4,653	Mrs E. Surber (1995)
Mary Erskine School, Edinburgh	1694	691‡	10,650	5,130	P. F. J. Tobin (Principal) (1989)
St George's School, Edinburgh	1888	550	10,905	5,580	Dr J. McClure (1994)
St Leonards School, St Andrews	1877	251†	14,430	7,950	Mrs M. James (1988)
St Margaret's School, Aberdeen	1846	200	—	4,536	Miss A. C. Ritchie (1998)
St Margaret's School and St Denis and Cranley, Edinburgh	1890	370	10,050	4,950	Miss A. Mitchell (1994)
CHANNEL ISLANDS					
The Ladies' College, Guernsey	1872	350	—	2,340	Miss M. E. Macdonald (Principal) (1992)

Health

	Under 1†	1–15	16–24	25–34	35–54	55–64	65–74	75 and over	All ages
Males									
Circulatory diseases	4	6	4	9	33	42	44	44	41
Cancer	1	15	7	11	27	36	34	22	27
Respiratory diseases	10	8	3	4	5	8	12	21	15
Injury and poisoning	5	31	66	53	15	3	1	1	4
Infectious diseases	9	5	2	3	2	1	1	—	1
Other causes	71	36	19	21	18	10	8	11	11
All males (number)	2,400	1,200	2,700	4,600	22,400	33,700	77,900	155,600	300,400
Females									
Circulatory diseases	3	5	7	10	17	28	38	46	41
Cancer	2	19	14	30	51	49	36	15	23
Respiratory diseases	14	8	6	5	6	9	13	20	17
Injury and poisoning	5	22	41	28	8	2	1	1	2
Infectious diseases	10	7	6	4	1	1	1	—	1
Other causes	67	40	26	24	17	12	11	17	16
All females (number)	1,900	900	1,000	2,000	14,700	21,000	55,700	232,200	329,300

* Percentages may not total 100 per cent because of rounding
† Excluding deaths at ages under 28 days
Source: The Stationery Office – *Social Trends 29* (Crown copyright)

NOTIFICATIONS OF INFECTIOUS DISEASES (UK) 1997

Measles	4,844
Mumps	2,264
Rubella	4,205
Whooping cough	3,669
Scarlet fever	4,639
Dysentery	2,427
Food poisoning	105,579
Typhoid and paratyphoid fevers	249
Hepatitis	3,601
Tuberculosis	6,367
Malaria	1,549

Source: The Stationery Office – *Annual Abstract of Statistics 1999* (Crown copyright)

HIV/AIDS AND SEXUALLY TRANSMITTED DISEASES (ENGLAND)

	1986	1996
HIV cases diagnosed	2,114	2,230
Exposure category		
Homosexual intercourse	76%	59%
Heterosexual intercourse	6%	29%
Injecting drug use	11%	6%
Blood products	4%	1%
Aids cases diagnosed	450	1,257
Sexually transmitted diseases (new cases)		
All, except HIV/Aids	—	424,300
Syphilis	2,400	1,200
Gonorrhoea	46,300	14,400
Chlamydia	—	44,700
Herpes	18,900	27,600
Wart virus	52,200	97,800

Source: The Stationery Office – *Health and Personal Social Services Statistics for England 1998* (Crown copyright)

PREVALENCE OF SMOKING CIGARETTES (ENGLAND)
Percentages among adults aged 16 and over, by sex

	1986	1997
Males		
Current smoker	34	30
Ex-regular smoker	33	27
Never smoked	33	42
Females		
Current smoker	31	29
Ex-regular smoker	18	19
Never smoked	51	52

Source: The Stationery Office – *All Change? The Health Education Monitoring Survey One Year On* (Crown copyright)

ALCOHOL CONSUMPTION - UNITS PER WEEK (ENGLAND) 1997
Percentage

Men	
Non-drinker	6
Under one	6
1–10	35
11–21	23
22–35	17
36–50	7
51 and over	6
Women	
Non-drinker	9
Under one	16
1–7	41
8–14	17
15–25	12
26–35	2
36 and over	3

Source: The Stationery Office – *All Change? The Health Education Monitoring Survey One Year On* (Crown copyright)

PEOPLE WHO HAVE USED DRUGS IN THE PAST YEAR
(ENGLAND AND WALES) 1997
by sex, age and type of drug
Percentage

Age	16–29	30–54	All aged 16–54
Men			
Cannabis	28	7	14
Hallucinants	18	2	7
Opiates	6	1	3
Other	3	1	1
Any drug	31	7	15
Women			
Cannabis	22	4	10
Hallucinants	10	1	4
Opiates	1	0	0
Other	1	0	0
Any drug	24	4	11

Source: The Stationery Office – *All Change? The Health Education Monitoring Survey One Year On* (Crown copyright)

HEALTH IN ENGLAND

A report, *Health in England 1996*, was published by the Health Education Authority and the Office for National Statistics in May 1997. In 1998 a follow-up survey, *All Change? The Health Education Monitoring Survey One Year On*, was published. It included the following main findings:
– 30 per cent of men and 29 per cent of women were cigarette smokers
– the mean alcohol consumption was 17.0 units a week for men and 7.3 units a week for women
– 26 per cent of respondents were sedentary
– 15 per cent of men and 11 per cent of women had taken drugs in the past year
– 16 per cent of men and 10 per cent of women aged 16–54 had had two or more sexual partners in the previous year

HEALTH TARGETS

In February 1997 the Government published a Green Paper, *Our Healthier Nation,* which identified four main areas of illness in England (heart disease and stroke, accidents, cancer and mental health) to be improved, and replaced the targets in *The Health of the Nation* (a White Paper published in 1992) with four main targets:
– a reduction in the number of deaths from coronary heart disease and strokes by two-fifths by 2010
– a reduction in the number of deaths from cancer by one fifth by 2010
– a reduction in the number of deaths by suicide by one sixth by 2010
– a reduction in the number of deaths from accidents by one fifth by 2010
Similar reviews are being undertaken in Wales and Northern Ireland. In Scotland a White Paper, *Towards a Healthier Scotland,* was presented in February 1999.

CONSUMPTION OF FOODS CONTAINING FIBRE AND STARCHY CARBOHYDRATES (ENGLAND) 1996 *by age and sex*
Percentage consuming each food

Age	16–24	25–34	35–44	45–54	55–64	65–74	Total
Men							
Eats wholemeal bread	7	14	16	21	23	22	17
Eats bread daily	83	77	87	84	89	92	84
Eats fruit, vegetables and salad daily	43	51	56	69	72	73	59
Eats potatoes, pasta or rice daily	35	51	55	56	63	66	53
Eats bread; fruit, vegetables and salad; and potatoes, pasta or rice daily	19	31	34	41	45	51	36
Women							
Eats wholemeal bread	16	23	24	30	29	34	25
Eats bread daily	76	75	79	83	83	93	81
Eats fruit, vegetables and salad daily	57	60	74	81	86	83	72
Eats potatoes, pasta or rice daily	44	51	55	62	67	64	56
Eats bread; fruit, vegetables and salad; and potatoes, pasta or rice daily	24	32	38	45	53	53	40

Source: The Stationery Office – *Health in England 1996* (Crown copyright)

FREQUENCY OF AT LEAST MODERATE-INTENSITY EXERCISE FOR 30 MINUTES OR MORE *by age and sex*
Percentages

Age	16–24	25–34	35–44	45–54	55–64	65–74	Total
Men							
Less than one day a week	9	19	20	26	38	42	24
1–2 days a week	21	20	25	25	23	29	23
3–4 days a week	14	12	12	11	7	14	12
5 or more days a week	56	48	43	39	32	14	41
Women							
Less than one day a week	20	18	19	22	37	46	26
1–2 days a week	29	27	33	28	33	28	30
3–4 days a week	18	15	14	14	9	11	14
5 or more days a week	32	39	34	35	21	14	31

Source: The Stationery Office – *Health in England 1996* (Crown copyright)

Social Welfare

National Health Service

The National Health Service (NHS) came into being on 5 July 1948 under the National Health Service Act 1946, covering England and Wales, and under separate legislation for Scotland and Northern Ireland. The NHS is now administered by the Secretary of State for Health (in England), the National Assembly for Wales, the Scottish Executive and the Secretary of State for Northern Ireland.

The function of the NHS is to provide a comprehensive health service designed to secure improvement in the physical and mental health of the people and to prevent, diagnose and treat illness. It was founded on the principle that treatment should be provided according to clinical need rather than ability to pay, and should be free at the point of delivery. However, prescription charges were provided for by legislation in 1949 and implemented in 1952, and charges for some dental and ophthalmic treatment have also been introduced.

The NHS covers a comprehensive range of hospital, specialist, family practitioner (medical, dental, ophthalmic and pharmaceutical), artificial limb and appliance, ambulance, and community health services. Everyone normally resident in the UK is entitled to use any of these services.

STRUCTURE

The structure of the NHS remained relatively stable for the first 30 years of its existence. In 1974, a three-tier management structure comprising Regional Health Authorities, Area Health Authorities and District Management Teams was introduced in England, and the NHS became responsible for community health services. In 1979 Area Health Authorities were abolished and District Management Teams were replaced by District Health Authorities.

The National Health Service and Community Care Act 1990 provided for more streamlined Regional Health Authorities and District Health Authorities, and for the establishment of Family Health Services Authorities (FHSAs) and NHS Trusts. The concept of the 'internal market' was introduced into health care, whereby care was provided through NHS contracts where health authorities or boards and GP fundholders (the purchasers) were responsible for buying health care from hospitals, non-fundholding GPs, community services and ambulance services (the providers).

NHS Trusts operate as self-governing health care providers independent of health authority control and responsible to the Secretary of State. Until 1999 they derived their income principally from contracts to provide services to health authorities and fund-holding GPs. In Northern Ireland, 20 health and social services trusts are responsible for providing health and social services in an organizational model unique to Northern Ireland.

The Act also paved the way for the Community Care reforms, which were introduced in April 1993 and changed the way care is administered for elderly people, the mentally ill, the physically handicapped and people with learning disabilities.

The eight Regional Health Authorities in England were abolished in April 1996 and replaced by eight regional offices which, together with the headquarters in Leeds, form the NHS Executive. The regional offices are part of the Department of Health, and their functions include financial and performance monitoring of local purchasers and providers, public health, regional research and development, and education programmes.

In April 1996 the District Health Authorities and Family Health Service Authorities were merged to form 100 unified Health Authorities (HAs) in England. The HAs are responsible for health and health services in their areas. They are also responsible for assessing the health care needs of the local population and developing integrated strategies for meeting these needs in partnership with GPs and in consultation with the public, hospitals and others. HAs' resources are allocated by the NHS Executive headquarters, to which they are also accountable for their performance. HA chairmen are appointed by the Health Secretary and non-executive members by the regional offices of the NHS Executive.

In Wales the chairman and non-executive members of the five HAs which replaced the former 17 HAs and FHSAs in April 1996 are appointed by the First Secretary. Health Solutions Wales provides a range of specialist services to the NHS in Wales. In Scotland there are 15 Health Boards with similar responsibilities to those of HAs. In Northern Ireland there are four Health and Social Services Boards.

There are also Community Health Councils (called Local Health Councils in Scotland and Health and Social Services Councils in Northern Ireland) throughout the UK; their role is to represent the interests of the public to health authorities and boards. The Government announced in March 1998 that public consultation and patient representation in the NHS would be increased.

Under the Health Act 1999 the NHS internal market in England was replaced by teams of GPs and community nurses working together in primary care groups (see page 481) from 1 April 1999. Long-term service agreements are beginning to replace annual contracts between primary care groups, health authorities, and NHS Trusts. A National Institute for Clinical Excellence has been established to produce new national guidelines and National Service Frameworks are being prepared to guarantee consistency in access to services. The first of these, to be published in late 1999, will address mental health and coronary heart disease services. A Commission for Health Improvement is being established in autumn 1999 to promote best practice. In Scotland, the Act replaced the internal market with Local Health Care Co-operatives (see page 481) from 1 April 1999. The NHS Trusts were reorganized into 13 primary care trusts and 15 acute care trusts, responsible to the Health Boards. In Wales the internal market was replaced by a system of Local Health Groups (see page 481). In Scotland the Scottish Health Technology Assessment Centre will provide guidelines to promote best practice.

FINANCE

UNITED KINGDOM

The NHS is still funded mainly (75.3 per cent in England for 1998–9) through general taxation, although in recent years more reliance has been placed on the NHS element of National Insurance contributions (13 per cent in England for 1998–9), patient charges and other sources of income.

Total UK expenditure on the NHS in 1998–9 was £49,125 million, of which £45,315 million was from public monies and £3,810 million from patient charges and other receipts. NHS expenditure represented 5.8 per cent of GDP. The total cost per head was £830. The planned expenditure for 1999–2000 is £52,376 million. The Government announced in July 1998 that an additional £21,000 million would be spent on the NHS between 1999 and 2002.

NATIONAL HEALTH CURRENT EXPENDITURE 1997–8

	£ million
National Health Service:	
Hospitals, Community Health Services and Family Health Services	40,993
Departmental administration	245
Other central services	3,242
Less payments by patients	−919
TOTAL	43,561

PERSONAL SOCIAL SERVICES CURRENT EXPENDITURE 1997–8

	£ million
Central government	73
Local authorities running expenses	10,484
Capital expenditure	213
TOTAL	10,770

Source: The Stationery Office – Annual Abstract of Statistics 1999 (Crown copyright)

WALES

CENTRAL GOVERNMENT HEALTH FUNDING 1997–8

	£ thousand
Central administration	6,904
Hospital, community and cash limited family health services	1,851,757
NHS Trusts	159,266
Demand-led (non-cash limited) family health services	425,705
Other health services	61,951
Welfare foods	12,773
TOTAL	2,518,356

Source: Welsh Office

SCOTLAND

NET COSTS OF THE NATIONAL HEALTH SERVICE 1996–7

	£ thousand
Central administration	8,378
Total NHS cost	4,377,923
NHS contributions	468,770
Net costs to Exchequer	3,909,153
Health Board administration	89,282
Hospital and community health services	3,108,575
Family practitioner services	986,616
Central health services	120,586
State hospital	22,400
Training	3,326
Research	10,517
Disabled services	2,331
Welfare foods	13,835
Miscellaneous health services	20,455
TOTAL	4,386,301

Source: Scottish Office – Annual Abstract of Statistics 1998 (Crown copyright)

ORGANIZATIONS

HEALTH AUTHORITIES (ENGLAND)

There are 100 health authorities in England. For details, contact the relevant NHS Executive regional office (see below).

NHS EXECUTIVE REGIONAL OFFICES

EASTERN, 6–12 Capital Drive, Linford Wood, Milton Keynes MK14 6QP. Tel: 01908-844400. *Chairman*, Mrs R. Varley; *Regional Director*, P. Houghton

LONDON, 40 Eastbourne Terrace, London W2 3QR. Tel: 0171-725 5300. *Chairman*, I. Mills; *Regional Director*, N. Crisp

NORTHERN AND YORKSHIRE, John Snow House, Durham University Science Park, Durham DH1 3YG. Tel: 0191-301 1325. *Chairman*, Mrs Z. Manzoor; *Regional Director*, P. Garland

NORTH WEST, 930–932 Birchwood Boulevard, Millennium Park, Birchwood, Warrington WA3 7QN. Tel: 01925-704000. *Chairman*, Prof. A. Breckenridge; *Regional Director*, Prof. R. Tinston

SOUTH EAST, 40 Eastbourne Terrace, London W2 3QR. Tel: 0171-725 2500. *Chairman*, Sir William Wells; *Regional Director*, B. Stocking

SOUTH WEST, Westward House, Lime Kiln Close, Stoke Gifford, Bristol BS34 8SR. Tel: 0117-984 1750. *Chairman*, Miss J. Trotter, OBE; *Regional Director*, A. Laurance

TRENT, Fulwood House, Old Fulwood Road, Sheffield S10 3TH. Tel: 0114-263 0300. *Chairman*, P. Hammersley; *Regional Director*, N. McKay

WEST MIDLANDS, Bartholomew House, 142 Hagley Road, Birmingham B16 9PA. Tel: 0121-224 4600. *Chairman*, C. Wilkinson; *Regional Director*, S. Day

HEALTH BOARDS (SCOTLAND)

ARGYLL AND CLYDE, Ross House, Hawkhead Road, Paisley PA2 7BN. Tel: 0141-842 7200. *Chairman*, M. D. Jones; *General Manager*, N. McConachie

AYRSHIRE AND ARRAN, PO Box 13, Boswell House, 10 Arthur Street, Ayr KA7 1QJ. Tel: 01292-611040. *Chairman*, Dr J. Morrow; *General Manager*, Mrs W.-Y. Hatton

BORDERS, Newstead, Melrose, Roxburghshire TD9 0SE. Tel: 01896-825500. *Chairman*, D. A. C. Kilshaw, OBE; *General Manager*, Dr L. Burley

DUMFRIES AND GALLOWAY, Grierson House, The Crichton, Bankend Road, Dumfries DG1 4ZG. Tel: 01387-272700. *Chairman*, J. Ross, CBE; *General Manager*, N. Campbell

FIFE, Springfield House, Cupar KY15 9UP. Tel: 01334-656200. *Chairman*, Mrs C. Stenhouse; *General Manager*, M. Murray

FORTH VALLEY, 33 Spittal Street, Stirling FK8 1DX. Tel: 01786-457248. *Chairman*, E. Bell-Scott; *General Manager*, D. Hird

GRAMPIAN, Summerfield House, 2 Eday Road, Aberdeen AB15 6RE. Tel: 01224-663456. *Chairman*, Dr C. E. MacLeod, CBE; *General Manager*, F. E. L. Hartnett, OBE

GREATER GLASGOW, Dalian House, PO Box 15329, 350 St Vincent Street, Glasgow G3 8YZ. Tel: 0141-201 4444. *Chairman*, Prof. D. Hamblen; *Chief Executive*, C. J. Spry

HIGHLAND, Beechwood Park, Inverness IV2 3HG. Tel: 01463-717123. *Chairman*, Mrs C. Thomson; *General Manager* (*acting*), E. Baigal

LANARKSHIRE, 14 Beckford Street, Hamilton, Lanarkshire ML3 0TA. Tel: 01698-281313. *Chairman*, I. Livingstone, CBE; *General Manager*, Prof. T. A. Divers

LOTHIAN, Deaconess House, 148 Pleasance, Edinburgh EH8 9RS. Tel: 0131-536 9000. *Chairman*, Mrs M. Ford; *General Manager*, T. Jones

ORKNEY, Garden House, New Scapa Road, Kirkwall, Orkney KW15 1BQ. Tel: 01856-885400. *Chairman*, I. Leslie; *General Manager*, J. Wellden

SHETLAND, Brevik House, South Road, Lerwick ZE1 0TG. Tel: 01595-696767. *Chairman*, J. Telford; *General Manager*, B. J. Atherton

TAYSIDE, Gateway House, Luna Place, Dundee Technology Park, Dundee DD2 1TP. Tel: 01382-561818. *Chairman*, Mrs F. Havenga; *General Manager*, T. Brett

WESTERN ISLES, 37 South Beach Street, Stornoway, Isle of Lewis HS1 2BN. Tel: 01851-702997. *Chairman*, A. Matheson; *General Manager*, M. Maclennan

HEALTH AUTHORITIES (WALES)

BRO TAF, 17 Churchill House, Churchill Way, Cardiff CF10 4TW. Tel: 01222-402402. *Chairman*, Mrs K. Thomas; *Chief Executive*, D. Hands

DYFED POWYS, St David's Hospital, Carmarthen SA31 3HB. Tel: 01267-225077. *Chairman*, Ms M. Price; *Chief Executive*, P. Stansbie

GWENT, Mamhilad House, Mamhilad Park Estate, Pontypool NP4 0YP. Tel: 01495-765065. *Chairman*, Mrs F. Peel; *Chief Executive*, G. Coomber

MORGANNWG, 41 High Street, Swansea SA1 1LT. Tel: 01792-458066. *Chairman*, D. H. Thomas; *Chief Executive*, Mrs J. V. Williams

NORTH WALES, Preswylfa, Hendy Road, Mold CH7 1PZ. Tel: 01352-700227. *Chairman*, Mrs E. Rowlands; *Chief Executive*, B. Jones

HEALTH SOLUTIONS WALES, National Assembly for Wales, Pierhead Street, Capital Waterside, Cardiff CF1 5XT. Tel: 01222-500500.

NORTHERN IRELAND HEALTH AND SOCIAL SERVICES BOARDS

EASTERN, Champion House, 12–22 Linenhall Street, Belfast BT2 8BS. Tel: 01232-321313. *Chairman*, J. D. Thompson, CBE; *Chief Executive*, Dr M. P. J. Kilbane, FRCP

NORTHERN, County Hall, 182 Galgorm Road, Ballymena BT42 1QB. Tel: 01266-653333. *Chairman*, R. J. Hanna; *Chief Executive*, J. S. MacDonell

SOUTHERN, Tower Hill, Armagh BT61 9DR. Tel: 01861-410041. *Chairman*, W. Gillespie; *Chief Executive*, B. P. Cunningham

WESTERN, 15 Gransha Park, Clooney Road, Londonderry BT47 6TG. Tel: 01504-860086. *Chairman*, R. G. Toland; *Chief Executive*, T. J. Frawley

HEALTH PROMOTION AUTHORITIES

HEALTH EDUCATION AUTHORITY, Trevelyan House, 30 Great Peter Street, London SW1P 2HW. Tel: 0171-222 5300. *Chair*, Ms Y. Buckland; *Chief Executive*, vacant. The Health Education Authority will be replaced by a new Health Development Agency in early 2000

NATIONAL ASSEMBLY FOR WALES HEALTH PROMOTION DIVISION, *see* page 349

HEALTH EDUCATION BOARD FOR SCOTLAND, Woodburn House, Canaan Lane, Edinburgh EH10 4SG. Tel 0131-536 5500. *Chairman*, D. R. Campbell; *Chief Executive*, Prof. A. Tannahill

HEALTH PROMOTION AGENCY FOR NORTHERN IRELAND, 18 Ormeau Avenue, Belfast BT2 8HS. Tel: 01232-311611

EMPLOYEES AND SALARIES

EMPLOYEES

HEALTH AND PERSONAL SOCIAL SERVICES WORKFORCE (*Great Britain*) *as at 30 September 1997*

General medical practitioners	35,206
General dental practitioners	19,598
Ophthalmic medical practitioners	*830
Ophthalmic opticians	*7,847
Medical staff	64,316
Dental staff	3,078
Nursing and midwifery staff	353,933
Professional and technical staff	107,158
Administrative and clerical staff	177,957
Health care assistants and support staff	91,774
Ambulance staff	16,424
Other Health Service staff	3,337
†Personal social services staff	229,439

* Figures for England and Wales relate to 31 December 1997. Figures for Scotland relate to 31 March 1997. Those with contracts with more than one authority/board will be counted more than once.
† England only
Source: The Stationery Office – *Annual Abstract of Statistics 1999* (Crown copyright)

SALARIES *as at 1 April 1999*

General Practitioners (GPs), dentists, optometrists and pharmacists are self-employed, and are employed by the NHS under contract. GPs are paid for their NHS work in accordance with a scheme of remuneration which includes a basic practice allowance, capitation fees, reimbursement of certain practice expenses and payments for out-of-hours work. Dentists receive payment for items of treatment for individual adult patients and, in addition, a continuing care payment for those registered with them. Optometrists receive approved fees for each sight test they carry out. Pharmacists receive professional fees from the NHS and are refunded the cost of prescriptions supplied.

Consultant	£47,345–£61,605
Specialist Registrar	£23,300–£33,965
Registrar	£23,300–£28,625
Senior House Officer	£20,845–£27,845
House Officer	£16,710–£18,860
GP	*£52,600
Nursing Grades G–I (Senior Ward Sister)	£20,145–£28,240
Nursing Grade F (Ward Sister)	£17,075–£20,925
Nursing Grade E (Senior Staff Nurse)	£15,395–£17,830
Nursing Grade D (Staff Nurse)	£14,400–£15,905
Nursing Grade C (Enrolled Nurse)	£11,735–£13,915
Nursing Grades A–B (Nursing Auxiliary)	£8,705–£11,735

* average intended net remuneration

HEALTH SERVICES

PRIMARY AND COMMUNITY HEALTH CARE

Primary and community health care services comprise the family health services (i.e. the general medical, personal medical, pharmaceutical, dental, and ophthalmic services) and community services (including preventive activities such as vaccination, immunization and fluoridation) commissioned by HAs and provided by NHS Trusts, health centres and clinics. Nursing services including practice nurses, district nurses and health visitors, community psychiatric nurses, school nurse and ante- and post-natal care are also an integral part of primary and community health care.

FAMILY DOCTOR SERVICE

In England and Wales the Family Doctor Service (or General Medical Service) is now the responsibility of the HAs. In late 1999 a pilot scheme of 19 walk-in centres, where people may consult a doctor without an appointment between the hours of 7 a.m. and 10 p.m., will begin operation. They are responsible to HAs and will work closely with primary care groups.

Any doctor may take part in the Family Doctor Service (provided the area in which he/she wishes to practise has not already an adequate number of doctors) and about 29,000 GPs in England and Wales do so. The distribution of GPs is controlled by the Medical Practices Committee, a statutory body. The average number of patients on a doctor's list in 1997 was:

England	1,878
Wales	1,706
Scotland	1,478

GPs may also have private fee-paying patients.

The Government has replaced the fundholding system by allowing the new primary care groups and trusts to assume one of four levels of responsibility. In April 1999 481 primary care groups became operational in England, covering populations of between 46,000 and 257,000. They operate as a committee of a Health Authority and are responsible for health improvement, primary and community health service development and commissioning secondary care services where appropriate. Primary care groups operate at one of two levels of responsibility. At level one, the group advises the Health Authority and is responsible for less than 40 per cent of the group's unified budget. Level two primary care groups are responsible for 40 per cent of the group's unified budget, rising to 60 per cent in their second year of operation. A board consisting of GPs, nurses, a social services officer, a health authority representative and a local member of the public administers each group.

From 1 April 2000, Primary Care Trusts will become operational in England. They will be free-standing statutory bodies undertaking many of the functions presently exercised by Health Authorities. They will operate at one of two levels. Level three Trusts will be able to commission services with greater scope than a level two primary care group, but not directly provide them. Those at level four will be able to commission and directly provide services and run community hospitals and health services.

In Scotland, fundholding was replaced by over 70 Local Health Care Co-operatives on 1 April 1999. These, consisting of GPs and others involved in primary care, are responsible for developing health care in their area.

In Wales 22 Local Health Groups were set up by the Health Authorities and began work in April 1999. They are coterminous with local authority areas. Initially they will advise Health Authorities but in the future they will assume responsibility for commissioning services and devising strategies for improved health. They will also integrate the delivery of primary and community care. A governing body including GPs and other health professionals, social services and community representatives administers each group.

Everyone aged 16 or over can choose their doctor (parents or guardians choose for children under 16); the doctor is free to accept a person or not. Should a patient have difficulty in registering with a doctor, HAs have powers to assign the patient to a GP. A person may change their doctor if they wish, by going to the surgery of a GP of their choice who is willing to accept them, and either handing in their medical card to register or filling in a form. When people are away from home they can still use the Family Doctor Service if they ask to be treated as temporary residents, and in an emergency, any doctor in the service will give treatment and advice. A number of drop-in medical centres are being set up where anyone can consult a doctor.

PHARMACEUTICAL SERVICE

Patients may obtain medicines, appliances and oral contraceptives prescribed under the NHS from any pharmacy whose owner has entered into arrangements with the HA to provide this service; the number of these pharmacies in England and Wales in March 1998 was about 10,500. There are also some appliance suppliers who only provide special appliances. In rural areas, where access to a pharmacy may be difficult, patients may be able to obtain medicines, etc., from their doctor.

Except for contraceptives (for which there is no charge), a charge of £5.90 is payable for each item supplied unless the patient is exempt and the declaration on the back of the prescription form is completed. Prepayment certificates (£30.80 valid for four months, £84.60 valid for a year) may be purchased by those patients not entitled to exemption who require frequent prescriptions.

The following people are exempt from prescription charges:

– children under 16
– full-time students under 19
– men and women aged 60 and over
– pregnant women who hold an exemption certificate
– women who have had a baby in the last 12 months and who hold an exemption certificate
– people suffering from certain medical conditions who hold an exemption certificate
– people who receive income support, full working families' tax credit or credit reduced by up to £70, full disabled person's tax credit or credit reduced by up to £70 or income-based jobseeker's allowance, and their partners
– people who are named on an HC2 certificate issued by the Health Benefits Division
– war pensioners (for their accepted disablements)

Booklet HC11, available from main post offices and local social security offices, gives further details.

The number of prescriptions dispensed in the community in 1998 was:

England	513,200,000
Wales	46,659,000
Scotland	35,670,000
Northern Ireland	22,171,000

DENTAL SERVICE

Dentists, like doctors, may take part in the NHS and also have private patients. About 17,000 dentists in England provide NHS general dental services. They are responsible to the HAs in whose areas they provide services.

Patients may go to any dentist who is taking part in the NHS and is willing to accept them. Patients are required to pay 80 per cent of the cost of NHS dental treatment. Since 1 April 1999 the maximum charge for a course of treatment has been £348. There is no charge for arrest of bleeding or repairs to dentures; home visits by the dentist or re-opening a surgery in an emergency are charged for as treatment given in the normal way. The following people are exempt from dental charges or have charges remitted:

– people under 18
– full-time students under 19
– women who were pregnant when accepted for treatment
– women who have had a child in the previous 12 months

– people who receive income support, full working families' tax credit or credit reduced by up to £70, full disabled person's tax credit or credit reduced by up to £70, or income-based jobseeker's allowance, and their partners
– people who are named on an HC2 certificate issued by the Health Benefits Division
Booklet HC11, available from main post offices and local social security offices, gives further details.

GENERAL DENTAL SERVICE 1998–9 (ENGLAND)

Number of dentists	17,319
Number of patients registered	
Adults	16,800,000
Children	6,900,000
Number of courses of treatment	
Adults	26,200,000
Expenditure (£ million)	
Gross expenditure	1,400
Paid by patients	400
Paid out of public funds	1,000

Source: NHS Executive

GENERAL OPHTHALMIC SERVICES

General Ophthalmic Services are administered by HAs. Testing of sight may be carried out by any ophthalmic medical practitioner or ophthalmic optician (optometrist). The optician must give the prescription to the patient, who can take this to any supplier of glasses to have them dispensed. Only registered opticians can supply glasses to children and to people registered as blind or partially sighted.

The NHS sight test costs £14.57. Those on a low income may qualify for help with the cost. The test is available free to:
– people aged 60 or over
– children under 16*
– full-time students under 19*
– people who receive income support, income-based jobseeker's allowance, full working families' tax credit or credit reduced by up to £70, full disabled person's tax credit or credit reduced by up to £70, and their partners*
– people who are named on an HC2 certificate issued by the Health Benefits Division*
– people prescribed complex lenses*
– people registered as blind or partially sighted*
– diagnosed diabetic and glaucoma patients
– people advised by an ophthalmologist that they are at risk of glaucoma
The categories indicated by * above are automatically entitled to help with the purchase of glasses under an NHS voucher scheme, as are people whose spectacles are lost or damaged as a result of illness. Booklet HC11, available from main post offices and local social security offices, gives further details.

Diagnosis and specialist treatment of eye conditions, and the provision of special glasses, are available through the Hospital Eye Service.

COMMUNITY CHILD HEALTH SERVICES

Pre-school services at GP surgeries or child health clinics provide regular monitoring of children's physical, mental and emotional health and development, and advice to parents on their children's health and welfare.

The School Health Service provides for the medical and dental examination of schoolchildren, and advises the local education authority, the school, the parents and the pupil of any health factors which may require special consideration during the pupil's school life. GPs are increasingly undertaking child health monitoring in order to improve the preventive health care of children.

HEALTH ACTION ZONES

Health Action Zones aim to improve health services and tackle health inequalities in certain areas, working with the primary care groups in their area. The first 11 zones were set up in April 1998 and by April 1999 a total of 26 were in existence. Each zone receives funding for seven years.

HOSPITALS AND OTHER SERVICES

Hospital, medical, dental, nursing, ophthalmic and ambulance services are provided by the NHS to meet all reasonable requirements. Facilities for the care of expectant and nursing mothers and young children, and other services required for the diagnosis and treatment of illness, are also provided. Rehabilitation services (occupational therapy, physiotherapy and speech therapy) may also be provided, and surgical and medical appliances are supplied where appropriate. Specialists and consultants who work in NHS hospitals can also engage in private practice, including the treatment of their private patients in NHS hospitals.

PRIVATE FINANCE INITIATIVE

The Private Finance Initiative (PFI) was launched in 1992, and involves the private sector in designing, building, financing and operating new hospitals, which are then leased to the NHS. In July 1997 a new programme of hospital building under the PFI was announced by the Government.

CHARGES

Certain hospitals have accommodation in single rooms or small wards which, if not required for patients who need privacy for medical reasons, may be made available to patients who desire it as an amenity for a small charge. These patients are still NHS patients and are treated as such.

In a number of hospitals, accommodation is available for the treatment of private in-patients who undertake to pay the full costs of hospital accommodation and services and (usually) separate medical fees to a specialist as well. The amount of the medical fees is a matter for agreement between doctor and patient. Hospital charges for private in-patients are set locally at a commercial rate.

There is no charge for drugs supplied to NHS hospital in-patients, but out-patients pay £5.90 an item unless they are exempt. With certain exceptions, hospital out-patients have to pay fixed charges for dentures, contact lenses and certain appliances. Glasses may be obtained either from the hospital or an optician, and the charge will be related to the type of lens prescribed and the choice of frame.

AMBULANCE SERVICE

The NHS provides emergency ambulance services free of charge via the 999 emergency telephone service. There are 37 ambulance services in the UK. Helicopter ambulances are used in some areas where access may be difficult or heavy traffic could hinder road progress, and an air ambulance service is available throughout Scotland. Non-emergency ambulance services are provided free of charge to patients who are deemed to require them on medical grounds.

In 1998–9 in England about 3,800,000 emergency calls were made to the ambulance service, an increase of 7.6 per cent on the previous year. There were about 2,700,000 emergency patient journeys. The Patients' Charter requires emergency ambulances to respond to 95 per cent of calls within 14 minutes in urban areas and 19 minutes in rural areas, and to reach 50 per cent of cases within eight minutes. In 1998–9 10 ambulance services met the Charter standard for responding to life-threatening emergencies and seven met the standard for non-life threatening emegencies. Of the 21 ambulance services whose calls are not prioritized, 10 achieved the Charter Standard.

NHS DIRECT

NHS Direct is a telephone service staffed by nurses which gives patients advice on how to look after themselves as well as directing them to the appropriate part of the NHS for treatment if necessary. The Government intends that the service will cover all parts of England by the end of 2000.

BLOOD SERVICES

There are four national bodies which co-ordinate the blood donor programme in each constituent country of the UK. About two million donations of blood are given each year; donors give blood at local centres on a voluntary basis.

NATIONAL BLOOD AUTHORITY, Oak House, Reeds Crescent, Watford, Herts WD1 1QH. Tel: 01923-486800. *Chairman*, M. Fogden, CB; *Chief Executive*, M. Gorham

SCOTTISH NATIONAL BLOOD TRANSFUSION SERVICE, 21 Ellens Glen Road, Edinburgh EH17 7QT. Tel: 0131-536 5701. *National Director*, A. McMillan-Douglas

WELSH BLOOD SERVICE, Ely Valley Road, Talbot Green, Pontyclun CF72 9WB. Tel: 01443-622000. *Director*, Dr F. G. Williams

NORTHERN IRELAND BLOOD TRANSFUSION SERVICE, Belfast City Hospital Complex, Lisburn Road, Belfast BT9 7TS. Tel: 01232-321414

HOSPICES

Hospice or palliative care may be available for patients with life-threatening illnesses. It may be provided at the patient's home or in a voluntary or NHS hospice or in hospital, and is intended to ensure the best possible quality of life for the patient during their illness, and to provide help and support to both the patient and the patient's family. The National Council for Hospices and Specialist Palliative Care Services co-ordinates NHS and voluntary services in England, Wales and Northern Ireland; the Scottish Partnership Agency for Palliative and Cancer Care performs the same function in Scotland.

NATIONAL COUNCIL FOR HOSPICE AND SPECIALIST PALLIATIVE CARE SERVICES, 7th Floor, 1 Great Cumberland Place, London W1H 7AL. Tel: 0171-723 1639. *Executive Director*, Ms E. S. Richardson

SCOTTISH PARTNERSHIP AGENCY FOR PALLIATIVE AND CANCER CARE, 1A Cambridge Street, Edinburgh EH1 2DY. Tel: 0131-229 0538. *Director*, Mrs M. Stevenson

NUMBER OF BEDS AND PATIENT ACTIVITY 1997

	England*	Wales
In-patients:		
Average daily available beds	199,000	15,200
Average daily occupation of beds	162,000	12,000
Persons waiting for admission at 31 March	†1,158,000	69,900
Day-case admissions	2,958,000	309,700
Ordinary admissions	8,381,000	521,100
Out-patient attendances:		
New patients	11,298,000	693,300
Total attendances	40,864,000	2,643,300
Accident and emergency:		
New patients	12,439,000	826,600
Total attendances	14,080,000	997,900
Ward attendances	1,027,000	n/a

* 1996 figures
† 1997 figure
n/a not available

SCOTLAND
In-patients:	
Average available staffed beds	38,400
Average occupied beds	30,900
Out-patient attendances:	
New patients	2,675,000
Total attendances	6,272,000

Source: The Stationery Office – *Annual Abstract of Statistics 1999* (Crown copyright)

WAITING LISTS

At the end of June 1999 the total number of patients waiting to be admitted to NHS hospitals in England was 1,094,300, a decrease of 15 per cent on the previous year. The number of patients who had been waiting more than one year was 48,700, a decrease of 32 per cent on the previous year. Some 70 per cent of elective patients are treated within three months of being placed on a waiting list. Under the Patient's Charter, patients are guaranteed admission within 18 months of being placed on a waiting list.

NHS CHARTERS

The original Patient's Charter was published in 1991 and came into force in 1992; an expanded version was published in 1995. The Charter sets out the rights of patients in relation to the NHS (i.e. the standards of service which all patients will receive at all times); and patients' reasonable expectations (i.e. the standards of service that the NHS aims to provide, even if they cannot in exceptional circumstances be met). The Charter covers areas such as access to services, personal treatment of patients, the provision of information, registering with a doctor, hospital waiting times, care in hospitals, community services, ambulance waiting times, dental, optical and pharmaceutical services, and maternity services. In England there are separate Patient's Charter leaflets setting out standards in relation to services for children and young people, maternity services, mental health services and blood donation.

The Government is developing a new NHS Charter and a consultation document is expected to be published in autumn 1999. The Charter is due to be issued in April 2000, with local charters in place by 2001. Further information is available free of charge from the national Health Information Service (Tel 0800-665544).

Health authorities and boards, NHS Trusts and GP practices may also have their own local charters setting out the standard of service they aim to provide.

COMPLAINTS

The Patient's Charter includes the right to have any complaint about the service provided by the NHS dealt with quickly, with a full written reply being provided by a relevant chief executive. There are two levels to the NHS complaints procedure: the first level involves resolution of a complaint locally, following a direct approach to the relevant service provider; the second level involves an independent review procedure if the complaint is not resolved locally. As a final resort, patients may approach the Health Service Commissioner or Ombudsman (*see* page 329) (in Northern Ireland, the Commissioner for Complaints if they are dissatisfied with the response of the NHS to a complaint.

In 1997–8 there were 88,757 written complaints about hospital and community health services, of which 65 per cent were resolved locally within the target period of four weeks; two per cent of complainants requested an independent review. There were 38,093 written complaints about family health services and in 1,390 cases the complainant requested an independent review.

NHS TRIBUNALS

The National Health Service Tribunal and the National Health Service Tribunal (Scotland) (*see* page 372) consider representations that the continued inclusion of a doctor, dentist, optician or pharmacist on the list of a health authority or health board would be prejudicial to the efficiency of the service concerned. The Mental Health Review Tribunals (*see* page 371) are responsible for reviewing the cases of patients compulsorily detained under the Mental Health Act 1983.

RECIPROCAL ARRANGEMENTS

Citizens of countries in the European Economic Area (EEA - *see* page 778) are entitled to receive emergency health care either free of charge or for a reduced charge when they are temporarily visiting other member states of the EEA. Form E111, available at post offices, should be obtained before travelling. Non-EEA nationals, or visitors receiving routine, non-emergency care, are normally required to pay for treatment in Britain. There are bilateral agreements with several other countries, including Australia and New Zealand, for the provision of urgent medical treatment either free of charge or for a reduced charge.

Personal Social Services

The Secretary of State for Health is responsible, under the Local Authority Social Services Act 1970, for the provision of social services for elderly people, disabled people, families and children, and those with mental disorders. Personal Social Services are administered by local authorities according to policies and standards set by central government. Each authority has a Director of Social Services and a Social Services Committee responsible for the social services functions placed upon them. Local authorities provide, enable and commission care after assessing the needs of their population. The private and voluntary sectors also play an important role in the delivery of social services, and an estimated six million people in Great Britain provide substantial regular care for a member of their family.

The Community Care reforms introduced in 1993 were intended to enable vulnerable groups to live in the community rather than in residential homes wherever possible, and to offer them as independent a lifestyle as possible.

At 31 March 1997, there were 519,115 places in residential and nursing care homes in England. About 240,000 residents were supported by local authorities (an increase of 12 per cent on the previous year). Of the local authority-supported residents, 24 per cent were in local authority-run homes (down from 29 per cent), 46 per cent were in independent residential care homes (up from 42 per cent) and 27 per cent were in independent nursing homes (the same percentage as in the previous year).

FINANCE

The Personal Social Services programme is financed partly by central government, with decisions on expenditure allocations being made at local authority level.

STAFF

STAFF OF LOCAL AUTHORITY SOCIAL SERVICES DEPARTMENTS 1997 (ENGLAND)
Full-time equivalents

Area office/field work staff	114,900
Residential care staff	65,400
Day care staff	30,800
Central/strategic HQ staff	16,400
Other staff	1,900
Total staff	229,400

Source: Department of Health

ELDERLY PEOPLE

Services for elderly people are designed to enable them to remain living in their own homes for as long as possible. Local authority services include advice, domestic help, meals in the home, alterations to the home to aid mobility, emergency alarm systems, day and/or night attendants, laundry services and the provision of day centres and recreational facilities. Charges may be made for these services. Respite care may also be provided in order to allow carers temporary relief from their responsibilities.

Local authorities and the private sector also provide 'sheltered housing' for elderly people, sometimes with resident wardens.

If an elderly person is admitted to a residential home, charges are made according to a means test; if the person cannot afford to pay, the costs are met by the local authority.

The Royal Commission on Long-Term Care reported in March 1999. Its proposals are being considered by the Government.

DISABLED PEOPLE

Services for disabled people are designed to enable them to remain living in their own homes wherever possible. Local authority services include advice, adaptations to the home, meals in the home, help with personal care, occupational therapy, educational facilities and recreational facilities. Respite care may also be provided in order to allow carers temporary relief from their responsibilities.

Special housing may be available for disabled people who can live independently, and residential accommodation for those who cannot.

FAMILIES AND CHILDREN

Local authorities are required to provide services aimed at safeguarding the welfare of children in need and, wherever possible, allowing them to be brought up by their families. Services include advice, counselling, help in the home and the provision of family centres. Many authorities also provide short-term refuge accommodation for women and children.

DAY CARE

In allocating day-care places to children, local authorities give priority to children with special needs, whether in terms of their health, learning abilities or social needs. They also provide a registration and inspection service in relation to childminders, play groups and private day nurseries in the local authority area. In England in 1997 there were 6,100 day nurseries providing 194,000 places, 98,500 registered child-minders providing 365,000 places, and 15,800 play groups providing 384,000 places.

A national child care strategy is being developed by the Government, under which day care and out-of-school child care facilities will be extended to match more closely the needs of working parents.

CHILD PROTECTION

Children considered to be at risk of physical injury, neglect or sexual abuse are placed on the local authority's child protection register. Local authority social services staff, school nurses, health visitors and other agencies work together to prevent and detect cases of abuse. In England at 31 March 1997 there were 16,400 boys and 15,700 girls on child protection registers. Of these, 38 per cent were at risk of neglect, 34 per cent of physical abuse, 23 per cent of sexual abuse and 16 per cent of emotional abuse.

LOCAL AUTHORITY CARE

Local authorities are required to provide accommodation for children who have no parent or guardian or whose parents or guardians are unable or unwilling to care for them. A family proceedings court may also issue a care order in cases where a child is being neglected or abused, or is not attending school; the court must be satisfied that this would positively contribute to the well-being of the child.

The welfare of children in local authority care must be properly safeguarded. Children may be placed with foster families, who receive payments to cover the expenses of caring for the child or children, or in residential care. Children's homes may be run by the local authority or by the private or voluntary sectors; all homes are subject to inspection procedures. In England at 31 March 1997, 51,600 children were in the care of local authorities. Of these, 65 per cent were placed with foster parents and 5 per cent were placed for adoption.

ADOPTION

Local authorities are required to provide an adoption service, either directly or via approved voluntary societies. In England and Wales in 1996, 6,000 children (3,000 boys and 3,000 girls) were adopted.

PEOPLE WITH LEARNING DISABILITIES

Services for people with learning disabilities (i.e. mental handicap) are designed to enable them to remain living in the community wherever possible. Local authority services include short-term care, support in the home, the provision of day care centres, and help with other activities outside the home. Residential care is provided for the severely or profoundly disabled.

MENTALLY ILL PEOPLE

Under the Care Programme Approach, mentally ill people should be assessed by specialist services and receive a care plan, and a key worker should be appointed for each patient. Regular reviews of the patient's progress should be conducted. Local authorities provide help and advice to mentally ill people and their families, and places in day centres and social centres. Social workers can apply for a mentally disturbed person to be compulsorily detained in hospital. Where appropriate, mentally ill people are provided with accommodation in special hospitals, local authority accommodation, or homes run by private or voluntary organizations. Patients who have been discharged from hospitals may be placed on a supervision register. In July 1998 the Government announced that the system of care for mentally ill people would be replaced. The Mental Health Act 1983 is under review. A Mental Health National Service Framework is due to be published in autumn 1999 and enter into force in spring 2000, introducing national standards of care throughout England. In Scotland a committee has been established to review mental health legislation and will report to the Scottish Parliament in mid-2000.

TOTAL PLACES IN RESIDENTIAL AND NURSING HOMES (ENGLAND) as at 31 March 1997

By client group

Elderly people	374,302
Physically/sensorily disabled adults	11,494
Elderly mentally infirm people	39,373
People with mental illness	22,646
People with learning disabilities	50,872
Other people	20,428
All client groups	519,115

Source: Department of Health

LOCAL AUTHORITY-SUPPORTED RESIDENTS IN STAFFED RESIDENTIAL AND NURSING CARE (ENGLAND) as at 31 March 1997

All staffed homes	236,335
Local authority	58,747
Independent residential care	111,530
Independent nursing care	66,058
Elderly people	180,471
Physically/sensorily disabled adults	8,628
People with mental health problems	17,271
People with learning disabilities	26,872
Other people	3,093

Source: The Stationery Office – *Health and Personal Social Services Statistics for England 1998* (Crown copyright)

LOCAL AUTHORITY PERSONAL SOCIAL SERVICES GROSS EXPENDITURE BY CLIENT GROUP 1996–7 (ENGLAND)
£ million

	Elderly	Children	Learning disability	Adults	Mental health	HQ costs	Total
HQ costs	—	—	—	—	—	123	123
Area officers/senior managers	95	143	21	23	25	—	308
Care management/care assessment	284	321	58	74	86	—	823
Residential care	2,685	657	665	181	185	—	4,373
Non-residential care	1,466	907	451	357	153	—	3,333
Field social work	44	113	14	16	19	—	207
Other	—	—	—	96	—	—	96
TOTAL	4,575	2,142	1,208	748	468	123	9,263

Source: The Stationery Office – *Health and Personal Social Services Statistics for England 1998* (Crown copyright)

National Insurance and Related Cash Benefits

NB All leaflets referred to in this section can be obtained from local social security offices unless an alternative source is given

The state insurance and assistance schemes, comprising schemes of national insurance and industrial injuries insurance, national assistance, and non-contributory old age pensions, came into force from 5 July 1948. The Ministry of Social Security Act 1966 replaced national assistance and non-contributory old age pensions with a scheme of non-contributory benefits. These and subsequent measures relating to social security provision in Great Britain were consolidated by the Social Security Act 1975, the Social Security (Consequential Provisions) Act 1975, and the Industrial Injuries and Diseases (Old Cases) Act 1975. Corresponding measures were passed for Northern Ireland. The Social Security Pensions Act 1975 introduced a new state pensions scheme in 1978, and the graduated pension scheme 1961 to 1975 has been wound up, existing rights being preserved. Under the Pensions Act 1995 the age of retirement is to be 65 for both men and women, this being phased in between 2010 and 6 April 2020. The Pensioners' Payments and Social Security Act 1979 provided for a Christmas bonus for pensioners in 1979 and in succeeding years. The Child Benefit Act 1975 replaced family allowances (introduced 1946) with child benefit and one-parent benefit. Some of this legislation has been superseded by the provisions of the Social Security Acts 1969 to 1992. The Government is reforming the social security system. The Welfare Reform and Pensions Bill was published in February 1999 and is expected to become law in autumn 1999. If it is enacted, changes in benefits will come into effect from April 2001. Details of proposed changes, where known, are included.

NATIONAL INSURANCE SCHEME

The National Insurance (NI) scheme operates under the Social Security Contributions and Benefits Act 1992 and the Social Security Administration Act 1992, and orders and regulations made thereunder. The scheme is financed by contributions payable by earners, employers and others (*see* below) and by a Treasury grant. Money collected under the scheme is used to finance the National Insurance Fund (from which contributory benefits are paid) and to contribute to the cost of the National Health Service.

NATIONAL INSURANCE FUND

Approximate receipts and payments of the National Insurance Fund for the year ended 31 March 1999 were:

Receipts	£'000
Balance, 1 April 1998 (provisional)	9,608,000
Contributions under the Social Security	
Acts (net of SSP and SMP)	48,934,000
Treasury grant	0
Compensation from Consolidated Fund for	
SSP and SMP recoveries	558,000
Compensation from Consolidated Fund for	
contribution holidays for employers	
taking on formerly long-term	
unemployed	3,000
Income from investments	675,000
State scheme premiums	88,000
Other receipts	115,000
	50,373,000

Payments	£'000
Benefits	44,337,000
Personal pensions contracted-out rebates	1,937,000
Age-related rebates for contracted-out	
money purchase schemes	80,000
Transfers to Northern Ireland	315,000
Administration	993,000
Redundancy payments (net)	106,000
Other payments	20,000
Balance, 31 March 1999	12,253,000
	60,041,000

CONTRIBUTIONS

There are six classes of NI contributions:

Class 1　paid by employees and their employers
Class 1A　paid by employers who provide employees with cars/fuel for private use
Class 1B　paid by employers in value of any items included on a PAYE settlement with the Inland Revenue
Class 2　paid by self-employed people
Class 3　voluntary contributions paid to protect entitlement to certain benefits
Class 4　paid by the self-employed on their taxable profits over a set limit

The lower and upper earnings limits and the percentage rates referred to below apply from 6 April 1999 to 5 April 2000.

CLASS 1

Class 1 contributions are paid where a person:
– is an employed earner (employee) or office holder (e.g. company director)
– is 16 or over and under state pension age
– earns at or above the lower earning limit of £66.00 per week (including overtime pay, bonus, commission, etc., without deduction of superannuation contributions)

Class 1 contributions are made up of primary and secondary contributions. Primary contributions are those paid by the employee and these are deducted from earnings by the employer. Primary contributions are not paid on earnings below the lower earnings limit. They are payable at the rate of 10 per cent on earnings between the lower earnings limit and the upper earnings limit of £500.00 per week (8.4 per cent for contracted-out employment, *see* page 488).

Some married women or widows pay a reduced rate of 3.85 per cent on earnings between the lower and upper earnings limits. It is no longer possible to elect to pay the reduced rate but those who had reduced liability before 12 May 1977 may retain it so long as certain conditions are met. *See* leaflet CA09 (widows) or leaflet CA13 (married women).

Secondary contributions are paid by employers of employed earners at the rate of 12.2 per cent on all earnings at or above the secondary earnings threshold of £83.00 per week. Employers operating contracted-out salary related schemes (*see* page 488) pay reduced contributions of 9.2 per cent; those with contracted-out money-purchase schemes (*see* page 488) pay 11.6 per cent. There is no upper earnings limit for employers' contributions. The contracted-out rate applies only to that portion of earnings between the lower and upper earnings limits. Employers' contributions below and above those respective limits are assessed at the appropriate not contracted-out rate.

CLASS 2

Class 2 contributions are paid where a person is self-employed and is 16 or over and under state pension age. Contributions are paid at a flat rate of £6.55 per week regardless of the amount earned. However, those with earnings of less than £3,770 a year can apply for Small Earnings Exception, i.e. exemption from liability to pay Class 2 contributions. Those granted exemption from Class 2 contributions may pay Class 2 or Class 3 contributions voluntarily. Self-employed earners (whether or not they pay Class 2 contributions) may also be liable to pay Class 4 contributions based on profits. There are special rules for those who are concurrently employed and self-employed.

Married women and widows can no longer choose not to pay Class 2 contributions but those who elected not to pay Class 2 contributions before 12 May 1977 may retain the right so long as certain conditions are met.

Class 2 contributions are collected by the National Insurance Contributions Office (NICO), an executive agency of the Inland Revenue, by direct debit or quarterly bills. See leaflets CA03 and CA02.

CLASS 3

Class 3 contributions are voluntary flat-rate contributions of £6.45 per week payable by persons over the age of 16 who would otherwise be unable to qualify for retirement pension and certain other benefits because they have an insufficient record of Class 1 or Class 2 contributions. This may include those who are not working, those not liable for Class 1 or Class 2 contributions or those excepted from Class 2 contributions. Married women and widows who on or before 11 May 1977 elected not to pay Class 1 (full rate) or Class 2 contributions cannot pay Class 3 contributions while they retain this right.

Class 3 contributions are collected by the NICO by quarterly bills or direct debit. See leaflet CA08.

CLASS 4

Self-employed people whose profits and gains are over £7,530 a year pay Class 4 contributions in addition to Class 2 contributions. This applies to self-employed earners over 16 and under the state pension age. Class 4 contributions are calculated at 6 per cent of annual profits or gains between £7,530 and £26,000. The maximum Class 4 contribution payable on £26,000 or more is £1,108.20.

Class 4 contributions are assessed and collected by the Inland Revenue together with Schedule D tax. It is possible, in some circumstances, to apply for exceptions from liability to pay Class 4 contributions or to have the amount of contribution reduced (where Class 1 contributions are payable on earnings assessed for Class 4 contributions). See leaflet CA03.

PENSIONS

The Social Security Pensions Act came into force in 1978. It aimed to:
- reduce reliance on means-tested benefit in old age, widowhood and chronic ill-health
- ensure that occupational pension schemes which are contracted out of the state scheme fulfil the conditions of a good scheme
- ensure that pensions are adequately protected against inflation
- ensure that men and women are treated equally in state and occupational schemes

Legislation and regulations introduced since 1978 go further towards fulfilling these aims and more changes came into effect in April 1997 (see below). One of the changes is to equalize the state pension age for men (currently 65 years) and women (currently 60 years) from 6 April 2020. The change will be phased in over the ten years leading up to 6 April 2020. As a result the state pension age is as follows:
- the pension age for men remains at 65
- the pension age for women born on or before 5 April 1950 remains at 60
- the pension age for women born on or after 6 April 1955 is now 65
- for women born after 5 April 1950 and before 6 April 1955, the pension age is 60 plus one month for every month, or part of a month, that their date of birth fell after 5 April 1950.

The Welfare Reform and Pensions Bill provides for the sharing of pensions between divorcing couples.

STATE PENSION SCHEME

The state pension scheme consists of the basic flat-rate pension and the state earnings-related pension scheme (SERPS), also known as additional pension.

The amount of basic pension paid is dependent on the number of 'qualifying years' a person has in their 'working life'. A 'qualifying year' is a tax year in which a person pays Class 1 (at the standard rate), 2 or 3 NI contributions for the whole year (see above). Those in receipt of invalid care allowance, disabled person's tax credit, jobseeker's allowance, incapacity benefit, severe disablement allowance or approved training have contributions credited to them for each week they receive benefit or fulfil certain other conditions. For those reaching pensionable age on or after 6 April 1999, a Class 3 credit of earnings will be awarded for each week from 6 April 1995 that family credit or, subsequently, working families tax credit, has been received. 'Working life' is counted from the start of the tax year in which a person reaches 16 to the end of the tax year before the one in which they reach pensionable age: for men this is normally 49 years and for women this varies between 44 and 49 years because the pension ages vary (see above). To get the full rate (100 per cent) basic pension a person must have qualifying years for about 90 per cent of their working life. To get the minimum basic pension (25 per cent) a person will need ten or eleven qualifying years. Married women who are not entitled to a pension on their own contributions may get a pension on their husband's contributions. It is possible for people who are unable to work because they care for children or a sick or disabled person at home to reduce the number of qualifying years required. This is called home responsibilities protection (HRP) and can be given for any tax year since April 1978; the number of years for which HRP is given is deducted from the number of qualifying years needed.

The amount of SERPS or additional pension paid depends on the amount of earnings a person has between the lower and upper earnings limits (see page 486) for each complete tax year between 6 April 1978 (when the scheme started) and the tax year before they reach state pension age. The right to additional pension does not depend on the person's right to basic pension. The amount of additional pension paid also depends on when a person reaches retirement; changes being phased in from 6 April 1999 mean that pensions will be calculated differently from that date. Women widowed before 6 April 2000 will inherit all their late husband's additional pension and women widowed on or after this date will inherit half of the husband's additional pension.

There are four categories of state pension provided under the Social Security Contributions and Benefits Act 1992:
- Category A, a contributory pension made up of basic and additional elements, payable to those of pensionable age who satisfy the entitlement conditions described above (see pages 490–1)

– Category B, a contributory pension made up of basic and additional elements, payable to married women and widows and based on their husband's contributions. This category of pension is to be extended to men whose wives were born after 5 April 1950 from 6 April 2010 (*see* pages 490–1)
– Category C, a non-contributory pension payable to those who reached pensionable age before 5 July 1948 (*see* page 492)
– Category D, a non-contributory pension for those over 80 (*see* page 492)

Graduated retirement benefit is also available to those who paid graduated NI contributions into the scheme when it existed between April 1961 and April 1975.

It is possible to find out how much basic and additional pension a person might receive by filling in form BR19, available from local social security offices or by telephoning 0191-225 5240.

The Welfare Reform and Pensions Bill proposes changes to pensions. SERPS will be replaced by a second state pension from 2002, subject to the legislation being passed. This will initially be earnings-related, but will subsequently be paid at a flat rate, targeted towards low earners. It will provide a guaranteed minimum income. Under certain circumstances, people not working (such as disabled people and those caring for children or sick relatives) will receive credits into the scheme as though they had earned £9,000 per year. As with SERPS, a person will be entitled to contract out into an occupational, personal or new stakeholder pension scheme. Subject to the passage of the Welfare Reform Bill, stakeholder pensions will be available from 2001. They will be targeted at those earning between £9,000 and £18,500 who have no occupational or appropriate personal scheme to join. Higher earners will also be able to join a stakeholder scheme if they wish.

CONTRACTED-OUT OCCUPATIONAL AND PERSONAL PENSION SCHEMES

Under the Pensions Schemes Act 1993, an employer can contract out of SERPS those employees who are members of an occupational scheme, so long as the occupational scheme satisfies certain conditions. The occupational pension took the place of the additional pension from April 1997 (previously it took the place of part of the additional pension); the state remains responsible for the flat rate state basic pension. Until April 1997 members of contracted-out occupational and personal pension schemes accrued additional pension in the same way as someone who is not contracted-out but the rate payable was reduced by contracted-out deductions. Since 5 April 1997, it has not been possible to accrue any SERPS while being a member of a contracted-out occupational or personal pension scheme. Members are still entitled to those rights earned before April 1997. Since April 1997 there have been age-related NI contribution rebates for people who leave SERPS and become members of either a COMP (*see* below) or an appropriate personal pension scheme; these will be lower for younger people and higher for older people.

There are three types of contracted-out occupational schemes.

Contracted-Out Salary-Related Scheme (COSR)

– this scheme must provide a pension related to earnings
– the pension provided must not be less than a person's guaranteed minimum pension (GMP), i.e. worth about the same as the additional pension provided by the state scheme had the member remained in the State scheme

– any notional additional pension earned from 6 April 1978 to 5 April 1997 will be reduced by the amount of GMP earned during that period (the contracted-out deduction)
– from 6 April 1997 these schemes no longer provide a GMP but do have to satisfy a new scheme-based test, certified by an actuary, before a contracting-out certificate can be issued

Contracted-Out Money Purchase Scheme (COMP)

– this scheme must provide a pension based on the value of the fund built up, i.e. the money paid in, along with returns from investment
– part of the pension, known as protected rights, takes the place of the additional pension. A contracted-out deduction, which may be more or less than the pension provided by the scheme, will be made from any additional pension earned from 6 April 1987 to 5 April 1997

In contracted-out occupational pension schemes, both the employee and employer pay lower NI contribution rates in recognition that SERPS will not be paid.

Contracted-Out Mixed Benefit Scheme (COMBS)

A mixed benefit scheme has two active sections, one salary-related and the other money purchase. Scheme rules set out which section individual employees may join and the circumstances (if any) in which members may move between sections. Each section must satisfy the respective contracting-out conditions for COSRs and COMPs.

Appropriate Personal Pension Schemes

The option of a personal pension scheme is open to all employees, even if their employer has an occupational pension scheme. A personal pension scheme must provide a pension based on the value of the fund built up, i.e. the money paid in, along with returns from investment. Part of the pension, known as protected rights, takes the place of the additional pension. A contracted-out deduction, which may be more or less than the pension provided by the scheme, will be made from any additional pension earned from 6 April 1987 to 5 April 1997.

Employees who are members of a personal pension plan and their employers pay NI contributions at the full rate and the Inland Revenue pays the difference between the full rate and the contracted-out rate into the personal pension scheme.

A Pensions Ombudsman deals with complaints about maladministration of pensions schemes. The Occupational Pensions Board, which supervised contracting-out and approved personal pension schemes, was abolished in April 1997 and replaced by the Occupational Pensions Regulatory Authority. *See* leaflet NP46.

BENEFITS

Leaflets relating to the various benefits and contribution conditions for different benefits are available from local social security offices; leaflets NI196 *Social Security Benefit Rates*, FB2 *Which Benefit?* and MG1 *A Guide to Benefits* are general guides to benefits, benefit rates and contributions.

The benefits payable under the Social Security Acts are:

CONTRIBUTORY BENEFITS
Jobseeker's allowance (contribution-based)
Incapacity benefit
Maternity allowance
Widow's benefit (comprising widow's payment, widowed mother's allowance and widow's pension)
Retirement pensions, categories A and B

NON-CONTRIBUTORY BENEFITS AND TAX CREDITS
Child benefit
Guardian's allowance
Jobseeker's allowance (income-based)
Invalid care allowance
Severe disablement allowance
Attendance allowance
Disability living allowance
Disabled person's tax credit
Retirement pensions, categories C and D
Income support
Working families tax credit
Housing benefit
Council tax benefit
Social fund

BENEFITS FOR INDUSTRIAL INJURIES AND
DISABLEMENT

OTHER
Statutory sick pay
Statutory maternity pay

TAX CREDITS

Under the Tax Credits Act 1999, Family Credit and Disability Working Allowance (both non-contributory benefits) were replaced by Working Families Tax Credit and Disabled Person's Tax Credit from 5 October 1999. . Both of these are administered by the Inland Revenue. The first payments will be made from April 2000. People receiving Family Credit or Disability Working Allowance on 5 October 1999 will continue to receive their benefits until the award expires, when they will be able to change to the new tax credits. Until March 2000 the tax credits will be paid directly to the applicant by the Inland Revenue. From April 2000 employees will receive the credits from their employer along with their wages or salary. Self-employed applicants will be paid direct by the Inland Revenue. Further information and application forms are available from Inland Revenue Tax Enquiry Centres, Benefits Agency offices, Jobcentres, post offices and Citizens' Advice Bureaux.

WORKING FAMILIES TAX CREDIT

Working Families Tax Credit is a system of tax credits paid to couples (married or unmarried) or lone parents who have at least one child living with them and where at least one partner works at least 16 hours per week. The credit is not payable if any savings exceed £8,000.

Working Families Tax Credit will usually be paid at the same rate for 26 weeks. There are four elements:
– a basic credit of £52.30 per family per week
– a credit of £11.05 per week where one earner works at least 30 hours per week
– a credit for each child at the rate of £19.85 per week from birth (rising by £1.10 plus inflation from April 2000), £20.90 from the September following their 11th birthday and £25.95 from the September following their 16th birthday up to the day before their 19th birthday
– a childcare credit (in certain circumstances) of up to 70 per cent of eligible childcare costs up to a maximum of £100 per week for one child and £150 per week for two or more children
If net income is below £90 per week, the maximum tax credit is payable. If net income exceeds £90 per week, the total tax credit is reduced by 55p for each £1.00 above £90.

DISABLED PERSON'S TAX CREDIT

Disabled Person's Tax Credit is a system of tax credits for people who are working at least 16 hours per week but

have an illness or disability which puts them at a disadvantage in getting a job. To qualify, a person must have one of the 'qualifying benefits' or have had them up to 182 days before applying. The credit is not payable if any savings exceed £16,000.

Disabled Person's Tax Credit will usually be paid at the same rate for 26 weeks. There are five elements:
– a basic credit of £54.30 per week for a single person or £83.55 for a couple
– a credit of £11.05 per week where one applicant works at least 30 hours per week
– a credit for each child at the rate of £19.85 from birth (rising by £1.10 plus inflation from April 2000), £20.90 from the September following their 11th birthday and £25.95 from the September following their 16th birthday up to the day before their 19th birthday
– a disabled child's tax credit of £21.90 per week
– a childcare credit (in certain circumstances) of up to 70 per cent of eligible childcare costs up to a maximum of £100 per week for one child and £150 per week for two or more children
If net income is below £70 per week for a single person or £90 per week for a couple or lone parent, the maximum tax credit is payable. If net income exceeds these thresholds, the total tax credit is reduced by 55p for each £1.00 above the threshold.

CONTRIBUTORY BENEFITS

Entitlement to contributory benefits depends on contribution conditions being satisfied either by the claimant or by some other person (depending on the kind of benefit). The class or classes of contribution which for this purpose are relevant to each benefit are:

Jobseeker's allowance (contribution-based)	Class 1
Incapacity benefit	Class 1 or 2
Maternity allowance	Class 1 or 2
Widow's benefits	Class 1, 2 or 3
Retirement pensions, categories A and B	Class 1, 2 or 3

The system of contribution conditions relates to yearly levels of earnings on which contributions have been paid.

JOBSEEKER'S ALLOWANCE

Jobseeker's allowance (JSA) replaced unemployment benefit and income support for unemployed people under pension age from 7 October 1996. There are two routes of entitlement. Contribution-based JSA is paid as a personal rate (i.e. additional benefit for dependants is not paid) to those who have made sufficient NI contributions in two particular tax years. Savings and partner's earnings are not taken into account and payment can be made for up to six months. Those who do not qualify for contribution-based JSA, those who have exhausted their entitlement to contribution-based JSA or those for whom contribution-based JSA provides insufficient income may qualify for income-based JSA. The amount paid depends on age and number of dependants and income and savings are taken into account. Income-based JSA may comprise three parts: a personal allowance for the jobseeker and his/her partner and one for each child or young person for whom they are responsible; premiums for groups of people with special needs; and housing costs. This is payable for the claimant and their dependants for as long as they satisfy the rules. Rates of jobseeker's allowance correspond to income support rates.

Claims for this benefit are made through Employment Service Jobcentres. A person wishing to claim jobseeker's allowance must be unemployed, capable of work and available for any work which they can reasonably be expected to do, usually for at least 40 hours per week.

They must agree and sign a 'jobseeker's agreement', which will set out each claimant's plans to find work, and must actively seek work. If they refuse work or training their benefit may be suspended for between two and six weeks.

A person will be disqualified from jobseeker's allowance if they have left a job voluntarily or through misconduct, if they refuse to take up an offer of employment or if they fail to attend a training scheme or employment programme. In these circumstances, it may be possible to receive hardship payments, particularly where the claimant or their family is vulnerable, e.g. if sick or pregnant, or for those with children or caring responsibilities. See leaflet JSAL5.

INCAPACITY BENEFIT

Incapacity benefit is available to those who are incapable of work but cannot get statutory sick pay from their employer. It is not payable to those over state pension age. However, people who are already in receipt of short-term incapacity benefit when they reach state pension age may continue to receive this benefit for up to 52 weeks. The Welfare Reform and Pensions Bill proposes restricting eligibility for incapacity benefit to people who have paid National Insurance contributions in the previous two years. The Bill also provides for the reduction of the amount of incapacity benefit payable where a claimant receives more than a specified amount of occupational or personal pension. Severely disabled people aged between 16 and 19 should receive incapacity benefit without meeting the national insurance contribution conditions under the Government's proposals. There are three rates of incapacity benefit:
- short-term lower rate for the first 28 weeks of sickness
- short-term higher rate from weeks 29 to 52
- long-term rate after week 52

The terminally ill and those entitled to the highest rate care component of disability living allowance are paid the long-term rate after 28 weeks. Incapacity benefit is taxable after 28 weeks.

Two rates of age addition are paid with long-term benefit based on the claimant's age when incapacity started. The higher rate is payable where incapacity for work commenced before the age of 35; and the lower rate where incapacity commenced before the age of 45. Increases for dependants are also payable with short and long-term incapacity benefit.

There are two medical tests of incapacity: the 'own occupation' test and the 'all work' test. Those who worked before becoming incapable of working will be assessed, for the first 28 weeks of incapacity, on their ability to do their own job. After 28 weeks (or from the start of incapacity for those who were not working) claimants are assessed on their ability to carry out a range of work-related activities. The 'all work' test applies to most former sickness and invalidity benefit claimants. The Government plans to replace the 'all work' test with a new 'personal capability assessment.' See leaflets IB202 and SD1.

MATERNITY ALLOWANCE

The maternity allowance (MA) scheme covers women who are self-employed or otherwise do not qualify for statutory maternity pay (see page 495). In order to qualify, the woman must have been working and paying standard rate NI contributions for at least 26 weeks in the 66-week period which ends with the week before the week in which the baby is due. A woman can choose to start receiving MA between the beginning of the 11th week before the week in which the baby is due and the Sunday after the baby is born, depending on when she stops working. MA is paid for a period of up to 18 weeks. MA is only paid while the woman is not working. See leaflet NI17A.

WIDOW'S BENEFITS

Only the late husband's contributions of any class count for widow's benefit in any of its three forms:

Widow's payment – may be received by a woman who at her husband's death is under 60, or whose husband was not entitled to a Category A retirement pension when he died. It is a single tax-free lump sum payable immediately the woman becomes a widow

Widowed mother's allowance – a taxable benefit payable to a widow if she is entitled or treated as entitled to child benefit, or if she is expecting her husband's baby

Widow's pension – a widow may receive this pension if aged 45 or over at the time of her husband's death (40 or over if widowed before 11 April 1988) or when her widowed mother's allowance ends. If aged 55 or over (50 or over if widowed before 11 April 1988) she will receive the full widow's pension rate

It is not possible to receive widowed mother's allowance and widow's pension at the same time, and widow's benefit in any form ceases upon remarriage or during a period in which a widow lives with a man as his wife. Different rules and conditions (other than those mentioned) apply to women widowed before 11 April 1988. The Welfare Reform and Pensions Bill proposes the replacement of widow's payment with a £2,000 bereavement payment and the introduction of widowed parent's allowance and bereavement allowance. All of the new benefits will be payable to both widowers and widows who are eligible. See leaflet NP45.

RETIREMENT PENSION: CATEGORIES A AND B

A Category A pension is payable for life to men and women who reach state pension age and who satisfy the contributions conditions (see page 486). A Category B pension is payable for life to a woman and is based on her husband's contributions. It becomes payable only when the husband has claimed his pension and the woman has reached state pension age. It is also payable on widowhood after 60 regardless of whether the late husband had qualified for his pension. There are special rules for those who are widowed before reaching pensionable age.

A person may defer claiming their pension for five years after state pension age. In doing so they may earn increments which will increase the weekly amount paid when they claim their pension. If a married man defers his Category A pension, his wife cannot claim a Category B pension on his contributions but she may earn increments on her pension during this time. A woman can defer her Category B pension, and earn increments, even if her husband is claiming his Category A pension.

The basic state pension is £66.75 per week plus any additional (earnings-related) pension the person may be entitled to (see page 486). An increase of £39.95 is paid for an adult dependant, providing the dependant's earnings do not exceed the rate of jobseeker's allowance for a single person (see below). It is also possible to get an increase of Category A and B pensions for a child or children. An age addition of 25p per week is payable if a retirement pensioner is aged 80 or over.

Since 1989 pensioners have been allowed to have unlimited earnings without affecting their retirement pension. Income support is payable on top of a pension where a pension does not give the person enough to live on and to those who are entitled to retirement pension but who have not claimed it. Pensioners may also be entitled to housing and council tax benefits.

GRADUATED RETIREMENT BENEFIT

Graduated NI contributions were first payable from 1961 and were calculated as a percentage of earnings between certain bands. They were discontinued in 1975. Any graduated pension which an employed person over 18 and under 70 (65 for a woman) had earned by paying graduated contributions will be paid when the contributor claims retirement pension or at 70 (65 for a woman), in addition to any retirement pension for which he or she qualifies. A wife can get a graduated pension in return for her own graduated contributions, but not for her husband's.

Graduated retirement benefit is at a weekly rate for each 'unit' of graduated contributions paid by the employee (half a unit or more counts as a whole unit); the rate varies from person to person. A unit of graduated pension can be calculated by adding together all graduated contributions and dividing by 7.5 (men) or 9.0 (women). If a person defers making a claim beyond 65 (60 for a woman), entitlement may be increased by one seventh of a penny per £1 of its weekly rate for each complete week of deferred retirement, as long as the retirement is deferred for a minimum of seven weeks.

WEEKLY RATES OF BENEFIT
from April 1999

Jobseeker's allowance (contribution-based)

Person under 18	£30.30
Person aged 18–24	39.85
Person over 25	50.35

Short-term incapacity benefit

Person under pension age – lower rate	48.80
*Person under pension age – higher rate	57.70
Increase for adult dependant	31.15
*Person over pension age	62.05
Increase for adult dependant	38.40

Long-term incapacity benefit

Person (under or over pension age)	64.70
Increase for adult dependant	39.95
Age addition – lower rate	6.80
Age addition – higher rate	13.60

Invalidity allowance: maximum amount payable

Higher rate	13.60
Middle rate	8.60
Lower rate	4.30

Maternity allowance

Employed	57.70
Self-employed or unemployed	50.10

Widow's benefits

Widow's payment (lump sum)	1,000.00*
†Widowed mother's allowance	66.75
†Widow's pension	66.75

Retirement pension: categories A and B

Single person	66.75
Increase for wife/other adult dependant	39.95

*These benefits attract an increase for each dependent child (in addition to child benefit) of £9.90 for the first or only child and £11.35 for each subsequent child
†To rise to £2,000 and be extended to widowers once Welfare Reform and Pensions Bill becomes law

NON-CONTRIBUTORY BENEFITS

These benefits are paid from general taxation and are not dependent on NI contributions. Unless otherwise stated, a benefit is tax-free and is not means tested.

CHILD BENEFIT

Child benefit is payable for virtually all children aged under 16, and for those aged 16 to 18 who are studying full-time up to and including A-level or equivalent standard. It is also payable for a short period if the child has left school recently and is registered for work or work-based training for young people at a careers office.

A higher rate of benefit (child benefit (lone parent)) may be paid to a person who is responsible for bringing up one or more children on his/her own. It is a flat rate benefit payable for the eldest child only. Since 6 July 1998 child benefit (lone parent) has not been available to new lone parents but it may still be payable in certain circumstances. *See* leaflets CH1 and CH11.

GUARDIAN'S ALLOWANCE

Where the parents of a child are dead, the person who has the child in his/her family may claim a guardian's allowance in addition to child benefit. In exceptional circumstances the allowance is payable on the death of only one parent. *See* leaflet NI14.

INVALID CARE ALLOWANCE

Invalid care allowance (ICA) is a taxable benefit payable to people of working age who give up the opportunity of full-time paid employment because they are regularly and substantially engaged (spending at least 35 hours per week as a carer) in caring for a severely disabled person. To qualify for ICA a person must be caring for someone in receipt of one of the following benefits:

– the middle or highest rate of disability living allowance care component
– either rate of attendance allowance
– constant attendance allowance, paid at not less than the normal maximum rate, under the industrial injuries or war pension schemes

See leaflets FB31 and SD1.

SEVERE DISABLEMENT ALLOWANCE

Persons who have been incapable of work for a continuous period of at least 28 weeks but who do not qualify for contributory incapacity benefit may be entitled to severe disablement allowance (SDA). This benefit is available to people over 16 and under 65. Those who are over 65 can only get SDA if they were entitled to it on the day before their 65th birthday. People who became incapable of work on or before their 20th birthday do not have to have their disability assessed but those who became incapable after their 20th birthday must be assessed as at least 80 per cent disabled. If the Welfare Reform and Pensions Bill is enacted, Severe Disablement Allowance will not be available to new claimants from April 2001. *See* leaflet NI252.

ATTENDANCE ALLOWANCE

This is payable to disabled people who claim after the age of 65 and who need a lot of care or supervision because of physical or mental disability for a period of at least six months. People not expected to live for six months because of an illness do not have to wait six months. The allowance has two rates: the lower rate is for day or night care, and the higher rate is for day and night care. *See* leaflets DS702 and SD1.

DISABILITY LIVING ALLOWANCE

This is payable to disabled people who claim before the age of 65 who have personal care and mobility needs because of an illness or disability for a period of at least three months and are likely to have those needs for a further six months or more. People not expected to live for six months because of an illness do not have to wait three months. The allowance has two components: the care component, which has three rates, and the mobility component, which has two rates. The rates depend on the care and mobility needs of the claimant. The mobility component is currently payable only to those aged five or over, but the Government plans to extend it to those aged over three. A Disability Income Guarantee will also be introduced. *See* leaflets DS704 and SD1.

RETIREMENT PENSION: CATEGORIES C AND D

A Category C pension is provided, subject to a residence test, for persons who were over pensionable age on 5 July 1948, and for the wives and widows of men who qualified if they are over pension age. A Category D pension is provided for people aged 80 and over if they are not entitled to another category of pension or are entitled to less than the Category D rate.

WEEKLY RATES OF BENEFIT
from April 1998

Child benefit

Eldest child	£14.40
Eldest child of certain lone parents	17.10
Each subsequent child	9.60

Guardian's allowance

Eldest child	7.30
Each subsequent child	11.35

*Invalid care allowance

	39.95
Increase for wife/other adult dependant	23.90

*Severe disablement allowance

†Basic rate	40.35
Under 40	14.05
40–49	8.90
50–59	4.45
Increase for wife/other adult dependant	23.95

Attendance allowance

Higher rate	52.95
Lower rate	35.40

Disability living allowance
Care component

Higher rate	52.95
Middle rate	35.40
Lowest rate	14.05

Mobility component

Higher rate	37.00
Lower rate	14.05

Retirement pension: categories *C and D

Single person	39.95
Increase for wife/other adult dependant	23.95
(not payable with Category D pension)	

*These benefits attract an increase for each dependent child (in addition to child benefit) of £9.90 for the first or only child and £11.35 for each subsequent child
†The age addition applies to the age when incapacity began

INCOME SUPPORT

Income support is a benefit for those aged 16 and over whose income is below a certain level. It can be paid to people who are not expected to sign on as unemployed (income support for unemployed people was replaced by jobseeker's allowance in October 1996) and who are:
– incapable of work due to sickness or disability
– bringing up children alone
– 60 or over
– looking after a person who has a disability
– registered blind

Some people who are not in these categories may also be able to claim income support.

Income support is also payable to people who work for less than 16 hours a week on average (or 24 hours for a partner). Some people can claim income support if they work longer hours.

Income support is not payable if the claimant, or claimant and partner, have capital or savings in excess of £8,000. For capital and savings in excess of £3,000, a deduction of £1 is made for every £250 or part of £250 held. Different limits apply to people permanently in residential care and nursing homes: the upper limit is £16,000 and deductions apply for capital in excess of £10,000.

Sums payable depend on fixed allowances laid down by law for people in different circumstances. If both partners are entitled to income support, either may claim it for the couple. People receiving income support may be able to receive housing benefit, help with mortgage or home loan interest and help with health care. They may also be eligible for help with exceptional expenses from the Social Fund. Special rates may apply to some people living in residential care or nursing homes. Leaflet IS20 gives a detailed explanation of income support.

In October 1998 the Government's voluntary New Deal for Lone Parents programme became available throughout the UK. All lone parents receiving income support are assigned a personal adviser at a jobcentre who will provide guidance and support with a view to enabling the claimant to find work.

INCOME SUPPORT PREMIUMS

Income support premiums are additional weekly payments for those with special needs. People qualifying for more than one premium will normally only receive the highest single premium for which they qualify. However, family premium, disabled child premium, severe disability premium and carer premium are payable in addition to other premiums.

People with children may qualify for:
– the family premium if they have at least one child (a higher rate is paid to lone parents, although from 6 April 1998 it has not generally been available to new claimants)
– the disabled child premium if they have a child who receives disability living allowance or is registered blind

Carers may qualify for:
– the carer premium if they or their partner are in receipt of invalid care allowance

Long-term sick or disabled people may qualify for:
– the disability premium if they or their partner are receiving certain benefits because they are disabled or cannot work; are registered blind; or if the claimant has been incapable of work or receiving statutory sick pay for at least 364 days (196 days if the person is terminally ill), including periods of incapacity separated by eight weeks or less
– the severe disability premium if the person lives alone and receives attendance allowance or the middle or higher rate of disability living allowance care component and no one receives invalid care allowance for caring for that person. This premium is also available to couples where both partners meet the above conditions

People aged 60 and over may qualify for:
– the pensioner premium if they or their partner are aged 60 to 74
– the enhanced pensioner premium if they or their partner are aged 75 to 79
– the higher pensioner premium if they or their partner are aged 80 or over. This is also available to people over 60 who receive attendance allowance, disability living allowance, long-term incapacity benefit or severe disablement allowance, or who are registered blind

WEEKLY RATES OF BENEFIT
from April 1999

Income support

Single person

under 18	£30.95
under 18 (higher)	40.70
aged 18–24	40.70
aged 25 and over	51.40
aged 18 and over and a single parent	51.40

Couples*

one or both aged 18 or over	80.65

For each child in a family

until September following 11th birthday	20.20
from September following 11th birthday	
to September following 16th birthday	25.90
†from September following 16th birthday	
to day before 19th birthday	30.95

Premiums

Family premium	13.90
Family (lone parent) premium	15.75
Disabled child premium	21.90
Carer premium	13.95
Disability premium	
Single	21.90
Couple	31.25
Severe disability premium	
Single	39.75
Couple (one person qualified)	39.75
Couple (both qualified)	79.50
Pensioner premium	
Single	23.60
Couple	35.95
Higher pensioner premium	
Single	30.85
Couple	39.20
Enhanced pensioner premium	
Single	25.90
Couple	39.20

*Where one or both partners are aged under 18, their personal allowance will depend on their situation
†If in full-time education up to A-level or equivalent standard

HOUSING BENEFIT

Housing benefit is designed to help people with rent (including rent for accommodation in guest houses, lodgings or hostels). It does not cover mortgage payments. The amount of benefit paid depends on:
– the income of the claimant, and partner if there is one, including earned income, unearned income (any other income including some other benefits) and savings
– number of dependants
– certain extra needs of the claimant, partner or any dependants
– number and gross income of people sharing the home who are not dependent on the claimant
– how much rent is paid

Housing benefit is not payable if the claimant, or claimant and partner, have savings of over £16,000. The amount of benefit is affected if savings held exceed £3,000. Housing benefit is not paid for meals, fuel or certain service charges that may be included in the rent. Deductions are also made for most non-dependants who live in the same accommodation as the claimant (and their partner).

The maximum amount of benefit (which is not necessarily the same as the amount of rent paid) may be paid where the claimant is in receipt of income support or income-based jobseeker's allowance or where the claimant's income is less than the amount allowed for their needs. Any income over that allowed for their needs will mean that their benefit is reduced.

Claims for housing benefit are made to the local council. Those who are also claiming income support or income-based jobseeker's allowance may claim housing benefit at the local benefits or employment services office. *See* leaflets RR1 and RR2.

COUNCIL TAX BENEFIT

Nearly all the rules which apply to housing benefit apply to council tax benefit, which helps people on low incomes to pay council tax bills. The amount payable depends on how much council tax is paid and who lives with the claimant. The benefit may be available to those receiving income support or income-based jobseeker's allowance or to those whose income is less than that allowed for their needs. Any income over that allowed for their needs will mean that their council tax benefit is reduced. Deductions are made for non-dependants.

The maximum amount that is payable for those living in properties in council tax bands A to E is 100 per cent of the claimant's council tax liability. This also applies to those living in properties in bands F to H who were in receipt of the benefit at 31 March 1998 if they have remained in the same property. From 1 April 1998 council tax benefit for new claimants living in property bands F to H (or existing claimants moving into these bands) was restricted to the level payable for band E.

If a person shares a home with one or more adults (not their partner) who are on a low income, it may be possible to claim a second adult rebate. Those who are entitled to both council tax benefit and second adult rebate will be awarded whichever is the greater. Second adult rebate may be claimed by those not in receipt of council tax benefit.

THE SOCIAL FUND

The Social Fund helps people with expenses which are difficult to meet from regular income. Regulated maternity and funeral payments are decided by Decision Makers; cold weather payments and winter fuel payments are made automatically. These payments are not limited by the district's Social Fund budget. Discretionary community care grants, and budgeting and crisis loans are decided by Social Fund Officers and come out of a yearly budget which is allocated to each district (1999–2000, grants £98 million; loans £436.7 million; £0.5 million set aside as a contingency reserve). *See* leaflet SB16.

REGULATED PAYMENTS

Maternity Payments

A payment of up to £100 for each baby expected, born, adopted, or the subject of a parental order (in the case of surrogacy). From April 2000 the Maternity Payment Scheme will be replaced by the State Maternity Grant Scheme. The payment will double to £200 and will be linked to the claimant seeking advice on the welfare of the baby. It is payable to people on income support, income-based jobseeker's allowance, disabled person's tax credit and working families tax credit and does not have to be repaid.

Funeral Payments

Payable for the necessary cost of burial or cremation, plus other funeral expenses reasonably incurred up to £600, to people receiving income support, income-based jobseeker's allowance, disabled person's tax credit, working families' tax credit, council tax benefit or housing benefit who have good reason for taking responsibility for the funeral expenses. These payments are recoverable from any estate of the deceased.

Cold Weather Payments

A payment of £8.50 when the average temperature over seven consecutive days is recorded as or forecast to be 0°C or below in their area. Payments are made to people on income support or income-based jobseeker's allowance and who have a child under five or whose benefit includes a pensioner or disability premium. They do not have to be repaid.

Winter Fuel Payments

An annual payment of £100 per household paid automatically to eligible pensioners. Payments are made before Christmas and do not have to be repaid.

DISCRETIONARY PAYMENTS

Community Care Grants

These are intended to help people on income support or income-based jobseeker's allowance (or those likely to receive these benefits on leaving residential or institutional accommodation) to live as independently as possible in the community; ease exceptional pressures on families; care for a prisoner or young offender released on temporary licence; help people set up home as part of a resettlement programme and/or assist with certain travelling expenses. They do not have to be repaid.

Budgeting Loans

These are interest-free loans to people who have been receiving income support or income-based jobseeker's allowance for at least 26 weeks, for intermittent expenses that may be difficult to budget for.

Crisis Loans

These are interest-free loans to anyone, whether receiving benefit or not, who is without resources in an emergency, where there is no other means of preventing serious damage or serious risk to their health or safety.

SAVINGS

Savings over £500 (£1,000 for people aged 60 or over) are taken into account for maternity and funeral payments, community care grants and budgeting loans. All savings are taken into account for crisis loans. Savings are not taken into account for cold weather or winter fuel payments.

INDUSTRIAL INJURIES AND DISABLEMENT BENEFITS

The industrial injuries scheme, administered under the Social Security Contributions and Benefits Act 1992, provides a range of benefits designed to compensate for disablement resulting from an industrial accident (i.e. an accident arising out of and in the course of an employed earner's employment) or from a prescribed disease due to the nature of a person's employment. Those who are self-employed are not covered by this scheme.

INDUSTRIAL INJURIES DISABLEMENT BENEFIT

A person must be at least 14 per cent disabled (except for certain respiratory diseases) in order to qualify for this benefit. The amount paid depends on the degree of disablement:

- those assessed as 14–19 per cent disabled are paid at the 20 per cent rate
- those with disablement of over 20 per cent will have the percentage rounded up or down to the nearest 10 per cent, e.g. a disablement of 44 per cent will be paid at the 40 per cent rate while a disablement of 45 per cent will be paid at the 50 per cent rate

Benefit is payable 15 weeks (90 days) after the date of the accident or onset of the disease and may be payable for a limited period or for life. The benefit is payable whether the person works or not and those who are incapable of work are entitled to draw statutory sick pay or incapacity benefit in addition to industrial injuries disablement benefit. It may also be possible to claim the following allowances:

- reduced earnings allowance for those who are unable to return to their regular work or work of the same standard and who had their accident (or whose disease started) before 1 October 1990
- retirement allowance for those who were entitled to reduced earnings allowance who have reached state pension age
- constant attendance allowance for those with a disablement of 100 per cent who need constant care. There are four rates of allowance depending on how much care the person needs
- exceptionally severe disablement allowance for those who are entitled to constant care attendance allowance at one of the higher rates and who need constant care permanently

See leaflets NI6 and N12.

OTHER BENEFITS

People who are disabled because of an accident or disease that was the result of work that they did before 5 July 1948 are not entitled to industrial injuries disablement benefit. They may, however, be entitled to payment under the workmen's compensation scheme or the pneumoconiosis, byssinosis and miscellaneous diseases benefit scheme. *See* leaflets WS1 and PN1.

WEEKLY RATES OF BENEFIT
from April 1999

*Disablement benefit/pension
Degree of disablement

100 per cent	£108.10
90	97.29
80	86.48
70	75.67
60	64.86
50	54.05
40	43.24
30	32.43
20	21.62
†Unemployability supplement	66.75
Addition for adult dependant (subject to earnings rule)	39.95
Reduced earnings allowance (maximum)	43.24
Retirement allowance (maximum)	10.81
Constant attendance allowance (normal maximum rate)	43.30
Exceptionally severe disablement allowance	43.30

*There is a weekly benefit for those under 18 with no dependants which is set at a lower rate
†This benefit attracts an increase for each dependent child (in addition to child benefit) of £9.90 for the first child and £11.35 for each subsequent child

---

CLAIMS AND QUESTIONS

With a few exceptions, claims and questions relating to social security benefits are decided in agencies. The decision makers act impartially. *See* leaflets GL24 and NI260(DMA).

Entitlement to benefit (including disablement questions) and regulated Social Fund payments is determined by decision makers. A claimant who is dissatisfied with that decision can ask for an explanation and review of the decision. If they are still dissatisfied they can go to the Appeals Service, an independent tribunal. There is a further right of appeal to a Social Security Commissioner against the tribunal's decision but leave to appeal must first be obtained. Appeals to the Commissioner must be on a point of law. Provision is also made for the determination of certain questions by the Secretary of State for Social Security.

Decisions on applications to the discretionary Social Fund are made by Social Fund Officers. Applicants can ask for a review within 28 days of the date on the decision letter. The Social Fund Review Officer will review the case and there is a further right of review to an independent Social Fund Inspector.

Reviews of housing and council tax benefit decisions are dealt with initially by the council. The claimant must ask for a review within six weeks of being told how much benefit they will receive. Further reviews are dealt with by an independent review board.

OTHER BENEFITS

STATUTORY SICK PAY

Employers usually pay statutory sick pay (SSP) to their employees for up to 28 weeks of sickness in any period of incapacity for work that lasts longer than four days. SSP is paid at £59.55 per week and is subject to PAYE tax and NI deductions. Employees who cannot obtain SSP may be able to claim incapacity benefit. Employers may be able to recover some SSP costs. See leaflets NI244 and NI245.

STATUTORY MATERNITY PAY

In general, employers pay statutory maternity pay (SMP) to pregnant women who have been employed by them full or part-time for at least 26 weeks before the end of the 'qualifying week', which is 15 weeks before the week the baby is due, and whose earnings on average at least equal the lower earnings limit applied to NI contributions. All women who meet these conditions receive payment of 90 per cent of their average earnings for six weeks, followed by a maximum of 12 weeks at £59.55. SMP can be paid from the beginning of the 11th week before the week in which the baby is due but women can decide to begin maternity leave later than this. SMP is not payable for any week in which the woman works. Employers are reimbursed for 92 per cent of the SMP they pay (105 per cent for those whose annual NI liability (excluding Class 1A) is £20,000 or less). *See* Leaflet NI17A.

War Pensions

The War Pensions Agency, an executive agency of the Department of Social Security (DSS), awards war pensions under The Naval, Military and Air Forces, Etc. (Disablement and Death) Service Pensions Order 1983 to members of the armed forces in respect of service after 4 August 1914. There is also a scheme for civilians and civil defence workers in respect of the 1939–45 war, and other schemes for groups such as merchant seamen and Polish armed forces who served under British command.

PENSIONS

War disablement pension is awarded for the disabling effects of any injury, wound or disease which is the result of, or has been aggravated by, conditions of service in the armed forces. It can only be paid once the person has left the armed forces. The amount of pension paid depends on the severity of disablement, which is assessed by comparing the health of the claimant with that of a healthy person of the same age and sex. The person's earning capacity or occupation are not taken into account in this assessment. A pension is awarded if the person has a disablement of 20 per cent or more and a lump sum is usually payable to those with a disablement of less than 20 per cent. No award is made for noise-induced sensorineural hearing loss where the assessment of disablement is less than 20 per cent.

War widow's pension is payable where the husband's death was due to, or hastened by, his service in the armed forces or where the husband was in receipt of a war disablement pension constant attendance allowance (or would have been had he not been in hospital). A war widow's pension is also payable if the husband was getting unemployability supplement at the time of his death and his pensionable disablement was at least 80 per cent. Most war widows receive a standard rank-related rate but a lower weekly rate is payable to war widows of men below the rank of Lieutenant-Colonel who are under the age of 40, without children and capable of maintaining themselves. This is increased to the standard rate at age 40. Allowances are paid for children (in addition to child benefit) and adult dependents. An age allowance may also be given when the woman reaches 65 and increased at age 70 and age 80.

A war widower's pension may be payable to a man whose wife died because of service in the armed forces, if he was dependent on his wife before her death and cannot support himself.

All war pensions and war widow's pensions are tax-free and pensioners living overseas receive the same amount as those resident in the UK.

SUPPLEMENTARY ALLOWANCES

A number of supplementary allowances may be awarded to a war pensioner which are intended to meet various needs which may result from disablement or death and take account of its particular effect on the pensioner or spouse. The principal supplementary allowances are unemployability supplement, allowance for lowered standard of occupation and constant attendance allowance. Others include exceptionally severe disablement allowance, severe disablement occupational allowance, treatment allowance, mobility supplement, comforts allowance, clothing allowance, age allowance and widow's age allowance. There is a rent allowance available on a war widow's pension.

SOCIAL SECURITY BENEFITS

Most social security benefits are paid in addition to the basic war disablement pension or war widow's pension. Any retirement pension for which a war widow qualifies on her own NI contribution record can be paid in addition to her war widow's pension.

A war pensioner or war widow who claims income support, working families tax credit or disabled person's tax credit has the first £10 a week of pension disregarded. A similar provision operates for housing benefit and council tax benefit; but the local authority may, at its discretion, disregard any or all of the balance.

CLAIMS AND QUESTIONS

To claim a war pension it is necessary to contact the nearest war pensioners' welfare service office, the address of which is available from local social security offices, or to write to the War Pensions Agency, Norcross, Blackpool FY5 3WP.

Regional Development

ENGLISH PARTNERSHIPS
16–18 Old Queen Street
London SWIH 9HP
Tel 0171-976 7070; fax 0171-976 7740

English Partnerships was established in April 1999 by the merger of the Commission for the New Towns (CNT) and the Urban Regeneration Agency (URA, formally known as English Partnerships). Its role is to work with central and local government, the regional development agencies (RDAs, *see* below), the private sector and other partners to bring about sustainable economic regeneration and development in the English regions. It has taken on the URA's responsibility for regenerating derelict, vacant and under-used land and buildings, and the CNT's responsibility for dealing with the residual assets and liabilities of the former new towns and urban development corporations in England. The regional assets and operations of the URA, with the exception of its London operation, were transferred to the RDAs on 1 April 1999.

Chairman, Sir Alan Cockshaw, FREng.
Non-Executive Board Members, Sir Idris Pearce, CBE, FRICS; M. Mallinson, CBE, FRICS; A. Fraser; Sir Brian Jenkins, GBE; W. Jordan, CBE; D. Mapp; Sir Dennis Stevenson, CBE; The Lord Thomas of Macclesfield, CBE
Chief Executive, Mrs P. Hay-Plumb
Corporate Strategy and Communications Director, T. Beattie
Commercial Director, J. Gill
Finance and Administration Directors, D. Hone (*CNT*); J. Walker (*EP*)
Development Director, D. Shelton

REGIONAL DEVELOPMENT AGENCIES

The creation of business-led regional development agencies in England was announced in a White Paper *Building Partnerships for Prosperity* in December 1997. The agencies were established in December 1998 and took on their responsibilities in April 1999. Their role is to improve regional economic performance and enhance regional competitiveness. They are the lead bodies at regional level for co-ordinating inward investment, raising people's skills, improving the competitiveness of business and bringing about social and physical regeneration. They will produce regional strategies and give advice to the Government. There are eight agencies in England outside London; a London agency will be set up at a later date. The regional operations (except those relating to London) of the former URA and the rural regeneration work of the former Rural Development Commission have been transferred to the agencies. Regional chambers are being established to provide a mechanism through which the RDAs can take account of regional views and account for their activities.

EASTERN
EAST OF ENGLAND DEVELOPMENT AGENCY, Compass House, Chivers Way, Histon, Cambridge CB4 9ZR. Tel: 01223-713900; fax: 01223-713910. *Chairman,* V. Watts; *Chief Executive,* W. Samuel

EAST MIDLANDS
EAST MIDLANDS DEVELOPMENT AGENCY, c/o East Midlands Development Company, 2–4 Weekday Cross, Nottingham NG1 2GB. Tel: 0115-952 7870; fax: 0115-958 5292. *Chairman,* D. Mapp; *Chief Executive,* M. Briggs

NORTH-EAST
ONE NORTH EAST, Great North House, Sandyford Road, Newcastle upon Tyne NE1 8ND. Tel: 0191-261 0026; fax 0191-232 9069. *Chairman,* J. Bridge; *Chief Executive,* M. Collier

NORTH-WEST
NORTH WEST DEVELOPMENT AGENCY, New Town House, Buttermarket Street, Warrington WA1 2LF. Tel: 01925-644683; fax: 01925-644671. *Chairman,* The Lord Thomas of Macclesfield, CBE; *Chief Executive,* M. Shields

SOUTH-EAST
SOUTH EAST ENGLAND DEVELOPMENT AGENCY (SEEDA), SEEDA Headquarters, Cross Lanes, Guildford GU1 1YA. Tel: 01483-484226; fax: 01483-484247. *Chairman,* A. Willett; *Chief Executive,* A. Dunnett

SOUTH-WEST
SOUTH WEST OF ENGLAND REGIONAL DEVELOPMENT AGENCY, The Gaunts' House, Denmark Street, Bristol BS1 5DR. Tel: 0117-922 0353; fax: 0117-922 0354. *Chairman,* Sir Michael Lickiss; *Chief Executive,* Ms J. Barrow

WEST MIDLANDS
ADVANTAGE WEST MIDLANDS, 2 Priestley Wharf, Holt Street, Aston Science Park, Birmingham B7 4BZ. Tel: 0121-380 3500; fax: 0121-380 3501. *Chairman,* A. Stephenson; *Chief Executive,* A. Cassidy

YORKSHIRE AND THE HUMBER
YORKSHIRE FORWARD, Westgate House, 100 Wellington Street, Leeds LS1 4LT. Tel: 0113-242 6268; fax: 0113-243 1088. *Chairman,* G. Hall; *Chief Executive,* M. Havenhand

---

DEVELOPMENT CORPORATIONS

URBAN DEVELOPMENT CORPORATIONS

Urban development corporations were established under the Local Government, Planning and Land Act 1980, as short-life public bodies. Their objectives were to bring land and buildings back into effective use; to develop existing and new industry and commerce; to improve the environment; and to ensure that housing and social facilities are available in the area. All the corporations in England have now been wound up.

CARDIFF BAY (1987), Baltic House, Mount Stuart Square, Cardiff CF1 6DH. Tel: 01222-585858. *Chairman,* Sir Geoffrey Inkin, OBE; *Chief Executive,* M. Boyce. Area, 1,094 hectares

LAGANSIDE (1989), Clarendon Building, 15 Clarendon Road, Belfast BT1 3BG. Tel: 01232-328507. *Chairman,* A. Hopkins; *Chief Executive,* M. Smith. Area, 200 hectares

OTHER DEVELOPMENT CORPORATIONS
Wales

DEVELOPMENT BOARD FOR RURAL WALES (1977), merged with Welsh Development Agency in October 1998 (*see* page 350)

The Water Industry

ENGLAND AND WALES

In England and Wales the Secretary of State for the Environment, Transport and the Regions and the National Assembly for Wales have overall responsibility for water policy and set the environmental and health and safety standards for the water industry. The Director-General of Water Services, as the independent economic regulator, is responsible for ensuring that the private water companies are able to fulfil their statutory obligation to provide water supply and sewerage services, and for protecting the interests of consumers.

The Minister of Agriculture, Fisheries and Food and the National Assembly for Wales are responsible for policy relating to land drainage, flood protection, sea defences and the protection and development of fisheries.

The Environment Agency is responsible for water quality and the control of pollution, the management of water resources and nature conservation. The Drinking Water Inspectorate and local authorities are responsible for the quality of drinking water.

THE WATER COMPANIES

Until 1989 nine regional water authorities in England and the Welsh Water Authority in Wales were responsible for water supply and the development of water resources, sewerage and sewage disposal, pollution control, freshwater fisheries, flood protection, water recreation, and environmental conservation. The Water Act 1989 provided for the creation of a privatized water industry under public regulation, and the functions of the regional water authorities were taken over by ten holding companies and the regulatory bodies.

Of the 99 per cent of the population of England and Wales who are connected to a public water supply, 78 per cent are supplied by the water companies (through their principal operating subsidiaries, the water service companies). The remaining 22 per cent are supplied by statutory water companies which were already in the private sector. Most of these have public limited company (PLC) status and many are now in foreign ownership or are part of larger multi-utility companies. They are represented by Water UK, which also represents the ten water service companies responsible for sewerage and sewage disposal in England and Wales, and the state-owned water authorities of Scotland and Northern Ireland. Water UK is the trade association for all the water service companies except Mid Kent Water.

Limited competition exists in the water industry, with large industrial customers being able to negotiate separate supply arrangements. Discussions are underway to determine the feasibility and future extent of competition.

WATER UK, 1 Queen Anne's Gate, London, SW1H 9BT. Tel: 0171-344 1844. *Chief Executive*, Ms P. Taylor

Water Service Companies

ANGLIAN WATER SERVICES LTD, Anglian House, Ambury Road, Huntingdon, Cambs PE18 6NZ

DWR CYMRU (WELSH WATER), Cambrian Way, Brecon, Powys LD3 7HP

NORTHUMBRIAN WATER LTD, Abbey Road, Pity Me, Durham DH1 5FJ

NORTH WEST WATER LTD, Dawson House, Liverpool Road, Great Sankey, Warrington WA5 3LW

SEVERN TRENT WATER LTD, 2297 Coventry Road, Sheldon, Birmingham B26 3PU

SOUTHERN WATER SERVICES LTD, Southern House, Yeoman Road, Worthing, W. Sussex BN13 3NX

SOUTH WEST WATER SERVICES LTD, Peninsula House, Rydon Lane, Exeter EX2 7HR

THAMES WATER UTILITIES LTD, Gainsborough House, Manor Farm Road, Reading RG2 0JN

WESSEX WATER SERVICES LTD, Wessex House, Passage Street, Bristol BS2 0JQ

YORKSHIRE WATER SERVICES LTD, Western House, Western Way, Halifax Road, Bradford BD6 2LZ

WATER SUPPLY AND CONSUMPTION 1997–8

	Supply		Consumption			
	Supply from treatment works (*Ml/day*)	Total leakage (*Ml/day*)	Household (*l/head/day*) Unmetered	Metered	Non-household (*l/prop/day*) Unmetered	Metered
WATER SERVICE COMPANIES						
Anglian	1,164.3	235.0	171.0	155.1	617.1	3,329.2
Dwr Cymru (Welsh)	990.0	336.7	168.2	169.6	776.9	2,832.1
North West	2,083.4	578.8	157.0	140.8	703.9	2,817.9
Northumbrian	788.8	184.5	164.7	130.0	922.8	5,037.8
Severn Trent	1,918.0	399.0	153.1	139.5	600.0	2,722.2
South West	445.1	101.1	177.1	127.2	1,113.4	1,757.3
Southern	603.4	98.8	173.8	148.0	837.7	2,769.8
Thames	2,664.7	905.5	191.8	166.3	767.9	3,602.6
Wessex	402.0	109.8	164.0	132.1	1,894.2	2,742.9
Yorkshire	1,292.1	368.1	155.3	135.7	127.4	2,864.3
Total	12,351.8	3,317.2	—	—	—	—
Average	—	—	167.0	146.7	745.6	3,000.6
WATER COMPANIES						
Total	3,331.0	664.3	—	—	—	—
Average	—	—	177.6	153.8	952.9	3,258.0

Source: Office of Water Services

REGULATORY BODIES

The Office of Water Services (Ofwat) (see page 350) was set up under the Water Act 1989 and is the independent economic regulator of the water and sewerage companies in England and Wales. Ofwat's main duty is to ensure that the companies can finance and carry out their statutory functions and to protect the interests of water customers. Ofwat is a non-ministerial government department headed by the Director-General of Water Services, who is appointed by the Secretary of State for the Environment, Transport and the Regions and the Secretary of State for Wales. Under the Competition Act 1998, from 1 March 2000 the Competition Commission (see page 291) will hear appeals against the regulator's decisions regarding anti-competitive agreements and abuse of a dominant position in the marketplace.

The Environment Agency (see page 299) has statutory duties and powers in relation to water resources, pollution control, flood defence, fisheries, recreation, conservation and navigation in England and Wales.

The Drinking Water Inspectorate is responsible for assessing the quality of the drinking water supplied by the water companies, inspecting the companies themselves and investigating any accidents affecting drinking water quality. The Chief Inspector presents an annual report to the Secretary of State for the Environment, Transport and the Regions and to the National Assembly for Wales.

METHODS OF CHARGING

In England and Wales, most domestic customers still pay for domestic water supply and sewerage services through charges based on the old rateable value of their property, although about 18 per cent of householders are now charged according to consumption, which is recorded by meter. Industrial and most commercial customers are charged according to consumption.

Under the Water Industry Act 1999, water companies can continue basing their charges on the old rateable value of property. Domestic customers can continue paying on an unmeasured basis unless they choose to pay according to consumption. After having a meter installed (which is free of charge), a customer can revert to unmeasured charging within 12 months. Domestic, school and hospital customers cannot be disconnected for non-payment.

In November 1999 Ofwat will decide the new pricing structure for 2000–2005. Both the Regulator and the Government have indicated that they expect charges to customers to be reduced.

SCOTLAND

Overall responsibility for national water policy in Scotland rested with the Secretary of State for Scotland until July 1999 when it was devolved to the Scottish Executive.

Until The Local Government etc. (Scotland) Act 1994, water supply and sewerage services were local authority responsibilities. The Central Scotland Water Development Board had the function of developing new sources of water supply for the purpose of providing water in bulk to water authorities whose limits of supply were within the board's area. Under the Act, three new public water authorities, covering the north, east and west of Scotland respectively, took over the provision of water and sewerage services from April 1996. The Central Scotland Water Development Board was then abolished. The new authorities were responsible to the Secretary of State for Scotland, and since July 1999 have been responsible to the Scottish Executive. The Act also established the Scottish Water and Sewerage Customers Council representing consumer interests. It monitored the performance of the authorities; approved

charges schemes; investigated complaints; and advised the Secretary of State. The Water Industries Act 1999, whose Scottish provisions were accepted by the Scottish Executive, abolished the Scottish Water and Sewerage Customers Council. It will be replaced in late 1999 by a Water Industry Commissioner who will promote the interests of customers. The Commissioner will make long-term recommendations about charging and efficiency to the Scottish Executive and will be advised by three water industry consultative committees (one for each water authority).

The Scottish Environment Protection Agency (SEPA) (see page 337) is responsible for promoting the cleanliness of Scotland's rivers, lochs and coastal waters. SEPA is also responsible for controlling pollution.

WATER RESOURCES 1997

	No.	Yield (Ml/day)
Reservoirs and lochs	287	3,018
Feeder intakes	27	—
River intakes	223	422
Bore-holes	35	77
Underground springs	103	46
Total	*676	3,562

* Including compensation reservoirs

WATER CONSUMPTION 1997

TOTAL (Ml/day)	2,336.3
Potable	2,320.3
Unmetered	1,781.7
Metered	538.5
Non-potable†	16.0
TOTAL (l/head/day)	468.6
Unmetered	357.4
Metered and non-potable†	109.9

† 'Non-potable' supplied for industrial purposes. Metered supplies in general relate to commercial and industrial use and unmetered to domestic use
Source: The Scottish Office

EAST OF SCOTLAND WATER AUTHORITY, Pentland Gait, 597 Calder Road, Edinburgh EH11 4HJ. Tel: 0131-453 7500. Chief Executive, R. Rennet
NORTH OF SCOTLAND WATER AUTHORITY, Cairngorm House, Beechwood Business Park, Inverness IV2 3ED. Tel: 01463-245400. Chief Executive, A. Findlay
SCOTTISH WATER AND SEWERAGE CUSTOMERS COUNCIL, Ochil House, Springkerse Business Park, Stirling FK7 7XE. Tel: 01786-430200. (The Council will be replaced by the Water Industry Commissioner at the same address)
WEST OF SCOTLAND WATER AUTHORITY, 419 Balmore Road, Glasgow G22 6NU. Tel: 0141-355 5333. Chief Executive, E. Chambers

METHODS OF CHARGING

The water authorities set charges for domestic and non-domestic water and sewerage provision through charges schemes which have to be approved by the Scottish Water and Sewerage Customers Council. The authorities must publish a summary of their charges schemes.

NORTHERN IRELAND

In Northern Ireland ministerial responsibility for water services lies with the Secretary of State for Northern Ireland. The Water Service, which is an executive agency of the Department of the Environment for Northern Ireland, is responsible for policy and co-ordination with regard to supply, distribution and cleanliness of water, and the provision and maintenance of sewerage services.

The Water Service (*see* page 328) is divided into four regions, the Eastern, Northern, Western and Southern Divisions. These are based in Belfast, Ballymena, Londonderry and Craigavon respectively.

On major issues the Department of the Environment for Northern Ireland seeks the views of the Northern Ireland Water Council, a body appointed to advise the Department on the exercise of its water and sewerage functions. The Council includes representatives from agriculture, angling, industry, commerce, tourism, trade unions and local government.

METHODS OF CHARGING

Usually householders do not pay separately for water and sewerage services; the costs of these services are allowed for in the Northern Ireland regional rate. Water consumed by industry, commerce and agriculture in excess of 100 cubic metres (22,000 gallons) per half year is charged through meters. Traders operating from industrially derated premises are required to pay for the treatment and disposal of the trade effluent which they discharge into the public sewerage system.

Energy

The main primary sources of energy in Britain are oil, natural gas, coal, nuclear power and water power. The main secondary sources (i.e. sources derived from the primary sources) are electricity, coke and smokeless fuels, and petroleum products. The Department of the Environment, Transport and the Regions is responsible for promoting energy efficiency.

INDIGENOUS PRODUCTION OF PRIMARY FUELS
Million tonnes of oil equivalent

	1997	1998p
Coal	31.5	27.0
Petroleum	140.4	145.2
Natural gas	86.2	90.3
Primary electricity		
Nuclear	22.99	23.28
Natural flow hydro	0.41	0.50
Total	281.9	286.2

p provisional

INLAND ENERGY CONSUMPTION BY PRIMARY FUEL
Million tonnes of oil equivalent, seasonally adjusted

	1997	1998p
Coal	42.9	43.1
Petroleum	77.0	76.7
Natural gas	88.7	92.2
Primary electricity	24.83	25.19
Nuclear	22.99	23.28
Natural flow hydro	0.42	0.50
Net imports	1.42	1.41
Total	233.5	237.2

p provisional

TRADE IN FUELS AND RELATED MATERIALS 1998

	Quantity*	Value†
IMPORTS		
Coal and other solid fuel	15.1	687
Crude petroleum	40.0	2,170
Petroleum products	17.8	1,414
Natural gas	0.4	43
Electricity	1.1	335
Total	74.5	4,648
Total (fob)‡	—	4,105
EXPORTS		
Coal and other solid fuel	0.9	69
Crude petroleum	79.6	4,441
Petroleum products	37.1	2,886
Natural gas	1.5	76
Electricity	—	3
Total	119.0	7,475
Total (fob)‡	—	7,475

* Million tonnes of oil equivalent
† £ million
‡ Adjusted to exclude estimated costs of insurance, freight, etc.
Source: Department of Trade and Industry – *Energy Trends May 1999*
(Crown copyright)

OIL

Until the 1960s Britain imported almost all its oil supplies. In 1969 oil was discovered in the Arbroath field of the UK Continental Shelf (UKCS). The first oilfield to be brought into production was the Argyll field in 1975, and since the mid-1970s Britain has been a major producer of crude oil.

Licences for exploration and production are granted to companies by the Department of Trade and Industry; the leading British oil companies are British Petroleum (BP) and Shell Transport and Trading. At the end of 1998, 1,021 offshore licences and 150 onshore licences had been awarded, and there were 121 offshore oilfields in production. In 1998 there were 10 oil refineries and four smaller refining units processing crude and process oils. There are estimated to be reserves of 1,800 million tonnes of oil in the UKCS. Royalties are payable on fields approved before April 1982 and petroleum revenue tax is levied on fields approved between 1975 and March 1993.

DRILLING ACTIVITY 1998

Number of wells started	Offshore	Onshore
Exploration and appraisal	80	14
Exploration	47	—
Appraisal	33	—
Development	281	21

VALUE OF UKCS OIL AND GAS PRODUCTION AND INVESTMENT
£ million

	1997	1998p
Total income	18,955	16,950
Operating costs	4,150	4,190
Exploration expenditure	1,194	762
Gross trading profits*	13,832	11,289
Percentage contribution to GDP	1.9	1.5
Capital investment	4,333	5,086
Percentage contribution to industrial investment	18	18

* Net of stock appreciation
p provisional

INDIGENOUS PRODUCTION AND REFINERY RECEIPTS

	1997	1998p
Indigenous production (thousand tonnes)	128,234	132,633
Crude oil	120,321	124,222
NGLs*	7,913	8,411
Refinery receipts (thousand tonnes)		
Indigenous	47,589	46,382
Other†	794	1,255
Net foreign imports	48,649	46,434

p provisional
* Natural gas liquids: condensates and petroleum gases derived at onshore treatment plants
† Mainly recycled products

DELIVERIES OF PETROLEUM PRODUCTS FOR INLAND CONSUMPTION BY ENERGY USE
Thousand tonnes

	1997	1998
Electricity generators	1,393	924
Gas works	46	47
Iron and steel industry	730	499
Other industries	5,751	5,678
Transport	47,317	47,831
Domestic	3,057	3,190
Other	3,253	3,042
Total	61,547	61,210

Source: Department of Trade and Industry – *Energy Trends May 1999*
(Crown copyright)

GAS

From the late 18th century gas in Britain was produced from coal. In the 1960s town gas began to be produced from oil-based feedstocks using imported oil. In 1965 gas was discovered in the North Sea in the West Sole field, which became the first gasfield in production in 1967, and from the late 1960s natural gas began to replace town gas. Britain is now the world's fourth largest producer of gas and in 1998 only 1.5 per cent of gas available for consumption in the UK was imported. From October 1998 Britain was connected to the continental European gas system via a pipeline from Bacton, Norfolk to Zeebrugge, Belgium.

By the end of 1998 there were 80 offshore gasfields producing natural gas and associated gas (mainly methane). There is estimated to be 1,795,000 million cubic metres of recoverable gas reserves. There are about 9,419 km of major submarine pipelines for transporting hydrocarbons, and onshore pipelines for carrying refined products and chemicals. Natural gas is transported around Britain by about 273,000 km of pipelines supplied by seven coastal terminals. This pipeline system is owned by Transco but BG's competitors are allowed access under a network code. New arrangements for trading within the pipeline system were introduced on 1 October 1999. Greater efficiency in balancing supply and demand is expected to achieve savings which will be reflected in lower prices.

The Office of Gas and Electricity Markets (see page 302) is the regulator for the gas industry. It was formed in 1999 by the merger of the Office of Gas Supply and the Office of Electricity Regulation. Under the Competition Act 1998, from 1 March 2000 the Competition Commission (see page 291) will hear appeals against the regulator's decisions regarding anti-competitive agreements and abuse of a dominant position in the marketplace.

The gas industry in Britain was nationalized in 1949 and operated as the Gas Council. The Gas Council was replaced by the British Gas Corporation in 1972 and the industry became more centralized. The British Gas Corporation was privatized in 1986 as British Gas PLC.

In 1993 the Monopolies and Mergers Commission found that British Gas's integrated business in Great Britain as a gas trader and the owner of the gas transportation system could be expected to operate against the public interest. In February 1997 British Gas demerged its trading arm and now operates as two separate companies: BG PLC, which runs the Transco pipeline business in Britain and oil and gas exploration and production in the UK and abroad; and Centrica PLC, which runs the trading, service and retail operations under the British Gas brand name in Great Britain.

Competition was gradually introduced into the industrial gas market from 1986. Supply of gas to the domestic market was opened to companies other than British Gas, starting in April 1996 with a pilot project in the West Country and Wales. From spring 1997 competition was progressively introduced throughout the rest of Britain in stages which were completed in May 1998. With the electricity market also open, many suppliers now offer their customers both gas and electricity. Some gas companies have become part of larger multi-utility companies, often operating internationally.

BG PLC, 100 Thames Valley Park Drive, Reading RG6 1PT. Tel: 0118-935 3222. *Chairman,* R. V. Giordano; *Chief Executive,* D. Varney

CENTRICA PLC, Charter Court, 50 Windsor Road, Slough, Berks SL1 2HA. Tel: 01753-758000. *Chief Executive,* R. Gardner

NATURAL GAS PRODUCTION AND SUPPLY
GWh

	1997	1998p
Gross gas production	998,343	1,048,353
Exports	21,666	31,604
Imports	14,062	10,582
Gas available	927,790	956,076
Gas transmitted‡	911,798	948,401

p provisional
‡ Figures differ from gas available mainly because of stock changes

NATURAL GAS CONSUMPTION
GWh

	1997	1998p
Electricity generators	243,361	253,348
Iron and steel industry	20,725	22,754
Other industries	174,763	175,747
Domestic	341,347	360,266
Public administration, commerce and agriculture	112,347	118,860
Total	892,544	930,975

p provisional
Source: Department of Trade and Industry – *Energy Trends May 1999* (Crown copyright)

COAL

Coal has been mined in Britain for centuries and the availability of coal was crucial to the industrial revolution of the 18th and 19th centuries. Mines were in private ownership until 1947 when they were nationalized and came under the management of the National Coal Board, later the British Coal Corporation. In addition to producing coal at its own deep-mine and opencast sites, of which there were 850 in 1955, British Coal was responsible for licensing private operators.

Under the Coal Industry Act 1994, the Coal Authority (see page 290) was established to take over ownership of coal reserves and to issue licences to private mining companies as part of the privatization of British Coal. The Coal Authority also deals with the physical legacy of mining, e.g. subsidence damage claims, and is responsible for holding and making available all existing records. The mines were sold as five separate businesses in 1994 and coal production in the UK is now undertaken entirely in the private sector. At the end of 1997 there were 20 large deep mines in operation.

The main UK customer for coal is the electricity supply industry, but the latter's demand for coal declined and National Power (see page 503) announced that it expected to close ten of its 18 coal-fired power stations by 2000. However, following a review of energy policy, the Government announced measures in its October 1998 Energy White Paper which included a freeze on new applications to build gas-fired power stations in order to increase opportunities for coal-fired power stations; there is a possibility that the EU might challenge the Government's plans. The Government also hopes that reform of the electricity wholesale market (the Pool, see below) will allow coal to compete better with other fuels.

COAL PRODUCTION AND FOREIGN TRADE
Thousand tonnes

	1997	1998p
Total production	48,495	41,428
Deep-mined	30,281	25,014
Opencast	16,700	15,033
Imports	19,756	21,233
Exports	1,147	944

p provisional

INLAND COAL USE
Thousand tonnes

	1997	1998p
Fuel producers		
Collieries	8	5
Electricity generators	47,058	48,521
Coke ovens	8,751	8,695
Other conversion industries	846	643
Total	63,075	63,039
Final users		
Industry	3,174	2,714
Domestic	2,587	2,182
Public administration, commerce and agriculture	651	279

p provisional
Source: Department of Trade and Industry

ELECTRICITY

The first power station in Britain generating electricity for public supply began operating in 1882. In the 1930s a national transmission grid was developed, and it was reconstructed and extended in the 1950s and 1960s. Power stations were operated by the Central Electricity Generating Board.

Under the Electricity Act 1989, 12 regional electricity companies (RECs), which are responsible for the distribution of electricity from the national grid to consumers, were formed from the former area electricity boards in England and Wales. Four companies were formed from the Central Electricity Generating Board: three generating companies (National Power PLC, Nuclear Electric PLC and PowerGen PLC) and the National Grid Company PLC, which owns and operates the transmission system. National Power and PowerGen were floated on the stock market in 1991. Nuclear Electric was split into two parts in 1995; the part comprising the more modern nuclear stations was incorporated into a new company, British Energy, which was floated on the stock market in 1996. Magnox Electric, which owns the magnox nuclear reactors, remained in the public sector and was integrated into British Nuclear Fuels (BNFL) in 1999. Ownership of the National Grid Company was transferred to the RECs and it was subsequently floated in 1995.

Generators sell the electricity they produce into an open commodity market (the Pool) from which buyers purchase. The Regulator and Government have announced their intention to replace the Pool. The introduction of competition into the domestic electricity market was completed in May 1999. With the gas market also open, many suppliers now offer their customers both gas and electricity.

Electricity companies can now also sell gas to their customers. Similarly, gas companies can also offer electricity. Some electricity companies have bought others, and there is a trend towards larger multi-utility companies, often operating internationally.

In Scotland, three new companies were formed under the Electricity Act 1989: Scottish Power PLC and Scottish Hydro-Electric PLC, which are responsible for generation, transmission, distribution and supply; and Scottish Nuclear Ltd. Scottish Power and Scottish Hydro-Electric were floated on the stock market in 1991 (the latter merged with Southern Electric in 1998 to become Scottish and Southern Energy PLC); Scottish Nuclear was incorporated into British Energy in 1995.

In Northern Ireland, Northern Ireland Electricity PLC was set up in 1993 under a 1991 Order in Council. It is responsible for transmission, distribution and supply and has been floated on the stock market. There is no Pool in Northern Ireland; three private companies are responsible for electricity generation and the electricity is sold to Northern Ireland Electricity under a series of power purchase agreements.

The Office of Gas and Electricity Markets (*see* page 302) is the regulator for the electricity industry. It was formed in 1999 by the merger of the Office of Electricity Regulation and the Office of Gas Supply. Under the Competition Act 1998, from 1 March 2000 the Competition Commission (*see* page 291) will hear appeals against the regulator's decisions regarding anti-competitive agreements and abuse of a dominant position in the marketplace.

The Electricity Association is the electricity industry's main trade association, providing representational and professional services for the electricity companies. EA Technology Ltd provides distribution and utilization research, development and technology transfer.

NUCLEAR POWER

Nuclear reactors began to supply electricity to the national grid in 1956. It is generated at six magnox reactors, seven advanced gas-cooled reactors (AGRs) and one pressurized water reactor (PWR), Sizewell 'B' in Suffolk. Nuclear stations now generate about 29 per cent of the UK's electricity.

In preparation for privatization, the nuclear industry was restructured in December 1995. A holding company, British Energy PLC, was formed with two operational subsidiaries, Nuclear Electric Ltd and Scottish Nuclear Ltd. Nuclear Electric operates the five AGRs and the PWR in England and Wales; Scottish Nuclear operates the two AGRs in Scotland. British Energy was floated on the stock market in 1996. The Magnox reactors were transferred to Magnox Electric PLC, and later to British Nuclear Fuels Ltd (BNFL, *see* above). BNFL is in public ownership, providing reprocessing, waste management and effluent treatment services. The UK Atomic Energy Authority (*see* page 283) is responsible for the decommissioning of nuclear reactors and other nuclear facilities used in research and development. UK Nirex, which is owned by the nuclear generating companies and the Government, is responsible for the disposal of intermediate and some low-level nuclear waste. The Nuclear Installations Inspectorate of the Health and Safety Executive (*see* page 306) is the nuclear industry's regulator.

ELECTRICITY UTILITIES

BRITISH ENERGY PLC, 10 Lochside Place, Edinburgh EH12 9DF. Tel: 0131-527 2000

BNFL MAGNOX GENERATION PLC, Berkeley Centre, Berkeley, Glos GL13 9PB. Tel: 01453-810451

EAST MIDLANDS ELECTRICITY PLC, PO Box 44, Wollaton, Nottingham NG8 1EZ. Tel: 0115-901 0101

EASTERN ELECTRICITY PLC, PO Box 40, Wherstead Park, Wherstead, Ipswich IP9 2AQ. Tel: 01473-688688

FIRST HYDRO COMPANY, Bala House, Lakeside Business Village, St David's Park, Ewloe CH5 3XJ. Tel: 01244-520234

GUERNSEY ELECTRICITY, PO Box 4, Electricity House, North Side, Vale, Guernsey GY1 3AD. Tel: 01481-46931

HYDER PLC, Newport Road, St Mellons, Cardiff CF3 9XW. Tel: 01222-792111

JERSEY ELECTRICITY, PO Box 45, Queens Road, St Helier, Jersey JE4 8NY. Tel: 01534-505000

LONDON ELECTRICITY PLC, Templar House, 81–87 High Holborn, London WC1V 6NU. Tel: 0171-242 9050

MANWEB PLC, Manweb House, Kingsfield Court, Chester Business Park, Chester CH4 9RF. Tel: 0845-272 3636

Manx Electricity Authority, PO Box 177, Douglas, Isle of Man IM99 IPS. Tel: 01624-687687

Midlands Electricity plc, Mucklow Hill, Halesowen, W. Midlands B62 8BP Tel: 0121-423 2345

National Grid Company plc, National Grid House, Kirby Corner Road, Coventry CV4 8JY. Tel: 01203-423000

National Power plc, Windmill Hill Business Park, Whitehill Way, Swindon, Wilts SN5 6PB. Tel: 01793-877777

Nigen Ltd., Kilroot Power Station, Larne Road, Carrickfergus, Co. Antrim BT38 7LX. Tel: 01960-351644

Northern Electric plc, Carliol House, Market Street, Newcastle upon Tyne NE1 6NE. Tel: 0191-210 2000

Northern Ireland Electricity plc, 120 Malone Road, Belfast BT9 5HT. Tel: 01232-661100

Norweb plc, Talbot Road, Manchester M16 0HQ. Tel: 0161-873 8000

PowerGen plc, Westwood Way, Westwood Business Park, Coventry CV4 8LG. Tel: 01203-424000

Premier Power Ltd, Ballylumford, Islandmagee, Larne, Co. Antrim BT40 3RS. Tel: 01960-381100

Scottish and Southern Energy plc, 10 Dunkeld Road, Perth PH1 5WA. Tel: 01738-455040

ScottishPower plc, 1 Atlantic Quay, Glasgow G2 8SP. Tel: 0141-248 8200

Seeboard plc, Forest Gate, Brighton Road, Crawley, W. Sussex RH11 9BH. Tel: 01293-565888

Sweb plc, 800 Park Avenue, Aztec West, Almondsbury, Bristol BS32 4SE. Tel: 01454-201101

Yorkshire Electricity Group plc, Wetherby Road, Scarcroft, Leeds LS14 3HS. Tel: 0113-289 2123

Electricity Association Ltd, 30 Millbank, London SW1P 4RD. Tel: 0171-963 5700

EA Technology Ltd, Capenhurst, Chester CH1 6ES. Tel: 0151-339 4181

Electricity Generation, Supply and Consumption
GWh

	1996	1997
Electricity generated: total	347,386	345,342
Major power producers: total	326,287	324,143
Conventional steam stations	160,565	133,132
Nuclear stations	94,671	98,146
Gas turbines and oil engines	226	459
Combined cycle gas turbine stations	65,880	86,974
Hydro-electric stations:		
Natural flow	2,801	3,337
Pumped storage	1,556	1,486
Renewables other than hydro	588	609
Other generators	21,099	21,199
Electricity used on works: total	17,728	16,369
Major generating companies	16,064	15,404
Other generators	1,664	956
Electricity supplied (gross): total	329,641	328,973
Major power producers: total	309,612	308,739
Conventional steam stations	153,170	127,075
Nuclear stations	85,820	89,341
Gas turbines and oil engines	216	436
Combined cycle gas turbine stations	65,604	86,609
Hydro-electric stations:		
Natural flow	2,763	3,299
Pumped storage	1,507	1,439
Renewables other than hydro	533	540
Other generators	20,028	20,234

Electricity used in pumping		
Major power producers	2,430	2,477
Electricity supplied (net): total	327,209	326,496
Major power producers	307,181	306,262
Other generators	20,028	20,234
Net imports	16,677	16,575
Electricity available	343,886	343,071
Losses in transmission, etc.	29,601	25,585
Electricity consumption: total	314,285	317,486
Fuel industries	8,629	8,235
Final users: total	305,656	309,251
Industrial sector	103,129	104,743
Domestic sector	107,513	104,455
Other sectors	95,014	100,053

Source: The Stationery Office – Annual Abstract of Statistics 1999

RENEWABLE SOURCES

Renewable sources of energy principally include biofuels, hydro, wind and solar. Renewable sources accounted for 2.7 million tonnes of oil equivalent of primary energy use in 1998; of this, about 1.7 million tonnes was used to generate electricity and about 0.9 million tonnes to generate heat.

The Non-Fossil Fuel Obligation (NFFO) Renewables Orders are the Government's principal mechanism for developing renewable energy sources. NFFO Renewables Orders require the regional electricity companies to buy specified amounts of electricity from specified non-fossil fuel sources. The technologies covered by NFFO Orders have been landfill gas, municipal and industrial waste, small-scale hydro, onshore wind and energy crops. The fifth NFFO Renewables Order was made in September 1998. In Scotland a similar system of Scottish Renewables Orders exists. The third Order was made in February 1999 and covers wave energy, the first time that this technology has been supported by a Renewables Order. Energy policy was devolved to the Scottish Parliament in July 1999.

The Government intends to achieve 10 per cent of the UK's electricity needs from renewables by 2010. Plans are also being made to determine how renewables can contribute to meeting commitments to future reductions in greenhouse gases.

Renewable Energy Sources 1998

	Percentages
Biofuels	79.8
Landfill gas	15.1
Sewage gas	6.9
Wood combustion	26.8
Straw combustion	2.7
Refuse combustion	21.4
Other biofuels	6.9
Hydro	16.9
Large-scale	16.3
Small-scale	0.6
Wind	2.9
Active solar heating	0.4
Total	100

Source: Department of Trade and Industry

Transport

CIVIL AVIATION

Since the privatization of British Airways in 1987, UK airlines have been operated entirely by the private sector. In 1998, total capacity on British airlines amounted to 40,017,000 tonne-km, of which 29,756,000 tonne-km was on scheduled services. British airlines carried 93.1 million passengers, 61.7 million on scheduled services and 31.4 million on charter flights.

Leading British airlines include British Airways, Britannia Airways, British Midland, Monarch Airlines and Virgin Atlantic.

There are 142 licensed civil aerodromes in Britain, with Heathrow and Gatwick handling the highest volume of passengers. BAA PLC owns and operates the seven major airports: Heathrow, Gatwick, Stansted, Southampton, Glasgow, Edinburgh and Aberdeen, which between them handle about 70 per cent of air passengers and 81 per cent of air cargo traffic in Britain. Many other airports, including Manchester, are controlled by local authorities or private companies. In the 1999 Budget, the Government announced it was setting up a review of competition in the airports sector.

The Civil Aviation Authority, an independent statutory body, is responsible for the economic regulation of UK airlines and for the safety regulation of the UK civil aviation industry. Through its wholly-owned subsidiary company National Air Traffic Services Ltd the CAA is also responsible for the provision of air traffic control services over Britain and its surrounding seas and at most major British airports. The Government has announced plans to privatize a majority holding in National Air Traffic Services.

The CAA is responsible for ensuring that UK airlines provide services at the lowest charges possible, given the requirement to meet stringent safety standards. It is also responsible for the economic regulation of the larger airports.

All commercial airline companies must be granted an Air Operator's Certificate, which is issued by the CAA to operators meeting the required safety standards. The CAA also issues airport safety licences, which must be obtained by any airport used for public transport and training flights. All British-registered aircraft must be granted an airworthiness certificate, and the CAA also issues professional licences to pilots, flight crew, ground engineers and air traffic controllers.

AIR PASSENGERS 1998*

ALL UK AIRPORTS: TOTAL	160,248,019
LONDON AREA AIRPORTS: TOTAL	102,216,797
Battersea Heliport	4,709
Gatwick (BAA)	29,173,130
Heathrow (BAA)	60,683,988
London City	1,360,187
Luton	4,132,818
Southend	4,063
Stansted (BAA)	6,862,611
OTHER UK AIRPORTS: TOTAL	58,026,513
Aberdeen (BAA)	2,662,960
Barra	9,045
Barrow-in-Furness	105
Belfast City	1,316,792
Belfast International	2,671,848
Benbecula (HIAL)	36,519
Biggin Hill	6,987
Birmingham	6,709,086
Blackpool	94,312
Bournemouth	315,537
Bristol	1,838,219
Cambridge	16,689
Campbeltown (HIAL)	9,595
Cardiff	1,263,225
Carlisle	966
Coventry	2,639
Dundee	10,583
East Midlands	2,142,005
Edinburgh (BAA)	4,588,507
Exeter	250,806
Glasgow (BAA)	6,566,927
Gloucestershire	2,246
Hawarden	6,394
Humberside	345,661
Inverness (HIAL)	340,742
Islay (HIAL)	21,282
Isle of Man	727,611
Kent International	2,269
Kirkwall (HIAL)	90,610
Leeds/Bradford	1,406,948
Lerwick (Tingwall)	4,029
Liverpool	873,172
Londonderry	49,146
Lydd	2,370
Manchester	17,351,162
Newcastle upon Tyne	2,984,724
Norwich	318,549
Penzance Heliport	119,800
Plymouth	139,930
Prestwick	564,043
St Mary's, Isles of Scilly	131,617
Scatsta	104,356
Sheffield City	46,527
Shoreham	2,156
Southampton (BAA)	737,463
Stornoway (HIAL)	96,070
Sumburgh (HIAL)	305,740
Teesside	655,218
Tiree (HIAL)	4,988
Tresco, Isles of Scilly (H)	35,475
Unst	1,806
Wick (HIAL)	41,057
CHANNEL IS. AIRPORTS: TOTAL	2,789,624
Alderney	77,198
Guernsey	963,674
Jersey	1,748,752

*Total terminal, transit, scheduled and charter passengers

Source: Civil Aviation Authority

RAILWAYS

Britain pioneered railways and a railway network was developed across Britain by private companies in the course of the 19th century. In 1948 the main railway companies were nationalized and were run by a public authority, the British Transport Commission. The Commission was replaced by the British Railways Board in 1963, operating as British Rail. On 1 April 1994, responsibility for managing the railway infrastructure passed to a newly-formed company, Railtrack; the British Railways Board continued as operator of all train services until they were sold or franchised to the private sector. All passenger activities have now been franchised and all British Rail's freight, technical support and specialist function businesses have been sold. The Board still has certain functions, including overall responsibility for the British Transport Police (*see* page 377).

PRIVATIZATION

Since 1 April 1994, ownership of operational track and land has been vested in Railtrack, which was floated on the Stock Exchange in 1996. Railtrack manages the track and charges for access to it and is responsible for signalling and timetabling. It does not operate train services. It owns the stations, and leases most of them out to the train operating companies. Infrastructure support functions are now provided by private sector companies. Railtrack invests in infrastructure principally using finance raised by track charges, and takes investment decisions in consultation with rail operators. Railtrack is also responsible for overall safety on the railways.

Proposals to privatize part of London Underground were announced in July 1997 with more details being given in June 1999. The Government intends the infrastructure to be run by private companies, with the operating company remaining in public ownership. In June 1999 the Government announced that the lines would be leased in three groups. The first group, lines close to the surface, would be leased to Railtrack with a view to integrating them into the national railway network. The remaining lines will be leased in two groups. In 1997–8 there were 832 million passenger journeys, including 384 million using season tickets.

RAIL REGULATOR

The independent Rail Regulator is responsible for the licensing of new railway operators, approving access agreements, promoting the use and development of the network, preventing anti-competitive practices (in conjunction with the Director General of Fair Trading) and protecting the interests of rail users. The Regulator will publish the conclusions of his review of Railtrack's funding arrangements in July 2000, for implementation in April 2001. He has indicated that he will seek to tighten the regime to promote improvements in the infrastructure. The White Paper *New Deal for Transport* contains proposals to strengthen the Regulator's power to impose sanctions and broaden the scope of his duties.

Separate regulations, which took effect on 28 June 1998, established licensing and access arrangements for certain international train services in Great Britain. These are overseen by the International Rail Regulator, a position held by the Rail Regulator.

The White Paper *New Deal for Transport*, published in July 1998, announced plans to establish a Strategic Rail Authority (SRA) to manage passenger railway franchising, take responsibility for increasing the use of the railways for freight transport, and lead strategic planning of passenger and freight rail services. In July 1999 the Government published its Railways Bill which will give the SRA its full powers.

The SRA began work in shadow form in April 1999, using the existing powers of the Franchising Director and British Rail.

SERVICES

For privatization, domestic passenger services were divided into 25 train-operating units, which have been franchised to private sector operators via a competitive tendering process overseen by the Director of the Office of Passenger Rail Franchising (OPRAF). The franchise agreements are for between five and 15 years. The Government continues to subsidize loss-making but socially necessary rail services. The Franchising Director is responsible for monitoring the performance of the franchisees, allocating and administering government subsidy payments, proposing closures to the Rail Regulator and designating experimental services.

There are currently 25 train operating companies: Anglia Railways; Cardiff Railway; Central Trains; Chiltern Railways; Connex South Central; Connex South Eastern; Eurostar (which is not subject to a franchise agreement); Gatwick Express; Great Eastern Railway; Great North Eastern Railway; Great Western Trains; Island Line (Isle of Wight); LTS Rail (London to Southend and Shoeburyness); Merseyrail Electrics; Midland Mainline; North Western Trains; Northern Spirit; Scotrail Railways; Silverlink Train Services (North London); South West Trains; Thameslink Rail; Thames Trains; Virgin Trains (which operates two franchises); Wales and West Passenger Trains; and West Anglia Great Northern Railway.

Railtrack publishes a national timetable which contains details of rail services operated over the Railtrack network, coastal shipping information and connections with Ireland, the Isle of Man, the Isle of Wight, the Channel Islands and some European destinations.

The national rail enquiries service offers information about train times and fares for any part of the country:

National Rail Enquiries	0345-484950
London Transport	0171-222 1234
Eurostar	0345-303030

Rail Users' Consultative Committees monitor the policies and performance of train and station operators in their area (there are nine, covering Great Britain). They are statutory bodies and have a legal right to make recommendations for changes. The London Regional Passengers Committee represents users of buses, the Underground and the Docklands Light Railway as well as users of rail services in the London area.

British Rail's passenger rolling stock was divided between three subsidiary companies, which were privatized in 1996. The companies lease rolling stock to passenger service operators. On privatization, British Rail's bulk freight haulage companies and Rail Express Systems, which carries Royal Mail traffic, were sold to English, Welsh and Scottish Railways, which also purchased Railfreight Distribution (international freight) in 1997. In 1997–8 an average 1,159,000 tonnes of freight was transported by an average of 1,900 trains a day.

BRITISH RAILWAYS BOARD, *see* page 285

RAILTRACK, Railtrack House, Euston Square, London NW1 2EE. Tel: 0171-557 8000. *Chairman*, Sir Robert Horton. *Chief Executive*, G. Corbett

ASSOCIATION OF TRAIN OPERATING COMPANIES, 40 Bernard Street, London WC1N 1BY. Tel: 0171-904 3010. *Chairman*, I. W. Warburton

OFFICE OF PASSENGER RAIL FRANCHISING (OPRAF), Golding's House, 2 Hay's Lane, London SE1 2HB. Tel: 0171-940 4200. *Franchising Director*, M. Grant

OFFICE OF THE RAIL REGULATOR (ORR) 1
Waterhouse Square, 138–142 Holborn, London
ECIN 2ST. Tel: 0171-282 2000. *Rail Regulator*, T. Winsor
SHADOW STRATEGIC RAIL AUTHORITY, 26 Old Queen
Street, London SW1H 9HP. Tel: 0171-960 1500. *Chairman*,
Sir Alastair Morton

RAILTRACK

At 31 March 1998, Railtrack had about 20,000 miles of
standard gauge lines and sidings in use, representing 10,343
miles of route of which 3,208 miles were electrified.
Standard rail on main line has a weight of 110 lb per yard.
Railtrack owns 2,495 stations, 90 light maintenance depots,
about 40,000 bridges, viaducts and tunnels, and over 9,000
level crossings.

Passenger journeys made in 1998–9 totalled 892.3
million, including 390 million made by holders of season
tickets. The average distance of each passenger journey on
ordinary fare was 28.97 miles; and on season ticket, 16
miles. Passenger stations in use numbered 2,500. The
number of ticket transactions in the year was 329.3 million,
earning a total ticket revenue of £3,100 million.

In 1998–9 Railtrack showed an operating profit of £471
million and a pre-tax profit of £428 million. On 31 March
1998 Railtrack employed 10,622 staff.

	£ million
Income	
Passenger	2,169
Freight	169
Property rental	131
Other	63
Total	2,573
Costs	
Production and management	547
Infrastructure maintenance	694
Joint industry costs	227
Depreciation	634
Total	2,102

RAIL SAFETY

The Railways (Safety Case) Regulations 1994 require
infrastructure controllers (e.g. Railtrack, London Underground) to have systems in place to manage safety on the
railway networks for which they are responsible.

The infrastructure controllers are required to present a
safety case to the Railway Inspectorate (part of the Health
and Safety Executive). The safety case must be accepted
by the Inspectorate, and is subsequently subject to regular
compliance audits.

The infrastructure controllers require companies bidding to operate services to present a safety case. The safety
case must be accepted by the infrastructure controller
before a service operator can receive a licence and begin
to provide services. If any variation is required, the safety
case must be re-presented. Safety cases must be reviewed
at least every three years. The Inspectorate may examine
the safety case of service operators as part of its compliance
audit of infrastructure operators.

ACCIDENTS ON RAILWAYS

	1996–7	1997–8
Train accidents: total	1,753	1,864
Persons killed: total	1	10
Passengers	1	7
Railway staff	0	0
Others	0	3
Persons injured: total	257	244
Passengers	182	190
Railway staff	61	39
Others	14	15

	1996–7	1997–8
Other accidents through movement of railway vehicles		
Persons killed	20	33
Persons injured	828	883
Other accidents on railway premises		
Persons killed	4	5
Passengers	3	3
Railway staff	0	0
Others	1	2
Persons injured	3,668	4,186
Trespassers and suicides		
Persons killed	251	264
Persons injured	106	136

THE CHANNEL TUNNEL

The earliest recorded scheme for a submarine transport
connection between Britain and France was in 1802.
Tunnelling has begun simultaneously on both sides of the
Channel three times: in 1881, in the early 1970s, and on 1
December 1987, when construction workers began to bore
the first of the three tunnels which form the Channel
Tunnel. They 'holed through' the first tunnel (the service
tunnel) on 1 December 1990 and tunnelling was completed
in June 1991. The tunnel was officially inaugurated by The
Queen and President Mitterrand of France on 6 May 1994.

The submarine link comprises three tunnels. There are
two rail tunnels, each carrying trains in one direction,
which measure 24.93 ft (7.6 m) in diameter. Between them
lies a smaller service tunnel, measuring 15.75 ft (4.8 m) in
diameter. The service tunnel is linked to the rail tunnels
by 130 cross-passages for maintenance and safety purposes.
The tunnels are 31 miles (50 km) long, 24 miles (38 km) of
which is under the sea-bed at an average depth of 132 ft
(40 m). The rail terminals are situated at Folkestone and
Calais, and the tunnels go underground at Shakespeare
Cliff, Dover, and Sangatte, west of Calais.

Passenger services (Eurostar) run from Waterloo station
in London and Ashford, Kent, to Paris, Brussels and Lille.
Connecting services from Edinburgh and Manchester via
London began in 1997. The introduction of through
services from these cities, not stopping in London, is the
subject of a government review, due to report in late 1999.
Vehicle shuttle services operate between Folkestone and
Calais.

RAIL LINKS

The route for the British Channel Tunnel Rail Link will
run from Folkestone to a new terminal at St Pancras
station, London, with new intermediate stations at Ebbsfleet, Kent, and Stratford, east London; at present services
run into a terminal at Waterloo station, London.

Construction of the rail link is financed by the private
sector with a substantial government contribution. A
private sector consortium, London and Continental Railways Ltd (LCR), is responsible for the design, construction
and ownership of the rail link, and comprises Union
Railways and the UK operator of Eurostar. Construction
was expected to be completed in 2003, but on 28 January
1998 LCR informed the Government that it was unable to
fulfil its obligations. On 3 June 1998 the Government
announced a new funding agreement with LCR. The rail
link will be constructed in two phases: phase one, from the
Channel Tunnel to Fawkham Junction (where an existing
connection allows trains to continue to Waterloo), began
in October 1998 and will be completed in 2003; phase two,
from Fawkham Junction to St Pancras, will be built between
2001 and 2007. Railtrack will buy phase one when it is
completed and has an option to buy phase two by 2003.

Infrastructure developments in France have been completed and high-speed trains run from Calais to Paris, linking the Channel Tunnel with the high-speed European network.

ROADS

HIGHWAY AUTHORITIES

The powers and responsibilities of highway authorities in England and Wales are set out in the Highways Acts 1980; for Scotland there is separate legislation.

Responsibility for trunk road motorways and other trunk roads in Great Britain rests in England with the Secretary of State for the Environment, Transport and the Regions, in Scotland with the Scottish Executive, and in Wales with the National Assembly for Wales. The costs of construction, improvement and maintenance are paid for by central government. The White Paper *New Deal for Transport*, published in July 1998, restated and revised the Highways Agency's responsibility for operating, maintaining and improving the trunk road network.

The highway authority for non-trunk roads in England, Wales and Scotland is, in general, the unitary authority, county council or London borough council in whose area the roads lie.

In Northern Ireland the Department of the Environment for Northern Ireland is the statutory road authority responsible for public roads and their maintenance and construction; the Roads Service executive agency (*see* page 328) carries out these functions on behalf of the Department.

FINANCE

The Government contributes towards capital expenditure through grants and credit approvals in England and Transport Grant (TG) in Wales. Grant rates are determined by the Secretary of State for the Environment, Transport and the Regions in England, the Scottish Executive and the National Assembly for Wales in each country respectively. Grant is paid at 50 per cent of expenditure accepted for grant in England and Wales.

In England Transport Supplementary Grant (TSG) is paid towards capital spending on highways, principal carriageways and the regulation of traffic; other capital spending is financed by credit approvals and specific grants. Current expenditure is funded by revenue support grant (i.e. central government grants to local authorities for non-specific services). TSG is also paid towards capital spending on bridge assessment and strengthening; towards structural maintenance on the primary route network; and towards all principal 'A' roads. In Wales TG is paid towards capital expenditure only; current expenditure is funded by revenue support grant.

For the financial year 1999–2000 local authorities in England will receive £158 million in TSG and £465 million in credit approvals. Total estimated expenditure on building and maintaining motorways and trunk roads in England in 1998–9 was £1,429 million; estimated outturn for 1999–2000 is £1,487 million.

For the financial year 1999–2000 local authorities in Wales will receive up to £18.8 million in TG. Total expenditure on motorways and trunk roads in Wales in 1998–9 was £114 million and estimated expenditure in 1999–2000 is £112.5 million.

Until 1999, the Scottish Office received a block vote from Parliament, and the Secretary of State for Scotland determined how much was spent on roads. Since 1 July 1999 all decisions on transport expenditure have been devolved to the Scottish Executive. Total expenditure on building and maintaining trunk roads in Scotland was estimated at £170 million in 1997–8.

In Northern Ireland estimated expenditure on roads for 1998–9 was £147.7 million and £155.6 million has been allocated for expenditure in 1999–2000.

The Government is currently considering the possibility of introducing tolls on certain roads. The White Paper *New Deal for Transport* contains proposals to enable local authorities to levy charges for driving cars in congested areas and for workplace parking; the income would be used to improve local transport.

PRIVATE FINANCE

Contracts have been let which allow greater involvement by the private sector in the design, finance, construction and operation of roads.

ROADS REVIEW

The Roads Review was published in July 1998 and the Government announced a reduction of over two-thirds in the road building programme in England. Greater emphasis is to be given to making better use of existing roads, including traffic management, network control and driver information. Thirty-seven schemes will go ahead and will be built by 2005 at a cost of £1,400 million (known as the Targeted Programme of Improvements (TPI)). The Government has begun studies to address trunk road problems not covered by the TPI. In Wales, a review resulted in four schemes going ahead, six being cancelled, eight being referred for further study and three deferred. A separate review of roads policy in Scotland is to be published in November 1998.

ROAD LENGTHS
(in miles) *as at April 1998*

	Total roads	Trunk roads (including motorways)	Motorways*
England	176,587	6,535	1,730
Wales	21,344	1,068	83
Scotland	32,999	2,019	212
N. Ireland	15,211	153†	82

*There were in addition 43.9 miles of local authority motorway in England
†1997 figure

MOTORWAYS

England and Wales:

M1	London to Yorkshire
M2	London to Faversham
M3	London to Southampton
M4	London to South Wales
M5	Birmingham to Exeter
M6	Catthorpe to Carlisle
M10	St Albans spur
M11	London to Cambridge
M18	Rotherham to Goole
M20	London to Folkestone
M23	London to Gatwick
M25	London orbital
M26	M20 to M25 spur
M27	Southampton bypass
M32	M4 to Bristol spur
M40	London to Birmingham
M41	London to West Cross
M42	South-west of Birmingham to Measham
M45	Dunchurch spur
M50	Ross spur
M53	Chester to Birkenhead
M54	M6 to Telford
M55	Preston to Blackpool
M56	Manchester to Chester
M57	Liverpool outer ring

M58	Liverpool to Wigan
M61	Manchester to Preston
M62	Liverpool to Hull
M63	Manchester southern ring road
M65	Calder Valley
M66	Manchester eastern ring road to Rochdale
M67	Manchester Hyde to Denton
M69	Coventry to Leicester
M180	South Humberside

Scotland:

M8	Edinburgh-Newhouse, Baillieston-West Ferry Interchange
M9	Edinburgh to Dunblane
M73	Maryville to Mollinsburn
M74	Glasgow-Paddy's Rickle Bridge, Cleuchbrae-Gretna
M77	Ayr Road Route
M80	Stirling to Haggs/Glasgow (M8) to Stepps
M90	Inverkeithing to Perth
M876	Dennyloanhead (M80) to Kincardine Bridge

Northern Ireland:

M1	Belfast to Dungannon
M2	Belfast to Antrim
M2	Ballymena bypass
M3	Belfast Cross Harbour Bridge
M5	M2 to Greencastle
M12	M1 to Craigavon
M22	Antrim to Randalstown

ROAD USE

ESTIMATED TRAFFIC ON ALL ROADS (GREAT BRITAIN) 1998

Million vehicle kilometres

All motor vehicles	459,400
Cars and taxis	375,900
Two-wheeled motor vehicles	4,000
Buses and coaches	5,000
Light vans	42,000
Other goods vehicles	32,100
Total goods vehicles	74,600
Pedal cycles	4,000

ROAD GOODS TRANSPORT (GREAT BRITAIN) 1998
Analysis by mode of working and by gross weight of vehicle

Estimated tonne kilometres (thousand million)	151.9
Own account	37.6
Public haulage	114.3
By gross weight of vehicle (billion tonne kilometres)	
Not over 25 tonnes	22.5
Over 25 tonnes	129.4
Estimated tonnes carried (millions)	1,630.0
Own account	589.0
Public haulage	1,041.0
By gross weight of vehicle (million tonnes)	
Not over 25 tonnes	382.0
Over 25 tonnes	1,248.0

ROAD PASSENGER SERVICES

Until 1988 most road passenger transport services in Great Britain were provided by the public sector; the National Bus Company was the largest bus and coach operator in England and Wales and the Scottish Bus Group the largest operator in Scotland. The privatization of the National Bus Company was completed in 1988 and that of the Scottish Bus Group in 1991. London Transport's bus operating subsidiaries were privatized by the end of 1994. Almost all bus and coach services in Great Britain are now provided by private sector companies.

Bus services outside London were deregulated in 1986, although local authorities can subsidise the provision of socially necessary services after competitive tendering. In London, London Transport retains overall responsibility for the provision of services.

The largest bus operators in Great Britain are Stagecoach Holdings, FirstGroup (formerly FirstBus) and Arriva (formerly Cowie British Bus), which between them account for over 50 per cent of all bus services (by turnover). There are also 17 municipal bus companies in England and Wales, and thousands of smaller private sector operators. National Express runs a national network of coach routes, mainly operating through franchises.

In Northern Ireland, almost all passenger transport services are provided by subsidiaries of Translink (formerly the Northern Ireland Transport Holding Company), which is publicly owned. The two main operators are Citybus Ltd (in Belfast) and Ulsterbus Ltd (outside Belfast). There are also about 75 small private sector operators.

The transport White Paper announced plans to promote bus use, primarily through agreements between local authorities and bus operators to improve the standard and efficiency of services in an area.

There are about 64,000 licensed taxis in Great Britain, of which about 19,000 are in London. There are also about 74,000 licensed private hire vehicles in Great Britain outside London, and an estimated 60,000 in London; an exact figure is not known because a new licensing system is to take effect in 1999.

BUSES AND COACHES (GREAT BRITAIN) 1997–8

Number of vehicles (31 March 1998)	76,200
Vehicle kilometres (millions)	4,191
Local bus passenger journeys (millions)	4,337
Passenger receipts (£ million)	3,778

ROAD SAFETY

The Government in 1987 set a target of reducing road traffic casualties by a third by the year 2000 compared to the average for 1981–5. Measures to achieve this were successful in reducing the number of deaths on the road by 36 per cent by 1997, and the number of serious casualties by 42 per cent. Over the same period the number of slight casualties increased by 16 per cent, but as road traffic increased by 52 per cent, the number of casualties per 100 km travelled has increased by only 1 per cent. In 1998, fatalities were reduced by 5 per cent from 1997, and all casualties decreased by 1 per cent.

Government consultations with local authorities, the police and road safety organizations in 1996 produced strong support for setting new road safety targets.

Proposals for discussion were produced in autumn 1997, and in autumn 1999 the Government will set new road safety targets for Britain for the period to 2010; similar targets are being set in Northern Ireland.

ROAD ACCIDENTS 1998

Road accidents	238,923
Vehicles involved:	
Pedal cycles	23,423
Motor vehicles	413,172
Total casualties	325,212
Pedestrians	44,886
Vehicle users	280,326
Killed*	3,421
Pedestrians	906
Pedal cycles	158
All two-wheeled motor vehicles	498
Cars and taxis	1,696
Others	163

*Died within 30 days of accident

	Killed	Injured
1965	7,952	389,985
1970	7,499	355,869
1975	6,366	318,584
1980	6,010	323,000
1985	5,165	312,359
1990	5,217	335,924
1995	3,621	306,885
1996	3,598	316,704
1997	3,599	323,945
1998	3,421	321,791

Source: Department of the Environment, Transport and the Regions

DRIVING LICENCES

It is necessary to hold a valid full licence in order to drive on public roads in the UK. Learner drivers must obtain a provisional driving licence before starting to learn to drive and must then pass theory and practical tests to obtain a full driving licence. Application forms for a driving licence (form D1) are available from post offices. A phased introduction of driving licences including the driver's photograph began in July 1998; all licences for newly qualified drivers will include a photograph, and qualified drivers will be issued with the new licence when their licence details need updating.

There are separate tests for driving motor cycles, cars, passenger-carrying vehicles (PCVs) and large goods vehicles (LGVs). Drivers must hold full car entitlement before they can apply for PCV or LGV entitlements. At 3 April 1999, 38 million people in the UK (20.9 male, 17.1 female) held a valid driving licence (full or provisional). The minimum age for driving motor cars, light goods vehicles up to 3.5 tonnes and motor cycles is 17 (moped, 16). Since June 1997, drivers who collect six or more penalty points within two years of qualifying lose their licence and are required to take another test. A leaflet, *What You Need to Know About Driving Licences* (form D100), is available from post offices.

The Driver and Vehicle Licensing Agency is responsible for issuing driving licences, registering and licensing vehicles, and collecting excise duty in Great Britain. In Northern Ireland the Driver and Vehicle Licensing Agency (Northern Ireland) has similar responsibilities.

DRIVING LICENCE FEES *as at 1 April 1999*

First provisional licence	£23.50
Changing a provisional to a full licence after passing a driving test	£8.50
Renewal of licence	£8.50
Renewal of licence including PCV or LGV entitlements	£28.50
Renewal after disqualification	£24.50
Renewal after drinking and driving disqualification	£33.50
Medical renewal	free
Medical renewal (over 70)	free
Duplicate Licence	£13.50
Exchange licence	£13.50
Removing endorsements	£13.50
Replacement (change of name or address)	free

DRIVING TESTS

The Driving Standards Agency is responsible for carrying out driving tests and approving driving instructors in Great Britain. In Northern Ireland the Driver and Vehicle Testing Agency (Northern Ireland) is responsible for testing drivers and vehicles.

In 1998–9, almost 1.2 million car driving tests were conducted in Great Britain, of which 45.9 per cent resulted in a pass. In addition over 49,000 lorry tests were undertaken, of which 51.9 per cent were successful. Over 83,000 motorcycle tests were undertaken, of which 67.9 per cent were successful. There were more than 7,600 bus tests, with a pass rate of 47.8 per cent. In the same period, 1.2 million theory tests were conducted. A new, longer driving test was introduced on 4 May 1999.

Since 1 March 1997 driving test candidates have been required to produce photographic confirmation of their identity.

*DRIVING TEST FEES (weekday rate/evening and Saturday rate) *as at 1 April 1999*

For cars	£36.75/£46
†For motor cycles	£45/£55
For lorries, buses	£73.50/£92

*Since 1 July 1996 most candidates for car and motor cycle tests have also been required to take a written driving theory test, for which there is a separate fee of £15.50. Theory tests for lorry and bus drivers were introduced on 1 January 1997

†Before riding on public roads, learner motor cyclists and learner moped riders are required to have completed Compulsory Basic Training, provided by DSA-approved training bodies. The Compulsory Basic Training certificate costs £8.00. All exemptions from CBT were removed on 1 January 1997

An extended driving test was introduced in 1992 for those convicted of dangerous driving. The fee is £73.50/£92 (car) or £90/£110 (motorcycle).

MOTOR VEHICLES

Vehicles must be licensed by the DVLA or the DVLNI before they can be driven on public roads. They must also be approved as roadworthy by the Vehicle Certification Agency. The Vehicle Inspectorate carries out annual testing and inspection of goods vehicles, buses and coaches.

There were 27.9 million vehicles registered at the DVLA at December 1998:

Private and light goods	24,840,942
Motor cycles, scooters, mopeds	701,692
Coaches and buses	80,862
Large goods vehicles	419,526
Electric vehicles	11,020
Others	1,926,884
Total	27,980,926

VEHICLE LICENCES

Registration and first licensing of vehicles is through local offices (known as Vehicle Registration Offices) of the Driver and Vehicle Licensing Agency in Swansea (*see* page 299). Local facilities for relicensing are available at any post office which deals with vehicle licensing. Applicants will need to take their vehicle registration document; if this is not available the applicant must complete form V62 which is held at post offices. Postal applications can be made to the post offices shown on form V100, available at any post office. This form also provides guidance on registering and licensing vehicles.

Details of the present duties chargeable on motor vehicles are available at post offices and Vehicle Registration Offices. The Vehicle Excise and Registration Act 1994 provides *inter alia* that any vehicle kept on a public road but not used on roads is chargeable to excise duty as if it were in use. All non-commercial vehicles constructed before 1 January 1973 are exempt from vehicle excise duty.

Vehicle Excise Duty Rates
from 10 March 1999

	Twelve months £	Six months £
Motor Cars		
Light vans, cars, taxis, etc.	155.00	85.25
Under 1100cc†	100.00	55.00
Over 1100cc†	155.00	85.25
Motor Cycles		
With or without sidecar, not over 150 cc	15.00	—
With or without sidecar, 150–250 cc	40.00	—
Others	60.00	33.00
Electric motorcycles (including tricycles)	15.00	—
Tricycles (not over 450 kg)		
Not over 150 cc	15.00	—
Others	60.00	33.00
*Buses**		
Seating 9–16 persons	160.00	88.00
	(155.00)	(85.25)
Seating 17–35 persons	210.00	115.50
	(155.00)	(85.25)
Seating 36–60 persons	320.00	176.00
	(155.00)	(85.25)
Seating over 60 persons	480.00	264.00
	(155.00)	(85.25)

*Figures in parentheses refer to reduced pollution vehicles.
†Rate from 1 June 1999

MoT Testing

Cars, motor cycles, motor caravans, light goods and dual-purpose vehicles more than three years old must be covered by a current MoT test certificate. The certificate must be renewed annually. The MoT testing scheme is administered by the Vehicle Inspectorate.

A fee is payable to MoT testing stations, which must be authorized to carry out tests. The maximum fees, which are prescribed by regulations, are:

For cars and light vans	£30.87
For solo motor cycles	£12.74
For motor cycle combinations	£21.28
For three-wheeled vehicles	£25.02
For non-public service vehicle buses	£38.68
For light goods vehicles between 3,000 and 3,500 kg	£32.77

Method of Travel to Work, *Great Britain (percentage*)*

	1993	1997
Car, van, minibus, works van	68	71
Bus, coach, private bus	9	8
Train (incl. Underground and light rail)	5	6
Walk	12	11
Other	5	5
All	100	100

*All figures are rounded
Source: DETR/The Stationery Office – *Focus on Personal Travel 1998* (Crown copyright)

SHIPPING AND PORTS

Since earliest times sea trade has played a central role in Britain's economy. By the 17th century Britain had built up a substantial merchant fleet and by the early 20th century it dominated the world shipping industry. In recent years the size and tonnage of the UK-registered trading fleet have declined; the UK-flagged merchant fleet now constitutes about 1 per cent of the world fleet. In December 1998 the Government published a document, *British Shipping: Charting a New Course*, which outlined strategies to promote the long-term interests of British shipping.

Freight is carried by liner and bulk services, almost all scheduled liner services being containerized. About 95 per cent by weight of Britain's overseas trade is carried by sea; this amounts to 75 per cent of its total value. Passengers and vehicles are carried by roll-on, roll-off ferries, hovercraft, hydrofoils and high-speed catamarans. There are about 57 million ferry passengers a year, of whom 36 million travel internationally. The leading British operators of passenger services are P. & O. Stena, Stena Line (which has a Swedish parent company) and P. & O. European Ferries.

Lloyd's of London provides the most comprehensive shipping intelligence service in the world. *Lloyd's Shipping Index*, published daily, lists some 25,000 ocean-going vessels and gives the latest known report of each.

Ports

There are about 70 commercially significant ports in Great Britain, including such ports as London, Dover, Forth, Tees and Hartlepool, Grimsby and Immingham, Sullom Voe, Milford Haven, Southampton, Felixstowe and Liverpool. Belfast is the principal freight port in Northern Ireland.

Broadly speaking, ports are owned and operated by private companies, local authorities or trusts. The largest operator is Associated British Ports (formerly the British Transport Docks Board, privatized in 1981), which owns 23 ports. Total traffic through British ports in 1998 amounted to 568 million tonnes, an increase of 2 per cent on the previous year.

Marine Safety

By 1 October 2002 all roll-on, roll-off ferries operating to and from the UK will be required to meet the new international safety standards on stability established by the Stockholm Agreement.

The Maritime and Coastguard Agency (MCA) was established on 1 April 1998 by the merger of the Coastguard Agency and the Marine Safety Agency. It is an executive agency of the Department of the Environment, Transport and the Regions. The Agency's aims are to develop, promote and enforce high standards of marine safety, to minimize loss of life amongst seafarers and coastal users, and to minimize pollution of the sea and coastline from ships. In 1998 HM Coastguard co-ordinated 11,553 incidents requiring search and rescue facilities. Assistance was rendered on 6,328 occasions and 249 lives were lost.

Locations hazardous to shipping in coastal waters are marked by lighthouses and other lights and buoys. The lighthouse authorities are the Corporation of Trinity House (for England, Wales and the Channel Islands), the Northern Lighthouse Board (for Scotland and the Isle of Man), and the Commissioners of Irish Lights (for Northern Ireland and the Republic of Ireland). Trinity House maintains 72 lighthouses, 13 major floating aids to navigation and more than 429 buoys; and the Northern Lighthouse Board 84 lighthouses, 116 minor lights and many buoys.

Harbour authorities are responsible for pilotage within their harbour areas; and the Ports Act 1991 provides for the transfer of lights and buoys to harbour authorities where these are used for mainly local navigation.

PRINCIPAL MERCHANT FLEETS 1998

Flag	No	Gross tonnage
Panama	6,143	98,222,372
Liberia	1,717	60,492,104
Bahamas	1,286	27,715,783
Greece	1,545	25,224,543
Malta	1,416	24,074,712
Cyprus	1,602	23,301,517
Singapore	1,677	20,370,399
Norway (NIS)	750	19,918,331
Japan	8,922	17,780,396
China (Taiwan)	3,214	16,503,355
*United States of America	5,626	11,851,660
Russia	4,723	11,089,922
Philippines	1,726	8,508,313
Germany	1,158	8,083,620
St Vincent	1,317	7,875,497
Italy	1,329	6,818,632
India	947	6,777,102
Marshall Islands	207	6,441,843
Turkey	1,135	6,251,395
Hong Kong, China	391	6,170,705
Korea (South)	2,381	5,694,216
China (Taiwan)	686	5,491,718
Malaysia	828	5,209,049
Denmark (DIS)	473	5,091,330
Bermuda	127	4,810,939
Netherlands	1,214	4,263,326
Isle of Man	207	4,202,970
Brazil	504	4,170,577
United Kingdom	1,421	4,084,970
Iran	382	3,347,429
Indonesia	2,359	3,252,093
Norway	1,575	3,218,007
Antigua and Barbuda	575	2,787,829
French Antarctic Territory	91	2,683,295
Sweden	562	2,552,365
Canada	835	2,501,274
Kuwait	202	2,459,004
Belize	1,308	2,382,478
Australia	617	2,188,146
Romania	389	2,088,166
Other countries	22,261	45,941,914
WORLD TOTAL	85,828	531,893,296

DIS   Danish International Register of Shipping – offshore registry
NIS   Norwegian International Ship Register – offshore registry
*Excluding ships of United States Reserve Fleet

Source: Lloyd's Register of Shipping

MERCHANT SHIPS COMPLETED 1998

Country of Build	No	Gross tonnage
Japan	561	10,206,334
Korea (South)	160	7,243,180
China (People's Republic)	130	1,440,184
Germany	77	1,049,545
Italy	37	811,571
Poland	48	696,929
Denmark	21	455,399
China (Taiwan)	22	447,046
Spain	107	435,903
Netherlands	96	291,267
Croatia	12	280,685
Finland	9	219,924
*United States of America	86	213,680
Norway	57	180,689
Singapore	39	170,355
France	15	148,345
United Kingdom	23	134,231
Romania	21	105,868
Bulgaria	8	93,774
Turkey	21	89,646
Brazil	4	86,077
Ukraine	4	75,135
Indonesia	22	69,485
Philippines	6	62,146
Russia	8	60,794
Other countries	132	229,305
For Registration in		
Panama	338	7,910,235
Liberia	93	2,921,791
Germany	127	1,699,035
Greece	23	1,307,404
Singapore	98	1,050,703
Hong Kong, China	29	917,874
Cyprus	37	699,300
Malaysia	35	695,162
Bahamas	26	637,977
Japan	163	636,824
Denmark (DIS)	16	597,782
Norway (NIS)	21	518,665
Netherlands	59	478,545
United Kingdom	39	459,961
Italy	33	429,056
China (People's Republic)	26	421,993
Kuwait	4	413,314
Malta	21	349,258
Philippines	21	288,746
Marshall Islands	7	246,327
Norway	43	206,239
China (Taiwan)	8	197,147
*United States of America	71	184,627
Sweden	10	151,916
Antigua and Barbuda	16	142,609
Other countries	362	1,735,007
WORLD TOTAL	1,726	25,297,497

DIS   Danish International Register of Shipping – offshore registry
NIS   Norwegian International Ship Register – offshore registry
*Excluding ships of United States reserve fleet

Source: Lloyd's Register of Shipping

UK-REGISTERED TRADING VESSELS OF 500
GROSS TONS AND OVER *as at end 1997*

Type of vessel	No	Gross tonnage
Tankers[1]	123	2,704,000
Bulk carriers[2]	35	1,408,000
Specialized carriers[3]	11	43,000
Container (fully cellular)	60	1,626,000
Ro-Ro[4]	85	827,000
Other general cargo	156	654,000
Passenger[5]	16	548,000
TOTAL	486	7,809,000

1 Includes oil, gas, chemical and other specialized tankers
2 Includes combination bulk carriers: ore/oil and ore/bulk/oil carriers
3 Includes livestock, car and chemical carriers
4 Roll-on, roll-off passenger and cargo vessels
5 Cruise liner and other passenger vessels

Source: The Stationery Office – *Annual Abstract of Statistics 1999*

SEABORNE TRADE OF THE UK 1996
EXPORTS (INCLUDING RE-EXPORTS) PLUS IMPORTS
BY SEA

	Million tonnes
By weight	
All cargo	354.3
Dry cargo	203.4
Tanker cargo	150.9
	£ million
By value	
All cargo	260,900
Dry cargo	244,700
Tanker cargo	16,300

Source: The Stationery Office – *Annual Abstract of Statistics 1999*

PASSENGER MOVEMENT BY SEA 1997p

*Arrivals plus departures at UK seaports by place of embarkation or landing**

All passenger movements	33,975,000
Irish Republic	4,055,000
Belgium	1,883,000
France†	26,960,000
Netherlands	1,934,000
Other EU countries	970,000
Other European and Mediterranean countries‡	172,000

p provisional
* Passengers are included at both departure and arrival if their journeys begin and end at a UK seaport
† Includes hovercraft passengers
‡ Includes North Africa and Middle East Mediterranean countries

Source: The Stationery Office – *Annual Abstract of Statistics 1999*

Communications

Postal Services

Responsibility for running postal services rests in the UK with the Post Office (*see* pages 330–1), which the Government plans to change from a public authority into a public limited company. All shares will be owned by the Government. An independent postal services regulator will be appointed. The Secretary of State for Trade and Industry has powers to suspend the letter monopoly of the Post Office in certain areas and to issue licences to other bodies to provide an alternative service. Non-Post Office bodies are permitted to transfer mail between document exchanges and to deliver letters, provided that a minimum fee of £1 per letter is charged. From 1 April 2000 this minimum fee will be reduced to 50 pence. Charitable organizations are allowed to carry and deliver Christmas and New Year cards.

INLAND POSTAL SERVICES AND REGULATIONS

INLAND LETTER POST RATES*

Not over	1st class†	2nd class†
60 g	26p	19p
100 g	39p	31p
150 g	52p	40p
200 g	66p	50p
250 g	77p	61p
300 g	88p	70p
350 g	£1.00	80p
400 g	£1.14	92p
450 g	£1.30	£1.05
500 g	£1.45	£1.20
600 g	£1.75	£1.40
700 g	£2.20	£1.60
750 g	£2.35	£1.70 (not
800 g	£2.55	admissible
900 g	£2.80	over 750 g)
1,000 g	£3.05	
Each extra 250 g or part thereof	75p	

UK PARCEL RATES

Not over	
1 kg	£2.85
2 kg	£3.90
4 kg	£5.95
6 kg	£6.45
8 kg	£7.40
10 kg	£7.95

*Postcards travel at the same rates as letter post
†There is a two-tier postal delivery system in the UK with first class letters normally being delivered the following day and second class post within three days

OVERSEAS POSTAL SERVICES AND REGULATIONS

Details of overseas parcel rates are available from Parcelforce Worldwide by telephoning 0800 884422.

STAMPS

Postage stamps are sold in values of 1p, 2p, 4p, 5p, 6p, 10p, 19p, 20p, 25p, 26p, 29p, 30p, 31p, 35p, 36p, 37p, 38p, 39p, 41p, 43p, 50p, 63p, £1, £1.50, £2.00, £5.00, and £10.00. Books or rolls of first and second class stamps are also available. Stamps are sold at Post Offices and some other outlets, including stationers and newsagents.

OVERSEAS SURFACE MAIL RATES

Letters

Not over		Not over	
20 g	34p	450 g	£3.04
60 g	56p	500 g	£3.36
100 g	80p	750 g	£4.96
150 g	£1.12	1,000 g	£6.59
200 g	£1.44	1,250 g	£7.84
250 g	£1.76	1,500 g	£9.76
300 g	£2.08	1,750 g	£11.36
350 g	£2.40	2,000 g	£12.96
400 g	£2.72		

Postcards travel at 20 g letter rate

AIRMAIL LETTER RATES

Europe: Letters

Not over		Not over	
20 g	30p	280 g	£1.95
40 g	44p	300 g	£2.07
60 g	56p	320 g	£2.20
80 g	69p	340 g	£2.32
100 g	82p	360 g	£2.45
120 g	94p	380 g	£2.57
140 g	£1.07	400 g	£2.70
160 g	£1.19	420 g	£2.82
180 g	£1.32	440 g	£2.95
200 g	£1.44	460 g	£3.08
220 g	£1.57	480 g	£3.20
240 g	£1.69	500 g	£3.33
260 g	£1.82	1,000 g	£6.50
		*2,000 g	£13.08

* Max. 2 kg
Postcards to Europe travel at 20 g letter rate

Outside Europe: Letters

	Not over 10 g	Not over 20 g	Over 20 g	Post-cards
Zone 1	44p	64p	varies	44p
Zone 2	44p	64p	varies	44p

For airmail letter zones outside Europe, *see* pages 518–19

PREPAID STATIONERY

Aerogrammes to all destinations are 37p, with a packet of six costing £2.05. Pictorial aerogrammes are 45p; a packet of six, £2.50. Forces aerogrammes are free to certain destinations.

Special Delivery prepaid envelopes:
Not over

500 g (C4 and C5 size)	£3.65

For items over 500g add additional payment

up to 1 kg	£1.10
2 kg	£2.35
10 kg	£11.35

Guaranteed services	Special Delivery	Registered	Registered Plus
C4, 500g	£3.65	£3.80	£4.85
C5, 250g	£3.20	£3.60	£4.55

Printed postage stamps cut from envelopes, postcards, newspaper wrappers, etc., may be used as stamps in payment of postage, provided that they are not imperfect or defaced.

POSTAL ORDERS

Postal orders (British pattern) are issued and paid at nearly all post offices in the UK and in many other countries.

Postal orders are printed with a counterfoil for denominations of 50p and £1, followed by £1 steps to £10, £15 and £20. Postage stamps may be affixed in the space provided to increase the value of the postal order by up to 49p. Charges (in addition to the value of the postal order): up to £1, 25p; £2–£4, 45p; £5–£7, 65p; £8–£10, 80p; £15, 90p; £20, 95p.

The name of the payee must be inserted on the postal order. If not presented within six months of the last day of the month of issue, orders must be sent to the local customer services manager of Post Office Counters Ltd (listed in the telephone directory) to ascertain whether the order may still be paid. If the counterfoil has been retained postal orders not more than four years out of date may be paid when presented with the counterfoil at a post office.

RESTRICTIONS

Articles which may not be sent in the post include offensive or dangerous articles (such as explosives, articles containing batteries, or aerosol products), packets likely to impede Post Office sorters, and certain kinds of advertisement. Certain other articles (such as biological specimens, liquids, or perishable foodstuffs) may be posted only if packed correctly. Advice is available from Royal Mail (tel: 0345-740740) for letters and small packets; Parcelforce (tel: 0800-224466) for parcels; or local post office counter staff.

The exportation of some goods by post is prohibited except under Department of Trade licence. Enquiries should be addressed to the Export Data Branch, Overseas Trade Divisions, Department of Trade and Industry, 1 Victoria Street, London SWIH OET. Tel: 0171-215 5000.

SPECIAL DELIVERY SERVICES

DATAPOST

A guaranteed service for the delivery of documents and packages: (i) Datapost Sameday offers same working day collection and delivery in many areas; (ii) Datapost 10 (for delivery before 10 a.m.) and Datapost 12 (for delivery before noon) offer next working day delivery nationwide and are available only to certain destinations. Items may be collected or handed in at post offices. There are also Datapost links with a number of overseas countries. Parcelforce 24 (next working day delivery) and 48 (delivery in two working days) offer a similar guaranteed service.

ROYAL MAIL SPECIAL DELIVERY

A guaranteed next working day delivery service by 12.30 p.m. to most UK destinations for first class letters and packets. The fee is £3.35. Compensation of up to £250 can be awarded for a 100 g item if next working day delivery is not achieved, provided that items are posted before latest recommended posting times. Details of other compensation levels can be obtained by telephoning 0345-740740.

SWIFTAIR

An express airmail service. Items are placed on the first available flight to the destination country. Although Swiftair mail receives priority treatment, delivery times are not guaranteed. Charge (in addition to postage): £2.85.

OTHER SERVICES

ADVICE OF DELIVERY

Written confirmation of delivery from the post office at the stated destination. Charge: 33p (inland); 40p (international); plus postage.

CERTIFICATE OF POSTING

Issued free on request at time of posting.

COMPENSATION (INLAND AND INTERNATIONAL)

Inland: compensation up to a maximum of £26 may be paid where it can be shown that a letter was damaged or lost in the post due to the fault of the Post Office, its employees or agents. The Post Office does not accept responsibility for loss or damage arising from faulty packing.

International: if a certificate of posting is produced, compensation up to a maximum of £26 may be given for loss or damage in the UK to uninsured parcels to or from most overseas countries. No compensation will be paid for any loss or damage due to the action of the Queen's Enemies.

INTERNATIONAL REPLY COUPONS

Coupons used to prepay replies to letters, exchangeable abroad for stamps representing the lowest airmail letter rate from the country concerned to the UK. Charge: 60p each.

NEWSPAPER POST

Copies of newspapers registered at the Post Office may be posted only by the publisher or their agents in open-ended wrappers or unsealed envelopes approved by the Post Office, or tied with string removable without cutting. Wrappers and envelopes must be prominently marked 'newspaper post' in the top left-hand corner. The only additional writing or printing permitted is 'with compliments', the name and address of sender, request for return if undeliverable, and a page reference. Items receive first class letter service.

POSTE RESTANTE

Poste Restante is solely for travellers and is for three months in any one town. A packet may be addressed to any post office, except town sub-offices, and should state 'Poste Restante' or 'to be called for' in the address. Redirection from a Poste Restante is undertaken for up to three months. Letters for an expected ship at a port are kept for two months, otherwise letters are kept for two weeks, or one month if from abroad. At the end of this period mail is treated as undeliverable or is returned.

PRIVATE BOX

Provides an alternative address (e.g. PO Box 123) and mail is held at the local delivery office for collection. Charges: £42 (six months); £52 (12 months).

RECORDED MAIL

Provides a record of posting and delivery of letters and ensures a signature on delivery. This service is recommended for items of little or no monetary value. All packets must be handed to the post office and a certificate of posting issued. Charges: 60p plus postage (inland); £2.60 plus postage (international).

REDIRECTION

By agent of addressee: mail other than parcels, business reply and freepost items may be reposted free not later than the day after delivery (not counting Sundays and public holidays) if unopened and if original addressee's name is unobscured. Parcels may be redirected free within the same time limits only if the original and substituted address are in the same local parcel delivery area (or the London postal area). Registered packets must be taken to a post office and are re-registered free up to the day after delivery.

By the Post Office: a printed form obtainable from the Post Office must be signed by the person to whom the letters are to be addressed. A fee is payable for each different surname on the application form. Charges: up to 1 calendar month, £6.00 (abroad, £12.00); up to 3 calendar months, £13.00 (£26.00); up to 12 calendar months, £30.00 (£60.00).

REGISTERED MAIL (INTERNATIONAL)

All packets must be handed to the post office and a certificate of posting obtained. Charges (plus postage):

Compensation up to	Registered fee plus postage
£500	£3.15
£2,200	£4.20

Compensation in respect of currency or other forms of monetary worth is given only if money is sent by registered letter post. Compensation cannot be paid in the case of any packet containing prohibited articles (see Restrictions). Compensation is only paid for well-packed fragile articles and not for exceptionally fragile or perishable articles.

SMALL PACKETS POST AND PRINTED PAPERS (INTERNATIONAL)

Permits the transmission of goods up to 2 kg to all countries, in the same mails as printed papers. Packets can be sealed and can contain personal correspondence relating to the contents. Registration is allowed as insurance as long as the item is packed in a way complying with any insurance regulations. A customs declaration is required and the packet must be marked with 'small packet' and a return address. Instructions for the disposal of undelivered packets must be given at the time of posting. An undeliverable packet will be returned to the sender at his/her expense.

Surface mail: worldwide

Not over		Not over		
100 g		54p	450 g	£1.80
150 g		72p	500 g	£1.98
200 g		90p	750 g	£2.70
250 g		£1.08	1,000 g	£3.78
300 g		£1.26	1,500 g	£5.58
350 g		£1.44	2,000 g	£7.38
400 g		£1.62		

Printed papers only, per extra 50 g, 17p

UNDELIVERED AND UNPAID MAIL

Undelivered mail is returned to the sender provided the return address is indicated either on the outside of the envelope or inside. If the sender's address is not available items not containing property are destroyed. If the packet contains something of value it is retained for up to three months. Undeliverable second class mail containing newspapers, magazines or commercial advertising is destroyed.

All unpaid or underpaid letters are treated as second class mail. The recipient is charged the amount of underpayment plus 15p per item. Parcels over 750 g are charged at first class rates plus 15p.

Public Telecommunications Services

Under the British Telecommunications Act 1981 British Telecom (now BT) was created to provide a national public telecommunications service. The Telecommunications Act 1984 removed BT's monopoly on running the public telecommunications system and BT was privatized in 1984.

The Telecommunications Act 1984 also established the Office of Telecommunications (Oftel) as the independent regulatory body for the telecommunications industry (see also Government Departments and Public Offices).

PUBLIC TELECOMMUNICATIONS OPERATORS

Until 1991 the three licensed fixed-link public telecommunications operators (PTOs) in the UK were BT, Mercury Communications Ltd, and Kingston Communications (Hull) PLC. In 1991 the Government announced that it was opening up the existing duopoly of the two major fixed-link operators, BT and Mercury, and would be encouraging applications for telecommunications licences. The Department of Trade and Industry has granted over 280 PTO licences.

BT's obligations under its operating licence continue to include the provision of a universal telecommunications service, including a service in rural areas; and essential services, such as public call boxes and emergency services.

Cable and Wireless Communications PLC (which was formed from the merger of Mercury Communications with other communications companies in 1997) is licensed to provide national and international public telecommunications services for residential and business customers. These services utilize the digital network created by Mercury. Cable and Wireless can also provide the following services: public and private telephone services; national and international switched voice and data services; electronic messaging (private circuits and networks (national and international), integrated voice and data); data network services; customer equipment cable television, Internet service provision and mobile communications services.

In December 1996 the Government liberalized international facilities licensing in the UK. The end of the BT/Mercury duopoly means that other operators are now able to apply for licences to own and operate their own international telecommunications networks. By July 1999, over 100 operators had been granted international facilities licences. In January 1998 the telecommunications market throughout the European Union was liberalized.

PREMIUM RATE TELEPHONE SERVICES

There are over 1,000 premium rate telephone companies which offer information on a variety of subjects such as the weather, stock market analysis, horoscopes, etc., on the various networks.

The lines and equipment are provided by telecommunications operators under condition that services adhere to the codes of practice of the Independent Committee for the Supervision of Standards of Telephone Information Services. Services are charged at different rates from 5p to £1.50 per minute.

MOBILE TELEPHONE SYSTEMS

Cellular telephone network systems allow calls to be made to and from mobile telephones. The four companies licensed by the Department of Trade and Industry to provide competing cellular telephone systems are BT Cellnet, jointly owned by BT and Securicor; One-2-One, jointly owned by Cable and Wireless and MediaOne; Orange; and Vodafone AirTouch.

INLAND TELEPHONES

An individual customer can install an extension telephone socket or apparatus in their own home without the need to buy the items from any of the licensed public telecommunications operators. Although an individual need not buy or rent an apparatus from a PTO, a telephone bought from a retail outlet must be of an approved standard compatible with the public network (indicated by a green disc on the label).

BT EXCHANGE LINE RENTALS
(including VAT)

	Per quarter
Residential, exclusive	£26.77
Light user scheme	from £9.24
Business, exclusive	£43.88

BT TELEPHONE APPARATUS RENTAL
Per quarter

Residential	from £4.47
Business	from £5.53
Private payphone	from £50.53

EXCHANGE LINE CONNECTION AND TAKE-OVER CHARGES
(including VAT)
BT

New line	£99.00
Removing customer	£0.00
Take-over of existing lines:	
Simultaneous (same day)	£0.00
Non-simultaneous	£0.00

Cable and Wireless

Monthly line rental	£7.98

RATES

BT and Cable and Wireless local and dialled national calls are charged by the second. Calls made from payphones are charged in 10p units. There is a 5p minimum charge on all BT calls and a minimum charge of at least 3.5p on Cable and Wireless calls depending on the charging package. All charges are subject to VAT, except those from payphones which are VAT inclusive. VAT charges on ordinary lines are calculated as a percentage of the total quarterly (BT)/monthly (Cable and Wireless) bill.

The charge per second depends on the time of day and the distance of the call:

BT	Cable and Wireless	
Daytime	Daytime	Monday to Friday 8 a.m. to 6 p.m.
Evening and night-time	Evening	Monday to Friday 6 p.m. to 8 a.m.
Weekend	Weekend	Midnight Friday to midnight Sunday

Local rate
Regional rate – up to 35 miles (56 km)
National rate – over 35 miles (56 km) (including Channel Islands and Isle of Man)
Calls to mobile phones

DIALLED CALL TIME
pence per minute charges (*including VAT*)*

BT	Local rate
Daytime	3.95
Evening and night-time	1.49
Weekend	1.00

Regional rate

Daytime	7.91
Evening and night-time	3.95
Weekend	2.95

National rate

Daytime	7.91
Evening and night-time	4.18
Weekend	2.95

Calls to mobile phones

	Daytime	Evening and night-time	Weekend
BT Cellnet	19.8	19.2	2.0
Vodafone AirTouch	20.6	15.0	7.4
One-2-One	25.3	17.9	8.0
Orange	24.8	17.8	7.9

*Cable and Wireless customers choose from a range of packages depending on the time of day they use the telephone most and the distance of their calls. Charges vary with each package.

OPERATOR-CONNECTED CALLS

Operator-connected calls from ordinary lines are generally subject to a one-minute minimum charge (and thereafter by the minute) which varies with distance and time of day. Operator-connected calls from payphones are charged in three-minute periods at the payphone tariff. There is also a £1.80 handling charge for operator-connected calls. For calls that have to be placed through the operator because a dialled call has failed, the charge is equivalent to the dialled rate, subject normally to the one-minute minimum.

Higher charges apply to other operator-connected calls, including special services calls and those to mobile phones, the Irish Republic and the Channel Islands.

PHONECARDS

BT phonecards to the value of £2, £5, £10 and £20 are available from post offices and other outlets for use in specially designated public telephone boxes. Each phonecard unit is equivalent to a 10p coin in a payphone. Special public payphones at major railway stations and airports also accept commercial credit cards.

INTERNATIONAL TELEPHONES

All UK customers have access to International Direct Dialling (IDD) and can dial direct to numbers on most exchanges in over 230 countries worldwide. Details about how to make calls are given in dialling code information and in the International Telephone Guide.

For countries without IDD, calls have to be made through the International Operator. All operator-connected calls are subject to a £1.80 handling charge. Thereafter the call is charged by the minute.

Countries which can be called on IDD fall into one of 18 international charge bands depending on location. Charges in each band also vary according to the time of day; cheap rate dialled calls are available to all countries at certain times, but there is no reduced rate for operator-connected calls. Details of current international telephone charges can be obtained from the International Operator.

For International Dialling Codes, *see* pages 518–19.

OTHER TELECOMMUNICATIONS SERVICES

TELEX SERVICE

There are now more than 240 countries that can be reached by the BT telex network from the UK. Calls can be sent to mobile terminals, including ships via the Inmarsat satellite service. Call charges start at 4.8p per minute for inland calls. International calls are charged by the second.

TELEMESSAGE

Telemessages can be sent by telephone or telex within the UK for 'hard copy' delivery the next working day, including Saturdays. To achieve this, a telemessage must be telephoned/telexed before 10 p.m. Monday to Saturday (7 p.m. Sundays and Bank Holidays). Dial 0800-190190 and ask for the Telemessage Service.

A telemessage costs £8.99 for the first 50 words and £5.00 for each subsequent group of 50 words – the name and address are free. A sender's copy costs £1.20. A selection of cards is available for special occasions at £1.00 per card. (All prices are include VAT.)

BT SERVICES

OPERATOR SERVICES – 100
  For difficulties
  For the following call services: alarm calls (booking charge £2.70); advice of duration and charge (charge £1.80); charge card calls (charge £1.50); freephone calls; international personal calls (charge £2.15–£4.30); transferred charge calls (charge £1.80); subscriber controlled transfer (All charges exclude VAT)

INTERNATIONAL OPERATOR – 155

DIRECTORY ENQUIRIES – 192 (35p charge per call)

INTERNATIONAL DIRECTORY ENQUIRIES – 153 (£1.10 charge per minute)

EMERGENCY SERVICES – 999
  Services include fire service; police service; ambulance service; coastguard; lifeboat; cave rescue; mountain rescue

FAULTS – 151 (residential), 154 (business)

TELEMESSAGE – 0800-190190

INTERNATIONAL TELEGRAMS – 100

MARITIME SERVICES – 100
  Includes Ship's Telegram Service and Ship's Telephone Service

BT INMARSAT SATELLITE SERVICE – 155

ALL OTHER CALL ENQUIRIES – 100

Airmail and IDD Codes

The table includes airmail letter zones for countries outside Europe, and destinations to which European and European Union airmail letter rates apply (*see also* page 513).
(*Source:* Post Office)

1   airmail zone 1
2   airmail zone 2
e   Europe

INTERNATIONAL DIRECT DIALLING (IDD)
International dialling codes are composed of four elements which are dialled in sequence:

(i)   the international code
(ii)   the country code (*see* below)
(iii) the area code
(iv)   the customer's telephone number

Calls to some countries must be made via the international operator. (*Source:* BT)

†   Connection is currently unavailable
‡   Calls must be made via the international operator
p   A pause in dialling is necessary whilst waiting for a
       second tone
*   Varies in some areas
**   Varies depending on carrier

Country	AZ	IDD from UK	IDD to UK
Afghanistan	1	†	†
Albania	*e*	00 355	00 44
Algeria	1	00 213	00*p*44
Andorra	*e*	00 376	00 44
Angola	1	00 244	00 44
Anguilla	1	00 1 264	011 44
Antigua and Barbuda	1	00 1 268	011 44
Argentina	1	00 54	00 44
Armenia	*e*	00 374	810 44
Aruba	1	00 297	00 44
Ascension Island	1	00 247	00 44
Australia	2	00 61	00 11 44
Austria	*e*	00 43	00 44
Azerbaijan	*e*	00 994	810 44
Azores	*e*	00 351	00 44
Bahamas	1	00 1 242	011 44
Bahrain	1	00 973	0 44
Bangladesh	1	00 880	00 44
Barbados	1	00 1 246	011 44
Belarus	*e*	00 375	810 44
Belgium	*e*	00 32	00 44
Belize	1	00 501	00 44
Benin	1	00 229	00*p*44
Bermuda	1	00 1 441	011 44
Bhutan	1	00 975	00 44
Bolivia	1	00 591	00 44
Bosnia-Hercegovina	*e*	00 387	00 44
Botswana	1	00 267	00 44
Brazil	1	00 55	00 44
British Virgin Islands	1	00 1 284	011 44
Brunei	1	00 673	00 44
Bulgaria	*e*	00 359	00 44
Burkina Faso	1	00 226	00 44
Burundi	1	00 257	90 44
Cambodia	1	00 855	00 44
Cameroon	1	00 237	00 44
Canada	1	00 1	011 44
Canary Islands	*e*	00 34	00 44
Cape Verde	1	00 238	0 44

Country	AZ	IDD from UK	IDD to UK
Cayman Islands	1	00 1 345	011 44
Central African Republic	1	00 236	19 44
Chad	1	00 235	15 44
Chile	1	00 56	00 44
China	2	00 86	00 44
Hong Kong	1	00 852	001 44
Colombia	1	00 57	009 44
Comoros	1	00 269	00 44
Congo, Dem. Rep. of	1	00 243	00 44
Congo, Republic of	1	00 242	00 44
Cook Islands	2	00 682	00 44
Costa Rica	1	00 506	00 44
Côte d'Ivoire	1	00 225	00 44
Croatia	*e*	00 385	00 44
Cuba	1	00 53	119 44
Cyprus	*e*	00 357	00 44
Czech Republic	*e*	00 420	00 44
Denmark	*e*	00 45	00 44
Djibouti	1	00 253	00 44
Dominica	1	00 1 767	011 44
Dominican Republic	1	00 1 809	011 44
Ecuador	1	00 593	00 44
Egypt	1	00 20	00 44
Equatorial Guinea	1	00 240	00 44
Eritrea	1	00 291	00 44
Estonia	*e*	00 372	800 44
Ethiopia	1	00 251	00 44
Falkland Islands	1	00 500	0 44
Faroe Islands	*e*	00 298	009 44
Fiji	2	00 679	05 44
Finland	*e*	00 358	00 44**
France	*e*	00 33	00 44
French Guiana	1	00 594	00 44
French Polynesia	2	00 689	00 44
Gabon	1	00 241	00 44
The Gambia	1	00 220	00 44
Georgia	*e*	00 995	810 44
Germany	*e*	00 49	00 44
Ghana	1	00 233	00 44
Gibraltar	*e*	00 350	00 44
Greece	*e*	00 30	00 44
Greenland	*e*	00 299	009 44
Grenada	1	00 1 473	011 44
Guadeloupe	1	00 590	00 44
Guam	2	00 1 671	001 44
Guatemala	1	00 502	00 44
Guinea	1	00 224	00 44
Guinea-Bissau	1	00 245	099 44
Guyana	1	00 592	001 44
Haiti	1	00 509	00 44
Honduras	1	00 504	00 44
Hungary	*e*	00 36	00 44
Iceland	*e*	00 354	00 44
India	1	00 91	00 44
Indonesia			001 44**
	1	00 62	00844**
Iran	1	00 98	00 44
Iraq	1	00 964	00 44
Ireland, Republic of	*e*	00 353	00 44
Israel	1	00 972	00 44**
Italy	*e*	00 39	00 44
Jamaica	1	00 1 876	011 44
Japan			001 44**
			004144**
	2	00 81	006144**
Jordan	1	00 962	00 44*
Kazakhstan	*e*	00 7	810 44
Kenya	1	00 254	00 44

Country	AZ	IDD from UK	IDD to UK	Country	AZ	IDD from UK	IDD to UK
Kiribati	2	00 686	00 44	Russia	*e*	00 7	810 44
Korea, North	2	00 850	00 44	Rwanda	1	00 250	00 44
Korea, South			001 44**	St Christopher and			
	2	00 82	00244**	Nevis	1	00 1 869	011 44
Kuwait	1	00 965	00 44	St Helena	1	00 290	0 44
Kyrgystan	*e*	00 996	00 44	St Lucia	1	00 1 758	011 44
Laos	1	00 856	00 44	St Pierre and			
Latvia	*e*	00 371	00 44	Miquelon	1	00 508	00 44
Lebanon	1	00 961	00 44	St Vincent and the			
Lesotho	1	00 266	00 44	Grenadines	1	00 1 784	001 44
Liberia	1	00 231	00 44	El Salvador	1	00 503	0 44
Libya	1	00 218	00 44	Samoa	2	00 685	0 44
Liechtenstein	*e*	00 423	00 44	Samoa, American	2	00 684	00 44
Lithuania	*e*	00 370	810 44	San Marino	*e*	00 378	00 44
Luxembourg	*e*	00 352	00 44	São Tomé and			
Macao	1	00 853	00 44	Princípe	1	00 239	00 44
Macedonia	*e*	00 389	99 44	Saudi Arabia	1	00 966	00 44
Madagascar	1	00 261	00 44	Senegal	1	00 221	00*p*44
Madeira	*e*	00 351 91	00 44*	Serbia	*e*	00 381	99 44
Malawi	1	00 265	101 44	Seychelles	1	00 248	00 44
Malaysia	1	00 60	00 44	Sierra Leone	1	00 232	00 44
Maldives	1	00 960	00 44	Singapore	1	00 65	001 44
Mali	1	00 223	00 44	Slovak Republic	*e*	00 421	00 44
Malta	*e*	00 356	00 44	Slovenia	*e*	00 386	00 44
Mariana Islands,				Solomon Islands	2	00 677	00 44
Northern	2	00 1 670	011 44	Somalia	1	00 252	16 44
Marshall Islands	2	00 692	011 44	South Africa	1	00 27	09 44
Martinique	1	00 596	00 44	Spain	*e*	00 34	00 44
Mauritania	1	00 222	00 44	Sri Lanka	1	00 94	00 44
Mauritius	1	00 230	00 44	Sudan	1	00 249	00 44
Mayotte	1	00 269	10 44	Suriname	1	00 597	00 44
Mexico	1	00 52	98 44	Swaziland	1	00 268	00 44
Micronesia, Federated				Sweden			007 44**
States of	2	00 691	011 44				00944**
Moldova	*e*	00 373	810 44		*e*	00 46	008744**
Monaco	*e*	00 377	00 44	Switzerland	*e*	00 41	00 44
Mongolia	2	00 976	00 44	Syria	1	00 963	00 44
Montenegro	*e*	00 381	99 44	Taiwan	2	00 886	002 44
Montserrat	1	00 1 664	011 44	Tajikistan	*e*	00 7	810 44
Morocco	1	00 212	00*p*44	Tanzania	1	00 255	00 44
Mozambique	1	00 258	00 44	Thailand	1	00 66	001 44
Myanmar	1	00 95	00 44	Tibet	1	00 86	00 44
Namibia	1	00 264	00 44	Togo	1	00 228	00 44
Nauru	2	00 674	00 44	Tonga	2	00 676	00 44
Nepal	1	00 977	00 44	Trinidad and Tobago	1	00 1 868	011 44
Netherlands	*e*	00 31	00 44	Tristan da Cunha	1	00 2 897	‡
Netherlands Antilles	1	00 599	00 44	Tunisia	1	00 216	00 44
New Caledonia	2	00 687	00 44	Turkey	*e*	00 90	00 44
New Zealand	2	00 64	00 44	Turkmenistan	*e*	00 993	810 44
Nicaragua	1	00 505	00 44	Turks and Caicos Is-			
Niger	1	00 227	00 44	lands	1	00 1 649	0 44
Nigeria	1	00 234	009 44	Tuvalu	2	00 688	00 44
Niue	2	00 683	00 44	Uganda	1	00 256	00 44
Norfolk Island	2	00 672	0101 44	Ukraine	*e*	00 380	810 44
Norway	*e*	00 47	00 44	United Arab Emirates	1	00 971	00 44
Oman	1	00 968	00 44	Uruguay	1	00 598	00 44
Pakistan	1	00 92	00 44	USA	1	00 1	011 44
Palau	2	00 680	011 44	Alaska		00 1 907	011 44
Panama	1	00 507	00 44	Hawaii		00 1 808	011 44
Papua New Guinea	2	00 675	05 44	Uzbekistan	*e*	00 998	810 44
Paraguay	1	00 595	00 44**	Vanuatu	2	00 678	00 44
			003 44**	Vatican City State	*e*	00 390 66982	00 44
Peru	1	00 51	00 44	Venezuela	1	00 58	00 44
Philippines	2	00 63	00 44	Vietnam	1	00 84	00 44
Poland	*e*	00 48	00 44	Virgin Islands (US)	1	00 1 340	011 44
Portugal	*e*	00 351	00 44	Yemen	1	00 967	00 44
Puerto Rico	1	00 1 787	011 44	Yugoslav Fed. Rep.	*e*	00 381	99 44
Qatar	1	00 974	00 44	Zambia	1	00 260	00 44
Réunion	1	00 262	00 44	Zimbabwe	1	00 263	00 44
Romania	*e*	00 40	00 44				

The Internet

The Internet is a rapidly-growing worldwide network of computer networks which use the same protocols (agreed methods of communication). It has its origins in the Advanced Research Projects Agency Network (ARPA-NET), a government-funded defence network in the USA, and other research and academic networks, such as the UK Joint Academic Network (JANET), a network linking universities and higher education institutions in the UK. JANET has extensive links to international and other national academic networks, and also to commercial and public network services. It is funded by the higher education funding agencies in the UK.

The main protocol used by the networks is Transmission Control Protocol/Internet Protocol (TCP/IP). Other protocols include:
- file transfer protocol (ftp), which allows files to be transferred between computers
- simple mail transfer protocol (smtp), which allows electronic mail (e-mail) to be sent
- hypertext transfer protocol (http), which allows hypertext facilities to be provided
- telnet, a facility which allows users to log on to other computers on the Internet

The most common uses of the Internet include:
- sending and receiving e-mail; text can be sent directly to another computer linked to the Internet
- playing computer games
- commercial transactions
- mailing lists, which enable users to send and receive information on specialist interests
- 'newsgroups' or bulletin boards, where messages on specialist interests can be left for users to read
- the publication of information

The World Wide Web (WWW or the Web) is a vast collection of computers able to support multi-media formats and accessible via Web 'browsers' (search and navigation tools). Data stored on these computers (servers) is organized into pages with hypertext links; each page has a unique address. It is estimated that 800 million pages of the Web are searchable, but the extent of the Internet which is indexed by search engines is diminishing rapidly and no engine is currently indexing more than about 16 per cent of the Web. For practical purposes the WWW and the Internet are now almost synonymous. The main Web browsers are Netscape Navigator and Internet Explorer. The Internet is increasingly used by commercial organizations for the conduct of electronic business. Policies and standards are being developed to ensure an appropriate level of privacy; tools include access control mechanisms, data labelling and cryptography standards.

The speed of access to Internet sources and of downloading information depends on the number of users on the system (which varies according to the time of day), the location of the information, and the amount of information being downloaded.

CONNECTIONS

Connection to the Internet usually requires access to a computer, a modem and a telephone line, although it is now possible to receive television-based Internet services. Internet service providers (ISPs) supply an Internet address and password, an electronic mailbox and some or all of the necessary software. Most providers provide only a connection to the Internet, but a few also offer more sophisticated on-line services which are usually easier to use but more expensive than direct Internet access. Leading service providers include AOL, CompuServe, Demon, UU net and Microsoft Network. Details of providers are available in computer magazines and specialist Internet publications.

The main methods of connecting to the Internet are by a dial-up connection or a leased-line connection. A dial-up connection may be made over standard telephone lines or over ISDN lines. There are two types of dial-up connection: an online account, which allows the user to log on to an account on a remote computer which is connected to the Internet; and a dial-up IP connection, where a full Internet connection is made from the user's computer. The latter requires more complicated software. A permanent leased-line connection (a data line requiring no modem) is likely to be used where there are a large number of potential users, e.g. where all the users on a local area network (LAN) are to be connected.

The total number of Internet users in the UK is estimated to exceed 12.5 million adults by the end of 1999. Some 15 per cent of the UK population have home access and 14 per cent work access. The number of people on-line worldwide is estimated to be about 179 million as at June 1999.

TERMS

Home page – the introductory section of a site on the Web

Hypertext mark-up language (HTML) – a standard document mark-up language used on the Web

Java – a programming language for writing client/server and networked applications; its uses include creating interactive Web sites

Search engine – a means of finding Web pages or other material on the Internet containing specific words or phrases

Server – a computer storing data and software which can be used by other computers on a network

Uniform/Universal resource locators (URLs) – the address system for the Web

Users' network (USENET) – a large bulletin board system on the Internet

Local Government

Major changes in local government were introduced in England and Wales in 1974 and in Scotland in 1975 by the Local Government Act 1972 and the Local Government (Scotland) Act 1973. Further significant alterations were made in England by the Local Government Acts of 1985 and 1992.

The structure in England was based on two tiers of local authorities (county councils and district councils) in the non-metropolitan areas; and a single tier of metropolitan councils in the six metropolitan areas of England and London borough councils in London.

Following reviews of the structure of local government in England by the Local Government Commission, 46 unitary (all-purpose) authorities were created between April 1995 and April 1998 to cover certain areas in the non-metropolitan counties. The remaining county areas continue to have two tiers of local authorities. The county and district councils in the Isle of Wight were replaced by a single unitary authority on 1 April 1995; the former counties of Avon, Cleveland, Humberside and Berkshire have been replaced by unitary authorities; and Hereford and Worcester was replaced by a new county council for Worcestershire (with district councils) and a unitary authority for Herefordshire.

The Local Government (Wales) Act 1994 and the Local Government etc. (Scotland) Act 1994 abolished the two-tier structure in Wales and Scotland with effect from 1 April 1996, replacing it with a single tier of unitary authorities.

Local authorities are empowered or required by various Acts of Parliament to carry out functions in their areas. The legislation concerned comprises public general Acts and 'local' Acts which local authorities have promoted as private bills.

ELECTIONS

Local elections are normally held on the first Thursday in May. Generally, all British subjects, citizens of the Republic of Ireland, Commonwealth and other European Union citizens who are 18 years or over and resident on the qualifying date in the area for which the election is being held, are entitled to vote at local government elections. A register of electors is prepared and published annually by local electoral registration officers.

A returning officer has the overall responsibility for an election. Voting takes place at polling stations, arranged by the local authority and under the supervision of a presiding officer specially appointed for the purpose. Candidates, who are subject to various statutory qualifications and disqualifications designed to ensure that they are suitable persons to hold office, must be nominated by electors for the electoral area concerned.

In England, the Local Government Commission is responsible for carrying out periodic reviews of electoral arrangements and making recommendations to the Secretary of State for changes found necessary. In Wales and Scotland these matters are the responsibility of the Local Government Boundary Commission for Wales and the Local Boundary Commission for Scotland respectively.

LOCAL GOVERNMENT COMMISSION FOR ENGLAND, Dolphyn Court, 10–11 Great Turnstile, Lincoln's Inn Fields, London WC1V 7JU. Tel: 0171-430 8400

LOCAL GOVERNMENT BOUNDARY COMMISSION FOR WALES, 1–6 St Andrew's Place, Cardiff CF1 3BE. Tel: 01222-395031

LOCAL GOVERNMENT BOUNDARY COMMISSION FOR SCOTLAND, 3 Drumsheugh Gardens, Edinburgh EH3 7QJ. Tel: 0131-538 7510

INTERNAL ORGANIZATION

The council as a whole is the final decision-making body within any authority. Councils are free to a great extent to make their own internal organizational arrangements. The Government has published a draft Local Government (Organization and Standards) Bill, proposing new management arrangements with a separate executive arm of the council.

Normally, questions of policy are settled by the full council, while the administration of the various services is the responsibility of committees of councillors. Day-to-day decisions are delegated to the council's officers, who act within the policies laid down by the councillors.

FINANCE

Local government in England, Wales and Scotland is financed from four sources: the council tax, non-domestic rates, government grants, and income from fees and charges for services. (For arrangements in Northern Ireland, see page 526.)

COUNCIL TAX

Under the Local Government Finance Act 1992, from 1 April 1993 the council tax replaced the community charge (which had been introduced in April 1989 in Scotland and April 1990 in England and Wales in place of domestic rates).

The council tax is a local tax levied by each local council. Liability for the council tax bill usually falls on the owner-occupier or tenant of a dwelling which is their sole or main residence. Council tax bills may be reduced because of the personal circumstances of people resident in a property, and there are discounts in the case of dwellings occupied by fewer than two adults.

In England, each county council, each district council and each police authority sets its own council tax rate. The district councils collect the combined council tax, and the county councils and police authorities claim their share from the district councils' collection funds. In Wales, each unitary authority and each police authority sets its own council tax rate. The unitary authorities collect the combined council tax and the police authorities claim their share from the funds. In Scotland, each island council and unitary authority sets its own rate of council tax.

The tax relates to the value of the dwelling. Each dwelling is placed in one of eight valuation bands, ranging from A to H, based on the property's estimated market value as at 1 April 1991.

The valuation bands and ranges of values in England, Wales and Scotland are:

England

A	Up to £40,000	E	£88,001–£120,000
B	£40,001–£52,000	F	£120,001–£160,000
C	£52,001–£68,000	G	£160,001–£320,000
D	£68,001–£88,000	H	Over £320,000

Wales

A	Up to £30,000	E	£66,001–£90,000
B	£30,001–£39,000	F	£90,001–£120,000
C	£39,001–£51,000	G	£120,001–£240,000
D	£51,001–£66,000	H	Over £240,000

Scotland

A	Up to £27,000	E	£58,001–£80,000
B	£27,001–£35,000	F	£80,001–£106,000
C	£35,001–£45,000	G	£106,001–£212,000
D	£45,001–£58,000	H	Over £212,000

The council tax within a local area varies between the different bands according to proportions laid down by law. The charge attributable to each band as a proportion of the Band D charge set by the council is approximately:

A	67%	E	122%
B	78%	F	144%
C	89%	G	167%
D	100%	H	200%

The band D rate is given in the tables on pages 543–8 (England), 555 (London), 558 (Wales), and 564 (Scotland). There may be variations from the given figure within each district council area because of different parish or community precepts being levied.

NON-DOMESTIC RATES

Non-domestic (business) rates are collected by billing authorities; these are the district councils in those areas of England with two tiers of local government and unitary authorities in other parts of England, in Wales and in Scotland. In respect of England and Wales, the Local Government Finance Act 1988 provides for liability for rates to be assessed on the basis of a poundage (multiplier) tax on the rateable value of property (hereditaments). Separate multipliers are set by the Secretary of State for the Environment, Transport and the Regions in England, the National Assembly for Wales and the Scottish Executive, and rates are collected by the billing authority for the area where a property is located. Rate income collected by billing authorities is paid into a national non-domestic rating (NNDR) pool and redistributed to individual authorities on the basis of the adult population figure as prescribed by the Secretary of State for the Environment, Transport and the Regions, the National Assembly for Wales or the Scottish Executive. The rates pools are maintained separately in England, Wales and Scotland. For the years 1995–6 to 1999–2000 actual payment of rates in certain cases is subject to transitional arrangements, to phase in the larger increases and reductions in rates resulting from the effects of the 1995 revaluation.

Rates are levied in Scotland in accordance with the Local Government (Scotland) Act 1975. For 1995–6, the Secretary of State for Scotland prescribed a single non-domestic rates poundage to apply throughout the country at the same level as the uniform business rate (UBR) in England. Rate income is pooled and redistributed to local authorities on a per capita basis. For the year 1995–6 payment of rates was subject to transitional arrangements to phase in the effect of the 1995 revaluation.

Rateable values for the 1995 rating lists came into force on 1 April 1995. They are derived from the rental value of property as at 1 April 1993 and determined on certain statutory assumptions by the Valuation Office Agency in England and Wales, and by Regional Assessors in Scotland. New property which is added to the list, and significant changes to existing property, necessitate amendments to the rateable value on the same basis. Rating lists (valuation rolls in Scotland) remain in force until the next general revaluation. Such revaluations take place every five years,

the next being in 2005. New rating lists come into force on 1 April 2000 based on rental levels as at 1 April 1998.

Certain types of property are exempt from rates, e.g. agricultural land and buildings, certain businesses and places of public religious worship. Charities and other non-profit-making organizations may receive full or partial relief. Empty property is liable to pay rates at 50 per cent, except for certain specified classes which are exempt entirely.

GOVERNMENT GRANTS

In addition to specific grants in support of revenue expenditure on particular services, central government pays revenue support grant to local authorities. This grant is paid to each local authority so that if each authority spends at the level of its standard spending assessment, all authorities in the same class can set broadly the same council tax.

COMPLAINTS

Commissioners for Local Administration in England, Wales and Scotland (*see* page 317) are responsible for investigating complaints from members of the public who claim to have suffered injustice as a consequence of maladministration in local government or in certain local bodies.

The Northern Ireland Commissioner for Complaints fulfils a similar function in Northern Ireland, investigating complaints about local authorities and certain public bodies.

Complaints are made to the relevant local authority in the first instance and complainants may approach the Commissioners if not satisfied. Complaints may also be made directly to the Commissioners.

THE QUEEN'S REPRESENTATIVES

The Lord-Lieutenant of a county is the permanent local representative of the Crown in that county. The appointment of Lord-Lieutenants is now regulated by the Lieutenancies Act 1997. They are appointed by the Sovereign on the recommendation of the Prime Minister. The retirement age is 75. The office of Lord-Lieutenant dates from 1557, and its holder was originally responsible for the maintenance of order and for local defence in the county. The duties of the post include attending on royalty during official visits to the county, performing certain duties in connection with armed forces of the Crown (and in particular the reserve forces), and making presentations of honours and awards on behalf of the Crown. In England, Wales and Northern Ireland, the Lord-Lieutenant usually also holds the office of *Custos Rotulorum*. As such, he or she acts as head of the county's commission of the peace (which recommends the appointment of magistrates).

The office of Sheriff (from the Old English shire-reeve) of a county was created in the tenth century. The Sheriff was the special nominee of the Sovereign, and the office reached the peak of its influence under the Norman kings. The Provisions of Oxford (1258) laid down a yearly tenure of office. Since the mid-16th century the office has been purely civil, with military duties taken over by the Lord-Lieutenant of the county. The Sheriff (commonly known as 'High Sheriff') attends on royalty during official visits to the county, acts as the returning officer during parliamentary elections in county constituencies, attends the opening ceremony when a High Court judge goes on circuit, executes High Court writs, and appoints under-sheriffs to act as deputies. The appointments and duties of the High Sheriffs in England and Wales are laid down by the Sheriffs Act 1887.

The serving High Sheriff submits a list of names of

possible future sheriffs to a tribunal which chooses three names to put to the Sovereign. The tribunal nominates the High Sheriff annually on 12 November and the Sovereign picks the name of the Sheriff to succeed in the following year. The term of office runs from 25 March to the following 24 March (the civil and legal year before 1752). No person may be chosen twice in three years if there is any other suitable person in the county.

CIVIC DIGNITIES

District councils in England may petition for a royal charter granting borough or 'city' status to the district. Local councils in Wales may petition for a royal charter granting county borough or 'city' status to the council.

In England and Wales the chairman of a borough or county borough council may be called a mayor, and the chairman of a city council a Lord Mayor. Parish councils in England and community councils in Wales may call themselves 'town councils', in which case their chairman is the town mayor.

In Scotland the chairman of a local council may be known as a convenor; a provost is the equivalent of a mayor. The chairmen of the councils for the cities of Aberdeen, Dundee, Edinburgh and Glasgow are Lord Provosts.

ENGLAND

There are currently 34 non-metropolitan counties; all are divided into non-metropolitan districts. In addition, there are 45 unitary authorities (13 created in April 1996, 13 in April 1997 and 19 in April 1998). At present there are 238 non-metropolitan districts. The populations of most of the new unitary authorities are in the range of 100,000 to 300,000. The non-metropolitan districts have populations broadly in the range of 60,000 to 100,000; some, however, have larger populations, because of the need to avoid dividing large towns, and some in mainly rural areas have smaller populations.

The main conurbations outside Greater London – Tyne and Wear, West Midlands, Merseyside, Greater Manchester, West Yorkshire and South Yorkshire – are divided into 36 metropolitan districts, most of which have a population of over 200,000.

There are also about 10,000 parishes, in 219 of the non-metropolitan and 18 of the metropolitan districts.

ELECTIONS

For districts, non-metropolitan counties and for about 8,000 parishes, there are elected councils, consisting of directly elected councillors. The councillors elect annually one of their number as chairman.

Generally, councillors serve four years and there are no elections of district and parish councillors in county election years. In metropolitan districts, one-third of the councillors for each ward are elected each year except in the year when county elections take place elsewhere. Non-metropolitan districts can choose whether to have elections by thirds or whole council elections. In the former case, one-third of the council, as nearly as may be, is elected in each year of metropolitan district elections. If whole council elections are chosen, these are held in the year midway between county elections.

FUNCTIONS

In non-metropolitan areas, functions are divided between the districts and counties, those requiring the larger area

or population for their efficient performance going to the county. The metropolitan district councils, with the larger population in their areas, already had wider functions than non-metropolitan councils, and following abolition of the metropolitan county councils were given most of their functions also. A few functions continue to be exercised over the larger area by joint bodies, made up of councillors from each district.

The allocation of functions is as follows:

County councils: education; strategic planning; traffic, transport and highways; fire service; consumer protection; refuse disposal; smallholdings; social services; libraries

Non-metropolitan district councils: local planning; housing; highways (maintenance of certain urban roads and off-street car parks); building regulations; environmental health; refuse collection; cemeteries and crematoria

Unitary councils: their functions are all those listed above, except that the fire service is exercised by a joint body

Concurrently by county and district councils: recreation (parks, playing fields, swimming pools); museums; encouragement of the arts, tourism and industry

The Police and Magistrates Court Act 1994 set up police authorities in England and Wales separate from the local authorities.

PARISH COUNCILS

Parishes with 200 or more electors must generally have parish councils, which means that over three-quarters of the parishes have councils. A parish council comprises at least five members, the number being fixed by the district council. Elections are held every four years, at the time of the election of the district councillor for the ward including the parish. All parishes have parish meetings, comprising the electors of the parish. Where there is no council, the meeting must be held at least twice a year.

Parish council functions include: allotments; encouragement of arts and crafts; community halls, recreational facilities (e.g. open spaces, swimming pools), cemeteries and crematoria; and many minor functions. They must also be given an opportunity to comment on planning applications. They may, like county and district councils, spend limited sums for the general benefit of the parish. They levy a precept on the district councils for their funds.

The Local Government and Rating Act 1997 gave additional powers to parish councils to spend money on community transport initiatives and crime prevention equipment.

FINANCE

Aggregate external finance for 1999–2000 was originally determined at £39,545 million. Of this, specific and special grants were estimated at £5,905 million; £19,902 million was in respect of revenue support grant and £13,612 million was support from the national non-domestic rate pool. Total standard spending by local authorities considered for grant purposes was £50,639 million.

The average council taxes, expressed in terms of Band D, two-adult properties for 1999–2000, were: inner London boroughs and the City of London £679; outer London boroughs £760; metropolitan districts £878; shire areas £792. The average for England was £664.

National non-domestic rate (or uniform business rate) for 1999–2000 is 48.9p. The provisional amount estimated to be raised from central, local and Crown lists is £12,700 million. Total rateable value held on draft local authority lists at 31 December 1998 was £29,300 million. The amount to be redistributed to authorities from the pool in 1999–2000 is £13,600 million.

Under the Local Government and Housing Act 1989, local authorities have four main ways of paying for capital expenditure: borrowing and other forms of extended credit; capital grants from central government towards some types of capital expenditure; 'usable' capital receipts from the sale of land, houses and other assets; and revenue.

The amount of capital expenditure which a local authority can finance by borrowing (or other forms of credit) is effectively limited by the credit approvals issued to it by central government. Most credit approvals can be used for any local authority service; these are known as basic credit approvals. Others (supplementary credit approvals) are for particular projects or services.

Generally, the 'usable' part of a local authority's capital receipts consists of 25 per cent of receipts from the sale of council houses. The balance has to be set aside as provision for repaying debt and meeting other credit liabilities. Since 1 September 1998, local authorities have been free to use all receipts from the sale of other property and assets.

EXPENDITURE

Local authority budgeted net revenue expenditure for 1999–2000 was (1999–2000 cash prices):

Service	£m
Education	22,564
Personal social services	9,673
Police	7,078
Highway maintenance	1,741
Fire	1,497
Civil defence and other Home Office services	577
Magistrates courts	316
Public transport and parking	685
Housing benefit administration	5,693
Non-housing revenue account housing	424
Libraries, culture and heritage	934
Sport	536
Local environmental services	5,933
Other services	415
Net current expenditure	58,066
Capital charges	2,137
Capital charged to revenue	762
Other non-current expenditure	2,303
Interest receipts	−767
Gross revenue expenditure	62,502
Specific and special grants outside AEF	−8,744
Revenue expenditure	53,758
Specific and special grants inside AEF	−2,340
Net revenue expenditure	51,418

AEF = aggregate external finance

LONDON

Since the abolition of the Greater London Council in 1986, the Greater London area has not had a single local government body. The area is divided into 32 borough councils, which have a status similar to the metropolitan district councils in the rest of England, and the Corporation of the City of London.

In March 1998 the Government announced proposals for a Greater London Authority (GLA) covering the area of the 32 London boroughs and the City of London, which would comprise a directly elected mayor and a 25-member assembly. A referendum was held in London on 7 May 1998; the turnout was approximately 34 per cent, of whom 72 per cent voted in favour of the GLA. The GLA will be responsible for transport, economic development, strategic planning, culture, health, the environment, the police and fire and emergency planning. The separately elected assembly will scrutinize the mayor's activities and approve plans and budgets. Fourteen of the assembly's members will be directly elected from constituencies made up of two or three London boroughs. The 11 additional members will be elected on a London-wide basis, either as independents or from party political lists on the basis of proportional representation. Parties or independent candidates must secure at least five per cent of the vote to be entitled to additional seats. Legislation to establish the GLA was introduced in Parliament in December 1998 and the Government plans to hold the first elections for the Mayor and Assembly on 4 May 2000, with the Authority assuming its responsibilities on 3 July 2000.

LONDON BOROUGH COUNCILS

The London boroughs have whole council elections every four years, in the year immediately following the county council election year. The next elections will be in 2002.

The borough councils have responsibility for the following functions: building regulations; cemeteries and crematoria; consumer protection; education; youth employment; environmental health; electoral registration; food; drugs; housing; leisure services; libraries; local planning; local roads; museums; parking; recreation (parks, playing fields, swimming pools); refuse collection and street cleansing; social services; town planning; and traffic management.

THE CORPORATION OF LONDON
(*see also* pages 550–2)

The Corporation of London is the local authority for the City of London. Its legal definition is 'The Mayor and Commonalty and Citizens of the City of London'. It is governed by the Court of Common Council, which consists of the Lord Mayor, 24 other aldermen, and 130 common councilmen. The Lord Mayor and two sheriffs are nominated annually by the City guilds (the livery companies) and elected by the Court of Aldermen. Aldermen and councilmen are elected from the 25 wards into which the City is divided; councilmen must stand for re-election annually. The Council is a legislative assembly, and there are no political parties.

The Corporation has the same functions as the London borough councils. In addition, it runs the City of London Police; is the health authority for the Port of London; has health control of animal imports throughout Greater London, including at Heathrow airport; owns and manages public open spaces throughout Greater London; runs the Central Criminal Court; and runs Billingsgate, Smithfield and Spitalfields markets.

THE CITY GUILDS (LIVERY COMPANIES)

The livery companies of the City of London grew out of early medieval religious fraternities and began to emerge as trade and craft guilds, retaining their religious aspect, in the 12th century. From the early 14th century, only members of the trade and craft guilds could call themselves citizens of the City of London. The guilds began to be called livery companies, because of the distinctive livery worn by the most prosperous guild members on ceremonial occasions, in the late 15th century.

By the early 19th century the power of the companies within their trades had begun to wane, but those wearing the livery of a company continued to play an important role in the government of the City of London. Liverymen still have the right to nominate the Lord Mayor and sheriffs, and most members of the Court of Common Council are liverymen (*see also* page 552).

GREATER LONDON SERVICES

After the abolition of the Greater London Council (GLC) in 1986, the London boroughs took over most of its functions. Successor bodies have also been set up for certain functions. The London Residuary Body (LRB) was set up in 1986 to deal with residual matters of the GLC. It completed its work and was wound up in 1995.

WALES

The Local Government (Wales) Act 1994 abolished the two-tier structure of eight county and 37 district councils which had existed since 1974, and replaced it, from 1 April 1996, with 22 unitary authorities. The new authorities were elected in May 1995. Each unitary authority has inherited all the functions of the previous county and district councils, except fire services (which are provided by three combined fire authorities, composed of representatives of the unitary authorities) and National Parks (which are the responsibility of three independent National Park authorities).

The Police and Magistrates Courts Act 1994 set up four police authorities with effect from 1 April 1995: Dyfed-Powys, Gwent, North Wales, and South Wales.

COMMUNITY COUNCILS

In Wales community councils are the equivalent of parishes in England. Unlike England, where many areas are not in any parish, communities have been established for the whole of Wales, approximately 865 communities in all. Community meetings may be convened as and when desired.

Community councils exist in 735 communities and further councils may be established at the request of a community meeting. Community councils have broadly the same range of powers as English parish councils. Community councillors are elected at the same time as a unitary authority election and for a term of four years.

FINANCE

Aggregate external finance for 1998–9 is £2,701.9 million. This comprises revenue support grant of £1,799.9 million, specific grants of £258.9 million, support from the national non-domestic rate pool of £612 million, and £31.2 million in council tax reduction grants. Total standard spending by local authorities considered for grant purposes is £3,090.5 million.

The average Band D council tax levied in Wales for 1998–9 is £555, comprising unitary authorities £513, police authorities £57, community councils £16 and an average grant reduction of £31.

National non-domestic rates (or uniform business rate) in Wales for 1998–9 is 42.9p. The amount estimated to be raised is £612 million. Total rateable value held on local authority lists at 31 December 1997 was £1,342 million.

EXPENDITURE

Local authority budgeted net revenue expenditure for 1999–2000 was (1999–2000 cash prices):

Service	£m
Education	1,427
Personal social services	616
Police	372
Highway maintenance	145

Fire	95
Probation and other Home Office services	35
Magistrates courts	19
Public transport and parking	18
Housing and council tax benefit	360
Non-housing revenue account housing	17
Libraries, museums and art galleries	50
Swimming pools and recreation	55
Local environmental services	314
Other services	97
Net current expenditure	3,620
Capital charges	259
Capital charged to revenue	19
Other non-current expenditure	11
Interest receipts	−20
Gross revenue expenditure	3,890
Specific grants outside AEF	−459
Revenue expenditure	3,431
Specific grants inside AEF	−68
Net revenue expenditure	3,362

AEF = aggregate external finance

SCOTLAND

The Local Government etc. (Scotland) Act 1994 abolished the two-tier structure of nine regional and 53 district councils which had existed since 1975 and replaced it, from 1 April 1996, with 29 unitary authorities on the mainland; the three islands councils remained. The new authorities were elected in April 1995. Each unitary authority has inherited all the functions of the regional and district councils, except water and sewerage (now provided by three public bodies whose members were appointed by the Secretary of State for Scotland; this power has now been devolved to the Scottish Executive) and reporters panels (now a national agency).

In July 1999 the Scottish Parliament assumed responsibility for legislation on local government. The Government had established a Commission on Local Government and the Scottish Parliament (the McIntosh Commission) to make recommendations on the relationship between local authorities and the new Parliament and on increasing local authorities' accountability. The Commission reported to the First Minister of the Scottish Parliament in June 1999. Among its recommendations were that joint working agreements and arrangements be set up between the Scottish Parliament, Scottish ministers and local councils; that councils should review their management and working practices with a view to becoming more accountable; and that councils should be elected for four years by proportional representation.

ELECTIONS

The unitary authorities consist of directly elected councillors. Elections take place every three years; the next elections are in 2002. In 1999 the register showed 4,027,433 electors in Scotland.

FUNCTIONS

The functions of the councils and islands councils are: education; social work; strategic planning; the provision of infrastructure such as roads; consumer protection; flood prevention; coast protection; valuation and rating; the police and fire services; civil defence; electoral registration; public transport; registration of births, deaths and marriages;

housing; leisure and recreation; development control and building control; environmental health; licensing; allotments; public conveniences; and the administration of district courts.

COMMUNITY COUNCILS

Unlike the parish councils and community councils in England and Wales, Scottish community councils are not local authorities. Their purpose as defined in statute is to ascertain and express the views of the communities they represent, and to take in the interests of their communities such action as appears to be expedient or practicable. Over 1,000 community councils have been established under schemes drawn up by district and islands councils in Scotland.

Since April 1996 community councils have had an enhanced role, becoming statutory consultees on local planning issues and on the decentralization schemes which the new councils have to draw up for delivery of services.

FINANCE

Figures for 1998–9 show total receipts from non-domestic rates of £441,126,663 (provisional) and £1,046 million from the council tax. The unified business rate for 1998–9 was 48p for property with a rateable value of less than £10,000 and 48.9p otherwise. The average Band D council tax payable was £827.

EXPENDITURE

Local authority current expenditure supported by aggregate external finance for 1999–2000 was (1999–2000 cash prices):

Service	£m
Tourism	8
Roads and transport	355
Housing	4
Other environmental services	749
Law, order and protective services	914
Education	2,875
Arts and libraries	115
Social work services	1,172
Housing benefit administration	30
Sheltered employment	10
Consumer protection	19
Total	6,251
Total excluding housing benefits, sheltered employment and consumer protection	6,192

NORTHERN IRELAND

For the purpose of local government Northern Ireland has a system of 26 single-tier district councils.

ELECTIONS

There are 582 members of the councils, elected for periods of four years at a time on the principle of proportional representation.

FUNCTIONS

The district councils have three main roles. These are:

Executive: responsibility for a wide range of local services including building regulations; community services; consumer protection; cultural facilities; environmental health; miscellaneous licensing and registration provisions, including dog control; litter prevention; recreational and social facilities; refuse collection and disposal; street cleansing; and tourist development

Representative: nominating representatives to sit as members of the various statutory bodies responsible for the administration of regional services such as drainage, education, fire, health and personal social services, housing, and libraries

Consultative: acting as the medium through which the views of local people are expressed on the operation in their area of other regional services, notably conservation (including water supply and sewerage services), planning and roads, provided by those departments of central government which have an obligation, statutory or otherwise, to consult the district councils about proposals affecting their areas

FINANCE

Local government in Northern Ireland is funded by a system of rates (a local property tax calculated by using the rateable value of a property multiplied by an amount per pound of rateable value). Rates are collected by the Rate Collection Agency, an executive agency within the Department of the Environment for Northern Ireland. A general revaluation of non-domestic properties became effective on 1 April 1997. As a result of this, separate regional rates are now made at standard uniform amounts by the Department of Finance and Personnel for both domestic and non-domestic sectors. District councils now make their individual district rates on the same basis.

In 1997–8 approximately £495 million was raised in rates. The average domestic poundage levied was 189.59p and the average non-domestic rate poundage was 41.37p.

Political Composition of Local Councils

AS AT END MAY 1999

Abbreviations:

C.	Conservative
Com.	Communist
Dem.	Democrat
Green	Green
Ind.	Independent
Lab.	Labour
Lib.	Liberal
LD	Liberal Democrat
MK	Mebyon Kernow
NP	Non-policital/Non-party
PC	Plaid Cymru
RA	Ratepayers'/Resident's Associations
SD	Social Democrat
SNP	Scottish National Party

ENGLAND

COUNTY COUNCILS

Bedfordshire	C. 25, Lab. 14, LD 10
Buckinghamshire	C. 38, LD 10, Lab. 5, Ind. 1
Cambridgeshire	C. 33, Lab. 10, LD 16
Cheshire	Lab. 19, C. 19, LD 10
Cornwall	LD 35, Ind. 27 C. 8, Lab. 8, MK 1
Cumbria	Lab. 43, C. 24, LD 12, Ind. 4
Derbyshire	Lab. 44, C. 12, LD 6, Ind. 2
Devon	LD 30, C. 14, Lab. 4, Ind. 3, Lib. 2, Ind. LD 1
Dorset	LD 21, C. 15, Lab. 5, Ind. 1
Durham	Lab. 52, Ind. 4, C. 2, LD 2, vacant 1
East Sussex	C. 20, LD 17, Lab. 7
Essex	C. 38, Lab. 24, LD 15, Ind. 2
Gloucestershire	LD 21, C. 22, Lab. 17, Ind. 3
Hampshire	C. 42, LD 22, Lab. 8, Ind. 2
Hertfordshire	C. 39, Lab. 29, LD 9
Kent	C. 45, Lab. 23, LD 16
Lancashire	Lab. 45, C. 23, LD 7, Other 2, vacant 1
Leicestershire	C. 25, Lab. 17, LD 11, others 1
Lincolnshire	C. 43, Lab. 19, LD 11, Ind. 3
Norfolk	C. 37, Lab. 33, LD 13, Ind. 1
Northamptonshire	Lab. 38, C. 27, LD 3
Northumberland	Lab. 42, Ind.C. 14, LD 8, Ind. 1, Green 1
North Yorkshire	C. 36, Lab. 11, Ind. 8, Ind. Lab. 19
Nottinghamshire	Lab. 42, C. 17, LD 4
Oxfordshire	C. 27, Lab. 22, LD 19, Green 2
Shropshire	C. 19, LD 13, Lab. 6, others 6
Somerset	LD 37, C. 17, Lab. 3
Staffordshire	Lab. 40, C. 20, LD 2
Suffolk	Lab. 31, C. 31, LD 15, Ind. 2, vacant 1
Surrey	C. 47, LD 17, Lab. 6, Ind. 3, RA 3
Warwickshire	Lab. 31, C. 21, LD 7, Ind. 2, other 1
West Sussex	C. 38, LD 23, Lab. 9, Ind. 1
Wiltshire	C. 23, LD 19, Lab. 4, Ind. 1
Worcestershire	C. 25, Lab 21, LD 8, Ind. 1, Lib. 1, Ind. Lab. 1

UNITARY COUNCILS

Barnsley	Lab. 57, Ind. 3, C. 2, LD 2 vacant 2
Bath and North-East Somerset	LD 30, Lab. 17, C. 16, Ind.Lab. 2
Birmingham	Lab. 77, C. 20, LD 16, Ind. 3, vacant 1
Blackburn with Darwen	Lab. 43, C. 16, LD 3
Blackpool	Lab. 33, C. 8, LD 3
Bolton	Lab. 41, C. 10, LD 9
Bournemouth	LD 19, C. 26, Ind. 6, Lab. 6
Bracknell Forest	C. 22, Lab. 18
Bradford	Lab. 54, C. 26, LD 10
Brighton and Hove	Lab. 45, C. 27, Green 3, LD 3
Bristol	Lab. 37, LD 23, C. 10
Bury	Lab. 37, C. 8, LD 3
Calderdale	Lab. 20, C. 19, LD 14, Ind. 1
Coventry	Lab. 44, C. 8, others 2
Darlington	Lab. 35, C. 15, LD 2
Derby	Lab. 34, C. 6, LD 4
Doncaster	Lab. 42, LD 9, Ind. 5, C. 5, Ind. Lab. 1, other 1
Dudley	Lab. 54, C. 8, LD 10
East Riding of Yorkshire	C. 27, LD 22, Lab. 12, Ind. 4, SDP 2
Gateshead	Lab. 49, LD 16, Lib. 1
Halton	Lab. 46, LD 8, C. 1, vacant 1
Hartlepool	Lab. 30, LD 10, C. 6, Ind. 1
Herefordshire	LD 31, Ind. 16, C. 8, Lab. 2, others 2, vacant 1
Isle of Wight	LD 16, C. 15, Ind. 9, Ind. Lab. 4, Lib. 2, others 2
Kingston upon Hull	Lab. 50, Ind. Lab. 4, LD 5, C. 1
Kirklees	Lab. 35, LD 23, C. 10, Green 3, Ind. 1
Knowsley Metropolitan Borough	Lab. 64, LD 2
Leeds	Lab. 70, C. 12, LD 14, Green 1, others 2
Leicester	Lab. 30, LD 16, C. 10
Liverpool	LD 59, Lab. 29, Lib. 5, Ind. 1, others 5
Luton	Lab. 36, LD 9, C. 3
Manchester	Lab. 79, LD 19, vacant 1
Medway	Lab. 39, LD 20, C. 21, other 1
Middlesbrough	Lab. 41, LD 7, C. 4, Ind. 1
Milton Keynes	Lab. 27, LD 19, C. 4, Ind. 1
Newcastle upon Tyne	Lab. 62, LD 15, vacant 1
North-East Lincolnshire	Lab. 22, LD 5, C. 11, Ind. 4
North Lincolnshire	Lab. 23, C. 19
North Somerset	C. 32, Lab. 13, LD 11, Ind. 4, others 1
North Tyneside	Lab. 39, C. 13, LD 8
Nottingham	Lab. 48, C. 4, LD 3
Oldham	Lab. 33, LD 26, C. 1
Peterborough	Lab. 26, C. 24, Ind. Lab. 1, Lib. 3, LD 2, other 1
Plymouth	Lab. 47, C. 13
Poole	LD 19, C. 17, Lab. 3
Portsmouth	Lab. 20, C. 10, LD 9
Reading	Lab. 36, LD 6, C. 3
Redcar and Cleveland	Lab. 32, LD 11, Ind. 2
Rochdale	Lab. 35, LD 18, C. 6, vacant 1
Rotherham	Lab. 63, C. 2, LD 1

Rutland	*Ind.* 8, *LD* 4, *C.* 1, *Lab.* 2, *Green* 1, *Ind. C.* 1, *others* 3
St Helens	*Lab.* 37, *LD* 14, *C.* 3
Salford	*Lab.* 56, *LD* 4
Sandwell	*Lab.* 61, *Lib.* 9, *C.* 2
Sefton	*Lab.* 30, *LD* 24, *C.* 15
Sheffield	*LD* 47, *Lab.* 39, *C.* 1
Slough	*Lab.* 32, *C.* 6, *Lib.*3
Solihull	*C.* 24, *Lab.* 15, *LD* 11, *Ind.* 1
Southampton	*Lab.* 27, *LD* 14, *C.* 4
South Gloucestershire	*LD* 37, *Lab.* 25, *C.* 7, *vacant* 1
Southend	*C.* 19, *LD* 12, *Lab.* 8
South Tyneside	*Lab.* 51, *LD* 6, *others* 3
Stockport	*LD* 32, *Lab.* 25, *Ind.* 4, *C.* 2
Stockton-on-Tees	*Lab.* 38, *C.* 12, *LD* 5
Stoke-on-Trent	*Lab.* 48, *LD* 4, *C.* 2, *Ind.* 6
Sunderland	*Lab.* 64, *C.* 8, *LD* 2, *Lib.* 1
Swindon	*Lab.* 39, *LD* 10, *C.* 5
Tameside	*Lab.* 48, *C.* 4, *LD* 2
Telford and Wrekin	*Lab.* 38, *C.* 8, *LD* 4, *Ind. C.* 1, *Ind.* 2, *RA* 1
Thurrock	*Lab.* 45, *C.* 4
Torbay	*LD* 20, *C.* 13, *Lab.* 2, *others* 1
Trafford	*Lab.* 33, *C.* 27, *LD* 3
Wakefield	*Lab.* 58, *C.* 3, *Ind.* 2
Walsall	*Lab.* 31, *C.* 22, *Lib.* 6, *Ind.* 1
Warrington	*Lab.* 45, *LD* 11, *C.* 4
West Berkshire	*LD* 38, *C.* 14, *Ind.* 1, *vacant* 1
Wigan	*Lab.* 70, *LD* 2
Windsor and Maidenhead	*LD* 30, *C.* 20, *Ind.* 7, *Lab.* 1
Wirral	*Lab.* 39, *C.* 17, *LD* 10
Wokingham	*C.* 30, *LD* 24
Wolverhampton	*Lab.* 39, *C.* 17, *LD* 3
York	*Lab.* 27, *LD* 22, *C.* 3, *Ind.* 1

DISTRICT COUNCILS

*Denotes councils where one-third of councillors retire each year except in the year of county council elections

*Adur	*Lab.* 15, *LD* 13, *C.* 9, *RA* 2
Allerdale	*Lab.* 33, *Ind.* 3, *others* 10, *LD* 7, *vacant* 3
Alnwick	*LD* 13, *Lab.* 2, *others* 1, *C.* 2, *Ind.* 12
Amber Valley	*Lab.* 32, *C.* 11
Arun	*C.* 35, *LD* 10, *Lab.* 8, *Ind.* 2, *vacant* 1
Ashfield	*Lab.* 29, *C.* 1, *Ind.* 2, *LD* 1
Ashford	*C.* 24, *LD* 9, *Lab.* 12, *Ind. C.* 1, *Ind.* 2, *others* 1
Aylesbury Vale	*LD* 26, *C.* 24, *Ind.* 7, *Lab.* 1
Babergh	*Ind.* 13, *C.* 10, *Lab.* 5, *LD* 13, *others* 1
*Barrow-in-Furness	*Lab.* 18, *C.* 17, *others* 3
*Basildon	*Lab.* 23, *LD* 8, *C.* 11
*Basingstoke and Deane	*C.* 24, *Lab.* 15, *LD* 14, *Ind.* 3, *others* 1
*Bassetlaw	*Lab.* 32, *C.* 12, *LD* 3, *Ind.* 2, *vacant* 1
*Bedford	*Lab.* 19, *LD* 18, *C.* 9, *Ind.* 7
Berwick-upon-Tweed	*LD* 18, *Ind.* 9, *C.* 1, *Lab.* 1
Blaby	*C.* 25, *LD* 8, *Lab.* 6
Blyth Valley	*Lab.* 36, *LD* 9, *Ind.* 3, *C.* 2
Bolsover	*Lab.* 32, *Ind.* 4, *RA* 1
Boston	*Lab.* 11, *Ind.* 6, *C.* 12, *LD* 3
Braintree	*Lab.* 31, *C.* 17, *Ind.* 7, *LD* 3, *Green* 2
Breckland	*C.* 34, *Lab.* 14, *Ind.* 3, *LD* 2

*Brentwood	*LD* 25, *C.* 10, *Lab.* 2, *Lib.* 1, *Ind. C.* 1
Bridgnorth	*Ind.* 9, *Lab.* 4, *LD* 4, *Ind. C.* 4, *C.* 4, *others* 8
Broadland	*C.* 25, *Lab.* 12, *LD* 9, *Ind.* 3
Bromsgrove	*C.* 30, *Lab.* 7, *RA* 2
*Broxbourne	*C.* 33, *Lab.* 5
Broxtowe	*Lab.* 27, *C.* 10, *LD* 11, *Ind.* 1
*Burnley	*Lab.* 31, *LD* 9, *Ind.* 5, *C.* 3
*Cambridge	*Lab.* 21, *LD* 3, *C.* 18
*Cannock Chase	*Lab.* 33, *LD* 5, *C.* 3, *vacant* 1
Canterbury	*LD* 17, *Lab.* 14, *C.* 18
Caradon	*Ind.* 20, *LD* 18, *Lab.* 2, *C.* 1
*Carlisle	*C.* 28, *Lab.* 16, *Ind.* 2, *LD* 6
Carrick	*LD* 27, *Ind.* 7, *C.* 9, *Lab.* 2
Castle Morpeth	*Ind.* 12, *Lab.* 9, *C.* 4, *LD* 7, *Green* 1
Castle Point	*Lab.* 24, *C.* 15
Charnwood	*Lab.* 24, *C.* 21, *LD* 6, *Ind.* 1
Chelmsford	*LD* 28, *C.* 21, *Lab.* 5, *Ind.* 2
*Cheltenham	*C.* 18, *LD* 17, *Lab.* 1, *others* 5
*Cherwell	*C.* 26, *Lab.* 19, *LD* 5, *Ind.* 2
Chesterfield	*Lab.* 28, *LD* 19
Chester-le-Street	*Lab.* 30, *C.* 1, *Ind.* 1, *Lib.* 1
*Chester	*Lab.* 22, *LD* 18, *C.* 18, *Ind.* 2
Chichester	*C.* 29, *LD* 19, *Ind.* 2
Chiltern	*C.* 29, *LD* 19, *RA* 2
*Chorley	*Lab.* 31, *C.* 9, *LD* 6, *Ind.* 2
Christchurch	*C.* 17, *Ind.* 3, *LD* 5
*Colchester	*LD* 26, *Lab.* 15, *C.* 18, *Ind.* 1
*Congleton	*LD* 38, *Lab.* 2, *C.* 8
Copeland	*Lab.* 31, *C.* 17, *Ind.* 2, *LD* 1
Corby	*Lab.* 27, *C.* 1, *LD* 1
Cotswold	*Ind.* 15, *LD* 7, *Ind. C.* 2, *Lab.* 2, *C.* 14, *others* 5
*Craven	*C.* 19, *LD* 5, *Ind.* 10
*Crawley	*Lab.* 25, *C.* 5, *LD* 2
*Crewe and Nantwich	*Lab.* 29, *C.* 20, *LD* 5, *Ind.* 2
Dacorum	*C.* 26, *Lab.* 20, *LD* 6
Dartford	*Lab.* 28, *C.* 14, *Ind. Lab.* 1, *others* 4
*Daventry	*C.* 20, *Lab.* 13, *LD* 3, *Ind.* 2
Derbyshire Dales	*C.* 21, *LD* 9, *Lab.* 6, *Ind.* 3
Derwentside	*Lab.* 47, *Ind.* 7, *others* 1
Dover	*Lab.* 28, *C.* 26, *LD* 1, *Ind.* 1
Durham	*Lab.* 33, *LD* 13, *Ind.* 3
Easington	*Lab.* 45, *Lib.* 1, *Ind.* 4, *Ind. Lab.* 1
*Eastbourne	*LD* 15, *C.* 15
East Cambridgeshire	*LD* 20, *Ind.* 8, *NP* 4, *Lab.* 4, *C.* 1
East Devon	*C.* 39, *LD* 14, *Ind.* 5, *Lab.* 1, *Lib.* 1
East Dorset	*C.* 26, *LD* 9, *Ind.* 1
East Hampshire	*C.* 22, *LD* 17, *Ind.* 3
East Hertfordshire	*C.* 31, *LD* 9, *Lab.* 8, *Ind.* 2
*Eastleigh	*LD* 29, *Lab.* 8, *C.* 7
East Lindsey	*Ind.* 28, *Lab.* 9, *LD* 7, *C.* 6, *Green* 1, *others* 8, *vacant* 1
East Northamptonshire	*C.* 20, *Lab.* 15, *Ind.* 1
East Staffordshire	*Lab.* 28, *C.* 15, *LD* 3
Eden	*Ind.* 30, *LD* 3, *C.* 3, *Lab.* 2
*Ellesmere Port and Neston	*Lab.* 37, *C.* 5, *LD* 1
*Elmbridge	*C.* 24, *RA* 21, *LD* 8, *Lab.* 6, *Ind.* 1
*Epping Forest	*C.* 19, *LD* 15, *Lab.* 14, *others* 8, *Ind.* 3
Epsom and Ewell	*RA* 27, *LD* 9, *Lab.* 3
Erewash	*Lab.* 29, *C.* 16, *LD* 4, *Ind.* 3
*Exeter	*Lab.* 22, *LD* 8, *C.* 3, *Lib.* 3

*Fareham	C. 23, LD 14, Lab. 5
Fenland	C. 28, Lab. 7, Ind. 3, LD 1, vacant 1
Forest Heath	C. 21, Ind. 1, LD 2, Lab. 1
Forest of Dean	Lab. 30, Ind. 12, LD 6, C. 1, NP 2
Fylde	C. 21, Lab. 2, LD 3, Ind. 12, others 11
Gedling	C. 28, Lab. 18, LD 7, others 3
*Gloucester	Lab. 23, LD 8, C. 8
*Gosport	Lab. 11, C. 10, others 2, LD 7
Gravesham	Lab. 29, C. 15
*Great Yarmouth	Lab. 29, C. 19
Guildford	LD 20, C. 17, Ind. 2, Lab. 6
Hambleton	C. 35, Ind. 6, Lab. 2, LD 4
Harborough	C. 16, LD 14, Lab. 3, Ind. 4
*Harlow	Lab. 34, LD 4, C. 4
*Harrogate	LD 41, C. 15, Lab. 3
*Hart	C. 16, LD 13, Ind. 4, Ind. C. 2
*Hastings	Lab. 19, LD 11, C. 2
*Havant	C. 16, LD 11, Lab. 9, Ind. 3, Ind. Lab. 2, Lib. 1
*Hertsmere	C. 20, Lab. 13, LD 6
High Peak	Lab. 27, LD 5, C. 10, Ind. 2
Hinckley and Bosworth	LD 14, Lab. 9, C. 11
Horsham	C. 24, LD 16, Ind. 3
*Huntingdonshire	C. 36, LD 14, vacant 1, Ind. 2
*Hyndburn	Lab. 23, C. 23, Ind. C. 1
*Ipswich	Lab. 36, C. 10, Ind. 1, LD 1
Kennet	C. 20, Ind. 11, Lab. 4, LD 4, Ind. C. 1
Kerrier	Ind. 18, Lab. 11, LD 11, C. 4
Kettering	Lab. 22, C. 18, Ind. 4, LD 1
King's Lynn and West Norfolk	Lab. 27, C. 26, LD 5, Ind. 2
Lancaster	Ind. 22, Lab. 17, C. 8, LD 6, Ind. C. 1, Green 1, NP 1
Lewes	LD 30, C. 16, Ind. 1, RA 1
Lichfield	C. 29, Lab. 24, LD 2, Ind. 1
*Lincoln	Lab. 31, C. 2
*Macclesfield	C. 37, Lab. 7, LD 13, others 3
*Maidstone	LD 22, Lab. 13, C. 15, Ind. 5
Maldon	C. 17, Ind. 6, Lab. 6, Ind. C. 1
Malvern Hills	LD 21, C. 10, Ind. 8, Lab. 1, Ind.C. 2
Mansfield	Lab. 39, C. 5, LD 2
Melton	Lab. 13, C. 7, Ind. 6
Mendip	LD 16, Lab. 10, C. 18, Ind. 2
Mid Bedfordshire	C. 34, Lab. 7, Ind. 6, LD 6
Mid Devon	Ind. 18, LD 18, Lab. 1, Lib. 1, C. 2
Mid Suffolk	LD 14, C. 14, Lab. 6, Ind. 3, Ind. Lab. 2, vacant 1
*Mid Sussex	C. 29, LD 21, Ind. 2, Lab. 2
*Mole Valley	C. 17, LD 16, Ind. 7, Lab. 1
Newark and Sherwood	Lab. 26, C. 20, LD 5, Ind. 3
*Newcastle under Lyme	Lab. 36, Lib. 12, C. 7, Ind. 1
New Forest	C. 30, LD 25, Ind. 3
Northampton	Lab. 28, LD 11, C. 8
North Cornwall	Ind. 24, LD 10, C. 3, MK 1
North Devon	LD 26, Ind. 12, NP 1, C. 5
North Dorset	C. 17, LD 10, Ind. 6
North East Derbyshire	Lab. 38, C. 9, LD 3, Ind. Lab. 1, Ind. 2
*North Hertfordshire	C. 28, Lab. 18, LD 3
North Kesteven	C. 14, LD 10, Ind. 9, Lab. 7
North Norfolk	Lab. 10, LD 12, others 17, Ind. 7
North Shropshire	Ind. 9, Lab. 5, LD 1, C. 9, others 16
North Warwickshire	Ind. Lab. 22, C. 9, Lib. 2, Lab. 1
North West Leicestershire	Lab. 31, C. 8, Ind. 1
North Wiltshire	LD 26, C. 20, Lab. 4, Ind. 2
*Norwich	Lab. 33, LD 15
*Nuneaton and Bedworth	Lab. 40, C. 5
*Oadby and Wigston	LD 22, C. 4
Oswestry	Ind. 11, Lab. 6, C. 4, LD 5, Ind. Lab. 3
*Oxford	Lab. 28, LD 16, Green 7
*Pendle	LD 23, Lab. 20, C. 7, Ind. 1
*Penwith	LD 9, C. 9, Ind. 8, Lab. 5, MK 2, vacant 1
*Preston	Lab. 28, C. 13, LD 13, Ind. Lab. 2, Ind. 1
*Purbeck	C. 13, LD 5, Ind. 5, Lab. 1
*Redditch	Lab. 20, C. 6, LD 3
*Reigate and Banstead	C. 22, Lab. 13, LD 8, RA 6
Restormel	LD 17, Ind. 12, Lab. 1, C. 13, MK 1
Ribble Valley	C. 19, LD 18, Ind. 2
Richmondshire	Ind. 18, LD 9, C. 6, SDP 1
*Rochford	LD 13, Lab. 12, C. 11, RA 3, Ind. 1
*Rossendale	Lab. 21, C. 15
Rother	C. 28, LD 8, Ind. 4, Lab. 5
*Rugby	Lab. 22, C. 11, LD 7, Ind. 6, others 2
*Runnymede	C. 25, Lab. 9, Ind. 6, LD 2
Rushcliffe	C. 31, Lab. 11, LD 11, Ind. 1
*Rushmoor	C. 20, Lab. 13, LD 12
Ryedale	Ind. 6, LD 5, C. 11, Lab. 1
*St Albans	LD 21, Lab. 16, C. 21
St Edmundsbury	C. 23, Lab. 16, LD 2, Ind. 3
Salisbury	LD 16, Lab. 11, C. 27, Ind. 4
Scarborough	C. 17, Lab. 13, Ind. 14, LD 5
Sedgefield	Lab. 43, Ind. 4, LD 2
Sedgemoor	C. 31, Lab. 16, LD 2, Ind. 1
Selby	Lab. 19, C. 15, Ind. 6, vacant 1
Sevenoaks	C. 33, LD 9, Lab. 9, Ind. 2
Shepway	C. 30, LD 13, Lab. 13
Shrewsbury and Atcham	Lab. 20, LD 11, C. 13, Ind. 4
*South Bedfordshire	LD 18, Lab. 16, C. 16, Ind. 3
South Bucks	C. 27, Ind. 10, LD 3
*South Cambridgeshire	C. 18, LD 14, Lab. 8, Ind. 14, vacant 1
South Derbyshire	Lab. 24, C. 9, Ind. C. 1
South Hams	C. 29, Ind. 4, LD 4, Lab. 3
South Holland	C. 20, Ind. 10, Lab. 3, Ind. Lab. 1, LD 1, NP 3
South Kesteven	C. 29, Ind. 14, Lab. 12, LD 3
*South Lakeland	LD 22, C. 17, Lab. 9, Ind. 4
South Norfolk	LD 27, C. 16, Lab. 2, Ind. 2
South Northamptonshire	C. 28, Lab. 7, Ind. 4, LD 3
South Oxfordshire	LD 20, Lab. 7, C. 20, Ind. 3
South Ribble	Lab. 21, C. 18, LD 12, others 3
South Shropshire	Ind. 16, LD 14, Green 2, others 8
South Somerset	LD 41, C. 13, Ind. 6
South Staffordshire	C. 37, Lab. 10, LD 1, Ind. 2
Spelthorne	C. 27, Lab. 9, LD 4
*Staffordshire Moorlands	Ind. C. 17, Lab. 15, RA 11, LD 9, Ind. 3, others 12
Stafford	Lab. 28, C. 23, LD 8, Ind. C. 1
*Stevenage	Lab. 33, LD 3, C. 3
*Stratford	C. 24, LD 20, Ind. 7, Lab. 4
*Stroud	Lab. 24, C. 17, LD 5, Ind. 4, Green 4, others 1
Suffolk Coastal	C. 36, Lab. 8, LD 10, Ind. 1
Surrey Heath	C. 22 LD 7, Lab. 7
*Swale	LD 23, Lab. 17, C. 9
*Tamworth	Lab. 27, C. 2, Ind. 1

*Tandridge — *C.* 18, *LD* 17, *Lab.* 7
Taunton Deane — *LD* 23, *C.* 21, *Lab.* 5, *Ind.* 4, *Green* 1
Teesdale — *Ind.* 12, *Lab.* 10, *NP* 8, *C.* 1
Teignbridge — *Ind.* 19, *LD* 16, *C.* 19, *Lab.* 2, *others* 2
Tendring — *Lab.* 23, *Ind.* 11, *C.* 17, *LD* 9
Test Valley — *C.* 28, *LD* 15, *others* 1
Tewkesbury — *C.* 13, *Ind.* 11, *LD* 4, *Lab.* 8
Thanet — *Lab.* 35, *C.* 16, *Ind.* 3
*Three Rivers — *LD* 26, *C.* 15, *Lab.* 7
*Tonbridge and Malling — *C.* 27, *LD* 21, *Lab.* 7
Torridge — *Ind.* 20, *LD* 12, *Lab.* 2, *C.* 1, *Green* 1
*Tunbridge Wells — *C.* 28, *LD* 12, *Lab.* 7, *Ind.* 1
Tynedale — *Lab.* 14, *LD* 10, *C.* 22, *Ind.* 6
Uttlesford — *LD* 18, *C.* 16, *Ind.* 6, *Lab.* 2
Vale of White Horse — *LD* 33, *C.* 15, *Lab.* 2, *Ind.* 1
Vale Royal — *Lab.* 33, *C.* 16, *LD* 8
Wansbeck — *Lab.* 25, *LD* 20
Warwick — *Lab.* 16, *C.* 10, *LD* 13, *Ind.* 6
*Watford — *Lab.* 19, *LD* 10, *C.* 7
*Waveney — *Lab.* 38, *C.* 5, *LD* 3, *Ind.* 2
Waverley — *C.* 31, *LD* 24, *Lab.* 2
Wealden — *C.* 34, *LD* 22, *Ind.* 2
Wear Valley — *Lab.* 30, *Ind.* 5, *LD* 5
Wellingborough — *Lab.* 20, *C.* 16
*Welwyn Hatfield — *Lab.* 24, *C.* 24
West Devon — *LD* 8, *Ind.* 13, *C.* 9
West Dorset — *C.* 22, *LD* 15, *others* 14, *Lab.* 4
*West Lancashire — *Lab.* 32, *C.* 21, *Ind.* 2
*West Lindsey — *LD* 16, *Ind.* 8, *Lab.* 3, *C.* 10
*West Oxfordshire — *C.* 19, *Ind.* 10, *LD* 13, *Lab.* 7
West Somerset — *C.* 17, *Ind.* 8, *Lab.* 5, *LD* 1
West Wiltshire — *LD* 27, *C.* 10, *Lab.* 2, *Ind.* 2, *others* 2
*Weymouth and Portland — *Lab.* 15, *LD* 12, *Ind.* 6, *C.* 2
*Winchester — *LD* 34, *C.* 12, *Ind.* 5, *Lab.* 4
*Woking — *LD* 14, *C.* 13, *Lab.* 7, *Ind.* 1
*Worcester — *Lab.* 20, *C.* 11, *Ind.* 3, *LD* 2
*Worthing — *C.* 20, *LD* 16
Wychavon — *C.* 31, *LD* 11, *Lab.* 5, *Ind.* 2
Wycombe — *C.* 42, *LD* 7, *Lab.* 9, *Ind.* 2
Wyre — *C.* 35, *Lab.* 19, *LD* 2
*Wyre Forest — *Lab.* 18, *LD* 4, *C.* 5, *Lib.* 3, *Ind.* 5, *others* 7

GREATER LONDON COUNCILS

Barking and Dagenham — *Lab.* 46, *RA* 3, *LD* 2
Barnet — *C.* 28, *Lab.* 26, *LD* 6
Bexley — *C.* 32, *Lab.* 24, *LD* 6
Brent — *Lab.* 43, *C.* 19, *LD* 4
Bromley — *C.* 29, *LD* 24, *Lab.* 7
Camden — *Lab.* 42, *C.* 11, *LD* 6
City of Westminster — *C.* 47, *Lab.* 13
Croydon — *Lab.* 38, *C.* 31, *LD* 1
Ealing — *Lab.* 53, *C.* 15, *LD* 3
Enfield — *Lab.* 43, *C.* 23
Greenwich — *Lab.* 52, *C.* 8, *LD* 2
Hackney — *Lab.* 29, *LD* 16, *C.* 13, *Green* 1, *Ind.* 1
Hammersmith and Fulham — *Lab.* 35, *C.* 14, *Ind.* 1
Haringey — *Lab.* 54, *LD* 3, *C.* 2
Harrow — *Lab.* 32, *C.* 20, *Lib.* 9, *Ind.* 2
Havering — *Lab.* 30, *RA* 16, *C.* 14, *LD* 3
Hillingdon — *C.* 33, *Lab.* 32, *LD* 4
Hounslow — *Lab.* 44, *C.* 11, *LD* 4, *Ind. Lab.* 1
Islington — *Lab.* 26, *LD* 26

Kensington and Chelsea — *C.* 39, *Lab.* 15
Kingston upon Thames — *C.* 21, *LD* 19, *Lab.* 10
Lambeth — *Lab.* 41, *LD* 18, *C.* 5
Lewisham — *Lab.* 59, *LD* 4, *C.* 2, *others* 1, *vacant* 1
Merton — *Lab.* 39, *C.* 12, *Ind.* 3, *LD* 3
Newham — *Lab.* 59, *Ind. Lab.* 1
Redbridge — *Lab.* 29, *C.* 24, *LD* 9
Richmond upon Thames — *LD* 34, *C.* 14, *Lab.* 4
Southwark — *Lab.* 32, *LD* 27, *C.* 4, *Ind.* 1
Sutton — *LD* 46, *C.* 5, *Lab.* 5
Tower Hamlets — *Lab.* 41, *LD* 9
Waltham Forest — *Lab.* 30, *C.* 14, *LD* 12, *Ind. C.* 1
Wandsworth — *C.* 50, *Lab.* 11

WALES

Anglesey — *Ind.* 27, *PC* 9, *Lab.* 4
Blaenau Gwent — *Lab.* 34, *RA* 4, *Ind.* 2, *Lib.* 1, *Ind. Lab.* 1
Bridgend — *Lab.* 42, *Ind.* 3, *C.* 1, *LD* 5, *Ind. Lab.* 1, *PC* 2
Caerphilly — *PC* 39, *Lab.* 28, *Ind.* 3, *LD* 3
Cardiff — *Lab.* 50, *LD* 18, *C.* 5, *PC* 1, *Ind. Lab.* 1
Carmarthenshire — *Lab.* 28, *Ind.* 25, *PC* 14, *Ind. Lab* 4, *RA* 2, *LD* 1
Ceredigion — *Ind.* 20, *LD* 7, *PC* 14, *Lab.* 1, *others* 2
Conwy — *Lab.* 19, *C.* 5, *Ind.* 14, *LD* 14, *PC* 7
Denbighshire — *Ind.* 17, *Lab.* 13, *PC* 8, *C.* 2, *LD* 1, *others* 5, *vacant* 1
Flintshire — *Lab.* 42, *LD* 7, *PC* 2, *others* 19
Gwynedd — *PC* 44, *Ind.* 19, *Lab.* 12, *LD* 6, *others* 2
Merthyr Tydfil — *Lab.* 16, *Ind.* 13, *PC* 4
Monmouthshire — *C.* 19, *Lab.* 18, *Ind.* 4, *LD* 1
Neath Port Talbot — *Lab.* 40, *PC* 10, *RA* 5, *Ind.* 3, *LD* 2, *SDP* 3, *Ind.Lab.* 1
Newport — *Lab.* 40, *C.* 5, *others* 2
Pembrokeshire — *Ind.* 38, *Lab.* 13, *LD* 3, *PC* 2, *vacant* 1, *C.* 3
Powys — *Ind.* 57, *Lab.* 7, *LD* 8, *C.* 1
Rhondda, Cynon, Taff — *PC* 42, *Lab.* 26, *Ind.* 5, *LD* 2
Swansea — *Lab.* 47, *Ind.* 8, *LD* 10, *C.* 4, *PC* 2, *others* 1
Torfaen — *Lab.* 39, *C.* 1, *Ind.* 3, *LD* 1
Vale of Glamorgan — *C.* 22, *Lab.* 19, *PC* 6
Wrexham — *Lab.* 26, *C.* 4, *Ind.* 8, *others* 2, *Ind. Lab.* 5, *LD* 7

SCOTLAND

Aberdeen City — *Lab.* 22, *LD* 12, *C.* 6, *SNP* 3
Aberdeenshire — *LD* 28, *SNP* 23, *Ind.* 10, *C.* 7
Angus — *SNP* 21, *Ind.* 3, *C.* 2, *LD* 2, *Lab.*1
Argyll and Bute — *Ind.* 19, *LD* 6, *SNP* 5, *C.* 4, *Lab.* 1, *NP* 1
City of Edinburgh — *Lab.* 31, *C.* 13, *LD* 13, *SNP* 1
Clackmannanshire — *SNP* 9, *Lab.* 8, *Com.*1
Dumfries and Galloway — *Ind.* 15, *Lab.* 13, *C.* 8, *LD* 6, *SNP* 5
Dundee City — *Lab.* 14, *SNP* 10, *C.* 4, *Ind. Lab.* 1

East Ayrshire	*Lab.* 17, *SNP* 14, *C.* 1
East Dunbartonshire	*Lab.* 11, *LD* 10, *C.* 3
East Lothian	*Lab.* 17, *C.* 5, *SNP* 1
East Renfrewshire	*Lab.* 9, *C.* 8, *LD* 2, *RA* 1
Eilean Siar/Western Isles	*NP* 22, *Lab.* 6, *SNP* 3
Falkirk	*Lab.* 15, *SNP* 9, *Ind.* 5, *C.* 2, *Ind. Lab.* 1
Fife	*Lab.* 43, *LD* 21, *SNP* 9, *Ind.* 2, *C.* 1, *Comm.* 1, *Dem. Left* 1
Glasgow City	*Lab.* 74, *SNP* 2, *C.* 1, *LD* 1, *other* 1
Highland	*Ind.* 50, *LD* 12, *Lab.* 10, *SNP* 8
Inverclyde	*Lab.* 11, *LD* 8, *C.* 1
Midlothian	*Lab.* 17, *LD* 1
Moray	*Ind.* 13, *Lab.* 6, *LD* 2, *SNP* 2, *Scottish Ind.* 2, *C.* 1
North Ayrshire	*Lab.* 25, *C.* 2, *SNP* 2, *Ind.* 1
North Lanarkshire	*Lab.* 56, *SNP* 12, *Ind.* 2
Orkney Islands	*Ind.* 20, *vacant* 1
Perth and Kinross	*SNP* 16, *C.* 11, *Lab.* 6, *LD* 6, *Ind.* 2
Renfrewshire	*Lab.* 21, *SNP* 15, *LD* 3, *C.* 1
Scottish Borders	*Ind.* 14, *LD* 14, *SNP* 4, *Lab.* 1, *C.* 1
Shetland Islands	*Ind.* 13, *LD* 8, *Ind. LD* 1
South Ayrshire	*Lab.* 17, *C.* 13
South Lanarkshire	*Lab.* 54, *SNP* 10, *C.* 2, *LD* 1
Stirling	*Lab.* 11, *C.* 9, *SNP* 2
West Dunbartonshire	*Lab.* 14, *SNP* 7, *Ind.* 1
West Lothian	*Lab.* 20, *SNP* 11, *C.* 1

England

The Kingdom of England lies between 55° 46' and 49° 57' 30" N. latitude (from a few miles north of the mouth of the Tweed to the Lizard), and between 1° 46' E. and 5° 43' W. (from Lowestoft to Land's End). England is bounded on the north by the Cheviot Hills; on the south by the English Channel; on the east by the Straits of Dover (Pas de Calais) and the North Sea; and on the west by the Atlantic Ocean, Wales and the Irish Sea. It has a total area of 50,351 sq. miles (130,410 sq. km): land 50,058 sq. miles (129,652 sq. km); inland water 293 sq. miles (758 sq. km).

POPULATION

The population at the 1991 census was 47,055,204 (males 22,812,889; females 24,242,315). The average density of the population in 1991 was 3.6 persons per hectare.

FLAG

The flag of England is the cross of St George, a red cross on a white field (cross gules in a field argent). The cross of St George, the patron saint of England, has been used since the 13th century.

RELIEF

There is a marked division between the upland and lowland areas of England. In the extreme north the Cheviot Hills (highest point, The Cheviot, 2,674 ft) form a natural boundary with Scotland. Running south from the Cheviots, though divided from them by the Tyne Gap, is the Pennine range (highest point, Cross Fell, 2,930 ft), the main orological feature of the country. The Pennines culminate in the Peak District of Derbyshire (Kinder Scout, 2,088 ft). West of the Pennines are the Cumbrian mountains, which include Scafell Pike (3,210 ft), the highest peak in England, and to the east are the Yorkshire Moors, their highest point being Urra Moor (1,490 ft).

In the west, the foothills of the Welsh mountains extend into the bordering English counties of Shropshire (the Wrekin, 1,334 ft; Long Mynd, 1,694 ft) and Hereford and Worcester (the Malvern Hills–Worcestershire Beacon, 1,394 ft). Extensive areas of highland and moorland are also to be found in the south-western peninsula formed by Somerset, Devon and Cornwall: principally Exmoor (Dunkery Beacon, 1,704 ft), Dartmoor (High Willhays, 2,038 ft) and Bodmin Moor (Brown Willy, 1,377 ft). Ranges of low, undulating hills run across the south of the country, including the Cotswolds in the Midlands and south-west, the Chilterns to the north of London, and the North (Kent) and South (Sussex) Downs of the south-east coastal areas.

The lowlands of England lie in the Vale of York, East Anglia and the area around the Wash. The lowest-lying are the Cambridgeshire Fens in the valleys of the Great Ouse and the River Nene, which are below sea-level in places. Since the 17th century extensive drainage has brought much of the Fens under cultivation. The North Sea coast between the Thames and the Humber, low-lying and formed of sand and shingle for the most part, is subject to erosion and defences against further incursion have been built along many stretches.

HYDROGRAPHY

The Severn is the longest river in Great Britain, rising in the north-eastern slopes of Plynlimon (Wales) and entering England in Shropshire with a total length of 220 miles (354 km) from its source to its outflow into the Bristol Channel, where it receives on the east the Bristol Avon, and on the

west the Wye, its other tributaries being the Vyrnwy, Tern, Stour, Teme and Upper (or Warwickshire) Avon. The Severn is tidal below Gloucester, and a high bore or tidal wave sometimes reverses the flow as high as Tewkesbury (13½ miles above Gloucester). The scenery of the greater part of the river is very picturesque and beautiful, and the Severn is a noted salmon river, some of its tributaries being famous for trout. Navigation is assisted by the Gloucester and Berkeley Ship Canal (16¾ miles), which admits vessels of 350 tons to Gloucester. The Severn Tunnel was begun in 1873 and completed in 1886 at a cost of £2 million and after many difficulties from flooding. It is 4 miles 628 yards in length (of which 2¼ miles are under the river). The Severn road bridge between Haysgate, Gwent, and Almondsbury, Glos, with a centre span of 3,240 ft, was opened in 1966.

The longest river wholly in England is the Thames, with a total length of 215 miles (346 km) from its source in the Cotswold hills to the Nore, and is navigable by ocean-going ships to London Bridge. The Thames is tidal to Teddington (69 miles from its mouth) and forms county boundaries almost throughout its course; on its banks are situated London, Windsor Castle, the oldest royal residence still in regular use, Eton College and Oxford, the oldest university in the kingdom.

Of the remaining English rivers, those flowing into the North Sea are the Tyne, Wear, Tees, Ouse and Trent from the Pennine Range, the Great Ouse (160 miles), which rises in Northamptonshire, and the Orwell and Stour from the hills of East Anglia. Flowing into the English Channel are the Sussex Ouse from the Weald, the Itchen from the Hampshire Hills, and the Axe, Teign, Dart, Tamar and Exe from the Devonian hills. Flowing into the Irish Sea are the Mersey, Ribble and Eden from the western slopes of the Pennines and the Derwent from the Cumbrian mountains.

The English Lakes, noteworthy for their picturesque scenery and poetic associations, lie in Cumbria, the largest being Windermere (10 miles long), Ullswater and Derwent Water.

ISLANDS

The Isle of Wight is separated from Hampshire by the Solent. The capital, Newport, stands at the head of the estuary of the Medina, Cowes (at the mouth) being the chief port. Other centres are Ryde, Sandown, Shanklin, Ventnor, Freshwater, Yarmouth, Totland Bay, Seaview and Bembridge.

Lundy (the name means Puffin Island), 11 miles north-west of Hartland Point, Devon, is about two miles long and about half a mile wide on average, with a total area of about 1,116 acres, and a population of about 20. It became the property of the National Trust in 1969 and is now principally a bird sanctuary.

The Isles of Scilly consist of about 140 islands and skerries (total area, 6 sq. miles/10 sq. km) situated 28 miles south-west of Land's End. Only five are inhabited: St Mary's, St Agnes, Bryher, Tresco and St Martin's. The population is 1,978. The entire group has been designated a Conservation Area, a Heritage Coast, and an Area of Outstanding Natural Beauty, and has been given National Nature Reserve status by the Nature Conservancy Council because of its unique flora and fauna. Tourism and the winter/spring flower trade for the home market form the basis of the economy of the Isles. The island group is a recognized rural development area.

EARLY HISTORY

Archaeological evidence suggests that England has been inhabited since at least the Palaeolithic period, though the extent of the various Palaeolithic cultures was dependent upon the degree of glaciation. The succeeding Neolithic and Bronze Age cultures have left abundant remains throughout the country, the best-known of these being the henges and stone circles of Stonehenge (ten miles north of Salisbury, Wilts) and Avebury (Wilts), both of which are believed to have been of religious significance. In the latter part of the Bronze Age the Goidels, a people of Celtic race, and in the Iron Age other Celtic races of Brythons and Belgae, invaded the country and brought with them Celtic civilization and dialects, place names in England bearing witness to the spread of the invasion over the whole kingdom.

THE ROMAN CONQUEST

The Roman conquest of Gaul (57–50 BC) brought Britain into close contact with Roman civilization, but although Julius Caesar raided the south of Britain in 55 BC and 54 BC, conquest was not undertaken until nearly 100 years later. In AD 43 the Emperor Claudius dispatched Aulus Plautius, with a well-equipped force of 40,000, and himself followed with reinforcements in the same year. Success was delayed by the resistance of Caratacus (Caractacus), the British leader from AD 48–51, who was finally captured and sent to Rome, and by a great revolt in AD 61 led by Boudicca (Boadicea), Queen of the Iceni; but the south of Britain was secured by AD 70, and Wales and the area north to the Tyne by about AD 80.

In AD 122, the Emperor Hadrian visited Britain and built a continuous rampart, since known as Hadrian's Wall, from Wallsend to Bowness (Tyne to Solway). The work was entrusted by the Emperor Hadrian to Aulus Platorius Nepos, legate of Britain from AD 122 to 126, and it was intended to form the northern frontier of the Roman Empire.

The Romans administered Britain as a province under a Governor, with a well-defined system of local government, each Roman municipality ruling itself and its surrounding territory, while London was the centre of the road system and the seat of the financial officials of the Province of Britain. Colchester, Lincoln, York, Gloucester and St Albans stand on the sites of five Roman municipalities, and Wroxeter, Caerleon, Chester, Lincoln and York were at various times the sites of legionary fortresses. Well-preserved Roman towns have been uncovered at or near Silchester (*Calleva Atrebatum*), ten miles south of Reading, Wroxeter (*Viroconium Cornoviorum*), near Shrewsbury, and St Albans (*Verulamium*) in Hertfordshire.

Four main groups of roads radiated from London, and a fifth (the Fosse) ran obliquely from Lincoln through Leicester, Cirencester and Bath to Exeter. Of the four groups radiating from London, one ran south-east to Canterbury and the coast of Kent, a second to Silchester and thence to parts of western Britain and south Wales, a third (later known as Watling Street) ran through Verulamium to Chester, with various branches, and the fourth reached Colchester, Lincoln, York and the eastern counties.

In the fourth century Britain was subject to raids along the east coast by Saxon pirates, which led to the establishment of a system of coastal defences from the Wash to Southampton Water, with forts at Brancaster, Burgh Castle (Yarmouth), Walton (Felixstowe), Bradwell, Reculver, Richborough, Dover, Lympne, Pevensey and Porchester (Portsmouth). The Irish (Scoti) and Picts in the north were also becoming more aggressive; from about AD 350 incursions became more frequent and more formidable. As the Roman Empire came under attack increasingly towards the end of the fourth century, many troops were removed from Britain for service in other parts of the empire. The island was eventually cut off from Rome by the Teutonic conquest of Gaul, and with the withdrawal of the last Roman garrison early in the fifth century, the Romano-British were left to themselves.

SAXON SETTLEMENT

According to legend, the British King Vortigern called in the Saxons to defend him against the Picts, the Saxon chieftains being Hengist and Horsa, who landed at Ebbsfleet, Kent, and established themselves in the Isle of Thanet; but the events during the one and a half centuries between the final break with Rome and the re-establishment of Christianity are unclear. However, it would appear that in the course of this period the raids turned into large-scale settlement by invaders traditionally known as Angles (England north of the Wash and East Anglia), Saxons (Essex and southern England) and Jutes (Kent and the Weald), which pushed the Romano-British into the mountainous areas of the north and west, Celtic culture outside Wales and Cornwall surviving only in topographical names. Various kingdoms were established at this time which attempted to claim overlordship of the whole country, hegemony finally being achieved by Wessex (capital, Winchester) in the ninth century. This century also saw the beginning of raids by the Vikings (Danes), which were resisted by Alfred the Great (871–899), who fixed a limit to the advance of Danish settlement by the Treaty of Wedmore (878), giving them the area north and east of Watling Street, on condition that they adopt Christianity.

In the tenth century the kings of Wessex recovered the whole of England from the Danes, but subsequent rulers were unable to resist a second wave of invaders. England paid tribute (*Danegeld*) for many years, and was invaded in 1013 by the Danes and ruled by Danish kings from 1016 until 1042, when Edward the Confessor was recalled from exile in Normandy. On Edward's death in 1066 Harold Godwinson (brother-in-law of Edward and son of Earl Godwin of Wessex) was chosen King of England. After defeating (at Stamford Bridge, Yorkshire, 25 September) an invading army under Harald Hadraada, King of Norway (aided by the outlawed Earl Tostig of Northumbria, Harold's brother), Harold was himself defeated at the Battle of Hastings on 14 October 1066, and the Norman conquest secured the throne of England for Duke William of Normandy, a cousin of Edward the Confessor.

CHRISTIANITY

Christianity reached the Roman province of Britain from Gaul in the third century (or possibly earlier); Alban, traditionally Britain's first martyr, was put to death as a Christian during the persecution of Diocletian (22 June 303), at his native town Verulamium; and the Bishops of Londinium, Eboracum (York), and Lindum (Lincoln) attended the Council of Arles in 314. However, the Anglo-Saxon invasions submerged the Christian religion in England until the sixth century when conversion was undertaken in the north from 563 by Celtic missionaries from Ireland led by St Columba, and in the south by a mission sent from Rome in 597 which was led by St Augustine, who became the first archbishop of Canterbury. England appears to have been converted again by the end of the seventh century and followed, after the Council of Whitby in 663, the practices of the Roman Church, which brought the kingdom into the mainstream of European thought and culture.

PRINCIPAL CITIES

BIRMINGHAM

Birmingham is Britain's second city. It is a focal point in national communications networks with a rapidly expanding international airport. The generally accepted derivation of 'Birmingham' is the *ham* (dwelling-place) of the *ing* (family) of *Beorma*, presumed to have been Saxon. During the Industrial Revolution the town grew into a major manufacturing centre and in 1889 was granted city status.

Despite the decline in manufacturing, Birmingham is still a major hardware trade and motor component industry centre. As well as the National Exhibition Centre and the Aston Science Park, recent developments include the International Convention Centre, the National Indoor Arena and Brindleyplace.

The principal buildings are the Town Hall (1834–50); the Council House (1879); Victoria Law Courts (1891); Birmingham University (1906–9); the 13th-century Church of St Martin-in-the-Bull-Ring (rebuilt 1873); Our Lady, Help of Christians Church; the Cathedral (formerly St Philip's Church) (1711) and the Roman Catholic Cathedral of St Chad (1839–41).

BRADFORD

Bradford lies on the southern edge of the Yorkshire Dales National Park, including within its boundaries the village of Haworth, home of the Brontë sisters, and Ilkley Moor.

Originally a Saxon township, Bradford received a market charter in 1251 but developed only slowly until the industrialization of the textile industry brought rapid growth during the 19th century; it was granted its city charter in 1897. The prosperity of that period is reflected in much of the city's architecture, particularly the public buildings: City Hall (1873), Wool Exchange (1867), St George's Hall (Concert Hall, 1853), Cartwright Hall (Art Gallery, 1904) and the Technical College (1882). Other chief buildings are the Cathedral (15th century) and Bolling Hall (14th century).

Textiles still play an important part in the city's economy but industry is now more broadly based, including engineering, micro-electronics, printing and chemicals. The city has a strong financial services sector, and a growing tourism industry.

BRISTOL

Bristol was a Royal Borough before the Norman Conquest. The earliest form of the name is *Bricgstow*. In 1373 Edward III granted Bristol county status.

The chief buildings include the 12th-century Cathedral (with later additions), with Norman chapter house and gateway, the 14th-century Church of St Mary Redcliffe, Wesley's Chapel, Broadmead, the Merchant Venturers' Almshouses, the Council House (1956), Guildhall, Exchange (erected from the designs of John Wood in 1743), Cabot Tower, the University and Clifton College. The Roman Catholic Cathedral at Clifton was opened in 1973.

The Clifton Suspension Bridge, with a span of 702 feet over the Avon, was projected by Brunel in 1836 but was not completed until 1864. Brunel's SS *Great Britain*, the first ocean-going propeller-driven ship, is now being restored in the City Docks from where she was launched in 1843. The docks themselves have been extensively restored and redeveloped and are becoming a focus for the arts and recreation.

CAMBRIDGE

Cambridge, a settlement far older than its ancient University, lies on the River Cam or Granta. The city is a county town and regional headquarters. Its industries include electronics, high technology research and development, and biotechnology. Among its open spaces are Jesus Green, Sheep's Green, Coe Fen, Parker's Piece, Christ's Pieces, the University Botanic Garden, and the Backs, or lawns and gardens through which the Cam winds behind the principal line of college buildings. East of the Cam, King's Parade, upon which stand Great St Mary's Church, Gibbs' Senate House and King's College Chapel with Wilkins' screen, joins Trumpington Street to form one of the most beautiful throughfares in Europe.

University and college buildings provide the outstanding features of Cambridge architecture but several churches (especially St Benet's, the oldest building in the city, and St Sepulchre's, the Round Church) are also notable. The Guildhall (1939) stands on a site of which at least part has held municipal buildings since 1224.

CANTERBURY

Canterbury, the Metropolitan City of the Anglican Communion, dates back to prehistoric times. It was the Roman *Durovernum Cantiacorum* and the Saxon *Cant-wara-byrig* (stronghold of the men of Kent). Here in 597 St Augustine began the conversion of the English to Christianity, when Ethelbert, King of Kent, was baptized.

Of the Benedictine St Augustine's Abbey, burial place of the Jutish Kings of Kent (whose capital Canterbury was), only ruins remain. St Martin's Church, on the eastern outskirts of the city, is stated by Bede to have been the place of worship of Queen Bertha, the Christian wife of King Ethelbert, before the advent of St Augustine.

In 1170 the rivalry of Church and State culminated in the murder in Canterbury Cathedral, by Henry II's knights, of Archbishop Thomas Becket. His shrine became a great centre of pilgrimage, as described in Chaucer's *Canterbury Tales*. After the Reformation pilgrimages ceased, but the prosperity of the city was strengthened by an influx of Huguenot refugees, who introduced weaving. The poet and playwright Christopher Marlowe was born and reared in Canterbury, and there are also literary associations with Defoe, Dickens, Joseph Conrad and Somerset Maugham.

The Cathedral, with architecture ranging from the 11th to the 15th centuries, is world famous. Modern pilgrims are attracted particularly to the Martyrdom, the Black Prince's Tomb, the Warriors' Chapel and the many examples of medieval stained glass.

The medieval city walls are built on Roman foundations and the 14th-century West Gate is one of the finest buildings of its kind in the country.

The 1,000-seat Marlowe Theatre is a centre for the Canterbury Arts Festival each autumn.

CARLISLE

Carlisle is situated at the confluence of the River Eden and River Caldew, 309 miles north-west of London and about ten miles from the Scottish border. It was granted a charter in 1158.

The city stands at the western end of Hadrian's Wall and dates from the original Roman settlement of *Luguvalium*. Granted to Scotland in the tenth century, Carlisle is not included in the Domesday Book. William Rufus reclaimed the area in 1092 and the castle and city walls were built to guard Carlisle and the western border; the citadel is a Tudor addition to protect the south of the city. Border disputes were common until the problem of the Debateable Lands was settled in 1552. During the Civil War the city remained Royalist; in 1745 Carlisle was besieged for the last time by the Young Pretender.

The Cathedral, originally a 12th-century Augustinian priory, was enlarged in the 13th and 14th centuries after the diocese was created in 1133. To the south is a restored Tithe Barn and nearby the 18th-century church of St Cuthbert, the third to stand on a site dating from the seventh century.

Carlisle is the major shopping, commercial and agricultural centre for the area, and industries include the manufacture of metal goods, biscuits and textiles. However, the largest employer is the services sector, notably in central and local government, retailing and transport. The city has an important communications position at the centre of a network of major roads, as a stage on the main west coast rail services, and with its own airport at Crosby-on-Eden.

CHESTER

Chester is situated on the River Dee, and was granted borough and city status in 1974. Its recorded history dates from the first century when the Romans founded the fortress of *Deva*. The city's name is derived from the Latin *castra* (a camp or encampment). During the Middle Ages, Chester was the principal port of north-west England but declined with the silting of the Dee estuary and competition from Liverpool. The city was also an important military centre, notably during Edward I's Welsh campaigns and the Elizabethan Irish campaigns. During the Civil War, Chester supported the King and was besieged from 1643 to 1646. Chester's first charter was granted *c.* 1175 and the city was incorporated in 1506. The office of Sheriff is the earliest created in the country (*c.* 1120s), and in 1992 the Mayor was granted the title of Lord Mayor. He/she also enjoys the title 'Admiral of the Dee'.

The city's architectural features include the city walls (an almost complete two-mile circuit), the unique 13th-century Rows (covered galleries above the street-level shops), the Victorian Gothic Town Hall (1869), the Castle (rebuilt 1788 and 1822) and numerous half-timbered buildings. The Cathedral was a Benedictine abbey until the Dissolution. Remaining monastic buildings include the chapter house, refectory and cloisters and there is a modern free-standing bell tower. The Norman church of St John the Baptist was a cathedral church in the early Middle Ages.

Chester is a thriving retail, business and tourist centre.

COVENTRY

Coventry is an important industrial centre, producing vehicles, machine tools, agricultural machinery, man-made fibres, aerospace components and telecommunications equipment. New investment has come from financial services, power transmission, professional services, leisure and education.

The city owes its beginning to Leofric, Earl of Mercia, and his wife Godiva who, in 1043, founded a Benedictine monastery. The guildhall of St Mary dates from the 14th century, three of the city's churches date from the 14th and 15th centuries, and 16th-century almshouses may still be seen. Coventry's first cathedral was destroyed at the Reformation, its second in the 1940 blitz (the walls and spire remain) and the new cathedral designed by Sir Basil Spence, consecrated in 1962, now draws numerous visitors.

Coventry is the home of the University of Warwick and its Science Park, Coventry University, the Westwood Business Park, the Cable and Wireless College, the Museum of British Road Transport and the Coventry Arena.

DERBY

Derby stands on the banks of the River Derwent, and its name dates back to 880 when the Danes settled in the locality and changed the original Saxon name of *Northworthy* to *Deoraby*.

Derby has a wide range of industries including aero engines, cars, pipework, specialized mechanical engineering equipment, textiles, chemicals, plastics and the Royal Crown Derby porcelain. The city is an established railway centre with rail research, engineering, safety testing, infrastructure and train-operating companies.

Buildings of interest include St Peter's Church and the Old Abbey Building (14th century), the Cathedral (1525), St Mary's Roman Catholic Church (1839) and the Industrial Museum, formerly the Old Silk Mill (1721). The traditional city centre is complemented by the Eagle Centre and 'out-of-centre' retail developments. In addition to the Derby Playhouse, the Assembly Rooms are a multi-purpose venue.

The first charter granting a Mayor and Aldermen was that of Charles I in 1637. Previous charters date back to 1154. It was granted city status in 1977.

DURHAM

The city of Durham is a district in the county of Durham and a major tourist attraction because of its prominent Norman Cathedral and Castle set high on a wooded peninsula overlooking the River Wear. The Cathedral was founded as a shrine for the body of St Cuthbert in 995. The present building dates from 1093 and among its many treasures is the tomb of the Venerable Bede (673–735). Durham's Prince Bishops had unique powers up to 1836, being lay rulers as well as religious leaders. As a palatinate Durham could have its own army, nobility, coinage and courts. The Castle was the main seat of the Prince Bishops for nearly 800 years; it is now used as a college by the University. The University, founded on the initiative of Bishop William Van Mildert, is England's third oldest.

Among other buildings of interest is the Guildhall in the Market Place which dates originally from the 14th century. Work has been carried out to conserve this area as part of the city's contribution to the Council of Europe's Urban Renaissance Campaign. Annual events include Durham's Regatta in June (claimed to be the oldest rowing event in Britain) and the Annual Gala (formerly Durham Miners' Gala) in July.

The economy has undergone a significant change with the replacement of mining as the dominant industry by 'white collar' employment. Although still a predominantly rural area, the industrial and commercial sector is growing and a wide range of manufacturing and service industries are based on industrial estates in and around the city. A research and development centre, linked to the University, also plays an important role in the local economy.

EXETER

Exeter lies on the River Exe ten miles from the sea. It was granted a charter by Henry II. The Romans founded *Isca Dumnoniorum* in the first century AD, and in the third century a stone wall (much of which remains) was built, providing protection against Saxon, and then Danish invasions. After the Conquest, the city led resistance to William in the west until reduced by siege. The Normans built the ringwork castle of Rougemont, the gatehouse and one tower of which remain, although the rest was pulled down in 1784. The first bridge across the Exe was built in the early 13th century. The city's main port was situated downstream at Topsham until the construction in the 1560s of the first true canal in England, the redevelopment of which in 1700 brought seaborne trade direct to the city. Exeter was the Royalist headquarters in the west during the Civil War.

The diocese of Exeter was established by Edward the Confessor in 1050, although a minster existed near the Cathedral site from the late seventh century. A new cathedral was built in the 12th century but the present building, which incorporates the Norman Towers, was begun c. 1275 and completed about a century later. The Guildhall dates from the 12th century and there are many other medieval buildings in the city, as well as architecture in the Georgian and Regency styles, and the Custom House (1680). Damage suffered by bombing in 1942 led to the redevelopment of the city centre.

Exeter's prosperity from medieval times was based on trade in wool and woollen cloth (commemorated by Tuckers Hall), which flourished until the late 18th century when export trade was hit by the French wars. Subsequently Exeter has developed as an administrative and commercial centre, notably in the distributive trades, light manufacturing industries and tourism.

KINGSTON UPON HULL

Hull (officially Kingston upon Hull) lies at the junction of the River Hull with the Humber, 22 miles from the North Sea. It is one of the major seaports of the United Kingdom, comprising 2,000 acres in four main dock installations. The port provides a wide range of cargo services, including ro-ro and container traffic, and handles a million passengers annually on daily sailings to Rotterdam and Zeebrugge. There is a variety of manufacturing and service industries, as well as increasing tourism and conference business.

The city, restored after heavy air raid damage during the Second World War, has good office and administrative buildings, its municipal centre being the Guildhall, its educational centres the University of Hull and the University of Lincolnshire and Humberside and its religious centre the Parish Church of the Holy Trinity. The old town area has been renovated and includes a marina and shopping complex. Just west of the city is the Humber Bridge, the world's longest single-span suspension bridge.

Kingston upon Hull was so named by Edward I. City status was accorded in 1897 and the office of Mayor raised to the dignity of Lord Mayor in 1914.

LEEDS

Leeds, situated in the lower Aire Valley, is a junction for road, rail, canal and air services and an important manufacturing and commercial centre. Seventy-three per cent of employment is in services, notably the distributive trades, public administration, medical services and business services. The main manufacturing industries are mechanical engineering, printing and publishing, metal goods and furniture.

The principal buildings are the Civic Hall (1933), the Town Hall (1858), the Municipal Buildings and Art Gallery (1884) with the Henry Moore Gallery (1982), the Corn Exchange (1863) and the University. The Parish Church (St Peter's) was rebuilt in 1841; the 17th-century St John's Church has a fine interior with a famous English Renaissance screen; the last remaining 18th-century church in the city is Holy Trinity in Boar Lane (1727). Kirkstall Abbey (about three miles from the centre of the city),

founded by Henry de Lacy in 1152, is one of the most complete examples of Cistercian houses now remaining. Temple Newsam, birthplace of Lord Darnley, was acquired by the Council in 1922. The present house was largely rebuilt by Sir Arthur Ingram in about 1620. Adel Church, about five miles from the centre of the city, is a fine Norman structure. The new Royal Armouries Museum houses the collection of antique arms and armour formerly held at the Tower of London.

Leeds was first incorporated by Charles I in 1626. The earliest forms of the name are *Loidis* or *Ledes*, the origins of which are obscure.

LEICESTER

Leicester is situated geographically in the centre of England. It dates back to pre-Roman times and was one of the Five Boroughs of the Danelaw. In 1589 Queen Elizabeth I granted a charter to the city and the ancient title was confirmed by letters patent in 1919.

The principal industries are hosiery, knitwear, footwear manufacturing and engineering. The growth of Leicester as a hosiery centre increased rapidly from the introduction there of the first stocking frame in 1670 and today it has some of the largest hosiery factories in the world.

The principal buildings are the Town Hall, the New Walk Centre, the University of Leicester, De Montfort University, De Montfort Hall, one of the finest concert halls in the provinces seating over 2,750 people, and the Granby Halls, an indoor sports facility. The ancient churches of St Martin (now Leicester Cathedral), St Nicholas, St Margaret, All Saints, St Mary de Castro, and buildings such as the Guildhall, the 14th-century Newarke Gate, the Castle and the Jewry Wall Roman site still exist. The Haymarket Theatre was opened in 1973 and The Shires shopping centre in 1992.

LINCOLN

Situated 40 miles inland on the River Witham, Lincoln derives its name from a contraction of *Lindum Colonia*, the settlement founded in AD 48 by the Romans to command the crossing of Ermine Street and Fosse Way. Sections of the third-century Roman city wall can be seen, including an extant gateway (Newport Arch), and excavations have discovered traces of a sewerage system unique in Britain. The Romans also drained the surrounding fenland and created a canal system, laying the foundations of Lincoln's agricultural prosperity and also of the city's importance in the medieval wool trade as a port and Staple town.

As one of the Five Boroughs of the Danelaw, Lincoln was an important trading centre in the ninth and tenth centuries and medieval prosperity from the wool trade lasted until the 14th century, enabling local merchants to build parish churches (of which three survive), and attracting in the 12th century a Jewish community (Jew's House and Court, Aaron's House). However, the removal of the Staple to Boston in 1369 heralded a decline from which the city only recovered fully in the 19th century when improved fen drainage made Lincoln agriculturally important and improved canal and rail links led to industrial development, mainly in the manufacture of machinery, components and engineering products.

The castle was built shortly after the Conquest and is unusual in having two mounds; on one motte stands a Keep (Lucy's Tower) added in the 12th century. It currently houses one of the four surviving copies of the Magna Carta. The Cathedral was begun c. 1073 when the first Norman bishop moved the see of Lindsey to Lincoln, but was mostly destroyed by fire and earthquake in the 12th century. Rebuilding was begun by St Hugh and completed over a century later. Other notable architectural features are the 12th-century High Bridge, the oldest in Britain still to carry buildings, and the Guildhall situated above the 15th–16th-century Stonebow gateway.

LIVERPOOL

Liverpool, on the right bank of the River Mersey, three miles from the Irish Sea, is the United Kingdom's foremost port for the Atlantic trade. Tunnels link Liverpool with Birkenhead and Wallasey.

There are 2,100 acres of dockland on both sides of the river and the Gladstone and Royal Seaforth Docks can accommodate Panamax-sized vessels. Approximately 31 million tonnes of cargo is handled annually. The main cargoes are crude oil, grain, fossil fuels, edible oils, timber, scrap metal, containers and break-bulk cargo. Liverpool Free Port, Britain's largest, was opened in 1984.

Liverpool was created a free borough in 1207 and a city in 1880. From the early 18th century it expanded rapidly with the growth of industrialization and the Atlantic trade. Surviving buildings from this period include the Bluecoat Chambers (1717, formerly the Bluecoat School), the Town Hall (1754, rebuilt to the original design 1795), and buildings in Rodney Street, Canning Street and the suburbs. Notable from the 19th and 20th centuries are the Anglican Cathedral, built from the designs of Sir Giles Gilbert Scott (the foundation stone was laid in 1904, and the building was completed only in 1980), the Catholic Metropolitan Cathedral (designed by Sir Frederick Gibberd, consecrated 1967) and St George's Hall (1838–54), regarded as one of the finest modern examples of classical architecture. The refurbished Albert Dock (designed by Jesse Hartley) contains the Merseyside Maritime Museum and Tate Gallery, Liverpool.

In 1852 an Act was obtained for establishing a public library, museum and art gallery; as a result Liverpool had one of the first public libraries in the country. The Brown, Picton and Hornby libraries now form one of the country's major libraries. The Victoria Building of Liverpool University, the Royal Liver, Cunard and Mersey Docks & Harbour Company buildings at the Pier Head, the Municipal Buildings and the Philharmonic Hall are other examples of the city's fine buildings.

MANCHESTER

Manchester (the *Mamucium* of the Romans, who occupied it in AD 79) is a commercial and industrial centre with a population engaged in the engineering, chemical, clothing, food processing and textile industries and in education. Banking, insurance and a growing leisure industry are among the prime commercial activities. The city is connected with the sea by the Manchester Ship Canal, opened in 1894, $35\frac{1}{2}$ miles long, and accommodating ships up to 15,000 tons. Manchester Airport handles 15 million passengers yearly.

The principal buildings are the Town Hall, erected in 1877 from the designs of Alfred Waterhouse, with a large extension of 1938; the Royal Exchange (1869, extended 1921); the Central Library (1934); Heaton Hall; the 17th-century Chetham Library; the Rylands Library (1900), which includes the Althorp collection; the University precinct; the 15th-century Cathedral (formerly the parish church) and G-MEX exhibition centre. Recent developments include the Manchester Arena, the largest indoor arena in Europe, and the Bridgewater Hall. Manchester is the home of the Hallé Orchestra, the Royal Northern College of Music, the Royal Exchange Theatre and seven public art galleries. Metrolink, the light rail system, opened in 1992.

The Commonwealth Games are to be held in Manchester in 2002 and new sports facilities include a stadium, a swimming pool complex and the National Cycling Centre.

The town received its first charter of incorporation in 1838 and was created a city in 1853.

NEWCASTLE UPON TYNE

Newcastle upon Tyne, on the north bank of the River Tyne, is eight miles from the North Sea. A cathedral and university city, it is the administrative, commercial and cultural centre for north-east England and the principal port. It is an important manufacturing centre with a wide variety of industries.

The principal buildings include the Castle Keep (12th century), Black Gate (13th century), Blackfriars (13th century), West Walls (13th century), St Nicholas's Cathedral (15th century, fine lantern tower), St Andrew's Church (12th–14th century), St John's (14th–15th century), All Saints (1786 by Stephenson), St Mary's Roman Catholic Cathedral (1844), Trinity House (17th century), Sandhill (16th-century houses), Guildhall (Georgian), Grey Street (1834–9), Central Station (1846–50), Laing Art Gallery (1904), University of Newcastle Physics Building (1962) and Medical Building (1985), Civic Centre (1963), Central Library (1969) and Eldon Square Shopping Development (1976). Open spaces include the Town Moor (927 acres) and Jesmond Dene. Nine bridges span the Tyne at Newcastle.

The city's name is derived from the 'new castle' (1080) erected as a defence against the Scots. In 1400 it was made a county, and in 1882 a city.

NORWICH

Norwich grew from an early Anglo-Saxon settlement near the confluence of the Rivers Yare and Wensum, and now serves as provincial capital for the predominantly agricultural region of East Anglia. The name is thought to relate to the most northerly of a group of Anglo-Saxon villages or *wics*. The city's first known charter was granted in 1158 by Henry II.

Norwich serves its surrounding area as a market town and commercial centre, banking and insurance being prominent among the city's businesses. From the 14th century until the Industrial Revolution, Norwich was the regional centre of the woollen industry, but now the biggest single industry is financial services and principal trades are engineering, printing, shoemaking, double glazing, the production of chemicals and clothing, food processing and technology. Norwich is accessible to seagoing vessels by means of the River Yare, entered at Great Yarmouth, 20 miles to the east.

Among many historic buildings are the Cathedral (completed in the 12th century and surmounted by a 15th-century spire 315 feet in height), the keep of the Norman castle (now a museum and art gallery), the 15th-century flint-walled Guildhall (now a tourist information centre), some thirty medieval parish churches, St Andrew's and Blackfriars' Halls, the Tudor houses preserved in Elm Hill and the Georgian Assembly House. The University of East Anglia is on the city's western boundary.

NOTTINGHAM

Nottingham stands on the River Trent and is connected by canal with the Atlantic Ocean and the North Sea. *Snotingabam* or *Notingeham*, literally the homestead of the people of Snot, is the Anglo-Saxon name for the Celtic settlement of *Tigguocobauc*, or the house of caves. In 878,

Nottingham became one of the Five Boroughs of the Danelaw. William the Conqueror ordered the construction of Nottingham Castle, while the town itself developed rapidly under Norman rule. Its laws and rights were later formally recognized by Henry II's charter in 1155. The Castle became a favoured residence of King John. In 1642 King Charles I raised his personal standard at Nottingham Castle at the start of the Civil War.

Nottingham is home to Notts County FC (the world's oldest football league side), Nottingham Racecourse and the National Watersports Centre. The principal industries include textiles, pharmaceuticals, food manufacturing, engineering and telecommunications. There are two universities within the city boundaries.

Architecturally, Nottingham has a wealth of notable buildings, particularly those designed in the Victorian era by T. C. Hine and Watson Fothergill. The City Council owns the Castle, of Norman origin but restored in 1878, Wollaton Hall (1580–8), Newstead Abbey (home of Lord Byron), the Guildhall (1888) and Council House (1929). St Mary's, St Peter's and St Nicholas's Churches are of interest, as is the Roman Catholic Cathedral (Pugin, 1842–4).

Nottingham was granted city status in 1897.

OXFORD

Oxford is a university city, an important industrial centre, and a market town. Industry played a minor part in Oxford until the motor industry was established in 1912.

It is for its architecture that Oxford is of most interest to the visitor, its oldest specimens being the reputedly Saxon tower of St Michael's church, the remains of the Norman castle and city walls, and the Norman church at Iffley. It is chiefly famous, however, for its Gothic buildings, such as the Divinity Schools, the Old Library at Merton College, William of Wykeham's New College, Magdalen College and Christ Church and many other college buildings. Later centuries are represented by the Laudian quadrangle at St John's College, the Renaissance Sheldonian Theatre by Wren, Trinity College Chapel, and All Saints Church; Hawksmoor's mock-Gothic at All Souls College, and the 18th-century Queen's College. In addition to individual buildings, High Street and Radcliffe Square, just off it, both form architectural compositions of great beauty. Most of the Colleges have gardens, those of Magdalen, New College, St John's and Worcester being the largest.

PLYMOUTH

Plymouth is situated on the borders of Devon and Cornwall at the confluence of the Rivers Tamar and Plym. The city has a long maritime history; it was the home port of Sir Francis Drake and the starting point for his circumnavigation of the world, as well as the last port of call for the *Mayflower* when the Pilgrim Fathers sailed for the New World in 1620. Today Plymouth is host to many international yacht races. The Barbican harbour area has many Elizabethan buildings and on Plymouth Hoe stands Smeaton's lighthouse, the third to be built on the Eddystone Rocks 13 miles offshore.

The city centre was rebuilt following extensive war damage, and comprises a large shopping centre, municipal offices, law courts and public buildings. The main employment is provided at the naval base, though many industrial firms and service industries have become established in the post-war period and the city is a growing tourism centre. In 1982 the Theatre Royal was opened. In conjunction with the Cornwall County Council, the Tamar Bridge was constructed linking the city by road with Cornwall.

PORTSMOUTH

Portsmouth occupies Portsea Island, Hampshire, with boundaries extending to the mainland. It is a centre of industry and commerce, including many high technology and manufacturing industries. It is the British headquarters of several major international companies. The Royal Navy base still has a substantial work-force, although this has decreased in recent years. The commercial port and continental ferry port is owned and run by the City Council, and carries passengers and vehicles to France and northern Spain.

A major port since the 16th century, Portsmouth is also a thriving seaside resort catering for thousands of visitors annually. Among many historic attractions are Lord Nelson's flagship, HMS *Victory*, the Tudor warship *Mary Rose*, Britain's first 'ironclad' warship, HMS *Warrior*, the D-Day Museum, Charles Dickens' birthplace at 393 Old Commercial Road, the Royal Naval and Royal Marine museums, Southsea Castle (built by Henry VIII), Fort Nelson on Portsdown Hill, the Sealife Centre and the Round Tower and Point Battery, which for hundreds of years have guarded the entrance to Portsmouth Harbour.

ST ALBANS

The origins of St Albans, situated on the River Ver, stem from the Roman town of *Verulamium*. Named after the first Christian martyr in Britain, who was executed here, St Albans has developed around the Norman Abbey and Cathedral Church (consecrated 1115), built partly of materials from the old Roman city. The museums house Iron Age and Roman artefacts and the Roman Theatre, unique in Britain, has a stage as opposed to an amphitheatre. Archaeological excavations in the city centre have revealed evidence of pre-Roman, Saxon and medieval occupation.

The town's significance grew to the extent that it was a signatory and venue for the drafting of the Magna Carta. It was also the scene of riots during the Peasants' Revolt, the French King John was imprisoned there after the Battle of Poitiers, and heavy fighting took place there during the Wars of the Roses.

Previously controlled by the Abbot, the town achieved a charter in 1553 and city status in 1877. The street market, first established in 1553, is still an important feature of the city, as are many hotels and inns which survive from the days when St Albans was an important coach stop. Tourist attractions include historic churches and houses, and a 15th-century clock tower.

The city now contains a wide range of firms, with special emphasis on information and legal services. In addition, it is the home of the Royal National Rose Society, and of Rothamsted Park, the agricultural research centre.

SHEFFIELD

Sheffield, the centre of the special steel and cutlery trades, is situated at the junction of the Sheaf, Porter, Rivelin and Loxley valleys with the River Don. Though its cutlery, silverware and plate have long been famous, Sheffield has other and now more important industries: special and alloy steels, engineering, tool-making, medical equipment and media-related industries (in its new Cultural Industries Quarter). Sheffield has two universities and is an important research centre.

The parish church of St Peter and St Paul, founded in the 12th century, became the Cathedral Church of the Diocese of Sheffield in 1914. The Roman Catholic Cathedral Church of St Marie (founded 1847) was created Cathedral for the new diocese of Hallam in 1980. Parts of the present building date from c.1435. The principal buildings are the Town Hall (1897), the Cutlers' Hall (1832), City Hall (1932), Graves Art Gallery (1934), Mappin Art Gallery, the Crucible Theatre and the restored 19th-century Lyceum theatre, which dates from 1897 and was reopened in 1990. Three major sports venues were opened in 1990 to 1991. The National Centre for Popular Music was opened in 1999.

Sheffield was created a city in 1893.

Master Cutler of the Company of Cutlers in Hallamshire 1998–9,
  D. B. Liversidge

SOUTHAMPTON

Southampton is the leading British deep-sea port on the Channel and is situated on one of the finest natural harbours in the world. The first charter was granted by Henry II and Southampton was created a county of itself in 1447. In 1964 it was granted city status.

There were Roman and Saxon settlements on the site of the city, which has been an important port since Anglo-Saxon times due to its natural deep-water harbour. The oldest church is St Michael's (1070) which has an unusually tall spire built in the 18th century as a landmark for navigators of Southampton Water. Other buildings and monuments within the city walls are the Bargate, the Tudor House Museum, God's House Tower, the Tudor Merchants Hall, the Weigh-house, West Gate, King John's House, Long House, Wool House, the ruins of Holy Rood Church, St Julien's Church and the Mayflower Memorial. The medieval town walls, built for artillery, are among the most complete in the UK. Public open spaces total over 1,000 acres and comprise 9 per cent of the city's area. The Common covers an area of 328 acres in the central district of the city and is mostly natural parkland. A recent addition to work in marine technology in Southampton is Europe's leading oceanography research centre, which is part of the University.

STOKE-ON-TRENT

Stoke-on-Trent, standing on the River Trent and familiarly known as The Potteries, is the main centre of employment for the population of North Staffordshire. The city is the largest clayware producer in the world (china, earthenware, sanitary goods, refractories, bricks and tiles) and also has a wide range of other manufacturing industry, including steel, chemicals, engineering and tyres. Extensive reconstruction has been carried out in recent years.

The city was formed by the federation of the separate municipal authorities of Tunstall, Burslem, Hanley, Stoke, Fenton, and Longton in 1910 and received its city status in 1925.

WINCHESTER

Winchester, the ancient capital of England, is situated on the River Itchen. The city is rich in architecture of all types but the Cathedral takes pride of place. The longest Gothic cathedral in the world, it was built in 1079–93 and exhibits examples of Norman, Early English and Perpendicular styles. The author Jane Austen is buried in the Cathedral. Winchester College, founded in 1382, is one of the most famous public schools, the original building (1393) remaining largely unaltered. St Cross Hospital, another great medieval foundation, lies one mile south of the city. The almshouses were founded in 1136 by Bishop Henry de Blois, and Cardinal Henry Beaufort added a new almshouse of 'Noble Poverty' in 1446. The chapel and dwellings are of great architectural interest, and visitors may still receive the 'Wayfarer's Dole' of bread and ale.

Excavations have done much to clarify the origins and development of Winchester. Part of the forum and several of the streets of the Roman town have been discovered; excavations in the Cathedral Close have uncovered the entire site of the Anglo-Saxon cathedral (known as the Old Minster) and parts of the New Minster which was built by Alfred's son Edward the Elder and is the burial place of the Alfredian dynasty. The original burial place of St Swithun, before his remains were translated to a site in the present cathedral, was also uncovered.

Excavations in other parts of the city have thrown much light on Norman Winchester, notably on the site of the Royal Castle (adjacent to which the new Law Courts have been built) and in the grounds of Wolvesey Castle, where the great house built by Bishops Giffard and Henry de Blois in the 12th century has been uncovered. The Great Hall, built by Henry III between 1222 and 1236 survives and houses the Arthurian Round Table.

YORK

The city of York is an archiepiscopal seat. Its recorded history dates from AD 71, when the Roman Ninth Legion established a base under Petilius Cerealis which later became the fortress of *Eburacum.* In Anglo-Saxon times the city was the royal and ecclesiastical centre of Northumbria, and after capture by a Viking army in AD 866 it became the capital of the Viking kingdom of Jorvik. By the 14th century the city had become a great mercantile centre, mainly because of its control of the wool trade, and was used as the chief base against the Scots. Under the Tudors its fortunes declined, though Henry VIII made it the headquarters of the Council of the North. Excavations on many sites, including Coppergate, have greatly expanded knowledge of Roman, Viking and medieval urban life.

With its development as a railway centre in the 19th century the commercial life of York expanded. The principal industries are the manufacture of chocolate, scientific instruments and sugar. It is the location of several government departments.

The city is rich in examples of architecture of all periods. The earliest church was built in AD 627 and, in the 12th to 15th centuries, the present Minster was built in a succession of styles. Other examples within the city are the medieval city walls and gateways, churches and guildhalls. Domestic architecture includes the Georgian mansions of The Mount, Micklegate and Bootham.

English Counties and Shires

LORD-LIEUTENANTS AND HIGH SHERIFFS

County/Shire	Lord-Lieutenant	High Sheriff, 1999–2000
Bedfordshire	S. C. Whitbread	C. R. Kilroy
Berkshire	P. L. Wroughton	M. J. B. Todhunter
Bristol	J. Tidmarsh, MBE	J. R. Pool
Buckinghamshire	Sir Nigel Mobbs	The Hon. Sir William McAlpine, Bt.
Cambridgeshire	J. G. P. Crowden	J. E. Heading
Cheshire	W. A. Bromley-Davenport	M. D. A. Clarke
Cornwall	Lady Holborow	Lt.-Cdr. N. J. Trefusis
Cumbria	J. A. Cropper	A. I. Bullough
Derbyshire	J. K. Bather	D. R. Penrose, MBE
Devon	E. Dancer, CBE	Sir Simon Day
Dorset	Capt. M. Fulford-Dobson, RN	A. G. Yeatman
Durham	Sir Paul Nicholson	F. Nicholson
East Riding of Yorkshire	R. Marriott, TD	A. L. Marr
East Sussex	Admiral Sir Lindsay Bryson, KCB, FRSE, FREng.	K. M. H. Millar
Essex	The Lord Braybrooke	G. R. Capel Cure
Gloucestershire	H. W. G. Elwes	The Hon. M. W. Vestey
Greater London	The Lord Imbert, QPM	R. J. L. Bramble
Greater Manchester	Col. J. B. Timmins, OBE, TD	N. K. Stoller
Hampshire	Mrs F. M. Fagan	V. A. L. Powell
Herefordshire	Sir Thomas Dunne, KCVO	Mrs R. J. Dawes
Hertfordshire	S. A. Bowes Lyon	H. M. Neal, CBE
Isle of Wight	C. D. J. Bland	S. H. G. Twining, LVO, OBE
Kent	The Lord Kingsdown, KG, PC	J. B. Sunley
Lancashire	The Lord Shuttleworth	Lady Shuttleworth
Leicestershire	T. G. M. Brooks	Mrs A. Grahame Wilson, CBE
Lincolnshire	Mrs B. K. Cracroft-Eley	F. J. F. M. Dymoke
Merseyside	A. W. Waterworth	D. H. Morris
Norfolk	Sir Timothy Colman, KG	N. W. D. Foster
Northamptonshire	Lady Juliet Townsend, LVO	D. Reynolds
Northumberland	The Viscount Ridley, KG, GCVO, TD	Mrs E. M. Fairbairn
North Yorkshire	The Lord Crathorne	A. V. Hudson
Nottinghamshire	Sir Andrew Buchanan, Bt.	A. M. Nall
Oxfordshire	H. L. J. Brunner	A. J. Feilden
Rutland	Air Chief Marshal Sir Thomas Kennedy, GCB, AFC	Mrs W. M. L. Goldring
Shropshire	A. E. H. Heber-Percy	J. R. B. Lovegrove-Fielden
Somerset	Lady Gass	T. A. H. Yandle
South Yorkshire	The Earl of Scarbrough	D. B. Shaw
Staffordshire	J. A. Hawley, TD	D. E. D. Johnson
Suffolk	The Lord Belstead, PC	Col. D. H. C. Gordon Lennox
Surrey	Mrs S. J. F. Goad	P. R. Nutting
Tyne and Wear	Sir Ralph Carr-Ellison, KCVO, TD	M. Bird
Warwickshire	M. Dunne	M. C. Fetherston-Dilke
West Midlands	R. R. Taylor, OBE	R. S. Burman, CBE
West Sussex	H. Wyatt	Mrs J. Buckland, MBE
West Yorkshire	J. Lyles, CBE	P. A. H. Hartley, CBE
Wiltshire	Lt.-Gen. Sir Maurice Johnston, KCB, OBE	P. J. Miles
Worcestershire	Sir Thomas Dunne, KCVO	Mrs R. J. Dawes

COUNTY COUNCILS: Area, Population, Finance

Council	Administrative headquarters	Area (hectares)	Population	Total demand upon collection fund 1999–2000
Bedfordshire	County Hall, Bedford	119,220	524,105	£92,756,000
Buckinghamshire	County Hall, Aylesbury	156,538	632,487	118,700,000
Cambridgeshire	Shire Hall, Cambridge	305,399	645,125	107,300,000
Cheshire	County Hall, Chester	208,344	956,616	171,543,844
Cornwall	County Hall, Truro	354,810	468,425	95,665,000
Cumbria	The Courts, Carlisle	681,000	483,163	106,644,000
Derbyshire	County Hall, Matlock	262,858	928,636	161,471,440
Devon	County Hall, Exeter	670,343	1,009,950	616,240,000
Dorset	County Hall, Dorchester	254,375	645,166	101,144,947
Durham	County Hall, Durham	223,180	593,430	94,113,602
East Sussex	Pelham House, St Andrew's Lane, Lewes	172,500	690,447	117,085,000
Essex	County Hall, Chelmsford	344,781	1,528,577	292,692,000
Gloucestershire	Shire Hall, Gloucester	265,535	528,370	369,000,000
Hampshire	The Castle, Winchester	367,915	1,541,547	280,805,000
Hertfordshire	County Hall, Hertford	164,306	975,829	238,025,212
Kent	County Hall, Maidstone	354,296	1,508,873	293,876,314
Lancashire	County Hall, Preston	289,780	1,383,998	260,156,000
Leicestershire	County Hall, Glenfield, Leicester	208,380	867,521	126,035,000
Lincolnshire	County Offices, Newland, Lincoln	588,000	584,534	433,411,000
Norfolk	County Hall, Norwich	537,234	745,613	161,910,340
Northamptonshire	County Hall, Northampton	236,737	578,807	118,053,000
Northumberland	County Hall, Morpeth	502,594	307,709	71,500,000
North Yorkshire	County Hall, Northallerton	830,399	556,200	122,900,000
Nottinghamshire	County Hall, Nottingham	208,510	993,872	174,592,555
Oxfordshire	County Hall, Oxford	260,595	547,584	131,000,000
Shropshire	The Shirehall, Shrewsbury	319,736	406,387	59,673,000
Somerset	County Hall, Taunton	345,233	460,368	103,551,885
Staffordshire	County Buildings, Stafford	262,355	1,031,135	150,640,000
Suffolk	County Hall, Ipswich	380,207	636,266	131,600,000
Surrey	County Hall, Kingston upon Thames	167,011	1,018,003	271,100,000
Warwickshire	Shire Hall, Warwick	198,054	484,247	115,333,810
West Sussex	County Hall, Chichester	199,025	702,290	175,870,000
Wiltshire	County Hall, Trowbridge	348,070	564,471	94,231,000
Worcestershire	County Hall, Worcester	173,529	531,909	107,497,073

COUNTY COUNCILS: OFFICERS AND CHAIRMEN

Council	Chief Executive	County Treasurer	Chairman of County Council
Bedfordshire	D. Cleggett	W. Dodds	J. Saunders
Buckinghamshire	I. Crookall	§S. Nolan	K. I. Ross
Cambridgeshire	A. Barnish	D. T. Earle	J. Eddy
Cheshire	C. Cheesman	A. Cope	D. Newton
Cornwall	J. F. Mills	F. P. Twyning	J. M. Philp
Cumbria	W. A. Swarbrick	°R. F. Mather	R. Watson
Derbyshire	A. R. N. Hodgson	P. Swaby	G. Bratt
Devon	P. Jenkinson	‡J. Glasby	K. J. Turner
Dorset	D. Jenkins	A. P. Peel	Mrs P. Hymers
Durham	K. W. Smith	J. Kirkby	J. Richardson
East Sussex	Mrs C. Miller	J. Howes	M. Skilton
Essex	K. W. S. Ashurst	K. D. Neale	Mrs J. E. Beard
Gloucestershire	R. Cockcroft	R. Cockcroft	Ms M. Rutter
Hampshire	P. C. B. Robertson	J. C. Pittam	F. A. J. Emery-Wallis
Hertfordshire	W. D. Ogley	*C. Sweeney	R. Smith
Kent	M. Pitt	*D. Lewis	F. Fox
Lancashire	G. A. Johnson	B. G. Aldred	Dr R. Henig
Leicestershire	J. B. Sinnott	A. Youd	G. Perkins
Lincolnshire	D. Bowles	†M. Spink	J. Fisher
Norfolk	T. J. Byles	*R. D. Summers	Mrs T. I. Paines
Northamptonshire	J. V. Picking	Mrs L. Charker (acting)	C. Kalyan
Northumberland	J. M. McCall (acting)	*C. Burns	L. B. Smith
North Yorkshire	J. Walker	J. S. Moore	Lt. Col. J. H. Jacob MC
Nottinghamshire	P. J. Housden	R. Latham	J. K. Stobbart
Oxfordshire	J. Harwood	C. Gray	H. Wyatt
Shropshire	N. T. Pursey	N. T. Pursey	Mrs P. Larney
Somerset	Dr D. Radford	C. N. Bilsland	R. B. Clark
Staffordshire	B. A. Price, CBE	R. G. Tettenborn, OBE	T. R. Wright
Suffolk	Mrs L. Homer	R. Whiteman	Dr A. D. Lower
Surrey	P. Coen	§M. Taylor	Mrs H. Hawker
Warwickshire	I. G. Caulfield	S. R. Freer	Mrs J. Tandy
West Sussex	D. P. Rigg	Mrs H. Kilpatrick	I. R. W. Elliott
Wiltshire	Dr K. Robinson	D. Chalker	Brig. R. J. Baddeley
Worcestershire	R. Sykes	M. Weaver	N. Knowles

* Director of Finance
° Director of Corporate Finance
† Director of Finance and Resources
‡ Director of Resources
§ Head of Finance

Unitary Councils

SMALL CAPITALS denote CITY status
§ Denotes Borough council

Council	Population	Band D charge 1999*	Chief Executive	Mayor (a)Lord Mayor (b)Chairman 1999–2000
§Barnsley	220,937	£818.93	J. Edwards, OBE	A. Whittaker
Bath and North-East Somerset	164,700	778.92	J. Everitt	J. Bailey
BIRMINGHAM	961,041	892.53	M. Lyons	(a) I. McArdle
§Blackburn with Darwen	136,612	914.84	P. S. Watson	S. R. Kiani
§Blackpool	151,200	683.07	G. E. Essex-Crosby	W. Burgess
§Bolton	258,584	885.49	B. Knight	J. Monaghan
§Bournemouth	160,700	737.56	D. Newell	J. Courtney
§Bracknell Forest	110,000	711.46	G. Mitchell	J. C. Finnie FRICS
BRADFORD	457,344	808.17	I. Stewart	(a) H. Mason
§Brighton and Hove	245,000	697.00	G. Jones	Ms J. Langston
BRISTOL	399,600	992.15	Ms L. de Groot	(a) G. Robertson
§Bury	176,760	811.20	D. Taylor	J. P. Costello
§Calderdale	191,585	876.19	P. Sheehan	P. Coles
COVENTRY	294,387	968.00	I. Roxburgh	(a) Mrs J. Wright
§Darlington	101,000	687.49	B. Keel	W. Dixon
DERBY	235,238	786.75	R. H. Cowlishaw	Ms S. F. Bolton
§Doncaster	288,854	760.86	A. M. Taylor	Mrs M. J. Robinson
§Dudley	304,615	779.19	A. Sparke	F. S. Hunt
East Riding of Yorkshire	310,800	857.37	D. Stephenson	(b) Ms D. Clark
§Gateshead	199,588	868.94	L. N. Elton	B. Coates
§Halton	123,038	678.81	M. Cuff	R. Gilligan
Hartlepool	92,000	976.82	B. J. Dinsdale	R. Watts
Herefordshire	167,000	729.11	N. Pringle	(b) G. Hyde
Isle of Wight	125,466	784.47	B. Quoroll	(b) Mrs B. Foster
KINGSTON UPON HULL	266,900	793.33	I. Crookham	(a) B. Wilkinson
§Kirklees	373,127	868.00	T. Elson	H. Fox
§Knowsley	152,091	948.87	D. G. Henshaw	J. King
LEEDS	680,722	687.00	P. Rogerson	(a) K. Parker
LEICESTER	270,493	791.80	R. Green	(a) P. Swift
LIVERPOOL	452,450	1,171.54	P. Bounds	(a) J. Devaney
§Luton	181,500	706.81	Mrs K. Jones	R. Saleem
§MANCHESTER	404,861	987.28	H. Bernstein	(a) A. Burns
Medway	239,978	670.47	Ms J. Armitt	D. Liyanage
Middlesbrough	144,500	805.81	¶ J. E. Foster	M. J. Carr
§Milton Keynes	204,415	742.00	H. Miller	K. Beeley
NEWCASTLE UPON TYNE	259,541	977.30	K. G. Lavery	(a) J. Cunningham
North-East Lincolnshire	168,000	864.53	R. Bentham	G. Mitchell
North Lincolnshire	152,423	983.97	Dr M. Garnett	Ms B. Martin
North Somerset	177,000	739.92	P. May	R. Moon
§North Tyneside	192,286	904.74	Executive Directorate	Ms M. Mulgrove
NOTTINGHAM	284,000	886.08	E. F. Cantle	(a) D. A. Jones
§Oldham	216,531	933.76	A. W. Kilburn	J. B. Battye
PETERBOROUGH	159,900	752.24	P. Martin	J. Bartlett
PLYMOUTH	255,800	701.89	Mrs A. Stone	(a) T. Savery
§Poole	139,200	702.99	J. Brookes	F. J. Wretham
PORTSMOUTH	190,400	680.31	N. Gurney	(a) D. Horne
§Reading	142,851	868.13	Ms J. Markham	S. Waite
Redcar and Cleveland	140,200	1,042.60	A. W. Kilburn	M. Stephen
§Rochdale	202,164	870.88	Mrs F. W. Done	D. Murphy
§Rotherham	251,637	808.96	A. G. Carruthers	M. G. Judge
Rutland	34,600	944.89	Dr J. R. Morphet	(b) Wg Cdr. R. D. Toy
§St Helens	178,764	962.88	Mrs C. Hudson	P. Jackson
SALFORD	220,463	1,198.02	J. C. Willis	W. B. Pennington
§Sandwell	290,091	856.01	F. N. Summers	J. Edwards
§Sefton	289,542	913.85	G. J. Haywood	R. J. Brennan
SHEFFIELD	501,202	883.50	R. W. Kerslake	(a) T. Bagshaw
§Slough	108,000	725.44	Ms C. Coppell	Mrs O. E. Mansell
§Solihull	199,859	894.63	Dr N. H. Perry	A. Harper

Council	Population	Band D charge 1999*	Chief Executive	Mayor (a)Lord Mayor (b)Chairman 1999–2000
SOUTHAMPTON	214,859	708.96	J. Cairns	D. Burke
South Gloucestershire	239,000	781.57	M. Robinson	(b) A. Adams
§Southend	172,300	675.75	J. K. M. Krawiec	A. S. North
§South Tyneside	154,697	884.25	‡P. J. Haigh	Ms M. Chenery
§Stockport	284,395	916.65	J. R. Schultz	Ms I. Shaw
§Stockton-on-Tees	179,000	852.87	G. Garlick	Mrs J. Kitchen
STOKE-ON-TRENT	254,300	750.97	B. Smith	(a) R. G. Booth
§SUNDERLAND	289,040	814.61	C. W. Sinclair, PH.D.	D. R.Wares
§Swindon	177,118	672.00	P. Doherty	Ms J. Brunt
§Tameside	216,431	898.20	M. J. Greenwood	F. Robinson
Telford and Wrekin	151,500	756.99	C. Barber (acting)	vacant
§Thurrock	132,283	672.48	K. Barnes	C. Morris
§Torbay	119,674	751.96	A. J. Hodgkiss	J. Turner
§Trafford	212,731	689.22	W. A. Lewis	R. Bowker
WAKEFIELD	310,915	742.52	†M. Pullan	B. Bullock
§Walsall	259,488	802.92	D. C. Winchurch	Mrs D. Farrell
§Warrington	187,000	738.48	S. Broomhead	T. Swift
West Berkshire	144,000	810.58	Ms S. Manzie	(b) J. Cottam
§Wigan	306,521	834.52	S. M. Jones	W. Smith
§Windsor and Maidenhead	132,465	743.73	D. C. Lunn	Mrs S. Hopkins
§Wirral	330,795	977.00	S. Maddox	H. Lloyd
Wokingham	142,767	820.61	Ms J. Earl	(b) Mrs P. Hellier-Symons
§Wolverhampton	242,190	954.72	D. Anderson	P. A. Bilson
YORK	175,925	691.43	D. Clark	(a) P. Vaughan

* For explanation of council tax, *see* pages 521–2
† The Chief Officer
‡ Head of Paid Service
¶ Managing Director

District Councils

SMALL CAPITALS denote CITY status
§ Denotes Borough status
For explanation of council tax, *see* pages 521–2
* Executive Director
** 1996 figure
† General Manager
‡ Head of Paid Service
¶ Managing Director

Council	Population	Band D charge 1999*	Chief Executive	Chairman (a)Mayor (b)Lord Mayor 1999–2000
Adur, W. Sussex	58,019	£797.44	I. Lowrie	G. Howitt
§Allerdale, Cumbria	95,702	856.45	C. J. Hart	(a) Mrs M. Snaith
Alnwick, Northumberland	30,081	901.27	L. A. B. St Ruth	G. R. Arckless
Amber Valley, Derbys	111,897	869.30	P. M. Carney	(a) M. B. Gent
Arun, W. Sussex	129,357	765.94	I. Sumnall	H. Parris
Ashfield, Notts	108,364	925.50	E. N. Bernasconi	Mrs C. Young
§Ashford, Kent	92,331	736.37	A. Baker	(a) Mrs B. A. Simmons
Aylesbury Vale, Bucks	145,931	762.05	B. Hurley	C. R. James
Babergh, Suffolk	79,632	765.34	P. Barnes	P. Jones
§Barrow-in-Furness, Cumbria	73,125	891.66	T. O. Campbell	(a) Mrs J. Waiting
Basildon, Essex	161,124	806.06	J. Robb	Mrs L. Gordon
§Basingstoke and Deane, Hants	144,790	749.08	Mrs K. E. P. Sporle	(a) L. Jones
Bassetlaw, Notts	103,979	930.00	J. Molloy	J. Napier
§Bedford, Beds	133,692	859.93	L. W. Gould	(a) Ms C. Ellis
§Berwick-upon-Tweed, Northumberland	26,731	890.31	E. O. Cawthorn, TD	(a) N. N. Ferguson

Council	Population	Band D charge 1999*	Chief Executive	Chairman (a)Mayor (b)Lord Mayor 1999–2000
Blaby, Leics	82,700	814.36	E. Hemsley	B. Garner
§Blyth Valley, Northumberland	79,584	883.06	G. Paul	(a) Mrs M. A. Parker
Bolsover, Derbys	70,437	904.50	J. R. Fotherby	R. Brooks
§Boston, Lincs	53,226	962.33	M. James	(a) P. Goodale
Braintree, Essex	118,883	761.04	Ms A. F. Ralph	F. Card
Breckland, Norfolk	107,167	735.31	R. N. Garnett	K. Martin
§Brentwood, Essex	70,597	760.77	C. P. Sivell	(a) H. Bailey
Bridgnorth, Salop	50,511	782.61	Mrs T. M. Elliott	Mrs M. Winckler
Broadland, Norfolk	106,292	777.15	J. Bryant	G. E. Debbage
Bromsgrove, Worcs	91,544	712.43	D. A. H. Bryant	R. J. Deeming
§Broxbourne, Herts	81,449	721.02	M. J. Walker	(a) R. L. Groucott
§Broxtowe, Notts	107,137	918.14	M. Brown	(a) F. Prince
§Burnley, Lancs	91,130	948.24	R. Ellis	(a) E. Fisk
Cambridge	91,933	737.49	R. Hammond	(a) R. Smith
Cannock Chase, Staffs	88,833	966.58	M. G. Kemp	A. B. Hill
Canterbury, Kent	123,947	752.00	C. Carmichael	(b) Miss J. Samper
Caradon, Cornwall	76,516	744.89	Dr J. Neal	T. G. Smale
Carlisle, Cumbria	100,562	883.39	R. S. Brackley	(a) J. R. Collier
Carrick, Cornwall	82,725	755.78	J. P. Winskill	Mrs S. C. Shaw
§Castle Morpeth, Northumberland	50,299	908.15	P. Wilson	(a) E. M. Coe
§Castle Point, Essex	86,560	797.13	B. Rollinson	(a) A. Hurd
§Charnwood, Leics	141,806	785.97	S. M. Peatfield	(a) J. B. Powell
§Chelmsford, Essex	152,418	774.35	M. Easteal	(a) M. J. Mackrory
§Cheltenham, Glos	103,115	703.71	L. Davison	(a) D. J. Banyard
Cherwell, Oxon	117,832	759.24	G. J. Handley	R. Laynes
§Chesterfield, Derbys	99,403	849.13	D. R. Shaw	(a) T. Gilby
Chester-le-Street, Co. Durham	52,641	830.27	J. A. Greensmith	Mrs I. Howey
Chester, Cheshire	115,971	860.08	P. F. Durham	(b) E. Plenderleath
Chichester, W. Sussex	101,358	749.12	J. S. Marsland	C. W. Spawton
Chiltern, Bucks	89,838	711.43	A. Goodrum	D. W. Phillips
§Chorley, Lancs	96,504	888.04	J. W. Davies	(a) Ms F. Molyneaux
§Christchurch, Dorset	40,865	816.02	M. A. Turvey	(a) R. J. R. McArthur
§Colchester, Essex	142,515	760.21	J. Cobley	(a) M. Hunt
§Congleton, Cheshire	84,525	857.17	P. Cooper	(a) R. Parry
§Copeland, Cumbria	71,296	852.00	†Dr J. Stanforth	(a) G. Blackwell
§Corby, Northants	53,044	765.59	N. Rudd	(a) E. Gordon
Cotswold, Glos	73,965	759.58	N. C. Abbott	B. I. Evans
Craven, N. Yorks	49,891	740.99	*Ms R. Mann (acting)	A. Dixon
§Crawley, W. Sussex	87,644	754.83	M. D. Sander	(a) R. Calcott
§Crewe and Nantwich, Cheshire	103,164	858.82	A. Wenham	(a) C. G. Thorley
§Dacorum, Herts	134,733	736.23	K. Hunt	(a) R. Jameson
§Dartford, Kent	79,439	750.10	C. R. Shepherd	(a) I. Jones
Daventry, Northants	62,886	719.63	P. Cook	Mrs I. Taylor
Derbyshire Dales, Derbys	67,562	877.56	D. Wheatcroft	Mrs J. N. Bevan
Derwentside, Co. Durham	86,046	897.58	vacant	Ms E. Wilson
Dover, Kent	103,216	744.38	J. P. Moir, TD	F. E. Woodbridge MBE
Durham	80,669	836.90	C. Shearsmith	(a) Mrs M. A. Adair
Easington, Co. Durham	97,824	921.83	vacant	G. Martin
§Eastbourne, E. Sussex	81,395	789.34	Mrs S. E. Conway	(a) Mrs B. Healy
East Cambridgeshire	60,416	703.25	R. C. Carr	Ms S. Friend-Smith
East Devon	115,873	761.07	F. J. Vallender	B. C. J. Hughes
East Dorset	78,698	837.15	A. Breakwell	G. W. Russell
East Hampshire	103,460	800.06	Miss J. Hunter	Dr J. Happel
East Hertfordshire	115,818	717.12	R. J. Bailey	R. Parker
§Eastleigh, Hants	105,999	784.00	C. Tapp	(a) Ms J. Welsh
East Lindsey, Lincs	116,957	755.45	P. Haigh	Mrs F. M. Martin
East Northamptonshire	67,686	681.29	R. K. Heath	M. L. Peacock
§East Staffordshire	97,105	790.14	F. W. Saunders	(a) D. Tilling
Eden, Cumbria	45,581	822.17	I. W. Bruce	Ms N. Walker
§Ellesmere Port and Neston, Cheshire	80,873	875.55	S. Ewbank	(a) S. M. Earley

Council	Population	Band D charge 1999*	Chief Executive	Chairman (a)Mayor (b)Lord Mayor 1999–2000
§Elmbridge, Surrey	114,479	779.56	M. Lockwood	(a) T. Stewart
Epping Forest, Essex	116,027	766.98	J. Burgess	S. Goodwin
§Epsom and Ewell, Surrey	67,007	748.95	D. J. Smith	(a) E. Kington
§Erewash, Derbys	106,101	854.71	G. A. Pook	(a) E. A. Bishop
EXETER, Devon	98,125	749.17	P. Bostock	(a) R. Hill
Fareham, Hants	99,262	762.84	A. A. Davies	(a) R. H. Price
Fenland, Cambs	74,426	728.00	N. R. Topliss	J. L. Baker
Forest Heath, Suffolk	54,843	719.21	‡D. W. Burnip	W. J. Bishop
Forest of Dean, Glos	75,351	759.25	Ms M. Holborow	W. Hobman
§Fylde, Lancs	70,999	885.46	J. R. Wilkinson	(a) Miss M. Procopides
§Gedling, Notts	110,133	903.27	D. Kennedy	(a) J. F. Glass
GLOUCESTER	101,608	758.65	G. Garbutt	(a) A. Meredith
§Gosport, Hants	75,061	786.22	M. Crocker	(a) K. P. J. Searle
§Gravesham, Kent	92,454	728.24	E. C. Anderson	(a) J. Jaggon
§Great Yarmouth, Norfolk	87,724	775.07	R. W. Packham	J. Barnes
§Guildford, Surrey	127,500	751.44	D. T. Watts	(a) R. E. Blundell
Hambleton, N. Yorks	79,425	695.29	P. Simpson	G. W. Ellis
Harborough, Leics	67,607	808.59	M. C. Wilson	P. R. Fewkes
Harlow, Essex	74,629	872.49	D. F. Byrne	J. McCree
§Harrogate, N. Yorks	143,526	760.22	P. M. Walsh	(a) G. Crowther OBE
Hart, Hants	80,921	779.32	G. R. Jelbart	J. Stocks
§Hastings, E. Sussex	80,820	813.35	R. Mawford	(a) R. Stevens
§Havant, Hants	119,697	775.08	R. D. Smith	(a) D. M. Farrow
§Hertsmere, Herts	87,590	747.85	P. H. Copland	(a) J. M. Donne
§High Peak, Derbys	87,900	865.61	R. P. H. Brady	(a) D. Bond
§Hinckley and Bosworth, Leics	96,201	763.43	J. Corry (acting)	(a) D. R. Bown
Horsham, W. Sussex	108,562	724.60	M. J. Pearson	E. D. Jenkins
Huntingdonshire, Cambs	144,075	695.15	D. Monks	Mrs P. Newbon
§Hyndburn, Lancs	78,390	939.87	M. J. Chambers	(a) B. Dawson
§Ipswich, Suffolk	116,956	828.63	J. D. Hehir	(a) J. C. Mowles
Kennet, Wilts	68,526	769.06	M. J. Boden	Mrs S. M. Findlay
Kerrier, Cornwall	87,566	757.00	G. G. Cox	M. Jeffery
§Kettering, Northants	78,200	773.94	P. Walker	(a) J. West
§King's Lynn and West Norfolk	131,000	775.19	Dr G. Taylor	(a) Dr P. Richards
LANCASTER, LANCS	123,856	883.88	D. Corker	(a) Mrs S. Rostron
Lewes, E. Sussex	87,389	811.45	J. N. Crawford	J. E. Lewry
Lichfield, Staffs	92,679	766.23	J. T. Thompson	J. A. Nichols
LINCOLN	81,987	800.67	A. Taylor	(a) Ms L. Woolley
§Macclesfield, Cheshire	151,590	852.40	B. W. Longden	(a) Miss C. M. Andrew
§Maidstone, Kent	137,000	797.20	J. D. Makepeace	(a) Ms F. Brown
Maldon, Essex	52,843	739.57	E. A. P. Plumridge	R. Pipe
Malvern Hills, Worcs	86,902	688.17	C. J. Bocock	R. J. Farmer
Mansfield, Notts	100,386	934.40	R. P. Goad	G. Harper
§Melton, Leics	45,112	799.21	P. M. Murphy	(a) R. Holt
Mendip, Somerset	95,603	779.02	G. Jeffs	C. Lockey
Mid Bedfordshire, Beds	109,801	858.81	C. A. Tucker	Ms F. Chapman
Mid Devon, Devon	64,258	794.16	M. I. R. Bull	D. F. Pugsley
Mid Suffolk, Suffolk	78,383	759.59	G. R. Chilton	Mrs W. Marchant
Mid Sussex, W. Sussex	126,000	762.72	W. J. H. Hatton	Mrs C. Field
Mole Valley, Surrey	79,220	748.58	Mrs H. Kerswell	Mrs B. Douglass
Newark and Sherwood, Notts	102,784	940.32	R. G. Dix	E. Jackson
§Newcastle under Lyme, Staffs	119,091	768.15	F. Harley	(a) Mrs B. Blaise
New Forest, Hants	160,456	799.25	¶I. B. Mackintosh	Mrs P. A. Wyeth
§Northampton	180,567	787.97	R. J. B. Morris	(a) A. McCutcheon
North Cornwall	73,800	720.01	D. Brown	R. W. Flower
North Devon	84,800	772.99	D. T. Cunliffe	A. E. Cook
North Dorset	52,110	808.67	vacant	Mrs D. Jones MBE
North East Derbyshire	97,570	905.13	‡Ms C. A. Gilby	J. A. Dargue
North Hertfordshire	111,994	758.89	S. Philp	D. Ashley
North Kesteven, Lincs	79,942	797.60	Mrs R. Marlow	Mrs B. Wells
North Norfolk	90,461	779.04	B. A. Barrell	C. Durrant

Council	Population	Band D charge 1999*	Chief Executive	Chairman (a)Mayor (b)Lord Mayor 1999–2000
North Shropshire	52,873	810.95	R. J. Hughes	Mrs P. A. Dee
§North Warwickshire	60,747	874.00	J. Hutchinson	(a) R. Spencer
North West Leicestershire	80,566	827.51	M. J. Diaper	S. D. Sheahan
North Wiltshire	111,974	789.64	R. Marshall	B. E. Atfield
NORWICH, Norfolk	120,895	817.70	J. R. Packer, OBE	(b) D. Underwood
§Nuneaton and Bedworth, Warks	117,052	850.93	Ms C. Kerr	(a) Ms M. Beaumont
§Oadby and Wigston, Leics	51,547	801.58	Mrs R. E. Hyde	(a) P. Swift
§Oswestry, Salop	33,508	800.71	B. D. Catton (acting)	(a) W. O. Jones
OXFORD	134,800	825.90	R. S. Block	(b) Ms V. Smith
§Pendle, Lancs	85,111	947.00	S. Barnes	(a) Mrs E. D. Sargeant
Penwith, Cornwall	59,251	738.46	‡D. H. Hosken	Mrs S. M. Menadue
§Preston, Lancs	126,082	958.52	J. E. Carr	(a) G. Threlfell Swabrick
Purbeck, Dorset	42,445	823.87	P. B. Croft	R. Anderson
§Redditch, Worcs	78,106	758.92	Ms K. Kerswell	(a) J. Witherspoon
§Reigate and Banstead, Surrey	117,777	707.00	M. Bacon	(a) B. Cowle
§Restormel, Cornwall	86,519	740.45	Mrs P. Crowson	J. Weller
§Ribble Valley, Lancs	51,767	897.99	D. G. Morris	(a) B. Collis
Richmondshire, N. Yorks	44,179	771.60	H. Tabiner	Ms H. Grant
Rochford, Essex	75,395	796.09	P. Warren	D. Helson
§Rossendale, Lancs	65,681	944.36	J. S. Hartley	(a) A. Neal
Rother, E. Sussex	81,683	777.95	D. F. Powell, FRICS	Mrs P. Bullock
§Rugby, Warks	81,683	839.39	Mrs D. M. Colley	(a) J. M. Roodhouse
§Runnymede, Surrey	71,789	688.59	T. N. Williams	(a) P. Poole
§Rushcliffe, Notts	97,567	882.52	K. Beaumont	(a) B. Nicholls
§Rushmoor, Hants	82,526	779.42	J. A. Lloyd	(a) D. E. Clifford
Ryedale, N. Yorks	47,981	778.97	H. W. Mosley	A. A. Aslett
ST ALBANS, Herts	128,700	763.78	E. A. Hackford	(a) M. Morrell
§St Edmundsbury, Suffolk	91,731	744.53	G. R. N. Toft	(a) Mrs M. M. L. Horbury
Salisbury, Wilts	105,318	778.68	R. Sheard	D. Parker
§Scarborough, N. Yorks	106,221	751.00	J. M. Trebble	(a) H. Dixon
§Sedgefield, Co. Durham	90,530	967.18	N. Vaulks	(a) Mrs A. Mumford
Sedgemoor, Somerset	97,763	760.68	A. G. Lovell	D. S. Alder
Selby, N. Yorks	89,428	744.65	M. Connor	D. N. Bain Mackay
Sevenoaks, Kent	109,742	765.27	N. Howells	Mrs S. Dunckley
Shepway, Kent	96,020	771.94	R. J. Thompson	Mrs S. Newlands
§Shrewsbury and Atcham, Salop	94,600	775.66	D. Bradbury	(a) R. Jones
South Bedfordshire	108,941	922.00	J. Ruddick	K. Sharer
South Bucks	62,482	757.17	C. R. Furness	R. Worrall
South Cambridgeshire	124,500	703.40	J. S. Ballantyne	A. W. Wyatt
South Derbyshire	71,772	848.97	D. J. Dugdale	K. Richards
South Hams, Devon	77,565	777.30	P. G. West (acting)	Mrs R. Rowe
South Holland, Lincs	70,386	795.28	C. J. Simpkins	J. Clark
South Kesteven, Lincs	108,945	767.84	C. Farmer	P. Taylor
South Lakeland, Cumbria	96,897	n/a	P. J. Cunliffe	Mrs J. S. Borer
South Norfolk	102,612	787.56	G. Rivers	W. Dinneen
South Northamptonshire	70,685	797.19	R. Tinlin	J. Byrom
South Oxfordshire	119,476	786.43	R. Watson	D. Turner
§South Ribble, Lancs	102,001	887.36	P. Halsall	(a) Mrs M. R. Smith
South Shropshire	38,230	820.17	G. C. Biggs, MBE	M. R. Williams
South Somerset	145,000	781.40	Ms E. Peters	N. Speakman, MBE, TD
South Staffordshire	105,487	655.40	L. T. Barnfield	Mrs C. Young
§Spelthorne, Surrey	89,748	761.39	M. B. Taylor	(a) E. O'Hara
Staffordshire Moorlands	95,072	965.00	B. J. Preedy	Ms S. Ralphs
§Staffordshire	117,788	754.70	D. Rawlings	(a) C. Baron
§Stevenage, Herts	75,147	625.18	I. Paske	(a) E. Webb
Stratford, Warks	109,400	771.26	I. B. Prosser	K. Lambert
Stroud, Glos	106,300	817.68	R. M. Ollin	Mrs L. Williams
Suffolk Coastal	107,970	752.85	T. K. Griffin	I. K. Jowers
§Surrey Heath	80,800	766.00	B. R. Catchpole	(a) K. Pedder
§Swale, Kent	115,769	744.40	C. Edwards	(a) Ms A. McLean
§Tamworth, Staffs	70,065	736.01	C. Moore	(a) Mrs P. Dix
Tandridge, Surrey	76,316	765.70	P. Thomas	Mrs W. Weston

Council	Population	Band D charge 1999*	Chief Executive	Chairman (a)Mayor (b)Lord Mayor 1999–2000
§Taunton Deane, Somerset	93,696	760.00	Mrs S. Douglas	(a) R. Parrish
Teesdale, Co. Durham	24,068	831.83	C. M. Anderson	J. L. Armstrong
Teignbridge, Devon	108,258	782.79	B. T. Jones	Mrs J. Collis
Tendring, Essex	130,900	769.40	J. Hawkins	Mrs R. Smith
§Test Valley, Hants	103,261	755.56	A. Jones	(a) Ms M. Kerley
§Tewkesbury, Glos	70,709	725.93	H. Davis	(a) Mrs B. A. Cromwell
Thanet, Kent	123,665	776.13	D. Ralls, CBE, DFC	R. Dickinson
Three Rivers, Herts	78,457	766.64	A. Robertson	I. Ambrose
§Tonbridge and Malling, Kent	101,763	748.13	T. Thompson	(a) Ms A. Oakley
Torridge, Devon	52,129	783.55	R. K. Brasington	J. Rawlinson
§Tunbridge Wells, Kent	99,538	769.41	R. J. Stone	(a) J. Ealden
Tynedale, Northumberland	57,275	878.93	A. Baty	W. Garrett
Uttlesford, Essex	67,500	795.72	K. Ivory	R. C. Dean
Vale of White Horse, Oxon	109,922	748.52	T. A. Stock	Mrs J. Hutchinson
§Vale Royal, Cheshire	114,700	850.94	J. W. Page	(a) Ms M. Bowhay-Merritt
Wansbeck, Northumberland	63,171	901.98	R. A. Stephenson	J. Young
Warwick	116,299	806.00	Miss J. M. Barrett	Mrs J. Compton
§Watford, Herts	74,566	831.51	Ms C. Hassan	(a) Ms R. Bell
Waveney, Suffolk	106,751	675.08	M. Berridge	J. Taylor
§Waverley, Surrey	113,212	776.51	Ms C. L. Pointer	(a) P. Betlem
Wealden, E. Sussex	130,214	821.90	D. R. Holness	Mrs S. M. Tidy
Wear Valley, Co. Durham	62,746	867.70	*Mrs C. Hughes	D. Kingston
§Wellingborough, Northants	**67,900	682.46	T. McArdle	(a) R. Cotter
Welwyn Hatfield, Herts	92,366	764.57	M. Saminaden	J. Mansfield
§West Devon	45,895	778.00	D. J. Incoll	(a) Mrs M. Gaston
West Dorset	85,463	831.46	R. C. Rennison	Mrs N. M. Penfold
West Lancashire	107,978	915.20	W. J. Taylor	S. J. Jones
West Lindsey, Lincs	76,218	799.39	R. W. Nelsey	A. D. Caine
West Oxfordshire	90,251	623.31	G. Bonner	A. Walker
West Somerset	31,651	776.54	C. W. Rockall	Mrs J. M. David
West Wiltshire	107,803	772.61	J. Ligo	R. J. Brice
§Weymouth and Portland, Dorset	61,233	679.96	T. Grainger	(a) Ms T. Roebuck
WINCHESTER, Hants	96,386	779.27	D. H. Cowan	(a) A. Mitchell
§Woking, Surrey	86,765	789.57	P. Russell	(a) I. D. F. Fidler
WORCESTER	89,481	730.86	D. Wareing	(a) Ms J. Hodges
§Worthing, W. Sussex	96,157	756.81	M. J. Ball	(a) B. McLuskie
Wychavon, Worcs	101,716	728.30	W. S. Nott	Mrs E. Hope
Wycombe, Bucks	162,000	768.77	R. J. Cummins	R. C. Pushman
§Wyre, Lancs	101,818	895.43	M. Brown	(a) H. Taylor
Wyre Forest, Worcs	94,814	748.79	W. S. Baldwin	J. Gordon

1. Stockton-on-Tees
2. Middlesbrough
3. Blackpool
4. Blackburn with Darwen
5. Bolton
6. Bury
7. Rochdale
8. Salford
9. Oldham
10. Liverpool
11. Knowsley
12. St Helens
13. Halton
14. Warrington
15. Trafford
16. Manchester
17. Tameside
18. Stockport
19. Nottingham
20. Telford and Wrekin
21. Wolverhampton
22. Walsall
23. Sandwell
24. Dudley
25. Birmingham
26. Solihull
27. Coventry
28. Peterborough
29. South Glos
30. Bristol
31. Bath and NE Somerset
32. Windsor and Maidenhead
33. Slough
34. Reading
35. Wokingham
36. Bracknell Forest
37. Thurrock
38. Southend
39. Medway
40. Plymouth
41. Torbay

LONDON

1. Hillingdon
2. Harrow
3. Barnet
4. Enfield
5. Waltham Forest
6. Redbridge
7. Barking and Dagenham
8. Havering
9. Ealing
10. Brent
11. Camden
12. Haringey
13. Islington
14. Hackney
15. Newham
16. Hounslow
17. Hammersmith and Fulham
18. Kensington and Chelsea
19. City of Westminster
20. City of London
21. Tower Hamlets
22. Richmond upon Thames
23. Wandsworth
24. Lambeth
25. Southwark
26. Lewisham
27. Greenwich
28. Bexley
29. Kingston upon Thames
30. Merton
31. Sutton
32. Croydon
33. Bromley

London

THE CORPORATION OF LONDON
(*see also* page 524)

The City of London is the historic centre at the heart of London known as 'the square mile' around which the vast metropolis has grown over the centuries. The City's residential population is 5,500. The civic government is carried on by the Corporation of London through the Court of Common Council.

The City is an international financial centre, generating over £20 billion a year for the British economy. It includes the head offices of the principal banks, insurance companies and mercantile houses, in addition to buildings ranging from the historic Roman Wall and the 15th-century Guildhall, to the massive splendour of St Paul's Cathedral and the architectural beauty of Wren's spires.

The City of London was described by Tacitus in AD 62 as 'a busy emporium for trade and traders'. Under the Romans it became an important administration centre and hub of the road system. Little is known of London in Saxon times, when it formed part of the kingdom of the East Saxons. In 886 Alfred recovered London from the Danes and reconstituted it a burgh under his son-in-law. In 1066 the citizens submitted to William the Conqueror who in 1067 granted them a charter, which is still preserved, establishing them in the rights and privileges they had hitherto enjoyed.

THE MAYORALTY

The Mayoralty was probably established about 1189, the first Mayor being Henry Fitz Ailwyn who filled the office for 23 years and was succeeded by Fitz Alan (1212–14). A new charter was granted by King John in 1215, directing the Mayor to be chosen annually, which has ever since been done, though in early times the same individual often held the office more than once. A familiar instance is that of 'Whittington, thrice Lord Mayor of London' (in reality four times, 1397, 1398, 1406, 1419); and many modern cases have occurred. The earliest instance of the phrase 'Lord Mayor' in English is in 1414. It was used more generally in the latter part of the 15th century and became invariable from 1535 onwards. At Michaelmas the liverymen in Common Hall choose two Aldermen who have served the office of Sheriff for presentation to the Court of Aldermen, and one is chosen to be Lord Mayor for the following mayoral year.

LORD MAYOR'S DAY

The Lord Mayor of London was previously elected on the feast of St Simon and St Jude (28 October), and from the time of Edward I, at least, was presented to the King or to the Barons of the Exchequer on the following day, unless that day was a Sunday. The day of election was altered to 16 October in 1346, and after some further changes was fixed for Michaelmas Day in 1546, but the ceremonies of admittance and swearing-in of the Lord Mayor continued to take place on 28 and 29 October respectively until 1751. In 1752, at the reform of the calendar, the Lord Mayor was continued in office until 8 November, the 'New Style' equivalent of 28 October. The Lord Mayor is now presented to the Lord Chief Justice at the Royal Courts of Justice on the second Saturday in November to make the final declaration of office, having been sworn in at Guildhall on the preceding day. The procession to the Royal Courts of Justice is popularly known as the Lord Mayor's Show.

REPRESENTATIVES

Aldermen are mentioned in the 11th century and their office is of Saxon origin. They were elected annually between 1377 and 1394, when an Act of Parliament of Richard II directed them to be chosen for life.

The Common Council, elected annually on the first Friday in December, was, at an early date, substituted for a popular assembly called the *Folkmote*. At first only two representatives were sent from each ward, but the number has since been greatly increased. The Corporation is reducing the number of Common Councilmen from 130 to 100 through natural wastage. The Government has introduced legislation to remove anomalies from the election system and to extend the non-resident franchise.

OFFICERS

Sheriffs were Saxon officers; their predecessors were the *wic-reeves* and *portreeves* of London and Middlesex. At first they were officers of the Crown, and were named by the Barons of the Exchequer; but Henry I (in 1132) gave the citizens permission to choose their own Sheriffs, and the annual election of Sheriffs became fully operative under King John's charter of 1199. The citizens lost this privilege, as far as the election of the Sheriff of Middlesex was concerned, by the Local Government Act 1888; but the liverymen continue to choose two Sheriffs of the City of London, who are appointed on Midsummer Day and take office at Michaelmas.

The office of Chamberlain is an ancient one, the first contemporary record of which is 1237. The Town Clerk (or Common Clerk) is mentioned in 1274.

ACTIVITIES

The work of the Corporation is assigned to a number of committees which present reports to the Court of Common Council. These Committees are: City Lands and Bridge House Grants Estates, Policy and Resources, Finance, Planning and Transportation, Central Markets, Billingsgate and Leadenhall Markets, Spitalfields Market, Police, Port and City of London Health and Social Services, Libraries, Art Galleries and Records, Board of Governors of City of London Freemen's School, Music and Drama (Guildhall School of Music and Drama), Establishment, Housing and Sports Development, Gresham (City side), Hampstead Heath Management, Epping Forest and Open Spaces, West Ham Park, Privileges, Barbican Residential and Barbican Centre (Barbican Arts and Conference Centre).

The City's estate, in the possession of which Corporation of London differs from other municipalities, is managed by the City Lands and Bridge House Grants Estates Committee, the chairmanship of which carries with it the title of Chief Commoner.

The Honourable the Irish Society, which manages the Corporation's estates in Ulster, consists of a Governor and five other Aldermen, the Recorder, and 19 Common Councilmen, of whom one is elected Deputy Governor.

THE LORD MAYOR 1998–9*

The Rt. Hon. the Lord Mayor, Lord Levene of Portsoken, KBE
  Secretary, Air Vice-Marshal M. Dicken, CB

THE SHERIFFS 1999–2000

R. G. Finch (*Alderman, Coleman Street*) and Mrs P. A. Halliday (*Councilman, Walbrook*); *elected,* 8 July 1999; *assumed office,* 29 September 1999

---

* The Lord Mayor for 1999–2000 was elected on Michaelmas Day. *See* Stop-press

OFFICERS, ETC

Town Clerk and Chamberlain, B. P. Harty
Chief Commoner (1999), Mrs P. B. Newman
Clerk, The Honourable the Irish Society, S. Waley, The Irish
Chamber, 1st Floor, 75 Watling Street, London
EC4M 9BJ

THE ALDERMEN

Name and Ward	CC	Ald.	Shff.	Lord Mayor
Sir Peter Gadsden, GBE, *Farringdon Wt.*	1969	1971	1970	1979
Sir Christopher Leaver, GBE, *Dowgate*	1973	1974	1979	1981
Sir Alan Traill, GBE, *Langbourn*	1970	1975	1982	1984
Sir David Rowe-Ham, GBE, *Bridge* and *Bridge Wt.*	—	1976	1984	1986
Sir Christopher Collett, GBE, *Broad Street*	1973	1979	1985	1988
Sir Alexander Graham, GBE, *Queenhithe*	1978	1979	1986	1990
Sir Brian Jenkins, GBE, *Cordwainer*	—	1980	1987	1991
Sir Paul Newall, TD, *Walbrook*	1980	1981	1989	1993
Sir Christopher Walford, *Farringdon Wn.*	—	1982	1990	1994
Sir John Chalstrey, *Vintry*	1981	1984	1993	1995
Sir Roger Cork, *Tower*	1978	1983	1992	1996
Richard Nichols, *Candlewick*	1983	1984	1994	1997
Lord Levene of Portsoken, KBE, *Portsoken*	1983	1984	1995	1998

All the above have passed the Civic Chair

	CC	Ald.	Shff.
Clive Martin, OBE, TD, *Aldgate*	—	1985	1996
David Howard, *Cornhill*	1972	1986	1997
James Oliver, *Bishopsgate*	1980	1987	1997
Peter Bull, *Cheap*	1968	1984	
Gavyn Arthur, *Cripplegate*	1988	1991	1998
Robert Finch, *Coleman Street*	—	1992	
Richard Agutter, *Castle Baynard*	—	1995	
Michael Savory, *Bread Street*	1980	1996	
David Brewer, *Bassishaw*	1992	1996	
Nicholas Anstee, *Aldersgate*	1987	1996	
Michael Everard, CBE, *Lime Street*	—	1996	
John Hughesdon, *Billingsgate*	1991	1997	

THE COMMON COUNCIL

Deputy: Each Common Councilman so described serves as
deputy to the Alderman of her/his ward.

Absalom, J. D. (1994)	*Farringdon Wt.*
Altman, L. P., CBE (1996)	*Cripplegate Wn.*
Angell, E. H. (1991)	*Cripplegate Wt.*
Archibald, *Deputy* W. W. (1986)	*Cornhill*
Ayers, K. E. (1996)	*Bassishaw*
Balls, H. D. (1970)	*Castle Baynard*
Barker, *Deputy* J. A. (1981)	*Cripplegate Wn.*
Barnes-Yallowley, H. M. F. (1986)	*Coleman Street*
Beale, *Deputy* M. J. (1979)	*Lime Street*
Bird, J. L., OBE (1977)	*Bridge*
Biroum-Smith, P. L. (1988)	*Dowgate*
Bowman, J. C. R. (1995)	*Aldgate*
Bradshaw, D. J. (1991)	*Cripplegate Wn.*
Bramwell, F. M. (1983)	*Langbourn*
Branson, N. A. C. (1996)	*Bassishaw*
Brewster, J. W., OBE (1994)	*Bassishaw*

Brighton, R. L. (1984)	*Portsoken*
Brooks, W. I. B. (1988)	*Billingsgate*
Byllam-Barnes, J. C. F. B. (1997)	*Cheap*
Caspi, D. R. (1994)	*Bridge*
Cassidy, *Deputy* M. J. (1989)	*Coleman Street*
Catt, B. F. (1982)	*Farringdon Wn.*
Chadwick, R. A. H. (1994)	*Tower*
Challis, G. H., CBE (1978)	*Langbourn*
Charkham, J. P. (1996)	*Farringdon Wt.*
Cohen, Mrs C. M. (1986)	*Lime Street*
Cole, Lt.-Col. Sir Colin, KCB, KCVO, TD (1964)	*Castle Baynard*
Cotgrove, D. (1991)	*Lime Street*
Currie, *Deputy* Miss S. E. M. (1985)	*Cripplegate Wt.*
Daily-Hunt, R. B. (1989)	*Cripplegate Wt.*
Darwin, G. E. (1995)	*Farringdon Wn.*
Davis, C. B. (1991)	*Bread Street*
Dove, W. H., MBE (1993)	*Bishopsgate*
Dunitz, A. A. (1984)	*Portsoken*
Eskenzi, *Deputy* A. N. (1970)	*Farringdon Wn.*
Eve, R. A. (1980)	*Cheap*
Everett, K. M. (1984)	*Candlewick*
Falk, F. A., TD (1997)	*Broad Street*
Farr, M. C. (1998)	*Walbrook*
Farrow, M. W. W. (1996)	*Farringdon Wt.*
Farthing, R. B. C. (1981)	*Aldgate*
Fell, J. A. (1982)	*Queenhithe*
FitzGerald, *Deputy* R. C. A. (1981)	*Bread Street*
Forbes, G. B. (1993)	*Bishopsgate*
Fraser, S. J. (1993)	*Coleman Street*
Fraser, W. B. (1981)	*Vintry*
Galloway, A. D. (1981)	*Broad Street*
Gillon, G. M. F. (1995)	*Cordwainer*
Ginsburg, S. (1990)	*Bishopsgate*
Gowman, Miss A. J. (1991)	*Dowgate*
Graves, A. C. (1985)	*Bishopsgate*
Green, C. (1994)	*Aldersgate*
Griffiths, Mrs R. M. (1996)	*Cripplegate Wt.*
Hall, B. R. H. (1995)	*Farringdon Wn.*
Halliday, Mrs P. (1992)	*Walbrook*
Hardwick, Dr P. B. (1987)	*Aldgate*
Harris, B. N. (1996)	*Broad Street*
Hart, *Deputy* M. G. (1970)	*Bridge*
Haynes, J. E. H. (1986)	*Cornhill*
Henderson, J. S., OBE (1975)	*Langbourn*
Henderson-Begg, M. (1977)	*Coleman Street*
Holland, *Deputy* J., CBE (1972)	*Aldgate*
Holliday, Mrs E. H. L. (1987)	*Vintry*
Horlock, *Deputy* H. W. S. (1969)	*Farringdon Wn.*
Jackson, L. St J. T. (1978)	*Bread Street*
Kellett, Mrs M. W. F. (1986)	*Tower*
Kemp, D. L. (1984)	*Coleman Street*
Knowles, S. K. (1984)	*Candlewick*
Lawrence, A. A. (1994)	*Farringdon Wt.*
Lawson, G. C. H. (1971)	*Portsoken*
Leck, P. (1998)	*Aldersgate*
Littlechild, Mrs V. (1998)	*Cripplegate Wt.*
Littlestone, N. (1993)	*Aldersgate*
Luder, I. D. (1998)	*Farringdon Wt.*
McGuinness, C. (1997)	*Castle Baynard*
MacLellan, *Deputy* A. P. W. (1989)	*Walbrook*
McNeil, I. D. (1977)	*Lime Street*
Malins, *Deputy* J. H., QC (1981)	*Farringdon Wt.*
Martinelli, *Deputy* P. J. (1994)	*Bassishaw*
Mayhew, Miss J. (1986)	*Queenhithe*
Mayhew, J. P. (1996)	*Aldersgate*
Mead, Mrs W. (1997)	*Farringdon Wt.*
Mitchell, *Deputy* C. R. (1971)	*Castle Baynard*
Mizen, *Deputy* D. H. (1979)	*Broad Street*
Mobsby, *Deputy* D. J. L. (1985)	*Billingsgate*

Mooney, B. D. F. (1998)	*Queenhithe*
Morgan, *Deputy* B. L., CBE (1963)	*Bishopsgate*
Moss, A. D. (1989)	*Tower*
Nash, *Deputy* Mrs J. C. (1983)	*Aldersgate*
Newman, Mrs P. B. (1989)	*Aldersgate*
O'Ferrall, P. C. K., OBE (1996)	*Aldgate*
Owen, Mrs J. (1975)	*Langbourn*
Owen-Ward, J. R. (1983)	*Bridge*
Parmley, A. C., PH.D. (1992)	*Vintry*
Pembroke, *Deputy* Mrs A. M. F. (1978)	*Cheap*
Platts-Mills, J. F. F., QC	*Farringdon Wt.*
Ponsonby of Shulbrede, *Deputy* Lady (1981)	*Farringdon Wt.*
Price, E. E. (1996)	*Farringdon Wt.*
Pulman, *Deputy* G. A. G. (1983)	*Tower*
Punter, C. (1993)	*Cripplegate Wn.*
Quilter, S. D. (1998)	*Cripplegate Wt.*
Regan, R. D. (1998)	*Farringdon Wn.*
Revell-Smith, *Deputy* P. A., CBE (1959)	*Vintry*
Rigby, P. P., CBE (1972)	*Farringdon Wn.*
Robinson, Mrs D. C. (1989)	*Bishopsgate*
Roney, *Deputy* E. P. T., CBE (1974)	*Bishopsgate*
Samuel, *Deputy* Mrs I., MBE (1971)	*Portsoken*
Sargant, K. A. (1991)	*Cornhill*
Saunders, *Deputy* R. (1975)	*Candlewick*
Scriven, R. G., CBE (1984)	*Candlewick*
Sellon, S. A., OBE, TD (1990)	*Cordwainer*
Shalit, D. M. (1972)	*Farringdon Wn.*
Sharp, *Deputy* Mrs I. M. (1974)	*Queenhithe*
Sherlock, M. R. C. (1992)	*Dowgate*
Snyder, *Deputy* M. J. (1986)	*Cordwainer*
Spanner, J. H., TD (1984)	*Broad Street*
Stevenson, F. P. (1994)	*Cripplegate Wn.*
Taylor, J. A. F., TD (1991)	*Bread Street*
Thorp, C. R. (1996)	*Billingsgate*
Thorp, D. A. R. (1998)	*Dowgate*
Trotter, J. (1993)	*Billingsgate*
Walsh, S. (1989)	*Farringdon Wt.*
Warner, D. W. (1994)	*Cripplegate Wn.*
White, Dr J. W. (1986)	*Cornhill*
Willoughby, P. J. (1985)	*Bishopsgate*
Wilmot, R. T. D. (1973)	*Cordwainer*
Wixley, G. R. A., CBE, TD (1964)	*Coleman Street*

The City Guilds (Livery Companies)

The constitution of the livery companies has been unchanged for centuries. There are three ranks of membership: freemen, liverymen and assistants. A person can become a freeman by patrimony (through a parent having been a freeman); by servitude (through having served an apprenticeship to a freeman); or by redemption (by purchase).

Election to the livery is the prerogative of the company, who can elect any of its freemen as liverymen. Assistants are usually elected from the livery and form a Court of Assistants which is the governing body of the company. The Master (in some companies called the Prime Warden) is elected annually from the assistants.

As at June 1998, 22,923 liverymen of the guilds were entitled to vote at elections at Common Hall.

The order of precedence, omitting extinct companies, is given in parenthesis after the name of each company in the list below. In certain companies the election of Master or Prime Warden for the year does not take place until the autumn. In such cases the Master or Prime Warden for 1998–9 is given.

THE TWELVE GREAT COMPANIES
In order of civic precedence

MERCERS (*1*). *Hall*, Ironmonger Lane, London EC2V 8HE. *Livery*, 253. *Clerk*, C. H. Parker. *Master*, P. R. Withers Green

GROCERS (*2*). *Hall*, Princes Street, London EC2R 8AD. *Livery*, 325. *Clerk*, P. P. Rawlins, MBE. *Master*, His Honour Judge S. Coltart

DRAPERS (*3*). *Hall*, Throgmorton Avenue, London EC2N 2DQ. *Livery*, 252. *Clerk*, A. L. Lang, MBE. *Master*, J. M. F. Padovan

FISHMONGERS (*4*). *Hall*, London Bridge, London EC4R 9EL. *Livery*, 363. *Clerk*, K. S. Waters. *Prime Warden*, The Earl of Clarendon

GOLDSMITHS (*5*). *Hall*, Foster Lane, London EC2V 6BN. *Livery*, 280. *Clerk*, R. D. Buchanan-Dunlop, CBE. *Prime Warden*, Sir Nigel Broackes

MERCHANT TAYLORS (*6/7*). *Hall*, 30 Threadneedle Street, London EC2R 8JB. *Livery*, 300. *Clerk*, D. A. Peck. *Master*, Alderman Sir Brian Jenkins, GBE

SKINNERS (*6/7*). *Hall*, 8 Dowgate Hill, London EC4R 2SP. *Livery*, 400. *Clerk*, Capt. D. Hart Dyke, CBE, LVO, RN. *Master*, Sir Andrew Wilson, KCB, AFC

HABERDASHERS (*8*). *Clerk*, Capt. R. J. Fisher, RN, *Hall*, *Livery*, 320. 39-40 Bartholomew Close, London EC1A 7JN. *Master*, M. D. G. Wheldon, FRICS

SALTERS (*9*). *Hall*, 4 Fore Street, London EC2Y 5DE. *Livery*, 165. *Clerk*, Col. M. P. Barneby. *Master*, The Hon. A. H. Todd

IRONMONGERS (*10*). *Hall*, Shaftesbury Place, Barbican, London EC2Y 8AA. *Livery*, 130. *Clerk*, J. A. Oliver. *Master*, Sir Richard Evans, KCMG, KCVO

VINTNERS (*11*). *Hall*, Upper Thames Street, London EC4V 3BG. *Livery*, 300. *Clerk*, Brig. M. Smythe, OBE. *Master*, A. J. Buchanan

CLOTHWORKERS (*12*). *Hall*, Dunster Court, Mincing Lane, London EC3R 7AH. *Livery*, 200. *Clerk*, M. G. T. Harris. *Master*, Sir John B. Hall, Bt.

OTHER CITY GUILDS
In alphabetical order

ACTUARIES (*91*). *Livery*, 187. *Clerk*, Mrs J. V. Evans, 81 Worrin Road, Shenfield, Brentwood, Essex CM15 8JN. *Master*, S. J. Green

AIR PILOTS AND AIR NAVIGATORS, GUILD OF (*81*). *Livery*, 500. *Grand Master*, HRH The Prince Philip, Duke of Edinburgh, KG, KT, OM, GBE, PC. *Clerk*, Air Vice-Marshal R. G. Peters, CB, Cobham House, 291 Grays Inn Road, London WC1X 8QF. *Master*, Capt J. C. Hutchinson

APOTHECARIES, SOCIETY OF (*58*). *Hall*, 14 Black Friars Lane, London EC4V 6EJ. *Livery*, 1700. *Clerk*, Lt.-Col. R. J. Stringer. *Master*, R. J. Parker

ARBITRATORS (*93*). *Livery*, 160. *Clerk*, Mrs G. Duffy, 13 Hall Gardens, Colney Heath, St Albans, Herts AL4 0QF. *Master*, J. Mackie

ARMOURERS AND BRASIERS (*22*). *Hall*, 81 Coleman Street, London EC2R 5BJ. *Livery*, 120. *Clerk*, Cdr. T. J. K. Sloane, OBE, RN. *Master*, G. Archer Garnett

BAKERS (*19*). *Hall*, Harp Lane, London EC3R 6DP. *Livery*, 390. *Clerk*, J. W. Tompkins. *Master*, C. Gilford

BARBERS (*17*). *Hall*, Monkwell Square, Wood Street, London EC2Y 5BL. *Livery*, 312. *Clerk*, Brig. A. F. Eastburn. *Master*, The Rt. Hon. The Lord McColl of Dulwich, CBE, FRCS

BASKETMAKERS (*52*). *Livery*, 317. *Clerk*, Maj. G. J. Flint-Shipman, TD, 48 Seymour Walk, London SW10 9NF. *Prime Warden*, Deputy G. A. G. Pulman

BLACKSMITHS (*40*). *Livery*, 237. *Clerk*, C. Jerl, 48 Upwood Road, London SE12 8AN. *Prime Warden*, H. A. E. Adams

BOWYERS (*38*). *Livery*, 108. *Clerk*, J. R. Owen-Ward, 11 Aldermans Hill, London N13 4YD. *Master*, W. P. Forrester

BREWERS (*14*). *Hall*, Aldermanbury Square, London EC2V 7HR. *Livery*, 140. *Clerk*, C. W. Dallmeyer. *Master*, R. H. B. Neame

BRODERERS (*48*). *Livery*, 168. *Clerk*, P. J. C. Crouch, 11 Bridge Road, East Molesey, Surrey KT8 9EU. *Master*, A. T. Peck

BUILDERS MERCHANTS (*88*). *Livery*, 185. *Clerk*, Miss S. M. Robinson, TD, 4 College Hill, London EC4R 2RB. *Master*, S. B. Tusting

BUTCHERS (*24*). *Hall*, 87 Bartholomew Close, London EC1A 7EB. *Livery*, 648. *Clerk*, G. J. Sharp. *Master*, G. A. Jackman

CARMEN (*77*). *Livery*, 430. *Clerk*, Cdr. R. M. H. Bawtree, OBE, RN, 35/37 Ludgate Hill, London EC4M 7JN. *Master*, J. M. Silbermann, OBE, FRSA

CARPENTERS (*26*). *Hall*, 1 Throgmorton Avenue, London EC2N 2JJ. *Livery*, 174. *Clerk*, Maj.-Gen. P. T. Stevenson, OBE. *Master*, N. B. C. Evelegh, MBE

CHARTERED ACCOUNTANTS (*86*). *Livery*, 340. *Clerk*, C. Bygrave, The Rustlings, Valley Close, Studham, Dunstable LU6 2QN. *Master*, D. T. Young

CHARTERED ARCHITECTS (*98*). *Livery*, 112. *Clerk*, J. Griffiths, 28 Palace Road, East Molesey, Surrey KT8 9DL. *Master*, Prof. P. Dale

CHARTERED SECRETARIES AND ADMINISTRATORS (*87*). *Livery*, 240. *Clerk*, Maj. I. F. Stewart, Sadler's Hall, 3rd Floor, 40 Gutter Lane, London EC2V 6BR. *Master*, W. C. Hammond, MBE

CHARTERED SURVEYORS (*85*). *Livery*, 350. *Clerk*, Mrs A. L. Jackson, 16 St Mary-at-Hill, London EC3R 8EE. *Master*, Miss D. F. Patman

CLOCKMAKERS (*61*). *Livery*, 230. *Clerk*, Gp Capt. P. H. Gibson, MBE, Room 66-67 Albert Buildings, 49 Queen Victoria Street, London EC4N 4SE. *Master*, Prof. A. Boksenberg, CBE, FRS

COACHMAKERS AND COACH-HARNESS MAKERS (*72*). *Livery*, 420. *Clerk*, Gp Capt. G. Bunn, CBE, Charlcote House, Burfield Road, Chorleywood, Herts WD3 5NS. *Master*, P. Ashfield

CONSTRUCTORS (*99*). *Livery*, 130. *Clerk*, L. L. Brace, 181 Fentiman Road, London SW8 1JY. *Master*, D. A. Hutchison, MBE

COOKS (*35*). *Livery*, 75. *Clerk*, M. C. Thatcher, Registry Chambers, The Old Deanery, Deans Court, London EC4V 5AA. *Master*, P. D. Herbage

COOPERS (*36*). *Hall*, 13 Devonshire Square, London EC2M 4TH. *Livery*, 265. *Clerk*, J. A. Newton. *Master*, M. J. Howell

CORDWAINERS (*27*). *Livery*, 163. *Clerk*, Lt.-Col. J. R. Blundell, RM, Eldon Chambers, 30 Fleet Street, London EC4Y 1AA. *Master*, Dr R. K. H. Parker

CURRIERS (*29*). *Livery*, 96. *Clerk*, Gp Capt. F. J. Hamilton, Kestrel Cottage, East Knoyle, Salisbury SP3 6AD. *Master*, C. W. Rome

CUTLERS (*18*). *Hall*, Warwick Lane, London EC4M 7BR. *Livery*, 100. *Clerk*, K. S. G. Hinde, OBE, TD. *Master*, C. M. Li Evans

DISTILLERS (*69*). *Livery*, 270. *Clerk*, C. V. Hughes, 71 Lincoln's Inn Fields, London WC2A 3JF. *Master*, R. H. Nicholson

DYERS (*13*). *Hall*, 10 Dowgate Hill, London EC4R 2ST. *Livery*, 123. *Clerk*, J. R. Chambers. *Prime Warden*, Lt. Col. M. A. Marshall

ENGINEERS (*94*). *Livery*, 282. *Clerk*, Cdr. B. D. Gibson, Kiln Bank, Bodle Street Green, Hailsham, E. Sussex BN27 4UA. *Master*, R. H. Rooley, FREng.

ENVIRONMENTAL CLEANERS (*97*). *Livery*, 235. *Clerk*, J. C. M. Chapman, Woodside Cottage, 44 New Road, Bengeo, Herts SG14 3JL. *Master*, D. A. S. Grant

FAN MAKERS (*76*). *Livery*, 202. *Clerk*, Lt.-Col. I. R. P. Green, 2 Bolts Hill, Castle Camps, Cambridge CB1 6TL. *Master*, M. H. Davis

FARMERS (*80*). *Hall*, 3 Cloth Street, London EC1A 7LD. *Livery*, 300. *Clerk*, Miss M. L. Winter. *Master*, J. H. Cossins, CBE

FARRIERS (*55*). *Livery*, 375. *Clerk*, Mrs C. C. Clifford, 19 Queen Street, Chipperfield, Kings Langley, Herts WD4 9BT. *Master*, R. J. Crocker

FELTMAKERS (*63*). *Livery*, 170. *Clerk*, Lt.-Col. C. J. Holroyd, Providence Cottage, Chute Cadley, Andover, Hants SP11 9EB. *Master*, Cdre I. R. Welsey-Harding

FLETCHERS (*39*). *Hall*, 3 Cloth Street, London EC1A 7LD. *Livery*, 108. *Clerk*, J. R. Owen-Ward. *Master*, R. H. Upton

FOUNDERS (*33*). *Hall*, Number One, Cloth Fair, London EC1A 7HT. *Livery*, 175. *Clerk*, A. J. Gillett. *Master*, L. W. Kemp

FRAMEWORK KNITTERS (*64*). *Livery*, 211. *Clerk*, H. W. H. Ellis, Whitegarth Chambers, 37 The Uplands, Loughton, Essex IG10 1NQ. *Master*, T. D. P. Turnbull

FRUITERERS (*45*). *Livery*, 262. *Clerk*, Lt.-Col. L. G. French, Chapelstones, 84 High Street, Codford St Mary, Warminster BA12 0ND. *Master*, L. S. Olins

FUELLERS (*95*). *Livery*, 66. *Clerk*, R. A. Riley, 22 Broadfields, Headstone Lane, Hatch End, Middx HA2 6NH. *Master*, V. M. F. Williams

FURNITURE MAKERS (*83*). *Livery*, 292. *Clerk*, Mrs J. A. Wright, Painters' Hall, 9 Little Trinity Lane, London EC4V 2AD. *Master*, J. A. Jacobs

GARDENERS (*66*). *Livery*, 247. *Clerk*, Col. N. G. S. Gray, 25 Luke Street, London EC2A 4AR. *Master*, The Revd Canon P. Delaney

GIRDLERS (*21*). *Hall*, Basinghall Avenue, London EC2V 5DD. *Livery*, 80. *Clerk*, Lt.-Col. R. Sullivan. *Master*, A. R. Westall

GLASS-SELLERS (*71*). *Livery*, 167. *Hon. Clerk*, B. J. Rawles, 43 Aragon Avenue, Thames Ditton, Surrey KT7 0PY. *Master*, The Rt. Revd J. Waine, KCVO

GLAZIERS AND PAINTERS OF GLASS (*53*). *Hall*, 9 Montague Close, London SE1 9DD. *Livery*, 240. *Clerk*, Col. D. W. Eking. *Master*, P. R. Batchelor

GLOVERS (*62*). *Livery*, 270. *Clerk*, Mrs M. Hood, 71 Ifield Road, London SW10 9AU. *Master*, Mrs M. Linton

GOLD AND SILVER WYRE DRAWERS (*74*). *Livery*, 310. *Clerk*, J. R. Williams, 50 Cheyne Avenue, London E18 2DR. *Master*, K. P. Kirby

GUNMAKERS (*73*). *Livery*, 268. *Clerk*, J. M. Riches, The Proof House, 48-50 Commercial Road, London E1 1LP. *Master*, Col. D. C. Munn

HORNERS (*54*). *Livery*, 244. *Clerk*, A. R. Layard. Whitethorns, Rannoch Road, Crowborough, E. Sussex TN6 1RA. *Master*, L. P. Smith

INFORMATION TECHNOLOGISTS (*100*). *Livery*, 300. *Clerk*, Mrs G. Davies, 30 Aylesbury Street, London EC1R 0ER. *Master*, P. Cropper

INNHOLDERS (*32*). *Hall*, 30 College Street, London EC4R 2RH. *Livery*, 129. *Clerk*, J. R. Edwardes Jones. *Master*, Dr R. Glover

INSURERS (*92*). *Hall*, 20 Aldermanbury, London EC2V 7HY. *Livery*, 380. *Clerk*, L. J. Walters. *Master*, M. J. Pickard

JOINERS AND CEILERS (*41*). *Livery*, 125. *Clerk*, Mrs A. L. Jackson, 75 Meadway Drive, Horsell, Woking, Surrey GU21 4TF. *Master*, R. W. E. Rogan

LAUNDERERS (*89*). *Hall*, 9 Montague Close, London Bridge, London SE1 9DD. *Livery*, 250. *Clerk*, Mrs J. Polek. *Master*, T. A. Elliott

LEATHERSELLERS (*15*). *Hall*, 15 St Helen's Place, London EC3A 6DQ. *Livery*, 150. *Clerk*, Capt. J. G. F. Cooke, OBE, RN. *Master*, R. S. Whitmore

LIGHTMONGERS (*96*). *Livery*, 145. *Clerk*, D. B. Wheatley, Crown Wharf, 11a Coldharbour, Blackwall Reach, London E14 9NS. *Master*, E. H. Ring

LORINERS (*57*). *Livery*, 353. *Clerk*, G. B. Forbes, 50 Cheyne Avenue, London E18 2DR. *Master*, E. I. Walker-Arnott

MAKERS OF PLAYING CARDS (*75*). *Livery*, 148. *Clerk*, M. J. Smyth, 6 The Priory, Godstone, Surrey RH9 8NL. *Master*, G. H. E. Robson

MARKETORS (*90*). *Livery*, 220. *Clerk*, Mrs G. Duffy, 13 Hall Gardens, Colney Heath, St Albans, Herts AL4 0PF. *Master*, Prof. J. A. P. Treasure

MASONS (*30*). *Livery*, 125. *Clerk*, P. F. Clark, 22 Cannon Hill, Southgate, London N14 6LG. *Master*, B. J. Rushton

MASTER MARINERS, HONOURABLE COMPANY OF (*78*). HQS Wellington, Temple Stairs, Victoria Embankment, London WC2R 2PN. *Livery*, 220. *Admiral*, HRH The Prince Philip, Duke of Edinburgh, KG, KT, OM, GBE, PC. *Clerk*, J. A. V. Maddock. *Master*, Capt G. M. Pepper

MUSICIANS (*50*). *Livery*, 359. *Clerk*, S. F. N. Waley, 75 Watling Street, London EC4M 9BJ. *Master*, Sir Alan Traill, QSD

NEEDLEMAKERS (*65*). *Livery*, 230. *Clerk*, M. G. Cook, 5 Staple Inn, London WC1V 7QH. *Master*, Sir Anthony Wilson

PAINTER-STAINERS (*28*). *Hall*, 9 Little Trinity Lane, London EC4V 2AD. *Livery*, 320. *Clerk*, Col. W. J. Chesshyre. *Master*, The Hon. M. Robson

PATTENMAKERS (*70*). *Livery*, 200. *Clerk*, Lt. Col. R. W. Murfin, TD, Vanguard House, Sutton Valence, Kent ME17 3JA. *Master*, R. P. Ziff

PAVIORS (*56*). *Livery*, 230. *Clerk*, J. L. White, 3 Ridgemount Gardens, Enfield, Middx EN2 8QL. *Master*, P. D. Marriott Gell

PEWTERERS (*16*). *Hall*, Oat Lane, London EC2V 7DE. *Livery*, 119. *Clerk*, Cdr. A. St J. Steiner, OBE, RN. *Master*, W. Grant

PLAISTERERS (*46*). *Hall*, 1 London Wall, London EC2Y 5JU. *Livery*, 205. *Clerk*, R. Vickers. *Master*, C. Towlson

PLUMBERS (*31*). *Livery*, 347. *Clerk*, Lt.-Col. R. J. A. Paterson-Fox, Room 28, 49 Queen Victoria Street, London EC4N 4SA. *Master*, J. H. Mayfield

POULTERS (*34*). *Livery*, 180. *Clerk*, A. W. Scott, 23 Orchard Drive, Chorleywood, Herts WD3 5QN. *Master*, C. R. S. Link

SADDLERS (*25*). *Hall*, 40 Gutter Lane, London EC2V 6BR. *Livery*, 75. *Clerk*, Gp Capt. W. S. Brereton Martin, CBE. *Master*, M. R. Quirk, OBE

SCIENTIFIC INSTRUMENT MAKERS (*84*). *Hall*, 9 Montague Close, London SE1 9DD. *Livery*, 235. *Clerk*, F. G. Everard. *Master*, M. T. Dixon

SCRIVENERS (*44*). *Livery*, 245. *Clerk*, G. A. Hill, HQS Wellington, Temple Stairs, Victoria Embankment, London WC2R 2PN. *Master*, N. Grimston

SHIPWRIGHTS (*59*). *Livery*, 400. *Permanent Master*, HRH The Prince Philip, Duke of Edinburgh, KG, KT, OM, GBE, PC. *Clerk*, Capt. R. F. Channon, RN, Ironmongers Hall, Barbican, London EC2Y 8AA. *Prime Warden*, P. Tudball, CBE

SOLICITORS (*79*). *Livery*, 260. *Clerk*, Miss S. M. Robinson, TD, 4 College Hill, London EC2R 2RB. *Master*, M. R. Mathews

SPECTACLE MAKERS (*60*). *Livery*, 230. *Clerk*, Lt.-Col. J. A. B. Salmon, OBE, LLB, Apothecaries' Hall, Black Friars Lane, London EC4V 6EL. *Master*, A. H. Chignell, FRCS

STATIONERS AND NEWSPAPER MAKERS (*47*). *Hall*, Ave Maria Lane, London EC4M 7DD. *Livery*, 446. *Clerk*, Brig. D. G. Sharp, AFC. *Master*, R. T. H. Harrison

TALLOW CHANDLERS (*21*). *Hall*, 4 Dowgate Hill, London EC4R 2SH. *Livery*, 180. *Clerk*, Brig. W. K. L. Prosser, CBE, MC. *Master*, Brig. N. H. Thompson, CBE

TIN PLATE WORKERS (ALIAS WIRE WORKERS) (*67*). *Livery*, 200. *Clerk*, M. Henderson-Begg, Bartholomew House, 66 Westbury Road, New Malden, Surrey KT3 5AS. *Master*, Dr B. T. K. Barry

TOBACCO PIPE MAKERS AND TOBACCO BLENDERS (*82*). *Livery*, 161. *Clerk*, N. J. Hallings-Pott, Hackhurst Farm, Lower Dicker, Hailsham, E. Sussex BN27 4BP. *Master*, The Hon. M. H. Richards

TURNERS (*51*). *Livery*, 190. *Clerk*, E. A. Windsor Clive, c/o Apothecaries' Hall, Black Friars Lane, London EC4V 6EL. *Master*, Dr J. M. Slater, BScM, PhD

TYLERS AND BRICKLAYERS (*37*). *Livery*, 126. *Clerk*, J. A. Norris, Hawthorns, Claygate Lane, Thames Ditton, Surrey KT7 0DT. *Master*, Sir Idris Pearce, CBE, TD

UPHOLDERS (*49*). *Livery*, 225. *Clerk*, J. P. Cody, Hall in the Wood, 46 Quail Gardens, Selsdon Vale, Croydon CR2 8TF. *Master*, C. B. Roffe

WAX CHANDLERS (*20*). *Hall*, Gresham Street, London EC2V 7AD. *Livery*, 119. *Clerk*, Cdr J. Stevens. *Master*, B. E. A. Reynolds

WEAVERS (*42*). *Livery*, 125. *Clerk*, Mrs F. Newcombe, Saddlers' House, Gutter Lane, London EC2V 6BR. *Upper Bailiff*, R. H. W. Graham-Palmer

WHEELWRIGHTS (*68*). *Livery*, 212. *Clerk*, P. J. C. Crouch, 11 Bridge Road, East Molesey, Surrey KT8 9EU. *Master*, T. W. P. Bridges

WOOLMEN (*43*). *Livery*, 135. *Clerk*, F. Allen, Hollands, Hedsor Road, Bourne End, Bucks SL8 5EE. *Master*, P. F. Valpy

FIREFIGHTERS (*No livery*). *Freemen*, 127. *Clerk*, G. P. Ellis, The Insurance Hall, 20 Aldermanbury, London EC2V 7GF. *Master*, Prof. D. E. Bland, OBE

PARISH CLERKS (*No livery*). *Members*, 95. *Clerk*, Lt. Col. B. J. N. Coombes, c/o 1 Dean Trench Street, London SW1P 3HB. *Master*, W. H. Dove, MBE

WATER CONSERVATORS (*No livery*). *Hall*, 16 St Mary-at-Hill, London EC2R 8EE. *Freemen. Hon. Clerk*, H. B. Berridge, MBE. *Master*, Dr E. W. Jackson

WATERMEN AND LIGHTERMEN (*No livery*). *Hall*, 16 St Mary-at-Hill, London EC3R 8EF. *Craft Owning Freemen*, 360. *Clerk*, C. Middlemiss. *Master*, J. Johnson

WORLD TRADERS (*No livery*). *Freemen*, 146. *Clerk*, N. R. Pullman, 36 Ladbroke Grove, London W11 2PA. *Master*, Sir Roger Cork

LONDON BOROUGH COUNCILS

Council	Municipal offices	Population	Band D charge 1999	Chief Executive (*Managing Director)	Mayor (a) Lord Mayor 1999–2000
Barking and Dagenham;	°Dagenham, RM10 7BN	143,681	£738.00	W. C. Smith	W. Dale
Barnet	†The Burroughs, Hendon, NW4 4BG	293,564	760.85	M. Caller	J. Cohen
Bexley	‡Bexleyheath, Kent DA6 7LB	215,615	750.18	C. Duffield	Mrs L. Bailey
Brent	†Forty Lane, Wembley, HA9 9EZ	243,025	678.46	G. Daniel	J. Lebor
Bromley	°Bromley, BR1 3UH	290,609	669.96	Dr M. Blanch	Ms S. Polydoru
§Camden	†Judd Street, WC1H 9JE	170,444	896.57	S. Bundred	R. Shaw
§CITY OF WESTMINSTER	City Hall, Victoria Street, SW1E 6QP	174,814	350.00	W. Roots	(a) A. Segal
Croydon	Taberner House, Park Lane, Croydon, CR9 3JS	313,510	758.39	D. Wechsler	S. Khan
Ealing	†Uxbridge Road, W5 2HL	275,257	643.00	Ms G. Guy	P. Portwood
Enfield	°Silver Street, Enfield, EN1 3XA	257,417	732.61	D. Plank	E. Smythe
§Greenwich	†Wellington Street, SE18 6PW	207,650	883.35	D. Brooks	J. Fahy
§Hackney	†Mare Street, E8 1EA	181,248	789.60	*S. Ebanja (acting)	J. Lobenstein, MBE
§Hammersmith and Fulham	†King Street, W6 9JU	148,502	827.02	*R. Harbord	A. Slaughter
Haringey	°High Road, N22 4LE	202,204	898.00	G. Singh	Ms M. Dewar
Harrow	°Harrow, HA1 2UJ	200,100	787.53	A. Redmond	Ms A. Groves
Havering	†Romford, RM1 3BD	229,492	724.00	H. W. Tinworth	Mrs M. Whitelock
Hillingdon	°High Street, Uxbridge, UB8 1UW	231,602	763.66	D. Leatham	M. Lancaster
Hounslow	°Lampton Road, Hounslow, TW3 4DN	204,397	795.43	D. Myers	G. Dhillon
§Islington	†Upper Street, N1 2UD	164,686	912.00	Ms L. Fullick	Ms J. Sands
§Kensington and Chelsea (RB)	†Hornton Street, W8 7NX	138,394	572.79	A. Taylor	Mrs P. Frazer
Kingston upon Thames (RB)	Guildhall, Kingston upon Thames, KT1 1EU	132,996	793.58	vacant	Ms J. Smith
§Lambeth	†Brixton Hill, SW2 1RW	244,834	642.00	Ms H. Rabbatts	S. Bourne
§Lewisham	†Catford, SE6 4RU	230,983	727.87	Dr B. Quirk	D. Sullivan
Merton	°London Road, Morden, SM4 5DX	168,470	784.24	R. Paine	Ms J. Paton
§Newham	†East Ham, E6 2RP	212,170	704.43	Dr W. Thomson	R. A. Mirza
Redbridge	†Ilford, IG1 1DD	226,218	750.00	M. Frater	F. Maravala
Richmond upon Thames	°Richmond Road, Twickenham, TW1 3BZ	160,732	834.44	Mrs G. Norton	M. Jones
§Southwark	†Peckham Road, SE5 8UB	218,541	808.60	R. Coomber	C. Cherrill
Sutton	‡St Nicholas Way, Sutton, SM1 1EA	168,880	748.62	Mrs P. Hughes	Ms S. Stears
§Tower Hamlets	107A Commercial Street, E1 6BG	160,064	674.02	Ms S. Pierce	Ms D. Jones
Waltham Forest	†Forest Road, Walthamstow, E17 4JF	212,033	840.29	A. Tobias	P. J. Dawe
§Wandsworth	†Wandsworth High Street, SW18 2PU	252,425	369.87	G. K. Jones	Mrs. L. Ayonrinde

§ Inner London Borough
RB Royal Borough
° Civic Centre
† Town Hall
‡ Civic Offices
For explanation of council tax, *see* pages 521–2

Wales

The Principality of Wales (Cymru) occupies the extreme west of the central southern portion of the island of Great Britain, with a total area of 8,015 sq. miles (20,758 sq. km): land 7,965 sq. miles (20,628 sq. km); inland water 50 sq. miles (130 sq. km). It is bounded on the north by the Irish Sea, on the south by the Bristol Channel, on the east by the English counties of Cheshire, Shropshire, Worcestershire and Gloucestershire, and on the west by St George's Channel.

Across the Menai Straits is the island of Anglesey (Ynys Môn) (276 sq. miles), communication with which is facilitated by the Menai Suspension Bridge (1,000 ft long) built by Telford in 1826, and by the tubular railway bridge (1,100 ft long) built by Stephenson in 1850. Holyhead harbour, on Holy Isle (north-west of Anglesey), provides accommodation for ferry services to Dublin (70 miles).

POPULATION

The population at the 1991 census was 2,835,073 (males 1,370,104; females 1,464,969). The average density of population in 1991 was 1.36 persons per hectare.

RELIEF

Wales is a country of extensive tracts of high plateau and shorter stretches of mountain ranges deeply dissected by river valleys. Lower-lying ground is largely confined to the coastal belt and the lower parts of the valleys. The highest mountains are those of Snowdonia in the north-west (Snowdon, 3,559 ft), Berwyn (Aran Fawddwy, 2,971 ft), Cader Idris (Pen y Gadair, 2,928 ft), Dyfed (Plynlimon, 2,467 ft), and the Black Mountain, Brecon Beacons and Black Forest ranges in the south-east (Carmarthen Van, 2,630 ft, Pen y Fan, 2,906 ft, Waun Fâch, 2,660 ft).

HYDROGRAPHY

The principal river rising in Wales is the Severn (see also page 532), which flows from the slopes of Plynlimon to the English border. The Wye (130 miles) also rises in the slopes of Plynlimon. The Usk (56 miles) flows into the Bristol Channel, through Gwent. The Dee (70 miles) rises in Bala Lake and flows through the Vale of Llangollen, where an aqueduct (built by Telford in 1805) carries the Pontcysyllte branch of the Shropshire Union Canal across the valley. The estuary of the Dee is the navigable portion, 14 miles in length and about five miles in breadth, and the tide rushes in with dangerous speed over the 'Sands of Dee'. The Towy (68 miles), Teifi (50 miles), Taff (40 miles), Dovey (30 miles), Taf (25 miles) and Conway (24 miles), the last named broad and navigable, are wholly Welsh rivers.

The largest natural lake is Bala (Llyn Tegid) in Gwynedd, nearly four miles long and about one mile wide. Lake Vyrnwy is an artificial reservoir, about the size of Bala, and forms the water supply of Liverpool; Birmingham is supplied from reservoirs in the Elan and Claerwen valleys.

WELSH LANGUAGE

According to the 1991 census results, the percentage of persons of three years and over able to speak Welsh was:

Clwyd	18.2	Powys	20.2
Dyfed	43.7	S. Glamorgan	6.5
Gwent	2.4	W. Glamorgan	15.0
Gwynedd	61.0		
Mid Glamorgan	8.5	Wales	18.7

The 1991 figure represents a slight decline from 18.9 per cent in 1981 (1971, 20.8 per cent; 1961, 26 per cent).

FLAG

The flag of Wales, the Red Dragon (Y Ddraig Goch), is a red dragon on a field divided white over green (per fess argent and vert a dragon passant gules). The flag was augmented in 1953 by a royal badge on a shield encircled with a riband bearing the words Ddraig Goch Ddyry Cychwyn and imperially crowned, but this augmented flag is rarely used.

EARLY HISTORY

The earliest inhabitants of whom there is any record appear to have been subdued or exterminated by the Goidels (a people of Celtic race) in the Bronze Age. A further invasion of Celtic Brythons and Belgae followed in the ensuing Iron Age. The Roman conquest of southern Britain and Wales was for some time successfully opposed by Caratacus (Caractacus or Caradog), chieftain of the Catuvellauni and son of Cunobelinus (Cymbeline). South-east Wales was subjugated and the legionary fortress at Caerleon-on-Usk established by about AD 75–77; the conquest of Wales was completed by Agricola about AD 78. Communications were opened up by the construction of military roads from Chester to Caerleon-on-Usk and Caerwent, and from Chester to Conwy (and thence to Carmarthen and Neath). Christianity was introduced during the Roman occupation, in the fourth century.

ANGLO-SAXON ATTACKS

The Anglo-Saxon invaders of southern Britain drove the Celts into the mountain stronghold of Wales, and into Strathclyde (Cumberland and south-west Scotland) and Cornwall, giving them the name of Waelisc (Welsh), meaning 'foreign'. The West Saxons' victory of Deorham (AD 577) isolated Wales from Cornwall and the battle of Chester (AD 613) cut off communication with Strathclyde and northern Britain. In the eighth century the boundaries of the Welsh were further restricted by the annexations of Offa, King of Mercia, and counter-attacks were largely prevented by the construction of an artificial boundary from the Dee to the Wye (Offa's Dyke).

In the ninth century Rhodri Mawr (844–878) united the country and successfully resisted further incursions of the Saxons by land and raids of Norse and Danish pirates by sea, but at his death his three provinces of Gwynedd (north), Powys (mid) and Deheubarth (south) were divided among his three sons, Anarawd, Mervyn and Cadell. Cadell's son Hywel Dda ruled a large part of Wales and codified its laws but the provinces were not united again until the rule of Llewelyn ap Seisyllt (husband of the heiress of Gwynedd) from 1018 to 1023.

THE NORMAN CONQUEST

After the Norman conquest of England, William I created palatine counties along the Welsh frontier, and the Norman barons began to make encroachments into Welsh territory. The Welsh princes recovered many of their losses during the civil wars of Stephen's reign and in the early 13th century Owen Gruffydd, prince of Gwynedd, was the dominant figure in Wales. Under Llewelyn ap Iorwerth (1194–1240) the Welsh united in powerful resistance to English incursions and Llewelyn's privileges and de facto independence were recognized in Magna Carta. His grandson, Llewelyn ap Gruffydd, was the last native prince; he was killed in 1282 during hostilities between the Welsh and English, allowing Edward I of England to establish his authority over the country. On 7 February 1301, Edward of Caernarvon, son of Edward I, was created Prince of Wales, a title which has subsequently been borne by the eldest son of the sovereign.

Strong Welsh national feeling continued, expressed in the early 15th century in the rising led by Owain Glyndŵr, but the situation was altered by the accession to the English throne in 1485 of Henry VII of the Welsh House of Tudor. Wales was politically assimilated to England under the Act of Union of 1535, which extended English laws to the Principality and gave it parliamentary representation for the first time.

EISTEDDFOD

The Welsh are a distinct nation, with a language and literature of their own, and the national bardic festival (Eisteddfod), instituted by Prince Rhys ap Griffith in 1176, is still held annually. These *Eisteddfodau* (sessions) form part of the *Gorsedd* (assembly), which is believed to date from the time of Prydian, a ruling prince in an age many centuries before the Christian era.

PRINCIPAL CITIES

CARDIFF

Cardiff, at the mouth of the Rivers Taff, Rhymney and Ely, is the capital city of Wales and a major administrative, commercial and business centre. The National Assembly for Wales was opened in Cardiff in 1999. It has many industries, including steel, and its flourishing port is within the Cardiff Bay area, subject of a major redevelopment continuing until the year 2000.

The many fine buildings include the City Hall, the National Museum of Wales, University Buildings, Law Courts, Welsh Office, County Hall, Police Headquarters, the Temple of Peace and Health, Llandaff Cathedral, the Welsh National Folk Museum at St Fagans, Cardiff Castle, the New Theatre, the Sherman Theatre and the Welsh College of Music and Drama. More recent buildings include St David's Hall, Cardiff International Arena and World Trade Centre, and the Welsh National Ice Rink. The Millennium Stadium is under construction for the 1999 rugby World Cup and the Centre for Visual Arts opened in 1999.

SWANSEA

Swansea (*Abertawe*) is a city and a seaport. The Gower peninsula was brought within the city boundary under local government reform in 1974. The trade of the port includes coal, steel products, containerized goods, petroleum products and petrochemicals.

The principal buildings are the Norman Castle (rebuilt *c*.1330), the Royal Institution of South Wales, founded in 1835 (including Library), the University of Wales Swansea at Singleton, and the Guildhall, containing Frank Brangwyn's British Empire panels. The Dylan Thomas Centre,

formerly the old Guildhall, was restored in 1995. More recent buildings include the County Hall, the new Maritime Quarter and Marina and the leisure centre.

Swansea was chartered by the Earl of Warwick, *c*. 1158–84, and further charters were granted by King John, Henry III, Edward II, Edward III and James II, Cromwell (two) and the Marcher Lord William de Breos.

LOCAL COUNCILS

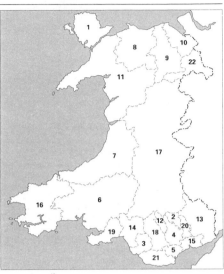

Key	Council
1	Anglesey
2	Blaenau Gwent
3	Bridgend
4	Gwynedd
5	Caerphilly
6	Cardiff
7	Carmarthenshire
8	Ceredigion
9	Conwy
10	Denbighshire
11	Flintshire
12	Merthyr Tydfil
13	Monmouthshire
14	Neath Port Talbot
15	Newport
16	Pembrokeshire
17	Powys
18	Rhondda, Cynon, Taff
19	Swansea
20	Torfaen
21	The Vale of Glamorgan
22	Wrexham

LORD-LIEUTENANTS AND HIGH SHERIFFS

County/Shire	Lord-Lieutenant	High Sheriff, 1999–2000
Clwyd	Sir William Gladstone, Bt., KG	D. E. Williams
Dyfed	Sir David Mansel Lewis, KCVO	J. M. G. Andrews
Gwent	Sir Richard Hanbury Tenison, KCVO	Mrs J. C. Johnson
Gwynedd	vacant	W. D. I. Edwards
Mid Glamorgan	M. A. McLaggan	D. H. Thomas, CBE
Powys	The Hon. Mrs E. S. Legge-Bourke, LVO	J. G. Coltman-Rogers
S. Glamorgan	Capt. N. Lloyd-Edwards	Mrs M. Watkins
W. Glamorgan	R. C. Hastie, CBE	H. A. Steane

LOCAL COUNCILS

SMALL CAPITALS denote CITY status
§ Denotes Borough status

Council	Administrative headquarters	Population	Band D charge 1999	Chief Executive	Chairman 1999–2000 (a) Mayor (b) Lord Mayor
Anglesey	Llangefni	67,055	£534.26¶	G. F. Edwards	R. J. Jones
Blaenau Gwent	Ebbw Vale	73,200	566.54	R. Leadbeter, OBE	(a) Mrs K. M. Williams
Bridgend	Bridgend	128,340	607.56	I. K. Lewis	(a) L. Jenkins
Caerphilly	Hengoed	69,100	637.00	M. Davies	D. Potter
CARDIFF	Cardiff	315,040	572.66	B. Davies	(b) R. Goodway
Carmarthenshire	Carmarthen	169,108	665.85	B. Roynon	K. Maynard
Ceredigion	Aberaeron	69,545	670.00	O. Watkin	W. T. K. Raw-Rees MBE
§Conwy	Conwy	110,600	487.52	C. D. Barker	G. Rees
Denbighshire	Ruthin	90,400	647.00	H. V. Thomas	E. Edwards
Flintshire	Mold	144,900	591.60	P. McGreevy	I. Roberts MBE
Gwynedd	Caernarfon	116,000	614.74	G. R. Jones	W. A. Evans
§Merthyr Tydfil	Merthyr Tydfil	58,100	711.43	G. Meredith	(a) L. C. Elliott
Monmouthshire	Cwmbran	86,248	490.24	Ms J. Redfearn	R. J. B. Wilcox
§Neath Port Talbot	Port Talbot	139,459	749.66	K. R. Sawyers	(a) M. Harris
§Newport	Newport	136,800	656.44	R. D. Blair	(a) F. J. Sweeting
Pembrokeshire	Haverfordwest	114,400	451.71	B. Parry-Jones	B. Phillips
Powys	Llandrindod Wells	124,400	551.98	Miss J. Tonge	G. Morgan
§Rhondda, Cynon, Taff	Tonypandy	240,117	671.92	K. Ryley	G. Beard
SWANSEA	Swansea	230,200	604.18	Ms V. Sugar	(b) R. Lloyd
§Torfaen	Pontypool	90,527	563.87	Dr C. Grace	(a) Ms B. Ryan
Vale of Glamorgan	Barry	119,500	522.00	D. Foster	T. H. Jarvie
§Wrexham	Wrexham	125,200	537.15	D. Griffin	(a) R. Davies

¶ Managing Director

THE NATIONAL ASSEMBLY FOR WALES
(see also pages 1280–91)

In July 1997 the Government announced plans to establish a National Assembly for Wales. In a referendum on 18 September 1997 about 50 per cent of the electorate voted, of whom 50.3 per cent voted in favour of the Assembly. Elections are to be held every four years. The first elections were held on 6 May 1999 when about 46 per cent of the electorate voted. The first session was held on 10 May 1999 and the Assembly was officially opened on 26 May at Crickhowell House, Cardiff; a new building to house the Assembly is under construction in Cardiff.

The Assembly has 60 members (including the Presiding Officer), comprising 40 constituency members and 29 additional regional members from party lists. It can introduce only secondary legislation and has no power to raise or lower income tax.

The National Assembly for Wales is responsible for education, health, training, environment, economic development, local government, housing, planning, financial assistance to industry, tourism, some transport, heritage and the arts, agriculture, forestry and food standards.

SALARIES FROM 1 APRIL 1999:

First Secretary	£64,308 (plus AM salary)
Ministers	£33,360 (plus AM salary)
AMs	£34,438*

* Reduced by two-thirds if the member is already an MP or an MEP

THE WELSH CABINET

First Secretary, The Rt. Hon. Alun Michael, MP, AM (*Lab.*)
Secretary for Economic Development, Rhodri Morgan, MP, AM (*Lab.*)
Secretary for Education Up to Age 16, Rosemary Butler, AM (*Lab.*)
Secretary for Post-16 Education and Training, Tom Middlehurst, AM (*Lab.*)
Secretary for Health and Social Services, Jane Hutt, AM (*Lab.*)
Secretary for Agriculture and the Rural Economy, Christine Gwyther, AM (*Lab.*)
Secretary for the Environment, Peter Law, AM (*Lab.*)
Trefnydd Manager, Andrew Davies, AM (*Lab.*)
Finance Secretary, Edwina Hart, AM (*Lab.*)

STATE OF THE PARTIES *as at May 1999*

	Constituency AMs	Regional AMs	Total
Labour	27	1	28
Plaid Cymru	8†	8	16†
Conservative	1	8	9
Liberal Democrats	3	3	6
Presiding Officer (The Lord Elis-Thomas, AM)	1	0	1

† Excludes the Presiding Officer, who has no party allegiance while in post

Scotland

The Kingdom of Scotland occupies the northern portion of the main island of Great Britain and includes the Inner and Outer Hebrides, and the Orkney, Shetland, and many other islands. It lies between 60° 51′ 30″ and 54° 38′ N. latitude and between 1° 45′ 32″ and 6° 14′ W. longitude, with England to the south, the Atlantic Ocean on the north and west, and the North Sea on the east.

The greatest length of the mainland (Cape Wrath to the Mull of Galloway) is 274 miles, and the greatest breadth (Buchan Ness to Applecross) is 154 miles. The customary measurement of the island of Great Britain is from the site of John o' Groats house, near Duncansby Head, Caithness, to Land's End, Cornwall, a total distance of 603 miles in a straight line and approximately 900 miles by road.

The total area of Scotland is 30,420 sq. miles (78,789 sq. km); land 29,767 sq. miles (77,097 sq. km), inland water 653 sq. miles (1,692 sq. km).

POPULATION

The population at the 1991 census was 4,998,567 (males 2,391,961; females 2,606,606). The average density of the population in 1991 was 0.65 persons per hectare.

RELIEF

There are three natural orographic divisions of Scotland. The southern uplands have their highest points in Merrick (2,766 ft), Rhinns of Kells (2,669 ft), and Cairnsmuir of Carsphairn (2,614 ft), in the west; and the Tweedsmuir Hills in the east (Hartfell 2,651 ft, Dollar Law 2,682 ft, Broad Law 2,756 ft).

The central lowlands, formed by the valleys of the Clyde, Forth and Tay, divide the southern uplands from the northern Highlands, which extend almost from the extreme north of the mainland to the central lowlands, and are divided into a northern and a southern system by the Great Glen.

The Grampian Mountains, which entirely cover the southern Highland area, include in the west Ben Nevis (4,406 ft), the highest point in the British Isles, and in the east the Cairngorm Mountains (Cairn Gorm 4,084 ft, Braeriach 4,248 ft, Ben Macdui 4,296 ft). The north-western Highland area contains the mountains of Wester and Easter Ross (Carn Eige 3,880 ft, Sgurr na Lapaich 3,775 ft).

Created, like the central lowlands, by a major geological fault, the Great Glen (60 miles long) runs between Inverness and Fort William, and contains Loch Ness, Loch Oich and Loch Lochy. These are linked to each other and to the north-east and south-west coasts of Scotland by the Caledonian Canal, providing a navigable passage between the Moray Firth and the Inner Hebrides.

HYDROGRAPHY

The western coast is fragmented by peninsulas and islands, and indented by fjords (sea-lochs), the longest of which is Loch Fyne (42 miles long) in Argyll. Although the east coast tends to be less fractured and lower, there are several great drowned inlets (firths), e.g. Firth of Forth, Firth of Tay, Moray Firth, as well as the Firth of Clyde in the west.

The lochs are the principal hydrographic feature. The largest in Scotland and in Britain is Loch Lomond (27 sq. miles), in the Grampian valleys; the longest and deepest is Loch Ness (24 miles long and 800 feet deep), in the Great Glen; and Loch Shin (20 miles long) and Loch Maree in the Highlands.

The longest river is the Tay (117 miles), noted for its salmon. It flows into the North Sea, with Dundee on the estuary, which is spanned by the Tay Bridge (10,289 ft)

opened in 1887 and the Tay Road Bridge (7,365 ft) opened in 1966. Other noted salmon rivers are the Dee (90 miles) which flows into the North Sea at Aberdeen, and the Spey (110 miles), the swiftest flowing river in the British Isles, which flows into Moray Firth. The Tweed, which gave its name to the woollen cloth produced along its banks, marks in the lower stretches of its 96-mile course the border between Scotland and England.

The most important river commercially is the Clyde (106 miles), formed by the junction of the Daer and Portrail water, which flows through the city of Glasgow to the Firth of Clyde. During its course it passes over the picturesque Falls of Clyde, Bonnington Linn (30 ft), Corra Linn (84 ft), Dundaff Linn (10 ft) and Stonebyres Linn (80 ft), above and below Lanark. The Forth (66 miles), upon which stands Edinburgh, the capital, is spanned by the Forth (Railway) Bridge (1890), which is 5,330 feet long, and the Forth (Road) Bridge (1964), which has a total length of 6,156 feet (over water) and a single span of 3,000 feet.

The highest waterfall in Scotland, and the British Isles, is Eas a'Chùal Aluinn with a total height of 658 feet (200 m), which falls from Glas Bheinn in Sutherland. The Falls of Glomach, on a head-stream of the Elchaig in Wester Ross, have a drop of 370 feet.

GAELIC LANGUAGE

According to the 1991 census, 1.4 per cent of the population of Scotland, mainly in the Highlands and western coastal regions, were able to speak the Scottish form of Gaelic.

LOWLAND SCOTTISH LANGUAGE

Several regional Lowland Scottish dialects, known variously as Scots, Scotch, Lallans or Doric, are widely spoken. The General Register Office (Scotland) has estimated that 1.5 million people, or 30 per cent of the population, are Scots speakers.

FLAG

The flag of Scotland is known as the Saltire. It is a white diagonal cross on a blue field (saltire argent in a field azure) and represents St Andrew, the patron saint of Scotland.

THE SCOTTISH ISLANDS

ORKNEY

The Orkney Islands (total area 375½ sq. miles) lie about six miles north of the mainland, separated from it by the Pentland Firth. Of the 90 islands and islets (holms and skerries) in the group, about one-third are inhabited.

The total population at the 1991 census was 19,612; the 1991 populations of the islands shown here include those of smaller islands forming part of the same civil parish.

Mainland, 15,128	Rousay, 291
Burray, 363	Sanday, 533
Eday, 166	Shapinsay, 322
Flotta and Fara, 126	South Ronaldsay, 943
Graemsay and Hoy, 477	Stronsay, 382
North Ronaldsay, 92	Westray, 704
Papa Westray, 85	

The islands are rich in prehistoric and Scandinavian remains, the most notable being the Stone Age village of Skara Brae, the burial chamber of Maeshowe, the many brochs (towers) and the 12th-century St Magnus Cathedral. Scapa Flow, between the Mainland and Hoy, was the war station of the British Grand Fleet from 1914 to 1919 and the scene of the scuttling of the surrendered German High Seas Fleet (21 June 1919).

Most of the islands are low-lying and fertile, and farming (principally beef cattle) is the main industry. Flotta, to the south of Scapa Flow, is the site of the oil terminal for the Piper, Claymore and Tartan fields in the North Sea.

The capital is Kirkwall (population 6,881) on Mainland.

SHETLAND

The Shetland Islands have a total area of 551 sq. miles and a population at the 1991 census of 22,522. They lie about 50 miles north of the Orkneys, with Fair Isle about half-way between the two groups. Out Stack, off Muckle Flugga, one mile north of Unst, is the most northerly part of the British Isles (60° 51′ 30″ N. lat.).

There are over 100 islands, of which 16 are inhabited. Populations at the 1991 census were:

Mainland, 17,596	Muckle Roe, 115
Bressay, 352	Trondra, 117
East Burra, 72	Unst, 1,055
Fair Isle, 67	West Burra, 857
Fetlar, 90	Whalsay, 1,041
Housay, 85	Yell, 1,075

Shetland's many archaeological sites include Jarlshof, Mousa and Clickhimin, and its long connection with Scandinavia has resulted in a strong Norse influence on its place-names and dialect.

Industries include fishing, knitwear and farming. In addition to the fishing fleet there are fish processing factories, while the traditional handknitting of Fair Isle and Unst is supplemented now with machine-knitted garments. Farming is mainly crofting, with sheep being raised on the moorland and hills of the islands. Latterly the islands have become a centre of the North Sea oil industry, with pipelines from the Brent and Ninian fields running to the terminal at Sullom Voe, the largest of its kind in Europe. Lerwick is the main centre for supply services for offshore oil exploration and development.

The capital is Lerwick (population 7,901) on Mainland.

THE HEBRIDES

Until the late 13th century the Hebrides included other Scottish islands in the Firth of Clyde, the peninsula of Kintyre (Argyll), the Isle of Man, and the (Irish) Isle of Rathlin. The origin of the name is stated to be the Greek *Eboudai*, latinized as *Hebudes* by Pliny, and corrupted to its present form. The Norwegian name *Sudreyjar* (Southern Islands) was latinized as *Sodorenses*, a name that survives in the Anglican bishopric of Sodor and Man.

There are over 500 islands and islets, of which about 100 are inhabited, though mountainous terrain and extensive peat bogs mean that only a fraction of the total area is under cultivation. Stone, Bronze and Iron Age settlement has left many remains, including those at Callanish on Lewis, and Norse colonization influenced language, customs and place-names. Occupations include farming (mostly crofting and stock-raising), fishing and the manufacture of tweeds and other woollens. Tourism is also an important factor in the economy.

The Inner Hebrides lie off the west coast of Scotland and relatively close to the mainland. The largest and best-known is Skye (area 643 sq. miles; pop. 8,868; chief town, Portree), which contains the Cuillin Hills (Sgurr Alasdair 3,257 ft), the Red Hills (Beinn na Caillich 2,403 ft), Bla Bheinn (3,046 ft) and The Storr (2,358 ft). Skye is also famous as the refuge of the Young Pretender in 1746. Other islands in the Highland council area include Raasay (pop. 163), Rum, Eigg and Muck.

Further south the Inner Hebridean islands include Arran (pop. 4,474) containing Goat Fell (2,868 ft); Coll and Tiree (pop. 940); Colonsay and Oronsay (pop. 106); Islay (area 235 sq. miles; pop. 3,538); Jura (area 160 sq. miles; pop. 196) with a range of hills culminating in the Paps of Jura (Beinn-

an-Oir, 2,576 ft, and Beinn Chaolais, 2,477 ft); and Mull (area 367 sq. miles; pop. 2,708; chief town Tobermory) containing Ben More (3,171 ft).

The Outer Hebrides, separated from the mainland by the Minch, now form the Eilean Siar Western Isles Islands Council area (area 1,119 sq. miles; population at the 1991 census 29,600). The main islands are Lewis with Harris (area 770 sq. miles, pop. 21,737), whose chief town, Stornoway, is the administrative headquarters; North Uist (pop. 1,404); South Uist (pop. 2,106); Baleshare (55); Benbecula (pop. 1,803) and Barra (pop. 1,244). Other inhabited islands include Bernera (262), Berneray (141), Eriskay (179), Grimsay (215), Scalpay (382) and Vatersay (72).

EARLY HISTORY

There is evidence of human settlement in Scotland dating from the third millennium BC, the earliest settlers being Middle Stone Age hunters and fishermen. Early in the second millennium BC, New Stone Age farmers began to cultivate crops and rear livestock; their settlements were on the west coast and in the north, and included Skara Brae and Maeshowe (Orkney). Settlement by the Early Bronze Age 'Beaker folk', so-called from the shape of their drinking vessels, in eastern Scotland dates from about 1800 BC. Further settlement is believed to have occurred from 700 BC onwards, as tribes were displaced from further south by new incursions from the Continent and the Roman invasions from AD 43.

Julius Agricola, the Roman governor of Britain AD 77–84, extended the Roman conquests in Britain by advancing into Caledonia, culminating with a victory at Mons Graupius, probably in AD 84; he was recalled to Rome shortly afterwards and his forward policy was not pursued. Hadrian's Wall, mostly completed by AD 30, marked the northern frontier of the Roman empire except for the period between about AD 144 and 190 when the frontier moved north to the Forth–Clyde isthmus and a turf wall, the Antonine Wall, was manned.

After the Roman withdrawal from Britain, there were centuries of warfare between the Picts, Scots, Britons, Angles and Vikings. The Picts, believed to be a non-Indo-European race, occupied the area north of the Forth. The Scots, a Gaelic-speaking people of northern Ireland, colonized the area of Argyll and Bute (the kingdom of Dalriada) in the fifth century AD and then expanded eastwards and northwards. The Britons, speaking a Brythonic Celtic language, colonized Scotland from the south from the first century BC; they lost control of south-eastern Scotland (incorporated into the kingdom of Northumbria) to the Angles in the early seventh century but retained Strathclyde (south-western Scotland and Cumbria). Viking raids from the late eighth century were followed by Norse settlement in the western and northern isles, Argyll, Caithness and Sutherland from the mid-ninth century onwards.

UNIFICATION

The union of the areas which now comprise Scotland began in AD 843 when Kenneth mac Alpin, king of the Scots from c.834, became also king of the Picts, joining the two lands to form the kingdom of Alba (comprising Scotland north of a line between the Forth and Clyde rivers). Lothian, the eastern part of the area between the Forth and the Tweed, seems to have been leased to Kenneth II of Alba (reigned 971–995) by Edgar of England c.973/4, and Scottish possession was confirmed by Malcolm II's victory over a Northumbrian army at Carham c.1016. At about this time Malcolm II (reigned 1005–34) placed his grandson Duncan on the throne of the British kingdom of Strathclyde, bringing under Scots rule virtually all of what is now Scotland.

The Norse possessions were incorporated into the kingdom of Scotland from the 12th century onwards. An uprising in the mid-12th century drove the Norse from most of mainland Argyll. The Hebrides were ceded to Scotland by the Treaty of Perth in 1266 after a Norwegian expedition in 1263 failed to maintain Norse authority over the islands. Orkney and Shetland fell to Scotland in 1468–9 as a pledge for the unpaid dowry of Margaret of Denmark, wife of James III, though Danish claims of suzerainty were relinquished only with the marriage of Anne of Denmark to James VI in 1590.

From the 11th century, there were frequent wars between Scotland and England over territory and the extent of England's political influence. The failure of the Scottish royal line with the death of Margaret of Norway in 1290 led to disputes over the throne which were resolved by the adjudication of Edward I of England. He awarded the throne to John Balliol in 1292 but Balliol's refusal to be a puppet king led to war. Balliol surrendered to Edward I in 1296 and Edward attempted to rule Scotland himself. Resistance to Scotland's loss of independence was led by William Wallace, who defeated the English at Stirling Bridge (1297), and Robert Bruce, crowned in 1306, who held most of Scotland by 1311 and routed Edward II's army at Bannockburn (1314). England recognized the independence of Scotland in the Treaty of Northampton in 1328. Subsequent clashes include the disastrous battle of Flodden (1513) in which James IV and many of his nobles fell.

THE UNION

In 1603 James VI of Scotland succeeded Elizabeth I on the throne of England (his mother, Mary Queen of Scots, was the great-granddaughter of Henry VII), his successors reigning as sovereigns of Great Britain. Political union of the two countries did not occur until 1707.

THE JACOBITE REVOLTS

After the abdication (by flight) in 1688 of James VII and II, the crown devolved upon William III (grandson of Charles I) and Mary II (elder daughter of James VII and II). In 1689 Graham of Claverhouse roused the Highlands on behalf of James VII and II, but died after a military success at Killiecrankie.

After the death of Anne (younger daughter of James VII and II), the throne devolved upon George I (great-grandson of James VI and I). In 1715, armed risings on behalf of James Stuart (the Old Pretender, son of James VII and II) led to the indecisive battle of Sheriffmuir, and the Jacobite movement died down until 1745, when Charles Stuart (the Young Pretender) defeated the Royalist troops at Prestonpans and advanced to Derby (1746). From Derby, the adherents of 'James VIII and III' (the title claimed for his father by Charles Stuart) fell back on the defensive and were finally crushed at Culloden (16 April 1746).

PRINCIPAL CITIES

ABERDEEN

Aberdeen, 130 miles north-east of Edinburgh, received its charter as a Royal Burgh in 1179. Scotland's third largest city, Aberdeen is the second largest Scottish fishing port and the main centre for offshore oil exploration and production. It is also an ancient university town and distinguished research centre. Other industries include engineering, food processing, textiles, paper manufacturing and chemicals.

Places of interest include King's College, St Machar's Cathedral, Brig o' Balgownie, Duthie Park and Winter Gardens, Hazlehead Park, the Kirk of St Nicholas, Mercat Cross, Marischal College and Marischal Museum, Provost Skene's House, Art Gallery, Gordon Highlanders Museum, Satrosphere Hands-On Discovery Centre, and Aberdeen Maritime Museum in Provost Ross's House.

DUNDEE

Dundee, a Royal Burgh, is situated on the north bank of the Tay estuary. The city's port and dock installations are important to the offshore oil industry and the airport also provides servicing facilities. Principal industries include textiles, computers and other electronic industries, lasers, printing, tyre manufacture, food processing, carpets, engineering, clothing manufacture and tourism.

The unique City Churches – three churches under one roof, together with the 15th-century St Mary's Tower – are the most prominent architectural feature. Dundee has two historic ships: the Dundee-built RRS *Discovery* which took Capt. Scott to the Antarctic lies alongside Discovery Quay, and the frigate *Unicorn*, the only British-built wooden warship still afloat, is moored in Victoria Dock. Places of interest include Mills Public Observatory, the Tay road and rail bridges, McManus Galleries, Barrack Street Museum, Claypotts Castle, Broughty Castle and Verdant Works (Textile Heritage Centre).

EDINBURGH

Edinburgh is the capital of and seat of government in Scotland. The city is built on a group of hills and contains in Princes Street one of the most beautiful thoroughfares in the world.

The principal buildings are the Castle, which now houses the Stone of Scone and also includes St Margaret's Chapel, the oldest building in Edinburgh, and near it, the Scottish National War Memorial; the Palace of Holyroodhouse; Parliament House, the present seat of the judicature; three universities (Edinburgh, Heriot-Watt, Napier); St Giles' Cathedral; St Mary's (Scottish Episcopal) Cathedral (Sir George Gilbert Scott); the General Register House (Robert Adam); the National and the Signet Libraries; the National Gallery; the Royal Scottish Academy; the National Portrait Gallery; and the Edinburgh International Conference Centre, opened in 1995. A new Scottish Parliament building is under construction at Holyrood.

GLASGOW

Glasgow, a Royal Burgh, is the principal commercial and industrial centre in Scotland. The city occupies the north and south banks of the Clyde, formerly one of the chief commercial estuaries in the world. The principal industries include engineering, electronics, finance, chemicals and printing. The city has also developed recently as a tourism and conference centre.

The chief buildings are the 13th-century Gothic Cathedral, the University (Sir George Gilbert Scott), the City Chambers, the Royal Concert Hall, St Mungo Museum of Religious Life and Art, Pollok House, the School of Art (Mackintosh), Kelvingrove Art Galleries, the Gallery of Modern Art, the Burrell Collection museum and the Mitchell Library. The city is home to the Scottish National Orchestra, Scottish Opera and Scottish Ballet.

LORD-LIEUTENANTS

Title	Name
Aberdeenshire	A. D. M. Farquharson
Angus	The Earl of Airlie, KT, GCVO, PC
Argyll and Bute	The Duke of Argyll
Ayrshire and Arran	Maj. R. Y. Henderson, TD
Banffshire	J. A. S. McPherson, CBE
Berwickshire	Maj.-Gen. Sir John Swinton, KCVO, OBE
Caithness	Maj. G. T. Dunnett, TD
Clackmannan	Lt.-Col. R. C. Stewart, CBE, TD
Dumfries	Capt. R. C. Cunningham-Jardine
Dunbartonshire	Brig. D. D. G. Hardie, TD
East Lothian	Sir Hew Hamilton-Dalrymple, Bt., KCVO
Eilean Siar/Western Isles	The Viscount Dunrossil, CMG
Fife	Mrs C. M. Dean
Inverness	The Lord Gray of Contin, PC
Kincardineshire	The Viscount of Arbuthnott, KT, CBE, DSC, FRSE
Lanarkshire	H. B. Sneddon, CBE
Midlothian	Capt. G. W. Burnet, LVO
Moray	Air Vice-Marshal G. A. Chesworth, CB, OBE, DFC
Nairn	E. Brodie
Orkney	G. R. Marwick
Perth and Kinross	Sir David Montgomery, Bt.
Renfrewshire	C. H. Parker, OBE
Ross and Cromarty	Capt. R. W. K. Stirling of Fairburn, TD
Roxburgh, Ettrick and Lauderdale	Dr June Paterson-Brown
Shetland	J. H. Scott
Stirling and Falkirk	Lt.-Col. J. Stirling of Garden, CBE, TD, FRICS
Sutherland	Maj.-Gen. D. Houston, CBE
The Stewartry of Kirkcudbright	Lt.-Gen. Sir Norman Arthur, KCB
Tweeddale	Capt. J. D. B. Younger
West Lothian	The Earl of Morton
Wigtown	Maj. E. S. Orr-Ewing

The Lord Provosts of the four city districts of Aberdeen, Dundee, Edinburgh and Glasgow are Lord-Lieutenants for those districts *ex officio*.

LOCAL COUNCILS

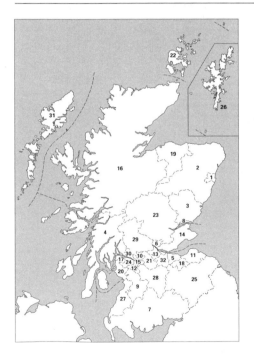

Key	Council
1	Aberdeen City
2	Aberdeenshire
3	Angus
4	Argyll and Bute
5	City of Edinburgh
6	Clackmannanshire
7	Dumfries and Galloway
8	Dundee City
9	East Ayrshire
10	East Dunbartonshire
11	East Lothian
12	East Renfrewshire
13	Eilean Siar/Western Isles
14	Falkirk
15	Fife
16	Glasgow City
17	Highland
18	Inverclyde
19	Midlothian
20	Moray
21	North Ayrshire
22	North Lanarkshire
23	Orkney
24	Perth and Kinross
25	Renfrewshire
26	Scottish Borders
27	Shetland
28	South Ayrshire
29	South Lanarkshire
30	Stirling
31	West Dunbartonshire
32	West Lothian

LOCAL COUNCILS

Council	Administrative headquarters	Population (latest estimate)	Band D charge 1999	Chief Executive	Chairman (a) Convener (b) Provost (c) Lord Provost
Aberdeen City	Aberdeen	213,070	£1,033.25	D. Paterson	(c) Ms M. Smith
Aberdeenshire	Aberdeen	226,260	719.00	A. G. Campbell	(a) R. Bisset
Angus	Forfar	110,070	938.60	A. B. Watson	(b) Mrs F. E. Duncan
Argyll and Bute	Lochgilphead	89,980	1,070.10	J. A. McLellan	(a) D. C. Currie
City of Edinburgh	Edinburgh	450,180	889.00	T. N. Aitchison	(c) Rt. Hon. E. Milligan
Clackmannanshire	Alloa	48,560	753.00	R. Allan	(b) W. McAdam
Dumfries and Galloway	Dumfries	147,300	766.00	P. N. Jones	(a) A. Campbell
Dundee City	Dundee	146,690	1,238.60	A. Stephen	(c) Rt. Hon. Ms H. W. Wright
East Ayrshire	Kilmarnock	121,300	1,037.80	D. Montgomery	(b) J. Boyd
East Dunbartonshire	Glasgow	109,570	830.00	Dr V. Nash	(b) R. McSkimming
East Lothian	Haddington	89,570	789.00	J. Lindsay	(a) P. O'Brien
East Renfrewshire	Giffnock	87,980	765.00	P. Daniels	(b) A. Steele
Eilean Siar/Western Isles	Stornoway	27,940	898.95	N. Galbraith (acting)	(a) A. A. Macdonald
Falkirk	Falkirk	144,110	892.00	Ms M. Pitcaithly	(b) D. Goldie
Fife	Glenrothes	348,900	986.50	D. Sinclair	(a) J. MacDougall
Glasgow City	Glasgow	619,680	1,263.10	J. Andrews	(c) A. Mosson
Highland	Inverness	208,300	799.00	A. D. McCourt	(a) D. Green
Inverclyde	Greenock	85,400	863.00	R. Cleary	(b) D. Roach
Midlothian	Dalkeith	80,860	936.00	T. Muir	(b) S. Campbell
Moray	Elgin	85,870	724.00	B. Stewart	(a) E. Aldridge
North Ayrshire	Irvine	139,660	977.10	B. Devine	(a) S. Taylor
North Lanarkshire	Motherwell	326,720	844.00	A. Cowe	(b) B. McCulloch
Orkney Islands	Kirkwall	19,550	624.00	A. Buchan	(a) H. Halcro-Johnston
Perth and Kinross	Perth	133,040	758.00	H. Robertson	(b) M. O'Malley
Renfrewshire	Paisley	177,830	972.10	T. Scholes	(b) J. McDowell
Scottish Borders	Newtown St Boswells	106,300	639.00	A. M. Croall	(a) A. L. Tulley
Shetland Islands	Lerwick	22,910	830.75	B. Bennett	(a) T. Stove
South Ayrshire	Ayr	114,440	792.00	G. W. F. Thorley	(b) Ms E. Foulkes
South Lanarkshire	Hamilton	306,860	880.00	vacant	(b) A. Dick
Stirling	Stirling	83,130	819.00	K. Yates	(b) T. Brookes
West Dunbartonshire	Dumbarton	94,880	1,170.10	T. Huntingford (acting)	(b) A. Macdonald
West Lothian	Livingston	153,090	1,044.00	A. M. Linkston	(b) J. Thomas

THE SCOTTISH PARLIAMENT (see also pages 1280–91)

In July 1997 the Government announced plans to establish a Scottish Parliament. In a referendum on 11 September 1997 about 62 per cent of the electorate voted of whom 74.3 per cent voted in favour of the Parliament and 63.5 per cent in favour of its having tax-raising powers. Elections are to be held every four years. The first elections were held on 6 May 1999 when about 59 per cent of the electorate voted. The first session was held on 12 May 1999 and the Scottish Parliament was officially opened on 1 July 1999 at the Edinburgh Assembly Hall; a new building to house the Parliament is under construction in Edinburgh.

The Scottish Parliament has 129 members (including the Presiding Officer), comprising 73 constituency members and 65 additional regional members from party lists. It can introduce primary legislation and has the power to raise or lower the basic rate of income tax by up to three pence in the pound.

The Scottish Parliament is responsible for education, health, law, environment, economic development, local government, housing, police, fire services, planning, financial assistance to industry, tourism, some transport, heritage and the arts, agriculture, forestry, food standards

SALARIES FROM 1 APRIL 1999:

First Minister	£64,308 (plus MSP salary)
Ministers	£33,360 (plus MSP salary)
Lord Advocate	£43,585
Solicitor-General for Scotland	£31,515
Junior Ministers	£17,305 (plus MSP salary)
MSPs	£40,092*
Presiding Officer	£33,360 (plus MSP salary)
Deputy Presiding Officers	£17,305 (plus MSP salary)

* Reduced by two-thirds (to £13,364) if the member is already an MP or an MEP

MSPs and officers are paid by the Scottish Parliamentary Corporate Body; ministers are paid out of the Scottish Consolidated Fund.

STATE OF THE PARTIES *as at May 1999*

	Constituency MSPs	Regional MSPs	Total
Scottish Labour Party	53	3	56
Scottish National Party	7	28	35
Scottish Conservative and Unionist Party	0	18	18
Scottish Liberal Democrats	12	4†	16†
Scottish Green Party	0	1	1
Scottish Socialist Party	0	1	1
Independent (Dennis Canavan)	1	0	1
Presiding Officer (Rt. Hon. Sir David Steel, PC, KBE, MSP)	0	1	1

† Excludes the Presiding Officer, who has no party allegiance while in post

Deputy Presiding Officers, George Reid, MSP (*SNP*); Patricia Ferguson, MSP (*Lab.*)

THE SCOTTISH EXECUTIVE

First Minister, The Rt. Hon. Donald Dewar, MP, MSP (*Lab.*)
Deputy First Minister and Minister for Justice, Jim Wallace, QC, MP, MSP (*LD*)
Finance Minister, Jack McConnell, MSP (*Lab.*)
Minister for Health and Community Care, Susan Deacon, MSP (*Lab.*)
Minister for Communities, Wendy Alexander, MSP (*Lab.*)
Minister for Transport and the Environment, Sarah Boyack, MSP (*Lab.*)
Minister for Enterprise and Lifelong Learning, Henry McLeish, MP, MSP (*Lab.*)
Minister for Rural Affairs, Ross Finnie, MSP (*LD*)
Minister for Education and Children, Sam Galbraith, MP, MSP (*Lab.*)
Minister for Parliament and Chief Whip, Tom McCabe, MSP (*Lab.*)
Lord Advocate, The Lord Hardie, QC (*Lab.*)

JUNIOR MINISTERS (NOT MEMBERS OF THE SCOTTISH EXECUTIVE)

Deputy Minister for Justice, Angus Mackay, MSP (*Lab.*)
Deputy Minister for Community Care, Iain Gray, MSP (*Lab.*)
Deputy Minister for Local Government, Frank McAveety, MSP (*Lab. Co-op.*)
Deputy Minister for Social Inclusion, Equality and the Voluntary Sector, Jackie Baillie, MSP (*Lab.*)
Deputy Minister for Enterprise and Lifelong Learning, Nicol Stephen, MSP (*LD*)
Deputy Minister for Highlands and Islands and Gaelic, Alasdair Morrison, MSP (*Lab.*)
Deputy Minister for Fisheries, John Home Robertson, MSP (*Lab.*)
Deputy Minister for Culture and Sport, Rhona Brankin, MSP (*Lab. Co-op.*)
Deputy Minister for Children and Education, Peter Peacock, MSP (*Lab.*)
Deputy Minister for Parliament and Whip, Iain Smith, MSP (*LD*)
Solicitor-General for Scotland, Colin Boyd, QC

Northern Ireland

Northern Ireland has a total area of 5,467 sq. miles (14,144 sq. km): land, 5,225 sq. miles (13,532 sq. km); inland water and tideways, 249 sq. miles (628 sq. km).

The population of Northern Ireland at the 1991 census was 1,577,836 (males, 769,071; females, 808,765). The average density of population in 1991 was 1.11 persons per hectare.

In 1991 the number of persons in the various religious denominations (expressed as percentages of the total population) were: Roman Catholic, 38.4; Presbyterian, 21.4; Church of Ireland, 17.7; Methodist, 3.8; others 7.7; none, 3.7; not stated, 7.3.

FLAG

The official national flag of Northern Ireland is now the Union Flag. The flag formerly in use (a white, six-pointed star in the centre of a red cross on a white field, enclosing a red hand and surmounted by a crown) has not been used since the imposition of direct rule.

PRINCIPAL CITIES

BELFAST

Belfast, the administrative centre of Northern Ireland, is situated at the mouth of the River Lagan at its entrance to Belfast Lough. The city grew, owing to its easy access by sea to Scottish coal and iron, to be a great industrial centre.

The principal buildings are of a relatively recent date and include the Parliament Buildings at Stormont, the City Hall, Waterfront Hall, the Law Courts, the Public Library and the Museum and Art Gallery.

Belfast received its first charter of incorporation in 1613 and was created a city in 1888; the title of Lord Mayor was conferred in 1892.

LONDONDERRY

Londonderry (originally Derry) is situated on the River Foyle, and has important associations with the City of London. The Irish Society was created by the City of London in 1610, and under its royal charter of 1613 it fortified the city and was for long closely associated with its administration. Because of this connection the city was incorporated in 1613 under the new name of Londonderry.

The city is famous for the great siege of 1688–9, when for 105 days the town held out against the forces of James II until relieved by sea. The city walls are still intact and form a circuit of almost a mile around the old city.

Interesting buildings are the Protestant Cathedral of St Columb's (1633) and the Guildhall, reconstructed in 1912 and containing a number of beautiful stained glass windows, many of which were presented by the livery companies of London.

CONSTITUTIONAL DEVELOPMENTS

Northern Ireland is subject to the same fundamental constitutional provisions which apply to the rest of the United Kingdom. It had its own parliament and government from 1921 to 1972, but after increasing civil unrest the Northern Ireland (Temporary Provisions) Act 1972 transferred the legislative and executive powers of the Northern Ireland parliament and government to the UK Parliament and a Secretary of State. The Northern Ireland Constitution Act 1973 provided for devolution in Northern Ireland

through an assembly and executive, but a power-sharing executive formed by the Northern Ireland political parties in January 1974 collapsed in May 1974; since then Northern Ireland has been governed by direct rule under the provisions of the Northern Ireland Act 1974. This allows Parliament to approve all laws for Northern Ireland and places the Northern Ireland department under the direction and control of the Secretary of State for Northern Ireland.

Attempts were made by successive governments to find a means of restoring a widely acceptable form of devolved government to Northern Ireland. In 1985 the governments of the United Kingdom and the Republic of Ireland signed the Anglo-Irish Agreement, establishing an intergovernmental conference in which the Irish government may put forward views and proposals on certain aspects of Northern Ireland affairs.

Discussions between the British and Irish governments and the main Northern Ireland parties began in 1991. It was agreed that any political settlement would need to address relationships within Northern Ireland, within the island of Ireland (north/south) and between the British and Irish governments (east/west). Although round table talks ended in 1992 the process continued from September 1993 as separate bilateral discussions with three of the Northern Ireland parties (the DUP declined to participate).

In December 1993 the British and Irish governments published the Joint Declaration complementing the political talks, and making clear that any settlement would need to be founded on principles of democracy and consent. The declaration also stated that all democratically mandated parties could be involved in political talks as long as they permanently renounced paramilitary violence.

The provisional IRA and loyalist paramilitary groups announced cease-fires on 31 August and 13 October 1994 respectively. The Government initiated exploratory meetings with Sinn Fein and loyalist representatives in December 1994.

In February 1995 the then Prime Minister (John Major) launched *A Framework for Accountable Government in Northern Ireland* and, with the Irish Prime Minister, *A New Framework for Agreement.* These outlined what a comprehensive political settlement might look like. The ideas were intended to facilitate multilateral dialogue involving the Northern Ireland parties and the British government.

In autumn 1995 the Prime Minister said that Sinn Fein would not be invited to all-party talks until the IRA had decommissioned its arms; the IRA ruled out any decommissioning of weapons in advance of a political settlement. An international body chaired by a former US senator, George Mitchell, reported in January 1996 that no weapons would be decommissioned before the start of all-party talks and that a compromise agreement was necessary under which weapons would be decommissioned during negotiations. The Prime Minister accepted the report and proposed the election of representatives to conduct all-party talks. On 9 February 1996 the IRA called off its cease-fire.

PEACE TALKS

Following elections on 30 May 1996, all-party talks opened at Stormont Castle on 10 June 1996 which included nine of the ten parties returned at the election; Sinn Fein representatives were turned away because the IRA had failed to reinstate its cease-fire. On 29 July 1996 the all-party talks were suspended after disagreements over the issue of decommissioning arms. An opening agenda for the talks was agreed in October 1996.

On 25 June 1997 the newly-elected Labour Government

said that substantive negotiations should begin in September 1997 with a view to reaching conclusions by May 1998. The British and Irish governments issued a joint paper outlining their proposals for resolving the decommissioning issue. The Government also indicated that if the IRA were to call a cease-fire, it would assess whether it was genuine over a period of six weeks, and if satisfied that it was so, would then invite Sinn Fein to the talks. An IRA cease-fire was declared on 20 July 1997.

When the UK Government announced in August 1997 that Sinn Fein would be present when the substantive talks opened on 15 September, the Unionist and loyalist parties, unhappy at the terms on which Sinn Fein had been admitted, boycotted the opening session. The Ulster Unionist Party, the Progressive Unionist Party and the Ulster Democratic Party re-entered the negotiations on 17 September. Full-scale peace talks began on 7 October. The parties had agreed to concentrate on constitutional issues, with the issue of decommissioning terrorist weapons to be handled by a new independent commission.

On 12 January 1998 the British and Irish governments issued a joint document, *Propositions on Heads of Agreement*, proposing the establishment of various new cross-border bodies; further proposals were presented on 27 January. A draft peace settlement was issued by the talks' chairman, Sen. George Mitchell, on 6 April 1998 but was rejected by the Unionists the following day. On 10 April agreement was reached between the British and Irish governments and the eight Northern Ireland political parties still involved in the talks (the Good Friday/Belfast Agreement). The agreement provided for an elected New Northern Ireland Assembly; a North/South Ministerial Council, and a British-Irish Council comprising representatives of the British, Irish, Channel Islands and Isle of Man governments and members of the new assemblies for Scotland, Wales and Northern Ireland. Further points included the abandonment of the Republic of Ireland's constitutional claim to Northern Ireland; the decommissioning of weapons; the release of paramilitary prisoners; and changes in policing.

Referendums on the agreement were held in Northern Ireland and the Republic of Ireland on 22 May 1998. In Northern Ireland the turnout was 81 per cent, of which 71.12 per cent voted in favour of the agreement. In the Republic of Ireland, the turnout was about 55 per cent, of which 94.4 per cent voted in favour of both the agreement and the necessary constitutional change. In the UK, the Northern Ireland Act 1998, enshrining the provisions of the Agreement, received Royal Assent in November 1998.

NORTHERN IRELAND ASSEMBLY

The Assembly has 108 members elected by single transferable vote (six from each of the 18 Westminster constituencies). The first elections took place on 25 June 1998 and members met for the first time on 1 July. Safeguards ensure that key decisions have cross-community support. The executive powers of the Assembly will be discharged by an executive committee comprising a First Minister and Deputy First Minister (jointly elected by the Assembly on a cross-community basis) and up to ten ministers with departmental responsibilities. Ministerial posts will be allocated on the basis of the number of seats each party holds.

The Assembly met in shadow form several times, pending the establishment of an Executive and the transfer of powers from Parliament. After devolution it will have executive and legislative authority over those areas formerly the responsibility of the Northern Ireland government departments (*see* page 326). Its powers might be extended further in future.

Power was initially due to be transferred to the new Executive on 10 March 1999, but disagreements emerged over whether Sinn Fein should be allowed to enter the Executive before IRA weapons had been decommissioned. Further deadlines of 2 April and 30 June were also missed. On 15 July the Assembly met to nominate ministers, with the transfer of power to follow on 18 July. However, as the decommissioning issue had still not been resolved, Unionists failed to nominate ministers (the UUP boycotting the meeting itself) and the process collapsed. On 20 July the British and Irish Governments initiated a review of the implementation of the Agreement and asked former Senator George Mitchell to act as facilitator. The review will resume in September 1999 with the aim of resolving the disagreements over decommissioning and formation of the Executive. (*See also* Events of the Year and Stop-press.)

Composition

Party	Seats
UUP	28
SDLP	24
DUP	20
Sinn Fein	18
Alliance Party	6
UK Unionist Party	5
Progressive Unionist Party	2
Northern Ireland Women's Coalition	2
Others	3

OTHER BODIES

Consultations between the First Minister and Deputy First Minister, the British and Irish Governments and the political parties concluded in early 1999 with an agreement to establish six areas for cross-border bodies and a further six areas for co-operation. Treaties between the British and Irish governments establishing the bodies and parallel domestic legislation to underpin them are now in place.

The intergovernmental conference established by the 1985 Anglo-Irish Agreement (*see* page 566) was replaced by a new British-Irish Intergovernmental Conference which will discuss all areas of mutual bilateral interest.

The British-Irish Council will operate on the basis of consensus and may reach agreements and pursue common policies in areas of mutual interest.

ECONOMY

FINANCE

Taxation in Northern Ireland is largely imposed and collected by the UK government. After deducting the cost of collection and of Northern Ireland's contributions to the European Union, the balance, known as the Attributed Share of Taxation, is paid over to the Northern Ireland Consolidated Fund. Northern Ireland's revenue is insufficient to meet its expenditure and is supplemented by a grant-in-aid.

	1998-9*	1999-2000**
Public income	£6,639,768,864	£7,541,000,000
Public expenditure	6,949,890,984	7,541,000,000

* Outturn
** Estimate

PRODUCTION

The products of the engineering and allied industries, which employed 29,500 persons in 1996, were valued at £4,403 million. The textiles industry (manufacture of textiles and textile products), employing about 25,200 persons, produced goods valued at approximately £1,266 million. The food products, beverages and tobacco industry, employing about 20,900 persons, produced goods valued at £3,512 million.

In 1998, 1,523 persons were employed in mining and quarrying operations in Northern Ireland and the minerals raised (22,356,000 tonnes) were valued at £58,989,000.

COMMUNICATIONS

The total tonnage handled by Northern Ireland ports in 1998 was 12.23 million. Regular ferry, freight and container services operate to ports in Great Britain and Europe from a number of ports, with most trade passing through Belfast (60 per cent of the total), Larne and Warrenpoint.

The Northern Ireland Transport Holding Company is largely responsible for the supervision of the subsidiary companies, Ulsterbus and Citybus (which operate the public road passenger services) and Northern Ireland Railways (collectively known as Translink). Road freight services are also provided by a large number of hauliers operating competitively under licence.

Belfast International Airport, owned by TBI International, provides scheduled and chartered services on domestic and international routes. In 1997–8 the airport handled approximately 2.5 million passengers and 41,000 tonnes of freight. Scheduled services also operate from Belfast City Airport (BCA, owned by Shorts Bombardier Aerospace) to 20 UK destinations. In 1997–8 the airport handled approximately 1.3 million passengers. City of Derry Airport (Londonderry, owned and operated by Derry City Council) provides services to 15 UK and European destinations and to Belfast, providing links to many of the locations serviced by BCA. In 1997–8 City of Derry Airport served approximately 68,000 passengers.

NORTHERN IRELAND COUNTIES

County	Area* (sq. miles)	Lord-Lieutenant	High Sheriff, 1999
Antrim	1,093	The Lord O'Neill, TD	Mrs P. Traill
Armagh	484	The Earl of Caledon	Mrs E. Cullen
‡Belfast City	25	Col. J. E. Wilson, OBE	R. Newton
Down	945	W. J. Hall	Mrs M. E. Crawford
Fermanagh	647	The Earl of Erne	Mrs P. G. Moore
†Londonderry	798	Sir Michael McCorkell, KCVO, OBE, TD	Mrs D. Hutchinson
‡Londonderry City	3.4	J. T. Eaton, CBE, TD	Mrs M. Hasson
Tyrone	1,211	The Duke of Abercorn, KG	Miss A. F. Colhoun

* Excluding inland waters and tideways
‡ Denotes County Borough
† Excluding the City of Londonderry

DISTRICT COUNCILS

SMALL CAPITALS denotes CITY status
§ Denotes Borough Council

Council	Population (September 1998)	Net Annual Value	Council Clerk	Chairman †Mayor 1999
§Antrim, Co. Antrim	47,500	£31,487,895	S. J. Magee	†P. Marks
§Ards, Co. Down	67,800	28,984,295	D. J. Fallows	†G. Ennis
§ARMAGH, Co. Armagh	53,200	20,155,297	D. R. D. Mitchell	†R. Turner
§Ballymena, Co. Antrim	58,200	34,032,137	M. G. Rankin	†J. Currie
§Ballymoney, Co. Antrim	24,900	8,786,335	J. Dempsey	†F. Campbell
Banbridge, Co. Down	37,700	14,406,488	R. Gilmore	S. Doyle
BELFAST, Co. Antrim and Co. Down	297,200	287,458,969	B. Hanna	D. Alderdice
§Carrickfergus, Co. Antrim	35,700	15,786,964	R. Boyd	†J. Cramsey
§Castlereagh, Co. Down	64,500	33,301,018	A. Donaldson	†J. Beattie
§Coleraine, Co. Londonderry	54,700	29,126,980	W. Moore	†J. McClure
Cookstown, Co. Tyrone	31,800	14,758,461	M. J. McGuckin	P. McAleer
§Craigavon, Co. Armagh	79,100	44,658,976	T. Reaney	†M. Carrick
DERRY, Co. Londonderry	104,700	59,358,072	T. J. Keanie	†J. Miller
Down, Co. Down	61,200	23,064,131	O. O'Connor	J. McIlhernon
Dungannon, Co. Tyrone	47,100	23,700,171	W. J. Beattie	J. Canning
Fermanagh, Co. Fermanagh	55,500	27,797,576	Mrs A. McGinley	P. McCaffrey
§Larne, Co. Antrim	30,300	17,373,878	C. McGarry	†Mrs J. Drummond
§Limavady, Co. Londonderry	30,800	11,886,598	J. K. Stevenson	†S. Gault
§Lisburn, Co. Antrim and Co. Down	106,600	58,153,699	N. Davidson	†P. O'Hagan
Magherafelt, Co. Londonderry	37,900	15,078,309	J. A. McLaughlin	R. A. Montgomery
Moyle, Co. Antrim	15,000	4,792,815	R. G. Lewis	H. Harding
Newry and Mourne, Co. Down and Co. Armagh	84,900	35,404,701	K. O'Neill	B. Curran
§Newtownabbey, Co. Antrim	79,600	43,371,929	N. Dunn	†N. Crilly
§North Down, Co. Down	73,500	38,920,296	T. Polley (acting)	†M. Fitzimons
Omagh, Co. Tyrone	47,000	22,308,485	J. P. McKinney	S. Clarke
Strabane, Co. Tyrone	36,800	13,265,922	D. McSorley	I. Barr

The Isle of Man

Ellan Vannin

The Isle of Man is an island situated in the Irish Sea, in latitude 54° 3′–54° 25′ N. and longitude 4° 18′–4° 47′ W., nearly equidistant from England, Scotland and Ireland. Although the early inhabitants were of Celtic origin, the Isle of Man was part of the Norwegian Kingdom of the Hebrides until 1266, when this was ceded to Scotland. Subsequently granted to the Stanleys (Earls of Derby) in the 15th century and later to the Dukes of Atholl, it was brought under the administration of the Crown in 1765. The island forms the bishopric of Sodor and Man.

The total land area is 221 sq. miles (572 sq. km). The report on the 1991 census showed a resident population of 69,788 (males, 33,693; females, 36,095). The main language in use is English. There are no remaining native speakers of Manx Gaelic but 643 people are able to speak the language.

CAPITAL – ΨDouglas; population (1991), 22,214. ΨCastletown (3,152) is the ancient capital; the other towns are ΨPeel (3,829) and ΨRamsey (6,496)

FLAG – A red flag charged with three conjoined armoured legs in white and gold

TYNWALD DAY – 5 July

GOVERNMENT

The Isle of Man is a self-governing Crown dependency, having its own parliamentary, legal and administrative system. The British Government is responsible for international relations and defence. Under the UK Act of Accession, Protocol 3, the island's relationship with the European Union is limited to trade alone and does not extend to financial aid. The Lieutenant-Governor is The Queen's personal representative in the island.

The legislature, Tynwald, is the oldest parliament in the world in continuous existence. It has two branches: the Legislative Council and the House of Keys. The Council consists of the President of Tynwald, the Bishop of Sodor and Man, the Attorney-General (who does not have a vote) and eight members elected by the House of Keys. The House of Keys has 24 members, elected by universal adult suffrage. The branches sit separately to consider legislation and sit together, as Tynwald Court, for most other parliamentary purposes.

The presiding officer in Tynwald Court is the President of Tynwald, elected by the members, who also presides over sittings of the Legislative Council. The presiding officer of the House of Keys is Mr Speaker, who is elected by members of the House.

The principal members of the Manx Government are the Chief Minister and nine departmental ministers, who comprise the Council of Ministers.

Lieutenant-Governor, HE Sir Timothy Daunt, KCMG
   ADC to the Lieutenant-Governor, C. J. Tummon
President of Tynwald, The Hon. Sir Charles Kerruish, OBE
Speaker, House of Keys, The Hon. N. Q. Cringle
The First Deemster and Clerk of the Rolls, His Honour T. W. Cain
Clerk of Tynwald, Secretary to the House of Keys and Counsel to the Speaker, Prof. T. St J. N. Bates
Clerk of Legislative Council and Clerk Assistant of Tynwald, T. A. Bawden
Attorney-General, W. J. H. Corlett, QC
Chief Minister, The Hon. D. J. Gelling
Chief Secretary, J. F. Kissack
Chief Financial Officer, J. A. Cashen

ECONOMY

Most of the income generated in the island is earned in the services sector with financial and professional services accounting for just over half of the national income. Tourism and manufacturing are also major generators of income whilst the island's other traditional industries of agriculture and fishing now play a smaller role in the economy.

Under the terms of Protocol 3, the island has tariff-free access to EU markets for its goods.

The island's unemployment rate is approximately 1.5 per cent and price inflation is around 2 per cent per annum.

FINANCE

The budget for 1999–2000 provided for net revenue expenditure of £287 million. The principal sources of government revenue are taxes on income and expenditure. Income tax is payable at a rate of 15 per cent on the first £9,900 of taxable income for single resident individuals and 20 per cent on the balance, after personal allowances of £7,350. These bands are doubled for married couples. The rate of income tax is 15 per cent on the first £100,000 of taxable income of companies, rising to 20 per cent on the balance. Non-residents are charged tax at the rate of 20 per cent. By agreement with the British Government, the island keeps most of its rates of indirect taxation (VAT and duties) the same as those in the United Kingdom, but this agreement may be terminated by either party. However, VAT on tourist accommodation is charged at 5 per cent. A reciprocal agreement on national insurance benefits and pensions exists between the governments of the Isle of Man and the United Kingdom. Taxes are also charged on property (rates), but these are comparatively low.

The major government expenditure items are health, social security and education, which account for 60 per cent of the government budget. The island makes a voluntary annual contribution to the United Kingdom for defence and other external services.

The island has a special relationship with the European Union and neither contributes money to nor receives funds from the EU budget.

The Channel Islands

The Channel Islands, situated off the north-west coast of France (at distances of from ten to 30 miles), are the only portions of the Dukedom of Normandy still belonging to the Crown, to which they have been attached since the Conquest. They were the only British territory to come under German occupation during the Second World War, following invasion on 30 June to 1 July 1940. The islands were relieved by British forces on 9 May 1945, and 9 May (Liberation Day) is now observed as a bank and public holiday.

The islands consist of Jersey (28,717 acres/11,630 ha), Guernsey (15,654 acres/6,340 ha), and the dependencies of Guernsey: Alderney (1,962 acres/795 ha), Brechou (74/30), Great Sark (1,035/419), Little Sark (239/97), Herm (320/130), Jethou (44/18) and Lihou (38/15) – a total of 48,083 acres/19,474 ha, or 75 sq. miles/194 sq. km. In 1991 the population of Jersey was 84,082; and of Guernsey, 58,867; Alderney, 2,297 and Sark, 575. The official languages are English and French but French is being supplanted by English, which is the language in daily use. In country districts of Jersey and Guernsey and throughout Sark a Norman-French *patois* is also in use, though to a declining extent.

GOVERNMENT

The islands are Crown dependencies with their own legislative assemblies (the States in Jersey, Guernsey and Alderney, and the Court of Chief Pleas in Sark), and systems of local administration and of law, and their own courts. Acts passed by the States require the sanction of The Queen-in-Council. The British Government is responsible for defence and international relations. The Channel Islands have trading rights alone within the European Union; these rights do not include financial aid.

In both Bailiwicks the Lieutenant-Governor and Commander-in-Chief, who is appointed by the Crown, is the personal representative of The Queen and the channel of communication between the Crown (via the Privy Council) and the island's government.

The government of each Bailiwick is conducted by committees appointed by the States. Justice is administered by the Royal Courts of Jersey and Guernsey, each consisting of the Bailiff and 12 elected Jurats. The Bailiffs of Jersey and Guernsey, appointed by the Crown, are President of the States and of the Royal Courts of their respective islands.

Each Bailiwick constitutes a deanery under the jurisdiction of the Bishop of Winchester (*see* Index).

ECONOMY

A mild climate and good soil have led to the development of intensive systems of agriculture and horticulture, which form a significant part of the economy. Equally important are invisible earnings, principally from tourism and banking and finance, the low rate of income tax (20p in the £ in Jersey and Guernsey; no tax of any kind in Sark) and the absence of super-tax and death duties making the islands a popular tax-haven.

Principal exports are agricultural produce and flowers; imports are chiefly machinery, manufactured goods, food, fuel and chemicals. Trade with the UK is regarded as internal.

British currency is legal tender in the Channel Islands but each Bailiwick issues its own coins and notes (*see* page 613). They also issue their own postage stamps; UK stamps are not valid.

JERSEY

Lieutenant-Governor and Commander-in-Chief of Jersey, HE Gen. Sir Michael Wilkes, KCB, CBE, *apptd* 1995
  Secretary and ADC, Lt.-Col. A. J. C. Woodrow, OBE, MC
Bailiff of Jersey, Sir Philip Bailhache, Kt.
Deputy Bailiff, F. C. Hamon
Attorney-General, M. C. St J. Burt, QC
Receiver-General, Gp Capt. R. Green, OBE
Solicitor-General, Miss S. C. Nicolle, QC
Greffier of the States, G. H. C. Coppock
States Treasurer, G. M. Baird

FINANCE

Year to 31 Dec.	1997	1998
Revenue income	£423,764,968	£442,434,776
Revenue expenditure	395,662,095	357,773,867
Capital expenditure	93,476,388	82,380,488
Public debt	0	0

CHIEF TOWN – ΨSt Helier, on the south coast of Jersey
FLAG – A white field charged with a red saltire cross, and the arms of Jersey in the upper centre

GUERNSEY AND DEPENDENCIES

Lieutenant-Governor and Commander-in-Chief of the Bailiwick of Guernsey and its Dependencies, HE Vice-Adm. Sir John Coward, KCB, DSO, *apptd* 1994
  Secretary and ADC, Capt. D. P. L. Hodgetts
Bailiff of Guernsey, de V. G. Carey
Deputy Bailiff, A. C. K. Day, QC
HM Procureur and Receiver-General, G. R. Rowland, QC
HM Comptroller, H. E. Roberts
States Supervisor, M. J. Brown

FINANCE

Year to 31 Dec.	1996	1997
Revenue	£182,016,695	£183,273,000
Expenditure	166,817,571	168,712,000

CHIEF TOWNS – ΨSt Peter Port, on the east coast of Guernsey; St Anne on Alderney
FLAG – White, bearing a red cross of St George, with a gold cross overall in the centre

ALDERNEY

President of the States, J. Kay-Mouat, OBE
Clerk of the States, D. V. Jenkins
Clerk of the Court, A. Johnson

SARK

Seigneur of Sark, J. M. Beaumont
The Seneschal, L. P. de Carteret
The Greffier, J. P. Hamon

OTHER DEPENDENCIES

Brechou, Lihou and Jethou are leased by the Crown. Herm is leased by the States of Guernsey.

The Environment

THE RIO EARTH SUMMIT

At the UN Conference on Environment and Development (UNCED) in Rio, Brazil, in 1992, 103 heads of state or government adopted the Rio Declaration, 27 principles intended to guide governments in pursuing economic development in ways that would benefit all and protect the environment. In particular the declaration stressed that the environment should be protected as part of development and that poorer developing countries should be helped to develop in ways that would minimize damage to the environment. The measures needed to ensure such sustainable development were outlined in the document *Agenda 21*. Neither the Rio Declaration nor Agenda 21 were binding agreements. The UN Commission on Sustainable Development was set up to monitor the progress of Agenda 21.

The second UNCED took place in New York in June 1997. It was found that progress towards the goals set at Rio had been slow. The UK agreed to reverse the decline in the amount of aid it was giving to developing countries and to reduce greenhouse gas emissions to 20 per cent below their 1990 levels by 2010.

CONVENTION ON BIOLOGICAL DIVERSITY

This binding agreement was adopted by 153 states at Rio, came into force in December 1993 and was ratified by the UK in June 1994. Its aim is to lessen the destruction of biological species and habitats, and parties to the convention are required to take inventories of their plants and animals, to protect endangered species and to ensure the diversity of species and habitats in the world. The convention is being implemented through a series of scientific advisory meetings and meetings of parties to the convention.

FRAMEWORK CONVENTION ON CLIMATE CHANGE

This convention, also a binding agreement, was adopted by 153 states at Rio, ratified by the UK in December 1993 and came into force in March 1994. It is intended to reduce the risks of global warming by limiting 'greenhouse' gas emissions. It recommended that industrialized countries reduce 'greenhouse' gas emissions to 1990 levels by 2000.

Progress towards the convention's targets is reviewed at regular conferences. The most recent of these was held in Kyoto, Japan, in December 1997 and the 159 countries represented agreed the Kyoto Protocol, which covers the six main 'greenhouse' gases (carbon dioxide, methane, nitrous oxide, hydrofluorocarbons (HFCs), perfluorocarbons (PFCs), sulphur hexafluoride (SF_6)). Under the protocol:
- 38 industrial countries agreed to legally binding targets for cutting their emissions of greenhouse gases to at least 5.2 per cent below 1990 levels between 2008 and 2012. EU members agreed to an 8 per cent reduction in emissions. The UK has agreed to a 12.5 per cent reduction
- nations are permitted to trade carbon permits, i.e. those close to their ceiling of allowed emissions could buy the right to pollute from those who had not used up their capacity
- nations can also offset emissions by using features such as forests that absorb carbon gases

Sanctions for those not meeting their targets are to be agreed at a later date. A timetable for implementing the protocol was agreed at Buenos Aires in November 1998. Trading in carbon permits will begin in 2000, when the Clean Development Mechanism will also be established. Developed countries will provide less polluting technology to developing countries, in return for carbon credits to offset their own emissions.

STATEMENT OF PRINCIPLES ON FORESTS

This non-binding agreement was intended to preserve tropical rain forests. It was recognized that forests must meet human needs (as a national resource providing timber and fuel) and that forests are important for absorbing carbon dioxide. The statement recommends the development of sustainable forest management policies and financial aid to developing countries so that they can preserve their forests.

EUROPEAN UNION PROGRAMMES

The first environmental action plan was adopted in 1972. These programmes are underpinned by the following principles: preventative action; the rectification of environmental damage at source where possible; and the 'polluter pays' principle (i.e. the polluter meets the full cost of the control of pollution). EU directives must be transposed into national law and policy to be effective.

The EC (now EU) Fifth Environmental Action Programme, called 'Towards Sustainability', was endorsed in December 1992 setting out a programme for sustainable development to 2000. It involves joint action by national and local government, private companies and individuals. A review of the programme, setting out priorities for further action, including further integration of environmental considerations into other policy areas, was completed in 1998.

The European Environment Agency was established in 1993 to monitor the state of the environment in the EU and to provide comparable environmental information.

UK MEASURES

The UK's international commitments on the environment have been incorporated into annual white papers called *This Common Inheritance*, summarizing the Government's commitments, achievements and future action and targets. Among the issues covered by the reports are climate change, wildlife and habitats, rural and urban development, air and water quality, pollution and waste, forestry and soil, and transport.

UK governments have increasingly seen environmental policy as part of the broader concept of sustainable development. This involves achieving environmental, economic and social objectives simultaneously, with environmental impact taken into account in all areas of policy rather than being considered in isolation. Government policy and operations are subject to scrutiny by the parliamentary environmental audit committee.

The UK produced its first national sustainable development strategy in 1994 and its first set of sustainable development indicators in 1996. A new strategy, 'A Better Quality of Life' was published in May 1999 which included revised indicators and targets. The Ministry of Agriculture, Fisheries and Food is working on a set of indicators of some of the pressures that agriculture exerts on the environment.

BIOLOGICAL DIVERSITY

The UK Biodiversity Group was set up after the Rio Earth Summit to identify and draw up costed action plans to protect the most threatened and declining species in the UK. The group's report, published in December 1995, identified 1,250 species and 38 key habitats which require action to protect them.

CLIMATE CHANGE AND POLLUTION

The Climate Change Impact Review Group was set up after Rio and in July 1996 published the *Review of the Potential Effects of Climate Change in the UK*, a sector by sector analysis of the impacts of climate change on sea level, the natural environment, energy and transport for the 2020s and 2050s in the UK. The Government intends to introduce legislation in the Finance Bill 2000 to provide for a climate change levy on businesses from April 2001.

The National Air Quality Strategy was adopted in March 1997. It is a framework for improving air quality. It sets quality standards for the main air pollutants and specific air quality objectives to be met by 2005, and outlines how industry, central and local government, transport and other sectors can contribute to improving air quality. A revised strategy was published in January 1999.

The draft UK Climate Change Consultation Paper was published in October 1998. It was followed by a period of consultation and a draft UK Climate Change Programme will be published in late 1999. The new programme is expected to be in place by 2001.

LOCAL AGENDA 21

Local authorities (and local communities) are being encouraged to play their part in meeting the UK's commitments under Agenda 21 and to a lesser degree the Biological Diversity and Climate Change Conventions. Under Local Agenda 21, local authorities draw up a sustainable development strategy for their areas. The main aims of the strategy are to protect and enhance the local environment, ensure prudent use of natural resources, meet social needs and promote economic success.

Each strategy should identify the local sustainability issues, set explicit objectives and priorities, state which organizations or sectors will take which actions, show how the objectives will be achieved and progress assessed, and outline the procedures for updating the strategy over time. Issues that might be covered by a local sustainability strategy include health, housing, home energy conservation, development plans, transport, air quality, biodiversity and recycling.

Local Agenda 21 is overseen in the UK by the Local Agenda 21 Steering Group, made up of representatives from the Local Government Association, the Convention of Scottish Local Authorities, the Association of Local Authorities of Northern Ireland, the TUC, the Advisory Committee on Business and the Environment, the World-Wide Fund for Nature, and other organizations. The International Council for Local Environmental Initiatives (ICLEI) is co-ordinating the international Local Agenda 21 initiative and the results of these efforts are reported via local government associations to the United Nations Commission on Sustainable Development.

Local authorities are under no statutory obligation to take part in Local Agenda 21 but a survey in 1998 found that 84 per cent of local authorities are engaged in or committed to Local Agenda 21. The Government wants all local authorities to adopt a Local Agenda 21 strategy by December 2000.

BUSINESSES

The Environmental Technology Best Practice Programme was set up in 1994 to help businesses to improve their environmental performance. The programme publishes free guides to good practice and case studies on low-cost waste minimization measures, cleaner technologies and on specific sectors and pollutants. The specific sectors covered so far are foundries, metal finishing, volatile organic compounds (solvents), textiles, paper and board, glass, printing, food and drink, chemicals, engineering, ceramics, plastics and packaging.

The Environment and Energy Helpline offers advice to business on any environmental issue.

UK TARGETS AND RECENT ACHIEVEMENTS
as at July 1999

Global Atmosphere

- reduce greenhouse gas emissions to 12.5 per cent below 1990 levels by 2010 (9 per cent reduction was achieved by 1997)
- reduce carbon dioxide emissions to 20 per cent below 1990 levels by 2010 (8 per cent reduction was achieved by 1997)
- phase out production and supply of CFCs by end of 1994 (achieved)
- return atmospheric chlorine and bromide to 1994 levels by 2012
- phase out HCFCs by 2015
- cut consumption of methyl bromide by 25 per cent by 1998 (*achieved*) and phase it out by 2005

Air Quality and Noise

- reduce sulphur dioxide emissions by 80 per cent on 1980 levels by 2010
- maintain emissions of oxides of nitrogen at 1987 levels from 1994 (*being achieved*)
- cut emissions from large combustion plants by 60 per cent between 1980 and 2003 (sulphur dioxide) and by 30 per cent between 1980 and 1988 (oxides of nitrogen)

Fresh Water and the Sea

- bring drinking water standards up to EC Directive standards by the mid-1990s (*largely achieved: in 1995, 99.5 per cent of tests in England and Wales met standards*)
- bring bathing waters fully up to EC Directive standards by the mid-1990s (*90 per cent of UK bathing waters met the standards in 1996*)
- phase out dumping of waste from collieries at sea by 1997 (*achieved in 1995*) and dumping of sewage sludge at sea by end of 1998
- halve atmospheric inputs of 17 harmful substances by 1999

Forestry

- double England's forest in the next 50 years (currently 7.5 per cent of total land area), subject to the necessary Common Agricultural Policy reform
- increase woodland cover in Wales by 50 per cent in next 50 years (currently 12 per cent of total land area)

Energy

- achieve energy savings of 250 petajoules per year by 2000
- achieve 15 per cent improvement in energy efficiency of government estate over five years to March 1996 (*achieved 14.5 per cent improvement*). New target set of 20 per cent improvement by 2000
- create 1500 MW of new electricity generating capacity from renewable resources by 2000

Waste

- reduce industrial and commercial waste going to landfill to 85 per cent of 1998 levels by 2005:

- recover 40 per cent of municipal waste by 2005, 45 per cent by 2010 and two-thirds by 2015
- recycle or compost 25 per cent of household waste by 2000
- 1 million tonnes of organic household waste a year to be composted by 2000, and 40 per cent of domestic properties with a garden to carry out composting by 2000
- 40 per cent of soil improvers and growing media in UK to be supplied by non-peat materials by 2005
- maintain at least 90 per cent recycling rate for waste lead-acid batteries
- increase use of waste/recycled materials as aggregates in England from about 30 to 55 million tonnes a year by 2006
- recover 50–65 per cent of packaging waste by 2001 and recycle 25–45 per cent by 2001 (minimum of 15 per cent for each material)
- ensure 40 per cent of UK newspaper feedstock to be waste paper by 2000
- recover 65 per cent of scrap tyres
- achieve easily accessible recycling facilities for 80 per cent of households by 2000

Housing

- reduce the proportion of homes lying empty to 3 per cent by 2005
- ensure that half of all new housing is built on re-used sites by 2005
- reduce number of government-owned empty homes.

ADDRESSES

ADVISORY COMMITTEE ON BUSINESS AND THE ENVIRONMENT, Floor 6/D9, Ashdown House, 123 Victoria Street, London SW1E 6DE. Tel: 0171-890 6624

ENVIRONMENT AGENCY, *see* page 299

ENVIRONMENTAL TECHNOLOGY BEST PRACTICE PROGRAMME, The Environment and Energy Helpline: 0800-585794. Web: http://www.environment.detr.gov.uk/bpp/helpline.htm

EUROPEAN ENVIRONMENT AGENCY, Kongens Nytorv 6, DK-1050 Copenhagen K, Denmark. Tel: Copenhagen 3336 7100. Web: http://www.eea.eu.int

GOVERNMENT PANEL ON SUSTAINABLE DEVELOPMENT, Zone 4/D9 Ashdown House, 123 Victoria Street, London SW1E 6DE. Tel: 0171-890 4962. Web: http://www.detr.gov.uk/environment

INTERNATIONAL COUNCIL FOR LOCAL ENVIRONMENTAL INITIATIVES (ICLEI), Sixteenth Floor, West Tower, City Hall, 100 Queen Street West, Toronto, Ontario M5H 2N2, Canada. Tel: Toronto 392 1462. Web: http://www.iclei.org

LOCAL AGENDA 21, Improvement and Development Agency, Layden House, 76-78 Turnmill Street, London EC1M 5QU. Tel: 0171-296 6599. Web: http://www.la21-uk.org.uk

ROYAL COMMISSION ON ENVIRONMENTAL POLLUTION, *see* page 300

SCOTTISH ENVIRONMENT PROTECTION AGENCY, *see* page 337

UK BIODIVERSITY GROUP, c/o Biodiversity Action Plan Secretariat, European Wildlife Division, Department of the Environment, Transport and the Regions, Room 902D Tollgate House, Houlton Street, Bristol BS2 9DJ. Tel: 0117-987 8974. Web: http://www.jncc.gov.uk/ukbg

UK ROUND TABLE ON SUSTAINABLE DEVELOPMENT, Zone 4/F4 Ashdown House, 123 Victoria Street, London SW1E 6DE. Tel: 0171-890 4962

UN COMMISSION ON SUSTAINABLE DEVELOPMENT, Division for Sustainable Development, Room DC2, 2220 United Nations, New York, NY 10017, USA. Tel: New York 963 3170

Conservation and Heritage

Conservation of the Countryside

NATIONAL PARKS

ENGLAND AND WALES

The ten National Parks of England and Wales were set up under the provisions of the National Parks and Access to the Countryside Act 1949 to conserve and protect scenic landscapes from inappropriate development and to provide access to the land for public enjoyment.

The Countryside Agency (established on 1 April 1999 from the merger of the Countryside Commission and the Rural Development Commission) is the statutory body which has the power to designate National Parks in England, and the Countryside Council for Wales is responsible for National Parks in Wales. Designations in England are confirmed by the Secretary of State for the Environment, Transport and the Regions and those in Wales by the National Assembly for Wales. The designation of a National Park does not affect the ownership of the land or remove the rights of the local community. The majority of the land in the National Parks is owned by private landowners (74 per cent) or by bodies such as the National Trust (7 per cent) and the Forestry Commission (7 per cent). The National Park Authorities own only 2.3 per cent of the land.

The Environment Act 1995 replaced the existing National Park boards and committees with free-standing National Park Authorities (NPAs). NPAs are the sole local planning authorities for their areas and as such influence land use and development, and deal with planning applications. Their duties include conserving and enhancing the natural beauty, wildlife and cultural heritage of the National Parks; promoting opportunities for public understanding and enjoyment of the National Parks; and fostering the economic and social well-being of the communities within National Parks. The NPAs publish management plans as statements of their policies and appoint their own officers and staff.

Membership of the NPAs differs slightly between England and Wales. In England membership is split between representatives of the constituent local authorities and members appointed by the Secretary of State (of whom one half minus one are nominated by the parish councils in the park), with the local authority representatives in a majority of one. The Countryside Agency advises the Secretary of State on appointments not nominated by the parish councils. In Wales two-thirds of NPA members are appointed by the constituent local authorities and one-third by the National Assembly for Wales, advised by the Countryside Council for Wales.

Central government provides 75 per cent of the funding for the parks through the National Park Grant. The remaining 25 per cent is supplied by the local authorities concerned. Approved net expenditure for all National Parks in 1999–2000 was £25,036,000 for England and £6,694,000 for Wales.

Two areas considered as having equivalent status are the Broads and the New Forest (*see* page 575).

The National Parks (with date designation confirmed) are:

BRECON BEACONS (1957), Powys (66 per cent)/Carmarthenshire/Rhondda, Cynon and Taff/Merthyr Tydfil/Blaenau Gwent/Monmouthshire, 1,351 sq. km/522 sq. miles – The park is centred on the Beacons, Pen y Fan, Corn Du and Cribyn, but also includes the valley of the Usk, the Black Mountains to the east and the Black Mountain to the west. There are information centres at Brecon, Craig-y-nos Country Park, Abergavenny and Llandovery, a study centre at Danywenallt and a day visitor centre near Libanus. *Information Office*, 7 Glamorgan Street, Brecon, Powys LD3 7DP. Tel: 01874–624437. *National Park Officer*, M. Fitton

DARTMOOR (1951 and 1994), Devon, 954 sq. km/368 sq. miles – The park consists of moorland and rocky granite tors, and is rich in prehistoric remains. There are information centres at Newbridge, Tavistock, Bovey Tracey, Steps Bridge, Princetown and Postbridge. *Information Office*, Parke, Haytor Road, Bovey Tracey, Devon TQ13 9JQ. Tel: 01626–832093. *National Park Officer*, N. Atkinson

EXMOOR (1954), Somerset (71 per cent)/Devon, 693 sq. km/268 sq. miles – Exmoor is a moorland plateau inhabited by wild ponies and red deer. There are many ancient remains and burial mounds. There are information centres at Lynmouth, County Gate, Dulverton and Combe Martin. *Information Office*, Exmoor House, Dulverton, Somerset TA22 9HL. Tel: 01398–23665. *National Park Officer*, K. Bungay

LAKE DISTRICT (1951), Cumbria, 2,292 sq. km/885 sq. miles – The Lake District includes England's highest mountains (Scafell Pike, Helvellyn and Skiddaw) but it is most famous for its glaciated lakes. There are information centres at Keswick, Waterhead, Hawkshead, Seatoller, Bowness, Grasmere, Coniston, Glenridding and Pooley Bridge, an information van at Gosforth and a park centre at Brockhole, Windermere. *Information Office*, Brockhole, Windermere, Cumbria LA23 1LJ. Tel: 01539–446601. *National Park Officer*, P. Tiplady

NORTHUMBERLAND (1956), Northumberland, 1,049 sq. km/405 sq. miles – The park is an area of hill country stretching from Hadrian's Wall to the Scottish Border. There are information centres at Ingram, Once Brewed, Rothbury, Housesteads, Harbottle and Kielder, and an information caravan at Cawfields. *Information Office*, Eastburn, South Park, Hexham, Northumberland NE46 1BS. Tel: 01434–605555. *National Park Officer*, G. Taylor

NORTH YORK MOORS (1952), North Yorkshire (96 per cent)/Redcar and Cleveland, 1,436 sq. km/554 sq. miles – The park consists of woodland and moorland, and includes the Hambleton Hills and the Cleveland Way. There are information centres at Danby, Pickering, Sutton Bank, Ravenscar, Helmsley and Hutton-le-Hole, and a day study centre at Danby. *Information Office*, The Old Vicarage, Bondgate, Helmsley, York YO6 5BP. Tel: 01439–70657. *National Park Officer*, D. Arnold-Forster

PEAK DISTRICT (1951), Derbyshire (64 per cent)/Staffordshire/South Yorkshire/Cheshire/West Yorkshire/Greater Manchester, 1,438 sq. km/555 sq. miles – The Peak District includes the gritstone moors

of the 'Dark Peak' and the limestone dales of the 'White Peak'. There are information centres at Bakewell, Edale, Fairholmes and Castleton, and information points at Torside (in the Longdendale Valley) and at Hartington (former station).
Information Office, Aldern House, Baslow Road, Bakewell, Derbyshire DE45 1AE. Tel: 01629-814321. *National Park Officer*, C. Harrison

PEMBROKESHIRE COAST (1952 and 1995), Pembrokeshire, 584 sq. km/225 sq. miles – The park includes cliffs, moorland and a number of islands, including Skomer. There are information centres at Tenby, St David's, Pembroke, Newport, Kilgetty, Haverfordwest and Broad Haven.
Information Office, Winch Lane, Haverfordwest, Pembrokeshire SA61 1PY. Tel: 01437-764636. *National Park Officer*, N. Wheeler

SNOWDONIA (1951), Gwynedd/Conwy, 2,142 sq. km/827 sq. miles – Snowdonia is an area of deep valleys and rugged mountains. There are information centres at Aberdyfi, Bala, Betws y Coed, Blaenau Ffestiniog, Conwy, Harlech, Dolgellau and Llanberis.
Information Office, Penrhyndeudraeth, Gwynedd LL48 6LF. Tel: 01766-770274. *National Park Officer*, I. Huws

YORKSHIRE DALES (1954), North Yorkshire (88 per cent)/Cumbria, 1,769 sq. km/683 sq. miles – The Yorkshire Dales are composed primarily of limestone overlaid in places by millstone grit. The three peaks of Ingleborough, Whernside and Pen-y-Ghent are within the park. There are information centres at Clapham, Grassington, Hawes, Aysgarth Falls, Malham and Sedbergh.
Information Office, Yorebridge House, Bainbridge, Leyburn, N. Yorks DL8 3BP. Tel: 01969-50456. *National Park Officer*, H. Hancock

Two other areas considered to have equivalent status to national parks are the Broads and the New Forest. The Broads Authority, a special statutory authority, was established in 1989 to develop, conserve and manage the Norfolk and Suffolk Broads (*see also* page 286). The Government declared in 1992 its intention of giving the New Forest a status equivalent to that of a National Park by declaring it an 'area of national significance'.

THE BROADS (1989), Norfolk, 303 sq. km/117 sq. miles – The Broads are located between Norwich and Great Yarmouth on the flood plains of the five rivers flowing through the area to the sea. The area is one of fens, winding waterways, woodland and marsh. The 40 or so broads are man-made, and are connected to the rivers by dykes, providing over 200 km of navigable waterways. There are information centres at Beccles, Hoveton, North-west Tower (Yarmouth), Ranworth and Toad Hole.
Broads Authority, Thomas Harvey House, 18 Colegate, Norwich NR3 1BQ. Tel: 01603-610734. *Chief Executive*, A. Clark

THE NEW FOREST, Hampshire, 376 sq. km/145 sq. miles – The forest has been protected since 1079 when it was declared a royal hunting forest. The area consists of forest, ancient woodland and heathland. Much of the Forest is managed by the Forestry Commission, which provides several camp-sites. The main villages are Brockenhurst, Burley and Lyndhurst, which has a visitor centre.
The Forestry Commission, Office of the Deputy Surveyor of the New Forest and the New Forest Committee, The Queen's House, Lyndhurst, Hants SO43 7NH. Tel: 01703-284149

SCOTLAND AND NORTHERN IRELAND

The National Parks and Access to the Countryside Act 1949 dealt only with England and Wales and made no provision for Scotland or Northern Ireland. Although there are no national parks in these two countries, there is power to designate them in Northern Ireland under the Amenity Lands Act 1965 and the Nature Conservation and Amenity Lands Order (Northern Ireland) 1985. In 1998 Scottish Natural Heritage submitted proposals to the Government for the designation of National Parks in Scotland. It will be for the Scottish Parliament to legislate in this area.

AREAS OF OUTSTANDING NATURAL BEAUTY

ENGLAND AND WALES

Under the National Parks and Access to the Countryside Act 1949, provision was made for the designation of Areas of Outstanding Natural Beauty (AONBs) by the Countryside Commission. The Countryside Agency is now responsible for AONBs in England and since April 1991 the Countryside Council for Wales has been responsible for the Welsh AONBs. Designations in England are confirmed by the Secretary of State for the Environment, Transport and the Regions and those in Wales by the National Assembly for Wales.

Although less emphasis is placed upon the provision of open-air enjoyment for the public than in the national parks, AONBs are areas which are no less beautiful and require the same degree of protection to conserve and enhance the natural beauty of the countryside. This includes protecting flora and fauna, geological and other landscape features. In AONBs planning and management responsibilities are split between county and district councils; where unitary authorities exist they have sole responsibility for planning and management. Several AONBs cross local authority boundaries. Finance for the AONBs is provided by grant-aid.

The 41 Areas of Outstanding Natural Beauty (with date designation confirmed) are:

ANGLESEY (1967), Anglesey, 221 sq. km/85 sq. miles
ARNSIDE AND SILVERDALE (1972), Cumbria/Lancashire, 75 sq. km/29 sq. miles
BLACKDOWN HILLS (1991), Devon/Somerset, 370 sq. km/143 sq. miles
CANNOCK CHASE (1958), Staffordshire, 68 sq. km/26 sq. miles
CHICHESTER HARBOUR (1964), Hampshire/West Sussex, 74 sq. km/29 sq. miles
CHILTERNS (1965; extended 1990), Bedfordshire/Hertfordshire/Buckinghamshire/Oxfordshire, 833 sq. km/322 sq. miles
CLWYDIAN RANGE (1985), Denbighshire/Flintshire, 157 sq. km/60 sq. miles
CORNWALL (1959; Camel estuary 1983), 958 sq. km/370 sq. miles
COTSWOLDS (1966; extended 1990), Gloucestershire/Wiltshire/Warwickshire/Worcestershire/Somerset, 2,038 sq. km/787 sq. miles
CRANBORNE CHASE AND WEST WILTSHIRE DOWNS (1983), Dorset/Hampshire/Somerset/Wiltshire, 983 sq. km/379 sq. miles
DEDHAM VALE (1970; extended 1978, 1991), Essex/Suffolk, 90 sq. km/35 sq. miles
DORSET (1959), 1,129 sq. km/436 sq. miles
EAST DEVON (1963), 268 sq. km/103 sq. miles
EAST HAMPSHIRE (1962), 383 sq. km/148 sq. miles
FOREST OF BOWLAND (1964), Lancashire/North Yorkshire, 802 sq. km/310 sq. miles

GOWER (1956), Swansea, 189 sq. km/73 sq. miles
HIGH WEALD (1983), Kent/Surrey/East Sussex/West Sussex, 1,460 sq. km/564 sq. miles
HOWARDIAN HILLS (1987), North Yorkshire, 204 sq. km/79 sq. miles
ISLE OF WIGHT (1963), 189 sq. km/73 sq. miles
ISLES OF SCILLY (1976), 16 sq. km/6 sq. miles
KENT DOWNS (1968), 878 sq. km/339 sq. miles
LINCOLNSHIRE WOLDS (1973), 558 sq. km/215 sq. miles
LLŶN (1957), Gwynedd, 161 sq. km/62 sq. miles
MALVERN HILLS (1959), Herefordshire/Worcestershire/Gloucestershire, 105 sq. km/40 sq. miles
MENDIP HILLS (1972; extended 1989), Somerset, 198 sq. km/76 sq. miles
NIDDERDALE (1994), North Yorkshire, 603 sq. km/233 sq. miles
NORFOLK COAST (1968), 451 sq. km/174 sq. miles
NORTH DEVON (1960), 171 sq. km/66 sq. miles
NORTH PENNINES (1988), Cumbria/Durham/Northumberland, 1,983 sq. km/766 sq. miles
NORTHUMBERLAND COAST (1958), 135 sq. km/52 sq. miles
QUANTOCK HILLS (1957), Somerset, 99 sq. km/38 sq. miles
SHROPSHIRE HILLS (1959), 804 sq. km/310 sq. miles
SOLWAY COAST (1964), Cumbria, 115 sq. km/44 sq. miles
SOUTH DEVON (1960), 337 sq. km/130 sq. miles
SOUTH HAMPSHIRE COAST (1967), 77 sq. km/30 sq. miles
SUFFOLK COAST AND HEATHS (1970), 403 sq. km/156 sq. miles
SURREY HILLS (1958), 419 sq. km/162 sq. miles
SUSSEX DOWNS (1966), 983 sq. km/379 sq. miles
TAMAR VALLEY (1995), Cornwall/Devon, 195 sq. km/115 sq. miles
NORTH WESSEX DOWNS (1972), Berkshire/Hampshire/Oxfordshire/Wiltshire, 1,730 sq. km/668 sq. miles
WYE VALLEY (1971), Monmouthshire/Gloucestershire/Herefordshire, 326 sq. km/126 sq. miles

NORTHERN IRELAND

The Department of the Environment for Northern Ireland, with advice from the Council for Nature Conservation and the Countryside, designates Areas of Outstanding Natural Beauty in Northern Ireland. At present there are nine and these cover a total area of approximately 284,948 hectares (704,121 acres).

ANTRIM COAST AND GLENS, Co. Antrim, 70,600 ha/174,452 acres
CAUSEWAY COAST, Co. Antrim, 4,200 ha/10,378 acres
LAGAN VALLEY, Co. Down, 2,072 ha/5,119 acres
LECALE COAST, Co. Down, 3,108 ha/7,679 acres
MOURNE, Co. Down, 57,012 ha/140,876 acres
NORTH DERRY, Co. Londonderry, 12,950 ha/31,999 acres
RING OF GULLION, Co. Armagh, 15,353 ha/37,938 acres
SPERRIN, Co. Tyrone/Co. Londonderry, 101,006 ha/249,585 acres
STRANGFORD LOUGH, Co. Down, 18,647 ha/46,077 acres

NATIONAL SCENIC AREAS

In Scotland, National Scenic Areas have a broadly equivalent status to AONBs. Scottish Natural Heritage recognizes areas of national scenic significance. At mid 1999 there were 40, covering a total area of 1,001,800 hectares (2,475,448 acres).

Development within National Scenic Areas is dealt with by local authorities, who are required to consult Scottish Natural Heritage concerning certain categories of development. Disagreements between Scottish Natural Heritage and local authorities are referred to the Scottish Executive. Land management uses can also be modified in the interest of scenic conservation.

ASSYNT-COIGACH, Highland, 90,200 ha/222,884 acres
BEN NEVIS AND GLEN COE, Highland/Argyll and Bute/Perth and Kinross, 101,600 ha/251,053 acres
CAIRNGORM MOUNTAINS, Highland/Aberdeenshire/Moray, 67,200 ha/166,051 acres
CUILLIN HILLS, Highland, 21,900 ha/54,115 acres
DEESIDE AND LOCHNAGAR, Aberdeenshire/Angus, 40,000 ha/98,840 acres
DORNOCH FIRTH, Highland, 7,500 ha/18,532 acres
EAST STEWARTRY COAST, Dumfries and Galloway, 4,500 ha/11,119 acres
EILDON AND LEADERFOOT, Scottish Borders, 3,600 ha/8,896 acres
FLEET VALLEY, Dumfries and Galloway, 5,300 ha/13,096 acres
GLEN AFFRIC, Highland, 19,300 ha/47,690 acres
GLEN STRATHFARRAR, Highland, 3,800 ha/9,390 acres
HOY AND WEST MAINLAND, Orkney Islands, 14,800 ha/36,571 acres
JURA, Argyll and Bute, 21,800 ha/53,868 acres
KINTAIL, Highland, 15,500 ha/38,300 acres
KNAPDALE, Argyll and Bute, 19,800 ha/48,926 acres
KNOYDART, Highland, 39,500 ha/97,604 acres
KYLE OF TONGUE, Highland, 18,500 ha/45,713 acres
KYLES OF BUTE, Argyll and Bute, 4,400 ha/10,872 acres
LOCH NA KEAL, MULL, Argyll and Bute, 12,700 ha/31,382 acres
LOCH LOMOND, Argyll and Bute/Stirling/West Dunbartonshire, 27,400 ha/67,705 acres
LOCH RANNOCH AND GLEN LYON, Perth and Kinross/Stirling, 48,400 ha/119,596 acres
LOCH SHIEL, Highland, 13,400 ha/33,111 acres
LOCH TUMMEL, Perth and Kinross, 9,200 ha/22,733 acres
LYNN OF LORN, Argyll and Bute, 4,800 ha/11,861 acres
MORAR, MOIDART AND ARDNAMURCHAN, Highland, 13,500 ha/33,358 acres
NORTH-WEST SUTHERLAND, Highland, 20,500 ha/50,655 acres
NITH ESTUARY, Dumfries and Galloway, 9,300 ha/22,980 acres
NORTH ARRAN, North Ayrshire, 23,800 ha/58,810 acres
RIVER EARN, Perth and Kinross, 3,000 ha/7,413 acres
RIVER TAY, Perth and Kinross, 5,600 ha/13,838 acres
ST KILDA, Western Isles, 900 ha/2,224 acres
SCARBA, LUNGA AND THE GARVELLACHS, Argyll and Bute, 1,900 ha/4,695 acres
SHETLAND, Shetland Islands, 11,600 ha/28,664 acres
SMALL ISLES, Highland, 15,500 ha/38,300 acres
SOUTH LEWIS, HARRIS AND NORTH UIST, Western Isles, 109,600 ha/270,822 acres
SOUTH UIST MACHAIR, Western Isles, 6,100 ha/15,073 acres
THE TROSSACHS, Stirling, 4,600 ha/11,367 acres
TROTTERNISH, Highland, 5,000 ha/12,355 acres
UPPER TWEEDDALE, Scottish Borders, 10,500 ha/25,945 acres
WESTER ROSS, Highland, 145,300 ha/359,036 acres

THE NATIONAL FOREST

The National Forest is being planted in about 200 square miles of Derbyshire, Leicestershire and Staffordshire. About 30 million trees, of mixed species but mainly broadleaved, will be planted over the next 20 years and beyond, and will eventually cover about one-third of the designated area. The project is funded by the Department of the Environment, Transport and the Regions. It was developed in 1992–5 by the Countryside Commission and is now run by the National Forest Company, which was established in April 1995. Since then almost 3 million trees have been planted on 1,518 hectares of land across 384 sites. Under the National Forest tender scheme, anybody wishing to undertake a project can submit a competitive bid to the National Forest Company.

NATIONAL FOREST COMPANY, Enterprise Glade, Bath Lane, Moira, Swadlincote, Derbys DE12 6BD. Tel: 01283-551211. *Chief Executive*, Miss S. Bell

Nature Conservation Areas

SITES OF SPECIAL SCIENTIFIC INTEREST

Site of Special Scientific Interest (SSSI) is a legal notification applied to land in England, Scotland or Wales which English Nature (EN), Scottish Natural Heritage (SNH), or the Countryside Council for Wales (CCW) identifies as being of special interest because of its flora, fauna, geological or physiographical features. In some cases, SSSIs are managed as nature reserves.

EN, SNH and CCW must notify the designation of a SSSI to the local planning authority, every owner/occupier of the land, and the Secretary of State for the Environment, Transport and the Regions, the Scottish Executive or the National Assembly for Wales. Forestry and agricultural departments and a number of other bodies are also informed of this notification.

Objections to the notification of a SSSI can be made and ultimately considered at a full meeting of the Council of EN or CCW. In Scotland an objection will be dealt with by the appropriate regional board or the main board of SNH, depending on the nature of the objection. Unresolved objections on scientific grounds must be referred to the Advisory Committee for SSSI.

The protection of these sites depends on the co-operation of individual landowners and occupiers. Owner/occupiers must consult EN, SNH or CCW and gain written consent before they can undertake certain listed activities on the site. Funds are available through management agreements and grants to assist owners and occupiers in conserving sites' interests. As a last resort a site can be purchased.

The number and area of SSSIs in Britain as at 31 March 1999 was:

	no.	hectares	acres
England*	4,012	980,539	2,422,912
Scotland	1,448	919,597	2,272,324
Wales	963	223,332	551,853

*Figures as at 30 September 1998

In Northern Ireland 161 Areas of Special Scientific Interest (ASSIs) have been established by the Department of the Environment for Northern Ireland. These cover a total area of 83,465.476 hectares (206,243.19 acres).

NATIONAL NATURE RESERVES

National Nature Reserves are defined in the National Parks and Access to the Countryside Act 1949 as land designated for the study and preservation of flora and fauna, or of geological or physiographical features.

English Nature (EN), Scottish Natural Heritage (SNH) or the Countryside Council for Wales (CCW) can designate as a National Nature Reserve land which is being managed as a nature reserve under an agreement with one of the statutory nature conservation agencies; land held and managed by EN, SNH or CCW; or land held and managed as a nature reserve by another approved body. EN, SNH or CCW can make by-laws to protect reserves from undesirable activities; these are subject to confirmation by the Secretary of State for the Environment, Transport and the Regions, the National Assembly for Wales or the Scottish Executive.

The number and area of National Nature Reserves in Britain as at 31 March 1999 was:

	no.	hectares	acres
England*	194	79,666	196,855
Scotland	71	114,277	282,378
Wales	62	23,308	57,594

*Figures as at 30 September 1998

NORTHERN IRELAND

National Nature Reserves are established and managed by the Department of the Environment for Northern Ireland, with advice from the Council for Nature Conservation and the Countryside. There are 45 National Nature Reserves covering 4,322.1 hectares (10,676 acres).

LOCAL NATURE RESERVES

Local Nature Reserves are defined in the National Parks and Access to the Countryside Act 1949 as land designated for the study and preservation of flora and fauna, or of geological or physiographical features. The Act gives local authorities in England, Scotland and Wales the power to acquire, declare and manage local nature reserves in consultation with English Nature, Scottish Natural Heritage and the Countryside Council for Wales. Conservation trusts can also own and manage non-statutory local nature reserves.

The number and area of designated Local Nature Reserves in Britain as at 31 March 1999 was:

	no.	hectares	acres
England	598	29,032	71,738
Scotland	29	9,297	22,973
Wales	41	4,283	10,583

An additional 38 km of linear trails are designated as Local Nature Reserves.

FOREST NATURE RESERVES

Forest Enterprise (an executive agency of the Forestry Commission) is responsible for the management of the

Commission's forests. It has created 46 Forest Nature Reserves with the aim of protecting and conserving special forms of natural habitat, flora and fauna. There are about 300 SSSIs on the estates, some of which are also Nature Reserves.

Forest Nature Reserves extend in size from under 50 hectares (124 acres) to over 500 hectares (1,236 acres). The largest include the Black Wood of Rannoch, by Loch Rannoch; Cannop Valley Oakwoods, Forest of Dean; Culbin Forest, near Forres; Glen Affric, near Fort Augustus; Kylerhea, Skye; Pembrey, Carmarthen Bay; Starr Forest, in Galloway Forest Park; and Wyre Forest, near Kidderminster.

Forest Enterprise also manages 18 Caledonian Forest Reserves in Scotland. These reserves are intended to protect and expand 16,000 hectares of native oak and pine woods in the Scottish highlands.

NORTHERN IRELAND

There are 36 Forest Nature Reserves in Northern Ireland, covering 1,759 hectares (4,346 acres). They are designated and administered by the Forest Service, an agency of the Department of Agriculture for Northern Ireland. There are also 15 National Nature Reserves on Forest Service-owned property.

MARINE NATURE RESERVES

The Secretary of State for the Environment, Transport and the Regions, the National Assembly for Wales and the Scottish Executive have the power to designate Marine Nature Reserves. English Nature, Scottish Natural Heritage and the Countryside Council for Wales select and manage these reserves. Marine Nature Reserves may be established in Northern Ireland under a 1985 Order.

Marine Nature Reserves provide protection for marine flora and fauna, and geological and physiographical features on land covered by tidal waters or parts of the sea in or adjacent to the UK. Reserves also provide opportunities for study and research.

The three statutory Marine Nature Reserves are:

LUNDY
(1986), Bristol Channel
SKOMER
(1990), Dyfed
STRANGFORD LOUGH
(1995), Northern Ireland

Two other areas proposed for designation as reserves are: the Menai Strait, and Bardsey Island and part of the Llŷn peninsula, both in Wales.

A number of non-statutory marine reserves have been set up by conservation groups.

EUROPEAN MARINE SITES

The 1992 EC Habitats Directive and the 1979 Birds Directive allow the UK government to establish Special Areas of Conservation (SACs) on land and at sea. Where the designated area includes sea or seashore it is described as a European marine site. The UK marine SACs project is a demonstration initiative, funded by the EU, to establish management schemes for twelve of the marine SACs in the UK.

Conservation of Wildlife and Habitats

The United Kingdom is party to a number of international conservation conventions.

RAMSAR CONVENTION

The Convention on Wetlands of International Importance especially as Waterfowl Habitat was adopted at Ramsar, Iran, in 1971 and ratified by the UK in 1976. By July 1999, 116 countries were party to promote the convention. The aim of the convention is to the conservation and wise use of wetlands (e.g. areas of marsh, fen) and their flora and fauna, especially waterfowl. Governments who are party to the convention are obliged to designate wetlands in their territory for inclusion in the List of Wetlands of International Importance and to include wetland conservation considerations in their national land-use planning. As at 10 May 1999, there were 148 sites in the UK.

RAMSAR CONVENTION BUREAU, Rue Mauverney 28, CH-1196 Gland, Switzerland. Tel: Gland 999 0170. Web: http://www.ramsar.org

BONN CONVENTION

The Bonn Convention on the Conservation of Migratory Species of Wild Animals was adopted in 1979 and came into force in the UK on 1 October 1979. The convention requires the protection of listed endangered migratory species and encourages international agreements covering these and other threatened species.

The United Kingdom has signed and ratified three regional agreements under the convention: the Agreement on the Conservation of Small Cetaceans of the Baltic and North Seas (ASCOBANS), protecting dolphins and porpoises, etc; the Agreement on the Conservation of Bats in Europe and the African-Eurasian Migratory Waterbird Agreement (AEWA), which is aimed at protecting migrant waterbirds, and is working towards becoming a signatory (on behalf of Gibraltar) to the Agreement on the Conservation of Cetaceans in the Mediterranean and Black Seas (ACCOBAMS).

UNEP/CMS SECRETARIAT, United Nations Premises in Bonn, Martin-Luther-King Strasse 8, D-53175 Bonn, Germany. Tel: Bonn 815 2401. Web: http://www.wcmc.org.uk/cms

BERN CONVENTION

The Convention on the Conservation of European Wildlife and Natural Habitats was adopted in 1979 and ratified by the UK in 1982. The aim of the convention is to conserve flora and fauna and their natural habitats in Europe. Particular emphasis is placed on the protection of endangered and vulnerable species (both endemic and migratory) and on those species and habitats whose conservation requires the co-operation of several states.

Parties to the convention undertake to maintain populations (or take steps to increase populations where necessary) of species covered by the convention while taking account of local cultural, economic and recreational requirements and the requirements of sub-species. They must also ensure that national and local planning and development policies take account of wildlife and fauna.

SECRETARIAT OF THE BERN CONVENTION STANDING COMMITTEE, Council of Europe, F-67075 Strasbourg Cedex, France. Tel: Strasbourg 8841 2253. Web: http://www.nature.coe.int

HABITATS DIRECTIVE

The Council (EC) Directive on the Conservation of Natural Habitats of Wild Fauna and Flora was adopted by the Council in 1992 and became law in the UK in 1994 as the Conservation (Natural Habitats) Regulations. Under this directive EU members are required to maintain or restore natural habitats and wild species (other than birds) and to designate Special Areas of Conservation (SACs). SACs are those areas that are considered to be of European-wide importance because they are rare, threatened or important for the maintenance of biological diversity in Europe. The directive specifies the habitat types and species which require site designation: 75 habitat types and 47 species are proposed for site designation in the UK.

Member states compile a national list from which a final list of European importance will be drawn by 2004. By June 1999 the UK had submitted a total of 340 candidate sites to the Commission.

BIRDS DIRECTIVE

The Council (EC) Directive on the Conservation of Wild Birds was adopted by the Council in 1979 and came into force in April 1981. Under this directive EU members are required to maintain populations of wild birds and to preserve the diversity and area of their habitats. The species that are to be protected are listed in Annex 1 to the directive and are those species that are in danger of extinction, rare, or vulnerable to changes in their habitat.

Members are also obliged, under the directive, to notify the Commission of sites which are of particular importance to the conservation of wild birds. These sites are designated as Special Protection Areas (SPAs). Any site that is to be designated as a SPA in the UK must first have been notified as a Site of Special Scientific Interest or Area of Special Scientific Interest (*see* page 577). Sites may be designated as SPAs if they are of national or international importance. New guidelines for the selection of SPAs were agreed in June 1999 and a definitive list of SPAs is expected to be published in spring 2000.

By June 1999, a total of 2,436 SPAs had been designated, of which 200 are in the UK. The UK designations cover over 930,000 hectares.

CITES

The Convention on Trade in Endangered Species of Wild Fauna and Flora (CITES) was agreed in 1973 and came into force in 1975. It aims to prevent international trade in wildlife and their products, e.g. skins, from species threatened with extinction. Plant and animal species subject to regulation are listed according to the degree of protection they need:

– appendix I is a list of species threatened with extinction that are, or may be, affected by trade. International trade in these species is prohibited
– appendix II is a list of species which might become threatened if trade in them is not controlled. A permit is required to trade in these species
– appendix III is a list of species, protected within individual countries, where the country has asked other parties to the convention to assist in controlling international trade. A permit is required to trade in these species

Approximately 30,000 species are covered by the regulations.

The Wildlife Licensing and Registration Service (Wildlife and Countryside Directorate) of the Department of Environment, Transport and the Regions (*see* page 297) is responsible for issuing permits and compiling annual trade

reports. The Joint Nature Conservation Committee (*see* page 326) and the Royal Botanic Gardens (*see* page 335) are the officially designated scientific authorities (on animals and plants respectively) who provide the expertise on which import and export approvals are based. CITES is financed by contributions from the member countries.
CITES SECRETARIAT, 15 Chemin des Anémones, CH-1219 Châtelaine, Geneva, Switzerland. Tel: Geneva 2979 9139

EUROPEAN WILDLIFE TRADE REGULATION

The Council (EC) Regulation on the Protection of Species of Wild Fauna and Flora by Regulating Trade Therein came into force in the UK on 1 June 1997. It is intended to standardize wildlife trade regulations across Europe and to improve the application of CITES. Approximately 30,000 plant and animal species are protected under the regulation.

UK LEGISLATION

The Wildlife and Countryside Act 1981 gives legal protection to a wide range of wild animals and plants. Subject to parliamentary approval, the Secretary of State for the Environment, Transport and the Regions may vary the animals and plants given legal protection. The most recent variation of Schedules 5 and 8 came into effect in March and April 1998.

Under Section 9 and Schedule 5 of the Act it is illegal without a licence to kill, injure, take, possess or sell any of the listed animals (whether alive or dead) and to disturb its place of shelter and protection or to destroy that place.

Under Section 13 and Schedule 8 of the Act it is illegal without a licence to pick, uproot, sell or destroy any of the listed plants and, unless authorized, to uproot any wild plant.

The Act lays down a close season for wild birds (other than game birds) from 1 February to 31 August inclusive, each year. Exceptions to these dates are made for:
Capercaillie and (except Scotland) *Woodcock* – 1 February to 30 September
Snipe – 1 February to 11 August
Wild Duck and *Wild Goose* (below high water mark) – 21 February to 31 August

Birds which may be killed or taken outside the close season (except on Sundays and on Christmas Day in Scotland, and on Sundays in prescribed areas of England and Wales) are the above-named, plus coot, certain wild duck (gadwall, goldeneye, mallard, pintail, pochard, shoveler, teal, tufted duck, wigeon), certain wild geese (Canada, greylag, pink-footed, white-fronted (in England and Wales only)), moorhen, golden plover and woodcock.

Certain wild birds may be killed or taken subject to the conditions of a general licence at any time by authorized persons: crow, collared dove, gull (great and lesser black-backed or herring), jackdaw, jay, magpie, pigeon (feral or wood), rook, sparrow (house), and starling. Conditions usually apply where the birds pose a threat to agriculture, public health, air safety, other bird species, and to prevent the spread of disease.

All other British birds are fully protected by law throughout the year.

Animals

‡Adder (*Vipera berus*)
Anemone, Ivell's Sea (*Edwardsia ivelli*)
Anemone, Starlet Sea (*Nematosella vectensis*)
Apus, Tadpole shrimp (*Triops cancriformis*)
Bat, Horseshoe (*Rhinolophidae*, all species)
Bat, Typical (*Vespertilionidae*, all species)
Beetle (*Graphoderus zonatus*)

Beetle (*Hypebaeus flavipes*)
Beetle, Lesser Silver Water (*Hydrochara caraboides*)
§§Beetle, Mire Pill (*Curimopsis nigrita*)
Beetle, Rainbow Leaf (*Chrysolina cerealis*)
*Beetle, Stag (*Lucanus cervus*)
Beetle, Violet Click (*Limoniscus violaceus*)
Beetle, Water (*Graphoderus zonatus*)
Beetle, Water (*Paracymus aeneus*)
Burbot (*Lota lota*)
*Butterfly, Adonis Blue (*Lysandra bellargus*)
*Butterfly, Black Hairstreak (*Strymonidia pruni*)
*Butterfly, Brown Hairstreak (*Thecla betulae*)
*Butterfly, Chalkhill Blue (*Lysandra coridon*)
*Butterfly, Chequered Skipper (*Carterocephalus palaemon*)
*Butterfly, Duke of Burgundy Fritillary (*Hamearis lucina*)
*Butterfly, Glanville Fritillary (*Melitaea cinxia*)
Butterfly, Heath Fritillary (*Mellicta athalia* (or *Melitaea athalia*))
Butterfly, High Brown Fritillary (*Argynnis adippe*)
Butterfly, Large Blue (*Maculinea arion*)
Butterfly, Large Copper (*Lycaena dispar*)
*Butterfly, Large Heath (*Coenonympha tullia*)
*Butterfly, Large Tortoiseshell (*Nymphalis polychloros*)
*Butterfly, Lulworth Skipper (*Thymelicus acteon*)
Butterfly, Marsh Fritillary (*Eurodryas aurinia*)
*Butterfly, Mountain Ringlet (*Erebia epiphron*)
*Butterfly, Northern Brown Argus (*Aricia artaxerxes*)
*Butterfly, Pearl-bordered Fritillary (*Boloria euphrosyne*)
*Butterfly, Purple Emperor (*Apatura iris*)
*Butterfly, Silver Spotted Skipper (*Hesperia comma*)
*Butterfly, Silver-studded Blue (*Plebejus argus*)
*Butterfly, Small Blue (*Cupido minimus*)
Butterfly, Swallowtail (*Papilio machaon*)
*Butterfly, White Letter Hairstreak (*Stymonida w-album*)
*Butterfly, Wood White (*Leptidea sinapis*)
Cat, Wild (*Felis silvestris*)
Cicada, New Forest (*Cicadetta montana*)
**Crayfish, Atlantic stream (*Austropotamobius pallipes*)
Cricket, Field (*Gryllus campestris*)
Cricket, Mole (*Gryllotalpa gryllotalpa*)
Damselfly, Southern (*Coenagrion mercuriale*)
Dolphin (*Cetacea*)
Dormouse (*Muscardinus avellanarius*)
Dragonfly, Norfolk Aeshna (*Aeshna isosceles*)
*Frog, Common (*Rana temporaria*)
Goby, Couch's (*Gobius couchii*)
Goby, Giant (*Gobius cobitis*)
Grasshopper, Wart-biter (*Decticus verrucivorus*)
Hatchet Shell, Northern (*Thyasira gouldi*)
Hydroid, Marine (*Clavopsella navis*)
Lagoon Snail (*Paludinella littorina*)
Lagoon Snail, De Folin's (*Caecum armoricum*)
Lagoon Worm, Tentacled (*Alkmaria romijni*)
Leech, Medicinal (*Hirudo medicinalis*)
Lizard, Sand (*Lacerta agilis*)
‡Lizard, Viviparous (*Lacerta vivipara*)
Marten, Pine (*Martes martes*)
Moth, Barberry Carpet (*Pareulype berberata*)
Moth, Black-veined (*Siona lineata* (or *Idaea lineata*))
Moth, Essex Emerald (*Thetidia smaragdaria*)
Moth, Fiery clearwing (*Bembecia chrysidiformis*)
Moth, Fisher's estuarine (*Gortyna borelii*)
Moth, New Forest Burnet (*Zygaena viciae*)
Moth, Reddish Buff (*Acosmetia caliginosa*)
Moth, Sussex Emerald (*Thalera fimbrialis*)
††Mussel, Fan (*Atrina fragilis*)
†Mussel, Freshwater Pearl (*Margaritifera margaritifera*)
Newt, Great Crested (or Warty) (*Triturus cristatus*)
*Newt, Palmate (*Triturus helveticus*)
*Newt, Smooth (*Triturus vulgaris*)

Otter, Common (*Lutra lutra*)
Porpoise (*Cetacea*)
Sandworm, Lagoon (*Armandia cirrhosa*)
††Sea Fan, Pink (*Eunicella verrucosa*)
Sea-Mat, Trembling (*Victorella pavida*)
Sea Slug, Lagoon (*Tenellia adspersa*)
‡‡Shad, Allis (*alosa alosa*)
§§Shad, Twaite (*alosa fallax*)
Shark, Basking (*Cetorhinus maximus*)
Shrimp, Fairy (*Chirocephalus diaphanus*)
Shrimp, Lagoon Sand (*Gammarus insensibilis*)
‡Slow-worm (*Anguis fragilis*)
Snail, Glutinous (*Myxas glutinosa*)
Snail, Sandbowl (*Catinella arenaria*)
‡Snake, Grass (*Natrix natrix* (*Natrix helvetica*))
Snake, Smooth (*Coronella austriaca*)
Spider, Fen Raft (*Dolomedes plantarius*)
Spider, Ladybird (*Eresus niger*)
Squirrel, Red (*Sciurus vulgaris*)
Sturgeon (*Acipenser sturio*)
*Toad, Common (*Bufo bufo*)
Toad, Natterjack (*Bufo calamita*)
Turtle, Marine (*Dermochelyidae* and *Cheloniidae*, all species)
Vendace (*Coregonus albula*)
§§Vole, Water (*Arvicola terrestris*)
Walrus (*Odobenus rosmarus*)
Whale (*Cetacea*)
Whitefish (*Coregonus lavaretus*)
* The offence relates to 'sale' only
** The offence relates to 'taking' and 'sale' only
† The offence relates to 'killing and injuring' only
‡ The offence relates to 'killing, injuring and sale'
§ The offence relates to 'killing, injuring and taking'
§§ The offence relates only to damaging, destroying or obstructing access to a shelter or protection
†† The offence relates to killing, injuring, taking, possession and sale
‡‡ The offence relates to killing, injuring, taking and damaging, etc., a shelter

Plants

Adder's tongue, Least (*Ophioglossum lusitanicum*)
Alison, Small (*Alyssum alyssoides*)
Blackwort (*Southbya nigrella*)
°Bluebell (*Hyacinthoides non-scripta*)
Broomrape, Bedstraw (*Orobanche caryophyllacea*)
Broomrape, Oxtongue (*Orobanche loricata*)
Broomrape, Thistle (*Orobanche reticulata*)
Cabbage, Lundy (*Rhynchosinapis wrightii*)
Calamint, Wood (*Calamintha sylvatica*)
Caloplaca, Snow (*Caloplaca nivalis*)
Catapyrenium, Tree (*Catapyrenium psoromoides*)
Catchfly, Alpine (*Lychnis alpina*)
Catillaria, Laurer's (*Catellaria laureri*)
Centaury, Slender (*Centaurium tenuiflorum*)
Cinquefoil, Rock (*Potentilla rupestris*)
Cladonia, Upright Mountain (*Cladonia stricta*)
Clary, Meadow (*Salvia pratensis*)
Club-rush, Triangular (*Scirpus triquetrus*)
Colt's-foot, Purple (*Homogyne alpina*)
Cotoneaster, Wild (*Cotoneaster integerrimus*)
Cottongrass, Slender (*Eriophorum gracile*)
Cow-wheat, Field (*Melampyrum arvense*)
Crocus, Sand (*Romulea columnae*)
Crystalwort, Lizard (*Riccia bifurca*)
Cudweed, Broad-leaved (*Filago pyramidata*)
Cudweed, Jersey (*Gnaphalium luteoalbum*)
Cudweed, Red-tipped (*Filago lutescens*)
Cut-grass (*Leersia oryzoides*)
Diapensia (*Diapensia lapponica*)
Dock, Shore (*Rumex rupestris*)
Earwort, Marsh (*Jamesoniella undulifolia*)

Eryngo, Field (*Eryngium campestre*)
Fern, Dickie's bladder (*Cystopteris dickieana*)
Fern, Killarney (*Trichomanes speciosum*)
Flapwort, Norfolk (*Leiocolea rutheana*)
Fleabane, Alpine (*Erigeron borealis*)
Fleabane, Small (*Pulicaria vulgaris*)
Fleawort, South stack (*Tephroseris integrifolia* (*ssp maritima*))
Frostwort, Pointed (*Gymnomitrion apiculatum*)
Fungus, Hedgehog (*Hericium erinaceum*)
Fungus, Oak polypore (*Buglossoporus pulvinus*)
Fungus, Royal bolete (*Boletus regius*)
Fungus, Sandy stilt puffball (*Battarraea phalloides*)
Galingale, Brown (*Cyperus fuscus*)
Gentian, Alpine (*Gentiana nivalis*)
Gentian, Dune (*Gentianella uliginosa*)
Gentian, Early (*Gentianella anglica*)
Gentian, Fringed (*Gentianella ciliata*)
Gentian, Spring (*Gentiana verna*)
Germander, Cut-leaved (*Teucrium botrys*)
Germander, Water (*Teucrium scordium*)
Gladiolus, Wild (*Gladiolus illyricus*)
Goosefoot, Stinking (*Chenopodium vulvaria*)
Grass-poly (*Lythrum hyssopifolia*)
Grimmia, Blunt-leaved (*Grimmia unicolor*)
Gyalecta, Elm (*Gyalecta ulmi*)
Hare's-ear, Sickle-leaved (*Bupleurum falcatum*)
Hare's-ear, Small (*Bupleurum baldense*)
Hawk's-beard, Stinking (*Crepis foetida*)
Hawkweed, Northroe (*Hieracium northroense*)
Hawkweed, Shetland (*Hieracium zetlandicum*)
Hawkweed, Weak-leaved (*Hieracium attenuatifolium*)
Heath, Blue (*Phyllodoce caerulea*)
Helleborine, Red (*Cephalanthera rubra*)
Helleborine, Young's (*Epipactis youngiana*)
Horsetail, Branched (*Equisetum ramosissimum*)
Hound's-tongue, Green (*Cynoglossum germanicum*)
Knawel, Perennial (*Scleranthus perennis*)
Knotgrass, Sea (*Polygonum maritimum*)
Lady's-slipper (*Cypripedium calceolus*)
Lecanactis, Churchyard (*Lecanactis hemisphaerica*)
Lecanora, Tarn (*Lecanora archariana*)
Lecidea, Copper (*Lecidea inops*)
Leek, Round-headed (*Allium sphaerocephalon*)
Lettuce, Least (*Lactuca saligna*)
Lichen, Alpine sulphur-tresses (*Alectoria ochroleuca*)
Lichen, Arctic kidney (*Nephroma arcticum*)
Lichen, Ciliate strap (*Heterodermia leucomelos*)
Lichen, Convoluted cladonia (*Cladonia convoluta*)
Lichen, Coralloid rosette (*Heterodermia propagulifera*)
Lichen, Ear-lobed dog (*Peltigera lepidophora*)
Lichen, Forked hair (*Bryoria furcellata*)
Lichen, Goblin lights (*Catolechia wahlenbergii*)
Lichen, Golden hair (*Teloschistes flavicans*)
Lichen, New Forest beech-lichen (*Enterographa elaborata*)
Lichen, Orange fruited Elm (*Caloplaca luteoalba*)
Lichen, River jelly (*Collema dichotomum*)
Lichen, Scaly breck (*Squamarina lentigera*)
Lichen, Stary breck (*Buellia asterella*)
Lichen, Upright mountain cladonia (*Cladonia stricta*)
Lily, Snowdon (*Lloydia serotina*)
Liverwort, Leafy (*Petallophyllum ralfsi*)
Liverwort, Lindenberg's (*Adelanthus lindenbergianus*)
Marsh-mallow, Rough (*Althaea hirsuta*)
Marshwort, Creeping (*Apium repens*)
Milk-parsley, Cambridge (*Selinum carvifolia*)
Moss (*Drepanocladius vernicosus*)
Moss, Alpine copper (*Mielichoferia mielichoferi*)
Moss, Anomodon, long-leaved (*Anomodon longifolius*)
Moss, Baltic bog (*Sphagnum balticum*)
Moss, Blue dew (*Saelania glaucescens*)

Moss, Blunt-leaved bristle (*Orthotrichum obtusifolium*)
Moss, Bright green cave (*Cyclodictyon laetevirens*)
Moss, Cordate beard (*Barbula cordata*)
Moss, Cornish path (*Ditrichum cornubicum*)
Moss, Derbyshire feather (*Thamnobryum angustifolium*)
Moss, Dune thread (*Bryum mamillatum*)
Moss, Flamingo (*Desmatodon cernuus*)
Moss, Glaucous beard (*Barbula glauca*)
Moss, Green shield (*Buxbaumia viridis*)
Moss, Hair silk (*Plagiothecium piliferum*)
Moss, Knothole (*Zygodon forsteri*)
Moss, Large yellow feather (*Scorpidium turgescens*)
Moss, Millimetre (*Micromitrium tenerum*)
Moss, Multifruited river (*Cryphaea lamyana*)
Moss, Nowell's limestone (*Zygodon gracilis*)
Moss, Polar feather-moss (*Hygrohypnum polare*)
Moss, Rigid apple (*Bartramia stricta*)
Moss, Round-leaved feather (*Rhyncostegium rotundifolium*)
Moss, Schleicher's thread (*Bryum schleicheri*)
Moss, Threadmoss, long-leaved (*Bryum neodamense*)
Moss, Triangular pygmy (*Acaulon triquetrum*)
Moss, Vaucher's feather (*Hypnum vaucheri*)
Mudwort, Welsh (*Limosella austeralis*)
Naiad, Holly-leaved (*Najas marina*)
Naiad, Slender (*Najas flexilis*)
Orache, Stalked (*Halimione pedunculata*)
Orchid, Early spider (*Ophrys sphegodes*)
Orchid, Fen (*Liparis loeselii*)
Orchid, Ghost (*Epipogium aphyllum*)
Orchid, Lapland marsh (*Dactylorhiza lapponica*)
Orchid, Late spider (*Ophrys fuciflora*)
Orchid, Lizard (*Himantoglossum hircinum*)
Orchid, Military (*Orchis militaris*)
Orchid, Monkey (*Orchis simia*)
Panneria, Caledonia (*Panneria ignobilis*)
Parmelia, New Forest (*Parmelia minarum*)
Parmentaria, Oil stain (*Parmentaria chilensis*)
Pear, Plymouth (*Pyrus cordata*)
Penny-cress, Perfoliate (*Thlaspi perfoliatum*)
Pennyroyal (*Mentha pulegium*)
Pertusaria, Alpine moss (*Pertusaria bryontha*)
Physcia, Southern grey (*Physcia tribacioides*)
Pigmyweed (*Crassula aquatica*)
Pine, Ground (*Ajuga chamaepitys*)
Pink, Cheddar (*Dianthus gratianopolitanus*)
Pink, Childing (*Petroraghia nanteuilii*)
Pink, Deptford (*Dianthus armeria*) (England and Wales only)
Plantain, Floating water (*Luronium natans*)
Pseudocyphellaria, Ragged (*Pseudocyphellaria lacerata*)
Psora, Rusty Alpine (*Psora rubiformis*)
Ragwort, Fen (*Senecio paludosus*)
Ramping-fumitory, Martin's (*Fumaria martinii*)
Rampion, Spiked (*Phyteuma spicatum*)
Restharrow, Small (*Ononis reclinata*)
Rock-cress, Alpine (*Arabis alpina*)
Rock-cress, Bristol (*Arabis stricta*)
Rustwort, Western (*Marsupella profunda*)
Sandwort, Norwegian (*Arenaria norvegica*)
Sandwort, Teesdale (*Minuartia stricta*)
Saxifrage, Drooping (*Saxifraga cernua*)
Saxifrage, Marsh (*Saxifrage hirulus*)
Saxifrage, Tufted (*Saxifraga cespitosa*)
Solenopsora, Serpentine (*Solenopsora liparina*)
Solomon's-seal, Whorled (*Polygonatum verticillatum*)
Sow-thistle, Alpine (*Cicerbita alpina*)
Spearwort, Adder's-tongue (*Ranunculus ophioglossifolius*)
Speedwell, Fingered (*Veronica triphyllos*)
Speedwell, Spiked (*Veronica spicata*)
Spike rush, Dwarf (*Eleocharis parvula*)

Star-of-Bethlehem, Early (*Gagea bohemica*)
Starfruit (*Damasonium alisma*)
Stonewort, Bearded (*Chara canescens*)
Stonewort, Foxtail (*Lamprothamnium papulosum*)
Strapwort (*Corrigiola litoralis*)
Turpswort (*Geocalyx graveolens*)
Violet, Fen (*Viola persicifolia*)
Viper's-grass (*Scorzonera humilis*)
Water-plantain, Ribbon-leaved (*Alisma gramineum*)
Wood-sedge, Starved (*Carex depauperata*)
Woodsia, Alpine (*Woodsia alpina*)
Woodsia, Oblong (*Woodsia ilvenis*)
Wormwood, Field (*Artemisia campestris*)
Woundwort, Downy (*Stachys germanica*)
Woundwort, Limestone (*Stachys alpina*)
Yellow-rattle, Greater (*Rhinanthus serotinus*)
° The sale of plants taken from the wild is prohibited; the sale of cultivated plants is still permitted

MOST UNDER THREAT

The animals and birds considered to be most under threat in Great Britain by the Joint Nature Conservation Committee are the high brown fritillary butterfly; violet click beetle; new forest burnet moth; corncrake; aquatic warbler; tree sparrow; wryneck; water vole; red squirrel; allis shad; and twaite shad.

Close Seasons and Times

GAME BIRDS

In each case the dates are inclusive:

Black game – 11 December to 19 August (31 August in Somerset, Devon and New Forest)
*Grouse – 11 December to 11 August
*Partridge – 2 February to 31 August
*Pheasant – 2 February to 30 September
*Ptarmigan – (Scotland only) 11 December to 11 August
*It is also unlawful in England and Wales to kill this game on a Sunday or Christmas Day

HUNTING AND GROUND GAME

There is no statutory close time for fox-hunting or rabbit-shooting, nor for hares. However, by an Act passed in 1892 the sale of hares or leverets in Great Britain is prohibited from 1 March to 31 July inclusive. The recognized date for the opening of the fox-hunting season is 1 November, and it continues till the following April.

DEER

The statutory close seasons for deer (all dates inclusive) are:

	England and Wales	Scotland
Fallow deer		
Male	1 May–31 July	1 May–31 July
Female	1 Mar.–31 Oct.	16 Feb.–20 Oct.
Red deer		
Male	1 May–31 July	21 Oct.–30 June
Female	1 Mar.–31 Oct.	16 Feb.–20 Oct.
Roe deer		
Male	1 Nov.–31 Mar.	21 Oct.–31 Mar.
Female	1 Mar.–31 Oct.	1 April–20 Oct.
Sika deer		
Male	1 May–31 July	21 Oct.–30 June
Female	1 Mar.–31 Oct.	16 Feb.–20 Oct.
Red/Sika hybrids		
Male	—	21 Oct.–30 June
Female	—	16 Feb.–20 Oct

ANGLING

GAME FISHING

Where local by-laws neither specify nor dispense with an annual close season, the statutory close times for game fishing are: Trout, 1 October to end February; Salmon, 1 November to 31 January. New national by-laws concerning salmon came into force from 15 April 1999. The main provisions are that angling for salmon before 16 June is only permitted with artificial fly or artificial lure and any salmon caught before 16 June must be returned to the water with minimum injury.

COARSE FISHING

Responsibility for the fisheries function of the National Rivers Authority, including licensing and regulation, passed to the Environment Agency on 1 April 1996. The statutory close season for coarse fish in England and Wales runs from 15 March to 15 June on all rivers, streams and drains. Close season arrangements for canals vary from region to region. The close season on all lakes, ponds and reservoirs is at the discretion of the fishery owner, except on the Norfolk Broads and certain Sites of Special Scientific Interest where the statutory close season still applies. It is necessary in all cases to check with the local Environment Agency office (telephone 0645-333111).

LICENCES

Purchase of a national rod fishing licence is legally required of anglers aged 12 or over wishing to fish with rod and line in all waters within the area of the Environment Agency.

	Salmon and sea trout	Non-migratory trout and coarse fish
Full	£57.00	£18.00
Concessionary	28.50	9.00
Eight-day	16.50	6.50
One-day	5.50	2.50

Concessionary licences are available for juniors (12–16 years), for senior citizens (65 years and over), and disabled who are in receipt of long-term incapacity benefit, short-term incapacity benefit (at the higher rate) or severe disablement allowance. Those in receipt of a war pension which includes unemployability supplements are also eligible. Licences can be purchased by telephone on 0870-166 2662.

Historic Buildings and Monuments

LISTING

Under the Planning (Listed Buildings and Conservation Areas) Act 1990, the Secretary of State for Culture, Media and Sport has a statutory duty to compile lists of buildings or groups of buildings in England which are of special architectural or historic interest. Under the Ancient Monuments and Archaeological Areas Act 1979 as amended by the National Heritage Act 1983, the Secretary of State is also responsible for compiling a schedule of ancient monuments. Decisions are taken on the advice of English Heritage (*see* page 296).

Listed buildings are classified into Grade I, Grade II* and Grade II. There are currently about 500,000 individual listed buildings in England, of which about 95 per cent are Grade II listed. Almost all pre-1700 buildings are listed, and most buildings of 1700 to 1840. English Heritage is carrying out thematic surveys of particular types of buildings with a view to making recommendations for listing, and members of the public may propose a building for consideration. The main purpose of listing is to ensure that care is taken in deciding the future of a building. No changes which affect the architectural or historic character of a listed building can be made without listed building consent (in addition to planning permission where relevant). Applications for listed building consent are normally dealt with by the local planning authority, although English Heritage is always consulted about proposals affecting Grade I and Grade II* properties. It is a criminal offence to demolish a listed building, or alter it in such a way as to affect its character, without consent.

There are currently about 22,500 scheduled monuments in England. English Heritage is carrying out a Monuments Protection Programme assessing archaeological sites with a view to making recommendations for scheduling, and members of the public may propose a monument for consideration. All monuments proposed for scheduling are considered to be of national importance. Where buildings are both scheduled and listed, ancient monuments legislation takes precedence. The main purpose of scheduling a monument is to preserve it for the future and to protect it from damage, destruction or any unnecessary interference. Once a monument has been scheduled, scheduled monument consent is required before any works are carried out. The scope of the control is more extensive and more detailed than that applied to listed buildings, but certain minor works, as detailed in the Ancient Monuments (Class Consents) Order 1994, may be carried out without consent. It is a criminal offence to carry out unauthorized work to scheduled monuments.

Under the Planning (Listed Buildings and Conservation Areas) Act 1990 and the Ancient Monuments and Archaeological Areas Act 1979, the Secretary of State for Wales is responsible for listing buildings and scheduling monuments in Wales on the advice of Cadw (*see* page 350), the Historic Buildings Council for Wales (*see* page 307) and the Ancient Monuments Board for Wales (*see* page 307). The criteria for evaluating buildings are similar to those in England and the same listing system is used. In April 1997 there were 19,161 listed buildings and 2,999 scheduled monuments in Wales.

Under the Planning (Listed Buildings and Conservation Areas) (Scotland) Act 1997 and the Ancient Monuments and Archaeological Areas Act 1979, the Secretary of State for Scotland is responsible for listing buildings and scheduling monuments in Scotland on the advice of

Historic Scotland (*see* page 338), the Historic Buildings Council for Scotland (*see* page 307) and the Ancient Monuments Board for Scotland (*see* page 308). The criteria for evaluating buildings are similar to those in England but an A, B, C grading system is used. There are about 44,462 listed buildings and about 7,035 scheduled monuments in Scotland.

Under the Planning (Northern Ireland) Order 1991 and the Historic Monuments and Archaeological Objects (Northern Ireland) Order 1995, the Department of the Environment for Northern Ireland (*see* page 327) is responsible for listing buildings and scheduling monuments in Northern Ireland on the advice of the Historic Buildings Council for Northern Ireland and the Historic Monuments Council for Northern Ireland. The criteria for evaluating buildings are similar to those in England but no statutory grading system is used. In March 1999 there were 8,563 listed buildings and 1,365 scheduled monuments in Northern Ireland.

OPENING TO THE PUBLIC

The following is a selection of the many historic buildings and monuments open to the public. The admission charges given are the standard charges for 1999–2000; many properties have concessionary rates for children, etc. Opening hours vary. Many properties are closed in winter and some are also closed in the mornings. Most properties are closed on Christmas Eve, Christmas Day, Boxing Day and New Year's Day, and many are closed on Good Friday. During the winter season, most English Heritage monuments are closed on Mondays and Tuesdays and monuments in the care of Cadw are closed on Sunday mornings. In Northern Ireland most monuments are closed on Mondays except on bank holidays. Information about a specific property should be checked by telephone.

*Closed in winter (usually November–March)
†Closed in winter, and in mornings in summer

ENGLAND

EH English Heritage property
NT National Trust property

*A LA RONDE (NT), Exmouth, Devon. Tel: 01395-265514. Closed Fri. and Sat. Adm. £3.20. Unique 16-sided house completed *c.*1796

†ALNWICK CASTLE, Northumberland. Tel: 01665-510777. Adm. £5.95. Seat of the Dukes of Northumberland since 1309; Italian Renaissance-style interior

ALTHORP, Northants. Tel: 01604-770107, ticket reservations 01604-592020. Open 1 July to 30 August. Adm £9.50. Spencer family seat. Diana, Princess of Wales memorabilia

†ANGLESEY ABBEY (NT), Cambs. Tel: 01223-811200. Closed Mon. (except Bank Holidays), Tues. and Good Friday. Gardens open daily July to Sept. Adm. £6.00 (£7.00 Sun. and Bank Holiday Mon.); gardens only, £3.50. House built *c.*1600. Outstanding grounds with unique statuary

APSLEY HOUSE, London W1. Tel: 0171-499 5676. Closed Mon. Adm. £4.50. Built by Robert Adam 1771–8, home of the Dukes of Wellington since 1817 and known as 'No. 1 London'. Collection of fine and decorative arts

†ARUNDEL CASTLE, W. Sussex. Tel: 01903-883136. Closed Sat. and Good Friday. Adm. £6.70. Castle dating from the Norman Conquest. Seat of the Dukes of Norfolk

AVEBURY (NT), Wilts. Tel: 01672-539250. Adm. free. Remains of stone circles constructed 4,000 years ago surrounding the later village of Avebury. Also *Alexander Keiller Museum*. Adm. £1.70

BANQUETING HOUSE, Whitehall, London SW1. Tel: 0171-930 4179. Closed Sun. and Bank Holidays. Adm. £3.60. Designed by Inigo Jones; ceiling paintings by Rubens. Site of the execution of Charles I

†BASILDON PARK (NT), Berks. Tel: 0118-984 3040. Closed Mon. (except Bank Holidays), Tues. and Good Friday. Adm. £4.10; grounds only, £1.80. Palladian house built in 1776–83

BATTLE ABBEY (EH), E. Sussex. Tel: 01424-773792. Adm. £4.00. Remains of the abbey founded by William the Conqueror on the site of the Battle of Hastings

BEAULIEU, Hants. Tel: 01590-612345. Adm. £9.00. House and gardens, Beaulieu Abbey and exhibition of monastic life, National Motor Museum (*see also* page 591)

BEESTON CASTLE (EH), Cheshire. Tel: 01829-260464. Adm. £2.80. Thirteenth-century inner ward with gatehouse and towers, and remains of outer ward

†BELTON HOUSE (NT), Grantham, Lincs. Tel: 01476-566116. Closed Mon. (except Bank Holidays), Tues. and Good Friday. Adm. £5.20. Fine 17th-century house in landscaped park

*BELVOIR CASTLE, nr Grantham, Lincs. Tel: 01476-870262. Closed Mon. (except Bank Holidays) and Fri.; also closed Mon.–Sat. in Oct. Adm. £5.00. Seat of the Dukes of Rutland; 19th-century Gothic-style castle

*BERKELEY CASTLE, Glos. Tel: 01453-810332. Opening times vary. Adm. £4.95. Completed 1153; site of the murder of Edward II (1327)

*BLENHEIM PALACE, Woodstock, Oxon. Tel: 01993-811325. Adm. £8.50. Seat of the Dukes of Marlborough and Winston Churchill's birthplace; designed by Vanbrugh

†BLICKLING HALL (NT), Norfolk. Tel: 01263-738030. Closed Mon. (except Bank Holidays) and Tues. Adm. £6.20; garden only, £3.50. Jacobean house with state rooms, temple and 18th-century orangery

BODIAM CASTLE (NT), E. Sussex. Tel: 01580-830436. Closed Mon. in winter. Adm. £3.50. Well-preserved medieval moated castle

BOLSOVER CASTLE (EH), Derbys. Tel: 01246-823349. Closed Mon. and Tues. in winter. Adm. £3.10. Notable 17th-century buildings

BOSCOBEL HOUSE (EH), Shropshire. Tel: 01902-850244. Closed Mon. and Tues. in winter; also closed in Jan. Adm. £4.00. Timber-framed 17th-century hunting lodge, refuge of fugitive Charles II

†BOUGHTON HOUSE, Northants. Tel: 01536-515731. House open Aug. only; grounds May to Sept. except Fri.; state rooms by prior booking. Adm. £6.00; grounds, £1.50. A 17th-century house with French-style additions

*BOWOOD HOUSE, Wilts. Tel: 01249-812102. Adm. £5.50. An 18th-century house in Capability Brown park, with lake, temple and arboretum

†BROADLANDS, Hants. Tel: 01794-505010. Open June-Sept. Adm. £5.50. Palladian mansion in Capability Brown parkland. Mountbatten exhibition

BRONTË PARSONAGE, Haworth, W. Yorks. Tel: 01535-642323. Closed 10 Jan.-4 Feb. 2000. Adm. £3.80. Home of the Brontë sisters; museum and memorabilia

BUCKFAST ABBEY, Devon. Tel: 01364-642519. Adm. free. Benedictine monastery on medieval foundations

*BUCKINGHAM PALACE, London SW1. Tel: 0171-839 1377. Open daily for eight weeks from early Aug. each year. Adm. £10.00. Purchased by George III in 1762, and the Sovereign's official London residence since 1837. Eighteen state rooms, including the Throne Room, and Picture Gallery

BUCKLAND ABBEY (NT), Devon. Tel: 01822-853607. Closed Thurs.; in winter open only weekend afternoons, closed 3 Jan.–18 Feb. 2000. Adm. £4.40; grounds only, £2.30. A 13th-century Cistercian monastery. Home of Sir Francis Drake

BURGHLEY HOUSE, Stamford, Lincs. Tel: 01780-752451. Adm. £6.10. Late Elizabethan house; vast state apartments

†CALKE ABBEY (NT), Derbys. Tel: 01332-863822. Closed Thurs. and Fri. Adm. £5.00, by timed ticket; garden only, £2.30. Baroque 18th-century mansion

CARISBROOKE CASTLE (EH), Isle of Wight. Tel: 01983-522107. Adm. £4.50. Norman castle; prison of Charles I 1647-8

CARLISLE CASTLE (EH), Cumbria. Tel: 01228-606000. Adm. £3.00. Medieval castle, prison of Mary Queen of Scots

*CARLYLE'S HOUSE (NT), Cheyne Row, London SW3. Tel: 0171-352 7087. Closed Mon. (except Bank Holidays), Tues. and Good Friday. Adm. £3.30. Home of Thomas Carlyle

CASTLE ACRE PRIORY (EH), Norfolk. Tel: 01760-755394. Closed Mon. and Tues. in winter. Adm. £3.10. Remains include 12th-century church and prior's lodgings

*CASTLE DROGO (NT), Devon. Tel: 01647-433306. Castle closed Fri. (except Good Friday). Adm. £5.30; grounds only, £2.50. Granite castle designed by Lutyens

*CASTLE HOWARD, N. Yorks. Tel: 01653-648444. Adm. £7.00; grounds only, £4.50. Designed by Vanbrugh 1699–1726; mausoleum designed by Hawksmoor

CASTLE RISING CASTLE (EH), Norfolk. Tel: 01553-631330. Closed Mon. and Tues. in winter. Adm. £2.75. A 12th-century keep in a massive earthwork with gatehouse and bridge

*CHARTWELL (NT), Kent. Tel: 01732-866368. Closed Mon. (except Bank Holidays) and Tues. (except July and Aug.). Adm. £5.50 by timed ticket; grounds only, £2.75. Home of Sir Winston Churchill

*CHATSWORTH, Derbys. Tel: 01246-582204. Adm. £6.50; garden only, £3.75. Tudor mansion in magnificent parkland

CHESTERS ROMAN FORT (EH), Northumberland. Tel: 01434-681379. Adm. £2.80. Roman cavalry fort

*CHYSAUSTER ANCIENT VILLAGE (EH), Cornwall. Tel: 0831-757934. Adm. £1.60. Romano-Cornish village, 2nd and 3rd century AD, on a probably late Iron Age site

CLIFFORD'S TOWER (EH), York. Tel: 01904-646940. Adm. £1.80. A 13th-century tower built on a mound

†CLIVEDEN (NT), Berks. Tel: 01628-605069. House open Thurs. and Sun. only, gardens daily. Adm. £5.00; £1.00 extra for house. Former home of the Astors, now an hotel set in garden and woodland

CORBRIDGE ROMAN SITE (EH), Northumberland. Tel: 01434-632349. Closed Mon. and Tues. in winter. Adm. £2.80. Excavated central area of a Roman town and successive military bases

CORFE CASTLE (NT), Dorset. Tel: 01929-481294. Adm. £4.00. Ruined former royal castle dating from 11th century

†CROFT CASTLE (NT), Herefordshire. Tel: 01568-780246. Closed Mon. (except Bank Holidays), Tues. and Good Friday; April and Oct. open weekends and Bank Holiday Mon. only; grounds open all year. Adm. £3.40; grounds only, £2.00 per car. Pre-Conquest border castle with Georgian-Gothic interior

DEAL CASTLE (EH), Kent. Tel: 01304-372762. Closed Mon. and Tues. in winter. Adm. £3.00. Largest of the coastal defence forts built by Henry VIII

DICKENS HOUSE, Doughty Street, London WC1. Tel: 0171-405 2127. Closed Sun. Adm. £3.50. House occupied by Dickens 1837–9; manuscripts, furniture and portraits

DR JOHNSON'S HOUSE, 17 Gough Square, London EC4. Tel: 0171-353 3745. Closed Sun. and Bank Holidays. Adm. £3.00. Home of Samuel Johnson

DOVE COTTAGE, Grasmere, Cumbria. Tel: 01539-435544. Closed Jan. and early Feb. Adm. £4.40; museum only, £2.20. Wordsworth's home 1799–1808; museum

DOVER CASTLE (EH), Kent. Tel: 01304-201628. Adm. £6.90. Castle with Roman, Saxon and Norman features; wartime operations rooms

DUNSTANBURGH CASTLE (EH), Northumberland. Tel: 01665-576231. Closed Mon. and Tues. in winter. Adm. £1.80. A 14th-century castle on a cliff, with a substantial gatehouse-keep

ELTHAM PALACE (EH), London SE9. Tel: 0181-294 2548. Closed Mon. (except Bank Holidays), Tues. and Sat. Adm. £5.50; grounds only, £3.30. 1930s house and remains of medieval palace

FARLEIGH HUNGERFORD CASTLE (EH), Somerset. Tel: 01225-754026. Closed Mon. and Tues. in winter. Adm. £2.30. Late 14th-century castle with two courts; chapel with tomb of Sir Thomas Hungerford

*FARNHAM CASTLE KEEP (EH), Surrey. Tel: 01252-713393. Adm. £2.00. Large 12th-century shell-keep

FOUNTAINS ABBEY (NT), nr Ripon, N. Yorks. Tel: 01765-608888. Closed Fri. Nov.-Jan.; deer park open daily all year. Adm. £4.30; visitor centre, deer park and St Mary's Church free. Ruined Cistercian monastery; 18th-century landscaped gardens of Studley Royal estate

FRAMLINGHAM CASTLE (EH), Suffolk. Tel: 01728-724189. Closed Mon. and Tues. in winter. Adm. £3.10. Castle (c.1200) with high curtain walls enclosing an almshouse (1639)

FURNESS ABBEY (EH), Cumbria. Tel: 01229-823420. Closed Mon. and Tues. in winter. Adm. £2.60. Remains of church and conventual buildings founded in 1123

GLASTONBURY ABBEY, Somerset. Tel: 01458-832267. Adm. £3.00. Ruins of a 12th-century abbey rebuilt after fire. Site of an early Christian settlement

GOODRICH CASTLE (EH), Herefordshire. Tel: 01600-890538. Adm. £3.10. Remains of 13th- and 14th-century castle with 12th-century keep

GREENWICH, London SE10. *Royal Observatory.* Tel: 0181-858 4422. Adm. £9.50 (joint ticket for Royal Observatory and National Maritime Museum). Former Royal Observatory (founded 1675) housing the time ball and zero meridian of longitude. *The Queen's House.* Tel: 0181-858 4422. Closed until Dec. 1999. Adm. charge. Designed for Queen Anne, wife of James I, by Inigo Jones. *Painted Hall and Chapel* (Royal Naval College). Visitors admitted to Sunday service (11 a.m.) in the chapel during college term

GRIME'S GRAVES (EH), Norfolk. Tel: 01842-810656. Closed Mon. and Tues. in winter. Adm. £1.85. Neolithic flint mines. One shaft can be descended

GUILDHALL, London EC2. Tel: 0171-332 1460. Closed Sun. in winter. Adm. free. Centre of civic government of the City. Built c.1440; facade built 1788-9

*HADDON HALL, Derbys. Tel: 01629-812855. Adm. £5.50. Well-preserved 12th-century manor house

HAILES ABBEY (EH), Glos. Tel: 01242-602398. Closed Mon. to Fri. in winter. Adm. £2.60. Ruins of a 13th-century Cistercian monastery

†HAM HOUSE (NT), Richmond, Surrey. Tel: 0181-940 1950. Closed Thurs. and Fri. Adm. £5.00. Garden open all year except Thurs. and Fri. Adm. £1.50. Stuart house with fine interiors

HAMPTON COURT PALACE, East Molesey, Surrey. Tel: 0181-781 9500. Adm. £10.00. A 16th-century palace with additions by Wren. Gardens with maze; Tudor tennis court (summer only)

†HARDWICK HALL (NT), Derbys. Tel: 01246-850430. Closed Mon. (except Bank Holidays), Tues. and Fri.; grounds open daily, all year. Adm. £6.00; grounds only, £3.00. Built 1591–7 for Bess of Hardwick; notable furnishings

*HARDY'S COTTAGE (NT), Higher Bockhampton, Dorset. Tel: 01305-262366. Closed Fri. (except Good Friday) and Sat. Adm. £2.60. Birthplace of Thomas Hardy

*HAREWOOD HOUSE, W. Yorks. Tel: 0113-288 6331. Adm. £6.95. An 18th-century house designed by John Carr and Robert Adam; park by Capability Brown

†HATFIELD HOUSE, Herts. Tel: 01707-262823. Closed Mon. (except Bank Holidays) and Good Friday. Adm. £6.00; grounds, £1.50. Jacobean house built by Robert Cecil; surviving wing of Royal Palace of Hatfield (1497)

HELMSLEY CASTLE (EH), N. Yorks. Tel: 01439-770442. Closed Mon. and Tues. in winter. Adm. £2.30. A 12th-century keep and curtain wall with 16th-century buildings. Spectacular earthwork defences

†HEVER CASTLE, Kent. Tel: 01732-865224. Adm. £7.30; gardens only, £5.80. A 13th-century double-moated castle, childhood home of Anne Boleyn

*HOLKER HALL, Cumbria. Tel: 015395-58328. Closed Sat. Adm. £6.00; grounds only, £3.35. Former home of the Dukes of Devonshire; award-winning gardens

†HOLKHAM HALL, Norfolk. Tel: 01328-710227. Closed Fri. and Sat. Adm. £4.00. Fine Palladian mansion

HOUSESTEADS ROMAN FORT (EH), Northumberland. Tel: 01434-344363. Adm. £2.80. Excavated infantry fort on Hadrian's Wall with extra-mural civilian settlement

†HUGHENDEN MANOR (NT), High Wycombe. Tel: 01494-532580. Closed Mon. (except Bank Holidays) and Tues.; open weekends only in March. Adm. £4.10. Home of Disraeli; small formal garden

JANE AUSTEN'S HOUSE, Chawton, Hants. Tel: 01420-83262. Closed Mon.-Fri. in Jan. and Feb. Adm. £2.50. Jane Austen's home 1809–17

*KELMSCOTT MANOR, nr Lechlade, Oxon. Tel: 01367-252486. Open Wed., afternoon of third Sat. in April, May, June and Sept., first and third Sat. in July and Aug., Thurs. and Fri. by appointment. Adm. £6.00. Summer home of William Morris, with products of Morris and Co.

KENILWORTH CASTLE (EH), Warks. Tel: 01926-852078. Adm. £3.50. Castle with building styles from 1155 to 1649

KENSINGTON PALACE, London W8. Closed Mon. and Tues. in winter. Adm. £8.50. Built in 1605 and enlarged by Wren; bought by William and Mary in 1689. Birthplace of Queen Victoria. Royal Ceremonial Dress Collection

KENWOOD (EH), Hampstead Lane, London NW3. Tel: 0181-348 1286. Adm. free; exhibitions, £3.50. Adam villa housing the Iveagh bequest of paintings and furniture. Open-air concerts in summer

*KEW, Surrey. Tel: 0181-332 5189. *Queen Charlotte's Cottage,* weekends and Bank Holidays in May-Sept. Adm. free (but £5.00 adm. to Kew Gardens)

†KINGSTON LACY HOUSE (NT), Dorset. Tel: 01202-883402. Closed Thurs. and Fri.; grounds open daily except Mon. to Thurs. in Nov. and Dec. Adm. £6.00; grounds only, £2.50. A 17th-century house with 19th-century alterations; important art collection

†KNEBWORTH HOUSE, Herts. Tel: 01438-812661. Adm. £6.00; grounds only, £5.00. Tudor manor house concealed by 19th-century Gothic decoration; Lutyens gardens

*KNOLE (NT), Kent. Tel: 01732-462100. Closed Mon. (except Bank Holidays) and Tues.; park open daily; garden open first Wed. of each month. Adm. £5.00; garden, £1.00; park free to pedestrians. House dating from 1456 set in parkland; fine art treasures

LAMBETH PALACE, London SE1. Tel: 0171-928 8282. Visits by written application. Official residence of the Archbishop of Canterbury. A 19th-century house with parts dating from the 12th century

*LANERCOST PRIORY (EH), Cumbria. Tel: 01697-73030. Adm. £2.00. The nave of the Augustinian priory church, c.1166, is still used; remains of other claustral buildings

*LANHYDROCK (NT), Cornwall. Tel: 01208-73320. Closed Mon. (except Bank Holidays). Garden open all year. Adm. £6.40; garden and grounds only, £3.20. House dating from the 17th century; 45 rooms, including kitchen and nursery

LEEDS CASTLE, Kent. Tel: 01622-765400. Adm. £9.30; grounds only, £7.30. Castle dating from 9th century, on two islands in lake

†LEVENS HALL, Cumbria. Tel: 01539-560321. Closed Fri. and Sat. Adm. £5.30; grounds only, £3.90. Elizabethan house with unique topiary garden (1694). Steam engine collection

LINCOLN CASTLE. Tel: 01522-511068. Adm. £2.50. Built by William the Conqueror in 1068

LINDISFARNE PRIORY (EH), Northumberland. Tel: 01289-389200. Open all year, subject to tide times. Adm. £2.80. Bishopric of the Northumbrian kingdom destroyed by the Danes; re-established in the 11th century as a Benedictine priory, now ruined

LITTLE MORETON HALL (NT), Cheshire. Tel: 01260-272018. Closed Mon. (except Bank Holidays) and Tues. March – Oct.; closed Mon. – Fri. 6 Nov. – 19 Dec. Adm. £4.20; joint adm. with Biddulph Grange Garden £6.00; free 4 – 19 Dec. Timber-framed moated manor house with knot garden

LONGLEAT HOUSE, Warminster, Wilts. Tel: 01985-844400. Open daily; safari park closed winter. Adm. £13.00; house only, £6.00. Elizabethan house in Italian Renaissance style

LULLINGSTONE ROMAN VILLA (EH), Kent. Tel: 01322-863467. Adm. £2.50. Large villa occupied for much of the Roman period; fine mosaics

MANSION HOUSE, London EC4. Tel: 0171-626 2500. Group visits only, by prior arrangement. Adm. free. The official residence of the Lord Mayor of London

MARBLE HILL HOUSE (EH), Twickenham, Middx. Tel: 0181-892 5115. Closed Mon. and Tues. in winter. Adm. £3.00. English Palladian villa with Georgian paintings and furniture

*MICHELHAM PRIORY, E. Sussex. Tel: 01323-844224. Closed Mon. and Tues. except in Aug. Adm. £4.20. Tudor house built onto an Augustinian priory

MIDDLEHAM CASTLE (EH), N. Yorks. Tel: 01969-623899. Closed Mon. and Tues. in winter. Adm. £2.30. A 12th-century keep within later fortifications. Childhood home of Richard III

†MONTACUTE HOUSE (NT), Somerset. Tel: 01935-823289. Closed Tues; grounds open all year. Adm. £5.40; grounds only, £3.00. Elizabethan house with National Portrait Gallery portraits from period

MOUNT GRACE PRIORY (EH), N. Yorks. Tel: 01609-883494. Adm. £2.80. Carthusian monastery, with remains of monastic buildings

NETLEY ABBEY (EH), Hants. Tel: 01703-453076. Adm. free. Remains of Cistercian abbey, used as house in Tudor period

OLD SARUM (EH), Wilts. Tel: 01722-335398. Adm. £2.00. Earthworks enclosing remains of the castle and the 11th-century cathedral

ORFORD CASTLE (EH), Suffolk. Tel: 01394-450472. Closed Mon. and Tues. in winter. Adm. £2.50. Circular keep of c.1170 and remains of coastal defence castle built by Henry II

*OSBORNE HOUSE (EH), Isle of Wight. Tel: 01983-200022. Adm. £6.90; grounds only, £3.50. Queen Victoria's seaside residence

†OSTERLEY PARK HOUSE (NT), Isleworth, Middx. Tel: 0181-568 7714. Closed Mon. (except Bank Holidays), Tues. and Good Friday; grounds open all year. Adm. £4.10; grounds free. Elizabethan mansion set in parkland

PENDENNIS CASTLE (EH), Cornwall. Tel: 01326-316594. Adm. £3.80. Well-preserved coastal defence castle built by Henry VIII

†PENSHURST PLACE, Kent. Tel: 01892-870307. Closed Mon.-Fri. in Mar. Adm. £5.70; grounds only, £4.20. House with medieval Baron's Hall and 14th-century gardens

†PETWORTH (NT), W. Sussex. Tel: 01798-342207. Closed Thurs. and Fri. (except Good Friday); grounds open all year. Adm. £5.50; grounds free. Late 17th-century house set in deer park

PEVENSEY CASTLE (EH), E. Sussex. Tel: 01323-762604. Closed Mon. and Tues. in winter. Adm. £2.50. Walls of a 4th-century Roman fort; remains of an 11th-century castle

PEVERIL CASTLE (EH), Derbys. Tel: 01433-620613. Closed Mon. and Tues. in winter. Adm. £2.00. A 12th-century castle defended on two sides by precipitous rocks

†POLESDEN LACEY (NT), Surrey. Tel: 01372-458203. Closed Mon. (except Bank Holidays) and Tues.; grounds open daily all year. Adm. £6.00; grounds only, £3.00. Regency villa remodelled in the Edwardian era. Fine paintings and furnishings

PORTCHESTER CASTLE (EH), Hants. Tel: 01705-378291. Adm. £2.70. Walls of a late Roman fort enclosing a Norman keep and an Augustinian priory church

*POWDERHAM CASTLE, Devon. Tel: 01626-890243. Closed Sat. Adm. £5.45. Medieval castle with 18th- and 19th-century alterations

†RABY CASTLE, Co. Durham. Tel: 01833-660202. Closed Sat. (except Bank Holiday weekends); open Wed. and Sun. only in May and June. Adm. 4.00; grounds only, £1.50. A 14th-century castle with walled gardens

*RAGLEY HALL, Warks. Tel: 01789-762090. Closed Mon.-Wed. (except Bank Holidays); grounds open daily in July and Aug. Adm. £5.00. A 17th-century house with gardens, park and lake

RICHBOROUGH ROMAN FORT (EH), Kent. Tel: 01304-612013. Closed Mon. and Tues. in Nov. and March, Mon.-Fri. Dec.-Feb. Adm. £2.50. Landing-site of the Claudian invasion in AD 43, with 3rd-century stone walls

RICHMOND CASTLE (EH), N. Yorks. Tel: 01748-822493. Adm. £2.30. A 12th-century keep with 11th-century curtain wall and domestic buildings

RIEVAULX ABBEY (EH), N. Yorks. Tel: 01439-798228. Adm. £3.00. Remains of a Cistercian abbey founded c.1131

ROCHESTER CASTLE (EH), Kent. Tel: 01634-402276. Adm. £3.50. An 11th-century castle partly on the Roman city wall, with a square keep of c.1130

†ROCKINGHAM CASTLE, Northants. Tel: 01536-770240. Open Sun. and Thurs. only (and Bank Holiday Mon. and Tues., and Tues. in Aug.). Adm. £4.20; gardens only, £2.70. Built by William the Conqueror

ROYAL PAVILION, Brighton. Tel: 01273-290900. Adm. £4.50. Palace of George IV, in Chinese style with Indian exterior and Regency gardens

†RUFFORD OLD HALL (NT), Lancs. Tel: 01704-821254. Closed Thurs. and Fri. Adm. £3.80; garden only, £2.00. A 16th-century hall with unique screen

ST AUGUSTINE'S ABBEY (EH), Canterbury, Kent. Tel: 01227-767345. Adm. £2.50. Remains of Benedictine monastery, with Norman church, on site of abbey founded AD 598 by St Augustine

ST MAWES CASTLE (EH), Cornwall. Tel: 01326-270526. Closed Thurs. in winter. Adm. £2.50. Coastal defence castle built by Henry VIII

ST MICHAEL'S MOUNT (NT), Cornwall. Tel: 01736-710507. Opening times vary. Adm. £4.40. A 12th-century castle with later additions, off the coast at Marazion

*SANDRINGHAM, Norfolk. Tel: 01553-772675. Closed for two weeks in summer and when the Royal Family is in residence. Adm. £5.00; grounds only, £4.00. The Queen's private residence; a neo-Jacobean house built in 1870

SCARBOROUGH CASTLE (EH), N. Yorks. Tel: 01723-372451. Closed Mon. and Tues. in winter. Adm. £2.30. Remains of 12th-century keep and curtain walls

†SHERBORNE CASTLE, Dorset. Tel: 01935-813182. Open Tues., Thurs., Sat., Sun. and Bank Holiday Mon. Adm. £4.80. Sixteenth-century castle built by Sir Walter Raleigh

*SHUGBOROUGH (NT), Staffs. Tel: 01889-881388. Open Sun. only in October; open for booked parties in winter. Adm. house, county museum and farm, £8.00; each site alone, £4.00. House set in 18th-century park with monuments, temples and pavilions in the Greek Revival style

SKIPTON CASTLE, N. Yorks. Tel: 01756-792442. Closed Sun. mornings. Adm. £4.00. D-shaped castle with six round towers and beautiful inner courtyard

†SMALLHYTHE PLACE (NT), Kent. Tel: 01580-762334. Closed Thurs. and Fri. (except Good Friday). Adm. £3.00. Half-timbered 16th-century house; home of Ellen Terry 1899-1928

†STANFORD HALL, Leics. Tel: 01788-860250. Open Sat.-Sun.; also Bank Holiday Mon. and Tues. following. Adm. £4.00; grounds only, £2.20. William and Mary house with Stuart portraits. Motorcycle museum

STONEHENGE (EH), Wilts. Tel: 01980-624715. Adm. £4.00. Prehistoric monument consisting of concentric stone circles surrounded by a ditch and bank

†STONOR PARK, Oxon. Tel: 01491-638587. Opening days vary. Adm. £4.50; gardens only, £2.50. Medieval house with Georgian facade. Centre of Roman Catholicism after the Reformation

†STOURHEAD (NT), Wilts. Tel: 01747-841152. Closed Thurs. and Fri. Gardens open daily all year. Adm. £4.50; gardens only, £4.50 (Nov. – Feb. £3.50); combined ticket £8.00. English Palladian mansion with famous gardens

*STRATFIELD SAYE HOUSE, Hants. Tel: 01256-882882. Closed Fri. June – Aug., Mon. – Fri. in Sept. Adm. £5.00. House built 1630-40; home of the Dukes of Wellington since 1817

STRATFORD-UPON-AVON, Warks. *Shakespeare's Birthplace* with Shakespeare Centre; *Anne Hathaway's Cottage*, home of Shakespeare's wife; *Mary Arden's House*, home of Shakespeare's mother; *Nash's House and New Place*, where Shakespeare died; and *Hall's Croft*, home of Shakespeare's daughter. Tel: 01789-204016. Adm. £11.00 for all buildings; £7.50 for *Shakespeare's Birthplace*, *Hall's Croft and Nash's House, and New Place*. Also *Grammar School* attended by Shakespeare, *Holy Trinity Church*, where Shakespeare is buried, *Royal Shakespeare Theatre* (burnt down 1926, rebuilt 1932) and *Swan Theatre* (opened 1986)

*SUDELEY CASTLE, Glos. Tel: 01242-602308. Adm. £6.00; grounds only, £4.50. Castle built in 1442; restored in the 19th century

SYON HOUSE, Brentford, Middx. Tel: 0181-560 0883. House closed Mon. (except Bank Holidays), Tues., Fri. and Sat. Adm. charges vary. Built on the site of a former monastery; Adam interior

TILBURY FORT (EH), Essex. Tel: 01375-858489. Closed Mon. and Tues. in winter. Adm. £2.50. A 17th-century coastal fort

TINTAGEL CASTLE (EH), Cornwall. Tel: 01840-770328. Adm. £2.80. A 12th-century cliff-top castle and Dark Age settlement site

TOWER OF LONDON, London EC3. Tel: 0171-709 0765. Adm. £10.50. Royal palace and fortress begun by William the Conqueror in 1078. Houses the Crown Jewels

*TRERICE (NT), Cornwall. Tel: 01637-875404. Closed Tues. and Sat. (except in Aug.). Adm. £4.00. Elizabethan manor house

TYNEMOUTH PRIORY AND CASTLE (EH), Tyne and Wear. Tel: 0191-257 1090. Closed Mon. and Tues. in winter. Adm. £1.80. Remains of a Benedictine priory, founded c.1090, on Saxon monastic site

†UPPARK (NT), W. Sussex. Tel: 01730-825415. Closed Fri. and Sat. Adm. £5.50 by timed ticket. Late 17th-century house, completely restored after fire. Fetherstonhaugh art collection

WALMER CASTLE (EH), Kent. Tel: 01304-364288. Closed Mon. and Tues. in winter; closed Jan.-Feb. and when the Lord Warden is in residence. Adm. £4.50. One of Henry VIII's coastal defence castles, now the residence of the Lord Warden of the Cinque Ports

WALTHAM ABBEY (EH), Essex. Tel: 01992-702200. Adm. free. Ruined abbey including the nave of the abbey church, 'Harold's Bridge' and late 14th-century gatehouse. Traditionally the burial place of Harold II (1066)

WARKWORTH CASTLE (EH), Northumberland. Tel: 01665-711423. Adm. £2.40. A 15th-century keep amidst earlier ruins, with 14th-century hermitage (open Wed., Sun. and Bank Holidays in summer, adm. £1.60) upstream

WARWICK CASTLE. Tel: 01926-406600. Adm. £10.50. Medieval castle with Madame Tussaud's waxworks, in Capability Brown parkland

WHITBY ABBEY (EH), N. Yorks. Tel: 01947-603568. Adm. £1.70. Remains of Norman church on the site of a monastery founded in AD 657

*WILTON HOUSE, Wilts. Tel: 01722-746720. Adm. £6.75. A 17th-century house on the site of a Tudor house and Saxon abbey

WINDSOR CASTLE, Berks. Tel: 01753-831118 for recorded information on opening times. Adm. £10.00, including the Castle precincts. Official residence of The Queen; oldest royal residence still in regular use. Also *St George's Chapel*

*WOBURN ABBEY, Beds. Tel: 01525-290666. Closed Mon.-Fri. in Oct. Adm. £7.50. Built on the site of a Cistercian abbey; seat of the Dukes of Bedford. Important art collection; antiques centre

WROXETER ROMAN CITY (EH), Shropshire. Tel: 01743-761330. Closed Mon. and Tues. in winter. Adm. £3.10. Second-century public baths and part of the forum of the Roman town of Viroconium

WALES

C Property of Cadw: Welsh Historic Monuments
NT National Trust property

BEAUMARIS CASTLE (C), Anglesey. Tel: 01248-810361. Adm. £2.20. Concentrically-planned castle

CAERLEON ROMAN BATHS AND AMPHITHEATRE (C), nr Newport. Tel: 01633-890104. Closed Sun. morning in winter. Adm. £2.00, joint ticket with Roman Legionary Museum £3.30. Rare example of a legionary bath-house and late 1st-century arena

CAERNARFON CASTLE (C). Tel: 01286-677617. Adm. £4.20. Important Edwardian castle built, with the town wall, between 1283 and 1330

CAERPHILLY CASTLE (C). Tel: 01222-883143. Adm. £2.50. Concentrically-planned castle (c.1270) notable for its scale and use of water defences

CARDIFF CASTLE. Tel: 01222-878100. Adm. charge. Castle built on the site of a Roman fort; spectacular towers and rich interior

CASTELL COCH (C), nr Cardiff. Tel: 01222-810101. Adm. £2.50. Rebuilt 1875-90 on medieval foundations

CHEPSTOW CASTLE (C). Tel: 01291-624065. Adm. £3.00. Rectangular keep amid extensive fortifications

CONWY CASTLE (C). Tel: 01492-592358. Adm. £3.50. Built by Edward I, 1283-7

*CRICCIETH CASTLE (C). Tel: 01766-522227. Adm. £2.20. Native Welsh 13th-century castle, altered by Edward I

DENBIGH CASTLE (C). Tel: 01222-500200. Adm. £2.00. Remains of the castle (begun 1282), including triple-towered gatehouse

HARLECH CASTLE (C). Tel: 01766-780552. Adm. £3.00. Well-preserved Edwardian castle, constructed 1283-90, on an outcrop above the former shoreline

PEMBROKE CASTLE. Tel: 01646-681510. Adm. £3.00. Castle founded in 1093; Great Tower built 1200; birthplace of King Henry VII

*PENRHYN CASTLE (NT), Bangor. Tel: 01248-353084. Closed Tues. Adm. £5.00; grounds only, £3.00. Neo-Norman castle built in the 19th century. Industrial railway museum

PORTMEIRION, Penrhyndeudraeth. Tel: 01766-770228. Adm. £4.00. Village in Italianate style

†POWIS CASTLE (NT), nr Welshpool. Tel: 01938-557018. Closed Mon. (except Bank Holidays) and Tues. (except July and Aug.). Adm. £7.50; garden only, £5.00. Medieval castle with interior in variety of styles; 17th-century gardens and Clive of India museum

RAGLAN CASTLE (C). Tel: 01291-690228. Adm. £2.40. Remains of 15th-century castle with hexagonal keep

ST DAVIDS BISHOP'S PALACE (C), St Davids. Tel: 01437-720517. Closed Sun. mornings in winter. Adm. £2.00. Remains of bishops palace built 1328-47

TINTERN ABBEY (C), nr Chepstow. Tel: 01291-689251. Adm. £2.40. Remains of 13th-century church and conventual buildings of a Cistercian monastery

*TRETOWER COURT AND CASTLE (C), nr Crickhowell. Tel: 01874-730279. Adm. £2.20. Medieval house with remains of 12th-century castle nearby

SCOTLAND

HS Historic Scotland property
NTS National Trust for Scotland property

ANTONINE WALL, between the Clyde and the Forth. Adm. free. Built about AD 142, consists of ditch, turf rampart and road, with forts every two miles

BALMORAL CASTLE, nr Braemar. Tel: 013397-42334. Open mid-April to end July. Adm. £4.00. Baronial-style castle built for Victoria and Albert. The Queen's private residence

BLACK HOUSE, ARNOL (HS), Lewis, Western Isles. Tel: 01851-710395. Closed Sun.; also Fri. in winter. Adm. £2.00. Traditional Lewis thatched house

*BLAIR CASTLE, Blair Atholl. Tel: 01796-481207. Adm. £6.00. Mid 18th-century mansion with 13th-century tower; seat of the Dukes of Atholl

*BONAWE IRON FURNACE (HS), Argyll and Bute. Tel: 01866-822432. Adm. £2.50. Charcoal-fuelled ironworks founded in 1753

†BOWHILL, Selkirk. Tel: 01750-22204. House open July only; grounds open April—June, Aug. except Fri., daily in July. Adm. £4.50; grounds only, £2.00. Seat of the Dukes of Buccleuch and Queensberry; fine collection of paintings, including portrait miniatures

BROUGH OF BIRSAY (HS), Orkney. Adm. £1.00 June—Sept. Free other times of year. Remains of Norse church and village on Birsay

CAERLAVEROCK CASTLE (HS), nr Dumfries. Tel: 01387-770244. Adm. £2.50. Fine early classical Renaissance building

CALANAIS STANDING STONES (HS), Lewis, Western Isles. Tel: 01851-621422. Adm. £1.50. Standing stones in a cross-shaped setting, dating from 3000 BC

CATHERTUNS (BROWN AND WHITE) (HS), nr Brechin. Adm. free. Two large Iron Age hill forts

*CAWDOR CASTLE, Inverness. Tel: 01667-404615. Adm. £5.40; grounds only, £2.80. A 14th-century keep with 15th- and 17th-century additions

CLAVA CAIRNS (HS), Highland. Adm. free. Late Neolithic or early Bronze Age cairns

*CRATHES CASTLE (NTS), nr Banchory. Tel: 01330-844525. Garden and grounds open all year. Adm. castle, garden and grounds, £5.00; each site, £2.10. A 16th-century baronial castle

*CULZEAN CASTLE (NTS), S. Ayrshire. Tel: 01655-760274. Country park open all year. Adm. £7.00; country park only, £3.50. An 18th-century Adam castle with oval staircase and circular saloon

DRYBURGH ABBEY (HS), Scottish Borders. Tel: 01835-822381. Closed Sun. mornings in Winter. Adm. £2.50. A 12th-century abbey containing tomb of Scott

*DUNVEGAN CASTLE, Skye. Tel: 01470-521206. Adm. £5.20; gardens only, £3.70. A 13th-century castle with later additions; home of the chiefs of the Clan MacLeod; trips to seal colony

EDINBURGH CASTLE (HS). Tel: 0131-225 9846. Adm. £6.50; war memorial free. Includes the Scottish National War Memorial, Scottish United Services Museum and historic apartments

EDZELL CASTLE (HS), nr Brechin. Tel: 01356-648631. Closed Sun. mornings, Thurs. afternoons and Fri. in winter. Adm. £2.50. Medieval tower house

*EILEAN DONAN CASTLE, Wester Ross. Tel: 01599-555202. Adm. £3.75. A 13th-century castle with Jacobite relics

ELGIN CATHEDRAL (HS), Moray. Tel: 01343-547171. Closed Sun. mornings, Thurs. afternoons and Fri. in winter. Adm. £2.80. A 13th-century cathedral with fine chapterhouse

*FLOORS CASTLE, Kelso. Tel: 01573-223333. Adm. £5.00. Largest inhabited castle in Scotland

FORT GEORGE (HS), Highland. Tel: 01667-462800. Closed Sunday mornings in winter. Adm. £3.00. An 18th-century fort

*GLAMIS CASTLE, Angus. Tel: 01307-840393. Adm. £5.40; grounds only, £2.50. Seat of the Lyon family since 1372

GLASGOW CATHEDRAL (HS). Tel: 0141-552 6891. Closed Sun. mornings. Adm. free. Medieval cathedral with elaborately vaulted crypt

GLENELG BROCH (HS), Highland. Adm. free. Two broch towers with well-preserved structural features

*HOPETOUN HOUSE, nr Edinburgh. Tel: 0131-331 2451. Adm. £5.00. House designed by Sir William Bruce, enlarged by William Adam

HUNTLY CASTLE (HS). Tel: 01466-793191. Closed Sun. mornings, Thurs. afternoons and Fri. in winter. Adm. £2.50. Ruin of a 16th- and 17th-century house

*INVERARAY CASTLE, Argyll. Tel: 01499-302203. Adm. £3.60. Gothic-style 18th-century castle; seat of the Dukes of Argyll

IONA ABBEY, Inner Hebrides. Tel: 01828-640411. Adm. £2.00. Monastery founded by St Columba in AD 563

*JARLSHOF (HS), Shetland. Tel: 01950-460112. Adm. £2.50. Remains from Stone Age

JEDBURGH ABBEY (HS), Scottish Borders. Tel: 01835-863925. Adm. £3.00. Romanesque and early Gothic church founded c.1138

KELSO ABBEY (HS), Scottish Borders. Adm. free. Remains of great abbey church founded 1128

LINLITHGOW PALACE (HS). Tel: 01506-842896. Adm. £2.50. Ruin of royal palace in park setting. Birthplace of Mary, Queen of Scots

MAES HOWE (HS), Orkney. Tel: 01856-761606. Closed Sun. mornings, Thurs. afternoons and Fri. in winter. Adm. £2.50. Neolithic tomb

*MEIGLE SCULPTURED STONES (HS), Angus. Tel: 01828-640612. Adm. £1.80. Celtic Christian stones

MELROSE ABBEY (HS), Scottish Borders. Tel: 01896-822562. Adm. £3.00. Ruin of Cistercian abbey

MOUSA BROCH (HS), Shetland. Adm. free. Finest surviving Iron Age broch tower

NETHER LARGIE CAIRNS (HS), Argyll and Bute. Adm. free. Bronze Age and Neolithic cairns

NEW ABBEY CORN MILL (HS), nr Dumfries. Tel: 01387-850260. Closed Sun. mornings, Thurs. afternoons and Fri. in winter. Adm. £2.80. Water-powered mill

PALACE OF HOLYROODHOUSE, Edinburgh. Tel: 0131-556 7371. Closed when The Queen is in residence. Adm. £5.50. The Queen's official Scottish residence. Main part of the palace built 1671-9

RING OF BROGAR (HS), Orkney. Adm. free. Neolithic circle of upright stones with an enclosing ditch

RUTHWELL CROSS (HS), Dumfries and Galloway. Adm. free. Seventh-century Anglian cross

ST ANDREWS CASTLE AND CATHEDRAL (HS), Fife. Tel: 01334-477196 (castle); 01334-472563 (cathedral). Adm. £2.50 (castle); £1.80 (cathedral); £3.50 (combined ticket). Ruins of 13th-century castle and remains of the largest cathedral in Scotland

*SCONE PALACE, Perth. Tel: 01738-552300. Adm. £5.40. House built 1802-13 on the site of a medieval palace

SKARA BRAE (HS), Orkney. Tel: 01856-841815. Adm. £3.20 (winter); £4.00 (summer, joint ticket with Skaill House). Stone-Age village near 17th-century house

*SMAILHOLM TOWER (HS), Scottish Borders. Tel: 01573-460365. Adm. £1.80. Well-preserved tower-house

STIRLING CASTLE (HS). Tel: 01786-450000. Adm. £5.00. Great Hall and gatehouse of James IV, palace of James V, Chapel Royal remodelled by James VI

TANTALLON CASTLE (HS), E. Lothian. Tel: 01620-892727. Closed Sun. mornings, Thurs. afternoons and Fri. in winter. Adm. £2.50. Fortification with earthwork defences and a 14th-century curtain wall with towers

*THREAVE CASTLE (HS), Dumfries and Galloway. Tel: 0411-223101. Adm. £1.80, including ferry trip. Late 14th-century tower on an island reached by boat

URQUHART CASTLE (HS), Loch Ness. Tel: 01456-450551. Adm. £3.80. Castle remains with well-preserved tower

NORTHERN IRELAND

DE Property in the care of the Northern Ireland Department of the Environment
NT National Trust property

CARRICKFERGUS CASTLE (DE), Co. Antrim. Tel: 01960-351273. Closed Sun. mornings. Adm. £2.70. Castle begun in 1180 and garrisoned until 1928

†CASTLE COOLE (NT), Enniskillen. Tel: 01365-322690. Closed Thurs., also Mon.-Fri. in April and Sept. (except Bank Holidays). Adm. house, £2.80; estate, £2.00 per car. An 18th-century mansion by Wyatt

†CASTLE WARD (NT), Co. Down. Tel: 01396-881204. Closed Thurs.; also closed Mon.-Fri. in April, Sept. and Oct.; grounds open all year. Adm. £2.60. An 18th-century house with Classical and Gothic facades

*DEVENISH ISLAND (DE), Co. Fermanagh. Closed Sun. mornings and Mon. Adm. £2.25. Island monastery founded in the 6th century by St Molaise

DOWNHILL CASTLE (NT), Co. Londonderry. Tel: 01265-848728. Adm. free. Ruins of palatial house in landscaped estate including Mussenden Temple. Opening times of temple vary

DUNLUCE CASTLE (DE), Co. Antrim. Tel: 012657-31938. Closed Sun. morning (except July and Aug.). Adm. £1.50. Ruins of MacDonnells' 16th-century stronghold

†FLORENCE COURT (NT), Co. Fermanagh. Tel: 01365-348249. Closed Tues.; also closed Mon.-Fri. (except Bank Holidays) in April and Sept.; grounds open all year. Adm. £2.80; estate £2.00 per car. Mid 18th-century house with rococo plasterwork

*GREY ABBEY (DE), Co. Down. Tel: 01247-788585. Closed Sun. morning and Mon. Adm £1.00. Substantial remains of a Cistercian abbey founded in 1193

HILLSBOROUGH FORT (DE), Co. Down. Closed Sun. mornings and Mon. Adm. free. Built in 1650

†MOUNT STEWART (NT), Co. Down. Tel: 012477-88387. Closed Tues.; also closed Mon.-Fri. in April and Oct. Adm. £3.50; garden only, £3.00. An 18th-century house, childhood home of Lord Castlereagh

NENDRUM MONASTERY (DE), Mahee Island, Co. Down. Closed Sun. mornings and Mon.; also Mon.-Fri. in winter. Adm. 75p. Founded in the 5th century by St Machaoi

*TULLY CASTLE (DE), Co. Fermanagh. Closed Sun. mornings and Mon. Adm. £1.00. Fortified house and bawn built in 1613

*WHITE ISLAND (DE), Co. Fermanagh. Closed Sun. mornings and Mon. Adm. £2.25. Tenth-century monastery and 12th-century church. Access by ferry

Museums and Galleries

There are more than 2,500 museums and galleries in the United Kingdom. Over 1,700 are registered with the Museums and Galleries Commission (*see* page 320), which indicates that they have an appropriate constitution, are soundly financed, have adequate collection management standards and public services, and have access to professional curatorial advice. Museums must achieve full or provisional registration status in order to be eligible for grants from the Museums and Galleries Commission and from Area Museums Councils. Over 700 of the registered museums are run by a local authority.

The national museums and galleries receive direct government grant-in-aid. These are: British Museum; Imperial War Museum; National Army Museum; National Galleries of Scotland; National Gallery; National Maritime Museum; National Museums and Galleries on Merseyside; National Museum of Wales; National Museums of Scotland; National Portrait Gallery; Natural History Museum; RAF Museum; Royal Armouries; Science Museum; Tate Gallery; Ulster Folk and Transport Museum; Ulster Museum; Victoria and Albert Museum; Wallace Collection. An online art museum (http://www.24hourmuseum.org.uk) has also been awarded national collection status.

Local authority museums are funded by the local authority and may also receive grants from the Museums and Galleries Commission. Independent museums and galleries mainly rely on their own resources but are also eligible for grants from the Museums and Galleries Commission.

The Museums and Galleries Commission has identified 26 non-national museum bodies which have pre-eminent collections of more than local or regional importance. Some of those designated are museum services with a wide variety of collections; others are small and more focused in a particular field. Ten Area Museum Councils in the UK, which are independent charities that receive an annual grant from the Museums and Galleries Commission, give advice and support to the museums in their area and may offer improvement grants. They also circulate exhibitions and assist with training and marketing.

OPENING TO THE PUBLIC

The following is a selection of the museums and art galleries in the United Kingdom. The admission charges given are the standard charges for 1999–2000, where a charge is made; many museums have concessionary rates for children, etc. Where no charge is shown, admission is free. Opening hours vary. Most museums are closed on Christmas Eve, Christmas Day, Boxing Day and New Year's Day; many are closed on Good Friday, and some are closed on May Day Bank Holiday. Some smaller museums close at lunchtimes. Information about a specific museum or gallery should be checked by telephone.

* Local authority museum/gallery
† Museum/gallery contains a collection designated pre-eminent

ENGLAND

BARNARD CASTLE, Co. Durham – *† *The Bowes Museum*, Westwick Road. Tel: 01833-690606. Adm. £3.90. European art from the late medieval period to the 19th century; music and costume galleries; English period rooms from Elizabeth I to Victoria; local archaeology

BATH – *American Museum in Britain*, Claverton Manor. Tel: 01225-460503. Closed mornings and Mon. (except Bank Holidays); also closed in winter (except on application). Adm. £5.00 (including house); grounds and galleries only, £2.50. American decorative arts from the 17th to 19th century

Museum of Costume, Bennett Street. Tel: 01225-477752. Adm. £3.90. Fashion from the 16th century to the present day

Roman Baths Museum, Abbey Church Yard. Tel: 01225-477774. Adm. (excluding 18th-century Pump Room, which is free) £6.70. Museum adjoins the remains of a Roman baths and temple complex

Victoria Art Gallery, Bridge Street. Tel: 01225-477772. Closed Bank Holidays. European Old Masters and British art since the 18th century

BEAMISH, Co. Durham – *† *Beamish, The North of England Open Air Museum*. Tel: 01207-231811. Closed Mon. and Fri. in winter. Adm. charge. Recreated northern town *c*.1900, with rebuilt and furnished local buildings, colliery village, farm, railway station, tramway, Pockerley Manor and horse-yard (set *c*.1800)

BEAULIEU, Hants – † *National Motor Museum*. Tel: 01590-612345. Adm. charge. Displays of over 250 vehicles dating from 1895 to the present day

BIRMINGHAM – *† *Aston Hall*, Trinity Road. Tel: 0121-327 0062. Closed mornings and in winter. Jacobean house containing paintings, furniture and tapestries from 17th to 19th century

* † *Barber Institute of Fine Arts*, off Edgbaston Park Road. Tel: 0121-472 0962. Closed Sun. morning. Fine arts, including Old Masters

Birmingham Nature Centre, Edgbaston. Tel: 0121-472 7775. Closed Mon.-Fri. in winter. Adm. £1.50. Indoor and outdoor enclosures displaying wildlife, especially British and European

*† *City Museum and Art Gallery*, Chamberlain Square. Tel: 0121-303 2834. Closed Sun. mornings. Adm. free (except Gas Hall). Includes notable collection of Pre-Raphaelites

*† *Museum of the Jewellery Quarter*, Vyse Street, Hockley. Tel: 0121-554 3598. Closed Sun. Adm. £2.50. Built around a real jewellery workshop

*† *Soho House*, Soho Avenue. Tel: 0121-554 9122. Closed Sun. mornings and Mon. (except Bank Holidays). Adm. £2.50. Eighteenth-century home of industrialist Matthew Boulton

BOVINGTON CAMP, Dorset – † *Tank Museum*. Tel: 01929-405096. Adm. £6.50. Collection of 300 tanks from the earliest days of tank warfare to the present

BRADFORD – * *Cartwright Hall Art Gallery*, Lister Park. Tel: 01274-493313. Closed Sun. mornings and Mon. (except Bank Holidays). British 19th- and 20th-century fine art

Industrial Museum and Horses at Work, Moorside Road. Tel: 01274-631756. Closed Sun. mornings and Mon. (except Bank Holidays). Engineering, textiles, transport and social history exhibits, including recreated back-to-back cottages, shire horses and horse tram-rides

National Museum of Photography, Film and Television. Tel: 01274-202030. Photography, film and television interactive exhibits. Features the UK's first IMAX cinema and the only public Cinerama screen in the world

BRIGHTON – *†*Booth Museum of Natural History,* Dyke Road. Tel: 01273-292777. Closed Sun. mornings and Thurs. Zoology, botany and geology collections; British birds in recreated habitats

*†*Brighton Museum and Art Gallery,* Church Street. Tel: 01273-290900. Closed Sun. mornings and Wed. Includes fine art and design, fashion, non-Western art, Brighton history

N.B. Rotational closure of galleries until 2001.

BRISTOL – *Arnolfini Gallery,* Narrow Quay. Tel: 0117-929 9191. Adm. free; charge for cinema and events. Contemporary visual arts, dance, performance, music, talks and workshops

*†*Blaise Castle House Museum,* Henbury. Tel: 0117-950 6789. Closed Thurs. and Fri.; also closed 1 Nov. to 31 Mar. Agricultural and social history collections in an 18th-century mansion

*†*Bristol Industrial Museum,* Prince Street. Tel: 0117-925 1470. Closed Thurs. and Fri.; closed Mon.-Fri. in winter. Industrial, maritime and transport collections

*†*City Museum and Art Gallery,* Queen's Road. Tel: 0117-922 3571. Includes fine and decorative art, oriental art, Egyptology and Bristol ceramics and paintings

CAMBRIDGE – *Duxford Airfield,* Duxford. Tel: 01223-835000. Adm. £7.20. Displays of military and civil aircraft, tanks, guns and naval exhibits

†*Fitzwilliam Museum,* Trumpington Street. Tel: 01223-332090. Closed Mon. (except August Bank Holidays) and Sun. mornings. Antiquities, fine and applied arts, clocks, ceramics, manuscripts, furniture, sculpture, coins and medals, temporary exhibitions

† *Sedgwick Museum of Geology,* Downing Street. Tel: 01223-333456. Closed Sat. afternoons and Sun. Extensive geological collection

† *University Museum of Archaeology and Anthropology,* Downing Street. Tel: 01223-333516. Closed Sun., Mon. and mornings. Archaeology and anthropology from all parts of the world

† *University Museum of Zoology,* Downing Street. Tel: 01223-336650. Closed Sat., Sun. and mornings. Extensive zoological collection

† *Whipple Museum of the History of Science,* Free School Lane. Tel: 01223-330906. Closed mornings and weekends. Scientific instruments from the 14th century to the present day

CARLISLE – *Tullie House Museum and Art Gallery,* Castle Street. Tel: 01228-534781. Adm. £3.75 to Border galleries only; ground floor, Old Tullie House and Jacobean galleries, adm. free. Prehistoric archaeology, Hadrian's Wall, Viking and medieval Cumbria, and the social history of Carlisle; also British 19th- and 20th-century art and English porcelain

CHATHAM – *World Naval Base.* Tel: 01634-823800. Closed Mon., Tues., Thurs. and Fri. in Feb., Mar. and Nov., also closed Dec.-Jan. Adm. charge. Maritime attractions including HMS *Cavalier,* the UK's last World War II destroyer

†*Royal Engineers Museum,* Brompton Barracks. Tel: 01634-406397. Closed Fri. Adm. £3.00. Regimental history, ethnography, decorative art and photography

CHELTENHAM – *†*Art Gallery and Museum,* Clarence Street. Tel: 01242-237431. Closed Sun. Paintings, arts and crafts

CHESTER – *Grosvenor Museum,* Grosvenor Street. Tel: 01244-321616. Closed Sun. mornings. Roman collections, natural history, art, Chester silver, local history and costume

CHICHESTER – † *Weald and Downland Open Air Museum,* Singleton. Tel: 01243-811348. Closed Mon.,Tues., Thurs., Fri. in winter. Adm. £5.20. Rebuilt vernacular buildings from south-east England; includes medieval houses, agricultural and rural craft buildings and a working watermill

COLCHESTER – *†*Colchester Castle Museum,* Castle Park. Tel: 01206-282931. Closed Sun. in winter, Sun. mornings in summer. Adm. £3.70. Largest Norman keep in Europe standing on foundations of roman Temple of Claudius; tours of the Roman vaults, castle walls and chapel with medieval and prison displays

COVENTRY – *Herbert Art Gallery and Museum,* Jordan Well. Tel: 01203-832381. Closed Sun. mornings. Local history, archaeology and industry, and fine and decorative art

*†*Museum of British Road Transport,* Hales Street. Tel: 01203-832425. Hundreds of motor vehicles and bicycles

CRICH, nr Matlock, Derbys – †*National Tramway Museum.* Tel: 01773-852565. Closed Mon. to Sat. in winter. Adm. £6.50 summer, £3.00 winter. Open-air working museum with tram rides

DERBY – *Derby Museum and Art Gallery,* The Strand. Tel: 01332-716659. Closed Bank Holiday and Sun. mornings. Includes paintings by Joseph Wright of Derby and Derby porcelain

Industrial Museum, off Full Street. Tel: 01332-255308. Closed Bank Holiday and Sun. mornings. Rolls-Royce aero engine collection and a railway engineering gallery

DEVIZES – †*Devizes Museum,* Long Street. Tel: 01380-727369. Closed Sun. Adm. £2.00. Natural and local history, art gallery, archaeological finds from Bronze Age, Iron Age, Roman and Saxon sites

DORCHESTER – *Dorset County Museum,* High West Street. Tel: 01305-262735. Closed Sun. (except July and Aug.). Adm. charge. Includes a collection of Thomas Hardy's manuscripts, books, notebooks and drawings

ELLESMERE PORT – †*Boat Museum,* South Pier Road. Tel: 0151-355 5017. Closed Thurs. and Fri. in winter. Adm. £5.50. Craft and boating history

EXETER – *†*Royal Albert Memorial Museum,* Queen Street. Tel: 01392-265858. Closed Sun. Natural history, archaeology, worldwide fine and decorative art including Exeter silver

GATESHEAD – *†*Shipley Art Gallery,* Prince Consort Road. Tel: 0191-477 1495. Closed Sun. mornings. Contemporary crafts

GAYDON, Warwick – *British Motor Industry Heritage Trust,* Heritage Motor Centre, Banbury Road. Tel: 01926-641188. Adm. charge. History of British motor industry from 1895 to present; classic vehicles; engineering gallery; Corgi and Lucas collections

GLOUCESTER, – †*National Waterways Museum,* Llanthony Warehouse, The Docks. Tel: 01452-318054. Adm. £4.75. Two-hundred-year history of Britain's canals and inland waterways

GOSPORT, Hants – *Royal Navy Submarine Museum,* Haslar Jetty Road. Tel: 01705-529217. Adm. £3.75. Underwater warfare, including the submarine *Alliance;* historical and nuclear galleries; and first Royal Navy submarine

GRASMERE, Cumbria – †*Dove Cottage* and the *Wordsworth Museum (see* page 586)

HALIFAX – *Eureka! The Museum for Children*, Discovery Road. Tel: 01426-983191. Adm. £5.75 (over age 12), £4.75 (ages 3-12), free (under age 3). Hands-on museum designed for children up to age 12

HULL – *Ferens Art Gallery*, Queen Victoria Square. Tel: 01482-613902. Closed Sun. mornings. European art, especially Dutch 17th-century paintings, British portraits from 17th to 20th century, and marine paintings

Town Docks Museum, Queen Victoria Square. Tel: 01482-613902. Closed Sun. mornings. Whaling, fishing and navigation exhibits

HUNTINGDON – *Cromwell Museum*, Grammar School Walk. Tel: 01480-375830. Closed Mon., and mornings (except Sat.) in winter. Portraits and memorabilia relating to Oliver Cromwell

IPSWICH – *Christchurch Mansion and Wolsey Art Gallery*, Christchurch Park. Tel: 01473-253246. Closed Sun. mornings and Mon. (except Bank Holidays). Tudor house with paintings by Gainsborough, Constable and other Suffolk artists; furniture and 18th-century ceramics. Art gallery for temporary exhibitions

LEEDS – *†City Art Gallery*, The Headrow. Tel: 0113-247 8248. Closed Sun. mornings and Bank Holidays. British and European paintings including English watercolours, modern sculpture, Henry Moore gallery, print room

Leeds Industrial Museum at Armley Mills, Canal Road, Armley. Tel: 0113-263 7861. Closed Sun. mornings and Mon.; also closed Jan.-Feb.Adm. £2.00. Largest woollen mill in world

†Lotherton Hall, Aberford. Tel: 0113-281 3259. Closed Sun. mornings and Mon.; also closed Jan.-Feb. Adm. £2.00. Costume and oriental collections in furnished Edwardian house; deer park and bird garden

Royal Armouries Museum, Armouries Drive. Tel: 0990-106666. Adm. £7.95. National collection of arms and armour f.om BC to present; demonstrations of foot combat in museum's five galleries; falconry and mounted combat in the tiltyard

†Temple Newsam House. Tel: 0113-264 7321. Closed Sun. mornings and Mon.; also closed Jan.-Feb. Adm. £2.00. Old Masters and 17th- and 18th-century decorative art in furnished Jacobean/Tudor house

LEICESTER – *Jewry Wall Museum*, St Nicholas Circle. Tel: 0116-247 3021. Closed Sun. mornings. Archaeology, Roman Jewry Wall and baths, and mosaics

New Walk Museum and Art Gallery, New Walk. Tel: 0116-255 4100. Closed Sun. mornings. Natural history, geology, ancient Egypt gallery, European art and decorative arts

Snibston Discovery Park, Coalville. Tel: 01530-510851. Adm. £4.75. Open-air science and industry museum on site of a coal mine; country park with nature trail

LINCOLN – *Museum of Lincolnshire Life*, Burton Road. Tel: 01522-528448. Closed Sun. mornings in winter. Adm. charge. Social history and agricultural collection and Royal Lincs Regiment memorabilia

Usher Gallery, Lindum Road. Tel: 01522-527980. Closed Sun. mornings. Adm. £2.00, free on Fri. Watches, miniatures, porcelain, silver; collection of Peter de Wint works; Lincolnshire topography; Tennyson memorabilia

LIVERPOOL – *Lady Lever Art Gallery*, Wirral. Tel: 0151-478 4136. Closed Sun. mornings. Adm. £3.00 for an 'Eight Pass' which is valid for 12 months and for all National Museums and Galleries on Merseyside. Paintings, furniture and porcelain

Liverpool Museum, William Brown Street. Tel: 0151-478 4399. Closed Sun. mornings. Adm. 'Eight Pass' as above. Includes Egyptian mummies, weapons and classical sculpture; planetarium, aquarium, vivarium and natural history centre

Merseyside Maritime Museum, Albert Dock. Tel: 0151-478 4499. Adm. 'Eight Pass' as above. Floating exhibits, working displays and craft demonstrations; incorporates *HM Customs and Excise National Museum*

Museum of Liverpool Life, Mann Island. Tel: 0151-478 4080. Adm. 'Eight Pass' as above. The history of Liverpool

Sudley House, Mossley Hill Road. Tel: 0151-724 3245. Closed Sun. mornings. Adm. 'Eight Pass' as above. Late 18th- and 19th-century British paintings in former shipowner's home

Tate Gallery Liverpool, Albert Dock. Tel: 0151-709 3223. Twentieth-century painting and sculpture

Walker Art Gallery, William Brown Street. Tel: 0151-478 4199. Closed Sun. mornings. Adm. 'Eight Pass' as above. Paintings from the 14th to 20th century

LONDON: GALLERIES – *Barbican Art Gallery*, Barbican Centre, EC2. Tel: 0171-382 7105. Adm. £5.00 or £6.00 according to exhibition. Temporary exhibitions

†*Courtauld Gallery*, Somerset House, Strand, WC2. Tel: 0171-848 2526. Closed Sun. mornings. Adm. £4.00. The University of London galleries

†*Dulwich Picture Gallery*, College Road, SE21. Tel: 0181-693 5254. Closed for refurbishment until May 2000. Closed Mon. (except Bank Holidays). Adm. £3.00 (free on Fri.). Built by Sir John Soane to house 17th- and 18th-century paintings

Hayward Gallery, Belvedere Road, SE1. Tel: 0171-928 3144. Adm. £6.00. Temporary exhibitions

National Gallery, Trafalgar Square, WC2. Tel: 0171-839 3321. Western painting from the 13th to 20th century; early Renaissance collection in the Sainsbury wing

National Portrait Gallery, St Martin's Place, WC2. Tel: 0171-306 0055. Closed Sun. mornings and some Bank Holidays. Adm. free (except for some special exhibitions). Portraits of eminent people in British history

Percival David Foundation of Chinese Art, Gordon Square, WC1. Tel: 0171-387 3909. Closed weekends and Bank Holidays. Adm. free (charge for use of reference library). Chinese ceramics from tenth to 18th century

Photographers Gallery, Great Newport Street, WC2. Tel: 0171-831 1772. Temporary exhibitions

The Queen's Gallery, Buckingham Palace, SW1. Tel: 0171-839 1377. Adm. £4.00. Closed from Oct. 1999 to Feb. 2002. Art from the Royal Collection

Royal Academy of Arts, Piccadilly, W1. Tel: 0171-300 8000. Adm. charge. British art since 1750 and temporary exhibitions; annual Summer Exhibition

Saatchi Gallery, Boundary Road, NW8. Tel: 0171-624 8299. Closed mornings and Mon.-Wed. Adm. £4.00. Contemporary art including paintings, photographs, sculpture and installations

Serpentine Gallery, Kensington Gardens, W2. Tel: 0171-298 1515. Temporary exhibitions of British and international contemporary art

Tate Gallery, Millbank, SW1. Tel: 0171-887 8000. Adm. free (charge for special exhibitions). British painting and 20th-century painting and sculpture. In 2000 the Millbank site will become the Tate Gallery of British Art, and the Tate Gallery of Modern Art will open on the South Bank, London SE1

Wallace Collection, Manchester Square, W1. Tel: 0171-935 0687. Closed Sun. mornings. Paintings and drawings, French 18th-century furniture, armour, porcelain, clocks and sculpture

Whitechapel Art Gallery, Whitechapel High Street, E1. Tel: 0171-522 7878. Closed Mon. Adm. free to most exhibitions. Temporary exhibitions of modern art

LONDON: MUSEUMS – *Bank of England Museum,* Threadneedle Street, EC2 (entrance from Bartholomew Lane). Tel: 0171-601 5545. Closed weekends and Bank Holidays. History of the Bank since 1694

Bethnal Green Museum of Childhood, Cambridge Heath Road, E2. Tel: 0181-983 5200. Closed Fri. Toys, games and exhibits relating to the social history of childhood

British Museum, Great Russell Street, WC1. Tel: 0171-636 1555. Closed Sun. mornings. Antiquities, coins, medals, prints and drawings

Cabinet War Rooms, King Charles Street, SW1. Tel: 0171-930 6961. Adm. £4.80. Underground rooms used by Churchill and the Government during the Second World War

Commonwealth Experience, Kensington High Street, W8. Tel: 0171-603 4535. Exhibitions on Commonwealth nations, visual arts and crafts; Interactive World

Cutty Sark, Greenwich, SE10. Tel: 0181-858 3445. Adm. £3.50. Restored and rerigged tea clipper with exhibits on board.

Design Museum, Shad Thames, SE1. Tel: 0171-378 6055. Adm. £5.50. The development of design and the mass-production of consumer objects

Geffrye Museum, Kingsland Road, E2. Tel: 0171-739 9893. Closed Mon.; also Sun. and Bank Holiday mornings. English urban domestic interiors from 1600 to present day; also paintings, furniture, decorative arts, walled herb garden and period garden rooms

HMS Belfast, Morgans Lane, Tooley Street, SE1. Tel: 0171-940 6300. Adm £4.70. Life on a warship, illustrated on World War II warship

†*Horniman Museum and Gardens,* London Road, SE23. Tel: 0181-699 1872. Museum of ethnography, musical instruments, natural history and aquarium; reference library; sunken, water and flower gardens

Imperial War Museum, Lambeth Road, SE1. Tel: 0171-416 5000. Reference departments closed Sat. (except by appointment) and Sun. Adm. £5.20. All aspects of the two world wars and other military operations involving Britain and the Commonwealth since 1914

†*Jewish Museum, Camden Town,* Albert Street, NW1. Tel: 0171-284 1997. Closed Fri., Sat., public and Jewish holidays. Adm. £3.00. Jewish life, history and religion

† *Jewish Museum, Finchley,* East End Road, N3. Tel: 0181-349 1143. Closed Fri., Sat., public and Jewish holidays. Adm. £2.00. Jewish life in London and Holocaust education

†*London Transport Museum,* Covent Garden, WC2. Tel: 0171-379 6344. Adm. £5.50. Vehicles, photographs and graphic art relating to the history of transport in London

MCC Museum, Lord's, NW8. Tel: 0171-289 1611. Open match days (closed most Sun. mornings); also conducted tours by appointment with Tours Manager. Adm. charge. Cricket museum

Museum of Garden History, Lambeth Palace Road SE1. Tel: 0171-401 8865. Closed Sat. and Dec.-Feb. Exhibition of aspects of garden history and re-created 17th-century garden

†*Museum of London,* London Wall, EC2. Tel: 0171-600 3699. Adm. £5.00 (ticket valid for one year); free after 4.30 p.m. History of London from prehistoric times to present day

National Army Museum, Royal Hospital Road, SW3. Tel: 0171-730 0717. Five-hundred-year history of the British soldier; exhibits include model of the Battle of Waterloo and *Army for Today* gallery

National Maritime Museum, Greenwich, SE10. Tel: 0181-858 4422. Reference library closed Sat. (except by appointment) and Sun. Adm. £7.50. Comprises the main building, the Royal Observatory and the Queen's House (*see page* 586). Maritime history of Britain; collections include globes, clocks, telescopes and paintings

Natural History Museum, Cromwell Road, SW7. Tel: 0171-938 9123. Adm. £6.50. Natural history collections

†*Petrie Museum of Egyptian Archaeology,* University College London. Tel: 0171-504 2884. Closed Sun., Mon. and mornings. Egyptian archaeology collection

Royal Air Force Museum, Colindale, NW9. Tel: 0181-205 2266. Adm. £6.50. National museum of aviation with over 70 full-size aircraft; aviation from before the Wright brothers to the present-day RAF; flight simulator

Royal Mews, Buckingham Palace, SW1. Tel: 0171-839 1377. Open Mon.-Thurs. afternoons. Adm. £4.00. Carriages, coaches, stables and horses

Science Museum, Exhibition Road, SW7. Tel: 0171-942 4454. Adm. £6.50. Science, technology, industry and medicine collections

Shakespeare Globe Exhibition, Bankside, SE1. Tel: 0171-902 1500. Adm. £6.00. Recreation of Elizabethan theatre using 16th-century techniques

Sherlock Holmes Museum, Baker Street, NW1. Tel: 0171-935 8866. Adm. £5.00. Recreated rooms of the fictional detective

Sir John Soane's Museum, Lincoln's Inn Fields, WC2. Tel: 0171-430 0175. Closed Sun. and Mon. Adm. free (groups by appointment only). Art and antiques

Theatre Museum, Russell Street, WC2. Tel: 0171-836 2330. Closed Mon. Adm. £4.50. History of the performing arts

*Tower Bridge Experience, SE1. Tel: 0171-378 1928. Adm. £6.15. History of the bridge and display of Victorian steam machinery; panoramic views from walkways

Victoria and Albert Museum, Cromwell Road, SW7. Tel: 0171-938 8500. Adm. £5.00. Includes National Art Library and Print Room (closed Sun. and Mon.). Fine and applied art and design, including furniture, glass, textiles, dress collections (British Galleries closed for refurbishment)

Wellington Museum, Apsley House, W1 (*see* page 584)

Wimbledon Lawn Tennis Museum, Church Road, SW19. Tel: 0181-946 6131. Closed Fri to Sun. before, middle Sun. and Mon. following Championships. Adm. £4.00. Tennis trophies, fashion and memorabilia; view of Centre Court

MANCHESTER – **Gallery of Costume,* Rusholme. Tel: 0161-224 5217. Exhibits from the 16th to 20th century

†*Manchester Museum,* Oxford Road. Tel: 0161-275 2634. Closed Sun. Archaeology, archery, botany, Egyptology, entomology, ethnography, geology, natural history, numismatics, oriental and zoology collections

†*Museum of Science and Industry,* Castlefield. Tel: 0161-832 2244. Adm. £6.50. On site of world's oldest passenger railway station; galleries relating to space, energy, power, transport, aviation, textiles and social history; interactive science centre

† *Pump House People's History Museum,* for *National Museum of Labour History,* Left Bank. Tel: 0161-228 7212. Adm. £1.00 (free on Fri.). Closed Mon. (except Bank Holidays). Political and and working life history

†*Whitworth Art Gallery,* Oxford Road. Tel: 0161-275 7450. Closed Sun. mornings. Watercolours, drawings, prints, textiles, wallpapers and 20th-century British art

MONKWEARMOUTH – **†Monkwearmouth Station Museum,* North Bridge Street. Tel: 0191-567 7075. Closed Sun. mornings. Victorian train station

NEWCASTLE UPON TYNE – *†*Hancock Museum,* Barras
Bridge. Tel: 0191-222 7418. Closed Sun. mornings.
Adm. charge varies. Natural history
*†*Laing Art Gallery,* New Bridge Street. Tel: 0191-232
7734. Closed Sun. mornings. British and European art,
ceramics, glass, silver, textiles and costume; *Art on
Tyneside* display
*†*Newcastle Discovery Museum,* Blandford Square. Tel:
0191-232 6789. Closed Sun. mornings. Science and
industry, local history, fashion and Tyneside's maritime
history; *Turbinia* (first steam-driven vessel) gallery
NEWMARKET – *National Horseracing Museum,* High Street.
Tel: 01638-667333. Closed Mon. (except July and Aug.)
and Nov.-March. Adm. £3.50. The Essential Horse
Millennium Exhibition, horseracing exhibits and tours
of local trainers' yards and studs
NORTHAMPTON – *†*Central Museum and Art Gallery,*
Guildhall Road. Tel: 01604-238548. Closed Sun.
mornings. Boot and shoe collection
NORTH SHIELDS – †*Stephenson Railway Museum,* Middle
Engine Lane. Tel: 0191-200 7144. Closed Mon. to Fri.
Locomotive engines and rolling stock
NOTTINGHAM – *Brewhouse Yard Museum,* Castle
Boulevard. Tel: 0115-915 3600. Adm. free (except
weekends and Bank Holidays). Daily life from the 17th
to 20th century
Castle Museum and Art Gallery. Tel: 0115-915 3700. Adm.
free (except weekends and Bank Holidays). Paintings,
ceramics, silver and glass; history of Nottingham
Industrial Museum, Wollaton Park. Tel: 0115-915 3910.
Adm. free (except weekends and Bank Holidays).
Lacemaking machinery, steam engines and transport
exhibits
Museum of Costume and Textiles, Castle Gate. Tel: 0115-
915 3500. Closed Mon. and Tues. Costume displays
from 1790 to the mid-20th century in period rooms
Natural History Museum, Wollaton Park. Tel: 0115-915
3900. Adm. free (except weekends and Bank Holidays).
Local natural history and wildlife dioramas
OXFORD – †*Ashmolean Museum,* Beaumont Street. Tel:
01865-278000. Closed Mon. (except Bank Holidays)
and Sun. mornings. European and Oriental fine and
applied arts, archaeology, Egyptology and numismatics
Museum of Modern Art, Pembroke Street. Tel: 01865-
722733. Closed Mon. Adm. £2.50. Temporary
exhibitions
†*Museum of the History of Science,* Broad Street. Tel: 01865-
277280. Closed mornings and Sun.-Mon. Displays
include early scientific instruments, chemical
apparatus, clocks and watches
†*Oxford University Museum of Natural History,* Parks Road.
Tel: 01865-272950. Closed mornings (except for school
parties by appointment). Entomology, geology,
mineralogy and zoology
†*Pitt Rivers Museum,* South Parks Road. Tel: 01865-
270927. Closed mornings (except by appointment) and
Sun. Ethnographic and archaeological artefacts. Check
for periods of closure in 1999-2000
PLYMOUTH – *†*City Museum and Art Gallery,* Drake
Circus. Tel: 01752-304774. Closed Mon. (except Bank
Holidays) and Sun. Local and natural history, ceramics,
silver, Old Masters, temporary exhibitions
The Dome, The Hoe. Tel: 01752-603300. Adm. £3.95.
Maritime history museum

PORTSMOUTH – *Charles Dickens Birthplace Museum,* Old
Commercial Road. Tel: 01705-827261. Closed 1 Oct. to
29 Nov. and 19 Dec. to 1 April, except 7 Feb. Adm.
£2.00. Dickens memorabilia
D-Day Museum, Clarence Esplanade. Tel: 01705-827261.
Closed Mon. morning Nov. to March. Adm. 4.75 (free
Monday afternoon Nov. to March). Includes the
Overlord Embroidery
Flagship Portsmouth, HM Naval Base. Incorporates the
Royal Naval Museum (tel: 01705-727562), HMS *Victory*
(tel: 01705-822034), HMS *Warrior* (tel: 01705-291379),
the †*Mary Rose* (tel: 01705-750521) and the *Dockyard
Museum.* Adm. charge to each (combined ticket
available). History of the Royal Navy and of the
dockyard and the trades in it
PRESTON – *Harris Museum and Art Gallery,* Market
Square. Tel: 01772-258248. Closed Sun. and Bank
Holidays. British art since the 18th century, ceramics,
glass, costume and local history; also contemporary
exhibitions
READING – †*Rural History Museum,* University of Reading.
Tel: 0118-931 8660. Closed Sun. and Mon. Adm. £1.00.
History of farming and the countryside over the last
200 years
ST ALBANS – *Verulamium Museum,* St Michael's. Tel:
01727-866100. Closed Sun. mornings. Adm. £3.00. Iron
Age and Roman Verulamium, including wall plasters,
jewellery, mosaics and room reconstructions
ST IVES, Cornwall – *Tate Gallery St Ives,* Porthmeor
Beach. Tel: 01736-796226. Opening times vary
seasonally; closed Mon. Oct.-March. Adm. £3.50.
Painting and sculpture by artists associated with St Ives
SALISBURY – †*Salisbury and South Wiltshire Museum,* The
Close. Tel: 01722-332151. Closed Sun., except July and
Aug. Archaeology collection
SHEFFIELD – *City Museum and Mappin Art Gallery,*
Weston Park. Tel: 0114-276 8588. Closed Mon.
Includes applied arts, natural history, Bronze Age
archaeology and ethnography, 19th- and 20th-century
art
Graves Art Gallery, Surrey Street. Tel: 0114-273 5158.
Closed Sun. Twentieth-century British art, Grice
Collection of Chinese ivories
Kelham Island Industrial Museum, off Alma Street. Tel:
0114-272 2106. Closed Fri. and Sat. Adm. £3.50. Local
industrial and social history
Ruskin Gallery and Ruskin Craft Gallery, Norfolk Street.
Tel: 0114-273 5299/203 9416. Closed Sun.
SOUTHAMPTON – *†*City Art Gallery, Civic Centre. Tel:
01703-832277. Fine art, especially 20th-century British
*†*Maritime Museum,* Town Quay. Tel: 01703-223941.
Southampton maritime history
*†*Museum of Archaeology,* Town Quay. Tel: 01703-635904.
Roman, Saxon and medieval archaeology
*†*Tudor House Museum and Garden,* Bugle Street. Tel:
01703-332513. Restored 16th century garden; social
history exhibitions
All of the above are closed Sun. mornings and Mon.
SOUTH SHIELDS – *†*Arbeia Roman Fort,* Baring Street. Tel:
0191-456 6612. Closed Sun. in winter, Sun. mornings in
summer. Excavated ruins
*†*South Shields Museum and Art Gallery,* Ocean Road. Tel:
0191-456 8740. Closed Sun. in winter, Sun. mornings in
summer. South Tyneside history, including
reconstructed street
STOKE-ON-TRENT – *Etruria Industrial Museum,* Etruria.
Tel: 01782-233144. Closed Mon. and Tues. Adm.
charge. Britain's sole surviving steam-powered potter's
mill

*Gladstone Pottery Museum, Longton. Tel: 01782-319232. Adm. charge. A working Victorian pottery.

*†Potteries Museum and Art Gallery, Hanley. Tel: 01782-232323. Closed Sun. mornings. Pottery, china and porcelain collections and a Mark XVI Spitfire. Pottery factory tours are available by arrangement Mon.-Fri., except during factory holidays, at the following: *Royal Doulton*, Burslem; *Spode*, Stoke; *Wedgwood*, Barlaston; *W. Moorcroft*, Cobridge; *H & R Johnson Tiles*, Tunstall; *Staffordshire Enamels*, Longton; *Royale Stratford China*, Fenton

STYAL, Cheshire – *Quarry Bank Mill.* Tel: 01625-527468. Closed Mon. in winter. Adm. £5.80. Working mill illustrating history of cotton industry; costumed guides at restored Apprentice House

SUNDERLAND – *†Sunderland Art Gallery, Borough Road. Tel: 0191-565 0723. Closed Sun. mornings. Fine and decorative art

WASHINGTON – †Washington 'F' Pit Museum, Albany Way. Tel: 0191-565 0723. Open Bank Holiday weekends only. Colliery-related collection

TELFORD – *†Ironbridge Gorge Museums. Tel: 01952-432166. Check opening times Nov. to March. Adm. charge £9.50 for all nine museums (ticket valid until all sites have been visited). Includes first iron bridge; Blists Hill (late Victorian working town); Museum of Iron; Jackfield Tile Museum; Coalport China Museum; Tar Tunnel; Broseley Pipeworks

TRING, Herts – *Tring Zoological Museum*, Akeman Street. Tel: 01442-824181. Closed Sun. mornings. Adm. £3.00. Display of more than 4,000 animal species

WAKEFIELD – *Yorkshire Sculpture Park*, West Bretton. Tel: 01924-830302. Open-air sculpture gallery including works by Moore, Hepworth, Frink and others in 300 acres of parkland

WORCESTER – *City Museum and Art Gallery*, Foregate Street. Tel: 01905-25371. Closed Thurs. and Sun. Includes a military museum, River Severn Gallery and changing art exhibitions
Museum of Worcester Porcelain and Royal Worcester Visitor Centre, Severn Street. Tel: 01905-23221. Factory tours

WROUGHTON, nr Swindon, Wilts – *Science Museum*, Wroughton Airfield. Tel: 01793-814466. Adm. charge. Aircraft displays and some of the Science Museum's transport and agricultural collection

YEOVIL, Somerset – *Fleet Air Arm Museum*, Royal Naval Air Station, Yeovilton. Tel: 01935-840565. Adm. £7.00. History of naval aviation; historic aircraft, including Concorde 002
Montacute House, Montacute (*see* page 587). Elizabethan and Jacobean portraits from the National Portrait Gallery

YORK – *Beningbrough Hall*, Shipton-by-Beningbrough. Tel: 01904-470666. Closed Thurs. and Fri. (except Good Friday and July-Aug.); also closed in winter. Adm. £4.75. Portraits from the National Portrait Gallery

*†Castle Museum. Tel: 01904-653611. Adm. £4.95. Reconstructed streets; costume and military collections

*†City Art Gallery, Exhibition Square. Tel: 01904-551861. European and British painting spanning seven centuries; modern pottery
Jorvik Viking Centre, Coppergate. Tel: 01904-643211. Adm. £5.35. Reconstruction of Viking York
National Railway Museum, Leeman Road. Tel: 01904-621261. Adm. £5.90. Includes locomotives, rolling stock and carriages

*†Yorkshire Museum, Museum Gardens. Tel: 01904-629745. Adm. £3.75. Yorkshire life from Roman to medieval times; geology gallery

WALES

BODELWYDDAN, Denbighshire – *Bodelwyddan Castle.* Tel: 01745-584060. Closed Fri. Adm. £4.30; grounds only £1.00. Portraits from the National Portrait Gallery, furniture from the Victoria and Albert Museum and sculptures from the Royal Academy

CAERLEON – *Roman Legionary Museum.* Tel: 01633-423134. Closed Sun. mornings. Adm. £3.30 museum and fortress, £2.10 museum only. Material from the site of the Roman fortress of Isca and its suburbs

CARDIFF – *National Museum and Gallery Cardiff*, Cathays Park. Tel: 01222-397951. Closed Mon. (except Bank Holidays). Adm. £4.50. Includes natural sciences, archaeology and Impressionist paintings
Museum of Welsh Life, St Fagans. Tel: 01222-573500. Adm. £5.50. Open-air museum with re-erected buildings, agricultural equipment and costume

DRE-FACH FELINDRE, nr Llandysul – *Museum of the Welsh Woollen Industry.* Tel: 01559-370929. Closed Sun., and Sat. in winter. Adm. £2.60. Exhibitions, a working woollen mill and craft workshops

LLANBERIS, nr Caernarfon –*Welsh Slate Museum.* Tel: 01286-870630. Closed in winter (except by appointment). Adm. £3.50. Former slate quarry with original machinery and plant; slate crafts demonstrations

LLANDRINDOD WELLS – *National Cycle Exhibition*, Automobile Palace, Temple Street. Tel: 01597-825531. Adm £2.50. Over 200 bicycles on display, from 1818 to the present day

SWANSEA – *Glynn Vivian Art Gallery and Museum*, Alexandra Road. Tel: 01792-655006. Closed Mon. (except Bank Holidays). Paintings, ceramics, Swansea pottery and porcelain, clocks, glass and Welsh art
Swansea Maritime and Industrial Museum, Museum Square. Tel: 01792-650351. Closed Mon. (except Bank Holidays). Includes a working woollen mill and historic boats afloat
*Swansea Museum, Victoria Road. Tel: 01792-653763. Closed Mon. (except Bank Holidays). Archaeology, social history, Swansea pottery

SCOTLAND

ABERDEEN – *Aberdeen Art Gallery, Schoolhill. Tel: 01224-523700. Closed Sun. mornings. Art from the 18th to 20th century
*Aberdeen Maritime Museum, Shiprow. Tel: 01224-337700. Adm. £3.50. Maritime history, including shipbuilding and North Sea oil

EDINBURGH – *Britannia*, Leith docks. Tel: 0131-555 5566. Former royal yacht with royal barge and royal family picture gallery. Tickets must be pre-booked
*City Art Centre, Market Street. Tel: 0131-529 3993. Closed Sun. Late 19th- and 20th-century art and temporary exhibitions
*Huntly House Museum, Canongate. Tel: 0131-529 4143. Closed Sun. Local history, silver, glass and Scottish pottery
*Museum of Childhood, High Street. Tel: 0131-529 4142. Closed Sun. Toys, games, clothes and exhibits relating to the social history of childhood
Museum of Flight, East Fortune Airfield, nr North Berwick. Tel: 01620-880308. Adm. £3.00. Display of aircraft

Museum of Scotland, Chambers Street. Tel: 0131-247 4422. Closed Sun mornings. Adm. £3.00. Scottish history from prehistoric times to the present
National Gallery of Scotland, The Mound. Tel: 0131-624 6200. Closed Sun. mornings. Paintings, drawings and prints from the 16th to 20th century, and the national collection of Scottish art
*The People's Story, Canongate. Tel: 0131-529 4057. Closed Sun. Edinburgh life since the 18th century
Royal Museum of Scotland, Chambers Street. Tel: 0131-225 7534. Closed Sun. mornings. Adm. £3.00. Scottish and international collections from prehistoric times to the present
Scottish Agricultural Museum, Ingliston. Tel: 0131-333 2674. Closed Sat. and Sun. in winter. History of agriculture in Scotland
Scottish National Gallery of Modern Art, Belford Road. Tel: 0131-624 6200. Closed Sun. mornings. Twentieth-century painting, sculpture and graphic art
Scottish National Portrait Gallery, Queen Street. Tel: 0131-624 6200. Closed Sun. mornings. Portraits of eminent people in Scottish history, and the national collection of photography
*The Writers' Museum, Lawnmarket. Tel: 0131-529 4901. Closed Sun. Robert Louis Stevenson, Walter Scott and Robert Burns exhibits
FORT WILLIAM – *West Highland Museum,* Cameron Square. Tel: 01397-702169. Closed Sun. Adm. £2.00. Includes tartan collections and exhibits relating to 1745 uprising
GLASGOW – **Burrell Collection,* Pollokshaws Road. Tel: 0141-649 7151. Paintings, textiles, furniture, ceramics, stained glass and silver from classical times to the 19th century
*Gallery of Modern Art, Queen Street. Tel: 0141-229 1996. Collection of contemporary Scottish and world art
*Glasgow Art Gallery and Museum, Kelvingrove. Tel: 0141-287 2699. Includes Old Masters, 19th-century French paintings and armour collection
Hunterian Art Gallery, Hillhead Street. Tel: 0141-330 5431. Closed Sun. Rennie Mackintosh and Whistler collections; Old Masters, Scottish paintings and modern paintings, sculpture and prints
*McLellan Galleries, Sauchiehall Street. Tel: 0141-331 1854. Adm. charge. Temporary exhibitions
*Museum of Transport, Bunhouse Road. Tel: 0141-287 2720. Includes a reproduction of a 1938 Glasgow street, cars since the 1930s, trams and a Glasgow subway station
*People's Palace Museum, Glasgow Green. Tel: 0141-554 0223. History of Glasgow since 1175
*St Mungo Museum of Religious Life and Art, Castle Street. Tel: 0141-553 2557. Explores universal themes through objects of all the main world religions

NORTHERN IRELAND

BELFAST – *Ulster Museum,* Botanic Gardens. Tel: 01232-383000. Closed weekend mornings. Irish antiquities, natural and local history, fine and applied arts
HOLYWOOD, Co. Down – *Ulster Folk and Transport Museum,* Cultra. Tel: 01232-428428. Closed Sun. mornings. Adm. £4.00. Open-air museum with original buildings from Ulster town and rural life *c.* 1900; indoor galleries including Irish rail and road transport and *Titanic* exhibitions
LONDONDERRY – *The Tower Museum,* Union Hall Place. Tel: 01504-372411. Closed Sun. and Mon. except July and Aug. Adm. £3.75. Tells the story of Ireland through the history of Londonderry
OMAGH, Co. Tyrone – *Ulster American Folk Park,* Castletown. Tel: 01662-243292. Closed in winter. Adm. £4.00. Open-air museum telling the story of Ulster's emigrants to America; restored or recreated dwellings and workshops; ship and dockside gallery

Lotteries and Gaming

Gaming and lotteries in the UK are officially regulated and may only be run by licensed operators or in licensed premises. Responsibility for policy and the laws on gaming and lotteries rests with the Home Secretary. The National Lottery (*see* below) is regulated by the National Lottery Commission, which replaced the Office of the National Lottery in April 1999. Supervision of other lottery operations and gaming is mostly the responsibility of the Gaming Board of Great Britain.

Most betting is on horseracing and greyhound racing, and may take place at racecourses and greyhound tracks, or at off-course betting offices. The amount spent on on-course betting is estimated to be about 10 per cent of the figures for off-course betting.

OFF-COURSE BETTING (UK)

	£ million
1996–7	6,718
1997–8	6,838p
1998–9	7,108p

p provisional
Source: Horserace Totalisator Board

Other forms of gaming and lotteries include the following:

Number of casinos operating	119
Total drop (1997–8)	£2,720m
Bingo clubs holding gaming licences	818
Amount staked (1997–8)	£1,019m
Gaming machines licensed	over 250,000
Society lottery schemes registered	614
Local authority lottery schemes registered	9
On-line lotteries held under registered schemes	1,927
Number of lotteries held under registered schemes	5,070
Total ticket sales (£ million)	c.£125m

In 1997–8 sales of society lottery tickets increased by 9 per cent to £125 million. Of this, £41.4 million (33 per cent) was spent on prizes, £32.6 million (26 per cent) on expenses and £50.8 million (41 per cent) went to good causes.
Source: Report of the Gaming Board for Great Britain 1997–8

THE NATIONAL LOTTERY

The National Lottery is currently run by a private company, Camelot Group PLC. The seven-year licence granted to Camelot expires in 2001. It is expected that the successful bidder for the next licence will be appointed by autumn 2000.

The five-member National Lottery Commission regulates the National Lottery's operations, licenses games promoted as part of the lottery and will appoint the operator of the next licence.

The first National Lottery tickets draw was made on 19 November 1994 and Instants (scratchcards) were introduced on 21 March 1995. A second weekly draw was introduced on Wednesday 5 February 1997, and on 12 June 1999 Thunderball, a third weekly draw, was introduced. Tickets for the main lottery game cost £1. If the jackpot prize is not won, it is 'rolled over' to the next draw. The highest win on a single ticket to date was £22,590,829 on 10 June 1995. By June 1999, 802 millionaires had been created.

SALES 1998–9

Average number of tickets (on-line and instants) sold per week	c.94.8m
Average number of people playing weekly	c.30m
% of adult population buying tickets regularly	c.55%
Amount raised by ticket sales, 1994 to June 1999	c.£23,000m

Sources: Camelot, Oflot

DISTRIBUTION OF PROCEEDS
over the seven-year licence period

Allocated to:	%
Prize money	50
Tax	13
Retailer commission	5
Camelot (operating costs and profit)	4
Good causes	28

The 'good causes' originally benefiting from lottery funds were the arts, sport, heritage, charities and the Millennium Commission. In July 1998 the National Lottery Act created a sixth good cause, the New Opportunities Fund, to fund health, education and environmental initiatives. The New Opportunities Fund announced its first awards in summer 1999. The Act also created a National Endowment for Science, Technology and the Arts (NESTA), a non-departmental public body whose objectives are: to help talented individuals; to enable inventions and ideas to be commercially exploited; and to promote public knowledge of science, technology and the arts. NESTA received an initial £200 million from the New Opportunities Fund but thereafter is to generate its own income.

From October 1997 the percentage of all the funds allocated to the good causes received by each cause is as follows: the arts, sport, heritage and charities 16.66 per cent each; the Millennium Commission 20 per cent; and the New Opportunities Fund 13.33 per cent. From October 1999 the share going to the Millennium Commission will be reduced to 13.33 per cent and that going to the New Opportunities Fund will rise to 20 per cent.

The cumulative amount allocated to the good causes from November 1994 to March 1999 was £7,304 million.

AWARDS 1998–9

Most awards are conditional on partnership funding being obtained from other sources.

	Number	Total value £
Total	12,932	3,192,005,425
Arts, total	1,345	163,146,724
Arts Council of England	497	120,370,829
Arts Council of Wales	577	14,236,149
Scottish Arts Council	185	20,001,747
Arts Council of Northern Ireland	86	8,537,999
Millennium Commission		
awards to projects	187	1,260,000,000
awards to schemes funding individuals	57	56,058,751
Heritage Lottery Fund	2,738	1,283,321,186
National Lottery Charities Board	7,079	281,453,961
Sport, total	1,526	148,024,803
Sport England	289	103,331,000
Sports Council for Wales	58	5,326,106
Scottish Sports Council	980	28,904,282
Sports Council for Northern Ireland	199	10,463,415

Countries of the World

The total population of the world in mid-1990 was estimated at 5,292 million, compared with 3,019 million in 1960 and 2,070 million in 1930.

Continent, etc.	Area sq. miles '000	sq. km '000	Estimated population mid-1990
Africa	11,704	30,313	642,000,000
North America[1]	8,311	21,525	276,000,000
Latin America[2]	7,933	20,547	448,000,000
Asia[3]	10,637	27,549	3,113,000,000
Europe[4]	1,915	4,961	498,000,000
Former USSR	8,649	22,402	289,000,000
Oceania[5]	3,286	8,510	26,500,000
TOTAL	52,435	135,807	5,292,000,000

[1] Includes Greenland and Hawaii
[2] Mexico and the remainder of the Americas south of the USA
[3] Includes European Turkey, excludes former USSR
[4] Excludes European Turkey and former USSR
[5] Includes Australia, New Zealand and the islands inhabited by Micronesian, Melanesian and Polynesian peoples
Source UN Demographic Yearbook 1990 (pub. 1992)

A United Nations report *The Sex and Age Distribution of the World Populations* (revised 1994) puts the world's population in the late 20th and the 21st centuries at the following levels (medium variant data):

1995	5,716.4m	2030	8,670.6m
2000	6,158.0m	2040	9,318.2m
2010	7,032.3m	2050	9,833.2m
2020	7,887.8m		

The population forecast for the years 2000 and 2050 is:

Continent, etc.	Estimated population (million) 2000	2050
Africa	831.596	2,140.844
North America[1]	306.280	388.997
Latin America[2]	523.875	838.527
Asia	3,753.846	5,741.005
Europe	729.803	677.764
Oceania	30.651	46.070
TOTAL	6,158.051	9,833.207

[1] Includes Bermuda, Greenland, and St Pierre and Miquelon
[2] Mexico and the remainder of the Americas south of the USA

AREA AND POPULATION BY CONTINENT

No complete survey of many countries has yet been achieved and consequently accurate area figures are not always available. Similarly, many countries have not recently, or have never, taken a census. The areas of countries given below are derived from estimated figures published by the United Nations. The conversion factors used are:

(i) to convert square miles to square km, multiply by 2.589988

(ii) to convert square km to square miles, multiply by 0.3861022

Population figures for countries are derived from the most recent estimates available. Accurate and up-to-date data for the populations of capital cities are scarce, and definitions of cities' extent differ. The figures given below are the latest estimates available.

Ψ seaport

AFRICA

COUNTRY/TERRITORY	AREA sq. miles	sq. km	POPULATION	CAPITAL	POPULATION OF CAPITAL
Algeria	919,595	2,381,741	29,168,000	Ψ Algiers	1,740,461
Angola	481,354	1,246,700	11,185,000	Ψ Luanda	475,328
Benin	43,484	112,622	5,563,000	Ψ Porto Novo	179,138
Botswana	224,607	581,730	1,490,000	Gaborone	286,779
Burkina Faso	105,792	274,000	10,780,000	Ouagadougou	634,479
Burundi	10,747	27,834	6,088,000	Bujumbura	235,440
Cameroon	183,569	475,442	13,560,000	Yaoundé	653,670
Cape Verde	1,557	4,033	396,000	Ψ Praia	61,644
Central African Republic	240,535	622,984	3,344,000	Bangui	473,817
Chad	495,755	1,284,000	6,515,000	N'Djaména	179,000
Comoros	863	2,235	632,000	Moroni	17,267
Congo, Dem. Rep. of	905,355	2,344,858	46,812,000	Kinshasa	2,664,309
Congo – Brazzaville, Rep. of	132,047	342,000	2,668,000	Brazzaville	596,200
Côte d'Ivoire	124,504	322,463	14,781,000	Yamoussoukro	126,191
Djibouti	8,958	23,200	617,000	Ψ Djibouti	62,000
Egypt	386,662	1,001,449	60,603,000	Cairo	6,800,000
Equatorial Guinea	10,831	28,051	410,000	Ψ Malabo	30,418
Eritrea	45,406	117,600	3,280,000	Asmara	358,100
Ethiopia	426,373	1,104,300	58,506,000	Addis Ababa	2,084,588

Country/Territory	Area sq. miles	sq. km	Population	Capital	Population of Capital
Gabon	103,347	267,668	1,106,000	Ψ Libreville	251,000
Gambia	4,361	11,295	1,141,000	Ψ Banjul	109,986
Ghana	92,098	238,533	18,885,616	Ψ Accra	1,445,515
Guinea	94,926	245,857	7,518,000	Ψ Conakry	763,000
Guinea-Bissau	13,948	36,125	1,091,000	Ψ Bissau	109,214
Kenya	224,081	580,367	31,806,000	Nairobi	1,400,000
Lesotho	11,720	30,355	2,078,000	Maseru	288,951
Liberia	43,000	111,369	2,820,000	Ψ Monrovia	421,053
Libya	679,362	1,759,540	4,389,739	Ψ Tripoli	1,000,000
Madagascar	226,658	587,041	15,353,000	Antananarivo	1,052,835
Malawi	45,747	118,484	10,114,000	Lilongwe	233,973
Mali	478,841	1,240,192	11,134,000	Bamako	809,552
Mauritania	395,956	1,025,520	2,351,000	Nouakchott	850,000
Mauritius	788	2,040	1,160,000	Ψ Port Louis	146,499
Mayotte (*Fr.*)	144	372	94,410	Mamoudzou	12,000
Morocco	172,414	446,550	27,623,000	Ψ Rabat	1,220,000
Western Sahara	102,703	266,000	256,000	Laayoune	20,010
Mozambique	309,496	799,380	16,916,600	Ψ Maputo	1,039,700
Namibia	318,261	824,292	1,575,000	Windhoek	147,056
Niger	489,191	1,267,000	9,465,000	Niamey	392,169
Nigeria	356,669	923,768	115,120,000	Abuja	378,671
Réunion (*Fr.*)	969	2,510	664,000	St Denis	121,999
Rwanda	10,169	26,338	5,397,000	Kigali	116,227
St Helena (*UK*)	47	122	5,157	Ψ Jamestown	884
Ascension Island (*UK*)	34	88	1,051	Ψ Georgetown	—
Tristan da Cunha (*UK*)	38	98	288	Ψ Edinburgh of the Seven Seas	—
São Tomé and Príncipe	372	964	135,000	Ψ São Tomé	5,714
Senegal	75,955	196,722	8,572,000	Ψ Dakar	1,641,358
Seychelles	176	455	76,000	Ψ Victoria	24,324
Sierra Leone	27,699	71,740	4,297,000	Ψ Freetown	469,776
Somalia	246,201	637,657	9,822,000	Ψ Mogadishu	230,000
South Africa	471,445	1,221,037	42,393,000	{ Pretoria / Ψ Cape Town	822,925 / 1,911,521
Sudan	967,500	2,505,813	27,291,000	Khartoum	947,483
Swaziland	6,704	17,364	938,000	Mbabane	38,290
Tanzania	362,162	938,000	30,799,000	Dodoma	85,000
Togo	21,925	56,785	4,201,000	Ψ Lomé	366,476
Tunisia	62,592	162,155	9,092,000	Ψ Tunis	1,830,634
Uganda	93,065	241,038	19,848,000	Kampala	750,000
Zambia	290,587	752,618	8,275,000	Lusaka	982,362
Zimbabwe	150,872	390,757	11,908,000	Harare	1,189,103

AMERICA

North America

Canada	3,849,674	9,970,610	29,964,000	Ottawa	1,010,498
Greenland (*Den.*)	840,004	2,175,600	58,000	Ψ Godthåb (Nuuk)	12,483
Mexico	756,066	1,958,201	96,578,000	Mexico City	15,047,685
St Pierre and Miquelon (*Fr.*)	93	242	7,000	Ψ St Pierre	5,416
United States of America	3,536,278	9,158,960	270,298,524	Washington DC	7,051,495

Central America and the West Indies

Anguilla (*UK*)	37	96	12,394	The Valley	2,400
Antigua and Barbuda	171	442	66,000	Ψ St John's	22,342
Aruba (*Neth.*)	75	193	87,000	Ψ Oranjestad	25,000
Bahamas	5,358	13,878	284,000	Ψ Nassau	172,196
Barbados	166	430	265,000	Ψ Bridgetown	108,000
Belize	8,763	22,696	222,000	Belmopan	44,087
Bermuda (*UK*)	20	53	64,000	Ψ Hamilton	2,277
Cayman Islands (*UK*)	102	264	38,000	Ψ George Town	20,000
Costa Rica	19,730	51,100	3,398,000	San José	1,209,045
Cuba	42,804	110,861	11,019,000	Ψ Havana	2,175,888
Dominica	290	751	74,000	Ψ Roseau	16,243

Country/Territory	Area sq. miles	sq. km	Population	Capital	Population of Capital
Dominican Republic	18,816	48,734	8,052,000	Ψ Santo Domingo	2,134,779
Grenada	133	344	92,000	Ψ St George's	4,788
Guadeloupe (*Fr.*)	658	1,705	431,000	Ψ Basse Terre	29,522
Guatemala	42,042	108,889	10,928,000	Guatemala City	1,675,589
Haiti	10,714	27,750	7,336,000	Ψ Port-au-Prince	846,247
Honduras	43,277	112,088	6,140,000	Tegucigalpa	670,100
Jamaica	4,243	10,990	2,491,000	Ψ Kingston	524,638
Martinique (*Fr.*)	425	1,102	384,000	Ψ Fort de France	133,920
Montserrat (*UK*)	39	102	4,500	Ψ Plymouth	1,478
Netherlands Antilles (*Neth.*)	309	800	207,333	Ψ Willemstad	50,000
Nicaragua	50,193	130,668	4,663,000	Managua	608,020
Panama	29,157	75,517	2,674,000	Ψ Panama City	458,490
Puerto Rico (*USA*)	3,427	8,875	3,736,000	Ψ San Juan	1,222,316
St Christopher and Nevis	101	261	41,000	Ψ Basseterre	14,161
St Lucia	240	622	144,000	Ψ Castries	56,000
St Vincent and the Grenadines	150	388	113,000	Ψ Kingstown	33,694
Salvador, El	8,124	21,041	5,796,000	San Salvador	1,200,000
Trinidad and Tobago	1,981	5,130	1,297,000	Ψ Port of Spain	46,222
Turks and Caicos Islands (*UK*)	166	430	23,000	Ψ Grand Turk	3,691
Virgin Islands					
British (*UK*)	58	151	19,000	Ψ Road Town	3,983
US (*USA*)	134	347	106,000	Ψ Charlotte Amalie	11,842
South America					
Argentina	1,073,518	2,780,400	35,220,000	Ψ Buenos Aires	11,298,030
Bolivia	424,165	1,098,581	8,140,000	La Paz	1,480,000
Brazil	3,300,171	8,547,403	157,872,000	Brasilia	1,737,813
Chile	292,135	756,626	14,419,000	Santiago	5,257,937
Colombia	439,737	1,138,914	35,626,000	Bogotá	5,398,998
Ecuador	109,484	283,561	11,698,000	Quito	1,444,363
Falkland Islands (*UK*)	4,700	12,173	2,221	Ψ Stanley	1,636
French Guiana (*Fr.*)	34,749	90,000	153,000	Ψ Cayenne	41,164
Guyana	83,000	214,969	838,000	Ψ Georgetown	250,000
Paraguay	157,048	406,752	4,955,000	Asunción	718,690
Peru	496,225	1,285,216	25,015,000	Lima	6,483,901
South Georgia (*UK*)	1,580	4,092	—	—	—
Suriname	63,037	163,265	423,000	Ψ Paramaribo	265,000
Uruguay	68,500	177,414	3,203,000	Ψ Montevideo	1,383,660
Venezuela	352,145	912,050	22,710,000	Caracas	2,784,042

ASIA

Country/Territory	Area sq. miles	sq. km	Population	Capital	Population of Capital
Afghanistan	251,773	652,090	20,883,000	Kabul	1,424,400
Bahrain	268	694	599,000	Ψ Manama	140,401
Bangladesh	55,598	143,998	120,073,000	Dhaka	3,397,187
Bhutan	18,147	47,000	1,812,000	Thimphu	15,000
Brunei	2,226	5,765	300,000	Bandar Seri Begawan	49,902
Cambodia	69,898	181,035	10,273,000	Ψ Phnom Penh	832,000
China[1]	3,705,408	9,596,961	1,232,083,000	Beijing (Peking)	7,362,426
Hong Kong (*China*)	415	1,075	6,687,200	—	—
India	1,269,346	3,287,590	970,930,000	New Delhi	301,297
Indonesia	735,358	1,904,569	196,813,000	Ψ Jakarta	9,160,500
Iran	634,293	1,648,195	61,128,000	Tehran	6,750,043
Iraq	169,235	438,317	20,607,000	Baghdad	3,841,268
Israel[2]	8,130	21,056	6,100,000	Tel Aviv	1,880,200
West Bank and Gaza Strip	2,406	6,231	1,635,000	Gaza City	120,000
Japan	145,870	377,801	125,761,000	Tokyo	11,680,296
Jordan	37,738	97,740	5,581,000	Amman	1,270,000
Kazakhstan	1,049,156	2,717,300	15,671,000	Astana	292,000
Korea, Democratic People's Republic	46,540	120,538	22,466,000	Pyongyang	2,741,260
Korea, Republic	38,368	99,373	46,430,000	Seoul	10,289,000
Kuwait	6,880	17,818	1,866,104	Ψ Kuwait City	400,000
Kyrgyzstan	76,641	198,500	4,575,000	Bishkek	585,800
Laos	91,429	236,800	5,035,000	Vientiane	132,253

Country/Territory	Area sq. miles	sq. km	Population	Capital	Population of Capital
Lebanon	4,015	10,400	3,084,000	Ψ Beirut	1,500,000
Macao (Port.)	7	18	440,000	Ψ Macao	241,413
Malaysia	127,320	329,758	20,581,000	Kuala Lumpur	1,145,342
Maldives	115	298	263,000	Ψ Malé	62,973
Mongolia	604,829	1,566,500	2,354,000	Ulaanbaatar	515,100
Myanmar	261,228	676,578	45,922,000	Ψ Yangon (Rangoon)	2,513,023
Nepal	56,827	147,181	21,127,000	Kathmandu	421,258
Oman	119,498	309,500	2,302,000	Ψ Muscat	400,000
Pakistan	307,374	796,095	134,146,000	Islamabad	350,000
Philippines	115,831	300,000	71,899,000	Ψ Manila	8,594,150
Qatar	4,247	11,000	558,000	Ψ Doha	217,294
Saudi Arabia	830,000	2,149,690	18,836,000	Riyadh	1,800,000
Singapore	239	618	3,044,000	—	—
Sri Lanka	25,332	65,610	18,354,000	Ψ Colombo	615,000
Syria	71,498	185,180	14,619,000	Damascus	1,549,000
Taiwan	13,800	35,742	21,854,273	Taipei	2,638,565
Tajikistan	55,251	143,100	5,919,000	Dushanbe	602,000
Thailand	198,115	513,115	60,206,000	Ψ Bangkok	5,882,000
Turkey[3]	299,158	774,815	62,697,000	Ankara	3,103,000
Turkmenistan	188,456	488,100	4,569,000	Ashgabat	407,000
United Arab Emirates	32,278	83,600	2,260,000	Abu Dhabi	450,000
Uzbekistan	172,742	447,400	24,000,000	Tashkent	2,200,000
Vietnam	128,066	331,689	75,181,000	Hanoi	3,056,146
Yemen	203,850	527,968	15,919,000	Sana'a	926,595

[1] Including Tibet
[2] Including East Jerusalem, the Golan Heights and Israeli citizens on the West Bank
[3] Including Turkey in Europe

EUROPE

Albania	11,099	28,748	3,670,000	Tirana	244,153
Andorra	175	453	65,877	Andorra la Vella	21,721
Armenia	11,506	29,800	3,893,000	Yerevan	1,254,400
Austria	32,378	83,859	8,106,000	Vienna	1,806,737
Azerbaijan	33,436	86,600	7,625,000	Ψ Baku	1,149,000
Belarus	80,155	207,600	10,203,000	Minsk	1,700,223
Belgium	11,783	30,519	10,159,000	Brussels	953,175
Bosnia-Hercegovina	19,735	51,129	4,510,000	Sarajevo	529,021
Bulgaria	42,823	110,912	8,356,000	Sofia	1,191,743
Croatia	21,824	56,538	4,501,000	Zagreb	867,717
Cyprus	3,572	9,251	756,000	Nicosia	188,800
Czech Republic	30,450	78,864	10,315,000	Prague	1,216,568
Denmark	16,639	43,094	5,262,000	Ψ Copenhagen	1,362,264
Faroe Islands	540	1,399	47,000	Ψ Tórshavn	16,218
Estonia	17,413	45,227	1,453,844	Tallinn	415,299
Finland	130,559	338,145	5,125,000	Ψ Helsinki	1,056,495
France	212,935	551,500	58,375,000	Paris	9,319,367
Georgia	26,911	69,700	5,411,000	Tbilisi	1,268,000
Germany	137,735	356,733	81,912,000	Berlin	3,472,009
Gibraltar (UK)	2.5	6.5	27,192	Ψ Gibraltar	—
Greece	50,949	131,957	10,475,000	Athens	3,072,922
Hungary	35,920	93,032	10,193,000	Budapest	2,002,121
Iceland	39,769	103,000	275,277	Ψ Reykjavík	107,764
Ireland, Republic of	27,137	70,284	3,626,087	Ψ Dublin	952,700
Italy	116,320	301,268	57,339,000	Rome	2,693,383
Latvia	24,942	64,600	2,491,000	Riga	805,997
Liechtenstein	62	160	31,320	Vaduz	4,975
Lithuania	25,174	65,200	3,701,300	Vilnius	581,500
Luxembourg	998	2,586	412,000	Luxembourg	77,400
Macedonia	9,928	25,713	2,174,000	Skopje	448,229
Malta	122	316	376,513	Ψ Valletta	7,146
Moldova	13,012	33,700	4,327,000	Chişinău	655,940
Monaco	0.4	1	32,000	Monaco	27,063
Netherlands	15,770	40,844	15,517,000	Ψ Amsterdam	1,101,629
Norway[1]	125,050	323,877	4,445,460	Ψ Oslo	499,693

Country/Territory	Area sq. miles	sq. km	Population	Capital	Population of Capital
Poland	124,808	323,250	38,628,000	Warsaw	1,643,203
Portugal[2]	35,514	91,982	9,920,760	Ψ Lisbon	2,561,225
Romania	92,043	238,391	22,520,000	Bucharest	2,027,500
Russia[3]	6,592,850	17,075,400	146,100,000	Moscow	8,598,896
San Marino	24	61	25,000	San Marino	4,357
Slovakia	18,928	49,035	5,374,000	Bratislava	452,278
Slovenia	7,821	20,256	1,991,000	Ljubljana	280,146
Spain[4]	195,365	505,992	39,270,000	Madrid	3,084,673
Sweden	173,732	449,964	8,843,000	Ψ Stockholm	1,148,953
Switzerland	15,940	41,284	7,076,000	Bern	321,932
Ukraine	233,090	603,700	51,094,000	Kiev	2,630,000
United Kingdom[5]	94,248	244,101	58,784,000	Ψ London	7,007,091
England	50,351	130,410	48,903,000	—	—
Wales	8,015	20,758	2,917,000	Ψ Cardiff	302,747
Scotland	30,420	78,789	5,137,000	Ψ Edinburgh	447,550
Northern Ireland	5,467	14,160	1,649,000	Ψ Belfast	296,700
Vatican City State	0.2	0.44	1,000	Vatican City	766
Yugoslavia	39,449	102,173	10,574,000	Belgrade	1,338,856

[1] Excludes Svalbard and Jan Mayen Islands (approx. 24,101 sq. miles (62,422 sq. km) and 3,000 population)
[2] Includes Madeira (314 sq. miles) and the Azores (922 sq. miles)
[3] Includes Russia in Asia
[4] Includes Balearic Islands, Canary Islands, Ceuta and Melilla
[5] Excludes Isle of Man (221 sq. miles (572 sq. km), 69,788 population), and Channel Islands (75 sq. miles (194 sq. km), 142,949 population)

OCEANIA

Country/Territory	Area sq. miles	sq. km	Population	Capital	Population of Capital
American Samoa (USA)	77	199	56,000	Ψ Pago Pago	3,519
Australia	2,988,902	7,741,220	18,871,800	Canberra	309,500
Norfolk Island (Aust.)	14	36	1,772	Ψ Kingston	—
Fiji	7,056	18,274	797,000	Ψ Suva	141,273
French Polynesia (Fr.)	1,544	4,000	223,000	Ψ Papeete	36,784
Guam (USA)	212	549	153,000	Agana	1,139
Kiribati	280	726	80,000	Tarawa	17,921
Marshall Islands	70	181	58,000	Dalap-Uliga-Darrit	20,000
Micronesia, Federated States of	271	702	109,000	Palikir	—
Nauru	8	21	11,000	Ψ Nauru	—
New Caledonia (Fr.)	7,172	18,575	189,000	Ψ Noumea	97,581
New Zealand	104,454	270,534	3,681,546	Ψ Wellington	326,900
Cook Islands	91	236	19,000	Rarotonga	9,281
Niue	100	260	2,000	Alofi	—
Ross Dependency[1]	175,000	453,248	—	—	—
Tokelau	5	12	2,000	—	—
Northern Mariana Islands (USA)	179	464	49,000	Saipan	52,706
Palau (USA)	177	459	17,000	Koror	10,493
Papua New Guinea	178,704	462,840	4,400,000	Ψ Port Moresby	173,500
Pitcairn Islands (UK)	2	5	54	—	—
Solomon Islands	11,157	28,896	391,000	Ψ Honiara	40,000
Tonga	288	747	99,000	Ψ Nuku'alofa	29,018
Tuvalu	10	26	10,000	Ψ Funafuti	2,856
Vanuatu	4,706	12,189	169,000	Ψ Port Vila	26,100
Wallis and Futuna Islands (Fr.)	77	200	15,000	Ψ Mata-Utu	—
Western Samoa	1,093	2,831	166,000	Ψ Apia	36,000

[1] Includes permanent shelf ice

Currencies of the World
AND EXCHANGE RATES AGAINST £ STERLING

Franc CFA = Franc de la Communauté financière africaine
Franc CFP = Franc des Comptoirs français du Pacifique

Country/Territory	Monetary Unit	Average Rate to £ 4 September 1998	Average Rate to £ 31 August 1999
Afghanistan	Afghani (Af) of 100 puls	Af 7947.70	Af 7429.49
Albania	Lek (Lk) of 100 qindarka	Lk 251.231	Lk 211.892
Algeria	Algerian dinar (DA) of 100 centimes	DA 98.4813	DA 105.034
American Samoa	Currency is that of the USA	US$ 1.6732	US$ 1.5878
Andorra	French and Spanish currencies in use	—	—
Angola	Readjusted kwanza (Kzrl) of 100 lwei	Kzrl 430226.7	Kzrl 4081484.3
Anguilla	East Caribbean dollar (EC$) of 100 cents	EC$ 4.5177	EC$ 4.2871
Antigua and Barbuda	East Caribbean dollar (EC$) of 100 cents	EC$ 4.5177	EC$ 4.2871
Argentina	Peso of 10,000 australes	Pesos 1.6720	Pesos 1.5872
Armenia	Dram of 100 louma	Dram 840.583	Dram 851.474
Aruba	Aruban florin	Florins 2.9950	Florins 2.8104
Ascension Island	Currency is that of St Helena	*at parity with £ sterling*	
Australia	Australian dollar ($A) of 100 cents	$A 2.8507	$A 2.5102
Norfolk Island	Currency is that of Australia	$A 2.8507	$A 2.5102
Austria	Schilling of 100 Groschen	Schilling 20.4216	Schilling 20.8988
Azerbaijan	Manat of 100 gopik	Manat 6609.14	Manat 6259.11
The Bahamas	Bahamian dollar (B$) of 100 cents	B$ 1.6732	B$ 1.5878
Bahrain	Bahraini dinar (BD) of 1,000 fils	BD 0.6308	BD 0.5986
Bangladesh	Taka (Tk) of 100 poisha	Tk 78.8078	Tk 78.5962
Barbados	Barbados dollar (BD$) of 100 cents	BD$ 3.3653	BD$ 3.1756
Belarus	Rouble of 100 kopeks	Roubles 402404.7	Roubles 500157.2
Belgium	Belgian franc (or frank) of 100 centimes (centiemen)	Francs 59.8839	Francs 61.2671
Belize	Belize dollar (BZ$) of 100 cents	BZ$ 3.3464	BZ$ 3.1756
Benin	Franc CFA	Francs 973.140	Francs 996.250
Bermuda	Bermuda dollar of 100 cents	$ 1.6732	$ 1.5878
Bhutan	Ngultrum of 100 chetrum (Indian currency is also legal tender)	Ngultrum 71.2156	Ngultrum 69.0693
Bolivia	Boliviano ($b) of 100 centavos	$b 9.3365	$b 9.3204
Bosnia-Hercegovina	Convertible marka	—	Marka 2.9385
Botswana	Pula (P) of 100 thebe	P 7.8389	P 7.3374
Brazil	Real of 100 centavos	Real 1.9711	Real 3.0653
Brunei	Brunei dollar (B$) of 100 sen (fully interchangeable with Singapore currency)	$ 2.9256	$ 2.6802
Bulgaria	Lev of 100 stotinki	Leva 2894.22	Leva 2.9555
Burkina Faso	Franc CFA	Francs 973.140	Francs 996.250
Burundi	Burundi franc of 100 centimes	Francs 747.541	Francs 969.612
Cambodia	Riel of 100 sen	Riel 6241.04	Riel 6020.84
Cameroon	Franc CFA	Francs 973.140	Francs 996.250
Canada	Canadian dollar (C$) of 100 cents	C$ 2.5605	C$ 2.3721
Cape Verde	Escudo Caboverdiano of 100 centavos	Esc 166.795	Esc 150.381
Cayman Islands	Cayman Islands dollar (CI$) of 100 cents	CI$ 1.3858	CI$ 1.3231
Central African Republic	Franc CFA	Francs 973.140	Francs 996.250
Chad	Franc CFA	Francs 973.140	Francs 996.250
Chile	Chilean peso of 100 centavos	Pesos 793.515	Pesos 817.479
China	Renminbi Yuan of 10 jiao or 100 fen	Yuan 13.8534	Yuan 13.1427
Hong Kong	Hong Kong dollar (HK$) of 100 cents	HK$ 12.9481	HK$ 12.3284
Colombia	Colombian peso of 100 centavos	Pesos 2585.26	Pesos 3055.72
The Comoros	Comorian franc (KMF) of 100 centimes	Francs 729.663	Francs 781.147
Congo, Dem. Rep. of	Congolese franc	CFr 230065.1	CFr 7.1451
Congo, Rep. of	Franc CFA	Francs 973.140	Francs 996.250
Costa Rica	Costa Rican colón (₡) of 100 céntimos	₡ 437.793	₡ 461.066
Côte D'ivoire	Franc CFA	Francs 973.140	Francs 996.250
Croatia	Kuna of 100 lipa	Kuna 10.5468·	Kuna 11.5632
Cuba	Cuban peso of 100 centavos	Pesos 38.4836	Pesos 33.3438
Cyprus	Cyprus pound (C£) of 100 cents	C£ 0.8558	C£ 0.8781
Czech Republic	Koruna (Kčs) of 100 haléřu	Kčs 51.6208	Kčs 55.6659
Denmark	Danish krone of 100 øre	Kroner 11.0523	Kroner 11.2892
Farøe Islands	Currency is that of Denmark	Kroner 11.0523	Kroner 11.2892

Country/Territory	Monetary Unit	Average Rate to £ 4 September 1998	Average Rate to £ 31 August 1999
Djibouti	Djibouti franc of 100 centimes	Francs 297.361	Francs 282.184
Dominica	East Caribbean dollar (EC$) of 100 cents	EC$ 4.5177	EC$ 4.2871
Dominican Republic	Dominican Republic peso (RD$) of 100 centavos	RD$ 25.7673	RD$ 25.1190
Ecuador	Sucre of 100 centavos	Sucres 9283.75	Sucres 17735.7
Egypt	Egyptian pound (£E) of 100 piastres or 1,000 millièmes	£E 5.7203	£E 5.4462
Equatorial Guinea	Franc CFA	Francs 973.140	Francs 996.250
Eritrea	Nakfa	—	—
Estonia	Kroon of 100 sents	Kroons 23.4228	Kroons 23.7512
Ethiopia	Ethiopian birr (EB) of 100 cents	EB 11.6923	EB 11.9355
Falkland Islands	Falkland pound of 100 pence	*at parity with £ sterling*	
Fiji	Fiji dollar (F$) of 100 cents	F$ 3.4536	F$ 3.1631
Finland	Markka (Mk) of 100 penniä	Mk 8.8297	Mk 9.0302
France	Franc of 100 centimes	Francs 9.7314	Francs 9.9625
French Guiana	Currency is that of France	Francs 9.7314	Francs 9.9625
French Polynesia	Franc CFP	Francs 176.887	Francs 181.171
Gabon	Franc CFA	Francs 973.140	Francs 996.250
The Gambia	Dalasi (D) of 100 butut	D 17.0918	D 18.6885
Georgia	Lari of 100 tetri	—	—
Germany	Deutsche Mark (DM) of 100 Pfennig	DM 2.9023	DM 2.9705
Ghana	Cedi of 100 pesewas	Cedi 3890.20	Cedi 4125.12
Gibraltar	Gibraltar pound of 100 pence	*at parity with £ sterling*	
Greece	Drachma of 100 leptae	Drachmae 501.358	Drachmae 495.902
Greenland	Currency is that of Denmark	Kroner 11.0523	Kroner 11.2892
Grenada	East Caribbean dollar (EC$) of 100 cents	EC$ 4.5177	EC$ 4.2871
Guadeloupe	Currency is that of France	Francs 9.7314	Francs 9.9625
Guam	Currency is that of USA	US$ 1.6732	US$ 1.5878
Guatemala	Quetzal (Q) of 100 centavos	Q 10.9173	Q 12.4287
Guinea	Guinea franc of 100 centimes	Francs 2079.79	Francs 2166.96
Guinea-Bissau	Franc CFA	Francs 973.140	Francs 996.250
Guyana	Guyana dollar (G$) of 100 cents	G$ 271.561	G$ 274.690
Haiti	Gourde of 100 centimes	Gourdes 27.5488	Gourdes 26.2257
Honduras	Lempira of 100 centavos	Lempiras 22.7555	Lempiras 22.8485
Hungary	Forint of 100 fillér	Forints 372.505	Forints 384.184
Iceland	Icelandic króna (Kr) of 100 aurar	Kr 118.496	Kr 116.751
India	Indian rupee (Rs) of 100 paisa	Rs 71.2156	Rs 69.0693
Indonesia	Rupiah (Rp) of 100 sen	Rp 18321.6	Rp 12067.3
Iran	Rial	Rials 5019.60	Rials 4763.40
Iraq	Iraqi dinar (ID) of 1,000 fils	ID 0.5202	ID 0.4933
Republic of Ireland	Punt (IR£) of 100 pence	IR£ 1.1582	IR£ 1.1962
Israel	Shekel of 100 agora	Shekels 6.4222	Shekels 6.7438
Italy	Lira of 100 centesimi	Lire 2866.48	Lire 2940.75
Jamaica	Jamaican dollar (J$) of 100 cents	J$ 59.9006	J$ 62.7975
Japan	Yen	Yen 224.769	Yen 177.357
Jordan	Jordanian dinar (JD) of 1,000 fils	JD 1.1913	JD 1.1297
Kazakhstan	Tenge	Tenge 132.518	Tenge 209.669
Kenya	Kenya shilling (Ksh) of 100 cents	Ksh 99.8064	Ksh 119.284
Kiribati	Australian dollar ($A) of 100 cents	$A 2.8507	$A 2.5102
Democratic People's Republic of Korea	Won of 100 chon	Won 3.6811	Won 3.4932
Republic of Korea	Won	Won 2247.11	Won 1877.57
Kuwait	Kuwaiti dinar (KD) of 1,000 fils	KD 0.5094	KD 0.4845
Kyrgyzstan	Som	—	—
Laos	Kip (K) of 100 at	K 4353.67	K 12146.7
Latvia	Lats of 100 santims	Lats 0.9952	Lats 0.9423
Lebanon	Lebanese pound (L£) of 100 piastres	L£ 2539.08	L£ 2394.41
Lesotho	Loti (M) of 100 lisente	M 10.4153	M 9.6697
Liberia	Liberian dollar (L$) of 100 cents	L$ 1.6732	L$ 1.5878
Libya	Libyan dinar (LD) of 1,000 dirhams	LD 0.6454	LD 0.7145
Liechtenstein	Swiss franc of 100 rappen (or centimes)	Francs 2.3816	Francs 2.4322
Lithuania	Litas	Litas 6.6946	Litas 6.3536
Luxembourg	Luxembourg franc (LF) of 100 centimes (Belgian currency is also legal tender)	LF 59.8839	LF 61.2671
Macao	Pataca of 100 avos	Pataca 13.3943	Pataca 12.7353
Macedonia	Dinar of 100 paras	Dinars 90.8466	Dinars 93.1193
Madagascar	Franc malgache (FMG) of 100 centimes	FMG 9035.28	FMG 10420.7

Country/Territory	Monetary Unit	Average Rate to £ 4 September 1998	Average Rate to £ 31 August 1999
Malawi	Kwacha (K) of 100 tambala	K 69.6029	K 69.1568
Malaysia	Malaysian dollar (ringgit) (M$) of 100 sen	M$ 6.3582	M$ 6.7005
Maldives	Rufiyaa of 100 laaris	Rufiyaa 19.6936	Rufiyaa 17.9263
Mali	Franc CFA	Francs 973.140	Francs 966.250
Malta	Maltese lira (LM) of 100 cents or 1,000 mils	LM 0.6432	LM 0.6442
Marshall Islands	Currency is that of the USA	US$ 1.6732	US$ 1.5878
Martinique	Currency is that of France	Francs 9.7314	Francs 9.9625
Mauritania	Ouguiya (UM) of 5 khoums	UM 338.932	UM 334.781
Mauritius	Mauritius rupee of 100 cents	Rs 40.7843	Rs 40.0682
Mayotte	Currency is that of France	Francs 9.7314	Francs 9.9625
Mexico	Peso of 100 centavos	Pesos 16.9704	Pesos 14.8952
Federated States of Micronesia	Currency is that of the USA	US$ 1.6732	US$ 1.5878
Moldova	Leu	Leu 8.0565	Leu 17.5174
Monaco	French franc of 100 centimes	Francs 9.7314	Francs 9.9625
Mongolia	Tugrik of 100 möngö	Tugriks 1368.03	Tugriks 1653.28
Montserrat	East Caribbean dollar (EC$) of 100 cents	EC$ 4.5177	EC$ 4.2871
Morocco	Dirham (DH) of 100 centimes	DH 15.8718	DH 15.7153
Mozambique	Metical (MT) of 100 centavos	MT 19233.4	MT 20166.7
Myanmar	Kyat (K) of 100 pyas	K 10.4604	K 9.9265
Namibia	Namibian dollar of 100 cents	*at parity with SA Rand*	
Nauru	Australian dollar ($A) of 100 cents	$A 2.8507	$A 2.5102
Nepal	Nepalese rupee of 100 paisa	Rs 114.330	Rs 109.130
The Netherlands	Gulden (guilder) or florin of 100 cents	Guilders 3.2753	Guilders 3.3470
Netherlands Antilles	Netherlands Antilles guilder of 100 cents	Guilders 2.9950	Guilders 2.8104
New Caledonia	Franc CFP	Francs 176.887	Francs 181.171
New Zealand	New Zealand dollar (NZ$) of 100 cents	NZ$ 3.3058	NZ$ 3.0924
Cook Islands	Currency is that of New Zealand	NZ$ 3.3058	NZ$ 3.0924
Niue	Currency is that of New Zealand	NZ$ 3.3058	NZ$ 3.0924
Tokelau	Currency is that of New Zealand	NZ$ 3.3058	NZ$ 3.0924
Nicaragua	Córdoba (C$) of 100 centavos	C$ 17.9869	C$ 19.0700
Niger	Franc CFA	Francs 973.140	Francs 966.250
Nigeria	Naira (N) of 100 kobo	N 36.6197	N 156.414
Northern Mariana Islands	Currency is that of USA	US$ 1.6732	US$ 1.5878
Norway	Krone of 100 øre	Kroner 12.8929	Kroner 12.6111
Oman	Rial Omani (OR) of 1,000 baisas	OR 0.6442	OR 0.6113
Pakistan	Pakistan rupee of 100 paisa	Rs 83.5680	Rs 82.2878
Palau	Currency is that of the USA	US$ 1.6732	US$ 1.5878
Panama	Balboa of 100 centésimos (US notes are also in circulation)	Balboa 1.6732	Balboa 1.5878
Papua New Guinea	Kina (K) of 100 toea	K 3.9376	K 4.6362
Paraguay	Guaraní (Gs) of 100 céntimos	Gs 4718.43	Gs 5255.62
Peru	New Sol of 100 cénts	New Sol 5.0966	New Sol 5.3509
The Philippines	Philippine peso (P) of 100 centavos	P 76.1189	P 63.1151
Pitcairn Islands	Currency is that of New Zealand	NZ$ 3.3058	NZ$ 3.0924
Poland	Złoty of 100 groszy	Złotys 6.1658	Złotys 6.3266
Portugal	Escudo (Esc) of 100 centavos	Esc 297.403	Esc 304.487
Puerto Rico	Currency is that of USA	US$ 1.6732	US$ 1.5878
Qatar	Qatar riyal of 100 dirhams	Riyals 6.0913	Riyals 5.7804
Réunion	Currency is that of France	Francs 9.7314	Francs 9.9625
Romania	Leu (Lei) of 100 bani	Lei 15038.7	Lei 25714.4
Russia	New rouble of 100 kopeks	Roubles 33.0877	Roubles 39.3933
Rwanda	Rwanda franc of 100 centimes	Francs 522.708	Francs 537.931
St Christopher and Nevis	East Caribbean dollar (EC$) of 100 cents	EC$ 4.5177	EC$ 4.2871
St Helena	St Helena pound (£) of 100 pence	*at parity with £ sterling*	
St Lucia	East Caribbean dollar (EC$) of 100 cents	EC$ 4.5177	EC$ 4.2871
St Pierre and Miquelon	Currency is that of France	Francs 9.7314	Francs 9.9625
St Vincent and the Grenadines	East Caribbean dollar (EC$) of 100 cents	EC$ 4.5177	EC$ 4.2871
El Salvador	El Salvador colón (₡) of 100 centavos	₡ 14.6489	₡ 13.8155
San Marino	San Marino and Italian currencies are in circulation	Lire 2866.48	Lire 2940.75
São Tomé and Príncipe	Dobra of 100 centavos	Dobra 3998.95	Dobra 3794.84
Saudi Arabia	Saudi riyal (SR) of 20 qursh or 100 halala	SR 6.2754	SR 5.9551
Senegal	Franc CFA	Francs 973.140	Francs 996.250

Country/Territory	Monetary Unit	Average Rate to £ 4 September 1998	Average Rate to £ 31 August 1999
Seychelles	Seychelles rupee of 100 cents	Rs 8.7007	Rs 8.4749
Sierra Leone	Leone (Le) of 100 cents	Le 2526.53	Le 2817.08
Singapore	Singapore dollar (S$) of 100 cents	S$ 2.9253	S$ 2.6802
Slovakia	Koruna (Sk) of 100 halierov	Kčs 58.8113	Kčs 67.1847
Slovenia	Tolar (SIT) of 100 stotin	Tolars 273.541	Tolars 298.428
Solomon Islands	Solomon Islands dollar (SI$) of 100 cents	SI$ 8.0261	SI$ 7.8226
Somalia	Somali shilling of 100 cents	Shillings 4383.79	Shillings 4160.04
South Africa	Rand (R) of 100 cents	R 10.4153	R 9.6697
Spain	Peseta of 100 céntimos	Pesetas 246.396	Pesetas 252.702
Sri Lanka	Sri Lankan rupee of 100 cents	Rs 110.808	Rs 114.115
Sudan	Sudanese dinar (SD) of 10 pounds	SD 305.526	SD 403.301
Suriname	Suriname guilder of 100 cents	Guilders 670.953	Guilders 1098.01
Swaziland	Lilangeni (E) of 100 cents (South African currency is also in circulation)	E 10.4153	E 9.6697
Sweden	Swedish krona of 100 öre	Kronor 13.2891	Kronor 13.2296
Switzerland	Swiss franc of 100 rappen (or centimes)	Francs 2.3816	Francs 2.4322
Syria	Syrian pound (S$) of 100 piastres	S£ 66.9280	S£ 71.4510
Taiwan	New Taiwan dollar (NT$) of 100 cents	NT$ 58.0508	NT$ 50.5794
Tajikistan	Tajik rouble (TJR) of 100 tanga	—	—
Tanzania	Tanzanian shilling of 100 cents	Shillings 1102.97	Shillings 1261.51
Thailand	Baht of 100 satang	Baht 68.2415	Baht 60.8049
Togo	Franc CFA	Francs 973.140	Francs 996.250
Tonga	Pa'anga (T$) of 100 seniti	T$ 2.8507	T$ 2.5102
Trinidad and Tobago	Trinidad and Tobago dollar (TT$) of 100 cents	TT$ 10.4441	TT$ 9.7162
Tristan da Cunha	Currency is that of the UK	—	—
Tunisia	Tunisian dinar of 1,000 millimes	Dinars 1.8806	Dinars 1.9094
Turkey	Turkish lira (TL) of 100 kurus	TL 464062.1	TL 710651.8
Turkmenistan	Manat of 100 tenesi		
Turks and Caicos Islands	US dollar (US$)	US$ 1.6732	US$ 1.5878
Tuvalu	Australian dollar ($A) of 100 cents	$A 2.8507	$A 2.5102
Uganda	Uganda shilling of 100 cents	Shillings 2098.19	Shillings 2322.16
Ukraine	Hryvna of 100 kopiykas	Hryvnas 5.1033	Hryvnas 7.0261
United Arab Emirates	UAE dirham (Dh) of 100 fils	Dirham 6.1457	Dirham 5.8316
United Kingdom	Pound sterling (£) of 100 pence	£1.00 £1.00	
United States of America	US dollar (US$) of 100 cents	US$ 1.6732	US$ 1.5878
Uruguay	Uruguayan peso of 100 centésimos	Pesos 17.9702	Pesos 18.5201
Uzbekistan	Sum of 100 tiyin	Sum 481.045	Sum 992.375
Vanuatu	Vatu of 100 centimes	Vatu 221.700	Vatu 207.288
Vatican City State	Italian currency is legal tender	Lire 2866.48	Lire 2940.75
Venezuela	Bolívar (Bs) of 100 céntimos	Bs 976.530	Bs 982.531
Vietnam	Dông of 10 hào or 100 xu	Dông 23270.0	Dông 22168.1
Virgin Islands, British	US dollar (US$) (£ sterling and EC$ also circulate)	US$ 1.6732	US$ 1.5878
Virgin Islands, US	Currency is that of the USA	US$ 1.6732	US$ 1.5878
Wallis and Futuna Islands	Franc CFP	Francs 176.887	Francs 176.887
Samoa	Tala (S$) of 100 sene	S$ 5.1546	S$ 4.8931
Yemen	Riyal of 100 fils	Riyals 219.173	Riyals 235.233
Yugoslavia	New dinar of 100 paras	New Dinars 17.5608	New Dinars 17.8645
Zambia	Kwacha (K) of 100 ngwee	K 3363.15	K 3842.49
Zimbabwe	Zimbabwe dollar (Z$) of 100 cents	Z$ 41.4120	Z$ 60.8129

Time Zones

Standard time differences from the Greenwich meridian

+   hours ahead of GMT
−   hours behind GMT
*   may vary from standard time at some part of the year (Summer Time or Daylight Saving Time)
h   hours
m   minutes

	h m
Afghanistan	+ 4 30
*Albania	+ 1
Algeria	+ 1
*Andorra	+ 1
Angola	+ 1
Anguilla	− 4
Antigua and Barbuda	− 4
Argentina	− 3
*Armenia	+ 4
Aruba	− 4
Ascension Island	0
*Australia	+10
*Broken Hill area (NSW)	+ 9 30
*Lord Howe Island	+10 30
Northern Territory	+ 9 30
*South Australia	+ 9 30
Western Australia	+ 8
*Austria	+ 1
*Azerbaijan	+ 4
*Azores	− 1
*Bahamas	− 5
Bahrain	+ 3
Bangladesh	+ 6
Barbados	− 4
*Belarus	+ 2
*Belgium	+ 1
Belize	− 6
Benin	+ 1
*Bermuda	− 4
Bhutan	+ 6
Bolivia	− 4
*Bosnia-Hercegovina	+ 1
Botswana	+ 2
Brazil	
Acre	− 5
central states	− 4
N. and NE coastal states	− 3
*S. and E. coastal states, including Brasilia	− 3
Fernando de Noronha Island	− 2
western states	− 5
British Antarctic Territory	− 3
British Indian Ocean Territory	+ 5
Diego Garcia	+ 6
British Virgin Islands	− 4
Brunei	+ 8
*Bulgaria	+ 2
Burkina Faso	0
Burundi	+ 2
Cambodia	+ 7
Cameroon	+ 1
Canada	
*Alberta	− 7
*British Columbia	− 8
*Labrador	− 4
*Manitoba	− 6
*New Brunswick	− 4
*Newfoundland	− 3 30
*Northwest Territories	
Nunavut	− 7
east of 85° W.	− 5
85° W.–102° W.	− 6
west of 102° W.	− 7
*Nova Scotia	− 4
*Ontario	
east of 90° W.	− 5
west of 90° W.	− 6
*Prince Edward Island	− 4
Quebec	
east of 63° W.	− 4
*west of 63° W.	− 5
Saskatchewan	− 6
*Yukon	− 8
*Canary Islands	0
Cape Verde	− 1
Cayman Islands	− 5
Central African Republic	+ 1
Chad	+ 1
*Chatham Islands	+12 45
*Chile	− 4
China	+ 8
Christmas Island (Indian Ocean)	+ 7
Cocos (Keeling) Islands	+ 6 30
Colombia	− 5
Comoros	+ 3
Congo (Dem. Rep.)	
east	+ 2
west	+ 1
Congo (Rep. of)	+ 1
Cook Islands	− 10
Costa Rica	− 6
Côte d'Ivoire	0
*Croatia	+ 1
*Cuba	− 5
*Cyprus	+ 2
*Czech Republic	+ 1
*Denmark	+ 1
Djibouti	+ 3
Dominica	− 4
Dominican Republic	− 4
Ecuador	− 5
Galápagos Islands	− 6
*Egypt	+ 2
El Salvador	− 6
Equatorial Guinea	+ 1
Eritrea	+ 3
*Estonia	+ 2
Ethiopia	+ 3
*Falkland Islands	− 4
*Faröe Islands	0
Fiji	+12
*Finland	+ 2
*France	+ 1
French Guiana	− 3
French Polynesia	−10
Marquesas Islands	− 9 30
Gabon	+ 1
The Gambia	0
Georgia	+ 3
*Germany	+ 1
Ghana	0
*Gibraltar	+ 1
*Greece	+ 2
*Greenland	− 3
Danmarkshavn	0
Mesters Vig	0
*Scoresby Sound	− 1
*Thule area	− 4
Grenada	− 4
Guadeloupe	− 4
Guam	+10
Guatemala	− 6
Guinea	0
Guinea-Bissau	0
Guyana	− 4
*Haiti	− 5
Honduras	− 6
*Hungary	+ 1
Iceland	0
India	+ 5 30
Indonesia	
Bali	+ 8
Flores	+ 8
Irian Jaya	+ 9
Java	+ 7
Kalimantan (south and east)	+ 8
Kalimantan (west and central)	+ 7
Molucca Islands	+ 9
Sulawesi	+ 8
Sumatra	+ 7
Sumbawa	+ 8
Tanimbar	+ 9
Timor	+ 8
*Iran	+ 3 30
*Iraq	+ 3
*Ireland, Republic of	0
*Israel	+ 2
*Italy	+ 1
Jamaica	− 5
Japan	+ 9
*Jordan	+ 2
*Kazakhstan	
western (Aktau)	+ 4
central (Atyrau)	+ 5
eastern	+ 6
Kenya	+ 3
Kiribati	+12
Line Islands	+14
Phoenix Islands	+13
Korea, North	+ 9
Korea, South	+ 9
Kuwait	+ 3
*Kyrgyzstan	+ 5
Laos	+ 7
*Latvia	+ 2
*Lebanon	+ 2
Lesotho	+ 2
Liberia	0
*Libya	+ 2
*Liechtenstein	+ 1
Line Islands not part of Kiribati	−10
*Lithuania	+ 1
*Luxembourg	+ 1
Macao	+ 8
*Macedonia (Former Yug. Rep. of)	+ 1
Madagascar	+ 3

	h m		h m
*Madeira	0	St Lucia	− 4
Malawi	+ 2	*St Pierre and Miquelon	− 3
Malaysia	+ 8	St Vincent and the	
Maldives	+ 5	Grenadines	− 4
Mali	0	Samoa	−11
*Malta	+ 1	Samoa, American	−11
Marshall Islands	+12	*San Marino	+ 1
Ebon Atoll	−12	São Tomé and Princípe	0
Martinique	− 4	Saudi Arabia	+ 3
Mauritania	0	Senegal	0
Mauritius	+ 4	Seychelles	+ 4
*Mexico	− 6	Sierra Leone	0
Nayarit, Sinaloa, Sonora,		Singapore	+ 8
S. Baja California	− 7	*Slovakia	+ 1
N. Baja California	− 8	*Slovenia	+ 1
Micronesia		Solomon Islands	+11
Caroline Islands	+10	Somalia	+ 3
Kosrae	+11	South Africa	+ 2
Pingelap	+11	South Georgia	− 2
Pohnpei	+11	*Spain	+ 1
*Moldova	+ 2	Sri Lanka	+ 6
*Monaco	+ 1	Sudan	+ 2
*Mongolia	+ 8	Suriname	− 3
Montserrat	− 4	Swaziland	+ 2
Morocco	0	*Sweden	+ 1
Mozambique	+ 2	*Switzerland	+ 1
Myanmar	+ 6 30	*Syria	+ 2
*Namibia	+ 1	Taiwan	+ 8
Nauru	+12	Tajikistan	+ 5
Nepal	+ 5 45	Tanzania	+ 3
*Netherlands	+ 1	Thailand	+ 7
Netherlands Antilles	− 4	Togo	0
New Caledonia	+11	Tonga	+13
*New Zealand	+12	Trinidad and Tobago	− 4
Nicaragua	− 6	Tristan da Cunha	0
Niger	+ 1	Tunisia	+ 1
Nigeria	+ 1	*Turkey	+ 2
Niue	−11	Turkmenistan	+ 5
Norfolk Island	+11 30	*Turks and Caicos Islands	− 5
Northern Mariana Islands	+10	Tuvalu	+12
*Norway	+ 1	Uganda	+ 3
Oman	+ 4	*Ukraine	+ 2
Pakistan	+ 5	United Arab Emirates	+ 4
Palau	+ 9	*United Kingdom	0
Panama	− 5	*United States of America	
Papua New Guinea	+10	Alaska	− 9
*Paraguay	− 4	Aleutian Islands, east of	
Peru	− 5	169° 30′ W.	− 9
Philippines	+ 8	Aleutian Islands, west	
*Poland	+ 1	of 169° 30′ W.	−10
*Portugal	0	eastern time	− 5
Puerto Rico	− 4	central time	− 6
Qatar	+ 3	Hawaii	−10
Réunion	+ 4	mountain time	− 7
*Romania	+ 2	Pacific time	− 8
*Russia		Uruguay	− 3
Zone 1	+ 2	Uzbekistan	+ 5
Zone 2	+ 3	Vanuatu	+11
Zone 3	+ 4	*Vatican City State	+ 1
Zone 4	+ 5	Venezuela	− 4
Zone 5	+ 6	Vietnam	+ 7
Zone 6	+ 7	Virgin Islands (US)	− 4
Zone 7	+ 8	Yemen	+ 3
Zone 8	+ 9	*Yugoslavia (Fed. Rep. of)	+ 1
Zone 9	+10	Zambia	+ 2
Zone 10	+11	Zimbabwe	+ 2
Zone 11	+12		
Rwanda	+ 2		
St Helena	0		
St Christopher and Nevis	− 4		

Source: reproduced with permission from data produced by HM Nautical Almanac Office

Nobel Prizes

For prize winners for the years 1901–95, *see* earlier editions of *Whitaker's Almanack*.

The Nobel Prizes are awarded each year from the income of a trust fund established by the Swedish scientist Alfred Nobel, the inventor of dynamite, who died on 10 December 1896 leaving a fortune of £1,750,000. The prizes are awarded to those who have contributed most to the common good in the domain of:

Physics – awarded by the Royal Swedish Academy of Sciences
Chemistry – awarded by the Royal Swedish Academy of Sciences
Physiology or Medicine – awarded by the Karolinska Institute
Literature – awarded by the Swedish Academy of Arts
Peace – awarded by a five-person committee elected by the Norwegian Storting
Economic Sciences (instituted 1969) – awarded by the Royal Swedish Academy of Sciences

The prizes are awarded every year on 10 December, the anniversary of Nobel's death. The first awards were made on 10 December 1901.

The Trust is administered by the board of directors of the Nobel Foundation, Stockholm, consisting of five members and three deputy members. The Swedish Government appoints a chairman and a deputy chairman, the remaining members being appointed by the awarding authorities.

The awards have been distributed as follows:

PHYSICS
American 68, British 20, German 19 (1948–90, West German 8), French 12, Soviet 7, Dutch 6, Swedish 4, Austrian 3, Danish 3, Italian 3, Japanese 3, Canadian 2, Chinese 2, Swiss 2, Indian 1, Irish 1, Pakistani 1

CHEMISTRY
American 43, German 27 (1948–90, West German 10), British 26, French 7, Swiss 5, Swedish 4, Canadian 3, Dutch 3, Argentinian 1, Austrian 1, Belgian 1, Czech 1, Finnish 1, Hungarian 1, Italian 1, Japanese 1, Mexican 1, Norwegian 1, Soviet 1

PHYSIOLOGY OR MEDICINE
American 78, British 23, German 15 (1948–90, West German 4), French 7, Swedish 7, Swiss 6, Danish 5, Austrian 4, Belgian 4, Australian 3, Italian 3, Canadian 2, Dutch 2, Hungarian 2, Russian 2, Argentinian 1, Japanese 1, Portuguese 1, South African 1, Spanish 1

LITERATURE
French 12, American 10, British 8, Swedish 7, German 6 (1948–90, West German 1), Italian 6, Spanish 5, Danish 3, Irish 3, Norwegian 3, Polish 3, Soviet 3, Chilean 2, Greek 2, Japanese 2, Swiss 2, Australian 1, Belgian 1, Colombian 1, Czech 1, Egyptian 1, Finnish 1, Guatemalan 1, Icelandic 1, Indian 1, Israeli 1, Mexican 1, Nigerian 1, Portuguese 1, South African 1, Trinidadian 1, Yugoslav 1, Stateless 1

PEACE
American 18, Institutions 18, British 11, French 9, Swedish 5, German 4 (1948–90, West German 1), South African 4, Belgian 3, Israeli 3, Swiss 3, Argentinian 2, Austrian 2, East Timorese 2, Irish 2, Norwegian 2, Soviet 2, Burmese 1, Canadian 1, Costa Rican 1, Danish 1, Dutch 1, Egyptian 1, Guatemalan 1, Italian 1, Japanese 1, Mexican 1, Palestinian 1, Polish 1, Tibetan 1, Vietnamese 1, Yugoslav 1

ECONOMICS
American 26, British 7, Norwegian 2, Swedish 2, Canadian 1, Dutch 1, French 1, German 1, Indian 1, Soviet 1

The Swedish Embassy can provide a full list of winners.

Prize	1996	1997	1998
Physics	Prof. D. Lee (American) Prof. D. Osheroff (American) Prof. R. Richardson (American)	Prof. S. Chu (American) Prof. C. Cohen-Tannoudji (French) Dr W. Phillips (American)	Prof. R. Laughlin (American) H. Störmer (American) Prof. D. Tsui (American)
Chemistry	Prof. R. Curl (American) Sir Harold Kroto, Kt., FRS (British) Prof. R. Smalley (American)	Dr J. Walker (British)	Prof. W. Kohn (American) Prof. J. Pople (British)
Physiology or Medicine	Prof. P. Doherty (Australian) Prof. R. Zinkernagel (Swiss)	Prof. S. Prusiner (American)	Prof. R. Furchgott (American) Prof. L. Ignarro (American) Prof. F. Murad (American)
Literature	W. Szymborska (Polish)	Dario Fo (Italian)	José Saramago (Portuguese)
Peace	Bishop Carlos Belo (East Timorese) J. Ramos-Horta (East Timorese)	The International Campaign to Ban Land-mines and the campaign co-ordinator, Jody Williams (American)	John Hume (Irish) David Trimble (British)
Economics	Prof. J. Mirrlees (British) Prof. W. Vickrey (Canadian)	Prof. M. Scholes (American) Prof. R. Merton (American)	Prof. A. Sen (Indian)

Events of the Year

1 September 1998 to 31 August 1999

SEPTEMBER 1998

2. Parliament was recalled from its summer recess (see Northern Ireland Affairs, below). 8. Sir David Rowland was appointed chairman of NatWest Group from April 1999. 9. The Labour MP for Renfrewshire West, Tommy Graham, was expelled from the Labour Party for misconduct and bringing the party into disrepute. 14. The TUC annual congress opened in Blackpool. 17. The Queen and the Duke of Edinburgh arrived in Brunei for a three-day state visit; on 20 September they arrived in Malaysia for a four-day state visit, during which The Queen closed the Commonwealth Games in Kuala Lumpur. 20. Camilla Carr and Jon James, British aid workers who were kidnapped by rebels in Chechenia in July 1997, were released from captivity. 21. The Liberal Democrat annual conference opened in Brighton. 24. Diplomatic relations between the UK and Iran were upgraded after the Iranian government said that it would not encourage or assist the murder of Salman Rushdie, the writer against whom Ayatollah Khomeini issued a *fatwa* in 1989 over his novel, *The Satanic Verses*. 27. The Labour Party conference opened in Blackpool.

OCTOBER 1998

1. The British embassy in Belgrade ordered Britons in Yugoslavia to leave the country because of the threat of UN air strikes over the massacre of Albanians in Kosovo. 4. Three Britons working in Chechenia were kidnapped. 5. The Prime Minister arrived in China for a five-day official visit. The Conservative Party conference opened in Bournemouth. The results of a ballot on party policy were announced: 58.9 per cent of members had voted, of which 84.4 per cent supported the policy of not joining a single European currency in the lifetime of this Parliament or the next. 13. The Committee on Standards in Public Life published a report which proposed reforms to the funding of political parties, a limit of £20 million on the amount a party can spend on a general election campaign, and new rules on the conduct of referendums. Phil Walker resigned as Editor of the *Daily Star* and was replaced by Peter Hill. 14. The Government announced that a Royal Commission would be set up on the second stage of reforming the House of Lords. 19. President Havel of the Czech Republic arrived in Britain at the start of a four-day official visit. 23–25. At least 12 people died as heavy rain caused severe flooding in Wales and western England. 27. Ron Davies resigned as Secretary of State for Wales over a 'serious lapse of judgment' after being robbed at knifepoint on 26 October by a stranger he had met on Clapham Common, London; he was replaced by Alun Michael. On 29 October Mr Davies resigned as the Labour Party's prospective candidate for First Minister of the National Assembly for Wales, although he denied that he had done anything improper or illegal. On 20 November the Crown Prosecution Service said that there was insufficient evidence to proceed with charges against a man suspected of having committed the robbery. President Menem of Argentina arrived in Britain at the start of a six-day official visit, the first by an Argentine president since the Falklands Conflict. 28–31. Severe flooding hit the Severn Valley, the Welsh border country and south-west England. 29. The Independent Commission on the Voting System set up by the Government and headed by Lord Jenkins of Hillhead published its report; it proposed a new system of electing members of the House of Commons which would combine an alternative vote system with a list system of proportional representation.

NOVEMBER 1998

2. The Prince of Wales arrived in Ljubljana at the start of an eight-day visit to Slovenia and the Balkans. 6. The Prince of Wales issued a statement strongly denying reports in a television documentary that he wished his mother to abdicate. 7. Following revelations in the tabloid press by a former lover, the Agriculture Minister, Nick Brown, acknowledged that he was gay. 11. The Queen took part in ceremonies in France and Belgium to mark the 80th anniversary of the end of the First World War, and joined with President Chirac to unveil a statue of Winston Churchill in central Paris. 14. The Prime Minister joined President Clinton in calling off imminent air strikes on Iraq because of a promise from the Iraqi president, Saddam Hussein, that he would co-operate with UN weapons inspectors. The Prince of Wales celebrated his 50th birthday. 16. The Agriculture Minister announced a £120 million aid package for farmers to cushion the effects of a collapse in the price of almost all agricultural produce. 18. The House of Lords defeated the Government's European Parliamentary Elections Bill, under which a 'closed list' system of proportional representation would be introduced for the 1999 elections to the European Parliament, for the fifth time; the Government announced that the legislation would be re-introduced in the new

parliamentary session under the Parliament Acts. 22. The Prince of Wales arrived in Greece for a two-day official visit. 23. EU agriculture ministers voted, subject to certain conditions, to lift the global ban on exports of British beef. 24. The state opening of parliament took place. 26. Tony Blair addressed both Houses of the Irish Parliament, the first British prime minister to do so. The North-East Scotland European Parliament by-election took place (*see* page 271).

DECEMBER 1998

1. The president of Germany, Roman Herzog, arrived in Britain for a four-day state visit. 2. The Leader of the Opposition (William Hague) sacked the Conservative leader in the House of Lords, Viscount Cranborne, for unilaterally reaching an agreement with the Government over an interim compromise arrangement for reform of the House of Lords, under which 91 hereditary peers would temporarily retain voting rights in the Upper House. Viscount Cranborne was replaced by the Earl of Strathclyde. On 3 December four Conservative peers (Lord Fraser of Carmyllie, Lord Bowness, Lord Pilkington and the Earl of Home) resigned as front-benchers in protest at the sacking of Lord Cranborne, and Baroness Strange and Baroness Flather resigned the Conservative whip. 8. Four hostages, including three Britons, who had been kidnapped in Chechenia on 3 October, were found beheaded after a failed rescue mission by Chechen special forces. 15. The House of Lords rejected the Government's European Parliamentary Elections Bill for the sixth time; it subsequently received royal assent under the Parliament Acts. The Government published a Green Paper outlining plans to abolish the State Earnings-Related Pension and encourage middle-income earners to take out personal pensions. 16. Cruise missiles were launched by US forces at military and security installations in Iraq in a joint US/British operation code-named Operation Desert Fox. The Labour MP Brian Sedgemore said in the House of Commons that the editor of the *Sunday Telegraph*, Dominic Lawson, had been named as an MI6 agent; Mr Lawson said that he was not an agent of MI6 or any other government agency. 17. An emergency debate on the crisis in Iraq was held in the House of Commons; RAF Tornado bombers later joined in the airstrikes on the country. 19. The Prime Minister said that Operation Desert Fox was over and that serious damage had been caused to Iraq's military capabilities. 21. The Trade and Industry Secretary (Peter Mandelson) admitted that he had borrowed £373,000 from the Paymaster-General (Geoffrey Robinson) in 1996 in order to buy a house; he denied that there was any conflict of interest since he had removed himself from involvement in the ongoing DTI investigation into Mr Robinson's financial affairs. On 23 December Peter Mandelson and Geoffrey Robinson both resigned from the Government and Stephen Byers was appointed

Trade and Industry Secretary. On 4 January 1999 Charlie Whelan, the Chancellor of the Exchequer's press secretary, resigned after denying persistent allegations that he had leaked information about Mr Mandelson's loan, and Dawn Primarolo was appointed Paymaster-General. 25. Richard Branson was forced to abandon his attempt to fly around the world in a balloon after 12,000 miles when the balloon hit a trough of low pressure over the Pacific. 28. Twelve Britons were among 16 tourists kidnapped by tribesmen in southern Yemen; on 29 December four of the hostages, including three Britons, were killed when government troops stormed the kidnappers' hideout.

JANUARY 1999

6. The Prince Edward announced his engagement to Sophie Rhys-Jones. The Prime Minister arrived in South Africa at the start of a three-day official visit. On 8 January in Cape Town police opened fire on armed Muslim demonstrators protesting against Britain's involvement in airstrikes against Iraq; four people were wounded. 9. A Briton was kidnapped in Yemen; he was released unharmed on 13 January. 16. A couple who had left their home in Ramsey, Cambs, with their two foster children in September 1998 because they had been told they would be unable to adopt the children returned home after Cambridgeshire social services agreed to put the matter in the hands of the courts. 17. Two British aid workers were among six people kidnapped in Yemen. They were released unharmed on 2 February. 20. The Government published a White Paper on reforming the House of Lords and a Bill to remove the right of hereditary peers to sit and vote in the House of Lords. Paddy Ashdown announced that he would resign as leader of the Liberal Democrats after the elections to the European Parliament in June 1999. 26. David Montgomery resigned as chief executive of the Mirror Group. 31. Six RAF Tornado bombers were involved in an attack on an air defence site south of Baghdad after an Iraqi fighter breached a no-fly zone. Tom Spencer, a Conservative MEP who had been caught carrying drugs and homosexual pornography at Heathrow airport on 17 January, said that he would not stand in the European elections in June 1999.

FEBRUARY 1999

8. The Prince of Wales and the Prime Minister attended the state funeral of King Hussein of Jordan in Amman. 9. The foreign affairs select committee of the House of Commons published a report highly critical of the role of Foreign Office officials in the 'arms to Sierra Leone' affair. 16. Hundreds of Kurds demonstrated outside the Greek Embassy in London after the rebel leader Abdullah Öcalan was arrested outside the Greek Embassy in Nairobi; a 15-year-old girl was taken to hospital after setting fire to herself. The protest ended on 18 February when 77 demonstrators who had occupied the embassy

surrendered to police. **20.** The Welsh Secretary Alun Michael was narrowly elected as Labour leader in Wales. **23.** The Prime Minister announced a 'national changeover plan' paving the way for the adoption of the euro in the UK.

MARCH 1999

1. Fourteen tourists, including five Britons, were kidnapped by Hutu rebels in the Bwindi Impenetrable National Park, Uganda; on 2 March eight of the tourists including four Britons were murdered. The Royal Commission on the Long-Term Care of the Elderly published its report, which recommended that the state should cover the costs of nursing and personal care for all elderly people who need it, and only those with assets above £60,000 should pay for the full costs of accommodation and food in residential and nursing homes. The Health Secretary (Frank Dobson) said that the recommendations would be put out to consultation until the end of 1999. **4.** An earthquake registering 4.0 on the Richter scale hit Arran, western Scotland. **7.** Four Britons were arrested in Kinshasa, Democratic Republic of Congo, and accused of espionage; on 10 March the Third Secretary at the British Embassy was also accused of spying and was expelled from the country. **8.** The Government announced plans to introduce a statutory 'right to roam' over millions of acres of private land in England and Wales. **9.** The Chancellor of the Exchequer (Gordon Brown) presented the Budget to the House of Commons (*see* page 275). The Prince of Wales arrived in Argentina at the start of a three-day official visit; he then visited Uruguay for two days before flying to the Falklands for a two-day visit. Heavy rain and melting snow caused the River Derwent to burst its banks, resulting in severe flooding in Malton and Norton, N. Yorks. **15.** Sir Leon Brittan and Neil Kinnock resigned as the UK's European Commissioners after the publication of a report detailing a culture of corruption and nepotism at the executive in Brussels; the other 18 Commissioners also resigned. **23.** The Prime Minister said that there was no alternative to military action by NATO forces against the Serbs in Kosovo. From 24 March British forces took part in bomb and missile attacks on Serb targets. **30.** Britain and other NATO leaders rejected an offer by President Milosević of Yugoslavia to start withdrawing troops from Kosovo and begin peace talks if NATO air strikes ceased.

APRIL 1999

6. An offer of an immediate cease-fire by President Milošević was rejected by NATO leaders. **10.** The Government announced that the aircraft carrier *Invincible* was to be deployed off the coast of Yugoslavia. **13.** The Prime Minister said in the House of Commons that a further 2,000 British troops, with tanks and artillery, would be sent to Macedonia to be part of an international force for eventual deployment in Kosovo; this brought the total number of British troops in Macedonia to

6,300. The House of Lords voted by a majority of 76 against giving a second reading to the Sexual Offences (Amendment) Bill, under which the gay age of consent would be reduced to 16; the Government said that it would reintroduce the Bill in the next session of Parliament and if necessary use the Parliament Acts to force the legislation through. **17.** About 50 people were injured when a nail bomb exploded in Brixton, London. **19.** The Queen and the Duke of Edinburgh arrived in Seoul, Republic of Korea, at the start of a four-day state visit. **22.** The Prime Minister held talks with President Clinton in Washington DC and said that NATO ground troops would be used in Yugoslavia if President Milošević did not accede to NATO's demands concerning Kosovo. **24.** Six people were injured when a nail bomb exploded in Brick Lane, London. **25.** The first refugees from the Balkan conflict to arrive in Britain landed at Leeds-Bradford airport. **27.** Michael Simmonds left his post as the Conservative Party's director of membership after details of a speech by the party's deputy leader, Peter Lilley, were leaked to the press; controversy continued within the party over whether the speech constituted a change of policy over the involvement of the market in the provision of public services. **30.** Three people were killed and 73 injured when a nail bomb exploded in a gay pub in Soho, London. On 2 May a man was charged with murder and causing explosions in relation to the bombs in Brixton, Brick Lane and Soho.

MAY 1999

3. The Prime Minister visited the border region between Kosovo and Macedonia. An American expedition on Mount Everest found the body of the British mountaineer George Mallory, who disappeared in 1924 less than 900 ft from the summit. **6.** Elections were held to the Scottish Parliament and the National Assembly for Wales; local elections were also held in Scotland, Wales and most parts of England except London. In Scotland the turnout was 59 per cent; Labour became the largest single party, with 56 seats, but failed to win an overall majority in the Parliament. In Wales the turnout was 46 per cent; Labour became the largest single party, with 28 seats, but failed to win an overall majority in the Assembly. In the local elections in England the turnout was 30 per cent; Labour won 36 per cent of the vote, the Conservatives 33 per cent and the Liberal Democrats 27 per cent. For full election results, *see* Local Government section. **8–9.** Demonstrators threw petrol bombs and bricks at the British embassy in Beijing in protest at the accidental bombing of the Chinese embassy in Belgrade by NATO planes on 7 May. **10.** Britain joined the USA and Germany in rejecting an offer by President Milošević to withdraw some of his forces from Kosovo. **11.** The House of Lords voted by 352 votes to 32 in favour of an amendment to the House of Lords Bill under which 92 hereditary peers would be allowed to remain in the House until the second stage of its reform. **12.** The Scottish Parliament sat for the first time; the Rt. Hon. Sir David Steel was elected Presiding Officer. The National Assembly for Wales met for the first time; Alun Michael was elected First Minister and named the eight other members of the Executive, and Lord Elis-Thomas was elected Presiding Officer. A list of serving MI6 agents was published illegally on the Internet. Chris Patten was appointed as one of Britain's two European Commissioners from September 1999. **13.** In the Scottish Parliament, Donald Dewar was elected First Minister; Labour and the Liberal Democrats agreed terms to form a coalition in the Parliament and the Liberal Democrat MSP Jim Wallace was named Deputy First Minister. **17.** Dr John Reid was appointed Scottish Secretary in place of Donald Dewar; Helen Liddell replaced Dr Reid as Transport Minister. Donald Dewar announced the members of the Scottish Executive. **20.** In the House of Commons 67 Labour MPs voted in favour of an amendment to the Welfare Reform and Pensions Bill aimed at blocking the Government's plans to means-test and restrict access to Incapacity Benefit. **25.** Cardinal Basil Hume was appointed by The Queen to the Order of Merit. **26.** The National Assembly for Wales was formally inaugurated by The Queen in Cardiff. **29.** The Prince of Wales represented The Queen at the inauguration of the first democratically elected president of Nigeria; the country also rejoined the Commonwealth.

JUNE 1999

9. Lt.-Gen. Sir Michael Jackson, in his role as NATO's commander in Kosovo, announced that the peace deal setting out terms for a Serb withdrawal from the area had been signed by Serb generals. On 12 June British troops entered Kosovo as part of the NATO-led peacekeeping operation. **10.** Elections were held to the European Parliament under the regional list system of proportional representation. The turnout was 23 per cent, with the Conservatives winning 36 seats, Labour 29, the Liberal Democrats 10, the UK Independence Party three, and the SNP, Plaid Cymru and the Green Party two each. For full results, *see* pages 269–271. The Leeds Central by-election was held; it was won by Labour with a reduced majority on a turnout of 19.6 per cent, the lowest in any post-war parliamentary election. **15.** William Hague reshuffled the Shadow Cabinet. John Prescott announced plans for Railtrack to control some London Underground lines. **16.** The Government published a series of hospital and health authority performance tables. **17.** The Public Health Minister (Tessa Jowell) said that tobacco advertising would be banned in the UK from December 1999. **18.** About 50 people were injured and 15 arrests were made during an anti-capitalist demonstration in the City of London. Thirty-six new life peers were created. **19.** The Queen conferred the earldom of Wessex and the viscountcy of Severn on the Prince Edward and said that he would be given the dukedom of Edinburgh

after the death of his parents. The Earl married Sophie Rhys-Jones at St George's Chapel, Windsor. **22.** President Göncz of Hungary began a four-day state visit to Britain. **25.** The funeral of Cardinal Basil Hume, the Archbishop of Westminster who died on 17 June, was held at Westminster Cathedral. **27.** The veteran Labour MP Tony Benn said that he would not stand for parliament at the next general election. **29.** The Home Secretary apologized for problems at the Passport Agency that were resulting in long delays in issuing passports. **30.** Janet Street-Porter was appointed editor of the Independent on Sunday.

JULY 1999

1. The Scottish Parliament was opened by The Queen. **7.** Britain resumed full diplomatic relations with Libya after the Libyan regime accepted responsibility for the murder of WPC Yvonne Fletcher outside the Libyan Embassy in London in 1984. **8.** The Government published proposals to reform the Post Office, including its conversion into a public limited company. **14.** The European Commission said that the ban on the export of British beef would be lifted on 1 August, but with severe restrictions still in force. **22.** The Conservatives won the Eddisbury by-election (*see* page 233). **28.** Paul Murphy was appointed Welsh Secretary in succession to Alun Michael, the First Secretary of the National Assembly for Wales; the Prime Minister also reshuffled a range of junior ministerial posts. **31.** The Prime Minister visited Priština, Kosovo.

AUGUST 1999

1. The European Union lifted its ban on the export of British beef; on 3 August the German health minister said that the ban would remain in place in Germany **4.** The Defence Secretary, George Robertson, was appointed secretary-general of NATO. Seven British soldiers acting as UN observers were taken hostage with 40 other people by rebels near Freetown, Sierra Leone; two of the soldiers were released in order to carry the rebel's demands to the Sierra Leonean government and the UN. On 8 August two more soldiers and 11 other hostages were released. On 9 August the remaining three soldiers were released. Queen Elizabeth the Queen Mother celebrated her 99th birthday. **9.** Charles Kennedy was elected leader of the Liberal Democrats. **11.** A total eclipse of the sun occurred at 11.11 a.m. over south-west England. Four British aid workers were abducted in Liberia; they were released on 13 August. **26.** John Stevens was appointed Commissioner of the Metropolitan Police from January 2000.

NORTHERN IRELAND AFFAIRS

1. The Sinn Fein president, Gerry Adams, said that for his party violence was 'a thing of the past'. 2. The British and Irish parliaments were recalled to debate anti-terrorist measures drawn up after the bombing at Omagh on 15 August. Sinn Fein agreed to appoint a delegate to the international body set up to oversee decommissioning of terrorist weapons. Two Scots Guardsmen who had been sentenced to life imprisonment for the murder of a teenager in Belfast in 1992 were released from prison. 3. President Clinton visited Northern Ireland. 5. A man who had been injured in the Omagh bombing on 15 August died, bringing the number of people killed to 29. 8. The Real IRA declared a permanent cease-fire. 11. The first seven prisoners to be released under the terms of the Belfast Agreement were freed from the Maze prison, Lisburn, and Magilligan prison, Londonderry. 12. Army patrols in Belfast ceased. 14. The New Northern Ireland Assembly met for the first time at Stormont.

OCTOBER 1998

6. A policeman who had been injured on 5 September in a bomb explosion during loyalist rioting in Portadown, Co. Armagh, died. 16. John Hume and David Trimble were awarded the Nobel peace prize. 20. Three INLA members were sentenced in Downpatrick to life imprisonment for the murder of Billy Wright, the leader of the LVF, at the Maze prison in December 1997. 31. A Roman Catholic man was shot dead by the dissident loyalist group the Red Hand Defenders.

NOVEMBER 1998

10. The Chief Inspector of Prisons (Sir David Ramsbotham) published a report highly critical of the regime at the Maze prison; the Government said that the prison would be closed by late 2000. 12. The Government formally recognized the cease-fire declared by the LVF in May 1998. 14. The Leader of the Opposition called for a halt to the release of terrorist prisoners until arms decommissioning had started.

DECEMBER 1998

18. Unionist and nationalist leaders reached agreement on new executive and cross-border bodies. The LVF surrendered some weapons to the Independent International Commission on Decommissioning.

JANUARY 1999

25. The Northern Ireland Secretary (Mo Mowlam) called for an end to punishment attacks by paramilitaries. 27. Eamon Collins, a former IRA terrorist turned informer, was found murdered in South Armagh.

FEBRUARY 1999

16. The New Northern Ireland Assembly voted for a 12-member executive on which Sinn Fein would be entitled to two seats, and ratified plans for a North-South ministerial council, six cross-border bodies, a civic forum and a British-Irish council.

MARCH 1999

8. In the face of continuing deadlock between the UUP and Sinn Fein over the issue of decommissioning weapons, the Government extended the deadline for the establishment of an executive from 10 March to 2 April. 11. The paratrooper Lee Clegg, who served four years in prison for the murder of a joyrider in Belfast in 1990 and who had his conviction quashed in the House of Lords in 1998, was acquitted of the murder at a retrial at Belfast Crown Court. 15. A leading nationalist lawyer, Rosemary Nelson, was killed by a bomb planted under her car in Lurgan, Co. Armagh. 17. A prominent loyalist, Frankie Curry, was shot dead in the Shankill Road area of Belfast. 22. The Home Secretary (Jack Straw) successfully sought a judicial review of the timing of the release from the Maze prison of four IRA prisoners under the terms of the Belfast Agreement; on 23 March the High Court in Belfast upheld the timing of their release. **30 March–1 April.** The British and Irish Prime Ministers and Northern Ireland's political leaders held talks at Hillsborough Castle aimed at breaking the deadlock over the issue of decommissioning weapons. On 1 April the talks were suspended until 13 April after the two Prime Ministers had put forward a detailed plan for decommissioning. The plan was formally rejected by Sinn Fein when the talks resumed.

MAY 1999

12. Loyalist gunmen shot and wounded a Roman Catholic man in Carrickfergus, Co. Antrim. 14. The Prime Minister held talks at Downing Street with Northern Ireland's political leaders aimed at breaking the deadlock over the implementation of the Belfast Agreement. On 16 May the British and Irish prime ministers set a final deadline of 30 June for devolution of powers to the New Northern Ireland Assembly. 28. The IRA left the body of Eamon Molloy, an IRA member shot dead by the IRA in 1975, in a graveyard in Faughart, Co. Louth; his was the first of nine bodies that the IRA had agreed to return to their families. On 1 June the IRA said it had been unable to locate the burial sites of the remaining eight bodies.

JUNE 1999

5. A Protestant woman married to a Roman Catholic man was killed when a bomb was thrown into her house in Portadown, Co. Armagh; five men believed to be loyalist extremists were later arrested in connection with the attack. 15. The Prime Minister said that decommissioning of weapons was not a

prerequisite for Sinn Fein to participate in Northern Ireland's government but that the party should either bring about decommissioning or condemn those who failed to bring it about. **17.** The High Court ruled that the decision of the forthcoming Saville inquiry, that 16 soldiers should not be granted automatic anonymity before giving evidence concerning the 'Bloody Sunday' shootings in Londonderry in 1972, was flawed. Martin McGartland, an IRA informer, was shot and seriously wounded at his home in Whitley Bay, Tyne and Wear. **22.** Patrick Magee, who was given eight life sentences in 1986 for the bomb attack on the Grand Hotel in Brighton which killed five people during the 1984 Conservative Party conference, was released from prison under the terms of the Belfast Agreement. David Trimble said that Mo Mowlam had lost the confidence of the Protestant community in Northern Ireland. **23.** The Prime Minister said that if the Belfast Agreement could not be implemented, violence would return to Northern Ireland. A former soldier was charged with the murder of the Roman Catholic solicitor Patrick Finucane in Belfast in 1989. **25.** The Prime Minister proposed that the IRA should commit itself to a timetable for decommissioning all its weapons by May 2000 in return for the agreement of the Unionists to the participation of Sinn Fein in the Executive of the New Northern Ireland Assembly. **28.** The Parades Commission ruled that the Orange Order could not march down the Garvaghy Road in Portadown on 4 July. **30.** Talks continued in Belfast aimed at breaking the deadlock over the issue of decommissioning. The deadline for the devolution of power to the Assembly passed with no agreement being reached.

JULY 1999

2. The Prime Minister and the Taoiseach put forward a new set of proposals aimed at breaking the deadlock over decommissioning; they said that a power-sharing executive could be formed in the middle of July and that the IRA would begin the process of decommissioning within days of power being devolved, with actual decommissioning starting within weeks. If any stage of the decommissioning obligations was not met, or if the Unionists did not co-operate in the devolution of power, the executive would be suspended. The talks were adjourned. **4.** The Prime Minister said that if the proposed decommissioning obligations were not met, the executive could be re-formed by the other parties without Sinn Fein. **12.** Emergency legislation to devolve power to a power-sharing executive was introduced into the House of Commons; under the legislation, the Government could suspend the executive and review its future if its proposed conditions were not met. The Unionists largely voted against the legislation on the grounds that it did not incorporate a clear timetable for the decommissioning of weapons and did not allow for Sinn Fein to be expelled immediately from the

executive should the IRA not disarm. **14.** The legislation was tabled in the House of Lords after the Prime Minister had introduced amendments to set out a timetable for decommissioning. The Unionists said that it was still party policy to refuse to sit on an executive with Sinn Fein unless the decommissioning process had begun. The legislation was therefore put on hold. **15.** The Unionists boycotted the session of the New Northern Ireland Assembly at which ministers were nominated for the power-sharing executive; the process therefore collapsed. The Deputy First Minister, Seamus Mallon, resigned in protest at the Unionists' actions. The Prime Minister announced a review of the implementation of the Belfast Agreement. **21.** The IRA said that the British government was responsible for the developing political crisis in Northern Ireland. **28.** The Court of Appeal ruled that the soldiers giving evidence to the forthcoming inquiry concerning the 'Bloody Sunday' shootings in Londonderry in 1972 should be granted anonymity.

AUGUST 1999

14. There were violent clashes between nationalist protesters and the RUC in Belfast and Londonderry as loyalist marches took place. **26.** Mo Mowlam said that in spite of the murder of a taxi driver in July 1999 and evidence of gun-running in the USA, in her judgement the IRA ceasefire was still intact; however she said that the continuing violence was deplorable and that the situation was deeply worrying. **28.** Four youths from Dungannon, Co. Tyrone, left Northern Ireland after receiving death threats from the IRA; a fifth youth left Belfast on 29 August.

ACCIDENTS AND DISASTERS

SEPTEMBER 1998

3. All 229 people on board a Swissair plane flying from New York to Geneva were killed when it crashed into the sea off Halifax, Nova Scotia. **13.** The death toll as a result of the flooding in Bangladesh rose to 950. **13–19.** Four hundred people died following torrential rains in Chiapas, Mexico. **18.** More than 120 people were missing feared drowned after a ferry sank near Manila, Philippines. **21–25.** Hurricane Georges hit the Caribbean and was reported to have left at least 300 people dead. **25.** Thirty-eight people were killed when an airliner bound for Melilla crashed into a mountain in Morocco.

OCTOBER 1998

8. At least 20 people drowned when a pleasure boat broke in two on Lake Banyoles, near Gerona, north-east Spain. **17.** Seven hundred people died when an oil pipeline in Nigeria caught fire. **23.** At least 82 people died and 250,000 were made homeless by typhoons in the Philippines. **28 October–**

2 November. Up to 20,000 people were killed in floods and mudslides and millions were left homeless when Hurricane Mitch hit central America. **30.** Sixty teenagers were killed and 190 were injured when fire broke out at a Hallowe'en discotheque in Gothenburg, Sweden.

NOVEMBER 1998

26. At least 205 people were killed in a train crash in the Punjab, India.

DECEMBER 1998

11. At least 100 people were killed when a Thai Airways airbus crashed in southern Thailand. **16.** Up to 40 people were killed when a five-storey block of flats collapsed in Rome, Italy.

JANUARY 1999

25. Up to 2,000 people were killed when an earthquake registering 6.0 on the Richter scale hit western Colombia.

FEBRUARY 1999

23–24. Thirty-eight people were killed when avalanches hit the ski resort of Galtür, Austria. **24.** All 64 people on board a China Southwest Airlines plane were killed when it exploded in mid-air near Wenzhou, eastern China.

MARCH 1999

16. At least 14 people were killed when a passenger train hit a lorry at Bourbonnias, USA. **24.** Forty people were killed after fire broke out in the Mont Blanc tunnel linking France and Italy. At least 32 people were killed when a train was derailed between Nairobi and Mombasa, Kenya. **29.** At least 85 people died when a series of earthquakes hit villages in northern India.

MAY 1999

4. At least 45 people were killed and hundreds injured when a tornado storm hit Oklahoma and Kansas, USA. **8.** At least 200 people were drowned when a ferry was sucked into a whirlpool in the Meghna River, Bangladesh. **21.** All 1,100 passengers and crew aboard a cruise liner were saved when the ship sank off the coast of Malaysia. **31.** Fifty-four people, mainly teenage girls, were killed in a stampede for shelter during a storm at a beer festival in Minsk, Belarus.

JUNE 1999

2. Nine people were killed and more than 80 injured when an American Airlines plane crashed and burst into flames on landing at Little Rock, Arkansas. **15.** At least 17 people were killed and hundreds were injured when an earthquake registering 6.7 on the Richter scale hit central Mexico. **23.** Thirty-one people were injured when a Virgin express train crashed into an empty commuter train on the West Coast main line route south of Winsford station, Cheshire. **30.** Twenty-three children were killed in

a fire in a summer camp dormitory in Hwasong, S. Korea.

JULY 1999

1. Twenty people were killed when a cable car fell onto the mountainside in the Alps near Saint-Etienne-en-Dévoluy, France. **8.** More than 1,100 passengers were rescued when a Norwegian ferry caught fire off the coast of Sweden. **27.** Twenty-one people were killed while canyoning near Wilderswil, Switzerland.

AUGUST 1999

2. At least 250 people were killed when two trains crashed head-on at Gaisal, eastern India. **5.** It was reported that 725 people had been killed and 5.5 million left homeless by flooding after the Yangtze River in China broke its banks. **17.** An estimated 40,000 people were killed when an earthquake registering at least 7.5 on the Richter scale hit western Turkey. **25.** A container ship caught fire after colliding with a cruise liner carrying 2,340 people in the English Channel; 29 people were slightly injured. **31.** At least 64 people were killed when a Boeing 737 crashed on take-off at Buenos Aires airport, Argentina.

ARTS, SCIENCE AND THE MEDIA

SEPTEMBER 1998

2. ITV lodged proposals with the Independent Television Commission to move the main evening news bulletin from 10 p.m. to 6.30 p.m. **9.** The Royal Opera House announced plans to shut down the Royal Opera company for 11 months of 1999 in order to save money. **14.** The Health Secretary (Frank Dobson) said that the anti-impotence drug Viagra would not be available on the NHS. **16.** The National Year of Reading was launched by the Education Secretary (David Blunkett). Michael Kaiser, the executive director of American Ballet Theatre, was appointed executive director of the Royal Opera House. **23.** Surgeons in Lyon, France, carried out the first ever arm transplant.

OCTOBER 1998

1. The first digital televisions went on sale to the public. **10.** Bernard Haitink said that he had resigned as music director of the Royal Opera House. He withdrew his resignation in December 1998 when the Arts Council announced increased funding to the House. **12.** The new Sadler's Wells Theatre in Islington, London, opened. **13.** A Briton, Prof. John Pople, was jointly awarded the Nobel prize for chemistry. **18.** Richard Bacon, one of the presenters of the children's television programme *Blue Peter*, was sacked after he admitted taking cocaine. **21.** The restored Albert Memorial in London was unveiled by The Queen. **25.** A controversial new biography of the Prince of Wales by Penny Junor began to be serialized in the *Mail on Sunday*; the Prince and Camilla Parker Bowles issued a joint statement saying that the book was not authorized, solicited or approved by them. **30.** The Royal Greenwich Observatory closed.

NOVEMBER 1998

19. The ITC approved a request from ITV to move its main evening news bulletin from 10 p.m. to 6.30 p.m. **20.** Five leading male dancers resigned from the Royal Ballet to join a new London-based ballet company. **30.** The Queen opened the new Museum of Scotland in Edinburgh. The Royal Exchange Theatre, Manchester, which was badly damaged by the IRA bomb that exploded in the city in June 1996, reopened after a £31 million refurbishment.

DECEMBER 1998

1. Chris Ofili won the Turner Prize for modern art. **2.** The Royal Court Theatre announced that it had secured sponsorship worth £3 million from the Jerwood Foundation and that its two auditoriums would in future carry the sponsor's name. **20.** A woman in Houston, Texas, gave birth to octuplets; one baby later died. **11.** Ted Hughes was awarded the T. S. Eliot Prize for Poetry posthumously for his book *Birthday Letters*. On 12 January he won the Whitbread Poetry Award for the same work, and on 26 January he won the Whitbread Book of the Year Award for it, becoming the first writer ever to win the award twice.

JANUARY 1999

19. A major exhibition of late paintings by Monet opened at the Royal Academy, London. Amanda Platell was sacked as editor of the *Express on Sunday*.

FEBRUARY 1999

11. The BBC suspended two producers and a researcher from *The Vanessa Show* after it emerged that four guests on the daytime chat show had been fakes. **16.** At the Brit Awards in London, Robbie Williams won the awards for best male singer, best single and best video.

MARCH 1999

5. The News at Ten was broadcast for the last time on ITV before moving to the new time of 6.30 p.m. **23.** Antonio Pappano was appointed music director of the Royal Opera from 2002. **24.** The former editor of the *Sunday Express*, Amanda Platell, was appointed press secretary to the Leader of the Opposition, William Hague.

MAY 1999

10. Quentin Blake was appointed the first 'Children's Laureate' with the aim of attracting more children to reading and writing. At Sotheby's in New York, Cezanne's *Still life with curtain, pitcher and bowl of fruit* sold for £36.8 million, a record for a work by the artist, and Seurat's *Island of the Grande Jatte* sold for £21.4 million, a record for a work by Seurat. The

private papers of Christopher Isherwood were acquired by the Huntington Library, Los Angeles. **13.** A memorial service for the late Poet Laureate, Ted Hughes, was held at Westminster Abbey. **18.** The Canadian billionaire Garry Weston gave the British Museum £20 million to enable it to complete its Great Court project. Paul Muldoon was appointed professor of poetry at Oxford University. **19.** Andrew Motion was appointed poet laureate. **26.** Buckingham Palace made a formal complaint to the Press Complaints Commission (PCC) following the publication by the *Sun* of a photograph of Prince Edward's fiancée Sophie Rhys-Jones topless in 1988; the *Sun* published an apology on 27 May. **27.** Leonardo da Vinci's *Last Supper* was unveiled in Milan for the first time after 22 years of restoration.

JUNE 1999

1. William Hague said that he had written to the chairman of the BBC to say that the broadcaster Greg Dyke would be a 'totally unacceptable' choice as director-general of the BBC in view of his donations totalling £50,000 to the Labour Party. **2.** Sir Anthony Dowell announced his resignation as director of the Royal Ballet from August 2001. **17.** The art collector Sir Denis Mahon donated his collection of Old Masters to the nation. **22.** The Royal Opera House said that its financial crisis was over. **24.** Greg Dyke was appointed director-general of the BBC from April 2000. **28.** At Sotheby's in London a Degas pastel, *Dancer at Rest*, sold for £17.6 million, a record for a work by the artist.

JULY 1999

8. A collection of art and antiques stolen by the Nazis from the Rothschild family in Austria in 1938 and recovered in 1945 sold for more than £57 million in an auction at Christie's in London. **20.** The Government announced an immunization programme against the C strain of meningitis.

AUGUST 1999

4. The director Alan Parker was appointed chairman of the new Film Council to be established by the Government in April 2000.

CRIMES AND LEGAL AFFAIRS

OCTOBER 1998

13. In the High Court 11-year-old Sam Mansell, who developed cerebral palsy after being deprived of oxygen at birth, was awarded record damages of £3.29 million. **17.** The former Chilean dictator Augusto Pinochet was arrested at a hospital in London under a warrant issued by the Spanish government; the request for his extradition to face charges of murdering Spanish citizens in Chile during his regime was refused in the High Court on 28 October on the grounds that he was entitled to sovereign immunity in respect of acts committed while he was head of state. On 25 November five Law Lords ruled by a majority of three to two that Gen. Pinochet was not entitled as a former head of state to immunity from extradition. On 9 December the Home Secretary (Jack Straw) ruled that extradition proceedings against Gen. Pinochet could proceed. **23.** Michael Stone was sentenced in Maidstone to life imprisonment for the murders of Lin and Megan Russell and the attempted murder of Josie Russell near Chillenden, Kent, in July 1996. **31.** Twenty-two-year-old Jennifer King was reported missing after failing to return home from a nightclub in Bristol; her body was found in nearby woodland on 3 November.

NOVEMBER 1998

3. Patrizia Reggiani, the former wife of the fashion heir Maurizio Gucci, was sentenced in Rome to 29 years' imprisonment for arranging his murder in 1995. **5.** Two police dog instructors were each sentenced in Chelmsford to four months' imprisonment for cruelty to dogs at their training centre at Sandon, Essex. **11.** Two small oil paintings by John Constable which had been in storage were reported to have been stolen from the Victoria and Albert Museum, London. **16.** In the High Court 17-year-old Helen Edwards, who suffered brain damage after being deprived of oxygen during an operation to remove a birthmark in 1986, was awarded record damages of £3.9 million. **17.** Paul Seddon was sentenced in Preston to life imprisonment for the murder of five-year-old Dillon Hull, who was killed by a bullet intended for his stepfather in a drug feud in Bolton in August 1997. **18.** A French court rejected a request from Britain to extradite David Shayler, the former MI5 officer who was arrested in Paris in August 1998 and wanted for allegedly leaking secrets to a newspaper; the court ruled that Mr Shayler's motives for revealing secret information were political and that there were therefore no grounds for his extradition. **23.** A social worker was stabbed to death at a hostel in Balham, London; a 'care in the community' patient she had been looking after was charged with the murder.

DECEMBER 1998

1. The gay activist Peter Tatchell was fined £18.60 at a magistrates' court in London for interrupting the Archbishop of Canterbury's sermon in Canterbury Cathedral on Easter Sunday 1998 with a protest about the Archbishop's views on the gay age of consent. **2.** The Lord Chancellor published a White Paper on reforming legal services in Britain. **17.** Five law lords overturned the ruling by five other law lords on 25 November that the former Chilean dictator Gen. Pinochet did not enjoy immunity from extradition; they reached their decision on the grounds that one of the law lords involved in the earlier ruling, Lord Hoffmann, had failed to disclose his links with Amnesty International, one of the organizations which had made representations to the law lords during the case.

The conviction of Gilbert 'Danny' McNamee, who was sentenced in 1987 to 25 years' imprisonment for making IRA bombs and who was released in November 1998 under the terms of the Belfast Agreement, was quashed by the Court of Appeal. **21.** In the High Court Martijn Biesheuvel, who was left paralysed after a car crash in Bath in May 1994, was awarded record damages of £9.2 million.

JANUARY 1999

19. Jonathan Aitken, the former Conservative Cabinet minister, admitted at the Central Criminal Court charges of perjury and perverting the course of justice in relation to his unsuccessful libel action against the *Guardian* and Granada Television in June 1997. On 8 June he was sentenced to 18 months' imprisonment. **27.** Mary Chipperfield, the circus trainer, was convicted in Andover of 12 charges to cruelty to animals; on 9 April she was fined £7,500.

FEBRUARY 1999

2. Jenny Cupit was sentenced in Chester to life imprisonment for the murder of Kathryn Linaker, with whose husband she had been having an affair, in April 1998. Louise Sullivan, an Australian nanny, was sentenced at the Central Criminal Court to fifteen months' imprisonment, suspended for two years, for the manslaughter of a six-month-old baby in her care in April 1997. **4.** A case involving the alleged smuggling of £14 million worth of cannabis was halted in Bristol after the judge said that customs officers had displayed a 'reckless disregard for the law' which would have prevented the ten defendants from having a fair trial. Nicholas Mullen, who had been sentenced in 1990 to 30 years' imprisonment for conspiracy to cause IRA explosions on the mainland, was released from prison after the Court of Appeal quashed his conviction on the ground that his deportation from Zimbabwe to England had been illegal. **15.** John Drewe was sentenced in London to six years' imprisonment for tampering with the records of national archives in order to create false histories for hundreds of fake copies of 20th-century works of art. **20.** The Home Secretary (Jack Straw) obtained an injunction to prevent the *Sunday Telegraph* from publishing leaked extracts from the report of the inquiry led by Sir William Macpherson of Cluny into the murder of Stephen Lawrence in London in 1993. On 21 February Mr Straw agreed that extracts already in the public domain could be reprinted and commented on. The full report was published on 24 February; it accused the Metropolitan Police of 'racism, professional incompetence and bad leadership' and made a series of recommendations aimed at eradicating racism from the criminal justice system and other areas of public life. On 25 February Sir William apologized for releasing the names and addresses of police informants in the case as part of the report.

MARCH 1999

6. Seven people including three children were killed in an arson attack on a house in Chingford, north-east London. **9.** The Chief Constable of Sussex Police was suspended over a raid in January 1998 during which an unarmed suspect was shot dead. **12.** Kenneth Peatfield was sentenced in Sheffield to life imprisonment for the murder of his lover, whose head was found in a block of concrete in his garage, in March 1998. **15.** The Commission of the European Court of Human Rights ruled that Jon Venables and Robert Thompson, who were convicted in 1993 of the murder of two-year-old James Bulger, did not receive a fair trial; the case was referred to the court for a full judgment. **19.** Four IRA members were sentenced in Belfast to an aggregate total of 640 years' imprisonment and three life terms for terrorist activities which led to the deaths of nine people. The Labour MP for Newark, Notts, Fiona Jones, was convicted in Nottingham of election expenses fraud in relation to her campaign at the 1997 general election; she was therefore immediately disqualified as an MP. On 15 April her conviction was quashed in the Court of Appeal. **24.** Seven law lords ruled that the former Chilean dictator Gen. Pinochet did not enjoy immunity as a former head of state from extradition on charges of torture, but that he could only face trial in Spain in relation to alleged crimes committed after 29 September 1988 when torture became an 'extraterritorial' crime in the UK after being incorporated in the Criminal Justice Act; this reduced the number of charges against him from 32 to three, and so the law lords referred the case back to the Home Secretary for a new ruling as to whether or not Gen. Pinochet should be extradited. On 15 April the Home Secretary ruled that extradition proceedings could begin. The anti-apartheid activist Allan Boesak was sentenced in Johannesburg, South Africa, to six years' imprisonment for the theft of more than £100,000 from his charity, the Foundation for Peace and Justice. **25.** The Labour MP for Glasgow Govan, Mohammed Sarwar, was acquitted in Edinburgh of bribing a rival candidate in the 1997 general election; two further charges of electoral fraud and understating his election expenses had been dropped during the trial. **26.** Jack Kevorkian, a doctor who had admitted assisting the suicide of terminally ill patients many times, was convicted in Michigan, USA, of second degree murder. On 13 April he was sentenced to between ten and 25 years' imprisonment.

APRIL 1999

5. Two Libyans, Abdel Basset Ali al-Megrahi and Lamen Khalifa Fhimah, arrived in Holland to face charges of bombing Pan Am flight 103 which crashed over Lockerbie, Scotland, in 1988; the trial was to be conducted at a former military air base, Camp Zeist, under Scottish law before three High Court judges sitting without a jury. **7.** At the Central Criminal Court, Edgar Pearce pleaded guilty to 20 charges including blackmail, assault, causing an explosion and possession of firearms; he had been known as the Mardi Gra bomber after planting home-made explosives near branches of Barclay's Bank and Sainsbury's between 1994 and 1998. On 14 April he was sentenced to 21 years' imprisonment. **13.** Seventeen-year-old Ashleigh Robinson, a pupil at Millfield school, was found murdered in Guildford, Surrey. **20.** Fourteen students and a teacher were killed and 24 people were injured when two teenagers entered their school in Colorado, USA, exploding bombs and firing indiscriminately. **23.** Darren Vickers, a bus driver, was sentenced in Manchester to life imprisonment for the murder of Jamie Lavis, an eight-year-old boy he had befriended, in May 1997. **26.** The television presenter Jill Dando was shot dead outside her home in Fulham, London. **27.** Neil Sayers and Graham Wallis were convicted in Maidstone of the murder of a fellow student at Hadlow Agricultural College, Kent, in May 1998. **28.** A man was arrested after shooting at police, hijacking four cars and taking refuge in a house in Feltham, London. **30.** Dame Shirley Porter, the former leader of Westminster city council who was found guilty of wilful misconduct and gerrymandering by the district auditor in 1996 and faced a surcharge of millions of pounds, was cleared of wrongdoing by the Court of Appeal.

MAY 1999

3. A former Israeli paratrooper, Daniel Okev, was sentenced in Beersheba, Israel to 20 years' imprisonment for murdering a British tourist and badly wounding his girlfriend in the Negev desert in August 1997. **11.** Dr David Moor, a GP, was cleared in Newcastle upon Tyne of murdering a terminally ill patient to whom he gave a fatal dose of a painkiller. **18.** Craig Smith was sentenced in Chester to life imprisonment for the murder of 13-year-old Claire Hart in Congleton, Cheshire, in June 1998. **19.** The Home Secretary (Jack Straw) put forward proposals for defendants in 'either way' cases to have the right to elect for trial by jury to be withdrawn. **25.** Shakeela Naz and her son Shazad were each sentenced in Nottingham to life imprisonment for the murder of her daughter Rukhsana, who was deemed to have brought disgrace on the family by conceiving a child as a result of an adulterous affair, in March 1998. **28.** Alan Hopkinson was sentenced in Lewes to nine terms of life imprisonment for abducting, imprisoning and assaulting two ten-year-old girls from Hastings in January 1999.

JUNE 1999

4. Kim Galbraith was sentenced in Glasgow to life imprisonment for the murder of her husband, who she claimed had subjected her to sexual and mental abuse, in January 1999. **6.** A British woman, Kathleen Morgan, was cleared in Dubai of unlawfully killing a Russian tourist in a jet ski accident. **27.** Two children, their mother and their grandmother were murdered in Clydach, near Swansea.

JULY 1999

17. The mutilated body of a woman was found in a suitcase in the car park at Heathrow airport; a man was later charged with the murder. **18.** A Radio 1 disc jockey, Tim Westwood, was shot in the arm when a gunman opened fire on his car in Kennington, south London. **21.** The Treasurer of the Conservative Party, Michael Ashcroft, started a libel action against *The Times* over articles it had published on his business activities in Belize. **23.** The pilot of an All Nippon Airways flight was stabbed to death by a hijacker after taking off from Tokyo airport; the hijacker was then overpowered by other crew members and arrested when the plane had returned to Tokyo. **26.** Thirty Greenpeace protesters, including its executive director, Lord Melchett, were arrested after starting to destroy a field of genetically modified maize in Lyng, Norfolk. **27.** Two 15-year-old girls were ordered in Manchester to be detained at Her Majesty's pleasure for the murder in September 1998 of an elderly woman in Failsworth, Gtr Manchester, whose body they dumped in the Rochdale Canal. At the Central Criminal Court, a record fine of £1.5 million was imposed on Great Western Trains over safety failures that contributed to the Southall crash in September 1997 in which seven people died. **29.** Twelve people were shot dead in Atlanta, Georgia, by a man who had lost money selling stocks and shares on the Internet.

AUGUST 1999

9. Eight British men were convicted in Yemen of plotting an Islamic fundamentalist bombing campaign in December 1998. **23.** A man was charged with murder after a 16-year-old boy was shot dead during a burglary at a farm in Emneth, Norfolk.

ECONOMIC AND BUSINESS AFFAIRS

SEPTEMBER 1998

1. The Dow Jones industrial average rose 288.36 points, the second-biggest one-day rise in its history. Scottish Hydro and Southern Electric announced a £4.9 billion merger. **3.** Shell and Texaco announced a joint venture in marketing and refining European oil. **4.** The Japanese electronics company Fujitsu announced that it was ceasing production at its factory in Newton Aycliffe, Co. Durham, with the loss of 570 jobs. **8.** The Dow Jones industrial average rose 380.53 points, the biggest one-day rise in its history. **15.** Microsoft replaced General Electric as the world's biggest company when its market worth reached US$267 billion. **23.** The Trade and Industry Secretary (Peter Mandelson) blocked the planned take-over of Coral by Ladbroke on the advice of the Monopolies and Mergers Commission. **24.** The

sale of the RAC roadside rescue business to the American marketing group Cendant was referred to the Monopolies and Mergers Commission. On 4 February 1999 Cendant pulled out of the sale.

OCTOBER 1998

4. The Group of Seven industrialized countries called for immediate interest rate cuts and a co-ordinated response to the prevailing financial crisis. **5.** Sterling closed at DM2.7638, its lowest level since May 1997. **6.** The Chancellor of the Exchequer (Gordon Brown) said that the British economy would suffer a significant slowdown in 1999 as a result of the economic crisis in Asia. **8.** The Bank of England cut bank base rates by 0.25 per cent to 7.25 per cent. **12.** The FT-SE 100 index closed 214.2 points up, the biggest ever points rise in a single day, at 5,037.6. **21.** Rover confirmed that it was seeking cost-cutting measures including 2,400 job cuts at its Longbridge plant in Birmingham. **30.** The Group of Seven industrialized countries announced a package of measures designed to restore confidence in the world financial markets.

NOVEMBER 1998

2. The Office for National Statistics suspended publication of monthly average earnings figures amid growing doubts about their reliability. **3.** The Chancellor of the Exchequer said that he would increase borrowing to compensate for lower than projected growth in 1999 but that there would be a return to strong economic growth in 2000. **5.** The Bank of England cut bank base rates by 0.5 per cent to 6.75 per cent. **23.** The Dow Jones industrial average rose 214 points to close at a record high of 9,374.27. **24.** America Online (AOL) announced a $4.2 billion agreed take-over bid for the Internet software company Netscape. **26.** Sir Richard Greenbury resigned as chief executive of Marks & Spencer to become its non-executive chairman; he was replaced as chief executive by Peter Salsbury. The company's deputy chairman, Keith Oates, resigned. **27.** Martin Taylor resigned as chief executive of Barclays Bank; Sir Peter Middleton was appointed interim chief executive. **30.** Deutsche Bank announced an agreed $10.1 billion take-over of Bankers Trust.

DECEMBER 1998

1. Exxon announced an agreed $82 billion take-over of Mobil. **2.** Walter Hasselkus resigned as chairman of Rover after heavy losses at the business; he was replaced by Werner Sämann. **3.** European central banks of the 11 countries due to join the single European currency on 1 January 1999 took co-ordinated action to cut interest rates. **7.** The Trade and Industry Secretary (Peter Mandelson) announced a set of proposals aimed at giving the Post Office greater commercial freedom. **9.** The British drugs company Zeneca announced a merger with the Swedish company Astra. **10.** The Bank of England cut bank base rates by 0.5 per cent to 6.25 per cent.

JANUARY 1999

1. The euro replaced the existing currencies in 11 European countries. 7. The Bank of England cut bank base rates by 0.25 per cent to 6 per cent. 8. The FT-SE 100 index closed at a record high of 6,195.6. 11. British American Tobacco and Rothmans International announced a £15 billion merger. 17. Vodafone announced an agreed £7.5 billion merger with the American company AirTouch. 19. British Aerospace announced a £7.7 billion merger with the Marconi Electronic Systems arm of GEC. The Internet service provider AtHome agreed to buy the Internet search company Excite for $6.7 billion. 21. January Investments bought the retailing group Sears, subject to shareholders' approval, in a deal worth £548 million. 22. International stock markets fell after Argentina confirmed that it was considering adopting the US dollar as its currency. 28. Ford agreed a £3.9 billion deal to buy Volvo's passenger car division.

FEBRUARY 1999

1. The French insurance company AXA acquired Guardian Royal Exchange (GRE) for £3.4 billion. 2. Pricewaterhouse Coopers, which as Coopers and Lybrand had acted as auditors to the group of companies controlled by the late Robert Maxwell, was fined £1.2 million and ordered to pay costs of £2.1 million by the accountancy Joint Disciplinary Tribunal for failures in its auditing of the companies. 4. The Bank of England cut bank base rates by 0.5 per cent to 5.5 per cent. 5. Bernd Pischetsrieder was ousted as chairman of BMW. 8. Ladbroke announced a £1.16 billion agreed take-over of the hotelier Stakis. 20. The flotation of the betting shop chain William Hill was cancelled after the company was bought by the venture capitalists Cinven and CVC Capital Partners in a deal worth £825 million. 24. The FT-SE 100 index closed at a record high of 6,307.6.

MARCH 1999

8. The World Trade Organization met in emergency session in Geneva; it urged the EU and the USA to resolve their dispute over sanctions imposed by the USA against some EU goods because of the EU's alleged protectionism in favouring bananas from the Caribbean over those from Latin America. 11. Prudential announced an agreed £1.9 billion take-over of M&G. 16. The Dow Jones Industrial Average rose to over 10,000 points for the first time when it reached 10,001.12. On 29 March it closed at over 10,000 points for the first time, at 10,006.78. 31. The future of the Rover car plant at Longbridge, Birmingham, was secured by a government aid package believed to be worth about £150 million.

APRIL 1999

6. The FT-SE 100 index closed at a record high of 6,415.3. 7. Sears sold the mail-order business Freemans to the German retailer Otto Versand in a deal believed to be worth £150–£200 million. The FT-SE 100 index closed at a record high of 6,473.2. 8. The Bank of England cut bank base rates by 0.25 per cent to 5.25 per cent. 12. The Ford Motor Company agreed to buy the Kwik-Fit car repair chain for about £1 billion. 13. The Norwegian company Kvaerner put the Govan and Clydebank shipyards in Glasgow and engineering and construction operations in the north-east and in Sheffield up for sale; the Government set up a task force aimed at finding a new buyer and safeguarding jobs. Mike O'Neill resigned as chief executive of Barclays for health reasons on his first day in the job. 16. The retail groups Kingfisher and Asda announced plans to merge (see 14 June below). 19. The FT-SE 100 index closed at a record high of 6,513.3. 27. The FT-SE 100 index closed at a record high of 6,593.6. 28. Keith Henry resigned as chief executive of National Power. 30. Lex Service announced an agreed £437 million take-over of the RAC's breakdown operation.

MAY 1999

3. The Dow Jones industrial average rose 225.65 points to close at a record high of 11,014.69. 4. The US investment bank Goldman Sachs floated on the New York stock exchange. 7. The Treasury said that the Bank of England would sell half of Britain's gold reserves over the medium term. 18. Marks and Spencer announced that pre-tax profits had fallen from £1.16 billion in 1997 to £546.1 million in 1998. 20. Barclays Bank announced 6,000 job losses. 24. WH Smith announced an agreed £185 million bid for the publishing company Hodder Headline. 25. British Airways announced that pre-tax profits had fallen by 61 per cent in the 1998–9 financial year. Allied Domecq sold its pubs business to Whitbread for £2.4 billion.

JUNE 1999

2. Sainsbury's announced pre-tax profits for 1998–9 of £756 million and said that it would cut 1,100 jobs. The euro fell to a new low against the pound of £0.6437. 10. The Bank of England cut bank base rates by 0.25 per cent to 5.0 per cent. 14. The American retailer Wal-Mart launched a £6.7 billion take-over bid for Asda. 17. Prudential Corporation announced 4,000 job losses. 23. Scottish Widows announced a £7 billion take-over by Lloyds TSB.

JULY 1999

1. The euro fell to a new low against the dollar of $1.0201. 5. Centrica made a £1.1 billion offer for the AA. 6. The price of gold fell to $257.60 per ounce, the lowest for 20 years, after the Government sold 25 tonnes of the UK's gold reserves at auction. 11. The commercial law firm Clifford Chance announced a merger with the American firm Rogers & Wells; a further merger was planned with the German firm Pünder, Volhard, Weber & Axster. 12. Kingston Communications, the telecoms business owned by Hull City Council, was floated on the

Stock Exchange; the Council retained a 49 per stake in the company. **13.** The Government announced plans to sell off 49 per cent of British Nuclear Fuels. About 1,200 jobs at the Govan shipyard, Glasgow, were safeguarded following a deal between its owners Kvaerner and the electronics company Marconi. **19.** Centrica announced the closure of its high street shops with the loss of 1,500 jobs. **26.** The Internet subsidiary of Dixons, Freeserve, floated on the Stock Exchange; its shares rose from 150p to close at 205p.

AUGUST 1999

4. The American congolomerate SFX Entertainment bought Apollo Leisure for £162 million. **6.** Deutsche Telekom bought the mobile phone operator One 2 One for £8.4 billion.

ENVIRONMENT

SEPTEMBER 1998

1. Government safety inspectors said that the Dounreay nuclear complex suffered from many chronic safety problems. **17.** Thousands of mink were released from a farm at Onneley, Staffs, by animal rights activists. **23.** The Environment Secretary (John Prescott) announced that the water companies would be required to treat all sewage discharged into the sea and to protect sites of special scientific interest (SSSIs).

OCTOBER 1998

1. The World Wide Fund for Nature published a report which said that a third of the Earth's natural resources had been lost in the previous 25 years.

NOVEMBER 1998

2. Researchers at the Institute of Terrestrial Ecology in Edinburgh said that billions of acres of tropical forests would turn into desert in the middle of the 21st century because of global warming. **11.** The Environment Secretary addressed a conference on climate change in Buenos Aires, Argentina.

JANUARY 1999

11. A large section of Beachy Head, E. Sussex, collapsed into the sea. **15.** The Milford Haven Port Authority was fined £4 million in Cardiff after admitting responsibility for the Sea Empress disaster in February 1996.

FEBRUARY 1999

12. The Prime Minister said that there was no scientific case for a moratorium on the sale of genetically modified foods in the UK. **19.** Greenabella Marsh, a Site of Special Scientific Interest in the Tees estuary, was contaminated by a major acid spill caused by a faulty drain at a company in Hartlepool.

MAY 1999

19. Environmentalists called for a five-year freeze on the planting of genetically modified (GM) crops in the UK. **27.** The Nuffield Council said that there was a 'compelling moral imperative' to develop GM foods.

JUNE 1999

7. A farmer in Wiltshire destroyed a test field of GM oil seed rape after pressure from the farm's trustees.

SPORT

For Sports results, *see* Sports section

SEPTEMBER 1998

5. Christian Gross was sacked as manager of Tottenham Hotspur FC. **7.** The satellite television group BskyB announced a £625 million agreement to buy Manchester United FC. On 9 April the Government accepted a recommendation by the Monopolies and Mergers Commission that the takeover should be blocked because it would damage the quality of British football. **26.** The Sheffield Wednesday striker Paolo Di Canio was suspended by his club for pushing over the referee after being sent off during a match against Arsenal at Hillsborough. On 23 October Di Canio was banned for 11 matches and fined £10,000 by the FA. **27.** Great Britain returned to the World Group of the Davis Cup after beating India 3–2 in Nottingham.

OCTOBER 1998

6. UEFA announced proposals to expand the European Champions' League and merge the UEFA Cup and the European Cup Winners' Cup. **14.** The first-class cricket counties and the MCC agreed changes to professional cricket in England and Wales from 1999–2000, including more international matches and the possible establishment of a two-division county championship. **15.** The BBC lost the right to televise Test and most one-day cricket matches. **27.** The England wicket-keeper Jack Russell announced his retirement from international cricket. **29.** The proposed take-over by BskyB of Manchester United FC was referred to the Monopolies and Mergers Commission.

NOVEMBER 1998

3. The West Indies cricket captain and vice-captain, Brian Lara and Carl Hooper, refused to join their team for a tour of South Africa because of a dispute over the fees to be paid to the players. On 4 November both players were dropped by the West Indies Cricket Board. On 5 November more players joined the protest. On 9 November the players reached agreement with the Board and Lara and Hooper were reinstated. **12.** Roy Evans resigned as joint manager of Liverpool FC, leaving Gerard

Houllier in sole charge. **14.** The England rugby union team set a new national record for the number of points scored in a match when they beat Holland 110–0 at Huddersfield; they also scored a record 16 tries during the match. **17.** David Hemery was elected the first president of Athletics UK. **21.** Roy Hodgson resigned as manager of Blackburn Rovers FC. **30.** Peter Johnson resigned as chairman of Everton FC.

DECEMBER 1998

3. The English county cricket clubs voted in favour of a two-division county championship from 2000. Brian Kidd was appointed manager of Blackburn Rovers FC. **8.** The Australian Cricket Board confirmed that Shane Warne and Mark Waugh had been fined in 1995 for giving information to an illegal Indian bookmaker in exchange for payment during a tour to Sri Lanka in late 1994. **13.** Michael Owen was named BBC Sports Personality of the Year. **15.** Graham Kelly resigned as chief executive of the FA for allegedly offering a £3.2 million loan to the Welsh FA without authorization. The FA's executive passed a unanimous vote of no confidence in its chairman, Keith Wiseman, over the same issue, but Mr Wiseman refused to resign. **22.** The Australian Open tennis champion Petr Korda was stripped of the prize-money and the world ranking points he won at Wimbledon in July 1998 because he had tested positive for steroids at the championships; he escaped being banned because an independent appeals committee accepted his evidence that he did not know he had taken the relevant substance. **27.** Six people, including the British Olympic yachtsman Glyn Charles, were missing presumed drowned when the Sydney-Hobart yacht race was hit by heavy storms. **29.** The Kent fast bowler Dean Headley took six wickets for 60 runs during the fourth Test between England and Australia at Melbourne; England won the match by 12 runs.

JANUARY 1999

2. Leeds United drew 0–0 with non-league Rushden and Diamonds in the third round of the FA Cup; Leeds United won the replay 3–1. On the first day of the fifth Test in Sydney, Darren Gough became the first England bowler for 100 years to take a hat-trick in an Ashes series. **7.** Supporters of Shiv Sena, a right-wing Hindu party, vandalized the pitch at New Delhi where the first Test between India and Pakistan was due to begin on 28 January. **15.** Terry Venables resigned as head coach of Crystal Palace FC. **17.** The former world heavyweight boxing champion Mike Tyson beat Francois Botha in his first fight since being banned for a year for biting off part of Evander Holyfield's ear in a fight in June 1997. **18.** England were expelled from the Five Nations Championship after a dispute over television rights; they were readmitted on 19 January. **23.** A row broke out after the Sri Lankan bowler Muttiah Muralitharan was no-balled by an umpire

during a one-day match against England in Adelaide; the Sri Lankan team walked to the edge of the pitch and a 15-minute delay ensued before the match resumed. **24.** An internal report by the International Olympic Committee acknowledged that members of the committee had accepted bribes in connection with the successful bid by Salt Lake City, Utah, to stage the 2002 Winter Olympics; three committee members had already resigned, and the report recommended that six more members be expelled. **26.** Dougie Walker, the European 200 metres champion, was revealed to have tested positive for drugs in December 1998; he denied having taking any banned substances but was suspended for two years by UK Athletics on 31 March. The new governing body for athletics in Britain, UK Athletics, was launched. **29.** On 2 February Glenn Hoddle was sacked after admitting a 'serious error of judgment' and Howard Wilkinson was appointed as acting coach.

FEBRUARY 1999

1. The Welsh Rugby Union rejected a proposal from the RFU to form an Anglo-Welsh league including five Welsh clubs. **7.** Amil Kumble, the India leg spinner, became only the second man in Test history to take ten wickets in an innings when he finished with figures of 10 for 74 in the second Test against Pakistan at Delhi. **13.** The Arsenal manager Arsène Wenger offered to replay an FA Cup tie against Sheffield United after his side won by a goal scored after breaking an unwritten rule that a ball put out of play because a player is injured should be returned to the opposition; the FA accepted the offer. The French solo yachtswoman Isabelle Autissier was rescued by a fellow competitor in the Around Alone single-handed round-the-world race after her boat had capsized in the South Pacific Ocean. **17.** Kevin Keegan was appointed England football coach on a part-time basis until June 1999.

MARCH 1999

1. The Government launched a £160 million regional network of sports facilities. **7.** Colin Prescot and Andy Elson set a new world record for a hot-air balloon flight when their balloon came down in the Pacific Ocean off Japan 18 days into an attempt to fly non-stop around the world. The London rugby league player Martin Offiah became the top English try-scorer in history when he scored his 447th try during a match against Huddersfield at the Stoop. **8.** West Indies were all out for 51, their lowest ever score, in the second Test against Australia in Port of Spain. **11.** Sir John Quinton resigned as chairman of the Premier League and Peter Leaver resigned as chief executive after allegedly exceeding their powers by giving lucrative consultancy contracts to two former BSkyB executives. Wembley Stadium was sold for £103 million to a consortium backed by the FA; the new owners said that the stadium would be demolished and rebuilt by 2003. **13.** The world heavyweight unification title fight between Evander Holyfield and Lennox Lewis in New York was declared a draw in spite of the widespread belief that it had been won by Lewis; on 15 March the three governing bodies involved said that a rematch should take place within six months. **20.** Brian Jones and Bertrand Piccard became the first people to fly non-stop round the world in a balloon when their British-made Breitling Orbiter 3 balloon reached Mauretania after 19 days in the air. The balloon landed in Egypt on 21 March. **23.** David Lloyd said that he would resign as the England cricket coach after the world cup in June 1999. **28.** The leading European rugby union countries and clubs agreed an eight-year format for European competition.

APRIL 1999

5. Richard Dunwoody became the most successful National Hunt jockey in history when he won the 1,679th race of his career in a meeting at Wincanton. **9.** The Liverpool striker Robbie Fowler was banned for six games and fined £32,000 by the FA for taunting the Chelsea defender Graeme Le Saux during a match in February, and for miming cocaine-sniffing after scoring a goal against Everton on 3 April. **25.** The seventh and final one-day cricket international between the West Indies and Australia in Bridgetown, Barbados, was disrupted by serious crowd trouble after the West Indies batsman Sherwin Campbell was controversially run out. David Ginola was named the Professional Football-ers' Association Player of the Year.

MAY 1999

1. Leeds Rhinos won the rugby league Challenge Cup final with the biggest ever score and by the biggest ever margin when they beat London Broncos 52–16 at Wembley; Leroy Rivett became the first player ever to score four tries in a Challenge Cup final. **2.** The referee of a match between Celtic and Rangers at Celtic Park was injured by a coin thrown from the crowd; there were further crowd distur-bances and three players were sent off during the match. **3.** Stephen Hendry became the first snooker player to win the world championship seven times when he beat Mark Williams in the final at Sheffield. **7.** The world motor cycling champion, Michael Doohan, was badly injured in a crash during qualifying for the Spanish Grand Prix in Jerez. **14.** The cricket world cup opened at Lord's. Kevin Keegan was confirmed as England football coach on a full-time basis. **16.** Manchester United won the football premiership for the fifth time in seven years. **23.** The *News of the World* published allegations that the England rugby union captain Lawrence Dallag-lio had sold drugs as a teenager and had taken drugs while on a British Lions tour in 1997. On 24 May Dallaglio denied the allegations but resigned as England captain and was replaced by Martin Johnson. On 25 August Dallaglio was fined £15,000 by the RFU for bringing the game into disrepute.

26. Manchester United became the first English club ever to win the league, FA Cup and European Cup when they beat Bayern Munich 2–1 in the European Cup final in Barcelona. On 27 May hundreds of thousands of people lined the streets in Manchester to welcome the team back. **30.** England was knocked out of the cricket world cup.

JUNE 1999

2. The Irish government refused to grant entry visas to the Yugoslav football team, which was due to play a European Championship qualifying match against the Republic of Ireland in Dublin on 5 June; the match was therefore called off. **5.** The leading Italian cyclist Marco Pantani was suspended for 15 days after failing a drugs test during the Giro D'Italia. **6.** Andre Agassi became the fifth man to win all four Grand Slam titles when he beat Andrei Medvedev to win the French Open in Paris. **7.** The Irish swimmer and former Olympic gold medallist Michelle De Bruin lost her appeal against a four-year ban imposed by FINA, the sport's international governing body, in 1998 after she had tested positive for drugs. **10.** Kenny Dalglish was appointed director of football operations and John Barnes was appointed head coach at Celtic. Ford announced that it had bought Jackie Stewart's grand prix team. **16.** In Athens the American athlete Maurice Greene set a new world record of 9.79 for the men's 100 metres. The former world motor racing champion Damon Hill announced his retirement from the sport. **17.** Australia qualified for the cricket world cup final after tying with South Africa in a semi-final at Edgbaston. **20.** Australia beat Pakistan in the cricket world cup final at Lord's. **22.** The women's top seed at Wimbledon, Martina Hingis, was knocked out of the tournament in the first round by a 16-year-old Australian qualifier, Jelena Dokić. **24.** Nasser Hus-sain was appointed England cricket captain in place of Alec Stewart. **26.** Geoff Thompson was elected chairman of the FA. **27.** The FA offered to exempt Manchester United from the 1999–2000 FA Cup to facilitate the club's participation in the inaugural FIFA World Team Championship in Brazil. On 30 June the club agreed to withdraw from the FA Cup.

JULY 1999

4. Pete Sampras won the men's singles title at Wimbledon for the sixth time, more than any other player in the 20th century, when he beat Andre Agassi in straight sets in the final. In the women's final, Lindsay Davenport won the title for the first time by beating Steffi Graf in straight sets. **5.** Chelsea FC bought Chris Sutton from Blackburn Rovers for £10 million. **7.** In Rome, the Moroccan athlete Hicham El Guerrouj set a new world record of 3 minutes 43.13 seconds for the mile. **13.** Granada bought a 9.9 per cent stake in Liverpool FC for £22 million. **18.** Paul Lawrie became the first Scotsman to win The Open golf championship in Scotland for 68 years when he won the tournament at Carnoustie after a four-hole play-off against Jean Van de Velde and Justin Leonard. **27.** The champion jockey Kieren Fallon was sacked as first jockey of the trainer Henry Cecil. **28.** The European 200 metres champion, Doug Walker, who had been suspended after failing a drugs test in March 1999, was reinstated after UK Athletics dropped the charges against him. **29.** Plans for a new £475 million Wembley Stadium designed by a team of architects headed by Lord Foster were unveiled.

AUGUST 1999

2. The BBC sports presenter Desmond Lynam announced that he was moving to ITV to present its live football coverage. **4.** The former Olympic 100 metres champion Linford Christie was suspended from athletics by the IAAF after failing a drugs test. The world high jump record-holder Javier Sotomayor was stripped of the gold medal he won at the Pan American Games in Canada in July 1999 after testing positive for cocaine. **5.** The Arsenal striker Nicolas Anelka was sold to Real Madrid for £22.5 million. **13.** The tennis champion Steffi Graf announced her retirement from the sport. **18.** The Jamaican sprinter Merlene Ottey withdrew from her country's squad for the World Championships after failing a drugs test. **25.** Colin Jackson became the first Briton to regain a world championship title when he won the 110 metres hurdles in Seville. **26.** At the World Championships in Seville, Michael Johnson set a new world record of 43.18 seconds for the 400 metres. **27.** Maurice Greene became the first athlete in the history of the World Championships to win both the 100 metres and the 200 metres titles. **28.** Ruud Gullit resigned as manager of Newcastle United FC.

AFRICA

SEPTEMBER 1998

7. The seven countries involved in fighting in the Democratic Republic of Congo held talks on the conflict and the future of the country. **13.** President Zeroual of Algeria called early presidential elections for February 1999 and announced that he would not be standing for re-election. **19.** Twenty-six people were killed and 125 injured in a bomb explosion in Zaroura, Algeria. **20.** Thirty-three people died in fighting between government forces and the troops of warlord Roosevelt Johnson in Monrovia, Liberia. **22.** Rioting broke out in Maseru, Lesotho, following intervention by South African troops to put down an attempted coup. **28.** More than 1,000 rebel soldiers in Lesotho surrendered to the South African-led Intervention Force.

OCTOBER 1998

1. The South African Development Community declared that it would attempt to destroy the Angolan rebel group UNITA because of its destabilizing influence in the region. **10.** Forty people were killed when rebel troops in the Democratic Republic of Congo shot down a Boeing 727. **18.** Fighting resumed in Guinea-Bissau between government forces and rebels. **19.** In Sierra Leone, 24 army officers were executed for their part in the 1997 coup. **20.** Sixteen Zimbabwean troops were captured by rebels in the Democratic Republic of Congo, the first evidence that Zimbabwe's forces were active in the country. **29.** The final report of South Africa's Truth and Reconciliation Commission was published; it blamed the successive white governments for years of atrocities but also criticized the African National Congress (ANC) for excessive violence.

NOVEMBER 1998

4. In Zimbabwe, thousands of protesters demonstrated against President Mugabe. **5.** The former president of Sierra Leone, Joseph Momoh, was sentenced to ten years' imprisonment for conspiracy in the 1997 coup. **6.** The Zambian opposition politician and possible presidential candidate, Ronald Penza, was shot dead. President Taki of the Comoros died. **10.** The family of the late Nigerian president, Sani Abacha, returned US$750 million of state funds he had illegally amassed. **11.** A one-day general strike was called in Zimbabwe to protest at price rises and the government's handling of the economy. **15.** Captain Blaise Compaoré was re-elected president of Burkina Faso; the election was boycotted by much of the opposition. **18.** A second one-day general strike was called in Zimbabwe. Following a compulsory purchase order by President Mugabe of Zimbabwe, 841 white farmers had their property seized.

DECEMBER 1998

5. The secretary-general of the UN, Kofi Annan, met Colonel Gaddafi of Libya to discuss the proposed trial of the Libyans suspected of the 1988 Lockerbie bombing. Four people died in heavy fighting on the island of Anjouan in the Comoros following a failed assassination attempt on the separatist leader Foundi Abdallah Ibrahim. In local elections in Nigeria, the People's Democratic Party won control of 459 of 751 councils. **6.** The presidential election in Gabon was won by the incumbent President Bongo. **7.** The death toll from fighting on Anjouan rose to between 30 and 40. **10.** Eighty-one people were killed by Muslim militants in the west of Algeria, bringing the number of deaths since the beginning of December to 200. **14.** Ahmed Ouyahia resigned as prime minister of Algeria. **16.** Civil war broke out again in Angola. **26.** A UN plane carrying 14 people crashed, possibly after being shot at, in Angola. **31.** Several hundred people died in the Republic of Congo following fighting between the army and the militia of Bernard Kolelas, the former prime minister.

JANUARY 1999

1. Five hundred civilians were killed by rebels in eastern areas of the Democratic Republic of Congo.

2. The UN suspended its flights to parts of Angola after a second UN plane was shot down. 9. State elections were held in Nigeria. 11. Nigerian troops launched a counter-offensive against rebel forces in Freetown, Sierra Leone. 12. The former president of Mali, Moussa Traoré, was sentenced to death by a court in Bamako, Mali, after being convicted of economic crimes. 13. Nigerian-led Economic Community of West African States' Monitoring Group (ECOMOG) troops drove rebel forces out of Freetown, Sierra Leone. 18. The UN announced that it would withdraw its personnel from Angola by 20 March, after fighting in the civil war escalated; Kofi Annan declared that 'there is no more peace to keep'. A cease-fire was declared in the Democratic Republic of Congo. The former president of Zimbabwe, Canaan Banana, was sentenced to ten years' hard labour for sodomy and assault. 23. Sifiso Nkabinde, the secretary-general of South Africa's United Democratic Movement, was murdered. 24. Eleven ANC supporters were murdered in a suspected revenge attack after Nkabinde's death. 27. In Angola, UNITA rebels captured the strategically important town of Mbanza-Congo. 28. At least 178 civilians were killed either by Hutu rebels or during clashes between rebels and government forces in Burundi. 31. Three of Zimbabwe's five judges of the Supreme Court wrote to President Mugabe asking him to condemn the illegal arrest and torture of two journalists, who had subsequently been freed.

FEBRUARY 1999

2. At least 35 people were killed in fighting between rebels and government forces in Guinea-Bissau. 6. Eritrean and Ethiopian forces clashed in renewed fighting along the border between the two countries. 8. President Kabbah of Sierra Leone announced that he would agree to talks with the rebel leader Foday Sankoh. 17. About 100 ECOMOG troops were arrested in Sierra Leone after allegations of 'summary executions'. 20. Parliamentary elections were held in Nigeria. 27. Presidential elections were held in Nigeria; they were won by General Olusegun Obasanjo, although independent observers identified 'many serious discrepancies' in the election process.

MARCH 1999

12. Britain recalled its ambassador in Kinshasa, Democratic Republic of Congo, after the arrest and subsequent expulsion of four British diplomats accused of espionage. 17. Eritrean troops claimed to have repelled a major attack by Ethiopian forces at Tsarona, 60 miles south of the Eritrean capital, Asmara. 21. Rebels massacred more than 250 civilians in the South Kivu region of the Democratic Republic of Congo. 26. Government and opposition parties in South Africa united to bid farewell to President Mandela when he addressed parliament for the last time before his retirement. Mr Mandela acknowledged the praise, but said that he was merely a product of his country's history.

APRIL 1999

5. UN sanctions against Libya were lifted after two suspected terrorists, Abdel Basset Ali al-Megrahi and Lamen Khalifa Fhimah were deported to the Netherlands to face trial over the 1988 Lockerbie disaster. The appeal court in Abuja, Nigeria, upheld the victory of Olusegun Obasanjo in February's presidential election. 9. President Ibrahim Bare Mainassara of Niger was assassinated by members of his personal security guard. Five former Rwandan politicians pleaded not guilty to 11 charges of genocide and crimes against humanity before the International Criminal Tribunal for Rwanda. 15. In Algeria, the presidential election took place; Abdelaziz Bouteflika, who was backed by the military, was the only candidate after the other six withdrew in protest against fraud in early voting. 16. Abdelaziz Bouteflika was proclaimed president of Algeria with 73 per cent of the vote. 17. Three former Rwandan government ministers implicated in the 1994 genocide of 800,000 people were arrested in Cameroon. 18. President Laurent Kabila of the Democratic Republic of Congo signed a peace agreement with President Museveni of Uganda. Rebels later dismissed the agreement, saying they wanted to talk directly to President Kabila. In Egypt, 20 Islamic militants were sentenced to death or life with hard labour. 21. ECOMOG said that rebels had hacked and burned to death scores of civilians as they retreated from Song, 27 miles east of Freetown, Sierra Leone. 30. The Government of the Comoros was overthrown in a bloodless military coup after three days of rioting.

MAY 1999

2. Militiamen of the warlord Hussein Mohamed Aidid counterattacked and recaptured the town of Baidoa, Somalia, from the Rahanwein resistance Army, which had overrun it on 1 May. 7. A military junta overthrew President Vieira of Guinea-Bissau; at least 70 people were killed. 14. Five people were sentenced to death for the 1993 assassination of Burundi's first democratically elected President, Melchior Ndadaye. 22. The African National Congress (ANC) and the Inkatha Freedom Party (IFP) in South Africa signed a pre-election peace pact. In Algeria's Tiaret province, troops killed 19 Muslim rebels suspected of murdering nine villagers. 24. In Sierra Leone, a cease-fire came into effect between government and rebel forces. 29. Olusegun Obasanjo was sworn in as Nigeria's president, ending more than 15 years of military rule. President Mandela addressed ANC supporters in the final rally before South Africa's general election.

JUNE 1999

3. South African voters returned the ANC to power with 266 seats in the 400-seat National Assembly, one seat short of a two-thirds majority. The Democratic Party became the official opposition with 38 seats and the IFP won 34 seats. The ANC

also won clear control of seven provinces in the parallel provincial election. **10.** The new South African president, Thabo Mbeki, consolidated his power by downgrading the office of deputy president and allying the ANC with a tiny opposition party, the Minority Front, which had won one seat in the election. The pact meant that the ANC had the two-thirds majority necessary to change the constitution. Several hundred Algerians who lost members of their family at the hands of Islamic extremists protested in Algiers against a government entente with the Islamic Salvation Army, the armed wing of the banned Islamic Salvation Front. **16.** In South Africa, Nelson Mandela handed over power to the new president, Thabo Mbeki **17.** President Mbeki named his first cabinet. **22.** Millers and bakers went on strike in Zimbabwe after the government issued new price controls. **25.** Violent protests followed the announcement that Bakili Muluzi had been re-elected as president of Malawi. In a separate election for parliament, opposition parties claimed the largest number of seats.

JULY 1999

1. Joshua Nkomo, the vice-president of Zimbabwe since 1990 and founder of the Zimbabwean African People's Union (ZAPU), died at the age of 83. **7.** The Sierra Leonean government reached a peace deal with the main rebel movement, under which its leader, Foday Sankoh, would become vice-president and head of the Mineral Resources Commission. **8.** The Swiss-based charity Christian Solidarity International claimed to have freed a record 2,035 slaves in a week in southern Sudan, bringing the number it had saved since 1995 to more than 11,000. **12.** Zimbabwe offered compensation to thousands of victims of the widespread massacres of the Ndebele tribe in 1982, in which at least 5,000 people died. **14.** The Truth and Reconciliation Commission implicated P. W. Botha, the former president of South Africa, in the murder of eight black activists in the 1980's. **19.** In Nigeria, hundreds of Hausa residents of Sagamu fled after heavy fighting with members of the Yoruba tribe left at least 66 people dead. Ethnic clashes between the two communities took place in other locations on 25 July, when some 30 people were killed. **23.** King Hassan II of Morocco died. **24.** In Angola, the authorities issued a warrant for the arrest of UNITA leader Jonas Savimbi, blaming him for the return to civil war. The Natal Law Society tendered a posthumous apology to Mahatma Gandhi for rejecting his application to become a South African lawyer in 1894 on racial grounds. **29.** A strike by 500,000 South African public sector workers began, threatening the strained alliance between the ANC and its trade union and Communist Party allies. **30.** A group of Kenyan MPs, including some from the ruling party, filed a no-confidence motion against the government, quoting evidence of senior officials' corruption.

AUGUST 1999

2. More than 12 people were killed in the Caprivi Strip, Namibia, in fighting between Namibian forces and the Caprivi Liberation Army seeking independence for the region. Namibian human rights activists later attempted to force President Nujoma to bring to court at least 300 people who disappeared in a round-up of suspects by paramilitary police. **3.** At least 15 people died and more than 25 were hurt after fighting between rival militia groups in Mogadishu, Somalia. **5.** The Sudanese government declared a two-month cease-fire in its conflict with southern rebels in order to allow aid to reach the region. In Nigeria, at least 700 people were thought to have died in local or ethnic fighting since May. **9.** The Zimbabwean Congress of Trade Unions announced it was to launch a political party. **11.** A former Rwandan minister for family and women's affairs, Pauline Nyiramasuhuko, was indicted for incitement to rape at the international tribunal sitting in Tanzania. **12.** Burundian villagers accused the Tutsi-led army of killing 147 Hutu civilians in revenge for a Hutu rebel attack **16.** Islamic extremists killed 29 people at Beni Ounif, Algeria. **21.** A bomb killed 17 people and wounded five near Ouzra, south of Algiers. **27.** The Roman Catholic bishop of Gikongoro diocese in Rwanda went on trial accused of genocide and crimes against humanity. In Uganda, King Ronald Muwenda Mutebi II of the Baganda tribe married British-born Sylvia Nagginda Luswata in Kampala Anglican Cathedral. **29.** President Mugabe demanded compensation from Britain for its part in colonizing Zimbabwe, saying that colonialism was an international criminal offence.

THE AMERICAS

SEPTEMBER 1998

3. Forest fires in Brazil were said to have destroyed more than three million acres of the Amazon rainforest. **11.** In the USA, the report of the investigation by the independent prosecutor Kenneth Starr into charges against President Clinton was published; it put forward 11 acts that might constitute grounds for the impeachment of the president. Brazil raised its interest rates by 20 per cent to 49.75 per cent and spent US$1.9 billion defending its currency. **21.** President Clinton's videotaped testimony to the grand jury investigating his alleged affair with Monica Lewinsky was broadcast in its entirety on US television. **30.** The IMF announced a rescue package for the Brazilian economy.

OCTOBER 1998

5. Fernando Cardoso was re-elected president of Brazil. **8.** The US House of Representatives voted 258–176 to authorize impeachment hearings into President Clinton's alleged misdemeanours. **26.**

Ecuador and Peru signed an agreement demarcating 48 km of common border, an issue that had led to three wars between the countries.

NOVEMBER 1998

2. In mid-term elections in the USA, the Republican majority in the House of Representatives was halved, though its majority in the Senate remained unchanged. 13. Paula Jones settled her sexual harassment case against President Clinton in return for $850,000. 19. Impeachment hearings against President Clinton began in the USA. 20. Tobacco companies reached a US$206 billion settlement with US states to pay for the treatment of smoking-related diseases. 25. Admiral Emilio Massera, the most notorious member of Argentina's military junta between 1976 and 1983, was arrested on charges of abducting children. 30. In Canada, the Quebec provincial election was won by the separatist Parti Québécois, but by a margin insufficient to force an immediate referendum on independence.

DECEMBER 1998

6. Hugo Chávez won the presidential election in Venezuela. 14. Puerto Rico voted to retain its status as a commonwealth within the USA. 16. Argentina and Chile signed an agreement settling their last territorial dispute in the Andes. 19. The US House of Representatives voted 228–206 to impeach President Clinton on charges of perjury before a grand jury and obstruction of justice.

JANUARY 1999

5. The US relaxed its trade embargo on Cuba. The senior military leader of the Shining Path rebel group was captured by Peruvian anti-terrorist forces in Lima. 7. The impeachment trial of President Clinton began in Washington DC. President Pastrana of Colombia held talks with the country's largest left-wing guerrilla group. 12. President Préval of Haiti said that he would appoint a government by decree, bypassing the country's parliament. 13. Brazil devalued its currency by 10 per cent. 22. The governor of Argentina's central bank said that his country was holding talks with the USA aimed at replacing the peso with the US dollar.

FEBRUARY 1999

2. Hugo Chávez was sworn in as president of Venezuela. Brazil sacked the governor of its central bank for the second time in a month when Francisco Lopes was fired. 12. The US Senate acquitted President Clinton of perjury and obstruction of justice. A Californian woman was awarded US$51 million damages against a tobacco company for its failure to warn her that smoking was addictive.

MARCH 1999

7. Francisco Flores won the presidential election in El Salvador. 8. President Préval and opposition party leaders agreed to create a provisional electoral council to organize elections in Haiti 22. The USA stepped up its trade dispute with the EU by threatening to impose punitive tariffs on $900 million worth of European agricultural exports in retaliation for the ban on its beef treated with growth hormones. 23. The vice-president of Paraguay, Luis Maria Argana, was assassinated in Asunción. 26. Jacques-Edouard Alexis took office as prime minister of Haiti and promised that elections would be held. 28. President Raul Cubas of Paraguay resigned and was granted asylum in Brazil. The first major sporting event between the USA and Cuba for 40 years was held when the Baltimore Orioles played the Cuban national baseball squad in Havana.

APRIL 1999

1. Nunavut, the new self-governing region of Canada, officially came into being. 6. Cuba condemned the American plan to house 20,000 Kosovar Albanians in the US naval base at Guantánamo Bay, saying it was a European problem. 12. In Colombia, left-wing rebels hijacked an Aviance plane on a domestic flight, forced it to land and herded away the 46 people on board. Police later found the empty plane. 16. Alabama's state house voted to repeal its constitutional ban on interracial marriages. 21. Four people died in rioting over fuel tax increases in Jamaica. The government later decided to halve the increases. 23. All cigarette billboards in the USA were removed under the terms of an agreement reached in 1998 between states and the tobacco industry. 28. According to a report in the New York Times, a scientist suspected of spying for China transferred huge amounts of data concerning nuclear weapons in the USA from a secret computer system to an unclassified network. The House of Representatives voted to limit President Clinton's freedom to deploy ground troops in Kosovo by insisting that congressional approval would have to be obtained first.

MAY 1999

3. Mireya Moscoso was elected president of Panama. 9. In the USA, the Energy Secretary Bill Richardson admitted that China had obtained nuclear secrets from the USA over the previous six years . 25. An Argentine delegation met a group of four councillors from the Falklands, the first meeting since the end of the conflict in 1982. They agreed to work together to conserve fish stocks and to co-operate over oil exploration as well as a range of regional issues. 25. A congressional inquiry in the USA reported that China had spent 40 years stealing nuclear technology and had spread it to unstable regimes around the world. The report by the Cox committee detailed what it described as the worst security lapse in American history. 28. The Colombian defence minister resigned in protest at a government decision to allow left-wing guerrillas to remain in control of a large area of jungle territory. 31. In Colombia, left-wing rebels held more than 100 worshippers from a church hostage. Four hostages were killed and 79 were later released.

JUNE 1999

1. Cuba demanded $181.1 billion (£113 billion) compensation for the deaths of 3,478 Cubans and injuries to 2,099 in 40 years of 'war' by the USA. 16. The American Vice-President Al Gore formally announced his bid for the presidency. The Republican George W. Bush also announced his candidacy. 30. Kenneth Starr ended his five-year Whitewater investigation into President and Mrs Clinton's financial dealings in Arkansas.

JULY 1999

9. Argentina applied for associate membership of NATO. 12. In Colombia, left-wing guerrillas launched their biggest offensive in 35 years of civil war. 13. In Peru, the last remaining commander of the Shining Path, a Maoist guerrilla movement, was captured. 16. The head of the US Chamber of Commerce, Thomas Donahue, visited Cuba; it was the first such visit in 40 years. 20. Cuba announced that it would claim US$181 billion in damages for the alleged deaths and injuries suffered by its citizens in four decades of American aggression against Cuba. 30. Venezuelan voters gave candidates backed by President Hugo Chávez an overwhelming majority in a constituent assembly that will draft a new constitution for the country. The USA announced it would pay $4.5 million in compensation for the three killed and 17 wounded at the Chinese embassy in Belgrade on 7 May 1999.

AUGUST 1999

2. Rebels from the Revolutionary Armed Forces of Colombia killed 19 villagers in Narion. 8. The first group of Argentine tourists to be allowed to visit the Falkland Islands since the 1982 conflict were given a cool reception. Islanders protested in Port Stanley after an Argentine flag was laid at a memorial on 11 August. 11. Buford Furrow, a member of the Aryan Nations white supremacist group, gave himself up to the FBI after shooting three children and two teachers at a Jewish community centre in Los Angeles. 25. The US Congress announced that it would investigate allegations that American financial institutions had helped to launder billions of dollars from Russia, including funds loaned by the IMF. 27. In Venezuela, the Constituent Assembly placed the opposition-controlled Congress in indefinite recess. The president of the Supreme Court resigned after the assembly voted to grant itself powers to sack judges.

ASIA

SEPTEMBER 1998

2. Thousands of students in Myanmar protested against the country's military rulers. 6. Iran moved thousands of troops to its border with Afghanistan following the deaths of Iranian diplomats and journalists during fighting in Mazar-i-Sharif, Afghanistan. 8. There were anti-government demonstrations in Jakarta, Indonesia and Phnom Penh, Cambodia. The Commonwealth Games opened in Malaysia. 11. The UN High Commissioner for Refugees confirmed that the Taleban militia in Afghanistan had massacred thousands of ethnic Hazara people during the battle for control of Mazar-i-Sharif in August 1998. Twelve people were killed when a bomb planted by Tamil Tiger rebels exploded in Jaffna, Sri Lanka. 20. Anwar Ibrahim, the former deputy prime minister of Malaysia, was arrested for demonstrating against the government. 27. More than 150,000 people demonstrated against the government in Kuala Lumpur, Malaysia. 28–29. More than 700 soldiers and Tamil Tigers were killed in fighting in northern Sri Lanka.

OCTOBER 1998

1. Tamil Tiger guerrillas captured the town of Kilinochi, northern Sri Lanka. 2. Sanjaasuregiin Zorig, the leader of Mongolia's transition to democracy and the man expected to be the country's next prime minister, was murdered. 8. Fighting was reported between Iranian and Taleban troops on the border between Iran and Afghanistan. Japan apologised to South Korea for the 'tremendous damage and suffering' caused during colonial rule. 9. Pakistan amended its constitution to make the Koran and the sayings of Muhammad supreme law. 10. Ten thousand Malaysians demonstrated in support of the imprisoned former deputy prime minister Anwar Ibrahim. 11. Presidential elections in Azerbaijan were won by the incumbent, Haidar Aliyev, although observers from the Organization for Security and Co-operation in Europe (OSCE) declared the election to be marred by fraud. 14. The Taleban militia in Afghanistan agreed to free all Iranian prisoners and to punish those responsible for killing Iranian diplomats and journalists. 14–19. China and Taiwan held their highest-level talks since 1949 when the semi-official Taiwanese envoy to the mainland met President Jiang Zemin in Beijing.

NOVEMBER 1998

2. The trial of Anwar Ibrahim opened in Malaysia. 4. Anti-government forces seized the airport and official buildings in Khodzhand, Tajikistan. 5. The Philippines complained to China after the latter had sent armed vessels to the disputed Spratly Islands in the South China Sea. 6. Talks between India and Pakistan opened with Pakistan rejecting a cease-fire offer. President Clinton agreed to further relax sanctions on India and Pakistan. 8. Fifteen former army officers and politicians in Bangladesh were sentenced to death for their involvement in the assassination of Sheikh Mujibir Rahman, Bangladesh's first president, in 1975. 12. Ninety people were injured in riots in Jakarta, Indonesia. 13. Hun Sen formed a coalition government in Cambodia. Fourteen protestors were killed following fighting in Indonesia. 20. China announced that it will open

all court trials to the public from December 1998. **25.** The IMF agreed a US$5.5 billion rescue package for Pakistan. President Jiang Zemin of China arrived in Tokyo for a state visit. **29.** The Congress Party in India won elections in three key states.

DECEMBER 1998

6. The ruling nationalist party Kuomintang increased its majority in Taiwan following parliamentary elections. **17.** South Korean troops sank a North Korean spy submarine during fighting in South Korean waters. One hundred and fifty students were injured in clashes with police in Jakarta, Indonesia. The Association of South-East Asian Nations (ASEAN) announced that Cambodia's membership would be delayed. The country's suspended UN membership was restored. **21.** Two Chinese dissidents, Xu Wenli and Wang Youcai, were jailed for more than ten years on charges of subversion. **22.** Qin Yongmin, a Chinese dissident who had attempted to set up the Chinese Democratic Party, was jailed for 12 years on charges of subversion.

JANUARY 1999

3. The prime minister of Pakistan, Nawaz Sharif, survived a suspected assassination attempt when a bridge was blown up shortly before he was due to cross it. **4.** Gunmen killed 16 Shi'ite Muslims at a mosque in Punjab province, Pakistan **10.** Nursultan Nazarbayev, the incumbent, won the presidential election in Kazakhstan, although the elections were described as 'grossly unfair' by human rights groups. **13.** Japan's ruling Liberal Democratic Party and an opposition group formed a coalition government. **16.** Afghan opposition forces captured the strategically important town of Yakaolang. **28.** Indonesia's House of Representatives passed a number of reforms liberalizing the country's political system. **31.** About 50 Tamil Tigers were killed in fighting in north-eastern Sri Lanka.

FEBRUARY 1999

2. Police in Pakistan attacked hundreds of journalists and press workers protesting at a government crackdown on the press. **5.** Leo Echegaray became the first person to be executed in the Philippines for 23 years after he was found guilty of raping his stepdaughter. **9.** The last remaining soldiers of the Khmer Rouge guerilla group formally joined the Cambodian army. **10.** The East Timorean leader Xanana Gusmão was moved from prison to house arrest to help shape the future of the disputed territory. **20.** The spiritual leader of Iraq's Shi'ite Muslims was shot dead in Najaf, Iraq. **21.** India and Pakistan agreed to inform each other of any future nuclear tests.

MARCH 1999

10. At least three people were killed and dozens injured as Muslims and Christians rioted in the Spice Islands, Indonesia, where religious violence had claimed 200 lives in the preceding two months.

14. The Taliban and the opposition in the north of Afghanistan reached an agreement to share power. **21.** Sri Lankan government forces captured the town of Madhu from Tamil Tiger control. Warring ethnic groups set fire to houses in Borneo after clashes in which at least 70 people were killed. **23.** Pakistan paraded long-range nuclear ballistic missiles capable of hitting targets deep inside India. **24.** Japanese ships fired shots for the first time in 46 years as two vessels, thought to be North Korean, were chased from Japanese waters.

APRIL 1999

11. India test-fired an Agni II ballistic missile, breaking a five-year period of restraint. **13.** Several million Sikhs gathered at Anandpur Sahib to celebrate the 300th anniversary of the formal founding of the Sikh brotherhood. **14.** Pakistan's successful test-firing of a Ghauri-II missile raised fears of a deterioration of security in South Asia. **15.** The former prime minister of Pakistan, Benazir Bhutto, and her husband were sentenced to five years' imprisonment and fined £5 million on corruption charges. Benazir Bhutto was absent. **17.** In India, Sonia Gandhi, the president of the Congress Party, tried to form a government after India's ruling coalition lost a confidence vote by one vote. **23.** More than 5,000 members of Nepal's Tibetan community demanded the release of the Panchen Lama, who was arrested by China in 1995. **25.** Mrs Gandhi met President Narayanan to tell him that she could not obtain a majority. **26.** Sultan Salahuddin Abdul Aziz Shah was installed as the 11th king of Malaysia under the system of rotating constitutional monarchs. President Narayanan dissolved India's lower house of parliament. **27.** Japan decided to legislate to allow military forces to provide support to US forces in case of emergency situations in areas surrounding Japan. Indonesia's President Habibie announced that he accepted the UN plan for a referendum to take place on 8 August giving East Timor a choice between autonomy and independence. **28.** China and Russia achieved a breakthrough in talks to map out their common 2,656-mile border, ending a 300-year-old dispute. An agreement was due to be signed later in 1999. The Congress Party announced that Sonia Gandhi would stand for election to parliament.

MAY 1999

1. Iran's culture minister, Ataollah Mohajerani, won a parliamentary vote of confidence after an attempt to unseat him by Islamic hard-liners **7.** China protested to the UN that the NATO bombing of the Chinese embassy in Belgrade was a war crime. Anti-Western demonstrations continued in Beijing for several days. **9.** Najam Sethi, the editor of Pakistan's *Friday Times*, was arrested on a sedition charge; he had called Pakistan a failed state and questioned the legitimacy of its creation. **17.** Mrs Gandhi resigned as president of India's Congress Party after three colleagues said that she was unfit to be a prime ministerial candidate because of her foreign origins. She retracted her resignation after they were expelled from the party. In Indonesia, the three leading reformist parties agreed to unite against President B.J. Habibie. 22. Pakistan launched eight-day celebrations to mark the first anniversary of its nuclear weapons tests. Benazir Bhutto declared that she would not return to Pakistan to fight her conviction for corruption and that she intended instead to settle in the UK. 26. Indian military officials said that MiG 21 and MiG 27 aircraft and helicopter gunships had inflicted 'heavy casualties' on about 500 separatist guerrillas who had infiltrated the disputed region of Kashmir from Pakistan. Squadrons of Pakistani aircraft were sent to front-line airfields in the first major confrontation involving aircraft since the war in 1971. 27. The government of the Philippines agreed to allow the American navy to resume port calls after a three-year suspension, and to resume joint military exercises using ground troops. Pakistan shot down two Indian MiG fighters over the Pakistani-controlled area of Kashmir. India declared that it would continue its airstrikes in spite of the loss. Shamshad Ahmad, Pakistan's foreign secretary, appealed to Western ambassadors to increase the strength of the UN Military Observers Group in Kashmir. 28. Pakistan-backed Muslim guerrillas in Kashmir shot down an Indian helicopter. India increased its troop numbers to more than 30,000, double the number of Pakistani troops in Kashmir. 29. Pakistan said its Foreign Minister, Sartaj Aziz, would visit New Delhi in an attempt to resolve the conflict in Kashmir.

JUNE 1999

1. India renewed air strikes and ground operations against Muslim guerrillas in the mountains of northern Kashmir. 7. Indonesians voted in the first democratic elections in the country in more than 40 years. Early poll returns showed that the main opposition party, Indonesian Democratic Struggle Party, had a commanding lead. 10. Pakistan returned the mutilated bodies of six Indian soldiers in northern Kashmir; the soldiers, from a 14-man patrol that had been captured, had apparently been tortured. 11. Pakistan claimed to have repulsed two major assaults by Indian troops in Kashmir. A four-day stand-off over fishing rights in the Yellow Sea was broken after South Korean Navy vessels rammed North Korean military boats; no shots were fired. 13. India's prime minister, Atal Behari Vajpayee, warned his country to be prepared for war with Pakistan. 15. North and South Korea fought a fierce naval battle at their disputed maritime border; five vessels on each side suffered damage. 18. The Beijing-appointed Panchen Lama returned to the Tibetan capital, Lhasa, in what was seen as an attempt to secure his acceptance over a rival nominated by the Dalai Lama. 22. The Indian Army began a huge offensive on a strategic peak and mountain range in Kashmir. 23. A UN-supervised

vote on the future of East Timor was delayed for two weeks because of the poor security situation in the province. 26. Pakistan's army chief, Pervez Musharraf, announced that Pakistan would not withdraw unilaterally from the battle zone of Kargil; this was the first admission by Pakistan that its forces had crossed the 1972 frontier. 27. More than 200 mainland Chinese protested in front of Hong Kong's Immigration Tower against China's reinterpretation of the territory's constitution, which took away their right of abode in the territory. 29. Amnesty International accused Myanmar's ruling military government of widespread abuses, including killings, torture and rape, against ethnic minorities.

JULY 1999

3. Pakistan called for UN mediation in the Kashmir conflict. Provisional results of the Indonesian general election were announced; the party of Megawati Sukarnoputri, daughter of Indonesia's founding president, gained the most votes 8. Five people died and dozens disappeared when the police and Islamic vigilantes in Tehran, Iran, broke up a student march. 9. The Pakistani Cabinet asked Muslim guerrillas fighting against Indian forces in Kashmir to withdraw. 12. Iran's reformist President Mohammed Khatami vowed to put down student protests in Tehran, which had spread from the university to the main commercial area. In Lahore, 15,000 people demonstrated to denounce what they saw as a betrayal by the Pakistani government in Kashmir. 13. Lee Teng-hui, the Taiwanese president, repudiated the One China policy, the pretence of a common goal of unification; he later declared that there would be one China only when the two sides had reunified as a democracy. Tens of thousands of Iranians marched through Tehran to show their support for the Islamic regime. 14. China declared that it had the technology to make neutron bombs. 20. Militants believed to be members of Laskar-i-Toiba (Army of the Pure) shot fifteen people dead in a Kashmiri village 28. The UN-sponsored referendum in East Timor on independence or greater autonomy within Indonesia was deferred until 30 August because of difficulties in registering voters.

AUGUST 1999

3. President Habibie of Indonesia declared the results of the parliamentary election valid and binding, clearing the way for a presidential election in November 1999. Hundreds of thousands of civilians fled fierce fighting in northern Afghanistan after a series of military victories by the Taliban militia. 5. South Korea and Japan conducted their first joint naval exercise. Afghan opposition forces launched a fierce counterattack against the Taliban, reversing its military gains. She Wanbao, a member of the China Democracy Party, was sentenced to 12 years' imprisonment for subversion; four other members of the banned party were given sentences

of between eight and 13 years. **9.** Beijing vetoed a proposed papal visit to Hong Kong, citing the Vatican's diplomatic ties with Taiwan. A Yemeni court convicted eight British men and two Algerians of plotting a fundamentalist bombing campaign in December 1998. **10.** Indian forces were put on alert after two of their combat planes shot down a Pakistani Navy aircraft, killing all 16 people on board. **12.** Priests accused the army of killing at least 25 Christians in Ambon, Indonesia; the armed forces launched an investigation the following day. **13.** The Japanese Cabinet approved research into an anti-ballistic missile defence system, to be run jointly with the USA; on 18 July the Taiwanese president said that Taiwan wished to participate in the project. **16.** The Indian Prime Minister Atal Bihari Vajpayee said that he would legislate to prevent those not born in India from holding the highest state offices. **24.** Presidents Yeltsin of Russia and Jiang Zemin of China met in Bishkek, Kyrgyzstan, with leaders of three Central Asian countries to discuss combating separatism, religious extremism and the narcotics and arms trades. Calcutta was officially renamed Kolkata. **25.** The largest pro-independence rally staged during more than two decades of Indonesian rule was held in East Timor. **30.** In East Timor, more than 90 per cent of the 450,000 electorate voted in a referendum on independence.

AUSTRALASIA AND THE PACIFIC

OCTOBER 1998

3. The ruling Liberal-National coalition led by John Howard won the general election in Australia.

MARCH 1999

23. The proposed new preamble to Australia's constitution was announced by the prime minister, John Howard **28.** The Labour government won a second term with an increased majority in the parliament of New South Wales, Australia.

APRIL 1999

12. The Australian foreign minister, Alexander Downer, denounced the Yugoslav government's claim that Steve Pratt, a captured aid worker, had been a spy.

JUNE 1999

10. In Australia, legislation was introduced under which a referendum on becoming a republic would be held on 6 November. **24.** Sitiveni Rabuka, the former prime minister of Fiji and a Commonwealth envoy, was taken hostage briefly whilst he tried to bring an end to the increasingly bitter civil war in the Solomon Islands.

JULY 1999

9. Papua New Guinea established diplomatic relations with Taiwan. **13.** Sir Mekere Morauta was elected prime minister of Papua New Guinea; he suggested that the controversial recognition of Taiwan, which had led to the fall of the previous government, would be cancelled. **18.** Luagalau Levaula Kamu, the Samoan minister of Public Works, was shot dead.

AUGUST 1999

12. Prime Minister John Howard of Australia was accused by opposition politicians of trying to engineer the defeat of the referendum on a republic which was due to be held in November 1999.

EUROPE

SEPTEMBER 1998

27. The German federal elections were won by Gerhard Schröder's Social Democrats who said that they would govern in coalition with the Green Party. Opposition parties won 93 of the 150 seats in the Slovakian election and said they would attempt to form a coalition government. **28.** Fatos Nano resigned as prime minister of Albania. **30.** Pandeli Majko, the leader of the Socialist Party, began to form a new government in Albania.

OCTOBER 1998

7. In Moscow, tens of thousands of protesters called for President Yeltsin to resign. **9.** Romano Prodi resigned as prime minister of Italy after losing a vote of confidence. **13.** Romano Prodi was asked to form a new coalition government in Italy. **15.** Prodi announced that he had failed to form a government and proposed that Massimo D'Alema, the leader of the Left Democrats, be appointed prime minister. **27.** Gerhard Schröder was inaugurated as chancellor of Germany. **29.** At the International Criminal Tribunal in The Hague, Goran Jelisić admitted to killing at least 14 Bosnians and Croats and pleaded guilty to 15 counts of crimes against humanity.

NOVEMBER 1998

3. The Spanish government announced that it was prepared to hold talks with ETA, the terrorist group that had announced a cease-fire in September. A new left-right coalition government was formed in Slovakia under Mikulas Dzurinda. **13.** Abdullah Öcalan, the head of the Kurdish terrorist organization the PKK, was arrested at Rome airport. **19.** Turkish importers announced a boycott on Italian goods after Rome refused to extradite Öcalan to face charges of terrorism in Turkey. **20.** Galina Starovoitova, Russia's most prominent female politician, was shot dead in St Petersburg. **25.** The Turkish government lost a vote of confidence following a corruption scandal in which the prime minister was implicitly accused of having links with organized crime. **27.** In Dublin, Paul Ward was convicted of the murder of journalist Veronica Guerin in June 1996.

DECEMBER 1998

1. NATO troops arrested General Radislav Krstić, the most senior member of the Serbian military to face charges of genocide in The Hague. **2.** Bülent Ecevit was appointed prime minister-designate in Turkey. **9.** Ruth Dreifuss became Switzerland's first female president. **16.** An Italian court of appeal ruled that Abdullah Öcalan should not be detained, although the Italian government said that he would remain under observation and could not leave Italy; on 17 January 1999 he was allowed to leave the country. **29.** The Cypriot government announced that it would not deploy Russian-made anti-aircraft systems on its territory, defusing tensions on the divided island. **30.** Juan José Ibarratxe of the moderate Basque Nationalist Party was elected president of the Basque region of Spain. **31.** Brane Miljus, a moderate, was named prime minister-designate of Republika Srpska, Bosnia-Hercegovina.

JANUARY 1999

11. Bülent Ecevit formed a new government in Turkey. Turkey's chief prosecutor called for the abolition of the main Kurdish party, Hadep, claiming that it was acting as a front for the outlawed Kurdistan Workers' Party.

FEBRUARY 1999

16. Abdullah Öcalan was captured by Turkish special forces in Kenya. **17.** Kurds across Europe held violent protests following the arrest of Öcalan. Greenland's governing Siumut Social Democratic Party won the largest number of seats in elections to the island's home-rule parliament. **18.** Three Greek ministers were dismissed following an outcry against the country's alleged role in the capture of Abdullah Öcalan.

MARCH 1999

5. Boris Berezovsky was sacked as head of the CIS. Nikola Poplasen was sacked as president of Republika Srpska. **7.** In the Estonian general election, the Centre Party won most seats but a coalition of centre-right parties formed the new government. **11.** Oskar Lafontaine resigned as finance minister of Germany and chairman of the Social Democratic Party. **13.** Two Kurdish groups claimed responsibility for the fire-bombing of an Istanbul shopping complex in which 13 people died. **20.** A bomb in the city of Vladikavkaz, the North Ossetian capital, killed 51 people and injured 154. **21.** President Aslan Maskhadov of the rebel Russian republic of Chechnya was the target of an assassination attempt. Finland's governing Social Democratic Party lost ground but retained the largest share of parliamentary seats in national elections. **31.** Finland's prime minister, Paavo Lipponen, tendered his government's resignation.

APRIL 1999

12. Dario Kordić, a former ally of President Tudjman of Croatia, went on trial before the International War Crimes Tribunal in The Hague, charged with 22 counts of war crimes in Bosnia in 1992 and 1993. In Germany, the Social Democratic Party confirmed Gerhard Schröder, the German Chancellor, as its leader. **16.** The Swedish finance minister, Erik Asbrink, resigned two days before he was to present a budget. **18.** A referendum was held in Italy on abolishing proportional representation; 90 per cent voted in favour, but the referendum was declared invalid as the number voting fell short of the required 50 per cent. Swiss voters approved changes to the constitution giving workers the right to strike for the first time. **28.** In Turkey, prosecutors formally demanded the death penalty for Abdullah Öcalan.

MAY 1999

4. Merve Kavakci, an Islamist deputy, caused uproar by wearing a headscarf to the Turkish Parliament; President Suleyman Demirel later stripped her of her Turkish citizenship for having taken up American citizenship without approval. **9.** Monaco celebrated the 50th anniversary of the accession of Prince Rainier. **12.** President Yeltsin sacked the prime minister, Yevgeny Primakov, and the rest of the government. The Duma later confirmed his nominee, Sergei Stepashin, as prime minister. **13.** Carlo Azeglio Ciampi was elected Italy's tenth president by an overwhelming majority in the first round of voting by the Italian Parliament. **22.** The Social Democrat Johannes Rau was elected president of Germany.

JUNE 1999

1. In Belgium, the public health minister, Marcel Colla, and the farm minister, Karel Pinxten, resigned after criticism that they had failed to act over animal feed contaminated with dioxin. The sale of Belgian poultry, eggs, beef and pork were later banned throughout the EU. **5.** The Pope began a 13-day tour of Poland in the city of Gdańsk, where he was welcomed by President Aleksander Kwasniewski. **10.** The Romanian Parliament voted to allow public access to the confidential files of the Securitate, the secret police during the communist era. **14.** Belgium's prime minister, Jean-Luc Dehaene, resigned after losing an election marked by public anger over the handling of the contaminated food crisis. **15.** Rudolf Schuster was sworn in as president of Slovakia, after a ballot which ended more than a year in which the country had been without a head of state. **29.** Abdullah Öcalan was sentenced to hang after he was convicted of treason against the Turkish state. **30.** Militant Kurds were suspected of fire-bombing ten Turkish businesses and an Islamic cultural centre in Germany in protest against the death sentence passed on Abdullah Öcalan.

JULY 1999

1. In Germany, Johannes Rau, the first Social Democratic President for 30 years, took office and promised to guide the country towards a more multicultural society. Turkish troops backed by helicopter gunships fought rebels loyal to Abdullah Öcalan after army positions in Tunceli province were attacked. **4.** Thousands of Belgian farmers marched through Brussels to demand more government aid to overcome the dioxin contamination crisis. **6.** British special forces soldiers arrested Radislav Brdjanin, who was a close political associate of Radovan Karadzić, the former Bosnian Serb leader accused of genocide, in Banja Luka, Bosnia-Hercegovina. **7.** Russia deployed helicopter gunships and armoured vehicles in a border battle against guerrillas from Chechnya equipped with mortars and grenade launchers on a bridge linking Chechnya and Dagestan. **8.** Turkey was convicted at the European Court of Human Rights of 13 instances of violating Kurds' free speech, and of two concerning torture and missing persons. **11.** In Belgium, King Albert II announced a new government led by liberal Guy Verhofstadt. **12.** The Dutch government voted to decriminalize euthanasia. **19.** Bülent Ecevit, the Turkish prime minister, ruled out any form of compromise over Cyprus; he was taking part in the 25th anniversary celebrations of the Turkish Republic of Northern Cyprus. **21.** The entire former executive of ETA, the Basque terrorist organization, was freed after Spain's Constitutional Court overturned seven-year jail sentences against them; they had been in prison for 20 months. **26.** Turkish and Greek leaders launched a week of consultations on a range of issues from trade to terrorism in an attempt to ease tensions. **27.** In Turkey, the Ankara State Security Council, which had imposed the death sentence on Abdullah Öcalan, sent its decision to the High Court of Appeals for review. **29.** The Autonomous Republic of Ingushetia declared its intention to legalize polygamy in defiance of the Russian government.

AUGUST 1999

9. President Yeltsin of Russia sacked the prime minister, Sergei Stepashin and appointed Vladimir Putin in his place. The appointment was approved by parliament on 16 August. Vinko Martinović, a Bosnian Croat, was handed over to the International Criminal Tribunal for the former Yugoslavia by the Croatian government to face trial on charges of ethnic cleansing. **10.** Islamic rebels in the republic of Dagestan declared it an independent Islamic state. **13.** Russia launched an offensive against Islamic rebels in Dagestan. **15.** A state of emergency was declared in Chechnya after Russia threatened to attack Islamic guerrilla bases located there. **17.** In response to Turkey's worst earthquake in 20 years, Greece sent emergency supplies, medical teams and pharmaceutical aid to the stricken area. In Bosnia-Hercegovina, a report by the anti-fraud unit of the Office of the High Representative of the European Union revealed 220 cases of fraud, naming several officials linked to various political parties. The report claimed that up to US$1 billion (£625 million) had been stolen from public funds and

international aid. **20.** The Danish Court of Appeal ordered the government to pay £44,000 in damages to Inuits who had been forced off land to expand the American airforce base at Thule, Greenland. **25.** Prime Minister Bülent Ecevit launched an appeal for the international community to come to Turkey's financial rescue. **26.** Russia claimed that it had recaptured all the villages seized by rebels in Dagestan. **29.** A Norwegian soldier with the NATO peacekeeping force was arrested by Macedonian authorities after his vehicle was involved in a crash in which Radovan Stojkoski, a government minister, was killed. **31.** A bomb blast in a Moscow shopping centre injured 29 people, five seriously. It was thought to be the work of Islamic militants from the Caucasus.

EUROPEAN UNION

OCTOBER 1998

1. The European Police Office (Europol) came into being in The Hague. **8.** The European Parliament voted by a large majority to lift the immunity of Jean-Marie Le Pen, the leader of the National Front in France, who was facing charges in Germany of trivializing the Holocaust. **27.** EU officials dropped non-military sanctions against Nigeria.

NOVEMBER 1998

10. The EU began formal enlargement talks with Hungary, Poland, the Czech Republic, Estonia, Slovenia and Cyprus. **13.** A report by the European Court of Auditors showed that 5 per cent of EU funds was misspent on schemes that were either mismanaged, poorly managed or fraudulent.

DECEMBER 1998

3. The European Parliament voted to end the process of allowing MEPs' salaries to be topped up by large expenses allowances. **11.** The Vienna summit opened. **17.** The European Parliament refused to clear the accounts of the European Commission.

JANUARY 1999

1. The euro became the standard currency of 11 European states, nicknamed 'Euroland'. Germany assumed the presidency of the EU **14.** MEPs rejected a motion of censure against the European Commission. **17.** EU ambassadors returned to Belarus following a six-month dispute over their residences.

FEBRUARY 1999

22. Thirty thousand European farmers clashed with riot police in Belgium in protest against the proposed reform of the Common Agricultural Policy.

MARCH 1999

11. The euro rose strongly after the resignation of the German finance minister, Oskar Lafontaine, who had been criticized for political interference in the affairs of the European Central Bank. **13.** Britain asked to be allowed to opt into parts of the Schengen agreement, but to be excluded from the requirements relating to border controls. **15.** European finance ministers met in Brussels to consider a 'withholding tax', a measure proposed by the Commission as part of moves towards tax harmonization. **16.** All the members of the European Commission resigned after an auditors' report concluded that fraud and corruption in the Commission had passed unnoticed. **24.** Romano Prodi was unanimously nominated to succeed Jacques Santer as president of the European Commission. **29.** The euro fell to a record low against the pound and the dollar, undermined by the intensifying conflict in the Balkans and fresh signs of European economic weakness.

APRIL 1999

8. The prospect of EU membership for all countries in the Balkan region was held out by EU foreign ministers as part of a strategy to promote peace. **13.** The European Parliament voted for the harmonization of criminal law for a limited range of serious offences. Romano Prodi, the president-designate of the European Commissions promised to use his term to create a single European economy and accelerate moves toward political unity. **28.** The final meeting of Schengen ministers took place before the Schengen Agreement became part of general EU law following the ratification of the Amsterdam Treaty.

MAY 1999

1. The Amsterdam Treaty came into force. **9.** Romano Prodi said that the creation of a European army was the logical next step in the integration of EU foreign policy.

JUNE 1999

2. EU leaders agreed an ambitious common defence and security policy giving it the means to respond to international crises independently of NATO. **4.** Javier Solana was appointed to the new position of EU High Representative for foreign and security policy. The European Commission placed restrictions on a wide range of Belgian foodstuffs, following fears of contamination by dioxins. **14.** The European People's party (EPP), an umbrella centre-right bloc, won the most seats in the European Parliament election, which was marked by a low turnout of voters. **25.** Tougher controls on the commercial release of genetically modified crops were agreed by EU environment ministers. **29.** The European Commission threatened to launch proceedings against Spain over delays imposed on people crossing the frontier to and from Gibraltar.

JULY 1999

1. The outgoing Commission rebuked the Industry Commissioner, Martin Bangeman, who had resigned

and accepted an employment offer from a telecommunications company. **6.** Pauline Green resigned as leader of the Socialist group in the European Parliament amid criticism of her leadership. **9.** Romano Prodi announced his team of 20 commissioners. **13.** A confidential report from the European Central Bank warned that governments of the countries participating in the euro were in danger of undermining the single currency by failing to take action to curb their budget deficits. Jacques Santer stepped down from his caretaker role as president of the Commission.

AUGUST 1999

19. The Italian authorities reopened a criminal investigation into the activities of Romano Prodi; the case involved a consulting company jointly owned by him and his wife, which he had failed to declare during his term as Italy's prime minister. **30.** Socialist MEPs declared that they would oppose the appointment of Loyola de Palacio as vice-president of the Commission.

THE BALKAN CONFLICT

SEPTEMBER 1998

28. International observers found evidence of systematic torturing and killing of ethnic Albanians by Serb forces in Kosovo, Yugoslavia.

OCTOBER 1998

12. President Milošević of Yugoslavia allowed international observers into Kosovo and agreed to talks on greater autonomy for the province.

DECEMBER 1998

14. Thirty-eight people died in fighting in Kosovo.

JANUARY 1999

8. Eight Serb soldiers were taken hostage by separatist soldiers in Kosovo; they were released on 12 January. **11.** Enver Maloku, a senior aide to the moderate ethnic Albanian leader Ibrahim Rugova, was shot dead outside his house in Priština, Kosovo. **16.** Serbian police forces broke the existing ceasefire and killed 45 Kosovars near the town of Racak, Kosovo. **18.** President Milošević expelled the chief observer of the OSCE and barred the head UN war crimes prosecutor from Kosovo as Serbian troops continued their attack on Racak. **21.** Following international pressure President Milošević backed down over the expulsion of the OSCE chief observer. **29.** NATO and Russia ordered the warring factions in Kosovo to attend a peace conference in Paris in February 1999.

FEBRUARY 1999

6. Peace talks over Kosovo began in Paris. **23.** The Kosovo peace talks broke up without a deal being agreed.

MARCH 1999

12. President Milošević repeated his opposition to any deployment of foreign troops in Kosovo after talks with Richard Holbrooke, the US special envoy. NATO's supreme commander, Gen. Wesley Clark, warned President Milošević that the alliance was prepared to strike Serbia if he blocked peace talks on Kosovo. **17.** Kosovar Albanians signed an international peace agreement in Paris that offered Kosovo broad autonomy within Serbia and provided for the deployment of a 28,000-strong NATO peacekeeping force. **19.** Western monitors evacuated Kosovo after peace talks were abandoned. **20.** Western embassies withdrew non-essential staff from Belgrade. **21.** Thousands fled their homes as Serbian forces advanced against a Kosovo Liberation Army (KLA) stronghold in the Drenica region. **22.** Richard Holbrooke met President Milošević in a final effort to avert military conflict. **23.** The Yugoslav government declared a state of emergency. The Russian prime minister, Yevgeni Primakov, denounced plans for 'unjustified' NATO attacks on Serb military targets. **24.** NATO air strikes against targets in Yugoslavia commenced. The German Luftwaffe flew into combat for the first time since the Second World War. President Yeltsin ordered an end to Russia's co-operation with NATO. **25.** Yugoslavia formally broke off diplomatic relations with the UK, the USA, France and Germany. Journalists from countries linked to the NATO air strikes were ordered to leave Yugoslavia. **26.** NATO forces shot down two Yugoslav MiG 29 aircraft after they flew into Bosnia's UN no-fly zone. **27.** NATO began low-level bombing missions against Serbian forces after reports of hundreds of Kosovo Albanian civilians being massacred in Kosovo. **28.** Albania appealed for international help to deal with tens of thousands of Kosovar refugees. NATO launched more air attacks against Serb military targets. **30.** NATO ambassadors met to consider extending the range of targets for the air strikes to include ministries in Belgrade and other key targets. Yevgeni Primakov visited Belgrade with the Russian foreign and defence ministers in a diplomatic mission aimed at ending the conflict in Kosovo.

APRIL 1999

2. President Milošević asked Russia to provide weapons to combat NATO's air attacks. **5.** NATO targeted oil storage sites inside Serbia. **6.** An offer from the Yugoslav government to begin a unilateral cease-fire in Kosovo was rejected by NATO. **7.** Macedonian troops forcibly evicted 30,000 refugees into Albania. Simultaneously, Serbian troops closed the border with Macedonia and ordered thousands of Kosovar Albanians back to Kosovo. Tony Blair and President Clinton warned President Milošević that the cessation of Serbia's ethnic cleansing policy was a precondition of Nato calling off its assault against Yugoslavia. **9.** President Yeltsin warned NATO not to send ground troops into Kosovo,

saying it would force Russia to become involved and could cause a European or even a world war. **11.** Paskal Milo, the Albanian foreign minister, said that his government was ready to accept ground troops from NATO and had decided to give NATO the right to control Albania's airspace, ports and other military infrastructure. President Djukanović of Montenegro warned that any attempt by Serbia to overthrow his government would result in civil war in Montenegro. **12.** The Yugoslav parliament voted overwhelmingly to apply for membership of a confederation with Russia and Belarus. **13.** Up to 100 Serb infantry crossed into Albania, seizing the villages of Kamenica and Padesh and setting fire to homes before retreating when engaged by the Albanian army. The Vatican criticized the distribution by UN agencies of the 'morning after' pill to Kosovar refugees who had been raped. **18.** NATO bombed a combined petrochemicals, fertilizer and refinery complex on the banks of the Danube in the northern outskirts of Belgrade, releasing clouds of poisonous gases and polluting the waters of the Danube. **21.** Tony Blair spoke on Russian television, appealing for support for NATO's actions and likening events in Kosovo to those in Nazi Germany. Dragan Burzan, the deputy prime minister of Montenegro, described the killing of Kosovar refugees as a crime against humanity and called for the perpetrators to be tried for war crimes. **22.** Romania granted NATO unrestricted use of its airspace. **28.** Vuk Drašković was dismissed as deputy prime minister of Yugoslavia after he told the government that Russia would not help Yugoslavia militarily and that the world's public opinion was against Yugoslavia.

MAY 1999

1. Serbian authorities reported that more than 40 people, mainly Kosovar Albanians, had been killed when NATO accidentally hit a bus in Luzane, Kosovo, during an air strike. **4.** Bulgaria's parliament voted to allow NATO access to its airspace for strikes against Yugoslavia. **7.** NATO forces accidentally bombed the Chinese embassy in Belgrade, killing three people. The Serb regime launched a fierce attack against opposition leaders, calling them 'traitors' and 'agents of NATO'. **9.** Britain, Germany and the USA rejected an offer from Yugoslavia to pull back part of its forces from Kosovo, saying that the offer fell far short of NATO's demand for a complete withdrawal to allow refugees to return. **12.** The EU appointed President Ahtisaari of Finland to represent its interests in negotiations alongside Russia's Viktor Chernomyrdin with President Milošević. **13.** President Milošević refused to meet Mary Robinson, the UN High Commissioner for Human Rights, who had planned to challenge him about ethnic cleansing. **14.** Ibrahim Rugova, the Kosovar leader, said that he was in talks with other exiled politicians to prepare for control of their homeland. **17.** President Djukanović of Montenegro appealed to the EU for emergency food and refugee relief. 20. Yugoslav soldiers blocked Montenegro's border with Croatia, confiscating Italian humanitarian aid. 22. Yugoslav troops briefly occupied a buffer zone of Albanian territory. Hundreds protested in the Serbian town of Raska, near the Kosovar border, after dozens of soldiers from the area were reported to have been killed by NATO bombing. 24. Serb forces launched a second wave of ethnic cleansing in Kosovo aimed at removing tens of thousands of Kosovar Albanians still living in Priština. 27. The UN War Crimes Tribunal indicted President Milošević of Yugoslavia, President Milutinović of Serbia, the Yugoslav deputy prime minister Nikola Sainović, the Yugoslav armed forces chief of staff Dragoljub Ojdanić, and the Serbian minister of the interior and commander of police, Vlajko Stojiljković, for crimes against humanity. 28. Viktor Chernomyrdin arrived in Belgrade for peace talks, saying the indictment of President Milošević had complicated his mission.

JUNE 1999

2. The EU and Russian negotiators met Slobodan Milošević, after the Yugoslav leader said that he accepted the general principles of the plan put forward by the G8 group of nations. The plan called for the withdrawal of all Serb military, police and paramilitary forces and the occupation of Kosovo by an international force. 3. President Milošević accepted the peace plan agreed by NATO and Russia after having obtained the approval of the Serb Parliament, but NATO insisted that the bombing would go on until there was clear evidence that Yugoslav troops were leaving Kosovo. 5. NATO commanders met Yugoslav generals on the Kosovo-Macedonia border to present them with a detailed military blueprint for the complete withdrawal of soldiers, police and paramilitary forces from Kosovo within seven days. 6. NATO accused Yugoslavia's generals of stalling on the deal to end the conflict and issued a warning that unless they agreed the details by the following day, the talks would be called off and the military campaign intensified. 8. Lt.-Gen. Sir Mike Jackson met Yugoslav officers at Kumanovo on the Kosovo-Macedonia border to obtain their formal acceptance of the withdrawal plan in line with the agreement reached a few hours earlier by the G8 foreign ministers in Cologne. 10. Yugoslav generals signed a military pact setting out terms for their forces' withdrawal from Kosovo, so paving the way for an end to NATO airstrikes. Dr Javier Solana, the NATO secretary-general, ordered the suspension of air operations following confirmation that the full withdrawal of the Yugoslav security forces from Kosovo had begun. The UN Security Council voted 14–0, with China abstaining, to adopt the peace plan prepared by the G8 powers. Europe, Russia and the USA launched a Stability Pact, which would offer billions of pounds for investment, market access and economic reform to the Balkan countries. 11. Russian troops, who had been based in Bosnia, seized control of Priština

airport. 13. British forces entered Priština and were hailed as liberators by the Kosovar Albanian population. 14. Three thousand refugees in Glogovac cheered the arrival of the first UN aid convoy to reach Kosovo. German and Italian forces arrived in their sector capitals, Pec and Prizren. Hungary and Bulgaria refused a Russian request for overflight rights, effectively cutting off the 200 Russian soldiers holding the airport in Priština. 15. Serb security forces withdrew from Priština. Their departure triggered a wave of revenge attacks by Kosovar Albanians on local Serbs while British peacekeepers tried to keep control. The Holy Synod of the Serbian Orthodox Church demanded the resignation of President Milošević. 18. Russia's defence and foreign ministers agreed with their American counterparts that Moscow would send about 3,000 soldiers to Kosovo. 20. All Yugoslav soldiers and policemen were declared to have withdrawn from Kosovo. President Yeltsin agreed with Western leaders to refuse any reconstruction aid to Serbia while President Milošević remained in power. 26. Patriarch Pavle, the head of the Serbian Orthodox Church travelled to Kosovo to persuade Serbs to remain in the province. 28. Crown Prince Alexander of Yugoslavia returned from exile in London and called for Milošević's removal; he backed demands from the Orthodox Church for the formation of a government of national salvation. 29. A crowd of 5,000 staged a demonstration in the Serbian town of Cacak, demanding the resignation of Slobodan Milošević and free elections in Serbia. Thousands of KLA troops rebels assembled at NATO-designated assembly points to hand in their weapons.

JULY 1999

1. The International Committee of the Red Cross claimed that thousands of Kosovar Albanians seized by Serb security forces were being held in Serbia and that the Serbian Ministry of Justice had refused to release a list of its detainees or their whereabouts. Tens of thousands of people poured onto the streets of Priština to celebrate the NATO Victory. 4. The President of the International Red Cross arrived in Serbia for a four-day assessment of the refugee crisis caused by tens of thousands of Serbs fleeing their homes in Kosovo. 5. Differences concerning the interpretation of the Helsinki agreement between Russia and NATO were resolved. The main contingent of the 3,600 Russian troops that were to take part in the KFOR peacekeeping force began arriving in Kosovo the day after differences between NATO and Russia were resolved. Zoran Djindjić, leader of the Democratic Party, returned to Belgrade from Montenegro. More than 20,000 people joined an anti-government march in the southern Serbian town of Leskovac. 7. French gendarmes and troops fought to keep order in Kosovska Mitrovica after escorting 7,000 Kosovar Albanians through its Serb section in a bid to reopen the divided city. 8. Kosovar Albanians demonstrated against the de-

ployment of Russian troops in Ohorovac. **13.** Serbia and Montenegro began two days of talks on constitutional issues after Montenegro demanded control of the military and the economy in its territory. **19.** EU sanctions against Kosovo and Montenegro were lifted. **24.** NATO appealed for calm after 14 Serbian men were murdered in the British-run sector of Kosovo near Gracko; British forces arrested four suspects on 28 July.

AUGUST 1999

4. Serbs in Kosovo claimed that Russian peacekeepers had failed to protect them. **5.** Montenegro declared that it wanted to abolish the Yugoslav Federation in favour of a loose partnership with Serbia, each with its own army, foreign ministry and currency. **11.** The UN refugee agency claimed that the Serb population of Priština had shrunk from about 40,000 to less than 2,000. **12.** British troops clashed with Kosovar Albanian extremists when two patrols thwarted an attack by an armed group who had fired automatic weapons and rocket-propelled grenades at a Serb-populated village, Dornja Brnica. Four of the five were arrested. Slobodan Milošević reshuffled the Yugoslav government, increasing the representation of the ultra-nationalist Serbian Radical Party and the United Left. **15.** Bernard Kouchner, the head of the UN mission in Kosovo, warned the KLA that the UN was not prepared to see the Serbs driven out of Kosovo. The UN estimated that 170,000 of 200,000 Serbs had left the province. **18.** General Agim Ceku, the KLA's military commander, denied responsibility for murders and attacks by Albanians that had forced Serbs and Gipsies to flee Kosovo. **19.** More than 100,000 people demonstrated in Belgrade, calling on President Milošević to resign. **20.** French troops began escorting Albanian families back to their homes in the Serb sector of the divided city of Kosovska Mitrovica. **22.** Serbs in Kosovo demanded the division of the province into ethnic cantons to protect them from the Albanians.

INTERNATIONAL RELATIONS

SEPTEMBER 1998

2. President Clinton arrived in Russia for talks on the country's economic crisis.

OCTOBER 1998

1. The UN Security Council condemned the massacres of ethnic Albanians being carried out in Kosovo, Federal Republic of Yugoslavia. **17.** The former Chilean dictator General Augusto Pinochet was arrested in London at the request of the Spanish government in connection with the murders of Spanish citizens in Chile during his regime.

NOVEMBER 1998

7–14. The USA withdrew most of the sanctions imposed on India and Pakistan following their

nuclear tests. **12.** The USA became the last major industrialized country to sign the Kyoto Protocol on 'greenhouse' gas emissions.

DECEMBER 1998

23. At a special court in Brussels, Willy Claes, the former secretary-general of NATO, was found guilty of corruption.

JANUARY 1999

11. Officials from China and the USA met in Washington DC to discuss human rights.

FEBRUARY 1999

25. China exercised its Security Council veto to end the UN mandate for its peacekeeping mission in the Former Yugoslav Republic of Macedonia following that country's extension of diplomatic recogntion to Taiwan.

MARCH 1999

3. The USA imposed sanctions on a range of EU goods in the so-called 'Banana War'(*see* Economic and Business Affairs). **12.** Poland, Hungary and the Czech Republic became members of NATO at a ceremony in Independence, Missouri. **26.** The UN Security Council rejected a Russian resolution demanding an immediate halt to NATO bombing in Yugoslavia. **29.** The UN High Commissioner for Refugees, Sadako Ogata, appealed to the international community to assist the Kosovar refugees.

APRIL 1999

7. The World Trade Organization (WTO) ruled that EU import regulations had given preferential treatment to bananas from former colonies of member states and discriminated unfairly against Latin American producers. The decision cleared the way for the USA to impose £120 million of punitive tariffs against unrelated EU exports to the USA as damages for lost business. **25.** At its 50th anniversary gathering, NATO offered a formal defence guarantee to Albania and Macedonia. It also agreed to give the EU a direct role in military matters. **29.** A Commonwealth working group recommended that Nigeria be readmitted to full membership on 29 May, when the democratically elected president, Olusegun Obansajo, was due to take over from the military government.

MAY 1999

28. A three-man group led by the former Swedish prime minister, Carl Bildt, was appointed by Kofi Annan to investigate the role of the UN in Rwanda during the 1994 genocide.

JUNE 1999

2. A request by Yugoslavia for emergency court orders against the UK and nine other NATO countries to stop their bombing was rejected by the International Court of Justice. Judges ruled that it lacked the jurisdiction to grant the provisional measures. **17.** The International Labour Organization voted for the *de facto* expulsion of Myanmar for using forced labour.

JULY 1999

4. NATO blocked two Russian military aircraft from flying to Kosovo with reinforcements, declaring that Russia had ignored an agreement on the deployment and responsibilities of its troops. Bulgaria, Hungary and Romania refused permission for the aircraft to cross their airspace. **13.** The Organization of African Unity committed itself to greater democracy by declaring that governments which came to power by military force would not be allowed to attend the next summit. **30.** Brazil suspended trade talks with Argentina and called for an emergency meeting of Mercosur officials after Argentina announced unilateral quotas on Brazilian textiles and shoes.

AUGUST 1999

8. George Robertson was confirmed as the new secretary-general of NATO. **11.** The UN Security Council appointed Switzerland's attorney-general, Carla Del Ponte, prosecutor at the UN War Crimes Tribunals for the Former Yugoslavia and Rwanda.

THE MIDDLE EAST

OCTOBER 1998

9. Ariel Sharon was appointed Israeli foreign minister. **15.** General Emile Lahoud was elected president of Lebanon. **23.** The Wye River Agreement, an interim peace plan for Palestine, was signed by Yasser Arafat and Binyamin Netanyahu; Israel agreed to withdraw its troops from a further 13.1 per cent of the West Bank in exchange for security guarantees from the Palestinian National Authority. **31.** The president of Iraq, Saddam Hussein, announced that all Iraqi co-operation with UN weapons inspectors would cease.

NOVEMBER 1998

14. Saddam Hussein agreed to co-operate with UN weapons inspectors after the USA sent troops to the Gulf. **20.** Israel withdrew troops from 2 per cent of the West Bank.

DECEMBER 1998

2. Salim al-Hoss was appointed prime minister of Lebanon. **10.** The Palestinian Central Committee voted to change the Palestinian Charter to remove references to the need for Israel's destruction. **12–15.** President Clinton visited Israel and Palestine.

JANUARY 1999

25. King Hussein of Jordan signed a royal decree naming his eldest son, Prince Abdullah ibn al-Hussein, as his successor in place of his youngest brother, Prince Hassan.

FEBRUARY 1999

7. King Hussein of Jordan died.

MARCH 1999

4. Abdel-Raouf Rawabdeh was named prime minister of Jordan. **6.** The Emir of Bahrain, Sheikh Issa, died of a heart attack; he was succeeded by his son, Sheikh Hamad al-Khalifa.

APRIL 1999

15. In Israel, Arieh Deri, the leader of the ultra-orthodox Shas party and an ally of Prime Minister Netanyahu, was jailed for four years for corruption. **21.** An end to years of strained relations between Syria and Jordan was signalled when the new Jordanian ruler, King Abdullah II, received a warm welcome from President Assad. **26.** In Egypt, more than 1,000 Islamic militants, all members of al-Gamaa al-Islamiya, were released from prison; the group had announced in March that it was halting all armed operations.

MAY 1999

4. The Emir of Kuwait dissolved parliament. **17.** Ehud Barak was elected prime minister of Israel; he promised to withdraw troops from Lebanon within a year, and offered to return the Golan Heights to Syria in return for a comprehensive peace settlement. **27.** Prime Minister Binyamin Netanyahu announced he would stand down from parliament.

JUNE 1999

8. Four judges were killed and five bystanders wounded when two gunmen sprayed a courtroom with machine gun fire in Sidon, Lebanon; Esmat al-Ansar, a Muslim fundamentalist group, was suspected of the attack. **21.** A Hezbollah mortar attack on northern Israel forced 250,000 people into bomb shelters.

JULY 1999

1. Ehud Barak, the prime minister-elect of Israel, formed a broad coalition of seven parties. **4.** In Kuwait, opposition liberals won 16 of the 50 National Assembly seats. Islamists won 20 seats and pro-government candidates' numbers halved. **7.** Ehud Barak assumed the premiership of Israel. **11.** Israel announced it would withdraw from 10 per cent of the West Bank, fulfilling the conditions of the Wye River agreement. **19.** Syrian-based dissident Palestinian and militant Muslim groups were ordered by the government to end their armed struggle against Israel.

Obituaries

Abraham, Sir Edward, CBE, FRS, biochemist, aged 85 – 8 May 1999

Adams, Rt. Revd James, suffragan bishop of Barking 1975–83, aged 83 – 11 May 1999

Ali Haidar, Jemadar, VC, aged 85 – 15 July 1999

Alport, Lord (Cuthbert), PC, former Conservative MP, High Commissioner in the Federation of Rhodesia and Nyasaland 1961–3, aged 86 – 28 October 1998

Ambler, Eric, OBE, novelist and screenwriter, aged 89 – 22 October 1998

Archer, Gen. Sir John, KCB, OBE, Commander-in-Chief UK Land Forces 1978–9, aged 75 – 12 March 1999

Autry, Gene, American actor and singer known as the 'singing cowboy', aged 91 – 2 October 1998

Bart, Lionel, composer and songwriter, aged 68 – 3 April 1999

Beloff, Lord (Max), FBA, aged 85 – 22 March 1999

Beriosova, Svetlana, Lithuanian-born ballerina, aged 66 – 10 November 1998

Blanchflower, Jackie, former Manchester United and Northern Ireland footballer, survivor of the 1958 Munich air disaster, aged 65 – 2 September 1998

Bogarde, Sir Dirk, actor and author, aged 78 – 8 May 1999

Box, Betty, OBE, film producer, aged 83 – 15 January 1999

Boxcar Willie, American country music singer, aged 67 – 12 April 1999

Brandon of Oakbrook, Lord (Henry), MC, PC, Lord Justice of Appeal 1972–81, Lord of Appeal in Ordinary 1981–91, aged 78 – 24 March 1999

Bristol, 7th Marquess of, aged 44 – 10 January 1999

Brooksby, John, CBE, FRS, veterinary virologist, aged 83 – 17 December 1998

Brown, Dennis, Jamaican reggae singer, aged 42 – 1 July 1999

Buckley, Sir Denys, PC, MBE, a Lord Justice of Appeal 1970–81, aged 92 – 13 September 1998

Budgen, Nicholas, Conservative MP for Wolverhampton South-West 1974–97, aged 60 – 26 October 1998

Butler, Sir Clifford, FRS, physicist and educational administrator, aged 77 – 30 June 1999

Cairncross, Sir Alec, KCMG, economist, aged 87 – 21 October 1998

Carmichael, Stokely (Kwame Ture), American civil rights leader, aged 57 – 15 November 1998

Carter, Betty, American jazz singer, aged 69 – 26 September 1998

Casey, Rt. Revd Patrick, Roman Catholic bishop of Brentwood 1969–79, aged 85 – 26 January 1999

Casson, Sir Hugh, CH, KCVO, architect, designer and artist, president of the Royal Academy 1976–84, aged 89 – 15 August 1999

Cathcart, Maj.-Gen. The 6th Earl, CB, DSO, MC, aged 79 – 15 June 1999

Cayzer, Lord (Nicholas), aged 89 – 16 April 1999

Chaudhuri, Nirad C., Indian author and broadcaster, aged 101 – 1 August 1999

Chebrikov, Viktor, head of the KGB 1982–8, aged 76 – 2 July 1999

Cockerell, Sir Christopher, CBE, FRS, inventor of the hovercraft, aged 88 – 1 June 1999

Crewe, Quentin, writer, aged 72 – 14 November 1998

Crombie, Prof. Leslie, FRS, chemist, aged 76 – 3 August 1999

Crowder, Petre, QC, Conservative MP for Ruislip-Northwood 1950–74 and for Hillingdon, Ruislip-Northwood 1974–9, aged 79 – 16 February 1999

Dalhousie, 16th Earl of, KT, GCVO, GBE, MC, governor-general of the Federation of Rhodesia and Nyasaland 1957–63, aged 84 – 15 July 1999

Dando, Jill, television presenter, aged 37 – murdered 26 April 1999

Darling, Gen. Sir Kenneth, GBE, KCB, DSO, aged 89 – 31 October 1998

Dean of Beswick, Lord (Joe), Labour MP for Leeds West 1974–83, aged 76 – 26 February 1999

Denning, Lord, OM, PC, Lord Justice of Appeal 1948–57, Lord of Appeal in Ordinary 1957–62, Master of the Rolls 1962–82, aged 100 – 5 March 1999

Devon, 17th Earl of, aged 82 – 19 November 1998

DiMaggio, Joe, American baseball player, aged 84 – 8 March 1999

Dunnett, Sir Alastair, editor of the *Daily Record* 1946–55 and of the *Scotsman* 1956–73, aged 89 – 2 September 1998

Dunsany, Lt.-Col. The 19th Lord, aged 92 – 6 February 1999

Eccles, 1st Viscount, PC, CH, KCVO, Conservative MP for Chippenham 1943–62, President of the Board of Trade 1957–9, Minister of Education 1959–62, Paymaster-General 1970–73, aged 94 – 24 February 1999

Erlichman, John, American lawyer involved in Watergate scandal, aged 73 – 15 February 1999

Evans, Godfrey, CBE, cricketer, aged 78 – 3 May 1999

Fairgrieve, Sir Russell, CBE, Conservative MP for Aberdeenshire West 1974–83, aged 74 – 17 February 1999

Fatchett, Derek, PC, Minister of State at the Foreign and Commonwealth Office since 1997, Labour MP for Leeds South 1982–3 and Leeds Central since 1983, aged 53 – 9 May 1999

Fifield, Elaine, Australian ballerina, aged 68 – 11 May 1999

Flanagan, Sir Jamie, CBE, Chief Constable of the RUC 1973–6, aged 85 – 4 April 1999

Fleming, Amaryllis, cellist, aged 73 – 27 July 1999

Fletcher, Air Chief Marshal Sir Peter, KCB, OBE, DFC, AFC, aged 82 – 2 January 1999

Foyle, Christina, bookseller, aged 88 – 8 June 1999

Frankel, Sir Otto, FRS, agricultural scientist, aged 98 – 21 November 1998

French, Leslie, actor and director, aged 94 – 21 January 1999

Gable, Christopher, CBE, dancer and actor, founder of the Central School of Ballet, director of Northern Ballet Theatre since 1987, aged 58 – 23 October 1998

Gardner, Andrew, newscaster, aged 66 – 2 April 1999

Giant Haystacks (Martin Ruane), wrestler, aged 52 – 29 November 1998

Gillard, Frank, CBE, broadcaster, BBC radio war correspondent 1942–5, aged 89 – 21 October 1998

Gillmore of Thamesfield, Lord (David), GCMG, Permanent Secretary at the Foreign and Commonwealth Office and Head of the Diplomatic Service 1991–4, aged 64 – 20 March 1999

Godden, Rumer, OBE, writer, aged 90 – 8 November 1998

Golding, John, Labour MP for Newcastle-under-Lyme 1969–86, junior employment minister 1976–9, General Secretary of the National Communications Union 1986–8, aged 67 – 20 January 1999

Goodchild, Rt. Revd Ronald, suffragan bishop of Kensington 1964–80, aged 88 – 28 December 1998

Goring, Marius, actor, aged 86 – 30 September 1998

Goulding, Cathal, chief of staff of the IRA 1962–9 and of the Official IRA 1969–80, aged 76 – 26 December 1998

Gowing, Prof. Margaret, CBE, FRS, FBA, historian, aged 77 – 7 November 1998

Grade, Lord (Lew), Russian-born film and television producer, aged 91 – 13 December 1998

Gray, Rt. Revd Joseph, Roman Catholic Bishop of Shrewsbury 1980–95, aged 79 – 7 May 1999

Griffith-Joyner, Florence, American athlete, winner of three gold medals at the 1988 Olympics, aged 38 – 21 September 1998

Grotowski, Jerzy, Polish theatre director, aged 65 – 14 January 1999

Guilford, 9th Earl of, aged 65 – 26 March 1999

Hale, Sir John, FBA, historian, aged 75 – 12 August 1999

Hassan II, King of Morocco since 1961, aged 70 – 23 July 1999

Hayes, Patricia, OBE, actress, aged 88 – 19 September 1998

Haynes, Frank, Labour MP for Ashfield 1979–92, aged 72 – 11 September 1998

Heron, Patrick, CBE, artist and writer, aged 79 – 20 March 1999

Hickson, Joan, OBE, actress, aged 92 – 17 October 1998

Hill, Sir James, Conservative MP for Southampton Test 1970–4 and 1979–97, aged 72 – 16 February 1999

Hobson, Valerie, actress, aged 81 – 13 November 1998

Hodgkin, Prof. Sir Alan, OM, KBE, FRS, biophysicist, joint winner of the Nobel prize for medicine 1963, aged 84 – 20 December 1998

Hodson, H. V., editor of the *Sunday Times* 1950–61, aged 92 – 27 March 1999

Hollenden, 3rd Baron, aged 85 – 12 April 1999

Howard de Walden, 9th Lord, TD, aged 86 – 9 July 1999

Hughes, Ted, OM, Poet Laureate since 1984, aged 68 – 28 October 1998

Hull, Rod, entertainer, aged 63 – 17 March 1999

Hume, Cardinal George Basil, OM, Roman Catholic Archbishop of Westminster since 1976, aged 76 – 17 June 1999

Hunt, Lord (John), KG, CBE, DSO, leader of the British expedition that conquered Everest in 1953, aged 88 – 8 November 1998

Hussein, King of Jordan since 1952, aged 63 – 7 February 1999

Jackson, Air Chief Marshal Sir Brendan, GCB, aged 63 – 19 November 1998

Jackson, Gen. Sir William, GBE, KCB, OBE, MC and Bar, aged 81 – 12 March 1999

Jenkins, Meg, actress, aged 81 – 5 October 1998

John, Rosamund, actress, aged 85 – 27 October 1998

Kane, Bob, American cartoonist, creator of Batman, aged 83 – 3 November 1998

Kane, Sarah, playwright, aged 27 – 20 February 1999

Karekin I, Supreme Patriarch and Catholicos of All Armenians since 1994, aged 66 – 29 June 1999

Keller, Prof. Andrew, FRS, polymer scientist, aged 73 – 7 February 1999

Kelley, DeForest, American actor, aged 79 – 11 June 1999

Kemball, Prof. Charles, CBE, FRS, chemist, aged 75 – 4 September 1998

Kemsley, 2nd Viscount, aged 89 – 28 February 1999

Kendall, Prof. Henry, physicist and Nobel laureate, aged 72 – 2 February 1999

Kennedy, John F., Jr, son of the late president of the USA, aged 38, in a plane crash – 16 July 1999

Killanin, 3rd Baron, president of the International Olympic Committee 1972–80, aged 84 – 25 April 1999

Kubrick, Stanley, American film-maker, aged 70 – 7 March 1999

Kurosawa, Akira, Japanese film director, aged 88 – 6 September 1998

Kurti, Prof. Nicholas, CBE, FRS, Hungarian-born physicist, aged 90 – 24 November 1998

Lanesborough, 9th Earl, aged 80 – December 1998

Lansdowne, 8th Marquess of, PC, aged 86 – 25 August 1999

Latey, Sir John, MBE (MIL), PC, High Court judge 1965–89, aged 85 – 24 April 1999

Leontief, Wassily, Russian-born economist, winner of the Nobel Prize for Economics 1973, aged 92 – 5 February 1999

Lewin, Admiral of the Fleet Lord, KG, GCB, LVO, DSC, Chief of the Defence Staff 1979–82, aged 78 – 23 January 1999

Love, Adrian, radio DJ, aged 54 – 10 March 1999

Lowry, Lord (Robert), PC, Lord Chief Justice of Northern Ireland 1971–88, Lord of Appeal in Ordinary 1988–94, aged 79 – 15 January 1999

Machin, Arnold, OBE, RA, sculptor who designed the portrait of The Queen which has appeared on postage stamps since 1967, aged 87 – 9 March 1999

Marais, Jean, French actor, aged 84 – 8 November 1998

March, Elspeth, actress, aged 88 – 29 April 1999

Marks of Broughton, 2nd Baron, aged 78 – 9 September 1998

Mars, Forrest, American confectionery maker who built the Mars chocolate empire, aged 95 – 1 July 1999

Mars-Jones, Sir William, MBE, High Court judge 1969–90, aged 83 – 10 January 1999

Marsden, Prof. David, FRS, neurologist, aged 60 – 29 September 1998

Martineau, Rt. Revd Robert, Bishop of Blackburn 1972–81, aged 85 – 28 June 1999

Masters, Rt. Revd Brian, area bishop of Edmonton since 1984, aged 65 – 23 September 1998

Mature, Victor, American film actor, aged 86 – 4 August 1999

McAdoo, Most Revd Henry, Church of Ireland Archbishop of Dublin and Primate of Ireland 1977–85, aged 82 – 10 December 1998

McCann, Donal, Irish actor, aged 56 – 17 July 1999

McCrea, Sir William, FRS, mathematician and astrophysicist, president of the Royal Astronomical Society 1961–3, aged 94 – 25 April 1999

McCrindle, Sir Robert, Conservative MP for Billericay 1970–4 and for Brentwood and Ongar 1974–92, aged 69 – 8 October 1998

McDowall, Roddy, actor, aged 70 – 3 October 1998

McGahey, Mick, former Scottish miners' leader, aged 73 – 30 January 1999

Mellon, Paul, American philanthropist, aged 91 – 2 February 1999

Menuhin, Lord (Yehudi), OM, violinist, conductor and philanthropist, aged 82 – 12 March 1999

Merryfield, Buster, actor, aged 78 – 23 June 1999

Mitchison, Naomi, CBE, author, aged 101 – 11 January 1999

Moore, Archie, American boxer, world light-heavyweight champion 1952–62, aged 84 – 9 December 1998

Moore, Brian, novelist, aged 77 – 11 January 1999

Moro, Peter, CBE, architect, associate designer of the Royal Festival Hall, London, aged 87 – 10 October 1998

Morris, Johnny, OBE, children's broadcaster, presenter of *Animal Magic* for 21 years, aged 82 – 6 May 1999

Mosey, Don, cricket journalist and broadcaster, aged 74 – 11 August 1999

Murdoch, Dame Iris, DBE, novelist and philosopher, aged 79 – 8 February 1999

Musin, Ilya, Russian conductor and teacher, aged 95 – 6 June 1999

Nedwell, Robin, comedy actor, aged 52 – 2 February 1999

Newborough, 7th Lord, DSC, aged 81 – 11 October 1998

Newley, Anthony, actor, singer and songwriter, aged 67 – 14 April 1999

Nimmo, Derek, actor and comedian, aged 68 – 25 February 1999

Nkomo, Joshua, vice-president of Zimbabwe since 1987, aged 82 – 1 July 1999

Nutting, Sir Anthony, Bt., PC, aged 79 – 23 February 1999

Orr-Ewing, The Lord, OBE, life peer and 1st baronet, aged 87 – 19 August 1999

Owen, Bill, actor, aged 85 – 12 July 1999

Pakula, Alan J., American film director, aged 70, in a car accident – 19 November 1998

Papadopoulos, George, dictator of Greece 1967–73, aged 80 – 27 June 1999

Paterson, Jennifer, television cook, aged 71 – 10 August 1999

Paton, Sir Angus, CMG, FRS, civil engineer, aged 93 – 7 April 1999

Peck, Bob, actor, aged 53 – 4 April 1999

Perry, Ernest, Labour MP for Battersea South 1964–79, aged 90 – 28 December 1998

Peters, Jim, marathon runner, aged 80 – 9 January 1999

Phillips of Ellesmere, Lord, KBE, FRS, scientist, aged 74 – 23 February 1999

Pillar, Adm. Sir William, GBE, KCB, aged 75 – 18 March 1999

Playfair, Sir Edward, KCB, Permanent Secretary at the Ministry of Defence 1960–61, aged 89 – 21 March 1999

Pliatzky, Sir Leo, KCB, Permanent Secretary at the Department of Trade 1977–9 and at the Civil Service Department 1979–80, aged 79 – 4 May 1999

Portman, 9th Viscount, aged 67 – 2 May 1999

Price, William, Labour MP for Rugby 1966–79, aged 64 – 6 May 1999

Pulman, John, world professional snooker champion 1957 and 1964–8, aged 75 – 25 December 1998

Puzo, Mario, American novelist, aged 78 – 2 July 1999

Quarry, Jerry, American heavyweight boxer, aged 53 – 3 January 1999

Ramsey, Sir Alf, England football manager 1963–74, aged 79 – 28 April 1999

Ray, Robin, actor, broadcaster and writer, aged 63 – 29 November 1998

Reed, Oliver, film actor, aged 61 – 2 May 1999

Rhodes James, Sir Robert, historian, Conservative MP for Cambridge 1976–92, aged 66 – 20 May 1999

Richards, Gordon W., national hunt trainer, aged 68 – 29 September 1998

Riches, Rt. Revd Kenneth, Bishop of Lincoln 1956–74, aged 90 – 15 May 1999

Robens of Woldingham, The Lord (Alfred), PC, former Labour MP, chairman of the National Coal Board 1961–71, aged 88 – 27 June 1999

Robinson, Betty, American athlete, the first woman to win an Olympic gold medal, aged 87 – 18 May 1999

Rodrigo, Joaquín, Spanish composer, aged 97 – 6 July 1999

Roe, Rt. Revd Gordon, suffragan bishop of Huntingdon 1980–97, aged 67 – 19 July 1999

Rollason, Helen, MBE, sports reporter, aged 43 – 9 August 1999

Rosier, Air Chief Marshal Sir Frederick, GCB, CBE, DSO, aged 82 – 10 September 1998

Rossington, Norman, actor, aged 70 – 21 May 1999

Rothermere, 3rd Viscount, proprietor of the *Daily Mail*, the *Mail on Sunday* and the *Evening Standard*, aged 73 – 2 September 1998

Rutland, 10th Duke of, CBE, aged 79 – 3 January 1999

Rybakov, Anatoli, Russian author, aged 87 – 23 December 1998

Sainsbury, Lord (Alan), chairman of Sainsbury's 1956–67, aged 96 – 21 October 1998

Sarazen, Gene, American golfer, first to win all four Majors, aged 97 – 13 May 1999

Schawlow, Arthur, American physicist, co-inventor of the laser, aged 77 – 28 April 1999

Seaborg, Prof. Glenn, American nuclear chemist who discovered plutonium, winner of the Nobel Prize for Chemistry 1951, aged 86 – 25 February 1999

Shacklock, Constance, OBE, opera singer, aged 86 – 29 June 1999

Sheikh Isa bin Sulman al-Khalifa, Emir of Bahrain since 1961, aged 65 – 6 March 1999

Soper, The Revd Lord, Methodist minister, aged 95 – 22 December 1998

Springfield, Dusty, OBE, pop singer, aged 59 – 2 March 1999

St Oswald, 5th Baron, aged 79 – 18 March 1999

Steinberg, Saul, American artist, aged 84 – 12 May 1999

Stephenson, Sir John, PC, Lord Justice of Appeal 1971–85, aged 88 – 1 November 1998

Stone, Jesse, rhythm and blues pioneer, aged 97 – 1 April 1999

Stoph, Willi, Chairman of the Council of Ministers (Prime Minister) of the German Democratic Republic 1964–73 and 1976–89, aged 84 – 13 April 1999

Stott, Lord (George), Lord Advocate 1964–7, Senator of the College of Justice in Scotland 1967–84, aged 89 – 12 April 1999

Stott, Roger, CBE, Labour MP for Westhoughton 1973–83 and for Wigan since 1983, aged 56 – 8 August 1999

Sutch, Screaming Lord, founder of the Official Monster Raving Loony Party, aged 58 – committed suicide 16 June 1999

Thomas, Adm. Sir Richard, KCB, KCVO, OBE, Gentleman Usher of the Black Rod 1992–5, aged 66 – 13 December 1998

Tilberis, Liz, magazine editor, aged 51 – 21 April 1999

Toms, Carl, OBE, theatrical designer, aged 72 – 4 August 1999

Tormé, Mel, American jazz singer and songwriter, aged 73 – 5 June 1999

Torney, Thomas, Labour MP for Bradford South 1970–87, aged 83 – 21 October 1998

Turnbull, Sir Richard, GCMG, governor of Tanganyika 1958–61, aged 89 – 21 December 1998

Vanneck, Air Cdre Hon. Sir Peter, GBE, CB, AFC, Conservative MEP for Cleveland 1979–84 and Cleveland and Yorks North 1984–9, aged 77 – 2 August 1999

Vick, Sir Arthur, OBE, vice-chancellor of Queen's University, Belfast 1966–76, aged 87 – 2 September 1998

Viollet, Dennis, former Manchester United footballer, survivor of the 1958 Munich air disaster, aged 65 – 6 March 1999

Wallace, George, former governor of Alabama and US presidential candidate, aged 79 – 13 September 1998

Waller, Sir George, PC, OBE, High Court judge 1965–76, a Lord Justice of Appeal 1976–84, aged 87 – 5 February 1999

Washbrook, Cyril, CBE, cricketer, aged 84 – 27 April 1999

Welch, Rt. Revd Neville, suffragan bishop of Bradwell 1968–73, aged 92 – 3 February 1999

West, Rt. Revd Francis, suffragan bishop of Taunton 1962–77, aged 89 – 2 January 1999

Whitelaw, 1st Viscount, KT, CH, MC, PC, Conservative MP for Penrith and the Border 1955–83, Leader of the House of Commons 1970–72, Northern Ireland Secretary 1972–3, Employment Secretary 1973–4, Chairman of the Conservative Party 1974–5, Home Secretary 1979–83, Leader of the House of Lords 1983–8, aged 81 – 1 July 1999

Winchilsea and Nottingham, The Earl of (16th Earl of Winchilsea and 11th Earl of Nottingham), aged 62 – June 1999

Wise, Ernie, OBE, comedian, aged 73 – 21 March 1999

Woolf, Sir John, film and television producer, aged 86 – 28 June 1999

Yang Shangkun, president of China 1988-92, aged 91 – 14 September 1998

Young, Freddie, OBE, cinematographer, aged 96 – 1 December 1998

Cost of Living and Inflation Rates

The first cost of living index to be calculated took July 1914 as 100 and was based on the pattern of expenditure of working-class families in 1914. The cost of living index was superseded in 1947 by the general index of retail prices (RPI), although the older term is still popularly applied to it.

GENERAL INDEX OF RETAIL PRICES

The general index of retail prices measures the changes month by month in the average level of prices of goods and services purchased by most households in the United Kingdom. The spending pattern on which the index is based is revised each year, mainly using information from the Family Expenditure Survey. The expenditure of certain higher income households and of households mainly dependent on state pensions is excluded.

The index is compiled using a selection of over 600 goods and services, and the prices charged for these items are collected at regular intervals in about 146 locations throughout the country. For the index, the price changes are weighted in accordance with the pattern of consumption of the average family.

INFLATION RATE

The twelve-monthly percentage change in the 'all items' index of the RPI is usually referred to as the rate of inflation. The percentage change in prices between any two months/years can be obtained using the following formula:

$$\frac{\text{Later date RPI} - \text{Earlier date RPI}}{\text{Earlier date RPI}} \times 100$$

e.g. to find the rate of inflation for 1988, using the annual averages for 1987 and 1988:

$$\frac{106.9 - 101.9}{101.9} \times 100 = 4.9\%$$

PURCHASING POWER OF THE POUND

Changes in the internal purchasing power of the pound may be defined as the 'inverse' of changes in the level of prices; when prices go up, the amount which can be purchased with a given sum of money goes down. To find the purchasing power of the pound in one month or year, given that it was 100p in a previous month or year, the calculation would be:

$$100p \times \frac{\text{Earlier month/year RPI}}{\text{Later month/year RPI}}$$

Thus, if the purchasing power of the pound is taken to be 100p in 1975, the comparable purchasing power in 1997 would be:

$$100p \times \frac{34.2}{157.5} = 21.71p$$

For longer term comparisons, it has been the practice to use an index which has been constructed by linking together the RPI for the period 1962 to date; an index derived from the consumers expenditure deflator for the period from 1938 to 1962; and the prewar 'cost of living' index for the period 1914 to 1938. This long-term index enables the internal purchasing power of the pound to be calculated for any year from 1914 onwards. It should be noted that these figures can only be approximate.

	Long-term index of consumer goods and services (Jan. 1987 = 100)	Comparable purchasing power of £1 in 1998	Rate of inflation (annual average)
1914	2.8	58.18	
1915	3.5	46.54	
1920	7.0	23.27	
1925	5.0	32.58	
1930	4.5	36.20	
1935	4.0	40.72	
1938	4.4	37.02	
There are no official figures for 1939–45			
1946	7.4	22.01	
1950	9.0	18.10	
1955	11.2	14.54	
1960	12.6	12.93	
1965	14.8	11.00	
1970	18.5	8.80	
1975	34.2	4.76	
1980	66.8	2.44	18.0
1981	74.8	2.18	11.9
1982	81.2	2.01	8.6
1983	84.9	1.92	4.6
1984	89.2	1.83	5.0
1985	94.6	1.72	6.1
1986	97.8	1.67	3.4
1987	101.9	1.60	4.2
1988	106.9	1.52	4.9
1989	115.2	1.41	7.8
1990	126.1	1.29	9.5
1991	133.5	1.22	5.9
1992	138.5	1.18	3.7
1993	140.7	1.16	1.6
1994	144.1	1.13	2.4
1995	149.1	1.09	3.5
1996	152.7	1.07	2.4
1997	157.5	1.03	3.1
1998	162.9	1.00	3.4

The RPI figures are published around the middle of each month. They are available as a recorded message which can be heard by telephoning 0171-533 5866. Each month an updated Consumer Price Indices bulletin is published by the Office of National Statistics.

OFFICE OF NATIONAL STATISTICS, 1 Drummond Gate, London SW1V 2QQ.
PUBLIC ENQUIRIES LINE: 0171-533 5874/6363/6364
WEB: http://www.ons.gov.uk

Index

Colleges *continued*
  theological, 463
Colne Valley, MP, 241
Commissary Office, HM, 365
Commissioner for Complaints, Northern
  Ireland, 329
Commissioner for Local Administration in
  Scotland, 318
Commissioner for Public Appointments,
  Office of, 287
Commissioners Commons, 370
Commissioners of Income Tax, Special,
  373
Commissioners Social Security and Child
  Support, 372
Commissioners of Northern Lighthouses,
  317
Commissioners Traffic, 373
Commission for Architecture and the Built
  Environment, 290
Commission for Integrated Transport, 290
Commission for Local Administration,
  England, 317–8
  Wales, 318
Commission for Racial Equality, 333
Commission for the New Towns, 496
Committee on Standards in Public Life,
  343
Common Entrance Examination, 428
Commons Commissioners, 370
Common Services Agency (Scotland), 339
Commonwealth Day, 9
Commonwealth Development
  Corporation, 290
Commonwealth Experience, 594
Commonwealth Institute, 322
Commonwealth Parliamentary Association,
  268
Commonwealth War Graves Commission,
  290
Communicable Diseases Surveillance
  Centre, 331
Communications,
  airmail zones, 518–9
  international dialling codes, 518–9
  Internet, 520
  postal services, 513–5
  telecommunications, 515–7
Communications Headquarters,
  Government (GCHQ), 340
Community charge, 521
Community councils,
  Scotland, 526
  Wales, 525
Companies Court, 355–6
  Registrar, 356
Companies House, 346
Companions of Honour, 173
Compass variation (magnetism), 77
Compensation Agency (Northern Ireland),
  327
Compensation Commission, Foreign, 302
Competition Commission, 291
Complementary Medicine, Professional
  Body, 461
Congleton, 528, 545
  MP, 241
Congo, Anglican Province, 413
Congregational Federation, 418
Connor, Bishop, 412
Connor, Down and, Bishop (RC), 416
Conservation,
  buildings, 584
  environmental, 574–8
  habitats, 579–80
  wildlife, 579–83
Conservative and Unionist Party, 224
  development, 223
  financial support, 223
  local representation, 527–31

Conservative and Unionist Party *continued*
  MEPs, 269–70
  MPs, 226–33
  Shadow Cabinet, 223
  whips, 224
Constabulary,
  Chief Constables, 375–6
  county, 375–6
  HM Inspectorate of, 309–10, 339, 374
Constants,
  astronomical, 75
  tidal, 97
Constellations, 16, 20, 24, etc., 71
Constituencies,
  by-elections, 233
  England, 236–61
  Northern Ireland, 267–8
  Scotland, 263–7
  Wales, 261–3
Constitution of UK, 215–6
Construction Service (Northern Ireland),
  327
Consumer Council, National, 324
Continents, 104–5
Contributory benefits, 489–91
Convention on Trade in Endangered
  Species of Wild Fauna and Flora,
  579–80
Conventions,
  biological diversity, 571
  climate change, 571
  conservation, 579–80
Conwy, 530, 558
  Education Authority, 441
  MP, 262
Cookstown, 568
Co-ordinated universal time, 73
Copeland, 528, 545
  MP, 241
Copyright Tribunal, 370
Corby, 528, 545
  MP, 241
Cork, Cloyne and Ross, Bishop, 413
Cork and Ross, Bishop (RC), 416
Cornwall, 527, 541, 542
  Archdeacon, 411
  Devon and, Police Authority, 375
  Duchy of, 294
  Education Authority, 439
  MPs, 241
  North, 529, 546
Coroners' courts, 354
Corporation of London, 524, 550– 2
  Aldermen, 550, 551
  Common Council, 551–2
  Lord Mayor, 550
  Records Office, 334
  Sheriffs, 550
Corporation of Trinity House, 317
Corpus Christi, 9, 83
Cost of living, 645
Cotswold, MP, 241–2
Cotswolds, 528, 545
Council for Nature Conservation and the
  Countryside (Northern Ireland), 328
Council on Tribunals, 348
Council tax, 521–2
  benefit, 493
  England, 521–2, 523–4, 541, 543–9
  London, 555
  Scotland, 522, 526, 564
  valuation bands, 521–2
  Wales, 521–2, 525, 558
Counsellors of State, 215
Countesses in own right, 144
  form of address, 135, 144
Countess of Wessex, 117
Counties,
  England, 540–1
  Northern Ireland, 568

Counties *continued*
  Wales, 556–7
Countries of the world, 599–603
Countryside Agency, 291
Countryside Council for Wales, 291
County councils,
  England, 521, 522, 541–2
  political composition, 527
Court of Session, 364–5
Court of the Lord Lyon, 280
Courts,
  Ecclesiastical, 368
  England and Wales, 353–63
  Northern Ireland, 366–7
  Scotland, 365
Courts administration,
  England and Wales, 318–9, 356–7
  Scotland, 364–5
Court Service, 319
Covent Garden Market Authority, 291
Coventry, 527, 535, 543
  airport, 504
  Archdeacon, 405
  Bishop, 164, 405
  Education Authority, 439
  MPs, 242
  University, 446
Craigavon, 568
Cranfield University, 446
Cranwell, Royal Air Force College, 456
Craven, 528, 545
  Archdeacon, 404
Crawley, 528, 545
  MP, 242
Crayford, Bexleyheath and, MP, 237
Crediton, Bishop (Suffragan), 406
Crewe and Nantwich, 528, 545
  MP, 242
Crime Squad, National, 374
Criminal Cases Review Commission, 291
Criminal Injuries Compensation Authority
  and Board, 291–2
Criminal Intelligence Service, National,
  374–5
Crofters Commission, 292
Cromarty, Ross and, Lord Lieutenant, 563
Crosby, MP, 242
Crown Agent, Scotland, 364
Crown Courts, 357–8
Crown Estate, 292
  Commissioners, 292
  Head of Scottish Estates, 292
Crown Office, 318
  Scotland, 364, 366
Crown of India, Imperial Order of, 172
Crown Prosecution Service, 362–3
Crown Solicitor, Northern Ireland, 367
Croydon, 530, 555
  Archdeacon, 410
  Bishop (Area), 410
  Education Authority, 441
  MPs, 242
Cuba, 105
  Bishop (Anglican), 413
Culture, Media and Sport, Department for,
  292–3
  Secretary of State
Cumbernauld and Kilsyth, MP, 264
Cumbria, 527, 541, 542
  Education Authority, 439
  Police Authority, 375
Cumnock, Carrick, and Doon Valley, MP,
  264
Cunninghame, MPs, 264
Curia (RC), 414–5
Currencies, exchange rates, 604– 7
Currencies of the world, 604–7
Curriculum,
  councils, 443
  schools, 428–30

Stop-press

CHANGES SINCE PAGES WENT TO PRESS

THE YEAR 2000

Amendments to the Hindu religious calendar:
Chaitra   5 April
Janmashtami   23 August
Sarasvati-puja   2 October
Diwali, last day 28 October

PEERAGE

Died: 2nd Viscount Caldecote; Baron Oram

BARONETAGE AND KNIGHTAGE

Rt. Hon. John Morris, QC, MP became a Knight Bachelor
Died: Sir Melville Arnott; Vice-Adm. Sir Ronald Buckley; Sir Philip Haddon-Cave; Sir Wilfred Cockcroft; Sir Piers Jacobs; Sir Robert Southern; Sir Gerald Staples; Sir Colin Walker

PRIVY COUNCIL

John Morris made a Knight Bachelor
Alan Clark died

PARLIAMENT

MPs – Rt. Hon. John Morris, QC, MP made a Knight Bachelor
Died: Roger Stott, Lab. Wigan and Rt. Hon. Alan Clark, C. Kensington and Chelsea
Bill Tynan (Lab.) won the Hamilton South by-election
Neil Turner (Lab.) won the Wigan by-election

GOVERNMENT DEPARTMENTS AND PUBLIC OFFICES

British Railways Board and Shadow Strategic Rail Authority – Lew Adams, OBE; Baron Bradshaw; D. Jefferies, CBE; P. Kent, CBE and D. Quarmby appointed members
Commonwealth Development Corporation – Dr A. R. Gillespie appointed Chief Executive
Office of Gas and Electricity Markets – C. Coulthard to be Deputy Director-General, Scotland; Ms J. Whittington appointed a Director
Highways Agency – L. J. Haynes resigned as Chief Executive
Office for National Statistics – A. Goldsmith appointed Director of Finance and Corporate Services
Science Museum – Prof. A. Dowling and M. Smith appointed Trustees

LAW COURTS AND OFFICES

Circuit judges – A. J. Worthington and A. J. Mills appointed (SE circuit); Judge M. K. Lee (Midland and Oxford) died
Special Commissioners of Income Tax – Dr A. N. Brice appointed
VAT and Duties Tribunals – Dr A. N. Brice appointed Chairman

DEFENCE

RAF – Air Chief Marshal Sir Peter Squire, KCB, DFC, AFC, to be Chief of the Air Staff from 21 April 2000

CHURCH OF ENGLAND

P. A. Delaney appointed Archdeacon of London

EDUCATION

The Council for Dance Education and Training has not recognized the teacher registration system of the Association of American Dancing.

HEALTH

White Paper Saving Lives: Our Healthier Nation published. Measures include improving the health of people on low incomes and public health observatories to be set up in each NHS region. Targets include:
– cancer deaths among under-75s to be reduced by 20 per cent over ten years
– heart disease and stroke rates among under-75s to be reduced by 40 per cent over ten years
– accidental deaths and suicides to be reduced by 20 per cent over ten years

THE WATER INDUSTRY

Ofwat issued plans for average reductions in bills of 14 per cent over five years.

ENERGY

The Government announced a partial privatization of BNFL, with 49 per cent of shares to be sold.

COMMUNICATIONS

Cable and Wireless Communications' residential cable telephone system to be sold to NTL and its business telecommunications and data services to be taken over by Cable and Wireless during 2000
One-2-One bought by Deutsche Telekom
BT is now the sole owner of BT Cellnet

LOCAL GOVERNMENT

Lord Mayor of London 1999–2000 – Alderman Clive Martin, OBE, TD, elected 29 September

OBITUARIES

September 1999
5 Alan Clark, Conservative MP for Plymouth, Sutton 1974-92, for Kensington and Chelsea 1997-99; government minister 1983-92, aged 71
10 Alfredo Kraus, opera singer, aged 71
14 Rt Revd Cyril Bowles, Bishop of Derby 1969-87, aged 83
15 Rt Revd William Westwood, Bishop of Peterborough 1984-95, aged 73
17 Frankie Vaughan, singer and entertainer, aged 71
20 Raisa Gorbachev, wife of the USSR's last president, Mikhail Gorbachev, aged 67
22 George C. Scott, American actor, aged 71

EVENTS – SEPTEMBER 1999

1. In Serbia, two Australian aid workers detained on spying charges were released. 4. An agreement between Israel and the PLO was signed, under which Israel agreed to withdraw from a further 11 per cent of the West Bank. The Final Status talks, to decide the boundaries of a Palestinian state, began on 13 September. 5. In Russia, Islamic rebels launched a second invasion of Dagestan. 6. Former US Senator George Mitchell, who chaired negotiations leading to the 1998 Good Friday Agreement, met with political parties in Belfast in an attempt to renew progress. 7. At

least 32 people were killed when an earthquake measuring 5.9 on the Richter scale struck Athens, Greece. **8.** The Bank of England raised bank base rates by 0.25 per cent to 5.25 per cent. **8-16.** Over 200 people were killed in a series of bombings in Russia. The Dagestan Liberation Army, a previously unknown group, later claimed responsibility. **9.** Chris Patten's commission on policing in Northern Ireland published its proposals, including re-naming the force the Northern Ireland Police Service and increasing the number of Roman Catholic officers. **14.** Hurricane Floyd caused extensive damage in the Bahamas before moving north to the eastern United States, where over three million people fled their homes by 16 September, although damage was less severe. **16.** Seven people, including four children, were killed when a man opened fire inside a church in Fort Worth, USA; the gunman also killed himself. In Bloomfontein, South Africa, an army officer killed seven colleagues before being shot dead himself. **17.** Fifty-nine soldiers were sentenced to death for taking part in a coup attempt against the democratically elected government of Zambia in October 1997. **20.** At least 2,000 people were killed when an earthquake measuring 7.6 on the Richter scale struck Taiwan. Powerful aftershocks caused more damage in subsequent days. UN Peacekeeping troops began to arrive in East Timor; violence had flared after the referendum on independence. The Agriculture Minister, Nick Brown, announced an extra £150m package to aid farmers. **22.** The political leader of Hamas, Khaled Meshaal, and two other senior Hamas officials were detained in Amman, Jordan.